EC COMPETITION LAW

EC COMPETITION LAW

TEXT, CASES, AND MATERIALS

Third Edition

ALISON JONES

Solicitor, Professor of Law, King's College London

AND

BRENDA SUFRIN

Solicitor, Professor of Law, University of Bristol

OXFORD

UNIVERSITY PRESS

OXFORD
UNIVERSITY PRESS

Great Clarendon Street, Oxford OX2 6DP

Oxford University Press is a department of the University of Oxford.
It furthers the University's objective of excellence in research, scholarship,
and education by publishing worldwide in

Oxford   New York

Auckland Cape Town Dar es Salaam Hong Kong Karachi
Kuala Lumpur Madrid Melbourne Mexico City Nairobi
New Delhi Shanghai Taipei Toronto

With offices in

Argentina Austria Brazil Chile Czech Republic France Greece
Guatemala Hungary Italy Japan Poland Portugal Singapore
South Korea Switzerland Thailand Turkey Ukraine Vietnam

Oxford is a registered trade mark of Oxford University Press
in the UK and in certain other countries

Published in the United States
by Oxford University Press Inc., New York

British Library Cataloguing in Publication Data

Data available

Library of Congress Cataloging in Publication Data

Data available

Typeset by Newgen Imaging Systems (P) Ltd, Chennai, India
Printed in Great Britain
on acid-free paper by
Ashford Colour Press Ltd, Gosport, Hants

ISBN 978-0-19-929904-1

10 9 8 7 6 5 4 3 2 1

PREFACE

The preface of the second edition of this book noted that the three years following publication of the first edition had seen the most far-reaching changes in EC competition law in its forty-year history. Although perhaps not quite as radical, EC competition law has continued to change at a rapid pace and evolve dramatically since 2004. Of particular importance has been DG Competition's publication in December 2005 of a Discussion Paper on the application of Article 82 of the Treaty to exclusionary abuses. In the previous ten years the working and application of both Article 81 and the EC Merger Regulation had been reviewed and overhauled and the failure to introduce any substantive change in approach to Article 82 or guidance on policy was conspicuous by its absence. Commentators complained that it was wrong that the influence that economic thinking had had on the Community rules applicable to agreements and mergers had not been felt to the same extent within the sphere of Article 82. The Discussion paper was intended to meet that criticism, to provoke debate as to how European markets are best protected from dominant companies' exclusionary conduct and to set out possible principles for the future application of Article 82 to exclusionary abuses. This review has been welcomed and, as will be seen in Chapters 5–7, has, as intended, provoked widespread and passionate debate and discussion. It remains to be seen what the outcome of the review will be, but the Commission may not adopt Guidelines and it is unlikely that it will take action, if any, until after the CFI hands down its judgment in *Microsoft* in September 2007.

In 2005, the Commission also published a Green Paper on Damages actions for breach of the EC antitrust rules. The purpose of the Green Paper, and an accompanying Commission Staff Working Paper, was to identify the main obstacles to a more efficient system of damages claims and to invite discussion on those obstacles and possible options formulated for overcoming them. A White Paper is anticipated around the New Year.

The last three years have also seen a stream of important case law from the ECJ and CFI, for example: *Volkswagen* on the meaning of 'agreement'; *FENIN* on the meaning of 'undertaking'; *Meca-Medina*, *O2* and *GlaxoSmithKline* on the meaning of a restriction of competition; *Confederación Espanola de Empresarios de Estaciones de Servicio v. Compania Espanola de Petróleos* and *DaimlerChrsyler* on agency; *France Télécom* and *British Airways* on the legitimacy of price discounting by dominant firms; *Manfredi* on the right to damages; crucial case law following the Commission's scrutiny of concentrations under the ECMR, for example, *Tetra Laval*, *Imapala* and *General Electric* and *Schneider*; and a raft of judgments dealing with fining and leniency policy and rights of defence in cartel cases. These judgments are discussed in the text. The Commission has also produced numerous decisions, published draft Guidelines on the assessment of non-horizontal mergers, updated some of the merger notices, published discussion papers, launched reviews, commissioned and conducted studies and reports as well as continuing to drive forward policy and international cooperation at both a bilateral and multilateral level. It has also been active in acting against protectionist interference from national government in cross-border merger cases.

This edition attempts, as before, to provide students and others interested in competition law with as comprehensive as possible a package of text, commentary, and materials as is possible given the confines of space. We have endeavoured to present the law in its economic context, trace the development of the rules, and to consider how the modernized regime works in practice. The developments since the last edition have required extensive rewriting, or a rigorous review, of most chapters of this book and has required some reordering of material. We read carefully the reviews and the comments on the second edition submitted to the publisher (for which we are very grateful) and have sought to incorporate these views in the new text. In particular, responding to the view of some we hope to publish online a separate chapter on state aids.

We have again decided not to rename this book 'EU Competition Law'. Until the Reform Treaty comes into force the competition rules remain the creature of the EC Treaty. After this time, however, the European Community will cease to exist and the rules will become EU Competition Law. The Reform Treaty was drawn up towards the end of June 2007, too late for us to incorporate a full discussion of it in the text. We have, however, briefly dealt with the Reform Treaty and its implications, if any, for competition law and policy in the relevant chapters and have given a fuller account of it in an Addendum which can be found at page 1399 of this book. The Treaty Articles we refer to in the text are those that result form the renumbering of the EC Treaty by the Treaty of Amsterdam. We have therefore referred in the text to Articles 81, 82, etc. throughout, even when discussing cases or events prior to 1 May 1999. In quotations and extracts we have replaced the old Article number with the new, but placed it in brackets, so 'Article [81]' denotes that the original said 'Article 85'. Where Regulation 17 and Regulation 1/2003 are concerned, however, we have left the original Regulation 17 numbers intact.

We would like to extend our thanks to everyone who has assisted us in the preparation of this edition. In particular, we wish to thank Eram Khan, our research assistant, and the Centre of European Law at King's College London. We also owe an enormous debt to Ruth Ballantyne, Matthew Baldwin, and their colleagues at Oxford University Press, and to our copy editor, Dan Liessner, whose helpfulness and efficiency have enabled us to produce this edition at this time amid so many seismic changes.

Our intention was to state the law as at 1 April 2007. With the cooperation and forbearance of OUP, however, we have been able to include a note of some later, important developments (such as the Reform Treaty) up until the middle of July 2007. Further developments may be found on a companion web site that accompanies this book. The main objective of the web site is to set out recent developments in the law and to provide links to helpful web sites where further information can be obtained. The web site will be updated twice per year and can be accessed at www.oxfordtextbooks.co.uk/orc/jones_sufrintcm3e/

Alison Jones would like to dedicate this edition to her Mother, Vivienne Jones, who died in 2004 and who is still missed enormously. Brenda Sufrin would like to dedicate this edition to the staff of the Bristol Bone Marrow Transplant Unit.

ALISON JONES
BRENDA SUFRIN
12 July 2007

OUTLINE CONTENTS

CONTENTS

ACKNOWLEDGEMENTS

Grateful acknowledgement is made to all the authors and publishers of copyright material which appears in this book, and in particular to the following for permission to reprint material from the sources indicated:

Extracts from UK Competition Law Reports (UKCLR) and Office of Fair Trading Research Paper 2: Barriers to Entry and Exit in Competition Policy are Crown copyright material and are reproduced under Class Licence Number C01P0000148 with the permission of the Controller of HMSO and the Queen's Printer for Scotland.

Extracts from the reports of the European Court of Justice and Court of First Instance (ECR) are taken from www.curia.europa.eu. These are unauthenticated reports and are reproduced free of charge. The definitive versions are published in Reports of Cases before the Court of Justice or the Official Journal of the European Union.

American Bar Association/ABA Publishing: extracts from Phillip Areeda: 'Essential Facilities: An Epithet in Need of Limiting Principles', 58 Antitrust Law Journal, No. 3, 841 (1989), copyright © 1989 by the American Bar Association; and Per Jebsen and Robert Stevens: 'Assumptions, Goals and Dominant Undertakings: The Regulation of Competition Under Article 86 of the European Union', 64 Antitrust Law Journal, No. 3, 443 (1996), copyright © 1996 by the American Bar Association. All rights reserved.

Basic Books, a member of Perseus Books Group: extracts from Robert H Bork: The Antitrust Paradox: A Policy at War with Itself (Basic Books, 1993), copyright © 1978 by Basic Books, LLC.

Blackwell Publishing Ltd: extract from W Bishop: 'Price discrimination under Article 86: Political economy in the European Court', 44 Modern Law Review 282 (1981).

Council of Europe, European Commission: DG Comp chart and extract from speech given by Commissioner Mario Monti at the Ecole des Mines, Paris 16.1.04 as published on the Commission's website www.europa.eu.int/comm/competition

Elsevier: extract from D Harbord and T Hoehn: 'Barriers to Entry and Exit in European Competition Policy', 14 international Review of Law & Economics 411 (1994), copyright © 1994.

Hart Publishing: extracts from G Amato: Antitrust and the Bounds of Power (Hart, 1997); R O'Donoghue and A J Padilla: The Law and Economics of Article 82 EC (Hart, 2006); and from G J Werden: 'Competition Policy on Exclusionary Conduct: Towards and Effect-based Analysis', 2 European Competition Journal 53 (2006).

Harvard Law Review Association via Copyright Clearance Center: extracts from W S Comanor: 'Vertical price-fixing, vertical market restrictions, and the new antitrust policy', 98 Harvard Law Review 983 (1985), copyright © 1985 The Harvard Law Review Association.

Houghton Mifflin Company: extracts from F M Scherer and David Ross: Industrial Market Structure and Economic Performance (3rd edn., Houghton Mifflin, 1990), copyright © 1990 by Houghton Mifflin Company.

Wolters Kluwer Law & Business: extracts from Common Market Law Review: D Edward and M Hoskins: 'Article 90: Deregulation and EC Law: Reflections arising from the XVI FIDE Conference', 32 CMLRev 157 (1995); L Hancher: 'Casenote on Corbeau', 31 CMLRev 105 (1994); B E Hawk: 'System Failure: Vertical restraints and EC Competition Law', 32 CMLRev (1995) 973; Giorgio Monti: 'Article 81 EC and Public Policy', CMLRev (2002) 1057, 'The Scope of Collective Dominance under Article 82C', 38 *CMLRev* (2001) 131; and extracts from World Competition: D Hildebrand: 'The European School in EC Competition Law', 25 World Competition 3 (2002); L Peeperkorn: 'IP Licences and Competition Rules: Striking the Right Balance', 26 World Competition (2003) 527; R Pardolesi and A Renda: 'The European Commissions' Case against Microsoft: Kill Bill?', 27 World Competition (2004) 513; and C Ritter: 'Refusal to Deal and Essential Facilities: Does Intellectual Property Require Special Deference compared to Tangible Property?', World Competition 3 (2005) 281.

The Michigan Law Review Association and the author: extracts from H Hovenkamp: 'Antitrust Policy After Chicago', 84 Mich. L Rev. 213 (1985), copyright © 1985 by Michigan Law Review Association.

New York University Law School: extract from Eleanor M Fox and Lawrence A Sullivan: 'Antitrust—Retrospective and Prospective: Where Are We Coming From? Where Are We Going?', 62 New York Univ. Law Review 936 (1987).

Oxford University Press: extracts from S D Anderman & J Kallauagher: Technology . Transfer and the New EU Competition Rules: Intellectual Property Licensing after Modernization (OUP, 2006); J Faull and A Nikpay {eds): The EC Law of Competition (2nd edn., OUP, 2007); and D Gerber: Law and Competition in Twentieth Century Europe: Protecting Prometheus (Clarendon Press, 1998).

Reed Elsevier (UK) Ltd trading as LexisNexis UK: extracts from All England Law Reports (All ER) and table from W Allan, M Furse and B Sufrin (eds): Butterworth's Competition Laws (Butterworths Looseleaf).

Sweet & Maxwell Ltd: extracts from S Bishop and M Walker: The Economics of EC Competition Law: Concepts, Application and Measurement (2nd edn., Sweet & Maxwell, 2002); and J Van den Bergh and P D Camesasca: European Law and Economics: A Comparative Perspective (2nd edn., Sweet & Maxwell, 2006); extracts from EC Law Review: J P Azevedo and M Walker: 'Dominance: Meaning and Measurement', ECLR 363 (2002); C D Ehlermann & B J Drijber: 'Legal Protection of Enterprises Administrative Procedure, in Particular Access to the File and Confidentiality', 7 ECLR 375 (1996); E Fox: 'The Merger Regulation and its Territorial Reach' ECLR 334 (1999); C Gauer and M Jaspers: 'Designing and European Solution for a "One Stop Leniency Shop" ', ECLR 685 (2006); A Jones and D Beard: 'Co-contractors, Damages and Article 81: The ECJ Finally Speaks' ECLR 246 (2002); and D Ridyard: 'Essential Facilities and the obligation to supply competitors', ECLR 438 (1996), and 'Exclutionary pricing and the price discrimination abuses under Article 82: An economic analysis', ECLR 286 (2002); extract from European Law Review: C W Baden Fuller: 'Article 86: Economic Analysis of the existence of a Dominant Position', 4 ELRev 423 (1979); and extracts from Common Market Law Reports (CMLR).

John Temple-Lang: extracts from J Temple Lang and R O'Donaghue: 'Defining legitimate competition: How to clarify pricing abuses under Article 82EC', 26 Fordham International Law Journal 83 (2002).

Thomson West: extracts from H Hovenkamp: Federal Antitrust Policy: The Law of Competition and its Practice (2nd edn., West, 1999).

University of Chicago Press: extracts from R A Posner: Antitrust Law (2nd edn., University of Chicago Press, 2001), copyright © 2001 by R A Posner.

Every effort has been made to trace and contact copyright holders prior to publication but this has not been possible in every case. If notified, the publisher will undertake to rectify any errors or omissions at the earliest opportunity.

TABLE OF EUROPEAN CASES

Page references in **bold** indicate that the item is given particular prominence in the text.

COMMISSION MERGER DECISIONS

COMMISSION DECISIONS (NON-MERGER)

COURT OF FIRST INSTANCE ALPHABETICAL TABLE

COURT OF FIRST INSTANCE NUMERICAL TABLE

EUROPEAN COURT OF JUSTICE

ALPHABETICAL TABLE

EUROPEAN COURT OF JUSTICE

NUMERICAL TABLE

EUROPEAN COURT OF HUMAN RIGHTS CASES

UNITED KINGDOM CASES

FRENCH CASES

SWEDISH CASES

TABLE OF INTERNATIONAL CASES

Page references in **bold** indicate that the item is given particular prominence in the text.

UNITED STATES CASES

TABLE OF LEGISLATION

Page references in **bold** indicate that the item is given particular prominence in the text.

EUROPEAN LEGISLATION

UK LEGISLATION

STATUTORY INSTRUMENTS

FOREIGN LEGISLATION

EIRE

GERMANY

TABLE OF EUROPEAN AND INTERNATIONAL TREATIES, CONVENTIONS AND CHARTERS

Page references in **bold** indicate that the item is given particular prominence in the text.

BIBLIOGRAPHY

The following are comprehensive general works on EC competition law which cover the material dealt with in this book. Specialized reading is listed at the end of each Chapter in the 'Further Reading' section.

ALBORS-LLORENS, A., *EC Competition Law and Policy* (Willan, 2002)

ALLAN, W., FURSE M., and SUFRIN B., (eds.), *Butterworths Competition Law* (Butterworths, looseleaf)

AMATO G. and EHLERMANN, C-D., *EC Competition Law, A Critical Assessment* (Hart Publishing, 2007)

BAEL, I. van and BELLIS, J-F., *Competition Law of the European Community* (4th edn., Kluwer, 2004)

BELLAMY, G., and CHILD, G., *European Community Law of Competition* (6th edn., Oxford University Press, 2007)

BISHOP, S. and WALKER, M., *The Economics of EC Competition Law* (3rd edn., Sweet & Maxwell, 2007)

FAULL, J., and NIKPAY, A. (eds.) *The EC Law of Competition* (2nd end., Oxford University Press, 2007)

FURSE, M., *Competition Law of the UK and EC* (5th edn., Oxford University Press, 2006)

GOYDER, D., *EC Competition Law* (3rd edn., Oxford University Press, 2003)

KORAH, V., *An Introductory Guide to EC Competition Law and Practice* (9th edn., Hart Publishing, 2007)

KORAH, V. (ed.), *Competition Law of the European Community* (2nd edn., Lexis Publishing, 2001, looseleaf)

LANE, R., *EC Competition Law* (Longman, 2001)

MONTI,, G., *EC Competition Law* (Cambridge University Press, 2007)

MOTTA, M., *Competition Policy: Theory and Practice* (Cambridge University Press, 2004)

RODGER, B., and MacCULLOCH, A., *Competition Law and Policy in the European Community and the United Kingdom* (3rd edn., Cavendish Publishing, 2004)

SLOT P. J., and JOHNSTON A., *An Introduction to Competition Law* (Hart, 2006)

WHISH, R., *Competition Law* (5th edn., Lexis Nexis Butterworths, 2003)

LIST OF ABBREVIATIONS

AC	Appeal Cases
AJIL	*American Journal of International Law*
All ER	All England Law Reports
Antitrust Bull	*Antitrust Bulletin*
Antitrust LJ	*Antitrust Law Journal*
AAC	average avoidable cost
ATC	average total cost
AVC	average variable cost
Bell J Econ	*Bell Journal of Economics*
BYIL	*British Yearbook of International Law*
CAT	Competition Appeal Tribunal
CDE	*Cahiers de Droit Européen*
CFI	Court of First Instance
CLP	*Current Legal Problems*
CMLR	Common Market Law Reports
CMLRev	*Common Market Law Review*
Colum LR	*Columbia Law Review*
CompAR	Competition Appeal Reports
Cornell LR	*Cornell Law Review*
Cowp	*Cowper's King's Bench Report*
DG Comp	EC Commission Competition Directorate-General
DGFT	Director General for Fair Trading
DOJ	Department of Justice (US)
EC	European Community
ECC	European Commercial Cases
EEC	European Economic Community
ECJ	European Court of Justice
ECLR	*European Competition Law Review*
ECMR	European Community Merger Regulation
ECN	European Competition Network
ECR	European Court Reports
ECSC	European Coal and Steel Community
Edinburgh LR	*Edinburgh Law Review*
EEA	European Economic Area
EFTA	European Free Trade Area
EG	*Estates Gazette*
EGLR	*Estates Gazette Law Reports*
EIPR	*European Intellectual Property Review*
ELRev	*European Law Review*
EMU	Economic and Monetary Union
ESA	EFTA Surveillance Authority
EU	European Union
EuLR	*European Law Reports*

EWCA Civ	England and Wales Court of Appeal (Civil)
EWHC	England and Wales High Court
Fordham Corp L Inst	*Fordham Corporate Law Institute*
Fordham Int'l LJ	*Fordham International Law Journal*
FTAIA	Foreign Trade Antitrust Improvements Act
FTC	Federal Trade Commission (US)
GWB	Gesetz gegen Wettbewerbsbeschrankungen (German competition law system)
Harvard LR	*Harvard Law Review*
HHI	Herfindahl-Hirschman index
HMG	Horizontal Merger Guidelines
HMT	Hypothetical Monopolist Test
ICLQ	*International and Comparative Law Quarterly*
ICN	International Competition Network
ILM	International Legal Materials
Indus & Corp Change	*Industrial and Corporate Change*
IO	industrial organization
IP	intellectual property
IPAC	International Competition Advisory Committee
IPRs	intellectual property rights
IRLR	Industrial Relations Law Reports
JIEL	*Journal of International Economic Law*
JO	Journal Officiel
LIEI	*Legal Issues in European Integration/Legal Issues in Economic Integration*
MES	minimum efficient scale
MLR	*Modern Law Review*
NCAs	national competition authorities
New York Univ LR	*New York University Law Review*
NHMG	Non-horizontal Merger Guidelines
OECD	Organization for Economic Co-operation and Development
OFT	Office of Fair Trading
OJ	Official Journal
PEC	promotion equalization charge
QB	Queen's Bench
Quart J of Econ	*Quarterly Journal of Economics*
R&D	research and development
RPM	resale price maintenance
RTPA	Restrictive Trade Practices Act 1976
SEA	Single European Act 1986
SIEC	significantly impede effective competition
SLC	substantial lessening of competition
SO	Statement of Objections
SRMC	short run marginal cost
Stan LR	*Stanford Law Review*
SSNIP	Small but Significant Non-transitory Increase in Price
TEU	Treaty on European Union ('Maastricht')
TTBER	Technology Transfer Block Exemption Regulation (Reg. 772/2004)
UCLA LR	*University of California Los Angeles Law Review*

UKCLR	United Kingdom Competition Law Reports
Univ Mich LR	*University of Michigan Law Review*
Univ Pa LR	*University of Pennsylvania Law Review*
UNCTAD	United Nations Conference on Trade and Development
WTO	World Trade Organization
Yale LJ	*Yale Law Journal*
YEL	Yearbook of European Law

1

INTRODUCTION TO COMPETITION LAW

1. CENTRAL ISSUES

1. Competition law is concerned with ensuring that firms (undertakings) operating in the free market economy do not restrict or distort competition in a way that prevents the market from functioning optimally.

2. The belief that competition amongst undertakings produces the best outcomes for society is based on economic theory that employs models of perfect competition and monopoly, and concepts of welfare and efficiency.

3. It is possible for systems of competition law to pursue objectives other than the economic ones of welfare and efficiency. Whether they should and, if so, what other objectives should be pursued, is extremely controversial.

4. Even if it is accepted that economics should be the sole or main goal of competition law, there is much debate as to how markets work and when, and on what basis, competition authorities should intervene. Three main 'schools' of

competition analysis are known as Harvard, Chicago, and Post-Chicago.

5. A system of competition law is provided for in the EC Treaty. Article 3 EC provides that the activities of the Community include 'a system ensuring that competition in the internal market is not distorted'.

6. A school of political theory in Europe (and more particularly, Germany) called Ordoliberalism contained ideas about competition law which were influential in the development of EC competition law.

7. Recently, EC competition law has been undergoing a process of modernization. This has led to the competition rules being applied in a more economically rigorous way, based on a consumer welfare standard.

8. Three central concepts used in competition law are market power, market definition and barriers to entry.

2. INTRODUCTION

The first question any book on competition law must address is, what is competition law?

The starting point is that competition law exists to protect competition in a free market economy—that is, an economic system in which the allocation of resources is determined solely by supply and demand in free markets and is not directed by government regulation.

States which adopt a market economy do so because, on the basis of neoliberal economic theory, they consider it to be the form of economic organization which brings the greatest benefits to society. The basis of a free market is competition between firms because such competition is believed, for the reasons explored below, to deliver efficiency, low prices, and innovation. At the other end of the spectrum is an economy which is run by central government planning, such as that which existed in Soviet Russia. Adherence to a belief in the market economy leads to great importance being attached to competition policy and the introduction of competition laws. Competition rules seek to promote effective and undistorted competition in the market. This does not mean that in a free market economy every sector is left to unbridled competition. Areas such as health services or the provision of basic utilities may, for example, be subject to governmental intervention or government controls. Different States may have different views about how far the free market should be tempered or supplemented by a social component and in the European Union agriculture is controlled by the common agricultural policy.[1] The terms competition *policy* and competition *law* are often used synonymously but they can be distinguished. The former is broader since it describes the way in which governments (or, in the case of the European Community (the EC), supranational organizations)[2] take measures to promote competitive market structures and behaviour. Competition *policy* will therefore encompass within it a system of competition *law*. Those rules will seek to implement competition policy by ensuring that firms operating in the market place do not act in a way that harms competition.[3]

At first sight it might perhaps seem ironic that competition laws seek to control and interfere with the freedom of conduct of firms in order to promote free competition. Similar paradoxes face democratic governments in other spheres: how far should the liberties of individuals be constrained in order to uphold liberty itself?

In the competition context regulatory rules are necessary to deal with market imperfections. In particular, left alone to determine their own conduct, firms are likely to combine or collude in a way which is profitable to those firms but which works to the detriment of society as a whole. As early as the eighteenth century Adam Smith,[4] who first identified the 'invisible hand' of competition as a force leading to the general good, described the tendency of those operating within the same trade to conspire to fix prices. Cartels are an age-old phenomenon. Further, competition between firms may produce a 'winner' which dominates the market, or 'natural' monopolies may exist on a market. In these situations it may be thought necessary for competition law to restrain the dominating firms' behaviour. Monopolies may also be created if competitors are allowed to merge freely with one another. Competition law may thus aim to preclude mergers where necessary to preserve the competitive process on the market.

The discussion above assumes that the sole goal of competition law is to achieve economic goals and to preserve the competitiveness of markets. The position is not this simple, however. Rather, there is much disagreement about what goals should be pursued through the application of the competition rules. Some argue that the economic goals should be the sole objective, others that a wider range of objectives should be pursued. The next section discusses the objectives of competition law.

---

[1] Although since the 1990's the system which manipulated the market through subsidizing products and intervention buying has been gradually reformed towards a more market-oriented, environmentally friendly policy which subsidizes farmers rather than products but often makes payments to farmers dependent on them attaining standards on matters such as food safety, animal welfare, and care of the environment: see Council Regulation 1184/2006 and http://ec.europa.eu/agriculture/publi/capexplained/cap_en.pdf.

[2] In this book we talk about EC rather than EU competition law since at present the competition rules are contained in the Treaty establishing the European Community and strictly pertain to the EC rather than the EU as such. If the Reform Treaty comes into force the EC will be subsumed into the EU (see Addendum, *infra* 1399). The competition rules also impact on the European Economic Area. See further *infra* Chap. 2.

[3] The adoption of competition *laws* has, however, sometimes pre-dated the adoption of a discernible policy, see, for example, the discussion of the Sherman Act in the USA, *infra* 19 ff.

[4] See Adam Smith, *The Wealth of Nations* (1776, reprinted Penguin, 1979).

As a matter of terminology it should be noted that in general parlance competition law is often called by its American name, 'antitrust law'. However, the EC Commission (the EC competition authority[5]) now uses the term 'antitrust' to denote the areas of competition law other than merger control and State Aids.[6] The reader will find, nevertheless, that many of the sources quoted in this book use 'antitrust' in its more general meaning.

3. THE OBJECTIVES OF COMPETITION LAW

A. ECONOMIC EFFICIENCY

(i) The Maintenance of Effective Competition

One possible objective of competition law, and the one which is currently in the ascendant, is economic efficiency. This section seeks to show why competition is thought to achieve efficiency and produce the greatest benefits to society. To facilitate the understanding of these issues it is useful to understand some basic concepts of micro-economics and welfare economics (welfare economics is the branch of economics which deals with the desirability of the social consequences of the arrangement of economic activities[7]). Reference should also be made to the EC Commission's own 'Glossary of terms used in EU competition policy'.[8]

(ii) Basic Economic Concepts

a. Demand Curves and Consumer and Producer Surplus

Consumers are all different. They place different values on things, have different preferences and different incomes, and will consequently be willing to pay different prices for a particular product. The maximum amount a consumer is willing to pay for a product is his reservation price.

Although suppliers might like to be able to charge each consumer his individual reservation price, in practice this is not normally feasible. The supplier must therefore consider the relationship between the consumer's willingness to pay and the quantity which will be bought on the market as a whole. If only buyers with very high reservation prices are supplied, the quantity produced will be smaller than if buyers with lower reservation prices are supplied. Conversely, if greater quantities are produced the price will have to fall to incorporate buyers with lower reservation prices. The relationship between price and supply is represented by the market demand curve. The demand curve normally slopes downwards from left to right.

---

[5] The organization and functions of the EC Commission in respect of competition law is explained *infra*, Chap. 2.

[6] See, for example, the web site of the Directorate General responsible for competition policy, http://www.europa.eu.int/ comm/competition/index_en.html.

[7] Welfare economics is described as 'normative' as it depends on value judgments about how well the economy works.

[8] Brussels, July 2002. Available also on the European Commission web site, http://www.europa.eu.int/ Commission/competition/publications/glossary_en.pdf and in on-line format at http://www.europa.eu.int/ Commission/competition/general_info/glossary_en.html. The Commission now subjects the Glossary to a rider that some of it is no longer valid after 1 May 2004 in view of the changes in enforcement procedures.

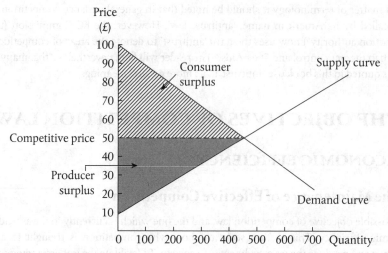

Figure 1.1 Demand curve and consumer and producer surplus

If we assume that the market price is £50 we can see that some consumers will be paying £50 for a product for which they would have paid more. This results in what is known as *consumer surplus* and is shown by the hatched area in Fig. 1. It is the difference between the buyers' reservation prices and the market price.[9]

The supply curve shows the marginal cost[10] of production. In Fig.1 we see that the producer is selling the output for more than it costs to produce. This results in what is known as *producer surplus* and is shown by the shaded area in Fig.1.

b. Elasticity of Demand (Own Price Elasticity)

The amount by which the quantity demanded increases as price reduces (and vice versa) will depend on the market in question and the elasticity of demand for the product.

Price elasticity of demand measures the sensitivity of the quantity demanded to the price. Demand is said to be *inelastic* if an increase in price leads to an insignificant fall in demand. For example, the demand for oil is inelastic since for many of its uses there are no substitutes which perform the same function. Conversely, demand is *elastic* if an increase in price leads to a significant fall in demand. The demand for foreign holidays is elastic.

Technically, price elasticity of demand is the percentage change in the quantity of a product demanded divided by the corresponding percentage change in its price. The result will be a negative figure as the fall in demand will be expressed as a negative figure from the starting point. If demand for widgets[11] falls by 2 per cent as a result of a 1 per cent price increase the change in demand will be expressed as −2 per cent. The demand elasticity is then −2 divided by

---

[9] The concept of consumer surplus was first described by Alfred Marshall, *Principles of Economics* (8th edn., Macmillan, 1920).

[10] See *infra* section iii.a. for an explanation of marginal cost.

[11] A widget is traditionally a mythical product with no specific characteristics used in competition law examples. Despite its recent metamorphosis into a device in the bottom of cans which introduces nitrogen into the liquid and therefore puts a head on canned beer (it won the Queen's Award for Industry in 1991, more than 100 million are made annually and in November 2003 it was reported in the *Daily Mirror* as coming top of a web site poll to find the 'greatest technological invention of the last 40 years') it still retains its characterless role as the Everyman of competition law discourse.

1 (the price increase), which is -2.[12] Typically, elasticity falls as one moves down the demand curve, so that at higher prices demand is more elastic. Economic theory puts the dividing line between elastic and inelastic demand at -1. Demand is elastic at a figure below, or more negative, than -1. It is inelastic between -1 and 0. In markets where demand is inelastic shortages will lead to higher prices. So a bad harvest may be better for food producers than a good one. This was true, for example, when a frost disaster struck the Brazil coffee harvest in 1995.[13]

The position of an individual firm on the market will be different from that of all producers on the market as a whole. Even if the demand for petrol is inelastic, the price for any individual brand will be elastic. If Esso puts up the price of its petrol but Shell does not, drivers will look for Shell garages and purchase the latter's petrol instead. If, however, all the sellers of petrol collectively agree to increase the price of their petrol the quantity demanded may not change significantly.[14]

c. Cross-elasticity of Demand

Elasticity of demand measures the relationship between the price of the product and the demand for it. In contrast, *cross price elasticity of demand* measures how much the demand for *one* product (A) increases when the price of *another* (B) goes up. It is measured by the percentage change in the quantity demanded of product A divided by the percentage increase in the price of B. Cross-elasticity of demand is crucial to market definition.[15]

Cross price elasticity is positive if the price increase in B leads to an increase in demand for A, and this suggests that A and B are substitute products. The Brazil coffee shortage, although leading to an increase in the price of coffee, did not cause consumers to stop purchasing coffee and to purchase tea instead. This indicated that consumers did not consider tea was a substitute for coffee and that the demand for coffee was inelastic. An important point to note is that when considering two products there may be cross price elasticity in one direction and not in the other. Although coffee drinkers may not purchase tea when the price of coffee increases, this does not mean that tea drinkers would not purchase coffee if there was a similar price rise in tea. So in *Microsoft*,[16] the Commission found that while a streaming media player was a substitute for a media player which delivered less functionality, substitution the other way round was not readily available as less performing media players did not satisfy consumer demand for features such as streaming or video playback.

If products are complements of each other, rather than substitutes, the cross price elasticity figure will be negative rather than positive. If the price of petrol goes up the demand for big-engine gas-guzzling cars may go down.

d. Profit Maximization

An assumption is made for the purposes of welfare economics that firms will act rationally and in a way which maximizes profits.[17] Whether firms really do always behave in this way may be

---

[12] Economists often express this figure without using the minus (as it is always negative). The bigger the negative number the 'higher' the elasticity, for example, elasticity of -5 is higher than elasticity of -1.

[13] D. Begg, S. Fischer, and R. Dornbusch, *Economics* (8th edn., McGraw-Hill, 2005), 53–4.

[14] The demand for petrol is not totally inelastic. Arguments about whether governments should take action on the environment by discouraging driving through higher petrol taxes are predicated on the assumption of some elasticity in the demand for petrol.

[15] See *infra* 60 ff.

[16] COMP/C-3/37.792, [2005] 4 CMLR 965, para. 415, on appeal Case T-201/04, *Microsoft* v. *EC Commission* (judgment pending).

[17] Profits represent the difference between the total cost of producing goods or providing a service and the revenue earned by selling them.

doubtful.[18] It will be seen below that, in particular, where a firm has a monopoly the managers may prefer a 'quiet life' to profit maximization. Nevertheless, welfare economics is predicated on this basis. It is certainly a safe assumption that a firm will be concerned not to make long-term *losses*, otherwise it will ultimately have to leave the market. It should also be remembered that a firm which does not deliver profits to its shareholders will be attractive to a predator and so vulnerable to a take-over bid.[19]

e. Economies of Scale and Scope

Economies of scale occur when the average cost of producing a commodity falls as more is produced. If a widget factory produces only one widget then that widget must bear the whole cost of establishing and running the factory. If it produces 100,000 widgets, however, the costs are spread over 100,000 widgets instead of one. Of course, some costs (variable costs) may increase with production (energy and labour for example, although they may not increase proportionately to the number of extra units). However, some costs may not increase at all: if a lorry is delivering widgets, for example, the driver will be paid the same, and the petrol will cost the same, whether the lorry is full or half empty.

Economies of scale result where efficiency in production is achieved as output is increased. There inevitably comes a point, however, when the average cost ceases to fall and economies of scale can no longer be reaped. That point is called the minimum efficient scale (MES). The MES is of great significance for competition law since it has very important repercussions for market structure. Where the MES is very large in relation to the market, i.e., a producer has to supply a large quantity of products on the market before the MES is reached, only a few firms, possibly only one, will be able to operate efficiently on the market. What is called a 'natural monopoly' is where it is less costly for just one firm to serve the market than for the market to be divided between more players. On a competitive market, however, the MES is low in comparison to overall demand so that numerous firms can operate efficiently on the market.

Economies of scope occur where it is cheaper to produce two different products jointly than each separately. This may result from factors such as shared assembly lines or shared personnel which enable the firm to make costs savings by producing a range of goods rather than the individual products on their own. Economies of scope may mean that a multi-product firm has lower unit costs than a single product firm.

---

[18] There is an enormous literature on this subject. The seminal work was A. A. Berle and G. C. Means, *The Modern Corporation and Private Property* (revised edn. 1968, Harcourt Brace and World, 1932). For an extensive discussion see J. E. Parkinson, *Corporate Power and Responsibility* (Oxford University Press, 1993), particularly chaps. 2–4. This doubt arises partly because of the separation of ownership from control in all but the smallest companies. In the layers of complex organization which make up modern businesses, decisions may be made by managers and executives facing uncertain future events and a large number of variables. Their expectations may be misplaced, they may be averse to risk-taking, and they may be most concerned with corporate or individual survival or the growth of the company rather than its profitability. Management may pursue of policy of 'satisficing'. This is a theory of firm behaviour that is contrary to that of profit maximization. 'Satisficing' is when management adopts certain goals for profits, sales, etc. and tries to meet, but not necessarily exceed, them. The goals may not be set high in the first place, so that management will not seem a failure if it does not achieve them, and it is unwilling to be in a position where the shareholders demand ever higher goals in the future. See H. A. Simon, 'Theories of Decision-making in Economic and Behavioral Sciences' (1959) 49 *American Economic Review* 253 and Parkinson, above, 66–7.

[19] See Parkinson, *supra*, n. 18, 113–32.

(iii) Perfect Competition and Efficiency

a. Perfect Competition

If competition rules are designed to achieve efficiency they should be utilized where there is no effective competition on the market. The theory of perfect competition presents a model of a market on which efficiency is maximized and cannot, therefore, be improved by the application of competition rules.

A perfectly competitive market is one in which there are a large number of buyers and sellers (firms with very small market shares can operate at minimal costs since the MES is small in comparison to the size of the market), the product is homogeneous, all the buyers and sellers have perfect information,[20] and there are no barriers to entry or exit. Sellers can come onto, and leave, the market freely.[21] The result of this state of affairs is that each seller is insignificant in relation to the market as a whole and has no influence on the product's price. Consequently, sellers are described as *price-takers*, not price-makers.

In a perfectly competitive market the price never exceeds marginal cost. The marginal cost to a firm is the cost of producing one extra unit of the product. So if it costs £100 to produce ten widgets but £105 to produce eleven, the marginal cost is £5. On such a market the firm will always be able to add to profit where the marginal cost of producing a unit is less than the price. The producer will therefore keep increasing the units it produces until the price obtained equals marginal cost. If the price is below marginal cost the firm will have to respond by reducing output. In other words, in a perfectly competitive market a firm's marginal revenue (the rise in what the firm earns by one extra unit of output) equals marginal cost.[22]

Where the price charged for a product is at marginal cost this does not mean that the firm makes no profit at that price. It does make a profit, but only a 'normal' one. All the factors of production used to make the product have to be taken into account when computing the cost, and this includes the capital. The firm has to make enough of a return on the capital employed in the business to make it worthwhile staying on the market. When economists talk of zero profits they mean that there is no profit above the 'normal' level, which is assessed in relation to the 'opportunity cost'. An opportunity cost is the value of what has to be given up to do something else. The capital employed in the business must therefore reap a profit to compensate the business for the profit which would come from a different outlay. If the firm does not do this it will leave the market.

The relationship between marginal and average cost is also an important one. The average cost is the costs of the firm evened out over all the units produced.[23] When the marginal cost of the next unit exceeds the average cost of the existing units, producing the next unit raises average costs. In that case the firm can decrease costs by reducing supply. If, on the other hand, the marginal cost of the next unit is less than the average cost of the existing units, an extra unit

---

[20] Buyers and sellers know of every change in price or demand and so respond immediately to such changes.

[21] For a discussion of barriers to entry, see *infra* 84 ff.

[22] The reason for this is that although the *industry's* demand curve is downward sloping, the demand curve for *each individual firm* is horizontal, which means that however much it sells it will get the market price. For further explanation of this, see D. Begg, S. Fischer, and R. Dornbusch, *Economics* (8th edn., McGraw-Hill, 2005), chap. 8; D. W. Carlton and J. M. Perloff, *Modern Industrial Organization* (4th edn., Pearson Addison Wesley, 2005), chap. 3.

[23] See further, *infra* Chap. 7 for a discussion of costs in relation to predatory pricing.

reduces average costs. In that case the firm can decrease costs by increasing supply. So the producer will produce at the point at which the average cost curve and the marginal cost curve intersect.

b. Allocative Efficiency

The fact that on a perfectly competitive market the market price equals the marginal cost is said to lead to *allocative efficiency*.

Allocative efficiency results from the fact that goods are produced in the quantities valued by society. The supplier will expand production to the point where market price and marginal cost coincide. The supplier will not make more but neither, if it is acting rationally to maximize profits, will it make less. Everyone who is willing and able to purchase the product at its cost of production will therefore be able to do so. The result is a market which is in equilibrium. Allocative efficiency is a state in which none of the players, sellers or buyers, could be made better off without someone being made worse off. It is sometimes known as *Pareto optimal* after the Italian economist, Vilfredo Pareto,[24] who first developed the theory.

c. Productive Efficiency

Similarly, *productive* (or technical) efficiency results from perfectly competitive markets. Goods are produced at the lowest possible cost. Every firm has to produce at minimum cost or it will lose its custom to others, make losses, and eventually will be obliged to leave the market. Given the perfect information in the market any cost-cutting techniques will be copied by the other firms and the market price will be lowered generally. There is therefore downward pressure on costs and cost reductions are passed on to customers because of the competitive pressure from other suppliers.

d. Dynamic Efficiency

Dynamic efficiency is a third type of efficiency. Allocative and productive efficiency describe static situations, but dynamic efficiency is concerned with how well a market delivers innovation and technological progress. The relation of dynamic efficiency to the concept of perfectly competitive markets is complex for, as we see below,[25] it can be argued that innovation may be better delivered by monopolistic rather than competitive markets and that the ability to achieve market power is an important spur to innovation.

(iv) Monopoly

At the opposite end of the spectrum to perfect competition lies monopoly. This is a market where there is only one seller. This may be because there are barriers which prevent other firms from entering the market (perhaps legal barriers) or because there is a natural monopoly, as the MES of production means that only one undertaking can operate profitably on the market.

The theory predicts that as the firm is not constrained by any competitors it will price as high as it possibly can. The monopoly price will be above the competitive market price. However, the price that the monopolist charges is still affected by demand and is constrained to some extent by products from outside the market. As the price rises some customers will not purchase the product but will use their resources to purchase something else instead. The firm usually faces

---

[24] 1848–1923.

[25] *Infra* 15.

a downward sloping demand curve, so the higher the price it charges the lower the demand for its product.

If a monopolist chooses to sell just one unit it may receive an extremely high price for that unit but that price is unlikely to cover its cost. The monopolist will therefore wish to produce more units but each time it sells one more unit it has to lower the price. Unless the monopolist can *price discriminate* between customers, the monopolist must lower the price on *all* units, not just the extra ones. The producer's marginal revenue is the extra amount the monopolist obtains from selling the extra unit, but because it involves lowering the price across the board the marginal revenue is less than the selling price. This means that the monopolist will sell units only up to the point at which the marginal revenue equals the marginal cost. A monopolist's marginal revenue is below the market price. This in turn means that the quantity supplied of the product will be less than that which would be supplied on a competitive market. Thus prices are higher than those resulting on a competitive market *and* output is restricted. This is illustrated by the following diagram.

Figure 2 shows that, in the absence of price discrimination, the marginal revenue curve is always under the demand curve.[26] Because price is above the competitive price the monopolist makes abnormal profits but some consumers who would have paid the competitive (marginal

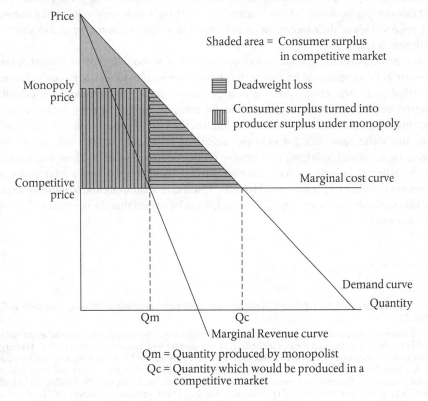

Figure 1.2 The deadweight loss due to monopoly

---

[26] If the monopolist is able to practise perfect price discrimination, that is, charge each customer his reservation price, the marginal revenue curve and the demand curve are the same.

cost) price are deprived of the product. Some of the consumer surplus identified in Figure 1 is therefore transferred to the producer as monopoly profit but some is lost altogether. The horizontally hatched area in the diagram shows this *deadweight loss of monopoly*, the loss of consumer surplus which is not turned into profit for the producer.

According to the above theory, therefore, the main distinction between perfect competition and pure monopoly is that the monopolist's price exceeds marginal cost, while the competitor's price equals marginal cost. This monopoly pricing leads to a transfer of wealth from consumer to producer. It is for this reason that firms operating on a competitive market may wish to emulate the effect of monopoly by colluding, for example, to set their prices at above the competitive level and by reducing output. From an efficiency point of view the transfer of wealth to the monopolist may be immaterial. The behaviour does not, however, simply lead to a redistribution of income but it also results in the misallocation in resources and a deadweight loss. It is this loss to efficiency as a whole that is of concern to economists.

This seeming technicality, so trivial at first glance, is the basis of the economist's most general condemnation of monopoly: it leads to an allocation of resources that is inefficient in the sense of failing to satisfy consumer wants as completely as possible.[27]

In economic theory, therefore, the objection to monopoly is not simply the one which would occur to most lay people—that the monopolist is able to charge excessively for its product—but that monopoly is inefficient.[28] Consumers who would have bought the product at the competitive price will spend their money on other things and welfare is not maximized as allocative inefficiency occurs.

Another important objection to monopoly is that a monopolist will not have the same pressure as firms operating on a perfectly competitive market to reduce its costs. This was identified by Leibenstein as, and has become known as, the 'X-inefficiency'. It describes internal inefficiencies and rising costs due, for example, to high salaries, excessive perks, over-manning, and the lack of need to minimize the cost of production.[29] A monopolist may also waste resources, for example, defending its monopoly position, maintaining excess capacity, and indulging in excessive product differentiation.[30] These inefficiencies will be reflected in higher prices. Another possible inefficiency is that a monopolist not subject to competitive pressures will have little incentive to innovate and to improve its production methods, but as we have already said, it can be argued that the opposite will be true on some markets.[31]

---

[27] F. M. Scherer and D. Ross, *Industrial Market Structure and Economic Performance* (3rd edn., Houghton Mifflin, 1990), 23.

[28] Economists have often sought to quantify the deadweight loss. The starting point was Harberger's article in 1954 in which he calculated the loss in the USA as less than 0.1% of national income: see A. C. Harberger, 'Monopoly and Resource Allocation' (1954) 44 *American Economic Review* 77–87. In a mass of further studies this has been found to be a great under-estimate (for the literature on this, see Scherer and Ross, *Industrial Market Structure and Economic Performance* (3rd edn., Houghton Mifflin, 1990), 661–7). Cowling and Mueller calculated it as 7%: see K. Cowling and D. C. Mueller, 'The Social Costs of Monopoly Power' (1978) 88 *Economic Journal* 724–48, although Scherer and Ross, *supra*, 665 describe these results as 'exaggerated'. In this, as in much else in economics, there are wide differences in views.

[29] H. Leibenstein, 'Allocative efficiency vs. "X-efficiency" ' (1966) 56 *American Economic Review* 392–415.

[30] See, e.g., R. Posner, 'The Social Costs of Monopoly and Regulation' (1975) *Journal of Political Economy* 83.

[31] And see *infra* 15.

(v) Oligopoly

Oligopoly is a type of market structure that lies between perfect competition and monopoly on the spectrum. An oligopolistic market is one on which there are only a few leading firms. Given their small number they know each other's identity and recognize that they are affected by the output and pricing decisions of the others. They are not only competitors but rivals too. The result of this mutual awareness may lead on some markets to tacit collusion (that is, understood or implied without being stated) between them. It may also lead them to collude expressly. However, other oligopolistic markets are characterized by fierce competition. Thus in some markets the price appears to be set above the competitive level and to approximate monopoly pricing, but in others it is not. A wealth of economic literature has been produced setting out economic models of oligopoly in an attempt to explain why this occurs. The differences in behaviour on these markets also cause problems for those responsible for drafting and applying the competition rules. The mainstream explanations of oligopolistic behaviour and the way in which EC competition law attempts to deal with oligopolistic markets are described in Chapter 11. It is important to note however, that many markets are oligopolistic and that since these markets may also lead to allocative and productive inefficiency they present a major problem for competition authorities.

(vi) Perfect Competition, Monopoly, and Competition in the Real World

Monopolies and oligopolies do exist. Monopolies may be created and maintained by government regulation (utilities and transport markets, for example) and/or may be natural. Pure monopoly is rare outside these circumstances but other markets, although not monopolized, may be dominated by one firm which holds a very large share of the market. Other markets may be oligopolistic, dominated by two, three, or four sellers. Even though there may be a fringe of smaller sellers on this type of market, they may present the same concerns for competition law as those arising on a monopolistic market, as explained in the preceding section.[32]

The analysis set out of perfectly competitive markets above does, however, present a number of problems. The main problem is that in the real world perfectly competitive markets hardly ever exist.[33] Rather, the model of perfect competition is just that—a model. It is a useful starting point because it demonstrates the concepts of productive and allocative efficiency. In reality, however, markets do not possess all the characteristics of perfect competition, and even if they did, the process of competition would tend to alter the situation. For example, goods are rarely homogeneous. Rather, players on competitive markets will usually strive to differentiate their products from those of their competitors, by improvements in quality or service, building up a brand image or adding individual features. They will seek to attract customers with better credit terms, delivery terms, or other conditions of sale. Further, it is very unlikely that an infinite number of firms will be operating at identical costs levels, that producers will not benefit from economies of scale, and that sellers and buyers have perfect information across an atomistic market.[34]

---

[32] For a more detailed discussion see, *infra* Chaps. 5–7 and Chap. 11.

[33] D. W. Carlton and J. M. Perloff, *Modern Industrial Organization* (4th edn., Pearson Addison Wesley , 2005), 84, suggest that the buying and selling of shares on the New York Stock Exchange comes close to satisfying the assumptions for perfect competition.

[34] Where markets are oligopolistic, on the other hand, with only a very small number of firms in the market, the position may be quite different, see *infra* Chap. 11.

Important caveats must thus be attached to the theory that the perfectly competitive market is superior. In particular, in most markets economies of scale make the attainment of perfect competition impossible. In some markets monopolies or different structures are 'natural' because of the MES. Further, it is not actually clear[35] that profit maximization is the policy which firms always pursue. In addition, as Scherer and Ross point out, it might not always be wise to rely on the sovereignty of the consumer.

F. M. Scherer and D. Ross, *Industrial Market Structure and Economic Performance* (3rd edn., Houghton Mifflin, 1990), 29–30

For one, the whole concept of efficient resource allocation is built upon the fundamental belief that the consumer is sovereign—that individual preferences are what count in the ledger of social values . . . . If, for example, consumers freely choosing in the market demonstrate that they would prefer at the margin to give up fifty bushels of grain to get an additional twenty hair shirts, we conclude that society is really better off because of the shift. Yet in practice our respect for consumer sovereignty is by no means universal—not, in any event, for infants, convicted criminals, dope addicts, the mentally ill, and others whose preferences cannot be trusted to generate rational choices. And in this age of widespread neuroses and psychoses, the line between rationality and irrationality is not all that easy to draw. One might even entertain doubts about the soundness of consumption decisions made by presumably normal, rational adults whose tastes (assumed in the standard theory of consumer behaviour to be stable) have been remolded under a barrage of advertising messages. Further qualms intrude when we recognize that there are external diseconomies in consumption, for example, that the purchase of a new hair shirt by Mr Willoughby may not only increase his utility, but simultaneously reduce the utility of envious neighbors. All this warns us that the theorems of welfare economics are erected upon sandy foundations. This does not mean that their conclusions are wrong. The demonstration of a competitive system's allocative efficiency makes considerable sense even when complications related to advertising, ignorance, and the like are introduced. But blind faith is also uncalled for.

The reality is that most markets lie somewhere between perfect competition and monopoly, in a state of 'imperfect' or 'monopolistic' competition where firms make differentiated or heterogeneous products[36] which consumers regard as imperfect substitutes, so that each firm has some degree of market power in that if it raises its prices it will not lose all its customers. The model of perfect competition is nonetheless still useful as a benchmark against which to measure the competitiveness of real markets. The difference between the perfectly competitive and monopolistic (or oligopolistic) market focuses attention on the crucial question: whether the firm or firms have sufficient market power to raise prices above the competitive level and keep them there.

---

[35] See *supra* n. 18.

[36] Or products which consumers think of as differentiated. The differentiation and heterogeneity may mainly be in their minds, perhaps as the result of clever branding or advertising (one can think of the results of blind tastings of different brands of cola drinks).

The value of any model lies not in the absolute fidelity of each element to real world phenomena, but in the model's ability to make useful predictions and, more importantly, its ability to give us meaningful verbal accounts of our observations.[37]

(vii) The Concept of Welfare: Total Welfare, Consumer Welfare and Efficiency Trade-offs

Welfare is the measure of how well a market is performing. A perfectly competitive market maximizes welfare because it leads to efficiency. However, there are different concepts of welfare: total welfare and consumer welfare.

We have seen above that producer surplus is the profit a producer makes by selling goods above the cost of production. Consumer surplus is the difference between what consumers would be prepared to pay for goods and what they do pay. Total welfare is the sum of these two surpluses. The objection to monopoly, it will be recalled, is that it does not just transfer some consumer surplus to producers but that some surplus (the deadweight) is totally lost to the market. That is a loss to total welfare. In a perfectly competitive market both producer and consumer surplus are maximized, but there are few perfectly competitive markets in the real world.

Although, as we will see below, it is arguable that EC competition law may have a more diffuse conception of the welfare of consumers,[38] consumer welfare can be defined for present purposes as consumer surplus (the aggregate measure of the surplus of all consumers).[39] If competition policy is concerned with consumer welfare rather than total welfare it will be concerned with the transfer of surplus from producers to consumers and consider it to be harmful.[40] However, *total* welfare may be maximized by such a transfer. In other words, prohibiting conduct and transactions which reduce consumer welfare may not allow efficiency gains which maximize total welfare. A competition policy which chooses to pursue total welfare as an objective is not concerned about the redistributive effects of efficiency gains (redistribution can be achieved by other policies, such as taxation). This is sometimes called 'the constant dollar' (or constant euro) philosophy, as no value judgment is made as to who, producer or consumer, has the dollar. It is worth remembering, when considering this idea, that in reality 'producers' and 'consumers' are often not separate entities. Consumers may also be shareholders, and many companies have institutional shareholders such as pension funds and life assurance firms whose members will benefit from increases in company profits. We are all consumers but we play other roles too.

Although theory accords prime position to allocative efficiency, improving overall efficiency may require a trade-off between different types of efficiencies and this may have an effect on the relationship between producer and consumer surplus. This is discussed in the following extract, which explains what is meant by a *potential Pareto improvement*.

---

[37] H. Hovenkamp, *Federal Antitrust Policy: The Law of Competition and its Practice* (3rd edn., West , 2005), 39.

[38] *Infra* 48.

[39] See M. Motta, *Competition Policy* (Cambridge University Press, 2004), 18.

[40] See R. J. Van den Bergh and P. D.Camesasca, *European Competition Law and Economics: A Comparative Perspective* (2nd edn., Sweet & Maxwell, 2006), 37.

R. J. Van den Bergh and P. D. Camesasca, *European Competition Law and Economics: A Comparative Perspective* (2nd edn., Sweet & Maxwell, 2006), 29–30

In some cases, allocative efficiency may conflict with other efficiency goals: productive efficiency and dynamic efficiency . . . Productive or technical efficiency implies that output is maximised by using the most effective combination of inputs; hence internal slack (also called X-inefficiency) is absent. The goal of productive efficiency implies that more efficient firms, which produce at lower costs, should not be prevented from taking business away from less efficient ones. Obviously, the achievement of productive efficiency is not a Pareto improvement since the less efficient firms are made worse off. Dynamic efficiency is achieved through the invention, development and diffusion of new products and production processes that increase social welfare. Whereas productive efficiency and allocative efficiency are static notions, progressiveness or dynamic efficiency refers to the rate of technological progress. Again, there will be losers in the dynamic competitive struggle, so that Pareto improvements cannot be reached. To enable policy decisions when the different efficiency goals are not consistent with each other, welfare economics offers the alternative criterion of Kaldor-Hicks efficiency.

A Kaldor-Hicks improvement allows changes in which there are both winners and losers, but requires that the gainers gain more than the losers lose. This condition being satisfied, the winners could compensate the losers . . . and still have a surplus left for themselves . . . A Kaldor-Hicks improvement is also referred to as a potential Pareto improvement, since actual compensation would again satisfy the Pareto criterion. The central value judgment underlying Kaldor-Hicks efficiency is that an exchange of money has a neutral impact on aggregate well-being, which may not be the case when the incomes of gainers and losers differ. By the using the Kaldor-Hicks criterion total welfare is maximised. This welfare notion may allow clearing mergers that enable the merging firms to achieve important scale economies and thus improve productive efficiency, but at the same time enable previously independent firms to collude and raise prices above competitive levels. In terms of total welfare, it is irrelevant that producers rather than consumers capture the surplus produced by achieving efficiencies, as the monopoly overcharge paid by purchasers to stockholders is treated as a transfer from one member of a society to another and so is ignored in the balance.

The question of trade-off between efficiencies and the relationship between efficiency and consumer welfare poses difficult problems for EC competition law and raises the issue of what is called the 'efficiency defence'. For example, a merger may put an undertaking in a position of market power, leading to a loss of allocative efficiency and higher prices for consumers, but also lower costs and increase productive efficiency (through economies of scale for instance). These issues are discussed further in the following chapters of this book.[41]

---

[41] See in particular Chap. 4 (Article 81(3)), Chap. 7 (in relation to abuses of a dominant position), and Chap. 12 (mergers).

(viii) Dynamic Competition

The trade-off between different types of efficiencies mentioned above is particularly acute when dynamic efficiencies are concerned:

... an improvement in terms of dynamic efficiency does not satisfy the Pareto criterion, since this will harm less innovative firms which will lose customers to their technically superior competitors. However, such improvements may satisfy the Kaldor-Hicks criterion since benefits both to pioneering firms and consumers may outweigh losses to non-innovative firms.[42]

It can be argued that monopolies have fewer incentives to innovate than firms in competitive markets but it is also possible that some degree of market power is an incentive to innovate. The Austrian economist Joseph Schumpeter took issue with the idea that competition is a better spur to innovation than monopoly. He considered that a monopolist may be more willing to bear the risks and costs of invention and technical development.[43]

Schumpeter's argument is that competition in innovation is more important than price competition because it is a more effective means of obtaining an advantage over one's competitors. This is known as 'Schumpterian rivalry', where firms compete in a constant race to bring new products on to the market in 'gales of creative destruction', competition is dynamic and positions of market power are short-term as further innovation hands the advantage to another player.

This involves accepting that short-term positions of significant market power may arise but that this is not necessarily inimical to consumer welfare. The following extract from an article by an economist explains why this is so.

D. Hildebrand, 'The European School in EC Competition Law' (2002) 25 *World Competition* 3, 8–9

In the static welfare analysis of market power, it is evidenced that a consumer surplus loss will occur where the consumer willing to pay the marginal cost is not supplied. Indeed this normally occurs when there is an unregulated monopoly that raises price above marginal cost of supply. A measure of the static inefficiency that results is analysed in terms of the actual cost of production in comparison with the minimum production cost (productive inefficiency), and in terms of price set above marginal cost of supply (allocative inefficiency) ... In this static analysis there is a clear total welfare loss associated with the exercise of market power. The static analysis, however, has no time dimension because it is looking at an equilibrium situation. Such an analysis is unable to explain or incorporate technological development or product and process innovation: it is concerned solely with the allocation of resources in the context of fixed technology and a given cost situation. In the real world, product markets evolve over time because of new technological discoveries and the introduction of new and improved products. Such innovation generates

---

[42] R. J. Van den Bergh and P. D. Camesasca, *European Competition Law and Economics: A Comparative Perspective* (2nd edn., Sweet & Maxwell, 2006), 31. And see Case T-168/01 P, *GlaxoSmithKline Services Unlimited v. Commission*, 27 September 2006, discussed *infra* Chap. 4, where it was argued that increased prices to consumers were outweighed by dynamic efficiencies resulting from the undertaking concerned having more profit to plough back into the research and development of pharmaceuticals.

[43] J. A. Schumpeter, *Capitalism, Socialism and Democracy* (Harper, 1942).

welfare gains due to dynamic efficiencies. This means that a proper welfare analysis of market power needs to take into account both the static and dynamic efficiencies—and any trade-off between them.

Where dynamic efficiency aspects are introduced into the competition analysis, it is evident that the presumption that market power leads to a loss of allocative efficiency and to a loss in consumer welfare is crucially predicated on the assumptions that the costs of the firm concerned do not fall due to production rationalization or that product innovation does not occur. According to the European School, the following conclusion can be drawn: market power may speed productivity and growth and reduce the costs of the growth process despite a tendency to a less than optimal allocation of resources in static equilibrium.

Dynamic efficiency is analysed in terms of how total surplus, consumer plus producer surplus, evolves over time with the introduction of a product of process innovation. A new product satisfied a demand that was not catered for before. If the product was supplied at its short run marginal production cost then none of the suppliers would recover their original research and development (R & D) investment. The anticipation of this by suppliers would mean that there would be no incentive to make the investment and develop a new product. Even in a competitive market situation, a firm invests in a project if the net present value of future returns matches the investment outlay and initial losses. The competitive firm's assessment will include the need for at least a normal rate of profit as an equilibrium condition. Suppliers are indifferent between investing and not, if they subsequently earn profits that exactly recover their outlay as well as the normal return on the investment. Product innovation only occurs if firms earn more than just enough to offset their investment. They will only actually invest if they anticipate making profits in excess. Such profits, however, mean pricing above short run minimal average total costs either because there are barriers to entry or because the innovating firm has market power. The market, when it is functioning well, solves this difficult balance by accommodating the creation of temporary positions of market dominance, the resulting super profits attracting all manner and types of entrepreneurial factor which bids away the excessive profit such that in equilibrium the marginal investment will be just offset by the present value of future normal profit.

Concepts of dynamic efficiency and dynamic competition are particularly important now in respect of what is called the 'new economy' of high technology markets.[44]

B. OTHER OBJECTIVES OF COMPETITION LAW

(i) Other Goals for Competition Law?

As we will see in the next section, competition laws have not always pursued, and still do not always pursue, the single goal of economic efficiency. Different jurisdictions may have different goals, and may change their goals over time. Even if one accepts that the goal of competition law is to achieve allocative efficiency and maximize consumer welfare there is the question whether this should be the *only* objective.

Once this has been resolved it will have to be decided what competition law should be adopted and *how* it should be applied in pursuit of these goals. We look first at what other goals competition law might pursue.

---

[44] See *infra* 54 ff.

(ii) Preservation of Liberty and Dispersal of Economic Power

The use of the competition rules to preserve competitive markets may achieve economic efficiency but may also uphold the foundations of liberal democracy. Competitive markets will generally preclude the creation of excessive private power.

G. Amato, *Antitrust and the Bounds of Power* (Hart Publishing, 1997), 2–3

Antitrust law was, as we know, invented neither by the technicians of commercial law (though they became its first specialists) nor by economists themselves (though they supplied its most solid cultural background). It was instead desired by politicians and (in Europe) by scholars attentive to the pillars of the democratic systems, who saw it as an answer (if not indeed 'the' answer) to a crucial problem for democracy: the emergence from the company or firm, as an expression of the fundamental freedom of individuals, of the opposite phenomenon of private power; a power devoid of legitimation and dangerously capable of infringing not just the economic freedom of other private individuals, but also the balance of public decisions exposed to its domineering strength. On the basis of the principles of liberal democracy, the problem was twofold and constituted a real dilemma. Citizens have the right to have their freedoms acknowledged and to exercise them; but just because they are freedoms they must never become coercion, an imposition on others. Power in liberal democratic societies is, in the public sphere, recognized only in those who hold it legitimately on the basis of law, while, in the private sphere, it does not go beyond the limited prerogatives allotted within the firm to its owner. Beyond these limits, private power in a liberal democracy (by contrast with what had occurred, and continues to occur, in societies of other inspirations) is in principle seen to be abusive, and must be limited so that no-one can take decisions that produce effects on others without their assent being given.

The question whether government regulation or the private power of the firm is more frightening is an ideological one which pervades many arguments in competition law, and is a fundamental dilemma of liberal democracy itself. However, one of the most important arguments in favour of a competitive market structure, where the individual sellers and buyers are insignificant in relation to the size of the market, is that it decentralizes and disperses private power and protects individual freedom.[45] This conception of the value of competition is central to the ideas of Ordoliberalism, as discussed below.[46]

(iii) Protecting Competitors and Fair Competition

The preservation of liberty supports competitive markets and may in some markets result in economic efficiency. In other cases the goals may be inimical. Competition laws which are aimed at the dispersal of power as a matter of ideology may favour small businesses and seek to protect them from big business. Instead of protecting *competition* the tendency may instead be to use the competition rules to protect *competitors*. For example, competition law could be used to protect

---

[45] See F. M. Scherer and D. Ross, *Industrial Market Structure and Economic Performance* (3rd edn., Houghton Mifflin, 1990), 18.

[46] *Infra* 34.

small firms from the dominant firm's (efficient) low pricing, or to force a dominant firm to give access to resources it controls to a smaller firm in order to allow the latter to compete with it.[47]

Such a policy may accord with popular sentiment which is distrustful of 'large' firms.[48] It is what is described by some schools of thought as 'populist', as we see below,[49] and can be seen as 'fair' rather than 'free' competition. It will, however, enable a government to nurture small businesses, and to promote a society in which citizens are encouraged to be their own boss, run their own business, and behave in an entrepreneurial manner. The dispersal of market power may prevent the redistribution of wealth from consumers to firms with market power but the protection of small and inefficient businesses may also take wealth from consumers.

(iv) Socio-political Issues

Competition law may also be used to service other policies, such as social, employment, industrial, environmental, and/or regional policy (for example, by prohibiting mergers which will cause job losses, or allowing restrictive agreements which will preserve declining industries for a little longer or produce environmental benefits). The pursuit of such policies may be inconsistent with the pursuit of efficiency.

(v) The EU Dimension

In the European Union there is an added dimension. The competition rules are at present set out within the Treaty establishing the European Community and when/if the new Reform Treaty comes into force they will be set out in the Treaty on the Functioning of the Union. The EU competition rules must therefore be viewed in their context and as one of the tools set out to achieve the aims and objectives of the European Treaties. The history of the EC Treaty, the European Community, and the European Union is explained in Chapter 2. The aims and tasks of the Community, the Union, and the competition rules are, however, introduced in section 5 below.

C. CONCLUSIONS

There seems to be a consensus at present that competition law should be adopted and applied in pursuit of economic efficiency. It will be seen in subsequent sections, however, that there are different views as to how competition law rules can best achieve this. Further, the extent to which competition laws should also be used to pursue goals other than efficiency such as the protection of competitors, jobs, or the environment is controversial.

The pursuit of these other goals may favour small firms, individuals or environmental concerns at the expense of consumer welfare.[50] Supporting small businesses for the sake of it at the

---

[47] See the issue of refusal to supply by dominant forms and the 'essential facilities' doctrine, *infra* Chap. 7, and in respect of intellectual property rights, Chap. 10.

[48] See *infra* p. 27 ff.

[49] *Infra* n. 60.

[50] A good example of the tension between a popular distrust of large and powerful firms coupled with sentimentality towards small businesses on the one hand, and a popular liking for low prices and plenty of choice on the other, can be seen in the debate in the UK over supermarkets which culminated in the market investigation reference of the grocery sector by the OFT to the Competition Commission under s. 131 of the Enterprise Act 2002 in May 2006; see *The Grocery Market, the OFT's reasons for making a reference to the the Competition Commission*, OFT 845. Similarly, although a society may object to the ability of a large company with market power to make excessive profits at the expense of consumers, the shareholders in the monopolist may be institutions such as pension funds and assurance companies which are investing on behalf of the consumers in their role as workers or policy-holders.

expense of more efficient competitors will be a drag on the economy. Similarly, the prevention of a merger which would result in efficiencies on the ground that it may save jobs in the short term may mean that the individual companies are unable to compete effectively on the market in the long run and a decision to allow an anti-competitive agreement between firms in an industry in historic decline may ensure the firm's survival for a time but may cause inefficiency. It may be better for nature to take its course. The most efficient will survive and the remaining resources can be used in new industries which will create future prosperity.

This is not to say that there should not be social, regional, employment, environmental, or other policies. It is a matter of whether, and to what extent, these may be or should be pursued as part of a *competition* policy and how far competition can be isolated from other policies. The question of what concerns competition law should encompass in addition to efficiency is ultimately a matter of political choice, and we return to it below when looking at the 'Chicago school' and at the current objectives of EC competition law.

4. US LAW

It is impossible to discuss competition law without some reference to US law because of the influence which American lawyers and economists, working with reference to the American system, have had on competition law thinking.

The USA was the first jurisdiction to adopt a proper 'modern' system of competition law.[51] The US Congress passed the Sherman Act in 1890.[52] It is still in force. Section 1[53] states:

Every contract, combination in the form of trust or otherwise, or conspiracy, in restraint of trade or commerce among the several States, or with foreign nations, is hereby declared to be illegal. Every person who shall make any contract or engage in any combination or conspiracy hereby declared to be illegal shall be deemed guilty of a felony . . .

Section 2 states:

Every person who shall monopolize, or attempt to monopolize, or combine or conspire with any other person or persons, to monopolize any part of the trade or commerce among several States, or with foreign nations, shall be deemed guilty of a felony . . .

None of the expressions used in the Sherman Act, such as 'in restraint of trade' or 'monopolize' were defined.

The most popular explanation for the passing of the Sherman Act is that it was to combat the power of the 'trusts'. It had become common for the owners of stocks held in competing companies to transfer those stocks to trustees who then controlled the activities of those competitors and consequently lessened competition between them (this is why it has become known as 'antitrust' law). The activities of the railroad companies gave rise to particular

---

[51] For a summary of the ways in which throughout the centuries the English Crown created monopolies and the spasmodic action taken against certain business practices, see M. Furse, *Competition Law of the UK and EC* (4th edn., Oxford University Press, 2004), 2–6; the UK courts developed a doctrine of restraint of trade at common law, but this never developed into a system of competition law: see *Chitty On Contracts* (29th edn., Sweet & Maxwell, 2006), Chap. 16.

[52] 'An Act to protect trade and commerce against unlawful restraints and monopolies', 15 USC, 2 July 1890. It was supplemented by later statutes, the Clayton Act (1914), the Federal Trade Commission Act (1914), the Robinson-Patman Act (1936), the Celler-Kefauver Act (1950) and the Hart-Scott-Rodino Antitrust Improvements Act 1976.

[53] See also *infra* Chap. 4.

concern. It is also claimed, however, that the Sherman Act was more of a protectionist measure passed in response to pressure by farmers, small businesses, or those desiring to stop the transfer of wealth from consumers to big business.[54] The Chicago school[55] view is that it was passed to preserve economic efficiency, but since the theories of allocative efficiency, dead-weight loss, and Pareto-efficiency had not then been invented it cannot have been articulated in exactly this way.[56] The argument about the conception of US antitrust is not merely about history, but is important when considering what the objective of that law is now and in the 'struggle for the soul of antitrust'. It may seem to the neutral observer that in passing the Sherman Act Congress made a law without a discernible policy behind it and that the policy only emerged later. Richard Posner, a leading exponent of the Chicago school, says that the motives of the legislators of 1890 are irrelevant. We explain below the meaning of the expression 'populist' which appears in this extract.

R. A. Posner, *Antitrust Law* (2nd edn., University of Chicago Press, 2001), 24–6

Populists would like the interpretation of the antitrust laws to be guided neither by the common-law background nor by economics, but instead by the prominent vein of populist thought that runs through the legislative history of all the major federal antitrust statutes. But the motive and meaning of legislation are different things. No doubt most of the legislators whose votes were essential to the enactment of these statutes cared more about the distribution of income and wealth and welfare of small business and particular consumer groups than they did about alloca-tive efficiency, especially since the economics profession itself had no enthusiasm for antitrust pol-icy ... But these legislators did not succeed in writing into the statutes standards that would have enabled judges to order these goals and translate them into coherent, administrable legal doc-trine without doing serious and undesired damage to the economy. For guidance the courts per-force turned elsewhere. After a century and more of judicial enforcement of the antitrust statutes, there is a consensus that guidance must be sought in economics. There is no generally accepted principle of statutory interpretation that shows that the courts were wrong to go this route.

The law developed in a series of judicial decisions in the half-century following the Sherman Act in a rather ad hoc manner, and reflected the experiences of the American economy as it went through an industrial revolution, the Depression, and the New Deal.[57] In the 1940s and 1950s the 'workable competition' hypothesis[58] was influential.[59] In the 1950s the

---

[54] See E. T. Sullivan (ed.), *The Political Economy of the Sherman Act* (Oxford University Press, 1991) for a collection of essays written between 1959 and 1989 on the Sherman Act, published to mark the centenary of the Act. The articles display the wide divergence of views between some of the most eminent names in antitrust thinking, as well as historians and Department of Justice officials.

[55] For the Chicago school, see *infra* 23. For Robert Bork's Chicago view of the intention of Congress see R. H. Bork, *The Antitrust Paradox* (Basic Books, 1978, reprinted with a new Introduction and Epilogue, 1993), chap. 2.

[56] Alfred Marshall's *Principles of Economics* (Macmillan, 1890) was first published only in 1890 and Pareto published his theory in 1909. For a good account of the history of the US legislation, see E. Gellhorn., W. E. Kovacic, and S. Calkins, *Antitrust Law and Economics* (5th edn., West, 2004) 22–36.

[57] The New Deal was a federal policy begun under President Roosevelt in 1933 to aid those thrown out of employment in the Depression.

[58] See *infra* 33.

[59] See the Report of the Attorney General's National Committee to Study the Antitrust Laws (1955).

Structure → Conduct → Performance paradigm was developed by what is called the Harvard School, particularly by J. S. Bain. This led to a belief that markets were fragile and to an antitrust policy which intervened to protect small businesses against large firms (a policy which Posner describes as 'populist' because he sees it as based on 'a hostility towards wealth and power and a suspicion of capitalism but a suspicion that falls short of an endorsement of socialism').[60] From the 1950s onwards, however, another school of thinking emerged, the Chicago school, which did *not* believe that markets were fragile. Chicago school thinking had a profound impact on the development of antitrust enforcement in the USA and has influenced the thinking about competition law in Europe and around the world. Later, a school of 'post-Chicago' thinking emerged. The Harvard, Chicago and post-Chicago schools are described in the next sections.

There are three particular features of US antitrust law which should be noted as differing from EC law.[61] These need to be borne in mind when looking at US cases or reading American commentators. First, the US competition authorities, the Department of Justice Antitrust Division (DOJ) and the Federal Trade Commission (FTC), enforce the antitrust laws by bringing actions before the ordinary federal courts: they are primarily prosecutors rather than decision-makers (although the FTC does have administrative adjudication powers and both agencies shape the application of the law by the issuing of guidelines, making speeches, negotiating settlements and so on). The DOJ may bring criminal as well as civil proceedings for violations of the Sherman Act. The state governments (through their attorneys general) may also prosecute federal antitrust infringements and the states have their own state antitrust laws too. This is in contrast to the EC competition authority, the Commission, which enforces the rules by taking decisions binding on the firms concerned, acting as both prosecutor and judge.[62] Secondly, in the US the antitrust laws are the subject of a very significant amount of private litigation, again before the ordinary federal courts. This contrasts with the position in Europe where private litigation has hitherto been relatively rare.[63] The result of these two factors is that US law has been developed on a case by case basis by the courts, while in the EC it has been primarily developed by an administrative authority with the Court acting only to review the legality of the authority's actions. The third matter to note at the outset is that s. 2 of the Sherman Act forbids monopolization and attempts to monopolize. It is thus crucially different from the corresponding provision in EC law, Article 82, which forbids the 'abuse of a dominant position'. The significance of the difference in these provisions is explored further in Chapter 7.

---

[60] R. A. Posner, *Antitrust Law* (2nd edn., University of Chicago Press, 2001), 24. 'Populism' is a term that has been attached to various political movements in different countries (for example, late nineteenth-century Russia) but in general means the preferences of 'ordinary people'. It is characterized by the defence of the little man against powerful organizations, such as governments, large firms, and trade unions.

[61] There are more than three differences of course (e.g., s. 1 of the Sherman Act is structured differently from the EC counterpart, Article 81) but the three mentioned here are particularly crucial.

[62] There is an appeal by way of judicial review to the Court of First Instance (CFI) and from there on a point of law to the European Court of Justice (ECJ). Since 1 May 2004, under Council Regulation 1/2003 [2003] OJ L1/1, all the Member States of the EU must empower their national competition authority (NCA) to apply and enforce the EC competition rules. In many Member States the NCAs have powers similar to those of the EC Commission, whereas in others the NCA prosecutes before the courts.

[63] The 'modernization' of EC law, which came into effect on 1 May 2004, aims, *inter alia*, to encourage greater private enforcement, and the EC Commission is reviewing how private actions may be facilitated: see further *infra* Chaps. 2 and 15.

5. SCHOOLS OF COMPETITION ANALYSIS

A. THE STRUCTURE → CONDUCT → PERFORMANCE PARADIGM AND THE HARVARD SCHOOL

The S → C → P paradigm is that the structure of the market determines the firm's conduct and that conduct determines market performance, for example, profitability, efficiency, technical progress, and growth. The model thus sought to establish that certain industry structures lead to certain types of conduct which then lead to certain kinds of economic performance. In particular, highly concentrated industries cause conduct which leads to poor economic performance, especially reduced output and monopoly prices.

These views stemmed mainly from work done at Harvard University. The initial work was done in the 1930s, particularly by E. S. Mason,[64] and was developed by his pupil J. S. Bain in the 1950s.[65] The theory was developed through empirical studies of American industries (twenty manufacturing industries were studied in the early 1950s) rather than from theoretical models. The conclusion that market structure dictated performance caused a belief that competition law should be concerned with *structural* remedies rather than *behavioural* remedies. The focus of attention was, therefore, on concentrated industries. Bain considered that most industries were more concentrated than was necessary (economies of scale were not substantial in most industries); that barriers to entry were widespread and very high and so new firms were prevented from entering markets; and that the monopoly pricing associated with oligopolies began to occur at relatively low levels of concentration. These influential conclusions coincided with a general trend of US Congressional policies which sought to protect small businesses and which were suspicious of business expansion. This led in the 1960s to an extremely interventionist antitrust enforcement policy in the US.[66] Criticism of the Bainian analysis, led by the Chicago school (below), centred particularly on the fact that the conclusions drawn from the empirical studies were flawed;[67] that they wrongly found barriers to entry to be pervasive and wrongly found economies of scale to be rare. Consequently, the policy of condemning so many business practices as anti-competitive was misconceived. Despite the rise of the Chicago school, the S → C → P paradigm remains a basic tool of competition analysis. Although mainstream

---

[64] See E. S. Mason, *Economic Concentration and the Monopoly Problem* (Harvard University Press, 1957).

[65] See J. S. Bain, *Barriers to New Competition* (Harvard University Press, 1956) and *Industrial Organization* (2nd edn., Wiley, 1968).

[66] e.g., *Brown Shoe Co v. United States*, 370 US 294, 82 S.Ct 1502 (1962); *FTC v. Consolidated Foods Corp* 380 US 592, 85 S.Ct 1220 (1965); *FTC v. Proctor & Gamble Co*, 386 US 568, 87 S.Ct 1224 (1967); *United States v. Arnold, Schwinn & Co*, 388 US 365, 87 S.Ct 1856 (1967).

[67] *Inter alia*, in that they used accounting rates of return to calculate profits although they are unreliable indicators of monopoly profits; that they used cross-sectional data rather than data on a particular industry; that they were not a proper test unless based on long-run rather than short-run performance; and that the researchers did not always consider that the structural variables were not exogenous i.e. that the concentration was itself determined by the economic conditions of the industry. There is modern work with the S → C → P model (notably by John Sutton) which takes account in particular of this last, very serious concern: see further D. W. Carlton and J. M. Perloff, *Modern Industrial Organization* (4th edn., Pearson Addison Wesley, 2005), 246–74.

economists no longer believe that structure *dictates* performance, it accepts that structure is important to the ability of firms to behave anti-competitively. As Hovenkamp says:

The S-C-P paradigm left certain marks that seem all but indelible—for example, the greatly increased attention to market definition, barriers to entry, and proof of market power that even the most convinced members of the Chicago School acknowledge to be important. Antitrust without structural analysis has become impossible, thanks largely to the S-C-P writers. To be sure, they may have gone too far in emphasizing structure over conduct, but that is a question of balance, not of basic legitimacy. Not even S-C-P's most vehement critics would roll the clock back completely.[68]

B. THE CHICAGO SCHOOL

'Chicago' is a school of monetarist and free-market economics, called after the University where many of its originators and adherents did their work.[69] Unlike the Harvard school the foundations of its competition analysis were rigorously theoretical rather than empirical. Even while the S → C → P paradigm was becoming established as the dominant ideology of the day Chicago scholars were loudly decrying it and developing an alternative model based on neo-classical price theory. Although the S → C → P model has never been entirely eclipsed, Chicago school economics produced a 'revolution' in competition thinking both in the US and (later) around the world.[70] Although, in its turn, it has been criticized and some of its most treasured shibboleths found not to withstand further analysis, its influence on competition law is profound. In the USA the ascendancy of Chicago during the 1970s and 1980s led to a change of direction in the application of antitrust law. [71]

The fundamental Chicago view[72] is that the pursuit of efficiency, by which is meant allocative efficiency[73] as defined by the market, should be the *sole* goal of competition law.[74] The school does not support sentimentality for small business or the corner store but places trust in the market. The identity of the winners or losers is irrelevant so long as efficiency is achieved. Indeed, since the writers consider that few barriers to entry exist, that industries frequently benefit from economies of scale, and that businesses are profit-maximizers, the Chicago school places much belief in the ability of the market to correct and achieve efficiency itself without interference from governments or competition laws.

Hovenkamp sets out the basic tenets of the Chicago school in the following extract from an article written in 1985. Although critical of some of the views, Hovenkamp nonetheless describes himself as a 'fellow traveler' [*sic*].

---

[68] H. Hovenkamp, *Federal Antitrust Policy: The Law of Competition and its Practice* (3rd edn., Thomson/West, 2005), 46.

[69] Milton Friedman was a leading figure of the Chicago school. The main proponents of its antitrust ideas include Stigler, Demsetz, Brozen, Posner, and Bork.

[70] See generally R. Posner, 'The Chicago School of Antitrust Analysis' 127 *Univ. Pa. LR.* 925 (1979).

[71] Chicago thinking was behind the entire 'Reaganomics' of the Reagan administration and Chicago School economics have had a profound and lasting influence on the economic policies of governments throughout the world.

[72] We can only describe here the views of Chicago school adherents generally. There are considerable divergences of view among them.

[73] Chicago theory holds that the market itself punishes those who are productively inefficient. As the conditions for Pareto-efficiency can rarely be fulfilled, Chicago usually uses 'potential' Pareto-efficiency as the guide, which means a policy whereby the total gains of all those who gain should be greater than the total losses of all those who lose, see *supra* 13 ff.

[74] Some Chicago adherents would hold that allocative efficiency should be the sole goal of *all* government policies.

H. Hovenkamp, 'Antitrust Policy After Chicago' [1985] *Univ. Mich. LR* 213, 226–9

...the following discussion summarizes a few of the model's basic assumptions and principles that have been particularly important in Chicago School antitrust scholarship.

(1) Economic efficiency, the pursuit of which should be the exclusive goal of the antitrust laws, consists of two relevant parts: allocative efficiency and productive efficiency... Occasionally practices that increase a firm's productive efficiency reduce the market's allocative efficiency. For example, construction of a large plant and acquisition of large market share may increase a firm's productive efficiency by enabling it to achieve economics of scale; however, these actions may simultaneously reduce allocative efficiency by facilitating monopoly pricing. A properly defined antitrust policy will attempt to maximize net efficiency gains...

(2) Most markets are competitive, even if they contain a relatively small number of sellers. Furthermore, product differentiation tends to undermine competition far less than was formerly presumed. As a result, neither high market concentration nor product differentiation are the anti-competitive problems earlier oligopoly theorists believed them to be...

(3) Monopoly, when it exists, tends to be self-correcting; that is, the monopolist's higher profits generally attract new entry into the monopolist's market, with the result that the monopolist's position is quickly eroded. About the best that the judicial process can do is hasten the correction process...

(4) 'Natural' barriers to entry are more imagined than real. As a general rule investment will flow into any market where the rate of return is high. The one significant exception consists of barriers to entry that are not natural—that is, barriers that are created by government itself. In most markets the government would be best off if it left entry and exit unregulated...

(5) Economies of scale are far more pervasive than economists once believed, largely because earlier economists looked only at intra-plant or production economics, and neglected economies of distribution. As a result, many more industries than were formerly thought may operate most economically only at fairly high concentration levels...

(6) Business firms are profit-maximizers. That is, their managers generally make decisions that they anticipate will make the firm more profitable than any alternative decision would. The model would not be undermined, however, if it should turn out that many firms are not profit maximizers, but are motivated by some alternative goal, such as revenue maximization, sales maximization, or 'satisficing.'...[75] The integrity of the market efficiency model requires only that a few firms be profit-maximizers. In that case, the profits and market shares of these firms will grow at the expense of other firms in the market...

(7) Antitrust enforcement should be designed in such a way as to penalize conduct precisely to the point that it is inefficient, but to tolerate or encourage it when it is efficient... During the Warren Court era,[76] antitrust enforcement was excessive, and often penalized efficient conduct...

(8) The decision to make the neoclassical market efficiency model the exclusive guide for antitrust policy is nonpolitical.

---

[75] For 'satisficing' see *supra* n. 18.

[76] Earl Warren was Chief Justice of the Supreme Court 1953–68.

A clear statement of the view that 'efficiency is all' is set out in Robert Bork's celebrated polemic, *The Antitrust Paradox*.

R. H. Bork, *The Antitrust Paradox: A Policy at War with Itself* (Basic Books, 1978, reprinted with a new Introduction and Epilogue, 1993), 90–1

Antitrust is about the effects of business behavior on consumers. An understanding of the relationship of that behavior to consumer well-being can be gained only through basic economic theory. The economic models involved are essential to all antitrust analysis, but they are simple and require no previous acquaintance with economics to be comprehended. Indeed, since we can hardly expect legislators, judges, and lawyers to be sophisticated economists as well, it is only the fact that the simple ideas of economics are powerful and entirely adequate to this field that makes it conceivable for the law to frame and implement useful policy.

Consumer welfare is greatest when society's economic resources are allocated so that consumers are able to satisfy their wants as fully as technological constraints permit. Consumer welfare, in this sense, is merely another term for the wealth of the nation. Antitrust thus has a built-in preference for material prosperity, but it has nothing to say about the ways prosperity is distributed or used. Those are matters for other laws. Consumer welfare, as the term is used in antitrust, has no sumptuary or ethical component, but permits consumers to define by their expression of wants in the marketplace what things they regard as wealth. Antitrust litigation is not a process for deciding who should be rich or poor, nor can it decide how much wealth should be expended to reduce pollution or undertake to mitigate the anguish of the cross-country skier at the desecration wrought by snowmobiles. It can only increase collective wealth by requiring that many lawful products, whether skis or snowmobiles, be produced and sold under conditions most favorable to consumers.

The role of the antitrust laws, then, lies at that stage of the economic process in which production and distribution of goods and services are organized in accordance with the scale of values that consumers choose by their relative willingness to purchase. The law's mission is to preserve, improve, and reinforce the powerful economic mechanisms that compel businesses to respond to consumers. 'From a social point of view,' as Frank H. Knight puts it, 'this process may be viewed under two aspects, (a) the assignment or *allocation* of the available productive forces and materials among the various lines of industry, and (b) the effective *co-ordination* of the various means of production in each industry into such groupings as will produce the greatest result.' . . .

These two factors may conveniently be called *allocative efficiency* and *productive efficiency* . . . . These two types of efficiency make up the overall efficiency that determines the level of our society's wealth, or consumer welfare. The whole task of antitrust can be summed up as the effort to improve allocative efficiency without impairing productive efficiency so greatly as to produce either no gain or a net loss in consumer welfare. That task must be guided by basic economic analysis, otherwise the law acts blindly upon forces it does not understand and produces results it does not intend.

Critics have argued that efficiency could not be the sole pursuit of competition law without becoming inconsistent with other government policies, such as those pursuing distributive goals.[77]

---

[77] The arguments are summed up in the Hovenkamp article an extract from which is set out *supra* 24.

Bork made a riposte to this in the Epilogue to his book reprinted in 1993:

R. H. Bork, *The Antitrust Paradox: A Policy at War with Itself* (Basic Books, 1978, reprinted with a new Introduction and Epilogue, 1993), 426–9

Of the two, the issue of the goals of antitrust seems to have fared somewhat better than the law's capacity to deal with economics. Fifteen years ago, the question of what goals antitrust serves, and hence what factors a judge may properly consider in deciding an antitrust case, had not been addressed in any systemic fashion. The answers given by courts and commentators were hardly more than slogans of a more or less appealing variety, depending on your taste for populist rhetoric. Though the preservation of competition was often cited as the aim of the law, there seemed no agreed definition of what, for the purposes of antitrust, competition is.

'Competition,' the courts assured us, meant the preservation or comfort of small businesses, the advancement of first amendment values, the preservation of political democracy, the preservation of local ownership, and so on ad infinitum. Judges could and did choose among the items they had invented and placed in this grab bag in order to legislate freely. Cornucopias have their attractions but, when it comes to finding and applying a policy to guide adjudication, horns of plenty make anything resembling a rule of law impossible.

The argument of this book, of course, is that competition must be understood as the maximization of consumer welfare or, if you prefer, economic efficiency. That requires economic reasoning because courts must balance, when they conflict, possible losses of efficiency in the allocation of resources with possible gains in the productive use of those resources. In a word, the goal is maximum economic efficiency to make us as wealthy as possible. The distribution of that wealth or the accomplishment of noneconomic goals are the proper subjects of other laws and not within the competence of judges deciding antitrust cases.

By and large, with some ambiguity at times, the more recent cases have adopted a consumer welfare model. Aside from some explicit statements to that effect, the best evidence for the proposition is that courts now customarily speak the language of economics rather than pop sociology and political philosophy. If the conversion from a multi-goal jurisprudence is not complete, it is nevertheless very substantial. Explicit opposition to the consumer welfare thesis comes less from judges than from the academics. The objections are generally of two kinds: denial that an exclusive consumer welfare focus is to be found in the various antitrust statutes; and insistence that such a policy is not desirable.

. . .

A different line of attack comes from those who observe, quite correctly, that people value things other than consumer welfare, and, therefore, quite incorrectly, that antitrust ought not be confined to advancing that goal. As non sequiturs go, that one is world class. There may be someone identified with the Chicago School who thinks all human activity can be analyzed in terms of economics and efficiency, but that is not true of most Chicagoans and certainly constitutes no part of my argument. No one body of law can protect everything that people value. If antitrust could, we would need no other statutes. If we trace the implications of the proposition, it results in judges deciding cases as if the Sherman Act said: 'A restraint of trade shall consist of any contract, combination, or conspiracy that fails to produce, in the eyes of the court, the optimum mix of consumer welfare and other good things that Americans want.' That is inevitably the result of bringing into judicial consideration an open-ended list of attractive-sounding goals to be weighed against consumer welfare.

Nor is there any force to the argument that the consumer welfare cannot be the exclusive mission of antitrust since that mission will be rendered less effective unless all other government policies pursue the same goal. Of course, antitrust will be less effective in promoting consumer welfare if government simultaneously subsidizes small business. A tariff policy designed to keep American companies viable will be less effective if government allows foreign competitors to set up manufacturing operations in the United States. That fact does not state a reason for a judge to alter the way he construes the tariff laws or other laws that apply to foreign companies' operations here. Many statutory policies conflict to some degree with other statutory policies. Whether or not they should do so, and to what degree, is a subject for legislation rather than adjudication.

In any event, no matter what policy goals or combination of goals one attributes to antitrust, the effectiveness of the law in forwarding those policies will be diminished by other public policies. That fact tells us nothing about how judges should go about deciding cases under the antitrust statutes.

Furthermore, in the following extract from the 2001 second edition of Posner's seminal book first published in 1976, he takes issue with the populist view that would seek still to use competition laws to promote goals other than efficiency.

R. A. Posner, *Antitrust Law* (2nd edn., University of Chicago Press, 2001), 24–5

Populists complain that monopolization transfers wealth from consumers to the stockholders of monopolistic firms, a redistribution that goes from the less to the more wealthy. The transfer, unlike the restriction in output that monopoly pricing entails, has no direct effect on efficiency, though some economists have long argued that, given diminishing marginal utility of income, a transfer of income from a wealthy to a poor person increases the utility of the poor person more than it reduces the utility of the wealthy person. The argument is plausible in extreme cases: a dollar surely confers more utility on an indigent person than on a billionaire. But applied to monopolies and cartels, it is undermined not only by the increasingly broad ownership of common stock, both directly and by virtue of pension-fund investments in the stock market, but also by the point made earlier that competition to become a monopolist will tend to transform the expected gains from the monopoly into social costs experienced as income by people not necessarily wealthier than the consumers of the monopoly's product. What is more, any windfall gains from monopolization will be enjoyed only by the first generation of the monopolist's shareholders, since anyone who buys their stock will pay a premium equal to the discounted present value of the expected monopoly profits, and so will earn only a normal, not a monopoly, return on his investment. In any event—and this is the most important point—the wealth-redistribution argument for antitrust has no implications for the content of antitrust policy. Whether the objection undergirding the policy is to the monopolist's distortion of output or to his profit, the measures required to meet the objection are the same.

A second populist concern is that monopoly, or more broadly any condition (such as concentration) that fosters cooperation among competing firms, will facilitate an industry's manipulation of the political process to obtain protective legislation aimed at increasing the industry's profits. Traditionally such protection took the form of controls over entry and price competition, coupled with exemption from the antitrust laws, that cartelized the industry much more effectively than could be done by private agreement. Once again, this is a concern that reinforces rather than contradicts the economic objection to monopoly. The legislation sought by an industry—a tariff, a tax on a substitute product, control of entry—will have economic effects similar to those of a private cartel agreement.

process, as well as directly through cartelization, thus implies no change in the character of an antitrust policy deduced from economic considerations. Nevertheless, it is not a solid argument. While monopoly or concentration reduces the costs of organizing effectively to manipulate the political process, it also reduces the demand for public assistance in suppressing competition. A firm that has a secure monopoly without public assistance or enjoys supracompetitive profits by reason of tacit collusion will have less incentive to expend resources on obtaining the aid of government in fending off competition than a highly competitive industry would have. The latter must incur higher costs of organizing to influence government, but it also has more to gain. The up-shot is that it's unclear as a matter of theory which type of industry, the monopolistic or the competitive, has more to gain from government intervention. This theoretical indeterminacy is mirrored in the empirical world, where we observe many unconcentrated industries—such as dairy farming, local broadcasting, taxi service, medicine, and law—enjoying governmental protection against competition.

A third populist argument has, in contrast, implications for antitrust policy that diverge sharply from those of the economic approach. The populist alternative to an antitrust policy designed to promote economic efficiency by limiting monopoly is a policy of restricting the freedom of action of large business firms in order to promote small business. The idea that there is some special virtue in small business compared to large is a persistent one, though the basis for the idea is obscure. While there may be a justifiable concern with the power of wealth to influence and perhaps deform the political process, the correlation between personal wealth and monopolization is weak. Among the wealthiest Americans today are trial lawyers, athletes, actors and actresses, other entertainers and media celebrities, and entrepreneurs few of whom owe their wealth to market power. Small businesses do not seem disadvantaged in lobbying relative to large, and large businesses are more likely to owe their size to economies of scale or scope, superior management, patents and copyrights, and other factors than even populists do not wish to bring under antitrust condemnation than to monopoly. Small businesses are not less likely than large to violate the antitrust laws or to seek and obtain protection from competition. Indeed, to the extent that small businesses tend to be found in small markets, they are as likely, even more likely, to collude to raise price above the competitive level. . . .

Antitrust enforcement is not only an ineffectual, but a perverse, instrument for trying to promote the interests of small business as a whole. Antitrust objectives and the objectives of small business people are incompatible at a very fundamental level. The best overall antitrust policy from a small-business standpoint is no antitrust policy. By driving a wedge between the prices and the costs of the larger firms in the market (a market cannot be effectively cartelized unless the large firms in it participate in the cartel), monopoly enables the smaller firms to survive even if their costs are higher than those of the large firms. The only kind of antitrust policy that would benefit small business would be one that sought to prevent large firms from underpricing less efficient small firms by sharing their lower costs with consumers in the form of lower prices. Apart from raising in acute form the question whether society should promote small business at the expense of the consumer, such a policy would be unworkable because it would require comprehensive and continuing supervision of the prices of large firms. There are no effective shortcuts. For example, if mergers between large firms are forbidden because of concern that they will enable the firms resulting from such mergers to take advantage of economies of scale and thereby underprice smaller firms operating at a less efficient scale, one or more of the larger firms will simply expand until the efficient scale of operation is reached.

Perhaps the most contentious of all Chicago school claims is that the pursuit of efficiency as the sole goal of competition law is non-political. The essential argument is that since competition policy is dictated only by micro-economics it is ideology-free. The adoption of such a policy is, however, in itself ideological. Chicago proclaims itself as neutral because it believes only in market forces. The idea that this is an apolitical stance is challenged by Fox and Sullivan in the following passages from an article in 1987.[78] In particular, the authors stress that the law should not only be economics. Rather, economics should be used as a tool to support the system which is aimed at supporting consumers and a dynamic system of competition law. The Chicagoans' view of economics itself reflects a vision of what society we should live in.

E. M. Fox and L. A. Sullivan, 'Antitrust—Retrospective and Prospective: Where Are We Coming From? Where Are we Going?' (1987) 62 *New York Univ LR* 936, 956–9

Economists have both praised and criticized mainstream antitrust law. Many economists, especially those with Chicago leanings, think that because antitrust is about markets, as is microeconomics, antitrust law should *be* economics. They react as though the law is out of kilter whenever it diverges from their particular economic insight; and they so react regardless of whether the law diverges because empirical processes have not validated factual assumptions, or because the law has identified social goals other than or in addition to allocative efficiency. Law is not economics. Nor were the antitrust laws adopted to squeeze the greatest possible efficiency out of business. Nonetheless, we would not want an antitrust system that hurts consumers rather than helps them. Most people agree that economics is a tool that can help keep the system on course to help consumers and to facilitate dynamic competition. Economic analysts have provided important insights into why business acts the way it does, and what the probable effect of a practice will be on the marketplace. Despite the consensus that economics can play a supporting role, the Chicago School, in the name of law and economics, has waged ideological warfare, assaulting antitrust itself. Commitment and belief fuel the debate on both sides. While others seem aware that the debate is about values, Chicagoans seem not to be. They often claim the imperative of science for their policy prescriptions. But on points of basic difference between Chicagoans on the one hand and realists or traditionalists on the other, the Chicago assertions are not provable. They are not matters of fact. They cannot be derived from economics. The basic difference between Chicagoans and traditionalists is a difference of vision about what kind of society we are and should strive to be . . .

. . .

The Chicago beliefs are compatible with only the most minimal law. In antitrust, the most minimal law, given the existence of the statutes, is law that proscribes only clear cartel agreements and mergers that would create a monopoly in a market that included all perceptible potential competition. Let us review the characteristics that underlie this minimalist approach to antitrust.

First, the Chicago School claims that it has the right prescription for efficiency. This is unprovable; some would say highly suspect, and others would say wrong. Economic experts have intense debates as to what scheme is likely to produce a more efficient or a more dynamic, inventive economy. Economics does not provide a conclusive answer. Within a wide range, the answer is indeterminate . . .

---

[78] One needs only to look at the USA in the 1980s. The economics of Chicago were those of the American Right. Robert Bork was President Reagan's nominee for the Supreme Court, but he was rejected by the Senate (although that had more to do with his conservative views on matters such as abortion than with his views on barriers to entry).

Second, the Chicago School always opts for norms that presuppose that markets are robust and that firms, imbued with perfect knowledge and risk neutrality, move their resources quickly and easily to the most profitable opportunity. Data about how people actually behave belie these assumptions . . . Yet Chicagoans continue to press for legal rules that accept these assumptions as true . . . It is this mind-set that led Judge Posner to dissent in a recent case in which a prisoner was blinded in jail and sued prison authorities for neglect . . . A majority of the appellate court thought that appointment of counsel was improperly denied to the prisoner, but Judge Posner disagreed . . . Assuming the existence of a market for lawyers that would function like a Chicago model market, Judge Posner argued that if the prisoner's case was any good, a lawyer would have taken it on contingency. The fact that no lawyer did 'proved' that the prisoner's case lacked merit . . . [79]

Third, the Chicago School defines competition in terms of efficiency; defines efficiency as the absence of inefficiency; defines inefficiency in terms of artificial output restraint; . . . and thus concludes that any activity that does not demonstrably limit output is efficient and therefore procompetitive. Thus, it 'proves' that almost all business activity is efficient—a neat trick.

Fox and Sullivan thus question the bases of many of the views on which the Chicago concept of efficiency is hung and hence challenge its utter faith in the ability of the market to correct itself. Criticisms have also been made in the Chicagoans' belief that barriers to entry are rare outside government regulation,[80] that potential competition polices the market as well as existing competitors because, in the absence of barriers to entry, monopolists will be challenged by new entrants if they reap monopoly profits, and that most markets are competitive. The Chicago model is criticized for being 'static' and concentrating too much on long-term effects rather than on short-term effects and of competition as a *process* Above all, it is argued that the neoclassical market efficiency model of Chicago is too simple to account for or predict business behaviour in the real world.

C. POST-CHICAGO

Whatever criticisms can be and have been made of the Chicago school, it undeniably changed competition law thinking profoundly. It placed rigorous economic analysis at the centre of competition law. After Chicago it is impossible to accept the S → C → P paradigm without qualification, or not to think of efficiency as a central concern. It shed new light on many matters.

More recently, however, there has been a synthesist of different strands of thought. Extreme Chicago ideas have been tempered by new insights. There is a general recognition that economics may give indications of what questions to ask, but does not always yield definitive answers, and certainly not answers which are necessarily value-free. What is called modern industrial organization theory or new industrial economics stresses the effect that the *strategic conduct* of firms can have in different market situations. It considers that firms may indulge in strategic entry deterrence, for example. So the belief that predatory pricing is rarely rational conduct, as Chicagoans said, is replaced with the idea that it can in some circumstances be adopted as a rational strategy to prevent new competitors entering the market.[81] Post-Chicago

---

[79] The case concerned was *Merritt v. Faulkner*, 697 F. 2d 761 (7th Cir). This story rather puts into the shade the classic Chicago school joke. A lawyer and a Chicago scholar walk along the pavement. The lawyer says 'Oh look, there's a £20 note lying on the pavement'. 'No', says the Chicago scholar, 'there can't be. If there was, someone would have picked it up'.

[80] See the discussion of barriers to entry *infra* 84 ff.

[81] See *infra* Chap. 7.

competition scholarship admits of more complexities than either the pure Harvard or Chicago approaches and 'helps observers understand why conduct thought benign in light of Chicago School teaching might in fact lessen competition'.[82] It also attempts to deal with the importance of dynamic competition.[83] Other ideas and theories which inform post-Chicago thinking include the following:

(i) Game Theory

Game theory is central to much modern industrial organization theory and stems from work done in the 1940's by von Neumann and Morgenstern.[84] It models the strategic interactions between firms—their conflict and cooperation—as 'games' in which each firm plans its own strategy, for example with regard to pricing or output, in the light of assumptions about the strategy which will be adopted by its competitors. Game theory is in particular an important tool in analysing the conduct of oligopolies and is dealt with further in that context in Chapter 14.

(ii) Contestable Markets

The theory of contestable markets[85] places the main emphasis on freedom of entry to, and exit from, a market. It attaches importance not to the structure of the market but to its contestability. So long as 'hit-and-run' entry by competitors is possible the behaviour of firms operating on the market will be constrained and they will perform efficiently and price competitively. The minimum conditions for a contestable market are instantaneous entry and costless exit and, crucially, the inability of the incumbent to respond to entry by another competitor by lowering its prices. This last point is vital because otherwise the incumbent firm can keep its prices at monopoly level and only lower them when it needs to respond to competition. In reality, again, the conditions for perfect contestability are not often found.[86] However, the term 'contestable market', meaning one with low barriers to entry and exit where the threat of entry does significantly constrain the incumbent, is used more loosely and is now often found in competition law discussion.[87]

(iii) Raising Rivals' Costs

Raising rivals' costs describes strategic behaviour of a firm which is designed to raise the costs of its rivals relative to its own.[88] It normally requires some degree of market power (or, for some strategies, political power or influence). It includes interfering with the production or selling methods of rivals, lobbying for or supporting government regulation which has a differential impact on the rivals' costs, raising the price of inputs, tying, raising switching costs (so that

---

[82] E. Gellhorn, W. Kovacic, S. Calkins, *Antitrust Law and Economics* (5th edn., West, 2004), 97.

[83] See *supra* 15.

[84] J. von Meumann and O. Morgenstern, *The Theory of Games and Economic Behaviour* (Princeton University Press, 1944).

[85] W. J. Baumol, J. Panzar, and R. Willig, *Contestable Markets and the Theory of Industry Structure* (Harcourt Brace Jovanovich, 1982); W. J. Baumol, 'Contestable Markets: An Uprising in the Theory of Industry Structure' (1982) 72 *Amer Economic Rev* 1.

[86] Sunk costs, for example, will be a hindering factor, see *infra* 88.

[87] S. Bishop and M. Walker, *The Economics of EC Competition Law* (2nd edn., Sweet & Maxwell, 2002), 3.33.

[88] T. G. Krattenmaker and S. C. Salop, 'Anticompetitive Exclusion; Raising Rivals' Costs to Achieve Power Over Price' 96 *Yale LJ* 209.

customers find it difficult or expensive to change to the rival's goods or services) and indulging in rapid product innovation in primary markets.[89] Some behaviour which raises rivals' costs may also increase welfare and whether competition law should sanction or allow it often depends on the particular circumstance of the case. In the following chapters of this book we will come across many examples of behaviour which can raise rivals' costs.[90]

(iv) Transaction Cost Economics

Transaction cost economics is based on the theory first developed by Ronald Coase in *The Nature of the Firm*.[91] Transaction costs are the costs a firm incurs by trading with other parties. Coase's argument was that a firm can choose to organize its activities by doing things itself (so internalising the costs) or by using other parties to do them (i.e. using the market). A firm producing widgets may therefore may have a choice between itself producing the inputs necessary for widget production and obtaining them from other parties. Similarly it may have a choice between doing its own distribution and using independent distributors. The first of these options in each case involves vertical integration while the second involves agreements with others. Which is chosen will depend on its comparative efficiency. The insight from transaction cost economics for competition law is that competition law should not be designed so as to force firms to take less efficient options for doctrinaire reasons of promoting more competitive markets.

Transaction cost research has identified efficiency reasons for which firms use various forms of internal organization and has underscored the importance of contractual techniques in curbing opportunistic behavior that, if left unchecked, undermines business arrangements that increase efficiency. By showing that the main purpose of many forms of economic organization—for example, joint ventures, vertical integration, and restrictive distribution contracts—often is to reduce costs, transaction costs scholars have spurred a reevaluation of antitrust doctrines that have treated such arrangements with hostility.[92]

Therefore, in contrast to other ideas taken on board by post-Chicago thinking, such as the anti-competitive effects of strategic behaviour, transaction cost economics point to a less expansive application of competition rules.

(v) Conclusion

Post-Chicago analysis is more complex than either the original S→C→P paradigm or pure Chicago. It accepts the efficiency goal but recognizes the real-life complications in devising competition rules to achieve this. As far as application and enforcement are concerned, post-Chicago analysis makes greater demands on competition authorities and decision-makers because of the very wealth of models and theories that may fall to be considered.

---

[89] See D. W. Carlton and J. M. Perloff, *Modern Industrial Organization* (4th edn., Pearson Addison Wesley, 2005), 371–9.

[90] See in particular Chaps. 7 and 12.

[91] *Economica* 4, 386 (1937). See also the work of Oliver Williamson, particularly 'Transaction Cost Economics' in R. Schmalensee and R. D. Willig (eds.), *1 Handbook of Industrial Organization* (1989) 135.

[92] E. Gellhorn, W. Kovacic, S. Calkins, *Antitrust Law and Economics* (5th edn., West, 2004), 101. See also R. J. Van den Bergh and P. D. Camesasca, *European Competition Law and Economics: A Comparative Perspective* (2nd edn., Sweet & Maxwell, 2006), 94–8; P. L. Joskow, 'The Role of Transaction Cost Economics in Antitrust and Public Utility Regulatory Policies' (1991) 7 JL Economic & Org 53.

D. OTHER SCHOOLS, THEORIES, AND CONCEPTS

The following should also be noted:

(i) Workable Competition

In the 1940's the theory of 'workable competition' was developed.[93] This was associated with the Harvard School and held that as perfect competition was usually impossible to attain competition policy should aim to produce the best competitive arrangement practically attainable. This too presented difficulties. The criteria by which workability can be assessed may be divided into structure, conduct and performance criteria but it may be hard to assess whether or not they have been satisfied in any particular industry; and if some are satisfied and some not, it may be hard to decide whether workability has been attained without making subjective value judgments.[94] Workable competition, in short, does not provide a very workable basis for developing a sound competition policy. The European Court of Justice (ECJ) referred to workable competition in 1976 in *Metro I*, equating it with 'the degree of competition necessary to ensure the observance of the basic requirements and the attainment of the objectives of the [EC] Treaty'.[95]

(ii) The Austrian School

The Austrian School embraces a theory of dynamic competition which goes beyond that advanced by Schumpeter.[96] As with Chicago, the Austrian School's conception of competition policy is just one facet of a wider school of economic theory,[97] one of whose most influential voices in the twentieth century was von Hayek.[98] Von Hayek believed in untrammelled free markets and the ability of potential competition to prevent the long-run exploitation of monopoly power. The implications of this were that competition laws should not interfere with the competitive process, not even by prohibiting cartels.[99]

(iii) Effective Competition

The concept of *effective competition* is found in EC competition law. The ECJ defines a dominant position for the purposes of Article 82[100] as involving an undertaking's power to 'prevent effective competition being maintained on the relevant market'[101] and under the EC Merger

---

[93] J. M. Clark, 'Towards a Concept of Workable Competition' (1940) 30 *American Economic Review* 241–56; see also S. Sosnick, 'A Critique of Concepts of Workable Competition' (1958) 72 *Quarterly Journal of Economics* 380–423.

[94] See further F. M. Scherer and D. Ross, *Industrial Market Structure and Economic Performance* (3rd edn., Houghton Mifflin, 1990) 52–5; R. J. Van den Bergh and P. D. Camesasca, *European Competition Law and Economics: A Comparative Perspective* (2nd edn., Sweet & Maxwell, 2006), 70–3.

[95] Case 26/76, *Metro v. Commission (No. 1)* [1977] ECR 1875, [1978] 2 CMLR 1, para. 20.

[96] See *supra* 15.

[97] Originating with Carl Menger, Professor of Economics at the University of Vienna, 1873–1903.

[98] Friedrich von Hayek held chairs from 1931 on at various universities: in London (the London School of Economics), Germany and Austria and, from 1950 to 1962, at the University of Chicago.

[99] See further R. J. Van den Bergh and P. D. Camesasca, *European Competition Law and Economics: A Comparative Perspective* (2nd edn., Sweet & Maxwell, 2006), 88.

[100] One of the two main competition law Articles. See *infra* Chaps. 5–7.

[101] Case 2/76, *United Brands v. Commission* [1978] ECR 207, [1978] 1 CMLR 429, para. 65; Case 85/76, *Hoffmann-La Roche & Co AG v. Commission* [1979] ECR 461, [1979] 3 CMLR 211, para. 38.

Regulation the grounds for the prohibition of a merger are that it would 'significantly impede effective competition'.[102] The Court of First Instance said in *GlaxoSmithKline* that 'the competition referred to in Article 3(1)(g) EC and Article 81 EC is taken to mean effective competition, that is to say, the degree of competition necessary to ensure that attainment of the objectives of the Treaty'.[103] Bishop and Walker suggest that 'effective competition' should be outcome-based.

S. Bishop and M. Walker, *The Economics of EC Competition Law* (2nd edn., Sweet & Maxwell, 2002), 16

2.10 ... The economic goal of EC competition law is the protection and promotion of effective competition. But this is a goal only because of the benefits that it delivers to European consumers. What matters therefore are the outcomes for consumers that competition in a particular market delivers—not the particular form that the competition process takes. Whether a market is characterized by effective competition or not therefore depends on the outcomes it produces.

This raises the question of what outcomes are produced by effective competition and how can they be distinguished from those produced by less than effective competition. The practical application of competition law ought to be interested less in outcomes that are desirable in some theoretical, abstract sense and more in outcomes that are feasible for regulatory intervention to achieve.... To draw this distinction requires consideration of the various economic models of competition and the implications each type of model has for consumer welfare.

---

6. ORDOLIBERALISM

Ordoliberalism is not a just school of competition or economic theory but an entire political and economic philosophy. However, it has important implications for competition policy and it is therefore convenient to mention it here before looking in the section below at its influence on the development of EC competition law.

Ordoliberalism was conceived in Germany in the 1930's and nurtured at the University of Freiburg during the Nazi era.[104] It became a key element of post-war thinking in Germany, envisaging a new relationship between law and the economic system and holding that competition is necessary for economic well-being and that economic freedom is necessary for political freedom.[105] It advocates an 'economic constitution' whereby competition and economic freedom are embedded into the law so that there is neither unconstrained private

---

[102] Council Regulation 139/2004 [2004] OJ L124/1, Art. 2(3). The previous Merger Regulation, Council Regulation 4064/89 [1990] OJ L257/13, also employed the concept of 'effective competition', see *infra* Chap. 12.

[103] Case T-168/01, *GlaxoSmithKline Services Unlimited* v. *Commission* [2006] ECR II-2969, [2006] 5 CMLR 1623, para. 109.

[104] Hence its alternative name of the 'Freiburg School'. The leading ordoliberal theorists were the economist Walter Eucken and the lawyers Franz Böhm and Hanns Grossmann-Doerth. See further D. Gerber, 'Constitutionalizing the Economy: German Neo-liberalism, Competition Law and the 'New Europe' (1994) 42 *American Journal of Comparative Law* 25.

[105] W. Möschel, 'Competition Policy from an Ordo Point of View' in A. Peacock and H. Willgerodt (eds.), *German Neo-Liberals and the Social Market Economics* (MacMillan, 1989), 142.

power nor discretionary governmental intervention in the economy. Competition law, it holds, should create and protect the conditions of competition. It follows from this that competition is a value in itself and not just a means by which purely economic objectives—such as efficiency—are to be achieved. An ordoliberal approach to competition policy leads to the protection of *competitors* and small and medium sized enterprises, regardless of the effects on efficiency, rather than the protection of *competition*, as it prizes the freedom of all citizens to be able to enter and compete on markets.

R. O'Donoghue and A. J. Padilla, *The Law and Economics of Article 82* (Oxford University Press, 2006), 9

Ordoliberal thinking on the goal of competition law was based on notions of "fairness" and that firms with market power should behave "as if" there was effective competition . . . This reflected a view that small and medium sized enterprises were important to consumer welfare and that they should receive some protection from the excesses of market power. Ordoliberal thought therefore considered that certain restrictions on dominant firm behaviour were necessary and appropriate. The basic notion was was that firms with economic power should not engage in conduct that unfairly limited rivals' access to markets or production. Of course, dominant firms had to be allowed the commercial freedom to compete on the merits. In this regard, ordoliberal thinking developed a notion of "performance-based competition" (*Leistungswettgewerb*). For example, non-predatory lower prices, better quality products, or better services were all considered as legitimate ways of excluding rival firms and should be permitted, whereas conduct that was not performance-based competition (e.g., below-cost prices) should be prohibited.

We see in later chapters of this book how ordoliberal thinking influenced the development of the law on Articles 81 and Article 82 of the EC Treaty.

7. EC COMPETITION LAW

A. GENERAL

The first 'European' competition rules were Articles 65 and 66 of the Treaty of Paris of 1951, which created the European Coal and Steel Community (ECSC).[106] The Treaty of Rome, which established the European Economic Community (EEC), and the competition rules set within it

---

[106] They were based on a draft prepared, at the behest of Jean Monnet, by the Harvard antitrust lawyer Robert Bowie, who was an adviser to John McCloy, the US High Commissioner for Germany and a close ally of Monnet. Monnet, a French economist and public official, Deputy Secretary-General of the League of Nations 1919–1923, is considered to be, with Robert Schuman, one of the founding fathers of the European Union. For an account of the history of the ECSC see D. Spiernburg and R. Poidevin, *The History of the High Authority of the European Coal and Steel Community: Supranationality in Operation* (Weidenfeld and Nicolson, 1994). The ECSC competition provisions were the pattern for the later EEC ones.

came into force in 1958.[107] However, the EEC competition rules were not enforced by the Community institutions until Regulation 17 was passed four years later.[108]

In a book published in 1998, Daniel Gerber, a comparative lawyer, argues that there is a rich tradition of thought in Europe about what we now call competition law, which has given European domestic competition laws, as well as EC law, a distinctive character of their own.

Gerber first of all summarizes what he calls the 'Competition Law Story' in Europe.

D. Gerber, *Law and Competition in Twentieth Century Europe: Protecting Prometheus* (Clarendon Press, 1998), 6–8

Europeans began to develop the idea of such a general law to protect competition almost a century ago. The idea took shape in the 1890s in Austria, where it was a product of Vienna's extraordinary creative intellectual life. Competition law proposals emerged in order to protect the competitive process from political and ideological onslaughts, and they relied heavily on bureaucratic application of a 'public interest' standard in doing so. One of these proposals gained significant political support, and a competition law was almost enacted—only to be barred by the disintegration of the Austrian legislative process.

Although political events blocked further development of competition law ideas in Austria, such ideas were intensely debated in both intellectual and political arenas in Germany during the decade that bracketed the turn of the century. These conflicts shaped a discourse from which Europe's early competition legislation drew much of its substance and without which its enactment is barely conceivable. Moreover, many elements of this discourse were to become fixtures of European competition law thought.

The first European 'competition law' was enacted in Germany in 1923 in response to the postwar inflation crisis. The system created to implement this legislation became an important factor of economic and legal life in Germany during the 1920s and established competition law as an operational reality rather than merely an idea. It was, however, too weak to withstand the pressures ranged against it, and it was eliminated during the 1930s.

German experience with this system was nevertheless influential in the spread of competition law ideas, and during the late 1920s competition law ideas were widely discussed throughout Europe. By the early 1930s, additional statutes along the lines of the German legislation had been enacted in several smaller European states. More importantly, these discussions and enactments generated a framework for thinking about the roles and characteristics of competition law that was to be used after the Second World War as the basis for competition legislation and that remains influential.

---

[107] On 1 January 1958 not only did the Treaty of Rome come into force but also, coincidentally, did a new German Competition Law system (the *Gesetz gegen Wettbewerbsbeschränkungen*). This was required by the American occupiers before they would return full sovereignty to the new German state. US officials considered that the concentrated and heavy cartelized nature of pre-war German industry had aided Hitler's rise to power and his military conquests and that US-style competition laws would help German democracy. Anti-cartelization statutes were first put into place in 1947. However, there was a domestic as well as an American impetus towards the adoption of a complete new system and Chancellor Adenauer's economics minister, Ludwig Erhard (who was himself Chancellor 1963–1966) pushed hard for it, although against strong opposition (which accounted for the delay until 1958). The GWB (which is still in place today) rapidly acquired an important role in Germany's economic and legal system. The institution primarily charged with enforcing it was (and is) the *Bundeskartellamt* (Federal Cartel Office).

[108] [1959–62] OJ Spec. Ed. 87. See *infra* Chap. 2.

After the end of the war, many European governments turned to competition law as a means of encouraging economic revival, undergirding recently re-won and still fragile freedoms and achieving political acceptance of post-war hardships. Virtually all of these competition law systems were based on the thought and experience of the interwar period. In most of them, however, competition law was imbedded in economic regulatory frameworks that impeded its effectiveness, and it was seldom supported by significant economic, political or intellectual resources. As a result, these systems remained a rather marginal component of general economic policy, and in this respect some have not fundamentally changed even today.

In postwar Germany, competition law took a different turn—one that was to play a key role in the process of European integration and to have extraordinary consequences for the course of postwar European history. This change of direction was prepared during the Nazi period by a group of neo-liberal thinkers who secretly and often at great personal risk developed ideas of how Germany should be reconstituted after the war. In their so-called 'ordoliberal' vision of society, economic freedom and competition were the sources not only of prosperity but also of political freedom. They represented the 'economic constitution' of society, and law, the ordoliberals said, had to protect and implement this constitution. In this view, therefore, competition law acquired a new importance because it was made a basic structure of the political system. It also acquired new characteristics: it was now to operate increasingly according to juridical principles and procedures rather than on the basis of administration discretion.

These ideas eventually fell on fertile soil in the years after the Second World War. Nourished by the desire for new social ideals and supported by the occupation authorities, neo-liberal reformers enacted a competition law in 1957 that achieved new prominence and a vastly greater economic and political role. Despite often intense opposition from 'big industry', competition law has become a 'pillar' of the 'social market economy', and as such it has played a key role in some of the postwar Europe's most impressive economic and political successes.

Gerber thus locates the spirit of European competition law in the ideas of *fin-de-siècle* Austria and in the German concept of ordoliberalism.[109] In fact, he goes further back, to nineteenth-century liberalism's conception of law as being necessary to create freedom by constraining power. In Europe, competition law is to be seen as part of an 'economic constitution' which embraces social justice and is part of the political system.[110] The UK, however, has in the recent past at least shared the American economic philosophy. One commentator has identified a dichotomy between what he calls 'neo-American' capitalism—individualistic, unregulated, based on short-term profits, and with a minimal social component—and 'Rhine model' capitalism—collective achievement, public consensus, social welfare.[111] Gerber considers that English legal culture led to distinctive features in the UK competition law model, which moved it away from the general 'European model' he identifies. Nevertheless the UK's use of administrative controls produced similarities which are important from the perspective of European integration 'because they have provided a common experiential base that has eased

[109] See *supra* 34. See further D. Gerber, 'Constitutionalizing the Economy: German Neo-liberalism, Competition Law and the 'New Europe' (1994) 42 *American Journal of Comparative Law* 25.

[110] For a recent example of the concern of many Member States for the 'social' aspect in competition policy, see the insertion into the Treaty of Article 16 (ex Art. 7) reiterating the value of 'services of general economic interest' in the Community. See further *infra* Chap. 8 and the Addendum, *infra* 1399.

[111] M. Albert, *Capitalism Against Capitalism* (Whurr Publishers Ltd, 1993).

mutual understanding and co-operation within EU institutions and forged important links between Member State governments and officials'.[112]

B. THE OBJECTIVES OF THE EUROPEAN COMMUNITY AND EC COMPETITION POLICY

(i) The Objectives of the European Community

An examination of the *raison d'être* of the European Community and European Union is beyond the scope of a book on competition law. As Craig and de Bùrca state, '[t]here are and always have been many different and contested views about the original aims and *raison d'être* of the EC and EU among its political actors, populace, and commentators. A complex range of historical, political, and economic forces and contingencies contributed to creating the entity which exists today'.[113] A brief discussion of the aims and objectives of the Community is, however, essential to understand the context within which the competition rules are set and the impact that these aims and objectives may have on the interpretation and application of those rules.

The Preamble to the Treaty of Rome[114] states that the Member States recognize, *inter alia*, 'that the removal of existing obstacles calls for concerted action in order to guarantee steady expansion, balanced trade and fair competition'. The objectives of the Treaty are set out in Article 2. The original Article 2 stated:

The Community shall have as its task, by establishing a common market and progressively approximating the economic policies of Member States, to promote throughout the Community a harmonious development of economic activities, a continuous and balanced expansion, an increase in stability, an accelerated raising of the standard of living and closer relations between the states belonging to it.

Article 2 has subsequently been amended, and since the Treaty of Amsterdam came into force on 1 May 1999 states:

The Community shall have as its task, by establishing a common market and an economic and monetary union and by implementing the common policies or activities referred to in Articles 3 and 4, to promote throughout the Community a harmonious, balanced and sustained development of economic activities, a high level of employment and of social protection, equality between men and women, sustainable and non-inflationary growth, a high degree of competitiveness and convergence of economic performance, a high level of protection and improvement of the quality of the environment, the raising of the standard of living and quality of life, and economic and social cohesion and solidarity among Member States.

The Community therefore has a number of wide-ranging and aspirational goals which have expanded during the life of the EC and which it seeks to achieve through economic integration. The creation of the common market is not therefore an end in itself, but a means (along with the establishment of economic and monetary union (EMU) and the implementation of common policies or activities) of achieving the promotion of the matters listed in Article 2. The 'common market', often used colloquially as a synonym for the Community, means an area where direct

---

[112] D. Gerber, *Law and Competition in Twentieth Century Europe: Protecting Prometheus* (Clarendon Press, 1998), 207.

[113] P. Craig and G. de Bùrca, *EU Law: Text, Cases and Materials* (3rd edn., Oxford University Press, 2003), 4.

[114] The adoption of this Treaty and its amendments are discussed *infra* Chap. 2.

and indirect barriers to trade between Member States are removed and a common import and export policy adopted toward the outside world as far as commercial transactions are concerned. In *Metro v. Commission*,[115] the Court of Justice said in 1976 that the objectives of the Treaty included the creation of a single market achieving conditions similar to those of a domestic market. The single market is the 'internal' aspect of the common market, and is now defined in Article 14(2):[116]

The internal market shall comprise an area without internal frontiers in which the free movement of goods, persons, services and capital is ensured in accordance with the provisions of this Treaty.

The economic integration of the Member States has been taken further by progress towards EMU. The third and final stage of EMU entailed the adoption of a single currency, the Euro (€).[117] The single internal market, however, remains the core concept on which economic integration is founded.

Article 3 of the Treaty sets out the 'activities' of the Community necessary for the purposes set out in Article 2. This has also expanded since 1958, reflecting the additions to Article 2. The present Article 3 states:

1. For the purposes set out in Article 2, the activities of the Community shall include, as provided in this Treaty and in accordance with the timetable set out therein:

   (a) the prohibition, as between Member States, of customs duties and quantitative restrictions on the import and export of goods, and of all other measures having equivalent effect;

   (b) a common commercial policy;

   (c) an internal market characterised by the abolition, as between Member States, of obstacles to the free movement of goods, persons, services and capital;

   (d) measures concerning the entry and movement of persons as provided for in Title IV;

   (e) a common policy in the sphere of agriculture and fisheries;

   (f) a common policy in the sphere of transport;

   (g) a system ensuring that competition in the internal market is not distorted;

   (h) the approximation of the laws of Member States to the extent required for the functioning of the common market;

   (i) the promotion of co-ordination between employment policies of the Member States with a view to enhancing their effectiveness by developing a co-ordinated strategy for employment;

   (j) a policy in the social sphere comprising a European Social Fund;

   (k) the strengthening of economic and social cohesion;

   (l) a policy in the sphere of the environment;

   (m) the strengthening of the competitiveness of Community industry;

---

[115] Case 26/76, *Metro v. Commission (No. 1)* [1977] ECR 1875, [1978] 2 CMLR 1, para. 20.

[116] Previously Article 7a. The concept of the 'internal market' was first formally enshrined in the Treaty by the Single European Act 1986 (SEA), which provided for its completion by the end of 1992.

[117] The adoption of the Euro began on 1 January 1999 and culminated in the introduction of the new coins and banknotes on 1 January 2002 and the withdrawal of national currencies at the end of February 2002. For the way in which the 'ECU' referred to in the Treaty became the 'Euro' without an amendment to the Treaty, see S. Weatherill and P. Beaumont, *EU Law* (3rd edn., Penguin, 1999), 776. Not all Member States have adopted the single currency. On 1 January 2007 the Member States in the eurozone were Belgium, Germany, Greece, Spain, France, Ireland, Italy, Luxembourg, the Netherlands, Austria, Portugal, Finland and Slovenia. Of the pre-2004 Member States, Denmark, Sweden and the UK remain outside it. Cyprus and Malta will join on 1 January 2008.

(n)   the promotion of research and technological development;

(o)   encouragement for the establishment and development of trans-European networks;

(p)   a contribution to the attainment of a high level of health protection;

(q)   a contribution to education and training of quality and to the flowering of the cultures of the Member States;

(r)   a policy in the sphere of development co-operation;

(s)   the association of the overseas countries and territories in order to increase trade and promote jointly economic and social development;

(t)   a contribution to the strengthening of consumer protection;

(u)   measures in the spheres of energy, civil protection and tourism.

The Community's activities are thus broad, encompassing the pursuit of a large number of policies and activities, including in Article 3(1)(g), 'a system ensuring that competition in the internal market is not distorted'.[118]

Further, Article 4(1), inserted into the Treaty by the TEU in 1993,[119] assumes that economic policies in the Community will be based on an open market economy with free competition:

For the purposes set out in Article 2, the activities of the Member States and the Community shall include, as provided in this Treaty and in accordance with the timetable set out therein, the adoption of an economic policy which is based on the close co-ordination of Member States' economic policies, on the internal market and on the definition of common objectives, and conducted in accordance with the principle of an open market economy with free competition.

This is taken up in Article 157(1) which deals with the Community's industrial policy,[120] and says that Community action shall be 'in accordance with a system of open and competitive markets'.

The abandoned Constitutional Treaty would have said that the EU offered its citizens '... a single market where competition is free and undistorted'. The June 2007 Council meeting, however, agreed that the EC wll be subsumed into the EU and a revised Treaty on European Union will refer to establishing an internal market but without the reference to free and undistorted competition. Article 3(1)(g) will disappear from the EC Treaty, which will be renamed the 'Treaty on the Functioning of the Union'. However, a Protocol on competition will be annexed to the new Treaties. EC competition law will become EU competition law. For details, see the Addendum.[121]

However, even if the over-arching objective of the competition rules is to advance the (present) aims of the EC as set out in Article 2 of the EC Treaty, that still leaves open the question of how exactly they are to do this. In other words, in the light of the discussion in the sections above, what are the goals which the application of EC competition law is designed to achieve in order to further the Community's mission?

---

[118] Until the TEU amendments in 1993 this provision was Article 3(f) and read: 'the institution of a system ensuring that competition in the common market is not distorted'. It was reworded by the TEU and became Article 3(g), and was again renumbered by the Treaty of Amsterdam to become the present Article 3(1)(g).

[119] As Article 3a under the previous numbering.

[120] 'Industrial policy' describes the very wide raft of policies to do with creating employment and investment opportunites and enhancing competitiveness (not necessarily the same as enhancing competition) and the output of industry.

[121] See *infra* 1399.

(ii) The Development of the Objectives of EC Competition Policy

As Bork wrote in relation to US law: 'Antitrust policy cannot be made rational until we are able to give a firm answer to one question: What is the point of the law—what are its goals?'.[122]

We said above[123] that EC law appears to be striving for 'effective competition'. We therefore need to ask, in the light of the preceding discussion, what effective competition entails. As noted above, competition policy has been included in the list of Community activities set out in Article 3 since the inception of the Community in 1958. It was embedded in the Treaty right from the start as a set of wider policy goals oriented towards the objective of European economic integration. It was necessary in order to underpin the internal market aspect of the common market because there was no point in dismantling, by means of the free movement provisions, State measures which divided the Community territorially and compartmentalized the market if private undertakings could erect and maintain barriers to trade between Member States by carving up markets between them and indulging in anti-competitive practices. Economic integration is therefore promoted both by free movement and by competition.[124] In general it is true to say that the free movement provisions apply to State measures and the competition provisions to those of private actors. However, this statement masks a number of complexities. First, in some cases the free movement provisions can bind private parties, in particular where 'collective' private action is concerned in the area of free movement of persons and services.[125] Secondly, some situations raise both free movement and competition issues. A good example of this is *Bosman*,[126] where the ECJ decided the case on free movement grounds and declined to deal with the (very interesting) competition arguments.[127] Thirdly, it is possible to impugn some State measures on competition grounds. Indeed, the application of the competition rules to State action has become a very significant aspect of competition law in the EU.[128]

The Community Courts have repeatedly stressed the fundamental nature of the competition rules. As the ECJ said in *Eco Suisse*:

However, according to Article [3(1)(g)] EC . . . , Article [81] of the Treaty constitutes a fundamental provision which is essential for the accomplishment of the tasks entrusted to the Community and, in particular, for the functioning of the internal market. [129]

---

[122] R. Bork, *The Antitrust Paradox: A Policy at War With Itself* (Basic Books, 1978, reprinted with a new Introduction and Epilogue, 1993), 50.

[123] *Supra* 34.

[124] See J. Baquero Cruz, *Between Competition and Free Movement: The Economic Constitutional Law of the European Community* (Hart Publishing, 2002).

[125] See Case 36/74, *Walrave & Koch* v. *Association Union Cycliste Internationale* [1974] ECR 1405 and Case 415/93, *Union Royal Belge des Sociétés de Football Association ASBL & others* v. *Jean-Marc Bosman* [1995] ECR I-4921, [1996] 1 CMLR 645 (both cases concerning the rules of sporting organizations).

[126] *Ibid. Bosman* is described in Chalmers, Hadjiemmanuil, Monti and Tomkins, *European Union Law* (Cambridge University Press, 2006), 708 as being '[o]utside the small world of Community lawyers, arguably the most famous cases in the history of Community law . . . '.

[127] The case dealt with the rights of professional football players to move between clubs when out of contract, and changed the transfer system. See also Case C-303/99, *Wouters* v. *Algemene Raad van de Nederlandse Orde van Advocaten* [2002] ECR I-1577, [2002] 4 CMLR 913, on the rules of the Dutch Bar, discussed *infra* Chap. 3.

[128] See *infra* 54 and Chap. 8.

[129] Case C-126/97, *Eco Swiss China Time Ltd* v. *Benetton International NV* [1999] ECR I-3055, [2000] 5 CMLR 816, para 36. Article 81 is one of the two main substantive competition articles. See also Case C-453/99, *Courage Ltd* v. *Crehan* [2001] ECR I-6297, [2001] 5 CMLR 28, para. 20; Case T-168/01, *GlaxoSmithKlineServices Unlimited* v. *Commission*, 27 September 2006, para. 118 ('indispensable for the achievement of the missions entrusted to the Community').

The role of competition policy as an instrument of single market integration is absolutely crucial to an understanding of EC competition law. It differentiates EC law from any system of domestic competition law, whether in the Member States, the USA, or elsewhere. EC competition law has been seen as serving two masters, the 'competition' one and (even more demanding) the imperative of single market integration. This second goal has sometimes dictated the entire development of the law, particularly, as we shall see, in respect of vertical restraints.[130] A good example of the use of the competition rules in advancing the single market was the adoption of the new block exemption Regulation on motor vehicle distribution in 2002.[131] The Regulation allows the dealers and manufacturers less leeway than the previous Regulation[132] because the Commission was concerned that they were still acting to maintain price differentials in different Member States. The Competition Commissioner, Mario Monti, said of the new Regulation:[133]

... The Commission also needs to play its role as an initiator of change where markets do not function satisfactorily in the light of the Treaty objectives. The adoption in July of new exemption regulation for motor vehicle distribution can serve as a concrete example. It is high time we had a genuine single market in cars, for the benefit of consumers but also in the interests of the competitiveness of European industry. A review had clearly shown that the market integration pursued by old regulation applicable to the sector had not been achieved to the extent hoped for, and that consumers were receiving their share of the benefits deriving from the exempted restrictions. Thus, a new system has been put in place to give a fresh boost to market integration, so that consumers can benefit from better prices, wider choice and improved services.[134]

As recently as 2000, the Commission's Annual Report on Competition Policy talked of the two objectives of competition policy:

Commission's XXIXth Report on Competition Policy (1999), Introduction, paras 2–3.

The first objective of competition policy is the maintenance of competitive markets. Competition policy serves as an instrument to encourage industrial efficiency, the optimal allocation of resources, technical progress and the flexibility to adjust to a changing environment. In order for the Community to be competitive on worldwide markets, it needs a competitive home market . . . .

The second is the single market objective. An internal market is an essential condition for the development of an efficient and competitive industry. As the Community has progressively broken down government erected trade barriers between Member States, companies operating in what they had regarded as "their" national markets were and are for the first time exposed to

---

[130] *Infra*, Chap. 9.

[131] Commission Regulation 1400/2000 [2002] OJ L203/30, [2002] 5 CMLR 777.

[132] Regulation 1475/95 [1995] OJ L145/25.

[133] Commission's *XXXIInd Report on Competition Policy* (Brussels, 2003), foreword, p. 5.

[134] Note also the swingeing fines imposed by the Commission on motor manufacturers found to have infringed the competition rules by attempting to prevent the parallel import of their cars between Member States, e.g., *Volkswagen* [1998] OJ L124/60, [1998] 5 CMLR 33 (€102 million, reduced by the CFI on appeal, Case T-62/98, *Volkswagen AG v. Commission* [2000] ECR II-2707, [2000] 5 CMLR 853 to €90 million, appeal to the ECJ dismissed, Case C-338/00P, *Volkswagen AG v. Commission* [2003] ECR I-9189, [2004] 4 CMLR 351).

competitors able to compete on a level playing field.... Moreover, the objectives of competition policy have been integrated into into the Commission's new strategy for the European single market adopted on 24 November.[135] The aim is to prevent anti-competitive practices from undermining the single market's achievements.

However, in 1999 the White Paper on Modernization in 1999 the Commission said that the focus of competition policy had changed:[136]

At the beginning the focus of [the Commission's] activity was on establishing rules on restrictive practices interfering directly with the goal of market integration ... The Commission has now come to concentrate more on ensuring effective competition by detecting and stopping cross-border cartels and maintaining competitive market structures.

As we will see below, the Commission has now formulated the objectives of competition law in a way which conceptualizes competition and market integration as serving a common end, rather than seeing competition as a means of advancing the single market.[137]

There was considerable German and ordoliberal influence on the drafting of the EC competition provisions (particularly noticeable in respect of Article 82 which is worded so as to prohibit 'the abuse ... of a dominant position' and gives specific examples of such abuse, including the charging of excessive prices[138]) and we have already seen that the development of EC competition law has been greatly influenced by ordoliberal ideas. Ordoliberalism, it will be recalled, prizes individual economic freedom and is hostile to monopoly not because of its effects on efficiency but because it embodies private economic power. The result of this is that EC law has often been interpreted and applied to protect the competitors themselves rather than the competitive process, to favour small or medium-sized enterprises, to keep markets open and to achieve' fairness'. Moreover, as well as serving to uphold the single market, competition policy has been called in aid to support or advance other Community policies such as liberalization.[139] We see in the subsequent chapters of this book how these purposes have sometimes conflicted, and how different ones have been favoured at different times and in different contexts. The question of to what extent, if at all, the EC competition rules should take on board socio-political issues such as the environment or employment has been, and remains, deeply controversial.

---

[135] This is a reference to the Commission's communication of 24 November 1999 (COM(1999)642, endorsed by the Helsinki Council, Bull. 12–1999), setting out the strategic objectives of the internal market for the next five years (2000–04), which were to improve the citizens' quality of life, enhance the efficiency of the EU's product and capital markets, improve the business environment and exploit the achievements of the internal market in a changing world.

[136] Commission White Paper on modernization of the rules implementing Articles 81 and 82 of the EC Treaty [1999] OJ C132/1, [1999] 5 CMLR 208, Executive Summary, pt. 8.

[137] See *infra* 51.

[138] The concept of a 'dominant position' is also central to EC merger regulation, see Council Regulation 139/2004 [2004] OJ L24/1 and *infra* Chap. 12, which shows the EC's fear of 'unilateral or collective acquisition of market power likely to undermine market mechanisms' (D. Gerard, 'Merger Control Policy: How to Give Meaningful Considerations to Efficiency Claims?' (2003) 40 *CMLRev* 1367, 1380).

[139] For example, in the liberalisation of the air transport and telecommunications markets: see further *infra* Chap. 7 and Chap. 8.

(iii) The 'Modernization' of EC Competition Law and the Consumer Welfare Standard

During the 1990's the Commission began to move towards a realignment of the goals of competition law in line with the modern economic thinking on competition described above.[140] The term 'modernization' is often used specifically to refer to the great reform of the enforcement of EC competition law which took place in 2004.[141] However, the modernization of EC competition law goes much wider and deeper than that, and encompasses also the gradual revolution in the interpretation and application of the substantive law which had taken place in the previous decade,[142] as well as developments subsequent to 2004.[143] The result of all this is to place the welfare of the consumer squarely at the heart of EC competition law discourse.

In fact, the word 'consumer(s)' appears twice in the text of the competition articles themselves. First, it is provided in Article 81(3) that a restrictive agreement may escape prohibition if it contributes to improving the production or distribution of goods or promoting technical or economic progress while, *inter alia*, 'allowing consumers a fair share of the resulting benefit'. Secondly, Article 82, which prohibits any abuse by undertakings of a dominant position, contains a (non-exhaustive) list of examples of abuses. The second of these (Article 82(b)) is 'limiting production, markets or technical development to the prejudice of consumers' (and the ECJ referred to Article 82(c) and (d) as being aimed at practices which cause damage to consumers in *Continental Can* in 1974[144]). In addition, consumers feature in the Merger Regulation (ECMR), Article 2(1)(b) of which says that in appraising a merger the Commission shall take into account, *inter alia*, '...the interests of the intermediate and ultimate consumers, and the development of technical and economic progress provided that it is to consumers' advantage and does form an obstacle to competition'.[145]

---

[140] *Supra* 13 ff.

[141] Council Regulation 1/2003 [2003] OJ L1/1 and the accompanying secondary legislation and Notices; see *infra* 119.

[142] This could be discerned first of all in the more 'economic' approach taken to some aspects the assessment of mergers under the regime which came into operation in 1990 (pursuant to the original European Merger Regulation, Council Regulation 4064/89 [1990] OJ L 257/13, now Regulation 139/2004 [2004] OJ L24/1, see *infra* Chap. 12); the first solid manifestation of it in the antitrust field was the adoption by the Commission of a Notice on the definition of the relevant market in 1997 (Commission Notice on the definition of the relevant market for the purposes of Community competition law [1997] OJ C372/51); then there was the Green Paper on vertical restraints (COM 96) 721 final) paving the way for the reform of the Commission's much-criticized policy towards vertical restraints in 1999 (Commission Regulation 2790/99 [1999] OJ L336/21 and the Commission Notice, Guidelines on vertical restrains [2000]OJ C291/1, see *infra* Chap.9), the 1999 White Paper on the modernization of enforcement and procedure (Commission White Paper on modernization of the rules implementing Articles 81 and 82 of the EC Treaty [1999] OJ C132/1), and new Guidelines and block exemptions on horizontal cooperation agreements in 2000 (Guidelines on the applicability of Article 81 of the EC Treaty to horizontal cooperation agreements [2001] OJ C3/2; Commission Regulation 2658/2000 on specialization agreements [2000] OJ L304/3; Commission Regulation 2659/2000 on categories of research and development agreements [2000] OJ L304/7).

[143] Such as the Commission review of Article 82, launched by the DG Comp Discussion Paper on the application of Article 82 of the Treaty to exclusionary abuses, Brussels, December 2005, and the Draft Guidelines on the assessment of non-horizontal mergers, 13 February 2007.

[144] Case 6/72, *Europemballage & Continental Can v. EV Commission* [1973] ECR 215, [1973] CMLR 199. para. 26, in which the ECJ made the important point that the provisions were aimed at practices which injured them indirectly as well as directly.

[145] Council Regulation 139/2004 [2004] OJ L24/1 (the ECMR). Exactly the same provision appeared in the original Merger Regulation, 4064/89 [1990] OJ L257/13. Note also that Recital 29 of Regulation 139/2004 refers to a merger's potential efficiencies counteracting the effects on competition and 'in particular the potential harm to consumers' (there was no similar recital in 4064/89).

As the modernization process progressed, the speeches and publications of the Commission proclaimed the belief that the competition rules should promote efficiency and consumer welfare. This was particularly so after the appointment of an economist, Mario Monti, as Commissioner responsible for competition in 1999. Furthermore, this theme appeared in 'soft law' documents emanating from the Commission.[146] The Commission Guidelines on vertical restraints, adopted in middle of 2000, state that '[T]he protection of competition is the primary objective of EC competition policy, as this enhances consumer welfare and creates an efficient allocation of resources'.[147] Monti elaborated on this later in 2000 when he described the EC approach in this way:

Enshrined in the Treaty.... [is] 'an open market economy with free competition'. Since its adoption more than 40 years ago, the Treaty acknowledges the fundamental role of the market and of competition in guaranteeing consumer welfare, encouraging the optimal allocation of resources and granting to economic agents the appropriate incentives to pursue productive efficiency, quality and innovation. Personally I believe that this principle of an open market economy does not imply an attitude of unconditional faith with respect to the operation of market mechanisms. On the contrary, it requires a serious commitment—as well as self-restraint—by public powers, aimed at preserving those mechanisms.[148]

Furthermore, in a speech in July 2001, he said:[149]

...the goal of competition policy, in all its aspects, is to protect consumer welfare by maintaining a high degree of competition in the common market. Competition should lead to lower prices, a wider choice of goods, and technological innovation, all in the interest of the consumer.

The fact that he said that the protection of consumer welfare was *the* goal rather than *a* goal was acclaimed by the then Deputy Assistant Attorney General of the US DOJ Antitrust Division who said that '[w]e in the United States applaud Commissioner Monti's bold leadership in embracing the consumer welfare model of competition policy'.[150]

The approach enunciated by Monti above, and reflected in the Verticals Guidelines, is one whereby competition laws protect the competitive structure and dynamic of the market: 'they protect openness of access to markets, and the right of market actors not to be fenced out by dominant firm strategies that are not based on competitive merits'.[151] Such an approach is likely to lead in some cases to a different outcome than that which is reached by a system concerned with efficiency seen exclusively in terms of whether or not output is limited, as is arguably currently the position in US law.[152] The importance accorded in the EC to the competitive

---

[146] Moreover, in a case in 1998 Advocate General Jacobs reminded the Court that 'the primary purpose of Article [82] is to prevent distortion of competition-and in particular to safeguard the interests of consumers-rather than to protect the position of particular competitors', Case C-7/97, *Oscar Bronner GmbH & Co KG v. Mediaprint* [1998] ECR I-7791, [1999] 4 CMLR 112, para. 58 of his Opinion, discussed *infra* Chap. 7.

[147] [2000] OJ C291/1 (the 'Verticals Guidelines), para 7.

[148] M. Monti, 'European Competition Policy for the 21st Century' in B. Hawk (ed.) [2000] *Fordham Corp L Inst*, chap. 15, (and available on the Commission's web site http://www.europa.eu.int/comm/competition/speeches/.

[149] 'The Future for Competition Policy in the European Union', Merchants Taylor's Hall, London, 9 July 2001, available on the Commission web site, http://www.europa.eu.int/comm/competition/speeches/index_speeches_by_the_commissioner.html.

[150] William J. Kolasky 'North Atlantic Competition Policy: Converging Towards What?', Address given at the BIICL 2nd Annual International and Comparative Law Conference, London, 17 May 2002, available on the DOJ web site, http://www.usdoj.gov/atr/public/speeches/speech_kolasky.htm.

[151] E. Fox, 'What is Harm to Competition? Exclusionary Practices and Anti-competitive Effect' (2002) 70 ALJ 371, 392.

[152] See *ibid.*, 380–91 and further *infra*, Chap. 7.

process is shown by the wording of the competition provisions themselves, as explained in the Commission's 2004 Guidelines on Article 81(3).[153] The Guidelines contain a statement of the objectives of Article 81 phrased differently to the statement in the Verticals Guidelines, but still talking of protecting competition as a means of enhancing consumer welfare:[154]

The objective of Article 81 is to protect competition on the market as a means of enhancing consumer welfare and of ensuring an efficient allocation of resources. Competition and market integration serve these ends since the creation and preservation of an open single market promotes an efficient allocation of resources throughout the Community for the benefit of consumers.

The Guidelines go on to deal with the question of the conditions which have to be fulfilled before agreements which are restrictive of competition may escape the prohibition against such agreements by the operation of Article 81(3).[155] The final condition under Article 81(3) is that the agreement must not 'afford the undertakings concerned the possibility of eliminating competition in respect of a substantial part of the products concerned'. The Commission's conclusion on this in the Guidelines is that in the end protecting competition trumps other considerations:

Ultimately the protection of rivalry and the competitive process is given priority over potentially pro-competitive efficiency gains which could result from restrictive agreements. The last condition of Article 81(3) recognises the fact that rivalry between undertakings is an essential driver of economic efficiency, including dynamic efficiencies in the shape of innovation. In other words, the ultimate aim of Article 81 is to protect the competitive process.[156]

Neelie Kroes, who took up office as Competition Commissioner in autumn 2004, continued to proclaim the goal of protecting competition as a means of ensuring efficiency and consumer welfare. For example, in a speech in London in September 2005 she said:[157]

Consumer welfare is now well established as the standard the Commission applies when assessing mergers and infringements of the Treaty rules on cartels and monopolies. Our aim is simple: to protect competition in the market as a means of enhancing consumer welfare and ensuring an efficient allocation of resources. An effects-based approach, grounded in solid economics, ensures that citizens enjoy the benefits of a competitive, dynamic market economy.

Further, her speech to the BEUC[158] in November 2006 was actually entitled 'Consumer Welfare is the Standard of Anti-trust Enforcement'.[159]

---

[153] [2004] OJ C101/97.

[154] *Ibid.*, para. 13.

[155] See *infra* Chap. 4.

[156] Guidelines on the application of Article 81(3) of the Treaty, para. 105.

[157] European Consumer and Competition Day, London, 15 September 2005, http://europa. eu/rapid/pressReleasesAction.do?reference=SPEECH/05/512&format=HTML&aged=0&language= EN&guiLanguage=en. The Commission's 'Competition Day' held twice yearly since 2000 became a 'Competition and Consumer Day' in September 2005 when it was held in London, and both the Competition Commissioner, Neelie Kroes and the Chairman of the OFT, John Vickers stressed that (in Vickers' words) '...consumer and competition policies must work together in tandem if not as one': see also http:// www.oft.gov.uk/NR/rdonlyres/1FA03036-F07D-42BE-858E-0B1194855CB0/0/sp0705.pdf.

[158] Bureau Européen des Unions de Consommateurs (the European Consumers' Organisation).

[159] Brussels, 16 November 2006, available at http://europa.eu/rapid/pressReleasesAction.do?reference= SPEECH/06/691&format=HTML&aged=0&language=EN&guiLanguage=en ('The consumer is at the heart of competition enforcement. We want markets to work better, not for an abstract notion of "free competition", but because better functioning markets provide consumers with better goods and better services, at better prices').

The imprimatur of the CFI has been given to the welfare of consumers as the objective of the competition rules. Although in 1976 the ECJ had referred to 'workable competition'[160] the Community Courts had not previously made pronouncements on the precise economic objectives of the rules. In the summer of 2006, however, the CFI gave two judgments[161] in which it identified the 'well-being' or 'welfare' of consumers as the objective. The first was *Österreichische Postsparkasse* in which the CFI said:

It should be pointed out in this respect that the ultimate purpose of the rules that seek to ensure that competition is not distorted in the internal market is to increase the well-being of consumers. That purpose can be seen in particular from the wording of Article 81 EC. Whilst the prohibition laid down in Article 81(1) EC may be declared inapplicable in the case of cartels which contribute to improving the production or distribution of the goods in question or to promoting technical or economic progress, that possibility, for which provision is made in Article 81(3) EC, is inter alia subject to the condition that a fair share of the resulting benefit is allowed for users of those products. Competition law and competition policy therefore have an undeniable impact on the specific economic interests of final customers who purchase goods or services. [162]

This was followed by the judgment in *GlaxoSmithKline* where the CFI said:[163]

However, as the objective of the Community competition rules is to prevent undertakings, by restricting competition between themselves or with third parties, from reducing the welfare of the final consumer of the products in question...

In *GlaxoSmithKline* this formulation of the objective of the rules was crucial to the one of the findings in the case, as it prevented an agreement from falling within the prohibition of anti-competitive agreements in Article 81(1). Although the object of the agreement was to restrict parallel trade that could not, on the facts of the case, be equated with the object of reducing the welfare of the final consumer.[164]

Two further interesting points should be noted. First, there is the meaning of 'consumers'. The word 'consumers' in Article 81(3) has long been interpreted in EC law as encompassing all indirect and direct users, and not just private (natural person) end-users, which is the popular conception of a 'consumer'.[165] However, *GlaxoSmithKline* (and to a lesser extent *Österreichische Postsparkasse*) considers the competition rules to be aimed at the welfare of the *final* consumer. This may be no more than a reflection of the facts in those cases. Nevertheless, there is undoubtedly a current rhetoric, illustrated by the Commissioner's speeches, that emphasises the benefits that the Commission's enforcement of the competition rules has for individuals. Moreover, the 2006 Leniency Notice (which sets out the rewards offered to cartel members who reveal the cartel to the Commission) justifies the leniency policy on the grounds that '[t]he interests of consumers *and citizens* in ensuring that secret cartels are detected and punished outweigh the

---

[160] Case 26/76, *Metro v. Commission (No. 1)* [1977] ECR 1875, [1978] 2 CMLR 1, para. 20, see *supra* 33.

[161] The judgments were given by different Chambers, with one judge in common. For the Court of First Instance, see Chap. 2.

[162] Cases T-213/01 and T-214/01, *Österreichische Postsparkasse AG v. Commission and Bank für Arbeit und Wirtschaft AG v. Commission* [2006] ECR II-1601, para. 115.

[163] Case T-168/01, *GlaxoSmithKlineServices Unlimited v. Commission*, 27 September 2006, para. 118.

[164] See further *infra*, Chap. 3.

[165] See Case T-29/92, *SPO v. Commission* [1996] ECR II-289; Merger Regulation, 139/2004, Art. 2(1)(b) (intermediate and ultimate consumers); Guidelines on the application of Article 81(3) [2004] OJ C101/97, para. 84 (...direct or indirect users...including producers that use the products as an input...In other words...customers of the parties to the agreement and subsequent purchasers).

interest in fining those undertakings that enable the Commission to detect and prohibit such practices'[166] (emphasis added). This suggests that European citizens have an interest in the enforcement of the competition rules that goes beyond their role as consumers.

Secondly, there is the question of what the 'welfare of the consumer' or 'consumer welfare' actually means. Because of the way that competition law works—in *prohibiting* agreements, abuses or mergers because of their anti-competitive effects—it will normally be the case that the competition authority will initially be concerned with identifying any consumer *detriment* that may arise from the conduct or transaction under review. The question may then arise as to whether this detriment is offset by any resulting consumer *benefit*. This is seen clearly in the operation of Article 81(3) of the EC Treaty, mentioned above.[167] What amounts to consumer detriment has never been precisely defined,[168] but appears to consist of higher prices, reduced output, less choice or lower quality of goods or services, or diminished innovation, while consumer *benefit* consists of the reverse (lower prices, greater output, greater choice, higher quality, more innovation).[169] EC law has not yet expressly equated 'consumer welfare' with 'consumer surplus' in the economic sense described earlier.[170] Certainly, the standard or objective of EC competition law does not appear to be 'total welfare'. It will be recalled from above[171] that the economic concept of total welfare is the sum of consumer surplus and producer surplus and that it does not encompass value judgments about how the surplus should be distributed. However, EC law demands in Article 81(3) that a 'fair share' of the efficiency gains resulting from anti-competitive agreements must be passed on to consumers if such agreements are not to be prohibited and, according to the Commission, the efficiency gains from anti-competitive mergers must likewise be passed on.[172] In other words, EC competition law is concerned not with the welfare effects on the whole economy but with the impact on consumers. The efficient allocation of resources must work to the benefit of consumers, or at the very least not make them worse off.

The pursuit of the objective of consumer welfare rather than, for example, the aims of competition policy identified by ordoliberalism, can have a decisive influence on the interpretation and application of the law. The last part of the EC competition rules to be subjected to 'modernization' is Article 82, the provision prohibiting the abuse of a dominant position.[173]

---

[166] Commission Notice on immunity from fines and reduction of fines in cartel cases [2006] OJ C298/17, para. 3.

[167] And see Chap. 4. It is also seen in the 'efficiency defence' in merger control, (*infra* Chap. 12) and in the suggested 'efficiency defence' in respect of Article 82 (see DG Comp Discussion Paper on the application of Article 82 of the Treaty to exclusionary abuses, Brussels, December 2005, paras. 84–92, *infra* Chap. 7). In Case C-95/04 P, *British Airways plc* v. *Commission*, 15 March 2007, para. 86, the ECJ said that it had to be determined whether the disadvantage to competition might be counterbalanced, or outweighed, by efficiency advantages which also benefited the consumer.

[168] See P. Marsden and P. Whelan, ' "Consumer Detriment and its Application in EC and UK Competition Law' [2006] *ECLR* 569.

[169] See e.g. Guidelines on the application of Article 81(3) [2004] OJ C101/97, particularly paras. 16, 21, 25; Guidelines on the assessment of horizontal mergers [2004] OJ C31/3, paras. 8, 80–1; DG Comp Discussion Paper on the application of Article 82 of the Treaty to exclusionary abuses, Brussels, December 2005, para. 4; Draft Guidelines on the assessment of non-horizontal mergers, 13 February 2007, paras. 71–72.

[170] *Supra* 3 ff.

[171] *Supra* 13.

[172] Commission Guidelines on Horizontal Mergers [2004] OJ C31/5, paras. 77 and 79 (see further *infra* Chap. 12); also, Discussion Paper on Article 82, paras. 84–90.

[173] The modernization of Article 82 was initiated by DG Comp's Discussion Paper on the application of Article 82 to exclusionary abuses, December 2005.

The question of whether competition law should protect competitors or competition is particularly relevant in respect of Article 82 and we will see in Chapters 5, 6, and 7 how the debate about the 'reform' of Article 82 necessitated a wide-ranging debate about the purposes of competition law. Older ideas linger on: the Advocate General's Opinion in *British Airways*, delivered in February 2006 described Article 82 as not being 'only or primarily designed to protect the immediate interests of individual competitors or consumers 'but to protect the structure of the market and thus competition as such (as an institution)… '.[174] The ECJ's judgment in that case, which took a very 'conservative' line towards the application of Article 82, did not gainsay that statement.[175]

(iv) Socio-Political or 'Non-efficiency' Factors and the Relationship of Competition with Other Community Policies

As already intimated, there has been a long controversy over how far, if at all, 'non-competition' issues should be taken into account in EC competition law. It will be seen in the subsequent chapters of this book that on numerous occasions in the past cases and decisions have taken account of socio-political factors,[176] particularly those embodied in other Community policies, but that contradictory messages on this have been sent out by the Community Courts and the Commission.

The adoption by the EC of the goal of promoting consumer welfare through allocative efficiency makes it difficult to simultaneously promote other objectives. Indeed, the whole philosophy of the modern 'economic' approach to competition policy is that it should be concerned only with efficiency. The EU and its Member States must obviously pursue other policies too, but these, it is argued, should not affect the ways in which the competition rules are interpreted and applied. Moreover, the 2004 reforms, which decentralized the enforcement of EC competition law to the national competition authorities of the Member States[177] and gave encouragement to the private enforcement of the competition rules in the national courts, made the exclusion of non-efficiency considerations attractive on expediency grounds. It is one thing for the Commission to balance competition against other Community policies, but quite another for national courts and authorities to do so.[178]

The problem with EC competition policy is that it can never stand alone in splendid isolation because, as seen above[179] it is stated in the EC Treaty to be one of a number of activities

---

[174] Opinion of Kokott A-G in Case C-95/04 P, *British Airways v. Commission*, delivered 23 February 2006, para. 86.

[175] Case C-95/04 P, *British Airways v. Commission*, 15 March 2007.

[176] See in particular the application of Article 81(3), *infra* Chap. 4.

[177] Council Regulation 1/2003 [2003] OJ L1/1; Commission Notice on cooperation with in the network of competition authorities [2004] OJ C101/43.

[178] In the Commission White Paper on modernization of the rules implementing Articles 81 and 82 of the EC Treaty [1999] OJ C132/1, the Commission first proposed decentralization and turned its face against using Article 81(3) to take into account socio-political factors: see *infra* Chap. 4. Member States do pursue objectives which do not fit with the efficiency approach. In 2006 Member State governments interfered with merger transactions in the energy sector in order to protect national companies from 'foreign' take-overs, thus incurring the wrath of the Commission which considered the actions contrary to the European Merger Regulation (ECMR) Regulation 139/2004 [2004] OJ L24/22. On 18 October 2006 the Commission opened infringement proceedings under Art 226 EC against Spain in respect of the conditions the Spanish energy regulator had imposed on the takeover of the Spanish energy company Endesa by the German company E.ON: see Press Release IP/06/1426, and further, Chap. 12.

[179] *Supra* 38 ff.

undertaken to achieve the objectives of the European project. The fact that the realm of EU activities is ever-widening complicates matters. The EC Treaty now contains a number of 'flanking'[180] provisions that provide that certain policies or objectives must be taken into consideration, or taken regard of, when other Community policies or activities are being pursued—the environment,[181] employment,[182] cultural aspects,[183] human health protection,[184] consumer protection,[185] economic and social cohesion,[186] and development co-operation.[187] There is no expressed hierarchy of these, except that the integration of environmental protection requirements into other Community policies and activities is stipulated in Article 6, in the 'Principles' section in Part One of the Treaty. It can be argued that it is possible to construct a hierarchy based on the legal nature of the provisions concerned, with for example, directly effective Treaty provisions taking precedence over secondary legislation,[188] and it should be noted that, as we have already seen, the ECJ has described the competition provisions as being 'fundamental' provisions.[189]

There are two possible ways in which non-efficiency issues and other Community policies can be taken into account.[190] A matter may be excluded from the scope of competition law altogether; or the matter may be covered by the competition rules but other considerations may affect their application. Examples of the former are the ECJ's exclusion of collective bargaining agreements between employer and employees on the ground that such arrangements fall within the ambit of social policy,[191] and cases finding that an entity is not an 'undertaking' and

---

[180] Or policy-linking or policy integration.

[181] Article 6 EC; the specific provisions on environment policy are in Articles 174–176. On the Commission's DG Comp (Competition Directorate General)'s website there is a page 'European Competition Policy and the Environment' which says 'Community law provides that environmental considerations must be integrated into all other Community policies. This includes European competition policy. In their turn both the national legislator and the industry have to respect competition law in putting in place environmental initiatives. Neither should they establish forms of collaboration, rules or practices that would constitute unjustified obstacles to competition'. See further, *infra* Chap. 4 and Chap. 13.

[182] Article 127(2) EC ('The objective of a high level of employment shall be taken into consideration in the formulation and implementation of Community policies and activities').

[183] Article 151(4) EC ('The Community shall take cultural aspects into account in its action under other provisions of this Treaty ...').

[184] Article 152(1) EC ('A high level of human health protection shall be ensured in the definition and implementation of all Community policies and activities').

[185] Article 153(2) EC ('Consumer protection requirements shall be taken into account in defining and implementing other Community policies and activities').

[186] Article 159 EC (Member States to conduct their economic policies to attain the objectives in Article 158, which provides for the Community to develop and pursue actions leading to strengthening of economic and social cohesion).

[187] Article 178 EC (Community to take account of the development cooperation objectives in Article 177 in implementing policies which are likely to affect developing countries).

[188] See J. Baquero Cruz, *Between Competition and Free Movement: The Economic Constitutional Law of the European Community* (Hart Publishing, 2002), 63–5; Odudu, O, *The Boundaries of EC Competition Law* (Oxford University Press, 2006), 169–70.

[189] Case C-126/97, *Eco Swiss China Time Ltd v. Benetton International NV* [1999] ECR I-3055, [2000] 5 CMLR 816, para. 36; Case C-453/99, *Courage Ltd v. Crehan* [2001] ECR I-6297, [2001] 5 CMLR 28, para. 20; J. Baquero Cruz, *op cit.* n. 188, 71.

[190] See generally Odudu, *op. cit.* n. 188, 159–174.

[191] Case C-67/96, *Albany International BV v. Stichting Bedrijfspensioenfonds Textielindustrie* [1999] ECR I-6025, [2000] 4 CMLR 446: see *infra* Chap. 3.

its agreements or conduct therefore not subject to the competition rules.[192] This manoeuvre preserves the purity of the 'only consumer welfare objective' approach to competition law by making competition law inapplicable, but is questionable.[193] Once within the scope of competition law, there is the possibility of taking account of non-efficiency considerations through the application of Article 81(3), or through what is categorized as an 'abuse of a dominant position' under Article 82. The present position is that Article 81(3) should not be used in this way,[194] and the approach to Article 82 is also being reformed in a direction that would exclude non-efficiency considerations (such as ordoliberal-inspired ones).[195] However, despite this general trend of restricting competition law to efficiency questions there continue to be instances where other considerations intrude. One difficult case is *Wouters*[196] in which the ECJ in 2002 held that the rules of the Dutch Bar did not infringe the prohibition against restrictive agreements because the rules pursued public interest objectives.[197]

As far as the objective of single market integration is concerned, it is noted above that the Commission now conceptualizes this and competition as serving the same ends. Those ends are consumer welfare and an efficient allocation of resources. If we look again at the statement of the objective of Article 81 set out in paragraph 13 of the Article 81(3) Guidelines[198] we see that that competition and market integration serve these ends as 'the creation and preservation of an open single market promotes an efficient allocation of resources throughout the Community for the benefit of consumers'. In this way competition policy is released from its role as the handmaid of market integration and the raison d'être of the single market identified as consumer welfare. No longer, as in the past, are there two separate objectives of competition policy.[199] Competition and single market integration converge as means to the same ends.[200]

There has also been a long-standing problem over the relationship between competition policy and the Community's industrial policy. In 2004 the Commission issued a Communication, *A pro-active competition policy for a competitive Europe*,[201] which set competition at

---

[192] For example, Case C-205/03 P, *Federación Nacional de Empresas de Instrumentación Científica, Médica, Técnica y Dental (FENIN) v. Commission*, 11 July 2006 (ECJ, affirming Case T-319/99 FENIN v. Commission [2003] ECR II-357, [2003] 5 CMLR 34); Cases C-264, 306, 354 & 355/01, *AOK Bundesverband and others v. Ichtyol-Gesellschaft Cordes and others* [2004] ECR I-2493: see further *infra* Chap. 3 and Chap. 8.

[193] There are also matters excluded from the competition rules by the Treaty itself: agriculture (Art. 36 EC and Council Regulation 26/62, [1959–62] OJ Spec.Ed. 129); national security (Art. 296 EC; for the application of this in the context of mergers, see *infra* Chap. 12); nuclear energy (inasmuch as it is covered by the Euratom Treaty, Art. 305(2) EC). For the position of undertakings entrusted with services of general economic interest see Art. 86(2) EC, discussed *infra* Chap. 8.

[194] *Infra* Chap. 4.

[195] *Infra* Chaps 5 and 7.

[196] Case C-309/99, *Wouters v. Algemene Raad van der Nederlandse Orde van Advocaten* [2002] ECR I-1577, [2002] 4 CMLR 913.

[197] Cf. Case C-519/04 P, *Meca-Medina and Majcen v. Commission*, 18 July 2006, [2006] 5 CMLR 1023, *infra* 111.

[198] *Supra*, 46.

[199] As said, for example, in the quotation from the Commission's XXIXth Report on Competition Policy set out *supra* 42.

[200] For the development of this convergence see C. D. Ehlermann, 'The Contribution of EC competition policy to the Single Market' (1992) 29 *CML Rev* 257; K. Mortelmans, 'Towards Convergence of the Rules on Free Movement and Competition' (2001) 38 *CML Rev* 613; R. O'Loughlin, 'EC Competition Rules and Free Movement Rules: An Examination of the Parallels and their furtherance by the ECJ *Wouters* Decision' [2003] *ECLR* 62; J. Baquero Cruz, *op. cit.* n. 188, *supra*. This does not mean, however, the single market does not have a *political* function as well.

[201] COM (2004) 293 final.

the heart of industrial policy rather than in opposition to it. The Commission said that '[T]he goal of a pro-active competition policy is to support the competitive process in the internal market and to induce firms to engage in competitive and dynamically efficiency-enhancing behavior'. The Commissioner elaborated on this in a speech in September 2006:

This afternoon I would like us to try to rethink industrial policy! I think it makes no sense to speak of industrial policy and competition policy as distinct one from the other, let alone as antagonistic policies. I would rather define industrial policy as one which frames the structural conditions necessary to ensure economic success in a globalising economy. And I therefore have no qualms in saying that competition policy forms—or should form—a central plank in any industrial policy.[202]

This explanation of the relationship between competition policy and industrial policy has to be seen in the context of the Lisbon Strategy[203] whereby the EU has set itself the strategic goal of becoming the most competitive and dynamic knowledge-based economy in the world by 2010, capable of sustainable economic growth and more and better jobs and greater social cohesion. The 2004 Communication said of competition and the Lisbon Strategy:

Competition policy is one of a number of Community policies impacting upon the economic performance of Europe. It is a key element of a coherent and integrated policy to foster the competitiveness of Europe's industries and to attain the goals of the Lisbon strategy.

The trumpeting of competition policy as advancing the Lisbon agenda highlights how the argument goes round in a (virtuous) circle: the application of competition law serves the 'economic' goal of consumer welfare/efficiency and does not take account of 'socio-political' concerns; the goal of consumer welfare/efficiency is to ensure that 'citizens enjoy the benefits of a competitive, dynamic economy';[204] and that economy will deliver to them 'sustainable growth with more and better jobs and greater social cohesion'[205]—surely a socio-political goal par excellence. As the Director General of DG Comp has said:[206]

Competition is not an end in itself, but an instrument designed to achieve a certain public interest object, consumer welfare. At the same time, competition policy can contribute to other objectives: in the EU context, for example, it can work towards the success of the strategy for growth and jobs, and form part of the public debate about the role of state intervention and regulation in industry.

C. THE LIMITS OF COMPETITION, PUBLIC SERVICES, AND REGULATION

(i) The Limits of Competition

At the beginning of this Chapter we said that even in a free market economy some areas may not be left to unbridled competition. In other words, there are 'limits to competition'. The provision of

---

[202] Neelie Kroes, *Industrial policy and competition law & policy*, speech at Fordham University School of Law, 14 September 2006.

[203] Originally declared at the Lisbon European Council in March 2000 and relaunched in February 2005 in the Communication of the Commission to the Spring European Council, *Working together for growth and jobs: A new start for the Lisbon Strategy* COM (2005) 24, 2 February 2005.

[204] See Neelie Kroes, London, 15 September 2005, n. 157, *supra*.

[205] *Ibid.*

[206] P. Lowe, (2006) 2 *EC Competition Policy Newsletter* 1 1.

some goods or services may be considered essential but unsuited to the rigours of the market and to the application of competition laws. Also, the liberal professions have historically operated closed shops replete with restrictive practices, claiming that this modus operandi is in the public interest.[207] The biggest area of contention relates to what can be called the 'public services'. There is much controversy inside Member States about how public services should be run, what should be privatized, and what should be a monopoly immune from competition and, not surprisingly, these are equally controversial matters at EC level. In EC law, some bodies are held to be outside the competition rules altogether, while in other cases the competition rules apply to them only to some extent or with dispensations. The question of what should be covered by the competition laws is a major issue and arises in a number of contexts throughout this book.[208]

(ii) Competition and Regulation

The last quarter of the twentieth century saw a revolution in the way in which public services were owned and run. Throughout Europe many State-owned monopolies were wholly or partly privatized and put into the private sector.[209] The opening up of sectors previously monopolized by State enterprises legally protected from competition is known as liberalization. However, such moves can lead, at least in the short term, to private monopolies replacing public ones. This does not necessarily benefit consumers. There are particular problems where the provision of services in a sector depends on the use of a network (such as railway lines) which cannot feasibly be duplicated. Moreover, these undertakings are often providing services which are essential and have to be provided 'universally' (the supply of water, sewage and basic postal and telephone services for example). One solution to these problems is to subject the liberalized sectors to 'regulation'. Regulation 'consists of public interventions which affect the operation of markets through command and control'[210] and typically involves setting up a body which implements controls on prices and quality, creates as far as possible conditions for competition to exist and then polices them, and oversees the social obligations of the undertaking such as the obligation to provide universal service.[211]

One difference between regulation and competition law is that regulation acts *ex ante* (in advance) whereas competition law may act *ex post* (reacting to conduct which is taking place or has taken place).[212] So, where prices are concerned, a regulator will set out in advance what the

---

[207] The EC Commission undertook a major review of competition law and the liberal professions in 2003, and reports were published in February 2004 (COM (2004) 83 final) and September 2005 (COM (2005) 451 final), available on the Commission's web site. A resolution of the European Parliament of 12 October 2006 supported the Commission's moves towards removing overly restrictive regulation in the professions. See also, e.g. Case C-309/99, *Wouters v. Algemene Raad van de Nederlandse Orde van Advocaten* [2002] ECR I-1577, [2002] 4 CMLR 913.

[208] But see in particular *infra* Chap. 3 and Chap. 8. The question of sport is dealt with in Chap. 2.

[209] Private rather than public ownership is a major plank of the 'neoliberal' ideology which at present drives globalized capitalism.

[210] T. Prosser, *Law and the Regulators* (Oxford University Press, 1997), 4.

[211] *Ibid.*, 5–6. Obviously this is a generality. The functions of the regulators differ between sectors and different states organize regulation differently. The regulators in the UK include OFWAT (water), OFGEM (energy), the Rail Regulator and, pursuant to the Communications Act 2003, OFCOM.

[212] Monopoly control is generally *ex post*, and so, in the current regime under Regulation 1/2003, is the control of anti-competitive agreements (although there is the possibility of interim measures or injunctions). Merger control is *ex ante* (the EC merger regime requires prior notification of mergers with a 'Community dimension', see Chap. 12). For the differences between competition and regulation, see further R. O'Donoghue and A. J. Padilla, *The Law and Economics of Article 82* (Hart Publishing, 2006), 1.4.5.

undertaking may charge while a competition authority will step in only if and when it appears that an undertaking's pricing infringes the competition rules. Regulation is far more *dirigiste* than competition law. Competition laws can apply to regulated sectors alongside regulatory regimes and numerous instances of where this has occurred in the EU will be seen in this book. Indeed, the Commission favours the application of competition law rather than regulation wherever possible.[213]

In the EC the European Commission has pursued a programme of liberalization and attempted to open up the transport, postal services, gas, electricity, and telecommunications markets. The telecommunications market is the most striking and ambitious example of this liberalization. It has been pursued both through Directives adopted under the special procedure laid down in Article 86(3) of the EC Treaty[214] and through Council harmonization Directives under Article 95 (which provides for measures necessary for the establishment of the internal market). The latter culminated in a package of measures adopted in 2002, the linchpin of which is the Framework Directive for electronic communications.[215] There are no EC regulators in the sense that we are discussing here[216] but the regulators in the Member States may have duties imposed upon them by EC law to implement Community policy. For example, the Framework Directive 'lays down tasks of national regulatory authorities and establishes a set of procedures to ensure the harmonised application of the regulatory framework throughout the Community'.[217] Perhaps the most significant point to note about the Framework is that only electronic communications markets where 'ordinary' competition law is not sufficient to remedy persistent market failures are to made subject to regulation. The Commission may ultimately veto the decision of a national regulatory authority to subject a particular market to *ex ante* regulation if it thinks it unnecessary. The regulated sectors are not specifically dealt with in this book but are discussed where relevant.[218]

D. THE NEW ECONOMY

We have seen that the regulation of telecommunications is now subsumed in the regulation of the electronic communications sector as a whole. This is because the telecommunications, media, and information technology sectors have converged to such an extent that they have to be regulated as a whole.[219] The electronic communications sector is part of what is termed the 'New Economy', an expression which also encompasses high technology industries such as Internet based businesses (for example B2B marketplaces),[220] computer software and

---

[213] In the UK the sector regulators have concurrent powers with the Office of Fair Trading to apply the Competition Act 1998 and the Enterprise Act 2002 in their sectors. See generally *Butterworths Competition Law* (Butterworths, Looseleaf), Div. IX.

[214] See *infra* Chap. 8.

[215] Directive on a common regulatory framework for electronic communications networks and services [2002] OJ L108/33. The Directive applies to all electronic communications, as explained in the following section.

[216] The expression 'regulator' is often used loosely to mean competition authority.

[217] Framework Directive, n. 215 *supra*, Art. 1.

[218] For example, some of the Notices in the telecommunications/electronic communications sector, as discussed in Chaps. 5 and 7.

[219] See European Commission, 'Towards an Information Society Approach', Green Paper on the convergence of the telecommunications, media and information technology sectors, and the implication for regulation, COM(97) 623 final (Brussels, 1997).

[220] Software systems whereby parties transact business online through a central node.

hardware, biotechnology and aerospace. The characteristics of these markets include very rapid technological change, the creation and exploitation of intellectual property rights, the need for complementary products to work together, and a high degree of technical complexity. In some markets such as electronic communications 'network externalities' (the service becomes more valuable to customers the more people who use it—mobile phones which can send and receive photos are no fun if your friends do not have one too) are an important feature. New economy industries pose particular problems for competition laws. For example, competition between undertakings is not so much on price as on innovation; the usual ways of defining markets may not work well;[221] and competition may not be *in* markets but *for* markets (markets may 'tip' towards one firm whose products become the standard, rendering the firm dominant—Microsoft is the obvious instance[222]—and competition will be aimed at replacing the dominant firm). Regulation can be applied to some markets, as in the case of electronic communications, to deal with some of the issues but there is much debate about the extent to which 'ordinary' competition law can be satisfactorily applied to the new economy.[223] The argument is that the application of competition rules should be revised to allow for the dynamic competition in these markets. Faull and Nikpay (a book written by a team of past and present officials of the EC Commission's Competition Directorate-General) concludes that in general such adjustment is unnecessary.[224]

In conclusion, there seems to be no important conflict between innovation and competition policy aimed at product market competition and there seems to be no fundamental flaw in competition policy. Competition policy, by defending competition and open markets, will in general have a positive impact on both static and dynamic efficiency. Companies under competition pressure will be less complacent and will have more incentive to innovate and gain market share. Product market competition and a strict competition policy generally work as an effective stick to promote innovative effort.[225]

In the later chapters of this book we will see many examples of cases and merger decisions involving new economy markets.

---

[221] For market definition tests, see *infra* 60 ff.

[222] Note also the battle in the early 1980s between the Betamax and VHS video formats, which was won by VHS to the total extinction of Betamax.

[223] See, e.g., J. Temple Lang 'European Community Antitrust Law—Innovation Markets and High Technology Industries' [1996] *Fordham Corp L Inst*, 519; C. Veljanovski, 'EC Antitrust in the New Economy: Is the European Commission's View of the Network Economy Right?' [2001] *ECLR* 115; C. Ahlborn, D. S. Evans, and A. J. Padilla, 'Competition Policy in the New Economy: Is European Competition Law up to the Challenge?' [2001] *ECLR* 156; M. Monti, 'Defining the Boundaries, Competition Policy in High Tech Sectors', speech at UBS Warburg Conference, Barcelona, 11 September 2001; D. S. Evans and R. Schmalensee, 'Some Economic Aspects of Antitrust Analysis in Dynamically Competitive Industries', NBER Working Paper 8268, May 2001; R. Lind and P. Muysert, 'Innovation and Competition Policy: Challenges for the New Millenium', [2003] *ECLR* 87.

[224] J . Faull and A. Nikpay (eds.), *The EC Law of Competition* (2nd edn., Oxford University Press, 2007, 1.123–1.129 (L. Peeperkorn and V. Verouden). The book is expressed to be the authors' personal opinions, rather than the official position, but is obviously of particular interest because of the connection with DG Comp.

[225] Faull and Nikpay, para. 1.129. This conclusion is reached after an analysis of, and in reliance on, the arguments of Evans and Schmalensee, *supra* n. 223. See also *Wanadoo*, COMP/38.233, [2005] 5 CMLR 120, upheld on appeal, Case T-340/03, *France Télécom SA v. Commission*, 30 January 2007.

8. COMPETITION LAW AND THE INTERNATIONAL CONTEXT

The effects of anti-competitive practices and the exercise of monopoly power can be felt in States far away from that in which the undertaking concerned is located. Indeed, many undertakings in todays globalized economy are truly 'multinational' in the sense that they have a presence throughout the world. One of the most important issues in competition law at present is the international application and enforcement of competition laws and there are (exciting) developments in international cooperation in competition matters. The international aspects of competition law arise in many places in this book, and are discussed as a whole in Chapter 16.

9. THE TECHNIQUES AND TOOLS OF COMPETITION LAW

A difficult question that must be faced by all authorities is how competition law should pursue its goals. The discussion above suggests that appropriate competition rules should be framed:

(i)   to deal with the prejudicial consequences of market power ;

(ii) to deal with oligopolistic markets;

(iii) to prevent mergers which lead to a concentration in market power;

(iv) to prevent restrictive agreements between competitors (horizontal agreements); and

(v)   to prevent restrictive vertical agreements which have anti-competitive consequences.

How such rules are interpreted and applied will also be crucial to the pursuit of those goals.

It is possible to adopt a system of competition law which takes a formalistic prohibitory approach based on the assumption that certain types of conduct are harmful. This was the position taken in the UK's restrictive trade practices legislation,[226] which has now been repealed and replaced by the Competition Act 1998. The legislation proscribed certain types of agreements between certain types of party concerning the matters listed in the Act. The Act did not admit the possibility of looking at the effect of agreements to see if they did in fact restrict competition. The matter was broadly denuded—deliberately—of economic content and the law reduced to a number of formal propositions. Judges did not, therefore, have to rule on economic matters.[227] The perverse result was a system which caught many harmless and even pro-competitive agreements but, conversely, allowed some which were seriously anti-competitive.[228]

---

[226] In its final form, the Restrictive Trade Practices Act (RTPA) 1976.

[227] The original Restrictive Trade Practices Act was enacted in 1956 and the judiciary did not wish to have to decide such matters.

[228] The best account of the Restrictive Trade Practices Acts was set out in the 3rd edition of R. Whish, *Competition Law* (Butterworths, 1993), chap. 5, 123, which stated that 'the formalism and technical conundra have multiplied and the present law is extremely complex and riddled with anomalies and unanswered questions'.

EC competition law does not take this type of extreme formalistic approach. It is essentially an 'effects-based' law. The provisions are drafted in broad terms. Thus Article 81 of the EC Treaty broadly aims to prevent 'restrictive' agreements (iv and v above); Article 82 broadly aims to prevent abuses of market power, in the terms of Article 82 a 'dominant position' (i above); and the Merger Regulation is intended to preclude mergers which would significantly impede effective competition, in particular by the creation or strengthening of a dominant position (ii and iii above).[229] Ironically, despite the economic base, the EC competition authorities have often been criticized for failing to take a sufficiently economically rigorous approach to the application of competition law and for having instead adopted a formalistic view. They, too, have sometimes operated on the assumption that certain things should be prohibited as a matter of course because they are bound to have an anti-competitive effect. More recently, the European Commission, which enforces the EC competition rules,[230] has displayed a greater determination to use rigorous economic analysis in its decision making. This was epitomized by the creation of the new post of Chief Competition Economist in 2003.[231]

Economic analysis is not, however, a panacea for all problems. It does not necessarily tell the competition authority what the outcome of any given agreement or conduct will be. It has already been seen that economists disagree over many things and economics do not provide the answer to every question. The applicability of a particular law may turn on the question whether or not a particular firm has market power. There may, however, be disagreement about what market that firm operates on (are pink widgets really substitutes for yellow widgets?) and about whether barriers to entry exist[232] to prevent other undertakings entering that market and challenging that firm's strong position. The economic view that monopoly is inefficient presents, therefore, only a starting-point to the application of the law in any particular case. Similarly, there may be disagreement about whether or not a particular agreement is or is not restrictive. A distribution agreement which decreases competition between A and B may in fact increase competition between X and Y. Thus a distribution agreement, for example, in which X grants A the sole right to distribute its brand of goods, to the exclusion of B, may encourage A to market the goods actively so that X's product competes vigorously on the market with Y's.[233] Furthermore, even if there is agreement that competition law should achieve consumer welfare, there can be disagreement about how allocative, productive and dynamic efficiencies should be weighed against one another, what are the welfare implications of certain practices or whether the protection of *competitors* in the short term is necessary to protect *competition*, and thus consumer welfare, in the longer term. We see these debates played out in the cases discussed in this book, especially those in Chapter 7 (abuse of a dominant position) and Chapter 12 (mergers). It is important to realize that over-enforcement of the competition rules (prohibiting agreements, conduct or mergers where there is no likely or actual harm to the market, so-called Type 1 errors, or 'false positives') is as harmful—some say *more* harmful—than under-enforcement (failing to prohibit where there is such harm, so-called Type 2 errors, or 'false negatives').[234]

---

[229] These Articles are described in greater detail *infra* in Chap. 2 and are discussed fully in subsequent chapters. The control of oligopolistic markets, outside the merger context, is problematic, although Article 82 can be employed in some situations: see *infra* Chap. 11.

[230] See *infra* Chap. 2.

[231] See *supra* Chap. 2.

[232] See *infra* 84 ff.

[233] For the approach of EC law to this scenario see *infra* Chaps. 3, 4, and 9.

[234] The way the terminology 'Type 1' and 'Type 2' errors is used is not standardized. Some writers use them the labels the other way round. However, this is how the terminology is used in this book.

It was seen in section 5 that there are fashions in economic theory and schools of antitrust analysis, and that today's orthodoxy may be overtaken by new ideas. Nevertheless, given that competition policy is concerned with economic structures, conduct, and effects, it must be correct that its application should be as economically literate as possible. Faull and Nikpay explains the advantages and limitations of economic analysis in competition cases:

J. Faull and A. Nikpay (eds.), *The EC Law of Competition* (2nd edn., Oxford University Press, 2007), 4

1.02 The growing acceptance and importance of economics in competition policy raises questions regarding the usefulness of economics, both for devising competition rules and for deciding on competition cases. A word of caution is appropriate in this respect. Economic thinking and economic models have proved not to be perfect guides.

1.03 Economic theories and models are built on and around assumptions. This approach has the benefit of making explicit the various elements relied upon in arriving at a particular conclusion or insight. At the same time, these assumptions by definition do not cover (all) real world situations. In addition, when the assumptions are changed the outcomes of the models may look very different. It is for these reasons that the application of economic theories may not always be able to give a clear and definitive answer, for example as to what will happen in a market when companies merge, or when companies try to collude or engage in specific types of conduct.

1.04 The best that the application of economic principles can do in general is to provide a coherent framework of analysis, to provide relevant lines of reasoning, to identify the main issues to be checked in the context of certain theories of competitive harm, and possibly to exclude certain outcomes. In other words, it helps to tell the most plausible story. In individual cases it will be necessary first to find the concepts and the model that best fit the actual market conditions of the case and then to proceed with the analysis of the actual or possible competition consequences. Economic insights can also be useful in the formulation of policy rules, indicating under what conditions anti-competitive outcomes are very unlikely, very likely, or rather likely, and helping to devise safe harbours.

In Section 10 we introduce some of the basic economic concepts used in antitrust analysis.

10. MARKET POWER, MARKET DEFINITION, AND BARRIERS TO ENTRY

A. MARKET POWER

It is clear from the discussion above that the key concern of competition law is with firms which can profitably raise prices above marginal cost.[235] This is what is meant by market power. It is firms which, individually or collectively, have market power that are able to restrict output, increase prices above the competitive level, and earn monopoly profits. They can raise prices without losing so many sales that the rise rise is unprofitable. Concomitantly, they can influence

---

[235] And see D. W. Carlton and J. M. Perloff, *Modern Industrial Organization* (4th edn., Pearson Addison Wesley, 2005), 642.

the variety or quality of goods or services, innovation, and the other parameters of competition.[236] Most firms have some market power in the short term,[237] but it is market power which endures for a significant period of time that matters. The exercise of such market power leads, as we have seen, to an inefficient result for society as a whole. In this section we introduce the concepts of market definition and barriers to entry which are central to the assessment of market power in EC competition law and to the discussion throughout this book.

In 1981 a seminal paper by William Landes and Richard Posner triggered a debate about the assessment of market power, and the point at which the degree of market power warrants antitrust proceedings, which continues today.[238] Landes and Posner advocated the use of the Lerner index to assess market power.[239] This expresses the concept of market power 'as the setting of price in excess of marginal cost by measuring the proportional deviation of price at the firm's profit- maximising output from the firm's marginal costs at that output'.[240]

There are two ways of measuring a firm's market power, 'direct' and 'indirect'. The 'direct' method involves estimating the market power by using econometric methods, particularly the residual demand curve (the demand curve facing a single firm[241]). However, this requires data which is often not available and even if it is the estimation of market power in this way may prove problematic.[242] The 'indirect' method involves a structural approach. First the 'relevant market' is defined and secondly the power on that market of the undertaking under review is assessed using market share and 'barriers to entry' analysis. *Barriers to entry* are vital to the determination of market power by this method since it is these which enable a firm already in the market to earn monopoly profits without attracting other firms to enter that market. The definition, identification, and significance of barriers to entry is one of the most controversial matters in antitrust economics. This issue is discussed below.[243] The 'indirect' method is the one commonly used by competition authorities throughout the world. It is used by the EC Commission. Moreover, it has the imprimatur of the ECJ.[244]

Under the 'indirect' method, therefore, the determination of the relevant market (or 'antitrust market'[245]) is of crucial importance. This raises the important question of how a market is identified and defined. This issue is discussed below.[246]

---

[236] DG Comp Discussion Paper on the application of Article 82 of the Treaty to exclusionary abuses, Brussels, December 2005 (hereafter 'Discussion Paper on Article 82') para. 24.

[237] As customers and competitors will need time to react to the price increase.

[238] W. M. Landes and R. A. Posner, 'Market Power in Antitrust Cases' (1981) 94 *Harvard L Rev* 937. See the discussion in J. Vickers, 'Market Power in Competition Cases' (2006) 2 *European Competition Journal* 3.

[239] A. P. Lerner, 'The Concept of Monopoly and the Measurement of Monopoly Power' (1934) *Rev. Economic Studies*, 157.

[240] RJ Van den Bergh and P.D.Camesasca, *European Competition Law and Economics: A Comparative Perspective* (2nd edn., Sweet & Maxwell, 2006), 110, who give the simplest formulation as L= (P-MC)/P. See also J. Vickers, 'Market Power in Competition Cases' (2006) 2 *European Competition Journal* 3, 4–6.

[241] Called 'residual' as it is demand not met by other firms in the market: see Carlton and Perloff *op. cit.*, n. 235, 66–9.

[242] M. Motta, *Competition Policy* (Cambridge University Press, 2004), 116–17; Vickers, *op cit.* n. 240, 7. See, however, J. B. Baker and T. F. Bresnahan, 'Estimating the Residual Demand Curve Facing a Single Firm' (1988) 6 *International Journal of Industrial Organization*, 283.

[243] See *Infra* 84 and Chap. 6.

[244] Case 6/72, *Europemballage Corp and Continental Can Co Inc* v. *Commission* [1973] ECR 215, [1973] CMLR 199, para. 32 and subsequent case law: see *infra* 61 and Chap. 6 .

[245] Including markets in merger cases, although, as noted *supra* 3, the Commission now uses 'antitrust' to denote areas of competition law other than mergers.

[246] See also, in particular, the discussion *infra* in Chap. 6.

The size of a firm's market share is, according to the Commission, 'an important indicator for the existence of market power'.[247] Market share measures 'the relative size of a firm in an industry or market, in terms of the proportion of total output, sales or capacity it accounts for'[248] and it is the starting point for assessing market power. It is not normally sufficient on its own for, as noted above, a more detailed analysis of the economic features of the market, such as barriers to entry, will also be required in order to determine the competitive constraints to which the firm is subject. However, in some areas of EC competition law market share stands proxy for market power. The current thinking of the Commission, in line with economic theory, is that many agreements between undertakings are not anti-competitive in the absence of a degree of market power,[249] although that degree of market power may be less than that required to put an undertaking into a 'dominant position' for the purpose of the competition rules.[250] Block exemption regulations, which exempt categories of agreements from the prohibition in Article 81(1) of the EC Treaty, are therefore drafted to apply only to situations in which the undertakings' market shares are below certain thresholds.[251] This approximation of market share with market power is simplistic but considered the most practicable way of enabling the block exemptions to be applied. The use of market share as the sole determinant is likely to over-estimate rather than under-estimate the market power of the undertakings concerned.[252]

B. MARKET DEFINITION AND EC COMPETITION LAW

(i) The Importance of Market Definition

It is only by defining the relevant market that a firm's market power can be assessed by the 'indirect' method. The purpose of defining the relevant market is to identify which products and services are such close substitutes for one another that they operate as a competitive constraint on the behaviour of the suppliers of those respective products and services. Suppose, for example, you are suspicious that Y, the only producer of yellow widgets, is exercising market power and engaging in monopoly pricing. A preliminary question which must be asked is whether or not the product has substitutes to which customers could easily turn. If it does, then if Y raises prices it will lose customers. If customers can instead buy blue widgets and pink widgets, which are perfect substitutes, from other firms a rise in the price of yellow widgets will lead customers to buy (cheaper) blue and pink ones instead. Saying that Y has a 'monopoly' over the sale of yellow widgets is meaningless in economic terms. Similarly, suppose Y is the sole manufacturer of all colours of widgets. Y will still not be able to raise prices without losing customers if blodgets, which are made by other firms, are perfect substitutes for widgets. The problem of market definition is that it is often difficult to decide which products or services *are* in the same market. It is obvious, for example, that steel beams and chewing-gum are not in the

---

[247] EC Commission Glossary of terms used in EU competition policy (Brussels, July 2002).

[248] *Ibid.*

[249] See *infra* Chaps. 9, 10, and 13.

[250] Under Article 82 of the EC Treaty undertakings in a 'dominant position' can infringe the rules by 'abusing' that position. See *infra* Chaps. 5–7.

[251] So below the threshold there is a 'safe harbour'. See Commission Reg. 2790/99 [1999] OJ L336/21 on vertical restraints, *infra* Chap. 9; Commission Reg. 2658/2000 [2001] OJ L304/3 on specialization agreements, Commission Reg. 2659/2000 [2001] OJ L304/7 on research and development agreements, *infra* Chap. 13; Commission Reg. 772/2004 [2004] OJ L123/11 on technology transfer agreements, *infra* Chap. 10.

[252] For the reasons why this is so see *infra* 84.

same market, but what about coffee and tea,[253] vodka and whisky, bananas and apples, Eurostar and cross-Channel ferries?

It is important to remember, however, that market definition is not an end in itself. Rather, it is 'a tool for aiding the competitive assessment by identifying those substitute products or services which provide an effective constraint on the competitive behaviour of the products or services being offered in the market by the parties under investigation'.[254] So the 'guiding principle' is that 'a relevant market is 'something which is worth monopolising'.[255]

In the next sections we consider how the relevant market has been defined for the purposes of Community competition law. We also outline the way in which the Community institutions go about, or should go about, actually determining what the relevant market is in any given case. Greater detail of the way in which the market has actually been determined by the Community authorities in specific contexts is set out in the relevant chapters later in this book.

(ii) Relevant Market Definition in the Case Law of the Court of Justice

The importance of market definition has been recognized by the European Court. The Court has stressed that it is necessary to define the relevant market before a breach of Article 82 of the EC Treaty can be established[256] as the application of that Article requires the existence of a dominant position in a given market 'which presupposes that such a market has already been defined'.[257] It is also generally essential to the application of the Merger Regulation.[258] In respect of Article 81 the determination of the market is ordinarily necessary before it can be determined whether or not an agreement has as its effect the prevention, restriction, or distortion of competition;[259] it is essential to the determination of whether or not an agreement *appreciably* restricts competition or trade, to the determination of whether or not an agreement substantially eliminates competition in the common market for the purposes of Article 81(3), and, in most cases, whether a block exemption is applicable or not. However, the CFI noted in the *Lombard Club* judgment[260] that market definition plays a different role in Article 81 cases from that in Article 82 cases. In Article 81 cases it serves to determine whether there is an effect on

---

[253] See discussion *supra* 5.

[254] S. Bishop and M. Walker, *The Economics of EC Competition Law: Concepts, Application and Measurement* (2nd edn., Sweet & Maxwell, 2002), 4.04.

[255] B. Owen and S. Wildman, *Video Economics* (Harvard University Press, 1992), quoted *ibid*.

[256] Case 6/72, *Europemballage Corp and Continental Can Co Inc v. Commission* [1973] ECR 215, [1973] CMLR 199, para. 32. On the other hand, if the conduct complained of would not amount to an abuse even if the undertaking concerned *was* in a dominant position it may not be necessary to define the market.

[257] Case T-62/98, *Volkswagen AG v. Commission* [2000] 5 CMLR 853, para. 231.

[258] Council Regulation 139/2004, [2004] OJ L24/1. See further *infra* Chap. 12. A merger's compatibility with the common market is dependent upon whether or not the merger leads to a significant impediment to effective competition, in particular as a result of the creation or strengthening of a dominant position (under the previous EC Merger Regulation, Reg. 4064/89 the test was whether the merger would create or strengthen a dominant position as a result of which effective competition would be significantly impeded in the common market).

[259] Cases T-374,375, 384 and 388/94, *European Night Services v. Commission* [1998] ECR II-3141, [1998] 5 CMLR 718, paras. 93–5 and 105.

[260] Cases T-259/02 to 264/02 and T-271/02, *Raiffeisen Zentralbank Österreich and others v. Commission*, 14 December 2006.

competition. So in the *Lombard Club* case, which concerned a horizontal cartel, it was justified for the Commission to use a broad market definition including many banking products that might in other contexts have belonged to separate markets, provided that an effect on competition in that market could be shown.

The Court defines the relevant market in terms of substitutability or interchangeability. It has thus adopted a definition of a relevant market which describes the market as consisting of products[261] which are interchangeable with each other but not (or only to a limited extent) interchangeable with those outside it. This interchangeability may be with other products (widgets as substitutes for blodgets) or with the same products from elsewhere (widgets from France as substitutes for widgets from England). The relevant market therefore has both a product aspect (the product market) and a geographical aspect (the geographic market).

The Court of Justice has set out the following definitions of the *relevant product market*:

. . . the definition of the relevant market is of essential significance, for the possibilities of competition can only be judged in relation to those characteristics of the products in question by virtue of which those products are particularly apt to satisfy an inelastic need and are only to a limited extent interchangeable with other products.[262]

The concept of the relevant market in fact implies that there can be effective competition between the products which form part of it and this presupposes that there is a sufficient degree of interchangeability between all the products forming part of the same market insofar as a specific use of such products is concerned.[263]

. . . for the purposes of investigating the possibly dominant position of an undertaking on a given market, the possibilities of competition must be judged in the context of the market comprising the totality of the products which, with respect to their characteristics, are particularly suitable for satisfying constant needs and are only to a limited extent interchangeable with other products.[264]

This approach to product market definition uses a 'functional interchangeability' yardstick based on the 'qualititave' criteria of characteristics, price and intended use. It will be seen in later chapters that in some cases this approach by the Court has led to it upholding controversial decisions of the Commission delineating very narrow markets. In *United Brands*, for example, the Court upheld the finding that the market for bananas was separate from the market for other fruit.[265] The Commission and the Court have been criticized in respect of the attention focused on characteristics and use. If too much attention is placed on factors which in reality tell us little about a relevant market then decisions are of course likely to be arbitrary. In particular, if the market is not determined scientifically, reference to factors such as product characteristics, intended use, and consumer preference may mean that too much subjectivity is introduced into the determination. In many circumstances this may result in the adoption of too narrow a market definition. In many cases, moreover, characteristics and intended use will not be particularly useful to the determination of the relevant market. They will not shed light when trying to determine, for example, whether or not sparkling mineral water is in the same market

[261] Or services. The words 'products' and 'product market' encompass both products and services, as appropriate.

[262] Case 6/72, *Europemballage Corp and Continental Can Co Inc v. Commission* [1973] ECR 215, [1973] CMLR 199, para. 32.

[263] Case 85/76, *Hoffmann-La Roche & Co AG v. EC Commission* [1979] ECR 461, [1979] 3 CMLR 211, para. 28.

[264] Case 322/81, *Nederlandsche Banden-Industrie Michelin v. Commission* [1983] ECR 3461, [1985] 1 CMLR 282, para. 37.

[265] See *infra* Chap. 6.

as still mineral water, tap water, orange juice, or tonic water. All of these products have similar characteristics and uses.[266]

In *United Brands* the Court set out the following definition of the *relevant geographic market*:[267]

The opportunities for competition under Article [82] of the Treaty must be considered having regard to the particular features of the product in question and with reference to a clearly defined geographic area in which it is marketed and where the conditions of competition are sufficiently homogeneous for the effect of the economic power of the undertaking concerned to be able to be evaluated.... The conditions for the application of Article [82] to an undertaking in a dominant position presuppose the clear delimitation of the substantial part of the Common Market in which it may be able to engage in abuses which hinder effective competition and this is an area where the objective conditions of competition applying to the product in question must be the same for all traders.

In some cases there may also be a temporal aspect, although this is usually considered as a feature of the product and therefore part of the delineation of the product market (for example, the provision of train services during the rush-hour rather than in the middle of the day).[268]

(iii) The Commission Notice on the Definition of the Relevant Market for the Purposes of Community Competition Law

a. The Publication of the Notice

The European Commission plays the key role in the enforcement of the EC competition rules.[269] It will be seen throughout this book that on many occasions the Commission has been criticized for having failed to take due account of economic arguments and, frequently, for having failed to take a realistic approach to market definition; in particular, that it failed to consider economic principles in defining the relevant market. A welcome step taken in this regard by the Commission was its publication in October 1997 of a Notice on the definition of the relevant market for the purposes of Community competition law (the 'Notice on market definition').[270] This Notice provides a framework for determining the relevant market which is based on economic principles. It was welcomed as a progressive and realistic approach to the matter and was hailed as an (early) indication of the 'modernization of DG IV'.[271]

The Notice states that its purpose is to 'provide guidance as to how the Commission applies the concept of relevant product and geographic market in its ongoing enforcement of Community competition law' (paragraph 1). The Commission states that market definition is a tool to identify and define the boundaries of competition between firms and that it serves to establish the framework within which the Commission applies competition policy (paragraph 2).

The Notice indicates that it seeks to render public the procedures the Commission follows and the evidence which it relies upon in reaching decisions on market definition. By doing this it hopes to increase transparency and assist undertakings (paragraph 3). The Notice thus

---

[266] See the *Nesté/Perrier* [1993] 4 CMLR M17 merger case, discussed in Chap. 12.

[267] Case 27/76, *United Brands v. Commission* [1978] ECR 207, [1978] 1 CMLR 429, paras. 11 and 44.

[268] See *infra* Chap. 6.

[269] See *infra* Chap. 2.

[270] [1997] OJ C372/5, [1998] 4 CMLR 177.

[271] See, e.g., W. Bishop, 'Editorial: The Modernisation of DGIV' [1997] 8 *ECLR* 481. DG IV was the previous number of the Competition Directorate-General of the Commission: see *infra* Chap. 2.

renders more transparent the Commission's practices and should lead to greater consistency in its decisions.

The Commission's approach set out in that Notice is outlined in this chapter since it describes economic principles which should be used to define the relevant market. It should be noted that the Notice describes a process which was not evident in many of the Commission's previous decisions or the Court's judgments[272] (in fact at times it seems to be at odds with the existing case law)[273]. Rather, it is more reflective of the new practice of the Commission which developed since the adoption of the EC Merger Regulation in 1989.[274] The Notice is 'soft law', not legislation,[275] and is 'without prejudice to the interpretation which may be given by the European Court of Justice or the European Court of First Instance'.[276] The case law of the Court and the relevant Commission decisions are described in their own contexts in subsequent chapters. The Commission's Notice is nevertheless of vital importance since it sets out the Commission's current approach to the matter.

b. The Definition of the Relevant Market in the Notice

The definition of the relevant market adopted by the Commission in the Notice on market definition is based on that of the Court of Justice set out above.

Commission Notice on the Definition of the Relevant Market for the Purposes of Community Competition Law [1997] OJ C372/5, [1998] 4 CMLR 177

7. ...A relevant product market comprises all those products and/or services which are regarded as interchangeable or substitutable by the consumer, by reason of the products' characteristics, their prices and their intended use.

8. ...The relevant geographic market comprises the area in which the undertakings concerned are involved in the supply and demand of products or services, in which the conditions of competition are sufficiently homogeneous and which can be distinguished from neighbouring areas because the conditions of competition are appreciably different in those areas.

The problem, of course, is to identify *what* products are considered substitutes by consumers.

(iv) Demand and Supply Substitution

We have seen that the relevant market depends on the determination of which products in which areas are substitutes for one another. If a product has perfect substitutes the sole producer of such a product has no market power, because if that supplier tries to exploit his monopoly by raising the price his customers will turn to the substitutes. There are two aspects

---

[272] At least in the context of Articles 81 and 82, see especially Chap. 6.

[273] e.g., the treatment of 'unique suitability' in para. 43 differs from that of the ECJ in Case 27/76, *United Brands v. Commission* [1978] ECR 207, [1978] 1 CMLR 429, discussed *infra* 77 and Chap. 6.

[274] See *infra* Chaps. 6 and 12.

[275] But note the effect the ECJ has ascribed to the Commission Notices, *infra* Chap. 2.

[276] Commission Notice on market definition, para. 6.

to substitutability. *Demand substitution* is concerned with the ability of users of the product to switch to substitute products. *Supply substitution* is concerned with the ability of producers of similar products to produce the product. *Potential competition* is also important. The behaviour of an undertaking on a market will be constrained if potential competitors are easily able to enter the market. Potential competition is, however, ordinarily taken into account not at the stage of market definition but later on in the competitive assessment when considering an undertaking's position on a market.[277]

When defining the relevant market both demand and supply substitutability have to be considered.[278] The Commission's Notice indicates however that the Commission mainly focuses on demand-side substitution.

Commission Notice on the Definition of the Relevant Market for the Purposes of Community Competition Law [1997] OJ C372/5, [1998] 4 CMLR 177

13. ... From an economic point of view, for the definition of the relevant market, demand substitution constitutes the most immediate and effective disciplinary force on the suppliers of a given product, in particular in relation to their pricing decisions. A firm or a group of firms cannot have a significant impact on the prevailing conditions of sale, such as prices, if its customers are in a position to switch easily to available substitute products or to suppliers located elsewhere. Basically, the exercise of market definition consists in identifying the effective alternative sources of supply for the customers of the undertakings involved, in terms both of products/services and of geographic location of suppliers.

14. The competitive constraints arising from supply side substitutability other than those described in paragraphs 20 to 23 and from potential competition are in general less immediate and in any case require an analysis of additional factors. As a result such constraints are taken into account at the assessment stage of competition analysis.

(v) Demand Substitution

a. Ways of Measuring Demand Substitution

Demand substitution identifies which products a consumer considers to be substitutes for another. Unless products are totally homogeneous there will be no perfect substitutes. On the other hand, most products do have substitutes of some kind. Whether or not products are substitutes for one another is dependent on a number of factors: in particular on customer preference, whether customers can switch immediately or need time to adapt, whether there is similarity in quality or price, and whether substitutes are available. The matter may be complicated if some customers can switch to substitutes but others cannot or if a product has several uses and there are substitutes for some of those uses but not for others. As explained above,[279]

---

[277] See *infra* Chap. 6.

[278] Case 6/72, *Europemballage Corp & Continental Can Co Inc v. Commission* [1973] ECR 215, [1973] CMLR 199 was lost by the Commission on the issue of demand substitution, see *infra* Chap. 6.

[279] *Supra*, 5.

products may be substitutes in one direction and not in the other. For example, in *Microsoft* [280] the Commission found that while a streaming media player was a substitute for a media player which delivered less functionality, substitution the other way round was not readily available as less performing media players did not satisfy consumer demand for features such as streaming or video playback.

b. The SSNIP Test

Interchangeability is gauged by measuring 'cross-elasticity of demand', as described above.[281] The primary method now adopted by the Commission for measuring the cross-elasticity of demand is set out in its Notice on market definition. The Commission relies upon the hypothetical monopolist test (HMT), put into effect by using the SSNIP test. This reflects the more economically rigorous approach adopted by the Commission to market definition. Subsequent chapters show that much Community authority is in fact indicative of a less scientific, 'qualitative' approach which in the past tended, at least in non-merger cases, to encourage the adoption of arbitrary and narrow market definitions.[282]

SSNIP stands for a Small but Significant Non-transitory Increase in Price. The test[283] has been adopted by competition authorities around the world, including the USA (where it was pioneered by the Department of Justice in 1982), Canada, New Zealand, Australia, and the UK.[284] Its adoption by the Commission is welcomed as an approach which reflects contemporary economic analysis. The test applies as follows: a small (5–10 per cent) rise in the price of widgets is assumed. It is then asked whether this price increase would cause widget customers to purchase blodgets, or to purchase widgets from another area, to such an extent that the price rise is unprofitable. If the answer is yes, then blodgets and/or widgets from the other area form part of the same market.

Commission Notice on the Definition of the Relevant Market for the Purposes of Community Competition Law [1997] OJ C372/5, [1998] 4 CMLR 177

15. The assessment of demand substitution entails a determination of the range of products which are viewed as substitutes by the consumer. One way of making this determination can be viewed as a speculative experiment, postulating a hypothetical small, lasting change in relative prices and evaluating the likely reactions of customers to that increase. The exercise of market

---

[280] COMP/C-3/37.792, [2005] 4 CMLR 965, para. 415, on appeal Case T-201/04, *Microsoft v EC Commission* (judgment pending).

[281] *Supra* 5.

[282] See in particular the criticism of Commission decisions and the case law of the ECJ set out *infra* in Chap. 6.

[283] R. J. Van den Bergh and P. D. Camesasca, *European Competition Law and Economics: A Comparative Perspective* (2nd edn., Sweet & Maxwell, 2006), 131, say that 'The so-called SSNIP test is not a test in itself but a conceptual framework, within which several quantitative tests can be emploted to address the market delineation question'.

[284] See the OFT Guideline 403, *Market Definition* setting out the principles of market definition for the purposes of the Competition Act 1998 and, further, the report prepared for the OFT by National Economic Research Associates (S. Bishop and S. Baker) *The role of market definition in monopoly and dominance inquiries* (Economic Discussion Paper 2, July 2001, OFT 342).

definition focuses on prices for operational and practical purposes, and more precisely on demand substitution arising from small, permanent changes in relative prices. This concept can provide clear indications as to the evidence that is relevant in defining markets.

16. Conceptually, this approach means that, starting from the type of products that the undertakings involved sell and the area in which they sell them, additional products and areas will be included in, or excluded from, the market definition depending on whether competition from these other products and areas affect or restrain sufficiently the pricing of the parties' products in the short term.

17. The question to be answered is whether the parties' customers would switch to readily available substitutes or to suppliers located elsewhere in response to a hypothetical small (in the range 5 to 10 per cent) but permanent relative price increase in the products and areas being considered. If substitution were enough to make the price increase unprofitable because of the resulting loss of sales, additional substitutes and areas are included in the relevant market. This would be done until the set of products and geographical areas is such that small, permanent increases in relative prices would be profitable. The equivalent analysis is applicable in cases concerning the concentration of buying power, where the starting point would then be the supplier and the price test serves to identify the alternative distribution channels or outlets for the supplier's products. In the application of these principles, careful account should be taken of certain particular situations as described within paragraphs 56 and 58.

18. A practical example of this test can be provided by its application to a merger of, for instance, soft-drink bottlers. An issue to examine in such a case would be to decide whether different flavours of soft drinks belong to the same market. In practice, the question to address would be whether consumers of flavour A would switch to other flavours when confronted with a permanent price increase of 5 to 10 per cent for flavour A. If a sufficient number of consumers would switch to, say, flavour B, to such an extent that the price increase for flavour A would not be profitable owing to the resulting loss of sales, then the market would compromise at least flavours A and B. The process would have to be extended in addition to other available flavours until a set of products is identified for which a price rise would not induce a sufficient substitution in demand.

19. Generally, and in particular for the analysis of merger cases, the price to take into account will be the prevailing market price. This may not be the case where the prevailing price has been determined in the absence of sufficient competition. In particular for the investigation of abuses of dominant positions, the fact that the prevailing price might already have been substantially increased will be taken into account.[285]

An economist explains the significance and advantages of the Commission's use of the SSNIP test when defining markets as follows:

The success of the SSNIP is no accident. The question that it asks goes to the core of why we care about market definition in the first place. We can only answer the question of whether, for instance, a 70 per cent share of a 'market' is likely to give a company market power if that 'market' is an economically meaningful market. The key question is whether substitution to other products or other geographic regions is a substantial, or only a trivial, limitation on the conduct of the parties offering those products. We want to include within the market everything that offers substitution to the products at issue for significant numbers of consumers and to exclude from the market all those things that are not realistic substitutes. The SSNIP test is a convenient way of doing this.[286]

---

[285] This is a recognition of the so-called 'cellophane fallacy'. See the discussion *infra* 70 ff.

[286] W. Bishop, 'Editorial: The Modernization of DGIV' [1997] *ECLR* 481. This was written when the Notice was in draft form. The final version, however, did not differ in any material respect relevant here.

The practical problem, however, is actually applying the SSNIP test. How are customers' reactions to the hypothetical price rise to be gauged?

The Commission attempts to answer this question in paragraphs 25–52 of the Notice. It stresses that it has an open approach to empirical evidence and recognizes that the types of evidence which will be relevant and influential will depend on the industry, product, or services in question. The Commission states that it can ordinarily establish the potential market from preliminary information available or submitted by firms involved. Frequently, the matter may boil down to a question as simple as 'is product A in the same market as product B?'. Where this is so, the case may be determined without a precise definition of the market being necessary. Where greater precision in market definition *is* necessary, the Commission may contact the main customers and companies in the industry, professional associations, and companies in upstream markets to ascertain their views. It may address written requests for information to the market players (including asking their views on reactions to hypothetical price increases and on market boundaries), enter into discussions with them, and even carry out visits to or inspections of the premises of the parties and/or their customers and competitors. Where consumers are concerned it is recognized that asking hypothetical questions may lead to biased results and that interviewees may behave in practice differently from how they answer survey questions.[287] Research on consumer behaviour has led economists to favour 'conjoint analysis' whereby the 'trade-offs' which consumers make when confronted with different products (between, e.g., price and quality, reliability and trendiness) can be built into the analysis.[288]

The Commission states in the Notice[289] that it will consider quantitative tests devised by economists for the purpose of delineating markets. These include elasticity estimates, tests based on similarity of price movements over time (price correlation analysis[290]), causality calculations,[291] and price convergence analysis. In particular, it will consider evidence of recent substitution in the past available as a result of actual events or shocks in the market ('shock analysis'), including the entry of other competitors into the market or the introduction of new products.[292] Indeed, the Commission indicates that 'this sort of information will normally be fundamental for market definition'.[293] Evidence of the consequences of past launches of new products on the sales of existing products is also described as useful.

---

[287] As anyone who has ever been asked to take part in a market research exercise will know. And see M. Hughes and N. Beale, 'Customer Surveys in UK Merger Cases—the Art and Science of Asking the Right People the Right Questions' [2005] *ECLR* 297.

[288] See B. Dunbow, 'Understanding Consumers: The Value of Stated Preferences in Antitrust Proceedings' [2003] 24 *ECLR* 141; D. Hildebrand, *The Role of Economics Analysis in the EC Competition Rules* (Kluwer Law International, 2002), 329–31; D. Hildebrand, 'The European School in EC Competition Law' (2002) 25 *World Competition* 3; D. Hidebrand, 'Using Conjoint Analysis for Market Definition: Application of Modern Market Research Tools to Implement the Hypothetical Monopolist Test' (2006) 29 *World Competition* (2) 315.

[289] Para. 39.

[290] See G. J. Stigler and R. A. Sherwin, 'The Extent of the Market' (1985) 28 *Journal of Law and Economics* 555.

[291] Causality tests try to determine if there is causation from one series of prices to another, or if they mutually determine each other. The most widely accepted testing procedure recently has been 'Granger causality', a method set out in C. Granger, 'Investigating Causal Relations by Econometric Models and Cross-Spectral Methods' (1969) 37 *Econometrica* 424, see Van den Bergh and Camesasca, *supra* n. 283 137.

[292] As well as things like natural disasters, strikes, sudden exchange rate changes, regulatory intervention, and the introduction of new technology.

[293] Para. 38. Economics is not an experimental science. The consequences of something happening which really affects the products available on the market (e.g., a shortage arising from a natural disaster) are therefore particularly significant.

The wide range of tests that can be employed in the attempt to define markets were discussed in a 1999 report prepared by an economics consultancy for the UK competition authority, the Office of Fair Trading (OFT).[294] The report demonstrated that there are problems of some kind with all the tests (although these are being continually refined and improved). For example:

Generally, tests based on price trends alone should be treated with caution, as they do not allow an assessment of whether prices could be profitably raised by market participants. However, the paucity of the data available often prevents the analyst from estimating more appropriate demand models, so that antitrust markets are defined on the basis of price tests alone.[295]

Bishop and Walker accept that price correlation analysis has several weaknesses[296] but consider that nevertheless it can provide useful information to aid market definition. One of its attractions is that it has 'relatively low information requirements and ease of use'[297] which is particularly important when, as in merger investigations, competition authorities are working to very tight deadlines.[298] There is general agreement that price correlation, Granger causality and cointegration[299] tests may identify economic markets but do not necessarily establish *antitrust* markets, i.e., do not answer the question 'is this market worth monopolising?'.[300] Critical loss analysis may also be employed:

This analysis compares the actual losses that are likely to result from a price increase with a threshold—the critical loss—which is equal to the level of sale losses for which a given price increase is just profitable . . . Thus, the critical loss is the point where the two opposing effects of a price increase offset each other so that the net effect in profits is nil. If the actual losses of a price increase exceed this threshold then the price increase is not profitable.[301]

---

[294] OFT 266, *Quantitative techniques in competition analysis*, Research Paper 17, prepared by LECG Ltd. See also the Lexecon report, *An Introduction to Quantitative Techniques in Competition Analysis* (2003), now available on the CRA web site, http://www.crai.com/ecp/publications/2003/index.htm.

[295] (OFT 266) para. 2.25.

[296] Price correlation analysis is based on the idea that if two products are in the same market their prices will move in the same way over time. Similarity, however, may result from products in different markets being subject to the same changes in external forces (common shocks), such as the increase in a raw material needed for both. This could result in a spurious correlation: see Motta, *supra*, n. 242, 108.

[297] S. Bishop and M. Walker, *The Economics of EC Competition Law* (2nd edn., Sweet & Maxwell, 2002), para. 11.01.

[298] See Chap. 12 for the time periods applicable under the EC Merger Regulation. Price correlation analysis was used, *inter alia*, in the leading merger cases of *Nesté/Perrier* [1993] 4 CMLR M17, *Guiness/Grand Metropolitan* [1997] 5 CMLR 760, and *Lonrho/Gencor* [1999] 4 CMLR 1076.

[299] Cointegration analysis looks at the relationship between economic data series, such as price series, and examines whether it is stable over the long run.

[300] OFT 266, para. 8.7, Bishop and Walker, n. 297 *supra*, para. 15.21; H. Wills, Market Definition: 'How Stationarity Tests Can Improve Accuracy' [2002] *ECLR* 4; Lexecon Report, n. 294 *supra*, paras. 3.1–3.4.

[301] O'Donoghue and Padilla, *supra* n. 212, 79. See also Van den Bergh and Camesasca, *supra* n. 283, 137–140; Faull and Nikpay, *supra* n. 224, 1.277–1.282; D. P. O'Brien and A. L. Wickelgreen, 'A Critical Analysis of Critical Loss Analysis' (2003) 70 *Antitrust Law Journal* 161; B. Harris and C. Veljanovski, 'Critical Loss Analysis: Its Growing Use in Competition Law' [2003] *ECLR* 213; I.Kokkoris, 'Critical Loss Analysis: Critically Ill?' [2005] *ECLR* 518. In respect of mergers, merger simulation analysis may be used, as it was in *Volvo/Scania* [2001] OJ L143/74.

As the OFT report concluded, although quantitative techniques are not 'magic bullets' they can, when used correctly and rigorously, be helpful tools.[302] Moreover, Faull and Nikpay conclude that:

In our view, the complexity of the SSNIP test should, however, not be overemphasised. The most important aspect of the SSNIP is its conceptual side, not its quantitative side...Even when no detailed data are available, it is useful to think of the market definition question in terms of SSNIP. By asking a question which is directly linked to the purpose of antitrust analysis (is the exercise of market power an issue for this collection of products or not?), it brings a certain structure and consistency to the market definition exercise. The SSNIP concept provides for a framework within which to consider the question of economic substitution.[303]

The Commission will not consider two *prima facie* demand substitutes as belonging to one market if it sees that there are obstacles which will prevent or hinder customers from changing. Paragraph 42 of the Notice discusses 'switching costs':

42. *Barriers and costs associated with switching demand to potential substitutes.* There are a number of barriers and costs that might prevent the Commission from considering two *prima facie* demand substitutes as belonging to one single product market. It is not possible to provide an exhaustive list of all the possible barriers to substitution and of switching costs. These barriers or obstacles might have a wide range of origins, and in its decisions, the Commission has been confronted with regulatory barriers or other forms of State intervention, constraints arising in downstream markets, need to incur specific capital investment or loss in current output in order to switch to alternative inputs, the location of customers, specific investment in production process, learning and human capital investment, retooling costs of other investments, uncertainty about quality and reputation of unknown suppliers, and others.

Switching costs are the price which consumers pay for changing to another product. They are not necessarily financial but cover inconvenience and hassle as well. Switching costs may also act as barriers to entry[304] and may be created or increased by incumbent firms as an exclusionary tactic.[305]

c. The Cellophane Fallacy

A major problem with the SSNIP test is that of the 'cellophane fallacy'. Paragraph 19 of the Notice[306] recognizes the difficulties presented by the cellophane fallacy (although it does not refer to it as such). The fallacy arises from the fact that the SSNIP test cannot identify whether the current price is already a monopoly price resulting from the exercise of market power. It is named after the subject-matter of an American case in which the Supreme Court is said to have failed to recognize it, in that it erroneously accepted Du Pont's argument that cellophane was not a separate relevant market but competed directly and closely with other flexible packaging materials such as aluminium foil, polythene, and wax paper.[307]

---

[302] OFT 266, para. 18.12.

[303] J. Faull and A. Nikpay, *The EC Law of Competition* (2nd edn., Oxford University Press, 2007), 1.147 (L. Peeperkorn and V. Verouden).

[304] See *infra* 84 ff.

[305] See *infra* 88.

[306] See *supra* 67.

[307] *United States v. El du Pont de Nemours & Co* 351 US 377 (1956).

The difficulty is that a profit-maximizing firm will price as high as it can. If X is the sole supplier of widgets it will normally set the price of widgets at a level where other products constrain it. If the marginal cost of a widget is £5 but blodgets, which perform the function as widgets, are sold at their marginal cost of £10, X will sell widgets at just under £10. That way X still makes a supra-normal profit and does not lose out to the blodget manufacturers. At the price of £10 blodgets and widgets are substitutes, and X can argue, as Du Pont did in the *Cellophane* case, that since it cannot raise the price without losing sales it must be operating on a competitive market. The fallacy arises, however, since X is *already* making a monopoly profit. It may have no substitutes at its competitive price of £5. There may be substitutes however at the price of £10. In the *Cellophane* case the Supreme Court found that the market was that for all flexible wrapping materials as other materials competed with cellophane at its current price. It did not ask, however, whether or not cross-elasticity between cellophane and other materials was only high *because Du Pont was already exercising market power*. The Notice recognizes this difficulty. The Commission states that using the prevailing market price as the base figure from which to hypothesize the 5–10 per cent price rise of the SSNIP test may be inappropriate where that price has been determined in the absence of competition. This means that great care will have to be exercised if using the SSNIP test to determine whether or not an incumbent on a market has a 'dominant position' (or market power) for the purposes of Article 82.[308]

In contrast, in merger cases it has only to be decided whether or not the merger will create or *increase* market power. The SSNIP test is thus much more reliable since the prevailing market price is used as the starting point.

The cellophane fallacy is a great problem because in very many markets prices do reflect some degree of market power and the failings of the SSNIP test in dealing with these is a serious limitation on its utility in non-merger cases. Furthermore, it is not just an issue where prices are already set *above* the competitive level, but also where the prevailing price is too low.[309] However, although the Notice recognizes the problem it makes no suggestions for dealing with it.[310]

In a UK case under the Competition Act 1998, *Aberdeen Journals*,[311] the alleged anti-competitive conduct was predatory pricing (pricing at a low level to drive out competitors)[312] of advertising space in newspapers.[313] The market definition question was which newspapers should be considered to be in the same market for this purpose. The DGFT[314] acknowledged the cellophane fallacy and considered that the prevailing price of advertising space in the *Herald and Post* might be below the competitive level. There were also other factors which made the application of the SSNIP test difficult.

---

[308] EC law terminology. See *infra* Chaps. 5 and 6.

[309] See P. Crocioni, 'The Hypothetical Monopolist Test: What it can and cannot tell you' [2002] *ECLR* 355.

[310] See, however, *infra* 73.

[311] *Predation by Aberdeen Journals Ltd* CA98/14/2002, [2002] UKCLR 740.

[312] The treatment of predatory pricing under EC law is dealt with *infra* Chap. 7.

[313] The case arose under the Chapter II prohibition of the Competition Act 1998 which is in effect identical (except that there is no requirement for an effect on inter-Member State trade) to Article 82 of the EC Treaty and which, by reason of s. 60 of the Act, has to be interpreted and applied consistently with the relevant EC case law.

[314] The functions of the Director General of Fair Trading (DGFT) were taken over by the OFT on 1 April 2003 pursuant to the provisions of the Enterprise Act 2002, s. 2. The OFT Guideline on market definition (OFT 403) paras. 5.4–5.6 recognizes the problem of the cellophane fallacy.

> ## *Predation by Aberdeen Journals Ltd* CA98/14/2002, [2002] UKCLR 740 *Director General of Fair Trading*
>
> 94. Such a test must be applied with caution, however, in cases involving markets where competition is being distorted (e.g., where there is a dominant undertaking), as market prices may already be at uncompetitive levels. In such a case, a 'small but significant' increase in prices that are already excessive may lead to large scale switching to products that would not be a viable substitute at normal price levels, whereas a similar increase in prices previously set at a predatory level may result in prices that are still below competition levels and thus result in little or no switching, despite the existence of alternative products that would be viable substitutes at normal price levels . . . Given the conduct of the *Herald & Post* in maintaining prices of its advertising space below the level required to cover its average variable cost up until the end of March 2000, the scope for applying such a substitution analysis in this is limited.
>
> 95. A variety of other aspects of newspaper advertising markets made it difficult to apply normal econometric analysis methods as an aid to market definition in this case. Due to extensive use of discounting, which may apply to bundles of advertising space covering different newspaper titles, different customers pay widely differing amounts to place the same type of advertisement in the same newspaper. As a result, prices are not transparent and it is not possible to generate meaningful data for analysis using ratecard prices alone. In addition, the tendency (noted at paragraph 33 above) of certain advertisers to react to price rises by altering the balance of their advertising spending between different newspapers, rather then switching outright, further complicated interpretation of the data, as did the difficulty of determining the extent to which space in the newspapers concerned may have been viewed by individual advertises as substitutes or complements, given relative prices at any moment in time.

Faced with these difficulties, the DGFT undertook a statistical analysis of the monthly revenues and advertising volumes of the various newspapers in an attempt to identify the degree of cross-price elasticity between the different newspapers and sought to deal with the lack of price transparency by analysing average yield data. He was unable to obtain any reliable statistically significant econometric results and therefore looked at other factors, in particular the conduct and statements of the undertakings concerned, to establish the relevant product market. On appeal the Competition Appeal Tribunal (CAT) upheld this way of proceeding, confirming that:

> . . . the fact that market conditions were already distorted, means that extreme caution must be exercised when dealing with the presence or absence of switching patterns. Such evidence is not a reliable guide to what would happen in normal competitive conditions.[315]

The DGFT also recognized that the cellophane fallacy would mean the SSNIP test yielding misleading results in *BSkyB*, where the fear, *inter alia*, was that the prices of BSkyB's programme packages containing live FA Premier League football matches were already at a monopoly level. In that case he relied instead on 'consideration of live FAPL football's characteristics and consumers' underlying preferences to permit assessment of whether other identified products can satisfy demand for such characteristics' as well as on relative price movements between products possibly in the same market.[316]

---

[315] *Aberdeen Journals Ltd* v. *OFT* [2003] CAT 11, [2003] CompAR 67, para. 262.

[316] Case CA98/20/2002, *BSkyB Investigation: Alleged Infringement of the Chapter II Prohibition* [2003] UKCLR 240, para. 97.

Some of the suggested solutions to the cellophane fallacy problem are set out in the extract below which draws on a number of sources, *inter alia* an Economic Discussion Paper prepared for the UK's competition authority.[317]

R. O'Donoghue and A. J. Padilla, *The Law and Economics of Article 82 EC* (Hart Publishing, 2006), 82–4

A number of solutions have been proposed to address the problem of the cellophane fallacy. Ultimately, however, there is no single, best solution. Much will depend on what evidence is available to estimate the extent to which prices already exceed the competitive level, including by reference to qualitative criteria and experience in comparable markets:

1. *Estimate the competitive price before undertaking a critical analysis.* One obvious solution in order to avoid drawing a wrong inference from the existence of supra-competitive prices is to estimate the competitive price level prior to engaging in a critical loss analysis. . . . But, in practice, this is not a very realistic alternative, given the enormous difficulties of estimating a competitive price in most industries. . . . These problems have plagued the analysis of excessive pricing under Article 82 EC and . . . no effective solution has emerged. A second difficulty is that estimating the competitive price level would transform the SSNIP test into a direct test of dominance. If, somehow, the competitive price level could be identified, then there would be no need to go through the whole process of defining relevant markets and assessing dominance on the basis of structural and behavioural proxies. . . .

2. *Use a combination of qualitative and quantitative evidence.* Another proposed solution is to adopt a qualitative approach based on the analysis of product characteristics and intended use, *but* taking into account the logic and principles of the SSNIP test and the critical loss analysis . . . . The SSNIP test forces analysts to take a structured view of the process of market definition and takes into account only those products that are potentially demand or supply-side substitutes of those forming part of the relevant market. A purely *ad hoc* market definition, which ignores these basic principles, is likely to produce overly narrow markets. What is important is not the difference in physical characteristics *per se*, but the manner in which these differences influence demand. Relying on the sound principles of the SSNIP test ensures that: (a) two physically similar products which, however, are not regarded as substitutes by consumers, are not included in the same market; and (b) two products with relatively dissimilar functionality, but which consumers regard as substitutes, are included in the same relevant product market. The Discussion Paper notes that: . . . . .

> "The SSNIP test at prevailing prices remains useful in the sense that it is indicative of substitution patterns at those prices. Products and areas that can be excluded from the relevant market at prevailing prices would also be excluded at any lower competitive price."

The application of the SSNIP test results in a putative relevant market, that may be defined too widely. The characteristics and intended use of the products included comprised in that putative market needs to be carefully examined to assess whether they are indeed substitutes.

3. *Use other comparable markets as a crosscheck.* A third alternative complements the critical loss analysis approach to market definition with: (a) the qualitative analysis of product

---

[317] S. Bishop and S. Baker, *The role of market definition in monopoly and dominance inquiries* (Economic Discussion Paper 2, July 2001, OFT 342), *supra* n. 284.

characteristics and customer needs; and (b) the study of competition in "comparable" markets, i.e. markets with similar structural and non-structural characteristics. Direct application of the critical loss analysis provides an upper bound to the scope of the relevant product market: all products that are found to be outside the relevant product market using a critical loss analysis at prevailing (high) prices can be safely excluded . . . The additional analysis of physical product characteristics could help to limit the size of the possibly overly wide market emerging from the critical loss analysis. Another possible way to refine the market definition resulting from the quantitative analysis is to investigate market conditions in similar markets that are more competitive than the one under investigation. If the price level in these markets is not significantly lower than in the market defined using a standard critical loss analysis, then it is unlikely that the cellophane fallacy plays a major role . . .

4. *Examine the competitive reactions of the allegedly dominant firm.* Another possibility is to investigate whether the allegedly dominant firm monitors and reacts to the price changes and new products introductions of its competitors. If it does, then those products are likely to be close substitutes for its own products. And the locations where those rivals operate are likely to be part of the same geographic market than the firm in the question . . .

5. *The small but significant non-transitory decrease in prices (SSNDP) test.* An alternative way to delineate the boundaries of the relevant market is to consider the impact on the volume sold by a hypothetical monopolist of a 5-10% *reduction* in the prevailing price (unlike an *increase* in the case of SSNIP) . . . . If the prevailing price was supra-competitive, the price reduction would lead to a relatively small increase in sales (otherwise, the price would not have been increased to its prevailing level in the first place). On the contrary, if the prevailing price was competitive, the output response to the price reduction would be large or small depending on the degree of substitution between the products in the candidate market and those outside it. Therefore, evidence that the response to a price reduction would trigger a significant output response suggests a broad market and a high degree of competition. On the other hand, if a small price reduction does not cause a significant increase in output, then the candidate market is likely to be a proper antitrust market where market power can be, or already is, exercised.

d. Characteristics and Intended Use

In paragraph 36 of the Notice the Commission recognizes the limited usefulness of analyzing the characteristics and intended use of a product when defining the market. The Notice indicates, however, that such an analysis may be useful as a preliminary step when considering the possible substitutes for a product.

Commission Notice on the Definition of the Relevant Market for the Purposes of Community Competition Law [1997] OJ C372/5, [1998] 4 CMLR 177

36. An analysis of the product characteristics and its intended use allows the Commission, as a first step, to limit the field of investigation of possible substitutes. However, product characteristics and intended use are insufficient to show whether two products are demand substitutes. Functional interchangeability or similarity in characteristics may not, in themselves, provide sufficient criteria, because the responsiveness of customers to relative price changes may be determined by other considerations as well. For example, there may be different competitive

constraints in the original equipment market for car components and in spare parts, thereby leading to a separate delineation of two relevant markets. Conversely, differences in product characteristics are not in themselves sufficient to exclude demand substitutability, since this will depend to a large extent on how customers value different characteristics.

However, as has already been noted, in the past an analysis of the characteristics and use of the product were the usual way of trying to identify substitutability and it was above all the experience of the Commission in defining markets for the purpose of merger control which led it to favour the more economic SSNIP test. The case law of the Court and the decisions of the Commission discussed in this book are replete with considerations of characteristics and use in market definition.[318] It is the examination of the characteristics of the product which have given rise to the greatest criticisms, as in the *United Brands* case, where the Court famously had to decide whether bananas were in a separate market from fruit.[319] In some cases, however, a consideration of the *use* of the product can be crucial because it can then be determined that it has no substitutes.[320] Since the publication of the Notice the Commission itself has continued to use characteristics and use where appropriate. For example, in *Van den Bergh Foods Ltd*[321] the Commission held that impulse ice-cream cream (bought as individual portions in shops for immediate consumption) and take-home ice-cream[322] (multi-packs of single items designed for storage and consumption at home) were in different markets. This was partly because the 'distinction on the basis of the consumer's intended purpose in purchasing the ice cream in turn determines the differences in characteristics and price between impulse and take-home products'.[323] Also, in its *Michelin* decision of 2001 (*Michelin II*),[324] the Commission held, without mentioning the SSNIP test, that the market for new replacement tyres for lorries and buses was separate to that for retreads. It took into account the 'analysis of their specific characteristics and their uses by final consumers'[325] based on surveys of those consumers (the haulier firms). In three more recent Article 82 decisions, *Microsoft*,[326] *Wanadoo*,[327] and *Clearstream*[328] the Commission relied heavily on qualitative analysis.[329] In short, it is difficult to envisage the

[318] See particularly *infra* Chap. 6.

[319] Case 2/76, *United Brands v. Commission* [1978] ECR 207, [1978] 1 CMLR 429.

[320] An example of this is the UK *Genzyme* decision by the OFT under the Competition Act 1998 in which a certain drug was identified as the relevant product market because there was no other drug which could effectively treat a rare disease (Gaucher's disease): Case CA98/3/03, [2003] UKCLR 950.

[321] [1998] OJ L246/1, [1998] 5 CMLR 530, particularly paras. 130–8, the decision was upheld on appeal, Case T-65/98, *Van den Bergh Foods Ltd v. Commission* [2004] 4 CMLR 1, *aff'd* Case C-552/03 P, *Unilever Bestfoods (Ireland) Ltd v. EC Commission* [2006] 5 CMLR 1494, where the definition of the market was not challenged.

[322] It also distinguished catering ice-cream (sold in bulk to catering establishments) from impulse and take-home ice-cream.

[323] Case T-65/98, para. 132. It also distinguished between the markets for industrial (produced for wide-scale distribution) and 'artisan' (produced, distributed, and consumed locally on a small scale) ice-cream.

[324] [2002] OJ L58/25, [2002] 5 CMLR 388, upheld by the CFI on appeal, Case T-203/01, *Michelin v. Commission* [2003] ECR II-4071, [2004] 4 CMLR 923. The case was, in effect, a sequel to the 1981 case, Case 322/81, *Nederlandsche Banden-Industrie Michelin v. Commission* [1983] ECR 3461, [1985] I CMLR 282: see further *infra* Chap. 6.

[325] *Michelin II*, para. 116.

[326] *Microsoft* [2005] 4 CMLR 965, on appeal Case T-201/04 *Microsoft v. EC Commission* (judgment pending).

[327] COMP/38.233, [2005] 5 CMLR 120, upheld on appeal, Case T-340/03, *France Télécom SA v. Commission*, 30 January 2007.

[328] COMP/38/096, [2005] 5 CMLR 1302.

[329] See further Chap. 6.

examination of characteristics and use being in practice confined to the 'first step' as suggested in paragraph 36 of the Notice, particularly in view of the very real difficulties caused by the cellophane fallacy in so many non-merger cases.[330] Moreover, the importance the Court has afforded to characteristics and use cannot be ignored for the Notice cannot overrule the case of the Court.

e. Chains of Substitution

Demand side substitutability can be complicated by the existence of a 'chain of substitution', where B is a substitute for A and C is a substitute for B, etc. This can occur in geographic as well as product markets.[331] For example, two shops may compete for the customers who live between them, but for customers who live the far side of either of them the substitute may be different:

Shop A ← customer 1 → **Shop B** ← customer 2 → **Shop C** ← customer 3 → **Shop D.**

In this example, shops A and B are substitutes for customer 1, B and C are substitutes for 2 and C and D are substitutes for 3. A and D, A and C, B and D are not direct substitutes for any customer. How then are the boundaries of the geographic market to be drawn? The Commission's Notice discusses the chain of substitution problem in paragraphs 57 and 58, and at the end of paragraph 57 concludes that the real question is how far the existence of substitutes has a constraining influence on an undertaking's pricing policy.

> 57. In certain cases, the existence of chains of substitution might lead to the definition of a relevant market where products or areas at the extreme of the market are not directly substitutable. An example might be provided by the geographic dimension of a product with significant transport costs. In such cases, deliveries from a given plant are limited to a certain area around each plant by the impact of transport costs. In principle, such an area could constitute the relevant geographic market. However, if the distribution of plants is such that there are considerable overlaps between the areas around different plants, it is possible that the pricing of those products will be constrained by a chain substitution effect, and lead to the definition of a broader geographic market. The same reasoning may apply if product B is a demand substitute for products A and C. Even if products A and C are not direct demand substitutes, they might be found to be in the same relevant product market since their respective pricing might be constrained by substitution to B.

> 58. From a practical perspective, the concept of chains of substitution has to be corroborated by actual evidence, for instance related to price inter-dependence at the extremes of the chains of substitution, in order to lead to an extension of the relevant market in an individual case. Price levels at the extremes of the chains would have to be of the same magnitude as well.

It is therefore possible to have a relevant market where some product or areas are indirect, rather than direct, substitutes for each other. Chains of substitution are discussed further in Chapter 6.[332]

f. Distinct Groups of Customers

Consumers as a whole have, of course, different preferences and priorities but exercises in market definition have to recognize that some consumers may be able to turn to a substitute in

---

[330] For example, the OFT's *BSkyB* decision, n. 316 *supra*, shows recourse by the UK authorities to 'live FAPL football's characteristics' where the use of the SSNIP test was rendered unreliable by the fact that the prevailing price was probably already a monopoly one. And see the discussion in the O'Donoghue and Padilla extract above.

[331] For geographic market definition, see further *infra* 81.

[332] *Infra* 364.

response to a price rise while for others it is impossible. A person who cannot drive, for example, cannot respond to an increase in rail fares by deciding to drive themselves in a car (at least, not legally). The most (in)famous case of this problem in EC law is the *United Brands*[333] case in which the ECJ confirmed the Commission's finding that there was a market for bananas separate from that for other fruit partly on the grounds that for some consumers (the very young, the old, and the sick) bananas were a uniquely suitable fruit (they can be mashed up for babies, are easily digestible, are easy to handle, and can be eaten by people with no teeth). This justification led, however, to widespread criticism of the judgment. The argument is that the fact that bananas satisfy a unique need of a particular class of customers does not mean that bananas constitute a separate market if other customers (the majority) are not so limited in their choice of fruit and can respond to a price rise in bananas by buying other fruit. Although it may be possible at point of sale to discriminate *in favour* of certain customers (such as students or old age pensioners) by charging them less than the standard price on production of identification, it is generally not possible to discriminate in the same way against individuals, for example pensioners, and to charge them a *higher* price. If it is impossible to discriminate against the 'infra-marginal' customers who cannot switch—the young, old, and sick[334]—by charging them a higher price, then the behaviour of marginal customers (who *are* able to switch) must be taken into account. It is the marginal customers who affect a supplier's pricing decisions and whose behaviour is, consequently, crucial in the determination of the market. One group of customers who have a particular need for the product is difficult to exploit *unless* it can somehow be kept separate from other customers and if those other customers can be prevented from making sales on to the special class.

In its Notice on market definition the Commission recognizes (despite the *United Brands* judgment) that a distinct group of customers will be relevant to market definition only where they, themselves, constitute a separate market and price discrimination between the different groups of customers is possible:

43. The extent of the product market might be narrowed in the presence of distinct groups of customers. A distinct group of customers for the relevant product may constitute a narrower, distinct market when such a group could be subject to price discrimination. This will usually be the case when two conditions are met: (a) it is possible to identify clearly which group an individual customer belongs to at the moment of selling the relevant products to him, and (b) trade among customers or arbitrage by third parties should not be feasible.

United Brands is examined in Chapter 6.[335]

g. Markets in the New Economy

We have already mentioned that particular problems arise in applying competition law to the 'new economy'.[336] One of these problems is the application of the usual principles of market definition. The SSNIP test tries to identify short term demand substitutability by positing a small but significant price rise. However, as we have seen,[337] the high technology markets of the new economy are characterized by dynamic competition, where the threat to existing products

---

[333] Case 2/76, *United Brands v. Commission* [1978] ECR 207, [1978] 1 CMLR 429.

[334] Or those buying to feed them.

[335] *Infra* 353 ff.

[336] See *supra* 54.

[337] See *supra* 55.

comes from *new* products. Concentrating on hypothetical price rises instead of the competitive constraints stemming from product innovation may lead to identifying markets which are too narrow. Market definition in the new economy is a particular problem in merger cases, where the merging parties may be hoping to produce innovative products which do not yet exist.[338]

h. The Structure of Supply and Demand

The structure of supply and demand may be important in determining the relevant market and may cause identical products to fall into different markets. As will be seen in Chapter 6, the structure of supply and demand was relevant to the determination of the market in *Michelin*.[339] In that case the ECJ upheld the Commission finding that identical new heavy vehicle tyres fell into different markets depending on whether they were supplied to vehicle manufacturers to fit as original equipment on the assembly line, or to dealers to be fitted as replacements. This was because the dynamics of the transactions were quite different.[340]

(vi) Primary and Secondary Markets (Aftermarkets)

Special problems of market definition arise where products are connected with one another but not substitutes. 'Aftermarket' is the expression used to describe a market comprising complementary products (or 'secondary' products) that are purchased after the purchase of another product (the 'primary product') to which they relate.[341] Many durable goods, such as cars, need compatible spare parts, and some, such as vacuum cleaners or photocopiers, also need a constant supply of 'consumables' in order to operate: some cleaners need bags or filters, photocopiers need toner cartridges and suitable paper, and so on. Furthermore, durables may need to be serviced and repaired. The customer may be 'locked in'—the owner of a Ford Fiesta needs spare parts which fit a Ford Fiesta, not those which fit a Nissan Micra. The Commission Notice, paragraph 56 says that this is an area 'where the application of the principles above has to be undertaken with care'. It recognizes that 'constraints on substitution imposed by conditions in the connected markets' must be taken into account. Although the normal approach to market definition may result in an aftermarket consisting of one brand of spare parts, however, that may not be, in certain situations, a 'relevant product market' for assessing market power.[342] There have been a number of EC cases involving primary and secondary markets and this issue is discussed further in Chapter 6.[343]

(vii) One Market or Two?

The issue of aftermarkets is one aspect of the general question of how far products or services can or should be seen as falling into separate markets. What about size 38 and size 42 shoes (they are not substitutes for one another, so does that mean there are separate product markets

---

[338] See *infra* Chap. 12. For further discussion of the issue in respect of Article 82 cases such as *Microsoft* (*supra* n. 280 and *Wanadoo* (*supra* n. 327), see Chap. 6.

[339] Case 322/81, *Nederlandsche Banden-Industrie Michelin v. Commission* [1983] ECR 3461, [1985] I CMLR 282.

[340] *Ibid.*, para. 44; see also Case C-333/94 P, *Tetra Pak International SA v. Commission* [1996] ECR I-5951, [1997] 4 CMLR 662, para. 13; *Van den Bergh Foods* [1998] OJ L246/1, [1998] 5 CMLR 530, para. 133, *supra* n. 321.

[341] Discussion Paper on Article 82, para. 243.

[342] Discussion Paper on Article 82, paras. 247–50.

[343] *Infra* 368. The Commission Discussion Paper on Article 82 devotes an entire section, paras. 243–65, to the issue of aftermarkets.

for each size of shoe?). Sometimes this is a matter of whether the product or service can be broken down into separate component parts which are in different markets. Is a pair of shoes one product or two (a right and left shoe are not substitutes for one another)? What about the shoes and the laces (again, they are not substitutes for one another)? The differentiation of products into separate markets can be crucial in cases concerning allegations of 'tying' or 'bundling' which can constitute an abuse of a dominant position contrary to Article 82 in some circumstances. The *Microsoft* case[344] is a perfect example of this: is the Windows operating system supplied with an inbuilt Windows media player one product or two products bundled together? If it is the latter then it is possible that Article 82 has been infringed.[345]

(viii) Two Sided Industries

A two-sided industry is one where the firms have to compete simultaneously for two groups of customers. O'Donoghue and Padilla[346] give the example of the manufacturers of video games, who must, in a 'chicken and egg' dilemma, persuade customers to buy the consoles and game developers to write games for the consoles (in return for royalties and/or fixed fees). A price rise to one group of customers (the console buyers) will lose sales to both groups (the console customers will buy less and the games developers will develop and sell less); with less choice of games, customers choosing a console will find that one less attractive, and so buy another. The conclusion is that the usual market definition tests are of little use in two-sided industries: if critical loss analysis is applied in the usual way it leads to the definition (incorrectly) of excessively narrow markets.[347]

(ix) Supply Substitution

The ECJ in *Continental Can*[348] stressed that the market must be defined by reference both to supply-side and demand side substitutability. If a manufacturer of one product can easily switch its production to another product then both products may be in the same market. A difficulty here is to distinguish supply-side substitutability from potential competition. The Commission considers this dilemma in the Notice and concludes that it is a question of time scale. If a producer of one product can switch production in the short term to produce another product, without significant cost or risk, then those two products will be found to be in the same market. If a producer can enter the market but only in the longer term and after incurring some cost, then that producer's presence is not relevant at the stage of market definition. Its presence will be crucial, however, when assessing market power: if the producer can enter the market then it is a potential competitor and its existence will have a constraining effect on those operating on the market.[349] Supply substitution is likely to be possible only where producers make products

---

[344] *Microsoft* [2005] 4 CMLR 965, on appeal Case T-201/04, *Microsoft v. EC Commission* (judgment pending).

[345] See Chaps. 6 and 7 for the *Microsoft* case. It can also be important in cases of refusal to supply, which depend on there being two markets involved: see Case C-418/01, *IMS Health GmbH & Co. OHG v NDC Health GmbH & Co. KG* [2004] ECR I-5039, [2004] 4 CMLR 1543, further Chaps. 6 and 7. For the issue in merger cases, see Chap. 12.

[346] R. O'Donoghue and A. J. Padilla, *The Law and Economics of Article 82 EC* (Hart Publishing, 2006), 2.5.4.

[347] *Ibid.*

[348] Case 6/72, *Europemballage Corp & Continental Can Co Inc v. Commission* [1973] ECR 215, [1973] CMLR 199.

[349] See *supra* 59.

which, while not substitutes for one another from the consumer's perspective are, nonetheless, similar. An example, given by the Commission in its Notice, is markets for paper.[350]

Commission Notice on the Definition of the Relevant Market for the Purposes of Community Competition law [1997] OJ C372/5, [1998] 4 CMLR 177

20. Supply-side substitutability may also be taken into account when defining markets in those situations in which its effects are equivalent to those of demand substitution in terms of effectiveness and immediacy. This means that suppliers are able to switch production to the relevant products and market them in the short term .... without incurring significant additional costs or risks in response to small and permanent changes in relative prices. When these conditions are met, the additional production that is put on the market will have a disciplinary effect on the competitive behaviour of the companies involved. Such an impact in terms of effectiveness and immediacy is equivalent to the demand substitution effect.

21. These situations typically arise when companies market a wide range of qualities or grades of one product; even if, for a given final customer or group of consumers, the different qualities are not substitutable, the different qualities will be grouped into one product market, provided that most of the suppliers are able to offer and sell the various qualities immediately and without the significant increases in costs described above. In such cases, the relevant product market will encompass all products that are substitutable in demand and supply, and the current sales of those products will be aggregated so as to give the total value or volume of the market. The same reasoning may lead to group different geographic areas.

22. A practical example of the approach to supply-side substitutability when defining product markets is to be found in the case of paper. Paper is usually supplied in a range of different qualities, from standard writing paper to high quality papers to be used, for instance, to publish art books. From a demand point of view, different qualities of paper cannot be used for any given use, i.e., an art book or a high quality publication cannot be based on lower quality papers. However, paper plants are prepared to manufacture the different qualities, and production can be adjusted with negligible costs and in a short time-frame. In the absence of particular difficulties in distribution, paper manufacturers are able therefore, to compete for orders of the various qualities, in particular if orders are placed with sufficient lead time to allow for modification of production plans. Under such circumstances, the Commission would not define a separate market for each quality of paper and its respective use. The various qualities of paper are included in the relevant market, and their sales added up to estimate total market value and volume.

23. When supply-side substitutability would entail the need to adjust significantly existing tangible and intangible assets, additional investments, strategic decisions or time delays, it will not be considered at the stage of market definition. Examples where supply-side substitution did not induce the Commission to enlarge the market are offered in the area of consumer products, in particular for branded beverages. Although bottling plants may in principle bottle different beverages, there are costs and lead times involved (in terms of advertising, product testing and

---

[350] In Case IV/M.166, *Torras/Sarrio* (1992) the Commission relied upon supply side substitution in considering a merger in the paper sector, see M. Furse, '*The Law of Merger Control in the EC and the UK*, (Hart Publishing, 2007), 33. See also Case IV/M.458, *Electrolux/AEG* (all models and sizes of washing machines found to be in the same market, ditto for dishwashers, fridges, microwaves and so on); Case T-65/96, *Kish Glass and Co Ltd* v. *Commission* [2000] ECR II-1885, aff'd Case C-241/00 P, *Kish Glass and Co Ltd* v. *Commission* [2001] ECR I-7159 where the market definition point was not pleaded, (different thicknesses of glass in the same market).

distribution) before the products can actually be sold. In these cases, the effects of supply-side substitutability and other forms of potential competition would then be examined at a later stage.

Whether supply-side issues are taken into account at the market definition stage can be of utmost importance, however, in cases where the *only* issue is market share and there is no 'later stage' as referred to at the end of paragraph 23 of the Notice. As explained above[351] the recent trend in block exemption regulations is to have them apply only to agreements where the parties have market shares below a particular threshold.[352] If supply side substitution is taken into account at the market definition stage it may widen the market and enable the parties concerned to take advantage of the block exemption, while with a narrower market they may have too large a share. Even post-modernization, where notification has been abolished, undertakings will prefer to know that a relevant block exemption applies to their agreement.[353] Such problems over market definition are one reason why market share thresholds in block exemptions are so unpopular with business people. As far as cases where the question being asked is whether an undertaking is in a dominant position are concerned, the Commission has sometimes been criticized for placing too little emphasis on supply-side substitutability. This may encourage too narrow definitions of the market to be adopted, a matter which is not necessarily remedied by taking into account potential competition at the next stage of the assessment of market power. In particular, a presumption of dominance is triggered at a market share of 50 per cent so the dynamics of the assessment may be skewed by omitting supply-side substitutability.[354]

(x) The Geographic Market

It is normally essential that the geographic market is defined. The ECJ in *United Brands* stressed the importance of defining the market from a geographic perspective.[355] Because market definition is determined by reference to substitutability it is possible that even firms producing identical products will not operate in the same market if they operate within mutually exclusive geographic areas. However where, for example, a customer in England may be able to substitute French widgets for English ones the English producer will not have market power if the small but significant price rise causes his customers to purchase French widgets instead. Whether or not geographic areas are mutually exclusive—whether the geographic market in a particular product is global,[356] local, or something in between—will depend on a number of factors, most notably the cost of transport, the nature of the product, and legal regulation. If transport costs

---

[351] *Supra* 351.

[352] See Commission Reg. 2790/99 [1999] OJ L336/21 on vertical restraints, *infra* Chap. 9; Commission Reg. 2658/2000 [2001] OJ L304/3 on specialization agreements, Commission Reg. 2659/2000 [2001] OJ L304/7 on research and development agreements, *infra* Chap. 13; Commission Reg. 772/2004 [2004] OJ L123/11 on technology transfer agreements, *infra* Chap. 10. The Notice on agreements of minor importance [2001] OJ C368/13, *infra* Chap. 3, 183 ff, also uses market share thresholds.

[353] See *infra* Chap. 2 and Chap. 4.

[354] For a more detailed discussion of this see *infra* Chap. 6.

[355] Case 27/76, *United Brands v. Commission* [1978] ECR 207, [1978] 1 CMLR 429.

[356] As it was, for example, in the merger case, Case IV/M.1069, *WorldCom/MCI* [1999] OJ L116/1, [1999] 5 CMLR 876.

are high relative to the value of the product, as in the case of paving slabs or concrete tiles, a geographic market may be small, perhaps even local. There may be chains of substitution in geographic markets, as explained above.[357]

The Commission sets out its approach to geographical market definition in the Notice. In paragraph 8[358] it describes the geographic market as comprising an area 'in which the conditions of competition are sufficiently homogeneous', faithfully following the ECJ's definition in *United Brands*,[359] although the rest of the Notice does not stress this aspect. Rather the Commission appears to recognize that the behaviour of undertakings may be constrained by imports from areas where the conditions of competition are not the same.[360] In *Deutsche Bahn*[361] the CFI held that 'the definition of the geographical market does not require the objective conditions of competition between traders to be perfectly homogenous. It is sufficient if they are "similar" or "sufficiently homogenous" and accordingly, only areas in which the objective conditions of competition are "heterogenous" may not be considered to constitute a uniform market'.

The Notice indicates the type of evidence the Commission considers to be relevant to the determination of the geographic market.

Commission Notice on the Definition of the Relevant Market for the Purposes of Community Competition Law [1997] OJ C372/5, [1998] 4 CMLR 177

28. The Commission's approach to geographic market definition might be summarized as follows: it will take a preliminary view of the scope of the geographic market on the basis of broad indications as to the distribution of market shares between the parties and their competitors, as well as a preliminary analysis of pricing and price differences at national and Community or EEA level. This initial view is used basically as a working hypothesis to focus the Commission's enquiries for the purposes of arriving at a precise geographic market definition.

29. The reasons behind any particular configuration of prices and market shares need to be explored. Companies might enjoy high market shares in their domestic markets just because of the weight of the past, and conversely, a homogeneous presence of companies throughout the EEA might be consistent with national or regional geographic markets. The initial working hypothesis will therefore be checked against an analysis of demand characteristics (importance of national or local preferences, current patterns of purchases of customers, product differentiation/brands, other) in order to establish whether companies in different areas do indeed constitute a real alternative source of supply for consumers. The theoretical experiment is again based on substitution arising from changes in relative prices, and the question to answer is again whether the customers of the parties would switch their orders to companies located elsewhere in the short term and at a negligible cost.

---

[357] See *supra* 76.

[358] See *supra* 64.

[359] Case 2/76, *United Brands* v. *Commission* [1978] ECR 207 [1978] 1 CMLR 429 at para. 11, see *supra* 63.

[360] See V. Korah, *An Introductory Guide to EC Competition Law and Practice* (7th edn., Hart Publishing, 2000), para. 3.2.1.2.

[361] Case T-229/94, *Deutsche Bahn AG* v. *Commission* [1997] ECR II-1689, [1998] 4 CMLR 220, para. 92; see also Case T-51/89, *Tetra Pak Rausing SA* v. *Commission* [1990] ECR II-309, [1991] 4 CMLR 334, paras. 91 and 92.

30. If necessary, a further check on supply factors will be carried out to ensure that those companies located in differing areas do not face impediments in developing their sales on competitive terms throughout the whole geographic market. This analysis will include an examination of requirements for a local presence in order to sell in that area the conditions of access to distribution channels, costs associated with setting up a distribution network, and the presence or absence of regulatory barriers arising from public procurement, price regulations, quotas and tariffs limiting trade or production, technical standards, monopolies, freedom of establishment, requirements for administrative authorizations, packaging regulations, etc. In short, the Commission will identify possible obstacles and barriers isolating companies located in a given area from the competitive pressure of companies located outside that area, so as to determine the precise degree of market interpenetration at national, European or global level.

. . .

44. The type of evidence the Commission considers relevant to reach a conclusion as to the geographic market can be categorized as follows:

45. *Past evidence of diversion of orders to other areas*. In certain cases, evidence on changes in prices between different areas and consequent reactions by customers might be available. Generally, the same quantitative tests used for product market definition might as well be used in geographic market definition, bearing in mind that international comparisons of prices might be more complex due to a number of factors such as exchange rate movements, taxation and product differentiation.

46. *Basic demand characteristics*. The nature of demand for the relevant product may in itself determine the scope of the geographical market. Factors such as national preferences or preferences for national brands, language, culture and life style, and the need for a local presence have a strong potential to limit the geographic scope of competition.

47. *Views of customers and competitors*. Where appropriate, the Commission will contact the main customers and competitors of the parties in its enquiries, to gather their views on the boundaries of the geographic market as well as most of the factual information it requires to reach a conclusion on the scope of the market when they are sufficiently backed by factual evidence.

48. *Current geographic pattern of purchases*. An examination of the customers' current geographic pattern of purchases provides useful evidence as to the possible scope of the geographic market. When customers purchase from companies located anywhere in the Community or the EEA on similar terms, or they procure their supplies through effective tendering procedures in which companies from anywhere in the Community or the EEA submit bids, usually the geographic market will be considered to be Community-wide.

49. *Trade flows/pattern of shipments*. When the number of customers is so large that it is not possible to obtain through them a clear picture of geographic purchasing patterns, information on trade flows might be used alternatively, provided that the trade statistics are available with a sufficient degree of detail for the relevant products. Trade flows, and above all, the rationale behind trade flows provide useful insights and information for the purpose of establishing the scope of the geographic market but are not in themselves conclusive.

50. *Barriers and switching costs associated to divert orders to companies located in other areas*. The absence of trans-border purchases or trade flows, for instance, does not necessarily mean that the market is at most national in scope. Still, barriers isolating the national market have to be identified before it is concluded that the relevant geographic market in such a case is national. Perhaps the clearest obstacle for a customer to divert its orders to other areas is the impact of transport costs and transport restrictions arising from legislation or from the nature of the relevant products. The impact of transport costs will usually limit the scope of the geographic market for bulky, low-value products, bearing in mind that a transport disadvantage might also be compensated by a comparative advantage in other costs (labour costs or raw materials). Access

to distribution in a given area, regulatory barriers still existing in certain sectors, quotas and custom tariffs might also constitute barriers isolating a geographic area from the competitive pressure of companies located outside that area. Significant switching costs in procuring supplies from companies located in other countries constitute additional sources of such barriers.

51. On the basis of the evidence gathered, the Commission will then define a geographic market that could range from a local dimension to a global one, and there are examples of both local and global markets in past decisions of the Commission.

52. The paragraphs above describe the different factors which might be relevant to define markets. This does not imply that in each individual case it will be necessary to obtain evidence and assess each of these factors. Often in practice the evidence provided by a subset of these factors will be sufficient to reach a conclusion, as shown in the past decisional practice of the Commission.

It will be seen in later chapters that the Community authorities' approach to the geographic market has often been criticized in the past for failing to give sufficient attention to substitutability between different geographic areas. As in the case of the product market the geographic market has often been drawn narrowly. One would expect further market integration in the EU, and particularly the adoption of the single currency, to broaden geographic markets in the EU.

C. BARRIERS TO ENTRY

(i) The Role of Barriers to Entry

Barriers to entry or expansion[362] are crucial when determining whether or not a firm is a monopolist or has significant market power on a market. Even a firm with a 100 per cent share of a market may not, in economic terms, have a monopoly. Market shares tell us nothing about *why* the firm has such a high market share or about potential competition. It tells us only about the current state of competition. A firm will not be able to charge monopoly prices if other firms can freely enter the market and compete with it. It is the monopoly prices which indicate to others that entry to the market is profitable. Whether or not a firm really does have a monopolist's power over price is, therefore, dependent on how vulnerable it is to new entrants. Whether or not a market is vulnerable to new entrants is dependent upon 'barriers to entry'. A firm can exercise market power for a significant time only if barriers to entry exist. As Bork states:[363] '[t]he concept of barriers to entry is crucial to antitrust debate ... The ubiquity and potency of the concept are undeniable.'

It is difficult to give even the loosest definition of what 'barriers to entry' means without participating in the debate which has raged for many years between different schools of economic thought.[364] To put it as neutrally as possible, however, a barrier to entry may be described as something which hinders the emergence of potential competition which would otherwise constrain the incumbent undertaking (the Commission's 'Glossary of terms used in

---

[362] The term 'barriers to entry' is used in this section to include barriers to entry *and* barriers to expansion, unless the context otherwise requires.

[363] R. Bork, *The Antitrust Paradox: A Policy at War With Itself* (Basic Books, 1978, reprinted with a new Introduction and Epilogue, 1993), 310–11.

[364] See *supra* 22 ff.

EU competition policy' describes entry barriers as 'factors that prevent or hinder companies from entering a specific market').[365] The difficulty of course is to determine *what* will deter potential competition from emerging in the market.

(ii) The Definition of a Barrier to Entry

As stated above, there is no single accepted definition of a 'barrier to entry'. The seminal work on barriers to entry was that of J. S. Bain[366] who belonged to the Harvard school.[367] Bain described barriers to entry as:

the extent to which, in the long run, established firms can elevate their selling prices above the minimal average costs of production and distribution . . . without inducing potential entrants to enter the industry.

This defines barriers to entry in an effects-based way. In contrast, Stigler, a leading exponent of the Chicago school,[368] adopted a narrower definition, focusing on the differences in demand and cost conditions suffered by incumbent firms and potential entrants respectively. He defined a barrier to entry as:

a cost of producing (at some or every rate of output) which must be borne by a firm which seeks to enter the industry but is not borne by firms already in the industry.[369]

The definition of Baumol and Willig[370] followed Stigler:

anything that requires an expenditure by a new entrant into an industry, but that imposes no equivalent costs upon an incumbent.

Von Weizsäcker[371] adopted the Stigler approach but added an economic welfare dimension:

A cost of producing which must be borne by a firm which seeks to enter an industry but is not borne by firms already in the industry and which implies a distortion on the allocation of resources from the social point of view.

---

[365] Even these statements are dangerous however, as they could include superior efficiency as a barrier to entry.

[366] J. S. Bain, 'Economies of Scale, Concentration, and the Condition of Entry in Twenty Manufacturing Industries' (1954) 44 *American Economic Review* 15, *Barriers to New Competition* (Harvard University Press, 1956), and *Industrial Organization* (2nd edn., John Wiley, 1968).

[367] See *supra* 22.

[368] See *supra* 23.

[369] G. J. Stigler, *The Organization of Industry* (Irwin, 1968), 67; D. Carlton, 'Why Barriers to Entry are Barriers to Understanding', *American Economic Review*, May 2004, 94(2), 466, 468, says that 'Although Stigler's definition of "barrier" as a differential cost is concise and unambiguous, it does raise the question of why it should be called a "barrier". Why not call it "differential cost advantage?" This may seem overly pedantic, but introduction of unnatural use of language can lead to confusion. Consider, for example, an industry where the government restricts the numbers of firms to 100. It issues 100 licences to operate that are then sold in an open market. The entry restriction is likely to be inefficient, but as long as all firms have access to the (artificially) scarce license at the market-clearing price, there is no entry barrier according to Stigler's definition. All firms earn a normal rate of return. Yet there is a restriction to entry. It seems to mangle the English language to refuse to call this entry restriction a "barrier to entry"'.

[370] W. Baumol and R. Willig, 'Fixed Costs, Sunk Costs, Entry Barriers and Sustainability of Monopoly' (1981) 95 *Quarterly Journal of Economics* 405, 408.

[371] C. von Weizsäcker, 'A Welfare Analysis of Barriers to Entry' (1980) 11 *Bell J Econ* 399, 400.

Another significant definition is that of Gilbert:[372]

a barrier to entry is a rent that is derived from incumbency. It is the additional profit that a firm can earn as a sole consequence of being established in an industry.

This approach follows Bain but emphasizes 'first-mover advantages', that is the advantage the firm derives simply from being on the market before its potential competitors, rather than absolute costs advantages.[373]

A wide spectrum of definitions has thus been suggested, each having different emphases and each incorporating different things within it. The essential debate still remains, however, over whether the definition adopted by Bain or by Stigler and the Chicago school is more appropriate or accurate. The Bain approach results in many things being identified as barriers. Conversely, the definition adopted by Stigler means that very few things constitute barriers to entry.[374] For example, Bain's approach, unlike Stigler's, accepts that market conduct may operate as a barrier to entry because the definition is effects-based.[375] Further, Bain's definition admits that economies of scale may operate as a barrier to entry, since they deter new entrants and so allow prices to remain above minimum unit cost. Stigler's definition does not, however, accept that economies of scale operate as a barrier since both incumbents and new competitors have to face them at the time they enter the market.[376] There is therefore no asymmetry which the Stigler definition demands.

It is the Bain approach which today has the greatest influence in industrial economics and which is ordinarily used in competition law decisions in both the EC and the US.[377] Herbert Hovenkamp in the extract below explains why this is so.

H. Hovenkamp, *Federal Antitrust Policy: The Law of Competition and Its Practice* (3rd edn., Thomson/West, 2005), 40–41

The difference between the two definitions of entry barriers can be quite substantial. For example, under the Bainian definition economies of scale is a qualifying barrier to entry. If scale economies are significant, then incumbent firms with established markets may have a large advantage over any new entrant, who will enter the market at a low rate of output. As a result, scale economies can permit incumbent firms to earn monopoly returns up to a certain point without encouraging new entry.

---

[372] R. Gilbert, 'Mobility Barriers and the Value of Incumbency' in R. Schmalensee and R. Willig (eds.), *Handbook of Industrial Organization* (North Holland, 1989), 478.

[373] See *infra* 89 ff.

[374] All Stiglerian entry barriers are Bainian entry barriers as well, but not vice versa.

[375] R. P. McAfee, H. M. Mialon and M. A. Williams, 'What is a Barrier to Entry?' *American Economic Review*, May 2004, 94(2), 461, 462 comment that 'Bain's definition is flawed in that it builds the consequences of the definition into the definition itself'.

[376] R. P. McAfee, H. M. Mialon and M. A. Williams, *supra* n. 375, 462, say that the present tense 'is' in Stigler's definition is confusing as '[l]iterally, the definition implies that a cost that only entrants (not incumbents) have to bear today is an entry barrier, even if incumbents had to bear it in the past (when they entered the market)'.

[377] And see the US *Horizontal Merger Guidelines* (1992, revised 1997) promulgated by the Department of Justice's Antitrust Division.

By contrast, scale economies are not a qualifying entry barrier under the Stiglerian definition. Both incumbent firms and new entrants had to deal with them at the time of entry; so scale economies are not a cost that applies only to new entrants.

The Stiglerian conception of entry barriers is based on a powerful analytic point: entry barrier analysis should distinguish desirable from undesirable entry. If prospective entrants face precisely the same costs that incumbents faced but still find entry unprofitable, then this market has probably already attained the appropriate number of players, even though monopoly profits are being earned. For example, suppose that minimum efficient scale (MES) in a market requires a 30% market share. Such a market has room for only three MES firms—and a three-firm market is quite likely to perform oligopolistically or else be conducive to collusion. The Stiglerian approach to entry barriers would say that, although monopoly profits are being earned in the industry, entry barriers should not be counted as high because entry by a fourth firm is not socially desirable. Additional entry would force at least one firm to be of suboptimal size, and eventually one of the four would probably exit the market. . . . The socially desirable solution to the problem of oligopoly performance in this market is not to force entry of a fourth, inefficiently small firm; but rather to look for alternative measures that make collusion more difficult.

Nevertheless, antitrust analysis has mainly used the Bainian rather than the Stiglerian definition of entry barriers. The Bainian definition is written into the 1992 Horizontal Merger Guidelines promulgated by the Justice Department's Antitrust Division and the Federal Trade Commission (FTC) . . . In all antitrust decisions except for a few in the FTC, tribunals have relied on the Bainian definition . . .

Although the Stiglerian approach to entry barriers offers a useful insight into the relationship between market structure and socially desirable entry, there are nevertheless good reasons for antitrust policy to prefer the Bainian approach. In particular, the Bainian definition is free of the value judgment of what constitutes socially desirable entry. This is important because the existence of entry barriers is not itself an antitrust violation. The antitrust policy maker does not use entry barrier analysis in order to consider whether further entry into a market is socially desirable; the market itself will take care of that question. Rather, the question is whether a particular practice is plausibly anti-competitive. This distinction is critically important because we know so little about the minimum efficient scale of operation in any given market.

The European Commission discussed the forms that barriers to entry can take in the Horizontal Merger Guidelines published in January 2004.[378] In the Notice the Commission takes a broad view of barriers to entry, considering that they can comprise legal or technical advantages or may exist because of the established position of the incumbent firms on the market. This reflects its decisional practice, not only in the merger context but also when applying Article 82 of the Treaty which prohibits abuse of a dominant position.[379] The debate about barriers to entry is not some theoretical discussion akin to mediaeval theologians debating the number of angels on the head of a pin. It is absolutely vital to the determination of market power. If factors are too readily identified as entry barriers a firm may be wrongly found to have market power and its conduct may then be constrained by competition laws. Similarly a merger between two firms may be prohibited even though it does not lead to the firms acquiring market power. This may mean that the competitive process is actually harmed by competition law since it interferes with and impedes the behaviour of firms operating on a competitive market. On the other hand,

---

[378] [2004] OJ C31/5. See *infra* Chap. 12. See also the Commission Guidelines on the application of Article 81(3) of the Treaty [2004] OJ C101/97, paras. 114–15.

[379] See further *infra* Chap. 6.

if the possibility of entry barriers is too easily dismissed, undertakings which *do* have market power might escape the prohibitions of competition law and mergers which create or strengthen market power might be allowed.

How barriers to entry are conceived is related to industrial organization theory. We have already seen above[380] that Bain was an important contributor to the development of the 'structure conduct performance' paradigm. This theory sought to show that certain industry structures dictate that the firms in the industry will engage in certain types of conduct which will in turn lead to a certain kind of economic performance. The paradigm was attacked by the Chicago school. Nonetheless it has had such an enduring influence on antitrust analysis that it is now clear that market structure can never be ignored.[381] However, modern industrial organization (IO) theory stresses the strategic competition of undertakings. This theory looks to the effect which conduct has on structure, rather than vice versa, and considers that whether a new entrant will enter a market will depend, at least in part, on the conditions of competition it will face post-entry. Thus predatory behaviour by the incumbent firm may constitute a barrier to entry. The theory also emphasizes the importance that 'sunk costs' may have on a firm's decision to enter a market. Sunk costs are costs which cannot be recovered on exiting a market.[382]

D. Harbord and T. Hoehn, 'Barriers to Entry and Exit in European Competition Policy' (1994) 14 *International Review of Law and Economics* 411, 413–15

2.2 Strategic Competition and Entry

Modern industrial organization theory, although based upon a large number of particular game-theoretic models and examples, has nevertheless succeeded in isolating a number of crucial factors from which a categorization or 'typology' of barriers to entry may be derived. At the most general level, the message of the new IO is that an analysis of business strategy, or strategic competition, is fundamental to the analysis of particular industries. The Bain paradigm, which analysed industries in terms of a causative chain from structure to conduct to performance, and in which structure was largely determined by technological factors, has been supplanted by an approach that emphasizes the effect of conduct (i.e., strategic interaction) on industry structure and performance. In brief, how firms compete partly determines how concentrated industries will be. Specifically, what is important for entry decisions is the nature of competition post-entry that potential entrants must factor into their decisions.

This has been expressed in a number of ways. Sutton (1991) uses the concept of the 'thoroughness of price competition' in classifying entry conditions in various industries, a concept that describes 'how prices change with market structure.' Bresnahan and Reiss (1990, 1991) suggest a function 'which determines how fast industry margins shrink with entry.' However, the important point is that no analysis of a market or industry, and in particular an assessment of market power and entry barriers, can avoid an analysis of strategic competition, because it is this

---

[380] *Supra* 22.

[381] *Supra* 30.

[382] See R. Schmalensee, 'Sunk Costs and Antitrust Barriers to Entry' *American Economic Review*, May 2004, 94(2),

that determines entrants' expectations of the profitability of entry, and ultimately their entry decisions. Thus

Lesson I. The analysis of strategic interaction is necessary to an understanding of industry structure and concentration, and in particular analysis of post-entry competition is fundamental to an assessment of entry conditions.

2.3 Sunk Costs and Commitments

The second lesson from modern IO theory is the crucial role played by sunk costs in entry (and exit) decisions. Sunk costs are costs that cannot be recovered on exiting an industry, and hence serve to commit a firm or firms to staying in the market. The U.S. Department of Justice Horizontal Merger Guidelines define sunk costs as 'the acquisition costs of tangible or intangible assets that cannot be recovered through redeployment of those assets outside the relevant market.' There are three important aspects of sunk costs that influence entry and exit decisions. First, sunk costs increase the risk of entering an industry because they cannot be recouped on exiting. Second, sunk costs create a cost asymmetry between entrants and incumbents. Once costs are sunk they are no longer a portion of opportunity costs of production, and hence an incumbent will require a lower return on costs in order to stay in an industry than will be required to enter. Asymmetries of this type have been modelled by Dixit (1979, 1981) and many others. Third, sunk costs can serve as a commitment by incumbent firms not to exit the industry. (For this reason Gilbert (1989) refers to them as 'exit costs.') Thus sunk costs are central to the calculations of potential entrants because if entry involves sunk costs it will be deterred if they are unlikely to be recouped, and incumbent firms may be able to exploit this fact strategically in a variety of ways.

The importance of sunk costs can be seen from a (much-discussed) simple example, which also illustrates the interaction of sunk costs with post-entry competition to create an entry barrier. Consider a market with two potential entrants, each of which face a sunk entry F and constant variable cost per unit of production c (i.e., there are no capacity constraints). If a single firm enters, it will charge the monopoly price Pm and earn monopoly profits. The second firm will then enter if and only if the expected price post-entry Pe, exceeds c +F/q, where q is the firm's expected post-entry output . . .

The above example is simple but illustrates clearly how sunk costs interact with post-entry competition to create a first-mover or incumbency advantage, even in the absence of strategic preemptive behaviour. The recent IO literature has also identified numerous means by which investments involving sunk costs can be used strategically to limit or deter entry in more complex environments . . . They may be roughly classified as follows.

- investments to lower the incumbent's costs relative to those of potential entrants, that is, capacity, patents, R&D, take or pay contracts with input suppliers, learning-by-doing, etc.

- investments to alter the cost structure of rivals, that is, take or pay contracts, sleeping patents, monopolization of inputs, vertical control, etc.

- investments to favourably alter demand conditions, that is, advertising, brand proliferation, long-term contracts with buyers, etc.

In all of these examples commitment is essential, and hence the importance of sunk costs. Thus

Lesson II. Sunk costs are fundamental to the calculations of potential entrants, and the identification of sunk costs that cannot be recovered on exiting an industry is crucial to the assessment of entry conditions. Strategic behaviour and post-entry competition combined with sunk costs are an important determinant of market structure via their effects on entry and exit decisions.

This industrial organization theory therefore stresses the importance of sunk costs. This means that barriers to entry can be separated into two classes: absolute (cost) advantages (which 'arise if some factor of production is denied to the potential entrant and, but for this omitted factor, the latter firm would be as efficient as the incumbent firm'[383]) and strategic entry barriers. This view is summarized in the conclusions of a 1994 report commissioned by the Office of Fair Trading from London Economics.[384]

Barriers to Entry and Exit in Competition Policy, OFT Research Paper 2, 57–9

5.1 Economic analysis of entry barriers

What is the key to the full analysis of entry barriers is therefore the careful appreciation and analysis of the entry conditions in a particular market.... [W]e distinguish between two types of asymmetries between incumbent firms and potential entrants which give rise to entry barrier, viz:

(i) *absolute* incumbent advantages, i.e., incumbent access to some factor of production that is denied (on equivalent terms) to potential contracts;

(ii) *strategic* incumbent advantages, typically arising from first-mover advantages in the presence of sunk costs and associated behaviour. These are related to:

  - economies of scale
  - product differentiation, advertising and goodwill
  - capital requirements
  - vertical foreclosure and exclusion
  - predatory behaviour

5.1.1 Absolute advantages

In considering absolute cost advantages it is important to take account of relevant *opportunity* costs. Some absolute advantages result from public policies designed to stimulate innovation activity. Dynamic incentive effects must also be considered in innovative industries, where an important issue is the degree of competition at the level of innovation.

In so-called '*contestable*' markets there are no absolute asymmetries, no sunk costs, and incumbents are constantly vulnerable to 'hit-and-run' entry threats. The relevance of contestable market theory to public policy is open to question, however, not least because the theory appears to be non-robust to the assumption of zero sunk costs, which will not be a good approximation to the bulk of industries where competition policy concerns are raised.

---

[383] Van den Bergh and Camesasca, *supra* n. 283, 142, referring to R. J. Gilbert, 'Mobility Barriers and the Value of Incumbency', in R. Schmalensee and R. D. Willig (Eds.), *The Handbook of Industrial Organization I* (North Holland, 1989), the article referred to in the Harbord and Hoehn extract above.

[384] The article by Harbord and Hoehn quoted above is based on the work done for that report.

5.1.2 Strategic entry barriers

Our classification of strategic entry barriers into five groups aids in the identification of factors which may create or strengthen 'first-mover' advantages:

Economies of scale may deter entry, even without strategic behaviour, in particular when these imply that entry:

(i) requires large sunk costs, and,

(ii) would cause tougher price competition. It is for these reasons, which strategic behaviour may add to, that *scale economies* can be entry barriers

However whenever entry involves the sinking of substantial costs, it is the expectations of entrants regarding **post-entry prices** that matter. Incumbents may be able to influence those expectations, in such a way as to deter entry, by altering future incumbents costs, raising rivals costs, future demand conditions, or potential entrants' beliefs about the likely response in the event of entry.

Product differentiation, advertising and goodwill can also be entry barriers, but for deeper reasons than have sometimes been suggested, relating to brand proliferation, scale economy and sunk cost effects of advertising, switching costs, pioneering brand advantages, and information asymmetries. Product differentiation can, of course, also be a means of entry.

Capital requirements more often reflect or are related to other barriers to entry (e.g., those associated with large sunk costs or predatory behaviour) than constituting entry barriers by themselves, though this is possible.

An important class of entry barriers relate to **vertical foreclosure and exclusion**. As was shown by the 'Chicago' school of antitrust analysis, the economics of vertical practices are complex, and superficially 'anti-competitive' vertical practices may in fact be pro-competitive and efficient. However, contrary to the Chicago School, practices such as refusal to supply, exclusive dealing, tying and vertical integration can create entry barriers under a range of circumstances, in particular where there is a horizontal market power in the upstream or downstream market. Such power can be extended vertically by means of vertical practices and hence they call for entry barrier analysis in many cases.

The Chicago School also argued that **predatory pricing** would be non-existent or very rare, on the grounds that it would not be in the incumbent's interests. Recent analysis of predatory behaviour in relation to financial market imperfections and reputation-for-toughness effects has shown that the possibility of predatory behaviour cannot be dismissed in this way.

5.2 Assessment of entry conditions in practise [sic]

Our discussion of the lessons from the theoretical literature of the past 10–15 years has important implications for the design of an appropriate methodology for the assessment of entry conditions in competition policy and practice, in the UK and elsewhere.

There is no single best or easy way to assess entry conditions or entry barriers. No single measure will capture all of the subtleties of strategic interaction, first-mover advantages and the nature of post-entry competition which combine with other factors to influence entry decisions.

We have therefore proposed a stepwise assessment which achieves two things: firstly, it allows for a quick identification of the circumstances in which it is not necessary to carry out a detailed or full evaluation of all factors; secondly, it systematically and comprehensively takes account of the major issues and factors which our overview of the theory and practice has identified as being crucial. These steps are:

Step 1: Market definition and entry by production substitutes

Step 2: Market conditions and historical entry

Step 3: Assessment of absolute (cost) advantages

Step 4: Assessment of strategic (first mover) advantages

Step 5:   Vertical foreclosure and exclusion

Step 6: Predatory behaviour

Step 7: Assessment of entry impediments.

The proposed procedure or methodology is both logical and parsimonious, and most importantly is informed by and consistent with the recent theoretical literature on barriers to entry. This subject has received a great deal of attention in the 'new industrial organisation' literature, which has addressed and clarified many of the issues which dominated the earlier debate between rival schools of thought, i.e., that associated with the 'Chicago school' on the one hand, and the so-called 'Harvard school' on the other... It is necessary to examine carefully the individual circumstances of particular markets in order to assess whether or not entry barriers are present, and whether or not a particular type of behaviour by an incumbent or incumbents, may lead to a divergence between private and public interests.

Many of the practices referred to in the above passage are explained in Chapter 7. For the present it should be noted that it is now commonly accepted that a firm's behaviour on the market can constitute a barrier to entry and deter and prevent other firms from entering it.

11. CONCLUSIONS

1. Competition law upholds the workings of the free market economy by policing the conduct of firms as they compete in the market. It is reactive, in that it does not order firms to merge or to engage in certain agreements or conduct as a matter of economic policy, but only intervenes to prevent them acting in a way that causes harm. Whether harm should be judged by the effects on competitors, on the competitive process itself, on consumers, on society in some broader sense, or by some combination of these, is a matter of long-standing debate and controversy.

2. There is currently a consensus in mainstream economics that competition law systems should be designed to maximize consumer welfare and efficiency. In the past (at least) EC competition law has sought to achieve a more diffuse range of objectives. The debate about the aims of EC competition law is affected by the fact that competition is but one of a range of policies by which the EC (which is one 'pillar' of the European Union) seeks to achieve the mission set out in the EC Treaty. At present the view of the Commission, the EC competition authority, is that competition law should be directed at the interests of consumers. Nevertheless, EC law recognizes that competition as a process should be protected as it is this that delivers consumer welfare.

3. The belief that competition produces the best outcomes for society is based on neoclassical economic theory. This teaches that in competitive markets prices are kept down, and other benefits flow to consumers, such quality, choice and innovation, whereas in markets which are monopolized output is reduced, prices rise, and consumers are deprived of choice, quality and innovation. Competition is said to produce 'efficiency'. The matter is complicated by the fact

that there are different aspects to efficiency and, in particular, the need to take account dynamic efficiencies may make the application of competition law in any specific situation a complex exercise. Even where there is agreement about the ultimate objectives of competition law there is much debate about how to achieve efficiency and maximize consumer welfare and in any particular case there may be room for argument about the analysis of the market, the effects of the transaction or conduct under review, and the desirability of intervention.

4. A central concept of competition law is 'market power'. Market power is the ability to profitably raise prices above the competitive level for a significant period of time.

5. Market definition and barriers to entry are both employed in assessing market power. There are difficulties involved in defining markets and identifying (and even defining) a barrier to entry. The imprecise nature of these concepts should be borne in mind in all cases where the application of competition rules is being considered. If markets are wrongly defined and barriers to entry imagined the application of the competition rules can take a wrong turn and prohibit conduct which might otherwise achieve economic efficiency.

12. FURTHER READING

A. BOOKS

AMATO, G., *Antitrust and the Bounds of Power* (Hart Publishing, 1997)

BAQUERO CRUZ, J., *Between Competition and Free Movement* (Hart Publishing, 2002)

BAIN, J. S., *Barriers to New Competition* (Harvard University Press, 1956)

—— *Industrial Organization* (2nd edn., John Wiley, 1968)

BEGG, D., FISCHER, S., and DORNBUSCH, R., *Economics* (8th edn., McGraw-Hill, 2005)

BISHOP, S., and WALKER, M., *The Economics of EC Competition Law: Concepts, Application and Measurement* (2nd edn., Sweet & Maxwell, 2002, 3rd edn. expected 2007)

BORK, R. H., *The Antitrust Paradox: A Policy at War with Itself* (Basic Books, 1978, reprinted with a new Introduction and Epilogue, 1993)

CAIRNCROSS, A., and others, *Economic Policy for the European Community* (MacMillan, 1974)

CARLTON, D. W., and PERLOFF, J. M., *Modern Industrial Organization* (4th edn., Pearson AddisonWesley, 2005)

CINI, M., and McGOWAN, L., *Competition Policy in the European Union* (Macmillan, 1998)

ELHAUGE, E., and GERADIN, D., *Global Competition Law and Economics* (Hart Publishing, 2007)

FAULL, J., and NIKPAY, A. (eds) *The EC Law of Competition* (2nd edn., Oxford University Press, 2007), chapter 1

GAL, M. S., *Competition Policy for Small Market Economies* (Harvard University Press, 2003)

GELLHORN, E., KOVACIC, W. E., and CALKINS, S., *Antitrust Law and Economics* (5th edn., West, 2004)

GERBER, D., *Law and Competition in Twentieth Century Europe: Protecting Prometheus* (Oxford University Press, 1998)

HAY, D., and VICKERS, J. (eds.), *The Economics of Market Dominance* (Oxford University Press, 1987)

HILDEBRAND, D., *The Role of Economics Analysis in the EC Competition Rules* (Kluwer Law International, 2002)

HOVENKAMP, H., *Federal Antitrust Policy: The Law of Competition and its Practice* (3rd edn., Thomson/West, 2005)

—— *The Antitrust Enterprise, Principle and Execution* (Harvard University Press, 2005)

JACQUEMIN, A. P., and DE JONG, H. W., *European Industrial Organisation* (MacMillan, 1997)

MERCURO, N., and MEDEMA, S. G., *Economics and the Law: From Posner to Post-Modernism* (Princeton University Press, 1999)

MÖSCHEL, W., 'Competition Policy from an Ordo Point of View' in A. Peacock and H. Willgerodt (eds.), *German Neo-Liberals and the Social Market Economics* (MacMillan, 1898), 142

MOTTA, M., *Competition Policy* (Cambridge University Press, 2004)

O'DONOGHUE, R., and PADILLA A. J., *The Law and Economics of Article 82 EC* (Hart Publishing, 2006), chapters 2 and 3

ODUDU, O, *The Boundaries of EC Competition Law* (Oxford University Press, 2006)

POSNER, R. A., *Antitrust Law* (2nd edn., University of Chicago Press, 2001)

SAUTER, W., *Competition Law and Industrial Policy in the EU* (Oxford University Press, 1997)

SCHERER, F. M., and ROSS, D., *Industrial Market Structure and Economic Performance* (3rd edn., Houghton Mifflin, 1990) chapters 1, 2, and 4

STIGLER, G. J., *The Organization of Industry* (Irwin, 1968)

VAN DEN BERGH, R. J., and CAMESASCA, P. D., *European Competition Law and Economics: A Comparative Perspective* (2nd edn., Sweet & Maxwell, 2006)

WILLIAMSON, O. E., *Anti-Trust Economics* (Basil Blackwell, 1987)

B. ARTICLES

BAIN, J. S., 'Economies of Scale, Concentration, and the Condition of Entry in Twenty Manufacturing Industries' (1954) 44 *American Economic Review* 15

CROCIONI, P., 'The Hypothetical Monopolist Test: What it can and cannot tell you' [2002] *ECLR* 355

DUNBOW, B., 'Understanding Consumers: The Value of Stated Preferences in Antitrust Proceedings' [2003] *ECLR* 141

FOX, E. M., 'The New American Competition Policy: From Antitrust to Pro-efficiency?' [1981] *ECLR* 439

—— 'The Modernisation of Antitrust: A New Equilibrium' (1981) 66 *Cornell LR*

—— 'Consumer beware Chicago' (1984–85) 84 *Mich LR* 1714

—— 'What is Harm to Competition? Exclusionary Practices and Anti-competitive Effect' (2002) 70 *ALJ* 371

—— and SULLIVAN, L. A., 'Antitrust—Retrospective and Prospective: Where Are We Coming From? Where Are we Going?' (1987) 62 *New York Univ LR* 936

FRAZER, T., 'Competition Policy after 1992: The Next Step' (1990) 53 *MLR* 609

GERBER, D., 'Constitutionalizing the Economy: German Neo-liberalism, Competition Law and the "New Europe"' (1994) 42 *American Journal of Comparative Law* 25

HARBORD, D., and HOEHN, T., 'Barriers to Entry and Exit in European Competition Policy' (1994) 14 *International Review of Law and Economics* 41

HILDEBRAND, D., 'The European School in EC Competition Law' (2002) 25 *World Competition* 3

HOVENKAMP, H., 'Antitrust after Chicago' (1984–85) 84 *Mich LR* 213

LANDES, W. M., and POSNER R. A., 'Market Power in Antitrust Cases' (1981) 94 *Harvard LR* 937.

LEIBENSTEIN, H., 'Allocative Efficiency vs. "X-efficiency"' (1966) 56 *American Economic Review* 392

POSNER, R., 'The Social Costs of Monopoly and Regulation' [1975] *Journal of Political Economy* 83

—— 'The Chicago School of Antitrust Analysis' 127 *Univ Pa LR* 925

WOOD, D. P., 'The Role of Economics & Economists in Competition Cases' [1999] *OECD Journal of Competition Law*

2

THE EUROPEAN COMMUNITY AND THE COMPETITION PROVISIONS

1. CENTRAL ISSUES

1. The entity now called the European Community (EC) was originally called the European Economic Community (EEC) and was created by the Treaty of Rome. The EC has developed greatly since 1958, both in membership and ambit, and is at present one 'pillar' of the European Union (EU). As the competition rules are contained in the Treaty of Rome, the competition rules are technically 'EC' rather than 'EU' law.

2. The Council has played a relatively minor role in the development of competition law. In 1962 Council Regulation 17 gave wide powers to enforce and apply the competition rules to the Commission. Regulation 17 was replaced by Regulation 1/2003, which took effect on 1 May 2004.

3. The Commission is divided into Directorates General. One of these, DG Comp, is responsible for competition policy. One Commissioner (currently Neelie Kroes) has responsibility for the competition portfolio.

4. The national competition authorities of the Member States and the national courts share the responsibility for the application and enforcement of the EC competition rules with the Commission.

5. The Community Courts (the European Court of Justice (ECJ) and the Court of First Instance (CFI)) play an important part in enforcing and developing the competition rules, both by hearing appeals from Commission decisions and (at present only as regards the ECJ) by hearing preliminary references from the national courts of the Member States. The Community Courts are responsible for the interpretation of the EC Treaty.

6. The doctrines of the Community legal order, such as direct applicability, supremacy and subsidiarity apply in the field of competition law as to all other areas of Community law. The general principles of Community law and fundamental human rights apply, and are particularly important in competition law, which entails the imposition of penalties and sanctions upon individual (usually legal) persons.

7. Two main Treaty provisions, Articles, 81 and 82, set out the competition rules. These have been amplified by rafts of delegated legislation, notices and other instruments, by Commission decisions in individual cases and by the case law of the Community courts.

8. The EU and three other states form the European Economic Area (EEA) and in effect the EC competition rules apply throughout the EEA, and not just to the EU.

9. The 'modernization' of EC competition law, of which the linch-pin is Regulation 1/2003, has taken EC competition law into a new era.

2. INTRODUCTION

The EC competition rules are set out in the Treaty establishing the European Community. The aims and objectives of this Treaty were introduced in Chapter 1 above. In this Chapter, in order to set the competition rules in context, we give a brief outline of the history of this Treaty, the European Community, and its institutions.[1] We then set out the competition provisions themselves and briefly explain the way in which those rules are applied and enforced. Procedure and enforcement of the competition rules are, however, more fully discussed in Chapters 14 and 15.

An important point to stress at the outset is that on 1 May 2004 a fundamental change took place to the way that EC competition law is applied and enforced. Council Regulation 17,[2] the first regulation implementing Articles 81 and 82, which had governed enforcement since 1962, was replaced by Council Regulation 1/2003.[3] Regulation 1/2003 is the main plank in the process of the 'modernization' of EC competition law enforcement which was first proposed by the Commission in a White Paper in 1999.[4] Other reforms, some of which were already in place,[5] some of which came into force on, or were applied from, 1 May 2004,[6] and some of which have been introduced since or are still ongoing,[7] are also part of the modernization programme.

3. INTRODUCTION TO THE EUROPEAN COMMUNITY

A. THE EUROPEAN UNION AND THE EUROPEAN COMMUNITY

Soon after the Second World War three European Communities were created. The Treaty of Paris in 1951 established the European Coal and Steel Community (the ECSC Treaty); the Euratom Treaty in 1957 created the European Atomic Energy Community; and the Treaty of

---

[1] For a more detailed discussion see, e.g., P. Craig and G. de Búrca, *EU Law: Text, Cases and Materials* (4th edn., Oxford University Press 2007), chap. 1. See also the addendum on the June 2007 Council, *infra* 1399.

[2] [1959–62] OJ Spec. Ed. 87.

[3] [2003] OJ L1/1.

[4] Commission White Paper on modernisation of the rules implementing Articles 81 and 82 of the EC Treaty [1999] OJ C132/1, [1999] 5 CMLR 208.

[5] Such as the reformed regime for vertical restraints, Commission Reg. 2790/99 [1999] OJ L336/21 and the accompanying Guidelines, [2000] OJ C291/1; and the new regime for horizontal cooperation agreements, Commission Reg. 2658/2000 [2001] OJ L304/3 on specialization agreements, Commission Reg. 2659/2000 [2001] OJ L304/7 on research and development agreements and the accompanying Guidelines, OJ [2001] C3/2. See further *infra* Chaps. 9 and 13.

[6] Commission Reg. 772/2004 [2004] OJ L123/11 on technology transfer agreements; Council Reg. 139/2004 [2004] OJ L24/1 on mergers; Guidelines on the assessment of horizontal mergers [2004] OJ C31/5; see *infra* Chap. 10 and Chap. 12. The Guidelines on the application of Article 81(3) [2004] OJ C 101/81, see *infra* Chap. 4, were also an important aspect of 'modernization'.

[7] Such as Draft Guidelines on the assessment of non-horizontal mergers, 27 February 2007, discussed *infra* Chap. 12; Review of Article 82 inaugurated by the DG Comp Discussion Paper on the application of Article 82 of the Treaty to exclusionary abuses, Brussels, December 2005, discussed *infra* Chaps. 5–7.

Rome in 1957 established the European Economic Community (EEC).[8] The ECSC Treaty was concluded for only twenty-five years and expired on 23 July 2002.[9]

In February 1992 the Member States of the EEC signed the Treaty on European Union (TEU, often called 'Maastricht'[10]). It entered into force on 1 November 1993. The TEU created a new entity, the European Union (EU), which marked a new stage in the process of European integration.[11] The EU comprised three 'pillars': the first was the existing three Communities, the second was co-operation in the Common Foreign and Security Policy (CFSP), and the third was co-operation in Justice and Home Affairs (JHA). The TEU expanded the ambit of the EEC to include more powers, particularly in the fields of economic and monetary union and citizenship, and renamed it the European Community (EC). The Treaty of Amsterdam, which came into force on 1 May 1999, removed some matters from the third pillar to the first, and the third pillar of the EU now encompasses mainly police and judicial co-operation in criminal matters (PJC).

A Treaty establishing a 'Constitution for Europe' was agreed in 2004 but abandoned after adverse referendum results in France and the Netherlands. Instead, the June 2007 Council meeting agreed on less ambitious 'Reform Treaty' which will amend both the TEU and the EC Treaty. The EC will be subsumed into the EU and the words 'European Community' will no longer be used. The amended EC Treaty will be known as the 'Treaty on the Functioning of the Union'. The timetable is for the Reform Treaty (which may become the 'Lisbon Treaty') to enter into force in mid-June 2009. In the meantime this book retains the use of the 'EC' terminology in accordance with the current situation. These developments are discussed in the Addendum, which explains that the substantive competition provisions will not change although there is some complication over the provisions on the objectives and activities of the Union.[12]

On 1 May 2004 ten new Member States[13] entered the Union, enlarging it to a membership of 25. The implications of this enlargement for the enforcement of EC competition law was one of the reasons for 'modernization' of the latter. Furthermore, Bulgaria and Romania entered the Union on 1 January 2007. Croatia opened accession negotiations in October 2005 and hopes to enter in 2009.[14]

---

[8] The original Member States were Belgium, France, Germany, Italy, Luxembourg and the Netherlands.

[9] For the effect of this on the competition rules applicable to the coal and steel sectors see *infra* 109 ff.

[10] After the Dutch town where it was signed. At the time the number of Member States had risen, through successive waves of accessions, to twelve.

[11] See generally, D. Chalmers, C. Hadjiemmanuil, G. Monti, A. Tomkins, *European Union Law* (Cambridge University Press, 2006), chap. 1.

[12] *Infra* 1399.

[13] Cyprus, the Czech Republic, Estonia, Hungary, Latvia, Lithuania, Malta, Poland, Slovakia, and Slovenia.

[14] Turkey opened accession negotiations at the same time, but the accession of Turkey is particularly problematic and the negotiations are likely to last a long time. Albania, Bosnia and Herzegovina, Serbia, Montenegro and, in the long run, former parts of the Soviet Union such as the Ukraine are also potential candidates. As at 1 January 2007 the membership of the EU (and therefore of the EC) were Austria, Belgium, Bulgaria, the Czech Republic, Cyprus, Denmark, Estonia, Finland, France, Germany, Greece, Hungary, Ireland, Italy, Latvia, Lithuania, Luxembourg, Malta, the Netherlands Poland, Portugal, Romania, Slovakia, Slovenia, Spain, Sweden and the United Kingdom.

B. THE SOURCES OF EUROPEAN COMMUNITY LAW

(i) Introduction

Community law is derived from several sources. The most important of these sources are the Treaties, Community acts (secondary legislation and other acts adopted by the Community institutions), the case law of the Court,[15] and the general principles of Community law.[16]

(ii) The Treaty Establishing the European Community

The Treaty of Rome establishing the European Community ('the Treaty') is a treaty of general application (its provisions are not confined to a specific sector). It is a framework, Treaty, providing the legal basis on which the Community operates and setting the limits of the competence of the institutions it creates. At the beginning it sets out the aims and objectives of the Community.[17] These aims and objectives provide an essential backdrop against which the other Treaty provisions and Community acts must be viewed. In particular, the single market objective of the Treaty has strongly influenced the way the competition rules have been interpreted and applied. It is the competition law set out in Articles 81–86 (ex Articles 85–91) of the Treaty which is the focus of this book.

The Treaty has been amended on several occasions. In particular,[18] significant amendments were made to it by the Single European Act of 1986, the TEU ('Maastricht'),[19] the Treaty of Amsterdam,[20] and the Treaty of Nice.[21] The Treaty of Amsterdam effected a complete renumbering of the provisions of both the EC Treaty and the TEU. The Reform Treaty will leave the present competition provisions, Articles 81–86 EC, unchanged except for an amendment to the procedural provision, Article 85. The competition articles will, however, be situated in the 'Treaty on the Functioning of the Union'.[22]

(iii) The EC Institutions

The Treaty establishes the Community's autonomous institutions and the rules governing those institutions. It also confers legislative, executive, and judicial powers upon them in order that the Community's tasks can be achieved. The five main institutions of the Community are set out in Article 7 of the Treaty: the European Parliament, the Council, the Commission, the Court of Justice, and the Court of Auditors. In this section we consider the roles of the Council

---

[15] The European Court of Justice (ECJ) and since 1989, the Court of First Instance (CFI).

[16] These sources are supplemented by international agreements entered into by the Community itself and by the individual Member States and by public international law.

[17] See in particular Articles 2 and 3, discussed *supra* in Chap. 1. These aims and objectives have been widened on each amendment of the Treaty.

[18] Accession agreements, for example, also amend the Treaties.

[19] *Supra* 97.

[20] *Ibid.*

[21] The Treaty of Nice was signed on 26 February 2001. It entered into force on 1 February 2003.

[22] See *supra* 97 and *infra* 1399.

and the Commission focusing particularly on the responsibilities of those institutions within the sphere of Community competition policy.[23]

a. The Council

The Council, which is comprised of representatives of the individual Member States, is in many respects the most powerful of the Community's political institutions. For example, it takes the final step in the passing of primary Community legislation,[24] concludes agreements with foreign countries, and plays a key role in the Community budget. In the sphere of Community competition policy it has, however, not played a great part on a day-to-day basis. Nonetheless, it has been responsible for the adoption of a number of very important pieces of legislation within the competition sphere. In particular, through Regulation 17 and Regulation 1/2003 it has conferred power on the Commission to enforce the competition rules.[25] Further, it has given the Commission power to adopt regulations exempting groups of agreements from the application of the competition rules (block exemptions),[26] and it adopted the Merger Regulation, conferring power on the Commission to rule on the compatibility with the common market of mergers with a Community dimension.[27]

The delegation of the routine enforcement of the rules to the Commission has had the advantage that the development of competition policy and the enforcement of the competition rules has not generally been subject to the delays and compromises that have been encountered in many other Community projects. Where the Council plays a significant role, the progress is generally dependent on the political will of the members and the differing views and interests of the individual Member States. The Commission has been vigorous in its enforcement of the competition rules since the early days of the Community. In contrast, the introduction of the original Merger Regulation[28] took sixteen years to reach the statute book. Even then the Regulation represented a political compromise and has required significant amendment.[29]

b. The Commission and DG Comp

The Commission is headed by the Commissioners, unelected individuals who represent the interests of the Community.[30] The Commission has a number of different functions. It formulates

[23] The role of the European Parliament in the legislative process in the sphere of competition policy is generally limited to a consultative role, see *infra* 103 and 114. Nonetheless, it can be influential. In adopting a block exemption for motor vehicle distribution agreements, Regulation 1400/2002, for example, the European Commission indicated that it had been greatly helped by the suggestions of the Parliament and that it had taken on board eighteen of the twenty-nine requests for modification it had made, see Introduction by Mario Monti, at http://europa.eu.int/comm/competition/car_sector/distribution/#addendum.

[24] In respect of many matters it does this with the European Parliament under the 'co-decision procedure' set out in Article 251 EC. In some cases it does so after 'consultation' with the Parliament and in others it does so after 'cooperation' with the Parliament under Article 252 EC.

[25] And, in Council Reg. 1/2003, on the national competition authorities of the Member States: see *infra* 114.

[26] See *infra* Chap. 4.

[27] Reg. 139/2004 [2004] OJ L24/1, replacing Reg. 4064/89 [1989] OJ L395/1.

[28] The legal basis for the merger regulations is EC Treaty, Article 83, which requires a qualified majority, and Article 308, which requires unanimous approval in the Council.

[29] See *infra* Chap. 12.

[30] The Commissioners are essentially appointed by the governments of the individual Member States but must be approved by the European Parliament: see EC Treaty, Art. 214. There are currently twenty-seven Commissioners, one from each Member State. From November 2009, when the next Commission takes office, the size of the Commission will be reduced. The size and composition of the Commission will be set by the Council acting unanimously. There will no longer be a Commissioner of each nationality and the Commissioners will be chosen 'according to a rotation system based on the principle of equality' among Member States (Art. 213 EC as amended by the Protocol on the Enlargement of the European Union, Art. 4 as amended by the Treaty of Accession of 16 April 2003, Art. 45, and by the Treaty of Accession 2005).

most proposals for legislation, mediates between the individual Member States, and as the 'guardian of the Treaty' is responsible for the enforcement of the Treaty rules. Its role as key enforcer of the competition rules has been a particularly important one. It has power, for example, to take decisions finding an infringement of the Treaty competition rules and fining those responsible. For over forty years, therefore, the Commission has both enforced the competition rules and played the central role in formulating and developing competition policy in the European Community.

One of the Commissioners has responsibility for competition. Neelie Kroes, a Dutch business woman and politician, was given the competition portfolio in 2004.[31] The three previous Competition Commissioners were Mario Monti, an Italian economist who held the portfolio between 1999 and 2004, Karel Van Miert and Sir Leon Brittan. Administratively the European Commission is divided into separate Directorates-General. Until the summer of 1999 the Directorate-General dealing with competition was called DG IV. Since then it has been called the Competition Directorate-General and is known as DG Comp. DG Comp is headed by a Director-General[32] and has three Deputy Directors-General[33] and a Chief Economist. It is now sub-divided into nine Directorates.[34] The organization of DG Comp and the responsibilities of each Directorate are set out in the diagram, figure 2.1. It will be noted that one of the Directorates is now dedicated to the investigation and prosecution of cartels.[35]

Although one Commissioner is responsible for the competition portfolio, formal decisions taken by the Commission must be adopted by the College of Commissioners as a whole,[36] subject to some limited possibilities for delegation.[37]

The office of Chief Economist was created in 2003, mainly in response to a series of CFI judgments annulling Commission merger decisions[38] which convinced the Commission that their decisions should be subjected to a more rigorous internal regime of economic oversight. The role of the Chief Economist and his team is to give guidance on methodological issues of economics and econometrics in the application of the competition rules; to give general guidance in individual competition cases from their early stages; to give detailed guidance in the most important competition cases involving complex economic issues, in particular those requiring sophisticated quantitative analysis; and to contribute to the development of general

---

[31] The term of the Commission appointed in 2004 terminates on 31 October 2009.

[32] The Director General at 1 June 2007 was Philip Lowe, who was appointed to the post on 1 September 2002.

[33] Responsible for Antitrust, Mergers and State Aids respectively.

[34] DG Comp was reorganized in the lead up to 1 May 2004. Initially it underwent a major reoganization in April 2003 (see Commission Press Release IP/03/603, 30 April 2003). A major change was the gradual incorporation of the previously separate Merger Task Force into the other Directorates. For the Merger Task Force see *infra* Chap. 12.

[35] A further reorganization in 2005 produced this dedicated 'cartel-busting' unit. For the problem of cartels and their investigation and punishment, see *infra* Chaps. 11 and 14.

[36] Decisions may be passed by a simple majority, EC Treaty, Art. 219. For the effect this may have on the adoption of a decision, see *infra* Chap. 12. The Legal Service of the Commission also plays an important role in competition matters.

[37] See Chap. 14.

[38] Case T-342/99, *Airtours plc v. Commission* [2002] ECR II-2585; Case T-310/01, *Schneider Electric SA v. Commission* [2002] ECR II-4071, [2003] 4 CMLR 768; Case T-5/02, *Tetra Laval BV v. Commission* [2002] ECR II-4381, [2002] 5 CMLR 1182, *aff'd* by the ECJ, Case C-12/03 P, *Commission v. Tetra Laval* [2005] ECR I-987. See further Chap. 12.

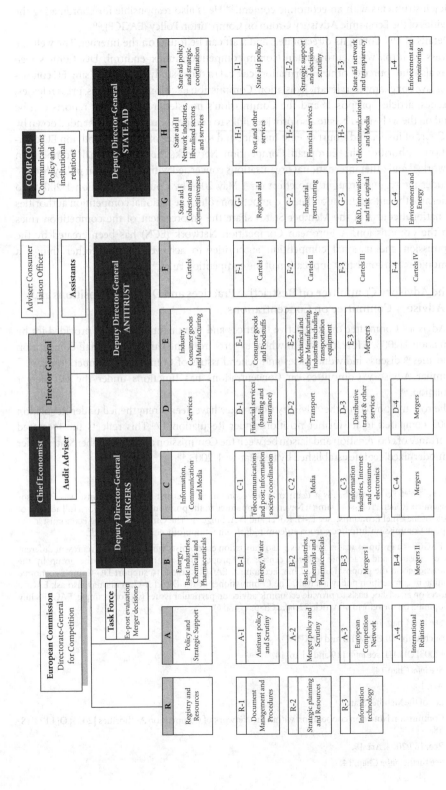

Figure 2.1 Organization of DG Comp

policy instruments with an economic content.[39] He is also responsible for coordinating the activities of the Economic Advisory Group on Competition Policy (EAGCP).[40]

Details of DG Comp, its directorates, and staff can be found on the Internet. The web site address is: http://www.europa.eu.int/comm/competition/index_en.html. DG Comp's web site is also the source of other information, critical to those studying or practising EC competition law. For example, relevant legislation, Commission decisions, daily news, press releases, speeches, articles, proposals and the Commission's newsletter and annual reports can be found on the web site. The site also provides links to competition judgments handed down by the Court of Justice and Court of First Instance and to the sites of other EU and non EU competition authorities, the European Competition Network, the International Competition Network,[41] and other international organisations concerned with competition policy.[42]

Under the regime brought into effect on 1 May 2004 by Council Regulation 1/2003[43] to modernize the enforcement of the EC competition rules, the national competition authorities and national courts of the Member States share the enforcement of the competition rules with the Commission. A European Competition Network (ECN) has been created by the Commission and national competition authorities to achieve, amongst other things, a harmonious and consistent application of the competition rules.[44]

c. The Advisory Committee on Restrictive Practices and Dominant Positions and the Advisory Committee on Concentrations

An Advisory Committee on Restrictive Practices and Dominant Positions is provided for by Regulation 1/2003.[45] It is 'the forum where experts from the various [national] competition authorities[46] discuss individual cases and general issues of Community competition law'.[47] A similar Advisory Committee on Concentrations has functions under the EC Merger Regulation.[48]

The role and powers of the Advisory Committee have been strengthened under Regulation 1/2003 compared to its former position under Regulation 17. This reflects the increased importance of coordination and liaison between the Commission and the Member States under the 'modernized' regime established by Regulation 1/2003.[49]

---

[39] The Chief Economist heads a team of 8–10 economists. The first Chief Economist was Professor Lars-Hendrik Röller. Professor Damien Neven was appointed to the position in July 2006. For a full account of the role of the Chief Economist, see L.-H. Röller and P. A. Buigues, 'The Office of the Chief Economist at the European Commission' http://ec.europa.eu/comm/dgs/competition/officechiefecon_ec.pdf.

[40] EAGCP is a group of academic industrial organisation economists whose members represent different fields of research and academic research centres in Europe. They are nominated to the group by the Commissioner on the proposal of the Chief Economist. EAGCP's role is to support DG Comp's economic reasoning in competition policy analysis. The Commissioner or the Director-General may also ask EAGCP members on an ad-hoc basis to provide economic advice on particular issues (see for example, EAGCP's July 2005 opinion on the reform of Article 82, *infra* Chaps. 5 and 6).

[41] See *infra* Chap. 16.

[42] Such as the OECD, WTO and UNCTAD.

[43] [2003] OJ L1/1: see *infra* 119 and Chap. 14.

[44] See *infra* Chap.14.

[45] Art. 14.

[46] i.e., of the Member States.

[47] Commission Notice on cooperation within the Network of Competition Authorities [2004] OJ L123/18, para. 58.

[48] Reg. 139/2004, Art. 19.

[49] See further *infra* Chap. 14.

(iv) Community Acts

Community acts adopted by the autonomous Community institutions (the Council, the Commission, and the European Parliament), such as regulations, directives decisions, recommendations, and opinions, flesh out the basic principles set out in the Treaty.[50] Most general legislative acts, intended to apply in all of the Member States, are adopted by regulation or directive.

It has already been seen that a number of Community regulations have been adopted by the Council to ensure that the objectives of the Treaty competition rules are carried out. In the field of competition the Commission has adopted a number of Regulations under powers delegated to it by the Council[51] and applies the competition rules to undertakings by means of decisions.[52]

(v) The Case Law of the Community Courts

The Community's judicial system comprises the Court of Justice (ECJ) and, since 1989, the Court of First Instance (CFI).[53] The ECJ is assisted by Advocates General. An Advocate General delivers an opinion on a case prior to the Court giving judgment.[54] The Court has the task of interpreting the law set out in the Treaty and secondary legislation and ensuring that the law is observed. The means of statutory interpretation adopted by the Court may seem unfamiliar or even unusual to an English lawyer. Because the Treaty is only a framework treaty its meaning is sometimes obscure. Furthermore, the difficulties of interpretation faced by the Court are compounded by the fact that each text of a Community provision is relevant to the determination (all provisions are translated into each of the twenty-three Community languages[55]). Each text has equal status and is equally authentic.[56] The approach of the Court is to adopt a 'teleological' interpretation of Treaty

---

[50] EC Treaty, Art. 249 defines the main characteristics of each of these measures. The ECJ has, however, recognized that other 'sui generis' acts adopted by one of the Community institutions may be capable of producing legal effects: Case 22/70, *Commission v. Council (ERTA)* [1971] ECR 263.

[51] See *infra* 114.

[52] The Commission also has powers under Article 86(3), which deals with public undertakings and those to whom Member States grant special or exclusive rights, to adopt directives (addressed to Member States) without the participation of the Council: see *infra* Chap. 8.

[53] 'The Court of Justice and the Court of First Instance, each within its own jurisdiction, shall ensure that in the interpretation and application of this Treaty the law is observed': EC Treaty, Art. 220. Under the Reform Treaty the Court of Justice will become the 'Court of Justice of the European Union' and the Court of First Instance the 'General Court'. Provision is also made for specialized courts. For the present Community Courts generally, see A. Arnull, *The European Union and its Court of Justice* (2nd edn., Oxford University Press, 2006); K. Lenaerts, D. Arts, I. Maselis (R. Bray, Eds,) *Procedural Law of the European Union* (2nd edn., Sweet & Maxwell, 2006).

[54] The Opinion is not binding but, particularly, when followed by the Court can be of acute importance to a better understanding of the case and the issues it raises.

[55] Bulgarian, Czech, Danish, Dutch, English, Estonian, Finnish, French, German, Greek, Hungarian, Irish, Italian, Latvian, Lithuanian, Maltese, Polish, Portuguese, Romanian, Spanish, Slovakian, Slovenian and Swedish. Irish became a full official and working language on 1 January 2007, following a Coreper (Committee of Permanent Representatives) agreement on 13 June 2005 (previously there was no Irish version of secondary legislation, but there was of the Treaty and Irish could be used as the language of procedure before the Court). The Romanian Commissioner, Leonard Orban, took up the multilingualism portfolio on 1 January 2007.

[56] Case 283/81, *CILFIT Srl and Lanificio de Gavardo SpA v. Ministry of Health* [1982] ECR 3415, [1983] CMLR 472, para. 18. See the discussion of the meaning of 'affect trade' in Article 81 of the Treaty, *infra* in Chap. 3, and the discussion of the meaning of an abuse of a dominant position, *infra* in Chap. 5.

provisions or Community acts which it construes, applying the Community provisions against the wider backdrop of the Treaty tasks and activities.[57] On occasion the Court has even gone so far as to ignore clear words of the Treaty or Community act if that construction will ensure an interpretation which best accords with the broad objectives of the Treaty.[58] A number of instances in which the Court has adopted an extremely broad interpretation of the competition rules or one which does not accord with the clear wording of the text will be seen in this book.[59]

The ECJ has no system of precedent. In practice, however, it strives for consistency.[60] It is only on rare occasions that it has seen fit expressly to reverse a previous ruling.[61] The CFI does not consider itself bound by its own previous decisions and neither generally does it consider itself bound by the ECJ.[62] As there is, however, an appeal from the CFI to the ECJ on a point of law, it is open to the ECJ to reverse the CFI if it does not agree with the lower court's departure from precedent. In a famous example of the CFI striking out on its own, *Jégo-Quéré*, the ECJ overturned the CFI on appeal and restored the status quo, but did not gainsay the CFI's right not to follow the ECJ's previous decisions.[63]

In the context of Community competition law the Court hears two main types of action. First, Article 230 (ex Article 173) of the Treaty specifically provides that the Court may review the legality of acts adopted by the Community institutions. This provision thus sets out a procedure for challenging the legality of the Commission's competition decisions.[64] Further, it also allows for challenge to a number of other administrative acts of the Commission which are capable of affecting the interests of individuals.[65] Since 1989 challenges are made in the first instance to the CFI.[66] A fast-track procedure is available in certain cases.[67] Appeals on points of

[57] Set out in Articles 2, 3, and 4 of the EC Treaty: see *supra* Chap. 1.

[58] See, e.g., Case C-70/88, *European Parliament v. Council ('Chernobyl')* [1990] ECR I-2041, [1992] 1 CMLR 91.

[59] See, e.g., *infra* Chaps. 3, 5, and 12.

[60] Case 4/73, *Nold v. Commission* [1974] ECR 491, [1974] CMLR 338. See also A. Arnull, 'Owning up to Fallibility: Precedent and the Court of Justice' (1993) 30 *CML Rev.* 247.

[61] See, e.g., Case C-70/88, *European Parliament v. Council ('Chernobyl')* [1990] ECR I-2041, [1992] 1 CMLR 91; Case C-10/89, *CNL-Sucal v. HAG GF AG ('Hag II')* [1990] ECR I-3711, [1990] 3 CMLR 571; and Cases C-267 and 268/91, *Keck and Mithouard, Criminal Proceedings Against* [1993] ECR I-6097, [1995] 1 CMLR 101, paras. 15–16. On some (unsatisfactory) occasions the ECJ has departed from its previous case law without explaining what it was doing but in others it has distinguished the case before it from the precedents in a way more familiar to common lawyers: see further Arnull, *op. cit.* n. 53, 625–633. The willingness of the ECJ to depart from its previous decisions may become as issue in respect of a modernized approach to Article 82, see *infra* Chap. 5.

[62] Unless there are exceptional circumstances, such as the previous judgment having the status of *res judicata*, or where the Statute of the Court decrees it, e.g. where the ECJ overturns a judgment of the CFI on a point of law and refers the case back to the CFI for judgment, Article 61 decrees that the CFI is bound by the ECJ on points of law. See Arnull, *op. cit.*, 633–637.

[63] Case T-177/01, *Jégo-Quéré v. Commission* [2002] ECR II-665, reversed by the ECJ, Case C-263/02 P, *Commission v. Jégo-Quéré* [2004] ECR I-3425. The case concerned the controversial matter of when an individual has standing under Article 230(4) of the EC Treaty to challenge an act of general application. The question of whether the ECJ could overturn the CFI where the CFI has followed the previous case law of the ECJ, but the ECJ wishes to depart from its own precedent, is considered *infra* Chaps. 7 and 14.

[64] EC Treaty, Art. 230. See discussion *infra* in Chap. 14.

[65] Case 60/81, *IBM v. Commission* [1981] ECR 2639, [1981] 3 CMLR 635. See also the discussion, *infra* Chap. 14.

[66] See EC Treaty, Art. 225(1) and the Protocol on the Statute of the Court of Justice, Article 51 as amended by Council Decision of 26 April 2004 [2004] OJ L132/5, see further Chap. 14 and Cases C-68/95 and C-30/95, *France v. Commission* [1998] ECR I-1375, [1998] 4 CMLR 829, *infra* Chap. 12.

[67] See the codified rules of the CFI [2003] OJ C193/41, [2003] 3 CMLR 25.

law can then be made to the ECJ.[68] The ECJ has taken a limited view of its role in such appeals[69] and it is often necessary to look at the CFI judgment rather than that of the ECJ to find a full analysis of the issues. Competition cases form a major part of the CFI's workload and the CFI is developing considerable competition law expertise.

Secondly, the national courts are frequently asked to apply the EC competition rules, which are directly applicable. Article 234 (ex Article 177)[70] of the Treaty provides a procedure for a national court or tribunal to request the ECJ to give a preliminary ruling on the interpretation of Community law where such a ruling is necessary to enable that court or tribunal to give judgment.[71] At present these references are still made directly to the ECJ and are not dealt with by the CFI.[72]

A severe problem for the Court is its volume of work and the consequent delays that may be experienced by litigants. This problem is particularly acute in the sphere of mergers where timing will be of the essence to the parties. The expedited procedure before the CFI to some extent ameliorated these difficulties but there is still criticism of the delays and calls for the creation of a specialist court to remedy the problem.[73] The Treaty of Nice contained procedures for changes to the structure and jurisdiction of the Court.[74] These included the creation of 'Judicial Panels' attached to the CFI, but the Civil Service Tribunal, which deals with staff cases, is so far the only one to have been established.

(vi) The General Principles of Community Law

The ECJ has developed and introduced a body of unwritten law, the general principles of law, as part of Community law.[75] These are rules, based on national laws of Member States and international treaties to which the Member States are signatories, especially the European Convention on Human Rights and Fundamental Freedoms, in accordance with which Community law is interpreted. The principles are important when determining the boundaries of proper and lawful action of the Community and national institutions (when the latter are acting within the sphere of Community law).[76]

---

[68] Protocol on the Statute of the Court of Justice, Art. 51: see Chap. 14.

[69] See *infra* Chap. 14.

[70] See *infra* Chap. 14.

[71] For a full discussion, see Craig and de Búrca, *supra* n. 1, Chap. 13.

[72] Article 225 was amended by the Treaty of Nice and Article 225(3) now provides that the CFI has jurisdiction to give preliminary rulings 'in specific areas laid down by the Statute'. The Statute of the Court has, however, not yet been amended to lay down such areas and all preliminary rulings therefore continue to go to the ECJ.

[73] The UK's Confederation of British Industry (CBI) has called for the creation of specialist competition panels in the CFI, see CBI Report, 15 June 2006. The question of whether there is a need for the creation of a distinct European competition court as a panel of the CFI has been examined by the House of Lords European Union Select Committee. See D.Trapp, 'Competition Court in the Dock' *Legal Week*, 26 October 2006, available at http//:www.freshfields.com/publications/pdfs/2006/LW_2610_p21.pdf. The Select Committee concluded that there is no such need at present (Select Committee on the European Union, 15th Report, 27 March 2007).

[74] Nice Treaty Art. 2(26).

[75] See generally T. Tridimas, *The General Principles of EU Law* (2nd edn., Oxford University Press, 2006).

[76] See, e.g., Case 5/88, *Wachauf* v. *Federal Republic of Germany* [1989] ECR 2609, [1990] 1 CMLR 328; Case C-260/89, *Ellinki Radiophonia Tileorassi—Anonimi Etairia (ERT-AE)* v. *Dimotiki Etairia Pliroforissis (DEP)* [1991] ECR I-2925, [1994] 4 CMLR 540.

The actions of institutions applying and enforcing the EC competition rules must respect the general principles of law, in particular, the principles of proportionality, legitimate expectations, and fundamental rights. This point is of special importance to the Commission which must ensure that when conducting competition investigations its administrative procedures comply with principles of human rights, rules of natural justice, and rights of defence, for example the right to be heard and to know the case against one. In many appeals from a Commission's competition decision the parties have alleged that the Commission has failed to observe these principles.[77] National authorities must also respect these principles when applying Articles 81 and 82.

The general principles were previously unwritten Community law, in the sense that they were to be found in the case law of the Court. However, a Charter of Fundamental Rights of the European Union was 'solemnly proclaimed' by the Council, Parliament, and Commission and politically approved by the Member States at the Nice European Council summit in December 2000.[78] The Charter, which 'could perhaps best be described as a creative distillation of the rights contained in the various European and international agreements and national constitutions on which the ECJ had for some years been drawing'[79] was not expressed to be legally binding, largely because of the opposition of certain Member States, notably the UK. As explained in the Addendum[80] the Charter will be annexed to the Treaties and become legally binding if (when) the Reform Treaty comes into force.[81]

The principle of subsidiarity, which is also a general principle of Community law, is now enshrined in Article 5 of the EC Treaty. This principle applies to all Community activity, including the implementation of Community competition policy. Article 5 provides:

In areas which do not fall within its exclusive competence, the Community shall take action, in accordance with the principle of subsidiarity, only if and insofar as the objectives of the proposed action cannot be sufficiently achieved by the Member States and can therefore, by reason of the scale or effects of the proposed action, be better achieved by the Community.

The Community competition rules apply only to firms' agreements and practices when they *affect trade between Members States* or to mergers that have a *Community dimension*. The rules thus incorporate the notion of subsidiarity. Moreover, the institutional arrangements set up to effect the modernization are expressed to be in accordance with the principle of subsidiarity.[82]

C. A NEW LEGAL ORDER OF INTERNATIONAL LAW

(i) Direct Effect

Although the European Communities are founded on international agreements, European Community law has developed its own unique legal system, with its own institutions and extremely effective enforcement mechanisms.

---

[77] See *infra* Chap. 14.

[78] [2000] OJ C364/1.

[79] Craig and de Bùrca, *supra* n. 1, 3rd edn., 359. The ECJ cited the Charter for the first time in Case C-540/03, *European Parliament v. Council* [2006] ECR I-5769, para. 38.

[80] See *infra* 1399.

[81] The UK is to have an opt-out, see *infra* 1399 ff.

[82] Council Reg. 1/2003 [2003] OJ L1/1, recital 34; see further 119.

International law and international treaties traditionally impose obligations only on States and do not impose obligations or confer rights on private individuals. It might perhaps have been assumed that Community law would merely create obligations between Member States. The Treaty specifically sets out a mechanism for both the European Commission and Member States to enforce Treaty obligations against recalcitrant Member States (see, in particular, Articles 226–8). However, very early in the Community's development the ECJ ruled that this would not be the limit of Community law. Rather, it has become clear that the rights and obligations created by European Community law are enforceable by and against private individuals and not just the Member States. In *Van Gend en Loos* v. *Nederlandse Administratie der Belastingen*[83] the ECJ ruled that individuals are entitled to rely on rights that they derive from Community measures (such as the Treaty competition rules) before national courts even if those measures have not been implemented by national legislation.[84] In addition, the rights conferred by Treaty Articles and regulations can be relied upon against a Member State or a state entity *and* against another individual or private party (they impose obligations on private entities and are capable of 'horizontal direct effect'[85]). The only requirement is that the Community measure is *capable of direct effect*. The provision relied upon must be sufficiently precise and unconditional.

The main competition provisions set out in the Treaty are directly applicable and can be relied upon by or against private individuals. One of these provisions, Article 81(3) of the Treaty, has only been directly applicable since 1 May 2004. The implications of the previous lack of direct applicability and the significance of the change made by Regulation 1/2003 are dealt with in other parts of this book, particularly Chapters 4 and 14.

(ii) Supremacy

Where there is a conflict between a directly effective Community provision and national law, the former must prevail.[86] The principle of supremacy ensures the full effectiveness and uniform application of directly effective Community law.[87]

---

[83] Case 26/62, *Van Gend en Loos* v. *Nederlandse Administratie der Belastingen* [1963] ECR 1, 12, [1963] CMLR 105, 129.

[84] European Communities Act 1972, s. 2(1) obliges English courts to recognize and enforce directly effective Community law. For present purposes 'directly applicable' and 'directly effective' can be considered interchangeable, unless one is speaking in respect of directives.

[85] Directives are not directly effective against private parties but only against the State and emanations of the State (they are capable only of 'vertical direct effect': see Case 152/84, *Marshall* v. *Southampton and South–West Hampshire Area Health Authority (Teaching)* [1986] ECR 723, [1986] 1 CMLR 688 and Case C-91/92, *Faccini Dori* v. *Recreb* [1994] ECR I-3325, [1995] 1 CMLR 665). The ECJ has given a wide interpretation to the term 'State': see Case C-188/89, *Foster* v. *British Gas plc* [1990] ECR I-3313, [1990] 2 CMLR 833. Even if a provision is not directly effective, however, a national court still has an obligation to interpret, in so far as it is possible, provisions of national law in conformity with that Community law (indirect effect): see, e.g., Case 14/83, *Von Colson and Kamann* v. *Land Nordrhein–Westfalen* [1984] ECR 1891, [1986] 2 CMLR 430 and Case C-106/89, *Marleasing SA* v. *La Comercial Internacional de Alimentacion SA* [1990] ECR I-4135, [1992] 1 CMLR 305. Further, a Member State may be liable for any loss caused by its failure to implement a directive or its failure to implement it correctly: Cases C-6 and 9/90; *Francovich* v. *Italy* [1991] ECR I-5357, [1993] 2 CMLR 66.

[86] Case 6/64, *Costa* v. *ENEL* [1964] ECR 585, 593–4, [1964] CMLR 425, 456.

[87] A national court faced with national rules or legislation that conflict with Community law has an obligation to give immediate precedence to the Community provisions. If necessary it must refuse to apply the provisions of national legislation even if subsequently adopted: see Case 106/77, *Amministrazione delle Finanze dello Stato* v. *Simmenthal SpA* [1978] ECR 629, [1978] 3 CMLR 263, para. 24.

Before 1 May 2004 the position was that the doctrine of supremacy did not ordinarily mean that national competition legislation could not be applied where Community competition rules applied,[88] but where there was a *conflict* between national and Community law, the latter had to prevail.[89] Regulation 1/2003, Article 3,[90] however, makes specific provision for the relationship between EC and national competition law in the sphere of anti-competitive agreements and conduct. The position under the new Regulation is discussed in Chapter 14.[91] The EC Merger Regulation also specifically deals with the relationship between Community and national merger regimes.[92]

(iii) Article 234 (Ex Article 177) of the EC Treaty

It is Article 234 of the EC Treaty which has enabled the enforcement of the Community rules at the national level through the principles of direct effect and supremacy without compromising the uniformity of Community law. It enables, and in some circumstances requires, national courts or tribunals to refer questions to the ECJ concerning, for example, the interpretation of the Treaty and Community acts where necessary to enable the national court to give judgment. The ECJ then gives preliminary rulings on those questions.[93] This procedure has been 'essential for the preservation of the Community character of the law established by the Treaty and has the object of ensuring that in all circumstances the law is the same in all states of the Community'.[94] It has been critical in the sphere of competition law.

4. THE COMPETITION PROVISIONS

A. GENERAL

(i) Article 3(1)(g) of the Treaty

The tasks and activities of the Community and the foundations of all Community policies are set out in Articles 2, 3, and 4 of the Treaty.[95] Article 3(1)(g)[96] provides that the activities of the Community shall include 'a system ensuring that competition in the internal market is not distorted'. This aim is crucial when interpreting the Treaty provisions which set out the competition

---

[88] But see the provisions dealing with mergers, *infra* Chap. 12.

[89] Case 14/68, *Walt Wilhelm* v. *Bundeskartellamt* [1969] ECR 1, [1969] CMLR 100. There were, however, potential complications where national law applied more strictly to agreements authorized by EC law, see the discussion in the 1st edn. of this book, pp. 1008–15.

[90] [2003] OJ L1/1.

[91] See *infra*, 1282 ff.

[92] *Infra* Chap. 12.

[93] See *supra* 105.

[94] Case 166/73, *Rheinmühlen-Düsseldorf* v. *Einfuhr und Vorratsstelle für Getreide und Futtermittel* [1974] ECR 33, [1974] 1 CMLR 523.

[95] See *supra* Chap. 1.

[96] Ex Article 3(f).

rules in greater detail. In *Continental Can*[97] the ECJ stated:

Article [82] is part of the Chapter devoted to the common rules on the Community's policy in the field of competition. This policy is based on Article [3(1)(g)] of the Treaty according to which the Community's activity shall include the institution of a system ensuring that competition in the Common Market is not distorted. The applicants' argument that this provision merely contains a general programme devoid of legal effect, ignores the fact that Article 3 considers the pursuit of the objectives which it lays down to be indispensable for the achievement of the Community's tasks. As regards in particular the aim mentioned in Article [3(1)(g)], the Treaty in several provisions contains more detailed regulations for the interpretation of which this aim is decisive.

(ii) The Main Treaty Provisions and The Merger Regulation

The main competition rules are contained in Chapter 1 of Title VI of the Treaty. Section 1 (Articles 81–86) deals with rules applying to undertakings.[98] Section 2 (Articles 87–89) deals with State Aids. The regulation of State Aids granted by Member States to industry is outside the scope of this book.[99] Article 31 deals with state monopolies of a commercial character. It is situated in Title I but the Commission treats it as part of the competition rules.[100] A general power to control mergers is not expressly contained in the Treaty.[101] Provision for merger control is, however, now set out in Council Regulation 139/2004.[102]

(iii) Special Sectors

The competition rules cover all areas of the economy. However, a few comments should be made about the special position of certain sectors.

a. Coal and Steel

Until 23 July 2002 the coal and steel industries were governed by the European Coal and Steel Community Treaty. The competition provisions set out in the ECSC Treaty were similar to those of the EC Treaty but had important differences.[103] Upon the expiry of that Treaty coal and steel

---

[97] Case 6/72, *Europemballage Corporation and Continental Can Co Inc* v. *Commission* [1973] ECR 215, [1973] CMLR 199, para. 23. For greater discussion of this case see Chap. 5. See also Case C-68/94, *French Republic* v. *Commission* [1998] ECR I-1375, [1998] 4 CMLR 829.

[98] Broadly, any entity engaged in commercial activities: see *infra* Chap. 3.

[99] But see the Online Resource Centre.

[100] See the Commission's Annual Reports on Competition Policy.

[101] Although in Case 6/72, *Europemballage Corporation and Continental Can Co Inc* v. *Commission* [1973] ECR 215, [1973] CMLR 199, the ECJ held that Article 82 did prohibit some mergers conducted by dominant undertakings: see *infra* Chaps. 5 and 12.

[102] [2004] OJ L24/1 replacing Council Regulation 4064/89 [1989] OJ L395/1, as amended by Council Reg. 1310/97 [1997] OJ L180/1.

[103] Under the ECSC Treaty the competition rules applied whether or not there was an effect on inter Member State trade whereas under the EC Treaty such an effect on trade is a prerequisite (see Chap. 3 pp. 191 ff, Chap. 5 pp. 339 ff; the ECSC provisions did not have direct effect (Case C-128/92, *H. J. Banks* v. *British Coal Corporation* [1994] ECR I-1209, [1994] 5 CMLR 30); under the ECSC regime all joint ventures, whether full-function or not, were regarded as being covered by the provisions on concentrations (under the EC merger regime only full-function joint ventures are treated as concentrations: see Chaps. 12 and 13); and the ECSC provisions gave the Commission exclusive jurisdiction over all concentrations and not only those above certain turnover thresholds as is the position under the EC Merger Regulation. The procedural rules had gradually been aligned (XXth Report on Competition Policy (Commission, 1990) part 122) but a few differences remained (under Article 66(7) of the ECSC Treaty the Commission could not proceed immediately to finding an abuse of a dominant

passed into the scope of the EC Treaty. The Commission issued a Communication in June 2002 explaining how the EC rules would now apply to coal and steel.[104] It stated that it did not intend to initiate proceedings under the EC rules in respect of agreements it had previously authorized under the ECSC regime unless 'owing to substantial factual or legal developments' they were clearly not eligible for exemption under the EC Treaty.[105]

b. Atomic Energy

The Euratom Treaty of 1957 established the European Atomic Energy Community in respect of the non-military use of nuclear energy. The competition provisions of the EC Treaty apply to nuclear energy insofar as they do not derogate from the Euratom Treaty.[106] The effect of this is that Articles 81 and 82 of the EC Treaty can be applied to the nuclear sector and the Commission has taken a number of decisions on horizontal cooperation agreements in the industry.[107]

c. Agriculture

In 1962 Regulation 26[108] modified the competition rules in respect of agriculture, and there is some tension between the objectives of the common agricultural policy (CAP) and competition policy.[109] Nevertheless, in 2006 the Council adopted Regulation 1184/2006[110] which provides that Articles 81 and 82 *do* apply to the production and trade of agricultural products. There are three exceptions to this general rule: (i) agreements, decisions and practices which form an integral part of national market organizations, (ii) agreements, decisions and practices which are necessary for the attainment of the objectives of the CAP and (iii) agreements between farmers or associations of farmers belonging to a single Member State not involving an obligation to charge identical prices. Also, some common market organisations such as those dealing with 'fruit and vegetables' or 'wine', containing specific provisions on interbranch organisations are outside the scope of Article 81, under certain conditions.[111]

d. Transport

The rules applicable to the transport sector have only gradually been brought within the general competition regime.[112]

position but had first to go through a recommendation procedure and consult the Member State concerned; the merger regime of the ECSC allowed notification at any time, in contrast to the prior authorization system under the EC Merger Regulation, 4064/89).

[104] Communication from the Commission concerning certain aspects of the treatment of competition cases resulting from the expiry of the ECSC Treaty [2002] OJ C152/5.

[105] *Ibid.*, paras. 28–9.

[106] EC Treaty, Art. 305(2).

[107] See *infra* Chap. 13.

[108] [1959–62] OJ Spec. Ed. 129.

[109] Article 33 (ex Art. 39).

[110] [2006] OJ L214/7.

[111] See http://ec.europa.eu/comm/competition/sectors/agriculture/overview_en.html. For cases concerning the application of the competition rules to agriculture even under the old regime, see e.g., Case 61/80, *Coöperative Stremsel- en Kleurselfabriek v. Commission* [1981] ECR 851, [1982] 1 CMLR 240; Case 71/74, *FRUBO v. Commission* [1975] ECR 563, [1975] 2 CMLR 123, Cases 40–8, 50, 54–6, 111, 113, and 114/73, *Suiker Unie v. EC Commission* [1975] ECR 1663, [1976] 1 CMLR 295; *French Beef* [2003] OJ L209/12, on appeal Cases T- 217/03 and T-245/03, *FNCBV v. Commission*, 13 December 2006.

[112] See *infra* 114 ff.

e. Sectors Subject to Liberalization

The Community has embarked on programmes of liberalization and/or harmonization of the energy, telecommunications, broadcasting, and financial services sectors with the aim of opening them up to greater competition.[113] There has been very little sympathy for the claims that these sectors should receive favourable treatment and should be protected from the competitive process.[114] The Commission is also currently much concerned with the application of the competition rules to professional services.[115]

f. Sport

Next, there is the question of sport.[116] Early case law concerned the application of the free movement provisions to sporting rules. The ECJ stated that the practice of sport was subject Community law only insofar as constituted an economic activity.[117] However, in the watershed case of *Bosman* the ECJ applied the free movement provisions to the football transfer system.[118] Competition law is applied to the undoubtedly commercial aspects of sport[119] and the Commission has particularly been concerned with the media rights to sporting events.[120] In a world in which sport is such very big business the distinction between the 'economic' and 'non-economic' has became harder and harder to draw. The current position of the ECJ is set out in *Meca-Medina*.[121] There the ECJ recognized that sporting regulatory bodies may have rules which

---

[113] See J. Faull and A. Nikpay (eds.), *The EC Law of Competition* (2nd edn., Oxford University Press, 2007) Chaps. 11–14.

[114] These industries may be the subject of regulatory regimes in the Member States and they may involve obligations of 'universal service'. See further *infra* Chap. 8. The Commission has undertaken sector enquiries under Regulation 1/2003, Article 17 in respect of the energy sector and the financial services sector (payment cards, retail banking and business insurance): see further Chap. 11. For energy markets, see P. Cameron, *Competition in Energy Markets* (2nd edn., Oxford University Press, 2007).

[115] The Commission has produced two reports: *Report on Competition in Professional Services* COM/2004/0083 final, February 2004; and *Professional Services—Scope for More Reform* COM/2005/0405 final, in September 2005. As a follow-up to these reports the European Parliament passed a resolution in December 2006 supporting the Commission's moves to rid the professional services sector of overly restrictive regulation (which is often put in place, or maintained, by the actions of Member States). For a discussion of the *Wouters* case on the regulation of the legal profession in the Netherlands, Case C-303/99, *Wouters v. Algemene Raad van de Nederlandse Order van Advocaten* [2002] ECR I-1577, [2002] 4 CMLR 913, see Chap. 4.

[116] See S. Van den Bogaert and A. Vermeersch, 'Sport and the EC Treaty: a tale of uneasy bedfellows?' (2006) 31 *ELRev* 821.

[117] Case 36/74, *Walrave and Koch v. Association Union Cycliste Internationale* [1974] ECR 1405; see also Case 13/76, *Donà v. Mantero* [1976] ECR 1333.

[118] Case C-415/93, *Union Royale Belge des Sociétés de Football Association v. Bosman* [1995] ECR I-4921, which fundamentally altered the professional game in Europe.

[119] See, e.g., the application of Article 82 to the ticketing arrangements for the 1998 World Cup in *1998 Football World Cup* [2000] OJ L5/55, [2000] 4 CMLR 963; the Commission dealt with Formula One racing in a lengthy investigation which culminated in a separation of the functions of the FIA and the FAO, IP/01/120.

[120] *Joint selling of the commercial rights of the UEFA Champions League* [2003] OJ L291/25, [2004] 4 CMLR 9; *Deutsche Bundesliga* [2005] OJ L134/46, [2005] 5 CMLR 1715; *FA Premier League* [2006] 5 CMLR 1430: see further *infra* Chaps. 11 and 13. The saga of litigation over the rules of the European Broadcasting Union (EBU) was largely to do with the television rights to sporting events: Cases T-528, 542, 543 and 546/93 *Métropole Télévision SA v. Commission* [1996] ECR II-649, [1996] 5 CMLR 386; Case T-206/99, *Métropole Télévision SA v. Commission* [2001] 4 CMLR 1423; Cases T-185, 216, 299 & 300/00 99, *Métropole Télévision SA (M6) v. Commission* [2003] 4 CMLR 707. For the sale of media rights, see T. Toft, 'Developments in European Law', Speech to the Sports and Law Congress, Berin, 28 April 2006, http://ec.europa.eu/comm/competition/speeches/text/sp2006_003_en.pdf.

[121] Case C-519/04, *Meca-Medina and Majcen v. Commission* [2006] ECR I-6991, [2006] 5 CMLR 1023. The case concerned the Olympic swimming doping rules and is discussed further in Chap. 4. For the

are necessary for regulating sporting activity even if they limit competition because such a limitation is 'inherent in the organisation and proper conduct of competitive sport and its very purpose is to ensure healthy rivalry between athletes'.[122] It nevertheless held that Community law must be the judge of whether they are compatible with the competition rules, in that they must comply with the principle of proportionality and not apply excessive penalties, for instance. There appears, therefore, to be no blanket exception from the competition rules for 'sporting' rules:

... it is apparent that the mere fact that a rule is purely sporting in nature does not have the effect of removing from the scope of the Treaty the person engaging in the activity governed by that rule or the body which has laid it down.

If the sporting activity in question falls within the scope of the Treaty, the conditions for engaging in it are subject to all the obligations which result from the various provisions of the Treaty.... [123]

g. Security

Article 296(1)(b)[124] provides that the Treaty provisions shall not preclude any Member State from taking 'such measures as it considers necessary for the protection of the essential interests of its security which are connected with the production of or trade in arms, munitions and war material'. This provision has, for example, been used by Member States to retain jurisdiction over mergers with a military significance.[125]

B. THE SUBSTANTIVE PROVISIONS OF THE TREATY

The substantive competition provisions of the Treaty are summarized here. The provisions are dealt with more fully in later Chapters.

Commission's policy on the competition rules and sport generally see Mario Monti, *Sport and Competition*, speech given at a Commission-organized conference on sports, Brussels, 17 Apr. 2000; Mario Monti, *Competition and Sport the Rules of the Game*, Conference on 'Governance in Sport', European Olympic Committee, Féderation Internationale de l'Automobile, Brussels, 26 Feb. 2001; Alexander Schaub, *Sports and Competition: Broadcasting Rights for SportsEvents*, European Competition Day, Madrid, 26 Feb. 2002: all available on DG Comp's web site.

[122] *Meca-Medina*, para. 45. See also *UEFA* [1999] OJ C363/2 where the Commission published an Article 19(3) Notice under Reg. 17 setting out its initial view that a UEFA rule precluding more than one club belonging to the same owner from taking part in the same competition did not fall within the competition rules.

[123] *Meca Medina*, paras. 27–8. So in this case the anti-doping rules of the IOC and FISA were subject to the competition rules. See further Case T-193/02, *Laurent Piau v. Commission* [2005] ECR II-209, *infra* 302; E. Szyszczak, 'Competition and Sport' (2007) 32 *ELRev* 95.

[124] Formerly Article 223(1)(b).

[125] See *infra* Chap. 12. It should be noted, however, that in December 2006 the Commission issued an Interpretative Communication on the application of Article 296 in the field of defence procurement (COM (2006) 779 final, published further to initiatives announced in December 2005, COM(2005) 626). This was promoted by Vice-President Verheugen, the Commissioner responsible for enterprise and industry, and was intended to herald a much tougher line towards Member States' reliance on the derogation in respect of defence procurement: 'It is the Member States' prerogative to define their essential security interests and their duty to protect them. The concept of essential security interests gives them flexibility in the choice of measures to protect those interests, but also a special responsibility to respect their Treaty obligations and not to abuse this flexibility. Member States must in particular keep in mind that the derogation under Article 296 TEC is only applicable in clearly defined cases and make sure that it does "not go beyond the limits of such cases" ...' (Interpretative Communication, section 5). This policy towards the application of Article 296 may well affect the impact of the derogation in respect of the competition rules. For Article 296 generally, see P. Koutrakos, *Trade, Foreign Policy and Defence in EU Constitutional Law* (Hart Publishing, 2001).

(i) Article 81 (Ex Article 85)

Article 81 is set out in three parts: Article 81(1) prohibits agreements, decisions of associations of undertakings and concerted practices which have as their object or effect the prevention, restriction, or distortion of competition and which may affect trade between Member States. Article 81(2) states that such agreements are void. Article 81(3) provides, however, that Article 81(1) may be 'declared inapplicable' in respect of agreements, decisions, or concerted practices or of categories of such agreements which are on balance beneficial since they satisfy the criteria set out in that provision. The provisions governing the analysis of an agreement are split, therefore, between Article 81(1) and Article 81(3). This 'bifurcation' of Article 81 has caused great difficulties.[126]

The wording in Article 81(3) that Article 81(1) 'may ... be declared inapplicable' to certain agreements left open, deliberately perhaps,[127] the question of how and by whom this declaration was to be made. The Council in 1962 conferred exclusive power on the Commission to exempt agreements from the prohibition of Article 81(1),[128] and later enabled it to adopt 'block exemption' regulations exempting categories of agreements from the prohibition.[129] In 1999, however, the Commission proposed in its White Paper on modernization[130] that the system of individual exemption should be abandoned. This proposal was adopted by the Council in Regulation 1/2003[131] and from 1 May 2004 Article 81(3) has had direct effect and is applied directly by the Commission, national courts, and national competition authorities as an exception to the Article 81(1) prohibition.

(ii) Article 82 (Ex Article 86)

Article 82 prohibits an undertaking which holds a dominant position in the common market, or a substantial part of it, from abusing that position in so far as it may affect inter-Member State trade. It contains no express provision for exception or exemption.

(iii) Articles 86 and 31 (Ex Articles 90 and 37)

Article 86 deals with the application of the competition rules (and other rules of the Treaty) to public undertakings and those given special or exclusive rights by Member States. It contains a limited exemption (Article 86(2)) from the Treaty rules for such undertakings. That limitation has, however, been construed narrowly.

Article 31 is situated in the part of the Treaty concerned with the free movement of goods. It requires Member States which have State monopolies of a commercial character to eliminate discrimination between nationals of Member States regarding the conditions under which goods are procured and marketed.

---

[126] See *infra* Chap. 4.

[127] See *infra* Chap. 14.

[128] Reg. 17 [1959–62] OJ Spec. Ed. 87, Art. 9.

[129] See *infra* Chap. 14.

[130] Commission White Paper on modernisation of the rules implementing Articles 81 and 82 of the EC Treaty [1999] OJ C132/1, [1999] 5 CMLR 208, paras. 11–13. See *infra* 119 and Chap. 14.

[131] [2003] OJ L1/1.

C. THE PROCEDURAL PROVISIONS

(i) Article 83 (Ex Article 87)

Article 83 confers a general power on the Council to adopt secondary legislation to give effect to the principles laid down in Articles 81 and 82. It provides:[132]

1. The appropriate regulations or directives to give effect to the principles set out in Articles 81 and 82 shall be laid down by the Council, acting by a qualified majority on a proposal from the Commission and after consulting the European Parliament.

2. The regulations or directives referred to in paragraph 1 shall be designed, in particular:

(a) to ensure compliance with the prohibitions laid down in Article 81(1) and in Article 82 by making provision for fines and periodic penalty payments;

(b) to lay down detailed rules for the application of Article 81(3), taking into account the need to ensure effective supervision on the one hand, and to simplify administration to the greatest possible extent on the other;

(c) to define, if need be, in the various branches of the economy, the scope of the provisions of Articles 81 and 82;

(d) to define the respective functions of the Commission and of the Court of Justice in applying the provisions laid down in this paragraph;

(e) to determine the relationship between national laws and the provisions contained in this Section or adopted pursuant to this Article.

a. Implementing Legislation

The Council has adopted regulations pursuant to Article 83 implementing Articles 81 and 82. The most important of these regulations is Regulation 1/2003, which replaced Regulation 17 of 1962 on 1 May 2004. Regulation 1/2003 confers power to enforce the competition rules on the Commission and on the national competition authorities of the Member States (NCAs). The exclusion of certain maritime transport services from Regulation 1/2003[133] was removed by Council Regulation 1419/2006.[134]

b. Block Exemptions

The Council has adopted regulations delegating power to the Commission to adopt regulations granting block exemptions, by which Article 81(1) is declared to be inapplicable to specified types of agreements.[135] The Commission has issued a number of block exemptions under these

---

[132] Article 83, formerly Article 87, was slightly amended by the Treaty of Amsterdam. It previously provided that the appropriate regulations or directives should be laid down 'within three years of the entry into force of this Treaty'. This requirement has been removed to make it clear that the Council has an ongoing power to adopt secondary legislation which gives effect to Articles 81 and 82.

[133] Article 32.

[134] [2006] OJ L269/1. Regulation 1419/2006 repeals Council Regulation 4056/86 [1986] OJ L378/4 and subjects international tramp vessel services and cabotage (maritime transport services taking place exclusively between ports in one and the same Member State) to Regulation 1/2003. The repeal of Regulation 4086/86 removes the special block exemption for liner conferences. Until Reg. 411/2004 [2004] OJ L68/1 the competition rules did not apply to aviation between the Community and third countries. Reg. 1/2003 applies to the inland transport sector, which is covered by Reg. 1017/68 [1968] OJ L175.

[135] See Chap. 4.

delegated powers. Some of these are general (such as those on vertical restraints[136] and technology transfer licences[137]) and some relate only to special sectors (such as motor vehicle distribution,[138] insurance[139] or aviation[140]).

c. Other Regulations and Measures Adopted by the Commission

The Commission has also adopted secondary legislation which implements Council Regulation 1/2003. For example, Regulation 773/2004[141] governs proceedings by the Commission, covering matters such as the Commission's powers while carrying out investigations under Reg. 1/2003, the handling of complaints[142] by the Commission, and the hearings that Regulation 1/2003 requires the Commission to carry out. Directives are rarely used in the area of competition policy. However, very unusually, the Commission has power under Article 86 to issue directives in order to ensure the application of that Article (directives are normally primary legislation issued by the Council).[143]

d. Notices and Guidelines

The Commission has also issued a number of notices (sometimes called 'guidelines').[144] These notices are important statements of how the Commission will deal with certain matters and help undertakings build an understanding of how the competition rules will be applied in practice. The notices called 'guidelines' tend to be those dealing with the way the Commission interprets the substantive law.[145] In many cases these notices are crucial to complete an overall picture of a particular competition rule. A number of notices were issued to accompany Regulation 1/2003 and its flanking legislation in order to flesh out the details of the new enforcement system.[146] The notices do not have legislative force and are sometimes referred to as 'soft law'.[147] However, that label underplays their real effects as the ECJ has held that they

---

[136] Commission Reg. 2790/99 [1999] OJ L336/21.

[137] Commission Reg. 772/2004 [2004] OJ L123/11 (replacing Commission Reg. 240/96 [1996] OJ L31/2).

[138] Commission Reg. 1400/2002 [2002] OJ L203/30.

[139] See Commission Reg. 358/2003 [2003] OJ L53/8, made pursuant to Council Reg. 1534/91 [1991] OJ L143/1 empowering the Commission to issue block exemptions for certain types of agreements in the insurance sector.

[140] See Commission Regulation 1459/2006 on the application of Article 81(3) to certain categories of agreements and concerted practices concerning consultations on passenger tariffs on scheduled air services and slot allocation at airports, [2006] OJ L272/3.

[141] [2004] OJ L123/18.

[142] This means complaints to the Commission that undertakings have infringed the competition rules. Complaints play an important role in the enforcement of competition law. See *infra* Chap. 14.

[143] Or by the Council and Parliament, see *supra* 98 ff. For Article 86, see Chap. 8.

[144] For example, the Notice on the definition of the relevant market [1997] OJ C372/5; Notice on agreements of minor importance [2001] OJ C368/13; Notice on remedies acceptable under the Merger Regulation [2001] OJ C168/3.

[145] Such as the Guidelines on vertical restraints [2000] OJ C291/1; Guidelines on horizontal cooperation agreements [2001] OJ C 3/2; Guidelines on the assessment of horizontal mergers [2004] C 31/5.

[146] Notice on cooperation within the network of competition authorities [2004] OJ C101/43; Notice on cooperation between the Commission and the courts of the EU Member States [2004] OJ C101/54; Notice on the handling of complaints by the Commission [2004] OJ C101/65; Notice on informal guidance relating to novel questions [2004] OJ C101/78; Notice on the effect on trade concept in Art. 81 and Art. 82 [2004] OJ C 101/81; Guidelines on the application of Art. 81(3) [2004] OJ C101/97.

[147] L. Senden, *Soft Law in European Community Law* (Hart Publishing, 2004); S. Lefevre, 'Interpretative Communications and the Implementation of Community Law at National Level' (2004) 29 *ELRev* 808.

may form rules of practice from which the administration may not depart in an individual case[148] and we see throughout this book instances in which cases before the Community Courts are fought on the issue of whether the Commission did or did not properly follow or apply one of more of its notices.[149] In practice they are very influential on the way in which firms conduct business.

(ii) Article 84 (Ex Article 88)

Article 84 enables Member States to apply Articles 81 and 82 in certain circumstances:

> Until the entry into force of the provisions adopted in pursuance of Article 83, the authorities in Member States shall rule on the admissibility of agreements, decisions and concerted practices and on abuse of a dominant position in the common market in accordance with the law of their country and with the provisions of Article 81, in particular paragraph 3, and of Article 82.

This Article confers power on 'authorities in Member States' to apply the competition rules prior to the Council's adoption of implementing rules. In *Nouvelles Frontières*[150] the ECJ held that the term authorities 'refers to either the administrative authorities entrusted, in most Member States, with the task of applying domestic legislation on competition subject to the review of legality carried out by competent courts, or else the courts to which, in other Member States, the task has been especially entrusted'. This provision does not, however, apply to an ordinary national court before which the direct effect of an EC competition provision is pleaded.[151]

Article 84 appears to have been designed as a transitional provision. It has, however, remained significant in conferring power on the national competition authorities to act whenever EC implementing legislation does not apply. A major example of this prior to 1 May 2004 was international flights between Community and non-Community airports.[152]

(iii) Article 85 (Ex Article 89)

Article 85 imposes a general duty on the Commission to ensure compliance with the competition rules:

> 1. Without prejudice to Article 84, the Commission shall ensure the application of the principles laid down in Articles 81 and 82. On application by a Member State or on its own initiative, and in co-operation with the competent authorities in the Member States, who shall give it their assistance,

---

[148] Cases C-189/02P, 202/02 P, 208/02 P and 213/02 P, *Dansk Rørindustri A/S and others v. Commission* [2005] ECR I-5425, [2005] 5 CMLR 796; Case C-397/03 P, *Archer Daniels Midland Company v. Commission* [2006] ECR I-4429; H. C. H. Hofman, *Negotiated and Non-Negotiated Administrative Rule-making: The Example Of EC Competition Policy*, 43 CML Rev. 153 (2006); Senden, *op. cit.* n. 147.

[149] Particularly in respect of the Fining Guidelines (currently[2006] OJ C210/2) and the Leniency Notice (currently [2006] OJ C298/17), see Chap. 14.

[150] Cases 209–213/84, *Ministère Public v. Lucas Asjes (Nouvelles Frontières)* [1986] ECR 1425, [1986] 3 CMLR 173, para. 55.

[151] Case 127/73, *BRT v. SABAM* [1974] ECR 51, [1974] 2 CMLR 23.

[152] The UK adopted regulations, the EC Competition Law (Arts. 88 and 89) Enforcement Regulations (SI 1996, No. 2199), to enable the competition authorities to act in such cases and asserted jurisdiction over the proposed alliance between British Airways and American Airlines on this basis. The Commission now enjoys powers of investigation and enforcement in respect to the applications of Articles 81 and 82 to air transport between the Community and third countries, under Reg. 411/2004, [2004] OJ L68/1.

the Commission shall investigate cases of suspected infringement of these principles. If it finds that there has been an infringement, it shall propose appropriate measures to bring it to an end.

2. If the infringement is not brought to an end, the Commission shall record such infringement of the principles in a reasoned decision. The Commission may publish its decision and authorise Member States to take the measures, the conditions and details of which it shall determine, needed to remedy the situation.

Article 85 was amended by the Treaty of Amsterdam. Previously it included the words 'as soon as it takes up its duties' between the words 'shall' and 'ensure' in the first line. This suggested that it was merely a transitional provision enabling the Commission to enforce Articles 81 and 82 prior to the adoption of implementing legislation. The change of wording recognizes that Article 85 is not a temporary measure, but in fact confers on the Commission an important and permanent residual power to intervene[153] which did not become redundant upon the adoption of the implementing legislation, Regulation 17 and now Regulation 1/2003.[154] Implementing rules governing the transport sector were introduced only gradually.[155] If the Commission wished to intervene in a transport case not covered by these regulations it had to rely on its powers under Article 85. Prior to 1 May 2004, the air transport Regulation, 3975/87, applied only to 'air transport between Community airports'[156] and not to air transport between a Community airport and a non-Member State. As a result of this the Commission was forced to assert jurisdiction under Article 85 when concerned about a proposed alliance between British Airways and American Airlines. The Commission's powers have now been expanded to cover air transport between the Community and third countries.[157]

D. THE MERGER REGULATION

The present Merger Regulation, 139/2004, was adopted by the Council pursuant to Article 83 and Article 308[158] of the Treaty. It replaced, with effect from 1 May 2004, the original Merger Regulation, Regulation 4064/89.[159] The Merger Regulation applies to concentrations with a 'Community dimension'.

E. OTHER RELEVANT TREATY PROVISIONS

Other provisions of the Treaty may interact with the competition provisions. For example, the Treaty provisions relating to the free movement of goods, Articles 28–30, and relating to the free movement of services, Articles 49–55. There is a significant interface between the free movement

---

[153] See C. Kerse, 'Enforcing Community Competition Policy under Articles 88 and 89 of the EC Treaty—New Powers for UK Competition Authorities' [1997] 1 *ECLR* 17.

[154] Reg. 1/2003, Art. 32.

[155] See *supra* n. 134 and accompanying text.

[156] Reg. 3975/87 [1987] OJ L374/1, Art. 1(2), repealed by Reg. 411/2004 [2004] OJ L68/1.

[157] See Reg. 411/2004 [2004] OJ L68/1 and Commission Notice concerning the Alliance Agreement between British Airways and American Airlines [1996] OJ C288/4; see *supra* n. 152. In Case C-466/98, *Commission v. UK* [2003] 1 CMLR 143 (the *Open Skies* case) the ECJ upheld the right of Member States to sign bilateral aviation service agreements with the US but held that this was subject to the Member States' obligation not to discriminate on grounds of nationality against other Community airlines.

[158] Ex Article 235.

[159] [1989] OJ L395/1, as amended by Council Reg. 1310/97 [1997] OJ L180/1. Article 308, the residual legislative power was used as one of the bases for both Reg. 4064/89 and Reg. 139/2004 as it was thought that, on its own, Article 83 was an inadequate basis for legislation to control mergers: see *infra* Chap. 12.

rules and the competition rules for both are instruments designed to increase competitiveness in the Community and to integrate the single market. The free movement rules are also of particular importance when dealing with intellectual property rights.[160] Articles 94 and 95 permit the Community institutions to adopt measures to achieve the approximation of national rules which affect the establishment and functioning of an internal market. Articles 96 and 97 also enable the Community institutions to act where measures in Member States are distorting competition in the common market. These latter two Articles have, however, rarely been used.[161]

5. THE COMPETITION RULES AND THE EUROPEAN ECONOMIC AREA

The agreement establishing the European Economic Area (EEA) came into force on 1 January 1994. The EEA creates a free trade area between the EC and the EFTA countries with the exception of Switzerland.[162] The competition rules in the EEA are modelled on those in the Treaty. References to trade between the contracting parties, however, replace references to trade between Member States. The agreement effectively extends to the territory of the relevant EFTA States the EC competition rules and all the rules governing the internal market, including intellectual property.

Article 53 EEA is modelled on Article 81 of the EC Treaty, Article 54 EEA is modelled on Article 82, Article 59 EEA is modelled on Article 86, and Article 57 EEA effectively applies the rules set out in the EC Merger Regulation to the EEA.

The EFTA Surveillance Authority (ESA) is entrusted, together with the Commission, with the enforcement of the EEA competition rules. The EEA Agreement sets out when the ESA or the Commission has jurisdiction over a particular case. Essentially the ESA has jurisdiction where:

(i) only trade between the EFTA states is affected; or

(ii) trade between one or more EFTA States and the EC is affected and the turnover of the undertakings concerned in the EFTA States is one-third or more of the total turnover of those undertakings in the EEA as a whole.[163]

Where, however, trade in the EC is affected to an appreciable extent the Commission and not the ESA has jurisdiction.[164] The Commission has jurisdiction in all other cases.

The EEA Agreement also established an EFTA Court. This court has jurisdiction in competition matters to deal with appeals from the ESA, infringement actions bought by the ESA against EFTA States, and the settlement of disputes between two or more EFTA States.[165]

---

[160] See *infra* Chap. 10.

[161] See P. J. G. Kapteyn and P. VerLoren van Themaat, *Introduction to the Law of the European Communities* (3rd edn. by L. R. Gormley, Kluwer, Deventer, 1998), 802–10.

[162] Switzerland did not join the EEA after membership was rejected in a referendum. As Austria, Finland, and Sweden joined the EU on 1 Jan. 1995, the only States which are in the EEA and not also in the EU are Liechtenstein, Iceland, and Norway.

[163] EEA Agreement, Art. 56(1)(a) and (b).

[164] *Ibid.*, Art. 56(1)(c) and (3).

[165] *Ibid.*, Art. 108(2).

6. MODERNIZATION

As already explained, on 1 May 2004, Council Regulation 1/2003[166] brought in a new era in EC competition law. Regulation 1/2003 is a decentralizing measure whereby a greater role than previously is given to the national competition authorities (NCAs) and national courts of the Member States to share with the Commission the enforcement and application of the competition rules.

Regulation 1/2003 does not, in itself, change the substantive law but, as will be seen throughout this book, the mechanisms for enforcement and application have impacted on the development of the substantive law and an appreciation of how the law is, and has been, enforced is necessary to a proper understanding of it. Many of the cases discussed in this book were decided under the previous enforcement system. The previous enforcement system, along with the reasons for its reform, is described in Chapters 14 and 15 where the context requires, when the present system is examined. In Chapter 4 we look at the linchpin of the reforms, the rendering of Article 81(3) directly applicable.

The 'modernization' contained in Regulation 1/2003 was a matter of great controversy. One striking feature, however, should be noted initially: Regulation 1/2003 contains the voluntary surrender by the EC Commission of some of its monopoly powers. It is rare for a body to initiate and orchestrate the divestment of its own monopoly. One has to admire the boldness of the Commission in conceiving the reforms and carrying them through. Nevertheless, it must be stressed that despite the changes brought into effect by Regulation 1/2003 the Commission remains at the heart of the system, at the centre of the development and application of EC competition law and policy, as it has been since 1962.[167]

7. CONCLUSIONS

1. The EC competition rules are primarily contained in Title VI, Chapter 1 of the EC Treaty (the Treaty of Rome) as amended.

2. The two main competition articles are Article 81 (which applies to agreements between undertakings) and Article 82 (which applies to the conduct of undertakings in a 'dominant position').

3. Articles 81 and 82 are supplemented by Article 86 (public undertakings and undertakings with special or exclusive rights) and by articles concerned with powers and procedures (Articles 83, 84 and 85).

4. The competition articles are a specific working out of Article 3(1)(g) EC.

5. The control of mergers is governed by Council Regulation 139/2004 (the ECMR) made under Articles 83 and 308 EC.

6. The EC competition rules are primarily enforced by administrative bodies by way of 'public' enforcement.

---

[166] [2003] OJ L1/1.

[167] Indeed, it has been argued that the Commission has in fact executed a 'strategic coup', by marginalizing national laws and in effect centralizing rather than decentralizing control of the application of the competition rules: see S. Wilkes, 'Agency Escape: Decentralization or Dominance of the European Commission in the Modernization of Competition Policy' (2005) *Governance*, 18, 3:431.

7. The EC Commission enforces the EC competition rules through DG Comp, the Competition Directorate General. However, the modernization embodied in Regulation 1/2003 decentralized enforcement to the national competition authorities (NCAs) of the Member States which form, together with the Commission, the European Competition Network (ECN).

8. The competition rules are directly applicable and can be enforced in national courts.

9. The enforcement and application of the competition rules must be seen in the context of the EC legal order as whole.

8. FURTHER READING

BOOKS

ARNULL, A., *The European Union and its Court of Justice* (2nd edn., Oxford University Press, 2006)

——, DASHWOOD, A., DOUGAN, M., ROSS, M., SPAVENTA, E., and WYATT, D., *Wyatt and Dashwood's European Union Law* (5th edn., Sweet & Maxwell, 2006)

CHALMERS, D., HADJIEMMANUIL, C., MONTI, G., and TOMKINS A, *European Union Law* (Cambridge University Press, 2006)

CRAIG, P., and DE BÚRCA, G., *EU Law: Text, Cases and Materials* (4th edn., Oxford University Press, 2007)

HARTLEY, T. C., *The Foundations of European Community Law* (5th edn., Oxford University Press, 2003)

3

ARTICLE 81: THE ELEMENTS

1. CENTRAL ISSUES

1. Chapters 3 and 4 set out and discuss the elements of Article 81.

2. The way that this provision applies to specific types of potentially anticompetitive business agreements (e.g. cartels, joint venture agreements, distribution agreements and, intellectual property licensing agreements) is discussed in greater detail in later chapters.

3. Article 81(1) prohibits collusion between two or more independent undertakings which has as its object or effect the prevention, restriction, or distortion of competition and which affects trade between Member States.

4. It applies only to agreements which appreciably affect competition and trade.

5. Article 81(3) provides that the prohibition may be declared inapplicable to agreements which fulfil its four criteria (two positive and two negative), broadly where beneficial aspects of the agreement outweigh its restrictive effect.

6. Chapter 3 focuses on the following issues:

    (a) *Who* Article 81 applies to, i.e. which enti-ties constitute an 'undertaking' and are consequently bound to comply with the competition rules;

    (b) What constitutes *joint* conduct caught by Article 81(1) and how this is distinguished from unilateral conduct falling outside of its scope;

    (c) When an agreement appreciably *affects trade* between Member States and so falls within the jurisdictional scope of Article 81(1).

7. Chapter 4 focuses on the question of *which* agreements are prohibited by Article 81 and the relationship between Article 81(1) and Article 81(3). In particular, it considers when:

    (a) An agreement 'restricts' competition for the purposes of Article 81(1); and

    (b) When the procompetitive aspects of the agreement enable it to satisfy the conditions of Article 81(3) and to 'trump' the anticompetitive effects identified under Article 81(1).

8. The question of what constitutes an appreciable restriction on competition is also considered in Chapter 3. Community law is not concerned with agreements that do not impact significantly on competition and trade.

2. INTRODUCTION

Article 81 (ex Article 85) precludes restrictive agreements between independent market operators, whether 'horizontal' (between parties operating at the same level of the economy, often actual or potential competitors) or 'vertical'[1] (between parties operating at different levels, for example, an agreement between a manufacturer and its distributor).

---

[1] See Cases 56 and 58/64, *Etablissements Consten SA & Grundig-Verkaufs-GmbH* v. *Commission* [1966] ECR 299, [1966] CMLR 418 and *infra* 150.

In this chapter the scheme of Article 81, the consequences of infringing it, and the key elements of Article 81(1) are considered. In Chapter 4 we focus on the relationship between Article 81(1) and Article 81(3) and consider when agreements will be considered to be so 'anti-competitive' that they contravene the Article. How the provisions are interpreted will depend, of course, upon the policy objectives being pursued in enforcement. As has already been seen, these objectives have evolved over time in Europe and the rules have been used to serve objectives which go beyond the simple maximization of consumer welfare and economic efficiency.[2] Although, therefore, in many cases Article 81 has been used to prohibit agreements which adversely affect the competition process, in others, it appears that the Community authorities have relied, not on economic analysis and the economic view of the impact of the agreement on competition but on the formal provisions of the agreement and the impact the agreement will have on other relevant objectives. In particular, the Commission, supported by the Court has, in the context of Article 81, been eager to prevent agreements which might be used to divide up the common market and thwart the single market project.[3]

It has also been seen, however, that the Commission has over the years shown a growing commitment to effective competition and has increasingly sought to focus the goal of Article 81 on consumer welfare. Indeed, in its 2004 Guidelines on the application of Article 81(3) of the Treaty ('the Article 81(3) Guidelines') it is stated:[4]

The objective of Article 81 is to protect competition on the market as a means of enhancing consumer welfare and of ensuring an efficient allocation of resources. Competition and market integration serve these ends since the creation and preservation of an open single market promotes an efficient allocation of resources throughout the Community for the benefit of consumers.[5]

This statement indicates that as far as the Commission is concerned the goal of Article 81 should be consumer welfare and that *both* competition *and* market integration will serve this end. It does not acknowledge, however, that pursuit of a consumer welfare and a market integration goal may not always pull in the same direction, although the statement may suggest that the single market goal should be pursued only where it enhances consumer welfare.[6] In addition, it should be noted that although the statement does not explicitly clarify whether this is the *sole* goal of competition law, the guidelines later suggest that these goals cannot be trumped by other public policy objectives.[7]

---

[2] *Supra* Chap 1.

[3] See, e.g., Cases 56 and 58/64, *Etablissements Consten SA & Grundig-Verkaufs-GmbH v. Commission* [1966] ECR 299, [1966] CMLR 418.

[4] [2004] OJ C101/97, para. 13.

[5] See Guidelines on the application of Articles 81(3) ('Article 81(3) Guidelines') [2004] OJ C101/97, para. 42. 'Effective competition brings benefits to consumers, such as low prices high quality products, a wide selection of goods and services, and innovation. Competition and market integration serve these ends since the creation and preservation of an open single market promotes an efficient allocation of resources throughout the Community for the benefit of consumers'. See also DG Competition Discussion Paper on the application of Article 82 of the Treaty to exclusionary abuses, December 2005, para. 4.

[6] But see e.g. discussion of Cases 56 and 58/64 *Etablissements Consten SA & Grundig-Verkaufs-GmbH v. Commission* [1966] ECR 299, [1966] CMLR 418 *infra* Chap. 4 and Case C-53/03, *Syfait v. Glaxosmithkline AEVE* [2005] ECR I-4609, [2005] 5 CMLR 1, Opinion of Jacobs AG. It appears that the single market goal may still influence the interpretation of Article 81, see especially Chaps. 4 and 9.

[7] Article 81(3) Guidelines, para. 42. As will be seen in Chap. 4 this latter point is critical to the scope of Article 81(3).

The Commission's view on objectives now gains support from the judgments of the CFI in *Österreichische Postsparkasse v. Commission*[8] and *GlaxoSmithKline Services Unlimited v. Commission*.[9] In the latter case the court stated that

the objective assigned to Article 81(1) EC, which constitutes a fundamental provision indispensable for the achievement of the missions entrusted to the Community, in particular for the functioning of the internal market . . . , is to prevent undertakings, by restricting competition between themselves or with third parties, from reducing the welfare of the final consumer of the products in question . . . . [10]

3. THE TEXT OF ARTICLE 81

Article 81 provides:

(1) The following shall be prohibited as incompatible with the common market: all agreements between undertakings, decisions by associations of undertakings and concerted practices which may affect trade between Member States and which have as their object or effect the prevention, restriction or distortion of competition within the common market, and in particular those which:

    (a) directly or indirectly fix purchase or selling prices or any other trading conditions;

    (b) limit or control production, markets, technical development, or investment;

    (c) share markets or sources of supply;

    (d) apply dissimilar conditions to equivalent transactions with other trading parties, thereby placing them at a competitive disadvantage;

    (e) make the conclusion of contracts subject to acceptance by the other parties of supplementary obligations which, by their nature or according to commercial usage, have no connection with the subject of such contracts.

(2) Any agreements or decisions prohibited pursuant to this Article shall be automatically void.

(3) The provisions of paragraph 1 may, however, be declared inapplicable in the cases of:

    — any agreement or category of agreements between undertakings;

    — any decision or category of decisions by associations of undertakings;

    — any concerted practice or category of concerted practices,

which contributes to improving the production or distribution of goods or to promoting technical or economic progress, while allowing consumers a fair share of the resulting benefit, and which does not:

    (a) impose on the undertakings concerned restrictions which are not indispensable to the attainment of these objectives;

    (b) afford such undertakings the possibility of eliminating competition in respect of a substantial part of the products in question.

---

[8] Case T-213/01, [2006] ECR II-1601, para. 115, see *supra* Chap. 1. In this case the CFI held that 'the ultimate purpose of the rules . . . is to increase the well-being of consumers'.

[9] Case T-168/01, 27 Sept. 2006, [2006] 5 CMLR 1623, Cases C-501, 513, 515 and 519/06 P (judgment pending).

[10] Case T-168/01, 27 Sept. 2006, [2006] 5 CMLR 1623, para. 118, Cases C-501, 513, 515 and 519/06 P (judgment pending).

4. THE SCHEME OF ARTICLE 81

A. THE THREE PARAGRAPHS

It can be seen from the text that Article 81 is in three parts.

(i) The Prohibition

Article 81(1) sets out the prohibition. It prohibits collusion between undertakings which has as its object or effect the prevention, restriction, or distortion of competition within the common market and which may affect trade between Member States. It sets out examples of such preventions, restrictions, or distortions. The list is illustrative, not exhaustive. For the prohibition in Article 81(1) to apply the following must be established:

(i) The existence of undertakings (or an association of undertakings);

(ii) Collusion (an agreement between undertakings, a decision by an association of undertakings or a concerted practice);

(iii) Collusion which has as its object or effect the prevention, restriction, or distortion of competition;

(iv) An appreciable effect on competition,[11] and

(v) An appreciable effect on trade between Member States.[12]

(ii) Nullity

Although Article 81(2) specifically states that an agreement, decision, or concerted practice prohibited by Article 81(1) is automatically void, the ECJ has held that the nullity affects *only* the clauses in the agreement prohibited by the provision.[13] The agreement as a whole is void only if the prohibited clauses cannot be severed from the remaining terms of the agreement. The nullity is automatic and is not dependent upon any prior decision to that effect.[14]

(iii) Legal Exception—Declaration of Inapplicability

The Article 81(1) prohibition may be declared inapplicable to an agreement, etc.[15] which fulfils the four criteria (two positive and two negative) set out in Article 81(3) (broadly where the beneficial aspects of the agreement outweigh its restrictive effect). Initially, agreements could benefit from Article 81(3) only if they were specifically 'exempted' from the Article 81(1) prohibition by virtue of **either** an *individual exemption*, granted by the Commission following notification of the agreement to it, **or** a *block exemption*, granted by Community regulation to

---

[11] Article 81 does not provide that the effect on competition and trade must be an appreciable one. The Court of Justice (ECJ) has, however, held that an agreement falls outside the prohibition if its effect on the market is insignificant, see *infra* 182 ff.

[12] *Ibid.*

[13] Case 56/65, *Société La Technique Minière v. Maschinebau Ulm GmbH* [1966] ECR 234, [1966] CMLR 357. See *infra* 201 and Chap. 15.

[14] See Reg. 1/2003, Art. 1.

[15] In this chapter unless the context otherwise requires or the discussion is specifically about one or other category of collusion the word 'agreement' is used as shorthand to cover agreements, decisions, and concerted practices.

certain categories of agreement. The Commission had *sole* power to declare Article 81(1) inapplicable to individual agreements pursuant to Article 81(3).[16] From 1 May 2004, however, it has not been possible to gain an individual exemption for an agreement (although block exemptions remain) and the Commission's exclusive competence to apply Article 81(3) has been removed.[17] The Commission, the national competition authorities (NCAs), or national courts may now apply Article 81(3) individually to agreements (no prior notification being possible) whenever an agreement's compatibility with the provision is raised.

B. THE CONSEQUENCES OF INFRINGEMENT

Severe consequences may result for parties to an agreement that contravenes Article 81(1) but which does not meet the four criteria set out in Article 81(3).

(i) Nullity and Private Proceedings between the Parties to a Contract

Provisions in an agreement that contravene Article 81(1) are automatically void where the agreement does not meet the conditions of Article 81(3). Article 81(2) may, therefore, render carefully negotiated clauses in an agreement void and unenforceable.[18]

(ii) Investigation, Detection, and Penalties—the Commission

The sanction of nullity will not be much of a threat to some parties to a prohibited agreement. Members of a cartel, for example, are unlikely to be concerned about their inability to enforce the agreement in court.[19] Cartels may, however, be deterred by the risk of investigation by the Commission and the likelihood of a fine if a breach is detected. The Commission has power to investigate suspected infringements of Article 81, to order those found to have violated the provision to put an end to the breach, and to impose fines on undertakings that have committed a breach of the competition rules.[20]

(iii) Investigation, Detection, and Penalties—the National Competition Authorities

Until 1 May 2004, it was principally the Commission that enforced Article 81. The NCAs and national courts played a relatively minor role in the enforcement process, partly at least, in

---

[16] This monopoly was conferred on the Commission by the Council in Reg. 17 [1959–62] OJ Spec. Ed. 87, Art. 9(1), see *infra* Chaps. 4 and 14.

[17] See Reg. 1/2003 and *infra* Chap. 14.

[18] See *infra* 201 and Chap. 15.

[19] They are likely to have their own mechanisms in place for the enforcement of the cartel, *infra* Chap. 11.

[20] Although breach of Article 81 is not a criminal offence, fines may be imposed of up to 10% of an undertaking's turnover in the preceding year of business, and in cases of serious violations of the rules have tended to be large, Reg. 1/2003, Art. 23, see *infra* Chap. 14. Changes introduced by Regulation 1/2003 are designed to facilitate the detection and prevention of severely anti-competitive practices. For example, the Regulation confers broader powers of investigation on the Commission. Further, the abolition of the notification system means that the Commission can refocus its resources on more seriously anti-competitive practices, see *infra* Chap. 14.

consequence of their inability to apply Article 81(3).[21] Regulation 1/2003, however, enables and in some circumstances requires the NCAs, and the national courts, to share in the enforcement of Article 81 and to apply it in its entirety.[22] NCAs may be able to impose fines, and/or other more severe sanctions, on undertakings or individuals found to have been involved in a breach of the rules. In the UK, for example, in addition to corporate fines, sanctions against *individuals* are available (imprisonment, fines, or disqualification from acting as a director) in certain circumstances.[23]

(iv) Damages and Other Private Proceedings

In addition, or alternatively, a claimant injured by the operation of a cartel or any other prohibited agreement may bring tortious or other proceedings before a national court. For example, an injunction and/or damages in respect of any loss suffered in consequence of the prohibited contract might be sought. Although there has been relatively little antitrust litigation in Europe to date, the Commission is taking steps to encourage 'private' enforcement of the rules and such claims are increasingly becoming a reality.[24] In *Courage Ltd* v. *Crehan*[25] the ECJ made it clear that an individual that has suffered loss due to another's breach of the competition rules must, in principle, be able to recover damages.[26]

C. BURDEN AND STANDARD OF PROOF

The ECJ has confirmed that 'the presumption of innocence resulting in particular from Article 6(2) of the ECHR is one of the fundamental rights which ... are protected in the Community legal order ... It must also be accepted that ... the presumption of innocence applies to the procedures relating to infringements of the competition rules applicable to undertakings that may result in the imposition of fines or periodic penalties payments'.[27] The burden is therefore clearly on the person or authority alleging an infringement of Article 81(1) to prove the same.

---

[21] Since the exclusive right to apply Article 81(3) was reserved to the Commission, see *supra* n. 17.

[22] Reg. 1/2003 provides that NCAs applying Articles 81 and 82 may adopt decisions ordering an infringement to be brought to an end, ordering interim measures, accepting commitments and imposing fines, periodic penalty payments, or imposing any other penalty provided for in their national law.

[23] Individuals who have caused their firm to make or to implement certain horizontal 'cartel' agreements may commit a criminal offence and be potentially liable to imprisonment for a period of up to five years and/or an unlimited fine, Enterprise Act 2002, Part 6. Even prior to the Enterprise Act 2002 it is possible that conclusion of a cartel constituted a conspiracy to defraud, see *infra* Chaps. 11 and 14. Further, directors of companies that have breached Article 81 (or Article 82) may be disqualified from acting in that capacity for up to 15 years Enterprise Act 2002, s. 204.

[24] See Chap. 15.

[25] Case C-453/99 *Courage Ltd* v. *Crehan* [2001] ECR I-6297, [2001] 5 CMLR 28. See also Cases 295–298/04 *Manfredi* v. *Lloyd Adriatico Assicurazioni SpA* [2006] ECR I-6619. When the *Crehan* case reverted to the English courts, however, it was eventually decided by the House of Lords *Inntrepreneur Pub Company* v. *Crehan* [2006] UKHL 38 that no breach of Article 81(1) had in fact been committed, see *infra* Chap. 15.

[26] See Chap. 15. In the UK, contractual and tortious claims have arisen before the High Court. Further, the UK's Enterprise Act 2002 introduced measures into the Competition Act 1998 designed to encourage private action (in particular, by allowing certain damages claims to be brought before a specialist Competition Appeal Tribunal. Such claims may be brought by individuals or consumer bodies on behalf of consumers where a breach of the competition rules has been established by the OFT or the European Commission and, essentially, where the avenues of appeal exhausted, see Competition Act 1998, ss. 47A and B).

[27] Case C-199/92 P, *Hüls AG* v. *Commission* [1999] ECR I-4287, [1999] 5 CMLR 1016, paras. 45, 149–50.

Once this is established, the burden shifts on to the undertakings claiming the benefit of Article 81(3) to establish that the agreement meets its criteria.[28]

The ECJ has held that for the Commission to establish a breach, 'sufficiently precise and coherent proof' must be produced.[29] It appears, therefore, that the Commission must establish breach of the competition rules only on the balance of probabilities and not more conclusively. The question of standard of proof applicable in competition proceedings brought by a regulator has been dealt with more comprehensively by the UK's Competition Appeal Tribunal ('CAT') when applying the UK Competition Act prohibitions (which are modelled on Articles 81 and 82). In its cases, the CAT has held that although Office of Fair Trading ('OFT') proceedings under the UK may lead to the imposition of a penalty (involving a 'criminal charge' for the purposes of Article 6 of the European Convention on Hunan Rights and Fundamental Freedoms) this does not mean that the standard of proof is proof beyond reasonable doubt (the criminal standard established in domestic cases). Rather, it has held that the standard of proof to be applied is the civil standard—the preponderance or balance of probabilities applied taking account of the gravity of the offence.[30]

5. THE INTERPRETATION AND APPLICATION OF ARTICLE 81(1)

A. GENERAL

In Chapter 2 it was explained that the Court's method of statutory interpretation, although drawing on those of the national courts, is an individual one. In particular, it adopts a 'teleological' approach construing Community acts in accordance with the broad system of Treaty aims and objectives set out in Articles 2 and 3. When construing the elements of Article 81 the ECJ has, therefore, tended to adopt an interpretation which best reflects the Treaty's aims and principles.[31]

---

[28] This position is specifically set out in Reg. 1/2003, Art. 2. In Cases C-204, 205, 211, 213, 217 and 219/00 P, *Aalborg Portland A/S v. Commission (Cement)* [2004] ECR I-123, [2005] 4 CMLR 251the ECJ stated: 'As the Council very recently stated in the fifth recital of Regulation (EC) No. 1/2003 of 16 Dec. 2002 on the implementation of the rules on competition laid down in Articles 81 and 82 of the Treaty ([2003] OJ L1/1), it should be for the party or the authority alleging an infringement of the competition rules to prove the existence thereof and it should be for the undertaking or association of undertakings invoking the benefit of a defence against a finding of an infringement to demonstrate that the conditions for applying such defence are satisfied, so that the authority will then have to resort to other evidence', para. 78.

[29] Cases 29 and 30/83, *Compagnie Royale Asturienne des Mines SA and Rheinzink GmbH v. Commission* [1984] ECR 1679, [1985] 1 CMLR 688. The standard of proof in civil litigation will be a matter for the national courts of the relevant Member State, see *infra* Chap. 15.

[30] See, e.g. Case 1022/1/1/03, *JJB Sports plc v. Office of Fair Trading* [2004] CAT 17, *aff'd* [2006] EWCA Civ 1318.

[31] See, in particular, Case 56/65, *Société La Technique Minière v. Maschinebau Ulm GmbH* [1966] ECR 235, [1966] 1 CMLR 357 (*supra* n. 13 and accompanying text), and Cases 56 and 58/64, *Etablissements Consten SA & Grundig-Verkaufs-GmbH v. Commission* [1966] ECR 299, [1966] CMLR 418, *infra* 193–4.

B. 'UNDERTAKING' AND 'ASSOCIATIONS OF UNDERTAKING'

(i) Every Entity Engaged in an Economic Activity: the Constituent Elements

Article 81 applies to agreements and concerted practices between *undertakings* and decisions by *associations of undertakings*. Undertaking has the same meaning for the purposes of both Article 81 and Article 82[32] so the concept determines 'the categories of actors to which the competition rules apply'.[33] The term 'undertaking' is not defined in the Treaty but has been widely construed by the European Court. In *Höfner and Elser v. Macrotron*[34] the ECJ held that 'the concept of an undertaking, encompasses every entity engaged in an economic activity, regardless of the legal status of the entity or the way in which it is financed'.[35] Entities engaged in economic activity must respect the principles of competition, whilst entities performing tasks in the public interest fall outside the scope of the rules.[36] The critical question is, therefore, what constitutes 'economic activity'. This question is explored in the series of cases discussed below. The fine distinctions that have been drawn have turned on the *functions* performed by the particular bodies involved in the case. The cases seem to establish, however, that the characteristic feature of an 'economic activity' is (1) the offering of goods or services on the market,[37] (2) where that activity 'could, at least in principle, be carried on by a private undertaking in order to make

---

[32] See Cases T-68, 77 and 78/89, *Società Italiana Vetro v. Commission* [1992] ECR II-1403, [1992] 5 CMLR 302. Many of the cases discussed below concerned Article 82, not Article 81, which prohibits any abuse by one or more undertakings of a dominant position.

[33] Case C-67/96, *Albany International BV v. Stichting Bedrijfspensioenfonds Textielindustrie* [1999] ECR I-5751, [2000] 4 CMLR 446, Jacobs AG, para. 206.

[34] See Case C-41/90, *Höfner and Elser v. Macroton GmbH* [1991] ECR I-1979, [1993] 4 CMLR 306. In *Polypropylene* [1986] OJ L230/1, [1988] 4 CMLR 347, para. 99 the Commission stated that '[t]he subjects of [EC] competition rules are undertakings, a concept which is not identical to the question of legal personality for the purposes of company law and fiscal law...It may, however, refer to any entity engaged in commercial activities'. For a helpful review of the Community case law in this area up to 2002, see the judgment of the UK's Competition Appeal Tribunal ('CAT') in *Bettercare Group Limited v. DGFT* [2002] CAT 7, [2002] CompAR 299.

[35] See Case C-41/90, *Höfner and Elser v. Macroton GmbH* [1991] ECR I-1979, [1993] 4 CMLR 306, para. 21. This definition has been consistently repeated by the Court, see, for example, Cases C-159–160/91, *Poucet and Pistre v. Assurances Générales de France* [1993] ECR I-637, para. 17; Case 364/92, *SAT Fluggesellschaft v. Eurocontrol* [1994] ECR I-43, [1994] 5 CMLR 208, para. 18, Cases C-180–184/98, *Pavlov v. Stichting Pensioenfonds Medische Specialisten* [2000] ECR I-6451, [2001] 4 CMLR 30, para. 74, Case C-218/00, *Cisal di Battistello Venanzio & Co v. Istituto Nazionale per L'Assicurazione Contro Gli fortuni Sul Lavoro (INAIL)* [2002] ECR I-691, [2002] 4 CMLR 24, para. 22.

[36] For the view that the Treaty contains a public/ private divide and that the different treatment of these entities is 'justified by a presumption underlying the rules of the private sphere that its occupants are self-interested and the presumption underlying rules of the public sphere that its occupants operate in pursuit of the public interest', see O. Odudu, *The Boundaries of EC Competition Law: The Scope of Article 81* (Oxford University Press, 2006), 45–56.

[37] See, for example, Case C-475/99, *Ambulanz Glöckner v. Landkreis Südwestpflaz* [2001] ECR I-8089, [2002] 4 CMLR 726, para. 19. See also, See also, Case C-35/96 *Commission v. Italy* [1998] ECR I-3851, [1998] 5 CMLR. 889, para. 36 and Case C-205/03 P, *FENIN v. Commission*, [2006] ECR I-6295, [2006] 5 CMLR 7, para. 25.

profits'.[38] If these requirements are satisfied it is irrelevant that the body is not in fact profit making[39] or that it is not set up for an economic purpose.[40]

(ii) The Notion of an Undertaking is a Relative Concept

The notion of undertaking focuses on the nature of the activity carried out by the entity concerned (a functional approach is adopted).[41] It is therefore 'a relative concept in the sense that a given entity might be regarded as an undertaking for one part of its activities while the rest fall outside the competition rules'.[42] In each case therefore it is necessary to identify the particular 'activity' carried out by the entity in question, since it may be an undertaking when carrying out some of its activities (which are economic) but not others. The case of *SELEX Sistemi Integrati SpA v. Commission*,[43] provides a good illustration of this point. In this case the Commission argued that Eurocontrol, (European Organisation for the Safety of Air Navigation) was not an undertaking, relying on a previous finding of the ECJ that '[t]aken as a whole, Eurocontrol's activities, by their nature, their aim and the rules to which they are subject, are connected with the exercise of powers relating to the control and supervision of air space which are typically those of a public authority.'[44] The CFI stressed, however, that, in arriving at this finding, the court had based its reasoning exclusively on a review of Eurocontrol's activities at issue, namely the creation and collection of route charges on behalf of the Contracting States from users of air navigation services. Since the Treaty provisions on competition applied to activities of an entity which could be severed from those in which it engages as a public authority, the various activities of Eurocontrol at issue in that case had to be considered individually to determine whether they were economic in nature. On the facts, the CFI considered that in exercising some of the relevant activities Eurocontrol was acting as an undertaking.[45]

[38] Case C-67/96, *Albany International BV v. Stichting Bedrijfspensioenfonds Textielindustrie*, [1999] ECR I-5751, [2000] 4 CMLR 446, Jacobs AG, para. 311. Cases C-180–184/98, *Pavlov v. Stichting Pensioenfonds Medische Specialisten* [2000] ECR I-6451, [2001] 4 CMLR 30, para. 201. In his book, O. Odudu argues that the three positive requirements of economic activity are that the entity must: 'offer goods or services to the market; bear the economic or financial risk of the enterprise; and have the potential to make profit from the activity', see O. Odudu, *The Boundaries of EC Competition Law: The Scope of Article 81* (Oxford University Press, 2006) 26–45.

[39] Case 96/82, *IAZ International Belgium SA v. Commission* [1983] ECR 3369, [1984] 3 CMLR 276; Case C-67/96, *Albany International BV v. Stichting Bedrijfspensioenfonds Textielindustrie* [1999] ECR I-5751, [2000] 4 CMLR 446 discussed *infra* 136. In the UK the OFT investigated price fixing by private schools, many of which are non-profit making charitable organizations. Interestingly, the OFT in the end entered into a settlement with the schools in which each school admitted that their information exchange had distorted competition in the market, agreed to pay a nominal penalty and to pay a £12,000 sum for five years into an independent charitable trust fund for the benefit of the pupils in the Schools in the relevant years of the infringement. Information on this case is available on the OFT's website, www.oft.gov.uk

[40] Case 155/73, *Italy v. Sacchi* [1974] ECR 409, [1974] 2 CMLR 177.

[41] For the view that an institutional, not a functional approach should be adopted, see A. Deringer, *The Competition Law of the European Economic Community: A Commentary on the EEC Rules of Competition (Articles 85 to 90) Including the Implementing Regulations and Directives* (New York: Commerce Clearing House, 1968), 5.

[42] Case C-475/99, *Ambulanz Glöckner v. Landkreis Südwestpflaz* [2001] ECR I-8089, [2002] 4 CMLR 726, Jacobs AG, para. 72. Some of the activities carried out by medical aid organizations in this case were economic in character and others were not (e.g., the power to grant or refuse authority for the provision of independent ambulance services).

[43] Case T-155/04 12 Dec. 2006, [2007] 4 CMLR 372, Case C-113/07 (judgment pending).

[44] Case C-364/92, *SAT Fluggesellschaft v. Eurocontrol* [1994] ECR I-43, [1994] 5 CMLR 208, para. 30, see *infra* 133.

[45] Case T-155/04 *SELEX Sistemi Integrati SpA v. Commission* 12 Dec. 2006, [2007] 4 CMLR 372, paras 50–94, Case C-113/07 (judgment pending).

(iii) The Legal Status or form or the Entity is Immaterial

The focus on the activities or functions of the entity also means that its legal personality is irrelevant so that natural persons, legal persons and State bodies are potentially caught. As well as companies and partnerships, individuals,[46] sporting bodies,[47] trade associations,[48] agricultural cooperatives,[49] P & I clubs,[50] and professional bodies[51] have been held to be undertakings for the purposes of the rules. The fact that the business occupation of a body is viewed as a liberal profession is not inconsistent with the fact that it may be an undertaking or an association of undertakings engaged in an economic activity.[52] In *Wouters* v. *Alegemene Raad van de Nederlandse Order van Advocaten*,[53] for example, the ECJ made it clear that members of the Bar which offered, for a fee, services in the form of legal assistance carried out an economic activity and so were undertakings for the purposes of the rules. Neither the complex and technical nature of the services provided nor the fact that the profession was regulated altered this conclusion.[54]

The importance of the function, and not the nature, of the entity is illustrated by a case concerning the 1990 World Cup. In this case the Commission held that sporting and other associations, the international football federation (FIFA), the Italian FA (FIGC), and the local organizing committee, which carried out economic activities, were undertakings within the meaning of Article 81(1).[55] Although in some circumstances it may be inappropriate to apply

---

[46] e.g., opera singers in *RAI/UNITEL* [1978] OJ L157/39, [1978] 3 CMLR 306, individual inventors in *Reuter/BASF* [1976] OJ L254/40, [1976] 2 CMLR D44 and farmers and slaughterers in *French Beef* [2003] OJ L209/12, [2005] 5 CMLR 891, *aff'd* (but fines reduced) in Cases T-217 and 245/03 *FNCBV* v. *Commission* 12 Dec. 2006, Cases C-101 and 110/07 *Coop de France Bétail and Viande* v. *Commission, FNSEA* v. *Commission* (judgment pending) but not, it seems, employees, see *infra* 139 and accompanying text, or purchasers, see *infra* 136–8. See also Case 42/84, *Remia BV and Verenigde Bedrijven Nutricia* v. *Commission* [1985] ECR 2545, [1987] 1 CMLR 1; *Vaassen BV /Moris* [1979] OJ L19/32, [1979] 1 CMLR 511.

[47] *Distribution of Package Tours During the 1990 World Cup* [1992] OJ L326/31, [1994] 5 CMLR 253, paras. 43–58.

[48] Case 96/82, *IAZ International Belgium NV* v. *Commission* [1983] ECR 3369, [1984] 3 CMLR 276.

[49] See Case C-250/92, *Gøttrup-Klim Grovvareforening and Others* v. *Dansk Landbrugs Grovvareselskab AmbA* [1994] ECR I-5641, [1996] 4 CMLR 191.

[50] Protection and Indemnity clubs, *P & I Clubs* [1985] OJ L376/2, [1989] 4 CMLR 178.

[51] See generally M. Monti, 'Competition in Professional Services: New Light and New Challenges', 21 March 2003, available on DG Comp's web site. At this time DG Comp launched a stocktaking exercise for professional services, see DG Comp's web site, at http://europa.eu.int/comm/competition/liberalization/conference/libprofconference.html.

[52] *AICIA* v. *CNSD* [1993] OJ L203/27, [1995] 5 CMLR 495, para. 40.

[53] Case C-309/99, [2002] ECR I-1577, [2002] 4 CMLR 913.

[54] Case C-309/99, [2002] ECR I-1577, [2002] 4 CMLR 913, paras. 46–9. The Court also held at para. 58 that when the Bar of the Netherlands adopted a regulation concerning partnerships between members of the bar and other professions it was acting as an association of undertakings and not a public authority. It was neither fulfilling a social function based on the principle of solidarity, nor exercising powers which were typically those of a public authority. 'It acts as the regulatory body of a profession, the practice of which constitutes an economic activity'. 'Such a regulation constitutes the expression of the intention of the delegates of the members of a profession that they should act in a particular manner in carrying on their economic activity, Case C-309/99, [2002] ECR I-1577, [2002] 4 CMLR 913, para. 64.

[55] *The Distribution of Package Tours During the 1990 World Cup* [1992] OJ L326/31, [1994] 5 CMLR 253. Note that the French organizers of the 1998 World Cup were also found to have infringed the competition rules. In this case it was found that they had abused their dominant position contrary to Article 82 by discriminating on grounds of nationality: *1998 World Cup Finals*, [2000] OJ L5/55, [2000] 4 CMLR 963.

the competition rules to functions carried out by sporting bodies,[56] they may apply where the body is carrying out economic activities.[57]

(iv) Public Bodies and Bodies Performing Public Functions

a. Distinction between Economic Activities and Activities which must Necessarily be Carried out by the State or which fulfil a Social Function[58]

The conclusion that any entity engaged in economic activity constitutes an undertaking raises the possibility that the agreements and conduct of public bodies or corporations can be scrutinized for compatibility with the rules. An entity may be an undertaking even where it does not have an independent legal personality but forms part of a State's general administration[59] in so far as it is engaged in 'economic' activities. The case law draws a sharp distinction between activities classified as 'economic' in character, and those where the entity 'acts in the exercise of official authority' (the latter activities falling outside the scope of the competition rules). An entity, public or private, which performs tasks of a public nature, connected with the exercise of public powers or in the exercise of official authority will not be an undertaking and will be immune from the application of the rules. Entities, public or private, engaged in economic activity and acting in a commercial context will need to comply with the competition rules *unless* the conditions set out in Article 86(2) of the Treaty are satisfied. Article 86(2) provides that undertakings entrusted with the operation of services of general economic interest or having the character of a revenue-producing monopoly are subject to the competition rules only in so far as the application of the rules does not obstruct the performance of the tasks assigned to them. Like all derogations from the main Treaty objectives, however, Article 86(2) has been construed narrowly.[60] A finding that an entity is not an undertaking obviates the need for reliance on Article 86(2). Article 86 is dealt with in Chapter 8.

It has been seen that the question of whether an entity is engaged in economic activities or tasks of a public natures appears to depend upon whether the offering of goods or services on the market could be carried out by a private firm to make a profit. 'If there were no possibility of a private undertaking carrying on a given activity, there would be no purpose in applying the competition rules to it'.[61] The tendency of States to contract out what were considered to be public tasks to private entities has made this distinction a difficult one to draw.

The following public or quasi-public bodies have, applying these criteria, been found *to be* undertakings: a German State-run employment agency;[62] the European Broadcasting Union;[63]

---

[56] For the discussion of when rules inherent in sport are subject to Article 81, see *supra* Chap. 2.

[57] *The Distribution of Package Tours During the 1990 World Cup* [1992] OJ L326/31, [1994] 5 CMLR 253, especially paras. 44–60. See also Case C-519/04 P, *Meca-Medina v. Commission* [2006] ECR I-6991, [2006] 5 CMLR 1023.

[58] See also the discussion *infra* Chap. 8.

[59] *Spanish Courier Services* [1990] OJ L233/19, [1991] 3 CMLR 560; *Aluminium Products* [1985] OJ L92/1, [1987] 3 CMLR 813. See also Case 118/85, *Commission v. Italy* [1987] ECR 2599, [1988] 3 CMLR. 255, paras. 7 and 8.

[60] In Case C-67/96, *Albany International BV v. Stichting Bedrijfspensioenfonds Textielindustrie* [1999] ECR I-5751, [2000] 4 CMLR 446, however, the ECJ accepted that the application of the competition rules would make it impossible for the pension fund to perform its tasks of an economic nature, see *infra* Chap. 8.

[61] Cases C-264, 306, 354, and 355/01, *AOK Bundesverband v. Ichthyol-Gesellschaft Cordes, Hermani & Co* [2004] ECR I-2493, [2004] 4 CMLR 1261, Jacobs AG, para. 27.

[62] Case C-41/90, *Höfner and Elser v. Macrotron GmbH* [1991] ECR I-1979, [1993] 4 CMLR 306. See also Case C-55/96, *Job Centre* [1997] ECR I-7119, [1998] 4 CMLR 708 where an Italian public placement office with an exclusive right to procure employment of employees in Italy was found to be an undertaking.

[63] *EBU* [1993] OJ L179/23, [1995] 4 CMLR 56.

independent customs agents in Italy;[64] the association of public broadcasting institutions in Germany;[65] a voluntary old-age pension scheme for agricultural workers in France;[66] a sectoral pension fund to which workers were compulsorily affiliated by government regulation;[67] medical aid organizations providing ambulance services in Germany,[68] the Spanish post office;[69] and public television broadcasting organizations.[70] In *Höfner and Elser* v. *Macrotron* the ECJ focused on the responsibilities of the relevant entity, holding that employment procurement activities were economic in nature since they had not always been, and are not necessarily, carried out by public entities.

Case C-41/90, *Höfner and Elser* v. *Macrotron* [1991] ECR I-1979, [1993] 4 CMLR 306

Under German law on the promotion of employment (the AFG) the Bundesanstalt für Arbeit (Federal Office for Employment, the Bundesanstalt), a public agency, had a monopoly in employment recruitment. Nevertheless the Bundesanstalt tolerated private agencies dealing with the recruitment of business executives. This case concerned a dispute which arose in the German courts between a private recruitment agency and a company for which it had provided recruitment services in breach of the Bundesanstalt's exclusive right. The private agency sought to recover fees payable under the terms of the recruitment contract. The German courts took the view that the claim should fail on the grounds that the contract had been concluded in breach of German law and was void. The German Civil Code provides that any legal act which infringes a statutory prohibition is void (the prohibition applies to employment procurement activities carried out in breach of the AFG). The Oberlandesgericht München nevertheless considered that the outcome of the dispute might be dependent on Community law and referred a number of questions to the Court of Justice under Article 234. In particular, it asked whether the Bundesanstalt had committed an abuse of a dominant position.[71] This necessitated consideration of whether the Bundesanstalt was an undertaking for the purposes of the competition rules.

Court of Justice

21. It must be observed, in the context of competition law, first that the concept of an undertaking encompasses every entity engaged in an economic activity, regardless of the legal status of the entity and the way in which it is financed and, secondly, that employment procurement is an economic activity.

---

[64] Case C-35/96, *Italy v. Commission* [1998] ECR I-3851, [1998] 5 CMLR 889, paras. 36–8.

[65] *Film Purchases by German Television Stations* [1989] OJ L284/96, [1990] 4 CMLR 841.

[66] Case C-244/94, *Fédération Française des Sociétés d'Assurance and others v. Ministère de l'Agriculture et de la Pêche* [1995] ECR I-4013, [1996] 4 CMLR 536: see discussion *infra* 136.

[67] Case C-67/96, *Albany International BV v. Stichting Bedrijfspensioenfonds Textielindustrie* [1999] ECR I-5751, [2000] 4 CMLR 446, see discussion *infra* 136. See also Cases C-180–184/98 *Pavlov v. Stichting Pensioenfonds Medische Specalisten* [2000] ECR I-6451, [2001] 4 CMLR 30.

[68] Case C-475/99, *Ambulanz Glöckner v. Landkreis Südwestpflaz* [2001] ECR I-8089, [2001] 4 CMLR 726. For a more detailed discussion of this case, see Chap. 8.

[69] *Spanish Courier Services* [1990] OJ L233/19, [1991] 4 CMLR 560.

[70] Case 155/73, *Italy v. Sacchi* [1974] ECR 409, [1974] 2 CMLR 177.

[71] This aspect of the case is discussed in Chaps. 7 and 8.

> 22. The fact that employment procurement activities are normally entrusted to public agencies cannot affect the economic nature of such activities. Employment procurement has not always been, and is not necessarily, carried out by public entities. That finding applies in particular to executive recruitment.
>
> 23. It follows that an entity such as a public employment agency engaged in the business of employment procurement may be classified as an undertaking for the purpose of applying the Community competition rules.
>
> 24. It must be pointed out that a public employment agency which is entrusted, under the legislation of a Member State, with the operation of services of general economic interest, such as those envisaged in Article 3 of the AFG, remains subject to the competition rules pursuant to Article [86(2) EC] unless and to the extent to which it is shown that their application is incompatible with the discharge of its duties: see Case 155/73, *Sacchi* [[1974] ECR 409].

In contrast, the following bodies have been found *not* to be undertakings and so not subject to the prohibitions set out in Article 81 or Article 82: an air traffic control organization involved in the maintenance and improvement of air navigation safety (*Eurocontrol* but see *SELEX Sistemi Integrati SpA v. Commission*);[72] a French body running a compulsory social security scheme (*Poucet et Pistre*);[73] a body governed by private law but entrusted by the public authorities with anti-pollution surveillance and control at the port of Genoa (*Diego Cali*);[74] French municipal authority giving exclusive concessions in respect of funeral services (*Bodson*);[75] an Italian institute providing insurance against accidents at work and occupational diseases (*Cisal v. INAIL*),[76] twenty-six organizations, including three ministries of the Spanish Government, which run the Spanish national health system (*FENIN*)[77], and groups of sickness funds (*AOK Bundesverband*).[78]

In *Bodson*,[79] the competition rules were not applicable because the local authority was carrying out an administrative duty, granting concessions for funeral services. The ECJ stressed that Article 81 would not apply to communes acting in their capacity as public authorities and entrusted with the 'operation of a public service'.[80] Similarly, in *Eurocontrol*, the ECJ indicated that the European air traffic control organization, which performed tasks which were in the public interest (maintaining and improving air navigation safety), was not an undertaking even though it collected route charges. The supervision of airspace was a duty typically reserved to public authorities. In the later case of *SELEX Sistemi Integrati SpA v. Commission*,[81] however, the CFI held that despite the conclusion in this previous judgment and although Eurocontrol's

---

[72] Case C-364/92, *SAT Fluggesellschaft v. Eurocontrol* [1994] ECR I-43, [1994] 5 CMLR 208. and Case T-155/04 *SELEX Sistemi Integrati SpA v. Commission* 12 Dec. 2006, [2007] 4 CMLR 372, Case C-113/07 (judgment pending), discussed *infra*.

[73] Case C-159/91, *Poucet et Pistre v. Assurances Générales de France* [1993] ECR I-637; see discussion *infra* 135.

[74] Case C-343/95, *Diego Cali v. SEPG* [1997] ECR I-1547, [1997] 5 CMLR 484.

[75] Case 30/87, *Corinne Bodson v. Pompes Funèbres des Régions Libérées SA* [1988] ECR 2479, [1989] 4 CMLR 984.

[76] Case C-218/00, *Cisal di Battistello Venanzio & Co v. Istituto Nazionale per L'Assicurazione Contro Gli Infortuni Sul Lavoro (INAIL)* [2002] ECR I-691, [2002] 4 CMLR 833.

[77] Case C-205/03 P, *FENIN v. Commission*, [2006] ECR I-6295, [2006] 5 CMLR 7.

[78] Cases C-264, 306, 354, and 355/01, *AOK Bundesverband v. Ichthyol-Gesellschaft Cordes, Hermani & Co* [2004] ECR I-2493, [2004] 4 CMLR 1261.

[79] Case 30/87, *Corinne Bodson v. Pompes Funèbres des Régions Libérées SA* [1988] ECR 2479, [1989] 4 CMLR 984.

[80] *Ibid.*, para. 18.

[81] Case T-155/04 12 December 2006, [2007] 4 CMLR 372, Case C-113/07 (judgment pending).

technical standardisation activities (for which there was no market) and research and development activities (acquisition of prototypes and the regime of intellectual property rights) were not economic activities, Eurocontrol did act as an undertaking when providing assistance to national administrations, such as assistance in public tender procedures. This latter activity was separable from Eurocontrol's tasks of air space management and development of air safety and involved offering services on the market for advice, a market on which private undertakings specialized in this area could very well participate.[82]

In *Diego Cali*,[83] the ECJ referred to *Eurocontrol* when dealing with a case concerning anti-pollution surveillance and intervention entrusted by the national port authority at Genoa to a *private* limited company, SEPG. A port user, Diego Cali, challenged charges levied on it by SEPG in respect of services provided, on the grounds that SEPG had abused its dominant position contrary to Article 82. The ECJ found that SEPG was not an undertaking since it carried out services relating to the protection of the environment which were not of an economic nature but which were essential functions of the State. The purpose of the activity was to guarantee safety and to protect the port environment and to ensure public assets were properly protected in the interest of the State and citizens.[84]

> 22. The anti-pollution surveillance for which SEPG was responsible in the oil port of Genoa is a task in the public interest which forms part of the essential functions of the State as regards protection of the environment in maritime areas.

> 23. Such surveillance is connected by its nature, its aim and the rules to which it is subject with the exercise of powers relating to the protection of the environment which are typically those of a public authority. It is not of an economic nature justifying the application of the Treaty rules on competition…

The outcome of *Eurocontrol*, and *Diego Cali* thus turned upon the ECJ's assessment that these tasks, in contrast to those carried out in *Höfner and Elser*, could only be performed by or on behalf of a public body.[85]

In a line of cases concerning pension funds and social security schemes, the ECJ has drawn a distinction between entities which operate in the same way as, or in competition with, ordinary commercial enterprises in the same sector and entities which fulfil an exclusively social function, carrying out an activity which is based on the principle of solidarity. The principle of solidarity has been described as: 'the redistribution of income between those who are better off and those who, in view of their resources…would be deprived'[86] or 'the inherently uncommercial act of involuntary subsidization of one social group by another'.[87]

---

[82] Case T-155/04 12 Dec. 2006, [2007] 4 CMLR 372, paras. 50–94, Case C-113/07 (judgment pending).

[83] Case C-343/95, *Diego Cali e Figli SrL v. SEPG* [1997] ECR I-1547, [1997] 5 CMLR 484.

[84] Case C-343/95, *Diego Cali e Figli SrL v. SEPG* [1997] ECR I-1547, [1997] 5 CMLR 484, Cosmas AG, paras. 44–46.

[85] Odudu states that it is not feasible to profit from the provision of public goods and services and that '[b]oth *Eurocontrol* and *Diego Cali* show recognition that effective provision of a public good is impossible absent the coercive power of the state'. He identifies the two characteristics of public goods that make profit impossible: such goods are non-rivalrous in consumption (once produced, an infinite number of consumers can enjoy them without increased production cost or diminished enjoyment by others); and the benefits are non-excludable (it is not possible to prevent people from enjoying the benefits once the good is produced, O. Odudu, *The Boundaries of EC Competition Law: The Scope of Article 81* (Oxford University Press, 2006), 42–5.

[86] Cases C-159–160/91, *Poucet et Pistre v. Assurances Générales de France* [1993] ECR I-637, para. 10 and see Chap. 8.

[87] Case C-70/95, *Sodemare v. Regione Lombardia* [1997] ECR I-3395, [1998] 4 CMLR 667, Fennelly AG, para. 29. In his book, Odudu considers that a number of elements possessed by redistributive activity can be identified: (a) compulsion; (b) control over cost; (c) control over price; and (d) absence of link between cost and

In *Poucet et Pistre*[88] it was held that a French body running a compulsory social security scheme was not an undertaking. In this case, benefits received under the scheme administered were not proportionate to contributions and contributions made were proportionate to income (there was an element of cross-subsidy).

18. Sickness funds, and the organizations involved in the management of the public social security system, fulfil an exclusively social function. That activity is based on the principle of national solidarity and is entirely non-profit-making. The benefits paid are statutory benefits bearing no relation to the amount of contributions.

19. Accordingly, that activity is not an economic activity and, therefore, the organizations to which it is entrusted are not undertakings within the meaning of Articles [81] and [82] of the Treaty.

Similarly, in *Cisal v. INAIL* the ECJ found that an institution providing compulsory insurance against accidents at work and occupational diseases applied the principle of solidarity and did not carry out an economic activity for the purposes of competition law. It was financed by contributions which were not systematically set at a rate proportionate to the risk insurance, the amount of benefits paid were not necessarily proportionate to earnings, there was no direct link between the contributions paid and the benefits granted, and the amount of benefits and contributions were, in the last resort, fixed by the State. The compulsory affiliation of the scheme was essential to its financial balance and for the application of the principle of solidarity.[89] By excluding such entities from the scope of the competition rules, Community law does not affect the power of the Member States to organize their social security systems.[90]

In *AOK Bundesverband*[91] the ECJ had to rule on the question of whether sickness funds that were direct providers of statutory sickness insurance were undertakings. The case involved claims brought by pharmaceutical companies against associations of funds which had set maximum amounts to be paid for certain medicinal products. In this case the Court found that the sickness funds, like the bodies in *Poucet and Pistre*, were involved in the management of the social security system. 'In this regard they fulfil an exclusively social function, which is founded on the principle of national solidarity and is entirely non-profit making'.[92] In particular, the funds were obliged to offer benefits to members which were not dependent upon the amount of contributions, and an equalization of costs and risks was operated between the funds. This conclusion was not affected by the fact that latitude was available to the funds when setting their contribution rate and that some competition with one another did exist.[93] Further, the Court

price. 'These features ... are more readily identified in Advocates General opinions that in decisions of the Court. A question mark must thus hang over whether the elements are ever relied upon by the Court and relied upon the in same way. Additionally, it remains unclear whether the elements are complete; cumulative; alternative, or simply a few of a number of factors to which weight is attached in determining whether profit can be made from an activity.' O. Odudu, *The Boundaries of EC Competition Law: The Scope of Article 81* (Oxford University Press, 2006), 39–42.

[88] Cases C-159–160/91, *Poucet et Pistre v. Assurances Générales de France* [1993] ECR I-637.

[89] Case C-218/00, *Cisal di Battistello Venanzio & Co v. Istituto Nazionale per L'Assicurazione Contro Gli Infortuni Sul Lavoro (INAIL)* [2002] ECR I-691, [2002] 4 CMLR 833, paras. 31–46, Jacobs AG, paras. 71–82.

[90] *Ibid.* para. 31 (relying in particular on Case C-158/96, *Kohl* [1998] ECR I-1931, [1998] 2 CMLR 928, para. 17).

[91] Cases C-264, 306, 354, and 355/01, *AOK Bundesverband v. Ichthyol-Gesellschaft Cordes, Hermani & Co* [2004] ECR I-2493, [2004] 4 CMLR 1261. The ECJ rejected the view of its Advocate General that the funds were undertakings and that their 'purchasing cartel' was subject to the competition rules unless exempt by virtue of Article 86(2). For further discussion of this case, see *infra* Chap. 8.

[92] *Ibid.*, para. 51.

[93] Contrast the Opinion of Advocate General Jacobs, para. 42.

held that the fixing of maximum purchasing amounts by the fund associations was linked to the funds' social functions and did not, therefore, constitute an activity of an economic nature.[94]

Conversely, in *Fédération Française des Sociétés d'Assurance*[95] a body operating a pension scheme was found to be an undertaking. Although it was non-profit-making it operated in the same way as other insurance companies, the rules were like those of private schemes and there was no mutuality or cross-subsidy between the beneficiaries. The ECJ further considered these cases in *Albany*.[96] This case concerned a supplementary pension fund. Essentially, affiliation to the fund was compulsory in the Textile Industry. A dispute broke out between the fund and Albany, a textile business, which wished to be exempted from the affiliation. On a reference to it the ECJ stressed the economic functions carried out by the pension fund. It found the fund to be an undertaking even though: affiliation to the scheme was compulsory; the supplementary pension scheme was designed to top up an extremely limited statutory pension; the sectoral pension fund was non-profit-making; and the pension fund was obliged to accept all workers without a medical examination.[97] The ECJ accepted that the social objectives which the pension fund were required to pursue might make the service it provided less competitive than those offered by other insurance companies. These factors did not, however, detract from the fact that the activities it engaged in were economic ones. The pension fund determined the amount of contributions made and benefits received (the latter were dependent upon the results of the investments made by it) and it could, in certain circumstances, grant exemption from affiliation to the fund. The social objectives were relevant, however, to the ECJ's finding that the public authority could nonetheless confer on a pension fund the exclusive right to manage a supplementary pension scheme in a given sector.[98]

b. Purchasing of Goods and Services by a Public Entity

In *Federación Nacional de Empresas de Instrumentación Científica, Médica, Técnica y Dental (FENIN) v. Commission*,[99] it had to be considered when 'purchasing' of goods and services by a public entity that discharges social functions might constitute economic activity. In this case, an association of the undertakings which marketed medical goods and equipments to bodies forming part of the Spanish Health Service (SNS), complained to the Commission that SNS were guilty of an abuse of a dominant position, in particular because they systematically took an average of 300 days to pay their debts. The Commission rejected the complaint on the ground that the organisations in question were not undertakings when they participated in the management of the national health service. Consequently, they were not acting as undertakings when they purchased medical goods and supplies. On appeal, the CFI affirmed that bodies forming part of

---

[94] See also the discussion of Case C-205/03 P, *FENIN v. Commission*, [2006] ECR I-6295, [2006] 5 CMLR 7 *infra*.

[95] Case C-244/94, *Fédération Française des Sociétés d'Assurance and Others v. Ministère de l'Agriculture et de la Pêche* [1995] ECR I-4013, [2000] 4 CMLR 446.

[96] Case C-67/96, *Albany International BV v. Stichting Bedrijfspensioenfonds Textielindustrie* [1999] ECR I-5751, [2000] 4 CMLR 446.

[97] *Ibid.*, paras. 77–87. In Cases C-180–184, *Pavlov v. Stichting Pensioenfonds Medische Specialisten* [2000] ECR I-6451, [2001] 4 CMLR 30 the ECJ also concluded that a pension fund which was compulsory for members of the Dutch medical profession was an undertaking. It was carrying out an economic activity. Again the Court found the facts that the Fund was non-profit-making and had solidarity aspects were not sufficient to relieve the Fund of its status as an undertaking.

[98] See discussion of the case *infra* Chap. 8.

[99] Case C-205/03 P, *FENIN v. Commission* [2006] ECR I-6295, [2006] 5 CMLR 7, Case T-319/99, [2003] ECR II-351, [2003] 5 CMLR 34.

the SNS did not act as an undertaking when *purchasing* medical goods and equipment for the purpose of using them for activities of a purely social nature (to provide free health services to SNS members) and not for the purpose of offering goods and services as part of an economic activity.[100] The Court stressed that it was the *supply* function (the offering of goods and services on a market) of the entity that was important when determining whether economic activity was carried out and not the purchasing function.[101] In the context of the former, SNS operated according to the principle of solidarity. It was funded from social security contributions and other State funding and it provided services free of charge to its members on the basis of universal cover. If the activity for which the entity purchased goods was not an economic one, it made no difference that the entity might wield very considerable economic power, even giving rise to a monopsony.[102] The CFI did not consider whether the fact that SNS did charge some patients (not covered by SNS) for care would alter the conclusion on the undertaking question. Although this point was raised on appeal it had not been put to the Commission and so was held not to be relevant for the purposes of reviewing the legality of the Commission's decision. [103]

On appeal, the ECJ,[104] in a very short judgment, upheld the CFI and rejected FENIN's argument that the CFI had adopted too narrow a definition of economic activity since it had failed to consider whether purchasing activity is in itself an economic activity which may be dissociated from the service subsequently provided or because the subsequent activity, the provision of medical treatment was itself an economic activity. Again, the ECJ stressed that the characteristic feature of an economic activity consists in offering of goods and services on a given market.

Case C-205/03, *Federación Nacional de Empresas de Instrumentación Científica, Médica, Técnica y Dental (FENIN)* v. *Commission* [2006] ECR I-6295

Court of Justice

23 In support of the first part of its plea, FENIN argues that the Court of First Instance adopted a definition of economic activity which is too narrow, holding that that activity necessarily consists of the offer of goods or services on a given market and excluding all purchasing activity from that definition. FENIN submits that the approach of the Court of First Instance would enable many bodies to avoid the competition rules of the Treaty, even though competition is affected by the conduct of such bodies.

24 The Commission submits that it is precisely the act of placing goods or services on a given market which characterises the concept of economic activity and not purchasing activity as such. Accordingly, there is no need to dissociate the purchase from the use to which the purchased goods are put.

---

[100] See also Cases C-264, 306, 354, and 355/01, *AOK Bundesverband* v. *Ichthyol-Gesellschaft Cordes, Hermani & Co* [2004] ECR I-2493, [2004] 4 CMLR 1261 discussed *supra* n. 92.

[101] Case T-319/99, [2003] ECR II-351, [2003] 5 CMLR 34, para. 36.

[102] Case T-319/99, *FENIN* v. *Commission* [2003] ECR II-351, [2003] 5 CMLR 34, para. 37. Contrast the view of Advocate General Jacobs in Case C-218/00, *Cisal di Battistello Venanzio & Co* v. *Istituto Nazionale per L'Assicurazione Contro Gli fortuni Sul Lavoro (INAIL)* [2002] ECR I-691, [2002] 4 CMLR 24, para. 71.

[103] Case T-319/99, *FENIN* v. *Commission* [2003] ECR II-351, [2003] 5 CMLR 34, paras. 40–43.

[104] Case C-205/03 P, *FENIN* v. *Commission* [2006] ECR I-6295, [2006] 5 CMLR 7.

Findings of the Court

25 The Court of First Instance rightly held, in paragraph 35 of the judgment under appeal, that in Community competition law the definition of an 'undertaking' covers any entity engaged in an economic activity, regardless of the legal status of that entity and the way in which it is financed (Case C-41/90 *Höfner and Elser* [1991] ECR I-1979, paragraph 21, and Joined Cases C-264/01, C-306/01, C-354/01 and C-355/01 *AOK-Bundesverband and Others* [2004] ECR I-2493, paragraph 46). In accordance with the case-law of the Court of Justice, the Court of First Instance also stated, in paragraph 36 of the judgment under appeal, that it is the activity consisting in offering goods and services on a given market that is the characteristic feature of an economic activity (Case C-35/96 *Commission* v *Italy* [1998] ECR I-3851, paragraph 36).

26 The Court of First Instance rightly deduced, in paragraph 36 of the judgment under appeal, that there is no need to dissociate the activity of purchasing goods from the subsequent use to which they are put in order to determine the nature of that purchasing activity, and that the nature of the purchasing activity must be determined according to whether or not the subsequent use of the purchased goods amounts to an economic activity.

27 It follows that the first part of the single plea raised by FENIN in support of its appeal, that the purchasing activity of the SNS management bodies constitutes an economic activity in itself, dissociable from the service subsequently provided and which, as such, should have been examined separately by the Court of First Instance, must be dismissed as unfounded.

The judgment in *FENIN* thus makes it clear that *purchasing* for consumption is not economic activity and that purchasing will only constitute an economic activity if the goods and services acquired are subsequently used as an input for an economic activity, the offering of goods and services on a market.[105] This means that public bodies (even if wielding substantial purchasing power) will escape the reach of competition law unless the goods or services are bought for an economic activity. In so concluding, the Court was perhaps mindful of the 'dangerous territory' it enters when seeking to determine whether an activity carried on by the State or a State entity is of an economic nature 'since it must find a balance between the need to protect undistorted competition on the common market and respect for the power of the Member States'.[106] The decision reached in this case will inevitably lead to difficult questions of when purchasing in a particular case is sufficiently closely linked to the provision of goods or services by the

[105] Contrast the view of the UK's CAT, in *Bettercare Group Limited* v. *DGFT* [2002] CAT 7, [2002] CompAR 299 where the CAT held that the conclusion of commercial contracts with private sector bodies was an economic activity and that it made no difference whether the entity acted as purchaser, rather than the supplier, of the services in question (especially where the purchaser was in a position to generate the effects which the competition rules seek to prevent).

[106] Case C-205/03 P, *FENIN* v. *Commission* [2006] ECR I-6295, [2006] 5 CMLR 7 Maduro AG, para. 26. For the view that economic activity depends equally on buyers and sellers so that there is no reason why the concept of an undertaking should apply only to one side of the equation, and that although this approach to public procurement might bring short-term savings (adopting unfair and anticompetitive practices to increase efficiency of its purchasing) it, may ultimately cause the disappearance of innovative and competitive suppliers in a number of areas of importance to public welfare, see J. Skilbeck, 'The EC Judgment in AOK: Can a major public sector purchaser control the prices it pays or is it subject to competition law' PPLR 2004, 44 NA95–97 and J. Skilbeck, 'Just When is a public body an "Undertaking": FENIN and Bettercare compared' PPLR 2003, 4, NA75–77. This conclusion is hard on suppliers, particularly in markets where there are few other customers, as arguably this means that they will be made to make sacrifices in the name of the principle of solidarity, see, e.g. L. Montana and J. Jellis, 'The Concept of Undertakings in EC Competition Law and its Application to Public Bodies: Can you Buy your way into Article 82?' [2003] Comp Law 110 and *infra* Chap. 8.

purchaser to constitute economic activity[107] and how purchasing should be treated when only some or a small proportion of the goods acquired are used in connection with an economic activity.[108]

(v) Employees and Trade Unions

Although individuals may act as independent economic actors and constitute an undertaking,[109] it seems that employees acting as employees are not undertakings for the purposes of the competition rules (although the actions of the employee may be attributable to the employer).[110] Rather, employees in an employment relationship do not bear the financial risks of the business and perform work for and under the direction of their employers which they are incorporated within. Such employees 'do not therefore in themselves constitute "undertakings" within the meaning of Community competition law'.[111] In *Albany* Advocate General Jacobs took the view that the competition rules were not designed to cover the activities of employees.[112] They were not structured to be applicable to employees and employees did not perform the 'functions' of undertakings. Rather, he considered work and labour to be distinct from the provision of goods or services. In addition, trade unions would not be characterized as undertakings in so far as they acted as agent for their members (employees).[113] This view inevitably creates the need for a difficult distinction to be drawn between self-employed persons and employees.[114]

Case C-67/96, *Albany International BV* v. *Stichting Bedrijfspensioenfonds Textielindustrie* [1999] ECR I-5751, [2000] 4 CMLR 446

Advocate General Jacobs

(a) Employees

. . .

211. Accordingly, the question arises how to classify the fact that employees offer labour against remuneration.

---

[107] See, e.g. Cases C-180–4/98, *Pavlov v. Stichting Pensioenfonds Medische Specialisten* [2000] ECR I-6451, [2001] 4 CMLR 30.

[108] See *infra* n. 104 and accompanying text.

[109] See *supra* n. 46.

[110] See *infra* 170.

[111] Case C-22/98, *Criminal Proceedings Against Becu* [1999] ECR I-5665, [2001] 4 CMLR 968, para. 26.

[112] See also his opinion in *Pavlov v. Stichting Pensioenfonds Medische Specialisten* [2000] ECR I-6451, [2001] 4 CMLR 30. The ECJ in Case C-67/96, *Albany International BV v. Stichting Bedrijfspensioenfonds Textielindustrie* [1999] ECR I-5751, [2000] 4 CMLR 446 did not rule specifically on whether or not, or when, employees or trade unions qualify as undertakings for the purposes of the competition rules. On the facts of the case it held that collective agreements concluded between trade unions and employers relating to conditions of employment and working conditions fell outside Article 81(1) altogether. These agreements were concluded to fulfil important social objectives which should not be frustrated by the application of Article 81(1), see *infra* 152.

[113] If the employee does not constitute an undertaking, the trade union could not constitute an association of undertakings.

[114] See *supra* n. 46.

212. One could argue that it is an economic activity similar to the sale of goods or the provision of services. From an economic point of view, that may—arguably—be true. However, I do not think that, from a legal perspective, the assertion is correct.

213. First, it is difficult to see how the term 'undertaking' could be understood in the sense of 'employee'. To interpret the Treaty in a manner that would include the latter term in the former would, in my view, exceed the limits which its wording imposes.

214. Secondly, the functional interpretation of the term 'undertaking' which the Court has adopted in its case-law leads to the same result. With respect to public bodies the Court examines whether the activity in question is—at least potentially—performed by private entities engaged in the supply of goods or services . . . Individuals, too, may be classified as undertakings . . . if they are independent economic actors on the markets for goods or services. The rationale underlying those cases is that the entities under scrutiny are fulfilling the 'function' of an undertaking. The application of Articles [81] and [82] is justified by the fact that those public bodies or individuals are operating on the same or similar markets and according to similar principles as 'normal' undertakings . . .

215. Dependent labour is by its very nature the opposite of the independent exercise of an economic or commercial activity. Employees normally do not bear the direct commercial risk of a given transaction. They are subject to the orders of their employer. They do not offer services to different clients, but work for a single employer. For those reasons there is a significant functional difference between an employee and an undertaking providing services. That difference is reflected in their distinct legal status in various areas of Community . . . or national law.

216. Thirdly, the system of Community competition law is not tailored to be applicable to employees. The examples of anti-competitive practices in Articles [81(1)] and [82] or the conditions for exemption in Article [81(3)] are clearly drafted with regard to economic actors engaged in the supply of goods or services. Article [81(1)(a)] for example refers to 'purchase or selling prices' and to 'other trading conditions'. Employees, on the contrary, are concerned with 'wages' and 'working conditions'. To apply Article [81(1)] to employees would therefore necessitate the use of uneasy analogies between the markets for goods and services and labour markets.

217. Accordingly, in my view, employees in principle fall outside the personal scope of the prohibition of Article [81(1)]. The future will probably show whether that principle applies also in certain borderline areas such as for example professional sport.

(b) Trade unions

218. Since employees cannot be qualified as undertakings for the purposes of Article [81], trade unions, or other associations representing employees, are not 'associations of undertakings'.

219. However, are trade unions themselves 'undertakings'?

220. The mere fact that a trade union is a non-profit-making body does not automatically deprive the activities which it carries on of their economic character . . .

221. A trade union is an association of employees. It is established that associations may also be regarded as 'undertakings' in so far as they themselves engage in an economic activity . . .

222. It must be borne in mind that an association can act either in its own right, independent to a certain extent of the will of its members, or merely as an executive organ of an agreement between its members. In the former case its behaviour is attributable to the association itself, in the latter case the members are responsible for the activity.

223. With regard to ordinary trade associations, the result of that delimitation is often not important, since Article [81] applies in the same way to agreements between undertakings and to decisions by associations of undertakings . . . It may be relevant when the Commission has to decide to whom to address its decision and whom to fine. . . .

224. However, in the case of trade unions that delimitation becomes decisive, since, if the trade union is merely acting as agent, it is solely an executive organ of an agreement between its members, who themselves—as seen above—are not addressees of the prohibition of Article [81(1)].

225. With regard to trade union activities one has therefore to proceed in two steps: first, one has to ask whether a certain activity is attributable to the trade union itself and if so, secondly, whether that activity is of an economic nature.

226. There are certainly circumstances where activities of trade unions fulfil both conditions. Some trade unions may for example run in their own right supermarkets, savings banks, travel agencies or other businesses. When they are acting in that capacity the competition rules apply.

227. However in the present cases the trade unions are engaged in collective bargaining with employers on pensions for employees of the sector. In that respect the trade unions are acting merely as agent for employees belonging to a certain sector and not in their own right. That alone suffices to show that in the present cases they are not acting as undertakings for the purposes of competition law.

(vi) Single Economic Entity

a. What is a Single Economic Entity?

Companies belonging to the same group and having the status of parent and subsidiary may have distinct legal personalities. In *Consten and Grundig*, however, the ECJ held that Article 81 intended to leave untouched the internal organization of an undertaking.[115] Thus, it has been held that if a subsidiary 'enjoys no economic independence'[116] or if the undertakings 'belong to the same concern' or have 'the status of parent company and subsidiary' and 'form an economic unit within which the subsidiary has no real freedom to determine its course of action on the market'[117] they are treated, for the purpose of Article 81, as a single economic entity. '[T]he unified conduct on the market of the parent company and its subsidiaries takes precedence over the formal separation between those companies as a result of their separate legal personalities'.[118] The relevant question is not therefore whether two given companies are separate legal persons but, rather, whether they behave together as a single unit on the market.[119] The doctrine also applies to relations between a company/principal and its commercial agent where the agent is an auxiliary organ which is integrated into the principal.[120]

In *Viho Europe BV v. Commission*,[121] the ECJ confirmed that the Commission had correctly found that a parent company and its 100 per cent owned subsidiaries were a single economic

---

[115] Cases 56 and 58/64, *Etablissements Consten SA & Grundig-Verkaufs-GmbH* v. *Commission* [1966] ECR 299, [1966] CMLR 418, set out *infra* 152.

[116] Case 22/71, *Béguelin Import* v. *GL Import-Export* [1971] ECR 949, [1972] CMLR 81, para. 8.

[117] Case 15/74, *Centrafarm BV and Adnaan De Peijper* v. *Sterling Drug Inc* [1974] ECR 1183, [1974] 2 CMLR 480, para. 41. See also Case 170/83, *Hydrotherm Gerätebau GmbH* v. *Compact de Dott Ing Mario Adredi & CSAS* [1984] ECR 2999, [1985] 3 CMLR 224, para. 11, Case T-11/89, *Shell* v. *Commission* [1992] ECR II-884, para. 311 and generally W. P. J. Wils, 'The Undertaking as Subject of E.C. Competition Law and the Imputation of Infringements to Natural or Legal Persons' (2000) 25 *ELRev* 99.

[118] Case T-102/92, *Viho Europe BV* v. *Commission* [1995] ECR II-117, [1997] 4 CMLR 469, para. 50. See also Case T-9/99, *HFB Holdings*, paras. 54–68.

[119] Case T-325/01, *Daimler Chrysler AG* v. *Commission* [2005] ECR II-3319, para. 85.

[120] Case C-217/05, *Confederación Espanola de Empresarios de Estaciones de Servicio* v. *Compania Espanola de Petróleos* 14 Dec. 2006, [2007] 4 CMLR 8661 and Case T-325/01, *Daimler Chrysler AG* v. *Commission* [2005] ECR II-3319, para. 86, see Chap. 9.

[121] Case C-73/95 P, *Viho Europe BV* v. *Commission* [1996] ECR I-5457, [1997] 4 CMLR 419.

unit. Consequently, agreements between these companies were not caught by Article 81(1): the activity was of a single enterprise and not the collusive action required to trigger Article 81.[122]

Case C-73/95 P, *Viho Europe BV* v. *Commission* [1996] ECR I-5457, [1997] 4 CMLR 419

Parker Pen Ltd is a company incorporated under English law which produces writing utensils. This case concerned a complaint made by a Dutch company, Viho, which marketed office equipment on a wholesale basis. Viho had been unable to obtain Parker products on conditions equivalent to those granted to Parker's subsidiaries and independent distributions. It complained to the Commission that Parker's distribution system (which prohibited exports between Member States, divided the common market into national markets, and maintained artificially high prices on those national markets) was in breach of Article 81(1). Parker sold its products in Europe through subsidiary companies in Germany, Belgium, France, Spain and the Netherlands of which it owned 100 per cent of the shares. Sales and marketing of the products through the subsidiaries were controlled by an area team of three directors.

After an investigation the Commission informed Viho that it was rejecting the complaint. Parker's subsidiary companies were wholly dependent on it, enjoyed no real autonomy, and the distribution system did not go beyond the normal allocation of tasks within a group of undertakings. Viho appealed against the Commission's rejection of the complaint to the Court of First Instance which upheld the decision (Case T-102/92 [1995] ECR II-17, [1995] 4 CMLR 299). Article 81(1) referred only to relations between economic entities which were capable of competing with one another. It did not cover agreements or concerted practices between entities belonging to the same group if they formed an economic unit. Viho appealed to the Court of Justice. The ECJ confirmed that the Commission and the CFI had correctly classified the Parker Group as one economic unit within which the subsidiaries did not enjoy real autonomy in determining their course of action in the market.

Court of Justice

13. The appellant claims that the fact that the conduct in question occurs within a group of companies does not preclude the application of Article [81(1)], since the division of responsibilities between the companies in the Parker group aims to maintain and partition national markets by means of absolute territorial protection. The evaluation of such conduct, which has harmful effects on competition, should not therefore depend on whether it takes place within a group or between Parker and its independent distributors. The appellant points out that such territorial protection prevents third parties such as itself from obtaining supplies freely within the Community from the subsidiary which offers the best commercial terms, so as to be able to pass such benefits on to the customer.

14. Consequently, the appellant considers that Article [81(1)], interpreted in the light of Articles 2 and [3(1)(c) and (g)] . . . of the E.C. Treaty must apply, since the referral policy in question goes far beyond a mere internal allocation of tasks within the Parker group.

---

[122] The US Supreme Court in *Copperweld Corp* v. *Independence Tube Corp.* 467 US 36, has held that since a parent and a wholly owned subsidiary have a complete unity of interest and because a parent can assert full control at any moment if a subsidiary fails to act in a parent's interest, the parent and subsidiary have a unity of purpose or common design that belies a section 1 Sherman Act of 1890 agreement.

15. It should be noted, first of all, that it is established that Parker holds 100 per cent of the shares of its subsidiaries in Germany, Belgium, Spain, France and the Netherlands and that the sales and marketing activities of its subsidiaries are directed by an area team appointed by the parent company and which controls, in particular, sales targets, gross margins, sales costs, cash flow and stocks. The area team also lays down the range of products to be sold, monitors advertising and issues directives concerning prices and discounts.

16. Parker and its subsidiaries thus form a single economic unit within which the subsidiaries do not enjoy real autonomy in determining their course of action in the market, but carry out the instructions issued to them by the parent company controlling them (Case 48/69, *ICI* v. *E.C. Commission*...; Case 15/74, *Centrafarm* v. *Sterling Drug*...; Case 16/74, *Centrafarm* v. *Winthrop*...; Case 30/87, *Bodson* v. *Pompes Funebres*...; and Case 66/86, *Ahmed Saeed Flugreisen and Others* v. *Zentrale zur Bekämpfung Unlauteren Wettbewerbs*...).

17. In those circumstances, the fact that Parker's policy of referral, which consists essentially in dividing various national markets between its subsidiaries, might produce effects outside the ambit of the Parker group which are capable of affecting the competitive position of third parties cannot make Article [81(1)] applicable, even when it is read in conjunction with Article 2 and Article [3(1)(c)] and (g) of the Treaty. On the other hand, such unilateral conduct could fall under Article [82] of the Treaty if the conditions for its application, as laid down in that article were fulfilled.

18. The Court of First Instance was therefore fully entitled to base its decision solely on the existence of a single economic unit in order to rule out the application of Article [81(1)] to the Parker group.

This case establishes that truly unilateral behaviour of an undertaking, even if within a group of connected companies, will escape the ambit of the competition rules unless that undertaking holds a dominant position and commits an infringement of Article 82.[123] In contrast, distribution arrangements concluded between independent undertakings will be caught by Article 81(1) if they restrict or distort competition. The complaints lodged by Viho about the arrangements between Parker and its *independent distributors,* i.e., firms which were not connected to Parker by any type of ownership or control, culminated with a Commission decision finding that the distribution arrangements were in breach of Article 81(1) and with the parties being fined.[124]

A difficulty is to determine the boundaries of the doctrine. The cases indicate that whether or not the entities constitute an economic unit or whether one has sufficient freedom of action to be considered a separate entity is a question of degree and will depend on a number of factors, for example, whether the parent has control of the board of directors, the amount of profit taken by the parent, and whether the subsidiary complies with directions given by the parent on matters such as marketing and investment. It appears therefore to boil down to the question of control. Where a parent has a majority shareholding, as in *Viho*, there is a presumption that the subsidiary is not independent and that the parent exercises decisive influence over it.[125] In contrast, where a subsidiary is not wholly owned it seems that the parent company must be able to influence the subsidiary's policy.[126] Thus in *Gosmé/Martell-DMP*,[127] the Commission found

---

[123] See Chap. 5, but see *infra* 155 ff.

[124] See the appeals to the CFI in Case T-66/92, *Herlitz AG* v. *Commission* [1994] ECR II-531, [1995] 5 CMLR 458 and Case T-77/92, *Parker Pen Ltd* v. *Commission* [1994] ECR II-549, [1995] 5 CMLR 435.

[125] See e.g. Case C-286/98 P, *Stora Kopparbergs Berlgslags AB* v. *Commission* [2000] ECR I-9925, para. 29. See also the Opinion of Warner AG in Cases 6 and 7/73, *Istituto Chemioterapico Italiano Spa and Commercial Solvents Corp* v. *EC Commission* [1974] ECR 223, [1974] 1 CMLR 309.

[126] See, e.g. Case 107/82, *AEG-Telefunken AG* v. *Commission* [1983] ECR 3151, [1984] 3 CMLR 325, para. 52.

[127] [1991] OJ L185/23, [1992] 5 CMLR 586.

that an agreement between a parent and its 50 per cent owned joint venture company fell within the scope of Article 81(1). The parent only jointly owned the company which was able to operate to a large extent autonomously of it.

There is not much decisional-practice or case law which sheds light on the question of when entities will be considered to form part of the same economic unit. It has been suggested, however, that Article 81 should not apply to agreements between entities which are linked in such a way that the creation of these links would amount to a merger or acquisition of sole control within the meaning of the EC Merger Regulation.[128] Aid in this respect may, therefore, possibly be derived from the EC Merger Regulation.

R. Whish, *Competition Law* (5th edn., Butterworths, 2003), 88–9

The crucial question, therefore, is whether parties to an agreement are independent in their decision-making or whether one has sufficient control over the affairs of the other that the latter does not enjoy 'real autonomy' in determining its course of action on the market. For these purposes it is necessary to examine various factors such as the shareholding that a parent company has in its subsidiary, the composition of the board of directors, the extent to which the parent influences the policy of or issues instructions to the subsidiary and similar matters. Where a parent has a majority shareholding, the presumption will be that it controls the subsidiary's affairs; the *Viho* case was a simple one, since Parker Pen held all the shares in the subsidiaries. What is less clear is whether a minority shareholder might be held to have sufficient control to negate autonomy on the part of the subsidiary. Under Article 3(3) of the EC Merger Regulation (hereafter 'the ECMR'), a minority shareholder which has the 'possibility of exercising decisive influence' over the affairs of another undertaking has sufficient control for there to be a concentration. The case law has yet to explain whether the notion of control in the ECMR should be applied to the 'single economic entity' doctrine under Article 81(1), or whether the notions of control differ as between those two provisions. There would seem to be much to be said for the adoption of a consistent approach.

---

b. Consequences of the Single Economic Entity Doctrine

It was seen from the case of *Viho Europe BV* v. *Commission* that one important consequence of the doctrine is that an arrangement between entities within an economic unit cannot amount to an agreement or concerted practice between undertakings[129] (although it is of course possible that the conduct of the undertakings is incompatible with Article 82).[130] Further, other consequences may flow from a finding that entities form a single economic unit.

---

[128] See W. P. J. Wils, 'The Undertaking as Subject of E.C. Competition Law and the Imputation of Infringements to Natural or Legal Persons' (2000) 25 *ELRev* 99, 106–8 and R. Whish, *Competition Law* (5th edn., Butterworths, 2003), 88–9. See *infra* Chap. 12.

[129] Although Article 81(1) does not catch agreements between a parent and a wholly owned subsidiary, it is unclear whether the single economic entity doctrine would exclude an agreement between two sister companies (both controlled by the same parent) from the ambit of Article 81(1). It would seem logical that such agreements should be excluded, as if the parent company controls both sister companies, it can ensure that they enter the agreement. In the US, although the Supreme Court has not ruled on the matter, most circuits are agreed that the *Copperweld* doctrine (*supra* n. 122) excludes agreements between sister corporations from the scope of section 1 of the Sherman Act of 1890, see e.g. *Eichorn* v. *AT&T Corp.* 248 F.3d 131 (3d Cir. 2001).

[130] See generally *infra* Chap. 5.

First, such entities are counted as only one party to an agreement. This can be relevant to the application of the technology transfer block exemption which permits only 'bilateral' agreements.[131]

Secondly, although Article 81 applies to undertakings, liability for its breach has to be imputed to a natural or legal person. The single economic entity suggests that companies can be held responsible for the acts of other entities, within the economic unit, such as subsidiaries found to be in breach of a Treaty provision even if they have not participated in the infringement. Where a subsidiary has infringed Article 81, therefore, it appears that liability may be imputed to, and a fine imposed upon, the subsidiary and/or the parent especially where the subsidiary does not decide independently its own conduct on the market, but carries out, in all material respects, the instructions given to it by the parent company. A competition authority may be particularly keen to attribute responsibility to a parent company where, for example, the subsidiary may be unable to pay any fine imposed. In *ICI v. Commission (Dyestuffs)*,[132] the Commission used the doctrine to impose liability on a parent company which operated the agreement, and concocted the breach, outside of the European Union. The ECJ rejected the applicant's argument that the Commission was not empowered to impose fines on it in respect of actions taken outside the Community. By the use of its power to control its subsidiaries established in the Community, the applicant had been able to ensure that its decisions were implemented on that market. The subsidiary did not enjoy autonomy and its actions could be attributed to the parent. In this way the single economic entity doctrine avoids the need for the extraterritorial application of EC competition law. The doctrine enables the competition rules to be applied to companies outside the jurisdiction without recourse to the more controversial 'implementation' or 'effects' doctrines.[133] It appears, however, that liability cannot be imputed to a parent which was able to exercise decisive influence over the policy of a subsidiary in breach but which did not in fact use this power i.e. imputation is dependent on a finding that management power was actually exercised.[134] Arguably, it would be reasonable to impose liability on a parent in this situation on the basis that it could have exercised control over the company and could perhaps have prevented the infringement from happening.[135]

Thirdly, in determining the appropriate level of the fine the Commission may impose fines 'from €1,000 to 1,000,000 ... or a sum in excess thereof but not exceeding 10 per cent of the turnover in the preceding business year of each of the undertakings participating in the infringement'. The reference to the total worldwide turnover of each undertaking thus includes turnover of all the entities within the corporate group and is not restricted to the entity in

---

[131] See Reg. 772/2004 [2004] OJ L123/11, Art. 2 (replacing Reg. 240/96 [1996] OJ L31/2) and Case 170/83, *Hydrotherm Gerätebau GmbH v. Compact de Dott Ing Mario Adredi & CSAS* [1984] ECR 2999, [1985] 3 CMLR 224. The 2004 technology transfer block exemption, however, specifically provides that the term undertaking includes 'connected undertakings' as defined therein, see *infra* Chap. 10, 809. See also Reg. 1983/83 [1993] OJ L173/1 and Reg. 1984/83 [1983] OJ L173/7, which were replaced on 1 June 2000 by the new verticals block exemption, Reg. 2790/1999, [1999] OJ L336/1, [2000] 4 CMLR 398, *infra* Chap. 9.

[132] Cases 48, 49, and 51–7/69 [1972] ECR 619, [1972] CMLR 557, paras. 125–46. See also, e.g. *Spanish Raw Tobacco* IP/04/1256, [2007] OJ L102/14 paras. 371 *et seq.* In Case T-24/05 *Standard Commercial v. Commission* (pending) one of the applicant's grounds of appeal is that the Commission had misapplied Article 81(1) in holding the applicant responsible for the conduct of its subsidiary.

[133] The extraterritorial application of the competition rules is discussed *infra* Chap. 16.

[134] See, e.g. Cases 48, 49, 51–7/69, *ICI v. Commission* [1972] ECR 619, [1972] CMLR 557, para. 137, Case 107/82, *AEG-Telefunken AG v. Commission* [1983] ECR 3151, [1984] 3 CMLR 325, para. 50, Case C-286/98 *Stora Kopparbergs Bergslags AB v. Commission* [2000] ECR I-9925, paras. 21–30 and Case T-109/02 *Bolloré SA v. Commission*, 26 April 2007, paras. 129–150, Cases C-322 and 327/07 (judgment pending).

[135] See W. P. J. Wils, 'The Undertaking as Subject of E.C. Competition Law and the Imputation of Infringements to Natural or Legal Persons' (2000) 25 *ELRev* 99. See also for a discussion of this issue, A. Montesa and A. Giraja, 'When Parents Pay for their Children's Wrongs: Attribution of Liability for EC Antitrust Infringements in Parent Subsidiary Scenarios' [2006] 29(4) *World Competition* 555.

breach or to the turnover earned in the market in which the infringement was committed.[136] In some cases both the parent company and the subsidiary may be liable for the breach of the competition rules. Where both are liable each can be fined under Council Regulation 1/2003, Article 23, and they will be jointly and severally liable.

Fourthly, Community secondary legislation and Commission Notices recognize a similar doctrine providing that the existence of entities within the same economic unit may affect their application. For example, most of the block exemptions[137] and the Commission's Notice on agreements of minor importance[138] apply only to firms which do not exceed specified market shares. These provisions require that, when calculating market shares, the shares of all entities closely 'connected' (as defined therein) to the body that actually entered into the agreement must be taken into account.[139] Similarly, the activities of the whole group must be considered when determining whether or not the parties to the agreement are competing undertakings.[140]

(vii) Associations of Undertakings

It has been seen that Article 81(1) applies not only to agreements and concerted practices between undertakings, but to decisions by associations of undertakings. It seems that the principle reason for such a reference is to enable 'those applying Article 81(1) to hold associations liable for the anti-competitive behaviour of their members'.[141] In *Wouters v. Alegemene Raad van de Nederlandse Order van Advocaten*,[142] Advocate General Léger stated the concept 'seeks to prevent undertakings from being able to evade the rules on competition on account simply of the form in which they coordinate their conduct on the market. To ensure that this principle is effective, Article [81(1)] covers not only direct methods of coordinating conduct between undertakings (agreements and concerted practices) but also institutionalised forms of cooperation, that is to say, situations in which economic operators act through a collective structure or a common body'.[143]

It appears that the concept of an association 'consists of undertakings of the same general type and makes itself responsible for representing and defending their common interests *vis-à-vis* other economic operators, government bodies and the public in general'.[144] Thus it applies to trade associations which may provide a forum for competitors in a particular industry to get together and to discuss matters which may be to their mutual interest and a perfect vehicle through which undertakings in a specific industry coordinate action, agricultural cooperatives,[145] a body set up by statute and with public functions if they represent the trading interests of the

---

[136] See Reg. 1/2003, Art. 23(2) and discussion of fines and fining policy *infra* in Chap. 14.

[137] See, e.g., Reg. 2790/1999 on the application of Article 81(3) of the Treaty to categories of vertical agreements or concerted practices, [1999] OJ L336/1, [2000] 4 CMLR 398, Art. 11.

[138] Commission Notice on agreements of minor importance which do not appreciably restrict competition under Article 81(1) [2001] OJ C368/13, [2002] 4 CMLR 699, para. 12.

[139] The term 'participating' or 'connected' undertaking are defined in the relevant provisions: see e.g. the Notice on agreements of minor importance [2001] OJ C368/13, [2002] 4 CMLR 699, para. 12, *infra* n. 288 and Reg. 2790/1999, [1999] OJ L336/1, [2000] 4 CMLR 398, Art. 11.

[140] See Reg. 2790/1999, [1999] OJ L336/1, [2000] 4 CMLR 398, Arts. 2(4) and 11.

[141] J. Faull and A. Nikpay (eds.), *The EC Law of Competition* (2nd edn., Oxford University Press, 2007), para. 3.102.

[142] Case C-309/99, [2002]ECR I-1577, [2002] 4 CMLR 913.

[143] Case C-309/99, *Wouters v. Alegemene Raad van de Nederlandse Order van Advocaten* [2002] ECR I-577, [2002] 4 CMLR 913, Léger AG, para. 62. Relying on M. Waelbroek and A. Frignani, *Commentaire J. Megret, Le Droit de la CE, Vol 4, Concurrence*, (Éditions de l'Université de Bruxelles, Bruxelles, 2nd edn., 1997), para. 128.

[144] Case C-309/99, *Wouters v. Alegemene Raad van de Nederlandse Order van Advocaten* [2002] ECR I-577, [2002] 4 CMLR 913, Léger AG, para. 61

[145] Case C-250/92, *Gøttrup-Klim Grovvareforening and Others v. Dansk Landbrugs Grovvaresel-skab AmbA* [1994] ECR I-5641, [1996] 4 CMLR 191.

members, even if there are some members appointed by the government or another public authority[146] and professional associations, even if governed by a public law statute.[147] Recommendations and other unilateral acts of such associations of undertakings designed to coordinate the behaviour of members are therefore brought within Article 81 without proof of a concerted practice or agreement between the individual members of the association.[148]

A further question arising is whether an association carrying out non-economic activity may be subject to the competition rules. After all if it were engaged in economic activity it would in any event be an undertaking and so subject to Article 81(1).[149] Case-law appeared to establish that for an entity to be classified as an association of undertakings, it is not necessary that it should itself carry on any economic activity.[150] Rather, Article 81(1) applies in so far as their activities or those of the undertakings affiliated to them are calculated to produce the results which it aims to suppress. In *Wouters v. Alegemene Raad van de Nederlandse Order van Advocaten*,[151] however, the ECJ suggests that a functional approach should be adopted to the concept of an association of undertakings in the same way as it applies to the concept of an undertaking. In that case it was argued that the Bar of the Netherlands, a body governed by public law, should not constitute an association of undertakings when exercising regulatory powers in order to perform a task of public interest. The ECJ held that 'the rules of competition do not apply to activity which, by its nature, its aim and the rules to which it is subject does not belong to the sphere of economic activity ... or which is connected with the exercise of the powers of a public authority ...' .[152] It held, however, that in adopting the regulatory rules the association was neither fulfilling a social function based on the principle of solidarity nor exercising powers which are typically those of a public authority. Rather, it was acting as the regulatory body of a profession, the practice of which constitutes an economic activity. It thus concluded that the Bar of the Netherlands must be regarded as an association of undertakings within the meaning of Article 81(1) when adopting a regulation such as one which prohibited certain multi-disciplinary partnerships. 'Such a regulation constitutes the expression of the intention of the delegates of the members of a profession that they should act in a particular manner in carrying on their economic activity.'[153]

---

[146] Case 123/83, *BNIC v. Clair* [1985] ECR 391, [1985] 2 CMLR 430.

[147] See Case C-35/96 *Commission v. Italy* [1998] ECR I-3851, paras. 36–8 (*CNSD*); (dealing with a professional association of custom agents), *Pavlov v. Stichting Pensioenfonds Medische Specialisten* [2000] ECR I-6451, [2001] 4 CMLR 30, paras. 73–7 and Case C-309/99, *Wouters v. Alegemene Raad van de Nederlandse Order van Advocaten* [2002] ECR I-577, [2002] 4 CMLR 913, para. 65.

[148] See *infra* 147.

[149] 'If the functional definition of undertaking given in *Höfner* captures all economic activity then associations of undertakings must be addressed when engaged in non-economic activity, otherwise the association would be an undertaking in its own right and 'associations of undertakings' otiose, O. Odudu, *The Boundaries of EC Competition Law: The Scope of Article 81* (Oxford University Press, 2006), 52–3.

[150] Cases 209–215 and 218/78 *Van Landewyck and Others v. Commission* [1980] ECR 3125, paras. 87–8; Cases 96–102, 104/82, 105/82, 108/82 and 110/82 *IAZ and Others v. Commission* [1983] ECR 3369, paras. 19–20 and Cases T-25, 26, 30–2, 34–9, 42–6, 48, 50–71, 87, 88, 103, and 104/95 *Cimenteries CBR SA v. Commission* [2000] ECR II-491, [2000] 5 CMLR 204, para. 1320.

[151] Case C-309/99, [2002] ECR I-1577, [2002] 4 CMLR 913.

[152] Case C-309/99, *Wouters v. Alegemene Raad van de Nederlandse Order van Advocaten* [2002] ECR I-577, [2002] 4 CMLR 913, para. 57.

[153] Case C-309/99, *Wouters v. Alegemene Raad van de Nederlandse Order van Advocaten* [2002] ECR I-577, [2002] 4 CMLR 913 para. 64. The Court found this view to be supported by the fact: that the governing bodies of the Bar was composed exclusively of members of the Bar elected solely by members of the profession; that when adopting regulatory measures it was not required to do so by reference to specified public-interest criteria (it was authorized to act where to do so would be in the interest of the proper practice of the profession); and given the influence the regulation had on the conduct of the members of the Bar of the Netherlands on the market in legal services (which indicated it did not fall outside the sphere of economic activity).

C. THE MEANING OF 'AGREEMENT', 'DECISION', AND 'CONCERTED PRACTICE'

(i) Introduction

Article 81(1) prohibits joint not individual conduct. The reference to 'agreements between undertakings, decisions by associations of undertakings and concerted practices' thus requires some element of 'collusion' between independent undertakings.

In effect, while that provision distinguishes between 'concerted practices', 'agreements between undertakings' and 'decisions by associations of undertakings', the aim is to have the prohibitions of that article catch different forms of coordination and collusion between undertakings (see Case C-49/92 P *Commission* v *Anic Partecipazioni* [1999] ECR I-4125, paragraph 112). Accordingly . . . a precise characterisation of the nature of the cooperation at issue in the main proceedings is not liable to alter the legal analysis to be carried out under Article 81 EC.'[154].

In many Article 81 cases the existence of an agreement is not in doubt. There may be doubt, however, as to the precise terms of the agreement[155] or as to whether the terms can be said to restrict competition. In other cases, frequently where it is suspected that a serious violation of the competition rules has been committed (for example, horizontal or vertical price fixing), evidence that independent undertakings agreed or concerted to fix prices will, effectively, prove a violation of Article 81(1). If detected, a large fine may be imposed on the undertakings proved to have been party to the infringement. In such cases, the parties who have been 'colluding' are likely to try and conceal its existence rather than attempt to try to defend the legitimacy of the practices under Article 81. The challenge for the competition authorities in such cases is therefore to uncover such covert operations and, where evidence is skimpy, to determine whether or not the behaviour on the market results from collusion, which is prohibited under Article 81, or independent behaviour, which is not.

Although the terms agreement, decision, and concerted practice may overlap and nothing turns legally on whether the conduct results from one or the other, collectively they draw a critical dividing line between lawful independent behaviour and illegitimate collusive practices. The terms are interpreted broadly but not so broadly that policy or behaviour that is determined *independently* on the market is incorporated within them.

(ii) Agreement

a. A Concurrence of Wills

The term 'agreement' has been given a liberal construction. In *Bayer AG* v. *Commission*[156] the CFI set out what has now become the classic definition of the concept, holding that proof of an agreement must be founded upon 'the existence of the subjective element that characterizes the very concept of the agreement, that is to say a concurrence of wills between economic operators on the implementation of a policy, the pursuit of an objective, or the adoption of a

---

[154] Case C-238/05, *Asnef-Equifax, Servicios de Información sobre Solvencia y Crédito, SL* v. *Asociación de Usuarios de Servicios Bancarios (Ausbanc)* [2006] ECR I-11125.

[155] See the discussion of unilateral conduct, *infra* 155 ff.

[156] Case T-41/96, [2000] ECR II-3383, [2001] 4 CMLR 126, *aff'd* on appeal Cases C-2 & 3/01 P, [2004] ECR I-23, [2004] 4 CMLR 653.

given line of conduct on the market'.[157] It is 'clear from the case-law that in order for there to be an agreement ... it is sufficient that the undertakings in question should have expressed their joint intention to conduct themselves on the market in a specific way'.[158]

Proof of an agreement must, therefore, be founded upon the direct or indirect finding of a concurrence of wills between economic operators. So long as there is a concurrence of wills, constituting the faithful expression of the parties' intention,[159] its form is unimportant. The concept catches agreements whether or not they amount to a contract under national rules, whether or not they are intended to be legally binding, whether or not sanctions are provided for a breach and whether they are in writing or oral.[160] It covers 'gentlemen's agreements',[161] standard conditions of sale,[162] trade association rules (which are treated as an agreement between the members to abide by the rules),[163] and agreements entered into to settle disputes, such as trade mark delimitation agreements.[164] An agreement exists once the parties agree on 'good neighbour rules' or 'establish practice and ethics' or 'certain rules of the game which it is in the interests of all of us to follow'.[165] Further, an agreement which has been terminated may be caught by Article 81(1) in respect of the period after termination if the effects of the agreement continue to be felt.[166] Agreements may be caught even if they are encouraged or approved by national law[167] or entered into after consultation with the national authorities.[168] It is no defence that an undertaking was bullied into concluding the agreement[169] or that an undertaking never intended to implement or to adhere to the terms of the agreement. This point was made forcefully by the Commission in *Industrial and Medical Gases*.[170] In this case, two of the undertakings alleged to be members of a cartel, Air Liquide and Westfalen, argued that they had

[157] *Ibid.*

[158] Case T-41/96, *Bayer AG v. Commission* [2000] ECR II-3383, [2001] 4 CMLR 126, *aff'd* on appeal Cases C-2 and 3/01 P, [2004] ECR I-23, [2004] 4 CMLR 653, relying on, e.g. Case 41/69, *ACF Chemiefarma NV v. Commission (the Quinine Cartel)* [1970] ECR 661, [1970] CMLR 43, para. 112

[159] Case T-41/96, *Bayer AG v. Commission* [2000] ECR II-3383, [2001] 4 CMLR 126, para. 69, *aff'd* on appeal Cases C-2 & 3/01 P, [2004] ECR I-23, [2004] 4 CMLR 653. See also Case T-62/98, *Volkswagen AG v. Commission* [2000] ECR II-2707, [2000] 5 CMLR 853, *aff'd* Case C-338/00 P, *Volkswagen AG v. Commission* [2003] ECR I-9189, [2004] 4 CMLR 7.

[160] See e.g. Case 28/77, *Tepea BV v. Commission* [1978] ECR 1391, [1978] 3 CMLR 392.

[161] Case 41/69, *ACF Chemiefarma NV v. Commission (the Quinine Cartel)* [1970] ECR 661, [1970] CMLR 43. In this case undertakings operated an export cartel but extended its terms within the EC through a gentlemen's agreement. The ECJ held that so long as the parties had declared themselves willing to abide by the gentleman's agreement that was sufficient.

[162] Case C-277/87, *Sandoz Prodotti Farmaceutici Spa v. Commission* [1990] ECR I-45, [1989] 4 CMLR 628.

[163] *Nuovo Cegam* [1984] OJ L99/29, [1984] 2 CMLR 484.

[164] See *infra* Chap. 10.

[165] Cases 209–15 and 218/78, *Van Landewyck v. Commission* [1980] ECR 3125, [1981] 3 CMLR 134, paras. 85 and 86 and *Cement* [1994] OJ L343/1, [1995] 4 CMLR 327, para. 45(6).

[166] Case T-7/89, *SA Hercules NV v. Commission* [1991] ECR II-1711, [1992] 4 CMLR 84. Whether or not an agreement has been terminated may be difficult to determine, see *Soda-ash—Solvay* [1991] OJ L152/1, [1994] 4 CMLR 645.

[167] See Cases 43 and 63/88, *VBVB & VBBB v. Commission* [1984] ECR 19, [1985] 1 CMLR 27; *Aluminium Imports from Eastern Europe* [1985] OJ L92/1, [1987] 3 CMLR 813; *AROW/BNIC* [1982] OJ L379/1, [1983] 2 CMLR 240.

[168] Cases 240–242, 261, and 262/82 *SSI v. Commission* [1985] ECR 3831, [1987] 3 CMLR 661. For the position where the State *requires* or encourages undertakings to enter into anti-competitive agreements, see *infra* 199–200 and Chap. 8.

[169] Case T-25/95, *Cimenteries CBR SA v. Commission* [2000] ECR II-491, para. 2557.

[170] [2003] OJ L 84/1, *aff'd* on appeal Case T-304/02 *Hoek Loos NV v. Commission* [2006] ECR II-1887, [2006] 5 CMLR 8.

not taken part in the agreements or implemented them. Rather, they had acted as a 'tough competitor' on the market or had pursued an 'aggressive commercial policy' towards competitors. The Commission rejected these arguments:

> 351. The Commission notes that the fact that Air Liquide and Westfalen participated in several meetings, and that the object of these meetings was to restrict competition, is confirmed by the documentary evidence in the Commission's file. The finding that the behaviour described constitutes agreements within the meaning of Article 81(1) of the Treaty is not altered even if it is established that one or more participants had no intention to implement the joint intentions expressed by them. Having regard to the manifestly anti-competitive nature of the meetings at which intentions were expressed, the undertakings concerned, by taking part without publicly distancing themselves, gave the other participants the impression that they subscribed to what was discussed and would act in conformity with it. The notion of 'agreement' is objective in nature. The actual motives (and hidden intentions) which underlay the behaviour adopted are irrelevant.

b. Horizontal and Vertical Agreements

Article 81(1) applies to agreements concluded between two or more undertakings (bilateral or multilateral agreements). It has already been seen that it is not applicable, however, where agreements are concluded between companies forming part of a single economic entity. Further it is not generally applicable to genuine agency agreements.[171] In the course of argument in *Consten and Grundig v. Commission*[172] it was suggested that, in a similar way, Article 81(1) should not be applied to agreements concluded between undertakings operating at different levels of the economy. If a producer could restrict the actions of its commercial representative without triggering the operation of Article 81(1) it should also be able to restrict the action of independent distributors. Article 81 should not be concerned with agreements concluded between entities which were not competitors and which were not on an equal footing. Rather, any conduct considered to be restrictive of competition should be dealt with under Article 82. The ECJ rejected these arguments, holding that Article 81(1) could apply to vertical arrangements.[173] The wording of the provision did not suggest that a distinction between horizontal and vertical agreements should be drawn. The agreement had not been concluded between a manufacturer and an entity integrated within it but had been concluded between independent undertakings. Further, the fact that the agreement was not concluded between competitors was immaterial. Article 81 applied to all agreements between undertakings which might distort competition within the common market.

Cases 56 and 58, *Etablissements Consten SA & Grundig-Verkaufs-GmbH v. Commission* [1966] ECR 299, 339–40, [1966] CMLR 418, 469–71

In 1957 Grundig, a German manufacturer of radios, tape recorders, dictaphones, and televisions, appointed Consten as its exclusive agent for France. Consten agreed, amongst other things, not

---

[171] Case C-73/95 P, *Viho Europe BV v. Commission* [1996] ECR I-5457, [1997] 4 CMLR 419 and Chap. 9.

[172] Cases 56 and 58/64, *Etablissements Consten SA & Grundig-Verkaufs-GmbH v. Commission* [1966] ECR 299, [1966] CMLR 418.

[173] Distribution agreements are discussed *infra* Chap. 9.

to handle any competing products, to order a minimum quantity of Grundig products, to stock accessories and spare parts and to provide after-sales services. In return, Grundig agreed not to deliver the product for sale in France and imposed export and re-export restrictions on all distributors in other Member States. The Grundig trade mark, Gint was registered in France in Consten's name. Under the agreements Consten, therefore, had absolute territorial protection. No-one else was entitled to sell Grundig products in France either actively or passively. In fact, UNEF, a Parisian company, started importing and selling Grundig products at more favourable prices in France. Consten commenced proceedings in the French courts contending that UNEF had failed to respect its contract with Grundig, that it was indulging in unfair competition and that it was infringing Consten's trade mark rights. It also brought proceedings against Leissner in Strasbourg which had also obtained Grundig products for resale in France. UNEF complained to the Commission and, in 1963, the agreement was notified to the Commission for examination. The French court adjourned its proceedings to await the Commission's decision.

The Commission concluded that the agreements did infringe Article 81(1) and could not be individually exempted under Article 81(3). Consten and Grundig appealed to the Court of Justice. One of their pleas was that Article 81(1) applied only to 'horizontal' and not 'vertical' agreements. This argument was supported by the Italian Government.

Court of Justice

The complaints concerning the applicability of Article [81(1)] to sole
distributorship contracts
The applicants submit that the prohibition in Article [81(1)] applies only to so-called horizontal agreements. The Italian Government submits furthermore that sole distributorship contracts do not constitute 'agreements between undertakings' within the meaning of that provision, since the parties are not on a footing of equality. With regard to these contracts, freedom of competition may only be protected by virtue of Article [82] of the Treaty.

Neither the wording of Article [81] nor that of Article [82] gives any ground for holding that distinct areas of application are to be assigned to each of the two Articles according to the level in the economy at which the contracting parties operate. Article [81] refers in a general way to all agreements which distort competition within the Common Market and does not lay down any distinction between those agreements based on whether they are made between competitors operating at the same level in the economic process or between non-competing persons operating at different levels. In principle, no distinction can be made where the Treaty does not make any distinction. Furthermore, the possible application of Article [81] to a sole distributorship contract cannot be excluded merely because the grantor and the concessionnaire are not competitors inter se and not on a footing of equality. Competition may be distorted within the meaning of Article [81(1)] not only by agreements which limit it as between the parties, but also by agreements which prevent or restrict the competition which might take place between one of them and third parties. For this purpose, it is irrelevant whether the parties to the agreement are or are not on a footing of equality as regards their position and function in the economy. This applies all the more, since, by such an agreement, the parties might seek, by preventing or limiting the competition of third parties in respect of the products, to create or guarantee for their benefit an unjustified advantage at the expense of the consumer or user, contrary to the general aims of Article [81].

It is thus possible that, without involving an abuse of a dominant position, an agreement between economic operators at different levels may affect trade between Member States and at the same time have as its object or effect the prevention, restriction or distortion of competition, thus falling under the prohibition of Article [81(1)].

In addition, it is pointless to compare on the one hand the situation, to which Article [81] applies, of a producer bound by a sole distributorship agreement to the distributor of his products with on the other hand that of a producer who includes within his undertaking the distribution of his own products by some means, for example, by commercial representatives, to which Article [81] does not apply. These situations are distinct in law and, moreover, need to be assessed differently, since two marketing organizations, one of which is [i]ntegrated into the manufacturer's undertaking whilst the other is not, may not necessarily have the same efficiency. The wording of Article [81] causes the prohibition to apply, provided that the other conditions are met, to an agreement between several undertakings. Thus it does not apply where a sole undertaking integrates its own distribution network into its business organization. It does not thereby follow, however, that the contractual situation based on an agreement between a manufacturing and a distributing undertaking is rendered legally acceptable by a simple process of economic analogy—which is in any case incomplete and in contradiction with the said Article. Furthermore, although in the first case the Treaty intended in Article [81] to leave untouched the internal organization of an undertaking and to render it liable to be called in question, by means of Article [82], only in cases where it reaches such a degree of seriousness as to amount to an abuse of a dominant position, the same reservation could not apply when the impediments to competition result from agreement between two different undertakings which then as a general rule simply require to be prohibited.

Finally, an agreement between producer and distributor which might tend to restore the national divisions in trade between Member States might be such as to frustrate the most fundamental objections of the Community. The Treaty, whose preamble and content aim at abolishing the barriers between States, and which in several provisions gives evidence of a stern attitude with regard to their reappearance, could not allow undertakings to reconstruct such barriers. Article [81(1)] is designed to pursue this aim, even in the case of agreements between undertakings placed at different levels in the economic process.

The submissions set out above are consequently unfounded.

c. Collective Bargaining Agreements

Article 81(1) *does not* apply to collective agreements between workers and employers intended to improve working conditions which belong to the realm of social policy. In *Albany International BV v. Stichting Bedrijfspensioenfonds Textielindustrie*[174] the ECJ held that agreements concluded by representatives of employers and workers in a sector would not be caught by Article 81(1) in so far as those agreements related to the improvement of conditions of work and employment. Not only was it an objective of the Treaty to ensure that competition in the common market was not distorted, but one of the Treaty's objectives was to achieve a high level of employment and social protection. The latter objective would be thwarted if Article 81(1) applied to agreements adopted by management and labour to improve conditions of work and employment. Consequently, such agreements fell outside the scope of Article 81(1) of the Treaty altogether.

---

[174] Case C-67/96, *Albany International BV v. Stichting Bedrijfspensioenfonds Textielindustrie* [1999] ECR I-5751, [2000] 4 CMLR 446. See also Cases C-115–117/97 *Bientjens' Handelsondernemig BV v. Stichting Bedrijfspensioenfonds voor de Handel in Bouwmaterialen* [1999] ECR I-6025.

Case C-67/96, *Albany International BV* v. *Stichting Bedrijfspensioenfonds Textielindustrie* [1999] ECR I-5751, [2000] 4 CMLR 446

Court of Justice

46. By its second question, which it is appropriate to consider first, the national court seeks essentially to ascertain whether Article [3(1)(g)] of the Treaty, Article 5 of the EC Treaty (now Article 10 EC) and Article [81] of the Treaty prohibit a decision by the public authorities to make affiliation to a sectoral pension fund compulsory at the request of organisations representing employers and workers in a given sector.

47. Albany contends that the request by management and labour to make affiliation to a sectoral pension fund compulsory constitutes an agreement between the undertakings operating in the sector concerned, contrary to Article [81(1)] of the Treaty . . .

52. It is necessary to consider first whether a decision taken by the organisations representing employers and workers in a given sector, in the context of a collective agreement, to set up in that sector a single pension fund responsible for managing a supplementary pension scheme and to request the public authorities to make affiliation to that fund compulsory for all workers in that sector is contrary to Article [81] of the Treaty.

53. It must be noted, first, that Article [81(1)] of the Treaty prohibits all agreements between undertakings, decisions by associations of undertakings and concerted practices which may affect trade between Member States and which have as their object or effect the prevention, restriction or distortion of competition within the common market. The importance of that rule prompted the authors of the Treaty to provide expressly in Article [81(2)] of the Treaty that any agreements or decisions prohibited pursuant to that article are to be automatically void.

54. Next, it is important to bear in mind that, under Article 3(g) and (i) of the EC Treaty (now, after amendment, Article 3(1)(g) and (j) EC), the activities of the Community are to include not only a 'system ensuring that competition in the internal market is not distorted' but also 'a policy in the social sphere'. Article 2 of the EC Treaty (now, after amendment, Article 2 EC) provides that a particular task of the Community is 'to promote throughout the Community a harmonious and balanced development of economic activities' and 'a high level of employment and of social protection'.

55. In that connection, Article 118 of the EC Treaty (Articles 117 to 120 of the EC Treaty have been replaced by Articles 136 EC to 143 EC) provides that the Commission is to promote close co-operation between Member States in the social field, particularly in matters relating to the right of association and collective bargaining between employers and workers.

56. Article 118b of the EC Treaty (Articles 117 to 120 of the EC Treaty having been replaced by Articles 136 EC to 143 EC) adds that the Commission is to endeavour to develop the dialogue between management and labour at European level which could, if the two sides consider it desirable, lead to relations based on agreement.

57. Moreover, Article 1 of the Agreement on social policy (OJ 1992 C 191, p. 91) states that the objectives to be pursued by the Community and the Member States include improved living and working conditions, proper social protection, dialogue between management and labour, the development of human resources with a view to lasting high employment and the combating of exclusion.

58. Under Article 4(1) and (2) of the Agreement, the dialogue between management and labour at Community level may lead, if they so desire, to contractual relations, including agreements, which will be implemented either in accordance with the procedures and practices

specific to management and labour of the Member States, or, at the joint request of the signatory parties, by a Council decision on a proposal from the Commission.

59. It is beyond question that certain restrictions of competition are inherent in collective agreements between organisations representing employers and workers. However, the social policy objectives pursued by such agreements would be seriously undermined if management and labour were subject to Article [81(1)] of the Treaty when seeking jointly to adopt measures to improve conditions of work and employment.

60. It therefore follows from an interpretation of the provisions of the Treaty as a whole which is both effective and consistent that agreements concluded in the context of collective negotiations between management and labour in pursuit of such objectives must, by virtue of their nature and purpose, be regarded as falling outside the scope of Article [81(1)] of the Treaty.

61. The next question is therefore whether the nature and purpose of the agreement at issue in the main proceedings justify its exclusion from the scope of Article [81(1)] of the Treaty.

62. First, like the category of agreements referred to above which derive from social dialogue, the agreement at issue in the main proceedings was concluded in the form of a collective agreement and is the outcome of collective negotiations between organisations representing employers and workers.

63. Second, as far as its purpose is concerned, that agreement establishes, in a given sector, a supplementary pension scheme managed by a pension fund to which affiliation may be made compulsory. Such a scheme seeks generally to guarantee a certain level of pension for all workers in that sector and therefore contributes directly to improving one of their working conditions, namely their remuneration.

64. Consequently, the agreement at issue in the main proceedings does not, by reason of its nature and purpose, fall within the scope of Article [81(1)] of the Treaty.

d. Complex Arrangements

An agreement can consist of a whole complex of arrangements spread over a period of time. This was the case in *Polypropylene*,[175] a case concerning a long lasting cartel in the petrochemical industry. Fifteen firms were held by the Commission to have infringed the competition rules by participating in a framework agreement to fix prices and sales volumes. The Commission considered that the cartel, which was based on a common and detailed plan, constituted a single continuing agreement for the purpose of Article 81(1). Some firms claimed they were not liable as they had not participated in all aspects of the arrangements. The CFI held that the Commission was justified in treating the entire course of the collusion as one single agreement. For there to be an 'agreement' for the purposes of Article 81(1) it was sufficient for the undertakings to have 'expressed their joint intention to conduct themselves on the market in a specific way'.[176] In this case the undertakings had, throughout the whole course of the arrangements, pursued the single economic aim of distorting the polypropylene market.

[175] *Polypropylene*, [1986] OJ L230/1, [1988] 4 CMLR 84; on appeal Cases T-1/89, *Rhône-Poulenc v. Commission* [1991] ECR II-867; T-2/89, *Petrofina SA v. Commission* [1991] ECR II-1087; T-3/89 *Atochem v. Commission* [1991] ECR II-1177; T-6/89, *Enichem Anic SpA v. Commission* [1991] ECR II-1623; T-7/89, *SA Hercules NV v. Commission* [1991] ECR II-1711, [1992] 4 CMLR 84, etc. The appeals by the companies to the ECJ were broadly dismissed: see Case C-51/92 P, *Hercules v. Commission* [1999] ECR I-4235, [1999] 5 CMLR 976; Case C-199/92 P, *Hüls v. Commission* [1999] ECR I-4287, [1999] 5 CMLR 1016, *ICI v. Commission* [1999] ECR I-4399, [1999] 5 CMLR 1110, etc., although the appeal by the Commission against the partial annulment of its Decision against Enichem was mainly successful, Case C-49/92 P *Commission v. Anic* [1999] ECR I-4125, [2001] 4 CMLR 17.

[176] *Ibid*. See especially Case T-1/89, *Rhone-Poulenc v. Commission* [1991] ECR II-867, para. 120, relying on Case 41/69, *ACF Chemiefarma NV v. Commission* [1970] ECR 661, [1970] CMLR 43, para. 112.

Similarly, in *PVC*[177] a plan setting out a framework for regular meetings to operate a cartel fixing prices and imposing restrictions on sales in the PVC market was uncovered. In its decision the Commission held that the undertakings had been party to collusive schemes, arrangements, and measures worked out within a framework of regular meetings which amounted to an agreement. Sufficient consensus had been reached on a plan which limited, or was likely to limit, the operators' commercial freedom on the market. It was not necessary that a legally binding agreement be shown to exist.

e. Vertical Agreements and Unilateral Conduct

It is clear that the word 'agreement' catches terms and conditions even if imposed by one party on another. If the terms are accepted the fact that one of the parties was unwilling to accept them does not prevent the agreement from being formed (although fines may be reserved for the principle beneficiaries of the activity involved[178]). In *BMW*[179] an agreement was found to have been concluded which incorporated export bans imposed on reluctant BMW dealers. A further related question is the extent to which the term agreement can encompass what, at first sight at least, appears to be a purely unilateral policy pursued by one of the parties to an agreement. The question of when behaviour is truly unilateral (where the aims can be achieved without participation of another) and when unilateral behaviour is merely *apparent* (receiving explicit or tacit acquiescence by another) is an important and difficult one which has provoked considerable litigation.[180] The former, even if restrictive of competition or hindering parallel imports, falls outside the scope of the competition rules unless conducted by a dominant firm.[181]

---

[177] [1994] OJ L239/3, upheld by the CFI on appeal in Cases T-305–7, 313–16, 318, 325, 328–9, and 335/94, *Limburgse Vinyl Maatschappij NV and Others v. Commission* [1999] ECR II-931, [1999] 5 CMLR 303 (*PVC Cartel II*). The 1994 decision replaced the original 1990 one [1989] OJ L74/1, [1990] 4 CMLR 345, annulled on appeal by the ECJ on procedural grounds: Case C-137/92 P, *Commission v. BASF and others* [1994] ECR I-2555 setting aside the judgment of the CFI in Cases T-79/89 etc., *BASF and Others v. Commission* [1992] ECR II-315, [1992] 4 CMLR 357 which had declared the decision non-existent. For this aspect of the case, see *infra* Chap. 14.

[178] The Commission may, therefore, decline to impose a fine on a party that has acted unwillingly, against its own economic interest, or under duress, see, e.g., *Volkswagen*, [1998] OJ L124/60, [1998] 5 CMLR 33, on appeal Case T-62/98, *Volkswagen AG v. Commission* [2000] ECR II-2707, [2000] 5 CMLR 853, the appeal to the ECJ was dismissed, Case C-338/00 P, *Volkswagen AG v. Commission* [2003] ECR I-9189, [2004] 4 CMLR 7. The Commission clearly recognizes that in some instances a smaller undertaking may be oppressed in a bargain concluded with a larger and more powerful undertaking and may have no choice other than to accept the terms offered and is fully aware of the pressure that producers or suppliers, for instance, may apply over their dealers/distributors. For example, Commission Regulation No. 1475/95 on the application of Article 85(3) [now Article 81(3)] to motor vehicle distribution and servicing agreements [1995] OJ L145/25 (which has now been replaced by Commission Regulation 1400/02) was intended amongst other things to take 'account of the need for a balance between the interests of the various parties involved' and to give dealers, the great majority of which are SMEs, greater commercial independence *vis-à-vis* manufacturers: see Commission communication of 23 February 1994 on the European automobile industry. The new motor vehicles block exemption, Regulation 1400/02 [2002] OJ L203/30, is also designed to ensure that car dealers retain independence *vis-à-vis* car manufacturers, see, e.g., Report on the evaluation of Regulation (EC) No. 1475/95 on the application of Article 85(3) [now Article 81(3)] of the Treaty to certain categories of motor vehicle distribution and servicing agreements, COM(2000)743, paras. 250–71. In some cases it could be the supplier that lacks bargaining power, for example, where an individual inventor wishes to license use of his invention to a large company, see *infra* Chap. 10. See also *infra* Chap. 14 for a discussion of the Commission's fining policy.

[179] Case 32/78, *BMW v. Commission* [1979] ECR 2435, [1980] 1 CMLR 370.

[180] Similarly, in the US, because resale price maintenance was, between 1911–2007, prohibited per se (without proof of anticompetitive harm and whatever the justification raised by the defendants, see *infra* Chap. 4) a frequently litigated question was whether or not a vertical price restraint formed was part of an agreement.

[181] Article 81 applies only to cases where there is an agreement or other concertation between two or more undertakings. Although Article 82 may apply to unilateral anti-competitive acts of an undertaking it does so *only* where the undertaking is dominant. The Treaty thus envisages that a non-dominant firm may act unilaterally, even if it thereby restricts competition or hinders parallel imports, without infringing either Article 81

Take, for example, a vertical agreement between a supplier and a dealer. Such agreements would now be most unlikely to incorporate provisions imposing resale price maintenance or incorporating an export ban as these constitute clear violations of Article 81(1).[182] What would be the position, therefore, if on its face an agreement appears to comply with Article 81 but the supplier subsequently unilaterally announces that it will not deal with dealers that do not adhere to minimum recommended prices or who sell outside of their allotted territory or it is understood that if dealers do not adhere to minimum recommended prices and/or if they sell outside their allotted territory, they will not be supplied. Can an agreement to adhere to minimum resale prices or an export ban between the supplier and dealers be established and/or can a dealer that continues to accept supply be said to have 'tacitly' acquiesced in the supplier's policy and to have agreed to adhere to the anti-competitive terms? Does it make any difference whether or not the dealers do in fact adhere to the terms or whether they price cut or make sales outside of their territory and/or whether the policy manifests itself before or after the agreement was concluded?

The Commission takes a broad view of agreement and has frequently been prepared to characterize what appears to be unilateral behaviour as behaviour attributable to an underlying agreement or concerted practice between the parties.[183] It has been prepared to infer the existence of an agreement, whether or not the provisions found to be an integral part of the agreement operate to the advantage of the other party to the contract. In *Bayer AG v. Commission*,[184] the court has made it clear that such a finding will not be upheld in the absence of evidence of a concurrence of wills. An early case is *AEG*.

Case 107/82, *AEG-Telefunken* v. *Commission* [1983] ECR 3151, [1984] 3 CMLR 325

AEG-Telefunken (a developer and manufacturer of consumer electronic products) notified its selective distribution system to the Commission. The system provided that it would supply its products to all distributors/resellers that satisfied certain objective criteria (e.g., on the suitability of its staff and trading premises).[185] In this case, the Commission indicated to AEG that the system did not infringe Article 81(1). Subsequently, however, the Commission received numerous complaints alleging that AEG was not operating the scheme in the manner notified. AEG had refused to

or Article 82. See also the discussion of Case C-73/95 P, *Viho Europe BV v. Commission* [1996] ECR I-5457, [1997] 4 CMLR 419, *supra* 141–3.

[182] Such agreements have as their object the restriction of competition, see *infra* Chap. 4. However, it will also have to be established that the agreement appreciably affects trade between Member States and competition (see *infra* 182–199).

[183] In the US, the Supreme Court accepted that a supplier is free to chose who to deal with and that a supplier who independently announces a pricing policy and refuses to do business with distributors who depart from it acts unilaterally, *United States v. Colgate & Co* 250 US 300, 307, 39 S.Ct 465 (1919). However, if a supplier goes further than this and takes affirmative active to achieve uniform adherence to the policy, joint conduct may be found, see *United States v. Parke Davis & Co* 362 US 29, 40 (1962). In such circumstances the distributor's acquiescence is not a matter of individual free choice. The effect of this latter case has, however, been weakened by subsequent cases. For a discussion of this issue see, e.g., H. Hovenkamp, *Federal Antitrust Policy: The Law of Competition and Its Practice* (3rd edn., Thomson/West, 2005), 464–71. The issue may assume less importance now the Supreme Court has held that resale price maintenance should be analysed under the rule of reason, see *Leegin Creative Leather Products Inc v. PSKS Inc DBA Kay's Kloset . . . Kay's Shoes*, 26 June 2007. See *infra* Chaps. 4 and 9.

[184] Case T-41/96, [2000] ECR II-3383, [2001] 4 CMLR 126, and Case C-2 and 3101 P, [2004] ECR I-23, [2004] 4 CMLR 653, *infra* 160.

[185] Selective distribution systems will be discussed *infra* Chap. 9.

supply certain resellers which satisfied the stipulated objective criteria, but which would not adhere to a policy of charging minimum prices. Had the agreement contained a clause imposing resale price maintenance the agreement would have fallen within Article 81(1) and would almost certainly have failed to meet the Article 81(3) criteria.[186] AEG argued that the acts complained of were not part of its agreement with resellers, but were decisions that it had taken unilaterally. Article 81(1) did not apply, since it caught only agreements *between* undertakings. Both the Commission and the Court rejected this argument.

Court of Justice

31. AEG contends that the acts complained of in the contested decision, namely the failure to admit certain traders and steps taken to exert an influence on prices, are unilateral acts and do not therefore, as such, fall within Article [81(1)], which relates only to agreements between undertakings, decisions by associations of undertakings and concerted practices.

32. In order properly to appreciate that argument it is appropriate to consider the legal significance of selective distribution systems.

33. It is common ground that agreements constituting a selective system necessarily affect competition in the common market. However, it has always been recognized in the case-law of the Court that there are legitimate requirements, such as the maintenance of a specialist trade capable of providing specific services as regards high-quality and high-technology products, which may justify a reduction of price competition in favour of competition relating to factors other than price. Systems of selective distribution, in so far as they aim at the attainment of a legitimate goal capable of improving competition in relation to factors other than price, therefore constitute an element of competition which is in conformity with Article [81(1)].

34. The limitations inherent in a selective distribution system are however acceptable only on condition that their aim is in fact an improvement in competition in the sense above mentioned. Otherwise they would have no justification inasmuch as their sole effect would be to reduce price competition.

35. So as to guarantee that selective distribution systems may be based on that aim alone and cannot be set up and used with a view to the attainment of objectives which are not in conformity with Community law, the Court specified in its judgment of 25 October 1977 (*Metro v Commission*, [1977] ECR 1875) that such systems are permissible, provided that resellers are chosen on the basis of objective criteria of a qualitative nature relating to the technical qualifications of the reseller and his staff and the suitability of his trading premises and that such conditions are laid down uniformly for all potential resellers and are not applied in a discriminatory fashion.

36. It follows that the operation of a selective distribution system based on criteria other than those mentioned above constitutes an infringement of Article [81(1)]. The position is the same where a system which is in principle in conformity with Community law is applied in practice in a manner incompatible therewith.

37. Such a practice must be considered unlawful where the manufacturer, with a view to maintaining a high level of prices or to excluding certain modern channels of distribution, refuses to approve distributors who satisfy the qualitative criteria of the system.

38. Such an attitude on the part of the manufacturer does not constitute, on the part of the undertaking, unilateral conduct which, as AEG claims, would be exempt from the prohibition contained in Article [81(1)] of the Treaty. On the contrary, it forms part of the contractual relations between the undertaking and resellers. Indeed, in the case of the admission of a distributor,

---

[186] See *infra* Chap. 4.

approval is based on the acceptance, tacit or express, by the contracting parties of the policy pursued by AEG which requires *inter alia* the exclusion from the network of all distributors who are qualified for admission but are not prepared to adhere to that policy.

39. The view must therefore be taken that even refusals of approval are acts performed in the context of the contractual relations with authorized distributors inasmuch as their purpose is to guarantee observance of the agreements in restraint of competition which form the basis of contracts between manufacturers and approved distributors. Refusals to approve distributors who satisfy the qualitative criteria mentioned above therefore supply proof of an unlawful application of the system if their number is sufficient to preclude the possibility that they are isolated cases not forming part of systematic conduct.

The Court thus found in this case that the systematic refusal by AEG to supply resellers, or to admit resellers to the network, which did not adhere to the pricing policy arose out of the agreement between AEG and its resellers. The resellers' admission to the network was dependent upon their acceptance, express or tacit, of AEG's policy.

A similar approach has been adopted in other cases, some involving export bans. In *Ford*,[187] the Commission refused an individual exemption to a selective distribution system for the distribution and sale of Ford products in Germany. Ford had stopped supplying right-hand drive cars to its German dealers in order to prevent those distributors from exporting the cars into the UK (where its car prices were higher). The Commission considered that Ford's act was an integral part of the agreements with its German dealers. This act was taken into account when determining whether or not Article 81(1) was infringed and whether the agreement should benefit from Article 81(3). The ECJ upheld the finding that the decision on the part of Ford formed part of the contractual relations between the undertakings and its dealers. Admission to the Ford AG dealer network implied acceptance by the contracting parties of the policy pursued by Ford with regard to the models delivered to the German market.

In *Sandoz*[188] the ECJ affirmed the Commission's view that Sandoz's policy of sending invoices to customers with the words 'export prohibited' upon it did not constitute unilateral conduct, but, on the contrary formed part of the general framework of commercial relations which the undertaking maintained with its customers. The Court stressed the uniform and systematic repetition of this practice noting that customers 'were sent the same standard invoice after each individual order... The repeated orders of the products and the successive payments without protest by the customer of the prices indicated on the invoice bearing the words "export prohibited", constituted a tacit acquiescence on the part of the latter in the clauses stipulated in the invoice'.[189]

In all of these cases the ECJ accepted that apparently unilateral conduct could be read into an agreement even though, in the export ban cases at least, it clearly did not operate to the dealer's advantage.[190] Although the Commission may look favourably on the dealer, when deciding

---

[187] Cases 228 and 229/82, *Ford Werke AG and Ford of Europe Inc v. Commission* [1984] ECR 1129, [1984] 1 CMLR 649. See also Case C-279/87, *Tipp-Ex v. Commission* [1990] ECR I-261.

[188] Case 277/87, *Sandoz Prodotti Farmaceutici SpA v. Commission* [1990] ECR I-45.

[189] *Ibid.*, paras. 7–12.

[190] In contrast it is arguable that the resale price maintenance in *AEG* operated to the advantage of the AEG dealers, which as a result did not face price competition from other retailers of the products. In some cases, however, a dealer may prefer to set its own prices and to cut prices in order to boost sales. If the distributors and the producer have met illicitly to discuss the fixing of prices or other prohibited conduct a concerted practice between the producer and distributors may be found: see the discussion of *Pioneer* [1980] OJ L60/1, [1980] 1 CMLR 457 *infra* 179.

whether to impose fines on a party to a contract which has been persuaded to act against its own economic interests,[191] the finding that the 'unilateral conduct' forms part of the agreement clearly characterizes the distributor as a party to the contract that has committed a breach of Article 81(1). That party could then become liable for damages to anyone which can prove loss suffered in consequence of the infringement.[192] Caution needs to be exercised therefore to ensure that an agreement is not found where none really exists.[193] If such caution is not exercised, the jurisdiction of the competition law is also enlarged since the Treaty does not prohibit unilateral conduct, however anti-competitive, engaged in by non-dominant undertakings.

The question of whether the Commission had been correct to characterize unilateral acts as an integral part of an agreement was raised again before the courts in *Bayer AG v. Commission*[194] and *Volkswagen v. Commission*.[195] In both of these cases the CFI annulled the Commission's decisions[196] and in both the CFI's judgments were upheld by the ECJ.[197]

In *Bayer/ADALAT*[198] the Commission had imposed a fine of €3 million on Bayer AG for taking action to prevent parallel imports in the pharmaceutical market. As parallel imports into the UK had apparently led to the sale of ADALAT by Bayer's UK subsidiary falling by almost a half, it acted, by reducing volumes of the drug supplied, to prevent its distributors in France and Spain from exporting types of the drug ADALAT into the UK. The Commission found that the export ban was an integral element in the continuous commercial relations between Bayer and its wholesalers. The wholesalers were aware of the purposes of Bayer and regularly placed and renewed orders for the product and aligned their conduct to the ban.

On appeal Bayer alleged that its conduct was *unilaterally* planned and that it had not imposed an export ban. In this case the CFI considered that the Commission had pushed the concept of an agreement too far, misjudging the concept of an agreement when it decided that the wholesalers' continuation of commercial relations with Bayer amounted to their acquiescence in its restrictive supply policy. In fact, their actual conduct was contrary to that policy. The CFI[199] thus annulled the Commission's decision, holding that a concurrence of wills between Bayer and its wholesalers,

[191] See *supra* n. 178.

[192] See *infra* Chap. 15.

[193] See, e.g., H. H. Lidgard, 'Unilateral Refusal to Supply: An Agreement in Disguise?' [1997] *ECLR* 354.

[194] Case T-41/96, *Bayer AG v. Commission* [2000] ECR II-3383, [2001] 4 CMLR 126, *aff'd* Cases C-2 & 3/01 P, [2004] ECR I-23, [2004] 4 CMLR 653.

[195] Case T-208/01, [2003] ECR II-5141, [2004] 4 CMLR 14, *aff'd* Case C-74/04P, [2006] ECR I-6585.

[196] See also, Case T-368/00, *General Motors Nederland BV and Opel Nederland BV v. Commission* [2003] ECR II-4491, *aff'd* Case C-551/03 P *General Motors BV v. Commission* [2006] ECR I-3173, *infra* n. 199 and T-67/01, *JCB Service v. Commission* [2004] ECR II-49, [2004] 4 CMLR 24, *aff'd*, Case C-167/04 *JCB Service v* Commission [2006] ECR I-8935, *infra* n. 209.

[197] Cases C-2 & 3/01 P, [2004] ECR I-23, [2004] 4 CMLR 653 and Case C-74/04P, [2006] ECR I-6585.

[198] [1996] OJ L201/1, [1996] 5 CMLR 416.

[199] Case T-41/96, [2000] ECR II-3383, [2001] 4 CMLR 126 *aff'd* Cases C-2 & 3/01 P, 6 [2004] ECR I-23, [2004] 4 CMLR 65. See also Case T-368/00, *General Motors Nederland BV and Opel Nederland BV v. Commission* [2003] ECR II-4491, *aff'd* Case C-551/03 P *General Motors BV v. Commission* [2006] ECR I-3173, where the Court recalled 'in the absence of agreements between undertakings, a unilateral act by one undertaking without the express or tacit participation of another does not fall within Article 81(1)', para. 58. Although the CFI essentially upheld the Commission's decision finding an infringement of Article 81(1) the CFI did not find that Opel Nederland had implemented a policy of restricting supply contrary to Article 81.The Commission had found that Opel Nederland had informed dealers identified as exporters that delivery volumes would be limited and that the decision was thus implemented. The Court, however, did not find sufficiently precise or coherent proof in the contested decision that the measure in question was communicated to the dealers or that the measure had entered into the field of contractual relations, paras. 78–89. As a result of this the amount of the fine imposed was reduced.

designed to prevent or limit exports of Adalat had not been established. A distinction had to be drawn between cases in which a genuinely unilateral measure had been adopted (without express or implied participation of another) and those in which the unilateral character of the measure was merely apparent, receiving at least the tacit acquiescence of the dealers.[200] It also held that Bayer could not rely on case-law precedents, in which a concurrence of wills had been found, to call into question its conclusion that neither agreement nor acquiescence in Bayer's policy had been established. In distinguishing *AEG* and *Ford* the CFI stressed that the practices of the manufacturers in those cases, refusing to approve distributors who satisfied the qualitative criteria, were not unilateral but part of the contractual relations between the manufacturers and resellers since *admission* to the selective distribution networks[201] was based on the acceptance, tacit or express, by the contracting parties of the policy pursued by supplier.[202]

Case T-41/96, *Bayer AG* v. *Commission* [2000] ECR II-3383, [2001] 4 CMLR 126

Court of First Instance

B. The concept of an agreement within the meaning of Article [81(1)] of the Treaty

66. The case-law shows that, where a decision on the part of a manufacturer constitutes unilateral conduct of the undertaking, that decision escapes the prohibition in Article [81(1)] of the Treaty (Case 107/82 *AEG* v. *Commission* [1983] ECR 3151, paragraph 38; Joined Cases 25/84 and 26/84 *Ford and Ford Europe* v. *Commission* [1985] ECR 2725, paragraph 21; Case T-43/92 *Dunlop Slazenger* v. *Commission* [1994] ECR II-441, paragraph 56).

67. It is also clear from the case-law in that in order for there to be an agreement within the meaning of Article [81(1)] of the Treaty it is sufficient that the undertakings in question should have expressed their joint intention to conduct themselves on the market in a specific way (Case 41/69 *ACF Chemiefarma* v. *Commission* [1970] ECR 661, paragraph 112; Joined Cases 209/78 to 215/78 and 218/78 *Van Landewyck and Others* v. *Commission* [1980] ECR 3125, paragraph 86; Case T-7/89 *Hercules Chemicals* v. *Commission* [1991] ECR II-1711, paragraph 256).

68. As regards the form in which that common intention is expressed, it is sufficient for a stipulation to be the expression of the parties' intention to behave on the market in accordance with its terms (see, in particular, *ACF Chemiefarma*, paragraph 112, and *Van Landewyck*, paragraph 86), without its having to constitute a valid and binding contract under national law (*Sandoz*, paragraph 13).

69. It follows that the concept of an agreement within the meaning of Article [81(1)] of the Treaty, as interpreted by the case-law, centres around the existence of a concurrence of wills between at least two parties, the form in which it is manifested being unimportant so long as it constitutes the faithful expression of the parties' intention.

70. In certain circumstances, measures adopted or imposed in an apparently unilateral manner by a manufacturer in the context of his continuing relations with his distributors have been

---

[200] Case T-41/96, [2000] ECR II-3383, [2001] 4 CMLR 126, paras. 66–71, *aff'd* Cases C-2 and 3/01 P, [2004] ECR I-23, [2004] 4 CMLR 653.

[201] A selective distribution system is one where the supplier limits the number or, more usually, the type of outlet that sells its products. They are discussed in greater detail, *infra* Chap. 9.

[202] Case 107/82, *AEG-Telefunken AG* v. *Commission* [1983] ECR 3151, [1984] 3 CMLR 325, para. 38.

regarded as constituting an agreement within the meaning of Article [81(1)] of the Treaty (Joined Cases 32/78, 36/78 to 82/78 *BMW Belgium and Others* v. *Commission* [1979] ECR 2435, paragraphs 28 to 30; *AEG*, paragraph 38; *Ford and Ford Europe*, paragraph 21; Case 75/84 *Metro* v. *Commission* ('*Metro II* [1986] ECR 3021, paragraphs 72 and 73; *Sandoz*, paragraphs 7 to 12; Case C-70/93 *BMW* v. *ALD* [1995] ECR I-3439, paragraphs 16 and 17).

71. That case-law shows that a distinction should be drawn between cases in which an undertaking has adopted a genuinely unilateral measure, and thus without the express or implied participation of another undertaking, and those in which the unilateral character of the measure is merely apparent. Whilst the former do not fall within Article [81(1)] of the Treaty, the latter must be regarded as revealing an agreement between undertakings and may therefore fall within the scope of that article. That is the case, in particular, with practices and measures in restraint of competition which, though apparently adopted unilaterally by the manufacturer in the context of its contractual relations with its dealers, nevertheless receive at least the tacit acquiescence of those dealers.

72. It is also clear from that case-law that the Commission cannot hold that apparently unilateral conduct on the part of a manufacturer, adopted in the context of the contractual relations which he maintains with his dealers, in reality forms the basis of an agreement between undertakings within the meaning of Article [81(1)] of the Treaty if it does not establish the existence of an acquiescence by the other partners, express or implied, in the attitude adopted by the manufacturer (*BMW Belgium*, paragraphs 28 to 30; *AEG*, paragraph 38; *Ford and Ford Europe*, paragraph 21; *Metro II*, paragraphs 72 and 73; *Sandoz*, paragraphs 7 to 12; *BMW* v. *ALD*, paragraphs 16 and 17).

The CFI held that the Commission had *not* shown that Bayer had sought to obtain agreement or acquiescence from its wholesalers to adhere to its policy or that the wholesalers had acquiesced explicitly or implicitly, in the policy.[203]

Case T-41/96, *Bayer AG* v. *Commission* [2000] ECR II-3383, [2001] 4 CMLR 126

The Court of First Instance

151. Examination of the attitude and actual conduct of the wholesalers shows that the Commission has no foundation for claiming that they aligned themselves on the applicant's policy designed to reduce parallel imports.

152. The argument based on the fact that the wholesalers concerned had reduced their orders to a given level in order to give Bayer the impression that they were complying with its declared intention thereby to cover only the needs of their traditional market, and that they acted in that way in order to avoid penalties, must be rejected, because the Commission has failed to prove that the applicant demanded or negotiated the adoption of any particular line of conduct on the part of the wholesalers concerning the destination for export of the packets of Adalat which it had supplied, and that it penalised the exporting wholesalers or threatened to do so.

153. For the same reasons, the Commission cannot claim that the reduction in orders could be understood by Bayer only as a sign that the wholesalers had accepted its requirements, or

[203] *Ibid*, paras. 66–185. In the context of a selective distribution system admission to the network may be based on acceptance by the distributors of the policy pursued by the producers, para. 170.

maintain that it is because they satisfied Bayer's requirements that they had to procure extra quantities destined for export from wholesalers who were not suspect' in Bayer's eyes and whose higher orders were therefore fulfilled without difficulty.

154. Moreover, it is obvious from the recitals of the Decision examined above that the wholesalers continued to try to obtain packets of Adalat for export and persisted in that line of activity, even if, for that purpose, they considered it more productive to use different systems to obtain supplies, namely the system of distributing orders intended for export among the various agencies on the one hand, and that of placing orders indirectly through small wholesalers on the other. In those circumstances, the fact that the wholesalers changed their policy on orders and established various systems for breaking them down or diversifying them, by placing them through indirect means, cannot be construed as evidence of their intention to satisfy Bayer or as a response to any request from Bayer. On the contrary, that fact could be regarded as demonstrating the firm intention on the part of the wholesalers to continue carrying on parallel exports of Adalat.

155. In the absence of evidence of any requirement on the part of the applicant as to the conduct of the wholesalers concerning exports of the packets of Adalat supplied, the fact that they adopted measures to obtain extra quantities can be construed only as a negation of their alleged acquiescence. For the same reasons, the Court must also reject the Commission's argument that, in the circumstances of the case, it is normal that certain wholesalers should have tried to obtain extra supplies by circuitous means since they had to undertake to Bayer not to export and thus to order reduced quantities, not capable of being exported.

156. Nor, finally, has the Commission proved that the wholesalers wished to pursue Bayer's objectives or wished to make Bayer believe that they did. On the contrary, the documents examined above demonstrate that the wholesalers adopted a line of conduct designed to circumvent Bayer's new policy of restricting supplies to the level of traditional orders.

157. The Commission was therefore wrong in holding that the actual conduct of the wholesalers constitutes sufficient proof in law of their acquiescence in the applicant's policy designed to prevent parallel imports.

3. The case-law precedents cited by the Commission

158. The Commission contends that the Decision entirely corresponds to its decision-making practice and to the case-law of the Court of Justice on the concept of an agreement, and maintains that in this case, as in a number of previous cases, there was an export ban inserted into a series of continuous commercial relations between the supplier and its customers, as witnessed by the fact that the wholesalers placed orders, were regularly supplied and received corresponding invoices, and that there was tacit consent on the part of the wholesalers, which the Commission maintains is established by the reduction in orders.

159. However, it cannot effectively rely on the case-law precedents referred to in order to call into question the analysis, which has led the Court to conclude that in this case acquiescence of the wholesalers in Bayer's new policy has not been established and that the Commission has therefore failed to prove the existence of an agreement.

160. The Commission relies first on *Sandoz*, in which it maintains that, as in this case, the distributors on the one hand tacitly consented to the export ban in order to maintain their commercial relations (paragraph 11 of the judgment) and, on the other hand, although they had no interest in abandoning exports, accepted the manufacturer's export ban because they wished to continue obtaining the goods.

161. That case concerned the penalty imposed by the Commission on a subsidiary of a multinational pharmaceutical company, Sandoz, which was guilty of inserting into invoices which it sent to customers (wholesalers, pharmacies and hospitals) the express words 'export

prohibited. Sandoz had not denied the presence of those words in its invoices, but had disputed that there was an agreement within the meaning of Article [81(1)] of the Treaty. The Court of Justice dismissed the action after replying to each of the applicant's arguments. It considered that the sending of invoices with those words did not constitute unilateral conduct, but, on the contrary, formed part of the general framework of commercial relations which the undertaking maintained with its customers. It reached that conclusion after examining the way in which the undertaking proceeded before authorising a new customer to market its products and taking into account the practices repeated and applied uniformly and systematically at each sales operation (paragraph 10 of the judgment). It was at that stage in its reasoning that the Court of Justice dealt with the question of the acquiescence of the commercial partners in the export ban, mentioned in the invoice, in the following terms:

> It should also be noted that the customers of Sandoz PF were sent the same standard invoice after each individual order or, as the case may be, after the delivery of the products. The repeated orders of the products and the successive payments without protest by the customer of the prices indicated on the invoices, bearing the words export prohibited, constituted a tacit acquiescence on the part of the latter in the clauses stipulated in the invoice and the type of commercial relations underlying the business relations between Sandoz PF and its clientele. The approval initially given by Sandoz PF was thus based on the tacit acceptance on the part of the customers of the line of conduct adopted by Sandoz PF towards them.

162. It was only after those findings that the Court of Justice concluded that the Commission was entitled to take the view that 'the whole of the continuous commercial relations, of which the export prohibited clause formed an integral part, established between Sandoz PF and its customers, were governed by a pre-established general agreement applicable to the innumerable individual orders for Sandoz products. Such an agreement is covered by the provisions of Article [81(1)] of the Treaty.

163. Although the two cases resemble each other in that they concern attitudes of pharmaceutical groups designed to prevent parallel imports of medicinal products, the concrete circumstances characterising them are very different. In the first place, unlike the situation in the present case, the manufacturer in Sandoz had expressly introduced into all its invoices a clause restraining competition, which, by appearing repeatedly in documents concerning all transactions, formed an integral part of the contractual relations between Sandoz and its wholesalers. Second, the actual conduct of the wholesalers in relation to the clause, which they complied with de facto and without discussion, demonstrated their tacit acquiescence in that clause and the type of commercial relations underlying it. On the facts of the present case, however, neither of the two principal features of Sandoz is to be found; there is no formal clause prohibiting export and no conduct of non-contention or acquiescence, either in form or in reality.

164. Second, the Commission relies on the judgment in Tipp-Ex v. Commission, cited above, in which the Court of Justice confirmed its decision penalising an agreement designed to prevent exports and in which, unlike the situation in Sandoz, there had not been a written stipulation concerning the export ban. It claims that Tipp-Ex, like the applicant in this case, had also argued before the Court of Justice that this was a unilateral measure that did not fall within the scope of Article [81(1)] of the Treaty, and that, since the supplies from the distributor to the parallel exporter had actually taken place, there was no common interest in parallel exports being terminated.

165. That case concerned an exclusive distribution agreement between Tipp-Ex and its French distributor, DMI, which had complied with the manufacturer's demand that the prices charged to a customer should be raised so far as was necessary to eliminate any economic interest on his part in parallel imports. Moreover, it had been established that the manufacturer carried out subsequent checks so as to give the exclusive distributor an incentive actually to adopt that conduct (recital 58 of Commission Decision 87/406/EEC of 10 July 1987 relating to a proceeding under

Article 85 of the EEC Treaty (OJ 1987 L 222, p. 1). Paragraphs 18 to 21 of the judgment show the reasoning followed by the Court of Justice, which, after finding the existence of a verbal exclusive distribution agreement for France between Tipp-Ex and DMI and recalling the principal facts, wished to examine the reaction of and, therefore, the conduct adopted by the distributor following the penalising conduct adopted by the manufacturer. The Court of Justice then found that the distributor 'reacted by raising by between 10 and 20 per cent the prices charged only to the undertaking ISA France. After the interruption of ISA France's purchases from DMI during the whole of 1980, DMI refused at the beginning of 1981 itself to supply Tipp-Ex products to ISA France. It was only after those findings with regard to the conduct of the manufacturer and the distributor that the Court of Justice arrived at its conclusion as to the existence of an agreement within the meaning of Article [81(1)] of the Treaty: 'it is therefore established that DMI acted upon the request of Tipp-Ex not to sell to customers who resell Tipp-Ex products in other Member States (paragraph 21 of the judgment).

166. In *Tipp-Ex*, therefore, unlike the situation in the present case, there was no doubt as to the fact that the policy of preventing parallel exports was established by the manufacturer with the cooperation of the distributors. As indicated in that judgment, that intention was already manifest in the oral and written contracts existing between the two parties (see paragraphs 19 and 20 concerning the distributor DMI and 22 and 23 concerning the distributor Beiersdorf) and, if there were any remaining doubt, analysis of the behaviour of the distributors, pressed by the manufacturer, showed very clearly their acquiescence in the intentions of Tipp-Ex in restriction of competition. The Commission had proved not only that the distributors had reacted to threats and pressure on the part of the manufacturer, but also the fact that at least one of them had sent the manufacturer proof of its cooperation. Finally, the Commission itself observes in this case that, in *Tipp-Ex*, in order to determine whether an agreement existed, the Court of Justice took the approach of analysing the reaction of the distributors to the conduct of the manufacturer running counter to parallel exports and that it was in assessing that reaction of the distributor that it concluded that there must be an agreement in existence between it and Tipp-Ex designed to prevent parallel exports.

167. It follows that that judgment, like *Sandoz*, merely confirms the case-law to the effect that, although apparently unilateral conduct by a manufacturer may lie at the root of an agreement between undertakings within the meaning of Article [81(1)] of the Treaty, this is on condition that the subsequent conduct of the wholesalers or customers may be interpreted as *de facto* acquiescence. As that condition is not fulfilled in this case, the Commission cannot rely on the alleged similarity between these two cases in support of its argument that acquiescence existed in this case.

168. For the same reasons, neither the Commission nor BAI may validly rely on the assessments carried out by the Court of Justice in *BMW Belgium, AEG* and *Ford and Ford Europe* in support of their argument that acquiescence by the wholesalers exists in this case.

169. In *BMW Belgium*, in order to determine whether there was an agreement within the meaning of Article [81(1)] of the Treaty between BMW and its Belgian dealers, the Court of Justice examined the measures capable of demonstrating the existence of an agreement, in that case circulars sent to BMW dealers, 'according to their tenor and in relation to the legal and factual context in which they [were] set, and concluded that the circulars in question 'indicate[d] an intention to put an end to all exports of new BMW vehicles from Belgium (paragraph 28). It added that 'in sending those circulars to all the Belgian dealers, BMW Belgium played the leading role in the conclusion with those dealers of an agreement designed to halt such exports completely (paragraph 29). Paragraph 30 of that judgment shows that the Court of Justice intended to confirm the existence of acquiescence by the dealers.

170. In *AEG*, in which the respective intentions of the manufacturer and the distributors do not appear clearly and in which the applicant expressly relied on the unilateral nature of its conduct, the Court of Justice considered that, in the context of a selective distribution system, a practice whereby the manufacturer, with a view to maintaining a high level of prices or to excluding certain modern channels of distribution, refused to approve distributors who satisfied the qualitative criteria of the system did 'not constitute, on the part of the undertaking, unilateral conduct which, as AEG claims, would be exempt from the prohibition contained in Article [81(1)] of the Treaty. On the contrary, it forms part of the contractual relations between the undertaking and resellers (paragraph 38). The Court of Justice then sought to determine the existence of acquiescence by the distributors by stating: 'Indeed, in the case of the admission of a distributor, approval is based on the acceptance, tacit or express, by the contracting parties of the policy pursued by AEG which requires *inter alia* the exclusion from the network of all distributors who are qualified for admission but are not prepared to adhere to that policy (paragraph 38). That approach has been confirmed in the other selective-distribution cases decided by the Court of Justice (*Ford and Ford Europe*, paragraph 21; *Metro II*, paragraphs 72 and 73; *BMW* v. *ALD*, paragraphs 16 and 17).

171. It follows that the Commission cannot rely on the case-law precedents which it has cited in order to establish the existence of an agreement in this case.

The CFI thus dismissed the Commission's conclusion that by not interrupting their business relations with Bayer, the wholesalers had agreed to its policy. Rather, proof of an agreement had to be based on a finding (direct or indirect) of a meeting of minds between the operators. The CFI stressed that the Commission was not at liberty to widen the scope of the rules in this way. It was not entitled to prohibit truly unilateral behaviour which did not abuse a dominant position, even if the aim of this conduct was to hinder parallel imports, to restrict competition, and affect trade between Member States. It was not 'open to the Commission to achieve a result, such as the harmonization of prices in the medicinal products markets, by enlarging or straining the scope' of the Treaty rules.[204]

The CFI's judgment was upheld by the ECJ. The ECJ started by stating that its judgment was confined to the question of whether there was an agreement within the meaning of Article 81. 'It should be made clear, therefore, that neither the possible application of other aspects of Article [81], nor Article [82] of the EC Treaty..., nor any other possible definitions of the relevant market are at issue in these proceedings'. The ECJ did not therefore deny that Article 82 proceedings might have been possible, if a position of dominance had been established. Like the CFI, the ECJ stressed that it was not open for the Commission automatically to assume that the expression of a unilateral policy by one of the parties established an agreement. Such a broad approach would confuse Article 81 with Article 82. It also considered that the CFI had been correct to find that the Commission could not rely on the case law precedents to call into question the analysis leading the CFI to conclude that, in this case, acquiescence by the wholesalers in Bayer's policy was not established. Again the Court distinguishes cases such as *AEG* and *Ford* on the basis that admission to the network in those cases was based on adherence to the manufacturer's policy.

---

[204] Case T-41/96, [2000] ECR II-3383, [2001] 4 CMLR 126, para. 179, *aff'd* Cases C-2 and 3/01 P, [2004] ECR I-23, [2004] 4 CMLR 653.

Cases C-2 and 3/01 P, *Bundesverband der Arzneimittel-Importeure EV and Commission* v. *Bayer AG* [2004] ECR I-23 [2004] 4 CMLR 653

Court of Justice

102. For an agreement within the meaning of Article [81(1)] of the Treaty to be capable of being regarded as having been concluded by tacit acceptance, it is necessary that the manifestation of the wish of one of the contracting parties to achieve an anti-competitive goal constitute an invitation to the other party, whether express or implied, to fulfil that goal jointly, and that applies all the more where, as in this case, such an agreement is not at first sight in the interests of the other party, namely the wholesalers.

103. Therefore, the Court of First Instance was right to examine whether Bayer's conduct supported the conclusion that the latter had required of the wholesalers, as a condition of their future contractual relations, that they should comply with its new commercial policy.

. . .

141. ... [I]t is important to note that this case raises the question of the existence of an agreement prohibited by Article [81(1)] of the Treaty. The mere concomitant existence of an agreement which is in itself neutral and a measure restricting competition that has been imposed unilaterally does not amount to an agreement prohibited by that provision. Thus, the mere fact that a measure adopted by a manufacturer, which has the object or effect of restricting competition, falls within the context of continuous business relations between the manufacturer and its wholesalers is not sufficient for a finding that such an agreement exists.

142. The case of *Sandoz* concerned an export ban imposed by a manufacturer in the context of continuous business relations with wholesalers. The Court of Justice held that there was an agreement prohibited by Article [81(1)] of the Treaty. However, as the Court of First Instance points out in paragraphs 161 and 162 of the judgment under appeal, that conclusion was based upon the existence of an export ban imposed by the manufacturer which had been tacitly accepted by the wholesalers. In that regard, at paragraph 11 of the *Sandoz* judgment, the Court of Justice held that [t]he repeated orders of the products and the successive payments without protest by the customer of the prices indicated on the invoices, bearing the words export prohibited, constituted a tacit acquiescence on the part of the latter in the clauses stipulated in the invoice and the type of commercial relations underlying the business relations between Sandoz PF and its clientele. The existence of a prohibited agreement in that case therefore rested not on the simple fact that the wholesalers continued to obtain supplies from a manufacturer which had shown its intention to prevent exports, but on the fact that an export ban had been imposed by the manufacturer and tacitly accepted by the wholesalers. Therefore, the appellants cannot usefully rely on the *Sandoz* judgment in support of their plea that the Court of First Instance erred in law by requiring acquiescence of the wholesalers in the measures imposed by the manufacturer.

143. Nor can the appellants rely on *AEG*, *Ford* and *BMW Belgium*, arguing that business relations in the wholesale trade in pharmaceutical products are comparable to a selective distribution system such as that which was at issue in those cases. As has been stated in paragraph 141 of this judgment, the relevant question is that of the existence of an agreement within the meaning of Article [81(1)] of the Treaty.

144. As has been stated in paragraph 106 of this judgment, in the *AEG* and *Ford* judgments the need to demonstrate the existence of an agreement within the meaning of Article [81(1)] of the Treaty was not at issue. The existence of an agreement capable of infringing that provision having already been established, the question raised was whether the measures adopted by the manufacturer formed part of that agreement and therefore had to be taken into account when

examining the compatibility of that agreement with Article [81(1)]. In that regard, the Court of First Instance rightly pointed out that, in those judgments, the Court of Justice had held that, at the time of a distributor's admission, its authorisation was based on its adherence to the policy pursued by the manufacturer . . .

145. A similar analysis must be drawn from the judgment in *BMW Belgium*, in which the question was whether Article [81(1)] of the [EC] Treaty must be interpreted as [prohibiting] a motor vehicle manufacturer which sells its vehicles through a selective distribution system from agreeing with its authorised dealers that they are not to supply vehicles to independent leasing companies where, without granting an option to purchase, those companies make them available to lessees residing or having their seat outside the contract territory of the authorised dealer in question, or from calling on such dealers to act in such a way (paragraph 14).

In *Volkswagen* v. *Commission*[205] the CFI also annulled a Commission decision. In this case the Commission had found that VW had set the selling price of the VW Passat in Germany.[206] The CFI reiterated the critical distinction between agreements (based on the concurrence of wills) and unilateral measures taken without the participation (explicit, tacit or implied) of the undertakings to which they were addressed.[207] It was not sufficient for the Commission to conclude that unilateral calls by the manufacturer, intended to influence the dealer,[208] provided sufficient evidence of an agreement between them. 'In doing so, the Commission is seeking to impose a new legal approach which not only enlarges the meaning of agreement, but also changes the rules on the burden of proof in its favour'.[209] Further, the CFI held that the Commission was wrong to conclude that acquiescence in the supplier's policy could be inferred simply from the dealer being part of a selective distribution network and that signature of an agreement which complies with competition law implied tacit acceptance of *future* unlawful variations of the agreement.[210] Rather, acquiescence and the existence of an agreement had to be established and the Commission had not done this in this case. In contrast: in *AEG*[211] such acquiescence had been established since admission to the network was on the basis of acceptance of AEG's policy; in *Ford*[212] the dealers had clearly implemented the terms of the circular sent by Ford and which

---

[205] Case T-208/01, [2003] ECR II-5141, [2004] 4 CMLR 14, *aff'd* Case C-74/04 P, [2006] ECR I-6585.

[206] [2001] OJ L 262/14, [2001] 5 CMLR 1309. It imposed a fine of €30.96 million on Volkswagen in respect of the infringement.

[207] Case T-208/01, [2003] ECR II-5141, [2004] 4 CMLR 14, paras. 30–5, *aff'd* Case C-74/04 P [2006] ECR I-6585.

[208] By definition the calls were intended to influence the dealer in the performance of the contract, *Ibid.*, para. 57.

[209] *Ibid.*, para. 19 *aff'd* on appeal Case C-74/04 [2006] ECR I-6585, para. 38. In Case T-67/01, *JCB Service* v. *Commission* [2004] ECR II-49, [2004] 4 CMLR 24 the CFI also annulled a Commission finding that a supplier's policy of drawing up lists of recommended retail prices amounted to resale price maintenance. The CFI considered that these prices scales were not binding and that there was nothing to indicate that JCB's efforts to influence dealers and discourage them from agreeing lower sales prices involved coercion, see especially paras. 121–33. This finding of the CFI was not challenged before the ECJ which broadly upheld the judgment of the CFI, Case C-167/04 *JCB Service* v. Commission [2006] ECR I-8935. In allowing the cross-appeal, however, the ECJ considered that the CFI had been wrong to cut the level of the fine imposed. Fining policy is discussed, *infra* Chap. 14. Note that the agreement in JCB was originally notified to the Commission in June 1973.

[210] The Commission's case amounted to a claim that a dealer who signed a dealership which complies with competition law is deemed to have accepted in advance a later unlawful variation of the contract.

[211] Case 107/82, *AEG-Telefunken AG* v. *Commission* [1983] ECR 3151, [1984] 3 CMLR 325.

[212] Cases 228–229/82, *Ford Werke AG and Ford of Europe Inc* v. *Commission* [1984] ECR 1129, [1984] CMLR 649.

was linked to the dealership agreement; and in *Volkswagen*[213] the Italian dealers had accepted the anti-competitive initiative and refused to sell to foreign customers and the dealership agreement provided for the possibility of limiting deliveries. On appeal, the Commission argued that it was 'settled' law that a call by a manufacturer to authorized dealers did not constitute a unilateral act but an agreement if it formed part of a set of continuous business relations governed by a general agreement drawn up in advance.[214] However, the ECJ[215] upheld the conclusion of the CFI (and the annulment of the Commission's decision), ruling that a call by manufacturer did not relieve the Commission of its obligation to prove that there was a concurrence of wills on the part of the parties to the dealership agreement (established either from the clauses of the dealership agreement or the conduct of the parties, in particular from tacit acquiescence by the dealers in the manufacturer's call).[216] Although the ECJ held that the CFI had erred in the law in making an assumption that contractual clauses complying with the competition rules could not regarded as authorising calls which are contrary to those rules,[217] it concluded that this error had not affected the soundness of the conclusion reached by the CFI.

Both the *Bayer* and *Volkswagen* judgments thus admonish the Commission for too easily finding an agreement where none exists and for so enlarging the scope of its jurisdiction. In the future clear evidence will be necessary to establish that a dealer has agreed or acquiesced, explicitly or tacitly, in any unilateral policy declared by a supplier. It is now apparent that simply continuing to participate in a selective distribution system or accepting supplies under the terms of a distribution agreement will not be sufficient to establish liability. A dealer that signs up to a distribution agreement or selective distribution network in no way binds itself to accept future variations in the way the agreement is operated. In such cases something more will have to be established, such as acceptance of the policy or adherence to the policy, before an agreement can be proved. Where, however, the dealer knows of the supplier's policy at the time it enters contractual relations, it may then be concluded that the contract was dependent upon the dealer accepting that policy.

f. Participation in Meetings

Any regular participant at a meeting at which an anti-competitive agreement is concluded will be taken to have participated in that agreement, unless it can establish that the undertaking did not have any anti-competitive intention when it attended the meeting, and that the other participants were aware of this.[218] It appears, therefore, that the participant tacitly accepts an

---

[213] This was a different Volkswagen case involving export bans, *Volkswagen* [1998] OJ L124/60, [1998] 5 CMLR 33, on appeal Case T-62/98, *Volkswagen AG v. Commission* [2000] ECR II-2707, [2000] 5 CMLR 853, the appeal to the ECJ was dismissed, Case C-338/00 P, *Volkswagen AG v. Commission* [2003] ECR I-9189, [2004] 4 CMLR 7. The case is discussed *infra* Chap. 9.

[214] It had been thought by many commentators that, at least as far as selective distribution systems were concerned, dealers involved in ongoing business relationships would be found to have agreed to whatever sale policies the manufacture had chosen to adopt by the very fact of agreeing to become part of a network, see J. Faull and A. Nikpay (eds.), *The EC Law of Competition* (2nd edn., Oxford University Press, 2007), para. 3.68.

[215] Case C-74/04 P, [2006] ECR I-6585.

[216] Case C-74/04 P, [2006] ECR I-6585, paras. 39–56. In this case the Commission had not attempted to show that the dealers had tacitly acquiesced in the manufacturer's call but had found that the concurrence was part of the dealership agreement.

[217] Rather, clauses had to be examined individually to determine whether the calls at issue were part of the overall commercial relationship between VW and its dealers.

[218] Case T-3/89, *Atochem v. Commission* [1991] ECR II-867, paras. 53–4. See also, e.g., *Steel Beams* (proceedings under Article 65 of the ECSC Treaty), Case T-141/94, *Thyssen Stahl AG v. Commission* [1999] ECR II-347, [1999] 4 CMLR 810, para. 177 *aff'd* Case C-194/99 P, [2003] ECR I-1082 and Case T-142/89 *Böel v. Commission* [1995] ECR II-867.

offer to collude by not publicly distancing itself. Further from the agreement. It is no defence that the participant did not put the initiatives into effect and evidence of prices or other behaviour not reflecting those discussed at the meeting would not be sufficient to prove that it had not participated in the scheme.[219] The ECJ set this position out clearly in *Cement*.[220]

Cases C-204, 205, 211, 213, 217 and 219/00 P, *Aalborg Portland AS v. Commission* [2004] ECR I-123, [2005] 4 CMLR 251

Court of Justice

81. According to settled case-law, it is sufficient for the Commission to show that the undertaking concerned participated in meetings at which anti-competitive agreements were concluded, without manifestly opposing them, to prove to the requisite standard that the undertaking participated in the cartel. Where participation in such meetings has been established, it is for that undertaking to put forward evidence to establish that its participation in those meetings was without any anti-competitive intention by demonstrating that it had indicated to its competitors that it was participating in those meetings in a spirit that was different from theirs (see Case C-199/92 P, *Hüls* v. *Commission* [1999] ECR I-4287, paragraph 155, and Case C-49/92 P, *Commission* v. *Anic* [1999] ECR I-4125, paragraph 96).

82. The reason underlying that principle of law is that, having participated in the meeting without publicly distancing itself from what was discussed, the undertaking has given the other participants to believe that it subscribed to what was decided there and would comply with it.

83. The principles established in the case-law cited at paragraph 81 of this judgment also apply to participation in the implementation of a single agreement. In order to establish that an undertaking has participated in such an agreement, the Commission must show that the undertaking intended to contribute by its own conduct to the common objectives pursued by all the participants and that it was aware of the actual conduct planned or put into effect by other undertakings in pursuit of the same objectives or that it could reasonably have foreseen it and that it was prepared to take the risk (*Commission* v. *Anic*, paragraph 87).

84. In that regard, a party which tacitly approves of an unlawful initiative, without publicly distancing itself from its content or reporting it to the administrative authorities, effectively encourages the continuation of the infringement and compromises its discovery. That complicity constitutes a passive mode of participation in the infringement which is therefore capable of rendering the undertaking liable in the context of a single agreement.

85. Nor is the fact that an undertaking does not act on the outcome of a meeting having an anti-competitive purpose such as to relieve it of responsibility for the fact of its participation in a cartel, unless it has publicly distanced itself from what was agreed in the meeting (see Case C-291/98 P, *Sarrió* v. *Commission* [2000] ECR I-9991, paragraph 50).

86. Neither is the fact that an undertaking has not taken part in all aspects of an anti-competitive scheme or that it played only a minor role in the aspects in which it did participate material to the establishment of the existence of an infringement on its part. Those factors must be taken into consideration only when the gravity of the infringement is assessed and if and when it comes to determining the fine (see, to that effect, *Commission* v. *Anic*, paragraph 90).

---

[219] Case T-3/89, *Atochem* v. *Commission* [1991] ECR II-867, para. 100.

[220] Cases C-204, 205, 211, 213, 217 and 219/00 P, *Aalborg Portland AS* v. *Commission* [2004] I-123, [2005] 4 CMLR 251.

g. Hub and Spoke Agreements

Anti-competitive agreements (or concerted practices) may have both horizontal and vertical elements. For example, collusion between retailers as to the price at which they will sell a particular product could be achieved directly or indirectly, through the intermediary of a supplier. In such a case it could be critical to determine both whether a vertical price fixing agreement exists (between the supplier and the relevant retailers) and/or whether there is in fact an agreement or a concerted practice between the supplier and retailers to fix the retail prices of the product. In the latter scenario, the violation has a horizontal element and becomes a more serious infringement of the competition rules.[221]

h. Agreements Concluded by Employees

An agreement (or concerted practice) can arise from the actions of employees acting within the scope of their employment. EC law holds that the undertaking will be liable even if the employees were not authorized or instructed to act in that way by senior management. This is particularly relevant in situations where employees have entered into secret collusive conspiracies to rig markets. Undertakings should have in place, and should enforce, a compliance programme to prevent breaches of the competition rules.[222] Although EC law does not provide sanctions (disqualification, fines and/or imprisonment) for the individual employees, such sanctions are available in some States.[223]

i. Recommendations by Bodies Constituted under Statutory Powers

Several cases have raised the question of whether there is an 'agreement' where undertakings are represented on a body constituted under statutory powers to make recommendations in respect of a certain industry, etc. The ECJ has held that there is not an agreement even when the trade representatives are in the majority on the committee, provided that the public authorities have not delegated their power of decision and that the matters to be fixed (e.g., tariffs) are fixed with due regard for public-interest criteria.[224]

j. Proving an Agreement

In addition to knowing how the concept of an agreement is defined it is essential to know how it is proved. The discussion above establishes that an agreement may be founded on a 'direct or indirect finding' of the existence of a concurrence of wills. Thus, both direct evidence,[225] which

---

[221] See e.g. discussion of Case 1022/1/1/03 *JJB Sports plc v. Office of Fair Trading* [2004] CAT 17, *aff'd* [2006] EWCA Civ 1318 at n. 273 and accompanying text.

[222] See further *infra* Chap. 14.

[223] In the UK directors may be disqualified where they are responsible for breaches of the competition rules (including Articles 81 and 82) and may be fined or sent to prison if found to have concluded a cartel agreement (see *supra* n. 23 and accompanying text). Further, employees who obstruct the OFT in its investigations may be sent to prison: see Competition Act 1998, ss. 42–4, see *infra* Chap. 14. Criminal sanctions are also available in, e.g., Canada, France, Germany (collusive tendering), Greece, Ireland, and the USA. In the USA a breach of certain of the competition rules (including section 1, Sherman Act 1890) is a felony.

[224] See, e.g., Case C-96/94, *Centro Servizi Spediporto v. Spedizioni Maritima del Golfo srl* [1995] ECR I-2883, [1996] 4 CMLR 613; Case C-38/97, *Autotrasporti Librandi v. Cuttica Spedizioni* [1998] ECR I-5955, [1998] 5 CMLR 966, see Chap. 8.

[225] i.e. smoking gun evidence which does not require inferences to establish the agreement alleged. Written or parol evidence may be used. The Commission has broad investigative powers which may help it uncover direct evidence of an agreement and the Commission's leniency programme is designed to encourage participants to come forward with direct evidence necessary to prove the existence of an agreement, see *infra* Chaps. 11 and 14.

will frequently be lacking in cases involving serious violations of the rules, and indirect evidence from which the agreement may be inferred may be relied upon to establish the concurrence of wills. The line of cases dealing with vertical agreements set out above, establishes that care must be taken when determining whether the requisite will can be found either from the clauses of the agreement in question and/or from the conduct of the parties in question.[226]

(iii) Decisions by Associations of Undertakings

a. Medium for a Cartel

Trade and other associations of course perform a plethora of legitimate functions which promote the competitiveness of the industry as a whole. However, membership of an association, particularly a trade association, may also tempt the members of undertakings meeting within its auspices to collude together and to coordinate their action. Indeed, studies have shown that where players wish to coordinate their action on a market, coordination through a trade association or some other vehicles may be critical when there are a relatively large number of players on the market.

Trade associations can play a particularly important role when [a] cartel involves a large number of firms. Hay and Delley (1974) found that trade associations were involved in more than 80 per cent of the cartels they studied that had more than 15 members, and in 100 per cent of cartels with more than 25 members.[227]

In *Re Belgian Roofing Felt Cartel*,[228] for example, an agreement was discovered between members of Belasco (Société Coopérative des Asphalteurs Belges) which was intended to ensure control of the Belgian roofing market. The parties had agreed, amongst other things, to adopt a common price list and minimum selling prices for roofing felt, to set quotas for sales on the Belgian market, and to advertise jointly their 'Belasco' products. The agreement was implemented by resolutions passed at the general meeting of Belasco. Belasco actively participated in the operations in a number of ways: in particular, it employed an accountant who monitored compliance with quotas at the end of each year so that penalties could be levied on members which had exceeded their quotas. Further, Belasco financed the joint advertising of the 'Belasco' trade mark which fostered users' impression of a homogeneous product. Members were not, therefore, able to compete by differentiating their products.

It may be that the conduct adopted by the members may be characterized as a decision or an agreement or a concerted practice. However, conduct may be prohibited even if technically speaking no agreement or concerted practice has been concluded. The prohibition of decisions as well as agreements and concerted practices may therefore facilitate the proof and prohibition of collusive devices operated through associations. The concept has been interpreted broadly to catch conduct designed to coordinate the conduct of the members contrary to Article 81(1),[229] whether engaged in through resolutions of the association, recommendations, the operation of certification schemes, or through the association's constitution itself.

---

[226] The ECJ stated in Case C-74/04, *Commission v. Volkswagen AG* [2006] ECR I-6585, para. 39 that the will of the parties might result both from the clauses of the agreement in question and from the conduct of the parties. See *supra* n. 216 and accompanying text.

[227] S. Bishop and M. Walker, *The Economics of EC Competition Law: Concepts, Application and Measurement* (2nd edn., Sweet & Maxwell, 2002), para. 5.19.

[228] Case 246/86, *Re Roofing Felt Cartel: BELASCO v. Commission* [1989] ECR 2117, [1991] 4 CMLR 96.

[229] Case 96/82, *IAZ International Belgium NV v. Commission* [1983] ECR 3369, [1984] 3 CMLR 276.

b. Trade Association Recommendations

A recommendation by an association to its members, which has no binding effect, will constitute a decision, if in reality it is intended to determine, or is likely to have the effect of determining, the members' conduct. In *IAZ*,[230] a recommendation made by an association of water-supply undertakings that its members should not connect 'unauthorized' appliances (without a conformity label supplied by another Belgian trade association) to the mains systems was held to be a binding decision capable of restricting competition within the meaning of Article 81(1). The practice discriminated against non-Belgian producers of the appliances. Similarly, in *FENEX*,[231] the Commission held that the recommendation of tariffs by a Dutch association to its member forwarding companies constituted a decision by an association of undertakings within the meaning of Article 81(1). Although the tariffs merely took the form of recommendations, the procedure for drawing up and circulating the tariffs was a habitual activity of the association and was accompanied by circulars drafted in more mandatory terms. The Commission concluded that the circulation of the tariffs had to be interpreted as a faithful reflection of the association's resolve to coordinate the conduct of its members on the relevant market.

c. Medium for Exchange of Information

More subtly, the association may simply collect and disseminate sensitive information and facilitate its exchange between competitors. Were the association to be used, for example, as a vehicle for exchanging information on the prices that the members intended to charge for their products, etc., the parties would inevitably be found to be operating a concerted practice.[232]

d. Certification Schemes

Certification schemes operated by members of an association may, in reality, be designed to exclude non-members from business opportunities or to preclude foreign undertakings from penetrating the domestic market of the association's members.[233] The word 'decision', in addition to catching acts of the association which are binding on its members, may also catch more informal methods of coordinating members' actions. In *Stichting Certificatie Kraanverhuurbedrijf and the Federatie van Nederlandse Krannverhuurbedrijven v. Commission*,[234] the Commission fined both FNK and SCK after an examination of agreements that they had notified.[235] Not only did the rules of FNK (the rules constituted a decision by an association of

---

[230] *Anseau* [1982] OJ L167/39, [1982] 2 CMLR 193, on appeal Case 96/82, *IAZ International Belgium NV v. Commission* [1983] ECR 3369, [1984] 3 CMLR 276.

[231] [1996] OJ L181/28, [1996] 5 CMLR 332.

[232] See Cases 40–8, 50, 54–6, 111, and 113–4/73, *Re the European Sugar Cartel; Cooperatiëve Vereniging 'Suiker Unie' UA v. Commission* [1975] ECR 1663, [1976] 1 CMLR 295. See also, *UK Agricultural Tractor Exchange* [1992] OJ L68/19, upheld on appeal, Case T-34/92, *Fiatagri and Ford New Holland v. Commission* [1994] ECR II-905, and Case T-35/92, *John Deere Ltd v. Commission* [1994] ECR II-957; on appeal to the ECJ Case C-7/95 P, *John Deere Ltd v. Commission* [1998] ECR I-3111, [1998] 5 CMLR 311, *infra* Chap 11.

[233] As in *Anseau* [1982] OJ L167/39, [1982] 2 CMLR 193, on appeal Case 96/82, *IAZ International Belgium NV v. Commission* [1983] ECR 3369, [1984] 3 CMLR 276. See also Case 8/72, *Vereeniging van Cementhandelaren v. Commission* [1972] ECR 977, [1973] CMLR 7.

[234] *Stichting Certificatie Kraanverhuurbedrijf and the Federatie van Nederlandse Krannverhuurbedrijven* [1995] OJ L312/79, [1996] 4 CMLR 565; on appeal Cases T-213/95 and T-18/96, *Stichting Certificatie Kraanverhuurbedrijf and the Federatie van Nederlandse Krannverhuurbedrijven v. Commission* [1997] ECR II-1739, [1998] 4 CMLR 259.

[235] After a preliminary examination of the agreements ([1994] OJ L117/30), the Commission had suspended the parties' immunity from fines that arose on the notification of an agreement to the Commission (Reg. 17 [1959–62] OJ Spec. Ed. 87, Art. 15(6)).

undertakings) providing for the charging of 'reasonable' rates by its members infringe Article 81(1), but SCK's rules on the certification of the crane-hire trade were also caught. The prohibition on the certificate holders from hiring cranes from non-affiliated firms without valid certification plates (and not affiliated to SCK) restricted competition between affiliated firms and substantially restricted access to the market by other firms.

The individual members themselves may be fined where membership coincides with participation in the agreement. Further, where the Commission finds that there has been a 'decision' by an association of undertakings, the association may be fined independently. In *Re Belgian Roofing Felt Cartel*,[236] for example, fines were imposed on both Belasco itself (ECU 15,000) and the individual members of the cartel (between ECU 50,000 and 420,000 each). In fixing those amounts, the Commission took account of the annual turnover of each undertaking concerned (and the turnover for supplies of roofing felt) and, in Belasco's case, its annual expenses.[237]

e. The Trade Association's Constitution

The constitution and rules of a trade association may themselves qualify as a decision (and an agreement) within Article 81(1).[238]

f. Governmental Intervention

The fact that a governmental body has either approved of or even imposed an obligation on an association to adopt a scale of compulsory tariffs for the association's members does not alter any resolution's (or other decision's) status as a decision of an association of undertakings.[239]

(iv) Concerted Practices

a. Description of a Concerted Practice

Article 81(1) is aimed at explicit collusion whatever form it takes, whether a formal agreement between undertakings to coordinate their behaviour and reduce effective competition between them or through more informal arrangements. The term concerted practice[240] is thus designed to provide a safety-net catching looser forms of collusion. It aims to forestall the possibility of undertakings evading the application of Article 81 by colluding in a manner falling short of an agreement. Classic descriptions of a concerted practice were set out by the ECJ in *ICI v. Commission (Dyestuffs)*[241] and *Suiker Unie*.[242] In *Dyestuffs* it held that the purpose of the term was to preclude:

co-ordination between undertakings which, without having reached the stage where an agreement, properly so called, has been concluded, knowingly substitutes practical co-operation between them for the risks of competition.[243]

---

[236] [1986] OJ L232/15, [1991] 4 CMLR 130; on appeal Case 246/86, *Re Roofing Felt Cartel: BELASCO v. Commission* [1989] ECR 2117, [1991] 4 CMLR 96.

[237] Reg. 1/2003 altered the fining system to make it more effective against trade associations, see *infra* Chap. 14.

[238] *National Sulphuric Acid* [1980] OJ L260/24, [1980] 3 CMLR 429.

[239] *AICIA v. CNSD* [1993] OJ L203/27, [1995] 5 CMLR 495, paras. 42–4, but see *infra* 199.

[240] The definition of concerted practice is further explored in Chap. 11.

[241] Cases 48, 49 and 51–7/69, *ICI v. Commission* [1972] ECR 619, [1972] CMLR 557.

[242] Cases 40–8, 50, 54–6, 111, and 113–4/73, *Re the European Sugar Cartel; Cooperatiëve Vereniging 'Suiker Unie' UA v. Commission* [1975] ECR 1663, [1976] 1 CMLR 295.

[243] Cases 48, 49, 51–7/69, *ICI v. Commission* [1972] ECR 619, [1972] CMLR 557, paras. 64 and 65.

In *Suiker Unie* it confirmed that the concept in no way required 'the working out of an actual plan'.[244] Further, that it did not deprive economic operators of a right to adapt themselves intelligently to existing and anticipated conduct of their competitors, but it did

preclude any direct or indirect contact between such operators, the object or effect whereof is either to influence the conduct on the market of an actual or potential competitor or to disclose to such a competitor the course of conduct which they themselves have decided to adopt or contemplate adopting on the market.[245]

Although, therefore, the concept does not require an actual plan it does seem to require *reciprocal* cooperation or contact, through direct or indirect contact, designed to influence the conduct of an actual or potential competitor or to disclose to them the course of conduct that will or may be adopted on the market.

b. The Need for the Concertation to be Implemented on the Market

One important difference between the concept of an agreement and the concept of a concerted practice is that the latter term implies a requirement that the concertation should be practiced or implemented on the market. This matter was raised in the appeals from the Commission's decision in *Polypropylene*[246] where the question arose as to whether or not it mattered whether the parties' conduct was characterized as an agreement or a concerted practice. One of the arguments raised by some of the parties was that although an agreement would be caught by Article 81(1) even if it was not implemented, as intended, on the market, direct or indirect conduct which has not been implemented on a market did not amount to a concerted practice. An agreement, however informal and whether or not successful or acted upon, is a consensual act. In contrast, the word 'practice' in the concept concerted practice implied proof not only of concertation but *also* of the fact that steps have been taken to give effect to the concertation. There would, therefore, be no actual concerted *practice* if the parties only *plotted* to coordinate their behaviour but did not carry out that plot by conduct on the market. The arguments supporting this view and academic writings on this issue are fully reviewed in the Opinion of Advocate General Vesterdorf designated by the President of the CFI.[247] The ECJ accepted that the concept of a concerted practice did require, both concertation between the undertakings *and* 'subsequent conduct on the market, and a relationship of cause and effect between the two'.[248] However, it held that once the Commission had adduced evidence of concertation it was for the undertaking to establish that concertation had not been followed by conduct on the market.

---

[244] Cases 40–8, 50, 54–6, 111, and 113–4/73, *Re the European Sugar Cartel; Cooperatiëve Vereniging 'Suiker Unie' UA v. Commission* [1975] ECR 1663, [1976] 1 CMLR 295, para. 173.

[245] Cases 40–8, 50, 54–6, 111, and 113–4/73, *Re the European Sugar Cartel; Cooperatiëve Vereniging 'Suiker Unie' UA v. Commission* [1975] ECR 1663, [1976] 1 CMLR 295, para. 174.

[246] *Polypropylene* [1986] OJ L230/1, [1988] 4 CMLR 347, appeals substantially dismissed both by the CFI and the ECJ: see, e.g., Case C-51/92 P, *SA Hercules NV v. Commission* [1999] ECR I-4235, [1999] 5 CMLR 976 and Case C-199/92 P, *Hüls AG v. Commission* [1999] ECR I-4287, [1999] 5 CMLR 1016.

[247] See [1991] ECR I-1711, 1923–1946, [1992] 4 CMLR 84, 141–64. The AG was appointed following the order of the ECJ referring this and other cases to the CFI soon after its establishment. It was the view of the AG that failed attempts to concert would not be caught by Article 81(1). The CFI did not specifically address this point, since it took the view that having participated in and having obtained information from meetings with competitors an undertaking would be bound to take it into account, directly or indirectly, when determining its conduct on the market. The Court assumed that information acquired as a result of a concerted practice always influences the market conduct of the participants: see, e.g., Case T-7/89, *SA Hercules NV v. Commission* [1991] ECR II-1711, [1992] 4 CMLR 84, para. 260.

[248] Case C-199/92 P, *Hüls AG v. Commission* [1999] ECR I-4287, [1999] 5 CMLR 1016, para. 161.

Case C-199/92 P, *Hüls AG* v. *Commission (Polypropylene)* [1999] ECR I-4287, [1999] 5 CMLR 1016

Court of Justice

158. The Court of Justice has consistently held that a concerted practice refers to a form of co-ordination between undertakings which, without having been taken to a stage where an agreement properly so-called has been concluded, knowingly substitutes for the risks of competition practical co-operation between . . .

159. The criteria of co-ordination and co-operation must be understood in the light of the concept inherent in the provisions of the Treaty relating to competition, according to which each economic operator must determine independently the policy which he intends to adopt on the market . . .

160. According to that case law, although that requirement of independence does not deprive economic operators of the right to adapt themselves intelligently to the existing and anticipated conduct of their competitors, it does however strictly preclude any direct or indirect contact between such operators, the object or effect whereof is either to influence the conduct on the market of an actual or potential competitor or to disclose to such a competitor the course of conduct which they themselves have decided to adopt or contemplate adopting on the market, where the object or effect of such contact is to create conditions of competition which do not correspond to the normal conditions of the market in question, regard being had to the nature of the products or services offered, the size and number of the undertakings and the volume of the said market . . .

161. It follows, first, that the concept of a concerted practice, as it results from the actual terms of Article [81(1)] E.C., implies, besides undertakings' concerting with each other, subsequent conduct on the market, and a relationship of cause and effect between the two.

162. However, subject to proof to the contrary, which the economic operators concerned must adduce, the presumption must be that the undertakings taking part in the concerted action and remaining active on the market take account of the information exchanged with their competitors for the purposes of determining their conduct on that market. That is all the more true where the undertakings concert together on a regular basis over a long period, as was the case here, according to the findings of the Court of First Instance.

163. Secondly, contrary to Hüls's argument, a concerted practice as defined above is caught by Article [81(1)] E.C., even in the absence of anti-competitive effects on the market.

164. First, it follows from the actual text of that provision that, as in the case of agreements between undertakings and decisions by associations of undertakings, concerted practices are prohibited, regardless of their effect, when they have an anti-competitive object.

165. Next, although the very concept of a concerted practice presupposes conduct by the participating undertakings on the market, it does not necessarily mean that that conduct should produce the specific effect of restricting, preventing or distorting competition.

166. Lastly, that interpretation is not incompatible with the restrictive nature of the prohibition laid down in Article [81(1)] E.C . . . since, far from extending its scope, it corresponds to the literal meaning of the terms used in that provision.

167. Consequently, contrary to Hüls's argument, the Court of First Instance was not in breach of the rules applying to the burden of proof when it considered that, since the Commission had established to the requisite legal standard that Hüls had taken part in polypropylene producers' concerting together for the purpose of restricting competition, it did not have to adduce evidence that their concerting together had manifested itself in conduct on the market or that it had had effects restrictive of competition; on the contrary, it was for Hüls to prove that that did not have any influence whatsoever on its own conduct on the market.

It can be seen from this extract that the Court emphasized that the question whether or not the parties had engaged in a concerted practice was completely distinct from the question whether or not that concertation had restricted competition.[249] It also set out a distinction between cooperation identified as a concerted practice and cooperation identified as an agreement. The former requires not only concertation *but also* subsequent conduct. In practice, however, since there is a presumption that concertation has been followed by conduct this is unlikely to make a material difference. It is hard to envisage circumstances in which an undertaking can establish that its conduct was *not* influenced by information acquired through concerting with others. The most important question appears to be whether or not there was collusion. 'The importance of the concept of a concerted practice does not thus result so much from the distinction between it and an agreement as from the distinction between forms of collusion falling under Article [81(1)] and mere parallel behaviour with no element of concertation'.[250]

The case law is summarized by the Commission in its *Belgian Beer* decision.

Interbrew and Alken-Maes [2003] OJ L200/1

Commission

222. Although it is clear from the actual terms of Article 81(1) of the EC Treaty that the concept of a concerted practice implies, besides undertakings' consulting with each other, subsequent conduct on the market, and a relationship of cause and effect between the two, the presumption must be, subject to proof to the contrary which the economic operators concerned must adduce, that the undertakings taking part in the consultation and remaining active on the market take account of the information exchanged with their competitors for the purposes of determining their conduct on that market. That is all the more true where the undertakings consult together on a regular basis over a long period of time. A concerted practice is caught by Article 81(1) even in the absence of anti-competitive effects on the market.

223. It is not necessary, particularly in the context of a complex infringement over a long period, for the Commission to classify the infringement as consisting exclusively of one or the other form of illegal behaviour. The concept of 'agreement' and 'concerted practice' are variable and may overlap. Realistically, it may even be impossible to make such a distinction, since an infringement may simultaneously have the characteristics of both forms of prohibited behaviour, whereas, taken separately, some of its elements may correctly be regarded as one rather than the other form. It would also be artificial from an analytical point of view to split what is clearly a continuous, collective enterprise with a single objective into several forms of infringement. A cartel may for instance constitute an agreement and a concerted practice at the same time.

224. In the PVC II case the Court of First Instance confirmed that 'the Commission cannot be expected to classify the infringement precisely, for each undertaking and for any given, as in any event both those forms of infringement are covered by Article [81] of the Treaty'.

225. The Court of Justice confirmed in the Anic case that it follows from the specific wording of Article 81(1) of the Treaty than an infringement may result not only from an isolated act but also from a series of acts or from continuous conduct.

---

[249] Where the object of the concerted practice is to restrict competition it is not necessary to show that the conduct has the *effect* of restricting, preventing, or distorting competition, see *infra* Chap. 4.

[250] *Polypropylene* [1986] OJ L230/1, [1988] 4 CMLR 347, para. 87.

226. A complex cartel can thus be regarded as a single continuous infringement for the period of its existence. The agreement may change from time to time, or its mechanisms may be adapted or strengthened to take account of new developments. The validity of this classification is not vitiated by the possibility that one or more elements of a series of acts or of continuous conduct could in themselves constitute a breach of Article 81(1) of the EC Treaty.

227. Although a cartel is a form of collective behaviour, each party to the agreement may play its own specific role. One or more of them may play a leading role. Internal conflicts and rivalries or even deceit may occur, but will not prevent the agreement from forming an agreement/ concerted practice within the meaning of Article 81(1), if the parties pursue a collective and continuous goal.

The following are examples of the type of conduct which might be used to establish that the parties involved have engaged in a 'concerted practice'.

c. Direct or Indirect Contact

If parties (however informally or loosely) agree to let other players know in advance of their anticipated future business moves, this may well amount to a concerted practice. As already seen the ECJ held in *Suiker Unie*,[251] the concept does not require a plan but precludes direct or indirect contact between competitors the object or effect of which is to influence the conduct on the market of an actual or potential competitor or to disclose to such a competitor the course of conduct which they themselves will or may on the market.[252]

In *Suiker Unie*, documents established that the parties had contacted each other and that they pursued the aim of removing in advance any uncertainty about the future conduct of their competitors. This conduct facilitated the coordination of their commercial behaviour.

In *PVC*,[253] the Commission considered that the term concerted practice was particularly apt to cover the involvement of some undertakings, for example Shell. Shell, whilst not a full member of the cartel, had cooperated with it. It was thus able to adapt its own market behaviour in the light of this contact. Similarly, in *Belgian Brewers*[254] the Commission took the view that in respect of one of the cartels it found to be operated on the Belgian market, the private label cartel, it could not establish an agreement from available evidence, but that a concerted practice was proven. Meetings between the brewers had clearly served to influence the market behaviour of the competitors and to report on market behaviour to competitors. 'At the meetings not only was information exchanged but prices and customers were discussed. From statements…it is clear that the aim of the meetings was, firstly, to prevent a price war and adopt a position on prices and, secondly, to share out customers by not making (real) offers to the customers of other brewers'.[255]

An acute difficulty might be to determine whether or not the players have intended to let each other know in advance what their intended business moves will be. For example, can

---

[251] Cases 40–8, 50, 54–6, 111, and 113–4/73, *Re the European Sugar Cartel; Cooperatiëve Vereniging 'Suiker Unie' UA v. Commission* [1975] ECR 1663, [1976] 1 CMLR 295.

[252] *Ibid.*, para. 174.

[253] [1994] OJ L239/14.

[254] [2003] OJ L200/1.

[255] [2003] OJ L200/1, para. 254.

undertakings be said to have concerted if they exchange information which is freely available to the public generally? It might be argued that the exchange of sensitive information, such as price lists, which is available to the public and, consequently to an undertaking's competitors should not be prevented under Article 81(1).[256] The purpose of Article 81(1) is, however, to ensure that where possible undertakings act 'independently' so that a spirit of competition is fostered on the market. It therefore seems inevitable that the exchange of information on prices to be charged should be caught by Article 81(1). Even if the parties have not actually agreed to exchange the price information the simple exchange may be prohibited where the behaviour of the undertakings eliminates 'the risks of competition and the hazards of competitors' spontaneous reactions by co-operation'.[257] Exchanges of information, designed to influence the conduct on the market of an actual or potential competitor, to disclose to a competitor the course of conduct which the sender has decided to adopt on a market or rendering the market artificially transparent will therefore be unacceptable,[258] at least where the recipient requests the information or at the very least, accepts it.[259] Indeed, the Commission has taken steps generally to discourage the exchange of less sensitive information on oligopolistic markets. It takes the view that the exchange exacerbates the problems of, and increases transparency on, oligopolistic markets where there is already limited opportunity for competition.[260]

In contrast, Article 81(1) does not ordinarily preclude unilateral decisions adopted by undertakings independently, for example, a decision to send its price list to the press for publication, unilateral price announcements in advance, or independently chosen parallel conduct in a narrow oligopolistic market. Such behaviour will be prohibited only if an agreement, an understanding, or direct or indirect contact between the parties (a concerted practice) is established. This point is stressed clearly by the ECJ in *Wood Pulp*.[261]

d. Participation in Meetings

In *Polypropylene*[262] although the Commission had concluded that an agreement existed between the undertakings, the CFI[263] confirmed that the Commission had been correct to classify the meetings in the alternative as a concerted practice. The clear purpose of the competing undertakings participating in meetings during which information was exchanged about, for example, the prices and sales volumes was to disclose to each other the course of conduct which

---

[256] Take, for example, four leading undertakings competing on a market which publish price lists setting out prices to be charged over the next quarter. Since each undertaking has only three main competitors, each will probably take steps to get hold of the others' price lists. For example, an employee may drive to the premises of the competitors and obtain price lists. Given the ease with which the information can be acquired can a decision by the undertakings to exchange this information be prohibited (after all it would save cost and reduce pollution if the lists were simply put in the post)?

[257] Cases 48, 49, and 51–7/69, *ICI v. Commission (Dyestuffs)* [1972] ECR 619, [1972] CMLR 557, para. 119.

[258] See also, Cases 40–8, 50, and 54–6/73, *Re the European Sugar Cartel: Cooperatiëve Verniging 'Suiker Unie' UA v. Commission* [1975] ECR 1663, [1976] 1 CMLR 295.

[259] Cases T-25, 26, 30–2, 34–9, 42–6, 48, 50–71, 87, 88, 103, and 104/95, *Cimenteries CBR SA v. Commission* [2000] ECR II-491, [2000] 5 CMLR 204.

[260] See *infra*, Chap. 11.

[261] Cases C-89, 104, 114, 116–17, and 125–29/85, [1993] ECR I-1307, [1993] 4 CMLR 407, discussed *infra* Chap. 11.

[262] *Polypropylene* [1986] OJ L230/1, [1988] 4 CMLR 347.

[263] The judgments of the ECJ focused mainly on procedural arguments, but see, e.g., Case C-199/92 P, *Hüls AG v. Commission* [1999] ECR I-4287, [1999] 5 CMLR 1016, discussed *supra* 174–5.

each of the producers itself contemplated adopting on the market.[264] Participants clearly had the aim of eliminating any uncertainty about the future conduct of their competitors. They were bound to take into account the course of conduct upon which other participants had decided.

e. Parallel behaviour and Information Exchanges

Market data may show that undertakings have acted in parallel (for example, that competing undertakings increased prices at the same moment, offered the same discounts and/or terms and conditions to customers etc). On an oligopolistic market (a market that contains only a few firms) or a market with oligopolistic tendencies, however, undertakings often operate in transparent conditions and know how their competitors are likely to behave and react to their actions. On such markets the operators may have no need to agree to disclose information giving away their contemplated course of conduct, since their actions are mutually interdependent. Alignment of conduct and parallel behaviour (tacit collusion) may be a rational response to characteristics of the relevant market even if the parties do not explicitly collude. The question of whether parallel behaviour, such as identical simultaneous price rises, constitutes a concerted practice or will furnish proof of a concerted practice and the ECJ's important judgment in *Woodpulp* is examined in Chapter 11. Further, Chapter 11 explores the extent to which exchanges of information between undertakings constitute an infringement of the rules.

f. Concerted Practice and Vertical Arrangments

A concerted practice may be operated horizontally between colluding competitors but also vertically between a manufacturer and its distributors. In *Pioneer*,[265] for example, the Commission found that Pioneer and its European exclusive distributors had engaged in concerted practices to prevent the parallel import of Pioneer products from the UK and Germany into France.[266]

g. The Nature of a Concerted Practice

The cases described above have sought to elucidate the meaning of a concerted practice. There is, however, still some uncertainty as to its exact definition and scope and how it differs from the broad definition of an agreement.[267] How, and to what extent, does the requirement of direct or indirect reciprocal contacts between undertakings differ from the requirement that there should be a 'concurrence of wills' which may be proved directly or indirectly (through conduct)?[268] Does the concept of a concerted practice catch collusion of "the same nature" as an

---

[264] e.g., Case T-7/89, *Hercules NV v. Commission* [1992] ECR II-1711, [1992] 4 CMLR 84, para. 259, see Case C-199/92 P, *Hüls v. Commission* [1999] ECR I-4287, [1999] 5 CMLR 1016, para. 155; Case C-49/92 P, *Commission v. Anic* [1999] ECR I-4125, [2001] 4 CMLR 17 para. 96; Case C-291/98 P *Sarrió v. Commission* [2000] ECR I-9991, para. 50.

[265] [1980] OJ L60/1, [1980] 1 CMLR 457. The finding that Pioneer had participated in the concerted practices was upheld on appeal: see Cases 100–103/80, *Musique Diffusion Française SA v. Commission* [1983] ECR 1825, [1983] 3 CMLR 528, see especially paras 75–6. See also Case 86/82, *Hasselblad (GB) Ltd v. Commission* [1984] ECR 883, [1984] 1 CMLR 559, paras 24–29 and Case T-43/92 *Dunlop Slazenger International Ltd v. Commission* [1994] ECR-II 441 and, in the UK, Case 1022/1/1/03, *JJB Sports plc v. Office of Fair Trading* [2004] CAT 17, paras 150–63, 637–70 *aff'd* [2006] EWCA Civ 1318.

[266] See also the discussion of the UK case of *JJB Sports plc v. Office of Fair Trading* discussed *infra* 180.

[267] Especially as it has been held that behaviour may display characteristics of both and it may be possible to categorize it as an agreement or, in the alternative, as concerted practices, see, e.g., Case T-1/89, *Rhone-Poulenc v. Commission* [1991] ECR II-867, paras. 118–24.

[268] In *Argos Limited and Littlewoods Limited v. OFT, JJB Sports plc v. OFT* [2006] EWCA Civ 1318, para. 22 the English Court of Appeal stated that both concepts required that there be a 'consensus' between the two or more undertakings said to be parties to the agreement or concerted practice but that concerted practices could take many different forms, and the courts had always been careful not to define or limit what might amount to a concerted practice for this purpose.

agreement but which is distinguishable by virtue of the intensity and the form in which it manifests itself (i.e. is it just a mechanism by which a broader, looser range conduct can be relied upon to *infer* a concurrence of wills) or does it catch a different, broader spectrum of conduct? In his book, *The Boundaries of EC Competition Law*, Odudu explores this question. He considers two concepts of concerted practice:

The first requires common intention,[269] but relies on different evidence than that used to show agreement. The second does not require common intention, but instead focuses on whether conduct reduces uncertainty as to the future conduct of others."

Odudu rejects the first interpretation, which would be based on a finding that the less probative the evidence is in showing common intention, the more likely that a concerted practice will be found,[270] on the grounds that the ECJ has clearly held that it does not require a working out of an actual plan and that this interpretation would render the concept of a concerted practice otiose. He thus concludes that the concept of concerted practice must be broader, and must also capture conduct which reduces the position of uncertainty of competitors' future conduct that exists on a competitive market and so enables the firms to act with greater knowledge and more or less justified expectations about other undertakings.

This latter interpretation of a concerted practice is extremely broad and potentially incorporates the situation where information is proffered by one undertaking to another without any commitment from the other as to how that information will be used. It thus requires a very expansive interpretation of reciprocal cooperation. This view is supported, however, by the cases on participation in meetings where concertation may be found even though only one firm has disclosed its future course of conduct to competitors. Others will be implicated unless they publicly distance themselves from the policy. The mere receipt of information may therefore in some circumstances provide the requisite reciprocal direct or indirect conduct.[271] Further, it seems that a concerted practice may be found where players on a market seek to ensure a division of markets by 'indirect' communication through an intermediary (e.g. where a distributor complains to supplier about other distributors selling into its territory and where that information is passed on by the supplier to the offending distributors).[272] The potential depths to which this concept could be stretched is illustrated by a judgment of the UK's Competition Appeal Tribunal (CAT) in *JJB Sports plc* v. *Office of Fair Trading*.[273] In this case, the appellant sought to challenge the Office of Fair Trading's finding that it unlawfully participated in various price fixing arrangements. In relation to an allegation that it had participated in indirect exchanges of price information with competing retailers through the intermediary of Umbro, the CAT held relying on *Cimenteries* and *Tate and Lyle* that:

642. The fact that only one participant reveals his future intentions or other competitive information does not exclude the possibility of a concerted practice, since the recipient of the information in question cannot morally fail to take that information into account when formulating its policy on the market.

---

[269] Odudu takes the view that the core of an agreement is 'common intention' and that it is both sufficient and necessary to establish an agreement within the meaning of Article 81. He thus equates it with a concurrence of wills.

[270] Written and parol evidence of common intention could establish agreement; and evidence of common intention inferred from conduct could establish concerted practice.

[271] See *supra* n. 263 and accompanying text.

[272] See *supra* n. 266 and accompanying text.

[273] Case 1022/1/1/03 [2004] CAT 17 (Judgment on Liability).

Building on this, the CAT later indicated that a concerted practice might be found where a retailer disclosed its pricing intentions to a supplier in circumstances where it was reasonably foreseeable that that information might be used to influence market conditions:

> 659. If one retailer A privately discloses to a supplier B its future pricing intentions in circumstances where it is reasonably foreseeable that B might make use of that information to influence market conditions, and B then passes that pricing information on to a competing retailer C, then in our view A, B and C are all to be regarded on those facts as parties to a concerted practice having as its object or effect the prevention, restriction or distortion of competition. The prohibition on direct *or indirect* contact between competitors on prices has been infringed.

> 660. As regards A, the position might in our view be different only if it could be shown that retailer A revealed its future pricing intentions to its supplier B for some legitimate purpose not related in any way to competition, and could not reasonably have foreseen that such information would be used by B in a way capable of affecting market conditions. It seems to us that such disclosure by a retailer to a supplier will rarely be legitimate, otherwise resale price maintenance could be reintroduced by the back door.

It is doubtful whether this broad interpretation of a concerted practice is consistent with the requirement set out in *Dyestuffs* that the parties to the concerted practice should *knowingly* substitute practical cooperation for the risks of competition and the requirement of reciprocal contact in concerted practices.[274] Indeed, on appeal, the Court of Appeal, although upholding the finding of liability, did indicate that this broad statement of the CAT, if taken out of context, went too far. The Court of Appeal considered that reasonable foresight was not enough to find a concerted practice. Rather, it favoured a more subjective test for the imposition of liability in which retailer A intended that the information be passed on by B and that retailer C knew that the information had been provided by A to B and used that information in setting its prices. 'The Tribunal may have gone too far if it intended that suggestion to extend to cases in which A did not, in fact, foresee that B would make use of the pricing information to influence market conditions or in which C did not, in fact, appreciate that the information was being passed to him with A's concurrence'.[275]

D. OBJECT OR EFFECT THE PREVENTION, RESTRICTION, OR DISTORTION OF COMPETITION

Whether or not an agreement has as its object or effect the prevention, restriction, or distortion of competition is the heart of Article 81(1). Agreements and other collusive practices are not prohibited unless they prevent, restrict, or distort competition within the meaning of Article 81(1). The way in which this phrase is interpreted determines the types of agreements which are prohibited and the scope of application of Article 81(1). Further, the way in which Article 81(1) is interpreted has a crucial impact on the role played and the interpretation of Article 81(3). Obviously there is only a need to consider Article 81(3) where an agreement is prohibited under Article 81(1). The relationship and interaction of these two paragraphs and the question of what issues should be considered under each Article has caused enormous controversy. The relationship of these two provisions is fully explored in Chapter 4 below.

---

[274] See generally A. Albors-Lorens 'Horizontal Agreements and Concerted Practices in EC Competition Law: Unalwful and Legitimate Contacts between Competitors' [2006] 51 *Ant Bull* 837.

[275] *Argos Limited and Littlewoods Ltd* v. *OFT, JJB Sports plc* v. *OFT* [2006] EWCA Civ 1318, para. 91. The Court of Appeal held, however, that the higher substantive test was satisfied on the facts.

As a preliminary issue, however, it should be stressed that Article 81(1) prohibits an agreement which has as its object *or* its effect the prevention, restriction, or distortion of competition.[276] The words 'object or effect' are read disjunctively. If, therefore, it is clear from the terms of the agreement that its object is to prevent, restrict, or distort competition there is no need to examine its effects.[277] Certain agreements containing hard-core restraints, for example, hard-core cartel agreements fixing prices, restricting output or sharing markets or vertical agreements fixing minimum resale prices or incorporating export bans, are considered to have as their object the restriction of competition and are prohibited unless they meet the Article 81(3) criteria. Where the object of the agreement cannot be said to restrict competition an analysis of the effect of the agreement on the market and in the context in which it occurs is necessary before it can be determined whether the agreement infringes Article 81(1).[278]

E. AN APPRECIABLE EFFECT ON COMPETITION

(i) *Völk v. Vervaecke*

The ECJ has held that 'in order to come within the prohibition imposed by Article [81], the agreement must affect trade between Member States and the free play of competition to an appreciable extent'.[279] The concept of appreciability was first accepted by the ECJ in *Völk v. Vervaecke*.

Case 5/69, *Völk v. Vervaecke* [1969] ECR 295, 302, [1969] CMLR 273, 282

The case concerned an exclusive distribution agreement concluded between Mr Völk, the owner of a company, Erd & Co, which manufactured washing machines, and Vervaecke, a Belgian company which distributed household electrical appliances. Under the agreement, Vervaecke had the exclusive right to sell Völk's products in Belgium and Luxembourg. According to the Commission, Erd & Co had only 0.08 per cent of the market for the production of washing machines Community wide, 0.2 per cent of the market in Germany and 0.6 per cent of the market in Belgium and Luxembourg. Following a dispute which raised the validity of the agreement before the German courts, the Oberlandesgericht in Munich made an Article 234 reference to the Community Court. In particular, it asked the Community Court whether, in considering if an agreement fell within Article 81(1), regard had to be had to the proportion of the market that the grantor had.

---

[276] Case 56/65, *Société Technique Minière v. Maschinebau Ulm GmbH* [1966] ECR 234, 249, [1966] CMLR 357. See also Case C-234/89, *Stergios Delimitis v. Henninger Bräu* [1991] ECR I-935, [1992] 5 CMLR 210, para. 13 and Cases T-374, 375, 384, and 388/94, *European Night Services v. Commission* [1998] ECR II-3141, [1998] 5 CMLR 718, para. 136, discussed *infra* Chap. 4.

[277] Cases 56 and 58/64, *Etablissements Consten SA & Grundig-Verkaufs-GmbH v. Commission* [1966] ECR 299, [1966] CMLR 418.

[278] Case C-234/89, *Stergios Delimitis v. Henninger Bräu* [1991] ECR I-935, [1992] 5 CMLR 210, para. 13 ff.

[279] Case 22/71, *Béguelin Import Company v. GL Import-Export SA* [1971] ECR 949, [1972] CMLR 81. The text of Article 81(1) does not require that the effect on competition or trade should be appreciable.

Court of Justice

If an agreement is to be capable of affecting trade between Member States it must be possible to foresee with a sufficient degree of probability on the basis of a set of objective factors of law or of fact that the agreement in question may have an influence, direct or indirect, actual or potential, on the pattern of trade between Member States in such a way that it might hinder the attainment of the objectives of a single market between States. Moreover the prohibition in Article [81(1)] is applicable only if the agreement in question also has as its object or effect the prevention, restriction or distortion of competition within the common market. Those conditions must be understood by reference to the actual circumstances of the agreement. Consequently an agreement falls outside the prohibition in Article [81] when it has only an insignificant effect on the markets, taking into account the weak position which the persons concerned have on the market of the product in question. Thus an exclusive dealing agreement, even with absolute territorial protection, may, having regard to the weak position of the persons concerned on the market in the products in question in the area covered by the absolute protection, escape the prohibition laid down in Article [81(1)].

This case makes it crystal clear that Community law is not concerned with agreements, even those containing hard-core restraints,[280] concluded between parties that hold a weak position on the market and which have an insignificant effect on intra-community trade and/or on competition. The insignificant position held by the undertakings causes the Community institutions to take the view that the agreement cannot possibly threaten the Community objectives.[281] The more serious the restraint, however, the more insignificant the position held by the undertakings must be.[282]

(ii) Commission Notice on Agreements of Minor Importance which do not Appreciably Restrict Competition under Article 81(1) (De minimis)

In *Völk v. Vervaecke* the undertakings involved had very small shares of the markets potentially affected by the agreement.[283] Although the ECJ, in the Article 234 reference, was not at liberty to apply Community law to the facts at issue in that case, in interpreting Article 81(1) it indicated that Article 81 would not in fact prohibit the agreement in question. In what other circumstances, however, might an agreement be considered to be insignificant on account of the weak position of the parties involved?

The concept of appreciability is obviously of huge practical importance to undertakings, particularly small and medium-sized ones. Because of this the Commission has, over the

---

[280] In *Völk* the distributor had been granted absolute territorial protection, which has as its object the restriction of competition, Case 5/69, *Völk v. Vervaecke* [1969] ECR 295, 302, [1969] CMLR 273, 282. See also Case C-306/96, *Javico International and Javico AG v. Yves Saint Laurent Parfums SA* [1998] ECR I-1983, [1998] 5 CMLR 172, para. 17. Similarly, it must be assumed that even horizontal price-fixing or market-sharing agreements concluded between undertakings with a weak market position may also be considered to be insignificant.

[281] Rather, it is more appropriate that they should be examined, if at all, within the framework of national competition legislation.

[282] See *infra* 186–9.

[283] *Supra* 182. The relevant geographical market in that case was not however actually defined. It was unclear whether the relevant product market was divided on national, Community, or some other line.

years, issued a series of notices indicating when, in its view, an agreement is likely to be considered to be of minor importance. Each notice has been intended to enable undertakings to be able to judge for themselves whether their agreements fall outside the Article 81(1) prohibition and to free up the Commission's resources to allow it to concentrate on serious infringement of the rules. The most recent notice was published in 2001 and replaces a notice published in 1997.[284] Unlike previous notices, the 2001 notice deals only with the question of whether the agreement appreciably restricts competition. It does not quantify what does not constitute an appreciable effect on trade (this is dealt with in the notice on the effect on trade concept).[285] The notice uses market share thresholds,[286] to quantify what is *not* likely to be an appreciable restriction of competition under Article 81 of the EC Treaty. In recognition of their differences, however, the notice makes a distinction between agreements between undertakings that are competitors (actual or potential) and agreements between undertakings that are not competitors.[287]

Paragraph 7 states that the Commission holds the view that agreements between competitors do not appreciably restrict competition where the aggregate market share held by the parties to the agreement does not exceed 10 per cent and that agreements between undertakings which are not competitors do not appreciably restrict competition if the market share held by each of the parties to the agreement does not exceed 15 per cent. Where it is difficult to classify the agreement as either an agreement between competitors or non-competitors the 10 per cent threshold applies. For the purposes of calculating market shares, the market shares of 'connected undertakings' are included.[288]

---

[284] Commission Notice on agreements of minor importance [2001] OJ C368/13, [2002] 4 CMLR 699. The first notice was published in 1970, [1970] OJ C64/1.

[285] See *infra* 197–9.

[286] One earlier notice (the 1986 Notice) was criticized as it indicated that an agreement would be of minor importance only if the parties satisfied two distinct criteria. The first was that the parties did not have more than 5% of the relevant market of the goods or services which were the subject of the agreement in the area of the common market affected by the agreement. The second was that the parties were required to show that the aggregate annual turnover of the participating undertakings did not exceed ECU 300 million. The necessity of satisfying the turnover criterion was argued to be irrelevant to the significance of the impact of the agreement on the market, see para. 7 of the 1986 Notice (the sum was increased from ECU 200 to 300 million by a Commission Notice of 23 December 1994). Taking heed of the criticism, the 2001 Notice (like the 1997 Notice) omits any reference to turnover thresholds and defines the term 'appreciable effect' on competition by using only quantative criteria. Appreciability (in the context of an appreciable effect on competition) is determined by reference to market shares thresholds alone (but see the notice dealing with an appreciable effect on trade *infra* 197–9).

[287] It does not distinguish between horizontal and vertical agreements like the 1997 Notice did.

[288] Commission Notice on Agreements of Minor Importance which do not Appreciably Restrict Competition under Article 81(1) [2001] OJ C368/13, para. 12. This is interpreted broadly to include (a) undertakings in which a party to the agreement directly or indirectly has the power to exercise more than half the voting rights; the power to appoint more than half the members of the board; or has the right to manage the undertaking's affairs; (b) undertakings which have such rights over a party to the agreement; (c) other undertakings in which an undertaking referred to in (b) has such rights over; (d) undertakings in which a party to the agreement together with any undertaking referred to in (a)-(c), or two of such undertakings, have such rights over; and (e) undertakings in which such rights are jointly held by parties to the agreement or their respective connected undertakings *or* one or more of the parties to the agreement or one or more of the connected undertakings and one or more third parties.

Commission Notice on Agreements of Minor Importance which do not Appreciably Restrict Competition Under Article 81(1) [2001] OJ C368/13, [2002] 4 CMLR 699

1. Article 81(1) prohibits agreements between undertakings which may affect trade between Member States and which have as their object or effect the prevention, restriction or distortion of competition within the common market. The Court of Justice of the European Communities has clarified that this provision is not applicable where the impact of the agreement on intra-Community trade or on competition is not appreciable.

2. In this notice the Commission quantifies, with the help of market share thresholds, what is not an appreciable restriction of competition under Article 81 of the EC Treaty. This negative definition of appreciability does not imply that agreements between undertakings which exceed the thresholds set out in this notice appreciably restrict competition. Such agreements may still have only a negligible effect on competition and may therefore not be prohibited by Article 81(1)(2).

3. Agreements may in addition not fall under Article 81(1) because they are not capable of appreciably affecting trade between Member States. This notice does not deal with this issue. It does not quantify what does not constitute an appreciable effect on trade. It is however acknowledged that agreements between small and medium-sized undertakings, as defined in the Annex to Commission Recommendation 96/280/EC(3), are rarely capable of appreciably affecting trade between Member States. Small and medium-sized undertakings are currently defined in that recommendation as undertakings which have fewer than 250 employees and have either an annual turnover not exceeding EUR 40 million or an annual balance-sheet total not exceeding EUR 27 million.

4. In cases covered by this notice the Commission will not institute proceedings either upon application or on its own initiative. Where undertakings assume in good faith that an agreement is covered by this notice, the Commission will not impose fines. Although not binding on them, this notice also intends to give guidance to the courts and authorities of the Member States in their application of Article 81.

5. This notice also applies to decisions by associations of undertakings and to concerted practices.

6. This notice is without prejudice to any interpretation of Article 81 which may be given by the Court of Justice or the Court of First Instance of the European Communities.

II

7. The Commission holds the view that agreements between undertakings which affect trade between Member States do not appreciably restrict competition within the meaning of Article 81(1):

(a) if the aggregate market share held by the parties to the agreement does not exceed 10 per cent on any of the relevant markets affected by the agreement, where the agreement is made between undertakings which are actual or potential competitors on any of these markets (agreements between competitors); or

(b) if the market share held by each of the parties to the agreement does not exceed 15 per cent on any of the relevant markets affected by the agreement, where the agreement is made between undertakings which are not actual or potential competitors on any of these markets (agreements between non-competitors).

In cases where it is difficult to classify the agreement as either an agreement between competitors or an agreement between non-competitors the 10 per cent threshold is applicable.

(iii) Networks of Agreements

Paragraph 8 provides that where competition in a market is restricted by the cumulative effect of agreements entered into by different suppliers and distributors, the ordinary thresholds do not apply. Rather, a reduced threshold of 5 per cent applies (both for agreements between competitors and non-competitors). Access to a market is unlikely to be foreclosed by the cumulative effect of parallel networks of agreements where they cover less than 30 per cent of the market. This paragraph will be of particular importance in the context of distribution agreements for example, beer supply agreements, which operate in a similar way to other agreements on the market.[289] The notice improves on the position set out in the previous 1997 notice which did not apply at all where the relevant market was restricted by the cumulative effects of parallel networks of similar agreements established by several manufacturers or dealers.

Commission Notice on Agreements of Minor Importance which do not Appreciably Restrict Competition Under Article 81(1) [2001] OJ C368/13, [2002] 4 CMLR 6998

8. Where in a relevant market competition is restricted by the cumulative effect of agreements for the sale of goods or services entered into by different suppliers or distributors (cumulative foreclosure effect of parallel networks of agreements having similar effects on the market), the market share thresholds under point 7 are reduced to 5 per cent, both for agreements between competitors and for agreements between non-competitors. Individual suppliers or distributors with a market share not exceeding 5 per cent are in general not considered to contribute significantly to a cumulative foreclosure effect. A cumulative foreclosure effect is unlikely to exist if less than 30 per cent of the relevant market is covered by parallel (networks of) agreements having similar effects.

(iv) Outgrowing the Notice

A possible difficulty is that parties may outgrow the notice by subsequently acquiring greater market shares or achieving increased turnovers. Paragraph 9 of the notice provides for some marginal relief.

9. The Commission also holds the view that agreements are not restrictive of competition if the market shares do not exceed the thresholds of respectively 10 per cent, 15 per cent and 5 per cent set out in point 7 and 8 during two successive calendar years by more than 2 percentage points.

(v) The Importance of Market Shares and Hard-core Restraints

The important part played by market shares means, of course, that the relevant product and geographic markets must be defined in each case.[290] This is an inherent (but inevitable) source of weakness of the notice. Although the notice (at paragraph 10) makes reference to the

---

[289] Beer supply agreements will not restrict competition at all if they do not significantly contribute to a cumulative effect caused by the network on the market, see Case 234/89, *Delimitis* v. *Henninger Bräu* [1991] ECR I-935, [1992] 5 CMLR 210, paras. 24–6. This aspect of the case is discussed *infra* Chap. 4.

[290] See Chap. 1.

Commission Notice on the definition of the relevant market for the purposes of Community competition law[291] the definition of the market is of course frequently uncertain.[292]

> 10. In order to calculate the market share, it is necessary to determine the relevant market. This consists of the relevant product market and the relevant geographic market. When defining the relevant market, reference should be had to the notice on the definition of the relevant market for the purposes of Community competition law. The market shares are to be calculated on the basis of sales value data or, where appropriate, purchase value data. If value data are not available, estimates based on other reliable market information, including volume data, may be used.

In addition, the Commission further detracts from the utility of the notice by stating, in paragraph 11, that these thresholds do not apply to agreement containing specified hard-core restrictions, for example:

(i) agreements between competitors which fix prices, limit output or sales or allocate markets or customers; or

(ii) agreements between non-competitors which impose fixed or minimum sale prices on buyers or restrict the territory into which, or the customers to whom, the buyer may sell.

The list of hard-core restraints mirror those set out in the horizontal and vertical block exemptions (see Chapters 13 and 9 respectively).

> 11. Points 7, 8 and 9 do not apply to agreements containing any of the following hardcore restrictions:
>
> (1) as regards agreements between competitors as defined in point 7, restrictions which, directly or indirectly, in isolation or in combination with other factors under the control of the parties, have as their object:
> (a) the fixing of prices when selling the products to third parties;
> (b) the limitation of output or sales;
> (c) the allocation of markets or customers;
>
> (2) as regards agreements between non-competitors as defined in point 7, restrictions which, directly or indirectly, in isolation or in combination with other factors under the control of the parties, have as their object:
> (a) the restriction of the buyer's ability to determine its sale price, without prejudice to the possibility of the supplier imposing a maximum sale price or recommending a sale price, provided that they do not amount to a fixed or minimum sale price as a result of pressure from, or incentives offered by, any of the parties;
> (b) the restriction of the territory into which, or of the customers to whom, the buyer may sell the contract goods or services, except the following restrictions which are not hardcore:
> — the restriction of active sales into the exclusive territory or to an exclusive customer group reserved to the supplier or allocated by the supplier to another buyer, where such a restriction does not limit sales by the customers of the buyer,
> — the restriction of sales to end users by a buyer operating at the wholesale level of trade,
> — the restriction of sales to unauthorised distributors by the members of a selective distribution system, and

---

[291] [1997] OJ C372/5, [1998] 4 CMLR 177.

[292] For the problems involved in defining a market, see *supra* Chap. 1.

> —the restriction of the buyer's ability to sell components, supplied for the purposes of incorporation, to customers who would use them to manufacture the same type of goods as those produced by the supplier;
>
> (c) the restriction of active or passive sales to end users by members of a selective distribution system operating at the retail level of trade, without prejudice to the possibility of prohibiting a member of the system from operating out of an unauthorised place of establishment;
>
> (d) the restriction of cross-supplies between distributors within a selective distribution system, including between distributors operating at different levels of trade;
>
> (e) the restriction agreed between a supplier of components and a buyer who incorporates those components, which limits the supplier's ability to sell the components as spare parts to end users or to repairers or other service providers not entrusted by the buyer with the repair or servicing of its goods;
>
> (3) as regards agreements between competitors as defined in point 7, where the competitors operate, for the purposes of the agreement, at a different level of the production or distribution chain, any of the hardcore restrictions listed in paragraph (1) and (2) above.

At first sight this paragraph seems to be contrary to the clear view expressed by the ECJ in *Völk* v. *Vervaeke* (where a restriction was imposed on the territory to which the buyer could sell).[293] It seems, however, that the exclusion of agreements containing hard-core restraints from the ambit of the notice does not mean that these agreements may never fall outside Article 81(1) on the ground that they do not appreciably restrict competition. Rather, this paragraph could reflect a view that where the agreement contains particularly serious restrictions of competition from a Community perspective the agreement will not be considered to be of minor importance unless the parties' market shares are considerably lower than that set out in the notice (the more serious the restraint the less likely it is to be insignificant). Although the approach taken in the notice is strict, conveying the seriousness with which the Commission views hardcore restraints, it seems unlikely that the Commission would allocate resources to cases in which market shares were small.[294]

J. Faull and A. Nikpay (eds.), *The EC Law of Competition* (2nd edn., Oxford University Press, 2007)

(b) Restriction by object and appreciability

3.158 An agreement which, *prima facie*, has as its object the restriction of competition can nevertheless escape the prohibition of Article 81(1) if it has only an insignificant effect on the market on or trade. Thus in *Società Italiana Vetro, Fabbrica Pisana and PPG Vernante Pennitalia* v. *Commission*, the CFI rejected the Commission's submission that the evidence of the agreements between the parties was so unambiguous and explicit that any investigation whatsoever into the structure of the market had been entirely superfluous. While acknowledging that the Commission was not required to discuss in its decisions all the arguments raised by undertakings, the CFI held that the Commission ought to have examined more fully the structure and the functioning of the market in order to show why the conclusions drawn by the applicants were groundless. in the ECJ affirmed this position in *Javico* where it held that: '... even an agreement imposing absolute

[293] Set out *supra* 182–3.

[294] See J. Faull and A. Nikpay (eds.), *The EC Law of Competition* (Oxford University Press, 2nd edn., 2007), para. 3.164.

territorial protection may escape the prohibition laid down in Article 85 [now Article 81] if it affects the market only insignificantly, regard being had to the weak position of the persons concerned on the market in the products in question.'

3.159 What is an *'insignificant effect'*? As a preliminary point it is worth noting that the Commission is not required to prove that an object restriction has or even could have the effect of raising prices or restricting output. European competition law assumes that object restrictions will potentially have this effect. Rather the issue is whether the effect is likely to be of sufficient magnitude to affect competition appreciably. For object restrictions this is largely assessed with reference to the market position of the parties. In its submissions in *Völk* v. *Vervaecke*, a case concerning absolute territorial protection, the Commission stated that the production of washing machines by Mr Völk's company represented 0.08 per cent of the total production of the common market and 0.2 per cent of production in the Federal Republic of Germany. Its market share of sales in Belgium and Luxembourg, the territory of its exclusive distributor Vervaecke, was approximately 0.6 per cent. On the basis of these small market shares the Commission accepted that the agreement did not appreciably restrict competition. On the other hand in *Miller*, which concerned a territorial restriction by object, the ECJ found that the company concerned, which had a market share of the German market in sound recordings which varied between 5 per cent and 6 per cent, could not be compared with the undertakings in the *Völk* case and that Article 81(1) was infringed.

3.160 These cases suggest that for *vertical* restrictions, shares below 1 per cent are likely to be 'insignificant' while above 5 per cent, the effect is likely to be appreciable and Article 81(1) is likely to apply. Between 1 per cent and 5 per cent is best described as a grey area.

3.161 As for *horizontal* cases, it seems highly unlikely that, even if applicable, market shares in this region would ever be relevant from a practical perspective: it is difficult to conceive of price fixing of market sharing agreements between entities with combined market shares in single digits on a properly defined market. In any even, given the general tenor of the case law on cartels, it would seem implausible that the European Courts would permit cartels to escape the Article 81 on the basis of low market shares alone.

The Commission is, however, more willing to accept that an agreement containing hard-core restraints may escape Article 81(1) on the ground that the agreement does not appreciably affect trade (see section F below).

(vi) Effect of the Notice

The Commission's notices are not legally binding on the ECJ or national courts. It seems however that they create legitimate expectations so that the Commission itself should not depart from them without reason.[295] Indeed, the Commission states at paragraph 4 of the notice that where an agreement falls within its ambit that it will not, generally, institute proceedings. Further, where undertakings assume in good faith that an agreement is covered by this notice, the Commission will not impose fines. The parties cannot, however, be saved from the consequence of nullity in the event of the agreement being found to contravene Article 81(1) although the notice is likely to guide the national courts in its application. Although, therefore, the market shares set out in the notice are useful in indicating the parties' position on the market they are not conclusive. Agreements between parties with smaller market shares may produce

---

[295] The ECJ has held that although Guidelines are not rules of law, 'they form rules of practice from which the administration may not depart in an individual case without giving reasons that are compatible with the principle of equal treatment' Case C-397/03 P, *Archer Daniels Midland Co* v. *Commission* [2006] ECR I-4429, [2006] 5 CMLR 4, para. 91 (see *supra* Chap. 2). In practice a national court would be likely to take it into account when assessing whether or not an agreement has an appreciable effect on competition and trade within the meaning of Article 81(1).

a significant impact. Conversely, agreements between undertakings with greater shares of the market may produce insignificant results.[296]

The Commission should, therefore, where it takes the view that an agreement infringes Article 81(1), take care to define the relevant markets and to set out the parties' share of that market. Where the parties to an agreement only slightly exceed the market shares set out in the notice the Commission must justify a finding that the agreement nonetheless has an appreciable effect on competition and trade. Where it fails to do so the Court may quash a decision holding that an agreement falls within Article 81(1).

Cases T-374, 375, 384 and 388/94, *European Night Services* v. *Commission* [1998] ECR II-3141, [1998] 5 CMLR 718

Court of First Instance

102. In any event, even if, as noted above, ENS's share of the tourist travel market was in fact likely to exceed 5 per cent on certain routes, attaining 7 per cent on the London–Amsterdam route and 6 per cent on the London–Frankfurt/Dortmund route, . . . it must be borne in mind that, according to the case-law, an agreement may fall outside the prohibition in Article [81(1)] of the Treaty if it has only an insignificant effect on the market, taking into account the weak position which the parties concerned have on the product or service market in question (Case 5/69, *Völk* v. *Vervaecke* [1969] ECR 295 paragraph [7].). With regard to the quantitative effect on the market, the Commission has argued that, in accordance with its notice on agreements of minor importance, . . . Article [81(1)] applies to an agreement when the market share of the parties to the agreement amounts to 5 per cent.[297] However, the mere fact that that threshold may be reached and even exceeded does not make it possible to conclude with certainty that an agreement is caught by Article [81(1)] of the Treaty. Point 3 of that notice itself states that 'the quantitative definition of "appreciable" given by the Commission is, however, no absolute yardstick and that "in individual cases . . . agreements between undertakings which exceed these limits may . . . have only a negligible effect on trade between Member States or on competition, and are therefore not caught by Article [81(1)]" (see also *Langnese-Iglo* . . .). It is noteworthy, moreover, if only as an indication, that that analysis is corroborated by the Commission's 1997 notice on agreements of minor importance ([1997] OJ C372, p. 13.) replacing the notice of 3 September 1986, . . . according to which even agreements which are not of minor importance can escape the prohibition on agreements on account of their exclusively favourable impact on competition.

103. That being so, where, as in the present case, horizontal agreements between undertakings reach or only very slightly exceed the 5 per cent threshold regarded by the Commission itself as critical and such as to justify application of Article [81(1)] of the Treaty, the Commission must provide an adequate statement of its reasons for considering such agreements to be caught by the prohibition in Article [81(1)] of the Treaty. Its obligation to do so is all the more imperative here, where, as the applicants stated in their notification, ENS has to operate on markets largely dominated by other modes of transport, such as air transport, and where, on the assumption of an increase in demand on the relevant markets and having regard to the limited possibilities for ENS to increase its capacity, its market shares will either fall or remain stable. In addition, such a statement of reasons is necessary in the present instance in view of the fact that,

---

[296] See Article 2 of the notice and, e.g., Case 319/82, *Société de Vente de Ciments et Bétons de l'Est SA* v. *Kerpen & Kerpen GmbH & Co KG* [1983] ECR 4173, [1985] 1 CMLR 511, para. 8.

[297] This was the threshold set out in the notice at the time.

as the Court of Justice held at paragraph 86 of its judgment in *Musique Diffusion Française*, . . . an agreement is capable of exercising an appreciable influence on the pattern of trade between Member States even where the market shares of the undertakings concerned do not exceed 3 per cent , provided that those market shares exceed those of most of their competitors.

104. There is, however, no such statement of reasons in the present case.

105. It must be concluded from the foregoing that the contested decision does not contain a sufficient statement of reasons to enable the Court to make a ruling on the shares held by ENS on the various relevant markets and, consequently, on whether the ENS agreements have an appreciable effect on trade between Member States, and the decision must therefore be annulled on that ground.

F. AN APPRECIABLE EFFECT ON TRADE BETWEEN MEMBER STATES

(i) Jurisdictional Limit

The concept of an effect on trade between Member States sets out a jurisdictional limit to the prohibition laid down in Article 81 (it is also a requirement that any abuse of a dominant position should affect trade for the purposes of Article 82).[298] The criterion confines the scope of the application of Articles 81 and 82 to agreements having a minimum level of cross-border effects within the Community, hence the practices must *appreciably* affect trade between Member States.[299] Since the requirement is merely viewed as a jurisdictional matter, it has been interpreted broadly, although it is accepted that the Community has no jurisdiction over cases in which the effects of an agreement, or conduct, are confined to one Member State.[300] The meaning of an effect on trade has been clarified in the case law. The Commission has also prepared a notice on the concept of effect on trade between Member States[301] which seeks to set out the principles developed by the Court and to spell out when agreements and conduct may 'appreciably' affect trade between Member States.[302] It aims 'to set out the methodology for the application of the effect on trade concept and to provide guidance on its application in frequently occurring situations'.[303] In paragraphs 58–109 of the Guidelines it applies the general principles set out in the cases to common types of agreements and abuses, for example: different types of agreements and abuse covering or implemented in several Member States; agreements and abuses covering a single or only part of a Member State; and agreements and abuses involving imports and exports with undertakings located in third countries; and agreements and practices involving undertakings located in third countries. The guidelines are, of course, without prejudice to the interpretation given to the concept by the ECJ or CFI.[304]

[298] The application of Article 81 to an agreement does not preclude the simultaneous application of national competition rules. For the relationship between Community and national law see the discussion of Reg. 1/2003, art. 3, *infra* 199 and Chap. 14.

[299] Guidelines on the effect on trade concept contained in Articles 81 and 82 of the Treaty [2004] OJ C101/81, para. 13.

[300] Case 22/78, *Hugin v. Commission* [1979] ECR 1869, [1970] 3 CMLR 345, see also *infra* 196–7 .

[301] [2004] OJL C101/81

[302] See *infra* 197–9.

[303] Guidelines on the effect on trade concept contained in Articles 81 and 82 of the Treaty [2004] OJ C101/81, para. 3.

[304] *Ibid.*, para. 5.

(ii) The Tests

The Commission's notice stresses, relying on case law of the Court,[305] that '[t]he concept of "trade" is not limited to traditional exchanges of goods and services across borders. It is a wider concept, covering all cross-border economic activity, including establishment. This interpretation, is consistent with the fundamental objective of the Treaty to promote free movement of goods, services, persons and capital'.[306] An agreement will be found to 'affect trade' if it interferes with the pattern of trade between Member States.[307] There must be an impact on the flow of goods and services or other relevant economic activities involving at least two Member States. An agreement or practice may also be found to affect trade if it is liable to interfere with the structure of competition in the common market, for example where it eliminates or threatens to eliminate a competitors operating within the Community. This latter structural test is more commonly used in the context of Article 82 than Article 81.[308]

(iii) Pattern of Trade Test

In *Société La Technique Minière* v. *Maschinenbau Ulm*, the ECJ set out a broad interpretation of the requirement that an agreement should affect trade so it is easily satisfied. All that is necessary is that 'it must be possible to foresee with a sufficient degree of probability on the basis of a set of objective factors of law or of fact that the agreement in question may have an influence, direct or indirect, actual or potential, on the pattern of trade between Member States ...'.[309]

The test requires the following to be shown:

(a) A sufficient degree of probability on the basis of a set of objective factors of law of fact;[310]

(b) An influence on the pattern of trade between Member States;[311]

(c) A direct or indirect, actual or potential influence on the pattern of trade.[312]

An agreement will, therefore, be caught even if it is not established that the agreement will affect the pattern of trade if it can be shown that it is *capable* of having such an effect,[313] for example, if it is anticipated that they will affect the pattern of trade in the future. As it is only a jurisdictional criterion it is not necessary to establish that it actually has cross-border effects. Relevant factors

---

[305] See, e.g., Case 172/80, *Züchner* [1981] ECR 2021, [1982] 1 CMLR 313, para. 18, and Case C-309/99, *Wouters* v. *Alegemene Raad van de Nederlandse Order van Advocaten* [2002] ECR I-1577, [2002] 4 CMLR 913, Case C-41/90, *Höfner and Elser* v. *Macroton* [1991] ECR I-1979, [1993] 4 CMLR 306.

[306] Guidelines on the effect on trade concept contained in Articles 81 and 82 of the Treaty, [2004] OJ C101/81, para. 19.

[307] Case 56/65, *Société La Technique Minière Ulm* v. *Maschinenbau* [1966] ECR 235, [1966] CMLR 357.

[308] See Case 6–7/73, *Istituto Chemioterapico Italiano SpA and Commercial Solvents Corp* v. *Commission* [1974] ECR 223, [1974] 1 CMLR 309, especially para. 5 and *infra* Chap. 5.

[309] Case 56/65, *Société La Technique Minière Ulm* v. *Maschinenbau* [1966] ECR 235, 249, [1966] CMLR 357, 375 and Case 5/69, *Völk* v. *Vervaecke* [1969] ECR 295, 302, [1969] CMLR 273, 282.

[310] Guidelines on the effect on trade concept contained in Articles 81 and 82 of the Treaty, [2004] OJ C101/81, paras. 25–32.

[311] *Ibid.*, paras. 33–5.

[312] *Ibid.*, paras. 36–43.

[313] *Ibid.*, para. 26.

to the determination will be: the nature of the agreement and practice; the nature of the products; and the position and importance of the undertakings involved.

The fact that the influence on trade need only be direct, indirect, actual, or potential means that a broad range of agreements will be caught including for example: agreements affecting goods or services that are not traded, but which are used in the supply of a final product, which is traded;[314] agreements which do not actually affect trade but which, taking account of foreseeable market developments, may affect trade in the future. In *AEG v. Commission*,[315] the ECJ held that the fact that there was little inter-State trade did not mean that Article 81(1) was inapplicable if it could reasonably be expected that the patterns of trade in the future might change. The Commission states, however, that the inclusion of indirect and potential effects in the analysis of effects on trade between Member States, does not mean that the analysis can be based on remote, hypothetical or speculative effects. 'For instance, an agreement that raises the prices of a product which is not tradable reduces the disposable income of consumers. As consumers have less money to spend they may purchase fewer products imported from other Member States. However, the link between such income effects and trade between Member States is generally in itself too remote to establish Community law jurisdiction'.[316]

(iv) An Increase in Trade

In *Consten and Grundig*, the parties argued before the ECJ that their distribution agreement did not produce an effect on trade within the meaning of Article 81(1) since it increased trade between Member States (in the absence of the agreement, Grundig products might not have been sold in France at all). This argument was partially supported by a textual analysis of the Treaty since, in at least one language (Italian), the text suggested that the effect on trade should be a harmful or prejudicial one. The ECJ[317] rejected this argument, ruling that 'the fact that an agreement encourages an increase, even a large one, in the volume of trade between states is not sufficient to exclude the possibility that the agreement may "affect" such trade ...'.[318] Rather, it examined the contract, which precluded anyone other than Consten from importing Grundig products into France, and prohibited Consten from re-exporting the products into other Member States, and concluded that it 'indisputably affects trade between Member States'. Instead of attempting to adopt a literal interpretation of the provision the ECJ adopted an interpretation which respected the aims and spirit of the Treaty. It was important that agreements such as the exclusive distribution agreement at issue in that case should be capable of being scrutinized under the provisions.[319] The aim of the Treaty was not to increase trade as an end in itself, but to create a system of undistorted competition. The ECJ concluded that Article 81

---

[314] Case 123/83, *BNIC v. Clair* [1985] ECR 391, [1985] 2 CMLR 430, para. 29.

[315] Case 107/82, [1983] ECR 3151, [1984] 3 CMLR 325, para. 60; see also *AEI/Reyrolle Parsons re Vacuum Interrupters* [1977] OJ L48/32, [1977] 1 CMLR D 67, discussed *infra* Chap. 13.

[316] Guidelines on the effect on trade concept contained in Articles 81 and 82 of the Treaty, [2004] OJ C101/81, para. 43.

[317] The argument was, however, supported by Roemer AG. He took the view that the effect on trade would have to be an unfavourable one before the prohibition applied.

[318] Cases 56 and 58/64, *Etablissements Consten SA & Grundig-Verkaufs-GmbH v. Commission* [1966] ECR 299, 341, [1966] CMLR 418, 472.

[319] The agreement was capable of bringing about a partition of the market in certain products between Member States, rendering more difficult the interpenetration of trade which the Treaty was intended to create and impeding the goal of single market integration.

applied to any agreement which might threaten the freedom of trade between Member States in a manner which might harm the attainment of the single market. The term pattern of trade is neutral, it is not a condition that trade is restricted or reduced.

Cases 56 & 58/64, *Etablissements Consten SA & Grundig-Verkaufs-GmbH* v. *Commission* [1966] ECR 299, 341, [1966] CMLR 418, 471–2

Court of Justice

The complaints relating to the concept of 'agreements...which may affect trade between Member States'.

The applicants and the German Government maintain that the Commission has relied on a mistaken interpretation of the concept of an agreement which may affect trade between Member States and has not shown that such trade would have been greater without the agreement in dispute.

The defendant replies that this requirement in Article [81(1)] is fulfilled once trade between Member State develops, as a result of the agreement, differently from the way in which it would have done without the restriction resulting from the agreement, and once the influence of the agreement on market conditions reaches a certain degree. Such is the case here, according to the defendant, particularly in view of the impediments resulting within the Common Market from the disputed agreement as regards the exporting and importing of Grundig products to and from France. The concept of an agreement 'which may affect trade between Member States' is intended to define, in the law governing cartels, the boundary between the areas respectively covered by Community law and national law. It is only to the extent to which the agreement may affect trade between Member States that the deterioration in competition caused by the agreement falls under the prohibition of Community law contained in Article [81]; otherwise it escapes the prohibition.

In this connexion, what is particularly important is whether the agreement is capable of constituting a threat, either direct or indirect, actual or potential, to freedom of trade between Member States in a manner which might harm the attainment of the objectives of a single market between States. Thus the fact that an agreement encourages an increase, even a large one, in the volume of trade between States is not sufficient to exclude the possibility that the agreement may 'affect' such trade in the abovementioned manner. In the present case, the contract between Grundig and Consten, on the one hand by preventing undertakings other than Consten from importing Grundig products into France, and on the other hand by prohibiting Consten from re-exporting those products to other countries of the Common Market, indisputably affects trade between Member States. These limitations on the freedom of trade, as well as those which might ensure for third parties from the registration in France by Consten of the GINT trade mark, which Grundig places on all its products, are enough to satisfy the requirement in question.

(v) Partitioning of the Common Market

Many vertical agreements are capable of an effect on trade between Member States because of their tendency to incorporate territorial restrictions and their ability to partition the common market. It was seen in the extract set out above that the ECJ in *Consten and Grundig* found that the nature of the territorial restrictions was to affect trade. Similarly, other agreements concerning imports or exports, containing provisions sharing markets between a manufacturer and its distributor or between distributors *inter se* are capable of affecting trade between Member States.[320]

Even an agreement covering third countries and undertakings located in third countries may appreciably affect trade between Member States where it is capable of affecting cross-border economic activity inside the Community, for example an agreement preventing a distributor appointed for a territory outside the EU from making sales outside its contractual territory (and, consequently, into the Community). If in the absence of the agreement, resale to the Community would be both possible and likely, it may be capable of affecting patterns of trade inside the Community.[321] Whether or not an agreement with an undertaking outside of the Community will affect trade will depend on factors such as the object of the agreement (is the object of the agreement to restrict competition within the Community), the prices for the contractual products charged in the Community and those charged outside the Community, the level of customs duties, and transport costs.[322] Further the product volumes exported compared to the total market for those products in the territory of the Common market must not be insignificant.[323]

It is also possible that an agreement may have an effect on trade even if it does not appear to at first sight. The impact on inter-State trade may be revealed on a closer examination of the agreement. In *Delimitis v. Henninger Bräu*,[324] for example, a beer-supply agreement between a German brewer and a German café proprietor imposed an obligation on the latter to purchase beer only from the brewer. In derogation from this obligation, however, it permitted the café proprietor to purchase competing beer from suppliers in other Member States. The ECJ ruled that the national court would have to examine the agreement in greater detail. It was critical to determine whether or not this 'access' clause was hypothetical or real. The contract obliged the café proprietor to purchase a specific quantity of the brewer's beer each year. It had to be determined, therefore, whether or not this clause stipulating the minimum quantity of the brewery's beer to be purchased in reality left the café proprietor with a real opportunity to purchase beer from brewers in other Member States. If it did not, the agreement would produce an effect on inter-State trade, despite the access clause. On the other hand, if the agreement left a real possibility for foreign brewers to supply the outlet, the agreement was not in principle capable of affecting trade between Member States.

---

[320] Case 161/86, *Pronuptia de Paris GmbH v. Pronuptia de Paris Irmgard Schillgallis* [1986] ECR 353, [1986] 1 CMLR 414, para. 27.

[321] Case C-306/96, *Javico International and Javico AF v. Yves Saint Laurent Parfums SA* [1998] ECR I-1983, [1998] 5 CMLR 172, paras. 15–29.

[322] *Ibid.* [1998] 5 CMLR 172.

[323] *Ibid.*, paras. 24–6.

[324] Case C-234/89, [1991] ECR I-935, [1992] 5 CMLR 210.

Case C-234/89, *Delimitis* v. *Henninger Bräu* [1991] ECR I-935, [1992] 5 CMLR 210

Court of Justice

The compatibility with Article [81(1)] of a beer supply agreement containing an access clause

28. A beer supply agreement containing an access clause differs from the other beer supply agreements normally entered into inasmuch as it authorizes the reseller to purchase beer from other Member States. Such access mitigates, in favour of the beers of other Member States, the scope of the prohibition on competition which in a classic beer supply agreement is coupled with the exclusive purchasing obligation. The scope of the access clause must be assessed in the light of its wording and its economic and legal context . . .

30. As far as its economic and legal context is concerned, it should be pointed out that where, as in this case, one of the other clauses stipulates that a minimum quantity of the beers envisaged in the agreement must be purchased, it is necessary to examine what that quantity represents in relation to the sales of beer normally achieved in the public house in question. If it appears that the stipulated quantity is relatively large, the access clause ceases to have any economic significance and the prohibition on selling competing beers regains its full force, particularly when under the agreement the obligation to purchase minimum quantities is backed by penalties.

31. If the interpretation of the wording of the access clause or an examination of the specific effect of the contractual clauses as a whole in their economic and legal context shows that the limitation on the scope of the prohibition on competition is merely hypothetical or without economic significance, the agreement in question must be treated in the same way as a classic beer supply agreement. Accordingly, it must be assessed under Article [81(1)] of the Treaty in the same way as beer supply agreements in general.

32. The position is different where the access clause gives a national or foreign supplier of beers from other Member States a real possibility of supplying the sales outlet in question. An agreement containing such a clause is not in principle capable of affecting trade between Member States within the meaning of Article [81(1)], with the result that it escapes the prohibition laid down in that provision.

(vi) Agreements Operating in One Member State

It tends to be assumed that an agreement between parties situated in different Member States affects trade between Member States.[325] It can be seen from *Delimitis* (an agreement between a German brewer and a German café proprietor) that an agreement which operates in only one Member State is also quite capable of affecting trade between Member States.

Similarly, national cartels, especially those dominating the whole or a large part of a market, tend to reinforce compartmentalization and make it more difficult for undertakings from other Member States to penetrate the market.[326] The ECJ has consistently held the fact that a cartel

---

[325] See, e.g., Guidelines on the effect on trade concept contained in Articles 81 and 82 of the Treaty, [2004] OJ C101/81, paras. 61–72.

[326] Case 8/72, *Vereeniging van Cementhandelaren* v. *Commission* [1972] ECR 997, [1973] CMLR 7. In Case C-N215/96, *Bagnasco* v. *Banca Popolare di Novarra (NPN) and Cassa di Risparmio di Genova e Imperia (Carige)* [1999] ECR I-135 [1999] 4 CMLR 624, paras. 38–53, however, the ECJ held that standard bank conditions relating to the provision of general guarantees required to secure the opening of current-account credit facilities in Italy did not have an appreciable effect on intra-Community trade within the meaning of Article 81(1), *infra* 197.

relates only to the marketing of products in a single Member State is not sufficient to exclude the possibility that trade between Member States might be affected.[327] Indeed, the cartel is likely to be successful only if the members can defend themselves against foreign competition. If they do not, and the product covered by the agreement is tradable, the cartel is likely to be undermined by competition from undertakings in other Member States. The agreement in *BELASCO*,[328] for example, specifically provided for protective and defensive measures to be taken against foreign undertakings. Where the relevant product or service affected by the cartel is easily transmissible across borders it is likely that an effect on trade will be found. A Dutch cartel agreement which operated in order to restrict competition in the market for mobile cranes was held to have an effect on intra-Community trade. Since the cranes could travel at speeds of between 63 and 78 kph, the agreement was likely to affect German and Belgian firms operating near the Dutch border.[329] The Commission reached a similar conclusion in *Luxembourg Brewers* in respect of a cartel designed to insulate the Luxembourg market against imports of beer from other Member States.[330]

In *Carlo Bagnasco* v. *BPN*[331] and *Dutch Banks*,[332] the ECJ and Commission respectively concluded that purely national banking agreements were not capable of affecting trade between Member States. Bagnasco, for example, concerned retail banking services (guarantees for current account credit facilities) and the ECJ considered that trade was not capable of being appreciably affected because the potential for trade in the products was very limited. The market was not particularly susceptible to imports and retail banking services were not an important factor affecting the choice made by undertakings from other Member States when determining whether or not to establish themselves in another Member State. Although somewhat out of line with other case law and decisions setting out extensive Community jurisdiction, the cases may be explicable by virtue of a reluctance to apply Community law to cases which essentially have a national impact and so can be dealt with at a national level. Post-modernization, of course, such cases may be appraised by the appropriate NCA under Article 81 (if an effect on trade is found) as well as domestic law.[333]

(vii) Restrictions on Competition and Restrictions on Trade

It is clear that so long as the agreement as a whole affects trade between Member States it is immaterial that the clause (or clauses) which restricts competition does not itself affect trade.[334]

(viii) Agreements which Appreciably Affect Trade between Member States

The Commission's notice dealing with the effect on trade concept also deals with the quantitative element of the criterion, the question of when an agreement will *appreciably* affect trade

---

[327] Case 246/86, *BELASCO* v. *Commission* [1989] ECR 2117, [1991] 4 CMLR 96, para. 33.

[328] *Ibid.*, paras. 35–8.

[329] *Stichting Certificatie Kraanberhuuvedrijf and the Federatie van Nederlandse Kraanverhuurvedrijven* [1995] OJ L312/79.

[330] [2002] OJ L253/21, paras. 77–81.

[331] Case C-215/96, [1999] ECR I-135, [1999] 4 CMLR 624. See also Guidelines on the effect on trade concept contained in Articles 81 and 82 of the Treaty [2004] OJ C101/81, para. 60.

[332] [1991] OJ L271/28, [2000] 4 CMLR 137.

[333] But see discussion of Reg. 1/2003, art. 3 *infra* 199 and Chap. 14.

[334] See Case 193/83, *Windsurfing International Inc* v. *Commission* [1986] ECR 611, [1986] 3 CMLR 489. This case is discussed *infra* Chap. 10.

between Member States.[335] It states that Community law limits jurisdiction to agreements and practices capable of having effects on trade of a certain magnitude. In particular, appreciability can be appraised by reference to the position and importance of the undertakings on the relevant market. The Commission considers that appreciability can be measured both in absolute terms (turnover) and in relative terms, comparing the position of the relevant undertakings with others on the market (market share).[336] In paragraphs 50–57 the Commission seeks to quantify appreciability, stressing however that the assessment depends on the circumstances of each individual case. It does, however, indicate when trade is normally not capable of being appreciably affected. It sets out a negative rebuttable presumption, defining the absence of an appreciable effect on trade between Member States (the NAAT-rule[337]). In contrast to its notice on agreements of minor importance, the Commission states that the rules applies to *all* agreements irrespective of the restrictions contained within it (i.e. applies even agreements containing hardcore restraints).[338] Agreements which do not fall within its negative definition of appreciability do not, however, necessarily appreciably affect trade.

At paragraph 52 the Commission states its view that 'in principle agreements are not capable of appreciably affecting trade between Member States when the following *cumulative* conditions are met' (emphasis added):[339]

(a) The aggregate market share of the parties on any relevant market within the Community affected by the agreement does not exceed 5 per cent , and

(b) In the case of horizontal agreements, the aggregate annual Community turnover of the undertakings concerned in the products covered by the agreement does not exceed 40 million Euro.[340] In case of agreements concerning joint buying of products the relevant turnover shall be the parties' combined purchases of the products covered by the agreement.

In the case of vertical agreements, the aggregate annual Community turnover of the supplier in the products covered by the agreement does not exceed 40 million Euro. In the case of licence agreements the relevant turnover shall be the aggregate turnover of the licensees in the products incorporating the licensed technology and the licensor's own turnover in such products. In cases involving agreements concluded between a buyer and several suppliers the relevant turnover shall be the buyer's combined purchase of the products covered by the agreement.

Paragraph 52 also provides marginal relief for those that outgrow the notice in two successive calendar years. In cases where the presumption applies the Commission will not normally

---

[335] Commission Guidelines on the effect on trade concept contained in Articles 81 and 82 of the Treaty, [2004] OJ C101/81, paras. 44–57.

[336] *Ibid.*, para. 46.

[337] The Commission does not define more specifically what this means in the notice but presumably it stands for No Appreciable Affect on Trade).

[338] *Ibid.*, para. 50.

[339] The NAAT-rule does not apply in emerging markets. In such cases appreciability may have to be assessed on the basis of the position of the parties on related product market or their strength in technologies relating to the agreement.

[340] The turnover threshold is calculated on the basis of total Community sales excluding tax during the last financial year by the undertakings concerned. Sales between entities that form part of the same undertaking are excluded, Commission Guidelines on the effect on trade concept contained in Articles 81 and 82 of the Treaty, [2004] OJ C101/87, para. 54.

institute proceedings. Further, where undertakings assumed in good faith that an agreement is covered by the negative presumption, the Commission will not impose fines.[341]

In contrast, paragraph 53 states that for agreements that, by their very nature, are capable of affecting trade between Member States, such as agreements concerning imports and exports or covering several Member States, the Commission states that there is a *rebuttable positive* presumption that the effects on trade are appreciable when the turnover of the parties exceeds €40 million. It may also often be presumed that effects are appreciable where the 5 per cent threshold is exceeded. These rebuttable presumptions will obviously be of central importance when these issues are litigated before national courts.

(ix) The Relationship between Community and National Law

The breadth of the effect on trade criterion determines the scope of Regulation 1/2003 Article 3, which determines the relationship between Articles 81 and 82 and national law. The affect on trade criterion can therefore have a substantive outcome. Essentially, Article 3 provides that whenever a NCA or national court applies national competition laws to an agreement or practice that affects trade between Member States it must also apply Articles 81 and 82. The application of national competition law may not, however, lead to the prohibition of agreements which affect trade between Member States but which do not restrict competition within the meaning of Article 81(1), or which fulfil the conditions of Article 81(3) of which are covered by a Community block exemption. Further, a national authority cannot authorize an agreement prohibited by Community law. The relationship between Community and national law is dealt with more fully *infra* Chapter 14.

G. AGREEMENTS REQUIRED BY NATIONAL LEGISLATION

Article 81 is concerned with the conduct of undertakings and not with laws or regulations of Member States.[342] Where national law requires an agreement or where national law creates a framework eliminating any possible competitive conduct there is no infringement of Article 81(1). In such a case the anti-competitive effect results from the national law and not the agreement.[343] A national authority is duty bound to disapply such national legislation.[344] Where, however, national law merely allows or even goes so far as to encourage an anti-competitive agreement, Article 81 applies. This position is clearly spelt out by the CFI in its judgment in *Atlantic Container Line.*

---

[341] *Ibid.*, para. 50.

[342] In Cases C-94 and 202/04 *Cipolla v. Fazari* [2006] ECR I-11421 the ECJ held that nonetheless, Articles 81 and 82, read in conjunction with Article 10 EC required Members States not to introduce or maintain in force measures which may render ineffective the competition rules applicable to undertakings. It held, however, that legislation which approves, on the basis of a draft produced by a professional body of lawyers, a scale fixing a minimum fee for members of the legal profession was not precluded by Articles 10, 81 and 82 of the Treaty.

[343] See, e.g. Cases C-94/04 and 202/04 *Cipolla v. Fazari* [2006] ECR I-1142. Articles 10 and 81 may be infringed 'where a Member State requires or encourages the adoption of agreements…contrary to Article 81 or reinforces their effects, or where it divests its own rules of the character of legislation by delegating to private economic operators responsibility for taking decisions affecting the economic sphere', para. 47.

[344] Case C-198/01, *Consorzio Industrie Fiammiferi (CIF) v. Autorità Garante della Concorrenza e del Mercato* [2003] ECR I-8055, discussed *infra* Chap. 14.

> ### Cases T-191 and 212–214/98, *Atlantic Container Line* v. *Commission* [2003] ECR II-3275, para. 1130
>
> *Court of First Instance*
>
> 1130. According to the case-law, Articles [81] and [82] of the Treaty apply only to anti-competitive conduct in which undertakings engage on their own initiative. If anti-competitive conduct is required of undertakings by national law or if the latter creates a legal framework eliminating any possibility of competitive conduct on their part, Articles [81] and [82] of the Treaty do not apply. In such a situation, the restriction of competition is not attributable, as is implied by those provisions, to the autonomous conduct of the undertakings. Articles [81] and [82] of the Treaty may apply, by contrast, if it is found that the national legislation does not preclude undertakings from engaging in autonomous conduct which prevents, restricts or distorts competition (Joined Cases C-359/95 P and C-379/95 P *Commission and France* v. *Ladbroke Racing* [1997] ECR I-6265, paragraph 33;…in Case C-198/01 *Consorzia Industrie Fiammiferi*, paragraphs 52 to 55, and Case C-207/01 *Altair Chimica*, paragraphs 30, 35 and 36; Case T-111/96 *ITT Promédia* v. *Commission* [1998] ECR II-2937, paragraph 96; *Irish Sugar*,…, paragraph 130; Case T-513/93 *Consiglio Nazionale degli Spedizionieri Doganali* v. *Commission* [2000] ECR II-1807, paragraphs 58 and 59; and Case T-154/98 *Asia Motor France and Others* v. *Commission* [2000] ECR II-3453, paragraphs 78 to 91). Consequently, if a national law merely allows, encourages or makes it easier for undertakings to engage in autonomous anti-competitive conduct, those undertakings remain subject to the Treaty competition rules (see *inter alia* Joined Cases 89/85, 104/85, 114/85, 116/85, 117/85 and 125/85 to 129/85 *Ahlström* v. *Commission* [1988] ECR 5193, paragraph 20, and *Consorzia Industrie Fiammiferi*, cited above, paragraph 56).

H. COMMISSION NOTICES

In addition to the Notice on agreements of minor importance and the Guidelines on the effect of trade concept, the Commission has issued other notices/guidelines which indicate that certain agreements may not infringe Article 81(1), in particular because they do not restrict competition. The Commission started issuing notices in 1962 in order to clarify specific matters arising under Article 81, including circumstances in which certain restrictive practices would fall outside Article 81(1). As in the case of the notices discussed above, these notices provide useful guidance for parties. Although they are not rules of law which the Commission (or a court) is always bound to observe, they nevertheless form rules of practice from which the administration itself may not depart without giving reasons that are compatible with the principle of equal treatment.[345] The following notices are of particular significance in determining the application of Article 81(1) to agreements:[346]

- Commission Notice concerning its assessment of certain subcontracting agreements;[347]
- Guidelines on Vertical Restraints;[348]

[345] See *supra* n. 295.

[346] See also, e.g., Notice on the application of the competition rules to the postal sector [1998] OJ C39/2, [1998] 5 CMLR 108 and the Commission's Consolidated Jurisdictional Notice under Council Regulation (EC) No 139/2004 on the control of concentrations between undertakings, 10 July 2007 (this notice explains when joint ventures are appraised under the ECMR and Article 81 respectively).

[347] [1979] OJ C1/2, [1979] 1 CMLR 819, see *infra* Chap. 9.

[348] The Guidelines on Vertical Restraints [2000] OJ C291/1, [2000] 5 CMLR 1074 also deal with agency agreements and replace the Notice on exclusive dealing contracts with commercial agents [1962] OJ L39/2921.

- Guidelines on the application of Article 81 to horizontal co-operation agreements;[349]
- Guidelines on the application of Article 81 of the EC Treaty to technology transfer agreements;[350]
- Commission Notice on restrictions directly related and necessary to the concentration;[351]
- Guidelines on the application of Article 81(3) of the Treaty.[352]

I. EXTRATERRITORIALITY

The question of when and in what circumstances the competition rules may be applied to the acts of overseas undertakings (which are not established in the EU) is controversial and politically sensitive. The answer to this question does, of course, have an impact on the scope of Article 81(1). The extraterritorial reach of Article 81(1) and the other EC competition rules is explored in Chapter 16.

6. ARTICLE 81(2)

It has already been seen[353] that despite the clear wording of Article 81(2), the nullity provided for in that provision applies only to individual *clauses* in the agreement affected by the Article 81(1) prohibition. In *Société La Technique Minière* v. *Maschinenbau Ulm GmbH*,[354] the ECJ held the agreement as a whole is void only where those clauses are not severable from the remaining terms of the agreement. It thus interpreted Article 81(2) with reference only to its purpose in Community law and to ensure compliance with the Treaty. The English Court of Appeal has taken the view that the nullity imposed by Article 81(2) is not absolute. Rather, it has only the same temporaneous or transient effect as the prohibition in Article 81(1) (an agreement will cease to be void if the agreement itself ceases to restrict competition or to affect trade within the meaning of Article 81(1)[355]).

The ECJ has held that the question whether any null clause or clauses in an agreement can be severed from the rest of the agreement must be decided by national, not Community, law.[356] Each national court will, therefore, have to apply its own national rules on severance to determine the impact of Article 81(2) on the agreement before it.

7. EXCLUSIONS

In the UK, the Competition Act 1998 provides that the Chapter I prohibition (modelled on Article 81(1)) does not apply to agreements 'excluded' by, or as a result of, other provisions of the

---

[349] [2001] OJ C3/2, [2001] 4 CMLR 819, see Chap. 13.

[350] [2004] OJ C101/2, see Chap. 10.

[351] [2005] OJ C56/24, Although this notice applies to merger cases, it provides guidance on the question of when contractual restraints fall outside Article 81(1) on the grounds that they are 'ancillary' to a pro-competitive merger or agreement, see *infra* Chap. 4.

[352] [2004] OJ C101/97, discussed *infra* Chap. 4.

[353] See *supra* 124.

[354] Case 56/65 [1966] ECR 234, 250, [1966] CMLR 357.

[355] *Passmore v. Morland plc* [1999] 3 All ER 1005.

[356] See also Case 319/82, *Société de Vente de Ciments et Bétons de l'Est v. Kerpen & Kerpen GmbH & Co KG* [1983] ECR 4173, [1985] 1 CMLR 511, para. 11. See *infra* Chap. 15.

Act.[357] For example, transactions that constitute mergers under the Enterprise Act 2002 merger regime or concentrations with a Community dimension under the EC Merger Regulation are excluded as are: agreements subject to competition scrutiny under special enactments;[358] land agreements;[359] agreements required to comply with planning obligations or a legal requirement; certain agreements made by an undertaking entrusted with the operation of services of general economic interest or of a revenue producing monopoly;[360] and certain agreements relating to agricultural products.[361]

Although Article 81 does not itself refer to any express exclusions, in practice a number of agreements are excluded from its scope in a similar way. For example, the scheme of the Merger Regulation is such that, with certain limited exceptions, merger transactions that constitute 'concentrations' are assessed either under any applicable national competition legislation, or, where the transaction has a Community dimension, under the provisions of the Merger Regulation itself. The idea is that concentrations, which includes certain joint venture agreements, should not generally be appraised under Article 81.[362] In addition, Regulation 1184/2006[363] provides that the competition rules shall not apply to certain agriculural agreements, for example, those of farmers, farmers' associations, or associations of such associations belonging to a single Member State which concern the production or sale of agricultural products or the use of joint facilities for the storage, treatment or processing of agricultural products, and under which there is no obligation to charge identical prices, (unless the Commission finds that competition is thereby excluded or that the objectives of Article 33 of the Treaty are jeopardised). Article 296(1)(b) of the Treaty provides that nothing in the Treaty shall preclude the application by Member States of measures 'it considers necessary for the protection of the essential interests of its security which are connected with the production of or trade in arms, munitions and war material'. Further, it has been mentioned that the Treaty itself (in Article 86(2)) provides that the competition rules do not apply to some activities of public bodies or bodies entrusted with public services. It should also be noted that in interpreting the elements of Article 81(1), the ECJ has excluded from its ambit agreements belonging to the realm of social policy,[364] agreements concluded by firms when carrying out tasks of a public or social nature[365] and matters which are of a purely sporting interest and, as such, has nothing to do with economic activity.[366]

---

[357] See especially s. 50 and Sched. 1–4 of the Act. See generally R. Whish *Competition Law* (5th edn., Butterworths, 2003), 323–36.

[358] See CA 1998, Sched. 2.

[359] See the Competition Act 1998 (Land and Vertical Agreements Exclusion) Order SI 2000/310 and the Competition Act 1998 (Land Agreements Exclusion and Revocation) Order 2004 SI 2004/1260.

[360] CA 1998, Sched. 3.

[361] *Ibid.*

[362] For discussion of the complicated question of which transactions fall to be assessed within the procedure of the Merger Reg., Council Reg. 139/2004 [2004] OJ L24/1 (replacing Council Reg. 4064/89 [1989] OJ L395/1, as amended by Council Reg. 1310/97 [1997] OJ L 180/1)) and not under Article 81 see *infra* Chaps. 12 and 13.

[363] [2006] OJ L 214/7.

[364] See *supra* 131ff.

[365] See Chap. 8

[366] See *supra* Chap. 1.

8. CONCLUSIONS

Agreements that infringe Article 81(1) and which do not meet the conditions of Article 81(3) are prohibited. Severe consequences potentially flow for those that violate Article 81. It is therefore of utmost importance for a firm to know whether any agreement it concludes may violate Article 81(1).

The following provides a checklist of agreements (or conduct) which may fall outside Article 81(1) and escape the prohibition altogether:

1. Agreements which are not concluded by two or more entities engaged in economic activity;

2. Agreements between entities which are part of the same economic unit, for example, parent and subsidiary;

3. Genuine agency agreements;[367]

4. Collective agreements between employers and workers;

5. Unilateral conduct not explicitly or tacitly accepted by another or by another party to a contract;

6. Agreements which constitute a 'concentration' within the meaning of the Merger Regulation.

7. Agreements which relate to the production or trade in certain agricultural products;

8. Agreements which do not have as their object or effect the prevention, restriction, or distortion of competition;[368]

9. Agreements which do not appreciably or significantly restrict competition;

10. Agreements which do not appreciably affect trade between Member States (although such agreements may be subject to national competition law);

11. Agreements which are necessary for the performance of a task of general economic interest entrusted to them by a Member State (see Article 86(2));

12. Agreements required by national law; and

13. Agreements which are truly extraterritorial.

9. FURTHER READING

BOOKS

ODUDU, O., *The Boundaries of EC Competition Law: The Scope of Article 81* (Oxford University Press, 2006)

---

[367] See Chap. 9.

[368] See Chap. 4. In addition to case law, various Commission Notices and Guidelines provide both general and specific guidance on this issue.

ARTICLES

ALBORS-LLORENS, A., 'Horizontal Agreements and Concerted Practices in EC Competition Law: Unlawful and Legitimate Contacts between Competitors' (2006) 51 *Ant Bull* 837

BLACK, O., 'Concerted Practices, Joint Action and Reliance' [2003] 24 *ECLR* 219

BURNLEY, 'Interstate Trade Revisited—The Jurisdictional Criterion for Articles 81 and 82 EC' [2002] 5 *ECLR* 217

DYEKJAER-HANSEN, K., and HØEGH, K., 'Succession for competition law infringements with special reference to Due Diligence and Warranty Claims' [2003] 24 *ECLR* 203

FAULL, J., 'Effect on Trade between Member States' [1991] *Fordham Corp L Inst* 485

JAKOBSEN, P. S., and BROBURG, M., 'The Concept of Agreement in Article 81(1) EC: On the Manufacturer's Right to Prevent Parallel Trade within the European Community' [2002] 23 *ECLR* 127

LASOK K. P. E., 'When Is an Undertaking Not an Undertaking' [2004] 25 *ECLR* 383

LIDGARD, H. H., 'Unilateral Refusal to Supply: an Agreement in Disguise?' [1997] *ECLR* 352

LOURI, V., ' "Undertaking" as a jurisdictional Element in EC Competition Rules' (2002) *LIEI* 143

MONTESA, A., and GIVAJA, A., 'When Parents Pay for their Children's Wrongs: Attribution of Liability for EC Antitrust Infringements in Parent-Subsidiary Scenarios' [2006] 29(4) *World Competition* 559.

WESSELY, T., 'Polyproplyene appeal cases' (2001) 38 *CMLRev* 739

WICKIHALDER., U., 'The distinction between an "agreement" within the meaning of Article 81(1) of the EC Treaty and unilateral conduct' [2006] *Euro CJ* 87

WILS W.P. J., 'The Undertaking as Subject of EC Competition Law and the Imputation of Infringements to Natural or Legal Persons' (2000) 25 *ELRev* 99.

4

THE RELATIONSHIP BETWEEN ARTICLE 81(1) AND ARTICLE 81(3) OF THE TREATY

1. CENTRAL ISSUES

1. Article 81(1) prohibits agreements between undertakings which appreciably affects trade between Member States and which have as their object or effect the restriction of competition. Article 81(3) provides that the prohibition may be declared inapplicable to any agreement which satisfies its four conditions.

2. In this chapter the relationship between Article 81(1) and Article 81(3) is explored. Essentially, it seeks to determine which agreements contravene the objectives of Article 81 and so should be prohibited.

3. It is of course essential, therefore, to consider the objective (or objectives) of Article 81. Is it designed simply to prevent agreements which harm consumer welfare or is also designed to prevent agreements which restrain economic freedom or harm Community or public policy concerns, such as the single market project? Is it possible to condone agreements which harm consumer welfare but which help achieve fulfil-ment of a Treaty or other objective, for example one that achieves environmental benefits or one which increases employment opportunities in a deprived region of the Community.

4. Once the objectives are identified, it is necessary to decide which part of the relevant analysis should be conducted under Article 81(1) and which part should be conducted under Article 81(3). This issue is of enormous importance, since the burden of proving a breach of Article 81(1) rests on the person alleging the same, whilst the burden of establishing that the Article 81(3) criteria are established rests on those undertakings claiming its benefit.

5. Acute difficulties in this area are that:
   - despite recent pronouncements by the CFI, the goals of Article 81 remain somewhat obscure;
   - different cases suggest different approaches to the analysis required under Article 81(1) and Article 81(3) respectively; and
   - the procedural framework between 1962–2004, conferring exclusive competence on the Commission to rule on the compatibility of Article 81(3) led to distortions in interpretation of both Article 81(1) and Article 81(3) which has further clouded these issues.

6. This means that there is no crystal clear answer to the question of which agreements are prohibited by Article 81 and, correspondingly, what analysis is required under Article 81(1) and Article 81(3).

7. The Commission now takes an economic approach to Article 81 based on a consumer welfare objective. It states that Article 81(1) is about identifying the anti-competitive effects of an agreement (agreements which adversely affect competition by restricting inter-brand or intra-brand competition) whilst Article 81(3) allows the balancing of offsetting efficiencies against these restrictive effects.

8. The case law of the ECJ, however, suggests that broader objectives may be relevant under both Article 81(1) and Article 81(3) and that Article 81(1) may play a fuller role than the Commission concedes.

2. INTRODUCTION AND BACKGROUND

A. ARTICLE 81(1) AND ARTICLE 81(3)

It was seen in Chapter 3 that Article 81 provides for a two-tier analysis of agreements between undertakings. First, an agreement between undertakings which appreciably affects trade between Member States must be scrutinized to determine whether it infringes Article 81(1), i.e. does it have as its object or effect the restriction of competition (the words 'prevention, restriction, or distortion' are intended to cover any interference with competition and are synonymous[1] so the term 'restriction' will be used as shorthand in this text to cover all three). If it does not, that is the end of the story. If it does, however, it must, secondly, be determined whether or not the agreement meets the criteria set out in Article 81(3). Article 81(1) may be declared inapplicable to any agreement which provides specified benefits (broadly, it improves the production or distribution of goods or services or promotes technical or economic progress[2]), allows consumers a fair share of the benefit, does not contain any indispensable restrictions, and does not eliminate competition in a substantial part of the products in question.

It will be remembered that prior to 1 May 2004, Article 81(1) could be declared inapplicable to an agreement under Article 81(3) only by virtue of an exemption, granted to certain categories of agreement by virtue of Community Regulations (block exemptions) or, following notification, by individual exemption granted by the European Commission.[3] This point is important. This set up significantly influenced the way in which Article 81 was interpreted and operated. Since 1 May 2004, the notification system set up in Regulation 17 has been abolished and Article 81(3) can be applied in individual cases *either* by the European Commission, a national competition authority (NCA) or a national court, whenever the compatibility of an agreement with Article 81 arises *or* to categories of agreements by way of block exemption. Regulation 1/2003 does not affect the validity and legal nature of block exemption regulations.[4]

The bifurcated structure of Article 81 suggests that substantive appraisal of an agreement may be undertaken in two places: first when determining whether it restricts competition; and/or second when determining whether it meets the Article 81(3) criteria and so is excepted from the Article 81(1) prohibition. This division has led to uncertainty as to the correct role for, and analysis required by, each part. Key questions arising, therefore, are what objectives influence the interpretation of Article 81 and what factors are taken into account at each stage i.e.: (i) what constitutes a restriction of competition for the purposes of Article 81(1); and (ii), in what circumstances should such restrictions be 'trumped' by Article 81(3) benefits. If many agreements are found to restrict competition within the meaning of Article 81(1) numerous agreements will be prohibited *unless* saved by Article 81(3) (which becomes the main vehicle for

---

[1] It is, therefore, unnecessary to decide whether competition is being restricted, prevented, or distorted.

[2] See *infra* 271–7.

[3] See Reg. 17 [1959–62] OJ Spec. Ed. 87, Art. 9(1).

[4] Commission's Notice Guidelines on the application of Article 81(3) of the Treaty [2004] OJ C101/97, para. 2.

authorizing agreements). If, however, a narrower interpretation is adopted when determining whether or not a contractual provision restricts competition and infringes Article 81(1), the role played by Article 81(3) is more limited. Finding the right balance between the application of Article 81(1) and Article 81(3) has proved to be an extremely difficult and tortuous one. Arguably, many additional complexities have arisen from the decision to set Article 81 out in this 'bifurcated' form.

B. POSSIBLE WAYS OF RECONCILING ARTICLE 81(1) AND 81(3)

The wording of Article 81(1) and (3) themselves do not define their relationship. A number of different approaches have been adopted, or advocated, as to how they should be reconciled. For example:

1. One way of reconciling the two parts could be to adopt a literal interpretation of Article 81(1), bringing many agreements within its net, and to conduct a more detailed analysis of the anti-competitive, pro-competitive and other aspects of the agreement within the more structured framework of Article 81(3). In this scenario the requirement that the agreement restricts competition would serve a jurisdictional function (bringing within its ambit all potentially problematic agreements which may, for example, unduly restrict the freedom of action of the parties or which may compartmentalize the common market). The rigorous substantive assessment would then be completed under Article 81(3).

2. A second approach could be to adopt an economic approach when determining whether an agreement 'restricts' competition within the meaning of Article 81(1) and to confine the role of Article 81(3). Thus an assessment of the anti- and pro-competitive effects and an impact of the agreement on consumer welfare could be made when determining whether it restricts competition and Article 81(3) could be utilized *both* to except agreements presumed to restrict competition (object cases)[5] *and*, perhaps, to allow other demonstrable public policy benefits (such as benefits to environment, health, industry, culture or employment) to be balanced against demonstrated anti-competitive effects.

3. A third approach could be to divide the substantive appraisal more evenly between the two parts. There are a number of ways in which this division could be effected, but one method could be to use Article 81(1) to identify presumed, actual or likely anti-competitive effects and Article 81(3) to enable the parties to establish that the agreement achieves offsetting pro-competitive effects. For example, Article 81(1) could become concerned with allocative efficiency (and, essentially, deadweight loss resulting from contrived restrictions of output) whilst Article 81(3) could become a productive and dynamic efficiency inquiry, available to allow the parties to demonstrate that the restraints in the agreement are necessary to achieve efficiencies which will be passed on to consumers and compensate them for the resulting allocative inefficiencies.[6]

The discussion in the next sections show that the Commission's approach to Article 81 and the objectives underlying it has evolved significantly over time, that its approach is not totally reconcilable with that adopted by the ECJ and that neither approach equates exactly to any of the scenarios outlined above.

---

[5] But which are in fact proved to have demonstrable pro-competitive effects.

[6] See, e.g., O. Odudu, *The Boundaries of EC Competition Law: The Scope of Article 81* (Oxford University Press, 2006), Chaps. 5–7.

C. THE INTERPRETATION OF 'OBJECT OR EFFECT IS THE PREVENTION, RESTRICTION, OR DISTORTION OF COMPETITION'—THE BROAD APPROACH

One of the most strident criticisms made of the Commission's application of the competition rules in the past was its failure to adopt a sufficiently realistic economic interpretation of Article 81(1), in particular, when determining whether or not an agreement restricts competition. The broad criticism was that, in accordance with the ordo-liberal philosophy, it tended to take the view that a restriction on a party's conduct (a restraint on economic freedom) was tantamount to a restriction on competition. Further, that any restriction which might interfere with the single market objective amounted to a restriction of competition.[7] In short, the Commission found, after a formalistic assessment, that many agreements were caught within the widely cast net of Article 81(1) but subsequently completed its analysis, and authorized many agreements, using Article 81(3). Arguably, the Commission conducted much of the analysis when scrutinizing an agreement for its compliance with the requirements set out in Article 81(3) which it could in fact have conducted earlier when determining whether or not the agreement restricted competition under Article 81(1).

This approach seems to have been motivated both by ideology and practicalities. The Commission utilized Article 81 to limit restrictions on conduct, to promote rivalry between undertakings operating on a market, and to prevent interferences with the single market project.[8] The Commission considered that rivalry between firms produced the best results, and was the best stimulant of economic activity.[9] Further, a broad jurisdictional interpretation of Article 81(1) cemented the Commission's central role in the development of EC competition policy since it had the exclusive right to apply Article 81(3) through the system of 'notification and exemption'.[10] This enabled it to influence the form and way in which agreements were operated through its application of Article 81(3). It was able to develop its own view of what goals EC Community competition law should serve. In contrast, had it adopted a narrower, more economic approach to Article 81(1), greater enforcement of agreements would have been delegated to the national level. The national competition authorities, together with the national and Community courts,[11] would have played a greater role in development of competition policy. The interpretation of Article 81 might then have evolved differently and the uniform interpretation of the competition rules might have been compromised.[12] The impact of this

---

[7] See *supra* Chap. 1 and e.g. J. Faull and A. Nikpay (eds.), *The EC Law of Competition* (2nd edn., Oxford University Press, 2007), paras. 3.132–3-144.

[8] See *supra* Chap. 1. These goals may be different from those of its US counterparts (see, e.g., the discussion of vertical restraints *infra* Chap. 9) and, as seen in Chap. 1, have changed over time.

[9] See, J. Faull and A. Nikpay (eds.), *The EC Law of Competition* (Oxford University Press, 2nd edn., 2007), paras. 3.132–3-134.

[10] See Reg. 17, 1959–62 OJ Spec. Ed. 87, Arts. 9(1) and 4. A broader interpretation of Article 81(1) could therefore, be adopted safe in the knowledge that the agreement can be authorized under Article 81(3). This undoubtedly affected the appraisal conducted at the Article 81(1) stage and calls into question the correct role of Article 81(3). Arguably, this approach led to distortions in the interpretation of Article 81 which have plagued its application ever since.

[11] Through Article 234 references.

[12] National courts may have adopted divergent views on whether an agreement restricted competition within the meaning of Article 81 and applied Article 81 differently to identical agreements or problems. Although Article 234 of the Treaty sets out a procedure for national courts to refer questions relating to the interpretation of Community law to the ECJ that provision does not guarantee that references will be made. Only courts from which there is no appeal are obliged to make such a reference. See *infra* Chap. 15.

arrangement has been enduring, both on the interpretation of Article 81 and on the Commission's special and influential role in the moulding and shaping of competition policy.[13]

The Commission thus initially considered that a broad category of agreements, whether distribution,[14] intellectual property licensing,[15] joint venture[16] or other horizontal collaboration agreements,[17] infringed Article 81(1) but then completed its assessment by authorizing (or exempting) many of these agreements under Article 81(3).

D. THE DRAWBACKS OF A BROAD INTERPRETATION OF ARTICLE 81(1): THE NEED FOR A MORE ECONOMIC APPROACH?

At first sight, it may appear immaterial whether or not the more rigorous scrutiny of the agreement is conducted under Article 81(1) or Article 81(3) if the outcome is the same. This is not just an academic point, however.

First, the broad approach raises conceptual difficulties: businesses have found it hard to understand why their agreement has been characterized as restrictive of competition, simply because it imposes restrictions on the conduct of one of the parties.[18] Secondly, up until 1 May 2004 when Regulation 1/2003 came into force, negative procedural consequences resulted both to the parties to the agreement and the Commission from this approach. Parties fearful that their agreement might infringe Article 81(1) had either to notify their agreement to the Commission[19] or draft it to fall within one of the block

---

[13] Although the ECJ and the CFI are charged with the interpretation and application of the Treaty (Art. 220 EC), the system of enforcement set up by Reg. 17 meant that relatively few Article 81 or 82 cases have been litigated either in the national courts or before the ECJ and that there is very little case law on the interpretation of Article 81(3). The Commission has therefore played the key role in the enforcement of the rules, and its policies, decisions, guidelines and notices are extremely influential in guiding interpretation and application of the rules by national courts and national competition authorities (*but* see, *e.g.*, the UK litigation in *Inntrepreneur Pub Co. v. Crehan* [2006] UKHL 38, where the UK courts differed from the Commission in their factual assessment of the UK beer market, so reaching a different conclusion as to whether the market was foreclosed and as to whether beer tie agreements might infringe Article 81(1)).

[14] See, e.g., *Goodyear Italiana-Euram*, [1975] OJ L38/10.

[15] See, e.g., *Campari*, [1978] OJ L70/ 69 para. 7, part IIA ('the exclusive nature of the licence entails a restriction upon Campari-Milan's freedom to use its mark as well as preventing third parties, particularly manufacturers of alcoholic beverages from using them as licensees, however much they may find it in their interests to do so.')

[16] See, e.g., *Vacuum Interrupters*, [1977] OJ L48/ 32; *De Laval-Stork*, [1977] OJ L215/11 para. 6 ('Even if an increase in competition between the joint venture and other companies in business on the relevant market results from the agreement, the effect of the agreement is to eliminate competition between the two parties on the same markets, both as regards research and as regards production and marketing'). In exempting the agreement, however, the Commission accepted that the parties to the joint venture had to compete with some very large groups which sold their goods throughout the world and had far greater sales capacities.

[17] See, e.g., *Beecham/Parke, Davis*, [1979] OJ L70/11.

[18] Especially if, in subsequently exempting the agreement, the Commission essentially accepted that the agreement was a pro-competitive one, see e.g. *supra* n. 16.

[19] Reg. 17 [1959–62] OJ Spec. Ed. 87, Art. 9(1). Notification was a time- and cost-consuming exercise but enabled the parties to apply for a negative clearance (a decision stating that the agreement does not fall within Article 81(1) at all) and/or to seek an individual exemption. The Commission could not grant more than a handful of exemptions each year and so was unable to deal satisfactorily with the notifications it received. In Case T-67/01, *JCB Service v. Commission* [2004] ECR II-49, [2004] 4 CMLR 1346 (Case *aff'd* Case C-167/04, *JCB Service v. Commission* [2006] ECR I-8935, [2006] 5 CMLR 23) the CFI considered an agreement that had been notified in 1973. The Commission had not rejected the application for an exemption until 2000, [2002] OJ L691, [2002] 4 CMLR 1458, when it looked again at the case following a complaint. In addition, the

exemptions.[20] Even if an agreement was notified to the Commission it was unable to deal with notifications within an acceptable time frame, and did not have the resources to grant individual exemptions (or other formal decisions) to all agreements potentially falling within Article 81(1). It had therefore to find other mechanisms for dissuading notifications and authorizing agreements falling within Article 81(1). This situation meant that the conclusion of agreements which were neutral from a competition perspective, or even pro-competitive, might have been deterred.[21] Thirdly, and critically, the interpretation of Article 81(1) impacts on the *scope* of Article 81(3). A broad approach to Article 81(1) leaves a fuller and more important role for Article 81(3). Because of these difficulties, the Commission was urged to take a more economically sophisticated approach in assessing whether or not an agreement restricted competition within the meaning of Article 81(1).[22] It was argued that Article 81(1) should not generally be applied formalistically to an agreement (or provisions within it) which did not have an appreciable adverse effect on competition. Rather, an analysis weighing anti- and pro-competitive effects, similar perhaps to rule of reason analysis adopted in the US, should be conducted.

A number of arguments were presented in support of a more sophisticated economic approach to Article 81(1). It was argued that:

• the legal rules followed by the Commission under Article 81(1) were overbroad and did not provide sufficiently precise and operable criteria to determine which agreements restricted competition;

• the approach led to the condemnation under Article 81(1) of innocuous agreements which did not in fact restrict competition through anti-competitive effects.[23] The analysis conducted by the Commission when scrutinizing an agreement for its compliance with the requirements set out in Article 81(3) was more appropriate to the determination of whether or not the

---

Commission's monopoly over Article 81(3) effectively excluded national courts and NCAs from the enforcement process and limited the role of the Luxembourg courts to judicial review (the Commission's decisions are subject to review under Article 230 EC, see *infra* Chap. 14. The Court did not, however, take a particularly interventionist stance when dealing with appeals against decisions taken under Article 81(3). In recognition of the complex economic assessments involved in decisions taken under Article 81(3) the review has generally been limited to an assessment of the facts and the legal conclusions drawn from those facts, Cases 56 and 58/64, *Etablissements Consten SA & Grundig-Verkaufs-GmbH v. Commission* [1966] ECR 299, [1966] CMLR 416.

[20] See *infra* 284–9. The original block exemptions were criticized for having a strait-jacketing effect and for leading to a formalistic and mechanistic treatment of agreements. Although the new block exemptions have adopted a more economic and less constraining formula, their broad, overarching terms can still be overly rigid and difficult to comply with, see, e.g. Chap. 10 and discussion of the Technology Transfer Block Exemption.

[21] If the parties did not wish to notify and their agreement did not fall within one of the Community block exemptions then they would have to take the risk that their agreement (or clauses in their agreement) might subsequently be found to be in contravention of Article 81(1) and void. The general rule was that an exemption could only be granted retrospectively to the date of application, Reg. 17 [1959–62] OJ Spec. Ed. 87, Art. 4, see Chap 14.

[22] See, e.g., R. Joliet, *The Rule of Reason in Antitrust Law* (Nijhof, 1967); I. Forrester and C. Norall, 'The Laïcization of Community Law: Self-help and the Rule of Reason: How Competition is and could be Applied' (1984) 21 *CMLRev* 11, V. Korah, 'EEC Competition Policy-Legal Form or Economic Efficiency?' [1986] *CLP* 85, B. E. Hawk, 'System Failure: Vertical Restraints and EC Competition Law' (1995) 32 *CMLRev* 973, James S. Venit, *Pronuptia: ancillary restraints or unholy alliances*, 11 *ELRev.* 213 (1986); R. Whish & B. Sufrin, 'Article 85 and the Rule of Reason,' (1987) *YEL* 1.

[23] Since many of the agreements prohibited created or increased competition they should not have required authorization under Article 81(3), see, e.g., the Opinion of Roemer AG in Cases 56 and 58/64, *Etablissements Consten SA & Grundig-Verkaufs-GmbH v. Commission* [1966] ECR 299, 348 [1966] CMLR 418.

agreement restricted competition under Article 81(1).[24] For example, in granting an exemption the Commission often recognized that the parties faced competition from others which would ensure that products were offered to consumers on the most favourable terms. Arguably, this type of factor should have been relied upon to demonstrate that the agreement did not have as its effect, the restriction of competition;

- the Commission's approach wrongly favoured the freedom of individual traders and competitors over consumer welfare;

- if a weighing of anti- and pro-competitive effects was conducted under Article 81(1), many of the procedural problems experienced in the application of Article 81 would fall away. Fewer agreements would need *either* to be notified and subjected to the interminable delay involved in gaining Commission authorization *or* drafted to comply with rigid block exemptions which encouraged formalism and treatment of agreement by category rather than effect. In addition, the Commission's resources would be freed to deal with the more serious violations of the competition rules and the rarer cases which would demand scrutiny under Article 81(3); and critically

- the advocated approach was necessitated by the case law of the ECJ which had not interpreted the concept of a restriction of competition under Article 81(1) so broadly as the Commission. Although it has been clear since the ECJ's judgment in *Etablissements Consten SA & Grundig-Verkaufs-GmbH v. Commission*[25] that there is no need to take account of the effects of an agreement if its *object* is to restrict competition, it was maintained that in 'effect' cases, a series of judgments commencing with *Société La Technique Minière v. Maschinenbau Ulm GmbH ('STM')*[26] (and including cases such as *Nungesser v. Commission*,[27] *Erauw-Jacquéry Sprl v. La Hesbignonne Société Coopérative*, [28] *Remia BV and NV Verenigde Bedrijven Nutricia v. Commission*,[29] *Pronuptia de Paris GmbH v. Pronuptia de Paris Irmgard Schillgallis*[30], *Brasserie de Haecht (No. 1)*,[31] *Gøttrup-Klim Grovvareforening*

---

[24] The emphasis on Article 81(3) also imposed a greater burden on the parties. Although the burden was not plainly stated under Reg. 17, 1959–62 OJ Spec. Ed. 87 to rest on the parties (as it is now, Reg. 1/2003, Art. 2) the Article 81(3) request had to be made and initially substantiated by the parties. In Cases 56 and 58/64, *Etablissements Consten SA & Grundig-Verkaufs-GmbH v. Commission* [1966] ECR 299, 348, [1966] CMLR 418, the ECJ stated that 'the undertakings are entitled to an appropriate examination by the Commission of their requests for Article [81(3)] to be applied, for this purpose the Commission may not confine itself to requiring from undertakings proof of the fulfilment of the requirements for the grant of the exemption but must, as a matter of good administration, play its part, using the means available to it, in ascertaining the relevant facts and circumstances.'). Further, an Article 81(3) decision was harder to challenge as the ECJ held that in judicially reviewing an exemption decision, account had to be taken of the discretion invested in the Commission by the exemption process ('the exercise of the Commission's powers necessarily implies complex evaluations on economic matters, a judicial review of these evaluations must take account of their nature by confining itself to an examination of the relevance of the facts and of the legal consequences which the Commission deduces therefrom', Cases 56 and 58/64, *Etablissements Consten SA & Grundig-Verkaufs-GmbH v. Commission* [1966] ECR 299, 348, [1966] CMLR 418).

[25] Cases 56 and 58/64, *Etablissements Consten SA & Grundig-Verkaufs-GmbH v. Commission* [1966] ECR 299, 348 [1966] CMLR 418.

[26] Case 56/65, *Société La Technique Minière v. Maschinenbau Ulm GmbH*, [1966] ECR 234, [1966] CMLR 357, discussed *infra* 246.

[27] Case 258/78, [1982] ECR 2015, [1983] 1 CMLR 278.

[28] Case 27/87, [1988] ECR 1999, [1988] 4 CMLR 576.

[29] Case 42/84, *Remia B.V. and N.V. Verenigde Bedrijven Nutricia v. Commission* [1985] ECR 2545, [1987] CMLR 1.

[30] Case 161/84, [1986] ECR 353, [1986] 1 CMLR 414.

[31] Case 23/67, *Brasserie de Haecht SA v. Wilkin (No. 1)* [1967] ECR 407, [1968] CMLR 26.

and *Others* v. *Dansk Landbrugs Grovvareselskab AmbA*[32] and *Delimitis* v. *Henninger Bräu*[33]) required the drawing up of a competition balance sheet and a weighing of anti and pro-competitive effects under Article 81(1).[34]

E. SECTION I OF THE SHERMAN ACT

In the US, section 1 of the Sherman Act 1890 provides that '[e]very contract, combination in the form of a trust or otherwise, or conspiracy, in restraint of trade or commerce among the several States, or with foreign nations, is declared to be illegal…'. The section contains no legal exception to the prohibition.

Since the main objective of a contract is to restrain the conduct of the parties to it, a literal interpretation of the section might have resulted in many agreements being held to be illegal.[35] 'Every agreement concerning trade, every regulation of trade, restrains. To bind, to restrain, is of their very essence'.[36] The US courts have, therefore, construed the section to mean that contracts must not restrain trade unreasonably.[37] Eventually, this has become an enquiry into the competitive significance of the restraint.[38] In determining whether or not an agreement does restrain competition unreasonably the courts have traditionally adopted two separate approaches.[39]

Some contracts are considered to be illegal *per se*. 'There are certain agreements or practices which because of their pernicious effect on competition and lack of any redeeming virtue are conclusively presumed to be unreasonable and therefore illegal without elaborate inquiries as to the prices, harm they have caused or the business excuse for their use'.[40] This bright line test focuses *solely* on whether the conduct took place, not on its effect. Some agreements, such as naked price-fixing among competitors,[41] are automatically held to restrain competition unreasonably. They are anti-competitive and the court will not waste time or resources hearing justifications for the agreement.

The presumptive and prevailing standard, however, is the 'rule of reason'. [42] Agreements are not assumed to be illegal but are assessed in their legal and economic context to determine

---

[32] Case C-250/92, [1994] ECR I-5641, [1996] 4 CMLR 191.

[33] Case C-234/89, [1991] ECR I-935, [1991] 5 CMLR 210.

[34] See *infra* 236 ff.

[35] But see the approach adopted in *United States* v. *Trans-Missouri Freight Assn.*, 166 US 290 (1897).

[36] *Chicago Board of Trade* v. *US*, 246 US 231 (1918), per Brandeis J.

[37] *Standard Oil Co of New Jersey* v. *US*, 221 US 1 (1911); *US* v. *American Tobacco Co*, 221 US 106 (1911). In the US here is no equivalent in the Sherman Act of Article 81(3). When interpreting section 1 Sherman Act it has, therefore, been of utmost importance that it is interpreted sensibly and reasonably. If an agreement is found to be in restraint of trade it is illegal. There is no scope for the beneficial aspects of the agreement to be taken into account later.

[38] *National Society of Professional Engineers* v. *United States* 435 US 679 (1978).

[39] As the law has developed, however, the boundary between the two categories has become increasingly blurred so that 'there is often no bright line separating per se from Rule of Reason analysis' *NCAA* v. *Board of Regents of Uni* v. *of Okla.*, 468 US 85, 104 (1984). This has led some courts to conclude that there has been a move away from fixed categories to a continuum, *Polygram Holding, Inc.*, v. *Federal Trade Commission*, 416 F.3d 29, 35 (D.C. Cir. 2005).

[40] *Northern Pac R Co* v. *United States*, 356 US 1, 5 (1958).

[41] *US* v. *Trenton Potteries Co*, 273 US 392 (1927); *US* v. *Socony-Vaccuum Oil Co*, 310 US 150 (1940).

[42] In the 1960s the US courts tended to take a formalistic approach to section 1 characterizing many contracts as illegal *per se*. For example, there was a time when the US courts took the view that almost all restraints in vertical agreements were illegal *per se*: see *infra* Chap. 9. In *Continental TV, Inc.* v. *GTE Slyvania Inc.*, 433

'whether the restraint imposed is such as merely regulates and perhaps thereby promotes competition or whether it is such as may suppress or even destroy competition. To determine that question the court must ordinarily consider the facts peculiar to the business to which the restraint is applied; its condition before and after the restraint was imposed; the nature of the restraint and its effect, actual or probable'.[43] In short, the anti- and pro-competitive aspects of the agreement are weighed before an agreement is condemned as illegal.[44]

Not all commentators agreed that EC case law supported an approach similar to the US rule of reason. Whish and Sufrin, for example, argued that it did little to suggest that it was even moving towards such an approach.[45] Although conceding that the case law did display an approach more rigorously based on economics than that of the Commission, they did not believe it to equate to that required in the US. Indeed, they saw little virtue in adopting a term borrowed from another system which was likely to do more to confuse than clarify. Not only might the term rule of reason be confused with the rule of reason conducted within the sphere of free movement of goods, but it would invite misleading comparison with antitrust analysis in the United States, the context of which was so dissimilar from that of the (then) EEC that comparative analysis should be conducted only with great caution. Their clear conclusion was that the term should be jettisoned.

F. MODERNIZATION

(i) Modernization and Regulation 1/2003

Eventually, the Commission realized that the status quo was no longer tenable: the notification system was failing and some change was obligatory. It set about reformulating its approach to agreements, accepting that there should be a shift from an approach based on form to one more focused on effects.[46] Further, it sought to resolve the procedural problems arising by proposing that its monopoly over Article 81(3) should be revoked. On 1 May 2004, Regulation 1/2003 abolished the Commission's exclusive right to rule on the compatibility of an agreement with

---

U.S. 36 (1977), however, the Supreme Court thus stressed that the per se category should be restricted to agreements having, or likely to have, a 'pernicious effect on competition' and which are lacking 'any redeeming virtue'. Departure from the rule-of-reason standard should be based only on demonstrable economic effect and not formalistic line drawing. The Supreme Court thus redrew, and cut back, the boundaries of the per se rule, which is now broadly confined to naked horizontal cartel arrangements (price fixing, market sharing, restraints on output and bid-rigging). The ruling also drew stark attention to the limitations of the 'dichotomy' model. The term 'rule of reason' should not be confused with the use of the same term which has been adopted in connection with Article 28 (ex Art. 30) EC on the free movement of goods.

[43] *Chicago Board of Trade* v. *US*, 246 US 231 (1918), per Brandeis J.

[44] Although there is negligible guidance from the Supreme Court as to how this analysis should be conducted, the lower federal circuits have adopted their own methods, essentially breaking down the assessment into four main stages: (1) The plaintiff is required to establish that the restraint or agreement has had, or is likely to have, substantial or significant anti-competitive effects, through a restraint on output or price. Where this burden is discharged: (2) The defendant must establish that the restraint or agreement achieves, or is likely to achieve, pro-competitive benefits (for example, that the restraints will improve technology or achieve technological efficiencies enabling the parties to lower costs, to create products or services that are cheaper or brought to the market faster or to construct new or improved products). If pro-competitive benefits are established, then it falls to the plaintiff to establish either: (3) That the conduct is not reasonably necessary to achieve the stated object; or (4) That the anti-competitive effects outweigh the pro-competitive effects for which the restraint is reasonably necessary.

[45] R. Whish and B. Sufrin, 'Article 85 and the Rule of Reason', (1987) *YEL* 1.

[46] See especially Chaps. 9, 10 and 13.

Article 81(3), rendering Article 81(3) directly applicable as a legal exception to Article 81(1).[47] It may, therefore, now be applied not only by the Commission,[48] but also by the national competition authorities of the 27 Member States[49] and the national courts.[50]

In rethinking its approach to agreements, the Commission has accepted that a more economic and less rigid approach to vertical, horizontal and technology transfer agreements under both Article 81(1) and Article 81(3) is requisite.[51] It has therefore gradually detached itself from its earlier more interventionist policy as it has moved towards an acceptance that consumer welfare should be the benchmark against which agreements are tested. The Commission, however, has not accepted that a 'rule of reason' style analysis balancing anti-and pro-competitive effects under Article 81(1), provides the solution. Rather, it is the Commission's view that it is Article 81(3) not Article 81(1) which provides the appropriate forum for weighing the restrictive effects of the agreement (identified at the Article 81(1) stage) against the economic benefits and efficiencies created by the agreement.[52] This position is set out clearly in its White Paper on Modernisation.

White Paper on the Modernisation of the Rules Implementing Articles 81 and 82 of the EC Treaty [1999] OJ C132/1, [1999] 5 CMLR 208

56. ...It would in a way mean interpreting Article [81(1)] as incorporating a 'rule of reason'...Such a system would ease the notification constraints imposed on undertakings, since they would not be required to notify agreements in order to obtain negative clearance.

57. The Commission has already adopted this approach to a limited extent and has carried out an assessment of the pro- and anti-competitive aspects of some restrictive practices under Article [81(1)]. This approach has been endorsed by the Court of Justice...However, the structure of

---

[47] Reg. 1/2003, Art. 1 provides that agreements which are caught by Article 81(1) and which do not satisfy the conditions of Article 81(3) are prohibited, no prior decision to that effect being required. Further that agreements which are caught by Article 81(1), but which satisfy the conditions of Article 81(3), are not prohibited, no prior decision to that effect being required.

[48] Reg. 1/2003, Arts. 7–10.

[49] Reg. 1/2003, Arts. 5 and 3.

[50] Although relatively rare, the Commission is seeking to encourage greater 'private' enforcement of EC competition law, see Green Paper Damages Actions for breach of the EC Antitrust rules, December 2005, see *infra* Chap. 15.

[51] In 1996, it published a Green Paper on vertical restraints in competition policy, COM (96) 721, instituting a review of its policy towards vertical agreements. This culminated in the adoption of a new broader Block Exemption for Vertical Agreements, Reg. 2790/1999, [1999] OJ L336/21, [2000] 4 CMLR 398, together with comprehensive, accompanying Guidelines on Vertical Restraints explaining both the operation of the block exemption, and analysis of vertical restraints that do not fall within it, [2000] OJ C291/1, [2000] 5 CMLR 1074. The Guidelines heralded a more 'economic approach in the application of Article 81 to vertical restraints' (the Commission promised that the scope of Art. 81 would be limited 'to undertakings holding a certain degree of market power where inter-brand competition may be insufficient', [2000] OJ C291/1, [2000] 5 CMLR 1074, para. 102). Modernization of the regime governing horizontal cooperation agreements followed later (see Reg. 2658/2000, [2000] OJ L304/3; Reg. 2659/2000, [2000] OJ L304/7; and the Commission's Guidelines on the applicability of Article 81 to horizontal co-operation agreements, [2001] OJ C3/ 2), and on 1 May 2004 changes to the regime governing technology transfer agreements were introduced, Commission Reg. 772/2004, [2004] OJ L123/11 and Guidelines on the application of Article 81 of the EC Treaty to technology transfer agreements, [2004] OJ C101/2. See especially Chaps. 9, 10 and 13.

[52] This view has now clearly been endorsed by the CFI, see *infra* 236–7.

Article [81] is such as to prevent greater use being made of this approach: if more systematic use were made under Article [81(1)] of an analysis of the pro- and anti-competitive aspects of a restrictive agreement, Article [81(3)] would be cast aside, whereas any such change could be made only through revision of the Treaty. It would at the very least be paradoxical to cast aside Article [81(3)] when that provision in fact contains all the elements of a 'rule of reason'... Lastly, this option would run the risk of diverting Article [81(3)] from its purpose, which is to provide a legal framework for the economic assessment of restrictive practices and not to allow application of the competition rules to be set aside because of political considerations.

In these paragraphs the Commission questions why Article 81(3) was included, if a full examination of the harmful and beneficial effects of the agreement (similar to the US rule of reason anlaysis) were intended to be made at the Article 81(1) stage. In its view such an approach would render Article 81(3) virtually redundant. It could then be used *only* to authorize restrictive agreements found to have as their object the restriction of competition *or* to authorize agreements resulting in non-economic benefits, for example, social, industrial, environmental, employment, cultural, and/or regional benefits. Whether or not these latter socio-political factors may, or should, be taken into account when making the assessment under Article 81(3) will be discussed below.[53]

In the extract from an article below, Giorgio Monti supports the Commission's view that Article 81(3) provides the main forum for authorizing agreements. He argues that such an approach accords with the ordoliberal background[54] of Article 81 and its bifurcated scheme.

G. Monti, 'Article 81 EC and Public Policy' (2002) *CMLRev* 1057–99, 1061

[T]he ordoliberal conception of competition is more consistent with the structure of Article 81. Under the first paragraph, an agreement which restricts competition (understood as an undue restriction of the economic freedom of the parties or a restriction on other market participants) is prohibited, but under the third paragraph the agreement is exempted if it increases efficiency, with two conditions: first, that the efficiencies resulting from the restrictive agreement be passed on to consumers (as a way of preventing too much wealth being accumulated by the parties to the agreement), and second that competition is not eliminated 'in a substantial part of the products in question' (signifying that the agreement cannot suffocate the economic freedom of the market participants). These conditions reflect the ordoliberal concern over the accumulation of economic power, which requires the Commission to grant exemptions based not only on utilitarian values of total efficiency, but also based on distributive justice.

(ii) The CFI's Judgment in *Métropole*

Although the discussion below will establish that the Community cases on this issue are difficult, if not impossible, to reconcile, the judgment of the CFI in *Métropole Télévision* v.

---

[53] See *infra* 273–7.

[54] See *supra* Chap. 1. See also G. Monti, *EC Competition Law* (Cambridge University Press, 2007), Chaps. 2–4.

Commission supports the view of the Commission that Article 81(3) provides the main forum for weighing anti and pro-competitive aspects of an agreement and, indeed, goes further.[55]

Métropole concerned an appeal from a Commission decision holding that the creation of the joint venture, Télévision par Satellite (TPS), did not infringe Article 81(1) but that certain clauses in the notified agreements infringed Article 81(1) and could be exempted under Article 81(3) *only* for a period of three years. Amongst other things, the applicants argued that the Commission had been wrong to exempt the clauses. Rather, the reasoning adopted by the Commission indicated that these clauses *favoured* competition and did not restrict it. Had the Commission, therefore, correctly applied Article 81(1) using the rule of reason, weighing the pro- and anti-competitive effects of the agreement, the Commission should have found that the agreement did not restrict competition within the meaning of Article 81 at all.[56] The CFI did not accept this argument, observing that contrary to the applicants' assertions the existence of such a rule had not been confirmed by the Community courts. Echoing the view of the Commission in its White Paper on Modernisation, that such an interpretation would be difficult to reconcile with the rules prescribed by Article 81, it stated that Article 81(3) provided the correct forum for weighing the pro and anti-competitive aspects of the agreement. The Court recognized that some Community cases, such as *STM*[57] had favoured a 'more flexible' interpretation of the Article 81(1) prohibition,[58] but held that they did not establish the existence of a rule of reason. Rather, such a rule had not been confirmed by the courts[59] and the cases simply formed part of a broader trend in the case-law according to which it is not necessary to hold, wholly abstractly, that any agreement restricting the freedom of action of one or more of the parties is necessarily caught by Article 81(1).

Case T-528/93, *Métropole Télévision SA* v. *Commission* [1996] ECR II-649, [1996] 5 CMLR 386

72. According to the applicants, as a consequence of the existence of a rule of reason in Community competition law, when Article [81(1)] of the Treaty is applied it is necessary to weigh the pro and anti-competitive effects of an agreement in order to determine whether it is caught by the prohibition laid down in that article. It should, however, be observed, first of all, that contrary to the applicants' assertions the existence of such a rule has not, as such, been confirmed by the Community courts. Quite to the contrary, in various judgments the Court of Justice and the Court

---

[55] Case T-528/93, *Métropole Télévision SA* v. *Commission* [1996] ECR II-649, [1996] 5 CMLR 386. See also Case T-65/98, *Van den Bergh Foods* v. *Commission* [2003] ECR II-4653, [2004] 4 CMLR 1, *aff'd* Case C-552/03 P, *Unilever Bestfoods* v. *Commission* [2006] OJ C294/19 and Case T-328/03, *O2 (Germany) GmbH & Co. OHG* v. *Commission* [2006] ECR II-1231, [2006] 5 CMLR 5.

[56] Case T-528/93, *Métropole Télévision SA* v. *Commission* [1996] ECR II-649, [1996] 5 CMLR 386, para. 72.

[57] Case 56/65, *Société La Technique Minière* v. *Maschinebau Ulm GmbH*, [1966] ECR 234, 249, [1966] CMLR 357. See also Case 258/78, *Nungesser and Eisile* v. *Commission* [1982] ECR 2015, [1983] 1 CMLR 278, Case 161/84, *Pronuptia de Paris GmbH* v. *Pronuptia de Paris Irmgard Schillgallis* [1986] ECR 353, [1986] 1 CMLR 414; Cases T-374, 375, 384 & 388/94, *European Night Services* v. *Commission* [1998] ECR II-3141, [1998] 5 CMLR 718; and Case C-250/92, *DLG*, [1994] ECR I-5641, paras. 31–35.

[58] Case T-528/93, *Métropole Télévision SA* v. *Commission* [1996] ECR II-649, [1996] 5 CMLR 386, para. 75.

[59] Case T-528/93, *Métropole Télévision SA* v. *Commission* [1996] ECR II-649, [1996] 5 CMLR 386, para. 72 set out *infra*.

of First Instance have been at pains to indicate that the existence of a rule of reason in Community competition law is doubtful (see Case C-235/92 P *Montecatini v Commission* [1999] ECR I-4539, paragraph 133 (... even if the rule of reason did have a place in the context of Article 85(1) of the Treaty), and Case T-14/89 *Montedipe v Commission* [1992] ECR II-1155, paragraph 265, and in Case T-148/89 *Tréfilunion v Commission* [1995] ECR II-1063, paragraph 109).

73. Next, it must be observed that an interpretation of Article [81(1)] of the Treaty, in the form suggested by the applicants, is difficult to reconcile with the rules prescribed by that provision.

74. Article 85 of the Treaty expressly provides, in its third paragraph, for the possibility of exempting agreements that restrict competition where they satisfy a number of conditions, in particular where they are indispensable to the attainment of certain objectives and do not afford undertakings the possibility of eliminating competition in respect of a substantial part of the products in question. It is only in the precise framework of that provision that the pro and anti-competitive aspects of a restriction may be weighed (see, to that effect, Case 161/84 *Pronuptia* [1986] ECR 353, paragraph 24, and Case T-17/93 *Matra Hachette v Commission* [1994] ECR II-595, paragraph 48, and *European Night Services and Others v Commission* . . . , paragraph 136). Article [81(3)] of the Treaty would lose much of its effectiveness if such an examination had to be carried out already under Article [81(1)] of the Treaty.

75. It is true that in a number of judgments the Court of Justice and the Court of First Instance have favoured a more flexible interpretation of the prohibition laid down in Article [81(1)] of the Treaty (see, in particular, *Société technique minière* and *Oude Luttikhuis and Others* . . . , *Nungesser and Eisele v Commission* and *Coditel and Others* . . . , *Pronuptia* . . . , and *European Night Services and Others v Commission* . . . , as well as the judgment in Case C-250/92 *DLG* [1994] ECR I-5641, paragraphs 31 to 35).

76. Those judgments cannot, however, be interpreted as establishing the existence of a rule of reason in Community competition law. They are, rather, part of a broader trend in the case-law according to which it is not necessary to hold, wholly abstractly and without drawing any distinction, that any agreement restricting the freedom of action of one or more of the parties is necessarily caught by the prohibition laid down in Article 85(1) of the Treaty. In assessing the applicability of Article [81(1)] to an agreement, account should be taken of the actual conditions in which it functions, in particular the economic context in which the undertakings operate, the products or services covered by the agreement and the actual structure of the market concerned (see, in particular, *European Night Services and Others v Commission* . . . , paragraph 136, *Oude Luttikhuis* . . . , paragraph 10, and *VGB and Others v Commission* . . . , paragraph 140, as well as the judgment in Case C-234/89 *Delimitis* [1991] ECR I-935, paragraph 31).

77. That interpretation, while observing the substantive scheme of Article [81] of the Treaty and, in particular, preserving the effectiveness of Article 85(3), makes it possible to prevent the prohibition in Article [81(1)] from extending wholly abstractly and without distinction to all agreements whose effect is to restrict the freedom of action of one or more of the parties. It must, however, be emphasised that such an approach does not mean that it is necessary to weigh the pro and anti-competitive effects of an agreement when determining whether the prohibition laid down in Article [81(1)] of the Treaty applies.

In *Métropole* the CFI appears, therefore, to reject both the first two of the possible approaches described above and to favour the third (one which divides the substantive appraisal between Article 81(1) and 81(3)).[60] It thus indicates that the Article 81 appraisal should be

---

[60] See *supra* n. 207, but for a different view see, e.g., G. Monti, 'Article 81 EC and Public Policy' (2002) *CMLRev* 1057.

divided into five parts: (1) the Commission (or other person seeking to demonstrate the same) must establish that the agreement restricts competition (identify the anti-competitive aspects); when this burden is discharged the parties (or other undertakings seeking the benefit of Article 81(3)) must establish (2) that the agreement achieves pro-competitive objectives; (3) that consumers attain a fair share of those benefits; (4) the agreement is indispensable to the attainment of the benefits; and (5) there is no possibility of an elimination of competition.[61]

This supposition leads to two further questions. Was the CFI correct to interpret previous case-law this way? If so, exactly how is the envisaged division in analysis to be made: in particular, what constitutes an 'anti-competitive effect' for the purpose of Article 81(1) and what 'pro-competitive' 'aspects of a restriction' can be weighed against them under Article 81(3)? In seeking to answer these questions the discussion in section 3 below indicates that the position is not as clear as the CFI in *Métropole* suggests.

G. THE IMPORTANCE OF THE DEBATE

The decision to render Article 81(3) directly applicable has meant that the procedural problems that followed as a result of the notification and authorization system have fallen away. In one sense, therefore, it does not matter if a broad interpretation of Article 81(1) is adopted, since the Article 81(3) appraisal can be conducted by the Commission, an NCA or a national court, i.e. wherever the issue arises.[62] In substantive and practical terms, however, the so-called 'rule of reason' debate still retains life. It is of paramount importance to know what appraisal should be conducted under Article 81(1) and Article 81(3) respectively. The analysis that must be conducted under Article 81(1) has a profound impact on the role and scope of Article 81(3),[63] the burden of proof imposed on the claimant and those claiming the benefit of Article 81(3) respectively (which may be critical to the outcome of a case),[64] and the risk the parties to the agreement are perceived to take in conclusion of an agreement. The operation of an agreement that falls within Article 81(1) and requires justification under Article 81(3) is perceived, commercially, to be of much greater risk than one falling outside of Article 81(1) altogether.

---

[61] These steps have similarities to the four steps taken in US rule of reason analysis, see A. Jones 'Analysis of Agreements under U.S. and EC Antitrust Law—Convergence or Divergence?' [2006] 51 *Ant Bull* 691.

[62] In one sense Article 81 has now been brought closer to its US counterpart, since the entire Article 81 appraisal may now be made both by competition authorities *and* the courts. Article 81 remains in two parts, however. The Article 81(1) assessment thus remains affected by the existence of Article 81(3).

[63] *See infra* section 4.B.

[64] The burden of proving a breach of Article 81(1) rests on the person alleging the same, whilst the burden of establishing that the Article 81(3) criteria are satisfied rests on those undertakings claiming its benefit, *see* Council Regulation (EC) 1/2003, [2003] OJ L1/1 ('Reg. 1/2003'), Art. 2.

3. ARTICLE 81(1), AGREEMENTS WHICH HAVE AS THEIR OBJECT OR EFFECT THE PREVENTION, RESTRICTION, OR DISTORTION OF COMPETITION

A. GENERAL

In section 2 above it was explained that, in the past, the Commission was criticized for failing to take a sufficiently economic approach when determining whether or not an agreement restricts competition within the meaning of Article 81(1) but that it is now more willing to embark on economic analysis at the Article 81(1) stage. In particular, the Commissions Guidelines on Article 81(3)[65] clearly set out the Commission's view that '[t]he objective of Article 81 is to protect competition on the market as a means of enhancing consumer welfare and of ensuring an efficient allocation of resources'[66] and that the purpose of Article 81(1) is to identify agreements that restrict inter-brand competition (competition between suppliers of competing brands) and intra-brand competition (competition between distributors of the same brand)[67] i.e. agreements which affect 'actual or potential competition to such an extent that on the relevant market negative effects on prices, output, innovation or the variety or quality of goods and services can be expected with a reasonable degree of probability'[68] or which restrict distributors from competing with each other.[69] In addition, it must not be forgotten that it is the Court, not the Commission, which is responsible for the interpretation of the Treaty.[70]

The sections below explore the case-law and consider to what extent it can be reconciled with the Commission's interpretation of Article 81(1) set out in its Article 81(3) Guidelines and the CFI's judgment in *Métropole*. Section B below explains more fully the distinction between object and effect cases. Section C looks at the object cases and section D examines what analysis must be conducted when determining whether or not an agreement has as its effect the restriction of competition.

---

[65] See Guidelines on the application of Article 81(3) of the Treaty [2004] OJ C101/97, paras. 13–31 and *infra* and Chaps. 9, 10 and 13.

[66] See Article 81(3) Guidelines at para. 42. 'Effective competition brings benefits to consumers, such as low prices, high quality products, a wide selection of goods and services, and innovation. Competition and market integration serve these ends since the creation and preservation of an open single market promotes an efficient allocation of resources throughout the Community for the benefit of consumers.' See also DG Competition Discussion Paper on the application of Article 82 of the Treaty to exclusionary abuses, December 2005, para. 4.

[67] See especially Chap. 9 and Guidelines on the application of Article 81(3) of the Treaty [2004] OJ C101/97, paras. 17 and 18.

[68] Article 81(3) Guidelines, para. 24.

[69] Thus according to the Commission two counterfactuals may need to be used one to determine whether the agreement restricts inter-brand competition (whether the agreement restricts actual or potential competition that would have existed without the agreement) and one to determine whether it restricts intra-brand competition (whether the agreement restricts actual or potential competition that would have existed in the absence of the contractual restraints), see Article 81(3) Guidelines, para. 18.

[70] Article 220 of the EC Treaty.

B. OBJECT OR EFFECT

(i) Alternative, not Cumulative, Requirements

The ECJ has held that the words 'object or effect' are to be read disjunctively. They are alternative, not cumulative, requirements. An agreement is caught if *either* its object *or* its effect is the restriction of competition.[71]

(ii) The Object of the Agreement

In the first instance it is necessary to look at the terms of the agreement to determine its object. This is determined by looking not at the common intention of the parties but by examining 'the aims pursued by the agreement ... in the light of the economic context in which the agreement is to be applied'.[72] Where the object of the agreement is to restrict competition there is no need to look further and to prove that its effect is the restriction of competition.

[F]or the purposes of applying Article [81(1)], there is no need to take account of the concrete effects of an agreement once it appears that it has as its object the prevention, restriction or distortion of competition.[73]

A finding that an agreement has as its object the restriction of competition for the purpose of Article 81(1) will not, therefore, be undermined by an argument that the agreement pursues a legitimate object since the agreement constitutes by its very nature a restriction of competition.[74] An agreement pursuing an anti-competitive 'object' cannot be justified by an analysis of the economic context of the anti-competitive conduct concerned.[75] The extract from the Commission's guidelines on the application of Article 81(3) below, explains that agreements are placed in the 'object category' where experience shows that the restraint is likely to lead to negative effects on the market, a reduction in output, an increase in prices and misallocation of resources.

---

[71] Case 56/65, *Société La Technique Minière* v. *Maschinebau Ulm GmbH* [1966] ECR 234, 249, [1966] CMLR 357. See also Case C-234/89, *Delimitis* v. *Henninger Bräu* [1991] ECR I-935, [1992] 5 CMLR 210, para. 13 and Cases T-374, 375, 384 and 388/94, *European Night Services* v. *Commission* [1998] ECR II-3141, [1998] 5 CMLR 718, para. 136.

[72] Cases 29 and 30/83, *Compagnie Royale Asturienne des Mines SA and Rheinzink GmbH* v. *Commission* [1984] ECR 1679, [1985] 1 CMLR 688, para. 26 and Case C-551/03 P, *General Motors BV* v. *Commission* [2006] ECR I-3173, para. 77. See also O. Odudu, 'Interpreting Article 81(1): object as subjective intention (2001) 26 *ELRev* 60 and O. Odudu. 'Interpreting Article 81(1): the Object Requirement Revisited (2001) 26 *ELRev* 379.

[73] Cases 56 and 58/64, *Etablissements Consten SA & Grundig-Verkaufs-GmbH* v. *Commission* [1966] ECR 299, [1966] CMLR 416. The other criteria of Article 81(1) must, of course, be satisfied. Thus the agreement must appreciably affect trade between Member States and appreciably restrict competition, *supra* Chap. 3.

[74] Case T-49/02, *Brasserie Nationale NA* v. *Commission* [2005] ECR II-3033, [2006] 4 CMLR 8, para. 85. 'Even supposing that those circumstances were established, the conclusion that the Agreement had the object of restricting competition within the common market cannot be invalidated by the supposed fact that it also pursued a legitimate object (see, to that effect, *IAZ and Others* v. *Commission*, para. 25). The applicants cannot rely to any purpose on *Delimitis*, because that judgment was delivered in a case relating to vertical relationships, whereas the present case concerns a horizontal agreement. Moreover, the reference made by Brasserie Nationale to *Cassis de Dijon* and *Wouters and Others* must be rejected. Once it has been established that the object of an agreement constitutes, by its very nature, a restriction of competition, such as a sharing of clientele, that agreement cannot, by applying a rule of reason, be exempted from the requirements of Article 81(1) EC by virtue of the fact that it also pursued other objectives, such as those at issue in those judgments'.

[75] Cases C-43 and 45/04 P, *Sumitomo Metal Industries Ltd* v. *Commission* 25 January 2007, para. 43 and Case C-551/03 P, *General Motors BV* v. *Commission* [2006] ECR I-3173, para. 64.

Commission Guidelines on the application of Article 81(3) [2004] OJ C101/97

21. Restrictions of competition by object are those that by their very nature have the potential of restricting competition. These are restrictions which in light of the objectives pursued by the Community competition rules have such a high potential of negative effects on competition that it is unnecessary for the purposes of applying Article 81(1) to demonstrate any actual effect on the market. This presumption is based on the serious nature of the restriction and on experience showing that restrictions of competition by object are likely to produce negative effects on the market and to jeopardize the objectives pursued by the Community competition rules. Restrictions by object such as price fixing and market sharing reduce output and raise prices, leading to misallocation of resources, because goods and services demanded by customers are not produced. They also lead to a reduction in consumer welfare, because consumers have to pay higher prices for the goods and services in question.

To this extent, the jurisprudence of the Court does support a formalistic approach to Article 81(1). In a similar way to the US courts, the ECJ applies a bright line test, finding that some restraints in particular types of agreement have such a 'pernicious' effect that they are automatically assumed to restrict competition. Proof is not required to demonstrate that they have this effect. Arguably, however, the parallel between the US *per se* and EC *object* cases should not be taken further than this. In contrast to the position in the US (i) any alleged economic justifications or pro-competitive aspects of the agreement may, in the EC, be weighed against the restrictive elements at the Article 81(3) stage (although in practice, it is rare for such agreements to meet Article 81(3) criteria[76] this possibility at least remains);[77] (ii) agreements characterized by the US courts as *per se* infringements are not identical to agreements held by the ECJ to have as their object the restriction of competition; and (iii) agreements in the EU will escape prohibition in the EU if the impact of the agreement is 'insignificant' or of minor importance.[78] These kinds of difference have led some to question whether it is useful to adopt the language of *per se* illegality at all under EC competition law.[79]

---

[76] *Infra* 271 ff. If the Commission discovers undertakings operating an agreement containing these types of clauses it is likely to impose a fine.

[77] Case T-17/93, *Matra Hachette* v. *Commission* [1994] ECR II-595, see *infra* 270.

[78] See Chap. 3.

[79] See *supra* section 2.F. These differences are actually more apparent than real and the agreement containing hardcore restraints in the EU are in fact treated in quite similar way to their US counterparts. First, agreements containing a hardcore restraint are most unlikely to escape the Article 81(1) prohibition on the grounds that they do not appreciably restrict competition, so difference (iii) is negligible. Second, the theoretical possibility of an agreement meeting the Article 81(3) criteria does not in fact create a great disparity, at least with regard to horizontal agreements. Because hardcore cartel agreements are naked the reality is that the parties will be incapable of justifying them (and do not generally seek to do so) under Article 81(3). They are, therefore, as they are in the US, effectively prohibited per se in the EU. Further, even though the Commission has on a number of occasions been prepared to exempt an agreement containing price and output restraints where those restraints are indispensable to the achievement of efficiencies, again this does not present a discrepancy. These types of restraint also escape per se categorization and are capable of justification in the US if ancillary to an efficiency enhancing integration, see, e.g. *Broadcast Music, Inc.* v. *Columbia Broadcasting Sys., Inc.,* 441 US 1 (1979) and *NCAA* v. *Bd. of Regents of the Uni v. of Okla.,* 468 US 85 (1984). This means that the theoretical difference created by (ii) is also negligible. It is only with regard to vertical agreements, that major differences are manifest. Although until 2007 the jurisdictions treated resale price

(iii) The Effect of the Agreement

If the object of the agreement cannot be said to restrict competition then, an agreement will not infringe Article 81(1) unless its effect can shown to be the restriction of competition.

Where . . . an analysis of the said clauses does not reveal the effect on competition to be sufficiently deleterious, the consequence of the agreement should then be considered and for it to be caught by the prohibition it is then necessary to find that those factors are present that show that competition has in fact been prevented or restricted or distorted to an appreciable extent. The competition in question must be understood within the actual context in which it would occur in the absence of the agreement in dispute.[80]

Whether or not an agreement falls within the object or effect category thus has a critical impact on the case and the burden of proof. Where it is shown that the object of the agreement is to restrict competition, the onus will shift to the parties to the agreement to defend it and to establish that it meets the criteria of Article 81(3).[81] Where it is not found that the object of the agreement is to restrict competition, however, the burden of proving that this is its *effect* is on the person alleging the breach. Only where this is established does the burden shift onto the parties to defend it under Article 81(3).

It is this determination of whether or not an agreement has as its effect the restriction of competition which presents one of the most difficult problems for EC competition law.[82] By their very nature, contracts restrict the conduct of the parties but restraints on *conduct* are not necessarily the same as restrictions on competition from an economic point of view. Further, even if an agreement creates a restriction of competition in one respect, that restriction may be outweighed by an increase in competition it creates in other respects, so that on balance the agreement is pro- rather than anti-competitive.[83] The objective pursued by Article 81 and the role played by Article 81(1) in pursuit of that objective is therefore of utmost importance to the answer to the question of when an agreement has as its effect the restriction of competition.

---

maintenance in a similar way the treatment of agreements conferring absolute territorial protection on a distributor has been in stark contrast since 1977. Since 1977 these latter agreements have not fallen within the per se category in the US and are, in fact, unlikely to be problematic in the absence of a demonstration that one or more of the parties to the agreement has market power. In the EU, such agreements, with the exception of intellectual property licensing agreements, have almost always been found automatically to infringe Article 81(1) and will be most unlikely to satisfy the conditions of Article 81(3). This approach appears to be motivated not by a pure consumer welfare objective but by tendency of such agreements to compartmentalize the internal market on national grounds, see *infra* 226–33 and Chap. 9.

[80] Case 56/65, *Société La Technique Minière v. Maschinebau Ulm GmbH* [1966] ECR 234, 249, [1966] 1 CMLR 357.

[81] Assuming the other conditions or Article 81(1) are proved to exist and no block exemption applies.

[82] But see also the difficulty of defining and identifying 'dominant' undertaking and 'abuses' of that dominant position for the purposes of Article 82: see *infra* Chaps. 5–7.

[83] See O. Odudu, 'Interpreting Article 81(1): Demonstrating Restrictive Effect' (2001) 26 *ELRev* 261, O. Odudu, 'A New Economic Approach to Article 81(1)?' (2001) 26 *ELRev* 100 and G. Amato, *Antitrust and the Bounds of Power* (Hart Publishing, 1997), 13.

C. AGREEMENTS THAT RESTRICT COMPETITION BY OBJECT

(i) Horizontal Agreements

It was explained above that a presumption of negative effects applies where experience shows that a restraint is likely to lead to a reduction of output and a misallocation of resources. In *European Night Services v. Commission*[84] the CFI held that agreements containing obvious restrictions of competition, such as provisions in agreements between competitors fixing prices or sharing markets, will automatically be held to restrict competition within the meaning of Article 81(1).[85] Thus hard-core cartel activities, where competitors agree or otherwise conspire to fix prices, share markets, impose quotas or otherwise limit output[86] have as their object the restriction of competition.

In some unusual horizontal cases, for example where an agreement involving price-fixing is not 'naked',[87] the Commission has decided that the provisions do not have as their *object* the restriction of competition. In *Visa International-Multilateral Interchange Fee*,[88] for example, the Commission considered that an agreement containing a provision to fix the 'Multilateral interchange fee' (MIF) paid by acquiring banks to issuing banks within the Visa system did not have as its object the restriction of competition[89] although it did find it to have this effect. The Commission *may* have considered that this conclusion made it easier for it to support its subsequent finding that the agreement met the Article 81(3) criteria,[90] since it takes the view that hardcore restraints falling within the object category are generally incapable of meeting the Article 81(3) conditions. Even if this were correct (1) the Commission went on quickly to find, without detailed consideration of the market power of the parties and analysis of the market, that the effect of the agreement was to restrict competition[91] and (2) it explicitly stated that

---

[84]   Cases T-374, 375, 384 and 388/94, [1998] ECR II-3141, [1998] 5 CMLR 718, para. 136 set out *infra* 242–3.

[85]   *Ibid*. Further, agreements to exchange price information may have as their object the restriction of competition, (at least where designed to facilitate the enforcement of a hard-core cartel agreement or to implement it), Cases T-25, 26, 30–2, 34–9, 42–6, 48, 50–71, 87, 88, 103, and 104/95, *Cimenteries CBR SA v. Commission*, [2000] ECR II-491, [2000] 5 CMLR 204, para. 1531, broadly *aff'd*, Cases C-204, 205, 211, 213, 217 & 219/00 P, *Aalborg Portland A/S v. Commission* [2004] ECR I-123, as may collective exclusive dealing agreements, *Nederlandse Federative Vereniging voor de Grootlandel op Elektrotechnisch Gebied and Tecnhische Unie (FEG and TU)*, [2000] OJ L39/1, 4, [2000] 4 CMLR 1208, para. 105.

[86]   Such agreements obviously have the same effect as agreements to restrict price. If the parties restrict output, the price automatically increases. Cartels are dealt with *infra* Chap. 11.

[87]   Agreements are naked where 'They seek to restrict competition without producing any objective countervailing benefits', Mario Monti, 'Fighting Cartels Why and How?' 3rd Nordic Competition Policy Conference Stockholm, 11–12 September 2000, *infra* Chap. 11.

[88]   [2002] OJ L318/17, [2003] 4 CMLR 283. See also *infra* n. 93.

[89]   '[T]he Commission does not consider the MIF agreement to be a restriction of competition by object, since a MIF agreement in a four-party payment system such as that of Visa has as its objective to increase the stability and efficiency of operation of that system...and indirectly to strengthen competition between payment systems...' [2002] OJ L318/17, [2003] 4 CMLR 283, para. 69.

[90]   It does not give this as its reason.

[91]   Since it restricted the freedom of banks individually to decide their own pricing polices, it distorted competition on the Visa issuing and acquiring markets and it distorted the behaviour of acquiring banks vis-à-vis their customers, [2002] OJ L318/17, [2002] 4 CMLR 283, paras. 61–71 (2003). In *National Bancard Corp. v. Visa U.S.A. Inc.*, 779 F.2d 592 (11th Cir. 1986), *cert. denied*, 479 U.S. 923 (1986), the Eleventh Circuit upheld the District Court's finding that Visa did not possess power in the relevant product market (all payment devices, including cash, checks, and all forms of credit cards) and that even if it did, the interchange fee was, on balance, pro-competitive in nature and reasonably cost related. See also discussion of Case T-168/01 *GlaxoSmithKline*

an agreement concerning prices was not always to be classified as a cartel and thus as inherently non-exemptible.[92]

Given these factors it is perhaps surprising that the Commission did not classify the restraints as restrictions by object, and so place the burden on the parties to defend them relying on the criteria set out in Article 81(3).[93] Indeed, this appears to be the approach the Commission subsequently took in *Reims II*[94] and *CECED*.[95] *Reims II* concerned an agreement on terminal dues (a multilateral system providing for remuneration for the costs of handling and delivering cross-border mail)[96] between EU postal operators. The Commission considered that by fixing the dues the parties had eliminated or reduced their freedom to determine the level of remuneration for the delivery of inward cross-border mail and so had jointly fixed prices. The agreement thus had 'as its object or effect to prevent, restrict or distort competition within the common market'. Further, in *CECED* the Commission held that an agreement between washing machine producers to refrain from producing or importing less energy efficient machines had as its object the restriction of competition. In both cases the Commission accepted that the agreement met the conditions of Article 81(3), and so merited an exemption.[97]

Visa nonetheless suggests that the assessment of whether the agreement has as its object the restriction of competition may require an enquiry that is broader than just an examination of the terms of the agreement.[98]

Guidelines on the application of Article 81(3) of the Treaty [2004] OJ C101/97

22. The assessment of whether or not an agreement has as its object the restriction of competition is based on a number of factors. These factors include, in particular, the content of the agreement and the objective aims pursued by it. It may also be necessary to consider the context in which it is (to be) applied and the actual conduct and behaviour of the parties on the market.

Services Unlimited v. Commission, 27 Sept. 2006, [2006] 5 CMLR 1623, Cases C-501, 513, 515 and 519/06 P (judgment pending) *infra* 231–3.

[92] When considering Art. 81(3) the Commission stated that it was not the case that an agreement concerning prices is always to be classified as a cartel and thus as inherently non-exemptible. [2002] OJ L318/17, [2003] 4 CMLR 283, para. 79.

[93] Contrast, the approach of the UK's Office of Fair Trading (the OFT) in *MasterCard UK Members Forum Limited* 6 September 2005 (although this decision was, in the end, set aside by the UK's Competition Appeal Tribunal (the 'CAT') essentially after the UK's Office of Fair Trading (the 'OFT') sought to defend the Decision on the basis of arguments not set out in the Decision itself, Cases 105401056/1/1/05, *MasterCard UK Members Forum Limited v. OFT* [2006] CAT 14) and the Eleventh Circuit in *National Bancard Corp. v. Visa U.S.A. Inc.*, 779 F.2d 592 (11th Cir. 1986), *cert. denied*, 479 U.S. 923 (1986), *supra* n. 91.

[94] *Reims II*, [1999] OJ L275/17 (renewal), [2004] OJ L56/76.

[95] 2000 OJ L187/47, [2000] 5 CMLR 635.

[96] The dues payable were fixed as a percentage of domestic tariffs. The agreement set dues for all the parties in a uniform way. Although it expressly allowed the parties to enter into bilateral or multilateral agreements between themselves the Commission considered it was unlikely they would do so as the agreement eliminated any incentive to do so, [2004] OJ L56/ 76, para. 65.

[97] See the discussion of Article 81(3) *infra*.

[98] This view gains support from the judgment of Case T-168/01, *GlaxoSmithKline Services Unlimited v. Commission*, 27 Sept. 2006, [2006] 5 CMLR 1623, Cases C-501, 513, 515 and 519/06 P (judgment pending), discussed *infra* 231–3.

> In other words, an examination of the facts underlying the agreement and the specific circumstances in which it operates may be required before it can be concluded whether a particular restriction constitutes a restriction of competition by object. The way in which an agreement is actually implemented may reveal a restriction by object even where the formal agreement does not contain an express provision to that effect. Evidence of subjective intent on the part of the parties to restrict competition is a relevant factor but not a necessary condition.

(ii) Vertical Agreements

a. General

The subject of vertical restraints, which is considered in Chapter 9 below, has caused as much, if not more, controversy as any other area of EC competition law. Since vertical agreements are not made between competitors and are *prima facie* less obviously anti-competitive than horizontal agreements,[99] some commentators have argued that competition law should only be concerned with vertical agreements where one of the parties to the agreement has market power. Indeed, some systems of competition law take a fairly relaxed or laissez-faire approach to vertical agreements.[100] This has not been the position in the EC where, until recently, an extremely interventionist approach was adopted. In Chapter 3 it was seen, that in *Consten & Grundig* the ECJ held that Article 81 applied to both horizontal and vertical agreements.[101] Further, it even went so far as to hold that certain vertical restraints have as their *object* the restriction of competition. An examination of cases dealing with vertical agreements suggests that the objectives of Article 81(1) run broader than pure consumer welfare objectives. Not only has the Court held that a provision imposing resale price maintenance[102] has as its object the restriction of competition, but it has persistently held that a provision granting a dealer an exclusive territory protected from all competition in the contract goods (absolute territorial protection)[103] will lead to a finding of anti-competitive object.[104]

---

[99] See *infra* Chap. 9.

[100] This was the position in the UK. Vertical agreements were not in general caught by the Restrictive Trade Practices Act 1976 (R. Whish, *Competition Law* (3rd edn., Butterworths, 1993), chap. 5), and vertical agreements (except for price-fixing agreements) were originally excluded from the Competition Act 1998's Chapter I prohibition (the provision modelled on Art. 81); see s. 50 of the Act and the Competition Act 1998 (Land and Vertical Agreements Exclusion) Order 2000/310. Post modernization, however, the Verticals Exclusion Order was repealed (from 1 May 2005) in order to bring UK law into line with EC law, see Competition Act 1998 (Land Agreements Exclusion and Revocation Order) 2004 and, e.g., 419 OFT Vertical Agreements. See also the approach adopted in the USA, discussed *infra* Chap. 9.

[101] In Cases 56 and 58/64, *Etablissements Consten SA & Grundig-Verkaufs-GmbH v. Commission* [1966] ECR 299, [1966] CMLR 418, the ECJ did not accept the argument that Article 81 should have no application to vertical agreements at all because they are analogous to relationships between a parent and its commercial representative or subsidiary and should be controlled, if at all, under Article 82: see *supra* Chap. 3.

[102] Case 234/83, *SA Binon & Cie v. S.A. Agence et Messageries de la Presse* [1985] ECR 2015, [1985] 3 CMLR 800, para. 44 ('provisions which fix the prices to be observed in contracts with third parties constitute, of themselves, a restriction on competition within the meaning of Article [81(1)]'). See also Case 161/84, *Pronuptia de Paris GmbH v. Pronuptia de Paris Irmgard Schillgallis* [1986] ECR 353, [1986] 1 CMLR 414.

[103] Agreements which prevent all parallel trade in the contract goods. See Cases 56 and 58/64, *Etablissements Consten SA & Grundig-Verkaufs-GmbH v. Commission* [1966] ECR 299, 348 [1966] CMLR 418; Case C-234/89, *Delimitis v. Henninger Bräu* [1991] ECR I-935, [1992] 5 CMLR 210; Case 161/84, *Pronuptia de Paris GmbH v. Pronuptia de Paris Irmgard Schillgallis,* [1986] ECR 353, [1986] 1 CMLR 414; Case T-77/92, *Parker Pen v. Commission* [1994] ECR II-549, [1995] 5 CMLR 435.

[104] The elimination of intra-brand price competition or a complete elimination of intra-brand competition between dealers, restricts competition within the meaning of Article 81(1) irrespective of the size of

b. Agreements Imposing Minimum Retail Prices on Distributors

Vertical, as well as horizontal, price restraints have as their object the restriction of competition.[105] In *Pronuptia de Paris GmbH v. Pronuptia de Paris Irmgard Schillgallis*[106] the ECJ, in setting out guidelines on the compatibility of distribution franchises with Article 81(1),[107] held that 'provisions which impair the franchisee's freedom to determine his own prices are restrictive of competition'[108] and in *SA Binon & Cie v. SA Agence et Messageries de la Presse*[109] the ECJ held that 'provisions which fix the prices to be observed in contracts with third parties constitute, of themselves, a restriction on competition within the meaning of Article [81(1)]'. Many take the view that resale price maintenance reduces competition between suppliers, leads to undue transparency in prices and, frequently, provides a simple mechanism for operating supplier or retailer cartels.[110]

c. Agreements Granting a Distributor Absolute Territorial Protection

It also appears clear that distribution agreements which prevent all parallel trade in the contract goods have as their object the restriction of competition.[111] This position was established by the ECJ in *Consten and Grundig*.[112]

It was seen in Chapter 3 that Consten and Grundig concerned an agreement concluded between Grundig, a German manufacturer of radios, tape recorders, dictaphones, and televisions, and Consten. Consten was appointed exclusive distributor of Grundig's products in France. The agreement obliged Consten not to handle competing products, to order a minimum quantity of Grundig products, to stock accessories and spare parts, to provide after-sales services, and not to sell Grundig products outside France. In return, Grundig agreed not to deliver the product for sale in France itself and to prohibit all other distributors from seeking sales, actively or passively, within France. To reinforce the territorial protection Grundig assigned to Consten the rights to the Grundig trade mark GINT, in France. The provisions in the agreement were therefore intended to confer *absolute territorial protection* upon Consten and to prevent all parallel trade in Grundig products. The parties argued that these restrictions on the conduct and/or the restriction on the sale of Grundig products by anyone else in France did not amount to restrictions of competition.

The Commission issued a decision finding that the agreement was designed to restrict and distort competition. The exclusive contract and ancillary arrangements (in particular, in relation to the trade mark) had the object of relieving Consten of the competition of other undertakings in so far as it involved the import or wholesale trade in Grundig products in

---

inter-brand competition on the market (but see discussion of appreciability *infra* 234–5). But see Case T-168/01 *GlaxoSmithKline Services Unlimited* v. *Commission*, 27 Sept. 2006, [2006] 5 CMLR 1623, Cases C-501, 513, 515 and 519/06 P (judgment pending).

[105] See the discussion of resale price maintenance (RPM), *infra* Chap. 9.

[106] Case 161/84, [1986] ECR 353, [1986] 1 CMLR 414.

[107] See *infra* 250 ff and Chap. 9.

[108] Case 161/84, *Pronuptia de Paris GmbH v. Pronuptia de Paris Irmgard Schillgallis* [1986] ECR 353, [1986] 1 CMLR 414, para. 25.

[109] Case 234/83, [1985] ECR 2015, [1985] 3 CMLR 800, para. 44.

[110] See Chap. 9.

[111] But see discussion of Case T-168/0, *GlaxoSmithKline Services Unlimited* v. *Commission*, 27 Sept. 2006, [2006] 5 CMLR 1623, Cases C-501, 513, 515 and 519/06 P (judgment pending).

[112] Cases 56 and 58/64, *Etablissements Consten SA & Grundig-Verkaufs-GmbH v. Commission* [1966] ECR 299, [1966] CMLR 416.

France. Further, an exemption was refused. The agreement created absolute territorial protection, prevented consumers obtaining a fair share of any of the benefits of the agreement, and contained restrictions which were not indispensable to the attainment of any benefit.

The parties appealed to the ECJ, challenging the Commission's decision on several grounds.[113] In particular, it was complained that the Commission had erred in its application of Article 81(1) since it had failed to base itself on the 'rule of reason'. It had been wrong simply to conclude that the object of its agreement was to restrict competition without considering its effect. Broadly, the parties' argument hinged on the fact that the agreement had been essential to enable Grundig to penetrate the French market and could not, therefore, be said to restrict competition.[114] The Commission had wrongly considered the transaction with hindsight, *ex post*, when matters had turned out well. If, however, it had taken account of the market at the time that the agreement was entered into, *ex ante*, when matters looked risky and uncertain, it would have been apparent that the distributor would not have proceeded without the territorial protection.[115] The exclusivity was crucial to prevent other distributors from taking a 'free ride'[116] on Consten's promotional and investment efforts. They would have been able to import the products more cheaply from Germany[117] (this is in fact exactly what UNEF, a Parisian company, and Leissner in Strasbourg had done).

The parties thus argued that despite the fact that the agreement resulted in the existence of only one distributor of Grundig products in France (there was a restriction of *intra-brand competition*), the agreement led to an increase in competition for electrical products in France (there was an increase in *inter-brand competition*). French consumers wishing to purchase such products now also had the option to purchase Grundig products in addition to those of the other manufacturers on the market. Consequently, the Commission had been wrong to focus solely on the restriction in intra-brand competition. It should instead have considered the effects of the disputed contract upon competition between Grundig and its competitor's products.[118]

The notion that the Commission's decision should have been marked with greater market analysis was supported by Advocate General Roemer.[119] The Advocate General was highly critical of the Commission's approach. The Commission should have considered both whether the agreement was necessary for Grundig to penetrate the French market and whether or not there was vigorous competition between producers of competing products. Article 81(1) should not have been applied on the basis of purely theoretical considerations to a situation which might, upon closer inspection, reveal no appreciable adverse effects on competition. Article 81(1) required a consideration of the effects of the agreement on the market. This could

---

[113] One of the grounds being that Article 81(1) did not apply to vertical agreements at all, see *supra* Chap. 3.

[114] In the absence of the promise of exclusivity, a distributor would not have been encouraged to take on the risky new venture and invest resources in promoting the new product on the French market. Such a distributor would have to persuade French consumers to purchase Grundig products instead of other competing brands of electrical products available and established on the French market.

[115] See, e.g., V. Korah, *An Introductory Guide to EC Competition Law and Practice* (7th edn., Hart Publishing, 2000), sect. 2.4.

[116] For a greater discussion of the free rider arguments, see *infra* Chap. 9.

[117] The German distributors did not, consequently, have to engage in such high levels of promotion and investment.

[118] See, e.g., V. Korah, *An Introductory Guide to EC Competition Law and Practice* (8th edn., Hart Publishing, 2004), para. 2.4.1.

[119] Cases 56 and 58/64, *Etablissements Consten SA & Grundig-Verkaufs-GmbH v. Commission* [1966] ECR 299, [1966] CMLR 418.

not be established without looking at the market *in concreto* and without taking account of competition between similar products. In a case like this one, where the agreement had already been implemented, the Commission should have made a comparison between two market situations: that after making the agreement and that which would have arisen had there been no agreement.[120] If Grundig would not have found an outlet for its products in the absence of supplying a sole concessionaire, the exclusive distribution agreement clearly promoted competition. It would have been necessary for Grundig to gain access to or penetrate the new market. In his view, therefore, Article 81(1) should not be applied if, in the absence of the agreement appointing a single distributor exclusively in France, Grundig would not have found an outlet for its products.

In this case the ECJ did not agree with its Advocate General but upheld the Commission's decision.[121] It held that the agreement giving Consten a monopoly over the sale of Grundig products in France (absolute territorial protection) had as its *object* the restriction of competition so that an assessment of its *effect* was unnecessary. The arguments of the parties thus fell on deaf ears.

Cases 56 and 58/64, *Etablissements Consten SA and Grundig-Verkaufs-GmbH* v. Commission [1966] ECR 299, 342–3, [1966] CMLR 418, 472–4

Court of Justice

The complaints concerning the criterion of restriction on competition

The applicants and the German Government maintain that since the Commission restricted its examination solely to Grundig products the decision was based upon a false concept of competition and of the rules on prohibition contained in Article [81(1)], since this concept applies particularly to competition between similar products of different makes; the Commission, before declaring Article [81(1)] to be applicable, should, by basing itself upon the 'rule of reason', have considered the economic effects of the disputed contract upon competition between the different makes. There is a presumption that vertical sole distributorship agreements are not harmful to competition and in the present case there is nothing to invalidate that presumption. On the contrary, the contract in question has increased the competition between similar products of different makes.

The principle of freedom of competition concerns the various stages and manifestations of competition. Although competition between producers is generally more noticeable than that between distributors of products of the same make, it does not thereby follow that an agreement tending to restrict the latter kind of competition should escape the prohibition of Article [81(1)] merely because it might increase the former.

Besides, for the purpose of applying Article [81(1)], there is no need to take account of the concrete effects of an agreement once it appears that it has as its object the prevention, restriction or distortion of competition.

---

[120] See the ECJ's judgment in Case 56/65, *Société La Technique Minière v. Maschinebau Ulm GmbH* [1966] ECR 234, [1966] 1 CMLR 357, discussed *infra* 246–7.

[121] Cases 56 and 58/64, [1966] ECR 299, [1966] CMLR 418.

Therefore the absence in the contested decision of any analysis of the effects of the agreement on competition between similar products of different makes does not, of itself, constitute a defect in the decision.

It thus remains to consider whether the contested decision was right in founding the prohibition of the disputed agreement under Article [81(1)] on the restriction on competition created by the agreement in the sphere of the distribution of Grundig products alone. The infringement which was found to exist by the contested decision results from the absolute territorial protection created [by] the said contract in favour of Consten on the basis of French law. The applicants thus wished to eliminate any possibility of competition at the wholesale level in Grundig products in the territory specified in the contra[c]t essentially by two methods.

First, Grundig undertook not to deliver even indirectly to third parties products intended for the area covered by the contract. The restrictive nature of that undertaking is obvious if it is considered in the light of the prohibition on exporting which was imposed not only on Consten but also on all the other sole concessionnaires of Grundig, as well as the German wholesalers.

Secondly, the registration in France by Consten of the GINT trade mark, which Grundig affixes to all its products, is intended to increase the protection inherent in the disputed agreement, against the risk of parallel imports into France of Grundig products, by adding the protection deriving from the law on industrial property rights. Thus no third party could import Grundig products from other Member States of the Community for resale in France without running serious risks.

The defendant properly took into account the whole distribution system thus set up by Grundig. In order to arrive at a true representation of the contractual position the contract must be placed in the economic and legal context in the light of which it was concluded by the parties. Such a procedure is not to be regarded as an unwarrantable interference in legal transactions or circumstances which were not the subject of the proceedings before the Commission.

The situation as ascertained above results in the isolation of the French market and makes it possible to charge for the products in question prices which are sheltered from all effective competition. In addition, the more producers succeed in their efforts to render their own makes of product individually distinct in the eyes of the consumer, the more the effectiveness of competition between producers tend to diminish. Because of the considerable impact of distribution costs on the aggregate cost price, it seems important that competition between dealers should also be stimulated. The efforts of the dealer are stimulated by competition between distributors of products of the same make. Since the agreement thus aims at isolating the French market for Grundig products and maintaining artificially, for products of a very well-known brand, separate national markets within the Community, it is therefore such as to distort competition in the Common Market.

It was therefore proper for the contested decision to hold that the agreement constitutes an infringement of Article [81(1)]. No further considerations, whether of economic data (price differences between France and Germany, representative character of the type of appliance considered, level of overheads borne by Consten) or of the corrections of the criteria upon which the Commission relied in its comparisons between the situations of the French and German markets, and no possible favourable effects of the agreement in other respects, can in any way lead, in the face of abovementioned restrictions, to a different solution under Article [81(1)].

The judgment in *Consten and Grundig* is one of the most important judgments in EC competition law. Apart from establishing that Article 81(1) applies to horizontal and vertical agreements, to all agreements which affect trade between Member States even if the effect on trade is not a

230 | EC COMPETITION LAW

prejudicial one,[122] and, potentially, to agreements relating to the licensing of intellectual property rights,[123] the ECJ held that Article 81(1) applied to an agreement which had as its object the restriction of competition irrespective of its alleged effects.[124] Although the ECJ recognized the importance of competition between producers (inter-brand competition) it held that agreements which restricted competition between distributors (intra-brand competition) could also restrict competition for the purposes of Article 81(1). It was important that competition between dealers should be stimulated, and intra-brand as well as inter-brand competition maintained. In particular, restrictions on intra-brand competition might facilitate brand differentiation and diminish competition between producers. The agreement in question eliminated any possibility of competition between distributors of Grundig products and led to the isolation of the French market and so distorted competition and infringed Article 81(1). The Commission had not, therefore, erred by failing to consider the effects of the agreement for the purposes of Article 81(1).

There seems little doubt that the Court's judgment in *Consten and Grundig* was influenced not so much by the pernicious effects of the agreement's provisions from a competition perspective, as by the effects of the agreement from the single market perspective. Whatever the economic justifications for the agreement the affront to the single market goal in this case was too severe.[125] It was this factor that led to the categorizing the agreement as an '*object*' case. The object of the agreement was to grant absolute territorial protection and to eliminate competition at a wholesale level in Grundig products in the territory. The French market had been isolated and the French distributor sheltered from all effective competition. The Court sent out a clear message: agreements which divide up the common market and preclude all cross-border trade in the contract product will not be tolerated. Provisions providing for such protection in an agreement will automatically infringe Article 81(1).

G. Amato, *Antitrust and the Bounds of Power* (Hart Publishing, 1997), 48–9

In the leading case in this area, *Consten & Grundig*, of 1966, . . . the Commission challenged the exclusive agreement for France that Grundig had given to Consten and had strengthened by barring its wholesale distributors in Germany and other countries from selling to France, where the price of Grundig products was kept higher than elsewhere, net of French tax. The parties maintained, first before the Commission itself and then before the Court of Justice, that Article [81] referred primarily to inter-brand competition, and that as far as intra-brand restrictions went, one had to presume efficiency in promoting inter-brand competition failing proof of the contrary. This argument copied word-for-word approaches of the Chicago School, which in fact at the time the American courts themselves had rejected, in the name of protection (dropped later in the *Sylvania* case) for the right of each distributor or retailer to exercise freedom of trade without restraint.

---

[122] The effect of the agreement in *Consten and Grundig* was that *more*, not less, of Grundig's products would flow from Germany to France and would compete there with other brands: see *supra* Chap. 3.

[123] The ECJ also went on to hold that the agreement relating to the GINT trade mark infringed Article 81(1). Otherwise, Consten could have used the trade mark to achieve the objectives of the prohibited exclusive distribution agreement: see *infra* Chap. 10.

[124] The object of the agreement was to restrict competition even though the parties might have been able to show that the agreement was necessary to ensure that the supplier found an outlet for its products.

[125] See *supra* Chap. 1.

Our court did not accept the arguments either, but for very different reasons. It accepted that inter-brand competition was the most relevant for the purposes of prohibition under Article [81], but added that this did not *a priori* exempt intra-brand restrictions, with the consequence—inconceivable today (and perhaps in earlier times too) for an American court—that the fact that the Commission was not concerned to ascertain the size of inter-brand competition was irrelevant. On this basis, the absolute territorial protection by which the exclusivity for France was guaranteed was illegitimate. It is indeed true, said the Court, that imports have an effect on the supply planning that Consten may engage in and on the organization of services it may offer customers. But a margin of risk is inherent in commercial activity, and in any case 'the more manufacturers isolate themselves from each other in consumers' eyes, the more competition among them is reduced. Moreover, competition among wholesale distributors of products of one and the same brand enlivens the downstream market of sales to final consumers'.

As we can see, these are very important assertions of principle that bring the decision close to the American ones of the 1960s. But there are two important differences, one explicit and the other implicit. The explicit one is that the need for intra-brand competition is based on protection not of an individual right (freedom of trade) but of a general and objective principle (competitiveness of the market in all its segments). The implicit one is that such a pervasive and rigorous principle is asserted to the extent that it serves to protect another principle, a higher one in 1966, that of market integration. For the territory protected by Consten's rigid exclusivity coincided with that of the French State, and both the Commission and the Court saw this protection as persistence of the segmentation of economic activities along national frontiers, violating the 'Grundnorm' of the whole Community system.

The ECJ has consistently reiterated this view that agreements which isolate national markets and preclude all cross-border trade automatically offend Article 81(1).[126] In this respect the single market objective has had a very special influence on the interpretation of what amounts to a restriction of competition for the purpose of Article 81(1). Only once, in exceptional circumstances, has a different conclusion been drawn. In *GlaxoSmithKline Services Unlimited v Commission*[127] the CFI held that since the objective of Article 81(1) was to prevent firms from reducing the welfare of the final consumer of the products in question, an agreement to limit parallel trade could only be considered to have as its object the restriction of competition, in so far as it could be presumed to deprive final consumers of those advantages. In that case the specific characteristics of the pharmaceutical sector, which led prices of medicine to be largely shielded from the free play of supply and demand by regulation, meant that *no* assumption could be made that parallel trade would reduce prices and increase the welfare of final consumers. It could not therefore be presumed that an agreement containing an export ban, dual pricing system or other limitation of parallel trade, would have a negative effect on competition so that it was to be regarded as having the object of restricting competition.

---

[126] See, e.g., Case C-234/89, *Delimitis v. Henninger Bräu* [1991] ECR I-935, [1992] 5 CMLR 210; Case 161/84, *Pronuptia de Paris GmbH v. Pronuptia de Paris Irmgard Schillgallis* [1986] ECR 353, [1986] 1 CMLR 414; Case T-77/92, *Parker Pen v. Commission* [1994] ECR II-549, [1995] 5 CMLR 435 and *infra* Chap. 9. To this limited extent the Court has, therefore, endorsed the Commission's view that distribution agreements pose a threat to the common market because of their ability to divide it.

[127] Case T-168/01, 27 Sept. 2006, [2006] 5 CMLR 1623, Cases C-501, 513, 515 and 519/06 P (judgment pending).

Case T-168/01, *GlaxoSmithKline Services Unlimited* v *Commission*, 27 September 2006, [2006] 5 CMLR 1623

The existence of an anti-competitive object

114. GSK does not dispute that Clause 4 of the General Sales Conditions was inserted with the intention of limiting the parallel trade between Spain and other Member States, in particular the United Kingdom, in 82 medicines sold by GW.

115. It follows from the case-law that agreements which ultimately seek to prohibit parallel trade must in principle be regarded as having as their object the restriction of competition (*Consten and Grundig* v *Commission*, paragraph 110 above, pp. 342 and 343; Case 19/77 *Miller International* v *Commission* [1978] ECR 131, paragraphs 7 and 18; Joined Cases 32/78, 36/78 and 82/78 *BMW Belgium* v *Commission* [1979] ECR 2435, paragraphs 20 to 28 and 31; and *Sandoz Prodotti Farmaceutici* v *Commission* . . . , paragraph 16).

116. It also follows from the case-law that agreements that clearly intend to treat parallel trade unfavourably must in principle be regarded as having as their object the restriction of competition (Joined Cases 96/82 to 102/82, 104/82, 105/82, 108/82 and 110/82 *IAZ and Others* v *Commission* [1983] ECR 3369, paragraphs 23 to 25; and Case C-551/03 P *General Motors* v *Commission* [2006] ECR I-0000, paragraphs 67 and 68).

117. However, GSK is correct to maintain that, having regard to the legal and economic context, the Commission could not rely on the mere fact that Clause 4 of the General Sales Conditions established a system of differentiated price intended to limit parallel trade as the basis for its conclusion that that provision had as its object the restriction of competition.

118. In effect, the objective assigned to Article 81(1) EC, which constitutes a fundamental provision indispensable for the achievement of the missions entrusted to the Community, in particular for the functioning of the internal market (Case C-126/97 *Eco Swiss* [1999] ECR I-3055, paragraph 36, and Case C-453/99 *Courage* v *Crehan* [2001] ECR I-6297, paragraph 20), is to prevent undertakings, by restricting competition between themselves or with third parties, from reducing the welfare of the final consumer of the products in question (Joined Cases T-213/01 and T-214/01 *Österreichische Postsparkasse and Bank für Arbeit und Wirtschaft* v *Commission* [2006] ECR II-0000, paragraph 115; see also, to that effect, *Consten and Grundig* v *Commission* . . . p. 493, and Case 28/77 *Tepea* v *Commission* [1978] ECR 1391, paragraph 56). At the hearing, in fact, the Commission emphasised on a number of occasions that it was from that perspective that it had carried out its examination in the present case, initially concluding that the General Sales Conditions clearly restricted the welfare of consumers, then considering whether that restriction would be offset by increased efficiency which would itself benefit consumers.

119. Consequently, the application of Article 81(1) EC to the present case cannot depend solely on the fact that the agreement in question is intended to limit parallel trade in medicines or to partition the common market, which leads to the conclusion that it affects trade between Member States, but also requires an analysis designed to determine whether it has as its object or effect the prevention, restriction or distortion of competition on the relevant market, to the detriment of the final consumer. As may be seen from the case-law cited at paragraphs 111 and 112 above, that analysis, which may be abridged when the clauses of the agreement reveal in themselves the existence of an alteration of competition, as the Commission observed at the hearing, must, on the other hand, be supplemented, depending on the requirements of the case, where that is not so (*Société technique minière*, paragraph 55 above, pp. 248 to 251, and *Consten and Grundig* v *Commission*, paragraph 110 above, pp. 342 and 343).

120. In particular, in *Consten and Grundig* v *Commission* . . . , which gave rise to the case-law cited at paragraphs 115 and 116 above, the Court of Justice, contrary to the Commission's contention in its written submissions, did not hold that an agreement intended to limit parallel trade

must be considered by its nature, that is to say, independently of any competitive analysis, to have as its object the restriction of competition. On the contrary, the Court of Justice merely held, first, that an agreement between a producer and a distributor which might tend to restore the national divisions in trade between Member States might be of such a kind as to frustrate the most fundamental objectives of the Community (p. 340), a consideration which led it to reject a plea alleging that Article 81(1) EC was not applicable to vertical agreements (pp. 339 and 340). The Court of Justice then carried out a competitive analysis, abridged but real, during the course of which it held, in particular, that the agreement in question sought to eliminate any possibility of competition at the wholesale level in order to charge prices which were sheltered from all effective competition, considerations which led it to reject a plea alleging that there was no restriction of competition (pp. 342 and 343).

121. While it has been accepted since then that parallel trade must be given a certain protection, it is therefore not as such but, as the Court of Justice held, in so far as it favours the development of trade, on the one hand, and the strengthening of competition, on the other hand (Case C-373/90, *X* [1992] ECR I-131, paragraph 12), that is to say, in this second respect, in so far as it gives final consumers the advantages of effective competition in terms of supply or price (*Tepea* v *Commission*, paragraph 118 above, paragraphs 43 and 56). Consequently, while it is accepted that an agreement intended to limit parallel trade must in principle be considered to have as its object the restriction of competition, that applies in so far as the agreement may be presumed to deprive final consumers of those advantages.

Despite the special characteristics of the pharmaceutical market, the conclusion drawn in this case is difficult to reconcile with other case law which establishes that certain agreements are in themselves considered to pursue an object restrictive of competition and fall within a category of agreements expressly prohibited by Article 81(1) and which cannot be justified by an analysis of the economic context of the anti-competitive conduct concerned.[128] Indeed, the Commission has appealed this aspect of the CFI's judgment maintaining that the Court's analysis confirming the existence of the restrictive 'effects' constitutes in reality an analysis of the restrictive 'object' of the agreement having due regard to the legal and economic context, and should have led the Court to confirm the Decision's finding that the agreement had an anti-competitive object.[129]

(iii) Intellectual Property Licensing Agreements

As in the case of vertical restraints, a strong argument may be presented to suggest that licences of intellectual property rights, which may be concluded between competitors or non-competitors, are not restrictive of competition at all and should not, therefore, be subjected to the control of Article 81(1). For example, the owner of a patent has the exclusive right to produce the patented product and to sell it at whatever price he wishes. The licensing of the right to exploit that patent in fact increases competition, in that a new licensee is introduced onto the market, and enables the new technology to be disseminated more widely. Further, like vertical agreements, restrictive clauses, such as a clause giving the licensee territorial protection, may be necessary in order to persuade the licensee to enter into the agreement.

---

[128] See *supra* n. 75 and accompanying text.

[129] Case 513/06 P (judgment pending). See also e.g. Case C-551/03 P, *General Motors BV v. Commission* [2006] ECR I-3173, paras. 64–80.

In accordance with its approach taken to vertical restraints, the ECJ takes the view that restrictions on the determination of prices for the licensed products[130] and, subject to limited exceptions,[131] provisions in a licence which impose absolute territorial protection on the licensee have as their *object* the restriction of competition within the meaning of Article 81(1).[132]

(iv) Restrictions by Object and 'Hard-Core' Restraints

The text above sets out the types of contractual provisions that have caused a finding that an agreement has as its object the restriction of competition.[133] These clauses correspond with an emerging list of 'hard-core' restraints, identified by the Commission in its Notice on agreements of minor importance;[134] block exemptions;[135] and guidelines on vertical restraints, horizontal cooperation agreements and technology transfer agreements.[136] This view is confirmed by the Commission in its Article 81(3) Guidelines.

Guidelines on the Application of Article 81(3) of the Treaty [2004] OJ C101/97

23. Non-exhaustive guidance on what constitutes restrictions by object can be found in Commission block exemption regulations, guidelines and notices. Restrictions that are black-listed in block exemptions or identified as hardcore restrictions in guidelines and notices are generally considered by the Commission to constitute restrictions by object. In the case of horizontal agreements restrictions of competition by object include price fixing, output limitation and sharing of markets and customers. As regards, vertical agreements the category of restrictions by object includes, in particular, fixed and minimum resale price maintenance and restrictions providing absolute territorial protection, including restrictions on passive sales.

It should be borne in mind, however, that this categorization may change over time with changes in economic thinking and other developments and that every agreement, even those containing hardcore restraints are capable of satisfying Article 81(3) if its conditions are fulfilled.

(v) Object Cases and Appreciability

The conclusion that an agreement has as its object the restriction of competition makes the simple assumption that, in the context in which the agreement is operated, it constitutes an

---

[130] See *supra* nn. 106 and 109 and accompanying text and *infra* Chap 10.

[131] See Case 27/87, *Erauw-Jacquéry Sprl v. La Hesbignonne Société Coopérative* [1988] ECR 1999, [1988] 4 CMLR 576. Cf. the special position of copyright exploited by performance: see Case 62/79, *Coditel v. Ciné Vog Films (Coditel I)* [1980] ECR 881, [1981] 2 CMLR 362, see Chap. 10.

[132] Case 258/78, *Nungesser v. Commission* [1982] ECR 2015, [1983] 1 CMLR 278.

[133] It should, however, be remembered that there are exceptions to the position set out above. See in particular *supra* nn. 127 and 131 and accompanying text.

[134] See *supra* Chap. 3, 187.

[135] See *infra* 284–9.

[136] Guidelines on vertical restraints [2000] OJ C291/1, [2000] 5 CMLR 1074, Guidelines on horizontal cooperation agreements [2001] OJ C3/2, [2001] 4 CMLR 819, Guidelines on technology transfer agreements [2004] OJ C101/2 discussed respectively in Chaps. 9, 13, and 10.

obvious restriction of competition irrespective of the market power of the parties involved and its actual effects. The person alleging the infringement is not, therefore, generally required to demonstrate of market power. The ECJ has, however, made it clear that 'in order to come within the prohibition imposed by Article [81(1)], the agreement must affect trade between Member States and the free play of competition to an appreciable extent'.[137] Community law is not concerned with agreements which have an 'insignificant effect on the market, taking into account the weak position which the persons concerned have on the market of the product in question'.[138] It has been seen in Chapter 3 that it is the Commission's view that it will be in rare circumstances that object cases will escape article 81(1) on this ground and its current guidance explaining when, in its view, an agreement may be of minor importance does not apply to an agreement containing 'hard-core' restraints.[139] The case law teaches, however, that these agreements may fall outside Article 81(1).[140] The exclusion of such restraints from the ambit of the notice thus appears to reflect the view that the more serious the restraint, the more insignificant the position held by the undertakings must be (so that lower thresholds than those set out in the Notice must apply) so that Article 81(1) applies unless the parties hold a negligible proportion of the relevant market.[141]

(vi) A Criticism?

The above restrictions are considered so serious that they are always viewed as restrictions of competition whatever the strength of the free rider argument, or other economic rationale for the restraint. Economic or other justifications may only be considered within the context of Article 81(3).[142]

Despite the clear textual support for such an approach (Article 81(1) specifically prohibits agreements which have as their object *or* effect the restriction of competition) and the possibility that Article 81(3) can be used to save such agreements, some commentators regret the fact that the Court, and more frequently the Commission, have adopted this formalistic interpretation of a provision drafted in terms of economic concepts.

One might have expected [it] to be applied only after a careful commercial and economic analysis of the market they affect... To see whether an agreement restricts competition, it is not enough to examine its provisions. One needs to know about the market and the commercial reasons for inserting restrictive provisions.[143]

Pragmatically, however, the finding that some contracts or contractual provisions have as their object the restriction of competition is sensible as it eradicates the need to prove, at cost, the

---

[137] Case 22/71, *Béguelin Import Co. v. GL Import-Export S.A.* [1971] ECR 949, [1972] CMLR 81. The text of Article 81(1) does not require that the effect on competition or trade should be appreciable.

[138] 'Thus an exclusive dealing agreement, even with absolute territorial protection, may, having regard to the weak position of the persons concerned on the market in the products in question in the area covered by the absolute protection, escape the prohibition laid down in Article [81(1)]'. Case 5/69, *Völk v. Vervaecke* [1969] ECR 295, 302, [1969] CMLR 273, 282.

[139] Commission Notice on agreements of minor importance which do not appreciably restrict competition under Article 81(1), [2001] OJ C368/13, [2002] 4 CMLR 699, para. 11.

[140] See *supra* Chap. 3.

[141] See *supra* Chap. 3 and *Völk v. Vervaecke* [1969] ECR 295, [1969] CMLR 273, paras. 5–7; Case T-77/92, *Parker Pen Ltd v. Commission* [1994] ECR II-549, [1994] 5 CMLR 435, para. 44.

[142] See Case 243/85, *SA Binon & Cie v. SA Agence et Messageries de la Presse* [1985] ECR 2015, [1985] 3 CMLR 800, *supra*, 226.

[143] V. Korah, 'EEC Competition Policy—Legal Form or Economic Efficiency?' [1986] *CLP* 85, 92–3.

adverse consequences of provisions which are in practice likely to lead to inefficiency and are unlikely to have any redeeming justification.[144] The burden is then shifted to the parties to prove its beneficial effects relying on Article 81(3).

D. AGREEMENTS THAT RESTRICT COMPETITION BY EFFECT

(i) General

In *Consten and Grundig* one of the arguments advanced by the parties was that the Commission had improperly applied Article 81(1) by failing to base itself on the rule of reason.[145] In this case the ECJ considered that no anaylsis of the effects of the agreement was necessary since its object was to restrict competition. The discussion of object cases above, however, establishes that a fairly limited category of restraints are considered by the ECJ to have as their object the restriction of competition. The question then arises as to what analysis is required in effect cases.

Suppose, for example, Consten had not been given *absolute* territorial protection but, rather, had been given some territorial protection (the German distributors had been forbidden from 'actively' seeking sales in France). Such an agreement would not have had as its object the restriction of competition[146] but could it be said to have that effect? The parties, supported by the Advocate General, would have argued no: the agreement was essential to enable Grundig to penetrate the French market. In the absence of some protection from parallel imports no distributor would have taken on the venture. The restriction on intra-brand competition was necessary to promote inter-brand competition.

(ii) A Rejection of the Rule of Reason

Ever since 1966, and its judgment in *Société La Technique Minière v. Maschinebau Ulm GmbH*,[147] the ECJ has recognized that agreements which do not have as their object the restriction of competition, should be assessed in their market context and an economic approach adopted when determining its effect. This position has been reiterated on many occasions. The courts have been accepting of economic justifications and explanations for restraints contained in an agreement when determining whether they restrict competition within the meaning of Article 81(1). It has been seen, however, that the CFI in *Métropole Télévision v. Commission*[148] expressly rejected the argument that these judgments required a US rule of reason style analysis but also held that Article 81(1) should not be applied abstractly to restrictions on freedom of action.[149] Despite

---

[144] See the discussion of *per se* prohibitions, *supra* 212.

[145] See *supra* 227.

[146] See Case 56/65, *Société La Technique Minière v. Maschinebau Ulm GmbH* [1966] ECR 234, [1966] 1 CMLR 357, *infra*.

[147] In Case 56/65, [1966] ECR 234, [1966] 1 CMLR 357, the ECJ held that a term conferring exclusivity on a distributor might not infringe Article 81(1) where it was a vital element in its decision to market a supplier's goods at all: see *infra* 246–7.

[148] Case T-528/93, *Métropole Télévision SA v. Commission* [1996] ECR II-649, [1996] 5 CMLR 386, see also Case T-65/98, *Van den Bergh Foods v. Commission* [2003] ECR II-4653, [2004] 4 CMLR 1, *aff'd* Case C-552/03 P, *Unilever Bestfoods v. Commission* [2006] OJ C294/19.

[149] Rather, account had to be taken of the impact of the agreement in the economic context in which the undertakings operated.

making these statements as to how Article 81(1) is *not* to be applied, the Court did little to elucidate how it is determined whether restrictions in an agreement are anti-competitive and caught by Article 81(1). What assessment then must be conducted at the Article 81(1) stage?

(iii) The Analytical Framework set out by the Commission in the Article 81(3) Guidelines

In its Guidelines on the application of Article 81(3), the Commission sets outs its interpretation, post *Métropole*, of the relationship between Article 81(1) and 81(3) and in light of its statement that the objective of Article 81 is to enhance consumer welfare and to ensure an efficient allocation of resources. It commences by stressing that in Article 81(1) 'effects' cases there is no presumption of anti-competitive effects rather the likely impact of the agreement on inter- or intra-brand competition must be determined.[150] This requires proof that the agreement either (1) affects 'actual or potential competition to such an extent that on the relevant market negative effects on prices, output, innovation or the variety or quality of goods and services can be expected with a reasonable degree of probability'[151] or (2) restricts a supplier's distributors from competing with each other since potential competition that could have existed between the distributors absent the restraint is restricted. If, following these principles, it is concluded that the transaction is not restrictive of competition, the Commission states that restraints 'ancillary' to the main non-restrictive transaction also fall outside Article 81(1).[152]

(iv) Restraints on Inter-Brand Competition: Appraisal of an Agreement in its Legal and Economic Context

The ECJ in *STM* and the CFI in *Métropole* emphasized the importance, where the object of an agreement is not to restrict competition, of considering the agreement in its market context.[153] Similarly, the ECJ stressed this need to examine agreements in context in *Brasserie de Haecht (No. 1)*.[154] This case concerned the compatibility of a beer supply agreement, containing a beer tie,[155] with Article 81(1). The ECJ held that in considering whether there was a restriction of

---

[150] Thus according to the Commission two counterfactuals may need to be used one to determine whether the agreement restricts inter-brand competition (whether the agreement restricts actual or potential competition that would have existed without the agreement) and one to determine whether it restricts intra-brand competition (whether the agreement restricts actual or potential competition that would have existed in the absence of the contractual restraints).

[151] Article 81(3) Guidelines, para. 24. This could be because the agreement restricts actual or potential competition between the parties or between any one of the parties and third parties that could have existed absent the agreement, Article 81(3) Guidelines, paras. 25–6.

[152] Article 81(3) Guidelines, paras. 28–31.

[153] Case 56/65, *Société La Technique Minière v. Maschinenbau Ulm GmbH ('STM')* [1966] ECR 234, 249–50, [1966] CMLR 357, 375–6, set out *infra.Société La Technique Minière v. Maschinenbau Ulm GmbH* [1966] ECR 234, [1966] CMLR 357.

[154] Case 23/67, *Brasserie de Haecht SA v. Wilkin (No. 1)* [1967] ECR 407, [1968] CMLR 26. See also Case 56/65, *Société La Technique Minière v. Maschinebau Ulm GmbH* [1966] ECR 234, 249, [1966] CMLR 357.

[155] In many Member States brewers conclude agreements with outlets such as public houses, which, in return for certain benefits from the brewer, oblige the outlet to purchase beer (and perhaps other drinks) exclusively from the brewer (or another named supplier). This obligation is frequently accompanied by a non-compete provision preventing the sale of competing products from the outlet. In many Member States the problems associated with such agreements result from networks of similar agreements being operated by all brewers on the market. In practice, this may mean that it is extremely difficult for a new brewer to gain access

competition, it was necessary to take account of the whole market context in which the beer supply agreement operated, including the simultaneous existence of similar contracts.

The ECJ built upon the foundations set in this case in *Delimitis v. Henninger Bräu*.[156] It held that the object of a commitment to purchase beer and other drinks exclusively from named suppliers was not to restrict competition. On the contrary, the Court specifically referred to the benefits which flowed from such an agreement, for example the guarantee for a supplier of an outlet for its product; the assurance that the retailer would concentrate its sales efforts on the distribution of the contract goods; the ability for the retailer to gain access to the market on favourable terms; and the guarantee for the retailer of supply of products. Since the object of the agreement was not to restrict competition, the agreement would only be prohibited by Article 81(1) if this was its effect.

Case C-234/89, *Delimitis* v. *Henninger Bräu* [1991] ECR I-935, [1992] 5 CMLR 210

Delimitis and a brewer concluded an agreement in which the brewer let a public house to Delimitis. In return, Delimitis undertook to obtain beer and soft drinks from the brewer or its subsidiaries. On the termination of the agreement a dispute arose as to the agreement's compatibility with Article 81. On a preliminary reference the Court of Justice set out guidelines in order to enable the national court to assess the compatibility of the agreement with Article 81. The extract below deals with Article 81(1).

Court of Justice

The compatibility of beer supply agreements with Article [81(1)] of the treaty

10. Under the terms of beer supply agreements, the supplier generally affords the reseller certain economic and financial benefits, such as the grant of loans on favourable terms, the letting of premises for the operation of a public house and the provision of technical installations, furniture and other equipment necessary for its operation. In consideration for those benefits, the reseller normally undertakes, for a predetermined period, to obtain supplies of the products covered by the contract only from the supplier. That exclusive purchasing obligation is generally backed by a prohibition on selling competing products in the public house let by the supplier.

11. Such contracts entail for the supplier the advantage of guaranteed outlets, since, as a result of his exclusive purchasing obligation and the prohibition on competition, the reseller concentrates his sales efforts on the distribution of the contract goods. The supply agreements, moreover, lead to co-operation with the reseller, allowing the supplier to plan his sales over the duration of the agreement and to organize production and distribution effectively.

12. Beer supply agreements also have advantages for the reseller, inasmuch as they enable him to gain access under favourable conditions and with the guarantee of supplies to the beer distribution market. The reseller's and supplier's shared interest in promoting sales of the contract

---

to the market or for any brewer to increase its market share. Access to the retail outlets is foreclosed. See also a series of cases dealing with ice-cream and the practice of freezer exclusivity, *infra* Chap. 9.

[156] Case C-234/89, [1991] ECR I-935, [1991] 5 CMLR 210. See V. Korah, 'The Judgment in *Delimitis*: A Milestone Towards a Realistic Assessment of the Effects of an Agreement or a Damp Squib' [1992] *EIPR* 167.

goods likewise secures for the reseller the benefit of the supplier's assistance in guaranteeing product quality and customer service.

13. If such agreements do not have the object of restricting competition within the meaning of Article [81(1)], it is nevertheless necessary to ascertain whether they have the effect of preventing, restricting or distorting competition.

14. In its judgment in Case 23/67 *Brasserie De Haecht* v. *Wilkin* [1967] ECR 407, the Court held that the effects of such an agreement had to be assessed in the context in which they occur and where they might combine with others to have a cumulative effect on competition. It also follows from that judgment that the cumulative effect of several similar agreements constitutes one factor amongst others in ascertaining whether, by way of a possible alteration of competition, trade between Member States is capable of being affected.

15. Consequently, in the present case it is necessary to analyse the effects of a beer supply agreement, taken together with other contracts of the same type, on the opportunities of national competitors or those from other Member States, to gain access to the market for beer consumption or to increase their market share and, accordingly, the effects on the range of products offered to consumers.

16. In making that analysis, the relevant market must first be determined. The relevant market is primarily defined on the basis of the nature of the economic activity in question, in this case the sale of beer. Beer is sold through both retail channels and premises for the sale and consumption of drinks. From the consumer's point of view, the latter sector, comprising in particular public houses and restaurants, may be distinguished from the retail sector on the grounds that the sale of beer in public houses does not solely consist of the purchase of a product but is also linked with the provision of services, and that beer consumption in public houses is not essentially dependent on economic considerations. The specific nature of the public house trade is borne out by the fact that the breweries organize specific distribution systems for this sector which require special installations, and that the prices charged in that sector are generally higher than retail prices.

17. It follows that in the present case the reference market is that for the distribution of beer in premises for the sale and consumption of drinks. That finding is not affected by the fact that there is a certain overlap between the two distribution networks, namely inasmuch as retail sales allow new competitors to make their brands known and to use their reputation in order to gain access to the market constituted by premises for the sale and consumption of drinks.

18. Secondly, the relevant market is delimited from a geographical point of view. It should be noted that most beer supply agreements are still entered into at a national level. It follows that, in applying the Community competition rules, account is to be taken of the national market for beer distribution in premises for the sale and consumption of drinks.

19. In order to assess whether the existence of several beer supply agreements impedes access to the market as so defined, it is further necessary to examine the nature and extent of those agreements in their totality, comprising all similar contracts tying a large number of points of sale to several national producers (judgment in Case 43/69 *Bilger* v. *Jehle* [1970] ECR 127). The effect of those networks of contracts on access to the market depends specifically on the number of outlets thus tied to national producers in relation to the number of public houses which are not so tied, the duration of the commitments entered into, the quantities of beer to which those commitments relate, and on the proportion between those quantities and the quantities sold by free distributors.

20. The existence of a bundle of similar contracts, even if it has a considerable effect on the opportunities for gaining access to the market, is not, however, sufficient in itself to support a finding that the relevant market is inaccessible, inasmuch as it is only one factor, amongst others, pertaining to the economic and legal context in which an agreement must be appraised (Case 23/67 *Brasserie De Haecht*, cited above). The other factors to be taken into account are, in the first instance, those also relating to opportunities for access.

21. In that connection it is necessary to examine whether there are real concrete possibilities for a new competitor to penetrate the bundle of contracts by acquiring a brewery already established on the market together with its network of sales outlets, or to circumvent the bundle of contracts by opening new public houses. For that purpose it is necessary to have regard to the legal rules and agreements on the acquisition of companies and the establishment of outlets, and to the minimum number of outlets necessary for the economic operation of a distribution system. The presence of beer wholesalers not tied to producers who are active on the market is also a factor capable of facilitating a new producer's access to that market since he can make use of those wholesalers' sales networks to distribute his own beer.

22. Secondly, account must be taken of the conditions under which competitive forces operate on the relevant market. In that connection it is necessary to know not only the number and the size of producers present on the market, but also the degree of saturation of that market and customer fidelity to existing brands, for it is generally more difficult to penetrate a saturated market in which customers are loyal to a small number of large producers than a market in full expansion in which a large number of small producers are operating without any strong brand names. The trend in beer sales in the retail trade provides useful information on the development of demand and thus an indication of the degree of saturation of the beer market as a whole. The analysis of that trend is, moreover, of interest in evaluating brand loyalty. A steady increase in sales of beer under new brand names may confer on the owners of those brand names a reputation which they may turn to account in gaining access to the public-house market.

23. If an examination of all similar contracts entered into on the relevant market and the other factors relevant to the economic and legal context in which the contract must be examined shows that those agreements do not have the cumulative effect of denying access to that market to new national and foreign competitors, the individual agreements comprising the bundle of agreements cannot be held to restrict competition within the meaning of Article [81(1)] of the Treaty. They do not, therefore, fall under the prohibition laid down in that provision.

24. If, on the other hand, such examination reveals that it is difficult to gain access to the relevant market, it is necessary to assess the extent to which the agreements entered into by the brewery in question contribute to the cumulative effect produced in that respect by the totality of the similar contracts found on that market. Under the Community rules on competition, responsibility for such an effect of closing off the market must be attributed to the breweries which make an appreciable contribution thereto. Beer supply agreements entered into by breweries whose contribution to the cumulative effect is insignificant do not therefore fall under the prohibition under Article [81(1)].

25. In order to assess the extent of the contribution of the beer supply agreements entered into by a brewery to the cumulative sealing-off effect mentioned above, the market position of the contracting parties must be taken into consideration. That position is not determined solely by the market share held by the brewery and any group, to which it may belong, but also by the number of outlets tied to it or to its group, in relation to the total number of premises for the sale and consumption of drinks found in the relevant market.

26. The contribution of the individual contracts entered into by a brewery to the sealing-off of that market also depends on their duration. If the duration is manifestly excessive in relation to the average duration of beer supply agreements generally entered into on the relevant market, the individual contract falls under the prohibition under Article [81(1)]. A brewery with a relatively small market share which ties its sales outlets for many years may make a significant contribution to a sealing-off of the market as a brewery in a relatively strong market position which regularly releases sales outlets at shorter intervals.

27. The reply to be given to the first three questions is therefore that a beer supply agreement is prohibited by Article [81(1)] of the [EC] Treaty, if two cumulative conditions are met. The first is that, having regard to the economic and legal context of the agreement at issue, it is difficult for

competitors who could enter the market or increase their market share to gain access to the national market for the distribution of beer in premises for the sales and consumption of drinks. The fact that, in that market, the agreement in issue is one of a number of similar agreements having a cumulative effect on competition constitutes only one factor amongst others in assessing whether access to that market is indeed difficult. The second condition is that the agreement in question must make a significant contribution to the sealing-off effect brought about by the totality of those agreements in their economic and legal context. The extent of the contribution made by the individual agreement depends on the position of the contracting parties in the relevant market and on the duration of the agreement.

In determining the effect of the agreement the ECJ stated that it is first necessary to define the relevant market. It must then be ascertained whether there is a concrete possibility for new competitors to penetrate the market or existing competitors to expand taking account of the number and size of producers operating on the market, the existence of networks of agreements, the saturation of the market, and brand loyalty, etc. If analysis shows that there is no denial of access to the market, an agreement cannot be found to restrict competition. Conversely, if access is inhibited it must then be assessed whether the agreement in question (which is taken to mean the agreements of that particular producer or brewer) contributes appreciably to that situation.

The analysis required by the ECJ in this case highlights the importance of looking at the contractual restraint, not abstractly as a restraint, but in the context in which it operates before its effect can be determined. Irrespective of the fact that the judgment in *Delimitis* dealt only with beer supply agreements it affirmed the general need for an economic approach when determining the compatibility of an agreement with Article 81(1) and an assessment of the impact of the agreement on inter-brand competition.

The position adopted by the ECJ in this case thus reflects a very different philosophy from that underpinning its judgment in *Consten and Grundig* (discussed above). Although the facts in *Delimitis* did not present such striking concerns from the single market perspective, the Court's focus shifted from restrictions on intra-brand competition to restrictions on inter-brand competition. In the extract below Amato underlines the importance of this shift in emphasis.

G. Amato, *Antitrust and the Bounds of Power* (Hart Publishing, 1997), 51–2

[T]he court expressed itself in terms now almost the same as the American ones following *Sylvania* . . . It no longer made explicit reference to the need for intra-brand competition, and told the trial judge to verify carefully whether there was room for new entrants, bearing in mind that entry was harder in saturated markets in which, moreover, consumers were faithful to a limited number of big manufacturers. Attention was henceforth, as we see, entirely on inter-brand competition; it would seem to be the case that as long as it is there and in the absence of import bans, intra-brand restrictions are of much less interest.

There is, then, as in the USA, an evolutionary course. However, it is a different course, even though the outcome is similar. In Europe too the starting point was protection of intra-brand competition, but this was done, as we have noted, not in the name of individual freedom (the trader's), something always ignored with us, but to protect a principle, competitiveness in market integration, which with time would become increasingly less pressing and in any case generate a

> *per se* illegality, that of import restrictions. It was consequently not vertical agreements limiting intra-brand competition that were to be prohibited *per se* (except for price fixing, which was never to be permitted in this context), but only agreements containing that specific type of restriction.

In *European Night Services*[157] the CFI also stressed the need for an economic approach to Article 81(1) in the context of horizontal agreements. In many cases parties operating at the same level of the economy may conclude an agreement which does not have the sole purpose of coordinating the parties' market conduct. For example, parties may create a joint venture[158] to pool their resources, perhaps to facilitate or speed up new entry into a market, to share financial risks, to achieve cost savings or even to enable entry into a new market (each undertaking individually may not have the necessary skills or technology to make entry feasible). Obviously, such agreements may cause concern to competition authorities[159] but in *European Night Services* v. *Commission* the CFI emphasized that where such an agreement does not contain obvious restrictions of competition, the actual conditions in which an agreement functions must be taken into account when considering whether or not it has the effect of restricting competition. In particular, account has to be taken of 'the economic context in which the undertakings operate, the products or services covered by the agreement and the actual structure of the market concerned'. The importance of examining the conditions of competition, including existing and *potential* competition was stressed. This was necessary 'in order to ascertain whether, in the light of the structure of the market and the economic and legal context within which it functions, there are real concrete possibilities for the undertakings concerned to compete among themselves or for a new competitor to penetrate the relevant market and compete with the undertakings already established'.[160]

Cases T-374, 375, 384 and 388/94, *European Night Services* v. *Commission* [1998] ECR II-3141, [1998] 5 CMLR 718

This case involved agreements notified to the Commission concerning the formation of European Night Services (ENS) by four undertakings, British Rail, Deutsche Bundesbahn, Nederlandse Spoorwegen, and Société Nationale des Chemis de Fer Français. The purpose of ENS was to provide and operate overnight passenger rail services between the UK and the Continent through the Channel Tunnel. The Commission had only exempted the agreements from the application of

---

[157] Cases T-374, 375 and 388/94, [1998] ECR II-3141, [1998] 5 CMLR 718.

[158] In some circumstances, the establishment of a joint venture amounts to a concentration for the purposes of EC Merger Regulation, Council Reg. 139/2004 [2004] OJ L24/1, replacing Council Reg. 4064/89 [1989] OJ L395/1, as amended by Council Reg. 1310/97 [1997] OJ L180/1, *infra* Chaps. 12 and 13.

[159] Although collaboration between such undertakings may enhance the position of the competitors on the market and lead to advantages on that market which the competitors may be unable to achieve on their own, joint venture agreements may cause concern. In particular, a competition authority may fear that: a joint venture agreement will make it easier for the parties to collude (in particular, the collaboration may spill over outside the field of the agreement); the relevant market may become foreclosed to third parties; the agreement will be more restrictive than is necessary to achieve the objectives achieved; or there will be a loss of actual or potential competition between the competitors.

[160] Cases T-374, 375, 384, and 388/94, *European Night Services* v. *Commission* [1998] ECR II-3141, [1998] 5 CMLR 718, paras. 136–7. For joint ventures generally, see *infra* Chap. 13.

Article 81(1) subject to the acceptance of stringent conditions. The applicants sought to have the decision annulled. On the facts the Court of First Instance annulled the Commission's decision. The decision had failed to give a sufficient statement of reasons as to how the ENS agreements could be said to restrict competition within the meaning of Article 81(1). It was not clear, consequently, that there was a need for exemption under Article 81(3).

Court of First Instance

135. According to the contested decision, the ENS agreements have effects restricting existing and potential competition (a) among the parent undertakings, (b) between the parent undertakings and ENS and (c) *vis-à-vis* third parties; furthermore (d), those restrictions are aggravated by the presence of a network of joint ventures set up by the parent undertakings.

136. Before any examination of the parties' arguments as to whether the Commission's analysis as regards restrictions of competition was correct, it must be borne in mind that in assessing an agreement under Article [81(1)] of the Treaty, account should be taken of the actual conditions in which it functions, in particular the economic context in which the undertakings operate, the products or services covered by the agreement and the actual structure of the market concerned (judgments in *Delimitis*, . . . *Gøttrup-Klim*, . . . Case C-399/93, *Oude Luttikhuis and Others* v. *Verenigde Coöperatieve Melkindustrie* [1995] ECR I-1415 paragraph 10 and Case T-77/94, *VGB and Others* v. *Commission* [1997] ECR II-759, paragraph 140), unless it is an agreement containing obvious restrictions of competition such as price-fixing, market-sharing or the control of outlets (Case T-148/89, *Tréfilunion* v. *Commission* ([1995] ECR II-1063, paragraph, 109)). In the latter case, such restrictions may be weighed against their claimed pro-competitive effects only in the context of Article [81(3)] of the Treaty, with a view to granting an exemption from the prohibition in Article [81(1)].

137. It must also be stressed that the examination of conditions of competition is based not only on existing competition between undertakings already present on the relevant market but also on potential competition, in order to ascertain whether, in the light of the structure of the market and the economic and legal context within which it functions, there are real concrete possibilities for the undertakings concerned to compete among themselves or for a new competitor to penetrate the relevant market and compete with the undertakings already established (*Delimitis* . . . paragraph 21). Furthermore, according to the Commission notice of 1993 concerning the assessment of cooperative joint ventures pursuant to Article [81] of the Treaty: 'The assumption of potential competitive circumstances presupposes that each parent alone is in a position to fulfil the tasks assigned to the [joint venture] and that it does not forfeit its capabilities to do so by the creation of the [joint venture]. An economically realistic approach is necessary in the assessment of any particular case'.

138. It is in the light of those considerations, therefore, that it is necessary to examine whether the Commission's assessment of the restrictive effects of the ENS agreements was correct.

In *O2 (Germany) GmbH & Co OHG* v. *Commission*[161] the CFI also stressed that the general method of analysis under Article 81(1) required an examination of the economic and legal context in which the agreement was concluded. In making the assessment, competition had to be understood in the context in which it would occur in the absence of the agreement in dispute.

The examination required in the light of Article 81(1) consists essentially in taking account of the impact of the agreement on existing and potential competition (see, to that effect, Case C-234/89, *Delimitis* . . .)

---

[161] Case T-328/03, [2006] ECR II-1231, [2006] 5 CMLR 5. See e.g. M. Marquis, 'O2 (Germany) v Commission and the exotic mysteries of Article 81(1) EC' [2007] *ELRev* 29.

and the competition situation in the absence of the agreement (*Société minière et technique* . . .), those two factors being intrinsically linked. The examination of competition in the absence of an agreement appears to be particularly necessary as regards markets undergoing liberalization or emerging markets . . . where effective competition may be problematic owing, for example, to the presence of dominant operator, the concentrated nature of the market structure or the existence of significant barriers to entry—factors referred to, in the present case, in the Decision.[162]

The *Delimitis, European Night Services* and *O2* cases are reflective of an 'economic approach' which support the Commission's view set out in its Article 81(3) Guidelines that a finding of anti-competitive effect is dependent on proof that the agreement has in fact led to a restraint on output or price increases or, is likely to do so.[163] Potential anti-competitive effects are determined through an examination of whether the parties individually or jointly have or obtain some degree of market power[164] and, if so, whether the agreement contributes to the creation, maintenance or strengthening of that market power or allows the parties to exploit it.[165] Where no such negative restrictive effects are identified, the agreement cannot be said to restrict competition.

Guidelines on the Application of Article 81(3) of the Treaty [2004] OJ C101/97

24. If an agreement is not restrictive of competition by object it must be examined whether it has restrictive effects on competition. Account must be taken of both actual and potential effects. In other words the agreement must have likely anti-competitive effects. In the case of restrictions of competition by effect there is no presumption of anti-competitive effects. For an agreement to be restrictive by effect it must affect actual or potential competition to such an extent that on the relevant market negative effects on prices, output, innovation or the variety or quality of goods and services can be expected with a reasonable degree of probability. Such negative effects must be appreciable. The prohibition rule of Article 81(1) does not apply when the identified anti-competitive effects are insignificant. This test reflects the economic approach which the Commission is applying. The prohibition of Article 81(1) only applies where on the basis of proper market analysis it can be concluded that the agreement has likely anti-competitive effects on the market. It is insufficient for such a finding that the market shares of the parties exceed the thresholds set out in the Commission's de minimis notice. Agreements falling within safe harbours of block exemption regulations may be caught by Article 81(1) but this is not necessarily so. Moreover, the fact that due to the market shares of the parties, an agreement falls outside the safe harbour of a block exemption is in itself an insufficient basis for finding that the agreement is caught by Article 81(1) or that it does not fulfil the conditions of Article 81(3). Individual assessment of the likely effects produced by the agreement is required.

---

[162] Case T-328/03, [2006] ECR II-1231, [2006] 5 CMLR 5, paras. 71–72. In this case the CFI found that the Commission had not carried out an economic analysis of the effect of the agreement on the competitive situation.

[163] Article 81(3) Guidelines, para. 27. 'Does the agreement restrict actual or potential competition that would have existed without the agreement?' Article 81(3) Guidelines, para. 18.

[164] Where competitive constraints are insufficient to maintain prices and output at competitive levels. It is thus usually necessary to define the market and to examine the nature of the products, the market position of the parties, the market position of competitors and buyers, and the existence of potential competitors and the level of barriers to entry, see Article 81(3) Guidelines, paras. 25–27 set out *infra*.

[165] Article 81(3) Guidelines, paras. 24–27 set out *infra*. The Guidelines thus recognize that it is usually necessary to define the market and to examine the nature of the products, the market position of the parties, the

25. Negative effects on competition within the relevant market are likely to occur when the parties individually or jointly have or obtain some degree of market power and the agreement contributes to the creation, maintenance or strengthening of that market power or allows the parties to exploit such market power. Market power is the ability to maintain prices above competitive levels for a significant period of time or to maintain output in terms of product quantities, product quality and variety or innovation below competitive levels for a significant period of time. In markets with high fixed costs undertakings must price significantly above their marginal costs of production in order to ensure a competitive return on their investment. The fact that undertakings price above their marginal costs is therefore not in itself a sign that competition in the market is not functioning well and that undertakings have market power that allows them to price above the competitive level. It is when competitive constraints are insufficient to maintain prices and output at competitive levels that undertakings have market power within the meaning of Article 81(1).

26. The creation, maintenance or strengthening of market power can result from a restriction of competition between the parties to the agreement. It can also result from a restriction of competition between any one of the parties and third parties, e.g. because the agreement leads to foreclosure of competitors or because it raises competitors' costs, limiting their capacity to compete effectively with the contracting parties. Market power is a question of degree. The degree of market power normally required for the finding of an infringement under Article 81(1) in the case of agreements that are restrictive of competition by effect is less than the degree of market power required for a finding of dominance under Article 82.

27. For the purposes of analysing the restrictive effects of an agreement it is normally necessary to define the relevant market. It is normally also necessary to examine and assess, inter alia, the nature of the products, the market position of the parties, the market position of competitors, the market position of buyers, the existence of potential competitors and the level of entry barriers. In some cases, however, it may be possible to show anti-competitive effects directly by analysing the conduct of the parties to the agreement on the market. It may for example be possible to ascertain that an agreement has led to price increases. The guidelines on horizontal cooperation agreements and on vertical restraints set out a detailed framework for analysing the competitive impact of various types of horizontal and vertical agreements under Article 81(1).

The scarcity of the case-law and economically reasoned Commission decisions in this area, however, make it difficult to draw conclusions as to the *degree* of market power required to establish anti-competitive effects. [166]The Article 81(3) Guidelines state only that the requisite degree is 'less than the degree of market power required for a finding of dominance under Article 82'.[167] This, combined with the moderately low market share thresholds, of between 20–30%, that are set out in the block exemptions,[168] which *exempt* agreements from the Article 81(1) prohibition, may cause firms to be concerned that market power issues will arise under Article 81(1) where relatively low market share thresholds are exceeded (between 10–20% for agreements between competitors and between 15–30% for agreements between non-competitors).[169]

market position of competitors and buyers, and the existence of potential competitors and barriers to entry. Such an assessment must ordinarily be made in the actual context in which competition occurs, *ibid.*, paras. 17–24.

[166] See the general discussion in J. Faull and A. Nikpay (Eds.) *The EC Law of Competition* (2nd edn., Oxford University Press, 2007), paras. 3.310–3.336.

[167] Article 81(3) Guidelines, para. 26. It is rare for a finding of dominance to be made where the dominant firm's market share is less than 40%, see, e.g., R. Whish, *Competition Law* (5th edn., LexisNexis, 2003) 178–83.

[168] See *infra* 288.

[169] Although the Commission makes it clear in its Guidelines accompanying the block exemptions, that the fact that the market share thresholds set out in the block exemptions (which operate as safe harbours) are

(v) Restraints on Intra-brand Competition

It has already been explained that the Commission's Guidelines state that when determining what constitutes a restriction of competition within the meaning of Article 81(1), it must *also* be determined whether the agreement, or its parts, restricts *intra-brand* competition.[170]

In *Société La Technique Minière v. Maschinenbau Ulm GmbH* ('STM'), for example, the ECJ dealt with an exclusive distribution agreement which, in contrast to that concerned in *Consten and Grundig*, did not confer absolute territorial protection (or a complete monopoly over the right to distribute in France) on the distributor. The contractual arrangements did admit the possibility of parallel imports from distributors in other Member States. In this case the ECJ did not hold that the object of the agreement was to restrict competition. Rather, accepting similar arguments to those raised by the parties in *Consten and Grundig*, it indicated that an exclusive distribution agreement would not restrict competition if the appointment of an exclusive distributor was necessary in order to enable a manufacturer to penetrate a new market. Before it could be determined whether the agreement restricted competition, the agreement should be examined in the light of the competition which would occur *if the agreement in question were not or had not been made*. In this case it seemed that the economic justifications for the agreement might outweigh the territorial restrictions inherent in the agreement.

Case 56/65, *Société La Technique Minière v. Maschinenbau Ulm GmbH* [1966] ECR 234, 249–50, [1966] CMLR 357, 375–6

The parties entered into an agreement by which a French company was given exclusive rights to distribute in France the equipment (levelling machines) of a German manufacturer. The French company was free to re-export the equipment outside France. The parties fell out, and in litigation in the French courts the French company claimed that the agreement was void under Article 81(2) because it infringed Article 81(1). The Cour d'Appel Paris asked the Court of Justice on a preliminary reference how it should assess the compatibility of this type of agreement with Article 81(1).

Court of Justice

The effects of the agreement on competition

... The competition in question must be understood within the actual context in which it would occur in the absence of the agreement in dispute. In particular it may be doubted whether there is an interference with competition if the said agreement seems really necessary for the penetration of a new area by an undertaking. Therefore, in order to decide whether an agreement containing a clause 'granting an exclusive right of sale' is to be considered as prohibited by reason of its object or of its effect, it is appropriate to take into account in particular the nature and quantity,

---

exceeded does not necessarily mean that Article 81(1) is infringed and that a full competition analysis will need to be completed to determine whether or not this is the case, it must still be questioned why these broad overarching block exemptions are necessary if the agreements covered would be unlikely to produce anti-competitive effects, see, e.g., the Guidelines on Vertical Restraints, [2000] OJ C291/ 1, 5, [2000] CMLR 1074, especially paras. 120–33.

[170] Article 81(3) Guidelines, paras. 17 and 18. See also the discussion of Cases 56 and 58/64, *Etablissements Consten SA & Grundig-Verkaufs-GmbH v. Commission* [1966] ECR 299, 348, [1966] CMLR 418 *supra*.

> limited or otherwise, of the products covered by the agreement, the position and importance of the grantor and the concessionnaire on the market for the products concerned, the isolated nature of the disputed agreement or, alternatively, its position in series of agreements, the severity of the clauses intended to protect the exclusive dealership or, alternatively, the opportunities allowed for other commercial competitors in the same products by way of parallel re-exportation and importation.

In line with *STM* the ECJ has also held that where exclusivity provisions do not give a licensee of intellectual property rights absolute territorial protection, restrictions in a licensing agreement may not infringe Article 81(1) if necessary to protect the investment of the licensee. In *Nungesser v. Commission*,[171] for example, the Court held that an open exclusive licence of new technology to produce maize seeds did not infringe Article 81(1). A licensee would not be prepared to take the licence and incur the risk/expense of producing the patented product without some protection from intra-brand competition. The Court developed this line of reasoning in *Erauw-Jacquéry Sprl v. La Hesbignonne Société Coopérative*[172] and accepted that in the context of the licensing of certain IP rights even export bans (absolute territorial protection) might, in certain circumstances, fall outside Article 81(1).[173]

In its Guidelines the Commission relies on this line of cases as authority for the proposition that that territorial or customer intra-brand restraints[174] are caught by Article 81(1) unless 'objectively necessary' for the existence of an agreement of that type or nature. 'The question is not whether the parties in their particular situation would not have accepted to conclude a less restrictive agreement, but whether given the nature of the agreement and the characteristics of the market a less restrictive agreement would not have been concluded by undertakings in a similar setting. For instance, territorial restraints in an agreement between a supplier and a distributor may for a certain period of time fall outside Article 81(1), if the restraints are objectively necessary in order for the distributor to penetrate a new market'.[175] This sweeping approach, appears to be motivated more by single market and/or economic freedom than pure competition concerns, and potentially brings many vertical and intellectual property licensing agreements within the ambit of Article 81(1) whether or not the parties have market power and/or the ability to affect prices or output on the market for example, by foreclosing access to supply or distribution channels to competitors.[176] This appears to underline 'the view that Community institutions continue to see merit in protecting, albeit to a significantly lesser degree than in the past, the process … of competition rather than focusing exclusively on the direct or probable economic effects of agreements. This means that in certain circumstances agreements which have a neutral or even *net positive* effect consumer welfare and allocative efficiency can fall within the scope of Article 81(1)'.[177]

---

[171] Case 258/78, [1982] ECR 2015, [1983] 1 CMLR 278.

[172] Case 27/87, [1988] ECR 1999, [1988] 4 CMLR 576.

[173] See Chap. 10.

[174] Falling short of absolute territorial protection, see discussion of Cases 56 and 58/64, *Etablissements Consten SA & Grundig-Verkaufs-GmbH v. Commission* [1966] ECR 299, 348, [1966] CMLR 418, *supra*.

[175] Article 81(3) Guidelines, para. 18(2). (See also the Guidelines on Vertical Restraints, [2000] OJ C291/ 1, [2000] 5 CMLR 1074, para. 119, rule 10 and paras. 161–174). This statement indicates that if not objectively necessary the intra-brand restraints will have as their effect the restriction of competition, irrespective of the amount of inter-brand competition on the market (subject to the principle of appreciability *supra*).

[176] This view explains the need for a broad overarching block exemptions for vertical and technology transfer agreements respectively.

[177] J. Faull and A. Nikpay (eds.), *The EC Law of Competition* (2nd edn., Oxford University Press, 2007), para. 3.142 and see *supra* Chap. 1.

It is not at all clear that such a sweeping approach is dictated by *STM* which clearly seems to require an assessment of the competitive situation in the absence of the agreement in dispute *and* a determination of the strength of the parties' position on the market prior to an assessment of the compatibility of an agreement with Article 81(1). Nonetheless, in *GlaxoSmithKline Services Unlimited* v. *Commission*[178] the CFI quickly assumed that a restraint on parallel trade between wholesalers would have as its actual or potential effect the restriction of competition. Although it held that a restriction of competition could not be assumed from the fact that the agreement had the effect of limiting parallel trade or from the fact that it restricted the freedom of action of the firms, it considered that it had been established that the agreement had reduced the welfare of final consumers: the provisions would prevent final consumers from taking advantage of reduced prices and costs which would otherwise be offered by exporting wholesalers.[179]

(vi) Ancillary Restraints

If a main transaction does not restrict inter- or intra-brand competition, the Commission states in its Article 81(3) Guidelines that individual restraints in the agreement ancillary to it (i.e. directly related and necessary to its implementation and proportionate to the main non-restrictive distribution or joint venture agreement) will also be compatible with Article 81(1).[180] Arguably, this 'doctrine' is derived from the following cases.

a. *Remia and Nutricia*

In *Remia and Nutricia* the ECJ recognized that a non-compete clause on the sale of a business[181] was likely to be an essential part of an agreement to sell a business. Viewed *ex post*, a non-compete clause may appear to restrict competition between the parties. However, when assessed *ex ante* it may become clear that competition is not restricted. No undertaking would be willing to purchase the business without an assurance from the vendor that it will not remain in business in such a way that it would still be able to exploit the goodwill and the customers of the business sold. Nonetheless, the Court held that the non-compete clause must be limited to what is necessary to make the transaction viable. If it is broader than required for the sale, for example, if it precludes the vendor from setting up any business within a wide geographic area for an indefinite period of time, it will restrict competition within the meaning of Article 81(1).

Case 42/84, *Remia BV and NV Verenigde Bedrijven Nutricia* v. *Commission* [1985] ECR 2545, [1987] 1 CMLR 1

This case concerned proceedings brought by Remia BV and NV Verenigde Bedrijven Nutricia (hereinafter referred to as 'Nutricia') under Article 230 of the EC Treaty for a declaration that a

---

[178] Case T-168/01, 27 Sept. 2006, [2006] 5 CMLR 1623, Cases C-501, 513, 515 and 519/06 P (judgment pending).

[179] See *supra* n. 178 and accompanying text.

[180] Article 81(3) Guidelines, paras. 28–9.

[181] Transactions that constitute a 'concentration' (or merger) may today be dealt with under the EC Merger Regulation rather than Article 81. The first Merger Regulation was not, however, adopted until 1989 and did not come into force until 1990, Council Reg. 4064/89 [1989] OJ L395/1, as amended by Council Reg. 1310/97 [1997] OJ L180/1. This regulation has now been replaced by Merger Regulation, Council Reg. 139/2004 [2004] OJ L24/1. Prior to this Articles 81 and 82 could, in certain circumstances, be used to scrutinize merger transactions, see *infra* Chap. 12.

Commission decision[182] relating to an agreement between them was void. Broadly this case concerned the sale by Nutricia (a manufacturer of health and baby foods) of two of its subsidiaries, Remia and Luycks. The sales agreements contained non-compete clauses designed to protect the purchasers from competition by the vendor on the same market for a period immediately after the transfer. Further, a provision in the sales agreements of Remia provided that neither Nutricia nor Luycks (engaged in the production of pickles and condiments) would engage directly or indirectly in the production of sale of sauces (Remia was principally engaged in sauce production,) on the Netherlands market. Further, Nutricia undertook to Luycks for a period of five years not to engage directly or indirectly in any production or sale of pickles or condiments in Europe. Campbell, the parent company of the undertaking purchasing Luycks considered that this clause infringed Article 81 of the Treaty and notified the two transfer agreements to the Commission requesting exemption. The Commission took the view that the duration and scope of the non-compete clauses were excessive and so restricted competition and were not eligible for exemption under Article 81(3). The applicants thus appealed to the Court of Justice seeking a declaration that the non-compete clause did not infringe Article 81(1) at all and in any case that the Commission had wrongly failed to apply Article 81(3).

Court of Justice

The application of Article [81(1)] of the [EC] Treaty

17. It should be stated at the outset that the Commission has rightly submitted—and the applicants have not contradicted it on that point—that the fact that non-competition clauses are included in an agreement for the sale of an undertaking is not of itself sufficient to remove such clauses from the scope of Article [81(1)] of the Treaty.

18. In order to determine whether or not such clauses come within the prohibition in Article [81(1)], it is necessary to examine what would be the state of competition if those clauses did not exist.

19. If that were the case, and should the vendor and the purchaser remain competitors after the transfer, it is clear that the agreement for the transfer of the undertaking could not be given effect. The vendor, with his particularly detailed knowledge of the transferred undertaking, would still be in a position to win back his former customers immediately after the transfer and thereby drive the undertaking out of business. Against that background non-competition clauses incorporated in an agreement for the transfer of an undertaking in principle have the merit of ensuring that the transfer has the effect intended. By virtue of that very fact they contribute to the promotion of competition because they lead to an increase in the number of undertakings in the market in question.

20. Nevertheless, in order to have that beneficial effect on competition, such clauses must be necessary to the transfer of the undertaking concerned and their duration and scope must be strictly limited to that purpose. The Commission was therefore right in holding that where those conditions are satisfied such clauses are free of the prohibition laid down in Article [81(1)].

21. However, without denying the basic principle of that reasoning, the applicants challenge the way in which it has been applied to their case on the ground, first, that the non-competition clause contained in the sauce agreement does not affect trade between Member States within the meaning of Article [81 (1)] of the Treaty, and, secondly, that in view of the special circumstances surrounding the transfer at issue the Commission did not provide an adequate statement of the grounds for its decision and wrongly assessed the facts in limiting to four years the permissible duration of the non-competition clause included in the transfer agreement...

---

[182] [1983] OJ L376/22.

25. On the second point, namely the limitation of the non-competition clause to four years, the applicants contend first that the statement of the reasons for the contested decision is inadequate and secondly that it contains errors of fact and is based on an erroneous assessment of the facts of the case as a whole . . .

35. In this instance the applicants have confined themselves to contending that the limitation of the duration of the non-competition clause to four years is based on a number of incorrect findings of fact and, essentially, on the Commission's incorrect appraisal of the specific circumstances of the case.

36. It cannot be inferred either from the documents before the Court or from the oral argument presented to it that by setting at four years the period beyond which the non-competition clause contained in the sauce agreement came within the prohibition laid down in Article [81 (1)] of the [EC] Treaty, the Commission based its decision on incorrect findings of fact or committed a manifest error in its appraisal of the facts of the case as a whole.

b. *Pronuptia*

In *Pronuptia de Paris GmbH* v. *Pronuptia de Paris Irmgard Schillgallis*[183] the ECJ set out guidelines for a national court ruling on the compatibility of a distribution franchising agreement with Article 81(1). It held that restrictions essential to the successful operation of a distribution franchise agreement, which provided a means for an undertaking to derive financial benefit from it expertise without investing its own capital and a means for traders who do not have expertise to benefit from the franchisor's experience and reputation, would not restrict competition. In particular, the franchisor should be able to communicate know-how without running the risk that it would be used to benefit competitors and to take measures necessary to maintain the identity and reputation of the network.[184] The Court thus considered that restrictions within the agreement would fall outside Article 81(1) if objectively necessary to the successful operation of the franchising transaction.

The ECJ did not consider, however, that all contractual restraints would be necessary to achieve these objectives. In particular, the Court considered that provisions which shared markets between the franchisor and franchisees or between the franchisees or which prevented the franchisees from engaging in price competition with one another would restrict competition.[185] Clauses in the agreement which conferred territorial exclusivity upon the franchisee were not essential to the functioning of the agreement and restricted competition. The combination of an exclusivity and location clause essentially gave the franchisees absolute territorial protection within their franchise area.[186]

G. Amato, *Antitrust and the Bounds of Power* (Hart Publishing, 1997), 50–1

In *Pronuptia* v. *Schillgallis*, . . . the Court was for the first time called on to speak on franchising contracts. It did so without going into the facts, since it was in a context of a preliminary ruling, that is,

---

[183] Case 161/84, [1986] ECR 353, [1986] 1 CMLR 414.

[184] *Ibid.*, paras. 16–17, *infra* Chap. 9.

[185] *Ibid.*, para. 23, *infra* Chap. 9.

[186] For franchise agreements generally, see *infra* Chap. 9.

merely supplying the national judge dealing with the case with the interpretation of Community law he has asked for pursuant to Article [234] of the EC Treaty. The question it was answering was whether the vertical restrictions inherent in the franchising relationship are compatible with Article [81], knowing that in this specific case the franchising generated exclusivity concerning not a whole Member State, but the Paris region only.

The Court accepted that the good functioning of franchising (the commercial utility of which it stressed) might require clauses protecting against competitors the know-how the producer transfers to the retailer, making the retailer subject to requirements as to the location and decor of points of sale, and as to the selection of products to sell, and even publicity. If however the contract were to provide both for an obligation to sell only at the points of sale indicated by the manufacturer and for the retailer's right to absolute exclusiveness on a given territory, then, said the Court, this would entail a division of the market contrary to Article [81], as decided in *Consten & Grundig* ... Moreover, no restraint should be imposed on the seller's freedom of pricing.

Pronuptia is a problematic decision, opening a sort of transition. The Court well understood that if it accepted the efficiency of franchising it would perforce have to accept also the restrictive clauses it requires, including exclusive agreements with territorial protection. Moreover, in the specific underlying case ... there was no national segmentation at stake. On the other hand, *Consten & Grundig* was there, and had set a general principle. The Court then on the one hand reaffirmed it, thus apparently from this viewpoint renewing its strength in still more expansive terms; on the other, however, it continued to circumscribe its scope to cases involving established brands, and let it be understood that territorial exclusivity, without absolute territorial protection, might be allowed to pass.

c. *Gøttrup-Klim*

In *Gøttrup-Klim Grovvareforening and Others* v. *Dansk Landbrugs Grovvareselskab AmbA*[187] the ECJ was asked by a Danish court whether a clause in the statutes of Dansk Landbrugs Grovvareselskab AmbA (a Danish cooperative association distributing farm supplies, 'DLG') restricted competition within the meaning of Article 81(1). The object of DLG was to provide its members with farm supplies (such as fertilizer) at the lowest possible prices and to offer its members other services, particularly in the area of finance. In 1988 the statutes of DLG were changed because of increasing competition from the claimants in this case. Essentially, the disputed clause precluded some of DLG's members from holding membership of, or any other kind of participation in, associations, societies, or other forms of cooperative organization in competition with DLG, with regard to the purchase and sale of fertilizers and plant protection products. The statutes provided that members which infringed this rule would be excluded from DLG (and some members were in fact excluded). DLG had notified the amendment to the Commission for negative clearance or exemption, but at the time of the proceedings before the ECJ, it had still not received an answer to the letter of notification. In the proceedings before the ECJ the Commission stated in reply to a question from the Court that the amendment to the statutes did not infringe the Article 81(1) prohibition.

DLG contended that the aim of the clause was not to restrict competition. On the contrary it (1) enabled the members to stand up to a few very large multinational producers of fertilizers and plant protection products in order to obtain lower purchase prices for Danish farmers and, (2) second, prevented competitors' representatives from taking part in the association's

[187] Case C-250/92, *Gøttrup-Klim Grovvareforening and Others* v. *Dansk Landbrugs Grovvareselskab AmbA* [1994] ECR I-5641, [1996] 4 CMLR 191.

management bodies (shareholders' committee and board of directors) in which business secrets were discussed. The Danish authorities did not take the view that the statutes as amended infringed Danish competition law. Nonetheless, the claimants challenged the compatibility of the provision with Article 81 of the Treaty and sought compensation and damages in respect of the loss sustained from their exclusion from DLG. The Danish court referred the matter to the ECJ using the procedure set out in Article 234 of the Treaty. In particular it asked whether a provision in the statues of a commercial cooperative society excluding members that participated in a cooperative organization which competed with it was contrary to Article 81(1). The ECJ replied that it would not so long as the provision was restricted to what was necessary to ensure that the cooperative functioned properly and maintained its contractual power in relation to producers.

Case C-250/92, *Gøttrup-Klim Grovvareforening and Others* v. *Dansk Landbrugs Grovvareselskab AmbA (DLG)* [1994] ECR I-5641, [1996] 4 CMLR 191

Court of Justice

18. In its order for reference, the Østre Landsret proceeds on the basis that DLG in essence sought to induce . . . members to stop purchasing fertilisers and plant protection products outside DLG, so that within the cooperative sector in Denmark there would be just one large association purchasing supplies on behalf of Danish farmers . . .

Restriction of competition

28. In the second set of questions, the national court seeks to ascertain whether a provision in the statutes of a cooperative purchasing association, the effect of which is to forbid its members to participate in other forms of organized cooperation which are in direct competition with it, is caught by the prohibition in Article [81(1)] of the Treaty.

29. The plaintiffs in the main proceedings claim that the object or effect of such an amendment to the statutes is to restrict competition, inasmuch as the objective pursued was to put an end to . . . members purchasing through LAG in competition with DLG, and thus to acquire a dominant position on the markets concerned.

30. A cooperative purchasing association is a voluntary association of persons established in order to pursue common commercial objectives.

31. The compatibility of the statutes of such an association with the Community rules on competition cannot be assessed in the abstract. It will depend on the particular clauses in the statutes and the economic conditions prevailing on the markets concerned.

32. In a market where product prices vary according to the volume of orders, the activities of co-operative purchasing associations may, depending on the size of their membership, constitute a significant counterweight to the contractual power of large producers and make way for more effective competition.

33. Where some members of two competing cooperative purchasing associations belong to both at the same time, the result is to make each association less capable of pursuing its objectives for the benefit of the rest of its members, especially where the members concerned, as in the case in point, are themselves cooperative associations with a large number of individual members.

34. It follows that such dual membership would jeopardize both the proper functioning of the co-operative and its contractual power in relation to producers. Prohibition of dual membership does not, therefore, necessarily constitute a restriction of competition within the meaning of Article [81(1)] of the Treaty and may even have beneficial effects on competition.

35. Nevertheless, a provision in the statutes of a cooperative purchasing association, restricting the opportunity for members to join other types of competing cooperatives and thus discouraging them from obtaining supplies elsewhere, may have adverse effects on competition. So, in order to escape the prohibition laid down in Article [81(1)] of the Treaty, the restrictions imposed on members by the statutes of cooperative purchasing associations must be limited to what is necessary to ensure that the cooperative functions properly and maintains its contractual power in relation to producers.

36. The particular features of the case at issue in the main proceedings, which are referred to in the questions submitted by the national court, must be assessed in the light of the foregoing considerations. In addition, it is necessary to establish whether the penalties for non-compliance with the statutes are disproportionate to the objective they pursue and whether the minimum period of membership is unreasonable.

37. First of all, the amendment of DLG's statutes is restricted so as to cover only fertilizers and plant protection products, the only farm supplies in respect of which a direct relationship exists between sales volume and price.

38. Furthermore, even after DLG has amended its statutes and excluded the plaintiffs, it is open to 'non-members' of the association, including the plaintiffs, to buy from it the whole range of products which it sells, including fertilizers and plant protection products, on the same commercial terms and at the same prices as members, except that 'non-members' are obviously not entitled to receive a yearly discount on the amount of the transactions carried out.

39. Finally, DLG's statutes authorize its members to buy fertilizers and plant protection products without using DLG as an intermediary, provided that such transactions are carried out otherwise than through an organized consortium. In that context, each member acts individually or in association with others but, in the latter case, only in making a one-off common purchase of a particular consignment or shipload.

40. Taking all those factors into account, it would not seem that restrictions laid down in the statutes, of the kind imposed on DLG members, go beyond what is necessary to ensure that the cooperative functions properly and maintains its contractual power in relation to producers.

41. As regards the penalties imposed on the plaintiffs as a result of their exclusion for infringing DLG's rules, these would not appear to be disproportionate, since DLG has treated the plaintiffs as if they were members exercising their right to withdraw.

42. So far as concerns the membership period, this has been reduced from ten to five years, which does not seem unreasonable.

43. It is significant, in the last analysis, that after their exclusion, the plaintiffs succeeded, through LAG, in competing vigorously with DLG, with the result that in 1990 their market share was similar to DLG's.

44. The other matters mentioned in the second set of questions referred by the national court are not such as to affect the analysis of the problem.

45. The answer to the second set of questions referred by the national court must therefore be that a provision in the statutes of a cooperative purchasing association, forbidding its members to participate in other forms of organized cooperation which are in direct competition with it, is not caught by the prohibition in Article [81(1)] of the Treaty, so long as the abovementioned provision is restricted to what is necessary to ensure that the cooperative functions properly and maintains its contractual power in relation to producers.

d. The Commission's Guidelines on Article 81(3) and *Métropole*

(i) *Remia and Nutricia v. Commission*[188]—the Court accepted that a reasonable non-compete clause in an agreement for the sale of a business would ensure that the transfer had the intended effect and did not restrict competition;[189]

(ii) *Pronuptia de Paris GmbH v. Pronuptia de Paris Irmgard Schillgallis*[190]—the Court held that restrictions on a party's conduct necessary for the successful operation of a franchising distribution agreement did not infringe Article 81(1); and

(iii) *Gøttrup-Klim*—the ECJ considered that the restraints necessary to enable the parties to set up an effective group purchasing association did not infringe Article 81(1).

The doctrine of ancillary restraints is not without difficulties. First, the utility of this doctrine is limited by the Court's failure to push it to its logical conclusion and to accept that restraints providing a distributor with absolute territorial protection may sometimes be ancillary to a non-restrictive agreement. In *Pronuptia* the Court concluded that provisions in a franchising agreement which led to the sharing of markets between the franchisor and the franchisees or between franchisees would restrict competition for the purpose of Article 81(1) and in *Consten and Grundig* the Court failed to accept that a distributor might only invest if intra-brand competition is completely eliminated within its territory. In both of these cases, it could be argued that the provisions were ancillary or objectively necessary to induce the agreement, but in both cases the impact of the provisions on the single market objective seemed to prevent the finding that the provisions would not restrict competition. Further, even leaving this issue aside, it is by no means easy to identify whether or not a particular restraint is objectively necessary or ancillary to the operation of the particular agreement so it may be hard to apply in practice.

The Commission has sought to explain how it approaches 'ancillary restraints' in its guidelines on the application of Article 81(3).

Commission's Guidelines on the application of Article 81(3) [2004] OJ C101/97

2.2.3. Ancillary restraints

28. Paragraph 18 above sets out a framework for analyzing the impact of an agreement and its individual restrictions on inter-brand and intra-brand competition. If on the basis of those principles it is concluded that the main transaction covered by the agreement is not restrictive of competition, it becomes relevant to examine whether individual restraints contained in the agreement are also compatible with Article 81(1) because they are ancillary to the main non-restrictive transaction.

29. In Community competition law the concept of ancillary restraints covers any alleged restriction of competition which is directly related and necessary to the implementation of a main

---

[188] [1985] ECR 2545, [1987] 1 CMLR 1.

[189] Without it, the vendor would be able to carry on its business as it had done previously and steal away the business of the transferee. The Court thus recognized the necessity of inserting such a clause into an agreement which would lead to an increase in competition on the market.

[190] [1986] ECR 353, [1986] 1 CMLR 414.

non-restrictive transaction and proportionate to it. If an agreement in its main parts, for instance a distribution agreement or a joint venture, does not have as its object or effect the restriction of competition, then restrictions which are directly related to and necessary for the implementation of that transaction, also fall outside Article 81(1). These related restrictions are called ancillary restraints. A restriction is directly related to the main transaction if it is subordinate to the implementation of that transaction and is inseparably linked to it. The test of necessity implies that the restriction must be objectively necessary for the implementation of the main transaction and be proportionate to it...

31. The assessment of ancillary restraints is limited to determining whether, in the specific context of the main non-restrictive transaction or activity, a particular restriction is necessary for the implementation of that transaction or activity and proportionate to it. If on the basis of objective factors it can be concluded that without the restriction the main non-restrictive transaction would be difficult or impossible to implement, the restriction may be regarded as objectively necessary for its implementation and proportionate to it. If, for example, a franchising agreement does not restrict competition, then restrictions, which are necessary for the proper functioning of the agreement, such as obligations aimed at protecting the uniformity and reputation of the franchise system, also fall outside Article 81(1). Similarly, if a joint venture is not in itself restrictive of competition, then restrictions that are necessary for the functioning of the agreement are deemed to be ancillary to the main transaction and are therefore not caught by Article 81(1). For instance in *TPS* the Commission concluded that an obligation on the parties not to be involved in companies engaged in distribution and marketing of televisions programmes by satellite was ancillary to the creation of the joint venture during the initial phrase. The restriction was therefore deemed to fall outside Article 81(1) for a period of three years. In arriving at this conclusion the Commission took account of the heavy investments and commercial risks involved in entering the market for pay-television.

Also of relevance is a Commission notice on restrictions directly related and necessary to concentrations,[191] which sets out guidance on how it is determined whether restrictions are ancillary to *concentrations* (merger transactions). Although specific to mergers, it appears from the CFI's judgment in *Métropole* that this notice will also provide guidance in pure Article 81 cases. Indeed, in *Métropole* the CFI drew on a previous notice on restrictions directly related and necessary to concentrations[192] when considering the parties' argument that two clauses should *not* have been found to infringe Article 81(1). In addition to the rule of reason argument set out above,[193] the parties argued that these clauses were 'ancillary' to the operation of the non-restrictive joint venture. The two clauses were an exclusivity clause, granting TPS the exclusive right to broadcast general-interest channels and a clause, essentially, granting TPS the right of first refusal with regard to special-interest channels produced by the parties. As the Commission had found that the joint venture did *not* infringe Article 81(1), it was argued that the ancillary clauses should also have been cleared. The CFI rejected this argument. It considered that the clauses were not objectively necessary for the operation and, even if they were, the Commission had not committed a manifest error in concluding that the restrictions were not proportionate to, or exceeded what was necessary for, the creation of the joint venture.

---

[191] [2005] OJ C26/4 discussed *infra* Chap. 12.

[192] 1990 Notice, [1990] OJ C203/5. This notice was replaced by a 2001 Notice, [2001] OJ C188/5, [2001] 5 CMLR 787 and then by a Notice in 2004, [2005] OJ C56/24.

[193] See *supra* 216.

Case T-112/99, *Métropole Télévision (M6)* v. *Commission* [2001] ECR II-2459, [2001] 5 CMLR 1236

Court of First Instance

(ii) The alternative claim, alleging that the exclusivity clause and the clause relating to the special-interest channels are ancillary restrictions...

—Findings of the court

103. It is necessary, first of all, to define what constitutes an ancillary restriction in Community competition law and point out the consequences which follow from classification of a restriction as ancillary. It is then necessary to apply the principles thereby established to the exclusivity clause and to the clause relating to the special-interest channels in order to determine whether, as the applicants assert, the Commission committed an error of appraisal in not classifying those commitments as ancillary restrictions.

The concept of ancillary restriction

104. In Community competition law the concept of an ancillary restriction covers any restriction which is directly related and necessary to the implementation of a main operation (see, to that effect, the Commission Notice of 14 August 1990 regarding restrictions ancillary to concentrations (OJ 1990 C 203, p. 5, hereinafter the notice on ancillary restrictions, point I.1[194]), the notice on cooperative joint ventures (point 65), and Articles 6(1)(b) and 8(2), second paragraph, of Regulation No. 4064/89).

105. In its notice on ancillary restrictions the Commission rightly stated that a restriction directly related to implementation of a main operation must be understood to be any restriction which is subordinate to the implementation of that operation and which has an evident link with it (point II.4).

106. The condition that a restriction be necessary implies a two-fold examination. It is necessary to establish, first, whether the restriction is objectively necessary for the implementation of the main operation and, second, whether it is proportionate to it (see, to that effect, *Remia* v. *Commission*, cited in paragraph 87 above, paragraph 20; see also points II.5 and II.6 of the notice regarding ancillary restrictions).

107. As regards the objective necessity of a restriction, it must be observed that inasmuch as, as has been shown in paragraph 72 et seq. above, the existence of a rule of reason in Community competition law cannot be upheld, it would be wrong, when classifying ancillary restrictions, to interpret the requirement for objective necessity as implying a need to weigh the pro and anti-competitive effects of an agreement. Such an analysis can take place only in the specific framework of Article [81(3)] of the Treaty.

108. That approach is justified not merely so as to preserve the effectiveness of Article [81(3)] of the Treaty, but also on grounds of consistency. As Article [81(1)] of the Treaty does not require an analysis of the positive and negative effects on competition of a principal restriction, the same finding is necessary with regard to the analysis of accompanying restrictions.

109. Consequently, as the Commission has correctly asserted, examination of the objective necessity of a restriction in relation to the main operation cannot but be relatively abstract. It is not a question of analysing whether, in the light of the competitive situation on the relevant market, the restriction is indispensable to the commercial success of the main operation but of determining

---

[194] This notice has now been replaced, see *supra* n. 192 and accompanying text.

whether, in the specific context of the main operation, the restriction is necessary to implement that operation. If, without the restriction, the main operation is difficult or even impossible to implement, the restriction may be regarded as objectively necessary for its implementation.

110. Thus, in the judgment in *Remia* v. *Commission*, . . . (paragraph 19), the Court of Justice held that a non-competition clause was objectively necessary for a successful transfer of undertakings, inasmuch as, without such a clause, and should the vendor and the purchaser remain competitors after the transfer, it is clear that the agreement for the transfer of the undertaking could not be given effect. The vendor, with his particularly detailed knowledge of the transferred undertaking, would still be in a position to win back his former customers immediately after the transfer and thereby drive the undertaking out of business.

111. Similarly, in its decisions, the Commission has found that a number of restrictions were objectively necessary to implementing certain operations. Failing such restrictions, the operation in question could not be implemented or could only be implemented under more uncertain conditions, at substantially higher cost, over an appreciably longer period or with considerably less probability of success (point II.5 of the notice regarding ancillary restrictions; see also, for example, Decision 90/410, point 22 et seq.)

112. Contrary to the applicants' claim, none of the various decisions to which they refer show that the Commission carried out an analysis of competition in classifying the relevant clauses as ancillary restrictions. On the contrary, those decisions show that the Commission's analysis was relatively abstract. Thus point 77 of Decision 1999/329 states as follows:

> Actually, a claim-sharing arrangement cannot function properly without at least one level of cover to be offered being agreed by all its members. The reason is that no member would be willing to share claims brought to the pool by other clubs of a higher amount than the ones it can bring to the pool.

113. Where a restriction is objectively necessary to implement a main operation, it is still necessary to verify whether its duration and its material and geographic scope do not exceed what is necessary to implement that operation. If the duration or the scope of the restriction exceed what is necessary in order to implement the operation, it must be assessed separately under Article [81(3)] of the Treaty (see, to that effect, Case T-61/89 *Dansk Pelsdyravlerforening* v. *Commission* [1992] ECR II-1931, paragraph 78).

114. Lastly, it must be observed that, inasmuch as the assessment of the ancillary nature of a particular agreement in relation to a main operation entails complex economic assessments by the Commission, judicial review of that assessment is limited to verifying whether the relevant procedural rules have been complied with, whether the statement of the reasons for the decision is adequate, whether the facts have been accurately stated and whether there has been a manifest error of appraisal or misuse of powers (see, to that effect, with regard to assessing the permissible duration of a non-competition clause, *Remia* v. *Commission*, cited in paragraph 87 above, paragraph 34).

Consequences of classification as an ancillary restriction

115. If it is established that a restriction is directly related and necessary to achieving a main operation, the compatibility of that restriction with the competition rules must be examined with that of the main operation.

116. Thus, if the main operation does not fall within the scope of the prohibition laid down in Article [81(1)] of the Treaty, the same holds for the restrictions directly related and necessary for that operation (see, to that effect, *Remia* v. *Commission*, cited in paragraph 87 above, paragraph 20). If, on the other hand, the main operation is a restriction within the meaning of Article [81(1)] but benefits from an exemption under Article [81(3)] of the Treaty, that exemption also covers those ancillary restrictions.

117. Moreover, where the restrictions are directly related and necessary to a concentration within the meaning of Regulation No. 4064/89, it follows from both Article 6(1)(b) and Article 8(2), second subparagraph, of that regulation that those restrictions are covered by the Commission's decision declaring the operation compatible with the common market.

(vii) Weighing Anti- and Pro-competitive Effects—Balancing under Article 81(1)?

Both the CFI in *Métropole* and the Commission in its Article 81(3) Guidelines, are emphatic that neither the ancillary restraints doctrine, nor the other case-law, implies a need to weigh the pro- and anti-competitive effects of an agreement in Article 81(1).[195] The view that the ancillary restraints doctrine (and other cases such as *STM*[196]) does not require any weighing is, however, difficult to accept.[197] This view relies on an alleged distinction between proportionate restraints objectively necessary to the implementation of a main non-restrictive operation (which are ancillary and fall outside Article 81(1)) and restraints which are indispensable to achieve efficiencies which offset anti-competitive effects of the transaction (which can be assessed only under Article 81(3)). On close examination, however, this distinction does not provide a satisfactory explanation of the 'ancillary restraints' cases. The problem with this approach to 'ancillary' restraints, is that it artificially separates the main transaction from the individual restraints forming part of the arrangement. The main transaction, however, cannot in most cases be divorced from these restraints. Rather, it is a product of them. Both *Consten and Grundig* and *STM* involved exclusive distribution agreements but one contained more severe territorial restraints than the other. This factor obviously affected the analysis of the agreement under Article 81(1) and the answer to the question of whether there was a restriction of competition.[198]

---

[195] Case T-112/99, [2001] CMLR II-2459, [2001] 5 CMLR 1236, para. 107 (2001); Article 81(3) Guidelines, para. 30. This position arguably represents a change in direction from the position set out by the CFI in Cases T-374, 375 & 388/94, *European Night Services* [1998] ECR II-3141, [1998] 5 CMLR 718 where the CFI indicated that a balancing under Article 81(1) might be required where restrictions by effect are involved. It stated at para. 136 that: 'in assessing an agreement under Article [81(1)] of the Treaty, account should be taken of the actual conditions in which it functions, in particular the economic context in which the undertakings operate, the products or services covered by the agreement and the actual structure of the market concerned . . . unless it is an agreement containing obvious restrictions of competition such as price-fixing, market-sharing or the control of outlets' (Case T-148/89, *Tréfilunion v. Commission* ([1995] ECR II-1063, para. 109)). In the latter case, such restrictions may be weighed against their claimed pro-competitive effects only in the context of Article [81(3)] of the Treaty, with a view to granting an exemption from the prohibition in Article [81(1)].
  The CFI only excludes the weighing of pro-competitive effects where restrictions by object are involved. See also the statement of the Commission in its White Paper.

[196] See also, e.g., Case 26/76, *Metro-SB-Grossmärkte GmbH v. Commission (No. 1)* [1977] ECR 1875, [1978] 2 CMLR 1 especially paras. 20–22.

[197] But see e.g. J. Faull and A. Nikpay (eds.), *The EC Law of Competition* (2nd edn., Oxford University Press, 2007), paras. 3.248–3.291. For the view that the doctrine is merely about 'administrative convenience, allowing the Commission to focus on the principal effects of an agreement, but also to control minor aspects if the ancillary restraints are excessive in duration or sege', see G. Monti, *EC Competition Law* (Cambridge University Press, 2007), 34–35.

[198] In the US, a doctrine of ancillary restraints has been used as a mechanism for distinguishing between naked restraints (demanding per se categorization) and those related to an efficiency-enhancing integration and reasonably necessary to achieve its pro-competitive benefits (analysed under the rule of reason). Under this doctrine it must be established that the restraints (which being severe are often by their very nature considered anti-competitive) are reasonably necessary for an integration which might generate plausible cognizable efficiencies. If so, rule of reason, not per se, analysis is applied. This approach clearly requires some weighing of anti- and pro-competitive benefits both when applying the doctrine and, subsequently, when conducting rule

If the CFI and Commission are simply stating that a disputed agreement, including these restraints, does not restrict inter- or intra-brand competition and so does not infringe Article 81(1) there is nothing controversial about this.[199] However, the case law suggests that in some situations the analysis goes beyond this and that there is in fact a need to weigh anti- and pro-competitive effects of the disputed restraint: anti-competitive restraints are permitted only if ancillary to some *pro-competitive* objective. In *Gøttrup-Klim Grovvareforening and Others v. Dansk Landbrugs Grovvareselskab AmbA*,[200] for example, the ECJ held that the compatibility of the statutes of a cooperative purchasing association was dependent upon the particular clauses of the statute and the conditions prevailing on the market. The ECJ recognized that provisions of a cooperative preventing members buying outside it would have adverse effects on competition. However, the Court also recognized that in a market where product prices varied according to the volume of orders, a cooperative purchasing association might constitute a significant counterweight to the contractual power of large producers and make way for more effective competition. It held that the compatibility of the exclusivity provision with Article 81(1) depended upon whether it was necessary to ensure the proper functioning of the cooperative and its contractual power in relation to others.[201] Similarly in *STM* the ECJ held that clauses conferring an exclusive right of sale on a distributor would not restrict competition if, taking account of the legal and economic context in which the agreement operated, it was necessary for the penetration of a new area by a firm.

It appears, therefore, that the ancillary restraints doctrine is hard, if not impossible, to square with the view that pro-competitive effects cannot be weighed against anti-competitive effects identified in the context of Article 81(1). Rather, it appears to hold that a restrictive clause which is necessary to achieve a pro-competitive purpose does not in fact have as its 'effect' the restriction of competition. This view is supported, for example, by Advocate General Léger who, in *Wouters v. Algemene Raad van de Nederlandse Order van Advocaten*,[202] relied on these cases as evidence of a limited application of the rule of reason. 'Confronted with certain classes of agreement . . . [the ECJ] has drawn up competition balance-sheet and, where the balance is positive, has held that the clauses necessary to perform the agreement fell outside the prohibition laid down by Article [81(1)] of the Treaty'.[203]

of reason analysis, see A. Jones, 'Analysis of Agreements under U.S. and EC Antitrust Law—Convergence or Divergence?' [2006] 51 *Ant Bull* 691.

[199] Arguably in Pronuptia, for example, the agreement and the 'ancillary restraints' did not restrict competition at all.

[200] Case C-250/92, [1994] ECR I-5641, [1996] 4 CMLR 191.

[201] Case C-250/92, [1994] ECR I-5641, [1996] 4 CMLR 191, paras. 33–5.

[202] Case C-309/99, [2002] ECR I-1577, [2002] 4 CMLR 913.

[203] Case C-309/99, [2002] ECR I-1577, [2002] 4 CMLR 913, Léger AG, para. 103. See also Case 1035/1/1/04, *The Racecourse Association (the 'RCA') v. OFT* [2005] CAT 29, where the UK's CAT confessed to have 'some difficulty in reconciling' the approach in *Gøttrup-Klim* and *Wouters* with that in *Métropole*. It considered that the analysis required under Article 81(1), or Chapter I therefore, by the ECJ in *Gøttrup-Klim* and *Wouters* was a rather more flexible exercise that the CFI had been willing to appreciate in Métropole. In determining the compatibility of that agreement with Chapter I of the Competition Act 1998 (based on and generally interpreted in accordance with Article 81(1), see s. 60 CA) the CAT held that it was not enough that an arrangement was apparently anti-competitive for it to have as its effect the restriction of competition. 'What those cases show is that ostensibly restrictive arrangements which are necessary to achieve a proper commercial objective will not, or may not, constitute an anti-competitive infringement at all. Whether or not they will do so requires an objective analysis of the particular arrangement entered into by the parties, assessed by reference to their subjective "wants" and against the evidence of the particular market in which they made their arrangement. The task then is to consider whether the restrictive arrangement of which complaint is made is "necessary" to achieve the objective', para. 167. A restriction could be regarded as objectively necessary for its implementation if the main operation was difficult or even impossible to implement without the restriction.

Also problematic to the non-weighing view is the judgment of the ECJ in *Wouters* v. *Algemene Raad van de Nederlandse Orde van Advocaten*,[204] which is simply ignored by the Commission in its discussion of Article 81(1) in the Article 81(3) Guidelines, and its judgment in *Meca-Medina* v. *Commission*.[205] Neither of these judgments refer to the CFI's judgment in *Métropole*.[206]

Wouters concerned rules adopted in the Netherlands which prohibited members of the Bar practising in full partnership with accountants. The question arose in national proceedings whether these rules were compatible with the Community rules on competition and freedom of establishment. Following a reference to it under Article 234 EC, the ECJ found that Regulations adopted by a body such as the Bar of the Netherlands had to be regarded as a decision adopted by an association of undertakings. Further, that the regulations did not have as their object or effect the restriction of competition.

Case C-309/99, *Wouters* v. *Algemene Raad van de Nederlandse Orde van Advocaten*, [2002] ECR I-1577, [2002] 4 CMLR 913

Court of Justice

73. By its second question the national court seeks, essentially, to ascertain whether a regulation such as the 1993 Regulation which, in order to guarantee the independence and loyalty to the client of members of the Bar who provide legal assistance in conjunction with members of other liberal professions, adopts universally binding rules governing the formation of multi-disciplinary partnerships, has the object or effect of restricting competition within the common market and is likely to affect trade between Member States.

. . . .

86. It appears to the Court that the national legislation in issue in the main proceedings has an adverse effect on competition and may affect trade between Member States.

87. As regards the adverse effect on competition, the areas of expertise of members of the Bar and of accountants may be complementary. Since legal services, especially in business law, more and more frequently require recourse to an accountant, a multi-disciplinary partnership of members of the Bar and accountants would make it possible to offer a wider range of services, and indeed to propose new ones. Clients would thus be able to turn to a single structure for a large part of the services necessary for the organisation, management and operation of their business (the 'one-stop shop' advantage).

88. Furthermore, a multi-disciplinary partnership of members of the Bar and accountants would be capable of satisfying the needs created by the increasing interpenetration of national markets and the consequent necessity for continuous adaptation to national and international legislation.

---

[204] Case C-309/99, [2002] ECR I-1577, [2002] 4 CMLR 913.

[205] Case C-519/04 P, *Meca-Medina* v. *Commission* [2006] ECR I-6991, [2006] 5 CMLR 1023.

[206] The cases dealing with selective distribution are also *sui generis*. In Case 26/76, *Metro-SB-Grossmärkte GmbH* v. *Commission (No. 1)* [1977] ECR 1875, [1978] 2 CMLR 1 the ECJ recognized that a producer of certain products, such as technically complex or high-quality products, may set up and operate a simple, purely qualitative, selective distribution system without infringing Article 81(1). Although the ECJ and the Commission have accepted that selective distribution systems may fall outside Article 81(1) altogether, the strict criteria which must be satisfied before an agreement can be held to escape Article 81(1) are hard to apply in practice and are difficult to explain on economic grounds. Selective distribution systems are dealt with *infra* Chap. 9.

89. Nor, finally, is it inconceivable that the economies of scale resulting from such multi-disciplinary partnerships might have positive effects on the cost of services.

90. A prohibition of multi-disciplinary partnerships of members of the Bar and accountants, such as that laid down in the 1993 Regulation, is therefore liable to limit production and technical development within the meaning of Article [81(1)(b)] of the Treaty.

91. It is true that the accountancy market is highly concentrated, to the extent that the firms dominating it are at present known as 'the big five' and the proposed merger between two of them, Price Waterhouse and Coopers & Lybrand, gave rise to Commission Decision 1999/152/EC of 20 May 1998 declaring a concentration to be compatible with the common market and the functioning of the EEA Agreement (Case IV/M.1016—Price Waterhouse/Coopers & Lybrand) (OJ 1999 L 50, p. 27), adopted pursuant to Council Regulation (EEC) No. 4064/89 of 21 December 1989 on the control of concentrations between undertakings (OJ 1989 L 395, p. 1), as amended by Council Regulation (EC) No. 1310/97 of 30 June 1997 (OJ 1997 L 180, p. 1).

92. On the other hand, the prohibition of conflicts of interest with which members of the Bar in all Member States are required to comply may constitute a structural limit to extensive concentration of law-firms and so reduce their opportunities of benefiting from economies of scale or of entering into structural associations with practitioners of highly concentrated professions.

93. In those circumstances, unreserved and unlimited authorisation of multi-disciplinary partnerships between the legal profession, the generally decentralised nature of which is closely linked to some of its fundamental features, and a profession as concentrated as accountancy, could lead to an overall decrease in the degree of competition prevailing on the market in legal services, as a result of the substantial reduction in the number of undertakings present on that market.

94. Nevertheless, in so far as the preservation of a sufficient degree of competition on the market in legal services could be guaranteed by less extreme measures than national rules such as the 1993 Regulation, which prohibits absolutely any form of multi-disciplinary partnership, whatever the respective sizes of the firms of lawyers and accountants concerned, those rules restrict competition.

95. As regards the question whether intra-Community trade is affected, it is sufficient to observe that an agreement, decision or concerted practice extending over the whole of the territory of a Member State has, by its very nature, the effect of reinforcing the partitioning of markets on a national basis, thereby holding up the economic interpenetration which the Treaty is designed to bring about (Case 8/72 *Vereeniging van Cementhandelaren* v. *Commission* [1972] ECR 977, paragraph 29; Case 42/84 *Remia and Others* v. *Commission* [1985] ECR 2545, paragraph 22; and *CNSD*, paragraph 48).

96. That effect is all the more appreciable in the present case because the 1993 Regulation applies equally to visiting lawyers who are registered members of the Bar of another Member State, because economic and commercial law more and more frequently regulates transnational transactions and, lastly, because the firms of accountants looking for lawyers as partners are generally international groups present in several Member States.

97. However, not every agreement between undertakings or every decision of an association of undertakings which restricts the freedom of action of the parties or of one of them necessarily falls within the prohibition laid down in Article [81(1)] of the Treaty. For the purposes of application of that provision to a particular case, account must first of all be taken of the overall context in which the decision of the association of undertakings was taken or produces its effects. More particularly, account must be taken of its objectives, which are here connected with the need to make rules relating to organisation, qualifications, professional ethics, supervision and liability, in order to ensure that the ultimate consumers of legal services and the sound administration of justice are provided with the necessary guarantees in relation to integrity and experience (see, to

that effect, Case C-3/95 *Reisebüro Broede* [1996] ECR I-6511, paragraph 38). It has then to be considered whether the consequential effects restrictive of competition are inherent in the pursuit of those objectives.

98. Account must be taken of the legal framework applicable in the Netherlands, on the one hand, to members of the Bar and to the Bar of the Netherlands, which comprises all the registered members of the Bar in that Member State, and on the other hand, to accountants.

99. As regards members of the Bar, it has consistently been held that, in the absence of specific Community rules in the field, each Member State is in principle free to regulate the exercise of the legal profession in its territory (Case 107/83 *Klopp* [1984] ECR 2971, paragraph 17, and *Reisebüro*, paragraph 37). For that reason, the rules applicable to that profession may differ greatly from one Member State to another.

100. The current approach of the Netherlands, where Article 28 of the Advocatenwet entrusts the Bar of the Netherlands with responsibility for adopting regulations designed to ensure the proper practice of the profession, is that the essential rules adopted for that purpose are, in particular, the duty to act for clients in complete independence and in their sole interest, the duty, mentioned above, to avoid all risk of conflict of interest and the duty to observe strict professional secrecy.

101. Those obligations of professional conduct have not inconsiderable implications for the structure of the market in legal services, and more particularly for the possibilities for the practice of law jointly with other liberal professions which are active on that market.

102. Thus, they require of members of the Bar that they should be in a situation of independence *vis-à-vis* the public authorities, other operators and third parties, by whom they must never be influenced. They must furnish, in that respect, guarantees that all steps taken in a case are taken in the sole interest of the client.

103. By contrast, the profession of accountant is not subject, in general, and more particularly, in the Netherlands, to comparable requirements of professional conduct.

104. As the Advocate General has rightly pointed out in paragraphs 185 and 186 of his Opinion, there may be a degree of incompatibility between the 'advisory' activities carried out by a member of the Bar and the 'supervisory' activities carried out by an accountant. The written observations submitted by the respondent in the main proceedings show that accountants in the Netherlands perform a task of certification of accounts. They undertake an objective examination and audit of their clients' accounts, so as to be able to impart to interested third parties their personal opinion concerning the reliability of those accounts. It follows that in the Member State concerned accountants are not bound by a rule of professional secrecy comparable to that of members of the Bar, unlike the position under German law, for example.

105. The aim of the 1993 Regulation is therefore to ensure that, in the Member State concerned, the rules of professional conduct for members of the Bar are complied with, having regard to the prevailing perceptions of the profession in that State. The Bar of the Netherlands was entitled to consider that members of the Bar might no longer be in a position to advise and represent their clients independently and in the observance of strict professional secrecy if they belonged to an organisation which is also responsible for producing an account of the financial results of the transactions in respect of which their services were called upon and for certifying those accounts.

106. Moreover, the concurrent pursuit of the activities of statutory auditor and of adviser, in particular legal adviser, also raises questions within the accountancy profession itself, as may be seen from the Commission Green Paper 96/C/321/01 'The role, the position and the liability of the statutory auditor within the European Union' (OJ 1996 C 321, p. 1; see, in particular, paragraphs 4.12 to 4.14).

107. A regulation such as the 1993 Regulation could therefore reasonably be considered to be necessary in order to ensure the proper practice of the legal profession, as it is organised in the Member State concerned.

108. Furthermore, the fact that different rules may be applicable in another Member State does not mean that the rules in force in the former State are incompatible with Community law (see, to that effect, Case C-108/96 *Mac Quen and Others* [2001] ECR I-837, paragraph 33). Even if multi-disciplinary partnerships of lawyers and accountants are allowed in some Member States, the Bar of the Netherlands is entitled to consider that the objectives pursued by the 1993 Regulation cannot, having regard in particular to the legal regimes by which members of the Bar and accountants are respectively governed in the Netherlands, be attained by less restrictive means (see, to that effect, with regard to a law reserving judicial debt-recovery activity to lawyers, *Reisebüro*, paragraph 41).

109. In light of those considerations, it does not appear that the effects restrictive of competition such as those resulting for members of the Bar practising in the Netherlands from a regulation such as the 1993 Regulation go beyond what is necessary in order to ensure the proper practice of the legal profession (see, to that effect, Case C-250/92 *DLG* [1994] ECR I-5641, paragraph 35).

110. Having regard to all the foregoing considerations, the answer to be given to the second question must be that a national regulation such as the 1993 Regulation adopted by a body such as the Bar of the Netherlands does not infringe Article [81(1)] of the Treaty, since that body could reasonably have considered that that regulation, despite the effects restrictive of competition that are inherent in it, is necessary for the proper practice of the legal profession, as organised in the Member State concerned.

The reasoning adopted by the ECJ in this case is difficult. It first stated that it appeared 'that the national legislation in issue...has an adverse effect on competition' since partnerships of lawyers and accountants would, for example, be able to offer a wider range of services, propose new ones, and result in economies of scale.[207] As such, the prohibition of multi-disciplinary partnerships was liable to limit production and technical development within the meaning of Article 81(1)(b) EC. The ECJ then went on to hold that not every agreement between undertakings that restricted the freedom of action of the parties necessarily fell within the prohibition of Article 81(1). Rather, account had to be taken of the *objectives* of the restrictions and the overall context in which they were adopted. In this case, the objective of the rules was to ensure that the ultimate consumers of legal services and the sound administration of justice were provided with the necessary guarantees in relation to integrity and justice.[208] For example, members of the Bar might not be in a position to advise and represent clients independently if they belonged to an organization which was also responsible for producing an account for the financial results of the transactions in respect of which their services were called upon and for certifying those accounts. The regulation therefore did not infringe Article 81(1) 'since the association could reasonably have considered that, despite its inherent restrictive effect on competition, it was necessary for the proper practice of the legal profession as organized in the Member States concerned'.[209]

---

[207] Case C-309/99, [2002] ECR I-1577, [2002] 4 CMLR 913, para. 86.

[208] The Bar clearly took the view that the restriction was necessary for the retention of the integrity of the legal profession.

[209] *Ibid.* at paras. 106–10. Contrast the opinion of Léger AG in this case who considered, at paras. 104–5, that the rule of reason in Community competition law was strictly confined to a '*purely competitive* balance-sheet of the effects of the agreement'. The reasoning in this case, however, required the introduction into the provisions of Article 81(1) considerations which were linked to the pursuit of a '*public-interest* objective'. He took the view, however, that social concerns and considerations connected with the pursuit of the public interest, were relevant to the Article 81(3) appraisal, see *infra* 273–7.

In this case, therefore, the ECJ, despite appearing to find that the agreement restricted competition, went on to conclude that the agreement did not infringe Article 81(1) as the restraints were necessary for the proper practice of the legal profession. It did not, as it had done with respect to collective bargaining agreements in *Albany*,[210] consider that reasonable rules relating to the regulation of the provision of professional services[211] should fall outside Article 81(1) altogether. Rather, at first sight, the Court seems to to weigh the anti-competitive effects of the agreement against benefits which are were *not* economic efficiency benefits.

If the Commission's analytical framework is correct, it might have been expected that the ECJ, having stated that the agreement had clear adverse effects on competition (in terms of the services that could be offered and economies of scope), would have gone on to find that the object or effect of the agreement was the restriction of competition.[212] The justifications raised by the parties could then have been appraised[213] when determining whether the rules of ethics could be excepted through the application of Article 81(3).[214] Indeed, this appears to be the route taken by the CFI in *Laurent Piau*[215] when it held that the actual principle of a licence required by FIFA as a condition for carrying on the occupation of players' agent, constituted a 'barrier to access to that economic activity and therefore necessarily affects competition'. The conduct could, consequently, be accepted 'only in so far as the conditions set out in Article 81(3) are satisfied'.[216] The ECJ did not, however, take this course in *Wouters*.[217] Had it done so the referring national court, which did not at this time have jurisdiction to rule on the compatibility of the agreement with Article 81(3),[218] would have been compelled to rule that the regulations,

---

[210] Case C-67/96, *Albany International BV v. Stichting Bedrijfspensioenfonds Textielindustrie* [1999] ECR I-5751, [2000] 4 CMLR 446. See *supra* Chap. 3, 152–4.

[211] The Commission is in fact concerned about the compatibility of many such regulatory rules with the EC competition provisions. In March 2003, DG Comp launched a stocktaking exercise for professional services. The purpose of the exercise is to consider the justification for and effects of restrictive rules and regulations in the professions. Details of this exercise are available on DG Comp's web site, at http://www.europa.eu.int/comm/competition/liberalization/conference/libprofconference.html.

[212] The ECJ had after all made it clear that the rules might have negative effects on prices, innovation and/or the variety or quality of goods and services that could be expected.

[213] See the discussion *infra* 4.E.

[214] Or, perhaps through Article 86(2) on the grounds that the rules were necessary to the task entrusted by statute to the Dutch Bar Council. The ECJ considered, however, that it was precluded from applying Article 86(2). The Bar Council was not an entrusted undertaking or group of undertakings within the meaning of Art. 86, Case C-309/99, [2002] ECR I-1577, 4 CMLR 913, paras. 111–116 (2002). *Contrast* the opinion of the Léger AG who considered that it was possible that professional rules aimed at the preservation, in the public interest, of certain essential features of the profession of lawyer may fall within the ambit of Article 86(2), see, e.g., paras. 114 and 201.

[215] Case T-193/02, *Laurent Piau v. Commission* [2005] ECR II-209, [2005] 5 CMLR 2, appeal dismissed by Order of the ECJ, Case C-171/05 P, [2006] ECR I-37.

[216] Case T-193/02, 25 January 2005, para. 101 (*aff'd* Case C-171/05 P, [2006] ECR I-37).

[217] Although it is possible to understand why the ECJ was unwilling to strike down reasonable national rules regulating the legal profession the problem is the analysis adopted. In the absence of Community rules, it would seem inevitable that the rules applicable to the profession will vary from Member State to Member State.

[218] At this time only the Commission could apply Article 81(3) in individual cases (Reg. 17, [1959–62] OJ Spec. Ed. 87, Art. 9). Further, the Commission could not have been called upon to apply Article 81(3) as the regulations had not been notified to it for exemption (and in this case an exemption could not be granted retrospectively, Reg. 17, [1959–62] OJ Spec. Ed. 87, Art. 4). In contrast, the ruling in *Piau* resulted from a rejection of a complaint on the basis that the agreement would have merited an exemption under Article 81(3). Whether and when non-competition benefits can be weighed under Article 81(3) against restrictive effects identified under Article 81(1) is discussed *infra* 273–7.

or at least the restrictive rules within them, were void.[219] The ECJ's clear view was that the Bar Association had not been unreasonable in considering that the restrictive rules were warranted by reference to the objective pursued.[220] The ECJ took a similar approach in *Meca-Medina*[221] ruling that restraints on freedom of action resulting from anti-doping rules would not constitute a restriction of competition[222] if inherent in, and justified by, a legitimate objective: in that case the organization and proper conduct of competitive sport. Restraints imposed by the rules had to be limited to what is necessary to ensure the proper conduct of competitive sport.[223]

These cases undoubtedly support the view that some weighing of anti-competitive and pro-competitive effects, and even *other* non-competition public interest objectives, should take place under Article 81(1).[224] With regard to *Wouters*, some commentators have argued that the judgment does not go this far. Professor Goyder states that:

What appears to have happened is that the two parts of the Article have been conflated and operated as if they were a single provision (in the same way as under section 1 of the Sherman Act in a case like *California Dental Association* v. *FTC*). This may become the usual method of applying Article 81 from 1 May [2004] once the modernization programme has been implemented and after the Commission has surrendered its monopoly of granting individual exemptions. It is certainly not to be regarded as an application of the 'rule of reason'.[225]

Arguably this view is supported by the Commission itself. In a report on competition in professional services it clearly takes the view that restraints on collaboration with other professions 'may have a negative economic impact'.[226] Although compelling, the difficulty is that the ECJ did in fact deal only with Article 81(1) and the national court (which made the reference) was not, at that time, at liberty to apply Article 81(3). The temptation to justify what the Court did by reference to something that is now possible should therefore be resisted. Even

---

[219] Even if the parties had notified the agreement to the Commission any exemption granted would not have taken effect retrospectively, see Reg. 17, [1959–62] OJ Spec. Ed. 87, Art 4.

[220] See *supra* n. 211.

[221] Case C-519/04 P, *Meca-Medina* v. *Commission* [2006] ECR I-6991, [2006] 5 CMLR 1023.

[222] The ECJ held that 'the penal nature of the anti-doping rules...are capable of producing adverse effects on competition because they could, if penalties were ultimately to prove unjustified, result in an athlete's unwarranted exclusion from sporting events.' Case C-519/04 P, *Meca-Medina* v. *Commission* [2006] ECR I-6991, [2006] 5 CMLR 1023, para. 47.

[223] Case C-519/04 P, *Meca-Medina* v. *Commission* [2006] ECR I-6991, [2006] 5 CMLR 1023, paras. 45–47. The ECJ set aside the judgment of the CFI which had held that the sporting rules had nothing to do with economic activity and so fell outside the scope of Article 81, Case T-313/02, [2004] ECR II-3291.

[224] It has been seen that Léger AG considered that the courts had drawn up a 'competition' balance-sheet, Case C-309/99, [2002] ECR I-1577, (2002) 4 CMLR 913, para. 103, see *supra* n. 203 and accompanying text. He took the view that public policy considerations were not relevant to the Article 81(1) assessment, see *supra* n. 209.

[225] D. G. Goyder, *EC Competition Law* (4th edn., Oxford University Press, 2003), 94–5.

[226] Communication from the Commission 'Report on Competition in Professional Services' COM (2004) 83 final (Brussels, 9 Feb. 2004), para. 60. For further discussion, see *infra* Chap. 11. The *Wouters* case is not discussed at all in the section dealing with Article 81(1) in the Commission's Guidelines on the application of Article 81(3) [2004] OJ C101/97.

if this approach is the correct one, the extent to which non-competition factors are relevant at the Article 81(3) stage is still uncertain.[227]

Professor Whish argues that the case is simply an application of the concept of ancillary restraints, endorsing the restraint on the grounds that it was ancillary not to some legitimate pro-competitive objective but to the regulatory aim of ensuring integrity and experience.[228]

R. Whish, *Competition Law* (5th edn., Butterworths, 2003), 121–2

[T]he judgment in *Wouters* does have a conceptual similarity to the cases discussed in section (iii) above, in that they are all concerned with the idea of ancillarity: restraints on conduct, even ones that, in a colloquial sense, appear to restrict competition, do not infringe Article 81(1) where they are ancillary to some legitimate purpose. What is of interest about *Wouters*, however, is that the restriction in that case was not necessary for the execution of a commercial transaction or the achievement of a commercial outcome on the market; instead it was ancillary to a regulatory function 'to ensure that the ultimate consumers of legal services and the sound administration of justice are provided with the necessary guarantees in relation to integrity and experience'. This seems to be a different application of the concept of ancillarity from that in the earlier case law: the *Wouters* case is concerned with 'regulatory' ancillarity, whereas earlier judgments were concerned with 'commercial' ancillarity; perhaps the use of these two terms would be useful in, first, demonstrating a continuity with the earlier case law, through the common idea of ancillarity, while also capturing the difference between the two situations, by distinguishing commercial and regulatory cases.

It has also been argued that the case is explicable by the fact that the rule was promulgated not by an undertaking but by an association of undertakings,[229] and that the ECJ transposed its analysis in free movement cases to the competition sphere, weighing non-discriminatory national rules against domestic mandatory requirements of public policy and allowing the Court to take account of non-competition factors which relate to domestic interests.[230]

---

[227] See *infra* 273–7. Arguably, Article 86(2) would provide a preferable mechanism, see *infra* Chap. 8.

[228] R. Whish *Competition* (5th edn., Butterworths, 2003), 121–22. The problem with this view is that as the restraint does not appear to be absolutely necessary to the implementation of the regulatory rules (multidisciplinary partnerships are permitted in other states) it does not seem to be truly ancillary in the sense described above (directly related and necessary to the implementation of the agreement). Further, it does still appear to involve the weighing of the impact of the restraint against the worthy objectives identified, something the CFI explicitly stated in *Métropole* should not be done under Article 81(1) (see *supra*).

[229] Had the rule been adopted by an undertaking, it would have fallen outside of Article 81 as the activity it was conducting was regulatory in nature (and regulation is not an economic activity). Once within Article 81 the ECJ had to find an appropriate standard by which to assess the non-economic, regulatory activity and that the principles applied were free-movement not competition ones, see and O. Odudu, *The Boundaries of EC Competition Law: The Scope of Article 81* (Oxford University Press, 2006), 53.

[230] G. Monti, 'Article 81 EC and Public Policy' (2002) *CMLRev* 1057, 1087–1088. See also G. Monti, *EC Competition Law* (Cambridge University Press, 2007), 110–113.

> ## G. Monti, 'Article 81 EC and Public Policy' (2002) *CMLRev* 1057, 1087–8
>
> This is a remarkable *ratio decidendi* for the Court intertwines principles of competition law and free movement. It is worth exploring in more detail how the Court reached its conclusion. In simple terms, the line of reasoning followed is this: we know from *Cassis de Dijon* that an indistinctly applicable domestic rule which is an obstacle to the free movement of goods does not fall under the prohibition in Article 28 if it is necessary to satisfy a mandatory requirement relating to, for example, fairness of commercial transactions or the defence of the consumer. The same approach has been applied in relation to other freedoms. In *Wouters*, the Court relies on this line of case law, specifically referring to *Reisbüro Vroede*, a case in relation to the regulation of the legal profession in the context of Article 49 (freedom to provide services) where it held that a non-discriminatory rule of German law which infringed Article 49 might be justified in the public interest. The Court then holds that the principle created by this case law (labelled by many commentators a 'rule of reason') applies *mutatis mutandis* to Article 81. Having transposed a rule from the free movement case law into the competition case law, the Court was free to say that the prohibition in Article 81 could not apply. This reasoning incorporates the rules of reason deployed in the free movement area as a mechanism for justifying an agreement otherwise unlawful under Article 81(1). It is ironic that while the Court (most explicitly in *Métropole*) has regularly refused to adopt an *American-style* rule of reason in Article 81 (whereby the legality of an agreement would depend upon whether, on balance it increased consumer welfare) it has in *Wouters* given strong indications that what I shall cal the *European-style rule of reason*, developed in the free movement field, can apply to competition cases so that an anti-competitive agreement necessary to preserve a domestic mandatory requirement of public policy is allowed to escape the application of Article 81. Thus *Wouters* is another in a line of cases that exemplifies what Mortelmans[231] labelled a 'convergence' in the application of the rules on free movement and competition. The purpose of convergence in this case is to allow the Court to take into account non-competition factors which relate to *domestic* interests.

There seems little doubt, however, that the case re-ignites the question of exactly what analysis is required under Article 81(1) and pours fuel on the view that Article 81(1) is *not* only about identifying undue restrictions on inter- or intra-brand competition.[232]

E. CONCLUSIONS ON THE APPROACH REQUIRED UNDER ARTICLE 81(1)

The Commission's view (supported by recent CFI judgments) that no weighing of anti- and pro-competitive effects is permitted under Article 81(1) in 'effect' cases, is not reconcilable with all of the case law. Rather, there seems to be a clear divide between this view and cases such as *STM*, *European Night Services*, *Gøttrup-Klim*, *Wouters* and *Meca-Medina* which are consistent with the view that weighing is required: justifications may be weighed against anti-competitive effects

---

[231] K. Mortelmans, 'Towards convergence in the application of the rules on free movement and on competition' (2001) *CMLRev* 613.

[232] See also the view of the UK's CAT set out *supra* n. 203.

identified.[233] Further, the latter two cases cast doubt on the correctness of the Commission's more recent statements on the objectives of Article 81.

The difficulty with a conclusion that weighing is required under Article 81(1), is that it does not mesh well with the current Article 81 scheme and it would seem to demand procedural and legislative changes which, it must be accepted, are most unlikely to occur. First, it has already been noted that this narrow interpretation of Article 81(1) would confer an extremely limited role on Article 81(3). It would be relevant only in object or public policy cases.[234] Not only does this interpretation of Article 81(3) not appear to fit with its broad wording, but the question of whether other public policy objectives should be relevant to the Article 81(3) appraisal is politically charged and highly controversial (especially as it is now applied by a plethora of national courts and competition authorities).[235] The Commission currently takes the view that these factors should not be taken into account in Article 81 cases. Secondly, the approach allocates similar analysis to different forums and sits awkwardly with the burden of proof allocated by Regulation 1/2003. In object cases, any justifications for the agreement could be considered only within the structured framework of Article 81(3) (where the onus lies with the parties[236]) whilst in effect cases, justifications would have to be raised and considered within the more amorphous framework of Article 81(1) (where the burden lies with the Commission or other person seeking to prove the breach).[237] Thirdly, the conclusion that anti- and pro-competitive effects must be weighed under Article 81(1) is incompatible with the existence of the current overarching block exemptions. These block exemptions do *not* apply to agreements containing hardcore restraints (agreements which have as their object the restriction of competition)[238] and would seem redundant, at least in their current form, in effect cases if the weighing of pro- and anti-competitive aspects of the agreement had already been concluded under Article 81(1).[239]

It is clear, therefore, why the Commission and CFI take the view that weighing of anti- and pro-competitive effects should be divided between Article 81(1) and Article 81(3). This view would seem to require, however, some clarification from the ECJ, and a significant evolution in the case-law. In addition, if such a division is to be adopted it is perhaps disappointing, in the light of the numerous steps taken by the Commission to 'modernize' the interpretation and application of Article 81(1) and to clarify its objectives, that it has not been prepared to accept that an even narrower analysis should be adopted under Article 81(1) than that suggested in its Guidelines (which focuses on both restraints on inter- and intra-brand competition). Although

---

[233] In contrast to the analysis conducted in the US, however, the case law indicates that in identifying anti-competitive effects, intra-brand restraints on parallel trade may be relevant, and that justifications may be broader than just efficiencies.

[234] See *supra* 3.B. If public policy issues may also be taken into account under Article 81(1) (as *Wouters* and *Meca-Medina* suggest) the role of Article 81(3) would be even more limited. The Court in *Wouters* was not at liberty to apply Article 81(3), see *supra* n. 218 and accompanying text.

[235] See *infra* 273.

[236] Reg 1/2003, art. 2.

[237] *But see* the approach suggested by the CAT, in Case 1035/1/1/04, *The Racecourse Association v. OFT* [2005] CAT 29 (discussed *supra* n. 203). Although it recognized that the burden under Chapter I (equivalent of Article 81(1)) was on the OFT, it stated that where the parties claimed any apparently anti-competitive effect identified by the OFT was justified by the necessity of such dealing, it would be for them to demonstrate this by evidence. Once that evidence was before the OFT, the overall legal burden still remained on the OFT to prove the infringement of Chapter I.

[238] *But see*, e.g., Council Reg. 4056/86 (which sets out a block exemption for liner shipping conferences allow them under certain conditions to fix prices and regulate capacity). This Regulation is currently under review.

[239] *But see* the discussion of the block exemptions *infra* 284–9 which are designed to provide safe harbours.

not binding, the Commission Guidelines are extremely influential on firms, their legal advisers and national authorities when considering the application of Article 81.[240]

4. ARTICLE 81(3)

A. GENERAL

Regulation 1/2003 allocates the burden of establishing the Article 81(3) criteria are met to those claiming its benefit.[241] Once those undertakings have submitted factual arguments and evidence to support an argument that Article 81(3) is satisfied, however, it is for the fact finder to examine whether, on the balance of probabilities, the agreement in question does meet these criteria. In *GlaxoSmithKline Services Unlimited* v. *Commission*,[242] the CFI held that the Commission had not adequately discharged its burden of examining the Article 81(3) arguments put forward, and refuting them by means of substantiated evidence.[243]

Case T-168/01 *GlaxoSmithKline Services Unlimited* v. *Commission*, 27 September 2006, [2006] 5 CMLR 1623

233. Any agreement which restricts competition, whether by its effects or by its object, may in principle benefit from an exemption (*Consten and Grundig* v *Commission*... 342, 343 and 347, and Case T-17/93 *Matra Hachette* v *Commission* [1994] ECR II-595, paragraph 85), as the Commission, moreover, observed at recital 153 to the Decision and at the hearing.

234. The application of that provision is subject to certain conditions, satisfaction of which is both necessary and sufficient (*Remia and Others* v *Commission*... paragraph 38, and *Matra Hachette* v *Commission*... paragraph 104). First, the agreement concerned must contribute to improving the production or distribution of the goods in question, or to promoting technical or economic progress; second, consumers must be allowed a fair share of the resulting benefit; third, it must not impose on the participating undertakings any restrictions which are not indispensable; and, fourth, it must not afford them the possibility of eliminating competition in respect of a substantial part of the products in question.

235. Consequently, a person who relies on Article 81(3) EC must demonstrate that those conditions are satisfied, by means of convincing arguments and evidence (Joined Cases 43/82 and 63/82 *VBVB and VBBB* v *Commission* [1984] ECR 19, paragraph 52, and *Aalborg Portland and Others* v *Commission*... paragraph 78).

---

[240] Although the CFI has annulled Commission exemption decisions for failure to provide an adequate Article 81(1) analysis (*see, e.g.,* Cases T-374, 375, 384 and 388/94, *European Night Services* v. *Commission* [1998] ECR II-3141, 5 CMLR 718 (1998) and Case T-328/03, *O2 (Germany) GmbH & Co OHG* v. *Commission* [2006] ECR II-1231, [2006] 5 CMLR 5, the central role played by the Commission in EU competition policy means that its guidelines, notices and decisions attain a prominent status.

[241] Reg. 1/2003, Art 2.

[242] Case T-168/01, 27 Sept. 2006, [2006] 5 CMLR 1623, paras. 247–252, Cases C-501 and 513, 515 and 519/06 P (judgment pending).

[243] In some respects the CFI held that the Commission had sought to reject the arguments on the basis of evidence which was, to say the least, fragmentary and of limited relevance or value. These omissions were particularly severe in a market, such as pharmaceuticals, where competition was distorted by the presence of national regulation.

236. The Commission, for its part, must adequately examine those arguments and that evidence (*Consten and Grundig v Commission* . . . 347), that is to say, it must determine whether they demonstrate that the conditions for the application of Article 81(3) EC are satisfied. In certain cases, those arguments and that evidence may be of such a kind as to require the Commission to provide an explanation or justification, failing which it is permissible to conclude that the burden of proof borne by the person who relies on Article 81(3) EC has been discharged (*Aalborg Portland and Others v Commission*, paragraph 55 above, paragraph 79). As the Commission agrees in its written submissions, in such a case it must refute those arguments and that evidence.

The burden imposed by Article 81(3) requires demonstration: (1) that the agreement achieves benefits, (2) that a fair share of those benefits are passed on to consumers, (3) that the agreement does not contain any indispensable restraints and (4) does not eliminate competition in respect of a substantial part of the products in question. The first two criteria of Article 81(3) are positive. The second two are negative. Any restrictive agreement is, in theory, capable of satisfying the criteria[244] but *all* four criteria must be satisfied.[245] The exception rule applies only for as long as the four conditions are met.[246]

It has been seen that the role of Article 81(3) relates to, and is affected by, the interpretation of Article 81(1). The answer to the question 'what is Article 81(3) *for*?' is thus dependent on the answer to the question 'what is Article 81(1) for' and which agreements does it prohibit. In its new analytical framework the Commission has narrowed the role of Article 81(1) to the identification of negative effects on competition.[247] It has also correspondingly, limited the role of Article 81(3)[248] to the determination of whether efficiencies achieved by the agreement outweigh negative effects, so that the agreement is on balance pro-competitive.[249]

[244] Case T-17/93, *Matra Hachette v. Commission* [1994] ECR II-595, para. 85. In practice, however, an agreement containing clauses which have as their object the restriction of competition or identified as 'hard-core' restraints in Community block exemptions or guidelines, will only do so in exceptional circumstances, see *infra* 280–1.

[245] The requirements are cumulative, Case T-528/93, *Métropole Télévision S.A. v. Commission*, [1996] ECR II-649, [1996] 5 CMLR 386, para. 86. In Case T-65/98, *Van den Bergh Foods v. Commission* [2003] ECR II-4653, [2004] 4 CMLR 1, para. 144, the CFI thus held that once it had concluded that the Commission had been correct to find that the first criterion of Art. 81(3) had not been met it was unnecessary to consider whether or not the other criteria had been satisfied (appeal dismissed, Case C-552/03 P, *Unilever Bestfoods v. Commission* [2006] OJ C294/19).

[246] It ceases to apply when that is no longer the case, Article 81(3) Guidelines, para. 44. In certain cases, the assessment will however have to be made on the basis of facts existing at the time of implementation, see Article 81(3) Guidelines, paras. 44–45. The parties will therefore have to continually review their agreement to ensure that is continues to satisfy the Art. 81(3) conditions. Under the old notification system an exemption would have been granted to an agreement for a period of time.

[247] It has also been seen in the section above, however, that the Commission in fact still casts the Article 81(1) net quite wide. Nonetheless, the Article 81(3) guidelines indicate that, when compared with the previous position, the burden on parties seeking to justify their agreement under Article 81(3) has been increased and that the bar, in terms of the level and sophistication of evidence required, has been raised.

[248] In early cases much of the Commission's analysis was focused on Art. 81(3), on account of the broad jurisdictional interpretation of Article 81(1). Despite this, published exemption decisions, especially the early ones, did not contain particularly lengthy or sophisticated analysis of the Article 81(3) criteria.

[249] 'The aim of the Community competition rules is to protect competition on the market as a means of enhancing consumer welfare and of ensuring an efficient allocation of resources. Agreements that restrict competition may at the same time have pro-competitive effects by way of efficiency gains. Efficiencies may create additional value by lowering the cost of producing an output, improving the quality of the product or

B. THE INTERPRETATION AND APPLICATION OF ARTICLE 81(3)

(i) Criterion 1: The Agreement must lead to an Improvement in the Production or Distribution of Goods or the Promotion of Technical or Economic Progress

a. Article 81(3) Benefits

This provision is broad, enabling the Commission to authorize agreements which: (1) lead to an improvement in the production of goods or services;[250] (2) lead to an improvement in the distribution of goods or services; (3) promote technical progress; and/or (4) promote economic progress. The benefits referred to are not subjective ones that result to the parties to the agreement. Rather, the ECJ has stressed that the improvement must 'show appreciable objective advantages of such a character as to compensate for the disadvantages which they cause in the field of competition'.[251] Given the broad nature of these four categories, it is possible that more than one, and occasionally all, will be applicable in some cases.

b. Efficiency Gains

This first limb permits the parties to establish that, despite the fact that the agreement restricts competition, efficiency gains, cost efficiencies,[252] and qualitative efficiencies, creating value in the form of new or improved products (dynamic efficiencies),[253] will result from the economic activity that forms the object of the agreement (there must be causal link between the agreement and the claimed efficiencies).[254] The Commission's guidelines on the application of Article 81(3) state that parties must substantiate efficiency claims by showing the nature of the claimed efficiencies, the link between the agreement and the efficiencies, the likelihood and magnitude of each claimed efficiency, and how and when each claimed efficiency would be achieved.[255]

---

creating a new product. When the pro-competitive effects of an agreement outweigh its anti-competitive effects the agreement is on balance pro-competitive and compatible with the objectives of the Community competition rules. The net effect of such agreements is to promote the very essence of the competitive process, namely to win customers by offering better products or better prices than those offered by rivals. This analytical framework is reflected in Article 81(1) and Article 81(3). The latter provision expressly acknowledges that restrictive agreements may generate objective economic benefits so as to outweigh the negative effects of the restriction of competition'. Article 81(3) Guidelines, para. 33. See also Case T-528/93, *Métropole Télévision SA v. Commission* [1996] ECR II-649, [1996] 5 CMLR 386, para. 86; Case T-65/98, *Van den Bergh Foods v. Commission* [2003] ECR II-4653, [2004] 4 CMLR 1, *aff'd* Case C-552/03 P, *Unilever Bestfoods v. Commission* [2006] OJ C294/19.

[250] Although Article 81(3) does not make specific reference to services, services are covered by analogy: see *P & I Clubs* [1985] OJ L376/2. Commission Guidelines on the application of Article 81(3) of the Treaty [2004] OJ C101/97, para. 48.

[251] Cases 56 and 58/64, *Etablissements Consten SA & Grundig-Verkaufs-GmbH v. Commission* [1966] ECR 299, 348 [1966] CMLR 418.

[252] Commission Guidelines on the application of Article 81(3) of the Treaty [2004] OJ C101/97, paras. 64–68.

[253] *Ibid.*, paras. 69–72.

[254] *Ibid.*, para. 45.

[255] Article 81(3) Guidelines, paras. 51 and 52–59. Examples of different types of efficiencies are given at paras. 59–72.

Parties may, therefore, establish that the agreement will improve production or distribution or promote technical or economic progress, for example, through cost reduction (such as those originating from: development of new production technologies and methods; synergies resulting from an integration of existing assets; economies of scale or scope; or better production planning[256]) and/or through improvement in the quality and choice of goods and services.[257] A number of joint venture agreements have, therefore, succeeded on the grounds that new or better products will be produced and that the cooperation permitted the parties to do so more quickly or cheaply and/or through the sharing of risk or cost, through the pooling of technical expertise and/or by making the venture financially viable.[258] In *Ford/Volkswagen*,[259] for example, the Commission held that the parties' creation of a joint venture company to develop and produce a multi-purpose vehicle ('MPV') in Portugal would improve the production of goods and promote technical development. It would rationalize product development and manufacturing and establish a new and modern manufacturing plant which would be using the latest production technology. In addition, the parties' pooling of technical knowledge would be converted into a significantly improved and innovative MPV. In the context of vertical and intellectual property licensing agreements the Commission has taken account of the fact that the agreement will improve production and distribution of products through, for example, permitting the increase in production capacity, conferring incentives to promote a product, conferring incentives to concentrate sales efforts and/or through reduction in transaction costs.[260] In *GlaxoSmithKline Services Unlimited* v. *Commission*[261] the CFI quashed a Commission decision declining an exemption to Glaxo in respect of an agreement designed to prevent parallel trade in its pharmaceutical products. Essentially, Glaxo argued that the agreement was necessary to stimulate and support costly and risky global R&D in a market where inter-brand competition was driven by innovation not price and where in many Member States the prices were controlled by public authorities. The agreement would thus encourage competition upstream by encouraging innovation and on the market itself, by optimising the distribution of medicines. In particular, it was stressed that the strong competitive pressure to innovate would ensure that any additional profits made would be ploughed into investment in R&D. The CFI considered that the Commission had been wrong to reject the evidence raised, which appeared 'relevant, reliable and credible' and, to some extent, to be corroborated by Commission documents.[262]

---

[256] Article 81(3) Guidelines, paras. 64–68.

[257] The enhancing potential of the agreement may not therefore be cost reduction but quality improvement resulting from technical and technological advance. Research and development, technology licensing and joint production, and distribution agreements may all be capable of realizing these qualitative efficiencies, Article 81(3) Guidelines, paras. 69–72.

[258] See, e.g., *Beecham/Parke, Davis* [1979] OJ L70/11 (research and development agreement would promote 'technical progress' by creating a product for the prevention or treatment of an impairment for which there was no known marketed compound and where the pooling of research capacities was a major factor in providing a reasonable likelihood of success); *De Laval-Stork* [1977] OJ L 215/11 (research and development agreement would enable the parties to penetrate a market more easily and quickly, enable the parties to reach optimal size, work at greater and to share latest technical advances).

[259] [1993] OJ L20/14, [1993] 5 CMLR 617.

[260] See, e.g., *Goodyear Italiana-Euram* [1975] OJ L38/10; *Campari* [1978] OJ L70/69.

[261] Case T-168/01, 27 Sept. 2006, [2006] 5 CMLR 1623, Cases C-501, 513, 515 and 519/06 P (judgment pending).

[262] Case T-168/01, 27 Sept. 2006, [2006] 5 CMLR 1623, Cases C-501, 513, 515 and 519/06 P (judgment pending), paras. 233–307.

c. Non-competition Factors

A controversial issue is whether the first head of Article 81(3) permits the parties to rely on broader public policy benefits achieved by the agreement. This question was of importance in the modernization debate and as to the question of whether the Commission should, or could, relinquish its exclusive right to rule on the compatibility of an agreement with Article 81(3). An acceptance that Article 81(3) permitted a balancing of public and private interests and/or of conflicting Community policies might have militated against the abolition of the notification and authorization and defeated the modernization proposals.[263] In its White Paper on Modernisation the Commission stated that Article 81(3) is intended 'to provide a legal framework for the economic assessment of restrictive practices and not to allow the application of the competition rules to be set aside because of political considerations'.[264] In its Article 81(3) Guidelines, the discussion of the first condition of Article 81(3) is headed 'Efficiency gains' and *only* efficiency gains are discussed within it.[265] Although it states that '[g]oals pursued by other Treaty provisions can be taken into account to the extent that they can be subsumed under the four conditions of Article 81(3)'[266] its reliance on the ruling of the CFI in *Matra Hachette* suggests that it considers that these factors may only be taken into account 'supererogatorily' where 'public policy considerations have been used to supplement the economic benefits which the agreement generates'.[267]

Case T-17/93, *Matra Hachette* v. *Commission* [1994] ECR II-595

139. As regards the argument based on the reference to 'exceptional circumstances', the Court observes that, although the Commission refers to them, in particular in paragraphs 23 and 28, and in paragraph 36, in which the Decision concludes its examination of the condition under review and considers the project's impact on public infrastructures and on employment, and its impact on European integration, the latter paragraph ends with the following sentence: 'This would not be enough to make an exemption possible unless the conditions of Article [81(3)] were fulfilled, but it is an element which the Commission has taken into account'. The Court considers that it is clear from the latter sentence that the 'exceptional circumstances' thus referred to in the Decision were taken into consideration by the Commission only supererogatorily. In other words, it is sufficiently established that, if those circumstances had not been referred to, the operative part of the

---

[263] If the application of Article 81(3) involves the consideration of socio-political issues, it might have been considered unwise to delegate this task to a multiplicity of bodies, including national courts.

[264] [1999] OJ C132/1, [1999] 5 CMLR 208, para. 56. *See*, for example, Claus-Dieter Ehlermann in *Objectives of Competition Policy* 480 (Ehlermann & Laudati, eds., 1998); Rein Wesseling, 'The Commission White Paper on Modernisation of EC Antitrust Law: Unspoken consequences and incomplete treatment of alternative options' [1999] *ECLR*. 420; G. Monti, 'Article 81 EC and Public Policy' (2002) *CMLRev* 1057.

[265] See also Case T-168/01, *GlaxoSmithKline Services Unlimited* v. *Commission*, 27 Sept. 2006, [2006] 5 CMLR 1623, Cases C-501, 513, 515, 519/06 P (judgment pending), where the CFI discussed evidence of a gain in 'efficiency' under the first head of Article 81(3), paras. 233–307.

[266] Article 81(3) Guidelines, para. 42. The following words incorporated in the draft guidelines were not repeated in the final version of the document: 'It is not, on the other hand, the role of Article 81 and the authorities enforcing this Treaty provision to allow undertakings to restrict competition in pursuit of general interest aims'.

[267] See J. Faull and A. Nikpay, *The EC Law of Competition* (2nd edn., Oxford University Press, 2007), para. 3.406.

> decision adopted would have been exactly the same as that of the contested Decision. It follows that the applicant's argument that, on the contrary, the individual exemption decision granted for the project in question was adopted only on the basis of the 'exceptional circumstances' surrounding the project must be rejected.

The Commission thus seems to take the view that past practice 'has never shown that the competition rules were "set aside" for political considerations ... rather public policy considerations have been used to supplement the economic benefits which the agreement generates'.[268]

A narrow view, that only improvements in economic efficiency can be taken into account under Article 81(3), is certainly the one which best sits with the Commission's view of Article 81's objectives and how Article 81(1) and (3) now interact. It is, however, arguably a somewhat disingenuous interpretation of past judgments and decisional practice. It has been seen that the ECJ has, when construing the Treaty competition provisions, adopted a teleological interpretation[269] so that it is conceivable that, despite its actual wording, the criteria set out in Article 81(3) might be interpreted broadly against the backdrop of the wider Community aims and objectives set out in Articles 2 and 3 of the Treaty.[270] Indeed, pursuit of a sole consumer welfare objective may produce results inconsistent with other Treaty policies and the Treaty specifically provides in some places that the formulation and implementation of *all* Community policies and actions should take account of certain 'policy-linking' clauses, such as environmental protection, employment, culture, health, consumer protection, industrial policy and/or the elimination of regional disparities.[271] In *Metro (No 1)*, the ECJ took the view that the fact that an agreement might lead to stability in the labour market, was a matter which could be taken into account within the first criterion of Article 81(3). The agreement in question constituted 'a stabilizing factor with regard to the provision of employment which, since it improves the general conditions of production, especially when market conditions are unfavourable, comes within the framework of the objective to which reference may be had pursuant to Article [81(3)]'.[272] Further, in *Métropole Télévision S.A.* v. *Commission*[273] the CFI stated that 'the

---

[268] G. Monti, 'Article 81 EC and Public Policy' (2002) *CMLRev* 1057, 1090–1. If the Commission is attempting to go further than this, however, and is seeking to deny even the more limited role of socio-political factors under Article 81(3), then the view is difficult, if not impossible, to square with previous decisional practice and case law. Such a view would require some *ex-post* rationalization of those decisions and judgments, see, e.g., R. Whish, *Competition Law* (5th edn., Butterworths, 2003), 154–5 and G. Monti, 'Article 81 EC and Public Policy' (2002) *CMLRev* 1057, 1091.

[269] See, e.g., Case 6/72, *Europemballage Corp. and Continental Can Co., Inc.* v. Commission [1973] ECR 215 (discussed *infra* Chap. 5); Cases C-68/94 & 30/95, *France* v. *Commission* [1998] ECR I-1375, [1998] 4 CMLR 829 (discussed *infra* Chaps. 11 and 12).

[270] Article 81(3) could therefore be construed to permit authorization of agreements which provide benefits, for example, from a regional, social, environmental, cultural, and/or industrial perspective, see G. Monti, 'Article 81 EC and Public Policy' (2002) *CMLRev* 1057; and see *supra* p. 268 and accompanying text.

[271] See, e.g., EC Treaty, arts. 6, 127(2), 151(4), 152(1), 153(2), 157(3), 159 and 178 (so called policy-linking, policy-integration or flanking clauses) (*supra* Chap. 1) and O. Odudu, *The Boundaries of EC Competition Law: The Scope of Article 81* (Oxford University Press, 2006), 161.

[272] Case 26/76, *Metro-SB-Grossmärkte GmbH* v. *Commission (No. 1)* [1977] ECR 1857, [1978] 2 CMLR 1, para. 43.

[273] Cases T-528, 542, 543 and 546/93, [1996] ECR II 649. See also Case T-193/02, *Laurent Piau* v. *Commission* [2005] ECR II-209, [2005] 5 CMLR 2 (appeal dismissed by Order of the ECJ, Case C-171/05P, [2006] ECR I-37), where the CFI considered that a licence system for players' agents required by FIFA resulted in an a qualitative selection, appropriate for the attainment of the objective of raising professional standards for the occupation of players' agents rather than a quantitative restriction on access to that occupation', para. 103.

Commission is entitled to base itself on considerations connected with the pursuit of the public interest in order to grant exemption under Article [81(3)] of the Treaty'.[274]

This attitude is also reflected in a number of the Commission's own decisions. In *Ford/Volkswagen*,[275] for example, the Commission noted, in exempting the agreement, that the joint venture would lead to the creation of a number of jobs and substantial foreign investment in one of the poorest regions of the Community.[276]

36. In the assessment of this case, the Commission also takes note of the fact that the project constitutes the largest ever single foreign investment in Portugal. It is estimated to lead, *inter alia*, to the creation of about 5 000 jobs and indirectly create up to another 10 000 jobs, as well as attracting other investment in the supply industry. It therefore contributes to the promotion of the harmonious development of the Community and the reduction of regional disparities which is one of the basic aims of the Treaty. It also furthers European market integration by linking Portugal more closely to the Community through one of its important industries. This would not be enough to make an exemption possible unless the conditions of Article [81(3)] were fulfilled, but it is an element which the Commission has taken into account.

Although the Commission emphasized that these broader factors would not have caused the agreement to merit an exemption had the other conditions of Article 81(3) not been fulfilled,[277] these factors do appear to have been relevant to its final decision.[278] Further, in an appeal from this decision the Commission argued that it was possible, when determining whether the agreement contributed to technical and economic progress,[279] to take into account factors such as the maintenance of employment.[280] Arguably, this decision is difficult to justify on pure efficiency grounds and it symbolizes the infiltrations of other policy objectives into EC competition law.[281]

In a series of decisions, the Commission also exempted agreements concluded between competitors which seek to ensure an orderly reduction of capacity between the undertakings which were operating in an industry in crisis (crisis cartels).[282] In *Synthetic Fibres*, for example, the Commission, in authorizing an agreement between competitors to reduce capacity, accepted that the decision to embark on an orderly reduction in output satisfied the first criteria of Article 81(3).[283]

---

[274] Cases T-528, 542, 543 and 546/93, [1996] ECR II 649, para. 118.

[275] [1993] OJ L20/14, [1993] 5 CMLR 617.

[276] The Commission found that the agreement would promote harmonious development, reduce regional disparities, and contribute to the integration of the European market [1993] OJ L20/14, [1993] 5 CMLR 617, paras. 23, 28, and 36; see also the Commission Press Release IP/92/1083 of 23 December 1992.

[277] [1993] OJ L20/14, [1993] 5 CMLR 617, para. 36.

[278] See *supra* n. 276.

[279] See *supra* n. 251 and accompanying text.

[280] Case T-17/93, *Matra Hachette v. Commission* [1994] ECR II-595, para. 96. The CFI considered that as the four criteria were fulfilled apart from the 'exceptional circumstances', there was no defect in the Decision, see *supra* 273.

[281] See G. Amato, *Antitrust and the Bounds of Power* (Hart Publishing, 1997), 58–63, and *infra* Chap. 13.

[282] Further, it is arguable that provisions in the Commission's specialization block exemption, which accept that production rationalization fulfils the Article 81(3) criteria, reflect industrial policy rather than competition thinking: G. Amato, *Antitrust and the Bounds of Power* (Hart Publishing, 1997), 63–4. In the early days competition policy was influenced by industrial policy to a greater extent than it is now. Note that Article 157 (ex Article 130, introduced by the Maastricht Treaty) states that the Community's industrial policy is to be conducted 'in accordance with a system of open and competitive markets'.

[283] [1984] OJ L207/17, [1985] 1 CMLR 787, paras. 30–1.

In a free market economy it ought to be principally a matter for the individual undertaking to judge the point at which overcapacity becomes economically unsustainable and to take the necessary steps to reduce it . . . In the present case, however, market forces by themselves had failed to achieve the capacity reductions necessary to re-establish and maintain in the longer term an effective competitive structure within the common market. The producers concerned therefore agreed to organise for a limited period and collectively, the needed structural adjustment.

The Commission thus recognized that ordinarily individual undertakings should make their own decision about reduction in capacity. However, in this case market forces had not achieved the reductions necessary. The agreement would enable the establishment and maintenance in the long term of effective competitive structures and would improve technical efficiency by enabling the undertakings to specialize. The eventual result would be to raise profitability and restore competitiveness. The 'coordination of plant closures will also make it easier to cushion the social effects of the restructuring by making suitable arrangements for the retraining and redeployment of workers made redundant. It can be concluded then that the agreement contributes to improving production and promoting technical and economic progress'.[284]

Similarly, in *Stichting Baksteen*[285] the Commission, when exempting an agreement for the restructuring of the Dutch brick industry, took account of the fact that the agreement allowed the restructuring to be carried out in acceptable social conditions and in a way which would lead to the redeployment of employees. The Commission held that the social advantages resulting to employees would promote economic progress for the purposes of Article 81(3).[286] In *Exxon/Shell*[287] the Commission held that a reduction in pollution would lead to a technological improvement for the purposes of Article 81(3). Further, in *European Council of Manufacturers of Domestic Appliances (CECED)*[288] it exempted an agreement concluded between 95 per cent of the producers and importers of washing machines operating on the EU market that restricted their freedom to manufacture or import the least energy-efficient washing machines. The agreement was found to restrict competition within the meaning of Article 81(1). The agreement, by restricting the parties' autonomy to produce or import less environmentally friendly machines,[289] had the object of controlling one important product characteristic on which there was competition, thereby restricting competition between the parties.[290] Nonetheless the Commission considered that the agreement met the criteria set out in Article 81(3). It would reduce the potential energy consumption of new machines and consequently lessen pollution, create more technically efficient machines and focus future research and

---

[284] *Ibid*, paras. 37–8.

[285] [1994] OJ L131/15, [1995] 4 CMLR 646.

[286] *Ibid.*, paras. 27–8.

[287] [1994] OJ L144/20.

[288] [2000] OJ L187/47, [2000] 5 CMLR 635. In J. Faull and A. Nikpay. *The EC Law of Competition* (2nd edn., Oxford University Press, 2007), para, 3.408 it is stated that the decision does not appear to reflect current Commission thinking as laid down in the Guidelines. See also *EACEM* [1998] OJ C12/2 (the Commission issued an Article 19(3) Notice setting out its intention to take a similar approach to environmental agreements for water heaters and dishwashers), *Eco-Emballages* [2001] OJ L233/37 (negative clearance) and *DSD* [2001] OJ L319/1, [2002] 4 CMLR 405 (exemption) and discussion of these latter cases *infra* Chap. 13.

[289] It did not directly restrict output as the agreement was only to cease to produce the least energy efficient machines. Limited effects on output might arise only indirectly, through reduced demand.

[290] It would result in a reduction of choice for consumers since fewer cheaper washing machines would be on the market.

development on furthering energy efficiency.[291] Upon approval by the Commission the Competition Commissioner, Mario Monti declared:

When I took office as Commissioner responsible for Competition, I stressed before the European Parliament that environmental concerns are in no way contradictory with competition policy. This decision clearly illustrates this principle, enshrined in the Treaty, provided that *restrictions of competition are proportionate and necessary to achieving the environmental objectives aimed at*, to the benefit of current and future generations [emphasis added].[292]

It also seems that the production of a product which increases safety for a consumer may constitute a technical improvement.[293]

(ii) Criterion 2: Allowing Consumers a Fair Share of the Resulting Benefit

Although the second criterion of Article 81(3) requires that it must be established that the agreement allows consumers a fair share of the benefit, the Article 81(3) Guidelines indicate that this condition should be considered only after it has been determined that the restrictions incorporated in the agreement are indispensable (see criterion 3 below). This is because the requirement that consumers receive a fair share of the benefits, 'implies a balancing of pro-competitive and anti-competitive effects. This balancing exercise should not include restrictions that in any event are unnecessary to achieve the efficiencies'.[294]

In early decisions (and especially where the Commission adopted a more formalistic approach under Article 81(1)), the Commission was often willing to assume that this criterion would be satisfied where the first and fourth criteria were satisfied (a benefit had been shown and where competition had not been eliminated, so that competition from competing products meant that the parties would not be interested in increasing prices or output). Under the 'modernized' approach, however, many of these agreements (previously dealt with under Article 81(3)) should, in theory at least, now fall outside Article 81(1) on the grounds that the agreement does not restrict competition at all.[295] The Article 81(3) Guidelines thus now require that the parties establish that the agreement allows consumers a fair share of the benefit, by showing that there is a pass-on of the cost and quality efficiencies to final, or intermediate, consumers.[296] This accords with the Commission's view that the objective of Article 81 is consumer not total welfare.[297]

---

[291] The Commission considered that the other elements of Article 81(3) were also satisfied, see *infra* Chap. 11.

[292] IP/00/148. This decision thus reflects the sentiment expressed in the Commission's *XXVth Report on Competition Policy* (1995) that 'in its scrutiny of individual cases pursuant to Article [81(3)]... it weighs up the restrictions on competition that result from the agreement and the environmental objectives to be attained', SEC(1997)628. Indeed, the Treaty of Amsterdam increased the European's Union commitment to the environment, EC Treaty, Art. 6.

[293] *BMW Belgium NV and Belgian BMW Dealers* [1978] OJ L46/33, [1978] 2 CMLR 126. See also *DSD* [2001] OJ L319/1, [2002] 4 CMLR 405.

[294] J. Faull and A. Nikpay *The EC Law of Competition* (2nd edn., Oxford University Press, 2007), para. 3.436.

[295] See the discussion *supra* 236 ff.

[296] Article 81(3) Guidelines, paras. 83–104.

[297] See *supra* Chap. 1.

a. Consumer

Consumer is interpreted broadly to include not only final consumers but also intermediate consumers, including wholesalers and retailers, that purchase products in the course of their trade or business.[298] Consumers can be undertakings or private individuals. It is clear that not all individual consumers need to derive a benefit from the agreement for Article 81(3) to apply. Rather it is the overall effect on consumers in the relevant markets that must be favourable. '[I]t is the beneficial nature of the effect on all consumers in the relevant markets that must be taken into consideration, not the effect on each member of that category of consumers'.[299]

b. Fair share

The Commission describes the concept of fair share in its Article 81(3) Guidelines.

85. The concept of 'fair share' implies that the pass-on of benefits must at least compensate consumers for any actual or likely negative impact caused to them by the restriction of competition found under Article 81(1). In line with the overall objective of Article 81 to prevent anti-competitive agreements, the net effect of the agreement must at least be neutral from the point of view of those consumers directly or likely affected by the agreement. If such consumers are worse off following the agreement, the second condition of Article 81(3) is not fulfilled. The positive effects of an agreement must be balanced against and compensate for its negative effects on consumers. When that is the case consumers are not harmed by the agreement. Moreover, society as a whole benefits because the efficiencies lead either to fewer resources being used to produce the output consumed or to the production of more valuable products and thus to a more efficient allocation of resources.

The Guidelines also explain that it is *not* necessary that consumers receive a share of each and every efficiency gain identified under the first condition, nor that the pass on must occur immediately or within a specified period of time.[300] Further, that the pass-on will have to be greater the greater the restriction of competition.[301]

Where consumers are forced to pay a higher price without attaining other benefits from the agreement, this criterion will not be satisfied.[302] In the context of vertical agreements, the Commission appears to accept that restraints on intra-brand competition may be excepted where the agreement leads to improvements in distribution and the existence of inter-brand competition ensures that the products will be offered to consumers on favourable terms.[303]

---

[298] *Kabel und Metallwerke Neumeyer AG and Etablissements Luchaire SA Agreement* [1975] OJ L222/34, [1975] CMLR D40.

[299] Case C-238/05 *Asnef-Equifax v. Asociaciónde Usuarios de Servicios Bancarios (Ausbanc)* [2006] ECR I-11125, [2007] 4 CMLR 6, para. 70.

[300] Commission Guidelines on the application of Article 81(3) of the Treaty [2004] OJ C101/97, paras. 86–9.

[301] *Ibid.*, paras. 90–1.

[302] See, e.g., *VBBB & VBVB* [1982] OJ L54/36, [1982] 2 CMLR 344, *aff'd* in Cases 43, 63/82, *VBVB & VBBB v. Commission* [1984] ECR 19, [1985] 1 CMLR 27, where the Commission held that the consumers would not benefit from the parties' agreement to fix the retail prices of books. On the contrary, consumers would be forced to pay a higher price and would be deprived of the opportunity to pay lower prices. See also, e.g., Case T-29/92, *SPO and others v. Commission* [1992] ECR II-289, para. 294.

[303] See, e.g., Reg. 2790/1999, [1999] OJ L 336/21, [2000] 4 CMLR 398 which block exempts vertical agreements (not containing hardcore restraints) where the supplier's market share does not exceed 30% of the relevant market. See also, e.g., *Goodyear Italiana-Euram* [1975] OJ L38/10, where the Commission seemed to consider that consumers would receive a fair share of the benefit as the parties faced intense competition from other competitors.

Some agreements have been refused an exemption on the ground that consumers will not receive a fair share of the benefit. For example, in *VBBB and VBVB*[304] the Commission held that the consumers would not benefit from the parties' agreement to fix the retail prices of books. On the contrary, consumers would be forced to pay a higher price and would be deprived of the opportunity to pay lower prices. The Commission also refused an exemption to an agreement that is clearly designed to restrict competition and force consumers to pay a higher price for products in the absence of other compensating benefits. In *SPO and others v. Commission*,[305] for example, the CFI heard an appeal against the Commission's refusal of an exemption to a Dutch building association. The purpose of the agreement in question was to protect the members from ruinous competition. The Court upheld the Commission's decision stating that 'by taking action to counteract what they regard as ruinous competition, the applicants necessarily restrict competition and therefore deprive consumers of its benefits'.[306] In contrast, however, to the decision it took in *SPO* the Commission in *Synthetic Fibres* concluded that consumers would benefit from an agreement between competitors on a market to reduce capacity. Although prices might rise initially, there was sufficient competition on the market and considerable countervailing purchasing power to limit these increases. Further, the agreement would result in a healthier more competitive industry in the long run.[307]

(iii) Criterion 3: Indispensable Restrictions

An agreement which satisfies the first two positive criteria set out in Article 81(3) must only contain restrictions which are indispensable to the achievement of the benefits shown to result from the agreement. The Commission states that this condition, an application of the Community principle of proportionality,[308] implies a two-fold test.

Commission's Guidelines on the Application of Article 81(3) [2004] OJ C101/97

73. According to the third condition of Article 81(3) the restrictive agreement must not impose restrictions, which are not indispensable to the attainment of the efficiencies created by the agreement in question. This condition implies a two-fold test. First, the restrictive agreement as such must be reasonably necessary in order to achieve the efficiencies.[309] Secondly, the individual restrictions of competition that flow from the agreement must also be reasonably necessary for the attainment of the efficiencies.

---

[304] [1982] OJ L54/36, [1982] 2 CMLR 344, *aff'd.* in Cases 43 & 63/82, *VBVB and VBBB v. Commission* [1984] ECR 19, [1985] 1 CMLR 27.

[305] Case T-29/92, [1992] ECR II-289.

[306] *Ibid.*, para. 294.

[307] [1984] OJ L207/17, [1985] 1 CMLR 787, paras. 39–41.

[308] The principle of proportionality essentially requires that an action (whether of the Community or of a state or, in this case, parties to an agreement) should not go beyond what is necessary to achieve the objectives of the Treaty, see discussion of principle in, e.g., P. Craig and G. De Burca, *EU Law Text, Cases and Materials* (3rd edn., Oxford University Press, 2003) Chap. 9 .

[309] Or, presumably, other non-economic benefits, in so far as they are relevant (see discussion *supra* 273–7).

> 74. In the context of the third condition of Article 81(3) the decisive factor is whether or not the restrictive agreement and individual restrictions make it possible to perform the activity in question more efficiently than would have been the case in the absence of the agreement or the restriction concerned. The question is not whether in the absence of the restriction the agreement would not have been concluded, but whether more efficiencies are produced with the agreement or restriction than in the absence of the agreement.[310]

Restrictions will not therefore be indispensable if the efficiencies specific to the agreement can be achieved by other practicable and less restrictive means, or if individual restrictions are not reasonably necessary to produce the efficiencies. Conversely, a restriction will be indispensable 'if its absence would eliminate or significantly reduce the efficiencies that follow from the agreement or make it significantly less likely that they will materialise'.[311] The assessment of indispensability must be made within the actual context in which the agreement operates.[312] In *P&O Stena Line*[313] the Commission granted an exemption to a joint venture which combined the parties' services on a particular ferry route. It accepted the argument that less restrictive alternatives, such as joint scheduling, or pooling, would not enable the parties to achieve the benefits, such as cost savings and increased frequency in service, of their joint venture. The Commission expended much effort in its exemption decisions in ensuring that agreements were not more restrictive than they needed to be to achieve their accepted benefits. Further, it takes the view that restrictions may be indispensable only for a period of time. It has been seen that the Commission seeks to distinguish this inquiry from that purportedly made under the doctrine of ancillary restraints by asking whether the restrictive agreement and restrictions make it possible to perform the activity in question more efficiently[314] i.e. 'if its absence would eliminate or significantly reduce the efficiencies that follow from the agreement or make it significantly less likely that they will materialize.'[315] Restrictions will not be indispensable if the efficiencies specific to the agreement can be achieved by other practicable and less restrictive means, or if individual restrictions are not reasonably necessary to produce the efficiencies e.g. the adoption of less restrictive clauses. It may therefore be rare for provisions which are 'restrictive by object' or for hard-core restraints prohibited in the block exemptions to be held indispensable.

> ## J. Faull and A. Nikpay (eds.), *The EC Law of Competition* (2nd edn., Oxford University Press, 2007)
>
> 3.441 Once it is found that the agreement in question is necessary in order to produce the efficiencies the indispensability of each restriction of competition flowing from the agreement must be assessed. A restriction is indispensable if its absence would eliminate or significantly

---

[310] See Commission Guidelines on the application of Article 81(3) of the Treaty [2004] OJ C101/97, para. 18.

[311] Contrast the ancillary restraints doctrine discussed *supra* 248.

[312] Guidelines on the application of Article 81(3) of the Treaty [2004] OJ C101/97, para. 80.

[313] [1999] OJ L163/61, [2000] 5 CMLR 646.

[314] Not whether the restraint is necessary to the implementation of the agreement, Article 81(3) Guidelines, para. 74.

[315] Article 81(3) Guidelines, para. 79. In *P&O Stena Line* [1999] OJ L163/61, [2000] 5 CMLR 646, the Commission granted an exemption to a joint venture which combined the parties' services on a particular ferry route. It accepted the argument that less restrictive alternatives, such as joint scheduling, or pooling,

> reduce the efficiencies achieved by the agreement or make it significantly less likely that they will materialise. The assessment of alternative solutions must take into account the actual and potential improvement in competition by the elimination of a particular restriction or the application of a less restrictive alternative. The third condition of Article 81(3) thus incorporates a sliding scale. The more restrictive the restraint, the stricter the test under the third condition. Restrictions that are black-listed in block exemption regulations or identified as hardcore restrictions in Commission guidelines and notices are unlikely to be considered indispensable.

In its Guidelines on the application of Article 81(3) the Commission states that '[r]estrictions that are black listed in block exemption regulations or qualified as hardcore restrictions in Commission guidelines and notices are only likely to be considered indispensable in exceptional circumstances'.[316] The black lists of the block exemptions thus provide useful guidance on the type of provisions that the Commission considers are dispensable and not essential to achieving the benefits produced by a particular type of agreement. For example, in the context of vertical agreements the Commission will not generally accept that a restriction on the distributor's freedom to determine prices is indispensable to the successful distribution system;[317] nor that the conferment of absolute territorial protection on a distributor is indispensable to the operation of, for example, an exclusive distribution agreement. However, it ordinarily permits a producer to protect an exclusive distributor within a territory from active selling by other distributors.[318]

It must be remembered, however, that *every* agreement is potentially capable of exemption. In later chapters of this book, examples will be given of some exceptional cases where it has been recognized that hardcore restraints may meet the Article 81(3) criteria.[319]

(iv) Criterion 4: The Agreement must not Afford the Parties the Possibility of Eliminating Competition

The last requirement is that the agreement as a whole must not lead to the elimination of competition. This criterion appears to reflect the view that short-term efficiency gains must not be outweighed by longer-term losses stemming from the elimination of competition.

The Commission states in the Article 81(3) Guidelines that '[u]ltimately the protection of rivalry and the competitive process is given priority over potentially pro-competitive efficiency gains which could result from restrictive agreements'.[320] Further, it sets out its view that rivalry between undertakings on the market should be preserved since rivalry is the essential driver of economic efficiency, including dynamic efficiency. 'When competition is eliminated the competitive process is brought to an end and short-term efficiency gains are outweighed by

---

would not enable the parties to achieve the benefits, such as cost savings and increased frequency in service, of their joint venture.

[316] *Ibid.*, para. 69. See also para. 46, these types of restraints are unlikely to satisfy the first two conditions of Article 81(3) since they neither create objective economic benefits nor benefit consumers.

[317] Reg. 2790/1999 [1999] OJ L336/21, [2000] 4 CMLR 398, Art. 4(a).

[318] See Reg. 2790/1999 [1999] OJ L336/21, [2000] 4 CMLR 398, Arts. 4(b)–(d).

[319] See, for example, Chap. 9, 761–4 and Chap. 11, 895–9. See also *supra* n. 244 and accompanying text.

[320] Commission Guidelines on the application of Article 81(3) of the Treaty [2004] OJ C101/97, para. 105. See *supra* Chap. 1, 46.

longer-term losses stemming *inter alia* from expenditures incurred by the incumbent to maintain its position (rent seeking), misallocation of resources, reduced innovation and higher prices'.[321]

This criterion thus requires an analysis of the competitive restraints imposed on the parties, the degree of competition existing prior to the agreement and the impact of the agreement on competition. Sources of competition, through actual and potential competitors, must be analysed along with the impact of the agreement on these competitive constraints.

The Commission considers, in its assessment, the market shares of the parties,[322] the incentives for actual competitors to compete, the impact of the agreement on the various parameters of competition, the actual market conduct of the parties (where the agreement has been implemented), past competitive interaction, the closeness of competition previously existing between the competitors, and the scope of potential competition.

When assessing barriers to entry the Commission stresses that it takes into account the real possibility for new entry into the market taking account, *inter alia*, of:[323]

(i) The regulatory framework with a view to determining its impact on new entry;

(ii) The cost of entry including sunk costs. Sunk costs are those that cannot be recovered if the entrant subsequently exits the market. The higher the sunk costs the higher the commercial risk for potential entrants.

(iii) The minimum efficient scale within the industry, i.e., the rate of output where average costs are minimised. If the minimum efficient scale is large compared to the size of the market, efficient entry is likely to be more costly and risky.

(iv) The competitive strengths of potential entrants. Effective entry is particularly likely where potential entrants have access to at least as cost efficient technologies as the incumbents or other competitive advantages that allow them to compete effectively. When potential entrants are on the same or an inferior technological trajectory compared to the incumbents and possess no other significant competitive advantage entry is more risky and less effective.

(v) The position of buyers and their ability to bring onto the market new sources of competition. It is irrelevant that certain strong buyers may be able to extract more favourable conditions from the parties to the agreement than their weaker competitors. The presence of strong buyers can only serve to counter a *prima facie* finding of elimination of competition if it is likely that the buyers in question will pave the way for effective new entry.

(vi) The likely response of incumbents to attempted new entry. Incumbents may for example through past conduct have acquired a reputation of aggressive behaviour, having an impact on future entry.

(vii) The economic outlook for the industry may be an indicator of its longer-term attractiveness. Industries that are stagnating or in decline are less attractive candidates for entry than industries characterized by growth.

(viii) Past entry on a significant scale or the absence thereof.

---

[321] Commission Guidelines on the application of Article 81(3) of the Treaty [2004] OJ C101/97, para. 105. See *supra* Chap. 1, 46.

[322] See *infra* n. 326. A definition of the relevant market (product and geographic) will therefore be an essential prerequisite to a determination under this fourth criterion. See *supra* Chap. 1. A decision of the Commission is likely to be annulled if the market has not been defined adequately: see, e.g., Cases 19 and 20/74, *Kali und Salz AG v. Commission* [1975] ECR 499, [1975] 2 CMLR 154.

[323] Guidelines on the application of Article 81(3) of the Treaty [2004] OJ C101/97, para. 115.

In certain decisions relating to crisis cartels the Commission has, occasionally, exempted agreements concluded between undertakings with a large share of the relevant market.[324] At paragraph 116 of the guidelines the Commission sets out some hypothetical examples of how this fourth condition is applied.

116. The above principles can be illustrated by the following hypothetical examples, which are not intended to establish thresholds:

Firm A is brewer, holding 70 per cent of the relevant market, comprising the sale of beer through cafés and other on-trade premises. Over the past 5 years A has increased its market share from 60 per cent. There are four other competitors in the market, B, C, D and E with market shares of 10 per cent, 10 per cent, 5 per cent and 5 per cent. No new entry has occurred in the recent past and price changes implemented by A have generally been followed by competitors. A concludes agreements with 20 per cent of the on-trade premises representing 40 per cent of sales volumes whereby the contracting parties undertake to purchase beer only from A for a period of 5 years. The agreements raise the costs and reduce the revenues of rivals, which are foreclosed from the most attractive outlets. Given the market position of A, which has been strengthened in recent years, the absence of new entry and the already weak position of competitors it is likely that competition in the market is eliminated within the meaning of Article 81(3).

Shipping firms A, B, C, and D, holding collectively more than 70 per cent of the relevant market, conclude an agreement whereby they agree to coordinate their schedules and their tariffs. Following the implementation of the agreement prices rise between 30 per cent and 100 per cent. There are four other suppliers, the largest holding about 14 per cent of the relevant market. There has been no new entry in recent years and the parties to the agreement did not lose significant market share following the price increases. The existing competitors brought no significant new capacity to the market and no new entry occurred. In light of the market position and the absence of competitive response to their joint conduct it can reasonably be concluded that the parties to the agreement are not subject to real competitive pressures and that the agreement affords them the possibility of eliminating competition within the meaning of Article 81(3).

A is a producer of electric appliances for professional users with a market share of 65 per cent of a relevant national market. B is a competing manufacturer with 5 per cent market share which has developed a new type of motor that is more powerful while consuming less electricity. A and B conclude an agreement whereby they establish a production joint venture for the production of the new motor. B undertakes to grant an exclusive licence to the joint venture. The joint venture combines the new technology of B with the efficient manufacturing and quality control process of A. There is one other main competitor with 15 per cent of the market. Another competitor with 5 per cent market share has recently been acquired by C, a major international producer of competing electric appliances, which itself owns efficient technologies. C has thus far not been active on the market mainly due to the fact that local presence and servicing is desired by customers. Through the acquisition C gains access to the service organisation required to penetrate the market. The entry of C is likely to ensure that competition is not being eliminated.

The guidelines also explore the relationship between this requirement (and Article 81(3) more generally) with Article 82.[325] The following principles are set out:

(i)   The application of Article 81(3) does not prevent the application of Article 82;

---

[324] See, e.g., *Synthetic Fibres* [1984] OJ L207/17, [1985] 1 CMLR 787 and *Bayer/BP Chemicals* [1988] OJ L150/35, [1989] 4 CMLR 24.

[325] Guidelines on the application of Article 81(3) of the Treaty [2004] OJ C101/97, para. 106.

(ii) Conduct which is abusive should not be permitted under Article 81(3).[326] This indicates that Article 81(3) could be used to authorize an agreement concluded by a dominant undertaking which does not constitute an abuse of a dominant position;[327]

(iii) Not all agreements infringing Article 81 constitute an abuse of a dominant position.

C. APPLICATION IN INDIVIDUAL CASES

It is, of course, no longer possible to get an individual exemption decision from the Commission. Article 81(3) can, however, be applied in individual cases in a variety of different ways. For example, the European Commission has to consider the application of Article 81(3) in infringement proceedings where it is raised by persons seeking to rely on it. It may also have to apply Article 81(3) when adopting commitment[328] or non-infringements decisions[329] or when providing 'informal guidance'.[330] Further, national competition authorities (NCAs) and national courts may, when considering the compatibility of an agreement with Article 81, apply that provision in its entirety.

D. BLOCK EXEMPTIONS

(i) General

A number of Community regulations grant exemption to categories of agreements. A majority of these regulations are Commission regulations adopted following authorization from the Council. Two block exemptions have, however, been adopted directly by the Council.

(ii) Current Block Exemptions

a. Council Regulations

The Council adopted two Regulations granting exemption to (1) agreements in road and inland waterway sectors and (2) liner conferences in the maritime transport sector. These were set out in Council Regulations 1017/68 and 4056/88 respectively.[331] The latter regulation is, however, to be repealed with effect from October 2008.[332]

---

[326] *Ibid.* The Guidelines state in footnote 92 that provisions in the Guidelines on vertical restraints and the Guidelines on horizontal cooperation agreements stating that, in principle, restrictive agreements concluded by dominant undertakings cannot be authorized under Article 81(3) should be understood in this way. In *Van den Bergh Foods* [1998] OJ L264/1, [1998] 5 CMLR 475, upheld on appeal Case T-65/98, *Van den Bergh Foods* v. *Commission* [2003] ECR II-4653, [2004] 4 CMLR 1, *aff'd* Case C-552/03 P, *Unilever Bestfoods* v. *Commission* [2006] OJ C294/19, the Commission declined to grant an exemption to conduct found to contravene Article 82. HB's dominant position was taken into account and influenced the Commission's decision that the agreement would substantially eliminate competition within the meaning of Article 81(3), see paras. 242–246.

[327] *Ibid.*

[328] Reg. 1/2003 [2003] OJ L1/1, Art. 9, see Chap. 14.

[329] *Ibid.*, Art. 10, see Chap. 14.

[330] Commission notice on informal guidance relating to novel questions concerning Articles 81 and 82 of the EC Treaty that arise in individual cases (guidance letters) [2004] OJ C101/78, see Chap. 14.

[331] Reg. 1017/68 [1968] OJ Spec. Ed. 302; Reg. 4056/86 [1986] OJ L378/14.

[332] See IP.06/1249, Regulation 1419/2006 [2006] OJ L269/1, MEMO/06/344 and generally, http://ec.europa.eu/comm/competition/antitrust/legislation/maritime/. The Commission is going to adopt guidelines on the type of information that undertakings can legitimately exchange in the maritime transport market.

b. Commission Regulations

Over the years the Commission has adopted a number of block exemptions which have applied to vertical, horizontal, technology transfer, and other particular agreements. Table 4.1 sets out the block exemptions currently in force.

Table 4.1 Block Exemptions adopted by the Commission currently in force

Regulation	Categories of Agreements Covered	Enabling legislation
Regulation 2790/1999[333]	Vertical agreements. Replacing: Exclusive distribution, Exclusive purchasing and Franchising regulations	Council Regulation 19/65[334] (amended by Council Regulation 1215/99)[335]
Regulation 1400/2002[336]	Vertical agreements and concerted practices in the motor vehicle sector	Council Regulation 19/65[337] (amended by Council Regulation 1215/99)[338]
Regulation 772/2004[339]	Technology transfer agreements	Council Regulation 19/65[340] (amended by Council Regulation 1215/99)[341]
Regulation 2658/2000[342]	Specialization agreements	Council Regulation 2821/75[343]
Regulation 2659/2000[344]	Research and development agreements	Council Regulation 2821/75[345]
Regulation 1459/2006[346] (exemptions do not apply after 31 october 2007)	Passenger transit consultations and slot allocations at airports, etc.	Council Regulation 3976/87[347]

[333] [1999] OJ L336/21, [2000] 4 CMLR 398.

[334] [1965–1966] OJ Spec. Ed., 35.

[335] [1999] OJ L148/1.

[336] [2002] OJ L203/30, [2002] 5 CMLR 777.

[337] [1965–1966] OJ Spec. Ed., 35.

[338] [1999] OJ L148/1.

[339] [2004] OJ L123/18.

[340] [1965–1966] OJ Spec. Ed., 35.

[341] [1999] OJ L148/1.

[342] [2000] OJ L304/3, [2001] 4 CMLR 800.

[343] [1971] OJ Spec. Ed. 1032.

[344] [2000] OJ L304/7, [2001] 4 CMLR 808.

[345] [1971] OJ Spec. Ed. 1032.

[346] [2006] OJ L272/3. This block exemption replaced an earlier Regulation, 1617/93 as amended by Regulation 1523/96 following consultation. The new block exemption has been adopted only for a short transitional period to allow undertakings sufficient time to adjust to self assessment.

[347] [1987] OJ L374/9. This regulation has been amended by Reg. 411/2004 [2004] OJ L68/1.

Table 4.1 (*Contd*)

Regulation	Categories of Agreements Covered	Enabling legislation
Regulation 3652/93[348]	Agreements relating to computerised reservation systems	Council Regulation 3976/87[349]
Regulation 358/2003[350]	Agreements in the insurance sector	Council Regulation 1534/91[351]
Regulation 823/2000[352]	Liner shipping consortia	Council Regulation 479/92[353]

A number of block exemptions which applied to exclusive distribution,[354] exclusive purchasing,[355] and franchising agreements[356] respectively were replaced on 1 June 2000 by a single block exemption applying more generally to vertical agreements, Regulation 2790/1999.[357] This block exemption did not, however, replace the block exemptions which then applied to motor car vehicle distribution agreements and to technology transfer agreements respectively.[358] Both of these block exemptions were subsequently reviewed. Regulation 1400/2002 now applies to motor car vehicle distribution agreements and Regulation 772/2004 applies to technology transfer agreements.

In 2000 two block exemptions applying to horizontal specialization and research and development agreements were replaced, by Regulation 2658/2000, which applies to specialisation agreements, and Regulation 2659/2000, which applies to research and development agreements.

The Commission has also adopted regulations which apply in the air transport and insurance sectors[359] and to liner shipping consortia.[360] It also has power to adopt block exemptions in the sphere of air transport between the EU and third countries.[361]

---

[348] [1993] OJ L333/37.

[349] [1987] OJ L374/9.

[350] [2003] OJ L53/8, [2003] 4 CMLR 734. This Regulation has been amended to provide an exception for the new EU countries. It provides that the 'prohibition in Article 81(1) of the Treaty shall not apply to agreements which were in existence at the date of accession of the Czech Rebublic, Estonia, Cyprus, Latvia, Lithuania, Hungary, Malta, Poland, Slovenia, and Slovakia, and which, by reason of accession, fall within the scope of Article 81(1) if, within six months from the date of accession, they are so amended that they comply with the conditions laid down in this Regulation.'

[351] [1991] OJ L143/1.

[352] [2000] OJ L100/24, [2000] 5 CMLR 92. This block exemption has been renewed until 25th April 2010, IP/05/477, see Regulation 611/2005 [2005] OJ L101/10.

[353] [1992] OJ L55/3.

[354] Reg. 1983/83 [1983] OJ L173/1.

[355] Reg. 1984/83 [1983] OJ L173/5.

[356] Reg. 4087/88 [1988] OJ L359/46.

[357] Reg. 2790/1999 [1999] OJ L336/21, [2000] 4 CMLR 398.

[358] Reg. 1475/95 [1995] OJ L145/25 and Reg. 240/96 [1996] OJ L31/2.

[359] In a hearing into the preliminary results of the inquiry into business insurance, the Competition Commissioner expressed doubt over whether there is a continued need for this insurance block exemption.

[360] The block exemption for liner shipping consortia has been extended until 25 April 2010, see *supra* n. 352.

[361] Council Reg. 411/2004 [2004] OJ L68/1, see Chap. 14.

c. The Format of a Block Exemption

Block exemptions typically commence with recitals explaining why the type of agreement covered by the block exemption merits exemption. These recitals may be relevant to the interpretation of the main body of the Regulation.

Until the adoption of Regulation 2790/1999[362] the Regulations tended to adopt the following format: a specification of the category of agreements covered, a list of restrictions which it is permissible for the agreement to contain ('white list'), and a list of prohibited restrictions ('black list'). The Regulation might then have included a list of clauses which, although probably not restrictive of competition at all, are specifically authorized for the sake of clarity. The new block exemptions, adopted since 1999, have sought to move away from this format, in an attempt to prevent the severe straitjacketing and limitations on the parties' autonomy which resulted from the previous formula. Reflecting the more economic approach, most now provide a rule of thumb that agreements concluded by undertakings which meet specified market share thresholds, satisfy specified conditions and which do not contain hardcore restraints are unlikely to raise competition problems (by listing only restrictions which may *not* be included within the agreement they allow the parties the freedom to determine what other provisions the agreement should include).[363]

The regulations also contain a number of miscellaneous provisions dealing with, for example, commencement and expiry dates of the regulation, withdrawal of the block exemption, and what entities are considered to be 'connected' to the agreements signatories.

(iii) Block Exemptions are Directly Applicable

Agreements falling within the ambit of one of the block exemptions are automatically exempt from the Article 81(1) prohibition and the national courts are, and always have been, free to apply the terms of the block exemption should the validity of the agreement be raised before such a court. Article 249 (ex Article 189) of the Treaty specifically provides that regulations are directly applicable.

If an agreement does not fall precisely within the scope of a block exemption the national court may not extend it to cover the agreement. The general rule is that if the conditions of the block exemption are not met the regulation ceases to apply in its entirety. However, in the block exemption applying to vertical and technology transfer agreements, for example, the Regulations distinguish between provisions which, if inserted, mean that the block exemption does not apply and provisions which are not covered by the block exemption but which do not prevent the remaining provisions of the agreement benefiting from the Regulation.

Where the conditions of a block exemption are not met, the national court will, of course, be bound to determine whether or not the agreement infringes Article 81(1) and, where it does, whether it individually meets the Article 81(3) criteria. An agreement which contains clauses

---

[362] [1999] OJ L336/21. See *infra* Chap. 9.

[363] Above those shares, however, there is a concern that the restraints may pose competition problems on account of the market power of the undertakings involved. An individual assessment is required. An agreement which contains clauses specifically prohibited by a regulation is, however, unlikely to satisfy the Article 81(3) criteria, see Case C-234/89, *Delimitis v. Henninger Bräu* [1991] ECR I-935, [1992] 5 CMLR 210, paras. 38–42 and see *supra* 281.

specifically prohibited by a regulation is, however, unlikely to satisfy Article 81(3).[364] As already indicated the 'black list' or hard-core restraints indicate the types of clauses which are unlikely to provide Article 81(3) benefits and which are unlikely to be considered to be indispensable to the successful operation of the agreement.

(iv) Market Share Thresholds

Most block exemptions now contain market share thresholds.[365] For example, Regulation 2790/1999, relating to vertical agreements, applies only where the relevant undertakings' market share is below 30 per cent, Regulation 772/2004, the technology transfer block exemption, applies only where the parties market shares do not exceed 20 or 30 per cent of the market (depending upon whether the parties are competitors or non-competitors), Regulation 2659/2000, the R&D block exemption, applies to agreements between competitors whose market shares do not exceed 25 per cent and Regulation 2658/2000 on specialization agreements applies provided the parties do not exceed a market share threshold of 20 per cent.

(v) Opposition Procedure

Some of the old block exemptions, which have now been replaced, contained an opposition procedure.[366] Essentially, this procedure enabled undertakings whose agreements fell outside the terms of the block exemption to notify the agreement and to expect exemption from the Commission unless the Commission opposed it within a specified period of time. Use of the opposition procedure was never popular and as there is no longer an individual exemption procedure, the new block exemptions do not contain such a procedure.

(vi) Withdrawal of Block Exemptions

Regulation 1/2003 makes provision for withdrawal of all block exemptions both by the Commission and by the competent authorities of the Member States.[367] Previously, withdrawal used to be specifically provided for in each individual block exemption.

Regulation 1/2003 now provides that the Commission may withdraw the benefit of any *Commission* block exemption when 'it finds that in any particular case an agreement, decision or concerted practice to which the exemption Regulation applies has certain effects which are incompatible with Article 81(3) of the Treaty'.[368] Withdrawal was threatened on several

---

[364] See Case C-234/89, *Delimitis v. Henninger Bräu* [1991] ECR I-935, [1992] 5 CMLR 210, paras. 38–42 and *supra* 241–3.

[365] Some of the older block exemptions which have now been replaced contained provisions which favoured agreements concluded between undertakings with combined turnovers which were below a specified threshold, e.g., Reg. 1983/83 [1983] OJ L173/1 (which expired on 31 May 2000) permitted the conclusion of a non-reciprocal distribution agreement between competitors where one of the undertakings involved had a market share below ECU 100 million. See also Reg. 2790/1999 [1999] OJ L336/21, [2000] 4 CMLR 398, Art. 2(4)(a).

[366] See Reg. 417/85, Art. 4; Reg. 418/85, Art. 7; Reg. 4087/88, Art. 6; and Reg. 240/96, Art. 4.

[367] Reg. 2790/99 [1999] OJ L336/21, [2000] 4 CMLR 398 on vertical restraints first provided that the benefit of block exemptions could be withdrawn not only by the Commission but also by a competent authority of a Member State, Reg. 2790/1999 [1999] OJ L336/21, [2000] 4 CMLR 398, Art. 7. This provision could be enacted only after Reg. 19/65 [1965–66] OJ Spec. Ed. 35, Art. 7 was amended to allow this by Reg. 1215/99 [1999] OJ L148/1.

[368] Reg. 1/2003 [2003] OJ L1/1, Art. 29(1).

occasions under some of the old Regulations[369] and actually occurred in *Langnese-Iglo*.[370] The ECJ made clear, however, that the benefit of the block exemption (in that case Regulation 1984/83 applying to exclusive purchasing agreements) could not be withheld in advance from *future* agreements.[371] The Verticals block exemption, however, specifically provides for the Commission to withdraw the benefit of the block exemption to specified categories of agreements (rather than individual agreements) by regulation.[372]

Regulation 1/2003 also provides NCAs with power to withdraw the benefit of any Commission block exemption where the agreement, to which the regulation applies has 'effects which are incompatible with Article 81(1) of the Treaty in the territory of a Member State, or in a part thereof, which has all the characteristics of a distinct geographic market'.[373]

(vii) Safe Harbours

The block exemptions are designed to provide legal certainty for undertakings. Undertakings know that agreements satisfying their conditions are valid and compatible with Article 81. Clearly, the introduction of market share thresholds somewhat detracts from this objective,[374] although their incorporation goes hand in hand with the more economic approach adopted by the Commission to Article 81. Further, the relatively low market share thresholds set out for those wishing to benefit from the safe harbour do not fit neatly within the analytical framework constructed by the Commission in its Article 81(3) guidelines. The block exemptions were initially adopted as an essential response to the broad interpretation given to Article 81(1). Exemption under Article 81(3) was vital to the validity of many agreements. Although it is understood that the Commission now intends the block exemptions to operate as safe harbours and considers that agreements which do not satisfy these requirements do not necessarily infringe Article 81(1),[375] it is arguable that agreements satisfying their conditions will be most unlikely to affect actual or potential competition to such an extent that a negative effect on prices, output, innovation or the variety or quality of goods and services can be expected on the market (and so arguably should not infringe Article 81(1)). The existence of the block exemptions, although providing welcome legal certainty, therefore concentrates attention on Article 81(3) and may confuse the question of what analysis is required under Article 81(1).

E. UNILATERAL ACTION AND ARTICLE 81(3)

It was seen in Chapter 3 that in certain circumstances seemingly unilateral conduct of one party to a contract might actually form part of the contractual arrangements between it and a co-contractor, for example where it has been explicitly or tacitly accepted by the latter.[376]

---

[369] See, e.g., *Tetra Pak/BTG* [1988] OJ L272/27, [1990] 4 CMLR 47.
[370] *Langnese-Iglo* [1993] OJ L183/19, [1994] 4 CMLR 51.
[371] Case C-279/95 P, *Langnese-Iglo v. Commission* [1998] ECR I-5609, [1998] 5 CMLR 933, paras. 207–9.
[372] See Chap. 9.
[373] Reg. 1/2003 [2003] OJ L1/1, Art. 29(2).
[374] See especially *infra* Chap. 10.
[375] See the Vertical Guidelines, para. 120.
[376] *Supra* Chap. 3.

In many cases the Commission has relied on such behaviour to find a breach of Article 81(1).[377] Similarly, in *Ford Werke AG v. Commission*[378] the Commission relied both on the terms of the agreement and on the way in which it was operated by Ford when it issued a decision refusing Ford an exemption for its selective distribution system. The ECJ held that the Commission was entitled when considering the terms of the agreement to take account not only of the written terms of the agreement but also the way the agreement was operated. In this case Ford had essentially refused to supply right-hand drive cars to its German dealers in order to protect the higher prices which the distributors charged in the UK. That apparently unilateral decision was, in that case, found to form part of the contractual arrangements since admission to the network involved implicit acceptance by the dealers of the terms imposed by Ford.

F. THE RELATIONSHIP BETWEEN ARTICLE 81(3) AND ARTICLE 82

The relationship between Article 81(3) and 82 is dealt with above and is discussed more fully in Chapter 5 below.

5. CONCLUSIONS

1. The challenge for a system of competition law is to design a set of transparent and predictable rules which can be used to determine as accurately as possible, and at a tolerable cost, which agreements are so restrictive of competition that they should be prohibited and deterred. It has been seen in this chapter that this challenge has been rendered particularly difficult in the EU both by the positioning of Article 81 in the EC Treaty and by the bifurcated structure of Article 81.

2. It is clear that the Commission has moved away from its broad, jurisdictional approach to Article 81(1) which created an expansive role for Article 81(3) and (at the time) a pressing need for block exemptions. It now adopts a more economic approach to Article 81(1) and Article 81(3) based on a consumer welfare objective.

3. In modernizing its approach to Article 81, the Commission has not accepted that Article 81(1) provides the correct forum for weighing anti- and pro-competitive effects on the basis that this approach would result in Article 81(3) being 'cast aside'. Rather, the Commission considers that Article 81(1) is about identifying restrictive effects on competition (it is for the Commission, or other person trying to prove the same, to demonstrate the restriction), whilst Article 81(3) provides the forum, for the person seeking to rely on it, to prove that counteracting efficiencies resulting from the agreement outweigh those restrictions.[379]

---

[377] *Supra* Chap. 3.

[378] Cases 228, 229/82, [1984] ECR 1129, [1984] 1 CMLR 649. *Ford* was, however, distinguished in Case T-41/96, *Bayer AG v. Commission* [2000] ECR II-3383, [2001] 4 CMLR 126, *aff'd* Cases C-2 and 3/01 P, [2004] 4 CMLR 653 and Case T-208/01, *Volkswagen v. Commission* [2003] ECR II-5141, [2004] 4 CMLR 72. In these cases the Commission's finding that unilateral measures formed an integral part of distribution arrangements was annulled, see *supra* Chap. 3, 155 ff.

[379] The weighing therefore within the framework of Article 81(3) rather than under Article 81(1).

4. The difficulty with this structure is that it requires an extremely strained view of the case law and past decisional practice. A number of judgments of the ECJ support the view that the weighing of anti-and pro-competitive effects should be conducted within the framework of Article 81(1) (restrictions of competition necessary and proportionate to a legitimate objective fall outside Article 81(1)).[380] Further, precedent indicates that public policy objectives may be taken into account when conducting the Article 81(3) appraisal. These cases suggest a quite different picture of the analysis to be conducted under Article 81, indicating a narrower interpretation of Article 81(1) and less emphasis on Article 81(3). Further, they suggests that both Article 81(1) and Article 81(3) may still have a role to play in the pursuit of public policy objectives.

6. FURTHER READING

A. BOOKS

AMATO, G., *Antitrust and the Bounds of Power* (Hart Publishing, 1997), chap. 4

BUTTERWORTHS, *Competition Law* (eds. B. Allen, B. Sufrin and M. Furse) (Butterworths, Looseleaf), Division I

KERSE, C. S., *EC Antitrust Procedure* (4th edn., Sweet & Maxwell, 1998), chap. 2

NEALE, A. D., and GOYDER, D. G., *The Antitrust Laws of the United States* (3rd edn., Cambridge University Press, 1981)

ODUDU, O., *The Boundaries of EC Competition Law: The Scope of Article 81* (Oxford University Press, 2006)

WESSELING, W., *The Modernisation of EC Antitrust Law* (Hart Publishing, 2000)

B. ARTICLES

BAILEY, D., 'Scope of Judicial Review under Article 81' (2004) 41 *CMLRev* 1327

BASRAN, H. R., 'How Should Article 81 EC Address Agreements that Yield Environmental Benefits?' [2006] *ECLR* 479

BLACK, O., 'Per Se Rules and Rules of Reason: What Are They?' [1997] *ECLR* 145

BROWN, A., 'Notification of Agreements to the EC Commission: Whether to Submit to a Flawed System' (1992) 17 *ELRev* 323

FORRESTER, I., and NORALL, C., 'The Laicization of Community Law: Self-help and the Rule of Reason: How Competition Law is and could be Applied' (1984) 21 *CMLRev* 11

HAWK, B. E., 'System Failure: Vertical Restraints and EC Competition Law' (1995) 32 *CMLRev* 973

JONES, A., 'Analysis of Agreements under U.S. and EC Antitrust Law—Convergence or Divergence?' [2006] 51 *Ant Bull* 691

KORAH, V., 'EEC Competition Policy—Legal Form or Economic Efficiency' [1986] *Current Legal Problems* 85

MARQUIS, M., 'O2 (Germany) v Commission and the exotic mysteries of Article 81(1) EC' [2007] *ELRev* 29

MONTI, G., 'Article 81 and Public Policy' (2002) *CMLRev* 1057

NAZZINE, R., 'Article 81 EC Between Time Present and Time Past: A Normative Critique of 'Restriction of Competition' in EU Law' (2006) 43 *CMLRev* 497

ODUDU, O., 'Interpreting Article 81(1): object as subjective intention' (2001) 26 *ELRev* 60

---

[380] But not the more recent judgments of the CFI.

ODUDU, O., 'Interpreting Article 81(1): demonstrating restrictive effect' (2001) 26 *ELRev* 261

SUFRIN, B., 'The Evolution of Article 81(3) of the EC Treaty' [2006] 51 *Ant Bull* 915

VOSSESTEIN A.J., 'Case Comment' (*Wouters*) (2002) 39 *CMLRev* 841

WESSELING, R., 'The Commission White Paper on Modernisation of EC Antitrust Law: Unspoken consequences and incomplete treatment of alternative options' [1999] *ECLR* 420

WHISH, R., and SUFRIN, B., 'Article 85 and the Rule of Reason' [1987] *YEL* 1

5

ARTICLE 82: THE ELEMENTS

1. CENTRAL ISSUES

1. Article 82 deals with the unilateral conduct of undertakings with market power.

2. Article 82 prohibits one or more undertakings which hold a dominant position in a substantial part of the common from abusing that dominant in so far as it may affect inter-Member State trade. For an infringement of Article 82 to be established, therefore, five cumulative elements must be established. Two of these elements, 'dominant position' and 'abuse' are particularly difficult both to define and establish. The holding of a 'dominant position' is not prohibited, only the 'abuse' of the dominant position.

3. The way in which the Commission and the Court have applied Article 82 has been extremely controversial. The Commission is currently reviewing its approach to Article 82. This review may culminate in the publication of some form of guidance, possibly 'Guidelines' like those on Article 81(3).

4. A 'dominant position' was defined by the ECJ cases in the 1970's and early 1980's in terms of the ability of the undertaking to act 'independently' rather than in terms of the ability to profitably raise prices.

5. Abuses can be categorised under various headings but a basic distinction drawn is between 'exploitative' and 'exclusionary' abuses (although some conduct can be both exploitative and exclusionary). The former focuses on behaviour which exploits the undertaking's position of market power (for example, the charging of supra-competitive prices) whilst the latter focuses on conduct which excludes other competitor's from the market and so

perpetuates the dominance problem. In 1979, the ECJ sought to set out a definition of an exclusionary abuse. The definition is inherently problematic in its wording but its effect is to distinguish 'competition on the merits' from conduct which is abusive.

6. As is the case with Article 81, an acute problem in the context of Article 82 is that its objectives remain somewhat obscure. In the past, it has undoubtedly been applied with the objective of preserving a particular market structure and protecting competitors from the behaviour of dominant firms, rather than with the objective of protecting consumer welfare and the competitive process. In this area, the influence of ordoliberalism on EC competition is clearly demonstrated.

7. A result of this influence is that a formalistic approach to the concept of abuse has been adopted, focusing on the form of the conduct and not its effect. This has dictated different results for conduct with similar or identical effects. In contrast an economic approach would demand an examination of the working of competition on the relevant market and an explanation of how the conduct harms consumers.

8. The current consensus of opinion, however, is that Article 82 should be applied only to enhance consumer welfare and the efficient allocation of resources and the Commission wishes to realign Article 82 to take a more effects-based approach. Nonetheless, there is no consistent requirement, even if more recent cases, that anticompetitive effects in an economic sense must be proved.

2. INTRODUCTION

Article 82 is designed to deal with monopoly and market power. It focuses not on agreements *between* undertakings (as Article 81 does) but on the unilateral behaviour of undertakings which hold a 'dominant position'. It constrains the behaviour of undertakings which are not sufficiently restrained by other competitors operating on the market by prohibiting the 'abuse' of a dominant position.

As we saw in Chapter 1, a monopolist is able to restrict output and increase prices without losing sales to competitors. It can reap monopoly profits. Article 82 prohibits an undertaking with a dominant position from exploiting that position, for example by charging unfair prices or by limiting production to the prejudice of consumers.[1] In addition, it is clear from the case law of the ECJ that the provision also prohibits dominant undertakings from engaging in anti-competitive conduct which reinforces their position and excludes actual or potential competitors from the market.[2] There is a fear that dominant undertakings will erect artificial barriers denying competitors the opportunity to compete. Article 82 therefore applies to so-called 'exclusionary' conduct as well as to conduct that exploits consumers directly.

The application of Article 82 by the Commission and the Court has often been highly controversial. This is principally due to:

- questionable findings that an undertaking is dominant for the purposes of the Article;
- an emphasis on the *form* that the behaviour of the dominant undertaking takes, rather than on its *effects*;
- an absence of coherent and consistent principle in the approach to Article 82: 'instead the Commission and the Community Courts have dealt with individual cases... seemingly without having any clear or general analytical or intellectual framework for doing so';[3]
- a failure to identify the policy objectives being pursued in the enforcement of the prohibition. As in the case of Article 81, the objectives pursued have a huge impact on the interpretation of the provision,[4] in particular whether or not behaviour is characterized as abusive. The application of Article 82 raises very starkly the question of whether the law should protect competitors for their own sake (in the interest of 'economic freedom' in the ordoliberal sense), competition as a process or even an 'institution' (and if so for whose benefit), consumer welfare (and if so, how), or some combination of these objectives. In the application of Article 82 and the debate surrounding it we thus see played out the arguments about the purposes of competition law which we noted in Chapter 1.
- the effect that the imperative of single market integration has played in some cases:

The... approach to the application of Article 82 cannot fully be understood without reference to the determination of the Community institutions to create and sustain the Single Market.[5]

---

[1] See *infra* Chap. 7.

[2] See Case 6/72, *Europemballage Corp and Continental Can Co Inc v. Commission* [1973] ECR 215, [1973] CMLR 199 and Chap. 7 *passim*.

[3] R. O'Donoghue and A. J. Padilla, *The Law and Economics of Article 82* (Hart Publishing, 2006), 17; J. Temple Lang and R. O'Donoghue, 'Defining Legitimate Competition: How to Clarify Pricing Abuses under Article 82EC' (2002) 26 *Fordham Int'l LJ* 83, 84.

[4] See *supra* Chap. 4.

[5] J. Faull and A. Nikpay, *The EC Law of Competition* (2nd edn., Oxford University Press, 2007), 4.14. See, e.g. Case 27/76, *United Brands Co and United Brands Continental BV v. Commission* [1978] ECR 207, [1978] 1 CMLR 429.

3. THE TEXT OF ARTICLE 82

Article 82 provides:

Any abuse by one or more undertakings of a dominant position within the common market or in a substantial part of it shall be prohibited as incompatible with the common market insofar as it may affect trade between Member States. Such abuse may, in particular, consist in:

(a) directly or indirectly imposing unfair purchase or selling prices or other unfair trading conditions;

(b) limiting production, markets or technical development to the prejudice of consumers;

(c) applying dissimilar conditions to equivalent transactions with other trading parties, thereby placing them at a competitive disadvantage;

(d) making the conclusion of contracts subject to acceptance by the other parties of supplementary obligations which, by their nature or according to commercial usage, have no connection with the subject of such contracts.

4. THE REFORM OF ARTICLE 82

In 2003 the Commission initiated an internal review of its policy on Article 82. This culminated in the publication in December 2005 of a Discussion Paper on the application of the article to exclusionary abuses,[6] which was put out for public consultation[7] and was intended to initiate a wide-ranging debate on Article 82. It this at least it succeeded spectacularly. The Commission received more than a hundred submissions in response,[8] and there was an outpouring of commentary about it. The Commission held a public hearing on the Discussion Paper in June 2006[9] at which the Director General said that the Commission was looking to take a decision about issuing draft Guidelines by the end of 2006.[10] At the time of writing no such draft has appeared but a draft text (which may or may not take the form of guidance) is expected to appear before the end of 2007. The proposals set out in the Discussion Paper are described in outline below and further dealt with in context in other parts of this chapter and in Chapters 6 and 7.

The purpose of the Commission's internal review, according to the Director General of DG Comp, was 'to evaluate policy, to assess how it could be made more effective, and to define ways in which we might make it more transparent'.[11] The Commission had recently reviewed its

---

[6] Brussels, December 2005, hereinafter 'the Discussion Paper'. The Discussion Paper was limited to exclusionary abuses, and did not deal with exploitative abuses such as excessive pricing and discrimination.

[7] The consultation period closed on 31 March 2006.

[8] Available on the Commission's website, which has a section dedicated to the Article 82 review, http://ec.europa.eu/comm/competition/antitrust/art82/index.html.

[9] A recording of the Public Hearing is available at http://ec.europa.eu/comm/competition/antitrust/art82/hearing.html.

[10] It is likely that they will also address 'exploitative' abuses.

[11] Speech by the Director General of DG Comp, Philip Lowe, at Fordham Corporate Law Institute 30th Annual Conference on International Antitrust Law and Policy, 23 Oct. 2003, published at 2003 Fordham Corp L Inst (B. Hawk, ed. 2004) 163, referring to the speech of (then) Commissioner Mario Monti at the 8th EU Competition Law and Policy Workshop, EUI, June 2003, published as C. D. Ehlermann and I. Atanasiu (eds.), *European Competition Law Annual 2003: What is an Abuse of a Dominant Position?* (Hart Publishing, 2006) 3, 9.

approach to Article 81[12] and mergers[13] and considered it time to look at Article 82. In particular this was thought desirable in the light of the modernization reforms whereby, under Regulation 1/2003, the national competition authorities have 'parallel competence' with the Commission to apply Article 82.[14] The Commission considered that 'a policy which is clear on the substantive interpretation of the Article is essential to make the system work'[15] and that a 'credible policy on abusive conduct must be compatible with mainstream economics'.[16] We will see throughout this Chapter and the two following that the policy on Article 82 has not always hitherto been so.

The Discussion Paper published by the Commission in December 2005 dealt only with the application of Article 82 to *exclusionary* abuses (defined as behaviour by a dominant undertaking which is likely to have a foreclosure effect on the market[17]) and not exploitative abuses (such as excessive pricing and non-exclusionary discrimination). As the types of abuse cannot always be neatly separated, however, the absence of the latter is unsatisfactory. The thrust of the Discussion Paper was to re-orientate the application of Article 82 in exclusionary abuse cases to an 'effects-based' analysis. Instead, therefore of asking 'what did the undertaking *do*?' (or 'what is it doing?'), which is a form-based analysis, the question will be 'what are the effects of what it has done/is doing?'.

The application of Article 82 has not in the past been devoid of effects based (or 'rule of reason')analysis but this has not been done in a systematic way and has been over-shadowed by the form-based approach to many types of conduct.[18] The Discussion Paper set out an analytical framework dealing with pervasive matters such as possible defences.[19] It then went through the main types of exclusionary abuse—predatory pricing, single branding and rebates, tying and bundling, refusal to supply, and problems on aftermarkets—explaining in turn how the Commission proposed applying an effects based assessment to them in future. The Commission stated that it is the effects on the market which would concern it, and not the protection of competitors. The Commission would apply Article 82 in order to protect competition as a means of enhancing consumer welfare and ensuring an efficient allocation of resources.[20]

The Discussion Paper also contained a short, and not altogether satisfactory, section on dominance.[21]

One problem with the principles set out in the Discussion Paper (and in any guidelines, guidance or other document that result from it) is how they relate to the case law of the Community Courts. The most crucial concepts in Article 82—'dominant position' and 'abuse'—are not defined in the EC Treaty but were defined by the ECJ in leading cases thirty years ago.[22] These

---

[12] With, e.g., the block exemption Regulation, 2790/99 on vertical agreements, [1999] OJ L336/21 and the accompanying Guidelines, [2000] OJ C291/1; block exemption Regulations 2658/2000 [2000] L304/3 on specialization agreements and 2659/2000 [2000] OJ L304/7 on research and development agreements and the accompanying Guidelines on horizontal co-operation agreements [2001] OJ C3/2; block exemption Reg. 772/2004 [2004] OJ L123/11 on technology transfer agreements and accompanying Guidelines [2004] OJ C101/2.

[13] Culminating in the new Merger Regulation, Council Regulation 139/2004 [2004] OJ L24/1.

[14] See *supra* Chap. 2 and *infra* Chap. 14.

[15] Philip Lowe at 30th Fordham Corporate Law Institute Conference, see n. 11 *supra*.

[16] *Ibid.*

[17] Discussion Paper, para. 1. For exclusionary abuses, see further *infra* 325.

[18] See Chap. 7.

[19] Discussion Paper, paras. 51–92.

[20] *Ibid.* 54.

[21] *Ibid.*, paras. 20–50, discussed *infra* 309 and Chap.6.

[22] Respectively Case 6/72, *Europemballage Corp and Continental Can Co Inc v. Commission* [1973] ECR 215, [1973] CMLR 199 and Case 85/76, *Hoffmann-La Roche & Co AG v. Commission* [1979] ECR 461, [1979] 3 CMLR 211.

definitions do not employ 'economic' terminology and sit uneasily with modern economic theory. However, they appear to be set in stone, in that the Community Courts continue to rely on them as the starting-point for all Article 82 analysis.[23] The Discussion Paper worked with the definitions of dominance and abuse laid down in the case law[24] but in some respects took a different approach to that previously taken by the Community Courts.[25] Where the modernized, more economics-based approach to Article 81 was concerned the Court had been in the vanguard, and the Commission was walking through an open door.[26] This is not so with regard to Article 82. Two months after the publication of the Discussion Paper Advocate General Kokott said, in giving her opinion in the *British Airways* appeal:

... it is immaterial how the Commission intends to define its competition policy with regard to Article 82 EC *for the future* ... Any reorientation in the application of Article 82 EC can be of relevance only for future decisions of the Commission, not for the legal assessment of a decision already taken. Moreover, even if its administrative practice were to change, the Commission would still have to act within the framework prescribed for it by Article 82 EC as interpreted by the Court of Justice.[27]

The subsequent judgment in *British Airways* in March 2007 took a highly conservative approach to the matter of rebates, at odds with that suggested by the Commission in the Discussion Paper.[28] This followed a judgment of the CFI a month earlier in *France Télécom*[29] in which the CFI faithfully followed the existing, much criticised, case law on predatory pricing.[30]

The path to modernizing what has been called 'the last of the steam-powered trains'[31] is therefore not straightforward. The Commission can certainly alter its approach to enforcement and can avoid taking decisions such as *Virgin/BA*[32] in future.[33] Any guidance it issues may be highly persuasive on the NCAs. However, national courts, applying the directly effective Article 82 in actions between private parties, or hearing appeals from NCA decisions, will normally look to the case law of the Community Courts.[34] Ultimately, the Commission needs the Court on board if the steam-powered train is to be transformed into the TGV.

---

[23] For example, Case T-219/99, *British Airways v. Commission* [2003] ECR II-5917, [2004] 4 CMLR 1008, *aff'd* by the ECJ, Case C-95/04 P *British Airways v. Commission*, 15 March 2007.

[24] Case 6/72, *Europemballage Corp and Continental Can Co Inc v. Commission* [1973] ECR 215, [1973] CMLR 199 and Case 85/76, *Hoffmann-La Roche & Co AG v. Commission* [1979] ECR 461, [1979] 3 CMLR 211, see *infra* 305 and 320 and Chaps. 6 and 7.

[25] Notably in respect of single branding and rebates.

[26] See Chap. 4.

[27] Case C-95/04 P, *British Airways v. Commission*, Opinion of A-G Kokott, 23 February 2006, para. 28.

[28] Case C-95/04 P, *British Airways v. Commission*, 15 March 2007 c.f. Discussion Paper, paras. 134–76.

[29] Case T-340/03, *France Télécom SA v. Commission*, 30 January 2007 (the appeal from the *Wanadoo* decision, COMP/38.233, 16 July 2003, [2005] 5 CMLR 120).

[30] In particular, in respect of the likelihood of recoupment.

[31] B. Sher, 'The Last of the Steam-Powered Trains: Modernising Article 82' [2004] *ECLR*, 243.

[32] [2000] OJ L30/1, [2000] 4 CMLR 999.

[33] Although complainants dissatisfied with the Commission's refusal to pursue their case may challenge that decision before the CFI, as in; e.g. Case T-193/02, *Laurent Piau v. Commission* [2005] ECR II-209.

[34] In accordance with the relationship of the Court with the national courts in the Community legal order, see, e.g. D. Chalmers, C. Hadjiemmanuil, G. Monti, A. Tomkins, *European Union Law* (Cambridge University Press, 2006) chap. 7. UK courts are constrained to follow the Court by the European Communities Act 1972, s. 3.

298 | EC COMPETITION LAW

5. THE SCHEME OF ARTICLE 82

A. THE PROHIBITION

Article 82 prohibits undertakings from committing an abuse of a dominant position held within a substantial part of the common market where that abuse has an effect on trade between Member States. Although sub-paragraphs (a) to (d) set out examples of abuses, they are illustrative only and do not provide an exhaustive list.[35] The essential elements of Article 82 are set out in its first sentence.

Article 82 thus prohibits dominant undertakings from engaging in certain conduct. The provision does not set out a procedure for declaring an undertaking to be dominant and so subject to Article 82. An undertaking is dominant simply when it satisfies the definition set out by the ECJ.[36] Its conduct then, automatically, becomes potentially subject to the prohibition.

Article 82 contains no express exception provision equivalent to that in Article 81(3).[37] It is, however, open to a dominant undertaking to plead that its conduct is 'objectively justified'.[38] Further, although it must be established that the dominant position is held 'in a substantial part of the common market' and there must be an *appreciable* effect on inter-Member State trade, there is no *de minimis* rule equivalent to that adopted by the ECJ in relation to Article 81(1).[39]

It can be seen from the text of Article 82 that five elements must be established before the prohibition applies. The five elements are:

(a) one or more undertakings;

(b) a dominant position;

(c) the dominant position must be held within the common market or a substantial part of it;

(d) an abuse; and

(e) an effect on inter-State trade.

It is often extremely difficult to determine whether or not these criteria have been satisfied, in particular whether an undertaking holds a 'dominant position' and/or whether it has committed an 'abuse' of that dominant position.

The question whether an undertaking is dominant requires, according to the case law of the ECJ, that the market on which the undertaking is alleged to be dominant is defined,[40] and the problems of market definitions are notorious.[41] The undertaking's position on the market must

---

[35] See Case 6/72, *Europemballage Corp and Continental Can Co Inc v. Commission* [1973] ECR 215, [1973] CMLR 199; Case C-333/94 P *Tetra Pak International SA v. Commission* [1996] ECR I-5951, [1997] 4 CMLR 662 (*Tetra Pak II*), para. 37; Case C-95/04 P *British Airways v. Commission*, 15 March 2007, para. 57. See the discussion *infra* 316 ff.

[36] See *infra*, 303.

[37] Although it was possible to apply for a negative clearance under Reg. 17, Art. 2 (JO 204/62, (1959–1962) OJ Spec. Ed. 87). It is possible under Reg. 1/2003, Art. 10 for the Commission to make a finding of inapplicability: see Chap.14.

[38] See *infra* 331 ff for the Discussion Paper proposals for, *inter alia*, an 'efficiency defence'.

[39] See Chap. 3. However, the effect on inter-Member State trade has to be appreciable. See Guidelines on the effect on trade concept contained in Articles 81 and 82 of the Treaty [2004] OJ C101/81, Case 22/78, *Hugin Kassaregister AB and Hugin Cash Registers Ltd v. Commission* [1979] ECR 1869, [1979] 3 CMLR 345, and *infra* 339.

[40] Case 6/72, *Europemballage Corp and Continental Can Co Inc v. Commission* [1973] ECR 215, [1973] CMLR. For the argument that market power may be able to be measured directly, rather than by going through the 'indirect method' via market definition, see Chap. 1, 59 and *infra* Chap. 6.

[41] See *supra* Chap. 1.

then be assessed. It is crucial that these definitions and assessments are made properly. It is not an offence to hold a dominant position (Article 82 does not prohibit the holding of a dominant position *per se* but only an abuse of that dominant position), but some behaviour which may be competitive, or at least neutral, from a competition perspective when engaged in by an undertaking on a competitive market may be prohibited when engaged in by a dominant undertaking.[42] An incorrect finding of dominance may consequently lead to a ruling that an undertaking's pro-competitive behaviour is abusive conduct prohibited by Article 82 (a Type 1 'false positive' error). In addition, if the concept of an abuse is found to encompass a wide spectrum of behaviour, Article 82 may come perilously close to forbidding the dominance itself. Furthermore, it was seen in Chapter 3 that a firm which unilaterally acts anticompetitively by imposing export bans[43] or resale prices[44] is not prohibited from doing so by Article 81(1), which applies only to agreements. If the undertaking concerned is not dominant the conduct falls outside Article 82 as well and is therefore legal. Dominant and non-dominant firms are in crucially different positions.

The question of what amounts to an 'abuse' is also a vexed one. It requires a determination of what conduct can and what conduct cannot legitimately be carried out by a dominant undertaking. This, of course, depends partly upon the purposes of the whole provision. As stated above, it has not always been entirely clear what objectives have been pursued in the enforcement of Article 82.[45]

This chapter, after setting out the consequences of infringing Article 82, considers the five elements of Article 82 in turn and deals with general issues concerning their scope, interpretation, and application, including the proposals for reform. Chapters 6 and 7 respectively consider in greater detail (1) how it is ascertained whether an undertaking holds a dominant position and (2) what conduct constitutes an abuse of a dominant position. It is important to realize, however, that the different elements of Article 82 cannot always be considered separately from one another. In particular, the questions whether an undertaking is in a dominant position and whether it has committed an abuse may be interrelated and intertwined.[46] We see below that it has even been argued that there should be no need to establish a preliminary and separate assessment of dominance, but that the analysis of dominance and abuse should be integrated.[47]

B. CONSEQUENCES OF INFRINGEMENT

(i) Investigation, Fines, and Other Remedies

The Commission may investigate undertakings it believes to have committed a breach of Article 82. Where the Commission finds that a violation of Article 82 has been committed, it can issue a decision ordering the undertaking to put an end to the abuse (by taking positive or negative measures) and can even, where certain conditions are met, impose structural remedies.[48] Further, it can impose fines on the undertaking of up to 10 per cent of its turnover in the

---

[42] See *infra* 316 ff.

[43] Cases C-2 and 3/01 P, *Bundesverband der Arzneimitte—Importeure EV and Commission v. Bayer AG* [2004] ECR I-23, 5141, [2004] 4 CMLR 653, see Chap. 3, 160.

[44] Case C-74/04 P, *Commission v. Volkswagen AG* [2006] ECR I-6585.

[45] See *infra* Chap. 7.

[46] And see T. Eilsmansberger, 'Dominance—The Lost Child? How the Effects-Based Rules Could and Should Change Dominance Analysis' (2006) 2 *European Law Journal* 15.

[47] Report by EAGCP, July 2005, see *infra* 311.

[48] Reg. 1/2003, Art. 7. See *infra* Chap. 14. The power to impose remedies of a structural nature, i.e., to order divestment and break up companies was introduced by Reg. 1/2003 and did not appear in Reg. 17.

preceding year of business. The Commission has imposed substantial fines on undertakings found to have committed a breach of Article 82. In *Microsoft*[49] the Commission imposed a fine of almost €500 million on a single undertaking.

The difficulties involved in determining whether or not an infringement of Article 82 has been committed and the controversy surrounding many of the Commission's decisions taken under Article 82 have rendered the Commission's willingness to impose heavy fines in respect of breaches of the Article extremely contentious. Moreover, as shown by *Microsoft*, behavioural remedies such as ordering an undertaking to supply may be more significant for the undertaking than even a large fine.[50]

Under Regulation 1/2003, Article 9 the Commission can take 'commitments decisions' whereby it accepts binding commitments from undertakings under investigation rather than proceeding to a final decision under Article 7.[51] Under the Regulation 17 regime the Commission had brought several Article 82 proceedings to a close by accepting commitments from the parties, but it could not make these binding.[52]

Regulation 1/2003 requires Member States to empower their designated competition authorities to apply Article 82 (and Article 81).[53] Article 5 provides that the NCAs shall have powers to take infringement, commitments and fining decisions and take interim measures. The Regulation itself does not give them the power to impose structural remedies.[54]

(ii) Private Action

Article 82, like Article 81, is directly effective.[55] It is possible, therefore, that an entity injured by a breach of Article 82 may bring proceedings before a national court seeking an injunction or damages in respect of loss resulting from the breach.[56]

Further, a party to a contract concluded with a dominant undertaking may claim that clauses within it are prohibited by Article 82 and consequently void or unenforceable.[57] That party may also bring proceedings to recover benefits conferred under a prohibited provision.[58]

---

[49] COMP/C-3/37. 792, [2005] 4 CMLR 965, on appeal Case T-201/04, *Microsoft v. EC Commission* (judgment pending).

[50] *Ibid*. See further Chap. 7 and Chap. 14.

[51] See *infra* Chap. 14, 1206.

[52] For example, *Digital Undertaking*, Commission Press Release IP/97/868. Up to the end of March 2007 the Commission had used Article 9 in two Article 82 cases, *Coca-Cola* [2005] OJ L253/21, and *De Beers/ALROSA* [2006] OJ L205/24, on appeal Case T-170/06, *ALROSA v. Commission*, 11 July 2007. See *infra* Chap. 7.

[53] Regulation 1/2003, Art. 35.

[54] See *infra* Chap. 14. National law may give the NCA such powers.

[55] See Case 127/73, *Belgische Radio en Televisie and Société belge des auteurs, compositeurs et editeurs v. SV SABAM and NV Fonior* [1974] ECR 313, [1974] 2 CMLR 238. The equivalent Article of the ECSC Treaty, Art. 66(7), did not have direct effect because it conferred sole jurisdiction on the Commission; see Case C-128/92, *H. J. Banks & Co Ltd v. British Coal Corp* [1994] ECR I-1209, [1994] 5 CMLR 30, paras. 18–19.

[56] See *infra* Chap. 15.

[57] In *English Welsh and Scottish Railway Ltd v. E.ON UK plc* [2007] EWHC 599, 23 March 2007, the England and Wales High Court (Field J.) ruled on the effect of a decision by the Office of Rail Regulation (which has concurrent powers with the OFT to apply Articles 81 and 82 in the regulated sector) on 17 November 2006 that EWS had abused a dominant position to Article 82 (and the equivalent domestic provision, the Chapter II prohibition of the Competition Act 1998) by entering into an exclusionary agreement with E.ON (a power generator) in respect of coal haulage. Field J. held that the exclusionary aspects of the agreement, being contrary to the competition rules, had been illegal and void since execution. The question was therefore whether they could be severed from the remainder, leaving the rest of the agreement standing (he concluded that they could not be). For the issue of severance, see *infra* Chap.15.

[58] *Ibid*.

6. THE INTERPRETATION AND APPLICATION OF ARTICLE 82

A. THE MEANING OF ONE OR MORE UNDERTAKINGS

(i) General

'Undertaking' is interpreted in the same way for the purpose of Article 82 as it is in the context of Article 81. It has been construed broadly and 'encompasses every entity engaged in an economic activity'.[59] If an entity is not engaged in an economic activity, the fact that the members who comprise it do carry out such activity will not render the entity itself an 'undertaking' for the purposes of Article 82. In *Wouters*[60] the ECJ thus held that the Dutch Bar was not itself an undertaking although the individual members of the Bar *were* undertakings for the purposes of Article 81.[61] Two points of particular importance arise when considering the meaning of the term 'undertaking' within the context of Article 82. First, since State regulation is a frequent source of an entity's market power, it is crucial to know to what extent public bodies or bodies with a special connection with the State will be characterized as undertakings and so potentially subject to Article 82. Secondly, it must be considered what is meant by 'one or more undertakings' in Article 82. So far, reference has been made to the problems caused by monopoly and market power held by an individual undertaking. It is clearly envisaged, however, that Article 82 should apply to the conduct of more than one undertaking. Is Article 82 confined to the conduct of undertakings which are part of the same single economic entity (in which a united policy may be pursued) or does Article 82 go further and prohibit the conduct of one or more independent undertakings?

(ii) Public Bodies and Bodies Performing Public Functions

The term 'undertaking' applies to any entity engaged in commercial activities whether or not it is a State entity, even if it has no identity separate from that of the State.[62] Further, it is clear from Articles 10 and 86(1) of the Treaty that the State itself cannot confer immunity upon undertakings from the application of those rules. The fact that an undertaking's market power has been created by State action is no defence to an action based on Article 82 unless the narrow exception set out in Article 86(2) applies. This provision states that '[u]ndertakings entrusted with the operation of services of general economic interest or having the character of a revenue-producing monopoly' are subject to the competition rules unless those rules 'obstruct the performance, in law or in fact, of the particular tasks assigned to them'. This topic is discussed in Chapter 8.

(iii) One or More Undertakings—Collective Dominance

Initially it was believed that the term 'one or more undertakings' referred only to bodies which were part of the same economic entity. The purpose of the term was to ensure that the conduct

---

[59] See *supra* Chap. 3.

[60] Case C-309/99 *Wouters v. Algemene Raad van de Nederlandse Orde van Advocaten* [2002] ECR I-1577, [2002] 4 CMLR 913, para. 112.

[61] See *supra* Chap. 3 and Chap. 4.

[62] See *supra* Chap. 3 and *infra* Chap. 8.

of all bodies within the corporate group was taken into account when assessing whether or not a breach of Article 82 had occurred. Thus circumstances such as those which arose in *Continental Can* and *Commercial Solvents* would be caught. In *Continental Can*,[63] for example, a US company held an 85.8 per cent share in a German company (SLW). It formed a wholly owned Belgian subsidiary through which it acquired a Dutch company which was a competitor of SLW. The Commission held that the American parent had, through SLW, a dominant position in a substantial part of the common market and that an abuse of the dominant position was committed when it used its Belgian subsidiary to take over the Dutch company.[64] Similarly, in *Commercial Solvents*[65] a US parent and its 51 per cent owned Italian subsidiary were involved in a refusal to supply a third party in Italy with a raw material produced by the parent. The subsidiary followed the policy laid down by the parent and both were held to have abused a dominant position. This belief that Article 82 might be confined to bodies forming part of the same economic unit or the same corporate group found support from a statement of the ECJ in *Hoffmann La-Roche*.[66]

Such an interpretation would, however, have meant that the term 'undertaking' in the context of Article 82 had a different meaning from that which it had in relation to Article 81. In Chapter 3 it was explained that the term 'undertaking' itself applied to all bodies which formed part of the same economic entity. Bodies within the same corporate group are treated as a single undertaking if those bodies 'form an economic unit within which the subsidiary has no real freedom to determine its course of action on the market, and if the agreements or practices are concerned merely with the internal allocation of tasks as between the undertakings'.[67] If interpreted in the same way, Article 82 would have applied to the behaviour of all bodies which formed an economic unit even if the Article had referred only to an abuse by *an* undertaking of a dominant position. So *what* interpretation should be given to the phrase 'one or more undertakings'?

It has now been established that 'one or more undertakings' can refer to legally independent undertakings which *together* hold a 'collective dominant position' on the market. Article 82 therefore applies to dominant positions held by single firms and, in certain circumstances, to those held collectively.[68] In other words, Article 82 can apply to oligopolies. Further, in *Laurent Piau* the CFI said that it was 'unrealistic' to claim that FIFA, (the international federation of football

---

[63] Case 6/72, *Europemballage Corp and Continental Can Co Inc* v. *Commission* [1973] ECR 215, [1973] CMLR 199, see discussion of this case *infra* at 318 ff.

[64] *Re Continental Can Co Inc* [1972] OJ L7/25, [1972] CMLR D11. The ECJ annulled the Commission's decision on the ground of an erroneous definition of the market (see *infra* Chap. 6) but the point about the aggregation of the activities of the group was not doubted.

[65] Cases 6 and 7/73, *Istituto Chemioterapico Italiano SpA and Commercial Solvents Corp* v. *Commission* [1974] ECR 223, [1974] 1 CMLR 309.

[66] Case 85/76, *Hoffmann-La Roche & Co AG* v. *Commission* [1979] ECR 461, [1979] 3 CMLR 211, para. 39.

[67] Case 15/74, *Centrafarm BV and Adriaan De Peijper* v. *Sterling Drug Inc* [1974] ECR 1147, [1974] 2 CMLR 480, para. 41, repeated in Case 30/87, *Bodson* v. *Pompes funèbres des régions libérées SA* [1988] ECR 2479, [1989] 4 CMLR 984, para. 19. See the discussion *supra* at Chap. 3. This seems to be a two-pronged test, but in Case C-73/95 P, *Viho Europe BV* v. *Commission* [1996] ECR I-5457, [1997] 4 CMLR 419, para. 16, the ECJ concentrated on the lack of freedom aspect. 'Parker and its subsidiaries thus form a single economic unit within which the subsidiaries do not enjoy real autonomy in determining their course of action in the market, but carry out the instructions issued to them by the parent company controlling them'. See further Cases C-395 and 396/96 P, *Compagnie Maritime Belge Transports SA* v. *Commission* [2000] ECR I-1365, [2000] 4 CMLR 1076 Opinion of Fennelly AG, para. 24.

[68] Cases T-68, 77, and 78/89, *Società Italiano Vetro SpA* v. *Commission* [1992] ECR II-1403, [1992] 5 CMLR 302, paras. 357–8, Cases C-395 and 396/96P *Compagnie Maritime Belge Transports SA* v. *Commission*, [2000] ECR I-1365, [2000] 4 CMLR 1076; Cases T-191/98 and 212–214/98, *Atlantic Container Line & Ors* v. *Commission* [2003] ECR II-3275, para. 595 (CFI).

associations) could not be in a collective dominant position in respect of the market for players' agents services. It was irrelevant that FIFA was not itself an economic operator buying agents' services as it was the emanation of the national associations and the clubs, which did.[69]

Collective dominance under Article 82 is examined in detail in Chapter 11 (and in respect of the application of the concept in the control of mergers, in Chapter 12).

B. DOMINANT POSITION

(i) What is meant by a 'Dominant Position'?

Whether or not an undertaking holds a 'dominant position' is of central importance to Article 82. Clearly the phrase is not intended only to refer to a complete monopolist (the sole undertaking on a relevant market). It is also intended to encompass undertakings which have a certain degree of market power.[70] The difficulty is to determine what degree of market power is necessary before Article 82 applies.

Perfect competition is rarely encountered outside textbooks; almost all firms have some market power, though most have very little. Accordingly, the relevant question in antitrust cases is not whether market power is present, but whether it is important.[71]

An initial problem for Article 82 is, therefore, to identify with sufficient clarity the point at which an undertaking becomes, and can know it becomes, dominant and so potentially subject to the prohibition. This point is likely to be defined by reference to policy considerations as much as scientific ones. The authorities identify the point on the spectrum of market power at which they wish to be able to intervene. Economists describe the ability of a firm to raise price above the competitive level without attracting new entrants and without losing sales to competitors so rapidly that the price increase is unprofitable and must be rescinded,[72] as substantial (or significant) market power (SMP). In US law, monopoly power for the purposes of section 2 of the Sherman Act has been defined as the power to control prices or to exclude competition.[73] However, this is not the way that 'dominant position' has been conceptualized in EC law.

In the extract below, Hawk suggests that the point at which undertakings are found to become subject to competition rules aimed at controlling the behaviour of firms with market power may, or may not, coincide with an economist's view. He also suggests that there may be some relationship between the degree of market power and what behaviour is held abusive.

---

[69] Case T-193/02, *Laurent Piau v. Commission* [2005] ECR II-209, paras. 112–16.

[70] Although the words 'monopoly' and 'monopolist' are sometimes used as a shorthand to cover both situations.

[71] R. Schmalensee, 'Another Look at Market Power' (1981–2) 95 *Harvard LR* 1789, 1790.

[72] See W. Landes and R. Posner, 'Market Power in Antitrust Cases' (1980–81) 94 *Harvard LR* 937, and see *supra* Chap. 1.

[73] See *Standard Oil Co of New Jersey v. United States*, 221 US 1 (1911); *United States v. E I du Pont de Nemours & Co*, 351 US 377 (1956); *United States v. Grinnell Corp*, 384 US 563 (1966).

> ## B. E. Hawk, *United States, Common Market and International Antitrust: A Comparative Guide* (2nd edn., Aspen Law & Business, 1990), II, 788–9
>
> Economics provides a variety of tools to measure degrees of market power. Market power is the power to raise prices by restricting output without a significant loss of sales—i.e., the power to fix prices or exclude competition. Any firm facing an inelastic demand or downward-sloping demand curve has some market power in an economic sense. But economics does not define—except at the extreme—at what point that market power becomes 'monopoly power'... Thus, economics does not provide the means to resolve the essentially legal question whether the market power of a firm is sufficiently great to constitute a 'dominant position' or 'monopoly power.' Like relevant market definition, 'dominant position' and 'monopoly power' are legal constructs based on policy considerations which suggest where the line should be drawn between acceptable market power and suspect monopoly power. For example, there could be an inverse sliding scale between the degree of power required and the invidiousness of the abusive or monopolizing conduct. Or broad definitions of what constitute abusive conduct might prompt a higher threshold of market power, particularly where broad definitions of abuse capture competitively ambiguous conduct and run the risk of inhibiting desirable competitive conduct (such as price reductions).

The definition of the term 'dominant position' should relate to the adverse consequences which result when an undertaking has market power. The traditional objection to an undertaking with market power is its inefficiency. Allocative inefficiency results from its ability to limit output and increase price, and productive inefficiency is likely to result from the ability to lead a quiet life. These problems will not arise if consumers have an alternative choice of products/services or suppliers. The increase in price or poor quality of the product or service will prompt consumers to look elsewhere. An undertaking should be found to be dominant, therefore, only if its conduct is not constrained by the existence of competitors producing competing products and services so that it is able to raise prices and reduce output.

(ii) The Definition of Dominant Position in the Case-law of the ECJ

Rather than focussing on power over price, the ECJ has defined dominance in terms of an undertaking's 'economic strength' and its ability to act independently on the market.

In *United Brands* the ECJ said that an undertaking would hold a dominant position where it could prevent effective competition being maintained by virtue of its ability to behave independently of the usual competitive constraints facing an entity operating on a market:

> The dominant position referred to in this Article relates to a position of economic strength enjoyed by an undertaking which enables it to prevent effective competition being maintained on the relevant market by giving it the power to behave to an appreciable extent independently of its competitors, customers and ultimately of its consumers.[74]

---

[74] Case 27/76, *United Brands Co and United Brands Continental BV v. Commission* [1978] ECR 207, [1978] 1 CMLR 429, para. 65. See also *Re Continental Can Co Inc* [1972] JO L7/25, [1972] CMLR D11, para. 3 where the Commission described dominance terms of independence and power over price:

'Undertakings are in a dominant position when they have the power to behave independently, which puts them in a position to act without taking into account their competitors, purchasers or suppliers. That is the position when, because of their share of the market, or of their share of the market combined with the availability of technical knowledge, raw materials or capital, they have the power to determine prices or to control

In *Hoffmann-La Roche* in 1979 the ECJ elaborated on this definition. It emphasized that a position of dominance did not preclude some competition and particularly focused on the ability of the undertaking to influence the conditions of competition occurring on the market. The definition of dominance in *Hoffmann-La Roche* has been followed ever since and become settled case-law. The Commission appears to accept that all discussion of what is meant by a dominant position has to start with *United Brands* and *Hoffmann-La Roche*.[75]

Case 85/76, *Hoffmann-La Roche & Co AG* v. *Commission* [1979] ECR 461, [1979] 3 CMLR 211, paras. 38–39

38. The dominant position thus referred to relates to a position of economic strength enjoyed by an undertaking which enables it to prevent effective competition being maintained on the relevant market by affording it the power to behave to an appreciable extent independently of its competitors, its customers and ultimately of its consumers.

39. Such a position does not preclude some competition, which it does where there is a monopoly or quasi-monopoly, but enables the undertaking which profits by it, if not to determine, at least to have an appreciable influence on the conditions under which that competition will develop, and in any case to act largely in disregard of it so long as such conduct does not operate to its detriment.

The definition presupposes a dominant *supplier*. However, it is clear that the dominant position may be on the buying, rather than the selling side. In that case the issue will be one of the independence of the undertaking from its suppliers. *British Airways* v. *Commission*, for example, concerned the position of BA as a dominant buyer of air travel agency services.[76]

The case law on the meaning of a dominant position was summed up by the CFI in *France Télécom*.

Case T-340/03, *France Télécom SA* v. *Commission*, 30 January 2007

Court of First Instance

99 As a preliminary point, it is appropriate to observe that, by virtue of settled case-law, a dominant position exists where the undertaking concerned is in a position of economic strength which

---

production or distribution for a significant part of the products in question. This power does not necessarily have to derive from an absolute domination permitting the undertakings which hold it to eliminate all will on the part of their economic partners, but it is enough that they be strong enough as a whole to ensure to those undertakings an overall independence of behaviour, even if there are differences in intensity in their influence on the different partial markets'. On appeal, Case 6/72, *Europemballage Corp and Continental Can Co Inc* v. *Commission* [1973] ECR 215, [1973] CMLR 199, the ECJ did not expressly comment on the Commission's formulation of dominance, but it was approved by Roemer AG at [1973] ECR 215, 257, [1973] CMLR 199, 209–10 and implicitly by the Court.

75 See Discussion Paper, para. 20. For the way in which the Commission argues on from that starting point, see *infra* 309.

76 Case C-95/04 P, *British Airways* v. *Commission*, 15 March 2007. See Chap. 6, 378 ff on the dominant position issue, and Chap. 7 on the abuse. See also, e.g., *Re Eurofirma* [1973] CMLR D217; Case 298/83, *CICCE* v. *Commission* [1985] ECR 1105, [1986] 1 CMLR 486.

enables it to prevent effective competition being maintained on the relevant market by giving it the power to behave to an appreciable extent independently of its competitors, its customers and, ultimately, consumers (*Michelin* v *Commission*, paragraph 78 above, paragraph 30, and Case T-65/98 *Van den Bergh Foods* v *Commission* [2003] ECR II-4653, paragraph 154). It should be noted at the outset that, in order to establish that a dominant position exists, the Commission does not need to demonstrate that an undertaking's competitors will be foreclosed from the market, even in the longer term.

100 Furthermore, although the importance of market shares may vary from one market to another, very large shares are in themselves, and save in exceptional circumstances, evidence of the existence of a dominant position (*Hoffmann-La Roche* v *Commission*, paragraph 80 above, paragraph 41, and Case T-221/95 *Endemol* v *Commission* [1999] ECR II-1299, paragraph 134). The Court of Justice held in Case C-62/86 *AKZO* v *Commission* [1991] ECR I-3359, paragraph 60, that this was so in the case of a 50% market share.

101 Even the existence of lively competition on a particular market does not rule out the possibility that there is a dominant position on that market, since the predominant feature of such a position is the ability of the undertaking concerned to act without having to take account of this competition in its market strategy and without for that reason suffering detrimental effects from such behaviour (*Hoffmann-La Roche* v *Commission*, paragraph 80 above, paragraph 70; see also, to that effect, Case 27/76 *United Brands* v *Commission* [1978] ECR 207, paragraphs 108 to 129). Thus, the fact that there may be competition on the market is a relevant factor for the purposes of ascertaining whether a dominant position exists, but it is not in itself a decisive factor in that regard.

(iii) Problems with the Definition of Dominant Position

The formulation of dominance in *Hoffmann-La* Roche is problematic. The ECJ test uses a concept of 'independence' which is wider and more nebulous than power over price and, particularly as the independence has to exist only 'to an appreciable extent' and is compatible with continuing competition on the market, it brings inherent uncertainty to the operation of Article 82. Commentators have questioned whether the reference both to the ability of the undertaking to impede effective competition—which means the power to exclude competition—and to behave independently are different tests or part of the same test. Further, it is argued that economic strength does not necessarily imply power over price, and that no successful firm can act 'independently of its consumers'.

V. Korah, *An Introductory Guide to EC Competition Law and Practice* (8th edn., Hart Publishing, 2004), para. 4.3

The power to behave independently sounds like the economists' concept of power over price. A monopolist, unconstrained by competitive pressures, enjoys a discretion in its pricing and other market decisions. The application of competition policy to the conduct of such a firm may protect those with whom it deals.

The concept of 'economic strength . . . which enables a firm to impede effective competition', however, may indicate a different idea: the ability to foreclose: to keep other firms out of the market. Such strategic behaviour may be restrained by the Commission to help a firm's competitors. Such strength does not necessarily imply power over price.

As Professor Korah also points out, the case-law has not been helpful 'in reconciling the two ideas', as we shall see in the subsequent two Chapters. In the following passage two economists argue that the 'act independently' criteria is inherently flawed and cannot distinguish satisfactorily between dominant and non-dominant firms. Note that they refer to the 'cellophane fallacy' problem, discussed in Chapter 1, in identifying the competitive price level.[77]

J. P. Azevedo and M. Walker, 'Dominance: Meaning and Measurement' [2002] *ECLR* 363, 364

Acting independently of consumers and customers

Our first criticism of the definition is that no successful firm anywhere can act to an appreciable extent independently of its consumers. This is because of what economists refer to as the discipline of the demand curve. Firms typically face downward sloping demand curves, indicating that the lower the price of their product, the more of it they sell. Conversely, if a firm raises its price, it will sell less. It is not open to the firm to raise prices and sell the same quantity as before. The demand curve facing a firm constrains its behaviour. If a firm raises its price, it has to accept that it will sell fewer units of its product. This is true of a dominant firm just as much as it is true of a non-dominant firm. One response to this might be to say that what the ECJ really meant was that a dominant firm can profitably raise prices higher than a non-dominant firm. This may well be true (see below), but it is important to note that this possibility is not dependent so much on the behaviour of consumers as on the existence and behaviour of competitors. A firm that faces many competitors will find it harder to raise prices profitably than a firm that faces no, or only weak, competitors. An example of this situation would be a cigarette manufacturer that knows that its consumers will not readily substitute cigarettes for other goods if the price of cigarettes is increased. We can say that it faces a very *inelastic* market demand. However, because it faces strong competition from other cigarette manufactures, this firm will not be able to significantly raise its price without losing sales to a close competitor. It is clear that what constrains the firm in this case is not consumers (the shape of the demand curve) but rather its competitors.

So it appears that trying to define dominance with respect to the ability of a firm to behave to an appreciable extent independently of its consumers will not distinguish adequately between dominant and non-dominant firms.

Acting independently of competitors

We have argued above that it is not economically coherent to think of firms acting independently of consumers to an appreciable extent. The next question is whether it makes sense economically to think of firms acting independently of their competitors. There is a sense in which it does, but here we run into a measurement problem. That is, we think that it may well make sense to think of firms acting independently of their competitors, but that it will be very hard to measure whether this is happening.

Every firm that faces competitors (i.e., all firms apart from true monopolists) is constrained to some extent by those competitors. This is clearly true of firms operating in a competitive market. In these circumstances firms cannot raise their prices above the competitive price level without losing so many sales to their competitors that the price rise is not profitable. Yet this is also true for a dominant firm. This is because a dominant firm will raise prices above the competitive level to the

---

point at which the constraints imposed on the firm by its competitors and its demand curve are binding. So the dominant firm does not act independently of its competitors. Rather, its behaviour is constrained by its competitors.

However, there is clearly an important sense in which the dominant firm has acted to an appreciable extent independently of its competitors: it has raised its price above the competitive price level. So it was not constrained from raising its prices above the competitive price level. This ability to price above the competitive price level strikes us as an important aspect of being dominant. So perhaps one test of a firm's dominance is whether the firm can profitably price above the competitive price level. However, there is a measurement problem here: how can we measure whether a firm has the ability to price above the competitive price level or to act independently of its competitors?

The competitive price level is virtually always impossible to calculate . . . , and of course if it could be routinely calculated then we would not need to worry about whether a firm was dominant. We would instead cut straight to the heart of the matter: was the firm pricing above the competitive price level by a significant amount? Further, we cannot ask the question 'could the firm profitably raise prices above the current price level' as a proxy because the answer to this question should always be 'no', regardless of whether the firm in question is dominant or not. A dominant firm, like a non-dominant firm, will raise its prices up to the point at which the constraints imposed on it by its competitors and demand curve bite and make a further price rise unprofitable.

This measurement issue is related to the *cellophane fallacy* . . . It has a very important implication for the ECJ's definition of dominance: an empirical test for dominance would never find that a dominant firm was acting independently of its competitors in its pricing decisions. Since it would be pricing at the profit maximizing level given the behaviour of its competitors, if its competitors changed their prices, it would change its prices. Hence the pricing policy even of a dominant firm is dependent on the pricing of its competitors.

In many cases this problem is more fundamental than just a measurement problem. In many cases it is not clear what the competitive price level is *as a matter of economic theory*, let alone practical measurement. Economists 'know' that the competitive price level is margin cost, but this statement begs more questions than its answers. Which margin cost—short-run/long-run? Whose marginal cost-the most efficient firm's or the least efficient firm's? What about in the case of large fixed costs (so that marginal cost will not cover the fixed costs except in the long-run)? How should fixed costs be allocated when they are incurred jointly by two or more products?

We have concentrated so far on price as being the important dimension of competition. This is clearly not always the case: in some markets the main focus of competition is in other dimensions, such as quality, service and innovation. However, our remarks above are equally applicable to markets of this type. Firms will act in such a way that they do face constraints from competitors in each of the dimensions of competition. With price that means raising prices up to the point a which further price rises would not be profitable. With quality it might be lowering quality (and hence costs), but not price up to the point at which further reductions in quality would not be profitable. With innovation it might be slowing the pace of innovation (and hence R&D expenditures) as far as it consistent with maintaining long run profits.

The authors of the above suggest that a better test would be 'the ability to restrict output substantially in the market-place'. This, they argue, would mean that the undertaking must have power over price. Also, the definition would be consistent with most of the standard factors usually considered relevant in the appraisal of dominance;[78] restricting output is the key to

---

[78] The market share of the leading firms, variability of market shares, existence of substitute products, barriers to entry, barriers to expansion, existence of spare capacity, and the nature of competitive interaction in the market: see further the discussion *infra* Chap. 6, 395 ff.

most anti-competitive behaviour; and concentrating on output limitation enables cases where the observation of prices and costs cannot be achieved to be dealt with more easily.[79]

Furthermore, the *Hoffmann-La Roche* definition rather strangely presents the prevention of effective competition as flowing from the independence. The implications of this are considered in the following passage.

T. Eilsmansberger, 'Dominance—The Lost Child? How the Effects-Based Rules Could and Should Change Dominance Analysis' (2006) 2 *European Law Journal* 15, 16

This formula possesses two remarkable elements. The first is that it refers to the two fundamental types of abuses pursued under Article 82 . . . Dominance is defined as the ability to exploit ("behave independently of competitors, customers and consumers") on the one hand and to exclude or hinder ("prevent effective competition") on the other. Dominance and abuse are presented as closely, if not intrinsically, linked concepts. This is entirely convincing.

The second element of this definition is much less persuasive. Through the words "by giving it the power", the Court in this passage establishes a connection between the potential to exclude and the ability to exploit; the former is assumed to result from the latter. The unfortunate consequence of this was that in exclusion cases, too, dominance has since then been regularly assessed with regard to the firm's potential to behave independently, ie to raise prices and reduce output. Accordingly, large market shares which the ECJ originally (and rightly) considered to be meaningful indicator's of a firm's capacity to behave independently . . . were treated as crucial evidence of a firm's capacity to exclude as well.

We discuss in Chapter 6 the way in which dominance is actually identified in EC law, and so come back to the matter of the 'large market shares' to which that Eilsmansberger refers.

In the Discussion Paper the Commission started its consideration of dominance with the *United Brands/Hoffmann-La Roche* definition. It then tried to analyse this into a rational formula as consisting of three elements, two of which are closely linked.

DG Competition discussion paper on the application of Article 82 of the Treaty to exclusionary abuses, Brussels, December 2005

21. This definition of dominance consists of three elements, two of which are closely linked: (a) there must be a position of economic strength on a market which (b) enables the undertaking(s) in question to prevent effective competition being maintained on that market by (c) affording it the power to behave independently to an appreciable extent.

22. The first element implies that dominance exists in relation to a market. It cannot exist in the abstract . . . It also implies that an undertaking either on its own or together with other undertakings must hold a leading position on that market compared to its rivals.

---

[79] Azevedo and Walker cite as an example the licensing of sports rights: for the action by the Commission over the licensing of Premier League football to BSkyB see *infra* Chap. 13, 1128 ff.

> 23. The second and third elements concern the link between the position of economic strength held by the undertaking concerned and the competitive process, i.e. the way in which the undertaking and other players act and inter-act on the market. Dominance is the ability to prevent effective competition being maintained on the market and to act to an appreciable extent independently of other players. The notion of independence, which is the special feature of dominance . . . , is related to the level of competitive constraint facing the undertaking(s) in question. For dominance to exist the undertaking(s) concerned must not be subject to effective competitive constraints. In other words, it thus must have substantial market power.
>
> 24. Market power is the power to influence market prices, output, innovation, the variety or quality of goods and services, or other parameters of competition on the market for a significant period of time. In this paper, the expression "increase prices" is often used as shorthand for the various ways these parameters of competition can be influenced to the harm of consumers. An undertaking that is capable of substantially increasing prices above the competitive level for a significant period of time holds substantial market power and possesses the requisite ability to act to an appreciable extent independently of competitors, customers and consumers. Unlike undertakings in a market characterised by effective competitive constraints is able to price above the competitive level. It can do so by reducing its own output or by causing rivals to reduce their output. The foreclosure of competitors may therefore allow the dominant company to further raise price or keep prices high.

It will be noted that in paragraph 22 the Commission introduced the notion of a 'leading position', but by the end of paragraph 23 it has reasoned that independence is related to the level of competitive constraint, dominance means the undertaking is not subject to effective competitive constraint and so 'in other words' the undertaking must have substantial market power. So, abracadabra, the *Hoffmann-La Roche* definition says that dominance equates with SMP.[80] The Commission then went on to explain SMP in the usual way.[81]

(iv) Effects-based Analysis and the Concept of Dominance

We explained above how the debate about the reform, or 'modernization', of Article 82 centres on the widely accepted idea that an effects-based analysis of Article 82 concerned only with

---

[80] In the published, extended version of a speech given in New York in September 2005, the Competition Commissioner said 'As an economist, it is natural for me to identify dominance with substantial market power': Neelie Kroes, 'Tackling Exclusionary Practices to Avoid Exploitation of Market Power: Some Preliminary Thoughts on on the Policy Review of Article 82' in 2005 *Fordham Corp. L. Inst.* (B. Hawk, ed. 2006), 381, 384.

[81] In the electronic communications sector the Commission had already equated dominance with significant market power. The Commission Guidelines on market analysis and the assessment of significant market power under the Community regulatory framework for electronic communications networks and services ([1997] OJ C165/6) refers to markets which are not effectively competitive as a result of which undertakings are in a position 'equivalent to dominance within the meaning of the EC Treaty'. It then continues: The notion of dominance has been defined in the case-law of the Court of Justice as a position of economic strength affording an undertaking the power to behave to an appreciable extent independently of its competitors, customers and ultimately consumers. Therefore, under the new regulatory framework . . . the Commission and the NRAs [national regulatory authorities] will rely on competition law principles and methodologies to define the markets to be regulated *ex-ante* and to assess whether undertakings have significant market power ('SMP') on those markets. (para. 5). However, para. 30 says designating an undertaking as having SMP for the purposes of *ex-ante* regulation does not automatically imply that it is also dominant for the purposes of Article 82 or similar national provisions. It has been suggested that this rider was added to prevent NRAs from applying Article 82 after defining markets too narrowly. See G. Monti, 'The Concept of Dominance in Article 82' (2006) 2 *European Competition Journal* 31, 33 and L. Garzantini, *Telecommunications, Broadcasting and the Internet* (2nd. edn., Sweet & Maxwell, 2003), 541.

consumer welfare should be adopted. It can be argued from this that if a rigorous economic approach is taken to determining whether the conduct of an undertaking harms consumers the preliminary question of whether an undertaking is in a dominant position need not be separately answered. This approach was urged by a report prepared for the Commission, during the internal review which led to the Discussion Paper, by the Economic Advisory Group on Competition Policy (EAGCP).[82] It will be noted that this was not a suggestion of 'abuse, *ergo* dominance' but a plea for an *integrated* examination of the issues as a whole.[83]

REPORT OF THE EAGCP, 'An Economic Approach to Article 82, Brussels, 14–15 July 2005, available at http://ec.europa.eu/comm/competition/publications/studies/eagcp_july_21_05.pdf

In proposing to reduce the role of separate assessments of dominance and to integrate the substantive assessment of dominance with the procedure for establishing competitive harm itself, we depart from the tradition of case law concerning Art. 82 of the Treaty, but *not*, we believe, from the legal norm itself. Art. 82 of the Treaty is concerned not just with dominance as such, but with abuses of dominance. The case law tradition of having separate assessments of dominance and of abusiveness of behaviour simplifies procedures, but this simplification involves a loss of precision in the implementation of the legal norm. The structural indicators which traditionally serve as proxies for "dominance" provide an appropriate measure of power in some markets, but not in others. In a market in which these indicators do not properly measure the firm's ability to impose abusive behaviour on others, the competition authority's intervention under traditional modes of procedure is likely to be inappropriate, too harsh in some cases and too lenient in others. Given that the Treaty itself does not provide a separate definition of dominance, let alone call for any of the traditionally used indicators as such, it seems more appropriate to have the implementation of the Treaty itself focus on the abuses and to treat the assessment of dominance in this context.

Lawyers are likely to have rather more trouble than economists with the inconvenient fact that for over thirty years, since *Continental Can* in 1974,[84] the Community Courts have said that, in applying Article 82, first dominance must be established and then the conduct under review judged abusive or not. However, commentators also disagreed with EAGCP's suggestion for other reasons, particularly arguing that it *is* possible for anti-competitive effects to be caused by the conduct of non-dominant undertakings,[85] that a dominance 'screen' is desirable for administrative reasons to avoid Type 1 'false positive errors', and that a requirement of a preliminary finding of dominance frees the vast majority of undertakings from the need to worry about accusations of abuse.[86]

---

[82] For EAGCP, see Chap. 2.

[83] J. Vickers, 'Market Power in Competition Cases' (2006) 2 *Competition Law Journal* 3, 11.

[84] See Case 6/72, *Europemballage Corp and Continental Can Co Inc v. Commission* [1973] ECR 215, [1973] CMLR 199.

[85] See, e.g. G. Monti, 'The Concept of Dominance in Article 82' (2006) 2 *European Competition Journal* 31, 45–6, discussing in particular predatory pricing.

[86] J. Vickers, 'Market Power in Competition Cases' (2006) 2 *Competition Law Journal* 3, 11–12; G. J. Werden, 'Competition Policy on Exclusionary Conduct: Towards an Effects-based Analysis' (2006) 2 *European Competition Journal* 53, 55–7.

(v) Assessing Dominance

It was explained in Chapter 1 that market power can be measured directly or indirectly. In EC law 'dominance' is measured by the indirect method, by defining the market and then assessing the undertaking's power on that market. In *Continental Can* the ECJ stated that 'the definition of the relevant market is of essential significance'[87] and the Community Courts have stressed this consistently ever since. Commission decisions applying Article 82 will be quashed if the market is not properly defined.[88]

The relevant market has three aspects, product (or service), geographic, and, in some cases, temporal, although the temporal aspect is usually seen as part of the product dimension.[89] Once the market is defined an analysis must be made of the competitive constraints which the allegedly dominant undertaking faces on the market. The Commission's practice, endorsed by the Community Courts, is to look at the undertaking's market share and then at other factors which may indicate whether it is dominant.

In some cases it may be difficult to separate these two stages in the process.[90] The two issues may be intertwined. Further to complicate matters, the question whether an undertaking is dominant may be intertwined with the issue of the allegedly abusive conduct.[91]

In Chapter 1 we described the principles of market definition generally and in Chapter 6 we set out how the Community authorities have defined the market and assessed market power in Article 82 cases. In many of the cases the findings of both the Court and the Commission have been controversial. The authorities have been criticized for defining markets too narrowly and for being too ready to find that an undertaking is dominant on a particular market, usually because they have placed too much reliance on market shares and/or have not taken a sufficiently rigorous view of what amounts to a barrier to entry. This approach, coupled with the wide interpretation that has been adopted in relation to the term 'abuse',[92] means that the EC competition authorities have played an interventionist, regulatory role. If a more stringent approach was taken to identifying abusive conduct, easy findings of dominance would not be so significant.

The concept of a 'dominant position' is also a term employed within the new Merger Regulation[93] as it was under the old one.[94] In applying the old Regulation the Commission relied on the definition of dominance set out in Article 82 cases.[95] The concept was interpreted in the same way for the purposes of both Article 82 and the Merger Regulation. In the draft proposal for the new Merger Regulation it was proposed to decouple the definition of dominance under

---

[87] Case 6/72, *Europemballage Corp and Continental Can Co Inc v. Commission* [1973] ECR 215, [1973] CMLR 199, para. 42.

[88] In Case 6/72, *Europemballage Corp and Continental Can Co Inc v. Commission* [1973] ECR 215, [1973] CMLR 199, the ECJ quashed the Commission's decision on account of its failure to define adequately the market from the supply side.

[89] See *infra* Chap. 6.

[90] See *ibid.*

[91] See *ibid.* This is why EAGCP, as noted above, proposed integrating the assessment of dominance with the assessment of abuse.

[92] See *infra* Chaps. 6 and 7.

[93] Council Reg. 139/2004 [2004] OJ L24/1. See *infra* Chap. 12.

[94] Council Reg. 4046/89 [1989] OJ L395/1, as amended by Council Reg. 1310/97 [1997] OJ L180/1. See *infra* Chap. 12.

[95] See Chap. 12 *infra*.

the Regulation from that employed for the purposes of Article 82[96] but ultimately that was not done.[97] It appears, therefore, that the concept remains the same under both provisions. It is important to note, however, that the concept is 'necessarily applied from two different perspectives'.[98] In the context of Article 82 a retrospective analysis is necessary (did the undertaking have a dominant position and did it abuse that position?). In contrast, a prospective analysis is usually necessary for the purposes of merger control (will this concentration lead to the creation or strengthening of a dominant position?).[99]

(vi) Super-dominance

It is possible that a concept of 'super-dominance' exists.[100] This may mean that there is an important relationship between the degree of market power and the types of behaviour characterized as abusive. A wider spectrum of conduct may be found to be abusive the closer the undertaking's position approximates to that of a complete monopolist.[101]

C. A DOMINANT POSITION WITHIN A SUBSTANTIAL PART OF THE COMMON MARKET

(i) Purpose of the Requirement

The dominant position of the undertaking must be held within the common market or within a substantial part of it. The purpose of this requirement is to exclude from the Article's scope purely localized monopoly situations in which there is no Community interest. Together with the necessity that the abuse of a dominant position has an effect on trade between Member States,[102] the requirement determines the limit of the Community jurisdiction.

(ii) Meaning of a Substantial Part of the Common Market

A 'substantial part' does not simply mean substantial in geographic terms. It is not a matter of counting hectares. In *Suiker Unie* the ECJ stated that:

[f]or the purpose of determining whether a specific territory is large enough to amount to a 'substantial part of the common market' within the meaning of Article [82] of the Treaty the pattern

---

[96] Commission proposal for a Council Regulation on the control of concentrations between undertakings, [2003] OJ C20/4, Art. 2(2) and recitals 55–7.

[97] For the reasons for this, see *infra* Chap. 12.

[98] J. Faull and A. Nikpay (eds.), *The EC Law of Competition* (2nd edn., Oxford University Press, 2007), para. 4.40.

[99] It is only very occasionally that the Commission has had to assess the compatibility with the merger rules of a concentration which has already been completed: see *infra* Chap. 12. The SSNIP test, employed in the determination of the relevant market, is more likely to be accurate where a prospective analysis is carried out than when a retrospective analysis is carried out. See the discussion of the SSNIP test and the *Cellophane* fallacy, *supra* Chap. 1.

[100] See, e.g., *1998 Football World Cup* [2000] OJ L5/55, [2000] 4 CMLR 963, para. 86; Cases C-395 and 396/96 P, *Compagnie Maritime Belge Transports SA v. Commission* [2000] ECR I–1365, [2000] 4 CMLR 1076, paras. 113–21, and Opinion of Fennelly AG, para. 136; *NDC Health/IMS Health: Interim Measures* [2002] OJ L59/18, [2002] 4 CMLR 111, para. 58; *Deutsche Post AG* [2001] OJ L331/40, [2002] 4 CMLR 598, paras. 103 and 124.

[101] Super-dominance is discussed in greater detail in Chaps. 6 and 7 *infra*.

[102] See *infra* 339 ff.

and volume of the production and consumption of the said product as well as the habits and economic opportunities of vendors and purchasers must be considered.[103]

(iii) Relevance of Volume of Production

In *Suiker Unie* the ECJ compared the volume of sugar production in Belgium, Luxembourg, and southern Germany to that of Community production overall. It held that each of those markets was a substantial part of the common market. The ECJ has never specified whether there is a particular percentage of the Community market which could automatically be said to satisfy the 'substantial' criterion. However, Advocate General Warner, in his Opinion in the *ABG Oil* case,[104] considered that the Dutch petrol market, which was approximately 4.6 per cent of the overall Community market, was substantial. He stated that:

[t]here is . . . in my opinion, in this kind of field, a danger in focusing attention exclusively on percentages. The opposite of 'substantial' is 'negligible', and what may seem negligible when looked at in the terms of a percentage may seem otherwise when looked at in absolute terms. The population of Luxembourg is, I believe, about 0.23 per cent of the population of the whole Community. I would however shrink from saying that one who had a monopoly, or near monopoly, of the Luxembourg market for a particular product was exempt from the application of Article [82].[105]

(iv) A Member State is likely to be a Substantial Part of the Common Market

In a number of cases individual Member States have been held to be a 'substantial part'[106] of the common market as have parts of Member States.[107] As the EU is enlarged the concept of what is a 'substantial part' of it may alter, with previously substantial parts becoming more insignificant so that older cases on this point may no longer be a reliable guide. It is difficult to imagine, however, that a single Member State would be held not to constitute a substantial part of the common market even in an EU of twenty-seven or more Member States. It would be politically insensitive. This attitude is reflected in the opinion of Advocate General Warner set out above (although at the time there were only nine Member States). As the process of European integration proceeds, however, the delineation of geographic markets is likely to become broader and it will become rarer for a position of dominance to be found to exist in a single Member State other than in the case of statutory monopoly.

---

[103] Cases 40–8, 50, 54–6, 111, 113, and 114/73, *Coöperatieve Vereniging 'Suiker Unie' UA v. Commission* [1975] ECR 1663, [1976] 1 CMLR 295, para. 371.

[104] Case 77/77, *Benzine en Petroleum Handelsmaatschappij BV v. Commission* [1978] ECR 1513, [1978] 3 CMLR 174.

[105] [1978] ECR 1513, 1537, [1978] 3 CMLR 174, 184. The ECJ held that the undertaking's conduct could not constitute an abuse and did not address the dominance issue: see further Chaps. 6 and 7.

[106] The UK was held to be a substantial part of the common market in Case 226/84, *British Leyland plc v. Commission* [1986] ECR 3263, [1987] 1 CMLR 185, as was Belgium in Case 127/73, *Belgische Radio en Televisie and Société belge des auteurs, compositeurs et editeurs v. SV SABAM and NV Fonior* [1974] ECR 313, [1974] 2 CMLR 238 and Case 26/75, *General Motors Continental NV v. Commission* [1975] ECR 1367, [1976] 1 CMLR 95.

[107] e.g., the south-east of England in Case 22/78, *Hugin Kassaregister AB and Hugin Cash Registers Ltd v. Commission* [1979] ECR 1869, [1979] 3 CMLR 345. A number of local markets in a Member State may be aggregated together to form a 'substantial part', as in Case C–323/93, *Société Civile Agricole du Centre d'Insémination de la Crespelle v. Coopérative d'Elevage et d'Insemination Artificielle du Département de la Mayenne* [1994] ECR I-5077, where there was a series of local statutory monopolies in bovine insemination services which together covered the whole of France. See also Case 30/87, *Bodson v. Pompes Funèbres des Régions Libérées* [1988] ECR 2479 [1989] 4 CMLR 984.

(v) Transport Cases

What constitutes a 'substantial part' of the common market may depend on the nature of the market in issue. For example, there have been a number of transport cases in which very small areas have been found to be substantial. In both *Sealink/B&I Holyhead: Interim Measures*[108] and *Sea Containers Ltd v. Stena Sealink Ports*[109] Holyhead Harbour was held to be a substantial part of the common market. In the former case the Commission stated:

40. ... The port of Holyhead constitutes a substantial part of the Common Market because it is a port providing one of the main links between two member-States; more especially, it provides the direct link between Great Britain and the capital city of Ireland. It should also be noted that this is, at least for passengers and cars, the most popular ferry route between Ireland and Great Britain.

In *Port of Roscoff*[110] the Commission emphasized the importance that might be played by the catchment area served by the port.

58. The market for the supply of port services does not exist in isolation. If there was no demand from consumers for transport services, there would be no demand for port services from ferry operators. The market for transport services between Ireland and Brittany must therefore be taken into account. The port services in Brittany are essential for the operation of ferry services between a Member State, Ireland, to which can be added part of another Member State, Northern Ireland (around five million inhabitants in total), and an important region of another Member State, Brittany (around three million inhabitants). These three regions form a substantial part of the common market. For Ireland, also, the port of Roscoff is an important entry point to the continent and the rest of the Community. It is already used by 25 per cent of ferry passengers between Ireland and France each year.

In *Merci Convenzionali* the Court looked to the volume of traffic handled by the port of Genoa. After stressing its importance in relation to the overall volume of imports and exports by sea to and from Italy the Court held that the market 'may be regarded as constituting a substantial part of the common market'.[111] The Commission has also found the activities at the port of Rødby[112] and various airports to involve substantial parts of the common market.[113]

The transport cases suggest, therefore, that, once it has been established that the routes or traffic concerned are significant in anything other than a purely domestic context, the 'substantial part' criterion will be satisfied.[114] Indeed, the full application of Article 82 to maritime and air transport would be impossible in the absence of such an interpretation.

---

[108] [1992] 5 CMLR 255, Commission's, *XXIInd Annual Report on Competition Policy* (Commission, 1992), point 219.

[109] [1994] OJ L15/8, [1995] 4 CMLR 84.

[110] Reported as *Irish Continental Group v. CCI Morlaix* [1995] 5 CMLR 177.

[111] Case C-179/90, *Merci Convenzionali Porto di Genova SpA v. Siderurgica Gabrielli SpA* [1991] ECR I-5889, [1994] 4 CMLR 422, para. 15; see also Case C-266/96, *Corsica Ferries France SA v. Gruppo Antichi Ormeggiatori del Porto di Genova Coop arl* [1998] ECR I-3949, [1998] 5 CMLR 402, para. 38.

[112] *Port of Rødby* [1994] OJ L55/52, [1994] 5 CMLR 457.

[113] e.g., *FAG-Flughafen Frankfurt/Main AG* [1998] OJ L72/30, [1998] 4 CMLR 779, *Alpha Flight Services/Aéroports de Paris* [1998] OJ L230/10, [1998] 5 CMLR 611; *Portugese Airports* [1999] OJ L69/31, on appeal Case C-163/99, *Portugal v. Commission* [2001] ECR I-2613, [2002] 2 CMLR 1319; *Ilmailulaitos/Luftfartsverket* [1999] OJ L69/24, [1999] 5 CMLR 90; *Spanish Airports* [2000] OJ L208/36, [2000] 5 CMLR 967.

[114] See Case 66/86, *Ahmed Saeed Flugreisen and Silver Line Reisebüro GmbH v. Zentrale zur Bekämpfung unlauteren Wettbewerbs eV* [1989] ECR 803, [1990] 4 CMLR 102; *British Midland v. Aer Lingus* [1992] OJ L96/34, [1993] 4 CMLR 596.

D. THE MEANING OF ABUSE

(i) Introduction

It has already been pointed out that Article 82 does not forbid the holding of a dominant position *per se* but only an abuse of it. The meaning of 'abuse' is, therefore, of vital importance. Although the term is not defined, Article 82 itself sets out an illustrative list of examples.[115]

(ii) Exploitative and Exclusionary (Anti-competitive) Abuses

The obvious objection to an undertaking with market power is its ability to 'exploit' its position in a way which would be impossible for an undertaking operating on a competitive market.[116] It is clearly the purpose of Article 82 to prevent such conduct as the provision refers specifically to ways in which market power may be exploited (for example, by prohibiting, *inter alia*, the dominant undertaking's imposition of unfair prices (Article 82(a)) and limiting production 'to the prejudice of consumers' (Article 82 (b)). It was questioned initially whether or not Article 82 went any further than this. In particular, the text of Article 82 in some language versions suggested that the Article was intended to forbid *only* the *exploitation* and *use of* the dominant position in certain ways. For example the French and German texts state that there should be an 'abusive exploitation'.[117]

Relying partly on the textual support, some commentators in the early days of EC competition law argued that Article 82 should be interpreted to catch only exploitative behaviour which harms consumers directly and should not prohibit conduct which has *structural* effects by excluding or disadvantaging other *competitors*.[118]

The Commission, however, considered that Article 82 *could* be applied to prohibit conduct affecting the structure of the market.[119] In conformity with this view in 1972 it issued its decision in *Continental Can*, finding that an undertaking which had merged with another had committed an abuse of a dominant position.[120] In the subsequent appeal the ECJ confirmed this broad view of what may constitute an abuse for the purposes of Article 82.[121]

Case 6/72, *Europemballage Corp and Continental Can Co Inc* v. *Commission* [1973] ECR 215, [1973] CMLR 199

Continental Can Co Inc was an American company which manufactured metal packaging. It acquired an 85.8 per cent share in a German metal can manufacturer, SLW. It then set about

---

[115] See *supra* 295.

[116] See *supra* 294.

[117] '... d'exploiter de façon abusive' in French, '*mißbräuchliche Ausnutzung*' in German.

[118] In particular, René Joliet, later a judge at the ECJ, argued that the prohibition of conduct because of its structural effects would be tantamount to the prohibition of the dominant position itself, which was not the purpose of Article 82, see R. Joliet, *Monopolization and Abuse of Dominant Position* (Nijhoff, 1970).

[119] *Le Problème de la Concentration dans le Marché Commun*, Etudes CEE, Série Concurrence No. 3, 1966, particularly paras. 25–7.

[120] *Re Continental Can Co Inc* [1972] OJ L7/25, [1972] CMLR D11. The Treaty of Rome contains no provisions which expressly enable the Commission to exercise merger control; for a full discussion of the current position in respect of EC merger control, see *infra* Chap. 12.

[121] Case 6/72, *Europemballage Corp and Continental Can Co Inc* v. *Commission* [1973] ECR 215, [1973] CMLR 199.

forming under Belgian law a wholly owned subsidiary, Europemballage, through which it planned to acquire a controlling interest in various other European can manufacturers. Only one of these transactions finally proceeded, the acquisition of a Dutch company, TDV. The Commission adopted a decision[122] holding that this was contrary to Article 82 on the grounds that through SLW Continental Can held a dominant position in a substantial part of the Common Market in the markets for light packaging for preserved meat, fish and crustacea and for metal caps for glass jars, and that by Europemballage's purchase of a majority shareholding in TDV Continental Can had abused this dominant position by practically eliminating competition in the relevant market. On appeal the Court of Justice annulled the decision on the grounds that the Commission had wrongly defined the relevant market because it had failed properly to take into account supply side substitutability.[123] Nevertheless, and contrary to the Opinion of Advocate General Roemer, the Court held that where there *was* a dominant position it was possible for a merger to amount to an abuse within Article 82.

Court of Justice

19. The applicants maintain that the Commission by its decision, based on an erroneous interpretation of Article [82] of the [EC] Treaty, is trying to introduce a control of mergers of under-takings, thus exceeding its powers. Such an attempt runs contrary to the intention of the authors of the Treaty, which is clearly seen not only from a literal interpretation of Article [82], but also from a comparison of the [EC] Treaty and the national legal provisions of the Member States. The exam-ples given in Article [82] of abuse of a dominant position confirm this conclusion, for they show that the Treaty refers only to practices which have effects on the market and are to the detriment of consumers or trade partners. Further, Article [82] reveals that the use of economic power linked with a dominant position can be regarded as an abuse of this position only if it constitutes the means through which the abuse is effected. But structural measures of undertakings—such as strengthening a dominant position by way of merger—do not amount to abuse of this position within the meaning of Article [82] of the Treaty. The decision contested is, therefore, said to be void as lacking the required legal basis.

20. Article [82] (1) of the Treaty says 'Any abuse by one or more undertakings of a dominant position within the common market or in a substantial part of it shall be prohibited as incompatible with the common market in so far as it may affect trade between Member States'. The question is whether the word 'abuse' in Article [82] refers only to practices of undertakings which may directly affect the market and are detrimental to production or sales, to purchasers or consumers, or whether this word refers also to changes in the structure of an undertaking, which lead to compe-tition being seriously disturbed in a substantial part of the Common Market.

21. The distinction between measures which concern the structure of the undertaking and practices which affect the market cannot be decisive, for any structural measure may influence market conditions, if it increases the size and the economic power of the undertaking.

22. In order to answer this question, one has to go back to the spirit, general scheme and wording of Article [82], as well as to the system and objectives of the Treaty. These problems thus cannot be solved by comparing this Article with certain provisions of the ECSC Treaty.

23. Article [82] is part of the chapter devoted to the common rules on the Community's policy in the field of competition. This policy is based on Article [3(1)(g)] of the Treaty according to which the Community's activity shall include the institution of a system ensuring that competition in the Common Market is not distorted. The applicants' argument that this provision merely contains a general programme devoid of legal effect, ignores the fact that Article 3 considers the pursuit of

[122] *Re Continental Can Co Inc* [1972] OJ L7/25, [1972] CMLR D11.
[123] See *infra* Chap. 6.

the objectives which it lays down to be indispensable for the achievement of the Community's tasks. As regards in particular the aim mentioned in [3(1)(g)], the Treaty in several provisions contains more detailed regulations for the interpretation of which this aim is decisive.

24. But if Article [3(1)(g)] provides for the institution of a system ensuring that competition in the Common Market is not distorted, then it requires a fortiori that competition must not be eliminated. This requirement is so essential that without it numerous provisions of the Treaty would be pointless. Moreover, it corresponds to the precept of Article 2 of the Treaty according to which one of the tasks of the Community is 'to promote throughout the Community a harmonious development of economic activities'. Thus the restraints on competition which the Treaty allows under certain conditions because of the need to harmonize the various objectives of the Treaty, are limited by the requirements of Articles 2 and 3. Going beyond this limit involves the risk that the weakening of competition would conflict with the aims of the Common Market.

25. With a view to safeguarding the principles and attaining the objectives set out in Articles 2 and 3 of the Treaty, Articles [81] to [86] have laid down general rules applicable to undertakings. Article [81] concerns agreements between undertakings, decisions of associations of undertakings and concerted practices, while Article [82] concerns unilateral activity of one or more undertakings. Articles [81] and [82] seek to achieve the same aim on different levels, *viz.* the maintenance of effective competition within the Common Market. The restraint of competition which is prohibited if it is the result of behaviour falling under Article [81], cannot become permissible by the fact that such behaviour succeeds under the influence of a dominant undertaking and results in the merger of the undertakings concerned. In the absence of explicit provisions one cannot assume that the Treaty, which prohibits in Article [81] certain decisions of ordinary associations of undertakings restricting competition without eliminating it, permits in Article [82] that undertakings, after merging into an organic unity, should reach such a dominant position that any serious chance of competition is practically rendered impossible. Such a diverse legal treatment would make a breach in the entire competition law which could jeopardize the proper functioning of the Common Market. If, in order to avoid the prohibitions in Article [81], it sufficed to establish such close connections between the undertakings that they escaped the prohibition of Article [81] without coming within the scope of that of Article [82], then, in contradiction to the basic principles of the Common Market, the partitioning of a substantial part of this market would be allowed. The endeavour of the authors of the Treaty to maintain in the market real or potential competition even in cases in which restraints on competition are permitted, was explicitly laid down in Article [81(3)(b)] of the Treaty. Article [82] does not contain the same explicit provisions, but this can be explained by the fact that the system fixed there for dominant positions, unlike Article [81(3)], does not recognize any exemption from the prohibition. With such a system the obligation to observe the basic objectives of the Treaty, in particular that of Article [3(1)(g)], results from the obligatory force of these objectives. In any case Articles [81] and [82] cannot be interpreted in such a way that they contradict each other, because they serve to achieve the same aim.

26. It is in the light of these considerations that the condition imposed by Article [82] is to be interpreted whereby in order to come within the prohibition a dominant position must have been abused. The provision states a certain number of abusive practices which it prohibits. The list merely gives examples, not an exhaustive enumeration of the sort of abuses of a dominant position prohibited by the Treaty. As may further be seen from letters (c) and (d) of Article [82] (2), the provision is not only aimed at practices which may cause damage to consumers directly, but also at those which are detrimental to them through their impact on an effective competition structure, such as is mentioned in Article [3(1)(g)] of the Treaty. Abuse may therefore occur if an undertaking in a dominant position strengthens such position in such a way that the degree of dominance reached substantially fetters competition, i.e., that only undertakings remain in the market whose behaviour depends on the dominant one.

27. Such being the meaning and the scope of Article [82] of the [EC] Treaty, the question of the link of causality raised by the applicants which in their opinion has to exist between the dominant position and its abuse, is of no consequence, for the strengthening of the position of an undertaking may be an abuse and prohibited under Article [82] of the Treaty, regardless of the means and procedure by which it is achieved, if it has the effects mentioned above.

The judgment in *Continental Can* is a seminal one for EC competition law. First, it clarified that Article 82 did not set out an exhaustive list of prohibited conduct and, on the contrary, it could prohibit a dominant undertaking from merging with another. The finding that the provision might prohibit mergers was crucial to the Commission since it had no direct means of controlling mergers until 1990.[124]

Secondly, the ECJ established that the conduct was prohibited irrespective of the fact that the dominant undertaking had not exploited, or otherwise used, its market power in concluding the merger transaction. Thus anti-competitive conduct which excludes competitors, strengthens the dominant position and weakens competition on the market *is* within the prohibition. The ECJ held that the object of Article 82 is not just to directly protect consumers from the dominant undertaking's exploitation of its market power, but to protect the competitive process itself. Conduct is prohibited if it threatens to weaken further the competitive structure of the market. In this case the ECJ accepted that a dominant undertaking could strengthen its position and eliminate competition by taking over its rival.[125] Nevertheless, it should be noted that in paragraph 26 of the judgment the ECJ is concerned with the impact on the competitive structure because of the (indirect) detriment to consumers.

Thirdly, the *way* in which it interpreted Article 82 is of both interest and importance. In determining the scope of the rule the Court looked to the basic objectives of the Community and construed Article 82 as a specific application of Article 3(1)(g). This 'teleological' reasoning was an early indication of how the Treaty and other Community rules, particularly the competition rules, would be interpreted in the future.[126] The Court has frequently referred to the broad Treaty aims and objectives. For example in *Commercial Solvents* the ECJ held that:

[t]he prohibitions of Articles [81] and [82] must in fact be interpreted and applied in the light of Article [3(1)(g)] of the Treaty, which provides that the activities of the Community shall include the institution of a system ensuring that competition in the Common Market is not distorted, and Article 2 of the Treaty, which gives the Community the task of promoting 'throughout the Community harmonious development of economic activities'. By prohibiting the abuse of a dominant position within the market in so far as it may affect trade between Member States, Article [82] therefore covers abuse which may directly prejudice consumers as well as abuse which indirectly prejudices them by impairing the effective competitive structure as envisaged by Article [3(1)(g)] of the Treaty.[127]

---

[124] See *infra* Chap. 12.

[125] On the facts, however, the ECJ quashed the Commission's decision because it had failed adequately to define the market and, consequently, to show that the undertaking was dominant.

[126] See *supra* Chap. 2. For another striking example in the competition field, see the interpretation of 'dominant position' in Article 2 of the Merger Reg. Council Reg. 4064/89 [1989] OJ L395/1, as amended by Council Reg. 1310/97 [1997] OJ L180/1, to encompass a collective dominant position in Cases C-68/94 and C-30/95, *France v. Commission* [1998] ECR I-1375, [1998] 4 CMLR 829, and Case T-102/96 *Gencor v. Commission* [2000] ECR II-753 [1999] 4 CMLR 971.

[127] Cases 6 and 7/73, *Istituto Chemioterapico Italiano SpA and Commercial Solvents Corp v. Commission* [1974] ECR 223, [1974] 1 CMLR 309, para. 32.

Since *Continental Can* the Commission and the Court have confirmed on numerous occasions that Article 82 applies both to exploitative and to exclusionary behaviour. In *Hoffmann La-Roche* the ECJ gave a description of the concept of an abuse which has been the foundation of the jurisprudence ever since.

Case 85/76, *Hoffmann-La Roche & Co AG* v. *Commission* [1979] ECR 461, [1979] 3 CMLR 211, para. 91

For the purpose of rejecting the finding that there has been an abuse of a dominant position the interpretation suggested by the applicant that an abuse implies that the use of the economic power bestowed by a dominant position is the means whereby the abuse has been brought about cannot be accepted. The concept of abuse is an objective concept relating to the behaviour of an undertaking in a dominant position which is such as to influence the structure of a market where, as a result of the very presence of the undertaking in question, the degree of competition is weakened and which, through recourse to methods different from those which condition normal competition in products or services on the basis of the transactions of commercial operators, has the effect of hindering the maintenance of the degree of competition still existing in the market or the growth of that competition.

The ECJ repeated this in *Michelin* in slightly different wording.

Case 322/81, *NV Nederlandsche Banden-Industrie Michelin* v. *Commission* [1983] ECR 3461, [1985] 1 CMLR 282, para. 70

. . . in prohibiting any abuse of a dominant position on the market . . . Article [82] covers practices which are likely to affect the structure of a market where, as a direct result of the presence of the undertaking in question, competition has already been weakened and which, through recourse to methods different from those governing normal competition in products or services based on traders' performance, have the effect of hindering the maintenance or development of the level of competition still existing on the market.

It should be noted that the definitions given in these cases describe *only* exclusionary (or 'anticompetitive' abuses). There have, in fact, been few cases in which an undertaking's exploitation of its dominant position has been prohibited[128] and the story of Article 82 is predominantly one of action against exclusionary abuses. This is partly because if a dominant undertaking can exploit its customers for a significant period of time there is something wrong with the market. For example, the ability to reap supra-competitive profits by charging excessive prices should in theory act as a spur to attract new competitors on to the market.[129] If that does not happen competition authorities, such as the Commission, may prefer to take action against anticompetitive practices which are preventing entry rather than tackle the high prices directly. Tackling high prices directly is an unattractive option for competition authorities. First, there are great

---

[128] See *infra* Chap. 7.
[129] See *infra*, Chap. 7, 586.

problems in identifying what is an excessive price and secondly there is the matter of the remedy. Competition authorities do not like acting as price regulators.[130] However, the Commission has made it clear that there is no question of Article 82 being applied *only* to anti-competitive abuses. 'Article 82 can properly be applied, where appropriate, to situations in which a dominant undertaking's behaviour directly prejudices the interests of consumers, notwithstanding the absence of any effect on the structure of competition'.[131] Moreover, as the imposition of 'unfair prices' is expressly listed as an abuse in Article 82(a) the Commission could not pursue a policy of never prosecuting excessive pricing and it will take action where the circumstances warrant it.[132] As a Commission official has put it: 'the [EEC] Founding Fathers' faith in competition as a process of rivalry between competitors was not strong enough to tolerate customer/consumer exploitation in the short run'.[133] This contrasts with the US Sherman Act, section 2, which (at least currently) is not applied to exploitative conduct.[134]

The prohibition of exclusionary behaviour may benefit consumers by protecting the competitive structure. The view that consumer welfare is the objective of competition law holds that consumer benefit is the *only* reason for doing this. However, such a prohibition also *directly* benefits competitors.[135] It prevents their exclusion from the market. The prohibition of exclusionary behaviour might, therefore, in some circumstances encourage the competition authorities to go beyond the objective of protecting the competitive process as a way of benefiting consumers. Indeed it appears that in some cases the Commission has acted with the purpose of protecting a *competitor* and not *competition* and that it is questionable whether preventing the exclusion of a competitor did, in fact, benefit consumers.[136] This raises again the question of what are and what should be the objectives of competition law.[137]

(iii) Categories of Abuse are not Mutually Exclusive

In addition to 'exploitative' and 'exclusionary ' abuses it has been suggested that there is a third category, 'reprisal' abuses. These are abuses which are specifically aimed at another undertaking and encompass steps taken to discipline or punish that other.[138]

[130] Some markets with high barriers to entry because of network effects or high minimum efficient scale may be candidates for price control by way of sector regulation. See further *infra* Chap. 7.

[131] *1998 World Cup* [2000] OJ L5/55, [2000] 4 CMLR 963, para. 100.

[132] See the (then) Competition Commissioner, Mario Monti, at the 8th EU Competition Law and Policy Workshop, EUI, June 2003, published as C. D. Ehlermann and I. Atanasiu (eds.), '*European Competition Law Annual 2003: What is an Abuse of a Dominant Position?*' (Hart Publishing, 2006) 3, 6–7; Director General of DG Comp, Philip Lowe, at Fordham Corporate Law Institute 30th Annual Conference on International Antitrust Law and Policy, 23 Oct. 2003, published as 2003 *Fordham Corp. L. Inst* (B. Hawk, ed. 2004) 163, 169–170. The cases on excessive pricing are discussed *infra* Chap. 7.

[133] L. Gyselen, 'Rebates: Competition on the Merits or Exclusionary Practice?' 8th EU Competition Law and Policy Workshop, EUI, June 2003,published as C.D.Ehlermann and I. Atanasiu (eds.), '*European Competition Law Annual 2003: What is an Abuse of a Dominant Position?*' (Hart Publishing, 2006) 287, 290.

[134] See *infra* 345.

[135] Clearly the prohibition of the exploitation of market power protects those with whom the monopolist or dominant undertaking deals, such as consumers. The objection to monopoly is based on its being less desirable for society as a whole than a more competitive market. See *supra* Chap. 1.

[136] See, e.g., Cases 6 and 7/73, *Istituto Chemioterapico Italiano SpA and Commercial Solvents Corp v. Commission* [1974] ECR 223, [1974] 1 CMLR 309; Case 22/78, *Hugin Kassaregister AB and Hugin Cash Registers Ltd v. Commission* [1979] ECR 1869, [1979] 3 CMLR 345, discussed *infra* Chap. 7.

[137] See *supra* Chap. 1.

[138] See J. Temple Lang, 'Monopolisation and the Definition of "Abuse" of a Dominant Position under Article 86 EEC Treaty' (1979) 16 *CMLRev* 345, 363–4. The best example of a 'reprisal' abuse is the termination of supply in Case 2/76 *United Brands* v. *EC Commission* [1978] ECR 207, [1978] 1 CMLR 429, discussed *infra* Chap. 7.

It must be emphasized that these categories of abuse—exploitative, exclusionary, and reprisal (if a separate category)—are not mutually exclusive. The same conduct may be both exploitative *and* make it more difficult for a competitor to gain access to the market. This might be the case where, for example, a firm charges discriminatory prices (prohibited by Article 82(c)). Those discriminatory prices might exploit one set of customers and exclude competitors by charging lower prices to customers which might otherwise purchase from the competitor.[139] Indeed, discrimination takes many forms, and there is a argument for classifying 'discrimination' as another category of abuse.[140] Limiting production and tying can also simultaneously exploit customers and exclude competitors. Similarly, it seems that reprisal abuses are really a sub-category of exclusionary abuses. In most cases they will exclude competitors from the market. They have an added element however since, as described above, they are 'calculated' to damage. It may, therefore, be possible to classify predatory pricing as a reprisal abuse where it is intended to punish a competitor.[141] However, it is also exclusionary since it is calculated to drive a competitor out of a market or to deter and prevent competitors from gaining access to the market.

(iv) The Broad Nature of the Concept of Abuse

a. Abuse Need not be Causally Connected to the Dominant Position

It has been seen in *Continental Can* that the Court adopted a broad view of what conduct may amount to an abuse of a dominant position for the purposes of Article 82. Further, it is clear from that judgment[142] and the extracts from the judgments in *Hoffmann-La Roche* and *Michelin* set out above that there is no need for a causal link to be established between the dominant position and the abuse. It is necessary only that the conduct strengthens the undertaking's dominant position and fetters competition on the market. By saying that there is no requirement for a causal link we mean that the dominant undertaking does not need to be *using* its dominance to commit the abuse. However, it is the fact that the undertaking is dominant that renders its behaviour abusive. The dominance means that the behaviour has effects which the behaviour of a non-dominant undertaking would not have. Since a dominant undertaking may be prohibited from some conduct even though it is not actually *using* its market power, some strategies possible for, and permitted to, non-dominant firms will be prohibited. This is because a dominant undertaking has a special responsibility on the market which it dominates. It may abuse its position by engaging in conduct which is acceptable when carried out by its competitors and irrespective of any intention to commit an abuse.[143]

---

[139] This can be seen from para. 26 of the *Continental Can* judgment (Case 6/72, *Europemballage Corp and Continental Can Co Inc v. Commission* [1973] ECR 215, [1973] CMLR 199) itself, where the conduct towards customers in headings (c) and (d) of Article 82 (discriminatory pricing and enforcing a tie) is described as having an impact on an effective competitive structure. See also Case C-95/04 P, *British Airways v. Commission*, 15 March 2007.

[140] See Chap. 7. R. O'Donoghue and A. J. Padilla, *The Law and Economics of Article 82* (Hart Publishing, 2006), 202–6, deals with discrimination in this way. The difficulty of pigeon-holing discrimination was illustrated by the Discussion Paper which, being restricted to 'exclusionary abuses' ended up discussing only some types of price discrimination and not others (it did not deal with Article 82(c)).

[141] See Case C-62/86, *AKZO Chemie BV v. Commission* [1991] ECR I-3359, [1993] 5 CMLR 215, discussed *infra* Chap. 7.

[142] Case 6/72, *Europemballage Corp and Continental Can Co Inc v. Commission* [1973] ECR 215, [1973] CMLR 199, particularly paras. 26–7. R. O'Donoghue and A. J. Padilla, *The Law and Economics of Article 82* (Hart Publishing, 2006), 217 suggest that the comments of the ECJ in *Continental Can* should be seen in the context of that case, where the Court was supporting the Commission's move to plug part of the gap in its armoury left, at the time, by the absence of a regime for merger control: see Chap. 12.

[143] C f. the position in the US under section 2 of the Sherman Act, *infra* 345.

b. The Special Responsibility of Dominant Undertakings

The issue of what conduct amounts to an abuse is governed by the fact that the ECJ has consistently stressed that although the finding that an undertaking is in a dominant position is not a reproach, dominant firms have a 'special responsibility' towards the competitive process and, implicitly, its competitors. This idea was first expressed by the Court in *Michelin*:

It is not possible to uphold the objections made against those arguments by Michelin NV, supported on this point by the French Government, that Michelin NV is thus penalized for the quality of its products and services. A finding that an undertaking has a dominant position is not in itself a recrimination but simply means that, irrespective of the reasons for which it has such a dominant position, the undertaking concerned has a special responsibility not to allow its conduct to impair genuine undistorted competition on the common market.[144]

This 'special responsibility' means that conduct which may at first sight look like ordinary business behaviour (such as in *Michelin* itself)[145] may be condemned as abusive. Article 82 thus prohibits what might otherwise be considered as normal methods of competition. The special responsibility arises 'irrespective of the reasons for which it has such a dominant position'.[146] The idea that dominant firms have a 'special responsibility' towards the competitive is an absolutely key element in the application of Article 82.[147] It imposes what is in effect a *positive*, or affirmative, duty on dominant firms. Article 82 regulates the conduct of dominant firms in a way that the US Sherman Act does not.[148] The consequences of this imposition of special responsibility will be seen in the discussion of what conduct amounts to an abuse in Chapter 7.

c. Super-dominance

It appears that the dominant undertaking's special responsibility increases with its degree of dominance. This was first suggested in *Tetra Pak II*[149] where the ECJ approved the CFI's statement that '[t]he actual scope of the special responsibility imposed on an undertaking in a dominant position must therefore be considered in the light of the specific circumstances of the case'.[150] The 'special circumstances' in that case included the undertaking's 'quasi-monopoly'.[151] In *Compagnie Maritime Belge* Fennelly A-G spoke of the 'super-dominance' of monopolists and quasi-monopolists and of the 'particularly onerous special responsibility' upon undertakings enjoying 'a position of dominance approaching a monopoly'.[152] Although the ECJ did not expressly endorse this view it did state that the scope of the special responsibility was affected by the circumstances of the case and the competition existing on the market. It indicated that an undertaking with a very large market share and only one competitor would be more likely to be

---

[144] Case 322/81, *NV Nederlandsche Banden-Industrie Michelin v. Commission* [1983] ECR 3461, [1985] 1 CMLR 282, para. 57; see also Case T-228/97, *Irish Sugar plc v. Commission* [1999] ECR II-2969; [1999] 5 CMLR 1300, para. 112.

[145] For the conduct found abusive in *Michelin*, see *infra* Chap. 7.

[146] See the discussion of super-dominance *supra* and *infra* in Chaps. 6 and 7.

[147] See, e.g. Case COMP/A.37.507.F3, *Generics/AstraZeneca*, 15 June 2005, IP /05/737.

[148] *Infra* 345.

[149] Case C-333/94 P, *Tetra Pak International SA v. Commission* [1996] ECR I-5951, [1997] 4 CMLR 662 *(Tetra Pak II)*, para. 24.

[150] Case T-83/91, *Tetra Pak International SA v. Commission* [1994] ECR II-755, [1997] 4 CMLR 726, para. 115.

[151] ECJ, *Tetra Pak II*, n. 149 *supra*, para. 31.

[152] Cases C-395 and 396/96 P, *Compagnie Maritime Belge Transports SA v. Commission* [2000] ECR I-1365, [2000] 4 CMLR 1076, Opinion of Fennelly AG, para. 137. This is the source of the term 'super-dominance'.

found to have abused its dominant position than a dominant undertaking with a lesser degree of market power.[153] The Commission was quite explicit in *Deutsche Post AG: Interception of Cross-Border Mail* when it said that the 'actual scope of the dominant firm's special responsibility must be considered in relation to the degree of dominance held by the firm and to the special characteristics of the market which may affect the competitive situation'.[154] It should be noted that such 'super-dominant' undertakings have featured in some of the most controversial applications of Article 82 finding selective price-cutting[155] and a refusal to license a copyright[156] to be abuses. Super-dominance as a concept has been criticised for having no basis in economics[157] and for adding further uncertainty to the application of Article 82.[158] Faull and Nikpay says, with reference to what it describes as Fennelly A-G's 'sliding scale' approach :

It is submitted that this graduated approach, which appears to imply that special rules may be applicable to some firms (which could be characterised as 'super-dominant') has certain drawbacks in terms of legal certainty. That said, the reference to the concept of super-dominance may be no more than acknowledgement of an obvious fact, namely that a firm with overwhelming market power will have enormous capacity and incentive to exploit that position to its advantage.[159]

d. Abuse as an Objective Concept

In *Hoffmann-La Roche*[160] the ECJ stressed that the notion of an abuse is an 'objective concept'. Although the Court has not elaborated on this statement it appears to reinforce the fact that it is not essential to a finding of an abuse that the dominant undertaking has used its dominant position.[161] Further, it appears to mean that the characterization of a dominant undertaking's conduct as abusive does not depend on the undertaking's subjective intent to exclude competitors or weaken competition. The competition authorities look to the effect (actual or potential[162]) of the conduct, not the reasons for it. An important *caveat* must be entered however. Although there are many cases in which an abuse has been found to have been committed without an investigation into the motives of the undertaking, there are some cases in which the undertaking's intent is of relevance. In particular, the ECJ has held that a dominant undertaking which prices its product between average variable and average total cost will be found to have engaged in predatory pricing and to have committed an abuse of Article 82 only if this level of pricing

---

[153] Cases C-395 and 396/96 P, *Compagnie Maritime Belge Transports SA v. Commission* [2000] ECR I-1365, [2000] 4 CMLR 1076, paras. 112–19, discussed *infra* Chap. 7.

[154] [2001] OJ L331/40, [2002] 4 CMLR 598. The term 'super-dominance' was used by the UK Competition Commission Appeal Tribunal (as it then was) when applying the Chapter II Prohibition of the Competition Act 1998 (which is the domestic equivalent of Article 82 and has to be interpreted consistently with the Article 82 case law) in Case 1001/1/01 *Napp Pharmaceutical Holdings Ltd v. DGFT* [2002] CompAR 13. At para. 343 it spoke of 'a question of "superdominance" amounting to a virtual monopoly'.

[155] See Case T-228/97, *Irish Sugar plc v. Commission* [1999] ECR II-2969, [1999] 5 CMLR 1300, confirmed on appeal to the ECJ, Case C-497/99P, *Irish Sugar plc v. Commission* [2001] ECR I-5333, [2001] 5 CMLR 1082; Cases C-395 and 396/96P, *Compagnie Maritime Belge Transports SA v. Commission* [2000] ECR I-1365, [2000] 4 CMLR 1076.

[156] Case C-418/01, *IMS Health GmbH & Co OHG v. NDC Health GmbH & Co KG* [2004] ECR I-5039; [2004] 4 CMLR 1543. The whole case is discussed *infra* Chap. 7.

[157] And, furthermore, it depends heavily on the undertaking's market share and over-reliance on market shares in the assessment of dominance is criticized: see *infra* Chap. 6.

[158] R. O'Donoghue and A. J. Padilla, *The Law and Economics of Article 82* (Hart Publishing, 2006), 167–8.

[159] J. Faull and A. Nikpay, *The EC Law of Competition* (2nd edn., Oxford University Press, 2007), 4.104.

[160] See *supra* 320.

[161] See Kirschner AG in Case T-51/89, *Tetra Pak Rausing SA v. Commission* [1990] ECR II-309, [1991] 4 CMLR 334, para. 64.

[162] See *infra* Chap. 7.

was adopted as part of a plan to eliminate competitors.[163] Further, the intent of the dominant undertaking may be crucial in cases of selective price cutting[164] and in some cases of refusal to supply.[165] According to the CFI, if the object pursued by the conduct of a dominant undertaking is to limit competition, that conduct will also be liable to have such an effect: establishing the anti-competitive object and the anti-competitive effect are one and the same thing.[166]

It should be noted that conduct may be abusive even if the dominant undertaking obtains no advantage, either financial or competitive, for itself. The behaviour of the French body which organized the 1998 World Cup was condemned as abusive in that it distributed tickets in a way which discriminated against fans who were not resident in France. It was accepted that the body had not gained any commercial or other advantage from its actions.[167]

(v) Exclusionary Abuses: Distinguishing Competition on the Merits From Exclusionary Behaviour

a. The Problem of Applying the Hoffmann-La Roche Definition

The finding that a dominant undertaking has a special responsibility to the competitive process and that any conduct which strengthens the dominant position/further weakens the competitive structure may be an abuse potentially brings within the prohibition an indefinite spectrum of conduct. The parameters of that spectrum have been the subject of judgments by the Court and decisions of the Commission (many of them highly contentious) ever since *Continental Can*. The difficulty is that anything done by a dominant undertaking may improve its market position in comparison to those of its competitors. New and attractive products, better quality, better service, good advertising, and low prices may all attract custom from the competitors. Should improving market share as a result of the dominant undertaking's increased efficiency and unbeatable products be forbidden? Obviously such a finding would be absurd.

The key to answering this question lies in the extracts of the judgments in *Hoffmann-La Roche* and *Michelin*, quoted above.[168] In these cases the Court speaks respectively of 'recourse to methods different from those which condition normal competition in products or services on the basis of the transactions of commercial operators' and 'recourse to methods different from those governing normal competition in products or services based on traders' performance'. The Court thus appears to distinguish between anti-competitive behaviour and 'competition on the merits' or 'competition on the basis of performance'.[169] A dominant undertaking providing a superior product at a low price which reflects its costs is competing on the merits. Its conduct is not prohibited even though its competitors, producing inferior products at less

---

[163] See Case C-62/86, *AKZO Chemie BV v. Commission* [1991] ECR I-3359, [1993] 5 CMLR 215, discussed *infra* in Chap. 7.

[164] See Case T-228/97, *Irish Sugar plc v. Commission* [1999] ECR II-2969, [1999] 5 CMLR 1300, confirmed on appeal to the ECJ, Case C-497/99 P, *Irish Sugar plc v. Commission* [2001] ECR I-5333, [2001] 5 CMLR 1082; Cases C-395 and 396/96 P *Compagnie Maritime Belge Transports SA v. EC Commission* [2000] ECR I-1365, [2000] 4 CMLR 1076. The Discussion Paper, paras. 127–29, plays down the likelihood of selective above-cost price-cutting being held abusive,

[165] Although a dominant undertaking does not always have a duty to supply, a refusal to supply may be found to be an abuse where it was carried out, for example, to discipline a customer, or to compete with a customer downstream: see *infra* Chap. 7, 529 ff.

[166] Case T-203/01, *Manufacture Française des Pneumatiques Michelin v. Commission* [2004] 4 CMLR 923, para. 241.

[167] *1998 World Cup* [2000] OJ L5/55, [2000] 4 CMLR 963, para. 102. For discrimination as an abuse, see *infra* Chap. 7, 594.

[168] See *supra* 320.

[169] See Korah, *An Introductory Guide to EC Competition Law and Practice* (7th edn., Hart Publishing, 2000), para. 3.3. The phraseology in English of *Hoffmann-La Roche* and *Michelin* is ungainly and unhelpful.

attractive prices, lose customers. This is the natural operation of the market. In contrast, a dominant undertaking which almost gives away its products, below cost, in order to attract customers from its competitors and to drive them out of business is not competing on the merits but acting anti-competitively. Often, however, the situation is not so clear-cut. The enduring difficulty with Article 82 is where the Court and the Commission draw the line between anti-competitive conduct and competition on the merits. In the following extract the authors[170] deplore the lack of clarification about what kind of conduct constitutes an abuse.

J. Temple Lang and R. O'Donoghue, 'Defining Legitimate Competition: How to Clarify Pricing Abuses under Article 82EC' (2002) 26 *Fordham Int'l LJ* 83, 83–4

Although a now universally-accepted distinction is drawn in the European Community ('Community') competition law between exploitative and exclusionary (or anti-competitive) abuses, . . . very little effort has been made to clarify the general principles about the kinds of behavior that are contrary to Article 82 of the Treaty Establishing the European Community ('Article 82') which prohibits abuse of a dominant position. The case law and practice has arisen pragmatically, and largely in response to complaints to the European Commission and appeals to the Community Courts against Commission decisions adopted on the basis of such complaints. With the exception of specialized Notices and guidance in the telecommunications and postal sectors, the Commission has not attempted to develop any kind of general or comprehensive statement on abusive behavior. There have been several consequences of this unplanned growth. First, the Commission and the Community Courts have dealt with individual cases that were said to raise questions of abuse by reference to the facts of the individual case, seemingly without having any clear general analytical or intellectual framework for doing so. Second, a number of basic questions have not been answered or even discussed, because due to the accidents of litigation or otherwise, they did not arise in any of the cases that have been decided. Finally, the influence that economic thinking has had on the Community rules on distribution, horizontal agreements, and mergers has not been felt, to the same extent or at all, in the interpretation and application of Article 82.

The Commission's initiative to 'modernize' the application of Article 82 to exclusionary abuses is an attempt to inject the missing intellectual coherence and interpret the vague and unscientific language of the Court in terms of rigorous economic principle. The Discussion Paper defined exclusionary abuses and then, crucially, set out what object should govern the application of Article 82 to exclusionary conduct.

DG Competition Discussion Paper on the Application of Article 82 of the Treaty to Exclusionary Abuses, Brussels, December 2005

1. . . . By exclusionary abuses are meant behaviours by dominant firms which are likely to have a foreclosure effect on the market, i.e. which are likely to completely or partially deny profitable

---

[170] The first author of this extract was for many years a senior Commission official but at the time of writing this was in private practice and an academic.

expansion in or access to a market to actual or potential competitors and which ultimately harm consumers. Foreclosure may discourage entry or expansion of rivals or encourage their exit.

. . .

54. The essential objective of Article 82 when analysing exclusionary conduct is the protection of competition on the market as a means of enhancing consumer welfare and of ensuring an efficient allocation of resources. The concern is to prevent exclusionary conduct of the dominant firm which is likely to limit the remaining competitive constraints on the dominant company, including entry of newcomers, so as to avoid that consumers are harmed. This means that it is competition, and not competitors as such, that is to be protected. Furthermore, the purpose of Article 82 is not to protect competitors from dominant firms' genuine competition based on factors such as higher quality, novel products, opportune innovation or otherwise better performance, but to ensure that these competitors are also able to expand in or enter the market and compete therein on the merits, without facing competition conditions which are distorted or impaired by the dominant firm.

Two particular points should be noted about these paragraphs. First, the Commission expressed the harm caused by exclusionary abuses in terms of the concept Of 'foreclosure'. Secondly, it said that the objective of Article 82 is the protection of competition as a means of enhancing consumer welfare and ensuring allocative efficiency. It firmly stated that it is competition, not competitors as such, that is to be protected. *Competition* is to be protected because of the benefits it brings to consumers. Insofar as that means protecting competitors, then they will be protected, but not for their own sake, This is not a world for sentimentalists. The Commissioner expressed this robustly:

I like aggressive competition—including by dominant companies—and I don't care if it may hurt competitors—as long as it ultimately benefits consumers. That is because the main and ultimate objective of Article 82 is to protect consumers, and this does, of course, require the protection of an undistorted competitive process on the market.[171]

There is much disagreement amongst lawyers, economists and other commentators, about some aspects of the identification and treatment of exclusionary abuses. However, in the following passage an economist sets out a number of precepts on which he says there is general consensus, and a further group on which there may be more divergence but a majority view can be discerned.

---

[171] Neelie Kroes, 'Preliminary Thoughts on Policy Review of Article 82', Speech at the Fordham Corporate Law Institute, New York, 23 September 2005, available at http://europa.eu/rapid/pressReleasesAction.do?reference=SPEECH/05/537&format=HTML&aged=0&language=EN&guiLanguage=en. A longer, and amended, version of this speech appears in the published volume of the proceedings as 'Tackling Exclusionary Practices to Avoid Exploitation of Market Power: Some Preliminary Thoughts on on the Policy Review of Article 82' in 2005 *Fordham Corp. L. Inst* (B. Hawk, ed. 2006), 381. Cf. Giuliano Amato (the author of *Antitrust and the Bounds of Power*' (Hart Publishing, 1997) extracted *supra* Chap. 1, 17) writing the foreword to the 2nd edition of J. Faull and A. Nikpay, *The EC Law of Competition* (2nd edn., Oxford University Press, 2007), viii, where he says 'We Europeans . . . are still convinced that competition is not only instrumental to efficiency, but also a goal in its own right. Furthermore we find it hard to abandon the idea that freedom—freedom of choice for the consumer and freedom of entrance for the producer—has a role to play in giving meaning to the type of welfare protected by competition law'.

G. J. Werden, 'Competition Policy on Exclusionary Conduct: Towards an Effects-based Analysis (2006) 2 *European Competition Journal* 53, 54–5

Views on important issues in competition policy may differ sharply, but on the most basic issues, there is remarkable agreement. Core beliefs forming the foundation of policy toward potentially exclusionary conduct by single competitors include the following 10 premises:

1. All competitors, even those that are dominant, are permitted and even encouraged to compete aggressively on the merits.

2. The conduct of a dominant competitor may harm consumers even when the same conduct by a non-dominant competitor would not.

3. Whether particular conduct benefits or harms consumers over the long term may be difficult to determine.

4. Competitor injury typically flows from conduct benefiting consumers, so effects on competitors are far from a sufficient basis for condemning single-competitor conduct.

5. Errors are inevitable in attempts to assess the effects of particular conduct, particularly when such effects are in the future.

6. False-positive determinations that conduct harms consumers chill conduct from which consumers may benefit significantly.

7. The more open-ended the enquiry into consumer effects, the greater the incidence of false positives.

8. A narrow focus on preventing consumer harm in the relatively near term may inappropriately deny competitors the fruits of their success and thus discourage innovation and risk taking.

9. Complex administrative proceedings are undesirable, as is business uncertainty about what conduct is permissible.

10. A remedy requiring frequent and detailed assessments of specific business decisions may be infeasible.

Views begin to diverge significantly when core beliefs are translated into prescriptions providing concrete guidance to agencies and courts in the implementation of competition policy toward single-competitor conduct. Nevertheless, a majority of interested observers likely would agree that:

- a dominance screen should be applied, requiring the demonstration of substantial and durable market power;

- safe harbours should be established to protect any conduct than can be categorically deemed "competition on the merits":

- conduct should be deemed lawful, even if potentially exclusionary, when there is no adequate and workable remedy;

- conduct should be evaluated under objective standards, with no role played by either intent to injure a rival or vague concepts like fairness;

- dominant-competitor conduct that is not in a safe harbour should be condemned if it injures competitors yet does not have any significant prospect of benefiting consumers; and

- dominant-competitor conduct that benefits consumers in the short term should not be condemned unless an agency (or private plaintiff) carries a heavy burden of demonstrating likely consumer harm over the longer term.

b. Tests for Determining what is 'Competition on the Merits'

Pinpointing exactly what amounts to 'competition on the merits' rather than exclusionary abusive behaviour remains difficult. While it is relatively easy to identify behaviour at the extremes of the spectrum as being one or the other, there are many more difficult behaviours in the middle. Economists have proposed a number of tests to aid identification. Each of these has its drawbacks, and they all have their advocates and critics, but nevertheless they can be useful as analytical tools.[172] The best known tests are:

• The 'as efficient competitor' test. The 'as efficient competitor' is a 'hypothetical competitor having the same costs as the dominant company'.[173] The idea behind this test is that conduct should be unlawful only if it is likely to exclude such a competitor, because only some kind of anti-competitive conduct can exclude equally efficient rivals. It has drawbacks if it is interpreted as allowing the exclusion of less efficient new competitors which could have in time become as efficient. Furthermore, conduct caught by the as efficient competitor test might nevertheless enhance consumer welfare (the test may not have the necessary correlation to consumer welfare), and the test is not useful in situations where the efficiency of competitors is not an issue.[174] The Commission's Discussion Paper suggested the 'as efficient competitor' test as the standard by which to assess price based exclusionary conduct.[175]

• The 'profit sacrifice' test. This examines the dominant undertaking's conduct to see if it involves sacrificing profits in circumstances where it would only be rational to do so if the undertaking was thereby able to exclude competitors. The obvious example is predatory pricing (when an undertaking prices below cost to drive competitors from the market). It does not however, capture other types of anti-competitive exclusionary conduct and can catch welfare-enhancing conduct such as investing in research and development (which if successful might result in an innovation so successful that competitors are eliminated).[176]

• The 'no economic sense' test. This is similar to the profit sacrifice test, but more inclusive as it does not depend on the one element of sacrificing profits. It says that conduct should be considered abusive only if it makes no economic sense except for its tendency to lessen or exclude competition. The test has recently been in favour with the US Department of Justice when arguing cases under section 2 of the Sherman Act.[177] Like the other tests it has its proponents and detractors.[178]

---

[172] See, e.g., OECD *Policy Brief* (2006) 'What is Competition on the Merits?' Available at http://www.oecd.org/dataoecd/10/27/37082099.pdf; J. Vickers, 'Abuse of Market Power' (2005) 115 *Economic Journal* F244; K. Fjell and L. Sørgard, 'How to Test for Abuse of Dominance?' (2006) 2 *European Law Journal* 69.

[173] OECD *Policy Brief* (2006), 4.

[174] For example, *Astra/Zeneca*, IP/05/737, *infra* Chap. 7 where the undertaking was held to have misused the patent system to exclude competitors.

[175] Discussion Paper, para. 63.

[176] See S. Salop, 'Exclusionary Conduct, Effect on Consumers, and the Flawed Profit-Sacrifice Standard' 73 *Antitrust LJ* (2005–6), 311; R. O'Donoghue and A. J. Padilla, *The Law and Economics of Article 82* (Hart Publishing, 2006), 185–7; E. Elhauge, 'Defining Better Monopolisation Standards' (2003–2004) 56 *Stan.L.Rev.* 253, 271 ('Sacrificing profits is neither sufficient nor necessary to show that conduct that excludes rivals is undesirable, nor does it even correlate well with the desirability of such conduct').

[177] e.g. in its briefs in *Microsoft*, available at http://www.doj.gov/atr/cases/f7200/7230.htm; *United States* v. *AMR Corp* 335 F.3d 1109 (*American Airlines*), available at http://www.usdoj.gov/atr/cases/f9800/9814.htm; *United States* v. *Dentsply International Inc* 399 F. 3d 181, available at http://www.doj.gov/atr/cases/f202100/ 202141.htm.

[178] The criticisms are summed up in R. O'Donoghue and A. J. Padilla, *The Law and Economics of Article 82* (Hart Publishing, 2006), 187–9; c.f. G. J.Werden, 'Competition Policy on Exclusionary Conduct: Towards an

• The consumer welfare balancing test. The various versions of this test involve balancing the positive and negative effects of the conduct on consumer welfare. As the OECD says, '[t]hey all have a degree of intuitive appeal because they attempt to use consumer welfare effects themselves, rather than indirect factors such as profit sacrifice, as the gauge of dominant firm conduct'.[179] O'Donoghue and Padilla conclude:

Although proponents of the consumer harm test have made its operational features as useful as possible, complex and precarious balancing acts are still likely to be necessary in marginal cases where the cost of error is likely to be high. Moreover, if issues of proportionality come into play, economics contributes very little by way of predictability and the outcomes will represent matters of policy rather than precision.[180]

• The test proposed by Professor Elhauge. In a leading article in 2003[181] Professor Elhauge proposed that the focus should be on asking whether the monopolist has improved its own efficiency by the conduct under review, or whether it has impaired a competitor's efficiency (regardless of whether it has impaired its own efficiency). The former would be permitted and the latter would be prohibited. This test seems to be most suitable where the alleged exclusionary conduct is of the 'refusal to deal' kind,[182] and it still requires a determination of whether the conduct is efficient or not.

c. Form or Effects Based Analysis

One of the most widespread criticisms made of the application of Article 82 over the years has been the use of 'form' rather than 'effects' based analysis. This has meant that the Community Courts and the Commission have condemned conduct as being an exclusionary abuse because it has taken a certain form, rather than examining the its effects. So, for example, exclusive requirements contracts entered into by dominant undertakings are akin to *per se* abuses,[183] and certain forms of rebate have been condemned because they were classified as 'loyalty' rather than as 'quantity' rebates.[184] We have seen in earlier chapters of this book how the approach to Article 81 has gradually been turned to a more 'effects based' or 'rule of reason' one, and it has long been argued that the application of Article 82 needs the same type of realignment. In the Discussion Paper the Commission firmly proposed taking in the future a more 'economic' approach with a clear effects-based analytical framework. It described the methodology:

This definition [i.e. *Hoffmann-La Roche*] implies that the conduct in question must in the first place have the capability, by its nature, to foreclose competitors from the market. To establish such capability it is in general sufficient to investigate the form and nature of the conduct in question. It secondly implies that, in the specific market context, a likely market distorting foreclosure effect must be established.[185]

The effects that matter, moreover, are the effects on the welfare of consumers.

Effects-based Analysis (2006) 2 *European Competition Journal* 53, who suggests that the 'no economic sense' test should generally be applied (note that, although writing in a personal capacity, Werden was at the time Senior Economic Counsel at the US DOJ).

[179] OECD *Policy Brief* (2006), 5.

[180] R. O'Donoghue and A. J. Padilla, *The Law and Economics of Article 82* (Hart Publishing, 2006), 194.

[181] E. Elhauge, 'Defining Better Monopolisation Standards' (2003–2004) 56 *Stan L Rev* 253.

[182] See Chap. 7, 529.

[183] See Chap.7, 476.

[184] See Chap. 7, 484.

[185] Discussion Paper, para. 58.

However, even the adoption of a general 'effects-based' philosophy leaves many questions to be decided in respect of its application. Amongst these are the following (which are closely related to each other). First, should there be any presumptions, or even absolute rules, that certain conduct is abusive or not abusive (in the latter case, this is sometimes called a 'screen')? For example, the current law on predatory pricing includes a presumption that prices below average variable cost are abusive.[186] On the other hand, the ECJ has upheld decisions finding that in certain circumstances even prices above total cost can be abusive, and many commentators critical of this would like there to be at least a strong presumption that they are not. Secondly, how are the effects to be assessed? Is it enough that a practice is *capable* of exclusionary effects, or do actual or likely concrete effects have to be demonstrated by the party alleging abuse?[187] Thirdly, is an exclusionary effect enough to trigger Article 82, or should it be 'measured' in some way to determine how much of the market is foreclosed to competitors? Fourthly, even if competitors are shown to be excluded by the conduct, should it be assumed that consumers are thereby harmed as a result? This is one of the most contentious issues of all and goes back to the reason for protecting the competitive structure by prohibiting exclusionary abuses. If the competition rules really do only protect competition as a means of protecting consumers, then exclusion which does not harm consumers should be permitted. Much of the criticism of the previous decisional practice of the Commission (and the case law of the Community Courts) centres around the tendency to assume detrimental effects on consumers from the exclusion of competitors.

The Discussion Paper, while adopting a general 'effects-based' approach, still maintained some 'form-based' elements in the shape of rules and presumptions, as we see when discussing specific abuses in Chapter 7. Many respondents to the Discussion Paper were critical of this and considered too much 'form-based' analysis lingered on. Some commentators, however, wanted more rules, at least insofar as they *removed* conduct from the risk of being found abusive (as to what percentage of the market a dominant undertaking can foreclose or what percentage of a customer's requirements can be supplied, without committing an abuse).[188] Furthermore, the Commission was criticised for adopting too much of a 'precautionary principle' in its attitude to effects analysis which 'appears to capture every constraint on competitive expansion and limits the scope for justification to the bare minimum'.[189]

d. Objective Justification, Meeting Competition, and Efficiency

The Court and Commission have developed the concept of 'objective justification' in order to distinguish between abusive conduct contrary to Article 82 and conduct which is pursued for legitimate commercial reasons. If conduct is objectively justified or 'objectively necessary' it is outside Article 82. The concept is problematic, however, for the Court and Commission (apart from the Discussion Paper) have hitherto not developed any theoretical framework for identifying conduct which is objectively justified. There is even some doubt about whether objective

---

[186] Case C-62/86, *AKZO Chemie* [1991] ECRI-3359, [1993] 5 CMLR 215; Case C-333/94 P, *Tetra Pak International SA v Commission* [1996] ECR I-5951, [1997] 4 CMLR 662 (*Tetra Pak II*); Case T-340/03, *France Télécom SA v. Commission*, 30 January 2007 where the CFI at para. 224 said such prices 'must always be considered abusive').

[187] This is the argument fought out in respect of rebates in the *Virgin/BA* case, which culminated in the ECJ judgment Case C-95/04 P, *British Airways v. Commission*, 15 March 2007, *infra* Chap. 7, 504.

[188] See the responses to the Discussion Paper, available at http://ec.europa.eu/comm/competition/antitrust/art82/index.html, and the speech by the Director General, Philip Lowe, at the Public Hearing on 14 June 2007, available at http://ec.europa.eu/comm/competition/antitrust/art82/hearing.html.

[189] B. Allan, 'Article 82: A Commentary on DG Competition's Discussion Paper', [2006] *Competition Policy International* 43 (reproduced in a Linklaters' publication, *Rethinking Article 82*).

justification renders the conduct not abusive in the first place, or justifies conduct which is abusive. The better view is that it is the former.[190]

There is no doubt that behaviour would be objectively justified if it consisted of legitimate business behaviour such as cutting off supplies to a bad debtor.[191] It appears that capacity constraints and safety issues could also be covered in appropriate situations[192] although in both *Hilti*[193] and *Tetra Pak II*[194] claims that tie-ins were justified on grounds of ensuring safety were rejected. The Court considers that safety is ensured by public authorities enforcing safety regulations and not by private undertakings indulging in exclusionary practices.

A more difficult issue is how far 'objective justification' also covers an undertaking protecting its own commercial interests, in particular where it is deliberately acting to ward off competition. The 'protection of commercial interests' point arose in *United Brands* where the undertaking cut off supplies to a distributor to discipline it for participating in a rival's promotion.

Case 27/76, *United Brands Co and United Brands Continental BV v. Commission* [1978] ECR 207, [1978] 1 CMLR 429

United Brands (UBC) was an undertaking found to be dominant in the market for bananas in several Member States.[195] One of the abuses UBC was found by the Commission to have committed was its decision to cut off supplies of its branded 'Chiquita' bananas to Oelsen. Oelsen was one of its ripener/distributors in Denmark. The distributor had, however, taken part in the advertising and promotion campaign of a rival producer's bananas, Dole. UBC claimed that it was justified in defending itself against attack from its main competitor. The Court of Justice, however, upheld the Commission's finding of abuse.

Court of Justice

189. Although it is true, as the applicant points out, that the fact that an undertaking is in a dominant position cannot disentitle it from protecting its own commercial interests if they are attacked, and that such an undertaking must be conceded the right to take such reasonable steps as it deems appropriate to protect its said interests, such behaviour cannot be countenanced if its actual purpose is to strengthen this dominant position and abuse it.

190. Even if the possibility of a counter-attack is acceptable that attack must still be proportionate to the threat taking into account the economic strength of the undertakings confronting each other.

---

[190] 'The analysis of the jurisprudence on objective justification demonstrates that this concept is not technically a defence. Rather it is used to explain the shifting of the evidential burden to the dominant undertaking once a prima facie case of abuse has been established' (R. Nazzini, 'The Wood Began to Move: An Essay on Consumer Welfare, Evidence and Burden of Proof in Article 82 EC Cases (2006) 31 *ELRev* 518, 535. The Court's judgments on refusals to supply (*infra* Chap. 7, 529.) as contrary to Article 82, for example, routinely include the finding that there was 'no objective justification' for the refusal. See further *infra* 337 ff.

[191] See *BBI/Boosey & Hawkes: Interim Measures* [1987] OJ L286/36, [1988] 4 CMLR 67.

[192] See *FAG-Flughafen-Frankfurt/Main* [1998] L65/19.

[193] Case T-30/89, *Hilti AG v. Commission* [1991] ECR II-1439, [1992] 4 CMLR 16, para. 118.

[194] Case C-333/94P, *Tetra Pak International SA v. Commission* [1996] ECR I-5951, [1997] 4 CMLR 662.

[195] See *infra* Chap. 6.

It is clear from this extract that, in order to be objectively justified, the conduct must be proportionate. The principle of proportionality is an established general principle of Community law, based on the German principle, *Verhältnismässigkeit*. It has been developed by the ECJ to judge both the validity of the actions of Community institutions (it is now embodied in Article 5 of the EC Treaty[196]) and, in some contexts, the actions of Member States.[197] The problems in its application are well known and its use to judge the legitimacy of a dominant undertaking's behaviour is equally problematic. Broadly, however, it involves the court weighing up the relationship between means and ends. When this is done in the context of the conduct of dominant undertakings it does not provide a definitive answer to the question 'is this an abuse?'. The application of proportionality to the facts of any given case does not help to predict the outcome.

The Court and Commission have often used the language of objective justification and proportionality when judging a dominant firm's claim that its allegedly abusive conduct was merely the protection of its own commercial interests.

BBI/Boosey & Hawkes: Interim Measures [1987] OJ L282/36, [1988] 4 CMLR 67

This Commission decision concerned interim measures ordering the musical instrument manufacturer Boosey & Hawkes to recommence supplies to two of its erstwhile distributors and repairers. Boosey & Hawkes stopped supplying them when they went into business together manufacturing instruments in competition with it. As in *United Brands* the dominant firm pleaded that it was only taking reasonable steps to protect itself. The Commission disagreed.

Commission

19. A dominant undertaking may always take reasonable steps to protect its commercial interests, but such measures must be fair and proportional to the threat. The fact that a customer of a dominant producer becomes associated with a competitor or a potential competitor of that manufacturer does not normally entitle the dominant producer to withdraw all supplies immediately or to take reprisals against that customer.

There is no obligation placed on a dominant producer to subsidise competition to itself. In the case where a customer transfers its central activity to the promotion of a competing brand it may be that even a dominant producer is entitled to review its commercial relations with that customer and on giving adequate notice terminate any special relationship. However, the refusal of all supplies to GHH and RCN, and the other actions B&H has taken against them as part of its reaction to the perceived threat of BBI, would appear in the circumstances of the present case to go beyond the legitimate defence of B&H's commercial interests.

In this case it seems to have been the undertaking's *immediate* withdrawal of supplies which was unacceptable. It was not *proportional* to the threat faced by Boosey & Hawkes. As in *United Brands* the dominant undertaking was held to have gone too far in the defence of its interests.

[196] Formerly, Article 3b. This Article was incorporated in to the EC Treaty by the TEU (the Maastricht Treaty).

[197] See *supra* Chap. 2, and D. Chalmers, C. Hadjiemmanuil, G. Monti, A. Tomkins, *European Union Law* (Cambridge University Press, 2006) 371–9; 448–454, T. C. Hartley, *The Foundations of European Community Law* (5th edn., Oxford University Press, 2003), 151–3; T.Tridimas, *The General Principles of EC Law* (2nd edn., Oxford University Press, 2006).

This requirement that any objectively justifiable conduct must be proportionate is crucial when assessing the compatibility with Article 82 of conduct which looks like 'normal' competitive behaviour. The actions of the dominant undertaking may be aimed not at extending its power, but at maintaining its market share in the face of aggressive competition—'meeting' competition rather than 'beating' it. A dominant undertaking which responds to competition by, for example, lowering its prices may be met with an accusation of abuse, but if it does nothing it will lose business. The question of what was meant by proportional in this context was explored by Advocate General Kirschner in *Tetra Pak I*.

Case T-51/89, *Tetra Pak Rausing SA* v. *Commission* [1990] ECR II-309, [1991] 4 CMLR 334

This case involved an appeal against a Commission decision finding that Tetra Pak's acquisition of an exclusive patent licence constituted an abuse.

Advocate General Kirschner

67. [Article 82] . . . contains four examples of abuses of a dominant position. The first two examples are concerned primarily about protecting parties to contracts with undertakings in dominant positions and consumers against exploitation of their dependence on the dominant undertaking, whilst the prohibition in subparagraph (d) on making the conclusion of contracts subject to the acceptance of supplementary obligations is clearly aimed at protecting competitors as well as contracting parties and example (c) prohibits discrimination as between the trading partners of the undertaking in a dominant position which would have an adverse impact on competition. The common feature shared by the first three examples is that the conduct to which they refer pursues the legitimate end of making profits through disproportionate means. Cases of abuse not expressly mentioned can be inferred from those examples. They point to limits which the undertaking in the dominant position must respect even in the case of activities which fall outside the examples, . . . namely the principle of proportionality . . . and the prohibition of discrimination.

68. In this case, the principle of proportionality is of primary importance, since the complaint relating to the acquisition of the exclusive licence (and only the exclusive licence) implies a complaint of disproportionate conduct. Applied to the conduct of an undertaking in a dominant position, that principle has the following meaning: the undertaking in a dominant position may act in a profit-oriented way, strive through its efforts to improve its market position and pursue its legitimate interests. But in so doing it may employ only such methods as are necessary to pursue those legitimate aims. In particular it may not act in a way which, foreseeably, will limit competition more than is necessary.

The 'meeting competition' plea is particularly relevant to cases in which the dominant undertaking has lowered its prices to a level where they are alleged to be 'predatory'.[198] In these cases the Court and the Commission have accepted that dominant undertakings do have the right to defend their commercial interests, but the permitted action is severely restricted. The judgments have not clearly distinguished between maintaining the dominant position and

---

[198] Cases T-24–6 and 28/93, *Compagnie Maritime Belge Transports SA* v. *Commission* [1996] ECR II-1201, [1997] 4 CMLR 273; Case T-228/97, *Irish Sugar plc* v. *Commission* [1999] ECR II-2969, [1999] 5 CMLR 1300; Case T-340/03, *France Télécom SA* v. *Commission*, 30 January 2007.

strengthening it. Further, the permissible level of action is sometimes related to the strength of the dominant position.[199]

There is also the issue of whether conduct can be justified because it produces efficiency gains which outweigh its detrimental effects. The first point to note is that there is no exception provision in Article 82 analogous to Article 81(3). In the absence of an express mechanism for weighing alleged efficiency gains against anticompetitive effects it is argued that the objective justification concept can play this role. Under Article 82 there has been no systematic treatment of the subject of efficiencies in the cases and decisions, whereas in the context of merger control there was considerable debate about an 'efficiency defence' which culminated in the Commission Guidelines on horizontal mergers recognizing the role of efficiencies in merger analysis[200]. Furthermore, the Commission Notice on the application of Article 81(3) equates Article 81(3) to an efficiency defence.[201] Nevertheless, the question of efficiencies has arisen in many Article 82 cases, as we see in Chapter 7.

The Discussion Paper attempted to define objective justification and give it a rational basis. It identified three types of objective justification defence: 'objective necessity', 'meeting competition' and 'efficiency'.

'Objective necessity' is where the dominant undertaking is 'able to show that that the conduct concerned is objectively necessary, for instance because of reasons of safety or health related to the dangerous nature of the product in question'. It must be 'based on objective factors that apply in general for all undertakings in the market' so that 'without the conduct the products concerned can not or will not be produced or distributed in that market. In these situations the Community Courts apply strictly the condition of indispensability'.[202]

The 'meeting competition' defence would apply only to individual behaviour that would otherwise constitute a pricing abuse and would be subject to strict conditions.[203]

The suggested 'efficiency defence' was formulated in terms almost identical to Article 81(3).

DG Competition Discussion Paper on the Application of Article 82 of the Treaty to Exclusionary Abuses, Brussels, December 2005

5.5.3 Efficiency Defence

84. For this defence the dominant company must demonstrate that the following conditions are fulfilled:

i)   that efficiencies are realised or likely to be realised as a result of the conduct concerned;

ii) that the conduct concerned is indispensable to realise these efficiencies;

iii) that the efficiencies benefit consumers;

iv) that competition in respect of a substantial part of the products concerned is not eliminated.

---

[199] See *infra*, Chap. 7, 435.

[200] [2004] OJ C31/5 paras. 76–88, discussed *infra* Chap. 12.

[201] [2004] OJ C31/5 discussed *supra* Chap. 4.

[202] Discussion Paper, para. 80. It added the strictures in *Hilti* and *Tetra Pak II, supra* 332, about what is not the proper role of private undertakings.

[203] See *infra*, Chap. 7, 474.

Where all four conditions are fulfilled the net effect of such conduct is to promote the very essence of the competitive process, namely to win customers by offering better products or better prices than those offered by rivals.

85. The dominant company must thus in the first place be able to show that the conduct is undertaken to contribute to improving the production or distribution of products or to promote technical or economic progress, for instance by improving the quality of its product or by obtaining specific cost reductions or other efficiencies. The Commission considers any substantiated efficiency claim in the overall assessment of the conduct, possibly along other defences put forward by the dominant company. Such claim may for instance concern the protection of client-specific investments made by the dominant company.

86. The dominant company must in the second place show that the conduct is indispensable to achieve the alleged efficiencies. It is for the dominant company to demonstrate that there are no other economically practical and less anticompetitive alternatives to achieve the claimed efficiencies, taking into account the market conditions and business realities facing the dominant company. The dominant company is not required to consider hypothetical or theoretical alternatives. The Commission will only contest the claim where it is reasonably clear that there are realistic and attainable alternatives. The dominant company must explain and demonstrate why seemingly realistic and less restrictive alternatives would be significantly less efficient.

87. In order to fulfil the third condition the dominant company needs to show that efficiencies brought about by the conduct concerned outweigh the likely negative effects on competition and therewith the likely harm to consumers that the conduct might otherwise have. This will be the case when the Commission on the basis of sufficient evidence is in a position to conclude that the efficiencies generated by the conduct are likely to enhance the ability and incentive of the dominant company to act pro-competitively for the benefit of consumers . . .

88. The Community competition rules protect competition on the market as a means of enhancing consumer welfare and of ensuring an efficient allocation of resources. This requires that the pass-on of benefits must at least compensate consumers for any actual or likely negative impact caused to them by the conduct concerned. If consumers in an affected relevant market are worse off following the exclusionary conduct, that conduct can not be justified on efficiency grounds.

89. In making this assessment it must be taken into account that the value of a gain for consumers in the future is not the same as a present gain for consumers. In general, the later efficiencies are expected to materialise in the future, the less weight the Commission can assign to them. This implies that, in order to be considered as a counteracting factor, the efficiencies must be timely.

90. The incentive on the part of the dominant company to pass cost efficiencies on to consumers is often related to the existence of competitive pressure from the remaining firms in the market and from potential entry. The greater the actual or likely negative effects on competition, the more the Commission has to be sure that the claimed efficiencies are substantial, likely to be realised, and to be passed on, to a sufficient degree, to consumers. It is therefore, when assessing the pass-on requirement, highly unlikely that the exclusionary conduct of a dominant company with a market position approaching that of a monopoly, or with a similar level of market power, can be justified on the ground that efficiency gains would be sufficient to outweigh its actual or likely anti-competitive effects and would benefit consumers. Similarly, in a market where demand is very inelastic it is highly unlikely that abusive conduct of a dominant company which strengthens its dominant position can be justified on the ground that efficiency gains would be sufficient to counteract the actual or likely anti-competitive effects and would benefit consumers.

91. The fourth condition is that competition in respect of a substantial part of the products concerned is not and will not be eliminated. When competition is eliminated the competitive

process is brought to an end and short-term efficiency gains are outweighed by longer-term losses stemming *inter alia* from expenditures incurred by the dominant company to maintain its position (rent seeking), misallocation of resources, reduced innovation and higher prices. This is recognition of the fact that rivalry between undertakings is an essential driver of economic efficiency, including dynamic efficiencies in the shape of innovation. Ultimately the protection of rivalry and the competitive process is given priority over possible pro-competitive efficiency gains. This is also required for a consistent application of Articles 81 and 82. It is therefore, also when assessing the no-elimination-of competition requirement, highly unlikely that abusive conduct of a dominant company with a market position approaching that of a monopoly, or with a similar level of market power, could be justified on the ground that efficiency gains would be sufficient to counteract its actual or likely anti-competitive effects.

92. A dominant company is in general considered to have a market position approaching that of a monopoly if its market share exceeds 75% and there is almost no competition left from other actual competitors in the market, for instance because they are producing at considerably higher costs and/or are severely capacity constrained for a longer period of time, and entry barriers are so substantial that relevant entry can not be expected in the foreseeable future . . .

The treatment of the efficiency defence was one of the most criticized parts of the Discussion Paper.[204] It was argued that the replication of the Article 81(3) conditions makes the efficiency defence almost impossibly difficult. In particular, there is an inherent problem in applying a 'no substantial elimination of competition' condition to the abuse of a dominant position, since Article 82 would not apply if the market was competitive, and under the approach advocated in the Discussion Paper there would be no abuse without a significant foreclosure effect. Furthermore, paragraph 92 would deny the benefit of the efficiency defence to an undertaking with a market share over 75percent (presumably the level at which 'super-dominance' might be identified). Since the conduct is already required to be 'indispensable' to the achievement of the efficiency gains, then consumers will be denied these benefits. It will be noted that in paragraph 91 the Commission repeated what it said in paragraph 105 of the Article 81(3) Guidelines, namely that in the last resort the protection of rivalry is preferred to pro-competitive efficiency gains.

Perhaps the most contentious point about an efficiency defence in Article 82 is the extent to which objective justification is really a 'defence' at all. In other words, do the countervailing efficiencies mean that the behaviour is not an abuse in the first place, or does it mean that the exclusionary conduct *is* an abuse but that it does not infringe Article 82. It matters, because if it is a 'defence' in the same way that Article 81(3) is a defence to an infringement of Article 81(1), the burden of proof will shift to the dominant undertaking . The view in the Discussion Paper was that objective justification, including the efficiency defence, should operate in the same way as Article 81:

Exclusionary conduct may escape the prohibition of Article 82 in case the dominant undertaking can provide an objective justification for its behaviour or it can demonstrate that its conduct produces efficiencies which outweigh the negative effect on competition ..The burden of proof for such an objective justification or efficiency defence will be on the dominant company.[205]

The main argument for countervailing efficiencies rendering the behaviour not an abuse in the first place is that the analysis of efficiencies should be integrated into the analysis of the effects

---

[204] See http://ec.europa.eu/comm/competition/antitrust/art82/index.html.

[205] Discussion Paper, para. 77.

of the behaviour as a whole, and the analysis should not be artificially divided into two separate questions. The bifurcation of Article 81 has led to endless conceptual problems[206] and it is certainly arguable that it is undesirable to replicate those problems in Article 82. The transfer of the burden of proof to undertakings pleading Article 81(3) is now enacted in Regulation 1/2003, Article 2, but that does not mean that it has to be similarly transferred for the purposes of an efficiency defence under Article 82. On the other hand, although the *evidential* burden of proof might shift to the defendant undertaking, it would still ultimately be for the competition authority or claimant to show that the conduct as a whole infringed Article 82.

R. Nazzini, 'The Wood Began to Move: An Essay on Consumer Welfare, Evidence and Burden of Proof in Article 82 EC Cases' (2006) 31 *ELRev* 518, 538

The DG Competition discussion paper on Art.82 proposes a model whereby the burden of proof appears to shift to the dominant undertaking once the Commission has established a "market distorting foreclosure effect" . . . The discussion paper does not distinguish between legal and evidential burden and may be read as suggesting that the dominant undertaking bears the legal burden to prove that its conduct is a legitimate way of competing on the merits or generates efficiencies that outweigh any reduction in consumer welfare . . . However, the proposed analytical model is only consistent with the consumer welfare objective of Art.82 and with Art.2 of Regulation 1/2003 if the establishment of a "market distorting foreclosure effect" based on the "tests" suggested in the discussion paper is simply a way of establishing a prima facie case of abuse as a result of which the dominant undertaking acquires the evidential burden to produce evidence to refute it. This would also appear to be required by the jurisprudence of the Community Court on Arts 81 and 82 and, to a certain extent, by the fair trial requirements of EU law and of the European Convention of Human Rights.

From a policy point of view, a model for the analysis of abusive conduct based on prima facie evidence and the shifting of the evidential burden has the clear advantage of maintaining the focus of Art.82 on consumer welfare and efficiencies. If the dominant undertaking adduces sufficient evidence to raise a serious issue as regards objective justification or efficiencies, the legal burden remains on the authority or claimant bringing the case to prove that the conduct in question does not generate efficiencies outweighing any (likely) reduction of consumer welfare. If this legal burden is not discharged, the infringement cannot be established. This minimises the risk of unwarranted regulatory intervention and of unacceptable levels of unfounded civil litigation.

The main argument for taking a 'bifurcated' approach to Article 82 is that there would be consistency between Articles 81 and 82 especially as it is possible to apply Articles 81 and 82 to the same conduct.[207]

---

[206] See *supra* Chap. 4.

[207] As, for example, in Case C-552/03 P, *Unilever Bestfoods (Ireland) Ltd v EC Commission* [2006] 5 CMLR 1494 (freezer exclusivity).

E. AN EFFECT ON TRADE BETWEEN MEMBER STATES

(i) General

Article 82 applies only if the abuse of a dominant position *appreciably* affects trade between Member States. As in the context of Article 81, this requirement marks the jurisdictional divide between Community and national law. The concept of an effect on trade is interpreted in the same way under the two Articles.[208] Thus an agreement or conduct will affect trade if it interferes with the pattern of trade between Member State or if it interferes with the structure of competition on the common market (even if there is no alteration to the flow of goods or services between Member States).[209] The latter test is more commonly utilized in Article 82 cases and was first adopted by the Court in an Article 82 case, *Commercial Solvents*.[210] This approach is particularly germane to Article 82 cases in which abusive conduct might result in a competitor leaving the market, which was indeed the position in *Commercial Solvents*. Zoja, an Italian pharmaceutical company, claimed it was being driven out of the market for a certain type of anti-TB drug by the conduct of the dominant supplier of the necessary raw material. At the time (the early 1970's) there was an insignificant incidence of TB in the EEC and Zoja was principally manufacturing for export to the developing world.[211] The ECJ said that whether or not there was trade between Member States in the drugs was immaterial:

> 33. The Community authorities must therefore consider all the consequences of the conduct complained of for the competitive structure in the Common Market without distinguishing between production intended for sale within the market and that intended for export. When an undertaking in a dominant position with[in] the Common Market abuses its position in such a way that a competitor in the Common Market is likely to be eliminated, it does not matter whether the conduct relates to the latter's exports or its trade within the Common Market, once it has been established that this elimination will have repercussions on the competitive structure within the Common Market.[212]

Hugin,[213] however, showed that not all abusive conduct in the common market affects trade. This case concerned the supply of cash register spare parts by a Swedish undertaking to a servicing and repair firm in south-east England at a time prior to Sweden joining the EU. The servicing firm's activities were confined to the London area and there was no inter-State trade in the spare parts. The ECJ quashed the Commission's decision on the ground that there was no effect on trade between Member States. The alteration in the competitive structure if the firm went out of business would not be felt outside one part of the UK. The ECJ stated:

> 17. ... The interpretation and application of the condition relating to effects on trade between Member States contained in Articles [81] and [82] of the Treaty must be based on the purpose of that condition which is to define, in the context of the law governing competition, the boundary between the areas respectively covered by Community law and the law of the Member States. Thus Community law covers any agreement or any practice which is capable of constituting a threat to freedom of trade

---

[208] See *supra* Chap. 3.

[209] See *ibid.*

[210] Cases 6 and 7/73, *Istituto Chemioterapico Italiano SpA and Commercial Solvents Corp* v. *Commission* [1974] ECR 223, [1974] 1 CMLR 309.

[211] Sadly, there is now a high and increasing incidence of TB in the EU.

[212] *Commercial Solvents*, n. 210 *supra*, para. 33.

[213] Case 22/78, *Hugin Kassaregister AB and Hugin Cash Registers Ltd* v. *Commission* [1979] ECR 1869, [1979] 3 CMLR 345.

between Member States in a manner which might harm the attainment of the objectives of a single market between the Member States, in particular by partitioning the national markets or by affecting the structure of competition within the common market. On the other hand conduct the effects of which are confined to the territory of a single Member State is governed by the national legal order.

This case established, therefore, that before trade between Member States will be affected the alteration in the competitive structure has to have some repercussion beyond the borders of a single Member State.

The meaning of an appreciable effect on inter-Member State trade for the purposes of Article 82 is now spelt out in the Commission's Guidelines on the effect on trade concept which it has adopted as part of the modernization programme.[214] The Guidelines explain how Article 82 applies where the dominant undertaking is pursuing several practices in an overall strategy not all of which have an effect on inter-Member State trade:

Commission's Guidelines on the Effect of Trade Concept Contained in Articles 81 and 82 of the Treaty [2004] OJ C101/81

17. In the case of Article 82 it is the abuse that must affect trade between Member States. This does not imply, however, that each element of the behaviour must be assessed in isolation. Conduct that forms part of an overall strategy pursued by the dominant undertaking must be assessed in terms of its overall impact. Where a dominant undertaking adopts various practices in pursuit of the same aim, for instance practices that aim at eliminating or foreclosing competitors, in order for Article 82 to be applicable to all the practices forming part of this overall strategy, it is sufficient that at least one of these practices is capable of affecting trade between Member States.

The Guidelines then deal with four situations: abuse of a dominant position covering several Member States; abuse of a dominant position covering a single Member State; abuse of a dominant position covering only part of a Member State; and abuses involving trade with third countries or practices involving undertakings in third countries. The principles set out in the Notice are basically a summing-up of the case law.

(ii) Abuse of a Dominant Positions Covering Several Member States

Not surprisingly, the Commission takes the view that both exclusionary and exploitative abuses[215] in which a dominant undertaking engages in more than one Member State are normally by their very nature capable of affecting trade between Member States.[216]

(iii) Abuse of a Dominant Position Covering a Single Member State

Where an undertaking has a dominant position which covers the whole of a Member State the Guidelines distinguish between exclusionary and exploitative abuses. Where exclusionary

---

[214] See further Chaps. 2, 3, and 14. The inter-Member State trade Notice is particularly dealt with in Chap. 3, 191 ff.

[215] For the difference between exclusionary and exploitative abuses, see *supra* 316.

[216] Guidelines on the effect on trade concept, paras. 73–6.

abuses are concerned, trade between Member States is normally capable of being affected because the abuse will generally make it more difficult for competitors from other Member States to penetrate the market.[217] There are a number of cases that illustrate this.[218] Also exclusionary abuses may affect the competitive structure in a Member State in a way that affects inter-Member State trade, as the Guidelines explain:

94. Exclusionary abuses that affect the competitive market structure inside a Member State, for instance by eliminating or threatening to eliminate a competitor, may also be capable of affecting trade between Member States. Where the undertaking that risks being eliminated only operates in a single Member State, the abuse will normally not affect trade between Member States. However, trade between Member States is capable of being affected where the targeted undertaking exports to or imports from other Member States . . . and where it also operates in other Member States . . . . An effect on trade may arise from the dissuasive impact of the abuse on other competitors. If through repeated conduct the dominant undertaking has acquired a reputation for adopting exclusionary practices towards competitors that attempt to engage in direct competition, competitors from other Member States are likely to compete less aggressively, in which case trade may be affected, even if the victim in the case at hand is not from another Member State.

In the case of exploitative abuses, such as price discrimination and excessive pricing, if only domestic customers are affected there will be no inter-Member State trade effect. But the Guidelines explain how, nevertheless, there may be an effect:

95. However, it may do so if the buyers are engaged in export activities and are disadvantaged by the discriminatory pricing or if this practice is used to prevent imports . . . . Practices consisting of offering lower prices to customers that are the most likely to import products from other Member States may make it more difficult for competitors from other Member States to enter the market. In such cases trade between Member States is capable of being affected.

The Guidelines explain that once the undertaking's *dominant position* covers a whole Member State it will normally not matter whether the *abuse* affects only some of the territory or only some customers:

96. As long as an undertaking has a dominant position which covers the whole of a Member State it is normally immaterial whether the specific abuse engaged in by the dominant undertaking only covers part of its territory or affects certain buyers within the national territory. A dominant firm can significantly impede trade by engaging in abusive conduct in the areas or vis-à-vis the customers that are the most likely to be targeted by competitors from other Member States. For example, it may be the case that a particular channel of distribution constitutes a particularly important means of gaining access to broad categories of consumers. Hindering access to such channels can have a substantial impact on trade between Member States. In the assessment of appreciability it must also be taken into account that the very presence of the dominant undertaking covering the whole of a Member State is likely to make market penetration more difficult. Any abuse which makes it more difficult to enter the national market should therefore be considered to appreciably affect trade. The combination of the market position of the dominant undertaking and the anti-competitive nature of its conduct implies that such abuses have normally by their very nature an appreciable effect on trade. However, if the abuse is purely local in nature or involves only an insignificant share of the sales of the dominant undertaking within the Member State in question, trade may not be capable of being appreciably affected.

---

[217] *Ibid.*, para. 93.

[218] e.g. Case 322/81, *NV Nederlandsche Banden-Industrie Michelin v. Commission* [1983] ECR 3461, [1985] 1 CMLR 282; Case T-65/89, *BPB Industries and British Gypsum* [1993] ECR II-389.

(iv) Abuse of a Dominant Position Covering only Part of a Member State

If a dominant position is held in only part of a Member State it will, of course, be a matter of whether that part is a 'substantial part of the common market'.[219] If so, then it is again a matter of deciding whether access by competitors from other Member States is made more difficult by the abuse. If it is, inter-Member State trade must normally be considered as being appreciably affected.[220] It should be remembered that a part of a Member State comprising only a port or airport is capable of being a substantial part of the common market.[221]

(v) Abuses Involving Trade with Third Countries

Abuses involving trade outside the EU will be caught by Article 82 if they are implemented in the EU.[222] If the conduct relates to imports or exports to and from the EU there may be an effect on cross-border activity. Imports into one Member State may affect the conditions of competition there, and this may have a knock-on effect in others.[223] Where the object is to restrict competition inside the Community the requisite effect on inter-Member State trade is more readily established than when it is predominantly to regulate competition outside it.[224] A more detailed analysis is necessary where the practice is not aimed at competition inside the Community, to identify exactly how, if at all, patterns of trade between Member States will be affected.[225] Thus, the conduct of liner conferences operating on routes between European ports and third countries was held to affect inter-Member State trade in that it obstructed the activities of competitors operating from ports in other Member States, limited the choice of services available to shippers in various Member States, and disturbed normal trade patterns in the common market.[226]

(vi) Regulation 1/2003, Article 3

The question of whether an effect on inter-Member State trade exists acquired an added significance after 1 May 2004. Regulation 1/2003, Article 3 provides that where a NCA applies national law to an abuse prohibited by Article 82 it *must* also apply Article 82. This means that if there is an effect on inter-Member State trade the NCA cannot deal with conduct which meets the other criteria of Article 82 by applying national law alone. On the other hand, it is important to note that Article 3 does allow national laws to be applied to conduct which affects inter-Member State trade but which is not caught by Article 82, i.e., national laws can be stricter or wider than Article 82. This point is of particular relevance to the UK, which has a market

---

[219] See *supra* 313.

[220] Guidelines on the effect on trade concept, para. 90

[221] *Ibid.*, para. 91, and *supra* 315.

[222] See *supra* Chap. 3, 195.

[223] Guidelines on the effect on trade concept, para. 101.

[224] *Ibid.*, para. 103

[225] *Ibid.*, paras. 106–9.

[226] So in *CEWAL* [1993] OJ L34/2, [1995] 5 CMLR 198 (on appeal Cases T-24–26 and 28/93, *Compagnie Maritime Belge Transports SA v. Commission* [1996] ECR II-1201, [1997] 4 CMLR 273, Cases C-395 and 396/96 P, *Compagnie Maritime Belge Transports SA v. EC Commission* [2000] ECR I-1365, [2000] 4 CMLR 1076) a liner conference operating between the North Sea ports and the coast of West Africa was held to have infringed Article 82. The inter-Member State trade point was not appealed.

investigation reference procedure under the Enterprise Act 2002 by which oligopolistic markets can be investigated.[227]

7. THE RELATIONSHIP BETWEEN ARTICLE 82 AND ARTICLE 81

Articles 81 and 82 are not mutually exclusive. In *Hoffmann-La Roche*[228] the ECJ confirmed that both Articles 81 and 82 may apply to the same contractual arrangements. When dealing with an exclusive requirements contract concluded by a dominant undertaking the Commission was, therefore, at liberty to proceed under either Article 81 or Article 82. The ECJ held that:

the question might be asked whether the conduct in question does not fall within Article [81] of the Treaty and possibly within its paragraph (3) thereof. However, the fact that agreements of this kind might fall within Article [81] and in particular within paragraph (3) thereof does not preclude the application of Article [82], since this latter article is expressly aimed in fact at situations which clearly originate in contractual relations so that in such cases the Commission is entitled, taking into account the nature of the reciprocal undertakings entered into and to the competitive position of the various contracting parties on the market or markets in which they operate to proceed on the basis of Article [81] or Article [82].[229]

The fact that Article 81 and Article 82 can be applied to the same agreements or practices is a powerful argument for aligning the approach to the two provisions.[230] One situation to be considered is that of dominant firms and block exemptions.[231] An agreement concluded by a dominant undertaking may benefit from a block exemption which does not restrict its ambit to undertakings with market shares below a specified threshold. Such block exemptions are, in fact, an increasingly rare phenomenon as the current trend is for block exemptions to contain thresholds.[232] However, where the agreement does qualify under a block exemption the Commission has power to withdraw the benefit of the exemption in particular cases.[233] It is possible, nonetheless, that even prior to the benefit of the block exemption being withdrawn a dominant undertaking may be found to have committed an abuse of a dominant position.

---

[227] This procedure is a reformulation of the monopoly provisions of the Fair Trading Act 1973. For the problems of the application of competition law to oligopolistic markets see *infra* Chap. 11.

[228] Case 85/76, *Hoffmann-La Roche & Co AG v. Commission* [1979] ECR 461, [1979] 3 CMLR 211. See also Cases C-395 and 396/96 P, *Compagnie Maritime Belge Transports SA v. EC Commission* [2000] ECR I-1365, [2000] 4 CMLR 1076, para. 33; Case T-65/98, *Van den Bergh Foods Ltd v. Commission* [2004] 4 CMLR 1.

[229] *Ibid.*, para. 116.

[230] See *Van den Bergh (Irish Ice Cream)* [1998] OJ L246/1, [1998] 5 CMLR 539, on appeal Case T-65/98, *Van den Bergh Foods Ltd v. EC Commission* [2003] ECR II-4653, [2004] 4 CMLR 1, aff'd Case C-552/03 P, *Unilever Bestfoods (Ireland) Ltd v. EC Commission* [2006] 5 CMLR 1494, and the discussion of exclusionary dealing and rebates, Chap. 7, 481 ff.

[231] For block exemptions generally see *supra* Chap. 5.

[232] Such as Reg. 2790/99 on vertical agreements [1999] OJ L336/21; Reg. 2658/2000 on specialization agreements, [2000] OJ L304/3; Reg. 2659/2000 on research and development agreements [2000] OJ L304/7; and Reg. 772/2004 [2004] OJ L123/11 on technology transfer agreements.

[233] Reg. 1/2003, Art. 29, and provisions in the particular exemption Regulations. In certain circumstances Member States may also withdraw the benefit of a block exemption with respect to their territory: see *infra* Chap. 14.

In *Tetra Pak I*[234] the Commission found that Tetra Pak had committed an abuse of a dominant position when it acquired an undertaking which held an exclusive patent licence. That patent licence was exempted under a block exemption. The CFI affirmed that an undertaking could commit an abuse of a dominant position by operating an agreement which was exempted under a block exemption even if the benefit of the block exemption had not been withdrawn. Otherwise an exemption under Article 81(3) would also operate as an exemption from Article 82.

When Regulation 17 was in force and individual exemptions were possible the Commission was in practice, of course, unlikely to grant a dominant undertaking an individual exemption in respect of an agreement the operation of which was likely to constitute an abuse of a dominant position. It was likely to take these aspects into account before granting an exemption.[235] Under Regulation 1/2003 there are no individual exemptions. The Notice on the application of Article 81(3) states[236] that the concept of the elimination of competition in respect of a substantial part of the products in question, which precludes the exception of an agreement from the Article 81(1) prohibition,[237] is an 'autonomous Community law concept specific to Article 81(3)'. The Notice refers to the judgment in *Atlantic Container Line*, where the CFI said that this is a narrower concept than that of a 'dominant position' and that therefore an agreement which established a dominant position might not go as far as eliminating competition within the meaning of Article 81(3).[238] The Notice reiterates the position established by the case law, that the application of Article 81(3) does not prevent the application of Article 82 and makes it clear that Article 81(3) cannot be applied to permit an agreement that constitutes an *abuse* of a dominant position.[239] Not all restrictive agreements entered into by dominant firms will, however, constitute an abuse. The Notice gives the example of a dominant firm's participation in non-full function joint venture. Interestingly, the Notice clarifies the meaning of various paragraphs in the Guidelines on vertical restraints[240] and the Guidelines on horizontal cooperation agreements[241] which might appear to equate the Article 81(3) 'substantial elimination' test with dominance. It says that these passages 'should be understood' to mean that agreements which *constitute an abuse* cannot be permitted by Article 81(3).[242]

The relationship between Articles 81 and 82 is also relevant in the context of undertakings found to be 'collectively dominant' for the purposes of Article 82. Both Article 81 and Article 82 may apply to the conduct of such undertakings. It is possible that the agreement between the parties will infringe Article 81 and that the behaviour conducted in consequence of the agreement will amount to an abuse of a collective dominant position. Moreover, the collective dominant position may arise from agreements between the parties. Collective dominance is discussed in Chapter 11.

---

[234] [1988] OJ L272/27, [1990] 4 CMLR 47.

[235] Under Article 8(3), Reg. 17 [1959–62] OJ Spec. Ed. 87, an individual decision could be revoked, *inter alia*, where it was based on incorrect information or induced by deceit, or where the facts basic to the decision had changed. (In Case C-279/95 P, *Langnese-Iglo GmbH v. Commission* [1998] ECR I-5609, [1998] 5 CMLR 933, the ECJ held that the Commission could 'revoke' a comfort letter because of a factual situation which had existed at the time the letter was sent but of which the Commission was unaware until later.) Where there were no Article 8(3) grounds for revocation the Commission had to take account of its earlier findings.

[236] [2004] COJ 101/97, para. 106.

[237] See *supra* Chap. 4, 281 ff.

[238] Case T-395/94, *Atlantic Container Line v. Commission* [2002] ECR II-875, [2002] 4 CMLR 1232, para. 330.

[239] Notice on the application of Article 81(3), para. 106.

[240] [2000] OJ C291/9, para. 135. See *infra* Chap. 9.

[241] [2001] OJ C3/2, paras. 36, 71, 105, 34, 135. See *infra* Chap. 13.

[242] Notice on the application of Article 81(3), n. 92.

8. COMPARISON BETWEEN ARTICLE 82 AND SECTION 2 OF THE US SHERMAN ACT

At various places in this book we refer to US antitrust law and, *inter alia*, to the Sherman Act. It is useful to look at section 2 of the Sherman Act, the US equivalent of Article 82, and consider how the two provisions differ, for a number of reasons.[243]

First, a comparison with the Sherman Act throws into relief what are the distinctive features of Article 82 and helps one to appreciate its nature as a regulatory tool. Secondly, some of the most trenchant criticism of the application of Article 82 has come from US commentators or from commentators who have been influenced by the American approach: Article 82 is therefore seen as the 'other' and it is helpful to understand what is the 'norm' to which it is being compared. Thirdly, the conduct of some undertakings may fall to be considered by both jurisdictions and the differences in the provisions being applied may lead to different outcomes. An example of this is the proceedings against Microsoft[244] and the different treatment in the two jurisdictions of Virgin's complaints about BA's incentive scheme for travel agents.[245] Fourthly (and this is connected with the previous point), competition law is becoming increasingly 'internationalized' and amid moves towards further cooperation between competition authorities, talk of international institutional mechanisms, and the adoption of competition law systems by more and more States[246] it is helpful to be clear about the differences between US and EC law.

Section 2 of the Sherman Act[247] states:

Every person who shall monopolize, or attempt to monopolize, or combine or conspire with any other person or persons, to monopolize any part of the trade or commerce among several States, or with foreign nations, shall be deemed guilty of a felony. . . .

It will be seen from this that section 2 encompasses three offences: (i) monopolization, (ii) attempted monopolization, and (iii) conspiracy to monopolize. The last one of these, conspiracy to monopolize, need not concern us here. Under US law conspiracies to monopolize are usually also violations of section 1 of the Sherman Act[248] and would be caught by Article 81 in the EC. As far as attempted monopolization is concerned, it was established in *Spectrum Sport Inc v. McQuillan*[249] that in an attempted monopolization case it is necessary for the plaintiff to prove that (1) the defendant has engaged in predatory or anticompetitive conduct with (2) a specific

---

[243] Although there is an important difference in the structure of Article 81 compared to its US equivalent, section 1 of the Sherman Act (see further *supra* Chap. 4), there is, apart from the consequences of the single market objective, less divergence in the way it is applied. See generally, A. Jones 'Refusal to Deal–EC and US Law Compared' in Marsden, P. (ed.) *Handbook of Research in Trans-Atlantic Antitrust* (Edward Elgar Publishing, 2006) chap. 8, 236–86.

[244] *United States* v. *Microsoft Corp* 147 F.3d 935 (D.C. Cir. 1998); *United States* v. *Microsoft Corp* 87 F.Supp.2d 30, (D.D.C. 2000), 253 F.3d 34 (D.C. Cir.). In the EC, Commission Decision of 24 March 2004, *Microsoft* COMP/C-3/37.792. See further *infra* Chap. 7.

[245] Case C-95/04 P, *British Airways* v. *Commission*, 15 March 2007; *Virgin Atlantic Airways Ltd* v. *British Airways plc*, 257 F.3d 256, (2d Cir. 2001), *infra* Chap. 7, 438.

[246] See *infra* Chap. 16.

[247] USC15.

[248] See the discussion in H. Hovenkamp, *Federal Antitrust Policy: The Law of Competition and Its Practice* (3rd edn., Thomson/West, 2005), 288–9.

[249] 506 US 447, 459 (1993).

intent to monopolize and (3) a dangerous probability of achieving monopoly power. In one sense at least, therefore, section 2 is broader than Article 82 as it prohibits conduct by a firm which does not have monopoly power but which threatens to acquire it. Article 82 does not prohibit attempts to obtain a dominant position but applies only once the threshold of dominance has been reached.[250]

Section 2 is not interpreted by the US courts as condemning 'mere' monopoly itself. In the context of a monopolization claim the prohibition is only infringed where a firm with monopoly power engages exclusionary *conduct*. The offence 'has two elements: the possession of monopoly power in the relevant market, and … the wilful acquisition or maintenance of that power as distinguished from growth or development as a consequence of a superior product, business acumen, or historical accident.'[251] Needless to say, the case law of what amounts to monopolization is vast and complex. Moreover it has developed over the years in line with changing objectives. It can, however, be summed up at present as prohibiting an undertaking with monopoly power from engaging in 'impermissable "exclusionary" practices with the design or effect of protecting or enhancing its monopoly position'.[252] These impermissable exclusionary practices constitute a narrower range of conduct than that caught by Article 82[253] and it seems that currently conduct only violates section 2 if it is 'output limiting'[254] as the limitation of output harms efficiency and consumer welfare. The root of the difference between section 2 and Article 82 lies in what is prohibited. In section 2 it is monopolization, in Article 82 the 'abuse' of a dominant position. The Sherman Act is not employed against 'exploitative abuses' such as excessive prices. Firms with monopoly power are not considered to have a 'special responsibility' towards the competitive process. However, the differences between the application of Article 82 and of section 2 may become less as a more economic and 'consumer welfare' standard is taken to Article 82. The differences of approach generally between section 2 and Article 82 is described in the following extract (by authors who, as can be seen, prefer the US to the EC approach).

P. Jebsen and R. Stevens, 'Assumptions, Goals and Dominant Undertakings: The Regulation of Competition Under Article 86 of the European Union' (1995–6) 64 *Antitrust LJ* 443, 487–91

Nothing distinguishes the U.S. and EU approaches more clearly than what transpires following the decision that an undertaking has monopoly power or a dominant position. Superficially, the United States and the European Union impose somewhat similar restraints upon the exercise of

---

[250] As the EC threshold of dominance is much lower, this may not be such a significant difference at it at first appears. Indeed, the absence of such a power in the EC could be one reason why the threshold is so much lower, see, e.g. T. Calvani and J. Fingleton 'Dominance: A Comparative Economic and Legal Analysis' in W. D. Collins (ed.) *Issues in Competition Law and Policy* (ABA, 2006).

[251] *United States v. Grinnell Corp.* 384 US 563, 571–2 (1966).

[252] Hovenkamp, n. 248 *supra*, 276.

[253] See William J. Kolasky 'North Atlantic Competition Policy: Converging Toward What?', speech at BIICL Second Annual Conference, 17 May 2002, available on the US Department of Justice web site, http://www.usdoj.gov/atr/public/speeches/11153.htm (Kolasky was at the time Deputy Assistant Attorney General in the Antitrust Division). The US courts demand proof of anti-competitive effects.

[254] See E. M. Fox, 'What is Harm to Competition—Exclusionary Practices and Anti-competitive Effect' (2002) 70 *Antitrust LJ* 371.

monopoly power; for instance, both prohibit predatory pricing or tie-ins. They diverge strikingly, however, in the standard of behavior that must be met before they will impose sanctions. The United States is much more reluctant to restrict what some perceive as monopoly power abuses; the European Union, with its *dirigiste* tradition, states that dominant undertakings bear a 'special responsibility' towards their competitors and must act accordingly. With such different philosophies it is not surprising that the two systems differ significantly in substance. A business that might continue to flourish under the U.S. approach may wither under the EU regime.

In *United States* v. *Grinnell Corp* . . . the Supreme Court stated that the 'offense of monopoly under § 2 of the Sherman Act has two elements: (1) the possession of monopoly power in the relevant market and (2) the willful acquisition or maintenance of that power as distinguished from growth or development as a consequence of a superior product, business acumen, or historic accident.' . . . The Court's inclusion of the qualifying phrase 'superior product, business acumen, or historic accident' captures the difference in tone and substance of the American approach. As stated by Judge Learned Hand in *United States* v. *Aluminum Co of America* . . . 'the successful competitor, having been urged to compete, must not be turned upon when he wins.' This concern animates many of the U.S. decisions.

In fact, the U.S. opinions take pains to resist condemning monopoly power per se. The American courts—at least in recent years—have not condemned the possession of monopoly power when it arises 'unexpectedly or unavoidably.' . . . In *United States* v. *United Shoe Machinery Corp* . . . the court emphasized that a monopolist is immune from statutory liability where:

it owes its monopoly solely to superior skill, superior products, natural advantages (including accessibility to raw materials or markets), economic or technological efficiency (including scientific research), low margins of profit maintained permanently and without discrimination, or licenses conferred by, and used within, the limits of law (including patents of one's own inventions, or franchises granted directly to the enterprise by a public authority). Businesses with monopoly positions may therefore pursue competitive advantage. In *Berkey Photo* . . . for instance, the court explained:

[A] large firm does not violate § 2 simply by reaping the competitive rewards attributable to its efficient size, nor does an integrated business offend the Sherman Act whenever one of its departments benefits from association with a division possessing a monopoly in its own market. So long as we allow a firm to compete in several fields, we must expect it to seek the competitive advantages of its broad-based activity—more efficient production, greater ability to develop complementary products, reduced transaction costs, and so forth. These are gains that accrue to any integrated firm, regardless of its market share, and they cannot by themselves be considered uses of monopoly power . . .

The EU approach presents a stark contrast. Reaping competitive rewards may give rise to an Article [82] violation. Moreover, in the European Union the decisions stress a form of strict liability—that an abuse of monopoly power may arise without there having been any intent to commit an abuse . . . The notion is alleged to be 'objective'. In *Hoffmann-La Roche* . . . the Court of Justice asserted:

The concept of abuse is an *objective* concept relating to the behavior of an undertaking in a dominant position which is such as to influence the structure of a market where, as a result of the very presence of the undertaking in question, the degree of competition is weakened and which, through recourse to methods different from those that condition normal competition in products or services on the basis of the transactions of commercial operators, has the effect of hindering the maintenance of the degree of competition still existing in the market or the growth of that competition . . .

> ...
>
> The notion of 'special responsibility' has taken on many manifestations and lies at the core of the EU authorities' attitudes towards a dominant entity's behaviour.
>
> ...
>
> The imposition of special responsibility notions in the area of monopoly power, and the willingness of the authorities to take actions beyond those which might be called for in situations of 'normal' competition, permit the EU competition regime to be regulatory in a fashion that the United States is not. Moreover, the notion applies not only in cases of pure monopoly, but also in oligopoly situations . . . The EU authorities are granted the power and ability to regulate competition without effective constraint in statute or precedent, since the standards by which these authorities implicitly regulate are nowhere laid down any more than they are readily deducible from the jurisprudence.

In one regard section 2 is broader than Article 82. As we have seen above Article 82 can be applied only to an undertaking which is already dominant. Unilateral behaviour by a non-dominant firm is caught neither by Article 82 nor by Article 81.[255] The second offence under section 2, however, can be committed by a firm *not* in a monopoly position. It condemns conduct whereby monopoly is achieved, or attempted to be achieved, through anti-competitive means. As Hovenkamp says, '[t]he offense of attempt to monopolize is one of the most complex of federal antitrust violations'.[256] It is worth bearing in mind therefore that US law under section 2 is not entirely less draconian than Article 82, although in general the offence of monopolization has been interpreted to impose further restrictions on individual firms.

9. CONCLUSIONS

1. Article 82 is a powerful regulatory tool. Undertakings held to be 'dominant'—itself an uncertain concept—are debarred from an open-ended range of conduct which goes beyond the bounds of 'normal competition'. Even if 'normal competition' is defined as 'competition on the merits' there is still much difficulty in distinguishing it from conduct which should be prohibited as an 'abuse'.

2. Article 82 has suffered from a lack of a proper theoretical framework and from confused policy goals. Protecting competitors for their own sake can lead to consumer detriment by penalizing efficient pro-competitive conduct. Even protecting competitors in order to protect competition has often been done without sufficient analysis of the real impact on consumers. It is argued that there is a danger of too many 'false positive' errors i.e. over-enforcement which chills competition and harms consumers.

3. The general consensus between economists and lawyers at present is that Article 82 should be applied only to enhance consumer welfare and efficiency and that this should be done by taking a rigorous 'effects-based' approach to the analysis, rather than prohibiting behaviour on the basis of the form it takes. This is the stance adopted by the Commission's 2005

---

[255] Cases C-2/01 and 301 P, *Bundesverband der Arzneimittel—Importeure EV and Commission v. Bayer AG* [2004] ECR I-23, [2004] 4 CMLR 653; Case T-208/01, *Volkswagen AG v. Commission* [2004] 4 CMLR 727: and see Chap. 3.

[256] Hovenkamp, n. 248. *supra*, 281.

Discussion Paper, although there has been much criticism of the details of this document ('the upswing is good but the downswing and the follow-through needs a lot of work'[257]).

4. This approach to Article 82 does not sit altogether comfortably with the case law of the Community Courts, and cases since the publication of the Discussion Paper show them taking a conservative approach, reluctant to depart from the existing jurisprudence.

10. FURTHER READING

A. BOOKS

FAULL, J., and NIKPAY, A. *The EC Law of Competition* (2nd edn., Oxford University Press, 2007)

HAWK, B. E. *United States, Common Market and International Antitrust: A Comparative Guide* (2nd edn., Aspen Law & Business, 1990)

JOLIET R., *Monopolization and Abuse of Dominant Position* (Nijhoff, 1970)

O'DONOGHUE R., and PADILLA A. J., *The Law and Economics of Article 82* (Hart Publishing, 2006)

B. ARTICLES

ALLAN B., 'Article 82: A Commentary on DG Competition's Discussion Paper', [2006] *Competition Policy International* 43

AZEVEDO, J. P., and WALKER, M. 'Dominance: Meaning and Measurement' [2002] *ECLR* 363

EILSMANSBERGER T., 'Dominance—The Lost Child? How the Effects-Based Rules Could and Should Change Dominance Analysis (2006) 2 *European Law Journal* 15

——— 'How to Distinguish Good from Bad Competition under Article 82 EC: In Search of Clearer and More Coherent Standards for Anti-competitive Abuses' (2005) *CMLRev* 129

ELHAUGE E., 'Defining Better Monopolisation Standards' (2003–2004) 56 *Stan.L.Rev.* 253

FOX E. M., 'What is Harm to Competition—Exclusionary Practices and Anti-competitive Effect' (2002) 70 *Antitrust LJ* 371

———, 'Abuse of Dominance and Monopolisation: How to Protect Competition Without Protecting Competitors' in C. D. Ehlermann and I. Atanasiu (eds.), *European Competition Law Annual(2003): What is Abuse of a Dominant Position* (Hart Publishing, 2006), 69

———, 'We Protect Competition, You Protect Competitors' (2003) 26(2) *World Competition* 149

FJELL K., and SØRGARD L., 'How to Test for Abuse of Dominance?' (2006) 2 *European Law Journal* 69

JEBSEN P., and STEVENS R., 'Assumptions, Goals and Dominant Undertakings: The Regulation of

Competition Under Article 86 of the European Union' (1995–96) 64 *Antitrust Law Journal* 443

KORAH V., 'Concept of a Dominant Position Within the Meaning of Article 86' (1980) 17 *CMLRev* 395

NAZZINI R., 'The Wood Began to Move: An Essay on Consumer Welfare, Evidence and Burden of Proof in Article 82 EC Cases (2006) 31 *ELRev* 518, 538

NEELIE KROES, 'Tackling Exclusionary Practices to Avoid Exploitation of Market Power: Some Preliminary Thoughts on on the Policy Review of Article 82' in 2005 *Fordham Corp L Inst.* (B. Hawk, ed. 2006), 381

SHER B., ' The Last of the Steam-Powered Trains: Modernising Article 82' [2004] *ECLR* 243

TEMPLE LANG J., 'Monopolisation and the Definition of "Abuse" of a Dominant Position under Article 86 EEC Treaty' (1979) 16 *CMLRev* 345

VICKERS J., 'How Does the Prohibition of Abuse of Dominance Fit with the Rest of Competition Policy?' in C. D. Ehlermann and I. Atanasiu (eds.), *European Competition Law Annual (2003): What is Abuse of a Dominant Position* (Hart Publishing, 2006), 147

——— 'Abuse of Market Power' (2005) 115 *Economic Journal* F244

WERDEN G. J., 'Competition Policy on Exclusionary Conduct: Towards an Effects-based Analysis' (2006) 2 *European Competition Journal* 53

---

[257] The Director General in Brussels, 14 June 2006, summing up the responses to the Discussion Paper.

6

ARTICLE 82: ESTABLISHING DOMINANCE

1. CENTRAL ISSUES

1. A 'dominant position' was defined by the ECJ in *Hoffmann-La Roche* and *United Brands* in terms of an undertaking's independence and ability to prevent effective competition. Article 82 can only apply to undertakings which, singly or collectively, are in such a position.

2. Dominance can be measured 'directly' or 'indirectly'. EC Law measures it 'indirectly' by defining the market and then assessing the undertaking's degree of market power on that market, as explained in Chapter 5.

3. Historically, the market has been defined in Article 82 cases by employing qualitative factors such as characteristics and intended use. The Commission now advocates the use of quantitative techniques such as the SSNIP test.

4. Once the market is defined, EC law relies heavily on market shares in order to assess the degree of market power.

5. The case law of the Court establishes that once an undertaking has 50 per cent of the market there is a presumption that it is dominant.

6. 'Other factors indicating dominance' (barriers to entry and expansion) are also taken into account and the lower the market share, the greater the importance that is attached to them. A wide range of 'factors indicating dominance' have been taken into account in the cases.

7. The cases do not establish a figure below which an undertaking cannot be found dominant.

8. In the Discussion Paper on the application of Article 82 to exclusionary abuses the Commission retained the heavy reliance on market share in the assessment of dominance. It maintained the position that undertakings with market shares below 40 per cent may be considered dominant.

9. It is often argued that the traditional way of assessing dominance is particularly unsuitable in new economy markets.

2. INTRODUCTION

In Chapter 5 it was seen that the Court, has, in defining dominance, focused on the ability of a dominant undertaking to act independently of its competitors, customers, and consumers and to prevent effective competition. In *Hoffmann-La Roche*[1] the ECJ stated:

> 38. The dominant position thus referred to relates to a position of economic strength enjoyed by an undertaking which enables it to prevent effective competition being maintained on the relevant

---

[1] Case 85/76, *Hoffmann-La Roche & Co AG v. Commission* [1979] ECR 461, [1979] 3 CMLR 211.

market by affording it the power to behave to an appreciable extent independently of its competitors, its customers and ultimately of its consumers.

39. Such a position does not preclude some competition, which it does where there is a monopoly or quasi-monopoly, but enables the undertaking which profits by it, if not to determine, at least to have an appreciable influence on the conditions under which that competition will develop, and in any case to act largely in disregard of it so long as such conduct does not operate to its detriment.

In this chapter we consider how the existence of a 'dominant position' is actually established, that is, how it is decided whether or not a particular undertaking is dominant. It will be seen that the criteria the Commission employs, and the way it applies them, have not always met with the approval of commentators or the approbation of economists. On the contrary, the Commission has often been criticized for finding that an undertaking occupies a 'dominant position' where, in reality, it has little market power.

In *Continental Can*[2] the ECJ stressed that dominance, or market power, exists only in relation to a particular market and not in the abstract. It held that 'the definition of the relevant market is of essential significance'[3] to the determination of whether or not an undertaking is dominant. In accordance with this judgment the practice of the Commission in ascertaining dominance is, first to identify the relevant market and then to assess the undertaking's position or power on that market. The position on the market is generally determined by looking at the market share of the undertaking concerned and at 'other factors indicating dominance'.

This two-stage procedure may, at times, be problematic. Not only are markets notoriously difficult to define,[4] but the process of market definition may be hard to separate from what is supposed to be the second step, assessing the undertaking's power on that market. It can be difficult to determine which factors should be taken into account when defining markets and which factors should be taken into account when considering the undertaking's position on the market.[5] For example, it may not be easy to decide whether account should be taken of the presence of a producer which can switch its production to making a particular product when defining the market or when assessing the competitive constraints that the allegedly dominant undertaking faces on a particular market.[6] Similarly, where a product has two distinct uses it may be difficult to determine whether the relevant market is for the product as a whole or whether there are two distinct markets, each of which is affected by competition on the other market.[7] In addition, the question whether a particular undertaking is dominant can be hard to disentangle from the question whether or not it has committed an abuse of its dominant position.[8]

Whatever the complexities involved, it is essential in EC law to define the market before it can be ascertained whether or not an undertaking holds a dominant position. When doing so it is

---

[2] Case 6/72, *Europemballage Corp and Continental Can Co Inc v. Commission* [1973] ECR 215, [1973] CMLR 199.

[3] *Ibid.*, para. 32.

[4] See *supra* Chap. 1.

[5] In *BPB Industries* [1989] OJ L10/50, [1990] 4 CMLR 464, for example, a question which arose was whether plasterboard and wet plastering formed part of the same market or whether there was a separate market for plasterboard alone. If the answer was the latter it was clear that the presence of undertakings operating on the market for wet plastering had to be taken into account when assessing an undertaking's position on the plasterboard market. The Commission found that there was a distinct plasterboard market: see para. 108.

[6] See also the discussion of supply side substitutability, *infra* 380 and *supra* in Chap. 1.

[7] See the Notice on the definition of the relevant market for the purposes of Community competition law [1997] OJ C372/5, discussed *supra* in Chap. 1.

[8] In some cases it has been indicated that the undertaking must be dominant, since if it was not it could not possibly have engaged in the conduct concerned: see *infra* 423.

important to remember that market definition is not an end in itself. Rather, it is a preliminary step and a tool necessary to answer the real question: does this firm have sufficient market power to occupy a dominant position for the purposes of Article 82?

It should be noted that the market must be defined anew, and a fresh analysis of the conditions of competition made, each time Article 82 is applied. The Commission cannot rely on findings of dominance in previous cases.[9]

3. MARKET DEFINITION

A. GENERAL

It was seen in Chapter 1 that the purpose of defining the relevant market is to identify those products and services that are such close substitutes for one another that they operate as a competitive constraint on the behaviour of the suppliers of those respective products and services. The relevant market has both a product aspect and a geographical aspect. The difficult question of how the relevant market is defined was discussed in the first chapter because it is central to all areas of competition law. In this chapter the discussion is generally confined to how the Commission and the Court have defined the relevant market in Article 82 cases. In most such cases the undertaking concerned will argue that the market is a wide one (for example, all fruit, rather than just bananas). The broader the market, the less likely the finding of dominance.[10] In contrast, the Commission has often been criticized for adopting too narrow a market definition.[11] In many instances this practice has made a finding of dominance inevitable. The assessment of the relevant market is therefore crucial. If defined too narrowly, an undertaking's position will be exaggerated and a finding of dominance made more likely.[12] Furthermore, there may be a question as to whether a 'market' exists at all.[13] The Commission Discussion Paper on the application of Article 82 to exclusionary abuses stated that:

The main purpose of market definition is to identify in a systematic way the immediate competitive constraints faced by an undertaking. The objective of defining a market in both its product and geographic dimension is to identify all actual competitors of the undertaking concerned that are capable of constraining its behaviour.[14]

[9] Cases T-125/97, etc. *Coca-Cola* v. *Commission* [2000] ECR II-1733, [2000] 5 CMLR 467, para. 82.

[10] Occasionally the undertaking argues for a narrow definition: e.g., in Case C-62/86, *AKZO Chemie BV* v. *Commission* [1991] ECR I-3359, [1993] 5 CMLR 215, the undertaking argued for a narrow market definition as in the narrow niche market it was relatively weak, but in the wider market as a whole it had a large market share. See *infra* 367.

[11] In merger cases the Commission has perhaps tended to be more objective in its definition of the market. In contrast, in Article 82 cases where the Commission is investigating what it considers to be a breach of Article 82 it may sometimes begin its case with a predisposition to a finding of dominance. This may encourage a narrow market definition.

[12] If defined too widely the undertaking's position will, of course, be underestimated. Narrow market definitions do not, however, give cause for concern where it is recognized that the undertaking may suffer competitive restraints from outside the market. This is important in the case of complementary products (such as cartons and machines for packaging products in cartons) where the markets are interlinked.

[13] See the discussion on 'input' markets, *infra* 367 and Case T-219/99, *British Airways plc* v. *Commission* [2004] 4 CMLR 1008, *aff'd* Case C-95/04 P, *British Airways* v. *Commission*, 15 March 2007, *infra* 378.

[14] Discussion Paper, Brussels 2005 (see Chap. 5), para. 12.

It was seen in Chapter 1 that in its Notice on market definition the Commission identifies three main competitive constraints that firms are subject to: demand substitutability, supply substitutability, and potential competition.[15] Demand and, to a more limited extent, supply substitutability are relevant to the determination of the market. Although potential competition may be relevant when considering supply substitutability it will more usually be relevant when considering the allegedly dominant undertaking's position on the relevant market once defined.

B. THE PRODUCT MARKET

(i) Demand Substitution

a. Interchangeability

When identifying the relevant market the Court has stressed the importance of the notion of *interchangeability* (or *substitutability*).[16] In the past, at least, both the Court and the Commission have placed importance on the characteristics and intended use of the product when considering their substitutability from a consumer's point of view. As we saw in Chapter 1, the Commission's Notice on market definition adopts the quantitative SSNIP test (which essentially asks whether a small (5–10 per cent) but non-transitory increase in price of one product (product A) will cause purchasers to purchase sufficient of another product instead (product B) to make the price increase unsustainable[17]) as the preferred mechanism for determining interchangeability.

b. Characteristcs, Price and Intended Use

The problems that identification using characteristics, price and intended use presents are illustrated by two of the most notorious and important Article 82 cases, *United Brands* and *Michelin*.[18]

c. The *United Brands* case

In *United Brands* the ECJ had to consider why people eat bananas and whether or not they are treated by consumers as reasonably interchangeable with other kinds of fresh fruit.[19] It decided that there was only a small degree of substitutability between bananas and other fruit, partly because of the unique appearance, taste, softness, seedlessness, and easy handling nature of the banana. The judgment does not make it clear why these distinctive characteristics should impact on the determination of the product market.

---

[15] Commission Notice on the definition of the relevant market for the purposes of Community competition law [1997] OJ C372/5, [1998] 4 CMLR 177, para. 13.

[16] See *supra* Chap. 1.

[17] *Supra* Chap. 1, 66.

[18] Case 27/76, *United Brands v Commission* [1978] ECR 207, [1978] 1 CMLR 429; Case 322/81, *NV Nederlandsche Banden-Industrie Michelin v. Commission* [1983] ECR 3461, [1985] 1 CMLR 282.

[19] Mayras AG confidently declared: 'As far as eating habits are concerned there is no doubt that a mother who gives her young child a fruit yoghurt will not give him a banana as well...' [1978] ECR 207, 312.

Case 27/76, *United Brands & Co and United Brands Continental BV v. Commission* [1978] ECR 207, [1978] 1 CMLR 429

United Brands Company was a US company which produced bananas. Its European subsidiary was United Brands Continental BV. The Commission found that United Brands had abused its dominant position on the banana market in a number of different ways, in particular by engaging in excessive and discriminatory pricing and refusal to supply. United Brands challenged the Commission's decision. One of the arguments raised was that the Commission had been wrong to find that there was a separate market for bananas. It claimed that, on the contrary, bananas formed part of a wider fresh fruit market. Bananas were reasonably interchangeable with other kinds of fresh fruit such as apples, oranges, grapes, peaches, and strawberries. The Commission contended that bananas were a separate market because of their unique physical, functional, and economic characteristics and because Food and Agriculture Organization studies had demonstrated only low cross-elasticity between bananas and other fruit.

Court of Justice

12. As far as the product market is concerned it is first of all necessary to ascertain whether, as the applicant maintains, bananas are an integral part of the fresh fruit market, because they are reasonably interchangeable by consumers with other kinds of fresh fruit such as apples, oranges, grapes, peaches, strawberries, etc. or whether the relevant market consists solely of the banana and is a market sufficiently homogeneous and distinct from the market of other fresh fruit.

13. The applicant submits in support of its argument that bananas compete with other fresh fruit in the same shops, on the same shelves, at prices which can be compared, satisfying the same needs: consumption as a dessert or between meals.

14. The statistics produced show that consumer expenditure on the purchase of bananas is at its lowest between June and December when there is a plentiful supply of domestic fresh fruit on the market.

15. Studies carried out by the Food and Agriculture Organization (FAO) (especially in 1975) confirm that banana prices are relatively weak during the summer months and that the price of apples for example has a statistically appreciable impact on the consumption of bananas in the Federal Republic of Germany.

16. Again according to these studies some easing of prices is noticeable at the end of the year during the 'orange season'.

17. The seasonal peak periods when there is a plentiful supply of other fresh fruit exert an influence not only on the prices but also on the volume of sales of bananas and consequently on the volume of imports thereof.

18. The applicant concludes from these findings that bananas and other fresh fruit form only one market and that UBC's operations should have been examined in this context for the purpose of any application of Article [82] of the Treaty.

19. The Commission maintains that there is a demand for bananas which is distinct from the demand for other fresh fruit especially as the banana is a very important part of the diet of certain sections of the community.

20. The specific qualities of the banana influence customer preference and induce him not to readily accept other fruits as a substitute.

21. The Commission draws the conclusion from the studies quoted by the applicant that the influence of the prices and availability of other types of fruit on the prices and availability of bananas on the relevant market is very ineffective and that these effects are too brief and too

spasmodic for such other fruit to be regarded as forming part of the same market as bananas or as a substitute therefor.

22. For the banana to be regarded as forming a market which is sufficiently differentiated from other fruit markets it must be possible for it to be singled out by such special features distinguishing it from other fruits that it is only to a limited extent interchangeable with them and is only exposed to their competition in a way that is hardly perceptible.

23. The ripening of bananas takes place the whole year round without any season having to be taken into account.

24. Throughout the year production exceeds demand and can satisfy it at any time.

25. Owing to this particular feature the banana is a privileged fruit and its production and marketing can be adapted to the seasonal fluctuations of other fresh fruit which are known and can be computed.

26. There is no unavoidable seasonal substitution since the consumer can obtain this fruit all the year round.

27. Since the banana is a fruit which is always available in sufficient quantities the question whether it can be replaced by other fruits must be determined over the whole of the year for the purpose of ascertaining the degree of competition between it and other fresh fruit.

28. The studies of the banana market on the Court's file show that on the latter market there is no significant long term cross-elasticity any more than—as has been mentioned—there is any seasonal substitutability in general between the banana and all the seasonal fruits, as this only exists between the banana and two fruits (peaches and table grapes) in one of the countries (West Germany) of the relevant geographic market.

29. As far as concerns the two fruits available throughout the year (oranges and apples) the first are not interchangeable and in the case of the second there is only a relative degree of substitutability.

30. This small degree of substitutability is accounted for by the specific features of the banana and all the factors which influence consumer choice.

31. The banana has certain characteristics, appearance, taste, softness, seedlessness, easy handling, a constant level of production which enable it to satisfy the constant needs of an important section of the population consisting of the very young, the old and the sick.

32. As far as prices are concerned two FAO studies show that the banana is only affected by the prices—falling prices—of other fruits (and only of peaches and table grapes) during the summer months and mainly in July and then by an amount not exceeding 20 per cent .

33. Although it cannot be denied that during these months and some weeks at the end of the year this product is exposed to competition from other fruits, the flexible way in which the volume of imports and their marketing on the relevant geographic market is adjusted means that the conditions of competition are extremely limited and that its price adapts without any serious difficulties to this situation where supplies of fruit are plentiful.

34. It follows from all these considerations that a very large number of consumers having a constant need for bananas are not noticeably or even appreciably enticed away from the consumption of this product by the arrival of other fresh fruit on the market and that even the personal peak periods only affect it for a limited period of time and to a very limited extent from the point of view of substitutability.

35. Consequently, the banana market is a market which is sufficiently distinct from the other fresh fruit markets.

It will be noted from the above extract that the ECJ was concerned with the question of whether the banana could be 'singled out by such special features distinguishing it from other fruits that it is only to a limited extent interchangeable with them and is only exposed to their competition in a way that is hardly perceptible' (paragraph 22). The 'special features' identified were first that the banana was a 'privileged fruit' (paragraph 25) in that it was not seasonal, and secondly that it had 'certain characteristics' making it suitable for the very young, the old, and the sick (paragraph 31). These characteristics, apart from constant availability, were appearance, taste, softness, seedlessness, and easy handling. This is a rather strange list. Softness, seedlessness, and easy handling may make bananas suitable for the young, old, and sick but it is difficult to see why their appearance does and it is never explained what is so special about their taste. Moreover, as we saw in Chapter 1,[20] it is unsatisfactory to conclude from the dependence of one group of customers that a product forms a separate market unless it is possible to price discriminate at the point of sale and to prevent arbitrage. This is now recognized in the Commission's Notice.[21] It may be that if the question arose again bananas would still be held to constitute a separate market, but it is most unlikely that this would be on the basis of their 'special suitability' for certain customers.[22] Rather, evidence would be sought from technology such as supermarket scanners, which would enable own-price and cross-price elasticities to be measured.[23]

d. The *Michelin* case

In *Michelin* the Commission found that Michelin had committed an abuse of a dominant position on the market for new replacement tyres for lorries, buses, and similar vehicles. Michelin claimed, *inter alia*, that the Commission's definition of the market was narrow and arbitrary and that Michelin did not hold a dominant position on the wider tyre market.[24] The ECJ had to determine whether or not the Commission had correctly defined the market. In considering this question a number of facts had to be taken into account: that lorries and buses need larger tyres than cars and vans; that there are different sizes of lorry and bus tyres; that tyre manufacturers supply their tyres separately to new lorry and bus manufacturers *and* to dealers who fit tyres on lorries and buses as replacements; and that tyre dealers also fit retreaded or remoulded tyres to vehicles whose owners do not want new replacement tyres. Which, if any, of these tyres were substitutes for each other so that they formed part of the same product market?

Case 322/81, *Nederlandsche Banden-Industrie Michelin* v. *Commission* [1983] ECR 3461, [1985] 1 CMLR 282

Court of Justice

(aa) The market in replacement tyres for heavy vehicles

35. The applicant claims that the definition of the relevant market on which the Commission based its decision is too wide, inasmuch as in the eyes of the consumer different types and sizes

---

[20] *Supra* 77.

[21] Para. 43.

[22] Moreover, changes in market conditions would affect the conclusion: many more fruits, for example, are now available in Europe all-year round, and kitchen equipment technology is such that few fruits cannot be pulped (although food processors were in fact readily available in the mid-1970s!).

[23] See R. O'Donoghue and A. J. Padilla, *The Law and Economics of Article 82* (Hart Publishing, 2006), 67.

[24] Michelin also challenged the definition of the geographic market as being the Netherlands. See *infra* 384.

of tyres for heavy vehicles are not interchangeable, and at the same time too narrow inasmuch as car and van tyres are excluded from it although they occupy similar positions on the market. It further argues that the Commission's reasoning in its decision is contradictory in so far as it puts itself alternately in the shoes of the ultimate consumer and in those of the dealer. However, at the level of dealers' total sales, the average proportion of sales of Michelin heavy-vehicle tyres represents only 12 to 18 per cent, which rules out the existence of any dominant position.

36. The Commission defends the definition of the relevant product market used in its decision by pointing out that with a technically homogeneous product it is not possible to distinguish different markets depending on the dimensions, size or specific types of products: in that connection the elasticity of supply between different types and dimensions of tyre must be taken into account. On the other hand the criteria of interchangeability and elasticity of demand allow a distinction to be drawn between the market in tyres for heavy vehicles and the market in car tyres owing to the particular structure of demand, which, in the case of tyres for heavy vehicles, is characterized by the presence above all of experienced trade buyers.

37. As the Court has repeatedly emphasized, most recently in its judgment of 11 December 1980 in Case 31/90 *NV L'Oreal and SA L'Oreal* v. *PVBA De Nieuwe AMCK* [1980] ECR 3775, for the purposes of investigating the possibly dominant position of an undertaking on a given market, the possibilities of competition must be judged in the context of the market comprising the totality of the products which, with respect to their characteristics, are particularly suitable for satisfying constant needs and are only to a limited extent interchangeable with other products. However, it must be noted that the determination of the relevant market is useful in assessing whether the undertaking concerned is in a position to prevent effective competition from being maintained and behave to an appreciable extent independently of its competitors and customers and consumers. For this purpose, therefore, an examination limited to the objective characteristics only of the relevant products cannot be sufficient: the competitive conditions and the structure of supply and demand on the market must also be taken into consideration.

38. Moreover, it was for that reason that the Commission and Michelin NV agreed that new, original-equipment tyres should not be taken into consideration in the assessment of market shares. Owing to the particular structure of demand for such tyres characterized by direct orders from car manufacturers, competition in this sphere is in fact governed by completely different factors and rules.

39. As far as replacement tyres are concerned, the first point which must be made is that at the user level there is no interchangeability between car and van tyres on the one hand and heavy-vehicle tyres on the other. Car and van tyres therefore have no influence at all on competition on the market in heavy-vehicle tyres.

40. Furthermore, the structure of demand for each of those groups of products is different. Most buyers of heavy-vehicle tyres are trade users, particularly haulage undertakings, for whom, as the Commission explained, the purchase of replacement tyres represents an item of considerable expenditure and who constantly ask their tyre dealers for advice and long-term specialized services adapted to their specific needs. On the other hand, for the average buyer of car or van tyres the purchase of tyres is an occasional event and even if the buyer operates a business he does not expect such specialized advice and service adapted to specific needs. Hence the sale of heavy-vehicle tyres requires a particularly specialized distribution network which is not the case with the distribution of car and van tyres.

41. . . .

42. The Commission rightly examined the structure of the market and demand primarily at the level of dealers to whom Michelin NV applied the practice in question. Michelin NV has itself stated, although in another context, that it was compelled to change its discount system to take account of the tendency towards specialization amongst its dealers, some of whom, such as garage owners, no longer sold tyres for heavy vehicles and vans. This confirms the differences

existing in the structure of demand between different groups of dealers. Nor has Michelin NV disputed that the distinction drawn between tyres for heavy vehicles, vans and cars is also applied by all its competitors, especially as regards discount terms, even if in the case of certain types of tyre the distinctions drawn by different manufacturers may vary in detail.

43. Nevertheless, it cannot be deduced from the fact that the conduct to which exception is taken in this case affects dealers that Michelin NV's position ought to be assessed on the basis of the proportion of Michelin heavy-vehicle tyres in the dealers' total turnover. Since it is a question of investigating whether Michelin NV holds a dominant position in the case of certain products, it is unimportant that the dealers also deal in other products if there is no competition between those products and the products in question.

44. On the other hand, in deciding whether a dominant position exists, neither the absence of elasticity of supply between different types and dimensions of tyres for heavy vehicles, which is due to differences in the conditions of production, nor the absence of interchangeability and elasticity of demand between those types and dimensions of tyre from the point of view of the specific needs of the user allow a number of smaller markets, reflecting those types and dimensions, to be distinguished, as Michelin NV suggests. Those differences between different types and dimensions of tyre are not vitally important for dealers, who must meet demand from customers for the whole range of heavy-vehicle tyres. Furthermore, in the absence of any specialization on the part of the undertakings concerned, such differences in the type and dimensions of a product are not a crucial factor in the assessment of an undertaking's market position because in view of their similarity and the manner in which they complement one another at the technical level, the conditions of competition on the market are the same for all the types and dimensions of the product.

45. In establishing that Michelin NV has a dominant position the Commission was therefore right to assess its market share with reference to replacement tyres for lorries, buses and similar vehicles and to exclude consideration of car and van tyres.

(bb) The taking into consideration of competition from retreads

46. In order to prove that its market share is less than the Commission claims the applicant also contends that the Commission arbitrarily excluded retreads from the relevant market; in the applicant's view these offer consumers a genuine alternative as regards both quality and price. To support that argument Michelin NV produces a number of calculations intended to show the competitiveness of retreads compared with new tyres.

47. In the Commission's view retreads must be excluded from the relevant market because they cannot replace new tyres. This, it argues, is first of all because consumers consider them inferior in terms of safety; secondly most retreads are produced to order for the transport undertakings themselves so that the market in question is one for the supply of services; lastly, since retreads are a secondary product as compared with new tyres, which are, as it were, the raw material for retreading, which largely prevents them from being replaced by retreads, competition must be assessed on the primary market, which is the key to the whole market.

48. In this regard it must first be recalled that although the existence of a competitive relationship between two products does not presuppose complete interchangeability for a specific purpose, it is not a pre-condition for a finding that a dominant position exists in the case of a given product that there should be a complete absence of competition from other partially interchangeable products as long as such competition does not affect the undertaking's ability to influence appreciably the conditions in which that competition may be exerted or at any rate to conduct itself to a large extent without having to take account of that competition and without suffering any adverse effects as a result of its attitude.

49. It is clear from the facts, as established from the parties' statements and those made by the witnesses examined at the hearing during the administrative procedure, that it cannot be denied that new tyres and retreads are interchangeable to some degree but only to a limited extent and not for all purposes. Although Michelin NV has produced calculations to show that the price and quality of retreads are comparable to those of new tyres and that a number of users do in fact consider the two groups of products interchangeable for their purposes; it has nevertheless admitted that in terms of safety and reliability a retread's value may be less than that of new tyre and, what is more, the Commission has shown that a number of users have certain reservations, which may or may not be justified, regarding the use of a retread, particularly on a vehicle's front axle.

50. In order to assess the effect of this limited competition from retreads on Michelin NV's market position it must be borne in mind that at least some retreads are not put on sale but are produced to order for the user as some transport undertakings attach importance to having their own tyre carcasses retreaded in order to be sure of not receiving damaged carcasses. It must be acknowledged that there has been no agreement between the parties as regards the percentage of tyres retreaded in this way as a form of service; the Commission has estimated it at 80 per cent to 95 per cent of retreads whereas Michelin NV maintains that it is only 15 to 20 per cent and that in most cases the order is placed in the name of the dealer and not that of the user. Despite that disagreement between the parties it may said that a proportion of retreads reaching the consumer stage are not in competition with new tyres because they involve a service provided directly by the retreading firms to the users.

51. Furthermore, in assessing the size of Michelin NV's market share in relation to its competitors' it must not be overlooked that the market in renovated tyres is a secondary market which depends on supply and prices on the market in new tyres since every retread is made from a tyre which was originally a new tyre and there is a limit to the number of occasions on which a tyre may be retreaded. Consequently a considerable proportion of demand will inevitably always be satisfied by new tyres. In such circumstances the possession by an undertaking of a dominant position in new tyres gives it a privileged position as regards competition from retreading undertakings and this enables it to conduct itself with greater independence on the market than would be possible for a retreading undertaking.

52. It is clear from the considerations set out above that the partial competition to which manufacturers of new tyres are exposed from retreading undertakings is not sufficient to deprive a manufacturer of new tyres of the economic power which he possesses by virtue of his dominant position on the market in new tyres. In assessing Michelin NV's position in relation to the strength and number of its competitors the Commission was therefore right to take into consideration a market share to 57 to 65 per cent on the market in new replacement tyres for heavy vehicles. Compared with the market shares of Michelin NV's main competitors amounting to 4 to 8 per cent, that market share constitutes a valid indication of Michelin NV's preponderant strength in relation to its competitors, even when allowance is made for some competition from retreads.

The ECJ thus upheld the Commission's decision in *Michelin*.[25] The Commission's decision itself was trenchantly criticized in an article by Korah. In the extract of that article set out below it is considered whether it was right to exclude retreads or remoulds from the relevant market.

[25] [1981] OJ L353/33, [1982] 1 CMLR 643.

V. Korah, 'The Michelin Decision of the Commission' (1982) 7 *ELRev* 130, 130–1

In order to decide whether a firm enjoys market power, it is necessary to analyse the market to see what competitive pressures constrain the ability of the firm to exploit its suppliers, customers or consumers. The Court has held in *Continental Can* that the Commission should define the relevant market and give reasons for its definition. In *Michelin* it was defined (para. 31) as new replacement tyres for trucks, buses and similar vehicles. The Commission excludes remoulds, as these are not adequate substitutes. Some users of heavy vehicles doubt the reliability of remoulds, and tend not to use them on the front, or driven axle for long distance transport or for the transport of rapidly perishable goods (para. 5). Moreover, most heavy vehicle users will use as remoulds only tyres that they themselves have used and which they know are not based on defective casings, so few buy these from dealers. Most have their own used tyres remoulded by specialists. Remoulds sell at a discount of at least 40 per cent of the price of new replacement tyres (we are not told what price—the retail price, the base price of the manufacturers or the net price paid by retailers after discount). At that relative price, contrary to the Commission's view, they must be substitutes for many vehicle users. Competitive pressures on market decisions may come from the supply of goods that are not identical, even if some customers would not switch. The possibility of losing the custom of those who would have their tyres remoulded must constrain Michelin Netherlands's pricing decisions . . . One of its reasons for excluding remoulds would be right, although it is not spelled out, but it is submitted that the other is wrong. The Commission limits its consideration of the relevant market to the 'level of the retailer' (para. 31). It seems that it is concerned with the retailer of replacement tyres being able to obtain adequate supplies. If one is concerned only with the welfare of retailers, the remoulders must by definition be excluded; but why should the inquiry be so limited? The interests of the remoulders is equally important, and to the extent that vehicle users prefer to have their tyres remoulded at a lower charge, the public interest in the efficient and competitive supply of usable tyres embraces both forms of supply.

The definition of the replacement tyre market was revisited 20 years later in a second decision of the Commission finding that Michelin had abused a dominant position in France by the discount and rebate system it operated.[26] The Commission concluded that new replacement tyres for trucks and buses in France and retreaded tyres for trucks and buses in France were two separate markets and that Michelin had a dominant position on both of them. On appeal to the CFI Michelin did not challenge the market definition or the finding of dominance.[27] The Commission's reasons for separating new tyres and retreads were essentially the same as they had been in 1981:[28] the supply and demand for the two types of tyre were different;[29] retreaders were skilled *service* providers who did not necessarily have any links to tyre dealers, whereas new tyres were supplied to dealers; the retread market was a secondary 'after-sales' market, in which new tyres were the raw material and the purpose was to prolong the life of the tyre to avoid purchasing another new one; and, finally, there was still a safety issue in that many final (haulier)

---

[26] *Michelin* [2001] OJ L143/1, [2002] 5 CMLR 388 (*Michelin II*). The abuse aspect of the case is discussed *infra* Chap. 7, 194.

[27] Case T-203/01, *Manufacture Française des Pneumatiques Michelin v. Commission* [2004] 4 CMLR 923, para 44.

[28] *Michelin II* decision, paras. 109–18.

[29] See *infra* 364.

customers perceived retreads as less safe ('the situation that prevailed in 1981 has thus not changed significantly').[30] The Commission did not employ the SSNIP test in *Michelin II*.

e. The SSNIP test

The SSNIP test and qualitative assessments of the characteristics and use of products may both be used to determine the market. In *Wanadoo*[31] the Commission defined the relevant market as the French market for high-speed internet access for residential customers (the products with which the infringement of predatory pricing was concerned were internet access services based on ADSL technology[32]). The Commission examined the differences in performance between high and low-speed internet access and concluded that the differences were clearly perceived by consumers, and that an analysis of price differences between them showed that consumers were prepared to pay a premium for the extra performance and convenience of high-speed.[33] On appeal, France Télécom (which had succeeded to the rights of Wanadoo Interactive (WIN) following a merger) pleaded, *inter alia*, that the Commission should have considered the market as comprising both high-speed and low-speed access.

Case T-340/03, *France Télécom SA* v. *Commission*, 30 January 2007

Court of First Instance

78. According to settled case-law (Case 322/81 *Michelin* v *Commission* [1983] ECR 3461, paragraph 37; Case T-65/96 *Kish Glass* v *Commission* [2000] ECR II-1885, paragraph 62; and Case T-219/99 *British Airways* v *Commission* [2003] ECR II-5917, paragraph 91), for the purposes of investigating the possibly dominant position of an undertaking on a given product market, the possibilities of competition must be judged in the context of the market comprising the totality of the products or services which, with respect to their characteristics, are particularly suitable for satisfying constant needs and are only to a limited extent interchangeable with other products or services. Moreover, since the determination of the relevant market is useful in assessing whether the undertaking concerned is in a position to prevent effective competition from being maintained and to behave to an appreciable extent independently of its competitors and, in this case, of its service providers, an examination to that end cannot be limited solely to the objective character-istics of the relevant services, but the competitive conditions and the structure of supply and demand on the market must also be taken into consideration.

79. If a product could be used for different purposes and if these different uses are in accordance with economic needs, which are themselves also different, there are good grounds for accepting that this product may, according to the circumstances, belong to separate markets which may present specific features which differ from the standpoint both of the structure and of the conditions of competition. However, this finding does not justify the conclusion that such a product, together with all the other products which can replace it as far as concerns the various uses to which it may be put and with which it may compete, forms one single market.

---

[30] *Michelin II* decision, para. 116.

[31] COMP/38.233, [2005] 5 CMLR 120.

[32] Asynchronous Digital Subscriber Line. It allows broadband services to be provided over the traditional telephone copper wire.

[33] COMP/38.233, para. 187.

80. The concept of the relevant market in fact implies that there can be effective competition between the products which form part of it and this presupposes that there is a sufficient degree of interchangeability between all the products forming part of the same market in so far as a specific use of such products is concerned (Case 85/76 *Hoffmann-La Roche* v *Commission* [1979] ECR 461, paragraph 28).

81. It is also apparent from the Commission Notice on the definition of the relevant market for the purposes of Community competition law (OJ 1997 C 372, p. 5, paragraph 7) that '[a] relevant product market comprises all those products and/or services which are regarded as interchangeable or substitutable by the consumer, by reason of the products' characteristics, their prices and their intended use'.

82. It must be stated that there is not a mere difference in comfort or quality between high- and low-speed access. It is clear from the evidence provided by the Commission (recital 175 of the decision), which was not contradicted by WIN, that some applications available with high-speed access are simply not feasible with low-speed access, including, for example, the downloading of very voluminous video files or interactive network games. WIN also confirmed, in its reply of 4 March 2002 to the first statement of objections, that there are 'audiovisual/multimedia activities . . . more specific to ADSL'. In addition, the study undertaken by the Centre de recherche pour l'étude et l'observation des conditions de vie (Research Centre for the Study and Monitoring of Living Standards) (Crédoc) on behalf of WIN which it presented in an annex to its application also describes new uses developed on the internet by the eXtense service and which are specific to high-speed access, that is, playing network games, listening to radio online, watching a video online and shopping online. According to that study, moreover, the subscriber with high-speed access goes online far more often and, on average, for considerably longer than the low-speed access user.

83. As regards the differences in technical features and performances, it is clear from the Commission's contentions (recitals 181 to 187 of the decision), which have not been denied by the applicant, that an important technical feature of high-speed internet access is the specific nature of the modems used. A high-speed internet access modem cannot be used for low-speed internet access and vice versa (recital 181 of the decision). In addition, in the case of high-speed access, the connection is always on and the telephone line always available for making calls.

84. In addition, in the case of the French market, it should be pointed out that, for the period investigated, the offers of high-speed access involved download speeds in the region of 512 kbits/s (recital 185 of the decision). The offers of traditional low-speed access (limited to 56 kbits/s) and of ISDN (integrated services digital network) (64 or 128 kbits/s) only allowed speeds of 4 to 10 times less. The ADSL offers with download speeds of 128 kbits/s, which, according to the applicant, bear witness to the continuity between low-speed and high-speed, only became available at the end of the period covered by the decision. In addition, even in the case of an offer of 128 kbits/s, the difference between low-speed and high-speed access is considerable. The difference in performance was therefore considerable during the period investigated.

85. In addition to the differences in use, features and performances, there is a significant price differential between low-speed and high-speed access (recitals 188 to 192 of the decision).

86. As regards the degree of substitutability, it is appropriate to recall, in addition to the case-law cited in paragraph 78 above, the criteria laid down by the Commission in its Notice on the definition of the relevant market for the purposes of Community competition law (see paragraph 81 above).

87. According to that notice, the assessment of demand substitution entails a determination of the range of products which are viewed as substitutes by the consumer. One way of making this determination can be viewed as a speculative experiment, postulating a hypothetical small but lasting change in relative prices and evaluating the likely reactions of customers to that increase. In paragraph 17 of the notice, the Commission states '[t]he question to be answered is whether

the parties' customers would switch to readily available substitutes...in response to a hypothetical small (in the range 5 to 10%) but permanent relative price increase in the products and areas being considered'.

88. In recital 193 of the decision, the Commission admits that low-speed and high-speed access indeed present some degree of substitutability. It adds in recital 194, however, that the operation of such substitutability is extremely asymmetrical, the migrations of customers from offers of high-speed to low-speed access being negligible compared with the migrations in the other direction. However, according to the Commission, if the products were perfectly substitutable from the point of view of demand, the rates of migration should be identical or at least comparable.

89. It should be pointed out, in this respect, that, first of all, it is clear from the information gathered by WIN and reproduced in Table 7 of the decision that the migration rates of high-speed subscribers to integral low-speed offers were very low during the period covered, in spite of the difference in price between those services, which should have prompted numerous internet users to turn to low-speed access. This large discrepancy in the rates of migration between low-speed and high-speed access and between high-speed and low-speed access does not lend credence to the argument that those services are interchangeable in the eyes of consumers. In the application, WIN also failed to adduce any evidence to cast doubt on that analysis.

90. Secondly, it transpires that, according to a survey carried out on behalf of the Commission and presented by WIN in an annex to its application, 80% of subscribers would maintain their subscription in response to a price increase in the range 5 to 10%. According to paragraph 17 of the Notice on the definition of the relevant market for the purposes of Community competition law (see paragraph 87 above), this high percentage of subscribers who would not abandon high-speed access in response to a price increase of 5 to 10% provides a strong indication of the absence of demand-side substitution.

91. Consequently, on the basis of all the foregoing, it should be held that the Commission was right to find that a sufficient degree of substitutability between high-speed and low-speed access did not exist and to define the market in question as that of high-speed internet access for residential customers.

It will be noted that in this judgment the CFI cited the case-law of the ECJ pertaining to identifying substitute products by reference to characteristics and use. However, it also referred to the Commission Notice and to the SSNIP test (paragraph 87) and to a survey showing that 80 per cent of subscribers to the high-speed service would be impervious to a 5–10 per cent price increase. The CFI concluded that this 'provides a strong indication' of the absence of demand-side substitution. This was hardly a rigorous analysis of the economic of the profitability of a price increase using critical loss analysis[34] but it was at least an acknowledgement of the hypothetical monopolist concept.[35]

f. The Cellophane Fallacy

The main problem with the application of the SSNIP test in Article 82 cases is the 'cellophane fallacy', as explained in Chapter I.[36] It will be recalled that erroneous market definitions can be reached if the hypothetical price rise is measured from a prevailing price which is *already* at a

---

[34] See Chap. 1, 69.

[35] Given that everyone in the case must have been familiar with the product at issue it may not have needed SSNIP tests to convince the Court that low-speed internet access is no substitute for high-speed.

[36] See *supra* Chap. 1, 70.

monopoly level. Given that Article 82 deals with dominant firms the cellophane fallacy is a very real limitation on the usefulness of the SSNIP test in ascertaining whether a firm is in a dominant position.

g. The Structure of Supply and Demand

The importance of considering the structure of supply and demand on the market was stressed in *France Télécom* (see paragraphs 78 and 79, extracted above). The structure of supply and demand may even cause identical products to fall into different markets. It was relevant to the determination of the market in *Michelin*. It is seen from the extract set out above[37] that the ECJ upheld the Commission finding that identical new heavy vehicle tyres and retreads formed two separate product markets and that the market for the supply of heavy vehicle tyres to vehicle manufacturers as original equipment was distinct from the market for the supply to dealers to be fitted as replacements. In both cases the Court stressed the difference in the dynamics of the transactions.[38] Conversely, the ECJ accepted (in paragraph 44) that different types of heavy vehicle tyres, although *not* substitutes for each other, *were* in the same market. This was because dealers[39] had to stock all tyres and the conditions of competition were the same for all types and dimensions. In *Michelin II* the Commission stressed that the structure of supply and demand for new replacement tyres and retreads was different in that the former were supplied to tyre dealers and the latter to retreaders.[40]

Similarly, in *Van den Bergh Foods* the Commission placed emphasis on the structure of supply and demand in finding that the markets for single wrapped individual ice cream and individual portions of soft ice cream were distinct. Although the consumer might perceive the two types of ice-cream to be reasonably interchangeable, the competitive conditions under which they were offered to the retail trade were different and distinct. Soft ice cream had, for example, to be processed by the retailer and so required the installation of special processing and dispensing machines; it was not self-service and was not normally branded.

The consumer's point of view is, . . . not in every instance the sole criterion in the determination of a product market; nor is an examination limited only to the objective characteristics of the products in question sufficient. The competitive conditions and the structure of supply and demand on the market must also be taken into consideration.[41]

h. Chains of Substitution and Products with Multiple Applications

It was explained in Chapter 1 that there can be 'chains of substitution' in both product and geographic markets, where a relevant market may be defined which comprises a group of products not all of which are direct substitutes for each other. The problem of a chain of substitution may arise where a product has more than one use, and there are substitutes for one use and not for others, or different substitutes for different uses.[42]

---

[37] *Supra* 356.

[38] See also Case C-333/94 P, *Tetra Pak International SA v. Commission* [1996] ECR I-5951, [1997] 4 CMLR 662, para. 13.

[39] For the abuse issues in *Michelin* see *infra* Chap. 7.

[40] *Michelin* [2001] OJ L143/1, [2002] 5 CMLR 388, para. 114.

[41] [1998] OJ L246/1, [1998] 5 CMLR 530, para. 133. The decision was upheld by the CFI on appeal, Case T-65/98, *Van den Bergh Foods Ltd v. Commission* [2003] ECR II-4653, [2004] 4 CMLR 1 (*aff'd* Case C-552/03 P, *Unilever Bestfoods (Ireland) Ltd v. EC Commission* [2006] 5 CMLR 1494), where the definition of the market was not challenged.

[42] See *supra* Chap. 1, 76.

This was illustrated in *Hoffmann-La Roche*.[43] Hoffmann-La Roche (HLR) challenged the Commission's finding that it had committed a number of abuses of dominant positions held on several separate vitamin markets. Two of the vitamins concerned, C and E, had two distinct uses. In each case the vitamin had a bio-nutritive use for which there were no substitutes, and an anti-oxidant use. Both vitamins C and E and other products could be used for the anti-oxidant use. Hoffmann-La Roche claimed that the two vitamins were in the same market for anti-oxidants together with these other products. The ECJ, concentrating on the bio-nutritive use, upheld the Commission's finding that the vitamins each constituted a separate market. The reasoning was not, however, entirely satisfactory. In particular, the judgment is criticized for the Court's failure to take account of the two distinct uses. If HLR could not profitably increase the price to customers in the bio-nutritive market without also losing customers in the anti-oxidant market, then arguably they should have been found to form part of the same market.[44]

Case 85/76, *Hoffmann-La Roche & Co AG* v. *Commission* [1979] ECR 461, [1979] 3 CMLR 211

Court of Justice

28. If a product could be used for different purposes and if these different uses are in accordance with economic needs, which are themselves also different, there are good grounds for accepting that this product may, according to the circumstances, belong to separate markets which may present specific features which differ from the standpoint both of the structure and of the conditions of competition. However this finding does not justify the conclusion that such a product together with all the other products which can replace it as far as concerns the various uses to which it may be put and with which it may compete, forms one single market. The concept of the relevant market in fact implies that there can be effective competition between the products which form part of it and this presupposes that there is a sufficient degree of interchangeability between all the products forming part of the same market in so far as a specific use of such products is concerned. There was no such interchangeability, at any rate during the period under consideration, between all the vitamins of each of the groups C and E and all the products which, according to the circumstances, may be substituted for one or other of these groups of vitamins for technological uses which are themselves extremely varied.

29. On the other hand there may be some doubt whether, for the purpose of delimiting the respective markets of the C and E groups of vitamins, it is necessary to include all the vitamins of each of these groups in a market corresponding to that group, or whether, on the contrary, each of these groups must be placed in a separate market, one comprising vitamins for bio-nutritive use and the other vitamins for technological purposes.

30. However, in order to calculate the market shares of Roche and its competitors correctly this question did not have to be answered because, as the Commission has rightly pointed out, if it had been necessary to draw this distinction, it would have to be drawn for Roche's competitors as well as for Roche itself, and—in the absence of any indication to the contrary by the applicant— in similar proportions with the result that the market shares in percentages would remain unchanged. Finally Roche, in answer to a question put to it by the Court, has stated that all the vitamins of each group, irrespective of the ultimate intended use of the product, were subject to

---

[43] Case 85/76, *Hoffmann-La Roche & Co AG* v. *Commission* [1979] ECR 461, [1979] 3 CMLR 211.

[44] See the discussion *supra* 65.

the same price system so that they could not be split up into specific markets. It follows from the foregoing that the Commission has correctly delimited the relevant markets in its contested decision.

The narrow definition adopted by the Commission and upheld by the Court in *Hoffmann-La Roche* is less troubling if it is remembered that market definition is not an end in itself, but a step towards assessing market power. As long as it is recognized that markets are not impermeable and may be subject to competitive pressures from *outside* the market, a narrow market definition is not serious. This point is made by Baden Fuller[45] in the extract below.

C. W. Baden Fuller, 'Article 86: Economic Analysis of the Existence of a Dominant Position' (1979) 4 *ELRev* 423, 425

The Court has said that it is necessary to define a market: economists would agree—for to point out dominance, one must say upon what market a firm is dominant. In *Roche* (paragraph 28) and *UBC* (paragraph 22), the Court defined the extent of a market by reference to the existence of substitutes on the demand side and in *Continental Can Company* to substitute on the supply side . . . For example, in *Roche* the defendants disputed whether Vitamins C and E should each be considered as part of one market. According to the Court (paragraphs 28 and 29), Vitamins C and E had two usages, one as additives to foodstuffs (called the bio-nutritive use), and the other as anti-oxydants, fermentation agents and additives (called the technological usage); in their first usage, C and E performed different functions and in this usage neither could be substituted for the other, and there was no other product which could perform as substitutes for either; in their second usage, C and E were not only interchangeable with each other, but there was a variety of other products which could also be interchanged with them. The notable aspect of the case was that it was not always possible for Roche to distinguish between customers who wanted Vitamins C and E for the different uses, because some buyers who used C or E in foodstuffs also required anti-oxydants for which C and E could be used interchangeably. An economist would argue that there were three markets defined from the demand side: the two separate bio-nutritive usage markets of C and E, and the technological usage market which included C, E and other anti-oxydants. It is obvious that a change in price of (say) Vitamin C would have little effect on the quantity of E sold for its bio-nutritive use. Economists would say that there is a low cross elasticity between C and E, and that these products were not substitutes (i.e they were in different markets). But a change in price of C would have a substantial effect on the quantity of E sold for its technological use, indicating a high cross elasticity, and that these products were substitutes (i.e in the same market). The Court ruled that Vitamins C and E were separate markets stressing their bio-nutritive uses. Here economists would agree with the Court, but would note that any analysis of these markets must also consider the technological market . . .

A narrower market definition may, however, be more likely to result in a finding of dominance.[46]

---

[45] And see, e.g., V. Korah, 'Concept of a Dominant Position within the Meaning of Art 86' (1980) 17 *CMLRev* 395.

[46] The higher the undertaking's market share, the more likely a finding of dominance: see *infra* 396 ff.

The Commission Notice on market definition, paragraph 57, which is set out in Chapter 1,[47] recognizes that where chains of substitution are possible practical problems may arise in determining both the geographic and the product market. It will be recalled that the Commission's conclusion is that the crucial question is the extent to which the existence of substitutes constrains an undertaking's pricing policy.[48]

In *AKZO*[49] AKZO Chemie was found to be dominant on the market for organic peroxides, which had multiple uses. The case shows how each of these situations has to be examined in the light of the particular circumstances.[50] Organic peroxides are used in polymer manufacture, where in some fields of application they have limited substitutes. The main organic peroxide, benzoyl peroxide, can also be used as a bleaching agent in flour-milling in the UK and Ireland. AKZO argued that the relevant market should be considered as that for flour additives (where it did not have a high market share). The Commission found that the relevant market was the organic peroxides market as a whole. Since AKZO concentrated its production on the polymer sector its share of the whole peroxides market was 50 per cent. The ECJ upheld the Commission's definition of the market because AKZO's conduct—lowering its prices in the flour-milling sector in order to protect its position in the polymer sector—as well as its internal documentation, showed that the undertaking itself treated the market as a single one.

i. Raw Materials

A raw material may constitute a separate product market even though the derivative product made from it forms part of a wide product market which has a number of substitutes. In *Commercial Solvents*, for example, it was held that a raw material, aminobutanol, used to produce ethambutol, an anti-TB drug, constituted a product market of its own.[51] In this case Zoja manufactured ethambutol from aminobutanol which had been manufactured by Commercial Solvents Corporation. Other anti-TB drugs existed on the market, which were not ethambutol based. The ECJ held that the relevant market was not the market for the derivatives (the drug) but the market for the raw material. There may have been substitute drugs which could be used to combat TB but a manufacturer of ethambutol, such as Zoja, could not operate without aminobutanol.[52]

Commercial Solvents was the first case to deal with the problems posed by derivative or ancillary markets. The concept developed in this case, that such markets can be distinguished from those for the primary product, has proved of great importance in the Article 82 jurisprudence, as the following paragraphs show.

j. Markets for 'Inputs'

The raw material in *Commercial Solvents* was an input in the production process for the TB drugs. It was a product which had been previously sold by Commercial Solvents to Zoja. The question has arisen, however, as to whether there can be a market in an 'input' which the producer of the 'input' does not offer for sale but uses only for its own purposes. This can become an issue in

[47] *Supra* 76.

[48] As it has demonstrated in a number of merger cases, such as *AstraZeneca/Novartis* COMP/M.1806.

[49] Case C-62/86, *AKZO Chemie BV v. Commission* [1991] ECR I-3359, [1993] 5 CMLR 215.

[50] *Ibid.*, para. 38.

[51] Cases 6 and 7/73, *Istituto Chemioterapico Italiano SpA and Commercial Solvents Corp v. Commission* [1974] ECR 223, [1974] 1 CMLR 309.

[52] Other possible ways of producing ethambutol, using thiophenol or butatone, were dismissed by the ECJ as they were uncertain and experimental and had not been used on an industrial scale.

cases where the alleged abuse of a dominant position is the refusal to supply something to which competitors in downstream markets seek access in order to serve customers there. In *Magill*[53] the ECJ upheld the Commission's definition of a market in 'television listings' although the broadcasting companies did not sell these for publication.[54] In *Bronner*[55] the ECJ accepted that there could be a market in schemes for the home delivery of newspapers even though the undertaking concerned had developed its scheme to distribute its own newspapers and did not 'sell' it independently. The most striking example is *IMS*[56] in which the ECJ said that there could be a 'potential' market in inputs which a monopoly undertaking decided not to market independently. In that case the 'input' was a system for representing pharmaceutical sales data over which the undertaking that created it claimed copyright. The undertaking used it to produce the sales reports it sold to pharmaceutical companies. There was no suggestion that the undertaking had ever contemplated 'selling' (licensing) the scheme to others. Nevertheless, the ECJ found that there could be a 'market' for the scheme.[57] The point can be of great importance in cases (such as *Magill*, *Bronner*, and *IMS*) where the alleged abuse is a refusal to supply, because it appears that there can be such an abuse only where two markets are involved.[58]

k. Aftermarkets

As explained in Chapter 1, an 'aftermarket' is a product or service which is complementary to, and follows on from, another, such as spare parts,[59] consumables or maintenance services.[60] Competition issues can arise when the supplier of the original (primary) product or equipment also supplies the product or service in the aftermarket (in some markets the producer makes more money from the sale of consumables than from the original product[61]). There are two possible scenarios.

First, the supplier may not be the only source of products or services in the aftermarket as the primary product may be compatible with different brands.[62] In this situation the supplier may try to ensure that its customers obtain the aftermarket goods or services from itself rather the competitors (it may or may not be dominant on the aftermarket). Where the supplier is in a

---

[53] Cases C-241–242/91 P, *RTE & ITP v. Commission (Television Listings/Magill)* [1995] ECR I-743 [1995] 4 CMLR 718.

[54] Their refusal to license them to publishers of independent 'composite' television magazines was the subject of the case, see *infra* Chap. 7, 557.

[55] Case C-7/97, *Oscar Bronner GmbH & Co KG v. Mediaprint* [1998] ECR I-7791, [1991] 4 CMLR 112.

[56] Case C-418/01, *IMS Health GmbH & Co OHG v. NDC Health GmbH & Co KG* [2004] ECR I-503, [2004] 4 CMLR 1543. The matter also arose in the Commission proceedings in the same matter, see *NDC Health/IMS: Interim Measures* [2002] OJ L 59/18, [2002] 4 CMLR 111 (suspended on appeal, Case T-184/01 R, *IMS Health v. Commission* [2001] ECR II-3193, [2002] 4 CMLR 58, confirmed by the President of the ECJ, Case C-481/01 P(R), *IMS Health v. Commission* [2002] ECR I-3401, [2002] 5 CMLR 44 and subsequently withdrawn because of developments in the copyright situation, *IMS Health/NDC Health: Interim Measures* [2003] OJ L268/69). IMS is discussed *infra* Chap. 7, 563.

[57] Case C-418/01, *IMS Health GmbH & Co OHG v. NDC Health GmbH & Co KG*, paras. 44–5.

[58] The issue of refusals to supply, and the essential facilities doctrine is discussed *infra* Chap. 7.

[59] A replacement for an integral part of the original product, produced by the supplier of that product and/or by independent manufacturers. Motor vehicle tyres have never been considered 'spare parts' in this sense.

[60] *Supra* 78.

[61] Compare the price of some video games with that of the games machine.

[62] This means that the primary product producer does not have intellectual property rights which prevent competitors making compatible spare parts or consumables. For the possibility of a refusal to license others to make compatible products constituting an abuse under Article 82, see Chap. 7, 535.

dominant position on the market for the primary product the steps it takes to this end may constitute the abuse of 'tying' or 'bundling'.[63] This was the situation in *Hilti*[64] and *Tetra Pak II*,[65] which are discussed below. The dominant manufacturer of the primary product may therefore seek to present itself as supplying an indivisible 'system' consisting of the durable primary product and e.g. an on-going supply of the consumable and a maintenance and repair service. If competition authorities take the view that there is one product market, consisting of the 'system', then tying or bundling is not an issue.

Secondly, the supplier may be the only source of products or services in the aftermarket which are compatible with the primary product. In that case owners of that brand of the primary product are dependent on the supplier for the products or services in the aftermarket. The one brand of spare parts, complements etc. has no substitutes. In this scenario there are two further possibilities:

- The supplier is dominant on the market for the primary product; or
- The supplier is not dominant on the market for the primary product.

Since the judgment in *Commercial Solvents*, in which the raw material market was distinguished from the ancillary market for the derivative product, the Commission has tended to define markets narrowly, finding that spare parts and consumables form part of a separate market from the original equipment supplied. The justification for this approach is that the original equipment and its spare parts or consumables are not substitutes for one another. The net result of such a division is that where only the supplier's brand in the aftermarket is compatible with the primary product an undertaking with a small share of the original equipment market may be found to be dominant in the aftermarket and find its behaviour constrained by Article 82.

The question whether the market for spare parts of a product might constitute a separate market for the purposes of EC competition law first arose in *Hugin*. This case concerned a refusal to supply by Hugin, a Swedish firm which produced and sold cash registers and their spare parts. It had approximately 12 per cent of the Community cash register market. Aftersales, maintenance, and repair services of Hugin machines were conducted by local subsidiaries, agents, and distributors in, *inter alia*, all the Member States. From October 1972 Hugin decided no longer to supply machines or their spare parts to Liptons, a small firm in south-east England which sold, leased, repaired, serviced, and reconditioned cash registers, including Hugin machines. Without the spare parts Liptons could not continue servicing and repairing Hugin machines. Liptons complained to the Commission and the Commission issued a decision holding that Hugin had committed an abuse of its dominant position on the spare parts market.[66] The ECJ held that the relevant market in this case was a narrow one. It was constituted only by Hugin spare parts which were required by independent undertakings that maintained and repaired Hugin cash registers. Since Hugin was the sole supplier of those spare parts it was held to be dominant on that market.[67]

---

[63] Effected through various pricing mechanisms, promises of favourable treatment or threats of unfavourable treatment: see further Chap. 7, 514 ff.

[64] Case T-30/89, *Hilti AG v. Commission* [1991] ECR II-439, [1992] 4 CMLR 16.

[65] Case C-333/94 P, *Tetra Pak International SA v Commission* [1996] ECR I-5951, [1997] 4 CMLR 662 (*Tetra Pak II*).

[66] See *infra* Chap. 7.

[67] See *infra* 425 ff.

Case 22/78, *Hugin Kassaregister AB and Hugin Cash Registers Ltd* v. *Commission* [1979] ECR 1869, [1979] 3 CMLR 345[68]

Court of Justice

5. To resolve the dispute it is necessary, first, to determine the relevant market. In this respect account must be taken of the fact that the conduct alleged against Hugin consists in the refusal to supply spare parts to Liptons and, generally, to any independent undertaking outside its distribution network. The question is, therefore, whether the supply of spare parts constitutes a specific market or whether it forms part of a wider market. To answer that question it is necessary to determine the category of clients who require such parts.

6. In this respect it is established, on the one hand, that registers are of such a technical nature that the user cannot fit the spare parts into the machine but requires the services of a specialized technician and, on the other, that the value of the spare parts is of little significance in relation to the cost of maintenance and repairs. That being the case, users of cash registers do not operate on the market as purchasers of spare parts, however they have their machines maintained and repaired. Whether they avail themselves of Hugin's after-sales service or whether they rely on independent undertakings engaged in maintenance and repair work, their spare part requirements are not manifested directly and independently on the market. While there certainly exists amongst users a market for maintenance and repairs which is distinct from the market in new cash registers, it is essentially a market for the provision of services and not for the sale of a product such as spare parts, the refusal to supply which forms the subject matter of the Commission's decision.

7. On the other hand, there exists a separate market for Hugin spare parts at another level, namely that of independent undertakings which specialize in the maintenance and repair of cash registers, in the reconditioning of used machines and in the sale of used machines and the renting out of machines. The role of those undertakings on the market is that of businesses which require spare parts for their various activities. They need such parts in order to provide services for cash register users in the form of maintenance and repairs and for the reconditioning of used machines intended for re-sale or renting out. Finally, they require spare parts for the maintenance and repair of new or used machines belonging to them which are rented out to their clients. It is, moreover, established that there is a specific demand for Hugin spare parts, since those parts are not interchangeable with spare parts for cash registers of other makes.

8. Consequently the market thus constituted by Hugin spare parts required by independent undertakings must be regarded as the relevant market for the purposes of the application of Article [82] [to] the facts of the case. It is in fact the market on which the alleged abuse was committed.

9. It is necessary to examine next whether Hugin occupies a dominant position on that market. In this respect Hugin admits that it has a monopoly in new spare parts. For commercial reasons any competing production of spare parts which could be used in Hugin cash registers is not conceivable in practice. Hugin argues nevertheless that another source of supply does exist, namely the purchase and dismantling of used machines. The value of that source of supply is disputed by the parties. Although the file appears to show that the practice of dismantling used machines is current in the cash register sector it cannot be regarded as constituting a sufficient alternative source of supply. Indeed the figures relating to Liptons' turnover during the years that

---

[68] The Commission Decision is reported at [1978] OJ L22/23, [1978] CMLR D19. The ECJ quashed the Commission's decision on the basis that it had not been established that there was an effect on inter-Member State trade.

Hugin refused to sell spare parts to it show that Liptons' business in the selling, renting out and repairing of Hugin machines diminished considerably, not only when expressed in absolute terms but even more so in real terms, taking inflation into account.

10. On the market for its own spare parts, therefore, Hugin is in a position which enables it to determine its conduct without taking account of competing sources of supply. There is therefore nothing to invalidate the conclusion that it occupies, on that market, a dominant position within the meaning of Article [82].

The ECJ's finding that the market was defined not as the market for spare parts needed by the owners of Hugin machines, but by general repairers and servicers of the machines has been criticized.

C. W. Baden Fuller, 'Article 86: Economic Analysis of the Existence of a Dominant Position' (1979) 4 *ELRev* 423, 426–7

In *Hugin* . . . , the Court defined the relevant market as Hugin spare parts required by independent undertakings. This definition of the market is conceptually different from that used in Roche and UBC. First, the Court defined the relevant market with respect to a brand, not a product. This is a minor point. Economists would have noted that spare parts could be made by independent concerns to fit Hugin machines. The Court . . . says that this was not the case, nor could ever be the case.

Second, the Court defined the relevant market without discussing the existence of possible substitutes on the demand side for independent undertakings. This is not a minor point. Consider those independent undertakings in the business of repairing, maintaining or refurbishing (but not renting or leasing) cash registers for independent customers. They often dealt in more than one brand of machine. Their engineers could, and did, repair more than one brand. In this respect, substitutes did exist on the demand side from the point of view of independent undertakings. The Court never discussed whether this substitution was easy, that is, whether the cross-elasticity was high or low. Hugin, in refusing to supply Liptons, apparently forced the latter to turn to servicing other machines. Liptons had said this shift was costly . . . The Commission in its Decision (paragraphs 27 and 28) did not show a proper analysis of this cost. Moreover, it did not even give figures on sales, costs or profits for Lipton's servicing business for outside customers separated from its other activities such as renting and leasing.

Without such an analysis it is not clear that the shift was so costly or difficult that it is reasonable to consider each brand of spare parts as forming a separate market. To me, the only sensible definitions of the relevant market are those which make specific reference to the owners of the machines. I believe the Court should have defined the market as: 'Spare parts required by those who are owners of Hugin machines.' One such owner would have been Liptons which owned machines as part of its business of renting and leasing and whose users were its customers. These spare parts could be obtained only from Hugin, directly or indirectly by means of maintenance contracts. A rise in the price of Hugin's spare parts and hence a concomitant rise in the price of the Hugin maintenance contracts (of which the costs of spare parts are but one component) does not lead to an easy substitution of any other spare parts for reasons noted. It is also unlikely to lead to a widescale scrapping of Hugin machines. (Incidentally, it is irrelevant but possibly correct to argue that increasing the price of such spare parts is likely to have adverse effects on Hugin's sales of new machines and hence Hugin's overall profits).

Despite this criticism, *Hugin* provides authority for the proposition that one brand of spare parts can constitute a separate product market for the purposes of Article 82. This principle has been applied and relied upon in a number of cases, in particular in two cases involving the motor industry, namely *Volvo*[69] and *Renault*.[70] In these cases it was held that spare parts for cars constitute a separate market from the cars themselves. A manufacturer of a car with a low market share may therefore find that it is dominant on the market for the supply of its spare parts.[71]

The *Hugin* principle was applied to consumables in *Hilti*. In that case the (dominant) manufacturer on the primary market was faced with competitors in the aftermarket.[72] Hilti made nail guns which were a technologically advanced way of making secure fastenings in the construction industry. The guns were used together with cartridges in cartridge strips and nails. The cartridges provided the explosive power which enabled the gun to fire the nails into different materials as required. Nails compatible with Hilti guns were made not only by Hilti but by a number of independent firms. These firms complained that Hilti was indulging in practices designed to ensure that purchasers of the guns bought only Hilti's own nails. The Commission held that these practices constituted an abuse.[73] Hilti argued that its nail gun and consumables formed a powder–actuated fastening system which was in competition with, and in the same market as, other forms of construction fastening system. Since the nail guns, cartridges, and nails were not in separate markets but formed one indivisible product, its conduct in 'tying' the sales together could not constitute an abuse. These arguments were rejected both by the CFI and the ECJ. The CFI set out its reasoning more fully:[74]

Case T-30/89, *Hilti AG* v. *Commission* [1991] ECR II-439, [1992] 4 CMLR 16

Court of First Instance

64. It should be observed at the outset that in order to assess Hilti's market position it is first necessary to define the relevant market, since the possibilities of competition can only be judged in relation to those characteristics of the products in question by virtue of which those products are particularly apt to satisfy an inelastic need and are only to a limited extent interchangeable with other products . . .

65. In order to determine, therefore, whether Hilti, as a supplier of nail guns and of consumables designed for them, enjoys such power over the relevant product market as to give it a dominant position within the meaning of Article [82], the first question to be answered is whether the relevant market is the market for all construction fastening systems or whether the relevant markets are those for PAF tools and the consumables designed for them, namely cartridge strips and nails.

---

[69] Case 238/87, *AB Volvo v. Erik Veng* [1988] ECR 6211, [1989] 4 CMLR 122.

[70] Case 53/87, *CICCRA v. Renault* [1988] ECR 6039, [1990] 4 CMLR 265.

[71] The *Volvo* and *Renault* cases are discussed further in Chap. 7.

[72] See *infra* Chap. 7, 518.

[73] *Eurofix-Bauco/Hilti* [1988] OJ L65/19, [1989] 4 CMLR 677. For the abuse issue, see Chap. 7.

[74] The ECJ in Case C-53/92 P *Hilti AG v. Commission* [1994] ECR I-667, [1994] 4 CMLR 614, confirmed the reasoning of the CFI.

66. The Court takes the view that nail guns, cartridge strips and nails constitute three specific markets. Since cartridge strips and nails are specifically manufactured, and purchased by users, for a single brand of gun, it must be concluded that there are separate markets for Hilti-compatible cartridge strips and nails, as the Commission found in its decision (paragraph 55).

67. With particular regard to the nails whose use in Hilti tools is an essential element of the dispute, it is common ground that since the 1960s there have been independent producers, including the interveners, making nails intended for use in nail guns. Some of those producers are specialized and produce only nails, and indeed some make only nails specifically designed for Hilti tools. That fact in itself is sound evidence that there is a specific market for Hilti-compatible nails.

68. Hilti's contention that guns, cartridge strips and nails should be regarded as forming an indivisible whole, 'a powder-actuated fastening system' is in practice tantamount to permitting producers of nail guns to exclude the use of consumables other than their own branded products in their tools. However, in the absence of general and binding statements or rules, any independent producer is quite free, as far as Community competition law is concerned, to manufacture consumables intended for use in equipment manufactured by others, unless in doing so it infringes a patent or some other industrial or intellectual property right. Even on the assumption that, as the applicant has argued, components of different makes cannot be interchanged without the system characteristics being influenced, the solution should lie in the adoption of appropriate laws and regulations, not in unilateral measures taken by nail gun producers which have the effect of preventing independent producers from pursuing the bulk of their business.

...

77. The conclusion must be that the relevant product market in relation to which Hilti's market position must be appraised is the market for nails designed for Hilti nail guns.

78. That finding is corroborated by the abovementioned letter of 23 March 1983 from Hilti to the Commission, in which the opinion was expressed that there were separate markets for guns, cartridge strips and nails. Although that did not, at the time, represent an interpretation of the term 'relevant market' for the purposes of Article [82] [EC], the content of the letter is nevertheless quite revealing as to Hilti's own commercial view of the markets in which it operated at the time. Hilti has explained that the letter was prepared by an in-house lawyer, in conjunction with an outside legal adviser and the product manager concerned. The letter was therefore drafted by persons who may be assumed to have had a sound knowledge of the undertaking and its business.

In paragraph 68 the Court states that independent producers are free, as far as Community competition law is concerned, to manufacture consumables. This statement is revealing of the policy behind the narrow market definition adopted in some of the cases. It is not, as the wording rather strangely suggests,[75] that Community competition law *allows* independents to manufacture but that Article 82 may preclude the producer of the original equipment from preventing others' access to the market. This prohibition is imposed in order to increase competition.[76]

The aftermarket issue also arose in *Tetra Pak II*,[77] one of the most complex Article 82 cases on market definition (an extract of the case is set out below[78]). Essentially in this case the

[75] The language of the case was English.

[76] See *infra* Chap. 7.

[77] *Elopak Italia/Tetra Pak* [1991] OJ L72/1, [1992] 4 CMLR 551, on appeal Case T-83/91, *Tetra Pak International SA v. Commission* [1994] ECR II-755, [1997] 4 CMLR 726, on appeal Case C-333/94 P, *Tetra Pak International SA v. Commission* [1996] ECR I-5951, [1997] 4 CMLR 662.

[78] *Infra* 389 ff.

Commission and the Court refused to accept that Tetra Pak operated on a market for systems in packaging liquid food. Rather it was found that it operated on four separate product markets: the market in machinery for the aseptic packaging of liquid foods in cartons and the corresponding market for cartons, and the market in machinery for the non-aseptic packaging of liquid foods in cartons and the corresponding market in cartons.

In *Info-Lab/Ricoh*,[79] however, the Commission declined to accept that there was a separate market for empty toner cartridges compatible with a specific (Ricoh) photocopy machine. This case concerned a complaint lodged by Info-Lab which made toner for photocopiers. It alleged that Ricoh, a manufacturer of photocopiers, was abusing its dominant position by refusing to supply Info-Lab with empty toner cartridges for Ricoh machines which Info-Lab could then fill with toner. Info-Lab could not make the cartridges itself without infringing Ricoh's intellectual property rights. It thus alleged that the empty cartridges, which could be filled with toner and sold to customers, constituted a separate product market and that Ricoh had abused its dominant position on this market. The Commission rejected the complaint, holding that the market identified by the complainant was not a separate product market. No producer or dealer produced or sold empty toner cartridges. There was no consumer demand for such a product. Rather, cartridge and powder were always sold together as a single product. The Commission went on to hold that Ricoh could not be forced to supply Info-Lab with empty cartridges.[80]

Servicing and maintenance may constitute an aftermarket. In *Digital*[81] the Commission took the view that there was a market for the maintenance services for Digital computer systems, separate from that for the computer systems themselves. Moreover, it considered that the maintenance services themselves fell into two separate markets: the market for hardware maintenance and the market for software maintenance services. The two services were not interchangeable with each other.

These narrow market definitions may perhaps seem alarming. However, the narrow definitions are not important if a realistic assessment is made when determining whether or not an undertaking operating on that market has market power. It will be seen in the discussion below that even a monopolist operating on a narrowly defined aftermarket may often not have market power. In many cases such a monopolist will not be able to exploit his position on the aftermarket (he will be unable to act with the 'independence' which the ECJ considers to be the mark of a dominant position) without compromising his position on the primary market. The need for compatible products or services may 'lock in' the purchaser of the original product but the supplier will ordinarily be constrained from exploiting this dependence. The question of market power in aftermarkets is discussed below.[82]

However, it may be that the interaction between the primary market and the aftermarket does not just affect the assessment of the supplier's market power but affects the definition of the market in the first place. The argument is that where a supplier's price increases in the aftermarket have the effect of customers switching to competitors in the primary market, then exploitation of the aftermarket is not possible. If an undertaking's behaviour on the aftermarket is constrained by the effects it has on the primary market, then the two markets may indeed be

---

[79] Case IV/36431, rejection of a complaint by decision: see *Competition Policy Newsletter* 1999, No. 1, 35.

[80] See *infra* 428 and Chap. 7.

[81] Commission Press Release IP/97/868. The Commission terminated its investigation following the acceptance of undertakings.

[82] See *infra* 425 ff.

one. This is recognized by the Commission in the Notice on market definition:

56. There are certain areas where the application of the principles above has to be undertaken with care. This is the case when considering primary and secondary markets, in particular, when the behaviour of undertakings at a point in time has to be analysed pursuant to Article [82]. The method of defining markets in these cases is the same, i.e., assessing the responses of customers based on their purchasing decisions to relative price changes, but taking into account as well, constraints on substitution imposed by conditions in the connected markets. A narrow definition of market for secondary products, for instance, spare parts, may result when compatibility with the primary product is important. Problems of finding compatible secondary products together with the existence of high prices and a long lifetime of the primary products may render relative price increases of secondary products profitable. A different market definition may result if significant substitution between secondary products is possible or if the characteristics of the primary products make quick and direct consumer responses to relative price increases of the secondary products feasible.[83]

1. One Product or Market or Two

It was seen above that an important consideration in market definition in the context of aftermarkets is that if there is only one product, and not two or more, there can be no question of 'tying' contrary to Article 82. A product cannot be tied to itself. The issue is broader than that of aftermarkets alone, and is illustrated by *Microsoft*.[84] There the Commission took action against Microsoft for infringing Article 82 by 'tying' in that it supplied its Windows desktop operating system with its Windows Media Player (WMP) ready installed. Microsoft claimed that it did not supply two separate product but one integrated one. The Commission disagreed.

Microsoft COMP/C-3/37.792, [2005] 4 CMLR 965

Commission

(800) The existence of distinct products is the second precondition for tying. Products that are not distinct cannot be tied in a way that is contrary to Article 82. Microsoft argues that WMP is an integral part of Windows and not a product distinct from Windows.

(801) Microsoft's proposition as to the existence of one integrated product does not correspond to the reality of the marketplace. Dominant companies often contest that two products are distinct, particularly when these products are used in conjunction with each other — thereby implying that a necessary condition for establishing tying according to competition law is not present. In *Tetra Pak II*..., Tetra Pak claimed that there was a natural link between the products it sold to its customers in combination (machines and cartons). The consequence in Tetra Pak's view was that it could lawfully combine the two products through contract. In *Hilti*, the producer of nail guns argued that the guns, cartridge strips and nails had to be regarded as belonging to one and the same relevant market.

(802) The Courts rejected these "integrative" approaches. In both cases, it pointed out that there existed independent manufacturers who specialised in the manufacture of the tied product, a fact which indicated that there was separate consumer demand and hence a distinct market for

---

[83] Commission Notice on the definition of the relevant market [1997] OJ C372/5, [1998] 4 CMLR 177. See also Discussion Paper, paras 247–9, O'Donoghue and Padilla, n. 23, *supra*, 103–4.

[84] COMP/C-3/37.792, [2005] 4 CMLR 965, on appeal Case T-201/04, *Microsoft v EC Commission* (judgment pending).

the tied product . . . Consequently, the Court held that the defendants had engaged in unlawful tying pursuant to Article 82.

(803) The distinctness of products for the purposes of an analysis under Article 82 therefore has to be assessed with a view to consumer demand. If there is no independent demand for an allegedly "tied" product, then the products at issue are not distinct and a tying charge will be to no avail.

(804) The fact that the market provides media players separately is evidence for separate consumer demand for media players, distinguishable from the demand for client PC operating systems . . . . There is, therefore, a separate market for these products. There are vendors who develop and supply media players on a stand-alone basis, separate from PC operating systems. Media players are often offered for download from the respective vendors' Web-sites. Microsoft itself states that *"there are a dozen of media players, of which RealNetworks' RealPlayer and Apple's QuickTime are only two of the most prominent."* . . .

(805) Microsoft's own practice to develop and distribute versions of WMP for Apple's Mac operating systems and Sun's Solaris client operating system . . . further indicates that operating systems and media players are not just parts of the same product. . . .

Also, Microsoft releases upgrades of WMP, distinct from Windows operating system releases or upgrades, as was the case with Microsoft's current WMP 9 (available as of 7 January 2003, while the latest operating system upgrade—Windows XP—was released on 25 October 2001) . . . .

(806) While Microsoft's tying and desktop ubiquity give it a substantial distribution advantage in this market, the fact that a not insignificant number of consumers choose to obtain media players separately from their operating system shows that informed consumers recognise them as separate products . . . . Microsoft continuously stresses the number of consumers who use RealPlayer, . . . a media player that clearly us separate from any operating system. RealNetworks does not develop and sell operating systems. . . .

(807) Some operating system users will not need or want a streaming media player at all . . . . There are companies, for example, which do not want their employees to use media players for instance because they could be used for non-work related purposes. . . .

(808) It may be true that the direct consumer demand test under a *per se* rule (as normally applied in US tying cases) *"focuses on historic consumer behaviour, likely before integration"* and therefore risks ignoring efficiency benefits deriving from new product integration . . . . In the case of WMP, however, there is non-significant consumer demand for alternative players some four years after Microsoft started tying its streaming media player with Windows . . . .

(809) Microsoft's argument to the effect that there is *"no demand for operating systems without media player technologies"* and that *"few consumerl* [sic] *would take Windows without WMP when offered a choice of Windows with and without WMP"* . . . as they would obtain *"operating systems that could nnot play music CDs or play music files downloaded from the Web"* . . . disregards the alternatives that would be available to customers if Microsoft did not bundle WMP and is for this reason invalid. If OEMs and consumers had the possibility to obtain Windows without WMP that would not mean that they would choose to obtain Windows without a media player. OEMs are likely to follow consumer demand for a pre-installed media player and offer a package which would include a media player on top of Windows, the difference being that it would not automatically be—although it could be—WMP.

(810) Microsoft also engages in promotion specifically dedicated to WMP, independent of the operating system. It refers, for example, to WMP as an "application" . . . . and cites a study it commissioned wherein "competing media players" are compared . . . . At another place it calls WMP a stand-alone technology . . . .

(811) Client PC operating systems and streaming media players are also different insofar as their functionality is concerned (see the description of the products in sections 5.1.1.1 and 5.1.1.3). And while it is correct that many consumers expect their PCs to be able to render

streaming media content—and media players do need to access an operating system to function—that does not make the two an integrated product any more than a nail gun and nails of the same brand are a single product. . . .

(812) Streaming media players and client PC operating systems involve different industry structures as can be seen from the fact that in the media player market, there still remain some competitors to Microsoft (RealNetworks and Apple), while in the client PC operating system market, Microsoft's competitors are insignificant. The price points of the two products are different too, in so far as media players are often distributed for less than USD 30 or for free . . . , while client PC operating systems are generally not.

(813) Last but not least, Microsoft applies SDK licensing agreements to Windows ("Platform SDK License Agreement") and Windows Media Technologies (for example "Windows Media Player SDK" and "Windows Media Format SDK") . . . .SDK stands for Software Developer's Kit and is a set of programs used by a computer programmer to write applications compatible with a particular product. Compared to the Platform SDK, Microsoft applies more restrictive licensing conditions to the Windows Media Technologies SDKs. For example, the standard term of the Windows Media Format SDK is one year . . .

It will be seen from this that the Commission's yardstick for determining whether the products were distinct or not was 'consumer demand' (paragraph 803). It took into account that media players are available separately (paragraph 804); that Microsoft distributed versions of the WMP to manufacturers of other operating systems (paragraph 805); that some consumers obtain media players separately (paragraph 806); that some operating systems users (e.g. kill-joy employers) did not want built-in media players (paragraph 807); that Microsoft engaged in WMP-specific promotion (paragraph 810); that operating systems and streaming media players have different functionality (paragraph 811); that they have different industry structures (paragraph 812); and that Microsoft applied different licensing arrangements (paragraph 813). Needless to say, both the Commission's arguments, and its conclusion, have been hotly contested. As the issue is inextricably bound up with that of tying, it is further pursued in Chapter 7.[85]

m. Markets Created by State Regulation

A relevant market may be affected by state regulation. Legislation may, for example, define a statutory market. Such regulation may mean that no substitutes are permitted for a particular product or service.

In *General Motors*[86] and *British Leyland*[87] national regulations required conformity or type-approval certificates from importers of motor vehicles and provided that they could only be issued by the vehicle manufacturer. In both cases the ECJ held that the provision of the certificates was a separate market and not part of the motor car market.

n. Markets in the New Economy

As noted in Chapter 1, competition in markets in the new economy is often by way of innovation rather than price. The implicit assumption underlying the SSNIP test, however, is that the products are homogeneous and competitors compete on price. However, in

---

[85] *Infra*, 522.

[86] Case 26/75, *General Motors v. Commission* [1975] ECR 1367, [1976] 1 CMLR 95.

[87] Case 226/84, *British Leyland v. Commission* [1986] ECR 3263, [1987] 1 CMLR 185.

dynamically competitive industries a price-based analysis can lead to distorted results:

> Application of the SSNIP test in an industry where competition is performance-based (almost always true when product innovation is present) rather than purely price-related is likely to create a downward bias in the definition of the size of the relevant product market, and a corresponding upward bias in the assessment of market power.[88]

It has therefore been argued that the importance of market definition should be down-played where new economy markets are concerned and that over-reliance on market shares should be avoided.[89] Dominance in new economy markets is considered further below.[90]

o. Markets on the Buying Side

We said in Chapter 5 that it is possible for a buyer to be in a dominant position.[91] The complications of market definition in such situations are illustrated by a case which concerned BA's system of rewards to travel agents for selling BA tickets.[92] BA is, of course, a supplier of services—air travel. However, like any other supplier it must also *purchase* goods and services as inputs into its business. The issue in the case was BA's relationship with travel agents. The Commission held that the travel agents supplied a service to BA by selling tickets for BA flights.[93] That service, 'air travel agency services' in the UK, was a relevant market. The Commission went on to hold that BA was the dominant buyer in this market and that it had abused its dominance. It concentrated not on BA as a provider of air transport services to persons wanting to fly, but on BA as a buyer of services from numerous travel agents. BA argued that the market identified by the Commission did not really exist and that even if it did it was not the relevant market to consider here. It claimed that the Commission should have looked instead at its position on the air transport market. The CFI upheld the Commission's definition of the market.[94]

Case T-219/99, *British Airways plc* v. *Commission* [2004] 4 CMLR 1008

Court of First Instance

89. The Commission took the view in the contested decision that the product market to be taken into consideration, for the purposes of establishing the dominant position of BA, is comprised by the services which airlines purchase from travel agents for the purposes of marketing and distributing their airline tickets (recital 72). In the Commission's view, that practice by airlines has the effect of creating a market for air travel agency services distinct from the air transport markets.

---

[88] D. Teece and M. Coleman, 'The meaning of Monopoly: Antitrust Analysis in High-technology Industries' [1998] *Antitrust Bull.* 801, 827–8.

[89] Over-reliance on market shares is criticized in relation to all markets, as discussed *infra* 405, but in the new economy context it is considered particularly damaging.

[90] *Infra*, 429.

[91] *Supra* 305.

[92] It came about as a result of a complaint by Virgin to the Commission.

[93] *Virgin/BA* [2000] OJ L30/1, [2000] 4 CMLR 999.

[94] And also the finding of a dominant position', see *infra* 400, and the Commission's controversial finding of abuse: see Chap. 7, 501 ff for that aspect of the case. The CFI's judgment was upheld by the ECJ, Case C-95/04 P, *British Airways* v. *Commission*, 15 March 2007, where the market definition point was not appealed.

90. The Commission has also taken the view that the relevant geographic market in this case was the territory of the United Kingdom, given the national dimension of travel agents' business.

91. According to settled case-law (Case 322/81 *Michelin* v. *Commission* [1983] ECR 3461, paragraph 37; Case T-65/96 *Kish Glass* v. *Commission* [2000] ECR II-1885, paragraph 62, confirmed on appeal by order of the Court of Justice in Case C-241/00 P *Kish Glass* v. *Commission* [2001] ECR I-7759), for the purposes of investigating the possibly dominant position of an undertaking on a given product market, the possibilities of competition must be judged in the context of the market comprising the totality of the products or services which, with respect to their characteristics, are particularly suitable for satisfying constant needs and are only to a limited extent interchangeable with other products or services. Moreover, since the determination of the relevant market is useful in assessing whether the undertaking concerned is in a position to prevent effective competition from being maintained and behave to an appreciable extent independently of its competitors and, in this case, its service providers, an examination to that end cannot be limited to the objective characteristics only of the relevant services, but the competitive conditions and the structure of supply and demand on the market must also be taken into consideration.

92. It is clear from BA's pleadings that it itself acknowledges the existence of an independent market for air travel agency services, since it states in paragraph 11.34 of its application that travel agents themselves operate in a competitive market, competing with each other to provide the best possible service to their customers.

93. In that regard, although travel agents act on behalf of the airlines, which assume all the risks and advantages connected with the transport service itself and which conclude contracts for transport directly with travellers, they nevertheless constitute independent intermediaries carrying on an independent business of providing services (see, to that effect, the judgment in *VVR*, . . . [95] at paragraph 20).

94. As the Commission states in recital 31 of the contested decision, that specific business of travel agents consists, on the one hand, in advising potential travellers, reserving and issuing airline tickets, (and) collecting the price of the transport and remitting it to the airlines, and, on the other hand, in providing those airlines with advertising and commercial promotion services.

95. In that regard, BA itself states that travel agents are and will remain, in the short term at least, a vital distribution channel for airlines, allowing them efficiently to sell seats on the flights they offer, and that there is a mutual dependence between travel agents and airlines which are not in themselves in a position to market their air transport services effectively.

96. As BA has also stated, travel agents offer a wider range of air routes, departure times and arrival times than any airline could. Travel agents filter information concerning various flights for the benefit of travellers faced with the proliferation of different air transport fare structures, which arise from the real-time pricing systems operated by airlines.

97. BA has further recognised that the role which travel agents play in the distribution of airline tickets explains why airlines seek to offer them advantages so that they sell seats on their flights. The irreplaceable nature of the services which travel agents provide to airlines is thus borne out by all the payments which the airlines make to them.

98. Finally, BA has itself emphasised that major travel agents individually negotiate agreements for the distribution of air tickets and that they are thus in a position to set the airlines in competition.

99. That specific nature of the services provided to airlines by travel agents, without any serious possibility of the airlines substituting themselves for the agents in order to carry out the same services themselves, is corroborated by the fact that, at the time of the events of which complaint

---

[95] This is a reference to Case 311/87, *VZW Vereniging van Vlaamse Reisbureaus* v. *VZW Sociale Dienst van de Plaatselijke en Gewestelijke Overheidsdiensten* [1987] ECR 3801, [1989] 4 CMLR 213, which concerned price-fixing amongst Belgian travel agents.

is made, 85 per cent of air tickets sold in the territory of the United Kingdom were sold through the intermediary of travel agents.

100. The Court therefore considers that the services of air travel agencies represent an economic activity for which, at the time of the contested decision, airlines could not substitute another form of distribution of their tickets, and that they therefore constitute a market for services distinct from the air transport market.

101. With regard to the fact that the restrictions on competition which the Commission imputes to BA's performance reward schemes arise from the position which BA holds in its capacity not as supplier but as purchaser of air travel agency services, this is irrelevant having regard to the definition of the market in question. Article 82 EC applies both to undertakings whose possible dominant position is established, as in this case, in relation to their suppliers and to those which are capable of being in the same position in relation to their customers.

102. BA itself acknowledged at the hearing, moreover, that it is possible both for a seller and for a purchaser to hold a dominant position within the meaning of Article 82 EC.

103. BA cannot therefore validly argue that, in order to define the product market in question, with a view to assessing the effects on competition of the financial advantages which it allows to travel agents established in the United Kingdom, it is necessary to determine whether a single supplier of air transportation services on a particular route can profitably increase its prices.

104. Such a parameter, which might be relevant in relation to each airline, is not of such a kind as to enable measurement of BA's economic strength in its capacity not as provider of air transport services but as purchaser of travel agency services, on all routes to and from United Kingdom airports, either in relation to all other airlines regarded in the same capacity as purchasers of air travel agency services or in relation to travel agents established in the United Kingdom.

105. BA's objections to the relevance of the product market adopted by the Commission, based on the possible marginalisation of the distribution of airline tickets through the intermediary of travel agents, on the exclusive specialisation of airlines by geographical destinations, and on the independent behaviour of an airline in a monopoly situation on certain routes, therefore have no bearing.

106. Those arguments are based on situations which are either hypothetical or foreign to the conditions of competition operating in the product market in question constituted by air travel agency services, both between the agents providing those services and between the airlines using them.

107. The Commission did not therefore make any error of assessment in defining the relevant product market as that for services provided by travel agents in favour of airlines, for the purposes of establishing whether BA holds a dominant position on that market in its capacity as bidder for those services.

The geographic aspect of the relevant market is discussed below.[96]

(ii) Supply Substitution

In *Continental Can*,[97] the ECJ held that the market must be defined not only from the demand side but from the supply side. In that case the Commission found three separate markets consisting of different types of metal containers for food packaging. The ECJ held that the Commission had

[96] *Infra* 387.

[97] Cases 6 and 7/72, *Europemballage Corp and Continental Can Co Inc v. Commission* [1973] ECR 215, [1973] CMLR 199.

not explained why these products were in separate markets and were not all part of a larger light metal container market. In particular, it had not set out why competitors could not enter the identified markets by a simple adaptation of their production facilities.

Case 6/72, *Europemballage Corp & Continental Can Co Inc* v. *Commission* [1973] ECR 215, [1973] CMLR 199

Court of Justice

32. For the appraisal of SLW's dominant position and the consequences of the disputed merger, the definition of the relevant market is of essential significance, for the possibilities of competition can only be judged in relation to those characteristics of the products in question by virtue of which those products are particularly apt to satisfy an inelastic need and are only to a limited extent interchangeable with other products.

33. In this context recitals Nos 5 to 7 of the second part of the decision deal in turn with a 'market for light containers for canned meat products', a 'market for light containers for canned seafood', and a 'market for metal closures for the food packing industry, other than crown corks', all allegedly dominated by SLW and in which the disputed merger threatens to eliminate competition. The decision does not, however, give any details of how these three markets differ from each other, and must therefore be considered separately. Similarly, nothing is said about how these three markets differ from the general market for light metal containers, namely the market for metal containers for fruit and vegetables, condensed milk, olive oil, fruit juices and chemico-technical products. In order to be regarded as constituting a distinct market, the products in question must be individualized, not only by the mere fact that they are used for packing certain products, but by particular characteristics of production which make them specifically suitable for this purpose. Consequently, a dominant position on the market for light metal containers for meat and fish cannot be decisive, as long as it has not been proved that competitors from other sectors of the market for light metal containers are not in a position to enter this market, by a simple adaption, with sufficient strength to create a serious counterweight.

The ECJ also held that the Commission should not have dismissed the possibility of the customers themselves commencing manufacture of their own cans.[98]

In cases subsequent to *Continental Can* the possibility of supply-side substitution has been considered. In *Michelin*[99] the ECJ held that there was no elasticity of supply between tyres for heavy vehicles and car tyres 'owing to significant differences in production techniques and in the plant and tools needed for their manufacture. The fact that time and considerable investment are required in order to modify production plant for the manufacture of light-vehicle tyres instead of heavy-vehicle tyres or vice versa means that there is no discernible relationship between the two categories of tyre enabling production to be adapted to demand on the market'. Similarly, in *Tetra Pak I*[100] the Commission dismissed the feasibility of

[98] *Ibid.*, para. 36.

[99] Case 322/81, *NV Nederlandsche Banden-Industrie Michelin* v. *Commission* [1983] ECR 3461, [1985] 1 CMLR 282, para. 41. The issue of supply substitutability was not addressed by the Commission in its decision, *Bandengroothandel Frieschebebrug BV/Nederlandsche Banden-Michelin NV* [1981] OJ L353/33, [1982] 1 CMLR 643.

[100] Commission decision in *TetraPak (BTG Licence)* [1988] OJ L272/27, [1990] 4 CMLR 47, paras. 36–8, upheld by the CFI Case T-51/89, *Tetra Pak Rausing SA* v. *Commission* [1990] ECR II-309, [1991] 4 CMLR 334 where the market definition was not challenged.

supply-side substitution. Manufacturers of other types of milk-packaging machinery were not readily able to switch to producing aseptic packaging machinery and cartons.

The difficulty when considering supply-side substitution is to distinguish undertakings that are able easily to switch production to produce another product from potential competitors. When is a potential competitor capable of switching production to be considered at the stage of market definition and when at the stage of assessing market power on the defined market?[101] In Chapter 1 it was seen that the Commission stipulates in its Notice on market definition, at paragraphs 20–23, that potential competition is relevant to market definition only when a supplier is able to switch production in the short term without incurring significant additional costs or risks. Only where the impact is effective and immediate is it equivalent to the demand substitution effect. The CFI said in *Atlantic Container Line*:

> Although potential competition and supply-side substitution are conceptually different issues, ... those issues overlap in part, as the distinction lies primarily in whether the restriction of competition is immediate or not.[102]

These difficulties once more illustrate how problematic it may be to divide market definition from the assessment of market power. Although it could be argued that it does not matter *when* the possibility of other producers switching is considered so long as it *is* considered, the heavy reliance EC law places on market shares makes the proper definition of the market crucial. The extract from Bishop and Walker set out below indicates that a more rigorous approach to supply side substitutability is desirable. Not only would it encourage less narrow market definitions to be adopted but it would make it less likely that wrong characterizations of dominance are made.

S. Bishop and M. Walker, *The Economics of EC Competition Law: Concepts, Application and Measurement* (2nd edn., Sweet & Maxwell, 2002), 112

4.58 It appears that the Commission's assessment of relevant product markets focuses, almost completely, on demand-side factors. In general, a failure to consider supply-side issues will lead to overly narrow relevant product markets. It may be that the Commission believes that it is following the lead of the U.S. Department of Justice (DoJ) and Federal Trade Commission (FTC) which also consider only demand-side responses when determining the relevant market. However, the DoJ and FTC do consider supply-side responses in some detail at later stages of its assessment, both in calculating market shares and in its assessment of competition. It does not matter whether supply-side responses are taken into account at the market definition stage or at the latter stage of interpreting the market share. Provided the competitive constraints provided by potential supply-side responses of firms are taken into account at some stage it should not matter precisely when. It is, however, important that a consistent approach is adopted.

An approach in which supply-side substitution is taken into account at the market definition stage has much to recommend it. First, supply-side considerations can be an important determinant of the elasticity of demand for a product. Secondly, we believe that one of the aims of market definition should be to make market shares meaningful and this is more likely to be the case if supply-side substitutability is taken into account at the market definition stage for

---

[101] See the problem in *BPB Industries, supra* n. 5.

[102] Cases T-191 and 212–14/98, *Atlantic Container Line* v. *EC Commission* [2003] ECR II-3275, para. 834.

the reasons discussed above. Thirdly, and most importantly, since supply-side substitution can provide an important source of competitive constraint, it would force the Commission to take account of these responses in a more systematic manner...

C. THE GEOGRAPHIC MARKET

We saw in Chapter 1 that the relevant market has a geographic as well as a product dimension. Obviously an undertaking will not be able to raise price above the competitive level if consumers are willing and able to purchase a substitute from another area. The Commission Notice on market definition explains at length how the geographic market is determined.[103] The breadth of the geographic market will depend on a number of factors, especially transport. Where products are valuable in relation to their transport costs, as with microchips or diamonds, the geographic market will tend to be wide. Conversely, where the cost of a product is low in relation to its transport cost, as in the case of bricks or roofing tiles, the geographic market is likely to be narrower.

The case law of the Court indicates that the geographic market will encompass all areas in which the conditions of competition are sufficiently homogeneous. In *United Brands*[104] the ECJ held that '[t]he opportunities for competition under Art, [82] of the Treaty must be considered... with reference to a clearly defined geographic area in which it is marketed and where the conditions of competition are sufficiently homogeneous for the effect of the economic power of the undertaking concerned to be able to be evaluated'. Thus 'the objective conditions of competition applying to the product in question must be the same for all traders'. In that case France, Italy, and the UK were excluded from the consideration of the banana market because they had special arrangements with their former colonies. In *Deutsche Bahn*[105] the CFI held that 'the definition of the geographical market does not require the objective conditions of competition between traders to be perfectly homogeneous. It is sufficient if they are "similar" or "sufficiently homogeneous" and accordingly, only areas in which the objective conditions of competition are "heterogeneous" may not be considered to constitute a uniform market'.

Although the Court has thus stressed the need for sufficiently homogeneous conditions of competition this requirement is not stressed in the Commission's Notice on market definition. Rather the Commission appears to recognize that the behaviour of undertakings may be constrained by imports from areas where the conditions of competition are not the same.[106]

It is clear from the case law that legal regulation may create national markets, as in the type-approval certificate cases.[107] Similarly, in *British Telecommunications*[108] BT was found to have a statutory monopoly and in *AKZO*[109] the geographic market was confined by the fact that the

---

[103] See *supra* Chap. 1.

[104] Case 27/76, *United Brands Co and United Brands Continental BV v. Commission* [1978] ECR 207, [1978] 1 CMLR 429, para. 11.

[105] Case T-229/94, *Deutsche Bahn AG v. Commission* [1997] ECR II-1689, [1998] 4 CMLR 220, para. 92; see also Case T-51/89, *Tetra Pak International SA v. Commission* [1994] ECR II-755, [1997] 4 CMLR 726, paras. 91 and 92.

[106] See V. Korah, *An Introductory Guide to EC Competition Law and Practice* (8th edn., Hart Publishing, 2004), 4.3.1.2.

[107] Case 26/75, *General Motors v. EC Commission* [1975] ECR 1367, [1976] 1 CMLR 95; Case 226/84, *British Leyland v. EC Commission* [1986] ECR 3263, [1987] 1 CMLR 185; see *infra* 588.

[108] [1982] OJ L360/36, [1983] 1 CMLR 457.

[109] Case C-62/86, *AKZO Chemie BV v. Commission* [1991] ECR I-3359, [1993] 5 CMLR 215.

UK and Ireland were the only Member States which permitted the use of bleaching agents in flour. With barriers to trade between Member States being further reduced as the internal market is completed, markets may be expected to become broader and to be EU-wide at least. However, narrower markets may be created through Community regulation (as is the case with sugar),[110] as a result of high transport costs, or as a result of consumer preference. The market may then be confined to a number of Member States,[111] to a single Member State, or to part of a Member State. In *Nestlé/Perrier*,[112] (a decision taken under the Merger Regulation, not Article 82), for example, the Commission found that the relevant geographic market for mineral water was limited to France. Irrespective of the integration of Europe, French consumers obstinately continued to choose local products.

In cases involving the transport sector narrow geographic markets have been defined (in these cases the geographic and product markets may in effect be the same). The Commission has, for example, defined as separate markets the air route between Dublin and Heathrow,[113] the air route between Brussels and Luton,[114] and in *Sealink/B&I Holyhead: Interim Measures* the ferry route between Holyhead and Dun Laoghaire.[115] In the latter decision the Commission distinguished the 'northern', 'southern', and 'central' corridor routes between Great Britain and Ireland. Further, within the 'central corridor' it distinguished the Liverpool and Holyhead routes, concluding that 'potential competition from Liverpool does not constrain the market power of Sealink at Holyhead'.

One of the most criticized cases on the geographic market is *Michelin*.[116] In this case the ECJ upheld the Commission's finding that there was a separate market for heavy vehicle new replacement tyres in the Netherlands.

Case 322/81, *Nederlandsche Banden-Industrie Michelin* v. *Commission* [1983] ECR 3461, [1985] 1 CMLR 282

Court of Justice

23. The applicant's first submission under this head challenges the Commission's finding that the substantial part of the common market on which it holds a dominant position is the Netherlands. Michelin NV maintains that this geographical definition of the market is too narrow. It is contradicted by the fact that the Commission itself based its decision on factors concerning the Michelin group as a whole such as its technological lead and financial strength which, in the applicant's view, relate to a much wider market or even the world market. The activities of Michelin NV's main competitors are world-wide too.

---

[110] See *Napier Brown-British Sugar* [1988] OJ L284/41, [1990] 4 CMLR 196; *Irish Sugar* [1997] OJ L258/1, [1997] 5 CMLR 666.

[111] Case 27/76, *United Brands Co and United Brands Continental BV* v. *Commission* [1978] ECR 207, [1978] 1 CMLR 429.

[112] *Nestlé/Perrier* [1992] OJ L356/1, [1993] 4 CMLR M17. See *infra* Chap. 12.

[113] *British Midland* v. *Aer Lingus* [1992] OJ L96/34, [1993] 4 CMLR 596.

[114] *London European-Sabena* [1988] OJ L317/47, [1989] 4 CMLR 662.

[115] [1992] 5 CMLR 255.

[116] Case 322/81, *NV Nederlandsche Banden-Industrie Michelin* v. *Commission* [1983] ECR 3461, [1985] 1 CMLR 282.

24. The Commission maintains that this objection concerns less the definition of the market than the criteria used to establish the existence of a dominant position. Since tyre manufacturers have on the whole chosen to sell their products on the various national markets through the intermediary of national subsidiaries, the competition faced by Michelin NV is on the Netherlands market.

25. The point to be made in this regard is that the Commission addressed its decision not to the Michelin group as a whole but only to its Netherlands subsidiary whose activities are concentrated on the Netherlands market. It has not been disputed that Michelin NV's main competitors also carry on their activities in the Netherlands through Netherlands subsidiaries of their respective groups.

26. The Commission's allegation concerns Michelin NV's conduct towards tyre dealers and more particularly its discount policy. In this regard the commercial policy of the various subsidiaries of the groups competing at the European or even the world level is generally adapted to the specific conditions existing on each market. In practice dealers established in the Netherlands obtain their supplies only from suppliers operating in the Netherlands. The Commission was therefore right to take the view that the competition facing Michelin NV is mainly on the Netherlands market and that it is at that level that the objective conditions of competition are alike for traders.

27. This finding is not related to the question whether in such circumstances factors relating to the position of the Michelin group and its competitors as a whole and to a much wider market may enter into consideration in the adoption of a decision as to whether a dominant position exists on the relevant product market.

28. Hence the relevant substantial part of the common market in this case is the Netherlands and it is at the level of the Netherlands market that Michelin NV's position must be assessed.

In this case it was not asked whether or not customers could easily have bought Michelin or other tyres outside the Netherlands. Rather, the geographic market appears to have been confined to the area in which the Commission found that the abuse had been committed.[117] The Commission's reasoning was criticized, *inter alia*, by Korah:[118]

The Commission defines the relevant geographic market as being the Netherlands, on the ground that this is where Michelin Netherlands operated and where the practice took place. Yet, that company would have no market power if the Dutch market could be flooded from Denmark, Germany or Belgium. The Commission merely states that dealers can obtain Michelin tyres only from retailers in the other Member States, and cannot obtain reliable and continuous supplies. Yet, were the Dutch subsidiary to attempt to exploit the Dutch dealers, the latter would not be able to pass the onus on to their customers if their customers could buy abroad directly, and so retailers would not agree to being exploited. If necessary, they would turn to selling other brands, or leave the market and sell completely different products. In that case, Michelin would not enjoy market power. The writer would have thought that many users of heavy vehicles must be well informed and able to shop around for new tyres in other Member States. In the U.S.A., Mr Baxter, currently in charge of antitrust in the Department of Justice, stated in his address to the Antitrust section of the A.B.A. in April 1981 that he treats a small percentage of imports as a welcome sign that the cost of transport is not too high to prevent a flood of imports if the local manufacturers restricted production to raise price. In *Bayer/Gist* . . . the Commission, quite rightly, relied on world statistics in order to assess the effect of the agreement on competition within the Common Market.

---

[117] S. Bishop and M. Walker, *The Economics of EC Competition Law: Concepts, Application and Measurement* (2nd edn., Sweet & Maxwell, 2002), para. 4.70.

[118] V. Korah, 'The Michelin Decision of the Commission' (1982) 7 *ELRev* 130, 131.

In some cases the ECJ has been more sceptical about narrowly drawn markets. In *Alsatel v. Novasam*,[119] for example, it did not accept that the evidence established that a particular region of France, rather than the country as a whole, was the geographic market for telephonic installations. In *BPB*,[120] however, a national market was found despite the existence of pressure from imports from elsewhere. The market was defined as being just the UK and Ireland.

In its 2001 *Michelin II* decision[121] the Commission was careful to devote considerable attention to the delineation of the geographic market. Taking into account the ECJ's judgment of 1983 the company argued that the new replacement tyre market was no longer national but had become international in the intervening years. The Commission refuted this claim. It said that what mattered was 'to assess the real capacity of dealers to obtain supplies from outside their national territory and the similarities or differences in the supply structure'.[122] Michelin argued that 'the structure of competition on the replacement tyre market is worldwide: the main players…compete on a world scale'.[123] The Commission denied that this situation implied that there were not national markets:

123. The argument that the largest international tyre producers compete in numerous countries and across the European Union in no way means that it can be supposed that the relevant geographic market is the world market. This situation is perfectly compatible with the existence of conditions of competition that are appreciably different in each of the relevant countries. This was already the situation in the tyre industry at the time, when the Court of Justice found that the Dutch new replacement tyre market was a national market.

The Commission took into account the fact that the large manufacturers still organized their distribution and sales along national lines;[124] that there were considerable differences in the large manufacturers' market shares from country to country which 'are hardly compatible with the theory of a European market characterised by homogeneous competition';[125] and that there were appreciable price differences from country to country.[126] It also rejected the argument that the hauliers could easily purchase their tyres from abroad if they wished: among the reasons for this was the structure of the road haulage industry in France which was composed in the main of small firms[127] which meant, *inter alia*, that they were unlikely to have the resources to surmount the linguistic obstacles to intra-Community trade.[128]

As far as the retread market was concerned the Commission held that since the retread market was a market for the provision of *services* rather than goods 'it is a national market and therefore at most of national dimension'. Moreover there were differences in the structure of demand within the Community which helped to set the French market apart, including the fact

[119] Case 247/86, [1988] ECR 5987, [1990] 4 CMLR 434.

[120] *BPB Industries* [1989] OJ L10/50, [1990] 4 CMLR 464, upheld in Case T-65/89, *BPB Industries and British Gypsum Ltd v. Commission* [1993] ECR II-389, [1993] 5 CMLR 32, and Case C-310/93 P, *BPB Industries plc and British Gypsum Ltd v. Commission* [1995] ECR I-865 [1997] 4 CMLR 238.

[121] *Michelin* [2001] OJ L143/1, [2002] 5 CMLR 388.

[122] *Ibid.*, para. 124.

[123] *Ibid.*, para. 121.

[124] *Ibid.*, paras. 125–31.

[125] *Ibid.*, para. 133.

[126] *Ibid.*, paras. 134–41.

[127] 'Micro-enterprises' in Community–speak, see *ibid.*, para. 144.

[128] *Ibid.*

that in France the predominant method of retreading in France was 'mould-cure' and custom retreading, rather than 'precure' treading.[129]

In *Virgin/BA* the CFI had to deal with the geographic market definition in a case involving the dominance of a buyer, not a supplier. It was seen above[130] that the CFI upheld the Commission's definition of the product market as being air travel agency services. The geographic market was defined as the UK.

Case T-219/99, *British Airways plc* v. *Commission* [2004] 4 CMLR 1008

Court of First Instance

108. As for the geographic market to be taken into consideration, consistent case-law shows that it may be defined as the territory in which all traders operate in the same or sufficiently homogeneous conditions of competition in so far as concerns specifically the relevant products or services, without it being necessary for those conditions to be perfectly homogeneous (Case T-83/91 *Tetra Pak* v. *Commission* [1994] ECR II-755, paragraph 91, confirmed on appeal by judgment in Case C-333/94 P *Tetra Pak* v. *Commission (Tetra Pak II)* [1996] ECR I-5951).

109. It can hardly be denied that, in the overwhelming majority of cases, travellers reserve airline tickets in their country of residence. Although BA has argued that not all tickets sold by travel agents in the United Kingdom are necessarily sold to residents of that country, it has acknowledged that transactions taking place outside the United Kingdom could not be quantified.

110. Moreover, as the Commission has stated in recital 83 of the contested decision, without challenge from BA, IATA's rules on the order of using the coupons in airline tickets prevent tickets sold outside the territory of the United Kingdom from being used for flights departing from United Kingdom airports.

111. Since the distribution of airline tickets takes place at national level, it follows that airlines normally purchase the services for distributing those tickets on a national basis, as is shown by the agreements signed to that end by BA with travel agents established in the United Kingdom.

112. Nor has any doubt been cast on the fact that airlines structure their commercial services at the national level, that travel agents' handling of air tickets is carried out in the context of IATA's national plans for bank settlement and, in this case, through the Billing and Settlement Plan for the United Kingdom (BSPUK).

113. Nor has BA challenged the Commission's statement that BA applies its performance reward schemes to travel agents established in the United Kingdom in a uniform manner over the whole of the territory of that Member State.

114. Nor has BA denied that the disputed financial incentives apply only to sales of BA tickets carried out in the United Kingdom, even if those incentives form part of agreements concluded with travel agents whose activities extend to more than one Member State.

115. Contrary to what BA maintains, the fact that BA concludes global agreements with certain travel agents is not capable of establishing that the latter increasingly deal with airlines on the

---

[129] *Ibid.*, para. 157. Mould–cure involves industrial retreading plants and, unlike the precure method, usually requires an intermediary between the retreader and the haulier.

[130] *Supra* 378.

> international level. As is shown in recital 20 of the contested decision, which BA has not challenged, those global agreements were signed with only three travel agents and only for the winter season 1992/1993. Moreover, those agreements were merely added to local agreements made in the countries concerned.
>
> 116. It does not therefore appear that the Commission erred in defining the relevant geographic market as the United Kingdom market, for the purposes of demonstrating that BA held a dominant position on that market in its capacity as the purchaser of air travel agency services provided by agents established in the United Kingdom.
>
> 117. The plea alleging incorrect definition of the relevant product and geographic market cannot therefore be accepted.

Again the difficulty involved in defining the geographic market, as is the case when defining product markets, can be tempered if competition from outside the market is taken into account when assessing market power. If that is done, over-narrow market definitions and the rather artificial distinction between market definition and market power assessment are not so misleading.

D. THE TEMPORAL MARKET

The temporal dimension of the market is often ignored and the Commission Notice does not refer to it. Many markets do not have a temporal dimension. It can, however, be relevant, for example when considering transport markets.[131] In such markets the temporal dimension may in fact be an inherent part of the definition of the product market.

In *United Brands*[132] there was evidence that the demand for bananas fluctuated from season to season depending on the availability of other fruits. This suggested that there were different seasonal markets and that in the summer at least bananas were part of a wider fruit market. The Commission disregarded this evidence and defined a single year-round market consisting only of bananas. The ECJ did not pursue the issue. In *ABG Oil*[133] the Commission looked at the oil market just in the period of the OPEC crisis in the 1970s.

E. THE *TETRA PAK II* CASE

The difficulties and complexities of market definition are illustrated by *Tetra Pak II*.[134] This case raised acute problems of demand substitutability and of aftermarkets. The CFI judgment was confirmed by the ECJ, but the arguments are more fully set out by the CFI.[135]

---

[131] In Cases T-374–5, 384 and 388/94, *European Night Services v. Commission* [1998] ECR II-3141, [1998] 5 CMLR 718, where the CFI annulled an Article 81 Commission decision on a joint venture, the Commission raised during the appeal the matter of confining the business transport market to early morning and late evening rather than all round the clock.

[132] Case 27/76, *United Brands Co and United Brands Continental BV v. Commission* [1978] ECR 207, [1978] 1 CMLR 429.

[133] [1977] OJ L117/1, [1977] 2 CMLR D1 (the decision was annulled on appeal but on abuse, not dominance, grounds: Case 77/77, *Benzine Petroleum Handelsmaatschappij BV v. Commission* [1978] ECR 1513, [1978] 3 CMLR 174, see *infra* Chap. 7).

[134] *Elopak Italia/Tetra Pak* [1992] OJ L72/1, [1992] 4 CMLR 551, confirmed by the CFI, Case T-83/91, *Tetra Pak International SA v. Commission* [1994] ECR II-755, [1997] 4 CMLR 726, confirmed by the ECJ, Case C-333/94 P, *Tetra Pak International SA v. Commission* [1996] ECR I-5951, [1997] 4 CMLR 662. The case is trenchantly criticized by V. Korah, 'The Paucity of Economic Analysis in the EEC Decisions on Competition—Tetra Pak II' [1993] *Current Legal Problems* 148.

[135] The abuse issues in the case are dealt with in Chap. 7.

Case T-83/91, *Tetra Pak Rausing* v. *Commission* [1994] ECR II-755, [1997] 4 CMLR 726

Tetra Pak produced aseptic cartons for packaging ultra-heat treated milk and the machines for processing the milk and filling the cartons. It also produced non-aseptic cartons for pasteurized (non-aseptic) milk and the machines for pasteurizing the milk and filling those cartons. The Courts confirmed the Commission's finding that there were four product markets concerned: aseptic packaging machines, aseptic cartons, non-aseptic machines, and non-aseptic cartons.

Court of First Instance

60. Before considering whether the definition of the four aseptic and non-aseptic markets given in the Decision is valid, the exact content of that definition in the aseptic sector must be determined.

61. Contrary to the applicant's arguments, the Decision seeks to encompass in the two aseptic markets, mentioned above, all aseptic machinery and cartons, whether used for the packaging of UHT milk or for the packaging under aseptic conditions of liquid foods not needing UHT treatment, such as fruit juice. The aseptic markets are expressly defined in recital 11 of the Decision as '(a) the market for machinery incorporating technology for the sterilization of cartons and the packaging in those cartons, under aseptic conditions, of UHT-treated liquid foods; and (b) the corresponding market for packaging cartons'. It is clear from this that those markets are determined exclusively by reference to the technological characteristics of machinery and cartons for packaging UHT-treated products, on the basis that the machinery and cartons with those characteristics are also used for the aseptic packaging on non-UHT-treated products. That interpretation is confirmed by Article 1 of the Decision, which simply finds the existence of a dominant position on the 'so-called aseptic markets in machines and cartons intended for the packaging of liquid foods', without making any reference to the use to which that equipment is put.

62. It is therefore for the Court to consider whether the four markets so defined by the Decision were indeed markets distinct from other sectors of the general market in systems for packaging liquid food products.

63. A preliminary point to note is that, according to settled case law, the definition of the market in the relevant products must take account of the overall economic context, so as to be able to assess the actual economic power of the undertaking in question. In order to assess whether an undertaking is in a position to behave to an appreciable extent independently of its competitors and customers and consumers, it is necessary first to define the products which, although not capable of being substituted for other products, are sufficiently interchangeable with its products, not only in terms of the objective characteristics of those products, by virtue of which they are particularly suitable for satisfying constant needs, but also in terms of the competitive conditions and the structure of supply and demand on the market: see Case 322/81, *Michelin* v. *EC Commission* . . .

64. In this case, the 'interchangeability' of aseptic packaging systems with non-aseptic systems and of systems using cartons with those using other materials must be assessed in the light of all the competitive conditions on the general market in systems for packaging liquid food products. Accordingly, in the specific context of this case, the applicant's approach of dividing that general market into differentiated sub-markets depending on whether the packaging systems are used for packaging milk, dairy products other than milk or non-dairy products by virtue of the specific characteristics of the packaging of those different categories of products, in which the possibility exists that various kinds of substitutable equipment may be used, would lead to a compartmentalization of the market which would not reflect economic reality. There is a comparable structure of supply and demand for both aseptic and non-aseptic machinery and cartons,

however they are used, since all belong to one sector, the packaging of liquid food products. Whether they are used for packaging milk or other products, aseptic and non-aseptic machinery and cartons not only share the same characteristics of production but also satisfy identical economic needs. In addition, a not insignificant proportion of Tetra's Pak's customers operate in both the milk sector and the fruit juice sector, as the applicant has admitted. In all those respects, therefore, this case is distinguishable from the situation contemplated in Case 85/76, *Hoffmann-La Roche* v. *EC Commission*. . . , relied on by the applicant, in which the Court of Justice had first considered the possibility of finding that there were two separate markets for one product which, unlike in this case, was used in two ways in wholly distinct sectors, one 'bio-nutritive' and the other 'technological'. . . . Furthermore, as both parties have submitted, Tetra Pak machinery and cartons of the same type were uniformly priced whether they were intended for packaging milk or other products, which confirms that they belong to a single product market. There is accordingly no need, contrary to the applicant's arguments, to find that there are differentiated sub-markets for packaging systems of the same type depending on whether they are used for packaging a particular category of products.

65. Accordingly, in order to ascertain whether the four markets defined in the Decision were indeed separate markets during the period in question, it is necessary—as the Commission submits—to determine in particular which products were sufficiently interchangeable with aseptic and non-aseptic machinery and cartons in the predominant milk sector. To the extent that the carton-packaging systems were used primarily for packaging milk, a dominant position in that sector was sufficient evidence, if relevant, of a dominant position on the market as a whole. Any such dominant position could not be called in question by the existence of substitutable equipment, alleged by the applicant, in the non-milk product packaging sector, since such equipment accounted for only a very small proportion of all products packaged in cartons during the period covered by the Decision. The predominance of the milk-packaging sector is clearly demonstrated by data given in the Decision (recital 6) and not disputed by the applicant, according to which in 1987 72 per cent of carton systems were used for packaging milk and only 7 per cent for packaging other milk products. According to the same source, in 1983 90 per cent of those systems were used for packaging milk and other dairy products. That pattern was even more marked in the case of the systems marketed by Tetra Pak. Tables produced by Tetra Pak in reply to a written question from the Court show that in the Community 96 per cent of the aseptic systems manufactured by it were used for packaging milk in 1976, 81 per cent in 1981, 70 per cent in 1987 and 67 per cent in 1991. Those figures indicate that, notwithstanding a decrease, the majority of Tetra Pak aseptic cartons were used for packaging milk during the period in question. As for non-aseptic cartons, 100 per cent were used for packaging milk until 1980 and 99 per cent thereafter, according to the same source. For all those reasons, the Commission was entitled to take the view that it was not necessary to carry out a separate analysis of the non-milk-packaging sector.

66. In the milk-packaging sector, the Commission correctly based itself, in this case, on the test of sufficient substitutability of the different systems for packaging liquid foods, as laid down by the Court of Justice: see in particular Case 6/72, *Europemballage and Continental Can* v. *EC Commission* . . . and Case 85/76 *Hoffmann La Roche* v. *EC Commission* . . . It is also in accordance with case-law (see Joined Cases 6 & 7/73, *Commercial Solvents* v. *EC Commission*) that the Commission applied the test of sufficient substitutability of products at the stage of the packaging systems themselves, which constitute the market in intermediate products on which Tetra Pak's position must be assessed, and not at the stage of the finished products, in this case the packaged liquid food products.

67. In order to assess the interchangeability for packers of the packaging systems, the Commission necessarily had to take account of the repercussions of the final consumers' demand on the packers' intermediate demand. It found that the packers could influence consumer habits

in the choice of types of product packaging only by promotion and publicity in a long and costly process, extending over several years, as Tetra Pak had expressly acknowledged in its reply to the statement of objections. In those circumstances, the various types of packaging could not be considered to be sufficiently interchangeable for packers, whatever their bargaining power, referred to by the applicant.

68. It is therefore exclusively to assess the effect of final demand on the packers' intermediate demand that the Commission referred to the lack of perfect substitutability, which concerned only the packaged products and not the packaging systems. In particular, the Commission correctly considered that, because of the small proportion of the retail price of milk accounted for by the cost of its packaging, 'small but significant changes in the relative price of the different packages would not be sufficient to trigger off shifts between the different types of milk with which they are associated because the substitution of different milks is less than perfect' (decision in *Tetra Pak I* . . .). The applicant's complaints that the Commission based itself on the model of perfect competition and defined the relevant markets solely by reference to consumer demand must accordingly be rejected.

69. The Court of First Instance therefore holds first that the Commission was entitled to find that during the period in question there was not sufficient interchangeability between machinery for aseptic packaging in cartons and machinery for non-aseptic packaging whatever the material used. At the level of demand, aseptic systems are distinguished by their inherent characteristics, satisfying specific consumer needs and preferences in relation to the duration and quality of conservation and to taste. Moreover, to move from packaging UHT milk to packaging fresh milk requires the setting up of a distribution system which ensures that the milk is continuously kept in a refrigerated environment. Furthermore, at the level of supply, the manufacture of machinery for the aseptic packaging of UHT milk in cartons requires complex technology, which only Tetra Pak and its competitor PKL have succeeded in developing and making operational during the period considered in the Decision. Manufacturers of non-aseptic machinery using cartons, operating on the market closest to the market in the aseptic machinery in question, were therefore not in a position to enter the latter market by modifying their machinery in certain respects for the market in aseptic machinery.

70. As for aseptic cartons, they also constituted a market distinct from that in non-aseptic packaging. At the level of the packers' intermediate demand, aseptic cartons were not sufficiently interchangeable with non-aseptic packages, including cartons, for the same reasons as those already set out in the preceding paragraph in relation to machinery. At the level of supply, the documents before the Court indicate that notwithstanding the absence of insurmountable technical problems, manufacturers of non-aseptic cartons were not in a position in the circumstances in question to adapt to the manufacture of aseptic cartons. The fact that on that market there was only one competitor of Tetra Pak, namely PKL, with only 10 per cent of the market in aseptic cartons during the period in question, demonstrates that the conditions of competition were such that in practice there was no possibility for manufacturers of non-aseptic cartons to enter the market in aseptic cartons, in particular given the lack of aseptic filling machines.

71. Secondly, the Court holds that, during the period in question, aseptic machinery and cartons were not sufficiently interchangeable with aseptic packaging systems using other materials. According to the data provided in the documents before the Court, which are not disputed by the applicant, no such substitutable equipment existed, with the exception of the arrival on the market towards the end of the relevant period of systems for aseptic packaging in plastic bottles, returnable glass bottles and pouches in France, Germany and Spain respectively. However, each of those new products was introduced in only one country and, what is more, accounted for only a marginal share of the UHT-milk-packaging market. According to information provided by the applicant, that share has been only 5 per cent of the market in France since 1987. In the Community as a whole, in 1976, all UHT milk was packaged in cartons. The observations submitted by the applicant in response to the statement of objections indicate that in 1987

approximately 97.7 per cent of UHT milk was packaged in cartons. At the end of the period in question, that is 1991, cartons still accounted for 97 per cent of the UHT-milk-packaging market, the remaining 3 per cent being held by plastic containers, as the applicant indicated in answer to a written question from the Court. The marginal share of the market thus held by aseptic containers made out of other materials demonstrates that those containers cannot be considered, even during the last years of the period covered by the Decision, as products which are sufficiently interchangeable with aseptic systems using cartons (see *Commercial Solvents* v. *EC Commission* . . .).

72. Thirdly, the Court finds that non-aseptic machinery and cartons constituted markets which were distinct from those in non-aseptic packaging systems using materials other than cartons. It has already been shown . . . that, because of the marginal proportion of the price of milk attributable to packaging costs, packers would have been led to consider that containers—in this case cartons, glass or plastic bottles and non-aseptic pouches—were easily interchangeable only if there had been an almost perfect substitutability of final consumer demand. In the light of their very different physical characteristics and the system of doorstep delivery of pasteurized milk in glass bottles in the UK, that form of packaging was not interchangeable for consumers with packaging in cartons. Moreover, the fact that environmental factors led some consumers to prefer certain types of packaging, such as returnable glass bottles, did not promote the substitutability of those containers with cartons. Consumers who were aware of those factors did not consider those containers to be interchangeable with cartons. The same applies to consumers who, conversely, were attracted to a certain convenience in using products packaged in cartons. As for plastic bottles and plastic pouches, they were on the market only in countries where consumers accepted that type of packaging, in particular, according to information in the Decision which is not disputed by the applicant, Germany or France. Furthermore, according to the same source, that packaging was used for only approximately one-third of pasteurised milk in France and 20 per cent in Germany. It follows that those products were not in practice sufficiently interchangeable with non-aseptic cartons throughout the Community during the period covered by the Decision.

73. Analysis of the markets in the milk-packaging sector thus shows that the four markets concerned, defined in the Decision, were indeed separate markets.

74. Moreover and in any event, the Court finds that an examination of the substitutability of the various packaging systems in the fruit-juice sector, fruit juices being the largest category of liquid foods other than milk, shows that in that sector also there was no sufficient interchangeability either between aseptic and non-aseptic systems or between systems using cartons and systems using other materials.

75. The market in the carton packaging of fruit juices was held mainly by aseptic systems during the period in question. In 1987, 91 per cent of cartons used for packaging fruit juice were aseptic. That proportion remained stable until 1991, when 93 per cent of all cartons were aseptic according to Tetra Pak's reply to a written question from the Court. The marginal share held by non-aseptic cartons for packaging fruit juice, which continued for several years as has been shown, demonstrates that in practice they were barely interchangeable with aseptic cartons.

76. Nor were aseptic machinery and cartons sufficiently interchangeable with equipment using other materials for packaging fruit juice. The tables provided by Tetra Pak in answer to a written question from the Court show that during the period in question the two major rival types of packaging in the fruit-juice sector were glass bottles and cartons. In particular, the tables indicate that in 1976 in the Community more than 76 per cent of fruit-juice (by volume) was packaged in glass bottles, 9 per cent in cartons and 6 per cent in plastic bottles. The share held by cartons reached approximately 50 per cent of the market in 1987 and 46 per cent in 1991. The share held by glass bottles increased from 30 to 39 per cent between those dates and the share held by plastic bottles remained negligible, decreasing from approximately 13 per cent to 11 per cent.

77. Taking into account their very different characteristics, concerning both price and presentation, weight and the way in which they are stored, cartons and glass bottles could not be considered to be sufficiently interchangeable. In relation particularly to comparative prices, both parties' answers to a written question from the Court show that the total cost to the packer of packaging fruit juice in non-returnable glass bottles is significantly higher by approximately 75 per cent than that of packaging in aseptic cartons.

78. It follows from all the above considerations that the Commission has established to the requisite legal standard that the markets in aseptic machinery and cartons and those in non-aseptic machinery and cartons were insulated from the general market in systems for packaging liquid foods.

2. The machinery and carton markets cannot be separated

Summary of the arguments of the parties

79. The applicant states that the relevant market must be defined as the integrated packaging-systems market, comprising machines for packaging liquid foods and the packaging itself. It argues that there is a natural and commercial link of the type referred to in Article 82(d) of the Treaty between the machines and the cartons. In particular, segregating aseptic filling machines and aseptic cartons may involve grave risks for public health and serious consequences for Tetra Pak's customers.

80. The applicant considers that the Commission took no account of the submissions of Tetra Pak's competitors, which support Tetra Pak's arguments, and adduced no evidence that the separate provision of machines and cartons reflected either the wishes of packers for independent suppliers of cartons or the wishes of the carton suppliers themselves.

81. The Commission disputes the link alleged by the applicant between machinery and cartons. It submits that Article 82 of the Treaty precludes the manufacturer of a complex product from hindering production by a third party of consumable products intended for use in its systems.

Assessment by the Court

82. First, and contrary to the arguments of the applicant, consideration of commercial usage does not support the conclusion that the machinery for packaging a product is indivisible from the cartons. For a considerable time there have been independent manufacturers who specialize in the manufacture of non-aseptic cartons designed for use in machines manufactured by other concerns and who do not manufacture machinery themselves. It is apparent in particular from the Decision, . . . and not disputed by the applicant, that, until 1987, Elopak, which was set up in 1957, manufactured only cartons and accessory equipment, for example handling equipment. Moreover, also according to the Decision . . . and not contested by the applicant, approximately 12 per cent of the non-aseptic carton sector was shared in 1985 between three companies manufacturing their own cartons, generally under licence and acting, for machinery, only as distributors. In those circumstances, tied sales of machinery and cartons cannot be considered to be in accordance with commercial usage, given that such sales were not the general rule of the non-aseptic sector and that there were only two manufacturers in the aseptic sector, Tetra Pak and PKL.

83. Furthermore, the applicants argument as to the requirements for the protection of public health and its interests and those of its customers cannot be accepted. It is not for the manufacturers of complete systems to decide that, in order to satisfy requirements in the public interest, consumable products such as cartons constitute, with the machines with which they are intended to be used, an inseparable integrated system. According to settled case-law, in the absence of general and binding standards or rules, any independent producer is quite free, as far as Community competition law is concerned, to manufacture consumables intended for use in equipment manufactured by others, unless in doing so it infringes a competitor's intellectual

property right: see Case T-30/89, *Hilti* v. *EC Commission*...and Case C-53/92P, *Hilti* v. *EC Commission*...

84. In those circumstances, whatever the complexity in this case of aseptic filling processes, the protection of public health may be guaranteed by other means, in particular by notifying machine users of the technical specifications with which cartons must comply in order to be compatible with those machines, without infringing manufacturers' intellectual property rights. Moreover, even on the assumption, shared by the applicant, that machinery and cartons from various sources cannot be used together without the characteristics of the system being affected thereby, the remedy must lie in appropriate legislation or regulations, and not in rules adopted unilaterally by manufacturers, which would amount to prohibiting independent manufacturers from conducting the essential part of their business.

85. It follows that the applicant's argument that the markets in machinery for packaging a product and those in packaging cartons are inseparable cannot be accepted.

4. ASSESSING MARKET POWER

A. GENERAL[136]

Once the market has been defined the power which the undertaking has on that market must be assessed in order to determine whether the undertaking is 'dominant'.

If legal regulation causes the undertaking concerned to have 100 per cent of the market and no competitors can enter the market, for example where a statutory monopoly over the market has been conferred upon it, then it may be a true monopoly. In other situations the matter will not be so clear.

It is possible, although rare in the absence of a statutory monopoly, for an undertaking to have 100 per cent of a market. It was seen in Chapter 1, however, that even an undertaking which has a 100 per cent share of the market does not, in the theory of industrial economics, necessarily occupy a dominant position or possess market power. Market shares do not indicate why that undertaking has 100 per cent of the market or tell us about potential competition. They do not explain, for example, whether the undertaking has a high market share because it produces the best products, most cheaply and most efficiently, or because the minimum efficient scale of production means that it is a 'natural' monopoly,[137] or whether that undertaking is vulnerable to market entry and to potential competition, or whether it is shielded from competition by barriers to entry. Whether or not an undertaking is vulnerable to such competition will be dependent upon whether or not there are 'barriers to entry' to the market. This is why the definition of a barrier to entry, discussed in Chapter 1, is such a central concept.

We saw in Chapter 1 that there is an ongoing debate about what constitutes a barrier to entry or expansion (in this Chapter 'barrier to entry' is used to cover both unless the context otherwise requires[138]), and even about how the term should be defined. It should also be noted that

---

[136] See D. Landes and R. A. Posner, 'Market Power in Antitrust Cases' (1981) 94 *Harvard LR* 937; R. Schmalensee, 'Another Look at Market Power' (1982) 95 *Harvard LR* 1789.

[137] See *supra* Chap. 1. *GVL* [1981] OJ L370/49, [1982] 1 CMLR 221 is an example of a monopoly which was in neither of those categories.

[138] Most barriers to entry are barriers to expansion as well, although Faull and Nikpay, *The EC Law of Competition* (2nd edn., Oxford University Press, 2007) 4.99, point out that barriers to expansion tend to be high in sectors where an increase in capacity would require a large investment.

there is an argument that the disciplining effect of potential, as distinct from existing, competitors can be exaggerated.[139] A major belief of the Chicago school,[140] however, is that there are few barriers to entry. Markets do not therefore need to be policed by competition authorities but will rectify themselves. Monopolies will endure only through superior efficiency. An extract from Bork's book sets out these arguments:

R. Bork, *The Antitrust Paradox: A Policy at War With Itself* (Basic Books, 1978), 195–6

The basic ambiguity of this concept has led to its misuse in antitrust analysis. If everything that makes entry more difficult is viewed as a barrier, and if barriers are bad, then efficiency is an evil. That conclusion is inconsistent with consumer-oriented policy. What must be proved to exist, therefore, is a class of barriers that do not reflect superior efficiency and can be erected by firms to inhibit rivals. I think it clear that no such class of artificial barriers exists. It is the same phenomenon as Judge Wyzanski's 'intermediate cases'—practices that are neither deliberately predatory nor efficiency creating, but are nevertheless somehow exclusionary. The idea is so transparent, so obviously lacking in substance, that one suspects it would never have been devised but for the desperate need to shore up a crumbling theory that markets allow unwarranted market shares to persist. Stigler states: 'Barriers to entry arise because of economies of scale, or differences in productive factors, or legal control of entry.' ... None of these, of course, is properly subject to attack by antitrust. There is in the list no 'artificial barrier' other than legal control of entry by government, and since we want the more efficient firm to have the extra share of the market its efficiency commands, there is no reason for concern over the other barriers.

Bork concludes that all the other 'artificial barriers' with which competition law is concerned are, in fact, activities that create efficiency.

Neither the Court nor the Commission appears to have followed any particular school of economic thought on this, and they certainly do not adhere to the Chicago view. In the past, a very wide variety of factors have been found to be barriers to entry or, in the terminology of the Court, 'other factors indicating dominance'.[141] The use of the term 'other factors indicating dominance' may be a recognition that not all the difficulties facing competitors entering a market can be described as barriers to entry under any definition. This eclectic approach means that in trying to ascertain whether an undertaking is likely to be held dominant for the purposes of Article 82 it is necessary carefully to study the case law of the Court and the Commission. It will be seen that this body of reasoning should perhaps be regarded as *sui generis*, rather than as economic theory.

---

[139] See E. M. Fox and L. A. Sullivan, 'Antitrust—Retrospective and Prospective: Where Are We Coming From? Where Are we Going?' (1987) 62 *New York Univ LR* 936, 975: 'Potential competition is not an existing alternative source of supply; it does not satisfy buyers' desires for choice or the opportunity for buyers to play one seller against another; and it is normally an inconsequential source of pressure to innovate.'

[140] See *supra* Chap. 1.

[141] 'Other' meaning factors other than market share. The Commission now uses the term 'barriers to entry': see, e.g., Commission Guidelines on the assessment of horizontal mergers under the Council Regulation on the control of concentrations between undertakings [2004] OJ C 31/5.

The sections below set out the approach of the Community authorities to date when determining whether or not an undertaking is dominant on a particular market. It will be seen that the authorities rely both on the market shares of the undertaking concerned and on 'other factors indicating dominance'. Throughout these sections it will be seen that a severe criticism of the case law and decisions taken under Article 82 has been their tendency to place too great an emphasis on market shares and the failure, at least in the past, to display rigorous economic analysis when dealing with barriers to entry. On the contrary, barriers to entry have often been seen as pervasive. When combined with the tendency to define markets narrowly, the importance attached to market shares and the broad approach to 'other factors indicating dominance' mean that an undertaking's market power may be considerably exaggerated. Undertakings which do not in reality have market power may, therefore, be precluded or deterred from engaging in conduct which is pro-competitive or at least neutral from a competition perspective (Type 1 errors). Competition law may then have the perverse effect of inhibiting the competitive process on the market.

Hitherto the Commission has not issued a general Notice on market power analagous to that on market definition although it has issued Guidelines on market analysis and the assessment of significant market power under the regulatory framework for electronic communications and services.[142] However, the matter was considered in the Discussion Paper, paras 34–40, although at less length than the abuse issue.

B. MARKET SHARES IN THE CASE OF SINGLE UNDERTAKING DOMINANCE

(i) General

If an undertaking has a statutory monopoly over a relevant market, that is the end of the matter. It is in a dominant position. In the absence of statutory monopoly the Court and Commission begin the assessment of market power by looking at market shares.

The calculation of market shares is dealt with in the Commission's Notice on market definition which explains that in some industries sales figures may not be the most appropriate basis for the calculation:

Commission Notice on the Definition of the Relevant Market for the Purposes of Community Competition Law [1997] OJ C372/5, [1998] 4 CMLR 177

53. The definition of the relevant market in both its product and geographic dimensions allows the identification of the suppliers and the customers/consumers active on that market. On that basis, a total market size and market shares for each supplier can be calculated on the basis of their sales of the relevant products in the relevant area. In practice, the total market size and market shares are often available from market sources, i.e., companies' estimates, studies commissioned from industry consultants and/or trade associations. When this is not the case, or when available

---

estimates are not reliable, the Commission will usually ask each supplier in the relevant market to provide its own sales in order to calculate total market size and market shares.

54. If sales are usually the reference to calculate market shares, there are nevertheless other indications that, depending on the specific products or industry in question, can offer useful information such as, in particular, capacity, the number of players in bidding markets, units of fleet in aerospace, or the reserves held in the case of sectors such as mining.

55. As a rule of thumb, both volume sales and value sales provide useful information. In cases of differentiated products, sales in value and their associated market share will usually be considered to better reflect the relative position and strength of each supplier.[143]

(ii) High Market Shares and the Presumption of Dominance

Although, as explained above, economic theory holds that in the absence of barriers to entry high market shares are not themselves indicative of dominance the Court has placed great emphasis on market share. The higher the market share the more likely a finding of dominance. In *Hoffmann-La Roche*[144] the Court, although recognizing that the significance of market shares may vary from market to market, and acknowledging the relevance of other factors, held that 'very large shares' are in themselves indicative of dominance unless there are 'exceptional circumstances'. The Court did, however, hold that the shares should be held 'for some time' as dominance requires power over time.

Case 85/76, *Hoffmann-La Roche & Co AG* v. *Commission* [1979] ECR 461, [1979] 3 CMLR 211

39. ...The existence of a dominant position may derive from several factors which, taken separately, are not necessarily determinative but among these factors a highly important one is the existence of very large market shares.

40. A substantial market share as evidence of the existence of a dominant position is not a constant factor and its importance varies from market to market according to the structure of these markets, especially as far as production, supply and demand are concerned....

41. Furthermore although the importance of the market shares may vary from one market to another the view may legitimately be taken that very large shares are in themselves, and save in exceptional circumstances, evidence of the existence of a dominant position. An undertaking which has a very large market share and holds it for some time, by means of the volume of production and the scale of the supply which it stands for—without those having much smaller market shares being able to meet rapidly the demand from those who would like to break away from the undertaking which has the largest market share—is by virtue of that share in a position of strength which makes it an unavoidable trading partner and which, already because of this secures for it, at the very least during relatively long periods, that freedom of action which is the special feature of a dominant position.

[143] In *Wanadoo*, COMP/38.233, [2005] 5 CMLR 120, on appeal Case T-340/03, *France Télécom SA v. Commission*, 30 January 2007, the Commission used the number of subscribers signed up to Wanadoo's high–speed internet service as a measure of market share.

[144] Case 85/76, [1979] ECR 461, [1979] 3 CMLR 211, para. 41.

In *Hoffmann-La Roche* itself the Court considered market shares, expressed both by value and quantity, over a three-year period. In respect of the various separate vitamin markets, market shares of:

(i) 75–87 per cent were found to be 'so large that they are in themselves evidence of a dominant position';[145]

(ii) 84–90 per cent were 'so large that they prove the existence of a dominant position';[146] and

(iii) '93–100 per cent had the result that it in fact has a monopoly'.[147]

In none of these instances did the Court look beyond the market shares figures.

Where the market share figures were lower in *Hoffmann-La Roche* (47 per cent,[148] 63–66 per cent,[149] and 54 per cent[150]) dominance was also found, but only after looking at other factors, particularly the market shares of the undertaking's competitors. The Court annulled the Commission's finding in respect of the Vitamin B3 market where in the three-year period only the share by value (51 per cent) in the last year had exceeded 42 per cent, saying:[151]

... the Commission, in the case of this particular market, has not indicated what the additional factors would be, which, together with the market share as corrected, nevertheless would be of such a kind as to admit of the existence of a dominant position.

These findings lead to the conclusion that, as far as concerns Vitamin B3, there is insufficient evidence of the existence of a dominant position held by Roche for the period under consideration.

The approach indicated in this case, therefore, is that where an undertaking has 'very high market shares' there is a *presumption* of dominance. In *Hilti*[152] and *Tetra Pak II*[153] the CFI held, citing *Hoffmann-La Roche*, that market shares respectively of 70–80 per cent and 90 per cent were in themselves evidence of a dominant position. In both cases, however, the Court also stated briefly that barriers to entry were high.

In *AKZO* the ECJ explained what was meant by a 'very high market share' within the meaning of the test set out in *Hoffmann-La Roche*. It interpreted it as 50 per cent of the market:

With regard to market shares the Court has held that very large shares are in themselves, and save in exceptional circumstances, evidence of the existence of a dominant position: Case 85/76 *Hoffmann-La Roche* v. *EC Commission*. That is the situation where there is a market share of 50 per cent such as that found to exist in this case.[154]

---

[145] Case 85/76, [1979] ECR 461, [1979] 3 CMLR, paras. 53–6 (Vitamin B2).

[146] *Ibid.*, paras. 59–60 (Vitamin B6).

[147] *Ibid.*, para. 67 (Vitamin H).

[148] *Ibid.*, paras. 50–2 (Vitamin A).

[149] *Ibid.*, paras. 61–3 (Vitamin C).

[150] *Ibid.*, paras. 64–6 (Vitamin E).

[151] *Ibid.*, para. 58.

[152] Case T-30/89, *Hilti AG* v. *Commission* [1991] ECR II-1439, [1992] 4 CMLR 16, paras. 91–4, upheld by the ECJ, Case C-53/92 P, *Hilti AG* v. *Commission* [1994] ECR I-667, [1994] 4 CMLR 614.

[153] Case T-83/91, *Tetra Pak International SA* v. *Commission* [1994] ECR II-755, [1997] 4 CMLR 726, paras. 109–10, upheld by the ECJ, Case C-333/94 P, *Tetra Pak International SA* v. *Commission* [1996] ECR I-5951, [1997] 4 CMLR 662.

[154] Case C-62/86, *AKZO Chemie BV* v. *Commission* [1991] ECR I-3359, [1993] 5 CMLR 215, para. 60.

In *AKZO* the Court added that the Commission had 'rightly pointed out that other factors confirmed AKZO's predominance in the market'. Nonetheless the significance of this case is enormous: once the market share is above 50 per cent there is, essentially, a presumption of dominance.[155] An undertaking is, of course, free to adduce evidence establishing that despite its high market share it has no market power. However, this will be a heavy burden to discharge.

When considering market shares of the undertaking concerned it is also important to consider the market shares of competitors: the Court said in *Hoffmann-La Roche* that 'the relationship between the market shares of the undertaking concerned and of its competitors, especially those of the next largest' was a relevant factor.[156] The market power of an undertaking with a market share of 51 per cent will be considerably different depending on whether, for example, it simply has one competitor with a 49 per cent share of the market, three competitors which have 16, 16, and 17 per cent of the market respectively or forty-nine competitors each with 1 per cent of the market. The differentials in market share are extremely important. A market where there are two undertakings, A with 51 per cent and B with 49 per cent, is an oligopoly. It is not dominated by A alone, although there may be a position of collective dominance with B.[157]

In *United Brands*[158] UBC was held to be dominant even though it had a market share of only 45 per cent. This share however was almost twice as large as that of its nearest competitor. In *Michelin*[159] Michelin was found to hold a share of 57–65 per cent of the relevant market but the remainder of the market was fragmented, the competitors each having only 4–8 per cent of the market. In *Michelin II* there was some uncertainty about Michelin's exact market share in France but it was taken as being over 50 per cent and thus over five times greater than that of its nearest competitor,[160] and in *Virgin/BA/BA*[161] BA's share was seven times greater. Once an undertaking has a market share as large as 70 per cent its share is bound to be at least twice the share of its nearest competitor. In these circumstances it will be very difficult indeed, given the importance accorded to market share and the attitude of the Court and Commission towards barriers to entry, for the undertaking to preclude a finding of dominance. There is no case where an undertaking with such a high market share has been held not to be dominant. It will therefore be appreciated why narrow market definitions may be fatal for undertakings and how important it is to make a realistic determination of the market.

(iii) Low Market Shares and Dominance

It is important to know the minimum market share at which an undertaking is likely to be found to be dominant. The crucial range is 40–50 per cent and the lower the market share of the undertaking the greater the significance which attaches to the other factors indicating dominance.

---

[155] See also Case T-395/94, *Atlantic Container Line AB and others* v. *Commission* [2002] ECR II-875, [2002] 4 CMLR 1008, para. 328.

[156] *Hoffmann-La Roche*, para. 48.

[157] For collective dominance in respect of Article 82 see *supra* Chap. 5, 301 and *infra* Chap. 11, 921 ff.

[158] Case 27/76, *United Brands Co and United Brands Continental BV* v. *Commission* [1978] ECR 207, [1978] 1 CMLR 429.

[159] Case 322/81, *Nederlandsche Banden-Industrie Michelin* v. *Commission* [1983] ECR 3461, [1985] 1 CMLR 282.

[160] *Michelin* [2001] OJ L143/1, [2002] 5 CMLR 388.

[161] [200] OJ L30/1, [2004] 4 CMLR 1008.

The lowest share at which an undertaking has been found dominant for the purposes of Article 82[162] is 39.7 per cent (in *Virgin/British Airways*). However, as we see below, the Commission has not (yet) ruled out finding that market shares considerably below this can support a finding a dominance. The market definition aspect of *Virgin/British Airways* is dealt with above.[163] As is apparent from the extract from the CFI judgment below, there were a number of special circumstances which led the CFI to uphold the Commission's finding that BA was dominant with such a low market share, and it should be borne in mind, that BA was held to be a dominant *buyer*, not supplier.

BA argued first that the Commission should not have found it dominant as a buyer without taking into account of the intense competition it faced as a supplier of air transport services; secondly, that the Commission had not explained how its dominance as a buyer of air travel agency services arose from its successful position; thirdly, that its market share did not establish a position of dominance, and moreover that the Commission had incorrectly assessed its share of the market;[164] fourthly, that its market share was falling; fifthly, that it was not an 'obligatory business partner' of the travel agents; and finally, that if it *were* dominant it would not have had to spend substantial sums on improving its services.

Case T-219/99, *British Airways* v. *Commission* [2003] ECR II-5917, [2004] 4 CMLR 1008

Court of First Instance

189. The dominant position referred to in Article 82 EC relates to a position of economic strength enjoyed by an undertaking which enables it to prevent effective competition being maintained on the relevant market by giving it the power to behave to an appreciable extent independently of its competitors, of its customers and ultimately of its consumers (Case T-128/98 *Aéroports de Paris* v. *Commission* [2000] ECR II-3929, paragraph 147).

190. ...it is on the United Kingdom market for air travel agency services, consisting in particular in the distribution of air tickets, supplied to airlines by travel agents established in the United Kingdom, that the Commission has chosen to establish the existence of a dominant position on the part of BA.

191. As has been pointed out in paragraph 101 above,[165] the fact that BA is to be regarded as an undertaking in a dominant position in its capacity as a purchaser of services, rather than as a provider of services, is irrelevant.

192. It follows that the number of seats offered on the services provided by BA on all routes to and from United Kingdom airports, which represent so many BA air tickets capable of being sold through the intermediary of travel agents established in the United Kingdom, is the appropriate criterion for measuring the economic strength which BA is capable of exercising in relation to those agents and the other companies which purchase the distribution services in question.

---

[162] Mergers are a different matter, see *infra* Chap. 12.

[163] *Supra* 378 ff and 387 ff.

[164] By, *inter alia*, including sales outside the UK, and not considering sales through non–travel agent channels such as the Internet.

[165] See *supra* 380.

193. BA itself has stated that the operation of its hub network in the territory of the United Kingdom allows it to offer many more flights to and from its hub airports, and therefore to carry a larger number of passengers than other airlines operating point-to-point services.

194. The Commission was therefore right, for the purposes of calculating BA's shares on the United Kingdom market for air travel agency services, to aggregate all BA tickets sold through travel agents established in the United Kingdom over all routes to and from United Kingdom airports.

195. In those circumstances, BA cannot profitably disregard the total number of air routes it operates in order to deny its capacity to act with an appreciable degree of independence in relation to its competitors on each of those routes, to travel agents, and to travellers, who have the ability to choose their airline.

196. Nor can BA validly accuse the Commission of failing to explain how its dominant position in the United Kingdom market for air travel agency services arises from its successes in air transport.

197. For the purposes of establishing whether BA holds a dominant position on the United Kingdom market for air travel agency services, there is no need to assess its economic strength on that market by reference to the competition between airlines providing services on each of the routes served by BA and its competitors to and from United Kingdom airports.

198. ...those various United Kingdom markets in air transport services are distinct from air travel agency services, including the distribution of air tickets in particular.

199. Concerning the alleged factual errors, BA cannot accuse the Commission of failing to take account of the impact of air ticket sales by telephone or internet, having regard to the specificity, as regards marketing procedures, of the services supplied by travel agents.

200. That specificity has, moreover, caused BA to state that travel agents are of vital importance, as intermediaries, for airlines. That specificity is, in addition, borne out by the fact that sales of air tickets handled by travel agents established in the United Kingdom represent 85 per cent of all air tickets sold in that Member State.

201. Nor can BA validly blame the Commission for taking account of sales of BA tickets outside the United Kingdom in determining its shares of the United Kingdom market for air travel agency services.

202. BA acknowledged, in reply to a question put by the Court, that it was impossible to quantify the transactions which took place outside the United Kingdom. The Commission was not therefore in a position to make a distinction according to whether or not the tickets were sold inside the United Kingdom. As examination of the third plea has shown, travellers normally reserve air tickets in their country of residence. Therefore, the applicant has not shown that the Commission's assessment related to a number of tickets capable of distorting its estimate of the market share held by BA on the United Kingdom market for air travel agency services.

203. BA's argument that BSPUK is unrepresentative is not convincing. Even if BSPUK [Billing and Settlement Plan for the United Kingdom] covers only 4,634 of the 7,000 travel agents established in the United Kingdom, it is undisputed that it is the largest among them that are members of that national settlement plan.

204. Considering the preponderant share of air ticket sales through BSPUK in the total of ticket sales through travel agents established in the United Kingdom, it appears that the Commission was right to hold that the shares of the six main airlines in those total sales of airline tickets could not be very different from those accounted for through BSPUK.

205. Moreover, as is shown by recital 34 of the contested decision, BA itself indicated during the administrative procedure that, between January and November 1998, it had sold 85 per cent of its air tickets issued in the United Kingdom through IATA travel agents and BSPUK. Recital 33 of the contested decision, not challenged on this point by the applicant, shows that 4,108 of the 4,634 agents participating in BSPUK, namely some 89 per cent, are accredited by IATA.

206. Nor is it disputed that BA ticket sales by IATA travel agents established in the United Kingdom represented 66 per cent of the sales of the top 10 airlines handled by BSPUK in the same financial year.

207. In those circumstances, the fact that 2,366 travel agents do not participate in BSPUK does not appear likely significantly to reduce BA's share in United Kingdom air ticket sales through travel agents.

208. The same applies to ticket sales by other companies using BA as an agent and not participating in the performance reward schemes at issue. As the Commission has stated, without being contradicted by BA, the latter merely stated that the amount of those sales might represent a percentage of 5 per cent or less.

209. The Court still needs to examine whether the reasoning followed by the Commission in order to establish BA's dominant position, on the basis of the evidence which it thus lawfully used, might not be vitiated by errors of assessment.

210. In that respect, account must be taken of the highly significant indicator which is the fact that the undertaking in question holds large shares of the market and of the ratio between the market share held by the undertaking concerned and that of its nearest rivals (*Hoffmann-La Roche*, . . . at paragraphs 39 and 48), particularly since the nearest rivals hold only marginal market shares (see, to that effect, Case 27/76 *United Brands* v. *Commission* [1978] ECR 207, paragraph 111).

211. As is shown by the table reproduced below, which is taken from recital 41 of the contested decision and the factual accuracy which BA has not been able to disprove (see paragraphs 199 to 208 above), not only is BA's market share in the total of air ticket sales handled by BSPUK to be regarded as large, but it invariably constitutes a multiple of the market shares of each of its five main competitors on the United Kingdom market for air travel agency services.

	1992	1993	1994	1995	1996	1997	1998
British Airways	46.3	45.6	43.5	42.7	40.3	42.0	39.7
American Airlines	–	5.4	7.3	7.7	7.6	3.6	3.8
Virgin	2.8	3.0	3.7	4.0	4.0	5.8	5.5
British Midland	3.6	3.4	3.2	3.0	2.7	–	–
Quantas	3.0	2.7	3.0	2.6	6.4	3.0	3.3
KLM	2.5	–	–	–	–	3.8	5.3

212. The economic strength which BA derives from its market share is further reinforced by the world rank it occupies in terms of international scheduled passenger-kilometres flown, the extent of the range of its transport services and its hub network.

213. According to BA's own statements, its network operations allow it, in comparison with its five competitors, to offer a wider choice of routes and more frequent flights.

214. It is further shown by recital 38 of the contested decision, not challenged by BA, that, in 1995, it operated 92 of the 151 international routes from Heathrow Airport and 43 of the 92 routes in service at Gatwick, that is to say several times the number of routes served by each of its three or four nearest rivals (operating) from those two airports.

215. As a whole, the services operated by BA on routes to and from United Kingdom airports have the cumulative effect of generating the purchase by travellers of a preponderant number of BA air tickets through agents established in the United Kingdom, and, correspondingly, at least as many transactions between BA and those agents for the purposes of supplying air travel agency services, particularly in the distribution of BA air tickets.

216. It necessarily follows that those agents substantially depend on the income they receive from BA in consideration for their air travel agency services.

217. BA is therefore wrong to deny that it is an obligatory business partner of travel agents established in the United Kingdom and to maintain that those agents have no actual need to sell BA tickets. BA's arguments are not capable of calling into question the finding, in recital 93 of the contested decision, that BA enjoys a particularly powerful position in relation to its nearest rivals and the largest travel agents.

218. The facts of this case therefore show that BA was in a position, unilaterally by circular of 17 November 1997, to impose a reduction as from 1 January 1998 of its rates of commission in force up to that date and to extend its new performance reward scheme to all travel agents established in the United Kingdom.

219. In those circumstances, neither the possibly modest size of the share of BA ticket sales in the business of some of the main agencies, which has moreover merely been alleged, nor the alleged fluctuations of BA's share in the total figure of air ticket sales by travel agents established in the United Kingdom can call into question the Commission's finding that BA holds a dominant position on the United Kingdom market for air travel agency services.

220. Nor are the great dependence of United Kingdom travel agents upon BA and BA's corresponding freedom of manoeuvre in relation to other companies using the services of air travel agencies capable of being called into question by the fact that those agents do not normally hold stocks of air tickets.

221. Such a purely logistical circumstance is not of such a kind as to affect the dominant position which BA derives from its preponderant weight on the United Kingdom market for air travel agency services.

222. The argument that, as an undertaking in a dominant position, BA would have no interest in spending considerable sums improving its services so as to compete more effectively with its rivals is irrelevant in that it concerns the United Kingdom air transport markets and not the United Kingdom market for air travel agency services which the Commission took to establish the dominant position of BA.

223. Finally, for the same reason, neither the decline in the percentage of BA air ticket sales nor the advance in market share of certain rival companies is sufficiently large to call into question the existence of BA's dominant position on the United Kingdom market for air travel agency services.

224. In this case, the reduction in BA's market share cannot, in itself, constitute proof that there is no dominant position. The position which BA still occupies on the United Kingdom market for air travel agency services remains very largely preponderant. As the table in paragraph 211 above shows, a substantial gap remained, during the whole of the period of the infringement found by the Commission, between, on the one hand, BA's market share and, on the other, both the market share of its closest rival and the cumulative shares of its five main competitors on the United Kingdom market for air travel agency services.

225. The Commission was therefore right to hold that BA held a dominant position on the United Kingdom market for air travel agency services.

It should also be noted that in *Gøttrup Klim* the ECJ did not dismiss the possibility of an undertaking with 36 and 32 per cent of two relevant markets being in a dominant position:

While an undertaking which holds market shares of that size may, depending on the strength and number of its competitors, be considered to be in a dominant position, those market shares cannot on their own constitute conclusive evidence of the existence of a dominant position.[166]

(iv) Market Shares and the Commission Discussion Paper

In the Discussion Paper the Commission stated that 'market shares provide useful first indications of the market structure and of the competitive importance of various undertakings active on the market'[167] and that it 'interprets market shares in the light of likely market conditions, for instance, whether the market is highly dynamic in character and whether the market structure is unstable due to innovation and growth'.[168] Further, it recognized that the significance of market share depends on the facts of each individual case and that market share is only a proxy for market power.[169] In particular, it stated that the importance of market shares may be affected by the degree of product differentiation in the market, as the greater the extent of product differentiation the less reliable market share data alone will be.[170] However, in a highly contentious passage it also said:

It is very likely that very high market shares, which have been held for some time, indicate a dominant position . . . This would be the case where an undertaking holds 50% or more of the market, provided that rivals hold a much smaller share of the market . . . In the case of lower market shares, dominance is more likely to be found in the market share range of 40% to 50% than below 40%, although also undertakings with market shares below 40% could be considered to be in a dominant position . . . However, undertakings with market shares of no more than 25% . . . are not likely to enjoy a (single) dominant position on the market concerned . . . [171]

The second sentence of this appears to misrepresent paragraph 60 of the *AKZO* judgment[172] as the ECJ did not limit the 'exceptional circumstances' rebutting the presumption of dominance at 50 per cent to a matter of the competitors holding much smaller market shares. It is highly unlikely that this will survive into any further communication from the Commission.

The second part of the paragraph was criticized in very many of the comments received on the Discussion Paper because it did not rule out dominance below 40 per cent and even went as far as saying that that undertakings with 25 per cent were merely 'not likely' to be dominant. This did not denote a change of policy by the Commission, as it had not previously ruled out the possibility of finding dominance at a market share of 20–40 per cent.[173] Many commentators

---

[166] Case C-250/92, *Gøttrup Klim v. KLG* [1994] ECR I-5641, [1996] 4 CMLR 191.

[167] Discussion Paper, para. 29

[168] *Ibid.*, para. 30.

[169] *Ibid.*, para. 32.

[170] *Ibid.*, para 33. And see Faull and Nikpay, n. 138 *supra*, 4.56.

[171] Discussion Paper, para. 31, citing *Hoffmann-La Roche*, *AKZO*, Case T-395/94, *Atantic Container Line AB* v. *Commission* [2002] ECR II-895, *United Brands*, and *Gøttrup Klim*.

[172] See *supra*, 398.

[173] See Commission's *Xth Report on Competition Policy* (Commission, 1981) part 150. The EC Merger Reg., Council Reg. 139/2004 [2004] OJ L24/1, recital 32, states a presumption that a concentration will not be liable to impede effective competition where the merging undertakings' aggregate market share is less than 25%. The Commission Guidelines on the assessment of significant market power under the regulatory framework for

would like to see a 'safe harbour' in respect of Article 82, similar to that provided by the block exemptions in respect to Article 81,[174] whereby a finding of dominance would be ruled out at, say, below a 40 per cent market share, and most certainly at 25 per cent. Such a 'dominance screen' could possibly allow some firms with market power to escape Article 82 but would, it is argued, generate legal certainty and avoid Type 1 errors (considered to be more damaging to consumer welfare where unilateral behaviour is concerned than Type 2 errors). The following extract, from the submission of an economics consultancy in response to the Discussion Paper, typifies the argument.

The Response of RBB Economics to the DG Competition Discussion Paper on the Application of Article 82 of the Treaty to Exclusionary Abuses, March 2006, 23[175]

One of the most striking points in this section of the DP is the suggestion that dominance could be found at market shares of 25% or less. Notwithstanding the profound problems of market definition, as a practical matter allowing for the possibility of dominance starting at such low levels of market share will extend the inherent uncertainty surrounding dominance to many more firms than currently perceive themselves to be at risk with the effective hurdle set at or around 40%. Whilst we would agree that a theoretical risk of significant market power arising at these levels may exist, the number of instances is likely to be small and the cost of widening the net, in terms of increased uncertainty for a potentially substantial number of businesses, is likely to be high. We would therefore see merit in the guidelines referring to a higher threshold, so as to introduce at least a degree of certainty into an intrinsically complex and unclear area. The cost of such an approach may be to limit the discretion of the Commission in those rare cases where market power may arise at lower levels, but this would appear justified given the benefits of relative clarity that this would provide for a considerable number of firms.

(v) Problems with the Role of Market Shares in the Assessment of Market Power

Critics of the present position of EC law in respect of the role of market shares argue that there is over-reliance on this factor compared to those taken into account at the next stage of the assessment of market power. They point to a number of specific problems, which include

---

electronic communications, networks and services (Guidelines on the assessment of significant market power under the Community regulatory framework for electronic communications, networks and services [2002] OJ C165/15) says : 'Although a high market share alone is not sufficient to establish the possession of significant market power (dominance), it is unlikely that a firm without a significant share of the relevant market would be in a dominant position. Thus, undertakings with market shares of no more than 25 per cent are not likely to enjoy a (single) dominant position on the market concerned … In the Commission's decision–making practice, single dominance concerns normally arise in the case of undertakings with market shares of over 40 per cent, although the Commission may in some cases have concerns about dominance even with lower market shares …, as dominance may occur without the existence of a large market share'. (para. 75).

[174] *Supra*, Chap. 4.

[175] Available at http://www.rbbecon.com/publications/downloads/RBB_Article82Response.pdf, and on the Commission website, http://ec.europa.eu/comm/competition/antitrust/art82/068.pdf.

the following:

- it all depends on the uncertain art of market definition;
- market definition is an 'in or out' (zero-one fallacy) game, whereas in reality products are often imperfect substitutes for one another and undertakings may be constrained by the existence of products which are outside the defined market;
- there is a presumption of dominance at 50 per cent of the market, which, it is argued, is too low. It should be noted that in applying section 2 of the Sherman Act US courts rarely find an offence of 'monopolization' to have been committed where an undertaking has less than 70 per cent of the market;
- as we saw above, there is an absence of a presumption of 'no dominance';
- market share analysis is 'static' and is not suited for application to dynamically competitive markets such as those in the new economy.[176]

As far as the second of these problems is concerned, the 'in or out' situation, an economist has suggested that it may be possible to devise a 'weighted market share' approach 'to take account of the fact that substitutability is a matter of degree in market power assessment'. This would involve taking into account imperfect substitutes when calculating the market share of a product but with a lesser weight than if it were a more perfect substitute.[177]

Unfortunately, to a large extent the heavy reliance on market share stems from the case law of the Court. That is probably why the Discussion Paper emphasised the importance of other factors but still contained paragraph 31. Nevertheless, the Competition Commissioner herself is as sceptical of over-dependence on market share analysis as any outside critic:

This means that I consider that high market shares are not—on their own—sufficient to conclude that a dominant position exists. Market share presumptions can result in an excessive focus on establishing the exact market shares of the various market participants. A pure market share focus risks failing to take proper account of the degree to which competitors can constrain the behaviour of the allegedly dominant company. That is not to say that market shares have no significance. They may provide an indication of dominance—and sometimes a very strong indication—but in the end a full economic analysis of the overall situation is necessary.[178]

C. MARKET SHARES IN THE CASE OF COLLECTIVE DOMINANCE

It must be stressed that what is said above about market shares relates to a position of *single* firm dominance. There may need to be higher market shares in order to sustain a finding of collective dominance. In the merger case *France v. Commission*[179] the ECJ annulled the Commission's

---

[176] See *infra*, 429.

[177] J. Vickers, 'Market Power in Competition Case' (2006) 2 *European Law Journal* 3, 8–10.

[178] Neelie Kroes, 'Preliminary Thoughts on Policy Review of Article 82', Speech at the Fordham Corporate Law Institute, New York, 23 September 2005, available at http://europa.eu/rapid/ pressReleasesAction.do? reference=SPEECH/05/537&format=HTML&aged=0&language=EN&guiLanguage=en. A longer, and amended, version of this speech (including a longer version of this passage) appears as 'Tackling Exclusionary Practices to Avoid Exploitation of Market Power: Some Preliminary Thoughts on on the Policy Review of Article 82' in 2005 *Fordham Corp. L. Inst* (B. Hawk, Ed. 2006), 381 at 384.

[179] Cases C 68/94 and C 30/95, *France v. Commission* [1998] ECR I-1375, [1998] 4 CMLR 829.

prohibition of a merger which had been made on grounds that it would lead to a position of collective dominance.[180] The merged company and its nearest competitor would have had a combined market share of 60 per cent and the ECJ held that this could not point conclusively to the existence of collective dominance. Developments in the collective dominance jurisprudence since then make it more likely that a collective dominant position requires the undertakings involved to hold between them a market share considerably in excess of 40 per cent.[181] Undertakings which hitherto have been held to be in a collective dominant position for the purposes of Article 82 have together had a 'quasi-monopoly'.[182]

D. OTHER FACTORS INDICATING DOMINANCE

(i) General

As explained above, a wide range of matters have been held by the Court and the Commission to constitute 'other factors indicating dominance'. In *United Brands* and *Hoffmann-La Roche* the ECJ held that a dominant position derives from a combination of several factors which, taken separately, are not necessarily determinative.[183] It should be noted that carrying out a full economic analysis before a finding of dominance is made would preclude any one factor (including market share) being determinative, so the inclusion of the word 'necessary' in this famous sentence is unfortunate.

The way in which dominance is derived from a combination of factors in addition to market share is illustrated by some of the leading cases on Article 82.

(ii) Some Leading Cases

a. *United Brands*

Case 27/76, *United Brands Co and United Brands Continental Bv* v. *Commission* [1978] ECR 207, [1978] 1 CMLR 429

The issues in *United Brands* were firstly whether bananas were a separate relevant market from other fruit (see above in the discussion on market definition) and if so, whether, secondly, United Brands was dominant on it.

---

[180] Case No. IV/M.308 *Kali+Salz/MDK/Treuhand* [1994] OJ L186/38.

[181] See *infra* Chap. 11.

[182] Case T-228/97, *Irish Sugar plc v. Commission* [1999] ECR II-2969, [1999] 5 CMLR 1300, confirmed on appeal to the ECJ, Case C-497/99 P, *Irish Sugar plc v. Commission* [2001] ECR I-5333, [2001] 5 CMLR 1082; Cases C-395 and 396/96P *Compagnie Maritime Belge Transports SA v. EC Commission* [2000] ECR I-1365, [2000] 4 CMLR 1076, discussed in Chap. 11.

[183] Case 27/76, *United Brands Co and United Brands Continental BV v. Commission* [1978] ECR 207, [1978] 1 CMLR 429, para. 66, Case 85/76, *Hoffmann-La Roche & Co AG v. Commission* [1979] ECR 461, [1979] 3 CMLR 211, para. 39.

Court of Justice

67. In order to find out whether UBC is an undertaking in a dominant position on the relevant market it is necessary first of all to examine its structure and then the situation on the said market as far as competition is concerned.

68. In doing so it may be advisable to take account if need be of the facts put forward as acts amounting to abuses without necessarily having to acknowledge that they are abuses.

. . . The structure of UBC

69. It is advisable to examine in turn UBC's resources for and methods of producing, packaging, transporting, selling and displaying its product.

70. UBC is an undertaking vertically integrated to a high degree.

71. This integration is evident at each of the stages from the plantation to the loading on wagons or lorries in the ports of delivery and after those stages, as far as ripening and sale prices are concerned, UBC even extends its control to ripener/distributors and wholesalers by setting up a complete network of agents.

72. At the production stage UBC owns large plantations in Central and South America.

73. In so far as UBC's own production does not meet its requirements it can obtain supplies without any difficulty from independent planters since it is an established fact that unless circumstances are exceptional there is a production surplus.

74. Furthermore several independent producers have links with UBC through contracts for the growing of bananas which have caused them to grow the varieties of bananas which UBC has advised them to adopt.

75. The effects of natural disasters which could jeopardize supplies are greatly reduced by the fact that the plantations are spread over a wide geographic area and by the selection of varieties not very susceptible to diseases.

76. This situation was born out by the way in which UBC was able to react to the consequences of hurricane 'Fifi' in 1974.

77. At the production stage UBC therefore knows that it can comply with all the requests which it receives.

78. At the stage of packaging and presentation on its premises UBC has at its disposal factories, manpower, plant and material which enable it to handle the goods independently.

79. The bananas are carried from the place of production to the port of shipment by its own means of transport including railways.

80. At the carriage by sea stage it has been acknowledged that UBC is the only undertaking of its kind which is capable of carrying two thirds of its exports by means of its own banana fleet.

81. Thus UBC knows that it is able to transport regularly, without running the risk of its own ships not being used and whatever the market situation may be, two thirds of its average volume of sales and is alone able to ensure that three regular consignments reach Europe each week, and all this guarantees it commercial stability and well being.

82. In the field of technical knowledge and as a result of continual research UBC keeps on improving the productivity and yield of its plantations by improving the draining system, making good soil deficiencies and combating effectively plant disease.

83. It has perfected new ripening methods in which its technicians instruct the distributor/ripeners of the Chiquita banana.

84. That is another factor to be borne in mind when considering UBC's position since competing firms cannot develop research at a comparable level and are in this respect at a disadvantage compared with the applicant.

85. It is acknowledged that at the stage where the goods are given the final finish and undergo quality control UBC not only controls the distributor/ripeners which are direct

customers but also those who work for the account of its important customers such as the Scipio group.

86. Even if the object of the clause prohibiting the sale of green bananas was only strict quality control, it in fact gives UBC absolute control of all trade in its goods so long as they are marketable wholesale, that is to say before the ripening process begins which makes an immediate sale unavoidable.

87. This general quality control of a homogeneous product makes the advertising of the brand name effective.

88. Since 1967 UBC has based its general policy in the relevant market on the quality of its Chiquita brand banana.

89. There is no doubt that this policy gives UBC control over the transformation of the product into bananas for consumption even though most of this product no longer belongs to it.

90. This policy has been based on a thorough reorganization of the arrangements for production, packaging, carriage, ripening (new plant with ventilation and a cooling system) and sale (a network of agents).

91. UBC has made this product distinctive by large-scale repeated advertising and promotion campaigns which have induced the consumer to show a preference for it in spite of the difference between the price of labelled and unlabelled bananas (in the region of 30 to 40 per cent) and also of Chiquita bananas and those which have been labelled with another brand name (in the region of 7 to 10 per cent).

92. It was the first to take full advantage of the opportunities presented by labelling in the tropics for the purpose of large-scale advertising and this, to use UBC's own words, has 'revolutionized the commercial exploitation of the banana' (Annex II to the application, p. 10).

93. It has thus attained a privileged position by making Chiquita the premier banana brand name on the relevant market with the result that the distributor cannot afford not to offer it to the consumer.

94. At the selling stage this distinguishing factor—justified by the unchanging quality of the banana bearing this label—ensures that it has regular customers and consolidates its economic strength.

95. The effect of its sales networks only covering a limited number of customers, large groups or distributor/ripeners, is a simplification of its supply policy and economies of scale.

96. Since UBC's supply policy consists—in spite of the production surplus—in only meeting the requests for Chiquita bananas parsimoniously and sometimes incompletely UBC is in a position of strength at the selling stage.

. . .

121. UBC's economic strength has thus enabled it to adopt a flexible overall strategy directed against new competitors establishing themselves on the whole of the relevant market.

122. The particular barriers to competitors entering the market are the exceptionally large capital investments required for the creation and running of banana plantations, the need to increase sources of supply in order to avoid the effects of fruit diseases and bad weather (hurricanes, floods), the introduction of an essential system of logistics which the distribution of a very perishable product makes necessary, economies of scale from which newcomers to the market cannot derive any immediate benefit and the actual cost of entry made up, *inter alia*, of all the general expenses incurred in penetrating the market such as the setting up of an adequate commercial network, the mounting of very large-scale advertising campaigns, all those financial risks, the costs of which are irrecoverable if the attempt fails.

123. Thus, although, as UBC has pointed out, it is true that competitors are able to use the same methods of production and distribution as the applicant, they come up against almost insuperable practical and financial obstacles.

124. This is another factor peculiar to a dominant position.

125. However UBC takes into account the losses which its banana division made from 1971 to 1976—whereas during this period its competitors made profits—for the purpose of inferring that, since dominance is in essence the power to fix prices, making losses is inconsistent with the existence of a dominant position.

126. An undertaking's economic strength is not measured by its profitability; a reduced profit margin or even losses for a time are not incompatible with a dominant position, just as large profits may be compatible with a situation where there is effective competition.

127. The fact that UBC's profitability is for a time moderate or non-existent must be considered in the light of the whole of its operations.

128. The finding that, whatever losses UBC may make, the customers continue to buy more goods from UBC which is the dearest vendor, is more significant and this fact is a particular feature of the dominant position and its verification is determinative in this case.

129. The cumulative effect of all the advantages enjoyed by UBC thus ensures that is has a dominant position on the relevant market.

b. *Hoffmann-La Roche*

Case 85/76, *Hoffmann-La Roche & Co AG* v. *Commission* [1979] ECR 461, [1979] 3 CMLR 211

The case concerned Hoffmann-La Roche's practices on various vitamin markets.

Court of Justice

48. . . . the relationship between the market shares of the undertaking concerned and of its competitors, especially those of the next largest, the technological lead of an undertaking over its competitors, the existence of a highly developed sales network and the absence of potential competition are relevant factors, the first because it enables the competitive strength of the undertaking in question to be assessed, the second and third because they represent in themselves technical and commercial advantages and the fourth because it is the consequence of the existence of obstacles preventing new competitors from having access to the market. As far as the existence or non-existence of potential competition is concerned it must, however, be observed that, although it is true—and this applies to all the groups of vitamins in question—that because of the amount of capital investment required the capacity of the factories is determined according to the anticipated growth over a long period so that access to the market by new producers is not easy, account must also be taken of the fact that the existence of considerable unused manufacturing capacity creates potential competition between established manufacturers. Nevertheless Roche is in this respect in a privileged position because, as it admits itself, its own manufacturing capacity was, during the period covered by the contested decision, in itself sufficient to meet world demand without this surplus manufacturing capacity placing it in a difficult economic or financial situation.

49. It is in the light of the preceding considerations that Roche's shares of each of the relevant markets, complemented by those factors which in conjunction with the market shares make it possible to show that there may be a dominant position, must be evaluated. Finally, it will also be necessary to consider whether Roche's submissions relating to the implication of its conduct on the market, mainly as far as concerns prices, are of such a kind as to alter the findings to which the examination of the market shares and the other factors taken into account might lead.

c. *Michelin*

Case 322/81, *Nederlandsche Banden-Industrie Michelin* v. *Commission* [1983] ECR 3461, [1985] 1 CMLR 282

As discussed above in relation to market definition, this case concerned Michelin's position on the tyre market. The Commission's definition of the market as being that for new replacement lorry and bus tyres was upheld. The alleged abuse concerned the terms Michelin offered its dealers. This part of the judgment deals with the assessment of dominance.

Court of Justice

53. The applicant challenges next the relevance of the other criteria and evidence used by the Commission to prove that a dominant position exists. It claims that it is not the only undertaking to have commercial representatives, that the numbers employed by its main competitors are even larger in relative terms and that its wide range of products is not a competitive advantage because the different types of tyre are not interchangeable and it does not require dealers to purchase its whole range of tyres.

54. It also claims that the Commission took no account of a number of evidential factors which were incompatible with the existence of a dominant position. For instance, dealers' net margins on Michelin tyres and competing tyres are comparable and the cost per mile of Michelin tyres is the most favourable for users. Since 1979 Michelin NV has made a loss. As its production capacity is insufficient, its competitors, which are also financially stronger and more diversified than the Michelin group, can at any moment replace the quantities which it supplies. Lastly, because users of heavy-vehicle tyres are experienced trade buyers they have the ability to act as a counterpoise to the tyre manufacturers.

55. In reply to those arguments it should first be observed that in order to assess the relative economic strength of Michelin NV and its competitors on the Netherlands market the advantages which those undertakings may derive from belonging to groups of undertakings operating throughout Europe or even the world must be taken into consideration. Amongst those advantages, the lead which the Michelin group has over its competitors in the matters of investment and research and the special extent of its range of products, to which the Commission referred in its decision, have not been denied. In fact in the case of certain types of tyres the Michelin group is the only supplier on the market to offer them in its range.

56. That situation ensures that on the Netherlands market a large number of users of heavy-vehicle tyres have a strong preference for Michelin tyres. As the purchase of tyres represents a considerable investment for a transport undertaking and since much time is required in order to ascertain in practice the cost-effectiveness of a type or brand of tyre, Michelin NV therefore enjoys a position which renders it largely immune to competition. As a result, a dealer established in the Netherlands normally cannot afford not to sell Michelin tyres.

57. It is not possible to uphold the objections made against those arguments by Michelin NV, supported on this point by the French Government, that Michelin NV is thus penalized for the quality of its products and services. A finding that an undertaking has a dominant position is not in itself a recrimination but simply means that, irrespective of the reasons for which it has such a dominant position, the undertaking concerned has a special responsibility not to allow its conduct to impair genuine undistorted competition on the common market.

58. Due weight must also be attached to the importance of Michelin NV's network of commercial representatives, which gives it direct access to tyre users at all times. Michelin NV has not disputed the fact that in absolute terms its network is considerably larger than those of its competitors or challenged the description, in the decision at issue, of the services performed by its network whose efficiency and quality of service are unquestioned. The direct access to users and the standard of service which the network can give them enables Michelin NV to maintain and strengthen its position on the market and to protect itself more effectively against competition.

59. As regards the additional criteria and evidence to which Michelin NV refers in order to disprove the existence of a dominant position, it must be observed that temporary unprofitability or even losses are not inconsistent with the existence of a dominant position. By the same token, the fact that the prices charged by Michelin NV do not constitute an abuse and are not even particularly high does not justify the conclusion that a dominant position does not exist. Finally, neither the size, financial strength and degree of diversification of Michelin NV's competitors at the world level nor the counterpoise arising from the fact that buyers of heavy-vehicle tyres are experienced trade users are such as to deprive Michelin NV of its privileged position on the Netherlands market.

60. It must therefore be concluded that the other criteria and evidence relevant in this case in determining whether a dominant position exists confirm that Michelin NV has such a position.

61. Michelin NV's submissions disputing that it has a dominant position on a substantial part of the common market are therefore unfounded.

d. *Eurofix-Bauco/Hilti*

Eurofix-Bauco/Hilti [1988] OJ L65/19, [1989] 4 CMLR 677[184]

For the market definition aspects of this case see the section on market definition above.[185] The case concerned the consumables (nails and cartridges) for Hilti's nail-guns.

Commission

69. In addition to the strength derived from its market share and the relative weakness of its competitors, Hilti has other advantages that help reinforce and maintain its position in the nail gun market:

— its biggest selling nail gun, the DX 450, has certain novel technically advantageous features which are still protected by patents,

— Hilti has an extremely strong research and development position and is one of the leading companies worldwide not only in nail guns but also other fastening technologies

— Hilti has a strong and well-organised distribution system—in the EEC it has subsidiaries and independent dealers integrated into its selling network who deal mostly direct with customers, and

— the market for nail guns is relatively mature, which may discourage new entrants since sales or market shares can only be obtained at the expense of existing competitors in the market for replacements.

---

[184] The appeals, Case T-30/89, *Hilti AG v. Commission* [1991] ECR II-1439, [1992] 4 CMLR 16 and Case C-53/92 P, *Hilti v. Commission* [1994] ECR I-667, [1994] 4 CMLR 614, confirmed the Commission.

[185] *Supra* 372.

70. The foregoing considerations lead to the conclusion that Hilti holds a dominant position in the EEC for nail guns, as well as the markets for Hilti-compatible nails and cartridge strips. These are the relevant markets for the purposes of this Decision. It should be stressed that, in this particular case, the relevant markets for Hilti compatible nails and cartridge strips are important because of Hilti's large share of sales of nail guns. Because of this large share, independent manufacturers of nails and cartridge strips must manufacture nails and/or cartridge strips which can be used in Hilti tools if they are to produce for more than a small segment of the market thus achieving the economies of scale necessary to be both competitive and profitable.

71. Hilti's market power and dominance stem principally from its large share of the sales of nail guns coupled with the patent protection for its cartridge strips. The economic position it enjoys is such that it enables it to prevent effective competition being maintained on the relevant markets for Hilti-compatible nails and cartridge strips. In fact Hilti's commercial behaviour, which has been described above and is analysed below, is witness to its ability to act independently of, and without due regard to, either competitors or customers on the relevant markets in question. In addition, Hilti's pricing policy also described above reflects its ability to determine, or at least to have an appreciable influence on the conditions under which competition will develop. This behaviour and its economic consequences would not normally be seen where a company was facing real competitive pressure. Therefore the Commission considers that Hilti holds a dominant position in the two separate relevant markets for Hilti-compatible nails and cartridge strips.

e. *Soda Ash–Solvay*

Soda Ash–Solvay [2003] OJ L10/10[186]

The case concerned the soda-ash market. This part of the Commission's decision also contains material on the definition of the market.

Commission

137. Solvay's own documentation recognises that it held a dominant position in western Europe. Its historic market share of some 70 per cent in continental western Europe over the whole of the period under consideration is in itself indicative of a significant degree of market power. Market share, while important, is only one of the indicators from which the existence of a dominant position may be inferred. Its significance may vary from case to case according to the characteristics of the relevant market.

138. To assess market power for the purposes of the present case, the Commission took into account all the relevant economic evidence, including the following elements:

(i)   Solvay's position as the only soda ash producer operating throughout the Community (with the exception of the United Kingdom and Ireland);

(ii) Solvay's manufacturing strength, with plants in Belgium, France, Germany, Italy, Spain and Portugal;

---

[186] This decision, of December 2000, replaced an earlier one, *Soda Ash-Solvay* [1991] OJ L152/21, [1994] 4 CMLR 645 which was annulled on appeal by the CFI on procedural grounds: Cases T-30/91, etc. *Solvay SA v. Commission* [1995] ECR II-1775, [1996] 5 CMLR 57 (see *infra* Chap. 14).

   (iii) Solvay's upstream integration in raw materials as the largest producer of salt in the Community;

   (iv) the absence of any competition from ICI, the only other Community producer of comparable market strength to Solvay;

   (v) Solvay's high market share in the Benelux countries, France and Germany and its monopoly or near-monopoly position in Italy, Spain and Portugal;

   (vi) Solvay's excellent market coverage as the exclusive or near-exclusive supplier to almost all the major customers in the Community;

   (vii) the improbability of any new producer of synthetic ash entering the market and setting up manufacturing facilities in the Community;

   (viii) the protection against non-Community producers afforded by the anti-dumping duties;

   (ix) Solvay's traditional role of price leader;

   (x) the perception of Solvay by other Community producers as the dominant producer and their reluctance to compete aggressively for Solvay's traditional customers.

139. In assessing the extent of Solvay's market power, the Commission took account of the possible substitutability of caustic soda for soda ash. Caustic soda (sodium hydroxide) is largely used for the production of paper and aluminium and may also in theory replace soda ash for certain manufacturing applications as a source of alkali particularly in the manufacture of detergents and in metallurgical processes. (NB: The reverse is also true: soda ash is in theory also an alternative for caustic soda in some processes.) In practice however the possible availability of caustic soda did not constitute a substantial limitation on Solvay's market power in the Community, which is principally based on supply to glass manufacturers, few if any of which were prepared to substitute caustic soda for soda ash.

140. Caustic soda is a co-product of the manufacture of chlorine, a basic raw material in the manufacture of PVC. Since long-term storage is not feasible, production of chlorine is tailored to current PVC demand. The supply of caustic soda inevitably fluctuates in line with that of chlorine. Demand for caustic soda on the other hand depends largely on the requirements of the paper industry. The price of caustic soda is therefore, unlike soda ash, subject to considerable fluctuation.

141. During the period under consideration caustic soda was 'short', i.e., the growth in demand for caustic soda exceeded that for chlorine: the product was in short supply and was likely to remain so for the foreseeable future. It was also considerably more expensive than the equivalent in soda ash. There was thus no incentive for soda ash users to switch to caustic soda. Further, conversion from soda ash to caustic requires a substantial capital investment. Even if caustic soda is 'long' at a particular time the cyclical nature of the alkali market and uncertainty as to future pricing acts as a deterrent to switching.

142. In the glass sector, the main consumer of soda ash, accounting for two-thirds of Solvay's sales in the period under consideration, caustic soda substitution is even less likely than in metallurgical and detergent applications. In theory up to 15 per cent of the alkali requirement of glassmakers may be provided by caustic soda. Again, capital investment in plant modification is required. In practice, by 1990 only one glassmaker had ever converted to caustic soda.

143. It should also be noted that the major soda ash producers (Solvay, ICI, Akzo) between them made around one third of the caustic soda produced in the Community.

144. Solvay has also argued that the availability of cullet (recycled broken glass) excluded its having a dominant position. A customer's requirements of soda ash in container glass manufacture can be reduced by up to 15 per cent by using cullet and with appropriate technology the proportion may be higher. It may well be that the use of cullet reduces the dependence of customers upon soda ash suppliers generally. It does not, however, reduce the ability of a powerful soda ash producer to exclude smaller producers of that product.

145. The possibilities of substitution did not therefore act as a significant constraint on the exercise of Solvay's market power vis-à-vis the other producers of soda ash.

146. The Commission assessed Solvay's market power in relation to the whole of the geographic area within which it operated, which in the present case consisted of those Member States in which it had production facilities. Solvay's own internal documentation shows that it tended to consider the nine 'directions nationales' as forming a homogeneous market. (This market delineation included two non-member countries, namely Switzerland and Austria, and excluded the United Kingdom and Ireland, which were traditional 'ICI' markets, and Denmark and Greece, which were 'non-producer' markets.)

147. However, even if each of the national markets particularly concerned by Solvay's exclusionary conduct were considered as a separate market, Solvay was still dominant in each one, and most of the considerations set out above apply equally.

148. On the basis of the above considerations the Commission concludes that throughout the period under consideration Solvay occupied a dominant position within the meaning of Article 82.

(iii) Summary of 'Other Factors Indicating Dominance'

It is possible from looking at the cases set out above and others to describe the main factors which the Court and the Commission do or do not consider indicate dominance

a. Statutory Monopoly, Legal Regulation, Intellectual Property Rights

State or regulatory measures which subject a market to licensing requirements, or grant to a particular undertaking a statutory monopoly, an exclusive concession (such as in the provision of undertaking services in *Bodson v. Pompes Funèbres*)[187] or exclusive access to finite resources (such as radio frequencies in *Decca Navigator*[188] or airport slots in *British Midland— Aer Lingus*)[189] are obvious barriers to entry. Even economists of the Chicago school recognize that governmental restrictions may operate as a barrier to entry. Most legal and regulatory barriers to entry would come under the heading of absolute cost advantages in the classification discussed in Chapter 1.[190] They are structural factors: characteristics inherent in the relevant market.[191] The Court and Commission have frequently held such measures to be factors indicating dominance and many cases on Article 82 concern statutory monopolists.[192]

Intellectual property rights are a particular type of legal right granted by national (or Community)[193] law. The ECJ has consistently held that the ownership of intellectual property

---

[187] Case 30/87, *Bodson v. Pompes Funèbres des Régions Libérées* [1988] ECR 2479, [1989] 4 CMLR 984.

[188] [1989] OJ L43/7, [1990] 4 CMLR 627.

[189] [1992] OJ L96/34, [1993] 4 CMLR 596.

[190] See the article by D. Harbord and T. Hoehn, 'Barriers to Entry and Exit in European Competition Policy' (1994) 14 *International Review of Law and Economics* 411 and the extract from the OFT report *supra* Chap. 1.

[191] Faull and Nikpay, n. 138 *supra*, 4.62.

[192] e.g., Case 311/84, *Centre Belge d'Etudes du Marché-Télémarketing v. Compagnie Luxembourgeoise de Télédiffusion SA and Information Publicité Benelux SA* [1985] ECR 3261, [1986] 2 CMLR 558; Cases C241–2/91 P, *RTE & ITP v. Commission (Magill)* [1995] ECR I-743, [1995] 4 CMLR 718; Case 226/84, *British Leyland v. Commission* [1986] ECR 3263, [1987] 1 CMLR 185; *Sealink/B&I Holyhead: Interim Measures* [1992] 5 CMLR 255, and other transport cases.

[193] As with the Community Trade Mark (1994) and the Community Plant Variety Right (1996). The Community Patent Convention (1975) is not yet in force. There is a regional trade mark regime covering the Benelux countries.

rights does not necessarily mean that the owner has a dominant position.[194] The legal monopoly may not equate to an economic monopoly if the relevant market is wider than the protected product. However, the fact that access to a market is protected by intellectual property rights may be relevant as a factor indicating dominance. This was found to be the case in *Hugin*,[195] (where the Court of Justice seemed to accept the argument that the spare parts were protected by the UK's Design Copyright Act 1968), *Eurofix-Bauco (Hilti)*[196] (above), and *Tetra Pak II*.[197] Again, economists classify intellectual property rights as absolute cost advantages.

b. Superior Technology and Efficiency

The superior technology of an undertaking has often been found to be a factor indicating dominance. This can be seen from the extracts set out from *United Brands, Hoffmann-La Roche, Michelin, Eurofix-Bauco (Hilti)*, and *Tetra Pak* above. It is, however, questionable from an economic point of view to hold that an undertaking's technological superiority operates as a barrier to entry *per se*. It is true that expenditure on technological development can be a sunk cost of entry but it is also true that a new entrant on to the market may not have to spend the same resources on research and development as the incumbent on the market: there is no need to reinvent the wheel.[198] Superior technology could not operate as a barrier to entry according to Stigler since it does not represent a cost to the new entrant which was not borne by the incumbent.[199]

The Court and the Commission have held in several cases that the overall efficacy of the undertaking's commercial arrangements contributed to and enhanced its dominant position. This is particularly marked in *United Brands* (above, paragraphs 75–95 of the judgment), in *Michelin* (above, paragraph 58) and in *Eurofix-Bauco* (above, paragraph 69) where the Court and Commission took into account the effectiveness of the undertakings' distribution networks. These judgments may, therefore, be criticized for failing to explain sufficiently *why* a new entrant could not replicate these arrangements. Otherwise, the authorities appear simply to be penalising the undertaking in respect of its efficiency.[200] In the Discussion Paper the Commission listed 'a highly developed distribution and sales network' as barriers to entry and expansion and simply stated that 'the allegedly dominant undertaking may have its own dense outlet network, established distribution logistics or wide geographical coverage that would be difficult for rivals to replicate'.[201]

---

[194] Case 24/67, *Parke Davis v. Probel* [1968] ECR 55, [1968] CMLR 47; Cases C-241–242/91 P, *RTE & ITP v. Commission (Magill)* [1995] ECR I-743, [1995] 4 CMLR 718. The issue here is with patents, copyrights and designs: it is unlikely that the holding of a trade mark alone would ever confer dominance although, as discussed below, the ownership of a popular brand name may constitute a barrier to entry.

[195] Case 22/78, *Hugin Kassaregister AB and Hugin Cash Registers Ltd v. EC Commission* [1979] ECR 1869, [1979] 3 CMLR 345.

[196] [1988] OJ L65/19, [1989] 4 CMLR 677.

[197] Case C-333/94 P, *Tetra Pak International SA v. Commission* [1996] ECR I-5951, [1997] 4 CMLR 662.

[198] See V. Korah, 'Concept of a Dominant Position Within The Meaning of Art. 86' (1980) 17 *CMLRev* 395, 408 and 410; D. Harbord and T. Hoehn, 'Barriers to Entry and Exit in European Competition Policy' (1994) 14 *International Review of Law and Economics* 411, 419; C. Baden Fuller, 'Article 86 EEC: Economic Analysis of the Existence of a Dominant Position' (1979) 4 *ELRev* 423, 437.

[199] See *supra* Chap. 1.

[200] Despite the ECJ's protestations in, *inter alia, Michelin* (para. 57) that finding an undertaking has a dominant position is not a reproach, the consequences are such that it is invariably to the undertaking's disadvantage.

[201] Discussion Paper, para. 40.

c. Vertical Integration

The Court and Commission have also found that vertical integration is a factor indicating dominance. Again this appears to condemn an undertaking in respect of its efficiency (see also (b) above). Further, economists generally argue that when vertical integration takes place the barriers to entry are only added up and are not multiplied. Vertical integration may therefore accompany monopoly but is not an indicator of it.[202] Nonetheless in *United Brands* UBC's vertical integration was an important factor for the Court in the finding of dominance. Clearly in the context of the growing and marketing of bananas, a highly perishable product, this vertical integration played an important part in UBC's ability to get its bananas across the world and into the hands of European distributors as quickly as possible. It is quite another thing, however, to hold that this vertical integration constituted a barrier to entry. There was no explanation in the case of why, or even if, the vertical integration was to be regarded as a barrier to entry. In *Soda-ash—Solvay*, as can be seen from the extract above,[203] the Commission gave Solvay's production of the raw material (salt) as a factor indicating its dominance.

d. Economies of Scale and Scope

In *United Brands* (above, para. 122) the ECJ recognized that economies of scale operate as a barrier to entry. It was seen in Chapter 1 that, according to the definition of barriers set out by Stigler, economies of scale do not operate as a barrier to entry. It was also explained, however, in the extract from the OFT Report,[204] that under modern industrial organization theory, economies of scale can operate as strategic entry barriers: these stem from first-mover advantages. According to this theory, economies of scale combined with large sunk costs can be a serious deterrent to market entry. In *United Brands*, the ECJ did refer to sunk costs when it spoke of 'costs which are irrecoverable if the attempt fails'.[205] It is also argued in the OFT Report that economies of scale would deter entry if they cause tougher price competition. Thus it seems that economies of scale will sometimes create a barrier to entry. Baden Fuller, for example, takes the view that the crucial impact of economies of scale is on the probability of lack of profits. Usually profits are unlikely to be high for a small entrant where the minimum efficient scale of production is high in relation to the market.[206]

The main criticism of the cases is that they do not explain why economies of scale or scope are considered to be a barrier to entry in the particular situation under consideration. In *BPB*, for example, the Commission merely stated that 'BPB enjoys substantial economies in producing on a large scale in integrated industrial complexes, extracting gypsum and producing plaster then plasterboard'.[207] In the Discussion Paper the Commission considered that it is a matter of

---

[202] See C. Baden Fuller, 'Art. 86 EEC: Economic Analysis of the Existence of a Dominant Position' (1979) 4 *ELRev* 423, 440 and the economic literature cited there; Harbord and Hoehn, *supra* n. 198, 419; V. Korah, 'Concept of a Dominant Position Within The Meaning of Art. 86' (1980) 17 *CMLRev* 395, 408.

[203] *Supra* 414.

[204] OFT Research Paper 2, 'Barriers to Entry and Exit in Competition Policy (OFT, 1994). See *supra* Chap. 1.

[205] Case 27/76, *United Brands Co and United Brands Continental BV v. Commission* [1978] ECR 207, [1978] 1 CMLR 429, para. 122.

[206] C. Baden Fuller, 'Article 86 EEC: Economic Analysis of the Existence of a Dominant Position' (1979) 4 *ELRev* 423, 429–33 and see also Korah, *supra* n. 202, 407.

[207] *BPB Industries* [1989] OJ L10/50, [1990] 4 CMLR 464, para. 116. The issue of dominance was not addressed in the appeals: Case T-65/89, *BPB Industries and British Gypsum Ltd v. Commission* [1993] ECR II-389, [1993] 5 CMLR 32; Case C-310/93 P, *BPB Industries and British Gypsum Ltd v. Commission* [1995] ECR I-865, [1997] 4 CMLR 238.

the minimum efficient scale in the market concerned: '[w]hen economies of scale or scope are important and require a substantial production capacity compared to the size of the market, efficient expansion or entry is more costly and risky'.[208]

e. Access to Financial Resources and the need for Investment

In *United Brands*[209] and *Hoffmann-La Roche*[210] the ECJ considered that the need for large-scale capital investment constituted a barrier to entry. In *Continental Can*[211] the Commission also appeared to consider that the undertaking's access to international capital markets was an indicator of its dominance. Bain considered that capital requirements could give rise to barriers to entry because of the amount a new entrant would need to enter the market at an efficient scale.[212] Whether or not this is correct however is questionnable. In Bork's view:[213]

> Capital requirements exist and certainly inhibit entry—just as talent requirements for playing professional football exist and inhibit entry. Neither barrier is in any sense artificial or the proper subject of special concern for antitrust policy.

Nonetheless, asymmetries between competitors in access to finance *can* constitute a barrier to entry. The Commission explained in the Discussion Paper that '...in some cases [financial strength] may be one of the factors that contribute to a finding of a dominant position, in particular in those cases where (i) finance is relevant to the competitive process in the industry under review; (ii) there are significant asymmetries between competitors in terms of their internal financing capabilities; and (iii) particular features of the industry make it difficult for firms to attract external funds.[214]

f. Access to Key Inputs

New entrants may be unable to enter the market because of lack of access to key inputs. This can cover items such as airport slots or things which are covered by intellectual property rights (see (a) above) but may also mean there is no access to raw materials. In *BPB*[215] a new entrant to the market would have needed access to the raw material, gypsum. There was no access to this in the UK without opening new mines. The only alternative was thus to import it. This would incur cost and risk and therefore relates to access to financial resources as discussed in (e) above. Where key inputs are unavailable to new entrants, refusals to supply can amount to strategic entry-deterring behaviour by the incumbent undertaking[216] and may amount to an abuse: see *Commercial Solvents* and the case law on refusal to supply and the essential facilities doctrine.[217]

---

[208] Discussion Paper, para. 40.

[209] Case 27/76, *United Brands Co and United Brands Continental BV v. Commission* [1978] ECR 207, [1978] 1 CMLR 429, para. 122.

[210] Case 85/76 [1979] ECR 461, [1979] 3 CMLR 211, para. 49.

[211] *Re Continental Can Co* [1972] JO L7/25, [1972] CMLR D11, para. 13.

[212] J. S. Bain, *Barriers to New Competition* (Harvard University Press, 1956) where he reported on a survey of twenty US industries. Capital requirements are therefore linked to economies of scale. See *supra* Chap. 1.

[213] R. H. Bork, *The Antitrust Paradox* (Basic Books, 1978), 320.

[214] Discussion Paper, para. 40.

[215] *BPB Industries* [1989] OJ L10/50, [1990] 4 CMLR 464, para. 120.

[216] See the discussion of conduct as a barrier to entry, *infra* 423.

[217] Cases 6 and 7/73, *Istituto Chemioterapico Italiano SpA and Commercial Solvents Corp v. Commission* [1974] ECR 223, [1974] 1 CMLR 309 and the concept of refusal to supply as an abuse and the essential facilities doctrine are discussed *infra* Chap. 7.

g. Advertising, Reputation, Product Differentiation

There is a large economics literature about the extent to which advertising, reputation, and goodwill, may operate as barriers to entry. There can be economies of scale in advertising and advertising expenditures will usually be sunk costs.[218] Bain considered advertising a barrier to entry.[219] Advertising builds up goodwill and reputation, and the first brand in the market may enjoy a classic first-mover advantage which will operate as a barrier to entry to later entrants.[220] Stigler's view, however, was that advertising is not a barrier to entry: it reduces consumer search costs and is pro-competitive.[221] In *United Brands* the ECJ considered that advertising and promotion had enhanced United Brands' large market share, because it had 'induced the customer to show a preference for' branded Chiquita bananas despite a large price differential with unlabelled and differently labelled bananas.[222] United Brands had 'thus attained a privileged position by making Chiquita the premier banana brand name'.[223] The Court did not appear to contemplate the possibility that consumers might have been swayed by the quality of the product rather than by advertising. The ECJ concluded that among the barriers faced by new competitors would be 'the mounting of very large-scale advertising campaigns'.[224] Similarly, in the merger case of *Nestlé/Perrier*[225] the Commission considered it relevant to the existence of a dominant position that any new entrant to the market would face formidable advertising and promotion requirements. In *BBI/Boosey & Hawkes*[226] the Commission relied on the goodwill and reputation enjoyed by Boosey & Hawkes, listing among 'other factors which tend ... to support a preliminary finding of dominance' the 'strong buyer preference for B&H instruments' and 'its close identification with the brass band movement'.

There is also a significant literature on brand proliferation and product differentiation as barriers to entry.[227] In the *Nestlé/Perrier* merger decision the Commission considered the difficulty of access to distribution outlets in a brand-crowded market and referred to the problem of shelf-space in retail stores. The following extract explains that the insights of modern industrial organization theory show that advertising and product differentiation can reduce consumer welfare in certain circumstances.

[218] Although a brand image built up by advertising might be deployable in a separate market, e.g., the name Virgin is applied to vastly different products and services. The Commission described advertising and promotion as sunk costs in the merger decision *Nestlé/Perrier* [1992] OJ L356/1, [1993] 4 CMLR M17, para. 97.

[219] J. S. Bain, *Barriers to New Competition* (Harvard University Press, 1956). See also M. Spence, 'Notes on Advertising, Economies of Scale and Entry Barriers' (1980) 95 *Quarterly Journal of Economics* 493; J. Sutton, *Sunk Costs and Market Structure: Price Competition, Advertising, and the Evolution of Concentration* (MIT Press, 1991).

[220] See R. Schmalensee, 'Entry Deterrence in the Ready–to–eat Breakfast Cereal Industry' (1978) 9 *Bell Journal of Economics* 305.

[221] G. Stigler, 'The Economics of Information' (1961) 69 J. Polit. Economy 213; see R. J. Van den Bergh and P. D. Camesasca, *European Competition Law and Economics: A Comparative Perspective* (2nd edn., Sweet & Maxwell, 2006), 144–5.

[222] Case 27/76, *United Brands Co and United Brands Continental BV v. Commission* [1978] ECR 207, [1978] 1 CMLR 429, para. 91.

[223] *Ibid.*, para. 93.

[224] *Ibid.*, para. 122.

[225] [1992] OJ L356/1, [1993] 4 CMLR M17 at recital 97. See *infra* Chap. 12.

[226] *BBI/Boosey & Hawkes* [1987] OJ L286/36, [1988] 4 CMLR 67, para. 18, where the product concerned was brass band instruments.

[227] See Bain, *supra* n. 219; R. Schmalensee, 'Product Differentiation Advantages of Pioneering Brands' (1981) 72 *American Economic Review* 349. See also *infra* Chap. 12. Bain considered product differentiation a barrier to entry but the Chicago school does not.

R. J. Van den Bergh and P .D. Camesasca, *European Competition Law and Economics: A Comparative Perspective* (2nd edn., Sweet & Maxwell, 2006), 145–6

Recent work in modern industrial organisation has further contributed to our understanding of product differentiation and advertising as entry barriers. It now appears that a cautious approach is warranted. Product differentiation and advertising can, under certain conditions, reduce consumer welfare. Advertising may be used either to increase the objective knowledge of products or to create consumers' preferences for a particular brand, thereby making the demand for those products less elastic and market entry by newcomers more difficult. However, to qualify as an entry barrier and not just as an entry impediment, the effects of advertising must last sufficiently long to enable incumbent firms to earn super-normal profits persistently. On the latter point the relevant empirical evidence is mixed: some researchers found that the effects of advertising lasted for several years, whereas others found that advertising effects are gone within a year.... Modern industrial organisation stresses the importance of sunk costs in assessing whether advertising may function as a barrier to entry. Sunk costs are central to the calculations of potential entrants: advertising costs to build consumer loyalty are normally sunk costs unless an exiting firm could either sell its brand name or use it somewhere else without a loss. The higher advertising and promotion expenditures that cannot be recovered on exiting a particular market, the more entry will be deterred.... Recent literature in industrial organisation on product differentiation also includes the view that it may be used as an instrument to obstruct market entry. To deter entrants looking for unfulfilled product design or brand image niches, established sellers might seek to crowd product space with enough brands (brand proliferation) so that no room for profitable new entry remains....

Moreover, the Discussion Paper stated:

...it may be difficult to enter an industry where experience or reputation is necessary to compete effectively, both of which may be difficult to obtain as an entrant. Factors such as consumer loyalty to a particular brand, the closeness of relationships between suppliers and customers, the importance of promotion or advertising, or other reputation advantages will be taken into account. Advertising and other investments in reputation are often sunk costs which cannot be recovered in the case of exit and which therefore make entry more risky.[228]

h. Overall Size and Strength and Range of Products

In its decision in *Hoffmann-La Roche* the Commission took into account the undertaking's position as the world's largest vitamin producer and leading pharmaceuticals producer and the wide range of vitamins it manufactured. The ECJ rejected the assertion that these factors were indicators of dominance, saying:[229]

45. The fact that Roche produces a far wider range of vitamins than its competitors must similarly be rejected as being immaterial. The Commission regards this as a factor establishing a dominant position and asserts that 'since the requirements of many users extend to several groups of vitamins,

---

[228] Discussion Paper, para. 40.

[229] [1976] OJ L223/27, [1976] 2 CMLR D25 at recitals 5, 6, and 21. On appeal Case 85/76, *Hoffmann La Roche & Co AG v. Commission* [1979] ECR 461, [1979] 3 CMLR 211.

Roche is able to employ a sales and pricing strategy which is far less dependent than that of the other manufacturers on the conditions of competition in each market.'

46. However, the Commission has itself found that each group of vitamins constitutes a specific market and is not, or at least not to any significant extent, interchangeable with any other group or with any other products (Recital 20 to the decision) so that the vitamins belonging to the various groups are as between themselves products just as different as the vitamins compared with other products of the pharmeceutical and food sector. Moreover, it is not disputed that Roche's competitors, in particular those in the chemical industry, market besides the vitamins which they manufacture themselves, other products which purchasers of vitamins also want, so that the fact that Roche is in a position to offer several groups of vitamins does not in itself give it any advantage over its competitors, who can offer, in addition to a less or much less wide range of vitamins, other products which are also required by the purchasers of these vitamins.

47. Similar considerations lead also to the rejection as a relevant factor of the circumstance that Roche is the world's largest vitamin manufacturer, that its turnover exceeds that of all the other manufacturers and that it is at the head of the largest pharmaceuticals group in the world. In the view of the Commission these three considerations together are a factor showing that there is a dominant position, because 'it follows that the applicant occupies a pre-ponderant position not only within the Common Market but also on the world market; it therefore enjoys very considerable freedom of action, since its position enables it to adapt itself easily to the developments of the different regional markets. An undertaking operating throughout the markets of the world and having a market share which leaves all its competitors far behind it does not have to concern itself unduly about any competitors within the Common Market.' Such reasoning based on the benefits reaped from economics of scale and on the possibility of adopting a strategy which varies according to different regional markets is not conclusive, seeing that it is accepted that each group of vitamins constitutes a group of separate products which require their own particular plant and form a separate market, in that the volume of the overall production of products which are different as between themselves does not give Roche a competitive advantage over its competitors, especially over those in the chemical industry, who manufacture on a world scale other products as well as vitamins and have in principle the same opportunities to set off one market against the other as are offered by a large overall production of products which differ from each other as much as the various groups of vitamins do.

Although size is not therefore *per se* an indicator of dominance on a particular market, the authorities have found it to be relevant in some situations. In *Michelin* the ECJ took into account the advantages Michelin NV derived from belonging to a group of undertakings which operated throughout Europe and the world.[230] In *Soda Ash–Solvay*[231] the Commission considered Solvay's manufacturing strength with plant in six other Member States to be part of the 'relevant economic evidence' to be taken into account in assessing dominance. The geographical spread of an undertaking's operations has also held to be an advantage where it makes it less vulnerable to natural disasters[232] and/or other fluctuations.[233]

It can be seen above that in *Hoffmann-La Roche* the ECJ overturned the Commission's finding that the wide range of vitamins produced by the undertaking was an indication of dominance because each vitamin was a separate market. It is otherwise if the undertaking benefits from the

---

[230] Although without specifying what these were: Case 322/81, *Nederlandsche Banden-Industrie Michelin* v. *Commission* [1983] ECR 3461, [1985] 1 CMLR 282, para. 55.

[231] [2003] OJ L10/10, para. 138.

[232] As with the banana plantations in *United Brands* [1978] ECR 207, [1978] 1 CMLR 429, para. 75.

[233] See *Elopak Italia/Tetra Pak* [1991] OJ L72/1, [1992] 4 CMLR 551, para. 101.

diversity of products. In *Tetra Pak II*[234] the Commission held that the diversity 'allows it, if necessary, to make financial sacrifices on one or other of its products without affecting the overall profitability of its operations'. This is a polite way of saying that a 'deep pocket' can facilitate practices such as predatory pricing.[235]

i. Profits

Since a monopolist can reap the benefits of its market power by earning monopoly profits, it is possible that these profits can be used as a means of identifying market power. However, it may be difficult to determine whether or not an undertaking is in fact earning monopoly profits. Perhaps for this reason profitability assessment has not hitherto been much used in EC cases as a tool to assist in the assessment of dominance, although in *Microsoft* the Commission was impressed by the fact that Microsoft was operating on a profit margin of approximately 81 per cent.[236] In UK domestic law, however, it has been employed quite regularly. In July 2003 a report prepared by an economics consultancy for the UK competition authority, the Office of Fair Trading, discussed ways of assessing profitability, *inter alia*, for the purpose of identifying a firm's market power.[237] The report concluded that useful results *could* be achieved if the methodology used the measures of internal rate of return (IRR) and net present value (NPV). The Community authorities have held that the fact that an undertaking is not earning profits at all, or a *lack* of profits, is not necessarily a contra-indication of dominance. In *United Brands*[238] and *Michelin*[239] the ECJ held that an undertaking's economic strength is not measured by profitability alone. Losses, at least if temporary, may demonstrate the economic strength of the undertaking which has the ability to absorb them.

j. Performance Indicators

The undertaking's economic performance has sometimes been held to be an indicator of dominance. In *Hoffmann-La Roche*[240] the ECJ took spare manufacturing capacity into account as a factor indicating dominance, although it did not distinguish between idle and excess capacity. Capacity is idle when its use would not be profitable because the market price is less than the cost of its use. It is found on both competitive and non-competitive markets. Excess capacity means that the undertaking is producing less output than the optimal output the plant is designed to produce, so that it could increase its output without its unit costs increasing.[241] The Discussion Paper states that competitors may have excess capacity which is so expensive to employ that the costs involved constitute a barrier to expansion.[242]

---

[234] See *Elopak Italia/Tetra Pak* [1991] OJ L72/1, [1992] 4 CMLR 551, para. 101.

[235] One of the abuses which was found in *Tetra Pak II*: see *infra* Chap. 7.

[236] As a percentage of revenues in year ending 30 June 2003, COMP/C-3/37.792, [2005] 4 CMLR 965, para. 464.

[237] OFT 657, 'Assessing profitability in competition policy analysis', prepared for the OFT by OXERA Consulting Ltd (Economic Discussion Paper 6). The other uses for profitability analysis are to assess whether a dominant undertaking has been charging excessive prices, or whether *low* profits suggest, e.g., predatory pricing or a margin squeeze: see *infra* Chap. 7.

[238] Case 27/76, *United Brands Co and United Brands Continental BV v. Commission* [1978] ECR 207, [1978] 1 CMLR 429, paras. 126–8.

[239] Case 322/81, *NV Nederlandsche Banden-Industrie Michelin v. Commission* [1983] ECR 3461, [1985] 1 CMLR 282, para. 59.

[240] Case 85/76, *Hoffmann-La Roche & Co AG v. Commission* [1979] ECR 461, [1979] 3 CMLR 211, para. 48.

[241] Excess capacity can be used against potential competitors as a form of strategic entry deterrence: see *infra* Chap. 7, 465.

[242] Discussion Paper, para. 40.

The ability of an undertaking to obtain premium prices was relevant in *United Brands*[243] and in *BBI/Boosey & Hawkes*.[244]

k. Opportunity Costs

Opportunity costs are the value of something which must be given up in order to achieve or acquire something else and can be classified as an absolute cost advantage for the incumbent undertaking. In *British Midland–Aer Lingus*[245] the Commission considered as a barrier to entry to the Heathrow–Dublin air route the opportunity costs involved in an airline having to divert its Heathrow airport slots, currently employed for other (profitable) routes, to service the less profitable Irish destination.

l. Switching Costs

Switching costs are costs which a customer would have to bear were it to move its custom to a competitor. They can include having to invest in new infrastructure, staff training or procedures or having to sacrifice advantages obtained from the existing supplier (such as frequent flyer programmes[246]). Network effects may make it unattractive to change supplier.[247] The costs to the customers in switching supplier were taken into account in, *inter alia*, *Tetra Pak I*,[248] *IMS/NDC*,[249] and *Microsoft*.[250] Switching costs arising from e.g. the loss of rebates or the privileges attached to long-term or exclusive supply contracts, may be strategic behaviour on the part of a dominant firm which constitutes an abuse.

m. The Undertaking's Own Assessment of its Position

The Court and the Commission have sometimes relied on an undertaking's own internal documentation as indicating its dominance. Such evidence was referred to in *BBI/Boosey & Hawkes* (' "automatic first choice" of all the top brass bands')[251] and *AKZO* ('AKZO regards itself as the world leader in the peroxides market')[252]. The opinions of managers, however, are not incontrovertible evidence of their truth. Managers may try to 'talk up' the undertaking's position to convince themselves, others, or both.[253]

n. Conduct

The undertaking's conduct may be taken as an indicator of dominance. In *United Brands* the Commission considered that the undertaking's geographical price-discrimination and export

---

[243] Case 27/76, *United Brands Co and United Brands Continental BV v. Commission* [1978] ECR 207, [1978] 1 CMLR 429, para. 91.

[244] *BBI/Boosey & Hawkes* [1987] OJ L286/36, [1988] 4 CMLR 67, para. 18.

[245] *British Midland—Aer Lingus* [1992] OJ L96/34, [1993] 4 CMLR 596.

[246] See Van den Bergh and Camescasca, n. 221 *supra*, 146.

[247] Network effects are particularly significant in new economy industries, see *infra* 429.

[248] [1988] OJ L272/37, [1990] 4 CMLR 97.

[249] *NDC Health/IMS: Interim Measures* [2002] OJ L59/18, [2002] 4 CMLR 111.

[250] COMP/C-3/37.792, [2005] 4 CMLR 965.

[251] *BBI/Boosey & Hawkes* [1987] OJ L286/36, [1988] 4 CMLR 67, para. 18.

[252] Case C-62/86, *AKZO Chemie BV v. Commission* [1991] ECR I-3359, [1993] 5 CMLR 215, para. 61.

[253] The same problem of taking account of internal documentation arises when it is used to show that an abuse has been committed: see *infra* Chap. 7.

bans were evidence of its dominance and the ECJ said that its economic strength had 'enabled it to adopt a flexible overall strategy directed against new competitors'.[254] In *Eurofix-Bauco* the Commission said that the undertaking's behaviour was 'witness to its ability to act independently of, and without due regard to, either competitors or customers ... This behaviour and its economic consequences would not normally be seen where a company was facing real competitive pressure'.[255]

This reasoning causes concern, however, on account of its circularity: the conduct leads to finding dominance which leads to finding the conduct is an abuse because the undertaking is dominant. It is justified, however, in some circumstances so long as caution is exercised. First, some conduct is impossible without market power. Secondly, some conduct may operate as a strategic entry barrier, as is discussed in the extracts from Harbord and Hoehn and the OFT Report.[256] If the conditions of post-entry competition are an important factor in undertakings' decisions about entering markets, predatory behaviour may deter entry, and exclusive dealing, tying, and similar practices may foreclose markets to new entrants.[257] Modern industrial organization theory, by emphasizing the analysis of strategic competition, makes the incumbent undertakings' conduct a major consideration in assessing dominance. Giving a prime place to conduct in the assessment of market power is a major reason why the issue of ascertaining whether an undertaking is dominant, and the issue of deciding whether it has abused that position, cannot be neatly separated.

o. An Unavoidable Trading Partner

In *Hoffmann-La Roche* the ECJ described the undertaking as being in a position *vis-à-vis* its customers where it was an 'unavoidable trading' partner.[258] The railway operators were described as being in a position of 'economic dependence' on the supplier of rail services in *Deutsche Bahn*.[259] In *British Airways v. Commission* the CFI confirmed the Commission's finding that BA was an 'obligatory business partner' for travel agents.[260] In view of BA's leading position on the UK air transport market it was imperative that travel agents could offer their customers BA tickets. In these situations there is no countervailing buyer (or, in the BA situation, supplier) power to dilute the power of the undertaking in question.

---

[254] Case 27/76, *United Brands* v. *Commission* [1978] ECR 207, [1978] 1 CMLR 429, para. 121.

[255] [1988] OJ L65/19, [1989] 4 CMLR 677 at recital 71. See similarly *ECS/AKZO* [1985] OJ L374/1, [1986] 3 CMLR 273 at recital 56, upheld in Case C-62/86, *AKZO Chemie BV* v. *Commission* [1991] ECR I-3359, [1993] 5 CMLR 215, para. 61.

[256] See *supra* Chap. 1.

[257] For a discussion of these practices as abuses under Article 82 see Chap. 7.

[258] Case 85/76, *Hoffmann-La Roche & Co AG* v. *Commission* [1979] ECR 461, [1979] 3 CMLR 211, para. 41, reproduced *supra* n. 397.

[259] Case T-229/94, *Deutsche Bahn* v. *Commission* [1997] ECR II-1689, [1998] 4 CMLR 220, para. 57.

[260] Case T-219/99, [2004] 4 CMLR 1008, para. 217: see *supra* 400, confirming *Virgin/BA* [2000] OJ L30/1, [2000] 4 CMLR 999, para. 92.

E. POWER OVER LOCKED-IN CUSTOMERS AND ON AFTERMARKETS

It was seen above[261] that in *Hugin*,[262] *Hilti*,[263] *Volvo*,[264] *Renault*,[265] and *Tetra Pak II*[266] it was held that aftermarkets may be part of a separate product market from the primary product. These cases recognize that customers may, having made a choice of product on a primary market, subsequently be 'locked in' on the secondary market and obliged to purchase compatible goods and services. Thus even though a primary market may be competitive (as in *Hugin*, *Volvo*, and *Renault*, for example) the Court and Commission have held that the undertaking which is the sole producer of the products on the aftermarket has a dominant position on that market. The question whether, and if so when, undertakings really *do* have market power on aftermarkets or over locked-in customers is, however, controversial.

Arguably, an undertaking cannot exploit its position over customers in a secondary market by raising prices if the primary market is competitive. This is due to the fact that:

(i)   a customer who has been exploited on an aftermarket will go elsewhere when the primary product (or 'installed base') needs replacing;

(ii) a customer may prefer to purchase another brand of product on the primary market rather than suffer continued exploitation on the aftermarket; and

(iii) when a customer decides, originally, to purchase the product in the primary product market its decision may be affected partly by the prices and conditions existing in the aftermarket, if the aftermarket is transparent.

In some markets the costs in the aftermarket over the lifetime of the primary product may exceed the price of the primary product. Customers choosing the original product may be sensitive to the 'lifetime cost' and make decisions accordingly. Undertakings may therefore only be able to exploit the aftermarket if the latter is not transparent and the costs there can be hidden at the time of the primary product purchase.[267]

Before it is determined whether or not an undertaking has market power on the aftermarket it should therefore be considered (1) whether customers can easily switch to a competing product in the primary market; and (2) what information is available to customers when making their initial decision to purchase the product in the primary market.

In earlier cases such as *Hugin*, *Volvo*, and *Renault* the Commission was criticized for having failed to take account of these factors. In *Pelikan v. Kyocera*,[268] however, the Commission took a more realistic view. This case concerned a complaint about the conduct of a Japanese manufacturer of printers. It was alleged that the manufacturer was abusing its dominant position on the

---

[261] *Supra* 368 ff.

[262] Case 22/78, *Hugin Kassaregister AB and Hugin Cash Registers Ltd v. EC Commission* [1979] ECR 1869, [1979] 3 CMLR 345.

[263] Case C-53/92 P, *Hilti v. Commission* [1994] ECR I-667, [1994] 4 CMLR 614.

[264] Case 238/87, *AB Volvo v. Erik Veng* [1988] ECR 6211, [1989] 4 CMLR 122.

[265] Case 53/87, *CICCRA v. Renault* [1988] ECR 6039, [1990] 4 CMLR 265.

[266] Case C-333/94 P, *Tetra Pak International SA v. Commission* [1996] ECR I-5951, [1997] 4 CMLR 662.

[267] M. Williams, 'Sega, Nintendo and Aftermarket Power: The Monopolies and Mergers Commission Report on Video Games' (1995) 5 *ECLR* 310 discusses these arguments in the context of a UK Monopolies and Mergers Commission report.

[268] Commission's *XXVth Report on Competition Policy* (Commission, 1995), part 87.

market for the supply of toner cartridges for its printers. In its *XXVth Report on Competition Policy* (1995) the Commission discussed the issue of secondary markets and set out how it had dealt with this case.

Commission's *XXVth Report on Competition Policy* (Commission, 1995)

86. Several complaints which the Commission received concern the alleged abuse of a dominant position in secondary product markets such as spare parts, consumables or maintenance services. These products are used in conjunction with a primary product and have to be technically compatible with it (e.g., software or hardware peripheral equipment for a computer). Thus, for these secondary products there may be no or few substitutes other than parts or services supplied by the primary product supplier. This prompts the question whether a non-dominant manufacturer of primary products can be dominant with respect to a rather small secondary product market, i.e., secondary products compatible with a certain type of that manufacturer's primary products.

The question raises many complex issues. Producers of primary equipment ex argue that there cannot be dominance in secondary products if there is lack of dominance in the primary product market because potential buyers would simply stop buying the primary products if the prices for parts or services were raised. This theory implies a timely reaction on the primary product market due to consumers' ability to calculate the overall life-time costs of the primary product including all spare parts, consumables, upgrades, services, etc. It furthermore implies that price discrimination is not possible between potentially new customers and 'old' captive customers or that switching costs for the latter are low. On the other hand, complainants who produce consumables or maintenance services assume dominance in the secondary product market if market shares are high in this market, i.e., this approach focuses only on the secondary products without analysing possible effects emanating from the primary product market.

In the Commission's view, neither of these approaches reflects reality sufficiently. Dominance has always been defined by the Commission as the ability to act to an appreciable extent independently of competitors and consumers. Therefore, an in-depth fact-finding exercise and analysis on a case-by-case basis are required. In order to assess dominance in this context the Commission will take into account all important factors such as the price and life-time of the primary product, transparency of prices of secondary products, prices of secondary products as a proportion of the primary product value, information costs and other issues partly mentioned above. A similar approach was taken by the US Supreme Court in its 1992 Kodak decision *Pelikan/Kyocera*.

87. The Commission took this approach when it rejected in 1995 the complaint of Pelikan, a German manufacturer of toner cartridges for printers, against Kyocera, a Japanese manufacturer of computer printers including toner cartridges for those printers. Pelikan's complaint alleged a number of practices by Kyocera to drive Pelikan out of the toner market and accused Kyocera, among others, of abusing its dominant position in the secondary market although Kyocera was clearly not dominant in the primary market. Apart from the fact that there was no evidence of behaviour that could be considered abusive, neither did the Commission find that Kyocera enjoyed a dominant position in the market for consumables. This was due to the particular features of the primary and secondary markets. Thus, purchasers were well informed about the price charged for consumables and appeared to take this into account in their decision to buy a printer. 'Total cost per page' was one of the criteria most commonly used by customers when choosing a printer. This was due to the fact that life-cycle costs of consumables (mainly toner

cartridges) represented a very high proportion of the value of a printer. Therefore, if the prices of consumables of a particular brand were raised, consumables would have a strong incentive to buy another printer brand. In addition, there was no evidence of possibilities for price discrimination between 'old'/captive and new customers.

The *Kodak* case referred to by the Commission is *Eastman Kodak Co v. Image Technical Services Inc*[269] in which, after much economic argument, the US Supreme Court ruled that it *was* possible for a manufacturer to have monopoly power over the spare parts for its equipment even if it did not have market power in the original market for that equipment. The Court held that although competition in the primary market *could* restrain power in the aftermarket there was no rule of law to that effect. Existing customers could be bound to the primary product supplier because it was too expensive to switch and there might not be sufficient transparency to give new customers enough information about the future costs in the aftermarket when making the original purchase. The *Kodak* case was controversial and has been argued to signify a shift in the Supreme Court's policy in antitrust matters.[270] Consequently, the Commission's action in *Pelikan/Kyocera* has been favourably compared to the *Kodak* judgment.[271] However, in *Digital*[272] the Commission considered that Digital was dominant in the software and hardware services market in its own systems despite the fact that the primary market for computer systems was intensely competitive. The Commission's Competition Policy Report for 1997 is not explicit about the reasons for the finding of market power[273] but the Commission's position was discussed by an official of the Competition Directorate in a Competition Policy Newsletter.[274] He gave four reasons why the Commission adopted a different position in *Digital* to that which was adopted in *Kyocera*:

(i) Digital had a large base of captive customers who could not easily replace their installed system with another brand;

(ii) It did not seem that Digital's customers usually based their decision about the purchase of the primary system on the total lifetime costs partly because evaluating those costs was difficult and there was a lack of transparency in the aftermarket;

(iii) The costs in the aftermarket were not large enough to influence the customer's choice in the primary market (unlike Kyocera where toner cartridges were a major expense);

(iv) The nature of the product meant that Digital had the possibility of offering well-informed new customers individual servicing conditions.

The Digital case did not proceed to a formal decision, but was settled. The Commission's views were not therefore set out in a decision or reviewed by the Court. The message from *Pelikan/Kyocera* and *Digital* is that dominance in aftermarkets will not be assumed but that the

---

[269] 504 US 451, 112 S.Ct 2072 (1992).

[270] See, e.g., H. Hovenkamp, 'Market Power in Aftermarkets: Antitrust Policy and the *Kodak* Case' (1993) 40 *UCLA LR* 1447; C. Shapiro, 'Aftermarkets and Consumer Welfare: Making Sense of Kodak' (1995) 63 *Antitrust LJ* 483. In his book Bork warns that the judgment 'may be as ominous a harbinger as *Sylvania* was a hopeful one': R. H. Bork, *The Antitrust Paradox: A Policy at War with Itself* (Basic Books, 1978, reprinted with a new Introduction and Epilogue, 1993), 430. See his discussion of the case at 436–9.

[271] D. Muldoom, 'The Kodak Case: Power in Aftermarkets' (1996) 8 *ECLR* 473.

[272] Commission Press Release IP/97/868 of 10 Oct. 1997.

[273] Commission's *XXVIIth Report* (Commission, 1997) parts 69 and 153.

[274] P. Chevalier, 'Dominance sur un marché de produits secondaires', Commission's Competition Policy Newsletter 1998/1, 26.

individual circumstances of each case will be subjected to a full economic analysis.[275] This view is affirmed by the Commission's decision rejecting a complaint, in *Info-Lab/Ricoh*,[276] that Ricoh had abused its dominant position by refusing to supply it with empty toner cartridges compatible for its photocopy machines.[277] The Commission concluded that even if there was a separate market for Ricoh toner cartridges, Ricoh did not have a dominant position on that market. Although it was the only supplier of the cartridges for Ricoh photocopiers it could not act independently in setting prices. The upstream photocopier market was competitive and, in accordance with the principles set out in *Pelikan/Kyocera*, this was a market in which the consumer was *able* to make an informed choice, appreciating the lifetime costs in the aftermarket; it was a market in which the consumer was *likely* to make an informed choice; potential new customers (of which there were a considerable number because of the short life-span of photocopiers) would be deterred by the exploitation of existing customers; and new customers could adapt their purchasing pattern within a reasonable span of time.

This decisional practice is reflected in the Discussion Paper.[278] As seen above,[279] it is possible that where the undertaking's behaviour on the aftermarket is constrained by the reactions of customers on the primary market, there is no separate aftermarket in the first place.

F. BUYER POWER

The Discussion Paper raised the issue of how far customers can constrain the behaviour of an allegedly dominant undertaking.[280] As the essence of dominance is defined as the independence of an undertaking from, *inter alia*, its customers,[281] it follows that an undertaking constrained by a powerful buyer may not be in a dominant position. However, as the Discussion Paper said, it is not enough that powerful buyers extract favourable terms from the supplier *for themselves*: in order to counter a finding of dominance they must be able to protect *the market itself* by defeating any price increase through paving the way for new entry or leading existing competitors to expand production.[282] This is possible, for example, where the buying side is highly concentrated.[283] It is possible that powerful buyers able to get a good deal for themselves could constitute a market for market definition purposes separate from that of other customers.[284]

---

[275] See also M. Dolmans and V. Pickering, 'The 1997 Digital Undertaking' [1998] *ECLR* 108; P. Andrews, 'Aftermarket Power in the Computer Services Market' [1998] *ECLR* 176; B. Bishop and C. Caffarra, 'Editorial, Dynamic Competition and Aftermarkets' [1998] *ECLR* 265 discuss the issue but mainly from the perspective of merger control.

[276] Case IV/36431, rejection of a complaint by decision, see Competition Policy Newsletter 1999, No. 1, 35.

[277] For the market definition aspect of this case, see *supra* 374.

[278] Paras. 251–63.

[279] *Supra*, 374.

[280] Paras. 41–2.

[281] Case 85/76, *Hoffmann-La Roche & Co AG v. Commission* [1979] ECR 461, [1979] 3 CMLR 211, para. 38.

[282] Discussion Paper, para. 41.

[283] As, e.g. in the merger cases, *Enso/Stora*, COMP.M/1225; *Behringwerke/Armour Pharmaceutical*, Case. No. IV/M.495.

[284] Discussion Paper, para. 42; the Notice on the definition of the relevant market, para. 43, acknowledges that the ability of an undertaking to price discriminate may put customers in different markets, see *supra* 77. For the technique of market definition where there is market power on the demand side, see I. Kokkoris, 'Buyer Power Assessment in Competition Law: A Boon or A Menace?' (2006) 29(1) *World Competition* 139; Dobson Consulting, 'Buyer Power and Its Impact in the Food Retail Distribution Sector of the European Union', 1999, available at http://ec.europa.eu/comm/competition/publications/studies/bpifrs/ (a paper version may also be made available at some point).

However, even a monopoly buyer may be unable to constrain the behaviour of a dominant firm. The perfect illustration of this is the UK case *Genzyme*[285] in which the producer of the only drug (Cerezyme) efficacious in treating a rare disease (Gaucher's Disease) was found to have infringed the Chapter II prohibition of the Competition Act 1998 (the domestic UK equivalent of Article 82) by a margin squeeze which excluded competitors in a downstream market. Given that there was no alternative to Cerezyme for Gaucher's Disease patients the monopoly buyer, the NHS, was in a 'relatively weak' bargaining position.[286]

Furthermore, powerful buyers may be in a dominant position *vis à vis* their suppliers and so capable of infringing Article 82. British Airways was found to be in such a position in *Virgin/BA*.[287]

G. DOMINANT POSITIONS IN THE NEW ECONOMY

As we have seen previously[288] competition in the new economy tends to be on innovation. Dominant positions are often temporary and fragile. In the following extract the authors (a lawyer and two economists) argue that market share is not a good basis from which to find dominance in new economy industries.

C. Ahlborn, D. Evans, and A. Padilla, 'Competition Policy in the New Economy: Is Competition Law Up To The Challenge' [2001] *ECLR* 156, 162

... [I]n new economy industries, the incumbent typically has a large market share since competition is often a matter of 'winner-takes-most'. Their large market share, however, is under permanent threat from innovating competitors and they are only able to retain their position if they continue to innovate. Imagine what Nokia's market share would be two years from now if it left the innovation to Ericsson, Siemens, Motorola or any of a dozen firms with the technical capacity to create mobile phones with a greater number of functionalities: it would plunge irremediably.

Equating high market shares with dominance in the case of these 'fragile monopolists' of the new economy is potentially very damaging to innovation and competition, as E.C. competition law imposes a 'special responsibility' to the market upon dominant firms... Apart from the fact that this special responsibility often prohibits welfare-enhancing action where it has a negative effect on rivals' profits, in the new economy it prevents companies with high market shares (which nevertheless are under competitive threat and do not have the power to act independently of competitors and customers) to compete vigorously on an equal footing with their rivals.

---

[285] *Genzyme Ltd* v. OFT [2004] CAT 4, [2004] CompAR 358 (Competition Appeal Tribunal, upholding *Genzyme* CA 98/03/03, [2003] UKCLR 950).

[286] *Ibid.*, para. 250. In fact, the answer in the UK to the monopoly pricing of a pharmaceutical company would be for the relevant authority, NICE (the National Institute for Health and Clinical Excellence) to refuse to license it for use in the NHS on financial grounds in the first place. The effect of cost on NICE's licensing practice is, unsurprisingly, a highly sensitive issue. See http://www.nice.org.UK.

[287] *Virgin/British Airways* [2000] OJ L30/1, [2000] 4 CMLR 999, upheld, Case T-219/99, *British Airways* v. *Commission* [2003] ECR II-5917, [2004] 4 CMLR 1008, *supra* 400. See also Case 298/83 *CICCE* v. *Commission* [1985] ECR 1105, [1986] 1 CMLR 486, *infra* Chap. 7, 594. And see further Kokkoris, n. 284, *supra*.

[288] *Supra* Chap. 1, 54 and *supra* 377.

> A better test of market power is contestability. If the market is contestable, as new economy markets often are..., a firm with a high market share does not enjoy a position of dominance because potential entry imposes an effective competitive constraint on its conduct; i.e., it cannot act independently of its (potential) competitors.[289]

It has also been argued that the Commission' statement in the Discussion Paper about the main purpose of market definition being to identify the *immediate* competitive constraints facing the undertaking and all *actual* competitors,[290] is particularly misconceived where dynamically competitive markets are concerned because of the importance there of *potential* competition.[291]

It has been suggested[292] that a multi-attribute SSNIP could be used to avoid the dangers of reaching over-narrow market definitions. This would involve asking whether a change in the *performance attributes* of one product, as well as in price, would induce substitution to or from another. Such a test is difficult to apply because of the problems in quantifying performance changes.[293] Questions of new economy market definition in EC law have arisen so far more in merger investigations than in the Article 82 context.[294]

A problem with some new economy markets is 'network externalities' (or 'network effects') as mentioned in Chapter 1.[295] The more users a network has, the more valuable it becomes to an individual user. Once a network has a certain number of users, therefore, the market may 'tip' towards that network That is why it is sometimes said that competition may be *for* rather than *in* the market (the winner takes *all* the market and the losers lose completely). The winner may be aided by the behaviour of the producers of complementary products, who will want to design products (such as software) which are compatible with the dominant network. More customers will attracted to the dominant network because of the large number of complementary products which can be used with it. So it becomes a vicious circle. The prime example of this effect is Microsoft, and its ubiquitous Windows operating system.[296] It can even be argued that the danger of network effects leads to the conclusion that competition authorities should intervene at an earlier moment, and not wait until one undertaking becomes dominant. On the other hand consumers may be better served by one network. Furthermore, some economists consider that the implications of network effects can be exaggerated.[297] There is often room for several networks and the crucial thing is whether they connect to each other. Mobile telephone

---

[289] See also C. Ahlborn, V. Denicolò, D. Deradin and A. J. Padilla, 'DG Comp's Discussion Paper on Article 82: Implications of the Proposed Framework and Antitrust Rules for Dynamically Competitive Industries' in Linklaters, *Rethinking Article 82* (B. Allan, C. Ahlborn and D. Bailey, eds.), 6, and available at http://papers.ssrn.com/sol3/papers.cfm?abstract_id=894466, 22, where the authors conclude that '[g]iven these problems, market definition should perhaps play a less significant role in the competitive assessment of uni-lateral behaviour in dynamically competitive industries. Market shares should not be blindly used as relevant indicators of market power in those industries, and supply–side constraints should be carefully considered at the assessment stage'.

[290] See *supra*, 352.

[291] Ahlborn et al., n. 289, 25.

[292] See, e.g., Teece and Coleman, n. 88, 853–7.

[293] Economists have, however, devised tests for doing this: see R. Hartman, D. Teece, W. Mitchell, and T. Jorde, 'Assessing Market Power in Regimes of Rapid Technological Change' (1993) 2 *Indus. & Corp Change* 317.

[294] See *infra* Chap. 12.

[295] *Supra*, 55.

[296] See *Microsoft*, Commission Decision 24 Mar. 2004, *infra* Chap. 7.

[297] See, for example, C. Veljanovski, 'Antitrust in the New Economy: Is the European Commission's View of the Network Economy Right?' [2001] *ECLR* 115.

networks, for example, connect with each other.[298] Moreover, the argument that once a network has 'won' it cannot be dislodged is not convincing. If a new product (or network) offers clearly superior benefits, consumers will be prepared to bear the switching costs, and there are always *new* consumers coming on stream. CDs replaced vinyl because consumers recognized the superiority and greater convenience of CDs,[299] despite having in many cases acquired large record collections on vinyl and expensive turntable equipment, while the younger generation of consumers could turn straight to CDs.[300] There is a general consensus, however, that competition authorities need to be sensitive to special characteristics of new economy markets and refrain from moving against dominant positions which are ephemeral.[301]

The Commission and the Community Courts have been quite robust in their treatment of new economy markets, as shown by the *Microsoft* decision.[302] In *France Télécom*[303] the applicant claimed that market shares were not a reliable indicator in the context of an emerging market. The CFI said that the fact that this was a fast-growing market could not preclude application of the competition rules.[304] It did, however, examine the claimant's contention that the market should be looked at from a dynamic perspective by assessing potential as well as actual competition, and found that the Commission had taken proper account of this.[305]

H. SUPER-DOMINANCE

As explained in Chapter 5, the concept of 'super-dominance' has appeared in some cases.[306] As this is inextricably bound up with what behaviour is categorised as an abuse, it is dealt with in context in Chapter 7.[307]

5. CONCLUSIONS

1. Article 82 case law on the ascertainment of dominance is often criticized for defining markets arbitrarily and too narrowly, overestimating undertakings' market power, and lacking sophisticated economic analysis.

2. Market definition is an inexact science (or perhaps art) which places products either in a market or outside it, whereas in reality there are degrees of substitution.

---

[298] Orange can talk to Vodafone without any trouble, although it is usually cheaper to talk on the same network.

[299] Although there are some *aficionados* who believe in the matchless superiority of the vinyl sound.

[300] An even newer generation is now going straight to downloading music and bypassing CDs.

[301] D. Teece and M. Coleman, 'The meaning of Monopoly: Antitrust Analysis in High–technology Industries' [1998] *Antitrust Bull.* 801; C. Ahlborn, D. S. Evans and A. J. Padilla, 'Competition Policy in the New Economy: Is European Competition Law up to the Challenge?' [2001] *ECLR* 156; R. Lind and P. Muysert, 'Innovation and Competition Policy: Challenges for the New Millenium' [2003] *ECLR* 87.

[302] COMP/C-3/37.792, [2005] 4 CMLR 965, discussed in Chap. 7.

[303] Case T-340/03, *France Télécom SA v. Commission*, 30 January 2007.

[304] *Ibid.*, para.107.

[305] *Ibid.*, paras. 110–13.

[306] See, e.g. Cases C-395 and 396/96 P, *Compagnie Maritime Belge Transports SA v. Commission* [2000] ECR I-1365, [2000] 4 CMLR 1076, paras. 113–21, and Opinion of Fennelly AG, para. 136; *NDC Health/IMS Health: Interim Measures* [2002] OJ L59/18, [2002] 4 CMLR 111, para. 58; *Deutsche Post AG* [2001] OJ L331/40, [2002] 4 CMLR 598, paras. 103 and 124.

[307] *Infra*, 435.

3. Despite this a great deal of reliance is placed on market share in assessing dominance, with a presumption of dominance operating at 50 per cent of the market. This tends to find undertakings in a dominant position when in reality they do not have significant market power. Further, market shares are a static measurement that does not reflect dynamic developments in the market and potential competition. The Commission is sometimes accused of taking a view which is too short-term.

4. The situation is exacerbated by the broad approach taken to barriers to entry and expansion.

5. Dominance is found in EC law at market shares of 40 per cent. Moreover, the Court and the Commission have hitherto not ruled out finding dominance below that point. There are good arguments for a dominance 'screen' or 'safe harbour' whereby undertakings with shares of the market below a certain point would have the legal certainty of knowing they were not subject to Article 82. The danger with Article 82 is considered by commentators to be its over, rather than under, inclusiveness (i.e. the danger is of Type I 'false positive' errors).

6. FURTHER READING

A. BOOKS

BAIN, J. S., *Barriers to New Competition* (Harvard University Press, 1956)

BISHOP, S., and WALKER, M., *The Economics of EC Competition Law: Concepts, Application and Measurement* (2nd edn., Sweet & Maxwell, 2002)

FAULL, J., and NIKPAY, A., *The EC Law of Competition* (2nd edn., Oxford University Press, 2007), chap. 4

MOTTA, M., *Competition Policy* (Cambridge University Press, 2004), chap.3

O'DONOGHUE, R., and PADILLA, A. J., *The Law and Economics of Article 82* (Hart Publishing, 2006), chaps. 2 and 3

SCHERER, F. M., and ROSS, D., *Industrial Market Structure and Economic Performance* (3rd edn., Houghton Mifflin, 1990), chaps. 4 and 16

SUTTON, J., *Sunk Costs and Market Structure: Price Competition, Advertising, and the Evolution of Concentration* (MIT Press, 1991)

VAN DEN BERGH, R. J., and CAMESASCA, P. D., *European Competition Law and Economics: A Comparative Perspective* (2nd edn., Sweet & Maxwell, 2006), chap. 4

B. ARTICLES

AHLBORN, C., EVANS, D. S., and PADILLA, A. J., 'Competition Policy in the New Economy: Is European Competition Law up to the Challenge?' [2001] *ECLR* 156

BADEN FULLER, C. W., 'Article 86 EEC: Economic Analysis of the Existence of a Dominant Position' (1979) 4 *ELRev* 423

BISHOP, W., 'Editorial: The Modernisation of DGIV' [1997] *ECLR* 481

—— and CAFFARRA, C., 'Editorial, Dynamic Competition and Aftermarkets' [1998] *ECLR* 265

FOX, E. M., and SULLIVAN, L. A., 'Antitrust—Retrospective and Prospective: Where Are We Coming From? Where Are We Going?' (1987) 62 *New York Univ LR* 936

GYSELEN, L., and KYRIAKIS, N., 'Article 86 EEC: The Monopoly Power Issue Revisited' (1986) 11 *ELRev* 134

HARBORD, D., and HOEHN, T., 'Barriers to Entry and Exit in European Competition Policy' (1994) 14 *International Review of Law and Economics* 411

HARTMAN, R., TEECE, D., MITCHELL, W., and JORDE, T., 'Assessing Market Power in Regimes of Rapid Tecnological Change' (1993) 2 *Indus & Corp Change* 317

KOKKORIS, I., 'Buyer Power Assessment in Competition Law: A Boon or A Menace?' (2006) 29(1) *World Competition* 139

KORAH, V., 'Concept of a Dominant Position within the Meaning of Article 86' (1980) 17 *CMLRev* 395

—— 'The Michelin Decision of the Commission' (1982) 7 *ELRev* 13

NEELIE KROES, 'Tackling Exclusionary Practices to Avoid Exploitation of Market Power: Some Preliminary Thoughts on on the Policy Review of Article 82', 2005 *Fordham Corp. L. Inst* (B. Hawk, ed. 2006), 381

—— 'The Paucity of Economic Analysis in the EEC Decisions on Competition—Tetra Pak II' [1993] *Current Legal Problems* 148

LANDES, D., and POSNER, R. A., 'Market Power in Antitrust Cases' (1981) 94 *Harvard LR* 937

LIND, R., and MUYSERT, P., 'Innovation and Competition Policy: Challenges for the New Millenium' [2003] *ECLR* 87

MULDOOM, D., 'The Kodak Case: Power in Aftermarkets' [1996] *ECLR* 473

SCHMALENSEE, R., 'Entry Deterrence in the Ready–to–eat Breakfast Cereal Industry' (1978) 9 *Bell J Econ* 305

—— 'Another Look at Market Power' (1981–2) 95 *Harvard LR* 1789

—— 'Product Differentiation Advantages of Pioneering Brands' (1981) 72 *American Economics Review* 349

—— 'Ease of Entry: Has the Concept Been Applied too Readily' (1987) 56 *Antitrust LJ* 41

SHAPIRO, C., 'Aftermarkets and Consumer Welfare: Making Sense of Kodak' (1995) 63 *Antitrust LJ* 483

SPENCE, M., 'Notes on Advertising, Economies of Scale and Entry Barriers' (1980) 95 *Quart. J of Econ* 493

TEECE, D., and COLEMAN, M., 'The meaning of Monopoly: Antitrust Analysis in High-technology Industries' [1998] *Ant Bull* 801

VELJANOVSKI, C., 'Antitrust in the New Economy: Is the European Commission's View of the Network Economy Right?' [2001] *ECLR* 115

VICKERS, J., 'Market Power in Competition Case' (2006) 2 *European Law Journal* 3

7

CONDUCT WHICH CAN BE AN ABUSE

1. CENTRAL ISSUES

1. The definition of (exclusionary) abuse was laid down by the ECJ *Hoffmann-La Roche*.

2. The main concern of the Commission in applying Article 82 has been with exclusionary rather than exploitative abuses.

3. The Court has held that dominant undertakings have a 'special responsibility' to the competitive process. That principle has had a major effect on the type of conduct which has been held abusive.

4. The Commission Discussion Paper published in December 2005 dealt only with the application of Article 82 to the main types of exclusionary abuses: predatory pricing, exclusive dealing (single branding), discounts and rebates, tying, and refusal to supply.

5. The EC predatory pricing rules centre on a costs-based test whereby some levels of pricing are presumed predatory and some depend on whether the dominant undertaking has an eliminatory intent. However, in some cases prices above the dominant undertaking's average total costs have been held to infringe Article 82.

6. The application of Article 82 to exclusive dealing, discounts and rebates has hitherto treated some of these practices as akin to a *per* se abuses. The Commission's Discussion Paper proposed to consider their effects rather than their form. However, there is still a question of how the effects are to be measured, and how far presumptions should be used to assess them. The ECJ has recently followed its previous case law and taken a conservative approach.

7. Some forms of tying have also been treated akin to *per se* abuses. The *Microsoft* decision involved a 'technological tie' whereby two elements are integrated into the product sold to the consumer.

8. The idea that it can be an abuse for a dominant undertaking to refuse to supply another party is contrary to fundamental notions of freedom of contract. There is also a danger that it may be harmful to consumer welfare as it may discourage innovation and investment. Nevertheless, the case law establishes that in certain situations it can be an abuse for a dominant undertaking to refuse to supply. There is particular controversy over whether dominant undertakings should be forced to license their intellectual property rights.

9. The Commission has paid less attention to exploitative abuses. One exploitative abuse is the charging of unfair prices. There is great difficulty in assessing whether a price is excessive. It is a question of assessing whether the price is excessive in relation to the 'economic value' of the product or service in issue.

10. Article 82(c) specifically prohibits discrimination which puts the other parties at a competitive disadvantage with one another. In general, however, price discrimination may be welfare enhancing or otherwise depending on the circumstances.

2. INTRODUCTION

In Chapter 5 it was seen that the concept of 'abuse' in Article 82 has been widely interpreted. The definition of abuse often repeated by the Court and the Commission is that set out in *Hoffmann-La Roche*:[1]

> The concept of abuse is an objective concept relating to the behaviour of an undertaking in a dominant position which is such as to influence the structure of a market where, as a result of the very presence of the undertaking in question, the degree of competition is weakened and which, through recourse to methods different from those which condition normal competition in products or services on the basis of the transactions of commercial operators, has the effect of hindering the maintenance of the degree of competition still existing in the market or the growth of that competition.

It was also noted that, although this definition describes only exclusionary (anti-competitive) abuses, Article 82 also prohibits exploitative abuses.

In this chapter we describe the types of conduct which have been held to constitute an abuse of a dominant position within the meaning of Article 82. It will be seen, however, that abuses cannot be pigeon-holed and do not fit into neat categories.

The ECJ first said in *Michelin*[2] that dominant firms have a 'special responsibility' towards the competitive process. The key concern of the Commission is with exclusionary abuses. The Commission's current policy towards conduct which excludes competitors from the market is based not on concepts of fairness towards, or protection of, competitors but on whether the exclusion will harm the welfare of consumers. It was not always clear in the past, however, whether the application of Article 82 was concerned with the exclusion only of *equally* efficient firms from the market or also of *less* efficient ones, whether the Commission wanted competition to be *fair* as well as free, and whether it wanted as many firms as possible in the market regardless of efficiencies. These questions should be borne in mind when reading the cases and decisions in this chapter. Many of the cases reflect the Commission's concern with *leverage*, which means the dominant undertaking's use of its market power in one market to affect competition in another.

The Commission Discussion Paper of December 2005 dealt only with (the main types of) exclusionary abuses and the proposals set out there are considered in the relevant places. Although it is impossible to completely separate exclusionary and exploitative abuses this chapter, will for convenience, deal with exclusionary abuses first (sections 6, 7 and 8) and then exploitative abuses (section 9).

Above all one must reflect on the Court's idea, in the definition of abuse quoted above, that an abuse is conduct which does not constitute 'normal competition'.

3. ABUSE AND THE DEGREE OF DOMINANCE

In Chapter 5 it was noted that a concept of 'super-dominance' has appeared in some cases. In several instances the Court, Advocate General, and Commission have variously alluded to the position of undertakings which are not merely dominant (within the usual *United Brands/*

---

[1] Case 85/76, *Hoffmann-La Roche v. Commission* [1979] ECR 461, [1979] 3 CMLR 211, para. 91; see also Case 322/81, *Nederlandsche Banden-Industrie Michelin v. Commission* [1983] ECR 3461, [1985] 1 CMLR 282, para. 70, set out *supra* Chap. 5, 320.

[2] Case 322/81, *Nederlandsche Banden-Industrie Michelin v. Commission* [1983] ECR 3461, [1985] 1 CMLR 282, para. 57.

Hoffmann-La Roche test) but which have a position of actual or quasi-monopoly. Advocate General Fennelly used the term 'super-dominant' in his opinion in *Compagnie Maritime Belge*.[3] Where an undertaking is in such a position it appears that its 'special responsibility' towards the competitive process is particularly onerous, and its conduct therefore more likely to be categorized as an abuse. When considering the types of conduct which can be abusive, therefore, it may be necessary to take account of the degree of dominance of the undertaking concerned.[4] The Commission, however, does not currently seem keen on the idea. It does not appear in the Discussion Paper [5] and Faull and Nikpay says:

> It is submitted that this graduated approach, which appears to imply that special rules may be applicable to some firms (which may be characterised as 'super-dominant') has certain drawbacks in terms of legal certainty. That said, the reference to the concept of super-dominance may be no more than acknowledgement of an obvious fact, namely that a firm with overwhelming market power will have enormous capacity and incentive to exploit that position to its advantage.[6]

4. DOMINANCE AND ABUSE ON DIFFERENT MARKETS

An undertaking may in some circumstances have a dominant position on one market and infringe Article 82 by its conduct on another. It may do this either to protect or strengthen its dominant position on the first market or to gain a competitive advantage on the second.

The earliest cases involved dominant undertakings which abused their position on one market in order to gain advantages on downstream, or ancillary, markets. The prevention of leverage on such markets has been a major theme in the application of Article 82, as the rest of this chapter reveals. In the leading case of *Commercial Solvents*[7] the dominant undertaking was held to have abused its position on a raw material market when it refused to supply it to a producer of a derivative drug because the dominant undertaking wished to enter the market in the derivative drug itself.

Télémarketing (or *CBEM*) was a highly significant case in the development of the application of Article 82 to abuses committed to affect competition on ancillary markets.[8] This case has frequently been relied on by the Court and the Commission in subsequent cases and in particular has featured in the development of the law on refusals to supply and the 'essential facilities' doctrine.[9]

---

[3] Cases C-395 and 396/96 P, *Compagnie Maritime Belge and Others v. Commission* [2000] ECR I-1365, [2000] 4 CMLR 1076, para. 137 of the Opinion.

[4] See Case C-333/94 P, *Tetra Pak International SA v. Commission* [1996] ECR I-5951, [1997] 4 CMLR 662; Cases C–395 and 396/96 P, *Compagnie Maritime Belge and Others v. Commission* [2000] ECR I-1365, [2000] 4 CMLR 1076: Case T–228/97, *Irish Sugar plc v. Commission* [1999] ECR II-2969, [1999] 5 CMLR 1300; *Football World Cup 1998* [2000] OJ L5/55, [2000] 4 CMLR 963, paras. 85–6.

[5] DG Comp Discussion Paper on the application of Article 82 of the Treaty to exclusionary abuses, Brussels, December 2005.

[6] J. Faull and A. Nikpay, *The EC Law of Competition* (2nd edn., Oxford University Press, 2007), 4.104.

[7] Cases 6 and 7/73, *Istituto Chemioterapico Italiano Spa & Commercial Solvents v. Commission*] [1974] ECR 223 [1974] 1 CMLR 309.

[8] See also Case C-260/89, *Elliniki Radiophonia Tileorasi (ERT) v. DEP* [1991] ECR I-2925, paras. 37–8 where the ECJ held that it was contrary to Article 82 for a television monopoly to pursue a discriminatory broadcasting policy which favoured its own programmes (the case also raised Article 86 issues which are discussed *infra* Chap. 8).

[9] See *Sealink/B&I Holyhead: Interim Measures* [1992] 5 CMLR 255 and *infra* 537 ff.

Case 311/84, *Centre Belge d'Etudes du Marché-Télémarketing* v. *Compagnie Luxembourgeoise de Télédiffusion SA and Information Publicité Benelux SA* [1985] ECR 3261, [1986] 2 CMLR 558

In 'tele-sales' or 'telemarketing' television advertisements carry a telephone number which viewers ring to order the goods or services or obtain further information. Luxembourg Television (CLT) stopped accepting advertisements on its television station unless the phone number used was that of its own subsidiary. Centre Belge, an independent company who ran a telesales operation could not therefore use its own number. It challenged CLT's behaviour in the Belgian courts and the Commercial Court made a reference for a preliminary ruling. CLT was a statutory monopolist and dominated the market in television advertising aimed at French-speaking viewers in Belgium as in Belgium itself there was at the time no advertising on national television stations.

Court of Justice

19. The second question asks whether an undertaking holding a dominant position on a particular market, by reserving to itself or to an undertaking belonging to the same group, to the exclusion of any other undertaking, an ancillary activity which could be carried out by another undertaking as part of its activities on a neighbouring but separate market, abuses its dominant position within the meaning of Article [82].

...

23. The Commission infers from the judgment of the Court of 6 March 1974 in Joined Cases 6 and 7/73 (*Commercial Solvents and Others* v. *Commission* [1974] ECR 223) that there is an abuse of a dominant position for the purposes of Article [82] where an undertaking which occupies a dominant position on a market and which is thus able to control the activities of other undertakings on a neighbouring market decides to establish itself on the second market and for no good reason refuses to supply the product or service in question on the market where it already occupies a dominant position to the undertakings whose activities are centred on the market which it is penetrating.

24. Even if the conduct in issue in the main proceedings were to be regarded not as a refusal to supply but as the imposition of a contractual condition, it would, in the Commission's view, be contrary to Article [82]. First, Information publicité, as a seller of television time, imposes on all other undertakings for telemarketing operations a condition which it does not impose on itself for the same operations, namely the condition that it must not use its own telephone number; that is an unfair trading condition within the meaning of Article [82(a)]. Secondly, Information publicité subjects the conclusion of contracts to the acceptance of supplementary obligations which have no connection with the subject of the contracts, and that is contrary to Article [82(d)].

25. In order to answer the national court's second question, reference must first be made to the aforesaid judgment of 6 March 1974 (*Commercial Solvents*), in which the Court held that an undertaking which holds a dominant position on a market in raw materials and which, with the object of reserving those materials for its own production of derivatives, refuses to supply a customer who also produces those derivatives, with the possibility of eliminating all competition from that customer, is abusing its dominant position within the meaning of Article [82].

26. That ruling also applies to the case of an undertaking holding a dominant position on the market in a service which is indispensable for the activities of another undertaking on another market. If, as the national court has already held in its order for reference, telemarketing activities constitute a separate market from that of the chosen advertising medium, although closely

associated with it, and if those activities mainly consist in making available to advertisers the telephone lines and team of telephonists of the telemarketing undertaking, to subject the sale of broadcasting time to the condition that the telephone lines of an advertising agent belonging to the same group as the television station should be used amounts in practice to a refusal to supply the services of that station to any other telemarketing undertaking. If, further, that refusal is not justified by technical or commercial requirements relating to the nature of the television, but is intended to reserve to the agent any telemarketing operation broadcast by the said station, with the possibility of eliminating all competition from another undertaking, such conduct amounts to an abuse prohibited by Article [82], provided that the other conditions of that article are satisfied.

27. It must therefore be held in answer to the second question that an abuse within the meaning of Article [82] is committed where, without any objective necessity, an undertaking holding a dominant position on a particular market reserves to itself or to an undertaking belonging to the same group an ancillary activity which might be carried out by another undertaking as part of its activities on a neighbouring but separate market, with the possibility of eliminating all competition from such undertaking.

The abuse in *Télémarketing* can be seen both as a refusal to supply and as an illegal tying arrangement. Either way, the statutory monopolist's purpose was to exclude other undertakings from competing with its own subsidiary on the ancillary market.

The purpose in *BPB Industries*,[10] on the other hand, was to protect the undertaking's dominant position in one market by conduct on another. In that case British Gypsum, which was dominant in the *plasterboard* market, promised priority delivery of *plaster* to plasterboard customers who stayed loyal to it and did not buy plasterboard from importers. This was held to be an abuse.[11] The two markets concerned were not vertically related, neither being downstream to the other, but were 'neighbouring' and the motive was to protect the dominant position. It is also clear that a dominant undertaking which abuses its dominant position in order to affect competition on another, 'neighbouring' but not vertically related, market may likewise be caught by Article 82.[12] The abuse of 'tying', where the dominant firm in one market uses its position to encourage customers also to buy from it products which fall into other markets, is a clear instance of this.[13]

British Airways was an interesting application of Article 82 where the dominant position and the abuse were on different markets. The two markets were related to each other but in a way which made the case unusual. Virgin Atlantic had complained to the Commission that BA was behaving anticompetitively in the means it employed to stop Virgin expanding in the air transport market. The impugned conduct was the way in which BA paid commission to travel agents selling its tickets, which was said to put pressure on the agents to push BA tickets, rather than those of rival airlines, to those intending to fly. The Commission did not try to prove that BA was dominant on any air route. Instead, it defined a market consisting of UK air travel agency services in which BA was dominant (as a *buyer*)[14] and held that it had abused this dominant position

[10] C-310/93 P, *BPB*, Case T-65/89, *BPB Industries and British Gypsum v. Commission* [1993] ECR II-389, [1993] 5 CMLR 32 (the appeal, Case C-310/93 P, *BPB Industries plc and British Gypsum Ltd v. Commission* [1995] ECR I-865, [1997] 4 CMLR 238 was only on procedural issues).

[11] See *infra* 477.

[12] See *De Poste-La Poste* [2002] OJ L61/32, [2002] 4 CMLR 1426 which concerned the statutory monopolist in the basic letter service trying to exclude competition on the business-to-business market.

[13] Which was what was happening in *Télémarketing*, discussed *supra* 437.

[14] See *supra* Chap. 6, 378.

in order to gain anti-competitive advantages in the air transport market. To this extent *British Airways* is an application of the original principle in *Commercial Solvents*. However, the reality was rather different. The case stemmed from the intense rivalry in air transport. The Commission found an abuse on one (arguably rather artificial) market, assessing BA as dominant (with an unprecedently low market share),[15] and identifying the effects of the abuse on another market where the powerful position of the undertaking was in effect the source of the dominance on the first market.[16] The CFI upheld the Commission.[17]

Case T-219/99, *British Airways* v. *Commission* [2003] ECR II-5917, [2004] 4 CMLR 1008

Court of First Instance

127. An abuse of a dominant position committed on the dominated product market, but the effects of which are felt in a separate market on which the undertaking concerned does not hold a dominant position may fall within Article 82 EC provided that separate market is sufficiently closely connected to the first (see, to that effect, Joined Cases 6/73 and 7/73 *Istituto Chemioterapico Italiano and Commercial Solvents* v. *Commission* [1974] ECR 223, paragraph 22, and Case 311/84 *CBEM* [1985] ECR 3261, paragraph 26).

128. In this case, the disputed performance reward schemes form part of a series of agreements which BA concluded with travel agents established in the United Kingdom, for the purposes of the provision of air transport agency services, including the issuing of its tickets to travellers and the provision of ancillary advertising and commercial promotion services.

129. As has been pointed out above, it is acknowledged that air travel agents carry out a retail function and that, in the short term at least, they will maintain that role and hence a vital importance for airlines.

130. The services which airlines thus sell to travellers through the intermediary of travel agents established in the United Kingdom are constituted by air transport services on scheduled flights which those airlines provide to and from United Kingdom airports.

131. The Court notes in that respect that, at the time of BA's disputed practices, 85 per cent of air tickets sold in the United Kingdom were sold through the intermediary of air travel agents.

132. There is therefore an undeniable close connection between, on the one hand, the air travel agency services supplied to airlines by agents established in the United Kingdom, and, on the other, the air transport services provided by those airlines on the United Kingdom air transport markets constituted by air routes to and from United Kingdom airports.

133. Furthermore, BA's line of argument rests on the premiss that such a close connection exists between the markets concerned. BA notes, . . . , that disinclination by an agent to promote BA's flights is likely to lead to an absolute loss of business for BA. Such a loss of revenue can come about only through a reduction in the number of BA tickets issued.

134. Conversely, BA notes . . . that, to the extent that they may lead to higher demand for an airline's services, advantages granted by airlines to travel agents result in significant cost savings.

---

[15] For the finding of dominance in this case, see *supra* Chap. 6.

[16] It also found that the abuse affected the air travel agency services market itself because it involved discrimination between travel agents: see *infra* 603.

[17] BA did not appeal the point to the ECJ in Case C-95/04 P, *British Airways* v. *Commission*, 15 March 2007. The details of the abuse, which are referred to in the following extract, are discussed *infra* 501 ff.

135. The Commission was therefore right to hold that the nexus required by Article 82 EC existed between the United Kingdom market for the travel agency services which airlines purchase from travel agents and the United Kingdom air transport markets.

136. In those circumstances, the fourth plea in law cannot succeed.

In *Tetra Pak II* it was held that Article 82 could catch a dominant undertaking's conduct on a market which was neighbouring rather than vertically related to the dominated one and where the conduct affected competition on the non-dominated market. In other words, a non-dominant undertaking's conduct on a market could be caught as an abuse *because the undertaking was dominant on another, separate market.* The difference between *Tetra Pak II* and *BPB Industries* is that in *Tetra Pak II* the dominant undertaking was not trying to protect its dominant position but to gain a competitive advantage on another market. Unlike tying cases the dominant undertaking was not directly *using* its dominance to commit the abuse. *Tetra Pak II*, which is discussed below[18] was an exceptional case,[19] concerned with predatory pricing.[20]

5. EXPLOITATIVE AND EXCLUSIONARY PRICING POLICIES

A. GENERAL

Many of the cases and decisions on Article 82 concern the pricing policies of dominant firms. One of the most serious consequences of a firm being found to be in a dominant position is that its pricing policies may be condemned as abusive. Although some pricing practices, such as excessive pricing, are impossible or at least unlikely in the absence of market power, others, such as discriminatory pricing in the form of discount and rebate schemes, can be practised by any firm, and in non-dominated markets may be applauded as lively competition. Abusive pricing policies cannot be completely separated from other forms of abuse, such as tying policies or exclusive contracts, since, as becomes apparent later in this chapter, the former are often pursued in furtherance of the latter.

For the convenience of the reader this chapter divides pricing abuses under various headings. However, it will soon be appreciated that many of these abuses are interrelated and that pricing policies may be characterized under more than one head and may arise in combination. Exclusionary pricing abuses are dealt with in section 6 and exploitative pricing abuses in section 8.

B. PRICE DISCRIMINATION

(i) What is Price Discrimination?[21]

Price discrimination occurs where the same commodity is sold at different prices to different customers despite identical costs, i.e., the sales have different ratios of price to marginal cost. It

---

[18] *Infra* 454.

[19] Its exceptional nature was stressed in the Discussion Paper, n. 67.

[20] So the fact that it was dominant in another market facilitated cross-subsidization.

[21] See F. M. Scherer and D. Ross, *Industrial Market Structure and Economic Performance* (3rd edn., Houghton & Mifflin, 1993), Chap. 13; L. Phlips, *The Economics of Price Discrimination* (Cambridge University Press, 1983); H. Varian, 'Price Discrimination' in R. Schmalensee and R. Willig (eds.), *Handbook of Industrial Organisation, Volume 1* (North Holland, 1989), chap. 10.

also covers sales at the same price despite different costs. Price discrimination covers a wide range of practices. As seen below, for example, predatory pricing and rebate policies may involve price discrimination.

Price discrimination is described as persistent when a supplier maintains a policy of obtaining a higher rate of return from some customers than from others. The ability to practise persistent price discrimination is a characteristic of market power. In a competitive market the customers who are 'disfavoured', i.e., charged the higher price, will be able to take their custom elsewhere. The fact that an undertaking can persistently discriminate against some customers shows that it is difficult or impossible for them to change suppliers. Price discrimination occurs in competitive markets too but it tends to be *sporadic*, i.e., it changes frequently and customers may be in a favoured group today and a disfavoured one tomorrow.

All customers have a 'reservation' 'price', the maximum price they will pay for the product.[22] In *perfect price discrimination* (first-degree discrimination) the dominant supplier charges each customer his reservation price. In the real world this is often impossible and the supplier can only practise *imperfect* price discrimination whereby he identifies different *groups* of customers with similar reservation prices and charges each group differently. In second-degree discrimination he does this by offering different 'deals' in the form of goods or services in different packages and lets the customer 'self-select' by choosing the one he wants. In third-degree discrimination the supplier identifies different groups of customers by some easily observable or ascertainable characteristic, such as old-age pensioners, students, residents of a particular country.[23] The information revolution has made price discrimination easier in some markets because 'suppliers often have detailed data on individual buyers. This lets them price discriminate, quoting different prices to different customers based on the actual or likely characteristics of the customers'.[24]

Price discrimination works only if arbitrage is not possible or feasible. Arbitrage is where the customers trade amongst themselves, which means the customers charged the lowest prices sell on to those charged more. There will be no incentive to do this if the difference in prices charged is not sufficient to recompense the selling customer for the transport, administrative, or other costs involved in selling on. In some cases arbitrage is not possible. In *United Brands*,[25] for example, it was difficult to transport bananas, a highly delicate and perishable product, between Member States. Price discrimination is easier in respect of services consumed on the spot than in respect of goods.[26]

The general consensus among economists is that price discrimination is welfare enhancing if it increases output.[27] Price discrimination may be pro-competitive in industries with high fixed (or sunk) costs and low marginal costs if an undertaking can charge above marginal cost to customers willing to pay in order to recover some fixed costs, while charging lower, marginal cost prices, to others.[28] This may in particular be a feature of high technology markets in the new economy. However, it is also possible for price discrimination to be anti-competitive and

[22] See *supra* Chap. 1.

[23] M. Motta, *Competition Policy* (Cambridge University Press, 2004), 492.

[24] D. Begg, S. Fischer, and R. Dornbusch, *Economics* (8th edn., McGraw-Hill, 2005), 247.

[25] Case 27/76, *United Brands v. Commission* [1978] ECR 207, [1978] 1 CMLR 429; see *infra* 597.

[26] D. Begg, S. Fischer, and R. Dornbusch, *Economics* (8th edn., McGraw-Hill, 2005), 138.

[27] There is a large literature on the economics of price discrimination, but see in particular R. Schmalensee, 'Output and Welfare Implications of Third Degree Price Discrimination' (1981) 71 *American Economic Review*, 242.

[28] See D. Ridyard, 'Exclusionary Pricing and Price Discrimination Abuses under Article 82—An Economic Analysis' [2002] *ECLR* 286, 287–8; J. Temple Lang and R. O'Donoghue, 'Defining Legitimate Competition: How to Clarify Pricing Abuses under Article 82EC' (2002) 26 *Fordham Int'l LJ* 83, 89–90.

produce adverse effects on efficiency. The problem for competition law is to develop the tools for distinguishing the situations in which price discrimination is welfare enhancing from those in which it is not. The complexity of the consumer welfare effects of price discrimination is summarised in the following passage.

> ## R. O'Donoghue and A. J. Padilla, *The Law and Economics of Article 82* (Hart Publishing, 2006), 561–2
>
> Price discrimination, if successful, increases firms' profits. What effect this has on consumer welfare, however, can only be decided in individual cases, since it is generally ambiguous. In thinking about effects arising from changes to producer welfare on consumer welfare, it is important to remember that the pattern of price discrimination paid by final customers may be very different from that faced by the intermediate supplier. For example, retailers may face complex non-linear tariffs (second degree price discrimination) when buying wholesale goods, but will often sell these goods on to final consumers at a constant unit price.
>
> Turning to the effects themselves, it is possible that consumers do benefit from price discrimination. Customers may buy more of an intermediate good if they are charged a different unit price depending on how many units they buy, according to a scheme that is tailored to them . . . . . These customers may face a lower marginal cost than they would if they paid the same price for all units, and they may pass on this lower marginal cost to their final customers in the form of lower unit retail price. If so, the practice is good for both economic efficiency and consumers.
>
> However, even in this relatively clear-cut case, there is another factor to take into account which could mean that consumers pay higher prices even though marginal costs have fallen. The problem arises from the different role played by marginal and average input costs. Non-linear tariffs for inputs mean that suppliers can have a high average input cost even though their marginal input cost is low. Low marginal costs encourage low prices, but if the resulting profits are too small to cover the average cost of inputs, some companies may be forced to exit the market, weakening the intensity of competition, and allowing the remaining companies to set higher prices and so earn higher margins.
>
> In practice, the outcome for consumers will be even more complex. If there are only limited differences in the non-linear tariff faced by different suppliers (i.e. the extent of third degree price discrimination is limited), then different suppliers will face different input costs for their marginal units. Whether this is good or bad for consumers depends on whether consumers can choose freely between the supplier with high costs and the supplier with low costs. If not, for example because consumers without a car have no option but to use the local shop, then those consumers that are "captive" to the high cost supplier will be disadvantaged, while those that can choose the low cost supplier will benefit. The balance could go either way.

(ii) Primary Line and Secondary Line Injury

Price discrimination may involve primary line or secondary line injury. Primary line injury prejudices the supplier's competitors. Price discrimination can cause primary line injury by having exclusionary (foreclosure) effects on competitors. For example, we see below that in *Irish Sugar*[29] and *Compagnie Maritime Belge*[30] the dominant undertakings pursued selective (and therefore

---

[29] Case T-228/97, *Irish Sugar plc v. Commission* [1999] ECR II-2969, [1999] 5 CMLR 1300, *infra* 471.

[30] Cases C-395 and 396/96 P, *Compagnie Maritime Belge and Others v. Commission* [2000] ECR I-1365, [2000] 4 CMLR 1076, *infra* 469.

discriminatory) low pricing policies in order to exclude their competitors. Secondary line injury is where the impact is in downstream markets, between the supplier's customers or third parties *inter se*. If a supplier sells a product to X cheaper than to Y, and X and Y are competing manufacturers who need the product as an input, then X's costs will be lower than Y's. The supplier will have distorted competition between them.

Primary and secondary line injury may arise from the same scenario. In *Virgin/BA*[31] the differential rebates given to travel agents for selling BA tickets were held to have both an excluding effect on BA's competitor airlines (primary line), and to cause distortions to competition between the agents (secondary line).[32]

Primary line injury through price discrimination is a major target of the Commission, as it can be exclusionary. Secondary line injury through discriminatory pricing is expressly listed as an abuse in Article 82(c).[33]

6. EXCLUSIONARY PRICING ABUSES AND TYING

A. PREDATORY PRICING

(i) General

Predatory pricing is the practice whereby an undertaking prices its product so low that competitors cannot live with the price and are driven from the market.[34] Once the competitors are excluded from the market the undertaking is able to increase prices to monopoly levels and recoup its losses. It is objectionable because, although it means low prices in the short term, its effects are to strengthen the power of the dominant undertaking to the prejudice of consumers. Competition policy should not be concerned with the exclusion of *less* efficient competitors from the market but the problem with predatory pricing is that it can exclude firms which are *equally efficient* to the predator.[35]

The intractable problem for competition authorities is to identify where robust price competition ends and predatory pricing begins. As one American commentator has stated: '[p]redatory pricing is one of the most daunting subjects confronting nations with competition policies'.[36] False positives (Type 1 errors, wrongfully identifying robust price competition as predatory pricing) and false negatives (Type 2 errors, wrongfully failing to identify predatory

---

[31] [2000] OJ L30/1, [20000] 4 CMLR 999, upheld on appeal, Case T-219/99, *British Airways v. Commission* [2003] ECR II-5917, [2004] 4 CMLR 1008 and Case C-95/04 P, *British Airways v. Commission*, 15 March 2007.

[32] Because they encouraged the agents to push BA tickets and they gave different rewards to agents for selling the same number of tickets, see *infra* 501 and 603.

[33] See *infra*, 594.

[34] See generally P. L. Joskow and A. K. Klevorick, 'A Framework for Analyzing Predatory Pricing Policy (1979) 89 *Yale LJ* 213. Conduct, other than low pricing, designed to drive competitors out of the market can also be described as 'predatory'.

[35] Although some economists argue that the efficiency of the entrant is irrelevant: what matters is whether there is room for another player in a non-cooperative Nash equilibrium (a market where all the participants are pursuing their best possible strategy given the strategies of all the others, see *infra* Chap. 11); see, e.g., L. Phlips, *Competition Policy: A Game-Theoretic Perspective* (Cambridge University Press, 1995), 233.

[36] E. Fox, 'Price Predation—US and EEC: Economics and Values' [1989] *Fordham Corp L Inst* 687, 687.

pricing when it occurs) are both prejudicial to consumer welfare, although many commentators argue that in respect of predatory pricing the avoidance of Type 1 errors should be the priority.

There are different opinions about how often predatory pricing actually occurs. The strategy of the predator is to sacrifice profit-maximization in the short term in order to reap monopoly profits in the long term. Some economists have argued that it is hardly ever a rational business strategy and that it is very, very rare. This view was famously adopted by Bork: '[i]t seems unwise...to construct rules about a phenomenon that probably does not exist or which, should it exist in very rare cases, the courts would have grave difficulty in distinguishing from competitive price behavior'.[37] Most economists do not take this position and consider that predatory pricing can be a rational strategy where the conditions are right. In particular, predatory pricing may be rational in new economy markets.[38]

One obvious condition for the rationality of predatory pricing generally is that there must be barriers to entry. Otherwise, it is argued, although one entrant is knocked out by the low prices others will enter when the incumbent raises them again. The incumbent will never be able to enjoy the fruits of its predation. However, it is important to appreciate that predatory pricing may itself *constitute* a barrier to entry. Industrial organization theory[39] suggests that the conditions of post-entry competition are a major factor in decisions about market entry and that the presence of a known predator on the market is a disincentive to entry. In this way predatory pricing not only drives out existing competitors, but also repels potential competition. This point should always be borne in mind. It may be easier to deter potential competitors through predatory pricing than to expel existing ones, as incumbents may have incurred sunk costs and have an incentive to remain on the market. Further, it is unlikely that all the actors on the market have perfect information. It can be argued that a predatory price may give the potential entrant erroneous signals about price levels in the market, which will deter entry as it will not appear worthwhile.

Predatory pricing is often considered to be feasible only where firms operate multi-market. It is argued that if the firm operates in only one market it is more rational for it to absorb the new entrant (by merger or take-over, insofar as that is permitted by the competition authorities), or to accommodate it, rather than incur greater losses by undercutting. Losses suffered by the predator are suffered *today*, and may be heavy: the profits above the competitive level are *tomorrow* if and when the predation strategy works, and are inherently uncertain. There is also the problem that in exiting the entrant may dispose of its assets to other competitors still on the market. Where a firm is multi-market, however, it may be able to off-set the losses on one market from the profits on another. Moreover, a firm which establishes a reputation for aggressive reaction to competition in one market may deter entrants into others, so predation in one market may protect several others. The firm may be multi-market in a geographical rather than

---

[37] R. Bork, *The Antitrust Paradox* (Basic Books, 1978, reprinted with new introduction and epilogue, Free Press, Macmillan, 1993), 154. This conclusion was based, *inter alia*, on a study in the USA by J. McGee, 'Predatory Price Cutting; The Standard Oil (New Jersey) Case' (1958)1 *Journal of Law and Economics* 137, described by R. T. Rapp, 'Predatory Pricing and Entry Deterring Strategies: the Economics of AKZO' [1986] *ECLR* 233, n. 1 as 'a work combining exceptionally bad economics and equally bad history' and its influence on US courts as showing 'that bad economic history can have a long, happy life'. For the influence on US courts see *Matsushita Elec. Indust. Co Ltd* v. *Zenith Radio Corp*, 475 US 574 (1986), where the Supreme Court, having quoted Bork, McGee, and others, said 'for this reason, there is a consensus among commentators that predatory pricing schemes are rarely tried, and even more rarely successful', before rejecting claims of predatory pricing by a cartel. The approach of US courts to predatory pricing is considered further *infra* 460 ff.

[38] See *infra* 464. Bork's thesis was formulated before the explosion of the new economy.

[39] See *supra* Chap. 1.

a product sense, so that a reputation for predation in one geographic market may deter entrants elsewhere.[40]

It can also be argued that predation can be a rational strategy only for a firm which is very dominant, in the sense that it has a very high market share:

Mere market power is not enough. The predator's sales must account for a sizeable fraction of market sales. If not, loss-making prices attract sales from the entire market which makes the strategy unworkably expensive. What is more, eliminating only one of many rivals leads to insufficient gains. All the incumbents stand to benefit from that turn of events and the prior investment by any one of them in loss-making prices never pays off.[41]

In short, there is great controversy about predatory pricing. Mainstream opinion can be summed up as saying that it can occur but only in certain conditions. The Commission and the Court consider that it can and does occur and that it infringes Article 82 when it does.

(ii) Cost Levels

If it is accepted that predatory pricing *does* occur the problem is to identify it. Most predatory pricing theory centres around costs levels. The basic concept of predatory pricing is that a dominant firm prices below cost. The difficulty with this is that a firm's costs are usually difficult to compute and so is the relationship between its costs and prices. Particular problems arise where a firm uses the same production capacity to make different products.

The terminology used is as follows:[42]

1. *Total cost* The total costs of production

2. *Average Total Cost (ATC)* The total costs involved in the production of one unit of output (i.e., total cost divided by the number of units produced).

3. *Total costs are of two kinds*:
   (a) Fixed costs Those which do not change with output over a given time period.
   (b) Variable costs Those which do change with output.

4. *Average Variable Cost(AVC)* The variable costs involved in the production of one unit (i.e., the variable costs added up and divided by the number of units produced).

5. *Marginal cost* The increase in total costs of a firm caused by increasing its output by one extra unit.

6. *Short-run Marginal Cost (SRMC)* The marginal cost based on a firm's existing plant and equipment, not on that which would be the most efficient.

7. *Avoidable costs* The costs that will not be incurred if an undertaking ceases a particular operation. Avoidable costs can include fixed costs but cannot included sunk costs (because sunk costs have already been spent and cannot be recovered).

8. *Average avoidable cost (AAC)* The avoidable cost involved in the production of one unit

9. *Long run average incremental cost (LRAIC)* The total long run average costs of supplying a specified additional unit of output, taking into account both capital and operating costs. The standard is useful in industries where there are large fixed costs but low, or even negligible, variable costs (because the main cost is the provision of a network for example, as is the case with telecommunications). It can be employed where there are fixed costs common to a number of different activities carried on by an undertaking.

---

[40] But see R. Selten, 'The Chain Store Paradox' (1978), *Theory and Decision* 9, 127–59 for a model of how predation in a series of geographic markets would be impossible.

[41] R. T. Rapp, 'Predatory Pricing and Entry Deterring Strategies: the Economics of *AKZO*' [1986] *ECLR* 233, 234; see also H. Hovenkamp, *Federal Antitrust Policy* (3rd edn., Thomson/West, 2005), 351.

[42] See also *supra* Chap. 1.

10. *Stand-alone costs* The costs which are involved in producing a product without taking into account that some of those costs are shared with the production of other products (ie that there are common costs).

The following should be noted:

(i) Average variable cost is always lower than average total cost.

(ii) Long run means a period of time long enough for all the factors of production to be cost-lessly varied (i.e., the period needed for complete adjustment).

(iii) Short run means a period of time so short that the factors of production cannot be costlessly varied (i.e., a period too short for complete adjustment).

(iii) The Areeda-Turner Test

In a seminal *Harvard Law Review* article Areeda and Turner put forward a test for identifying preda-tory pricing.[43] Under this test a price lower than reasonably anticipated short-run marginal cost is predatory, whilst a price equal to or higher than reasonably anticipated short-run marginal cost is not predatory. 'Reasonably anticipated' means that a firm's conduct is not judged *ex post facto*. The marginal cost is judged by what seemed reasonable at the time. If the SMRC turned out higher than anticipated the firm should not be condemned for predatory pricing.

SRMC is, however, almost impossible to compute in practice, as it is a question of looking back to determine what the firm's marginal cost was during a past period of time. The Areeda–Turner test therefore uses average variable cost (AVC) as a surrogate for SRMC. The test is stated as follows:

A price at or above reasonably anticipated AVC should be conclusively presumed lawful.

A price below reasonably anticipated AVC should be conclusively presumed unlawful.

(iv) Problems with the Areeda-Turner Test

The formulation of the Areeda–Turner test provoked a lively debate amongst lawyers and econ-omists.[44] Particular criticisms of the test which have been made are:

• SRMC is not the right level from which to measure predatory pricing as some above SRMC-level pricing may also be predatory. One argument is that the test does not accommodate 'limit pricing'[45] where pricing is geared to potential entrants rather than existing competitors;

• AVC is an unsatisfactory substitute for SRMC, because the AVC cost curve tends to be U-shaped and gives the undertaking a lot of room for manoeuvre. Marginal cost rises and falls more dramati-cally than AVC because AVC averages out the cost of one additional unit over the entire output being produced. The assumption that SRMC and AVC are equivalent holds good only in the long-run;[46]

• It is difficult to draw a rigid demarcation line between fixed and variable categories (as was demonstrated in the leading EC case, *AKZO*.[47]) Classification is dependent upon the industry and the time period in issue. The longer the time period, the more costs that become variable.

---

[43] P. Areeda and D. Turner, 'Predatory Pricing and Related Practices Under Section 2 of the Sherman Act' (1975) 88 *Harvard. LR* 697.

[44] See the summary in J. Brodley and D. Hay, 'Predatory Pricing: Competing Economic Theories and the Evolution of Legal Standards' (1981) 66 *Cornell LR* 738.

[45] See *infra* 465.

[46] S. Bishop and M. Walker, *The Economics of EC Competition Law* (2nd edn., Sweet & Maxwell, 2002), para. 6.92.

[47] Case C-62/86, *AKZO Chemie BV v. Commission* [1991] ECR I-3359, [1993] 5 CMLR 215, discussed *infra* 447. See also Case T-340/03, *France Télécom SA v. Commission*, 30 January 2007, *infra* 452.

Areeda and Turner recognized this problem and proposed[48] that certain costs should always be considered fixed (interest on debt, depreciation, taxes which do not vary with output);

- In certain markets where AVC (or SRMC) may be minimal (such as intellectual property markets, many markets in the new economy and/or where networks are involved) the test does not work.[49]

Despite the perceived flaws in the test it has been highly influential in antitrust thinking and some version of it is commonly used in US antitrust cases.[50] It formed the basis for the discussion in *AKZO*.

(v) The AKZO Case

The Commission first considered predatory pricing in *AKZO*.[51]

ECS was a small UK firm based in Epsom and Gloucester which produced benzoyl peroxide. Benzoyl peroxide is used as a catalyst in plastics production and also (in the UK and Ireland) as a bleaching agent in flour-milling. ECS concentrated on the flour sector, where its major customer was Allied Mills. AKZO, a multinational chemicals company also produced benzoyl peroxide but concentrated on the plastics sector. The facts as found by the Commission were that ECS decided to expand its operations in the plastics sector (capturing one of AKZO's largest customers), whereupon AKZO retaliated by threatening to attack ECS's business in the UK flour sector by reducing prices. It then set about supplying benzoyl peroxide to the UK flour sector at low prices, offering large discounts to ECS's best customers. ECS originally obtained an interim injunction in the High Court in London to prevent AKZO from implementing its threats, and those proceedings were terminated by agreement. ECS then complained to the Commission, which first granted interim relief[52] and subsequently adopted a final decision[53] holding that AKZO had abused a dominant position contrary to Article 82.

The Commission found that AKZO was dominant in the organic peroxides market as a whole[54] and had infringed Article 82 by pursuing a course of predation against ECS designed to drive it from the the plastics sector. It fined AKZO ECU 10 million and ordered it to terminate the infringement. The order required AKZO to refrain from offering or applying prices which would result in customers in respect of whose business it was competing with ECS paying prices dissimilar to those applied to comparable customers. The Commission decision finding predation focused on AKZO's threats[55] and its eliminatory intent. The decision did not adopt

[48] P. Areeda and D. Turner, *Antitrust Law* (Little Brown, 1978), para. 715c.

[49] See *infra* 464.

[50] In *US v. AMR Corporation and American Airlines* 335 F.3d 1109 (2003) the US Ct of Appeals (10th Circuit) rejected the argument that some test of incremental cost should be used in place of AVC. It held that all the suggested ways of measuring incremental cost were flawed, and as American Airlines did not price below AVC the government's case against it was dismissed. Hovenkamp criticizes this because the court refused to take into account the opportunity costs incurred by the airline (it had switched aircraft from more profitable routes to those on which it faced competition from smaller airlines), see H. Hovenkamp, *The Antitrust Enterprise: Principle and Execution* (Harvard University Press, 2005) 165–167; but c. f. E. Elhauge 'Why Above-Cost Price Cuts to Drive Out Entrants are not Predatory—And the Implications for Defining Costs and Market Power' 112 *Yale L.J.* 681 (2003).

[51] *ECS/AKZO* [1985] OJ L374/1, [1986] 3 CMLR 273; on appeal Case C-62/86, *AKZO Chemie BV v. Commission* [1991] ECR I-3359, [1993] 5 CMLR 215.

[52] [1983] OJ L252/13, [1983] 3 CMLR 694.

[53] [1985] OJ L374/1, [1986] 3 CMLR 273.

[54] See *supra* Chap. 6 for the market definition aspects of the case.

[55] It uncovered the evidence of these to support ECS's contentions when it conducted a Reg. 17, Article 14(3) investigation on AKZO's premises (for Commission investigations, see *infra* Chap. 14).

the Areeda–Turner rule or lay down specific rules about the point at which low prices become predatory, and abusive. It suggested that even prices above ATC could be predatory.[56]

AKZO appealed to the Court. It argued that it could not be guilty of an abuse since it had not reduced its prices below AVC, and that under the Areeda–Turner test its prices were therefore not predatory. The Court confirmed the Commission's definition of the market and the finding of dominance. It did accept AKZO's arguments that some costs which the Commission had classified as variable were, in this case, fixed. The Court confirmed that AKZO had been guilty of predatory pricing,[57] but set out a more structured, costs-based test for identifying it.

Case C-62/86, *AKZO Chemie BV* v. *Commission* [1991] ECR I-3359, [1993] 5 CMLR 215

The Court of Justice

66. AKZO disputes the relevance of the criterion of lawfulness adopted by the Commission, which it regards as nebulous or at least inapplicable. It maintains that the Commission should have adopted an objective criterion based on its costs.

67. In that respect, it states that the question of the lawfulness of a particular level of prices cannot be separated from the specific market situation in which the prices were fixed. There is no abuse if the dominant undertaking endeavours to obtain a optimum selling-price and a positive coverage margin. A price is optimum if the undertaking may reasonably expect that the offer of another price or the absence of a price would produce a less favourable operating profit in the short term. Furthermore, coverage margin is positive if the value of the order exceeds the sum of the variable costs.

68. According to AKZO, a criterion based on an endeavour to obtain an optimal price in the short term cannot be rejected on the grounds that it would jeopardise the viability of the undertaking in the long term. It is only after a certain time that the undertaking in the question could take measures to eliminate the losses or withdraw from a loss-making branch of business. In the meantime the undertaking would have to accept 'optimum orders' in order to reduce its deficit and to ensure continuity of operation.

69. It should be observed that, as the Court held in Case 85/76, *Hoffmann-La Roche* v. *E.C. Commission* [1979] ECR 461, paragraph 91, the concept of abuse is an objective concept relating to the behaviour of an undertaking in a dominant position which is such as to influence the structure of a market where, as a result of the very presence of the undertaking in question, the degree of competition is weakened and through recourse to methods which, different from those which condition normal competition in products or services on the basis of the transactions of commercial operations, has the effect of hindering the maintenance of the degree of competition still existing in the market or the growth of that competition.

70. It follows that Article [82] prohibits a dominant undertaking from eliminating a competitor and thereby strengthening its position by using methods other than those which come within the scope of competition on the basis of quality. From that point of view, however, not all competition by means of price can be regarded as legitimate.

71. Prices below average variable costs (that is to say, those which vary depending on the quantities produced) by means of which a dominant undertaking seeks to eliminate a competitor

[56] *ECS/AKZO* [1985] OJ L374/1, [1986] 3 CMLR 273, para. 79.

[57] It annulled the Commission's decision in respect of offers made to one particular customer and reduced the fine to ECUs 7.5 million.

must be regarded as abusive. A dominant undertaking has no interest in applying such prices except that of eliminating competitors so as to enable it subsequently to raise its prices by taking advantage of its monopolistic position, since each sale generates a loss, namely the total amount of the fixed costs (that is to say, those which remain constant regardless of the quantities produced) and, at least, part of the variable costs relating to the unit produced.

72. Moreover, prices below average total costs, that is to say, fixed costs plus variable costs, but above average variable costs, must be regarded as abusive if they are determined as part of a plan for eliminating a competitor. Such prices can drive from the market undertakings which are perhaps as efficient as the dominant undertakings but which, because of their smaller financial resources, are incapable of withstanding the competition waged against them.

73. These are the criteria that must be applied to the situation in the present case.

74. Since the criterion of legitimacy to be adopted is a criterion based on the costs and strategy of the dominant undertaking itself, AKZO's allegation concerning the inadequacy of the Commission's investigation with regard to the cost structure and the pricing policy of its competitors must be rejected at the outset.

It can be seen from the Court's judgment that the costs-based test it adopted differs significantly from the Areeda–Turner test. The test set out in AKZO states that prices below AVC 'must be regarded as abusive' because there is no profit-maximizing reason for them. The only explanation for them is that they are directed at eliminating competitors. This appears to set out a *presumption*, albeit a very strong one, that pricing below AVC is abusive.[58] The Court went on to hold that above AVC but below ATC prices can also be abusive if they are part of a plan to eliminate competitors (under the Areeda–Turner test there is no predation where prices are above AVC). There appears to be no presumption as to the undertaking's intention, so the onus is on the Commission.[59] Eliminatory intent was found in *AKZO* from the direct threats and from the price cuts the dominant firm introduced.

The Court did not expressly deal with the situation where prices are at or above ATC. Nor did it say anything *expressly* about the dominant undertaking's possibility of recouping its losses, although it can be argued that it is implicit in paragraph 71.[60]

The test in *AKZO* can be summed up as follows:

(i) Prices below AVC are presumed to be predatory.

(ii) Prices above AVC but below ATC (the 'grey' area) are not *presumed* predatory but are predatory if they are part of a plan to eliminate a competitor.

The *AKZO* test has been subjected to much criticism, and presents a number of problems as discussed below. It was reaffirmed in *Tetra Pak II*[61] and followed and applied by the CFI in *France Télécom*,[62] a judgment delivered after the debate on the reform of Article 82 was well under way.

---

[58] Although see Case C-333/94 P, *Tetra Pak International SA v. Commission* [1996] ECR I-5951, [1997] 4 CMLR 662, discussed *infra*, where the language of the Court is arguably more absolute.

[59] But see the Commission's attitude in the *Digital Undertaking* (Commission Press Release IP/97/868), *infra* 465.

[60] Fennelly AG argued this in his opinion in *Compagnie Maritime Belge*, see *infra*. For the question of recoupment generally, see *infra* 459.

[61] Case C-333/94 P, *Tetra Pak International SA v. Commission* [1996] ECR I-5951, [1997] 4 CMLR 662.

[62] Case T-340/03, *France Télécom SA v. Commission*, 30 January 2007, para. 130.

(vi) Some Problems with the Criteria Laid Down in *AKZO*

a. Problems with Costs Based Tests

As noted above, when discussing the Areeda–Turner test, costs–based criteria are inherently problematic. It was noted there that AVC is in any case an inadequate substitute for SRMC and that classification of costs can be difficult. In *AKZO* itself the parties submitted to the Court very different calculations of AKZO's costs. The Court stated that 'an item of cost is not fixed or variable by nature' and overruled the Commission's classification of the labour costs as variable rather than fixed. In this case there was no direct correlation between labour costs and quantities produced.[63] The Court gave no guidance on how costs are to be allocated in multi-product firms,[64] nor did it address known problems such as stepwise or semi-variable costs. In *Wanadoo*[65] the Commission classified the advertising of the undertaking's residential broadband services as a variable rather than a fixed cost, which the undertaking disputed.[66]

b. Rational Reasons for below AVC Pricing

There *are* sometimes rational, non-predatory reasons for pricing under AVC: for example the launch of new lines, obsolete stock clearance, and using continuous production facilities. It may be better for an undertaking to sell temporarily at a loss and make *some* return, than to make none at all. If paragraph 71 of the Court's judgment *does* only set out a presumption then circumstances such as these could be recognized and the presumption rebutted.

c. Ascertaining Intention between AVC and ATC

Under the *AKZO* test the intention of the undertaking becomes the crucial factor when prices are in the 'grey' area between AVC and ATC. This part of the test accepts that pricing at that level can be a rational, non-predatory strategy in certain circumstances because the undertaking will be covering the variable costs and at least some part of the fixed costs on every unit sold. However, reliance on intention is problematic, as in one sense all undertakings might be said to intend to eliminate their competitors by the very fact that they are participating in the struggle for custom in the market place. The Court presumably means intending to eliminate competitors by competition which is not on the basis of performance (a better widget, better service, etc.), and therefore not, in the words of *Hoffmann-La Roche*, 'normal' competition,[67] but the distinction between 'normal' price competition and predatory pricing is the very thing this test is trying to identify. The formulation 'determined as part of a plan' seems to denote some degree of systematic and deliberate strategy. In *AKZO* the anti-competitive intentions were derived partly from company documentation, but words may be open to different interpretations and what seemed like an exhortationary address to the troops in the sales department at the time may read like threats of ruthless predatory intent months or years afterwards.[68] *AKZO* itself

---

[63] Case C-62/86, *AKZO Chemie BV v. Commission* [1991] ECR I-3359, [1993] 5 CMLR 215, para. 95.

[64] This question was addressed by the Commission in its decision in *Deutsche Post* [2001] OJ L125/27, [2001] 5 CMLR 99, see *infra* 456.

[65] COMP/38.233, [2005] 5 CMLR 120.

[66] The CFI dismissed the appeal on this point in *France Télécom*, on procedural grounds. The undertaking's arguments that the Commission had calculated its recovery of costs incorrectly were likewise dismissed.

[67] See the definition of 'abuse' in Case 85/76, *Hoffmann-La Roche v. Commission* [1979] ECR 461, [1979] 3 CMLR 211, para. 91; see *supra* Chap. 5.

[68] See, e.g., *Napier Brown/British Sugar* [1988] OJ L284/41, [1990] 4 CMLR 196 where an internal memo which said '[i]f we are to succeed in seeing off the Whitworths threat, we MUST attack on all fronts. It is time to get nasty!' did not go down well with the Commission.

may make proving intent more difficult as undertakings are now advised to be more careful in what they record. Nevertheless, in *Wanadoo* the Commission was able to rely upon on a number of internal documents to show that the undertaking had dropped its price for residential high-speed broadband access in order to 'pre-empt' the developing market. The undertaking disputed the scope and significance of the documents, alleging that some of them were merely informal or impromptu. The CFI, however, pointed out that some of the incriminating words and phrases came from management level staff and were expressed in the context of formal presentations for the taking of a decision or of a very detailed framework letter.[69] It did not think the phrase 'our pre-emption of the ASDL market is imperative' could be read as anything other than an intention to 'pre-empt'.[70]

Documentary evidence from the allegedly predating undertaking is 'direct evidence' of an intention to predate. 'Indirect' evidence can also be used. In *Tetra Pak II* factors such as the duration and scale of the losses, and the tactics of specially importing the products into Italy in order to sell them at a loss there, wer taken into account in identifying a predatory strategy. In the Discussion Paper the Commission said that the following elements will be particularly relevant to showing a plausible scheme of predation.

DG Competition Discussion Paper on the Application of Article 82 of the Treaty to Exclusionary Abuses, Brussels, December 2005

115. In case there is no direct evidence of a predatory strategy a case will have to be built on indirect evidence of such a strategy to predate. In arguing such a case the following elements will be of particular relevance to show a plausible scheme of predation: does the pricing behaviour only make commercial sense as part of a predatory strategy or are there also other reasonable explanations, is there an actual or likely exclusionary effect, the scale, duration and continuity of the low pricing, does the dominant company actually incur specific costs in order for instance to expand capacity which enables it to react to entry, are certain customers selectively targeted, is there concurrent application of other exclusionary practices, does the dominant company have the possibility to off-set its losses with profits earned on other sales, does it have the possibility to recoup the losses in the foreseeable future through (a return to) high prices, can predation on one market have a reputation effect on other markets, is the prey particularly dependent on external financing and does the prey have counter strategies. The relevance of the different elements for individual cases may not always be the same and it is not possible to define in the abstract and in advance what is exactly required in an individual case to show a predatory strategy with such indirect evidence. However the following can be said on the importance of the various elements.

116. If the pricing behaviour only makes commercial sense as part of a predatory strategy and there are no other reasonable explanations, such will normally suffice to show a strategy to predate, certainly if also other exclusionary practices are applied by the dominant company. In such a case it will not be necessary to show that a foreclosure effect is likely.

117. In all other cases it is at least necessary to show that a foreclosure effect is likely in view of the scale, duration and continuity of the low pricing before predatory pricing can be found to exist. In general it will not suffice to show only the likely foreclosure effect. The investigation of more elements is usually necessary before a strategy to predate can be convincingly shown.

---

[69] *France Télécom*, para. 202.

[70] *Ibid.*, para. 206.

d. Intention not Effect

The emphasis in *AKZO* is placed on intention, not on effect. It can be argued, however, that the firm which embarks on a process of price-cutting to exclude its rivals *and does not succeed* benefits its customers and harms only itself. In *AKZO* the customers were presumably happy to have the lack of price competition between AKZO and ECS in the flour sector replaced with some robust soliciting of their custom. On the other hand it is not sensible for competition authorities (and courts) to stand back and refuse interim relief while a firm is driven from the market by exclusionary conduct which will ultimately harm consumers and, in driving prices below costs, the dominant undertaking may cause harm to competitors short of elimination and cause other distortions in the market which may affect third parties including consumers.[71] At the end of the day it is the effect of the predator's behaviour, rather than the intention, which should be the decisive matter. In *France Télécom*, the CFI reiterated the traditional approach to predatory pricing.

Case T-340/03, *France Télécom SA* v. *Commission*, 30 January 2007

130. It is clear from the case-law on predatory pricing that, first, prices below average variable costs give grounds for assuming that a pricing practice is eliminatory and that, if the prices are below average total costs but above average variable costs, those prices must be regarded as abusive if they are determined as part of a plan for eliminating a competitor (*AKZO* v *Commission*, paragraph 100 above, paragraphs 71 and 72; Case T-83/91 *Tetra Pak* v *Commission* [1994] ECR II-755, paragraphs 148 and 149, upheld by the Court of Justice in Case C-333/94 P *Tetra Pak* v *Commission* [1996] ECR I-5951, paragraph 41 (together, 'the *Tetra Pak* cases').

195. … As regards the conditions for the application of Article 82 EC and the distinction between the object and effect of the abuse, it should be pointed out that, for the purposes of applying that article, showing an anti-competitive object and an anti-competitive effect may, in some cases, be one and the same thing. If it is shown that the object pursued by the conduct of an undertaking in a dominant position is to restrict competition, that conduct will also be liable to have such an effect. Thus, with regard to the practices concerning prices, the Court of Justice held in *AKZO* v *Commission*, paragraph 100 above, that prices below average variable costs applied by an undertaking in a dominant position are regarded as abusive in themselves because the only interest which the undertaking may have in applying such prices is that of eliminating competitors, and that prices below average total costs but above average variable costs are abusive if they are determined as part of a plan for eliminating a competitor. In that case, the Court did not require any demonstration of the actual effects of the practices in question (see, to that effect, Case T-203/01 *Michelin* v *Commission* [2003] ECR II-4071, paragraphs 241 and 242).

196. Furthermore, it should be added that, where an undertaking in a dominant position actually implements a practice whose object is to oust a competitor, the fact that the result hoped for is not achieved is not sufficient to prevent that being an abuse of a dominant position within the meaning of Article 82 EC (*Compagnie maritime belge transports and Others* v *Commission*, paragraph 104 above, paragraph 149, and Case T-228/97 *Irish Sugar* v *Commission* [1999] ECR II-2969, paragraph 191).

---

[71] See H. Hovenkamp, *Federal Antitrust Policy* (3rd edn., Thomson/West, 2005), chap. 8.

e. Recoupment

In *AKZO* the ECJ did not expressly address the issue of recoupment. The rationality of predatory pricing hinges on the possibility that the predator can recoup its losses, i.e., that short-term loss of profitability is more than compensated for by long-run profitability when, after the competitor's exit, the undertaking can raise prices to monopoly level. If there are no barriers to entry to the market the undertaking will not be able to recoup if it is continually having to price low in order to fight off new competitors (although one must remember that predation may constitute a barrier to entry). The Court did not expressly consider whether predation was a plausible strategy for AKZO.[72] Recoupment is discussed further below.[73]

f. Unsuitability for some Industries

The rules may need to be different in certain industries. In network industries, common and joint costs are large and cost structures are not the same as in other industries. The Commission accepted this in its Notice on the Application of the Competition Rules to Access Agreements in the Telecommunications Sector, where it said that in the case of telecommunications variable cost may be substantially lower than the price the operator needs to cover the cost of providing the service. The Commission therefore contemplates using long-run average incremental cost (the cost of each increment of output) as the cost floor for examining predatory pricing in this sector.[74]

(vii) The *AKZO* Test and the Reform of Article 82

In the Discussion Paper the Commission proposed retaining the structure of the *AKZO* cost-based test but using average avoidable cost (AAC) as the measure, rather than AVC. The retention of the *AKZO* test was perhaps inevitable, despite its problems and critics, given the unambiguous case-law of the Court. The Discussion Paper managed to discuss the *AKZO* test using AAC in place of AVC without mentioning the fact that it was thereby departing from the *AKZO* standard. The Discussion Paper states that;

108. The AAC benchmark is the appropriate and practical answer to the question about avoidable losses . . . Often the AAC benchmark will be the same as the AVC benchmark as in many cases only variable costs can be avoided. However, if the dominant company, for instance, had to expand capacity in order to predate, then also fixed or sunk investments made for this extra capacity will have to be taken into account and will filter into the AAC benchmark. In the latter case AAC will, for good reasons, exceed AVC.

(viii) Predatory Pricing where Dominance and Abuse are on Different Markets

In *Tetra Pak II* an undertaking was held to have infringed Article 82 by predatory pricing where it was dominant on one market and the predatory pricing took place on another. The case involved two carton markets: aseptic and non-aseptic. They were held to be separate, distinct

---

[72] But see Case C-333/94 P, *Tetra Pak International SA v. Commission* [1996] ECR I-5951, [1997] 4 CMLR 662.

[73] *Infra*, 459.

[74] [1998] OJ C265/2, paras. 114 and 115.

markets. Neither was ancillary to the other or upstream or downstream of the other.[75] The Commission held that Tetra Pak was dominant on the aseptic market but made no finding of dominance with regard to the non-aseptic market. It held, however, that Tetra Pak had abused its dominant position on the aseptic market by its conduct on the non-aseptic market which was designed to obtain a competitive advantage on the non-aseptic market. The Commission's decision was upheld by the Court of First Instance,[76] which was affirmed by the Court of Justice.

Case C-333/94 P, *Tetra Pak International SA v. Commission* [1996] ECR I-5951, [1997] 4 CMLR 662

Court of Justice

24. It must first be stressed that there can be no question of challenging the Court of First Instance's assessment, at paragraph 113 of its judgment, that Article [82] gives no explicit guidance as to the requirements relating to where on the product market the abuse took place. That Court was therefore correct in stating, at paragraph 115, that the actual scope of the special responsibility imposed on a dominant undertaking must be considered in the light of the specific circumstances of each case which show a weakened competitive situation.

25. In that regard, the case-law cited by the Court of First Instance is relevant. Joined Cases 6/73 and 7/73 *Commercial Solvents* v. *Commission* [1974] ECR 223 and Case 311/84 *CBEM* v. *CLT and IPB* [1985] ECR 3261 provide examples of abuses having effects on markets other than the dominated markets. In Case C–62/86 *AKZO* v. *Commission* [1991] ECR I-3359 and Case T-65/89 *BPB Industries and British Gypsum* v. *Commission* [1993] ECR II-389, the Community judicature found certain conduct on markets other than the dominated markets and having effects on the dominated markets to be abusive. The Court of First Instance was therefore right in concluding from that case-law, at paragraph 116 of the judgment under appeal, that it must reject the applicant's arguments to the effect that the Community judicature had ruled out any possibility of Article [82] applying to an act committed by an undertaking in a dominant position on a market distinct from the dominated market.

26. Nor, for the reasons set out by the Advocate General at point 61 of his Opinion, can Tetra Pak derive any support from the judgments in Case 85/76 *Hoffmann-La Roche* v. *Commission* [1979] ECR 461 or *Michelin* v. *Commission*, cited above.

27. It is true that application of Article [82] presupposes a link between the dominant position and the alleged abusive conduct, which is normally not present where conduct on a market distinct from the dominated market produces effects on that distinct market. In the case of distinct, but associated, markets, as in the present case, application of Article [82] to conduct found on the associated, non-dominated, market and having effects on that associated market can only be justified by special circumstances.

28. In that regard, the Court of First Instance first considered, at paragraph 118 of its judgment, that it was relevant that Tetra Pak held 78 per cent of the overall market in packaging in both aseptic and non-aseptic cartons, that is to say seven times more than its closest competitor. At paragraph 119, it stressed Tetra Pak's leading position in the non-aseptic sector. Then, in paragraph 121, it found that Tetra Pak's position on the aseptic markets, of which it held nearly a 90 per cent share, was quasi-monopolistic. It noted that that position also made Tetra Pak a favoured supplier of non-aseptic systems. Finally, at paragraph 122, it concluded that, in the circumstances of the

---

[75] For market definition in *Tetra Pak II*, see *supra* Chap. 6.

[76] Case T-83/91, *Tetra Pak Rausing v. Commission* [1994] ECR II-755, [1997] 4 CMLR 726.

case, application of Article [82] was justified by the situation on the different markets and the close associative links between them.

29. The relevance of the associative links which the Court of First Instance thus took into account cannot be denied. The fact that the various materials involved are used for packaging the same basic liquid products shows that Tetra Pak's customers in one sector are also potential customers in the other. That possibility is borne out by statistics showing that in 1987 approximately 35 per cent of Tetra Pak's customers bought both aseptic and non-aseptic systems. It is also relevant to note that Tetra Pak and its most important competitor, PKL, were present on all four markets. Given its almost complete domination of the aseptic markets, Tetra Pak could also count on a favoured status on the non-aseptic markets. Thanks to its position on the former markets, it could concentrate its efforts on the latter by acting independently of the other economic operators.

30. The circumstances thus described, taken together and not separately, justified the Court of First Instance, without any need to show that the undertaking was dominant on the non-aseptic markets, in finding that Tetra Pak enjoyed freedom of conduct compared with the other economic operators on those markets.

31. Accordingly, the Court of First Instance was right to accept the application of Article [82] of the Treaty in this case, given that the quasi-monopoly enjoyed by Tetra Pak on the aseptic markets and its leading position on the distinct, though closely associated, non-aseptic markets placed it in a situation comparable to that of holding a dominant position on the markets in question as a whole.

32. An undertaking in such a situation must necessarily be able to foresee that its conduct may be caught by Article [82] of the Treaty. Thus, contrary to the appellant's argument, the requirements of legal certainty are observed.

It was rather strange of the Court to cite *AKZO* in paragraph 25 since ultimately only one relevant market was held to exist in that case, so the dominant position and the abuse were actually on the same market.[77] *Tetra Pak II* extended the previous law because the abuse was committed on a non-dominated market, unrelated vertically to the dominated one, in order to gain an advantage in the former. The Court stated in paragraph 27 that Article 82 can be applied to conduct by a dominant undertaking on a distinct, non-dominated market only where it is justified by 'special circumstances'. The special circumstances in this case were the 'close associative links' between the two markets, the quasi-monopolistic position held by Tetra Pak on the dominated market (where it had a 90 per cent market share), and the leading position on the non-dominated market. Both types of carton were used for packaging the same basic liquid, and many customers bought on both markets. Its powerful position on the dominated market therefore meant that Tetra Pak could concentrate its efforts on the associated market where it enjoyed a greater freedom of action than its competitors. It was thus in a position comparable to that of holding a dominant position on the two markets as a whole (paragraph 31). *Tetra Pak II*, therefore, does *not* mean that dominance on one market can always be abused by conduct on another, distinct, market. It *does* mean that it is a possibility where the markets are associated and there are particular circumstances pertaining which mean that the undertaking's dominance gives it significant advantages on the second market. What amounts to 'special circumstances' will vary from case to case. The importance accorded in *Tetra Pak II* to the quasi-monopolistic position should, however, be noted. This possibly reflects the added responsibility of undertakings which enjoy a position of 'super-dominance'.

[77] Case C-62/86, *AKZO Chemie* [1991] ECR I-3359, [1993] 5 CMLR 215. Organic peroxides had various uses but the Court accepted that it was all one market: see *supra* Chap. 6, 367.

The abuse at issue in this part of *Tetra Pak II* was predatory pricing. It was found that Tetra Pak had priced below ATC in the non-aseptic carton market to eliminate competitors. In the Discussion Paper the Commission was keen to downplay the significance of *Tetra Pak II*. It said:

In general predatory pricing will only be dealt with as an abuse under Article 82 if the dominant company applies it to protect or strengthen its dominant position. Usually it will do so by applying predatory pricing on the market where it has a dominant position. . . . Predatory pricing by a dominant company in an unrelated market where it is not dominant and where the predation will only have effects in this unrelated market will normally not be an abuse under Article 82.[78]

At this point the Commission referred to *Tetra Pak II* in a footnote, saying that:

The case can however be considered wholly exceptional because the markets of aseptic and non-aseptic cartons were strongly linked and the Court and Commission considered that due to the quasi-monopolistic position of Tetra Pak on the aseptic markets and its leading position on the closely associated non-aseptic markets it enjoyed a quasi dominant position also on the latter markets.[79]

(ix) Cross-Subsidies, Incremental Costs, and Multi-Product Firms

In *Deutsche Post* the Commission applied an incremental cost standard, instead of the *AKZO* AVC threshold, when it dealt with a statutory monopolist which was also active on a competitive market.

Deutsche Post AG [2001] OJ L125/27, [2001] 5 CMLR 99

Deutsche Post (DPAG) had a statutory monopoly in Germany over the basic letter post (of letters weighing less than 200g). Further, it had a universal service obligation in over the counter parcel services (OTC), where parcels are brought by individuals to the post office.[80] It also operated in the mail-order parcel market, which was open to competition. UPS, a competitor in the mail-order sector, complained to the Commission that, *inter alia*, DPAG was using revenue from its profitable letter post monopoly to sustain a policy of below cost selling in the mail-order parcels sector, i.e., that it was cross-subsidizing the activity open to competition from its monopoly. One problem in the case was how DPAG's costs in the mail-order parcel sector were to be calculated, since it could use its OTC infrastructure for its mail-order operation. How therefore could the real cost of providing the mail-order service be determined?

Commission

E. The economic concept of cross subsidies

(5) The applicant's main allegation is that DPAG offers its commercial parcel service at below-cost prices with the aim of ousting competitors from the market. DPAG covers the resultant losses

---

[78] Discussion Paper, para. 101.

[79] Discussion Paper, n. 67.

[80] 'Universal service' means that a product or service must be provided throughout a particular territory at a certain price to all those who require it. Universal service obligations are commonly imposed on undertakings given special or exclusive rights which provide the utilities or other 'services of general economic interest'. The concept is discussed further in Chap. 8.

with the aid of the profits made in the reserved area. This means that DPAG hinders competition by cross- subsidising commercial parcel services through the reserved letter-post services.

The relevant cost concepts

(6) From an economic point of view cross-subsidisation occurs where the earnings from a given service do not suffice to cover the incremental costs of providing that service and where there is another service or bundle of services the earnings from which exceed the stand-alone costs . . . The service for which revenue exceeds stand-alone cost is the source of the cross subsidy and the service in which revenue does not cover the incremental costs is its destination. The reserved area is a likely and permanent source of funding as . . . overall revenues in the reserved area exceed its stand-alone costs . . . [81]

(7) This means that, when establishing whether the incremental costs incurred in providing mail-order parcel services are covered, the additional costs of producing that service, incurred solely as a result of providing the service, must be distinguished from the common fixed costs, which are not incurred solely as a result of this service.

The impact of DPAG's public service obligation

(8) When calculating the share of the common fixed costs it must be borne in mind that DPAG is required by law to maintain a capacity reserve large enough to cover any peak demands that may arise in over-the-counter parcel services while meeting statutory service quality standards for those services . . . Even if DPAG were no longer to offer mail-order parcel services, it would still be obliged vis-a-vis every mail-order customer to provide catalogues and parcels over the counter within a specified delivery target. This follows from the universal service obligation whereby every potential postal user is entitled to receive from DPAG over-the-counter parcel services of the pre-scribed quality at uniform prices. If DPAG were to stop offering a specific parcel service, it could not, unlike a private firm such as UPS, cut back on staff and equipment in perfect proportion to the reduction in volume. Even if the specific parcel service were stopped, staff and equipment could not be reduced to the full extent of the cut in service, as some staff and equipment are also needed to provide over-the-counter services that meet statutory quality standards (D +2 for 80 per cent of the consignments). This obligation to maintain a reserve capacity is known in economic terms as the carrier of last resort . . .

(9) Where DPAG maintains an infrastructure to fulfil its public service mission, a distinction must be made between the cost of maintaining capacity and the specific incremental costs of producing individual services:

— The costs of maintaining capacity arise independently of the services provided and the vol-ume of parcels processed only as a consequence of maintaining capacity to allow everyone the standard option of having their parcels sent over-the-counter in the normal way. The legal obliga-tion to remain ready to offer a standard parcel delivery service at a uniform tariff increases the pro-portion of common fixed costs that a carrier of last resort bears in comparison with companies who do not have this obligation. Costs arising from the legal obligation to maintain an option for everyone to have parcels carried at a geographically averaged tariff also arise even if commercial parcels not dealt with at the postal counter are discontinued. This means that these capacity costs are not attributable to a specific service and must be treated as DPAG's common fixed costs . . . Common fixed costs cease to exist only where the statutory obligation no longer applies,

[81] This is called the 'combinatorial test': see R. O'Donoghue and A. J. Padilla, *The Law and Economics of Article 82* (Hart Publishing, 2006), 266–8 and the economics literature cited there.

— On the other hand costs that are attributable to a specific service arise only where services other than over-the-counter parcel services are provided. These costs, which are dependent on the volume posted and arise solely as a function of the specific service, cease to exist if the service at issue is stopped.

(10) To avoid subsidising mail-order parcel services by using revenue from the reserved area, DPAG must earn revenue on this parcel service which at least covers the costs attributable to or incremental to producing the specific service. Emphasising the coverage of costs attributable to a particular service also makes it possible to take account of the additional burden incurred by DPAG as a result of fulfilling its statutory obligation of maintaining network reserve capacity . . . As this emphasis is expressly intended to take account of network capacity costs as an additional burden. DPAG is required only to cover the costs attributable to the provision of mail-order parcel services. This means that these operations are not burdened with the common fixed cost of providing network capacity that DPAG incurs as a result of its statutory universal service obligation . . .

. . .

(35) Predatory pricing occurs where a dominant firm sells a service below cost with the intention of eliminating competitors or deterring entry, enabling it to further increase its market power. Such unjustifiably low prices infringe Article 82 of the EC Treaty According to the case-law of the European Court of Justice, pricing below average variable costs must be regarded as abusive (. . . AKZO . . . and . . . BPB Industries . . .). This principle was established in AKZO, where the Court defined average variable costs as 'costs which vary depending on the quantities produced' (paragraph 71 of the judgment). In determining which costs vary depending on the quantities produced, the division between common fixed costs and costs attributable to a specific service set forth earlier must be borne in mind in DPAG's favour. Given the public universal service obligation, only the additional costs of providing a particular service vary with volume produced.

(36) On the basis of relationship between the costs of maintaining capacity and the incremental costs of providing a particular service, the following may be said about DPAG's activities other than its over-the-counter business: In the period 1990 to 1995 DPAG's revenue from mail-order parcels was below the incremental costs of providing this specific service . . . This means that in the period 1990 to 1995 every sale by DPAG in the mail-order parcel services business represented a loss which comprises all the capacity-maintenance costs and at least part of the additional costs of providing the service. In such circumstances, every additional sale not only entailed the loss of at least part of these additional costs, but made no contribution towards covering the carrier's capacity-maintenance costs. In the medium term, such a pricing policy is not in the carrier's own economic interest. This being so, DPAG had no economic interest in offering such a service in the medium term. DPAG could increase its overall result by either raising prices to cover the additional costs of providing the service or—where there is no demand for this service at a higher price—to discontinue providing the service, because revenue gained from its provision is below the additional costs incurred in providing it. However, DPAG, by remaining in this market without any foreseeable improvement in revenue restricted the activities of competitors which are in a position to offer this service at a price that covers their costs.

In this decision the Commission started from the principle of identifying the 'incremental cost', which it describes (in a footnote) as comprising 'costs incurred in providing a specific parcel service. They do not include the fixed costs not incurred only as a result of providing a specific service (common fixed costs)'. This means that the Commission looked at the cost of providing the mail-order parcels service and deducted from it the costs which it shared with those services in respect of which it had a universal service obligation. The incremental cost is that additional cost which DPAG incurred *solely* as a result of the mail-order service. In disregarding the common fixed costs shared with the 'universal' services the Commission was being generous to DPAG. The result of this calculation was a low level of cost but, even so, DPAG did not earn enough from its mail-order service to cover it and was operating at a loss. It seems from paragraph 9 of the decision that the removal of the common fixed costs from the equation was because of the universal service obligations (which increased the costs of the OTC service as DPAG had to maintain enough spare capacity to deal with surges in demand while maintaining the statutory standards imposed upon it). It must not be assumed that the same concession would be made to an undertaking which did not have to sustain universal service. The common costs might then have to be allocated on some appropriate basis.[82] It is vital to note that the 'incremental cost' in *Deutsche Post* included *fixed* as well as variable costs. The incremental cost level is different from the crucial costs threshold in the *AKZO* test which, as we saw above, takes account only of *variable* costs. *Deutsche Post* was the first case in which the Commission expressly dealt with cross-subsidization, although it was implicit in the *Tetra Pak II* decision[83] that Tetra Pak had been financing its losses in the non-aseptic carton sector from profits in the aseptic sector.[84] The Commission gave a definition of cross-subsidization in paragraph 6 of *Deutsche Post* and concluded that the mail-order service was being subsidized from the letter monopoly.

There is nothing in *Deutsche Post* to suggest that cross-subsidization is an abuse *in itself*. It is the below cost, predatory pricing which is the abuse. Cross-subsidization merely allows that to be effected. In *UPS Europe* the CFI said that 'the mere fact' that an undertaking with a statutory monopoly on one market used funds derived from that market to acquire control of an undertaking active in a neighbouring market did not in itself constitute an infringement of Article 82.[85] It would be otherwise if the funds had derived from excessive or discriminatory prices, or other abusive practices, in the reserved market.[86]

(x) Recoupment

The notion of predatory pricing rests on the assumption that the predator sacrifices short-term profits for future gains. It will be able to charge prices above the competitive level and make profits which will more than compensate for its losses during the period of predation. The economics literature emphasizes that this ability to recoup is central to recognizing that predatory pricing can, in certain, conditions, be a rational strategy. It is another matter, however, to say

---

[82] 'In the absence of a universal service obligation, however, the incremental-costs-only approach would be too favorable to the dominant company because it would create or legitimize a barrier to entry into the competitive market. In the absence of any objective criterion such as the universal service obligation, the dominant company would have too much freedom to decide which of its costs in the competitive market were incremental and which were not. A rule should not be adopted if its application would lie essentially within the discretion of the company to be bound by the rule. The dominant company's incremental costs (because they can include some fixed costs) are likely to be higher than the average variable costs of its operations in the competitive market. If it is accepted that the incremental-costs-only approach is not appropriate in the absence of a universal service obligation (or the equivalent for some other reason), then it seems that the right approach would be to require allocation of common costs on some appropriate basis. What the best basis should be will depend on the circumstances.' J. Temple Lang and R. O'Donoghue, 'Defining Legitimate Competition: How to Clarify Pricing Abuses under Article 82EC' (2002) 26 *Fordham Int'l LJ* 83, 156.

[83] *Tetra Pak* [1992] OJ L72/1, [1992] 4 CMLR 551; on appeal to the CFI Tetra Pak denied it had been cross-subsidizing, but the Court said that the application of Article 82 did not depend on cross-subsidization having taken place, and did not rule on the issue,

[84] Case T-83/91, *Tetra Pak Rausing v. Commission* [1994] ECR II-755, [1997] 4 CMLR 726, para. 186.

[85] Case T-175/99, *UPS Europe SA v. Commission* [2002] ECR II-1915, [2002] 5 CMLR 67, para. 61.

[86] *Ibid.*, para. 55.

that it should be necessary for a competition authority[87] to show that recoupment is possible or likely[88] before predatory pricing can be held to have occurred.

The present position in the US is that the courts do not find predatory pricing to have occurred unless the plaintiff[89] demonstrates that the alleged predator had a dangerous probability of recouping its investment in below-cost prices. This stems from the Supreme Court ruling in *Brooke Group Ltd* v. *Brown & Williamson Tobacco Corp* in 1993.[90] It means in effect that even if the plaintiff can show below cost prices[91] and an anti-competitive intent, there will be no antitrust violation.[92] The result of this, especially when wedded to the sceptical judicial attitude to predatory pricing shown in the *Matsushita* case,[93] is that it is very hard for predatory pricing actions to succeed in the US courts. It is not difficult for a properly advised defendant to raise sufficient doubts as to the possibility of recoupment.[94]

The position in EC law is different. The question of whether a possibility or likelihood of recoupment is part of the test for predatory pricing was raised in the leading case of *Tetra Pak II* and answered in the negative—at least in the circumstances of that case.

The principles laid down in *AKZO* were confirmed and developed in *Tetra Pak II*.[95] Tetra Pak's share of the dominated market (aseptic cartons) was over 90 per cent although, as discussed above, the impugned pricing conduct took place on the unrelated non-dominated market.

In *Tetra Pak II* the Commission imposed a fine of ECU 75 million in respect of various abuses found to have been committed. One of the abuses was that Tetra Pak had engaged in predatory pricing in the non-aseptic carton market. This included selling at below AVC in Italy. On appeal Tetra Pak argued before the Court that economic theory found predatory pricing to be plausible only if losses can be recouped after the competitor's exit. The Commission had not found that it did have a reasonable chance of recoupment: *ergo* it could not be guilty of predation. The Court said that the Commission did not have to prove that Tetra Pak could recoup.

Case C-333/94 P, *Tetra Pak International SA* v. *Commission* [1996] ECR I-5951, [1997] 4 CMLR 662

Court of Justice

39. In its fourth plea, Tetra Pak submits that the Court of First Instance erred in law when, at paragraph 150 of the judgment under appeal, it characterised Tetra Pak's prices in the non-aseptic

---

[87] Or for a plaintiff where the claim of predatory pricing is made in litigation.

[88] Depending on the standard of proof which is applied.

[89] As explained in Chap. 1, US antitrust laws are enforced in the ordinary courts with either the enforcement agencies or private parties as plaintiff.

[90] 509 US 209, 113 S.Ct 2578.

[91] They were below AVC in *Brooke Group*.

[92] *Brooke Group* was an action brought under the Robinson—Patman Act, 15 U.S.C. § 13(a) on price discrimination but the analysis applies equally to section 2 of the Sherman Act. See J. B. Baker, 'Predatory Pricing after *Brooke Group*: An Economic Perspective (1994) 62 *Antitrust LJ* 585.

[93] *Supra* n. 37.

[94] The question of how courts can judge the possibility of recoupment is discussed in C. Scott Hemphill, 'The Role of Recoupment in Predatory Pricing Analyses' (2001) *Stan LR* 1581. He argues for a 'narrow-but-deep' examination of structure and says that the court should not consider the alleged predator's conduct.

[95] Case C-333/94 P, *Tetra Pak International SA* v. *Commission* [1996] ECR I-5951, [1997] 4 CMLR 662, confirming Case T-83/91, *Tetra Pak Rausing* v. *Commission* [1994] ECR II-755, [1997] 4 CMLR 726, and Commission decision [1992] OJ L72/1, [1992] 4 CMLR 551.

sector as predatory without accepting that it was necessary for that purpose to establish that it had a reasonable prospect of recouping the losses so incurred.

40. Tetra Pak considers that the possibility of recouping the losses incurred as a result of predatory sales is a constitutive element in the notion of predatory pricing. That is clear, it claims, from paragraph 71 of the *AKZO* judgment. Since, however, both the Commission and the Court of First Instance accept that sales below cost took place only on the non-aseptic markets, on which Tetra Pak was not found to hold a dominant position, it had no realistic chance of recouping its losses later.

41. In *AKZO* this Court did indeed sanction the existence of two different methods of analysis for determining whether an undertaking has practised predatory pricing. First, prices below average variable costs must always be considered abusive. In such a case, there is no conceivable economic purpose other than the elimination of a competitor, since each item produced and sold entails a loss for the undertaking. Secondly, prices below average total costs but above average variable costs are only to be considered abusive if an intention to eliminate can be shown.

42. At paragraph 150 of the judgment under appeal, the Court of First Instance carried out the same examination as did this Court in *AKZO*. For sales of non-aseptic cartons in Italy between 1976 and 1981, it found that prices were considerably lower than average variable costs. Proof of intention to eliminate competitors was therefore not necessary. In 1982, prices for those cartons lay between average variable costs and average total costs. For that reason, in paragraph 151 of its judgment, the Court of First Instance was at pains to establish—and the appellant has not criticized it in that regard—that Tetra Pak intended to eliminate a competitor.

43. The Court of First Instance was also right, at paragraphs 189 to 191 of the judgment under appeal, to apply exactly the same reasoning to sales of non-aseptic machines in the United Kingdom between 1981 and 1984.

44. Furthermore, it would not be appropriate, in the circumstances of the present case, to require in addition proof that Tetra Pak had a realistic chance of recouping its losses. It must be possible to penalize predatory pricing whenever there is a risk that competitors will be eliminated. The Court of First Instance found, at paragraphs 151 and 191 of its judgment, that there was such a risk in this case. The aim pursued, which is to maintain undistorted competition, rules out waiting until such a strategy leads to the actual elimination of competitors.

In paragraph 44 the Court stressed that the important factor in the determination of predation is the risk that competitors will be eliminated. This could be shorthand for saying that once that happened Tetra Pak would be able to raise prices. Economic theory, however, suggests that the possibility of recoupment can only be judged after a thorough analysis of the structure of the market and other factors. In fact, the Court does not say in paragraph 44 that it would *never* be necessary to show the feasibility of recoupment, but only that it would not be appropriate *in the circumstances of the present case*. Those circumstances included the fact that Tetra Pak had a quasi-monopoly and that the alleged predation was on a market distinct from the dominated one (so that Tetra Pak could cross-subsidize). Further, there was clear evidence from the data uncovered by the Commission that Tera Pak was pursuing a deliberate strategy of eliminating competitors.

In his Opinion in *Compagnie Maritime Belge* Advocate General Fennelly considered that the possibility of recoupment should be an essential part of the test for predatory pricing.[96] He

[96] Para. 136 of his Opinion in Cases C-395 and 396/96 P, *Compagnie Maritime Belge and others* v. *Commission* [2000] ECR I-1365, [2000] 4 CMLR 1076.

thought it was implicit in paragraph 71 of the Court's judgment in *AKZO*.[97] In the *Compagnie Maritime Belge* judgment the Court did not address the point.[98]

There are good arguments against making feasibility of recoupment part of the legal test. There are problems wherever the burden of proof is placed, predicting recoupment is difficult, and the 'recoupment' gained by the firm may, for example, consist of deterring entrants in other markets, as discussed above,[99] which is impossible to measure. In the following extract the authors approve of the present position of EC law in not having a strict recoupment requirement.

J. Temple Lang and R. O'Donoghue, 'Defining Legitimate Competition: How to Clarify Pricing Abuses under Article 82EC' (2002) 26 *Fordham Int'l LJ* 83, 144–5

There are, however, reasons to treat a strict recoupment requirement with caution. First, it is often difficult to prove what the dominant company could do successfully at an unspecified time in the future. It would be necessary to show that there would be no entry by more competitive or more determined rivals, and that when the dominant company increased its price, it would not attract new entry. It would also be necessary to show that the price elasticity of the product was such that, although buyers were accustomed to low prices, they would be willing to pay significantly higher ones in the future. All of this suggests that the burden of proof is crucial. If the burden of proof was on the party alleging illegal low prices, it would make it difficult to bring a successful case. If the burden of proof was on the dominant company, it would be obliged to prove a negative, that is, to prove that it would be unable to recoup its losses if it tried to do so.

Second, predatory pricing by a dominant company may have anti-competitive effects even if the dominant company does not or could not recoup its losses. The most effective form of predatory pricing is one where a company discourages market entry, or causes exit, by signaling to actual or potential competitors that their profitability in the market in question will be low as long as the dominant company is price leader in that market. This signaling would be more effective, and the effects of it would last longer, if the dominant company did not have to recover its losses, but held its prices only a little above competitive levels. This discouraging or signaling effect is particularly likely to be important if the dominant company is active on several markets, because predatory pricing on one market may discourage market entry on the others. This is particularly important in air transport, where predatory pricing, if it occurred on one route, would discourage entry on the other routes on which the dominant airline was operating.

Finally, predatory pricing may have anti-competitive effects even if the rival is not forced out of the market, but instead decides to raise its prices to approximately the prices of the dominant company. In particular, in a concentrated market predatory pricing may demonstrate the dominant company's ability and willingness to retaliate against aggressive pricing by a competitor, and so may give rise to oligopolistic pricing. In such circumstances it would be extremely difficult to prove that recoupment had occurred, even if it had.

In the Discussion Paper the Commission was constrained by the clear case law of the court in *Tetra Pak II* holding that proof of recoupment is not always required. On the other hand, it was faced with strong arguments from many quarters that condemning low pricing involving a

[97] In that the ECJ said that 'A dominant undertaking has no interest in applying such prices except that of eliminating competitors so as to enable it subsequently to raise its prices ...'. See *supra* 448.

[98] Cases C-395 and 396/96 P, *Compagnie Maritime Belge and Others* v. *Commission* [2000] ECR I-1365, [2000] 4 CMLR 1076.

[99] *Supra* 444.

sacrifice of profits, without any proof that the undertaking would be able to exercise its increase in market power by increasing prices and recouping its sacrifice, would be more likely to harm consumer welfare than advance it. The Commission therefore concluded as follows.

DG Competition Discussion Paper on the Application of Article 82 of the Treaty to Exclusionary Abuses, Brussels, December 2005

122. The issue of recoupment concerns the question whether the negative effect on (the growth of) competition in the market makes the sacrifice of the temporarily incurred losses a good 'investment' from the dominant company's perspective. Is it reasonable to assume that the predation and its exclusionary effect will allow the dominant company to have higher prices in the future than it otherwise would have had and can it thus recoup its losses? This does not require that the dominant company will be able to increase its prices above the level persisting in the market before the predation. For recoupment it is sufficient that the predation avoids or delays a decline in prices that would otherwise occur as a result of the increased competition that would have come from the companies that are now eliminated, disciplined or whose entry is prevented. It may often be possible to exactly quantify the likely price and profit effects . . . . It will in general be sufficient to show the likelihood of recoupment by investigating the entry barriers to the market, the (strengthened) position of the company and foreseeable changes to the future structure of the market. As dominance is already established this normally means that entry barriers are sufficiently high to presume the possibility to recoup. The Commission does therefore not consider it is necessary to provide further separate proof of recoupment in order to find an abuse . . . . In case it is observed that the dominant company's price that was lowered upon entry is again increased after exit or disciplining of the entrant, this may be an indication that recoupment is likely and can help to convincingly show the existence of a predatory strategy. In case of disciplining it should then be observed that also the entrant is raising its price after the dominant company's lowering of price.

The thinking of DG Competition may have moved on since the publication of the Discussion Paper, particularly in the light of the debate which has happened since. It may well conclude in any further guidance it issues that recoupment must be present for predation, but that once the other elements are established the burden is on the dominant undertaking to prove it cannot recoup. However, there is still the problem of the Community Courts. In *France Télécom* the CFI reviewed the case law, cited paragraph 44 of *Tetra Pak II* and concluded as follows.

Case T-340/03, *France Télécom SA* v. *Commission*, 30 January 2007

227. In line with Community case-law, the Commission was therefore able to regard as abusive prices below average variable costs. In that case, the eliminatory nature of such pricing is presumed (see, to that effect, Case T-83/91 *Tetra Pak v Commission*, paragraph 130 above, paragraph 148). In relation to full costs, the Commission had also to provide evidence that WIN's predatory pricing formed part of a plan to 'pre-empt' the market. In the two situations, it was not necessary to establish in addition proof that WIN had a realistic chance of recouping its losses.

228. The Commission was therefore right to take the view that proof of recoupment of losses was not a precondition to making a finding of predatory pricing.

It should be noted, however, that the CFI was specifically referring to cases in which the prices were below AVC.

(xi) Predatory Pricing in New Economy Markets

We have noted previously the particular characteristics of markets in the new economy.[100] One of these is the 'tipping' effect, whereby the competitor who wins takes most (or all) of the market because its product or service becomes the standard. Predatory pricing may therefore be a highly rational strategy in such markets: low pricing may achieve the critical mass of customers which results in the undertaking winning the competition 'for' the market. Further, high technology markets commonly have very high fixed costs and very low variable costs (it costs Microsoft a great deal to develop a new software product and very little to reproduce another copy of it once it is on the market) which may confuse predatory pricing tests based on average variable cost.

Wanadoo, already mentioned above,[101] concerned the pricing of Wanadoo's ADSL services.[102] Wanadoo was a 72 per cent owned subsidiary of France Télécom which at the relevant time had almost 100 per cent of the wholesale ADSL services for Internet service providers. The Commission found that in one period (until August 2001) Wanadoo's prices were below AVC and thereafter they were above AVC but still below ATC.[103] It also found that that the undertaking deliberately pursued a pricing policy which made losses but 'was designed to take the lion's share of a booming market at the expense of other competitors'.[104] Indeed, one competitor went out of business. Wanadoo claimed that its conduct was perfectly rational, in that its pricing attracted new customers who would be profitable in the end (in less than five years). It said that this was a rational way of developing a new market and reaching profitability in the medium term. The Commission, however, saw this reasoning as demonstrating that the pricing *was* predatory, '[i]ndeed, the recoupment of initial losses over a certain period of time is in the most common settings the very objective of a predatory pricing behaviour...Admitting Wanadoo's reasoning in this respect would have led to the conclusion that by essence predatory pricing can simply not exist'.[105] The Commission also rejected the argument that it was inappropriate for it to intervene in a market at a nascent stage.[106] The Commission fined Wanadoo €10.35 million. Seven months later it placed Wanadoo's accounts under review until the end of 2006, to ensure month by month that its prices were not anti-competitive.

The decision was significant in that the demonstrated the Commission's disinclination to alter the fundamentals of the predatory pricing rules to take account to the peculiar characteristics of a new economy market. The Commission stood firm against the argument that it should adopt a 'hands off' approach while the ADSL market developed. The decision was upheld by the CFI in *France Télécom*.[107]

---

[100] *Supra* Chap. 1, 54 and Chap 6.

[101] COMP/38.233, [2005] 5 CMLR 120, IP/03/1025; for some aspects of this case, see *supra* 452. See also R. Klotz and J. Fehrenbach (2003) Competition Policy Newsletter No. 3 (Autumn 2003), 10.

[102] Asynchronous Digital Subscriber Line. It allows broadband services to be provided over the traditional telephone copper wire.

[103] The Commission calculated the costs in a way which it claimed was highly favourable to Wanadoo, for example treating customer acquisition costs as capital expenditures. This lowered Wanadoo's AVC (and therefore the significant cost level for the *AKZO* test).

[104] IP/03/1025; Klotz and Fehrenbach, n. 101, 11.

[105] *Ibid.*, 12.

[106] See *supra* Chap. 1, 55.

[107] Case T-340/03, 30 January 2007.

(xii) The Digital Undertaking

In *Digital Undertaking*[108] the Commission accepted undertakings from a company alleged to be dominant in the software support services market for its own computer systems. It supplied a 'package' consisting of software support and hardware maintenance together.[109] In the undertakings given by Digital to settle the proceedings it undertook, *inter alia*, to ensure a non-discriminatory and transparent discount policy and that 'all discounted prices will remain above average total costs'. Digital reserved the right to grant non-standard price reductions to meet competition but undertook that they would be proportionate and not foreclose or distort competition. It expressly acknowledged that the Commission could initiate proceedings if in specific cases allowances resulted in service prices below its average total costs. This case shows that the Commission recognizes that even dominant firms must be allowed to 'meet' competition.[110] However, the suggestion that the Commission might initiate proceedings if prices were below ATC does not seem to reflect the Court's judgment in *AKZO*. There was nothing in the undertaking about below ATC prices having to be part of a plan to eliminate competition. The answer may be that the Commission was concerned about *selective* price-cutting and that this *would* be practised in order to exclude competitors.[111] Selective price cutting is dealt with further below.[112]

(xiii) Limit Pricing

There is as yet no Community jurisprudence on what is known as 'limit pricing'. Neither the Areeda–Turner test nor the *AKZO* test makes any reference to limit pricing, which is a form of strategic entry deterrence aimed at potential entrants rather than existing competitors. It can occur when the dominant undertaking creates excess capacity and uses this to deter entrants without ever lowering its price below ATC, for if entry is attempted the dominant firm can increase its production and lower its price without going below cost.[113]

(xiv) Transformation Costs and 'Price' or 'Margin' Squeezing

Where an undertaking operates in both upstream (where it is dominant) and downstream markets it should not pursue a pricing policy which means that its competitors are unable to operate profitably downstream. The abuse of price squeezing was described by the CFI in *Industrie des poudres sphériques* [114]:

Price squeezing may be said to take place when an undertaking which is in a dominant position on the market for an unprocessed product and itself uses part of its production for the manufacture of a more processed product, while at the same time selling off surplus unprocessed product on the

---

[108] Commission Press Release IP/97/868; see *supra* Chap. 6.

[109] For the tying aspects of the case see *infra* 521.

[110] See *infra* 474 ff.

[111] As indeed it was in *AKZO* itself. See further, P. Andrews, 'Aftermarket Power in the Computer Services Market: The Digital Undertaking' [1998] *ECLR* 176, 180.

[112] *Infra* 466.

[113] For the economics of this, see F. M. Scherer and D. Ross, *Industrial Market Structure and Economic Performance* (3rd edn., Houghton & Mifflin, 1993), Chap. 4.

[114] Case T-5/97, *Industrie des poudres sphériques SA* v. *Commission of the European Communities* [2000] ECR II-3755, para. 178.

market, sets the price at which it sells the unprocessed product at such a level that those who purchase it do not have a sufficient profit margin on the processing to remain competitive on the market for the processed product.

Basically, a dominant undertaking may try to squeeze out the competitors in two ways (or a combination of them): by low pricing of its own products in the downstream market, or by charging high prices upstream to the competitors. *Napier Brown-British Sugar*[115] was a case of the former. The Commission held that British Sugar abused its dominant position in the upstream, industrial sugar, market. British Sugar also operated in the downstream, retail sugar, market but the margin between its two prices was below its own repackaging and selling costs. Its competitor in the retail market, Napier Brown, which was dependant on British Sugar for its supplies, could not therefore viably operate. The Commission considered this part of a deliberate strategy to force Napier Brown out of the market. In *Deutsche Telekom*,[116] on the other hand, the dominant undertaking effected the margin squeeze by charging its competitors so excessively in the wholesale market that the competitors could not possibly supply customers in the retail market at a price less than the dominant undertaking was charging there. In fact, Deutsche Telekom's wholesale prices were higher than its retail prices.[117] The Discussion Paper says that price or margin squeeze can be characterized as a refusal to supply, in that it may amount to the termination of an existing supply relationship.[118]

B. SELECTIVE LOW PRICING

As can be seen from *AKZO*, predatory pricing may involve not just across-the-board low prices but price discrimination[119]—targeting the low prices on certain customers so that they are charged less than others for the same product. The cases indicate that in some situations the EC authorities are concerned with low prices which are *not* below cost but which are part of a deliberate plan to eliminate competitors through selective price-cutting. These cases can be seen as a species of predatory pricing. However, if predatory pricing is defined as below-cost pricing to eliminate competitors, or as a pricing strategy in which short-term losses are incurred to make long-term gains, then these cases are not instances of predatory pricing. The essential factor in these cases where selective low prices have been held abusive is that *the prices did not involve the dominant undertakings in making losses* (although they may have made less profit than previously). The crucial question is whether it is possible to identify when selective price-cutting constitutes an abuse. This affects the extent to which dominant undertakings may *defend* themselves against competition rather than act to *increase* their dominance.

The first relevant case is *Eurofix–Bauco*.[120] In this case the Commission found that the dominant undertaking, Hilti, had lowered its prices in order to tie customers for its nail-guns into buying its consumables also.[121]

---

[115] [1988] OJ L284/41, [1990] 4 CMLR 196.

[116] [2003] OJ L263/9.

[117] The case is subject to appeal in the CFI, Case T-271/03, judgment pending.

[118] Discussion Paper, para. 220. For a full treatment of margin squeezes, see R. O'Donoghue and A. J. Padilla, *The Law and Economics of Article 82* (Hart Publishing, 2006), chap. 6. Telefonica was fined more than €151 million for a margin squeeze in July 2007, IP/07/1011.

[119] For price discrimination generally, see *supra* 440 ff.

[120] *Eurofix-Bauco* [1988] OJ L65/19, [1989] 4 CMLR 677, on appeal (on the dominance issue only) Case T-30/89, *Hilti v. Commission* [1991] ECR II-1439, [1992] 4 CMLR 16 and Case C-53/92 P *Hilti v. Commission* [1994] ECR I-667, [1994] 4 CMLR 614.

[121] See *infra* 518.

Eurofix-Bauco [1988] OJ L65/19, [1989] 4 CMLR 677

Commission

80. The evidence presented shows that Hilti has a policy designed illegally to limit the entry into the market of competitors producing Hilti-compatible nails. On several occasions Hilti singled out some of the main customers of these competitors and offered them especially favourable conditions in order to attract their loyalty, going in certain cases so far as to give away products free of charge. These conditions were selective and discriminatory in that other customers of Hilti buying similar or equivalent quantities did not benefit from these special conditions. The customers of Hilti who did not receive these special offers are discriminated against and effectively bear the cost of the lower prices to other customers. These special offers were not a direct defensive reaction to competitors, but reflected Hilti's pre-established policy of attempting to limit their entry into the market for Hilti-compatible nails. Only a dominant undertaking such as Hilti could carry out such a strategy because it is able, through its market power, to maintain prices to all its other customers unaffected by its selectively discriminatory discounts.

81. An alternative strategy devised by Hilti to illegally limit its competitors' sales is through its carefully orchestrated policy to damage seriously or even eliminate certain of these competitors' main customers. Internal Hilti documentation fully supports Firth's views that its business was singled out in this way, on the one hand by creating difficulties in supplying Firth and by reducing its discount to uneconomic levels, and on the other hand applying the above described favourable and selective discrimination to Firth's customers.

Application of such a policy not only damages the business of Hilti's competitors and their customers directly, but also has a disciplinary and anti-competitive effect on other potential customers for the independents' nails, in that they can be threatened with similar policies which would then discourage them from buying non-Hilti nails. An aggressive price rivalry is an essential competitive instrument. However, a selectively discriminatory pricing policy by a dominant firm designed purely to damage the business of, or deter market entry by, its competitors, whilst maintaining higher prices for the bulk of its customers, is both exploitive of these other customers and destructive of competition. As such it constitutes abusive conduct by which a dominant firm can reinforce its already preponderant market position. The abuse in this case does not hinge on whether the prices were below costs (however defined—and in any case certain products were given away free). Rather it depends on the fact that, because of its dominance, Hilti was able to offer special discriminatory prices to its competitors' customers with a view to damaging their business, whilst maintaining higher prices to its own equivalent customers.

In this case the Commission was not concerned with the relationship between the undertaking's prices and its costs.[122]

In *CEWAL*[123] the Commission found that undertakings in a collective dominant position had engaged in predatory conduct through selective low pricing targeted at a competitor's customers. The undertakings in this case were parties to a liner conference[124] (CEWAL) which was

---

[122] Although Hilti sought annulment of the Commission decision, this point was not raised in those proceedings (Case T-30/89, *Hilti v. Commission* [1991] ECR II-1439, [1992] 4 CMLR 16; Case C-53/92 P, *Hilti v. Commission* [1994] ECR I-667, [1994] 4 CMLR 614).

[123] *CEWAL* [1993] OJ L34/20, [1995] 5 CMLR 198.

[124] A 'liner conference', according to the UNCTAD Liner Code, is a group of two or more vessel-operators providing international liner services for carrying cargo on a particular route or routes within specified geographical limits, which has an agreement or arrangement within the framework of which they operate under

confronted with competition from an independent shipping line (G & C). Among the practices it adopted to counter this threat was the use of so-called 'fighting ships', which were specially designated CEWAL vessels whose sailing dates were close to those of G & C ships. CEWAL dropped the rates on fighting ships to match those of G & C. The Commission condemned this conduct as an abuse of CEWAL's collective dominant position[125] without an analysis of CEWAL's costs. The prices caused the members of CEWAL some revenue losses, but did not appear to have been below their total costs. The shipping lines appealed, *inter alia*, on the grounds that their prices were not an abuse as they were not predatory within the *AKZO* test.

The Commission decision was upheld by the CFI, focusing on CEWAL's intent to eliminate G & C and the possible effect of its actions.[126] The CFI rejected the argument that CEWAL was merely trying to *meet* rather than *beat* the competition and said that its response to the threat from G & C was not reasonable and proportionate.[127] The Commission was therefore justified in holding that the response by CEWAL's members was an abuse of their collective dominant position. In the appeal to the ECJ the shipping lines argued that the CFI 'erred in law in refusing to recognise that a dominant undertaking may, in reaction to price competition from a new undertaking wishing to penetrate the market, devise a plan designed to eliminate that undertaking by using selective price-cutting, so long as the prices it quotes are not abusive, within the definition given by the ECJ in... *AKZO*... the mere fact that the aim of that price competition was to drive a competitor from the market cannot render legitimate competition lawful'.[128]

Advocate General Fennelly took the view that this was a case of a 'super-dominant' entity setting out to exclude a competitor. In such a situation targeted, selective price cuts designed to eliminate would be an abuse regardless of the relationship of the prices to costs.

Cases C-395 and 396/96 P, *Compagnie Maritime Belge and Others* v. *Commission* [2000] ECR I-1365, [2000] 4 CMLR 1076

Advocate General Fennelly

137. In all these circumstances, the Court of First Instance committed no error of law in finding that the response of Cewal members to the entrance of G & C was not 'reasonable and proportionate'. To my mind, Article [82] cannot be interpreted as permitting monopolists or quasi-monopolists to exploit the very significant market power which their superdominance confers so as to preclude

uniform or common freight rates and other agreed conditions. At the time of the case Council Reg. 4056/86, [1986] OJ L378/4, provided a block exemption for liner conferences which, *inter alia*, allowed horizontal price-fixing between the members of the conference. As Faull and Nikpay said, 'This is without question the most generous exemption which exists in Community competition law especially as it is unlimited in time and is granted regardless of market shares' (*The EC Law of Competition* (Oxford University Press, 1999), 12.108). Reg. 4056/86 was repealed by Council Regulation 1419/2006, [2006] OJ L 269/1. Article 8 of Regulation 4056/86 provided that an abuse of a dominant position within Article 82 was prohibited and that the Commission had power to withdraw the benefit of the exemption if the exemption brought about effects incompatible with Article 82. This provision was referred to by the CFI in Cases T-68/89, etc. *Società Italiana Vetro Spa* v. *EC Commission* [1992] ECR II-1403, [1992] 5 CMLR 302, para. 359, as support for interpreting Article 82 as applying to collective dominance.

[125] For the collective dominance aspects of this case, see *infra* Chap. 11.

[126] Case T-24/93, etc. *Compagnie Maritime Belge Transports* v. *Commission* [1996] ECR II-1201, [1997] 4 CMLR 273.

[127] *Ibid.*, para. 148, and see the discussion *supra* in Chap. 5.

[128] Cases C-395 and 396/96 P, *Compagnie Maritime Belge and Others* v. *Commission* [2000] ECR I-1365, [2000] 4 CMLR 1076, paras. 96–7.

the emergence either of a new or additional competitor. Where an undertaking, or group of undertakings whose conduct must be assessed collectively, enjoys a position of such overwhelming dominance verging on monopoly, comparable to that which existed in the present case at the moment when G & C entered the relevant market, it would not be consonant with the particularly onerous special obligation affecting such a dominant undertaking not to impair further the structure of the feeble existing competition for them to react, even to aggressive price competition from a new entrant, with a policy of targeted, selective price cuts designed to eliminate that competitor. Contrary to the assertion of the appellants, the mere fact that such prices are not pitched at a level that is actually (or can be shown to be) below total average (or long-run marginal) costs does not, to my mind, render legitimate the application of such a pricing policy.

The ECJ held that the prices charged were abusive,[129] but its judgment was couched in narrower terms than the wide sweep of the Advocate General's Opinion. It concentrated on the actual situation, i.e., that this was the conduct of a liner conference.

Cases C-395 and 396/96 P, *Compagnie Maritime Belge and Others* v. *Commission* [2000] ECR-1365, [2000] 4 CMLR 1076

Court of Justice

111. The third ground of appeal concerns the question whether the alleged abuse, as defined in the contested decision and the defence, can properly be so characterised.

112. It is settled case-law that the list of abusive practices contained in Article [82] of the Treaty is not an exhaustive enumeration of the abuses of a dominant position prohibited by the Treaty (Case 6/72 *Europemballage and Continental Can* v. *Commission* . . . paragraph 26).

113. It is, moreover, established that, in certain circumstances, abuse may occur if an undertaking in a dominant position strengthens that position in such a way that the degree of dominance reached substantially fetters competition (*Europemballage and Continental Can*, paragraph 26).

114. Furthermore, the actual scope of the special responsibility imposed on a dominant undertaking must be considered in the light of the specific circumstances of each case which show that competition has been weakened (Case C-333/94 P *Tetra Pak* v. *Commission* . . . , paragraph 24).

115. The maritime transport market is a very specialised sector. It is because of the specificity of that market that the Council established, in Regulation No. 4056/86, a set of competition rules different from that which applies to other economic sectors. The authorisation granted for an unlimited period to liner conferences to co-operate in fixing rates for maritime transport is exceptional in light of the relevant regulations and competition policy.

116. It is clear from the eighth recital in the preamble to Regulation No. 4056/86 that the authorisation to fix rates was granted to liner conferences because of their stabilising effect and their contribution to providing adequate efficient scheduled maritime transport services. The result may be that, where a single liner conference has a dominant position on a particular market, the user of those services would have little interest in resorting to an independent competitor, unless the competitor were able to offer prices lower than those of the liner conference.

---

[129] The fines on the shipping lines were, however, annulled for procedural reasons as the Commission had not stated in its Statement of Objections that it intended to impose fines on the individual members: see *infra* Chap. 14.

117. It follows that, where a liner conference in a dominant position selectively cuts its prices in order deliberately to match those of a competitor, it derives a dual benefit. First, it eliminates the principal, and possibly the only, means of competition open to the competing undertaking. Second, it can continue to require its users to pay higher prices for the services which are not threatened by that competition.

118. It is not necessary, in the present case, to rule generally on the circumstances in which a liner conference may legitimately, on a case by case basis, adopt lower prices than those of its advertised tariff in order to compete with a competitor who quotes lower prices, or to decide on the exact scope of the expression 'uniform or common freight rates' in Article 1(3)(b) of Regulation No. 4056/86.

119. It is sufficient to recall that the conduct at issue here is that of a conference having a share of over 90 per cent of the market in question and only one competitor. The appellants have, more-over, never seriously disputed, and indeed admitted at the hearing, that the purpose of the conduct complained of was to eliminate G & C from the market.

120. The Court of First Instance did not, therefore, err in law, in holding that the Commission's objections to the effect that the practice known as 'fighting ships', as applied against G & C, constituted an abuse of a dominant position were justified. It should also be noted that there is no question at all in this case of there having been a new definition of an abusive practice.

121. The grounds of appeal concerning fighting ships must therefore be rejected as inadmissible or unfounded.

The Court stated that the 'special responsibility' of dominant undertakings has to be considered in the light of the circumstances in each case (paragraph 114) citing *Tetra Pak II*. However, it confined its remarks thereafter to the facts of the case and stressed the specialized nature of the maritime transport sector (paragraph 115).[130] In that context selective price-cutting deliberately made in order to meet the prices of the only competitor was an abuse. The Court expressly declined to say (paragraph 118) when a liner conference *could* legitimately drop its prices from its advertised tariff in order to compete with a competitor, let alone to say when this is *generally* permissible. The general question posed by the case, i.e., when is above-cost price competition designed to eliminate a new competitor illegitimate, remains unanswered. However, it should be noted that in paragraph 119 the Court remarked that the conference had over 90 per cent of the market, and its comments about liner conferences in paragraphs 116–17, read with the reference to *Tetra Pak II*, confirm that undertakings in a monopolistic or quasi–monopolistic position do have a particularly heavy responsibility towards the competitive process.

Selective price cutting arose again in the Commission decision, *Irish Sugar*.[131] Irish Sugar was the sole producer of sugar beet in Ireland and Northern Ireland. It reacted to increasing imports from other Member States by a variety of pricing practices.[132] In particular it dropped its prices to customers identified as most vulnerable to the imports although the reductions do not seem to have taken prices below total cost. As in *CEWAL* the Commission held that the conduct was abusive because of the intent to exclude competition (shown by company documents) and the selective, targeted nature of the price cuts. Again, the undertaking appealed to the CFI on the grounds that it was only defending its position as it was entitled to do, and that its pricing policy could not be considered an abuse.

---

[130] And thus the liner conference had already been given a lot of leeway by the competition rules in the shape of Reg. 4056/86, [1986] OJ L378/4.

[131] [1997] OJ L258/1, [1997] 5 CMLR 666.

[132] See further in the discussion of discriminatory pricing and rebates and discounts, *infra*, 493.

Case T-228/97, *Irish Sugar plc* v. *Commission* [1999] ECR II-2969, [1999] 5 CMLR 1300

Court of First Instance

111. The case law shows that an 'abuse' is an objective concept referring to the behaviour of an undertaking in a dominant position which is such as to influence the structure of a market where, as a result of the very presence of the undertaking in question, the degree of competition is already weakened and which, through recourse to methods different from those governing normal competition in products or services on the basis of the transactions of commercial operators, has the effect of hindering the maintenance of the degree of competition still existing in the market or the growth of that competition (*Hoffmann-La Roche*, paragraph 91 . . .) It follows that Article [82] of the Treaty prohibits a dominant undertaking from eliminating a competitor and thereby reinforcing its position by having recourse to means other than those within the scope of competition on the merits. From that point of view, not all competition on price can be regarded as legitimate (*AKZO*, paragraph 70 . . .). The prohibition laid down in Article [82] is also justified by the consideration that harm should not be caused to consumers (*Continental Can*, paragraph 26; *Suiker Unie*, paragraphs 526 and 527 . . .).

112. Therefore, whilst the finding that a dominant position exists does not in itself imply any reproach to the undertaking concerned, it has a special responsibility, irrespective of the causes of that position, not to allow its conduct to impair genuine undistorted competition on the Common Market (*Michelin* paragraph 57 . . .). Similarly, whilst the fact that an undertaking is in a dominant position cannot deprive it of its entitlement to protect its own commercial interests when they are attacked, and whilst such an undertaking must be allowed the right to take such reasonable steps as it deems appropriate to protect those interests, such behaviour cannot be allowed if its purpose is to strengthen that dominant position and thereby abuse it (*United Brands*, paragraph 189; *BPB Industries*, paragraph 69; Case 83/91 *Tetra Pak II*, paragraph 147; Case T-24/93 *CMB*, paragraph 107 . . .).

. . .

189. Thus, even if the existence of a dominant position does not deprive an undertaking placed in that position of the right to protect its own commercial interests when they are threatened (see paragraph 112 above), the protection of the commercial position of an undertaking in a dominant position with the characteristics of that of the applicant at the time in question must, at the very least, in order to be lawful, be based on criteria of economic efficiency and consistent with the interests of consumers. In this case, the applicant has not shown that those conditions were fulfilled.

It should be noted that this case concerned, once again, an undertaking with a very high market share. In paragraph 189 the CFI specifically refers to an undertaking 'with the characteristics of that of the applicant at the time in question' and relates the abuse to that. It is clear from this judgment at least that the ability of 'super-dominant' undertakings to react to encroachments on their market position is limited, and that they have to act in a way 'based on criteria of economic efficiency' and consistent with consumers' interests. If one looks at the cases in which selective low-but-above-cost pricing has been held abusive this feature of 'super-dominance' is a common element. If such firms are to be held to different pricing standards than other dominant undertakings it would be desirable for the threshold for the status to be clarified and for the economic basis for condemning above-cost pricing to be spelt out. Another element in the cases is the identification of an exclusionary intent (which is similar to the second part of the

AKZO test, where eliminatory intent is relevant in the 'grey' area between AVC and ATC) but it is a serious matter to say that intent can render otherwise perfectly legal above ATC pricing illegal. A third common element in the cases is that they all involved a range of exclusionary practices, so that there was a cumulative effect from a number of abuses. In *Hilti* the dominant firm was pursuing a tying policy by a variety of means,[133] in *Compagnie Maritime Belge* the collectively dominant liner conference, *inter alia*, engaged in the predatory scheduling practice of operating 'fighting ships'[134], and in *Irish Sugar* the undertaking engaged in a number of other abusive practices, including discriminatory, fidelity and target rebates,[135] and product swaps.[136] Lastly, both *Compagnie Maritime Belge* and *Irish Sugar* involved situations of collective dominance.

The Discussion Paper treated the idea that pricing above ATC can be an abuse with circumspection as such pricing can usually only exclude less efficient competitors.[137] It said that it would be an abuse only in exceptional situations. Examples were where 'companies in a collective dominant situation apply a clear strategy to collectively exclude or discipline a competitor by selectively undercutting the competitor and therby putting pressure on its margins, while collectively sharing the loss of revenues'[138] (as in *Compagnie Maritime Belge* itself). Furthermore:

> 129. Another example of such an exceptional situation where price cuts above average total costs could be deemed predatory is where a single dominant company operates in a market where it has certain non-replicable advantages or where economies of scale are very important an entrants necessarily will have to operate for an initial period at a significant cost disadvantage because entry can practically only take place below the minimum efficient scale. In such a situation the dominant company could prevent entry or eliminate entrants by pricing temporarily below the average total cost of the entrant while staying above its own average total cost. For such price cut to be assessed as predatory it ahs to be shown that the incumbent dominant company has a clear strategy to exclude, that the entrant will only be less efficient because of these non-replicable or scale advantages and that entry is being prevented because of the disincentive to enter resulting from specific price cuts.

It will be noted that strict conditions for this exception are laid down in the last sentence. Commentators remarked on paragraph 129:

R. O'Donoghue and A. J. Padilla, *The Law and Economics of Article 82* (Hart Publishing, 2006)

The second example presented in the Discussion Paper is more controversial. It states that price cuts above ATC may be predatory where a single dominant company operates in a market where it has certain non-replicable advantages of where economies of scale are very important and entrants necessarily will have to operate for an initial period at a significant cost disadvantage because entry can practically only take place below the minimum efficient scale.... By pricing above its own ATC, but below that of an entrant, the Discussion Paper states that a dominant frim

---

133 See further *infra* 518.
134 For other aspects of this case, see Chap. 11.
135 See *infra* 493.
136 See *infra* 580.
137 Discussion Paper, para. 127.
138 *Ibid.*, 128.

may commit an abuse. It adds that, for such price cut to be assessed as predatory, it has to be shown that the dominant firm has a clear strategy to exclude, that the entrant will only be less efficient because of these non-replicable or scale advantages, and that entry is being prevented because of the disincentive to enter resulting from specific price cuts.

This example has some theoretical attraction, but its implementation in practice raises significant concern. The basic point suggested is that a dominant firm should refrain from price cuts above ATC where rivals have not yet reached the minimum efficient scale and price cuts above ATC by the dominant firm would prevent them from doing so. Several problems arise. First, it is not clear how a dominant firm can be expected to know that its rivals have not yet reached the minimum efficient sale, or at what point they will in the future. Second, it will usually be very difficult, it not impossible, for the dominant firm to know whether it is pricing below the entrant's ATC and at what point price cuts above the dominant firm's ATC, but below that of rivals, would deny the entrant sufficient scale. (It may also be illegal for the dominant firm to seek such information.) Third, if the entrant can achieve scale over time, capital markets, though imperfect, should find it rational to fund entrants that will become as efficient as the dominant firm. Entrants that are, and will remain, less efficient confer no benefit on consumers and there is harm to consumer welfare in the short and long term in protecting them. Finally, and most importantly, the rule proposed in the Discussion Paper is not sufficiently precise and runs a very significant risk of deterring legitimate price competition.

Furthermore, an eminent US commentator concludes that above cost price-cuts should never be held predatory, but that care should be taken in measuring costs.

E. Elhauge, 'Why Above-Cost Price Cuts to Drive Out Entrants are not Predatory—And the Implications for Defining Costs and Market Power' (2003)112 *Yale LJ* 681, 826–7

Even when incumbents do have market power, restrictions on their ability to adopt reactive above-cost price cuts are unlikely to achieve the objective of encouraging and protecting entry because less efficient entrants cannot survive in the long run, and entrants who are (or will predictably become) more efficient need no encouragement or protection. Further, such restrictions will have harmful effects by raising prices and lowering productive efficiency during any period of price restriction, inflicting wasteful transition and entry costs, as well as distorting innovation and price flexibility in response to changing market conditions. And the restrictions will discourage the creation of more efficient incumbents and entrants, which is ultimately far more important.

This analysis reaffirms the wisdom of the position that antitrust law should not recognize any claim of above-cost predatory pricing. It also helps specify just what should count as costs. Costs should be defined in whatever way assures that an incumbent pricing at cost could not deter or drive out an equally efficient entrant. This test should be met by a cost measure that includes all costs that are varied by the allegedly predatory increase in output, since short-term threats or pricing strategies that exceed short-term costs should not be able to deter long-term investments or entry. Alternatively, if short-term pricing could deter such long-term decisions, this test would be met by a cost measure that reflected the magnitude of predator costs for the sorts of costs that are variable to the rival during the period of entry or investment decisions influenced by the short-term existence or threat of such pricing.

C. THE MEETING COMPETITION DEFENCE

It was seen in the sections above that undertakings accused of abusive low pricing may claim that they are just trying to 'meet' competition, and that although the Court has accepted the right of dominant undertakings to protect their own commercial interests in theory, actions taken in pursuit of this strategy have generally been found abusive. The present position was restated by the CFI in *France Télécom*, in response to WIN's argument that it had the right to align its prices with those of its competitors, even if that led to it charging below cost.

Case T-340/03, *France Télécom SA* v. *Commission*, 30 January 2007

Court of First Instance

176. It must be pointed out first of all that the Commission is in no way disputing the right of an operator to align its prices on those previously charged by a competitor. It states in recital 315 of the decision that '[w]hilst it is true that the dominant operator is not strictly speaking prohibited from aligning its prices on those of competitors, this option is not open to it where it would result in its not recovering the costs of the service in question'.

177. WIN takes the view, however, that the Commission thereby disregards its previous decisions and the case-law of the Court of Justice.

178. In that regard, it should be observed that, in the previous cases relied on by WIN, the conferral on a dominant undertaking of a right to align its conduct was limited. That observation applies both to Decision 83/462 making an order for interim measures and the subsequent judgment of the Court of Justice (*AKZO* v *Commission*, paragraph 100 above, paragraph 134).

179. Indeed, in Decision 83/462, the Commission did not permit AKZO to align its prices generally on those of its competitors but only, in respect of a particular customer, to align its prices on those of another supplier ready and able to supply to that customer. In addition, that authorisation to align prices in very precise circumstances was not contained in the final decision adopted in that case (Commission Decision 85/609/EEC of 14 December 1985 relating to a proceeding under Article [82 EC] (IV/30.698—ECS/AKZO Chemie); OJ 1985 L 374, p. 1).

180. WIN therefore cannot claim on that basis alone that, in its previous decisions, the Commission recognised the right of a dominant undertaking to align its prices on those of its competitors, even where that leads it to charge prices below cost.

181. In *AKZO* v *Commission*, paragraph 100 above, which is the only example by way of case-law referred to by WIN in support of its argument, the Court of Justice admittedly did not call into question, as a matter of principle, the right of a dominant undertaking to align its conduct. However, having held that the Commission was right to find that there was no competing offer in the particular case, the Court did not have to rule on the lawfulness of an alignment of prices by a dominant undertaking on those of its competitors where such alignment involved pricing below cost.

182. It is therefore not possible to assert that the right of a dominant undertaking to align its prices on those of its competitors is absolute and that it has been recognised as such by the Commission in its previous decisions and in the relevant case-law, in particular where this right would in effect justify the use of predatory pricing otherwise prohibited under the Treaty.

183. In the present case, the Commission takes the view that a dominant undertaking should not be permitted to align its prices where the costs of the service in question would not be recovered by the dominant undertaking.

184. It is therefore appropriate to examine whether that restriction is compatible with Community law.

185. It should be recalled that, according to established case-law, although the fact that an undertaking is in a dominant position cannot deprive it of the right to protect its own commercial interests if they are attacked and such an undertaking must be allowed the right to take such reasonable steps as it deems appropriate to protect those interests, such behaviour cannot be countenanced if its actual purpose is to strengthen this dominant position and abuse it (*United Brands* v *Commission*, paragraph 101 above, paragraph 189; Case T-65/89 *BPB Industries and British Gypsum* v *Commission* [1993] ECR II-389, paragraph 117; and *Compagnie maritime belge transports and Others* v *Commission*, paragraph 104 above, paragraph 146).

186. The specific obligations imposed on undertakings in a dominant position have been confirmed by the case-law on a number of occasions. The Court stated in Case T-111/96 *ITT Promedia* v *Commission* [1998] ECR II-2937, paragraph 139, that it follows from the nature of the obligations imposed by Article 82 EC that, in specific circumstances, undertakings in a dominant position may be deprived of the right to adopt a course of conduct or take measures which are not in themselves abuses and which would even be unobjectionable if adopted or taken by non-dominant undertakings.

187. WIN cannot therefore rely on an absolute right to align its prices on those of its competitors in order to justify its conduct. Even if alignment of prices by a dominant undertaking on those of its competitors is not in itself abusive or objectionable, it might become so where it is aimed not only at protecting its interests but also at strengthening and abusing its dominant position.

In the Discussion Paper the Commission discussed a 'meeting competition defence' which would apply to only behaviour which would otherwise constitute a pricing abuse. This would recognize a dominant undertaking's right to minimize short run losses resulting directly from competitors' actions, and would apply only if there were no other economically practicable and less anti-competitive alternatives. It would be subject to a proportionality test which would require 'with a view to protect the consumers' interest, a case by case weighing of the interest of the dominant company to minimise its losses and the interest of the competitors to enter or expand'.[139] The defence would normally not apply if the prices were below AAC and the Discussion Paper states that the conditions are unlikely to be fulfilled even if prices are above AAC.[140]

D. EXCLUSIVE DEALING (SINGLE BRANDING) CONTRACTS

(i) General

An exclusive dealing contract is an arrangement by which a customer is obliged to obtain all or most of its requirements for the relevant product from one supplier.[141] In *Hoffmann-La Roche* the

---

[139] Discussion Paper, paras. 81–3.

[140] *Ibid.*, para. 83.

[141] See P. Lugard, 'Eternal Sunshine on a Spotless Policy? Exclusive Dealing under Article 82 EC' (2006) 2 *European Competition Journal*, 163.

ECJ spoke in terms which suggest that exclusive dealing is *per se* abusive when entered into by dominant suppliers:

An undertaking which is in a dominant position on the market and ties purchasers—even if it does so at their request—by an obligation or promise on their part to obtain all or most of their requirements exclusively from the said undertaking abuses its dominant position within the meaning of Article [82] of the Treaty . . . [142]

The objection to exclusive purchasing commitments (which are also called requirements contracts and, particularly since the Commission's reform of the law of vertical restraints, single branding or non-compete obligations) involving dominant suppliers is that they may be exclusionary and foreclose competitors from the market. The argument against having virtually a *per se* rule against them is that they should be judged by their effect on the market in the specific context of the case. What should matter is whether they directly or indirectly harm *consumers*. They should not be condemned *per se*.

In the Guidelines on Vertical Restraints[143] the Commission says:

Dominant companies may not impose non-compete obligations on their buyers unless they can objectively justify such commercial practice within the context of Article 82.

Objective justification may be possible where 'the anti-competitive effects are kept to the minimum necessary for the attainment of some economic advantage' as, for example, where they provide the customer with the benefit of security of supply.[144]

In *Hoffmann-La Roche* the Court referred to an exclusive purchasing obligation covering 'all or most' of the customer's requirements. In *Soda-Ash–ICI*[145] the Commission said that an obligation or promise on the part of customers to 'obtain the whole or substantially the whole of their requirements' exclusively from the dominant undertaking will constitute an infringement of Article 82. Guidance as to what this means can be derived from the Verticals Regulation where a non-compete obligation is defined as including an obligation on a buyer to purchase 80 per cent of its requirements from one source.[146]

Exclusivity can be stipulated in the contract. In that case the customer will be contractually bound to obtain his requirements solely from the dominant supplier. However, the same result can be reached by the supplier offering inducements to the customer, typically some form of 'loyalty rebate' by which the customer is rewarded for not buying elsewhere. This was the situation in *Hoffmann-La Roche* itself. We see in the section below that the exclusionary nature of rebates and discounts is a controversial topic in the application of Article 82 and closely bound up with the issue of exclusive dealing. It should be noted that the abusive nature of exclusive contracts and loyalty rebates is not removed by the presence of an 'English clause'. This is a clause in a supply contract whereby the customer is allowed to switch suppliers without penalty if the dominant undertaking cannot or will not match more favourable terms offered by another supplier. In *Hoffmann-La Roche*[147] the dominant firm argued that the English clause denuded the loyalty rebate provision of its anti-competitive effect so that there was no abuse.

---

[142] Discussion Paper, para. 89.

[143] [2000] OJ C291/1, para. 141.

[144] J. Faull and A. Nikpay (eds.), *The EC Law of Competition* (2nd edn., Oxford University Press, 2007), para. 4.321. And see the settlement of the proceedings in the soda-ash market, Commission's *XIth Report on Competition Policy* (Commission, 1981), parts 73–6.

[145] [2003] OJ L10/33, para. 142.

[146] [1999] OJ L336/21, Art. 1(b): for the Verticals Regulation, see *infra* Chap. 9.

[147] Case 85/76, *Hoffmann-La Roche v. Commission* [1979] ECR 461, [1979] 3 CMLR 211.

The Court held that, on the contrary, the clause exacerbated the abuse by enabling Hoffmann-La Roche to learn of its competitors' offers.[148] In the Guidelines on Vertical Restraints the Commission says that Article 82 specifically prevents dominant companies from applying English clauses.[149]

In *Hoffmann-La Roche*[150] Article 82 was infringed by exclusive purchasing induced by loyalty rebates. In *BPB Industries* the incentives to exclusivity were not only loyalty rebates[151] but also priority deliveries at times of shortage. The Commission's condemnation of this as an abuse[152] was upheld by the CFI.

Case T-65/89, *BPB Industries and British Gypsum Ltd* v. *Commission* [1993] ECR II-389, [1993] 5 CMLR 32

Court of First Instance

94. As regards the abusive nature of the practice in question, the Court observes that, whilst, as the applicants maintain, it is open to an undertaking in a dominant position and is also a matter of normal commercial policy, in times of shortage, to lay down criteria for according priority in meeting orders, those criteria must be objective and must not be discriminatory in any way. They must be objectively justified and observe the rules governing fair competition between economic operators. Article [82] . . . prohibits a dominant undertaking from strengthening its position by having recourse to means other than those falling within competition based on merits . . . That requirement is not met by the criterion adopted in this case by BG, which was based on a distinction between, on the one hand, customers who marketed plasterboard imported and produced by certain of its competitors and, on the other, 'loyal' customers who obtained their supplies from BG. Such a criterion, which results in the provision of equivalent services on unequal terms, is in itself anti-competitive by reason of the discriminatory purpose which it pursues and the exclusionary effect which may result from it.

Article 82 can be infringed where the supply arrangements do not stipulate exclusivity, or offer rewards in exchange for exclusivity, but the nature of the arrangements is such that exclusivity results, i.e., there is *de facto* exclusivity. This was considered in a lengthy case concerned with freezer cabinets for ice-cream. Freezer exclusivity is the practice whereby frozen goods suppliers (ice cream manufacturers) provide retail outlets with freezers but stipulate that no other supplier's brand can be stored there.[153] It is argued that this creates a strategic barrier to the entry of new competition and reduces the intensity of competition between incumbent firms, because in practice it is impractical for a retailer to make room for a second freezer and he has no incentive to do so.[154]

---

[148] *Ibid.*, paras. 107–8. the Commission objected to an English clause in *IRI/Nielsen, XXXVIth Report on Competition Policy* (1996) part 64.

[149] [2000] OJ C 291/1, para. 152.

[150] Case 85/76, *Hoffmann-La Roche* v. *Commission* [1979] ECR 461, [1979] 3 CMLR 211.

[151] See *infra* 488.

[152] *BPB Industries* [1989] OJ L10/50, [1990] 4 CMLR 464, paras. 141–7.

[153] The issue relates to 'impulse ice cream', that is ice cream sold in individual wrapped portions for immediate consumption, not ice cream bought in multi-packs from supermarkets.

[154] The practice was considered in the UK under the Fair Trade Act 1973 by the MMC in its report, *Ice Cream: A report on the Supply in the UK of Ice Cream for Immediate Consumption*, Cm. 2524 (TSO, 1994), and by the Competition Commission in its report, *The Supply of Impulse Ice Cream* Cm. 4510 (TSO, 2000). In the latter, but

In *Van den Bergh Foods*[155] HB Ice Cream Ltd (which in the course of the proceedings became Van den Bergh Foods and subsequently Unilever Bestfoods) entered into distribution agreements for its impulse ice cream with retailers in Ireland. Under the terms of the agreement a freezer cabinet was made available to the retailer for the storage and display of HB's ice cream at the point of sale. The cabinet was either loaned with no direct charge or leased for a nominal sum which was not collected, and the maintenance and repair of the cabinet was done by HB. The cabinet had to be used exclusively for HB's products. These agreements were found by the Commission to infringe Article 81 and not to satisfy the criteria for exemption in Article 81 (3).[156] The Commission also found that HB held a dominant position in the Irish impulse ice cream market (its market share was 75 per cent) and that its distribution arrangements infringed Article 82.

HB put forward certain arguments which were equally relevant to both Article 81 and Article 82. It argued that the application of Article 81 to the exclusivity provisions in the freezer agreements would be tantamount to interference with its property rights, contrary to Article 295 of the EC Treaty, in that it would permit other manufacturers' products to be stored in its property. The Commission replied[157] that, although the Community legal order recognizes the right to property in Article 295,[158] it is recognized in the constitutions of all Member States that the exercise, as distinct from the essence, of property rights may be restricted in the public interest to the necessary extent. This distinction between the existence and exercise of property rights is a familiar one in EC jurisprudence,[159] particularly in the field of intellectual property rights.[160] It sounds plausible, but the distinction is not theoretically convincing and is difficult to apply in practice. In *Van den Bergh* the Commission said that its condemnation of exclusivity could not be construed as an interference with HB's property rights. In essence, the retailer was paying for the freezer as part of the ice cream price and yet the exclusivity was for HB's benefit. Van den Bergh appealed to the CFI. After reciting the definition of an exclusionary abuse from *Hoffmann-La Roche* and repeating the mantra from *Michelin I* about the special responsibility of a dominant firm not to allow its conduct to impair genuine undistorted competition on the common market, the CFI continued as follows and upheld the Commission's decision.[161]

---

not the former, the practice was held to operate against the public interest. See A. Robertson and M. Williams, 'The Law and Economics of Freezer Exclusivity' [1995] 1 *ECLR* 7 (written after the MMC report) but cf. W. Sibree 'Ice Cream War: In Defence of the MMC' [1995] *ECLR* 203.

[155] [1998] OJ L246/1, [1998] 5 CMLR 530. The decision was suspended by Order of the President of the CFI pending the appeal; Case 65/98 R [1998] 5 CMLR 475. The Commission had originally addressed a Statement of Objections to HB, the ice cream supplier, in July 1993 in which it considered that HB's distribution system infringed both Article 82 and 81. HB therefore modified its distribution system and the Commission was for a time satisfied (see [1995] OJ C211/4). In 1997 the Commission decided that the distribution system still raised competition problems and it addressed a new Statement of Objections to HB on 22 January 1997, which in due course led to the 1998 Decision. In the meantime proceedings initiated in the Irish High Court by Mars, which was a competitor of HB on the Irish ice cream market, asking for a declaration that HB's cabinet exclusivity agreements breached Articles 81 and 82, reached the Irish Supreme Court, which, three months after the decision decided to refer the issue to the Court under Article 234. The ensuing judgment, Case C-344/89, *Masterfoods Ltd v. HB Ice Cream Ltd* [2000] ECR I–1369, [2001] 4 CMLR 449, clarified the status of Commission decisions in national proceedings: for this aspect of the case see *infra* Chap. 15.

[156] See paras. 130–254 of the decision.

[157] Para. 212.

[158] Article 295 (ex Art. 222) EC says '[t]his Treaty shall in no way prejudice the rules in Member States governing the system of property ownership'.

[159] See Case 44/79, *Hauer v. Land Rheinland Pfalz* [1979] ECR 3727, [1980] 3 CMLR 42.

[160] See *infra* Chap. 10.

[161] For the Article 81 aspects of this judgment see *infra* Chap.9.

Case T-65/98, *Van den Bergh Foods Ltd* v. *Commission* [2003] ECR II-4653, [2004] 4 CMLR 1

Court of First Instance

159. The Court finds, as a preliminary point, that HB rightly submits that the provision of freezer cabinets on a condition of exclusivity constitutes a standard practice on the relevant market . . . In the normal situation of a competitive market, those agreements are concluded in the interests of the two parties and cannot be prohibited as a matter of principle. However, those considerations, which are applicable in the normal situation of a competitive market, cannot be accepted without reservation in the case of a market on which, precisely because of the dominant position held by one of the traders, competition is already restricted. Business conduct which contributes to an improvement in production or distribution of goods and which has a beneficial effect on competition in a balanced market may restrict such competition where it is engaged in by an undertaking which has a dominant position on the relevant market. With regard to the nature of the exclusivity clause, the Court finds that the Commission rightly held in the contested decision that HB was abusing its dominant position on the relevant market by inducing retailers who, for the purpose of stocking impulse ice-cream, did not have their own freezer cabinet, or a cabinet made available by an ice-cream supplier other than HB, to accept agreements for the provision of cabinets subject to a condition of exclusivity. That infringement of Article [82] takes the form, in this case, of an offer to supply freezer cabinets to the retailers and to maintain the cabinets free of any direct charge to the retailers.

160. The fact that an undertaking in a dominant position on a market ties de facto—even at their own request—40 per cent of outlets in the relevant market by an exclusivity clause which in reality creates outlet exclusivity constitutes an abuse of a dominant position within the meaning of Article [82] of the Treaty. The exclusivity clause has the effect of preventing the retailers concerned from selling other brands of ice cream (or of reducing the opportunity for them to do so), even though there is a demand for such brands, and of preventing competing manufacturers from gaining access to the relevant market. It follows that HB's contention, set out in paragraph 149 above, that the percentage of outlets potentially likely to be inaccessible owing to the provision of freezer cabinets does not exceed 6 per cent, is incorrect and must be rejected.

164. HB submits that the application of the competition rules in the contested decision constitutes an unjustified and disproportionate infringement of its rights to property, as recognised in Article [295] of the Treaty. It accepts that the right to property is not absolute but says that any restriction on that right must not constitute a disproportionate and intolerable interference with the rights of the owner (see Case 44/79 *Hauer* [1979] ECR 3727). The result of the prohibition of the exclusivity clause is to permit freezer cabinets paid for and maintained by HB to be used for the stocking of ice creams supplied by third parties and that seriously affects its property rights in the cabinets and more generally its economic interests. HB submits that, contrary to the Commission's statement in recital 219 of the contested decision, its property rights could not be appropriately protected by the levying of a separate rental fee for the freezer cabinet. It observes that the management and levying of a rental fee would involve substantial operating costs and that rental would not compensate for the economic dysfunctions which would be caused to its distribution system by the stocking of third-party ice creams in its cabinets. Moreover, it would be placed at a manifest disadvantage in comparison with its competitors, who could continue to make freezer cabinets available without charge.

. . .

170. It is settled case-law that, although the right to property forms part of the general principles of Community law, it is not an absolute right but must be viewed in relation to its social

function. Consequently, its exercise may be restricted, provided that those restrictions in fact correspond to objectives of general interest pursued by the Community and do not constitute a disproportionate and intolerable interference, impairing the very substance of the rights guaranteed (Hauer, paragraph 23; Case 265/87 *Schräder* [1989] ECR 2237, paragraph 15, Case C-280/93 Germany v. Commission [1994] ECR I-4973, paragraph 78). Article 3(g) of the EC Treaty (now, after amendment, Article 3(1)(g) EC) provides that in order to achieve the aims of the Community, its activities are to include a system ensuring that competition in the internal market is not distorted. It follows that the application of Articles [81] and [82] of the Treaty constitutes one of the aspects of public interest in the Community (see, to that effect, the Opinion of Advocate General Cosmas in Masterfoods and HB, at p. I-11371). Consequently, pursuant to those articles, restrictions may be applied on the exercise of the right to property, provided that they are not disproportionate and do not affect the substance of that right.

The appeal to the ECJ was shortly dismissed by Order.[162]

The CFI judgment in *Van den Bergh* marked an interesting stage in the development of the approach of EC law to exclusive dealing. The Commission had held that the agreements infringed Article 81 as well, and the CFI considered their actual effects on the market very carefully, applying the principle in *Delimitis*,[163] before upholding that finding. When it came to Article 82 it can be seen from paragraph 160 that the CFI did not simply view the arrangements as *per se* abusive but held that they breached Article 82 because of their *effects* in preventing competitors gaining access to the market. In fact, the CFI considered it significant that 40 per cent of the retail outlets were foreclosed by HB's freezer policy. It is clearly rational that where Articles 81 and 82 are both applied to the same scenario that the same approach is taken. The economic effects approach under Article 81 thus leads to a more economic approach under Article 82.[164] This way of applying Article 82 to exclusive dealing is further developed in the Discussion Paper, where it is dealt with alongside loyalty (or what the Commission calls there 'conditional') rebates. Shortly, the Discussion Paper states that the Commission is likely to conclude that an exclusive dealing (single branding) obligation has a market distorting foreclosure effect and thus constitutes an abuse; however, the Commission will consider not only the capability of the obligation to do this but also the likely and actual foreclosure effects.[165] In other words, an effects analysis should replace the *per se* approach. Further, exclusive dealing would be able to be justified under the 'efficiency defence', as discussed in Chapter 5.[166]

Exclusive contracts can also be a problem where they limit customers' avenues of supply. This is illustrated by *DeBeers/Alrosa*[167] De Beers is the world's leading diamond mining company. Its current market share is omitted from the decision, but for much of the twentieth century it controlled over 80 per cent of the world supply of rough diamonds. Alrosa, a Russian company, accounts for over 98 per cent of Russian diamond production and is the world's second largest diamond producer. De Beers and Alrosa entered into an agreement by which De Beers undertook to purchase substantial amounts of rough diamonds ($800 million per annum)

---

[162] Case C-552/03 P, *Unilever Bestfoods (Ireland) Ltd* v. *EC Commission* [2006] 5 CMLR 1494.

[163] Case C-234/89 *Stergios Delimitis* v. *Henniger Brau* [1991] ECR I-935, [1992] 5 CMLR 210, see Chap. 4.

[164] O'Donoghue and Padilla, n. 81, 359–60.

[165] Discussion Paper, paras. 149 and 144.

[166] *Supra* 331.

[167] COMP/B-2/38.381, 22 February 2006.

from Alrosa for five years. The Commission took the view that De Beers is in a dominant position on the rough diamond market and that the agreement was the outcome of a long relationship between De Beers and Alrosa aimed at jointly regulating the volume, assortment and prices of rough diamonds on the world market. The Commission considered that the agreement would lead to *de facto* distribution exclusivity for De Beers. Alrosa would be prevented from acting as an alternate and independent supplier outside the Russian Federation. The Commission's concerns were settled by De Beers giving commitments[168] to phase out its purchases from Alrosa by reducing the maximum amount from 2006 to 2008 and thereafter ceasing to purchase altogether. The CFI annulled the decision.[169]

E. DISCOUNT AND REBATE SCHEMES

(i) General

The granting of discounts and rebates[170] is a common fact of commercial life and a major way in which suppliers compete on price and try to attract customers to themselves and away from competitors. The ability to grant discounts is not a characteristic of market power, but the case law on Article 82 establishes that where undertakings *are* dominant their discounting policies will be severely constrained. This is a classic case of the difficult line between competition on the merits and abusive conduct.

Although, as we will see below, Article 82(c) has been applied to discrimination affecting downstream markets, the concern of the Commission and the Court over discount policies has concentrated on the exclusionary primary line injury they are perceived to cause. Such policies have been held to foreclose the market and make it more difficult for smaller competitors to compete. It is possible to see such exclusionary effects as specifically covered by Article 82(b), which forbids 'limiting production, markets or technical development to the prejudice of consumers'.[171] Discounts and rebates are a highly contentious area in which the stance taken by EC law has been widely criticized. In brief, the criticisms are that the law has distinguished between different types of discounts and rebates in a way that makes no economic sense; that it has condemned certain types of rebates as 'loyalty-inducing', and therefore an abuse *per* se, without any analysis of the effects on the market; that it has assumed that an exclusionary effect on competitors means consumer harm; and that it has taken no account of the reasons why undertakings adopt certain discounting and rebating practices and the fact that these might be pro-competitive.[172] In 1999 and 2001 the Commission adopted two decisions, *Virgin/British Airways*[173] and *Michelin II*,[174] which were as controversial as ever. It was widely thought that the

[168] For commitments decisions under Regulation 1/2003, Art. 9, see Chap. 14, 1206.

[169] Alrosa has appealed the commitments decision to the CFI, Case T-170/06, *Alrosa v. Commission* and the CFI annulled it, mainly on grounds of lack of proportionality, judgment 11 July 2007.

[170] Technically a discount is a deduction from a price list and a rebate is refund granted later, but the terms are used more or less synonymously in competition cases.

[171] See J. Temple Lang and R. O'Donoghue, 'Defining Legitimate Competition: How to Clarify Pricing Abuses under Article 82EC' (2002) 26 *Fordham Int'l LJ* 83.

[172] See, e.g J. Temple Lang and R. O'Donoghue, *ibid*; J. Kallaugher and B. Sher, 'Rebates Revisited: Anti-competitive Effects and Exclusionary Abuse under Article 82' [2004] *ECLR* 263; C. Ahlborn and D. Bailey, 'Discounts, Rebates and Selective Pricing by Dominant Firms: A Trans-Atlantic Comparison' (2006) 2 *European Competition Journal* 101; D. Spector, 'Loyalty Rebates: An Assessment of Competition Concerns and a Proposed Structured Rule of Reason' (2005) 1(2) *Competition Policy International* 89.

[173] [2000] OJ L30/1, [2000] 4 CMLR 999.

[174] [2002] OJ L143/1, [2002] 5 CMLR 388.

CFI might overturn these decisions, and take the opportunity to review the law, placing it on what the critics consider a more economically rigorous footing. In the event, at the end of 2003 both decisions were upheld by the CFI and the previous trends in the case law confirmed, and even extended.[175] Furthermore, in March 2007, fifteen months after the publication of the Discussion Paper, which proposed a new dispensation in the treatment of discounts and rebates[176] the CFI *British Airways* judgment was upheld by the ECJ.[177]

Before turning to the case law it is useful to understand what kinds of discount an undertaking may give. In the following extract an economist describes different types of discount and why they might be adopted. He also makes some comment about their treatment under Article 82 which we elaborate upon below. Note that in the last paragraph he describes the type of selective price cutting that we have met above in *Compagnie Maritime Belge* and *Irish Sugar*.[178]

D. Ridyard, 'Exclusionary Pricing and Price Discrimination Abuses Under Article 82—An Economic Analysis' (2002) *ECLR* 286, 288–90

Key categories of pricing, discount and rebate structures

To focus the analysis in this article specifically on price discrimination—i.e., non-cost-related discounts—we consider here some of the various categories of discounts that might be operated by a firm whose business is characterised by fixed cost recovery problems. For the purposes of the illustration below, we take the case of a simply homogenous product industry with fixed per unit production costs, so that any variation in price we observe amounts to price discrimination.

Volume rebate schemes

Perhaps the simplest form of rebate scheme is a system of standard volume rebates, for example offering a 10 per cent discount to all customers whose purchases exceed a certain threshold level. In a very loose way, one could argue that the volume rebates encourage customers to buy more of the firm's product, but such incentives only really apply to customers whose purchases are within reach of the sales level threshold that triggers the volume rebate.

Standard volume rebates tend to be a comparatively blunt instrument for encouraging customers to increase their purchases. Their existence is as much a reflection of large buyer power rather than any seller objective or initiative. Large buyers expect to obtain better terms than smaller buyers, and they can often recognise that the seller's fixed cost recovery problem translates to a negotiating weakness when it comes to large buyers. For suppliers, even those who enjoy significant market power, who have low marginal costs of supply and high fixed costs, any threat of withdrawal of purchases or goodwill by a large buyer carries a significant business risk. Volume discounts are often a reaction to this risk.

---

[175] Case T-203/01, *Manufacture Française des Pneumatiques Michelin* [2003] ECR II-4071, [2004] 4 CMLR 923; Case T-219/99, *British Airways v. Commission* [2003] ECR II-5917, [2004] 4 CMLR 1008.

[176] Discussion Paper, paras. 134–176, *infra* 510 ff.

[177] Case C-95/04 P, *British Airways v. Commission*, 15 March 2007. One can but speculate why the Commission carried on defending the *British Airways* decision before the courts whilst proposing radical changes in the treatment of rebates.

[178] *Supra* 466 ff.

This kind of volume-based rebate is commonly found in real world markets. Many non-economists would characterise such discounts as being 'non-discriminatory' since they treat all like customers in the same way (i.e., there is no 'dissimilar treatment for equivalent transactions', to use the Article 82 wording), and the criteria for achieving the volume discounts are transparent and open to anyone whose purchase volumes meet them. In terms of competition law, such volume discounts are invariably deemed unexceptionable. Yet there is almost no plausible cost function that would make this kind of discount scheme 'cost-related' in the sense that the differences in price were explained by differences in the costs of supply . . .

Sales target rebate schemes

Another commonly observed discount scheme involves sales target rebates. An example would be a small discount to any customer whose purchases in the current year exceed its previous year's purchases by some sales growth target.

The purpose of such a target rebate scheme is to persuade customers to increase their purchases of the firm's product. Since, in an industry characterised by high fixed costs, typical price-cost margins are quite high, even small incremental sales expansions could have big positive effects on the supplier's profits, and this explains the motivation for target rebates.

Target rebates again involve some degree of price discrimination. Indeed, they could lead to a situation where a smaller customer who qualified for the target rebate could achieve a lower purchase price than a big one who did not.

Compared to volume rebate schemes, target rebate schemes of this kind are more specifically focused on growing the firm's sales, since basing the payment of the rebate on an expansion on last year's purchases is designed to induce the customer to try a little harder to increase the amount of business it does with the supplier . . . As such, it is an attempt by the firm to identify an elastic part of demand and to target lower prices at that elastic section of demand in order to induce additional volumes.

. . . there are numerous examples of such target rebates being found to be objectionable by the competition authorities. The reason for the harsher competition law treatment for this form of price discrimination is closely linked to the fact that target rebates are a more intelligent, commercially driven mechanism. They are attractive to the suppliers in question because, properly constructed, they provide incentives to the customer where it matters most, at the margin, to buy more of that supplier's product. But that is precisely the factor that leads such discount schemes to be criticised in competition terms because of their tendency to harm competitor interests by 'rewarding loyalty', 'foreclosing competitors' and acting in other potentially exclusionary ways.

Discounts in return for exclusivity

A third discount scheme a firm might practice is one of exclusivity discounts, whereby the supplier provides an extra discount to the customer who undertakes to purchase all its requirements of the product in question from the firm. Exclusivity discounts are in reality a limiting case of requirements discounts in which discounts are offered in return for a set percentage of that customer's purchases . . .

There are of course several prominent Article 82 cases in which such contracts have been found to be abusive when practiced (sic) by dominant firms. The potential for such discounts to be exclusionary is evident from the nature of the contract. The customer who accepts the dominant firm's exclusivity discount is by definition thereby closing itself off as a potential customer for rival suppliers.

Discounts or rebates 'targeted' against competing suppliers

Finally, the firm might well choose to offer special discounts targeted at a certain class of customer that is perceived as being most likely to switch to a competing supplier. There are various ways in

484 | EC COMPETITION LAW

which this selection of target customers might be made—it could be done on the basis of location (for example, if competing products are imported, customers located close to the border might be most at risk); or on the basis of customer requirements (for example, if competitor products were inferior in quality, those customers with lower quality requirements might be targeted); or simply on the basis of past experience (for example, selecting those customers who currently buy from the competing suppliers).

Aggregated rebates are schemes whereby discounts are given on aggregated purchases of products belonging to different product markets. The objection to this practice is that the scheme acts as a tie-in. If the dominant supplier of widgets also supplies blodgets, and offers a discount scheme whereby purchases of blodgets (for which the customer is not dependent on the supplier) are aggregated with those of widgets for discount purposes, the customer will have an incentive to buy the blodgets from the dominant widget supplier. Aggregated rebates were condemned in *Hoffmann-La Roche*[179] and *Tetra Pak II*.[180] Tie-ins are discussed below.[181]

(ii) Quantity (Volume) Discounts and Loyalty Rebates

The basic distinction made in the cases is between quantity (volume) discounts relating to objective amounts (such as ten widgets for the price of nine) offered on equal terms to all customers without discrimination, and 'loyalty' ('fidelity') rebates.

Loyalty rebates are bound up with the issue of exclusive contracts.[182] As we have seen above, provisions whereby a customer contractually commits himself to buying all his requirements of a product from a dominant supplier have hitherto been treated as virtually *per se* abuses (i.e., always forbidden).[183] As Ridyard explains in the extract above, however, a supplier may offer a customer a rebate if he commits himself to buying all his requirements for the product from that supplier, or a rebate system may be set up so that it rewards customers who *do* buy exclusively.[184] Other rebate schemes, while not actually rewarding exclusivity, may strongly encourage the customer to stay with the supplier. A rebate such as a sales target, for example, may induce a customer to buy a large amount of the product from the dominant undertaking without the customer being contractually bound to do so. Historically at least, the Commission has been extremely concerned about discounts and rebates offered by dominant firms which induce such 'loyalty'. Loyalty means that the customer stays with the dominant firm and competitors cannot win its business. Of course, a customer may choose to stay with an existing supplier because it prefers the product or considers that it gets better service, etc. Loyalty inducing discounts, however, are seen in the Article 82 cases as going beyond this type of competition on the merits. Rather, they enmesh the customer into deals with the dominant supplier with which equally efficient competitors cannot compete. They have an exclusionary effect and foreclose the market. A fundamental question about the application of Article 82 to discounts and rebates is which, if any, discounting practices have such a pernicious effect when adopted

---

[179] Case 85/76, *Hoffmann-La Roche v. Commission* [1979] ECR 461, [1979] 3 CMLR 211.

[180] *Elopak Italia/Tetra Pak* [1991] OJ L72/1, [1992] 4 CMLR 551.

[181] See *infra* 514 ff.

[182] In the terminology now employed by the Commission, 'single branding' or 'non-compete' obligations. See *infra*, Chap. 9.

[183] Case 85/76, *Hoffmann-La Roche v. Commission* [1979] ECR 461, [1979] 3 CMLR 211.

[184] Or a large proportion.

by dominant firms that they are *per se* abuses or at least subject to a strong presumption of illegality, or whether every case should be judged individually to identify any exclusionary effects. The Commission Guidelines on Vertical Restraints[185] baldly state, reflecting the case law, that 'Article 82 specifically prevents dominant companies from applying ... fidelity rebate schemes.' However, current emphasis on economic analysis and on consumer harm as the test for whether the behaviour of the dominant firm amounts to an abuse suggests two things: first, that the actual or likely exclusionary effects in a particular case should be assessed, rather than presumed and secondly, that it should not be presumed that the exclusion of *competitors* harms *consumers*.

The starting-point in the cases has traditionally been that a dominant firm can give quantity discounts without infringing Article 82. However, that simple proposition must be treated with caution as the position of quantity discounts has become increasingly problematic. It was demonstrated in *Portuguese Airports*[186] that to be non-abusive a quantity discount must be non-discriminatory, not just on paper but in fact. Otherwise it will be an abuse contrary to Article 82(c) even if it is not exclusionary. *Portuguese Airports* also raised the issue of whether quantity discounts are legal only to the extent that they reflect efficiencies/economies of scale/costs savings. The ECJ said in that case:

52. None the less, where as a result of the thresholds of the various discount bands, and the levels of discount offered, discounts (or additional discounts) are enjoyed by only some trading parties, giving them an economic advantage which is not justified by the volume of business they bring or by any economies of scale they allow the supplier to make compared with their competitors, a system of quantity discounts leads to the application of dissimilar conditions to equivalent transactions.

Although *Portuguese Airports* concerned a discriminatory, rather than exclusionary, abuse,[187] the statements of the ECJ made there, particularly in paragraph 52, have been relied upon in subsequent cases in both contexts.

The distinction between quantity discounts and loyalty rebates has become increasingly blurred. In *Michelin II*, a quantity rebate scheme (one which was based on standardized targets) was held to be an abuse as it was loyalty inducing. In the sections below we set out the major cases on discounts and rebates[188] and consider what rules (if any) are discernible therefrom. We then look at the suggestions for reform.

(iii) The Cases

a. The *European Sugar Cartel* Case: Rebates in Return for Exclusive Purchasing

The *European Sugar Cartel* case[189] was mainly concerned with a cartel between the European sugar producers but the Commission also found the rebate scheme of one dominant producer to be an abuse. The scheme gave an 'annual quantity rebate' to customers who purchased their annual requirements only from that producer. If the customer purchased elsewhere at all it lost the rebate on the entire year's purchases. The ECJ upheld the decision, and for the first time

---

[185] [2000] OJ C291/1, para. 152. For the Guidelines generally, see *infra* Chap. 9.

[186] Case C-163/99 *Portugal v. EC Commission* [2001] ECR I-2613, [2002] 4 CMLR 1319.

[187] *Portuguese Airports* involved discrimination among airlines using an airport, contrary to Article 82(c). See further *infra* 396.

[188] *Irish Sugar* is mainly dealt with *supra* 471 in the context of selective low pricing: Case T-228/97, *Irish Sugar plc v. Commission* [1999] ECR II-2969, [1999] 5 CMLR 1300 (the Case was appealed to the ECJ, Case C-497/99 P, [2001] ECR I-5333, [2001] 5 CMLR 1082 but only on procedural grounds and the finding of collective dominance).

[189] Cases 40/73, etc. *Suiker Unie v. EC Commission* [1975] ECR 1663, [1976] 1 CMLR 295.

made a distinction between true quantity rebates and loyalty rebates and classified this as the latter:

> ...the rebate at issue is not to be treated as a quantity rebate exclusively linked with the volume of purchases from the producer concerned but has rightly been classified by the Commission as a loyalty rebate designed, through the grant of a financial advantage, to prevent customers obtaining their supplies from competing producers.[190]

The loyalty rebate was an abuse for two reasons. It discriminated against purchasers who did not buy exclusively from the dominant firm (the main thrust of the Commission's objections and an application of Article 82(c)) and it excluded competitors (who would have to offer a low enough price to compensate the customer for the loss of its whole year's rebate).

b. *Hoffmann-La Roche*: The Abusive Nature of Loyalty Rebates

In the seminal case of *Hoffmann-La Roche* the ECJ elaborated on the distinction between quantity rebates and loyalty rebates and laid down the basis for the treatment of loyalty rebates which remains the foundation of the law.

Case 85/76, *Hoffmann-La Roche* v. *Commission* [1979] ECR 461, [1979] 3 CMLR 211

Hoffmann-La Roche (HLR) supplied a number of vitamins. The Commission held that it was in a dominant position[191] and had abused its position by giving loyalty rebates to 22 large customers. HLR appealed. The Court dealt with three arguments on the question of the loyalty rebates: whether such rebates are an abuse, what was the nature of the rebates in this case, and whether they were saved from infringing Article 82 by the presence in the contracts of an 'English clause'.[192]

Court of Justice

89. An undertaking which is in a dominant position on the market and ties purchasers—even if it does so at their request—by an obligation or promise on their part to obtain all or most of their requirements exclusively from the said undertaking abuses its dominant position within the meaning of Article [82] of the Treaty, whether the obligation in question is stipulated without further qualification or whether it is undertaken in consideration of the grant of a rebate. The same applies if the said undertaking, without tying the purchasers by a formal obligation, applies, either under the terms of agreements concluded with these purchasers or unilaterally, a system of fidelity rebates, that is to say discounts conditional on the customer's obtaining all or most of its requirements—whether the quantity of its purchases be large or small—from the undertaking in a dominant position.

90. Obligations of this kind to obtain supplies exclusively from a particular undertaking, whether or not they are in consideration of rebates or of the granting of fidelity rebates intended to give the purchaser an incentive to obtain his supplies exclusively from the undertaking in a dominant position, are incompatible with the objective of undistorted competition within the Common Market, because—unless there are exceptional circumstances which may make an

---

[190] *Ibid.*, para. 513.
[191] For the dominance aspects of this case see *supra* Chap. 6.
[192] For 'English clauses' see *supra* 476.

> agreement between undertakings in the context of Article [81] and in particular of paragraph (3) of that Article, permissible—they are not based on an economic transaction which justifies this burden or benefit but are designed to deprive the purchaser of or restrict his possible choice of sources of supply and to deny other producers access to the market. The fidelity rebate, unlike quantity rebates exclusively linked with the volume of purchases from the producer concerned, is designed through the grant of a financial advantage to prevent customers from obtaining their supplies from competing producers. Furthermore, the effect of fidelity rebates is to apply dissimilar conditions to equivalent transactions with other trading parties in that two purchasers pay a different price for the same quantity of the same product depending on whether they obtain their supplies exclusively from the undertaking in a dominant position or have several sources of supply. Finally, these practices by an undertaking in a dominant position and especially on an expanding market tend to consolidate this position by means of a form of competition which is not based on the transactions effected and is therefore distorted.

The most controversial issue in the famous passage above is that it seems to say that dominant firms cannot enter into exclusive purchasing agreements and cannot operate rebate schemes which have the same effect as an exclusive purchasing agreements: in other words, these are *per se* abusive. It does not depend on assessing the effect of the rebate in the particular case, as it is assumed that if a dominant firm rewards customers for not buying elsewhere, rather than for buying certain amounts from itself (so rewarding negative rather than positive behaviour) it is bound to have an exclusionary effect on competitors. This may have been justifiable in *Hoffmann-La Roche* itself, where on the facts the dominant supplier had designed a system intended to have the same effect as an exclusive (or near-exclusive) purchasing obligation.[193] However, as we see below, the statements in *Hoffmann-La Roche* have been heavily relied upon in subsequent cases where the factual situation and the form of the rebates were different. Moreover, it will be noted that the effect of the assumed exclusion of competitors on *consumers* is not mentioned at all.

The hostility to loyalty as distinct from quantity rebates has led undertakings to present their rebates as related to objective volumes. In *Hoffmann-La Roche* itself the ECJ detected that what appeared at first sight to be quantity discounts were in fact disguised loyalty rebates.[194] The obvious tactic is to calculate the anticipated requirements of the customer for the product and to offer the customer a discount based on that quantity. This failed to get past the Commission in *Deutsche Post*, for example, where the Commission once again stressed that quantity rebates are fixed objectively and applicable to all possible purchasers and that rebates linked to an estimate of each customer's presumed capacity of absorption are loyalty rebates.[195]

c. *BPB Industries*: Quantity Discounts and Loyalty Rebates to Fight New Competition

BPB Industries illustrates very well the traditional distinction between quantity and loyalty rebates. The Commission held that one set of discounts were legal quantity discounts, and the undertaking therefore did not appeal this part of the decision to the Court. The finding that other rebates were unlawful loyalty rebates was appealed.

---

[193] See J. Temple Lang and R. O'Donoghue, 'Defining Legitimate Competition: How to Clarify Pricing Abuses under Article 82EC' (2002) 26 *Fordham Int'l LJ* 83, 94, 110–11.

[194] Case 85/76, *Hoffmann-La Roche v. Commission* [1979] ECR 461, [1979] 3 CMLR 211, paras. 95–101.

[195] [2001] OJ L125/27, [2001] 5 CMLR 99, para. 33.

BPB, through its subsidiary British Gypsum (BG), supplied plasterboard in the UK and Ireland. From 1982 onwards it faced increasing competition from imports from France and Spain and the importers complained to the Commission about the pricing practices BG adopted. The Commission held that BPB/BG was dominant in the plasterboard market in the UK and Ireland. One of the practices it considered was BG's introduction of a 'Super Schedule A' discount whereby all customers (builders merchants) in Hampshire and Dorset were offered special discounts for plasterboard delivered in particularly large lorry loads. The discount was greater than the costs savings actually made.

BPB Industries [1989] OJ L10/50, [1990] 4 CMLR 464

Commission

131. From August 1984 to April 1987, BG operated a scheme of discounts for merchants buying in large loads, in a limited geographical area, the counties of Hampshire and Dorset, where BG was facing particular price competition from Lafarge. Though initially designed, at least in part, as a test exercise to gain experience in the delivery of larger loads than previously, the scheme was subsequently maintained as a competitive measure. Only a part of the price reduction by BG was offset by the cost savings which were actually made. Another part of the price reduction corresponded to additional savings which might have been made had the scheme been operated nationally. This part may therefore be regarded as objectively justified during the initial experimental phase.

132. In any event, the part of the price reduction which was not objectively justified, whether in the initial phase or later, amounted to a small price reduction. Furthermore, the offer was open to all customers albeit, in a fairly limited geographical area. In the area, BPB was facing competition from relatively lower zone prices charged by Lafarge or low prices charged by Lafarge to certain large customers.

133. There has been no suggestion that the Super Schedule A prices were in themselves predatory, nor that they were part of any scheme of systematic alignment. There was a single price reduction to a level broadly equivalent to or slightly below those of Lafarge until April 1985, when Lafarge increased its prices.

134. On the basis of the matters stated above and the arguments presented by BG during the procedure on these points, the Commission concludes that BG's geographically selective Super Schedule A prices in Hampshire and Dorset did not constitute an abuse of BG's dominant position.

It is notable here that the part of the price reduction which was *not* objectively justified was not, on the facts, held to be an abuse, although the reasons for this are unclear.[196] The question of how far quantity rebates must be justified by costs savings is pursued below.[197]

Further in *BPB Industries*, the managing director asked the marketing director how the company could 'reward the loyalty of merchants who remained exclusively with us'.[198] The company then devised a system of payments for promotional and advertising expenses to customers who bought exclusively from it. These were condemned for infringing Article 82, as was the scheme put in place in Northern Ireland for offering rebates to those buying exclusively

---

[196] See M. Waelbroeck, 'Price Discrimination and Rebate Policies under EU Competition Law' [1995] *Fordham Corp L Inst* 147, 159.

[197] *Infra* 501.

[198] [1989] OJ L10/50, [1990] 4 CMLR 464, para. 58.

from BG and not dealing with the importers.[199] The Commission's decision was upheld by the CFI and ECJ. BG argued that the promotional payments were normal commercial practice, made in response to growing buyer power, and that BG was entitled to take steps to protect its legitimate commercial interests.

Case T-65/89, *BPB Industries and British Gypsum Ltd* v. *Commission* [1993] ECR II-389, [1993] 5 CMLR 32

Court of First Instance[200]

The abusive nature of the exclusive purchasing arrangements

65. The Court considers, *in limine*, that the applicants are correct in their view that the making of promotional payments to buyers is a standard practice forming part of commercial co-operation between a supplier and its distributors. In a normal competitive market situation, such contracts are entered into in the interest of both parties. The supplier thereby seeks to secure its sales by ensuring loyalty of demand, whereas the distributor, for his part, can rely on security of supply and related commercial facilities.

66. It is not unusual for commercial co-operation of that kind to involve, in return, an exclusive purchasing commitment given by the recipient of such payments or facilities to his supplier. Such exclusive purchasing commitments cannot, as a matter of principle, be prohibited. As the Court of First Instance stated in Case T-61/89, *Dansk Pelsdyravlerforening* v. *E.C. Commission*, . . . appraisal of the effects of such commitments on the functioning of the market concerned depends on the characteristics of that market. As the ECJ held in Case C-234/89, *Delimitis* v. *Henninger Brau*, . . . it is necessary, in principle, to examine the effects of such commitments on the market in their specific context.

67. But those considerations, which apply in a normal competitive market situation, cannot be unreservedly accepted in the case of a market where, precisely because of the dominant position of one of the economic operators, competition is already restricted. An undertaking in a dominant position has a special responsibility not to allow its conduct to impair genuine undistorted competition in the common Market (Case 322/81 *Michelin* v. *Commission*, paragraph 57 . . .).

68. As regards the nature of the contested obligation, the Court observes that, as the ECJ has held, an undertaking which is in a dominant position in a market and ties purchasers—even if it does so at their request—by an obligation or promise on their part to obtain all or most of their requirements exclusively from the said undertaking abuses it dominant position within the meaning of Article [82] . . . , whether the obligation in question is stipulated without further qualification or whether it is undertaken in consideration of the grant of a rebate (Case 85/76 *Hoffmann-La Roche* v. *Commission*, paragraph 89 . . . , Case C-62/86 *AKZO* v. *Commission*, paragraph 149 . . .). That solution is justified by the fact that where, as in the present case, an economic operator holds a strong position in the market, the conclusion of exclusive supply contracts in respect of a substantial proportion of purchases constitutes an unacceptable obstacle to entry to that market. The fact—even if it were established—that the promotional payments represented a response to requests and to the growing buying power of merchants does not, in any case, justify the inclusion in the supply contracts in question of an exclusivity clause. Consequently, the applicants cannot maintain that the Commission has not established the abusive nature of the practice at issue, and it is unnecessary to give a decision on the dispute between the parties as to the meaning of

[199] The company also put in place a system of priority deliveries for loyal customers.
[200] The judgment of the ECJ merely confirmed that of the CFI.

exclusivity in regard to purchasing since it is in any event clear from the documents before the Court that the contractual condition at issue related to all or nearly all the customers' purchases.

69. Whilst the fact that an undertaking is in a dominant position cannot disentitle it from protecting its own commercial interests if they are attacked and whilst such an undertaking must be conceded the right to take such reasonable steps as it deems appropriate to protect its said interests, such behaviour cannot be countenanced if its actual purpose is to strengthen this dominant position and abuse it (Case 27/76 *United Brands* v. *Commission* . . .). It follows that neither the argument that BG was under a duty to ensure continuity and reliability of supplies nor the argument relating to Iberian's commercial practices can be upheld (Case T-30/89 *Hilti* v. *Commission*, paragraph 118 . . . , Case 226/84 *British Leyland* v. *Commission* . . .).

70. The Court further observes that the concept of abuse is an objective one (Case 85/76 *Hoffmann-La Roche* v. *Commission*, paragraph 91 . . .) and that, accordingly, the conduct of an undertaking in a dominant position may be regarded as abusive within the meaning of Article [82]. even in the absence of any fault. Consequently, the applicants' argument according to which BG never had any intention to discourage or weaken Iberian has no bearing on the legal classification of the facts.

71. Even if it is conceded that one of the aims of that system might, as maintained by the applicants, have been to promote plaster products in general, it must nevertheless be stated that it leads to the grant of payments which are strictly conditional upon exclusive loyalty to BG and are therefore abusive, irrespective of the merits of the argument that brand loyalty is lacking.

72. Similarly, the applicants' reference to their competitors' supply difficulties cannot justify the exclusive supply arrangements which they brought into being, since they cannot reasonably contend that their customers were not in a position to adjust their marketing policy to take account of those difficulties.

73. The argument that the merchants were entitled to discontinue their contractual relations with BG at any time has no force since the right to terminate a contract in no way prevents its actual application until such time as the right to terminate it has been exercised. It should be observed that an undertaking in a dominant position is powerful enough to require its customers not only to enter into such contracts but also to maintain them, with the result that the legal possibility of termination is in fact rendered illusory.

. . .

The practices carried out in Ireland and Northern Ireland

119. . . . the Court considers, first, that it is sufficiently clear from the documentary evidence not contested on this point submitted to it, as previously analysed in connection with the presentation of the Decision, that BG decided to withdraw the 4 per cent rebate that it was granting to Northern Ireland merchants which, it learned, intended to import plasterboard from Spain. At the same time, it decided to grant a rebate of 5 per cent to the merchants who agreed to obtain their supplies exclusively from BG. Such a practice, by virtue of its discriminatory nature, was clearly intended to penalize those merchants who intended to import plasterboard and to dissuade them from doing so, thus further supporting BG's position in the plasterboard market.

120. The Court points out, secondly, that, as the Court of Justice has held (in the judgment in *Michelin*, . . .), the application by a supplier who is in a dominant position, and upon whom as a result the customer is more or less dependent, of any form of loyalty rebate through which the supplier endeavours, by means of financial advantages, to prevent its customers from obtaining supplies from competitors constitutes an abuse within the meaning of Article [82] of the Treaty. In the present case, the rebates granted between June and December 1985 to Northern Irish builders' merchants were indeed intended to prevent them from obtaining products from competing suppliers, it being sufficiently proved that those rebates, being conditional on exclusivity,

necessarily implied that the recipients were not to handle imported plasterboard. It is of little importance, in that regard, whether, as the applicants maintain, the exclusive supply arrangements on which the benefit of the discounts at issue was conditional merely constituted one of several conditions imposed on the merchants.

d. The *Soda Ash* Cases: Top-Slice Rebates

In the *Soda Ash* cases[201] the Commission condemned a pricing structure based on 'top slice' rebates, whereby customers got the basic tonnage, which would have been bought from the dominant undertaking anyway, at the normal price, but were offered substantial discounts on extra amounts above that. These amounted to exclusionary loyalty rebates. They were also discriminatory contrary to Article 82(c) in that the basic tonnage was set at a different figure for each customer, so giving them different costs.[202]

e. *Michelin*: Target Discounts

Target discounts are rebates awarded when customers reach targets in their purchases from the supplier. The customer receives a discount on his purchases if he buys more than a certain amount in a certain period (the reference period). They are seen as loyalty inducing in that they put pressure on the customer to stay with the supplier in order to ensure that the discount at the end of the reference period is obtained. The target may be set according to the customer's perceived capacity to absorb the goods, and often requires the customer to buy a certain amount in excess of his purchases in the past.

Target discounts were first considered, and held to be an abuse on account of their exclusionary effect, in the first *Michelin* case.

Case 322/81, *Nederlandsche Banden-Industrie Michelin* v. *Commission* [1983] ECR 3461, [1985] 1 CMLR 282

Michelin supplied heavy vehicle new replacement tyres to tyre dealers who sold both Michelin tyres and competing brands. It ran a fixed invoice discount and a cash discount for early payment, which were the same for all dealers. These were not found to infringe Article 82. Michelin also offered a discount linked to an annual sales target which was personal to each dealer. A proportion of this variable discount was paid in advance, initially every month and then every four months as an advance on the annual sum. The full sum became payable only if the dealer attained a predetermined sales target. The target was fixed for each dealer by a Michelin sales representative at the beginning of each year. The discount was basically geared to turnover and to the proportion of Michelin tyres sold and the aim was to ensure that the dealer sold more Michelin tyres than he had in the year before although if times were hard it might be sufficient to equal the previous year. Towards the end of each sales year Michelin's sales representative would urge the dealer to place an order big enough to obtain the full discount. The Commission held that the scheme infringed Article 82. This finding was upheld by the Court of Justice.

---

[201] *Soda Ash–Solvay* [2003] OJ L10/10 and *Soda Ash–ICI* [2003] OJ L10/33, replacing *Soda Ash–ICI* and *Soda Ash–Solvay* [1991] OJ L152/40 and 152/21, [1994] 4 CMLR 645; annulled for procedural reasons, Cases T-30/91, etc. *Solvay v. Commission* [1995] ECR II-1775, [1996] 5 CMLR 57 and 91 and Cases C-286–8/96 P, *Commission v. Solvay* [2000] ECR I-2391, [2000] 5 CMLR 454.

[202] [2003] OJ L10/10, paras. 181–2.

Court of Justice

71. In the case more particularly of the grant by an undertaking in a dominant position of discounts to its customers the court has held in its judgments of 16 December 1975 in Joined Cases 40 to 48, 50, 54, to 56, 111, 113 and 114/73 *Cooperatieve Vereniging 'Suiker Unie' UA and others* v. *Commission* (1975) ECR 1663 and of 13 February 1979 in Case 85/76 *Hoffmann-La Roche* v. *Commission* (1979) ECR 461 that in contrast to a quantity discount, which is linked solely to the volume of purchases from the manufacturer concerned, a loyalty rebate, which by offering customers financial advantages tends to prevent them from obtaining their supplies from competing manufacturers, amounts to an abuse within the meaning of Article [82] of the treaty.

72. As regards the system at issue in this case, which is characterized by the use of sales targets, it must be observed that this system does not amount to a mere quantity discount linked solely to the volume of goods purchased since the progressive scale of the previous year's turnover indicates only the limits within which the system applies. Michelin NV has moreover itself pointed out that the majority of dealers who bought more than 3 000 tyres a year were in any case in the group receiving the highest rebates. on the other hand the system in question did not require dealers to enter into any exclusive dealing agreements or to obtain a specific proportion of their supplies from michelin NV, and that this point distinguishes it from loyalty rebates of the type which the court had to consider in its judgment of 13 February 1979 in *Hoffmann-la Roche*.

73. In deciding whether Michelin NV abused its dominant position in applying its discount system it is therefore necessary to consider all the circumstances, particularly the criteria and rules for the grant of the discount, and to investigate whether, in providing an advantage not based on any economic service justifying it, the discount tends to remove or restrict the buyer's freedom to choose his sources of supply, to bar competitors from access to the market, to apply dissimilar conditions to equivalent transactions with other trading parties or to strengthen the dominant position by distorting competition.

74. It is in the light of those considerations that the submissions put forward by the applicant in answer to the two objections raised in the contested decision to the discounted system in general, namely that Michelin NV bound tyre dealers in the Netherlands to itself and that it applied to them dissimilar conditions in respect of equivalent transactions, must be examined.

. . .

81. The discount system in question was based on an annual reference period. However, any system under which discounts are granted according to the quantities sold during a relatively long reference period has the inherent effect, at the end of that period, of increasing pressure on the buyer to reach the purchase figure needed to obtain the discount or to avoid suffering the expected loss for the entire period. In this case the variations in the rate of discount over a year as a result of one last order, even a small one, affected the dealer's margin of profit on the whole year's sales of Michelin heavy-vehicle tyres. In such circumstances, even quite slight variations might put dealers under appreciable pressure.

82. That effect was accentuated still further by the wide divergence between Michelin NV's market share and those of its main competitors. If a competitor wished to offer a dealer a competitive inducement for placing an order, especially at the end of the year, it had to take into account the absolute value of Michelin NV's annual target discount and fix its own discount at a percentage which, when related to the dealer's lesser quantity of purchases from that competitor, was very high. Despite the apparently low percentage of Michelin NV's discount, it was therefore very difficult for its competitors to offset the benefits or losses resulting for dealers from attaining or failing to attain Michelin NV's targets, as the case might be.

83. Furthermore, the lack of transparency of Michelin NV's entire discount system, whose rules moreover changed on several occasions during the relevant period, together with the fact that

neither the scale of discounts nor the sales targets or discounts relating to them were communicated in writing to dealers meant that they were left in uncertainty and on the whole could not predict with any confidence the effect of attaining their targets or failing to do so.

84. All those factors were instrumental in creating for dealers a situation in which they were under considerable pressure, especially towards the end of a year, to attain Michelin NV's sales targets if they did not wish to run the risk of losses which its competitors could not easily make good by means of the discounts which they themselves were able to offer. Its network of commercial representatives enabled Michelin NV to remind dealers of this situation at any time so as to induce them to place orders with it.

85. Such a situation is calculated to prevent dealers from being able to select freely at any time in the light of the market situation the most favourable of the offers made by the various competitors and to change supplier without suffering any appreciable economic disadvantage. It thus limits the dealers' choice of supplier and makes access to the market more difficult for competitors. Neither the wish to sell more nor the wish to spread production more evenly can justify such a restriction of the customer's freedom of choice and independence. The position of dependence in which dealers find themselves and which is created by the discount system in question, is not therefore based on any countervailing advantage which may be economically justified.

86. It must therefore be concluded that by binding dealers in the Netherlands to itself by means of the discount system described above Michelin NV committed an abuse, within the meaning of Article [82] of the Treaty, of its dominant position in the market for new replacement tyres for heavy vehicles. The submission put forward by the applicant to refute that finding in the contested decision must therefore be rejected.

The particular objections to the *Michelin* scheme were therefore that it required the customer to purchase more than in the preceding period, it set a different target for each customer based on exceeding the previous purchases (i.e., it was individualized), it had a long reference period (a year), and it was not transparent. On this basis it could be argued that a more transparent scheme, with a short reference period and less discriminatory targets, would be less likely to infringe Article 82. However, in *Irish Sugar*[203] the Commission unequivocally condemned rebate schemes which are conditional on the customer buying more than in a previous period because they tie the customers to the supplier and foreclose the market to competitors. Although it found that the lack of transparency in Irish Sugar's entire rebate scheme was in itself an abuse (paragraph 150 of the decision) it is clear from *Irish Sugar* that the Commission had fundamental objections to this type of target. The Commission rejected the contention that they are a species of quantity discount. The CFI upheld the Commission's decision:

...the Commission has not committed an error of assessment in taking the view that a rebate granted by an undertaking in a dominant position by reference to an increase in purchases made over a certain period, without that rebate being capable of being regarded as a normal quantity discount (point 153), as the applicant does not deny, constitutes an abuse of that dominant position, since such a practice can only be intended to tie the customers to which it is granted and place competitors in an unfavourable competitive position. The Court would also observe that the reference period used to calculate the target rebates in question, namely the period from April to September 1993, began before the launching, during the summer of 1993, of new brands of sugar by sugar packers competing with the applicant (point 152). As the Commission states, the choice of such a reference period implied that 'the volume-related discounts that [the applicant] granted in spring 1994 and

203 [1997] OJ L258/1, [1997] 5 CMLR 666.

October 1994 . . . must have been closely related to the customer's total requirements for retail sugar (point 1).[204]

In *Coca Cola*,[205] the Commission dealt with the distribution arrangements of Coca Cola's Italian subsidiary. The Commission settled the proceedings by taking undertakings by which the company undertook not to include in agreements concluded with distributors in Member States 'clauses which make the granting of rebates subject to the joint contracting party's purchasing quantities of "Coca-Cola" set individually during a period of more than three consecutive months'. Individually set targets of less than three months were accepted because the Commission considered that the new scheme did not substantially impede the customers from switching suppliers.[206] In 1999, in *Virgin/British Airways*,[207] the Commission for the first time condemned a target scheme in the services sector and on the buying side. As the CFI judgment in the appeal from this decision was not given until four years later it and the subsequent ECJ judgment are dealt with after the *Michelin II* judgment.

f. *Michelin II*: Standardized Volume Targets and other Loyalty-Inducing Payments

In 2001 the Commission adopted another decision holding Michelin to have infringed Article 82, *Michelin II*.[208] This time Michelin was operating a wide range of pricing schemes in respect of the supply of replacement tyres for heavy vehicles in France rather than the Netherlands. The details of these schemes were complex. One of them involved a 'progress bonus'[209] in which the tyre dealer was rewarded if he increased his purchases of Michelin tyres compared to the previous year. The 'target' at which the dealer had to aim was therefore individualised, varying from dealer to dealer, as in *Michelin I*. The Commission roundly condemned it:

> 263. This individualised bonus corresponds exactly to that the Court ruled against in the . . . *Michelin* judgment . . . An undertaking in a dominant position cannot require dealers to exceed, each year, their figures for the previous years and thus automatically increase its market shares by taking advantage of its dominant position.
>
> 264. Here again, the bonus was unfair, because of the requirement imposed by Michelin to increase purchases and because of the insecurity brought about by the individualised determination of the minimum base. The bonus was also loyalty-inducing and market-partitioning since it applied only to purchases made from Michelin France.[210]

In addition to the individualized target rebates, other forms of discounts, rebates, and payments were at issue in *Michelin II*. These were primarily quantity rebates based on standardized volume targets (*rappels quantitatifs*); a 'service bonus' scheme; and arrangements known as the 'Michelin Friends Club'.

---

[204] Case T-228/97, *Irish Sugar plc v. Commission* [1999] ECR II-2969, [1999] 5 CMLR 1300, para. 213. For other aspects of *Irish Sugar* see *supra* 471.

[205] *XIXth Report on Competition Policy* (Commission, 1989), part 50.

[206] The Commission's clearance in 1997 of the *Coca Cola/Amalgamated Beverages* merger [1997] OJ L218/15 was on the basis that Coca-Cola undertook to adopt the 1989 undertakings (para. 212 of the decision).

[207] [2000] OJ L30/1, [2000] 4 CMLR 999.

[208] [2002] OJ L143/1, [2002] 5 CMLR 388.

[209] Some of the schemes changed in their detail during the period under review. The 'progress bonus' became an 'achieved-target' bonus in 1997–8 but essentially it worked in the same way.

[210] The finding against the individualized target scheme was not specifically appealed to the CFI. Michelin did, however, contend in respect of *all* its impugned practices that the Commission should have carried out a specific analysis of their effects. This plea was dismissed.

The quantity rebates were given according to a grid. Rebates were a percentage of the tyre dealers' annual turnover and increased with the volumes purchased during the reference period (a year). The target volumes were not based on estimates of each dealer's purchase requirements. The grid had a large number of 'steps'. When a dealer went up a step by hitting a particular target the extra discount was 'rolled back' and he obtained not just an extra payment on the last tranche but on all previous purchases in the reference period. *Michelin II* was the first time that the Commission had made a decision on a standardized target scheme (rather than an individualized scheme like that in *Michelin I*). The Commission held that it infringed Article 82. The most significant passage in the decision is paragraph 216:

216. Quantity rebates took the form of an annual rebate as a percentage of total turnover (trucks, cars and vans) achieved with Michelin France. To be eligible, the dealer had to achieve the turnover thresholds provided for in the rebate grids. In the first Michelin case . . . , and consistently in more recent cases, the Court of Justice has ruled against the granting of quantity rebates by an undertaking in a dominant position where the rebates exceed a reasonable period of three months (as is the case here) on the grounds that such a practice is not in line with normal competition based on prices. Merely buying a small additional quantity of Michelin products made the dealer eligible for a rebate on the whole of the turnover achieved with Michelin and this was greater than the fair marginal or linear return on the additional purchase, which clearly creates a strong buying incentive effect. In the Court's view, a rebate can only correspond to the economies of scale achieved by the firm as a result of the additional purchases which consumers are induced to make.

In this paragraph the Commission made two highly contentious statements. First, it stated that in *Michelin I* 'and consistently in more recent cases' the Court had ruled that a dominant undertaking cannot grant quantity discounts with a reference period of more than three months. Secondly it stated that a rebate 'can only correspond' (meaning is only legally allowed if it corresponds)[211] to the economies of scale achieved as a result of the customer's extra purchases.[212] Michelin appealed to the CFI, *inter alia*, on the grounds that the Commission was wrong on both these points.

The next objection of the Commission was to the 'service bonus'. Under this scheme the dealer earned 'points' for compliance with various commitments entered into with Michelin. The operation of the scheme left considerable discretion to Michelin. Points could be earned at various times when the scheme was running, for achieving a minimum percentage of purchases of Michelin products,[213] and for the dealer committing himself to systematically returning used Michelin tyres to Michelin for retreading. The Commission said the service bonus scheme was unfair, loyalty-inducing, and (in some parts) equivalent to tied sales.

The 'Michelin Friends Club' was an arrangement by which larger dealers could enter into a closer relationship with Michelin in return for additional payments. The dealers undertook not to divert 'spontaneous demand' away from Michelin; to carry enough Michelin stock to always be able to respond immediately to customers' needs; and to give Michelin certain sales forecasts and statistics. This was to do with the maintenance of the dealer's 'température Michelin'. The Commission found the Club terms to be abusive as they were loyalty-inducing. In rather

---

[211] This may be clearer in the French 'La Cour insiste sur le fait qu'un rabais ne peut que correspondre aux économies d'echelle . . .'.

[212] The Commission had already stated this publicly in two occasions, in a Press Releases on the day of the *Virgin/British Airways* decision (IP/99/504), when it laid down its principles on airline ticket commissions, and in a statement made by the Competition Commissioner when he ordered 'dawn raids' (see *infra* Chap. 14) on the premises of three Coca-Cola bottlers (MEMO/99/42).

[213] At one time the dealer could earn extra points if his purchases of new products amounted to a specific percentage in relation to the regional share of such products.

dramatic terms the Commission said that the dealers were left completely dependent on Michelin, 'Certainly the members of the Club all shared the feeling that there could be no turning back...The commitment they had all entered into could fairly be described as a lifetime one'.[214]

Michelin appealed to the CFI, primarily in respect of the quantity rebates, the service bonus, and Friends Club. It appealed against the progress bonus only insofar as it claimed that the Commission was wrong to find that the combination of all the discount systems together had a further impact, and that it had wrongfully failed to carry out an analysis of the *effects* of the discounting practices.[215] The CFI upheld the Commission's decision in its entirety, despite admitting, in paragraph 85, that the Commission was wrong in suggesting in paragraph 216 that the Court of Justice had expressly held that a reference period could not exceed three months.

The CFI (paragraphs 54 and 55 of the judgment) rehearsed again the definition of abuse from *Hoffmann-LA Roche*, and the special responsibility of dominant undertakings laid down in *Michelin I*. It said again that dominant undertakings may protect their own commercial interests when they are attacked but cannot abuse their dominant position in so doing.[216] It then continued as set out below.

Case T-203/01, *Manufacture Française Des Pneumatiques Michelin* v. *Commission* [2004] 4 CMLR 923

Court of First Instance

...

56. With more particular regard to the granting of rebates by an undertaking in a dominant position, it is apparent from a consistent line of decisions that a loyalty rebate, which is granted in return for an undertaking by the customer to obtain his stock exclusively or almost exclusively from an undertaking in a dominant position, is contrary to Article 82 EC. Such a rebate is designed through the grant of financial advantage, to prevent customers from obtaining their supplies from competing producers (Joined Cases 40/73 to 48/73, 50/73, 54/73 to 56/73, 111/73, 113/73 and 114/73 *Suiker Unie and Others* v. *Commission* [1975] ECR 1663, paragraph 518; *Hoffmann-La Roche* v. *Commission*..., paragraphs 89 and 90; *Michelin* v. *Commission*... paragraph 71; and Case T-65/89 *BPB Industries and British Gypsum* v. *Commission*...paragraph 120).

57. More generally, as the applicant submits, a rebate system which has a foreclosure effect on the market will be regarded as contrary to Article 82 EC if it is applied by an undertaking in a dominant position. For that reason, the Court has held that a rebate which depended on a purchasing target being achieved also infringed Article 82 EC (*Michelin* v. *Commission*...).

58. Quantity rebate systems linked solely to the volume of purchases made from an undertaking occupying a dominant position are generally considered not to have the foreclosure effect prohibited by Article 82 EC (see *Michelin* v. *Commission*..., paragraph 71, and Case C-163/99 *Portugal* v. *Commission* [2001] ECR I-2613, paragraph 50). If increasing the quantity supplied results in lower costs for the supplier, the latter is entitled to pass on that reduction to the customer in the form of a more favourable tariff (Opinion of Advocate General Mischo in *Portugal*

---

[214] *Michelin II*, para. 326.
[215] Michelin also appealed against the amount of the fine.
[216] Citing *United Brands, BPB Industries, Compagnie Maritime Belge*: and *Irish Sugar*.

v. *Commission* . . . , at ECR I-2618, point 106). Quantity rebates are therefore deemed to reflect gains in efficiency and economies of scale made by the undertaking in a dominant position.

59. It follows that a rebate system in which the rate of the discount increases according to the volume purchased will not infringe Article 82 EC unless the criteria and rules for granting the rebate reveal that the system is not based on an economically justified countervailing advantage but tends, following the example of a loyalty and target rebate, to prevent customers from obtaining their supplies from competitors (see *Hoffmann-La Roche* v. *Commission*, cited at paragraph 54 above, paragraph 90; *Michelin* v. *Commission* . . . , paragraph 85; *Irish Sugar* v. *Commission* . . . , paragraph 114; and *Portugal* v. *Commission* . . . , paragraph 52).

60. In determining whether a quantity rebate system is abusive, it will therefore be necessary to consider all the circumstances, particularly the criteria and rules governing the grant of the rebate, and to investigate whether, in providing an advantage not based on any economic service justifying it, the rebates tend to remove or restrict the buyer's freedom to choose his sources of supply, to bar competitors from access to the market, to apply dissimilar conditions to equivalent transactions with other trading parties or to strengthen the dominant position by distorting competition (see *Hoffmann-La Roche* v. *Commission* . . . , paragraph 90; *Michelin* v. *Commission* . . . , paragraph 73; and *Irish Sugar* v. *Commission* . . . , paragraph 114).

. . . .

62. . . . the Court points out that the mere fact of characterising a discount system as quantity rebates does not mean that the grant of such discounts is compatible with Article 82 EC. It is necessary to consider all the circumstances, particularly the criteria and rules governing the grant of the discounts, and to investigate whether, in providing an advantage not based on any economic service justifying it, the quantity rebates tend to remove or restrict the buyer's freedom to choose his sources of supply, to bar competitors from access to the market, to apply dissimilar conditions to equivalent transactions with other trading parties or to strengthen the dominant position by distorting competition (see the case-law cited at paragraph 60 above).

. . .

64. It is apparent from the contested decision that the Commission considers that the quantity rebate system applied by the applicant constitutes an infringement of Article 82 EC because it is unfair, it is loyalty-inducing and it has a partitioning effect . . .

65. However, it may be inferred generally from the case-law that any loyalty-inducing rebate system applied by an undertaking in a dominant position has foreclosure effects prohibited by Article 82 EC (see paragraphs 56 to 60 above), irrespective of whether or not the rebate system is discriminatory. In *Michelin* v. *Commission* . . . , the Court, when considering the lawfulness of Commission Decision 81/969/EEC of 7 October 1981 . . . (. . . *Bandengroothandel Frieschebrug BV/NV Nederlandsche Banden-Industrie Michelin*) (OJ 1981 L 353, p. 33, the NBIM Decision), did not uphold the Commission's claim that the rebate system applied by Michelin was discriminatory but nevertheless held that it infringed Article 82 EC because it placed dealers in a position of dependence in relation to Michelin.

66. This Court considers that it is necessary, first, to consider whether the Commission had good reason to conclude, in the contested decision, that the quantity rebate system was loyalty-inducing or, in other words, that it sought to tie dealers to the applicant and to prevent them from obtaining supplies from the applicant's competitors. As the Commission acknowledges in its defence, moreover, the alleged unfairness of the system was closely linked to its loyalty-inducing effect. Furthermore, it must be held that a loyalty-inducing rebate system is, by its very nature, also partitioning, since it is designed to prevent the customer from obtaining supplies from other manufacturers.

— . . .

95. It follows from all of the foregoing that a quantity rebate system in which there is a significant variation in the discount rates between the lower and higher steps, which has a reference period of one year and in which the discount is fixed on the basis of total turnover achieved during the reference period, has the characteristics of a loyalty-inducing discount system.

96. Admittedly, as the applicant points out, the aim of any competition on price and any discount system is to encourage the customer to purchase more from the same supplier.

97. However, an undertaking in a dominant position has a special responsibility not to allow its conduct to impair genuine undistorted competition on the common market (*Michelin* v. *Commission* . . . , paragraph 57). Not all competition on price can be regarded as legitimate (*AKZO* v. *Commission* . . . , paragraph 70, and *Irish Sugar* v. *Commission* . . . , paragraph 111). An undertaking in a dominant position cannot have recourse to means other than those within the scope of competition on the merits (*Irish Sugar* v. *Commission* . . . , paragraph 111).

98. In those circumstances, it is necessary to consider whether, in spite of appearances, the quantity rebate system applied by the applicant is based on a countervailing advantage which may be economically justified (see, in that regard, *Michelin* v. *Commission* . . . , paragraph 73; *Irish Sugar* v. *Commission* paragraph 114; and *Portugal* v. *Commission* . . . , paragraph 52) or, in other words, if it rewards an economy of scale made by the applicant because of orders for large quantities. If increasing the quantity supplied results in lower costs for the supplier, the latter is entitled to pass on that reduction to the customer in the form of a more favourable tariff (Opinion of Advocate General Mischo in *Portugal* v. *Commission* . . . , point 106).

. . .

100. It must be borne in mind that, according to settled case-law, discounts granted by an undertaking in a dominant position must be based on a countervailing advantage which may be economically justified (*Michelin* v. *Commission* . . . , paragraph 85; *Irish Sugar* v. *Commission* . . . , paragraph 114; and *Portugal* v. *Commission* . . . , paragraph 52). A quantity rebate system is therefore compatible with Article 82 EC if the advantage conferred on dealers is justified by the volume of business they bring or by any economies of scale they allow the supplier to make (*Portugal* v. *Commission*, paragraph 52).

. . .

107. It is then necessary to examine whether the applicant has established that the quantity rebate system, which presents the characteristics of a loyalty-inducing rebate system, was based on objective economic reasons (see, in that regard, *Irish Sugar* v. *Commission* . . . , paragraph 188, and *Portugal* v. *Commission* . . . , paragraph 56).

108. It must be stated that the applicant provides no specific information in that regard. It merely states that orders for large amounts involve economies and that the customer is entitled to have those economies passed on to him in the price that he pays (point 57 of the application). It also refers to its reply to the statement of objections and to the transcript of the hearing (reply, point 91). Far from establishing that the quantity rebates were based on actual cost savings (Opinion of Advocate General Mischo in *Portugal* v. *Commission* . . . , point 118), the applicant merely states generally that the quantity rebates were justified by economies of scale in the areas of production costs and distribution (transcript of the hearing, p. 62).

109. However, such a line of argument is too general and is insufficient to provide economic reasons to explain specifically the discount rates chosen for the various steps in the rebate system in question (see, in that regard, *Portugal* v. *Commission* . . . , paragraph 56).

110. It follows from all of the foregoing that the Commission was entitled to conclude, in the contested decision, that the quantity rebate system at issue was designed to tie truck tyre dealers in France to the applicant by granting advantages which were not based on any economic justification. Because it was loyalty-inducing, the quantity rebate system tended to prevent dealers from being able to select freely at any time, in the light of the market situation, the most

advantageous of the offers made by various competitors and to change supplier without suffering any appreciable economic disadvantage. The rebate system thus limited the dealers' choice of supplier and made access to the market more difficult for competitors, while the position of dependence in which the dealers found themselves, and which was created by the discount system in question, was not therefore based on any countervailing advantage which might be economically justified (see *Michelin* v. *Commission* . . . , paragraph 85).

111. The applicant cannot find support in the transparent nature of the quantity rebate system. A loyalty-inducing rebate system is contrary to Article 82 EC, whether it is transparent or not. Furthermore, the quantity rebates formed part of a complex system of discounts, some of which on the applicant's own admission constituted an abuse . . . The simultaneous application of various discount systems—namely, the quantity rebates, the service bonus, the progress bonus, and the bonuses linked to the PRO Agreement and the Michelin Friends Club—which were not obtained on invoice, made it impossible for the dealer to calculate the exact purchase price of Michelin tyres at the time of purchase. That situation inevitably put dealers in a position of uncertainty and dependence on the applicant.

. . .

113. It follows from the foregoing that the Commission was correct to find that the quantity rebate system applied by the applicant infringed Article 82 EC, *inter alia*, because it was loyalty-inducing.

. . .

140. The granting of a discount by an undertaking in a dominant position to a dealer must be based on an objective economic justification (*Irish Sugar* v. *Commission* . . . , paragraph 218). It cannot depend on a subjective assessment by the undertaking in a dominant position of the extent to which the dealer has met his commitments and is thus entitled to a discount. As the Commission points out in the contested decision (recital 251), such an assessment of the extent to which the dealer has met his commitments enables the undertaking in a dominant position to put strong pressure on the dealer . . . and allow[s] it, if necessary, to use the arrangement in a discriminatory manner.

141. It follows that a discount system which is applied by an undertaking in a dominant position and which leaves that undertaking a considerable margin of discretion as to whether the dealer may obtain the discount must be considered unfair and constitutes an abuse by an undertaking of its dominant position on the market within the meaning of Article 82 EC (see, in that regard, *Hoffmann-La Roche* v. *Commission* . . . , paragraph 105). Because of the subjective assessment of the criteria giving entitlement to the service bonus, dealers were left in uncertainty and on the whole could not predict with any confidence the rate of discount which they would receive by way of service bonus (see, in that regard, *Michelin* v. *Commission* . . . , paragraph 83).

. . .

219. The fact remains that, by its arguments, the applicant merely accepts the conclusion which the Commission reached in the contested decision, namely that the obligations imposed on dealers to provide information and the obligation to accept the list of areas suggested by Michelin only reflect Michelin's desire to supervise distribution in detail (recital 322 of the contested decision). Although some of that information (the balance-sheet and income statement) is public, most of it is not. The applicant's sole aim in imposing on dealers obligations to communicate detailed information on turnover, statistics and sales forecasts, future strategies and the development of Michelin market shares is to obtain information about the market which is not public and which is of value for the carrying out of its own marketing strategy (see, in that regard, *Hoffmann-La Roche* v. *Commission* . . . , paragraph 107). Furthermore, the applicant's right, by way of exception, to examine in detail the activities of the Club members must inevitably increase the dependence on Michelin of the Club members, who, in exchange for fulfilling those obligations,

receive financial advantages (recitals 104 to 106 of the contested decision). Dealers are no longer able to increase the market share of products of rival brands without Michelin being aware of the fact.

220. The obligations referred to at paragraph 215 above are therefore designed to monitor the Club members, to tie them to the applicant and to eliminate competition from other manufacturers. The Commission was therefore correct to characterise those obligations as abusive in the contested decision.

. . .

232. The applicant points out that, in recital 274 of the contested decision, the Commission states that the combination and interaction of the various conditions helped to reinforce their impact and thus the abusive nature of the system considered as a whole. The applicant contends that lawful discounts cannot become unlawful as a result of the cumulative or contagious effect produced by the coexistence of several parallel discount systems. In any event, the Commission has failed to state the reasons why a lawful discount becomes unlawful solely because another discount exists alongside it.

233. The premiss on which the applicant bases its argument is misconceived. In the contested decision, the Commission established that the various discount systems applied by the applicant were unlawful. The Commission did not therefore, in the contested decision, infer the unlawful nature of the system applied by Michelin from the combination of discount systems which were lawful in themselves.

. . .

237. The Court points out that Article 82 EC prohibits, in so far as it may affect trade between Member States, any abuse of a dominant position within the common market or in a substantial part thereof. Unlike Article 81(1) EC, Article 82 EC contains no reference to the anti-competitive aim or anti-competitive effect of the practice referred to. However, in the light of the context of Article 82 EC, conduct will be regarded as abusive only if it restricts competition.

238. In support of its argument, the applicant refers to the consistent line of decisions which show that an abuse is an objective concept referring to the behaviour of an undertaking in a dominant position which is such as to influence the structure of a market where, as a result of the very presence of the undertaking in question, the degree of competition is already weakened and which, through recourse to methods different from those governing normal competition in products or services on the basis of the transactions of commercial operators, has the effect of hindering the maintenance of the degree of competition still existing in the market or the growth of that competition (*Hoffmann-La Roche* v. *Commission* . . ., paragraph 91; *Michelin* v. *Commission* . . ., paragraph 70; *AKZO* v. *Commission* . . ., paragraph 69; and *Irish Sugar* v. *Commission*, . . ., paragraph 111; emphasis added).

239. The effect referred to in the case-law cited in the preceding paragraph does not necessarily relate to the actual effect of the abusive conduct complained of. For the purposes of establishing an infringement of Article 82 EC, it is sufficient to show that the abusive conduct of the undertaking in a dominant position tends to restrict competition or, in other words, that the conduct is capable of having that effect.

240. Thus, in *Michelin* v *Commission* (cited at paragraph 54 above), the Court of Justice, after referring to the principle reproduced at paragraph 238 above, stated that it is necessary to consider all the circumstances, particularly the criteria and rules for the grant of the discount, and to investigate whether, in providing an advantage not based on any economic service justifying it, the discount tends to remove or restrict the buyer's freedom to choose his sources of supply, to bar competitors from access to the market, to apply dissimilar conditions to equivalent transactions with other trading parties or to strengthen the dominant position by distorting competition

(paragraph 73). It concluded that Michelin had infringed Article 82 EC, since its discount system [was] calculated to prevent dealers from being able to select freely at any time in the light of the market situation the most favourable of the offers made by the various competitors and to change supplier without suffering any appreciable economic disadvantage (paragraph 85).

241. It follows that, for the purposes of applying Article 82 EC, establishing the anti-competitive object and the anti-competitive effect are one and the same thing (see, in that regard, *Irish Sugar* v *Commission*, cited at paragraph 54 above, paragraph 170). If it is shown that the object pursued by the conduct of an undertaking in a dominant position is to limit competition, that conduct will also be liable to have such an effect.

The judgment firmly links the legality of quantity rebates to efficiencies. At paragraph 58 the CFI stated that quantity rebates are 'deemed' to lower suppliers' costs, and in paragraph 59 that quantity rebates are not an abuse 'unless' the system is not based on an economically justified countervailing advantage. When this was applied to Michelin's system, however, Michelin was found to have infringed Article 82 because it did not establish what exactly were the costs savings (paragraphs 108–9). This seems to put the burden of proof on the dominant undertaking. The CFI relies on paragraph 56 of the ECJ's *Portuguese Airports* judgment for this. However, *Portuguese Airports* concerned a blatant case of discriminatory pricing by a statutory monopolist which distorted competition downstream, contrary to Article 82(c). It is arguable that the principle stated there should not be extrapolated wholesale into the exclusionary abuse scenario of *Michelin II* without further reasoning.

According to *Michelin II* discounts and rebates given by dominant undertaking therefore fall into one of two categories: economically justified quantity rebates (lawful) and loyalty-inducing rebates (unlawful). Quantity rebates which are not linked to a demonstrable economic justification are loyalty-inducing. All loyalty-inducing rebates are classed with the exclusivity linked discounts condemned in *Hoffmann-La Roche* and appear to be *per se* abuses. The 'effect' of hindering the maintenance of the degree of competition still existing on the market, referred to in the definition of the abuse concept in *Hoffmann-La Roche* and *Michelin I*,[217] does not have to relate to an *actual* effect (*Michelin II*, paragraph 239). It can be presumed by showing that the conduct is capable of it. Moreover, anti-competitive object and anti-competitive effect are the same thing for the purposes of Article 82 (paragraph 241, echoing what the CFI had already said in *Irish Sugar*,[218] albeit not so clearly).

g. *Virgin/British Airways*: Target Incentives on the Buying Side

In *Virgin/British Airways*[219] the Commission for the first time dealt with a loyalty-inducing target scheme in the services sector and on the buying side. The decision resulted from complaints made to the Commission by the rival airline Virgin that the incentives which BA gave travel agents to push its tickets to their customers were anti-competitive and had exclusionary effects. The matter was an episode in the on-going war between BA and Virgin.[220] As explained in Chapter 6[221] the Commission found BA to be in a dominant position by defining a market consisting of air travel agency services in which BA was the dominant buyer. British Airways

[217] At paras. 91 and 70 respectively. See *supra* 435 and Chap. 5, 320.

[218] Case T-228/97, *Irish Sugar plc* v. *Commission* [1999] ECR II-2969, [1999] 5 CMLR 1300, para. 170.

[219] [2000] OJ L30/1, [2000] 4 CMLR 999.

[220] Virgin also mounted an action in the US: for the fate of which see *infra* 514.

[221] *Supra* 378.

(BA) was fined €6.8 million for offering travel agents commission schemes which included extra payments in return for meeting or exceeding their previous year's sales of BA tickets. The Commission particularly noted that the schemes all had one feature in common: meeting its target meant that the agent received an increase in commission not just on the tickets sold thereafter, but on *all* the tickets it had sold in the reference period (payments were 'rolled back'). This meant that 'when a travel agent is close to one of the thresholds for an increase in commission rate selling relatively few extra BA tickets can have a large effect on his commission income. Conversely a competitor of BA who wishes to give a travel agent an incentive to divert some sales from BA to the competing airline will have to pay a much higher rate of commission than BA on all of the tickets sold by it to overcome this effect'.[222] The Commission held that the schemes were exclusionary as 'they represent loyalty discounts as condemned in the *Michelin* . . . and *Hoffmann-La Roche* cases'.[223] It said that the fact that BA's competitors had nevertheless been able to gain market share from BA could not indicate that the schemes had had no effect as 'it can only be assumed that competitors would have had more success in the absence of these abusive commission schemes'.[224] Moreover, at the time of the decision the Commission issued a statement setting out the principles it considered applied to such practices by airlines: target discounts (or commissions) and indeed any discounts not reflecting costs savings or differences in value, were not allowed.[225] The Commission decision also condemned the commission schemes for being discriminatory, contrary to Article 82(c), in that the different levels of commission the travel agents received distorted competition between them.[226]

British Airways appealed, and the CFI gave judgment over four years later.[227] The CFI judgment upheld the Commission decision in *Virgin/British Airways* in its entirety.

In the part of the judgment concerning the exclusionary effect on competitors the CFI judgment followed very closely *Michelin II*. In particular, paragraphs 241–7 were almost identical[228] to paragraphs 54–9 of *Michelin II* (except that paragraph 244 of *BA* refers to rebates having the *effect* of preventing customers going to rival producers rather than being *designed* to do so as paragraph 56 of *Michelin II* said). The CFI then said as follows.

Case T-219/99, *British Airways* v. *Commission* [2003] ECR II-5917, [2004] CMLR 1008

248. It can be deduced from that case-law generally that any fidelity-building rebate system applied by an undertaking in a dominant position tends to prevent customers from obtaining supplies from competitors, in breach of Article 82 EC, irrespective of whether the rebate system is discriminatory. The same applies to a fidelity-building performance reward scheme practised by a purchaser in a dominant position in relation to its suppliers of services . . .

271. It needs to be determined in this case whether the marketing agreements and the new performance reward scheme had a fidelity-building effect in relation to travel agents established

---

[222] *Ibid.*, para. 29.

[223] *Ibid.*, para. 96.

[224] *Ibid.*, para. 107.

[225] Principles concerning travel agents' commissions: Press Release IP/99/504, 14 July 1999.

[226] *Virgin/British Airways*, paras. 108–11.

[227] The decision was dated 14 July 1999, the judgment was delivered on 17 December 2003.

[228] Save for the occasional grammatical detail and the fact that the text is divided into paragraphs slightly differently.

in the United Kingdom and, if they did, whether those schemes were based on an economically justified consideration (see, to that effect, *Michelin*, paragraph 73; *Portugal* v. *Commission*, cited in paragraph 246 above, paragraph 52, and *Irish Sugar*, paragraph 114).

...279. Concerning, secondly, the question whether the performance reward schemes applied by BA were based on an economically justified consideration, it is true that the fact that an undertaking is in a dominant position cannot deprive it of its entitlement, within reason, to perform the actions which it considers appropriate in order to protect its own commercial interests when they are threatened (*Irish Sugar*, paragraph 112).

280. However, the protection of the competitive position of an undertaking which, like BA, occupies a dominant position must, at the very least, in order to be lawful, be based on criteria of economic efficiency (*Irish Sugar*, paragraph 189).

281. In this case, BA does not appear to have demonstrated that the fidelity-building character of its performance reward schemes was based on an economically justified consideration.

. . . .

293. Finally, BA cannot accuse the Commission of failing to demonstrate that its practices produced an exclusionary effect. In the first place, for the purposes of establishing an infringement of Article 82 EC, it is not necessary to demonstrate that the abuse in question had a concrete effect on the markets concerned. It is sufficient in that respect to demonstrate that the abusive conduct of the undertaking in a dominant position tends to restrict competition, or, in other words, that the conduct is capable of having, or likely to have, such an effect.

294. Moreover, it appears not only that the disputed practices were indeed likely to have a restrictive effect on the United Kingdom markets for air travel agency services and air transport, but also that such an effect has been demonstrated in a concrete way by the Commission.

295. Since, at the time of the conduct complained of, travel agents established in the United Kingdom carried out 85 per cent of all air ticket sales in the territory of the United Kingdom, BA's abusive conduct on the United Kingdom market for air travel agency services cannot fail to have had the effect of excluding competing airlines (to their detriment) from the United Kingdom air transport markets, by reason of the close nexus existing between the markets in question, as has been established in the examination of the fourth plea.

296. By reason of that effect produced by the reward schemes applied by BA on the United Kingdom air transport markets, the Court cannot accept BA's argument that the contested decision contains no analysis of the air transport markets or empirical proof of the damage which its financial incentive schemes caused to competitor airlines or to travellers.

297. Furthermore, where an undertaking in a dominant position actually puts into operation a practice generating the effect of ousting its competitors, the fact that the hoped-for result is not achieved is not sufficient to prevent a finding of abuse of a dominant position within the meaning of Article 82 EC.

298. Moreover, the growth in the market shares of some of BA's airline competitors, which was modest in absolute value having regard to the small size of their original market shares, does not mean that BA's practices had no effect. In the absence of those practices, it may legitimately be considered that the market shares of those competitors would have been able to grow more significantly (see, to that effect, *Compagnie Maritime Belge Transports*, paragraph 149).

299. The Commission did not therefore make any errors of assessment in holding that BA contravened Article 82 EC by applying to air travel agents in the United Kingdom performance reward schemes that were both discriminatory against some of their beneficiaries in relation to others and had as their object and effect, without any economically justified consideration, the reward of the loyalty of those agents to BA and thereby the ousting of rival airlines both from the United Kingdom market for air travel agency services and, as a necessary consequence, from the United Kingdom air travel markets.

> . . .
>
> 311. Since Article 82 EC is aimed at penalising even an objective detriment to the structure of competition itself (Case 6/72 *Europemballage and Continental Can* v. *Commission* [1973] ECR 215, paragraph 26), BA's argument that there is no proof of damage caused to consumers by its reward schemes cannot be accepted.

There is an interesting difference with *Michelin II*. That case (no doubt because of the facts) considered economic justification such as costs savings only in respect of quantity discounts. In paragraph 271 of the *British Airways* judgment however, the CFI said that *loyalty-inducing rebates* infringe Article 82 unless they are based on 'economically justified considerations'. This suggested that not all loyalty-inducing rebates are *per se* abuses. A dominant undertaking could presumably, on this basis, justify such a rebate. This is a less black and white world than that conjured up by *Michelin II*. Of course, British Airways failed to show such justification. Again, the CFI agreed with the Commission that concrete effects on the market did not have to be proved (paragraph 293). In perhaps the most striking passage in the judgment the CFI agreed with the Commission that the fact that the market shares of some of BA's competitors had actually increased during the relevant period did not disprove the exclusionary effect of the commission payments (paragraph 298). The CFI cited its own judgment in *Compagnie Maritime Belge* for this approach. Finally, in paragraph 311 the CFI considered that Article 82 is aimed at the protection of the competitive structure and so dismissed the argument that there was no proof of consumer harm.

BA appealed to the ECJ. As already noted, there had in the intervening three years been an ever more intensive debate about the EC's approach to rebates, and a general consensus had emerged that it needed to be realigned towards a concern with effects on consumers rather than with formalistic analysis and presumptions. An innovative way of assessing the exclusionary effects of rebates was set out in the Discussion Paper. Nevertheless, the *British Airways* judgment was upheld by the ECJ, largely on the basis of its previous case-law.

Case C-95/04 P, *British Airways* v. *Commission*, 15 March 2007

British Airways began by arguing that 'in order to distinguish between legitimate competition on price and unlawful anti-competitive or exclusionary conduct, the Court of First Instance should have applied subparagraph (b) of the second paragraph of Article 82 EC, according to which practices constituting an abuse of a dominant position may, in particular, consist in limiting production, markets or technical development to the prejudice of consumers. It should therefore have verified whether BA had actually limited the markets of rival airlines and whether a prejudice to consumers had resulted'.

Court of Justice

57. Concerning, first, the plea that the Court of First Instance wrongly failed to base its argument on the criteria in subparagraph (b) of the second paragraph of Article 82 EC in assessing whether the bonus schemes at issue were abusive, the list of abusive practices contained in Article [82] EC is not exhaustive, so that the practices there mentioned are merely examples of abuses of a dominant position (see, to that effect, Case C-333/94 P *Tetra Pak* v *Commission* [1996] ECR I-5951, paragraph 37). According to consistent case-law, the list of abusive practices contained in that

provision does not exhaust the methods of abusing a dominant position prohibited by the EC Treaty (Case 6/72 *Europemballage and Continental Can* v *Commission* [1973] ECR 215, paragraph 26; Joined Cases C-395/96 P and C-396/96 P *Compagnie maritime belge transports a.o.* v *Commission* [2000] ECR I-1365, paragraph 112).

58. It follows that discounts and bonuses granted by undertakings in a dominant position may be contrary to Article 82 EC even where they do not correspond to any of the examples mentioned in the second paragraph of that article. Thus, in determining that fidelity discounts had an exclusionary effect, the Court based its argument in *Hoffmann-La Roche* and *Michelin* on Article [82] ... .in its entirety, and not just on subparagraph (b) of its second paragraph. Moreover, in its judgment in Joined Cases 40/73 to 48/73, 50/73, 54/73 to 56/73, 111/73, 113/73 and 114/73 *Suiker Unie and Others* v *Commission* [1975] ECR 1663, paragraph 523, concerning fidelity rebates, the Court expressly referred to subparagraph (c) of the second paragraph of Article 86 of the EEC Treaty, according to which practices constituting abuse of a dominant position may consist, for example, in applying dissimilar conditions to equivalent transactions with other trading parties, thereby placing them at a competitive disadvantage.

59. The plea that the Court of First Instance erred in law by not basing its argument on the criteria in subparagraph (b) of the second paragraph of Article 82 EC is therefore unfounded.

60. Nor does it appear that the Court's assessment of the exclusionary effect of the bonus schemes in question was based on a misapplication of the case-law of the Court of Justice.

61. In the *Hoffmann-La Roche* and *Michelin* judgments, the Court of Justice found that certain discounts granted by two undertakings in a dominant position were abusive in character.

62. The first of those two judgments concerned discounts granted to undertakings whose business was the production or sale of vitamins, and the grant of which was, for most of the time, expressly linked to the condition that the co-contractor obtained its supplies over a given period entirely or mainly from Hoffmann-La Roche. The Court found such a discount system an abuse of a dominant position and stated that the granting of fidelity discounts in order to give the buyer an incentive to obtain its supplies exclusively from the undertaking in a dominant position was incompatible with the objective of undistorted competition within the common market (*Hoffmann-La Roche*, paragraph 90).

63. In *Michelin*, unlike in *Hoffmann-La Roche*, Michelin's co-contractors were not obliged to obtain their supplies wholly or partially from Michelin. However, the variable annual discounts granted by that undertaking were linked to objectives in the sense that, in order to benefit from them, its co-contractors had to attain individualised sales results. In that case, the Court found a series of factors which led it to regard the discount system in question as an abuse of a dominant position. In particular, the system was based on a relatively long reference period, namely a year, its functioning was non-transparent for co-contractors, and the differences in market share between Michelin and its main competitors were significant (see, to that effect, *Michelin*, paragraphs 81 to 83).

64. Contrary to BA's argument, it cannot be inferred from those two judgments that bonuses and discounts granted by undertakings in a dominant position are abusive only in the circumstances there described. As the Advocate General has stated in point 41 of her Opinion, the decisive factor is rather the underlying factors which have guided the previous case-law of the Court of Justice and which can also be transposed to a case such as the present.

65. In that respect, *Michelin* is particularly relevant to the present case, since it concerns a discount system depending on the attainment of individual sales objectives which constituted neither discounts for quantity, linked exclusively to the volume of purchases, nor fidelity discounts within the meaning of the judgment in *Hoffmann-La Roche*, since the system established by Michelin did not contain any obligation on the part of resellers to obtain all or a given proportion of its supplies from the dominant undertaking.

66. Concerning the application of Article 82 EC to a system of discounts dependent on sales objectives, paragraph 70 of the *Michelin* judgment shows that, in prohibiting the abuse of a dominant market position in so far as trade between Member States is capable of being affected, that article refers to conduct which is such as to influence the structure of a market where, as a result of the very presence of the undertaking in question, the degree of competition is already weakened and which, through recourse to methods different from those governing normal competition in products or services on the basis of the transactions of commercial operators, has the effect of hindering the maintenance of the degree of competition still existing in the market or the growth of that competition.

67. In order to determine whether the undertaking in a dominant position has abused such a position by applying a system of discounts such as that described in paragraph 65 of this judgment, the Court has held that it is necessary to consider all the circumstances, particularly the criteria and rules governing the grant of the discount, and to investigate whether, in providing an advantage not based on any economic service justifying it, the discount tends to remove or restrict the buyer's freedom to choose his sources of supply, to bar competitors from access to the market, to apply dissimilar conditions to equivalent transactions with other trading parties or to strengthen the dominant position by distorting competition (*Michelin*, paragraph 73).

68. It follows that in determining whether, on the part of an undertaking in a dominant position, a system of discounts or bonuses which constitute neither quantity discounts or bonuses nor fidelity discounts or bonuses within the meaning of the judgment in *Hoffmann-La Roche* constitutes an abuse, it first has to be determined whether those discounts or bonuses can produce an exclusionary effect, that is to say whether they are capable, first, of making market entry very difficult or impossible for competitors of the undertaking in a dominant position and, secondly, of making it more difficult or impossible for its co-contractors to choose between various sources of supply or commercial partners.

69. It then needs to be examined whether there is an objective economic justification for the discounts and bonuses granted. In accordance with the analysis carried out by the Court of First Instance in paragraphs 279 to 291 of the judgment under appeal, an undertaking is at liberty to demonstrate that its bonus system producing an exclusionary effect is economically justified.

70. With regard to the first aspect, the case-law gives indications as to the cases in which discount or bonus schemes of an undertaking in a dominant position are not merely the expression of a particularly favourable offer on the market, but give rise to an exclusionary effect.

71. First, an exclusionary effect may arise from goal-related discounts or bonuses, that is to say those the granting of which is linked to the attainment of sales objectives defined individually (*Michelin*, paragraphs 70 to 86).

72. It is clear from the findings of the Court of First Instance in paragraphs 10 and 15 to 17 of the judgment under appeal that the bonus schemes at issue were drawn up by reference to individual sales objectives, since the rate of the bonuses depended on the evolution of the turnover arising from BA ticket sales by each travel agent during a given period.

73. It is also apparent from the case-law that the commitment of co-contractors towards the undertaking in a dominant position and the pressure exerted upon them may be particularly strong where a discount or bonus does not relate solely to the growth in turnover in relation to purchases or sales of products of that undertaking made by those co-contractors during the period under consideration, but extends also to the whole of the turnover relating to those purchases or sales. In that way, relatively modest variations—whether upwards or downwards—in the turnover figures relating to the products of the dominant undertaking have disproportionate effects on co-contractors (see, to that effect, *Michelin*, paragraph 81).

74. The Court of First Instance found that the bonus schemes at issue gave rise to a similar situation. Attainment of the sales progression objectives gave rise to an increase in the commission

paid on all BA tickets sold by the travel agent concerned, and not just on those sold after those objectives had been attained (paragraph 23 of the judgment under appeal). It could therefore be of decisive importance for the commission income of a travel agent as a whole whether or not he sold a few extra BA tickets after achieving a certain turnover (paragraphs 29 and 30 of the grounds for the Commission's decision, reproduced in paragraph 23 of the judgment under appeal). The Court of First Instance, which describes that characteristic and its consequences in paragraphs 272 and 273 of the judgment under appeal, states that the progressive nature of the increased commission rates had a 'very noticeable effect at the margin' and emphasises the radical effects which a small reduction in sales of BA tickets could have on the rates of performance-related bonus.

75. Finally, the Court took the view that the pressure exerted on resellers by an undertaking in a dominant position which granted bonuses with those characteristics is further strengthened where that undertaking holds a very much larger market share than its competitors (see, to that effect, *Michelin*, paragraph 82). It held that, in those circumstances, it is particularly difficult for competitors of that undertaking to outbid it in the face of discounts or bonuses based on overall sales volume. By reason of its significantly higher market share, the undertaking in a dominant position generally constitutes an unavoidable business partner in the market. Most often, discounts or bonuses granted by such an undertaking on the basis of overall turnover largely take precedence in absolute terms, even over more generous offers of its competitors. In order to attract the co-contractors of the undertaking in a dominant position, or to receive a sufficient volume of orders from them, those competitors would have to offer them significantly higher rates of discount or bonus.

76. In the present case, the Court of First Instance held in paragraph 277 of the judgment under appeal that BA's market share was significantly higher than that of its five main competitors in the United Kingdom. It concluded, in paragraph 278 of that judgment, that the rival airlines were not in a position to grant travel agents the same advantages as BA, since they were not capable of attaining in the United Kingdom a level of revenue capable of constituting a sufficiently broad financial base to allow them effectively to establish a reward scheme similar to BA's (paragraph 278 of the judgment under appeal).

77. Therefore, the Court of First Instance was right to examine, in paragraphs 270 to 278 of the judgment under appeal, whether the bonus schemes at issue had a fidelity-building effect capable of producing an exclusionary effect.

At this point the ECJ refused BA's plea that it review the CFI's finding that the bonus scheme had an exclusionary effect, and that it had a very noticeable effect at the margin, as it will not review the CFI's findings of fact. This plea was therefore inadmissible. It continued by examining the CFI's assessment of the objective justification for the scheme.

84. Discounts or bonuses granted to its co-contractors by an undertaking in a dominant position are not necessarily an abuse and therefore prohibited by Article 82 EC. According to consistent case-law, only discounts or bonuses which are not based on any economic counterpart to justify them must be regarded as an abuse (see, to that effect, *Hoffmann-La Roche*, paragraph 90, and *Michelin*, paragraph 73).

85. As has been held in paragraph 69 of this judgment, the Court of First Instance was right, after holding that the bonus schemes at issue produced an exclusionary effect, to examine whether those schemes had an objective economic justification.

86. Assessment of the economic justification for a system of discounts or bonuses established by an undertaking in a dominant position is to be made on the basis of the whole of the circumstances of the case (see, to that effect, *Michelin*, paragraph 73). It has to be determined whether the exclusionary effect arising from such a system, which is disadvantageous for competition, may be counterbalanced, or outweighed, by advantages in terms of efficiency which also benefit the consumer. If the exclusionary effect of that system bears no relation to advantages for the market and consumers, or if it goes beyond what is necessary in order to attain those advantages, that system must be regarded as an abuse.

87. In this case, correctly basing its examination upon the criteria thus inferred from the case-law, the Court of First Instance examined whether there was an economic justification for the bonus schemes at issue. In paragraphs 284 and 285 of the judgment under appeal, it adopted a position in relation to the arguments submitted by BA, which concerned, in particular, the high level of fixed costs in air transport and the importance of aircraft occupancy rates. On the basis of its assessment of the circumstances of the case, the Court of First Instance came to the conclusion that those systems were not based on any objective economic justification.

Again, the ECJ refused to review the CFI's findings of fact on this issue, stating the plea was to that extent inadmissible. It confined itself to stating that the CFI had not committed an error of *law*.

90. The Court of First Instance did not therefore make any error of law in holding that the bonus schemes at issue had a fidelity-building effect, that they therefore produced an exclusionary effect, and that they were not justified from an economic standpoint.

96. Concerning BA's argument that the Court of First Instance did not examine the probable effects of the bonus schemes at issue, it is sufficient to note that, in paragraphs 272 and 273 of the judgment under appeal, the Court of First Instance explained the mechanism of those schemes.

97. Having emphasised the very noticeable effect at the margin, linked to the progressive nature of the increased commission rates, it described the exponential effect on those rates of an increase in the number of BA tickets sold during successive periods, and, conversely, the disproportionate reduction in those rates in the event of even a slight decrease in sales of BA tickets in comparison with the previous period.

98. On that basis, the Court of First Instance was able to conclude, without committing any error of law, that the bonus schemes at issue had a fidelity-building effect. It follows that BA's plea accusing the Court of not examining the probable effects of those schemes is unfounded.

99. Moreover, in paragraph 99 of its appeal, BA acknowledges that, in its judgment, the Court of First Instance rightly held that travel agents were given an incentive to increase their sales of BA tickets. In addition, in paragraph 113 of its appeal, it states that, if the Court of First Instance had examined the actual or probable impact of the bonus schemes at issue on competition between travel agents, it would have concluded that that impact was negligible.

100. It follows that BA is not seriously denying that those schemes had a fidelity-building effect on travel agents and thus tended to affect the situation of competitor airlines.

Again, the ECJ rejected as inadmissible the plea that the CFI had taken insufficient account of BA's evidence of the lack of exclusionary effects. It then dealt with BA's plea that the CFI should have examined whether BA's conduct involved a 'prejudice [to] consumers' within Article 82(b).

105. It should be noted first that, as explained in paragraphs 57 and 58 of this judgment, discounts or bonuses granted by an undertaking in a dominant position may be contrary to Article 82 EC even where they do not correspond to any of the examples mentioned in the second paragraph of that article.

106. Moreover, as the Court has already held in paragraph 26 of its judgment in *Europemballage and Continental Can*, Article 82 EC is aimed not only at practices which may cause prejudice to consumers directly, but also at those which are detrimental to them through their impact on an effective competition structure, such as is mentioned in Article 3(1)(g) EC.

107. The Court of First Instance was therefore entitled, without committing any error of law, not to examine whether BA's conduct had caused prejudice to consumers within the meaning of subparagraph (b) of the second paragraph of Article 82 EC, but to examine, in paragraphs 294 and 295 of the judgment under appeal, whether the bonus schemes at issue had a restrictive effect on competition and to conclude that the existence of such an effect had been demonstrated by the Commission in the contested decision.

108. Having regard to those considerations, the third plea must be dismissed as unfounded.

In this judgment the ECJ appeared to consider that a quantity discount system is not abusive; that a system whereby the rebate is conditional on purchasing mainly or exclusively from the dominant undertaking is abusive in principle, on the basis of *Hoffmann-La Roche* (paragraph 62); and that other types of discount or rebate such as that in *Michelin I* (paragraph 65) must be judged in the light of the circumstances, but in particular in the light of two criteria (paragraph 67). These are i) whether the discounts or bonuses are *capable* of producing an exclusionary effect (see also paragraph 77) in that they make market entry very difficult or impossible for competitors and make it more difficult or impossible for the other party to choose other sources of supply (paragraph 68) and ii) whether there is objective economic justification for the system (paragraph 69).

In assessing the *capability* of a scheme to cause exclusion (paragraph 73) the ECJ particularly stressed the effect of a 'roll-back' provision, whereby the bonus applies not only to the sales or purchases above the target, but extends backwards to all the previous sales or purchases during the reference period once the target is hit. The ECJ referred here to the 'very noticeable effect at the margin' which the roll-back feature of the BA schemes produced.

The ECJ looked at the second criteria, the objective economic justification, in terms of countervailing efficiencies which produce benefits for consumers (paragraph 86).

The ECJ did not actually state whether or not a concrete effect on the market has to be shown. It said that the CFI had explained the mechanism of the schemes, their effect at the margin and so on (paragraph 97) and so had been able to conclude that they did have a 'fidelity-building effect'. The ECJ refused to review the CFI's actual assessment of whether the schemes were exclusionary on the basis of lack of jurisdiction.

It should be noted that the ECJ rejected the plea that the CFI should have examined whether the schemes infringed Article 82(b) which refers to 'prejudice to consumers' on the grounds that the list of abuses in Article 82 is not exhaustive (paragraphs 57 and 58) and that in order to show a detrimental effect on consumers it is only necessary to conclude that there is a restrictive effect on *competition* (paragraphs 106 and 107).

F. REFORM OF THE LAW ON SINGLE BRANDING, DISCOUNTS AND REBATES

(i) General

The law set out above draws hard lines about when single branding, discounts, rebates and bonus schemes infringe Article 82. It assumes exclusionary effects from certain types of discounts and rebates, assumes that exclusion of competitors leads to detriment to consumers and pays insufficient regard to the pro-competitive aspects of these practices. The case law and the Commission's decisional practice has been much criticized.[229]

The Commission's Discussion Paper proposed a new methodology for dealing with single branding (as it called exclusive dealing), rebates and discounts. This was the most radical section of the Discussion Paper. The single branding obligations and rebate systems dealt with in that section are those that have their possible negative effects in the market on which the undertaking concerned is dominant. Where the effects are on other markets they are dealt with under the tying and bundling section.[230]

The Discussion Paper accepted that suppliers use single branding obligations and rebate systems for efficiency enhancing reasons and for anti-competitive reasons and that they may have efficiency enhancing effects and anti-competitive effects.[231] It started from the premise that as the supplier is dominant buyers will generally buy a large part or even most of their purchases from the dominant supplier, even without loyalty enhancing measures, and that the brand may be a 'must stock' item.[232] It stated that the Commission 'will make its assessment of the obligation or system in the light of the likely and actual foreclosure effects'. [233]

(ii) Single Branding And The Discussion Paper

However, the Discussion Paper also contained a general statement about the nature of single branding obligations and what appeared to be a presumption that a single branding obligation on a 'good part' of the market is likely to be abusive. It said that in general a short duration does not limit its likely foreclosure effect.

Where the dominant company applies a single branding obligation to a good part of its buyers and this obligation therefore affects, if not most, at least a substantial part of market demand, the Commission is likely to conclude that the obligation has a market distorting foreclosure effect and thus constitutes an abuse of its dominant position. In its assessment the Commission will however

---

[229] See, e.g. B. Sher, 'Price Discounts and *Michelin II*; What Goes Around, Comes Around' [2002] *ECLR* 482; J. Temple Lang and R. O'Donoghue, 'Defining Legitimate Competition: How to Clarify Pricing Abuses under Article 82EC' (2002) 26 *Fordham Int'l LJ* 83; J. Kallaugher and B. Sher, 'Rebates Revisited: Anticompetitive Effects and Exclusionary Abuse under Article 82' (2004) 25(5) *European Competition Law Journal* 263; D. Spector, 'Loyalty Rebates: An Assessment of Competition Concerns and a Proposed Structured Rule of Reason' (2005) 1(2) *Competition Policy International*, 89; C. Ahlborn and D. Bailey, 'Discounts, Rebates and Selective Pricing by Dominant Firms' (2006) 2 *European Competition Journal* 101. For a defence of the more traditional position, see L. Gyselen, 'Rebates: Competition on the Merits or Exclusionary Practice?', Speech at 8th EU Competition Law and Policy Workshop, EUI, Florence, 3 June 2003, published in D. D. Ehlermann and I. Atanasiu, *European Competition Law Annual 2003: What is an Abuse of a Dominant Position* (Hart Publishing, 2006), 287.

[230] Discussion Paper, para. 142.

[231] *Ibid.*, para. 135.

[232] *Ibid.*, para. 143.

[233] *Ibid.*, para. 144.

not only look at the capablility of the obligation, the degree of dominance and the level of the tied market share, but will also take into account evidence why for particular reasons no market distorting foreclosure effect may result. For instance, whereas in general a short duration or a right to terminate the single branding obligation does not limit its likely foreclosure effect, under particular circumstances a short duration or right to terminate at short notice may make a market distorting foreclosure effect unlikely . . .'.[234]

The Discussion Paper takes the same approach to 'English clauses'.[235]

(iii) Rebates and the Discussion Paper: Unconditional and Conditional Rebates

On rebates, the Discussion Paper jettisoned categories of 'quantity', 'loyalty' and 'target' rebates and so on, and adopted instead a classification of 'unconditional' and 'conditional' rebates:

(i) an unconditional rebate is one granted only to particular customers (otherwise it would be a general price reduction[236]), but independently of their purchasing behaviour. So, although unconditional rebates are granted to some customers and not others, it depends on some other characteristic (such as their geographical location which makes them susceptible to foreign imports etc);

(ii) a conditional rebate is one granted to customers to reward certain (purchasing) behaviour, such as the amount purchased in a preceding period, or the percentage of total requirements bought from the supplier in a preceding period (i.e. a target or loyalty rebate). Conditional rebates differentiate the purchase price for each customer depending on its behaviour.[237]

Unconditional rebates can have both exclusionary and exploitative effects, As far as the exclusionary effects are concerned the Discussion Paper proposed dealing with them under the predatory pricing rules.[238] The Discussion Paper did not cover exploitative abuses, but unconditional rebates can have exploitative effects in that they can discriminate between customers and cause secondary line injury, contrary to Article 82(c).[239] Their exploitative effects would therefore be dealt with as abusive discrimination, discussed below.[240]

The Discussion Paper proposed a complex methodological framework for assessing the exclusionary effects of conditional rebates. Crucially, conditional rebates were sub-divided into two categories:

(i) Conditional rebates granted on *all* purchases in the reference period once a certain threshold is exceeded (i.e. where the rebate is 'rolled-back'). The Commission is particularly concerned with the 'suction' effect, or 'effect at the margin', whereby the nearer the customer gets to the threshold the stronger the incentive to stay with the dominant supplier in order to obtain the rebate on the previous purchases.[241]

(ii) Conditional rebates granted only on the incremental purchases above the threshold.

---

[234] *Ibid.*, para. 149.

[235] *Ibid.*, para. 150.

[236] *Ibid.*, n. 85.

[237] *Ibid.*, para. 137.

[238] *Ibid.*, para. 171.

[239] See *supra*, 440.

[240] *Infra*, 595.

[241] As seen in the cases, *Michelin I*, *Michelin II*, and *British Airways*, *supra* 491ff.

In respect of the former (rebates on all purchases), the Commission's methodology was based on the concept of the 'contestable share'. This reflects the idea that as the supplier is dominant there is no alternative to it for part of the customer's requirements i.e. that part of the customer's requirements are 'non-contestable'. It is over the remaining, 'contestable' part that foreclosure effects may be of concern. The concept of the 'required share', and the 'commercially viable' share were also deployed. The 'required share' is the share of the customer's requirements which a competitor needs to capture so that the effective price resulting from the application of the rebate equals the dominant undertaking's ATC. The 'commercially viable share' is the share of the customer's requirements which an efficient entrant can reasonably be expected to capture. The 'required share' and the 'commercially viable share' have to be compared. If the 'required share' is greater than the 'commercially viable share' the Discussion Paper stated that the rebate system is likely to have a foreclosure effect.[242] The Commission would also take into account a number of other factors such as whether the conditional rebate is standardized or individual-ized;[243] whether the customers are left in uncertainty about the rebate;[244] and the length of the reference period.[245]

In respect of conditional rebates only on incremental purchases above a threshold and where the threshold is set in terms of a percentage of total requirements or an individualized volume target the Discussion Paper said that the Commission would only conclude that the rebate system constituted an abuse if the resulting price after the rebate was a predatory one (judged under the principles set out in the Discussion Paper's section on predatory pricing). However, if the resulting price was under ATC and 'the part of demand to which the rebate is applied is important enough to create a foreclosure effect' an abuse would be considered likely.[246]

Finally, it should be remembered that all of this would be subject to the general 'efficiency defence' proposed in the Discussion Paper.[247] However, the efficiency defence as proposed there is narrow and in particular would demand that the scheme is 'indispensable' to the generation of the efficiencies, which is a high hurdle to surmount where rebates are concerned.

The general reception of the Discussion Paper proposals on single branding and rebates was favourable in principle, in that it was welcomed as moving the assessment away from *per se* rules and unhelpful categorisations. However, there was considerable criticism of the details of the proposals outlined above. In particular, there was criticism of the extensive use still made of presumptions,[248] of the use of ATC as the costs standard, and of the complexity of the framework for assessing conditional rebates. The latter, although grounded in economic theory, was thought to be almost impossibly difficult to implement in practice, particularly in respect of the assessment of the commercially viable share.[249] It is important that the principles adopted

---

[242] Because the effective price over the commercially viable share will be below the dominant supplier's ATC, see Discussion Paper, para. 156.

[243] *Ibid.*, paras. 158–9.

[244] *Ibid.*, para. 160; as in *Michelin I*, see *supra*, 491.

[245] *Ibid.*, para. 161.

[246] *Ibid.*, para. 168. Where the rebate is set in terms of a standardised volume target it is unlikely to have a loyalty enhancing effect, but it will depend on the facts, see *ibid.*, para.169.

[247] See *supra*, Chap. 5.

[248] E.g., the comments of White and Case on the Discussion Paper, 9 ('...a more economic approach in the application of Article 82 EC to rebates should leave no room for the existence of presumptions and inferences of abuse'), http://ec.europa.eu/comm/competition/antitrust/art82/077.pdf; Linklaters' comments, pps. 13–16, http://ec.europa.eu/comm/competition/antitrust/art82/127.pdf

[249] e.g., the comments by Ashurst, p. 23, http://ec.europa.eu/comm/competition/antitrust/art82/066.pdf; O'Donoghue and Padilla, n. 81. *supra*, 399.

on the application of Article 82 to rebates or exclusivity clauses deliver legal certainty, predictability and workability and do not discourage undertakings from entering into arrangements whose effects are pro-competitive. It is likely that any future guidance from the Commission will contain an amended version of the Discussion Paper proposals.

In 2006 the Commission took a decision which applied Article 82 to the exclusive dealing and rebate schemes of Tomra, a firm holding market shares of more than 80 per cent in various national markets in the supply of 'reverse vending machines' (used by supermarkets to collect empty drink containers from consumers and return the deposit to them). The practices condemned by the decision included agreements which (i) granted Tomra the status of an exclusive supplier of the machines, and (ii) imposed individualized quantity targets, or retroactive rebate schemes, the thresholds of which usually corresponded to total or almost total machine requirements of its customers.[250] The individualized target scheme included a 'roll-back' element. The article in the Commission's Competition Policy Newsletter says that the 'likely and actual effect of foreclosing the market, was analysed following the previous case law of the European Court of Justice, in addition to being based and supported by economic analysis in the spirit of the recently publicised DG Competition Discussion Paper...'. The Commission did analyse the suction effect of the rebate and concluded that it had a foreclosure effect. RBB Economics commented that:

The Tomra decision has been portrayed as a case in which the Commission has applied an effects-based approach to rebates. However, from the description of the case in the Newsletter it is unclear whether the Commission has satisfied the tests for foreclosure that were proposed in the Article 82 Discussion Paper. The specific reasons given in the Newsletter for rejection of Tomra's defence appear to rely on a very localised result that does little more than re-state the traditional form-based objections to rebates.

Perhaps the published version of the Decision will reveal a richer and more convincing foreclosure story. If not, this would be a disappointing start to the promised new era of effects-based analysis.[251]

One point worth noting is that it appears that the foreclosure identified by the Commission affected only 32 per cent of demand. Tomra are appealing, *inter alia* on the grounds that the Commission committed a manifest error in law by holding exclusivity agreements, individualised quantity commitments and individualized retroactive rebates unlawful *per se* under Article 82 EC.[252] It shows how difficult the brave new world of effects based analysis in this most problematic area is in practice.

G. COMPARISON WITH US LAW ON DISCOUNTS AND REBATES UNDER SECTION 2 OF THE SHERMAN ACT

A different approach is taken to discounts and rebates by US courts applying section 2 of the Sherman Act. This is an area where the two systems of law diverge. US law generally sees any

---

[250] *Prokent/Tomra*, COMP/38.113, IP/06/398, 29 March 2006. Tomra was fined €24 million and has appealed, Case T-155/06, judgment pending. At the time of writing no public version of the decision is available, but see the article in the Commission's Competition Newsletter, F. Maier-Rigaud and D. Vaigauskaite, 'Prokent/Tomra, a Textbook Case? Abuse of Dominance under Perfect Information' (2006) 2 *EC Competition Policy Newsletter*, 19.

[251] RBB Economics, Brief 21, February 2007, available at http://www.rbbecon.com/publications/downloads/rbb_brief21.pdf.

[252] [2006] OJ C190/24.

price reduction by a leading firm as pro-competitive (at least so long as prices are not predatory, which in US law means proving that the prices were below an appropriate measure of cost and that there was a reasonable prospect of the firm recouping its losses[253]) and rebates are normally not held to infringe section 2. The contrast was dramatically illustrated by the fact that Virgin brought an action in the US against BA's commission scheme at the same time as its complaint to the Commission under EC Law. The trial court in the US granted summary judgment in favour of BA and this was upheld by the Second Circuit Court of Appeals. The American courts said that Virgin had failed to show that BA's incentive scheme harmed consumers.[254] The difference between this outcome and the judgment in *British Airways*, discussed above, could not be starker. However, in *LePage's Inc* v. *3M*[255] a majority in the 3rd Circuit Court of Appeals held that a bundled discount scheme did violate section 2, as although it did not amount to predatory pricing it resulted in *de* facto exclusivity.[256] The Supreme Court refused permission to appeal.[257]

H. TYING

(i) General

Article 82 (d) specifically lists as an example of abuse:

making the conclusion of contracts subject to acceptance by the other parties of supplementary obligations which, by their nature or according to commercial usage, have no connection with the subject of such contracts.

This describes tying, the practice of supplying something on condition that the customer obtains something else from the supplier as well.[258] Suppose X makes both widgets and blodgets. X is the monopoly supplier of widgets but the blodget market is competitive. Customers for widgets need to buy blodgets as well. If X refuses to supply widgets unless the customers buy its blodgets as well the other manufacturers of blodgets may be squeezed out of the market. Tying can apply to both products and services and the tying of services to products has become a particular issue in competition law.

Competition policy is concerned with tying because it may result in the foreclosure of competitors from the market. Tying can work because the supplier is dominant in the market for the *tying* product, so the customer has difficulty going elsewhere for it and therefore does not shop around for the *tied* product. Competition authorities may fear that the dominant supplier can extract two monopoly prices, one from the tying and one from the tied product.[259] The Chicago

---

[253] According to the Supreme Court ruling in *Brooke Group Ltd* v. *Brown & Willianmson Tobacco Corp* 509 US 209 (1993): for US law on predation, see *supra* 460.

[254] *Virgin Atl. Airways Ltd* v. *British Airways plc*, 257 F.3d 256 (2d Cir. 2001).

[255] 324 F3d 141 (3d Cir 2003).

[256] C. Ahlborn and D. Bailey, 'Discounts, Rebates and Selective Pricing by Dominant Firms' (2006) 2 *European Competition Journal* 101, 125, and see also H.Hovenkamp, *The Antitrust Enterprise* (Harvard University Press, 2005, 172–3.

[257] 124 S Ct 2932 (2004), after the DOJ and FTC submitted a brief to the Supreme Court urging it not to take the case on the grounds that this was not an appropriate case in which to examine the subject. There are suggestions that the agencies may now be regretting this, as it has left in place a judgment which leaves it unclear when bundling of discounts will or should be section 2 violations. The US courts are generally very concerned to avoid false positive (Type 1) errors.

[258] Tying can arise as an issue in distribution arrangements which do not involve dominant firms (see *infra* Chap. 9) and in technology transfer agreements, such as patent licensing (see *infra* Chap. 10).

[259] The Commission considered in *Eurofix-Bauco* [1988] OJ L65/19, [1989] 4 CMLR 677, that Hilti was trying to raise prices in the market for the consumables (the nails).

school argued that this is not possible ('the single monopoly profit theorem'), but post-Chicago economists have demonstrated that it *is* possible unless the two products are used in fixed proportions and the market for the tied good would be competitive if it were not for the tying.[260] The economics of tying (and bundling, described below) are complex, and ultimately show that these practices may have both pro- and anti-competitive effects. Everything will depend on the facts of each case.[261] Where the dominant undertaking will not supply the tying product without the tied product this may be seen as constituting an infringement of Article 82 as a *refusal to supply* as well as a tie, although as we will see, the competition rules apply differently to tying and refusal to supply. It can also be a form of price discrimination.

Tying can be economic as well as contractual. Instead of providing that the customer must obtain the tied product from him in order to be supplied with the tying product the supplier may offer a deal which induces the customer to obtain both. Such offers will usually amount to discriminatory pricing. If the normal unit price for widgets is £10 and the competitive unit price for blodgets is £5 the supplier may offer widgets for £8 if both are bought from him. Competitors on the blodget market will have to reduce the price to £3 per unit in order to compete. This is known as '*mixed bundling*' (the supplier is willing to supply each product separately but the customer gets a financially advantageous deal if he buys both together). '*Pure bundling*' occurs where the elements of the package are *only* supplied together. For example, where services are tied to products the supplier may quote a price for the product which includes the service (such as repair and maintenance). If the customer does not want the service he will still have to pay the full price (or be offered only a reduction which does not reflect the true cost of the service element). In either case he has an incentive to obtain the service from the supplier of the product rather than from an independent service provider. The inducements offered may be non-financial, such as refusing to honour guarantees on the tying product[262] or offering priority delivery to customers who take both products.[263] In the *cause célèbre* merger decision *GE/Honeywell* the fear (*inter alia*), that the merged entity might bundle its products in the future and thereby exclude competitors caused the Commission to prohibit the transaction.[264] *Technological tying* (a form of pure bundling) is where the supplier physically integrates the products in some way, so that one is not available without the other.[265]

In *Microsoft*[266] the Commission stated that tying prohibited under Article 82 requires the presence of the following elements:

(i)   the tying and the tied goods are two separate products;

(ii) the undertaking concerned is dominant in the tying product market;

(iii) the undertaking concerned does not give customers a choice to obtain the tying product without the tied product; and

(iv) tying forecloses competition.

[260] For the economics of this, see S. Bishop and M. Walker, *The Economics of EC Competition Law* (2nd edn., Sweet & Maxwell, 2002), paras. 6.54–6.68; M. Motta, *Competition Policy* (Cambridge University Press, 2004), 7.3, R. J. Van den Bergh and P. D. Camesasca, *European Competition Law and Economics: A Comparative Perspective* (2nd edn., Sweet & Maxwell, 2006), 265–70.

[261] O'Donoghue and Padilla, n. 81, *supra*, 480.

[262] See *Eurofix-Bauco v. Hilti* [1988] OJ L65/19, [1989] 4 CMLR 677, para. 44.

[263] See Case T-65/89, *BPB Industries and British Gypsum Ltd v. Commission* [1993] ECR II-389, [1993] 5 CMLR 32.

[264] Case COMP/M.2220, 3 July 2001, reversed on this point on appeal to the CFI, Cases T-209 and 210/01, *General Electric and Honeywell v. Commission* [2005] ECR II-5575, [2006] 4 CMLR 686 discussed *infra* Chap. 12.

[265] As in *Microsoft*, COMP/C-3/37.792, [2005] 4 CMLR 965, on appeal Case T-201/04, judgment pending.

[266] COMP/C-3/37.792, [2005] 4 CMLR 965, para. 794. See also Faull and Nikpay, n. 6 *supra*, 4.241–4.256.

(ii) Commercial Reasons for Tying

Tying is a strategy which may make good commercial sense for reasons which are not necessarily anti-competitive. It can be used as a method for obtaining royalties or fees for the use of a process or product i.e. as a metering device. A good example is the patent licensing case *Vaassen/Moris*[267] where the inventor of a device for filling *saucissons de Boulogne* supplied it royalty free but on the condition that customers bought their sausage skins from him. This was an easy way of monitoring, and charging for, the use of the device. Tying can also allow the supplier to achieve economies of scale which are then reflected in the price reduction offered to customers, to 'spread the risk' when trying to penetrate a new market, or to offer a 'bundle' which is more attractive (and of greater value) to consumers than the sum of its separate parts. Suppliers may also tie products or services together in order to ensure their optimal performance and maintain the supplier's reputation, or to ensure safety, although the Court and Commission have not proved receptive to this justification for tying.[268]

(iii) Single or Distinct Products

Where an undertaking dominant in one market ties in a product (or service) in another market it may be an instance of a practice which the Court and Commission have repeatedly held to infringe Article 82—leverage, the projection of dominance from one market to another. The *Télémarketing* case,[269] where the television company tied the use of its own sales agents to the sale of its advertising slots, is a clear example of this. The delivered pricing policy in *Napier Brown— British Sugar*[270] was condemned as an abuse because, by providing the product and the delivery together, the dominant undertaking was excluding competition on the separate although ancillary market. However, the whole concept of tying presupposes that different products are being tied together. If what is supplied consists of one product there cannot be a tie as one cannot tie something to itself. Whether products or services are components of a single product or service or are distinct is a difficult issue, and one that goes back to questions of market definition.[271] As seen in Chapter 6, the tendency of the Court and Commission is to separate products and then to condemn the supplier's attempts to ensure that the customer buys them all as a package. It should be noted that in the Discussion Paper the Commission points out that tying does not depend on the distinct products being in different *markets*, as in a market with differentiated products two products may be sufficiently differentiated that the undertaking can be said to be tying or bundling two distinct products.[272] Further, Article 82(d) specifically prohibits

---

[267] [1979] OJ L19/32, [1979] 1 CMLR 511. The tie was condemned by the Commission as contrary to Article 81(1).

[268] See the *Hilti* and *Tetra Pak II* cases (*infra* 518 ff). In Case T-30/89, *Hilti v. Commission* [1991] ECR II-1439, [1992] 4 CMLR 16, para. 118, the CFI said 'As the Commission has established, there are laws in the United Kingdom attaching penalties to the sale of dangerous products and to the use of misleading claims as to the characteristics of any product. There are also authorities vested with powers to enforce those laws. In those circumstances it is clearly not the task of an undertaking in a dominant position to take steps on its own initiative to eliminate products which, rightly or wrongly, it regards as dangerous or at least as inferior in quality to its own products'.

[269] See *supra* 437. The Court treated this as a refusal to supply scenario: see *infra* 524.

[270] [1988] OJ L284/41, [1990] 4 CMLR 196.

[271] It was the issue at the heart of the *Microsoft* litigation in the USA which culminated in the final order of 3 April 2000, and of the Commission's *Microsoft* decision of 24 March 2004, *infra* 523.

[272] Discussion Paper, para. 185. However, for Article 82 to apply the undertaking concerned must be dominant by virtue of selling one of the products (the tying product) on its own).

supplementary obligations which 'by their nature or according to commercial usage, have no connection with the subject of such contracts' which suggests that there will be no abuse if there is an inherent or customary link between the products. However, as is seen in *Tetra Pak II*[273] the Court has interpreted this narrowly.

The Commission's test for whether there are distinct products is 'consumer demand'—is there actual or potential consumer demand for the tied product on a stand-alone basis? This test appears in the Guidelines on vertical restraints:

> What is to be considered as a distinct product is determined first of all by the demand of the buyers. Two products are distinct if, in the absence of tying, from the buyers' perspective, the products are purchased by them on two different markets. For instance, since customers want to buy shoes with laces, it has become commercial usage for show manufacturers to supply shoes with laces. Therefore, the sale of shoes with laces is not a tying practice. Often combinations have become accepted practice because the nature of the product makes it technically difficult to supply one product without the supply of another product.[274]

The problem is that almost any product can be broken down into smaller parts:

> A coat can be sold without its buttons, a desk without its drawers . . . The market would come to a standstill, however, if the antitrust laws gave every customer a legal right to atomize his purchases as much as he chose.[275]

Moreover, this is a situation which can change over time. New products can be brought on to the market but may gradually become commonly integrated into others, or products may be introduced which in time are broken down and the elements sold separately. Where new products are concerned, the 'commercial usage' test in Article 82(d)[276] will not be useful. There may always be consumers whose wants are different from those of the majority but the consumer welfare test has to ensure that *most* consumers are better off and that consumer gains exceed consumer losses. If one bears in mind that the purpose of the rules on tying should be the welfare of consumers, rather than the welfare of competitors, then the enquiry about distinct products is just part of the overall assessment of whether 'the efficiencies of tying outweighs the inherent reduction in choice for the consumer'.[277]

(iv) Lack of Customer Choice

The lack of customer choice referred to as an element of the abuse in *Microsoft*[278] is sometimes described as 'coercion'.[279] It can arise from the refusal of the dominant undertaking to sell the tying product without the tied one, either as a contractual clause or *de facto*; from the unavailability of the products separately; from pressure exerted on the customer through the promise of favourable treatment to customers who take both products or threats to those who do not; or

---

[273] *Infra*, 520.

[274] [2000] OJ C 291/1, para. 216.

[275] H. Hovenkamp, *Federal Antitrust Policy: The Law of Competition and its Practice* (3rd edn., Thomson/West, 2005), 399.

[276] Case C-333/94 P, *Tetra Pak International SA v. Commission* [1996] ECR I-5951, [1997] 4 CMLR 662, *infra* 520.

[277] See the comments of Linklaters on the Discussion Paper, http://ec.europa.eu/comm/competition/antitrust/art82/127.pdf, p. 17.

[278] *Supra*, 515.

[279] See Faull and Nikpay, n. 6 *supra*, 4.247.

from pricing incentives which may be 'so powerful that no rational customer would choose to buy the products separately'.[280]

(v) The Case Law

There has been comparatively little case law and decisional practice on tying and bundling. However, two leading cases, *Hilti* and *Tetra Pak II*, established contractual tying as virtually a *per se* abuse. In both of these cases the Commission found an abuse after very little analysis of the market. Once it had found dominance, separate products and no objective justification, the finding of abuse followed almost automatically. In both cases the appeals to the Community Courts concentrated on the issues of market definition and objective justification.

Eurofix-Bauco/Hilti [1988] OJ L65/19, [1989] 4 CMLR 677

Hilti was dominant in the supply of nail guns, the biggest selling models of which were protected by patents. It supplied the cartridge strips which were also protected by patents. The nails which were fired out of the cartridge strips in the guns were not, however, covered by patents and there were some small, independent manufacturers of Hilti-compatible nails. Hilti followed a number of practices to ensure that customers who bought its cartridges also bought its nails and did not buy nails from the independent suppliers: i) making the sale of patented cartridge strips conditional upon taking a corresponding complement of nails; ii) reducing discounts on cartridges where the customer did not order nails as well; iii) inducing its distributors not to supply certain customers so that the independent nail producers could not get hold of Hilti cartridges; iv) refusing supplies of cartridges to long-standing customers who might resell to independent nail producers; v) frustrating or delaying applications for licences of right of the cartridge strip technology so that the independent producers could not obtain non-Hilti cartridges; vi) refusing to honour guarantees on nail guns if non-Hilti nails had been used with them.

The Commission held that the nail-guns, cartridges, and nails each constituted a separate relevant product market and that Hilti was dominant in the EEC in all of them.[281] It held that Hilti had infringed Article 82 by the practices above which were designed to tie the nails to the cartridges and thus to prevent or limit the entry of independent producers of Hilti-compatible consumables into the markets. Hilti claimed that the practices were objectively justified because it was necessary for safety reasons to ensure that Hilti guns were only used with Hilti consumables and that the nails produced by the independents were sub-standard. The Commission rejected this, pointing out that Hilti had never communicated its safety concerns to the independents or taken steps to alert the UK Trading Standards Departments or the Health and Safety Executive about any danger and that there had never been any report of safety difficulties stemming from the use of non-Hilti nails. Hilti appealed to the Court of First Instance both on the issue of market definition[282] and on the finding of abuse.

Commission

74. Hilti has abused its dominant position in the EEC in the relevant market for nail guns and most importantly the markets for Hilti-compatible cartridge strips and nails. It has done this principally through its attempts to prevent or limit the entry of independent producers of Hilti-compatible

---

[280] Faull and Nikpay, 4.250.
[281] See *supra* Chap. 6.
[282] See *supra* Chap. 6.

consumables into these markets. Hilti's attempts to block or limit such entry went beyond the means legitimately available to a dominant company. The different aspects of Hilti's commercial behaviour were designed to this effect and were aimed at preventing Hilti-compatible cartridge strips from being freely available. Without such availability of Hilti-compatible cartridge strips, for which in the EEC Hilti until recently enjoyed protection afforded by patents, independent producers of Hilti-compatible nails have been severely restricted in their penetration of the market. Furthermore, customers have been obliged to rely on Hilti for both cartridges and nails for their Hilti nail guns. By limiting the effective competition from new entrants Hilti has been able to preserve its dominant position. The ability to carry out its illegal policies stems from its power on the markets for Hilti-compatible cartridge strips and nail guns (where its market position is strongest and the barriers to entry are highest) and aims at reinforcing its dominance on the Hilti-compatible nail market (where it is potentially more vulnerable to new competition) . . . Most of the abuses took place in or were centred on the UK which constitutes a substantial part of the common market. However, at least one of these abuses had direct effects in another Member State and in addition the strategy of Hilti was aimed indirectly at the whole EEC in its attempt both to stop new entrants into the market (who might start exporting) and to prevent otherwise profitable arbitrage.

75. Making the sale of patented cartridge strips conditional upon taking a corresponding complement of nails constitutes an abuse of a dominant position, as do reduced discounts and other discriminatory policies described above on cartridge-only orders. These policies leave the consumer with no choice over the source of his nails and as such abusively exploit him. In addition, these policies all have the object or effect of excluding independent nail makers who may threaten the dominant position Hilti holds. The tying and reduction of discounts were not isolated incidents but a generally applied policy.

The CFI[283] upheld the decision, dismissing pleas about the products forming a 'system' and refusing to accept that Hilti's conduct was justified by safety concerns.[284] The judgment was affirmed by the ECJ.[285]

The facts of *Tetra Pak II* have already been described.[286] The Commission held that aseptic packaging machines, aseptic cartons, non-aseptic machines, and non-aseptic cartons were four separate relevant markets, and that Tetra Pak was dominant on the markets for aseptic machines and cartons and had committed abuses on the associated non-aseptic markets.[287] One of the ways the Commission held that Tetra Pak had infringed Article 82[288] was by tying the supply of its non-aseptic packaging machines to the supply of cartons which the machines filled. Tetra Pak either sold or leased the machines and imposed a contractual condition on its customers that obliged them to purchase only Tetra Pak cartons. The contract also obliged customers to obtain the cartons only from Tetra Pak itself or from a company it designated (although as there were no independent distributors the Commission pointed out that this clause was superfluous). Customers were obliged to obtain all maintenance and repair services and the supplies of

[283] Case T-30/89, *Hilti v. Commission* [1991] ECR II-1439, [1992] 4 CMLR 16.

[284] *Supra*, 516.

[285] Case C-53/92 P, *Hilti AG v EC Commission* [1994] ECR I-667, [1994] 4 CMLR 614.

[286] See *supra* Chap. 6 and *supra* 454.

[287] For a discussion of the issue of the dominant position and the abuse being on different markets see *supra* 454.

[288] *Elopak Italia/Tetra Pak* [1991] OJ L72/1, [1992] 4 CMLR 551.

spare parts from Tetra Pak. Tetra Pak claimed that the machines and the cartons formed 'integrated distribution systems' and that in any event the tie was justified for technical reasons, considerations of public liability and health, and by the need to protect its reputation. The Commission's rejected these arguments and said that the system of tied sales 'which again limits outlets and makes contracts subject to acceptance of conditions (the purchase of cartons) which have no connection with their purpose (the sale of machines), constitutes a serious infringement of Article [82]'.[289] The CFI upheld this, referring to the tied-sales clause intending to 'strengthen Tetra Pak's dominant position by reinforcing its customers' economic dependence on it'. [290]

Tetra Pak appealed to the ECJ, claiming that the CFI erred in law in holding that the tied sales of cartons and filling machines were contrary to Article 82. In particular, it said that Article 82(d) prohibited tying only where the supplementary obligations imposed had by their nature, or according to commercial usage, no connection with the subject of the contract. The ECJ confirmed the CFI's judgment. It held that the reasoning of the CFI, holding that there was no natural link, was correct. It also held that, as the examples in Article 82 are not exhaustive, a tie may constitute an abuse even if there *is* a natural link or the tied sale is in accordance with commercial usage.

Case C-333/94 P, *Tetra Pak International SA* v. *Commission* [1996] ECR I-5951, [1997] 4 CMLR 662

Court of Justice

34. In its third plea, Tetra Pak submits that the Court of First Instance erred in law in holding that the tied sales of cartons and filling machines were contrary to Article [82] in circumstances where there was a natural link between the two and tied sales were in accordance with commercial usage.

35. Tetra Pak interprets Article [82] (d) of the Treaty as prohibiting only the practice of making the conclusion of contracts dependent on acceptance of additional services which, by nature or according to commercial usage, have no link with the subject-matter of the contracts.

36. It must be noted, first, that the Court of First Instance explicitly rejected the argument put forward by Tetra Pak to show the existence of a natural link between the machines and the cartons. In paragraph [82] of the judgment under appeal, it found: 'consideration of commercial usage does not support the conclusion that the machinery for packaging a product is indivisible from the cartons. For a considerable time there have been independent manufacturers who specialise in the manufacture of non-aseptic cartons designed for use in machines manufactured by other concerns and who do not manufacture machinery themselves'. That assessment, itself based on commercial usage, rules out the existence of the natural link claimed by Tetra Pak by stating that other manufacturers can produce cartons for use in Tetra Pak's machines. With regard to aseptic cartons, the Court of First Instance found, at paragraph [83] of its judgment, that 'any independent producer is quite free, as far as Community competition law is concerned, to manufacture consumables intended for use in equipment manufactured by others, unless in doing so it infringes a competitor's intellectual property right'. It also noted, at paragraph [138], rejecting the argument based on the alleged natural link, that it was not for Tetra Pak to impose certain measures on its own initiative on the basis of technical considerations or considerations relating to

---

[289] *Ibid.*, para. 117.
[290] Case T-83/91, *Tetra Pak v. Commission* [1994] ECR II-755, para. 140.

product liability, protection of public health and protection of its reputation. Those factors, taken as a whole, show that the Court of First Instance considered that Tetra Pak was not alone in being able to manufacture cartons for use in its machines.

37. It must, moreover, be stressed that the list of abusive practices set out in the second paragraph of Article [82] of the Treaty is not exhaustive. Consequently, even where tied sales of two products are in accordance with commercial usage or there is a natural link between the two products in question, such sales may still constitute abuse within the meaning of Article [82] unless they are objectively justified. The reasoning of the Court of First Instance in paragraph [137] of its judgment is not therefore in any way defective.

It is clear from *Tetra Pak II* that, once it is shown that the products or services tied together are distinct, a dominant undertaking cannot rely on the words about nature and commercial usage in Article 82(d). 'Commercial usage' may merely have been established by the dominant undertaking itself[291] and the Court has stressed the non-exhaustive character of the particular examples listed in the Article, thereby emasculating the conditions in that sub-paragraph. EC law on tying in both *Hilti* and *Tetra Pak II* was driven by concerns about the structure of the market, not about the extraction of monopoly profits or the protection of consumers. In *Tetra Pak II* the monopoly profit could have been extracted from the tying product (the machines), had Tetra Pak wished.[292] The concern was with the ability of smaller firms to compete. This was a matter of policy and is summed up in paragraph 36 of the *Tetra Pak II* judgment, quoting the CFI, where the ECJ says 'any independent producer is quite free, as far as Community competition law is concerned, to manufacture consumables intended for use in equipment manufactured by others'. This is rather strange wording but means not so much that independents are *free* to manufacture but that Community competition law will positively *help* them to do so by constraining the conduct of dominant undertakings for whose equipment they wish to provide products or services. This is a policy not so much about efficiency and free competition as the protection of small firms and competitors.

(vi) Mixed Bundling

There have been some cases and settlements concerning mixed bundling. Two of these involved Coca-Cola. In *Coca-Cola Italia Undertaking* (1989)[293] the Commission issued a Statement of Objections alleging that Coca-Cola's practice of offering discounts to retailers based on a package of cola and non-cola was an abuse. Coca-Cola agreed not to make discounts on cola conditional on the retailers buying non-cola, and the case was settled on that basis. In *Coca-Cola Undertaking* (2005)[294] Coca-Cola agreed, *inter alia*, to no longer offer a rebate to its customers if the customer agreed to buy other products together with its best-selling products or to reserve shelf space for the entire group of products.

In the aftermarket case, *Digital Undertaking*,[295] the primary product market of computer systems was competitive and the aftermarket consisted of both hardware maintenance services

---

[291] See V. Korah, 'The Paucity of Economic Analysis in the EEC Decisions on Competition: Tetra Pak II' [1993] *CLP* 150.

[292] See *ibid*.

[293] Commission's *XIXth Report on Competition Policy* (Commission, 1989), para. 50.

[294] [2005] OJ L253/21

[295] Commission Press Release IP/97/868. Cf. the *Pelikan/Kyocera* case, *XXVth Report on Competition Policy* (Commission, 1995) pt. 87: see *supra* Chap. 6. See also D. Maldoom: 'The Kodak Case: Power in Aftermarkets' [1996] *ECLR* 473; M. Dolmans and V. Pickering: 'The 1997 Digital Undertaking' [1998] 2 *ECLR* 108; P. Andrews, 'Aftermarket Power in the Computer Services Market: The Digital Undertaking' [1998] 3 *ECLR* 176.

and software support services for Digital systems. The Commission alleged that Digital had abused its dominant position on the software support market for Digital systems by offering customers a 'package' of software support plus hardware maintenance. The Commission considered that the price of the software support alone was high, but the price was 'considerably more attractive when included in a hardware and software package than when sold on a stand-alone basis'. This meant it was uneconomic for customers to buy the hardware from a third party, so companies in the hardware maintenance market were excluded from servicing Digital systems. The Commission issued a Statement of Objections and following negotiations Digital undertook:[296]

to offer hardware maintenance services for Digital systems on a stand-alone basis and to implement a pricing policy for its software-support services based on a single flat fee per Central Processing Unit. Whereas it will continue to offer a software and hardware service package (so-called 'DSS' package), the price of the DSS package will not be less than 90 per cent of the sum of the list prices of the individual component services; the difference of up to 10 per cent allows costs savings or other benefits to be passed on to system users while ensuring the maintenance of effective competition in the supply of hardware services. In addition, Digital will introduce a new software service package consisting of software support and license [sic] update services.

Digital will make its price list publicly available and will include in all customer quotations for Digital's DSS package separate quotations for each of the individual components thereof.

Digital undertakes to ensure a transparent and non-discriminatory discount policy and to publish or otherwise make known the eligibility provisions for all discount programs. When offering a discount for its DSS package, it will also offer the same discount on the component services of the package if taken separately. All discounted prices will remain above average total costs.[297]

The terms of the *Digital* undertaking show that the Commission will allow a dominant undertaking to pass on costs savings stemming from the efficient packaging together of different products or services. However, it also shows that the Commission will in some circumstances interfere in an undertaking's activities on the aftermarket of its own product even if that primary product market is intensely competitive. Moreover, the discount on a package of products and/or services is liable to infringe Article 82 whenever an undertaking is dominant over one of the elements of the package and it is uneconomical for customers to go to third parties for any of the elements as a result of the discount, unless the discount can be objectively justified on costs savings grounds.

(vii) Technological Tying and the *Microsoft* Case

In 1984 the Commission came to a settlement with IBM after it had alleged that IBM had infringed Article 82 by, *inter alia*,[298] tying various computer products together. This involved not offering System/370 central processing units (CPUs) without a capacity of main memory included in the price ('memory bundling'); and not offering System/370 CPUs without the basic software included in the price ('software bundling'). IBM did not admit it had a dominant position or that it had committed an abuse but nevertheless undertook to offer its System/370 CPUs

---

[296] Commission Press Release IP/97/868.

[297] For the predatory pricing aspects of these proceedings, see *supra* 465.

[298] IBM was also alleged to have committed an abuse by failing to disclose interface information, see *infra* 571, and by discriminating between users of IBM software, i.e., refusing to supply certain software installation services to users of non-IBM CPUs.

in the EEC either without main memory or with only such capacity as was strictly required for testing.[299]

The Commission returned to the issue of tying in software markets when it took action against Microsoft for supplying its Windows Media Player (WMP) as a package with its Windows desktop operating system. When the purchaser turned on Windows, there was the WMP, pre-installed. This meant, according to the Commission's final statement of objections[300] that competition from other media players (such as RealPlayer) was stifled as it led to a vicious circle by which the ubiquity of the WMP caused companies such as content suppliers and software developers to develop products geared to the WMP, which thereby became even more desirable to consumers. Microsoft's conduct, said the Commission, 'weakens competition on the merits, stifles product innovation, and ultimately reduces consumer choice'.[301]

Meanwhile, in the US the competition authorities charged Microsoft with an illegal tie by bundling its own browser (Internet Explorer) with its Windows operating system, a claim which gave rise an argument over market definition. Were the operating system and the browser really one product rather than two (as Tetra Pak unsuccessfully argued in *Tetra Pak II*)? The District Court judge (Judge Jackson) held that they were two products and that the browser/operating system package constituted a *per se* illegal tie-in.[302] However, the Court of Appeals (DC Circuit) reversed and remanded this finding.[303] It sent it back to the court below to try it under a rule of reason analysis. The US Department of Justice then withdrew the tying claim, so it was not retried.[304] The Court of Appeals was concerned that the bundling of the system and browser served consumer welfare, in that consumers welcome being able to buy a computer with a browser ready installed, rather than having to shop around for one. This approach follows the general approach of US law towards monopoly leveraging, which is more tolerant than that of EC law, insofar as US law does not usually disapprove of an undertaking using monopoly power in one market to gain competitive advantages in another unless it thereby maintains its existing monopoly or creates a dangerous probability of gaining a monopoly in the second market.[305]

The Commission, however, came to a different conclusion over tying. In March 2004 the Commission adopted a decision finding that Microsoft had infringed Article 82 by bundling the WMP with Windows.[306]

Microsoft, Commission DecisionCOMP/C-3/37.792, [2005] 4 CMLR 965

Commission

(794) Tying prohibited under Article 82 of the Treaty requires the presence of the following elements: (i) the tying and tied goods are two separate products; (ii) the undertaking concerned is

---

[299] See *XIVth Report on Competition Policy* (Commission, 1984) parts 94–5.

[300] IP/03/1150.

[301] *Ibid.*

[302] 87 F. Supp. 2d 30 (DDC 2000).

[303] 253 F.3d 34. A number of other practices *were* held illegal, including co-mingling the browser and operating system codes.

[304] The States which were also plaintiffs followed the DOJ and withdrew their claims.

[305] See *supra* Chap. 5, 345.

[306] The decision also found Microsoft's refusal to disclose interface information to its competitors to be an abuse. For that aspect of *Microsoft* see *infra* 572; *Microsoft* has appealed, Case T-201/04.

dominant in the tying product market; (iii) the undertaking concerned does not give customers a choice to obtain the tying product without the tied product; and (iv) tying forecloses competition.

(841) There are indeed circumstances relating to the tying of WMP which warrant a closer examination of the effects that tying has on competition in this case. While in classical tying cases, the Commission and the Courts considered the foreclosure effect for competing vendors to be demonstrated by the bundling of a separate product with the dominant product, in the case at issue, users can and do to a certain extent obtain third party media players through the internet, sometimes for free. There are therefore indeed good reasons *not* to assume without further analysis that tying WMP constitutes conduct which by its very nature is liable to foreclosure competition.

. . .

(978) The Commission does not purport to pass judgment as to the desirability of one unique media player or set of media technologies (for example DRM, formats) coming to dominate the market. However, the manner in which competition unfolds in the media player market, which may or may not bring about such a result, is of competitive concern. Article 82 must be read in the light of its underlying objective which is to ensure that competition in the internal market is not distorted (see Article 3 (g) of the Treaty) . . . To maintain competitive markets so that innovations succeed or fail on the merits is an important objective of Community competition policy.

(979) Through tying WMP with Windows, Microsoft uses Windows as a distribution channel to anti-competitively ensure for itself a significant competition advantage in the media player market. Competitors, due to Microsoft's tying, are *a priori* at a disadvantage irrespective of whether their products are potentially more attractive on the merits.

(980) Microsoft thus interferes with the normal competitive process which would benefit users in terms of quicker cycles of innovation due to unfettered competition on the merits. Tying of WMP increases the content and applications barrier to entry which protects Windows and it will facilitate the erection of such a barrier for WMP. A position of market strength achieved in a market characterised by network effects—such as the media player market—is sustainable, as once the network effects work in favour of a company which has gained a decisive momentum, they will amount to entry barriers for potential competitors . . .

(981) This shields Microsoft from effective competition from potentially more efficient media player vendors which could challenge its position. Microsoft thus reduces the talent and capital invested in innovation of media players, not least its own . . . and anti-competitively raises barriers to market entry. Microsoft's conduct affects a market which could be a hotbed for new and exciting products springing forth in a climate of undistorted competition.

(982) Moreover, tying of WMP allows Microsoft to anti-competitively expand its position in adjacent media-related software markets and weaken effective competition to the eventual detriment of consumers.

(983) Microsoft's tying of WMP also sends signals which deter innovation in any technologies which Microsoft could conceivably take interest in and tie with Windows in the future. . . Microsoft's tying instils actors in the relevant software markets with a sense of precariousness thereby weakening both software developers. incentives to innovate in similar areas and venture capitalists' proclivity to invest in independent software application companies . . . A start-up intending to enter or raise venture capital in such a market will be forced to test the resilience of its business model against the eventuality of Microsoft deciding to bundle its own version of the product with Windows . . .

(984) There is therefore a reasonable likelihood that tying WMP with Windows will lead to a lessening of competition so that the maintenance of an effective competition structure will not be ensured in the foreseeable future. For these reasons, tying WMP with Windows violates the prohibition to abuse a dominant position enshrined in Article 82 of the Treaty and in particular point (d) of the second paragraph thereof.

The Commission fined Microsoft €497,196,304. The fine included that for the other abuse investigated.[307] More seriously for Microsoft it ordered that it should offer PC manufacturers a version of the Windows client PC operating system without the WMP. The manufacturers can choose a 'package' of Windows plus the WMP or one of Windows alone. If they choose the latter they can install a rival media player. Consumers will have a choice of which media player to have when they buy their PC. Microsoft is not allowed to offer any technological, commercial or contractual term or inducement to make the bundled version the more attractive, and a monitoring trustee ensured that the unbundled version of Windows works as well as the bundled version.

Microsoft is appealing against the Commission decision.[308] In the meantime the remedy is proving difficult. Microsoft argued that it should not be ordered to supply a 'degraded' product i.e. Windows with the WMP stripped out and events since the decision have shown that there is no demand amongst computer manufacturers for a version of Windows without WMP.

The Commission's decision raised a number of difficult and controversial issues. Among these is the fact that the Commission's conclusions were based on the premise that there were two products, desktop operating systems and media players. Microsoft argued that it was relevant whether there was consumer demand for the tying product (Windows) without the tied product (WMP). It also argued that the tie did not restrict consumer choice because consumers could download other media players for free. Therefore there was no restriction of *actual* (rather than *hypothetical*) customer choice. Another issue is how far even dominant suppliers should be free to develop new versions of their products with 'built in' features. Economists explain the problem of technological tying and the perceived shortcomings of the Commission decision in the following passages.

D. S. Evans and A. J. Padilla, 'Tying Under Article 82 and the Microsoft Decision' (2004) 27 *World Competition* 4, 503, 511–12[309]

The Commission's single-product test also does not capture those product configurations that are the source of the competitive distortion they believe tying law should remedy. A firm has engaged in tying under their analysis if it offers customers *AB* without also offering customers *A*. If there is no material demand for *A* then the failure to offer *A* cannot have any competitive consequences. Material demand for *A and B* is required for the decision to offer only *AB* to restrict consumer choice in a way that is meaningful. Indeed, lack of material demand for *A* is the test that is needed to eliminate cases such as shoes with shoelaces and cars with tyres that people view as integrated products . . .

That brings us back to a fundamental problem with the Commission's analysis. Having asserted that Windows including media player technologies is not a single product based on a test equivalent

---

[307] Refusal to supply interface information. The Commission said that as regards the tying/bundling abuse it was not applying a new rule but that *Hilti* and *Tetra Pak II* should been sufficient guidance to Microsoft in making it clear that that its conduct infringed Article 82: 'the software industry is not exempted from the application of competition law' (*Microsoft*, para. 1057).

[308] Case T-201/04, *Microsoft* v. *Commission*, judgment pending. Microsoft's application to have the remedies imposed by the decision suspended was dismissed, Case T-201/04 R, *Microsoft* v. *Commission*, Order of the President of the CFI (Judge Vesterdorf), 22 December 2004.

[309] This was written in reply to M. Dolmans and T. Graf, 'Analysis of Tying under Article 82 EC' (2004) 27 *World Competition* 2, 225. It should perhaps be pointed out Dolmans and Graf were with the firm which represented RealNetworks in the case, whereas Evans and Padilla acted as consultant economists for Microsoft.

to Dolmans-Graf, it never investigated whether there was any (let alone material) demand for client PC operating systems without media player technologies ... Significant demand seems doubtful both for commonsense reasons and given that all commercial operating systems come with media player technologies included ... Without knowing whether there is material demand for Windows without media player technologies, the Commission had no way of assessing whether the failure to offer that alternative: (a) foreclosed competition or otherwise distorted the market; or (b) represented normal pro-competitive commercial conduct.

Far from applying settled law, the Commission appears to advocate an extension of tying law in the EC to a vast set of products that are built from components and to numerous products that are based on technological integration of new features ... It does so at the same time that the US courts have rejected the application of mechanical approaches to tying, especially when it comes to technologically sophisticated products or ones for which the courts have had a little experience. Such an extension of tying law would not, in our view, be a good thing in the promoting of the Lisbon Agenda, ... and in particular its goal of making the European Union the most technologically advanced and fastest-growing economy in the world.

R. Pardolesi and A. Renda, 'The European Commission's Case Against Microsoft: Kill Bill? (2004) 27(4) *World Competition* 513, 560–1, 562–3

Even if Microsoft's conduct is found to satisfy the four-step screen normally applied by the European Commission in order to detect anticompetitive tying, we must live with the fact that technological integration is quite different from standard tying ... In other words, in most cases technological integration was found to create more appealing and efficient products, therefore enhancing consumer welfare. For such reason, US courts have gradually abandoned the *per se rule* approach normally adopted for tying claims, and upheld a more careful rule of reason approach, aimed at ascertaining whether the integrated product is more valuable to end users than the sum of its parts ...

In other words, the Commission has never directly addressed the problem of consumer harm in assessing the competitive impact of Microsoft's conduct in the streaming media market. Authoritative commentators have recently denounced an increasing attitude towards neglecting the issue of consumer harm in antitrust policy, and considered weaker, "edentulous" consumer harm standard adopted in cases like *Intel*, *Microsoft* or *Visa* to represent "economically unsound policy" ... Such attitude dangerously brings the Commission back to the resounding *j'accuse* moved by US commentators and policy enforcers in the aftermath of the *GE/Honeywell* decision: that the Commission ends up "protecting competitors, not competition" ...

Economists have also clearly pointed out that technological integration should be treated differently from traditional tying allegations by competition authorities. Under the Chicago school approach, economists have gradually acknowledged that tying can exert in most cases a beneficial impact on consumers. First, a technological tie-in can lead to beneficial removal of the deadweight loss, by allowing better price-discrimination. Secondly, tying can reduce consumer risk. Thirdly, tying can in most cases respond to a need to control the quality of a system good. And, whereas traditional tie-ins can be seen as anticompetitive when they impose additional costs on consumers, software integration normally does not impose any additional charge on end users, since the tied product is in most cases priced at zero, i.e. in line with the marginal cost of most software products. This was the case for Microsoft's tie-in of Internet Explorer with Windows, and is the case for Microsoft's decision to integrate Windows with WMP.

In summary, US enforcers, lawyers and economists have gradually reached the conclusion that technological tying devices deserves a more relaxed approach when subject to antitrust scrutiny, and certainly should be freed from the *per se* rule. The European Commission seems to have completely neglected the premises and underpinnings of such a twenty year long debate. Had the Commission applied sound economic theory, we doubt that unbundling of the media player would have reaped such a wide consensus in Brussels.

The US Department of Justice made it clear that it did not like the Commission decision on the media player point. It will be recalled that the US action against Microsoft in regard to tying was dropped. In a statement on the day of the decision the US Assistant Attorney General for Antitrust explained why the DOJ thought the Commission's action was not pro-competitive.

Assistant Attorney General for Antitrust, R. Hewitt Pate, Issues Statement on the EC'S Decision in its Microsoft Investigation, 24 March 2004[310]

The EC has today pursued a different enforcement approach by imposing a 'code removal' remedy to resolve its media player concerns. The U.S. experience tells us that the best antitrust remedies eliminate impediments to the healthy functioning of competitive markets without hindering successful competitors or imposing burdens on third parties, which may result from the EC's remedy. A requirement of 'code removal' was not at any time—including during the period when the U.S. was seeking a breakup of Microsoft prior to the rejection of that remedy by the court of appeals—part of the United States' proposed remedy.

Imposing antitrust liability on the basis of product enhancements and imposing 'code removal' remedies may produce unintended consequences. Sound antitrust policy must avoid chilling innovation and competition even by 'dominant' companies. A contrary approach risks protecting competitors, not competition, in ways that may ultimately harm innovation and the consumers that benefit from it. It is significant that the U.S. district court considered and rejected a similar remedy in the U.S. litigation.

While the imposition of a civil fine is a customary and accepted aspect of EC antitrust enforcement, it is unfortunate that the largest antitrust fine ever levied will now be imposed in a case of unilateral competitive conduct, the most ambiguous and controversial area of antitrust enforcement. For this fine to surpass even the fines levied against members of the most notorious price fixing cartels may send an unfortunate message about the appropriate hierarchy of enforcement priorities.

However, whatever criticisms are made of the *Microsoft* tying decision, the Commission did take a more effects-based or 'rule of reason' approach than it has done in the past. The tying was not condemned *per se*, as can be seen from paragraph 841. The fact that the Commission's

---

[310] Available on the DOJ web site, http://www.usdoj.gov/atr/public/press_releases/2004/202976.htm.

conclusions are open to criticism should not mask the fact that the framework for the decision departed from previous practice.

(viii) The Discussion Paper Proposals

The Discussion Paper section on tying and bundling was written in the shadow of the *Microsoft* litigation. The Commission stated the four elements required for practices to be abusive under Article 82: dominance in the tying market, two distinct products, a likely market distorting foreclosure effect and no justification objectively or by efficiencies.[311]

The Discussion Paper proposed that in the situation of new product development there will only be a single product where consumer demand has shifted so that there is 'no more independent demand for the tied product'.[312]

On the foreclosure issue, the Commission would first ask 'which customers are "tied" in the sense that competitors to the dominant company cannot compete for their business', and then establish 'whether these customers "add up" to a sufficient part of the market being tied'.[313] Then, where the Commission 'finds that the dominant company ties a sufficient part of the market, the Commission is likely to reach the rebuttable conclusion that the tying practice has a market distorting foreclosure effect and thus constitutes the abuse of a dominant position'.[314]

In respect of the first part of the analysis, in the case of (contractual) tying and pure bundling the individual customers are clearly foreclosed. In the case of mixed bundling the Discussion Paper set out a price-cost measurement analysis, essentially aimed at discovering whether the difference between the price of the bundle and the individual products is sufficient to cover the incremental cost of supplying the tied product. [315] In ascertaining whether the market as a whole is foreclosed, the Discussion Paper lists a number of factors the Commission would take into account.[316] The Discussion Paper recognized that combining two independent products into one new one might be an innovative way to market them and might satisfy an efficiency defence.[317]

In respect of aftermarkets the Discussion Paper said that once dominance has been established,[318] the Commission presumes it is abusive for the undertaking to reserve the aftermarket for itself by excluding competitors (either by tying or refusing to deal).[319]

The Discussion Paper's embrace of an effects based analysis of tying and bundling was generally welcomed, although the detail, particularly its continued reliance on a number of presumptions, was disapproved of in a number of respects. Further guidance from the Commission is likely to reflect the outcome of the next stage of the *Microsoft* case, which is the pending judgment of the CFI.

[311] Para. 183.
[312] Para. 187.
[313] Para. 188.
[314] *Ibid.*
[315] Para. 195.
[316] Paras. 196–203.
[317] Para. 205.
[318] *Supra*, Chap. 6, 428.
[319] Discussion Paper, para. 264.

7. REFUSALS TO SUPPLY

A. GENERAL

A number of cases on Article 82 have concerned a dominant undertaking's refusal to supply its products or services or to grant access to its facilities. The CFI said in *Bayer*:[320]

> 180. . . . under Article [82] refusal to supply, even where it is total, is prohibited only if it constitutes an abuse. The case-law of the Court of Justice indirectly recognises the importance of safe-guarding free enterprise when applying the competition rules of the Treaty where it expressly acknowledges that even an undertaking in a dominant position may, in certain cases, refuse to sell . . .

The Court has never said that all dominant undertakings have an absolute duty to supply all those who request them to do so. However, it is clear that in certain situations a refusal to supply is an abuse. Refusals to supply are exclusionary abuses, in that the dominant undertaking's behaviour denies the other party the tools it need to compete on the market. Unsurprisingly, refusals to supply based on grounds of nationality have been held to infringe Article 82.[321]

The idea that a dominant undertaking has a duty to supply, in that a refusal to do so will be an abuse, is contrary to deep-seated notions of freedom of contract which decree that one should be free to deal with whom one chooses. The Court and Commission have developed their notions of when and why, in the name of competition, that freedom should be limited through a steady stream of decisions and judgments since *Commercial Solvents*[322] in 1973. The theme which pervades much Article 82 jurisprudence, that firms dominant on one market should not use their position to gain competitive advantages on others (leverage),[323] has been prominent in this case law. It has made it difficult for undertakings wishing to integrate vertically or to operate downstream, and it has laid the foundations for the 'essential facilities' doctrine.

The Commission indicated in its 1983 Report that refusal to supply includes making supplies conditional on control over further processing or marketing and 'refusal to supply' includes supplying only on discriminatory and unfair conditions, or 'constructive refusals' where the offer is such that the supplier knows it is unacceptable.[324] Conduct which can be described under some other heading of abuse, such as tying, can also be seen as a refusal to supply. In *Télémarketing*[325] the condition that advertisers could buy advertising time on television only if

---

[320] Case T-41/96, *Bayer AG v. Commission* [2000] ECR II-3383, [2001] 4 CMLR 126, confirmed Cases C-2 and 3/01, *Bundesverband der Arzneimittel-Importeure EV and the Commission v. Bayer AG* [2004] ECR I-23, [2004] 4 CLMR 653. See also *XIIIth Report on Competition Policy* (Commision, 1983), pt. 157 in the context of the *Polaroid/SSI* investigation where Polaroid was alleged to have refused to supply a customer with the quantities ordered because of concerns that SSI intended to export some of the products. Polaroid agreed to supply the full amount and the Commission closed its file.

[321] Case 7/82, *GVL v. Commission* [1983] ECR 483, [1983] 3 CMLR 645, which concerned the German collecting society's refusal to offer its services to artists established outside Germany unless they were of German nationality.

[322] Cases 6, 7/73, *Istituto Chemioterapico Italiano SpA and Commercial Solvents Corp v. EC Commission* [1974] ECR 223, [1974] 1 CMLR 309.

[323] See Case 311/84, *Centre Belge d'Etudes du Marché-Télémarketing v. Compagnie Luxembourgeoise de Télédiffusion SA and Information Publicité Benelux SA* [1985] ECR 3261, [1986] 2 CMLR 558.

[324] For example, in *Napier Brown British Sugar* [1988] OJ L284/41, [1990] 4 CMLR 196 the downstream competitor asked for industrial sugar, but British Sugar was prepared to offer only 'special grain' sugar and at so high a price that the competitor could not use it; in *Deutsche Post AG—Interception of cross-border mail* [2001] OJ L331/40, [2002] 4 CMLR 558 (see *infra* 588) DPAG refused to deliver certain cross-border mail unless the British Post Office paid an excessively and unacceptably high surcharge.

[325] See *supra* 437.

530 | EC COMPETITION LAW

they used the television company's own telesales agency was both a refusal to supply and a tie, and so was the delivered pricing policy in *Napier Brown/British Sugar*.[326]

The cases show how difficult it is for a dominant undertaking to prove that a refusal to supply an existing customer is objectively justified. The defence did succeed, however, in *BP v. Commission*[327] where, during the OPEC oil boycott in 1973, an oil supplier dealt with the shortage by supplying its regular, long-term rather than occasional customers. The Commission found that the refusal to deal with occasional customers on the basis of what they ordered in a previous period was an abuse.[328] However, the Court held that the supply strategy was reasonable in the circumstances and that the refusal to supply ABG was justified.

A finding that a refusal to supply is an abuse raises the question of what is the appropriate remedy. Article 3 of Regulation 17[329] stated that where the Commission finds an infringement of Article 82 'it may by decision require the undertakings...concerned to bring such infringement to an end'. In *Commercial Solvents* the Court established that this did not restrict the Commission to prohibiting actions or practices which are contrary to the Treaty. It allowed it to order an undertaking positively to do certain acts or to provide certain advantages which have been wrongfully withheld, including making specific orders about what exactly the dominant undertaking should supply to whom. This continues to be the position under Article 7 of Regulation 1/2003.[330]

The issue of refusal to supply as a way of hindering parallel trade is dealt with in Section 10 below.

B. THE *COMMERCIAL SOLVENTS* CASE: REFUSAL TO SUPPLY IN ORDER TO EXCLUDE COMPETITORS FROM ANCILLARY MARKETS

Commercial Solvents was the first case in which a refusal to supply was held to be capable of infringing Article 82.

Cases 6 and 7/73, *Istituto Chemioterapico Italiano Spa and Commercial Solvents Corp* v. *Commission* [1974] ECR 223, [1974] 1 CMLR 309

Commercial Solvents (CSC) supplied aminobutanol, a raw material from which a derivative, ethambutol, could be produced. CSC had an Italian subsidiary, Istituto, which resold aminobutanol in Italy to Zoja, an Italian pharmaceuticals company which used it to make ethambutol based anti-TB drugs. In 1970 Zoja cancelled its orders for aminobutanol from Istituto as independent distributors were supplying it cheaper. When these alternative supplies proved unsatisfactory Zoja placed new orders with Istituto. However, CSC had decided no longer to supply aminobutanol to the EEC but

---

[326] *Napier Brown British Sugar* [1988] OJ L284/41, [1990] 4 CMLR 196: see *infra* 601.

[327] Case 77/77, *BP v. Commission* [1978] ECR 1513, [1978] 3 CMLR 174.

[328] *ABG Oil* [1977] OJ L117/1, [1977] 2 CMLR D1. The Commission held that for the duration of the crisis each supplier was in a dominant position in respect of its former customers, a point on which it was upheld by the Court.

[329] See *infra* Chap. 14.

[330] [2003] OJ L1/1.

only an upgraded product, dextroaminobutanol, which Istituto would convert into ethambutol itself, manufacturing its own ethambutol based drugs. Zoja was therefore refused supplies. Zoja found it impossible to obtain supplies on the world market as all its searches led back to CSC. Zoja complained to the Commission. The Commission held that CSC was dominant in the market for aminobutanol and had abused its position by refusing to supply it to Zoja, a refusal which would lead to the elimination of one of the principal manufacturers of ethambutol in the common market. CSC appealed to the Court, which upheld the finding of dominance on the raw material market[331] and the finding of abuse.[332]

Court of Justice

23. The applicants state that they ought not to be held responsible for stopping supplies of aminobutanol to Zoja for this was due to the fact that in the spring of 1970 Zoja itself informed Istituto that it was cancelling the purchase of large quantities of aminobutanol which had been provided for in a contract then in force between Istituto and Zoja. When at the end of 1970 Zoja again contacted Istituto to obtain this product, the latter was obliged to reply, after consulting CSC, that in the meantime CSC had changed its commercial policy and that the product was no longer available. The change of policy by CSC was, they claim, inspired by a legitimate considera-tion of the advantage that would accrue to it of expanding its production to include the manufac-ture of finished products and not limiting itself to that of raw material or intermediate products. In pursuance of this policy it decided to improve its product and no longer to supply aminobutanol save in respect of commitments already entered into by its distributors.

24. It appears from the documents and from the hearing that the suppliers of raw material are limited, as regards the EEC, to Istituto, which, as stated in the claim by CSC, started in 1968 to develop its own specialities based on ethambutol, and in November 1969 obtained the approval of the Italian government necessary for the manufacture and in 1970 started manufacturing its own specialities. When Zoja sought to obtain further supplies of aminobutanol, it received a negative reply. CSC had decided to limit, if not completely to cease, the supply of nitropropane and aminobutanol to certain parties in order to facilitate its own access to the market for the derivatives.

25. However, an undertaking being in a dominant position as regards the production of raw material and therefore able to control the supply to manufacturers of derivatives, cannot, just because it decides to start manufacturing these derivatives (in competition with its former cus-tomers) act in such a way as to eliminate their competition which in the case in question, would amount to eliminating one of the principal manufacturers of ethambutol in the Common Market. Since such conduct is contrary to the objectives expressed in Article [3(1)(g)] of the Treaty and set out in greater detail in Articles [81] and [82], it follows that an undertaking which has a dominant position in the market in raw materials and which, with the object of reserving such raw materials for manufacturing its own derivatives, refuses to supply a customer, which is itself a manufacturer of these derivatives, and therefore risks eliminating all competition on the part of this customer, is abusing its dominant position within the meaning of Article [82]. In this context it does not matter that the undertaking ceased to supply in the spring of 1970 because of the cancellation of the pur-chases by Zoja, because it appears from the applicants' own statement that, when the supplies provided for in the contract had been completed, the sale of aminobutanol would have stopped in any case.

---

[331] See *supra* Chap. 6.

[332] It also upheld the finding that there was an effect on inter-Member State trade on the basis that although few of Zoja's ethambutol-based drugs were exported to other Member States the elimination of Zoja as a competitor would affect the competitive structure of the common market: see *supra* Chap. 5.

26. It is also unnecessary to examine, as the applicants have asked, whether Zoja had an urgent need for aminobutanol in 1970 and 1971 or whether this company still had large quantities of this product which would enable it to reorganize its production in good time, since that question is not relevant to the consideration of the conduct of the applicants.

27. Finally CSC states that its production of nitropropane and aminobutanol ought to be considered in the context of nitration of paraffin, of which nitropropane is only one of the derivatives, and that similarly aminobutanol is only one of the derivatives of nitropropane. Therefore the possibilities of producing the two products in question are not unlimited but depend in part on the possible sales outlets of the other derivatives.

28. However the applicants do not seriously dispute the statement in the Decision in question to the effect that 'in view of the production capacity of the CSC plant it can be confirmed that CSC can satisfy Zoja's needs, since Zoja represents a very small percentage (approximately 5–6 per cent) of CSC's global production of nitropropane'. It must be concluded that the Commission was justified in considering that such statements could not be taken into account.

29. These submissions must therefore be rejected.

According to paragraph 25, the factors leading to the finding of abuse were that CSC was using its dominant position on the raw material market to affect competition on the derivatives market, that it refused to supply an existing customer[333] because it wanted to compete with it downstream, and that the refusal risked eliminating the customer from the downstream market.

CSC had, in effect, decided to integrate vertically. The Court did not consider, however, whether this strategy might produce efficiencies, and there is no discussion in the judgment about the possible benefits to the end user, the consumer. It appears to be an instance of the competition authorities protecting the situation of the 'small' competitor and it may even have been significant that Zoja was a small *Italian* competitor suffering at the hands of an American multinational.

C. REFUSAL TO SUPPLY IN RESPONSE TO AN ATTACK ON THE DOMINANT UNDERTAKING'S COMMERCIAL INTERESTS

It has been held that a dominant undertaking may infringe Article 82 by refusing to supply as a response to a perceived threat to its commercial interests. In *United Brands*[334] the Commission held that UBC had abused its dominant position on the banana market by refusing to continue supplying its Chiquita bananas to its Danish ripener/distributor, Oelsen. The refusal was made in response to Oelsen taking part in an advertising and promotion campaign for a rival brand, Standard Fruit's 'Dole' bananas. Oelsen was not under an exclusive purchasing obligation but UBC argued that Oelsen had sold fewer and fewer Chiquitas in comparison to Doles, and had taken less trouble in ripening them. Without gainsaying UBC's allegations, the Court upheld the Commission's finding that there was no objective justification for the refusal to supply and that it infringed Article 82.

---

[333] It was not material that Zoja had previously cancelled its purchases from Istituto (see para. 25, last sentence).

[334] [1976] OJ L95/1, [1976] 1 CMLR D28.

Case 27/76, *United Brands* v. *Commission* [1978] ECR 207, [1978] 1 CMLR 429

Court of Justice

182. ... [i]t is advisable to assert positively from the outset that an undertaking in a dominant position for the purpose of marketing a product—which cashes in on the reputation of a brand name known to and valued by the consumers—cannot stop supplying a long standing customer who abides by regular commercial practice, if the orders placed by that customer are in no way out of the ordinary.

183. Such conduct is inconsistent with the objectives laid down in Article [3(1)(g)] of the Treaty, which are set out in detail in Article [82], especially in paragraphs (b) and (c), since the refusal to sell would limit markets to the prejudice of consumers and would amount to discrimination which might in the end eliminate a trading party from the relevant market.

...

189. Although it is true, as the applicant points out, that the fact that an undertaking is in a dominant position cannot disentitle it from protecting its own commercial interests if they are attacked, and that such an undertaking must be conceded the right to take such reasonable steps as it deems appropriate to protect its said interests, such behaviour cannot be countenanced if its actual purpose is to strengthen this dominant position and abuse it.

190. Even if the possibility of a counter-attack is acceptable that attack must still be proportionate to the threat taking into account the economic strength of the undertakings confronting each other.

191. The sanction consisting of a refusal to supply by an undertaking in a dominant position was in excess of what might, if such a situation were to arise, reasonably be contemplated as a sanction for conduct similar to that for which UBC blamed Olesen.

192. In fact UBC could not be unaware of that fact that by acting in this way it would discourage its other ripener/distributors from supporting the advertising of other brand names and that the deterrent effect of the sanction imposed upon one of them would make its position of strength on the relevant market that much more effective.

193. Such a course of conduct amounts therefore to a serious interference with the independence of small and medium sized firms in their commercial relations with the undertaking in a dominant position and this independence implies the right to give preference to competitors' goods.

194. In this case the adoption of such a course of conduct is designed to have a serious adverse effect on competition on the relevant banana market by only allowing firms dependant upon the dominant undertaking to stay in business.

195. The applicant's argument that in its view the 40 per cent fall in the price of bananas on the Danish market shows that competition has not been affected by the refusal to supply Olesen cannot be upheld.

196. In fact this fall in prices was only due to the very lively competition—called at the time the 'banana war'—in which the two transnational companies UBC and Castle and Cooke engaged.

This is a prime example of the objective justification issue in the context of Article 82. Whilst affirming that dominant undertakings are justified in acting to prevent attacks on their commercial interests, the Court nevertheless judged UBC's response here to be disproportionate. It reached this conclusion despite recognizing that the company was in the midst of a 'banana war'.[335] It is not clear, given Oelsen's conduct, what the Court meant when it stated, in paragraph 182, that a dominant undertaking could not stop supplying a regular customer who 'abides by regular commercial practice'. Jebsen and Stevens argue[336] that 'the Court of Justice inferred an anti-competitive motive on United Brands' part, without, as far as one can see, a scintilla of evidence, and then condemned United Brands for having had this improper motive'. In their view the case results in the Court effectively precluding dominant undertakings 'from refusing to supply customers who either directly or indirectly wage an assault on their businesses'. The Discussion Paper saw United Brands' behaviour as aimed at reinforcing exclusive dealing and suggested it should be analysed in that context.[337]

A similar situation arose in *Boosey & Hawkes*[338] where B&H, which the Commission held to be dominant in the narrowly defined British-style brass band instrument market, refused to have further dealings with two firms, one a distributor of its instruments and the other a repairer, who formed a company to manufacture and market instruments which competed with B&H's. The Commission took interim measures, ordering B&H to recommence supplies to its two customers. Again, the Commission recognized the right of dominant undertakings to protect their interests when attacked but refused to accept the conduct here was justified and proportionate.

BBI/Boosey & Hawkes: Interim Measures [1987] OJ L286/36, [1988] 4 CMLR 67

Commission

19. A course of conduct adopted by a dominant undertaking with a view to excluding a competitor from the market by means of other than legitimate competition on the merits may constitute an infringement of Article [82].

In the present case the documentary evidence indicates that B&H embarked on a course of conduct intended to remove the competitive threat from BBI, and that its withdrawal of supplies from GHH and RCN was part of that plan.

It is well established that refusal of supplies by a dominant producer to an established customer without objective justification may constitute an abuse under Article [82] (Case 27/76 *United Brands* v. *Commission*; Cases 6/73 and 7/73 *Commercial Solvents* . . .).

On the facts of the present case, the dependence of GHH and RCN on B&H products is such that there was a substantial likelihood of their going out of business as a result of the withholding of supplies.

The injury to competition would be aggravated where (as is alleged here) the stated purpose of the action is indirectly to prevent the entry into the market of a potential competitor to the dominant producer.

A dominant undertaking may always take reasonable steps to protect its commercial interests, but such measures must be fair and proportional to the threat. The fact that a customer of a dominant producer becomes associated with a competitor or a potential competitor of that manufacturer does not normally entitle the dominant producer to withdraw all supplies immediately or to take reprisals against that customer.

---

[335] In para. 196. As discussed *supra* in Chap. 6, UBC was found dominant with 45% of a narrowly drawn market (bananas rather than fruit) despite evidence of what the Court itself here calls 'very lively competition'.

[336] P. Jebsen and R. Stevens, 'Assumptions, Goals, and Dominant Undertakings: The Reg. of Competition Under Art. 86 of the European Union' (1996) 64 *Antitrust LJ* 443, 510–11.

[337] Discussion Paper, para. 208.

[338] *BBI/Boosey & Hawkes* [1987] OJ L 286/36, [1988] 4 CMLR 67. There were other alleged abuses by B&H, such as engaging in vexatious litigation (see *infra* 582).

> There is no obligation placed on a dominant producer to subsidize competition to itself. In the case where a customer transfers its central activity to the promotion of a competing brand it may be that even a dominant producer is entitled to review its commercial relations with that customer and on giving adequate notice terminate any special relationship. However, the refusal of all supplies to GHH and RCN, and the other actions B&H has taken against them as part of its reaction to the perceived threat of BBI, would appear in the circumstances of the present case to go beyond the legitimate defence of B&H's commercial interests.

B&H took the measures it did to retaliate against its customers for entering into competition with it. Had the new company been successful it could have seriously threatened B&H's position in a highly specialized, narrowly-defined market. The Commission saw here a dominant undertaking trying to exclude others from the market and seemed only reluctantly to admit that in the circumstances which arose in this case 'even a dominant producer is entitled to review its commercial relations'. It shows, like *United Brands*, how seriously a finding of dominance limits an undertaking's conduct.

D. THE REFUSAL TO SUPPLY SPARE PARTS

A firm which refuses to supply spare parts may infringe Article 82 even though it is not dominant in the primary product market, but only in the market for its own spare parts. This was established in *Hugin*.

Hugin AB was a Swedish manufacturer of cash registers. Hugin's share of the cash register market was 12–14 per cent. Liptons was a UK firm which had been Hugin's exclusive distributor in the UK and had built up a business of servicing and repairing Hugin machines and renting them out, for which it required a constant supply of Hugin spare parts. Hugin supplied Liptons with spare parts until 1972 when it established a UK subsidiary to deal with its products in the UK and ceased to supply Liptons with spare parts. Liptons said that it was likely to go out of business as a result. The Commission held that in refusing to carry on supplying Liptons Hugin had abused its dominant position in the market for its own spare parts.[339] The Court annulled the decision, ruling that there was no effect on inter-Member State trade, but it confirmed the finding of dominance.[340] The Court did not rule on the finding of abuse but in the light of other developments in the cases on refusal to supply the Commission's decision was significant.

> ### *Liptons Cash Registers/ Hugin* [1978] OJ L22/23, [1978] 1 CMLR D19
>
> #### Commission
>
> 63. In cases in which an undertaking holding a dominant position within the Common Market or in a substantial part of it for the supply of certain products, and in particular where the dominant position is a monopoly:
>
> (a) refused without objective justification to supply those products to existing substantial customers for and users of the products, and the refusal to supply seriously injures the latter

---

[339] For the dominant position aspect of this case, see *supra* Chap. 6.
[340] See *supra* Chap. 6.

> in their business by interfering with and ultimately preventing them from continuing to offer a service or to carry on a line of business, thereby ultimately eliminating all competitors independent of the dominant undertaking from the market for that service or that line of business; and
>
> (b) prohibits its subsidiaries and dealers from supplying those products outside its own distribution network and in particular to buyers in other member-States, thereby making the refusal to supply more effective by denying those products to the customers and users in question.
>
> such conduct amounts to an abuse of a dominant position, where it causes competition to be substantially restricted and trade between member-States to be affected appreciably.

Hugin was not dominant on the cash register market, and the case raised the issues of power in aftermarkets and tying in aftermarkets.[341] Hugin, like Commercial Solvents, wanted to integrate vertically. The Commission rejected its claim of objective justification and (at paragraph 63(a)) said that the refusal to supply was an abuse because it would lead to an existing customer being unable to carry out a particular line of business. As in *Commercial Solvents* the Commission did not consider questions of efficiencies or the advantages to owners of Hugin machines of the vertical integration but looked at the situation from the perspective of Liptons. It seems that the Commission's objective was Lipton's continued presence on the market: the protection of competitors rather than competition.

The Court did deal, obliquely, with the refusal to supply spare parts in two Article 234 references concerning the licensing of intellectual property rights covering car parts, *Renault*[342] and *Volvo*.[343] In *Volvo* the Court held that a refusal by the car manufacturer to license did not necessarily constitute an abuse, but would do so if it gave rise to 'certain abusive conduct...such as the arbitrary refusal to deliver spare parts to independent repairers'.[344]

E. REFUSAL TO SUPPLY AND THE 'ESSENTIAL FACILITIES' CONCEPT

(i) General

In *Commercial Solvents* and *Télémarketing* it was found that an outright refusal to supply, or a refusal to supply unless tied products or services were accepted, constituted an abuse. In both cases the refusal interfered with competition on a downstream market. The principle in those cases has been expanded upon and applied subsequently. A good example of a refusal to supply as a deliberate move to remove a competitor from a downstream market is *Napier Brown/British Sugar*,[345] where the dominant supplier of industrial sugar, which itself produced the derivative retail sugar, refused to supply industrial sugar to a competitor on the downstream market who was an existing customer.

---

[341] See *supra* Chap. 6 and *supra*, 514 ff.

[342] Case 53/87, *CICCRA v. Renault* [1988] ECR 6039, [1990] 4 CMLR 265.

[343] Case 238/87, *AB Volvo v. Erik Veng* [1988] ECR 6211, [1989] 4 CMLR 122.

[344] Case 53/87, *CICCRA v. Renault. supra* n. 333, para. 16. The case is considered further *infra*, 555 and Chap. 10.

[345] *Napier Brown British Sugar* [1988] OJ L284/41, [1990] 4 CMLR 196.

(ii) Access to Facilities and Resources

A number of Commission decisions concerning refusal to supply have led to the development in EC law of what is called an 'essential facilities doctrine'. These decisions have concerned not the supply of products but the grant of access to some kind of facility or resource controlled by the dominant undertaking.[346] One of these decisions was *London-European Sabena*.[347] In this case the Belgian airline Sabena was dominant in Belgium in the computer reservation services market. It refused to give London-European, a competing airline, access to the system (although it had spare capacity). The Commission found that the refusal, which was to pressurize London-European either to withdraw from the London-Brussels route or to raise prices and also to punish London-European for its failure to use Sabena's ground-handling services, was an abuse. The Commission said that Sabena's conduct could equally be seen as a desire to limit production, markets, or technical development to the prejudice of consumers, contrary to Article 82(b), and as enforcing a tie contrary to Article 82(d). In this case, therefore, the Commission required a dominant undertaking to share its facilities with a competitor. As is seen below, in many of the cases where access to facilities or resources has been denied the undertaking refusing access has been dominant in consequence of a legal or statutory monopoly. The issue has particularly arisen in the transport sector, but it is also very important in the liberalization of sectors such as telecommunications.[348]

(iii) The Development of the 'Essential Facilities' Doctrine in EC Law

a. General

The definition of an 'essential facility' is fraught with difficulty. However, the central idea is that it is something owned or controlled by a dominant undertaking to which other undertakings need access in order to provide products or services to customers. It is sometimes called a 'bottleneck monopoly'. A refusal to grant access to an essential facility may be a breach of the competition rules.

The essential facilities doctrine originated in US law, where it has proved to be highly contentious. When the Commission started using the expression it was therefore employing a concept which was familiar to competition lawyers and the subject of much debate in the US context. The present position in US law is described below.[349]

b. The Commission Decisions on Essential Facilities

The Commission did not use the expression 'essential facility' until *Sealink/B&I Holyhead*[350] in 1992. It is possible, however, particularly with hindsight, to see that the doctrine manifested itself in earlier cases discussed above and in the Commission decision *British-Midland/Aer Lingus*.[351]

[346] This is one reason why it is sometimes preferable to use the expression 'refusal to deal', rather than 'refusal to supply'.

[347] [1988] OJ L317/47, [1989] 4 CMLR 662.

[348] See *infra* 342.

[349] *Infra* 575.

[350] *Sealink/B&I Holyhead: Interim Measures* [1992] 5 CMLR 255.

[351] See J. Temple Lang, 'Defining Legitimate Competition: Companies' Duties to Supply Competitors and Access to Essential Facilities' (1994) 18 *Fordham Int'l LJ* 437 and the Commission's citation of cases in *Sealink/B&I*.

British Midland/Aer Lingus [1992] OJ L96/34, [1993] 4 CMLR 596

Interlining is a standard practice in the air transport industry, operated by IATA through a multilateral agreement to which interested airlines become parties, whereby airlines are authorised to sell each other's services. As a result a single ticket can be issued which comprises segments to be performed by different airlines. The issuing airline collects the price for all segments from the passenger and pays the fare due to the carrying line. The system enables a passenger to use a ticket issued by one airline for a return journey on another. Aer Lingus, which was held by the Commission to be in a dominant position on the London (Heathrow)-Dublin air-route, withdrew from its interlining arrangements with British Midland when British Midland started to operate a Heathrow-Dublin service. In a press statement at the time Aer Ligus said 'We have established ourselves as the dominant carrier on the routes between the two capitals, and intend to remain so . . . , British Midland does not have the resources to offer a similar frequency or service, so they want us to provide product for them via an interline agreement'.[352] The Commission held that the refusal to interline was an abuse of Aer Lingus's dominant position, fined it ECU 750,000 and ordered it to interline with British Midland on the Heathrow-Dublin route for two years.

Commission

24. Abusive conduct is defined as 'practices which are likely to affect the structure of a market where, as a result of the presence of the undertaking in question, competition has already been weakened and which, through recourse to methods differing from those governing normal competition in goods or services based on traders' performance, have the effect of hindering the maintenance or development of the level of competition existing on the market' (Case 85/76, *Hoffmann-La Roche* v. *E.C. Commission* . . .).

25. Refusing to interline is not normal competition on the merits. Interlining has for many years been accepted industry practice, with widely acknowledged benefits for both airlines and passengers. A refusal to interline for reasons other than problems with currency convertibility or doubts about the creditworthiness of the beneficiary airline is a highly unusual step and has up to now not been considered by the European airline industry as a normal competitive strategy. Aer Lingus itself has maintained interline agreements with the other airlines competing with it on London-Dublin services, British Airways and Dan Air.

Aer Lingus has argued that, whereas interlining in most circumstances is beneficial to all participating airlines, it would suffer from interlining with British Midland by losing several points of market share to the new entrant. Even if this could be demonstrated, the argument that interlining would result in a loss of revenue would not in itself make the refusal legitimate. Aer Lingus has not argued that interlining with British Midland would have a significant effect on its own costs, whereas there is evidence that a refusal to interline would impose a significant handicap on British Midland.

26. Both a refusal to grant new interline facilities and the withdrawal of existing interline facilities may, depending on the circumstances, hinder the maintenance or development of competition. Whether a duty to interline arises depends on the effects on competition of the refusal to interline; it would exist in particular when the refusal or withdrawal of interline facilities by a dominant airline is objectively likely to have a significant impact on the other airline's ability to start a new service or sustain an existing service on account of its effects on the other airline's costs and revenue in respect of the service in question, and when the dominant airline cannot give any

---

[352] Para. 7.

objective commercial reason for its refusal (such as concerns about creditworthiness) other than its wish to avoid helping this particular competitor. It is unlikely that there is such justification when the dominant airline singles out an airline with which it previously interlined, after that airline starts competing on an important route, but continues to interline with other competitors.

27. When an airline commences a new service, it will normally expect to incur some losses during an initial period, during which it will have to organise economic operation of its service and to attract sufficient interest from the travel trade and from travellers. It cannot expect to attain the load factors and the revenue necessary to ensure profitable operations from the beginning of the service. Therefore new entry will always be difficult.

Denying interline facilities is likely to increase that difficulty. A new entrant without interlining facilities is likely to be considered in this respect as a second-rate airline by travel agents and by travellers alike, which will make it more difficult to attain the commercial standing required to operate profitably. Travel agents wish to avoid the loss of time, the extra work and the potential loss of revenue caused by issuing tickets for transport on an airline without interline facilities. Furthermore a significant number of passengers consider the possibility to change tickets and to organise complex journeys on a single ticket as necessary; a refusal to interline will have the effect of diverting many of these passengers away from the new entrant airline. In this respect, a refusal to interline affects in particular the well-informed business travellers who require fully flexible tickets and who make a disproportionately large contribution to the revenue of the new entrant; significantly reducing this revenue will have a serious affect on the economics of the new entrant's operations . . .

28. A refusal to interline also hinders the maintenance or development of competition when it imposes a significant cost on competitors . . .

29. It is true that Aer Lingus' strategy in the event has not resulted in British Midland's departure from the route, and that British Midland has succeeded in building up a reasonable schedule and in obtaining a significant market share . . .

The fact that British Midland has been able to continue operations notwithstanding the handicap imposed on it by Aer Lingus, is due in the first place to British Midland's determination to succeed in the face of unusual difficulties; it does not mean that the refusal had no effect on competition. There is no doubt that at the time the practice was implemented, the refusal to interline was intended and was likely to hinder the development of competition. The lawfulness of the refusal at the time when it occurred cannot depend on whether the competitor was later willing and able to remain on the route in spite of the disadvantages imposed on it.

30. Consequently, Aer Lingus has pursued a strategy which (even if not wholly effective) is both selective and exclusionary and restricts the development of competition on the London (Heathrow)–Dublin route.

The refusal to interline in this case essentially consists in the imposition, contrary to normal industry practice, of a significant handicap on a competitor by raising its costs and depriving it of revenue. Aer Lingus has not been able to point to efficiencies created by a refusal to interline nor to advance any other persuasive and legitimate business justification for its conduct. Its desire to avoid loss of market share, the circumstance that this a route of vital importance to the company and that its operating margin in under pressure do not make this a legitimate response to new entry.

In this case the refusal to supply affected competition on the market on which the dominant position existed, and not on a downstream market. The Commission did not condemn refusals to interline *per se* but only where they have significant effects on competition (paragraph 26) and are not objectively justified. In this case, in fact, Aer Lingus's strategy had *not* resulted in

British Midland's departure from the route, and it is difficult to see that the interlining could be classified as an essential facility. It was not *essential* to the competitor's operations.[353] However, the mode of reasoning is similar both to the American cases and to the Commission decisions which succeeded it. It was a case of a clear intention of refusing to supply in order to exclude a competitor, although Aer Lingus was dominant only because of the narrowly defined market and no more than a minnow in the wider European airline market.[354] The case well illustrates the point that it does not matter if the new competitor is a powerful player on *another* market (a similar situation arose in *Irish Sugar*[355] where the undertaking dominant in Ireland was trying to exclude the dominant French supplier from the Irish market). *British-Midland* needs to be seen in context, however, as part of the Commission's drive to liberalize the European air transport sector.[356]

The first express reference to the essential facilities doctrine in EC law was made in *B&I/Sealink*:

Sealink/B&I Holyhead: Interim Measures [1992] 5 CMLR 255

Sealink Harbours was the owner and operator of the port at Holyhead, in Wales, and as such was held by the Commission to be in a dominant position on the market on the British side for port facilities for ferry services on the 'central corridor' route between Wales and Ireland (i.e., Holyhead to Dublin and Dun Laoghaire). It ran ferries on that route. B&I also ran ferries from the port. B&I used a particular berth, the Admiralty Pier, and the limitations of the harbour were such that whenever Sealink's ferries passed the berth the drawing away of water and turbulence meant that B&I had to cease all loading and unloading activity. B&I complained that Sealink intended to introduce a new timetable which would cause greater disruption to B&I's schedules in this way. The Commission adopted a decision providing for interim measures, ordering Sealink to return to its previous timetable. The matter never went to a final decision as the dispute was settled.

Commission

41. A dominant undertaking which both owns or controls and itself uses an essential facility, i.e., a facility or infrastructure without access to which competitors cannot provide services to their customers, and which refuses its competitors access to that facility or grants access to competitors only on terms less favourable than those which it gives its own services, thereby placing the competitors at a competitive disadvantage, infringes Article [82], if the other conditions of that Article are met....[357] A company in a dominant position may not discriminate in favour of its own activities in a related market (Case C-260/89 *Elliniki Radiophonia*, paragraphs 37–38)... The owner

[353] It would not fulfill the criteria laid down by the ECJ in Case C-7/97, *Oscar Bronner GmbH & Co KG v. Mediaprint* [1998] ECR I-7791, [1999] 4 CMLR 112, discussed *infra* at 547.

[354] A point which was made in a question about the decision put to the Competition Commissioner by an Irish MEP: E.P. Deb. 3-418/222 (13 May 1992), question No. H-0464/92, [1992] 5 CMLR 209.

[355] Case T-228/97, *Irish Sugar plc v. Commission* [1999] ECR II-2969, [1999] 5 CMLR 1 300, confirmed Case C-497/99 P, *Irish Sugarplc v. Commission* [2001] ECR I-5333, [2001] 5 CMLR 1082.

[356] The Commission said of the case: 'This decision is evidence of the Commission's determination to act against airlines holding dominant positions, if they attempt to prevent the development or maintenance of competition. At a time when the European air transport industry is being liberalized, airlines making use of the new opportunities for competition should be given a fair chance to develop and sustain their challenge to established carriers. Airlines holding dominant positions should not penalize this competition. They should not withold facilities which the industry traditionally provides to all other airlines, and they should take care to compete strictly on the merits of their own services.' (Commission's *XXIInd Report on Competition Policy* (Commission, 1992), para. 218.

[357] The Commission here cited Cases 6 and 7/73 *Istituto Chemioterapico Italiano Spa and Commercial Solvents Corp v. EC Commission* [1974] ECR 223, [1974] 1 CMLR 309; Case 311/84, *Centre Belge d'Etudes du*

of an essential facility which uses its power in one market in order to strengthen its position in another related market, in particular, by granting its competitor access to that related market on less favourable terms than those of its own services, infringes Article [82] where a competitive disadvantage is imposed upon its competitor without objective justification.

. . .

42. The owner of the essential facility, which also uses the essential facility, may not impose a competitive disadvantage on its competitor, also a user of the essential facility, by altering its own schedule to the detriment of the competitor's service, where, as in this case, the construction or the features of the facility are such that it is not possible to alter one competitor's service in the way chosen without harming the other's. Specifically, where, as in this case, the competitor is already subject to a certain level of disruption from the dominant undertaking's activities, there is a duty to the dominant undertaking not to take any action which will result in further disruption. That is so even if the latter's actions make, or are primarily intended to make its operations more efficient. Subject to any objective elements outside its control, such an undertaking is under a duty not to impose a competitive disadvantage upon its competitor in the use of the shared facility without objective justification, as seemed to be accepted by SHL in 1989.

In the first sentence of paragraph 41 the Commission laid down the basic principle that an owner of an essential facility may have to provide non-discriminatory access to it to a competitor. The Commission developed the theme in three further decisions concerning ports, *Sea Containers Ltd v. Stena*,[358] *Port of Rødby (Euro-port) v. Denmark*,[359] and *Morlaix (Port of Roscoff)*.[360] In *Sea Containers* Stena Sealink (previously Sealink, the port authority and ferry operator involved in *Sealink/B I Holyhead*), refused to give the requested access to a company wanting to operate a new fast ferry service on the Wales-Ireland central corridor route by lightweight catamaran. The Commission, repeating the *B&I* decision held this was an abuse.

The *Sea Containers/Stena* decision made it clear that the duty to supply essential facilities set out in *Sealink/B&I* applies to *new* as well as to existing customers. This was also shown in another decision taken on the same day, *Port of Rødby*, in which the Commission held that Denmark had infringed Article 86(1) in conjunction with Article 82.[361]*Morlaix (Port of Roscoff)*[362] dealt with a

Marché-Télémarketing v. Compagnie Luxembourgeoise de Télédiffusion SA and Information Publicité Benelux SA [1985] ECR 3261, [1986] 2 CMLR 558; Case 53/87 *CICCRA v. Renault* [1988] ECR 6039, [1990] 4 CMLR 265; Case 238/87, *AB Volvo v. Erik Veng* [1988] ECR 6211, [1989] 4 CMLR 122; Case C-260/89, *Elliniki Radiophonia Tileorasi (ERT) v. DEP* [1991] ECR I-2925; Cases T-69–70/89, *RTE, ITP, BBC v. EC Commission (Magill)* [1991] ECR II-485, [1991] 4 CMLR 586, (the ECJ judgment had not yet been given); Case C-18/88, *LRTT v. GB-INNO-BM SA* [1991] ECR I-5941; and the Commission decisions *National Carbonising* [1976] OJ L35/6, [1976] 1 CMLR D82; *London-European/Sabena* [1988] OJ L317/47, [1989] 4 CMLR 662.; *British Midland/Aer Lingus* [1992] OJ L 96/34, [1993] 4 CMLR 596.

358 *Sea Containers Ltd/Stena Sealink* [1994] OJ L15/8, [1995] 4 CMLR 84.

359 [1994] OJ L55/52, [1994] 5 CMLR 457.

360 [1995] 5 CMLR 177.

361 *Port of Rødby* [1994] OJ L55/52, [1994] 5 CMLR 457. The port of Rødby in Denmark was owned and managed by a publicly owned port authority (DSB) which operated the only ferry between there and Puttgarden in Germany jointly with German national railways (DB). Two other companies, Euro-Port and Scan-Port wanted to run a ferry on the same route. The Danish Government refused either to grant them access to the port or to grant permission to build another terminal on the immediate vicinity. The Commission held that DSB was a public undertaking in a dominant position on the market for the organization of port services in Denmark for ferries on the Rødby-Puttgarden route and that the double refusal had the effect of eliminating a potential competitor and infringed Article 82. '... [A]n undertaking that owns or manages an essential port facility from which it provides a maritime transport service may not, without objective justification, refuse to grant a shipowner wishing to operate on the same maritime route access to that facility without infringing Article [82]' (*Port of Rødby*, para. 12). For Article 86, which deals with the application of the competition rules to public undertakings, see *infra* Chap. 8.

362 [1995] 5 CMLR 177.

slightly, though significantly, different situation. Irish Continental Group (ICG) wanted to run a ferry service from Ireland to Brittany and needed access to the port of Roscoff, which was managed by CCI Morlaix, a French administrative body granted a concession by the State for that purpose. CCI Morlaix did *not* run ferries itself, although it did have a shareholding of about 5 per cent in Brittany Ferries, which at the time operated the only ferry running from Ireland to Brittany. The Commission found that CCI Morlaix's difficult behaviour over the negotiations for access amounted to a refusal to supply and that the refusal would have been an abuse *even if the authority had had no interest in Brittany Ferries*.

c. Issues in the Essential Facilities Doctrine

The recognition of the concept of essential facilities is just the beginning. Even if the doctrine is accepted many questions follow which have to be answered: what exactly constitutes an essential facility? when does access have to be given? to whom does it have to be given? on what terms must it be given?

In *B&I/Sealink* essential facilities were defined as 'a facility or infrastructure without access to which competitors cannot provide services to their customers'. This definition provides only a starting point. The definition should, however, be narrowly confined, since a finding that an undertaking is dominant over essential facilities may result in that undertaking being forced to share its facilities or assets with its competitors. This represents a severe interference with an undertaking's rights which can only be justified where there would otherwise be a serious effect on competition which cannot be remedied by less intrusive measures.

There has to be some way of identifying assets to which access by competitors is truly 'essential' rather than merely desirable. Even when these are identified there may be practical problems about access or sharing. Some facilities (ports for example) have limited physical capacity, and the question arises *which* competitors should be given access. There is also the matter of the *terms* on which access is given. If the parties are left to settle their own terms the owner of the facility may be able to impose a price which is prohibitively high.[363] If the terms are to be set by an authority such as the Commission, however, the authority ends up acting as a price regulator.

It will be noted that the Commission decisions mentioned above concern the transport sector. The development of the essential facilities doctrine in EC law was closely bound up with liberalization in that sector. This is no coincidence. The Commission used the doctrine to encourage competition where there had previously been monopoly. The essential facilities doctrine has a particular relevance to liberalization in transport and in the utilities sectors,[364] which across the Community have been opened up to competition. Competition, however, is possible only if new competitors are granted access to existing facilities, such as networks, which cannot feasibly be replicated and which may originally have been developed with public money. Even where replication is possible it may be against the public interest on other grounds, such as environmental considerations. On the other hand, an over-enthusiastic approach to essential facilities may result in undertakings having to share with competitors assets which they have developed over many years at great expense. Robbing firms of the fruits of their endeavours may be injurious to the public interest as it removes incentives to innovation.

---

[363] See Case C-242/95, *GT–Link A/S v. De Danske Statsbaner (DSB)* [1997] ECR I-4449, [1997] 5 CMLR 601, where the ECJ held that excessive duties levied by a public undertaking on a ferry company in breach of Article 86, in conjunction with Article 82, must be repaid.

[364] See the Notice on the Application to Access Agreements in the Telecommunications Sector [1998] OJ C265/2.

These issues and the difficulties inherent in the recognition of the essential facilities doctrine are discussed in the following extracts. The first author is an economist and the second was an eminent American commentator.

D. Ridyard: 'Essential Facilities and the Obligation to Supply Competitors' [1996] *ECLR* 438, 447–8, 450, 451

Identifying the essential facility

Essential facilities cases invariably originate from a complaint by a firm that feels disadvantaged by a competitor's position. Unless a complete revolution in competition policy enforcement is envisaged, however, it does not make sense to treat 'disadvantage to a competitor' as a sufficient condition for the existence of an essential facility. This would lead to intervention as soon as any firm gained a competitive advantage that its rivals envied.

Equally, 'disadvantage to consumers' is likely to be a poor or unworkable criterion despite its superficial appeal. The tension between static and dynamic incentives for efficiency within a market economy will always entail unrealised potential consumer gains remaining untapped at any point in time if the market is working effectively. Any competition policy action that focuses exclusively on the immediate short-term impact on consumers, whether in essential facility or other circumstances, stands to do considerable economic damage. . . .

To gain a proper perspective, it is necessary to stand back from specific concerns of consumers and competitors, and instead to ask where essential facilities issues fit into the general objective of competition rules to protect effective competition. This suggests that the key to the problem is to assess whether the owner of the allegedly essential facility is subject to effective competitive pressure, either in the form of existing assets also competing at the up-stream level, or in the form of potential assets that other firms might create. Any rational standard of effective or workable competition must acknowledge that some competitive activity will be very highly rewarded, so assets created through the competitive process will be highly sought after by others. But it is only where competition has seriously broken down or cannot be expected to operate that a case for compulsion arises.

In the great majority of cases, this approach will confine the existence of essential facilities to natural monopoly activities that, quite apart from it being commercially infeasible, one would not even want competitors to replicate . . .

The identification of an essential facility using this test has important consequences that must be acknowledged in full if a rational policy is to emerge. Once it is acknowledged that it is neither feasible nor even desirable for competitors to replicate the asset concerned, it follows that the essential facility is a monopoly asset, and that if the competition rules are used to impose a duty on the owner to share the asset with competitors, these powers must also be used to regulate the terms on which that access is granted.

This need for the regulator to enter into price decisions does imply an unattractive degree of intervention in the market, but one that logically must be unavoidable once it is decided that an essential facility must be shared. A recognition of the difficulties that the competition body must resolve once it has identified the essential facility should serve to provide a sharp reminder not to take up essential facilities cases too readily.

Negotiation between the owner of the essential facility and the complainant

Free negotiation cannot be expected to provide a satisfactory solution. If the essential facility is indeed a monopoly, the outcome of free negotiation between a monopoly asset owner and a competitive complainant must also be unsatisfactory. Indeed, refusal to supply or deal is itself equivalent to the asset owner setting an access price that is prohibitively high, and any asset owner subject to free negotiation will be able to replicate this outcome by quoting a sufficiently high price.

There are several reasons why it may be pro-competitive and welfare enhancing for an asset owner to retain joint control of both up-stream and down-stream activities, and thus impose access terms that are prohibitive. Reasons include the possible existence of scope economics, and adverse effects on the asset owner's reputation if a third party fails to meet the same standards as the in-house operator.

. . .

Optimal access pricing requires the competition authority or regulator to reach a view on the appropriate asset value for the essential facility. That appropriate value will correspond to the value the asset would command if it were subject to effective competition from rival assets. If the asset in question is indeed an essential facility, the appropriate asset value will always be less than the value of the essential facility if the owner is free to exploit the asset to maximise profits without regulatory constraint. The difference between the appropriate and the unconstrained asset values will be the excess profit or monopoly component of the property right that is being confiscated by the competition policy intervention.

Access pricing to the essential facility should be set such as to provide a revenue stream (including both in-house and third party use of the asset) that will remunerate the appropriate value of the asset, but no more.

When the problem is put in these terms it is easy to see why competition authorities choose to evade the question of access prices. Even for a relatively stable essential facility such as BG's [British Gas] UK network of gas pipes, reasonable people can and do hold widely divergent views on the appropriate asset value. In cases where the existence of the essential facility is more contentious, and where the value of the asset in question is more susceptible to shifts in market circumstances, the scope for varying outcomes is even wider.

However, evading the problem does not make it disappear. It simply makes the solutions adopted more difficult to interpret and less likely to form part of a rational and consistent response to the essential facilities problem.

Ridyard discusses several fundamental points here. He stresses that access to a facility should be required only where competition in the downstream market has seriously broken down, that the concept of an 'essential facility' should be very narrowly defined, that there are difficult problems of access pricing to be faced, and that competition authorities may as a result of the doctrine end up as price regulators.

The second comment is the conclusion from Areeda's critical survey of the essential facilities doctrine in US law. He considers it a concept which should be treated with the greatest circumspection, in particular because it is a dangerous disincentive to innovation. Obviously, his remarks relate to the doctrine in US law at the time of writing.

P. Areeda, 'Essential Facilities: An Epithet in Need of Limiting Principles' (1990) 58 *Antitrust LJ*, 841, 852–3

I conclude by offering six principles that should limit application of the essential facilities concept.

(1) There is no general duty to share. Compulsory access, if it exists at all, is and should be very exceptional . . .

(2) A single firm's facility, as distinct from that of a combination, is 'essential' only when it is both critical to the plaintiff's competitive vitality and the plaintiff is essential for competition in the marketplace. 'Critical to the plaintiff's competitive vitality' means that the plaintiff cannot compete effectively without it and that duplication or practical alternatives are not available.

(3) No one should be forced to deal unless doing so is likely substantially to improve competition in the marketplace by reducing price or by increasing output or innovation. Such an improvement is unlikely (a) when it would chill desirable activity; (b) the plaintiff is not an actual or potential competitor; (c) when the plaintiff merely substitutes itself for the monopolist or shares the monopolist's gains; or (d) when the monopolist already has the usual privilege of charging the monopoly price for its resources . . .

(4) Even when all these conditions are satisfied, denial of access is never per se unlawful; legitimate business purpose always saves the defendant. What constitutes legitimacy is a question of law for the courts. Although the defendant bears the burden of coming forward with a legitimate business purpose, the plaintiff bears the burden of persuading the tribunal that any such claim is unjustified.

(5) The defendant's intention is seldom illuminating, because every firm that denies its facilities to rivals does so to limit competition with itself and increase its profits. Any instruction on intention must ask whether the defendant had an intention to exclude by *improper* means. To get ahead in the marketplace is not, itself the kind of intention that contaminates conduct . . .

(6) No court should impose a duty to deal that it cannot explain or adequately and reasonably supervise. The problem should be deemed irremedial by antitrust law when compulsory access requires the court to assume the day-to-day controls characteristic of a regulatory agency. Remedies may be practical (a) when admission to a consortium is at stake, especially at the outset, (b) when divestiture is otherwise appropriate and effective, or (c) when, as in *Otter Tail*, a regulatory agency already exists to control the terms of dealing. However, the availability of a remedy is not reason to grant one. Compulsory sharing should remain exceptional.

The first two sentences of paragraph 5 were cited with approval by the US Supreme Court in *Verizon v. Trinko*.[365]

(iv) The *European Night Services* Case

The Commission decision in *European Night Services*,[366] was taken under Article 81 of the Treaty. It raised similar issues to the Article 82 cases although the *Commission* did not actually use the expression 'essential facilities'. Railway undertakings in the UK, France, Germany, and the Netherlands formed a joint venture (ENS) to provide overnight passenger rail services between the UK and the Continent via the Channel Tunnel. The Commission granted an exemption on condition that the parent companies should provide locomotives, train crews and train paths to any other undertaking wishing to compete in the running of a similar service, on the same terms as they gave to the joint venture. The CFI annulled the decision on various grounds.[367]

---

[365] 124 S.Ct. 872 (13 Jan. 2004): see *infra* 575.

[366] [1994] OJ L259/20, [1995] 5 CMLR 76.

[367] Cases T-374–5, 384 and 388/94, *European Night Services v. Commission* [1998] ECR II-3141, [1998] 5 CMLR 718. Other aspects of this case are dealt with in Chaps. 3, 4, and 13. The requirement that train paths should be provided was quashed because it was based on false premises to do with the relevant transport directive (91/440 [1991] OJ L237–25).

The condition as regards the locomotives and train crews was quashed because the Commission had not properly analysed why the requirement to supply was appropriate and had not supplied adequate reasoning for imposing this condition. In this case the CFI expressly referred to essential facilities. It stressed that a facility can be essential only if there are no substitutes. Mere advantage to the competitor is not enough.

Cases T-374–5, 384 and 388/94, *European Night Services* v. *Commission* [1998] ECR II-3141, [1998] 5 CMLR 718[368]

Court of First Instance

215. As the applicants have argued, the contested decision does not contain any analysis demonstrating that the locomotives in question are necessary or essential. More specifically, it is not possible to conclude from reading the contested decision that third parties cannot obtain them either directly from manufacturers or indirectly by renting them from other undertakings. Nor has any correspondence between the Commission and third parties, demonstrating that the locomotives in question cannot be obtained on the market, been produced before the Court. As the applicants have stated, any undertaking wishing to operate the same rail services as ENS through the Channel Tunnel may freely purchase or rent the locomotives in question on the market. It is clear, moreover, from the papers before the Court that the contracts for the supply of locomotives entered into between the notifying undertakings and ENS do not involve any exclusively in favour of ENS, and that each of the notifying undertakings is thus free to supply the same locomotives to third parties and not only to ENS.

216. It must further be pointed out in that regard that the Commission has not denied that third parties may freely purchase or rent the locomotives in question on the market; it has merely asserted that the possibility is in fact purely theoretical and that only the notifying undertakings actually possess such locomotives. That argument cannot, however, be accepted. The fact that the notifying undertakings have been the first to acquire the locomotives in question on the market does not mean that they are alone in being able to do so.

217. Consequently, the Commission's assessment of the necessary or essential nature of the special locomotives designed for the Channel Tunnel and, thus, the obligation imposed on the parent undertakings to supply such locomotives to third parties are vitiated by an absence or, at the very least, an insufficiency of reasoning.

. . .

221. As regards the supply to ENS of special locomotives and crew for the Channel Tunnel, the mere fact of its benefiting from such a service could impede access by third parties to the downstream market only if such locomotives and crew were to be regarded as essential facilities. Since, for the reasons set out above, . . . they cannot be categorized as such, the fact that they are to be supplied to ENS under the operating agreements for night rail services cannot be regarded as restricting competition *vis-à-vis* third parties. That aspect of the Commission's analysis of restrictions of competition *vis-à-vis* third parties is therefore also unfounded.

This judgment showed a disinclination to apply the essential facilities concept too widely.

---

[368] The judgment was delivered after the opinion of Jacobs A-G in Case C-7/97, *Oscar Bronner GMBH & Co KG* v. *Mediaprint* [1998] ECR I-7791, [1999] 4 CMLR 112, see *infra* 547.

(v) The *Oscar Bronner* Case

Bronner arose before the ECJ on an Article 234 reference.[369] It is a leading judgment in which the Court set out the limited circumstances in which access to a facility will be ordered. Before looking at the case it is important to note that both the Advocate General and the Court refer to the 1995 judgment of the ECJ in the *Magill* case,[370] which concerned intellectual property rights. Refusals to supply which involve intellectual property rights raise particular problems, and the intellectual property rights cases are dealt with together below.[371] However, it is necessary to have some idea of the judgment in *Magill* in order to understand the reference points in *Bronner*, so a brief outline is given here.[372]

Magill concerned an Irish publisher who wanted to publish a composite television listings magazine. However, the broadcasters whose programmes could be received in Ireland at the time refused to allow him to publish their schedules, which were protected by copyright under Irish and UK law. The ECJ found that in exceptional cases a refusal to supply material protected by an intellectual property right could be an abuse. The exceptional circumstances in *Magill* were that there was no substitute for a weekly television guide, the refusal to supply was preventing the appearance of a new product for which there was consumer demand, there was no justification for the refusal, and the refusal was excluding competition on a secondary market by denying access to the indispensable raw material.

Bronner was notable for a thoughtful Opinion in which Advocate General Jacobs discussed the necessity of confining the essential facilities concept within strict limits. Extracts from the Opinion as well as from the judgment are therefore reproduced below.

Case C-7/97, *Oscar Bronner GmbH & Co KG* v. *Mediaprint* [1998] ECR I-7791, [1999] 4 CMLR 112

Bronner published a newspaper, *Der Standard* which had approximately 3.6 per cent of the daily newspaper market in Austria in terms of circulation and 6 per cent in terms of advertising revenue. Mediaprint published two daily newsapapers in Austria, *Neue Kronen Zeitung* and *Kurier* which together had a combined market share of 46.8 per cent of circulation and 42 per cent of advertising revenues. For the distribution of its newspapers Mediaprint had established a nationwide home-delivery scheme. Bronner wanted Mediaprint to include *Der Standard* in its delivery scheme but Mediaprint refused. Mediaprint did include another newspaper it did not publish in its scheme but it did the whole of the printing and distribution in respect of that paper. Bronner sought an order from the Austrian courts requiring Mediaprint to cease abusing its alleged dominant position on the home-delivery market and requiring it to include *Der Standard* in its home-delivery service in return for reasonable remuneration. It claimed that other methods of sale, such as postal delivery, were less advantageous than home-delivery and that given the small circulation of *Der Standard* it would be entirely unprofitable for it to organise its own home-delivery service.

---

[369] The case actually involved a question of Austrian law (there was no appreciable effect on inter-Member State trade) but the referring court was concerned not to apply the law in a way which conflicted with Community law. It therefore asked for an interpretation of Article 82. The ECJ held the reference to be admissible, see paras. 12–22 of the judgment.

[370] Cases C-241–242/91 P, *RTE & ITP v. Commission* [1995] ECR I-743, [1995] 4 CMLR 718.

[371] *Infra* 553 ff.

[372] For a fuller treatment of *Magill*, see *infra* 557.

The Austrian court referred to the ECJ two questions as to whether the conduct in issue amounted to an abuse of a dominant position. Although the situation related only to trade inside Austria, the Austrian court asked for the reference because it wished to avoid a conflict between the interpretation of domestic and EC law. The ECJ held that the reference was admissible.

Advocate General Jacobs

56. First, it is apparent that the right to choose one's trading partners and freely to dispose of one's property are generally recognized principles in the laws of the Member States, in some cases with constitutional status. Incursions on those rights require careful justification.

57. Secondly, the justification in terms of competition policy for interfering with a dominant undertaking's freedom to contract often requires a careful balancing of conflicting considerations. In the long term it is generally pro-competitive and in the interest of consumers to allow a company to retain for its own use facilities which it has developed for the purpose of its business. For example, if access to a production, purchasing or distribution facility were allowed too easily there would be no incentive for a competitor to develop competing facilities. Thus while competition was increased in the short term it would be reduced in the long term. Moreover, the incentive for a dominant undertaking to invest in efficient facilities would be reduced if its competitors were, upon request, able to share the benefits. Thus the mere fact that by retaining a facility for its own use a dominant undertaking retains an advantage over a competitor cannot justify requiring access to it.

58. Thirdly, in assessing this issue it is important not to lose sight of the fact that the primary purpose of Article [82] is to prevent distortion of competition—and in particular to safeguard the interests of consumers—rather than to protect the position of particular competitors. It may therefore, for example, be unsatisfactory, in a case in which a competitor demands access to a raw material in order to be able to compete with the dominant undertaking on a downstream market in a final product, to focus solely on the latter's market power on the upstream market and conclude that its conduct in reserving to itself the downstream market is automatically an abuse. Such conduct will not have an adverse impact on consumers unless the dominant undertaking's final product is sufficiently insulated from competition to give it market power.

...

61. It is on the other hand clear that refusal of access may in some cases entail elimination or substantial reduction of competition to the detriment of consumers in both the short and long term. That will be so where access to a facility is a precondition for competition on a related market for goods or services for which there is a limited degree of interchangeability.

62. In assessing such conflicting interests particular care is required where the goods or services or facilities to which access is demanded represent the fruit of substantial investment. That may be true in particular in relation to refusal to license intellectual property rights. Where such exclusive rights are granted for a limited period, that in itself involves a balancing of the interest in free competition with that of providing an incentive for research and development and for creativity. It is therefore with good reason that the Court has held that the refusal to license does not of itself, in the absence of other factors, constitute an abuses.

63. The ruling in *Magill* can in my view be explained by the special circumstances of that case which swung the balance in favour of an obligation to license. First, the existing products, namely individual weekly guides for each station, were inadequate, particularly when compared with the guides available to viewers in other countries. The exercise of the copyright therefore prevented a much needed new product from coming on the market. Secondly, the provision of copyright protection for programme listings was difficult to justify in terms of rewarding or providing an incentive for creative effort. Thirdly, since the useful life of programme guides is relatively short, the

exercise of the copyright provided a permanent barrier to the entry of the new product on the market. It may incidentally be noted that national rules on intellectual property themselves impose limits in certain circumstances through rules on compulsory licensing.

64. While generally the exercise of intellectual property rights will restrict competition for a limited period only, a dominant undertaking's monopoly over a product, service or facility may in certain cases lead to permanent exclusion of competition on a related market. In such cases competition can be achieved only by requiring a dominant undertaking to supply the product or service or allow access to the facility. If it is so required the undertaking must however in my view be fully compensated by allowing it to allocate an appropriate proportion of its investment costs to the supply and to make an appropriate return on its investment having regard to the level of risk involved. I leave open the question whether it might in some cases be appropriate to allow the undertaking to retain its monopoly for a limited period.

65. It seems to me that intervention of that kind, whether understood as an application of the essential facilities doctrine or, more traditionally, as a response to a refusal to supply goods or services, can be justified in terms of competition policy only in cases in which the dominant undertaking has a genuine stranglehold on the related market. That might be the case for example where duplication of the facility is impossible or extremely difficult owing to physical, geographical or legal constraints or is highly undesirable for reasons of public policy. It is not sufficient that the undertaking's control over a facility should give it a competitive advantage.

66. I do not rule out the possibility that the cost of duplicating a facility might alone constitute an insuperable barrier to entry. That might be so particularly in cases in which the creation of the facility took place under non-competitive conditions, for example, partly through public funding. However, the test in my view must be an objective one: in other words, in order for refusal of access to amount to an abuse, it must be extremely difficult not merely for the undertaking demanding access but for any other undertaking to compete. Thus, if the cost of duplicating the facility alone is the barrier to entry, it must be such as to deter any prudent undertaking from entering the market. In that regard it seems to me that it will be necessary to consider all the circumstances, including the extent to which the dominant undertaking, having regard to the degree of amortisation of its investment and the cost of upkeep, must pass on investment or maintenance costs in the prices charged on the related market (bearing in mind that the competitor, who having duplicated the facility must compete on the related market, will have high initial amortisation costs but possibly low maintenance costs).

67. It is in my view clear that in the present case there can be no obligation on Mediaprint to allow Bronner access to its nation-wide home-delivery network. Although Bronner itself may be unable to duplicate Mediaprint's network, it has numerous alternative—albeit less convenient—means of distribution open to it. That conclusion is borne out by the claims made in *Der Standard* itself that 'the "Standard" is enjoying spectacular growth in terms of both new subscriptions (an increase of 15 per cent) and placement of advertisements (an increase of 30 per cent by comparison with last year)' . . . Such a claim hardly seems consistent with the view that Mediaprint's home-delivery system is essential for it to compete on the newspaper market.

68. Moreover, it would be necessary to establish that the level of investment required to set up a nation-wide home distribution system would be such as to deter an enterprising publisher who was convinced that there was a market for another large daily newspaper from entering the market. It may well be uneconomic, as Bronner suggests, to establish a nation-wide system for a newspaper with a low circulation. In the short term, therefore, losses might be anticipated, requiring a certain level of investment. But the purpose of establishing a competing nation-wide network would be to allow it to compete on equal terms with Mediaprint's newspapers and substantially to increase geographical coverage and circulation.

69. To accept Bronner's contention would be to lead the Community and national authorities and courts into detailed regulation of the Community markets, entailing the fixing of prices and

conditions for supply in large sectors of the economy. Intervention on that scale would not only be unworkable but would also be anti-competitive in the longer term and indeed would scarcely be compatible with a free market economy.

70. It seems to me therefore that the present case falls well short of the type of situation in which it might be appropriate to impose an obligation on a dominant undertaking to allow access to a facility which it has developed for its own use.

The judgment of the ECJ followed the thrust of the Advocate General's argument, although it was less expansive.

Court of Justice

38. Although in *Commercial Solvents* v. *Commission and CBEM*, cited above, the ECJ held the refusal by an undertaking holding a dominant position in a given market to supply an undertaking with which it was in competition in a neighbouring market with raw materials (*Commercial Solvents* v. *Commission*, paragraph 25) and services (*CBEM*, paragraph 26) respectively, which were indispensable to carrying on the rival's business, to constitute an abuse, it should be noted, first, that the Court did so to the extent that the conduct in question was likely to eliminate all competition on the part of that undertaking.

39. Secondly, in *Magill*, at paragraphs 49 and 50, the Court held that refusal by the owner of an intellectual property right to grant a licence, even if it is the act of an undertaking holding a dominant position, cannot in itself constitute abuse of a dominant position, but that the exercise of an exclusive right by the proprietor may, in exceptional circumstances, involve an abuse.

40. In *Magill*, the Court found such exceptional circumstances in the fact that the refusal in question concerned a product (information on the weekly schedules of certain television channels) the supply of which was indispensable for carrying on the business in question (the publishing of a general television guide), in that, without that information, the person wishing to produce such a guide would find it impossible to publish it and offer it for sale (paragraph 53), the fact that such refusal prevented the appearance of a new product for which there was a potential consumer demand (paragraph 54), the fact that it was not justified by objective considerations (paragraph 55), and that it was likely to exclude all competition in the secondary market of television guides (paragraph 56).

41. Therefore, even if that case-law on the exercise of an intellectual property right were applicable to the exercise of any property right whatever, it would still be necessary, for the *Magill* judgment to be effectively relied upon in order to plead the existence of an abuse within the meaning of Article [82] of the Treaty in a situation such as that which forms the subject-matter of the first question, not only that the refusal of the service comprised in home delivery be likely to eliminate all competition in the daily newspaper market on the part of the person requesting the service and that such refusal be incapable of being objectively justified, but also that the service in itself be indispensable to carrying on that person's business, inasmuch as there is no actual or potential substitute in existence for that home-delivery scheme.

42. That is certainly not the case even if, as in the case which is the subject of the main proceedings, there is only one nationwide home-delivery scheme in the territory of a Member State and, moreover, the owner of that scheme holds a dominant position in the market for services constituted by that scheme or of which it forms part.

43. In the first place, it is undisputed that other methods of distributing daily newspapers, such as by post and through sale in shops and at kiosks, even though they may be less advantageous

for the distribution of certain newspapers, exist and are used by the publishers of those daily newspapers.

44. Moreover, it does not appear that there are any technical, legal or even economic obstacles capable of making it impossible, or even unreasonably difficult, for any other publisher of daily newspapers to establish, alone or in co-operation with other publishers, its own nationwide home-delivery scheme and use it to distribute its own daily newspapers.

45. It should be emphasised in that respect that, in order to demonstrate that the creation of such a system is not a realistic potential alternative and that access to the existing system is therefore indispensable, it is not enough to argue that it is not economically viable by reason of the small circulation of the daily newspaper or newspapers to be distributed.

46. For such access to be capable of being regarded as indispensable, it would be necessary at the very least to establish, as the Advocate General has pointed out at point 68 of his Opinion, that it is not economically viable to create a second home-delivery scheme for the distribution of daily newspapers with a circulation comparable to that of the daily newspapers distributed by the existing scheme.

47. In the light of the foregoing considerations, the answer to the first question must be that the refusal by a press undertaking which holds a very large share of the daily newspaper market in a Member State and operates the only nationwide newspaper home-delivery scheme in that Member State to allow the publisher of a rival newspaper, which by reason of its small circulation is unable either alone or in co-operation with other publishers to set up and operate its own home-delivery scheme in economically reasonable conditions, to have access to that scheme for appropriate remuneration does not constitute abuse of a dominant position within the meaning of Article [82] of the Treaty.

It is significant that in this judgment the ECJ continued to avoid using the term 'essential facilities'. It referred back again to *Commercial Solvents*. In paragraph 41 the ECJ listed four factors which would have to be present before the refusal could be an abuse. First, the refusal would have to be likely to eliminate all competition in the downstream market from the person requesting access; secondly, the refusal must be incapable of objective justification; thirdly, the access must be indispensable to carrying on the other person's business; and, fourthly, there must be no actual or potential substitute for it. These criteria were patently not fulfilled in *Bronner*.

In *Bronner* the Court took a restrictive view of the obligation to grant access to facilities. It stressed that the refusal must be likely to *eliminate* all competition from the undertaking requesting access. It was not sufficient that the refusal would just make it harder for it to compete. Access must also be *indispensable*, not desirable or convenient, since there must be no actual or potential substitute for the requesting undertaking. Moreover, in paragraphs 45–6 the Court held that in the case before it access could have been indispensable only if it was not economically viable to create a home-delivery system for a newspaper *with a comparable circulation to the dominant firm's*. It was not enough to show it was not viable for a small-circulation paper.[373] Arguably, the Commission decisions in *British Midland/Aer Lingus*[374] and *London European/ Sabena*[375] would not have passed the Court's more stringent test in *Bronner*.[376] *Bronner* left many questions unanswered. It did not address the problems about pricing, for example, or how

---

[373] See M. A. Bergman, 'Editorial: The Bronner Case—A Turning Point for the Essential Facilities Doctrine?' [2000] *ECLR* 59.

[374] See *supra* 538.

[375] See *supra* 537.

[376] L. Hancher, 'Case Note on Oscar Bronner' (1999) 36 *CMLRev* 1289, 1306–7.

the facility owner should deal with competing claims for access, or the role of competition authorities in essential facilities scenarios. The judgment itself rather coyly (paragraph 41) side-stepped the question whether the case law on intellectual property rights (i.e., *Magill*), is applicable to other property rights. It did, however, make quite clear that an obligation to grant access to a facility will arise only in exceptional circumstances. *Bronner*, of course, was an easy case for the Court. It concerned a facility built up by a private undertaking with its own resources and a situation in which the other undertaking was operating satisfactorily on the downstream market without access to it. If the Court had considered that it was a situation suitable for the application of the essential facilities doctrine then all dominant firms owning or controlling a facility someone else might have found useful should have been worried, and incentives to innovation would have been seriously undermined. However, it was made apparent that facilities are not lightly to be termed 'essential' or access lightly required. The essential facilities doctrine was 'reined in' by the Court.

The Commission recognized the Court's restrictive approach to the issue in the *Info-Lab* decision.[377] A producer of toner for photocopiers complained to the Commission that Ricoh, a photocopier manufacturer, refused to supply it with empty cartridges compatible with Ricoh machines so that it could fill them with toner and compete with Ricoh in the market for filled toner cartridges. Ricoh did not make empty cartridges. The Commission held that Ricoh did not have a dominant position[378] but considered that even if it had, in the light of *Bronner* such forced cooperation could be envisaged only under exceptional circumstances which did not pertain here.

In the EC the most likely markets for the application of the essential facilities doctrine are transport infrastructures and/or infrastructures originally developed with public money. The Commission decisions discussed above demonstrate how the essential facilities concept is used to open up transport markets.[379] In some cases, where competition is being brought on to markets which have previously been statutory monopolies, duplication of facilities, such as networks, is not feasible in the real world. Liberalization therefore cannot take place unless the new competitors are given access to the established facilities. The Commission has dealt specifically with access agreements in the telecommunications sector,[380] and it also intervened in the financial services sector, and issued a notice on cross-border credit transfers, because it considered that access to payment systems is vital if banks are to compete on relevant markets.[381] In special sectors, therefore, the Commission applies the concept of an essential facility through regulation. The *Bronner* case, however, shows that the Court is alive to the harm to competition which can arise from an over-enthusiastic application of a duty to deal in other markets.

(vi) Refusal to Supply in the Financial Industry

The Commission took its first decision on a refusal to supply in the financial sector in *Clearstream*.[382] Clearstream Banking AG was the Central Securities Depository (CSD) for securities

---

[377] Case IV/36431, see Competition Policy Newsletter, 1999, No. 1, 35.

[378] See *supra* Chap. 6.

[379] And see also *GVG/FS* [2004] OJ L11/17, [2004] 4 CMLR 1446 (Italian state-owned railway company (FS) abused dominant position on Italian passenger rail market by refusing to enter into an international grouping with a German railway company. FS gave undertakings to grant access).

[380] Commission Notice on access agreements in the telecommunications sector [1998] OJ C265/2.

[381] Commission Notice on the application of the competition rules to cross-border credit transfers [1995] OJ C251/3; see also *SWIFT*, XXVIIth Report on Competition Policy (Commission, 1997), 143.

[382] Case COMP/38.096, *Clearstream Banking AG and Clearstream International SA*, IP/04/705, 2 June 2004; and see *Clearstream: Questions and Answers on Commission Decision*, MEMO/04/705, available on the Commission's web site, http://www.europa.eu.int/comm/competition/antitrust/cases/decisions/38096/clearstream_en.pdf., on appeal to the CFI, Case T-301/04, *Clearstream v. Commission*.

issued under German Law and kept in collective safe custody, which is the only significant form of custody for securities traded. The Commission found it was in a dominant position in the market for the provision of primary clearing and settlement services for securities issued according to German law to CSDs in other Member States and to international CSDs. The Commission held that Clearstream Banking and its parent had infringed Article 82 in denying Euroclear Bank clearing and settlement services for two years (and, for a period, in charging it discriminatory prices which were higher than those charged to other security depositories outside Germany). Although the infringement had ceased the Commission adopted the decision (without imposing a fine) 'to make it clear that the competition rules are being applied in the financial industry'.[383] The Commission said that Clearstream's behaviour qualified as a refusal to supply contrary to Article 82 because: it was an unavoidable trading partner, new entry into its activity being unrealistic for the foreseeable future; Euroclear could not duplicate the requested services; and Clearstream's behaviour had the effect of impairing Euroclear's ability to provide efficient cross-border clearing and settlement services to clients. The Commission referred to Euroclear's 'legitimate expectation' that it would be supplied with services within a reasonable period of time. The Commission stated that anti-competitive practices committed by market players in the area of cross-border clearing and settlement 'are a major source of inefficiencies that harm consumers', thereby emphasizing that the application of Article 82 in this case was for the protection of consumer welfare, not of competitors.[384]

F. REFUSAL TO SUPPLY AND INTELLECTUAL PROPERTY RIGHTS

(i) General

The question whether it is an abuse to refuse to supply others with intellectual property rights has become intertwined with the question of essential facilities and the debate about the interaction of competition law and intellectual property is one of the most hotly disputed in competition law discourse. Neither the Court nor Commission has applied the phrase 'essential facilities' to intellectual property rights but the leading case on intellectual property rights, *Magill*,[385] featured significantly in *Bronner*,[386] the leading ECJ judgment on essential facilities and, in turn, *Bronner* was relied upon in the intellectual property case *IMS*.[387] The arguments on this matter centre around the fact that the law has already put in place a regime to deal with intellectual property; that compulsory licensing of intellectual property rights is a dangerous disincetive to innovation; and that the law to date has not properly explained why some situations are so 'exceptional' that the normal rights of an intellectual property right owner to exclude others should be eroded. In the following extract one sceptic questions whether intellectual property rights *should* be treated differently from other forms of property.

---

[383] Commissioner Monti, IP/04/705.

[384] MEMO/04/705, n. 382 *supra*.

[385] Cases C-241–242/91 P, *RTE & ITP v. Commission* [1995] ECR I-743, [1995] 4 CMLR 718, on appeal from Cases T-69–70/89, 76/89, *RTE, ITP, BBC v. EC Commission* [1991] ECR II-485, [1991] 4 CMLR 586.

[386] Case C-7/97, *Oscar Bronner GmbH & Co KG v. Mediaprint* [1998] ECR I-7791, [1999] 4 CMLR 112; see *supra* 547.

[387] Case C-418/01, *IMS Health GmbH & Co OHG v. NDC Health GmbH & Co KG* [2004] ECR I-5039, [2004] 4 CMLR 1543.

C. Ritter, 'Refusal to Deal and Essential Facilities: Does Intellectual Property Require Special Deference compared to Tangible Property?' (2005) *World Competition* (3) 281, 291 and 298

There are at least four more or less strong arguments why IP probably does *not* deserve "special deference" compared to tangible property . . . First, before moving on to policy arguments and economic arguments, it is useful to bear in mind that the "special deference" approach does not have any legal foundation. The law does not exempt IP owners from antitrust scrutiny. The "right to property" and the right to protection of *intellectual* property, which are both protected under EU law and under the European Convention on Human Rights . . . are strictly parallel, meaning that IP does not require *more* protection than physical property. Moreover, under EU law as well as under the ECHR, neither physical property rights nor IP rights are absolute . . . Second, any difference in treatment favouring IP compared to physical facilities would induce dominant firms to incorporate *some* IP into their valuable input or facility or interface in order to make sure it benefits from higher standard that applies to IP, compared to physical facilities . . . Third, IP infringement or, rather, the limitation of an IPR by means of compulsory license is in many cases more practical and productive than mandating access to somebody else's physical property. This is due to the very nature of IP rights, which are "non-rivalrous" (i.e., your use of an IPR does not interfere with my use of that IPR; we can both use it at the same time and it does not deteriorate as a result of use). The fourth reason is that—contrary to the current wisdom—limiting certain IP rights through compulsory licensing does not *necessarily* discourage innovation . . . .

In any event innovation competition, just like price competition, is merely an intermediate goal in order to improve consumer welfare (one of the end goals, if not *the* end goal of competition policy). Even if compulsory licensing were found to reduce innovation incentives, and therefore dynamic efficiency, this negative effect may be outweighed by the "static" gains in allocative efficiency, so that on the whole, consumer welfare is increased . . . (And, again, I readily acknowledge that dynamic efficiency is more important than allocative efficiency). On the basis of this broader framework, it is perfectly possible that, on balance, compulsory access to physical facilities may be appropriate in "certain circumstances" (to quote from *Trinko*).[388] For the various reasons outlined above, it is submitted that (a) in the area of essential facilities, IP cases and "tangible property" cases should be governed by the same legal standard; and (b) the counter-argument based on the "innovation incentives" should be taken with a pinch of salt.

Nonetheless, as we see below, EC law does apply different rules to refusal to supply intellectual property rights.

(ii) The Car Parts Cases

It is obvious that the existence of intellectual property rights will prevent undertakings competing on certain markets. Although the Court has held that the ownership of intellectual property rights does not necessarily mean that an undertaking holds a dominant position,[389] some rights can nonetheless constitute a barrier to entry under any conception of that term.[390]

[388] *Verizon v. Trinko* is discussed *infra*, 575.
[389] See *supra* Chap. 6.
[390] See *supra* Chap. 1.

Another undertaking cannot usually produce something which is protected by intellectual property rights without the consent of the rights holder. Intellectual property rights owners often *do* license their rights to others and Chapter 10 deals with the application of Article 81 to such agreements. Article 82 may be relevant, however, when the rights holder *is* in a dominant position and refuses to give licences to those wanting them.

The matter first came before the ECJ in two Article 234 references, *AB Volvo v. Erik Veng*[391] and *CICCRA v. Renault*[392] which were decided on the same day. The specific questions asked by the national courts were formulated differently, but amounted in essence to the same thing: is it an abuse for a car manufacturer to refuse to license the design rights on its car parts to third parties wishing to manufacture and sell such parts? The cases arose as the Court in *Hugin* had confirmed that an undertaking may be dominant on the market for its own spare parts even if the primary product market is competitive.[393] The Court held that a refusal to license was not *per se* an abuse, but might become so in certain circumstances.

Case 238/87, *AB Volvo* v. *Erik Veng* [1988] ECR 6211, [1989] 4 CMLR 122

Court of Justice

8. It must also be emphasized that the right of the proprietor of a protected design to prevent third parties from manufacturing and selling or importing, without its consent, products incorporating the design constitutes the very subject-matter of his exclusive right. It follows that an obligation imposed upon the proprietor of a protected design to grant to third parties, even in return for a reasonable royalty, a licence for the supply of products incorporating the design would lead to the proprietor thereof being deprived of the substance of his exclusive right, and that a refusal to grant such a licence cannot in itself constitute an abuse of a dominant position.

9.[394] It must however be noted that the exercise of an exclusive right by the proprietor of a registered design in respect of car body panels may be prohibited by Article [82] if it involves, on the part of an undertaking holding a dominant position, certain abusive conduct such as the arbitrary refusal to supply spare parts to independent repairers, the fixing of prices for spare parts at an unfair level or a decision no longer to produce spare parts for a particular model even though many cars of that model are still in circulation, provided that such conduct is liable to affect trade between Member States.

The references in the judgments to the 'very subject-matter of the exclusive right' and the 'exercise of an exclusive right' are to concepts which the Court had already developed to deal with the tension between intellectual property rights and Community law, mainly in the area of the free movement of goods and services.[395] The outcome of their application in *Volvo* and *Renault* was that the Court held that a refusal to grant licences would be an abuse only if it involved or gave rise to 'certain abusive conduct'. In effect the car makers were given a choice: either they could license third parties, or they could retain their monopoly and ensure, *inter alia*, that they did not

[391] Case 238/87, *AB Volvo v. Erik Veng* [1988] ECR 6211, [1989] 4 CMLR 122.

[392] Case 53/87, *CICCRA and Maxicar v. Renault* [1988] ECR 6039, [1990] 4 CMLR 265.

[393] Case 22/78, *Hugin Kassaregister AB v. EC Commission* [1979] ECR 1869 [1979] 3 CMLR 345; see *supra* Chap. 6.

[394] Para. 9, with only insignificant changes in wording, was repeated in the *Renault* judgment at para. 16.

[395] See *infra* Chap. 10.

arbitrarily refuse to supply independent repairers, did not charge unfairly and continued to supply parts for old models. One way of looking at this is to see an order to license as a *remedy* for other abuses.[396] The examples of abusive conduct give rise to difficulties, however.

First, to be an abuse the refusal to supply independents would have to be 'arbitrary'. What constitutes arbitrariness? Does it mean the same as not objectively justified? The concern of the Court here was really to ensure that no distortions of competition in the car servicing market arose. Korah asks:[397]

Is a refusal to supply body panels to an independent repairer arbitrary if it is costly to test his ability to fit the parts properly, and the car producer wants to maintain the reputation of his brand without incurring that cost by supplying only his franchised dealers whose skills and stock of tools and parts he controls? Is it more arbitrary if the brand owner wants to ensure sufficient turnover for his network of appointed dealers in order to persuade them to make the necessary investment in personnel, equipment and spares? He may even have promised his dealers to supply only them in an area.

The striking thing about categorizing the refusal to supply spare parts to independent repairers as an abuse is that it involves the supply of *products* to *new*, rather than existing, customers.

Secondly, with regard to the unfair prices, the Court stated in *Renault*:

17. With reference more particularly to the difference in prices between components sold by the manufacturer and those sold by the independent producers, it should be noted that the Court has held (Case 24/67, *Parke Davis*) . . . that a higher price for the former than for the latter does not necessarily constitute an abuse, since the proprietor of protective rights in respect of an ornamental design may lawfully call for a return on the amounts which he has invested in order to perfect the protected design.

The Court recognized here that the holder of an intellectual property right is entitled to charge in a way that recompenses him for his development efforts. In his Opinion in the case Advocate General Mischo considered that the car producer should be able to allocate his costs between the whole car and the individual parts, as all are protected.[398] The whole point of granting protection to a design or patent is to reward innovation and provide incentives and it is difficult to determine what is an 'unfair' price for the protected product.[399] The difficulties of determining at what level a price becomes 'unfair' are discussed below.[400] Further, the extent to which a car manufacturer has power to charge excessively in the aftermarket for spare parts without affecting sales in the competitive foremarket is questionable.[401]

The third example, prematurely terminating the production of spare parts, may or may not be a real problem. It can be argued that if the car maker itself is not interested in further production it will not object to a third party manufacturing the parts and may be happy to profit through licensing: on the other hand the car maker may have an interest in obsolescence and not want old models to be repairable.[402] In any event, the yardstick 'many cars still in production' is too vague to provide a properly applicable criterion.

---

[396] See the discussion in J. Temple Lang, 'Anti-competitive Non-Pricing Abuses under European and National Antitrust Law' in B. Hawk (ed.) [2003] *Fordham Corp L Inst* 235, 292–301.

[397] V. Korah, 'No Duty to License Independent Repairers to Made Spare Parts: The Renault, Volvo and Bayer and Hennecke Cases' [1988] *EIPR* 381, 382 (the *Bayer-Hennecke* case was about no challenge clauses in licence agreements (see *infra* Chap. 10) and is not relevant here).

[398] At para. 31.

[399] See I. Govaere, *The Use and Abuse of Intellectual Property Rights in EC Law* (Sweet & Maxwell, 1996), paras. 8.55–8.56.

[400] *Infra* 585.

[401] See *supra* Chap. 6.

[402] Korah, *supra* n. 397, cf. Govaere, *supra* at n. 399, paras. 8.57–8.59.

(iii) The *Magill* Case

Magill[403] concerned copyright in 'television listings' (television programme schedules). Under UK and Irish law copyright protects not only literary works which result from creative or intellectual endeavour but also compilations of information resulting from 'skill, judgment and labour' or the 'sweat of the brow', including listings of programmes to be broadcast.[404] Such compilations are not protected by intellectual property laws in the other Member States of the EU, where copyright covers only the fruits of creative or intellectual effort. The EU has not (yet) harmonized the substantive copyright laws of the Member States[405] but the Court has said on several occasions that where intellectual property laws are not harmonized Community law recognizes the *existence* of rights granted by the Member States.

In 1985 RTE had a statutory monopoly over television broadcasting in Ireland and the BBC and IBA had a statutory duopoly in the UK (including Northern Ireland). Most television viewers in Ireland and Northern Ireland could receive the channels of all three television authorities. RTE and the BBC owned the copyright in the programme listings for their respective channels and Independent Television Publications (ITP) owned the copyright in the programme listings of the IBA franchised channels. RTE, the BBC, and ITP each published a weekly TV guide containing only their own individual weekly programme listings. They also gave listings information to the press to be published according to strictly enforced licensing conditions. An Irish publisher, Magill, started to publish a comprehensive weekly TV guide giving details of all programmes available to viewers in Ireland and Northern Ireland, but the television companies obtained injunctions against it in national legal proceedings. Magill complained to the Commission that the television companies, by refusing to give out reliable advance listings information and protecting their listings by enforcing their copyright, were infringing Article 82.

Nowhere else in the Community but the UK and Ireland did copyright laws protect TV listings, and in the rest of the Community comprehensive composite TV guides were popular and common. These facts seem to have influenced the approach of the Court and Commission to the case.[406] The case became perceived as a battle between the protection of national intellectual property rights and competition law, for if the TV companies' refusal to deal with Magill *was* an abuse the only remedy was, in effect, to order them to give the publisher a licence of their copyrights. This raised the spectre of compulsory licensing of intellectual property rights more generally. If the Commission found an abuse, did this mean that in future pharmaceutical companies holding a dominant position on a particular market might have to license their

---

[403] Cases C-241–2/91 P, *RTE & ITP* v. *Commission* [1995] ECR I-743, [1995] 4 CMLR 718 on appeal from Cases T-69–70/89, 76/89, *RTE, ITP, BBC* v. *EC Commission* [1991] ECR II-485, [1991] 4 CMLR 586, on appeal from *Magill TV Guide* [1989] OJ L78/43, [1989] 4 CMLR 757.

[404] The relevant UK law is now the Copyright Designs and Patents Act 1988 s. 3 (1), although at the time of the *Magill* decision it was still the Copyright Act 1956. The protection of programme listings by copyright in the UK was confirmed by *Independent Television Publications* v. *Time Out* [1984] FSR 64. The Broadcasting Act 1990 s. 176 specifically provides that persons broadcasting television and radio programmes in the UK have to make information about the programme schedules available to any person in the UK who wants to publish it: the actual dispute in *Magill* therefore became a dead issue as regards the UK during the course of the case, which is why the BBC was not party to the appeal to the ECJ.

[405] See *infra* Chap. 10.

[406] See particularly the Commission's submissions to the CFI, [1991] ECR II-485, summarized in paras. 43–59 of the judgment, culminating in the Commission's statement in para. 59 that 'copyright should not subsist in compilations of banal information'.

patents to third parties wanting to use them to manufacture?[407] If so, the risk of removing incentives for innovation, discussed by Areeda and Ridyard (in the passages reproduced above), which intellectual property rights are particularly designed to protect, would be acute.

The Commission did hold that the television companies had infringed Article 82. It held that the companies were each dominant in the market for their weekly listings and that their policies in restricting the availability of the information were driven by a desire to protect their own individual weekly guides in the downstream market. The Commission's decision was upheld by the CFI, which related its discussion of Article 82 to the case law of the Court on intellectual property rights in the context of the free movement of goods and services.[408] RTE and ITP appealed to the ECJ. The ECJ confirmed the finding of abuse but its judgment was strikingly narrow. It concentrated on the specific scenario in issue and eschewed extended discussion about the nature of intellectual property rights and their relationship to the competition rules.[409] The ECJ treated the matter as a straightforward refusal to supply and applied the principles laid down in previous Article 82 case law.

Cases C-241–1/91 P, *RTE & ITP* v. *Commission* [1995] ECR I-743, [1995] 4 CMLR 718

Court of Justice

(a) Existence of a dominant position

46. So far as dominant position is concerned, it is to be remembered at the outset that mere ownership of an intellectual property right cannot confer such a position.

47. However, the basic information as to the channel, day, time and title of programmes is the necessary result of programming by television stations, which are thus the only source of such information for an undertaking, like Magill, which wishes to publish it together with commentaries or pictures. By force of circumstance, RTE and ITP, as the agent of ITV, enjoy, along with the BBC, a *de facto* monopoly over the information used to compile listings for the television programmes received in most households in Ireland and 30–40 per cent. of households in Northern Ireland. The appellants are thus in a position to prevent effective competition on the market in weekly television magazines. The CFI was therefore right in confirming the Commission's assessment that the appellants occupied a dominant position (*Michelin, paragraph 30*)

(b) Existence of abuse

48. With regard to the issue of abuse, the arguments of the appellants and IPO wrongly pre-suppose that where the conduct of an undertaking in a dominant position consists of the exercise of a right classified by national law as 'copyright', such conduct can never be reviewed in relation to Article [82] of the Treaty.

49. Admittedly, in the absence of Community standardization or harmonization of laws, determination of the conditions and procedures for granting protection of an intellectual property right

---

[407] Compulsory licensing of patents is provided for in the patent legislation, but only in clearly defined circumstances.

[408] There were three separate judgments, but the crucial paras. are the same in all three: see *RTE* v. *Commission* para. 71, *BBC* v. *Commission* para. 58, *ITP* v. *Commission*, para. 56.

[409] See particularly para. 58 of the judgment. The Court did not follow the opinion of Gulmann AG, who recommended setting aside the CFI judgment, primarily to uphold the inviolability of intellectual property rights.

is a matter for national rules. Further, the exclusive right of reproduction forms part of the author's rights, so that refusal to grant a licence, even if it is the act of an undertaking holding a dominant position, cannot in itself constitute abuse of a dominant position (*Volvo* v. *Veng*, paragraphs 7 and 8).

50. However, it is also clear from that judgment (paragraph 9) that the exercise of an exclusive right by the proprietor may, in exceptional circumstances, involve abusive conduct.

51. In the present case, the conduct objected to is the appellants' reliance on copyright conferred by national legislation so as to prevent Magill—or any other undertaking having the same intention—from publishing on a weekly basis information (channel, day, time and title of programmes) together with commentaries and pictures obtained independently of the appellants.

52. Among the circumstances taken into account by the CFI in concluding that such conduct was abusive was, first, the fact that there was, according to the findings of the Court of First Instance, no actual or potential substitute for a weekly television guide offering information on the programmes for the week ahead. On this point, the CFI confirmed the Commission's finding that the complete lists of programmes for a 24-hour period—and for a 48-hour period at weekends and before public holidays—published in certain daily and Sunday newspapers, and the television sections of certain magazines covering, in addition, 'highlights' of the week's programmes, were only to a limited extent substitutable for advance information to viewers on all the week's programmes. Only weekly television guides containing comprehensive listings for the week ahead would enable users to decide in advance which programmes they wished to follow and arrange their leisure activities for the week accordingly. The CFI also established that there was a specific, constant and regular potential demand on the part of consumers (see the *RTE* judgment, paragraph 62, and the *ITP* judgment, paragraph 48).

53. Thus the appellants—who were, by force of circumstance, the only sources of the basic information on programme scheduling which is the indispensable raw material for compiling a weekly television guide—gave viewers wishing to obtain information on the choice of programmes for the week ahead no choice but to buy the weekly guides for each station and draw from each of them the information they needed to make comparisons.

54. The appellants' refusal to provide basic information by relying on national copyright provisions thus prevented the appearance of a new product, a comprehensive weekly guide to television programmes, which the appellants did not offer and for which there was a potential consumer demand. Such refusal constitutes an abuse under heading (b) of the second paragraph of Article [82] of the Treaty.

55. Second, there was no justification for such refusal either in the activity of television broadcasting or in that of publishing television magazines (*RTE* judgment, paragraph 73, and *ITP* judgment, paragraph 58).

56. Third, and finally, as the CFI also held, the appellants, by their conduct, reserved to themselves the secondary market of weekly television guides by excluding competition on that market (*Commercial Solvents*, paragraph 25) since they denied access to the basic information which is the raw material indispensable for the compilation of such a guide.

57. In the light of all those circumstances, the CFI did not err in law in holding that the appellants' conduct was an abuse of a dominant position within the meaning of Article [82] of the Treaty.

58. It follows that the plea in law alleging misapplication by the CFI of the concept of abuse of a dominant position must be dismissed as unfounded. It is therefore unnecessary to examine the reasoning of the contested judgments in so far as it is based on Article [30] of the Treaty.

It can be seen that in this judgment the ECJ said (paragraph 48) that while it is not true that the exercise of intellectual property rights can *never* be reviewed under Article 82, a refusal to grant a licence to reproduce cannot *in itself* constitute an abuse of a dominant position (paragraph 49).

It cited *Volvo* as establishing that a refusal might constitute an abuse in exceptional circumstances. In this case the exceptional circumstances were:

— there was no substitute for a composite weekly television guide, for which there was a specific, constant, and regular potential demand on the part of consumers;

— the appellants' refusal to supply prevented the appearance of a new product for which there was a potential consumer demand[410] (this constituted an abuse under Article 82 (b), in 'limiting production, markets or technical development to the prejudice of consumers');

— there was no justification for such refusal;

— the appellants were reserving to themselves the secondary market of weekly television guides by excluding all competition on the market.

The 'list' of exceptional circumstances in *Magill* acquired great significance. It was not clear whether the circumstances were cumulative. In particular it was not clear whether the hindrance of a new product is a necessary or a separate and sufficient ground for holding the refusal to supply to be abusive. If the television companies had already produced their *own* composite guides by cross-licensing each other, the composite guide of a third party would not have been a new product, but the undertakings would still have reserved for themselves a special position on the secondary market. In the extract from his article, above,[411] Ridyard takes issue with the idea that competition authorities should intervene just because there are unrealized potential consumer gains. He argues that such intervention will cause economic damage because it upsets the tension between static and dynamic incentives for efficiency. Nevertheless, whether or not the hindrance or prevention of a new product is a necessary condition for finding a refusal to supply abusive in cases involving intellectual property rights became a major issue, as is seen from the subsequent case law discussed below.

The following points about the *Magill* judgment should also be noted:

• The ECJ based its finding of dominance on the fact that the TV companies had a *de facto* monopoly over the listings, i.e., they were responsible for producing the TV schedules and were the only source of advance information about them (paragraph 47). The Commission (paragraph 22) based the finding of dominance on both the *de facto* monopoly and the legal monopoly stemming from the copyright. The CFI based it on the legal monopoly (paragraph 63 of the *RTE* judgment). The ECJ did not even *mention* the existence of the intellectual property rights in its discussion of dominance in paragraph 47.

• The ECJ (paragraphs 53 and 56) described the companies' conduct in terms of refusal to supply a raw material. It did not use essential facilities terminology.

• The ECJ referred back to the early case of *Commercial Solvents* (paragraph 56) seeing the present case as an example of the established abuse of an undertaking dominant on one market trying to exclude competition on a downstream market.

• Unlike the car makers in *Volvo* and *Renault* the television companies were not given a choice of how they could avoid committing an abuse. Although the judgment did not mention compulsory licensing there was only one way in which the abuse could be remedied.[412]

---

[410] The AG on the other hand (paras. 93–102 of the Opinion) thought that the fact that the product Magill wanted to produce was new and would compete with the right holders' own products was a reason to find that the refusal to supply was *not* abusive.

[411] D. Ridyard, 'Essential Facilities and the Obligation to Supply Competitors' [1996] *ECLR* 438, 447; see *supra* 543.

[412] The existence of the Copyright Tribunal in the UK meant that the Commission itself did not have to become involved in price-setting.

The narrow terms in which this judgment was couched did not indicate that the Court was likely to embark on wholesale condemnation of refusals to license patents. It established that the norm, as exemplified in *Volvo* and *Renault,* was that refusal to license is *not* generally an abuse. The judgment was less of an assault on intellectual property rights than it was on the exploitation of compilations of information gained as a by-product of an undertaking's main business. The case is thus of a piece with all the previous cases on interference with ancillary markets: a significant difference between *Magill* and the car parts cases is that in the latter the would-be licensee wished to compete with the dominant undertaking in the core area of its business. In contrast, the television companies were not set up to publish magazines. It is true that *British Midland* also concerned competition with the dominant undertaking's core business, but that case did not involve intellectual property rights and was bound up with the liberalization of the air transport market.

It is possible to see *Magill* as a limitation of the power wielded by statutory monopolists. The power of the television companies in respect of the TV guides arose as a result of their privileged position on the broadcasting market. In a market which had more numerous television channels they would probably have been glad to provide their programme details to composite magazines: although consumers may buy two or three guides, they will not buy fifty, and television companies *need* to advertise their programme schedules.

(iv) The *Ladbroke* Case

In the next case concerning a refusal to license intellectual property rights, *Tiercé Ladbroke,* the CFI's judgment was couched in an essential facilities type of terminology. The CFI appeared to be limiting the application of that doctrine.

Case T-504/93, *Tiercé Ladbroke SA v. Commission* [1997] ECR II-923, [1997] 5 CMLR 309

Ladbroke ran betting shops in Belgium taking bets on horse races run abroad, including France. The French race course societies (sociétés de courses) and their associated companies (PMU and PMI) had exclusive responsibility for organising off-course betting in France, taking bets abroad on French races, taking bets in France on races run abroad and exploiting outside France televised pictures of, and information about, French horse races. PMI granted exclusive rights to show televised broadcasts of French horse races in Germany and Austria to DSV. PMI and PMU refused to supply broadcasts to Ladbroke's outlets in Belgium and DSV refused to retransmit to them. Ladbrokes complained to the Commission that this was an infringement of Article 82 (and Article 81) but the Commission rejected the complaint. Ladbroke challenged the decision rejecting the complaint before the Court of First Instance. The CFI held that the geographic market was Belgium alone, and not a wider area including at least Belgium, France and Germany. It rejected the appeal.

Court of First Instance

128. It must be pointed out, however, that, if the refusal to supply the applicant with French sound and pictures in Belgium does not constitute an abuse because, as the Court has just found, it involves no discrimination as between operators on the Belgian market, that refusal likewise cannot be held to be an abuse merely because outlets operating on the German market have French sound and pictures available to them. There is no competition between betting outlets operating in Belgium and those operating in Germany.

129. Moreover, neither the absence of technical barriers to the transmission of French sound and pictures in Belgium nor the fact that the applicant might be regarded, from an overall perspective, as a potential competitor of the *sociétés de courses* is sufficient for the refusal to supply sound and pictures to be regarded as constituting an abuse of a dominant position since the *sociétés de courses* themselves are not present in the separate geographical market on which the applicant operates and, secondly, they have not granted any licence to other operators on that market.

130. The applicant cannot rely on the *Magill* judgment to demonstrate the existence of the alleged abuse, since that decision is not in point. In contrast to the position in *Magill*, where the refusal to grant a licence to the applicant prevented it from entering the market in comprehensive television guides, in this case the application is not only present in, but has the largest share of, the main betting market on which the product in question, namely sound and pictures, is offered to consumers whilst the *sociétés de courses*, the owners of the intellectual property rights, are not present on that market. Accordingly, in the absence of direct or indirect exploitation by the *sociétés de courses* of their intellectual property rights on the Belgian market, their refusal to supply cannot be regarded as involving any restriction of competition on the Belgian market.

131. Even if it were assumed that the presence of the *sociétés de courses* on the Belgian market in sound and pictures were not, in this case, a decisive factor for the purposes of applying Article [82] of the Treaty, that provision would not be applicable in this case. The refusal to supply the applicant could not fall within the prohibition laid down by Article [82] unless it concerned a product or service which was either essential for the exercise of the activity in question, in that there were no real or potential substitute, or was a new product whose introduction might be prevented, despite specific, constant and regular potential demand on the part of consumers (see in that connection Joined Cases C-241–242/91P, *RTE and ITP* v. *E.C. Commission* . . .

132. In this case, as moreover the Commission and the interveners have pointed out, the televised broadcasting of horse races, although constituting an additional, and indeed suitable, service for bettors, it is not in itself indispensable for the exercise of bookmakers' main activity, namely the taking of bets, as is evidenced by the fact that the applicant is present on the Belgian betting market and occupies a significant position as regards bets on French races. Moreover, transmission is not indispensable, since it takes place after bets are placed, with the result that its absence does not in itself affect the choices made by bettors and, accordingly, cannot prevent bookmakers from pursuing their business.

133. For the same reasons, the applicant likewise cannot rely on the *London European* v. *Sabena* decision and the *ICI and Commercial Solvents* v. *E.C. Commission* and *CBEM* judgments . . . In the *London European* v. *Sabena* decision, the action taken to exclude a competitor related to a market in which both Sabena and that competitor, London European, were operating, whereas in this case the *sociétés de courses* are not present on the Belgian market. The same applies to the two judgments relied upon. In *ICI and Commercial Solvents* v. *E.C. Commission*, the abuse consisted in the refusal by a company occupying a dominant position on the market in raw materials to provide those materials to a customer producing derivatives in order to keep those raw materials for its own production of derivatives, and so the company in a dominant position, like its customers, was present on the downstream market, namely the market in derivatives. In contrast, in this case the *sociétés de courses* are not present on the Belgian market in French sound and pictures. In the *CBEM* judgment, the ECJ held that an undertaking abuses a dominant position where, without any objective necessity, it reserves to itself or to an undertaking belonging to the same group an ancillary activity which might be carried out by another undertaking as part of its activities on a neighbouring but separate market. However, in this case the *sociétés de courses* have not reserved the Belgian market in French sound and pictures to themselves and have not granted access to that market to a third-party undertaking or to an undertaking belonging to them.

In this case the CFI distinguished the situation before it from that in *Magill*. The *sociétés de courses* did not operate betting shops in Belgium, so the downstream market issue did not arise. Showing films of the races was not essential to providing services in betting shops. The copyright owners were not discriminating (contrary to Article 82(c)) in that they did not supply *anybody* with licences in the relevant market (Belgium). The refusal to supply could constitute an abuse (paragraph 131) only if *either* the product or service was essential to the activity in question *or* the introduction of a new product demanded by consumers was being prevented. The CFI thus suggested, claiming to follow *Magill*, that a refusal to supply which precluded the introduction of a new product might constitute an abuse for that reason alone, even if the access demanded was not 'essential'. This suggestion means that Article 82 can be employed to enable assumed consumer demand to be satisfied: this is refusal to supply characterized as an exploitative abuse capable of harming consumers directly, by depriving them of things they want (i.e., in the words of Article 82(b) it limits production, etc. to the prejudice of consumers). On the other hand, if the refusal to license concerned a product or service which was essential, that too would be sufficient. In other words, the CFI read the 'exceptional circumstances' in *Magill* as severable, not cumulative.

The concern about the essential facilities doctrine detectable in *Tiercé Ladbroke* was expressly addressed by the ECJ in *Bronner*, as seen above.[413]

(v) The *IMS* Case

a. The Sequence of Events in *IMS*

Because of the convoluted proceedings in this case, the sequence of events in *IMS* is set out here before the issues raised in the case are considered.

The *IMS* case concerned the '1860 brick structure', a system for representing regional pharmaceutical sales data in Germany over which IMS claimed copyright. On a complaint from competitors the Commission made an interim decision ordering IMS to grant a licence for the brick structure.[414] IMS appealed and the President of the CFI granted interim measures suspending the execution of the decision.[415] The President of the ECJ dismissed the appeal and upheld the suspension.[416] In the meantime, litigation between IMS and NDC had been proceeding in the German courts. In July 2001, nine days after the Commission's interim decision, the Landgericht Frankfurt am Main made a preliminary reference to the ECJ asking questions about the interpretation of Article 82 in the context of IMS's refusal to licence. Before this case was heard by the ECJ, however, the Oberlandsgericht Frankfurt am Main gave a judgment on the issue of IMS's claim to copyright in the brick structure.[417] It held that although the brick structure was protected by copyright this did not prevent other parties from developing a similar structure. Moreover, NDC began to compete more successfully with IMS. As a result of these developments, in August 2003 the Commission decided not to proceed to a final decision and

---

[413] *Supra* 547.

[414] *NDC Health/IMS: Interim Measures* [2002] OJ L59/18, [2002] 4 CMLR 111 (Commission Decision 2002/165/EC of 3 July 2002).

[415] Case T-184/01 R, *IMS Health v. Commission*, [2001] ECR II-3193, [2002] 4 CMLR 58 (26 Oct. 2001, confirming an earlier interim suspension on 10 Aug. 2001, [2002] 4 CMLR 46). It was suspended until such time as the CFI had given judgment in the main action. For the power of the Commission to grant interim measures and the power of the Court to suspend Commission decisions see *infra* Chap 14.

[416] Case C-481/01 P(R), *IMS Health v. Commission* [2002] ECR I-3401, [2002] 5 CMLR 44 (11 Apr. 2002).

[417] 17 Sept. 2002.

withdrew the interim measures.[418] The ECJ gave its ruling on the preliminary reference from the Landgericht in April 2004. [419]

b. The Commission's *IMS/NDC* Decision

The '1860 brick structure' employed a grid superimposed on the map of Germany, breaking down the country into small geographical areas (bricks) based on factors including postcodes, administrative and political boundaries and the location of doctors and pharmacies.[420] IMS collected pharmaceutical sales information from wholesalers and formatted it in accordance with the brick structure, so enabling it to be analysed in various ways. IMS then provided sales reports to its customers, the pharmaceutical companies. The 1860 brick structure had been developed over many years, in collaboration by IMS with the pharmaceutical industry (there was considerable dispute about the extent of this collaboration) and the Commission found that it had become the *de facto* industry standard. IMS's competitors[421] attempted to develop similar brick structures but IMS claimed that these infringed its copyright and obtained interim injunctions in the German courts to restrain their use. The competitors complained to the Commission that IMS's refusal to license the 1860 brick structure meant that it was impossible for them to provide pharmaceutical data services to customers as they could not present data in a way which was acceptable to the customers without infringing IMS's copyright and there was no prospect of the customers changing to a radically different structure. The Commission upheld the complaint and found that the use of the 1860 brick structure was indispensable to carrying on business in the relevant market as there was no actual or potential substitute for it; there was no objective justification for IMS's refusal to licence; and that there were 'exceptional circumstances' in the *Magill* sense. It ordered *IMS* to give a licence on request and on a non-discriminatory basis to all undertakings currently on the German regional sales data services market.[422] The most contentious points in the case were that there was not obviously a 'new product' involved, and that it did not appear to be a leverage situation as there was (arguably) only one market. The Commission seemed to be requiring IMS to help a horizontal competitor compete with it on the primary market and share a competitive advantage. There was no allegation that IMS was engaged in other abusive conduct in addition to the refusal to supply.

In its decision, the Commission surveyed the existing case law and continued:

NDC Health/IMS: Interim Measures [2002] OJ L59/18, [2002] 4 CMLR 111

Commission

70. Therefore the criteria for the establishment of abuse under Article 82 in cases relating to the exercise of a property right, as further clarified by the Court in Bronner, are whether:

— the refusal of access to the facility is likely to eliminate all competition in the relevant market;

---

[418] Commission Decision 2003/741/EC, 13 Aug. 2003, [2003] OJ L268/69; IP 03/1159.

[419] Case C-418/01, *IMS Health GmbH & Co OHG v. NDC Health GmbH & Co KG*.

[420] There are around 21,500 pharmacies and 287,000 doctors in Germany (*IMS/NDC* [2002] OJ L59/18, para. 14). German privacy laws prevent the production of data which can identify sales in individual pharmacies.

[421] One of the competitors, PII, was founded by a former director of IMS, and later taken over by NDC.

[422] [2004] OJ L59/18, Art. 1. The Commission ordered the royalties to be fixed by agreement between the parties within two weeks, failing which recourse was to be had to independent expert(s) appointed by the parties. If the parties could not agree on the expert(s) within a further week the Commission would make the appointment (Art. 2).

— such refusal is not capable of being objectively justified; and

— the facility itself is indispensable to carrying on business, inasmuch as there is no actual or potential substitute in existence for that facility.

...

179. The Commission considers that this case meets the requirements for the establishment of abuse under Article 82 as developed in ECJ and CFI jurisprudence, beginning with the *Commercial Solvents* and *Volvo* judgements and taken further in *Magill, Ladbroke* and *Bronner*.

180. The Commission considers that there are 'exceptional circumstances' in this case within the meaning of the phrase used by the ECJ in *Magill* (paragraph 50) read in conjunction with the *Ladbroke* and *Bronner* cases. IMS has created, in collaboration with the pharmaceutical industry over a long period of time, a brick structure which has become the *de facto* industry standard for the presentation of regional data services and which the Frankfurt Court has found is its intellectual property right. IMS is now excluding all competition from the market for regional data services by refusing, without objective justification, to licence this structure to competitors. As clarified in the *Ladbroke* judgement, there is no requirement for a refusal to supply to prevent the emergence of a new product in order to be abusive.

181. It is clear that refusal of access to the 1,860 brick structure is likely to eliminate all competition in the relevant market, since without it is not possible to compete on the relevant market. IMS'S reasons for its refusal to licence are not capable of being objectively justified. Moreover, use of the 1,860 structure is indispensable to carrying on business on the relevant market; there is no actual or potential substitute for it. These exceptional circumstances meet the test set out in *Bronner* for a refusal to supply to be considered an abuse of a dominant position.

182. IMS makes a number of arguments attacking the legal analysis set out in the Statement of Objections. It says that there is no suggestion that IMS has engaged in any abusive conduct or has tried to use its control of intellectual property to monopolise downstream or related markets. IMS is entitled to refuse licences of its copyright to competitors for the market to which copyright relates (cf. the *Volvo* case). A refusal is only abusive if coupled with additional abusive behaviour, and there is none here.

183. Furthermore, IMS does not consider that the 1,860 brick structure is an essential facility, since there is no second related market on which competition is restricted.

184. As regards the first of these two arguments, ECJ and CFI case law subsequent to the *Volvo* case makes clear that in exceptional circumstances the refusal to licence an intellectual property right itself can be considered to be an abuse under Article 82. As described above in paragraphs 75–174, such circumstances exist here. A dominant company has negotiated over a long period with its customer industry so as to produce a structure on which the industry is now very highly dependent, to the extent that they consider it a de facto industry standard, and which a national court has now found is the dominant company's intellectual property. This dominant company now refuses to licence this structure to competitors, so that no competing products based on this structure can be produced. On the second argument, the fact that the case considered by the ECJ and CFI to which IMS refers involved two markets does not preclude the possibility that a refusal to licence an intellectual property right can be contrary to Article 82. In the *Magill* case cited above, the basic information about TV programmes was considered to be an indispensable input to allow an undertaking to compete in a downstream market (that for television listings magazines). The circumstances are similar in this case, in that use of the 1,860 brick structure is an indispensable input to allow undertakings to compete in the market for regional sales data services in Germany. As explained above in paragraphs 15–16, there is an important distinction between the product, which is regional sales data services, and the brick structure in which data used to create these services is formatted. In this case, in the specific and exceptional circumstances in which the '1,860 brick structure' was developed and copyright was asserted and found to subsist, the work

> in question for the technical, legal and economic constraints referred to above is incapable of being replicated by means of a non-infringing parallel creation.
>
> 185. The finding here is that there is a prima facie case that use of the 1,860 brick structure is indispensable to compete on the relevant market. The input which the pharmaceutical companies have made to the structure have contributed greatly to its status as a de facto industry standard and to their current dependence on this structure as a format for the receipt of regional sales data services. It is therefore the case that refusing access to this structure to competitors on the relevant market would exclude all competition from this market, and that therefore IMS's refusal to licence the 1,860 brick structure involves abusive conduct.

It will be noted that on the 'new product' issue the Commission categorically stated (paragraph 180) that *Ladbroke* had 'clarified' that there is no requirement for a refusal to supply to prevent the emergence of a new product in order to be abusive. In other words, the list in *Magill* is not cumulative. As for the 'one or two markets issue', the Commission separated the brick structure from the provision of the data reports. The brick structure was an indispensable 'input' into the data, and those competing on the data market needed access to the brick structure (paragraph 184). It drew an analogy with *Magill* where the programme listings are described as an indispensable input in respect of the television listings magazines market. It will also be noted that the Commission applied the principles laid down in *Bronner* to an intellectual property rights scenario.

IMS appealed, applying for interim relief. It claimed that the decision contradicted settled Community case law and previous Commission decisions, in that it deprived it of the very essence of its copyright and went beyond the conception of 'exceptional circumstances' in *Magill*. The President of the CFI[423] suspended the decision on the ground that the status quo should be maintained pending the CFI's judgment in the appeal. He was concerned that the decision did, indeed, go beyond *Magill*.[424]

As explained above, the ECJ gave judgment in April 2004, not on appeal from the Commission decision but on an Article 234 reference. The judgment, which largely followed the Opinion of Advocate General Tizzano, set out the conditions in which a refusal to supply a copyright (the judgment did not discuss other intellectual property rights) is an abuse, and left the German court to decide whether the conditions were satisfied in the situation before it.

Case C-418/01, *IMS Health GmbH & Co OHG* v. *NDC Health GmbH & Co KG* [2004] ECR I-5039, [2004] 4 CMLR 1543

The Landgericht Frankfurt am Main asked three questions:

- first, whether it was an abuse not to grant a licence in a situation where the competitor was seeking access to the same geographical and product market and the customers would only accept a product based on material protected by the copyright;

---

[423] Confirmed by the President of the ECJ. For the suspension of decisions, see further *infra* Chap. 14, 1267.

[424] It was held that the balance of interests favoured preserving the copyright unimpaired during the appeal proceedings: there was potentially serious and irreparable harm to IMS in having to license its copyright and the copyright should not be devalued by reducing it to a purely economic right to receive financial compensation: the conditions for granting interim relief were therefore fulfilled. Case T-184/01 R, *IMS Health* v. *Commission*, [2001] ECR II-3193, [2002] 4 CMLR 58, para. 125, confirmed by the President of the ECJ, Case C-481/01 P(R), *IMS Health* v. *Commission* [2002] ECR I-3401, [2002] 5 CMLR 44.

- secondly, was the participation of the customers in developing the copyright material relevant;
- thirdly, were the costs which the customers would occur in switching to a product protected by a different data bank relevant.

The Court held that the second and third questions both concerned factors which had to be taken into consideration in determining whether the protected structure was indispensable for the relevant marketing studies. The following extract is the part of the judgment dealing with the first question.

Court of Justice

34. According to settled case-law, the exclusive right of reproduction forms part of the owner's rights, so that refusal to grant a licence, even if it is the act of an undertaking holding a dominant position, cannot in itself constitute abuse of a dominant position (judgment in Case 238/87 Volvo, . . . paragraph 8, and Magill, paragraph 49).

35. Nevertheless, as is clear from that case-law, exercise of an exclusive right by the owner may, in exceptional circumstances, involve abusive conduct (Volvo, paragraph 9, and Magill, paragraph 50).

36. The Court held that such exceptional circumstances were present in the case giving rise to the judgment in Magill, in which the conduct complained of by the television channels in a dominant position involved invoking the copyright conferred by national legislation on the weekly listings of their programmes in order to prevent another undertaking from publishing information on those programmes together with commentaries, on a weekly basis.

37. According to the summary of the Magill judgment made by the Court at paragraph 40 of the judgment in Bronner, the exceptional circumstances were constituted by the fact that the refusal in question concerned a product (information on the weekly schedules of certain television channels), the supply of which was indispensable for carrying on the business in question, (the publishing of a general television guide), in that, without that information, the person wishing to produce such a guide would find it impossible to publish it and offer it for sale (paragraph 53), the fact that such refusal prevented the emergence of a new product for which there was a potential consumer demand (paragraph 54), the fact that it was not justified by objective considerations (paragraph 55), and was likely to exclude all competition in the secondary market (paragraph 56).

38. It is clear from that case-law that, in order for the refusal by an undertaking which owns a copyright to give access to a product or service indispensable for carrying on a particular business to be treated as abusive, it is sufficient that three cumulative conditions be satisfied, namely, that that refusal is preventing the emergence of a new product for which there is a potential consumers demand, that it is unjustified and such as to exclude any competition on a secondary market.

39. In light of the order for reference and the observations submitted to the Court, which reveal a major dispute as regards the interpretation of the third condition, it is appropriate to consider that question first.

The third condition, relating to the likelihood of excluding all competition on a secondary market

40. In that regard, it is appropriate to recall the approach followed by the Court in the Bronner judgment, in which it was asked whether the fact that a press undertaking with a very large share of the daily newspaper market in a Member State which operates the only nationwide newspaper home-delivery scheme in that Member State refuses paid access to that scheme by the publisher of a rival newspaper, which by reason of its small circulation is unable either alone or in cooperation with other publishers to set up and operate its own home-delivery scheme under economically reasonable conditions, constitutes the abuse of a dominant position.

· 41. The Court, first of all, invited the national court to determine whether the home delivery schemes constituted a separate market (Bronner, paragraph 34), on which, in light of the circumstances of the case, the press undertaking held a de facto monopoly position and, thus, a dominant position (paragraph 35). It then invited the national court to determine whether the refusal by the owner of the only nationwide home-delivery scheme in a Member State, which used that scheme to distribute its own daily newspapers, to allow the publisher of a rival daily newspaper access to it deprived that competitor of a means of distribution judged essential for the sale of its newspaper (paragraph 37).

42. Therefore, the Court held that it was relevant, in order to assess whether the refusal to grant access to a product or a service indispensable for carrying on a particular business activity was an abuse, to distinguish an upstream market, constituted by the product or service, in that case the market for home delivery of daily newspapers, and a (secondary) downstream market, on which the product or service in question is used for the production of another product or the supply of another service, in that case the market for daily newspapers themselves.

43. The fact that the delivery service was not marketed separately was not regarded as precluding, from the outset, the possibility of identifying a separate market.

44. It appears, therefore, as the Advocate General set out in points 56 to 59 of his Opinion, that, for the purposes of the application of the earlier case-law, it is sufficient that a potential market or even hypothetical market can be identified. Such is the case where the products or services are indispensable in order to carry on a particular business and where there is an actual demand for them on the part of undertakings which seek to carry on the business for which they are indispensable.

45. Accordingly, it is determinative that two different stages of production may be identified and that they are interconnected, the upstream product is indispensable in as much as for supply of the downstream product.

46. Transposed to the facts of the case in the main proceedings, that approach prompts consideration as to whether the 1860 brick structure constitutes, upstream, an indispensable factor in the downstream supply of German regional sales data for pharmaceutical products.

47. It is for the national court to establish whether that is in fact the position, and, if so be the case, to examine whether the refusal by IMS to grant a licence to use the structure at issue is capable of excluding all competition on the market for the supply of German regional sales data on pharmaceutical products.

The first condition, relating to the emergence of a new product

48. As the Advocate General stated in point 62 of his Opinion, that condition relates to the consideration that, in the balancing of the interest in protection of copyright and the economic freedom of its owner, against the interest in protection of free competition the latter can prevail only where refusal to grant a licence prevents the development of the secondary market to the detriment of consumers.

49. Therefore, the refusal by an undertaking in a dominant position to allow access to a product protected by copyright, where that product is indispensable for operating on a secondary market, may be regarded as abusive only where the undertaking which requested the licence does not intend to limit itself essentially to duplicating the goods or services already offered on the secondary market by the owner of the copyright, but intends to produce new goods or services not offered by the owner of the right and for which there is a potential consumer demand.

50. It is for the national court to determine whether such is the case in the dispute in the main proceedings.

The second condition, relating to whether the refusal was unjustified

51. As to that condition, on whose interpretation no specific observations have been made, it is for the national court to examine, if appropriate, in light of the facts before it, whether the refusal of the request for a licence is justified by objective considerations.

52. Accordingly, the answer to the first question must be that the refusal by an undertaking which holds a dominant position and is the owner of an intellectual property right over a brick structure which is indispensable for the presentation of data on regional sales of pharmaceutical products in a Member State, to grant a licence to use that structure to another undertaking which also wishes to supply such data in the same Member State, constitutes an abuse of a dominant position within the meaning of Article 82 EC where the following conditions are fulfilled:

— the undertaking which requested the licence intends to offer, on the market for the supply of the data in question, new products or services not offered by the copyright owner and for which there is a potential consumer demand;

— the refusal is not justified by objective considerations;

— the refusal is such as to reserve to the copyright owner the market for the supply of data on sales of pharmaceutical products in the Member State concerned by eliminating all competition on that market.

In this judgment the ECJ laid down (paragraphs 38 and 52) that three *cumulative* conditions must be fulfilled to render a refusal to license a copyright abusive (it said that this was 'clear from the case law', which is rather questionable). Contrary to the Commission's decision there must, first, be a new product involved. Secondly, access to the protected material must be 'indispensable' so that the refusal will exclude *any* (paragraph 38) or *all* (paragraph 52) competition on a secondary market. Thirdly, the refusal must be unjustified.

There are two ways of looking at this judgment, analogous to the 'is the glass half full or half empty' conundrum. One can view it as the Court coming down firmly on the 'side' of the intellectual property right holder, in that there is a presumption against the licence (see paragraph 48). The Court repeated that a refusal to grant a licence cannot in itself constitute an abuse (paragraph 34). It allowed for the possibility of compulsory licences but only in 'exceptional circumstances' (paragraph 35). It incorporated into the exceptional circumstances the requirement of 'indispensability' in the *Bronner* sense, which as we saw above,[425] put the bar at a high level, and demanded that the party requiring the licence intends to offer new goods and services for which there is a potential consumer demand. On the other hand, the nature of the 'indispensable' and 'new product' requirements are such that everything will turn on the application of these conditions to the facts of the case by the national court or competition authority concerned. In *IMS* the ECJ referred everything back to the national court without giving any indication as to whether the requirements were in fact satisfied in the case. This can be contrasted with *Bronner*, where the ECJ made it absolutely clear that that the conditions laid down there were *not* satisfied.[426] In *IMS* there was in fact some room for argument about whether NDC was providing a 'new product' and the Commission stated in its Decision that the sales reports of the firms 'differ markedly'.[427] It comes down to a matter of whether this would fulfill

---

[425] *Supra* 551.

[426] *Magill* was an appeal from a Commission decision under Article 230.

[427] According to the customers the coverage of parts of Germany was more complete and they provided more detail on types of information, Commission Decision [2002] OJ L59/18, para. 15.

the condition of not 'essentially duplicating' the right holder's product. The key to this is the interests of consumers. In paragraph 48 the Court said that the only situation in which free competition can override the rights of the copyright holder is where the refusal prevents the development of the secondary market *to the detriment of consumers*. The licence is not ordered to protect the competitor but to protect consumers .

The Court did require that the development of a *secondary* market be affected. As the Commission had done it spelt two markets out of the situation in *IMS*. The Court said (paragraph 44) that it is enough if a 'potential or even hypothetical' market can be identified upstream. It only required that 'two different stages of production' can be identified.[428] The question here of course is how hypothetical can the market for the input be. The upstream market in *IMS* was a very artificial one: IMS only developed the brick structure in order to produce its own sales reports. It was different in *Magill* where the television listings existed as a by-product of the broadcasting activities and would have existed whether or not the broadcasters had published their own magazines. As one commentator said (critically) of the Commission decision in *IMS*, it was enough 'even if the input is a competitive advantage of a kind which has never previously been marketed or licensed by any company, and which it would not be economically rational to license to a direct competitor'.[429] There are few production processes that cannot be divided as in *IMS* if one thinks hard enough and anything protected by an intellectual property right could on this basis form an upstream market. One can compare *IMS* on this point with the judgment of the US Supreme Court in *Verizon* v. *Trinko*,[430] discussed below, where the fact that 'the services allegedly witheld are not otherwise marketed or available to the public' and existed 'only deep in the bowels of Verizon' was a factor in holding the refusal to deal lawful. Moreover *IMS* did not involve leveraging. IMS was not leveraging its dominance from the upstream to the downstream market. The Court appears therefore, not to require leveraging as an element of refusal to supply.[431]

The *IMS* judgment gives little flavour of the underlying factual situation. It is necessary to read the Commission decision to fully appreciate that *IMS*, like *Magill*, involved a 'weak' copyright. Indeed, the Commission seemed to consider that IMS had more or less hi-jacked the industry standard.[432] If *IMS* could be taken as turning on the particular facts of how the brick structure had been developed and the copyright acquired it could be viewed as a response to a quirk of national law (which the Court could do nothing about as it respects copyright as recognized by the relevant national law). Some commentators consider that the cases should be viewed in this light—as exceptional responses to unsatisfactory copyright laws—and that there is no reason to suppose that the same approach would be taken to strong patent rights, for example.[433] If so, the danger to innovation (insofar one accepts there *is* a danger to innovation)

---

[428] It can be argued that by saying that it was a matter of whether two *stages of production* can be identified the Court was abandoning the requirement of two *markets*: it is enough that there are two *products*. See J. Venit, 'The IP/Antitrust Interface After *IMS Health*', in C. D. Ehlermann and I. Atanasiu (eds.), *European Competition Law Annual 2005: The Interaction Between Competition Law and Intellectual Property Law* (Hart Publishing, 2007) 609, 625.

[429] J. Temple Lang, 'Anti-competitive Non-Pricing Abuses under European and National Antitrust Law' in B. Hawk (ed.) [2003] *Fordham Corp L Inst* 235, 307.

[430] 124 S.Ct 872, see *infra*.

[431] See Venit, n. 428, *supra*.

[432] And see F. Fine, 'NDC/IMS: A Logical Application of the Essential Facilities Doctrine' [2002] *ECLR* 457; *ibid*., 'NDC/IMS: In Response to Professor Korah (2002) 70 *Antitrust LJ* 247.

[433] See, e.g. M. Delrahim, 'Forcing Firms to Share the Sandbox: Compulsory Licensing of Intellectual Property Rights and Antitrust', BIICL conference, 10 May 2004, available at http://www.usdoj.gov/atr/public/speeches/203627.htm (Delrahim was at the time US Deputy Assistant Attorney General, DOJ Antitrust Division).

is minimized. As far as the indispensability requirement is concerned it should be noted that the Commission withdrew its interim decision in August 2003 because the situation had changed, in that NDC had succeeded in concluding contracts with some larger pharmaceutical companies and there was no longer a threat that it might be eliminated from the market. The Commission stated that its decision was without prejudice to whether the improvement in NDC's position had been caused by the judgment of the Oberlandesgericht on the copyright.[434] If it was not caused by this it would throw doubt on how indispensable the 1,860 brick structure was in the first place. In the application of the principles laid down in both *IMS* and *Bronner*, everything ultimately turns on the assessment of indispensability.

G. INTEROPERABILITY

A particular kind of refusal to supply arises in the information technology sector in respect of 'interface information'. Providers of software need to be able to make products which operate with other systems and programs. This is known as 'interoperability'.[435] For this they require interface information, i.e., information about the systems and programs of other producers with which they want their products to be compatible and usable. This information may be protected by intellectual property rights (copyright). It may be obtainable by decompilation (reverse engineering) but this can be impossible or not practically or economically feasible.[436] Where the software market is dominated by an undertaking with significant market power it may be essential to the competitive viability of other providers that their products are compatible with those of the dominant undertaking.

The Commission first addressed this issue in 1984 when it dealt with a number of IBM's practices.[437] It alleged that IBM had abused its dominant position by failing to supply other manufacturers with interface information needed to make competitive products work with IBM's System/370. The Commission and IBM reached a settlement by which IBM, while not admitting the existence of a dominant position or any abuse thereof, undertook to disclose sufficient interface information to enable competitors in the EEC to attach hardware and software products of their own design to System/370.[438]

The Commission began an investigation into the software company Microsoft in 1998 on a complaint lodged by Sun Microsystems. Sun complained that Microsoft refused to disclose to Sun (and others) who provided server operating systems sufficient interface information to enable them to create 'workgroup' server operating systems that would operate with Microsoft's Windows desktop and server operating systems. Microsoft has approximately a 95 per cent share of the PC operating systems market and consumers buying workgroup server operating systems naturally want products that are compatible with Windows and Microsoft's applications products. Five years and three statements of objections later the Commission held that Microsoft had abused its dominant position on the PC operating systems market. It fined it €497,196,304[439] and ordered that within 120 days it should make the relevant interface infor-

---

[434] See *supra* 563.

[435] See *infra* Chap. 10 for the right of decompilation in software licences for the purposes of interoperability contained in Dir. 91/250 [1991] OJ L122/42.

[436] For the arguments about the possibilities of reverse engineering in *Microsoft*, see *infra* 512.

[437] For the tying aspects, see *supra* 522.

[438] See *XIVth Report on Competition Policy* (Commission, 1984) parts 94–5.

[439] The fine was also in respect of the abuse Microsoft had committed in tying its media player to Windows, see *supra* 525.

mation available to undertakings on the work group server operating system market and should ensure that the information was kept updated on an ongoing basis and in a timely manner.[440]

Although the facts of *Microsoft* were highly complex[441] the decision came down in the end to applying the principles of the refusal to supply cases discussed above to this particular situation. Microsoft argued that reverse engineering was a means of its competitors accessing information necessary for interoperability. The Commission held that reverse engineering programs such as Windows required 'considerable efforts with uncertain chances of success'[442] and that the viability of products produced by reverse engineering depended on Microsoft not breaking the compatibility (for instance by upgrading the operating system). 'Reverse engineering is therefore an unstable basis for a business model'.[443] The Commission said that under *Bronner* and *Magill*[444] it was necessary to show that supply is indispensable to carry on business in the market, which means that there is no realistic actual or potential substitute to it[445] and it held that in this case the refusal to supply 'puts Microsoft's competitors at a strong competition disadvantage . . . to an extent where there is a risk of elimination of competition'.[446] This would impact on technical development to the prejudice of consumers (the Commission was at pains to show that it was protecting competition in the interests of consumers and not just competitors).[447] The Commission (adopting this decision before the *IMS* judgment) said that 'there is no persuasiveness to an approach that would advocate the existence of an exhaustive checklist of exceptional circumstances'.[448] It considered it to be relevant ('of interest') that this was a case of the disruption of previous levels of supply, i.e. like *Commercial Solvents*.[449] The Commission rejected Microsoft's argument that its refusal to supply could be justified by its need for incentives to innovate.

Microsoft, Commission Decision, 24 March 2004, COMP/C-3/37.792, [2005] 4 CMLR 965

Commission

(694) ... [The lack of interoperability] limits the prospect for such competitors to successfully market their innovation and thereby discourages them from developing new products.

. . .

(700) In a longer term perspective, if Microsoft's strategy is successful, new products other than Microsoft's work group server operating systems will be confined to niche existences or not be viable at all. There will be little scope for innovation—except possibly for innovation coming from Microsoft . . .

---

[440] To be enforced by the appointment of a 'monitoring trustee' to ensure that the disclosures are complete and accurate.

[441] Especially to anyone without an expert knowledge of information technology.

[442] *Microsoft*, para. 685.

[443] *Ibid.*, para. 686.

[444] The decision was adopted a month before the judgment of the ECJ in Case C-418/01, *IMS v. NDC* [2004] ECR I-5039, [2004] 4 CMLR 1543.

[445] *Microsoft*, para. 585.

[446] *Ibid.*, para. 589.

[447] *Ibid.*, 692.

[448] *Ibid.*, para. 555.

[449] *Ibid.*, para. 555.

. . .

(724) . . . . When analysing how an obligation to disclose the interface information requested by Sun would impact on Microsoft's incentives to innovate, account must be taken of Microsoft's incentives to innovate its products as a whole, not only in the design of its products' interfaces. Furthermore, such an assessment must be conducted *in comparison* to the alternative situation where Microsoft's anti-competitive behaviour remains unfettered.

(725) In the latter situation, there is a serious risk that Microsoft will succeed in eliminating all effective competition in the work group server operating system market . . . This would have a significant negative effect on its incentives to innovate as regards its clients PC and work group server operating system products. Microsoft's research and development efforts are indeed spurred by the innovative steps its competitors take in the work group server operating system market. Were such competitors to disappear, this would diminish Microsoft's incentives to innovate. By contrast, were Microsoft to supply Sun and other work group server operating systems with the interoperability information at stake in this case, the competitive landscape would liven up as Microsoft's work group server operating system products would have to compete with implementations interoperable with the Windows domain architecture. Microsoft would no longer benefit from a lock-in effect that dirves consumers towards a homogeneous Microsoft solution, and such competitive pressure would increase Microsoft's own incentives to innovate.

. . .

(779) Microsoft has been enjoying a dominant (quasi-monopoly) position on the client PC operating system market for many years. This position of market strength enables Microsoft to determine to a large extent and independently of its competitors the set of coherent communications rules that will govern the *de facto* standard for interoperability in work group networks. As such, interoperability with the Windows domain architecture is necessary for a work group server operating system vendor in order to viably stay on the market.

(780) Microsoft has diminished the level of disclosures that it makes concerning information necessary to achieve such interoperability. Microsoft has turned down a formal request by Sun concerning such interoperability information.

(781) The data collected by the Commission show that there is a risk of elimination of competition in the work group server operating system market. Microsoft's market share has increased swiftly. The company has reached a dominant position in the relevant market. This position continues to be reinforced. Technologies that will lead to a further lock-in into Microsoft's products at the work group server and client PC level are quickly gaining traction in the market. The Commission's investigation has also produced evidence that establishes a causal link between the market evolution and the interoperability advantage enjoyed by Microsoft. Furthermore, there is no actual or potential substitute to disclosures by Microsoft of interoperability information.

(782) Microsoft's refusal to supply has the consequence of stifling innovation in the impacted market and of diminishing consumers. choices by locking them into a homogeneous Microsoft solution. As such, it is in particular inconsistent with the provisions of Article 82 (b) of the Treaty.

(783) The major objective justification put forward by Microsoft relates to Microsoft's intellectual property over Windows. However, a detailed examination of the scope of the disclosure at stake leads to the conclusion that, on balance, the possible negative impact of an order to supply on Microsoft's incentives to innovate is outweighed by its positive impact on the level of innovation of the whole industry (including Microsoft). As such, the need to protect Microsoft's incentives to innovate cannot constitute an objective justification that would offset the exceptional circumstances identified. Microsoft's other objective justification, which is that it has no incentive to engage in anti-competitive conduct with respect to interoperability, is not supported . . . and in fact is largely contradicted . . . by the evidence in this case.

(784) In conclusion, Microsoft's refusal to supply interoperability information violates Article 82 of the Treaty.

Three aspects of the decision should particularly be noted. Firstly, the criterion of 'indispensability' did not appear satisfied. The interface information might be greatly more convenient for the competitors, but they *were* functioning on the market.[450] Secondly, the 'new product' criterion, afterwards held essential in *IMS* in respect of intellectual property rights, did not appear satisfied, as in, e.g. paragraph 724 the Commission refers to innovation still coming from Microsoft and the competitors operating in niche markets. Moreover, there is no *specific* new product for which actual or potential consumer demand is identified. Thirdly, (paragraph 783) the Commission concluded that the balancing of the incentives/disincentives to innovation come down on the side of forcing access. The decision is on appeal to the CFI. [451] As far as the application of the existing case law is concerned, insofar as the interface information is covered by intellectual property rights the principles laid down in *IMS* are relevant In respect of other information *Bronner*[452] (which does not demand a 'new product') is relevant. However, as we see below, the Discussion Paper states that interoperability situations are *sui generis*.

The author of the article extracted at the start of this discussion on intellectual property rights says of the innovation disincentives in *Microsoft* and in the US judgment:

C. Ritter, 'Refusal to Deal and Essential Facilities: Does Intellectual Property Require Special Deference compared to Tangible Property?' (2005) *World Competition* (3) 281, 298

In the *Microsoft* cases, both the European Commission and the US Department of Justice looked at industry-wide innovation incentives. The Commission's *Microsoft* decision states that "on balance, the possible negative impact of an order to supply on Microsoft's incentives to innovate is outweighed by its positive impact on the level of innovation of the whole industry (including Microsoft)...Similarly, one of the DOJ's economic experts testified that Microsoft's conduct "reduces the expected profits that outside innovators can expect to earn from developing technologies that threaten to create additional competition for Microsoft's operating system monopoly....Because outsiders are such an important source of innovative energy, Microsoft's threatening message reduced the rate of innovation in the software industry as a whole."...Some commentators have asked whether antitrust agencies are well-equipped to carry out this kind of industry-wide balancing of incentives...but this is a biased formulation. The real question is: is the risk of antitrust agencies erring in evaluating the need for compulsory licenses so great that we should generally prefer no compulsory licenses at all? Those who argue that false convictions are more damaging to the economy than false acquittals...have so far failed to produce evidence supporting their position. Even so, it would be necessary to show that the cumulative cost of false convictions is *so* great (given their rate of occurrence) that it would be preferable to have no enforcement at all.

...

---

[450] See D. Ridyard, 'Compulsory Access under EC Competition Law—A New Doctrine of 'Convenient Facilities' and the Case for Price Regulation' [2004] *ECLR* 670.

[451] Case T-201/04, *Microsoft v. EC Commission* (judgment pending).

[452] Case C-7/97, *Oscar Bronner GmbH & Co KG v. Mediaprint* [1998] ECR I-7791, [1999] 4 CMLR 112.

H. THE ESSENTIAL FACILITIES DOCTRINE IN US LAW

It was said above[453] that the essential facilities doctrine originated in US law. Section 2 of the Sherman Act prohibits the acquisition or maintenance of monopoly power. In *United States* v. *Colgate & Co*,[454] however, the Supreme Court said that in the absence of any purpose to create or maintain a monopoly a private trader may freely 'exercise his own independent discretion as to parties with whom he may deal' and the US courts have consequently been generally reluctant to condemn refusals to deal. However, they have held that such refusals do come within section 2, by way of exception to the *Colgate* principle, in certain limited circumstances, and some courts have applied an 'essential facilities' doctrine.[455] There has been controversy in US antitrust law as to whether the doctrine is really part of the recognized exceptions to the *Colgate* principle, or whether it is a separate principle.[456] In any event, many American commentators are highly critical of the doctrine. We have already seen that Areeda expressed caution about it[457] and Hovenkamp says the 'so-called essential facilities doctrine is one of the most troublesome, incoherent and unmanageable bases for Sherman section 2 liability. The antitrust world would almost certainly be a better place if it were jettisoned, with a little fine tuning of the general doctrine of the monopolist's refusal to deal to fill in the resulting gaps'.[458] In 2004 a case concerning a refusal to supply where the essential facilities doctrine was raised finally came before the Supreme Court. The case concerned the telecommunications sector, which complicated the issues. Nevertheless, the Supreme Court dismissed the claim that there was a refusal to deal under section 2 and was less than enthusiastic about the essential facilities doctrine. The extracts below rehearse again (albeit in the context of the US provisions) the dangers of forcing undertakings to share with or supply competitors and should be compared with the similar arguments of Advocate General Jacobs in *Bronner*.[459]

Verizon Communications Inc v. *Trinko LLP* 124 S.Ct. 872

Customers who received local telephone services from competing local exchange carriers (LEC) brought an action against the incumbent LEC alleging that it had breached its duty to share under the Telecommunications Act 1996 and that its failure to share violated section 2 of the Sherman Act. The Supreme Court held that the duties under the 1996 Act could not be enforced through a section 2 claim, but the Act did not affect any liability which the LEC had under general antitrust law. It therefore examined the customers' claims under antitrust law. The Court held (paragraph 6) that even if the essential facilities doctrine existed it served no purpose here as the question of access was taken care of by the 1996 Act.

---

[453] *Supra* 537.

[454] 250 US 300, 39 S.Ct 465 (1919).

[455] The leading cases are discussed by the Supreme Court in *Verizon* v. *Trinko, infra* 576 ff.

[456] See L. Hancher, 'Case note on *Oscar Bronner*' (1999) 36 *CMLRev* 1289.

[457] P. Areeda, 'Essential Facilities: An Epithet in Need of Limiting Principles' [1990] *Antitrust LJ* 841, extracted *supra* 544.

[458] H. Hovenkamp, *Federal Antitrust Policy* (3rd edn., Thomson/West, 2005), 309, and see generally Chap. 7. Jacobs A-G, reviewing the US position in Case C-7/97, *Oscar Bronner GmbH & Co KG* v. *Mediaprint* [1998] ECR I-7791, [1999] 4 CMLR 112, para. 46 of his Opinion, pointed out that section 2 of the Sherman Act and Article 82 protect competition in different ways. The Sherman Act prohibits the acquisition or maintenance of monopoly power, whereas Article 82 regulates the actions of companies in dominant positions.

[459] *Supra* 548 ff.

Supreme Court of the United States (Justice Scalia delivered the opinion of the Court)

III

[2] The complaint alleges that Verizon denied interconnection services to rivals in order to limit entry. If that allegation states an antitrust claim at all, it does so under § 2 of the Sherman Act, 15 U.S.C. § 2, which declares that a firm shall not 'monopolize' or 'attempt to monopolize.' *Ibid*. It is settled law that this offense requires, in addition to the possession of monopoly power in the relevant market, 'the willful acquisition or maintenance of that power as distinguished from growth or development as a consequence of a superior product, business acumen, or historic accident.' *United States* v. *Grinnell Corp*, 384 U.S. 563, 570–571, 86 S.Ct. 1698, 16 L.Ed.2d 778 (1966). The mere possession of monopoly power, and the concomitant charging of monopoly prices, is not only not unlawful; it is an important element of the free-market system. The opportunity to charge monopoly prices—at least for a short period—is what attracts 'business acumen' in the first place; it induces risk taking that produces innovation and economic growth. To safeguard the incentive to innovate, the possession of monopoly power will not be found unlawful unless it is accompanied by an element of anti-competitive *conduct*.

[3] Firms may acquire monopoly power by establishing an infrastructure that renders them uniquely suited to serve their customers. Compelling such firms to share the source of their advantage is in some tension with the underlying purpose of antitrust law, since it may lessen the incentive for the monopolist, the rival, or both to invest in those economically beneficial facilities. Enforced sharing also requires antitrust courts to act as central planners, identifying the proper price, quantity, and other terms of dealing—a role for which they are ill-suited. Moreover, compelling negotiation between competitors may facilitate the supreme evil of antitrust: collusion. Thus, as a general matter, the Sherman Act 'does not restrict the long recognized right of [a] trader or manufacturer engaged in an entirely private business, freely to exercise his own independent discretion as to parties with whom he will deal.' *United States* v. *Colgate & Co*, 250 U.S. 300, 307, 39 S.Ct. 465, 63 L.Ed. 992 (1919).

[4] However, '[t]he high value that we have placed on the right to refuse to deal with other firms does not mean that the right is unqualified.' *Aspen Skiing Co* v. *Aspen Highlands Skiing Corp*, 472 U.S. 585, 601, 105 S.Ct. 2847, 86 L.Ed.2d 467 (1985). Under certain circumstances, a refusal to cooperate with rivals can constitute anti-competitive conduct and violate § 2. We have been very cautious in recognizing such exceptions, because of the uncertain virtue of forced sharing and the difficulty of identifying and remedying anti-competitive conduct by a single firm. The question before us today is whether the allegations of respondent's complaint fit within existing exceptions or provide a basis, under traditional antitrust principles, for recognizing a new one.

[5] The leading case for § 2 liability based on refusal to cooperate with a rival, and the case upon which respondent understandably places greatest reliance, is *Aspen Skiing, supra*. The Aspen ski area consisted of four mountain areas. The defendant, who owned three of those areas, and the plaintiff, who owned the fourth, had cooperated for years in the issuance of a joint, multiple-day, all-area ski ticket. After repeatedly demanding an increased share of the proceeds, the defendant canceled the joint ticket. The plaintiff, concerned that skiers would bypass its mountain without some joint offering, tried a variety of increasingly desperate measures to re-create the joint ticket, even to the point of in effect offering to buy the defendant's tickets at retail price. *Id., at 593–594, 105 S.Ct. 2847*. The defendant refused even that. We upheld a jury verdict for the plaintiff, reasoning that '[t]he jury may well have concluded that [the defendant] elected to forgo these short-run benefits because it was more interested in reducing competition...over the long run by harming its smaller competitor.' *Id.*, at 608, 105 S.Ct. 2847.

Aspen Skiing is at or near the outer boundary of § 2 liability. The Court there found significance in the defendant's decision to cease participation in a cooperative venture. See *id.*, at 608, 610–611, 105 S.Ct. 2847. The unilateral termination of a voluntary (*and thus presumably profitable*) course of dealing suggested a willingness to forsake short-term profits to achieve an anti-competitive end. *Ibid.* Similarly, the defendant's unwillingness to renew the ticket *even if compensated at retail price* revealed a distinctly anti-competitive bent.

The refusal to deal alleged in the present case does not fit within the limited exception recognized in *Aspen Skiing*. The complaint does not allege that Verizon voluntarily engaged in a course of dealing with its rivals, or would ever have done so absent statutory compulsion. Here, therefore, the defendant's prior conduct sheds no light upon the motivation of its refusal to deal—upon whether its regulatory lapses were prompted not by competitive zeal but by anti-competitive malice. The contrast between the cases is heightened by the difference in pricing behavior. In *Aspen Skiing*, the defendant turned down a proposal to sell at its own retail price, suggesting a calculation that its future monopoly retail price would be higher. Verizon's reluctance to interconnect at the cost-based rate of compensation available under § 251(c)(3) tells us nothing about dreams of monopoly.

The specific nature of what the 1996 Act compels makes this case different from *Aspen Skiing* in a more fundamental way. In *Aspen Skiing*, what the defendant refused to provide to its competitor was a product that it already sold at retail—to oversimplify slightly, lift tickets representing a bundle of services to skiers. Similarly, in *Otter Tail Power Co v. United States*, 410 U.S. 366, 93 S.Ct. 1022, 35 L.Ed.2d 359 (1973), another case relied upon by respondent, the defendant was already in the business of providing a service to certain customers (power transmission over its network), and refused to provide the same service to certain other customers. *Id.*, at 370–371, 377–378, 93 S.Ct. 1022. In the present case, by contrast, the services allegedly withheld are not otherwise marketed or available to the public. The sharing obligation imposed by the 1996 Act created 'something brand new'—'the wholesale market for leasing network elements.' *Verizon Communications Inc v. FCC*, 535 U.S., at 528, 122 S.Ct. 1646. The unbundled elements offered pursuant to § 251(c)(3) exist only deep within the bowels of Verizon; they are brought out on compulsion of the 1996 Act and offered not to consumers but to rivals, and at considerable expense and effort. New systems must be designed and implemented simply to make that access possible—indeed, it is the failure of one of those systems that prompted the present complaint . . . [460]

[6] We conclude that Verizon's alleged insufficient assistance in the provision of service to rivals is not a recognized antitrust claim under this Court's existing refusal-to-deal precedents. This conclusion would be unchanged even if we considered to be established law the 'essential facilities' doctrine crafted by some lower courts, under which the Court of Appeals concluded respondent's allegations might state a claim. See generally Areeda, Essential Facilities: An Epithet in Need of Limiting Principles, 58 Antitrust L.J. 841 (1989). We have never recognized such a doctrine, see *Aspen Skiing Co*, 472 U.S., at 611, n. 44, 105 S.Ct. 2847; *AT & T Corp v. Iowa Utilities Bd.*, 525 U.S., at 428, 119 S.Ct. 721 (opinion of BREYER, J.), and we find no need either to recognize it or to repudiate it here. It suffices for present purposes to note that the indispensable requirement for invoking the doctrine is the unavailability of access to the 'essential facilities'; where access exists, the doctrine serves no purpose. Thus, it is said that 'essential facility claims should . . . be denied where a state or federal agency has effective power to compel sharing and to regulate its scope

---

[460] The footnote here reads, 'Respondent also relies upon *United States v. Terminal Railroad Assn. of St. Louis*, 224 U.S. 383, 32 S.Ct. 507, 56 L.Ed. 810 (1912), and *Associated Press v. United States*, 326 US 1, 65 S.Ct 1416, 89 L.Ed. 2013 (1945). These cases involved *concerted* action, which presents greater anti-competitive concerns and is amenable to a remedy that does not require judicial estimation of free-market forces: simply requiring that the outsider be granted nondiscriminatory admission to the club.'

and terms.' P. Areeda & H. Hovenkamp, Antitrust Law, p. 150, ∂ 773e (2003 Supp.). Respondent believes that the existence of sharing duties under the 1996 Act supports its case. We think the opposite: The 1996 Act's extensive provision for access makes it unnecessary to impose a judicial doctrine of forced access. To the extent respondent's 'essential facilities' argument is distinct from its general § 2 argument, we reject it.

IV

[7] Finally, we do not believe that traditional antitrust principles justify adding the present case to the few existing exceptions from the proposition that there is no duty to aid competitors. Antitrust analysis must always be attuned to the particular structure and circumstances of the industry at issue. Part of that attention to economic context is an awareness of the significance of regulation . . .

Against the slight benefits of antitrust intervention here, we must weigh a realistic assessment of its costs. Under the best of circumstances, applying the requirements of § 2 'can be difficult' because 'the means of illicit exclusion, like the means of legitimate competition, are myriad.' *United States* v. *Microsoft Corp*, 253 F.3d 34, 58 (C.A.D.C.2001) (en banc) *(per curiam)*. Mistaken inferences and the resulting false condemnations 'are especially costly, because they chill the very conduct the antitrust laws are designed to protect.' *Matsushita Elec. Industrial Co* v. *Zenith Radio Corp*, 475 U.S. 574, 594, 106 S.Ct. 1348, 89 L.Ed.2d 538 (1986). The cost of false positives counsels against an undue expansion of § 2 liability . . .

Even if the problem of false positives did not exist, conduct consisting of anti-competitive violations of § 251 may be, as we have concluded with respect to above-cost predatory pricing schemes, 'beyond the practical ability of a judicial tribunal to control.' *Brooke Group Ltd* v. *Brown & Williamson Tobacco Corp*, 509 U.S. 209, 223, 113 S.Ct. 2578, 125 L.Ed.2d 168 (1993). Effective remediation of violations of regulatory sharing requirements will ordinarily require continuing supervision of a highly detailed decree. We think that Professor Areeda got it exactly right: 'No court should impose a duty to deal that it cannot explain or adequately and reasonably supervise. The problem should be deemed irremedia[ble] by antitrust law when compulsory access requires the court to assume the day-to-day controls characteristic of a regulatory agency.' Areeda, 58 Antitrust L.J., at 853. In this case, respondent has requested an equitable decree to '[p]reliminarily and permanently enjoi[n] [Verizon from providing access to the local loop market . . . to [rivals] on terms and conditions that are not as favorable' as those that Verizon enjoys. App. 49–50. An antitrust court is unlikely to be an effective day-to-day enforcer of these detailed sharing obligations.

In paragraph 6 Justice Scalia points out that the Supreme Court has never recognized the essential facilities doctrine, which has been 'crafted by some lower courts'. Given that it could not apply here he states that there is 'no need either to recognize or repudiate it here'.[461] However, the tenor of the judgment is not sympathetic towards it. Earlier he is careful to confine the Court's existing refusal to deal precedents such as the famous *Aspen Skiing*, and *Otter Tail* cases to their own facts. Even taking into account the ECJ's conservative approach in *Bronner*, it appears that refusals to deal and essential facilities are an area of divergence between US and EC law. Some commentators argue strongly that the EC should take the same

---

[461] Thus disappointing many people. The Supreme Court's pronouncement on the essential facilities doctrine had been eagerly awaited.

robust approach to demands for access to the facilities of others as the Supreme Court has taken.[462]

I. REFUSAL TO SUPPLY IN THE DISCUSSION PAPER

In the Discussion Paper the Commission, citing the case law discussed above, divided refusals to supply into four categories, termination of an existing supply relationship; refusal to start supplying an input; refusal to license intellectual property rights; and refusal to supply information needed for interoperability.[463]

1. Termination of an existing relationship. The Commission said that there are normally four conditions to be fulfilled before the refusal to supply is abusive:[464]

   (a) behaviour can properly be characterized as a termination;

   (b) refusing undertaking is dominant;

   (c) refusal is likely to have a negative effect on competition;

   (d) refusal is not justified objectively or by efficiencies.

   One problem here is with the second condition. In *Commercial Solvents*[465] it was a matter of the probable *elimination* of the competitor. 'Negative effect on competition' is much weaker. Moreover, there was no requirement that the product or access is *indispensable*.

2. Refusal to start supplying input. There are normally five conditions to be fulfilled:[466]

   (a) behaviour can properly be characterized as a termination;

   (b) refusing undertaking is dominant;

   (c) input is indispensable;

   (d) the refusal is likely to have a negative effect on competition;

   (e) the refusal is not objectively justified.

   The same comment applies here. *Bronner*, talked about *elimination* of the competition, not just 'negative effect'. However, the 'indispensability' criterion appears here. The Discussion Paper therefore maintained an arguably unjustifiable distinction between terminations of existing supply relationships and refusals to start new ones. That would give perverse incentives to firms not to start supplying in the first place.

3. Refusal to licence intellectual property rights. The same five conditions as in (ii) apply, plus the refusal to licence prevents the production of a new new goods and services for which there is potential consumer demand,[467] Further, the Discussion Paper said that an 'IPR

---

[462] See in particular D. Geradin, 'Limiting the Scope of Article 82 EC: What Can the EU Learn from the Supreme Court's Judgment in *Trinko*, in the Wake of *Microsoft*, *IMS* and *Deutsche Telekom*?' (2004) 41 *CMLRev* 1526.

[463] For a critical analysis of the proposals on refusal to supply in the Discussion Paper, see R. Incardona, 'Modernization of Article 82 EC and Refusal to Supply' (2006) 2 *European Competition Journal* 337.

[464] Discussion Paper, para. 218.

[465] Cases 6 & 7/73, *Istituto Chemioterapico Italiano Spa & Commercial Solvents v. EC Commission* [1974] ECR 223, [1974] 1 CMLR 309.

[466] Discussion Paper, para. 9.2.2.

[467] *Ibid.*, para. 239.

technology which is indispensable as a basis for follow-on innovation by competitors may be abusive even if the licence is not sought to directly incorporate the technology in clearly identifiable new goods and services'.[468] This widened the 'new product' condition (which was not otherwise explained in the Discussion Paper) in a way which one commentator claimed 'could annihilate the incentives of firms engaging in radical, first-generation innovations for the sake of protecting firms that are merely engaged in exploiting the technological breakthroughs of their competitors'.[469]

4. Information needed for interoperability. The Discussion Paper placed this in a separate category, describing this as a 'special case'. The Commission thereby acknowledged that the *Microsoft* decision may not have met the conditions set out in *Bronner*, *Magill*, and *IMS*.

241. . . . Although there is no general obligation even for dominant companies to ensure operability, leveraging market power from one market to another by refusing interoperability information may be an abuse of a dominant position.

242. Even if such information may be considered a trade secret it may not be appropriate to apply to such refusals to supply information the same high standards for intervention as those described in the previous subsections.

8. OTHER EXCLUSIONARY PRACTICES

A. GENERAL

It is clear that any conduct which excludes competitors from the market *may* be capable of constituting an exclusionary abuse, whatever form it takes. The extent to which concrete foreclosure effects have to be demonstrated or measured is the subject of the current debate, as discussed throughout the preceding parts of this chapter. It is also possible that the *intent* to exclude may be relevant to characterizing the behaviour as an abuse. We saw above[470] that intent is relevant to some situations of predatory pricing but that abuse is described as an 'objective concept'.[471] However, in *AstraZeneca* athe Commission's finding that AstraZeneca intended to exclude competitors seems to have been key to the outcome of the case.[472] Miscellaneous exclusionary conduct which has come before the Court or Commission includes alleging to third parties that a competitor is a bad debtor,[473] buying up a competitor's machines,[474] and monopolizing the specialist advertising media.[475] In *Irish Sugar*[476] the dominant undertaking in the Irish sugar market persuaded certain

---

[468] Discussion Paper, para. 240.

[469] D, Geradin, 'Refusal to Supply and Article 82' Paper delvered at Commission's public hearings on the Discussion Paper, 14 June 2006, available at http://ec.europa.eu/comm/competition/antitrust/art82/geradin.pdf.

[470] *Supra* 448.

[471] Case 85/76, *Hoffmann-La Roche & Co AG v. Commission* [1979] ECR 461, [1979] 3 CMLR 211, para. 91.

[472] Case COMP/A.37.507.F3, *Generics/AstraZeneca*, 15 June 2005, IP /05/737, see *infra* 581–2, paras. 628, 632, 648, 789, 908.

[473] *BBI/Boosey & Hawkes* [1987] OJ L286/36, [1988] 4 CMLR 67.

[474] *Elopak Italia/Tetra Pak* [1991] OJ L72/1, [1992] 4 CMLR 551, para. 165.

[475] *Ibid.*

[476] Case T-228/97, *Irish Sugar plc v. Commission* [1999] ECR II-2969, [1999] 5 CMLR 1300.

wholesalers and retailers to swap the sugar they had bought from a competitor for its own. This conduct was found to be an abuse. Irish Sugar also put pressure on a shipping line to stop carrying the competitor's product by threatening to withdraw its own custom if this continued. The Commission commented that '[p]utting pressure on a carrier to prevent him from transporting competing goods cannot be considered to constitute a normal business practice'.[477] In TACA[478] the Commission held that a liner conference had committed an abuse by 'inducing' a competitor shipping line to join it. This in effect neutralized the competition by turning the competitor into one of the club. On appeal the CFI held that the Commission had not proved that there had been the alleged 'inducement' and overturned the decision.[479]

In the following sections we discuss specific exclusionary practices which have been held to infringe Article 82.

B. THE ACQUISITION OF INTELLECTUAL PROPERTY RIGHTS

It was seen in Chapter 5 that in *Tetra Pak*[480] the acquisition by a dominant undertaking of an exclusive patent licence was held to be an abuse even though the licence agreement did not infringe Article 81 as it fell within the block exemption regulation.[481] The CFI said that although the acquisition of an exclusive licence by a dominant undertaking is not an abuse *per se*, it may be so, and was on the facts of this case. The principle in *Tetra Pak I*, is a striking example of the onerous nature of the 'special responsibility' towards the competitive process imposed on dominant firms.[482]

C. THE MISUSE OF INTELLECTUAL PROPERTY RIGHTS OR OTHER REGULATORY PROCEDURES

It can be an abuse for a dominant undertaking to 'misuse' the patent system and drug marketing authorisation procedures. The Commission fined AstraZeneca €60 million for (i) misrepresenting certain dates to national patent offices in order to obtain extra patent protection to which it would otherwise not have been entitled and (ii) misusing marketing authorisation procedures by switching drugs from capsule to tablet form in order to hinder generic versions of the drugs coming onto the market, and also to hinder parallel imports. The decision demonstrates a broad approach to the concept of abuse, striking at AstraZeneca's commercial strategy and stressing its intent.

---

[477] Commission Decision, [1997] OJ L258/1, [1997] 5 CMLR 666, paras. 120–2.

[478] *Transatlantic Conference Agreement (TACA)* [1999] OJ L95/1, [1999] 4 CMLR 1415.

[479] Cases T-191/98 and T-212–14/98, *Atlantic Container Line AB v. Commission*, [2003] ECR II-3275.

[480] Case T-51/89, *Tetra Pak Rausing v. Commission* [1990] ECR II-309, [1991] 4 CMLR 334.

[481] Reg. 2349/84, [1984] OJ L219/15, on patent licensing agreements (replaced by 240/96, [1996] OJ L31/2, on Technology Transfer Agreements and subsequently by Reg. 772/2004 [2004] OJ L123/11 (see *infra* Chap. 10)).

[482] The principle has been applied subsequently in cases which were settled informally to the Commission's satisfaction: *Carlsberg/Interbrew*, XXIVth Report on Competition Policy (Commission, 1994), parts 209 and 213; *Svenska Tobaks*, XXVIIth Report on Competition Policy (Commission, 1997), part 66. See J. Faull and A. Nikpay (eds.), *The EC Law of Competition* (2nd edn., Oxford University Press, 2007), paras. 4.355–4.356.

Conduct that may otherwise be permissible even on the part of a dominant undertaking may be rendered abusive if its purpose is anti-competitive, in particular if it is part of a plan to eliminate competition.[483]

The decision, however, should be seen in the on-going battle in the EU over generic drugs. The Competition Commissioner stated:

I fully support the need for innovative products to enjoy strong intellectual property protection so that companies can recoup their R & D expenditure and be rewarded for their innovative efforts. However, it is not for a dominant company but for the legislator to decide which period of protection is adequate. Misleading regulators to gain longer protection acts as a disincentive to innovate and is a serious infringement of EU competition rules. Health care systems throughout Europe rely on generic drugs to keep costs down. Patients benefit from lower prices. By preventing generic competition AstraZeneca kept Losec prices artificially high. Moreover, competition from generic products after a patent has expired itself encourages innovation in pharmaceuticals.[484]

D. PURSUIT OF LEGAL PROCEEDINGS, VEXATIOUS LITIGATION, AND ENFORCING LEGAL RIGHTS

It may be an infringement of Article 82 for a dominant undertaking to pursue legal proceedings against a competitor. This was suggested by *BBI/Boosey & Hawkes*[485] where it was alleged that Boosey & Hawkes had pursued unjustified breach of copyright actions in the UK and actions for 'slavish copying' in the German courts against a new competitor it was trying to exclude from the market. The Commission did not pursue these allegations but concentrated its decision on the refusal to supply aspect.[486] The matter arose again in *ITT Promedia v. Commission*.[487] Promedia, which was engaged in a dispute with Belgacom, the dominant supplier of voice telephony services in Belgium, about the publication of telephone directories complained to the Commission that Belgacom was abusing its dominant position by entering into national litigation against it. The Commission rejected the complaint as it considered that the conduct of litigation by a dominant firm could be abusive only if two cumulative criteria were met, and that these criteria had not been met in this case. Promedia appealed to the CFI. The judgment of the CFI is unsatisfactory in some respects because Promedia alleged that the Commission had *applied the criteria incorrectly* but did not challenge the *criteria themselves*. The CFI expressly said that it was not necessary for it to rule on the correctness of the criteria[488] and confined itself to holding that they had been properly applied. The implication of the CFI judgment, however, is that the criteria themselves are correct.

---

[483] Case COMP/A.37.507.F3, *Generics/AstraZeneca*, 15 June 2005, para. 327, on appeal Case T-321/05, judgment pending.

[484] IP /05/737.

[485] *BBI/Boosey & Hawkes* [1987] OJ L286/36, [1988] 4 CMLR 67.

[486] See *supra* 534.

[487] Case T-111/96, *ITT Promedia NV v. Commission* [1998] ECR II-2937, [1998] 5 CMLR 491.

[488] *Ibid.*, at para. 57.

Case T-111/96, *ITT Promedia* v. *EC Commission* [1998] ECR II-2937, [1998] 5 CMLR 491

Court of First Instance

60. ... [a]s the Commission has rightly emphasised, the ability to assert one's rights through the courts and the judicial control which that entails, constitute the expression of a general principle of law which underlies the constitutional traditions common to the Member States and which is also laid down in Articles 6 and 13 of the European Convention for the Protection of Human Rights and Fundamental Freedoms of 4 November 1950 (see Case 222/84, *Johnson* v. *Chief Constable of the Royal Ulster Constabulary* ...). As access to the Court is a fundamental right and a general principle ensuring the rule of law, it is only in wholly exceptional circumstances that the fact that legal proceedings are brought is capable of constituting an abuse of a dominant position within the meaning of Article [82] of the Treaty.

61. Second, since the two cumulative criteria constitute an exception to the general principle of access to the courts, which ensures the rule of law, they must be construed and applied strictly, in the manner which does not defeat the application of the general rule (see, *inter alia*, Case T-105/95, *WWF UK* v. *E.C.Commission* ...).

...

72. According to the first of the two cumulative criteria set out by the Commission in the contested decision, legal proceedings can be characterised as an abuse, within the meaning of Article [82] of the Treaty, only if they cannot reasonably be considered to be an attempt to assert the rights of the undertaking concerned and can therefore only serve to harass the opposing party. It is therefore the situation existing when the action in question is brought which must be taken into account in order to determine whether that criterion is satisfied.

73. Furthermore, when applying that criterion, it is not a question of determining whether the rights which the undertaking concerned was asserting when it brought its action actually existed or whether that action was well founded, but rather of determining whether such an action was intended to assert what that undertaking could, at that moment, reasonably consider to be its rights. According to the second part of that criterion, as worded, it is satisfied solely when the action did not have that aim, that being the sole case in which it may be assumed that such action could only serve to harass the opposing party.

The Commission based its criteria on human rights—the rights of access to the courts. The test is not whether the right claimed exists, but whether the dominant undertaking may reasonably consider that it does. The CFI judgment confirms that vexatious litigation *can* be an abuse, but only in limited circumstances. Moreover, the CFI held that Belgacom was entitled to rely on its rights under national law unless and until the Court ruled that the national law had been invalidated:

93. The purpose of Belgacom's first two actions must therefore be regarded as the assertion of what Belgacom, at the moment when it brought those two actions, could reasonably consider, on the basis of the Belgian provisions governing the publishing of telephone directories, to be its rights. Consequently, the first of the Commissions two cumulative criteria was not satisfied.

94. In such circumstances, an examination of the question whether the relevant Belgian provisions governing the publishing of telephone directories were compatible with Community law could not have shown that the objective of Belgacom's first two actions was not to assert what Belgacom, at the moment when it brought those actions, could reasonably consider to be its rights under those

provisions and that the two actions therefore served only to harass the applicant. Consequently, that question fell to be considered in the examination of the merits, which was a matter for the national court hearing Belgacom's first two actions.

95. In that context, the Court rejects the applicant's argument that the Commission should have examined whether the relevant Belgian provisions were, at least apparently, compatible with Community law. Such an interpretation of the first of the two cumulative criteria would make it practically impossible for undertakings in a dominant position to have access to the courts. In order to avoid the risk of infringing Article [82] of the Treaty solely because they had brought an action before the courts, those undertakings would have to ensure beforehand that the relevant provisions on which they based their rights were compatible with Community Law.

The CFI also held that a dominant undertaking which sought performance of a contract would commit an abuse only if the claim went beyond what it could reasonably expect from the contract.[489] However, the ECJ held that it was an abuse for the dominant liner conference in *Compgnie Maritime Belge*[490] to insist on the Zaïrean authorities keeping strictly to the terms of the exclusive contract they had signed. This meant that Zaïre could not continue giving a small amount of trade to a new competitor.

E. VERTICAL AND HORIZONTAL INTEGRATION

Although it is not an infringement of Article 82 for a dominant undertaking to integrate vertically, it has been seen that actions taken in pursuit of a policy of vertical integration may infringe. Many cases finding a refusal to supply[491] or tying[492] to infringe Article 82 involved actions taken by a dominant undertaking which would enable it to integrate vertically.

In *Continental Can*[493] it was established that Article 82 could apply to mergers whereby an undertaking strengthened its dominant position. Since the EC Merger Regulation regime has been in force, however, the general rule is that the Regulation alone applies to mergers falling within its scope.[494]

F. STRATEGIC ENTRY DETERRENCE AND RAISING RIVALS' COSTS

Exclusionary behaviour is often described, particularly in the USA, as 'strategic entry deterrence'. This can be used to cover practices such as tying on which, as is seen above, there is considerable EC case law. There is as yet no EC jurisprudence on what is called predatory product or process innovation. This occurs when a dominant undertaking introduces a

[489] *Ibid.*, para. 129.

[490] Cases C-395 and 396/96 P, *Compagnie Maritime Belge Transports SA v. EC Commission* [2000] ECR I-1365, [2000] 4 CMLR 1076, paras. 72–88.

[491] Such as Cases 6, 7/73, *Istituto Chemioterapico Italiano Spa and Commercial Solvents Corp v. EC Commission* [1974] ECR 223, [1974] 1 CMLR 309 and Case 22/78, *Hugin Kassaregister AB v. EC Commission* [1979] ECR 1869, [1979] 3 CMLR 345.

[492] E.g., the *Digital Undertaking*, Commission Press Release IP/97/868; see *supra* 521.

[493] Case 6/72, *Europemballage Corp & Continental Can Co Inc v. EC Commission* [1973] ECR 215, [1973] CMLR 199; see Chaps. 5 and 12.

[494] Council Regulation Reg. 139/2004 [2004] OJ L24/1, replacing Council Regulation 4064/89 [1989] L395/1. For a discussion of this, see *infra* Chap. 12.

product or process which appears to present no technological, æsthetic, or other improvement, but is introduced merely to exclude existing competitors, for example where a product is redesigned with the purpose of making it incompatible with a complementary product offered by a competitor. Nor is there as yet specific case law on other practices much discussed in economics literature, such as predatory advertising and excessive product differentiation. This type of practice may particularly deter new entrants and operate as a barrier to entry. Existing competitors may fight to stay in the market because they have incurred sunk costs. Many types of abusive conduct which have arisen in the EC case law and which are discussed in this chapter can be classed as behaviour which 'raises rivals' costs'. Practices such as tying, refusals to deal,[495] exclusive dealing, discriminatory pricing, and vexatious litigation may all raise the competitor's costs relative to those of the dominant undertaking and result in inefficiencies for the competitor. The essence of raising rivals' costs is that the dominant undertaking raises the competitor's costs relative to its own, resulting in inefficiencies for the competitor. In 'non-price predation' the line between normal competition and abusive conduct is difficult to draw. As Rapp says:[496]

Non-price predation is said to take a variety of different forms whose common characteristics is that they raise costs for rivals. Excessive advertising and building excess capacity (with its implied threat that the dominant firm will flood the market in response to the entry or expansion of smaller firms) are two of the forms most often discussed. Even partisans for the theory of non-price predation admit that the line between normal competitive behaviour and anti-competitive action is so hard to distinguish in most cases that the risk of harm from enforcement often may outweigh the possible benefits to competition.

9. EXPLOITATIVE ABUSES

A. UNFAIRLY HIGH OR LOW PRICING

(i) Unfairly High Prices

Article 82 (a) specifically provides that an abuse may consist in 'directly or indirectly imposing 'unfair purchase or selling prices or other unfair trading conditions'. On the selling side 'excessive' prices may be 'unfair'.[497] Excessive pricing is the most obvious way in which a monopolist can exploit its position. Economic theory demonstrates[498] that monopoly prices are likely to be higher than those in competitive markets and excessive prices match the popular conception of the evils of monopoly. However, it is often argued that the free market economy needs the lure of monopoly pricing: '[t]he opportunity to charge monopoly prices—at least for a short period—is what attracts 'business acumen' in the first place; it induces risk taking that produces

---

[495] e.g., in *British Midland/Aer Lingus* [1992] OJ L96/34, [1993] 4 CMLR 596, para. 30, the Commission described the refusal to interline as raising the competitor's costs.

[496] R. Rapp, 'Predatory Pricing and Entry Deterring Strategies: the Economics of AKZO' [1986] *ECLR* 233, 235.

[497] In Case 78/70, *Deutsche Grammophon v. Metro* [1971] ECR 487, [1971] CMLR 631, the Court spoke of prices which were 'excessive and consequently unfair'.

[498] See *supra* Chap. 1.

innovation and economic growth'.[499] Furthermore, excessive prices may be pro- rather than anti-competitive because high prices and profits may act as a signal to attract new competitors on to the market. Where this cannot happen because barriers to entry are high the spectre of competition authorities acting as price regulators arises. Price regulation, however, is the antithesis of the free market and, as we saw in Chapter 5, the Commission has not much concerned itself with excessive prices,[500] appearing to agree with the view that interference with high prices and profits *per se* is a disincentive to innovation and investment. Price regulation is better restricted to situations of natural or legal monopoly, where it may be applied in a system of *ex ante* regulation.[501] It may be preferable to solve the problem of excessive pricing in other situations by taking vigorous action against exclusionary conduct whereby dominant firms seek to preserve their dominance. The Commission explained this in its 1994 Competition Report:[502]

The existence of a dominant position is not itself against the rules of competition. Consumers can suffer from a dominant company exploiting this position, the most likely way being through prices higher than would be found if the market were subject to effective competition. However, the Commission in its decision-making practice does not normally control or condemn the high level of prices as such. Rather it examines the behaviour of the dominant company designed to preserve its dominance, usually directed against competitors or new entrants who would normally bring about effective competition and the price level associated with it.

It is, in any case, difficult to decide what constitutes an excessive or unfair price. Ascertaining what the price might have been in a more competitive market is rarely possible in practice, so what other yardstick can be used? In *United Brands* the Commission condemned UBC for charging excessive prices for Chiquita bananas in Germany, Denmark, and Benelux. It compared the prices with those for unbranded bananas, competitors' bananas, and with the price of Chiquitas in Ireland, and it said that the prices were 'excessive in relation to the economic value of the product supplied'. The Court annulled the Commission's decision that unfair prices had been charged.

Case 27/76, *United Brands* v. *Commission* [1978] ECR 207, [1978] 1 CMLR 429

Court of Justice

248. The imposition by an undertaking in a dominant position directly or indirectly of unfair purchase or selling prices is an abuse to which exception can be taken under Article [82] of the Treaty.

---

[499] *Verizon Communications Ltd* v. *Trinko* 124 S.Ct 872 (2004), para. 2 (Scalia J).

[500] Although note the special sector of telecommunications. For example, the investigation into prices in mobile telephone services in the EC (Press Releases IP/98/141, IP 98/707, IP (98) 1036). The Commission found fourteen cases of discrimination and high prices but closed its files when prices were reduced or there was action by the domestic regulator. Furthermore, in the postal sector in 2001 the Commission took a decision finding that Deutsche Post had imposed excessive prices on cross-border mail: *Deutsche Post AG—Interception of cross-border mail* [2001] OJ L331/40, [2002] 4 CMLR 558, see *infra* 588.

[501] For the position of public undertakings and other statutory monopolists, see *infra* Chap. 8. For example, in Cases C-147–148/97, *Deutsche Post AG* v. *Gesellschaft für Zahlungssysteme mbH (GZS) and Citicorp Kartenservice GmbH* [2000] ECR I-825, [2000] 4 CMLR 838, an Article 234 reference concerning the German postal monopoly, the ECJ said that the monopolist would commit an abuse if it charged the full internal rate for forwarding international mail without offsetting the 'terminal dues' to which it was entitled.

[502] *XXIVth Report on Competition Policy* (Commission, 1994), part 207.

249. It is advisable therefore to ascertain whether the dominant undertaking has made use of the opportunities arising out of its dominant position in such a way as to reap trading benefits which it would not have reaped if there had been normal and sufficiently effective competition.

250. In this case charging a price which is excessive because it has no reasonable relation to the economic value of the product supplied would be such an abuse.

251. This excess could, *inter alia*, be determined objectively if it were possible for it to be calculated by making a comparison between the selling price of the product in question and its cost of production, which would disclose the amount of the profit margin; however the Commission has not done this since it has not analysed UBC's costs structure.

252. The questions therefore to be determined are whether the difference between the costs actually incurred and the price actually charged is excessive, and, if the answer to this question is in the affirmative, whether a price has been imposed which is either unfair in itself or when compared to competing products.

253. Other ways may be devised—and economic theorists have not failed to think up several—of selecting the rules for determining whether the price of a product is unfair.

254. While appreciating the considerable and at times very great difficulties in working out production costs which may sometimes include a discretionary apportionment of indirect costs and general expenditure and which may vary significantly according to the size of the undertaking, its object, the complex nature of its set up, its territorial area of operations, whether it manufactures one or several products, the number of its subsidiaries and their relationship with each other, the production costs of the banana do not seem to present any insuperable problems.

. . .

258. The Commission bases its view that prices are excessive on an analysis of the differences—in its view excessive—between the prices charged in the different Member States and on the policy of discriminatory prices which has been considered above.

. . .

260. Having found that the prices charged to ripeners of the other Member States were considerably higher, sometimes by as much as 100 per cent, than the prices charged to customers in Ireland it concluded that UBC was making a very substantial profit.

. . .

264. However unreliable the particulars supplied by UBC may be . . . the fact remains that it is for the Commission to prove that the applicant charged unfair prices.

265. UBC's retraction, which the Commission has not effectively refuted, establishes beyond doubt that the basis for the calculation adopted by the latter to prove the UBC's prices are excessive is open to criticism and on this particular point there is doubt which must benefit the applicant, especially as for nearly 20 years banana prices, in real terms, have not risen on the relevant market.

266. Although it is also true that the price of Chiquita bananas and those of its principal competitors is different, that difference is about 7 per cent, a percentage which has not been challenged and which cannot automatically be regarded as excessive and consequently unfair.

267. In these circumstances it appears that the Commission has not adduced adequate legal proof of the facts and evaluations which formed the foundation of its finding that UBC had infringed Article [82] of the Treaty by directly and indirectly imposing unfair selling prices for bananas.

268. Article 1 (c) of the decision must therefore be annulled.

The Commission's decision on excessive pricing was thus quashed because the Commission had failed to do its homework properly. It had not presented sufficient evidence and had not analysed UBC's costs.

In *United* Brands therefore, the Court accepted that excessive prices can constitute an abuse and that charging a price which has no relation to the product's 'economic value' would be excessive (paragraph 250). But what is the economic value of a banana other than what a customer is prepared to pay for it? The Court thought the excess might be determined by comparing the selling and production costs (the 'cost + standard'), which would disclose the profit margin (paragraph 251), but it did not suggest the level at which the profit would become excessive. If undertakings' profit margins are attacked under Article 82 then undertakings may be discouraged from costs savings. Further, high profits may be necessary to provide a fair return on the costs of innovation, or to act as a spur to further innovation in a dynamic market. However, in paragraph 252 the Court said that finding the price is 'excessive' by these means is not the end of the matter: it must then be determined whether the price is *unfair*. So a finding that prices are high in relation to the costs of production is not a sufficient condition for an infringement of Article 82.

The notion that the price charged should relate to the 'economic value' of the product or service was first discussed by the ECJ in *General Motors*.[503] In this case a car company was charging a high price for the production of documentation without which car owners could not bring their cars into Belgium. The documentation was obviously cheap to produce, but in fact the 'value' to the customers was great since without the certificate the car could not be imported. On the facts the Court accepted that no abuse had been committed[504] and so the meaning of 'economic value' or excessive prices did not need to be more specifically defined. After *United Brands*, a similar case arose. In *British Leyland*[505] the manufacturer demanded a high price for type-approval certificates as a way of discouraging individuals from importing cars from Member States where they were cheaper. The price was condemned as 'excessive and discriminatory' but viewed by the Court as a part of a policy of maintaining price differentials and compartmentalizing the common market rather than as a simple garnering of monopoly profits.

In *United Brands* the Court referred to 'other ways' devised by economists for identifying unfair prices (paragraph 253) but did not identify them. It did however consider that a comparison with the price of other products (paragraph 252) was valid. In *Deutsche Post—Interception of Cross-Border Mail*[506] DPAG had a statutory monopoly which encompassed, *inter alia*, the forwarding and delivery of cross-border mail in Germany. It (wrongfully) classified certain categories of incoming mail from the UK as unauthorized remail[507] and levied a charge which the British Post Office had to pay before the mail was released for delivery. The Commission said that when judging whether a price is excessive in a market which is open to competition, the normal test is to compare the prices of the dominant operator with those charged by competitors. Given the undertaking's wide-ranging monopoly in this case such a comparison was impossible, and in

---

[503] Case 26/75, *General Motors v. Commission* [1975] ECR 1367, [1976] 1 CMLR 95.

[504] Because the high price had been a temporary blip while national procedures were changed.

[505] Case 226/84, *British Leyland v. EC Commission* [1986] ECR 3263, [1987] 1 CMLR 185.

[506] [2002] OJ L331/40, [2002] 4 CMLR 598. The case raised issues in respect of competition rules and undertakings granted monopoly rights by the State, and the application of Article 86(2): see *infra* Chap. 8.

[507] DPAG's policy towards remailing was also the subject of a preliminary reference to the ECJ, Cases C-147–8/97, *Deutsche Post AG v. Gesellschaft für Zahlungssysteme mbH (GZS) and Citicorp Kartenservice GmbH* [2000] ECR I-825, [2000] 4 CMLR 838, discussed *infra* Chap. 8.

the absence of 'reliable cost accounting' the Commission compared the cross-border tariff with the domestic tariff and held the former to be excessive as it had 'no sufficient or reasonable relationship to real costs or to the real value of the service provided'.[508]

The ECJ also said in *United Brands* that a comparison could be made with prices in other areas. It dismissed the comparison with Ireland for lack of proper analysis, not because it rejected the comparison as a technique. In *Bodson* v. *Pompes Funèbres des Régions Libérées*,[509] which concerned funeral services in areas of France where there were monopoly concessions granted by local authorities, the Court talked of whether the price was 'fair' in comparison with prices in areas where there were no such concessions. In *Ministère Public* v. *Tournier*[510] it said in the context of a complaint about the high charges imposed by the French copyright collecting society, SACEM, that:

38. When an undertaking holding a dominant position imposes scales of fees for its services which are appreciably higher than those charged in other member-States and where a comparison of the fee levels has been made on a consistent basis, that difference must be regarded as indicative of an abuse of a dominant position. In such a case it is for the undertaking in question to justify the difference by reference to objective dissimilarities between the situation in the member-State concerned and the situation prevailing in all the other member-States.

In *Deutsche Grammophon*[511] the Court said that the fact that the price of the product in one Member State was different from that when re-imported from another did not necessarily constitute an abuse, but it would be a determining factor if the difference was very marked and unjustified by any objective criteria. In *Alsatel* v. *Novasam* the Court said that a rental increase of 25 per cent for telephone installations might 'constitute unfair trading conditions'.[512] The Court has also considered excessive pricing in references concerning intellectual property rights. In *Parke, Davis*[513] it said that the higher price of a patented compared with a non-patented product did not necessarily mean that an abuse had been committed. In *Renault*,[514] however, it suggested that a car manufacturer which refused to license its intellectual property rights in respect of its spare parts to other manufacturers might commit an abuse if it charged 'unfair prices' for its own parts. The idea that intellectual property rights owners are not entitled to extract the maximum return from their monopoly position, however, raises serious questions about the value of such rights, If the competition authorities are to look at a cost-price

---

[508] *Ibid.*, paras. 159–67. In the UK case, *Napp Pharmaceutical Holdings Ltd* the Director General of Fair Trading held that Napp had charged excessive prices for sustained release morphine (MST) in the community sector (i.e., to patients not in hospital), contrary to the Chap. II prohibition of the Competition Act 1998. The DGFT demonstrated that the difference between costs actually incurred and prices actually charged was excessive by relying on a range of comparisons (Napp's MST prices against those of its competitors; MST prices over time; Napp's MST prices to hospitals as against those to the community market and those in the export market; Napp's profitability on sales to hospitals compared to those to the community market; and Napp's margins as against those of its competitors). The Competition Commission Appeal Tribunal held that no serious criticism could be made of this approach: Case 1/1/1/01 *Napp Pharmaceutical Holdings Ltd* v. *DGFT* [2002] CAT 1, 386–442. The excessive prices in this case were at the expense of the NHS. Napp had over 90% of the MST market, there were high barriers to entry, and MST is an essential pain relief technique.

[509] Case 30/87, [1988] ECR 2479, [1989] 4 CMLR 984, para. 31.

[510] Case 395/87, [1989] ECR 2521, [1991] 4 CMLR 248, para. 38.

[511] Case 78/70, *Deutsche Grammophon* v. *Metro* [1971] ECR 487, [1971] CMLR 631.

[512] Case 247/86, *Alsatel* v. *Novasam* [1988] ECR 5987, [1990] 4 CMLR 434. *Deutsche Grammophon, Bodson,* and *Tournier* were all Article 234 references.

[513] Case 24/67, *Parke, Davis & Co* v. *Probel* [1968] ECR 55, [1968] CMLR 47.

[514] Case 53/87, *CICCRA* v. *Renault* [1988] ECR 6039, [1990] 4 CMLR 265, para. 16.

comparison in order to detect excessive pricing they will need to consider the undertaking's past research costs, including research costs which do not result in commercially exploitable products.[515] That is particularly true in high technology markets in the new economy. Large resources may be devoted to the development of new products by a number of competitors and the undertaking which 'wins' the market may reap huge rewards (for a time at least). The incentive of that level of profit is, it is often argued, necessary to persuade undertakings to incur research and development costs which may never be recovered.

The Commission's reluctance to bring excessive pricing cases has led to a dearth of decisional practice on this issue,[516] but in 2004 it adopted a decision rejecting complaints of such pricing[517] in which it took the opportunity to systematically analyse the *United Brands* judgment and explain when a price is 'unfair' and constitutes an abuse within the meaning of Article 82. The complaints were lodged by two ferry operators and related to the port fees charged by the Port authority at Helsingborg, Sweden, in relation to the services provided to ferry operators active on the Helsingborg-Elsinore route between Sweden and Denmark. The Commission saw the central question, derived from *United Brands*, as being the relation between the price and the economic value of the product or service provided. Although *United Brands* referred to several ways of determining whether prices are excessive/unfair, the Commission adopted the methodology set out in paragraph 252 of the case: the first question to be determined is whether the difference between cost and price is excessive and *if it is*, then the second question is whether the price unfair in itself or when compared to competing products. The Commission rejected the contention that it was just a question of 'cost +' i.e. of determining the supplier's costs, adding a profit margin and considering any price above this 'unfair'. Rather, the economic value had to be determined with regard to the particular circumstances of the case and taking into account non-cost related factors.[518]

Scandlines Sverige v. *Port of Helsingborg*, COMP/36.568, [2006] 4 CMLR 1298

Commission

145. In the *United Brands* judgment, the Court referred to several possibilities to determine whether prices are unfair:

— In para. [251], the Court mentions the possibility, inter alia, to make a comparison between the selling price of the product in question and its cost of production, which could disclose the amount of the profit margin.

— In para. [252], the Court makes clear that the questions to be determined are "whether the difference between the costs actually incurred and the price actually charged is excessive,

---

[515] See *Duales System Deutschland AG (DSD)* [2001] OJ L166/1, [2001] 5 CMLR 609 upheld Case T-151/01, judgment 24 May 2007, for a case where an excessive price for a trade mark licence was held to be an abuse.

[516] In *DSD* [2001] OJ L166/1, para. 111 the Commission simply said that an infringement of Article 82(a) exists where the price charged for a service is 'clearly disproportionate to the cost of supplying it'.

[517] Where the Commission decides not to pursue the matter complained of the complainant is entitled to a challengeable act explaining the reasons. See Chap. 14.

[518] See also the comment on this decision in (2004) 3 *EC Competition Policy Newsletter*, 40 (M. Lamalle, L. Lindström-Rossi and A. C. Teixara). The complainants withdrew their appeal against the decision to the CFI.

and, if the answer to this question is in the affirmative, whether a price has been imposed which is either unfair in itself or when compared to competing products."

— In para.[253], the Court acknowledges that there may be "other ways [. . . .] of selecting the rules for determining whether the price of a product is unfair."

146. In this light, the Commission finds that the most appropriate methodology in the present decision is the one set out by the Court in para. [252] of the *United Brands* judgment.

147. The questions to be determined are as follows:

(i) "whether the difference between the costs actually incurred and the price actually charged is excessive and, *if the answer to this question is in the affirmative*, (emphasis added);

(ii) "whether a price has been imposed which is either unfair in itself or when compared to the price of competing products."

149. In para. [252] of the *United Brands* judgment, the Court made a clear distinction between, on the one hand, the question whether the difference between the price and the production costs—the profit margin—is "excessive" and, on the other hand, the question whether the price is unfair. Had it been otherwise, there would have been no reason for the Court, once the first question has been answered in the affirmative, to proceed to the question whether the price is unfair in itself or when compared to the price of competing products.

150. A comparison between the price charged and the costs incurred (in the present case, the *approximate* incurred costs) can only serve as a first step in an analysis of excessive or unfair pricing. The *United Brands* judgment made clear (in para. [250]) that such an abuse can only be established where the price bears no reasonable relation to the economic value of the product concerned.

171. According to case law and the decisional practice of the Commission, the contested price may however be compared to: (i) other prices charged by the dominant company on a market different from the relevant market; or (ii) prices charged by other firms providing similar products/services on other relevant markets.

172. In the former alternative above, two profitable prices that the dominant company charges for the same product/service, respectively on the relevant market and on another market, may be compared. This would notably address the situation of an undertaking charging, for the same product/service, higher prices on a market where it holds a dominant position than on other markets where it faces competition . . . . This approach was followed by the Commission in *General Motors* . . . and *British Leyland* . . . and implicitly endorsed by the Court in *United Brands*. Such a comparison is made in section II.B.2.2.b) below where the prices charged by HHAB to the ferry-operators on the relevant market (where HHAB holds a monopoly position) is compared to the prices it charges to cargo vessels, on a competitive market.

214. As explained in s.II.B.2.1.d, an analysis of excessive or unfair pricing abuse must focus on the price charged, and its relation to the *economic value* of the product. While a comparison of prices and costs, which revelas the profit margin of a particular company may serve as a first step in such an analysis, this in itself cannot be conclusive as regards the existence of an abuse.

215. In line with what the Court has stated in para.[252] of the *United Brands* judgment, a distinction must be made between the assessment of the difference between the price and the production costs—the profit margin—and the assessment of whether the price is unfair.

216. At the end of s.II.B.2.1.d, the Commission concluded that in any event, even if it were to be assumed that the profit margin of HHAB is high or even "excessive", this would not be sufficient to conclude that the price charged bears no reasonable relation to the economic value of the services provided.

217. The case law of the Court of First Instance and the European Court of Justice as well as the decisional practice of the Commission provide little guidance on how to determine whether a price must be considered unfair in itself.

218. While the ECJ in *United Brands* stated that:

"*[c]harging a price which is excessive because it has no reasonable relation to the economic value of the product supplied would be such an abuse*". . . .

it provided no further details on how to determine this 'economic value' of the product/service provided.

228. As a consequence, even if it were to assume that there is a positive difference between the price and the production costs exceeding what Scandlines claims as being a reasonable margin (whatever that may be), the conclusion should not necessarily be drawn that the price is unfair, provided that this price has a reasonable relation to the economic value of the product/service supplied. The assessment of the reasonable relation between the price and the economic value of the product/service must also take into account the relative weight of non-cost related factors.

232. In the present case, the economic value of the product/service cannot simply be determined by adding to the approximate costs incurred in the provision of this product/service as assessed by the Commission, a profit margin which would be a pre-determined percentage of the production costs. The economic value must be determined with regards to the particular circumstances of the case and take into account also non-cost related factors such as the demand for the product/service.

233. As a consequence, finding a positive difference between the price and the approximate production costs exceeding what Scandlines claims as being a reasonable margin, would not necessarily lead to the conclusion that the price is unfair, provided that this price has a reasonable relation to the economic value of the product/service supplied.

A perfect example of the problem of ascertaining the 'economic value' of a product or service arose in the UK courts shortly after *Scandlines*. In *Attheraces Ltd* v. *The British Horseracing Board Ltd*[519] ATR, a supplier of websites, TV channels and other audio-visual media relating to British racing which are used by bookmakers and punters, challenged the price the British horse racing authorities (BHB) charged it for the supply of pre-race data,[520] claiming it was an abuse contrary to both Article 82 and the Chapter II prohibition (s.18) of the Competition Act 1998. At first instance the judge found the abuse proved. He concluded that '[t]he economic value of BHB's pre-race data is not more, or significantly more, than the competitive price',[521] that the competitive price should be ascertained by cost +, and that 'BHB's charges to ATR . . . have been so far in excess of any justifiable allocation of the cost of production and a reasonable return (in effect, the competitive price) that they are, in my judgment, plainly excessive'.[522] The Court of Appeal reversed this. One feature of the case was that the pre-race data was not a 'stand-alone' product, but a secondary product (or by-product) of the BHB's policing and administration of the horse-racing industry, and an application of the cost + formula was not favourable to the BHB. The Court of Appeal, however, held that cost + was not conclusive of the matter as, applying *United Brands*, it was only a first step in analysing 'economic value'.

---

[519] [2005] EWHC 3015 (Ch), on appeal, [2007] EWCA Civ 38.

[520] It includes the name and time of race, the course where the race will be run, the race distance, the criteria for entry in the race, the names of the horses entered and declared runners, their saddlecloth and stall numbers, their ages, weights, official ratings, jockeys', trainers' and owners' names, [2007] EWCA Civ 38, para. 47.

[521] [2005] EWHC 3015 (Ch), para. 300.

[522] *Ibid.*, para. 305.

There was money to be made in exploiting the data in the in the overseas betting market and there was no reason why competition law should ensure that this went to the broadcaster rather than the racing authorities.

Attheraces Ltd v. *The British Horseracing Board Ltd* [2007] EWCA Civ 38

Court of Appeal

204. The judge correctly stated the law as laid down in *United Brands* (cited above) that a fair price is one which represents or reflects the economic value of the product supplied. A price which significantly exceeds that will be prima facie excessive and unfair. But the formulation begs a fundamental question: what constitutes economic value?

205. On the one hand, the economic value of a product in market terms is what it will fetch. This cannot, however, be what Article 82 and section 18 envisage, because the premise is that the seller has a dominant position enabling it to distort the market in which it operates.

206. On the other hand, it does not follow that whatever price a seller in a dominant position exacts or seeks to exact is an abuse of his dominant position.

207. How is the critical judgment of the economic value of the pre-race data to be made? That has to be determined before deciding whether BHB is seeking to charge ATR a price which abuses its dominant position by trying to obtain substantially more than the economic value of the prerace data. There is nothing in the Article or its jurisprudence to suggest that the index of abuse is the extent of departure from a cost + criterion. It seems to us that, in general, cost + has two other roles: one is as a baseline, below which no price can ordinarily be regarded as abusive: the other is as a default calculation, where market abuse makes the existing price untenable.

. . .

213. . . . the Commission's decision in *Scandlines* supports the view that the exercise under Article 82, while it starts from a comparison of the cost of production with the price charged, is not determined by the comparison. This in itself is sufficient to exclude a cost +test as definitive of abuse . . .

214. As the expert witnesses in the present case agreed, economic theory recognises the relevance of externalities to price. The judge rejected BHB's argument that the benefit of the system to overseas bookmakers was a relevant externality. But it was incontestable that the overseas bookmakers were paying ATR, in a competitive market, amounts which afforded it a handsome profit which it wanted, so far as possible, to keep. The facts found by the judge do not suggest that anybody is going to go out of business as a result of the alleged abuse of dominant position. Despite its elaborate legal and economic arguments and the high levels of moral indignation, the case is about who is going to get their hands on ATR's revenues from overseas bookmakers. There is no need to classify the benefit derived by the bookmakers from the deployment of part of BHB's products as a "positive externality" in order to recognise that it has a bearing on whether their pricing is excessive.

215. This said, we accept that there is moral force in ATR's position. ATR adds value (in the form of pictures of the races) to the pre-race data and has the task of collecting overseas bookmakers' payments. It is taking all the risks and, as the judge found, will have to absorb most or all of the costs, while BHB seeks to take half of what they make. This may be thought to be unfair, but it cannot alone make it an abuse of BHB's dominant position. As Jacobs A-G said in

> *Bronner* . . . [523], the principal object of Article 82 of the Treaty is the protection of consumers, in this case the punters, not of business competitors. In our judgment, this is correct, even if it is the competitors and not the consumers who are alleging abuse of dominant position. We need to look beyond ATR's immediate interests to the market served by ATR. There is little, if any, evidence that competition in the market is being distorted by the demands made by BHB upon ATR.

It will be noted that the Court of Appeal considered this matter in the light of the object of Article 82 being the protection of consumers. The BRB was not exploiting consumers. Had ATR succeeded in obtaining the pre-race data at a lower price there was no suggestion that it would have charged the customers less. Any 'unfairness' to ATR is not a concern of competition law (see paragraph 215). It is interesting to compare *Attheraces* with other aspects of *United Brands*, where the ECJ's judgment suggested that the profit extracted from consumers should go the distributor rather than to the producer.[524]

(ii) Low Prices on the Buying Side

Although there is little case law on it, it is possible that unfairly low purchase prices may constitute an abuse where the dominant position is on the buying side. *CICCE v. Commission*[525] concerned a complaint about the allegedly low prices paid as licence fees for the showing of films on French television. The Commission dismissed the complaint on the ground that the complainant had produced insufficient evidence but did not deny that low prices *could* constitute an abuse. This may become more of an issue in future, as in several Member States there is disquiet about the power of large retail groups.[526]

B. DISCRIMINATION CONTRARY TO ARTICLE 82(C)

(i) General

Article 82 states that an abuse may, in particular, consist in:

applying dissimilar conditions to equivalent transactions with other trading parties, thereby placing them at a competitive disadvantage.

Price discrimination generally is discussed above.[527] This is a clear reference to secondary line injury. 'Dissimilar conditions' obviously includes dissimilar prices. There are, however, problems in the application of Article 82(c). For example, 'equivalent transactions' refers to the fact that price discrimination involves different prices for the same thing. However, the elements

---

[523] This is a reference to Case C-7/97, *Oscar Bronner GmbH & Co KG v Mediaprint* [1998] ECR I-7791, [1991] 4 CMLR 112, see *supra* 547.

[524] See *infra*, 598.

[525] Case 298/83, *CICCE v. Commission* [1985] ECR 1105, [1986] 1 CMLR 486, upholding the Commission.

[526] The Commission noted the matter in its *XVIth Report on Competition Policy* (Commission, 1986), parts 345–8. In the UK the prices and conditions offered to suppliers by supermarkets was raised in the market investigation reference under the Enterprise Act 2002, Groceries, which commenced in 2006.

[527] *Supra* 440.

which make up a transaction may be complex and identifying equivalence can be difficult. Is the sale of a train ticket for a journey during the weekday rush-hour equivalent to the sale of a ticket for the same journey on a Sunday morning? The Court and Commission have sometimes assumed that transactions are equivalent without a great deal of analysis.[528] Furthermore, it appears from the case law that discriminatory pricing may be found to constitute an abuse even if nobody is put at a competitive disadvantage.

(ii) The Application of Article 82(c) to Discounts and Rebates

Price discrimination in downstream markets may be effected by giving different discounts and rebates to different customers or by adopting discount and rebate schemes which impact unequally on different customers. EC law has more often been concerned more with the exclusionary capacity of discounts and rebates, as discussed above. [529] It should be noted, however, that the discriminatory pricing imposed in the transport sector and/or by statutory monopolists discussed in the following paragraphs has often been effected through discounting practices.

(iii) Article 82(c) and the Transport Sector

The Commission has taken a number of decisions finding the operators of transport infrastructures guilty of abusive conduct by charging discriminatory prices contrary to Article 82(c). For example in the first *Corsica Ferries* case[530] the port operator in Genoa charged different prices for pilotage services depending on whether the vessels were sailing between two domestic (Italian) ports[531] or were on an international route; in *Deutsche Bahn*[532] a national rail operator applied different prices in respect of railway traffic via German ports and traffic via Belgian and Dutch ones; and in *Aeroports de Paris*[533] the airport authority at Orly and Charles de Gaulle in Paris charged different levels of fees to companies it licensed to provide groundhandling services. In none of these cases was there found to be any objective justification for the differentials.[534] In the leading case *Portuguese Airports* the airport authority applied a seemingly uniform system of quantity discounts which was so constructed that it gave larger discounts to Portuguese airlines than to others. This was found to infringe Article 82(c) and the ECJ took the opportunity to discuss the application of Article 82(c) to quantity discounts.

The airport operator, *inter alia*, gave discounts on landing fees to airlines depending on the number of planes they landed. There were a number of discount bands and the highest rate of discount could be earned only by airlines with a very large number of landings. The only

---

[528] e.g., railway traffic via German ports and via Belgian and Dutch ones (Case T-229/94, *Deutsche Bahn AG v. Commission* [1997] ECR II-1689, [1998] 4 CMLR 220, upheld on appeal, Case C-436/97 *Deutsche Bahn AG v. Commission* [1999] ECR I-2387, [1999] 5 CMLR 776) and transactions with exclusive and non-exclusive customers (in the loyalty rebate cases, see *supra* 481 ff).

[529] *Supra*, 481.

[530] Case C-18/93, *Corsica Ferries Italia Srl v. Corporazione dei Piloti del Porto di Genova* [1994] ECR I-1783.

[531] This is known as maritime cabotage.

[532] Case T-229/94, *Deutsche Bahn AG v. Commission* [1997] ECR II-1689, [1998] 4 CMLR 220.

[533] Case T-128/98, *Aeroports de Paris v. Commission* [2000] ECR II-3929, [2001] 4 CMLR 611, upheld by the ECJ, Case C-82/01, [2002] ECR I-9297, [2003] 4 CMLR 609.

[534] See also *Brussels National Airport (Zaventem)* [1995] OJ L216/8, [1996] 4 CMLR 232; *Ilmailulaitos/ Luftsfartverket (Finnish Airports)* [1999] OJ L69/24, [1999] 5 CMLR 90; *Spanish Airports* [2000] OJ L208/36.

airlines to qualify for this high rate were the two Portuguese carriers, TAP and Portugalia. The ECJ said that while it was inherent in any quantity discount system that the largest buyers obtained the highest reductions, nevertheless it could be discriminatory if the system included thresholds that only a few very large users could reach and which gave them disproportionate rewards.

Case C-163/99, *Portugal* v. *Commission: Landing Fees at Portuguese Airports* [2001] ECRI-2613, [2002] 4 CMLR 1319

Court of Justice

49. The Commission accepts that an undertaking in a dominant position is entitled to grant quantity discounts. Such discounts must, however, be justified on objective grounds, that is to say, they should enable the undertaking in question to make economies of scale. The Portuguese authorities have not mentioned any economy of scale in this case. It is common ground that aircraft require the same landing and take-off services, regardless of how many aircraft belong to the same company.

50. An undertaking occupying a dominant position is entitled to offer its customers quantity discounts linked solely to the volume of purchases made from it (see, *inter alia*, Case 322/81 *Michelin* v. *Commission* [1983] ECR 3461, paragraph 71). However, the rules for calculating such discounts must not result in the application of dissimilar conditions to equivalent transactions with other trading parties within the meaning of subparagraph (c) of the second paragraph of Article [82] of the Treaty.

51. In that connection, it should be noted that it is of the very essence of a system of quantity discounts that larger purchasers of a product or users of a service enjoy lower average unit prices or—which amounts to the same—higher average reductions than those offered to smaller purchasers of that product or users of that service. It should also be noted that even where there is a linear progression in quantity discounts up to a maximum discount, initially the average discount rises (or the average price falls) mathematically in a proportion greater than the increase in purchases and subsequently in a proportion smaller than the increase in purchases, before tending to stabilise at or near the maximum discount rate. The mere fact that the result of quantity discounts is that some customers enjoy in respect of specific quantities a proportionally higher average reduction than others in relation to the difference in their respective volumes of purchase is inherent in this type of system, but it cannot be inferred from that alone that the system is discriminatory.

52. None the less, where as a result of the thresholds of the various discount bands, and the levels of discount offered, discounts (or additional discounts) are enjoyed by only some trading parties, giving them an economic advantage which is not justified by the volume of business they bring or by any economies of scale they allow the supplier to make compared with their competitors, a system of quantity discounts leads to the application of dissimilar conditions to equivalent transactions.

53. In the absence of any objective justification, having a high threshold in the system which can only be met by a few particularly large partners of the undertaking occupying a dominant position, or the absence of linear progression in the increase of the quantity discounts, may constitute evidence of such discriminatory treatment.

54. In this case, the Commission has established that the highest discount rate (32.7 per cent at Lisbon Airport and 40.6 per cent at other airports) was enjoyed only by the airlines TAP and Portugalia. The figures given by the Commission in the contested decision also show that the

increase in the discount rate is appreciably greater for the highest band than for the lower bands (except for the lowest band for all airports apart from Lisbon Airport), which, in the absence of any specific objective justification, leads to the conclusion that the discount for the highest band is excessive in comparison with the discounts for the lower bands.

55. It is apparent that, in order to justify the system in question, the Portuguese Republic has submitted only general arguments relating to the advantage for airports of operating a system of quantity discounts on landing charges and has done no more than claim that the system was open to all airlines.

56. In a situation where, as the Commission has observed, the system of discounts appears to favour certain airlines, in this case de facto the national airlines, and where the airports concerned are likely to enjoy a natural monopoly for a very large portion of their activities, such general arguments are insufficient to provide economic reasons to explain specifically the rates chosen for the various bands.

57. In such circumstances the conclusion must be that the system in question discriminates in favour of TAP and Portugalia.

(iv) Article 82(c) and Statutory Monopolists

The operators of transport infrastructures, such as those in the cases mentioned above, are likely to be statutory monopolists—either public undertakings or undertakings which are given special or exclusive rights in respect of the facility concerned. Discriminatory conduct by statutory monopolists in other sectors has also been condemned. In *Deutsche Post—Interception of Cross-Border Mail*,[535] for example, the German postal authority was held to have discriminated without objective justification between different types of mail coming into Germany. Statutory monopolists entrusted with a 'service of general economic interest' have a limited exemption from the competition rules under Article 86(2) of the Treaty. This is discussed in Chapter 8. However, in none of the transport cases above, nor in *Deutsche Post*, did Article 86(2) excuse the undertaking's discriminatory pricing.

(v) Geographical Price Discrimination

Geographical price discrimination means charging different prices for the same products or services in different geographical territories. It is more of an issue in EC competition law than in national systems because its most obvious form—different prices in different Member States—may be contrary to the objectives of market integration and not just a competition issue. Artificial price differences across the Community should be eliminated or reduced by arbitrage and parallel trade, but this may be impeded by other factors. If these factors are measures taken by the dominant undertaking to buttress the pricing policy the prices will be an abuse in themselves and the buttressing measures are also likely to infringe Article 82. In both leading cases on geographical price discrimination, *United Brands*[536] and *Tetra Pak II*,[537] Article 82(c) was applied and the dominant undertaking was found to have taken measures to prevent parallel trade.

---

[535] [2002] OJ L331/40, [2002] 4 CMLR 598.

[536] Case 27/76, *United Brands v. Commission* [1978] ECR 207, [1978] 1 CMLR 429.

[537] Case C-333/94 P, *Tetra Pak International SA v. Commission* [1996] ECR I-5951, [1997] 4 CMLR 662.

Case 27/76, *United Brands* v. *Commission* [1978] ECR 207, [1978] 1 CMLR 429

United Brands shipped its bananas across the Atlantic and unloaded them at Rotterdam and Bremerhaven. At those ports it sold them to its approved ripener/distributors from various Member States at different prices. The prices reflected the different prices in the retail markets in the Member States. The contractual conditions under which the bananas were sold contained a prohibition on the distributors reselling the bananas while they were still green (the 'green banana' clause). The Commission concluded that this clause was simply a tactic to reinforce the price differences because once the bananas had started to turn yellow they were so perishable that it was not possible to export them to other Member States. The Commission also found that United Brands' practice of supplying the distributors with less than they ordered made them sell locally instead of in other markets. The Commission held that these practices infringed Article 82. United Brands appealed.[538]

Court of Justice

204. All the bananas marketed by UBC under the brand name 'Chiquita' on the relevant market have the same geographic origin, belong to the same variety (Cavendish Valery) and are of almost the same quality.

205. They are unloaded in two ports, Rotterdam and Bremerhaven, where unloading costs only differ by a few cents in the dollar per box of 20 kilogrammes, and are resold, except to Scipio and in Ireland, subject to the same conditions of sale and terms of payment after they have been loaded on the buyer's wagons or lorries, the price of a box amounting on average to between 3 and 4 dollars and going up to 5 dollars in 1974.

206. The costs of carriage from the unloading ports to the ripening installations and the amount of any duty payable under the Common Customs Tariff are borne by the purchaser except in Ireland.

207. This being so all those customers going to Rotterdam and Bremerhaven to obtain their supplies might be expected to find that UBC offers them all the same selling price for 'Chiquita' bananas.

208. The Commission blames the applicant for charging each week for the sale of its branded bananas—without objective justification—a selling price which differs appreciably according to the Member State where its customers are established.

209. This policy of charging differing prices according to the Member States for which bananas are intended has been applied at least since 1971 in the case of customers of the Federal Republic of Germany, the Netherlands and the BLEU and was extended in January 1973 to customers in Denmark and in November 1973 to customers in Ireland.

. . .

227. Although the responsibility for establishing the single banana market does not lie with the applicant, it can only endeavour to take 'what the market can bear' provided that it complies with the rules for the regulation and co-ordination of the market laid down by the Treaty.

228. Once it can be grasped that differences in transport costs, taxation, customs duties, the wages of the labour force, the conditions of marketing, the differences in the parity of currencies, the density of competition may eventually culminate in different retail selling price levels according to the Member States, then it follows those differences are factors which UBC

[538] United Brands also appealed against the finding that the relevant market was bananas and that it was dominant in the Member States in issue. See *supra* Chap. 6.

only has to take into account to a limited extent since it sells a product which is always the same and at the same place to ripener/distributors who—alone—bear the risks of the consumer's market.

229. The interplay of supply and demand should, owing to its nature, only be applied to each stage where it is really manifest.

230. The mechanisms of the market are adversely affected if the price is calculated by leaving out one stage of the market and taking into account the law of supply and demand as between the vendor and the ultimate consumer and not as between the vendor (UBC) and the purchaser (the ripener/distributor).

231. Thus, by reason of its dominant position UBC, fed with information by its local representatives, was in fact able to impose its selling price on the intermediate purchaser. This price and also the 'weekly quota allocated' is only fixed and notified to the customer four days before the vessel carrying the bananas berths.

232. These discriminatory prices, which varied according to the circumstances of the Member States, were just so many obstacles to the free movement of goods and their effect was intensified by the clause forbidding the resale of bananas while still green and by reducing the deliveries of the quantities ordered.

233. A rigid partitioning of national markets was thus created at price levels, which were artificially different, placing certain distributor/ripeners at a competitive disadvantage, since compared with what it should have been competition had thereby been distorted.

234. Consequently the policy of differing prices enabling UBC to apply dissimilar conditions to equivalent transactions with other trading parties, thereby placing them at a competitive disadvantage, was an abuse of a dominant position.

This part of the *United Brands* judgment contains some unconvincing reasoning which has been savagely criticized.

W. Bishop, 'Price Discrimination under Article 86: Political Economy in the European Court' (1981) 44 *MLR* 282, 284–6[539]

B. Supply and demand

The 'law of supply and demand' referred to in [229] is a 'law' of economics in the sense that the fundamental theorem of micro-economics is that price is determined by supply of and demand for a good. This theorem has been empirically confirmed as having considerable predictive power. It is a descriptive law and not a prescriptive or normative one. What can be meant by the statement that firms in setting prices should only 'apply' the law 'to each stage where it is really manifest'? To speak of applying a descriptive law is odd. Surely the court has not made the elementary blunder of confusing descriptive and prescriptive concepts of law?

The court seems to have thought that when a producer faces separate regional markets, and consumer demand is stronger in one than in the other, then this demand is 'really manifest' only in the retail market and not in the wholesale market. But this is in fact wrong. Demand in the retail market will be transmitted by retailers through implicit or explicit bids for various price and

---

[539] See also L. Zanon, 'Price Discrimination under Article 82 of the EEC Treaty: A Comment on the UBC Case' (1982) 31 *ICLQ* 36; M. Siragusa, 'The Application of Article 86 to the Pricing Policy of Dominant Companies: Discriminatory and Unfair Prices' (1979) 16 *CMLRev* 179.

quantity combination in the wholesale and ripener-distributor markets. It truly will be, 'really manifest' in those markets.

The court might have meant by this strange language to say that a firm should set its prices at the same level as it would if it faced keen competition. Alternatively the court might have meant to say that a producer should behave as if there were one market where no price discrimination is possible. If the court intended either of these it should have said so clearly. To call either 'applying the law of supply and demand' is a travesty of language and is pregnant with confusion for the future.

C. Bearing risks

The court said that in setting prices the firm should take into account different retail demand conditions in different markets to only a 'limited extent,' since UBC did not 'bear the risks of the consumers' market.' This reasoning is wholly novel and wholly bad. The test of 'bearing risks' is misconceived in principle, undesirable in its consequences and misapplied on the facts before the court.

The existence of risk in retailing may lead to a level of normal profit to each retailer that is higher or lower than in other industries, because risk is different. This may happen if investors are risk averse over the relevant range...The court seems to regard monopoly profit as a reward for risk. That is an error. Many risky industries are competitive and many non-risk ones are monopolistic.

Confusion is bad enough. Worse follows from use of the 'bearing the risks' criterion. Why should a firm be allowed to consider demand conditions if it is a retailer, or combines both manufacturing and retai[l]ing, but not if it is only manufacturer? Apparently a vertically integrated firm can use differential pricing because its wholesaling or retailing division 'bears risks'. This creates an incentive for a manufacturer to integrate an industry vertically. This is an artificial incentive that will have costly effects and consume resources. It will be attractive to firms intent on harvesting some part of those monopoly profits, derived from discrimination, of which the *United Brands* judgment seeks to deprive them. In future a manufacturer may find it profitable to undertake local distribution himself so that he can claim to be 'bearing risks'—even if the net cost of distributing himself is higher than selling to local distributors. This is inefficiency created solely by legal decision. Furthermore no one, neither consumers nor anyone else, benefits. It is pure waste.

Even if the consideration of 'bearing risks' were not irrelevant or undesirable, the criterion was misapplied by the court. On the facts UBC probably did bear all the risks of changes in demand in consumer markets. It did not sell to ripeners at prices and quantities fixed long in advance, but announced weekly prices a few days before the ships were due. Even if UBC had wished to shift to its dealers all the risks from time of shipment it would probably have been unable to sell such long term forward contracts profitably, because ripeners are probably not as well placed as UBC to assess changes in retail market conditions and would therefore have to be given price inducements to enter long term contracts. Also ripeners were probably less liquid and more risk averse than UBC. Ripeners bore risks only for a very short period and even then UBC may have been the real risk bearer. For if a contract of sale turned out badly for a ripener, UBC would probably find it too costly to hold a ripener to that contract since his bankruptcy would deprive UBC of continuity of outlet ...

The real Community objection to the price discrimination in *United Brands* was of course that it offended against the concept of the single market.

In *Tetra Pak II* the Commission found wide disparities in the prices that Tetra Pak charged for its milk packaging machinery and cartons in different Member States despite the fact that the geographical market was Community-wide. It held these prices differences to be due to artificial partitioning of the market and not to objective market conditions.[540] The decision was upheld by the CFI, which found that 'those disparities in price could not be attributed to objective market conditions'.[541]

Whether or not geographical price discrimination is an abuse in the absence of measures taken by the dominant undertaking to partition the separate geographical areas is less clear. In *Tetra Pak II* the CFI reiterated that setting different prices could be justified by local conditions. In *United Brands*, however, local conditions did not justify variations in retail prices. This suggests that once the Member States are held to be in the same geographic market and costs are the same, objective justification for price discrimination between them may be hard to prove.[542]

What has been described as a 'peculiar form of geographical price discrimination'[543] was condemned in *Irish Sugar*.[544] The dominant undertaking operated a system of 'sugar export rebates', granted on sales of industrial sugar to companies exporting to other Member States. The Commission found that this practice discriminated against customers of industrial sugar supplying the domestic Irish market. The CFI upheld the Commission's finding that this was an abuse, holding that market mechanisms were distorted by pricing according to the location of the customers' buyers.

(vi) Delivered Pricing

Delivered pricing is a method of pricing where the supplier quotes a price for the product which includes delivery and does not offer an *ex works* or *ex factory* price which allows the customer the choice of making its own transport arrangements. The Commission has condemned it as an infringement of Article 82 because it distorts competition on the downstream market in transport and means that the dominant undertaking is using its position in one market to strengthen its position in another.[545] It is therefore an example of leverage. Delivered pricing may however be *uniform*, which means that all customers are charged the same delivered price irrespective of their distance from the place from which they are being supplied. It is discriminatory as the same price is being charged for transactions which entail different costs: the proximate customers subsidize those which are far off and competition on the downstream market between the customers is thereby distorted. This is a classic case of putting a trading party at a competitive disadvantage contrary to Article 82(c).

---

[540] e.g., customers for the machines could purchase cartons only from Tetra Pak itself or a company designated by it, and so customers in high price countries were not free to purchase from third parties in lower price areas.

[541] Case T-83/91, *Tetra Pak Rausing v. Commission* [1994] ECR II-755, [1997] 4 CMLR 726, para. 170. See also Case T-168/01, *GlaxoSmithKline Services Unlimited v. Commission* [2006] ECR II-2969, para. 177.

[542] J. Faull and A. Nikpay (eds.), *The EC Law of Competition* (2nd edn., Oxford University Press, 2007), para. 4.407 says that arguably the case law gives dominant companies the responsibility for implementing public policy.

[543] *Ibid.*, para. 4.409.

[544] [1997] OJ L258/1, [1997] 5 CMLR 666.

[545] *Napier Brown–British Sugar* [1988] OJ L284/41, [1990] 4 CMLR 196.

(vii) Competitive Disadvantage and Article 82(c)

The abuse set out in Article 82(c) is the application of dissimilar conditions to equivalent trans-actions with other trading parties 'thereby placing them at a competitive disadvantage'. In respect of the export rebates in *Irish Sugar* mentioned in the previous paragraph, the CFI did not accept that the non-export customers suffered no competitive disadvantage.[546] However, it was probably immaterial either way as in effect the need for a 'competitive disadvantage' has been read out of Article 82(c). In *United Brands* the ECJ applied Article 82(c) even though the ripener/distributors from different Member States were not in competition with one another and greengrocers in Ireland certainly did not compete with those in Germany. Likewise, in *Corsica Ferries I* the ECJ applied Article 82(c) regardless of the fact that the domestic and international shipping lines were not competing with each other.[547] In *Deutsche Post— Interception of Cross-Border Mail*, however, the Commission did address the issue. Answering the argument that customers were not put at a competitive disadvantage by having to pay more than others for their cross-border mail the Commission pointed out that the list in Article 82 is not exhaustive:

In any event, the Court of Justice has stated that the list of abuses mentioned in Article 82 itself is not exhaustive and thus only serves as examples of possible ways for a dominant firm to abuse its market power ... Article 82 may be applied even in the absence of a direct effect on competition between undertakings on any given market. This provision may be also be applied in situations where a domin-ant undertakings behaviour causes damage directly to consumers ... The senders of the disputed mailings are consumers of postal services. Due to the behaviour of DPAG, these consumers are affected negatively by having to pay prices for these services which are higher than those charged to other senders and by having their mailings delayed significantly. Likewise, the German addressees are to be regarded as consumers who are affected in a negative manner by the behaviour of DPAG. Having their incoming mail delayed may prevent the addressees from benefiting from commercial offers made by the senders.[548]

The Commission here is saying that directly damaging consumers may infringe Article 82, although of course consumers will usually not be 'in competition' with one another. Since Deutsche Post was a statutory monopolist the consumers had no alternative supplier: nor indeed did the shipping lines in *Corsica Ferries*. Moreover, both *Deutsche Post* and *Corsica Ferries* involved discrimination in the context of inter Member State transactions, while *United Brands*, as we have seen, involved compartmentalizing the common market. In such situations one can expect that EC law will disapprove of discriminatory behaviour.[549]

In *British Airways* the bonus/commission scheme operated by British Airways was found by the Commission to infringe Article 82 because of its capability to exclude competitors.[550] It was also held to specifically infringe Article 82(c) because it discriminated between the travel agents. This was upheld by the CFI[551] and the ECJ.

---

[546] Case T-228/97, *Irish Sugar plc v. Commission* [1999] ECR II-2969, [1999] 5 CMLR 1300, paras. 140–9.

[547] Case C-18/93, *Corsica Ferries Italia Srl v. Corporazione dei Piloti del Porto di Genova* [1994] ECR I-1783. The ECJ did not mention the issue at all: the AG did, but stated that it did not matter, para. 34 of the Opinion of AG Van Gerven.

[548] [2002] OJ L331/40, [2002] 4 CMLR 598, para. 133.

[549] For further consideration of discrimination as an abuse, see *infra* 605.

[550] *Virgin/British Airways* [2000] OJ L30/1, [2000] 4 CMLR 999, see *supra* 501.

[551] Case T-219/99, *British Airways v. Commission* [2003] ECR II-5917, [2004] CMLR 1008.

Case C-95/04 P, *British Airways* v. *Commission*, 15 March 2007

Court of Justice

133. Subparagraph (c) of the second paragraph of Article 82 EC prohibits any discrimination on the part of an undertaking in a dominant position which consists in the application of dissimilar conditions to equivalent transactions with other trading parties, thereby placing them at a competitive disadvantage (Case C-163/99 *Portugal* v *Commission* [2001] ECR I-2613, paragraph 46).

134. In the present case, it is undisputed that BA applied different commission rates to travel agents operating in the United Kingdom according to whether or not they had achieved their sales objectives by comparison with the reference period.

135. It remains to be examined, first, whether the Court of First Instance was right to rely on the equivalence of the travel agents' services in order to conclude that the bonus schemes at issue, being capable of entailing the application of different rates of commission to agents who had sold the same number of BA tickets, were discriminatory, and, secondly, whether, without committing an error of law, that Court could dispense with detailed findings concerning the existence of a competitive disadvantage.

136. In the first part of its fifth plea, BA criticises the analysis by the Court of First Instance of the comparability of the services carried out by travel agents who attained their objectives in BA ticket sales and those carried out by agents who did not attain those objectives. In particular, BA accuses the Court of First Instance of failing to take account of the greater economic usefulness from the airline's point of view of the services of travel agents who attained their sales objectives or increased their turnover.

137. On that latter point, which concerns the assessment by the Court of First Instance of the circumstances of this case from which it might be possible to deduce the comparability or otherwise of travel agents' services for an airline such as BA, it is sufficient to point out that the assessment of facts and evidence is a matter for the Court of First Instance alone. It is thus not for the Court of Justice, on an appeal, to substitute its own assessment of market data and the competitive position for that of the Court of First Instance. This claim is therefore inadmissible.

138. As for the second claim, that the Court of First Instance erred in law in relation to subparagraph (c) of the second paragraph of Article 82 EC, by holding that transactions involving a travel agent who had increased his sales of BA tickets and transactions involving an agent who had not increased them constituted 'equivalent transactions' within the meaning of that provision, it should be noted that, in paragraph 234 of the judgment under appeal, the Court of First Instance pointed out that attainment by United Kingdom travel agents of their BA ticket sales growth targets led to an increase in the rate of commission paid to them by BA not only on BA tickets sold after the target was reached but also on all BA tickets handled by the agents during the period in question.

139. The Court of First Instance logically inferred therefrom that the bonus schemes at issue led to the sale of an identical number of BA tickets by United Kingdom travel agents being remunerated at different levels according to whether or not those agents had attained their sales growth targets by comparison with the reference period.

140. The Court of First Instance does not therefore appear to have erred in law by regarding as equivalent the services of travel agents whose sales of BA tickets had, in absolute terms, been at the same level during a given period. This second claim is therefore unfounded.

141. Therefore, the first part of the fifth plea must be dismissed as in part inadmissible and in part unfounded.

142. In the second part of its fifth plea, BA argues that, for the purposes of correctly applying subparagraph (c) of the second paragraph of Article 82 EC, the mere finding of the Court of First Instance, in paragraph 238 of the judgment under appeal, that travel agents, in their capacity to compete with each other, are 'naturally affected by the discriminatory conditions of remuneration

inherent in BA's performance reward schemes' is not sufficient, since concrete evidence of a competitive disadvantage was required.

143. The specific prohibition of discrimination in subparagraph (c) of the second paragraph of Article 82 EC forms part of the system for ensuring, in accordance with Article 3(1)(g) EC, that competition is not distorted in the internal market. The commercial behaviour of the undertaking in a dominant position may not distort competition on an upstream or a downstream market, in other words between suppliers or customers of that undertaking. Co-contractors of that under-taking must not be favoured or disfavoured in the area of the competition which they practise amongst themselves.

144. Therefore, in order for the conditions for applying subparagraph (c) of the second para-graph of Article 82 EC to be met, there must be a finding not only that the behaviour of an under-taking in a dominant market position is discriminatory, but also that it tends to distort that competitive relationship, in other words to hinder the competitive position of some of the business partners of that undertaking in relation to the others (see, to that effect, *Suiker Unie*, paragraphs 523 and 524).

145. In that respect, there is nothing to prevent discrimination between business partners who are in a relationship of competition from being regarded as being abusive as soon as the behaviour of the undertaking in a dominant position tends, having regard to the whole of the circumstances of the case, to lead to a distortion of competition between those business partners. In such a situ-ation, it cannot be required in addition that proof be adduced of an actual quantifiable deteriora-tion in the competitive position of the business partners taken individually.

146. In paragraphs 237 and 238 of the judgment under appeal, the Court of First Instance found that travel agents in the United Kingdom compete intensely with each other, and that that ability to compete depended on two factors, namely 'their ability to provide seats on flights suited to travellers' wishes, at a reasonable cost' and, secondly, their individual financial resources.

147. Moreover, in the part of the judgment under appeal relating to the examination of the fidelity-building effect of the bonus schemes at issue, the Court of First Instance found that the latter could lead to exponential changes in the revenue of travel agents.

148. Given that factual situation, the Court of First Instance could, in the context of its examination of the bonus schemes at issue having regard to subparagraph (c) of the second paragraph of Article 82 EC, move directly, without any detailed intermediate stage, to the conclu-sion that the possibilities for those agents to compete with each other had been affected by the discriminatory conditions for remuneration implemented by BA.

149. The Court of First Instance cannot therefore be accused of an error of law in not verifying, or in verifying only briefly, whether and to what extent those conditions had affected the compet-itive position of BA's commercial partners. The Court of First Instance was therefore entitled to take the view that the bonus schemes at issue gave rise to a discriminatory effect for the purposes of subparagraph (c) of the second paragraph of Article 82 EC. The second part of the fifth plea is therefore unfounded.

C. IMPOSING UNFAIR TRADING CONDITIONS AND ENTERING INTO RESTRICTIVE AGREEMENTS

A number of provisions imposed by dominant undertakings on their customers have been condemned as abuses because they were unfair, and some of these have been dealt with above under other heads of abuse. Article 82(a) expressly condemns unfair conditions as well as prices, and Article 82(c) condemns discriminatory conditions as well as prices. In *Tetra Pak II*[552] the terms on which the dominant undertaking dealt with its customers (in pursuance of a marketing policy which aimed to restrict supply and compartmentalize national markets) were found by the Commission to be unfairly onerous. The conditions included placing limitations on the purchasers' use of the machines, binding purchasers to Tetra Pak's repair and maintenance services, and reserving to Tetra Pak the right to make surprise inspections. The Commission held that these conditions deprived the purchaser of certain aspects of its property rights. Although it accepted that stipulations in the terms upon which the supplier *leased* machines, such as prohibitions on modifying or moving the equipment, were not *in themselves* abusive, it held they were in this case. The rental payments were so high in comparison to sale prices that the supplier had to be taken to have relinquished its property rights to the hirer. Lease terms which exceeded the technological (though not the physical) life of the machine were abusive. Further, clauses imposing penalties for breach of any of the terms of the agreements at Tetra Pak's discretion also infringed Article 82, as these were aimed at ensuring the customers complied with terms of the agreements which were in themselves abuses. In *AAMS v. Commission*[553] the terms of the distribution agreements which the dominant wholesale distributor of cigarettes in Italy imposed on foreign producers were held to be unfair. They were also objectionable in that they limited the foreign producers' access to the Italian market, contrary to the imperative of the single market.[554]

In 1994 the Commission launched an investigation into Microsoft's licensing practices. In particular it was concerned that Microsoft's standard agreements for licensing software to PC manufacturers excluded competitors from selling their products. For example, Microsoft: (a) used 'per processor' 'per system' licences which required payment of royalties on every computer made by a PC manufacturer either containing a particular processor type or belonging to a particular model series, whether or not the computer was shipped with Microsoft software pre-installed; (b) used 'minimum commitment' clauses which required licensees to pay for a minimum number of copies of a product regardless of actual use; and (c) had excessively long licence agreements. The Commission (and the US Department of Justice) reached a settlement with Microsoft.[555] Microsoft undertook not to enter licence contracts of more than one year's duration, not to impose minimum commitments, and not to use per processor clauses: per system clauses would be allowed if the licensees were given flexibility not to buy Microsoft products and not to have to pay for what they did not buy.

In a number of cases concerning performing rights societies the Commission has found the society to have committed abuses by virtue of the terms on which the society did business. For example, in *GEMA*[556] the society wished to prevent members leaving it and entering into direct relationships with undertakings such as record companies. Its rules took the rights to works even after the member's resignation, provided for long periods of withdrawal and made payments to the social fund payable only to members of twenty years' standing.[557]

---

[552] [2001] OJ 1166/1, Para. 112, *aff'd* on appeal, Case T-151/01, *Der Grüne Punkt—Duales System Deutschland*, 24 May 2007.

[553] Case T-139/98, *Amministrazione Autonoma dei Monopoli di Stato (AAMS) v. Commission* [2001] ECR II-3413, [2002] 4 CMLR 302.

[554] See *infra* 607.

[555] *Microsoft*, IP (94) 653 of 17 July 1994, [1994] 5 CMLR 143. The US Federal Trade Commission was investigating similar concerns over Microsoft at the same time.

[556] [1971] OJ L134/15, [1971] CMLR D35.

[557] The subject of collecting societies is currently under review by the Commission, see Communication from the Commission to the Council, European Parliament and Economic and Social Committee on The Management of Copyright and Related Rights in the Internal Market, COM(2004) 261 final.

GEMA also discriminated on grounds of nationality, always a heinous offence in EC law.[558] Discriminatory treatment of other trading parties on *any* grounds without objective justification is expressly prohibited by Article 82 (c) and is a policy which the dominant undertaking is likely to have adopted in pursuance of some other abusive practice. Discriminatory pricing is dealt with above.[559] As seen above, in *BPB Industries*[560] the company gave priority of delivery of *plaster* to customers who were 'loyal' to BPB and did not buy imported *plasterboard*. The purpose of this provision, which discriminated between customers for plaster, was to ensure exclusive purchasing of plasterboard by the customers and to make it more difficult for the competitors to penetrate the market.[561] When a dominant undertaking enters into restrictive agreements it may be caught by both Article 81 and Article 82. In *Ahmed Saeed*[562] the Court, in the context of an agreement fixing air tariffs, said that what appeared to be an agreement could really be the imposition on the other party of the dominant undertaking's will, the agreement simply constituting 'the formal measure setting the seal on an economic reality characterised by the fact that an undertaking in a dominant position has succeeded in having the tariffs in question applied by other undertakings'.

In *FENIN*[563] a group of suppliers to the bodies which run the Spanish national health service (SNS) complained to the Commission that SNS was abusing its position as a dominant buyer by persistently paying its debts late (an average of 300 days). The suppliers said that the bodies took advantage of the fact that the suppliers could exert no commercial pressure on them. The CFI and ECJ upheld the Commission's view that the SNS organizations were not 'undertakings' for the purpose of Article 82[564] and therefore the question of whether a practice such as late payment could constitute an abuse was not addressed.

In *DSD* the Commission found that the creator of the 'Green Dot' recycling trade mark had abused its dominant position in Germany in charging licence fees in circumstances where the trade mark was not actually being used. This was an infringement of Article 82(a) as '[u]nfair commercial terms exist where an undertaking in a dominant position fails to comply with the principle of proportionality'.[565]

The fact that there are not more cases and decisions on the imposition of unfair trading conditions can be explained by the prevalence of other legislative regimes, such as consumer

---

[558] Which is of course contrary to Article 12 EC where it relates to citizens of the Union; see also Case 7/82, *GVL v. Commission* [1983] ECR 483, [1983] 3 CMLR 645. See also *1998 Football World Cup* [2000] OJ L5/55, [2000] 4 CMLR 963.

[559] See *supra* 594 ff.

[560] Case T-65/89, *BPB Industries and British Gypsum Ltd v. Commission* [1993] ECR II-389, [1993] 5 CMLR 32; on appeal Case C-310/93 P, *BPB Industries plc and British Gypsum Ltd v. Commission* [1995] ECR I-865, [1997] 4 CMLR 238.

[561] The company had applied dissimilar conditions to equivalent transactions on one market in order to strengthen its dominance on the other: see on this point, *supra* 438.

[562] Case 66/86, *Ahmed Saeed Flugreisen and Silver Line Reiseburo GmbH v. Zentrale zur Bëkämpfung Unlauteren Wettwerbs eV* [1989] ECR 803, [1990] 4 CMLR 102.

[563] Case T-319/99, *Federación Nacional de Empresas de Instrumentación Científica, Médica, Técnica y Dental (FENIN)* v. *Commission* [2003] ECRII-357, [2003] 5 CMLR 34 and Case C-205/03 P, *Federación Española de Empresas de Tecnología Sanitaria (FENIN) v. Commission* [2006] ECR I-6295.

[564] See the discusssion of the concept of an undertaking for the purposes of Articles 81 and 82, *supra* Chap. 3.

[565] [2001] OJ L166/1, para. 112, upheld on appeal, Case T-151/01, judgment 24 May 2007.

protection and unfair competition and general contract and tort laws. Some of rules have been enacted at EU level.[566]

D. INEFFICIENCY

Article 82 (b) prohibits 'limiting production, markets, or technical development to the prejudice of consumers'. This has been applied to dominant undertakings operating inefficiently and unable to meet demand, particularly public undertakings with statutory monopolies where Article 82 has applied in conjunction with Article 86.[567] In *Port of Genoa*[568] the Court held that an undertaking with the exclusive right to organize dock work at Genoa, which refused to use modern technology and thus raised costs and caused delays, was in breach of Article 82. In *Höfner v. Macroton*[569] the Court held that a state employment agency which was unable to meet the demand for its services would infringe Article 82. This type of abuse can, however, also be committed by private undertakings. In *P and I Clubs*,[570] which concerned associations providing marine insurance, the Commission stated that it would intervene in situations only where there is 'clear and uncontroversial evidence that a very substantial share of the demand is being deprived of a service that it manifestly needs'.[571]

10. EXPORT BANS AND OTHER CONDUCT HINDERING INTER-MEMBER STATE TRADE

Any type of conduct dividing markets or hindering exports and imports in the EC will be abusive not just on competition grounds but also as it is contrary to single market integration.[572] The excessive prices charged for the type approval certificates in *British Leyland*[573] were held to be an abuse because they both hindered parallel imports and exploited consumers. In *United Brands*[574] UBC imposed on its ripener/distributors the obligation not to resell the bananas while

---

[566] Such as Council Directive 93/13/EEC [1993] OJ L95/29. For a general discussion of this point, see O'Donoghue and Padilla, n. 81 *supra*, 646–58.

[567] See further Chap. 8.

[568] Case C-179/90, *Merci Convenzionali Porto di Genova v. Siderurigica Gabrielle* [1991] ECR I-5889, [1994] 4 CMLR 422.

[569] Case C-41/90, *Höfner v. Macroton* [1991] ECR I-1979, [1993] 4 CMLR 306; Case C-55/96, *Job Centre Co-op. arl* [1998] 4 CMLR 708 was a similar case from Italy.

[570] [1999] OJ L125/12.

[571] *Ibid.*, para. 128. The Commission's Statement of Objections stated that the undertaking had abused its (collective) dominant position by offering only a single insurance product. The undertaking amended its arrangements and the Decision found that there was no longer any question of an infringement of Article 82.

[572] See, e.g., Case 40/73, *Suiker Unie v. EC Commission* [1975] ECR 1663, [1976] 1 CMLR 295, *Eurofix-Bauco* [1988] OJ L65/19, [1989] 4 CMLR 677; Case C-333/94 P, *Tetra Pak International SA v. Commission* [1996] ECR I-5951, [1997] 4 CMLR 662; Case C-310/93 P, *BPB Industries PLC and British Gypsum Ltd v. Commission* [1995] ECR I-865, [1997] 4 CMLR 238; Case T-228/97, *Irish Sugar plc v. Commission* [1999] ECR II-2969, [1999] 5 CMLR 1300.

[573] Case 226/84, *British Leyland v. EC Commission* [1986] ECR 3263, [1987] 1 CMLR 185.

[574] Case 27/76, *United Brands v. Commission* [1978] ECR 207, [1978] 1 CMLR 429.

they were still green. This was treated by the Court and Commission as tantamount to an export ban (as bananas once yellow were so perishable that exporting them was not feasible) which reinforced UBC's policy of geographical price discrimination.[575] UBC claimed throughout that the necessary measure of quality control and had never been understood, applied, or enforced as an export ban, but it was nevertheless held to infringe Article 82. The unfair distribution terms imposed by the dominant undertaking in AAMS[576] hindered the trade in cigarettes between Member States.

However, the issue of whether a refusal to supply in order to hinder inter-Member State parallel trade is a *per se* abuse was raised in *Syfait*,[577] an Article 234 reference from the Greek Competition Commission. Greek pharmaceutical wholesalers claimed that GlaxoSmithKline were refusing to fulfill all their orders in respect of certain pharmaceuticals in order to prevent them exporting to other Member States in which prices were higher.[578] Advocate General Jacobs considered that in the context of the European pharamacetical sector it was not necessarily an abuse.[579] He said that there were special circumstances pertaining to trade in pharmaceuticals. First, the price differentials between Member States were due to pervasive and diverse State intervention; secondly, Community and Member State regulation imposed obligations on pharmaceutical undertakings and wholesalers to ensure adequate stocks; thirdly, parallel trade could have potentially negative consequences on research and development incentives; and fourthly, that end consumers could not be assumed to benefit from parallel trade, given that the Member States' public authorities are the main purchasers and that parallel trade does not necessarily result in any price competition discernible to the end consumers. In the circumstances, therefore, a refusal to supply that aimed thereby to limit parallel trade was capable of objective justification and thus of not constituting an abuse. The Advocate General was careful to say that his conclusion was 'highly specific'to the peculiarities of the European pharmaceutical market and did not generalise about refusals to supply and parallel trade.[580] Unfortunately the ECJ did not give a judgment on the issue as it held the reference inadmissible on the grounds that the Greek Competition Commission is not a 'court or tribunal of a Member State' within Article 234 from which the ECJ can accept a reference.[581] The Advocate General's opinion, however, shows both a reluctance to widen the ambit of refusal to supply abuses simply on single market grounds,[582] and a sympathetic stance towards the pharmaceutical

---

[575] See *supra* 598.

[576] Case T-139/98, *Amministrazione Autonoma dei Monopoli di Stato (AAMS) v. Commission* [2001] ECR II-3413, [2002] 4 CMLR 302.

[577] Case C-53/03, *Synetairismos Farmakopoion Aitolias & Akarnanias (Syfait) v. GlaxoSmithKline plc and GlaxoSmithKline AEVE* [2005] ECR I-4609.

[578] Such a strategy on the part of a pharmaceutical company was also at issue in *Bayer*, Cases C-2 & 3/01P, *Bundesverband der Arzneimittel-Importeure eV and the Commission* v. *Bayer AG* [2004] ECR I-23, [2004] 4 CMLR 653, discussed *supra*, Chap. 3, where it was held that there was no breach of Article 81(1) as the refusal was a unilateral act and did not constitute an agreement. In *Syfait* it was alleged that it respect of at least one of the pharmaceuticals concerned GlaxoSmithKline was in a dominant position and so Article 82 could apply.

[579] Case C-53/03, *Synetairismos Farmakopoion Aitolias & Akarnanias (Syfait) v. GlaxoSmithKline plc and GlaxoSmithKline AEVE* [2005] ECR I-4609, Opinion, paras 77–104.

[580] *Ibid.*, paras. 101–2.

[581] Subsequently, the Greek Competition Authority gave its decision, ruling that the decision of a dominant pharmaceutical firm to stop supplying the wholesalers and distribute the pharmaceuticals itself breaches Greek competition law but not Article 82 (1 September 2006). Furthermore, a number of wholesalers commenced private damages actions before the Greek courts, and the Efetio Athinon has referred questions to the ECJ about the compataibilty of GlaxoSmithKline's practices with Article 82, Case C-468/06, *Sot. Lelos kai Sia EE* v. *GlaxoSmithKline AEVE FP*, judgment pending.

[582] *Syfait*, Opinion, para. 53.

industry. This should now be seen in the light of the Article 81 judgment in *GlaxoSmithKline*, where the CFI held that the restriction of parallel trade in pharmaceuticals did not necessarily prejudice consumers, and that the argument that pharmaceutical undertakings need to curb parallel trade in order to maintain the level of profit needed for research and development had to be taken seriously.[583]

11. ABUSE AND COLLECTIVE DOMINANCE

It was explained in Chapter 5 that a 'dominant position' may be held by a single undertaking or by one or more independent undertakings which hold a collective dominant position. This concept and its application are explored below in Chapter 11, in the context of cartels and oligopolies, and in Chapter 12 in the context of mergers. In some of the cases discussed in this chapter, the dominant position being abused was a collective one.[584] It should be noted here, however, that in *Irish Sugar* the CFI said that it was not necessary for the collective dominant position to be *abused* collectively. It is possible therefore that an undertaking may individually commit an abuse of a dominant position held collectively with other undertakings, at least insofar as the abuse is committed to protect the collective dominant position.[585] In *Laurent Piau*, where a complainant was impugning the FIFA player's agents regulations, the CFI held that the regulations were not quantitative restrictions on access to the occupation, but justifiable qualitative ones.[586]

12. CONCLUSION

1. The matter of what behaviour on the part of a dominant undertaking can consitute an infringement of Article 82 needs to be put on a sound and consistent economic footing. Behaviour should be judged by its effects on the market, not on its form.

2. Even if such a 'effects based' or 'rule of reason' policy is adopted, however, there are still many difficulties. There are many different views about what effects flow from certain types of behaviour and about the best rules to adopt.

3. Undertakings need legal certainty in that they need to be able to adopt commercial policies in the knowledge that their conduct is legal. However theoretically sound, effects-based rules that are too complex or impractical are not a good basis on which to build a sound competition policy.

4. It is unlikely that there will ever be agreement about the effects on innovation and consumer welfare of the compulsory licensing of intellectual property rights. The disputes that have arisen in this area have, however, been on very particular facts.

---

[583] Case T-168/01, *GlaxoSmithKlineServices Unlimited* [2006] 5 CMLR 1623, see *supra* Chap. 4. For argument that the pharmaceutical sector does not necessarily warrant the special treatment suggested by the Advocate General in *Syfait*, see R. O'Donoghue and A. J. Padilla, *The Law and Economics of Article 82* (Hart Publishing, 2006), 472–6.

[584] Cases C-395 and 396/96 P, *Compagnie Maritime Belge and others v. Commission* [2000] ECR I-1365, [2000] 4 CMLR 1076.

[585] Case T-228/97, *Irish Sugar plc v. Commission* [1999] ECR II-2969, [1999] 5 CMLR 1300, para. 66.

[586] Case T-193/02, *Laurent Piau v. Commission* [2005] ECR II-209.

13. FURTHER READING

A. BOOKS

BEGG, D., FISCHER, S., and DORNBUSCH, R., *Economics* (8th edn., McGraw-Hill, 2005)

BISHOP, S., and WALKER, M., *The Economics of EC Competition Law: Concepts, Application and Measurement* (2nd edn., Sweet & Maxwell, 2002, new edition expected 2007)

BORK, R., *The Antitrust Paradox* (Basic Books, 1978, reprinted with a new Introduction and Epilogue, 1993), chap. 7

CARLTON, D. W., and PERLOFF, J. M., *Modern Industrial Organization* (4th edn., Pearson Addison Wesley, 2005)

HOVENKAMP, H., *Federal Antitrust Policy* (3rd edn., Thomson/West, 2005), chaps. 6, 7, 8, and 10

MOTTA, M., *Competition Policy* (Cambridge University Press, 2004), chaps. 2 and 7

O'DONOGHUE, R. and PADILLA, A. J., *The Law and Economics of Article 82* (Hart Publishing, 2006)

PHLIPS, L., *The Economics of Price Discrimination* (Cambridge University Press, 1983)

POSNER, R. A., *Antitrust Law*, (2nd edn., University of Chicago Press, 2001), chaps. 7 and 8

SCHERER, F. M., and ROSS, D., *Industrial Market Structure and Economic Performance* (3rd edn., Houghton Mifflin, 1990), chaps. 13 and 16

VAN DEN BERGH R. J., and CAMESASCA, P. D., *European Competition Law and Economics: A Comparative Perspective* (2nd edn., Sweet & Maxwell, 2006), chap. 7

B. ARTICLES

AHLBORN C. and BAILEY D., 'Discounts, Rebates and Selective Pricing by Dominant Firms: A Trans-Atlantic Comparison' (2006) 2 *European Competition Journal* 101

—— EVANS D., and PADILLA J., 'The Logic and Limits of Exceptional Circumstances Test in *Magill* and *IMS Health* (2005) *Fordham International Law Journal* 1062

ANDREWS, P., 'Aftermarket Power in the Computer Services Market: The Digital Undertaking' [1998] *ECLR* 176

AREEDA, P., 'Essential Facilities: An Epithet in Need of Limiting Principles' (1990) 58 *Antitrust LJ* 841

—— and TURNER, D., 'Predatory Pricing and Related Practices under Section 2 of the Sherman Act' (1975) 88 *Harvard LR* 697

BERGMAN, M. A., 'Editorial: The Bronner case—A Turning Point for Essential Facilities' [2000] *ECLR* 59

BISHOP, W., 'Price Discrimination under Article 86: Political Economy in the European Court' (1981) 66 *MLR* 282

BRODLEY, J., and HAY, D., 'Predatory Pricing: Competing Economic Theories and the Evolution of Legal standards' (1981) 66 *Cornell LR* 738

Bundeskartellamt/Competition Law Forum Debate on Reform of Article 82: A "Dialectic" on Competing Approaches (2006) 2 *European Competition Journal*, 211

CAPOBIANCO, A., 'The Essential Facility Doctrine: Similarities and Differences between the American and European Approaches' (2001) 26 *ELRev* 548

COLLEY L., and BURNSIDE S., 'Margin Squeeze Abuse' (2006) 2 *European Competition Journal*, 185

DOHERTY, B., 'Just What Are Essential Facilities?' (2001) 38 *CMLRev* 397

FJELL K., and SØRGARD L., 'How to Test for Abuse of Dominance?' (2006) 2 *European Competition Journal*, 69

FINE, F., 'NDC/IMS: A Logical Application of the Essential Facilities Doctrine' [2002] *ECLR* 457;

—— 'NDC/IMS: In Response to Professor Korah (2002) 70 *Antitrust LJ* 247.

FOX, E., 'Price Predation—US and EEC: Economics and Values' [1989] *Fordham Corp L Inst* 687

—— 'What is Harm to Competition? Exclusionary Practices and Anti-competitive Effect' (2002) 70 *Antitrust LJ* 371

—— Fox, E., 'Price Predation—US and EEC: Economics and Values' [1989] *Fordham Corp L Inst* 687

Geradin, D., 'Limiting the Scope of Article 82 EC: What Can the EU Learn from the Supreme Court's Judgment in *Trinko*, in the Wake of *Microsoft*, *IMS* and *Deutsche Telekom*?' (2004) 41 *CMLRev* 1526

Grimes, W. S., 'The Antitrust Tying Law Schism: 'A Critique of *Microsoft III* and a Response to Hylton and Salinger' (2002) 70 *Antitrust LJ* 199

Hancher, P., 'Case Note on Oscar Bronner' (1999) 36 *CMLRev* 1289

Incardona, R., 'Modernization of Article 82 EC and Refusal to Supply' (2006) 2 *European Competition Journal* 337

Jebsen, P., and Stevens, R., 'Assumptions, Goals and Dominant Undertakings: The Regulation of Competition Under Article 86 of the European Union (1996) 64 *Antitrust LJ* 443

Jones, A., 'Distinguishing Predatory Prices from Competitive Ones' [1995] *EIPR* 252

—— 'Refusal to Deal—EC and US Law Compared' in Marsden, P (ed.) *Handbook of Research in Trans-Atlantic Antitrust* (Edward Elgar Publishing, 2006), Chapter 8, 236–86

Kallaugher, J., and Sher, B., 'Rebates Revisited: Anti-Competitive Effects and Exclusionary Abuse Under Article 82' [2004] *ECLR* 263

ten Kate, A., and Niels, G., 'On the Rationality of Predatory Pricing: The Debate between Chicago and Post-Chicago' (2002) *Antitrust Bull* 1

Klein, B., and Shepard Wiley, J., 'Competitive Price Discrimination as an Antitrust Justification for IP Refusals to Deal' (2003) 70 *Antitrust LJ* 599

Korah, V., 'The Paucity of Economic Analysis in the EEC Decisions on Competition: Tetra Pak II' [1993] *Current Legal Problems* 150

—— 'The Interface between Intellectual Property and Antitrust: the European Experience (2002) 69 *Antitrust LJ* 801

Lianos, I., 'Competition Law and Intellectual Property Rights: Is the Property Rights Approach Right?' (2005–6) 8 *Cambridge Yearbook of European Legal Studies*

Lugard, P., 'Eternal Sunshine on a Spotless Policy? Exclusive Dealing under Article 82 EC' (2006) 2 *European Competition Journal*, 163

McGee, J., 'Predatory Price Cutting: The Standard Oil (New Jersey) Case' (1958) 1 *Journal Law and Economy* 137

Maier-Rigaud, F., 'Article 82 Rebates: Four Common Fallacies' (2006) 2 *European Competition Journal*, 85

Maldoom, D., 'The Kodak Case: Power in Aftermarkets' [1996] *ECLR* 473

Monti, M., 'European Competition Policy for the 21st Century' in B. Hawk (ed.) [2000] *Fordham Corp L Inst*, chap. 15

Pitofsky, R., Patterson, D., and Hooks, J., 'The Essential Facilities Doctrine under US Antitrust Law' (2002) 70 *Antitrust LJ* 443

Rapp, R. T., 'Predatory Pricing and Entry Deterring Strategies: The Economics of AKZO' [1986] *ECLR* 233

Ridyard, D., 'Essential Facilities and the Obligation to Supply Competitors' [1996] *ECLR* 438

—— 'Exclusionary Pricing and Price Discrimination Abuses under Article 82—An Economic Analysis' [2002] *ECLR* 286

—— 'Compulsory Access under EC Competition Law—A New Doctrine of 'Convenient Facilities' and the Case for Price Regulation' [2004] *ECLR* 670

Ritter, C., 'Refusal to Deal and Essential Facilities: Does Intellectual Property Require Special Deference compared to Tangible Property?' (2005) *World Competition* (3) 281, 298

Robertson, A., and Williams, M., 'The Law and Economics of Freezer Exclusivity' [1995] *ECLR* 7.

Rousseva, E., 'Modernizing by Eradicating: How the Commissions's New Approach to Article 81 EC Dispenses with the Need to Apply Article 82 EC to Vertical Restraints' (2005) 42 *CMLRev* 587.

Scott Hemphill, C., 'The Role of Recoupment in Predatory Pricing Analyses' (2001) *Stan LR* 1581

Sher, B., 'Price Discounts And *Michelin II*; What Goes Around, Comes Around' [2002] *ECLR* 482

Siragusa, M., 'The Application of Article 86 to the Pricing Policies of Dominant Companies' (1979) 16 *CMLRev* 179

Spector, D., 'Loyalty Rebates: An Assessment of Competition Concers and a Proposed Structured Rule of Reason' (2005) 1(2) *Competition Policy International* 89

—— 'From Harm to Competitors to Harm to Competition: One More Effort, Please!' (2006) 2 *European Competition Journal*, 145

Temple Lang, J.,'The Principle of Essential Facilities in European Community Competition Law—The Position since *Bronner*' (2000) 1 *Journal of Network Industries*, 375

TEMPLE LANG, J., 'Defining Legitimate Competition: Companies' Duties to Supply Competitors and Access to Essential Facilities' (1994) 18 *Fordham Int'l LJ* 437

—— and O'DONOGHUE, R., 'Defining Legitimate Competition: How to Clarify Pricing Abuses under Article 82EC' (2002) 26 *Fordham Int'l LJ* 83

—— 'Anti-competitive Non-Pricing Abuses under European and National Antitrust Law' in B. Hawk (ed.) [2003] *Fordham Corp L Inst* 235

SCHMALENSEE, R., 'Output and Welfare Implications of Third Degree Price Discrimination' (1981) 71 *American Economic Review*, 242.

WERDEN, G. 'Competition Policy on Exclusionary Analysis: Towards an Effects-based Analysis?' (2006) 2 *European Competition Journal*, 53.

8

COMPETITION, THE STATE, AND PUBLIC UNDERTAKINGS: ARTICLE 86

1. CENTRAL ISSUES

1. Article 86 EC addresses the matter of the application of the competition rules (and other rules of the Treaty) to State measures in respect of public undertakings and to undertakings granted special or exclusive rights, and to undertakings entrusted with services of general economic interest.

2. Article 86(1) is a prohibition addressed to Member States. Its object is to prevent Member States from depriving the Treaty rules of their effectiveness by the measures they adopt in respect of public undertakings and those to which they grant special or exclusive rights.

3. There is some uncertainty as to what measures violate Article 86(1). Some cases suggest that it is infringed only if, in merely exercising the exclusive rights, the undertaking cannot avoid abusing its dominant position. Other cases have suggested that the very granting of special or exclusive rights is contrary to Article 86(1).

4. Article 86(2) provides a derogation from, *inter alia*, the competition rules for undertakings entrusted with services of general economic interest if otherwise they would be obstructed in the performance of their tasks. However, in some cases entities are removed from the ambit of the competition rules by being held not to be undertakings engaged in an economic activity for the purposes of Article 81 or Article 82 in the first place. In several cases this has been because the entity has been found to operate on the basis of 'solidarity'.

5. It may be an important factor in the application of Article 86(2) that the undertaking has 'universal service' obligations. It may also be important to shield an undertaking from competition so that it can cross-subsidize from profitable sectors to uneconomic ones and competitors cannot come in and 'cherry pick' the profitable parts of the operation.

6. Article 86(3) provides the Commission with special supervisory and policing powers to ensure the application of the Article. It can adopt directives as well as issue decisions,

7. Article 16 EC was added to the EC Treaty by the Treaty of Amsterdam. It establishes that services of general economic interest have a place in the 'shared values of the Union'. The Commission has also produced Green and White Papers on services of general interest.

2. INTRODUCTION[1]

A. GENERAL

In this chapter we consider how competition law applies to the actions of the State when it intervenes in the market through undertakings which it controls or owns or which it places in a privileged position. We do not deal with the subject of State Aids, which is outside the scope of this book.[2]

A competition policy which did not deal with the State in the market place would be incomplete and would disadvantage other undertakings. The State plays some part in the market place, directly or indirectly, in all the Member States, although the means and extent of this varies. The means and extent have also changed over time since the inception of the European Community. In 1957 there was still a fashion for nationalization, and it will be remembered that the leading case on the supremacy of Community law, *Costa v. ENEL*,[3] concerned the nationalization of the Italian electricity industry. Since then there has been a move in Europe away from public ownership, and indeed a revolution in the way that public services are delivered. There has been increasing 'marketisation' whereby Member States have turned to the market to provide services to the public, and an erosion of the distinction between public and private providers. This is due not only to shifts in ideology but also to technological and economic advances which have meant that the arguments for publicly owned monopolies in sectors such as telecommunications and electricity generation have been transformed.[4] As well as public ownership, however, distortions to the competitive structure may be caused by monopolies created by privatization and by other undertakings which, although not in public ownership, are given an exclusive or protected position. Here again, new technology has eroded many of the arguments for maintaining such arrangements. One problem with national monopolies is that they maintain the compartmentalization of the common market. The programme of liberalization upon which the Community has embarked (in the telecommunications sector, for example) is inspired as much by the desire to increase the integration of the market as that of increasing competition.[5]

E. Szyszczak, 'Public Service Provision in Competitive Markets' (2001) 20 *Yearbook of European Law* 35, 36

The economic, political, and social world has been shaped by a number of processes in recent years: most significantly by rapid technological change, globalization of economic activity, the development of capital markets, the liberalization and restructuring of product and service

---

[1] For an analysis of the development of the law in this area, see L. Hancher, 'Community, State and Market' in P. Craig and G. de Búrca (eds.), *The Evolution of EU Law* (Oxford University Press, 1999), 721. And see generally J. Faull and A. Nikpay (eds.), *The EC Law of Competition* (2nd edn., Oxford University Press, 2007), chap. 6; J. L. Buenida Sierra, *Exclusive Rights and State Monopolies in EC Law* (Oxford University Press, 1999); T. Prosser, *The Limits of Competition Law* (Oxford University Press, 2005.)

[2] But a chapter on State Aids will be available on the companion web site.

[3] Case 6/64, *Flaminio Costa v. ENEL* [1964] ECR 585, [1964] CMLR 425.

[4] See G. Amato, *Antitrust and the Bounds of Power: The Dilemma of Liberal Democracy in the History of the Market* (Hart Publishing, 1997); 88–9, E. Szyszczak, 'Public Service Provision in Competitive Markets' (2001) 20 YEL 35.

[5] See Hancher, *supra* n. 1, 722.

markets and deregulation of markets. Governments and privates companies alike have persuaded their electorates and consumers of the capacity of markets to provide not only private goods and services, but also what have traditionally been viewed as publicly provided services . . . The belief in free markets is premised on the view not only that private enterprise is more efficient than state provision but that it may also be more responsive to consumer wishes. This change in attitude towards free markets has complemented other goals being pursued by governments, particularly the exercise of tighter fiscal discipline on public spending and the embracing of new forms of public management by neo-liberal governments seeking to provide a climate in which markets can develop and flourish . . . Such beliefs are particularly prevalent in the EU; indeed liberalization of the public sector has been viewed by one Commissioner responsible for competition, Van Miert, as an *unavoidable* consequence of the establishment of the Internal Market:

> It is obvious that a market based on competition and free circulation of goods, services, people and capital is at odds with systems based on national monopolies. Our liberalisation policy was therefore conceived as an indispensable instrument for the establishment of the internal market.[6]

. . .

 The result has been a radical restructuring of the relationship between the State and the market.

The original version of the Treaty of Rome was neutral as between public and private ownership. Article 295[7] states that the Treaty in no way prejudices the rules in Member States governing the system of property ownership. That Article, which has been important in the formulation of Community law on intellectual property rights,[8] is unchanged, but it is arguable that the insertion by the Treaty of European Union of what is now Article 4 of the EC Treaty,[9] represents a shift in policy which favours private over public ownership. Article 4 says that the activities of the Member States and the Community shall be conducted 'in accordance with the principle of an open market economy with free competition'. Article 4, in contrast to Article 295, is among the 'Principles' set out in Part One of the EC Treaty. Article 4 is elaborated upon in Article 157 which provides that the 'Community and Member States shall ensure that the conditions necessary for the competitiveness of the Community's industry exist' and that their action in this respect which should be aimed, *inter alia*, at encouraging an environment favourable to initiative and the development of small and medium-sized undertakings, should be in accordance 'with a system of open and competitive markets'. One commentator has said of Article 4 that '[t]his provision elevated a policy directed at effective competition to the level of a constitutional imperative, loosing competition policy for the first time from its traditional role as a handmaid of integration concerns'.[10]

The fundamental question is in what, if any, areas the normal principles of competition law should not apply. The answer to this should be found in the political, rather than the legal, realm. However, the original Treaty of Rome contained nothing about the limits to competition

---

[6] K. Van Miert, 'Liberalization of the Economy of the European Union: The Game is not (yet) Over' in D. Geradin (ed.), *The Liberalization of State Monopolies in the European Union and Beyond* (Kluwer, 2000), 1.1.

[7] Ex Art. 222.

[8] See *infra* Chap. 10.

[9] Ex Art. 3a(2).

[10] L. Flynn, 'Competition Policy and Public Services in EC Law after the Maastricht and Amsterdam Treaties' in D. O'Keefe and P. Twomey (eds.), *Legal Issues of the Amsterdam Treaty* (Hart Publishing, 1999), 185, 188.

law and the provision of public services, save for a provision about State Aids in the inland transport sector in respect of 'certain obligations inherent in the concept of a public service' being permitted,[11] and a derogation in Article 86(2)[12] pertaining to 'services of general economic interest'. The 'services of general economic interest' concept was not defined and appeared nowhere else in the Treaty or in secondary legislation. Before 1990[13] the application of competition law to State owned, State controlled, or State privileged undertakings was not a significant issue. It has become so because of the technological, ideological, social, and economic changes noted above, the increasing sophistication and reach of EC competition law, and the more aggressive enforcement of competition law.

As will be seen in this chapter, the case law of the Court has sometimes been inconsistent and confusing. The political debate about the relationship between competition law and public services, conducted in the shadow of that case law, resulted in the introduction into the Treaty of Rome by the Treaty of Amsterdam of what is now Article 16,[14] and the inclusion in the Charter of Fundamental Rights of the European Union of Article 36, both of which proclaim the value and importance of 'services of general economic interest'.[15] The Commission has complemented these provisions with 'soft law' in a series of Communications on services of general interest.[16] In May 2004 the Commission published a White Paper on services of general interest,[17] as a follow up to its Green Paper of 2003.[18] The Commission, and many commentators, now see the provision of services of general (economic) interest[19] as 'one of the pillars of the European model of society'.[20] The question of the application of competition law to such services is therefore a major factor in shaping the character of the post-enlargement European Union.

B. THE LIMITS OF COMPETITION LAW

There are two ways in which the application of EC competition law to public services can be limited. First, the activity can be found not to be 'economic', and therefore not subject to Articles 81 and 82 in the first place. Secondly, it can be found to be economic but allowed

---

[11] Art. 73 (ex Art. 77). The Article was at issue in Case C-280/00, *Altmark Trans GmbH, Regierungspräsidium Magdeburg v. Nahverkehrsgesellschaft Altmark GmbH* [2003] ECR I-7747 on whether compensation for services of general economic interest is a State Aid: see *infra* 671.

[12] Ex Art. 90(2).

[13] The early 1990s saw the four major Article 234 rulings, Case C-41/90, *Höfner v. Macrotron* [1991] ECR I-1979, [1993] 4 CMLR 306; Case C-179/90, *Merci Convenzionali v. Porto di Genova* [1991] ECR I-5889, [1994] 4 CMLR 422. Case C-260/89, *Elliniki Radiophonia Tileorasi (ERT) v. DEP* [1991] ECR I-2925, [1994] 4 CMLR 540; and Case C-18/88, *RTT v. GB-INNO-BM SA* [1991] ECR I-5973; and the telecommunications cases between the Commission and Member States, Case C-202/88, *France v. Commission* [1991] ECR I-1223 and Cases C-271, 281, and 289/90, *Spain, Belgium & Italy v. Commission* [1992] ECR I-5833.

[14] Ex Art. 7d.

[15] See *infra* 671.

[16] Communication on Services of General Interest in Europe, [1996] OJ C281/03; Communication on Services of General Interest, [2001] OJ C17/4. The difference between services of *general economic interest* and services of *general interest* is discussed *infra* 621.

[17] COM (2003) 270, 12 May 2004; see *infra* 676.

[18] COM (2003) 270 final. The Green Paper suggested the possibility of a framework directive or other general instrument on services of general interest, but the White Paper came down against this: see *infra* 677.

[19] It is tempting to use the term 'public services' but the Commission considers that term too imprecise and expressly declined to use it in the White Paper (Annex 1), See also Green Paper COM (2003) 270 final, para. 19.

[20] White Paper, para. 2.1 Green Paper, para. 2.

to take advantage of a derogation from the rules (in particular, the derogation provided in Article 86(2)).

Whether or not an activity is economic in the first place goes back to the definition of 'undertaking' which was discussed in Chapter 3.[21] Articles 81 and 82 apply only to 'undertakings', and denying a body the status of an undertaking removes it from the ambit of the competition rules. It will be recalled that 'undertaking' is a Community concept and that it is immaterial how the entity is regarded in national law. The fundamental question is whether it carries out commercial activities and not whether it is governed by public law or is non-profit-making. The Court held in *Höfner v. Macrotron* that in regard to competition law 'the concept of an undertaking encompasses every entity engaged in an economic activity, regardless of the legal status of the entity and the way it is financed'.[22] In that case the fact that employment procurement was normally entrusted to public agencies could not affect the economic nature of the activity the entity carried out. It was not always an activity carried out by public entities and it followed that a public employment agency could be classified as an undertaking.[23]

It was also seen in Chapter 3 that bodies which exercise powers which can be seen as part of the prerogatives of the State, such as the air traffic control in *Eurocontrol*[24] and the anti-pollution surveillance in *Diego Cali*,[25] are not engaging in activities of an economic nature.

Particular problems, however, have arisen in determining the status of various types of social security and health insurance funds. Here the Court has considered not whether the services are such that they may potentially be provided on the market (health insurance can undoubtedly be provided on the market and is therefore 'economic' in nature), but whether the details of the schemes demonstrate 'solidarity'. The principle of solidarity, the 'inherently uncommercial act of involuntary subsidization of one social group by another'[26] has been used by the Court to distinguish economic from non-economic activities.[27] It can take various forms, depending on the type of scheme in issue. *Inter alia*, it can involve low risk persons subsidizing high risk persons, the richer subsidizing the poorer, one generation subsidizing another, or more profitable schemes subsidizing less profitable ones.[28] A number of cases have involved bodies being classified as undertakings or not on this basis.[29] A striking recent example of this is *AOK Bundesverband*, in which the ECJ held the German *Krankenkassen* (sickness funds) not to be undertakings and therefore to be outside Article 81.

---

[21] *Supra* 131.

[22] Case C-41/90, *Höfner v. Macrotron* [1991] ECR I-1979, [1993] 4 CMLR 306, para. 21.

[23] *Ibid.*, paras. 22–3.

[24] Case C-364/92, *SAT Fluggesellschaft v. Eurocontrol* [1994] ECR I-43, [1994] 5 CMLR 208 but c.f Case T-155/04, SELEX *Sistemi Integrati v. Commission*, 12 December 2006.

[25] Case C-343/95, *Diego Cali v. SEPG* [1997] ECR I-1547, [1997] 5 CMLR 484.

[26] Case C-70/95, *Sodemare v. Regione Lombardia* [1997] ECR I-3395, [1998] 4 CMLR 667, Opinion of Fennelly AG, para. 29.

[27] See N. Boeger, 'Solidarity and EC Competition Law' (2007) 32 *ELRev* 319.

[28] See A. Winterstein, 'Nailing the Jellyfish: Social Security and Competition Law' [1999] *ECLR* 324.

[29] See *Poucet and Pistre v. Assurances Générales de France* [1993] ECR I-637; Case C-244/94, *Fédération Française des Sociétés d'Assurance and Others v. Ministère de l'Agriculture et de la Pêche* [1995] ECR I-4013, [1996] 4 CMLR 536; Case C-67/96, *Albany International BV v. Stichting Bedrijfspensioenfonds Textielindustrie* [1999] ECR I-5751, [2000] 4 CMLR 446; Cases C-180–4/98, *Pavlov v. Stichting Pensioenfonds Medische Specialisten* [2000] ECR I-6451, [2001] 4 CMLR 30; Case C-218/00 *Cisal di Battistello Venanzio & Co v. Istituto Nazionale per L'Assicurazione Contro Gli Infortuni Sul Lavoro (INAIL)* [2002] ECR I-691, [2002] 4 CMLR 833, discussed *supra* Chap. 3, 134 ff.

Cases C-264/01, 306/01, 354/01, and 355/01, *AOK Bundesverband and Others* v. *Ichtyol-Gesellschaft Cordes and others* [2004] 4 CMLR 1261

In Germany statutory health insurance is provided by sickness funds (*Krankenkassen*). The great majority of employees are required to belong to the statutory health insurance system by joining one of these funds and making compulsory contributions. The contributions are calculated on the basis of the employee's wage or salary, not on the basis of sex, age, health risk, or any other consideration. The employee's insurance also covers unemployed family members. Employees whose income exceeds a certain level are not required to join and some groups of workers (in particular civil servants) belong to a separate statutory scheme. On the other hand, self-employed persons and any others may join if they wish. The funds are organized regionally and sectorally into associations. The dispute in this case concerned the role of the sickness funds in setting maximum prices to be paid for medicines. Under German law a Federal Committee of doctors and sickness funds determines the groups of medicines for which fixed maximum amounts must be laid down, and sets the maximum amounts. Patients have to bear their own costs if they choose medicines which cost more than the fixed maximum amount, and cannot get the extra reimbursed by the sickness funds. Pharmaceutical companies brought an action in the German courts challenging the way in which the maximum prices were fixed. One issue was whether Article 81 applied. This involved deciding whether the sickness funds were acting as 'undertakings'. Advocate General Jacobs (Opinion, 22 May 2003) decided that they were. He considered that although they operated on the basis of solidarity there was also an element of competition in their activities. He thought it relevant that the funds determined the employees' levels of contributions, that the funds could compete among themselves on the basis of what they offered, and that they were in competition for the business of persons for whom membership was not compulsory.

Court of Justice

46. The concept of an undertaking in competition law covers any entity engaged in economic activity, regardless of the legal status of the entity or the way in which it is financed (Case C-41/90 *Höfner and Elser* [1991] ECR I-1979, paragraph 21, and Case C-218/00 *Cisal* [2002] ECR I-691, paragraph 22).

47. In the field of social security, the Court has held that certain bodies entrusted with the management of statutory health insurance and old-age insurance schemes pursue an exclusively social objective and do not engage in economic activity. The Court has found that to be so in the case of sickness funds which merely apply the law and cannot influence the amount of the contributions, the use of assets and the fixing of the level of benefits. Their activity, based on the principle of national solidarity, is entirely non-profit-making and the benefits paid are statutory benefits bearing no relation to the amount of the contributions (Joined Cases C-159/91 and C-160/91 *Poucet and Pistre* [1993] ECR I-637, paragraphs 15 and 18).

48. The fact that the amount of benefits and of contributions was, in the last resort, fixed by the State led the Court to hold, similarly, that a body entrusted by law with a scheme providing insurance against accidents at work and occupational diseases, such as the Istituto nazionale per l'assicurazione contro gli infortuni sul lavoro (the Italian National Institute for Insurance against Accidents at Work), was not an undertaking for the purpose of the Treaty competition rules (see *Cisal*, cited above, paragraphs 43 to 46).

49. On the other hand, other bodies managing statutory social security systems and displaying some of the characteristics referred to in paragraph 47 of the present judgment, namely being non-profit-making and engaging in activity of a social character which is subject to State rules that

include solidarity requirements in particular, have been considered to be undertakings engaging in economic activity (see Case C-244/94 *Fédération française des sociétés d'assurance and Others* [1995] ECR I-4013, paragraph 22, and Case C-67/96 *Albany* [1999] ECR I-5751, paragraphs 84 to 87).

50. Thus, in *Fédération française des sociétés d'assurance and Others*, at paragraph 17, the Court held that the body in question managing a supplementary old-age insurance scheme engaged in an economic activity in competition with life assurance companies and that the persons concerned could opt for the solution which guaranteed the better investment. In paragraphs 81 and 84 of *Albany*, concerning a supplementary pension fund based on a system of compulsory affiliation and applying a solidarity mechanism for determination of the amount of contributions and the level of benefits, the Court noted however that the fund itself determined the amount of the contributions and benefits and operated in accordance with the principle of capitalisation. It deduced therefrom that such a fund engaged in an economic activity in competition with insurance companies.

51. Sickness funds in the German statutory health insurance scheme, like the bodies at issue in *Poucet and Pistre*, cited above, are involved in the management of the social security system. In this regard they fulfil an exclusively social function, which is founded on the principle of national solidarity and is entirely non-profit-making.

52. It is to be noted in particular that the sickness funds are compelled by law to offer to their members essentially identical obligatory benefits which do not depend on the amount of the contributions. The funds therefore have no possibility of influence over those benefits.

53. In its orders for reference, the Bundesgerichtshof states in this regard that the sickness funds are joined together in a type of community founded on the basis of solidarity ('Solidargemeinschaft') which enables an equalisation of costs and risks between them. In accordance with paragraph 265 et seq. of SGB V, an equalisation is thus effected between the sickness funds whose health expenditure is lowest and those which insure costly risks and whose expenditure connected with those risks is highest.

54. The sickness funds are therefore not in competition with one another or with private institutions as regards grant of the obligatory statutory benefits in respect of treatment or medicinal products which constitutes their main function.

55. It follows from those characteristics that the sickness funds are similar to the bodies at issue in *Poucet and Pistre* and *Cisal* and that their activity must be regarded as being non-economic in nature.

56. The latitude available to the sickness funds when setting the contribution rate and their freedom to engage in some competition with one another in order to attract members does not call this analysis into question. As is apparent from the observations submitted to the Court, the legislature introduced an element of competition with regard to contributions in order to encourage the sickness funds to operate in accordance with principles of sound management, that is to say in the most effective and least costly manner possible, in the interests of the proper functioning of the German social security system. Pursuit of that objective does not in any way change the nature of the sickness funds' activity.

57. Since the activities of bodies such as the sickness funds are not economic in nature, those bodies do not constitute undertakings within the meaning of Articles 81 EC and 82 EC.

58. However, the possibility remains that, besides their functions of an exclusively social nature within the framework of management of the German social security system, the sickness funds and the entities that represent them, namely the fund associations, engage in operations which have a purpose that is not social and is economic in nature. In that case the decisions which they would be led to adopt could perhaps be regarded as decisions of undertakings or of associations of undertakings.

59. It must therefore be examined whether determination of the fixed maximum amounts by the fund associations is linked to the sickness funds' functions of an exclusively social nature or whether it falls outside that framework and constitutes an activity of an economic nature.

60. In the submission of the pharmaceutical companies, the fund associations adopt decisions of associations of undertakings, of an economic nature, when they determine the fixed maximum amounts.

61. However, as is apparent from the documents before the Court, when the fund associations determine the fixed maximum amounts they merely perform an obligation which is imposed upon them by paragraph 35 of SGB V in order to ensure continuance of operation of the German social security system. That paragraph also lays down in detail the applicable procedure for determining the amounts and specifies that the fund associations must observe certain requirements as to quality and profitability. SGB V also provides that if the fund associations do not succeed in determining fixed maximum amounts, the competent minister must then decide them.

62. Thus, only the precise level of the fixed maximum amounts is not dictated by legislation, but decided by the fund associations having regard to the criteria laid down by the legislature. Furthermore, while the fund associations have a certain discretion in this regard, the discretion relates to the maximum amount paid by the sickness funds in respect of medicinal products which is an area where the latter do not compete.

63. It follows that, in determining those fixed maximum amounts, the fund associations do not pursue a specific interest separable from the exclusively social objective of the sickness funds. On the contrary, in making such a determination, the fund associations perform an obligation which is integrally connected with the activity of the sickness funds within the framework of the German statutory health insurance scheme.

64. It must accordingly be found that, in determining the fixed maximum amounts, the fund associations merely perform a task for management of the German social security system which is imposed upon them by legislation and that they do not act as undertakings engaging in economic activity.

It will be noted that in this judgment the Court disagreed with its Advocate General. It decided that the role of the sickness funds was essentially to manage the social security system (paragraph 51). It stressed the application of the solidarity principle and did not consider that the factors identified by the Advocate General detracted from this. Significantly, in paragraph 56 it says that the element of competition introduced in to the operation of the funds did not render their activity economic. It will also be noted that the Court asked itself two questions. First, were the funds undertakings, and secondly, were they in fact engaging in an economic function *when they were fixing the maximum amounts* (paragraphs 58 and 59). The Court decided that they were not so engaged but rather intriguingly says in paragraph 58 that, if they had been, their decisions 'could perhaps' be regarded as decisions of undertakings.

The ruling in *AOK Bundesverband*, which was contrary to the Opinion of the Advocate General and to the views of distinguished commentators,[30] can perhaps be seen as part of a policy, along with the CFI's judgment in *FENIN*,[31] to remove the operation of the health services in the

---

[30] See P. J. Slot, 'Applying the Competition Rules in the Healthcare Sector' [2003] *ECLR* 580; J. W. van de Gronden, 'Purchasing Care: Economic Activity or Service of General Economic Interest?' [2004] *ECLR* 87.

[31] Case T-319/99, *Federación Nacional de Empresas de Instrumentación Científica, Médica, Técnica y Dental (FENIN)* v. *Commission* [2003] 5 CMLR 34, *aff'd* by the ECJ, Case C-205/03 P, *FENIN* v. *Commission* [2006] ECR I-6295.

Member States from the application of competition law.[32] The Advocate General's approach was to bring the sickness funds within Article 81 but then to classify them as services of general economic interest and apply the Article 86(2) derogation. This would have meant, however, a greater degree of scrutiny as the national court would have had to determine whether the conditions in Article 86(2) were fulfilled.

C. SOME CONCEPTS

The concept of 'solidarity' has already encountered above and in Chapter 3. It is useful before proceeding further to note some other concepts which are employed in this area of law. Further discussion of their meaning and application is found later in this chapter.

(i) Services of General Economic Interest

The phrase 'services of general economic interest' appears, as explained above, in Article 86(2) of the Treaty. Article 86(2) gives a limited derogation from (*inter alia*) the competition rules to undertakings entrusted with such services, in certain circumstances. What amounts to a service of general economic interest is the subject of a considerable body of case law.[33] The phrase is an unhappy one because of the placing of the word 'economic'. It is the *service* to which the word 'economic' really applies, rather than the 'interest'. In the 2000 Communication the Commission defines services of general economic interest as

...market services which the Member States or the Community subject to specific public service obligations by virtue of a general interest criterion. This would tend to cover such things as transport networks, energy and communication.[34]

The White Paper describes the term in the same way except that it uses the expression 'services of an economic nature' instead of 'market services' and makes it clear that the term includes any economic activity subject to public service obligations.[35] For the meaning of 'economic' one must turn to the case law on the meaning of 'undertaking' which has already been discussed.[36] Services of general economic interest are therefore services which belong to the market, but to which other, 'non-market', values are applied.

In the Green Paper the Commission also suggested that existing (sector specific) Community legislation 'contains a number of common elements that can be drawn on to define a useful Community concept of services of general economic interest. These elements include in particular: universal service, continuity, quality of service, affordability, as well as user and consumer protection'.[37]

---

[32] This should be compared with the pre-*FENIN* judgment of the UK Competition Appeal Tribunal holding an NHS Trust to be an 'undertaking' for the purpose of the Chapter I prohibition of the Competiiton Act 1998 (the UK equivalent to Article 81) in *Bettercare Group Limited v. DGFT* [2002] CAT 6, [2002] CompAR 229.

[33] See *infra* 653 ff.

[34] Communication on services of general economic interest [2001] OJ C17/4, Annex II.

[35] White Paper, Annex 1.

[36] *Supra*, 617 and Chap. 3.

[37] Green Paper, para. 49.

(ii) Services of General Interest

This term does not appear anywhere in the Treaty (even post Amsterdam) or in the Charter. It is, however used by the Commission in its Communication of 2000.[38] It is defined there and in the White Paper to mean:

Market and non-market services which the public authorities class as being of general interest and subject to specific public service obligations.[39]

It is therefore an umbrella term encompassing both services of general economic interest (market services) which are subject to the competition rules unless some kind of derogation applies, and non-economic (non-market) services, to which the competition rules do not apply in the first place. Into which category a service falls depends on the application of the concept of an 'economic activity'. Therefore services provided as part of the prerogatives of the State; services such as the basic national education and social security systems; and those organizations operating on the basis of 'solidarity' which we have seen from the case law are not 'economic' activities, are services of general interest but not services of general *economic* interest.

In the Green Paper the Commission doubted that it is either desirable or possible to develop a single comprehensive European definition of the content of services of general interest, as distinct from services of general *economic* interest.[40] Indeed the Court has sometimes used the terms interchangeably.[41]

(iii) Public Services

'Public services' is not a term of art. It is usually used (and is in this book) to denote services whose delivery is generally considered to be in the public interest and which may be either regulated, provided or financed by the State. The Commission tends to avoid the term, which it thinks confusing,[42] and prefers the specifically Community terminology of services of general economic interest or services of general interest. The term 'public service obligations' is used in the White Paper to refer to 'specific requirements that are imposed by public authorities on the provider of the service in order to ensure that certain public interest objectives are met, for instance, in the matter of air, rail and road transport and energy'.[43]

(iv) Universal Service

Universal service is the obligation on a supplier of goods and services to provide them at an affordable cost and guaranteed quality to all who require them. It is particularly relevant to the suppliers of the basic postal service and the utilities. It is described in the Commission's Green Paper on services of general interest as follows:

50. The concept of universal service refers to a set of general interest requirements ensuring that certain services are made available at a specified quality to all consumers and users throughout the

---

[38] [2001] OJ C17/4.

[39] *Ibid.*, Annex II, White Paper, Annex I.

[40] Green Paper, para. 49.

[41] Case C-393/92, *Gemeente Almelo* [1994] ECR I-1477; J. Faull and A. Nikpay, *The EC Law of Competition* (2nd edn., Oxford University Press, 2007), 6.140.

[42] See Green Paper, para. 19.

[43] White Paper, Annex 1.

territory of a Member State, independently of geographical location, and, in the light of specific national conditions, at an affordable price... It has been developed specifically for some of the network industries (e.g., telecommunications, electricity and postal services). The concept establishes the right for every citizen to access certain services considered as essential and imposes obligations on industries to provide a defined service at specified conditions, including complete territorial coverage. In a liberalised market environment, a universal service obligation guarantees that everybody has access to the service at an affordable price and that the service quality is maintained and, where necessary, improved.

51. Universal service is a dynamic concept. It ensures that general interest requirements can take account of political, social, economic and technological developments and it allows these requirements, where necessary, to be regularly adjusted to the citizens' evolving needs.

Universal service obligations are of crucial importance in the application of Article 86(2) to services of general economic interest.

3. ARTICLE 10

Article 10 states the principle of Community loyalty. It requires Member States to take all appropriate measures to ensure fulfilment of their Treaty obligations, facilitate the achievement of the Community's tasks, and abstain from measures which could jeopardize the attainment of the Treaty's objectives. The Court held in *INNO v. ATAB*, and has consistently stated ever since, that the Treaty imposes a duty on Member States not to adopt or maintain in force measures which could deprive the competition provisions of their effectiveness. It is an infringement of Articles 10 and 81, for example, for a Member State to require or favour the adoption of agreements, decisions, or concerted practices contrary to Article 81, or to reinforce their effect.[44]

Case 13/77, *NV GB-INNO-BM* v. *ATAB* [1977] ECR 2115

The Court was asked by the Belgian Court of Cassation about the compatibility with Community law of Belgian rules prohibiting the sale of tobacco at less than the price fixed by the manufacturers or importers.

Court of Justice

28. First, the single market system which the Treaty seeks to create excludes any national system of regulation hindering directly or indirectly, actually or potentially, trade within the Community.

29. Secondly, the general objective set out in Article [3(1)(g)] is made specific in several Treaty provisions concerning the rules on competition, including Article [82], which states that any abuse by one of more undertakings of a dominant position shall be prohibited as incompatible with the Common Market in so far as it may affect trade between Member States.

30. The second paragraph of Article [10] of the Treaty provides that Member States shall abstain from any measure which could jeopardize the attainment of the objectives of the Treaty.

31. Accordingly, while it is true that Article [82] is directed at undertakings, nonetheless it is also true that the Treaty imposes a duty on Member States not to adopt or maintain in force any measure which could deprive that provision of its effectiveness.

---

[44] Case 267/86, *Van Eycke v. ASPA NV* [1988] ECR 4769, [1990] 4 CMLR 330, para. 16; Cases C-140–142/94, *DIP and Others v. Commune di Bassano del Grappa and Commune di Chioggia* [1995] ECR I-3257, [1996] 4 CMLR 157, para. 15.

32. Thus Article [86] provides that, in the case of public undertakings and undertakings to which Member States grant special or exclusive rights, Member States shall neither enact nor maintain in force any measure contrary, *inter alia*, to the rules provided for in Articles [81] to [89].

33. Likewise, Member States may not enact measures enabling private undertakings to escape from the constraints imposed by Articles [81] to [89] of the Treaty.

34. At all events, Article [82] prohibits any abuse by one or more undertakings of a dominant position, even if such abuse is encouraged by a national legislative provision.

35. In any case, a national measure which has the effect of facilitating the abuse of a dominant position capable of affecting trade between Member States will generally be incompatible with Articles [28] and [29], which prohibits quantitative restrictions on imports and exports and all measures having equivalent effect.

4. ARTICLE 86

The application of Community rules to public undertakings and those granted special or exclusive rights is dealt with in Article 86 (ex Article 90). Article 86 states:

1. In the case of public undertakings and undertakings to which Member States grant special or exclusive rights, Member States shall neither enact nor maintain in force any measure contrary to the rules contained in this Treaty, in particular to those rules provided for in Article 12 and Articles 81 to 89.

2. Undertakings entrusted with the operation of services of general economic interest or having the character of a revenue producing monopoly shall be subject to the rules contained in this Treaty, in particular to the rules on competition, insofar as the application of such rules does not obstruct the performance, in law or in fact, of the particular tasks assigned to them. The development of trade must not be affected to such an extent as would be contrary to the interests of the Community.

3. The Commission shall ensure the application of the provisions of this Article and shall, where necessary, address appropriate directives or decisions to Member States.

A. THE OBJECTIVES OF ARTICLE 86

As will be appreciated from its wording, Article 86 is normally applied in conjunction with another Article of the Treaty, since its function is to limit the ways in which State measures protecting certain undertakings hinder the operation of the Treaty. Thus Article 86 does not deal only with competition, despite its position in the Treaty. It deals rather with the application of *all* the rules in the EC Treaty, although it mentions in particular the competition rules (Articles 81–9) and the prohibition on discrimination on the grounds of nationality (Article 12, ex Article 6). Apart from those, the rules most likely to be concerned are those on free movement and State monopolies.[45] Article 86 does, however, have particular relevance to the competition provisions and especially Article 82, because public undertakings and undertakings granted special or exclusive rights frequently hold a dominant position.[46]

[45] See *Spanish Transport Fares to the Balearic and Canary Islands* [1987] OJ L194/28; *Flemish Television Advertising* [1997] OJ L244/18; Case C-260/89, *Elliniki Radiophonia Tileorasi (ERT) v. DEP* [1991] ECR I-2925, [1994] 4 CMLR 540.

[46] But not inevitably: the usual criteria of dominance apply, and the exclusive right has to be over a relevant market: see Case 30/87, *Bodson v. Pompes Funèbres des Régions Libérées* [1988] ECR 2479, [1989] 4 CMLR 984, paras. 26–9.

Article 86 is a specific manifestation of the duty of Community loyalty contained in Article 10.

B. THE FORMAT OF ARTICLE 86

Article 86 contains three interrelated provisions.

(i) Article 86(1): Prohibition Addressed to Member States

The prohibition in Article 86(1) is addressed to Member States, not to undertakings. It prohibits Member States from enacting or maintaining in force any measures in relation to public undertakings and undertakings to which they have granted special or exclusive rights which are contrary to the rules of the Treaty. It is designed to prevent Member States from depriving the Treaty rules of their effectiveness through the measures they adopt in respect of public undertakings or through measures which enable private undertakings to escape the constraints of the competition provisions.

(ii) Article 86(2): Provision Addressed to Undertakings Providing for Limited Immunity from the Treaty Rules

Article 86(2) is addressed to the undertakings themselves. It gives a limited derogation from the Treaty rules to 'undertakings entrusted with the operation of services of general economic interest or having the character of a revenue producing monopoly' in so far as that is necessary for the carrying out of their tasks. Despite being addressed to undertakings, Article 86(2) can be invoked by Member States in relation to exclusive rights they have granted.[47]

(iii) Article 86(3): Policing and Legislative Powers of the Commission

Article 86(3) provides that the Commission may address decisions to Member States to ensure the observance of Article 86. This is an expedited enforcement mechanism which does not have to comply with the procedures of the general enforcement provision, Article 226, which provides for infraction proceedings brought by the Commission against Member States.

It also gives the Commission power to issue directives to Member States to ensure the application of the Article. This power does not have to be exercised within the detailed procedural framework ordinarily applicable to the adoption of directives, which involves other Community institutions and is set down in Articles 250 to 252.

The Commission's exercise of these special powers under Article 86(3) has led to challenges by Member States claiming that the situation concerned was not one to which Article 86(3) applied, that the Commission was acting *ultra vires* and/or that some other legislative base should have been used.[48]

---

[47] See *infra* 652 ff.

[48] Cases 188-90/88, *France, Italy and the UK v. Commission* [1982] ECR 2545 (the *Transparency Dir.* case); Cases C-271, 281 and 289/90, *Spain, Belgium & Italy v. Commission* [1992] ECR I-5833 (the *Telecommunications Services* case); Case C-202/88, *France v. Commission* [1991] ECR I-1223 (the *Telecommunications Equipment* case).

C. ARTICLE 86(1)

(i) Definitions

When considering Article 86(1) it is first necessary to determine the meaning of the concepts it employs, in particular the terms 'public undertakings', 'granted special or exclusive rights', and 'measures'.

a. 'Public Undertakings'

Determining the meaning of 'public undertakings' is a two-step procedure. First, one must ask whether a particular body is an 'undertaking' and secondly, if it is, whether it is a 'public undertaking'.

The answer to the first question, what constitutes an undertaking, has already been considered in the context of Articles 81 and 82[49] and above.[50] The second question is whether an undertaking is a 'public' undertaking. Again, this is a Community concept[51] because Article 86(1) would be deprived of its effect if Member States were free to choose their own conception of 'public undertaking'. State participation in the ownership or running of undertakings comes in an almost indefinite range of guises and the Community concept must embrace them all.

The concept of a 'public undertaking' was clarified by the Court in the *Transparency Directive* case.[52] This case arose as a result of a directive issued by the Commission pursuant to Article 86(3) aimed at creating greater transparency in the financial relationship between the Member States and public undertakings.[53] Article 2 defined 'public undertaking' as:

any undertaking over which the public authorities may exercise, directly or indirectly, a dominant influence by virtue of their ownership of it, their financial participation therein or the rules which govern it. A dominant influence is to be presumed when the public authority holds the major part of the undertaking's subscribed capital, controls the majority of votes attached to the shares issued or can appoint more than half of the members of the undertaking's administrative, managerial or supervisory body.

Various Member States challenged the directive, *inter alia*, on the ground that the Commission was not entitled to amplify the concept of public undertaking contained in Article 86(1). The Court upheld the definition set out in the directive.[54]

The key to the concept is therefore control by the State. This can be through ownership or through some contractual, financial, or structural connection between the State and the undertaking.

---

[49] *Supra* Chaps. 3 and 5; and see Case 82/71, *Pubblico Ministero della Repubblica Italiana v. Società Agricola Industria Latte (SAIL)* [1972] ECR 119; Case 155/73, *Sacchi* [1974] ECR 409, [1974] 2 CMLR 177; Case 52/76, *Benedetti v. Munari* [1977] ECR 163; Case 123/83, *BNIC v. Clair* [1985] ECR 391; *European Broadcasting Union* [1993] OJ L179/23, [1995] 4 CMLR 56; Case C-364/92, *SAT Fluggesellschaft v. Eurocontrol* [1994] ECR I-43, [1994] 5 CMLR 208; Case C-159/91, etc. *Poucet* [1993] ECR I-637; Case C-343/95, *Diego Cali v. Servizi Ecologici Porto di Genova* [1997] ECR I-1547, [1997] 5 CMLR 484.

[50] *Supra* 617.

[51] See the Opinion of Reischl AG in Cases 188-90/88, *France, Italy and the UK v. Commission* [1982] ECR 2545, para. 9 (the *Transparency Directive* case).

[52] Cases 188–190/88, *France, Italy and the UK v. Commission* [1982] ECR 2545.

[53] Commission Dir. 80/723 [1980] OJ L195/35, amended by Commission Dir. 85/413. [1985] OJ L229/20.

[54] For Article 86(3) see the discussion *infra* 668 ff.

b. Undertakings Granted Special or Exclusive Rights

Special or exclusive rights may be granted in the whole of a national territory or in only part of it.[55] Undertaking is defined as discussed above and in Chapters 3 and 5, but difficulties have arisen over the definition of 'special and exclusive rights'. Two categories are involved here: 'special' and 'exclusive' are not synonymous. Entities with such rights may or may not be public undertakings.

Exclusive rights are the most easily identified. They exist where a monopoly has been granted by the State to one entity to engage in a particular economic activity on an exclusive basis. They have been held to have been conferred, for example, upon broadcasting monopolies,[56] and upon undertakings granted the sole right to operate employment recruitment services,[57] the sole right to operate on a particular air route,[58] the sole right to supply unloading services at a port,[59] and the sole right to provide bovine insemination services.[60] The rights granted to the television duopoly in the Greek television case, *ERT*,[61] were designated as 'special or exclusive'. Rather strangely, however, the Court described the three firms who were entitled to collect waste for recycling in Copenhagen, as holding 'exclusive' rights.[62] It is important to note that the grant of intellectual property rights does not entail the granting of exclusive rights for the purposes of Article 86(1) because it involves laws which lay down criteria which any undertaking is free to satisfy: there is no question of a closed class.

What amounts to 'special rights' has been determined by the Court as a result of a series of challenges brought by Member States to directives issued by the Commission under Article 86(3) in pursuance of its objective to liberalize the telecommunications market. This liberalization inevitably meant ensuring the removal of the protection hitherto given by Member States to national telecommunications operators.

The *Telecommunications Equipment Case*[63] concerned the challenge by France to Directive 88/301 on competition in the markets in telecommunications terminal equipment.[64] According to Article 2, Member States which had granted special or exclusive rights to undertakings for the importation, marketing, connection, bringing into service of telecommunications terminal equipment, and/or maintenance of such equipment were to ensure that those rights were withdrawn. The Court held that Article 2 was void in so far as it concerned the

---

[55] E.g., Case 30/87, *Bodson v. Pompes Funèbres des Régions Libérées* [1988] ECR 2479, [1989] 4 CMLR 984 (funeral services in particular French communes); Case C-179/90, *Merci Convenzionali v. Porto di Genova* [1991] ECR I-5889, [1994] 4 CMLR 422 (unloading services in the port of Genoa); Case C-323/93, *Société Civile Agricole du Centre d'Insémination de la Crespelle v. Coopérative d'Elevage et d'Insémination Artificielle du Département de la Mayenne* [1994] ECR I-5077 (exclusive rights to provide bovine insemination services in defined areas of France).

[56] Case 155/73, *Sacchi* [1974] ECR 409, [1974] 2 CMLR 177.

[57] Case C-41/90, *Höfner v. Macrotron* [1991] ECR I-1979, [1993] 4 CMLR 306.

[58] Case 66/86, *Ahmed Saeed Flugreisen and Silver Line Reiseburo GmbH v. Zentrale zur Bëkampfung Unlauteren Wettwerbs eV* [1989] ECR 803, [1990] 4 CMLR 102; *Sterling Airways/SAS Denmark*, Commission's *Xth Report on Competition Policy* (Commission, 1980), paras 136–8.

[59] Case C-179/90, *Merci Convenzionali v. Porto di Genova* [1991] ECR I-5889, [1994] 4 CMLR 422.

[60] Case C-323/93, *Société Civile Agricole du Centre d'Insémination de la Crespelle* [1994] ECR I-5077.

[61] Case C-260/89, *Elliniki Radiophonia Tileorasi (ERT) v. DEP* [1991] ECR I-2925, [1994] 4 CMLR 540.

[62] Case C-209/98, *Entreprenørforeningens Affalds (FFAD) v. Københavns Kommune* [2000] ECR I-3743, [2001] 2 CMLR 936.

[63] Case C-202/88, *France v. Commission* [1991] ECR I-1223.

[64] [1988] OJ L131/73.

withdrawal of *special* rights because:

45. . . . neither the provisions of the directive nor the preamble thereto specify the type of rights which are actually involved and in what respect the existence of such rights is contrary to the various provisions of the Treaty.

46. It follows that the Commission has failed to justify the obligation to withdraw special rights regarding the importation, marketing, connection, bringing into service and/or maintenance of telecommunications terminal equipment.

The *Telecommunications Services*[65] case concerned a similar challenge by Spain, Belgium, and Italy to Directive 90/388 on competition in the markets for telecommunications services.[66] Again the Court annulled the provisions concerning the requirement to withdraw all special rights. In this directive the Commission had defined 'special or exclusive rights' in Article 1 as being 'rights granted by a Member State or a public authority to one or more private or public bodies through any legal, regulatory or administrative instrument reserving them the right to provide a service or undertake an activity'. The Court held that this was inadequate as it did not make it possible 'to determine the type of special rights with which the directive is concerned or in what respect the existence of those rights is contrary to the various provisions of the Treaty'.[67]

As a result of these cases, the Commission set out an extended definition of the meaning of 'special rights' in the field of telecommunications in the Preamble to Directive 94/46[68] stating that special rights (in field of telecommunication services) are:

rights that are granted by a Member State to a limited number of undertakings through any legislative, regulatory or administrative instruments which, within a given geographical area, limits to two or more, otherwise than according to objective, proportional and non-discriminatory criteria, the number of undertakings which are authorised to provide any such service, or designates, otherwise than according to such criteria, several competing undertakings, as those which are authorised to provide any such service, or confers on any undertaking or undertakings otherwise than according to such criteria, legal or regulatory advantages which substantially affect the ability of any other undertaking to provide that same telecommunications service in the same geographical area under substantially equivalent conditions.

Although this definition is set out in a directive relating to telecommunications there is no reason to suppose that it is not also applicable in other fields. What it does is to identify as 'special rights' those which are given by the State to a limited number of undertakings chosen in a subjective and discretionary manner.[69] This is borne out by the contrast with those cases in which it has been held that special or exclusive rights do not exist. So in *NV-GB-INNO v. ATAB* the Court doubted whether special or exclusive rights could result from allowing manufacturers and importers of a particular product to impose resale price maintenance.[70] In *Banchero*[71] it

---

[65] Cases C-271, 281 and 289/90, *Spain, Belgium & Italy v. Commission* [1992] ECR I-5833.

[66] [1990] OJ L192/10.

[67] [1992] ECR I-5833, para. 31.

[68] Directive amending Dir. 88/301 and 90/388 in particular with regard to satellite communications [1994] OJ L268/15.

[69] See also the Commission's statement at the hearing in the *Telecommunications Services* case, Cases C-271, 281, and 289/90, *Spain, Belgium & Italy v. Commission* [1992] ECR I-5833, quoted by Jacobs AG at para. 50 of his Opinion.

[70] Case 13/77, [1977] ECR 2115, [1978] 1 CMLR 283: the point did not actually have to be answered because of the reply given to an earlier question.

[71] Case C-387/93, *Banchero* [1995] ECR I-4663.

held that Italian laws on the distribution of tobacco did not entail special or exclusive rights as, although they governed access to the market, all undertakings were treated in the same way. Further, in *GEMA*[72] the Commission held that an authors' rights society did not enjoy special or exclusive rights even though legislation required authors to exercise their rights through such a society, because there was no limit on the number of rights societies which could exist. As with exclusive rights, special rights involve the creation of some sort of limited, closed class.

c. 'Measures'

The word 'measures' also appears in Article 10 which obliges Member States to fulfil their Treaty obligations and not to jeopardize Treaty objectives, and in Article 28 (ex Article 30) which prohibits, *inter alia*, measures having an equivalent effect to quantitative restrictions on imports between Member States. In Directive 70/50[73] the Commission defined measures as 'laws, regulations, administrative provisions, administrative practices, and all instruments issued from a public authority, including recommendations' and both Articles 10 and 28 have been interpreted to give a very wide interpretation to the word. The best illustration of this point is provided by the *Buy Irish* case[74] in which a number of steps taken by the Irish Government to encourage the public to buy home-produced goods were condemned as contrary to Article 28. The Court held that 'measures' do not have to have a binding effect.[75] 'Measures' does not, however, cover the actions of private undertakings rather than the State actions which allow or authorize them, so that anti-competitive conduct engaged in by undertakings on their own initiative must be dealt with by Articles 81 and 82.[76]

(ii) Measures which are Forbidden by Article 86(1)

There is some uncertainty about what measures violate Article 86(1). In some cases there is clearly a violation in that some aspect of the State's arrangements inherently infringes a Treaty rule in itself. A good example, which does not involve the competition rules, is *Merci Convenzionali*,[77] where Italian laws reserved the loading and unloading of ships at an Italian port to certain dock-work companies whose worker-members had to be of Italian nationality. This infringed Article 39 (ex Article 48) on the free movement of workers, which specifically applies Article 12 forbidding nationality discrimination in situations governed by Community law.[78] In other cases the measures taken by the Member State *result in* violations of the Treaty. The problem is that where the measures result in violations of the competition rules there are suggestions in some cases that the *very fact of granting monopoly rights* may itself be a violation. If this is so, the neutrality as to the organization of economic activities within the Member States discussed at the beginning of the Chapter is truly eroded and the right of Member States to make certain economic choices is limited.

---

[72] [1971] OJ L134/15, [1971] CMLR D35.

[73] On the abolition of measures which have an effect equivalent to quantitative restrictions on imports and are not covered by other provisions [1970] OJ Spec. Ed. 17.

[74] Case 249/81, *Commission v. Ireland* [1982] ECR 4005, [1983] 2 CMLR 104.

[75] *Ibid.*, para. 28.

[76] Case C-202/88, *France v. Commission* [1991] ECR I-1223, para. 55.

[77] Case C-179/90, *Merci Convenzionali Porto di Genova v. Siderurgica Gabrielli SpA* [1991] ECR I-5889, [1994] 4 CMLR 422.

[78] *Ibid.*, paras. 10–13.

It has been clear since the *Telecommunications Equipment* case in 1991 that Member States do not have unassailable rights to create legal monopolies under any conditions they choose:

Case C-202/88, *France* v. *Commission* [1991] ECR I-1223

France challenged the Telecommunications Terminal Equipment Directive, 88/301, *inter alia*, on the grounds that the Commission had no competence to adopt it on the basis of Article 86(3) (ex Article 90(3)). France claimed that Article 86 did not allow the Commission to interfere with the granting of special or exclusive rights by Member States because Article 86(1) presupposed the existence of special or exclusive rights so the granting of such rights could not itself constitute a 'measure' within the Article.

Court of Justice

21. ...it must be held in the first place that the supervisory power conferred on the Commission includes the possibility of specifying, pursuant to Article [86(3)], obligations arising under the Treaty. The extent of that power therefore depends on the scope of the rules with which compliance is to be ensured.

22. Next, it should be noted that even though that article presupposes the existence of undertakings which have certain special or exclusive rights, it does not follow that all the special or exclusive rights are necessarily compatible with the Treaty. That depends on different rules, to which Article [86(1)] refers.

As Edward and Hoskins say:[79]

It follows from *France* v. *Commission* that Member States have not retained complete sovereignty in relation to the creation of legal monopolies. Rather, the creation of such monopolies must be balanced with the principle of free competition. However, the precise point at which the balance is to be struck is less clear.

It is therefore important to look at the cases to try to determine the point at which that balance is to be struck. Guidance can be derived in particular from *Höfner* v. *Macrotron*, *Merci Convenzionali*, *ERT*, *RTT*, *Corbeau*, and *La Crespelle*.

Case C-41/90, *Höfner* v. *Macrotron* [1991] ECR I-1979, [1993] 4 CMLR 306

A dispute arose in a German court, the Oberlandsgericht München, between a company and the recruitment consultants it had employed to find it a sales director. In a dispute about fees the company claimed that the contract between the parties was void as it infringed the German law on the promotion of employment, the Arbeitsförderungsgesetz (the AFG). The AFG conferred on the Bundesanstalt, the Federal Office for Employment, the exclusive right to put prospective

---

[79] D. Edward and M. Hoskins, 'Art. 90: Deregulation and EC Law. Reflections Arising from the XVI FIDE Conference' (1995) 32 *CMLRev* 157, 160.

employees and employers in contact with one another. Nevertheless, to some extent the Budesanstalt tolerated the existence and activities of independent recruitment consultants and it appeared that the Bundesanstalt was unable, on its own, to meet the demand for executive recruitment. The questions referred by the Oberlandsgericht raised the issue of whether there was an abuse of a dominant position involved and whether Article 86(1) was infringed by the exclusive rights. The Court first held that the Bundesanstalt was an undertaking for the purposes of Articles 82 and 86.[80] It then considered the possible infringements.

Court of Justice

24. It must be pointed out that a public employment agency which is entrusted, under the legislation of a Member State, with the operation of services of general economic interest, such as those envisaged in Article 3 of the AFG, remains subject to the competition rules pursuant to Article [86(2)] of the Treaty unless and to the extent to which it is shown that their application is incompatible with the discharge of its duties (see judgment in Case 155/73 *Sacchi* . . .).

25. As regards the manner in which a public employment agency enjoying an exclusive right of employment procurement conducts itself in relation to executive recruitment undertaken by private recruitment consultancy companies, it must be stated that the application of Article [82] of the Treaty cannot obstruct the performance of the particular task assigned to that agency in so far as the latter is manifestly not in a position to satisfy demand in that area of the market and in fact allows its exclusive rights to be encroached on by those companies.

26. Whilst it is true that Article [82] concerns undertakings and may be applied within the limits laid down by Article [86(2)] to public undertakings or undertakings vested with exclusive rights, or specific rights, the fact nevertheless remains that the Treaty requires the Member States not to take or maintain in force measures which could destroy the effectiveness of that provision (see judgment in Case 13/77 *Inno* . . . paragraphs 31 and 32). Article [86(1)] in fact provides that the Member States are not to enact or maintain in force, in the case of public undertakings and the undertakings to which they grant special or exclusive rights, any measure contrary to the rules contained in the Treaty, in particular those provided for in Articles [81] to [89].

27. Consequently, any measure adopted by a Member State which maintains in force a statutory provision that creates a situation in which a public employment agency cannot avoid infringing Article [82] is incompatible with the rules of the Treaty.

28. It must be remembered, first, that an undertaking vested with a legal monopoly may be regarded as occupying a dominant position within the meaning of Article [82] of the Treaty (see judgment in Case 311/84 *CBEM*, [1985] ECR 3261) and that the territory of a Member State, to which that monopoly extends, may constitute a substantial part of the common market (judgment in Case C 322/81 *Michelin* . . . , paragraph 28).

29. Secondly, the simple fact of creating a dominant position of that kind by granting an exclusive right within the meaning of Article [86(1)] is not as such incompatible with Article [82] of the Treaty (see Case 311/84 *CBEM*, above, paragraph 17). A Member State is in breach of the prohibition contained in those two provisions only if the undertaking in question, merely by exercising the exclusive right granted to it, cannot avoid abusing its dominant position.

30. Pursuant to Article [82(b)], such an abuse may in particular consist in limiting the provision of a service, to the prejudice of those seeking to avail themselves of it.

31. A Member State creates a situation in which the provision of a service is limited when the undertaking to which it grants an exclusive right extending to executive recruitment activities is

---

[80] See *supra* Chap. 3.

manifestly not in a position to satisfy the demand prevailing on the market for activities of that kind and when the effective pursuit of such activities by private companies is rendered impossible by the maintenance in force of a statutory provision under which such activities are prohibited and non-observance of that prohibition renders the contracts concerned void.

32. It must be observed, thirdly, that the responsibility imposed on a Member State by virtue of Articles [82] and [86(1)] of the Treaty is engaged only if the abusive conduct on the part of the agency concerned is liable to affect trade between Member States. That does not mean that the abusive conduct in question must actually have affected such trade. It is sufficient to establish that the conduct is capable of having such an effect (see Case 322/81 *Michelin*, above, paragraph 104).

33. A potential effect of that kind on trade between Member States arises in particular where executive recruitment by private companies may extend to the nationals or to the territory of other Member States.

34. In view of the foregoing considerations, it must be stated in reply to the fourth question that a public employment agency engaged in employment procurement activities is subject to the prohibition contained in Article [82] of the Treaty, so long as the application of that provision does not obstruct the performance of the particular task assigned to it. A Member State which has conferred an exclusive right to carry on that activity upon the public employment agency is in breach of Article [86(1)] of the Treaty where it creates a situation in which that agency cannot avoid infringing Article [82] of the Treaty. That is the case, in particular, where the following conditions are satisfied.

— the exclusive right extends to executive recruitment activities;

— the public employment agency is manifestly incapable of satisfying demand prevailing on the market for such activities;

— the actual pursuit of those activities by private recruitment consultants is rendered impossible by the maintenance in force of a statutory provision under which such activities are prohibited and non-observance of that prohibition renders the contracts concerned void;

— the activities in question may extend to the nationals or to the territory of other Member States.

In *Höfner* v. *Macrotron* the Court reiterated (at paragraph 29) that the fact of creating a dominant position by granting exclusive rights is not *as such* incompatible with the Treaty. However, a Member State *will* infringe the Treaty if the undertaking in question, merely by exercising the exclusive right granted to it, *cannot avoid* abusing its dominant position. In this case the criterion was fulfilled as German law had given the undertaking a monopoly over executive recruitment services, the demand for which it was incapable of satisfying. Such limitation of the service offered to customers constituted an abuse under Article 82(b), and so the Member State had created a situation in which the agency could not avoid infringing the Article.[81]

---

[81] See para. 27 of the judgment. See also the similar judgment of the Court in respect of the public placement office monopoly in Italy, Case C-55/96, *Job Centre Coop. arl* [1997] ECR I-7119, [1998] 4 CMLR 708. The Commission came to a similar conclusion in *Spanish Courier Services* [1990] OJ L233/19 (courier services reserved to Post Office which could not offer complete services). For inefficiency and the limitation of production and services as an abuse, see *supra* Chap. 7.

In *ERT*, the Court took a slightly different approach:

Case C-260/89, *Elliniki Radiophonia Tileorassi Anonimi Etaira (ERT)* v. *Dimotiki Etairia Pliroforissis (DEP)* [1991] ECR I-2925, [1994] 4 CMLR 540

The Thessaloniki Regional Court referred to the Court under Article 234 various questions concerning the position of the Greek radio and television undertaking (ERT) to which the Greek government had granted exclusive rights in regard to the original broadcasting and retransmitting of programmes in Greece. Greek law prohibited any person from engaging in activities for which ERT had an exclusive right without ERT's authorisation. The Mayor of Thessaloniki and a municipal company, DEP, set up a television station and began to broadcast television programmes. ERT sought an injunction and the seizure of the new station's technical equipment.

Court of Justice

10. In Case C-155/73 *Sacchi* . . . , paragraph 14, the Court held that nothing in the Treaty prevents Member States, for considerations of a non-economic nature relating to the public interest, from removing radio and television broadcasts from the field of competition by conferring on one or more establishments an exclusive right to carry them out.

11. Nevertheless, it follows from Article [86(1) and (2)] of the Treaty that the manner in which the monopoly is organized or exercised may infringe the rules of the Treaty, in particular those relating to the free movement of goods, the freedom to provide services and the rules on competition.

12. The reply to the national court must therefore be that Community law does not prevent the granting of a television monopoly for considerations of a non-economic nature relating to the public interest. However, the manner in which such a monopoly is organized and exercised must not infringe the provisions of the Treaty on the free movement of goods and services or the rules on competition.

. . .

27. As a preliminary point, it should be observed that Article [3(1)(g)] of the Treaty states only one objective for the Community which is given specific expression in several provisions of the Treaty relating to the rules on competition, including in particular Articles [81], [82] and [86].

28. The independent conduct of an undertaking must be considered with regard to the provisions of the Treaty applicable to undertakings, such as, in particular, Articles [81], [82] and [86(2)].

29. As regards Article [81], it is sufficient to observe that it applies, according to its own terms, to agreements 'between undertakings'. There is nothing in the judgment making the reference to suggest the existence of any agreement between undertakings. There is therefore no need to interpret that provision.

30. Article [82] declares that any abuse of a dominant position within the common market or in any substantial part of it is prohibited as incompatible with the common market in so far as it may affect trade between Member States.

31. In that respect it should be borne in mind that an undertaking which has a statutory monopoly may be regarded as having a dominant position within the meaning of Article [82] of the Treaty (see the judgment in Case C-311/84 *CBEM* v. *CLT and IBP* . . . , paragraph 16) and that the territory of a Member State over which the monopoly extends may constitute a substantial part of the common market (see the judgment in Case C-322/81 *Michelin* v. *Commission* . . . , paragraph 28).

32. Although Article [82] of the Treaty does not prohibit monopolies as such, it nevertheless prohibits their abuse. For that purpose Article [82] lists a number of abusive practices by way of example.

33. In that regard it should be observed that, according to Article [86(2)] of the Treaty, undertakings entrusted with the operation of services of general economic interest are subject to the rules on competition so long as it is not shown that the application of those rules is incompatible with the performance of their particular task (see in particular, the judgment in *Sacchi*, cited above, paragraph 15).

34. Accordingly it is for the national court to determine whether the practices of such an undertaking are compatible with Article [82] and to verify whether those practices, if they are contrary to that provision, may be justified by the needs of the particular task with which the undertaking may have been entrusted.

35. As regards State measures, and more specifically the grant of exclusive rights, it should be pointed out that while Articles [81] and [82] are directed exclusively to undertakings, the Treaty none the less requires the Member States not to adopt or maintain in force any measure which could deprive those provisions of their effectiveness (see the judgment in Case C-13/77 *INNO* v. *ATAB* . . . , paragraphs 31 and 32).

36. Article [86(1)] thus provides that, in the case of undertakings to which Member States grant special or exclusive rights, Member States are neither to enact nor to maintain in force any measure contrary to the rules contained in the Treaty.

37. In that respect it should be observed that Article [86(1)] of the Treaty prohibits the granting of an exclusive right to retransmit television broadcasts to an undertaking which has an exclusive right to transmit broadcasts, where those rights are liable to create a situation in which that undertaking is led to infringe Article [82] of the Treaty by virtue of a discriminatory broadcasting policy which favours its own programmes.

38. The reply to the national court must therefore be that Article [86(1)] of the Treaty prohibits the granting of an exclusive right to transmit and an exclusive right to retransmit television broadcasts to a single undertaking, where those rights are liable to create a situation in which that undertaking is led to infringe Article [82] by virtue of a discriminatory broadcasting policy which favours its own programmes, unless the application of Article [82] obstructs the performance of the particular tasks entrusted to it.

In *ERT* the Court said that the Treaty does not prevent the granting of a monopoly (*in casu* a television monopoly) but stressed, as it had in *INNO* v. *ATAB*, that the Treaty prohibits Member States from adopting measures which deprive the competition rules of their effectiveness. This means that the *manner in which the monopoly is organized* may infringe the rules of the Treaty (paragraph 11). The Court therefore concluded that the Treaty prohibits the granting of an exclusive right to retransmit TV broadcasts to an undertaking which has exclusive rights to transmit broadcasts *where those rights are liable to create a situation in which that undertaking is led to infringe Article 82* by virtue of a discriminatory broadcasting policy which favours its own programmes (paragraphs 37 and 38). This is different from the situation in *Höfner*, where the infringement was unavoidable because the State had given monopoly rights to a body manifestly unable to deal with the demand for its services. In *ERT* the cumulation of rights in the hands of the monopolist did not result in an *unavoidable* infringement of Article 82 but to a situation where the monopolist was *led to* infringe the Article because it would inevitably discriminate in favour of retransmitting its own programmes rather than anyone else's.

The theme of the monopolist being led to an infringement was taken up in the next case, *Merci Convenzionali*:

Case C-179/90, *Merci Convenzionali Porto di Genova* v. *Siderurgica Gabrielli SpA* [1991] ECR I-5889, [1994] 4 CMLR 422

By Italian law Merci had the exclusive right to organize the loading, unloading, and other handling of goods within the Port of Genoa through a dock-work company.[82] There was a delay in unloading Siderurgica's ship, caused in particular by the dock-work company's workers being on strike. The exclusive rights meant that the vessel's crew were not able to do the work themselves. Siderurgica demanded compensation for the damage it suffered due to the delay and the reimbursement of the charges it had paid to Merci, which it claimed were unfair given the service it had received, or rather, not received. The Tribunale di Genoa made an Article 234 reference, asking, *inter alia*,[83] whether Article [86(1)] in conjunction with Article 82 precluded the Italian rules. The Court confirmed in paragraph 14 that an undertaking with a statutory monopoly over a substantial part of the Common Market[84] could be regarded as having a dominant position within Article 82.

Court of Justice

16. It should next be stated that the simple fact of creating a dominant position by granting exclusive rights within the meaning of Article [86(1)] of the Treaty is not as such incompatible with Article [82].

17. However, the Court has had occasion to state, in this respect, that a Member State is in breach of the prohibitions contained in those two provisions if the undertaking in question, merely by exercising the exclusive rights granted to it, cannot avoid abusing its dominant position (see the judgment in Case C-41/90 *Höfner*, cited above, paragraph 29) or when such rights are liable to create a situation in which that undertaking is induced to commit such abuses (see the judgment in Case C-260/89 *ERT*, cited above, paragraph 37).

18. According to subparagraphs (a), (b) and (c) of the second paragraph of Article [82] of the Treaty, such abuse may in particular consist in imposing on the persons requiring the services in question unfair purchase prices or other unfair trading conditions, in limiting technical development, to the prejudice of consumers, or in the application of dissimilar conditions to equivalent transactions with other trading parties.

19. In that respect it appears from the circumstances described by the national court and discussed before the Court of Justice that the undertakings enjoying exclusive rights in accordance with the procedures laid down by the national rules in question are, as a result, induced either to demand payment for services which have not been requested, to charge disproportionate prices, to refuse to have recourse to modern technology, which involves an increase in the cost of the operations and a prolongation of the time required for their performance, or to grant price reductions to certain consumers and at the same time to offset such reductions by an increase in the charges to other consumers.

---

[82] For another case involving Italian law on dock-work companies, see Case C-163/96, *Silvano Raso* [1998] ECR I-533, [1998] 4 CMLR 737.

[83] For the nationality discrimination issue, see *supra* 629.

[84] The Court held (para. 15) that the Port of Genoa was a substantial part: for this aspect of Article 82 see *supra* Chap. 5.

> 20. In these circumstances it must be held that a Member State creates a situation contrary to Article [82] of the Treaty where it adopts rules of such a kind as those at issue before the national court, which are capable of affecting trade between Member States as in the case of the main proceedings, regard being had to the factors mentioned in paragraph 15 of this judgment relating to the importance of traffic in the Port of Genoa.

In this judgment the Court quoted *Höfner* and *ERT* and cited the latter for the proposition that a Member State infringes Article 82 where it grants rights which are liable to *induce* the undertaking to commit abuses (paragraphs 17 and 19). So we reach the position that although, as the Court said in *Merci* (paragraph 16), the simple fact of creating a dominant position by granting exclusive rights is not incompatible with Article 86 the granting of rights which induce or lead to the undertakings committing abuses *is* incompatible.[85] The question then is: what rights induce abuses? The problem is that any dominant position enables the undertaking to conduct itself in ways which would not be feasible on a more competitive market, but the existence of a statutory monopoly puts an undertaking in an even stronger position. A statutory monopolist does not have to worry, for example, that excessive or discriminatory pricing may ultimately attract new entrants into the market, for the barriers to entry are absolute. Can we not argue, therefore, that *all* undertakings with exclusive rights are being led or induced by their special position to commit abuses since they are safe from competition? *ERT* (above) was less to do with the *fact* of abusive conduct than with the *possibility* of it. This is also shown in *RTT* below. Both *ERT* and *RTT* involved the cumulation of rights, a matter of particular concern.[86]

Case C-18/88, *RTT* v. *GB-INNO-BM SA* [1991] ECR I-5973

Under Belgian law RRT held a monopoly over the establishment and operation of the public telephone system. The law also provided that only equipment supplied by RTT or approved by it could be connected to its network. GB-INNO sold in its shops telephones which had not been approved by RTT. RTT brought proceedings in the Commercial Court for an order that GB-INNO should not sell telephones without informing the purchasers that they were not approved. The Commercial Court asked the Court, *inter alia*, whether Articles 3(1)(g), 82, and 86 precluded a Member State from granting to the company operating the public telephone network the power to lay down the standards for telephone equipment and to check that economic operators meet those standards when it is competing with those operators on the market for terminals.

Court of Justice

15. Under Belgian law, the RTT holds a monopoly for the establishment and operation of the public telecommunications network. Moreover, only equipment supplied by the RTT or approved by it can be connected to the network. The RTT thus has the power to grant or withhold authorization

---

[85] See also Case C-18/93, *Corsica Ferries Italia Srl* v. *Corpo dei Piloti del Porto di Genovo* [1994] ECR I-1783.

[86] Although note that in Cases C-67/96, 115–17/97 and 219/97, *Albany International BV* v. *Stichting Bedrijfspensioenfonds Textielindustrie* [1999] ECR I-5751, [2000] 4 CMLR 446, paras. 112–21, the Court, unlike Advocate General Jacobs in his Opinion (paras. 441–68), was not concerned that the pension funds with the exclusive rights were also the authority able to grant exemptions from compulsory participation in the pension schemes.

to connect telephone equipment to the network, the power to lay down the technical standards to be met by that equipment, and the power to check whether the equipment not produced by it is in conformity with the specifications that it has laid down.

16. At the present stage of development of the Community, that monopoly, which is intended to make a public telephone network available to users, constitutes a service of general economic interest within the meaning of Article [86(2)] of the Treaty.

17. The Court has consistently held that an undertaking vested with a legal monopoly may be regarded as occupying a dominant position within the meaning of Article [82] of the Treaty and that the territory of a Member State to which that monopoly extends may constitute a substantial part of the common market (judgments in Case C-41/90 *Höfner* . . . , paragraph 28, and in Case C-260/89 *ERT* . . . , paragraph 31).

18. The Court has also held that an abuse within the meaning of Article [82] is committed where, without any objective necessity, an undertaking holding a dominant position on a particular market reserves to itself an ancillary activity which might be carried out by another undertaking as part of its activities on a neighbouring but separate market, with the possibility of eliminating all competition from such undertaking (judgment in Case 311/84 *CBEM* . . .).

19. Therefore the fact that an undertaking holding a monopoly in the market for the establishment and operation of the network, without any objective necessity, reserves to itself a neighbouring but separate market, in this case the market for the importation, marketing, connection, commissioning and maintenance of equipment for connection to the said network, thereby eliminating all competition from other undertakings, constitutes an infringement of Article [82] of the Treaty.

20. However, Article [82] applies only to anti-competitive conduct engaged in by undertakings on their own initiative (see judgment in Case C-202/88 *France* v. *Commission* 'Telecommunications terminals', . . .), not to measures adopted by States. As regards measures adopted by States, it is Article [86(1)] that applies. Under that provision, Member States must not, by laws, regulations or administrative measures, put public undertakings and undertakings to which they grant special or exclusive rights in a position which the said undertakings could not themselves attain by their own conduct without infringing Article [82].

21. Accordingly, where the extension of the dominant position of a public undertaking or undertaking to which the State has granted special or exclusive rights results from a State measure, such a measure constitutes an infringement of Article [86] in conjunction with Article [82] of the Treaty.

22. The exclusion or the restriction of competition on the market in telephone equipment cannot be regarded as justified by a task of a public service of general economic interest within the meaning of Article [86(2)] of the Treaty. The production and sale of terminals, and in particular of telephones, is an activity that should be open to any undertaking. In order to ensure that the equipment meets the essential requirements of, in particular, the safety of users, the safety of those operating the network and the protection of public telecommunications networks against damage of any kind, it is sufficient to lay down specifications which the said equipment must meet and to establish a procedure for type-approval to check whether those specifications are met.

23. According to the RTT, there could be a finding of an infringement of Article [86(1)] of the Treaty only if the Member State had favoured an abuse that the RTT itself had in fact committed, for example by applying the provisions on type-approval in a discriminatory manner. It emphasizes, however, that the order for reference does not state that any abuse has actually taken place, and that the mere possibility of discriminatory application of those provisions by reason of the fact that the RTT is designated as the authority for granting approval and is competing with the undertakings that apply for approval cannot in itself amount to an abuse within the meaning of Article [82] of the . . . Treaty.

24. That argument cannot be accepted. It is sufficient to point out in this regard that it is the extension of the monopoly in the establishment and operation of the telephone network to the market in telephone equipment, without any objective justification, which is prohibited as such by Article [82], or by Article [86(1)] in conjunction with Article [82], where that extension results from a measure adopted by a State. As competition may not be eliminated in that manner, it may not be distorted either.

25. A system of undistorted competition, as laid down in the Treaty, can be guaranteed only if equality of opportunity is secured as between the various economic operators. To entrust an undertaking which markets terminal equipment with the task of drawing up the specifications for such equipment, monitoring their application and granting type-approval in respect thereof is tantamount to conferring upon it the power to determine at will which terminal equipment may be connected to the public network, and thereby placing that undertaking at an obvious advantage over its competitors (judgment in Case C-202/88, paragraph 51).

26. In those circumstances, the maintenance of effective competition and the guaranteeing of transparency require that the drawing up of technical specifications, the monitoring of their application, and the granting of type-approval must be carried out by a body which is independent of public or private undertakings offering competing goods or services in the telecommunications sector (judgment in Case C-202/88, paragraph 52).

27. Moreover, the provisions of the national regulations at issue in the main action may influence the imports of telephone equipment from other Member States, and hence may affect trade between Member States within the meaning of Article [82] of the Treaty.

28. Accordingly, it must first be stated, in reply to the national court's questions, that Articles [3(1)(g)], [86] and [82] of the . . . Treaty preclude a Member State from granting to the undertaking which operates the public telecommunications network the power to lay down standards for telephone equipment and to check that economic operators meet those standards when it is itself competing with those operators on the market for that equipment.

It will be noticed here that there was no allegation that RTT had actually behaved improperly in its authorization of equipment. The objection was that the State measures in effect extended the monopoly position from one market to another, a situation which, if brought about by the conduct of an undertaking rather than by State measures, would have constituted an abuse, as the Court pointed out at paragraphs 18–20.[87] The rights conferred on the undertakings in both ERT and RTT were found to be contrary to Article 86 since they created a conflict of interest.[88] State measures cannot 'bundle' regulatory functions and commercial activities together.

In the case of *Corbeau*, however, the Court appeared to go further and suggest that the very granting of special or exclusive rights, even where the elements in the cases discussed above are

---

[87] See Case 311/84, *Centre Belge d'Etudes du Marché—Télémarketing v. Compagnie Luxembourgeoise de Télédiffusion SA and Information Publicité Benelux SA* [1985] ECR 3261, [1986] 2 CMLR 558 (quoted in para. 18 of the RTT judgment) and the cases discussed *supra* in Chap. 7.

[88] See also Case C-163/96, *Silvano Raso* [1998] ECR I-533, [1998] 4 CMLR 737, where an Italian law, which gave the exclusive right to supply temporary labour to other dock-work companies operating in a port to an undertaking which was also authorized to carry out dock-work itself, was held to infringe Article 86(1).

not present, might be contrary to Article 86(1):

Case C-320/91, *Corbeau* [1993] ECR I-2533, [1995] 4 CMLR 621

Belgian law conferred a monopoly on the Belgian Post Office, the Regie des Postes, in respect of the collection, transporting, and delivery throughout the Kingdom of various forms of correspondence. Criminal sanctions were imposed for infringing the monopoly. Corbeau set up his own postal service in the Liège area, whereby personal collection would be made from the sender's premises and delivery made before noon next day in the same area, although deliveries outside the area were made by putting the items in the ordinary post. Corbeau was prosecuted for infringing the Post Office's monopoly. The Liège court referred questions to the Court concerning the compatibility of the post office monopoly with Articles 81, 82, and 86, whether the monopoly should be modified to comply with Article 86(1), the application of Article 86(2) and whether the post office was in a dominant position. (The part of the judgment concerning Article 86(2) is reproduced later).

Court of Justice

7. With regard to the facts in the main proceedings, the questions referred to the Court must be understood as meaning that the national court is substantially concerned with the question whether Article [86] of the Treaty must be interpreted as meaning that it is contrary to that Article for the legislation of a Member State which confers on a body such as the Régie des Postes the exclusive right to collect, carry and distribute mail to prohibit an economic operator established in that State from offering, under threat of criminal penalties, certain specific services on that market.

8. To reply to that question, as thus reformulated, it should first be pointed out that a body such as the Régie des Postes, which has been granted exclusive rights as regards the collection, carriage and distribution of mail, must be regarded as an undertaking to which the Member State concerned has granted exclusive rights within the meaning of Article [86(1)] of the Treaty.

9. Next it should be recalled that the Court has consistently held that an undertaking having a statutory monopoly over a substantial part of the Common Market may be regarded as having a dominant position within the meaning of Article [82] of the Treaty (see the judgments in Case C-179/90 *Merci Convenzionali Porto di Genova* . . . , paragraph 14 and in Case C-18/88 *RTT* v. *GB-Inno-BM* . . . , paragraph 17).

10. However, Article [82] applies only to anti-competitive conduct engaged in by undertakings on their own initiative, not to measures adopted by States (see the *RTT* v. *GB-Inno-BM* judgment, cited above, paragraph 20).

11. The Court has had occasion to state in this respect that although the mere fact that a Member State has created a dominant position by the grant of exclusive rights is not as such incompatible with Article [82], the Treaty none the less requires the Member States not to adopt or maintain in force any measure which might deprive those provisions of their effectiveness (see the judgment in Case C-260/89 *ERT* . . . , paragraph 35).

12. Thus Article [86(1)] provides that in the case of public undertakings to which Member States grant special or exclusive rights, they are neither to enact nor to maintain in force any measure contrary to the rules contained in the Treaty with regard to competition.

13. That provision must be read in conjunction with Article [86(2)] which provides that undertakings entrusted with the operation of services of general economic interest are to be subject to the rules on competition in so far as the application of such rules does not obstruct the performance, in law or in fact, of the particular tasks assigned to them.

> 14. That latter provision thus permits the Member States to confer on undertakings to which they entrust the operation of services of general economic interest, exclusive rights which may hinder the application of the rules of the Treaty on competition in so far as restrictions on competition, or even the exclusion of all competition, by other economic operators are necessary to ensure the performance of the particular tasks assigned to the undertakings possessed of the exclusive rights.

There was no suggestion in *Corbeau* that the Régie des Postes had acted abusively. The challenge raised by Corbeau's defence to the criminal charges was to the monopoly itself.[89] The Court answered this in paragraphs 7–12 of the judgment. It repeated there (paragraph 11) its usual mantra about the mere grant of exclusive rights not in itself being incompatible with the Treaty but said that Member States are not to adopt or maintain provisions which may deprive the provisions of their effectiveness. It then quoted Article 86(1). It never clearly identified which, if any, features of the Belgian legislation were contrary to Article 86(1) and Article 82.[90] This case did not concern an undertaking accused of acting abusively, the extension of the monopoly into a neighbouring market, a conflict of interest, or the bundling of regulatory functions with entrepreneurial activities. It did however, as Hancher notes,[91] appear to suggest that, in order to ensure the *effet utile* or effectiveness of Articles 86(1) and 82 and, despite the Court's statement to the contrary at paragraph 11, the very existence of national rules conferring a dominant position on an undertaking is unacceptable unless the rights at issue can be justified under Article 86(2) (see paragraphs 13 and 14). In effect, it reversed the burden of proof: exclusive rights are not *prima facie* legal, but *prima facie* illegal unless they are objectively justified or fulfill the Article 86(2) criteria.[92]

Edward and Hoskins argue that it is a question whether the Court chooses to take a 'limited sovereignty' or 'limited competition' approach. Under the limited sovereignty approach, the Member States are free to grant legal monopolies provided that the operation of the monopoly does not have the *necessary* consequence of contravening the competition rules of the Treaty. This is illustrated by *Höfner v. Macroton* and by the post-*Corbeau* case, *La Crespelle* (below). Under the Limited Competition approach, however:[93]

> ...the creation of a legal monopoly must: (a) be justified by a legitimate national objective and (b) satisfy the principle of proportionality, that is, the consequent restriction of competition must not exceed what is necessary in order to attain the objective... The underlying rationale for this approach is that the creation of a legal monopoly will necessarily produce restrictive effects on competition so such monopolies should be permitted only where there is a particular justification for their existence...

[89] It should be noted that since *Corbeau* the postal sector has been liberalized, partly as a result of the judgment in *Corbeau*. See Directive 97/67/EC, [1998] OJ L15/14, Commission Notice on the Application of the Competition Rules to the Postal Sector [1998] OJ C39/2 and Directive 2002/39 [2002] OJ L176/21.

[90] As Jacobs AG pointed out in his Opinion in Cases C-67/96, 115–17/97, and 219/97, *Albany International BV v. Stichting Bedrijfspensioenfonds Textielindustrie* [1999] ECR I-5751, [2000] 4 CMLR 446, para. 417.

[91] See L. Hancher, 'Casenote on *Corbeau*' (1994) 31 *CMLRev* 105, 111.

[92] See J. Faull and A. Nikpay (eds.), *The EC Law of Competition* (2nd edn., Oxford University Press, 2007), para. 6.80.

[93] D. Edward and M. Hoskins 'Art. 90: Deregulation and EC Law. Reflections Arising from the XVI FIDE Conference' (1995) 32 *CMLRev* 157, 164, and 167.

The Limited Competition approach starts from the presumption that the restriction of competition inherent in legal monopolies is illegal. The *onus* is placed squarely on the Member State to prove that the existence of a particular legal monopoly is justified and that the consequent restriction of competition is limited to what is necessary to achieve the relevant objective.

If we accept that legal monopolies by definition hinder free competition since they prevent other undertakings from entering the reserved market, and that Member States may choose to create or maintain such monopolies for reasons such as bare protectionism, the Limited Competition approach would appear to be more in keeping with the purpose and aims of the EC Treaty.

Both these authors and Hancher in the extract below argue that one way of looking at the dilemma about the status of legal monopoly itself is to take the time factor into account. Market conditions change and therefore Member States have an obligation to keep legal monopolies under review.[94]

L. Hancher, 'Casenote on Corbeau' (1994) 31 *CMLRev* 105, 115–16

Before jumping to the conclusion that **all** state measures conferring exclusive rights or creating national monopolies must now be considered as prima facie illegal, an assertion which would conflict with the first sentence of Article [86(1)], one should bear in mind certain aspects of the market for postal services. As the Advocate General had pointed out in his Opinion, this market has been the subject of quite recent development in the sense that demand for 'added-value' services by certain types of consumer, including personal collection, tracing and tracking services has grown rapidly. At the time when the monopoly to provide postal services was conferred on national postal administrations in the majority of the Member States demand for this sort of service simply did not exist. The relevant question was then whether the initial grant of general monopoly rights to the national postal administrations could be legitimately interpreted as covering these new added value services as well as the more traditional basic services. From this perspective, neither the Member State nor the postal monopoly had actively abused a dominant position, for example by illegally extending an existing monopoly into new markets or through the accumulation of additional exclusive rights. The essence of the problem was whether the original monopoly should now be redefined and circumscribed to take account of the changing nature of demand for postal services . . .

In addressing this issue, the Advocate General took the Court's ruling in Case C-18/88, *RTT*, as his point of departure. This case, it will be recalled, dealt with the active extension of one monopoly right into a related market. Advocate General Tesauro argued that the same reasoning should apply to measures which create a monopoly (para. 14)—measures actively extending the scope of the exclusivity are no different from those which institute that exclusivity in the first place. Either way then, the effectiveness of the Treaty rules on competition would be limited. The relevant question was whether the scope of the original monopoly could be said to meet objective justifications given the current nature of the market.

The Advocate General's reasoning has been dealt with at some length because it helps to cast some light on the novelty of the case before the Court in *Corbeau*. The Court was effectively being asked to rule upon the compatibility with Community competition rules of a measure which had conferred an exclusive right in general terms on an undertaking, almost forty years previously to a market situation which had altered fundamentally with the passage of time. The abuse, if any, lay

---

[94] *Ibid.*, at 167–8.

in the failure on the part of the Member State to respond to such changes, by refining the scope of the initial right. Thus inaction could be considered a violation of Article [86(1)]. This was obviously the essence of the second question referred by the national court. If this interpretation is correct, then the first part of the *Corbeau* ruling represents a significant extension of the Court's jurisprudence on the effet utile of the Treaty's competition rules to situations where the development of competition is restricted because the market itself has changed, and not necessarily as a result of any independent action on the part of either the Member State or the statutory monopoly. The first part of the Court's reasoning in *Corbeau* suggests that failure to redefine a right conferring a wide-ranging exclusivity can indeed amount to a breach of Articles [86(1)] and [82], unless there are objective justifications for maintaining a monopoly of this scope. These justifications are to be sought in Article [86(2)].

The Court subsequently retreated from the position it adopted in *Corbeau*. In *La Crespelle* it again held that a Member State contravenes the Treaty only if, in merely exercising the exclusive right granted to it, the undertaking cannot avoid abusing its dominant position:[95] it is not possible automatically to impute the abuse to the existence of the right. In this case, where the exclusive right concerned bovine insemination centres, there was nothing in the grant of exclusive rights which made an abuse (excessive pricing) unavoidable.

Case C-323/93, *Société Civile Agricole du Centre d'Insémination de la Crespelle* v. *Coopérative d'Elevage et d'Insemination Artificielle du Département de la Mayenne* [1994] ECR I-5077

French law conferred on certain bovine insemination centres the exclusive right to provide insemination services over a particular geographical area. It was alleged that the centres charged excessively for their services.

Court of Justice

15. So far as concerns the relevant provisions of the Treaty, Article 10 requires Member States to carry out their Community obligations in good faith. However, the Court has consistently held that that provision cannot be applied independently when the situation concerned is governed by a specific provision of the Treaty, as in the present case (see the judgment in Joined Cases C-78/90 to C-83/90 *Compagnie Commerciale de l'Ouest and Others* [1992] ECR I-1847, paragraph 19). The question must therefore be considered in the light of Articles [86(1)] and [82] of the Treaty.

16. Article [86(1)] of the Treaty provides that, in the case of public undertakings and undertakings to which Member States grant special or exclusive rights, Member States may neither enact nor maintain in force any measure contrary to the rules contained in the Treaty, in particular to those rules provided for in Article [12] and Articles [81] to [89].

17. In this case, by making the operation of the insemination centres subject to authorization and providing that each centre should have the exclusive rights to serve a defined area,

95 See also Case C-387/93, *Banchero* [1995] ECR I-4663.

the national legislation granted those centres exclusive rights. By thus establishing, in favour of those undertakings, a contiguous series of monopolies territorially limited but together covering the entire territory of a Member State, those national provisions create a dominant position, within the meaning of Article [82] of the Treaty, in a substantial part of the common market.

18. The mere creation of such a dominant position by the granting of an exclusive right within the meaning of Article [86(1)] is not as such incompatible with Article [82] of the Treaty. A Member State contravenes the prohibitions contained in those two provisions only if, in merely exercising the exclusive right granted to it, the undertaking in question cannot avoid abusing its dominant position (see the judgments in Case C-41/90 *Höfner and Elser*..., paragraph 29, and most recently, in Case C-179/90 *Merci Convenzionali Porto di Genova*..., paragraph 17).

19. The alleged abuse in the present case consists in the charging of exorbitant prices by the insemination centres.

20. The question to be examined is therefore whether such a practice constituting the alleged abuse is the direct consequence of the national Law. It should be noted in this regard that the Law merely allows insemination centres to require breeders who request the centres to provide them with semen from other production centres to pay the additional costs entailed by that choice.

21. Although it leaves to the insemination centres the task of calculating those costs, such a provision does not lead the centres to charge disproportionate costs and thereby abuse their dominant position.

22. The answer to this part of the question must therefore be that Articles [86(1)] and [82] of the Treaty do not preclude a Member State from granting to approved bovine insemination centres certain exclusive rights within the defined area.

The same approach can be seen in *Corsica Ferries*,[96] where the Court held that the grant of the exclusive right to offer compulsory piloting services in a port was not in itself an infringement of Article 86(1) but the approval of the discriminatory tariffs, which were contrary to Article 82(c), *was* an infringement.

The Court has continued to state the principle that the creation of a dominant position through the grant of exclusive rights within Article 86(1) is not itself incompatible with Article 82, but will become so if the rights make an abuse unavoidable, or if they create a situation whereby the undertaking, merely by exercising its rights, is led to commit an abuse.[97] Where this is the position, it can only be justified under Article 86(2).[98]

---

[96] Case C-18/93, *Corsica Ferries Italia Srl* v. *Corpo dei Piloti del Porto di Genova* [1994] ECR I-1783.

[97] Case C-55/96, *Job Centre Coop. arl* [1997] ECR I-7119, [1998] 4 CMLR 708; Case C-260/89, *Elliniki Radiophonia Tileorasi (ERT)* v. *DEP* [1991] ECR I-2925, [1998] 4 CMLR 737; Case C-163/96, *Silvano Raso* [1998] ECR I-533, [1998] 4 CMLR 737; Case C-266/96, *Corsica Ferries France SA* v. *Gruppo Artichi Ormeggiatori del Porto di Genovo Coop and Others* [1998] ECR I-3949, [1998] 5 CMLR 402; Case C-67/96, *Albany International BV* v. *Stichting Bedrijfspensioenfonds Textielindustrie* [1999] ECR I-5751, [2000] 4 CMLR 446; Cases C-147–8/97, *Deutsche Post AG* v. *Gesellschaft für Zahlungssysteme mbH (GZS) and Citicorp Kartenservice GmbH* [2000] ECR I-825, [2000] 4 CMLR 838; Case C-209/98, *Entreprenørforeningens Affalds (FFAD)* v. *Københavns Kommune* [2000] ECR-3743, [2001] 2 CMLR 936; Cases C-180–4/98, *Pavlov* v. *Stichting Pensioenfonds Medische Specialisten* [2000] ECR I-6451, [2001] 4 CMLR 30; Case C-475/99, *Ambulanz Glöckner* v. *Landkreis Südwestpfalz* [2001] ECR I-8089, [2002] 4 CMLR 726.

[98] See L. Gyselen 'Case note on *Albany, Brentjens'* and *Drijvende Bokken*' (2000) 37 *CML Rev* 425 and *infra* 652.

Albany concerned the Dutch regime of compulsory affiliation to sectoral pension funds:

Case C-67/96, *Albany International BV* v. *Stichting Bedrijfspensioenfonds Textielindustrie* [1999] ECR I-5751, [2000] 4 CMLR 446

Under Dutch law pension provision included a system whereby, at the request of the representatives of employers and employees in a particular sector of the economy, affiliation to a sectoral pension fund was made compulsory for all undertakings in that sector. This was to provide a pension supplementary to the basic State pension. Various undertakings brought proceedings in the Dutch courts challenging the compulsory affiliation regime on the grounds that they provided equivalent supplementary pension schemes themselves. The Dutch courts referred to the Court of Justice the question, *inter alia*, whether the exclusive rights conferred on the sectoral pension funds infringed the Treaty.[99]

Court of Justice

90. It must be observed at the outset that the decision of the public authorities to make affiliation to a sectoral pension fund compulsory, as in this case, necessarily implies granting to that fund an exclusive right to collect and administer the contributions paid with a view to accruing pension rights. Such a fund must therefore be regarded as an undertaking to which exclusive rights have been granted by the public authorities, of the kind referred to in Article [86(1)] of the Treaty.

91. Next, it should be noted that according to settled case-law an undertaking which has a legal monopoly in a substantial part of the common market may be regarded as occupying a dominant position within the meaning of Article [82] of the Treaty (see Case C-179/90 *Merci Convenzional Porto di Genova* [1991] ECR I-5889, paragraph 14, and Case C-18/88 *GB-Inno-BM* [1991] ECR I-5941, paragraph 17).

92. A sectoral pension fund of the kind at issue in the main proceedings, which has an exclusive right to manage a supplementary pension scheme in an industrial sector in a Member State and, therefore, in a substantial part of the common market, may therefore be regarded as occupying a dominant position within the meaning of Article [82] of the Treaty.

93. It must not be forgotten, however, that merely creating a dominant position by granting exclusive rights within the meaning of Article [86(1)] of the Treaty is not in itself incompatible with Article [82] of the Treaty. A Member State is in breach of the prohibitions contained in those two provisions only if the undertaking in question, merely by exercising the exclusive rights granted to it, is led to abuse its dominant position or when such rights are liable to create a situation in which that undertaking is led to commit such abuses (*Höfner and Elser*, cited above, paragraph 29; Case C-260/89 *ERT* [1991] ECR I-2925, paragraph 37; *Merci Convenzionali Porto di Genova*, cited above, paragraphs 16 and 17; Case C-323/93 *Centre d'Insémination de la Crespelle* . . . , paragraph 18; and Case C-163/96 *Raso and Others* . . . , paragraph 27).

94. Albany contends in that connection that the system of compulsory affiliation to the supplementary pension scheme managed by the Fund is contrary to the combined provisions of Articles

---

[99] See also Cases C-115–17/97, *Brentjens' Handelsonderneming BV* v. *Stichting Bedrijfspensioenfonds voor de Handel in Bouwmaterialen* [1999] ECR I-6025, [2000] 4 CMLR 566 and Case C-219/97, *Maatschappij Drijvende Bokken BV* v. *Stichting Pensioenfonds voor de Vervoer-en Havenbedrijven* [1999] ECR I-6121, [2000] 4 CMLR 599, which raised the same issue. The cases also raised questions about the application of the Treaty rules to collective agreements between employers and employees. For these aspects, see *supra* Chap. 3.

[82] and [86] of the Treaty. The pension benefits available from the Fund do not, or no longer, match the needs of the undertakings. The benefits are too low, are not linked to wages and, consequently, are generally inadequate. Employers have therefore to make other pension arrangements. The system of compulsory affiliation deprives those employers of any opportunity of arranging for comprehensive pension cover from an insurance company. Pension arrangements spread over a number of insurers would increase administrative costs and reduce efficiency.

95. It should be remembered that, in *Höfner and Elser*, cited above, paragraph 34, the Court held that a Member State which conferred on a public employment agency an exclusive right of recruitment was in breach of Article [86(1)] of the Treaty where it created a situation in which that office could not avoid infringing Article [82] of the Treaty, in particular because it was manifestly incapable of satisfying the demand prevailing on the market for such activities.

96. In the present case, it is important to note that the supplementary pension scheme offered by the Fund is based on the present norm in the Netherlands, namely that every worker who has paid contributions to that scheme for the maximum period of affiliation receives a pension, including the State pension under the AOW, equal to 70 per cent of his final salary.

97. Doubtless, some undertakings in the sector might wish to provide their workers with a pension scheme superior to the one offered by the Fund. However, the fact that such undertakings are unable to entrust the management of such a pension scheme to a single insurer and the resulting restriction of competition derive directly from the exclusive right conferred on the sectoral pension fund.

98. It is therefore necessary to consider whether, as contended by the Fund, the Netherlands Government and the Commission, the exclusive right of the sectoral pension fund to manage supplementary pensions in a given sector and the resultant restriction of competition may be justified under Article [86(2)] of the Treaty as a measure necessary for the performance of a particular social task of general interest with which that fund has been charged.

The Court then went on to consider whether the exclusive right and the restriction of competition could indeed be justified under Article 86(2). This part of the judgment is reproduced below.[100]

It can be seen from the above extract that the Court said once again that the granting of exclusive rights is not contrary to the Treaty unless merely by exercising the right the undertaking is led to commit an abuse (paragraph 93) or unless an abuse is unavoidable (paragraph 95). However, the Court did not proceed to consider whether the undertaking here *was* put in such a position, but instead turned to see whether the justification under Article 86(2) applied.[101]

The *Deutsche Post* case concerned the German post office, Deutsche Post (a State monopoly with the exclusive right to collect, carry, and deliver certain categories of mail in Germany), and the obligations flowing from the Universal Postal Convention (UPC).

---

[100] See *infra* 662.

[101] See L. Gyselen, 'Case note on *Albany, Brentjens'* and *Drijvende Bokken*' (2000) 37 *CMLRev* 425 and *infra* 662. In other cases too the Court has expressly left open the question of the position brought about by the exclusive right before considering whether or not Article 86(2) applied: see for example Case C-209/98, *Entreprenørforeningens Affalds (FFAD) v. Københavns Kommune* [2000] ECR-3743, [2001] 2 CMLR 936.

Cases C-147–8/97, *Deutsche Post AG* v. *Gesellschaft für Zahlungssysteme mbH (GZS) and Citicorp Kartenservice GmbH* [2000] ECR I-825, [2000] 4 CMLR 838

Under the Universal Postal Convention 1989 the contracting states are obliged to forward and deliver international mail addressed to persons resident in their country which is passed to them by the postal services of other contracting parties. The Convention provides for the receiving state to charge a fixed fee for the costs of delivering the mail (terminal dues). The Convention also provides, *inter alia*, that where senders resident in country A cause mail addressed to addressees in country A to be posted in bulk in country B, country A is entitled to either charge its full internal rate for the items or to return them to their origin (Article 25). Various credit-card companies based in Germany electronically transmitted the data for their customers' bills to processing centres outside Germany which prepared the German customers' bills and posted them back to Germany. In one case this resulted in the bills being posted in Denmark, where the rate for international mail is lower than the internal rate in Germany. Deutsche Post was merely paid the terminal dues. It demanded the full internal rate. The credit companies refused to pay. In the course of the subsequent litigation the German courts referred to the Court questions about whether it was contrary to Article 86 and Article 82 (and Article 49, which was also relevant since the situation involved the freedom to provide services) for Deutsche Post to exercise its rights under Article 25 of the Convention to charge the internal postage rate.

Court of Justice

36. ... the national court is to be understood in the first three questions as essentially asking whether it is contrary to Article [86] of the Treaty, read in conjunction with Articles [82] and [49] thereof, for a body such as Deutsche Post to exercise the right provided for by Article 25(3) of the UPC to charge, in the cases referred to in the second sentence of Article 25(1) and Article 25(2), internal postage on items of mail posted in large quantities with the postal services of a Member State other than the Member State to which that body belongs.

37. To reply to that question, as reformulated, it should first be noted that a body such as Deutsche Post, which has been granted exclusive rights as regards the collection, carriage and delivery of mail, must be regarded as an undertaking to which the Member State concerned has granted exclusive rights within the meaning of Article [86(1)] of the Treaty (Case C-320/91 *Corbeau* ..., paragraph 8).

38. Also, it is settled case-law that an undertaking having a statutory monopoly over a substantial part of the common market may be regarded as holding a dominant position within the meaning of Article [82] of the Treaty (see Case C-179/90 *Merci Convenzionali Porto di Genova* v. *Siderurgica Gabrielli* ..., paragraph 14, Case C-18/88 *RTT* v. *GB-Inno-BM* ..., paragraph 17, and *Corbeau*, cited above, paragraph 9).

39. The Court has had occasion to state in this respect that although the mere fact that a Member State has created a dominant position by the grant of exclusive rights is not as such incompatible with Article [82], the Treaty none the less requires the Member States not to adopt or maintain in force any measure which might deprive that provision of its effectiveness (see Case C-260/89 *ERT* [1991] ECR I-2925, paragraph 35, and *Corbeau*, cited above, paragraph 11).

40. Article [86(1)] of the Treaty thus provides that in the case of undertakings to which Member States grant special or exclusive rights, they are neither to enact nor to maintain in force any measure contrary, in particular, to the rules contained in the Treaty with regard to competition (see *Corbeau*, paragraph 12).

41. That provision must be read in conjunction with Article [86(2)] which provides that undertakings entrusted with the operation of services of general economic interest are to be subject to

the rules contained in the Treaty in so far as the application of such rules does not obstruct the performance, in law or in fact, of the particular tasks assigned to them.

42. A final point to note is that the UPC proceeds on the basis of a market in letter-post where the postal services of the various Contracting States of the Universal Postal Union are not in competition.

43. In that context, the UPC is designed to establish rules ensuring that international items of mail addressed to residents of a Contracting State and passed on by the postal services of other Contracting States are forwarded and delivered. One of the fundamental principles of the UPC, set out in Article 1 thereof, is the obligation of the postal administration of the Contracting State to which international mail is sent to forward and deliver it to addressees resident in its territory using the most rapid means of its letter post. In that regard, the States which have adopted the Convention of the Universal Postal Union constitute a single postal territory, in which the freedom of transit of reciprocal international mail is in principle guaranteed.

44. For the postal services of the Member States, performance of the obligations flowing from the UPC is thus in itself a service of general economic interest within the meaning of Article [86(2)] of the Treaty.

45. In the present case, German legislation assigns the operation of that service to Deutsche Post.

46. As has been noted in paragraph 5 of this judgment, postal services initially delivered international mail without being paid for that task. However, when it became apparent that the flows of postal traffic between two Contracting States frequently did not balance out, so that the postal services of the various Contracting States had to process quantities of international mail which differed greatly, specific provisions were laid down in that regard, one of which is Article 25 of the UPC.

47. Under Article 25(3) of the UPC, the postal services of the Contracting States may in particular, in the cases referred to in Article 25(1) and (2), charge postage on items of mail at their internal rates.

48. The grant to a body such as Deutsche Post of the right to treat international items of mail as internal post in such cases creates a situation where that body may be led, to the detriment of users of postal services, to abuse its dominant position resulting from the exclusive right granted to it to forward and deliver those items to the relevant addressees.

49. It is accordingly necessary to examine the extent to which exercise of such a right is necessary to enable a body of that kind to perform its task of general interest pursuant to the obligations flowing from the UPC and, in particular, to operate under economically acceptable conditions.

50. If a body such as Deutsche Post were obliged to forward and deliver to addressees resident in Germany mail posted in large quantities by senders resident in Germany using postal services of other Member States, without any provision allowing it to be financially compensated for all the costs occasioned by that obligation, the performance, in economically balanced conditions, of that task of general interest would be jeopardised.

51. The postal services of a Member State cannot simultaneously bear the costs entailed in the performance of the service of general economic interest of forwarding and delivering international items of mail, which is their responsibility by virtue of the UPC, and the loss of income resulting from the fact that bulk mailings are no longer posted with the postal services of the Member State in which the addressees are resident but with those of other Member States.

52. In such a case, it must be regarded as justified, for the purposes of the performance, in economically balanced conditions, of the task of general interest entrusted to Deutsche Post by the UPC, to treat cross-border mail as internal mail and, consequently, to charge internal postage.

. . .

54. Article [86(2)] of the Treaty therefore justifies, in the absence of an agreement between the postal services of the Member States concerned fixing terminal dues in relation to the actual costs of processing and delivering incoming trans-border mail, the grant by a Member State to its postal services of the statutory right to charge internal postage on items of mail where senders resident in that State post items, or cause them to be posted, in large quantities with the postal services of another Member State in order to send them to the first Member State.

. . .

> 56. On the other hand, in so far as part of the forwarding and delivery costs is offset by terminal dues paid by the postal services of other Member States, it is not necessary, in order for a body such as Deutsche Post to fulfil the obligations flowing from the UPC, that postage be charged at the full internal rate on items posted in large quantities with those services.
>
> 57. It is to be remembered that a body such as Deutsche Post which has a statutory monopoly over a substantial part of the common market may be regarded as holding a dominant position within the meaning of Article [82] of the Treaty.
>
> 58. Thus, the exercise by such a body of the right to demand the full amount of the internal postage, where the costs relating to the forwarding and delivery of mail posted in large quantities with the postal services of a Member State other than the State in which both the senders and the addressees of that mail are resident are not offset by the terminal dues paid by those services, may be regarded as an abuse of a dominant position within the meaning of Article [82] of the Treaty.
>
> 59. In order to prevent a body such as Deutsche Post from exercising its right, provided for by Article 25(3) of the UPC, to return items of mail to origin, the senders of those items have no choice but to pay the full amount of the internal postage.
>
> 60. As the Court has stated in relation to a refusal to sell on the part of an undertaking holding a dominant position within the meaning of Article [82] of the Treaty, such action would be inconsistent with the objective laid down by Article [3(1)(g)] of the EC Treaty] . . . , as explained in Article [82], in particular in subparagraphs (b) and (c) of its second paragraph (Case 27/76 *United Brands* v. *Commission* [1978] ECR 207, paragraph 183).

In this judgment the Court said that Deutsche Post had been granted exclusive rights within the meaning of Article 86(1), and that Article 86(1) had to be read in conjunction with Article 86(2). In saying this (paragraphs 40–1), the Court repeated the wording in paragraphs 12–13 of the *Corbeau* judgment. The performance of the obligations of the UPC was a service of general economic interest within the meaning of Article 86(2) (paragraph 44). The Court held that granting Deutsche Post the right under the UPC to treat international mail as internal mail *did* create a situation where 'it may be led, to the detriment of users of postal services, to abuse its dominant position' (paragraph 48). The Court therefore said it must examine whether the exercise of the right was necessary to perform its task of general interest 'under economically acceptable conditions' (paragraph 49). It concluded that it *was* necessary, because of the financial loss Deutsche Post would otherwise incur.[102] However, it would be an abuse of a dominant position if Deutsche Post were to charge the full internal postage without offsetting the terminal dues against the money demanded from the senders.

A similar approach to the application of Article 86(1) was taken in *Ambulanz Glöckner*.

Case C-475/99, *Ambulanz Glöckner* v. *Landkreis Südwestpfalz* [2001] ECR I-8089, [2002] 4 CMLR 726

The provision of the public ambulance service in Germany is governed by legislation referred to in the judgment below as the 'RettDG 1991'. This distinguishes between 'emergency transport' and 'patient transport' (non-emergency). Emergency transport in the *Land* of Rheinland-Pfalz was

---

[102] See *infra* 664.

entrusted to two medical aid organizations which also ran a non-emergency service. Ambulanz Glöckner had previously also provided a non-emergency service. However, when it applied to the relevant public authority for a renewal of its permit, the two medical aid organizations objected, claiming that competition on the non-emergency market would affect their ability to provide the emergency service. As a result the public authority refused Ambulanz Glöckner a permit.

Court of Justice

39. It must be borne in mind that the mere creation of a dominant position through the grant of special or exclusive rights within the meaning of Article [86(1)] of the Treaty is not in itself incompatible with Article [82] of the Treaty. A Member State will be in breach of the prohibitions laid down by those two provisions only if the undertaking in question, merely by exercising the special or exclusive rights conferred upon it, is led to abuse its dominant position or where such rights are liable to create a situation in which that undertaking is led to commit such abuses (see *Pavlov*, cited above, paragraph 127).

40. It is settled case-law that an abuse within the meaning of Article [82] of the Treaty is committed where, without any objective necessity, an undertaking holding a dominant position on a particular market reserves to itself an ancillary activity which could be carried out by an other undertaking as part of its activities on a neighbouring but separate market, with the possibility of eliminating all competition from that undertaking (judgment in Case C-18/88 *GB-INNO-BM* [1991] ECR I-5941, paragraph 18). Where the extension of the dominant position of an undertaking to which the State has granted special or exclusive rights results from a State measure, such a measure constitutes an infringement of Article 90 in conjunction with Article 86 of the Treaty (*GB-INNO-BM*, paragraph 21, and Case C-203/96 *Dusseldorp and Others* [1998] ECR I-4075, paragraph 61).

41. In the present case, the argument put forward by Ambulanz Glöckner is indeed that it is excluded from the market for patient transport as a result of the application of Paragraph 18(3) of the RettDG 1991, which, in its submission, enables the medical aid organisations, acting in concertation with the public authorities, to restrict access to that market.

42. The Commission also contends that the extension of the dominant position on the urgent transport market to the related, but separate, market for patient transport is due to the changes made in the federal legislation governing the latter type of transport, then in the legislation of the Land of Rheinland-Pfalz and, in particular, to the adoption of Paragraph 18(3) of the RettDG 1991. Such a restriction of competition, it contends, constitutes a breach of Article [86] of the Treaty in conjunction with Article [82] thereof.

43. As far as those arguments are concerned, it must be concluded that, in enacting Paragraph 18(3) of the RettDG 1991, the application of which involves prior consultation of the medical aid organisations in respect of any application for authorisation to provide non-emergency patient transport services submitted by an independent operator, the legislature of the Land of Rheinland-Pfalz gave an advantage to those organisations, which already had an exclusive right on the urgent transport market, by also allowing them to provide such services exclusively. The application of Paragraph 18(3) of the RettDG 1991 therefore has the effect of limiting markets . . . to the prejudice of consumers within the meaning of Article [82(b)] of the Treaty, by reserving to those medical aid organisations an ancillary transport activity which could be carried on by independent operators.

The Court then went on to consider whether Article 86(2) applied.[103]

---

[103] *Infra* 665.

(iii) Summary of the Measures which Make Abuse Unavoidable or Create a Situation in which the Undertaking is Led to Abuse its Dominant Position

It is not possible to neatly categorize the types of measure whose results infringe Article 86(1). Furthermore, it must be stressed that even if it were, the categories would not be closed. However, looking at the case law, one can identify general themes.

First, inability to meet demand. It is clear from *Höfner v. Macroton*[104] that Article 86(1) is infringed where a statutory monopoly is set up in such a way that it is incapable of meeting the demand in the reserved sector. This was also the case in *Job Centre Coop. arl.*[105] *Merci Convenzionali* showed that Article 86(1) is infringed where the monopolist is enabled to behave inefficiently, exploit customers, and not modernize.[106] In *Amblanz Glöckner* the Advocate General discussed the possible causes for inefficiency or inability to meet demand. He considered that a Member State is only liable under Article 86(1) if the fault is in the system it has set up, and not where the only reason that an organization is 'manifestly not able to satisfy demand' is inefficient management.[107] The Court did not address this point in its judgment. There are a number of cases in the postal[108] and telecommunications[109] sectors which were the subject of Article 86(3) decisions[110] because of an inability to meet demand. The abuses at issue under this head are a violation of Article 82(b), 'limiting production, markets or technical development to the prejudice of consumers'.

Secondly, there are a number of cases where the cumulation of rights conferred on an undertaking create a conflict of interest. As seen above[111] this was a problem in *RTT*[112] and *ERT*[113] where a 'regulatory' function was given to the monopoly, enabling it to disadvantage competitors in a downstream market. In *Silvano Raso*[114] a dockers' company was given a monopoly over the supply of temporary labour to authorized port operators although it competed with them in the market for port services. The Court said that the company would have 'a conflict of interest':[115]

29. That is because merely exercising its monopoly will enable it to distort in its favour the equal conditions of competition between the various operators on the market in dock-work services (Case C-260/89, *ERT* v. *DRP* . . . and Case C-18/88, *GB-INNO-BM*).

30. The result is that the company in question is led to abuse its monopoly by imposing on its competitors in the dock-work market unduly high costs for the supply of labour or by supplying them with labour less suited to the work to be done.

---

[104] *Supra* 630.

[105] Case C-55/96, [1997] ECR I-7119, [1998] 4 CMLR 708.

[106] *Supra* 635.

[107] Case C-475/99, *Ambulanz Glöckner v. Landkreis Südwestpfalz* [2001] ECR I-8089, [2002] 4 CMLR 726, Opinion of Jacobs AG, para. 148.

[108] See *Dutch Express Delivery Services* [1994] OJ L10/47; *Spanish Express Courier Services* [1990] OJ L233/19.

[109] See *Italian GSM* [1995] OJ L280/49; *Spanish GSM* [1997] OJ L79/19.

[110] See *infra* 668.

[111] *Supra* 636 ff.

[112] Case C-18/88, *RTT v. GB-INNO-BM SA* [1991] ECR I-5973.

[113] Case C-260/89, *Elliniki Radiophonia Tileorasi (ERT) v. DEP* [1991] ECR I-2925.

[114] Case C-163/96, *Silvano Raso* [1998] ECR I-533, [1998] 4 CMLR 737.

[115] *Ibid.*, para. 28.

The Court did not appear to find the dual role of the pension funds in *Albany* (as both managers of the scheme and as the authority with power to grant exemptions whereby companies could be allowed to insure with other undertakings) to constitute a conflict of interest. The Court held the situation justified because '[e]xercise of that power of exemption involves an evaluation of complex data relating to the pension schemes involved and the financial equilibrium of the fund, which necessarily implies a wide margin of appreciation'.[116] In that case, however, the Court concentrated on the application of Article 86(2) rather than Article 86(1) and, as we noted above,[117] passed rather quickly over the issue of Article 86(1) altogether. It is therefore unclear whether there was no infringement of Article 86(1) or whether the Court was applying Article 86(2) at this point.

Thirdly, there are cases where the problem is that the undertaking with exclusive rights is enabled to extend its monopoly into neighbouring markets. *RTT* can also be classified under this head, as can *ERT*. The postal and telecommunication cases mentioned above[118] are likewise examples of this. In *Ambulanz Glöckner* the Court said that the fact that the medical aid organizations providing emergency transport were consulted by the authorities about the permit applications of other undertakings wishing to operate in the non-emergency market gave the aid organizations an advantage in the latter. The 'essential facilities' case, *Port of Rødby*,[119] concerned an infringement of Article 86(1) as the port authority was able to refuse access to the port it controlled, thus eliminating competition from a competitor ferry company.

Fourthly, undertakings with exclusive rights may be enabled to commit pricing abuses. Indeed, price discrimination has featured in a number of cases concerning the conduct of undertakings given control over transport infrastructures.[120] *GT-Link*, where the port authority was guilty of price discrimination in waiving harbour duties in respect of its own ferry services and those of its partners but charging them to its competitors on the ferry market, is also a case where there was a cumulation of rights and where the undertaking was extending its monopoly into a downstream market.[121]

Fifthly, the undertaking may refuse to supply. This may be in a case involving 'essential facilities', as in *Port of Rødby*. The refusal to deliver incoming cross-border mail in *Deutsche Post*[122] unless extra payments were made was treated as a refusal to supply.

However, there are some cases in which the nature of the abusive conduct was not altogether clear. This is true, for instance, of *Albany*, where the Court concentrated on the application of Article 86(2). The most striking case, however, is *Corbeau*, where as was seen above[123] the Court

---

[116] Case C-67/96, *Albany International BV v. Stichting Bedrijfspensioenfonds Textielindustrie* [1999] ECR I-5751, [2000] 4 CMLR 446, para. 119. Advocate General Jacobs was not so sanguine and considered that Article 86(1) was infringed, see paras. 441–68 of the Opinion.

[117] *Supra* 645.

[118] *Supra* n. 108 and 109.

[119] [1994] OJ L 55/52, [1994] 5 CMLR 457, see *supra* Chap. 7, 541.

[120] See, e.g., Case C-266/96, *Corsica Ferries France SA v. Gruppo Antichi Ormeggiatori del Porto di Genova* [1998] ECR I-3949, [1998] 5 CMLR 402 (discussed *infra* 660); Case C-163/99, *Portugal v. Commission* [2002] ECR I-2613, [2002] 4 CMLR 1319 (concerning the landing fees at Portugese airports, and discussed *supra* Chap. 7, 596).

[121] Case C-242/95, *GT-Link A/S v. Danske Staatsbaner (DSB)* [1997] ECR I-4449, [1997] 5 CMLR 601. In this case the Court in effect imposed on undertakings in this position, an obligation to maintain a transparent accounting system demonstrating that they did not favour their own operations. Otherwise they will not be able to avoid a finding of abuse.

[122] Cases C-147–8/97, *Deutsche Post AG v. Gesellschaft für Zahlungssysteme mbH (GZS) and Citicorp Kartenservice GmbH* [2000] ECR I-825, [2000] 4 CMLR 838. See *supra* 646 *and infra* 664.

[123] *Supra* 646.

appeared to consider that a monopoly which was too wide infringed Article 86(1) for that reason alone and did not identify any abusive conduct.

D. ARTICLE 86(2)

(i) The Purpose of Article 86(2)

Article 86(2) provides a limited derogation from the rules of the Treaty in order to deal with the activities of undertakings entrusted by the State with certain tasks. It provides that the Treaty rules shall apply to two sorts of undertaking—revenue-producing monopolies and those entrusted with services of general economic interest—only in so far as that does not obstruct the performance of their tasks. It is subject to the proviso that the exception should not affect trade to an extent contrary to the interests of the Community. Unlike Article 86(1), Article 86(2) is addressed to undertakings themselves and not to Member States, although Member States may rely on Article 86(2)[124] and, as we have seen above, the two provisions may be applied together. As with Article 86(1), the competition rules are singled out for special mention and Article 86(2) is particularly important in relation to the application of Article 82, to which no other exemption or derogation applies.[125] Article 86(2) is therefore the only defence to an Article 82 abuse.

The Treaty does not say in Article 86(2) what value is to be accorded to services of general economic interest and in particular does not say that 'universal service' should be protected or promoted.[126] In the past the Court tended to construe the provision narrowly (as with other derogations from the Treaty) and so preserve the widest possible application of the competition rules.[127] Nevertheless, from the case of *Corbeau* in 1993 onwards, the Court has been more willing to accept that providers of public services may need to be protected from the full rigours of competition and has become more flexible in the way in which it applies the criteria in Article 86(2).

(ii) Undertakings having the Character of a Revenue Producing Monopoly

This is a reference to undertakings which exploit their exclusive rights to raise revenue for the State. They may constitute commercial monopolies and so be subject to the rules laid down in Article 31 of the EC Treaty. Article 31 appears among the free movement provisions, but the Court has said that it aims to eliminate distortions in competition in the common market as well as discrimination against the products and trade of other Member States.[128]

---

[124] See, e.g., Case C-203/96, *Chemische Afvalstoffen Dusseldorp BV v. Minister van Volkshuisvesting, Ruimtelijke Ordening en Milieubeheer* [1998] ECR I-4075, [1998] 3 CMLR 873.

[125] Unlike Article 81, which contains an exception in Article 81(3) and the free movement provisions which are subject to the mandatory requirements doctrine and to the exceptions in Articles 30, 39(3), 45, and 46.

[126] See M. Ross, 'Art. 16 EC and Services of General Interest: From Derogation to Obligation?' (2000) 25 *ELRev* 22, 24. 'Universal service' is discussed *supra* 622.

[127] See Case 127/73, *BRT v. SABAM* [1974] ECR 313, [1974] 2 CMLR 238.

[128] For a discussion of Article 31 see J. Faull and A. Nikpay, *The EC Law of Competition* (2nd edn., Oxford University Press, 2007), 6.106–6.121.

(iii) Undertakings Entrusted with the Operation of Services of General Economic Interest

a. 'Undertakings Entrusted With ...'

'Undertaking' has the meaning previously discussed.[129] The legal status of the undertaking in national law is immaterial. It can be a public or private undertaking, but the important thing is that the State has assigned it certain tasks by a positive act conferring on it certain functions or by granting it a concession. Merely tolerating, approving, or endorsing its activities is insufficient. So according to the Commission the Member States' approval of the Eurocheque system did not mean that Article 86(2) applied to the banks concerned,[130] and an authors' rights society was not within the provision merely because it was subject to obligations imposed on all monopolies by national law.[131] In *Dusseldorp* the Advocate General said that an undertaking is 'entrusted with' a service where 'certain obligations are imposed on it by the State in the general economic interest'.[132]

b. Operation of Services of General Economic Interest

Not surprisingly, the Court has held that 'services of general economic interest' is a Community concept, and must be uniformly applied by the Member States.[133] The word 'services' is construed to cover the widest spectrum of activities and is not limited to the meaning of the term as used in Title III, Chapter 3, of the Treaty on free movement. 'Services of general economic interest' denotes activities that need to be carried out in the public interest. As the Advocate General said in *Dusseldorp*:[134]

The reason for the assignment of particular tasks to undertakings is often that the tasks need to be undertaken in the public interest but might not be undertaken, usually for economic reasons, if the service were to be left to the private sector.

In the *Telecommunications Equipment* case the Court explained that Article 86(2) reconciles the interests of Member States and Community:[135]

In allowing derogations to be made from the general rules of the Treaty in certain circumstances, that provision seeks to reconcile the Member States' interest in using certain undertakings, in particular in the public sector, as an instrument of economic or fiscal policy with the Community's interest in ensuring compliance with the rules on competition and the preservation of the unity of the common market.

---

[129] See *supra* 617 and Chaps. 3 and 5.

[130] *Uniform Eurocheques* [1985] OJ L35/43, [1985] 3 CMLR 434.

[131] *GEMA* [1971] OJ L134/15.

[132] Opinion of Jacobs AG, para. 103, in Case C-203/96, *Chemische Afvalstoffen Dusseldorp BV v. Minister van Volkshuisvesting, Ruimtelijke Ordening en Milieubeheer* [1998] ECR I-4075, [1998] 3 CMLR 873.

[133] Case 10/71, *Ministère Public of Luxembourg v. Muller* [1971] ECR 723, paras. 14–15. Faull and Nikpay n. 92 *supra* (J. L. Buenida Sierra), 6.146, says that the concept should be understood as a maximum standard beyond which the Member States cannot go.

[134] Opinion of Jacobs AG in Case C-203/96, *Chemische Afvalstoffen Dusseldorp BV v. Minister van Volkshuisvesting, Ruimtelijke Ordening en Milieubeheer* [1998] ECR I-4075, [1998] 3 CMLR 873, para. 105.

[135] Case C-202/88, *France v. Commission* [1991] ECR I-1223 (the *Telecommunications Equipment* case), para. 12; see also Case C-157/94, *Commission v. Netherlands (Re Electricity Imports)* [1997] ECR I-5699, para. 39.

Further, this passage refers to undertakings which are used as instruments of economic or fiscal policy. In *Albany International* the Court applied the same principle to social policy.[136] The most obvious candidates for recognition as services of general economic interest on this basis are the utilities, as the Commission stated in its *XXth Report on Competition Policy*.[137] The definition of services of general economic interest', and of the 'universal service' which they often involve, is given above.[138] The Court has accepted as services of general economic interest the administration of major waterways;[139] the operation of non-economically viable air routes;[140] the operation of the electricity supply network;[141] the operation of the basic, as distinct from extra 'added-value', postal service;[142] mooring services in ports;[143] the treatment of waste;[144] sectoral supplementary pension funds;[145] the performance of obligations flowing from the Universal Postal Convention;[146] and the provision of emergency ambulance services.[147] It will be seen from this list that the Court has expanded the application of the concept of services of general economic interest way beyond the basic utilities. It did not, however, accept that commercial port operations are services of general economic interest[148] and it has sometimes left open the status of the services provided, and said that even if they were of general economic interest the other criteria in Article 86(2) were not fulfilled.[149] Extracts from the judgments in the leading cases on what amounts to a service of general economic interest are set out in the section below as they usually deal also with the question of whether non-compliance with the Treaty rules is essential to the fulfilment of the entrusted tasks.

c. Obstruct the Performance of the Particular Tasks Assigned to Them

Even if an activity is accepted as a service of general economic interest it still has to be shown that compliance with the Treaty rules would 'obstruct the performance' of the particular tasks assigned to the undertaking. As Article 86(2) is a derogation from the normal rules it is for those claiming its benefit to show that its terms are satisfied.

---

[136] Case C-67/96, *Albany International BV v. Stichting Bedrijfspensioenfonds Textielindustrie* [1999] ECR I-5751, [2000] 4 CMLR 446, paras. 103–5.

[137] (Commission, 1990), Introduction, 12.

[138] *Supra* 621.

[139] Case 10/71, *Ministère Public of Luxembourg v. Muller* [1971] ECR 723.

[140] Case 66/86, *Ahmed Saeed Flugreisen and Silver Line Reiseburo GmbH v. Zentrale zur Bёkampfung Unlauteren Wettwerbs eV* [1989] ECR 803, [1990] 4 CMLR 102.

[141] Case C-393/92, *Gemeente Almelo* [1994] ECR I-1477; in Case C-157/94, *Commission v. Netherlands (Re Electricity Imports)* [1997] ECR I-5699 the Commission did not contest that the monopoly electricity distributor in the Netherlands provided a services of general economic interest.

[142] *Dutch Courier Services* [1990] OJ L10/47, [1990] 4 CMLR 947; *Spanish Courier Services* [1990] OJ L233/19, [1991] 4 CMLR 560; Case C-320/91, *Corbeau* [1993] ECR I-2533, [1995] 4 CMLR 621.

[143] Case C-266/96, *Corsica Ferries France SA v. Gruppo Antichi Ormeggiatori del Porto di Genova* [1998] ECR I-3949, [1998] 5 CMLR 402.

[144] Case C-203/96, *Dusseldorp* [1998] ECR I-4075, [1998] 3 CMLR 873.

[145] Case C-67/96, *Albany International BV v. Stichting Bedrijfspensioenfonds Textielindustrie* [1999] ECR-5751, [2000] 4 CMLR 446.

[146] Joined Cases C-147–8/97, *Deutsche Post AG v. Gesellschaft für Zahlungssysteme mbH (GZS) and Citicorp Kartenservice GmbH* [2000] ECR I-825, [2000] 4 CMLR 838.

[147] Case C-475/99, *Ambulanz Glöckner v. Landkreis Südwestpfalz* [2001] ECR I-8089, [2002] 4 CMLR 726. Jacobs AG considered that non-emergency ambulance services were also services of general economic interest, see Opinion, para. 175.

[148] Case C-179/90, *Merci Convenzionali Porto di Genova v. Siderurigica Gabrielle* [1991] ECR I-5889, [1994] 4 CMLR 422; Case C-242/95, *GT–Link v. De Danske Statsbaner (DSB)* [1997] ECR I-4449, [1997] 5 CMLR 601.

[149] e.g., Case C-203/96, *Chemische Afvalstoffen Dusseldorp BV v. Minister van Volkshuisvesting, Ruimtelijke Ordening en Milieubeheer* [1998] ECR I-4075, [1998] 3 CMLR 873.

Until 1993 the Court took a very strict view of the 'obstruct the performance' test. Thus, in *Höfner* v. *Macrotron* the Court accepted that the Bundesanstalt had been entrusted with services of general economic interest but said that such an undertaking remained subject to the competition rules 'unless and to the extent to which it is shown that their application is *incompatible* [emphasis added] with the discharge of its duties';[150] in *Merci Convenzionali*[151] it said that even if services of general economic interest had been involved it would not have been necessary for the undertaking to infringe the Treaty rules; in *British Telecom*[152] it said that Italy had failed to establish that compliance by BT with the competition rules would obstruct it in carrying out its tasks; and in *RTT*[153] it did not accept that the undertaking entrusted with the public telephone network also needed power to lay down the standards for telephone equipment and to check rival equipment suppliers' compliance with them.[154]

The Court changed its approach in *Corbeau*,[155] and recognized that Article 86(2) contains what is in effect a proportionality requirement. The facts of *Corbeau* are given above. It will be recalled that the Court considered both Article 86(1) and Article 86(2) and seemed to say that Member States may grant special or exclusive rights only in so far as they entrust undertakings with services of general economic interest and the criteria in Article 86(2) are fulfilled.[156] The Court went on to consider the application of Article 86(2):

Case C-320/91, *Corbeau* [1993] ECR I-2533, [1995] 4 CMLR 621

Court of Justice

15. As regards the services at issue in the main proceedings, it cannot be disputed that the Régie des Postes is entrusted with a service of general economic interest consisting in the obligation to collect, carry and distribute mail on behalf of all users throughout the territory of the Member State concerned, at uniform tariffs and on similar quality conditions, irrespective of the specific situations or the degree of economic profitability of each individual operation.

16. The question which falls to be considered is therefore the extent to which a restriction on competition or even the exclusion of all competition from other economic operators is necessary in order to allow the holder of the exclusive right to perform its task of general interest and in particular to have the benefit of economically acceptable conditions.

17. The starting point of such an examination must be the premise that the obligation on the part of the undertaking entrusted with that task to perform its services in conditions of economic equilibrium presupposes that it will be possible to offset less profitable sectors against the profitable sectors and hence justifies a restriction of competition from individual undertakings where the economically profitable sectors are concerned.

18. Indeed, to authorize individual undertakings to compete with the holder of the exclusive rights in the sectors of their choice corresponding to those rights would make it possible for them

---

[150] Case C-41/90, *Höfner* v. *Macroton* [1991] ECR I-1979, [1993] 4 CMLR 306, para. 24.

[151] Case C-179/90, *Merci Convenzionali Porto di Genova* v. *Siderurigica Gabrielle* [1991] ECR I-5009, [1994] 4 CMLR 422.

[152] Case 41/83, *Italy* v. *Commission* [1985] ECR 873, [1985] 2 CMLR 368.

[153] Case C-18/88, *RTT* v. *GB-INNO-BM SA* [1991] ECR I-5973.

[154] See also Case 66/86, *Ahmed Saeed Flugreisen and Silver Line Reiseburo GmbH* v. *Zentrale zur Bëkampf Unlauteren Wettwerbs eV* [1989] ECR 803, [1990] 4 CMLR 102; Commission Decision, *Dutch Courier Services* [1990] OJ L10/47, [1990] 4 CMLR 947.

[155] Case C-320/91, *Corbeau* [1993] ECR I-2533, [1995] 4 CMLR 621.

[156] *Ibid.*, para. 14: see *supra* 640.

to concentrate on the economically profitable operations and to offer more advantageous tariffs than those adopted by the holders of the exclusive rights since, unlike the latter, they are not bound for economic reasons to offset losses in the unprofitable sectors against profits in the more profitable sectors.

19. However, the exclusion of competition is not justified as regards specific services dissociable from the service of general interest which meet special needs of economic operators and which call for certain additional services not offered by the traditional postal service, such as collection from the senders' address, greater speed or reliability of distribution or the possibility of changing the destination in the course of transit, in so far as such specific services, by their nature and the conditions in which they are offered, such as the geographical area in which they are provided, do not compromise the economic equilibrium of the service of general economic interest performed by the holder of the exclusive right.

20. It is for the national court to consider whether the services at issue in the dispute before it meet those criteria.

21. The answer to the questions referred to the Court by the Tribunal Correctionnel de Liége should therefore be that it is contrary to Article [86] of the EEC Treaty for legislation of a Member State which confers on a body such as the Régie des Postes the exclusive right to collect, carry and distribute mail, to prohibit, under threat of criminal penalties, an economic operator established in that State from offering certain specific services dissociable from the service of general interest which meet the special needs of economic operators and call for certain additional services not offered by the traditional postal service, in so far as those services do not compromise the economic equilibrium of the service of general economic interest performed by the holder of the exclusive right. It is for the national court to consider whether the services in question in the main proceedings meet those criteria.

In this judgment the Court accepted that the operation of a basic postal system providing a universal service is a service of general economic interest and that the normal principles of competition law will not apply to the extent necessary to preserve it through cross-subsidy. The undertaking must have 'economically acceptable conditions' (paragraph 16) and be able to perform its task in 'conditions of economic equilibrium' (paragraph 17). If competitors are allowed to come in and 'cherry-pick' or 'cream-skim' the most profitable parts of the system the holder of the exclusive right required to operate the universal service cannot operate under economically acceptable conditions. The Court said, however, in paragraph 19 that this does not justify the exclusion of competition from additional services, separable from the basic public service, if these could be offered by other undertakings without compromising the economic viability of the latter. *Corbeau* is a paradoxical case: it is the high water-mark of hostility by the Court to the very existence of statutory monopoly in the context of Article 86(1) but the dawn of a much more flexible and generous (to incumbents) interpretation of Article 86(2).

The Court elaborated on the *Corbeau* ruling in *Commission v. Netherlands*. It said again that the entrusted undertaking must be allowed 'economically acceptable conditions'. It also said that the undertaking does not have to prove that there is no other way but the impugned measure whereby it could carry out its task.[157]

---

[157] Cf. the Opinion of Darmon AG in Case C-393/92, *Gemeente Almelo and others v. Energiebedrijf Ijsselmij NV* [1994] ECR I-1477, on this point.

Case 157/94, *Commission* v. *Netherlands (Re Electricity Imports)* [1997] ECR I-5699

Court of Justice

52. ...it is not necessary, in order for the conditions for the application of Article [86(2)] to be fulfilled, that the financial balance or economic viability of the undertaking entrusted with the operation of a service of general economic interest should be threatened. It is sufficient that, in the absence of the rights at issue, it would not be possible for the undertaking to perform the particular tasks entrusted to it, defined by reference to the obligations and constraints to which it is subject.

53. Moreover, it follows from the *Corbeau* judgment ..., that the conditions for the application of Article [86(2)] are fulfilled in particular if maintenance of those rights is necessary to enable the holder of them to perform the tasks of general economic interest assigned to it under economically acceptable conditions.

...

58. Whilst it is true that it is incumbent upon a Member State which invokes Article [86(2)] to demonstrate that the conditions laid down by that provision are met, that burden of proof cannot be so extensive as to require the Member State, when setting out in detail the reasons for which, in the event of elimination of the contested measures, the performance, under economically acceptable conditions, of the tasks of general economic interest which it has entrusted to an undertaking would, in its view, be jeopardized, to go even further and prove, positively, that no other conceivable measure, which by definition would be hypothetical, could enable those tasks to be performed under the same conditions.

In *Corbeau* the Court did not consider whether the universal service provision could be achieved by a less extreme measure than granting a monopoly. Universal service and cross-subsidization are not inseparable: it is possible for the State to subsidize the universal service, for example. It will be noted that it was left (paragraph 21) to the national court actually to determine whether or not the additional services *were* severable and able to be operated by other undertakings without prejudicing the economic equilibrium of the traditional postal service. This left the national court with a difficult task involving extensive economic analysis. It had to decide the extent of the cross-subsidization, and how far this was necessary to maintain the 'economic equilibrium'.[158] Cross-subsidization is a problematic issue, particularly in respect of network monopolies.

D. Edward and M. Hoskins, 'Article 90: Deregulation and EC Law. Reflections Arising from the XVI FIDE Conference' (1995) 32 *CMLRev* 157, 179–81[159]

In *Corbeau*, the Court of Justice assumed that the *Régie des postes* should be permitted to use profitable activities to subsidize less profitable activities. However, in future cases, it will be necessary to examine further the situations in which cross-subsidization is incompatible with EC competition law.

---

[158] See L. Hancher, 'Casenote on *Corbeau*' (1994) 31 *CMLRev* 105 at 119–20. For the issue of the direct effect of Article 86, see *infra* 667.

[159] See also L. Hancher and J. L. Buendia Sierra, 'Cross-subsidization and EC Law' (1998) 35 *CMLRev* 901.

The Commission has defined cross-subsidization as meaning 'that an undertaking allocates all or part of the costs of its activity in one product or geographic market to its activity in another product or geographic market' (Commission's Guidelines on the Application of EEC Competition Rules in the Telecommunications Sector at paragraph 102 (O.J. 1991 C 233/2). Thus, cross-subsidization may lead to a distortion in competition as it enables an undertaking to provide goods or services at a price lower than their true market price or even lower than their production cost.

The issues raised by cross-subsidization in the context of universal providers and legal monopolies are complex. As a starting point, if a particular undertaking has an obligation to provide a universal service *at a standard price* to all consumers, then it necessarily follows that geographical cross-subsidization must be permitted. Consumers in profitable urban areas will be obliged to subsidize consumers in unprofitable rural areas.

This assumption was confirmed by the Commission in its Telecommunications Guidelines:

> 'Cross-subsidization does not lead to predatory pricing and does not restrict competition when it is the costs of reserved activities which are subsidized by the revenue generated by other reserved activities. This form of subsidization is even necessary, as it enables the TOs [Telecommunications Organizations] holders of exclusive rights to perform their obligation to provide a public service universally and on the same conditions to everybody. For instance, telephone provision in unprofitable rural areas is subsidized through revenues from telephone provision in profitable urban areas or long-distance calls.'

The Commission stated that the same reasoning could be applied to the subsidizing of reserved services by means of activities which are subject to competition. However, it is very important to ensure that third party value-added service providers have access to the network on equitable terms, since there will be an incentive for the universal provider to try to improve its competitive position in the market for value-added services by imposing detrimental conditions of access to the network on its competitors.

The Commission also considered that subsidization of activities which are subject to competition by activities which are subject to a monopoly is likely to distort competition in violation of Article [82]. However, there is a strong argument that Article [82] should not be applied inflexibly to such cross-subsidization. Certainly, legal monopolies should not be permitted to use such cross-subsidization to finance predatory pricing in competitive markets. But it would be inefficient to prevent legal monopolies from using their resources to enter other, competitive markets under any circumstances.

A final point to note is that it is often very difficult to identify whether there has in fact been any cross-subsidization. This is because subsidies can be provided in a number of ways. For example, in setting the price to be charged to customers for a non-reserved value-added service, the universal provider may not take full account of the actual cost of access to the network involved in providing that service. Any shortfall can be absorbed by increasing the price of monopoly services. Furthermore, a universal provider may be able to obtain loan capital at a lower rate than normal private undertakings due to the financial security which it enjoys as a result of its legal monopoly. If such capital is then used to subsidize activities which are not covered by its legal monopoly, this may give the universal provider an unfair advantage over its competitors, for whom borrowing money is more expensive.

The existence of cross-subsidization can be controlled to a certain extent by ensuring that universal providers use transport accounting techniques which take full account of true cost allocations. The judgment of the Court of Justice in Case 66/86 *Ahmed Saeed* . . . recognizes the need for transparency in order to ensure the effective application of the competition rules. However, detailed rules (for example, in relation to accountancy practices to be followed) can be introduced only through legislation.

Issues similar to those in *Corbeau* arose in *Almelo* where the Court dealt with a preliminary reference from a Dutch court seised of litigation between regional and local electricity distributors concerning, *inter alia*, the legality of an exclusive purchasing clause:

Case C-393/92, *Gemeente Almelo and Others* v. *Energiebedrijf Ijsselmij NV* [1994] ECR I-1477

Court of Justice

46. Article [86(2)] of the Treaty provides that undertakings entrusted with the operation of services of general economic interest may be exempted from the application of the competition rules contained in the Treaty in so far as it is necessary to impose restrictions on competition, or even to exclude all competition, from other economic operators in order to ensure the performance of the particular tasks assigned to them (see the judgment in Case C-320/91 *Corbeau* . . . , paragraph 14).

47. As regards the question whether an undertaking such as IJM has been entrusted with the operation of services of general interest, it should be borne in mind that it has been given the task, through the grant of a non-exclusive concession governed by public law, of ensuring the supply of electricity in part of the national territory.

48. Such an undertaking must ensure that throughout the territory in respect of which the concession is granted, all consumers, whether local distributors or end-users, receive uninterrupted supplies of electricity in sufficient quantities to meet demand at any given time, at uniform tariff rates and on terms which may not vary save in accordance with objective criteria applicable to all customers.

49. Restrictions on competition from other economic operators must be allowed so far as they are necessary in order to enable the undertaking entrusted with such a task of general interest to perform it. In that regard, it is necessary to take into consideration the economic conditions in which the undertaking operates, in particular the costs which it has to bear and the legislation, particularly concerning the environment, to which it is subject.

50. It is for the national court to consider whether an exclusive purchasing clause prohibiting local distributors from importing electricity is necessary in order to enable the regional distributor to perform its task of general interest.

Here again, the Court accepted that the undertaking provided a service of general economic interest and that Article 86(2) allows the restrictions of competition necessary for the performance of its universal service obligations (although it was for the national court to make the decision whether the actual restriction at issue in the case was necessary for that purpose). Ross comments that *Almelo*, reinforcing *Corbeau*, was a movement towards recognizing the value of public service independently of its economic viability because 'it clearly indicated that the availability of the derogation was to be measured by a balancing exercise based upon competing priorities rather than inhibiting that choice by insisting upon narrow economic tests to be satisfied before the normal market rules can be disapplied'.[160]

In *Dusseldorp*,[161] however, where the Court was dealing with an undertaking with a monopoly over certain waste incineration, it was less flexible and reverted to a previous, more stringent

---

[160] M. Ross, 'Art. 16 EC and Services of General Interest: From Derogation to Obligation' (2000) 25 *ELRev* 22, 25.

[161] Case C-203/96, *Chemische Afvalstoffen Dusseldorp BV* v. *Minister van Volkshuisvesting, Ruimtelijke Ordening en Milieubeheer* [1998] ECR I-4075, [1998] 3 CMLR 873.

approach. It said that even if the task could constitute a task of general economic interest it was for the Dutch Government to show to the satisfaction of the national court that the objective could not be equally achieved by other means, and that Article 86(2) could apply only if it shown that without the contested measure the undertaking could not carry out its entrusted task.[162]

In some cases, unlike *Corbeau* and *Almelo*, the Court has not left the decision to the national court but has actually decided that the conditions in Article 86(2) were satisfied. This can be seen in *Corsica Ferries France, Albany*, and *Deutsche Post*.

Case C-266/96, *Corsica Ferries France SA* v. *Gruppo Antichi Ormeggiatori del Poro di Genovo Coop. and Others* [1998] ECR I-3949, [1998] 5 CMLR 402

Under Italian law ships from other Member States were required to use the services of local mooring companies who held exclusive concessions in each port. Corsica Ferries claimed that the Genoa and La Spezia mooring groups were abusing their dominant positions by preventing shipping companies using their own staff to carry out mooring operations, in the excessive nature of the price of the service which bore no relation to the actual cost of the service provided, and in fixing tariffs that varied from port to port for equivalent services. The Italian court asked, *inter alia*, whether the Treaty prohibited national measures which put the mooring companies in the position to act in this way.

Court of Justice

36. The national court asks whether there is an abuse, on the part of the Genoa and La Spezia mooring groups, of their dominant position on a substantial part of the Common Market by virtue of the exclusive rights conferred upon them by the Italian public authorities.

37. There are three aspects of the abuse alleged in this case. It is said to reside in the grant of exclusive rights to local mooring groups, preventing shipping companies from using their own staff to carry out mooring operations, in the excessive nature of the price of the service, which bears no relation to the actual cost of the service provided, and in the fixing of tariffs that vary from port to port for equivalent services.

38. As regards the definition of the market in question, it appears from the order for reference that it consists in the performance on behalf of third persons of mooring services relating to container freight in the ports of Genoa and La Spezia. Having regard, *inter alia*, to the volume of traffic in those ports and their importance in intra-Community trade, those markets may be regarded as constituting a substantial part of the Common Market (Case C-179/90, *Merci Convenzionali Porto di Genova* . . . And Case C-163/96, *Raso and Others* . . .

39. As far as the existence of exclusive rights is concerned, it is settled law that an undertaking having a statutory monopoly in a substantial part of the Common Market may be regarded as having a dominant position within the meaning of Article [82] of the Treaty (Case C-41/90, *Höfner and Elser* v. *Macrotron* . . . , Case C-260/89, *ERT* v. *DEP* . . . , *Merci Convenzionali Porto di Genova* . . . and *Raso and Others* . . .

40. Next, it should be pointed out that although merely creating a dominant position by granting exclusive rights within the meaning of Article [86(1)] of the Treaty is not in itself incompatible with Article [82], a Member State is in breach of the prohibitions contained in those two provisions if the undertaking in question, merely by exercising the exclusive rights granted to

---

[162] *Ibid.*, para. 67.

it, is led to abuse its dominant position or if such rights are liable to create a situation in which that undertaking is led to commit such abuses (Case C-41/90, *Höfner and Elser* v. *Macrotron* ... ; Case C-260/89, *ERT* v. *DEP* ... ; *Merci Convenzionali Porto di Genova* ... ; Case C-323/93, *Centre d'Insemination de la Crespelle* ... ; *Raso and others* ...).

41. It follows that a Member State may, without infringing Article [82] of the Treaty, grant exclusive rights for the supply of mooring services in its ports to local mooring groups provided those groups do not abuse their dominant position or are not led necessarily to commit such an abuse.

42. In order to rebut the existence of such abuse, the Genoa and La Spezia mooring groups rely on Article [86(2)] of the Treaty, which provides that undertakings entrusted with the operation of services of general economic interest are to be subject to the competition rules contained in the Treaty only in so far as their application does not obstruct the performance, in law or in fact, of the particular tasks assigned to them. Article [86(2)] of the Treaty further provides that, in order for it to apply, the development of trade must not be affected to such an extent as would be contrary to the interests of the Community.

43. They maintain that the tariffs applied are indispensable if a universal mooring service is to be maintained. On the one hand, the tariffs include a component corresponding to the additional cost of providing a universal mooring service. On the other hand, the difference in the tariffs from one port to another, which, according to the file, result from account being taken, when the tariffs are calculated, of corrective factors reflecting the influence of local circumstances—which would tend to indicate that the services provided are not equivalent—are justified by the characteristics of the service and the need to ensure universal coverage.

44. It must therefore be considered whether the derogation from the rules of the Treaty provided for in Article [86(2)] of the Treaty may fall to be applied. To that end, it must be determined whether the mooring service can be regarded as a service of general economic interest within the meaning of that provision and, if so, first, whether performance of the particular tasks assigned to it can be achieved only through services for which the charge is higher than their actual cost and for which the tariff varies from one port to another, and secondly, whether the development of trade is not affected to such an extent as would be contrary to the interests of the Community (see, to that effect, Case C-157/94, *E.C. Commission* v. *Netherlands* ...).

45. It is evident from the file on the case in the main proceedings that mooring operations are of general economic interest, such interest having special characteristics, in relation to those of other economic activities, which is capable of bringing them within the scope of Article [86(2)] of the Treaty. Mooring groups are obliged to provide at any time and to any user a universal mooring service, for reasons of safety in port waters. At all events, Italy could properly have considered that it was necessary, on grounds of public security, to confer on local groups of operators the exclusive right to provide a universal mooring service.

46. In those circumstances it is not incompatible with Articles [82] and [86(1)] of the Treaty to include in the price of the service a component designed to cover the cost of maintaining the universal mooring service, inasmuch as it corresponds to the supplementary cost occasioned by the special characteristics of that service, and to lay down for that service different tariffs on the basis of the particular characteristics of each port.

47. Consequently, since the mooring groups have in fact been entrusted by the Member State with managing a service of general economic interest within the meaning of Article [86(2)] of the Treaty, and the other conditions for applying the derogation from application of the Treaty rules which is laid down in that provision are satisfied, legislation such as that at issue does not constitute an infringement of Article [82] of the Treaty, read in conjunction with Article [86(1)].

As in *Corbeau*, the Court considered that the exclusive rights could escape the prohibition in Article 86(1) if they satisfied Article 86(2). However, the Court did not leave this determination to the national court, but said that the mooring operations were services of general economic interest provided on a universal basis and that it was, in the circumstances, not incompatible with the Treaty to include supplementary costs related to the running of that service and to charge varying tariffs (paragraph 46). Therefore there was no infringement of Article 86(1). There is no explanation of how the Court reached its conclusions in paragraph 46, or of how the supplementary costs arose or what cross-subsidization was taking place.

The ECJ also made a clear decision on the application of Article 86(2) in *Albany*. It will be remembered from the discussion of Article 86(1) above[163] that the case concerned the Dutch regime of compulsory affiliation to sectoral pension schemes. The Court considered whether the derogation in Article 86(2) applied, and held that it did because the scheme involved a service of general economic interest which had to operate under 'economically acceptable conditions'.

Case C-67/96, *Albany International BV* v. *Stichting Bedrijfspensioenfonds Textielindustrie* [1999] ECR I-5751, [2000] 4 CMLR 446

Court of Justice

102. It is important to bear in mind first of all that, under Article [86(2)] of the Treaty, undertakings entrusted with the operation of services of general economic interest are subject to the rules on competition in so far as the application of such rules does not obstruct the performance, in law or in fact, of the particular tasks assigned to them.

103. In allowing, in certain circumstances, derogations from the general rules of the Treaty, Article [86(2)] of the Treaty seeks to reconcile the Member States' interest in using certain undertakings, in particular in the public sector, as an instrument of economic or fiscal policy with the Community's interest in ensuring compliance with the rules on competition and preservation of the unity of the common market (Case C-202/88 *France* v. *Commission* . . . , paragraph 12, and Case C-157/94 *Commission* v. *Netherlands* . . . , paragraph 39).

104. In view of the interest of the Member States thus defined they cannot be precluded, when determining what services of general economic interest they entrust to certain undertakings, from taking account of objectives pertaining to their national policy or from endeavouring to attain them by means of obligations and constraints which they impose on such undertakings (*Commission* v. *Netherlands*, cited above, paragraph 40).

105. The supplementary pension scheme at issue in the main proceedings fulfils an essential social function within the Netherlands pensions system by reason of the limited amount of the statutory pension, which is calculated on the basis of the minimum statutory wage.

106. Moreover, the importance of the social function attributed to supplementary pensions has recently been recognised by the Community legislature's adoption of Council Directive 98/49/EC of 29 June 1998 on safeguarding the supplementary pension rights of employed and self-employed persons moving within the Community (OJ 1998 L 209, p. 46).

107. Next, it is not necessary, in order for the conditions for the application of Article [86(2)] of the Treaty to be fulfilled, that the financial balance or economic viability of the undertaking

[163] *Supra* 644.

entrusted with the operation of a service of general economic interest should be threatened. It is sufficient that, in the absence of the rights at issue, it would not be possible for the undertaking to perform the particular tasks entrusted to it, defined by reference to the obligations and constraints to which it is subject (*Commission v. Netherlands*, cited above, paragraph 52) or that maintenance of those rights is necessary to enable the holder of them to perform tasks of general economic interest which have been assigned to it under economically acceptable conditions (Case C-320/91 *Corbeau* [1993] ECR I-2533, paragraphs 14 to 16, and *Commission v. Netherlands*, cited above, paragraph 53).

108. If the exclusive right of the fund to manage the supplementary pension scheme for all workers in a given sector were removed, undertakings with young employees in good health engaged in non-dangerous activities would seek more advantageous insurance terms from private insurers. The progressive departure of 'good' risks would leave the sectoral pension fund with responsibility for an increasing share of 'bad' risks, thereby increasing the cost of pensions for workers, particularly those in small and medium-sized undertakings with older employees engaged in dangerous activities, to which the fund could no longer offer pensions at an acceptable cost.

109. Such a situation would arise particularly in a case where, as in the main proceedings, the supplementary pension scheme managed exclusively by the Fund displays a high level of solidarity resulting, in particular, from the fact that contributions do not reflect the risk, from the obligation to accept all workers without a prior medical examination, the continuing accrual of pension rights despite exemption from the payment of contributions in the event of incapacity for work, the discharge by the Fund of arrears of contributions due from an employer in the event of insolvency and the indexing of the amount of pensions in order to maintain their value.

110. Such constraints, which render the service provided by the Fund less competitive than a comparable service provided by insurance companies, go towards justifying the exclusive right of the Fund to manage the supplementary pension scheme.

111. It follows that the removal of the exclusive right conferred on the Fund might make it impossible for it to perform the tasks of general economic interest entrusted to it under economically acceptable conditions and threaten its financial equilibrium.

. . .

123. The answer to the third question must therefore be that Articles [82] and [86] of the Treaty do not preclude the public authorities from conferring on a pension fund the exclusive right to manage a supplementary pension scheme in a given sector.

It is important to note that, again, the Court (paragraph 107) did not demand that the economic viability of the entrusted undertaking should be threatened without the exclusive right. Article 86(2) can apply where it is necessary to provide economically acceptable conditions. Here again this meant preventing 'cherry-picking': without the exclusive rights other insurers would be able to offer a better deal to companies with predominantly young, healthy workforces.

The cross-subsidy argument did not succeed, however, in *Air Inter* where the proportionality requirement was not satisfied. There the Commission challenged the granting of exclusive rights on two internal French air routes to Air Inter. The undertaking claimed that domestic air transport in France was based on cross-subsidy between profitable and unprofitable routes, but the Commission and the CFI were not convinced.

Case T-260/94, *Air Inter* v. *Commission* [1997] ECR II-997, [1997] 5 CMLR 851

Court of First Instance

138. The application of those articles could, however, be excluded only in as much as they 'obstructed' performance of the tasks entrusted to the applicant. Since that condition must be interpreted strictly, it was not sufficient for such performance to be simply hindered or made more difficult. Furthermore, it was for the applicant to establish any obstruction of its task (see, to that effect, Case 155/73, *Sacchi*...).

139. In that regard, the applicant merely asserts that the organization of domestic air transport was based on a system of cross-subsidy between profitable routes and unprofitable routes and that the exclusivity which had been granted to it on the Orly–Marseille and Orly–Toulouse routes was justified by its obligation to operate the unprofitable routes regularly and at tariffs that were not prohibitive, in order to contribute to regional development. It does not put a figure on the probable loss of revenue if other air carriers are allowed to compete with it on the two routes in question. Nor has it shown that that loss of income will be so great that it will be forced to abandon certain routes forming part of its network.

140. In any event, the domestic air network system combined with the internal cross-subsidy system to which the applicant refers in support of its case did not constitute an aim in themselves, but were the means chosen by the French public authorities for developing the French regions. The applicant has not argued and still less established that, following the entry into force of Regulation 2408/92, there was no appropriate alternative system capable of ensuring that regional development and in particular of ensuring that loss-making routes continue to be financed (see also the order of the President of the Court in Case C-174/94 R, *France* v. *E.C.Commission*...).

141. Consequently, the applicant has not shown that the contested decision would obstruct the performance in law or in fact of the particular task assigned to it. It follows that the plea of infringement of Article [86(2)] of the Treaty cannot be accepted either.

In *Deutsche Post*,[164] the facts of which are given above,[165] the ECJ had to consider a statutory monopolist's exercise of a right (charging for international mail as though it were internal mail) stemming from an international convention. It held that the German Post Office was justified in doing this. Fulfilling the obligations under the UPC was a service of general economic interest and the Court simply stated without further explanation that levying the charges in issue was necessary to the performance of the task in economically balanced conditions. Otherwise the task would be jeopardized.[166] Bartosch points out that this was very favourable treatment of Deutsche Post. He argues that the need for cross-subsidization should have been more closely examined.

---

[164] Cases C-147–8/97, *Deutsche Post AG v. Gesellschaft für Zahlungssysteme mbH (GZS) and Citicorp Kartenservice GmbH* [2000] ECR I-825, [2000] 4 CMLR 838.

[165] *Supra* 646.

[166] Cases C-147–8/97, *Deutsche Post AG v. Gesellschaft für Zahlungssysteme mbH (GZS) and Citicorp Kartenservice GmbH* [2000] ECR I-825, [2000] 4 CMLR 838, para. 50.

A. Bartosch, 'Casenote on Cases C-147–148/97, *Deutsche Post AG v. Gesellschaft für Zahlungssysteme mbH (GZS) and Citicorp Kartenservice GmbH*' (2001) 38 *CMLRev* 195, 207–8

. . . a postal administration cannot be regarded as entitled to ask for the derogation provided for in Article 86(2) EC for each individual element of such a universal service. Deutsche Post AG can consequently on the one hand not be asked to use revenues generated from services dissociable from the universal service concept to cross-subsidize the burdens associated with such universal service, the burden of which has been entrusted to it by the Federal Republic of Germany . . . On the other hand, it has to use revenues from activities that do fall under this universal service to cross-subsidize other less profitable parts of the same. If it were permitted to split up the whole of the universal service into its different elements for the purposes of applying Article 86(2) EC, it would become possible for the entrusted undertaking to compete effectively with regard to those elements that can be operated profitably and to ask for a derogation from the application of the Treaty's competition rules wherever this is not feasible. Article 86(2) EC could therefore be relied on for each individual operation within the universal service that can be shown to operate at a loss. This is exactly why the Court in the . . . *Corbeau* case distinguished between universal services and those which are clearly dissociable from them.

In *Ambulanz Glöckner*, however, the Court again took an approach to the cross-subsidization issue which greatly favoured the incumbent. It identified the emergency ambulance service as being a service of general economic interest subject to universal service but held the extension of provider's exclusive rights to the non-emergency market was justified so that it could subsidize the emergency from the non-emergency service.

Case C-475/99, *Ambulanz Glöckner* v. *Landkreis Südwestpfalz* [2001] ECR I-8089, [2002] 4 CMLR 726

Court of Justice

55. With regard to those arguments, the medical aid organisations are incontestably entrusted with a task of general economic interest, consisting in the obligation to provide a permanent standby service of transporting sick or injured persons in emergencies throughout the territory concerned, at uniform rates and on similar quality conditions, without regard to the particular situations or to the degree of economic profitability of each individual operation.

56. However, Article [86(2)] of the Treaty, read in conjunction with paragraph (1) of that provision, allows Member States to confer, on undertakings to which they entrust the operation of services of general economic interest, exclusive rights which may hinder the application of the rules of the Treaty on competition in so far as restrictions on competition, or even the exclusion of all competition, by other economic operators are necessary to ensure the performance of the particular tasks assigned to the undertakings holding the exclusive rights (Case C-320/91 *Corbeau* [1993] ECR I-2533, paragraph 14).

57. The question to be determined, therefore, is whether the restriction of competition is necessary to enable the holder of an exclusive right to perform its task of general interest in economically acceptable conditions. The Court has held that the starting point in making that determination must be the premiss that the obligation, on the part of the undertaking entrusted

with such a task, to perform its services in conditions of economic equilibrium presupposes that it will be possible to offset less profitable sectors against the profitable sectors and hence justifies a restriction of competition from individual undertakings in economically profitable sectors (*Corbeau*, paragraphs 16 and 17).

58. In the case before the national court, for the reasons advanced by the Landkreis, the ASB, the Vertreter des öffentlichen Interesses, Mainz, and the Austrian Government, which are set forth in paragraph 53 above and which are for the national court to assess, it appears that the system put in place by the RettDG 1991 is such as to enable the medical aid organisations to perform their task in economically acceptable conditions. In particular, the evidence placed before the Court shows that the revenue from non-emergency transport helps to cover the costs of providing the emergency transport service.

59. It is true that, in paragraph 19 of *Corbeau*, the Court held that the exclusion of competition is not justified in certain cases involving specific services, severable from the service of general interest in question, if those services do not compromise the economic equilibrium of the service of general economic interest performed by the holder of the exclusive rights.

60. However, that is not the case with the two services now under consideration, for two reasons in particular. First, unlike the situation in *Corbeau*, the two types of service in question, traditionally assumed by the medical aid organisations, are so closely linked that it is difficult to sever the non-emergency transport services from the task of general economic interest constituted by the provision of the public ambulance service, with which they also have characteristics in common.

61. Second, the extension of the medical aid organisations' exclusive rights to the non-emergency transport sector does indeed enable them to discharge their general-interest task of providing emergency transport in conditions of economic equilibrium. The possibility which would be open to private operators to concentrate, in the non-emergency sector, on more profitable journeys could affect the degree of economic viability of the service provided by the medical aid organisations and, consequently, jeopardise the quality and reliability of that service.

62. However, as the Advocate General explains in point 188 of his Opinion, it is only if it were established that the medical aid organisations entrusted with the operation of the public ambulance service were manifestly unable to satisfy demand for emergency ambulance services and for patient transport at all times that the justification for extending their exclusive rights, based on the task of general interest, could not be accepted.

63. In this regard, Ambulanz Glöckner contends that Paragraph 18(3) of the RettDG 1991 does indeed promote the creation of a situation in which the medical aid organisations are not always able to satisfy all demand for patient transport services at acceptable prices (see, by analogy, Case C-41/90 *Höfner and Elser* [1991] ECR I-1979, paragraph 31, and Case C-55/96 *Job Centre* [1997] ECR I-7119, paragraph 35). On the other hand, the Landkreis and the ASB maintain that the public ambulance service is incontestably able to satisfy both demand for emergency transport and that for patient transport, even without private undertakings.

64. It is for national court to determine whether the medical aid organisations which occupy a dominant position on the markets in question are in fact able to satisfy demand and to fulfil not only their statutory obligation to provide the public emergency ambulance services in all situations and 24 hours a day but also to offer efficient patient transport services.

65. Consequently, a provision such as Paragraph 18(3) of the RettDG 1991 is justified under Article [86(2)] of the Treaty provided that it does not bar the grant of an authorisation to independent operators where it is established that the medical aid organisations entrusted with the operation of the public ambulance service are manifestly unable to satisfy demand in the area of emergency transport and patient transport services.

(iv) No Effect on Trade Contrary to the Interests of the Community

Article 86(2) contains the proviso that 'the development of trade must not be affected to such an extent as would be contrary to the interests of the Community'. This is similar to the proviso in Article 30 that the derogation from the free movement provisions should not be 'a means of arbitrary discrimination or a disguised restriction on trade between Member States', but unlike that proviso the tailpiece to Article 86(2) has not so far been of importance. It was pleaded by the Commission in the electricity cases[167] but the Court held that the Commission had provided no explanation to demonstrate such an effect on trade. The proviso must denote something more than the phrase 'affect trade between Member States' in Articles 81 and 82 because without such an effect on trade those Articles cannot apply at all. It may, however, simply be a further proportionality requirement. In *De Post-La Poste*[168] the Commission held that the undertaking with a statutory monopoly over the general letter mail in Belgium had infringed Article 82 by operating a tying policy in order to exclude competitors from the neighbouring business-to-business (B2B) market. The undertaking did not rely on Article 86(2) in its defence, but the Commission went out of its way to say that, if it had, the sealing off of a national market would have impeded trade to an extent contrary to the Community interest.

E. THE DIRECT EFFECT OF ARTICLE 86(1) and (2)

(i) Article 86(1)

As Article 86(1) prohibits Member States from enacting or maintaining measures contrary to rules contained in the Treaty it applies, as we have seen, only in conjunction with some other rule. Whether or not individuals may invoke Article 86(1) before a national court, i.e., whether Article 86(1) is directly effective, therefore depends on whether the rule infringed by the Member State is itself directly effective. In *Höfner* v. *Macrotron*, for example, the litigant was able to claim in the German court that the German laws breached Article 86(1) because they led to an infringement of Article 82, which is directly effective. The litigant was therefore able to rely on the Articles in conjunction with one another.

(ii) Article 86(2)

There are four questions raised by Article 86(2): is the undertaking 'entrusted' with a task; is that task a 'service of general economic interest'; would the task be obstructed by complying with the Treaty rules; and would a derogation from the Treaty rules have an effect on trade contrary to the interests of the Community.

As far as the first two questions are concerned, the Court confirmed long ago that Article 86(2) is directly effective in that a national court may decide whether or not an undertaking has been entrusted with a service of general economic interest.[169]

---

[167] Case 157/94, *Commission v. Netherlands (Re Electricity Imports)* [1997] ECR I-5699, paras. 66–72; Case C-159/94, *Commission v. France (Re Electricity and Gas Imports)* [1997] ECR I-5815, paras. 109–16.

[168] [2002] OJ L61/32.

[169] Case 127/73, *BRT v. SABAM* [1974] ECR 313, [1974] 2 CMLR 238.

As for the third question, whether the task would be obstructed, for a long time it appeared from the judgment in *Muller*[170] that the national courts were not competent to answer it and that only the Community institutions could decide the point in favour of the undertaking. However, the position has changed and the Court expressly said at paragraph 34 of the *ERT* judgment[171] that it is for the national court to verify whether the application of the competition rules would obstruct the undertaking's task. As can be seen above, the Court also left this determination to the national court in *Corbeau* and *Almelo*.

The fourth question is more problematic as it requires an assessment of whether the *interests of the Community* would be adversely affected. At first sight the issue seems more suited to a decision by the Commission than to a judgment by a national court. However, it may be that this is not an additional requirement at all, but part of the overall proportionality requirement to which the first sentence is subject.[172] If this is so Article 86(2) as a whole has direct effect. On the other hand, it can also be argued that only the first sentence of Article 86(2) has direct effect and that the Commission alone has competence to declare that the interest of the Community is being infringed.[173] There is as yet no definitive Court ruling on the point.

F. ARTICLE 86(3)

(i) The Ambit of the Provision

Article 86(3) provides that the Commission shall ensure the application of the Article[174] and gives it the supervisory and policing powers with which to do this. These powers are in addition to the general powers conferred upon the Commission elsewhere in the Treaty. Under Article 86(3) the Commission can adopt two types of measure, decisions addressed to Member States (not to the undertakings themselves, in respect of whom the Commission must use its powers under Regulation 1/2003) and directives. The Commission may use these powers either to deal with some existing infringement of the Treaty rules or to take steps to prevent future infringements. The adoption of directives to deal with the latter has proved particularly contentious.

(ii) Decisions

The power to issue decisions addressed to Member States provides the Commission with an enforcement mechanism in respect of infringements of the Treaty in addition to the general power in Article 226.[175] However, the Commission still has to comply with the general

---

[170] Case 10/71, *Ministère Public of Luxembourg v. Muller* [1971] ECR 723; see also Case 155/73, *Sacchi* [1974] ECR 409, Case 172/82, *Syndicat National des Fabricants Raffineurs d'Huile de Graissage v. Inter Huiles* [1983] ECR 555; Guidelines on the Application of EC Competition Rules in the Telecommunications Sector [1991] OJ C233/2, para. 23.

[171] Case C-260/89, *Elliniki Radiophonia Tileorasi (ERT) v. DEP* [1991] ECR I-2925; see *supra* 17; see also Case 66/86, *Ahmed Saeed Flugreisen and Silver Line Reiseburo GmbH v. Zentrale zur Bëkampf Unlauteren Wettwerbs eV* [1989] ECR 803, [1990] 4 CMLR 102, paras. 55–7.

[172] See J. Faull and A. Nikpay (eds.), *The EC Law of Competition* (2nd edn., Oxford University Press, 2007), para. 6.205.

[173] *Ibid.*, 6.206.

[174] This is a specific manifestation of the Commission's general duty of enforcement and supervision under Article 211.

[175] Cases C-48 and 66/90, *Netherlands and Koninklijke PTT Netherland v. Commission* [1992] ECR I-565, [1993] 5 CMLR 316.

principles of Community law, such as giving reasons and allowing the addressee to be heard, and failure to do so means that the decision can be quashed.[176] In *max.mobil*[177] the CFI held that the Commission was under an obligation to examine complaints based on Article 86 diligently and objectively. However, the ECJ overruled the CFI and held that the Commission's refusal to act under Article 86(3) is not susceptible to judicial review.[178]The Commission has adopted Article 86(3) decisions in several of the cases mentioned in the sections above and in Chapter 7, such as *Spanish Courier Services*,[179] *ANA*,[180] and the essential facilities case, *Port of Rødby*.[181]

(iii) Directives

The reason that the adoption of directives under Article 86(3) is so contentious is that the Commission can thereby legislate alone, without going through any of the usual legislative procedures laid down in Articles 249 to 252 involving other Community institutions. The Member States therefore do not have any opportunity to vote against the measures in the Council, and the Commission can act where there is no political consensus. This has become an issue with regard to liberalization where there is a thin line to be drawn between harmonization under Articles 94 and 95 and preventing infringements of the competition rules under Article 86(3). Directives adopted under Article 86(3) have been challenged by Member States claiming that the wrong legal base was used for their adoption. The Commission used its Article 86(3) powers for the first time in adopting the Transparency Directive[182] which was challenged by France, Italy, and the UK. The Court confirmed that the Commission was entitled to proceed under Article 86(3) in adopting the Directive, a preventive measure which was aimed at creating greater transparency in the financial relationship between Member States and public undertakings, as it was necessary to its duty of surveillance under the Article.[183]

The Commission used Article 86(3) as the legal basis for two directives in the telecommunications sector, on telecommunications equipment[184] and telecommunications services,[185] both of which were challenged by Member States.[186] In the *Telecommunications Equipment* case the Court held that Article 86(3) does not give the Commission a general legislative power, but a

---

[176] *Ibid.*

[177] Case T-54/99, *max.mobil* [2002] ECR II-313.

[178] Case C-141/02 P, *max.mobil* [2005] ECR I-1283.

[179] [1990] OJ L233/19.

[180] [1999] OJ L69/31, [1999] 5 CMLR 103, confirmed on appeal, Case C-163/99, *Portugal v. Commission* [2001] ECR I-2613, [2002] 4 CMLR 1319, concerning discriminatory landing charges at Portuguese airports, discussed *supra* Chap. 7.

[181] [1994] 5 CMLR 457, discussed *supra* in Chap. 7.

[182] 80/723/EEC [1980] OJ L195/35 as amended [1985] OJ L229/20.

[183] Cases 188–90/80, *France, Italy and the UK v. Commission* [1982] ECR 2545, [1982] 3 CMLR 144.

[184] Dir. 88/301/EEC [1988] OJ L131/73.

[185] Dir. 90/388 [1990] OJ L192/10.

[186] For other aspects of the litigation, see *supra* 627 ff.

specific one to deal with State measures concerning legal monopolies:

Case C-202/88, *France* v. *Commission (Telecommunications Equipment)* [1991] ECR I-1223, [1992] 5 CMLR 552

Court of Justice

23. As regards the allegation that the Commission has encroached on the powers conferred on the Council by Articles [83] and [95] of the Treaty, those provisions have to be compared with Article [86], taking into account their respective subject-matter and purpose.

24. Article [95] is concerned with the adoption of measures for the approximation of the provisions laid down by law, regulation or administrative action in Member States which have as their object the establishment and functioning of the internal market. Article [83] is concerned with the adoption of any appropriate regulations or directives to give effect to the principles set out in Articles [81] and [82], that is to say the competition rules applicable to all undertakings. As for Article [86], it is concerned with measures adopted by the Member States in relation to undertakings with which they have specific links referred to in the provisions of that article. It is only with regard to such measures that Article [86] imposes on the Commission a duty of supervision which may, where necessary, be exercised through the adoption of directives and decisions addressed to the Member States.

25. It must therefore be held that the subject-matter of the power conferred on the Commission by Article [86(3)] is different from, and more specific than, that of the powers conferred on the Council by either Article [95] or Article [83].

26. It should also be noted that, as the Court held in Joined Cases 188 to 190/80 (*France, Italy and United Kingdom* v. *Commission*...paragraph 14), the possibility that rules containing provisions which impinge upon the specific sphere of Article [86] might be laid down by the Council by virtue of its general power under other articles of the Treaty does not preclude the exercise of the power which Article [86] confers on the Commission.

27. The plea in law alleging lack of powers on the part of the Commission must therefore be rejected.

In this case, although the Court upheld the Commission's power to legislate over telecommunications equipment it did annul Article 7 of the Directive, which required Member States to ensure the telecommunications monopolies did not enter into certain types of long-term contracts. The Court said that 'anti-competitive conduct engaged in by undertakings on their own initiative' could be dealt with only by individual decisions adopted under Articles 81 and 82 and that Article 86(3) was not an appropriate basis. Likewise in the *Telecommunications Services* case[187] the Court upheld the Commission's right to use Article 86(3) for measures which were necessary for its surveillance function.[188]

The Member States look jealously at the Commission's use of its Article 86(3) powers and the Commission strives to distinguish its surveillance and supervisory powers from other measures. The Open Network Provision Directive,[189] to which the Services Directive was an

---

[187] Cases C-271, 281 and 289/90, *Spain, Belgium & Italy* v. *Commission* [1992] ECR I-5833.

[188] Although Article 8 was annulled on the same grounds as Article 7 of the Equipment Dir., Dir. 88/301/EEC [1988] OJ L131/73 and the provisions on special rights were annulled for inadequacy of reasons; for this aspect see *supra* 628.

[189] Council Dir. 90/387/EEC [1990] OJ L192/1.

accompaniment, was adopted under Article 95 (ex Article 100a), because it was a harmonization measure, dealing with the conditions for access to, and use of, public networks and services.

5. SERVICES OF GENERAL ECONOMIC INTEREST AND STATE AIDS

This book does not cover State Aids, but it should be noted here that there a major issue over the financing of services of general economic interest and State Aids. It particular the question is whether, or in what circumstances, compensation for services of general economic interest is to be considered a State Aid under Article 87. A series of cases[190] culminated in the ruling in *Altmark*,[191] where the Court established that compensation that does not exceed what is necessary to cover the minimum possible costs incurred in the discharge of public service obligations is not a State Aid.[192] Commission decision (EC) 2005/842 now specifies that certain types of compensation paid by Member States to undertakings dealing with services of general economic interest are compatible with Article 86(2) and exempt from the State Aid notification obligation under Article 88.[193]

6. SERVICES OF GENERAL (ECONOMIC) INTEREST AND POLITICAL AND LEGAL DEVELOPMENTS

A. ARTICLE 16 EC

(i) The Background To Article 16

It will be apparent from the discussion in this Chapter that much of the case law on Article 86(2) is inconsistent. That may be inevitable. Although it accepts that the (Community) goals of free markets and unrestricted competition may have to give way to the imperative of the (Member States') delivery of public services, Article 86(2) gives little guidance on how the balance is to be struck. This is not, however, an area where the Commission and the Member States line up against each other, for the Member States differ among themselves. Some States (such as France) have different values and priorities from others (such as the UK), and in modern economies the divide between public and private has become increasingly blurred.[194] Ultimately the whole issue comes down to one question: when do non-market considerations trump market concerns?

---

[190] Case 240/83, *ADBHU* [1985] ECR 531; Case T-106/95, *Fédération Française des Sociétés d'assurances (FFSA)* [1997] ECR II-0229; Case C-53/00, *Ferring* [2001] ECR I-9067.

[191] Case C-280/00, *Altmark Trans GmbH, Regierungspräsidium Magdeburg v. Nahverkehrsgesellschaft Altmark GmbH* [2003] ECR I-7747.

[192] See S. Santamato and N. Pesaresi, 'Compensation for Services of General Economic Interest: Some Thoughts on the *Altmark* Ruling' [2004] *Competition Policy Newsletter*, No. 1, p. 1.

[193] [2005] OJ L312/67 (adopted under Article 86(3)).

[194] See E. M. Garcia, 'Public Service, Public Services, Public Functions, and Guarantees of the Rights of Citizens: Unchanging Needs in a Changed Context' in M. Freedland and S. Sciarra (eds.), *Public Services and Citizenship in European Law* (Clarendon Press, 1998), 57.

There was a lively debate in the European Union about liberalization, how public services should be delivered, and how far competition principles should be modified as regards public services, in the period leading up to the Intergovernmental Conference in 1996. In September 1996 the Commission produced a Communication, *Services of General Interest in Europe*,[195] stressing the importance of services of general interest to the European citizen and the role which they play in promoting social and economic cohesion. Part of the Communication read:[196]

A. Serving the public

1. Shared values

5. The Community's involvement with services of general interest is within the context of an open economy which is based on a commitment to mutual assistance ('solidarity' for short), social cohesion and market mechanisms.

6. European societies are committed to the general interest services they have created which meet basic needs. These services play an important role as social cement over and above simple practical considerations. They also have a symbolic value, reflecting a sense of community that people can identify with. They form part of the cultural identity of everyday life in all European countries.

7. The roles assigned to general interest services and the special rights which may ensue reflect considerations inherent in the concept of serving the public, such as ensuring that needs are met, protecting the environment, economic and social cohesion, land-use planning and promotion of consumer interests. The particular concern of consumers is to obtain high-quality services at prices they can afford. The sector-specific economic characteristics of the activities they cover also enter into the equation, since they have considerable knock-on effects for the economy and society as a whole and may require the use of scarce resources or large-scale long-term investment. This implies certain basic operating principles: continuity, equal access, universality and openness.

8. Central to all these issues are the interest of the public, which in our societies involves guaranteed access to essential services, and the pursuit of priority objectives.

. . .

The Commission concluded that the provision of public interest services is central to the values on which the European model of society is based.[197] The Communication elevated general interest services from merely a ground of derogation to a core element of European culture and a factor promoting European cohesion and solidarity. The Commission suggested (paragraphs 71–4) that a new paragraph should be inserted into Article 3 of the EC Treaty, adding 'a contribution to the promotion of services of general interest' to the activities of the Community.

(ii) Article 16 and its Place in the Treaty

In the event, the Commission's suggested amendment was not taken up. Instead, the Treaty of Amsterdam added a new 'Principle', now Article 16, to the EC Treaty:

Without prejudice to Articles 73, 86 and 87,[198] and given the place occupied by services of general economic interest in the shared values of the Union as well as their role in promoting social and

---

[195] [1996] OJ C281/3.

[196] There are sections in the Communication relating to specific sectors such as telecommunications, postal services, transport, electricity, and broadcasting (paras. 33–53).

[197] *Ibid.*, para. 70.

[198] Article 73 concerns transport policy, Article 87 concerns State Aids.

territorial cohesion, the Community and the Member States, each within their respective powers and within the scope of application of this Treaty, shall take care that such services operate on the basis of principles and conditions which enable them to fulfil their missions.

The Article is accompanied by a Declaration:

The provisions of Article [16][199] of the Treaty establishing the European Community on public services shall be implemented with full respect for the jurisprudence of the Court of Justice, *inter alia*, as regards the principles of equality of treatment, quality and continuity of such services.

The Treaty of Amsterdam also added a Protocol dealing with public service broadcasting to the EC Treaty:[200]

The provisions of the Treaty establishing the European Community shall be without prejudice to the competence of Member States to provide for the funding of public service broadcasting insofar as such funding is granted to broadcasting organisations for the fulfilment of the public service remit as conferred, defined and organised by each Member State, and insofar as such funding does not affect trading conditions and competition in the Community to an extent which would be contrary to the common interest, while the realisation of the remit of that public service shall be taken into account.

(iii) The Interpretation and Meaning of Article 16

Article 16 has been described as initially appearing 'a triumph for ambiguous drafting and diplomacy insofar as it appears to support any interpretation along a spectrum running from defensive protection by Member States of their existing national public sector influence to the creation of a new *communautaire* concept of public service capable of horizontal application throughout Community law and policy'.[201]

The first thing to notice is that it is placed in the Treaty among the fundamental principles of the Community and so cannot be dismissed as an insignificant side-show. This can be contrasted with the rather confused placing of Article 86 which, as we saw at the beginning of this Chapter, appears among the competition provisions despite being expressed to apply to all the rules of the Treaty. It can also be contrasted with Article 295, on national rules of property ownership, which languishes among the 'general and final provisions'. Whatever Article 16 means, the governments of the Member States have accorded it prominence.

The second thing to remark is that it assumes an existing state of affairs. It says '*given* the place occupied by services of general economic interest in the shared values of the Union as well as their role in promoting social and territorial cohesion' (emphasis added), thus accepting as a fact the vision described by the Commission in the 1996 Communication.

One interpretation of Article 16 is that, despite its place in the Treaty, it is ultimately no more than political window-dressing, changing nothing of substance. The Article says that it is 'without prejudice' to the existing case law and the annexed Declaration says it must be implemented with 'full respect' for the Court's jurisprudence. However, as we have noted above, the existing case law is far from clear, although the recent trend, from *Corbeau* onwards,[202] is to

---

[199] Article 7D before the renumbering took effect.

[200] In addition a Declaration on public credit institutions in Germany was adopted, and one by Austria and Luxembourg on credit institutions was annexed to the Final Act.

[201] M. Ross, 'Article 16 EC and Services of General Interest: From Derogation to Obligation' (2000) 25 *ELRev* 22, 22.

[202] And see also Case C-70/95, *Sodemare v. Regione Lombardia* [1997] ECR I-3395, [1998] 4 CMLR 667, where the Court said that Italian rules which provided that only non-profit-making private undertakings could be reimbursed by public authorities for running old people's homes were not against the competition rules.

interpret the derogation generously. Article 16 could be interpreted as simply giving Member States and entrusted undertakings more ammunition for justifying the latters' privileges and sending a message to the Court to continue on its present path. The Commission's view was that Article 16 reinforced the existing position:[203]

> The new Treaty, while retaining the provisions of Article [86], thus reinforces the principle whereby a balance must be struck between the competition rules and the fulfilment of the public services' missions . . .
>
> Regarding competition policy, a new legitimacy has thus been conferred on the main institutional and legal balances in the Treaty of Rome by the provisions contained in the Treaty of Amsterdam, particularly those of the new Article [16].

A further examination of the wording of Article 16, however, reveals that there is a crucial difference from Article 86(2). The latter Article is a derogation, whereas Article 16 puts a positive obligation on both Member States and the Community to ensure that entrusted undertakings are enabled to fulfill their missions by the principles and conditions under which they operate. Ross argues[204] that, although on one level Article 16 may simply be a 'seal of approval' for the existing law on Article 86(2), it may also represent a step forward. In elevating the support of services of general interest to an obligation owed by both the Community institutions and the Member States in the interests of solidarity and social cohesion, it realigns the Community's priorities and values. This point of view is also taken by Flynn.

L. Flynn, 'Competition Policy and Public Services in EC Law after the Maastricht and Amsterdam Treaties' in D. O'Keefe and P. Twomey (eds.), *Legal Issues of the Amsterdam Treaty*, 185, 197–8

Article 16, in essence, imposes a duty of solicitude on the Community and the Member States in respect of public services which are described, using language adopted from Article 86(2), as 'services of general economic interest'. This duty rests on two distinct, underpinning grounds. The first, putatively a general observation on the nature of the socio-political values of the Member States, is a normative claim, contending that services of general economic interest occupy a common position within the 'shared values of the Union', while the second, their role in promoting territorial and social cohesion, is chiefly instrumental. The former, irrespective of its accuracy, marks a shift in attempts to define 'Europe' in a formal fashion. It is clear that, post-Maastricht, the idea that the process of European integration can proceed as though it were no more than a functionalist and technocratic matter has lost its dominant character. This check has seen calls for the development of a political European Union, although it is clear that many central features of such an emerging polity have yet to be defined . . . Article 16 offers one thread to be woven into that wider picture, although not without raising uncomfortable questions about the lack of precision in the formulae used. To point only to one of these, while it is not possible to dispute the prosaic truisms that such services occupy 'some' place in the shared values of the Union (whatever these may prove to be), it is not clear from the new provision whether this place is significant, or marginal, developing or stagnant, and so on.

---

[203] Commission's *XXVIIth Report on Competition Policy* (Commission, 1997), parts 97 and 100.

[204] M. Ross, 'Article 16 EC and Services of General Interest: From Derogation to Obligation' (2000) 25 *ELRev* 22, 31–4.

B. ARTICLE 36 OF THE CHARTER

Article 16 is in effect repeated in Article 36 of the Charter of Fundamental Rights of the European Union which states:

The Union recognizes and respects access to services of general economic interest as provided for in national laws and practices, in accordance with the Treaty establishing the European Community, in order to promote the social and territorial cohesion of the Union.

Article 36 appears in Chapter IV of the Charter, 'Solidarity', and elevates access to services of general economic interest to the status of a fundamental right.[205]

C. THE COMMISSION'S 2000 COMMUNICATION ON SERVICES OF GENERAL INTEREST

The Commission's Communication of September 2000[206] replaced that of 1996.[207] The Commission described the Communication as, *inter alia*, giving 'perspectives on how, building upon Article 16, the Community in partnership with local, regional and national authorities can develop a proactive policy at European level to ensure that all the citizens of Europe have access to the best services'.[208] It locates services of general interest at the heart of the concept of European citizenship.

Communication on Services of General Interest

2. The Mission of Services of General Interest

8. At the heart of Community policy on services of general interest lies the interest of citizens. Services of general interest make an important contribution to the overall competitiveness of European industry and to economic, social and territorial cohesion. As users of these services, European citizens have come to expect high quality services at affordable prices. It is thus users and their requirements that are the main focus of public action in this domain. The Community protects the objectives of general interest and the mission of serving the public.

9. In order to fulfill their mission, it is necessary for the relevant public authorities to act in full transparency, by stipulating with some precision the needs of users for which services of general interest are being established, who is in charge of setting up and enforcing the relevant obligations and how these obligations are going to be fulfilled. Action at the appropriate level, Community, national, regional or local level, needs to be taken to establish criteria for services of general interest. Such action must be mutually supportive and coherent.

10. The needs of users should be defined widely. Those of consumers clearly play an important role. For consumers, a guarantee of universal access, high quality and affordability constitutes the

---

[205] *Supra* 106.
[206] [2001] OJ C 17/4.
[207] [1996] OJ 281/3.
[208] [2001] OJ C17/4, Executive Summary.

basis of their needs. Enterprises, and in particular, small and medium-sized enterprises, are also major users of services of general interest, whose needs must be met. Citizens' concerns are also of a wider nature, such as:

— that for a high level of environment protection,

— specific needs of certain categories of the population, such as the handicapped and those on low incomes,

— complete territorial coverage of essential services in remote or inaccessible areas.

. . .

64. The special place of services of general economic interest in the shared values of the Union, recognized by Article 16 of the Treaty, calls for a parallel recognition of the link between access to services of general interest and European citizenship. While Member States retain ample freedom as to means by which the objectives of solidarity served by services of general interest are to be accomplished, a core common concept of such general interest may be necessary to sustain allegiance to the Union. The Commission considers the provisions on access to services of general economic interest in the draft Charter of Fundamental Rights[209] as an important step in this direction.

The Commission stated that three principles underlie the application of Article 86:[210] neutrality, freedom to define, and proportionality. *Neutrality* is neutrality as regards the public or private ownership of companies guaranteed by Article 295. *Freedom to define* means that Member States are primarily responsible for defining what they regard as services of general economic interest and that this definition can only be subject to control for manifest error. *Proportionality under Article 86(2)* 'implies that the means to used to fulfil the general interest mission shall not create unnecessary distortions of trade'. The Commission 'exercises this control of proportionality, subject to the judicial review of the Court of Justice, in a way that is reasonable and realistic . . .'.[211] Furthermore, 'the principles formulated in Article 86 allow for a flexible and context-sensitive balance that takes account of the Member States' different circumstances and objectives as well as the technical constraints that vary from one sector to another'.[212]

D. THE COMMISSION'S GREEN PAPER OF 2003

The European Parliament suggested that the Commission should present a proposal for a framework directive on services of general interest and the Council also asked the Commission to look into this.[213] The Green Paper of May 2003 officially launched that debate. The Commission was concerned with the following questions:

(i) The scope of possible Community action that implements the Treaty in full respect of the principle of subsidiarity,

(ii) The principles that could be included in a possible framework directive or another general instrument concerning services of general interest and the added value of such an instrument,

[209] The Communication preceded the proclaimation of the Charter by three months.
[210] *Ibid.*, paras. 21–4.
[211] *Ibid.*, para. 23.
[212] *Ibid.*, para. 24.
[213] Presidency Conclusions of the Barcelona European Council, 15 and 16 Mar. 2002, para. 42 and of the Brussels European Council, 20 and 21 Mar. 2003, para. 26.

(iii) The definition of good governance in the area of organization, regulation, financing, and evaluation of services of general interest in order to ensure greater competitiveness of the economy and efficient and equitable access of all persons to high-quality services that are satisfying their needs,

(iv) Any measures that could contribute to increasing legal certainty and to ensuring a coherent and harmonious link between the objective of maintaining high-quality services of general interest and rigorous application of the internal market rules.[214]

E. THE COMMISSION'S WHITE PAPER OF 2004 AND SUBSEQUENT DEVELOPMENTS

The Green Paper initiated a broad debate on services of general interest and the Commission presented its conclusions in the White Paper of May 2004.[215] Following the public consultation the Commission was doubtful whether a horizontal framework directive was the most appropriate way forward and decided not to present a proposal for such a directive at present but to continue with the existing sector-specific legislation.[216] However, the White Paper highlighted the fact that the responsibilities in the area of services of general interest are shared between the European Union and the Member States and stressed the role of national, regional and local authorities in defining, organizing, financing and monitoring services of general interest. The White Paper defined the guiding principles of the Commission's approach to services of general interest as: enabling public authorities to operate close to the citizens; achieving public service objectives within competitive open markets; ensuring cohesion and universal access; maintaining a high level of quality, security and safety; ensuring consumer and user rights; monitoring and evaluating performance; respecting diversity of services and situations; increasing transparency; and providing legal certainty (without prejudice to the case law of the Court).[217]

For developments in respect of services of general economic interest at the Council Meeting of June 2007, see the Addendum at the end of this book.

7. CONCLUSION

1. Since 1990 the question of the relationship between competition law and public services has gone from being a side issue to a matter of central concern.

2. The thinking of the Commission about the role of services of general economic interest has developed to the point where it sees them as core unifying factor in the enlarged Union.

3. The Court has used the concept of solidarity to remove some undertakings from the ambit of the competition rules altogether.

4. The case law on Article 86 is not easy to reconcile. It reflects the tensions that exist within the EU and between Member States on the different choices that can be made in respect of the delivery of public services and to what extent they can be fully marketized.

---

[214] Green Paper, COM(2003)270 final, para. 12.

[215] COM (2004) 374, IP/04/638.

[216] But note Decision 2005/842, n. 193 *supra* on public service compensation and State Aid, and also the Community framework for State Aid in the form of public service compensation [2005] OJ C 297/4.

[217] White Paper, section 3.

8. FURTHER READING

A. BOOKS

BARNARD, C., 'EU Citizenship and the Principle of Solidarity' in M. Dougan and E. Spaventa (eds) *Scial Welfare and the Law* (Hart Publishing, 2005)

BOEGER, N., ' "New" Social Democracy before the Court of Justice' in J.Bell and C.Kilpatrick (eds), *Cambridge Yearbook of European Legal Studies 8* (2005–6), chap. 5

BUENIDA SIERRA, J. L., *Exclusive Rights and State Monopolies in EC Law* (Oxford University Press, 1999)

FAULL, J., and NIKPAY, A., *The EC Law of Competition* (2nd edn., Oxford University Press, 2007), chap. 6 (J. L. Buenida Sierra)

PROSSER, T., *The Limits of Competition Law* (Oxford University Press, 2005)

B. ARTICLES

BARTOSCH, A., Casenote on Cases C-147–8/97, *Deutsche Post AG v. Gesellschaft für Zahlungssysteme mbH (GZS) and Citicorp Kartenservice GmbH* (2001) 38 *CMLRev* 195

BOEGER, N., 'Solidarity and EC Competition Law' (2007) 32 *ELRev* 319

EDWARD, D., and HOSKINS, M., 'Article 90: Deregulation and EC Law. Reflections Arising from the XVI FIDE Conference' (1995) 32 *CMLRev* 157

FLYNN, L. 'Competition Policy and Public Services in EC Law after the Maastricht and Amsterdam Treaties' in D. O'Keefe and P. Twomey (eds.), *Legal Issues of the Amsterdam Treaty* (Hart Publishing, 1999)

GARCIA, E. M., 'Public Service, Public Services, Public Functions, and Guarantees of the Rights of Citizens: Unchanging Needs in a Changed Context' in M. Freedland and S. Sciarra (eds.), *Public Services and Citizenship in European Law* (Clarendon Press, 1998)

GYSELEN, L., 'Case note on *Albany, Brentjens'* and *Drijvende Bokken*' (2000) 37 *CMLRev* 425

HANCHER, L., 'Casenote on *Corbeau*' (1994) 31 *CMLRev* 105

—— 'Community, State and Market' in P. Craig and G. de Búrca (eds.), *The Evolution of EU Law* (Oxford University Press, 1999)

—— and BUENDIA SIERRA, J. L., 'Cross-Subsidization and EC Law' (1998) 35 *CMLRev* 901

PROSSER, T. 'Public Service and the Limits to Competition Law' in C. Graham and F. Smith (eds.), *Competition, Regulation and the New Economy* (Hart Publishing, 2004)

ROSS, M., 'Article 16 EC and Services of General Interest: From Derogation to Obligation?' (2000) 25 *ELRev* 22

SANTAMATO, A., and PESARESI, N., 'Compensation for Services of General Economic Interest: Some Thoughts on the *Altmark* Ruling' [2004] *Competition Policy Newsletter*, No. 1 p. 1

SAUTER, W., 'Universal Service Obligations and the Emergence of Citizens' Rights in European Telecommunications Liberalization' in M. Freedland and S. Sciarra (eds.), *Public Services and Citizenship in European Law* (Clarendon Press, 1998)

SLOT, P. J., 'Applying the Competition Rules in the Healthcare Sector' [2003] *ECLR* 580

SZYSZCZAK, E., 'Public Service Provision in Competitive Markets' (2001) 20 *Yearbook of European Law* 35 (Oxford University Press)

TESAURO, G., 'The Community's Internal Market in the Light of the Recent Case-law of the Court of Justice' (1995) 15 *YEL* 1

VAN DE GRONDEN, J. W., 'Purchasing Care: Economic Activity or Service of General Economic Interest?' [2004] *ECLR* 87

VAN MIERT, K., 'Liberalization of the Economy of the European Union: The Game is not (yet) Over' in D. Geradin (ed.), *The Liberalization of State Monopolies in the European Union and Beyond* (Kluwer, 2000)

9

DISTRIBUTION AGREEMENTS

1. CENTRAL ISSUES

1. Vertical agreements are agreements concluded between firms which operate at different levels of the production and supply chain. Vertical agreements provide the links in the distribution chain from raw material to the final consumer.

2. Parties to vertical agreements generally produce complementary products or services, not competing products or services.

3. Initially, an extremely formalistic approach was taken by the Commission when determining whether vertical agreements infringed Article 81. This led to treatment of agreement by category, rather than economic effect. This approach may have deterred the conclusion of procompetitive agreements, innovative distribution methods and may have encouraged firms to integrate forward.

4. The recognition that restraints in distribution agreements are frequently procompetitive has, however, provoked a more economic approach to Article 81. The Commission overhauled and modernized its approach to vertical agreements in 2000.

5. A key issue considered in this chapter is when vertical agreements appreciably restrict competition by object or effect. It will be seen that the Commission no longer assumes that restraints on economic freedom equate to a restriction of competition. Case law and Commission guidelines provide guidance as to how the determination is made.

6. Even if an agreement infringes Article 81(1), an overarching block exemption exempts all vertical agreements that meet specified conditions from the Article 81(1) prohibition: in particular, the block exemption applies so long as the 30 per cent market share threshold is not exceeded and the agreement does not contain any hardcore restraints.

7. The block exemption operates as a 'safe harbour' exempting agreements even if they infringe Article 81(1).

8. The existence of the block exemption means that, despite the adoption of a more economic approach to Article 81(1), legal analysis still tends to be focused on Article 81(3) rather than Article 81(1).

2. INTRODUCTION

A. GENERAL

A manufacturer of a product is not solely concerned with manufacturing. If it does not itself use that product as an input, it must also plan for its distribution. Generally, the manufacturer will wish to minimize the costs of distribution and to ensure that its products are distributed in the most efficient manner. Broadly, this may be achieved either by doing it itself or by delegating the task to a third party (for example, an independent distributor or an agent). Similarly, a supplier of a service will need to decide how best to distribute its services.

This chapter starts by outlining the choices available to a supplier when deciding how best to market and sell its products or services to customers and the impact that the competition rules may have on a supplier's choice. The discussion focuses, however, on distribution agreements concluded between vertically related firms, for example, a manufacturer and an independent wholesaler or retailer[1] (the terms supplier and distributor will generally be used to describe the upstream and downstream parties respectively in this chapter), and the competition law problems that such agreements raise.[2] These problems differ significantly from those raised in relation to horizontal agreements since the agreements are not usually concluded by competitors (actual or potential), but by suppliers of complementary products or services. In this first section we outline the main pro-competitive and anti-competitive effects that may result from vertical restraints and the heated debate that their compatibility with the competition rules has provoked. In section 3 we outline the Community approach to vertical restraints, stressing the impact that the single market project and the Regulation 17 notification and exemption system has had on the Article 81 analysis. Further, we chart the key changes introduced by the Commission when it adopted a new block exemption on vertical restraints, Regulation 2790/1999 (the 'Verticals Regulation')[3] and published its Guidelines on Vertical Restraints (the 'Guidelines').[4] The enactment of this block exemption and the accompanying Guidelines heralded a new, more economic, approach to vertical agreements and initiated the Community's broader modernization programme. In sections 4 and 5 we set out in detail how Article 81(1) and Article 81(3) (including the Verticals Regulation) respectively apply to vertical restraints. In section 6 we consider subcontracting agreements, in section 7 we outline how Article 82 may apply to vertical restraints and in section 8 some conclusions are set out.

B. METHODS OF DISTRIBUTION

(i) Factors Affecting Choice

The method of distribution selected by a supplier is likely to be determined after consideration of a wide range of factors. In particular, the nature of the product or service, the nature of the market, the size and resources of the supplier, and any tax or legal implications will be relevant to the assessment. In addition, the decision may be affected by competition rules.[5] This is possible where the rules are applied more stringently to some distribution arrangements than to others.

(ii) Vertical Integration

A supplier which wishes to retain maximum control over distribution may take charge of it itself. This may be appealing to a supplier with considerable resources seeking to sell a highly

---

[1] An agreement between a manufacturer of a component and a producer of a product that uses that component is also a vertical agreement.

[2] It will focus on the way Article 81 applies to such agreements. Although clauses inserted into a distribution agreement by a dominant supplier may infringe Article 82 this issue is not discussed in detail in this chapter but is dealt with *supra* Chap. 7.

[3] [1999] OJ L336/21, [2000] 4 CMLR 398.

[4] [2000] OJ C291/1, [2000] 5 CMLR 1074.

[5] But see discussion of transaction cost economics and Coase Theory, *supra* Chap. 1.

complex product or to a supplier seeking to sell a high volume of low-margin products. This has perhaps become more popular since the Internet has taken off as a mode of distribution. The supplier may set up a distribution arm (internal growth) or may acquire an undertaking that is already in the distribution business (external growth).

A decision to move into distribution may, however, be impractical and/or an inefficient use of a firm's resources. There may not be a close fit between the supplier's product and the retailer's scope, the firm may become less efficient and management may find it harder to keep track of what their employees are doing as it grows, or the firm may simply not have the resources to move into retailing.

Retailers commonly secure economies of scope by offering the consumer under one roof dozens or even thousands of products, often gathered together from a diversity of manufacturers. It would be prohibitively costly for the manufacturer of paper towels, crescent wrenches, or anti-biotics to establish its own retail distribution facilities in order to control the conditions under which its product is resold to consumers. And even when there is a reasonably close fit between manufacturer product line and retail outlets' scope, as in automobiles, major appliances, or photo supplies, the two stages require quite different skills, attitudes, and spans of managerial focus, and the advantages of specialization typically require that retailers be kept separate organizationally from their primary suppliers.[6]

In many cases a supplier may, therefore, consider it preferable to leave distribution to entities that are experienced in retailing and which know more about the markets and customers to be targeted. In particular, local distributors may be able to penetrate foreign markets more quickly and effectively.

(iii) Agency

Whether or not a supplier decides to appoint an agent or an independent distributor will be dependent mainly on the independence it wishes the third party to be given, the risk it wishes to bear, and the responsibilities of the supplier on the termination of the relationship. Ordinarily, the functions of an agent are restricted and limited to negotiating sales or purchasing agreements on behalf of the principal.[7]

If any agent appointed satisfies the definition of a 'commercial agent', Directive 86/653 may provide the agent with some protection.[8] The objective of this directive is to ensure that principals and agents compete on an equal footing throughout the Community and to provide agents with minimum protection. Amongst other things the directive contains provisions on the

---

[6] F. M. Scherer and D. Ross, *Industrial Market Structure and Economic Performance* (3rd edn., Houghton Mifflin, 1990), 542.

[7] In its Guidelines the Commission defines agency agreements to cover '[T]he situation in which a legal or physical person (the agent) is vested with the power to negotiate and/or conclude contracts on behalf of another person (the principal), either in the agent's own name or in the name of the principal, for the purchase of goods or services by the principal, or sale of goods or services supplied by the principal', Guidelines on Vertical Restraints ('Guidelines') [2000] OJ C291/1, [2000] 5 CMLR 1074, para. 12. It will be seen below that what constitutes a genuine agency agreement is key to the competition law assessment.

[8] A commercial agent is defined as a self-employed intermediary who has continuing authority to negotiate the sale or purchase of goods on behalf of another person (his principal) or to negotiate and conclude such transactions on behalf of and in the name of the principal, Council Dir. 86/653 on the coordination of the laws of the Member States relating to self-employed commercial agents [1986] OJ L382/17, Art. 1(2). See also the UK implementing legislation, the Commercial Agents (Council Directive) Reg. 1993, SI 1993/3053. For further detail on the terms of the directive see, e.g., J. Goyder, *EU Distribution Law* (4th edn., Hart Publishing, 2005), para. 6.4.

remuneration payable to the agent during the term of the agreement and on indemnification or compensation on the termination or expiration of the agency contract.[9] This could, of course, act as a disincentive to appointing an agent. Another drawback may be that agents are 'often less entrepreneurial, and may use less initiative in marketing than an independent dealer'.[10]

(iv) Distribution through Independent Distributors

Alternatively, distribution may be left to a distributor that will itself sell, or use, the goods or supply the services.[11] Efficiency in distribution through independent distributors was transformed by the information technology revolution. 'Just in time' principles have enabled consumer demand to pull products towards the market instead of products being manufactured and stored in anticipation of customer demand. This in turn has forced firms to address inefficiencies in supply and has led to closer cooperative relationships being formed between suppliers and their distributors respectively. This 'revolution' is described in the Commission's Green Paper on Vertical Restraints.

Green Paper on Vertical Restraints in Competition Policy, COM(96) 721

40. Traditional distribution channels consisting of independent manufacturers, wholesalers and retailers are in decline. These traditional channels consist of independent operators acting at arms' length and seeking to maximize their own profit rather than those of the channel as a whole.

41. The whole nature of distribution has been changed by the information technology revolution. Information systems have forced companies to re-evaluate and adapt their commercial relationships with both customers and suppliers and have enabled them to adopt more tightly managed and efficient business practices. The adoption of Just-in-time (JIT) principles by manufacturing industry and their extension to traditional distribution systems has had a profound effect on the whole distribution chain. JIT is based upon the principle that no products should be made, no components ordered, until there is downstream demand. Combined with modern technology (i.e., computers, automation, laser scanning, etc.) JIT has facilitated a shift from 'push' (i.e., where products are manufactured and stored in anticipation of demand) to 'pull' (i.e., where consumer demand pulls products towards the market and behind those products the flow of components is also determined by that same demand) in the supply chain. The disadvantage of the 'push' system is that it frequently results in stock levels being higher or lower than necessary. The adoption of JIT techniques reduces stock holdings and forces companies to address inefficiencies or bottlenecks in the supply chain. JIT also involves a shift from large shipments towards smaller and more frequent shipments, a factor which forces both suppliers and customers to search for consolidation (i.e., JIT deliveries from a number of supplies are consolidated into one delivery, thus cutting down on transport and other costs arising from smaller and more frequent nature of batches).

42. Quick response logistics (QR) a further refinement of JIT, is a concept used to describe the capturing of demand in as close to real times as possible and as close to the final consumer as

---

[9] Council Dir. 86/653 [1986] OJ L382/17, Art. 19.

[10] V. Korah and D. O'Sullivan, *Distribution Agreements under the EC Competition Rules* (Hart Publishing, 2002), para. 2.8.4.

[11] In some cases the distributor will not just resell the product supplied but may use a raw material or component to produce another product.

possible. The implementation of QR has been facilitated by electronic data interchange (EDI), efficient replenishment (ER), bar coding, laser scanners, etc. The most recent evolution of these concepts in retailing is called efficient consumer response (ECR) the aim of which is to provide consumes with the best possible value, service and variety of products through a collaborative approach to improving the supply chain.

43. The adoption of JIT, QR and ECR systems in distribution involve a shift from the traditional arms' length relationship between manufacturers, wholesalers and retailers towards a relationship of co-operation, particular in the area of logistics. Although well advanced in the U.S. it has been suggested that co-operation between product manufacturers and retailers in the supply chain is still in its infancy in the EC due to a number of obstacles, including the traditional conflict between branded manufacturers and large multiples who would rather sell their own branded goods, and differing national terms and conditions of business. One of the most commonly quoted examples of co-operation involving a branded manufacturer and a retailers is the 'partnership' in the US between Procter & Gamble (P&G) and Wal-Mart, one of North America's largest retailers, whereby the former receives sales data directly from the check-out counters of the latter. P&G and uses this information to match its production to Wal-Mart's demand. The benefits of such a system for both manufacturers and retailers is that they can reduce the levels of stocks while improving consumer availability. While the fully integrated 'partnership' concept as between P&G and Wal-Mart may still be in its infancy in Europe, we are now starting to see the emergence of integrated logistics systems that link the operations of the entire supply chain.

Where distribution through an independent undertaking is chosen, a distribution agreement will, of course, be necessary. A supplier may simply wish to ensure that its products or services are distributed through as many outlets as possible. Alternatively or additionally restrictions and obligations limiting the number or type of distributors or restricting the conduct of the distributors may be considered necessary to make the distribution agreement commercially viable and/or acceptable.[12] Vertical restraints restrict the commercial freedom of one or more of the parties to the agreement. For example, a contractual provision may seek to restrict the freedom of how the distributor deals with the contract goods or services by limiting:

• the area within which the distributor can resell (territorial restrictions) or the customers to whom the distributor may resell (customer restraints). Frequently, such restraints may accompany the grant to a distributor of an exclusive territory in which to sell the product or to provide the service (exclusive distribution);

• the price at which the products may be resold, for example a fixed or a minimum resale price (*resale price maintenance*) or a maximum resale price (*maximum resale price maintenance*) may be imposed;

• the type or number of outlets in which the supplier's products are sold may be limited and the distributors restricted from selling to unauthorized distributors outside of the network (*selective distribution*).

These types of restriction limit *intra-brand* competition (competition between distributors of the supplier's product or service). They do not, *directly*[13] at least, limit *inter-brand* competition

---

[12] For the positive effects and the justifications for imposing vertical restraints, see *infra* 689 ff.

[13] Although such restraints do not directly foreclose competitors of competing brands from the market, they may dampen competition between distributors and facilitate collusion (explicit or tacit) between suppliers or distributors, see *infra* 692–8.

(competition between the supplier and producers of competing products). On the contrary, their main purpose may be to encourage distributor's to concentrate their selling efforts on the suppliers products and so to increase inter-brand competition. Frequently, such restraints may be accompanied by obligations on distributors to make specific services available to customers or to engage in active promotion of the products.

Vertical restraints may also seek to limit where the distributor purchases the contract products or products that compete with it. Clearly, these restraints may directly impact on competition between the supplier and its competitors by precluding distributors from handling competitor's products. For example:

- the distributor may be obliged or have incentives to purchase a specific brand of product exclusively from the supplier (in the *Guidelines on Vertical Restraints* the Commission describes this kind of obligation as an *exclusive purchasing commitment*. The exclusive purchasing commitment does not preclude the distributor from purchasing or selling competing goods or services from another supplier);[14]

- the distributor may be precluded from manufacturing, buying, marketing and/or selling competing products or services (*non-compete* or *non-competition obligations*) or required to purchase a specific percentage or a specific amount of its requirements of a type of product from the supplier (*quantity forcing* or *requirements contracts*);[15]

- the distributor may be required to purchase a second distinct (tied) product as a condition of purchasing the first (tying) product (*tying*);

- distributors may be required not to open a competing business for a certain period after the distribution agreement has been terminated. Such an obligation may be of particular importance in, for example, a *franchising agreement* where a supplier, a franchisor, grants the right to a distributor, a franchisee, to exploit a franchise and to set up a business marketing specified goods or services as part of a uniform business network established by the franchisor. The franchising agreement will ordinarily authorize the use of intellectual and industrial property rights, such as trade marks and know-how, to enable and to aid the franchisee to resell the goods and services.

It has been seen in Chapter 7 that non-competition and tying provisions may create competition law problems where the firm imposing the provisions is dominant.

C. COMPETITION RULES AND DISTRIBUTION

(i) The Impact of the Competition Rules on Methods of Distribution

It will be seen from the discussion below that a decision to distribute products through an independent distributor raises most problems from an EC competition law perspective and has

---

[14] The Commission describes 'exclusive purchasing agreements' in its the Guidelines as 'where an obligation or incentive scheme agreed between the supplier and the buyer makes the latter purchase it requirements for a particular product, for instance beer of brand X, exclusively from the designated supplier'. The exclusive purchasing obligation thus prohibits the buyer from buying that particular brand of the product from anyone other than the designated supplier but theoretically leaves the buyer free to purchase and sell competing products, for instance competing brands of beer. In practice, however, an exclusive purchasing obligation is frequently backed by a non-compete obligation, a prohibition on selling competing products: see, e.g., Case C-234/89, *Delimitis* v. *Henninger Bräu* [1991] ECR I-935, [1992] 5 CMLR 210, para. 10.

[15] See the definition of non-compete obligation in Reg. 2790/1999, Art. 1(b), set out *infra* 741. Distribution agreements may also include exclusive supply provisions, precluding the supplier from supplying other distributors, see *supra*.

raised significant difficulties in the past. This may therefore mean that competition law is a relevant factor when business is deciding how to distribute. Arguably, this should not be the case. Rather, '[u]nless there is a good reason, businessmen should be left to select the most cost effective method with as little distortion as possible induced by the competition rules and other kinds of legal measure'.[16] In particular, if the competition rules on distribution are too severe when compared with the treatment of vertical integration there is a danger that this policy might sharply accelerate the trend towards vertical integration of the distribution process.

(ii) Vertical Integration

A supplier that sets up its own distribution arm is unlikely to encounter difficulties with EC competition law. Article 81(1) does not apply to an agreement concluded between a supplier and distributor forming part of the same economic unit (in these circumstances the conduct is considered to be the unilateral workings of an economic unit and not joint conduct).[17] It is therefore necessary to look beyond the legal identities of the persons involved in the contract, and to determine whether they behave together as a single unit on the market. Where they do, distribution arrangements will fall outside Article 81(1) but might contravene Article 82 where one of the undertakings is dominant on a relevant market. Further, integration through external growth will rarely cause competition law difficulties. Although 'vertical' mergers between undertakings may be notifiable to the European Commission, the Commission is only likely to intervene where one of the parties has significant market power and there is a risk of serious foreclosure effects.[18]

(iii) Agency

a. Genuine and Non-Genuine Agency Agreements

The relationship between a principal and his agent, like the relationship between a parent and its subsidiary, may be characterised by 'economic unity' so that Article 81 does not catch genuine agency agreements concluded between them[19] (there is no agreement between undertakings for the purposes of Article 81(1)).[20] The separate legal status of the principal and agent is not, therefore, decisive. Rather, the critical issue is whether the so-called agent operates as:

- an 'auxiliary organ' 'forming an integral part of the principal's undertaking'[21] (a genuine agent); or

---

[16] V. Korah and D. O'Sullivan, *Distribution Agreements under the EC Competition Rules* (Hart Publishing, 2002), para. 1.1. See also discussion of transaction cost economics and Coase Theory, *supra* Chap. 1.

[17] See Case 15/74, *Centrafarm BV and Adnaan De Peijper v. Sterling Drug Inc* [1974] ECR 1183, [1974] 2 CMLR 480 and discussion of the single economic entity doctrine, *supra* Chap. 3. It will be remembered that an undertaking designates an economic unit even if in law that economic unit consists of several persons, natural or legal, see, e.g. Case 170/83, *Hydrotherm v. Compact* [1985] ECR 3016, para. 11.

[18] See *infra* Chap. 12.

[19] Cases 40–8, 50, 54–6, 111, 113–4/73, *Re the European Sugar Cartel: Cooperatiëve Vereniging 'Suiker Unie' UA v. Commission* [1975] ECR 1663, [1976] 1 CMLR 295, para. 480. In Case T-325/01, *DaimlerChrysler v. Commission* [2005] ECR II-3319, para. 86, the CFI also confirmed that the single economic entity doctrine was not restricted to cases where companies were in a parent-subsidiary relationship but could also apply to relations between a principal and its agent. An agent working for the benefit of its principal could in principle be treated as an auxiliary organ forming an integral part of the latter, who must carry out his principal's instructions and, like a commercial employee, forms an economic unit with this undertaking.

[20] See *supra* nn. 17 and 19 and Case C-217/05 *Confederación Espanola de Empresarios de Estaciones de Servicio v. Compania Espanola de Petróleos*, 14 Dec, 2006 [2007] 4 CMLR 866.

[21] See Case 311/85, *ASBL Verenging van Vlaamse Reisbureaus v. ASBL Sociale Diense van de Plaatselijke en Gewestelijke Overheidsdiensten* [1987] ECR 3801, [1989] 4 CMLR 213, paras. 19–20 and Case C-266/93,

- an independent economic operator assuming financial and commercial risks linked to sale or the performance of contracts entered into with third parties.

The question of what constitutes a genuine agency agreement, equated with internal allocations of the working of the firm rather than joint conduct, is therefore of critical importance. Although the JIT principle,[22] has rendered it easier for suppliers to distribute through agents, since the shift from push to pull from consumers has made it less important for distributors to hold stocks and to accept distribution risks,[23] it is clear that in assessing the relationship the real economic situation, rather than the parties' contractual classification of the relationship is determinative.[24] Guidance on this issue can be found both in the case law and in the Commissions' *Guidelines on Vertical Restraints*. The strands of case law and the Guidelines are, however, not entirely easy to reconcile with one another.

In 2006, the ECJ held in *Confederación Espanola de Empresarios de Estaciones de Servicio v Compania Espanola de Petróleos*[25] that the decisive factor for the purposes of determining whether an entity (in that case a service-station operator) constituted an independent economic operator or an auxiliary part of the principal, was to be found in the agreement concluded with the principal and, in particular, in the clauses relating to the assumption of financial and commercial *risks* linked to sales of goods to third parties (such as the risks relating to financing of stocks (in that case fuel stocks) and those linked to investments specific to the market).[26] If the operator bore more than a negligible proportion of those risks Article 81 would be applicable. The following factors are relevant to the appraisal: whether the distributor takes possession of goods prior to selling them to a third party; whether the distributor assumes costs linked to distribution of goods, such as transport costs; whether the distributor maintains stocks at his own expense; who assumes responsibility for any damage caused to the goods or by the goods to third parties; allocation of financial risk in the case of not finding a purchaser or deferred payment; and who pays for investments to premises, equipment and advertising campaigns.[27]

This approach is extremely similar to, and thus appears to endorse, that set out by the Commission in its *Guidelines on Vertical Restraints*.[28] The Guidelines accept that selling or purchasing function of an agent may form 'part of the principal's activities, despite the fact that the agent is a separate undertaking',[29] and that the decisive factor in the determination is 'the financial or commercial risk borne by the agent in relation to the activities for which he has been

---

Bundeskartellamt v. Volkswagen AG and VAG Leasing GmbH [1995] ECR I-3477, para. 19. See also the Commission's Guidelines on Vertical Restraints which replace the Commission's 1962 Notice on exclusive dealing contracts with commercial agents, Notice on exclusive dealing contracts with commercial agents [1962] JO L39/2921, see Guidelines, n. 7.

[22] See *supra* 682.

[23] See e.g. Faull and A. Nikpay *The EC Law of Competition* (2nd edn., Oxford University Press, 2007), para. 9.171.

[24] *Ibid*, paras. 46–9.

[25] Case C-217/05, *Confederación Espanola de Empresarios de Estaciones de Servicio v. Compania Espanola de Petróleos* [2006] 14 Dec. 2006, [2007] 4 CMLR 866.

[26] *Ibid*. para. 46.

[27] *Ibid*. paras 50–61.

[28] Where it is recognized that, in certain circumstances, agents play an auxiliary function similar to that played by an employee

[29] Guidelines, para. 15.

appointed as an agent by the principal'.[30] The agency will be genuine where the agent does not bear any or only insignificant risk, and non-genuine where it does accept the risk.

First there are the risks which are directly related to the contracts concluded and/or negotiated by the agent on behalf of the principal, such as financing of stocks. Secondly, there are the risks related to market-specific investments. These are investments specifically required for the type of activity for which the agent has been appointed by the principal, i.e., which are required to enable the agent to conclude and/or negotiate this type of contract. Such investments are usually sunk, if upon leaving that particular field of activity the investment cannot be used for other activities or sold other than at a significant loss.[31]

Although the Commission states that the question of risk must be assessed on a case-by-case basis,[32] it states that Article 81(1) is unlikely to apply where the property in the contract goods bought or sold on behalf of the principal does not vest in the agent or the contract services are not supplied by the agent and where a number of other conditions are satisfied.[33] The Guidelines also make it clear that an agent may act for more than one principal.

In 2001, in *Mercedez Benz*,[34] the Commission applied the approach set out in its Guidelines when considering the application of Article 81 to restrictions of competition, namely restrictions on the export of new Mercedes-Benz vehicles, agreed by a supplier with German 'commercial agents'. The Commission rejected the view that the relevant agreements were genuine agency agreements. In its view the Mercedes-Benz agents bore a number of risks, which went beyond the scope of a genuine commercial agent contract. It did not consider this view to be affected by the fact that the agents formed an integral part of the Mercedes-Benz organization. 'The criterion of integration is, unlike risk allocation, not a separate criterion for distinguishing a commercial agent from a dealer.'[35] The CFI, however,[36] adopting perhaps a slightly stricter approach than that manifest in earlier case law,[37] annulled this part of the decision, holding that the German agents were genuine agents so that an agreement between undertakings had not been substantiated. It stressed that in considering whether an entity constituted an independent distributor or an agent, it had to be determined whether the entity bore any of the risks resulting from the contracts negotiated on behalf of the principal and operated as an auxiliary organ forming an integral part of the principal's undertaking. On the facts, it considered that the Commission had wrongly assessed the risk and held that Mercedes-Benz did in fact bear the risk

---

[30] Guidelines, para. 13. Paragraphs 12–17 provide more detailed guidance on how to distinguish between 'genuine' and 'non-genuine' agency agreements.

[31] Guidelines, para. 14. Risks connected with the provision of agency services, such as agency income, are not relevant.

[32] The Commission looks to the economic reality, not the form of the agency.

[33] A non-exhaustive list of relevant factors is set out in the Guidelines. It may be important, for example, that the agent does not incur the costs relating to the supply/purchase of the contract goods or services (such as transport), does not invest in sales promotion, does not maintain at its own cost or risk stocks of the contract goods, does not create and/or operate at its own cost an after-sales, repair or warranty service, does not make market-specific investments, does not incur product liability, and does not take responsibility for the customers' non-performance of the contract, see Guidelines, paras. 16 and 17.

[34] [2002] OJ L257/1, [2003] 4 CMLR 95.

[35] Ibid., para. 163, relying on Case C-266/93, *Bundeskartellamt v. Volkswagen AG and VAG Leasing GmbH* [1995] ECR I-3477, paras. 4 and 9.

[36] Case T-325/01, *DaimlerChrysler v. Commission* [2005] ECR II-3319, para. 86.

[37] See V. Korah and D. O'Sullivan, *Distribution Agreements under the EC Competition Rules* (Hart Publishing, 2002), 101–3.

associated with the contract and the purchase of new cars and not the commercial agents which operated, acting on the instructions of the principal, as an auxiliary organ integrated into the principal's business. Title in the cars passed direct from Mercedez-Benz to the customer and the agent had no authority to negotiate rebates except out of its own commission.[38] The fact that the agents bore responsibility for some activities and financial obligations on separate markets (such as transportation of the cars, purchase of demonstration cars and provision of after-sales guarantee services) did not detract from this conclusion. This approach seems to place importance on the degree of integration of the agent within the principal and whether the agent acts autonomously or as an auxiliary organ to the principal in relation to the market concerned (in this case the sale of the new cars).[39]

In its Guidelines the Commission also states that even if the agency is a genuine one, only obligations inherent in the agency agreement such as those imposed on the agent in relation to the contracts concluded and/or negotiated on behalf of the principal (including territorial, customer, and price restraints), and, possibly, exclusive agency provisions (provision preventing the principal from appointing other agents in respect of a given type of transaction, customer, or territory) fall outside Article 81(1).[40] Thus even a genuine agency agreement may infringe Article 81(1) if it contains provisions preventing the agent from acting as an agent or distributor of undertakings which compete with the principal (non-compete provisions) and leads to foreclosure on the relevant market[41] or where it facilitates collusion.[42] Intuitively, this latter conclusion may at first sight seem irreconcilable with the judgments in *DaimlerChrsyler* and *Confederación Espanola de Empresarios de Estaciones de Servicio v Compania Espanola de Petróleos* which indicate that agreements between principal and agent constitute the unilateral conduct of a single economic entity (or undertaking) falling outside the scope of Article 81(1) altogether. Nonetheless, the ECJ approved this conclusion in *Confederación Espanola de Empresarios de Estaciones de Servicio v Compania Espanola de Petróleos* stating at paragraph 62 that:

only the obligations imposed on the intermediary in the context of the sale of the goods to third parties on behalf of the principal fall outside the scope of that article. As the Commission submitted, an agency contract may contain clauses concerning the relationship between the agent and the principal to which that article applies, such as exclusivity and non-competition clauses. In that connection it must be considered that, in the context of such relationships, agents are, in principle, independent economic operators and such clauses are capable of infringing the competition rules in so far as they entail locking up the market concerned.

(iv) Distribution Agreements

a. Restraints on Conduct and Restrictions of Competition—The Problem

It has already been seen that vertical agreements concluded between suppliers and independent distributors operating at different levels of the supply chain generally contain restraints on the conduct or commercial freedom of one or more of the parties.[43] A key question arising is

---

[38] Case T-325/01, *DaimlerChrysler v. Commission* [2005] ECR II-3319, paras. 93 and 94.

[39] Nonetheless the Commission's Guidelines state that a genuine agent may act for more than one principal.

[40] *Ibid.*, paras. 18–19.

[41] *Ibid.*, para. 19.

[42] This could for instance be the case when a number of principals use the same agents while collectively excluding others from using these agents, or when they use the agents to collude on marketing strategy or to exchange sensitive market information between the principals, *Ibid.*, para. 20.

[43] See *supra* n. 683–4 and accompanying text.

whether or not these restraints on conduct should be characterized as restrictions of competition for the purposes of Article 81(1) or, indeed, whether or not vertical agreements should fall within that provision at all.[44] Although economic theory supports a suspicion of horizontal agreements '[e]conomists are much more equivocal about vertical agreements, between firms at different stages of the value-added chain'.[45]

b. The Positive Effects of Vertical Restraints

From the late 1960s lawyers and economists in the Chicago school argued that competition law should rarely, if at all, be troubled by vertical restraints which lead to increased sales and to the minimization of distribution costs. In particular, they propounded the view that a supplier will impose vertical restraints on intra-brand competition only where necessary to enhance sales of its product and to encourage inter-brand competition.

One of the main arguments is that vertical restraints are frequently necessary to enable a supplier to protect its distributors from *free riders*. For example, vertical agreements imposing resale price maintenance, awarding a distributor an exclusive distribution territory, or restricting supplies to selected retailers may be essential to encourage distributors to provide additional services necessary to boost sales and to persuade consumers to purchase more of the supplier's product. In the absence of such restraints,[46] distributors might be unwilling to incur the cost of providing additional services since other distributors would be able to take a 'free ride' on their investment.

Bork went further, arguing that not only was the rationale for the imposition of *all* vertical restraints[47] obvious, but their implication for economic efficiency was clear. A supplier would only ever impose vertical restraints in order to achieve distributive efficiency and to increase its output.[48] If the supplier wrongly required distributors to provide services that customers did not want, or did not consider to be worth the increase in price, those consumers would purchase rival products instead. The market itself would provide retribution for a supplier's mistaken belief that a vertical restraint was desirable. Where it did not, the problem would be the monopoly power of the supplier, not the vertical restraint.

The extract below from an article by Comanor explains these free-rider and distributive efficiency arguments more fully.

W. S. Comanor, 'Vertical Price-fixing, Vertical Market Restrictions, and the New Antitrust Policy' (1985) 98 *Harvard LR* 983, 986–90

Building on earlier studies . . . Lester Telser offered a detailed explanation of why manufacturers benefit from resale price maintenance [L. Telser, 'Why Should Manufacturers Want Fair Trade?, 3 *J.L. & E.* 86 (1960)] As he observed, because the quantity sold of a manufacturer's product

---

[44] See *supra* Chap. 4.

[45] F. Fishwick, *Making Sense of Competition Policy* (Kogan Page, 1993), 56.

[46] Such as the grant of an exclusive distribution territory or the imposition of resale price maintenance.

[47] Not only restraints on intra-brand competition, but restraints that encourage distributors to deal only with one supplier (single-branding agreements, for example, where the distributor agrees to purchase, or deal in, only the supplier's product).

[48] See *infra* 689–90.

depends on the final price paid by consumers, the manufacturer normally stands to gain from competition among dealers that limits the distribution margin. Only if other factors intervene can the manufacturer benefit from restraints on competition among his dealers . . .

Telser's primary explanation centered on the distributor's role in furnishing 'services' along with the manufactured product. By 'services,' Telser referred not only to delivery, credit, and repair, but also to selling, advertising, and promotional activities . . . In short . . . all factors supplied by the distributor that may influence demand for the manufacturer's product. The provision of these services benefits the manufacturer as long as the positive effect on demand outweighs the depressing effect of the accompanying rise in price.

The manufacturer, however, can influence the level of services furnished only by limiting competition among his distributors. He cannot simply lower his price in the hope that distributors will use their increased revenues to finance the appropriate services. Even if some distributors will do so—recognizing that greater sales result from providing services jointly with the product—others will not, and might compete by setting a lower price. The result is the classic 'free rider' problem:

> Sales are diverted from the retailers who do provide the special services at the higher price to the retailers who do not provide the special services and offer to sell the product at the lower price. The mechanism is simple. A customer, because of the special services provided by one retailer, is persuaded to buy the product. But he purchases the product from another paying the latter a lower price. In this way the retailers who do not provide the special services get a free ride at the expense of those who have convinced consumers to buy the product . . .

In order to remain competitive with free riders, other distributors will cease to provide the requisite services . . . Thus, fewer services will be offered and total sales of the product will be lower than they would be otherwise . . . The solution, according to Telser, is for manufacturers to establish minimum retail prices, forcing retailers 'to compete by providing special services,' . . . and thereby eliminating the free-rider problem . . .

Telser's analysis explains why manufacturers would wish to impose vertical restraints. What it does not do, nor claim to do, is answer the question whether dealers' provision of additional services is efficient—that is, whether the additional services justify the higher price charged for the product . . .

Judge Bork wrote the first article directly addressing the implications of vertical restraints for economic efficiency [R. H. Bork, *The Rule of Reason and the per se* Concept: Price Fixing and Market Division (pt. 2) 75 *Yale LJ*, 373 (1966)]. His test was simple: restrictions on output are anticompetitive, and increases in output are procompetitive. Using this criterion, Bork concluded that all restraints imposed by manufacturers *must* be efficiency-enhancing and procompetitive . . .

According to Bork, because a manufacturer will impose vertical restraints only if they lead to increased output and, in turn, to increased profits, such restraints must be procompetitive . . . his position assumes that the interests of manufacturers and consumers fully coincide.

The reasoning behind Bork's theory, which appears to have gained acceptance among both lawyers and economists, is that manufacturers will not find it profitable to impose vertical restraints when customers do not find the value of the new services exceeds their incremental cost. Otherwise a rival manufacturer would surely offer the product without the additional services and lure customers away.

The government's . . . brief in *Spray-Rite* adopts precisely this position. Monsanto, the manufacturer whose products were distributed by Spray-Rite, believed that demand for its products was unnecessarily low because many potential customers understood neither which Monsanto herbicides were appropriate for particular farming needs, nor the proper method of applying the products. To spur the dissemination of information and avoid free-rider problems, the company initiated a policy of vertical restraints. The government argued that the restraints were pro-competitive:

> [A]lthough vertical restrictions increase both dealer costs and price, such restrictions will be unprofitable for the manufacturer unless they also increase the quantities of product that dealers sell. This is the critical, pro-competitive respect in which such vertical restrictions differ from a mere widening of dealer margins, which would increase price but *reduce* quantities of product sold. Indeed, the manufacturer usually will anticipate that its marketing program will enable its dealers to increase their prices, precisely so that they can recover their added costs. That is true whether the manufacturer uses restricted sales territories, location clauses, exclusive dealing arrangements, or some other vertical restriction. [Brief for the United States as Amicus Curiae in Support of Petitioner, *Spray-Rite* (No. 82-914)]

This extract stresses the positive effects that may result from vertical restraints, even price restraints imposing resale price maintenance. The imposition of resale prices may be necessary to encourage retailers to compete on non-price criteria, such as service and promotion, to protect a retailer's reputation for providing high-quality services and stocking high-quality products and to facilitate market entry by a new competitor or an undertaking producing a new product. In each case the imposition of resale prices prevents other retailers from free riding on the retailer's efforts.

The Commission in its *Guidelines on Vertical Restraints* shows that it is fully aware of the benefits that vertical restraints may bring, recognizing that '[f]or most vertical restraints, competition concerns can only arise if there is insufficient inter-brand competition, i.e., if there is some degree of market power at the level of the supplier or the buyer or at both levels'. 'When a company has no market power, it can only try to increase its profits by optimising its manufacturing or distribution processes'.[49] Consequently, it accepts that vertical restraints may be essential to the realization of efficiencies and the development of new markets. In paragraphs 115–118 it summarizes the positive effects that vertical restraints may bring, especially the promotion of non-price competition and the improved quality of service.

In paragraph 116 a number of justifications for the imposition of certain vertical restraints are listed (which does not purport to be complete or exhaustive). In particular, the following justifications are recognized:

(i) to 'solve a "free-rider" problem', to prevent free riding on pre-sales services, for example by the allocation of an exclusive territory to a distributor, or the imposition of a non-compete obligation;[50]

(ii) to 'open up or enter new markets', to induce a distributor to engage in sufficient investment to enable a manufacturer to enter a new geographic market, for example, by the allocation of an exclusive territory to a distributor;

(iii) the 'certification free-rider issue', to introduce a new product on a market particularly by selling through retailers that have a reputation for selling only 'quality' products, for example, by appointing an exclusive distributor or establishing a selective distribution system;

---

[49] Guidelines, paras. 6 and 115.

[50] A supplier who funds a distributor's promotional expenses may also demand that the distributor purchase exclusively from it in order to prevent other supplier's free-riding or benefiting from its promotional effort.

(iv) to deal with the 'hold-up problem' and encourage client-specific investment and innovation, for example, a distributor may require exclusivity in distribution if it is to contribute to the cost of developing a manufacturer's new product;

(v) to deal with the 'specific hold-up problem that may arise in the case of transfer of substantial know-how', to protect know-how transferred under a distribution agreement, for example, by the imposition of non-compete restrictions;

(vi) to enable a manufacturer to exploit 'economies of scale in distribution' and to realize lower prices, for example, by using exclusive or selective distribution systems or quantity forcing provisions;[51]

(vii) to deal with 'capital imperfections', to provide security in respect of loans made in the terms of the agreement, for example, through the use of exclusivity provisions; and/ or

(viii) to achieve 'uniformity and quality standardization', to increase sales by creating a brand image and increasing the attractiveness of a product to the final consumer, for example, through the use of selective distribution or franchising agreements.

In addition a vertical restraint may be required in some cases to solve a 'double marginalization' problem. For example, a supplier may consider that exclusive distribution of its product is efficient. It may, however, wish to impose a maximum price cap on the product, in order to ensure that the distributor is not able to exploit its market power.

Many of these restraints discussed will ensure the distributor's commitment to the sale of its products.[52]

c. The Negative Effects of Vertical Restraints

The fact that vertical restraints might provide positive effects does not, however, mean that all commentators take the view that the imposition of vertical restraints is always justified and that such restraints will inevitably result in distributive efficiency.[53]

[E]conomists are becoming more cautious in their assessment of vertical restraints with respect to competition policy and less willing to make sweeping generalisations, and vertical restraints cannot all be regarded as *per se* beneficial for competition.[54]

Comanor, for example, criticized Bork's assumption that restraints would always lead to the most efficient result. The theory failed to attach sufficient importance to the different preferences of consumers for extra dealer-provided services and to distinguish between marginal and infra-marginal consumers.

---

[51] The limitation of the number of distributors within the system will reduce the costs of distribution and of monitoring any promotional efforts required of distributors.

[52] Obligations requiring a distributor to purchase all of its requirements of a product from the supplier (an exclusive purchasing commitment) and not to handle competing goods (a non-compete obligation) encourage distributors to promote the supplier's product actively.

[53] 'As on several other fronts, the debate over vertical restraints can be characterized with only mild imprecision as a contest between the University of Chicago...and the rest of the world. And as in other areas, the "Chicago school" has through superior organization, fervor,...and timing, if not superior access to revealed truth, sent the rest of the world reeling. But as competing in the marketplace of ideas continued, serious weaknesses in the Chicago position materialized': F. M. Scherer and D. Ross, *Industrial Market Structure and Economic Performance* (3rd edn., Houghton Mifflin, 1990), 541.

[54] European Commission, Green Paper on Vertical Restraints in EC Competition Policy, COM(96)721, para. 54. See, e.g., W. S. Comanor, 'Vertical Price-Fixing, Vertical Market Restrictions, and the New Antitrust Policy' (1984–1985) 98 *Harvard LR* 983 and J. J. Flynn, 'The "Is" and "Ought" of Vertical Restraints After Monsanto Co v. Spray-Rite Service Corp' (1985–1986) 71 *Cornell LR* 1095.

The 'marginal consumer' is one whose valuation of the product approximates to its current price. This consumer is, therefore, sensitive to improvements leading to an increase in the market price of a product. He will purchase more of the product only if he considers that the improvement in service or quality of the product is worth the increase in its price. If he does not he will generally purchase less. In contrast 'infra-marginal consumers' are consumers that place a value on the product substantially higher than the original price. Such consumers are relatively insensitive to increases in price. They will, therefore, not refrain from purchasing the product on an increase in price even if, in their view, the improvement in the quality of the products did not merit that increase in price.[55]

In the view of Comanor 'societal gains or losses from changes in the product depend on the preferences of *all* consumers, not merely those at the margin. To the extent that such alterations fail to reflect the preferences of infra-marginal consumers, the interests of consumers in general may not be served'.[56]

W. S. Comanor, Vertical Price-fixing, Vertical Market Restrictions, and the New Antitrust Policy [1985] 98 *Harvard LR* 983, 992–9

Suppose, for example, that the service in question is the provision of information about how to use a product. Consumers who are 'ignorant' about the product value this information and are willing to pay more for it. For 'knowledgeable' consumers—those already familiar with the product—the opposite is true: this class of consumers is unwilling to pay the increased price for the product necessary to fund the information services.

Assume further that a large number of infra-marginal consumers are 'knowledgeable.' Many of the consumers in this class may be previous customers who originally learned about the product from outside sources or from advertising provided directly by the manufacturer. The 'ignorant' consumers, we may assume, are largely marginal. Perhaps they value the product less than 'knowledgeable' consumers do simply because they are uncertain of its merits.

Because marginal consumers desire the information services, the manufacturer will impose vertical restraints. But this action may not lead to an efficient result: the interests of 'knowledgeable' infra-marginal consumers must also be taken into account. If they are great in number, the harm caused by making them pay for unwanted services may exceed the benefit derived by marginal consumers. Thus, the mere fact that the services are profitable for the manufacturer is not sufficient evidence that all—or even most—consumers benefit from their supply ... In short, these services may be oversupplied in relation to the consumer optimum ...

Economic theory alone cannot predict whether the imposition of vertical restraints—and dealers' provision of additional services—will benefit consumers and enhance efficiency. Whether consumers benefit depends on whether gains to marginal consumers outweigh losses to their infra-marginal counterparts. Because such losses may predominate—particularly when the restraints are used to support services for established products—consumer harm may result.

---

[55] W. S. Comanor, 'Vertical Price-Fixing, Vertical Market Restrictions, and the New Antitrust Policy' (1984–5) 98 *Harvard LR* 983, 991.

[56] *Ibid.*

In this extract Comanor stresses, therefore, that vertical restraints which are profitable to a manufacturer may not always achieve economic efficiency. They may lead to a reduction in consumer welfare as a whole. In particular, vertical restraints imposed to promote the sale of established products may induce distributors to supply an excessive level of information services. In contrast, where consumers must be persuaded to purchase new products vertical restraints are less likely to harm consumer welfare. Consumers will require more information to entice them to purchase the products.

Several other concerns also cause scepticism about the necessity or legitimacy in all cases of vertical restraints, even those that limit only intra-brand competition.[57]

In the Community, there is a unique concern that agreements which impose territorial restrictions on dealers whilst restricting only intra-brand competition lead to the division of markets on national lines in contravention of the single market objective. This is an extremely important point, since this factor has affected the Community institutions' approach to vertical restraints when applying Article 81(1), (3), and Article 82.[58] The extract below from the Commission's Green Paper on Vertical Restraints[59] explains that the Commission is unwilling to allow undertakings to re-erect, through agreements, the barriers to trade between Member States that it has worked so hard to dismantle.

Green Paper on Vertical Restraints in Competition Policy, COM(96) 721

70. The ongoing integration process of the Single Market adds an extra dimension to the analysis of vertical restraints. The 1992 programme was the result of a widely held conviction that the failure to achieve a single market has been costing European industry millions in unnecessary costs and lost opportunities. The exact title of the Cecchini Report, 'The cost of Non-Europe' . . . is a clear reflection of this. The efforts made since the entry into force of the EEC Treaty in 1958 had not exhausted by the mid-1980's all the potential gains to be expected from the full economic integration of the economies of the Member States. Now that more steps have been taken to eliminate the remaining obstacles to the free movement of goods, services and factors of production, it is still apparent that further efforts are necessary to achieve the maximum possible level of integration . . .

78. The EC experience shows that the removal of non-tariff barriers is not sufficient for the full development of parallel trade, arbitrage and changes in distribution across Europe. For the complete success of economic integration it is necessary that producers, distributors and consumers, find it profitable to move towards the new market situation and do not take actions to avoid or counteract the effects of the Single Market measures. The elimination of barriers to trade may not achieve its objectives if producers and/or distributors introduce practices contrary to integration. Unfortunately in many cases it is likely that they have strong incentives to do so.

---

[57] 'When the market is concentrated and manufacturers or distributors have market power, vertical restraints may be used to exploit consumers directly, or to put costs on competitors or raise barriers to entry, thus creating market power and inducing exploitation. The manufacturer may use the distributor to help it exploit the customer, and the manufacturer and distributor may share the extra gains': G. A. Bermann, R. J. Goebel, W. J. Davey, and E. M. Fox, *Cases and Materials on European Community Law* (West Publishing Company, 1993), 720.

[58] See *supra* Chaps. 1 and 4. Another reason for its 'overbroad' application of Article 81(1) was the Commission's tendency to focus on restraints on conduct rather than the impact that the restraint at issue would have on competition in the consumer welfare sense of economics, see generally B. E. Hawk, 'System Failure: Vertical Restraints and EC Competition Law' (1995) 32 *CMLRev* 973 and extract *infra* 704.

[59] European Commission, Green Paper on Vertical Restraints in EC Competition Policy, COM(96)721.

Further, and more generally, it is feared that restrictions on intra-brand competition may reinforce horizontal agreements, push up prices, and weaken inter-brand competition. The imposition of minimum resale prices (RPM), for example, may reinforce horizontal agreements, at either the manufacturers' or distributors' level. They may preclude distributors from pushing manufacturers for lower prices and provide a simple way for suppliers to prevent cheating on a cartel. Alternatively, they may be imposed as a result of colluding retailers cajoling or coercing suppliers.[60] There has also been concern that the free rider argument, used to justify many vertical restraints on intra-brand competition is frequently exaggerated and in fact applies to only relatively few products.[61] In addition, if practices such as resale price maintenance,[62] exclusive and selective distribution are widespread, retailers engaging in significant price discounts will be eliminated from the market, consumers may be deprived of innovative retailing and price discounting so that prices may increase,[63] price competition between suppliers may be softened, and tacit collusion between suppliers may result.

Another vital concern is that vertical restraints may actually affect and stifle inter-brand competition more directly. Exclusive dealership where a manufacturer sells his products in outlets that stock only his products affects inter-brand competition by removing other brands from the outlet. Obligations requiring dealers not to handle competing goods or, as a condition of purchasing a tying product, requiring the dealer to purchase tied products from the supplier may foreclose the market to competitors.[64] Some writers have suggested that the foreclosure resulting from the imposition of vertical restraints should be the sole concern for competition authorities:

Overall, the contribution of the economic literature on vertical restraints has been to establish that there should be no competition policy intervention, except where they are used strategically by the incumbent to foreclose the market to a new entrant, essentially by reducing rival manufacturers' access to downstream distributors.[65]

---

[60] F. M. Scherer and D. Ross, *Industrial Market Structure and Economic Performance* (3rd edn., Houghton Mifflin, 1990), 550.

[61] It applies only to pre-sales services (not post-sales services). Pre-sales services are unnecessary where the consumer knows what he wants to buy (see the extract from W. S. Comanor, 'Vertical Price-Fixing, Vertical Market Restrictions, and the New Antitrust Policy' (1984–1985) 98 *Harvard LR* 983 set out *supra*) and the free-rider argument is justified only in purchases of relatively high value. 'The consumer who secures from her friendly local hardware store a ten-minute demonstration of a $1.79 potato peeler's merits and then makes a special trip to the discount house to buy one is a candidate for something other than center stage in the economic theory of shopping behaviour', F. M. Scherer and D. Ross, *Industrial Market Structure and Economic Performance* (3rd edn., Houghton Mifflin, 1990), 552.

[62] S. Bishop and M. Walker, *The Economics of EC Competition Law: Concepts, Application and Measurement* (2nd edn., Sweet & Maxwell, 2002), para. 5.48.

[63] T. R. Overstreet, *Resale Price Maintenance: Economic Theories and Empirical Evidence* (Federal Trade Commission Bureau of Economics staff report, Nov. 1983). This report indicated that the more widespread practice of resale price maintenance in Europe delayed the arrival of supermarkets. For a detailed discussion of the pro- and anti-competitive effects of RPM, see the majority and dissenting opinions of Kennedy and Breger JJ respectively in *Leegin Creative Leather Products Inc v. PSKS Inc., DBA Kay's Kloset ... Kay's Shoes*, 26 June 2007.

[64] Provisions in a contract which require a distributor to purchase a product only from the supplier and not to purchase for resale competing goods, or other similar tying and requirements contracts, may preclude competitors from gaining access to retail outlets. Similarly exclusive supply contracts may preclude the buyer's competitors from gaining access to an essential source of supply.

[65] London Economics, *Competition in Retailing* (OFT Research Paper No. 13, 1997).

The Commission indicates in the Guidelines that its anxieties about vertical restraints are relatively broad. In particular, it fears that vertical restraints may foreclose the market, reduce rivalry and facilitate collusion between undertakings operating on the market, reduce intra-brand competition, and create obstacles to the single market.

103. The negative effects on the market that may result from vertical restraints which EC competition law aims at preventing are the following:

(i) Foreclosure of other suppliers or other buyers by raising barriers to entry;

(ii) Reduction of inter-brand competition between the companies operating on a market, including facilitation of collusion amongst suppliers or buyers . . . ;

(iii) Reduction of intra-brand competition between distributors of the same brand;

(iv) The creation of obstacles to market integration, including, above all, limitations on the freedom of consumers to purchase goods or services in any Member State they may choose.

104. Such negative effects may result from various vertical restraints. Agreements which are different in form may have the same substantive impact on competition. To analyse these possible negative effects, it is appropriate to divide vertical restraints into four groups: a single branding group, a limited distribution group, a resale price maintenance group and a market partitioning group . . .

In order to assess the effects of vertical restraints the Commission thus divides distribution agreements into four different categories that include similar types of restraints, single branding, limited distribution, resale price maintenance, and market partitioning groups, and analyses the competition problems that each type of agreement may pose. Previously, the Commission had been severely criticized for dealing with agreements by category and not looking at the effect of the restraint. The approach in the Guidelines recognizes that it is not the form of the vertical restraint that is important, but its effect on competition. Many different types of vertical restraint can have the same effect.

The Commission describes *single branding* agreements as those in which a buyer is induced to concentrate orders for a type of product with one supplier. This category includes agreements containing clauses that result in a buyer purchasing products or their substitutes only from one supplier such as non-compete or quantity forcing provisions.[66] The Commission is concerned that these agreements may foreclose the market to competitors, make market shares more rigid, facilitate collusion between suppliers, limit in-store inter-brand competition, and lead to higher prices for buyers.

107. There are four main negative effects on competition: (1) other suppliers in that market cannot sell to the particular buyers and this may lead to foreclosure of the market or, in the case of tying, to foreclosure of the market for the tied product; (2) it makes market shares more rigid and this may help collusion when applied by several suppliers; (3) as far as the distribution of final goods is concerned, the particular retailers will only sell one brand and there will therefore be no inter-brand competition in their shops (no in-store competition); and (4) in the case of tying, the buyer may pay a higher price for the tied product than he would otherwise do. All these effects may lead to a reduction in inter-brand competition.

108. The reduction in inter-brand competition may be mitigated by strong initial competition between suppliers to obtain the single branding contracts, but the longer the duration of the non-compete obligation, the more likely it will be that this effect will not be strong enough to compensate for the reduction in inter-brand competition.

---

[66] Full-line forcing, tie-in sales, and bundling can also have this effect if the distributor has no room left to stock competing products.

Limited distribution agreements are those in which the producer sells to only one or a limited number of buyers, for example, exclusive distribution, exclusive supply (where an obligation or incentive scheme makes the supplier sell only or mainly to one buyer), or selective distribution arrangements. The Commission notes that these agreements may foreclose the purchase market, may facilitate collusion between suppliers or distributors; and, by severely limiting intra-brand competition, weaken inter-brand competition.

110. There are three main negative effects on competition: (1) certain buyers within that market can no longer buy from that particular supplier, and this may lead in particular in the case of exclusive supply, to foreclosure of the purchase market, (2) when most or all of the competing suppliers limit the number of retailers, this may facilitate collusion, either at the distributor's level or at the supplier's level, and (3) since fewer distributors will offer the product it will also lead to a reduction of intra-brand competition. In the case of wide exclusive territories or exclusive customer allocation the result may be total elimination of intra-brand competition. This reduction of intra-brand competition can in turn lead to a weakening of inter-brand competition.

The Commission also considers that agreements obliging or inducing a buyer not to sell below a certain price, at a certain price or not above a certain price, the *resale price maintenance* group, will both reduce intra-brand competition and lead to increased transparency on prices. These factors may make horizontal collusion between manufacturers or distributors easier, especially in concentrated markets.

112. There are two main negative effects of RPM on competition: (1) a reduction in intra-brand price competition, and (2) increased transparency on prices. In the case of fixed or minimum RPM, distributors can no longer compete on price for that brand, leading to a total elimination of intra-brand price competition. A maximum or recommended price may work as a focal point for resellers, leading to a more or less uniform application of that price level. Increased transparency on price and responsibility for price changes makes horizontal collusion between manufacturers or distributors easier, at least in concentrated markets. The reduction in intra-brand competition may, as it leads to less downward pressure on the price for the particular goods, have as an indirect effect a reduction of inter-brand competition.

In the extract below, Korah and O'Sullivan sum up some of the reasons for being suspicious of resale price maintenance.

V. Korah and D. O'Sullivan, *Distribution Agreements under the EC Competition Rules* (Hart Publishing, 2002)

2.8.5. Resale price maintenance

Economists have differed widely over time and between countries as to whether vertical rpm is anti-competitive. The practice may alleviate the free rider problem . . . , in as much as a dealer providing the services will be protected from under-cutting by those that do not. It may restrain intra-brand competition less than an exclusive territory since competition on non-price items within the same area may be permitted.

On the other hand, in many trades the practice has originated in a horizontal cartel at the dealers' level.

Secondly, even in the absence of such a cartel, it may produce horizontal effects . . .

Thirdly, there is no assurance that the dealer given a firm margin over the price it pays will use it to provide the services the supplier hopes to induce. The dealer may prefer to promote less, but keep the high margin, relying on other dealers to provide pre-sales services.

Fourthly, . . . where it is only a few marginal consumers who desire the services, consumer welfare may not be increased by the increased demand.

Fifthly, resellers may compete away their assured margin by providing services that cost more than they are worth to customers; although if that be the case, one would expect the supplier to abrogate the practice.

Sixthly, where competition is not acute, it may enable the supplier to increase its share of the distribution margin in a way that increases the price to final buyers and reduces production.

Seventhly, rpm may be used to maintain the status of a premium brand rather than to induce the provision of services.

It will be seen later in this chapter that the Commission's concerns have, despite any potential efficiency justifications, led it, supported by the Court, to adopt a very strict policy against resale price maintenance so that it is treated as, virtually, unlawful per se. In the US, there was a call for the Supreme Court to abandon the per se rule against resale price maintenance and in June 2007 the court did overrule a nearly century old per se prohibition against it.[67] The Supreme Court's decision to subject resale price maintenance to the rule of reason, might lead to a call for the adoption of a more flexible approach in Europe.

Finally, the Commission expresses the belief that agreements within the *market partitioning* groups, in which the buyer is restricted in where it either sources[68] or resells[69] a particular product, may reduce intra-brand competition and help the supplier to partition the market and to hinder market integration. Further, the limitation of sourcing or resale possibilities of buyers may facilitate collusion at both the distributors' and suppliers' level.

114. The main negative effect on competition is a reduction of intra-brand competition that may help the supplier to partition the market and thus hinder market integration. This may facilitate price discrimination. When most or all of the competing suppliers limit the sourcing or resale possibilities of their buyers this may facilitate collusion, either at the distributors' level or at the suppliers' level.

In this section we have seen that vertical restraints enable efficiencies to be achieved but can also result in an anti-competitive outcome. These pro- and anti-competitive effects have caused many competition lawyers and economists to disagree violently about when vertical restraints cause anti-competitive harm and as to how any such harm should be reconciled with the efficiencies that vertical restraints may generate.

Before we summarize the Community approach to vertical restraints a brief look at the experience in the USA is helpful. The approach of the US courts, and authorities, has provoked and reflected much of the economic debate concerning the legitimacy of vertical restraints.

d. *Per Se* Illegality and the Rule of Reason—The Approach in the US

In the USA, as in the European Community, the analysis of vertical restraints on intra-brand competition has been the subject of excited debate.[70]

---

[67] *Leegin Creative Leather Product, Inc.* v. *PSKS, Inc. DBA Kay's Kloset . . . Kay's Shoes*, 26 June 2007. The US, in a brief as amicus curiae, urged the Supreme Court to overrule *Dr Miles* and to subject resale price maintenance to the rule of reason, see *infra* n. 88.

[68] The Commission places 'exclusive purchasing agreements' within the 'market partitioning' group. Exclusive purchasing agreements are frequently backed up by a non-compete provision, see nn. 14 and 15.

[69] e.g., where an agreement includes 'territorial resale restrictions, the allocation of an area of primary responsibility, restrictions on the location of a distributor and customer resale restrictions': Guidelines, para. 113.

[70] The treatment of tying and restraints on dealers handling competing products (exclusive dealing) has been rather different, see, e.g. *Jefferson Parish Hospital District No. 2* v. *Hyde* 466 US 2 (1984), *Illinois Tool Works Inc.* v. *Independent Ink, Inc* No. 04-1329 (2006) and *Tampa Electric Co* v. *Nashville Coal Co* 365 US 320 (1961).

US law on the permissibility of vertical restraints has had an unusually tumultuous history, marked by abrupt changes in legislated policy and judicial interpretations. Paralleling these changes, and sometimes influencing them, have been sharply conflicting interpretations of the economic motivations for, and consequences of, vertical restraints. Since the 1960s, few questions in the field of industrial organization economics have been debated more heatedly.[71]

In 1911, the Supreme Courts ruled in *Dr Miles Medical Co v. John D Park & Sons Co*[72] that resale price maintenance was illegal *per se*.[73] Justice Hughes stated:

If there be an advantage to the manufacturer in the maintenance of fixed prices, the question remains whether it is one which he is entitled to secure by agreements restricting the freedom of trade on the part of dealers who own what they sell. As to this, the complainant can fare no better with its plan of identical contracts than could the dealers themselves if they formed a combination and endeavored to establish the same restrictions, and thus to achieve the same result, by agreement with each other. If the immediate advantage they would obtain would not be sufficient to sustain a direct agreement, the asserted ulterior benefit to the complainant cannot be regarded as sufficient to support its system.[74]

In 1967, in *United States v. Arnold Schwinn & Co*,[75] the Supreme Court extended the *per se* rule to other vertical non-price restraints on intra-brand competition:

Under the Sherman Act, it is unreasonable without more for a manufacturer to seek to restrict and confine areas or persons with whom an article may be traded after the manufacturer has parted with dominion over it . . . Such restraints are so obviously destructive of competition that their mere existence is enough.

It has been seen that commentators, particularly those from the Chicago school, stressed the benefits for competition that result from vertical restraints. The decisions in *Dr Miles* and *Schwinn* were, therefore, subjected to fervent criticism. Indeed, Bork described Justice Hughes' decision to equate horizontal cartel behaviour with vertical price fixing as 'one decisive misstep that has controlled a whole body of law'. A manufacturer would not have the same motives in imposing resale price maintenance as distributors would in forming a cartel. The consequences for consumers were not the same. A manufacturer would have no interest in creating a monopoly profit for its distributors. A rule of *per se* illegality had, therefore, been created on an 'erroneous economic assumption'.[76]

---

[71] F. M. Scherer and D. Ross, *Industrial Market Structure and Economic Performance* (3rd edn., Houghton Mifflin, 1990), 541.

[72] 220 US 373 (1911). Under the 'Colgate' doctrine (*US v. Colgate & Co*, 250 US 300 (1919)) a supplier has been able to recommend prices and refuse to deal with those who do not adhere to the recommended prices if it acts *unilaterally*. Further, in many States resale price maintenance has been permitted at various periods since 1931. In 1937 (Miller–Tydings Act) and 1952 (McGuire Act) Congress passed legislation approving the practice of resale price maintenance. However, in 1975 the legislation was repealed so that, effectively, the ruling of *Dr Miles* was restored. In 2007, the Supreme Court overruled *Dr Miles* and subjected resale price maintenance to the rule of reason see *infra* n. 88.

[73] For a discussion of *per se* illegality and the rule of reason in relation to the Sherman Act see *supra* Chap. 4.

[74] 220 US 373 (1911), 407–8 per Justice Hughes.

[75] 388 US 365 (1967). In *White Motor Co v. United States* 372 U.S. 253 (1963) the Supreme Court had ruled just four years earlier that it knew too little of the actual impact non-price vertical restraints to extend the *per se* rule to vertical territorial and customer restraints.

[76] R. H. Bork, *The Antitrust Paradox: A Policy at War with Itself* (Basic Books, 1978, reprinted with a new Introduction and Epilogue, 1993), 32–3.

R. H. Bork, *The Antitrust Paradox: A Policy at War with Itself* (Basic Books, 1978, reprinted with a new Introduction and Epilogue, 1993), 289–90

Vertical restraint law has reached its present unhappy state because the Supreme Court is struggling with the logical results of an incorrect premise laid down sixty years ago by Justice Hughes in the *Dr. Miles* opinion. That premise . . . holds that there is no more reason to permit a manufacturer to eliminate rivalry among his retailers than there is to permit the retailers to eliminate rivalry by agreement among themselves. The premise is wrong. Retailers who agree to a horizontal restraint that the manufacturer does not desire are almost certainly attempting to restrict output for the sake of monopoly gains. If such a restraint would increase efficiency, the manufacturer would not only favor it but would impose it himself. When a manufacturer wishes to impose resale price maintenance or vertical division of reseller markets, or any other restraint upon the rivalry of resellers, his motive cannot be the restriction of output and, therefore, can only be the creation of distributive efficiency. That motive should be respected by the law . . . .

Schwinn's vertical price fixing . . . and vertical market division did not eliminate the rivalry of any other bicycle manufacturer with itself. These vertical restraints could not, therefore, create any additional power in Schwinn to restrict output. This would be true whether Schwinn had 1 or 100 percent of the bicycle market. If it had any power to restrict output, it would exercise that power directly and take the monopoly profits itself. There is no need for vertical restraints on retailers or wholesalers. The vertical restraint could not be anti-competitive for any effect they might have on the manufacturer's level of the industry

But by maintaining its retailers' prices and dividing its wholesalers' markets, did Schwinn simply give retailers and wholesalers the power to restrict output? That is so unlikely as not to be worth consideration. No manufacturer or supplier will ever use either resale price maintenance or reseller market division for the purpose of giving the resellers a greater-than-competitive return. The extra return would be money out of his pocket for no good reason, and we may safely assume that manufacturers are not moved to engage in that peculiar form of philanthropy. The manufacturer shares with the consumer the desire to have distribution done at the lowest possible cost consistent with effectiveness. That is why courts need never weigh the opposing forces of lessened intrabrand and heightened interbrand competition. When the manufacturer chooses, he chooses on criteria that also control consumer welfare. No court is likely to make a more accurate assessment than does a businessman with both superior information and the depth of insight that only self-interest can supply.

Since vertical restraints are not means of creating restriction of output, we must assume that they are means of creating efficiencies, and it is perfectly clear that they are. The Court in *Schwinn* admitted as much. The most obvious efficiency is the purchase of increased sales and service efforts by the reseller. A retailer whose price is controlled will have to vie for business by sales and service effort. In the absence of resale price maintenance, the problem of the free ride may arise . . . Customers will be able to go to the retailer who offers a display of the full line, explanation of the product, and so forth, and then purchase from the retailer who offers none of these things but gives a lower price. The result will be a diminution in the amount of sale and service effort by all retailers. When this is to the manufacturer's disadvantage, he may wish to employ either resale price maintenance or vertical division of territories to get the performance he wants.

The decision in *Schwinn* 'marked the apex of the trend toward prohibiting vertical restraints . . . Since that time, however, the law has moved in the opposite direction'.[77] In 1977 in *Continental TV Inc* v. *GTE Slyvania Inc*,[78] the Supreme Court, recognizing that vertical restraints, especially those restricting only intra-brand competition, might promote inter-brand competition, overruled *Schwinn*. Instead, the Court ruled that the scope of *per se* illegality should be narrow in the context of vertical restraints. A rule of reason approach should be adopted in relation to vertical non-price restraints.

[T]he market impact of vertical restrictions is complex because of their potential for a simultaneous reduction of intrabrand competition [rivalry between sellers of the same brand] and stimulation of interbrand competition [rivalry with sellers of other brands] . . . vertical restrictions promote interbrand competition by allowing the manufacturer to achieve certain efficiencies in the distribution of his products.[79]

The Court's ruling did not affect the *per se* illegality for vertical price fixing set out in *Dr Miles*. In maintaining a distinction between price and non-price restrictions the judgment did not go as far as some commentators would have liked.[80] Nevertheless, the judgment was welcomed, in particular, for the high degree of economic sophistication it displayed and for the recognition that as long as there was competition at the inter-brand level, the redeeming benefits of the agreement would outweigh the necessarily less significant limitation on intra-brand rivalry.[81] Subsequently, the lower courts, in applying the rule of reason, recognized that violations of the Act[82] would be unlikely in the absence of market power.[83] They have thus tended to decline to find an infringement unless the manufacturer imposing the restraint had substantial market share. In *Valley Liquors Inc* v. *Renfield Importers Ltd*,[84] for example, Judge Posner stated:

The plaintiff in restricted distribution cases must show that the restriction he is complaining of was unreasonable because, weighing effects on both intrabrand and interbrand competition, it made consumers worse off.

---

[77] W. S. Comanor, 'Vertical Price-Fixing, Vertical Market Restrictions, and the New Antitrust Policy' (1984–5) 98 *Harvard LR* 983, 985.

[78] 433 US 36 (1977).

[79] The Supreme Court upheld the validity of a location clause precluding the franchisee of a manufacturer of colour television sets, Sylvania, from selling the television sets from a new location.

[80] The Court did, however, provide a justification for the difference in treatment. In particular, it considered there to be support for the view that vertical price restraints would reduce *inter*-brand competition because they would facilitate cartelizing. In contrast support for the cartel-facilitating effect of non-price restraints was lacking, 433 US 36, 52 at n. 18 quoting R. Posner, 'Antitrust Policy and the Supreme Court: An Analysis of the Restricted Distribution, Horizontal Merger and Potential Competition Decisions' (1975) 75 *Colum LR* 282, 294. However, Justice White recognized that, given that price restraints might be used to achieve the same result as non-price restraints, the logical conclusion of the ruling might be that price restraints should also be subject to the rule of reason. 'The effect, if not the intention, of the Court's opinion is necessarily to call into question the firmly established *per se* rule against price restraints': 433 US 36 (1977), 69–70 per Justice White (concurring in the judgment).

[81] See, e.g. E. Gellhorn and W. E. Kovacic, *Antitrust Law and Economics* (5th edn., West Publishing Co, 2004), 365–6.

[82] The move from *per se* illegality to rule of reason analysis of course led to uncertainty and left, and still leaves, open difficult questions. In particular, how the rule of reason is to be applied.

[83] Since market power cannot easily be measured by the methods of litigation, it is normally inferred from possession of a substantial percentage of the sales in the relevant product or geographic market.

[84] 678 F.2d 742 (7th Cir. 1982), 745. Since the Supreme Court's ruling in Slyvania US Courts have rarely found agreements incorporating non-price vertical restraints to be in unreasonable restraint of trade.

Admittedly, this test of illegality is easier to state than to apply, the effects to be weighed being so difficult to measure or even estimate by the methods of litigation. The courts have therefore looked for shortcuts. A popular one is to say that the balance tips in the defendant's favor if the plaintiff fails to show that the defendant has significant market power...

A firm that has no market power is unlikely to adopt policies that disserve its consumers; it cannot afford to. And if it blunders and does adopt such a policy, market retribution will be swift. Thus its mistakes do not seriously threaten consumer welfare... Even if there is some possibility that the distribution practices of a powerless firm will have a substantial anti-competitive effect, it is too small a possibility to warrant trundling out the great machinery of antitrust enforcement.

The emphasis on the distribution efficiencies brought about by vertical restraints prompted an almost complete U-turn in the attitude of the judicial and enforcement authorities to vertical restraints. 'By the early 1980's the position had swung from regarding them as suspect for competition, to a generalised perception that they were innocuous for competition (the Chicago school.)'[85] In the 1980s the Department of Justice was rarely interested in vertical restraints,[86] even price restraints. The anecdote set out below emphasizes the striking nature of this change in policy:

I am... struck by an anecdote told by Mr Schroeter, the draftsman of the [EC] Regulations dealing with vertical restraints. When discussing the first Community Regulation for vertical restraints (67/67) with American friends in the FTC and the D of J he was severely criticised in that by exempting non-absolute territorial exclusivity and other vertical restraints he was permitting pernicious anti-competitive practices. Fifteen years later when drafting the renewal Regulation... he was also criticised from Washington for bothering at all with vertical restraints as clearly they were all pro-competitive. These criticisms referred to the same restraints and a very similar policy approach adopted by the Commission.[87]

In 2007, the U-turn was made complete when the Supreme Court in *Creative Leather Product, Inc.* v. *PSKS, Inc, DBA Kay's Kloset... Kay's Shoes*,[88] by a majority of 5-to-4 overruled *Dr Miles* and held that agreements incorporating resale price maintenance provisions should be analysed under the rule of reason. Neither the reasoning in *Dr Miles*, nor the economic effects, nor administrative convenience, nor the principle of state decisis compelled continued adherence to the *per se* rule.

3. THE COMMUNITY APPROACH—AN OVERVIEW

A. THE BACKGROUND: SINGLE MARKET PROJECT AND RESTRICTIONS ON ECONOMIC FREEDOM

It has been mentioned in earlier Chapters of this book that the Commission's historical approach to Article 81(1), and in particular to vertical distribution agreements, sparked huge controversy

---

[85] European Commission Green Paper on Vertical Restraints in EC Competition Policy, COM (96) 721, 17.

[86] See its non-price vertical restraint guidelines published in 1985 Fed. Reg. 6263 (1985) (these guidelines are no longer in force). The Guidelines declared certain vertical agreements, such as selective distribution agreements, to be *per se* lawful.

[87] D. Deacon, 'Vertical Restraints under EU Competition Law: New Directions' [1995] Fordham Corp L Inst 307, para. 8.

[88] 26 June 2007, see *supra* n. 72. Although the DOJ and FTC urged the Supreme Court to overrule the *per se* prohibition two of the FTC Commissioners dissented from the decision to support the DOJ brief, see in particular the open letter to the Supreme Court of Pamela Jones Harbour, available at http://www. ftc.gov/ speeches/harbour/070226verticalminimumpricefixing.pdf. See also the powerful dissenting opinion of Breger J with whom Stevens, Souter and Ginsburg JJ joined.

and intense debate. For many years the European Commission appeared unwilling to recognize the distribution efficiencies resulting from vertical restraints. Rather, it adopted a strict and extremely interventionist approach when dealing with them. It has already been explained that one of the key causes of the Commission's pre-occupation with vertical restraints has been that they often demarcate territories between distributors, isolate national markets, erect barriers to trade, and maintain price differences between Member States. The Commission has intervened to prevent agreements that thwart the single market objective and has tried to ensure in so far as is possible that agreements admit the possibility of *some* parallel trade.

The often bitter debate on vertical restraints has an added dimension in the Community because competition policy not only has a goal of undistorted competition but also market integration. This has led to a two-way tug on policy makers. On the one hand vertical restraints including territorial exclusivity were recognised as necessary to give both producers and distributors the protection and certainty needed for them to make the investments to launch new products or launch their products on the markets of other Member States outside their home markets. The pro-competitive arguments in favour of such restrictions are well rehearsed. On the other hand territorial exclusivity in particular was considered as contrary to one of the fundamental aims of the Community—the creation of real internal/single market. Such restrictions appeared to contribute both to the continued division of the market along national lines and the maintenance of price differences between Member States.[89]

Even where a distribution agreement did not impact on the single market project the Commission was concerned about agreements that restrained the parties' 'economic freedom'.[90] It sought to encourage and to nurture the process of rivalry between undertakings and to foster the freedom and right of initiative of the individual economic operator and the spirit of enterprise.[91] It took the view, often without serious analysis of the effect of the agreement on the competitive process that restrictions on parties' freedom of action, such as price or non-price restraints or non-compete clauses, amounted to restrictions of competition.[92] It thus took a broad view of what constituted a restriction of competition within the meaning of Article 81(1). In addition, it adopted a strict and formalistic approach when applying the Article 81(3) criteria.

The chief criticism made of the Commission in its approach to vertical restraints was its failure to take a sufficiently realistic view of whether an agreement restricted competition for the purposes of Article 81(1). Not only was this approach considered difficult conceptually, the main objective of an agreement being to bind the parties and to restrict their freedom of action,[93] but it caused the Commission to deal with agreements by category, applying certain

---

[89] D. Deacon, 'Vertical Restraints under EU Competition Law: New Directions' [1995] *Fordham Corp L Insts* 307, para. 8.

[90] 'Vertical restraints are more strictly treated under EC competition law than is the case in most other jurisdictions. This strictness is a product of extreme hostility toward restrictions that threaten to interfere with trade between Member States. The strictness also results from a concern with restraints on so-called "economic freedom" where the restraints frequently have no harmful effect on consumer welfare and may even promote consumer welfare through enhancing economic efficiency.' B. E. Hawk, 'System Failure: Vertical Restraints and EC Competition Law' (1995) 32 *CMLRev* 973.

[91] See *supra* Chap. 4.

[92] D. Deacon, 'Vertical Restraints under EU Competition Law: New Directions' [1995] *Fordham Corp L Inst* 307, para. 9.

[93] *Supra* Chap. 4, section 1. 'There can be no doubt that the challenged practices of the NCAA constitute a "restraint of trade" in the sense that they limit members' freedom to negotiate and enter into their own television contracts. In that sense, however, every contract is in restraint of trade, and…the Sherman Act was intended to prohibit only unreasonable restraints of trade': *National Collegiate Athletic Ass'n v. Board of Regents of University of Oklahoma*, 468 US 85, 98 (1984).

rules to one type of agreement and different rules to others. It also meant, with the host of accompanying drawbacks, that businesses felt the need to secure exemptions for their distribution agreements.[94] At the time, and partly because the block exemptions preceding Regulation 2790/1999 were rigid and more difficult to satisfy, this policy imposed an enormous, and, arguably, unnecessary, burden on firms wishing to conclude distribution agreements. It meant that in practice firms would often have to seek an individual exemption for their agreement, or more realistically since exemptions were rarely granted, rely on a comfort letter.[95]

B. CRITICISMS OF THIS APPROACH

Although the Commission introduced devices to try and deal with the problems experienced[96] the approach was widely criticized by practitioners and academic commentators. In the extract from the article below, Hawk fiercely criticized the Commission, especially for its broad and inconsistent application of Article 81(1). In his view the approach had caused the whole notification system to fail. It had led to legal uncertainty, proliferation of block exemptions, and to rigid analysis of agreements by category rather than by economic effect. This article is perceived to have been the straw (or at least one of the straws) which broke the camel's back and which finally convinced the Commission that its approach to vertical restraints would have to change.[97]

B. E. Hawk, 'System Failure: Vertical Restraints and EC Competition Law' (1995) 32 *CMLRev* 973, 974–86

2. System failure

The Commission's approach to vertical restraints evidences more fundamental institutional issues. Bluntly put, the notification system set up in 1962 in Regulation 17 has failed. The following flow-chart illustrates this system failure:

Step A Overly broad application of Article [81(1)] (incoherent rationale, inconsistency with Court judgments and inadequate economic analysis)

↓

Step B Generation of Extraordinary Legal Uncertainty

---

[94] 'A broad definition of restriction of competition under Art. [81(1)] shifts most of the inquiry over to Art. [81(3)] where only the Commission has the power to grant exemptions, thus requiring notification and excluding the national courts from the more important part of the antitrust analysis': B. E. Hawk, 'The American (Anti-Trust) Revolution: Lessons for the EEC' [1988] *ECLR* 53, 65.

[95] 'Only a limited number of formal decisions can be rendered each year for cases under Articles [81] and [82]. . . . In most cases of application for negative clearance or individual exemption, the Commission declares by simple letter known as a "comfort letter"': European Commission Green Paper on Vertical Restraints COM(96) 721, 30.

[96] For example, the Commission developed the doctrine of appreciability within the context of Article 81(1), and introduced block exemptions to exempt distribution agreements from the prohibition of Article 81(3). The old block exemptions, which applied until 31 May 2000, restricted the type of distribution agreement which parties could conclude and imposed severe limitations on the types of clauses that could be contained within them, *infra* 738–9.

[97] See also D. Deakin, 'Vertical Restraints under EU Competition Law: New Directions' [1995] *Fordham Corporate L Inst* 307.

↓

Step C Proliferation of Block Exemptions to Attempt to Reduce Legal Uncertainty

↓

Step D Legal Formalisms and 'Analysis' by Categories

↓

Step E De-emphasis on or Lack of Substantive (Economic) Analysis

2.1 Overbroad application of Article [81(1)]

The most fundamental, and most trenchant, criticism is that the Commission too broadly applies Article [81(1)] to agreements having little or no anti-competitive effects. This criticism rests on three pillars: 1) an inadequate economic analysis under Article [81(1)]; 2) an unpersuasive rationale for this overbroad application of [81(1)], notably the 'economic freedom' notion; and 3) the Commission's historical and continuing resistance to Court judgments evidencing a more nuanced economics-based interpretation of [81(1)].

2.1.1 Inadequate analysis under [81(1)]

The majority of the Commission decisions fail adequately to consider whether the restraint at issue harms competition in the consumer welfare sense of economics, i.e., effect on price or output. Concomitantly, market power, which should be the threshold issue, frequently is hardly examined (let alone given a central role) or is simply found to exist in a conclusory fashion under the rubric of 'appreciability.'

Market power is perhaps the most fundamental factor in a competition analysis. Market power is just as important under Article [81] as it is under Article [82]. The fact that the *legal* thresholds for the requisite degree of market power differ under Article [81] and [82] should not obscure that fact. There are no separate economics for Article [81(1)], (3) and [82].

It is essential to emphasize that a more rigorous economic analysis under [81(1)], does not mean that there must be only a 'rule of reason' under Article [81(1)]. There is room for both a *per se* rule and a rule of reason under Article [81(1)] . . .

The anaemic nature of the economic analysis under [81(1)] . . . can be seen in . . . examples . . .

Perhaps the most striking example is the Commission's (almost) automatic placement of *exclusive distributorships* or *exclusive supply obligations* under [81(1)] without any inquiry into actual anti-competitive effects or market power. But exclusive distributorships ordinarily pose no risk of anti-competitive effects where interbrand competition is healthy (i.e., the supplier lacks significant market power) and distributors and consumers have a range of similar products from which to choose. This automatic condemnation is particularly troublesome given the broad variety of efficiencies that can result from exclusive distribution.

A second example of anaemic economic analysis under Article [81] concerns *selective distribution*. Specific provisions appear to be simply catalogued under [81(1)] or [81(3)] with little economic basis or analysis. There are exceptions, notably the Commission's decision in *Villeroy & Boch* [[1985] OJ L 376/15]. The Community Courts have engaged in a more economic analysis of selective distribution, an irony to some given that the Courts are intended to provide judicial review of an administrative body enjoying special antitrust expertise and experience.

A third example can be seen in the stark contrast between the Court of Justice's insistence on foreclosure and entry barrier analysis in examining *exclusive purchasing* and the Commission's begrudging and narrow use of foreclosure analysis . . .

Economic analysis of vertical arrangements in the United States has profoundly affected legal attitudes towards vertical arrangements. Vertical restraints are no longer viewed with suspicion.

The most important threshold issue is the existence of market power: in most instances, the absence of market power means that competition is effective, that consumers have adequate choices available to them and that the market will correct temporary deficiencies far more efficiently than the law. Also, the existence of procompetitive or legitimate business justifications may validate a restraint even where there is market power . . .

2.1.2 The Commission's rationale under [81(1)] is unpersuasive

The first explanation for the inadequate economic analysis under [81(1)] lies in the Commission's stubborn (in the face of Court judgments) adherence to the definition of a restriction on competition as a restriction on the 'economic freedom' of operators in the marketplace. The principal weaknesses of the Freiburg School notion of restriction on economic freedom are (1) its failure to generate precise operable legal rules (i.e., failure to provide an analytical framework); (2) its distance from and tension with (micro) economics which does provide an analytical framework; (3) its tendency to favour traders/ competitors over consumers and consumer welfare (efficiency) and (4) its capture under Article [81(1)] of totally innocuous contract provisions having no anti-competitive effects in an economic sense.

The restriction on economic freedom notion could literally cover most if not all contractual agreements on the reasoning that the contract contains provisions which limit or 'restrict' the freedom of the parties as it existed prior to the contract . . .

Under U.S. law, an effect on competition is necessary; harm to the plaintiff or to a particular trader is not sufficient. This is clearly accepted. . . .

The economic freedom notion also fails to provide operable criteria to determine which agreements restrict competition. This is reflected in the handful of Court and Commission decisions finding that certain 'restrictions' do not fall within Article [81(1)] despite the fact that they clearly limit 'economic freedom.' These decisions do not provide a clear, consistent rationale to distinguish the 'exceptions' from the vast majority of 'restrictions' which have been held to fall within Article [81(1)] . . .

The breadth of coverage resulting from the economic freedom concept effectively shifts the analysis from [81(1)] to [81(3)] whenever notification of the agreement is required as a condition for the granting of an individual exemption. The Commission may find this shift of analysis and the resultant notification attractive because it appears to offer greater Commission surveillance and control.

Although the Court decisions are not entirely clear or consistent, it is fair to conclude that the Court has not accepted unequivocally the Commission's economic freedom definition.

Criticism of the Commission's overreaching under Article [81(1)] also comes from the highly interesting perspective of competition authority officials charged with enforcing mini-Article [81]s that have been exported to them. The head of the Venezuelan Authority stated that the Authority found the Article [81] bifurcation artificial and the consequent notification system infeasible. Despite the statutory language, Venezuela has gone to a unitary substantive analysis under their mini-[81]. Ferenc Vissi, head of the Hungarian competition authority, asked the following (rhetorical) question: does it make more sense to condemn all vertical restrains and then (block) exempt 90 per cent à la Brussels, or to accept 90 per cent and condemn only 10 per cent (à la Budapest).

These reactions suggest that the export of Article [81] is not carrying with it the Commission's interpretation of Article [81(1)]. . . .

A second explanation for the frequently sparce economic analysis under Article [81] (both (1) and (3)) derives form the market integration goal which impels both the Commission and the Community courts, according to the critics, to emasculate the economic analysis by rejecting in principle efficiency arguments/ justifications and by favouring intrabrand competition over interbrand competition. This criticism is most relevant with respect to territorial restraints. I shall limit myself here to only one comment. The economic freedom notion above and the market integration goal raise very different issues. The former effectively eliminates economics and should be discarded; the latter requires a more sophisticated economic analysis whose task is to reconcile the consumer welfare (efficiency) considerations with the market integration goal (e.g., an assessment of distributional (in the economic sense) variance among the different Member States).

A third possible explanation for some of the anaemic economics under Article [81] is a Commission desire to protect small and medium firms. For example, the treatment of exclusive distributorships, exclusive purchasing and intellectual property licensing appears partially motivated by a desire to protect smaller resellers and licensees from larger suppliers and licensors . . .

The protection of small and medium firms is often justified on the assumption that this promotes competition in the long run. Although this assumption might often be true, it should be put to the test with economic analysis in individual cases. Does a vertical restriction that would threaten the survival of certain small firms (a) harm competition by preventing them from becoming more formidable competitors in the future or (b) promote competition by exposing them to legitimate market forces?

A final explanation asserted by some critics of the Commission's overbroad [81(1)] approach is that it furthers the Commission's institutional interests; more specifically, it reinforces its monopoly to grant [81(3)] exemptions. If an economic analysis were made under Article [81(1)], far fewer vertical arrangements would be subject to the Commission's exclusive jurisdiction to grant individual exemption under Article [81(3)]. Economic analysis also would be within the competence of national courts when applying Article [81(1)].

2.1.3 Commission refusal to follow Community Courts

The Court of Justice and Court of First Instance have taken a more nuanced approach toward vertical arrangements under Article [81(1)]. The Courts have increasingly required an economic analysis of economic effects, particularly the possibility of foreclosure. This approach has largely been ignored or distinguished by the Commission, which adheres to its non-economics based application of Article [81(1)], i.e., restriction on economic freedom.

. . .

2.2 Step B—generation of extraordinary legal uncertainty

The overbroad application of Article [81(1)] generates extraordinary legal uncertainty about common contractual provisions that frequently raise little or no risk of anti-competitive effect in an economics sense, i.e., no effect on harm to consumer welfare in terms of price or output effects. The practical consequences cannot be exaggerated. Counsel's analysis of nonterritorial vertical arrangements under Article [81] is largely a matter of identifying for each party the clauses it may have difficulty enforcing, weighing the business interests involved and considering, on purely formalistic grounds, alternative that may fit more neatly within the Commission's maze of rules. This alters the content of agreements, upsets the bargain struck by agreements and undermines incentives necessary either to enter arrangements in the first place or to induce more specific forms of investment in distribution.

The Commission's fining policy also is important in this regard. Many agreements fall within Article [81(1)] and the parties are unable to obtain greater certainty without notifying the agreement to the Commission. If fines are unlikely, the decision largely comes down to an assessment of the timing and enforceability risks for each party with respect to each suspect clause. This situation is very common because significant fines are typically reserved for territorial restrictions, horizontal cartels and Article [82] cases.

2.3 Step C—proliferation of block exemptions

The Commission has attempted to reduce the legal uncertainty generated by its overbroad application of [81(1)] by resorting to block exemptions . . .

2.4 Step D—legal formalisms and 'analysis' by pigeonholing

The Commission largely applies Article [81(1)] to distribution arrangements according to formal legal categories. One set of rules applies to exclusive distribution, another to selective distribution, another to franchising, and a chaotic array of considerations apply to distribution arrangements that are not neatly pigeonholed. . . .

2.5 Lack of substantive analysis

The legal formalisms described above ultimately eliminate what should be the heart of the matter: and antitrust (i.e., economics/law) substantive analysis of a particular agreement or practice, i.e., its competitive harms and benefits. Competition law is economic law, and economics must play a predominant (if not exclusive) role in the examination of particular agreements. That is why the Commission's frequent inattention to market power and effects on price and output is so sorely criticized.

The legal formalisms under Article [81] contrast starkly with U.S. antitrust counselling practice. When dealing with non-territorial restraints under EC law, lawyers spend the great majority of their time in pigeonholing exercises and in textual exegesis of block exemptions and interpretative guidelines. It is shocking how little time is devoted to assessing the competitive risks and benefits for the vertical restraints at issue. The practice under the Sherman Act is exactly the opposite. It is difficult to believe that EC competition policy is furthered where there is far more attention and intellectual resources devoted to doctrinal formalisms than to substantive analysis.

C. THE NEW MORE ECONOMIC APPROACH: THE BLOCK EXEMPTION AND REFORM

The relentless stream of criticism that the Commission's approach to vertical restraints provoked, charging it with a failure to take a sufficiently economic approach and stultifying innovation in the distribution process, eventually led the Commission to take heed of the criticisms and to introduce changes. In 1996 it issued a Green Paper on Vertical Restraints in EC Competition Policy in which it discussed possible ways for developing and ameliorating its approach to vertical restraints. The Paper canvassed and sought opinion upon four possible options for reform.[98] A fifth option, to adopt a more realistic approach when assessing the agreement's compatibility with Article 81(1), was not discussed within the Paper but attracted much attention in the discussion that the Paper provoked.

Following the introduction of that Paper a follow-up document to the Green Paper was published and several significant changes were introduced to the way in which vertical restraints are

---

[98] Maintaining the existing system; maintaining the system but making the, then, existing block exemptions more flexible; limiting the existing block exemption to agreements concluded between undertakings with a share of less than 40% of the market and introducing an assumption that agreements concluded between undertakings with less than 20% of the market do not infringe Article 81(1); and making changes to the existing block exemptions.

dealt with under Article 81 of the Treaty. On 22 December 1999, the Commission adopted the new Verticals Regulation, which exists for all vertical agreements that may fall within Article 81(1).[99] It embraces a more flexible approach than its predecessors,[100] requiring a new Council Regulation to extend the Commission's *vires* to adopt it.[101] Primarily, it seeks to avoid the straight-jacketing that resulted from the preceding regulations. It thus applies more broadly to *all* vertical agreements that satisfy the requirements set out in the regulation. Essentially this depends upon the parties not exceeding a specified market share threshold (of 30%) and on the agreement not containing any hardcore vertical restraints.

Where a vertical agreement is not exempted by the Verticals Regulation, or another block exemption, the parties to the agreement may, of course, no longer seek negative clearance of an individual exemption from the Commission.[102] Rather, they will have to make their own determination[103] whether or not the agreement infringes Article 81(1) at all and, if it does, whether or not it meets the criteria set out in Article 81(3).[104] In May 2000 the Commission published 'Guidelines' explaining both the operation of the block exemption, and its analysis of vertical restraints that do not fall within it, and its analysis of agency agreements.[105] These Guidelines now have to be read alongside the Commission's Article 81(3) Guidelines which set out general guidance on how it interprets Article 81(1) and Article 81(3) and how they interrelate to one another.[106] The Vertical Guidelines promise that the Commission 'will adopt an economic approach in the application of Article 81 to vertical restraints' and that the scope of Article 81 will be limited 'to undertakings holding a certain degree of market power where inter-brand competition may be insufficient'.[107] The Guidelines recognize that even agreements concluded between undertakings with more than 30 per cent of the relevant market (and hence falling outside of the block exemptions safe harbour) may not fall within Article 81(1).[108] It has also issued a number of decisions adopting a more economically realistic approach.[109]

D. METHODOLOGY

The Commission's modernized approach to vertical agreements signals, in line with the case law of the Court, that many such agreements will not infringe Article 81(1) at all. Further, that even if they do, or may, the Article 81(3) criteria are to be applied more flexibly.

---

[99] [1999] OJ L336/21, [2000] 4 CMLR 398.

[100] The regulation replaced three regulations that exempted certain exclusive distribution, exclusive purchasing, and franchising agreements respectively, *infra* 738–9.

[101] The previous Council Regulation, Reg. 19/65 [1965–6] OJ Spec. Ed. 85. conferring such authority was too limited. Reg. 1215/99 [1999] OJ L148/1 thus extended the legislative power of the Commission, conferring authority on the Commission to adopt a broader exemption.

[102] See *supra* Chaps. 2 and 4.

[103] Relying on decisional practice and the Guidelines.

[104] Should the agreement's compatibility with Article 81 become important, the full Article 81 assessment can be made wherever the question arises, whether before a national court, a national competition authority or the Commission.

[105] [2000] OJ C291/1, [2000] 5 CMLR 1074.

[106] See generally Chap. 4. The Article 81(3) Guidelines also stress that the primary goal of Article 81 is the enhancement of consumer welfare, see *supra* Chaps. 1 and 4.

[107] Guidelines, para. 102.

[108] Where the parties to the agreement do not have more than 15% of the relevant market, the agreement is likely to be '*de minimis*' so long as there are no network effects and it does not contain hard-core restraints, see *supra* Chap. 3.

[109] See, e.g., *Spring* [2000] OJ L195/49, [2000] 5 CMLR 948, *Whitbread* [1999] OJ L88/26, [1999] 5 CMLR 118, upheld on appeal Case T-131/99, *Shaw v. Commission* [2002] ECR II-2023, [2002] 5 CMLR 81 and *Bass* [1999] OJ

Logically, the first question that should be addressed in a verticals case is, does this agreement infringe Article 81(1) at all?[110] Many vertical agreements will fall outside Article 81(1) on account of their minor importance, because they do not appreciably affect trade between Member States and/or, in the absence of hard-core restraints, because they do not actually have the 'effect' of appreciably restricting competition. Practically, however, where an agreement appreciably affects trade and is not of minor importance the parties may prefer to rely on the 'safe haven' of the block exemption, rather than going through the full economic analysis required to determine whether or not the agreement has as its effect the restriction of competition. It is for this reason perhaps that the Commission states, in its Guidelines at paragraph 120, that the first question for undertakings to ask is whether or not the agreement falls within the block exemption, *not* whether the agreement actually falls within Article 81(1) and so requires scrutiny under Article 81(3).

(1) First, the undertakings involved need to define the relevant market in order to establish the market share of the supplier or the buyer, depending on the vertical restraint involved . . .

(2) If the relevant market share does not exceed the 30 per cent threshold, the vertical agreement is covered by the BER, subject to the hardcore restrictions and conditions set out in that regulation.

(3) If the relevant market share is above the 30 per cent threshold, it is necessary to assess whether the vertical agreement falls within Article 81(1).

(4) If the vertical agreement falls within Article 81(1), it is necessary to examine whether it fulfils the conditions for exemption under Article 81(3).[111]

Although this approach clearly represents sensible, pragmatic advice, this methodology turns Article 81 on its head as theoretically, of course, undertakings should not feel the need to comply with the block exemption or Article 81(3) criteria if the agreement does not infringe Article 81(1).

In this Chapter we thus start with the question of whether the agreement infringes Article 81(1) before going on to consider the terms of the block exemption and how Article 81(3) applies to vertical agreements which do not benefit from the block exemption. It should be remembered, however, that in most cases it may, in practice, be preferable when determining the compatibility of an existing or proposed distribution arrangement with Article 81, to side step the more complex Article 81(1) analysis and to start as the Commission suggests with the question: is this agreement covered by the block exemption and so exempted from Article 81(1) if within it?

The flowchart in Figure 9.1 opposite illustrates a sequence of questions that are likely to be relevant as a preliminary issue when examining a vertical agreement or a proposed vertical agreement.

L186/1, [1999] 5 CMLR 782, upheld on appeal Case T-231/99, *Joynson v. Commission* [2002] ECR II-2085, [2002] 5 CMLR 123.

[110] Assuming that there is an agreement between two or more undertakings (and not, e.g., an agreement between a parent and subsidiary) and that the agreement is not a genuine agency agreement.

[111] Guidelines, para. 120.

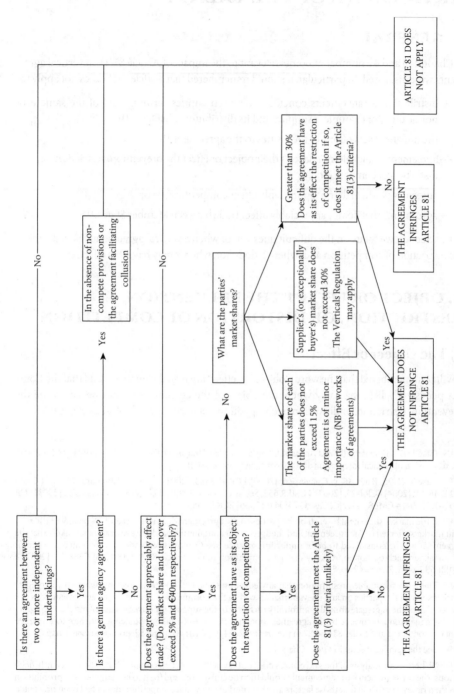

Figure 9.1 Analysis of Vertical Agreements under Article 81

4. DISTRIBUTION AGREEMENTS AND ARTICLE 81(1) OF THE TREATY

A. GENERAL

In Chapters 3 and 4 a number of points relevant to the impact of Article 81(1) on vertical agreements were discussed. In particular, it should remembered that Article 81(1) does not apply to:

— distribution arrangements concluded between entities forming part of the same economic unit, for example, a supplier and its distributor subsidiary;[112]

— the unilateral acts of one of the parties to the agreement;[113]

— agreements which do not have as their object or effect the prevention, restriction, or distortion of competition;

— agreements which do not appreciably affect competition;[114] or

— agreements that do not appreciably affect trade between Member States.[115]

In this Section we focus on the difficult question of when a vertical agreement has as its object the restriction of competition and, where it does not, when it may have this effect.

B. OBJECT OR EFFECT THE PREVENTION, RESTRICTION, OR DISTORTION OF COMPETITION[116]

(i) The Object or Effect

It will be remembered that the words 'object' or 'effect' are read disjunctively and that the Court has persistently held that only where the object of the agreement cannot be said to be the prevention, restriction, or distortion of competition is it necessary to look at its effect.[117]

---

[112] Case 15/74, *Centrafarm BV and Adnaan De Peijper* v. *Sterling Drug Inc* [1974] ECR 1183, [1974] 2 CMLR 480. See discussion of vertical integration and also of agency, *supra* 680 ff.

[113] Case T-41/96, *Bayer AG* v. *Commission*, [2000] ECR II-3383, [2001] 4 CMLR 126, para. 173 *aff'd* Cases C-2 & 3/01 P, [2004] ECR I-23, [2004] 4 CMLR 653. See also Case T-208/01, *Volkswagen* v. *Commission* [2003] ECR II-5141, [2004] 4 CMLR 727, *aff'd* Case C-74/04 P, [2006] ECR I-6585.

[114] If the market share held by each of the parties to the agreement does not exceed 15% on any of the relevant markets affected by the agreement and the agreement contains no 'hard-core restraints' it is likely that the agreement will be considered to be of minor importance, see Commission Notice on agreements of minor importance which do not appreciably restrict competition under Article 81(1) [2001] OJ C368/13, [2002] 4 CMLR 699, para. 7, *supra* Chap. 3.

[115] There is a rebuttable presumption that any effect on trade will not be appreciable where the aggregate market share of the parties on any relevant market within the Community affected by the agreement does not exceed 5% *and* the aggregate annual Community turnover of the supplier (or buyer in case of purchasing agreements) in the products covered by the agreement does not exceed €40 million, Guidelines on the effect on trade concept contained in Articles 81 and 82 of the Treaty [2004] OJ C101/81, para. 52, discussed *supra* Chap. 3.

[116] See the detailed discussion *supra* Chap. 4.

[117] 'Where ... an analysis of the said clauses does not reveal the effect on competition to be sufficiently deleterious, the consequence of the agreement should then be considered and for it to be caught by the prohibition it is then necessary to find that those factors are present that show that competition has in fact been prevented or restricted or distorted to an appreciable extent'. Case 56/65, *Société La Technique Minière* v. *Maschinenbau Ulm* [1966] ECR 235, 249, [1966] CMLR 357, 375.

In the absence of certain serious restraints the Court has been prepared to accept that many restrictions on conduct do not have as their effect the restriction of competition for the purposes of Article 81(1).[118] Some of the cases illustrating this point are set out and analysed in Chapter 4. Several cases dealt with there are discussed again here because of their importance to the question of whether and when Article 81(1) applies to distribution agreements. The full extracts of the cases which are set out in that Chapter should, however, be read again on account of their importance to this discussion.

(ii) Vertical Agreements which have as their Object the Prevention, Restriction, or Distortion of Competition

a. Absolute Territorial Protection and Export Bans

The ECJ has, when dealing with distribution agreements, held that two types of clauses, certain territorial and price restraints, have as their object the restriction of competition. In *Consten and Grundig*[119] the Court held that clauses resulting in the isolation of a national market and/or maintaining separate national markets distorted competition and constituted an infringement of Article 81(1). The ECJ did not accept the view of its Advocate General[120] that Article 81(1) required, in all cases, an examination of the market to determine whether or not the agreement was likely to promote or restrict competition. In that case it held that the object of an agreement was the restriction of competition since it sheltered the distributor from all intra-brand competition and led to the division of national markets.[121] It will be remembered, that this case provides a clear example of the Court struggling to balance the Community policy of market integration against competition and efficiency.

G. Monti, 'Article 81 EC and Public Policy' *(2002) CMLRev* 1057–99, 1065–6

The more complex question is how to balance market integration with competition and efficiency, especially in the context of distribution agreement. The problem manifests itself because it has been argued (contrary to the Commission's position) that territorial protection is a means to increase competition in the market. This well-know argument can be summarized by reference to the decision in *Consten and Grundig*: Grundig's attempt to isolate the French market so as to give its exclusive distributor in France the opportunity to devote resources to market a new product

---

[118] E.g., restraints necessary or ancillary to the operation of a pro-competitive agreement or essential to persuade a distributor to take on the risk of distribution or necessary to the operation of a selective distribution agreement or which do not restrict inter-brand competition, *supra* Chap. 4.

[119] Cases 56 and 58/64, *Etablissements Consten SA & Grundig-Verkaufs-GmbH v. Commission* [1966] ECR 299, [1966] CMLR 418 (see extract set out in Chap. 4). See also, e.g., Case T-77/92 *Parker Pen v. Commission* [1994] ECR II-559, [1995] 5 CMLR 435. But see, e.g., Case 262/81, *Coditel II* [1982] ECR 3382, [1983] 1 CMLR 49, and *infra* Chap. 10.

[120] See extract set out in Chap. 4.

[121] The Court has, however, accepted in the context of intellectual property licensing agreements that in exceptional circumstances export bans may fall outside Article 81(1) altogether, see Case 27/87, *Erauw-Jacquéry Sprl v. La Hesbignonne Société Coopérative* [1988] ECR 1999, [1988] 4 CMLR 576. See also the discussion of Case T-168/01, *GlaxoSmithKline Unlimited v. Commission*, 27 Sept. 2006, [2007] 5 CMLR 1623, Cases C-501, 513, 515 and 519/06 P (judgment pending).

was held unlawful the ECJ being deaf to the argument that without territorial protection, no reasonable distributor would have taken the risk of sinking costs into a new and uncertain market if he
knew that a free rider would later enter and sell goods taking advantage of its marketing efforts.

Some economists would argue that in this situation, territorial protection is a necessary incentive to convince a distribution to market goods to remove the free-rider effect. Instead, under EC
competition law, as Gyselen once memorably put it, the free rider is a 'hero' because he integrates
markets by selling across borders. Pardoxically, this hard line may result in less competition and less
integration: there would be less competition because firms might decide to integrate vertically,
thus reducing the number of distributors in a Member State, to the possible disadvantage of new
manufacturers who might find it harder to distribute their products; alternatively firms might decide
not to export at all if they fear that commercial success will not materialize with an unprotected distributor, diminishing both competition and integration; or they might waste resources trying to find
other means to prevent free riding without infringing competition provisions. These considerations
suggest that territorial restrictions should be looked upon generously and that preference for market integration is counterproductive. However, economic learning and evidence from the United
States suggests that absolute territorial protection does not *always* yield an efficient outcome.
Comanor for example has argued that while with resale price maintenance agreements distributors
are still able to compete against each other on things other than price, with territorial segregation
all competition among rival distributors is lost, meaning that the increased prices set by distributors are not necessarily designed to recoup the costs of additional services provided to consumers,
but are evidence of a welfare loss. Even in an integrated market like the United States, there is evidence that a lack of intra-brand competition can lead to anti-competitive results.

Therefore, economic evidence shows that it is impossible to state either that all territorial
restraints by firms which lack market power are efficiency- enhancing (as some Chicago School
lawyers would contend) nor that they are all inefficient (as *Consten and Grundig* suggests). This
ambiguity poses a difficulty for competition authorities: the best approach would be to analyse
territorial restrictions on a case-by-case basis to determine what the right amount of territorial
protection is: however, this would lead to undesirable delay and uncertainty. The second-best
solution is to devise some rule of thumb with draws a clear distinction between those territorial
restrictions that are lawful and those that are unlawful which is a close as possible to the economic
evidence but which allows parties to implement agreements speedily and with certainty. The rules
of thumb deployed in the EC are stricter than those in the U.S. but, as will be demonstrated below,
the Commission has become increasingly willing to relax its tough stance against market
partitioning agreement when this results in greater efficiencies.

The Commission, supported by the Court, has maintained a strict policy against any measure
inserted in an agreement, or imposed unilaterally by the supplier and explicitly or tacitly
accepted by the distributor,[122] which directly, or indirectly, divides the EU market on territorial
lines and totally prevents parallel imports and parallel trade.[123] An agreement which does not
explicitly contain an export ban or confer absolute territorial protection on a distributor will

[122] See *supra* Chap. 3. But see, in particular, Case T-41/96, *Bayer AG v. Commission*, [2000] ECR II-3383, [2001]
4 CMLR 126, *aff'd* Cases C-2 and 3/01 P, [2004] ECR I-23, [2004] 4 CMLR 653. See also Case T-208/01, *Volkswagen
v. Commission* [2003] ECR II-5141, [2004] 4 CMLR 727, *aff'd* Case C-74/04 P, [2006] ECR I-6585.

[123] There is an important distinction between absolute territorial protection and qualified territorial protection, see *infra* 723–4 and 751–4. But see Case T-168/01, *GlaxoSmithKline Unlimited v. Commission* 27 Sept. 2006,
[2007] 5 CMLR 1623, Cases C-501, 513, 515 and 519/06 P (judgment pending), discussed *supra* Chap.3.

thus be found to restrict competition if this is its purpose,[124] for example:[125] where circulars are sent discouraging[126] or prohibiting[127] export; where export is permitted but only if the consent of the producer is obtained;[128] where the producer must be contacted before exporting via the Internet;[129] where goods are supplied to distributors but the invoice for supply bears the words 'export prohibited';[130] where insufficient quantities of goods are supplied with the objective of precluding export;[131] where performance bonuses are dependent upon dealers not exporting;[132] where exported products are bought back by the manufacturer;[133] where products supplied are marked so that parallel importers can be identified;[134] where guarantees are limited to the Member State in which the product was purchased;[135] where discriminatory prices are charged to discourage export;[136] where an agreement requires a distributor to pass on any customer enquiries coming from outside the contract territory to the producer;[137] where a producer threatens to terminate or actually terminates contractual arrangements with distributors or dealers which sell outside of their allotted territory;[138] where financial support is contingent on products supplied to distributors being used only within a distributor's allotted territory;[139] or where foreign customers are required to pay a deposit to the producer not required of national consumers.[140]

---

[124] An export ban will be prohibited even if it is stipulated to be applicable only 'unless prohibited by law', *Novalliance/Systemform* [1997] OJ L47/11, [1997] 4 CMLR 876.

[125] See also the discussion of hard-core restraints prohibited by the Verticals Reg., *infra* 751 ff.

[126] *Konica* [1988] OJ L78/34, [1988] 4 CMLR 848.

[127] *Mercedes-Benz* [2002] OJ L257/1, [2003] 4 CMLR 95. This aspect of the case was annulled on appeal, Case T-325/01, *DaimlerChrysler v. Commission* [2005] ECR II-3319, on the grounds that the German commercial agents were genuine agents. The conduct therefore lacked the necessary duality to trigger the application of Article 81 see *supra* 687–8.

[128] Case T-77/92, *Parker Pen v. Commission* [1994] ECR II-559, [1995] 5 CMLR 435; Case 19/77, *Miller v. Commission* [1978] ECR 131, [1978] 2 CMLR 334.

[129] *Yamaha* IP/03/1028.

[130] Case C-227/87, *Sandoz Prodotti Farmaceutici SpA v. Commission* [1990] ECR I-45, [1990] 4 CMLR 242.

[131] See *Volkswagen* [1998] OJ L124/60, [1998] 5 CMLR 33, on appeal Case T-62/98, *Volkswagen AG v. Commission* [2000] ECR II-2707, [2000] 5 CMLR 853, the appeal to the ECJ was dismissed, see Case C-338/00 P, *Volkswagen AG v. Commission* [2003] ECR I-9189, [2004] 4 CMLR 351 and, e.g. *Peugeot* IP/05/1227 but see *infra* n. 142 and accompanying text.

[132] *Peugeot* IP/05/1227. In this case the discriminatory bonus system was backed up by a threat to reduce supplies to exporting dealers.

[133] Cases T-38 and 43/92, *Dunlop Slazenger v. Commission* [1994] ECR II-441, [1993] 5 CMLR 352.

[134] *Tretorn* [1994] OJ L378/45, [1997] 4 CMLR 860, *Hasselblad AG* [1982] OJ L161/18, [1982] 2 CMLR 233.

[135] *Zanussi* [1978] OJ L322/26, [1979] 1 CMLR 81; Case 31/85, *ETA Fabriques d'Ebauches v. DK Investments SA* [1985] ECR 3933, [1986] 2 CMLR 674. Guarantees can be limited to products sold by an authorized distributor of a selective distribution system, however, see Case C-372/02, *Metro v. Cartier* [1994] ECR I-15, [1994] 5 CMLR 331, paras. 32–4.

[136] *The Distillers Company Limited* [1978] OJ L50/16, [1978] 1 CMLR 400; on appeal Case 30/78, *Distillers Company v. Commission* [1980] ECR 2229, [1980] 3 CMLR 121; and see *Distillers Company plc (Red Label)* [1983] OJ C245/3, [1983] 3 CMLR 173; *Newitt/Dunlop Slazenger International* [1992] OJ L131/32, [1993] 5 CMLR 352, on appeal Cases T-38 and 43/92, *Dunlop Slazenger v. Commission* [1994] ECR II-441, [1993] 5 CMLR 352.

[137] Cases T-175/95, *BASF Coating AG v. Commission* [1999] ECR II-1581, [2000] 4 CMLR 33.

[138] *Volkswagen* [1998] OJ L124/60, [1998] 5 CMLR 33, on appeal Case T-62/98, *Volkswagen AG v. Commission* [2000] ECR II-2707, [2000] 5 CMLR 853, and Case C-338/00 P, *Volkswagen AG v. Commission* [2003] ECR I-9189, [2004] 4 CMLR 351.

[139] *JCB* [2002] OJ L69/1, [2002] 4 CMLR 1458. This aspect of the decision was upheld on appeal, Case T-67/01, *JCB Service v. Commission* [2004] ECR II-49, [2004] 4 CMLR 1346, *aff'd* Case C-167/04 *JCB Service v. Commission* [2006] ECR I-8935.

[140] *Mercedes-Benz* [2002] OJ L257/1, [2003] 4 CMLR 95. This aspect of the case was annulled on appeal, Case T-325/01, *DaimlerChrysler v. Commission* [2005] ECR II-3319, see supra n. 127.

The Commission takes these kinds of practices very seriously and, where it can establish that the practice is a result of an agreement or concerted practice and is not simply a policy unilaterally pursued by one of the parties,[141] undertakings in breach can expect high fines.[142] For example: in *VW*[143] the Commission imposed fines of €102 million (reduced to €90 million on appeal[144]) in respect of a wide range of contractual practices designed to prevent distributors selling outside of their contractual territory; and in *Nintendo*,[145] the Commission imposed a fine of €167.8 million on Nintendo and seven of its European distributors for colluding through agreements and/or concerted practices to prevent exports from low-priced to high-priced countries. The Commission stated: 'Contrary to the Commission's policy in respect of exclusive distribution that passive sales are always to be allowed, the territorial protection awarded to exclusive distributors was thereby enhanced to a state of absolute territorial protection and in each territory all competition facing the distributor of the products in that territory was eliminated. As a result, intra-brand competition was severely restricted and the single market partitioned ... Because their object is to restrict competition, it is not necessary to consider the actual effects upon competition'.[146]

Only once, in *GlaxoSmithKline Services Unlimited v Commission*,[147] has it been held that indirect export bans (operated through a dual pricing system) did not have as their object the restriction of competition. In this case, however, exceptional factors (the fact that medicine prices were largely shielded from ordinary competition by regulation) led the CFI to conclude that it could not be presumed that the agreement to limit parallel trade would reduce the welfare of the final consumers and the CFI went on to conclude that the effect of the agreement was to restrict competition.[148] It was seen in Chapter 4, however, that this decision is somewhat difficult to reconcile with other case-law and that the Commission has appealed this aspect of the CFI's judgment maintaining that the Court's analysis confirming the existence of the restrictive "effects" constitutes in reality a finding that the agreement was restrictive by object.[149]

b. Resale Price Maintenance

The economic arguments in favour of resale price maintenance have been explored above.[150] Despite these economic arguments, the Commission takes the view that a provision setting out minimum retail prices to be charged by distributors has as its object the restriction of

---

[141] See Case T-41/96, *Bayer AG v. Commission*, [2000] ECR II-3383, [2001] 4 CMLR 126, *aff'd* Cases C-2 & 3/01 P, [2004] ECR I-23, [2004] 4 CMLR 653, *supra* Chap. 3, 155 ff.

[142] The Commission fined Topps, a company which produces collectible Pokemon stickers and cards, €1,590,000 for hindering cross–border trade in these products, see Commission press release, IP/04/682.

[143] *Volkswagen* [1998] OJ L124/60, [1998] 5 CMLR 33.

[144] Case T-62/98, *Volkswagen AG v. Commission* [2000] ECR II-2707, [2000] 5 CMLR 853 (essentially the fine was reduced because the CFI did not consider that the breach had been established for the full period found by the Commission), the appeal to the ECJ was dismissed, see Case C-338/00 P, *Volkswagen AG v. Commission* [2003] ECR I-9189, [2004] 4 CMLR 351.

[145] [2003] OJ L255/33 Case T-13/03 (judgment pending). Nintendo itself received a fine of €149.128 million and has contested the decision in so far as it imposes an unusually large fine upon it.

[146] *Ibid.*, para. 331. In April 2007, the Commission sent a statement of objections to the major record companies and Apple, alleging that agreements imposing territorial restrictions with respect to iTunes infringe Article 81.

[147] Case T-168/01 27 Sept. 2006, [2006] 5 CMLR 1623, Cases C-501, 513, 515 and 519/06 P (judgment pending). For further discussion of the case see *supra* Chap. 4.

[148] But see the discussion of the case *supra* Chap. 4.

[149] See *supra* Chap. 4 and Case C-513/06 P (judgment pending). See also e.g. Case C-551/03 P, *General Motors BV v. Commission* [2006] ECR I-3173, paras. 64–80.

[150] See *supra* 688–702.

competition. It believes that the practice leads to the ossification of distribution networks and horizontal effects.[151]

Although, this view may come under attack in Europe now that the Supreme Court has ruled that resale price maintenance must be analysed under the rule of reason in the USA,[152] the approach is supported by the jurisprudence of the Court. In *Pronuptia de Paris v. Schillgalis* the ECJ, in setting out guidelines on the compatibility of distribution franchises with Article 81(1),[153] held that 'provisions which impair the franchisee's freedom to determine his own prices are restrictive of competition'.[154] In *Metro v. Commission (No. 1)*, an appeal from a Commission decision authorizing the operation of a selective distribution system pursuant to Article 81, the Court stated that 'price competition is so important that it can never be eliminated'[155] and in *SA Binon & Cie v. SA Agence et Messageries de la Presse* the Court specifically held that 'provisions which fix the prices to be observed in contracts with third parties constitute, of themselves, a restriction on competition within the meaning of Article [81(1)]'.[156]

The cases thus establish that, where an agreement between the supplier and distributor can be established,[157] a provision fixing minimum resale prices to be charged by distributors will be held to have as its object the restriction of competition. Despite this strict approach it seems acceptable for a franchisor, and other suppliers, to provide 'franchisees with price-guidelines, so long as there is no concerted practice between the franchisor and the franchisees or between the franchisees themselves for the actual application of the prices'.[158] Further, a producer may operate a selective distribution system in which 'price competition is not generally emphasized either as an exclusive or indeed as a principal factor'. In *Metro v. Commission* the Court accepted that price competition 'does not constitute the only effective form of competition or that to which absolute priority must in all circumstances be afforded'.[159] Thus the provision of price guidelines or the operation of a selective distribution system may be compatible with Article 81(1) so long as it is not operated in a way which precludes price discounting.[160] Further, it seems that maximum prices may not infringe Article 81(1) so long as they do not operate as a 'focal point for the resellers' and which will be followed by them.[161] Recommended resale

[151] See *supra* 688 ff.

[152] See *supra* 698–702. It seems unlikely, however, that this will lead to any dramatic change in approach in Europe, in the short term at least. Indeed, despite Slyvania, a strict approch has been maintained in respect of non-price restraints. The Supreme Court's opinion may, however, serve to remind people that resale price maintenance provisions may provide efficiencies which may be used to build a convincing case that the agreement meets the Article 81(3) criteria.

[153] See *infra* 734–7.

[154] Case 161/84, *Pronuptia de Paris GmbH v. Pronuptia de Paris Irmgard Schillgallis* [1986] ECR 353, [1986] 1 CMLR 414, para. 25.

[155] Case 26/76, *Metro-SB-Grossmärkte GmbH v. Commission (No. 1)* [1977] ECR 1875, [1978] 2 CMLR 1, para. 21.

[156] Case 234/83 [1985] ECR 2015, para. 44.

[157] Case T-208/01, *Volkswagen v. Commission* [2003] ECR II-5141, [2004] 4 CMLR 727, *aff'd* Case C-74/04 P, [2006] ECR I-6585, the CFI quashed a Commission decision condemning resale price maintenance on the grounds that the Commission had failed to establish that the distributors had agreed to or acquiesced in the supplier's policy of resale price maintenance. In Australia, for example, it is simply an offence for a corporation or other person to 'engage in the practice of resale price maintenance', Trade Practices Act 1974, ss. 48, 96–100. Although the provisions clearly prohibit agreements between a supplier and a reseller providing that the latter will not advertise or sell below a specified price it applies more widely to other conduct designed to force or induce the resellers not to sell or advertise at below a specified price.

[158] Case 161/84, *Pronuptia de Paris GmbH v. Pronuptia de Paris Irmgard Schillgallis* [1986] ECR 353, [1986] 1 CMLR 414, para. 25.

[159] Case 26/76, *Metro-SB-Grossmärkte GmbH v. Commission (No. 1)* [1977] ECR 1875, [1978] 2 CMLR 1, para. 21.

[160] Case 107/82, *AEG-Telefunken v. Commission* [1983] ECR 3151, [1984] 3 CMLR 325.

[161] Guidelines, para. 226.

prices, selective distribution and maximum prices may also be covered by the Verticals Regulation.[162]

The Commission's enforcement policy indicates that it also takes resale price maintenance very seriously and that it will impose significant fines on those found to have participated in such a practice. For example: in *Yamaha*[163] the Commission imposed fines for practices designed to partition the single market and for fixing resale prices of its products in certain EU countries; and in *JCB*[164] the Commission found that JCB had imposed resale prices on Community distributors of its construction and earthmoving equipment. This aspect of its finding was, however, annulled by the CFI on appeal on the grounds that the manufacturer's suggested retail prices 'although strongly indicative, were nonetheless not binding'.[165] Similarly in *Volkswagen*[166] the Commission imposed fines of €30.96 million on VW for resale price maintenance in Germany. This decision was, however, annulled by the CFI on the grounds that the Commission had failed to establish that the distributors had agreed to, or acquiesced in, the manufacturer's policy of resale price maintenance.[167] The ECJ[168] upheld the annulment ruling that a call by manufacturer would only be prohibited by Article 81(1) if the Commission established concurrence of wills on the part of the parties to the dealership agreement.[169] These cases establish that the Commission has a heavy burden to discharge before it can establish that an actual agreement to fix minimum resale prices exists. Article 81 does not prevent a supplier from pursuing a policy of minimum resale prices if that policy is not accepted by its distributors.[170]

(iii) Agreements which have as their Effect the Prevention, Restriction, or Distortion of Competition

a. Introduction

In all other cases, that is, where the agreement does not contain clauses imposing severe territorial or price restraints, it is necessary to look at the *effect* of the agreement.[171] Only then can it be determined whether or not competition has in fact been restricted. Despite the strict approach taken by the Commission initially, more recent decisions, the guidelines on Vertical Restraints and the Guidelines on the application of Article 81(3) of the Treaty demonstrate that,

---

[162] See *infra* 739 ff.

[163] *Yamaha* IP/03/1028, 16 July 2003.

[164] [2002] OJ L691, [2002] 4 CMLR 1458.

[165] Case T-67/01, *JCB Service* v. *Commission* [2004] ECR II-49, [2004] 4 CMLR 1346, para. 130. This finding was not challenged before the ECJ which broadly upheld the judgment of the CFI, Case C-167/04 *JCB Service* v. *Commission* [2006] ECR I-8935 In allowing the cross-appeal, however, the ECJ considered that the CFI had been wrong to cut the level of the fine imposed. Fining policy is discussed, infra Chap. 14. Note that the agreement in JCB was originally notified to the Commission in June 1973!

[166] [2001] OJ L162/14. It imposed a fine of €30.96 million on Volkswagen in respect of the infringement, the decision was annulled on appeal, Case T-208/01, *Volkswagen* v. *Commission* [2003] ECR II-5141, [2004] 4 CMLR 727, *aff'd* Case C-74/04P, [2006] ECR I-6585.

[167] Case T-208/01, *Volkswagen* v. *Commission* [2003] ECR II-5141, [2004] 4 CMLR 727, *aff'd* Case C-74/04 P, [2006] ECR I-6585, see *supra* Chap. 3.

[168] Case C-74/04 P, [2006] ECR I-6585.

[169] Case C-74/04 P, [2006] ECR I-6585, paras. 39–56. In this case the Commission had not attempted to show that the dealers had tacitly acquiesced in the manufacturer's call but had found that the concurrence was part of the dealership agreement.

[170] For a discussion of unilateral conduct and agreements, see *supra* Chap. 3, 155–168.

[171] See Case 56/65, *Société La Technique Minière* v. *Maschinenbau Ulm GmbH* [1966] ECR 234, [1966] CMLR 357 and *supra* Chap 4. But see the discussion of hardcore restraints *infra* 749–55.

in line with case-law, a more principled economic approach is adopted when applying Article 81(1). In particular, the Article 81(3) Guidelines indicate that in effect cases it must be established that the agreement affects inter-brand or intra-brand competition i.e. that it affects 'actual or potential competition to such an extent that on the relevant market negative effects on prices, output, innovation or the variety or quality of goods and services can be expected with a reasonable degree of probability'[172] or it restricts, without objective justification, distributors from competing with each other.[173] Further that if, following these principles, the transaction is not restrictive of competition, restraints 'ancillary' to the main non-restrictive transaction also fall outside Article 81(1).[174]

In paragraphs 100–229 of the *Guidelines on Vertical Restraints* the Commission sets out its enforcement policy in relation to vertical restraints in individual cases (i.e., in relation to those agreements which will not benefit from the new Verticals Regulation). In this section the Commission explicitly recognizes that '[v]ertical restraints are generally less harmful than horizontal restraints'[175] and states that it will adopt an economic approach in its application of Article 81. It rehearses the *positive* effects of vertical restraints, accepting that restraints may be essential to the realization of efficiencies and the development of new markets by, for example, solving a 'free rider' problem and opening up or facilitating entry to new markets and that, where there is sufficient inter-brand competition and there are no cumulative effects, vertical restraints are unlikely to cause competition concerns.[176] Further, it accepts that vertical restraints restricting inter-brand competition are more harmful than vertical restraints that reduce intra-brand competition.[177] The Commission concedes that vertical restraints may be warranted and essential to achieve efficiency, particularly where the restraints are 'of a limited duration which help the introduction of new complex products or protect relationship-specific investments'. The Commission also recognizes however that '[a] vertical restraint is sometimes necessary for as long as the supplier sells its product to the buyer'.[178]

In paragraphs 121–33 the Commission sets out the factors it considers to be most important when assessing whether or not an agreement appreciably restricts competition under Article 81(1). The central enquiry focuses on the *market power* of the undertakings concerned:

121. ... The following factors are the most important to establish whether a vertical agreement brings about an appreciable restriction of competition under Article 81(1):

a) market position of the supplier;

b) market position of competitors;

c) market position of the buyer;

---

[172] Article 81(3) Guidelines, para. 24. This could be because the agreement restricts actual or potential competition between the parties or between any one of the parties and third parties that could have existed absent the agreement, paras. 25–26.

[173] Thus according to the Commission two counterfactuals may need to be used one to determine whether the agreement restricts inter-brand competition (whether the agreement restricts actual or potential competition that would have existed without the agreement) and one to determine whether it restricts intra–brand competition (whether the agreement restricts actual or potential competition that would have existed in the absence of the contractual restraints).

[174] Article 81(3) Guidelines, paras. 28–31. But see the discussion of restriction by effect and ancillary restraints *supra* Chap. 4.

[175] Guidelines, para. 100.

[176] *Supra* 688 ff.

[177] Guideline, para. 119, sets out general rules for the evaluation of vertical restraints. The hard-core restraints prohibited by the Verticals Register, however, all focus on restrictions on intra-brand competition.

[178] Guidelines, para. 117.

d) entry barriers;

e) maturity of the market;

f) level of trade;

g) nature of the product;

h) other factors.

122. The importance of individual factors may vary from cases to case and depends on all other factors. For instance, a high market share of the supplier is usually a good indicator of market power, but in the case of low entry barriers it may not indicate market power. It is therefore not possible to provide strict rules on the importance of the individual factors.

The sections below consider the case-law, decisional practice, and guidance on the question of how Article 81(1) applies to specific types of vertical agreements and restraint. These judgments indicate that many restraints, when viewed in context, do not restrict competition or may be regarded as 'ancillary' to an agreement that does not itself infringe Article 81(1).[179] It is stressed again, however, that the complex analysis demanded in effect cases will ordinarily be circumvented where the parties' market shares do not exceed 30%, since in nearly all cases the block exemption should apply.

b. Single Branding Agreements and *Delimitis*

One of the most important of all of the Court's judgments in the context of distribution agreements is *Delimitis v. Henninger Bräu*.[180] In this case the Court had to give guidance to a national court asked to rule on the compatibility of a beer supply agreement with Article 81(1). It will be remembered that the contract obliged the café proprietor to obtain his beer requirements from the brewer, Henninger Bräu (although once a fixed quantity had been bought, Delimitis was free to purchase beer from other Member States). Agreements such as this which oblige a buyer to obtain all, most, or a certain percentage or amount of its requirements from a named supplier frequently lead to efficiencies in distribution. A supplier is enabled to plan the number of sales it will make with greater precision, and distributors are encouraged actively to promote the supplier's product. Further, suppliers often confer reciprocal benefits (such as loans at below market rates, training, business and financial advice) on distributors which agree not to purchase a competitor's products. Obviously the supplier will wish to ensure that these benefits are not used to assist sales of competitors' products.

Since, however, these non-compete or quantity forcing agreements prohibit or deter distributors from handling competitors' products, there is a concern that that these agreements, or networks of similar agreements, might tie up outlets and preclude competitors from gaining access to the retail market. This worry is particularly acute in markets where access to the market is not easy on account of the existence of barriers to entry, such as planning restrictions or licensing requirements.[181] Further, there is a concern that such agreements may restrict inter-brand competition by facilitating collusion or by limiting in-store inter-brand competition.[182]

In *Delimitis*[183] the ECJ recognized that an obligation imposed on the café proprietor to purchase most of its beer requirements from the brewer entailed advantages for both the

---

[179] See Chap. 4.

[180] Case C-234/89, *Delimitis v. Henninger Bräu* [1991] ECR I-935, [1992] 5 CMLR 210. See also Chap. 4, 205–12.

[181] See *supra* 688 ff.

[182] See Guidelines, paras. 106–8.

[183] Case C-234/89, *Delimitis v. Henninger Bräu* [1991] ECR I-935, [1992] 5 CMLR 210. The relevant paragraphs of the judgment are set out *supra* Chap. 4.

supplier and the reseller. It set out guidelines for the national court to determine whether or not the effect of such an agreement foreclosed access to the market and so prevented, restricted, or distorted competition. This could be determined by, first, defining the relevant market and considering whether or not that market was foreclosed to other competitors or precluded expansion by existing competitors. If it was, secondly, it had to be determined whether or not the agreement in question restricted competition. It would only do so if the agreements concluded by that producer appreciably contributed to the foreclosure effect.

This case clearly demonstrates that in the absence of territorial exclusivity or resale price maintenance a careful analysis of the impact of the agreement on the market should be made. The Court focused its enquiry on the important question whether or not the agreement, alone or in conjunction with a network of similar agreements, would lead to a restriction of inter-brand competition. The Court considered that only where the agreement contributed to the foreclosure of the market and to a restriction of inter-brand competition would it be found to restrict competition within the meaning of Article 81(1).

The CFI has adopted a similar approach in respect of agreements affecting the market for ice creams for impulse purchase. In *Langnese-Iglo GmbH v. Commission*,[184] the CFI upheld a finding of the Commission that an agreement providing for the exclusive sale of ice creams for impulse purchase in retail outlets infringed Article 81(1) and could not be exempted under Article 81(3).[185] Similarly, in *Van den Bergh Foods v. Commission*[186] the CFI upheld a finding that freezer exclusivity operated by HB in Ireland infringed Article 81(1) and did not meet the criteria of Article 81(3). The freezer exclusivity had the same effect as outlet exclusivity. In respect to the analysis required under Article 81(1) the CFI reiterated that a *Delimitis* type analysis was required:

83. In order to determine whether HB's exclusive distribution agreements fall within the prohibition contained in Article [81(1)] of the Treaty, it is appropriate, in accordance with the case-law, to consider whether all the similar agreements entered into in the relevant market and the other features of the economic and legal context of the agreements at issue, show that those agreements cumulatively have the effect of denying access to that market to new competitors. If, on examination, that is found not to be the case, the individual agreements making up the bundle of agreements cannot impair competition within the meaning of Article [81(1)] of the Treaty. If, on the other hand, such examination reveals that it is difficult to gain access to the market, it is then necessary to assess the extent to which the agreements at issue contribute to the cumulative effect produced, on the basis that only those agreements which make a significant contribution to any partitioning of the market are prohibited (*Delimitis*, paragraphs 23 and 24, and *Langnese-Iglo v. Commission*, paragraph 99).

84. It follows that, contrary to HB's submission, the contractual restrictions on retailers must be examined not just in a purely formal manner from the legal point of view, but also by taking into account the specific economic context in which the agreements in question operate, including the particular features of the relevant market, which may, in practice, reinforce those restrictions and thus distort competition on that market contrary to Article [81(1)] of the Treaty.

85. In that regard, it must be remembered that the exclusivity clause in HB's distribution agreements was part of a set of similar agreements concluded by manufacturers on the relevant market and was an established practice not only in Ireland but also in other countries (see paragraph 79 above).

[184] Case T-7/93 [1995] ECR II-1583, [1995] 5 CMLR 602.

[185] *Langnese-Iglo GmbH* [1993] OJ L183/19, [1994] 4 CMLR 51, see especially paras. 94–5 and 101. See also the Commission's decision in *Schöller Lebensmittel GmbH & Co KG* [1993] OJ L183/1, [1994] 4 CMLR 51.

[186] Case T-65/98, [2003] ECR II-4653, [2004] 4 CMLR 1, *aff'd* Case C-552/03 P, *Unilever Bestfoods v. Commission* [2006] OJ C294/19.

On the facts the Court considered that the Commission had proved to the required legal standard that there was evidence of demand for ice creams of other manufacturers but that freezer exclusivity had prevented retailers from stocking such competing ice creams. The network of HB's agreements and their supply of exclusive freezer cabinets had 'a considerable dissuasive effect on retailers with regard to the installation of their own cabinet or that of another manufacturer and operate de facto as a tie on sales outlets that have only HB freezer cabinets'.[187] It thus concluded that it was 'clear from an examination of the entirety of the similar distribution agreements concluded on the relevant market, and other evidence of the economic and legal context of which those agreements form part, that the distribution agreements concluded by HB are liable to have an appreciable effect on competition for the purposes of Article [81(1)] of the Treaty and contribute significantly to a foreclosure of the market'.[188]

The Commission's approach in the guidelines is consistent with the Court's case-law.[189] In particular, the Commission stresses the central importance in the appraisal of single branding agreements of examining: the market position of the supplier (considering the market power of the supplier and the market position of its competitors); and the extent to and the duration for which the supplier applies a non-compete obligation.[190] The foreclosure will be more significant the greater the tied market share and the longer the duration of the non-compete obligation. The Commission takes the view that non-compete obligations for under one year by non-dominant companies are in general not considered to give rise to appreciable anti-competitive effects, non-compete clauses in excess of five years are generally unnecessary and will outweigh claimed efficiencies,[191] and clauses imposing non-compete obligations of between one and five years will require a proper balancing of the pro- and anti-competitive effects.[192]

The Commission states that it does not anticipate a single or cumulative anti-competitive effect where the market share of the largest supplier is below 30 per cent and the market share of the five largest suppliers is below 50 per cent.[193] The Commission states that it will also take into account entry barriers, countervailing buyer power and the level of trade.[194]

In a series of cases subsequent to *Delimitis*, the Commission dealt with single branding agreements notified to it for exemption. In some decisions it has been found that single branding agreements infringe Article 81(1) and do not meet the criteria of Article 81(3),[195] in some cases it has been found that the agreements infringe Article 81(1) but meet the criteria of

---

[187] Case T-65/98, [2003] ECR II-4653, [2004] 4 CMLR 1, *aff'd* Case C-552/03 P, *Unilever Bestfoods v. Commission* [2006] OJ C294/19., para. 98.

[188] *Ibid.*, para. 118.

[189] See also, e.g., Case C-214/99, *Neste Markkinointi Oy v. Yötuuli* [2000] ECR I-1121, [2000] 4 CMLR 993.

[190] Guidelines, paras. 140–1.

[191] The Verticals Reg. allows for longer periods where the property occupied by the distributor is owned by the supplier, *infra* 756. See also the ruling of the EFTA court in Case E-7/01, *Hegelstad Eindomsselskap Arvid B. Hegeltad v. Hydro Texaco AS*, [2002] EFTA Court Reports 310 where it held that a petrol supply agreement between a fuel supplier and a service station operator for 15 years would only infringe Article 53(1) EFTA where it made a significant contribution to the cumulative closing off effect caused by the totality of the agreements on the market.

[192] Guidelines, para. 141. The Commission states controversially view that '[d]ominant companies may not impose non-compete obligations on their buyers unless they can objectively justify such commercial practice within the context of Article 82', but it may now have retreated from this position see *supra* Chap. 4, 283–4.

[193] Guidelines, para. 143.

[194] *Ibid.*, 141.

[195] See, e.g., the Commission's decision in *Langnese-Iglo GmbH* [1993] OJ L183/19, [1994] 4 CMLR 51 and *Schöller Lebensmittel GmbH & Co KG* [1993] OJ L183/1, [1994] 4 CMLR 51, in which the Commission appeared to adopt an extremely narrow construction of the Court's judgment in Case C-234/89, *Delimitis v. Henninger Bräu* [1991] ECR I-935, [1992] 5 CMLR 210.

Article 81(3),[196] and in some cases it has been found that such agreements do not infringe Article 81(1) at all.[197] A fairly remarkable example of the latter is *Interbrew*[198] where the Commission found that beer supply agreements concluded by Interbrew, which had 56 per cent[199] of the Belgian horeca market[200] did not, as amended following negotiations with the Commission, infringe Article 81(1). Essentially the amended agreements gave Belgian horeca outlets extended freedom to carry other beers not brewed by Interbrew. Although the agreements did incorporate non-compete obligations (clauses forcing the outlets to serve exclusively Interbrew's beer) these were essentially limited to draught pils and, in the case of loan-tie agreements, the agreements could be terminated more easily.[201]

c. Exclusive Distribution Agreements and *STM*

Exclusive distribution agreements, in which a manufacturer appoints a sole distributor for a particular area, have a number of positive effects and may consequently stimulate the competitive process. For example: efficiencies flow from the manufacturer's decision to deal only with one distributor in a particular territory; transaction costs are saved; customer feedback may be more easily obtained; and such an agreement may be essential to solve a free-rider problem. If the distributor is sheltered from intra-brand competition it will be encouraged to incur expenditure promoting and advertising the product, safe in the knowledge that other distributors will not be able to 'free ride' on that expenditure.[202]

In drawing up an exclusive distribution agreement varying degrees of immunity from intra-brand competition can be granted. The manufacturer may agree only to refrain from distributing the product itself within the distributor's territory. Additionally or alternatively, protection may be given from the selling efforts of other distributors. Distributors may be prohibited from actively seeking sales outside their own territory (qualified territorial protection) or from making any sales outside their territories at all (absolute territorial protection).[203] *Consten and Grundig* makes it clear that where the territorial protection granted to the distributor is absolute the affront to the single market objective is too severe. In consequence, the agreement will be found to have as its object the restriction of competition.[204]

[196] See, e.g., *Bass* [1999] OJ L186/1, [1999] 5 CMLR 782 and *Whitbread* [1999] OJ L88/26, [1999] 5 CMLR 118. But see the discussion of *Inntrepreneur Pub Company v. Crehan* [2006] UKHL 38, *infra* Chap. 15.

[197] See *Roberts/Greene King* IP/98/967 where the Commission concluded that Greene King's network of agreements did not make a significant contribution to the foreclosure of the market of the distribution on beer in establishments selling alcoholic beverages for consumption on the premises in the UK. The decision was upheld on appeal Case T-25/99, *Roberts v. Commission* [2001] ECR II-1881, [2001] 5 CMLR 828.

[198] IP/03/545.

[199] As a result Interbrew was the only Belgian brewer whose exclusivity arrangements were clearly not covered by the Verticals Reg., see *infra* 738 ff.

[200] Horeca outlets are those that have concluded loan agreements or lease/sublease agreements with a brewer.

[201] In its Press Release that Commission stated that it had kept the Belgian competition authority informed throughout the procedure. Further, that it had responded to a request from the Dutch competition authority, the NMA, to obtain guidance from it in the context of its handling of similar brewery contracts notified by Heineken which had a leading position in the Dutch market with shares in excess of 30%. The Commission specifically referred to the need to intensify contacts with the National Competition Authorities through the European Competition Network, *infra* Chap. 14.

[202] See *supra* 688 ff.

[203] Absolute territorial protection may be reinforced by the grant of intellectual property rights: see, e.g., Cases 56 and 58, *Etablissements Consten SA & Grundig-Verkaufs-GmbH v. Commission* [1966] ECR 299, [1966] CMLR 418.

[204] *Supra* 713–6.

The case law of the ECJ clearly recognizes, however, the benefits for the competitive process that potentially flow from exclusive distribution agreements and accepts that in the absence of absolute territorial protection such agreements may not infringe Article 81(1). In *Société La Technique Minière* v. *Maschinenbau Ulm GmbH*[205] the ECJ held that exclusive distribution agreements will not restrict competition if the appointment of the exclusive distributor is necessary to enable the manufacturer to penetrate a new market. The Court accepted that a restraint necessary to persuade the distributor to take on the commercial risk inherent in the agreement would not constitute a restriction of competition within the meaning of Article 81(1).

The Commission's approach to exclusive distribution agreements is summarized in paragraphs 161–76 of its Guidelines. When considering the effect of these agreements on competition, the Commission looks at the market position of the supplier, the position of its competitors, barriers to trade, buying power, the maturity of the market, and the level of trade. The Commission states that 'the loss of intra-brand competition can only be problematic if inter-brand competition is limited. The stronger the "position of the supplier", the more serious is the loss of intra-brand competition'.[206] In its Article 81(3) Guidelines, however, the Commission appears to display a stricter approach to these types of restraint stating that territorial or customer intra-brand restraints[207] are caught by Article 81(1) unless 'objectively necessary' for the existence of an agreement of that type or nature.[208] This approach, potentially brings many vertical agreements containing territorial or customer restraints within Article 81(1) whether or not the parties have market power and/or the ability to affect prices or output on the market for example, by foreclosing access to supply or distribution channels to competitors.[209]

To encourage concentration of selling efforts exclusive distribution agreements are often combined with a commitment on the part of the distributor not to purchase the products of competitors for resale.[210] Single branding provisions can of course foreclose other suppliers.[211] The Commission deals with the combination of exclusive distribution and single branding in its guidelines.

171. The combination of exclusive distribution with single branding may add the problem of foreclosure of the market to other suppliers especially in case of dense network of exclusive distributors with small territories or in case of a cumulative effect. This may necessitate application of the principles set out . . . on single branding. However, when the combination does not lead to significant foreclosure, the combination of exclusive distribution and single branding may be pro-competitive by increasing the incentive for the exclusive distributor to focus his efforts on the particular brand. Therefore, in the absence of such a foreclosure effect, the combination of exclusive distribution with non-compete is exemptable for the whole duration of the agreement, particularly at the wholesale level.

---

[205] Case 56/65, 1966] ECR 234, [1966] CMLR 357. See extract set out in Chap. 4, 246.

[206] Guidelines, para. 163. The Commission notes, however, that if the number of competitors becomes small and their market position is rather similar, there is a risk of collusion, para. 164. But see the Guidelines on Vertical Restraints, para. 119, rule 10 and paras. 161–74.

[207] Falling short of absolute territorial protection, see *supra* n. 204.

[208] Article 81(3) Guidelines, para. 18(2) and see *supra* Chap. 4.

[209] This view explains the need for a broad overarching block exemptions for vertical and technology transfer agreements respectively.

[210] See *infra* 710–3.

[211] *Ibid.*

d. Selective Distribution Agreements and *Metro*

A supplier wishing to project an image for its goods and/or to ensure that sales are accompanied by the provision of specific services may decide to establish a selective distribution system. Under such a system the supplier will select its retailers, perhaps by number or by reference to quality or location of the distributor. Where the supplier wishes to portray and enhance a luxury image and to capitalize on consumers' desires to purchase a luxury product it may restrict supplies to retailers selling from a high quality location. Alternatively, a supplier may agree only to supply retailers that will comply with certain obligations as to service, sales promotion, or regular ordering. It may wish to ensure that consumers purchasing its product receive a minimum level of pre-sales services and are fully informed about the product's qualities and capabilities. If such a system is to be effective both the supplier and the distributors will wish to ensure that non-authorized retailers, which will detract from the image they are attempting to create or which will free-ride on the pre-sales services provided, are not supplied.

A prohibition on the supply of retailers that have not been authorized to sell the products impacts on *intra-brand* competition and may be aimed at promoting inter-brand competition. In an ideal world a consumer who does not value the luxury image or the additional services imposed will purchase other competing products instead. Nonetheless, in some cases it may be arguable that the justifications for a selective distribution system are not as strong as the supplier suggests and that, especially where networks of similar agreements are operated, the practice may in fact weaken inter-brand competition, facilitate horizontal coordination, and lead to higher prices.[212]

Despite the similarities between franchising agreements and selective distribution systems[213] they have been afforded, at least prior to the Verticals Regulation, quite different treatment under EC law. In *Pronuptia* the Court accepted that many clauses essential to the operation of a franchising agreement do not infringe Article 81(1). Further, Regulation 4087/88[214] (which has now expired) provided, from 1988, a block exemption for those franchising agreements that did infringe Article 81(1). In contrast, until 1 June 2000 there was no Community block exemption for selective distribution systems. Although many selective distribution systems are now block exempted from Article 81(1) by the Verticals Regulation, prior to its adoption the question of whether such a system infringed Article 81(1) was of extreme importance. It is important to remember, however, that since 2000, the compatibility of selective distribution systems with Article 81(1) is only likely to be of key importance where the conditions of the block exemption are not satisfied.

The ECJ has recognized that certain qualitative selective distribution systems may escape the Article 81(1) prohibition but has been less willing than it has in the context of franchising agreements to accept that clauses do not fall within Article 81(1).[215] The leading case on the

---

[212] See *supra* 688 ff.

[213] In each case the supplier wishes to project a certain image for its product or to ensure that specific services are provided by the distributor. It may therefore wish to control the distributors operating within the system and the location and/or the get-up of the premises. In each case the assignment of intellectual property rights might be essential to the successful operation of the agreement

[214] [1988] OJ L35/46, see *infra* 738–9.

[215] 'The Commission (and the Court) generally accord more favourable treatment to restrictive clauses in franchising agreements as compared to distributions agreements...For example, dealer location clauses, minimum purchasing obligations and stocking requirements in franchise agreement do not even fall within Art. [81(1)], while in selective distribution agreements the same clauses not only fall within Art. [81(1)] but might also be denied an exemption under Art. [81(3)]. This is problematic: many distribution agreements have

compatibility of selective distribution systems with Article 81(1) is *Metro-SB-Grossmärkte GmbH v. Commission (No. 1)*.[216] The principles set out in this case relating to the compatibility of selective distribution networks with Article 81(1) are different from those adopted in relation to other vertical agreements, and as such should perhaps be considered *sui generis*.[217] The Court has developed a particular jurisprudence on this type of distribution which is at times hard to comprehend or rationalize fully.[218] Nonetheless, the judgment throws interesting light on the Court's thinking. It appears to indicate that certain restrictions in the selective distribution network are not caught by Article 81(1) because they are necessary in pursuance of a desirable end.

Case 26/76, *Metro-SB-Grossmärkte GmbH* v. *Commission (No. 1)* [1977] ECR 1875, [1978] 2 CMLR 1

SABA manufactured televisions, radios, and tape-recorders, which it distributed through a selective distribution network (SDN), whereby only specialist dealers who met certain criteria sold the products.[219] The Commission held that some aspects of the SDN were outside Article 81(1). Other provisions it held to be within Article 81(1) but it granted an exemption. Metro was a self-service dealer who SABA refused to admit to the network because it did not fulfill all the criteria. It appealed to the Court of Justice under Article 230 against the grant of the exemption to SABA.[220]

Court of Justice

19. The applicant maintains that Article 2 of the contested decision is vitiated by misuse of powers inasmuch as the Commission has failed to recognise 'what is protected under Article [81] [namely] freedom of competition for the benefit of the consumer, not the coincident interests of a manufacturer and a given group of traders who wish to secure selling prices which are considered to be satisfactory by the latter'. Furthermore, if it were to be considered that an exemption from the prohibition might be granted in respect of the distribution system in dispute pursuant to Article [81(3)], the applicant maintains that the Commission has misapplied that provision by granting an exemption in respect of restrictions on competition which are not indispensable to the attainment of the objectives of improving production or distribution or promoting technical or economic progress and which lead to the elimination of competition from self-service wholesale traders.

A Misuse of powers

20. The requirement contained in Articles [3(1)] and [81] of the [EC] Treaty that competition shall not be distorted implies the existence on the market of workable competition, that is to say the degree of competition necessary to ensure the observance of the basic requirements and the

---

elements that are characteristic of franchises, ... i.e., the transfer of commercial know-how to independent parties operating under the supplier's trademark and not dealing in certain competing goods'. B. E. Hawk, 'System Failure: Vertical Restraints and EC Competition Law' [1995] 32 *CMLRev* 973, 985.

[216] Case 26/76, [1977] ECR 1875, [1978] 2 CMLR 1. The Court's judgment was given soon after the US Supreme Court's judgment in *Sylvania* which overruled *Schwinn*: see *supra* 698–102.

[217] See *supra* Chap. 4.

[218] See Case 75/84, *Metro-SB-Grossmärkte GmbH* v. *Commission (No. 2)* [1986] ECR 3021, [1987] 1 CMLR 118; Case T-19/92, *Groupement d'Achat Edouard Leclerc* v. *Commission* [1996] ECR II-1851, [1997] 4 CMLR 968.

[219] Selective distribution system is defined in the Verticals Reg., *infra* 741.

[220] For the *locus standi* under Article 230 of an undertaking in Metro's position, see *infra* Chap. 14.

attainment of the objectives of the Treaty, in particular the creation of a single market achieving conditions similar to those of a domestic market. In accordance with the requirement the nature and intensiveness of competition may vary to an extent dictated by the products or services in question and the economic structure of the relevant market sectors. In the sector covering the production of high quality and technically advanced consumer durables, where a relatively small number of large- and medium-scale producers offer a varied range of items which, or so consumers may consider, are readily interchangeable, the structure of the market does not preclude the existence of a variety of channels of distribution adapted to the peculiar characteristics of the various producers and to the requirements of the various categories of consumers. On this view the Commission was justified in recognising that selective distribution systems constituted, together with others, an aspect of competition which accords with Article [81(1)], provided that resellers are chosen on the basis of objective criteria of a qualitative nature relating to the technical qualifications of the reseller and his staff and the suitability of his trading premises and that such conditions are laid down uniformly for all potential resellers and are not applied in a discriminatory fashion.

21. It is true that in such systems of distribution price competition is not generally emphasised either as an exclusive or indeed as a principal factor. This is particularly so when, as in the present case, access to the distribution network is subject to conditions exceeding the requirements of an appropriate distribution of the products. However, although price competition is so important that it can never be eliminated, it does not constitute the only effective form of competition or that to which absolute priority must in all circumstances be accorded. The powers conferred upon the Commission under Article [81(3)] show that the requirements for the maintenance of workable competition may be reconciled with the safeguarding of objectives of a different nature and that to this end certain restrictions on competition are permissible, provided that they are essential to the attainment of those objectives and that they do not result in the elimination of competition for a substantial part of the Common Market. For specialist wholesalers and retailers the desire to maintain a certain price level, which corresponds to the desire to preserve, in the interests of consumers, the possibility of the continued existence of this channel of distribution in conjunction with new methods of distribution based on a different type of competition policy, forms one of the objectives which may be pursued without necessarily falling under the prohibition contained in Article [81(1)], and, if it does fall thereunder, either wholly or in part, coming within the framework of Article [81(3)]. This argument is strengthened if, in addition, such conditions promote improved competition inasmuch as it relates to factors other than prices.

In this case the ECJ thus recognized that a simple, purely qualitative, selective distribution system is compatible with Article 81(1). Although recognizing that selective distribution limits price competition it accepted that price competition does not necessarily constitute the only form of competition.[221] It is clear, however, from the Court's judgments,[222] reiterated in the Commission's guidelines,[223] that Article 81(1) is only inapplicable if certain conditions are satisfied:

(i)   the characteristics or nature of the product in question necessitate a selective distribution system;

---

[221] Case 26/76, *Metro-SB-Grossmärkte GmbH* v. *Commission (No. 1)* [1977] ECR 1875, [1978] 2 CMLR 1, para. 21.

[222] *Ibid.*, paras. 20, 33–4 and Case T-19/92, *Groupement d'Achat Edouard Leclerc* v. *Commission* [1994] ECR II-441, [1997] 4 CMLR 995, para. 112.

[223] Guidelines, para. 185.

(ii) the distributors are chosen by reference to objective criteria of a qualitative nature which are set out uniformly and are not used arbitrarily to discriminate against certain retailer; and

(iii) the criteria set out do not go beyond what is necessary for the product in question.[224]

Even a system complying with these requirements may infringe Article 81(1) if the market is tied up with a network of similar agreements.[225]

The Nature of the Product

In Metro[226] the Court stated that the operation of a selective distribution system was justified in 'the sector covering the production of high quality and technically advanced consumer durables'. It is accepted that two categories of products justify a selective distribution system: technically complex products and luxury or branded products.

In the context of technically complex products it is necessary to determine whether or not the technology involved is so complex as to justify a distribution network involving specialized wholesalers and retailers.[227] In the case of luxury products it is necessary to assess the need for the producer to preserve its brand image and the need to safeguard, in the mind of the consumer, the aura of exclusivity and prestige of the product. In such cases appropriate marketing and a setting and presentation in line with the luxurious and exclusive nature and brand image of the product is essential.[228]

It has been found that the following products justify such a system: televisions,[229] hi-fis,[230] cameras,[231] personal computers,[232] clocks and watches,[233] high-quality gold and silver products,[234] perfumes,[235] dinner services,[236] and cars[237] (a specific block exemption applies for motor vehicle distribution agreements).[238] It has been doubted whether plumbing fittings are technically advanced products that necessitate a selective distribution system.[239] It also seems

---

[224] Case 31/80, L'Oréal NV aud L'Oréal SA v. De Nieuwe AMCK Puba [1980] ECR 3775, [1981] 2 CMLR 235 and Case T-19/91, Société d'Hygiène Dermatologique de Vichy v. Commission [1992] ECR II-415. The restrictions must be objectively necessary to protect the quality of the products in question: see, e.g., Grohe [1985] OJ L19/17, [1988] 4 CMLR 612.

[225] See Case 75/84, Metro v. Commission (No. 2) [1986] ECR 3021, [1987] 1 CMLR 118, discussed infra.

[226] Case 26/76, Metro-SB-Grossmärkte GmbH v. Commission (No. 1) [1977] ECR 1875, [1978] 2 CMLR 1.

[227] Case 75/84, Metro v. Commission (No. 2) [1986] ECR 3021, [1987] 1 CMLR 118.

[228] Case T-19/92, Groupement d'Achat Edouard Leclerc v. Commission [1994] ECR II-441, [1997] 4 CMLR 995, para. 116.

[229] Case 75/84, Metro v. Commission (No. 2) [1986] ECR 3021, [1987] 1 CMLR 118.

[230] Grundig [1985] OJ L233/1, renewed [1994] OJ L20/15, [1995] 4 CMLR 658.

[231] Hasselblad [1982] OJ L161/18, [1982] 2 CMLR 233.

[232] IBM [1984] OJ L118/24, [1984] 2 CMLR 342.

[233] Junghans [1977] OJ L30/10, [1977] 1 CMLR D 82; cf. Case 31/85, ETA Fabriques d'Ebauches v. DK Investments SA [1985] ECR 3933, [1986] 2 CMLR 674.

[234] Murat [1983] OJ L348/20, [1984] 1 CMLR 219.

[235] Parfums Givenchy [1992] OJ L236/11, [1993] 5 CMLR 579; Yves Saint Laurent [1992] OJ L12/24, [1993] 4 CMLR 120, partially annulled on appeal Case T-19/92, Groupement d'Achat Edouard Leclerc v. Commission [1994] ECR II-441, [1997] 4 CMLR 995. The Yves Saint Laurent selective distribution system now satisfies the terms of the Verticals Reg., see IP/01/713.

[236] Villeroy & Bosch [1985] OJ L376/15, [1998] 4 CMLR 461.

[237] BMW [1975] OJ L29/1, [1975] 1 CMLR D44.

[238] Reg. 1400/2002.

[239] Grohe [1985] OJ L19/17, [1988] 4 CMLR 612.

that 'selective distribution systems which are justified by the specific nature of the products or the requirements for their distribution may be established in other economic sectors'.[240] In *SA Binon & Cie v. SA Agence et Messageries de la Presse*,[241] for example, it was accepted that newspapers and periodicals would constitute a suitable product for selective distribution, partly because of the limited shelf life which each had:

Such a system may be established for the distribution of newspapers and periodicals, without infringing the prohibition in Article [81(1)], given the special nature of those products as regards their distribution. As AMP rightly pointed out, newspapers and periodicals can, as a general rule, only be sold by retailers during an extremely limited period of time whereas the public expects each distributor to be able to offer a representative selection of press publications, in particular those of the national press. For their part, publishers undertake to take back unsold copies and this gives rise to a continuous exchange of products between publishers and distributors.

It may be hard to persuade the Commission or a court that a product merits a selective distribution system if such a system if not operated in all jurisdictions in which the product is sold.

Qualitative not Quantitative Criteria Applied Uniformly

The Court in *Metro* stated clearly that a selective distribution system in which 'resellers are chosen on the basis of objective criteria of a qualitative nature relating to the technical qualifications of the reseller and his staff and the suitability of his trading premises and that such conditions are laid down uniformly for all potential resellers and are not applied in a discriminatory fashion'[242] would accord with Article 81. Any distributor satisfying the qualitative criteria should be supplied.

An immediate problem is to determine whether or not criteria are qualitative or quantitative in nature. The distinction is a difficult one since qualitative restrictions inevitably lead to restrictions on the number of resellers selected. It seems however that the distinction is between criteria designed to select dealers on the basis of their objective suitability to distribute a particular kind of good (qualitative criteria) and criteria which 'more directly limit the potential number of dealers by, for instance, requiring minimum or maximum sales, by fixing the number of dealers, etc'[243] (quantitative criteria). The Court's judgments and Commission's decisions indicate the types of restrictions likely to be held to be qualitative and the types of restrictions likely to be found to be quantitative. Unfortunately, the cases are not always entirely consistent.

It is clear from *Metro* itself that criteria relating to the technical qualification of the reseller and its staff and suitability of trading premises are of a qualitative nature. Further, it seems that obligations precluding the sale of goods that would detract from the product's brand image[244] and requiring dealers to provide after-sales services[245] are qualitative and compatible with Article 81(1). In some cases the Commission has found an obligation requiring a dealer to stock a wide or an entire range of products to be qualitative and in others it has found them to be

---

[240] Case T-19/92, *Groupement d'Achat Edouard Leclerc v. Commission* [1994] ECR II-441, [1997] 4 CMLR 995, para. 113.

[241] Case 243/85, [1985] ECR 2015, [1985] 3 CMLR 800, para. 32.

[242] Case 26/76, *Metro-SB-Grossmärkte GmbH v. Commission (No. 1)* [1977] ECR 1875, [1978] 2 CMLR 1, para. 20.

[243] Guidelines, para. 185.

[244] *Parfums Givenchy* [1992] OJ L236/11, [1993] 5 CMLR 579.

[245] *Grundig* [1985] OJ L233/1, renewed [1994] OJ L20/15, [1995] 4 CMLR 658; *Villeroy & Bosch* [1985] OJ L376/15, [1998] 4 CMLR 461.

quantitative. It seems that the classification of the obligation as qualitative or quantitative may turn upon the nature of the product involved.[246]

An obligation precluding members of the system from supplying unauthorized retailers does not infringe Article 81(1) since it is the corollary of the essential system of selective distribution.[247] Further, a provision precluding wholesalers from supplying private customers does not infringe Article 81(1).[248]

Other Restrictions

In contrast, quantitative restrictions will infringe Article 81(1). Although the exact meaning of the term quantitative is elusive, the purpose appears to be to catch all provisions that protect approved network members from the competition of other retailers meeting the qualitative criteria. It is thus broader than where a simple numerical limit is placed on the number of distributors in a particular area, although a clause fixing the number of distributors for a specific area[249] is of course prohibited. The following have also been held to be quantitative restrictions which infringe Article 81(1):[250] clauses restricting sales to specific types of stores;[251] or clauses requiring distributors to maintain specific amounts of stocks,[252] to promote the manufacturers product, to stock an entire range of products,[253] or to have a minimum annual turnover.[254]

Further, provisions directly or indirectly aimed at resale price maintenance[255] or preventing approved retailers from selling to each other (bans on cross-suppliers)[256] or to consumers in other Member States[257] will infringe Article 81(1).

---

[246] In *Grundig* OJ [1985] L 233/1, renewed [1994] OJ L20/15, [1995] 4 CMLR 658 the Commission found a requirement that retailers had to carry and stock a whole range of products went beyond what was necessary for the distribution of products and was an impediment to competition (the agreement was, however, granted an exemption under Article 81(3)). In contrast, in *Villeroy & Bosch* [1985] OJ L376/15, [1998] 4 CMLR 461, the requirement that the retailer had to display and stock a sufficiently wide and varied range of products did not infringe Article 81(1) and the system was granted negative clearance. In this case sales targets were not imposed, the requirement did not prevent retailers stocking competing products and inter-brand competition was high. In the Guidelines, para. 185, the Commission states that an obligation requiring distributors to sell a certain range of the products is purely of a qualitative nature.

[247] Case 26/76, *Metro-SB-Grossmärkte GmbH v. Commission (No. 1)* [1977] ECR 1875, [1978] 2 CMLR 1, para. 27.

[248] *Ibid.*

[249] In, e.g., *Hasselblad* [1982] OJ L161/18, [1982] 2 CMLR 233 the supplier supplied only a few of those distributors which satisfied the criteria set out.

[250] Such clauses may also limit the freedom of a distributor to purchase other supplier's products.

[251] Case T-19/92, *Groupement d'Achat Edouard Leclerc v. Commission* [1994] ECR II-441, [1997] 4 CMLR 995 (it is not justifiable to have a provision precluding supermarkets or hypermarkets becoming part of the network). See also *Vichy* [1991] OJ L75/57, on appeal Case T-19/91, *Société d'Hygiène Dermatologique de Vichy v. Commission* [1992] ECR II-415.

[252] Case 26/76, *Metro-SB-Grossmärkte GmbH v. Commission (No. 1)* [1977] ECR 1875, [1978] 2 CMLR 1.

[253] See *supra* n. 246.

[254] *Parfums Givenchy* [1992] OJ L236/11, [1993] 5 CMLR 579, *Yves Saint Laurent* [1992] OJ L12/24. [1993] 4 CMLR 120, partially annulled on appeal Case T-19/92, *Groupement d'Achat Edouard Leclerc v. Commission* [1994] ECR II-441, [1997] 4 CMLR 995. The CFI annulled part of the decision which raised indirect obstacles to sale in supermarket. The system was then modified to permit sales of perfume in multi-product sales points.

[255] Case 243/85, *SA Binon & Cie v. SA Agence et Messageries de la Presse* [1985] ECR 2015, [1985] 3 CMLR 800 and Case 107/82, *AEG-Telefunken v. Commission* [1983] ECR 3151, [1984] 3 CMLR 325.

[256] *Hasselblad* [1982] OJ L161/18, [1982] 2 CMLR 233.

[257] See Cases 228 and 229/82, *Ford Werke AG and Ford of Europe Inc v. Commission* [1984] ECR 1129, [1984] 1 CMLR 649; Case 32/78, *BMW v. Commission* [1979] ECR 2435, [1980] 1 CMLR 370; *Kodak* [1970] JO L142/24, [1970] CMLR D19. Guarantees granted on sale in one Member State must be honoured by distributors in other Member States: Case 31/85, *ETA Fabriques d'Ebauches v. DK Investments SA* [1985] ECR 3933, [1986] 2 CMLR 674.

Provisions setting out a difficult or lengthy procedure for retailers to join the network may also infringe Article 81(1).[258]

Discriminatory Application of the Criteria and Refusal to Supply

Article 81(1) will apply if the supplier precludes network members from supplying other members of the system[259] or if the supplier itself, acting in agreement with its distributors (and not unilaterally),[260] refuses to supply those that meet its requirements. A breach of Article 81 may therefore be committed if a supplier refuses to supply distributors known, for example, to sell at prices below those recommended by the supplier or outside their territory. This will only be the case, however, if an 'agreement' is established. Distributors which are part of the network but which understand that they will not be supplied if they do not adhere to the manufacturer's policy may be taken to have agreed, explicitly or implicitly, to these terms.[261]

Where a supplier is found to be operating a selective distribution system in a discriminatory manner in breach of Article 81(1) it appears that the Commission may *not* make an order for supply. In *Automec v. Commission (No. 2)* the CFI indicated that the Commission did not have power to order supply[262] and to insist on contractual arrangements when other suitable means were available to ensure that the infringement was terminated.[263] The Commission[264] may declare that the relevant agreement infringes Article 81(1), consider whether or not the agreement meets the conditions of Article 81(3) (where the system is being operated so as to deter distributors from selling outside their territory or to interfere with their freedom to set resale prices the Article 81(3) criteria will also almost certainly not be met) and, where appropriate, fine the parties in breach.[265] If the supplier is dominant it is possible that a refusal to supply may constitute an abuse of a dominant position and that an order for supply will be made.[266]

The Criteria must not go beyond What is Necessary

In *Metro (No. 1)*[267] the ECJ held that there must be a relationship between the goods protected by the selective distribution system and the restrictions imposed on distributors: the restrictions

---

[258] *Parfums Givenchy* [1992] OJ L236/11, [1993] 5 CMLR 579; *Yves St Laurent* [1992] OJ L12/24, [1993] 4 CMLR 120; on appeal Case T-19/92, *Groupement d'Achat Edouard Leclerc v. Commission* [1994] ECR II-441, [1997] 4 CMLR 995.

[259] See *supra* n. 256.

[260] For the difficulty of proving that a distributor has agreed to or acquiesced in a supplier's illegal policy see *supra* Chap. 3, 155–68.

[261] See Case 107/82, *AEG-Telefunken v. Commission* [1983] ECR 3151, [1984] 3 CMLR 325; Cases 228 and 229/82, *Ford Werke AG and Ford of Europe Inc v. Commission* [1984] ECR 1129, [1984] 1 CMLR 649 and Case T-41/96, *Bayer AG v. Commission* [2000] ECR II-3383, [2001] 4 CMLR 126, *aff'd* Cases C-2 and 3/01 P, [2004] ECR I-23, [2004] 4 CMLR 653. See also C Case T-208/01, *Volkswagen v. Commission* [2003] ECR II-5141, [2004] 4 CMLR 727, *aff'd* Case C-74/04 P, [2006] ECR I-6585. Only truly unilateral behaviour escapes the Article 81(1) prohibition: see discussion of unilateral conduct and agreements, *supra* Chap. 3, 155–68.

[262] See *supra* Chap. 7.

[263] Case T-24/90, [1992] ECR II-2223, [1992] 5 CMLR 431, para. 51. This aspect of *Automec II* is discussed in Chaps. 14 and 15.

[264] National competition authorities and national courts also, of course, have power to enforce the rules, *infra* Chaps. 14 and 15.

[265] See *infra* Chap. 14.

[266] See *supra* Chap. 7. In Case 75/84, *Metro v. Commission (No. 2)* [1986] ECR 3021, [1987] 1 CMLR 118) the argument that SABA was dominant was rejected. The market for TVs and other such goods was competitive and SABA's market share was less than 10%.

[267] Case 26/76, [1977] ECR 1875, [1978] 2 CMLR 1.

are permissible provided that they are essential to protect the 'quality' of the relevant product. Restrictions that go beyond this will infringe Article 81(1). In *Vichy v. Commission*,[268] for example, the CFI held that 'the requirement of the status of dispensing chemist, which is a pre-condition for admission to the distribution network for Vichy products, is certainly not necessary for the proper distribution of those [cosmetic] products'. Rather such a requirement in relation to cosmetic products was 'entirely unnecessary' and 'disproportionate'.[269]

Networks of Agreements

In *Metro (No. 2)* the ECJ held that even a simple selective distribution system will fall within Article 81(1) where a network of similar agreements exist which tie up the market and leave no room for other methods of distribution.

Case 75/84, *Metro-SB-Grossmärkte GmbH & Co.KG* v. *Commission (No. 2)* [1986] ECR 3021, [1987] 1 CMLR 118

Following the expiry of its exemption, SABA applied for its renewal. Metro again objected, this time asserting that market conditions had changed significantly since the grant of the last exemption. It pointed out that many other electronics companies now operated selective distribution systems and that the market had become much more rigid. Although the Court accepted that it is necessary to determine whether or not the existence of other systems lead to rigidity in the market it agreed with the Commission that the systems in issue had not led to rigidity in price structures.

Court of Justice

40. It must be borne in mind that, although the Court has held in previous decisions that 'simple' selective distribution systems are capable of constituting an aspect of competition compatible with Article [81(1)], there may nevertheless be a restriction or elimination of competition where the existence of a certain number of such systems does not leave any room for other forms of distribution based on a different type of competition policy or results in a rigidity in price structure which is not counterbalanced by other aspects of competition between products of the same brand and by the existence of effective competition between different brands.

41. Consequently, the existence of a large number of selective distribution systems for a particular product does not in itself permit the conclusion that competition is restricted or distorted. Nor is the existence of such systems decisive as regards the granting or refusal of an exemption under Article [81(3)], since the only factor to be taken into consideration in that regard is the effect which such systems actually have on the competitive situation. Therefore the coverage ratio of selective distribution systems for colour television sets, to which Metro refers, cannot in itself be regarded as a factor preventing an exemption from being granted.

42. It follows that an increase in the number of 'simple' selective distribution systems after an exemption has been granted must be taken into consideration, when an application for renewal of that exemption is being considered, only in the special situation in which the relevant market was already so rigid and structured that the element of competition inherent in 'simple' systems is not sufficient to maintain workable competition. Metro has not been able to show that a special situation of that kind exists in the present case.

---

[268] Case T-19/91, [1992] ECR II-415.
[269] *Ibid.*, para. 69.

> ...
> 46. Therefore Metro's submission based on the growth of selective distribution systems in the consumer electronics sector must be rejected.

It is possible therefore that a simple selective distribution system may fall within Article 81(1) and be refused an exemption where the existence of networks of other similar agreements leads to excessive rigidity on the market.

Although it is true that, especially where selective distribution systems are commonplace throughout a market, they may lead to an increase in consumer prices[270] and the judgment displays a willingness to embark on economic analysis, the case has raised several practical difficulties.[271] In particular, given the Court's unwillingness to embrace a realistic economic analysis to selective distribution systems in *Metro (No. 1)*, it seems peculiar to add an economic layer later, the effect of which is to bring more agreements within the net of Article 81(1). The usual argument advanced is that a more realistic approach should be adopted to ensure that more agreements fall outside of Article 81(1) altogether.[272]

Difficulties in Applying the Metro Criteria and Article 81(3)

Although a welcome recognition that selective distribution systems may enhance inter-brand competition the principles set out are frustrating. First, the requirement that the product should fall within one of two categories that the Commission and/or the Court has ruled should be able to benefit from such a system seem inappropriate. Although it may be true that the need for a selective distribution system has sometimes been exaggerated, a producer operating on a competitive market will be punished by consumers if they do not believe that the product in question merits the system. Secondly, the requirement that retailers should be selected by reference only to *qualitative* criteria makes no economic sense. If a retailer has to comply with stringent qualitative criteria this may involve considerable expense which may demand that a quantitative limit on distributors is imposed. Apart from being economically indefensible it has been seen that the requirement has proved difficult to apply in practice and that identical restrictions have been labelled as qualitative in some cases and quantitative in others.

The Court's view that some restrictions of conduct imposed on dealers do not restrict competition is welcome, but the narrowness of the tests was regretted. The rules are nonsense commercially and economically speaking. It is very difficult for the holder of a prestigious brand to become master of its retail outlets. The rules encouraged a firm that is concerned about the services offered by retailers to integrate forward, and sell as far down the distribution chain as it could manage. This policy did not increase competition and may well reduced inefficiency. Moreover, it could not be adopted by small firms.[273]

The net outcome has been selective distribution systems have not, in the context of Article 81(1), adequately been assessed to determine whether or not it has led to an anti-competitive

---

[270] Although distributors still compete on the basis of enhanced services there are fears that the operation of selective distribution systems throughout a market will lead to tacit or explicit co-ordination of suppliers' or distributors' behaviour, higher consumer prices, and limited discounting on the market.

[271] See, e.g., R. J. Goebel, 'Metro II's Confirmation of the Selective Distribution Rules: Is This the End of the Road?' (1987) *CMLRev* 605.

[272] See R. Whish, *Competition Law* (3rd edn., Butterworths, 1993), 594.

[273] V. Korah, *An Introductory Guide to EC Competition Law and Practice* (8th edn., Hart Publishing, 2004), para. 9.4.

outcome on the market.[274] This problem was rectified in the past by the Commission accepting that many quantitative restrictions, for example, an obligation to engage in sales promotions, met the criteria of Article 81(3).[275] Now most selective distribution systems can benefit from the Verticals Regulation.[276] Where the Verticals Regulation does not apply, however, guidance on the application of Article 81(1) and 81(3) will still have to be sought from the case law and Guidelines on Vertical Restraints.[277] This indicates that that factors such as the nature of the product (which is not relevant to the application of the block exemption), the supplier's market position, the competitor's market position, barriers to entry, buying power and the maturity of the market will be relevant to the appraisal.

e. Franchising Agreements and *Pronuptia De Paris*

The Commission describes franchise agreements in its Guidelines on Vertical Restraints:

> 199. Franchise agreements contain licences of intellectual property rights relating in particular to trade marks or signs and know-how for the use and distribution of goods or services. In addition the licence of IPRs, the franchisor usually provides the franchisee during the life of the agreement with commercial or technical assistance. The licence and the assistance are integral components of the business method being franchised. The franchisor is in general paid a franchise fee by the franchisee for the use of the particular business method. Franchising may enable the franchisor to establish, with limited investments a uniform network for the distribution of his products. In addition to the provision of the business method, franchise agreements usually contain a combination of different vertical restraints concerning the products being distributed, in particular selective distribution and/or non-compete and/or exclusive distribution or weaker forms thereof.

Franchising arrangements in which a franchisee, or franchisees, is appointed and established as part of a uniform business network, may have a positive impact on competition on a market. Franchise arrangements assist the entry of new competitors to a market and lead to an increase in inter-brand competition. They enable a franchisor to expand its reputation and network without engaging in substantial investment. A franchisee is also enabled to set up and to enter a market with the assistance of an entrepreneur whose business has already been tried and tested on the market.

In *Pronuptia de Paris GmbH v. Pronuptia de Paris Irmgard Schillgallis*[278] the ECJ held that two categories of clauses essential to the successful operation of distribution *franchise agreements* did not constitute restrictions of competition for the purposes of Article 81(1): first the franchisor had to be able to communicate his know-how to franchisees and to protect it from use by competitor and second the franchisor had to be able to maintain the identity and reputation of its network.[279] The Court thus held that a restriction on the ability of a franchisee:

(1) to open a shop of a similar nature during the period of the contract and for a reasonable period thereafter; and

(2) to sell the shop without the franchisor's consent

---

[274] But see Case 75/84, *Metro v. Commission (No. 2)* [1986] ECR 3021, [1987] 1 CMLR 118.

[275] See Case 26/76, *Metro-SB-Grossmärkte GmbH v. Commission (No. 1)* [1977] ECR 1875, [1978] 2 CMLR 1; *Grundig* [1985] OJ L233/1, renewed [1994] OJ L20/15, [1995] 4 CMLR 658; *Parfums Givenchy* [1992] OJ L236/11, [1993] 5 CMLR 579.

[276] See *infra* 739 ff.

[277] Guidelines, paras. 187–98.

[278] Case 161/84, *Pronuptia de Paris GmbH v. Pronuptia de Paris Irmgard Schillgallis* [1986] ECR 353, [1986] 1 CMLR 414.

[279] *Ibid.*, paras. 16–17.

will not restrict competition where essential to protect the know-how and assistance provided under the terms of the contract. Similarly, clauses requiring the franchisee:

(1) to apply and to use the franchisor's business methods and know how;

(2) to locate, lay out and decorate the sales premises according to the franchisor's instructions;

(3) to gain the franchisor's approval prior to an assignment of the franchise;

(4) to sell only products supplied by the franchisor; and

(5) to gain the franchisor's approval for all advertising

may also be essential to preserve the identity and the reputation of the network and so fall outside Article 81(1).[280]

The Court did not, however, totally embrace an economic approach to franchise agreements.[281] It would not accept that: (1) clauses effecting a division of territories between the franchisor and franchisees or between the franchisees *inter se*,[282] or (2) preventing price competition between them, were essential to the operation of the franchise agreement. These are the types of clauses, discussed above, which automatically restrict competition. Arguments raised justifying their imposition can be considered only when determining their compatibility with Article 81(3).

Case 161/84, *Pronuptia de Paris GmbH* v. *Pronuptia de Paris Irmgard Schillgallis* [1986] ECR 353, [1986] 1 CMLR 414

A franchise agreement had been concluded between Pronuptia de Paris and Mrs Schillgalis. The latter had the exclusive right to use the 'Pronuptia de Paris' trademark in specific territories. Pronuptia assisted Mrs Schillgalis with the commercial aspects of her business. In exchange Mrs Schillgalis had undertaken to equip her shop in accordance with the franchisor's instructions, not to move its location, to purchase 80 per cent of her wedding dresses and accessories from the franchisor and to pay royalties, etc. Following a dispute between the parties, the compatibility of the agreement with Article 81(1) was raised before the German courts. The Bundesgerichtshof, considering that the outcome of the case depended on the interpretation of Community law, made an Article 234 reference to the Court of Justice. The first question it asked was whether Article 81(1) was applicable to franchise agreements such as the contract between the parties.

Court of Justice

16. First, the franchisor must be able to communicate his know-how to the franchisees and provide them with the necessary assistance in order to enable them to apply his methods, without running the risk that know-how and assistance might benefit competitors, even indirectly. It follows that provisions which are essential in order to avoid that risk do not constitute restrictions on competition for the purposes of Article [81(1)]. That is also true of a clause prohibiting the

---

[280] See paras. 16–22, set out *infra*.

[281] See *supra* Chap. 4.

[282] This has created difficulties since many franchisees are not willing to make the requisite investment without such protection.

franchisee, during the period of validity of the contract and for a reasonable period after its expiry, from opening a shop of the same of a similar nature in an area where he may compete with a member of the network. The same may be said of the franchisee's obligation not to transfer his shop to another party without the prior approval of the franchisor; that provision is intended to prevent competitors from indirectly benefiting from the know-how and assistance provided.

17. Secondly, the franchisor must be able to take the measures necessary for maintaining the identity and reputation of the network bearing his business name or symbol. It follows that provisions which establish the means of control necessary for that purpose do not constitute restrictions on competition for the purposes of Article [81(1)].

18. The same is true of the franchisee's obligation to apply the business methods developed by the franchisor and to use the know-how provided.

19. That is also the case with regard to the franchisee's obligation to sell the goods covered by the contract only in premises laid out and decorated according to the franchisor's instructions, which is intended to ensure uniform presentation in conformity with certain requirements. The same requirements apply to the location of the shop, the choice of which is also likely to affect the network's reputation. It is thus understandable that the franchisee cannot transfer his shop to another location without the franchisor's approval.

20. The prohibition of the assignment by the franchisee of his rights and obligations under the contract without the franchisor's approval protects the latter's right freely to choose the franchisees, on whose business qualifications the establishment and maintenance of the network's reputation depend.

21. By means of the control exerted by the franchisor on the selection of goods offered by the franchisee, the public is able to obtain goods of the same quality from each franchisee. It may in certain cases—for instance, the distribution of fashion articles—be impractical to lay down objective quality specifications. Because of the large number of franchisees it may also be too expensive to ensure that such specifications are observed. In such circumstances a provision requiring the franchisee to sell only products supplied by the franchisor or by suppliers selected by him may be considered necessary for the protection of the network's reputation. Such a provision may not however have the effect of preventing the franchisee from obtaining those products from other franchisees.

22. Finally, since advertising helps to define the image of the network's name or symbol in the eyes of the public, a provision requiring the franchisee to obtain the franchisor's approval for all advertising is also essential for the maintenance of the network's identity, so long as that provision concerns only the nature of the advertising.

23. It must be emphasized on the other hand that, far from being necessary for the protection of the know-how provided or the maintenance of the network's identity and reputation, certain provisions restrict competition between the members of the network. That is true of provisions which share markets between the franchisor and franchisees or between franchisees or prevent franchisees from engaging in price competition with each other.

24. In that regard, the attention of the national court should be drawn to the provision which obliges the franchisee to sell goods covered by the contract only in the premises specified therein. That provision prohibits the franchisee from opening a second shop. Its real effect becomes clear if it is examined in conjunction with the franchisor's undertaking to ensure that the franchisee has the exclusive use of his business name or symbol in a given territory. In order to comply with that undertaking the franchisor must not only refrain from establishing himself within that territory but also require other franchisess to give an undertaking not to open a second shop outside their own territory. A combination of provisions of that kind results in a sharing of markets between the franchisor and the franchisees or between franchisees and thus restricts competition within the network. As is clear from the judgment of 13 July 1966 (Joined Cases 56 and 58/64 *Consten and*

> *Grundig* v. *Commission* [1966] ECR 299), a restriction of that kind constitutes a limitation of competition for the purposes of Article [81(1)] if it concerns a business name of symbol which is already well-known. It is of course possible that a prospective franchisee would not take the risk of becoming part of the chain, investing his own money, paying a relatively high entry fee and undertaking to pay a substantial annual royalty, unless he could hope, thanks to a degree or protection against competition on the part of the franchisor and other franchisees, that his business would be profitable. That consideration, however, is relevant only to an examination of the agreement in the light of the conditions laid down in Article [81(3)].
>
> 25. Although provisions which impair the franchisee's freedom to determine his own prices are restrictive of competition, that is not the case where the franchisor simply provides franchisees with price guidelines, so long as there is no concerted practice between the franchisor and the franchisees or between the franchises themselves in the actual application of such prices.

The Commission has scrutinized a number of franchise agreements in the past and frequently takes a favourable view of such agreements. Ordinarily, however, following the approach of the ECJ in *Pronuptia*, the Commission has taken the view that certain clauses in the agreement (ordinarily clauses involving market sharing between the franchisor and franchisees or the franchisees *inter se*) infringe Article 81(1). It has therefore completed its assessment under Article 81(3).[283] In its guidelines it indicates that franchising agreements may fall outside Article 81(1) altogether.[284]

f. Tying

Although there have been relatively few cases which have dealt with tying under Article 81 (but see the discussion of when tying may constitute an abuse of a dominant position in Chapter 7), paragraphs 215–24 of the Guidelines deal with tying under Article 81. In particular, the Commission is concerned that tying may result in foreclosure on the market for the tied product (single branding for the tied product) and /or may create entry barriers into both the tying and tied product market. The Guidelines state that the three main criteria for determining the effects of tying under Article 81 are: the market position of the supplier on the tying market; the market position of its competitor's on the tying market; and the power of buyers on the market.

g. Other Restraints

The Commission's Guidelines also give specific guidance on the following restraints: exclusive customer allocation (treated in a similar, but not identical, way as exclusive distribution);[285] exclusive supply (i.e., where one distributor only is appointed within the European Community and where the main competition risk of such agreement is foreclosure of other buyers);[286] and recommended or maximum resale prices.[287]

---

[283] See, e.g., *Pronuptia* [1987] OJ L13/39, [1989] 4 CMLR 355, *Yves Rocher* [1987] OJ L8/49, [1988] 4 CMLR 592, *ServiceMaster* [1988] OJ L332/38, [1989] 4 CMLR 581 and *Charles Jourdan* [1989] OJ L35/31, [1989] 4 CMLR 591.

[284] Guidelines, para. 201.

[285] *Ibid.*, paras. 178–83.

[286] *Ibid.*, 202–14.

[287] See *supra* 716–8.

5. ARTICLE 81(3)

A. GENERAL

The broad view taken of Article 81(1) in the past has meant that many vertical agreements have been dealt with under Article 81(3). The procedural difficulties that were involved in gaining an individual exemption (or comfort letter)[288] meant that the block exemptions were of utmost importance. An agreement drafted to fall within the terms of a block exemption of course benefits from automatically being exempted from the Article 81(1) prohibition. The complex assessment required to determine whether or not an agreement infringes Article 81(1) or meets the Article 81(3) criteria is likely to mean that the importance of the block exemptions will be retained. In practice, a business concerned that its agreement may infringe Article 81(1) may prefer, or be advised, to draft its agreement to fall within a block exemption. Only where one does not apply will it be necessary to determine, in an individual case, whether or not the agreement meets the criteria of Article 81(3) (or whether it in fact, infringes Article 81(1) at all).

B. THE OLD BLOCK EXEMPTIONS

The Verticals Regulation replaced three block exemptions which applied to three different categories of distribution agreement:

(i) Regulation 1983/83[289] applied to exclusive distribution agreements;

(ii) Regulation 1984/83 applied to exclusive purchasing agreements (the regulation contained special provisions for beer supply and petrol agreements);[290] and

(iii) Regulation 4087/88[291] applied to franchising agreements.

It did not replace the motor vehicles block exemption (considered below). These three Regulations formed a vital part of the Commission's policy towards distribution agreements and through them the Commission was able to mould and influence the content of distribution agreements. Although the exclusive distribution, exclusive purchasing, and franchising block exemptions (the 'old block exemptions') were, in contrast to those available to horizontal agreements,[292] moderately successful, that success was at cost. Distribution agreements did not always fit neatly within one of these categories which the Commission, not business, has identified or within the mould that the Commission set out within those regulations. The old block exemptions thus restricted the *type* of arrangement that parties to a distribution agreement could make. This structure (is this an exclusive distribution, exclusive purchasing, or franchise agreement?) did not cater for the variety of arrangements that suppliers sought to use to distribute their products or services. In particular, the regulations did not apply at all to selective distribution arrangements, even though they were very similar in effect and in their impact on competition to franchising agreements. This approach stultified the diversity of distribution arrangements within the European Union.

---

[288] See *supra* Chap. 4.

[289] [1988] OJ L173/1.

[290] Regs. 1983/83 [1983] OJ L173/1 and 1984/83 [1983] OJ L173/7 were the successors of Reg. 67/67 [1967] OJ Spec. Ed. 10.

[291] [1988] OJ L359/46.

[292] See *infra* Chap. 13.

Further, even within the confines of one of these types of agreements, the parties' freedom of contract was curtailed. Each block exemption applied only if they related to goods for resale, set out categories of clauses that were permissible (a white list)[293] and categories of clauses[294] that were not (a black list of hard-core restraints). Any restriction on conduct not specifically exempted by the regulation would compromise and risk the validity of the agreement.[295] The bargaining ability of the parties was thus constrained and, instead, distribution agreements tended to be drafted in similar, if not identical, ways.

The Commission has sought to address these problems and criticisms of the old regimes in the new Verticals Regulation Adopted in 1999.

C. THE VERTICALS REGULATION—REGULATION 2790/1999[296]

(i) The Background

The background to the adoption of this new block exemption has already been discussed.[297] The Commission's treatment of vertical agreements had attracted so much criticism that the Commission adopted a Green Paper espousing reform. The changes culminating from that Paper have already been outlined. A most significant change has been the recognition that the existing block exemptions were not working and the consequent adoption of the Verticals Regulation, which seeks to provide an umbrella block exemption applying to vertical agreements generally. The new Regulation came into force on 1 January 2000[298] and has applied since 1 June 2000. It replaced the block exemptions dealing with exclusive distribution, exclusive purchasing, and franchising agreements but exists alongside the motor vehicle distribution block exemption, Regulation 1400/02.[299] The Verticals Regulation provides a safe harbour, or presumption of legality, for distribution agreements, whether for goods or services, where a market share threshold of 30 per cent is not exceeded. Not surprisingly, the Regulation reflects the old concerns manifest from the practice of the Commission, the case law of the Court, and the old block exemptions. Clauses conferring absolute territorial protection or imposing resale prices will therefore prevent the block exemption from applying. It seeks, however, to avoid the rigidity of its predecessors.

---

[293] These block exemptions applied only where one party agreed to supply the other with 'goods for resale'. They did not therefore apply to agreements relating to services or to intermediate goods that the distributor had to finish or prepare for resale. This obviously severely limited the scope of application of the block exemptions. The Verticals Reg. applies to goods (whether for resale or use by the distributor) and services.

[294] The impact of having a white list (of clauses that were exempted in so far as they infringed Article 81(1)) was that if the agreement contained any other clause that constituted a restriction of competition within the meaning of Article 81(1) the benefit of the block exemption would be lost. Thus the insertion of a restriction, even one which was not specifically prohibited by the Black list would lead to a risk that the block exemption did not apply. This meant that, in practice, parties to an agreement would attempt to limit the restrictions on conduct and obligations imposed to the clauses explicitly permitted by the white list. Of course, this imposed a significant constraint on the clauses that the parties could include in the agreement.

[295] See n. 294.

[296] Guidelines, paras. 21–70 deal with the application of the block exemption Regulation.

[297] See *supra* 702–12.

[298] Art. 13, *infra* 759.

[299] See *infra* 759–60.

Figure 9.2 Application of the Verticals Regulation (VR)

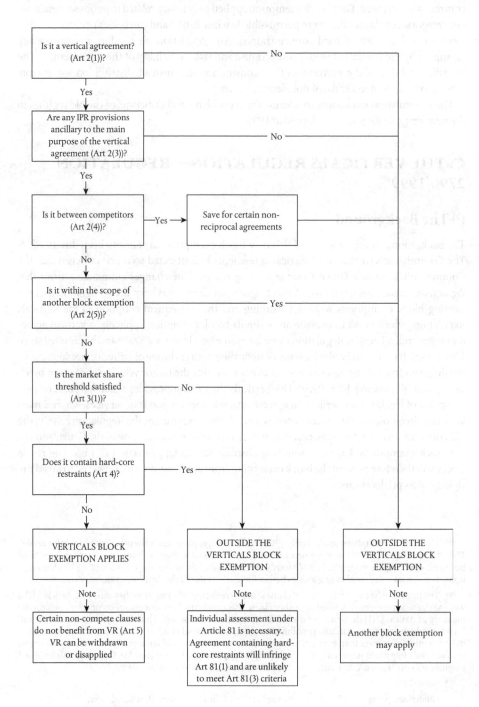

The flowchart above, figure 9.2, explains the principal provisions of the block exemption. The subsequent commentary sets out and explains the main provisions of the block exemption, drawing on the commentary set out in the Commission's guidelines.

(ii) The Recitals

The block exemption contains seventeen recitals that set out the background to the Regulation. Of particular importance is the Commission's recognition in the recitals that vertical agreements 'can improve economic efficiency in a chain of production or distribution' and that the 'likelihood that such efficiency-enhancing will outweigh any anti-competitive effects due to restrictions contained in vertical agreement depends on the degree of market power of the undertakings concerned'.[300]

(iii) Article 1—Definitions

Article 1 defines concepts relevant to the remainder of the block exemption: competing undertakings, non-compete obligation, exclusive supply obligation, selective distribution system, intellectual property rights, know-how, and buyer. There is no definition of franchising agreements.[301]

Article 1

For the purposes of this Regulation:

(a) 'competing undertakings' means actual or potential suppliers in the same product market; the product market includes goods or services which are regarded by the buyer as interchangeable with or substitutable for the contract goods or services, by reason of the products' characteristics, their prices and their intended use;

(b) 'non-compete obligation' means any direct or indirect obligation causing the buyer not to manufacture, purchase, sell or resell goods or services with compete with the contract goods or services, or any direct or indirect obligation on the buyer to purchase from the supplier or from another undertaking designated by the supplier more than 80 per cent of the buyer's total purchases of the contract goods or services and their substitutes on the relevant market, calculated on the basis of the value of its purchases in the preceding calendar year;

(c) 'exclusive supply obligation' means any direct or indirect obligation causing the supplier to sell the goods or services specified in the agreement only to one buyer inside the Community for the purposes of a specific use or for resale;

(d) 'Selective distribution system' means a distribution system where the supplier undertakes to sell the contract goods or services, either directly or indirectly, only to distributors selected on the basis of specified criteria and where these distributors undertake not to sell such goods or services to unauthorised distributors;

(e) 'intellectual property rights' includes industrial property rights, copyright and neighbouring rights;

---

[300] Verticals Reg., recitals 6 and 7.

[301] It seems likely that there is no definition of franchising agreement as, in contrast to selective distribution agreements, there are no provisions in the regulation that specifically affect these agreements. The application of the Verticals Reg. to franchising agreements is, however, discussed in some detail in the Guidelines.

(f) 'know-how' means a package of non-patented practical information, resulting from experience and testing by the supplier, which is secret, substantial and identified: in this context,
'secret' means that the know-how, as a body or in the precise configuration and assembly of its
components, is not generally known or easily accessible; 'substantial' means that the know-how
includes information which is indispensable to the buyer for the use, sale or resale of the contract
goods or services; 'identified' means that the know-how must be described in a sufficiently comprehensive manner so as to make it possible to verify that it fulfils the criteria of secrecy and substantiality;

(g) 'buyer' includes an undertaking which, under an agreement falling within Article 81(1) of
the Treaty, sells goods or services on behalf of another undertaking.

(iv) Article 2—The Main Exemption

a. An Umbrella Exemption Applying to all Vertical Agreements

Vertical Agreements

The Regulation is much broader than the previous Regulations since it exempts *all* distribution
agreements which meet its requirements, whether for goods *or* services (it is not restricted to
agreements relating to goods for resale),[302] and whatever their main objective is exclusive distribution, exclusive purchasing, franchising, selective distribution, *or* some other. The Regulation
thus applies to selective distribution systems which did not previously benefit from any
Community block exemption. By providing an umbrella block exemption that is potentially
applicable to all vertical restraints it seeks to answer the objection that the Commission's previous practice resulted in bizarre and unjustified pigeon-holing and categorization of agreements. The Regulation contains some provisions that apply only to certain types of agreements.
Some categorization thus seems inevitable, but the focus of the Regulation is more on the
restrictive nature of the clause than the type of the agreement involved. The emphasis is on
substantive effect and not form.[303]

The key definition of vertical agreements is set out not in Article 1 but in Article 2. Article 2(1)
states that Article 81(1)[304] shall not apply to:

agreements or concerted practices entered into between two or more undertakings each of which
operates, for the purposes of the agreement, at a different level of the production or distribution
chain, and relating to the conditions under which the parties may purchase, sell or resell certain
goods or services.

---

[302] Contrast the position in Reg. 1983/83, for example.

[303] In the Guidelines, the Commission states at para. 104 that agreements which are different in form may
have the same substantive impact on competition.

[304] In so far as Article 81(1) applies at all of course.

Agreements between Two or More Undertakings

The exemption applies to agreements concluded between two or more undertakings[305] so long as *each* undertaking operates, for the purposes of the agreement,[306] at different levels of the production of distribution chain (for example, supplier, wholesaler, and retailer).[307] Unlike its predecessors the regulation is not confined to bilateral agreements.

Agreements Relating to the Conditions Under which the Parties may Purchase, Sell or Resell Certain Goods or Services

The block exemption covers purchase and distribution agreements.

These are agreements which concern the conditions for the purchase, sale or resale of the goods or services supplied by the supplier and/or which concern the conditions for the sale by the buyer of the goods or services which incorporate these goods or services. For the application of the BER [block exemption regulation] both the goods or services supplied by the supplier and the resulting goods or services are considered to be contract goods or services. Vertical agreements relating to all final and intermediate goods and services are covered...the goods or services provided by the supplier may be resold by the buyer or may be used as an input by the buyer to produce its own goods or services.[308]

The regulation does not exempt agreements or restrictions or obligations that do *not* relate to the purchase, sale, or resale of goods or services, such as rent or leasing agreements or clauses preventing parties from carrying out independent research and development.[309]

b. Association of Retailers of Goods

Article 2(2) provides:

The exemption provided for in paragraph 1 shall apply to vertical agreements entered into between an association of undertakings and its members, or between such an association and its suppliers, only if all its members are retailers of goods and if no individual member of the association, together with its connected undertakings, has a total annual turnover exceeding EUR 50 million; vertical agreements entered into by such associations shall be covered by this Regulation without prejudice to the application of Article 81 to horizontal agreements concluded between the members of the association or decisions adopted by the association.

This provision permits vertical agreements concluded between an association of retailers[310] (no member of which, together with its connected undertakings, has a total turnover of more than €50 million) and its members or between an association and its supplier. Any horizontal agreements concluded between the members or any decisions adopted by the association must however be assessed separately for their compatibility with Article 81.

---

[305] The exemption applies therefore only where the agreement is concluded between undertakings (see discussion of that term, *supra* Chap. 3). It would not apply to agreements concluded between a supplier and a final consumer which does not operate as an undertaking, but of course such agreements would not be caught by Article 81 at all since the article applies only to agreements between undertakings, see Guidelines, para. 24.

[306] The general rule is that agreements concluded between competitors will not benefit from the block exemption.

[307] It does not, therefore, apply to an agreement between a supplier and two wholesalers, for example.

[308] Guidelines, para. 24.

[309] *Ibid.*, 25.

[310] *Ibid.*, para. 28 the Commission states that retailers 'are distributors reselling goods to final consumers'.

c. Provisions Relating to the Assignment of Intellectual Property Rights (IPRS)

Article 2(3)[311]

Article 2(3) provides:

The exemption provided for in paragraph 1 shall apply to vertical agreements containing provisions which relate to the assignment to the buyer or use by the buyer of intellectual property rights, provided that those provisions do not constitute the primary object of such agreements and are directly related to the use, sale or resale of goods or services by the buyer or its customers. The exemption applies on condition that, in relation to the contract goods or services, those provisions do not contain restrictions of competition having the same object or effect as vertical restraints which are not exempted under this Regulation.

The assignment of IPRs, such as trade marks, copyright, or know-how, may be essential or extremely useful to the effective performance of a vertical agreement. The exemption therefore applies to vertical agreements containing ancillary provisions relating to the assignment or use of IPRs which are directly related to the use, sale, or resale of goods or services by the buyer or its customers. This provision is of importance to all vertical agreements but is particularly relevant to franchise agreements that ordinarily involve the assignment or licensing of IPRs.

The Five Conditions

The Commission sets out the five conditions which must be fulfilled before the block exemption applies to vertical agreements containing IPR provisions in paragraph 30 of the Guidelines.

The BER applies to vertical agreements containing IPR provisions when five conditions are fulfilled:

— the IPR provisions must be part of a vertical agreement, i.e., an agreement with conditions under which the parties may purchase, sell or resell certain goods or services;

— the IPRs must be assigned to or for use by the buyer;

— the IPR provisions must not constitute the primary object of the agreement;

— the IPR provisions must be directly related to the use, sale or resale of goods or services by the buyer or his customers. In the case of franchising where marketing forms the object of the exploitation of the IPRs, the goods or services are distributed by the master franchisee or the franchisees;

— the IPR provisions, in relation to the contract goods or services, must not constrain restrictions of competition having the same object or effect as vertical restraints which are not exempted under the BER.

The block exemption will not therefore apply unless:

(i) the agreement is a vertical one and not, for example, an assignment of IPRs for the manufacture of goods or licensing agreements;[312]

(ii) the assignment of the IPRs is made by the supplier to the buyer and not vice versa;

(iii) the IPR provisions are *ancillary* to the implementation of the vertical agreement and not its primary object;

---

[311] Guidelines, paras. 30–44.

[312] Reg. 772/2004 [2004] OJ L123/11, which applies to technology transfer agreements may apply to such agreements; see *infra* Chap. 10. Para. 32 of the Guidelines set out some examples of agreements which would not benefit from the Verticals Reg.

(iv) the IPR provisions are directly related to the use, sale, or resale of goods or services by the buyer or its customers, for example, where the licensing of a trade mark or know how is necessary for the marketing of a good.

It is also essential that:

(v) the clauses relating to the IPRs must not have the same object or effect as restrictions that are not exempted under the regulation. For example, territorial exclusivity, which is prohibited by Article 4, cannot be circumvented by arrangements involving licensing or assignment of IPRs.[313]

Franchise Agreements

Franchise agreements, which no longer benefit from their own independent regime, are dealt with in some detail in paragraphs 42–4 of the Guidelines. In particular, the Guidelines indicate that franchise agreements will ordinarily meet all five of the conditions set out in Article 2(3) as:

the franchisor provides goods and/or services, in particular commercial or technical assistance services, to the franchisee. The IPRs help the franchisee to resell the products supplied by the franchisor or by a supplier designated by the franchisor or to use these products and sell the resulting goods or services.[314]

Franchise agreements that do not fall within the block exemption on the ground that they principally concern the licensing of IPRs will be treated in a similar way to those dealt with under the block exemption.

Paragraph 44 of the Guidelines sets out the type of obligations related to IPRs which are likely to benefit from the block exemption:

44. The following IPR-related obligations are generally considered to be necessary to protect the franchisor's intellectual property rights and are, if these obligations fall under Article 81(1), also covered by the BER:

(a) an obligation on the franchisee not to engage, directly or indirectly, in any similar business;

(b) an obligation on the franchisee not to acquire financial interests in the capital of a competing undertaking such as would give the franchisee the power to influence the economic conduct of such undertaking;

(c) an obligation on the franchisee not to disclose to third parties the know-how provided by the franchisor as long as this know-how is not in the public domain;

(d) an obligation on the franchisee to communicate to the franchisor any experience gained in exploiting the franchise and to grant it, and other franchisees, a non-exclusive licence for the know-how resulting from that experience;

(e) an obligation on the franchisee to inform the franchisor of infringements of licensed intellectual property rights, to take legal action against infringers or to assist the franchisor in any legal actions against infringers;

(f) an obligation on the franchisee not to use know-how licensed by the franchisor for purposes other than the exploitation of the franchise;

(g) an obligation on the franchisee not to assign the rights and obligations under the franchise agreement without the franchisor's consent.

---

[313] Reg. 2790/1999, Art. 2(3); see also Cases 56 and 58, *Etablissements Consten SA & Grundig-Verkaufs-GmbH* v. *Commission* [1966] ECR 299, [1966] CMLR 418, para. 48.

[314] Guidelines, para. 43.

d. Agreements between Competing Undertakings

It has already been noted that the block exemption applies to vertical agreements concluded between undertakings which *for the purposes of the* agreement operate at different levels of the production or distribution chain. This broad definition suggests that an agreement between two competing manufacturers could fall within it. Suppose, for example, manufacturer A in Member State A appoints a competing manufacturer, B, in neighbouring State, B, as its exclusive distributor in State B. That transaction is a vertical agreement within the meaning of Article 2(1) as for the purpose of the agreement A is acting as supplier and B is acting as distributor. If B then appoints A as its exclusive distributor in Member State A that agreement is also a vertical one. However, it can be seen from these examples that the agreements might give rise to concern that there is some form of horizontal agreement between A and B rather than truly vertical arrangements. Article 2(4) of the Verticals Regulation prevents the Block exemption applying to horizontal agreements. It states that the Regulation generally *does not apply* to agreements concluded between competing undertakings (even if operating for the purposes of the agreement at different levels of the production or distribution chain), *however* :

it shall apply where competing undertakings enter into a non-reciprocal vertical agreement and:

(a) the buyer has a total annual turnover not exceeding EUR 100 million, or

(b) the supplier is a manufacturer and a distributor of goods, while the buyer is a distributor not manufacturing goods competing with the contract goods,[315] or

(c) the supplier is a provider of services at several levels of trade, while the buyer does not provide competing services at the level of trade where it purchases the contract services.

Article 1 defines competing undertakings to mean actual or potential suppliers in the same product market, irrespective of whether or not they operate in the same geographic market.[316] A potential supplier is a supplier who could and would be likely to produce a competing product or service in response to a small and permanent increase in relative prices. The Commission promises in its guidelines that this assessment will be made on realistic grounds and that a theoretical possibility of entering a market is not enough. The supplier should be able to make the necessary investments and enter the market within a period of year.[317]

e. Agreements falling within the Scope of another Block Exemption

Article 2(5) states that the Regulation does not apply to vertical agreements the subject matter of which falls within the scope of another block exemption.[318] Agreements potentially falling within the technology transfer Regulation[319] or the motor vehicle distribution Regulation[320] and vertical agreements concluded in connection with horizontal agreements that may potentially benefit from a block exemption[321] are, therefore, excluded. The exclusion is for types of agreements so, for example, a technology transfer agreement which does not meet the criteria

---

[315] Dual distribution, 'the manufacturer of particular goods also acts as a distributor of the goods in competition with independent distributors of his goods': Guidelines, para. 27.

[316] See *supra* 741.

[317] Guidelines, para. 26.

[318] The reference to another block exemption regulation means that future block exemptions are covered as well. Agreements falling within the scope of a block exemption adopted after Reg. 2790/1999, therefore, do not benefit from the Verticals Reg. either.

[319] Reg. 772/2004 [2004] OJ L123/11.

[320] Reg. 1400/02, [2002] OJ L203/30, [2002] 5 CMLR 777.

[321] See *infra* Chap. 13.

of the technology transfer block exemption cannot be exempted by virtue of the Verticals Regulation.[322] As it is of a different type it falls within the scope of the technology transfer regime, not the verticals regime.

(v) Article 3—The Market Share Cap

a. The 30 per cent Threshold

A new feature introduced in the Verticals Regulation and which was not used in the old block exemptions (which applied, unless withdrawn, whatever the market shares of the parties), is the introduction of a market share cap of 30 per cent. Article 3 imposes the cap. The general rule is that the block exemption will not apply where the supplier's market share exceeds this amount.[323] Article 3(1) states:

Subject to paragraph 2 of this Article, the exemption provided for in Article 2 shall apply on condition that the market share held by the supplier does not exceed 30 per cent of the relevant market on which it sells the contract goods or services.

This reflects the Commission's view that vertical restraints are unlikely to pose competition problems, where inter-brand competition is strong[324] or, to put the point another way, that the vertical restraints may pose competition problems where imposed by a firm with significant market power:[325]

where the share of the relevant market accounted for by the supplier does not exceed 30 per cent, vertical agreements which do not contain certain types of severely anti-competitive restraints generally lead to an improvement in production or distribution and allow consumers a fair share of the resulting benefits.[326]

Where there is an exclusive supply obligation,[327] where a supplier agrees to supply only one buyer inside the Community,[328] the relevant market share is that of the buyer, not the supplier. The exemption applies only if the market share held by the buyer does not exceed 30 per cent of the market on which it purchases the goods or services (not the market on which the buyer sells the goods or services). Article 3(2) states:

In the case of vertical agreements containing exclusive supply obligations, the exemption provided for in Article 2 shall apply on condition that the market share held by the buyer does not exceed 30 per cent of the market on which it purchases the contract goods or services.

Where the vertical agreement is concluded between three parties each at different level of trade the market shares at both levels are relevant. Thus where, for example, an agreement is concluded between a supplier, a wholesaler (or an association of retailers), and retailers, the relevant market shares are those of both the manufacturer and the wholesaler.[329]

---

[322] Technology transfer agreements are defined broadly as a patent licensing agreement, a know-how licensing agreement, a software copyright licensing agreement or a mixed patent, know how or software copyright licensing agreement Reg. 772/2004 [2004] OJ L128/11.

[323] See *Interbrew supra* nn. 198 and 199 and accompanying text.

[324] So long as the agreement does not contain hard-core restraints, see Article 4, *infra* 749–55.

[325] The Commission recognizes that firms that do not hold a dominant position may, nonetheless, have significant market power, *supra* Chap. 1.

[326] Verticals Reg., recital 8.

[327] See Verticals Regulation, Art 1(c), set out *supra* 741.

[328] *Ibid.*

[329] Guidelines, para. 93.

b. Defining the Market

The Commission Notice on definition of the relevant market provides general guidance on market definition.[330] Further, the Commission's decisions and Court judgments taken under Article 81, 82, and the Merger Regulation[331] provide useful guidance on how markets have been defined in the past. The Guidelines also set out information, on market definition and market share calculation issues, which is specifically focused on distribution cases.[332]

The introduction of a market share test inevitably introduces an element of uncertainty into the block exemption which, arguably, was principally intended to provide legal certainty. The Commission abandoned a proposal to incorporate a market share test within the 1996 Technology Transfer Regulation because of the uncertainty that it was feared such a provision would create. The new technology transfer regulation, however, now incorporates market share thresholds which differ depending on whether or not the parties to the agreements are competing undertakings.[333]

Given the call for greater economic analysis in its approach to vertical restraints it is difficult to be too critical of the imposition of the market share cap (although market shares do not of course necessarily equate to market power).[334] Many commentators would perhaps, however, have preferred to see the more economic approach manifested at the Article 81(1) stage of assessment, rather than when exempting the agreement under Article 81(3).

c. Exceeding the Market Shares

Because of the inherent uncertainty which the market share test brings, it has already been explained that the Guidelines address the Commission's enforcement policy in respect of individual agreements exceeding the 30 per cent threshold. In such cases there is no presumption that the agreement infringes Article 81(1). Where it does, it may be possible to establish that the agreement satisfies the Article 81(3) criteria.[335]

Where an agreement has been operated in breach of Article 81 in consequence of an assumption, held in good faith, that the market share threshold was not exceeded, the Commission states in its Guidelines that fines will not be imposed.[336] The Regulation also provides for the situation where the agreement satisfies the market share thresholds initially but subsequently exceeds them.[337]

---

[330] See *supra* Chap. 1.

[331] Council Reg. 139/2004 [2004] OJ L24/1. In particular, the Commission makes it possible to find merger decisions in various different ways, e.g., by parties' names, case number, or by industry sector (nace code, see Chap. 12). This latter classification group is particularly helpful when trying to determine the relevant market in a particular case. Past findings on market definition are not, however, binding Cases T-125 and 127/97, *Coca-Cola v. Commission* [2000] ECR II-1733, [2000] 5 CMLR 467.

[332] Guidelines, paras. 88–99.

[333] See *infra* Chap. 10.

[334] See *supra* Chap. 1.

[335] Guidelines, paras. 121–229.

[336] *Ibid.*, 65. The Commission actually states that it will not fine an undertaking that has failed to notify an agreement because they assumed in good faith that they had not exceeded the 30% market share threshold. 'Presumably, the Commission will adhere to this policy even if the notification procedure is abolished', V. Korah and D. O'Sullivan, *Distribution Agreements under the EC Competition Rules* (Hart Publishing, 2002).

[337] Verticals Reg., Art. 9, *infra* 758–9.

d. Portfolio of Products Distributed through the Same Distribution System

Where the supplier uses the same distribution system to distribute several goods or services some of which are, and some of which are not, in view of the market share thresholds, covered by the block exemption the block exemption exempts only the former.[338]

(vi) Article 4—Hard-Core Restrictions[339]

a. The Block Exemption is not Applicable to Vertical Agreements Containing Hard-Core Restraints

Article 4 sets out a list of clauses, similar to the black list set out in the old block exemptions, which prevent the block exemption from applying. Unlike the earlier block exemptions the regulation does not contain a list of permissible restrictions. The strait-jacketing effect of the Regulation is therefore minimized. Vertical agreements may be exempted whatever restrictions or obligations they contain so long as they are not prohibited by Article 4.[340] The insertion of just one of these clauses precludes the entire vertical agreement from benefiting from the block exemption.[341]

The BER exempts vertical agreements on condition that no hardcore restriction, as set out in Article 4, is contained in or practised with the vertical agreement. If there are one or more hardcore restrictions, the benefit of the BER is lost for the entire vertical agreement. There is no severability for hardcore restrictions.[342]

Article 4 focuses on clauses, such as those imposing resale price maintenance or territorial restraints, which restrict intra-brand competition.[343] It prohibits all clauses which, *directly or indirectly*, have as their object certain restrictions specified in paragraphs (a)–(e) of the Article.

Article 4

The exemption provided for in Article 2 shall not apply to vertical agreements which, directly or indirectly, in isolation or in combination with other factors under the control of the parties, have as their object:

(a) the restriction of the buyer's ability to determine its sale price, without prejudice to the possibility of the supplier's imposing a maximum sale price or recommending a sale price, provided that they do not amount to a fixed or minimum sale price as a result of pressure from, or incentives offered by, any of the parties;

---

[338] Guidelines, para. 68.

[339] *Ibid.*, paras. 46–56 deals with hard-core restrictions under the block exemption. See also discussion of vertical agreements which have as their object the restriction of competition, *supra* 713.

[340] But see also the discussion of Art. 5 *infra* 755–7.

[341] In contrast, clauses infringing Article 5 do not benefit from the block exemption, but the remainder of the agreement may benefit, see *infra* 755–7.

[342] Guidelines, para. 66.

[343] The Commission takes the view, however, that such restraints may restrict inter-brand competition by facilitating collusion, see *supra* 688–702. The whole premise of the block exemption is that it should apply where the supplier does not have significant market power so that, ordinarily, inter-brand competition will be reasonably effective in the absence of facilitating practices (but see, e.g., Arts 5–8 discussed *infra*).

(b)   the restriction of the territory into which, or of the customers to whom, the buyer may sell the contract good or services, except;

— the restriction of active sales into the exclusive territory or to an exclusive customer group reserved to the supplier or allocated by the supplier to another buyer, where such a restriction does not limit sales by the customers of the buyer,

— the restriction of sales to end users by a buyer operating at the wholesale level of trade,

— the restriction of sales to unauthorised distributors by the members of a selective distribution system, and

— the restriction of the buyer's ability to sell components, supplied for the purposes of incorporation, to customers who would use them to manufacture the same type of goods as those produced by the supplier;

(c)   the restriction of active or passive sales to end users by members of a selective distribution system operating at the retail level of trade, without prejudice to the possibility of prohibiting a member of the system from operating out of an unauthorised place of establishment;

(d)   the restriction of cross-supplies between distributors within a selective distribution system, including between distributors operating at different level of trade;

(e)   the restriction agreed between a supplier of components and a buyer who incorporates those components, which limits the supplier to selling the components as spare parts to end-users or to repairers or other service providers not entrusted by the buyer with the repair or servicing of its goods.

b. Article 4(a): Fixed or Minimum Sales Prices

Article 4(a) prohibits clauses resulting in the establishment of a fixed or minimum resale price or a fixed or minimum price level to be observed by the buyer. Recommended or maximum prices may be imposed so long as they do not amount to indirect means of achieving resale price maintenance.[344] Examples of price fixing through indirect means and measures facilitating direct or indirect price fixing are set out in paragraph 47 of the Guidelines:

[F]ixing the distribution margin, fixing the maximum level of discount the distributor can grant from a prescribed price level, making the grant of rebates or reimbursement of promotional costs by the supplier subject to the observance of a given price level, linking the prescribed resale price to the resale prices of competitors, threats, intimidation, warnings, penalties, delay or suspension of deliveries or contract terminations in relation to observance of a given price level. Direct or indirect means of achieving price fixing can be made more effective when combined with measures to identify price-cutting distributors, such as the implementation of a price monitoring system, or the obligation on retailers to report other members of the distribution network who deviate from the standard price level. Similarly, direct or indirect price fixing can be made more effective when combined with measures which may reduce the buyer's incentive to lower the resale price, such as the supplier printing a recommended resale price on the product or the supplier obliging the buyer to apply a most-favoured-customer clause. The same indirect means and the same 'supportive' measure can be used to make maximum or recommended prices work as RPM. However, the provision of a list of recommended prices or maximum prices by the supplier to the buyer is not considered in itself as leading to RPM.

---

[344]   The Commission lists some means of indirectly imposing resale prices in the Guidelines, para. 47.

In paragraph 48 the Commission also objects, where agency agreements do fall within Article 81(1), to contractual provisions preventing or restricting the agent from sharing commission with the customer. As the principal sets the price, the agent should be 'free to lower the effective price paid by the customer without reducing the income for the principal'.

c. Article 4(b): Restrictions of the Territory or the Customers to Whom the Buyer may Sell

Article 4(b) prohibits clauses that directly or indirectly restrict the territory into which, or the customers to whom, the buyer may sell the contract goods or services. The provision prohibits both direct restrictions and indirect provisions that, in practice, prevent or deter a distributor from making sales outside of specific territories or customer groups.

This hardcore restriction relates to market partitioning by territory or by customer. This may be the result of direct obligations, such as the obligation not to sell to certain customers or to customers in certain territories or the obligation to refer orders from these customers to other distributors. It may also result from indirect measures aimed at inducing the distributor not to sell to such customers, such as refusal or reduction of bonuses or discounts, refusal to supply, reduction of supplied volumes or limitation of supplied volumes to the demand within the allocated territory or customer group, threat of contract termination of profit pass-over obligations. It may further result from the supplier not providing a Community-wide guarantee service, whereby all distributors are obliged to provide the guarantee service and are reimbursed from this service by the supplier, even in relation to products sold by other distributors into their territory.[345]

Restrictions are not prohibited, however, if they relate to the display of the supplier's brand name or if there is *objective justification* for the provision that relates to the product. A ban on sales to certain customers could therefore be justified, for example, by health and safety considerations.[346]

Article 4 itself sets out four exceptions to the prohibition:

(1) Restrictions on Active Sales into Exclusive Territories or to an Exclusive Customer Group Reserved to Another

The first exception allows a supplier to restrict active sales by a distributor into an exclusive territory or to an exclusive consumer group reserved either to itself or another buyer.[347] It thus allows a supplier to reserve both exclusive territories *and/or* exclusive customer groups to a distributor.[348] A distributor can be appointed to supply a certain customer group in a certain territory and can be precluded from actively selling both into other territories reserved to another *and* to a customer group reserved to another within its territory.[349]

---

[345] Guidelines, para. 49.

[346] *Ibid.*, para. 49.

[347] This provision is similar, but has important differences, to the provisions in Reg. 1983/83 that authorized a supplier to prevent an exclusive distributor from *seeking* sales outside its territory.

[348] Reg. 1983/83 authorized only the allocation of exclusive territories. In consequence, in contrast to the position under Reg. 1983/83, it is possible to appoint more than one distributor in a particular territory.

[349] Reg. 1983/83 enabled the supplier to prohibit its exclusive distributors from making any active sales outside its territory. In practice, this is unlikely to be a material distinction, since if the supplier does not appoint a buyer for a particular area it can reserve it for itself.

The Regulation thus permits the supplier only to prohibit the buyer from making 'active' sales to another's customers or customers in another's territory.[350] The Commission makes the corollary clear in the Guidelines, a prohibition on the making of 'passive' sales into another's territory or to another's customer group is not permitted in the context of exclusive distribution and exclusive customer allocation. The agreement must admit the possibility of some parallel trade in the goods or services. The distinction between active and passive sales is clearly very important, since it defines the border between what is and what is not permissible. The Guidelines explain that the prohibition on active sales is intended to prohibit a distributor from mailing, visiting, or targeting advertising on other customer groups or customers within another's territory or setting up a warehouse or distribution outlet in another's territory. No prohibition is permitted, however, on sales made in response to unsolicited orders.

A point which is of acute importance is whether or not distributors are entitled to advertise on the Internet—does this amount to active selling? It seems at first sight that this would amount to active selling by advertising to customers located in a different territory, especially if the web site advertises in languages other than that of the territory in which it is selling. The Commission, however, takes the opposite view. It states in its Guidelines that use of the Internet to advertise does not amount to active sales. On the contrary, it is a reasonable way to reach every customer, and the fact that it may have effects outside the distributor's own territory is a result of the technology. The sending of unsolicited emails to individual customers or to customer groups does, however, amount to active selling.

Guidelines on vertical restraints [2000] OJ C 291/1, [2000] 5 CMLR 1074

50. . . . —'Active' sales mean actively approaching individual customers inside another distributor's exclusive territory or exclusive customer group by for instance direct mail or visits; or (2) actively approaching a specific customer group or customers in a specific territory allocated exclusively to another distributor through advertisement in media or other promotions specifically targeted at that customer group or targeted at customers in that territory; or establishing a warehouse or distribution outlet in another distributor's exclusive territory.

— 'Passive' sales mean responding to unsolicited requests from individual customers including delivery of goods or services to such customers. General advertising or promotion in media or on the Internet that reaches customers in other distributors' exclusive territories or customer groups but which is a reasonable way to reach customers outside those territories or customer groups, for instance to reach customers in non-exclusive territories or in one's own territory, are passive sales.

51. Every distributor must be free to use the Internet to advertise or to sell products. A restriction on the use of the Internet by distributors could only be compatible with the BER to the extent that promotion on the Internet or sales over the Internet would lead to active selling into other distributors' exclusive territories or customer groups. In general, the use of the Internet is not considered a form of active sales into such territories or customer groups, since it is a reasonable way to reach every customer. The fact that it may have effects outside one's own territory or customer

---

[350] This is similar to Reg. 1983/83 which authorized an obligation on the exclusive distributor to refrain from 'seeking' customers, establishing a branch, or maintaining a distribution depot outside its allotted territory.

group results from the technology, i.e., the easy access from everywhere. If a customer visits the web site of a distributor and contacts the distributor and if such contact leads to a sale, including delivery, then that is considered passive selling. The language used on the web site or in the communication plays normally no role in that respect. Insofar as a web site is not specifically targeted at customers primarily inside the territory or customer group exclusively allocated to another distributor, for instance with the use of banners or links in pages of providers specifically available to these exclusively allocated customers, the web site is not considered a form of active selling. However, unsolicited e-mails sent to individual customers or specific customer groups are considered active selling. The same considerations apply to selling by catalogue. Notwithstanding what has been said before, the supplier may require quality standards for the use of the Internet site to resell his goods, just as the supplier may require quality standards for a shop or for advertising and promotion in general. The latter may be relevant in particular for selective distribution. An outright ban on Internet or catalogue selling is only possible if there is an objective justification. In any case, the supplier cannot reserve to itself sales and/or advertising over the Internet.

The table below seeks to summarize the differences between 'active' and 'passive' selling.

Active sales	Passive sales
Approaching individual customers in another territory or customer group by direct mail, telephone, or in person	Delivery of goods or services to another territory or customer group on unsolicited request
Unsolicited emails sent to specific customers or customer group	General advertising in the media in a way which is reasonable to reach customers
Unsolicited product catalogues sent to specific customers or customer groups	in own or non-exclusive territory or group
Establishing a warehouse or distribution outlet in another territory	Use of the Internet so long as it is not specifically targeted at customers primarily inside the territory or customer group of another
Advertising or promotion targeted at another territory or customer group	

(2) Restrictions on wholesalers

The second exception permits a prohibition on a buyer at the wholesale level of trade from making active or passive sales to end users.

(3) The restriction on sales to unauthorised distributors by the members of a select distribution system

This provision reiterates that where a selective distribution system is operated it is possible to prohibit members of the system from selling (actively or passively) to unauthorized distributors. In the absence of such a provision the system would obviously break down. The way in which the Verticals Regulation applies to selective distribution systems is discussed further below.

(4) Buyers of components

A supplier may preclude a buyer of components for incorporation into another product selling (actively or passively) to a customer who would use them to manufacture a product which competes with that produced by the supplier.

d. Article 4(c) and (d): Restrictions in Selective Distribution Systems

It has been seen that as an exception to the rule that suppliers may not restrict the customers to whom or the territories in which the buyers sell the contract goods, Article 4(b) provides that members of a selective distribution system can be precluded from making sales to unauthorized distributors outside of the system and wholesalers can be prohibited from making sales to end users. Articles 4(c) and (d) impose further limits on sales restraints that may be imposed on authorized members of the network. Article 4(c) provides that members of a selective distribution system at the retail level of the trade may not be precluded from making active or passive sales to end users, whether professional end user or final customers.[351] Article 4(d) provides that members of a system may not be precluded from making cross-supplies *inter se*.

It appears therefore that, in so far as a selective distribution system is caught by Article 81(1) at all, the main constraints on the operation of a selective distribution system are that: the relevant party does not exceed the 30 per cent market share threshold set out; resale price maintenance is not directly or indirectly imposed; retail members are not restrained from making sales to any end user;[352] and members are not restrained from making sales to another member of the network. In *B&W Loudspeakers*,[353] the Commission objected to price restraints, restraints on cross-supplies between dealers and restraints on distant selling via the Internet in a selective distribution system notified to it under the old notification system. Eventually, however, it granted a comfort letter after the parties agreed to remove the hardcore restraints. The members may not, therefore, be required to purchase products only from the supplier but must be able to get them from other members of the network. Although therefore an exclusive purchasing obligation is *not* permitted, Article 5 makes it clear that non-compete obligations are permissible so long as they are not excessive in time and are not targeted at specific suppliers.[354]

Restraints can be imposed on the location and nature of the distributors' premises[355] and on sales being made to unauthorized distributors (often essential features of a selective distribution system).[356] Further, in contrast to the position under Article 81(1) it is not necessary to establish that the products concerned merit selective distribution system nor that the members of the system are chosen only by reference to qualitative criteria. Quantitative criteria may be used to select distributors. The Guidelines make it clear that selective distribution may be combined with exclusive distribution. The supplier may decide to appoint only one or a few selected distributors that meet specific criteria in a particular territory.[357] In contrast to where

---

[351] Guidelines, para. 53.

[352] They should be free to advertise and sell with the help of the Internet, Guidelines, para. 53.

[353] See IP/00/1418 (opening of proceedings) and IP/02/916 (comfort letter).

[354] Verticals Reg., Art. 5(c), *infra* 758.

[355] *Ibid.*, Art. 4(c).

[356] *Ibid.*, Art. 4(b).

[357] Guidelines, para. 53. Although permitted under the old motor vehicles block exemption, the new block exemption does not permit suppliers to use a combination of exclusive distribution and selective distribution, Reg. 1400/02 on motor vehicle distribution, [2002] OJ L203/30, [2002] 5 CMLR 777, *infra* 759–60.

an exclusive distribution system is set up, however, a single selected distributor must be able to make both passive and active sales to end users.[358]

e. Article 4(e): Restrictions on Suppliers of Components

Where a supplier supplies a buyer with components which the latter incorporates into its goods, a restriction may not be imposed which prevents the supplier from selling the components to customers or repairers which have not been authorized by the buyer to repair or service its goods.

(vii) Article 5—Severable, Non-Exempted Obligations

a. Obligations Which are not Exempted but Which are Severable

Article 5, in comparison with Article 4, focuses on non-compete clauses[359] that are capable of foreclosing the market and restricting inter-brand competition directly. In contrast to the provision in Article 4 and to provisions in previous block exemptions, Article 5 provides that where an agreement contains a non-compete obligation which goes beyond its provisions, that *clause* does not benefit from the block exemption. The insertion of such a clause does not, therefore, necessarily prevent the possibility of the remaining provisions of the agreement benefiting from the Regulation. It will only do so where the offensive clauses violate Article 81 and are *not* severable from the remaining provisions of the agreement. It seems that whether or not the offending clauses can be severed is a question of national, not Community, law.[360]

Article 5

The exemption provided for in Article 2 shall not apply to any of the following obligations contained in vertical agreements;

(a) any direct or indirect non-compete obligation, the duration of which is indefinite or exceeds five years. A non-compete obligation which is tacitly renewable beyond a period of five years is to be deemed to have been concluded for an indefinite duration. However, the time limitation of five years shall not apply where the contract goods or services are sold by the buyer from premises and land owned by the supplier or leased by the supplier from third parties not connected with the buyer, provided that the duration of the non-compete obligation does not exceed the period of occupancy of the premises and land by the buyer;

(b) any direct or indirect obligation causing the buyer, after termination of the agreement, not to manufacture, purchase, sell or resell goods or services, unless such obligation:

— relates to goods or services which compete with the contract goods or services, and

— is limited to the premises and land from which the buyer has operated during the contract period, and

— is indispensable to protect know-how transferred by the supplier to the buyer. and provided that the duration of such non-compete obligation is limited to a period of one year

---

[358] Guidelines, para. 53.

[359] See the definition of non-compete obligations in the Verticals Reg., Art. 1(b), set out *supra* 741 The term non-compete includes both obligations not to purchase or manufacture the contract goods or services and their substitutes and obligations to purchase more than 80% of requirements of contract goods and services and their substitutes from the supplier or other designated supplier.

[360] See Chaps. 3 and 15.

> after termination of the agreement; this obligation is without prejudice to the possibility of imposing a restriction which is unlimited in time on the use and disclosure of know-how which has not entered the public domain;
>
> (c) any direct or indirect obligation causing the members of a selective distribution system not to sell the brands of particular competing suppliers.

b. Article 5(a): Non-Compete Obligations

Article 5(a) provides that the exemption does not apply to non-compete obligations imposed (or tacitly renewable) in excess of five years. An exception applies, however, where the buyer of the goods or services operates from premises owned by the supplier or leased by it from a third party not connected with the buyer. In this case the non-compete obligation can be imposed for the duration of the buyer's occupancy of the land. It thus seems, for example, that brewers leasing premises to a publican will be able to impose a non-compete obligation for the entire duration of the lease. The reason for this latter exception is that 'it is normally unreasonable to expect a supplier to allow competing products to be sold from premises and land owned by the supplier without its permission'. But '[a]rtificial ownership constructions intended to avoid the five-year duration limit cannot benefit from this exception'.[361]

c. Article 5(b): Non-Compete Obligations after the Termination of the Agreement

Article 5(b) states that the exemption does not apply to obligations imposed on the buyer which prevents it from manufacturing, purchasing, or selling or reselling goods or services after the termination of the agreement *unless* the prohibition: relates to competing goods or services; is limited to the premises and land from which the buyer has operated during the agreement; is indispensable to protect know-how[362] transferred by the supplier under the agreement; and is limited to a period of one year. A restriction which is unlimited in time may be possible, however, where essential to prevent the use or disclosure of know-how which has not entered the public domain.

d. Article 5(c): Non-Compete Obligations and Selective Distribution Systems

It can be seen from Article 5(a) above that the block exemption covers 'the combination of selective distribution with a non-compete obligation, obliging the distributor not to resell competing brands in general'. Article 5(c) provides, however, that the exemption will not apply where the supplier prevents distributors from buying products for resale from *specific* competing suppliers.

The objective of the exclusion of this obligation is to avoid a situation whereby a number of suppliers using the same selective distribution outlets prevent one specific competitor or certain specific competitors from using these outlets to distribute their products (foreclosure of a competing supplier which would be a form of collective boycott).[363]

---

361 Guidelines, para. 59.
362 Verticals Reg., Art. 1(f).
363 Guidelines, para. 61; see *Parfums Givenchy* [1992] OJ L236/11, [1993] 5 CMLR 579.

(viii) Article 6—Withdrawal of the Block Exemption by the Commission

Article 6 permits the Commission to withdraw the benefit of the block exemption where it considers that an *individual* agreement[364] does not give rise to objective advantages to compensate for the damage which it causes to competition, so that it is not in fact compatible with Article 81(3). This provision has now been superceded by a provision in Regulation 1/2003 that provides the Commission with a general right to withdraw the benefit of any Commission exemption regulation[365] which has effects incompatible with Article 81(3).

Where the Commission wishes to so withdraw the benefit of the Verticals Regulation it will have to prove that the agreement infringes Article 81(1) and does not fulfil all four conditions set out in Article 81(3).[366] The Commission may, for example, do so where foreclosure occurs as a result of parallel networks of vertical agreements. Responsibility for anti-competitive effects identified will be attributed to the undertakings which make an appreciable contribution to it. The Guidelines set out the kind of factors likely to cause the Commission to withdraw the benefit of the block exemption.[367] A withdrawal does not apply retrospectively, it only has *ex nunc* effect. The validity and enforceability of an agreement are not affected in the period prior to the withdrawal becoming effective.[368]

(ix) Article 7—Withdrawal of the Block Exemption by a National Competition Authority (NCA)

Article 7 sets out a provision, novel at the time, enabling the *authorities of a Member State*, authorized under national law to do so, to withdraw the benefit of the block exemption 'under the same conditions as provided in Article 6'.[369] Again, Regulation 1/2003 now provides NCAs with a general power to withdraw the benefit of any Commission block exemption from an agreement which has effects incompatible with Article 81(3) in their territory.[370] It can do this in respect of vertical agreements where effects incompatible with Article 81(3) are felt in the territory of its State, or in part of it, 'which has all the characteristics of a distinct geographic market'. National decisions of withdrawal are taken in accordance with national procedures and have effect only within the territory of that State. A national authority should not act where it would, by doing so, prejudice the uniform application of the competition rules and measures adopted in implementation of them.[371]

Where the geographic market is wider than the territory of a single Member State the Commission has the sole power to withdraw the benefit of the block exemption. Where

---

[364] See Art. 8, discussed *infra* 758.

[365] Reg. 1/2003, Art. 29(1).

[366] Guidelines, para. 72.

[367] *Ibid.*, paras. 71–5.

[368] *Ibid.*, para. 75.

[369] Presumably this means that the national authority may withdraw the benefit of the block exemption in the same sorts of circumstances as the Commission would withdraw the benefit of the block exemption, in particular where the market is foreclosed.

[370] Reg. 1/2003, Art. 29(2), see Chap. 4.

[371] Guidelines, para. 78. See discussion of principle of the supremacy of Community law *infra* Chap. 14. The consultation mechanisms set out in the Commission's Notice on cooperation within the Network of Competition Authorities [2004] OJ C101/43 should avert the risk of conflicting decisions and duplication of procedures.

the geographic market is confined to a single Member State, or a part thereof, the Commission and the national authorities have concurrent powers of withdrawal. In the latter case, and save in cases of particular Community interest, the national competition authority should act.[372]

(x) Article 8—Regulations to Deal with Networks of Agreements

This Article also introduced a novel feature to block exemptions. It permits (but does not require) the Commission to declare by regulation that the exemption should not apply to agreements containing specified restraints in cases where more than 50 per cent of the relevant market is covered by networks of similar vertical restraints.[373] Any such regulation, fully restoring the application of Article 81 to the restraints and markets concerned,[374] could not take effect earlier than six months following its adoption[375] and does not affect the exempted status of the agreements concerned for the period preceding its coming into force.[376]

In paragraph 83 of the Guidelines the Commission states that disapplication may be appropriate when it is likely that access to the relevant market or competition therein is appreciably restricted. In each such case it is likely to be necessary for the Commission to determine whether withdrawal of the block exemption would be more appropriate. This will depend on the number of competing undertakings contributing to the cumulative effects and the number of affected geographic markets.[377]

Because the Regulation must specify the scope of the Regulation both in relation to the relevant product and geographic markets to which it applies and to the vertical restraints in respect of which the Verticals Regulation will not apply, the Regulation may not apply to all agreements concluded on an affected market. Rather:

the Commission may modulate the scope of its regulation according to the competition concern which it intends to address. For instance, while all parallel networks of single-branding type arrangements shall be taken into account in view of establishing the 50 per cent market coverage ratio, the Commission may nevertheless restrict the scope of the disapplication regulation only to non-compete obligations exceeding a certain duration. Thus, agreements of a shorter duration or of a less restrictive nature might be left unaffected, in consideration of the lesser degree of foreclosure attributable to such restraints. Similarly, when on a particular market selective distribution is practiced in combination with additional restraints such as non-compete or quantity-forcing on the buyer, the disapplication regulation may concern only such additional restraints.[378]

(xi) Articles 9, 10, and 11—Market Share, Turnover, Transitional Provisions, and Connected Undertakings

Articles 9 and 10 contain provisions relating to the calculation of market share and turnover for the purposes of the Regulation. In particular, Article 9(2)(d) makes provision to exempt

---

[372] Guidelines, para. 78. See also discussion of the application of the competition rules by NCAs, *infra* Chap. 14.

[373] The Commission considers that restraints normally produce similar effects when the restraints come within one of the four groups dealt with in paras. 100–14 of the Guidelines, para. 82, see *supra* 696–8.

[374] *Ibid.*, 81.

[375] Art. 8(2).

[376] Guidelines, para. 87.

[377] *Ibid.*, 84.

[378] *Ibid.*, 85.

agreements for a period of one to three years which satisfy the 30 per cent threshold initially but subsequently exceed it.

Article 11 makes it clear that the terms undertaking, supplier, and buyer also include their respective connected undertakings. For the purposes of the regulation the turnover and market shares of these undertakings must, therefore, also be taken into account.

(xii) Article 12—The Old Block Exemptions

Article 12 extended the application of the exclusive distribution, exclusive purchasing and franchising block exemptions until 31 May 2000. Further it provided transitional relief until 31 December 2001 to agreements concluded on or before 31 May 2000 which satisfied the conditions set out in one of those regulations.

(xiii) Article 13—Commencement and Expiry

Article 13 provides that the block exemption entered into force on 1 January 2000, applied from 1 June 2000,[379] and expires on 31 May 2010.

D. THE MOTOR VEHICLE DISTRIBUTION BLOCK EXEMPTION

Regulation 1400/02[380] applies specifically to motor vehicle distribution agreements. It replaces the previous motor vehicles block exemption, Regulation 1475/95[381] and is not affected by the Verticals Regulation.[382]

Controversy surrounded the application of the previous motor vehicle block exemption, many believing it to be too lenient.[383] Further, the Commission was concerned that it conferred too much power on manufacturers (correspondingly limiting the freedom of dealers), it had not achieved the integration of national markets, and had not been properly implemented by the

---

[379] Except for the provision extending the application of the block exemption which has applied since 1 January 2000.

[380] [2002] OJ L203/30, [2002] 5 CMLR 777.

[381] Reg. 1475/95, [1995] OJ L145/25.

[382] Verticals Reg., Art. 2(5).

[383] For example, the UK Competition Commission's report on new cars published in April 2000 suggested that the block exemption was responsible, partly at least, for the high car prices in the UK. Following this report, the UK's Secretary of State for Trade and Industry negotiated with the Commission for drastic measures to be taken. In the meantime an Order was made under national law. The Competition Commission suggested in its report, *New Cars: A Report on Supply of New Motor Cars within the UK*, Cm. 4660 (TSO, 2000) that both selective and exclusive distribution agreements should be prohibited in the car sector. The UK authorities took steps to bring about greater competition in the supply and selling of cars, lower prices and increased sales: see SI 2000/2088. The British Consumers' Association in particular adopted the view that British car buyers were being ripped off in comparison to their European counterparts. The association forwarded 20,000 protest notes to Mario Monti, the Commissioner for Competition: see M. Monti, *Who Will be in the Driver's Seat*, Forum Europe Conference, Brussels, 11 May 2000. For the relationship between community and national law see *infra* Chap. 14.

manufacturers.[384] The new Regulation was adopted following an extensive process of fact-finding, consultation and the publication of the Commission's own evaluation report.[385]

The new Regulation, which entered into force on 1 October 2002, seeks to address some of the difficulties identified in the application of the old block exemption, whilst recognizing the special features of the motor vehicle sector.[386] In particular, it seeks to encourage competition between dealers, make cross-border purchase of new vehicles easier, and to introduce greater price competition. At the same time it seeks to avoid the straitjacket effect of the previous Regulation and to allow the development of innovative distribution formats. The Regulation deals not only with distribution of motor vehicles but also with issues of repair and maintenance and the supply of spare parts (it aims to inject competition to all level of car distribution). It has been drafted to follow the same approach as the Verticals Regulation (it contains a market share cap and a list of hard-core restraints but no white list) although the Commission did not consider it to be appropriate to bring motor vehicle agreements within the general regime. It believed that the general regime did not have sufficient safeguards to remedy the problems identified in its evaluation report. It is, therefore, stricter in some respects than Regulation 2790/1999,[387] for example, it does not allow the combination of exclusive distribution and selective distribution (dealers must chose between the systems); it does not exempt location clauses; and it takes a stricter approach to non-compete provisions by not exempting, as a general rule, restrictions on the sale of motor vehicles of different brands by a dealer. The Commission has published a detailed explanatory brochure to accompany the new block exemption.[388] In 2006, the Commission closed two investigations into BMW's and General Motor's distribution and servicing agreements following changes to bring them into line with the motor vehicle block exemption.[389]

E. ARTICLE 81(3)—INDIVIDUAL ASSESSMENT

(i) Introduction

In the past, drafting within the confines of one of the block exemptions was not always an appealing or possible option. Given the greater flexibility introduced in the new Verticals

---

[384] A number of Article 81 infringement actions have been brought against car manufacturers in respect of restraints imposed in vertical agreements, particularly restraints seeking to impose direct or indirect export bans or to achieve resale price maintenance, see, e.g., *Volkswagen* [1998] OJ L124/60, [1998] 5 CMLR 33, on appeal Case T-62/98, *Volkswagen AG v. Commission* [2000] ECR II-2707, [2000] 5 CMLR 853, the appeal to the ECJ was dismissed, see Case C-338/00 P, *Volkswagen AG v. Commission* [2003] ECR I-9189, [2004] 4 CMLR 351, *Opel Nederland* [2001] OJ L59/1, partially annulled and fine reduced on appeal, Case T-368/00, *General Motors Nederland BV and Opel Nederland BV v. Commission* [2003] ECR II-4491, *aff'd* Case C-551/03 P, *General Motors BV v. Commission* [2006] ECR I-3173, *VW-Passat* [2001] OJ L262/14, [2001] 5 CMLR 1309, annulled on appeal, Case T-208/01, *Volkswagen v. Commission* [2003] ECR II-5141, [2004] 4 CMLR 727, *aff'd* Case C-74/04 P, [2006] ECR I-6585, and *Mercedes-Benz* [2002] OJ L257/1, [2003] 4 CMLR 95, partially annulled on appeal Case T-325/01, *DaimlerChrysler v. Commission* [2005] ECR II-3319.

[385] Report on the evaluation of Regulation (EC) No. 1475/95 on the application of Article 85(3) [now 81(1)] of the Treaty to certain categories of motor vehicle distribution and servicing agreements, COM (2000) 743.

[386] The block exemption contains a one-year transitional arrangement to allow for the adaptation of existing contracts. A longer transition period of five years applies to the phasing out of location clauses in selective distribution systems.

[387] It is also stricter than its predecessor.

[388] The document is available at: http://www.europa.eu.int/comm/competition/car_sector.

[389] IP/06302 and IP/06/303.

Regulation there should now be fewer cases in which block exemption is not a realistic possibility. Where, however, the parties will not or cannot ensure that their agreement benefits from either the Verticals Regulation (most likely when the market share threshold is exceeded)[390] or the motor vehicle distribution block exemption and the risk of infringing Article 81(1) is real, it may still be important to consider the application of Article 81(3) to an agreement. Since May 2004, it is necessary for the parties to the agreement to make their own assessment of whether the four conditions of Article 81(3) are satisfied. It will be remembered that any restrictive agreement is, in theory, capable of satisfying the criteria[391] but *all* four criteria must be satisfied.[392]

(ii) Hard-Core Restraints

A supplier or distributor may perceive territorial and/or price restraints to be essential to the operation of a distribution agreement. In particular, territorial restraints and resale price maintenance restrict only *intra-brand* competition and may be imposed in order to induce a distributor to invest in pre-sales services, marketing, and advertising and to prevent free-riding on those investments and/or to enable a supplier to penetrate a market and to increase *inter-brand* competition on a market. Nonetheless, these restrictions are considered to be so serious in Europe that they have consistently been held to have as their object the restriction of competition for the purposes of Article 81(1) and have been listed as hard-core restraints in the block exemptions.[393] Any economic justification explaining the need for the provision may, however, always be relied upon by the parties when seeking to argue that the agreement meets the criteria set out in Article 81(3).[394] Despite this, Article 4 of the Verticals Regulation indicates the types of clauses that the Commission considers to be unlikely to satisfy the terms of Article 81(3) except in the most rare cases. Indeed, the Commission has been unwilling in its decisional practice to accept that agreements which confer resale price maintenance[395] or confer absolute territorial protection on a distributor or which otherwise operate to prevent parallel imports meet the requirements of Article 81(3) (where the Commission discovers that such agreements are being operated in contravention of Article 81 it generally imposes large fines).[396] It will be remembered that in *Grundig*[397] it was the clauses resulting in Consten being granted the exclusive right to sell led Grundig's products in France which caused the Commission to find both that the agreement infringed Article 81(1) and did not meet the Article 81(3) criteria (it refused an exemption).[398] The Commission has not therefore proved receptive to any argument that these

---

[390] It is unlikely that hard-core restrictions will meet the criteria of Article 81(3), *infra*.

[391] Case T-17/93, *Matra Hachette v. Commission*, 1994 ECR II-595, para. 85, see *supra* Chap. 4.

[392] The requirements are cumulative, Case T-528/93, *Métropole Télévision S A v. Commission* [1996] ECR II-649, 5 CMLR 386, para. 86.

[393] See *supra*.

[394] All agreements are eligible for exemption, Case T-17/93, *Matra Hachette v. Commission* [1994] ECR II-595, discussed *supra* Chap. 4.

[395] See e.g. *B&W Loudspeakers supra* n. 353.

[396] See, e.g., *Volkswagen* [1998] OJ L124/60, [1998] 5 CMLR 33, on appeal Case T-62/98, *Volkswagen AG v. Commission* [2000] ECR II-2707, [2000] 5 CMLR 853, the appeal to the ECJ was dismissed, see Case C-338/00 P, *Volkswagen AG v. Commission* [2003] ECR I-9189, [2004] 4 CMLR 351.

[397] [1964] CMLR 489.

[398] See *supra* 713 and Chap. 4.

types of clauses may be essential to prevent free-riding on the distributors' services or to ensure that a product is successfully launched in a new market.[399]

In *Nintendo*,[400] the Commission specifically relied on *Grundig* when it stated that agreements conferring absolute territorial protection, would not meet the criteria of Article 81(3) (the provisions were not indispensable to realize the potential benefits of the exclusive distribution system). 'Instead, in regard to the goods in question territories are hermetically sealed off, making interpenetrating of national markets impossible, thereby bringing to nought economic integration'.[401] Further, in *Distillers* the Commission was unwilling to accept that absolute territorial protection was necessary to, enable penetration of a new geographic market. In this case Distillers wished to promote certain of its products, in particular whisky, on a number of the European markets. Distributors in those countries would have to engage in considerable promotion to encourage local consumers to purchase whisky instead of other popular local products. Distillers wished to shelter local distributors from the competition of distributors in the UK, where whisky was already established on the market. These distributors did not consequently have to incur such heavy promotional expenses. The Commission issued a decision holding that provisions in Distillers' agreements with its UK distributors prohibiting export or imposing dual price terms (which allowed rebates etc. for home trade) infringed Article 81(1) and did not meet the Article 81(3) criteria.[402] Distillers accepted that the prohibition on exports would not satisfy the conditions of Article 81(3), but argued that the dual price provisions were capable of doing so. Although Distillers' view gained support from Advocate General Warner,[403] who acknowledged that dual pricing, which did not completely exclude the possibility of export, might be necessary to protect the promotional efforts of the Continental distributors, the Court rejected the plea on the grounds that the agreement had not been notified and so was not eligible for exemption by the Commission under Article 81(3).[404] The result was that Distillers was forced either to withdraw products it wished to promote on the Continent from the UK market or to raise the UK prices to such an extent that they almost ceased to sell. Consequently, different brands were sold in the UK and on the Continent and it seems that in '[t]he year after it split its brands, Distillers' turnover on the Continent for those brands, the price of which in England had not been raised and which ceased to be worth promoting on the Continent, increased less than its turnover for those that suffered no parallel imports and whose price was higher'.[405]

---

[399] See *supra* 713 and Chap. 4.

[400] [2003] OJ L255/33, Case T-13/03, *Nintendo v. Commission*, (judgment pending).

[401] *Ibid.*, para. 338.

[402] *The Distillers Company Limited* [1978] OJ L50/16, [1978] 1 CMLR 400. The Commission considered that it did not have to rule on Article 81(3) in respect of the latter since it had not been notified correctly in accordance with Reg. 17.

[403] Case 30/78, *Distillers Company* v. *Commission* [1980] ECR 2229, [1980] 3 CMLR 121, paras. 89–121.

[404] *Ibid.*, 24. At the time an exemption could be granted only if notification had been made to the Commission, Reg. 17, Art. 4(2).

[405] V. Korah, *An Introductory Guide to EC Competition Law and Practice* (8th edn., Hart Publishing, 2004), para. 7.6.1. In the end, Distillers was allowed a period of grace in which to launch one of its products on the Continental market. Distillers made a further notification seeking exemption for agreements providing for the institution of a 'promotion equalization charge' (PEC) for its brand, Johnnie Walker Red Label. The PEC was an amount, calculated on the basis of the average expenditure by exclusive distributors in other Member States less an amount corresponding to the parallel trader's own marketing expenditure, which was to be levied on purchases of Red Label for export. The monies collected were to be spent on the promotion of Red Label in the EC, other than the UK. Because of the exceptional circumstances which existed (Red Label had been withdrawn from the UK market) the Commission stated that it would consider (no final decision was ever taken) granting

More recently, in *GlaxoSmithKline Services Unlimited* v. *Commission*,[406] the CFI held that the Commission's decision to refuse an exemption to a dual pricing system operated by Glaxo was fundamentally flawed. Essentially, Glaxo had argued that parallel trade reduced its ability to innovate (by reducing its usable funds), and therefore reduced the efficiency of competition on the market where inter-brand competition was driven by innovation rather than price. It argued that its ability to engage in price differentiation increased efficiency by allowing the cost of R&D to be recovered from those customers who were willing to pay for it through higher prices. The CFI held that the arguments raised were 'relevant, reliable and credible' (and supported in part by the Commission's own publications) and that the Commission had not discharged its burden of examining those arguments and refuting them by means of substantiated evidence.[407] The CFI thus annulled the Commission's decision insofar as the decision had rejected the exemption application and had ordered Glaxo to bring the infringements to an end. It should be stressed, however, that the CFI did not find that the Article 81(3) conditions had been met, only that the Commission had not adequately discharged its duty under Article 81(3).

The Commission has also taken a rigid view of provisions imposing resale price maintenance. Thus despite any economic justifications which might be raised to justify the vertical price restraints, and which might be similar to those used to justify other non-price vertical restraints,[408] the Commission has found that such agreements infringe Article 81(1) and do not meet the conditions of Article 81(3).[409] The ECJ has recognized, in one case, however, that an agreement imposing minimum resale prices might meet the Article 81(3) criteria. In *Binon*, the ECJ indicated that the Commission might have to consider whether or not an agreement, where a publisher fixed the prices of its newspapers and periodicals, fulfilled the requirements of Article 81(3).[410]

---

an exemption which 'if given, would be conditional upon the progressive reduction of the PEC during the short period of time necessary to allow for the adaptation of marketing conditions for Red Label in the common market to the consequences of its large-scale re-introduction in one member-State' [1983] 3 CMLR 173, para. 12. The Commission made it clear that no similar arrangements could be made in respect of other brands. See also *Transocean Marine Paint Associations* [1967] OJ L/10.

[406] Case T-168/01, 27 Sept. 2006, [2006] 5 CMLR 1623, Cases C-501, 513, 515 and 519/06 P (judgment pending). For further discussion of the case see *supra* Chap. 4.

[407] Rather, in some respects the CFI held that the Commission had relied on evidence which was, to say the least, fragmentary and of limited relevance or value. Thorough reasoning by the Commission was all the more necessary when considering the application of Article 81(3) in markets, such as the pharmaceuticals industry, where competition is distorted by national regulations.

[408] See *supra* 688–702.

[409] The Commission states in its Green Paper on Vertical Restraints, COM(96) 721, para. 226 that resale price maintenance is unlikely to benefit from an exemption. See *Hennessy/Henkell* [1980] OJ L383/11, [1981] 1 CMLR 601; Case 161/84, *Pronuptia de Paris GmbH* v. *Pronuptia de Paris Irmgard Schillgallis* [1986] ECR 353, [1986] 1 CMLR 414; Cases 43 and 63/82, *VBBB and VBVB* v. *Commission* [1984] ECR 19, [1985] 1 CMLR 27; *cf.* Case C-360/92 P, *Publishers' Association* v. *Commission* [1995] ECR I-23; [1995] 5 CMLR 33.

[410] In a subsequent notice the Commission did suggest, without giving reasons, that it might be willing to grant the agreement, including the resale maintenance provisions, an exemption under Article 81(3): *Agence et Messageries de la Presse* [1987] OJ L164/2.

Case 243/85, *SA Binon & Cie* v. *SA Agence et Messageries de la Presse* [1985] ECR 2015, [1985] 3 CMLR 800

44. It should be observed in the first place that provisions which fix the prices to be observed in contracts with third parties constitute, of themselves, a restriction on competition within the meaning of Article [81(1)] . . .

45. In those circumstances, where an agreement which establishes a selective distribution system and which affects trade between Member States includes such a provision, an exemption from the prohibition contained in Article [81(1) of the [EC] Treaty may only be granted by means of a decision adopted by the Commission in the conditions laid down by Article [81(3)].

46. If, in so far as the distribution of newspapers and periodicals is concerned, the fixing of the retail price by publishers constitutes the sole means of supporting the financial burden resulting from the taking back of unsold copies and if the latter practice constitutes the sole method by which a wide selection of newspapers and periodicals can be made available to readers, the Commission must take account of those factors when examining an agreement for the purposes of Article [81(3)].

The net effect of the Commission's and Court's extremely strict approach to territorial and price restraints may mean, in some cases, that undertakings are encouraged to avoid distribution agreements and to seek other alternatives, perhaps vertical integration, instead. In the USA, the Supreme Court has also recognized that 'the *per se* illegality of vertical restraints would create a perverse incentive for manufacturers to integrate vertically into distribution'.[411]

(iii) Non-Compete Provisions and Other Restraints

In other cases, it is extremely important when drafting agreements to look both generally at the Article 81(3) Guidelines and,[412] more specifically, at the Guidelines on Vertical Restraints which set out how the Commission will enforce Article 81 in respect of individual agreements not covered by the block exemption and containing specified restraints (such as: single branding; exclusive distribution and customer allocation; selective distribution; franchising; exclusive supply; and/or recommended and maximum prices).[413] Past decisional practice of the Commission when granting or refusing individual exemptions should also be examined.[414] Article 5 of the Verticals Regulation also gives an indication of how Article 81(3) will apply to non-compete provisions. On occasions, however, it may be possible to argue that a non-compete provision for longer than that permitted in Article 5 is indispensable to the operation of the agreement.[415]

---

[411] *Business Electronics Corp* v. *Sharp Electronics Corp*, 485 US 717, 725, per Justice Scalia. See also discussion *supra* 698–702.

[412] [2004] OJ C101/97.

[413] See, especially, paras. 131–6 and 139–226.

[414] An agreement strengthening a firm's position in a foreclosed market and serving as a barrier to entry may well not meet the conditions of Article 81(3). In Case T-65/98, *Van den Bergh Foods* v. *Commission* [2003] II-4653, [2004] 4 CMLR 1, *aff'd* Case C-552/03 P *Unilever Bestfoods* v. *Commission* [2006] OJ C294/19, the CFI refused to interfere with the Commission's finding that HB's provisions providing for freezer exclusivity did not satisfy the first condition of Article 81(3). The Commission considered that the arrangements did not present appreciable objective advantage that compensated for the disadvantages to competition.

[415] See, e.g., Guidelines, paras. 155 (longer periods may be possible where significant investment is required), and 158 and 171 (a non-compete provision may be permitted for the duration of an exclusive distribution agreement).

When deciding whether or not an agreement meets the criteria of Article 81(3), in particular whether a restriction is indispensable to the operation of the agreement, the Guidelines make it clear that the determination must be made with regard to the *justification* for the vertical restraints (for example, whether or not it is necessary to help solve a free-rider problem, to create brand-image, or to deal with a hold-up problem).

An example of a case in which a non-compete provision was found not to meet the criteria of Article 81(3) is *Van den Bergh Foods*.[416] In this case the CFI rejected the applicants, assertion that the Commission had erred in the law in applying Article 81(3), in particular, by wrongly concluding that the restrictive effects of its freezer exclusivity agreements outweighed the advantages flowing from the distribution efficiency they produced. The CFI held that as the agreement did not satisfy the first condition of Article 81(3), the Commission was entitled to refuse an exemption.[417] The advantages produced by the agreement were not objective ones but ensued to the parties to the agreement.[418]

Case T-65/98, *Van den Bergh Foods Ltd* v. *Commission* [2003] ECR II-4653, [2004] 4 CMLR 1[419]

Court of First Instance

138. The Court finds that, contrary to HB's submission in paragraph 123 above, it is clear from the contested decision that the Commission carried out a detailed analysis of the HB distribution agreement in the light of each of the four conditions laid down by Article [81(3)] of the Treaty (see recitals 221 to 254 of the contested decision).

139. As regards the first of those conditions, the agreements capable of being exempted are those which contribute to improving the production or distribution of goods or to promoting technical or economic progress. The Court would point out in that regard that it is settled law of the Court of Justice and of the Court of First Instance that the improvement cannot be identified with all the advantages which the parties obtain from the agreement in their production or distribution activities. The improvement must in particular display appreciable objective advantages of such a character as to compensate for the disadvantages which they cause in the field of competition (Joined Cases 56/64 and 58/64 *Consten and Grundig* v. *Commission* [1966] ECR 299, at 348, and *Langnese-Iglo*, paragraph 180).

140. The first condition is examined in recitals 222 to 238 of the contested decision. The Commission acknowledged in particular that the agreements whereby freezer cabinets are made

---

[416] Case T-65/98, *Van den Bergh Foods* v. *Commission* [2003] ECR II-4653, [2004] 4 CMLR 1, *aff'd* Case C-552/03 P *Unilever Bestfoods* v. *Commission* [2006] OJ C294/19.

[417] Under the old notification and exemption system the Court reiterated that 'the review carried out … of the complex economic assessments undertaken by the Commission in the exercise of the discretion conferred on it by Article [81(3)] of the Treaty in relation to each of the four conditions laid down therein, must be limited to ascertaining whether the procedural rules have been complied with, whether proper reasons have been provided, whether the facts have been accurately stated and whether there has been any manifest error of appraisal or misuse of powers (see, to that effect, Joined Cases T-39/92 and T-40/92, *CB and Europay* v. *Commission* [1994] ECR II-49, para. 109; *Matra Hachette* v. *Commission*, para. 104, and Case T-29/92, *SPO and others* v. *Commission* [1995] ECR II-289, para. 288). It is not for the Court of First Instance to substitute its own assessment for that of the Commission', Case T-65/98, *Van den Bergh Foods* v. *Commission* [2003] ECR II-4653, [2004] 4 CMLR 1, para. 135, *aff'd* Case C-552/03 P, *Unilever Bestfoods* v. *Commission* [2006] OJ C294/19.

[418] The CFI held that rather than improving distribution of promoting progress, the effect of the agreements was to strengthen the strong position of HB on the market.

[419] *Aff'd* Case C-552/03 P, *Unilever Bestfoods* v. *Commission* [2006] OJ C294/19.

available might secure some or all of the benefits described in the fifth recital to Regulation No. 1984/83 for HB itself and for the retailers who are the other parties to the agreements, and that the distribution method currently used by HB might offer it and its retailers certain advantages in terms of efficiency of planning, organisation and distribution. Therefore, the Commission held that those arrangements did not present appreciable objective advantages of such a character as to compensate for the disadvantages caused to competition. In support of that assertion, it pointed out that the freezer cabinet agreements in question considerably strengthened HB's position in the relevant market, especially vis-à-vis potential competitors. It rightly observed in that regard that the strengthening of an undertaking which is as important on the market as HB leads not to more but to less competition because the network of that undertaking's agreements constitutes a major barrier to the entry of others into the market, as well as to expansion within the market by its existing competitors (see in particular recitals 225 and 236 of the contested decision, and, by analogy, *Langnese-Iglo* v. *Commission*, paragraph 182). It must also be pointed out that the level of foreclosure of the relevant market is in the order of 40 per cent (see paragraph 98 above) and not 6 per cent as HB submits . . .

141. Consequently, the Court finds that, contrary to HB's contention . . . , the Commission rightly took into consideration the barriers to entry to the relevant market resulting from the exclusivity clause, and the consequent weakening of competition, when it assessed HB's distribution agreement in the light of the first condition laid down by Article [81(3)] of the Treaty (see, by analogy, *Consten and Grundig* v. *Commission* at p. 348, and *Langnese-Iglo* v. *Commission*, paragraph 180). It follows that the Court cannot accept HB's argument . . . to the effect that recitals 222 to 225 of the contested decision contain a fundamental logical flaw with regard to the relationship between Article [81(1)] and Article [81(3)] of the Treaty, as the Commission was obliged, pursuant to settled case-law on the subject, to ascertain whether there were objective advantages of such a character as to compensate for the disadvantages which an agreement creates for competition.

142. The Court also notes that HB's distribution agreements have two particular aspects, namely, first, they make freezer cabinets available without charge to retailers and, second, the retailers undertake to use those cabinets to stock HB ice creams only. The benefits ensured by the agreements in question are the result of the first aspect and can therefore be achieved even without the exclusivity clause.

143. The Court also accepts the Commission's argument in recital 227 of the contested decision that although the wide availability in outlets of freezer cabinets intended for the sale of impulse ice-creams, covering the entire geographic market and consisting mainly of HB's cabinets, could be considered an objective advantage in the distribution of those products in the public interest, it is nevertheless unlikely that HB would definitely cease to supply freezer cabinets to retailers, whatever the conditions, except in small number of cases, if its power to impose an obligation of exclusivity in respect of those freezers were to be restricted. HB has not shown that the Commission committed a manifest error in taking the view that business reality for a company such as HB, which wishes to maintain its position on the relevant market, is to be present in the maximum number of outlets possible (see recital 228 and paragraph 125 above). Contrary to HB's submission, the Commission did not merely assume continuity of provision by HB of freezer cabinets on the relevant market, but carried out a prospective analysis of the operation of the market after the adoption of the contested decision. Furthermore, contrary to HB's argument (see paragraph 125 above), the Commission could validly rely on the argument that manufacturers competing with HB might adopt a policy of supplying freezer cabinets to sales outlets whose turnover in impulse ice-creams is too low to be of interest to HB, and do so upon more advantageous conditions than those which the retailers might expect to obtain themselves if HB ceased to supply freezer cabinets to certain sales outlets. Similarly, the Commission could validly point to the possibility that cabinets would be installed by independent resellers who would obtain supplies from

various sources and satisfy demand from all the sales outlets from which HB had withdrawn its equipment or to which it decided not to supply equipment. HB cannot claim that the Commission's prospective analysis is vitiated by a manifest error of assessment unless it does so on the basis of concrete evidence, which HB has failed to adduce in the present case.

144. As HB's distribution agreements do not satisfy the first of the conditions laid down by Article 85(3) of the Treaty, the third plea must therefore be rejected and it is not necessary to consider whether the Commission committed a manifest error in regard to its assessment of the other conditions laid down by that provision. If any one of the four conditions is not satisfied, the exemption must be refused.

In *Telenor/Canal+/Canal Digital*,[420] the European Commission granted negative clearance, in combination with an exemption, to complex contractual arrangements providing for the exclusive distribution by Canal Digital of pay-TV premium content channels and pay-per-view and near-video-on demand ('PPV'/'NVOD') channels in the Nordic region.[421] The agreements also imposed non-compete obligations which, broadly, prohibited Canal Digital from owning, operating or retailing any other pay-TV premium content or PPV/NVOD channels.

In order to gain approval for the agreements the parties agreed to modify the agreements and: to mitigate foreclosure of potential entrants in the downstream direct to home (DTH) pay-TV market by reducing the duration and scope of Canal Digital's exclusivity; to alleviate foreclosure of potential entrants on the supply-side in the upstream market for the wholesale supply of pay-TV by reducing the duration of the pay-TV non-compete obligations on Canal Digital; and to alleviate foreclosure of potential entrants on the supply-side in the upstream market for the provision of transponder capacity for TV broadcasting by reducing non-compete obligations on Canal+.[422]

The Commission took the view that most of the clauses, even in their revised form, appreciably restricted competition within the meaning of Article 81(1).[423] Further, the Commission noted that the Verticals block exemption was not available to the parties, both because the primary purpose of the exclusivity and non-compete arrangement was the use by the buyer of IPRs and because of Canal+'s strong market position, which exceeded the 30 per cent threshold. The Commission stressed, however, that this did not mean that there was a presumption that the vertical agreement was illegal. 'Rather the agreements need individual examination by the Commission in the application of Article 81(3) of the Treaty'.[424]

---

[420] 29 Dec. 2003.

[421] The notified agreements also related to the divestiture by Canal + of its 50% shareholding in Canal Digital, previously jointly run with Telenor Broadband Services ('TBS'), and its acquisition by TBS. The distribution agreements related to the distribution by Canal Digital of Canal +Nordic's pay-TV premium content channels and PPV/NVOD channels via Direct to home (DTH) satellite platform, satellite master antenna television system networks (SMATV) and small cable networks in the Nordic region. Essentially, the agreements aimed to ensure continuity of the pay-TV content supply and distribution that had previously been secured within the vertically integrated company structure. Under the new arrangements there was a vertical relationship between the independent upstream supplier of pay-TV premium content, Canal+ Nordic, and an independent downstream DTH platform for the distribution of pay-TV to end-consumers, Canal Digital.

[422] The parties also took steps to address horizontal cooperation concerns and to avoid foreclosure in related market segments.

[423] It granted negative clearance, however, to the clauses governing exclusive distribution by Canal Digital of Canal+ Nordic's PPV/NVOD channels, 29 Dec. 2003, paras. 170–8.

[424] 29 Dec. 2003, para. 196.

The Commission found that the modified exclusivity and non-compete provisions generated efficiencies and contributed to the improvement in distribution and the promotion of economic progress within the meaning of Article 81(3) and that consumers received a fair share of the benefits. Although the Commission accepted that the provisions were indispensable to attain the efficiencies, this was only so subject to a strict limitation period in time, for example: of four years duration for the pay-TV channel exclusivity provisions; and of three years in respect of the obligation on Telenor/Canal Digital not to own, operate or distribute via DTH any other pay-TV premium content channels. The Commission concluded that the various contractual arrangements did not eliminate competition in the affected markets during the term of their validity. The Cooperation for a limited period would maintain competition with the second satellite pay-TV distributor in the Nordic region, MTV/VIASAT and preserve the possibility of market entry in the Nordic pay-TV segments in the mid- to long-term. It thus granted an exemption to the provisions found to infringe Article 81(1) for a five-year period.[425]

6. SUBCONTRACTING AGREEMENTS

Subcontracting agreements, under which a contractor entrusts the manufacture of goods or the supply or services to a sub-contractor, are vertical in nature.[426] Goods or services in subcontracting agreements are provided, on the instructions of the contractor, to that contractor or, on its behalf, to a third party. The arrangement may also involve a licence of intellectual property rights from the contractor to the sub-contractor.

A Commission Notice concerning the assessment of certain subcontracting agreements in relation to Article 81(1) of the Treaty (the 'Subcontracting Notice) recognizes that these agreements are frequently procompetitive. It thus indicates that certain clauses in subcontracting agreements are unlikely to restrict competition and infringe Article 81(1). For example, a requirement that: (1) technology or equipment provided by the contractor (a) may not be used except for the purposes of the subcontracting agreement and (b) may not be made available to third parties; and (2) goods or services resulting from such technology or equipment may be supplied only to the contractor or performed on his behalf, will fall outside Article 81(1) on condition that the technology or equipment provided is necessary to enable the subcontractor to manufacture the goods or supply the serivces or to carry out the work in accordance with the contractor's instructions.[427] Further, paragraph 3 provides that the following provisions are unlikely to violate Article 81(1): (1) an obligation that a specified 'trade mark, trade name or get-up' provided under the contract be used by the sub-contractor only as a means of identification in relation to the contract goods, services or work; (2) an undertaking by either party not to reveal secret know-how (which has not become public knowledge) given by the other party during the negotiation and performance of the agreement; (3) an undertaking by the

---

[425] The Commission took due account of Telenor's/Canal Digital's and Canal+ Nordic's legitimate interest in achieving a reasonable return on their investment in their pay-TV business so far.

[426] See Notice of 18 December 1978 concerning its assessment of certain subcontracting agreements in relation to Article [81(1)] (the 'Subcontracting Notice'), [1979] OJ C1/2, para 1. Guidelines on the applicability of Article 81 Horizontal Cooperation Agreements [2001] OJ C3/2, para. 79 and Guidelines on the application of Article 81 of the EC Treaty to technology transfer agreements OJ [2004] C 101/2, para. 44 and Guidelines on Vertical Restraints [2000] OJ C291/1. [2000] 5 CMLR 1074. In para 1 of the Subcontracting Notice it is recognized that to carry out certain subcontracting agreements in accordance with the contractor's instructions, the subcontractor may have to make use of particular technology or equipment provided by the contractor.

[427] The Subcontracting Notice, para. 2.

sub-contractor not to make use, even after expiry of the agreement, of secret know-how (which has not become public knowledge) received during the currency of the agreement; and (4) an undertaking by the sub-contractor to pass on to the contractor on a non-exclusive basis technical improvements or patentable inventions relating to improvements and/or new applications of the original invention, discovered during the currency of the agreement.

Where there is concern that the subcontracting agreements may violate Article 81(1), the agreement may be able to benefit from the Verticals Regulation.[428] It has been seen in the discussion above, however, that this block exemption is not generally applicable if the agreement is between competitors[429] or if the subject matter of the agreement falls within the scope of another block exemption.[430] Further, it does not cover the licensing or assignment of intellectual property rights unless they are assigned to the buyer, in this case, the *contractor*. In practice, therefore, although some subcontracting agreements may benefit from the Verticals Regulation, such as agreements between non-competitors whereby the contractor provides only specifications to the subcontractor describing the goods or services to be supplied, many will in fact fall outside of its scope. Nonetheless, where, the primary object of the agreement is to enable the subcontractor to use licensed technology exclusively for the production of products for the contractor, the technology transfer block exemption may apply. Technology transfer agreements are discussed in Chapter 10. Alternatively, if the agreement is between competitors and, if any provisions concerning the assignment or use of intellectual property rights do not constitute the primary object of the agreement, the subcontracting agreement might constitute a specialization agreement (capable of benefiting from the specialization block exemption) or a production agreement, dealt with in the Commission's Guidelines on horizontal cooperation agreements. Horizontal Cooperation agreements are discussed in Chapter 13.

7. ARTICLE 82 AND DISTRIBUTION

Where the supplier has a market share approaching 40 per cent a finding of dominance within the meaning of Article 82 is possible. In such cases, it should be considered whether provisions within a vertical agreement, such as clauses imposing unfair or discriminatory selling prices, exclusive purchasing commitments or non-compete provisions, tying provisions, or granting discounts and rebates to purchasers,[431] may infringe Article 82 as well as Article 81.[432] Conduct that amounts to an abuse of a dominant position is unlikely to meet the criteria of Article 81(3).[433]

---

[428] Since the agreement is between undertakings which operate, for the purposes of the agreement, at different level of the production or distribution chain, and which relates to the conditions under which the parties may purchase, sell or sell certain goods or services.

[429] See *supra* 746.

[430] See *supra* 746–7.

[431] See Chap. 7.

[432] Where there is an exclusive supply agreement the relevant market share is that of the buyer, see *supra* 747.

[433] See Chap. 4. 283–4.

8. CONCLUSIONS AND THE FUTURE

1. The Verticals Regulation and Guidelines indicate that the Commission now adopts a more economic approach to vertical agreements. The Verticals Regulation sets out a presumption that vertical agreements which do not incorporate hard-core restraints and which are concluded between undertakings which do not exceed a 30 per cent market share threshold are compatible with Article 81.

2. The centrality of the Verticals Regulation and the Commission's recommended methodology of approach[434] means that the main focus of attention is still on whether or not a vertical agreement or restraint is compatible with Article 81(3), not whether it is compatible with Article 81(1), i.e., whether it restricts competition within the meaning of that provision.

3. Although both the Guidelines and the Article 81(3) Guidelines indicate that the Commission will take a more realistic approach at the Article 81(1) stage, in particular, it is acknowledged that Article 81(1) may not apply even where the 30 per cent market share threshold set out in the Verticals Regulation is exceeded, no explanation is offered as to why such a broad overarching block exemption is necessary if a more economic approach is required at the *Article 81(1)* stage. Such an approach would surely mean that most vertical agreements do not require block exemption at all.

4. Although the Verticals Regulation provides legal certainty and is intended to operate as a safe harbour, its existence clouds the water when trying to rationalize and understand the analysis required under Article 81(1) and Article 81(3) respectively.[435] The Commission has not therefore adequately met the criticism that it does not make a realistic economic assessment of agreements under Article 81(1).[436] The inevitable result must be that businesses feel the need to comply, where possible, with the terms of the block exemption.

5. The Verticals Regulation does represent a significant improvement on the old block exemptions and removes some of the arbitrary and unconvincing restrictions that those exemptions imposed on parties concluding vertical agreements. Nonetheless the existence of the hard-core and non-exemptible but severable restraints provides pitfalls for undertakings when drafting their agreements. The hardcore restraints in particular reflect the Commission's old intolerance to agreements containing territorial and price restraints that impact, directly at least, only on intra-brand competition. Whatever the free rider or other rationale for these restraints, agreements containing such clauses, which affect competition and trade to an appreciable extent, are generally precluded.

6. Although no further changes to the Commission's approach to vertical restraints can be anticipated prior to its review of the Verticals Regulation before its expiry in 2010, subtle changes may result now that the national courts and national competition authorities have been given the opportunity to rule on an agreement's compatibility with the provisions of both Article 81(1) and Article 81(3). Regulation 1/2003 means that greater enforcement and litigation at the national level is likely. Those authorities may be more willing to accept,

---

[434] See Guidelines, para. 120 set out *supra* 710.

[435] See *supra* Chap 4.

[436] Although the Commission states that agreements which are not capable of appreciably affecting competition or trade are not caught by Article 81(1), this is an entirely separate issue from the question whether the agreement restricts competition: see *supra* Chap. 3.

in accordance with the Court's case law, that an agreement does not infringe Article 81(1) at all[437] or that, in exceptional circumstances, agreements containing price[438] or territorial restraints[439] satisfy the requirements of Article 81(3).

7. FURTHER READING

A. BOOKS

BORK, R. H., *The Antitrust Paradox: A Policy at War with Itself* (Basic Books, 1978, reprinted with a new Introduction and Epilogue, 1993), chap. 14

GOYDER, J., *EU Distribution Law* (4th edn., Hart Publishing, 2005)

KORAH, V., and O'SULLIVAN, D., *Distribution Agreements under the EC Competition Rules* (Hart Publishing, 2002)

SCHERER, F. M., and ROSS, D., *Industrial Market Structure and Economic Performance* (3rd edn., Houghton Mifflin, 1990), chap. 15

B. ARTICLES

CHARD, J. S., 'The Economics of the Application of Article 85 to Selective Distribution Systems' (1982) 7 *ELRev* 83

COMANOR, W. S., 'Vertical Price-Fixing, Vertical Market Restraints, and the New Antitrust Policy' (1984–1985) 98 *Harvard LR* 983

DEACON, D., 'Vertical Restraints under EU Competition Law: New Directions' [1995] *Fordham Corp L Inst* 307

EASTERBROOK, F. H., 'Vertical Arrangements and the Rule of Reason' (1984) 53 *Antitrust LJ* 135

FLYNN, J. J., 'The "Is" and "Ought" of Vertical Restraints After Monsanto Co v. Sprayrite Service Corp' (1985–1986) 1 *Cornell LR* 1095

GOEBEL, R. J., 'Metro II's Confirmation of the Selective Distribution Rules: Is this the End of the Road?' (1987) 24 *CMLRev* 605

GYSELEN, L., 'Vertical Restraints in the Distribution Process: Strengths and Weaknesses of the Free Rider Rationale under EEC Competition Law' (1984) 21 *CMLRev* 647

HAWK, B. E., 'The American (Antitrust) Revolution: Lessons for the EEC' [1998] *ECLR* 53

—— 'System Failure: "Vertical Restraints and EC Competition Law"' (1995) 32 *CMLRev* 973

KORAH, V., 'Goodbye Red Label: Condemnation of Dual Pricing by Distillers' (1978) *ELRev* 62

—— 'Selective Distribution' [1994] *ECLR* 101

PITOFSKY, R., 'In Defense of Discounters: The No-Frills Case for a Per Se Rule against Vertical Price Fixing' 71 *Geo. LJ.* 1487 (1983)

SUBIOTTO, R., and AMATO, G., 'The Reform of European Competition Policy concerning Vertical Restraints' (2001–02) 69 *Antitrust LJ* 147

VENIT, J., 'Pronuptia: Ancillary restraints or Unholy Alliances?' (1986) 11 *ELRev* 213

WHISH, R., 'Regulation 2790/1999: the Commission's "New Style" Block Exemption for Vertical Agreements' (2000) 37 *CMLRev* 887.

[437] See, for example, the rather exceptional ruling of the High Court in *Crehan v. Inntrepreneur Pub Company* [2003] 27 EG 138 where, applying *Delimitis*, Park J found, despite Commission decisions indicating a contrary conclusion, that the *Delimitis* conditions were not satisfied so the brewery agreement did not infringe Article 81(1) at all. Although this finding was overturned by the Court of Appeal, it was later upheld by the House of Lords, see *Inntrepreneur Pub Company v. Crehan* [2006] UKHL 38. This case and its background is discussed in greater detail, *infra* Chap. 15.

[438] In most Member States resale price maintenance is considered to be a serious infringement of the competition rules.

[439] But see the UK Office of Fair Trading's draft opinion on Newspaper and Magazine Distribution, OFT 851, July 2006, available on OFT's website www.oft.gov.uk (replacing an earlier opinion, OFT450, published in May 2005).

10

INTELLECTUAL PROPERTY RIGHTS

1. CENTRAL ISSUES

1. Intellectual property rights, such as patents, trade marks, copyrights and designs, grant the holder of the right an exclusionary, and sometimes exclusive, right to the exploitation of an emanation of the human intellect. They are designed to provide an incentive for innovation and invention.

2. Intellectual property rights are still generally granted at the national level (although there are some Community rights).

3. The existence and exercise of intellectual property rights (especially national rights) has sometimes created tension with the Community rules both on free movement and competition.

4. This chapter focuses on the compatibility of intellectual property licensing agreements with Article 81.

5. Like vertical agreements, the Commission's policy towards intellectual property licensing agreements has been a tumultuous one. The policy has evolved from a permissive approach, to a more interventionist and formalistic one, to the current more economic approach reflected in a 2004 block exemption for technology transfer agreements (the 'TTBER') and accompanying guidelines.

6. The 2004 TTBER provides a block exemption (or safe harbour) for bilateral technology transfer

agreements concluded between parties which do not exceed specified market shares and which do not contain specified hardcore restraints. Certain other specified provisions in the contract are excluded and not covered by the block exemption.

7. The introduction of market share thresholds into the TTBER means that, in practice, it provides less legal certainty than previous block exemptions governing licensing of intellectual property rights.

8. The framework for Article 81 analysis set out in the Technology Transfer Guidelines is thus of utmost importance. These guidelines set out a general principles concerning Article 81 and intellectual property rights, explain the provisions and application of the TTBER and explain the application of Article 81(1) and Article 81(3) to technology transfer agreements outside the scope of the TTBER.

9. Trade mark and copyright (except software copyright) licensing agreements are not technology transfer agreements and are not covered by the technology transfer block exemption or guidelines.

2. INTRODUCTION

A. GENERAL

Intellectual property rights are those rights which may be asserted in respect of the product of the human intellect. They are recognized and protected in some way in all developed countries and encompass a broad spectrum of different rights. For example, they safeguard the creators of aesthetic and artistic works from having their creations distorted and purloined by others, they provide an incentive for invention and innovation by enabling those who develop new products and processes to reap the financial rewards of their efforts, and they allow those who develop brand names to exploit the reputation attached to the brand. The importance of intellectual property rights in the modern commercial world is incontrovertible, but their interaction with Community law is complex. They raise problems not only for competition law but also for the free movement of goods and services and the operation of the single market. This is because:

(a) Despite the introduction of some Community-wide rights[1] intellectual property rights are still typically granted by national laws and enforced on a national basis, conferring protection within national territories. This inevitably leads to a conflict with the Community provisions governing the free movement of goods and services.

(b) Intellectual property rights may erect barriers to entry to a market and thus affect the determination of whether an undertaking is in a dominant position for the purposes of Article 82.[2] In addition, the use by a dominant undertaking of its intellectual property rights may constitute an abuse.

(c) Transactions involving intellectual property rights may be agreements falling within Article 81. Holders of intellectual property rights often exploit them by licensing others to use them. The terms of such licences may involve restrictions of competition, including territorial restrictions which divide the common market.

This chapter starts by looking at some of the different types of intellectual property rights before outlining the relationship between intellectual property and both Community competition law and the Community free movement rules. The Chapter focuses, however, on intellectual property licensing agreements and their treatment under Article 81. The application of Article 81 to intellectual property licensing agreements has changed dramatically over the years and, especially, since modernization in 2004. In particular, on 1 May 2004 a new Technology Transfer block exemption, Regulation 772/2004 (the 'TTBER'), came into force exempting certain 'technology transfer agreements' (patent, design, knowhow and/or software copyright licensing agreements) from Article 81(1).[3] The TTBER is accompanied by Technology Transfer Guidelines (the 'Guidelines') which explain in detail the Commission's approach to technology transfer agreements.[4] The development of Community competition policy to intellectual

---

[1] E.g., the Community Trade Mark, provided for by Council Reg. 40/94, [1994] OJ L11/1, and administered by the Office for Harmonization in the Internal Market (Trade Marks and Designs) in Alicante, Spain. The Community Patent Convention (76/76/EEC of 15 Dec. 1975) annexed to the Agreement relating to Community Patents [1989] OJ L401/1, providing for a Community-wide patent, never came into force having been ratified by only seven Member States. The Commission re-activated the process in 1997, resulting in the Proposal for a Council Regulation on the Community Patent (COM (2000) 412 final of 1 Aug. 2000, but the EU Council of Ministers at its meeting on 18 May 2004 could not agree on issues such as the translation of claims. The possibility of introducing a Community patent is still under discussion, however, see Commission consultation on future patent policy in Europe to create an EU-wide system of protection (16 January 2006) and Preliminary findings of consultation of future patent policy (12 July 2006). The European Patent Convention (EPC, 1973, entered into force October 1977) is not an EU instrument. It is administered by the European Patent Office (EPO) in Munich and enables a bundle of *national* patents to be granted on a single application. The EPO is the executive arm of the European Patent Organisation, an intergovernmental body set up under the EPC, whose members are the EPC contracting states.

[2] See *supra* Chap. 6.

[3] Reg. 772/2004 on technology transfer agreements (the TTBER) [2004] OJ L123/11.

[4] Guidelines on the application of Article 81 of the EC Treaty to technology transfer agreements [2004] OJ C101/2.

property licensing agreements is traced in section 3 whilst sections 4 and 5 examine the TTBER and the Guidelines in close detail. Sections 6, 7 and 8 deal with trade mark licences, trade mark delimitation agreements and copyright licences not covered by the TTBER and Guidelines. Section 9 considers software licences and interoperability whilst section 10 outlines issues arising in cases involving intellectual property rights under Article 82. In section 11 some conclusions are drawn.

B. TYPES OF INTELLECTUAL PROPERTY RIGHTS

(i) The Nature of Intellectual Property Rights

Intellectual property rights give the holder an exclusionary, and sometimes exclusive, right to the exploitation of an emanation of the intellect. The nature of the right varies from one type of intellectual property to another. Intellectual property rights vary in duration. Some arise only upon registration, while others arise from the act of creation itself. In the absence of harmonization, Community law does not regulate the conditions upon which national law grants intellectual property rights,[5] although it may curtail the *exercise* of them.[6] This section briefly describes the main types of intellectual property rights.[7]

(ii) Patents

Patents relate to inventions. The grant of a patent confers on the holder (the patentee), normally for a maximum period of twenty years,[8] a monopoly over a new and inventive product or process, and the right to prevent others from making, disposing of, using, or importing a product which is the subject of the patent or derived from it, or from using the patented process itself. Patents protect applied technology, not abstract ideas. Patents are granted in respect of the product or process disclosed in the specification when the patent is applied for, and on the expiry of the patent anyone else in the world may use the information contained in the specification.

(iii) Trade Marks

A trade mark is a mark or sign used to identify and differentiate a product or service. Registration of a trade mark gives the holder an exclusive right to use it as such, although if it is a non-invented word it does not take the word out of general use, but only prevents its use by others as a trade mark.[9] Other parties remain free to offer competing goods and services under

---

[5] See, e.g., Case 144/81, *Keurkoop v. Nancy Kean Gifts* [1982] ECR 2853, [1983] 2 CMLR 47; Cases C-241–2/91 P, *RTE & ITP v. Commission* [1995] ECR I-743, [1995] 4 CMLR 718, para. 49.

[6] See *infra* 781 ff.

[7] See further L. Bently and B. Sherman, *Intellectual Property Law* (2nd edn., Oxford University Press, 2004); W. Cornish and D. Llewelyn, *Intellectual Property: Patents, Copyright, Trade Marks and Allied Rights* (5th edn., Sweet & Maxwell, 2003).

[8] The maximum 20-year term is common throughout the EU because of the European Patent Convention (*supra* n. 1). Council Reg. 1768/92, [1992] OJ L182/1, on the creation of supplementary protection certificates for medicinal products, enables a period not exceeding five years to be added to this in respect of delays in regulatory approval.

[9] And the use of a *similar* mark or sign on identical or similar goods or services where there is a likelihood of confusion, Dir. 89/104/EEC [1989] OJ L40/1 (Council Directive to approximate the laws of the Member States relating to Trade Marks, the First Trade Marks Directive), Art. 4(1)(b).

other marks and brand names. If renewal procedures are complied with trade mark registration can continue indefinitely. Trade mark law in the EU was harmonized by the First Trade Marks Directive of 21 December 1988.[10]

Marks and brand names which are not registered may also be protected by other means. In the UK this is by the law on passing-off, and in many other EU countries by laws on unfair competition.

(iv) Copyright

Copyright protects 'works' such as literary, dramatic, musical and artistic works, films, sound recordings, and broadcasts from unauthorized exploitation by third parties. Unlike a patent, copyright does not confer a monopoly because it prevents only *copying*: if a third party independently comes up with the same melody or words, he will not be liable for breach of copyright. Copyright does not depend on registration or formal procedures but arises automatically when the work is set down or recorded in some form. Copyright in the EU lasts for the lifetime of the author plus seventy years.[11]

There are greater differences between the laws of EU Member States in respect of copyright than there are with other forms of intellectual property. Common law notions of copyright emphasize the right of the author to prevent others exploiting his or her work for commercial gain whereas the civil law emphasizes the right of the creator of a work to be recognized as such and to be morally entitled to protect its integrity.[12] UK copyright law covers performers' rights, and similar rights but in most EU countries there is a distinction drawn between 'author's right' and 'neighbouring rights' (those accorded to sound recordings, broadcasts, and performers). Under UK law works created by the 'sweat of the brow', such as compilations of information, are accorded copyright protection, whereas civil law systems require a greater degree of creativity: this difference seemed to be a material issue in the Article 82 case on television listings, *Magill*.[13] The Information Society Directive has harmonized national laws on certain aspects of the protection of copyright owners' rights to control reproduction, distribution, and communication (primarily on the Internet).[14]

(v) Designs

Under the Berne Convention[15] countries are free to choose the way in which they protect industrial designs. In the UK a design which has features which in the finished article 'is new and has

---

[10] Council Dir. 89/104/EEC to approximate the laws of the Member States relating to Trade Marks [1989] OJ L40/1 implemented in the UK by the Trade Marks Act 1994. The Directive leaves to Member States the procedural details for applying for or revoking a mark or bringing infringement proceedings. See also Council Regulation 40/94 on the Community trade mark [1994] OJ L11/1, *supra* n 1.

[11] Under Dir. 93/98 [1993] OJ L290/9, harmonizing the term of protection of copyright and related rights.

[12] The Copyright Designs and Patents Act 1988 ss. 77–85, introduced express 'moral rights' into UK law, partly to come into line with the Berne Convention for the Protection of Literary and Artistic Works, 1886.

[13] Cases C-241–242/91 P, *RTE & ITP* v. *Commission* [1995] ECR I-743, [1995] 4 CMLR 718; see Chap. 7. Specific protection is now accorded to databases under Dir. 96/9 [1996] OJ L77/20.

[14] Directive 2001/20/EC on Copyright and Related Rights in the Information Society [2001] OJ L167/10. The Directive was adopted to fulfil the EU's obligations under the WIPO (World Intellectual Property Organization) Copyright Treaty 1996 and the WIPO Performances and Phonograms Treaty 1996. It has been implemented in the UK by the Copyright and Related Rights Regulations 2003, SI 1996/2967.

[15] Berne Convention for the Protection of Literary and Artistic Works, 1886 (as subsequently revised).

individual character' can be registered.[16] Registration gives the proprietor a monopoly over its use for a maximum of twenty-five years, in respect of articles for which it has been registered. UK law also recognizes unregistered design rights in respect of the original design of any aspect of the shape or configuration of an article.[17] The right is analogous to copyright in that it arises automatically when the design is created, but it lasts for a maximum of fifteen years. Like copyright it protects the holder against *copying*, not against independent creation, whereas registered design right is like a patent in protecting against independent creation. The 1998 Directive on the legal protection of designs[18] dealt only with registered designs and is a partial harmonization measure only. Under the Directive protection is for twenty-five years and entitles the holder to prevent the making, offering, putting on the market, importing, exporting, and stocking of a product incorporating the design.

(vi) Know-how

Strictly speaking, know-how is not an intellectual property right, but it often features in commercial transactions such as licensing arrangements to which Article 81 applies. Know-how is confidential, technical, commercially valuable information which is not patented or registered in any way.[19] Know-how is defined in the TTBER[20] and is protected by contractual provisions and breach of confidence laws.

(vii) Miscellaneous

a. Plant Breeders' Rights

Plant breeders' rights are given in respect of the creation of new plant varieties. They are similar to patents in that they confer a monopoly. Council Regulation 2100/94 on plant variety rights created a Community plant variety right which co-exists with national regimes.[21]

b. Semi-conductor Topographies

The protection of the topography of semi-conductor chips was the subject of harmonization in Directive 87/54.[22]

c. Databases

Databases were the subject of specific harmonization in the 1996 Database Directive[23] which creates a *sui generis* right for their protection. Previously, Member States' copyright laws differed according to the extent of the protection that was afforded to databases.

---

[16] Registered Designs Act 1949 s.1B(1), as amended by the Copyright Designs and Patents Act 1988, s. 265 and SI 2001/3949 and SI 2003/550.

[17] Copyright Designs and Patents Act 1988 s. 213. There are a number of exceptions: e.g., design right does not subsist in surface decoration, or features which enable the article to fit with or match another article.

[18] Dir. 98/71 [1998] OJ L289/28. There is a proposal to amend the directive to harmonize design protection for spare parts, see Proposal for a Directive amending Directive 98/71 on the legal protection of designs (COM/2004/582). See also Council Regulation 6/2002 on Community designs [2002] OJ L3/1.

[19] Usually because it does not fulfil the necessary criteria for patentability, but sometimes the creator chooses not to patent in order to keep the information out of the public domain.

[20] Reg. 772/2004 [2004] OJ L123/11, Art. 1(1)(i), further explained in Commission Guidelines on the application of Article 81 to technology transfer agreements, [2004] OJ C101/2, para. 47; see *infra* 810.

[21] [1994] OJ L227/1.

[22] [1987] OJ L24/36. In the UK semiconductor topography is protected as an unregistered design. See the Design Right (Semi-conductor Topographies) Regulations 1989, SI 1989/1100.

[23] Dir. 96/9 on the legal protection of databases [1996] OJ L77/20.

d. Computer Software

Before the implementation of the Software Directive[24] Member States varied in their ways of protecting software. The Directive requires them to do it by way of copyright as a literary work within the meaning of the Berne Convention. However, the Commission proposed that software programs should also qualify for patent protection in all Member States.[25] In May 2004 the Council agreed on a common position on a proposed directive to extend patent protection to computer-implemented inventions.[26]

C. THE RELATIONSHIP BETWEEN INTELLECTUAL PROPERTY RIGHTS AND COMPETITION LAW

The relationship between intellectual property rights and competition law has sometimes been an uneasy one. In the EC, this has particularly been the case in the (rather rare) instances where competition law has required unwilling dominant firms to license their rights to others.[27] The underlying issue, however, is whether intellectual property rights and competition law are fundamentally in conflict or whether they are different routes to the same goals. It appears to be generally accepted at present that intellectual property rights and competition law do not have conflicting aims but that, on the contrary, both pursue the promotion of consumer welfare. This view is set out in the extracts below, one written by a Commission official, Luc Peeperkorn[28] and the other by Anderman and Kallaugher in their book on technology transfer agreements.

L. Peeperkorn, 'IP Licences and Competition Rules: Striking the Right Balance' (2003) 26 *World Competition* 527, 527–8

II. Do IP and competition law have conflicting aims?

Recognising that early copying of an innovation and free riding on an innovator's efforts under-mine the incentive to innovate, IP laws (intellectual property laws) grant the innovator a legal monopoly. They provide the innovator the right to exclusively exploit the innovation and exclude others from exploiting it. This legal monopoly may, depending on the availability of substitutes in the relevant market, in turn lead to market power and even monopoly as defined under competi-tion law. This has given rise to the alleged source of conflict often mentioned: that competition law would take away what IP law is providing.

However, in principle this is only an apparent source of conflict. At the highest level of analysis IP and competition law are complementary because they both aim at promoting consumer welfare.

---

[24] Council Dir. 91/250 on the legal protection of computer programs, [1991] OJ L122/42.

[25] See Commission Communication 'Promoting Innovation through Patents: the Follow-up to the Green Paper on the Community Patent System in Europe' COM(1999)42.

[26] 18 May 2004, IP/04/659.

[27] See *supra* Chap. 7.

[28] L. Peeperkorn was one of the officials in DG Comp responsible for conducting the review of the EC intellectual property licensing regime and which resulted in the adoption of the new block exemption on technology transfer agreements in April 2004, Reg. 772/2004 on technology transfer agreements [2004] OJ L123/11.

The objective of IP laws is to promote technical progress to the ultimate benefit of consumers. This is done by striking a balance, hopefully the right one, between over- and under-protection of innovators' efforts. The aim is not to promote the individual innovator's welfare. The property right provided by IP laws is awarded to try to ensure a sufficient reward for the innovator to elicit its creative or inventive effort while not delaying follow-on innovation or leading to unnecessary long periods of high prices for consumers. A delay in follow-on innovation may result when the innovation consists of an improvement on earlier ideas that have been granted patent protection already. Unnecessary long periods of high prices will result when the innovation allows the IPR holder to obtain market power in the antitrust market(s) where the IPR is exploited and where the IPR protects this monopoly position longer than is required to elicit the innovative effort.

In order to correctly strike the balance between under- and over-protecting innovators' efforts, intellectual property rights differ from and are usually less absolute than 'normal' property rights: they are often limited in duration (patents, copyright), not protected against parallel creation by others (copyright, know how) or lose their value once they become public (know how).

Competition policy aims at promoting consumer welfare by protecting competition as the driving force of efficient markets, providing the best quality products at the lowest prices. Companies under competitive pressure will be less complacent and will have more incentive to innovate and gain market share. Product market competition and a strict competition policy work as an effective stick to promote innovative effort. The relevant question is therefore not one of conflict but of complementarity and possibly adjustment in the individual case.

S. D. Anderman and J. Kallaugher *Technology Transfer and the New EU Competition Rules: Intellectual Property Licensing after Modernisation* (Oxford University Press, 2006)

B. Background — the Relationship between Competition Law and IP

1.11 The introduction of the new EC paradigm comes at a time when advocates of competition policy and proponents of intellectual property have reached an accommodation that recognises that both competition law and intellectual property rights legislation constitute complementary components of a modern industrial policy. Although both policies pursue the common aim of improving innovation and consumer welfare each does so using rather different means. Intellectual property rights legislation such as patent, copyright and design rights laws offer intellectual property right holders a period of exclusive rights to exploit their property right as both a reward to the individual and as an incentive to the wider process of innovation and R&D investment. Trademarks perform a different function. Their exclusivity is meant to protect the consumer as well as to reward the originator. Modern competition policy attempts to keep markets innovative and competitive by maintaining effective competition. The means it uses to pursue this aim include maintaining access to markets and preventing 'foreclosure' or monopolisation of markets.

1.12 At first sight there may seem to be a potential clash in the methods used by the two systems of legal regulation to achieve their common aim. The concern to maintain access to markets appears to be implacably opposed to the concept of exclusive rights to make, use and sell a product. And indeed, there was a period when the misunderstanding of the economic effects of intellectual property rights led EC competition law and policy to attempt to place overly strict limits on the exercise of intellectual property rights, particularly in the filed of patent licensing. Today, however, the interrelationship between the two systems of law is characterised more by its accommodations than by its conflict. These accommodations tend to occur most often as an incidental result of the ordinary doctrines of each system. Thus, intellectual property laws make a contribution to effective competition and maintaining access to market by devices within their own internal doctrine that strive to maintain a balance between 'initial' inventors and creators and 'follow-on' invention and creation. Good examples are the 'fair use' doctrine in copyright laws, the doctrine of 'non-obviousness' and the provision of compulsory licensing in patent law and interoperability imperatives and decompilation rights in the computer program directive. On rare occasions, as in the EC database directive, the accommodation will be explicitly spelt out in the intellectual property law itself.

1.13 Within EC competition law the accommodation also tends to occur more owing to the incidental effect of the logic of the general doctrines of competition law rather that in the form of special treatment. When one looks at EC competition law the most obvious example of special treatment is the 'exceptional circumstances' test embedded within the abuse of refusal to supply under Article 82 . . .

1.14 This observation offers a good perspective for viewing the relationship between Article 81 and intellectual property licensing under the new post-modernised legal framework. The accommodation with intellectual property rights in the new Technology Transfer Block Exemption Regulation (TTBER) and Guidelines occurs almost entirely within the logic of the doctrines of competition law. Most of the accommodation takes place as an incidental benefit of the ordinary interpretation of Article 81 under the modernisation programme. In the Guidelines and Recitals there is evidence that the competition authorities have made a considerable effort to understand the nature of intellectual property rights and intellectual property rights licensing. Thus, they acknowledge that the creation of intellectual property rights often entails substantial investment and that it is often a risky endeavour. They state plainly that '[I]n order not to reduce dynamic competition and to maintain the incentive to innovate the innovator must not be unduly restricted in the exploitation of the IPR that turn out to be valuable'. In particular, they must be able to seek compensation for successful projects that takes failed projects into account. The Commission also acknowledges that technology licensing may required the licensee to make considerable sunk investment in the licensed technology and production assets necessary to exploit it. Moreover, the Guidelines have accepted that the great majority of licensing agreements are pro-competitive and compatible with Article 81.

1.15 This approach represents a conscious rejection of the argument that a special self-contained regime (like the old block exemptions) is necessary to satisfy the special requirements of intellectual property licensing. As the Guidelines confidently proclaim '[in] assessing licensing agreements under Article 81, the existing analytical framework is sufficiently flexible to take due account of the dynamic aspects of technology licensing'. The new framework clearly harmonises the treatment of licensing agreements with that of other commercial agreements under Article 81 and, on the whole, this results in a reasonable treatment of intellectual property licensing. However, as we shall see, the process of harmonisation has not been complete; the analytical framework has had to make certain adjustments to take due account of the special features of technology licensing.

D. RELEVANT PROVISIONS OF THE EC TREATY OTHER THAN THE COMPETITION ARTICLES

Perhaps surprisingly for a document purporting to lay down the foundations for a single market, the EC Treaty itself contains very little about intellectual property. Article 295 (ex Article

222), however, contains a general rule about property rights:

This treaty shall in no way prejudice the rules in Member States governing the system of property ownership.

Community law therefore recognizes the existence and ownership of rights given by national law. Nevertheless, there is a fundamental conflict between this and the principle of the free movement of goods. Article 28 (ex Article 30), the basic provision on the free movement of goods, states:

Quantitative restrictions on imports and all measures having equivalent effect shall, without prejudice to the following provisions, be prohibited between Member States.

However, if widgets made in France by F cannot be imported into Germany because they would infringe G's German patent, the market is divided along national lines. Not only that, but G may wish to use its German patent to prevent its *own* widgets, which it has manufactured in the UK, from being imported into Germany by a parallel importer. In both these examples national intellectual property rights can seriously impede the free circulation of goods.

Intellectual property rights are specifically dealt with in Article 30 (ex Article 36), which provides a derogation from Article 28. It is the only place in the Treaty where they are mentioned. Article 30 provides:

The provisions of Articles 28 and 29 shall not preclude prohibitions or restrictions on imports, exports or goods in transit justified on grounds of public morality, public policy or public security; the protection of health and life of humans, animals or plants; the protection of national treasures possessing artistic, historic or archaeological value; or the protection of industrial and commercial property.[29] Such prohibition or restrictions shall not, however, constitute a means of arbitrary discrimination or a disguised restriction on trade between Member States.

Community law therefore accepts that restrictions on free movement may be justified to protect national intellectual property rights. However, Article 30 contains a final proviso in the last sentence. The restrictions are not to constitute 'a means of arbitrary discrimination or a disguised restriction' on inter-Member State trade. This 'sting in the tail'[30] has been used to justify many of the limitations which the ECJ has placed on the exercise of national intellectual property rights.

Intellectual property rights can also affect the free movement of services. Article 49 (ex Article 59) is the basic provision on services:

Within the framework of the provisions set out below, restrictions on freedom to provide services within the Community shall be prohibited in respect of nationals of Member States who are established in a State of the Community other than that of the person for whom the services are intended.

Article 49 does not have a derogation equivalent to Article 30, but the ECJ has held that the principle in Article 30 should be applied to it by analogy.[31] Restrictions on the movement of services may therefore be justified by the need to protect intellectual property rights in the same way as they are justified in respect of the movement of goods.

---

[29] It could be argued that the phrase 'industrial and commercial' property does not cover copyright, but the ECJ has held that it does: see Case 78/70, *Deutsche Grammophon v. Metro* [1971] ECR 487, [1971] CMLR 631 and Cases 55 and 57/80, *Musik-Vertrieb Membran v. GEMA* [1981] ECR 147, [1981] 2 CMLR 44. 'Intellectual property' is the generic phrase now used both at Community and international level.

[30] V. Korah, *An Introductory Guide to EC Competition Law and Practice* (8th edn., Hart Publishing, 2004), para. 10.3.

[31] See Case 62/79, *Coditel v. Ciné Vog Films* [1980] ECR 881, [1981] 2 CMLR 362 (*Coditel I*); Case 262/81, *Coditel v. Ciné Vog Films* [1982] ECR 3381, [1983] 1 CMLR 49 (*Coditel II*).

E. THE CASE LAW OF THE COURT: EXISTENCE, EXERCISE, AND THE EXHAUSTION OF RIGHTS

In its case law concerning both the free movement and the competition provisions the ECJ has attempted to reconcile the conflicting demands of the economic integration of the single market and the protection of intellectual property rights. It has developed a number of inter-linking concepts by which to do this:

(a) It has drawn a dichotomy between the *existence* of intellectual property rights and their *exercise*: the existence of rights is unaffected by the EC Treaty but their exercise may be.

(b) It developed the idea that there is a 'specific subject-matter' of each kind of right, the protection of which is justified even if it leads to restrictions on inter-Member State trade: the exercise of intellectual property rights which partitions the market will be allowed in so far as it is necessary to protect the 'specific subject matter' of that right.

(c) It has built up a jurisprudence on the 'exhaustion of rights'. Once a rights holder has consented to the marketing of the protected product within the Community,[32] the rights encompassed in the 'specific subject-matter' are exhausted and the holder cannot rely on national rights to prevent the movement of the goods between Member States.

The distinction between the existence and exercise of rights is not convincing. A property right which cannot be exercised has no value.[33] Intellectual property rights are valuable because they enable the holder to exercise rights which prevent third parties from committing infringing acts. If Community law limits the holder's ability to control third parties then the value of the right is diminished, and the fact that the 'existence' of the right is untouched is of little comfort. Arguably the existence/exercise dichotomy is simply a flexible tool developed by the ECJ which enables it to make policy decisions under the guise of principle.

The distinction between existence and exercise was first introduced by the ECJ in 1966 in *Consten & Grundig*.[34] It will be remembered that this was a case about an exclusive distribution agreement, which primarily concerned the competition rather than the free movement provisions. Grundig appointed Consten to be its exclusive distributor in France and allowed Consten to register its trade mark GINT in France. The provisions of the agreement and the registration of the trade mark conferred absolute territorial protection on Consten by enabling it to repel parallel imports of Grundig's products into France through proceedings for trade mark infringement. The Court held that the Commission's condemnation of these arrangements did not affect the grant of the trade mark rights but 'only limits their exercise'.

---

[32] 'The Community' should be interpreted in this context to mean the whole EEA. The EEA (see *supra* Chap. 2) is the relevant area by virtue of Protocol 28 of the EEA Agreement, which provides for exhaustion throughout the EEA in accordance with the case law of the Court.

[33] See the Opinion of Fennelly AG, para. 95 in Cases C-267 and 268/95, *Merck and Co Inc v. Primecrown Ltd (Merck II)*. [1996] ECR I-6285, [1997] 1 CMLR 83.

[34] Cases 56 and 58/64, *Consten & Grundig v. Commission* [1966] ECR 229, [1966] CMLR 418. The case is considered at length, *supra*, Chaps. 3 and 4.

Cases 56 and 58, *Etablissements Consten SA & Grundig-Verkaufs-GmbH* v. *Commission* [1966] ECR 299, [1966] CMLR 418

Court of Justice

46. Consten's right under the contract to the exclusive user in France of the GINT trade mark, which may be used in a similar manner in other countries, is intended to make it possible to keep under surveillance and to place an obstacle in the way of parallel imports. Thus, the agreement by which Grundig, as the holder of the trade-mark by virtue of an international registration, authorized Consten to register it in France in its own name tends to restrict competition.

47. Although Consten is, by virtue of the registration of the GINT trade-mark, regarded under French law as the original holder of the rights relating to that trade-mark, the fact nevertheless remains that it was by virtue of an agreement with Grundig that it was able to effect the registration.

48. That agreement therefore is one which may be caught by the prohibition in Article [81(1)]. The prohibition would be ineffective if Consten could continue to use the trade-mark to achieve the same object as that pursued by the agreement which has been held to be unlawful.

49. Articles [30], [295] and [307] of the Treaty relied upon by the applicants do not exclude any influence whatever of Community law on the exercise of national industrial property rights.

50. Article [30], which limits the scope of the rules on the liberalization of trade contained in Title I, Chapter 2, of the Treaty, cannot limit the field of application of Article [81]. Article [295] confines itself to stating that the 'Treaty shall in no way prejudice the rules in Member States governing the system of property ownership'. The injunction contained in Article 3 of the operative part of the contested decision to refrain from using rights under national trade-mark law in order to set an obstacle in the way of parallel imports does not affect the grant of those rights but only limits their exercise to the extent necessary to give effect to the prohibition under Article [81(1)]. The power of the Commission to issue such an injunction for which provision is made in Article 3 of Regulation No. 17/62 of the Council is in harmony with the nature of the Community rules on competition which have immediate effect and are directly binding on individuals.

51. Such a body of rules, by reason of its nature described above and its function, does not allow the improper use of rights under any national trade-mark law in order to frustrate the Community's law on cartels.

52. Article [307] which has the aim of protecting the rights of third countries is not applicable in the present instance.

This distinction drawn between the grant of rights and their exercise was further elaborated in *Deutsche Grammophon.*

Case 78/70, *Deutsche Grammophon Gesellschaft* v. *Metro-SB-Großmärkte GmbH* [1971] ECR 487, [1971] CMLR 631

Deutsche Grammophon (DGG) marketed its records in France through its French subsidiary, Polydor, under the designation 'Polydor'. A quantity of records was pressed by DGG in Germany and supplied to Polydor in Paris. Polydor supplied them to an undertaking in a third country which resold them to a firm in Germany which resold them to Metro. Metro then marketed them in

Germany, undercutting DGG's standard price for its records there. DGG sued Metro in the German courts for breach of its copyright. The Hamburg court made an Article 234 reference to the Court of Justice, asking whether the exercise of the intellectual property right infringed the Community provisions on free movement.

Court of Justice

4. It is clear from the facts recorded by the Hanseatisches Oberlandesgericht, Hamburg, that what it asks may be reduced in essentials to the question whether the exclusive right of distributing the protected articles which is conferred by a national law on the manufacturer of sound recordings may, without infringing Community provisions, prevent the marketing on national territory of products lawfully distributed by such manufacturer or with his consent on the territory of another Member State. The Court of Justice is asked to define the tenor and the scope of the relevant Community provisions, with particular reference to the second paragraph of Article [10] or Article [81(1)].

5. According to the second paragraph of Article [10] of the Treaty, Member States 'shall abstain from any measure which could jeopardize the attainment of the objective of this Treaty'. This provision lays down a general duty for the Member States, the actual tenor of which depends in each individual case on the provisions of the Treaty or on the rules derived from its general scheme.

6. According to Article [81(1)] of the Treaty 'The following shall be prohibited as incompatible with the common market: all agreements between undertakings, decisions by associations of undertakings and concerted practices which may affect trade between Member States and which have as their object or effect the prevention, restriction or distortion of competition within the Common Market'. The exercise of the exclusive right referred to in the question might fall under the prohibition set out by this provision each time it manifests itself as the subject, the means or the result of an agreement which, by preventing imports from other Member States of products lawfully distributed there, has as its effect the partitioning of the market.

7. If, however, the exercise of the right does not exhibit those elements of contract or concerted practice referred to in Article [81(1)] it is necessary, in order to answer the question referred, further to consider whether the exercise of the right in question is compatible with other provisions of the Treaty, in particular those relating to the free movement of goods.

8. The principles to be considered in the present case are those concerned with the attainment of a single market between the Member States, which are placed both in Part Two of the Treaty devoted to the foundations of the Community, under the free movement of goods, and in Article 3 [(1)(g)] of the Treaty which prescribes the institution of a system ensuring that competition in the common market is not distorted.

9. Moreover, where certain prohibitions or restrictions on trade between Member States are conceded in Article [30], the Treaty makes express reference to them, providing that such derogations shall not constitute 'a means of arbitrary discrimination or a disguised restriction on trade between Member States'.

10. It is thus in the light of those provisions, especially of Articles [28], [30], [81] and [82], that an appraisal should be made as to how far the exercise of a national right related to copyright may impede the marketing of products from another Member State.

11. Amongst the prohibitions or restrictions on the free movement of goods which it concedes Article [30] refers to industrial and commercial property. On the assumption that those provisions may be relevant to a right related to copyright, it is nevertheless clear from that article that, although the Treaty does not affect the existence of rights recognized by the legislation of a Member State with regard to industrial and commercial property, the exercise of such rights may nevertheless fall within the prohibitions laid down by the Treaty. Although it permits prohibitions or restrictions on the free movement of products, which are justified for the purpose of protecting industrial and commercial property, Article [30] only admits derogations from that freedom to the

extent to which they are justified for the purpose of safeguarding rights which constitute the specific subject-matter of such property.

12. If a right related to copyright is relied upon to prevent the marketing in the Member State of products distributed by the holder of the right or with his consent on the territory of another Member State on the sole ground that such distribution did not take place on the national territory, such a prohibition, which would legitimize the isolation of national markets, would be repugnant to the essential purpose of the Treaty, which is to unite national markets into a single market.

That purpose could not be attained if, under the various legal systems of the Member States, nationals of those States were able to partition the market and bring about arbitrary discrimination or disguised restrictions on trade between Member States.

13. Consequently, it would be in conflict with the provisions prescribing the free movement of products within the common market for a manufacturer of sound recordings to exercise the exclusive right to distribute the protected articles, conferred upon him by the legislation of a Member State, in such a way as to prohibit the sale in that State of products placed on the market by him or with his consent in another Member State solely because such distribution did not occur within the territory of the first Member State.

In this case, unlike *Consten & Grundig*, there was no agreement between any of the parties which could be caught by Article 81. The Court was thus faced with a stark conflict between the exercise of intellectual property rights and the free movement of goods in a situation where, in order to protect its higher price level in Germany, the holder was trying to use its German rights to prevent the import into Germany of its own records, which it had originally placed on the market itself. Like many of the cases in this area the scenario involved the activities of parallel importers. It can be seen from the judgment that the Court considered that the exercise of the right to prevent the imports in this situation would go beyond the protection of the 'specific subject-matter' of the right. Although *Deutsche Grammophon* did not expressly mention the principle of exhaustion of rights it is implicit in the judgment: DGG had exercised its German rights by putting the records on the market, and any further exercise of the rights was not permitted by Community law—its rights were exhausted. The Court did not explain what constituted the 'specific subject-matter' of the right in issue, but in subsequent cases it has defined the concept in relation to different rights and developed a complex case law on the exhaustion of rights.[35]

3. EXPLOITING INTELLECTUAL PROPERTY RIGHTS BY LICENSING

A. GENERAL

The owner of an intellectual property right has a choice of ways in which to benefit from the right commercially. He may exploit it himself, assign it to a third party, or license it. The method

---

[35] See further C. Barnard, *The Substantive Law of the EU* (Oxford University Press, 2004), Chap. 8; L. Bently and B. Sherman, *Intellectual Property Law* (2nd edn., Oxford University Press, 2004), 10–13, 880–96; W. Cornish and D. Llewelyn, *Intellectual Property: Patents, Copyright, Trade Marks and Allied Rights* (5th edn., Sweet & Maxwell, 2003), Chap. 18 and W. Allan, M. Furse and B. Sufrin (eds.), *Butterworths Competition Law* (Butterworths, looseleaf), Div V, Chap. 2.

chosen will depend on a number of factors. These include the resources available to the owner, the type of right concerned, the nature of the product and its life cycle, manufacturing costs and complexity, the overall commercial strategy of the owner, local conditions in the territory in which the right is held, and taxation considerations. Some rights may be able to be carved up: for example the owner of copyright in a book may deal separately with the rights to make a television programme of it, the rights to film it, the rights to serialize it in a newspaper, and the rights to make an audio tape or other recordings of it.

An *assignment* involves the outright transfer of the right to a third party. After transfer the original owner is excluded from using it without a licence from the new owner. An assignment may be gratuitous or by way of sale or swap. It may be made pursuant to a contract of employment when an employee assigns to the employer rights which he acquires in the course of employment. Rights are commonly sold on the transfer or take-over of a business, when they pass to the new owner along with the other assets. In contrast, a *licence* involves the owner of an intellectual property right conferring permission upon another party to exploit the owner's legally protected exclusive right. The advantages of licensing include:

(i) the owner (the licensor) has continuing control of the use of the rights (in so far as this is not limited by competition law);

(ii) the ability to carve up the rights is normally greater with licensing than assignment;

(iii) the owner can obtain a continuing revenue stream from the exploitation and can benefit from the licensee's success;

(iv) the owner can continue to exploit the right himself.

The TTBER treats certain assignments of patents, designs, know-how, and software copyright as licences where part of the risk associated with their exploitation remains with the assignor. This is particularly so where the consideration is related to the turnover the assignee obtains from the products produced with the assigned technology or the quantity of the products the assignee produces (or the number of operations he carries out) with the licensed technology.[36]

B. COMMERCIAL CONSIDERATIONS IN LICENCES

(i) General

A number of intellectual property rights may be licensed together, for example patents, know-how, and trade marks. Whatever the licence consists of, the licensor will normally be concerned with maximizing the financial return. The licensor may also wish to incorporate provisions in a licence agreement relating to, for example: safeguarding confidential information; ensuring quality control; supplying essential components or other goods to the licensee; ensuring (in the case of patents and know-how) that the licensor benefits from improvements made by the licensee; safeguarding the licensor from challenges by the licensee to the validity of the rights;[37] limiting what the licensee may do with the goods or services produced under the licence; ensuring that the licensee does not compete with the licensor; and providing for termination. Licensees will be concerned with the same issues but from the other side. How far such commercial requirements can be met will depend, in part, on competition law. In this section we

---

[36] TTBER, Art. 1(1)(b) *infra* 810–1.

[37] With a patent, a licensee working it will be in the best position to identify the weaknesses in it: see further *infra* 788–9.

look briefly at some of the terms commonly found in licensing agreements that may raise competition law concerns.[38]

(ii) Royalties

Payment by the licensee for the licence will be by way of royalty obligations which may, for instance, take the form of lump sum payments, a percentage of the selling price or a fixed amount for each product incorporating the licensed technology.[39] 'Running royalties' means royalties calculated on the basis of individual product sales. Where royalties are calculated on the basis of the licensee's products which incorporate the licensed technology the licensor may wish to stipulate that a minimum number are produced.

(iii) Territorial Restrictions on Production: Exclusive and Sole Licences

Licences can be exclusive, sole or non-exclusive.

A licence is *exclusive* as regards a particular territory where it provides that the licensor will not grant further licences for that territory to other parties and will not itself exploit the licensed intellectual property rights in the territory. It means that only the licensee can exercise the licensed rights in the territory covered by the licence.

A *sole* licence is where the licensor undertakes not to grant other licences for the territory but remains free to exploit the rights there itself. The rights can therefore be exploited in the territory by the licensor, the licensee, and no-one else.

A *non-exclusive* licence is where the licensor remains free to grant other licences if it wishes and to exploit the licence in the territory itself.

Exclusive and sole licences are a common phenomenon. Licensees will often be interested in taking a licence only if they are assured of exclusivity. An undertaking may be interested in taking a licence of X's French patent, for example, only if it can be certain that having invested large resources in tooling up to exploit the patented process it will not face competition from other licensees in France or from the licensor itself operating in France. In the EU, however, clauses conferring such protection may raise serious concerns on account of the fact that they compartmentalize the single market. The concern will be particularly acute where they are coupled (as they frequently are) with territorial sales restrictions, whereby the licensor and/or the licensee are limited as to where they may *sell* the products produced with or incorporating the licensed technology. Sales restrictions are dealt with below.

In EC law the term 'exclusive licence' has often used in the past to cover both exclusive and sole licences, without distinction. The correct use of the terminology is now set out in the Guidelines on technology transfer agreements.[40]

---

[38] See further W. Cornish and D. Llewelyn, *Intellectual Property: Patents, Copyright, Trade Marks and Allied Rights* (5th edn., Sweet & Maxwell, 2003), 7–19–7–29.

[39] See Commission Notice, Guidelines on the application of Article 81 of the EC Treaty to technology transfer agreements [2004] OJ C101/2 (hereinafter 'Guidelines'), para. 156.

[40] Guidelines, para. 162.

(iv) Sales Restrictions

A licence may include restrictions as to where the licensor and/or licensee may sell (territorial restrictions) or to whom they may sell (customer allocation).

a. Territorial Sales Restrictions

A licensee may be unwilling to take a licence unless he can be protected not only from the licensor and/or other licensees *producing* in the same territory as him, but also from them *selling* there. This is similar to the wish of a distributor to be protected from intra-brand competition which we discussed in Chapter 9. Indeed, the reasons for a licensee requiring such protection may be stronger than in the case of a mere distributor because the licensee may have to invest very heavily in order to tool up to exploit the licensed technology. A licensee may therefore want protection from sales by the licensor and other licensees and for the licensor to impose export bans on other licensees. On the other side, the licensor may not be willing to disseminate his technology through licensing unless he can stop the licensees selling their production in territories where he sells himself. As with distribution agreements, sales bans can be of two kinds, active or passive (soliciting sales and responding to unsolicited sales respectively).[41] Moreover, provisions such as quantity restrictions on output can amount to indirect sales bans. EC competition law, not surprisingly, takes a strict view of territorial sales restrictions, particularly those which attempt to give the parties absolute territorial protection.

b. Customer Allocation

Provisions limiting the customers or customer groups to which parties can sell are another form of sales restriction. The licensor may wish to keep certain customers as his own preserve, or grant a licence to a licensee to service only particular customers. Again, these restrictions may be in respect of active and passive sales, or only active sales.[42]

(v) Field of Use Restrictions

Field of use restrictions confine the licensee to exploitation of the technology within certain technical fields of application. Technology may be exploited in different ways, for example, a patented chemical may be used to produce both fertilizers and pesticides. A licensor may wish to grant a licence to exploit only one or some of the uses, or to grant licences for different uses to different licensees.[43]

Field of use restrictions may be difficult to distinguish from, and have the same effect as, customer allocation as different customers may require the technology for different purposes. Thus in *French State/Suralmo*,[44] the Commission objected to provisions dividing the exploitation of engine technology for use in military equipment and use in civilian equipment respectively. The Commission explains the distinction in the Guidelines on technology transfer agreements.[45]

---

[41] See *supra* Chap. 9.

[42] A licence is unlikely *only* to ban passive sales.

[43] Guidelines, para. 179.

[44] Commission's *IXth Report on Competition Policy* (Commission, 1979), part 114.

[45] Guidelines, para. 180, see *infra* n. 265 and accompanying text.

(vi) Tying and Bundling

Tying and bundling on the part of dominant undertakings was discussed in Chapter 7.[46] In the context of the licensing of intellectual property rights it is described in the Guidelines on technology transfer agreements as follows:

In the context of technology licensing tying occurs when the licensor makes the licensing of one technology (the tying product) conditional upon the licensee taking a licence for another technology or purchasing a product from the licensor or someone designated by him (the tied product). Bundling occurs where two technologies or a technology and a product are only sold together as a bundle. In both cases, however, it is a condition that the products and technologies involved are distinct in the sense that there is distinct demand for each of the products and technologies forming part of the tie or the bundle. This is normally not the case where the technologies or products are by necessity linked in such a way that the licensed technology cannot be exploited without the tied product or both parts of the bundle cannot be exploited without the other . . . [47]

The licensor may use tying and bundling in order to exercise quality control over the licensee's output and maintain standards by ensuring that the licensee uses only certain inputs in his production process. It may be necessary for the licensee to use these inputs to ensure the proper exploitation of the intellectual property right. On the other hand it may also be a means of giving the licensor a guaranteed outlet for products not covered by intellectual property rights and foreclosing competitors from the licensee's custom.

(vii) Non-Compete Obligations

The licensor may wish to ensure that the licensee does not also use his own (or a third party's) technology to produce goods in competition with those produced under the licence. Limiting the licensee's ability to do this is one way of ensuring that the licensee produces a minimum amount under the licence and generates adequate royalties.

(viii) No-Challenge Clauses

The owner of a valid intellectual property right is able to sue anyone who infringes his right. What amounts to an infringing act depends on the nature of the intellectual property right. As explained above, a licence entitles another party to use the technology or other matter protected by the intellectual property right without infringing. However, he can only use it in accordance with the terms of the licence and these will normally entail the payment of royalties. Were the intellectual property right not valid he would be able to produce without payment and be free from the terms of the licence. A licensee exploiting licensed technology is in a good position to detect anything which might render the intellectual property right invalid (for example, that the subject-matter of a patent is obvious in the light of prior art and therefore not novel). Licensors, knowing this, often wish to insert 'no-challenge clauses' into licences which make it a breach of contract (and therefore actionable by damages) for the licensee to challenge the validity of the licensed intellectual property right or even to challenge the validity of *any* of the licensor's intellectual property rights. It should be noted, however, that it is not necessarily in the licensee's interest to establish the invalidity of the right because then anyone else may freely

---

[46] *Supra* 514 ff.
[47] Guidelines, para. 191.

use the hitherto protected subject matter (although the licensee may have a great advantage on the market in being already tooled up and producing).

(ix) Improvements

While exploiting the licensed technology the licensee may well develop improvements or further know-how. These may be severable or non-severable. A severable improvement is one which can be exploited without infringing the licensed technology. Unless prevented by the terms of the licence therefore the licensee could continue using it after the licence has expired and/or could license or assign it to third parties. Licensors, however, frequently want exclusive access to the improvements and want terms in the licence which oblige the licensee to 'grant back' severable improvements. This enables them to improve their own technology, prevent third parties gaining access to the improvements, and, perhaps, prevent the licensee from becoming a stronger competitor. They may also want to 'feed-on' improvements made by one licensee to the others.[48] Competition law may be concerned to limit the terms of severable improvements clauses. Non-severable improvements do not raise the same issues as they can be used only with the licensor's technology.

C. DEVELOPMENT OF COMPETITION POLICY TOWARDS LICENSING OF INTELLECTUAL PROPERTY RIGHTS

(i) General

The licensing of intellectual property rights helps to disseminate new technology, brings new competitors on to the market, and increases the rewards for innovation. Its effects are generally pro-competitive and beneficial to consumer welfare. It can be argued that since a licence of intellectual property rights allows a third party to exploit the rights, allowing it to do what would otherwise be unlawful, the grant of a licence opens up markets and does not restrict competition. It should not therefore infringe Article 81(1). However, it has been seen that licence agreements commonly contain provisions which go beyond a bare permission for the licensee to exploit the right.[49] Competition law has to decide whether, and in what circumstances, these further obligations have the effect of restricting competition.

The Commission's policy to intellectual property licensing agreements has developed and varied significantly over the years. Initially, a fairly permissive approach was adopted but, gradually, the Commission's attitude hardened and a more formalistic and interventionist approach was taken. The TTBER and Technology Transfer Guidelines, however, have heralded a more economic and effects based approach to these types of agreements. The Commission has played an extremely influential role in the development of policy in this area, especially as there have been comparatively few Court decisions on licensing. This is due to a number of factors, in

---

[48] The dynamics of this are complex. Feed-on arrangements disseminate technology but licensees will only be happy with the arrangements if they are getting as much out of them as they put in. If one licensee does all the innovation and the others get the benefits while contributing little to the common knowledge the first licensee may lose the incentive to innovate and will certainly not be keen to reveal his improvements. See further W. Cornish and D. Llewelyn, *Intellectual Property: Patents, Copyright, Trade Marks and Allied Rights* (5th edn., Sweet & Maxwell, 2003), 7–26.

[49] See discussion of such clauses *supra*.

particular that: parties granted an Article 81(3) exemption had little incentive to challenge the decision (even if they had to change the agreement to obtain the exemption); and because from 1984 onwards block exemptions covered patent licences (and mixed patent/know-how licences and later pure know-how licences too).[50] Therefore after 1984 the name of the game was for the parties to enter into licensing arrangements which were covered by the block exemptions wherever possible. The importance of the block exemptions has meant that an enormous amount of lobbying and discussion has gone on whenever new block exemptions have been drawn up, as exemplified by the activity which preceded the adoption of the latest TTBER, Regulation 772/2004.[51] The judgments of the Court which *have* been given, however, are of great importance. This is particularly true of the judgment of the ECJ in *Nungesser* (the *Maize Seeds* case)[52] which was significant in the development not only of the law on licensing but also on the question of what amounts to a restriction of competition for the purposes of Article 81(1) generally.[53]

(ii) The Evolution of the Commission's Policy towards Licensing Agreements

The Commission's early attitude, illustrated by its 1962 notice on patent licensing agreements (the so-called Christmas Message)[54] was that even exclusive patent licensing agreements did not fall within Article 81(1) so long as the restrictions did not go beyond the 'scope of the patent'.[55]

Later, however, the Commission's attitude began to change and it moved towards the position that exclusive licences, unless *de minimis*, always fell within Article 81 and that many common non-territorial restraints also went beyond the scope of the patent and violated Article 81(1). This essentially led to the position that a patent (or other) licence which went beyond a simple right to exploit a patented invention against payment of royalties would violate Article 81(1) and require exemption.[56] The Commission's sharp change in attitude was triggered by the development of the exhaustion of rights doctrine and the elaboration of the existence/exercise dichotomy[57] as more intellectual property rights issues came before the Court and were notified to the Commission. Significant to this change, was the ECJ's judgment in *Consten & Grundig*[58] in which it dealt with a trade mark licence which had been used as a mechanism to create absolute territorial protection for the distributor/licensee and to seal off the French market. The Commission became acutely conscious of the potential of exclusive licensing agreements for isolating markets. It was haunted by the idea that if the licensor had not given an *exclusive* licence he might have given a *non-exclusive* one, which would have led to competition between the different licensees in the same territory.

---

[50] See *infra* 797–8.

[51] [2004] OJ L123/11.

[52] Case 258/78, *Nungesser* v. *Commission* [1982] ECR 2015, [1983] 1 CMLR 278. See *infra* 791.

[53] See *supra* Chap. 4.

[54] 24 Dec. 1962 [1962–3] JO 2922/62, finally withdrawn in 1984 [1984] OJ C220/14. The same approach could be seen in Art. 4(2)(b) of Reg. 17, [1959–62] OJ Spec.Ed.87, as amended by Council Reg. 1216/1999 [1999] OJ L148/5, which classed a narrow category of licensing agreements as non-notifiable.

[55] See further See further S. Anderman, *EC Competition Law and Intellectual Property Rights* (Clarendon Press, 1998), 53–4.

[56] See, e.g., The Commission Fourth Report on Competition Policy (1974), point 20.

[57] See *supra* 781–4.

[58] *Ibid.*

In the real world, however, licensees will frequently not entertain any licence but an exclusive (or at least a sole) one. The commercial risk is too great. The choice is often therefore between an exclusive licence and no licence, not between an exclusive or a non-exclusive one. The Commission was frequently criticized for considering matters with hindsight, *ex post*, rather than *ex ante*, as the parties would have done, when the transaction might well have looked risky.[59] Nevertheless, throughout the 1970s the Commission held in a series of decisions that exclusive licences were restrictive of competition and so came within Article 81(1). However, so long as the parties were willing to modify the exclusivity clauses and other provisions held to be restrictions (such as tie-ins, no-challenge clauses and grant-backs of improvements), the Commission would exempt them under Article 81(3).[60]

The broad interpretation of Article 81(1) of course created a pressing need for some form of block exemption.[61] With the experience it gained from handling notified licensing agreements, the Commission set about constructing a block exemption regulation on patent licences. The first draft was produced in 1979 but there were lengthy negotiations with Member States, business, and other interested parties. The Commission also waited to take account of the ECJ's judgment in *Nungesser*, the appeal from its 1978 decision in *Maize Seeds*.[62] The first intellectual property licensing block exemption was finally adopted in 1984.[63]

(iii) Exclusivity and Territorial Restrictions in the Case Law of the Court

The ECJ never endorsed such a strict approach to exclusivity as that adopted by the Commission. This is shown by its judgment in *Nungesser* (*Maize Seeds*), the first judgment after *Consten & Grundig* in which it had to deal with an exclusive licence. The case concerned plant breeders' rights but the principles set out in the judgment are not limited to this type of right.[64]

Case 258/78, *Nungesser* v. *EC Commission* [1982] ECR 2015, [1983] 1 CMLR 278

INRA, a French State research institute, developed new strains of hybrid maize seed of great importance in European agriculture. Acting through FRAESMA, a French company set up to deal with INRA's seed varieties, it gave Kurt Eisele (later Nungesser KG) the exclusive right to produce and distribute INRA varieties in Germany. INRA agreed with Eisele not to import its seed into Germany itself and to prevent others from doing so. Eisele relied on the rights in Germany to

---

[59] See discussion of Cases 56 and 58 164, *Etablissements Consten SA & Grundig-Verkaufs-GmbH* v. *Commission* [1966] ECR 299, [1966] CMLR 418, *supra* Chap. 4.

[60] See, e.g. *Re the Agreements of Davidson Rubber Co* [1972] OJ L143/31 [1972] CMLR D52; *Burroughs/Deplanque* [1972] OJ L13/50 [1972] CMLR D67; *Raymond/Nagoya* [1972] OJ L143/39, [1972] CMLR D45; *Bronbemaling* v. *Heidemaatschappij* [1975] OJ L249/27, [1975] 2 CMLR D67; *AOIP* v. *Beyrard* [1976] OJ L6/8, [1976] 1 CMLR D14.

[61] See *supra* Chaps 2–4.

[62] [1978] OJ L286/23, [1978] 3 CMLR 434.

[63] Commission Reg. 2349/84 on patent licences, [1984] OJ L219/15.

[64] See *infra* 794. Plant breeders' rights were excluded from the scope of block exemption Reg. 2349/84 [1984] OJ L219/15 on patent licensing but were covered by the block exemption on technology transfer agreements, Commission Reg. 240/96: [1996] OJ L31/2, and are now covered by Reg. 772/2004 (the TTBER).

prevent parallel importers from importing seed obtained from another source in France. One importer settled the action, but another complained to the Commission.

The Commission held that the exclusivity and territorial protection provisions were caught by Article [81(1)] and could not be exempted. Eisele/Nungesser appealed.

Court of Justice

41. Th[e] synopsis of the German legislation shows that seeds certified and approved for marketing are subject to quality control on the part of the public authorities and that that control extends to the stability of the variety. However, breeders' rights are not intended to substitute for controls carried out by the competent authorities, controls carried out by the owner of those rights, but to confer on the owner a kind of protection, the nature and effects of which all derive from private law. From that point of view the legal position of a breeder of seeds is not difficult from that of the owner of patent or trade mark rights over a product subject to strict control by the public authorities, as is the case with pharmaceutical products.

. . . .

43. It is therefore not correct to consider that breeder's rights are a species of commercial or industrial property right with characteristics of so special a nature as to require, in relation to the competition rules, a different treatment from other commercial or industrial property rights. That conclusion does not affect the need to take into consideration, for the purposes of the rules on competition, the specific nature of the products which form the subject-matter of breeders' rights.

. . .

48. The statement of reasons on which the decision is based refers to two sets of circumstances in order to justify the application of Article [81(1)] to the exclusive licence in question (II, No. 3). The accuracy of the facts thus stated has not been challenged.

49. The first set of circumstances is described as follows . . .

'By licensing a single undertaking to exploit his breeders' rights in a given territory, the licensor deprives himself for the entire duration of the contract of the ability to issue licences to other undertakings in the same territory . . .'

'By undertaking not to produce or market the product himself in the territory covered by the contract the licensor likewise eliminates himself, as well as Frasema and its members, as suppliers in that territory.'

50. Corresponding to that part of the statement of reasons is Article 1(b) of the decision, which in its first and second indents declares the exclusive nature of the licence granted by the 1965 contract to be contrary to Article [81(1)] of the Treaty in so far as it imposes:

An obligation upon INRA or those deriving rights through INRA to refrain from having the relevant seeds produced or sold by other licensees in German, and An obligation upon INRA or those deriving rights through INRA to refrain from producing or selling the relevant seed in Germany themselves.

51. The second set of circumstances referred to in the decision is described as follows:

'The fact that third parties may not import the same seed [namely the seed under licence] from other Community countries into Germany, or export from Germany to other Community countries, leads to market sharing and deprives German farmers of any real room for negotiation since seed is supplied by one supplier and one supplier only.'

52. That part of the statement of reasons is also reflected in Article 1 (b) of the decision, which in its third and fourth indents declares the exclusive nature of the licence granted by the 1965

contract to be contrary to Article [81(1)] of the Treaty in so far as it imposes:

> An obligation upon INRA or those deriving rights through INRA to prevent third parties from exporting the relevant seeds to Germany without the licensee's authorization for use or sale there, and Mr Eisele's concurrent use of his exclusive contractual rights and his own breeder's rights to prevent all imports into Germany or exports to other Member States of the relevant seeds.

53. It should be observed that those two sets of considerations relate to two legal situations which are not necessarily identical. The first case concerns a so-called open exclusive licence or assignment and the exclusivity of the licence relates solely to the contractual relationship between the owner of the right and the licensee, whereby the owner merely undertakes not to grant other licences in respect of the same territory and not to compete himself with the licensee on that territory. On the other hand, the second case involves an exclusive licence or assignment with absolute territorial protection, under which the parties to the contact propose, as regards the products and the territory in question, to eliminate all competition from third parties, such as parallel importers or licensees for other territories.

54. That point having been clarified, it is necessary to examine whether, in the present case, the exclusive nature of the licence, in so far as it is an open licence, has the effect of preventing or distorting competition with the meaning of Article [81(1)] of the Treaty.

55. In that respect the Government of the Federal Republic of Germany emphasized that the protection of agricultural innovations by means of breeders' rights constitutes a means of encouraging such innovations and the grant of exclusive rights for a limited period, is capable of providing a further incentive to innovative efforts.

From that it infers that a total prohibition of every exclusive licence, even an open one, would cause the interest of undertakings in licences to fall away, which would be prejudicial to the dissemination of knowledge and techniques in the Community.

56. The exclusive licence which forms the subject-matter of the contested decision concerns the cultivation and marketing of hybrid maize seeds which were developed by INRA after years of research and experimentation and were unknown to German farmers at the time when the co-operation between INRA and the applicants was taking shape. For that reason the concern shown by the interveners as regards the protection of new technology is justified.

57. In fact, in the case of a licence of breeders' rights over hybrid maize seeds newly developed in one Member State, an undertaking established in another Member State which was not certain that it would not encounter competition from other licensees for the territory granted to it, or from the owner of the right himself, might be deterred from accepting the risk of cultivating and marketing that product; such a result would be damaging to the dissemination of a new technology and would prejudice competition in the Community between the new product and similar existing products.

58. Having regard to the specific nature of the products in question, the Court concludes that in a case such as the present, the grant of an open exclusive licence, that is to say a licence which does not affect the position of third parties such as parallel importers and licensees for other territories, is not in itself incompatible with Article [81(1)] of the Treaty.

59. Part B of the third submission is thus justified to the extent to which it concerns that aspect of the exclusive nature of the licence.

. . .

76. It must be remembered that under the terms of Article [81(3)] of the Treaty an exemption from the prohibition contained in Article [81(1)] may be granted in the case of any agreement between undertakings which contributes to improving the production or distribution of goods or to promoting technical progress, and which does not impose on the undertakings concerned restrictions which are not indispensable to the attainment of those objectives.

> 77. As it is a question of seeds intended to be used by a large number of farmers for the pro-
> duction of maize, which is an important product for human and animal foodstuffs, absolute territo-
> rial protection manifestly goes beyond what is indispensable for the improvement of production or
> distribution or the promotion of technical progress, as is demonstrated in particular in the present
> case by the prohibition, agreed to by both parties to the agreement of any parallel imports of INRA
> maize seeds into Germany even if those seeds were bred by INRA itself and marketed in France.
>
> 78. It follows that the absolute territorial protection conferred on the licensee, as established
> to exist by the contested decision, constituted a sufficient reason for refusing to grant an exemp-
> tion under Article [81(3)] of the Treaty. It is therefore no longer necessary to examine the other
> grounds set out in the decision for refusing to grant such an exemption.

In this judgment the ECJ distinguished between 'open' and 'closed' exclusive licences (paragraph 53). On the one hand there is an 'open' licence which pertains only to the position between licensor and licensee. The licensor agrees not to grant further licences in the same territory and not to operate there itself. On the other hand there is a licence containing provisions which affect third parties and which create absolute territorial protection.[65]

The distinction between 'open' licences and others is not completely clear as the Court did not expressly deal with a situation where the provisions fall short of granting absolute terri-torial protection, for example where restrictions on the licensee's activities outside the licensed territory are imposed. Presumably a provision whereby the licensee undertakes not to compete with the *licensor* in the latter's territory is covered by the 'open' designation, as it 'relates solely to the contractual relationship between the owner of the right and the licensee'. However, it appears that any further limitation on the licensee, other than an obligation not to *produce* out-side its allocated territory, renders the licence closed rather than open.[66] The Commission held in *Boussois/Interpane*[67] that a licence which prohibited a licensee from selling outside its territory was closed.

As far as open licences are concerned, the Court did not conclude in *Nungesser* that the exclu-sivity provisions automatically infringed Article 81(1), as the Commission had done. Instead the Court looked at the licence in its economic context: if the exclusivity provisions were necessary to induce the licensee to enter the transaction then competition was not restricted. It should be noted that the Court's realistic approach was limited. In paragraphs 77 and 78 the Court con-demned outright the clauses leading to the imposition of absolute territorial protection without considering their possible economic justifications.[68] Not only were these provisions automat-ically caught by Article 81(1), they did not qualify for exemption under Article 81(3).

The principles in *Nungesser* apply to other kinds of 'manufacturing' licences involving the licensing of patents and know-how, and not just to plant breeders' rights. The general applic-ability of *Nungesser* to such transactions is manifest from the Court's rationale for holding the open exclusive licence outside Article 81(1), (i.e., the need to provide incentives for investment by the licensee). This can apply equally to other kinds of right. However, it can be seen from paragraph 58 of *Nungesser* that, in deciding whether or not Article 81(1) applies, regard has to be

---

[65] See the discussion of exclusive and sole licences and sales restrictions *supra* section 5.B.

[66] See M. Siragusa, 'EEC Technology Transfers—A Private View' [1982] *Fordham Corp L Inst* 95, 116–18.

[67] [1987] OJ L50/30, a know-how rather than a patent licence, but the difference does not appear to have been relevant.

[68] See further the discussion of the application of Article 81(3) generally, *supra* Chap. 4.

had to the specific nature of the *products* in question. In the subsequent case of *Erauw-Jacquéry* the nature of the products concerned was crucial to the Court's finding that even an export ban could be outside Article 81(1). *Erauw-Jacquéry* concerned basic seed, which is seed which can lawfully be used to propagate further seed, as distinct from the certified seed sold to produce crops. Plant breeders' rights in basic seeds are particularly vulnerable as they can easily be lost.[69]

Case 27/87, *Erauw-Jacquéry* v. *La Hesbignonne* [1988] ECR 1919, [1988] 4 CMLR 576

The owner of plant breeders' rights licensed them to a co-operative on the terms that the co-operative could propagate basic seed and sell seed of the first or second generation but could not sell or export basic seed. The Court of Justice recognized the need for quality control and for assuring the proper handling of the basic seed by those allowed to propagate it. Advocate General Mischo likened the situation to one of a franchise, where the franchisor is justified in preventing its know-how benefiting competitors.

Court of Justice

8. In the first place the national court seeks to ascertain whether the provision prohibiting the holder of the licence for propagating basic seed from selling, assigning or exporting that seed falls within Article [81(1)] of the Treaty.

9. The Commission and the breeder maintain that the provision prohibiting the sale and exportation of E2 basic seed, which is placed at the disposal of the growers only for the purposes of propagation, is not contrary to Article [81(1)] of the Treaty. Such a provision falls within the ambit of the plant breeder's rights.

10. In this respect, it must be pointed out that, as the Court acknowledged in its judgment of 8 June 1982 (in Case 258/78 *Nungesser* v. *Commission* [1982] ECR 2015), the development of the basic lines may involve considerable financial commitment. Consequently, a person who has made considerable efforts to develop varieties of basic seed which may be the subject-matter of plant breeders' rights must be allowed to protect himself against any improper handling of those varieties of seed. To that end, the breeder must be entitled to restrict propagation to the growers which he has selected as licensees. To that extent, the provision prohibiting the licensee from selling and exporting basic seed falls outside the prohibition contained in Article [81(1)].

11. Therefore, the answer to the first part of the question referred by the national court must be that a provision of an agreement concerning the propagation and sale of seed, in respect of which one of the parties is the holder or the agent of the holder of certain plant breeders' rights, which prohibits the licensee from selling and exporting the basic seed is compatible with Article [81(1)] of the Treaty in so far as it is necessary in order to enable the breeder to select the growers who are to be licensees.

The Court in this case stressed the need to protect the licensor's investment. The Court recognized the particularly fragile nature of basic seed and was prepared to hold that in these special circumstances absolute territorial protection was not within Article 81(1). The Court referred

---

[69] They are subject to cancellation if they cease to be stable or uniform. See in the UK the Plant Varieties and Seeds Act 1997 ss. 4(2) and 22 and, in respect of Community plant variety, Articles 8, 9, and 21 of Reg. 2100/94 [1994] OJ L227/1.

to *Nungesser*, but in that case, where certified rather than basic seed was concerned, the absolute territorial protection caused the agreement both to infringe Article 81(1) and to be denied exemption pursuant to Article 81(3).[70]

(iv) Non-Territorial Restraints

The Commission also took the view that many non-territorial restraints in licences restricted competition within the meaning of Article 81(1). Its approach is exemplified by the *Windsurfing* case.[71]

Windsurfing International (WI), an American company founded by Hoyle Schweitzer, granted a number of non-exclusive licences of its German patent for windsurfing equipment to firms within the Community. Litigation was current in Germany over whether or not the patent covered both the rig and the board, but the Commission proceeded on the basis that it covered only the rig. The Commission found that the following provisions concerning quality control, tying, licensed-by notices, no-challenge clauses, and royalty calculation, infringed Article 81(1):

- an obligation on the licensee to mount the patented rig only on boards approved by the licensor; the Commission rejected WI's contention that this was a permissible measure of quality control, as the controls did not relate to a product covered by the patent and were not laid down in advance on the basis of objectively verifiable criteria;

- an obligation on the licensee to sell the rigs only as part of a complete sailboard, and not separately; the Commission held that an obligation arbitrarily placed on a licensee to sell the patented product only in conjunction with a product outside the scope of the patent was not indispensable to the exploitation of the patent;

- an obligation on the licensee to pay royalties calculated on the net selling price of the whole sailboard and not just the rig; the Commission held that this method of calculation could be justified only where 'the number of items manufactured or consumed or their value are difficult to establish separately in a complex production process or ... there is for the patented item on its own no separate demand which the licensee would be prevented from satisfying through such a method of calculation';

- an obligation on the licensee to affix to boards manufactured and marketed in Germany a notice saying 'licensed by Hoyle Schweitzer' or 'licensed by Windsurfing International'; the Commission said that this created the false impression that the board as well as the rig was covered by the patent;

- an obligation on the licensees to acknowledge the word marks 'Windsurfer' and 'Windsurfing' as well as a design mark or logo as valid trade marks; the Commission considered this tantamount to a no-challenge clause to the validity of the trade mark, while WI claimed it was part of an attempt to stop its trade mark being used as a generic designation;

---

[70] The Commission emphasized the special nature of basic seeds in its comment on the case in the *XVIII Report on Competition Policy Commission*, (1989) part 103; in *Sicasov* [1999] OJ L4/27, [1999] 4 CMLR 192 the Commission applied *Erauw-Jacquery* to another licence of basic seed.

[71] *Windsurfing International* OJ [1982] L229/1, [1984] 1 CMLR 1, Case 193/83, *Windsurfing International v. EC Commission* [1986] ECR 611, [1986] 3 CMLR 489. Note, that although the Commission no longer adopts such a formatistic approach, it cites *Windsurfing* in the Guidelines, para. 81, when explaining why price-fixing within the hardcore restriction list in Article 4(1)(a) includes agreements whereby royalties are calculated on the basis of all product sales irrespective of whether the licensed technology is being used.

- an obligation on the licensees to restrict production of the licensed product to specific manufacturing plant in Germany; the Commission rejected the plea that this was a measure of quality control and held that it limited freedom of competition by means of a clause which had nothing to do with the patent; neither the Commission nor the Court dealt with the position of a prohibition relating only to territories where there was patent protection;

- an obligation on the licensees not to challenge the validity of the licensed patents; the Commission had long held that no-challenge clauses restrict competition and that it is in the public interest that invalid patents should be challenged.

The ECJ, which agreed that the Commission was justified in treating the patent as covering only the rig, upheld all of the Commission's findings except for (c), where it held that the global calculation of royalties on the complete sailboard was not a restriction of competition on the sale of separate *rigs*, although it was on the sale of *boards*. Like the Commission, the ECJ took a highly formalistic approach and condemned the other provisions for going beyond the 'scope of the patent' and the 'specific subject-matter of the patent' without engaging in any economic analysis. As one critical commentator put it, the judgment as a whole is 'based on the assumptions that there is something inherently anti-competitive in the patent monopoly and that patent licenses [*sic*], even when arguably vertical in nature, differ fundamentally from distribution arrangements and warrant stricter treatment'.[72]

As the agreements had not been notified to the Commission, the ECJ did not have to rule on the compatibility of the agreement with Article 81(3) and whether the Commission had been correct to hold that the agreement could not have been exempted. Between the date of the decision in *Windsurfing* and the judgment the Commission had adopted the block exemption Regulation on patent licensing agreements, 2349/84.[73] Both the decision and the judgment reflected the approach taken by the Commission in the block exemption.

(v) The Block Exemptions on Patent Licensing and Know-How Licensing Prior to 1 May 2004

Despite the urgent need for block exemptions caused by the broad interpretation of Article 81(1) in the field of intellectual property licensing agreements, the first block exemption was not adopted until 1984. Regulation 2349/84[74] applied to pure patent licensing agreements or to mixed patent and know-how licensing agreements where the patent was the predominant element. The second block exemption, Regulation 556/89,[75] applied to pure know-how licensing agreements and to mixed know-how and patent licensing agreements where know-how was the predominant element. Both exemptions applied only to bilateral agreements. The two Regulations were very similar: Article 1 set out the type of agreement covered and exempted certain restrictions of competition, mainly relating to exclusivity; Article 2 contained a 'white list' of provisions which did not normally restrict competition but were exempted just in case; Article 3 contained the 'black list' of provisions whose inclusion in an agreement took it outside the exemption; and Article 4 contained the opposition procedure.[76]

---

[72] J. Venit, 'In the Wake of Windsurfing: Patent Licensing in the Common Market' [1986] *Fordham Corp L Inst* 517, 560–1.

[73] [1984] OJ L219/15.

[74] [1984] OJ L219/15.

[75] [1989] OJ L61/1.

[76] See *supra* Chap. 4, 88.

Patents and know-how are commonly licensed together and which element, if any, predominates depends on the precise terms of the agreement. Although they were very similar, there were material differences in the Regulations, some of which favoured the licensor and some the licensee. Lawyers could sometimes structure their clients' agreements to produce one sort of transaction rather than another in order to exploit these differences. Both Regulations were replaced in 1996 by a single block exemption, Regulation 240/96 on technology transfer agreements.[77] The title denoted that it encompassed any transaction in which the predominant element was the licensing of patents or know-how. Compared to the previous Regulations it had a shortened 'black-list' of prohibited clauses and a longer 'white-list', reflecting the Commission's further experience of licensing arrangements and a more sophisticated view of what really restricts competition and could not be exempted. More agreements fell within this exemption, therefore, than within the earlier regulations. Regulation 240/96 applied to agreements concluded after 31 March 1996. It was replaced on 1 May 2004 by Regulation 772/2004 on technology transfer agreements (the TTBER).[78]

D. THE ADOPTION OF THE TTBER AND THE TECHNOLOGY TRANSFER GUIDELINES

(i) The Commission's Review Process and the Adoption of the New Measures

In December 2001 the Commission adopted a mid-term review Report on the application of Regulation 240/96, pursuant to Article 12 of that Regulation.[79] The report concluded that the Regulation was too formalistic, narrow and 'straitjacketing', catching some pro-competitive agreements while missing anti-competitive ones, and that it was out of line with the approach of newer block exemptions.

> ## Evaluation Report on the Transfer of Technology Block Exemption Regulation No. 240/96
>
> (175) Firstly, the TTBE is generally considered overly formalistic and too complex and in addition too narrow in scope. It does not cover a number of licensing arrangements that do not pose great risks to competition and this problem seems to increase with new trends in licensing. In some cases, by imposing on companies an unnecessary compliance burden and forcing industry into a legal straitjacket, the TTBE may skew enforcement towards overdeterrence, which may have a negative impact on dynamic efficiency.
>
> (176) Secondly, it does not seem to place sufficient weight on inter-brand issues and does not follow a consistent approach as regards the competitive relationship between licensors and licensees. It thereby may cover certain licensing arrangements that do not deserve coverage because they may work to the detriment of competition and result in a reduction of dynamic and allocative efficiency.
>
> (177) Lastly, the TTBE is out of line with the recent reforms concerning vertical and horizontal agreements, which affects the coherence of Community competition policy and the predictability of the rules.

[77] [1996] OJ L31/2.

[78] [2004] OJ L123/11.

[79] *Evaluation Report on the Transfer of Technology Block Exemption Regulation No. 240/96*, on the Commission's web site, http://www.europa.eu.int/comm/competition/antitrust/technology_transfer/en.pdf.

The reforms to which reference was made in paragraph 177 were the 'new generation' block exemptions, the Verticals Regulation (1999)[80] and the block exemptions for specialization agreements[81] and for research and development (R&D) agreements[82] (2000). Less than four years separated Regulation 240/96 from the Verticals Regulation but in that period the Commission had adopted a new pattern of block exemptions and a more economic approach to the assessment of agreements. The new Regulations had moved away from a legalistic approach based on form, to a more economic one, focussed on the effects of the agreement. Moreover, it had become apparent by 2001 that the Commission's proposals for modernizing the system for applying the competition rules[83] were likely to be adopted. The Commission began to think that although Regulation 240/96 was not due to expire until 2006 it would be desirable for a more 'modern' block exemption on technology transfer to be put in place.[84]

The Commission invited (and received) comments on the Evaluation Report[85] and decided to produce a new block exemption and accompanying guidelines. It put out a draft of each of these on 1 October 2003. There followed a period of heated debate and much lobbying. The Commission received over seventy submissions on its proposals.[86]

The critics were most concerned that the draft proposed a 'safe harbour' only for undertakings whose market shares were below certain thresholds. The block exemption would not apply where these thresholds were exceeded. Although a market share cap was in line with the other new block exemptions it caused particular consternation in respect of IP licences. Market share is notoriously difficult to assess in many IP licensing situations because, primarily, of the market definition problems and is in any case arguably an inappropriate and arbitrary indicator of the real competitive situation in technology markets.[87] Moreover, the draft proposed a different threshold according to whether the agreement was between 'competitors' or 'non-competitors'.[88] The narrower reach of the proposed block exemption combined with the proposed removal of the notification system meant that companies would face less legal certainty, and *ex post* control of the agreements by the Commission, NCAs or (much more likely in respect of licensing agreements) national courts if the validity of the licence was challenged. Furthermore, there were great concerns about other provisions in the draft. For example, although the Commission proposed a more flexible block exemption than Regulation 240/96

---

[80] Reg. 2790/99 [1999] OJ L336/21, discussed *supra* Chap. 9.

[81] Reg. 2658/2000 [2000] OJ L304/3, discussed *infra* Chap. 13.

[82] Reg. 2659/2000 [2000] OJ L 304/7, discussed *infra* Chap. 13.

[83] Commission's White Paper on modernisation of the rules implementing Articles 85 and 86 [now 81 and 82] of the EC Treaty [1999] OJ C132/1.

[84] The 'opposition procedure' in Reg. 240/96, Article 4 (see *supra* n. 78) would, anyway, not have worked in a system without provision for the notification of agreements. Also, with the abolition of notification and exemption, guidelines were desirable to assist undertakings make their own assessment of agreements outside the block exemption.

[85] Published on the Commission's web site on 19 July 2002.

[86] From industry, trade associations, law and IP societies, individual law firms, national authorities, individual companies, universities and consultants, still available on DGComp's web site, http://ec.europa.eu/comm/competition/antitrust/technology_transfer_2/. And see also the speech by Commissioner Mario Monti, 'The New EU Policy on Technology Transfer Agreements', Ecole des Mines, Paris, 16 Jan. 2004, available on the Commission's web site, http://www.europa.eu.int/comm/competition/speeches/index_speeches_by_the_commissioner.html.

[87] See, e.g., the submission of the International Chamber of Commerce to the Commission, available on the Commission's web site, but c.f. M. Monti, speech of 16 Jan. 2004, *supra* n. 86 + *infra* n. 91 and accompanying text.

[88] There was also concern that parties might start life as non-competitors but move into the competitor category during the lifetime of the agreement, with serious consequences for its validity.

the draft contained a list of hardcore restrictions which in some respects was more severe than the blacklist in 240/96, and a list of 'excluded' restrictions.[89] The Guidelines too were criticized, in particular for their approach to incentives to innovation.[90]

The Commission accepted some, but by no means all, of these criticisms. The Competition Commissioner explained the Commission's response to the consultation exercise in a speech in Paris.[91] Above all, the Commission adhered to its decision to impose market share thresholds despite pressure to drop them:

> The use of market share thresholds is mainly opposed because it is considered that market shares are of no relevance in high tech sectors, that the assessment of market shares throughout the life of the agreement decreases legal certainty and is costly and furthermore that relevant product and geographic markets are often difficult to define.
>
> Let me first recall that the TTBER applies to all sectors not just high tech ones. It is fair to state that most sectors are mature and that even sectors that are in such a state of flux are so usually only for a limited period. Therefore in most sectors, and that also means in most sectors where licensing takes place, market shares do matter. In addition, usually licensing concerns products that either will continue to compete with existing products or that will replace existing products. There are not many products which cater to a human need for which nothing existed before. Therefore market definition in case of licensing will not be markedly more difficult than market definition for most other agreements.[92]

The Commission had, in any event, a limited time in which to prepare the final version of the new regulation and guidelines as time's wingèd chariot brought 1 May 2004 ever nearer.[93] The new block exemption, Regulation 772/2004 on the application of Article 81(3) of the Treaty to categories of technology transfer agreements (hereafter the TTBER), was adopted, and accompanying Guidelines published, on 7 April 2004.[94] Regulation 772/2004 came into force on 1 May 2004.

(ii) Methodology

The TTBER and the Guidelines must be considered as a whole. The TTBER obviously provides the key block exemption for technology transfer agreements but the Guidelines go further, doing three things. First, they set out a framework of general principles concerning Article 81 and intellectual property rights. Secondly, they explain the provisions and application of the TTBER. Thirdly, they explain the application of Article 81(1) and Article 81(3) to agreements

---

[89] For example, the territorial and customer restrictions were stricter. For the meaning of 'excluded' restrictions, see *infra* 825 and *supra* Chap. 9.

[90] See, e.g., Charles River Associates Ltd, *Competition Policy Discussion Papers 8* (Nov. 2003), available at http://www.crai.co.uk and on the Commission's web site as a submission to the Commission's consultation on the draft. Charles Rivers Associates was the consultants responsible for the preparation of the Commission report, *Multiparty Licensing* (April 2003), available on http://www.crai.uk and on www.europa.eu.int/comm/competition/antitrust/legislation/multiparty_licensing.pdf.

[91] Mario Monti, 'The New EU Policy on Technology Transfer Agreements', Ecole des Mines, Paris, 16 Jan. 2004.

[92] *Ibid.*

[93] There was no legal necessity to adopt the new measures by 1 May 2004, but the Commission had imposed the target on itself and wished the technology transfer reforms to be part of the whole modernization package.

[94] Regulation 772/2004 [2004] OJ L 123/11 (the Regulation is stated there to be 'of 27 April 2004' and signed by Commissioner Monti on behalf of the Commission on that date but this was subject to a corrigendum in [2004] OJ L127/58 stating that the date should have been 7 April 2004); Commission Guidelines on the application of Article 81 of the EC Treaty to technology transfer agreements [2004] OJ C101/2.

outside the scope of the TTBER. This latter role is of utmost importance in the regime post modernization as the new TTBER now plays a reduced role compared with that played by the previous IP licensing block exemptions. The introduction of market share thresholds into the TTBER means that it provides less legal certainty than its predecessors and operates more as a 'safe harbour' providing, along with the Guidelines, a framework for analysis.[95] Where individual analysis is required, further insight into the Commission's thinking can be found in the Article 81(3) Guidelines[96] which set out general guidance on Article 81(1), Article 81(3) and their interrelationship. Anderman and Kallaugher explain the central importance of the Guidelines in the 2004 framework.

S. D. Anderman and J. Kallaugher, *Technology Transfer and the New EU Competition Rules: Intellectual Property Licensing after Modernisation* (Oxford University Press, 2006)

1.19 The Guidelines are the real centrepiece of the reformed treatment of technology transfer under Article 81. The Guidelines commence with a summary of the general principles applicable under the new paradigm. The Guidelines continue with a detailed and useful summary of the TTBER and the conditions for its application. They then law out a 'general framework for analysis'-applying the general principles set out in the first section to intellectual property licensing. They conclude by applying this analytical framework to a host of specific restrictions commonly found in IP licences. The central theme of the Guidelines is the need to identify competitive harm and to identify economic benefits that might outweigh those competitive harms in order to determine whether a licence agreement raised Article 81 issues.

1.20 The system of assessment created by the Guidelines entails a fundamental change in the way that practitioners must address competition law issues in the intellectual property context. In place of a purely legalistic evaluation of the contents of licensing agreements, the new system demands a new type of legal and economic assessment of individual agreements. The old system offered legal certainty and this was important for technology transfer agreement because of the ever present risk that licensees might go into competition with their licensors once they mastered the problems of efficient manufacture of the new technology. However, it also created a tight corset or legal straitjacket. The parties had to adjust their commercial arrangements to fit the legal rules or forgo the benefits of legally certain enforceability of the commercial agreement throughout its duration. For those commercial agreement whose curves could fit within the corset of the BER, there were considerably benefits. However, for those commercial agreements whose contours were either too angular or too plump to fit within the golden corset, there was a form of legal limbo.

1.21 The new reform entails some benefits to intellectual property owners. First, the Commission has finally recognised that 'vertical' licensing agreements, or agreements between non-competitors should systematically be treated more leniently than 'horizontal' licensing agreements, agreements between competitors. A lighter regulatory burden on purely vertical

---

[95] 'Previous BERS in the IP licensing field conferred an exemption on parties without market share and subject only to a formal power of withdrawal by the Commission or a national competition authority. If there was a blacklisted provision in the agreement, the agreement was unexemptable and unenforceable. In the current group of BERs, including the TTBER, the BER takes a reduced role within the legal framework'. S. D. Anderman and J. Kallaugher *Technology Transfer and the New EU Competition Rules: Intellectual Property Licensing after Modernisation* (Oxford University Press, 2006), 1.16.

[96] Guidelines on the application of Article 81(3) of the Treaty [2004] OJ C101/2.

licensing agreements is entirely appropriate because such agreements present fewer risks to competition. Secondly, there are benefits for the parties to licensing in the reduced list of hard core restrictions in the new TTBER. These changes have meant that the new framework offers considerably greater flexibility to the parties to draft intellectual property licensing agreements to reflect their preferred underlying commercial bargain. No longer is it so necessary to distort commercial arrangements to fit the strictly defined categories offered by the existing BERs. The Guidelines to the interpretation of the TTBER as well as to the more general application of Article 81 to licensing agreements outside the scope of the TTBER are also an improvement in the regulatory framework.

1.22 However, these improvements in the regulatory structure are accompanied by serious costs. First, and most obvious, has been the loss of legal certainty in the applicability of the safe harbour of the TTBER owing to its market share limits. Under the previous TTBER an agreement normally retained its exemption for its entire duration. This allowed lawyers to enjoy the authority to determine the lawfulness of the licensing agreement with some finality. That type of legal certainty has disappeared to be replaced by a legal structure requiring a methodology to ensure continued legal enforceability for intellectual property licensing agreements.

1.23 Second, the new legal methodology itself requires a considerable adjustment by lawyers to a new methodology for assessing licensing agreements for the purposes of exemption. Since the TTBER has practically no value other than as a reference for identifying hard core restraints, effective counselling requires lawyers to learn the new skills required by the new paradigm as applied in the Guidelines. This in turn requires lawyers to accept the need to combine legal and economic analysis in vetting licensing agreements under Article 81.

Despite the limitations of the new TTBER, as with vertical agreements[97] the mere existence of the TTBER turns the appraisal of the agreement under Article 81 on its head. It encourages undertakings to consider first whether their agreement falls (or can be made to fall) within the safe harbour of the TTBER:

... many licence agreements fall outside Article 81(1), either because they do not restrict competition at all or because the restriction of competition is not appreciable ... To the extent that such agreements would anyhow fall within the scope of the TTBER, there is no need to determine whether they are caught by Article 81(1) ... [98]

Only if a technology transfer agreement does not fall within the TTBER (because, for instance, the market share threshold is exceeded) is it necessary to consider the application of Article 81(1) and 81(3).

In the next sections the general principles applicable to intellectual property rights and the general principles and framework for the assessment of technology transfer agreements set out in the Guidelines are considered. The provisions of the TTBER are then analysed prior to looking at how Article 81 applies to technology transfer agreements falling outside the safe harbour TTBER.[99]

It is important to remember that the Guidelines are not binding but might influence interpretation by a national competition authority or court in so far as they are consistent with the judgments of the ECJ.[100]

---

[97] See *supra* Chap. 9.

[98] The Guidelines, para. 36.

[99] The TTBER and the Guidelines apply by analogy to other types of agreement too, see *infra* 829.

[100] As the Commission recognizes in Guidelines, para. 4. See also discussion of nature of Commission notices and guidance *supra* Chaps. 2 and 3.

(iii) General Principles: Application of Article 81 to Intellectual Property Rights

The Commission sets out the general principles by which it approaches the application of Article 81 to intellectual property rights at the beginning of the Guidelines on the application of Article 81 to technology transfer agreements.[101] This section of the Guidelines considers the value of intellectual property rights and the relationship of intellectual property rights and competition law.[102]

1. Article 81 and intellectual property rights

5. The aim of Article 81 as a whole is to protect competition on the market with a view to promoting consumer welfare and an efficient allocation of resources. Article 81(1) prohibits all agreements and concerted practices between undertakings and decisions by associations of undertakings . . . which may affect trade between Member States . . . and which have as their object or effect the prevention, restriction or distortion of competition . . . As an exception to this rule Article 81(3) provides that the prohibition contained in Article 81(1) may be declared inapplicable in the case of agreements between undertakings which contribute to improving the production or distribution of products or to promoting technical or economic progress, while allowing consumers a fair share of the resulting benefits and which do not impose restrictions which are not indispensable to the attainment of these objectives and do not afford such undertakings the possibility of eliminating competition in respect of a substantial part of the products concerned.

6. Intellectual property laws confer exclusive rights on holders of patents, copyright, design rights, trademarks and other legally protected rights. The owner of intellectual property is entitled under intellectual property laws to prevent unauthorised use of his intellectual property and to exploit it, *inter alia*, by licensing it to third parties. Once a product incorporating an intellectual property right has been put on the market inside the EEA by the holder or with his consent, the intellectual property right is exhausted in the sense that the holder can no longer use it to control the sale of the product . . . (principle of Community exhaustion). The right holder has no right under intellectual property laws to prevent sales by licensees or buyers of such products incorporating the licensed technology . . . The principle of Community exhaustion is in line with the essential function of intellectual property rights, which is to grant the holder the right to exclude others from exploiting his intellectual property without his consent.

7. The fact that intellectual property laws grant exclusive rights of exploitation does not imply that intellectual property rights are immune from competition law intervention. Articles 81 and 82 are in particular applicable to agreements whereby the holder licenses another undertaking to exploit his intellectual property rights (See, e.g., Joined Cases 56/64 and 58/64, *Consten and Grundig* [1966] ECR 429.). Nor does it imply that there is an inherent conflict between intellectual property rights and the Community competition rules. Indeed, both bodies of law share the same basic objective of promoting consumer welfare and an efficient allocation of resources. Innovation constitutes an essential and dynamic component of an open and competitive market economy. Intellectual property rights promote dynamic competition by encouraging undertakings to invest in developing new or improved products and processes. So does competition by putting pressure

[101] [2004] OJ C101/2.

[102] See also *supra* Section 2. .

on undertakings to innovate. Therefore, both intellectual property rights and competition are necessary to promote innovation and ensure a competitive exploitation thereof.

8. In the assessment of licence agreements under Article 81 it must be kept in mind that the creation of intellectual property rights often entails substantial investment and that it is often a risky endeavour. In order not to reduce dynamic competition and to maintain the incentive to innovate, the innovator must not be unduly restricted in the exploitation of intellectual property rights that turn out to be valuable. For these reasons the innovator should normally be free to seek compensation for successful projects that is sufficient to maintain investment incentives, taking failed projects into account. Technology licensing may also require the licensee to make significant sunk investments in the licensed technology and production assets necessary to exploit it. Article 81 cannot be applied without considering such ex ante investments made by the parties and the risks relating thereto. The risk facing the parties and the sunk investment that must be committed may thus lead to the agreement falling outside Article 81(1) or fulfilling the conditions of Article 81(3), as the case may be, for the period of time required to recoup the investment.

9. In assessing licensing agreements under Article 81, the existing analytical framework is sufficiently flexible to take due account of the dynamic aspects of technology licensing. There is no presumption that intellectual property rights and licence agreements as such give rise to competition concerns. Most licence agreements do not restrict competition and create pro-competitive efficiencies. Indeed, licensing as such is pro-competitive as it leads to dissemination of technology and promotes innovation. In addition, even licence agreements that do restrict competition may often give rise to pro-competitive efficiencies, which must be considered under Article 81(3) and balanced against the negative effects on competition. The great majority of licence agreements are therefore compatible with Article 81.

(iv) Points of General Importance in the Application of Article 81 to Technology Transfer Agreements

The appraisal of agreements falling outside of the TTBER are discussed in section 5 below. However, it is useful at the outset to note a few points of general importance stressed in the Guidelines.

First, there is no presumption of illegality for a technology transfer agreement falling outside the TTBER so long as it does not contain hardcore restrictions on competition.

Secondly, there is a negative presumption that a technology transfer agreement, which does not contain hardcore restraints, will be compatible with Article 81 where four or more independently controlled substitutable technologies exist in addition to those controlled by the parties.

Thirdly, in paragraphs 10 to 18 of the Guidelines the Commission states, in line with its approach set out in the Article 81(3) Guidelines, that in applying Article 81 to technology transfer agreements it is concerned both with restrictions on inter-technology competition (competition between undertakings using different technologies) and restrictions on intra-technology competition (competition between undertakings using the same technology). This underpins the reliance upon *two* different 'counterfactuals' i.e. benchmarks against which the restriction of competition is measured.[103] The tests are set out paragraphs 12(a) and (b) of the Guidelines. Both may be applied to the same restraint.

---

[103] See L. Peeperkorn, 'IP Licences and Competition Rules: Striking the Right Balance' (2003) 26 *World Competition* 527.

Paragraph 12(a) asks 'does the licence agreement restrict actual or potential competition that would have existed *without the contemplated agreement?*':

Does the licence agreement restrict actual or potential competition that would have existed without the contemplated agreement? If so, the agreement may be caught by Article 81(1). In making this assessment it is necessary to take into account competition between the parties and competition from third parties. For instance, where two undertakings established in different Member States cross licence competing technologies and undertake not to sell products in each other's home markets, (potential) competition that existed prior to the agreement is restricted. Similarly, where a licensor imposes obligations on his licensees not to use competing technologies and these obligations foreclose third party technologies, actual or potential competition that would have existed in the absence of the agreement is restricted.

It can be seen that this paragraph is dealing with inter-technology competition, by asking whether the agreement restricts competition between existing technologies by, for example, sales bans in cross-licensing agreements between undertakings holding competing technologies or non-compete obligations.

Paragraph 12(b) asks 'does the agreement restrict actual or potential competition that would have existed *in the absence of the contractual restraint(s)?*' (emphasis added).

Does the agreement restrict actual or potential competition that would have existed in the absence of the contractual restraint(s)? If so, the agreement may be caught by Article 81(1). For instance, where a licensor restricts its licensees from competing with each other, (potential) competition that could have existed between the licensees absent the restraints is restricted. Such restrictions include vertical price fixing and territorial or customer sales restrictions between licensees. However, certain restraints may in certain cases not be caught by Article 81(1) when the restraint is objectively necessary for the existence of an agreement of that type or that nature (See in this respect the judgment in *Société Technique Minière* . . . and Case 258/78, *Nungesser* [1982] ECR 2015). Such exclusion of the application of Article 81(1) can only be made on the basis of objective factors external to the parties themselves and not the subjective views and characteristics of the parties. The question is not whether the parties in their particular situation would not have accepted to conclude a less restrictive agreement, but whether, given the nature of the agreement and the characteristics of the market, a less restrictive agreement would not have been concluded by undertakings in a similar setting. For instance, territorial restraints in an agreement between non-competitors may fall outside Article 81(1) for a certain duration if the restraints are objectively necessary for a licensee to penetrate a new market. Similarly, a prohibition imposed on all licensees not to sell to certain categories of end users may not be restrictive of competition if such a restraint is objectively necessary for reasons of safety or health related to the dangerous nature of the product in question. Claims that in the absence of a restraint the supplier would have resorted to vertical integration are not sufficient. Decisions on whether or not to vertically integrate depend on a broad range of complex economic factors, a number of which are internal to the undertaking concerned.

Paragraph 12(b) focuses on restrictions on intra-technology competition. It looks at the competitive situation arising from the agreement and compares it with less restrictive alternatives. It is seen in Chapter 4, that the Article 81(3) Guidelines state that Article 81(1) is applied to restraints on intra-brand unless 'objectively necessary' for the existence of an agreement of that type or nature (as in *Nungesser* itself). It does not ask, as 12(b) makes clear, whether these particular parties would have concluded a less restrictive agreement, but whether undertakings 'in a similar setting' would have done so. This is because the issue is what is *objectively* necessary.

This concern with intra-technology restrictions (and intrabrand competition more generally) distinguishes EC from US law (the US federal agencies employ a counterfactual in licensing situations which is analogous to the paragraph 12(a) test).[104] This concern still supports a relatively interventionist approach to technology transfer agreements under Article 81 and influences the interpretation of both Article 81(1) and Article 81(3). The Commission remains unapologetic about this, however, as a Commission official explained in 2003.[105]

L. Peeperkorn, 'IP Licences and Competition Rules: Striking the Right Balance' (2003) 26 *World Competition* 527, 538–9

The proposed new block exemption regulation and guidelines maintain a stricter EU approach, stricter than the United States, towards intra-technology restrictions contained in agreements between non-competitors. The reasons for this divergence with the United States are threefold:

First, territorial restrictions are paid more attention in particular because of the additional market integration objective which EC competition policy has. Secondly, it reflects the higher importance EC competition policy attaches to intra-brand and intra-technology competition in general. It is considered important to protect intra-brand and intra-technology competition as a useful and sometimes essential complement to inter-brand competition. For instance, production costs of licensees and distribution costs of distributors make up a good deal of the end price of most products and competition between licensees or distributors may help to reduce these costs. It is also recognition of the fact that restraints are almost never only affecting intra-brand competition. There is no neat distinction between intra-brand and inter-brand restrictions. Reduced intra-brand competition may facilitate collusion and restrict inter-brand competition, especially in cases of cumulative use.

Thirdly, sales restrictions may be used to prevent arbitrage and support price discrimination between different markets, what economists call third degree price discrimination. This will in general lead to a loss of consumer welfare. While some consumers will pay a higher price and others will pay a lower price, collectively consumers will have to pay more to finance the extra profits obtained by the supplier (its motive to do price discrimination) and to cover the extra costs of supporting the price discrimination scheme and prevent arbitrage. Consumer welfare will also decline because of the loss of allocative efficiency because the marginal consumer in the high price market is willing to pay more than the marginal consumer in the low price market. Therefore consumer welfare will in general decline unless it can be clearly shown that otherwise the lower priced market would not be served at all and that therefore the price discrimination will lead to an undisputable increase of output. It is only in the latter case that consumer welfare may actually increase.

---

[104] See M. Delrahim (US Deputy Assistant Attorney General), 'US and EU Approaches to the Antitrust Analysis of Intellectual Property Licensing: Observations from the Enforcement Perspective' ABA Antitrust Section Meeting, Washington, 1 Apr. 2004, available on the DOJ web site, http://www.usdoj.gov/atr/public/ speeches and 1995 Department of Justice and Federal Trade Commission Antitrust Guidelines for the Licensing of Intellectual Property (The 'Intellectual Property Guidelines').

[105] The following extract is from a paper which contains the usual disclaimer that the views expressed are the author's and do not necessarily represent those of the Commission or DG Comp.

4. REGULATION 772/2004, THE TECHNOLOGY TRANSFER BLOCK EXEMPTION

A. GENERAL

As explained above, the TTBER was born in controversy. It is at once both more flexible and more strict than Regulation 240/96. It is more flexible as, like the other 'new' block exemptions, it does not contain lists of 'white' or 'grey' clauses. All provisions which are not in the list of hardcore restrictions or the list of excluded restrictions are permitted. Therefore it does not force parties into such a straightjacket as its predecessor, Regulation 240/96. Recital 4 of the TTBER explains:

It is appropriate to move away from the approach of listing exempted clauses and to place greater emphasis on defining the categories of agreements which are exempted up to certain levels of market power and on specifying the restrictions or clauses which are not to be contained in such agreements.

The TTBER also covers a wider range of agreements and draws an important distinction between agreements between competitors and agreements between non-competitors. On the other hand, the new lists of hardcore and excluded restrictions decrease, in some respects, the parties' contractual freedom in comparison to the previous position. In addition, and most importantly, the decision to introduce market share thresholds into the sphere of technology transfer render the TTBER far less useful to many undertakings as the passionate objections to the proposal to incorporate them pointed out. The practical effect is that numerous agreements have been cast adrift on a sea of uncertainty as it will frequently be unclear whether or not the TTBER applies.[106] As there is now no possibility of notification of an agreement to the Commission, parties to technology transfer agreements face greater uncertainty, greater risk of litigation and other allegations that their licensing agreements violate Article 81.

B. THE SCHEME OF THE TTBER

The TTBER comprises twenty recitals and eleven articles.

Article 1 contains definitions of the most important terms in the regulation.

Article 2 contains the exemption for bilateral technology transfer agreements which fall within it.

Article 3 contains the market share thresholds which limit the application of the regulation. Thus technology transfer agreements can only benefit from the 'safe harbour' of the block exemption if the relevant market shares (of 20 per cent, for agreements between competitors, and 30 per cent, for agreements between non-competitors) are satisfied.

Article 4 contains the list of hardcore restrictions. The presence in the agreement of any of these restrictions removes the entire agreement from the protection of the block exemption, including provisions which would otherwise have been exempted.[107]

---

[106] See extract from S. D. Anderman and J. Kallaugher *Technology Transfer and the New EU Competition Rules: Intellectual Property Licensing after Modernisation* (Oxford University Press, 2006), paras. 1.19–1.23 set out *supra* 801–2.

[107] Pursuant to the judgment of the Court in Case C-234/89, *Delimitis* [1991] ECR I-935.

Article 5 contains the list of excluded restrictions. These restrictions are not exempted by the TTBER but their presence in an agreement does not remove the remainder of the agreement from the protection of the block exemption. The effect of including an excluded restraint is, therefore, as in the application of the Verticals Regulation, quite different from including a hard-core restraint.

Article 6 provides that the Commission and national competition authorities may withdraw the benefit of the TTBER from a particular agreement in certain circumstances.

Article 7 provides that the Commission may by regulation declare the TTBER inapplicable in situations where parallel networks of similar technology transfer agreements cover more than 50 per cent of a market.

Article 8 contains provisions about the calculation of the market share thresholds and provides for some marginal relief where market share increases during the lifetime of the agreement.

Article 9 repeals Regulation 240/96.

Article 10 contains the transitional provisions. Agreements in force on 30 April 2004 which satisfied the conditions for exemption in Regulation 240/96 remained exempt from Article 81(1) until 31 March 2006. After that they are not block exempted unless they comply with the TTBER. Undertakings were therefore given two years in which to examine existing licensing agreements.

Article 11 provides that the TTBER enters into force on 1 May 2004 and expires on 30 April 2014.

C. PRINCIPAL FEATURES OF THE TTBER

Certain features of the TTBER should be noted at the outset:

- The category of agreements covered by the TTBER is wider than that covered by Regulation 240/96 in that the TTBER covers not only patents and know-how licensing but also licences of computer software and of designs;[108]

- As already mentioned, the TTBER applies only where certain market share thresholds are not exceeded;[109]

- Throughout the TTBER a distinction is drawn between agreements between competitors and agreements between non-competitors.[110] The market share thresholds, the hardcore restrictions[111] and the excluded restrictions[112] differ depending on whether the agreement is between competitors or non-competitors;

- In respect of some types of provision the TTBER draws a distinction between reciprocal and non-reciprocal obligations.[113]

- In applying the TTBER two markets need to be taken into account: the *technology* market (consisting of the licensed technology and its substitutes) and the *product or service* market (consisting of the market for the product or service incorporating the licensed technology).[114]

---

[108] Reg. 772/2004, Art. 1(1)(b) and 1(1)(h). Designs are brought into the scope by the definition of 'patent' in Article 1(h).

[109] TTBER, Art. 3.

[110] See *infra* 816–7.

[111] TTBER, Art. 4.

[112] *Ibid.*, Art. 5.

[113] For example, in the active and/or passive sales provisions in Article 4.

[114] Guidelines, paras. 19–22, *infra* 814–5.

D. SCOPE OF THE TTBER

(i) Agreements to which the TTBER may Apply

a. Bilateral Technology Transfer Agreements

Article 2 of the TTBER exempts from Article 81(1) bilateral technology transfer agreements permitting the production of contract products. It states:

Pursuant to Article 81(3) of the Treaty and subject to the provisions of this Regulation, it is hereby declared that Article 81(1) of the Treaty shall not apply to technology transfer agreements entered into between two undertakings permitting the production of contract products.

This exemption shall apply to the extent that such agreements contain restrictions of competition falling within the scope of Article 81(1). The exemption shall apply for as long as the intellectual property right in the licensed technology has not expired, lapsed or been declared invalid or, in the case of know-how, for as long as the know-how remains secret, except in the event where the know-how becomes publicly known as a result of action by the licensee, in which case the exemption shall apply for the duration of the agreement.

b. The Number of Parties

The TTBER is limited to bilateral agreements i.e. agreements between two undertakings. It does not therefore cover agreements between three or more undertakings.[115] When counting the parties to an agreement, however, each group of 'connected undertakings' are counted as a single party.[116] The TTBER itself defines 'connected undertaking.[117] The two party limitation does not prevent an agreement which affects third parties from falling within the TTBER however. For example, an agreement may require the licensee to impose obligations on resellers of the product produced under the licence.[118]

---

[115] Council Reg. 19/65 OJ Spec. Ed. Series I 1965–6, p. 35, the relevant enabling Regulation, only empowers the Commission to block exempt technology transfer agreements between two undertakings.

[116] See also the discussion of the single economic entity doctrine, *supra* Chap. 3.

[117] TTBER, Art. 1(2), (the same definition as Reg. 2790/99 on vertical agreements [1999] OJ L336/21, Art. 11(2); Reg. 2658/2000 on specialization agreements [2000] OJ L304/3, Art. 2(3); Reg. 2659 on research and development agreements [2000] OJ L304/7, Art. 2(3)). The definition is: '"Connected undertakings" means:

(a) undertakings in which a party to the agreement, directly or indirectly:
  (i) has the power to exercise more than half the voting rights, or
  (ii) has the power to appoint more than half the members of the supervisory board, board of management or bodies legally representing the undertaking, or
  (iii) has the right to manage the undertaking's affairs;
(b) undertakings which directly or indirectly have, over a party to the agreement, the rights or powers listed in (a);
(c) undertakings in which an undertaking referred to in (b) has, directly or indirectly, the rights or powers listed in (a);
(d) undertakings in which a party to the agreement together with one or more of the undertakings referred to in (a), (b) or (c), or in which two or more of the latter undertakings, jointly have the rights or powers listed in (a);
(e) undertakings in which the rights or the powers listed in (a) are jointly held by:
  (i) parties to the agreement or their respective connected undertakings referred to in (a) to (d), or
  (ii) one or more of the parties to the agreement or one or more of their connected undertakings referred to in (a) to (d) and one or more third parties.'

[118] Guidelines, para. 39.

c. Definition of Technology Transfer Agreement

The definition of a technology transfer agreement is set out in the TTBER, Article 1(1)(b):

'technology transfer agreement' means a patent licensing agreement, a know-how licensing agreement, a software copyright licensing agreement or a mixed patent, know-how or software copyright licensing agreement, including any such agreement containing provisions which relate to the sale and purchase of products or which relate to the licensing of other intellectual property rights or the assignment of intellectual property rights, provided that those provisions do not constitute the primary object of the agreement and are directly related to the production of the contract products; assignments of patents, know-how, software copyright or a combination thereof where part of the risk associated with the exploitation of the technology remains with the assignor, in particular where the sum payable in consideration of the assignment is dependent on the turnover obtained by the assignee in respect of products produced with the assigned technology, the quantity of such products produced or the number of operations carried out employing the technology, shall also be deemed to be technology transfer agreements . . .

Article 1(1)(b) thus makes it clear that a technology transfer agreement can comprise:

• A pure patent licensing agreement. 'Patent' is defined in Article 1(1)(h) to cover patents, patent applications, utility models, applications for registration of utility models, designs, topographies of semiconductor products, supplementary protection certificates for medicinal products or other products for which such supplementary protection certificates may be obtained and plant breeder's certificates;

• A pure know-how licensing agreement. Know-how is defined in Article 1(1)(i) as: a package of non-patented practical information, resulting from experience and testing, which is:

(i) secret, that is to say, not generally known or easily accessible,
(ii) substantial, that is to say, significant and useful for the production of the contract products, and
(iii) identified, that is to say, described in a sufficiently comprehensive manner so as to make it possible to verify that it fulfils the criteria of secrecy and substantiality.

The meaning of 'secret', 'substantial' and 'identified' are further elaborated upon in paragraph 47 of the Guidelines.

• A pure software copyright licence. Such licences are brought within a block exemption for the first time. Other forms of copyright are not covered by the TTBER;[119]

• A pure design licence (as noted above, the definition of 'patent' means that design licences are for the first time covered by a block exemption);

• A 'mixed' agreement, by which two or more of the above rights (patents, know-how, software copyright, designs) are licensed together (it is very common, for example, to license know-how together with a patent);

• An agreement which comprises a licence of one of the above rights and *other* intellectual property rights not covered by the TTBER, provided that the licence of the other right(s) is only ancillary to the licence of the covered rights and not the 'primary object' of the agreement.[120]

---

[119] But the provisions apply by analogy to some other copyright licensing: see Guidelines, paras. 52-2, and *infra* 849–52.

[120] This point is well illustrated by the *Moosehead/Whitbread* decision, [1990] OJ L100/32, [1991] 4 CMLR 391 in which a Canadian brewer granted to Whitbread an exclusive know-how and trade mark licence to produce,

The TTBER also covers licences which contain provisions about the sale and purchase of goods provided the sale and purchase is not the 'primary object'.[121]

The TTBER only covers agreements whereby technology is *transferred*, meaning that technology 'flows from one undertaking to another', i.e., normally where the licensor grants a licensee the right to use his technology against the payment of royalties. It also covers a sub-licence by the licensee for the exploitation of the technology,[122] assignments where the licensor retains the risk[123] and subcontracting, where the licensee uses the licensed technology exclusively to produce products for the licensor or where the licensor supplies equipment to be used in the production of goods and services covered by the agreement.[124]

d. The Agreement must Concern the Production of Contract Products

Article 2 provides that the TTBER exempts technology transfer agreements 'permitting the production of contract products'. The point of the licence must be to allow the licensee to use the licensed technology to produce goods or services (the word 'goods' is hereafter used in this chapter to denote both goods and services unless the context otherwise requires). The TTBER does not therefore cover:

- 'Technology pools' whereby two or more parties agree to pool their respective technologies and licensee them as a package;[125]

- Agreements which are in effect 'master licensing' agreements of which the primary object is sub-licensing;[126]

- Agreements whose object is to enable the licensee to carry out R&D rather than produce goods or services. For an agreement to be covered by the TTBER there must be 'a direct link between the licensed technology and an identified contract product'.[127] The TTBER does not cover R&D sub-contracting whereby the licensee carries out R&D for the licensor and returns the improved technology package to the licensor;

- Agreements whose primary object is the sale and purchase of products (rather than their production).[128]

On the other hand the TTBER *does* cover agreements:

- which *permit* the licensee to sub-license as distinct from where sub-licensing is the purpose of the agreement;[129]

---

promote, market, and sell in the UK beer under the name 'Moosehead' using Mooseheadís know-how. The Commission held that the agreement was not covered by Reg. 556/89 on know-how agreements because the exploitation of the *trade mark* was the crucial element in the deal and it was not ancillary to the know-how licence. See further *infra* 846–8.

[121] As explained in Guidelines, paras. 49–50.

[122] Guidelines, para. 48.

[123] See also *supra* 785.

[124] For a fuller discussion of subcontracting agreements, see *supra* Chap. 9.

[125] Guidelines, para. 31. There is a lengthy section of the Guidelines (paras. 210–35) on technology pools: see *infra* 841–3. In any event such agreements are likely to be 'bilateral' and the parties are unlikely to meet the market share thresholds of the TTBER.

[126] Guidelines, 42.

[127] *Ibid.*, 45

[128] *Ibid.*, 49.

[129] *Ibid.*, 42.

- which are entered into to settle disputes over intellectual property rights within the scope of the TTBER (called 'settlement' or 'non-assertion' agreements), including cross-licensing;[130]

- which are sub-contracting agreements whereby the technology is licensed in order for the licensee to produce certain products exclusively for the licensor;[131]

- whereby the licensee has to carry out development work before obtaining a product or process that can be commercially exploited, provided that a contract product has been identified and the primary purpose of the agreement is not R&D (see above).[132]

(ii) Relationship with other Block Exemptions

Specialisation, research and development and vertical agreements may involve the transfer of technology between the contracting parties. In such cases it is important to know whether a particular agreement is in essence of technology transfer agreement potentially covered by the TTBER and the Guidelines or a horizontal cooperation or vertical agreement potentially covered by one of the other block exemptions and guidelines.[133] Broadly:

- Licensing of technology used in the production of products produced by a joint venture is normally subject to Regulation 2658/2000,[134] the specialization block exemption, and not the TTBER. Regulation 2658/2000 does not, however, apply to the situation where the joint venture engages in licensing technology to a third party. That amounts to a technology pool.[135]

- Licensing between parties for joint research and development and joint exploitation of results of such activities will normally be covered by Regulation 2659/2000, the research and development block exemption, and not the TTBER;[136] and

- The umbrella block exemption on vertical restraints, Regulation 2790/1999[137] applies to vertical agreements involving licences of intellectual property so long as the licence is ancillary to the vertical agreement and IP rights are assigned to the buyer for the purpose of using or selling the goods or services supplied under the agreement.[138] Regulation 2790/1999 is of particular relevance to franchise agreements.[139] Further, the Verticals Regulation may apply where a licensee sells products incorporating licensed technology to a buyer. Thus even though the TTBER will block exempt an agreement (within the safe harbour) a technology transfer agreement requiring a licensee to distribute the products in a particular way, e.g. through an exclusive or selective distribution system such agreements will be vertical and subject to Regulation

---

[130] Guidelines, paras. 43, and 204–9.

[131] Guidelines, 44. If the licensor supplies the licensee with equipment for this purpose the TTBER will not apply if the supply of the equipment rather than the supply of the technology is the primary purpose of the agreement. According to the 1979 Notice on sub-contracting agreements, [1979] OJ C1/20032, sub-contracting agreements whereby the sub-contractor only undertakes to produce certain products exclusively for the contractor generally fall outside Article 81(1).

[132] Guidelines, para. 45.

[133] Ibid., paras. 56–64.

[134] [2000] OJ L304/3. See infra Chap. 13.

[135] Guidelines, para. 58. Technology pools are not within the scope of the TTBER but are dealt with in the Guidelines, paras. 210–35. See discussion of technology pools infra 841–3.

[136] Guidelines, 59–60.

[137] [1999] OJ L336/21. See supra Chap. 9.

[138] See [1999] OJ L336/21, Arts 2(3)(5).

[139] Franchise agreements are intended to be covered by Reg. 2790/1999 despite the view of the ECJ in Case 161/84, Pronuptia de Paris GmbH v. Pronuptia de Paris Irmgard Schillgallis [1986] ECR 353, [1986] 1 CMLR 414 that the essence of a franchise is that it is a transaction concerning intellectual property rights.

INTELLECTUAL PROPERTY RIGHTS | 813

2790/1999 and the Guidelines on Vertical Restraints.[140] Paragraph 64 of the Guidelines addresses the situation where the licensees sell under a common brand name:

Furthermore, distributors must in principle be free to sell both actively and passively into territories covered by the distribution systems of other licensees producing their own products on the basis of the licensed technology. This is because for the purposes of Regulation 2790/1999 each licensee is a separate supplier. However, the reasons underlying the block exemption contained in that Regulation may also apply where the products incorporating the licensed technology are sold by the licensees under a common brand belonging to the licensor. When the products incorporating the licensed technology are sold under a common brand identity there may be the same efficiency reasons for applying the same types of restraints between licensees' distribution systems as within a single vertical distribution system. In such cases the Commission would be unlikely to challenge restraints where by analogy the requirements of Regulation 2790/1999 are fulfilled. For a common brand identity to exist the products must be sold and marketed under a common brand, which is predominant in terms of conveying quality and other relevant information to the consumer. It does not suffice that in addition to the licensees' brands the product carries the licensor's brand, which identifies him as the source of the licensed technology.

E. SAFE HARBOUR: THE MARKET SHARE THRESHOLDS

(i) The Market Share Thresholds

Article 3 provides that the block exemption applies on condition that specified market share thresholds are not exceeded on affected technology and product markets. Where the parties are competitors the relevant market share is 20 per cent. Where the parties are non-competitors the relevant market is 30 per cent. Article 3 thus sets out the market share thresholds which provide the 'safe harbour'.[141]

Article 3

Market-share thresholds

1. Where the undertakings party to the agreement are competing undertakings, the exemption provided for in Article 2 shall apply on condition that the combined market share of the parties does not exceed 20 per cent on the affected relevant technology and product market.
2. Where the undertakings party to the agreement are not competing undertakings, the exemption provided for in Article 2 shall apply on condition that the market share of each of the parties does not exceed 30 per cent on the affected relevant technology and product market.

The Commission explains Article 3(1) and (2) in paragraph 69 of the Guidelines 69:

69. In the case of agreements between competitors the market share threshold is 20 per cent and in the case of agreements between non-competitors it is 30 per cent (cf. Article 3(1) and (2) of the

---

[140] Guidelines, paras. 62–3.

[141] In para. 131 of the Guidelines the Commission states that Article 81 is unlikely to be infringed in where there are a number of other independently controlled technologies, see *infra* 830. Although this is referred to as a 'second safe harbour' it is important to remember that in the TTBER itself there is only *one* safe harbour and that it is expressed in terms of market share.

TTBER). Where the undertakings party to the licensing agreement are not competitors the agreement is covered if the market share of neither party exceeds 30 per cent on the affected relevant technology and product markets. Where the undertakings party to the licensing agreement are competitors the agreement is covered if the combined market shares of the parties do not exceed 20 per cent on the relevant technology and product markets. The market share thresholds apply both to technology markets and markets for products incorporating the licensed technology. If the applicable market share threshold is exceeded on an affected relevant market, the block exemption does not apply to the agreement for that relevant market. For instance, if the licence agreement concerns two separate product markets or two separate geographic markets, the block exemption may apply to one of the markets and not to the other.

It should be noted that with regard to competitors it is the *combined* market share which is relevant, but in the case of non-competitors it is the market share of *each* of the parties that is relevant.

Where the thresholds are exceeded the TTBER does not apply. If the parties' market shares are below the thresholds at the time the agreement is entered into, but subsequently increase so that they exceed it, the agreement will cease to be covered by the TTBER. The matter is not settled once and for all at the outset. This means that the parties (and their lawyers) need to keep the agreement under review. Article 8 provides for some marginal relief, providing that the TTBER will continue to apply for two consecutive calendar years following the year in which the relevant threshold is first exceeded.

In order to determine whether the market share thresholds it is therefore ordinarily necessary to determine the relevant markets, to calculate market shares and to determine whether or not the parties are competitors.

(i) Market Definition

The normal principles of market definition as set out in the Commission Notice on market definition apply.[142] However, the Guidelines provide guidance on specific issues which arise in the technology transfer context.[143] For technology transfer agreements, both the technology market and the product market need to be considered. It has already been explained that market definition raises acute difficulties in this area.[144]

a. The Technology Market

The technology market is the licensed technology and any other technology that the licensees consider to be interchangeable with, or substitutable for, the technology by reason of the technologies' characteristics, their royalties and their intended use. Paragraph 22 of the Guidelines state that the objective is therefore to identify competing technologies to which licensees could switch in response to a small but permanent increase in prices (which in this context means the royalties). This is an application of the SSNIP test.[145] Paragraph 22 of the Guidelines also provides 'an alternative approach' to defining the technology market, which looks to the market

---

[142] Commission Notice on the definition of the relevant market [1997] OJ C372/5, see Chap. 1.

[143] Guidelines, para. 19.

[144] See *supra* 799.

[145] See *supra* Chap. 1.

for products incorporating the licensed technology.[146] This method is discussed below in the section dealing with the calculation of market shares.

b. The Product Market

The term 'product' market in the TTBER is shorthand for the product *and* geographical dimensions of goods and services markets. The term is used in contradistinction to the technology market. The relevant product market comprises products regarded as interchangeable with or substitutable for the contract products incorporating the licensed technology by reason of the products' characteristics, price, and intended use.[147] Occasionally, it may be necessary to define an innovation market, in particular, where the agreement affects innovation aimed at creating new products and research and development poles can be identified.[148]

(iii) Market Shares

a. Means of Calculation

Where it is available, market share is to be calculated on the basis of market sales value data. Otherwise 'other reliable market information' including market sales volume data may be used.[149]

b. The Technology Market

The Guidelines suggest more than one method of calculating market shares on the technology market. One solution is to calculate the market shares by reference to the licensed technology and its substitutes. Market share can then be calculated on the basis of each technology's share of total licensing income from royalties. In practice, however, this test is hard to apply especially as companies are unlikely to know the level of royalty income derived by their competitors. Article 3(3) thus provides that the market share can be defined with regard to the presence of the licensed technology on the relevant product market. This means looking at the sales on the downstream market of products incorporating the licensed technology produced by the licensor and licensee, and calculating what share of the product market they have taking into account products which use substitute technologies.[150] The advantages of this method are:

• it takes account of 'captive use', which means undertakings producing products using their own technology which they do not license out at present (but could start licensing if there was a small but significant increase in licence prices);

• it takes account of the fact that a licensor's market power may be constrained if the downstream product market is competitive, because what the license can be made to pay will be limited if an increase in his costs would make him less able to compete on that downstream market.

The licensor's market share of the relevant technology market is the combined market share of the contract products produced by the licensor and all its licensees.[151] Where the parties are

---

[146] It refers to para 23 of the Guidelines which discusses the method adopted by the Article 3(3) TTBER, for *calculating shares* on the technology market, which 'is defined in terms of the presence of the licensed technology on the relevant product market'.

[147] TTBER, Art. 1(1)(j)(ii) and Guidelines, para. 21.

[148] Guidelines, para. 25.

[149] TTBER, Art. 8(1). The calculation is on the basis of the preceding year.

[150] Explained in Guidelines, para. 23, which is not clearly written.

[151] TTBER, Art. 3(3) and Guidelines, para. 70.

competitors on the technology market, sales of products incorporating the licensee's own technology are added to the sales of products incorporating the licensed technology.[152] The Commission states that it may use both methods when assessing agreements falling outside the safe harbour thresholds of the TTBER.[153]

c. The Product Market

Market shares on the product market are assessed in the usual way, using sales data value if available.[154] The licensee's market share is the total sales of the licensee on the product market, i.e., products incorporating the licensor's technology and competing products. The licensor's sales (if any) on the product market must be included, but not those of other licensees.[155]

(iv) The Distinction between Competitors and Non-competitors (Competing and Non-competing Undertakings)

The provisions of the TTBER are based on the premise that agreements between competitors are likely to be more dangerous to the competitive process than agreements between non-competitors.[156] Thus not only are the market share thresholds lower for agreements between competitors but a different, stricter set of hardcore restraints applies. Paragraph 27 of the Guidelines explains:

In order to determine the competitive relationship between the parties it is necessary to examine whether the parties would have been actual or potential competitors in the absence of the agreement. If without the agreement the parties would not have been actual or potential competitors in any relevant market affected by the agreement they are deemed to be non-competitors.

Article 1(1)(j) of the TTBER defines competing undertakings as undertakings that compete on the relevant technology market and/or the relevant product market.

(i) competing undertakings on the relevant technology market, being undertakings which license out competing technologies without infringing each others' intellectual property rights (actual competitors on the technology market); . . .

(ii) competing undertakings on the relevant product market, being undertakings which, in the absence of the technology transfer agreement, are both active on the relevant product and geographic market(s) on which the contract products are sold without infringing each others' intellectual property rights (actual competitors on the product market) or would, on realistic grounds, undertake the necessary additional investments or other necessary switching costs so that they could timely enter, without infringing each others' intellectual property rights, the(se) relevant product and geographic market(s) in response to a small and permanent increase in relative prices (potential competitors on the product market) . . .

It can be seen from this definition that as far as product markets are concerned, both actual and potential competitors are treated as competitors. As far as technology markets are concerned, however, only actual competitors are relevant. If the licensor and licensee are both active on the same technology or product market, without infringing each other's intellectual property

---

[152] *Ibid.* The market share will be zero where no products have yet been made incorporating the technology.

[153] *Ibid.*

[154] *Ibid.*

[155] Guidelines, para. 71.

[156] *Ibid.*, para. 26.

rights, they are actual competitors on the market. They are potential competitors on the product market if, in the absence of the agreement and without infringing intellectual property rights, they would be likely to undertake the necessary investments required to enter the market within a short period (one to two years) in response to a small but permanent increase in price.[157] On technology markets the parties will be considered actual competitors if the licensee is already licensing out his technology and the licensor enters the technology market by granting a licence for a competing technology to the licensee.[158] Outside the safe harbour of the TTBER potential competitors on the technology market are taken into account.[159]

The reference in Article 1(1)(j) to parties being competing undertakings only where they are both active on the technology market or product market 'without infringing each others' intellectual property rights' means that if there is a one-way (one party cannot exploit its technology without infringing the other's intellectual property rights) or two-way (neither party can exploit its technology without infringing the other's intellectual property rights) blocking situation, the parties will *not* be characterised as competitors. The Commission is, however, alive to the fact that the parties will usually prefer to be classified as non-competitors and will examine blocking claims carefully.[160] In addition, the parties will not be competitors where the licensor is neither an actual nor potential supplier of products on the product market and the licensee does not license out a competing technology.[161]

The Guidelines state that in cases of 'drastic innovation' parties should be classed as non-competitors even though they produce competing products. This will be the case where the licensed technology represents such a technological breakthrough that the licensee's technology becomes obsolete or uncompetitive (for example, the replacement of LP vinyl technology with CD technology).[162] Often, however, it will not be possible to draw this conclusion at the time the agreement is concluded. If it is *not* obvious at this time the parties will be clasified as competitors initially but can be recognized as non-competitors later.[163]

It is extremely important when deciding whether the parties are competitors or non-competitors to remember that activities of their 'connected undertakings' must be taken into account.[164]

(v) Non-competitors which Subsequently become Competitors

What is the position if the parties are not competitors, *ex ante* at the time the agreement is concluded but subsequently become competitors? Article 4(3) of the TTBER provides that the more liberal black-list of hard-core restrictions for agreements between non-competitors will apply during the life-time of the agreement even if the parties later become competitors *unless the*

---

[157] *Ibid.*

[158] *Ibid.*, 28.

[159] See Guidelines, 66. This does not lead to the application of the hardcore list of restrictions relating to agreements between competitors.

[160] Guidelines, para. 32. Where opinions of independent experts are relied upon the Commission will 'closely examine how the expert has been selected'!

[161] Guidelines, paras. 30 and 68.

[162] *Ibid.*, para. 33.

[163] *Ibid.* This was a major concession by the Commission, which had originally intended that the agreement would have to be reassessed if the relationship of the parties subsequently changed to that of competitors. It was persuaded to change its mind on this print.

[164] See *supra* n. 117.

agreement is amended 'in any material respect' (in which case restraints previously block exempted may become hardcore restraints).[165] Neither Article 4(3) nor the Guidelines comment, however, on the position if the 20 per cent market share threshold is exceeded (i.e. whether or not the TTBER ceases to apply if the parties combined market shares exceed 20 per cent). This suggests that subject to the two-year transitional relief provided by Article 8(2), the benefit of the TTBER will be lost where parties become competitors and their combined market shares exceed the 20 per cent threshold.

F. HARD-CORE RESTRICTIONS

(i) General

The hardcore restraints are set out in Article 4 of the TTBER.[166] As is the case in the context of vertical agreements, a restraint will be hardcore whether achieved directly or indirectly. The presence in the agreement of any one of the hardcore restrictions takes the entire agreement out of the safe harbour of the block exemptions. Indeed, the Commission's view is that hardcore restraints are restrictive of competition by object and are most unlikely even *individually* to satisfy the Article 81(3) conditions.[167] As already noted, there are two separate lists of hardcore restrictions: those applying to agreements between competitors (Article 4(1)) and those applying to agreements between non-competitors (Article 4(2)). In addition, the list of hardcore restraints in agreements between competitors may differ depending upon whether the agreement is reciprocal or non-reciprocal. These terms are defined in TTBER, Article 1(1)(c) and (d). Essentially, an agreement is reciprocal where the parties cross-license competing technologies or technologies which can be used for the production of competing products.

(ii) Agreements between Competing Undertakings

The list of hardcore restraints applicable to agreements between competitors is set out in Article 4(1). It focuses, subject to specified exceptions, on: price fixing; limitations of output; allocation of markets or customers; restrictions on the licensee's ability to exploit its own technology; and provisions restraining either party from carrying out research and development unless indispensable to prevent disclosure of the licensed technology.

Article 4(1)

1. Where the undertakings party to the agreement are competing undertakings, the exemption provided for in Article 2 shall not apply to agreements which, directly or indirectly, in isolation or in combination with other factors under the control of the parties, have as their object:

   (a) the restriction of a party's ability to determine its prices when selling products to third parties;

---

[165] As would be the case if the licensee developed and began to exploit a competing technology, or if the licensor subsequently entered the product market on which the licensee was active. See Guidelines, para. 31.

[166] The TTBER, with the objective of minimizing the straitjacketing effect of the block exemption does not contain a list of permissible restrictions. As is the case for the Verticals Regulation, the idea is that if it is not prohibited, the restraint is exempted by the block exemption.

[167] Guidelines, paras. 74–6. See generally on this point, *supra* Chap. 4 and see *infra* 831.

(b) the limitation of output, except limitations on the output of contract products imposed on the licensee in a non-reciprocal agreement or imposed on only one of the licensees in a reciprocal agreement;

(c) the allocation of markets or customers except:

   (i) the obligation on the licensee(s) to produce with the licensed technology only within one or more technical fields of use or one or more product markets,

   (ii) the obligation on the licensor and/or the licensee, in a non-reciprocal agreement, not to produce with the licensed technology within one or more technical fields of use or one or more product markets or one or more exclusive territories reserved for the other party,

   (iii) the obligation on the licensor not to license the technology to another licensee in a particular territory,

   (iv) the restriction, in a non-reciprocal agreement, of active and/or passive sales by the licensee and/or the licensor into the exclusive territory or to the exclusive customer group reserved for the other party,

   (v) the restriction, in a non-reciprocal agreement, of active sales by the licensee into the exclusive territory or to the exclusive customer group allocated by the licensor to another licensee provided the latter was not a competing undertaking of the licensor at the time of the conclusion of its own licence,

   (vi) the obligation on the licensee to produce the contract products only for its own use provided that the licensee is not restricted in selling the contract products actively and passively as spare parts for its own products,

   (vii) the obligation on the licensee, in a non-reciprocal agreement, to produce the contract products only for a particular customer, where the licence was granted in order to create an alternative source of supply for that customer;

(d) the restriction of the licensee's ability to exploit its own technology or the restriction of the ability of any of the parties to the agreement to carry out research and development, unless such latter restriction is indispensable to prevent the disclosure of the licensed know-how to third parties.

Article 4(1)(a)—Price Restrictions

Price fixing between competitors is treated more strictly than price fixing in agreements between non-competitors.[168] Article 4(1)(a) prohibits agreements 'that have as their object the fixing of prices' whether in the form of fixed, minimum, maximum, or recommended prices.[169] An obligation on the licensee to pay a certain minimum royalty does not in itself amount to price fixing.[170] However, indirect price restraints, for example, through disincentives to deviate from a certain price level or through provisions for the royalty rate to increase if prices are reduced below a certain level, are prohibited.[171]

---

[168] *Infra* 823.

[169] Guidelines, para. 79.

[170] A licensor is entitled to ensure that he obtains a certain minimum return for the licence.

[171] Guidelines, paras. 79–81.

Article 4(1)(b)—Output Limitations

An output restriction is a limitation on how much a party may produce and sell. Article 4(1)(b) permits output limitations on the licensee in a non-reciprocal agreement or on only one licensee in a reciprocal agreement. This means, in effect, that reciprocal output restrictions and output restrictions on the licensor in respect of his own technology constitute hard-core restrictions.[172] Provisions which have the effect of output restrictions, such as disincentives to produce more than a certain amount, are also caught by Article 4(1)(b).[173]

Article 4(1)(c)—Market or Customer Allocation

Article 4(1)(c) seeks to reconcile the need to ensure that competitors are not able to share markets between themselves with an acceptance that in certain circumstances a licensee will require an exclusive or sole licences and protection from sales into its territory.[174] It prohibits agreements between competitors that share markets or customers unless they fall within one of seven very important exceptions:

(i) Article 4(1)(c)(i)

Field of use and product market restrictions[175] may be imposed on the licensee in a reciprocal or non-reciprocal agreement. This means that a licensee can be restricted to using the technology for a specific purpose.

(ii) Article 4(1)(c)(ii)

In a non-reciprocal agreement only, the licensor and/or the licensee can agree not to produce within one or more fields of use, product markets or exclusive territories reserved to the other party.[176] This provides a licensee with an incentive to invest in and develop the technology. Note that this exception relates to production and not to sales.

(iii) Article 4(1)(c)(iii)

The licensor may agree not to give another licence of the same technology in the same territory. This permits the grant of a sole licence and protects the licensee from competition from other licensees *producing* in the same territory. The exception applies to both reciprocal and non-reciprocal agreements but must not affect the parties' ability to exploit their own technology in the respective territories.[177]

(iv) Article 4(1)(c)(iv)

In a *non-reciprocal* licence both licensor and licensee can be restricted from making both *active* and *passive* sales into an exclusive territory or to the exclusive customer groups reserved to the other.

(v) Article 4(1)(c)(v)

In a *non-reciprocal* licence the licensee can be prohibited from making *active* sales (but *not* passive sales) into exclusive territories or to customer groups allocated to another licensee (so long as that other licensee was not a competitor of the licensor when he was given his licence). If the

---

[172] Guidelines, para. 82.

[173] *Ibid.*

[174] It considers that agreements between customers sharing markets or customers have as their object the restriction of competition, Guidelines, para. 84.

[175] See *supra* 787–8.

[176] See Guidelines, para. 86.

[177] *Ibid.*, para. 88.

licensees agree among themselves not to actively or passively sell into each other's territories or customers this clearly goes beyond what is permitted and indeed amounts to market sharing clearly prohibited by Article 81.[178]

(vi) Article 4(1)(c)(vi)

This exception permits licensing where the licensee takes a licence in order to make products for his own use (known as captive use restrictions).[179] It enables the licensor to limit the licensee to making components to be incorporated into the licensee's own products and to prohibit him from selling them to others. The licensee must, however, not be restricted from selling the components as spare parts.

(vii) Article 4(1)(c)(vii)

A non-reciprocal licence granted specifically to create a source of supply for a customer, may restrict the licensee to producing the contract products only for that customer. This is called a 'second source' provision. The restriction is permitted as the whole point of the agreement is to provide a particular customer with an alternative source of the products. It is possible, however, for more than one licensee to be given a licence in respect of the same customer (so the latter gets a third or even fourth source of supply).[180]

A list of permissible market or customer restraints in agreement between competitors is summarized in a table in Butterworths *Competition Law*.

W. Allan, M. Furse and B. Sufrin (eds.), *Butterworths Competition Law* (Butterworths, looseleaf), Division V Chapter 3, para. 575

Table of Permissible Market or Customer Restraints in agreements between Competitors under the TTBER

RESTRAINT	PERMITTED IN A RECIPROCAL AGREEMENT?	PERMITTED IN A NON-RECIPROCAL AGREEMENT?
Obligation on the licensee to produce with licensed technology within one or more technical fields	Yes, so long as restriction does not got beyond scope of licensed technology and does not limit use of licensee's own technology	Yes, so long as restriction does not got beyond scope of licensed technology and does not limit use of licensee's own technology
Obligation on the licensor and/or licensee not to use technology to produce within one or more technical fields of use, product markets or exclusive territories reserved to the other	No	Yes, licensor can grant exclusive licence to product and agree not to produce itself

---

[178] Guidelines, para. 89. 'Active' and 'passive' sales have the same meaning as in respect of vertical agreements (see *supra* Chap. 9), 752–3.

[179] Guidelines, para. 92.

[180] *Ibid.*, para. 93.

822 | EC COMPETITION LAW

RESTRAINT	PERMITTED IN A RECIPROCAL AGREEMENT?	PERMITTED IN A NON-RECIPROCAL AGREEMENT?
An obligation on the licensor not to license the technology to another licensee in a particular territory	Yes	Yes
Ban on active or passive selling into territory or exclusive customer group reserved to other (licensor or licensee)	No	Yes
Ban on active selling into territory of, or to exclusive customer group reserved to, another licensee	No	Yes, as long as other licensee was not a competitor of the licensor at the time the agreement was concluded
Ban on passive selling into territory of, or to exclusive customer group reserved to, another licensee	No	No
Captive use restriction	Yes, so long as can sell as spare parts	Yes, so long as can sell as spare parts
Second source provision (obligation on licensee to produce for a single customer)	No	Yes, if the licence was granted specifically to create a source of supply for that customer

Article 4(1)(d)—Limitations on Technology Exploitation or R&D

Whether the agreement is reciprocal or non-reciprocal neither party to the agreement can be restricted from carrying out R&D unless it is to prevent the licensed know-how being disclosed to third parties (in which case the restriction must be proportionate and necessary).[181] In addition, the licensee must not be prevented from exploiting his own technology.

(iii) Agreements between Non-Competing Undertakings

Where the parties are non-competitors they are allowed more leeway. The list of hardcore restraints is briefer and less limiting. To some extent, it resembles the list contained in Article 4 of the Verticals Regulation, focussing on fixed or minimum resale price maintenance and, subject to specified exceptions, restrictions on the territory into which, or the customers to whom, the licensee may sell the contract product.

---

[181] Guidelines, para. 94.

Article 4(2)

Where the undertakings party to the agreement are not competing undertakings, the exemption provided for in Article 2 shall not apply to agreements which, directly or indirectly, in isolation or in combination with other factors under the control of the parties, have as their object:

(a) the restriction of a party's ability to determine its prices when selling products to third parties, without prejudice to the possibility of imposing a maximum sale price or recommending a sale price, provided that it does not amount to a fixed or minimum sale price as a result of pressure from, or incentives offered by, any of the parties;

(b) the restriction of the territory into which, or of the customers to whom, the licensee may passively sell the contract products, except:

   (i) the restriction of passive sales into an exclusive territory or to an exclusive customer group reserved for the licensor,

   (ii) the restriction of passive sales into an exclusive territory or to an exclusive customer group allocated by the licensor to another licensee during the first two years that this other licensee is selling the contract products in that territory or to that customer group,

   (iii) the obligation to produce the contract products only for its own use provided that the licensee is not restricted in selling the contract products actively and passively as spare parts for its own products,

   (iv) the obligation to produce the contract products only for a particular customer, where the licence was granted in order to create an alternative source of supply for that customer,

   (v) the restriction of sales to end-users by a licensee operating at the wholesale level of trade,

   (vi) the restriction of sales to unauthorised distributors by the members of a selective distribution system;

(c) the restriction of active or passive sales to end-users by a licensee which is a member of a selective distribution system and which operates at the retail level, without prejudice to the possibility of prohibiting a member of the system from operating out of an unauthorised place of establishment.

Article 4(2)(a)—Price Restrictions

It will be noted that the prohibition of resale price maintenance does not, unlike the hardcore competitor list, cover maximum or recommended prices so long as they do not really amount to fixed or minimum prices. This clause is the same as that in the Verticals Regulation.[182] Like the Verticals Regulation it covers indirect means of fixing selling prices.[183]

Article 4(2)(b)—Passive Sales Restrictions Imposed on the Licensee

The point of this clause is to identify as hardcore restrictions 'agreements or concerted practices that have as their direct or indirect object the restriction of passive sales by licensees of products incorporating the licensed technology'.[184] It therefore includes provisions in agreements which are a disincentive to make unsolicited sales, such as financial measures and monitoring systems. The Commission does not assume that quantity limitations are imposed as passive sales restrictions but indications that this is so will be examined.[185] It is important to note that Article

---

[182] Reg. 2790/99 [1999] OJ L336/21, Art. 4(a), see *supra* Chap. 9, 750–1. In respect of the TTBER see Guidelines, para. 97.

[183] See Guidelines, para. 97.

[184] *Ibid.*, para. 98.

[185] *Ibid.*

4(2)(b) does not black-list any sales restrictions on the *licensor* or *active* sales restrictions on the *licensee*. Therefore sales restrictions on the licensor and active sales restrictions on the licensee (except those falling within Article 4(2)(b)(vi), discussed below) are block exempted.[186] There are, moreover, a number of major exceptions to the ban on licensees making passive sales outside their allocated territory or customer group which are listed in Article 4(2)(b).

(i) Article 4(2)(b)(i)
The licensee can be prevented from making passive sales into an exclusive territory or to a customer group which the licensor has reserved for himself. If the licensor could not prevent this he might not disseminate the technology through licensing in the first place.[187]

(ii) Article 4(2)(b)(ii)
The licensee can be restricted from making passive sales into the exclusive territory, or to a customer group, allocated by the licensor to another licensee. However, this restriction is only block exempted for a period of the first two years in which the other licensee is serving that territory or customer group. Indeed, paragraph 101 of the Guidelines indicates that such a clause will often fall outside Article 81(1) for the first two years because the licensee needs the protection it affords to persuade him to take the licence. This passive sales exemption for licensees is less generous than in Regulation 296/96, which allowed five years.

(iii) Article 4(2)(b)(iii)
This clause exempts captive use restrictions, as in the hardcore competitor list.[188] The licensee can, therefore be required to produce the product only for his own use provided he is not restricted from selling the products as spare parts.

(iv) Article 4(2)(b)(iv)
This clause exempts second source provisions, as in the hardcore competitor list.[189] The licensee can therefore be required to produce only as an alternative source for a specified customer.

(v) Article 4(2)(b)(v)
The block exemption permits the maintenance of a distinction between wholesale and retail levels of trade. The licensor can give the wholesale distribution function to a licensee and prohibit him from serving the end customers.[190]

(vi) Article 4(2)(b)(vi)
As under the Verticals Regulation[191] this provision allows members of a selective distribution system to be restricted from selling to unauthorized distributors, thereby preserving the integrity of the system.

The table below, set out in Butterworths *Competition Law,* provides in tabular form the passive sales restraints that may be imposed on licensees in a licence agreement between non competitors.

---

186 See Guidelines, para. 99.
187 See further Guidelines, para. 100.
188 See *supra* 821.
189 *Ibid.*
190 Guidelines, para. 104.
191 Reg. 2790/99, Art. 4(b).

W. Allan, M. Furse, and B. Sufrin (eds.), *Butterworths Competition Law* (Butterworths, looseleaf), Division V Chapter 3, para. 591

Table of permissible restraints in the context of agreements between non-competitors on the territory into which or the customer to whom the licensee can passively sell the contract products

Restraint	Permissible?
Passive sales into an exclusive territory or an exclusive customer group reserved to the licensor	Yes
Restriction on passive sales into an exclusive territory or to an exclusive customer group reserved to another licensee	Yes, for a period of 2 years after the licensee first starts selling the contract products
Captive use restriction	Yes, the licensee can be required to produce the product only for its own use provided he can sell as spare parts to customers or third parties performing after sales services
Second source provision	Yes, an obligation on the licensee to produce the products only for a specified customer is permissible where the licence was granted to create an alternative source of supply
Sales to end users	Yes, where the licensee operates at the wholesale level
Sales to unauthorised distributors within a selective distribution system	Yes, but unless the licensee operates at the wholesale level, the licensee must be able to make sales (actively or passive) to end users

Article 4(2)(c)—Active or Passive Sales Bans to End Users within Selective Distribution Systems

A licensee who operates at the retail level of a selective distribution system cannot be prevented from active or passive selling to any end-users. Again, this is similar to the Verticals Regulation.[192]

G. EXCLUDED RESTRICTIONS

(i) Introduction

Article 5 sets out the 'excluded restrictions'. These are restrictions which are not exempted by the TTBER but whose inclusion does not remove the protection of the TTBER from the remainder of the agreement. Individual assessment is required to determine whether the

---

[192] *Ibid.*

excluded restraints infringe Article 81 and, if they do, whether they can be severed from the rest of the agreement.[193]

Article 5

Excluded restrictions

1. The exemption provided for in Article 2 shall not apply to any of the following obligations contained in technology transfer agreements:
   (a) any direct or indirect obligation on the licensee to grant an exclusive licence to the licensor or to a third party designated by the licensor in respect of its own severable improvements to or its own new applications of the licensed technology;
   (b) any direct or indirect obligation on the licensee to assign, in whole or in part, to the licensor or to a third party designated by the licensor, rights to its own severable improvements to or its own new applications of the licensed technology;
   (c) any direct or indirect obligation on the licensee not to challenge the validity of intellectual property rights which the licensor holds in the common market, without prejudice to the possibility of providing for termination of the technology transfer agreement in the event that the licensee challenges the validity of one or more of the licensed intellectual property rights.

2. Where the undertakings party to the agreement are not competing undertakings, the exemption provided for in Article 2 shall not apply to any direct or indirect obligation limiting the licensee's ability to exploit its own technology or limiting the ability of any of the parties to the agreement to carry out research and development, unless such latter restriction is indispensable to prevent the disclosure of the licensed know-how to third parties.

(ii) Improvements

Article 5(1)(a) and (b) deals with improvements made by the licensee to the licensed technology. Article 5(1)(a) and (b) exclude from the ambit of the block exemption a provision by which the licensee is obliged to give an exclusive licence (grant back) over, or to assign to, the licensor (or a designated third party) any severable improvements he has made to the licensed technology or any new applications of it he has developed (even if the grant or assignment is compensated).[194] The reason for excluding these restrictions is to preserve the licensee's incentives to innovate.[195] Such an incentive might be undermined if the licensee is prevented from exploiting its own innovation.

It should be noted that Article 5 does not cover (so that the block exemption does cover) *non-exclusive* grant back provisions even if they are non-reciprocal (i.e., the licensor does not have to license his improvements to the licensee).[196] Further, it does not prevent provisions allowing the licensor to feed-on the severable improvements to other licensees.[197] It does not, therefore, prevent a licence from providing for an exclusive grant back of non-severable

---

[193] See also the discussion of excluded but severable restraints in Chap. 9 in the context of the Verticals Regulation.

[194] See *supra* 840–1 for an explanation of severable improvements.

[195] Guidelines, para. 108.

[196] *Ibid.*, para. 109.

[197] *Ibid.*, paras. 110–11.

improvements, a non-exclusive grant back of severable improvements and feed on of any such improvements by the licensor to other licensees.

(iii) No Challenge Clauses

Article 5(1)(c) excludes no-challenge clauses, whereby the licensee is prohibited from challenging the validity of *any* intellectual property rights which the licensor holds in the common market, from the coverage of the TTBER.[198] However, this is expressed to be without prejudice to the licensor reserving the right to terminate the licence in the event of a challenge to *the licensed rights*. The licensor is therefore not obliged to carry on dealing with a party who is trying to challenge the very subject matter of the agreement. The fact that the licence can be terminated in the event of a challenge is obviously a disincentive to the licensee to challenge, but it is not as great as if it also faced an action for breach of contract.[199]

(iv) Limitations on Technology Exploitation or R&D

Although restrictions on the licensee's ability to exploit its own technology or on either party's ability to carry out R&D are not hardcore restraints in agreements between non-competitors, Article 5(2) provides that such restraints are excluded restraints and are not exempted by the TTBER.[200]

H. WITHDRAWAL AND DISAPPLICATION OF THE BLOCK EXEMPTION

(i) Withdrawal

Regulation 1/2003, Article 29(1) provides that the Commission has a general right withdraw the benefit of a block exemption from any agreement which has effects which are incompatible with Article 81(3). Article 29(2) of Regulation 1/2003 also confers power on the national authorities of the Member States to withdraw the benefit of the TTBER where the agreement has restrictive effects incompatible with Article 81(3) in the territory of their Member State. The TTBER, Article 6(1) and 6(2) indicate that withdrawal may be appropriate in respect of technology transfer agreements where foreclosure effects result from networks of similar agreements[201] or where the parties do not exploit the licensed technology so that no efficiency enhancing activity takes place and the rationale of the block exemption disappears.[202] Thus withdrawal may be proper where:

(a) access of third parties' technologies to the market is restricted, for instance by the cumulative effect of parallel networks of similar restrictive agreements prohibiting licensees from using third parties' technologies;

---

[198] See *supra* 840 for an explanation of no-challenge clauses.

[199] See Guidelines, para. 113 and *infra* 840.

[200] See *supra* 822.

[201] Guidelines, para. 121.

[202] And where this happens in the context of an agreement between competitors the Commission may suspect that the arrangement is really a disguised cartel, see *ibid.*, para. 122.

(b) access of potential licensees to the market is restricted, for instance by the cumulative effect of parallel networks of similar restrictive agreements prohibiting licensors from licensing to other licensees;

(c) without any objectively valid reason, the parties do not exploit the licensed technology.

Withdrawal may only be made prospectively (it has *ex nunc* effect and does not affect prior validity). Further, where the Commission or a national authority wishes to withdraw the benefit of the block exemption, it must issue an infringement decision (finding that the agreement infringes Article 81(1) *and* that it does not meet the conditions of Article 81(3)[203]) or a decision making commitments binding on the undertakings concerned.[204]

(ii) Disapplication

As is the case for the Verticals Regulation, the TTBER, Article 7, provides that the Commission may, by regulation, exclude from the scope of the TTBER parallel networks of similar agreements containing specified restraints, which cover more than 50 per cent of a relevant market. Whereas withdrawal under Article 6 is by decision addressed to specific undertakings, disapplication under Article 7 is by a regulation describing a certain type of agreement to which it applies. Disapplication does not therefore operate as an infringement decision but simply restores the possibility of Article 81(1) applying to the affected agreements. The circumstances in which the Commission would consider exercising this power are discussed in paragraphs 123–9 of the Guidelines.

I. DURATION OF THE EXEMPTION

Article 2(1) sets out the length of time for which the TTBER exemption applies:

This exemption shall apply to the extent that such agreements contain restrictions of competition falling within the scope of Article 81(1). The exemption shall apply for as long as the intellectual property right in the licensed technology has not expired, lapsed or been declared invalid or, in the case of know-how, for as long as the know-how remains secret, except in the event where the know-how becomes publicly known as a result of action by the licensee, in which case the exemption shall apply for the duration of the agreement.

This is different from Regulation 240/96 which exempted some provisions in pure know-how agreements for a maximum of ten years.

---

[203] The burden of proving that the agreement satisfies the conditions is not then as it usually is on the persons seeking to rely on Article 81(3), see Guidelines, para. 19 (compare Regulation 1/2003, Art. 2).

[204] See *infra* Chap. 14.

5. THE APPLICATION OF ARTICLE 81 TO AGREEMENTS FALLING OUTSIDE THE TTBER

A. GENERAL PRINCIPLES

(i) Technology Transfer Agreements Outside the TTBER

Agreements may fall outside the TTBER because:

- they are not bilateral technology transfer agreements under Article 1(1)(b);
- they exceed the market share thresholds;
- they contain hardcore restrictions.

In addition, individual provisions may be outside the TTBER because they are excluded restrictions under Article 5.

The Guidelines provide guidance as to how Article 81 applies to agreements falling outside of the TTBER because they exceed the market share thresholds or contain hardcore restraints and to agreements containing excluded restraints. Although the principles applied in the TTBER and the Guidelines do not apply to agreements that do not constitute technology transfer agreements, the Guidelines indicate that these principles will apply by analogy to: technology transfer agreements to which more than two undertakings are party;[205] 'master licensing agreements';[206] and the licensing of copyright for the purposes of the reproduction and distribution of the protected work.[207] In the case of other licensing agreements that do not constitute technology transfer agreements, however, such as: R&D sub-contracting;[208] licensing of rights in performance and other rights related to copyright (other than software licensing and licensing of copyright for the purposes of the reproduction and distribution of the protected work),[209] and trade mark licences,[210] guidance must be sought from other sources: the Case law of the court; the Commission's decisional practice; and the Commission's Article 81(3) Guidelines.

(ii) No Presumption of Illegality

The general framework for analysis of technology transfer agreements falling outside of the TTBER is set out in paragraphs 130–2 of the Guidelines. The basic principle is that there is no presumption of illegality for agreements that fall outside the TTBER provided they do not contain hard-core restrictions. In particular, there is no presumption that Article 81(1) applies just because the market share thresholds are exceeded.

---

[205] Guidelines, para. 40.
[206] See *supra* n. 126 and accompanying text, Guidelines, para. 42.
[207] Guidelines, para. 51.
[208] *Ibid.*, para. 45.
[209] *Ibid.*, para. 52.
[210] *Ibid.*, para. 53.

(iii) The Second Safe Harbour

The Commission sets out in Guideline 131 the 'second safe harbour'. It states:

Article 81 is unlikely to be infringed in the absence of hardcore restrictions where there are four or more independently controlled technologies in addition to the technologies controlled by the parties to the agreement that may be substitutable for the licensed technology at a comparable cost to the users.

The fact that the agreement falls outside the second safe harbour does not imply that the agreement is caught by Article 81(1) and, if so, that Article 81(3) is not satisfied. The safe harbour merely creates a negative presumption that, in the stipulated circumstances, the agreement is not prohibited. The basis for determining whether the technologies are sufficiently substitutable is discussed in paragraph 131 of the Guidelines.

(iv) The Approach to the Analysis of Individual Agreements

a. Article 81(1)

The general approach to the application of Article 81 to technology transfer agreements is described in paragraphs 10–18 of the Guidelines .[211]

The first question to be asked is, of course, whether or not the agreement has as its object or effect the prevention, restriction, or distortion of competition.[212] In making this determination the relevant case law of the Court is of utmost importance. Guidance can also be sought from the Commission's decision and Guidelines. The Technology Transfer Guidelines seek to bring together the principles derived from these sources and to provide a coherent structure for the appraisal.

It has already been seen that in determining what constitutes a restriction of competition for the purposes of Article 81(1), restraints on both inter -technology and intra-technology competition are relevant. The Commission is concerned that a licensing agreement will lead to negative effects from:

1. reduction of inter-technology competition between companies operating on a technology market or on a market for products incorporating the technologies in question, including facilitation of collusion, both explicit and tacit;

2. foreclosure of competitors by raising their costs, restricting their access to essential inputs or otherwise raising barriers to entry; and

3. reduction of intra-technology competition between undertakings that produce products on the basis of the same technology.[213]

Guidance on what constitutes a restraint by object can be found in the list of hardcore restrictions set out in the TTBER, Article 4.[214] Where the object of the agreement is not to

---

[211] *Supra* 804 ff.

[212] Article 81(1) also only applies if the agreement appreciably restricts competition and appreciably affects trade between Member States, see *supra* Chap. 3.

[213] Guidelines, para. 141.

[214] See also, e.g. Cases T-374, 375, 384 & 388/94, *European Night Services v. Commission* [1998] ECR II-3141, [1998] 5 CMLR 718, Case 234/83, *SA Binon & Cie v. S.A. Agence et Messageries de la Presse*, [1985] ECR 2015, [1985] 3 CMLR 800, Case T-168/01, *GlaxoSmithKline Services Unlimited v. Commission*, 27 Sept. 2006, [2006] 5 CMLR 1623, Cases 505, 513, 515 and 519 (judgment pending) (discussed *supra* Chap. 4) and Case 27/87, *Erauw-Jacquéry*

restrict competition, it must be established that this is its effect. Essentially, this will require proof that the licence agreement: affects competition to such an extent that a negative effect on prices, output, innovation or variety of quality of goods or services has occurred or is likely; forecloses competitors; and/or restricts competition between licensees where not objectively necessary to the existence of an agreement of that type or nature.

b. Article 81(3)

Agreements that restrict competition will be excepted from the Article 81(1) prohibition if they satisfy the Article 81(3) criteria. Thus, restrictions of competition identified under Article 81(1) must be balanced against pro-competitive effects in the context of Article 81(3).[215] The Commission recognises in the Guidelines that restrictive licence agreements will frequently produce pro-competitive effects in the form of efficiencies.[216]

Licence agreements, however, also have substantial pro-competitive potential. Indeed, the vast majority of licence agreements are pro-competitive. Licence agreements may promote innovation by allowing innovators to earn returns to cover at least part of their research and development costs. Licence agreements also lead to a dissemination of technologies, which may create value by reducing the production costs of the licensee or by enabling him to produce new or improved products. Efficiencies at the level of the licensee often stem from a combination of the licensor's technology with the assets and technologies of the licensee. Such integration of complementary assets and technologies may lead to a cost/output configuration that would not otherwise be possible. For instance, the combination of an improved technology of the licensor with more efficient production or distribution assets of the licensee may reduce production costs or lead to the production of a higher quality product. Licensing may also serve the pro-competitive purpose of removing obstacles to the development and exploitation of the licensee's own technology. In particular in sectors where large numbers of patents are prevalent licensing often occurs in order to create design freedom by removing the risk of infringement claims by the licensor. When the licensor agrees not to invoke his intellectual property rights to prevent the sale of the licensee's products, the agreement removes an obstacle to the sale of the licensee's product and thus generally promotes competition.[217]

The burden of Article 81(3) is on those seeking its benefit. The Guidelines provide that hardore restraints will rarely satisfy the conditions of Article 81(3). It will be remembered, however, that all agreements are, theoretically, capable of satisfying the Article 81(3) conditions and that in exceptional circumstances even hardcore restraints may do so.[218] The burden of satisfying the Article 81(3) conditions is an onerous one requiring proof that: efficiency gains, such as the creation of new and improved products or production at lower cost) will result from the activity that forms the object of the agreement;[219] that the restrictions are indispensable to the attainment of the efficiencies (in particular 'whether individual restrictions make it possible to perform the activity in question more efficiently than would have been the case in the absence of the restriction concerned');[220] that consumers receive a fair share of benefit through

---

Sprl v. *La Hesbignonne Société Coopérative* [1988] ECR 1999, [1988] 4 CMLR 576 and Case 258/78, *Nungesser and Eisile* v. *Commission* [1982] ECR 2015, [1983] 1 CMLR 278.

[215] Guidelines, para. 18.

[216] *Ibid.*, para. 146.

[217] *Ibid.*, para. 17.

[218] See *supra* Chap. 4.

[219] Guidelines, para. 148. For the conditions in of Art. 81(3) generally see *supra* Chap. 4, 271 ff.

[220] *Ibid.*, para. 149.

off-setting the likely negative impact of the agreement on prices, output and other relevant matters;[221] and that the agreement does not afford the parties the possibility of eliminating competition in respect of a substantial part of the products concerned. The remaining competitive pressures on the market must therefore be analyzed to ensure that the parties are not afforded the possibility of eliminating competition.[222] An *ex ante* approach is taken, assessing the position at the time the contract was concluded.[223] The Article 81(3) exception lasts for as long as its conditions are fulfilled.[224]

(v) Relevant Factors

The Guidelines discuss factors which are particularly relevant to the application of Article 81 in individual cases.[225]

a. The Nature of the Agreement

The agreement must be analysed in terms of the competitive relationship between the parties and the analysis must go beyond the express terms of the agreement.[226]

b. The Market Position of the Parties

The higher the market share of the parties the greater their market power is likely to be. They may also enjoy first mover advantages, hold essential patents, or have superior technology.[227] Even where the parties are not competitors it is relevant whether or not the licensee owns a competing technology.[228]

c. The Market Position of Competitors

The stronger the actual competitors are, and the more numerous they are, the less risk there is of the parties individually exercising market power.[229]

d. The Market Position of the Buyers of the Licensed Product

Buyer power may prevent the licensor and/or licensee from exercising market power, thereby solving a competition problem which might otherwise have existed, but whether this is so will depend on the conduct of the buyers in question.[230] A good indicator of buyer power is the buyer's market share of the purchase market.

e. Entry Barriers

Entry barriers will be relevant to an assessment of the parties' market power but the Commission states that 'actual competition is in general more effective and will weigh more heavily in the assessment of a case than potential competition'.[231]

---

[221] Guidelines, para. 150.

[222] *Ibid.*, 151, and see the general discussion of Art. 81(3), *supra* Chap. 4, 271 ff.

[223] Guidelines, para. 147.

[224] See *supra* Chap. 4.

[225] Guidelines, para. 132.

[226] *Ibid.*, para. 133.

[227] *Ibid.*, para. 134.

[228] *Ibid.*, para. 135.

[229] *Ibid.*, para. 136.

[230] *Ibid.*, para. 137.

[231] *Ibid.*, para. 138.

f. The Maturity of the Market

A market is said to be mature when it has existed for some time, the technology used is well-known, widespread and not changing very much, and demand is relatively stable or declining. In mature markets restrictions on competition are more likely to have negative effects.[232]

g. Other Factors

Other factors which may be taken into account include the coverage of the market by similar agreements (cumulative effects), the duration of the agreement, the regulatory environment, and behaviour that may indicate or facilitate collusion.[233]

B. THE APPLICATION OF THE TTBER AND THE GUIDELINES TO SPECIFIC PROVISIONS

It is essential to remember that within the safe harbour of the TTBER any restriction not in the list of hardcore or excluded restrictions is permitted. The Guidelines provide guidance on the compatibility of specific restraints in technology transfer agreements which do *not* benefit from the safe harbour of the block exemption. The Guidelines do not, however, provide further guidance on hardcore restraints as the Commission consider that such restraints automatically infringe Article 81(1) and are most unlikely to satisfy the Article 81(3) conditions.

(i) Provisions not Generally Restrictive of Article 81(1)

Paragraph 155 of the Guidelines sets out a list of obligations in licence agreements which are generally not restrictive of competition within the meaning of Article 81(1). These are:

- confidentiality obligations;
- obligations on licensees not to sub-licence;
- obligations not to use the licensed technology after the expiry of the agreement, provided that the licensed technology remains valid and in force;
- obligations to assist the licensor in enforcing the licensed intellectual property rights;
- obligations to pay minimum royalties or to produce a minimum quantity of products incorporating the licensed technology;
- obligations to use the licensor's trade mark or indicate the name of the licensor on the product.

(ii) Royalty Obligations

a. Agreements between Competitors

Provisions relating to royalty payments are not normally caught by Article 81(1)[234] even if the royalty obligations extend beyond the validity of the licensed intellectual property right.[235]

---

[232] *Ibid.*, para. 139.

[233] *Ibid., para.* 140.

[234] *Ibid.*, paras. 155 and 156.

[235] *Ibid.*, para. 159. Once the intellectual property right has expired third parties can legally compete with the parties to the agreement so such a provision is unlikely to have appreciable anti-competitive effects.

In agreements between competitors, the Guidelines state[236] that occasionally royalty clauses could amount to price-fixing arrangements, which constitute a hard-core restriction (under TTBER, Article 4(1)(a)). This will be so, for example, if the competitors provide for reciprocal running royalties[237] in circumstances in which the licence is a sham to disguise price fixing[238] or if royalties have to be paid on products produced solely with the licensee's own technology (see Article 4(1)(a) and Article 4(1)(d)).[239] If the royalty provisions do not amount to hardcore restraints, they will of course be block exempted if the parties market shares do not exceed the 20 per cent threshold. Outside of the safe harbour, however, the Guidelines indicate that Article 81 may be infringed where competitors cross-license and the running royalties are 'clearly disproportionate' to the market value of the licence or where running royalties per unit increase as output increases[240]

b. Agreements between Non-competitors

In agreements between non-competitors the TTBER covers agreements whereby royalties are calculated on the basis of both products produced with the licensed technology and those produced with technology licensed from third parties. Outside the 30 per cent safe harbour, however, such a provision must be analysed for appreciable foreclosure effects (similar to a non-compete provision) which would bring the agreement within Article 81(1) and make the fulfilment of Article 81(3) unlikely.[241]

(iii) Exclusive and Sole Licences

The grant of exclusive and sole licences is often accompanied by sales restrictions (discussed below).[242]

a. Agreements between Competitors

The effect of the TTBER is that sole licensing and *non-reciprocal* exclusive licensing are exempted up to the 20 per cent market share threshold. The effect of Article 4(1)(c), however, is to make reciprocal exclusive licensing between competitors a hardcore restriction as it amounts to market sharing.[243]

Outside the safe harbour, a non-reciprocal exclusive licence must be analysed for likely anti-competitive effect. The licence will result in either the licensor leaving the market altogether (if the licence is worldwide) or ceasing to produce inside a particular territory (if the licence is limited to a territory). The key issue, therefore, is the competitive significance of the licensor leaving the market in question. It may be that where the licensor is insignificant (e.g., a small research undertaking active only on the technology market) Article 81(1) may not be infringed

---

[236] Guidelines, para. 157.

[237] See *supra* 819.

[238] The language of Guideline 157 is toned down from the aspersions cast upon reciprocal running royalties in the draft of the Guidelines: see Commissioner Mario Monti, 'The New EU Policy on Technology Transfer Agreements', Ecole des Mines, Paris, 16 Jan. 2004, available on the Commission's web site.

[239] Guidelines, para. 81 cites Case 193/83, *Windsurfing International v. Commission* [1986] ECR 611, [1986] 3 CMLR 489, *supra* 796, as authority for this.

[240] Guidelines, para. 158.

[241] *Ibid.*, para. 160.

[242] See *supra* 820.

[243] Guidelines, para. 163.

in the first place.[244] Reciprocal sole licensing may facilitate collusion where the parties have market power.[245]

b. Agreements between Non-competitors

To the extent that exclusive or sole licensing between non-competitors is caught by Article 81(1) at all[246] it is exempted by the TTBER up to the 30 per cent threshold. Outside the safe harbour, the Guidelines accept that exclusive licensing agreements between non-competitors may not infringe Article 81(1) and will usually fulfil the Article 81(3) conditions because of the need to give the licensee sufficient incentive to invest. The Commission 'will therefore only exceptionally intervene' irrespective of the territorial scope of the licence. A reason for intervention might be that there is a foreclosure problem because the licensee obtains an exclusive licence to crucial competing technologies.[247]

c. Cross Licences

The Commission is also concerned that where parties cross-license each other and undertake not to license third parties it could lead to the creation of a closed *de facto* industry standard. Such arrangements are treated accorded to the same principles as technology pools discussed below. Normally, to satisfy the conditions of Article 81(3) it will be necessary for technology supporting such a standard to be licensed to third parties on fair, reasonable and non-discriminatory terms.[248]

(iv) Sales Restrictions

a. Agreements between Competitors

In a reciprocal agreement between competitors, restrictions on active or passive sales of products incorporating the licensed technology into another territory or to another customer group are hardcore restrictions.[249] As such provisions amount to market sharing, they are unlikely to fulfil the Article 81(3) conditions when they are individually assessed.[250]

In non-reciprocal agreements, restrictions on active or passive sales by either party to customer groups or territories of the other are block exempted by the TTBER.[251] Restrictions on active (but not passive) sales by the licensee into another licensee's territory or to his customer group are exempted too, but only if the latter licensee was not a competitor of the licensor at the time his own licence agreement was concluded.[252]

Outside the safe harbour active and passive sales restrictions are likely to fall within Article 81(1) where either party has a significant degree of market power. However, the conditions of Article 81(3) could be fulfilled if the restrictions are indispensable to protect substantial investments made by the licensee and the dissemination of the technology.[253]

---

[244] Guidelines, para. 164.

[245] *Ibid.*

[246] See Case 258/78, *Nungesser v. EC Commission* [1982] ECR 2015, [1983] 1 CMLR 278, discussed *supra* 791 ff.

[247] Guidelines, paras. 165 and 166.

[248] *Ibid.*, 167.

[249] TTBER, Art. 4(1)(c).

[250] Guidelines, paras. 12(b), 77, and 169.

[251] TTBER, Art. 4(1)(c)(iv).

[252] *Ibid.*, Art. 4(1)(c)(v).

[253] Guidelines, paras. 170–1.

b. Agreements between Non-competitors

The TTBER exempts all restrictions on active sales in agreements between non-competitors.

The TTBER also exempts passive sales restrictions on the licensor and passives sales restrictions which protect the licensor from the licensee.[254] Outside the safe harbour, restrictions on the licensee selling into the territory of the licensor are unlikely to fall within Article 81(1) if without them the licensing would not occur.[255] Sales restrictions on the licensor are likely, if they do fall within Article 81(1) to satisfy the Article 81(3) criteria unless there are no real alternatives to the licensor's technology exists.[256]

The TTBER exempts restrictions on passive sales by a licensee into the territory, or to the customers of another licensee only for the first two years that the other licensee is selling the contract products.[257] Restrictions lasting for more than two years are hardcore restraints and are likely to be caught by Article 81(1) and are unlikely to satisfy Article 81(3).[258]

Above the 30 per cent threshold active sales restrictions are likely to be caught by Article 81(1) if the licensee has significant market power (because they limit intra-technology competition) but may satisfy the Article 81(3) conditions where necessary to prevent free riding and to induce investment by the licensee.[259]

(v) Output Restrictions

a. Agreements between Competitors

Output limitations in agreements between competitors are hard-core restrictions under the TTBER, Article 4(1)(b) but this is subject to two exceptions. They are exempted up to the 20 per cent threshold first, where they are imposed on the licensee in a non-reciprocal agreement and secondly, where they are imposed on only one of the licensees in a reciprocal agreement. Above the thresholds, restrictions on the licensee may restrict competition where the parties have significant market power. Article 81(3) may apply, however, where the licensor's technology is substantially better than the licensee's and the licensee's output under the agreement substantially exceeds his previous output. The key issue in the application of Article 81(3) is whether the licensor would be willing to disseminate his technology to licensees in the absence of output limitations on the licensee (including site licences).[260]

b. Agreements between Non-competitors

Output restrictions in agreements between non-competitors are exempted by the TTBER up to the 30 per cent threshold (they do not appear in the hardcore list at all). Above the threshold the Commission is concerned that restraints on quantities will restrain intra-technology competition between licensees.[261] However, again it is recognized that the licensor may only be prepared to licence his technology if output restrictions are possible.[262] The Commission

---

[254] TTBER, Art. 4(2)(b)(i) (ii).

[255] Guidelines, para. 172

[256] *Ibid.*, para. 173.

[257] TTBER, Art. 4(2)(b)(ii).

[258] Guidelines, para. 174.

[259] *Ibid.*

[260] Guidelines, para. 175. A site licence is where the licence may be exploited only on one site.

[261] *Ibid.*, para. 176.

[262] *Ibid.*, para. 178.

nevertheless considers that output restrictions combined with exclusive territory or customer group provisions increases the likelihood of the agreement partitioning markets.[263]

(vi) Field of Use Restrictions

a. General

The distinction between field of use restrictions and customer allocation provision is explained above.[264] The Guidelines stress the importance of this distinction and that field of use restrictions are frequently pro-competitive.

Given that field of use restrictions are block exempted and that certain customer restrictions are hardcore restrictions under Articles 4(1)(c) and 4(2)(b) of the TTBER, it is important to distinguish the two categories of restraints. A customer restriction presupposes that specific customer groups are identified and that the parties are restricted in selling to such identified groups. The fact that a technical field of use restriction may correspond to certain groups of customers within a product market does not imply that the restraint is to be classified as a customer restriction. For instance, the fact that certain customers buy predominantly or exclusively chipsets with more than four CPUs does not imply that a licence which is limited to chipsets with up to four CPUs constitutes a customer restriction. However, the field of use must be defined objectively by reference to identified and meaningful technical characteristics of the licensed product.[265]

b. Agreements between Competitors

Field of use restrictions constitute a form of 'allocation of markets and customers' within the meaning of Article 4(1)(c) of the TTBER. Thus, field of use restrictions imposed on licensors in reciprocal agreements between competitors are hard-core restrictions. Article 4(1)(c)(i), however, exempts field of use restrictions on licensees up to the 20 per cent threshold, so long as the restrictions do not go beyond the scope of the licensed technology and the licensee is not limited in the use of his own technology.[266] Field of use restrictions on licensors are block exempted below the threshold only in non-reciprocal agreements where the field of use is reserved to the licensee. Outside of the safe harbour, the Commission's main concern is that the licensee ceases to be a competitive force outside the licensed field of use and considers the risk of this greatest where the parties cross-license and the restrictions are asymmetrical (the parties are licensed for different fields of use). The agreement is likely to be caught by Article 81(1) if it is likely to lead to the licensee reducing output outside the licensed field of use. Where there are symmetrical restrictions (the parties each license the other to use their technology in the same field of use) the agreement is unlikely to be caught by Article 81(1).[267]

c. Agreements between Non-competitors

Field of use restrictions imposed on the licensor and licensee are block exempted by the TTBER up to the 30 per cent threshold. Outside of the safe harbour the Guidelines indicate that allowing the licensor to limit the licensee to certain fields of use will generally be pro-competitive since it enables the licensor to license exploitation of the technology in fields which he does not

[263] Guidelines, para. 177.
[264] *Supra* 787 and Guidelines, para. 179.
[265] Guidelines, para. 180.
[266] See Guidelines, paras. 77 and 90.
[267] Guidelines, para. 183.

want to exploit himself.[268] In agreements between non-competitors the licensor may normally grant sole or exclusive licences to different licensees for different fields of use.[269]

(vii) Captive Use Restrictions

a. Agreements between Competitors

Captive use restrictions[270] are block exempted in agreements between competitors up to the 20 per cent threshold. Outside of the safe harbour there is concern that the provision will prevent the licensee from supplying components to third party producers. The Article 81 analysis is thus affected by the question of whether or not the licensee was an actual or potential supplier of components to third parties. If he was not, the captive use restriction does not change anything. If he was a supplier, the impact of the restriction must be examined, as competition which existed prior to the agreement is restricted.[271]

b. Agreements between Non-competitors

Captive use restrictions in agreements between non-competitors are block exempted up to the 30 per cent threshold. Outside of the block exemption, two main competitive risks arise: first, the provision may restrict intra-technology competition on the market for inputs; and secondly, the provision may exclude arbitrage between licensees, which may enable the licensor to impose discriminatory royalties on the licensees.[272] If the licensor is himself a component supplier the restriction may be pro-competitive as otherwise he would not give the licence, being unwilling to create competition for his own components. In that case the restriction may not be caught by Article 81(1), and, if it is, it may satisfy the conditions of Article 81(3).[273] Where, however the licensor is not a supplier of components a captive use restriction normally infringes Article 81 since it not necessary for the dissemination of the technology.[274]

(viii) Tying and Bundling

Tying and bundling in technology transfer agreements is explained above.[275] Tying (the expression is used in the Guidelines to cover both tying and bundling) is block exempted by the TTBER in both agreements between competitors and non-competitors where the market share thresholds are satisfied. The market share thresholds apply to any relevant technology or product market affected by the agreement including that for the tied product. Outside of the thresholds the pro and anti-competitive effects have to be balanced.

The key concern with tying is the foreclosure of competing suppliers from the tied market. It may also enable a licensor to maintain market power in the tying market.

The main restrictive effect of tying is foreclosure of competing suppliers of the tied product. Tying may also allow the licensor to maintain market power in the market for the tying product by raising

---

[268] While retaining for himself fields in which he does want to operate. *Ibid.*, 184.

[269] Guidelines, para. 185.

[270] See *supra* 821.

[271] Guidelines, para. 187.

[272] *Ibid.*, para. 188.

[273] *Ibid.*, para. 189.

[274] *Ibid.*, para. 190.

[275] *Supra* 788.

barriers to entry since it may force new entrants to enter several markets at the same time. Moreover, tying may allow the licensor to increase royalties, in particular when the tying product and the tied product are partly substitutable and the two products are not used in fixed proportion. Tying prevents the licensee from switching to substitute inputs in the face of increased royalties for the tying product. These competition concerns are independent of whether the parties to the agreement are competitors or not. For tying to produce likely anti-competitive effects the licensor must have a significant degree of market power in the tying product so as to restrict competition in the tied product. In the absence of market power in the tying product the licensor cannot use his technology for the anti-competitive purpose of foreclosing suppliers of the tied product. Furthermore, as in the case of non-compete obligations, the tie must cover a certain proportion of the market for the tied product for appreciable foreclosure effects to occur. In cases where the licensor has market power on the market for the tied product rather than on the market for the tying product, the restraint is analysed as non-compete or quantity forcing, reflecting the fact that any competition problem has its origin on the market for the 'tied' product and not on the market for the 'tying' product . . . [276]

On the other hand, tying may be a source of efficiency gains and may be necessary to protect the reputation of the licensor and the products produced with the licensed technology.[277] This will particularly be so when it is necessary for the licensee to use the tied product in order to exploit the technology in a technically satisfactory way, in order to ensure conformity to quality standards or to exploit the licensed technology more efficiently. In these cases tying will not normally infringe Article 81.

(ix) Non-Compete Obligations

Non-compete obligations are obligations on the licensee not to use third party technologies which compete with the licensed technology. Obligations covering products, or additional technologies supplied by the licensor are dealt with under the tying section (above).

Non-compete obligations do not constitute hardcore restraints and are block exempted by the TTBER up to the relevant thresholds. Outside the thresholds the Commission's main concern, in regard to both agreements between competitors and non-competitors, is the risk of foreclosure of third parties who may not be able to find outlets for their technology and/or, in cases of cumulative use, that the agreements may facilitate collusion between licensors. Foreclosure may arise where a single licensor has a significant degree of market power or a number of licensors conclude similar agreement that cumulatively have the effect of foreclosing the market to competitors (unlikely if less than 50 per cent of the market is tied) and where barriers to entry for new licensees are relatively high.[278] Even if a substantial part of the market is not covered by non-compete obligations the risk may be high if the non-compete obligations are targeted at those undertakings most likely to license competing technologies.[279]

On the other hand, non-compete obligations may have pro-competitive effects. The Guidelines accept that they: may promote the dissemination of technology by reducing the misappropriation of licensed technology (particularly know-how); may ensure that the licensee has an incentive to invest in and exploit the licensed technology effectively (possibly in combination with an exclusive territory); and may induce the licensor to make specific

---

[276] Guidelines, para. 193.

[277] *Ibid.*, para. 194.

[278] *Ibid.*, para. 199.

[279] *Ibid.*, para. 200.

investments (such as training the licensee or tailoring the technology to his needs). However, the Commission considers that this can often be achieved by less restrictive means (such as charging directly by way of a lump sum).[280]

(x) No-Challenge Clauses

No-challenge clauses, which prohibit a challenge to the licensor's technology, are 'excluded restrictions' within the meaning of Article 5[281] since it is generally considered to be in the interests of undistorted competition, and of the intellectual property rights system, that invalid intellectual property rights should be eliminated. 'Invalid intellectual property stifles innovation rather than promoting it'.[282] The licensee is normally in the best position to spot the invalidity of the rights because he is actually working with the technology. The Guidelines state that no-challenge clauses are likely to violate Article 81 where the licensed technology is valuable. However, with regard to know-how, a more favourable attitude to these clauses is adopted, as once know-how has been disclosed it is often impossible or difficult to recover it (the genie cannot be put back in the bottle). A no-challenge clause may therefore in these circumstances promote the dissemination of new technology, for example, by preventing stronger licensees absorbing the know-how of weaker licensors and then challenging it.[283]

It will be recalled, however, that the TTBER does not exclude clauses permitting the licensor to terminate the licence if the licensee challenges *the licensed technology*.[284] The licensor is not forced to continue to deal with a licensee that challenges the subject matter of the licence and, following termination of the agreement, the use of the technology will be at the licensee's own risk.

No-challenge clauses in settlement and non-assertion agreements will normally fall outside Article 81(1).[285]

(xi) Improvements

Article 5 also excludes from the benefit of the TTBER exclusive grant backs or assignments of severable improvements to the licensor.[286] When such provisions are individually assessed under Article 81 the existence and level of consideration given for the improvements may be relevant. If the licensee is to obtain compensation he will have greater incentive to innovate. The market position of the licensor will also be relevant, as the stronger the licensor's position the more likely it is that that exclusive grant backs will have restrictive effects on competition in innovation. In addition, there may be negative effects on competition where there are parallel networks of licence agreements containing such obligations.[287]

---

[280] Guidelines, para. 201–3.

[281] *Supra* 827.

[282] Guidelines, para. 112.

[283] *Ibid.*

[284] TTBER, Art. 5(2) and Guideline 113.

[285] Guidelines, para. 209, see *infra* 841.

[286] Article 5 does not cover *non-exclusive* grant back obligations, even if the grant back is not reciprocal (i.e., only imposed on the licensee) and where the licensor is entitled to feed-on the severable improvements to other licensees. Non-reciprocal grant back may be pro-competitive because of its effect on the licensor, Guidelines, para. 109 *supra* 826–7.

[287] Guidelines, para. 110.

The Commission is concerned that where competitors cross-license each other with grant back obligations neither can gain a competitor advantage over the other because they will be sharing improvements.[288]

Grant backs of non-severable improvements are not restrictive of competition within Article 81(1) since the licensee cannot exploit them without the licensor's permission as they cannot be separated from the licensed technology.[289]

(xii) Settlement and Non-assertion Agreements

The TTBER covers settlement and non-assertion agreements insofar as they do not contain hardcore restrictions. Outside of the safe harbour, the approach of the Commission is set out in paragraph 204 of the Guidelines:

Licensing may serve as a means of settling disputes or avoiding that one party exercises his intellectual property rights to prevent the other party from exploiting his own technology. Licensing including cross licensing in the context of settlement agreements and non-assertion agreements is not as such restrictive of competition since it allows the parties to exploit their technologies post agreement. However, the individual terms and conditions of such agreements may be caught by Article 81(1). Licensing in the context of settlement agreements is treated like other licence agreements. In the case of technologies that from a technical point of view are substitutes, it is therefore necessary to assess to what extent it is likely that the technologies in question are in a one-way or two-way blocking position (cf. paragraph 32 above). If so, the parties are not deemed to be competitors.

If the parties cross-license under the agreement, have a significant degree of market power, and the restrictions clearly go beyond what is required to unblock, the arrangement is likely to be caught by Article 81(1).[290] Where the agreement entitles the parties to use each other's technology and extends to future developments the Commission will be concerned with the impact of the agreement on the parties' incentives to innovate. If they have a significant degree of market power and the agreement prevents them from gaining a competitive lead over one another the agreement is likely to be caught by Article 81(1) and not satisfy Article 81(3).[291] No-challenge clauses will generally be outside Article 81(1) in settlement and non-assertion agreements since the whole point of the agreement is to settle disputes and avoid future ones.[292]

C. TECHNOLOGY POOLS

Agreements setting up technology pools, where two or more parties come together to assemble a 'package' of technology that is then licensed to the contributors to the pool and possibly third parties,[293] are not covered by the TTBER (although it may cover a licence granted by a technology pool to a third party). However, they are specifically dealt with in the Guidelines.[294] The

---

[288] This is also a concern over clauses in settlement or non-assertion agreements, where the parties settle disputes by, *inter alia*, agreeing to share future technological developments: see Guidelines, para. 208.

[289] Guidelines, para. 109.

[290] *Ibid.*, para. 207.

[291] *Ibid.*, para. 208.

[292] *Ibid.*, para. 209.

[293] Technology pools can be simple arrangements but may also be very elaborate, with the pooled technology entrusted to a separate entity, Guidelines, 210.

[294] Particularly Guidelines, paras. 210–35.

Commission has indicated that it will closely monitor existing or new technology pools, in particular those that support or establish a *de facto* or *de jure* industry standard.[295]

The competitive risks of technology pools, resulting from collusion and/or exclusion, have to be balanced against their efficiency enhancing potential, for example, the ability to facilitate dissemination of technology, to reduce costs, to clear blocking-positions and to provide one-stop licensing of technologies. In assessing the competing risks and efficiency potentials account must taken of: the nature of the pooled technologies, and whether they are (a) complementary[296] or substitutes[297] and (b) essential[298] or non-essential;[299] and the institutional framework of the pool.[300] The way in which this assessment is carried out is explained in paragraphs 217–22 of the Guidelines. In assessing individual restraints commonly found in technology pools the Commission applies three guiding principles:

- The stronger the market position of the pool the greater the risk of anti-competitive effects;
- Pools that hold a strong position on the market should be open and non-discriminatory;
- Pools should not unduly foreclose third party technologies or limit the creation of alternative pools.[301]

Where a technology pool compatible with Article 81 is created, all provisions ancillary to the establishment of the standard or pool, such as royalty provisions, also fall outside Article 81. Where, however, the pool has a dominant position, the Guidelines indicate that closer scrutiny of the licensing provisions will be necessary and, for example, that the licensing and royalty provisions should be fair, non-discriminatory and non-exclusive.[302]

The Guidelines provide no information on patent ambushes. Patent ambushes occur where an undertaking withholds or does not reveal information in a standard setting procedure but later asserts patent claims against other undertakings which have adopted and are using the standard. In the US, a number of cases have been brought alleging, for example, fraudulent behaviour in a standard setting organization. In *Rambus*,[303] for example, the FTC found that Rambus Inc, a computer technology company, had monopolized the market for computer memory technologies

---

[295] IP/06/139. In this press release the Commission announced that it had closed an investigation into the practices of Philips Electronics which had offered European manufacturers of CD-Recordable disks a joint portfolio licence which included both its own CD-Recordable disc patents and those of Sony and Taiyo Yuden. The Commission closed the investigation once Philips undertook to discontinue the joint patent portfolio licence in Europe and to offer revised individual licences limited to its own patents.

[296] Both technologies are required to produce the product or carry out in process in question.

[297] Either technology allows the holder to produce the product or carry out the process.

[298] There are no substitutes for the technology inside or outside the pool and the technology in question constitutes a necessary part of the package of technologies for the purposes of producing the product(s) or carrying out the process(es) to which the pool relates.

[299] Guidelines, paras. 215–16. Broadly, the creation of a pool composed of only essential complementary technology pools is likely to fall outside Article 81(1). In contrast, a pool of substitute technologies will constitute a price fixing arrangement which violates Article 81(1) and is unlikely to satisfy the conditions of Article 81(3). A pool comprising non essential substitute technologies may foreclose third party competing technologies, Guidelines paras. 219–22.

[300] Factors such as whether participation in the pool is open, whether experts are involved, how information exchange is dealt with and how disputes should be resolved are relevant, Guidelines, paras. 230–5.

[301] Guidelines, para. 224.

[302] *Ibid.*, paras. 225–9.

[303] *In the Matter of Rambus Incorporated*, FTC Docket No. 9302, available at http://www.ftc.gov/os/adjpro/d9302/index.htm.

when it participated in the work of a standard setting organisation (Joint Electron Device Engineering Council) without revealing to other members that it possessed and was developing patents and patent applications for technologies adopted in the relevant standards. In its final order not only did the FTC bar Rambus from making misrepresentations or omissions to any standard setting organisation, but it imposed obligations to license certain technology and maximum royalty rates that Rambus could charge firms implementing standards.

6. TRADE MARK LICENCES

A. GENERAL

There is no block exemption which specifically covers trade mark licences. In the discussion of the TTBER above, however, it is seen that where the licence of a trade mark is ancillary to a licence of patents, know-how, designs or software the TTBER may apply.[304] In this situation the trade mark licence may enable the licensee to exploit the licensed technology better. The licence may authorize the licensee to use his trade mark on products incorporating the licensed technology. This will help consumers make the link between the licensee's products and the licensed technology and may promote the dissemination of the licensed technology by allowing the licensor to identify himself as its source.[305] In other situations the TTBER does not cover trade mark licensing and, because the trade mark licences are not sufficiently linked to the dissemination of technology, the principles developed in the TTBER and the Guidelines do *not* apply by analogy.[306]

Trade mark licences may also be ancillary to a vertical agreement, such as a franchising agreement.[307] The Verticals Regulation, Regulation 2790/1999, which applies to agreements between two or more undertakings each of which operates at a different level of the production or distribution chain and which relates to the conditions under which the parties may purchase, sell or resell certain goods or services,[308] covers agreements containing provisions relating to the assignment to the buyer or use by the buyer of trade marks where these provisions do not constitute the primary object of the agreement and where they are directly related to the use, sale or resale of the goods by the buyer of its customers.[309]

Where the block exemptions are not applicable, however, it will be necessary to seek guidance from the case law of the ECJ, Commission decisions, the Article 81(3) Guidelines and, where appropriate, the Technology Transfer and Vertical Guidelines. The paucity (and age) of the case law and decisional practice mean that frequently principles to be applied in the Article 81 analysis may have to be derived more broadly from the case law and the relevant Commission Guidelines.

In *Consten & Grundig*[310] it was held that an agreement seeking to confer absolute territorial protection on the licensee of a trade mark would infringe Article 81(1). Further, the

---

[304] Reg. 772/2004, [2004] OJ L123/11, Art. 1(1)(b).

[305] Guidelines on technology transfer agreements [2004] OJ C101/2, para. 50.

[306] Guidelines, para. 53.

[307] As the Guidelines recognize, see para. 53.

[308] Franchising agreements were formerly dealt with in a specific block exemption, Reg. 4087/88 [1988] OJ L359/46: see *supra* Chap. 9.

[309] Reg. 2790/1999 [1999] OJ L336/21, Art. 2(3): see *supra* Chap. 9.

[310] Cases 56 and 58 164, *Etablissements Consten SA & Grundig-Verkaufs-GmbH* v. *Commission* [1966] ECR 299, [1966] CMLR 418, see *supra* 781 and Chap. 4.

844 | EC COMPETITION LAW

Commission's two formal decisions relating to trade mark licences, *Campari* and *Moosehead/ Whitbread*,[311] demonstrate that the Commission took a strict approach to exclusivity provisions[312] and applied broadly the same principles to trade mark licences as it did *at the time* in its decisions to patent and know-how licences. As the Commission's thinking has evolved considerably since this time, the reasoning in these cases, which support a formalistic approach to restraints on economic freedom, should be treated with some caution.

B. THE *CAMPARI* DECISION[313]

The *Campari* transaction is difficult to classify but the trade mark licence was a predominant element. The aperitifs Bitter Campari and Cordial Campari were made by mixing alcohol with a secret herbal concentrate. Campari-Milano set up a network of licensees to manufacture and sell its products in all Community countries except the UK and Ireland.[314] Under the agreements the licensees purchased the secret concentrate and colouring matter from the licensor and manufactured the drink in compliance with the licensor's instructions. The resulting bottles of aperitif were then sold under the licensor's Campari trade mark. The licences were exclusive, prevented the licensees from manufacturing or handling competing products or pursuing an active sales policy outside their territory, banned exports outside the common market and provided that only the original Italian product could be supplied to certain customers/outlets. There were also provisions about manufacture only at approved sites, confidentiality, advertising, and non-assignment. The Commission held that the following provisions were outside Article 81(1): the ban on exports outside the common market, as in the circumstances there was little chance of this indirectly affecting inter-Member State trade; the restriction of the licence to those plants capable of guaranteeing the quality of the product; the obligation to follow the licensor's manufacturing instructions and to buy secret raw materials from the licensor, as this was central to the product being of proper 'Campari' quality;[315] the confidentiality of the know-how; the minimum advertising commitments and the prohibition on assignment. Other clauses, including the exclusivity and the active sales ban, were held to infringe Article 81(1).

The Commission granted an exemption however. This part of the decision is a particularly good illustration of how the four criteria in Article 81(3) are, or were, applied. Note that in paragraph 71 the Commission distinguishes between the effects of a non-competition clause in a trade mark licence and one in a patent licence.

---

[311] *Re the Agreement of Davide Campari-Milano SpA* [1978] OJ L70/69, [1978] 2 CMLR 397, *Moosehead/Whitbread* [1990] OJ L100/32, [1991] 4 CMLR 391.

[312] Even though this approach bore 'no relation to the reality that no lager brewer would contemplate developing and marketing a new brand in competition with one of its rivals', N. Green and A. Robertson, *Commercial Agreements and Competition Law* (2nd edn., Kluwer, 1997), 931.

[313] *Re the Agreement of Davide-Campari-Milano SpA* [1978] OJ L70/69, [1978] 2 CMLR 397.

[314] The UK and Ireland were covered by a straightforward distribution agreement which fell within the block exemption then in force, Reg. 67/67[1967] OJ Spec. Ed. 10.

[315] Certain other ingredients did not necessarily have to be bought from the licensor but had to be sourced on the basis of objective quality considerations.

Re the Agreement of Davide-Campari-Milano SpA [1978] OJ L70/69, [1978] 2 CMLR 397

Commission

III APPLICABILITY OF ARTICLE [81(3)] OF THE EC TREATY

. . .

A. The restrictions of competition mentioned at points 1 to 4 of item II A satisfy the tests of Article [81(3)].

1. The exclusivity granted by Campari-Milano contributes to improving the production and distribution of the products. By giving each licensee a guarantee that no other undertaking will obtain a licence within its allocated territory, and that in this territory neither Campari-Milano nor any other licensee may manufacture products bearing the licensor's trade mark this commitment confers upon each licensee an advantage in its allotted territory. This territorial advantage is such as to permit a sufficient return on the investment made by each licensee for the purpose of manufacturing the product bearing the trade mark under conditions acceptable to the licensor and holder of the trade mark, and it enables the licensee to increase its production capacity and constantly to improve the already long-established distribution network.

In practice the exclusivity granted has allowed each licensee to improve its existing plant and to build new plant. It has also enabled each licensee to strengthen its efforts to promote the brand, doubling the total volume of sales in the Benelux countries and Germany over the last six years, and, by establishing a multistage distribution network, to secure a constantly increasing number of customers and thus to ensure supplies throughout the allotted territory.

2. The ban on dealing in competing products also contributes to improving distribution of the licensed products by concentrating sales efforts, encouraging the build-up of stocks and shortening delivery times.

The restriction on the licensees' freedom to deal in other products at the same time as the products here in question prevents the licensees from neglecting Campari in the event of conflict between the promotion of Campari sales and possible interest in another product. Although a non-competition clause in a licensing agreement concerning industrial property rights based on the result of a creative activity, such as a patent, would constitute a barrier to technical and economic progress by preventing the licensees from taking an interest in other techniques and products, this is not the case with the licensing agreements under consideration here. The aim pursued by the parties, as is clear from the agreements taken as a whole, is to decentralise manufacture within the EEC and to rationalise the distribution system linked to it, and thus to promote the sale of Campari-Milano's Bitter, manufactured from the same concentrates provided by Campari-Milano, according to the same mixing process and using the same ingredients, and bearing the same trade mark, as that of the licensor.

The prohibition on dealing in competing products, therefore, makes for improved distribution of the relevant product in the same way as do exclusive dealing agreements containing a similar clause, which are automatically exempted by Regulation 67/67/EEC; a declaration that the prohibition in Article [81(1)] is inapplicable to this clause is accordingly justified.

3. Distribution will also be improved by the prohibition against the parties engaging in an active sales policy outside their respective territories. This restriction on the licensees will help to concentrate their sales efforts, and provide a better supply to consumers in their territories for which they have particular responsibility, without preventing buyers elsewhere in the Community from securing supplies freely from any of the licensees. Application of the same restriction to Campari-Milano encourages the efforts made by the each territory allotted; the licensees thus have the benefit of a certain protection relative to Campari-Milano's strong market position.

4. The obligation on licensees to supply the original Italian product rather than that which they themselves manufacture, when selling to diplomatic corps, ships' victuallers, foreign armed

forces and generally speaking all organisations with duty-free facilities, also helps to promote sales of Campari-Milano's Bitter. By restricting licensees' freedom to supply the products they manufacture themselves it makes sure that particular categories of consumers, who are deemed to be outside the licensee's territory and are usually required to move frequently from one territory to another, can always purchase the same original product with all its traditional features as regards both composition and outward appearance. Even though quality standards are observed, it is impossible in particular to avoid differences in taste between the products of the various manufacturers. This obligation is thus designed to prevent these consumers from turning to other competing products and to ensure that they continue to buy Bitter Campari, with the facility of being able to obtain stocks from their local dealer. Further, such consumers are not prevented from freely obtaining the licensees' own products even though any such purchase would be on the normal trading conditions applicable to non-duty free purchasers.

B. The licensing agreements have increased the quantities of Bitter Campari available to consumers and improve distribution, so that consumers benefit directly. There are other producers of bitter on the market, and effective competition will be strengthened by the growing quantities produced by Campari-Milano's licensees, so that it can be assumed that the improvements resulting from the agreements and the benefits which the licensees obtain from them are shared by consumers.

As buyers may secure supplies of Bitter from other territories through unsolicited orders, they are in a position to exert pressure on the prices charged by the exclusive licensee in their territory if these should be too high.

C. The restrictions of competition imposed on the parties must be considered indispensable to the attainment of the benefits set out above. None of the restrictions could be omitted without endangering the parties' object of promoting sales of Bitter Campari by concentrating the activities of the licensees on this product and offering the same original product to certain customers. In particular, none of the licensees and in all probability no other undertaking in the spirituous liquors industry would have been prepared to make the investment necessary for a significant increase in sales of Bitter if it were not sure of being protected from competition from other licensees or Campari-Milano itself.

D. The licensing agreements which are the subject of this Decision do not give Campari-Milano or its licensees the possibility of eliminating competition in respect of a substantial part of the Bitter products in question. In the EEC there exists a fairly large number of other well-known brands of bitter, which are all able to compete against Bitter Campari. Campari-Milano's licensees and Campari-Milano itself are also free to sell the Campari products in question within the Common Market but outside their territory for which they have particular responsibility.

C. THE *MOOSEHEAD*/*WHITBREAD* DECISION[316]

This case concerned the manufacture in the UK of a lager produced by the Canadian brewer Moosehead. According to the Commission, it had a taste typical of Canadian lagers.[317] Under the agreement Moosehead granted to the British brewer, Whitbread, the sole and exclusive right to produce and promote, market, and sell beer manufactured for sale under the name 'Moosehead' in the UK using Moosehead's secret know-how. Moosehead gave Whitbread an exclusive licence of its UK trade mark rights and agreed to provide it with all the relevant know-how (the know-how licence was non-exclusive) and to supply it with the necessary yeast.

---

[316] *Moosehead/Whitbread* [1990] OJ L100/32, [1991] 4 CMLR 391.
[317] *Ibid.*, para. 3.

Whitbread agreed not to make active sales outside its territory, not to produce or promote any other beer identified as a Canadian beer, not to contest the ownership or validity of the trade mark, to comply with Moosehead's directions in relation to the know-how and to buy the yeast only from Moosehead or a designated third party.

The Commission held that the exclusivity provisions and the active sales ban in the trade mark licence were caught by Article 81(1). It did not consider the no-challenge clause to the *ownership* of the mark was caught because whoever's name it was registered in any other parties would be prevented from using it. A no-challenge clause in respect of *validity*, however, was another matter. The Commission held that whether such clauses *may* infringe Article 81(1) would depend on the circumstances, but in this case it did not:

15.4. In relation to the trade mark non-challenge clause:

(a) in general terms, a trade mark non-challenge clause can refer to the ownership and/or the validity of the trade mark:

— The ownership of a trade mark may, in particular, be challenged on grounds of the prior use or prior registration of an identical trade mark.

— A clause in an exclusive trade mark licence agreement obliging the licensee not to challenge the ownership of a trade mark, as specified in the above paragraph, does not constitute a restriction of competition within the meaning of Article [81(1)]. Whether or not the licensor or licensee has the ownership of the trade mark, the use of it by any other party is prevented in any event, and competition would thus not be affected.

— The validity of a trade mark may be contested on any ground under national law, and in particular on the grounds that it is generic or descriptive in nature. In such an event, should the challenge be upheld, the trade mark may fall within the public domain and may thereafter be used without restriction by the licensee and any other party.

Such a clause may constitute a restriction of competition within the meaning of Article [81(1)], because it may contribute to the maintenance of a trade mark that would be an unjustified barrier to entry into a given market.

Moreover in order for any restriction of competition to fall under Article [81(1)], it must be appreciable. The ownership of a trade mark only gives the holder the exclusive right to sell products under that name. Other parties are free to sell the product in question under a different trade mark or trade name. Only where the use of a well-known trade mark would be an important advantage to any company entering or competing in any given market and the absence of which therefore constitutes a significant barrier to entry, would this clause which impedes the licensee to challenge the validity of the trade mark, constitute an appreciable restriction of competition within the meaning of Article [81(1)].

(b) In the present case Whitbread is unable to challenge both the ownership and the validity of the trade mark.

As far as the validity of the trade mark is concerned it must be noted that the trade mark is comparatively new to the lager market in the territory. The maintenance of the 'Moosehead' trade mark will thus not constitute an appreciable barrier to entry for any other company entering or competing in the beer market in the United Kingdom. Accordingly, the Commission considers that the trade mark non-challenge clause included in the agreement, in so far as it concerns its validity (see the second indent of point 15.4 above), does not constitute an appreciable restriction of competition and does not fall under Article [81(1)].

The Commission granted an exemption to the agreement, holding that the exclusivity provisions, active sales ban, and non-competition clauses met the Article 81(3) criteria, particularly in view of the amount of inter-brand competition on the UK beer market.

D. THE CURRENT POSITION

Although the Commission's decisions in *Campari* and *Moosehead* are reflective of the more formalistic approach to Article 81(1) it pursued prior to modernization, they are useful in: (1) confirming that some types of clauses, such as non-challenge clauses, confidentiality provisions, provisions dealing with quality control and manufacturing standards may fall outside Article 81(1): and (2) setting out when provisions that may infringe Article 81(1) (such as exclusive licences, sales restraints and non-compete provisions) are likely to satisfy the conditions of Article 81(3). It must not be forgotten, however, that the Commission (or a national court or national competition authority) analyzing a case today would now be likely to adopt a more economic approach, in particular when applying Article 81(1). Although caselaw could be interpreted to support the Commission's view that exclusive licences, especially if accompanied by sales restraints, violate Article 81(1), it is likely that fuller analysis would now be required before it could be determined whether other provisions such as non-compete clauses restrict competition within the meaning of Article 81(1).

7. TRADE MARK DELIMITATION AGREEMENTS

Trade mark delimitation agreements are entered into in order to settle disputes.[318] They usually occur where one party opposes the other's application for, or use of, a mark on the ground that it is confusingly similar to one owned by the first party for similar products. The trade mark delimitation agreement may be adopted to settle protracted litigation. The ECJ and Commission have made it clear that the provisions in such agreements may infringe Article 81(1)[319] in the same way as they might in any other agreement. The context in which the agreement is made does not therefore mean that it is immune from the application of Article 81(1). Delimitation agreements may restrict the class of products for which a party may use the mark, or the territories in which he may use the mark, or a party may accept a no-challenge obligation in relation to certain products or territories. In *BAT v. Commission*[320] the Court took a more liberal attitude to delimitation agreements than the Commission had done previously. The position now appears to be that an agreement will be outside Article 81(1) if there is a genuine risk of confusion between the parties, and it is not just a ploy for market-sharing, and if the agreement does not divide markets within the EC (at least if there is no less restrictive means of dealing with the dispute).[321]

---

[318] See *supra* for non-assertion and settlement agreements in respect of intellectual property rights covered by the TTBER.

[319] See Case 65/86, *Bayer AG and Maschinenfabrik Hennecke v. Heinz Süllhöfer* [1988] ECR 5249, [1990] 4 CMLR 182 concerning a no-challenge clause.

[320] Case 35/83, *BAT v. Commission* [1985] ECR 363, [1985] 2 CMLR 470, the appeal from *Toltecs/Dorcet* [1982] OJ L379/19, [1983] 1 CMLR 412.

[321] See also *Sirdar/Phildar* [1976] 1 CMLR D93; *Hershey/Schiffers*, Commission Press Release IP(90)87; *Chiquita/Fyffes* Commission Press Release IP(92)461; *Synthex/Synthelabo* [1990] 4 CMLR 343. See also W. Allan, M. Furse, and B. Sufrin (eds.), *Butterworths Competition Law* (Butterworths, looseleaf), Div V, Chap. 4.

8. COPYRIGHT LICENCES OTHER THAN SOFTWARE LICENCES

A. GENERAL

Software licences are 'technology transfer agreements' and are thus governed by the TTBER and the accompanying Guidelines. Licences of other types of copyright, however, do not benefit from the TTBER or the Verticals Regulation, unless the licence is ancillary to a technology transfer or vertical agreement.[322] In discussing copyright licensing the Technology Transfer Guidelines distinguish between the licensing of copyright for the purpose of reproduction and distribution of the protected work, i.e., the production of copies for resale on the one hand, and the licensing of rights in performances (such as film, television and radio broadcasts) and other rights related to copyright on the other. The principles set out in the TTBER and the Guidelines will, as a general rule, be applied to licensing for the purpose of reproduction and distribution.[323] Because the licences in this situation relate to the production and sale of a physical product embodying the work (such as a book or audio cassette), the view is taken that such licensing is of a similar nature to technology transfer. The principles set out in the TTBER and Guidelines will not be applied, however, to licences involving 'performance' and other rights,[324] which raise particular issues.

B. PERFORMANCE COPYRIGHT

In the case of exploitation through performance, the ECJ held in *Coditel II*[325] that an exclusive licence (amounting in effect to absolute territorial protection) did not in itself infringe Article 81(1). The Court recognized the special nature of the product and rights concerned. In *Coditel I*[326] the Court considered the application of the exhaustion of rights doctrine to copyright in films and concluded that the owner's rights were not exhausted by the first showing of the film because the specific subject-matter was the entitlement of the owner to charge each time the film was shown. The same facts (a Belgian cable company relaying in Belgium the transmission of a film (Chabrol's 'Le Boucher') shown in Germany for which Ciné Vog had exclusive distribution rights in Belgium) gave rise to a second case in which the cable company claimed that the exclusive licence granted to Ciné Vog infringed Article 81(1).

Case 262/81, *Coditel* v. *SA Ciné Vog Films (Coditel II)* [1982] ECR 3381, [1983] 1 CMLR 49

Court of Justice

10. It should be noted, by way of a preliminary observation, that Article [30] permits prohibitions or restrictions on trade between Member States provided that they are justified on grounds, *inter alia*, of the protection of industrial and commercial property, a term which covers literary and

---

[322] TTBER, Art. 1(1)(b).

[323] Guidelines, para. 51.

[324] *Ibid.*, para. 52.

[325] Case 262/81, *Coditel v. SA Ciné Vog Films (Coditel II)* [1982] ECR 3381, [1983] 1 CMLR 49.

[326] Case 62/79, *SA Compagnie Générale pour la Diffusion de la Télévision, Coditel v. Ciné Vog Films (Coditel I)* [1980] ECR 881, [1981] 2 CMLR 362.

artistic property, including copyright, whereas the main proceedings are concerned with the question of prohibitions or restrictions placed upon the free movement of services.

11. In this regard, as the Court held in its judgment of 18 March 1980 (*Coditel v. Ciné-Vog Films* [1980] ECR 881), the problems involved in the observance of a film producer's rights in relation to the requirements of the Treaty are not the same as those of which arise in connection with literary and artistic works the placing of which at the disposal of the public is inseparable from the circulation of the material form of the works, as in the case of books or records, whereas the film belongs to the category of literary and artistic works made available to the public by performances which may be infinitely repeated and the commercial exploitation of which comes under the movement of services, no matter whether the means whereby it is shown to the public be the cinema or television.

12. In the same judgment the Court further held that the right of the owner of the copyright in a film and his assigns to require fees for any showing of that film is part of the essential function of copyright.

13. The distinction, implicit in Article [30], between the existence of a right conferred by the legislation of a Member State in regard to the protection of artistic and intellectual property, which cannot be affected by the provisions of the Treaty, and the exercise of such right, which might constitute a disguised restriction on trade between Member States, also applies where that right is exercised in the context of the movement of services.

14. Just as it is conceivable that certain aspects of the manner in which the right is exercised may prove to be incompatible with Articles [49] and [50] it is equally conceivable that some aspects may prove to be incompatible with Article [81] where they serve to give effect to an agreement, decision or concerted practice which may have as its object or effect the prevention, restriction or distortion of competition within the common market.

15. However, the mere fact that the owner of the copyright in a film has granted to a sole licensee the exclusive right to exhibit that film in the territory of a Member State and, consequently, to prohibit, during a specified period, its showing by others, is not sufficient to justify the finding that such a contract must be regarded as the purpose, the means or the result of an agreement, decision or concerted practice prohibited by the Treaty.

16. The characteristics of the cinematographic industry and of its markets in the Community, especially those relating to dubbing and subtitling for the benefit of different language groups, to the possibilities of television broadcasts, and to the system of financing cinematographic production in Europe serve to show that an exclusive exhibition licence is not, in itself, such as to prevent, restrict or distort competition.

17. Although copyright in a film and the right deriving from it, namely that of exhibiting the film, are not, therefore, as such subject to the prohibitions contained in Article [81], the exercise of those rights may, none the less, come within the said prohibitions where there are economic or legal circumstances the effect of which is to restrict film distribution to an appreciable degree or to distort competition on the cinematographic market, regard being had to the specific characteristics of that market.

18. Since neither the question referred to the Court nor the file on the case provides any information in this respect, it is for the national court to make such inquiries as may be necessary.

19. It must therefore be stated that it is for national courts, where appropriate, to make such inquiries and in particular to establish whether or not the exercise of the exclusive right to exhibit a cinematographic film creates barriers which are artificial and unjustifiable in terms of the needs of the cinematographic industry, or the possibility of charging fees which exceed a fair return on investment, or an exclusivity the duration of which is disproportionate to those requirements, and whether or not, from a general point of view, such exercise within a given geographic area is such as to prevent, restrict or distort competition within the common market.

> 20. Accordingly, the answer to be given to the question referred to the Court must be that a contract whereby the owner of the copyright in a film grants an exclusive right to exhibit that film for a specific period in the territory of a Member State is not, as such, subject to the prohibitions contained in Article [81] of the Treaty. It is, however, where appropriate, for the national court to ascertain whether, in a given case, the manner in which the exclusive right conferred by that contract is exercised is subject to a situation in the economic or legal sphere the object or effect of which is to prevent or restrict the distribution of films or to distort competition within the cinematographic market, regard being had to the specific characteristics of the market.

The Court therefore accepted that the absolute territorial protection given by the exclusive right was not *of itself* prohibited by Article 81(1), given the nature of the protected work and the characteristics of the film industry. It did not, nevertheless, rule out the possibility that in certain circumstances the exercise of the exclusive right might fall within Article 81(1). However, the criteria in the qualifications in paragraphs 17 and 19 as to when exclusivity *will* infringe the prohibition (the exclusivity might create artificial and unjustifiable barriers to trade, lead to excessive prices, or be for an excessive duration) are imprecise and uncertain.[327] Some indication of how the Commission will apply them was given in its decision in *Film Purchases by German Television Stations*.[328] In this case an exclusive broadcasting licence of MGM/UA films was granted to a group of German TV stations for fifteen years with a further 'selection period' which preceded this.[329] The Commission held that the agreement was within Article 81(1) because of the number of films covered by the transaction[330] and the long duration of the arrangements which excluded third parties for a length of time which was described as 'disproportionate within the *Coditel II* judgment of the Court of Justice' and 'an artificial barrier to other undertakings'.[331] The agreement was exempted after provision was made for third-party broadcasters in Germany to apply for licences to show the films at times which did not clash with those of the licensees. The Commission held that Article 81(3) was satisfied because the arrangements as a whole allowed more films to be shown to German audiences and to be dubbed into German.

In the Guidelines the Commission cites *Coditel II* and recognizes the special factors that arise in connection with this type of copyright:

... In the case of the various rights related to performances value is created not by the reproduction and sale of copies of a product but by each individual performance of the protected work. Such exploitation can take various forms including the performance, showing or the renting of protected material such as films, music or sporting events. In the application of Article 81 the specificities of the work and the way in which it is exploited must be taken into account (See in this respect Case 262/81, *Coditel (II)* ...). For instance, resale restrictions may give rise to less competition concerns whereas particular concerns may arise where licensors impose on their licensees to extend to each of the licensors more favourable conditions obtained by one of them. The Commission will therefore not

---

[327] Para. 19 provides that a relevant factor is whether the rewards are excessive, although no indication is given of how the national court is to make such judgments in the context of the film industry.

[328] [1989] OJ L284/36.

[329] In fact the Commission left open whether the transaction amounted to a licence 'in the legal and technical sense' or an assignment of rights for a limited period and to a limited extent. In either case the Commission considered that there was a restriction of competition: *ibid.*, para. 41.

[330] And the fact that many of them were important or noteworthy or had 'particular mass appeal such as the James Bond films': *ibid.*, para. 43.

[331] *Ibid.*, para. 44.

apply the TTBER and the present guidelines by way of analogy to the licensing of these other rights.[332]

There is almost no other precedent which indicates how other provisions in performance copyright licences will be appraised under Article 81. Further, as the Commission has not expanded the Guidance in the Technology Transfer Guidelines and Guidelines on Vertical Restraintsto include these agreements, caution must be exercised in determining whether they are helpful in assessing the compatibility of provisions in performance copyright licences with Article 81.[333] In 2004, the Commission indicated that it might be suspicious of favoured nation clauses incorporated in such contracts. In a press release, it reported that it had closed an investigation into contracts concluded by certain of the major Hollywood studios. These contracts, providing for the sale of their entire film production to European pay-TV broadcasters, had originally included most favoured nation clauses, giving the studios the right to enjoy the most favourable terms agreed between a pay-TV company and any one of them. The Commission considered that the cumulative effect of these clauses was an alignment of prices paid to the studios for the broadcasting rights. It closed its investigation into the contracts of six of the studios after they withdrew the clauses.[334]

9. SOFTWARE LICENCES AND INTEROPERABILITY

We have seen above that the licensing of software copyright amounts to a technology transfer agreement for the purposes of the TTBER[335] and the Guidelines on technology transfer agreements.[336] Council Directive 91/250 on the legal protection of computer programs[337] was adopted in order to harmonize the way in which Member States protect software. It stipulates that this should be done through copyright. Article 1(1) states:

Member States shall protect computer programs, by copyright, as literary works within the meaning of the Berne Convention for the Protection of Literary and Artistic Works.

Software licensing is very common as software is usually licensed rather than sold. This is because it is expensive to create software but easy and cheap to copy it. The author of the software therefore needs to control copying in order to obtain a proper financial return and tries to do this by only licensing its use and by hedging the use around with restrictions. Other features of software licensing are the speed of developments in the industry, so that the producer will be looking for a return in the short rather than the long term, and the fact that it is often necessary for the user (or a third party on its behalf) to modify the software for its own needs, in which case the producer may licence the software specifically for the licensee to modify it for particular purposes. Directive 91/250 contains some provisions relevant to copyright licensing. Article 4

---

[332] Guidelines, para. 52.

[333] For a Fuller discussion of how individual clauses may be appraised under Article 81 see, W. Allan, M. Furse, and B. Sufrin (eds.), *Butterworths Competition Law* (Butterworths, looseleaf), Div V, Chap. 5.

[334] IP/04/1314.

[335] Reg. 772/2004 on technology transfer agreements [2004] OJ L123/11, Art. 1(1)(b).

[336] [2004] OJ C101/2.

[337] [1991] OJ L122/42.

sets out what constitute the 'exclusive rights' of the rightholder, Article 5 provides for exceptions and Article 6 gives licensees a special right of decompilation.

Council Directive 91/250 on the legal protection of computer programmes [1991] OJ L122/42

Article 4

Restricted acts

Subject to the provisions of Articles 5 and 6, the exclusive rights of the rightholder within the meaning of Article 2, shall include the right to do or to authorize:

(a) the permanent or temporary reproduction of a computer program by any means and in any form, in part or in whole. Insofar as loading, displaying, running, transmission or storage of the computer program necessitate such reproduction, such acts shall be subject to authorization by the rightholder;

(b) the translation, adaptation, arrangement and any other alternation of a computer program and the reproduction of the results thereof, without prejudice to the rights of the person who alters the program;

(c) any form of distribution to the public, including the rental, of the original computer program or of copies thereof. The first sale in the Community of a copy of a program by the rightholder or with his consent shall exhaust the distribution right within the Community of that copy, with the exception of the right to control further rental of the program or a copy thereof.

Article 5

Exceptions to the restricted acts

1. In the absence of specific contractual provisions, the acts referred to in Article 4 (a) and (b) shall not require authorization by the rightholder where they are necessary for the use of the computer program by the lawful acquirer in accordance with its intended purpose, including for error correction.

2. The making of a back-up copy by a person having a right to use the computer program may not be prevented by contract insofar as it is necessary for that use.

3. The person having a right to use a copy of a computer program shall be entitled, without the authorization of the rightholder, to observe, study or test the functioning of the program in order to determine the ideas and principles which underlie any element of the program if he does so while performing any of the acts of loading, displaying, running, transmitting or storing the program which he is entitled to do.

Article 6

Decompilation

1. The authorization of the rightholder shall not be required where reproduction of the code and translation of its form within the meaning of Article 4 (a) and (b) are indispensable to obtain the information necessary to achieve the interoperability of an independently created computer program with other programs, provided that the following conditions are met:

(a) these acts are performed by the licensee or by another person having a right to use a copy of a program, or on their behalf by a person authorized to do so;

(b) the information necessary to achieve interoperability has not previously been readily available to the persons referred to in subparagraph (a); and

(c) these acts are confined to the parts of the original program which are necessary to achieve interoperability.

   2. The provisions of paragraph 1 shall not permit the information obtained through its application:

(a) to be used for goals other than to achieve the interoperability of the independently created computer program;

(b) to be given to others, except when necessary for the interoperability of the independently created computer program; or

(c) to be used for the development, production or marketing of a computer program substantially similar in its expression, or for any other act which infringes copyright.

Article 4 in effect sets out what comprises the 'specific subject-matter' of copyright in computer programs and it may reasonably be assumed that, although the Directive cannot actually affect the application of the competition rules, any clause in a licence safeguarding those rights would not fall foul of Article 81(1) unless it contradicted the exceptions in Articles 5 and 6. Article 6 is a crucial provision in that the licensee is given the right to decompile the licensed program (i.e., to run the program in order to reverse engineer and reduce the object code in the program to a form that approximates with the source code)[338] where it is necessary to achieve 'interoperability', i.e., to ensure that independently created programs can be used with 'other programs' (Article 6(1)). 'Other programs' covers not only the licensed program itself but also software which *competes* with the licensed program.

Interoperability has become a major issue in the field of computer technology and recital 27 of the Directive provides that its provisions are without prejudice to the application of Articles 81 and 82 if a dominant supplier refuses to make available information which is necessary for interoperability[339] (although it must be noted that Article 6 applies whether or not the copyright holder is dominant). The Commission applied Article 82 to Microsoft's refusal to reveal interface information in the *Microsoft* decision of March 2004.[340] The issue was Microsoft's refusal to supply interface information to developers wishing to create 'workgroup' server operating systems that interoperate with Microsoft's Windows system.[341] In its defence, Microsoft argued, *inter alia*, that if the Commission found its refusal to supply interoperability information abusive it would upset the 'careful balance between copyright and competition policies' struck

---

[338] Decompilation involves intermediate copying of the program which would otherwise involve *prima facie* copyright infringement. See L. Bently and B. Sherman, *Intellectual Property Law* (2nd edn., Oxford University Press, 2004), 220. Article 6 does not provide a defence if decompilation leads to the writing and production of a program which infringes the copyright in the original. Article 6 was implemented in UK by an amendment to the Copyright, Designs and Patents Act, 1988 (s. 50B) which slightly adapted Article 6 (a matter with which the Commission was unhappy, see *Report from the Commission on the implementation and effects of Directive 91/250/EEC on the legal protection of computer programs* COM(2000) 199 final, 14). One authority on intellectual property law says of this, 'It might have been more discreet to tread this bloody and treacherous battlefield exactly in the footsteps of the Directive; but our valiant draftsman struck out for himself': W. Cornish and D. Llewelyn, *Intellectual Property: Patents, Copyright, Trade Marks and Allied Rights* (5th edn., Sweet & Maxwell, 2003), 774.

[339] See further *supra* Chap. 7.

[340] COMP/C-3/37. 792, *Microsoft* [2005] 4 CMLR 965, on appeal Case T-201/04, *Microsoft v EC Commission* (judgment pending).

[341] See *supra* Chap. 7.

by the Software Directive.[342] Microsoft pleaded an ingenious interpretation of Article 6 of Directive 91/250 according to which it was already disclosing sufficient information (and therefore should not be held to have committed an abuse). It argued that the 'full interoperability' required by the Directive was satisfied when all of the functionality of the developer's program could be accessed from a Windows client operating system. The Commission rejected this argument and held that 'information necessary to ensure that the decompiled program works as intended in interoperating with the independently created program is information covered by the derogation provided by Article 6'.[343] Microsoft further argued that if it was required to disclose interface information beyond that which could be ascertained through reverse engineering under Article 6 it would amount to a compulsory licence which was not consistent with the Community's obligations under TRIPS.[344] Again, this argument was rejected.[345]

10. THE APPLICATION OF ARTICLE 82 TO INTELLECTUAL PROPERTY RIGHTS

There are two facets to the relationship between Article 82 and intellectual property rights. First, there is the extent to which the ownership of intellectual property rights puts the holder in a dominant position. Secondly, there is the question whether the holding, acquisition, or exploitation of intellectual property rights can constitute an abuse of a dominant position, and if so in what circumstances.

The application of Article 82 to intellectual property rights is dealt with in Chapters 6 and 7 because it is impossible to divorce these questions about intellectual property rights from the operation of Article 82 as a whole. Looking at them in isolation from other developments in Article 82 jurisprudence can lead to an incomplete and distorted picture. Reference should therefore be made to those chapters. Nonetheless, a few important points dealt with in those chapters are reiterated here:

- The monopoly conferred by an intellectual property right (a legal monopoly) cannot automatically be equated with a finding of dominance (an economic monopoly) under Article 82: 'so far as a dominant position is concerned, it is to be remembered at the outset that mere ownership of an intellectual property right cannot confer such a position'.[346] If the protected product is part of a wider market the intellectual property right will not in itself create dominance, but if the market is narrowed to comprise only the product covered by the intellectual property right then there will be a *de facto* monopoly, because the intellectual property right will constitute a barrier to entry preventing supply substitution or new entrants coming onto the market.

- The CFI has held, upholding the Commission, that it can be an abuse for a dominant undertaking to acquire an exclusive patent licence.[347]

---

[342] Microsoft's submission of 17 Nov. 2000, see [2005] 4 CMLR, para. 743 *Microsoft*.

[343] *Microsoft* [2005] 4 CMLR 965, para. 762, on appeal Case T-201/04 *Microsoft v EC Commission* (judgment pending).

[344] The Agreement on Trade-Related Aspects of Intellectual Property Rights.

[345] *Microsoft*, [2005] 4 CMLR, para. 1050.

[346] Cases C-241–242/91 P, *RTE & ITP v. Commission* [1995] ECR I-743, [1995] 4 CMLR 718, para. 46: see also Case 78/70, *Deutsche Grammophon v. Metro* [1971] ECR 487, [1971] CMLR 631, para. 16.

[347] Case T-51/89, *Tetra Pak Ravsing SA v. Commission* [1990] ECR II-309, [1991] 4 CMLR 334, on appeal from *Tetra Pak (BTG Licence)* [1988] OJ L272/27, [1990] 4 CMLR 47: the case was not appealed from the CFI to the ECJ.

• In a series of extremely controversial cases it has been held that the exercise of an exclusive right conferred by an intellectual property right, such as the charging of excessive prices or refusal to license, may in certain circumstances constitute an abuse of a dominant position.[348]

• Collecting societies, such as performers' rights societies, are organizations which collectively manage copyrights on behalf of rights holders. They exist because of the impracticality of performers, musicians, etc. individually giving permission for their work to be performed or collecting royalties. Performers' rights societies are usually organized on a national basis and often have a *de facto* monopoly. Their activities have often given rise to competition law problems, particularly in respect of Article 82. The Commission is concerned to address the issue of collecting societies as a whole and published a Communication on this in 2004.[349]

11. CONCLUSIONS

1. The TTBER and Guidelines indicate that the Commission now adopts a more economic approach to intellectual property licensing agreements. The TTBER sets out a presumption that technology transfer agreements which do not incorporate hard-core restraints and which are concluded between undertakings which do not exceed the market share thresholds are compatible with Article 81.

2. As with the approach to vertical agreements, the centrality of the TTBER means that the main focus of attention is still on whether or not a technology transfer agreement is compatible with Article 81(3), not whether it is compatible with Article 81(1), i.e., whether it actually restricts competition.

3. In contrast with the position for vertical agreements, however, in practice it is likely to be much harder for firms to be sure about compliance with the provisions of the TTBER. Not only is it inherently more difficult to define technology markets but the cocktail of hardcore and excluded restraints are more complex than those set out in the Verticals Regulation.

4. The practical reality is, therefore, that in many situations parties to intellectual property licensing agreements will have to rely on self-assessment to determine their agreement's compatibility with Article 81. As there is relatively little decisional practice and case law dealing with intellectual property licensing agreements, reliance on the Technology Transfer Guidelines and Article 81(3) Guidelines will be essential. As trade mark and copyright licences are generally not covered by the TTBER and guidelines, recourse to general Article 81 principles will be necessary in such cases.

---

[348] See Case 238/87, *AB Volvo v. Erik Veng* [1988] ECR 6211, [1989] 4 CMLR 122, Case 53/87, *CICCRA v. Renault* [1988] ECR 6039, [1990] 4 CMLR 265, Cases C-241–242/91 P, *RTE & ITP v. Commission* [1995] ECR I-743, [1995] 4 CMLR 718, on appeal from Cases T-69–70/89, 76/89, *RTE, ITP, BBC v. EC Commission* [1991] ECR II-485, [1991] 4 CMLR 586, on appeal from *Magill TV Guide* [1989] OJ L78/43, [1989] 4 CMLR 757, Case T-198/98, *Micro Leader v. Commission* [1999] ECR II-3989, [2000] 4 CMLR 886. (The CFI annulled a Commission decision rejecting a complaint as there was enough evidence of the copyright owner (Microsoft) practising excessive pricing to have warranted the Commission examining that point.), Case C-418/01, *IMS Health GmbH & Co OHG v. NDC Health GmbH & Co KG* [2004] 4 CMLR 1543.

[349] Communication from the Commission to the Council, European Parliament and ESC on the Management of Copyright and Related Rights in the Internal Market COM(2004) 261 final. See also, e.g. the commitments adopted in relation to the Cannes Agreement, see IP/06/1311.

12. FURTHER READING

A. BOOKS

ANDERMAN, S.D., *EC Competition Law and Intellectual Property Rights* (Clarendon Press, 1988)

—— and KALLAUGHER, J., *Technology Transfer and the New EU Competition Rules: Intellectual Property Licensing after Modernisation* (Oxford University Press, 2006)

CRAIG, P. and DE BÚRCA, G., *EU Law: Text, Cases and Materials* (3rd edn., Oxford University Press, 2003)

GOVAERE, I., *The Use and Abuse of Intellectual Property Rights in EC Law* (Sweet & Maxwell, 1996)

KORAH, V., *Intellectual Property rights and the EC Competition Rules* (Hart Publishing, 2006)

B. ARTICLES

AITMAN, D., and JONES A., 'Competition and Copyright: has the copyright owner lost control?' [2003] *EIPR* 137

ANDERMAN, S. D., 'Substantial Convergence: the US influence on the development of the regulatory framework for IP licensing in the EC' in Marsden, P., (ed.) *Handbook of Research In Trans-Atlantic Antitrust* (Edward Elgar Publishing, 2007)

—— 'EC Competition Law and Intellectual Property Rights in the New Economy' [2002] *Antitrust Bull* 285

COTTER, T. F., 'Intellectual Property and the Essential Facilities Doctrine' [1999] *Antitrust Bull* 211

DOLMANS, M., and, PIILOLA, A., 'The New Technology Transfer Block Exemption, A Welcome Reform After All' [2004] 27(3) *World Competition* 351

KORAH, V., 'Draft Block Exemption for Technology Transfer' (2004) *ECLR* 247

PEEPERKORN, L., 'IP Licences and Competition Rules: Striking the Right Balance' (2003) 26 *World Competition* 527

VENIT, J., 'In the Wake of Windsurfing: Patent Licensing in the Common Market' [1986] *Fordham Corp L Inst* 517

For other Articles on Article 82, see the Further Reading for Chapter 7, *supra* 610.

11

CARTELS AND OLIGOPOLY

1. CENTRAL ISSUES

1. This chapter deals with explicit and tacit collusion. Explicit and tacit collusion are most likely to occur on oligopolistic markets, that is markets on which there only a few suppliers.

2. Explicit collusion occurs where firms conclude naked agreements to fix prices, restrict output, share markets or rig bids (hardcore cartels).

3. Hardcore cartel activity leads to higher prices, deadweight loss, and reduced incentives for firms to keep costs low and to innovate, leading to productive inefficiency and dynamic harm.

4. There has been a dramatic change in policy towards hardcore cartels in Europe since the 1990s. The Commission increasingly focuses its scarce resources on detecting cartels and fining undertakings involved. The number of cartel decisions adopted each year and the fines imposed have increased dramatically since 2000. In some Member States, as in the US, cartel activity constitutes a criminal offence.

5. Another problem for consumer welfare is tacit collusion (or tacit coordination).

6. Economic theory predicts that, on some oligopolistic markets, the players will recognize that the profitability of what they do is dependent on the behaviour of other firms operating on the market, and that they are all better off if they charge higher prices and earn greater profits. They are thus able to coordinate their behaviour in a similar way to those operating a cartel, without explicitly agreeing to do so. Such coordination is known as tacit collusion or tacit coordination.

7. A problem for competition law is how to deal with tacit collusion. This Chapter explores the tools that the EC competition rules offer. In particular, whether *ex post* Articles 81 or 82 can be used to condemn the behaviour of firms engaged in tacit collusion. Further, whether *ex ante* the EC Merger Regulation can be used to prohibit or deter mergers likely to create conditions conducive to tacit collusion (see also Chapter 12) and/or whether Article 81 can be used to condemn agreements which may facilitate tacit collusion on a market.

2. INTRODUCTION

A. CARTELS AND OLIGOPOLY

This chapter examines explicit collusion and tacit collusion (or tacit coordination[1]). Both explicit and tacit collusion may result in a reduction of consumer welfare, mainly through the raising of prices and the restriction of output. These practices may also damage variety and innovation on a market.

---

[1] See *infra* 872.

Explicit collusion occurs where undertakings agree, collectively, to exploit their joint economic power and to improve their profitability by raising prices, restricting output, sharing markets or rigging bids. Successful cartels raise the joint profits of all the firms in the industry, maintain the parties' respective position on the market and achieve pricing stability or an increase in prices. They thus enable the member firms to enjoy market power and profits over and beyond what would otherwise result and to reproduce artificially the market outcomes and welfare loss arising on a monopolized market. Hardcore cartel activity is most likely to be successful on oligopolistic markets (markets having only a small number of producers or sellers).[2]

Tacit collusion occurs where undertakings operating on some oligopolistic markets, set their prices "as if" there had been some explicit collusion between them. Oligopolists may recognize their interdependence and, without explicitly agreeing to do so, align their conduct and charge supra-competitive prices as a rational response to market circumstances. Market conditions may therefore dictate that, without any communication between the undertakings, they align their behaviour in a manner which maximizes the profits of the players involved.[3]

This chapter will consider EC competition law applying both to undertakings operating cartels and undertakings that tacitly coordinate their behaviour on an oligopolistic market. We start by looking at the difference between 'explicit' and 'tacit' collusion. Section 3 then deals with cartels and other agreements which may be used to bolster cartels or which may facilitate explicit or tacit collusion on a market. Section 4 deals with the problem of tacit collusion and whether, in particular, Articles 81 and 82 operate as effective mechanisms for dealing with the problem. It also considers other options that EC competition law might offer to deal with tacit collusion, either *ex ante* or *ex post*.

B. EXPLICIT AND TACIT COLLUSION

(i) Cartels and Explicit Collusion

a. Introduction

In Chapter 13 it is seen that some horizontal cooperation between undertakings operating at the same level of the market may be highly beneficial to the competitive structure of that market. A joint venture agreement may, for example, seek to improve the parties' competitive position on a market by pooling resources and know-how and sharing the financial risk necessary to launch a new, better, cheaper and/or more innovative product on that market. In this chapter, however, we focus on cooperation between producers which is purely intended to maximize the joint profits of the parties to the agreement. The objective of a cartel is to maintain the parties' respective positions on the market and to achieve pricing stability or an increase in prices. The parties thus deliberately set out to interfere with free competition (the best environment for ensuring the optimum allocation of resources and continuous economic progress) and to act instead to protect the prosperity of the industrial group as a whole. Such cartels 'diminish social welfare, create allocative inefficiency and transfer wealth from consumers to the participants in the cartel'.[4] The formation and successful operation of a cartel is easier for firms operating in an

---

[2] See *infra* 862–4. The word oligopoly is derived from the Greek word for a few sellers.

[3] See discussion *infra*, 871–3.

[4] Commission *XXXIInd Report on Competition Policy* (2002), part 26.

oligopolistic market, where each firm's profits are strongly dependent upon the course of action chosen by its competitors.

b. The Prisoner's Dilemma and Theory of Games

In the 1940s the pioneering work of von Neumann and Morgenstern[5] laid the foundation for the development of a new branch of economics, 'game theory', which deals with the strategic inter-action of firms and which is now highly developed. Game theory is a helpful tool used to explain and predict the behaviour of firms on an oligopolistic market.

The basic model applied to illustrate decision-making on such a market is the 'prisoners' dilemma'. It clearly demonstrates that on an oligopolistic market, both cooperative and non-cooperative outcomes may result. It explains the incentives that exist for firms operating on a market to agree to coordinate their behaviour and to charge prices which are higher than those which would occur on a competitive market. It also illustrates, through the Nash non-cooperative equilibrium, the practical difficulties involved in operating such an agreement. The Nash non-cooperative equilibrium arises 'when, given the behaviour of all other firms in the market, no firm wishes to change its behaviour (i.e., each firm maximizes profit, given the behaviour of all the other firms').[6] The theory thus helps to predict which market conditions are likely to result in price levels above the competitive price. In the extract below, Van den Bergh and Camesasca explain insights from game theory and how it is relevant to the study of oligopoly.

R. Van den Bergh and P. Camesasca, *European Competition Law and Economics: A Comparative Perspective* (2nd edn., Sweet & Maxwell, 2006)

5.2.2.2 Basic insights from game theory

...Game theory distinguishes between cooperative and non-cooperative games. Under the former the parties can make binding agreements. In the latter this is not possible and strategic interaction may lead to an outcome which is suboptimal in comparison to what would be feasible if agreements were allowed. The game providing the most relevant insights thereto is the classic one-shot prisoners' dilemma. Two criminals, who together committed a crime, are caught and put in separate cells. Not having enough direct evidence, the police needs a confession from one of them in order to convict both of them for the crime and impose a high sentence. The criminals are questioned separately and each prisoner is told that if he or she testifies against the other, he or she will receive a lighter sentence. Neither prisoner can speak with the other before making the decision whether to talk or remain silent. The best solution for both prisoners is that neither of them testifies. Having insufficient evidence, the pubic prosecutor will not be able to ask for a high sentence. However, if one prisoner talks, it is better for the other to testify as well in order to escape a more severe punishment. If the other remains silent, testifying is also the best choice since it once again guarantees a lighter punishment. In the jargon of game theory, testifying is the dominant strategy. As a result, both prisoners will be severely punished. The optimal outcome from the prisoners' perspective would have been a lighter sentence because of lack of evidence; but this will not be obtained, as the two criminals cannot make a prior binding agreement.

---

[5] J. von Neumann and O. Morgenstern, *The Theory of Games and Economic Behaviour* (Princeton University Press, 1944). See now e.g. J. Tirole, *The Theory of Industrial Organization* (MIT Press, 1988) and *supra* Chap. 1.

[6] S. Bishop and M. Walker, *The Economics of EC Competition Law: Concepts, Application and Measurement* (2nd edn., Sweet & Maxwell, 2002), para. 2.29.

5.2.2.3 The prisoners' dilemma in oligopolistic markets

The above analysis can be extended to the study of oligopolies. Given the existing interdependencies as a result of which a firm's actions depend on a rival's decisions, oligopolistic markets are characterised by strategic behaviour. Firms will have a choice between cooperative and non-cooperative strategies (collusion or cheating). On the one hand, they will recognise the possibility of earning higher profits jointly through coordinating their activities. Price agreements or joint decisions to restrict output will achieve the goal. On the other hand, though, the collective incentive to collude will be opposed by the strong private incentives of each individual firm to cheat on its fellow cartel members. If other firms respect the price agreement, the cheating firm will achieve additional profits. The example in Box 5.1 shows the different pay-offs for two firms which both face a choice between collusion (obeying the cartel agreement) and cheating (price undercutting or output expansion to attract additional customers). The numbers in each box denote the profits resulting from the outcome of the two firms' decisions. The first number shows the profits which Firm A makes and the second the profits which Firm B obtains. Considering the various outcomes, both firms would prefer an outcome in which both charged a high price (top left quadrant) to that in which they both charged a low price (bottom right quadrant). However, the duopoly is characterised by a prisoner's dilemma so that the outcome (Nash equilibrium) will be that both firms cheat.

Box 5:1 The prisoner's dilemma: profit opportunities in a duopoly

		Firm B	
		Collude	Cheat
Firm A	Collude	20, 20	15, 22
	Cheat	22, 15	17, 17

If both firms coordinate their behaviour and collude, they will charge higher prices (or restrict output) and obtain joined profits amounting to €40 with each firm individually earning €20. If one firm cheats on the other by price undercutting (or expanding production) while the other firm adheres to the cartel agreement, the cheating firm will earn €22 while the other firm's profit declines to €15. Clearly, both firms are better off collectively if they collude. The joint collusive profits equal €40 and exceed the joined profits of €34 in case of price undercutting (or output expansion) by both firms. It is equally clear, however, that each firm has an incentive to forsake collusion and improve its own position through cheating. On the one hand, the latter option will increase profits by an additional €2 (€22 compared with 20) if the second duopolist does not cheat as well. On the other hand, if the rival cheats, adhering to the cartel agreement reduces profits by €3 (€17 compared with 20). Given the extra profit in the case of cheating and the fear of losing money if the rival cheats, each duopolist will decide to cheat. In game-theoretic terms, the non-cooperative strategy will be dominant. To the duopolist the final outcome of the game (joined profits of €34) is worse than the cooperative outcome (joined profits of €40). To avoid this non-cooperative outcome the duopolists must be able to detect and punish cheating.

The fact that firms do meet in practice makes a collusive outcome more likely. Even in the absence of explicit agreements, non-cooperative games that are subject to repeated interaction (suggesting an infinite repetition of the prisoners' dilemma) may lead to a collusive outcome. In industries which only a few firms compete over a long period under stable demand and costs conditions cooperation prevails, even though no contractual arrangements are entered into. Thus, if antitrust laws require hard evidence to show the existence of concerted practices, they may fall short of adequately controlling serious anti-competitive concerns.

The model illustrates that firms operating on a market realize that the profitability of what they do is dependent on the behaviour of other firms operating on the market. If firms compete vigorously with one another and charge low prices their overall profits will be considerably less than if they increase prices and increase profits. They are all better off if they coordinate their behaviour and charge higher prices. As Adam Smith noted in *The Wealth of Nations*:

people of the same trade seldom meet together, even for merriment and diversion, but the conversation ends in a conspiracy against the public, or in some contrivance to raise prices.

A player on the market nevertheless knows that if its competitor charges a high price, it will be better off if it charges a low price (and cheats on any cartel agreement).[7] The Nash equilibrium for a one shot game is, therefore, for the two firms to lower prices: it is better for both firms to charge a low price, whatever the other one does. Where, however, the game is repeated, it may be possible through recurring market interaction for collusion at the high price to be sustained.

It can be seen from this theory, that achieving and sustaining a cartel and coordinated behaviour is difficult. The success of a cartel is dependent upon the parties being able to:

(i)   align their behaviour (the competitors must reach an understanding on prices, output or another factor of competition);

(ii) monitor the market so that deviations from the collusive strategy can quickly be detected (it is the fear of retaliation and punishment that makes the collusion sustainable); and

(iii) punish those that cheat on the cartel agreement.

c. Alignment, Detection, and Punishment of Deviation

Clearly it will be easier to align behaviour on some market than others: for example, alignment is more feasible where there are fewer players on the market; the players are of similar sizes; their products are very similar (there is little non-price competition for the product); and their cost structures are similar (there will then be less disagreement as to the collusive price to be charged).

Further, the cartel members will need to be able to monitor the market and detect cheating on the collusive arrangement, and to find a mechanism for punishing those that cheat so that cheating becomes unprofitable. Cheating on a cartel is obviously easier the less transparent the markets, the greater the number of firms, where products are differentiated, and where demand is unpredictable. The incentive to cheat is also affected by the 'punishment' that can be levied on a firm that cheats. Punishment usually takes the form of a promise of loss of profits once the collusion is uncovered: i.e. the other firms lower price and expand output so that prices revert to the non-collusive or competitive price.

The operation of internal enforcement mechanisms is inevitably time-consuming and expensive and on some markets may be impossible. These difficulties will become more acute the larger the number of participants and the greater the differentiation in their products. The more elaborate the monitoring and enforcement devices, the more vulnerable the cartel is to detection by competition authorities.[8]

---

[7] 'The benefits of cheating are the extra profits that a firm can earn by selling significantly more units as a result of undercutting the collusive price.' S. Bishop and M. Walker, *The Economics of EC Competition Law: Concepts, Application and Measurement* (2nd edn., Sweet & Maxwell, 2002), para. 5.21 and *supra* 860–1.

[8] See discussion of the types of market which particularly lend themselves to collusion below.

d. Markets Prone to Explicit Collusion

The discussion above indicates that markets with the following characteristics are more likely to support the successful operation of a cartel:

Fewer Firms and Higher Market Concentration

The fewer the number of operators on the market, or controlling the market, the simpler it is to coordinate actions, the cheaper the costs of collusion, the easier it is to detect cheating and the easier it is to keep the arrangement secret.[9] Further, the larger the market share that each undertaking has the greater the potential profits to be earned from successful collusion (the bigger the share that each will receive of the collusive pie!). The greater the anticipated rewards the more likely they are to outweigh the risks of detection. Oligopolistic markets are therefore particularly prone to cartelization.

Barriers to Entry

Barriers to entry[10] are important to the successful operation of a cartel. In the absence of barriers, an increase in price will attract new competitors into the market.

Homogeneous Goods

It will be much easier for firms to collude where products are similar and where the main dimension of competition is price competition (competition is not multidimensional). Where goods are homogeneous the costs of collusion are reduced and the likelihood of successful collusion increased. The possibility for non-price competition through product differentiation is, of course, reduced. Many of the Commission's decisions prohibiting the operation of a cartel have been taken against undertakings whose products offer little scope for differentiation, for example, steel tubes, vitamins, sugar, cement, cartonboard, pvc, soda ash, polypropylene.[11] In *BELASCO*[12] cartel members actually took steps, for example, through standardization and joint advertising to foster an impression in consumers that their products were homogeneous in order to limit the scope of competition by means of product differentiation.

Firms with Similar Cost Structures or Operating Efficiencies and Market Shares

The more similar cost structures, the easier it is for the firms to cooperate on prices to be charged. For example, where costs are not similar, lower cost firms are likely to want lower prices than other cartel members.[13]

---

[9] The larger the number of firms involved the more likely that a trade association, or some other similar body, might be involved in the cartel, see *supra* Chap. 3, 171.

[10] See *supra* Chaps. 1 and 6 for a discussion of barriers to entry.

[11] See, e.g., *British Sugar plc, Tate & Lyle plc, Napier Brown & Company Ltd, James Budgett Sugars Ltd (British Sugar)* [1999] OJ L76/1, [1999] 4 CMLR 1316, substantially upheld by the CFI, Case T-208/98, *Tate & Lyle v. Commission* [2001] ECR II-2035, [2001] 5 CMLR 859, Case C-359/01, [2004] ECR I-4933, [2004] 5 CMLR 329 and *Polypropylene* [1988] OJ L230/1, [1988] 4 CMLR 347, appeals substantially dismissed both by the CFI and the ECJ: see, e.g., Case C-51/92 P, *SA Hercules NV v. Commission* [1999] ECR I-4235, [1999] 5 CMLR 976 and Case C-199/92 P, *Hüls AG v. Commission (Polypropylene)* [1999] ECR I-4287 [1999] 5 CMLR 1016.

[12] [1986] OJ L232/15, [1991] 4 CMLR 130, *aff'd* on appeal, Case 246/86, *Re Roofing Felt Cartel: BELASCO v. Commission* [1989] ECR 2117, [1991] 4 CMLR 96.

[13] It might be possible to deal with these kinds of issues through side payments (e.g., to compensate high cost firms for not producing so much). In practice, however, this is likely to increase the chances of detection.

Market Transparency

The more transparent the market, the easier it will be for firms to monitor what their competitors are doing and to detect cheating on, or deviation from, any cartel arrangement.

Mechanisms for Coordination

Cartel members often, in addition to price fixing, agree to share markets and/or to adhere to quotas (restriction of output is ordinarily essential to sustain a price rise). The allocation of markets, customers, and quotas may also facilitate coordination. An undertaking will be likely to cheat on the cartel only where it can do so for a relatively long period of time without detection. The effective operation of a cartel requires that some credible enforcement mechanism be in place. It may be easier to detect if firms are not complying with quotas or are selling to customers outside their allotted territory. In BELASCO,[14] for example, a trade association of which the parties to the cartel were members took steps to monitor compliance with a price- and quota-fixing cartel. Indeed, it employed an accountant which fined undertakings which exceeded the quota allocated to it under the terms of the cartel agreement. Other agreements between firms may also facilitate collusion between them, for example, by rendering the market more transparent through agreements to exchange information or vertical agreements containing provisions such as meeting competition clauses[15] or resale price maintenance.[16]

Dispersed Buyers with No Controlling Purchasing Power

Where buyers are numerous and dispersed it is almost impossible to advertise price-cuts or reductions and, consequently, to cheat on the cartel without it being brought to the attention of the other members. Further, it will be easier to operate a cartel where individual buyers do not have controlling purchasing power.

Demand Patterns

Cyclical changes in demand may lead to the breakdown of a cartel. In these circumstances undertakings may find it difficult to determine whether the decline in demand for their products is due to a reduction in demand as a whole or to another member cheating on the cartel. This uncertainty may cause the members to deviate from the terms of the cartel. Further, where large orders are put in for a product occasionally (rather than on a regular basis) there may be a greater temptation for cheating since the gains will obviously be greater.

Depressed Conditions or Low Innovation Rate

Firms operating in industries in recession or suffering from declining demand may be tempted to adopt price-fixing or other collusive agreements to maintain profits (see, for example, the arguments raised in Polypropylene).[17]

---

[14] [1986] OJ L232/15, [1991] 4 CMLR 130, aff'd on appeal, Case 246/86, Re Roofing Felt Cartel: BELASCO v. Commission [1989] ECR 2117, [1991] 4 CMLR 96.

[15] A clause providing that a seller will meet any lower price offered to the buyer by a competing seller. This obviously deters cartel members from cheating on a collusive outcome, since deviations from the agreed price will be instantly detected by competitors and in any even the other seller will retaliate by matching the lower price offered.

[16] A most favoured nation clause which requires the supplier to offer any price reduction offered to one buyer to all buyers, may deter deviation from a collusive price. However, the scope for retaliation is also reduced because the retaliator will have to reduce prices to all customers, not just those deviating from the norm.

[17] See infra n. 134 and accompanying text. The fact that an agreement is intended to combat the effect of over-capacity does not deprive the agreement of its anti-competitive effect. It might, however, encourage the Commission to be more sympathetic when considering any fines to be imposed in respect of the breach of Article 81(1).

In a speech, the then Competition Commissioner Mario Monti referred to these types of factors as those likely to lead to collusive arrangements between market operators. He stated his belief, however, that cartel agreements might also operate outside industries with these traditional characteristics, and a number of the cartels unearthed bear this statement out.

M. Monti, 'Fighting Cartels Why and How? Why should we be concerned with cartels and collusive behaviour?' 3rd Nordic Competition Policy Conference, Stockholm, 11–12 Sept. 2000

As we all know, cartels do not occur with the same frequency in all sectors. Indeed, some sectors have been particularly prone to cartelisation. These sectors are generally characterised by a relatively high degree of concentration, significant barriers to entry, homogeneous products, similar cost structures and mature technologies. In such stable sectors it is easier to reach consensus on the collusive outcome and to maintain it. The steel, cement and chemical industries can be mentioned as examples of sectors that fit this description and in which the Commission has in the past uncovered cartels.

However, our experience shows that cartel behaviour is not limited to such traditional industries. Recent investigations concerning the banking sector and the liberal professions demonstrate that we should certainly not lose sight of other sectors. In the case of the liberal professions collusion has generally involved the fixing of tariffs. In these sectors it is often quite difficult to assess with precision the level of quality. Price competition is therefore quite an important aspect of competition. It is also interesting to note that in these cases the cartels have virtually always been operated by a trade association. The involvement of an association is necessary due to the large number of operators. One study has found that trade associations were involved in most of the cases that involved more than 10 undertakings. Moreover, in the case of the liberal professions the rules of the association can be a very effective weapon in maintaining discipline.

---

e. The Desire to Combat and Eliminate Cartels

It is arguable that in the long run most cartels will break down without the intervention of any competition authority. The Commission has, however, uncovered a number of cartels that have been operated successfully over long periods of time: for example, the market sharing agreement in *Soda Ash*[18] was thought to have been in operation since the nineteenth century and the cartel in *Peroxygen Products*[19] for a period of at least twenty years.[20] In *Sorbates*[21] the Commission found that the investigation had established, beyond any doubt, that the cartel had been operated 'between the end of December 1978 and 31 October 1996'[22] and in *Organic Peroxides*[23] the

---

[18] [1991] OJ L152/1, [1994] 4 CMLR 454, annulled on procedural Grounds Case T-30/91, *Solvay SA v. Commission* [1995] ECR II-1775, [1996] 5 CMLR 57 (*infra* Chap. 14) but readopted [2003] OJ L10/1, see Case T-57/01, *Solvay v. Commission* (judgment pending).

[19] [1985] OJ L35/1, [1985] 1 CMLR 481.

[20] In the US a series of cases were taken between 1988 and 1997 against bid-rigging on school milk markets. In some cases, it was thought that the bid-rigging had occurred since the late 1960s, see, e.g., Department of Justice Press Release, 25 Apr. 1997 'Minnesota, Iowa Dairies agreed to plead guilty and will each pay $1 million for participating in milk price fixing conspiracy'.

[21] IP/03/1330.

[22] *Ibid.*

[23] [2005] OJ L110/44, *aff'd*, Case T-120/04, etc *Peróxiidos Orgánicos SA v. Commission* 16 Nov. 2006, [2007] 4 CMLR 4.

cartel was found to have lasted twenty-nine years. In the meantime loss to society as a whole is suffered. It is thus widely accepted that cartels should be deterred.[24] Of all agreements, cartels most contradict the principles of the free market economy as the operators specifically attempt to eliminate or limit the free play of competition. Further, they differ from other agreements considered in this book,[25] in that they are 'naked'. 'They seek to restrict competition without producing any objective countervailing benefits.'[26] They lead to higher prices (customer harm), deadweight loss (consumer welfare loss) and, probably, productive inefficiency and dynamic harm resulting from reduced incentives to innovate and to strive for efficiency.[27]

Cartels harm consumers and have pernicious effects on economic efficiency. A successful cartel raises price above the competitive level and reduces output. Consumers (which include businesses and governments) chose either to pay the higher price for some or all of the cartelized product that they desire thus forgoing the product, or they pay the cartel price and thereby unknowingly transfer wealth to the cartel operators. Further, a cartel shelters its members from full exposure to market forces, reducing pressures on them to control costs and to innovate. All of these effects harm efficiency in a market economy.[28]

Cartels have, therefore, provoked strong and hostile reactions from competition enforcement authorities and are generally considered to be 'the most egregious violations of competition law'.[29] In Europe, (then) Competition Commissioner Mario Monti described them as 'cancers on the open market economy'.[30]

It is clear today that most competition authorities are agreed, that one of the, if not the, most important objective of the competition rules is to detect, punish, prevent, and eliminate the operation of 'hard-core cartels'. In a Recommendation of the OECD Council Concerning Effective Action Against Hard Core Cartels, a hard-core cartel was defined as:

an anti-competitive agreement, anti-competitive concerted practice, or anti-competitive arrangement by competitors to fix prices, make rigged bids (collusive tenders), establish output restrictions or quotas, or share or divide markets by allocating customers, suppliers, territories or lines of commerce.[31]

---

[24] The Chicago school accepts that the key focus of the antitrust laws should be applied to deter hard-core cartels: see e.g. R. H. Bork, *The Antitrust Paradox* (Basic Books, 1978, reprinted with a new Introduction and Epilogue, 1993), 67.

[25] See especially Chaps. 9 and 13.

[26] M. Monti, 'Fighting Cartels Why and How?' 3rd Nordic Competition Policy Conference Stockholm, 11–12 Sept. 2000. As they are intrinsically detrimental to the competitive process and are not reasonably related to the lawful realisation of cost-reducing or output enhancing efficiencies they cannot be held lawful under competition law, see J. Faull and A. Nikpay *The EC Law of Competition* (2nd edn., Oxford University Press, 2007), para. 8.02.

[27] 'Collusion ... directly raises price and causes a wealth transfer from consumers to the cartel as well as a deadweight loss (allocative inefficiency). From society's perspective, the costs of forming and enforcing the cartel ("rent seeking") are also welfare-reducing In addition, the prospect of profits that are easy to make may reduce incentives to keep production costs low (productive inefficiency) or to innovate (dynamic inefficiencies).' R. Van den Bergh and P. Camesasca *European Competition Law and Economics: A Comparative Perspective* (2nd edn., Sweet & Maxwell, 2006), 5.2.1.2 See, OFT 386, 'The development of targets for consumer savings arising from competition policy', Chap. 5 (Cartels: By how much do they raise price, and how long do they last?).

[28] 'Hardcore Cartels, Recent Progress and Challenges Ahead' (OECD, 2003), and 'Hardcore Cartels—Harm and Effective Sanctions' (OECD Policy Brief, May 2002), both available at www.oecd.org.

[29] 'Recommendation of the Council Concerning Effective action Against Hard-Core Cartels' OECD Publication C(98)35/FINAL, of May 1998, available on the OECD's web site.

[30] M. Monti, 'Fighting Cartels Why and How?' 3rd Nordic Competition Policy Conference, Stockholm, 11–12 September 2000.

[31] OECD Publication C(98)35/FINAL, of May 1998, available on the OECD's web site.

In a subsequent report prepared by the OECD in 2000, *Hard Core Cartels*, urging an OECD anti-cartel programme,[32] it was estimated that cartels cost society $ billions and thwart the gains sought to be achieved through global market liberalization.[33] 'The average increase from price fixing is estimated to amount to 10% of the selling price and the corresponding reduction of output to be as high as 20 percent. In some recent big cases prices have been increased by the cartel participants 30 percent (graphite electrodes) and 50 percent (citric acid).'[34] In a 2002 report on the nature and impact of cartels, it provided:

Cartels harm consumers and have pernicious effects on economic efficiency. A successful cartel raises prices above the competitive level and reduces output. Consumers choose either not to pay the higher price for some or all of the cartelised product . . . thus forgoing the product, or they pay the cartel price and thereby unknowingly transfer wealth to the cartel operators. A cartel shelters it members from full exposure to market forces, reducing pressure on them to control costs and innovate.

At the EC level, cartels of course also thwart attempts to liberalize and integrate European markets.[35]

Cartels thus pose a serious threat to economies and consumers. Many competition authorities now work together through formal and informal bilateral and multilateral arrangements to combat such cartels,[36] are prepared to coordinate searches and investigations across jurisdictions, are increasingly allocating their scare resources towards the detection and elimination of cartels, and are imposing hefty sanctions on the undertakings found to be in breach. Further, an increasing number of countries have introduced, or are introducing, criminal or other sanctions for *individuals* involved in, or responsible for, the operation of a cartel. Although the operation of a cartel is not a criminal offence in the EU, it is in a number of the Member States[37] and there is a view that those responsible for violation of the EC cartel rules should be punished

[32] The findings of this programme were published in 'Hard Core Cartels, Recent Progress and Challenges Ahead' (OECD, 2003), available on the OECD's web site.

[33] For example, it estimated that the Graphite electrodes cartel affected $6 billion in commerce worldwide and the estimated harm of such cartel was up to 65% of this sum, in 'Hard Core Cartels, Recent Progress and Challenges Ahead' (OECD, 2003), 97. See also OFT 386, 'The development of targets for consumer savings arising from competition policy', Economic Discussion Paper 4, June 2002. In conclusion this report suggests that bid rigging cartels lead to price increases of between 10–20%, whilst price fixing cartels did not lead so consistently to higher prices, but when they did, the price rises were often well in excess of 10%.

[34] M. Monti, 'Fighting Cartels Why and How? Why should we be concerned with cartels and collusive behaviour?' 3rd Nordic Competition Policy Conference, Stockholm, 11–12 Sept. 2000.

[35] 'It is essential to ensure that the removal of State measures that have shielded companies from competition is not replaced by collusion, having the same effect. Companies that have been used to the absence of effective competition, may have a particularly strong incentive to collude rather than to compete. Indeed, liberalization of markets and removal of other regulatory obstacles to effective competition increases competition and thereby the payoffs from successful collusion. The higher the degree of competition in a market, the greater the incentive to form a cartel and the greater the harm to the economy and consumers', M. Monti, 'Fighting Cartels Why and How? Why should we be concerned with cartels and collusive behaviour?' 3rd Nordic Competition Policy Conference, Stockholm, 11–12 Sept. 2000.

[36] An International Anti-Cartel Enforcement Workshop has been held each year since 1999 for cartel investigators and prosecutors, see, e.g., 'Status Report: An Overview of Recent Developments in the Antitrust Division's Criminal Enforcement Program' Department of Justice Antitrust Division, 25 Feb. 2004. The EU has concluded formal cooperation agreements with the US, Canada, and Japan. For example, the agreements provide for reciprocal notification of cases; coordination of enforcement activities; and mutual assistance and requests to the other jurisdiction to take enforcement action. For a list of all the bilateral arrangements concluded by the Commission, see http://ec.europa.eu/comm/competition/international/bilateral/bilateral.html. In some cases, parallel dawn raids are concluded internationally. International cooperation is discussed, *infra* Chap. 16.

[37] The more states that have criminal regimes the harder it will be for an individual to avoid extradition to a jurisdiction in which a criminal cartel offence was committed. In the UK the criminal cartel offence is an extraditable offence, Enterprise Act 2002, s. 191.

individually.[38] In the UK,[39] for example, it is an offence for an individual to dishonestly agree with one or more other persons that two or more undertakings will engage in specified cartel arrangements fixing prices, limiting production or supply, sharing markets, or rigging bids.[40] The offence applies to agreements concluded outside the UK if implemented within it. In the UK it is also possible for directors of companies in breach of the competition rules to be disqualified from acting as directors for a period of up to fifteen years where they contributed to a breach or knew, or should have known, of the breach.[41]

In the US, Richard Posner has commented that '[t]he elimination of the formal cartel from ... industries is an impressive, and remains the major, achievement of American antitrust law'.[42] Hardcore cartel activity is prosecuted criminally in the US and, since the mid-1990s, the Department of Justice has concentrated its enforcement resources on international cartels that victimize American consumers and businesses. Huge fines are now imposed on corporations and executives, and executives are sent to prison for long periods. The DOJ takes the view that individual jail sentences are the most effective deterrent to cartel activity.[43] Further, firms in breach may be liable to treble damages to persons injured by the violation.[44] Damages paid may exceed any fine imposed by a competition agency.[45] In the UK, the elimination of the cartel is a major preoccupation of the competition authorities.[46] If the European Commission once felt

[38] See *infra* n. 43 and accompanying text. Criminal law and criminal procedure does not ordinarily fall within the sphere of the Community's competence. The Community legislature could, however, require Member States to impose criminal penalties for European cartel offences. For a discussion of this issue see, e.g. J. Faull and A. Nikpay (eds.), *The EC Law of Competition* (2nd edn., Oxford University Press, 2007), paras. 8.868–8.874 and W. Wils, 'Does the Effective Enforcement of Articles 81 and 82 Require Not Only Fines on Undertakings But Also Individual Penalties, In Particular Imprisonment' in C. D. Ehlermann (ed.) *European Competition Law Annual 2001: Effective Private Enforcement of EC Antitrust Law* (Hart Publishing, 2002), P. H. Roshowicz, 'The Appropriateness of Criminal Sanctions in the Enforcement of Competition Law' [2004] *ECLR* 12 and G. J Werden and M. J. Simon, 'Why Price Fixers should go to Prison' (1987) 32 *Ant Bull* 917. Criminal sanctions may increasingly become a reality in Europe since criminal regimes exist in a number of Member States.

[39] Criminal regimes also exist, e.g., in France, Austria, Ireland, and the Slovak Republic and bid-rigging is an offence in Germany. Criminal regimes also exist in the US, Canada, Brazil, Japan, and Norway.

[40] Enterprise Act 2002, Part 6. It may also be an offence at common law. The statutory offence applies *only* in respect of horizontal agreements (between undertakings operating at the same level of the supply chain). Following consultation, the Government decided against extending the offence to any types of vertical agreements (between undertakings at different level of the supply chain), such as resale price maintenance.

[41] Enterprise Act 2002, s. 204 (amending the Company Directors Disqualification Act 1986), see Chap. 14.

[42] R. A. Posner, *Antitrust Law* (University of Chicago Press, 1976), 39.

[43] 'Once convicted, defendants are paying a heavy price for their illegality. Over the past six years, the Division has obtained more than $2 billion in fines against corporations convicted of engaging in cartel conduct. Individual cartelists also have paid a heavy price for their illegal conduct. In the last fiscal year, the average jail sentence imposed in Antitrust Division cases was over 18 months—a Division record', 'Anti-cartel enforcement: the core antitrust mission', R. Hewitt Pate, (then) Acting Assistant Attorney General, Antitrust Division, US Department of Justice, 16 May 2003. The average jail sentence reached a high of 21 months in fiscal year 2003, 'Status Report: An Overview of Recent Developments in the Antitrust Division's Criminal Enforcement Program' Department of Justice Antitrust Division, 25 Feb. 2004. See, also, for example J. Griffin, 'A Summary Overview of the Antitrust Division's Criminal Enforcement Programme' (August 2003), available on the DOJ's web site at www.usdoj.gov and S. D. Hammond 'An Update on the Antitrust Division's Criminal Enforcement Program' speech before the ABA section of Antitrust Law Cartel Enforcement, 16 November 2005.

[44] Clayton Act, s. 4.

[45] In the *Vitamins* cartel case, for example, the defendants agreed to pay US customers more than $1billion in damages, see 'Status Report: An Overview of Recent Developments in the Antitrust Division's Criminal Enforcement Program' Department of Justice Antitrust Division, 25 Feb. 2004. The question of whether, and if so when, European claimants can bring class actions cases in the US is dealt with infra Chap. 16.

[46] One of the major reasons for reforming the UK competition rules and for introducing the Chap. I prohibition into the UK Competition Act 1998 was to ensure that the UK's Office of Fair Trading could effectively combat the operation of cartels. Under the Restrictive Trade Practices Act 1976 the authorities had extremely limited investigatory powers and fines could not be imposed in respect of agreements operated in

inhibited about acting against national champions and industrial giants engaged in the operation of cartels, this can no longer be said to be the case. In its annual competition reports it has indicated that it is determined to take vigorous action against cartels, believing that their effect is to deprive consumers of the benefits of undistorted competition. It seems clear that the fight against cartels is now one of the, if not the, principal concerns of the Commission.[47] It has resolved to deploy all the resources necessary to take effective action against them despite the major effort in terms of manpower and lengthy procedure that their identification and combating involves.[48] This attitude has been reflected by a number of factors, for example:

- increasing numbers of decisions have been adopted prohibiting cartels (ten in 2001, nine in 2002, five in 2003, seven in 2004, five in 2005 and seven in 2006).[49] Well over half of the cartel decisions adopted by the Commission have been adopted since 1998.

- increasing fines[50] are imposed on cartel members. The fines imposed by the Commission in 2001 totalled more than €1.8 billion, and, for example, total fines in *Vitamins*,[51] *Plasterboard* and *Carbonless Paper*[52] amounted to €855.23, €478.32 and €313.69 million respectively. In 2002, the Commission imposed fines totalling more than €944 million, in 2003 fines totalling more than €404 million, in 2004, fines totalling more than €390 million, in 2005 fines totalling more than €683 million and in 2006 fines totally more than €1,846 million.[53] Table 11.1 below sets out the ten largest fines imposed by the Commission in its cartel cases between 1969 and the end of March 2007;

- in 1998, the Commission introduced Guidelines on the Methods for setting fines indicating that fines will increase the more serious the violation and the longer the duration (cartel members know that the clock is ticking).[54] The notice was replaced in 2006 with the aim of further

contravention of the Act. The Enterprise Act 2002 bolsters the Competition Act 1998 by providing for the disqualification of the directors that commit breaches of the competition rules (Articles 81 or 82 or the UK Chapter I or II prohibitions) and are unfit to act as directors and by introducing a criminal cartel offence. The latter is a criminal offence and individuals convicted of infringing it may be imprisoned for up to 5 years and/or may be subjected to an unlimited fine (see *supra* n. 40).

[47] See M. Monti, 'Fighting Cartels Why and How? Why should we be concerned with cartels and collusive behaviour?' 3rd Nordic Competition Policy Conference, Stockholm, 11–12 Sept. 2000.

[48] See, e.g., *XXIIIrd Report on Competition Policy* (Commission, 1993), part 209.

[49] See cartel statistics for the period 2002–2007, available on DGComp's website at: http://ec.europa.eu/comm/competition/cartels/statistics/statistics.pdf

[50] In its 2002 report the OECD looked at a number of cartels in a number of different States and in some considered how much the fines were in proportion to the estimated harm of the cartel, OECD Cartels, 2002, 96–8. In only four cases of those where fines were assessed as a percentage of the estimated harm, did it appear that the fine exceeded the gains made by the cartel members. It must be questioned, therefore, to what extent fines, given the small chance of detection, operate as an effective deterrent. For this reason, some Member States believe that the possibility of brining criminal prosecutions against individuals operates as a more effective deterrent, see, e.g., *supra* n. 43 and accompanying text.

[51] [2003] OJ L6/1, [2003] 4 CMLR 1030, see Case T-15 and 26/02, *BASF* v. *Commission* [2006] ECR II-497, [2006] 5 CMLR 2 (reducing some of the fines).

[52] [2004] OJ L15/1, Cases T-109/02, etc. *Bolloré* v. *Commission*, 27 April 2007 Cases C-322 and 327/07 (judgment pending).

[53] The figures are slightly lower once corrected to take account of court judgments adjusting the relevant fines, see the cartel statistics available on DGComp's web site at: http://ec.europa.eu/comm/competition/cartels/statistics/statistics.pdf

[54] The 1998 guidelines aimed to retain the Commission's broad discretion in this area but to improve transparency, to strengthen the coherence of the policy of the Commission as regards fines, whilst maintaining the deterrent character of the sanctions. Broadly, the Commission determined a basic fine calculated by reference to the gravity and duration of the infringement (without reference to turnover). This sum could be raised where aggravating circumstances exist and may be reduced to take account of attenuating circumstances, see Chap. 14.

developing and refining policy and to provide more effective sanctions and deterrents to the operation of cartels, not only by sanctioning those involved but also through deterrence of others, and to ensure adequate punishment of repeat offenders. Extra sums are imposed to deter hardcore cartel agreements and, repeat offenders may expect an increase of 100 percent for each such infringement established;[55]

• increased international co-operation focused on the elimination of international hardcore cartel activity;

• the introduction in 1996 of a successful leniency programme encouraging parties to blow the whistle and to confess to their participation in an illegal cartel. The Commission thus adopts a 'carrot and stick' policy: imposing large fines on those found to violate the rules but rewards for those who come forward with information on cartels. The programme was revised in 2002 to address defects in the original system and again in 2006 with the objective of strengthening, clarifying and improving it;[56]

• the abolition of the notification and authorization system set up in Regulation 17. The changes introduced by Regulation 1/2003 on 1 May 2004 enable the Commission to refocus its activities and to divert resources from scrutinising (mainly innocuous) notified agreements to uncovering the most serious infringements of competition law, especially the detection and prevention of cross-border cartels. It has also acquired broader powers to investigate breaches of the rules;

• the Commission's initiative to encourage greater private enforcement of the competition rules. The Commission wants to make exercising the right to claim damages for breach of Community competition law easier and to ensure compensation of victims of cartels. In 2005, it published a Green Paper (available on its web site), opening a debate about private enforcement and setting out a number of possible options to facilitate private damages actions. The Commission is now preparing a follow-up White Paper for publication at the end of 2007 or early in 2008. Each Commission press release announcing fines in a cartel case now contains a reminder that any person or firm affected by the anti-competitive behaviour described can seek damages submitting elements of the published decision as evidence that the behaviour took place and was illegal;[57]

• the creation of an entire cartel directorate (Directorate F) within DG competition to focus on cartel activity; and

• the Commission's willingness to consider whether direct settlements of a cartel case may provide an effective and speedy mechanism for resolving cartel cases.[58]

---

[55] Fining policy are discussed *infra* Chap. 14.

[56] The leniency rules are discussed *infra* 878–9 (in outline) and, more fully, in Chap. 14.

[57] See Chap. 15.

[58] This issue is discussed *infra* Chap. 14 but see, e.g. speech by N. Kroes, 'Reinforcing the fight against cartels and developing private antitrust damage actions: two tools for a more competitive Europe', 8 March 2007 and the UK settlement of the investigation of price fixing by independent schools, available at: http://www.oft.gov.uk/ advice_and_resources/resource_base/ca98/decisions/schools. A discussion paper on this issue is anticipated towards the end of 2007.

Table 11.1 Highest cartel fines per case 1969–March 2007

Commission Decision	Approximate Total Fines
Lifts and Escalators[59]	€992 million (including a fine of €480 million on ThyssenKrupp)
Vitamins[60]	€855.23 million[61] (including a fine of €462 million and 236.8 million on Hoffman La-Roche and BASF AG respectively)
Gas Insulated Switchgear[62]	€750 million (including a fine of more than €396 million on Siemens)
Synthetic Rubber[63]	€519 million (including a fine of €272 million on Eni SpA)
Plasterboard[64]	€478.32 million (including a fine of €249 million for Lafarge SA)
Bleaching Chemicals[65]	€388.1 million
Methacrylates[66]	€344.5 million
Copper Fitting producers[67]	€314.7 million
Carbonless paper[68]	€313.69 million
Plastic Industrial Bags[69]	€290 million

(ii) Tacit Collusion, Coordinated Effects on an Oligopolistic Market

In Chapter 1 it was seen that in the 1930s and 1940s an ascendant view was that the structure of a market affected outcome on that market and that concentrated markets delivered poorer outcomes for consumers and higher profitability for firms.[70] Game theory, however, indicates that although in some oligopolistic markets players may coordinate their behaviour, coordination will not always occur.[71] On the contrary, there are oligopolistic markets where both price and/or non-price competition is intense. Although therefore, undertakings operating on a market on which there are only a few players *may* align their conduct and charge supra-competitive

---

[59] IP/07/209.

[60] *Vitamins* [2003] OJ L6/1, [2003] 4 CMLR 1030, *aff'd* (but some of fines were reduced) Cases T-15 etc /02, *BASF AG v. Commission* [2006] ECR II-497, [2006] 5 CMLR 2.

[61] Total fines reduced on appeal to approximately €790 million, see *supra* n. 60.

[62] IP/07/80.

[63] IP/06/1851, Cases T-44 and 45/07, *Kaucuk v. Commission* (judgment pending).

[64] *Plasterboard* [2005] OJ L166/8, see Case T-50/03, *Gyproc Benelux v Commission* (judgment pending).

[65] IP/06/560, Cases T-192, etc/06, *Cafarro v. Commission* (judgment pending).

[66] IP/06/698, Case T-214/06, *Imperial Chemical Industries v. Commission* (judgment pending).

[67] IP/06/1222, Cases T-378/06, *IMI v. Commission* (judgment pending).

[68] [2004] OJ L15/1, Cases T-109/02, etc. *Bolloré v. Commission*, 27 April 2007, Cases C-322 and 32/07 (judgment pending).

[69] IP/05/1508, Case T-51/06, *Fardem Packaging v. Commission* (judgment pending).

[70] See e.g. E. H. Chamberlain, *The Theory of Monopolistic Competition* (Harvard University, 1933).

[71] G. Stigler, 'A Theory of Oligopoly' (1964) 72 *Journal of Political Economy* 44.

prices as a rational response to market circumstances, this is by no means an inevitable outcome. The prisoners' dilemma provides a framework for understanding when an oligopolistic market may be conducive to collusion and when it may not.

The Prisoners' Dilemma, set out on pages 860–861 above, illustrates how, even without contractual arrangements or other explicit collusion between the parties, collusion (tacit collusion) may occur on an oligopolistic market. A and B know, even without conferring together, that if they both choose a high price they will, collectively, maximize their profits (by raising their prices and restricting their output). However, A is aware that if B charges a high price, A can increase its profits, at B's expense, by reducing its price and attracting away B's customers. B is also aware that it can achieve substantial profits by reducing its price and soliciting A's customers. In the event that both A and B end up lowering their prices or having a price war, prices will be driven down to a lower level. In the first game, therefore, A and B may reduce price and achieve a result that is disadvantageous for both parties.[72] Where, however, the game is played continually, A and B may reconsider their situation independently, without meeting and agreeing, and realize that they are both much better off if they decide to charge a high price. Oligopolists thus have heightened awareness of other firms' presence on the market. They are likely to monitor the behaviour of their competitors (a reduction in one's price will swiftly attract away the others' customers) and to recognize their interdependence. They may realize, without the need for communication, that the most efficient course of conduct is for them all to set their prices at a profit-maximizing level and to behave 'as if' they have agreed to act in a manner which maximizes the profits of the market players and 'tacitly' to coordinate their behaviour. Tacit collusion thus occurs where, without any formal arrangement, firms simply understand that if they compete less vigorously they will be able to earn higher profits and that conversely, cutting prices will simply lead to its rivals following suit. Because economists consider the outcome or effects to be similar to explicit collusion, they generally describe this behaviour as tacit collusion. Because collusion is the evil against which Article 81 acts, however, lawyers may feel unhappy with this terminology as it is not neutral and suggests the existence of a conspiracy between the parties. Richard Whish, for example, prefers to use the term tacit coordination 'since this at least eliminates the pejorative word 'collusion' whilst retaining the notion of parallel behaviour which is beneficial to the collectively dominant operators on the market and disadvantageous to customers and consumers'.[73] In this chapter, the terms tacit collusion and tacit coordination are used interchangeably.

To be conducive to such tacit collusion, tacit coordination or oligopolistic interdependence the market must possess features which make tacit collusion feasible or likely. Thus, it is necessary for the firms to have the incentive to avoid competing, to realize their mutual interdependence, to be able successfully to engage in a common form of behaviour i.e. to align their conduct (this is of course more difficult to achieve without explicit collusion), to monitor what their competitors are doing on the market, and to realize that if they deviate from the common behaviour they will be punished or disciplined (with low prices and low profits). These markets are likely to have similar characteristics as those on which explicit collusion is possible. For example, the market is likely to be transparent and characterized by high concentration, barriers to entry, homogenous products,[74] firms with similar cost and demand structures and a common high valuation of future profits, some mechanism for alignment (either through

---

[72] See *supra* 860–1.

[73] R. Whish, *Competition Law* (5th edn., Butterworths, 2003), 508–9.

[74] Parallel pricing will have little impact where the undertakings are also competing on factors such as the quality of their product and brand image.

signalling[75] or a focal point),[76] and a mechanism for punishing those deviating from parallelism (perhaps through a costly price wars or expansion of output). In contrast, markets characterized by differentiated products, volatile demand or demand booms, the existence of large and sophisticated buyers, ease of entry or cost asymmetries are likely to make coordination more unlikely.[77]

(iii) Unilateral (or Non-Coordinated) Effects

In Chapter 12 it is seen that economic theory[78] predicts that when the number of firms on an oligopolistic market decrease, because two of the parties operating on the market merge, prices may increase unless the merger results in large efficiency gains.[79] The theories envisage that, even in the absence of the remaining firms operating on the oligopolistic market engaging in tacit collusion or explicitly coordinating their behaviour, prices will be higher than before the merger. The firms on the market do not raises prices by coordinating their behaviour (explicitly or tacitly) but by reacting independently to their competitors' anticipated behaviour (non-coordinated effects). As a merger triggers this situation, any potential adverse outcome on a market may be dealt with *ex ante* through the application of merger rules. The extent to which the EC Merger Regulation (the 'ECMR') can, or should, be used to prevent mergers which will lead to these unilateral, or non-coordinated, effects on a market is discussed in Chapter 12.

C. COMPETITION LAW AND COLLUSION (EXPLICIT AND TACIT)

Where undertakings agree to fix or otherwise *explicitly collude* in fixing prices, restricting output, and/or sharing markets there will be sufficient cooperation between the undertakings to constitute an agreement, decision or concerted practice and so to trigger the operation of Article 81(1) (assuming of course that the other requirements of Article 81 are satisfied).

The difficulty with *tacit* collusion is that although the impact of such coordination on the market is the same, or at least similar, as where it is explicit (consumer welfare is harmed), the parties have not in fact *agreed* or otherwise explicitly cooperated with each other to coordinate their behaviour. How then should the competition rules deal with tacit collusion?

In the EC, the European Commission has utilized the merger rules to try and prevent mergers between firms, which are likely to *create* a market situation in which tacit collusion between the parties is likely, or more likely.[80] Further, Article 81 may be used to prevent practices which may facilitate tacit or explicit collusion on a market, for example, by rendering the market more transparent through the exchange of information or the incorporation of meeting competition clauses into sales agreements.[81] But what can be done about markets which are already

---

[75] By signalling, for example, making price announcements in advance, firms may be able to indicate what their future pricing policy will be. It will be a question of degree whether or not this type of conduct can be characterized as concerted behaviour contrary to Article 81(1), see *infra* 916–8.

[76] A practice of recommending prices can operate as a focal point and facilitate alignment of behaviour. So too can historical price leadership.

[77] See *supra* and R. Van den Bergh and P. Camesasca *European Competition Law and Economics: A Comparative Perspective* (2nd edn., Sweet & Maxwell, 2006), 5.2.3.

[78] The Cournot and Betrand models. See also, *infra*, Chap. 12, especially 1007–9 and 1018–37.

[79] See *infra* Chap. 12.

[80] It has the power to prevent mergers that will significantly impede effective competition by leading to coordinated and unilateral or non-coordinated effects, see Chap. 12.

[81] See *supra* n. 15.

concentrated and on which tacit collusion is, or may be, occurring? What action can be taken *ex post* as opposed to *ex ante*? As the tacit collusion stems from the *structure* of the market, should the Commission adopt a structural solution and try to deconcentrate the market, perhaps by ordering the firms operating on the market to sell off parts of its business?[82] In the US, in the 1960s there was significant support for the view that unreasonable market power should be condemned and that there should be power to dissolve firms found to possess it.[83] Indeed, in 1968 a White House Task Force on Antitrust Policy proposed legislation that would permit deconcentration of markets where four or fewer firms had a combined market share of 70 percent or more *unless* the defendant could establish that such a step would reduce efficiency.[84] Support for this kind of legislation was, however, abandoned following 'post-1970s scepticism about ambitious governmental interventions in the economy'.[85] Deconcentration would, of course, be extremely controversial and, arguably, grossly inappropriate given how difficult it is to determine whether or not tacit collusion is occurring and that it is adopted as a rational response to market conditions.

Alternatively, should tacit collusion be seen as a problem stemming from the anti-competitive *behaviour* of the oligopolists?[86] Since the effects of tacit collusion are similar to cases in which there is explicit collusion and the firms' decisions are not taken truly unilaterally (but rather taking into account the anticipated reaction of its competitors), could parallel behaviour or conscious parallelism, without any proof of actual collusion between the undertakings, be prohibited as an illegal concerted practice under Article 81? In the US, Richard Posner was a proponent of the view that the concepts of contract, combination or conspiracy in section 1 of the Sherman Act 1890 were capable of reaching, and an appropriate mechanism for dealing with, tacit collusion.[87] This view did not, however, gain acceptance in the US courts and such[88] an approach has also been rejected by the ECJ, Alternatively, could Article 82, which applies to firms that 'collectively' hold a dominant position, be used to condemn tacit behaviour (or other

---

[82] Such an outcome is, since 1 May 2004, now theoretically possible but only so long as a breach of Article 81 or 82 is established, see Reg. 1/2003, Art. 7 and discussion *infra* Chap. 14. In the UK the competition authorities can look more broadly at features of the market (which is not just restricted to an assessment of the behaviour of the firms on the market) to determine whether they prevent, restrict, or distort competition in the UK. Where an adverse effect on competition is identified, a broad range of remedies are available to remedy the problems identified, including divestiture, see *infra* section 4.

[83] See, e.g., C. Kaysen and D. Turner Antitrust Policy (1959), 110–19 and 266–72. See the criticisms of these 'startling' conclusions set out in R.H. Bork, The Antitrust Paradox: A Policy at War with Itself (Basic Books, 1978, reprinted with a new Introduction and Epilogue, 1993), 176.

[84] The White House Task Force Report on Antitrust Policy (the Neale Report), 1968 recommended adoption of this Concentrated Industries Act (it was endorsed by eleven of its thirteen members).

[85] R. Posner Antitrust Law (2nd edn., University of Chicago Press, 2001), 102. The author takes the view that deconcentration would confer few benefits and even if were effective its social costs would exceed its social benefits.

[86] A third alternative 'would be to introduce direct regulation of oligopolistic industries so that prices would be fixed at what might be considered to be a "competitive", or at any rate a "reasonable", level by a Government agency...However, there are problems with the regulatory approach to oligopoly. Direct regulation is enormously cumbersome and requires extensive bureaucratic resources. It is also difficult to establish what a competitive or reasonable price should be: in so far as it is possible, it is preferable to let the market itself determine this issue rather than a Governmental body or competition authority', R. Whish, *Competition Law* (5th edn., Butterworths, 2003), 513.

[87] See R. Posner, 'Oligopoly and the Antitrust Laws: A Suggested Approach' 21 Stan. L. Rev 1562 (but see now R. Posner *Antitrust Law* (2nd edn., University of Chicago Press, 2001)). But contrast, e.g. D. F. Turner 'The Definition of Agreement under the Sherman Act: Conscious Parallelism and Refusals to Deal' [1962] 75 *Harv L Rev* 655.

[88] See, in particular, *Theatre Enterprises v. Paramount Film Distributing Corp.* 346 US 537 (1954).

behaviour of tacitly colluding oligopolists) as an abuse of a collective dominant position? Or is it inappropriate to characterize tacit collusion, which is a consequence of the structure of the market (and not as the term collusion perhaps suggests a consequence of a conspiracy between the firms),[89] as illegal under either Article 81 or 82? Section 3 below considers the extent to which Article 81 or 82 may be applied as an effective tool against tacit collusion on a market. It also considers the extent to which those Articles can be used to prevent *other* behaviour of oligopolistic firms operating on the market, for example practices which might lead to or encourage tacit collusion. The extent to which the ECMR can be used to prevent mergers that will increase concentration on a market and lead to coordinated or unilateral (non-coordinated) effects is considered in Chapter 12.

3. CARTELS

A. INTRODUCTION

It is Article 81, of course, which prohibits the creation and operation of cartels. Article 81(1) prohibits all 'agreements between undertakings, decisions by associations of undertakings and concerted practices' which both affect trade between Member States and have as their object or effect the prevention, restriction, or distortion of competition.[90]

B. SCOPE OF ARTICLE 81

(i) Article 81(1)

In order to ensure that detrimental collusion between undertakings does not escape the ambit of the competition rules, the requirements of Article 81(1) have been interpreted broadly.

In Chapter 3 it was seen that the terms agreement, decision, and concerted practice have been interpreted generously to catch all illicit cooperation (agreements whatever their form, complex arrangements, the activities of trade associations, and other conduct of firms designed to substitute cooperation for the risks of competition) between firms. Further, in Chapter 4 it was seen that in most cartel cases, in contrast with distribution, intellectual property licensing, or horizontal cooperation cases, the question of whether any established agreement, decision, or concerted practice has as its *object or effect* the prevention, restriction, or distortion of competition is usually uncontroversial. Hard-core cartel activities, price-fixing and market-sharing agreements or agreement to restrict output or rig bids have as their *object* the restriction of competition.[91] Further agreements to exchange price information may have as their object the restriction of competition both in itself and where facilitating the enforcement of a hard-core

---

[89] For this reason some prefer to use a term such as 'conscious parallelism' or 'tacit coordination' which avoid reference to the term collusion, see, e.g., R. Whish, *Competition Law* (5th edn., Butterworths, 2003), 508–9 set out *supra* 872.

[90] See *supra* Chap. 3.

[91] See, e.g., *BELASCO* [1986] OJ L232/15, [1991] 4 CMLR 130, *aff'd* on appeal, Case 246/86, *Re Roofing Felt Cartel: BELASCO v. Commission* [1989] ECR 2117, [1991] 4 CMLR 96, Case 96/82, *IAZ International Belgium NV v. Commission* [1983] ECR 3369, [1984] 3 CMLR 276; and Case T-7/89, *SA Hercules NV v. Commission* [1991] ECR II-1711, [1992] 4 CMLR 84 and Cases T-374, 375, 384 and 388/94, *European Night Services v. Commission* [1998] ECR II-3141, [1998] 5 CMLR 718. Only where a horizontal agreement is not naked will it be necessary to determine whether or not its effect is to restrict competition.

cartel agreement or implementing it.[92] The object of the agreement is not affected by the fact that: the agreement has proved difficult to apply in practice (and may not, therefore, have had the effect of restricting competition);[93] a participant always intended to ignore the terms of the agreement and that it did, in fact, cheat on the cartel (when cheating the undertaking inevitably relies on the existence of the agreement or concerted practice and will not gain unless the others adhere to its terms);[94] the agreement has been rendered lawful by national legislation[95] or that price control is in place;[96] or the market is in crisis or decline, or plagued with over-capacity. The fact that the market is 'characterised over a period of several years by under-utilisation of capacity, with attendant losses by the producers, does not relieve the agreement of its anti-competitive object'.[97] In most cartel cases the effect of the agreement will, therefore, be relevant only when determining whether its impact on competition or trade is appreciable,[98] whether it meets the criteria set out in Article 81(3), or, where a breach of the rules is established, to the determination of the fine, if any, imposed.[99]

In addition, it should be remembered that many cartel arrangements, even national cartels, will have an appreciable affect on trade between Member States as in order to be successful, cartels will need to make it difficult for undertakings, including undertakings from other Member States, to penetrate the market.[100]

The difficulty for the Commission is ordinarily to establish the existence of an agreement or concerted practice between undertakings or a decision by an association of undertakings.[101]

---

[92] Cases T-25, 26, 30–2, 34–9, 42–6, 48, 50–71, 87, 88, 103, and 104/95 *Cimenteries CBR SA* v. *Commission* [2000] ECR II-491, [2000] 5 CMLR 204, para. 1531 (at least where it underpins another anti-competitive agreement), broadly *aff'd* Cases C-204, 205, 211, 213, 217 and 219/00 P, *Aalborg Portland A/S* v. *Commission* [2004] ECR I-123, [2005] 4 CMLR 251. See also *IFTRA Glass* [1974] OJ L160/1. See discussion *infra* especially *infra* 880 ff.

[93] *Ferry Operators* [1997] OJ L26/23, [1997] 4 CMLR 789.

[94] See *BELASCO* [1986] OJ L232/15, [1991] 4 CMLR 130, *aff'd* on appeal, Case 246/86, *Re Roofing Felt Cartel: BELASCO* v. *Commission* [1989] ECR 2117, [1991] 4 CMLR 96.

[95] See *infra* 889.

[96] See *Belgian Brewers* [2003] OJ L 200/1, para. 247, *aff'd* Case T-38/02 *Groupe Danone* v. *Commission* [2005] ECR II-4407 (small reduction in fine) *aff'd* Case C-3/06 P, *Groupe Danone* v. *Commission*, 8 Feb. 2007.

[97] See *Polypropylene* [1986] OJ L230/1, [1988] 4 CMLR 347, para. 89; appeals substantially dismissed both by the CFI and the ECJ, see, e.g., Case C-51/92 P, *SA Hercules NV* v. *Commission* [1999] ECR I-4235, [1999] 5 CMLR 976 and Case C-199/92 P, *Hüls AG* v. *Commission (Polypropylene)* [1999] ECR I-4287, [1999] 5 CMLR 1016. Occasionally, the difficulties faced by undertakings have been taken into account as mitigation in assessing the fine See, e.g., *Polypropylene* [1986] OJ L230/1, [1988] 4 CMLR 347, para. 108.

[98] These types of agreement are not covered by the Commission's Notice on Agreements of Minor Importance, *supra* Chap. 3. In practice, these serious restrictions of competition are most unlikely to be considered to be insignificant, see *supra* Chap. 3.

[99] Case 246/86, *Re Roofing Felt Cartel: BELASCO* v. *Commission* [1989] ECR 2117, [1991] 4 CMLR 96.

[100] It is possible, however, that a cartel affecting only a local geographic market may not have an effect on inter-state trade, see *supra* Chap. 3.

[101] In a number of cartels uncovered by the Commission, a significant role has been played by a trade association or a fiduciary company. Where this is the case the trade association or fiduciary company may be held responsible for the breach and fined, see, e.g. Case 246/86, *Re Roofing Felt Cartel: BELASCO* v. *Commission* [1989] ECR 2117, [1991] 4 CMLR 96 and *Organic Peroxides* [2005] OJ L110/44, *aff'd*, Case T-120/04 etc *Peróxiidos Orgánicos SA* v. *Commission*, 16 Nov. 2006, [2007] 4 CMLR 4. In the latter case a Swiss company, AC Treuhand, was found to have played a key role in the organization of the cartel, helping to administer the meetings and reimbursing travel expenses of participants in order to avoid them leaving traces of the illegal meetings. It was fined a mere €1,000 for its participation, however, on the grounds that this was the first time the Commission had imposed a fine in these circumstances. It warned, however, that organizers of facilitators could expect heavy sanctions in the future.

(ii) Establishing a Breach of Article 81(1)

a. General

In cartel cases it is normally the detection of cartels, rather than the legal intricacies of Article 81, which presents the main difficulty. Because of the serious nature of such infringements, proof of collusion is likely to prove the breach. Even though, therefore, the terms have been interpreted broadly parties are likely to operate any arrangements covertly in order to make detection difficult. A competition authority's task of proving the existence of the cartel is an onerous one.

M. Monti, 'Fighting Cartels Why and How? Why should we be Concerned with Cartels and Collusive Behaviour?' 3rd Nordic Competition Policy Conference, Stockholm, 11–12 Sept. 2000

Fighting cartels is not an easy business to be in. Companies operating cartels are of course very much aware of the illegality of their conduct under the antitrust laws. For that reason, cartels are typically operated in secrecy and considerable efforts are devoted by the participants to avoiding detection by the authorities. Meetings are held in exotic places around the globe. Incriminating documents are destroyed or stored outside the premises of the companies. Practices are arranged so as to simulate normal market behaviour and so on.

In order to be successful a competition authority must be able to play a number of different cards. In particular, a successful fight against cartels presupposes an effective leniency programme, effective enforcement powers and sanctions, and close cooperation amongst competition authorities.

In 1996 the Commission adopted for the first time a Leniency Programme. The first experience shows that it has led to a substantial increase in the number of cartels that have been uncovered and punished.

The programme provides a strong incentive for companies to come forward and to co-operate. Companies which provide information on a secret cartel before the Commission has opened an investigation can benefit even from total immunity from fines. Moreover, companies which cooperate with the Commission in the course of a pending investigation can benefit from a substantial reduction of their fines . . . Such substantial reductions of the fines are based on the premise that the public interest in detection and prohibition of cartels is higher than the interest in fining colluding companies.

---

b. Standard of Proof, Powers, and Leniency

The burden of proof is on the Commission, or other person alleging a breach, to prove that Article 81(1) has been infringed.[102] Regulation 1/2003 does not deal with the standard of proof but the ECJ has held that the evidence produced by the Commission must be 'sufficiently precise and coherent' to prove an infringement.[103] The Court will have no hesitation in annulling a decision of the Commission where a breach has not been proved to the requisite standard.[104] Regulation 1/2003 confers broad powers of enforcement and investigation on the Commission.

---

[102] Reg. 1/2003 [2003] OJ L1/1, Art. 2 and see Chap. 3.

[103] Cases 29 and 30/83, *Compagnie Royale Asturienne des Mines SA and Rheinzink GmbH v. Commission* [1984] ECR 1679, [1985] 1 CMLR 688, see Chaps. 3 and 14.

[104] See Chap. 14, 1299 ff and Chap. 12 1084 ff.

It extended the Commission's powers with the express objective of facilitating investigations of suspected serious breaches of the rules. For example, the Commission has the power to seal premises during its investigations, to take statements from persons relating to the investigation, and, in addition to its powers to conduct dawn raids at business premises, a power to inspect other premises, including the homes of individuals thought to be responsible for a cartel.[105] Despite the existence of broad investigative powers, difficulties remain in uncovering covertly operated cartels. Many competition authorities now encourage undertakings to cooperate with them prior to or during cartel investigations through the operation of 'leniency' regimes. Leniency regimes have become a key part of policy in the fight against cartels. Authorities operating such regimes believe that the public interest in terminating and eradicating cartels outweighs the public interest in punishing those involved in the operation of cartels.[106]

The Commission has operated a leniency regime since 1996.[107] It offered the possibility of fines not being imposed or being seriously or significantly reduced (possible reductions from 100–10 per cent) in return for cooperation. The Commission considered, however, that the scheme could be improved and in 2002 the Commission adopted a new Notice,[108] which aimed both to make it easier for firms to receive *total* immunity in return for their cooperation *and* to provide greater legal certainty for cooperating firms.[109] The Notice was further amended and improved in 2006.[110] Central to both the 2002 and 2006 Notices is the provision that total immunity is only available to the *first* undertaking to submit evidence to the Commission (subject to other conditions also being satisfied).[111] This provides a strong incentive for a cartel member to blow the whistle prior to its co-collaborators and destabilizes the game of collusion set up by the members.[112] The leniency regime has been extremely successful and firms have cooperated with the Commission in a high proportion of the cases occurring since 1996.

---

[105] See Chap. 14.

[106] e.g., jurisdictions with leniency regimes apart from the EC itself and the majority of its Member States (see further Chap. 14) were, as at April 2006, Australia, Brazil, Canada, EFTA, Israel, Japan, Romania (which joined the EU on 1 January 2007), South Korea, New Zealand, South Africa, and the US (see the website of the International Competition Network (ICN, discussed infra Chapter 16), www.internationalcompetitionnetwork.org). Details of leniency regimes operated by EU states is available on DG Camp's website. For suggestions as to how an effective leniency programme should be operated see 'Report on Leniency Programs to Fight Hard Core Cartels' (OECD, 2001), and the 'Anti-Cartel Enforcement Manual' of the ICN's Cartel Working Group, April 2006, available at www.internationalcompetitionnetwork.org/media/library/conference_5th_capetown_2006/FINALFormattedChapter2-modres.pdf. See also the ECN Model Leniency Programme explained infra 880.

[107] Notice on the non-imposition of fines in cartel cases [1996] OJ C207/4.

[108] [2002] OJ C45/3.

[109] In 1993, the Department of Justice revised its leniency policy reducing its discretion and making the leniency provisions more generous. It seems that leniency applications have risen since then from one per year to one per month (initially), to more than two per month (2001–2), to more than four per month (2002–3). Further, in 25–50% of cases parties now ask for amnesty plus (amnesty in respect of other cartels).

[110] Commission Notice on immunity from fines and reduction of fines in cartel cases [2006] OJ C298/17.

[111] Total immunity was granted, for example, in *Fine Art Auction Houses (Christie's and Sotheby's)* IP/02/1744, [2006] 4 CMLR 90. In this case Sotheby's received a fine of €20.4 million (6% of its worldwide turnover) whilst Christie's, the first to provide crucial evidence, escaped a fine. Similarly, in *Methylglucamine* [2004] OJ L38/18, [2004] 4 CMLR 1591, Merck was granted total immunity from a fine despite there only being one other undertaking in the cartel, Aventis Pharma SA and its subsidiary Rhone-Poulenc Biochemie SA. Such cases send out a clear signal that it is worth being the first member of the cartel to come forward and provide the Commission with information relating to it, see Chap. 14.

[112] Reductions in fines are also available to those who are not eligible for total immunity but who nevertheless provide the Commission with evidence that represents significant added value. Essentially greater reductions are offered to those that provide evidence first, see Chap. 14.

Between 1996 and 1998 none of the on site inspections carried out by the European Commission was based on a leniency request. However, as the EC policy became more widely known the position changed dramatically. Between 2001 and 2003 nearly two-thirds of inspections were based on leniency requests. Another striking fact is that throughout the eight year period to 2003 there were generally three or four inspections a year that were not based on leniency requests. But inspections based on leniency applications rose steadily from one in 1999 to 14 in the first nine months of 2003. This demonstrates the strong ability of leniency programmes to uncover cartels. Almost all the Commission inspections since 1996 have resulted in decisions.[113]

Total immunity from fines has now been granted in a number of cases, For example, it was granted in *Fine Auction Houses (Christie's and Sotheby's)* (where Sotheby's received a fine of €20.4 million (6 percent of its worldwide turnover) whilst Christie's, the first to provide crucial evidence, escaped a fine),[114] *Vitamins, Luxembourg Brewers, Methionine, Methylglucamine, Food flavour enhancers, Specialty graphites, Sorbates, Carbon and graphite products, Organic Peroxides, Copper plumbing tubes, Needles and haberdashery, Industrial bags; Rubber chemicals; Bleaching chemicals; Acrylic glass; Road bitumen in the Netherlands, Copper fittings, Synthetic rubber, Gas insulated switchgear* and *Lifts and Escalators*.[115] In each of these cases, except for sorbates and gas insulated switchgear, reductions of up to 50 pecent were also granted to other members of the cartel.

This fact has had an effect on the nature of cartel decisions and appeals: in many cases the dispute now revolves around the nature and duration[116] of the infringement, which firms should be given what credit for cooperation under the relevant Leniency Notice, and the amount of the fine.[117]

The leniency regime is dealt with fully in Chapter 14. It is worth mentioning here, however, that despite the success it has had the Notice does have some limitations. In particular, the Notice cannot give whistle-blowers immunity from the civil law consequences of its participation in an illegal agreement. A third party injured by the cartel's actions may therefore, commence civil proceedings. Having provided evidence incriminating itself and others, a whistle-blower will obviously have difficulty defending such proceedings successfully. This was perceived to be a particular problem in the US where, generally, treble damages are available to those who can establish that they have suffered loss in consequence of another's breach of the competition rules. In 2004 a new Act was adopted which reduces damages to 'single' damages from corporations that participate in the 'amnesty' programme and cooperate with the claimants in their damages actions.[118] In some jurisdictions, the fact that an *individual* might gain immunity from criminal prosecution may encourage leniency applications to be brought, irrespective of the possibility of civil damages.[119]

---

[113] M. Bloom, UAE Symposium, VI Conference, Antitrust between EC law and national law, 13 and 14 May 2004, Treviso. See also, O. Guersent, 'The fight against secret Horizontal Agreement in EC Competition Policy', 2003 Fordham Corp. L. Inst. 43 (B. Hawk, ed. 2004).

[114] Christie's approached both the US and EC competition authorities in January 2000 (the original EC leniency rules thus applied, see *supra* n. 111).

[115] Details of some of these cases are provided *infra* (see especially 883–4) and can be found on DG Competition's web site in the cartels section.

[116] In *Methylglucamine* [2004] OJ L38/18, [2004] 4 CMLR 1591, for example, the Commission found that, where the exact finishing date for the cartel was unclear, the cartel should be treated as having determined on the last day of the validity for the list prices agreed at the last cartel meeting (not the date of the meeting itself).

[117] See Chap. 14.

[118] The Antitrust Criminal Penalty Enhancement and Reform Act 2004. The Act also increases the maximum Sherman Act corporate and individual fines, and maximum jail term. The 'detrebling' provision is designed to remove the disincentive to submitting amnesty applications.

[119] For the question of criminal liability, see *infra* Chap.14.

Another potential problem is that a leniency application to the Commission does not constitute an application to any other competition authority within the European Competition Network ('ECN') or elsewhere. An undertaking applying for leniency will, therefore, need to consider simultaneous applications in all states where leniency programmes are operated and where a breach of the rules may have been committed. This may lead to problems where differences between the programmes exist.[120] The ECN has considered various ways of dealing with difficulties arising and, adopted a Model Leniency Programme in 2006.[121] The purpose of this is to encourage the alignment of Member States' leniency policies so that potential leniency applicants are not discouraged from applying as a result of discrepancies between them.[122]

(iii) Article 81(3)

Where an infringement of Article 81(1) is established, the parties to the agreement may seek to show that the agreement meets the criteria of Article 81(3). It is very unlikely, however, that hard-core cartel activity will satisfy all, or any, of the four criteria set out therein.

C. PRICE FIXING, RESTRICTIONS ON OUTPUT, MARKET SHARING, AND COLLUSIVE TENDERING

(i) General

It has been seen that classic 'hard-core cartels' are operated by fixing prices and/or by imposing quotas on the members and/or by sharing markets between them. In some situations, cartel members may limit price competition and share the market between them by engaging in collusive tendering.

(ii) Article 81(1)

a. Price-fixing Agreements

Selling prices

Article 81(1) specifically provides that agreements 'directly or indirectly fixing purchase or selling prices or any other trading conditions' may infringe Article 81(1) of the Treaty. In *Dyestuffs*,[123] the ECJ stressed that:

The function of price competition is to keep prices down to the lowest possible level . . . Although every producer is free to change his prices, taking into account in so doing the present or foreseeable conduct of his competitors, nevertheless it is contrary to the rules on competition contained in the Treaty for a producer to co-operate with his competitors, in any way whatsoever, in order to determine a co-ordinated course of action relating to a price increase and to ensure its success by prior elimination of all uncertainty as to each other's conduct regarding the essential elements of that action, such as the amount, subject-matter, date and place of the increases.[124]

---

[120] See C. Gauer and M. Jaspers, 'Designing a European Solution for a 'One-stop Leniency Shop'' [2006] ECLR 685.

[121] http://ec.europa.eu/comm/competition/ecn/model_leniency_en.pdf.

[122] See *infra* Chap. 14.

[123] Cases 48, 49, and 51–7/69, *ICI v. Commission (Dyestuffs)* [1972] ECR 619, [1972] CMLR 557.

[124] *Ibid.*, paras. 115 and 118.

In many cartel cases investigated by the Commission, and discussed below, it has uncovered and condemned price-fixing arrangements between cartel members. Often the price fixing is accompanied by other provisions which strengthen the operation of the cartel, such as market sharing or information sharing provisions or the imposition of quotas or output restraints.

Target Prices and Indirect Price Fixing

Not only are agreements to fix prices prohibited, but the discussion and implementation of target prices will be condemned:

[I]f a system of imposed selling prices is clearly in conflict with that provision [Article 81], the system of [target prices] is equally so. It cannot in fact be supposed that the clauses of the agreement concerning the determination of target prices are meaningless. In fact the fixing of a price, even one which merely constitutes a target, affects competition because it enables all the participants to predict with a reasonable degree of certainty what the pricing policy pursued by their competitors will be.[125]

Other agreements which may directly or indirectly facilitate level pricing will also be condemned, for example, agreements fixing or prohibiting discounts, rebates[126] or other financial concessions,[127] agreements to consult on price lists,[128] to restrict advertising,[129] to exchange information and give warning of price increases to provide reassurance that a price war will not break out,[130] to pursue a collaborative strategy of higher pricing,[131] or to exchange price information.[132]

It is contrary to the provisions of Article [81(1)]... for a producer to communicate to his competitors the essential elements of his price policy such as price lists, the discounts and terms of trade he applies, the rates and date of any change to them and the special exceptions he grants to specific customers.[133]

Obviously there is little incentive to make a price cut to attract business from a competitor if that information must be disclosed to the competitor.

In *Polypropylene*[134] the Commission fined producers of polypropylene approximately €57 million for their participation in an agreement and/or concerted practice to implement price

---

[125] Case 8/72, *Cementhandelaren v. Commission* [1972] ECR 977, [1973] CMLR 7, para. 21.

[126] Case 311/85, *VZW Vereniging van Vlaamse Reisbureaus v. VZW Sociale Dienst van de Plaatselijke en Grewestelijke Overheidsdiensten* [1987] ECR 3801, [1988] 4 CMLR 755. See also *Dutch Beer*, IP/07/309.

[127] e.g., *IFTRA Rules on Glass Containers* [1974] OJ L160/1, [1974] 2 CMLR D50.

[128] Re *Cast Iron Steel Rolls* [1983] OJ L 317/1.

[129] See *infra* 901–2.

[130] See *Plasterboard* [2005] OJ L166/8, see Case T-50/03, *Gyproc Benelux v Commission* (appeal pending).

[131] *British Sugar plc, Tate & Lyle plc, Napier Brown & Company Ltd, James Budgett Sugars Ltd* (*British Sugar*) [1999] OJ L76/1, [1999] 4 CMLR 1316, substantially upheld by the CFI, Case T-208/98, *Tate & Lyle v. Commission* [2001] ECR II-2035, [2001] 5 CMLR 859, on appeal Case C-359/01 [2004] ECR I-4933, [2004] 5 CMLR 329. In this case the Commission did not find that the parties had specifically fixed prices but that they had engaged in a collaborative and coordinative strategy of higher pricing.

[132] Cases T-25, 26, 30–2, 34–9, 42–6, 48, 50–71, 87, 88, 103, and 104/95, *Cimenteries CBR SA v. Commission* [2000] ECR II-491, [2000] 5 CMLR 204, para. 1531 (at least where it underpins another anti-competitive agreement), broadly *aff'd* Cases C-204, 205, 211, 213, 217, and 219/00 P, *Aalborg Portland A/S v. Commission* [2004] ECR I-123;, [2005] 4 CMLR 251. See also *IFTRA Rules on Glass Containers* [1974] OJ L160/1, [1974] 2 CMLR D50.

[133] *IFTRA Rules on Glass Containers* [1974] OJ L160/1, [1974] 2 CMLR D50.

[134] *Polypropylene* [1986] OJ l230/1, [1988] 4 CMLR 347, appeals substantially dismissed both by the CFI and the ECJ see, e.g., Case C-51/92 P, *SA Hercules NV v. Commission* [1999] ECR I-4235, [1999] 5 CMLR 976 and Case C-199/92 P, *Hüls AG v. Commission (Polypropylene)* [1999] ECR I-4287, [1999] 5 CMLR 1016.

initiatives, to set target prices, and to operate production and sales quotas.[135] In a series of cases both the CFI and the ECJ, broadly, dismissed the appeals.[136] However, in a few cases, where the Court found that the Commission had not sufficiently proved the period of time during which an undertaking had participated in the collusion, the amount of the fine was reduced.[137]

In *FENEX*,[138] the Commission held that tariffs recommended by a Dutch association to its members constituted a decision by an association of undertakings.

Buying Prices

Price fixing amongst buyers can have quite different effects to price fixing by sellers. Whilst the latter is clearly likely to be designed to maximize sellers' profits and to extract higher prices from purchasers, the former may be designed to achieve lower prices for members which may then be passed on to their customers.[139] Nonetheless, horizontal agreements restricting the parties' freedom to negotiate buying prices might be prohibited by Article 81. For example, agreement by cartel members on the purchase price of a key raw material may facilitate the operation of the cartel at the downstream level.[140] In both the Spanish and Italian raw tobacco cases,[141] the Commission imposed fines on companies active in raw tobacco processing for colluding on the prices paid to (as well as the quantities bought from) tobacco growers.

Joint Selling

Joint selling is likely to be condemned under Article 81(1) although in certain circumstances the Commission has been prepared to accept that joint selling may meet the criteria of Article 81(3).[142]

Agreements between Distributors and Resale Price Maintenance

It is, of course, also an infringement of Article 81(1) for distributors of a product to agree to fix prices. Collusion between distributors as to selling prices achieved indirectly, through the intermediary of a supplier is also prohibited.[143] The Commission has also condemned horizontal agreements by suppliers to impose resale prices in so far as they have an impact on inter-State trade. In particular, it has been unsympathetic to the arguments in favour of collective resale

---

[135] *Polypropylene* [1986] OJ L230/1, [1988] 4 CMLR 347, appeals substantially dismissed both by the CFI and the ECJ: see Case T-7/89 etc., *SA Hercules NV v. Commission* [1991] ECR II-1711, [1992] 4 CMLR 84 and Case C-51/92 P, etc., *SA Hercules/ Hüls/ICI/Shell v. Commission* [1999] ECR I-4235, [1999] 5 CMLR 976, 1016, 1110, 1142.

[136] See, e.g., Case T-7/89, *SA Hercules NV v. Commission* [1991] ECR II-1711, [1992] 4 CMLR 84, Case T-11/89, *Shell International Chemical Co Ltd v. Commission* [1992] ECR II-757; Case T-13/89, *Imperial Chemical Industries plc v. Commission* [1992] ECR II-757; Case C-51/92 P, *SA Hercules NV v. Commission* [1999] ECR I-4235, [1999] 5 CMLR 976; Case C-199/92P, *Hüls AG v. Commission* [1999] ECR I-4287, [1999] 5 CMLR 1016; Case C-200/92 P, *Imperial Chemical Industries plc v. Commission* [1999] 5 CMLR 1110; Case C-234/92 P, *Shell International Chemical Co Ltd v. Commission* [1999] ECR I-4501, [1999] 5 CMLR 1142.

[137] e.g., Case T-2/89, *Petrofina v. Commission* [1991] ECR II-1087 and Case T-11/89, *Shell v. Commission* [1991] ECR II-757.

[138] [1996] OJ L181/28, [1996] 5 CMLR 332.

[139] See Research Paper prepared by RBB for the OFT on cooperation by purchasers; 'The Competitive Effects of Buyer Groups', Jan 2007.

[140] See, e.g., *Zinc Producer Group* [1984] OJ L220/7, [1985] 2 CMLR 108.

[141] IP/04/1256 *Spanish Raw Tobacco*, Cases T-37/05 etc *World Wide Tobacco España v Commission* (judgment pending). IP/05/1315 *Italian Raw Tobacco*, Cases T-11–12/06 *Romana Tabacchi v. Commission* (judgment pending).

[142] See, e.g., the Commission's Guidelines on the application of Article 81 to horizontal cooperation agreements [2001] OJ C3/2, [2001] 4 CMLR 819 and *infra* 895 ff.

[143] See e.g. discussion of Case 1022/1/1/03, *JJB Sports Plc v. Office of Fair Trading* [2004] CAT 17, *aff'd* [2006] EWCA Civ 1318 *supra* Chap. 3.

price maintenance in the book industry.[144] Both the Commission and the Court have also found that agreements directly or indirectly imposing individual resale price maintenance infringe Article 81(1). Individual resale price maintenance is discussed in Chapter 9, which deals generally with vertical restraints.

Supplementary Provisions

Other devices, such as information exchanges,[145] or meeting competition clauses[146] aimed at strengthening the operation of the cartel frequently supplement price-fixing agreements.

Some Examples of Price-fixing Agreements

It has already been explained that in more recent years the Commission has adopted numerous cartel decisions, adopting between 5–10 decisions per year since 2001. Most of these have involved some element of price fixing, either alone or together with other anti-competitive practices. In *Cartonboard*[147] the Commission fined nineteen producers of cartonboard (used primarily for the manufacture of folding cartons for packaging food and non-food consumer goods) for their participation in a price-fixing cartel. The producers had met secretly but regularly in order to plan and implement uniform and regular price increases within the Community, to plan and coordinate price initiatives in advance, to freeze market shares, to control output, and to organize the exchange of confidential information.[148]

The Commission found incriminating documentation that disclosed evidence of collusion at the premises of a number of the participants. The collusion was complex and long, having lasted at least since mid-1986 (although one of the undertakings, Stora, had informed the Commission that the parties had been cooperating since 1975, the Commission had no documentary evidence to corroborate these statements). The documents established that implementation of uniform price increases for each grade of cartonboard was closely monitored. Failure to cooperate would be the subject of discussion and laggards would be strongly urged to support the increases. Although not entirely watertight, the agreement caused considerable harm to competition.

Further, the Commission has found price-fixing, for example, by French federations in the beef sector[149] and by undertakings selling: stainless steel,[150] synthetic rubber,[151] bleaching

---

[144] *VBVB/VBBB* [1982] OJ L54/36, [1982] 2 CMLR 344. Its view was upheld by the ECJ in Cases 43 and 63/82, *VBVB and VBBB v. Commission* [1984] ECR 19, [1985] 1 CMLR 27. See *Publishers' Association—Net Book Agreement* [1989] OJ L22/12, [1989] 4 CMLR 825 (Commission); Case T-66/89, *Publishers' Association v. Commission* [1992] ECR II-1995, [1992] 5 CMLR 120 (CFI), and Case C-360/92 P, *Publishers' Association v. Commission* [1995] ECR I-23, [1995] 5 CMLR 33 (ECJ).

[145] See *infra* 902–10.

[146] See *supra* n. 15.

[147] [1994] OJ L243/1, [1995] 5 CMLR 547. The decision was broadly upheld by the CFI. On appeal the ECJ reduced three fines, referred two cases back to the CFI for reassessment, and dismissed the remainder of the appeals: see, e.g., Case C-286/98 P, *Stora Kopparbergs Bergslags AB v. Commission* [2000] ECR I-9641.

[148] In a series of cases, see in particular Case T-334/94, *Sarrio SA v. Commission* [1998] ECR II-1439, [1998] 5 CMLR 195, the CFI broadly upheld the fines imposed (one firm, Enzo, had its fine annulled but most of the fines on the ringleaders remained unchanged).

[149] *French Beef* [2003] OJ L209/12, [2005] 5 CMLR 891, *aff'd* (but fines reduced) in Cases T-217 and 245/03, *FNCBV v. Commission* [2004] ECR II-239, [2005] 5 CMLR 12, Cases C-101 and 110/07, *Coop de France Bétail and Viande v. Commission, FNSEA v. Commission* (judgment pending).

[150] IP/06/1851.

[151] IP/06/1851, Cases T-44 and 45/07 *Kaucuk v. Commission* (judgment pending).

chemicals,[152] acrylic glass,[153] road bitumen,[154] copper fittings,[155] methylglucamine;[156] Dutch industrial gases;[157] zinc phosphates;[158] carbonless paper;[159] vitamin products;[160] graphite electrodes;[161] lysine[162] and plasterboard.[163] In many of the cases, the price fixing was supplemented by other restrictive operations such as measures designed: to limit imports;[164] to allocate sales quotas;[165] to share markets;[166] to share customers;[167] to fix other trading conditions (such as transport costs);[168] and to share customers.[169] Some of these cartels have been global ones where European proceedings followed high profile criminal proceedings and private litigation in the US. For example, Hoffman-la Roche and BASF were fined £500 million and $225 million in the US in 1999 for their participation in the Vitamins cartel.[170] Subsequently, in *Vitamins*[171] the Commission imposed fines on the companies involved, totalling €855.2 million. The parties agreed target and minimum prices, agreed quotas (agreeing to maintain the status quo in respect of market shares) and provided for compensation payments to be paid in case quotas

[152] IP/06/560, Cases T-192, etc/06, *Cafarro v. Commission* (judgment pending).

[153] IP/06/698, Case T-190/06, *Total and Elf Aquitaine v. Commission* (judgment pending).

[154] IP/06/1179, Cases T-370 etc/06, *Kuwait Petroleum Corp v. Commission* (judgment pending).

[155] IP/06/1222, Case T-378/06, *IMI v. Commission* (judgment pending).

[156] [2004] OJ L38/18.

[157] *Dutch Industrial Gases* [2003] OJ L84/1, *aff'd* on appeal Cases T-303 and 304/02, *Hoek Loos NV v. Commission* [2006] ECR II-1887, [2006] 5 CMLR 8.

[158] [2003] OJ L 153/1, *aff'd* Case T-33/02, *Britannia Alloys v. Commission* [2005] ECR II-4973.

[159] [2004] OJ L15/1, Cases T-109/02, etc. *Bolloré v. Commission*, 27 April 2007, Cases C-322 and 327/07 (judgment pending).

[160] [2003] OJ L6/1, [2003] 4 CMLR 1030, see Case T-15 and 26/02, *BASF v. Commission* [2006] ECR II-497, [2006] 5 CMLR 2 (reducing some of the fines).

[161] *Graphite Electrodes* [2002] OJ L100/1, [2002] 5 CMLR 829, on appeal Cases T-236/01, *Tokai Carbon v. Commission* [2004] ECR II-1181, [2004] 5 CMLR 28 (some of the fines reduced on appeal), Cases C-301/04 and 308/04, *SGL v. Commission* [2006] ECR I-5915, [2006] 5 CMLR 15 (fine increased on SGL).

[162] [2001] OJ L152/24, [2001] 5 CMLR 322, see, e.g., Case T-220/00, *Cheil Jedang Corp v. Commission*, 9 July 2003 (fine reduced on appeal).

[163] In *Plasterboard* [2005] OJ L166/8, see Case T-50/03, *Gyproc Benelux v Commission* (appeal pending), the Commission imposed fines totalling €478 million on four companies for a long-run cartel designed to prevent damaging "price wars" breaking out on the plasterboard market. Top representatives of the companies met to ensure that price rises were applied and co-ordinated.

[164] *French Beef* [2003] OJ L209/12, [2005] 5 CMLR 891, *aff'd* (but fines reduced) in Cases T-217 and 245/03, *FNCBV v Commission* [2004] ECR II-239, [2005] 5 CMLR 12, Cases C-101 and 110/07 *Coop de France Bétail and Viande v. Commission*, *FNSEA v. Commission* (judgment pending). See also, e.g. *Gas Insulated Switchgear* IP/07/80.

[165] *Zinc Phosphate* [2003] OJ L153/1.

[166] See, e.g., *Methylglucamine* [2004] OJ L38/18, *Carbonless Paper* [2004] OJ L115/1, *Vitamins* [2003] OJ L6/1, [2003] 4 CMLR 1030, *Graphite Electrodes* [2002] OJ L100/1, [2002] 5 CMLR 829, on appeal Cases T-236/01, *Tokai Carbon v. Commission* [2004] ECR II-1181, [2004] 5 CMLR 28 (some of the fines reduced on appeal), Cases C-301/04 and 308/04, *SGL v. Commission* [2006] ECR I-5915, [2006] 5 CMLR 15 (fine increased on SGL).

[167] *Synthetic Rubber* IP/06/1851, Cases T-44 and 45/07 *Kaucuk v. Commission* (judgment pending).

[168] *Dutch Industrial Gases* [2003] OJ L84/1, *aff'd* on appeal Cases T-303 and 304/02 *Hoek Loos NV v. Commission* [2006] ECR II-1887, [2006] 5 CMLR 8.

[169] *Ibid.*

[170] The defendants also agreed to pay US customers more than $1billion in damages, see 'Status Report: An Overview of Recent Developments in the Antitrust Division's Criminal Enforcement Program' Department of Justice Antitrust Division, 25 Feb. 2004. High fines were also imposed on companies such as SGL Carbon and Archer Daniels Midland for their participation in the graphite electrode and lysine cartels respectively.

[171] [2003] OJ L6/1, [2003] 4 CMLR 1030, see Case T-15 and 26/02, [2006] ECR II-497, [2006] 5 CMLR 2 (reducing some of the fines).

were exceeded. Elaborate provisions for monitoring and enforcing the agreements were also established and a formal structure and management were involved in the operation of the agreements, including most senior levels of management. In the case of Hoffmann-La Roche the Commission considered that the arrangements were part of a strategic plan to control the world market in vitamins by illegal means.

Price Fixing in the Services Sector

Article 81(1) also applies, of course, to agreements operated in the services sector. Although occasionally the Commission has tempered the rigorous application of the rules in certain service sectors, for example banking and insurance,[172] in *Eurocheque: Helsinki Agreement*[173] the Commission imposed heavy fines on French banks and Eurocheque for operating a scheme under which the same commission was charged for both Eurocheque transactions and for the use of Carte Bleu. The Commission considered that the scheme eliminated the positive features of the Eurocheque system (that it was free to the payee). Further, it eliminated competition between Eurocheques and Carte Bleu. Fines have also been imposed on banks in *German Banks*[174] and *Austrian Banks ('Lombard Club')*.[175] In the latter case, the Commission found that the Austrian banks had concluded agreements about interest rates and charges/fees and by meeting regularly had 'coordinated their conduct with respect to every essential factor of competition.'[176]

In *Fine Art Auction Houses*[177] the Commission found that Christie's and Sotheby's had fixed commission fees and other trading conditions between 1993 and 2000. A significant fine was imposed on Sotheby's, although Christie's escaped a fine in consequence of its cooperation with the Commission.

Price Fixing and Liberal Professions

The Commission is concerned that high levels of regulation (including state or self-regulation) within the sphere of professional services in Europe serve to restrict competition. Although the Commission accepts that some carefully targeted regulation may be necessary to deal with specific issues arising in this sphere, such as asymmetry of information between customers and service providers, externalities, and to ensure adequate and sufficient supply of these services, it has paid close attention to the professions and has adopted two reports on the subject, a 'Report on Competition in Professional Services'[178] and 'Professional Services—Scope for more reform'.[179] These reports focus on the question of whether the regulatory regimes existing for lawyers, notaries, accountants, architects, engineers and pharmacies can be adapted or

---

[172] See *infra* 895 ff.

[173] [1992] OJ L95/50, [1993] 5 CMLR 323, partially annulled and fines reduced on appeal, see Case T-39/92, *Groupement des Cartes Bancaires v. Commission* [1994] ECR II-49, [1995] 5 CMLR 410. But see *Uniform Eurocheques* [1985] OJ L35/43, [1985] 3 CMLR 434; *infra*, n. 896.

[174] [2003] OJ L15/1, [2003] 4 CMLR 842, annulled on appeal Case T-44/02, *Dresdner Bank v. Commission* [2004] OJ C314/13.

[175] [2004] OJ L56/1, *aff'd* on appeal (but fine reduced on Osterrechische Postssparkasse AG) see Cases T-259–264 and 271/02, *Raiffeisen Zentralbank Osterreich v. Commission*, 14 Dec. 2006, Case C-125/07 (judgment pending).

[176] *Ibid.*, para. 1.

[177] IP/02/1585.

[178] Communication from the Commission 'Report on Competition in Professional Services' COM(2004) 83 final (Brussels, 9 Feb. 2004), available on DG Comp's web site. Table 1 indicates that professions with fixed, minimum of maximum prices exist in Austria, Belgium, France, Germany, Greece, Italy, Luxembourg, Netherlands, and Spain.

[179] Professional Services—Scope for more reform. Follow-up on Competition in Professional services SEC(2005) 1064.

modernised to spur economic growth and value to consumers. The Commission is particularly concerned about regulation, involving the fixing of prices or recommended prices,[180] and believes that such practices, which may infringe Article 81, are widespread in the liberal professions.[181] In the first report the Commission states that 'within an otherwise competitive market, price regulation is unlikely to ensure prices that are lower than competitive levels'.[182] Further, that price recommendations 'like fixed prices, may have a significant negative effect on competition. First, recommended prices may facilitate the coordination of prices between service providers. Secondly, they can mislead consumers about reasonable price levels'.[183] It believes that competition in this sphere is often additionally, or alternatively, restricted by advertising restrictions, entry restrictions and reserved tasks and business structure regulation (for example, the scope for collaboration with other professions).[184] Recognizing the complex issues involved in this area, however, the Commission called, at first instance, for these restrictions to be reviewed and, where not objectively justified, removed or replaced by less restrictive rules.[185] Further, it considers that, since in most cases the professional rules have their origin and effect in a single Member State, they should be dealt with at the national level, with progress being monitored and coordinated through the European Competition Network.[186] The 2005 report comments on the progress that has been made at the national level.

The Commission will itself also consider infringement procedures. In particular, it takes the view that rules relating to price are likely to constitute automatic violations of Article 81(1), even though in practice an increase in price may be very difficult to sustain in this sphere.[187] In *Belgian Architects*,[188] the Commission sent out a clear message that restrictive practices operated by members of the liberal professions should be eliminated and reform promoted. The Commission fined the Belgian Architects' Association in respect of its operation of a recommended minimum fee scale. The fee scale recommended the laying down of fees as a percentage of the value of work realized. The Commission considered that this practice infringed Article 81 and had as its object to the restriction of competition since it sought to co-ordinate the pricing behaviour of architects which was unnecessary for the proper practice of the profession. Rather, the architects should have been free to charge a fee commensurate with their skills, efficiency, costs and reputation.

---

[180] Communication from the Commission 'Report on Competition in Professional Services' COM(2004) 83 final (Brussels, 9 Feb. 2004), available on DG Comp's web site, table 2. The table indicates that professions with recommended prices exist in Austria, Belgium, Denmark, Greece, Ireland, Luxembourg, Portugal, and Spain.

[181] Occupations requiring special training in the liberal arts or sciences, for examples lawyers notaries, accountants, architects, engineers, and pharmacists, *ibid.*, para. 1. The OECD is also carrying out ongoing work on competition in professional services, including some professions not dealt with by the Commission in its report.

[182] *Ibid.*, para. 32.

[183] *Ibid.*, para. 37.

[184] *Ibid.*, paras. 42–64. See *infra* 890–1.

[185] *Ibid.*, para. 90.

[186] *Ibid.*, paras. 93–102.

[187] It has been noted that there is not perfect harmony with the treatment of price fixing cartels as virtually illegal per se and economic insights as a full-scale economic analysis could show that prices are not above competitive levels where a price fixing cartel exists (i.e. that the cartel is ineffective). 'Another example is recommended fees in the sector of the liberal professions. Since the number of practitioners in these markets is high, cartel discipline is difficult to maintain and cheating very attractive. The non-sustainability of price cartels under such circumstances is also confirmed by empirical evidence... Current European competition law, however allows the relevant economic evidence to be pushed aside if the objective to fix prices or control output can be proven, and the (lack of) economic impact on the market will only be taken into account when determining the ultimate fine.' R. Van den Bergh and P. Camesasca, *European Competition Law and Economics: A Comparative Perspective* (2nd edn., Sweet & Maxwell, 2006), 5.3.1.1.

[188] [2005] OJ L004/10.

Some commentators are critical of the Commission's approach, believing that specific problems will result from trying to introduce competition in markets for professional services in the ordinary way.

R. Van den Bergh and P. Camesasca, *European Competition Law and Economics: A Comparative Perspective* (2nd edn, Sweet & Maxwell, 2006)

Box 5.3 Application of the European competition rules to the liberal professions

The sector of the liberal professions (such as lawyers, notaries, architects, accounts and engineers) is characterised by high levels of regulation, which are often a mix of state regulation and self-regulation. The regulatory framework includes exclusive rights to perform certain professional services, regulation of fees, restrictions on advertising and regulation governing business structure and multidisciplinary practices. The European Commission is of the opinion that many of these rules unnecessarily restrict competition. It has invited regulatory authorities in the Member States and professional bodies to review existing rules, taking into consideration whether those rules are beneficial for society in general and proportionate to the public interest goal to be achieved. The European Commission accepts that some carefully targeted regulation of professional services can be necessary. However, restrictions on prices and advertising restrictions should be removed quickly. The analysis here will show that this is too rapid a conclusion. The specific characteristics of the markets for professional services make the design of the "optimal" regulation, which not unnecessarily restricts competition, very difficult. Consequently, all limitations of competition, including fee and advertising restrictions, must be more carefully assessed.

A vast economic literature has shown that free markets for professional services will not produce efficient outcomes. There are three market failures that may impede a full satisfaction of consumers' wishes. A first major problem is asymmetric information. Professional services require a high level of technical knowledge that many consumers do not have. Free markets will only achieve efficient outcomes if a significant number of consumers is able to make purchase decisions on the basis of complete and undistorted price-quality judgments. Many consumers cannot judge the quality of the services offered by the professions before purchase (no search qualities). At most, some quality assessment may be possible after the services have been bought (experience qualities), but in many cases the buyers will never be able to perform a reliable quality judgment (credence qualities). As a consequence, free markets for professional services will fail due to adverse selection (overall deterioration of quality) and moral hazard (supplier induced demand). Regulation of quality is a response to this problem. A second problem is that bad performance of contracts between sellers and buyers of professional services will cause negative externalities to third parties and society at large. For example, an inaccurately drafted will will harm the heirs of the testator and a poorly constructed bridge will jeopardise traffic safety. In a free market, these negative externalities are not internalised in the decision-making process of the suppliers. The third market failure is known as the "pubic good" problem. Professional services generate important positive externalities that are of great value for society in general. Examples include a proper administration of justice (lawyers) and increased legal certainty (notaries), as well as a high quality urban environment (architects). In a free market, suppliers of services who do not get any reward from persons (other than the contract parties) profiting from these benefits may not supply or inadequately supply public goods.

From these arguments, it become clear that introducing competition in the sector of the liberal professions will not necessarily be welfare increasing. If there are no limitations on price fixing and advertising, the risk exists that competition will be mainly on price and quality dimensions that buyers of services can easily access, such as the location of the offices and the friendliness of the professionals. By contrast, in markets plagued by severe information asymmetries, professionals will not be able to credibly signal the intrinsic high quality of the services provided. The consequence of price advertising may thus be a process of adverse selection leading to an overall deterioration of quality. Introducing price competition maybe counterproductive if it is not accompanied by adequate measures to improve the quality assessment in markets for professional services. Also, the provisions of public goods may be jeopardised by increasing competitive pressures. In a regulated market, less profitable services may be cross-subsidised by gains on more lucrative market segments. Deregulation will cause prices to sink in the profitable market segments ("cream skimming") but lead to price increases for the previously cross-subsidised services. The deregulation of the market for notaries in the Netherlands confirms this outcome: whereas prices decreased for authenticating transfer of property, prices in the family practice (wills, matrimonial contracts) increased. As a consequence, fewer people will ask the notary's assistance, which in turn will decrease legal certainty and harm society at large. In sum, competition between professional may be counterproductive if no accompanying measures to improve quality assessment and guarantee provision of public goods are taken.

Guaranteeing quality may be a difficult task for government agencies lacking specific knowledge of the professions. An important benefit of self-regulation is the possibility of using the information advantage of professions. Other benefits include greater flexibility, allowing easy adaptation to changed consumer preferences, and internalisation of regulatory costs within the profession. Disadvantages of self-regulation are its lack of democratic legitimacy and the risk that professions may abuse their self-regulatory powers to restrict competition. Self-regulatory bodies are not accountable through normal democratic channels and third parties do not usually participate in establishing the self-regulatory regime. On top of these problems, self regulatory rules may create entry barriers and enable the professions to achieve super-competitive profits. The problem of disproportionate regulation, which is stressed by the European Commission, can be seen as an example of an anti-competitive entry barrier. It thus seems to be the case that curing one market imperfection (information asymmetry) creates another market imperfection (super-competitive prices). A possible way out of this conundrum may be to create scope for competition between self-regulatory bodies (competitive self-regulation). In this way, the information advantage of the professions is kept intact and competition between the professional bodies impedes excessive profits. Under a system of competitive self-regulation, there remains a role for the state as a referee. Professional bodies may be required to get approval of their rules (accreditation) before they are allowed to enter the market; in this way the risk of a "race to the bottom" is contained. Aside from a few exceptions (for example, competition between English barristers and solicitors to plead cases in the higher courts), the regulatory framework of the EC Member States provides no scope for competitive self-regulation. Also, the European Commission seems to have set the wrong priorities. Abolishing restrictions on fees and advertising may be counterproductive in markets characterised by serious information asymmetries. By contrast, abolishing reserved rights and creating scope for competition between accredited professional groups may be the best available method to guarantee quality at competitive prices.

b. Output Restrictions and Restrictions Limiting or Controlling Production

Beneficial collaboration between competitors or potential competitors may involve restrictions on production.[189] Where, however, restrictions on output are 'naked', competition law is likely to be hostile. A restriction in output automatically creates an imbalance between supply and demand and causes an increase in market prices. Indeed, volume control is an indispensable condition and inevitable consequence of any price initiative adopted. Article 81(1)(b) specifically provides that agreements which 'limit or control production ... or investment' may restrict competition within the meaning of that provision.

A number of the cases discussed in the section dealing with price fixing above involved collusion to fix both prices and sales quotas. In many cases the implementation of quotas is easier

---

[189] See *infra* Chap. 13.

to operate than adherence to a pricing policy: no undertaking can benefit from price-cutting if it is obliged to adhere to sales restrictions, and the adherence to quotas may be easier to monitor. Further, a decision to adhere to quotas may facilitate collusion where participants with different cost structures cannot agree on the prices to be charged for their products. The Organization of Petroleum Exporting Countries (OPEC) cartel, for example, operated simply by the members voluntarily restricting their outputs following the negotiation of quotas in 1973. As a result of the output restrictions, the world price of oil nearly quadrupled within a year. The increase in wealth to the participants was so enormous that, initially at least, there was little temptation to cheat on the cartel.

The *Quinine Cartel* was the first case in which the Commission fined undertakings for the operation of a cartel which raised prices by means of the restriction of output.[190] In particular, certain French companies had agreed not to manufacture synthetic quinidine. The parties contended that, in any event, the companies did not have either the expertise or the resources to manufacture quinidine. The Court dismissed those arguments:

The fact relied upon that, when the gentlemen's agreement was concluded, the French undertakings were not in a position to manufacture synthetic quinidine does not render lawful such a restriction which entirely precluded them from taking up this activity.[191]

In *BELASCO*,[192] an accountant appointed by BELASCO monitored compliance with quotas at the end of each year. Undertakings which had exceeded these quotas were required to pay penalties.

The *Polypropylene*[193] cartel not only operated price initiatives and set target prices but operated production and sales quotas. The CFI in *Hercules v. Commission* had no hesitation in holding that the object of meetings to fix target prices and sale volume targets was anti-competitive.[194]

In *Zinc Producer Group*[195] the Commission held that an agreement to fix prices, to adhere to production quotas, and to refrain from the building of new production capacity without the consent of the Group infringed Article 81(1). The purpose of the agreement was to substitute its common zinc producer price for the London Metal Exchange (LME) price. Production controls precluded producers from supplying surplus zinc to the LME or zinc producers at lower prices. The fact that the practices had been tolerated/approved by Member States could not be used as a defence to the operation of the EC competition rules (the position might be different, however if the conduct is required of the undertakings by national law).[196]

---

[190] *Quinine Cartel* [1969] OJ L192/5, [1969] CMLR D41.

[191] Case 41/69, *ACF Chemiefarma NV v. Commission* [1970] ECR 661.

[192] [1986] OJ L232/15, [1991] 4 CMLR 130, on appeal, Case 246/86, *Re Roofing Felt Cartel: BELASCO v. Commission* [1989] ECR 2117, [1991] 4 CMLR 96.

[193] *Polypropylene* [1986] OJ 1230/1, [1988] 4 CMLR 347, appeals substantially dismissed both by the CFI and the ECJ: see, e.g., Case C-51/92 P, *SA Hercules NV v. Commission* [1999] ECR I-4235, [1999] 5 CMLR 976 and Case C-199/92 P, *Hüls AG v. Commission (Polypropylene)* [1999] ECR I-4287, [1999] 5 CMLR 1016. See also, e.g. *Cartonboard* [1994] OJ L243/1.

[194] *Ibid.*

[195] [1984] OJ L220/27, [1985] 2 CMLR 108. See also e.g. *Amino Acid* [2001] OJ L152/24, appeal dismissed in part Case T-224/00, *Archer Daniels Midlands Company and Archer Daniels Ingredients Ltd v. Commission* [2003] ECR II-2597, *aff'd* Case C-397/03 P, *Archer Daniels Midlands Company and Archer Daniels Ingredients Ltd v. Commission* [2006] ECR I-4429.

[196] *Ibid.*

Allocation of market share quotas was also the central plank of the *Zinc Phosphate* cartel.[197] The parties calculated initial market shares. Each cartel member then had to adhere to its allotted market share, and sales quotas were allocated at the European level. A monitoring system was set up to ensure that the parties adhered to the terms of the agreement. Pressure was brought to bear on members those that did not and customer allocation was used as a form of compensation for a company which had not achieved its quota. On an annual basis the market shares of the producers did in fact closely follow their specified shares.[198] The parties also agreed on 'bottom' prices, and on some occasions, the allocation of customers. The cartel in this case, in operation from 1994, appeared to have been concluded in response to a prior period of low prices, aggressive price-cutting and targeting of mutual customers.

A practice in the professions which can cause significant reductions in competition in the spectrum of services offered are business structure regulations. It will be remembered that in *Wouters v. Algemene Raad van de Nederlandse Order van Advocaten*[199] the ECJ had to deal with a professional rule that prevented lawyers from working in partnership with accountants. In Chapter 4 it was seen that the ECJ did not treat this agreement as one that had as its object the restriction of competition, Further, that the ECJ held that such a provision, despite constituting a restriction on production and technical development within the meaning of Article 81(1)(b) EC, did not have as its *effect* the restriction of competition. Rather, it held that restrictions required to ensure the proper practice of the profession as organized in a Member State, and which did not go beyond what was necessary to ensure the proper practice of the legal profession, did not infringe Article 81(1). In the section above it was seen that the Commission has issued a report on competition in professional services. The view set out in that report does not seem to support such a robust view as that set out by the ECJ in *Wouters*. Rather, the Commission clearly takes the view that such restrictions 'may have a negative economic impact',[200] particularly where collaboration is prevented between members of the same profession or between professions where there is no overriding need to protect independence or ethical standards.

Communication from the Commission 'Report on Competition in Professional Services' COM(2004) 83 final (Brussels, 9 Feb. 2004)

4.5 Business structure regulations

59. A number of professions are subject to sector-specific regulations on business structure. These regulations can restrict the ownership structure of professional services companies, the scope for collaboration with other professions and, in some cases, the opening of branches, franchises or chains.

60. Business structure regulations may have a negative economic impact if they inhibit providers from developing new services or cost-efficient business models. For example, these regulations might inhibit lawyers and accountants from providing integrated legal and accountancy advice for

---

197 [2003] OJ L153/1, para. 66.

198 [2003] OJ L153/1, paras. 65–72.

199 Case C-309/99, [2002] ECR I-1577, [2002] 4 CMLR 913.

200 Communication from the Commission 'Report on Competition in Professional Services' COM(2004) 83 final (Brussels, 9 Feb. 2004), para. 60.

tax issues or prevent the development of one-stop shops for professional services in rural areas. Certain ownership regulations such as prohibition of incorporation can also reduce access to capital in professional services markets, hindering new entry and expansion.

61. On the other hand, it is argued that business structure and ownership regulation may be necessary to ensure practitioner's personal responsibility and liability towards clients and avoid conflicts of interest. It has also been suggested that these regulations may be necessary to ensure practitioners' independence. If professional service companies were controlled or influenced by non-professionals, this might compromise practitioners' judgement or respect for professional value.

62. In the Commission's view business structure regulations appear to be least justifiable in cases where they restrict the scope for collaboration between members of the same profession. Collaboration between members of the same profession would appear less likely to reduce the profession's independence or ethical standards

63. Business structure regulations appear likewise to be less justifiable in professions where there is no overriding need to protect practitioners' independence. The architectural and engineering professions, for example, function effectively without these regulations in most Member States. It therefore appears unlikely that business structure regulations are essential to protect consumers of these services.

64. Business structure regulations appear to be more justifiable in markets where there is a strong need to protect practitioners' independence or personal liability. There might however be alternative mechanisms for protecting independence and ethical standards which are less restrictive of competition. In some markets, stringent ownership restrictions might therefore be replaced or partially replaced by less restrictive rules.

c. Market or Customer Sharing

Market-sharing agreements also have restrictive effects on competition and Article 81(1)(b) and (c) specifically prohibit collusive practices which 'limit or control … markets' or 'share markets and sources of supply'. Like sales quotas, market-sharing agreements may provide an extremely effective means of operating a cartel. Exclusivity in a particular geographical area, or over a particular customer group, obviously grants an undertaking a monopoly within that area or over that group which it is free to exploit. No price or non-price competition between the parties to the agreement thus operates at all. From the perspective of the Commission, geographical market-sharing agreements are viewed particularly seriously. In addition to restricting competition, such agreements thwart the objective of integrating the single market by dividing up the common market. The Commission is likely to punish such infringements particularly severely. The Commission has stated:

Market sharing agreements are particularly restrictive of competition and contrary to the achievement of a single market. Agreements or concerted practices for the purpose of market-sharing are generally based on the principle of mutual respect of the national markets of each Member State for the benefit of producers resident there. The direct object and result of their implementation is to eliminate the exchange of goods between the Member States concerned. The protection of their home market allows producers to pursue a commercial policy—particularly a pricing policy—in that market which is insulated from the competition of other parties to the agreement in other Member States, and which can sometimes only be maintained because they have no fear of competition from that direction.[201]

---

[201] Commission's *Ist Report on Competition Policy* (Commission, 1971), para. 2.

The Commission and Court have acted against all forms of geographical market sharing: whether through agreements to refrain from exporting from home markets; agreements to make sales only through the home manufacturer; agreements to limit sales to home markets; or agreements between EC and non-EC undertakings to protect the EC market from low-priced imports.[202]

In *Cement*[203] the Commission found that Community cement producers had operated a systematic and well-policed policy of, amongst other things, dividing markets on the basis of the 'home market principle' (refraining from exporting to other Member States). The agreements showed that the parties made concerted efforts to stem cross-frontier flows and to reduce trade between Member States. A number of bilateral and multilateral agreements were concluded in order to back up the main agreement, for example, to exchange sensitive price information. The agreement which aimed to ensure the non-trans shipment of products to home markets of Member States and the regulation of sales to other Member States' markets was clearly prohibited by Article 81(1), market sharing being expressly referred to in Article 81(1).[204]

In *Peroxygen Products*[205] the Commission fined producers of hydrogen peroxide a total of €9 million for operating agreements which included a 'home market' rule. The agreement provided that undertakings would confine their activities to their traditional home markets. It had eliminated all competition between the competitors and excluded virtually all trade between Member States (prices varied enormously between States).

In *Soda Ash*[206] the Commission imposed large fines (of approximately € 7 million) on ICI and Solvay, the two largest producers of synthetic soda ash in the Community, for the operation of an agreement under which ICI was exclusively to supply the UK and Ireland and Solvay was exclusively to supply continental Europe. Although the formal written agreement had been abandoned in 1972 (on the UK's accession to the Community) the Commission found that the agreement/concerted practice in fact continued unaltered. This decision was annulled on procedural grounds[207] but the Commission subsequently readopted it.[208]

In *SAS/Maersk*[209] the Commission imposed fines of €52.5 million for market sharing in the air transport sector. In this case, the parties had notified a co-operation agreement to the Commission. The Commission became suspicious that the agreements were more far-reaching

---

[202] See, e.g. *Seamless Steel Tubes* [2003] OJ L140/1, on appeal Case T-44/00, *Mannesmannröhren-Werke AG v. Commission* [2004] ECR II-2223 (fine reduced), Cases C-403 etc/04, *Sumitomo Metal Industries Ltd v. Commission*, 25 Jan 2007.

[203] [1994] OJ L343/1, [1995] 4 CMLR 327, *aff'd* Case T-25/95, etc., *Cimenteries CBR SA v. Commission*, [2000] ECR II-491, [2000] 5 CMLR 204, broadly *aff'd* Cases C-204, etc/00, *Aalborg Portland v. Commission* [2004] ECR I-123, [2005] 4 CMLR 251.

[204] The Commission imposed fines totalling approximately €248,000,000 on the cement producers. On appeal the CFI found that there *was* a single agreement between all the applicants that was designed to ensure no transhipment to the companies' home markets. However, the Court found that the Commission had not adequately proved the participation of all of the undertakings in the agreement, and in the case of others the duration of the participation was not as long as the Commission had found. The total fines were reduced to around €110 million, Case T-25/95 etc., *Cimenteries CBR SA v. Commission*, [2000] ECR II-491, [2000] 5 CMLR 204, broadly *aff'd* Cases C-204 etc/00, *Aalborg Portland v. Commission* [2004] ECR I-123, [2005] 4 CMLR 251. Some of the fines were annulled for procedural flaws: see *infra* Chap. 14.

[205] [1985] OJ L35/1, [1985] 1 CMLR 481.

[206] [1991] OJ L152/1, [1994] 4 CMLR 454, annulled on procedural grounds Case T-30/91, *Solvay SA v. Commission* [1995] ECR II-1775, [1996] 5 CMLR 57 (*infra* Chap. 14) but readopted [2003] OJ L 10/1, see Case T-57/01, *Solvay v. Commission* (judgment pending).

[207] Case T-30/91, *Solvay SA v. Commission* [1995] ECR II-1775, [1996] 5 CMLR 57; see further *infra* Chap. 14.

[208] [2003] OJ L10/1, see Case T-57/01 *Solvay v. Commission* (judgment pending).

[209] [2001] OJ L265/15, [2001] 5 CMLR 1119, *aff'd* Case T-241/01, *Scandinavian Airlines System AB v. Commission* [2005] ECR II-2917, [2005] 5 CMLR 18.

than the notified agreements made out. Following investigations at the parties' premises, the Commission discovered that the parties had omitted to provide information relating to a broad market sharing agreement under which, essentially, the parties would withdraw from each other's routes and would share out domestic routes.

Market sharing, through customer allocation, is also prohibited. In *Methylglucamine*,[210] for example, the parties sought to maintain the status quo of 50 per cent market share for both companies operating on the market. In particular, they tried to prevent switching by their respective customers from one to the other supplier and agreed not to compete for each other's customers.

A more unusual case of market sharing was that condemned by the Commission in both *Luxembourg Brewers*[211] and *Belgian Brewers*.[212] It has been seen in Chapters 3, 4, and 9 that it is common in beer markets for brewers to require publicans or café proprietors to purchase beer exclusively from them (beer ties). In *Luxembourg Brewers*, four Luxembourg brewers had agreed in 1985 (in signed writing!)[213] not to supply beer, for an unlimited duration, to any customer tied to another by an exclusive purchasing commitment or beer tie. When taking on a new customer, each would consult one another to check that a beer tie did not bind the customer to another. Further, the parties had measures in place that impeded trade from other Member States, and which were designed to keep foreign brewers out of the market. The Commission held that this agreement had as its object the restriction of competition. In *Belgian Brewers* Interbrew and Danone also shared out their distribution channels and pursued a policy of non-aggression.

d. Collusive Tendering or Bid Rigging

Collusive tendering occurs where undertakings collaborate on responses to invitations to tender for the supply of goods and services. The practice limits price competition between the parties and amounts to an attempt by the tenderers to share markets between themselves. Instead of competing to submit the lowest possible tender at the tightest possible margin, the parties may agree on the lowest offer to be submitted or agree amongst themselves who should be the most successful bidder. The practice will automatically infringe Article 81(1).

In a system of tendering, competition is of the essence. If the tenders submitted by those taking part are not the result of individual economic calculation, but of knowledge of the tenders by other participants or of concertation with them competition is prevented, or at least distorted and restricted.[214]

[210] [2004] OJ L38/18. See also, e.g. *Synthetic Rubber* IP/06/1851, Cases T-44 and 45/07 *Kaucuk v. Commission* (judgment pending).

[211] [2002] OJ L253/21, [2002] 5 CMLR 1279, *aff'd* Case T-49/02, *Brasserie National SA v. Commission* [2005] ECR II-3033.

[212] [2003] OJ L 200/1, para. 247, *aff'd* Case T-38/02, *Groupe Danone v. Commission* [2005] ECR II-4407 (small reduction in fine) *aff'd* Case C-3/06 P, *Groupe Danone v. Commission* 8 Feb. 2007. 'After the Commission, on its own initiative, uncovered a cartel on the Belgian beer market, InBev provided information under the auspices of the Commission's leniency policy that it was also involved in cartels in other European countries. This led to surprise inspections on brewers in France, Luxembourg, Italy and the Netherlands. These investigations led to decisions condemning cartels in Belgium (see IP/01/1739 upheld by the CFI and ECJ, see CJE/07/13), France (see IP/04/1153, not appealed) and Luxembourg (see IP/01/1740, upheld by the CFI). The Italian investigation was closed without charges being brought' IP/07/309. The Netherlands cartel decision was adopted on 18 April 2007, IP/07/309.

[213] The agreement was subject to a 12-month notice period. No party had given notice when Interbrew disclosed details of the cartel to the Commission in 2000, following an investigation into its practices on the Belgian beer market, see *Belgian Brewers* [2003] OJ L 200/1, para. 247, *aff'd* Case T-38/02, *Groupe Danone v. Commission* [2005] ECR II-4407 (small reduction in fine) *aff'd* Case C-3/06 P, *Groupe Danone v. Commission* 8 Feb. 2007. In *Belgian Brewers* there was also an agreement to respect each other's beer ties.

[214] *Re The European Sugar Cartel* [1973] OJ L140/17, [1973] CMLR D65, para. 42.

Despite the relative paucity of EC bid rigging cases, evidence suggests that bid rigging, at least in some countries, may be rather widespread, in particular in government procurement cases.[215] Further, that they may lead to greater price increases than ordinary price fixing. The extract from an OFT discussion paper in the UK makes this point:

OFT 386 'The Development of Targets for Consumer Savings Arising from Competition Policy', Economic Discussion Paper 4, June 2002, chapter 5, paras. 5.3–5.8

Evidence from us bid rigging cases

5.3 Froeb, Koyak and Werden (1993) noted that in the five years to 1993, 70 per cent of the cartel cases investigated by the US Department of Justice (DoJ) involved bid rigging rather than price fixing, bid rigging in government procurement being typical. Perhaps for this reason, much of the empirical literature on the effect of cartels concentrates on bid rigging. While there are exceptions, in general, the evidence suggests that cartels lead to prices well in excess of 10 per cent, and sometimes in excess of 20 per cent, of competitive levels.

School milk markets

5.4 Some recent papers refer to bid rigging cartels in school milk markets. These markets lend themselves to collusion for several reasons set out in Porter and Zona (1999):

- Price competition is the only dimension of competition,

- Demand is inelastic and stable,

- Firms face similar costs of production:

- Building a new plant would be unattractive solely on the basis of higher margins made on school milk contracts, and this reduces the scope for new entry,

- Markets tend to be concentrated and localized (transport costs reduce the scope of supply side substitution) which facilitates market sharing,

- The 'game' is repeated year by year and multi-market contact is enhanced by disaggregated contracts staggered throughout the year,

- Although tendering is by sealed bid auctions, immediately after contracts are won, bids and bidders are made public so cheating can be observed,

- Competitors can obtain each other's list prices for sales of milk to retail customers which may facilitate signalling, and

- Parties often meet through trade associations or by being customers of each other.

...

Bid rigging cases in Europe

5.8 The European Commission imposed record fines for bid rigging in the Pre-Insulated Pipe cartel. The Commission does not provide a formal analysis of how much higher prices were during the periods when the conspiracy had effect. However, there is a suggestion that the cartel inflated prices in Denmark by 15–20 per cent or more, whilst information from one of the cartel meetings suggests that prices in most other markets were inflated by about the same amount. Given the US evidence of bid rigging against the public sector, price rises of 15–20 per cent would certainly seem plausible.

---

[215] In Germany, for example, bid rigging is a specific criminal offence, which can be punished by imprisonment for up to 5 years and/or by the imposition of a fine, see s. 298 of the Criminal Code.

In the *Pre-Insulated Pipe Cartel*[216] the Commission imposed fines in excess of €92 million on ten undertakings it had found to be engaged in market-sharing, price-fixing, and bid rigging in the market for pipes used for district heating systems (contracts for the supply of pipes were almost all awarded on the basis of competitive tendering procedures). The parties had also tried to squeeze out of the market the only competitor that had refused to participate in the cartel and had deliberately flouted the EU Public Procurement Rules. The large fines imposed reflected the deliberate nature, the gravity, and duration of the infringement (in particular, the fact that the parties had continued to operate the cartel after the Commission investigation had commenced). Further, in *Lifts and Escalators*[217] the Commission imposed record fines on €992 million on four firms for operating a number of bid rigging cartels for the installation and maintenance of lifts and escalators in Belgium, Germany, Luxembourg and the Netherlands. The Commission was particularly outraged by this cartel since it affected a vast market for the sale, installation, maintenance and modernization of lifts and escalators, the cartel would have long-term effects because of the maintenance contracts which lasted decades and because the cartel had affected the installation of lifts and escalators in the buildings of the Commission itself and the courts in Luxembourg!

e. Bolstering Provisions

Provisions designed to reinforce or bolster the operation of a hard-core cartel, such as: measures designed to block imports;[218] refusals to supply or boycott customers who purchase from sellers outside of the cartel; boycotts of competitors refusing to participate in the cartel arrangements,[219] collective exclusive dealing;[220] or information sharing arrangements, especially agreements to exchange price information,[221] are likely to infringe Article 81(1).

(iii) Article 81(3)

a. The Possibility of Meeting the Article 81(3) Criteria

All agreements may, in theory, meet the criteria of Article 81(3).[222] In practice, however, naked agreements to fix prices, share markets, restrict output or rig bids are the sorts of agreement which are totally prohibited under Article 81 and are extremely unlikely to do so.

---

[216] *Pre-Insulated Pipe* [1999] OJ L24/1, [1998] 4 CMLR 402; decision substantially upheld on appeal (although some fines reduced) Case T-9/99 etc., *HFB Holdings v. Commission* [2002] ECR II-1487, [2001] 4 CMLR 1066 *aff'd* Cases C-189/02 P *Dansk Røindustri A/S* [2005] ECR I-5425. See also *Building and Construction Industry in the Netherlands* [1992] OJ L92/1, [1993] 5 CMLR 135, *aff'd* Case T-29/92, *SPO v. Commission* [1995] ECR II-289.

[217] IP/07/209. See also Gas Insulated Switchgear IP/07/80.

[218] See, e.g. *Meldoc* [1986] OJ L348/50, *Luxembourg Brewers* [2002] OJ L253/21, [2002] 5 CMLR 1279, *aff'd* Case T-49/02, *Brasserie National SA v. Commission* [2005] ECR II-3033.

[219] *Pre-Insulated Pipe* [1999] OJ L24/1, [1998] 4 CMLR 402; decision substantially upheld on appeal (although some fines reduced) Case T-9/99, etc., *HFB Holdings v. Commission* [2002] ECR II-1487, [2001] 4 CMLR 1066 *aff'd* Case C-189/02 P, *Dansk Røindustri A/S* [2005] ECR I-5425. See also *Building and Construction Industry in the Netherlands* [1992] OJ L92/1, [1993] 5 CMLR 135, *aff'd* Case T-29/92, *SPO v. Commission* [1995] ECR II-289.

[220] See, e.g. *Nederlandse Federative Vereniging voor de Grootlandel op Elektrotechnisch Gebied and Tecnhische Unie (FEG and TU)* [2000] OJ L39/1, [2000] 4 CMLR 1208.

[221] Cases T-25, 26, 30–2, 34–9, 42–6, 48, 50–71, 87, 88, 103, and 104/95, *Cimenteries CBR SA v. Commission* [2000] ECR II-491, [2000] 5 CMLR 204, para. 1531, broadly *aff'd* Cases C-204, 205, 211, 213, 217, and 219/00 P, *Aalborg Portland A/S v. Commission* [2004] ECR I-123, [2005] 4 CMLR 251, *IFTRA Rules on Glass Containers* [1974] OJ L160/1, [1974] 2 CMLR D50.

[222] Case T-17/93, *Matra Hachette v. Commission* [1994] ECR II-595, *supra* Chap. 4.

b. Price-fixing Agreements

Price-fixing agreements generally fall into 'the category of manifest infringements under Article [81(1)] which it is always impossible to exempt under Article [81(3)] because of the total lack of benefit to the consumer'.[223] Even in cases concerning 'crisis cartels'[224] the Commission would not extend its benevolent approach to terms fixing prices.

Some restrictions on pricing have, however, on rare occasions been accepted. Strikingly, Council Regulation 4056/86 block exempts certain liner conference agreements, refers to the 'stabilising effect of liner conferences' on pricing.[225] This block exemption is, however, to be repealed with effect from October 2008.[226]

Further, the Commission has also been prepared in the past to grant an exemption to agreements incorporating terms which limit price competition where the agreements are not 'naked', but pursue some efficiency enhancing objective. A key issue in these types of case (see Chapter 4), is whether such agreements have as their 'object' the restriction of competition (and so are prohibited unless the parties establish that they satisfy the Article 81(3) criteria) or whether a recognition that the agreement is not naked, means that the agreement falls outside of the object category, requiring the Commission, or other person seeking to demonstrate the same, to establish that the 'effect' of the agreement is to restrict competition.[227]

In *Uniform Eurocheques*,[228] the Commission was prepared to exempt for a limited period an agreement which fixed commissions for the cashing of Eurocheques. Although the uniformity of prices and conditions for Eurocheque services led to a restriction of competition between banks in different countries in cashing Eurocheques, the Commission found that the agreement (i) improved payment methods and (ii) benefited users (all currencies were available and interest-free credit was available whilst the cheques were being cleared). The restrictions were essential in the circumstances and did not lead to an elimination of competition. Customers using the facilities knew that they would be charged a uniform amount throughout the EC. Similarly, in *Visa International-Multilateral Interchange Fee*[229] the Commission held that an agreement containing a provision to fix the 'Multilateral interchange fee' paid by issuing banks to acquiring banks within the Visa system, which had as its effect the restriction of competition, met the Article 81(3) criteria.[230] In *Reims II*[231] the Commission exempted price fixing with 'unusual

[223] Commission's *Xth Report on Competition Policy* (Commission, 1980), 115.

[224] See *supra* Chap. 4 and *infra* 898.

[225] For further discussion of liner conferences, see e.g. discussion of Cases C-395 and 396/96 P, *Compagnie Maritime Belge Transports SA v. Commission* [2000] ECR I-1365, [2000] 4 CMLR 1076, *supra* Chap. 7 and *infra*.

[226] See IP 06/1249,Regulation 1419/2006 [2006] OJ L269/1, MEMO/06/344 and generally, http://ec.europa.eu/comm/competition/antitrust/legislation/maritime/. The Commission is going to adopt guidelines on the type of information that undertakings can legitimately exchange in the maritime transport market.

[227] See *supra* Chap. 4 and also *infra* Chap. 13.

[228] [1985] OJ L35/43, [1985] 3 CMLR 434. But see *Eurocheque: Helsinki Agreement* [1992] OJ L95/50, [1993] 5 CMLR 323, partially annulled and fines reduced on appeal, see Case T-39/92, *Groupement des Cartes Bancaires v. Commission* [1994] ECR II-49, [1995] 5 CMLR 410.

[229] [2002] OJ L318/17.

[230] See more detailed discussion of the case, *supra* Chap. 223–4.

[231] [1999] OJ L275/17, [2000] 4 CMLR 704. The 1999 notification only received exemption until the end of 2001. The Commission exempted the agreement again in 2003 following renotification [2004] OJ L56/76 (effective until 31 Dec. 2006).

characteristics'. The Commission held that fixing of terminal dues[232] payable by post offices for the delivery of letters in other Member States would lead to an improvement in efficiency[233] and would eliminate cross-subsidy. In none of the cases were the price restraints exempted 'naked'.

On a number of occasions, the Commission has also granted exemption to joint distribution, joint selling, or collective licensing arrangements. The Commission is ordinarily hostile to joint selling or sales joint ventures as they restrict competition between the parents on the supply-side and limit purchaser's choice. They effectively operate as horizontal price fixing agreements. Particularly when dealing with copyright, or other neighbouring rights, however, the Commission has been persuaded that joint selling or licensing may be beneficial and meet the criteria of Article 81(3).

In *UIP*,[234] for example, the Commission granted an exemption to agreements creating United International Pictures BV (UIP) a joint film distribution company established by Paramount Pictures Corporation, Universal Studios Inc and Metro-Goldwyn Mayer Inc. UIP distributed and licensed on an exclusive basis feature motion pictures, short subjects and trailers produced by the parties for showing in cinemas. Following modifications to the agreement, in particular by limiting the effect of the exclusivity provisions by allowing UIP only a right of first refusal to the parent companies' films,[235] the Commission was prepared to accept the Article 81(3) requirements were met. The Commission accepted that the cooperation produced economic benefits for the production and distribution of motion pictures and for consumers, which could not be achieved in the absence of the joint venture and which outweighed its disadvantages. In particular, the creation of UIP made possible a more effective and rationalized distribution of the parents' products, avoiding duplication of distribution organizations, and creating an economically viable distribution network in a deteriorating market where high financial risks were present. When the parties applied for an extension of the exemption the Commission required further amendments to the agreements before issuing a comfort letter.[236]

In *IFPI*[237] the International Federation of the Phonic Industry notified a reciprocal agreement in the name of national collecting societies of music record companies. The main objective of the agreement was to facilitate the grant of a multi-territorial licence[238] which broadcasters could exploit *globally*, and not just nationally, by simulcasting sound recordings onto the global digital network of the Internet. The agreement would therefore facilitate the creation of a new type of licence and ensure effective administration and protection of producers' rights in the face of global Internet exploitation and provide broadcasters with an alternative of obtaining a licence from the local society in every country in which their Internet transmissions could be accessed. Although the agreement did involve some prices restrictions between the parties, the Commission concluded that the restrictions were indispensable to the agreement, would lead to substantial economic benefits, and would improve the distribution of music, which would benefit consumers.

[232] The remuneration that public postal operators (PPO) pay each other for the delivery of incoming cross-border mail. The receiving PPO is remunerated by the sending PPO for the delivery of the latter's mail.

[233] The agreement would lead to a correlation between the terminal dues paid and cost and improve the quality of service for cross-border mail.

[234] [1989] OJ L226/35, [1990] 4 CMLR 749.

[235] This meant that the parent company concerned had first to offer its product for distribution in the EC to UIP but if UIP elected not to distribute a picture, the parent company could impose its distribution to UIP or to distribute the film independently, either itself or through a third party.

[236] IP/99/681.

[237] [2003] OJ C107/58.

[238] Ordinarily, collecting societies have the right to grant licences for exploitation of sound recordings in their territory only.

Broadcasting rights to sports matches or competitions are frequently sold collectively on behalf of clubs or participants by sports associations. The agreements in the sporting sector also frequently involve exclusivity, which leads to concern as it distorts competition between broadcasters, encourages media concentration, and stifles the development of new products and services such as Internet sports services and new generation mobile phones.[239] The Commission has therefore taken a keen interest in such cases.[240]

In *Joint Selling of commercial rights to the UEFA Champions League*[241] the Commission, following revision of their terms, exempted regulations concerning the joint selling of the commercial rights to the UEFA Champion League on behalf of the clubs participating in the league. The Commission accepted that the new joint selling arrangements would improve production and distribution of the League by the creation of a quality branded content product and creating a single point of sale for the acquisition of a packaged league product.

c. Output Restrictions and Restrictions Limiting or Controlling Production

The Commission has been prepared to accept that agreements which restrict output meet the Article 81(3) criteria. For example, where a restriction of output is ancillary to a beneficial research and development or specialization agreement the terms in such agreements may, in certain circumstances, satisfy the terms of Article 81(3).[242] Further, in the past, where there has been serious over-capacity in an industry, the Commission has occasionally been sympathetic to parties that notified 'crisis cartels' (for example, restructuring agreements) for exemption.[243] It permitted undertakings operating in industries suffering severe difficulties to conclude cooperation agreements providing, for example, for an orderly reduction in over-capacity where the economic effect of the improved rationalization outweighs the disadvantages of the reduced competition in the short term. However, it would not allow the restructuring to be achieved by unacceptable means such as price-fixing or market-sharing. Further, it would regard the restrictions as indispensable only if the agreement was concerned solely with the reduction of capacity and was limited from the outset to a period necessary for its setting up and implementation. It permitted several agreements in the petro-chemical and thermo-plastics sector.[244]

In another case the Commission granted an exemption to an agreement which did not restrict output but which restricted the type of goods that the parties to the agreement could produce or import. In *European Council of Manufacturers of Domestic Appliances*[245] the Commission exempted an agreement concluded between 95 per cent of the producers and importers of

---

[239] The Commission is concerned that exclusivity agreements do not lead to other broadcasters being excluded from the market altogether. Thus a long duration of exclusivity may be prohibited if there is a risk that a broadcaster might prevent its competitors gaining access.

[240] See Chap. 13.

[241] [2003] OJ L291/25.

[242] See *infra* Chap. 13.

[243] One of the Commission's objectives was to ensure the elimination of over-capacity in an industry and to enable the industry to recover its profitability, *XXIst Report on Competition Policy* (Commission, 1991), 207 ff.

[244] For example, in *ENI/Montedison* [1987] OJ L5/13, [1988] 4 CMLR 444, the Commission exempted for 15 years an agreement between two large petrochemical groups for rationalization of their production capacities and transfer of certain businesses leading to a *de facto* specialization by each party. The Commission considered that the agreement would enable the parties to slim down operations and concentrate on modernizing their plant and benefit consumers who would be ensured a continued supply of products, cost-saving in the medium term, and better products in the long term generated by the parties' ability to finance new research and development. The radical reorganization could not be achieved without the restrictions and workable competition would not be eliminated by the agreement. See also the discussion of crisis cartels *supra* Chap. 4.

[245] [2000] OJ L 187/47, [2000] 5 CMLR 635. See also IP/01/1659 where the Commission indicated its intention to take a similar approach to environmental agreements for water heaters and dishwashers.

washing machines operating on the EU market that restricted their freedom to manufacture or import the least energy-efficient washing machines. The agreement was found to restrict competition within the meaning of Article 81(1).[246] Nonetheless the Commission considered that the agreement met the criteria set out in Article 81(3) since it would reduce the potential energy consumption of new machines and consequently lessen pollution, create more technically efficient machines, and focus future research and development on furthering energy efficiency. Such economic and technical progress would benefit society and consumers. The Commission considered that the restrictions were indispensable to the agreement which would not substantially eliminate competition.

d. Market Sharing Agreements

It is particularly unlikely market-sharing agreements will meet the Article 81(3) criteria. The Commission has stated its opinion that:

in principle, exemption from the prohibition cannot be considered for market-sharing agreements. The elimination of a competitor from a market—either in whole or in part—cannot be justified objectively on economic or technical grounds or in the interests of the consumer.[247]

e. Collusive Tendering

As with other hard-core cartel activity it is unlikely that bid rigging would meet the Article 81(3) criteria.[248] In *FIEC/CEETB*,[249] however, the Commission indicated that it would take a favourable view of an agreement designed to standardize and reduce the cost of the tendering process between building contractors and sub-contractors but which would not in any way limit either the firms who could tender or the prices at which they could tender.

D. RESTRICTIONS ON NON-PRICE TRADING CONDITIONS, ADVERTISING, AND PROMOTION AND INFORMATION SHARING AGREEMENTS

(i) General

Agreements relating to non-price trading conditions or relating to advertising or promotion may not have such a serious impact on competition as the agreements discussed in the section above. They may, nonetheless, restrict important methods of competition between undertakings operating on the market. Further, such restraints may chill competition between firms operating on the market and may, in some circumstances, be used to complement and facilitate the operation of a hard-core cartel agreement or may have the effect of facilitating tacit collusion between firms operating on the market. Although these types of restraints do not generally have as their object the restriction of competition, they may have to be carefully scrutinized to consider whether or not they have that effect and, if so, whether or not they meet the criteria of Article 81(3).

---

[246] See *supra* Chap. 4.

[247] *Ist Report on Competition Policy* (Commission, 1971), 3.

[248] See, e.g., *Cast Iron and Steel Rolls* [1983] OJ L317/1, [1984] 1 CMLR 694.

[249] [1998] OJ C52/2.

(ii) Restrictions on Non-price Trading Conditions

a. Introduction

Because non-price competition may also be an important part of competition between undertakings Article 81(1)(a) prohibits, as incompatible with the common market, collusive practices which 'directly or indirectly fix...any other trading conditions'. Restraints on such trading conditions may also bolster other hard-core cartel activities. In *Fine Art Auction Houses*,[250] for example, Christie's and Sotheby's not only fixed the commissions that they charged but other conditions, such as payment conditions, guarantees, and advances. In some cases, however, it may be advantageous for undertakings to have access to suitably drafted terms and conditions and/or the adoption of common quality or technical standards. In such cases, it is possible that the agreements will not infringe Article 81(1) at all or that they will meet the criteria of Article 81(3).[251]

b. Uniform Terms and Conditions

The use of printed forms setting out standard terms and conditions to be applied by undertakings will not necessarily infringe Article 81(1). However, where the terms and conditions relate to 'important secondary aspects of competition',[252] that is, to any aspect of a supplier's offer which has economic value in the eyes of the customer, they may infringe Article 81(1).

In *Fabricants de Papiers Peints de Belgique*,[253] the Commission found that general conditions of sale concluded by Belgian manufacturers of wallpaper, which related to terms of delivery, returns policy, lengths of rolls, etc. infringed Article 81(1) and did not satisfy the conditions of Article 81(3).

c. Customer Services

Prohibitions on parties to an agreement offering customers special services such as the loan of products or special delivery arrangements are likely to cause an infringement of Article 81(1).[254]

d. Product Quality

The adoption of a common quality label (establishing that products meet a minimum quality standard) will not necessarily infringe Article 81(1). However, a provision restricting suppliers from producing products of a different, inferior standard (and limiting the quality of products supplied) is likely to infringe Article 81(1).[255]

e. Technical Development

Similarly, the adoption of a label identifying products that achieve a certain common technical standard will not infringe Article 81(1) where the quality mark is freely available and the parties are free to market products of a different or inferior standard.[256] There may, however, be an

---

[250] IP/02/1585.

[251] *Concordato Incendio* [1990] OJ L15/27, [1991] 4 CMLR 199.

[252] *Vimpoltu* [1983] OJ L200/44, [1983] 3 CMLR 619.

[253] [1974] OJ L237/3, [1974] 2 CMLR D102.

[254] See, e.g., *VCH* [1972] OJ L13/34, [1973] CMLR D16.

[255] *Belgian Association of Pharmacists* [1990] OJ L160/1. But see also *European Council of Manufacturers of Domestic Appliances* [2000] OJ L187/47, [2000] 5 CMLR 635, *supra* n. 245 and accompanying text and Case C-309/99, *Wouters v. Algemene Raad van de Nederlandse Order van Advocaten* [2002] ECR I-1577, [2002] 4 CMLR 913, *supra* n. 199 and accompanying text.

[256] Notice on Cooperation Agreements [1968] JO C75/3, para. II(8).

infringement of Article 81(1) where the agreement limits technical development[257] or is used to hinder imports, as in *IAZ*.[258]

In *IAZ* a Belgian trade association agreed with Belgian manufacturers and sole importers for washing machines and dishwashers that only appliances with a 'conformity' label could be connected to the mains. To receive a conformity label the appliances had to comply with technical standards laid down by Belgian law. In fact, the label was available only to Belgian manufacturers or sole importers of products. Thus parallel imports of the appliances were made impossible in practice.

(iii) Restrictions on Advertising and Promotion

The advertising and promotion of a product may be an extremely important aspect of competition between undertakings. It may be a vital means of distinguishing the products, in the eyes of the consumer, from those of competitors and may draw attention to the different characteristics, prices, and qualities of the relevant products. It can also provide an important mechanism for entering a new market.

The Commission has indicated that restrictions on the ability of parties to an agreement to advertise is likely to be seen as a restriction on their competitive freedom and competition.[259] The Commission is concerned about restrictions on advertising in the liberal professions.

Communication from the Commission, 'Report on Competition in Professional Services' Com (2004) 83 final (Brussels, 9 Feb. 2004)

42. A large number of the EU professions are subject to sector-specific advertising regulation . . . in some cases advertising as such is prohibited. In others, specific media or advertising methods such as radio advertising, televisions advertising or 'cold calling' or specific types of advertising content are proscribed. In certain cases, there is a lack of clarity in existing advertising regulations which, in itself, may deter professions from employing certain advertising methods.

43. According to economic theory, advertising may facilitate competition by informing consumers about different products and allowing them to make better informed purchasing decisions. Advertising restrictions may thus reduce competition by increasing the costs of gaining information about different products, making it more difficult for consumers to search for the quality and price that best meets their needs. It is also widely recognized that advertising, and in particular comparative advertising, can be a crucial competitive tool for new firms entering the market and for existing firms to launch new products.

44. The proponents of advertising restrictions emphasise the asymmetry of information between practitioners and consumers of professional services. According to this argument, consumers find it difficult to assess information about professional services and therefore need particular protection from misleading or manipulative claims.

45. There is, however, an increasing body of empirical evidence which highlights the potentially negative effects of some advertising restrictions. This research suggests that restrictions may under certain circumstances increase the fees for professional services without having a positive

---

[257] See, e.g., *Video Cassette Recorders* [1978] OJ L47/42, [1978] 2 CMLR 160.

[258] *Anseau* [1982] OJ L167/39, [1982] 2 CMLR 193; on appeal Case 96/82, *IAZ International Belgium NV v. Commission* [1983] ECR 3369, [1984] 3 CMLR 276.

[259] Notice on Cooperation Agreements [1968] JO C75/3, para. 11(7).

effect on the quality of those services. The implication of these findings is that advertising restrictions as such do not, necessarily, provide an appropriate response to asymmetry of information in professional services. Conversely, truthful and objective advertising may actually help consumers to overcome the asymmetry and to make more informed purchasing decisions.

In general, where parties agree jointly to advertise industry products or products of a common brand, there is no infringement of Article 81(1) so long as the parties are also free to advertise individually. However, different rules may apply in an oligopolistic market where product differentiation and advertising may play a more vital role.[260]

In *Milchförderúngsfonds*,[261] the German dairy industry established a milk promotion fund. The fund was financed by a voluntary levy on milk delivered to dairies. The purpose of the fund was to promote the export of milk products. Brand advertising campaigns and subsidized sales were conducted abroad. The Commission considered that the campaign distorted competition within Article 81(1) and artificially strengthened the position of German exporters abroad. Although generic advertising, which did not commend the products solely on the ground of their national origin and did not disparage foreign products, would have benefited all exporters, brand-oriented advertising appreciably reduced the possibility of sales for competing brands. Individual manufacturers benefited from the campaign without having to suffer a corresponding cost which otherwise would have been reflected in the sales price.

In *BELASCO*,[262] Belgian manufacturers jointly advertised and promoted their products, which were sold under a common trade mark, through the association, BELASCO. The Commission considered that the purpose of the standardization of the products and the joint advertising was to reinforce the other provisions of the agreement which provided for a common price list and sales quotas. The fostering of an impression in consumers that their products were homogeneous limited the scope of competition by means of product differentiation.

The Commission has on occasions accepted that it may be advantageous for undertakings to rationalize and coordinate their advertising efforts, particularly in the context of trade fairs.[263]

(iv) Information Sharing Agreements

a. Exchange of Information between Competitors

The dissemination and exchange of information between competitors and the creation of a transparent market may be harmless or even highly beneficial to the competitive structure of the market. Trade associations frequently collect industry data on prices, outputs, capacity, and investment and circulate information to their members. Detailed market data may make it easier for undertakings to plan their own business strategies (e.g., data may avoid the creation of overcapacity in an industry based on false expectations). Further, the theory of perfect competition rests upon the assumption that there is perfect freedom of information. A market characterized by many buyers and sellers should, therefore, positively benefit from such transparency. Where information is available generally, consumers with complete knowledge of what is on offer may fully utilize their choice. Competition will be maximized. Where the exchange of opinion or experience is harmless or beneficial to competition, it will not infringe Article 81(1).[264]

---

[260] *Ibid.*, in particular, para. 11(7).

[261] [1985] OJ L35/35, [1985] 3 CMLR 101.

[262] [1986] OJ L232/15, [1991] 4 CMLR 130.

[263] See, e.g., *UNIDI* [1984] OJ L322/10, [1985] 2 CMLR 38.

[264] See, e.g., *Eudim* [1996] OJ C111/8. This case concerned an information exchange on the market for installation machines. The market was fragmented and there were around a million products on the market.

However, information exchanges present a danger. The ECJ and the Commission have consistently stressed the importance of competitors acting independently. Exchanges of very sensitive information, for example, on capacity and price may be used as a mechanism for implementing or monitoring compliance with a cartel agreement. The exchange may thus make it easier for competitors to act in concert. Where the information is exchanged to support price-fixing or other hard-core cartel activity the Commission or other enforcing authority will obviously take a dim view.[265] In *Methylglucamine*,[266] for example, cartel meetings (where price increases and customer allocation were agreed) normally started with an exchange of information and views on the worldwide demand for the product, referring to the volumes sold to the respective main clients during the previous year. In this case, however, the Commission concluded that this practice had not materialized into a full systematic exchange of sales data.[267] Further, it is possible that exchange of price information may in *itself* be sufficient to establish a price fixing agreement or concerted practice which is restrictive by object in violation of Article 81(1).[268]

Information exchanges may also exacerbate the problems of, and increase the transparency on, oligopolistic markets where there is already limited opportunity for competition and facilitate the alignment of behaviour and tacit coordination. Where information exchanges do not have as their object the restriction of competition, an appraisal of the effect of the agreement will be required, taking into consideration of course the actual context to which they belong.[269] The compatibility of such information exchanges with Article 81(1) cannot therefore be determined abstractly, but must be determined taking into account the economic conditions on the relevant markets. This point is spelt out clearly by the ECJ in *Asnef-Equifax, Servicios de Información sobre Solvencia y Crédito, SL v. Asociación de Usuarios de Servicios Bancarios (Ausbanc)*.[270]

Accordingly . . . the compatibility of an information exchange system . . . with the Community competition rules cannot be assessed in the abstract. It depends on the economic conditions on the relevant markets and on the specific characteristics of the system concerned, such as, in particular, its purpose and the conditions of access to it and participation in it, as well as the type of information exchanged—be that, for example, public or confidential, aggregated or detailed, historical or current—the periodicity of such information and its importance for the fixing of prices, volumes or conditions of service.

Two issues, in particular, are crucial to the making of such a determination: the type of information exchanged and the market structure.[271]

b. The Type of Information Exchanged

Statistical information which enables undertakings to assess the level of demand and output in the market or the costs of its competitors may be beneficial and is not of itself objectionable.[272] Similarly, exchange of technical or other information that does not restrict the parties' freedom to determine their market behaviour independently should not be objectionable. However, exchanges of information on individuals' pricing intentions,[273] or information about: capacity

---

[265] See, e.g., *Building and Construction Industry in the Netherlands* [1992] OJ L92/1, aff'd, Case T-29/92, SPO v. *Commission* [1995] ECR II-289.

[266] [2004] OJ L38/18.

[267] *Ibid.*, paras. 76–82.

[268] See, e.g. Case T-141/94, *Thyssen Stahl v. Commission* [1999] ECR II-347, [1999] 4 CMLR 810, paras. 379–92.

[269] Case C-238/05, *Asnef-Equifax, Servicios de Información sobre Solvencia y Crédito, SL v. Asociación de Usuarios de Servicios Bancarios (Ausbanc)* [2006] ECR I-11125, [2007] 4 CMLR 6, paras. 48–9.

[270] Case C-238/05, [2006] ECR I-11125, [2007] 4 CMLR 6, para. 54.

[271] See generally E. Biscolli, 'Trade Associations and Information Exchange under US and EC Competition Law' [2000] 23(1) *World Competition* 29. L. Boulter and T. Bendell, 'Competition Risks in Benchmarking' [1999] *ECLR* 434.

[272] Case T-334/94, *Sarrio SA v. Commission* [1998] ECR II-1439, [1998] 5 CMLR 195.

[273] *Supra* n. 92 and accompanying text.

increases;[274] investment plans;[275] research projects; individual output and sales figures;[276] or other business secrets are likely to infringe Article 81(1).

c. The Market Structure

It has already been mentioned that information exchanges in competitive markets may be beneficial. However, information exchanges in markets which are prone to cartelization or oligopolistic are likely to be scrutinized by the Commission with care. Individualized market data may facilitate the identification of those cheating on a cartel. Alternatively, they may facilitate tacit collusion or conscious parallel behaviour by enabling undertakings to react rapidly to one another's actions:

> In assessing information agreements the Commission also pays close attention to the structure of the relevant market. The tendency for firms to fall in line with the behaviour of their competitors is particularly strong in oligopolistic markets. The improved knowledge of market conditions aimed at by information agreements strengthens the connection between the undertakings, in that they are enabled to react very efficiently to one another's actions, and thus lessens the intensity of competition.[277]

The effect of such exchanges is likely to be less serious (a) where consumers also have access to the information, and (b) where the agreement provides for post-notification of historic information rather than pre-notification of information. In *UK Agricultural Tractor Registration Exchange*, the Commission condemned the exchange of information relating to past transactions.[278] Where demand was stable, a forecast of a competitor's future actions could be largely determined on the basis of past transactions. The forecast would be more effective the more accurate and recent the information was. The exchange of information could, however, truly be categorized as historic from a certain period of time (e.g., if it was more than one year old).[279]

d. Notice on Cooperation Agreements and Guidelines on Horizontal Cooperation

In 1968 the Commission published a Notice that set out certain cooperation agreements which would fall outside the ambit of Article 81(1).[280] For example, where the sole object of the agreements is:

- to exchange opinion and experience, joint market research, joint comparative studies of industries;
- to cooperate in accounting.

The Notice indicated that the Commission would be wary of agreements on an oligopolistic market for homogeneous products. In *UK Agricultural Tractor Registration Exchange*,[281] the Commission stated that in more concentrated or oligopolistic markets there was already limited opportunity for competition and '[u]ncertainty and secrecy between suppliers [was] ...

---

[274] See, e.g., *Re Cimbell* [1972] OJ L303/24.

[275] See, e.g., *Zinc Producer Group* [1984] OJ L220/27, [1985] 2 CMLR 108.

[276] See *UK Agricultural Tractor Registration Exchange, infra* 905.

[277] Commission's VIIth Report on Competition Policy (Commission, 1977), part 7(2).

[278] [1992] OJ L 68/19, [1994] 3 CMLR 358; on appeal Case T-34/92, *Fiatagri & Ford New Holland v. Commission* [1994] ECR II-905 and Case T-35/92, *John Deere Ltd v. Commission* [1994] ECR II-957; on appeal to the ECJ, Case C-7/95 P, *John Deere Ltd v. Commission* [1998] ECR I-3111, [1998] 5 CMLR 311.

[279] See also *CEPI/Cartonboard* [1996] OJ C310/3.

[280] [1968] OJ C75/3.

[281] [1992] OJ L68/19, [1993] 4 CMLR 358.

vital'[282] to it. The 1968 Notice has been replaced by the Guidelines on Horizontal Cooperation adopted on 29 November 2000.[283] The new Guidelines do not, however specifically deal with information agreements.

e. Agreement or Concerted Practice Essential

Agreements to exchange information on prices to be charged or output to be produced (often through trade associations) will be caught by Article 81(1). Even if it cannot be established that an agreement which is restrictive of competition has been concluded, Article 81(1) prohibits behaviour which eliminates 'the risks of competition and the hazards of competitors' spontaneous reactions by co-operation'.[284] Exchanges of information, the object or effect of which is to influence the conduct on the market of an actual or potential competitor, to disclose to a competitor the course of conduct which the sender has decided to adopt on a market, or to render the market artificially transparent, will therefore be unacceptable.[285] Where no agreement or concerted practice exists no infringement of Article 81(1) is of course committed. In *Wood Pulp*,[286] the ECJ found that there was no infringement of Article 81 where undertakings had announced their price increases in advance. The increases had been rapidly transferred between both buyers and sellers by means of publication in the trade press and by agents which dealt with a number of buyers and sellers and no agreement or concerted practice between the producers to exchange the information had been established.[287]

f. *Cobelpa/VNP* and *UK Agricultural Tractor Registration Exchange*

In *Cobelpa/VNP*,[288] the Commission held that although there was nothing wrong in a trade association exchanging information on industry output and sales, in this case, where the information exchanged identified the output and sales of individual undertakings, the practice was prohibited. By exchanging information about matters normally regarded as confidential (especially where the information was not available to consumers) the parties were replacing practical co-operation for the normal risks of competition. It would make no difference that the information could have been obtained from elsewhere.

In *UK Agricultural Tractor Registration Exchange*,[289] eight UK manufacturers and importers of agricultural tractors operated, through the Agricultural Engineers Association, an information exchange agreement called the UK Agricultural Tractor Registration Exchange. The information identified the volume of retail sales and market shares of each of the eight manufacturers individually. In condemning the agreement under Article 81(1) and refusing to exempt it under Article 81(3) (after an initial Commission investigation the Exchange had been notified to it) the Commission took account of the fact that:

(i) the market was highly concentrated, (the eight manufacturers/importers had approximately 87–88 per cent of the relevant market);

---

[282] *Ibid.*, para. 37.

[283] [2001] OJ C3/2, [2001] 4 CMLR 819, see *infra* Chap. 13.

[284] Cases 48, 49, and 51–7/69, *ICI v. Commission (Dyestuffs)* [1972] ECR 619, [1972] CMLR 557, para. 119. See *supra* Chap. 3.

[285] See also Cases 40–8, 50, and 54–56/73, *Re the European Sugar Cartel: Cooperatiëve Verniging 'Suiker Unie' UA v. Commission* [1975] ECR 1663, [1976] 1 CMLR 295.

[286] Cases C-89, 104, 114, 116–17, and 125–9/85, *Re Wood Pulp Cartel: Ahlström Oy (Wood Pulp II) v. Commission (Wood Pulp II)* [1993] ECR I-1307, [1993] 4 CMLR 407.

[287] See further, *infra* 913–5.

[288] [1977] OJ L242/10, [1977] 2 CMLR D28.

[289] *Ibid.*

(ii) there were high barriers to entry into the market;

(iii) there were insignificant extra-Community imports;

(iv) the information exchanged was detailed and identified the exact retail sales and shares of the undertakings which were generally trade secrets between competitors; and

(v) the members met regularly.

First, the Commission held that the exchange of information prevented hidden competition by creating transparency on a market which was already highly concentrated and largely shielded from outside competition. Although it recognized that there were benefits of transparency in a competitive market, in this case the concentration of the market was not low and the market transparency was not in any way directed towards the benefit of consumers. The information in this case enabled each participant accurately to establish its rivals' market position and to see immediately if a rival increased its market share (e.g., by price reductions or other marketing incentives). It limited price competition since competitors would be able to react quickly to changes in market positions (this would, of course, mean that there was little incentive for a potential initiator to take steps to improve its position). Information would thus limit the possibility of surprise or secrecy if a rival received information disclosing sensitive information about his competitors. It would then be able to react quickly and eliminate any possible advantage to be gained by the initiator.

Secondly, the information would also be likely to increase barriers to entry since participants would know immediately of new market entrants and would be able to react accordingly.

The Commission's analysis was upheld by the CFI in *John Deere Ltd v. Commission*.[290] The Court accepted that a truly competitive market would benefit from transparency but that exchanges of precise information at short intervals on a highly concentrated market would be likely to impair the competition which existed between the traders.

Case T-35/92, *John Deere Ltd* v. *Commission* [1994] ECR II-957

Court of First Instance

51. The Court observes that, as the applicant points out, the Decision is the first in which the Commission has prohibited an information exchange system concerning sufficiently homogeneous products which does not directly concern the prices of those products, but which does not underpin any other anti-competitive arrangement either. As the applicants correctly argue, on a truly competitive market transparency between traders is in principle likely to lead to the intensification of competition between suppliers, since in such a situation, the fact that a trader takes into account information made available to him in order to adjust his conduct on the market is not likely, having regard to the atomized nature of the supply, to reduce or remove for the other traders any uncertainty about the foreseeable nature of its competitors' conduct. On the other hand, the Court considers that, as the Commission argues this time, general use, as between main suppliers and, contrary to the applicant's contention, to their sole benefit and consequently to the exclusion of the other suppliers and of consumers, of exchanges of precise information at short intervals, identifying registered vehicles and the place of their registration is, on a highly concentrated oligopolistic market such as the market in question and on which competition is as a result already greatly reduced and exchange of information facilitated, likely to impair substantially the competition which exists between traders (see paragraph 81, below). In such circumstances, the

[290] Case T-35/92 [1994] ECR II-957.

sharing, on a regular and frequent basis, of information concerning the operation of the market has the effect of periodically revealing to all the competitors the market positions and strategies of the various individual competitors.

52. Furthermore, provision of the information in question to all suppliers presupposes an agreement, or at any rate a tacit agreement, between the traders to define the boundaries of dealer sales territories by reference to the United Kingdom postcode system, as well as an institutional framework enabling information to be exchanged between the traders through the trade association to which they belong and, secondly, having regard to the frequency of such information and its systematic nature, it also enables a given trader to forecast more precisely the conduct of its competitors, so reducing or removing the degree of uncertainty about the operation of the market which would have existed in the absence of such an exchange of information. Furthermore, the Commission correctly contends, at points 44 to 48 of the Decision, that whatever decision is adopted by a trader wishing to penetrate the United Kingdom agricultural tractor market, and whether or not it becomes a member of the agreement, that agreement is necessarily disadvantageous for it. Either the trader concerned does not become a member of the information exchange agreement and, unlike its competitors, then forgoes the information exchanged and the market knowledge which it provides; or it becomes a member of the agreement and its business strategy is then immediately revealed to all its competitors by means of the information which they receive.

53. It follows that the pleas that the information exchange agreement at issue is not of such a nature as to infringe the Community competition rules must be dismissed.

. . .

81. Secondly, with regard to the type of information exchanged, the Court considers that, contrary to the applicant's contention, the information concerned, which relates in particular to sales made in the territory of each of the dealerships in the distribution network, is in the nature of business secrets. Indeed, this is admitted by the members of the agreement themselves, who strictly defined the conditions under which the information received could be disseminated to third parties, especially to members of their distribution network. The Court also observes that, as stated above (in paragraph 51), having regard to its frequency and systematic nature the exchange of information in question makes the conduct of a given trader's competitors all the more foreseeable for it in view of the characteristics of the relevant market as analyzed above, since it reduces, or even removes, the degree of uncertainty regarding the operation of the market, which would have existed in the absence of such an exchange of information, and in this regard the applicant cannot profitably rely on the fact that the information exchanged does not concern prices or relate to past sales. Accordingly, the first part of the plea, to the effect that there is no restriction of competition as a result of alleged 'prevention of hidden competition', must be dismissed.

An appeal before the ECJ against the judgment of the CFI was unsuccessful.[291]

The Commission in *Wirtschaftsvereinigung Stahl*[292] also condemned, under Article 65 ECSC, information sharing in a market that was concentrated and had high barriers to entry. This decision was, however, annulled by the CFI essentially on the grounds that the Commission's decision was marred by errors of fact.[293] In contrast to these cases the Commission considered in *Eudim*[294]

---

[291] See Case C-7/95 P, *John Deere Ltd v. Commission* [1998] ECR I-3111, [1998] 5 CMLR 311.

[292] [1998] OJ L1/10, [1998] 4 CMLR 450.

[293] Case T-16/98, [2000] ECR II-1217, [2001] 5 CMLR 3.

[294] [1996] OJ C111/8, [1996] 4 CMLR 871.

that information sharing in an agreement that was competitive on both the purchasing and selling side did not infringe Article 81(1).

g. Asnef-Equifax, Servicios De Información sobre Solvencia Y Crédito, SL v. Asociación de Usuarios de Servicios Bancarios (Ausbanc)[295]

In this case Ausbanc had challenged the exchange of information between financial institutions on the solvency of customers and borrower default. Following an Article 234 reference to it the ECJ set out guidance for the referring court to determine the compatibility of the provisions for exchange with Article 81(1). With regard to the question of whether the agreement had as its effect the restriction of competition the ECJ stressed the importance of considering whether supply on the market was highly concentrated, whether information identified competitors individually and whether access to the information was available in a non-discriminatory manner to all operators.

Case C-238/05, *Asnef-Equifax, Servicios de Información sobre Solvencia y Crédito, SL v. Asociación de Usuarios de Servicios Bancarios (Ausbanc)* [2006] ECR I-11125, [2007] 4 CMLR 6

55. As indicated at paragraph 47 of this judgment, registers such as the one at issue in the main proceedings, by reducing the rate of borrower default, are in principle capable of improving the functioning of the supply of credit. As the Advocate General observed, in substance, at point 54 of his Opinion, if, owing to a lack of information on the risk of borrower default, financial institutions are unable to distinguish those borrowers who are more likely to default, the risk thereby borne by such institutions will necessarily be increased and they will tend to factor it in when calculating the cost of credit for all borrowers, including those less likely to default, who will then have to bear a higher cost than they would if the institutions were in a position to evaluate the probability of repayment more precisely. In principle, registers such as that mentioned above are capable of reducing such a tendency.

56. Furthermore, by reducing the significance of the information held by financial institutions regarding their own customers, such registers appear, in principle, to be capable of increasing the mobility of consumers of credit. In addition, those registers are apt to make it easier for new competitors to enter the market.

57. None the less, whether or not there is in the main proceedings a restriction of competition within the meaning of Article 81(1) EC depends on the economic and legal context in which the register exists, and in particular on the economic conditions of the market as well as the particular characteristics of the register.

58. In that regard, first of all, if supply on a market is highly concentrated, the exchange of certain information may, according in particular to the type of information exchanged, be liable to enable undertakings to be aware of the market position and commercial strategy of their competitors, thus distorting rivalry on the market and increasing the probability of collusion, or even facilitating it. On the other hand, if supply is fragmented, the dissemination and exchange of information between competitors may be neutral, or even positive, for the competitive nature of the market (see, to that effect, *Thyssen Stahl v Commission*, paragraphs 84 and 86). In the present case, it is common ground, as may be seen from paragraph 10 of this judgment, that the referring court premi[s]ed its reference for a preliminary ruling on the existence of 'a fragmented market', which it is for that court to verify.

---

[295] Case C-238/05 [2006] ECR I-11125, [2007] 4 CMLR 6.

59. Secondly, in order that registers such as that at issue in the main proceedings are not capable of revealing the market position or the commercial strategy of competitors, it is important that the identity of lenders is not revealed, directly or indirectly. In the present case, it is apparent from the decision for referral that the Tribunal de Defensa de la Competencia imposed on Asnef-Equifax, which accepted it, a condition that the information relating to lenders contained in the register not be disclosed.

60. Thirdly, it is also important that such registers be accessible in a non-discriminatory manner, in law and in fact, to all operators active in the relevant sphere. If such accessibility were not guaranteed, some of those operators would be placed at a disadvantage, since they would have less information for the purpose of risk assessment, which would also not facilitate the entry of new operators on to the market.

61. It follows that, provided that the relevant market or markets are not highly concentrated, that the system does not permit lenders to be identified and that the conditions of access and use by financial institutions are not discriminatory, an information exchange system such as the register is not, in principle, liable to have the effect of restricting competition within the meaning of Article 81(1) EC.

62. While in those conditions such systems are capable of reducing uncertainty as to the risk that applicants for credit will default, they are not, however, liable to reduce uncertainty as to the risks of competition. Thus, each operator could be expected to act independently and autonomously when adopting a given course of conduct, regard being had to the risks presented by applicants. Contrary to Ausbanc's contention, it cannot be inferred solely from the existence of such a credit information exchange that it might lead to collective anti-competitive conduct, such as a boycott of certain potential borrowers.

63. Furthermore, since, as the Advocate General observed, in substance, at point 56 of his Opinion, any possible issues relating to the sensitivity of personal data are not, as such, a matter for competition law, they may be resolved on the basis of the relevant provisions governing data protection. In the main proceedings, it is apparent from the documents before the Court that, under the rules applicable to the register, affected consumers may, in accordance with the Spanish legislation, check the information concerning them and, where necessary, have it corrected, or indeed deleted.

The ECJ in *Asnef-Equifax* also recognized that the referring court might need to carry out an Article 81(3) reference in order to resolve the dispute at issue.[296] For example, the court might be required to determine whether objective economic advantages, such as helping to prevent over indebtedness for consumers of credit and leading to a greater overall availability of credit, might be such as to offset the disadvantages of any restriction of competition identified. The ECJ stressed that in making the Article 81(3) determination, it was not necessary that all consumers should benefit from the system. Rather, it was not inconceivable that some applicants for credit would be faced with increased interest rates or refused credit. This circumstance was not in itself sufficient to prevent the condition that consumers be allowed a fair share of the benefit from being satisfied since 'it is the beneficial nature of the effect on all consumers in the relevant markets that must be taken into consideration, not the effect on each member of that category of consumers'.[297] Indeed, the exchange in this situation might be capable of leading to a greater

---

[296] But see, e.g., *International Energy Program* [1983] OJ L376/30.

[297] Case C-238/05, *Asnef-Equifax v. Asociación Usuarios de Servicios Bancarios (Ausbanc)* [2006] ECR I-11125, [2007] 4 CMLR 6, para.70.

overall availability of credit, including for applicants for whom interest rates might be excessive if lenders did not have appropriate knowledge of their personal system.

h. B-2-B Exchanges

B-2-B e-marketplaces, which allow industrial buyers and sellers to transact business online over the Internet, have exploded in recent years.[298] Although such market places may create huge efficiency gains in purchasing and supply chain management there has also been a concern that such markets would create an ideal climate for collusion, due to increased communication and transparency in the market,[299] exchange of confidential information and foreclosure. The Commission, however, recognizes the clear advantages that may result from such market places and has sought to develop a coherent approach to their assessment and has in many cases accepted that such agreements do not infringe Article 81(1) at all.[300] In *Covisint*,[301] for example, the Commission sent a comfort letter clearing the creation of the Covisint Automotive Internet Marketplace (the agreement did not infringe Article 81(1)). Six car manufacturers notified a joint venture to the Commission to serve the procurement needs of major car makers and suppliers and to reduce costs and improve efficiency in the supply chain. The Commission noted in its press release that in general B-2-B marketplaces should have pro-competitive effects by creating more transparency, integrating markets, creating marketing efficiencies by reducing search and information costs and improving inventory management, leading ultimately to lower prices for the end consumer. In this case the Commission was satisfied that potential competition concerns had been eliminated: 'Covisint is open to all firms in the industry on a non-discriminatory basis, is based on open standards, allows both shareholders and other users to participate in other B-2-B exchanges, does not allow joint purchasing between car manufacturers or for automotive-specific products, and provides for adequate data protection, including firewalls and security rules.' It has also sent negative clearance comfort letters in relation to B-2-B electronic marketplaces set up in other sectors.[302] In an article by a Commission official in the competition policy newsletter several guidelines are set out for companies considering setting up e-market places.[303]

---

[298] J. Lüking, 'B2B e-marketplaces and EC competition law: where do we stand?' Competition Policy Newsletter, Oct. 2001, 14. See also S. Stroux, 'B2B E-market-places: The Emerging Competition Law Issues' [2001] 24 *World Competition* 125 and D. Lancefield, 'The regulatory Hurdles Ahead in B2B' [2001] *ECLR* 9.

[299] *E-Commerce and Its Implications for Competition Policy* OFT 308, para. 6.54.

[300] See, e.g., M. Monti, 'European Competition Policy for the 21st century' [2000] *Fordham Corp L Inst* (ed. B. E. Hawk), Chap. 15 and 'Competition in the New Economy' 10th International Conference on Competition of the Bundeskartellamt, Berlin, 21 May 2001.

[301] IP/01/1155 (a negative clearance comfort letter).

[302] See *Eutilia/Endorsia* IP/01/1775, *Eurex* IP/02/4, *Inreon* IP/02/761, *Centradia* IP 02/943, *Water Portal* IP/02/956, and J. Lüking, 'B2B e-marketplaces and EC competition law: where do we stand?' Competition Policy Newsletter, Oct. 2001.

[303] *Ibid.*, 15–16.

4. OLIGOPOLY

A. OLIGOPOLY AND ARTICLE 81

(i) The Oligopoly Problem

It has been explained that in some oligopolistic markets the players may, without explicit communication, coordinate their behaviour, aligning their conduct and setting their prices at supra-competitive levels ('tacit collusion'). Because there are only a few players on the market, oligopolists' awareness of each other's presence is automatically heightened and the undertakings react to each other's behaviour as a rational response to market circumstances. An undertaking is bound to monitor the behaviour of its competitors since a reduction in price by a competitor may swiftly attract away the former's customers. Oligopolists may, therefore, recognize their interdependence and realize, without needing to agree to do so, that the most efficient course of conduct is for them all to set their prices at a profit-maximizing level. This section and section B below consider whether tacit collusion is, or maybe, prohibited by either Article 81 or 82

(ii) Tacit Collusion and Concerted Practices

a. The Problem

Oligopolists engaged in tacit collusion have not got together and actually agreed to increase prices and restrict output. A question which has arisen, however, is whether the concept of a concerted practice in Article 81 is broad enough to catch tacit collusion since the firms do not behave totally unilaterally, but determine their strategy by taking account of the likely response of their competitors (see *supra* 874). It will be remembered that the term concerted practice has been construed broadly to catch all:

co-ordination between undertakings which, without having reached the stage where an agreement, properly so called, has been concluded, knowingly substitutes practical co-operation between them for the risks of competition.[304]

The purpose is to catch undertakings which have not agreed but which determine their market policy in co-operation with other undertakings, for example, through direct or indirect conduct, and not *independently*. A key issue is, therefore, whether tacit collusion constitutes practical cooperation between undertakings or independent behaviour outside the scope of Article 81(1). In addition, if tacit collusion cannot be *equated* with a concerted practice a further question arising, is whether parallel conduct by firms operating on an oligopolistic market can ever be used as circumstantial evidence to justify a finding that an agreement or concerted practice existed between the undertakings.

The answer to these questions appears to have been provided in the ECJ's judgment in *Wood Pulp*.[305] First, it makes clear that tacit collusion is not in itself prohibited by Article 81(1). Secondly, that although parallel behaviour may furnish proof of explicit collusion it will not do so if the behaviour can be explained by the conditions of competition on the market, for example,

---

[304] Cases 48, 49, and 51–7/69, *ICI v. Commission* [1972] ECR 619, [1972] CMLR 557, paras. 64 and 65.

[305] Cases C-89, etc. 85 [1993] ECR I-1307, [1993] 4 CMLR 407.

that the conditions have led to tacit collusion of the undertaking's behaviour. Before looking at the Court's judgment in *Wood Pulp* it is, however, useful to consider some of the Court's previous rulings, in particular in *Dyestuffs*, *Suiker Unie*, and *Züchner*.

b. The *Dyestuffs* Case

In *Dyestuffs*, three general and uniform increases in the prices of dyestuffs had taken place within the common market over a period of years. The first, in 1964, took place on the markets in Italy, Holland, Belgium, and Luxembourg, the second in 1965 on the market in Germany, and in 1967 uniform increases took place in Germany, Holland, Belgium, Luxembourg, and France (the latter at a different rate, since prices had previously been frozen by the Government there).

In this case the Commission concluded that the increases had occurred as a result of a concerted practice operating between ten producers (it had discovered significant evidence of actual direct/indirect contact between the parties).[306]

The ECJ upheld the decision. The behaviour constituted a concerted practice prohibited by Article 81(1) of the Treaty. In particular, the Court relied upon the fact that price increases had been announced in advance (the announcements eliminating all uncertainty between them as regards their future conduct and the risk inherent in any independent change in conduct) and that the announcements rendered the market transparent as regards the rates of increases. Further, given the number of producers on the European dyestuffs market, it did not consider that it was possible to say, as the applicants had alleged, that the market was an oligopolistic one. Price competition should have been able to play a substantial role. It was not plausible, therefore, that the parallel conduct could have been brought into effect within a period of two to three days without prior concertation. The Court concluded that, taking into account the nature of the market in the products in question, the conduct of the undertakings was designed to replace both the risks of competition and the hazards of competitors' spontaneous reactions with cooperation.

There were suggestions and concern after the Court's judgment that its interpretation of the term 'concerted practice' would be used broadly to catch rational, and purely parallel, market behaviour.[307] The Court had relied mainly on market data to support its finding that the parties had cooperated, without conducting a thorough study of the market. In particular, it characterized behaviour as apparently innocuous as making price announcements in advance as an impermissible means of indirect communication.[308]

The Commission had, however, in fact discovered significant evidence of actual direct/indirect contact between the parties. It had not relied on economic evidence of parallel behaviour alone. Apart from the similarity in rates and dates of increases, the Commission found proof of concertation from the similarity of the content of the orders sent by the producers to their subsidiaries or representatives on the various markets, to make the increases. The orders were on occasion sent on the same day (at the same hour), were couched in similar terms, and showed a very great similarity in drafting. Some messages contained exactly identical phrases which, the Commission concluded, could not be explained in the absence of prior concertation between the undertakings involved. The Commission also discovered records of meetings of the producers in Basel and London. The records disclosed that not only was the question of prices discussed but that on occasion the dates and timings of intended price increases were announced.

---

[306] *Re Cartel in Aniline Dyes* [1969] CMLR D23.

[307] e.g., see V. Korah, 'Concerted Practices' (1973) 36 *MLR* 260; R. Joliet, 'La notion de pratique concertée et l'arrêt I.C.I. dans une perspective comparative' [1974] *CDE* 251.

[308] See *infra* 916–8.

Further, the ECJ specifically stated that 'parallel behaviour may not by itself be identified with a concerted practice' although it could provide 'strong evidence of such a practice if it leads to conditions of competition which do not correspond to the normal conditions of the market, having regard to the nature of the products, the size and number of the undertakings, and the volume of the said market'.[309] This would be the case where prices were stabilized at a level different from that to which competition would otherwise have led. A producer was thus 'free to charge his prices, taking into account in so doing the present or foreseeable conduct of his competitors'. In contrast, he was precluded from cooperating 'with his competitors, in any way whatsoever, in order to determine a coordinated course of action relating to a price increase to ensure its success by prior elimination of all uncertainty as to each other's conduct'.[310] However, '[a]s Professor Joliet pointed out, the judgment was not so much worrying because of its definition of a concerted practice but more because it so easily assumed, without a detailed study of the market characteristics and without evidence of concertation, that parties had cooperated. Although the Court recognized the need to consider the specific features of the market in weighing the evidence, . . . it only did so superficially'.[311]

c. *Suiker Unie* and *Züchner*

In both *Suiker Unie*[312] and *Züchner*[313] the ECJ stressed that Article 81(1) did not prevent an undertaking from adapting its behaviour intelligently to the existing or anticipated conduct of competitors. In accordance with these judgments the Commission, in *Zinc Producer's Group*,[314] accepted the legitimacy of parallel/oligopolistic behaviour. It held that:

parallel pricing behaviour in an oligopoly producing homogeneous goods [would] not in itself be sufficient evidence of a concerted practice.[315]

Thus, parallel action explicable in terms of barometric price leadership (that is to say, linked to a change in the market conditions, for example, an increase in the price of the main raw material) would not be sufficient evidence of a concerted practice.

d. *Wood Pulp*

The ECJ in *Re Wood Pulp Cartel: Ahlström Oy v. Commission (Wood Pulp II)*[316] delivered the clearest judgment on the relationship between conscious parallelism (or tacit collusion) and concerted practices. The Commission had investigated alleged restrictive practices and agreements between pulp producers operating on the bleached sulphate wood pulp market. The Commission found several breaches of Article 81(1) and levied fines on forty-three wood pulp

---

[309] Cases 48, 49, and 51–7/69 [1972] ECR 619, [1972] CMLR 557, para. 66; see Annex 4.

[310] *Ibid.*, para. 118.

[311] G. van Gerven and E. N. Varona, 'The Wood Pulp Case and the Future of Concerted Practices' (1994) 31 *CMLRev* 575, 590 and R. Joliet, 'La notion de pratique concertée et l'arrêt I.C.I. dans une perspective comparative' [1974] *CDE* 251.

[312] Cases 40–8, 50, 54–6, 111, and 113–4/73, *Re the European Sugar Cartel: Cooperatiëve Vereniging 'Suiker Unie' UA v. Commission* [1975] ECR 1663, [1976] 1 CMLR 295.

[313] Case 172/80, *Züchner v. Bayerische Vereinsbank* [1981] ECR 2021, [1982] 1 CMLR 313.

[314] [1984] OJ L220/27, [1985] 2 CMLR 108.

[315] *Ibid.*, paras. 75–6.

[316] Cases C-89, 104, 114, 116–17, and 125–9/85 [1993] ECR I-1307, [1993] 4 CMLR 407.

producers.[317] In particular, it found that concertation between many of the Finnish, US, and Canadian undertakings with regard to both announced and transaction prices in the pulp market had led to prices which were both artificially high and rigid. The Commission considered that the parallel behaviour was not explicable as rational behaviour.[318] It could not be explained as independently chosen parallel conduct in a narrow oligopolistic market (the market was characterized by a large number of producers, customers, and products; the market was not inherently transparent, but was only so as a result of the producers' deliberately chosen strategy of making price announcements in advance and there was no clear price leader etc.). The parties sought annulment of the Commission's decision before the ECJ.

The Court annulled much of the Commission's decision and many of the fines on substantive grounds. It considered two separate points: first whether or not the price announcements were in themselves prohibited by Article 81(1)[319] and secondly whether they provided evidence of a concerted practice and concertation in advanced prices.

The Court reiterated its previous statements that parallel conduct could not be used to establish the existence of a concerted practice unless, taking account of the nature of the products, the size and the number of undertakings, and the volume of the market in question, it could not be explained otherwise than by concertation. Parallel behaviour would furnish proof of concertation only where it constituted the only plausible explanation for such conduct. Every producer was free to react intelligently to market forces and to alter its course of action, taking into account in so doing the present or foreseeable conduct of his competitors.

The Court was not prepared to reject, as the Commission had done, the protestations that the undertaking's behaviour was a consequence, not of a concerted practice, but of non-collusive interdependence or conscious parallelism. It commissioned two independent reports from economic experts to analyse the wood pulp market and the evidence involved. The reports were extremely damaging to the Commission's case. On the facts and relying on experts' reports, the Court found that the system of quarterly price announcements did not, of itself, amount to an infringement of Article 81(1)[320] and that this system and the parallelism of announced prices were not evidence of concertation. It could not be conclusively stated that the system of advance price announcements and parallel behaviour was a result of a concerted practice. The Commission had failed sufficiently to appreciate that the wood pulp market had oligopolistic tendencies, being characterized by oligopolies and oligopsonies (on the buying side), in particular pulp types. Also the market was inherently transparent. Paper manufacturers were in constant touch with a number of pulp suppliers and exchanged price information amongst themselves and the transparency was reinforced both by a number of common agents that operated throughout the market and an active trade press.

The system of advanced announced prices was, therefore, explicable as a rational response to the fact that the pulp market was a long-term one and met a legitimate business concern of customers.

[317] [1985] OJ L85/1, [1985] 3 CMLR 474.

[318] Although the Commission relied on some documentary evidence to supplement its finding this was excluded by the Court.

[319] See infra 916–8.

[320] Ibid.

Cases C-89, 104, 114, 116–17 and 125–9/85, *Re Wood Pulp Cartel: Ahlström Oy* v. *Commission (Wood Pulp II)* [1993] ECR I-1307, [1993] 4 CMLR 407

Court of Justice

70. Since the Commission has no documents which directly establish the existence of concertation between the producers concerned, it is necessary to ascertain whether the system of quarterly price announcements, the simultaneity or near-simultaneity of the price announcements and the parallelism of price announcements as found during the period from 1975 to 1985 constitute a firm, precise and consistent body of evidence of prior concertation.

71. In determining the probative value of those different factors, it must be noted that parallel conduct cannot be regarded as furnishing proof of concertation unless concertation constitutes the only plausible explanation for such conduct. It is necessary to bear in mind that, although Article [81] . . . prohibits any form of collusion which distorts competition, it does not deprive economic operators of the right to adapt themselves intelligently to the existing and anticipated conduct of their competitors (see *Suiker Unie*, . . . paragraph 174).

72. Accordingly, it is necessary in this case to ascertain whether the parallel conduct alleged by the Commission cannot, taking account of the nature of the products, the size and the number of the undertakings and the volume of the market in question, be explained otherwise than by concertation.

. . .

126. Following that analysis, it must be stated that, in this case, concertation is not the only plausible explanation for the parallel conduct. To begin with, the system of price announcements may be regarded as constituting a rational response to the fact that the pulp market constituted a long-term market and to the need felt by both buyers and sellers to limit commercial risks. Further, the similarity in the dates of price announcements may be regarded as a direct result of the high degree of market transparency, which does not have to be described as artificial. Finally, the parallelism of prices and the price trends may be satisfactorily explained by the oligopolistic tendencies of the market and by the specific circumstances prevailing in certain periods. Accordingly, the parallel conduct established by the Commission does not constitute evidence of concertation.

127. In the absence of a firm, precise and consistent body of evidence, it must be held that concertation regarding announced prices has not been established by the Commission. Article 1(1) of the contested decision must therefore be annulled.

e. Conclusions on Article 81 and Parallel Behaviour

It is clear that purely parallel oligopolistic behaviour is not prohibited *per se* by Article 81(1). Rather, the requirement of concertation appears to demand *reciprocal* cooperation, through direct or indirect contact, designed to influence the conduct of an actual or potential competitor or to disclose to them the course of conduct that will or may be adopted on the market.[321]

Where direct evidence of reciprocal is not available, parallel behaviour may, however, furnish circumstantial proof of an agreement or concerted practice if it is not the kind of behaviour which would be anticipated on the market involved (whether the parallel conduct alleged by the Commission cannot, taking into account the nature of the products, the size and number of the

---

[321] See *supra* Chap. 3 and, e.g. see generally A. Albors-Lorens 'Horizontal Agreements and Concerted Practices in EC Competition Law: Unlawful and Legitimate Contacts between Competitors' [2006] 51 *Ant. Bull* 837 and A. Jones, 'Wood Pulp: Concerted Practice and/or Conscious Parallelism' [1993] *ECLR* 273, 275–6.

undertakings, and the volume of the market in question, be explained otherwise than by concertation) and if there is no other plausible explanation for the conduct.[322] In *Wood Pulp* the ECJ's judgment describes the market characteristics in meticulous detail. In particular, it seems clear that the number of undertakings on the market, the homogeneity of the product, and the transparency of the market will be relevant to the analysis. The market structure may, therefore, provide a plausible explanation for the behaviour. It can be seen from *Wood Pulp* itself that explanations may well be available outside a tight oligopoly situation.

It is unclear whether, on the proof of parallel behaviour, the burden shifts onto the accused to establish that there *is* a plausible explanation for the conduct. In *Wood Pulp*, the Advocate General appeared to consider that '[t]he burden of proof cannot be shifted simply by a finding of parallel conduct. Unless the Court can be satisfied by a set of presumptions having a solid basis, concertation is not established'.[323] If, as seems correct, the onus does not shift it is impossible to imagine how the Commission (or any other) could establish that there is no other plausible explanation for the parallel conduct. It would thus seem inadvisable to rely solely on economic evidence to establish the existence of a cartel. Rather, other evidence should be used to corroborate a case.[324] Indeed, in *Cartonboard* the Commission stated:

Had they been challenged, the producers could as a result of this elaborate scheme of deception have attributed the series of uniform, regular and industry-wide price increases in the cartonboard sector to the phenomenon of 'oligopoly behaviour'. They could argue that it made sense for all the producers to decide of their own volition to copy an increase initiated by one or other of the market leaders as soon as it became publicly known; unlawful collusion as such would not necessarily be indicated. Customers might well suspect and even accuse them of operating a cartel; and given the relatively large number of producers, economic theory would be stretched to its limits and beyond, but unless direct proof of collusion were forthcoming—and they went to some lengths to ensure it was not—the producers must have had hopes of defeating any investigation into their pricing conduct by the competition authorities by invoking the defence of oligopolistic interdependence.[325]

(iii) Concerted Practices and Unilateral Price Announcements in Advance

Price announcements in advance on a market may signal to other players on the market what a firm's future price policy will be and may facilitate alignment of their behaviour and tacit collusion on an oligopolistic market. Could price announcements in advance constitute indirect contact with a competitor sufficient to establish a concerted practice to fix prices? In *Dyestuffs*, the ECJ considered that advance price communications provided, in the circumstances, proof of a concerted practice. It held that the announcements rendered the market artificially transparent and eliminated all uncertainty between the operators as regards the rates of increase, future conduct, and the risks inherent in an independent change of conduct. The Court commented:

... the undertakings taking the initiative ... announced their intentions of making an increase some time in advance, which allowed the undertakings to observe each other's reactions on the different

---

[322] See *supra* 915.

[323] [1993] ECR I-1307, [1993] 4 CMLR 407, Darmon AG, para. 195.

[324] Cartel members thus have a strategic advantage in cartel investigations in the sense that, if guilty, they can nonetheless destroy incriminating evidence making the detection, prosecution, and final repression of the cartel extremely difficult.

[325] *Cartonboard* [1994] OJ L243/1, [1994] 5 CMLR 547, para. 73.

markets, and to adapt themselves accordingly. By means of these advance announcements the various undertakings eliminated all uncertainty between them as to their future conduct and, in doing so, also eliminated a large part of the risk usually inherent in any independent change of conduct on one or several markets. This was all the more the case since these announcements, which led to the fixing of general and equal increases in prices for the markets in dyestuffs, rendered the market transparent as regard the percentage rates of increase. Therefore, by the way in which they acted, the undertakings in question temporarily eliminated with respect to prices some of the preconditions for competition on the market which stood in the way of the achievement of parallel uniformity of conduct.[326]

This case must now be assessed in the light of its own particular facts and the judgment of the ECJ in *Wood Pulp*. In the latter case the Commission found concertation in respect of both announced and actual transaction prices. The ECJ, however, held that price announcements in advance did not, *per se*, constitute an infringement of Article 81(1).

64. In this case, the communications arise from the price announcements made to users. They constitute in themselves market behaviour which does not lessen each undertaking's uncertainty as to the future attitude of its competitors. At the same time when each undertaking engages in such behaviour, it cannot be sure of the future conduct of the others.

65. Accordingly, the system of quarterly price announcements on the pulp market is not to be regarded as constituting in itself an infringement of Article [81](1).

Further, the Court held that it had not been established that the system amounted to a means of indirect communication between the competitors. The announcements served the need of customers desiring the information to plan the cost of their paper products. This provided a plausible or alternative explanation for the parallel behaviour (see the discussion on parallel behaviour *supra*).

In the light of these two cases it is conceivable that, where advanced price announcements or other price signalling do not correspond to a legitimate business justification, the conduct might amount to indirect contact between the undertakings and an illegitimate concerted practice prohibited by Article 81.[327]

G. van Gerven and E. N. Varona, 'The Wood Pulp Case and the Future of Concerted Practices' (1994) 31 *CMLRev* 575, 595

It is clear that in deciding whether price signalling is illegal, one should not overlook the circumstances. In the *Wood pulp* case, it was established that (i) there was a clear lawful business justification for advance price communications, since the price of wood pulp constituted a major proportion of the cost of paper and it was the paper producers themselves which had requested prior announcement; (ii) the announcements were made to customers. If, given the high transparency of the market, firms become aware of the prospective pricing of their competitors, so be it. If a rival adapts its pricing to the information it has obtained, it merely 'adapts intelligently to existing or anticipated conduct of its competitors' as allowed by the *Dyestuffs* and *Suiker Unie* judgments.

---

[326] Cases 48, 49, and 51–7/69, *ICI v. Commission (Dyestuffs)* [1972] ECR 619, [1972] CMLR 557, paras. 100–3.

[327] See the Opinion of Darmon AG in Cases C-89, 104, 114, 116–17, and 125–9/85, *Re Wood Pulp Cartel: Ahlström Oy v. Commission(Wood Pulp II)* [1993] ECR I-1307, [1993] 4 CMLR 407, para. 251. For greater discussion, see G. van Gerven and E. N. Varona, 'The Wood Pulp Case and the Future of Concerted Practices' (1994) 31 *CMLRev* 575.

> Firstly, as Advocate Darmon pointed out in his opinion, if price signalling does not correspond to a legitimate business justification, such advance announcements may very well be considered as an illegal exchange of information. In the end, as so often in antitrust law, the decisive question in practice may be whether there is a valid business reason for the particular market conduct. In the *Wood pulp* judgment, the Court had no difficulty finding such a valid business reason for the price announcements and, therefore, it was easy and correct to conclude that the system of price announcements did not give rise to a concerted practice. However, price signalling, if not warranted by any legitimate explanation and clearly not in the individual (non-collusive) self-interest of the individual companies may constitute sufficient evidence of concertation.
>
> Secondly, in *Wood pulp*, it appeared that the trade press was also very rapidly informed of the advance price announcements but the Court went out of its way to state that most of the wood pulp producers did not send as a matter of course their announced prices to the trade press and that if, sporadically, this was done, such communications were made at the request of the press. Thus the Court implicitly rejected the Commission's claim that wood pulp producers had deliberately made the market transparent or increased transparency by talking to the press.

In the *Cartonboard* case, where the producers, twice a year, announced price increases several months in advance, the Commission took care to produce documentary evidence establishing that the undertakings had agreed the date and sequence of advance price increases.

The Commission will inevitably be sensitive to attempts by oligopolists to make the market artificially more transparent than it otherwise would be. The section above indicates that agreements which have this effect may violate Article 81(1).

B. OLIGOPOLY AND ARTICLE 82

(i) 'One or More Undertakings'

a. Introduction

It has been seen in Chapter 5 that Article 82 prohibits as incompatible with the common market, in so far as trade between Member States is affected, '[a]ny abuse by one or more undertakings of a dominant position'. Article 82 thus lends itself to a broad interpretation, and the view that Article 82 might be used both to control the behaviour of a single undertaking that is 'dominant', and also 'abuses' by duopolists or oligopolists which 'collectively' hold a dominant position on a market. Despite early doubts, it is now well established that Article 82 does apply to independent undertakings that collectively hold a dominant position on the market. The answer to the question of what exactly constitutes a collective dominant position and how it is established has, however, had a long and rather tortuous evolution.

b. The Acceptance of a Concept of Collective or Joint Dominance[328]—the Judgment in *Flat Glass*

In Chapter 5 it was explained that, initially at least, it was believed that the term 'one or more undertakings' referred only to bodies which were within the same corporate group or which

---

[328] The terms collective, joint, and oligopolistic dominance are used interchangeably. See generally on this subject R. Whish, 'Collective Dominance' in D. O'Keefe and M. Andenas (eds.), *Liber Amicorum for Lord Slynn* (Kluwer, 2000) and J. Temple-Lang, 'Oligopolies and Joint dominance in Community Antitrust Law' [2002] *Fordham Corp L Inst* (ed. B. E. Hawk), chap. 12.

formed part of the same economic entity.[329] In *Hoffmann La-Roche* v. *Commission*, the ECJ stated:

A dominant position must also be distinguished from parallel courses of conduct which are peculiar to oligopolies in that in an oligopoly the courses of conduct interact, while in the case of an undertaking occupying a dominant position the conduct of the undertaking which derives profits from that position is to a great extent determined unilaterally.[330]

Such an interpretation would, however, have been inconsistent with the interpretation of the term 'undertaking' adopted for the purposes of Article 81[331] and in *Flat Glass* the CFI confirmed that the term 'undertaking' had the same meaning within the context of both Article 82 and 81. Article 82 could apply where a dominant position was held collectively by one or more *economically independent* undertakings. Article 82 was not confined to the activities of one or more undertakings within the same corporate group.

Cases T-68, 77, and 78/89, *Società Italiana Vetro SpA* v. *Commission* ('*Flat Glass*') [1992] ECR II-1403, [1992] 5 CMLR 302

In *Flat Glass* the Commission found that three Italian producers of flat glass had all infringed Article 81(1) (by concluding agreements to fix prices and sales quotas for their products, etc.) and infringed Article 82 by abusing their collective dominant position (although the Commission did not adduce any evidence to establish the latter infringement above that relied on to establish the breach of Article 81).[332] On appeal, the Court of First Instance quashed the Commission's decision that there had been an abuse of a joint dominant position. It was not sufficient simply to recycle the facts constituting an infringement of Article 81 in order to deduce that their behaviour constituted an abuse of a collective dominant position.

The Court, however, finally expressed its view that Article 82 could apply to independent undertakings and that Article 82 was not confined to the activities of one or more undertakings within the same corporate group.

Court of First Instance

357. The Court notes that the very words of the first paragraph of Article [82] provide that 'one or more undertakings' may abuse a dominant position. It has consistently been held, as indeed all the parties acknowledge, that the concept of agreement or concerted practice between undertakings does not cover agreements or concerted practices among undertakings belonging to the same group if the undertakings form an economic unit . . . It follows that when Article [81] refers to agreements or concerted practices between 'undertakings', it is referring to relations between two or more economic entities which are capable of competing with one another.

---

[329] Case 85/76, *Hoffmann-La Roche* v. *Commission* [1979] ECR 461, [1979] 3 CMLR 211, para. 39.

[330] *Ibid.*

[331] Case 15/74, *Centrafarm* v. *Sterling Drug* [1974] ECR 1147, [1974] 2 CMLR 480, para. 41, repeated in Case 30/87, *Bodson* v. *Pompes Funèbres des Régions Libérées* [1988] ECR 2479, [1989] 4 CMLR 984, para. 19. See discussion *supra* in Chap. 3.

[332] [1989] OJ L33/44, [1990] 4 CMLR 535.

358. The Court considers that there is no legal or economic reason to suppose that the term 'undertaking' in Article [82] has a different meaning from the one given to it in the context of Article [81]. There is nothing in principle, to prevent two or more independent economic entities from being, on a specific market, united by such economic links that, by virtue of that fact, together they hold a dominant position *vis-à-vis* the other operators on the same market. This could be the case, for example, where two or more independent undertakings jointly have, through agreements or licences, a technological lead affording them the power to behave to an appreciable extent independently of their competitors, their customers and ultimately of their consumers (*Hoffmann-La Roche* [Case 102/77, [1978] ECR 1139], paragraphs [38] and [48]).

359. The Court finds support for that interpretation in the wording of Article 8 of Council Regulation 4065/86 . . . laying down detailed rules for the application of Articles [81] and [82] [EC] to maritime transport. Article 8(2) provides that the conduct of a liner conference benefiting from an exemption from a prohibition laid down by Article [81(1)] [EC] may have effects which are incompatible with Article [82] [EC]. A request by a conference to be exempted from the prohibition laid down by Article [81(1)] necessarily presupposes an agreement between two or more independent economic undertakings.

The Court thus clearly held in paragraph 358 that there is nothing, in principle, to prevent two or more independent economic entities from being, on a specific market, united by such economic links that, by virtue of that fact, together they hold a dominant position *vis-à-vis* the other operators on the same market. The Court gave examples of when such economic links would exist, for example, where two or more independent undertakings jointly have, through agreements or licences, a technological lead affording them the power to behave to an appreciable extent independently of their competitors, their customers, and ultimately of their consumer.

The judgment, despite recognizing that a collective dominant position can be held by independent economic entities, was not, however, as helpful as it might have been. The requirement in paragraph 358 that the entities be united by '*economic links*' arguably supports a wide view of Article 82. Such links might, for example, be derived from the structure of the market which dictates that the undertakings operating upon it may tacitly collude.[333] However, the Court, by subsequently referring to 'agreements or licences' operating between independent undertakings as an example of economic links, cast doubt on this broad view. The reference to such contractual, structural or more tangible links between the parties caused speculation that Article 82 would not apply unless something *more* than mutual interdependence existed between the undertakings, perhaps an agreement or some other special relationship between the parties. This latter narrower view of the concept was supported by the Court's reliance on Article 8(2) of Council Regulation 4056/86 which provides that Article 82 may be applied to agreements between undertakings even though they have been exempted under the Regulation.[334]

If this latter position had been the correct one it is hard to see how much the concept of an abuse of a joint or collective dominant position could usefully have added to the Commission's

---

[333] [1986] OJ L378/1. See discussion of the kind of markets on which might be prone to collusion between undertakings, *supra* 862–5.

[334] [1986] OJ L378/1. This Council Regulation lays down the substantive and procedural rules for the application of Articles 81 and 82 to maritime transport services from or to a Community port (excluding tramp vessel services). Part of the Regulation (see especially Article 3) provides exemption for 'liner conference agreements' from the Article 81(1) prohibition. Article 8(2) of the Regulation provides that the Commission may withdraw the benefit of the block exemption where it considers that an agreement benefiting from it has effects incompatible with Article 82 and take measures to bring the infringement to an end.

armoury. Agreements between undertakings could, in any event, be controlled under Article 81 (the concept would be useful only to act against agreements between the undertakings which fall outside Article 81(1) or which meet the Article 81(3) criteria). It seemed unlikely, therefore, that the Court intended to confine the term 'economic links' to circumstances in which an agreement existed between the undertakings. Nonetheless, the judgment left it far from clear what exactly it did mean when it said that the undertakings should be united by 'economic links'. Although the Commission decisions and Court judgments delivered soon after *Flat Glass* did not add much clarity to the picture, subsequent case law now confirms that both Article 82 and the ECMR will apply where the only link between the parties is the 'economic interdependence' which independent undertakings have with each other on an oligopolistic market.

b. The Development of the Concept of Collective Dominance under Article 82

The early authorities proceeded cautiously. In a series of decisions, the Commission applied the concept of collective dominance to undertakings which were bound together by contractual links. For example, in three cases, *French-West African Shipowners' Committees*,[335] *CEWAL*,[336] and *Trans-Atlantic Conference Agreement* (TACA),[337] the Commission used collective dominance in relation to shipowners that were members of liner conferences, and which had concluded agreements regulating the operation of trade on shipping routes. In *French-West African Shipowners' Committees*,[338] for example, the Commission imposed fines on shipowners that had participated in cargo-sharing systems on routes between France and eleven West African States. The Committee monitored the quota systems and imposed penalties on those that exceeded the quotas without approval. The Commission found that the agreements infringed Article 81(1)[339] and could not be exempted under Article 81(3).[340] In addition, the Commission considered that the shipowners had infringed Article 82. As a result of the conference, the shipowners had presented themselves with a united front to shippers and, consequently, the position of the shipowners on the market for cargo between France and the eleven African States had to be assessed collectively. Since the committees had been set up by a group of shipowners covering virtually the entire market, the agreement resulted in the creation of a collective dominant position to their advantage. Their practices, which endeavoured to eliminate effective competition for non-committee shipping lines, also constituted an abuse of a dominant position within the meaning of Article 82(b) by limiting the supply of liner services available to shippers.[341]

---

[335] [1992] OJ L134/1, [1993] 5 CMLR 446.

[336] [1993] OJ L34/20, [1995] 5 CMLR 198. The finding of collective dominance was upheld on appeal: Cases T-24/93 etc., *Compagnie Maritime Belge Transports SA v. Commission* [1996] ECR II-1201, [1997] 4 CMLR 273 and Cases C-395 and 396/96 P, *Compagnie Maritime Belge Transports SA v. Commission* [2000] ECR I-1365, [2000] 4 CMLR 1076.

[337] *Transatlantic Conference Agreement* [1999] OJ L95/1, [1999] 4 CMLR 1415: on appeal, Case T-191/98. 30 Sept. 2003.

[338] [1992] OJ L134/1, [1993] 5 CMLR 446.

[339] The object and effect of the agreements was to share markets amongst the members and to limit the supply of transport services available, contrary to Article 81(1)(c) and (b) respectively.

[340] Further, and because the objective of the agreements was not to fix common rates of the participants, it did not fall within the terms of the block exemption dealing with 'liner conferences' in Regulation 4056/86 (the Regulation provides a block exemption for carriers providing international carrier services that agree to operate on particular routes under certain terms and conditions).

[341] Both the practice of imposing penalties on shipowners which had exceeded their quotas and the application of conditions protecting their own interests against those of newcomers wishing to serve the routes infringed Article 82.

Similarly, in both *CEWAL* (on appeal *Compagnie Maritime Belge*) and *TACA*[342] the Commission found that members of a liner conference were collectively dominant on certain shipping routes between ports in Northern Europe and Zaïre, and Northern Europe and the US/Canada respectively. In these cases the agreements enabled the undertakings to present a 'united front' to shippers and were crucial to the finding of a collective dominant position. Although it does not seem that it was strictly necessary to use Article 82, since Article 81 was applicable (Article 82 would only have been vital had the agreement been block exempted under Article 3 of Regulation No. 4056/86), the cases fitted neatly within CFI's formulation in *Flat Glass*. The parties were undoubtedly united by 'economic links'.[343] In *Irish Sugar*[344] the Commission found Irish Sugar and one of its distributors to be collectively dominant. In this case the producer and the distributor were linked *vertically* by agreements and other factors which created a clear parallelism of interest, such as a significant equity holding which Irish Sugar held in the distributor.

In *Almelo*, the ECJ stated that 'in order for such a collective dominant position to exist, the undertakings in the group must be linked in such a way that they adopt the same conduct on the market'.[345] This interpretation lent support to the view that the purpose of requiring links between the undertakings is simply to determine whether the parties are likely to engage in a coordinated course of conduct on the market (such as tacit collusion). However, the judgment did not elaborate on what links were necessary between undertakings before they could be found, collectively, to hold a dominant position on the market so did not clarify the position.

Since *Almelo*, however, the Court has developed the concept of collective dominance in a series of cases adopted in the context of both the ECMR and Article 82. Before going on to consider the latter, the developments that have occurred within the sphere of the ECMR are outlined as they are also relevant to the interpretation of Article 82.[346]

C. Collective Dominance and the Merger Regulation

The discussion in this Chapter has indicated that even in the absence of explicit collusion, oligopolistic markets might not deliver the low prices and efficient outcome that is expected on competitive markets. Rather, firms may be able to tacitly coordinate their behaviour and earn supra-competitive profits (coordinated effects)[347] or increase price and restrict output in response to a merger which makes the market more concentrated (non-coordinated effects). The question of whether the ECMR authorizes the Commission to prevent mergers which

---

[342] [1999] OJ L95/1, [1999] 4 CMLR 1415. The Commission found that the TACA members held a collective dominant position on the relevant market and that they abused that collective dominant position between 1994 and 1996, first, by entering into an agreement to place restrictions on the availability and content of service contracts and secondly by altering the competitive structure of the market so as to reinforce the TACA's dominant position. It imposed substantial fines which were annulled on appeal, see Cases T-191 and 214–16/98, *Atlantic Container Line AB v. Commission* [2003] ECR II-3275, [2005] 4 CMLR 20.

[343] See *French-West African Shipowners' Committees* [1992] OJ L134/1, [1993] 5 CMLR 446.

[344] [1997] OJ L25/1, [1997] 5 CMLR 668. The CFI upheld the finding of collective dominance: Case T-228/97, *Irish Sugar plc v. Commission* [1999] ECR II-2969, [1999] 5 CMLR 1300.

[345] 'It is for the national court to consider whether there exist between the regional electricity distributors in the Netherlands links which are sufficiently strong for there to be a collective dominant position in a substantial part of the common market', Case C-393/92, *Almelo v. NV Energiebedrijf Ijsselmij* [1994] ECR I-1477, paras. 42–3. This interpretation was reiterated by the Court on a number of occasions, see, e.g., Case C-96/94, *Centro Servizi Spediporto Srl v. Spedizioni Marittima de Glofo Srl* [1995] ECR I-2883, [1996] 4 CMLR 613, Case C-70/95 *Sodeamare SA v. Regione Lombardia* [1997] ECR I-3395, [1997] 3 CMLR 591, and in Cases T-24/93 etc., *Compagnie Maritime Belge Transports SA v. Commission* [1996] ECR II-1201, [1997] 4 CMLR 273, but see the ruling of the ECJ, *infra* 924–6.

[346] The ECMR developments are of course also discussed in greater detail in Chap. 12.

[347] These markets are also easy to cartelize and may make explicit collusion more likely.

might result in these effects has thus been of critical importance. Prior to substantive changes introduced to the ECMR in 2004,[348] it seemed possible that the ECMR could not prevent mergers which would result in unilateral effects.[349] The ECMR was, however, interpreted in a way which authorized the Commission to prevent mergers which would lead to coordinated effects by construing it to prohibit mergers which would lead to the creation or strengthening of a *collective* dominant position (and not just the creation or strengthening of a dominant position held individually by one firm).[350]

Although the wording of the Regulation, as originally drafted, made it unclear whether or not it authorized the prohibition of mergers leading to the creation or strengthening of a collective dominant position,[351] the Commission, undeterred by this ambiguity, took the view that it did so apply and applied it to such situations almost from the outset.[352] This view was upheld by the ECJ in *France v. Commission, Société Commerciale des Potasses et de l'Azote v. Commission*.[353] The Court held that the ECMR did preclude mergers which 'lead to a situation in which effective competition in the relevant market is significantly impeded by the undertakings involved in the concentration and one or more other undertakings which together, in particular because of factors giving rise to a connection between them, are able to adopt a common policy on the market and act to a considerable extent independently of their competitors, customers, and also of consumers'.[354]

Like *Almelo*, this judgment did not clarify whether or not the merger provisions would apply to the creation of collective dominance in the absence of contractual or other, more formal, structural links between the 'collectively dominant' undertakings operating on the market. This point, which was critical to the success of the provisions, was finally resolved in *Gencor Ltd v. Commission*[355] where the CFI confirmed that such links between the undertakings were not necessary for a finding of collective dominance. Rather, a 'relationship of interdependence existing between the parties to a tight oligopoly' which would make alignment of conduct likely constituted an economic link sufficient for a finding of collective dominance. In *Airtours plc v. Commission*[356] the CFI built on *Gencor* stating that a collective dominant position would exist where each member of a dominant oligopoly would 'consider it possible, economically rational, and hence preferable, to adopt on a lasting basis a common policy on the market with the aim of selling at above competitive prices, without having to enter into an agreement or resort to a concerted practice within the meaning of Article 81 . . .'. It considered that a finding of collective dominance could be established if: first, each firm knew how other members were behaving (they could monitor the market to see if they were adopting the common policy); secondly, tacit co-ordination was sustainable over time, (i.e., there was not an incentive to depart from the common policy on the market); and thirdly, the foreseeable reactions of

---

[348] Reg. 4064/89 [1989] OJ L395/1, as amended by Reg. 1310/97 [1997] OJ L180/1. This Regulation has now been replaced by Reg. 139/2004, [2004] OJ L24/1.

[349] See *infra* Chap. 12.

[350] The meaning and interpretation of collective dominance has therefore also been of central importance to the ECMR. Under the new substantive test set out in the ECMR the concept of collective dominance may no longer be so important, see *infra* Chap. 12.

[351] See *infra* Chap. 12.

[352] Case IV/M190, *Nestlé/Perrier* [1992] OJ L356/1 discussed *infra* Chap. 12.

[353] Cases C-68/94 and C-30/95 [1998] ECR I-1375, [1998] 4 CMLR 829, para. 178 (Commission decision, Case IV/M308 [1994] OJ L186/30).

[354] *Ibid.*, para. 221.

[355] Case T-102/96, *Gencor Ltd v. Commission* [1999] 4 CMLR 971.

[356] Case T-342/99, [2002] ECR II-2585, [2002] 5 CMLR 317. See also, Case T-464/04, *Independent Music Publishers and Labels Association (Impala) v. Commission* [2006] ECR II-2289, [2006] 5 CMLR 19 discussed below.

competitors (actual and potential) and customers would not jeopardize the results expected from the common policy.

In the context of the ECMR therefore, it is clear that a collective dominant position would be created where the market structure would provoke the undertakings *to align their conduct* on the market; and where the links between the undertakings are such that tacit coordination on the market could be expected.

d. Alignment of the Tests: The Judgments in *Irish Sugar, Compagnie Maritime Belge, Taca* and *Laurent Piau*

Although the concept of collective dominance may, argrably, be of less importance in the context of the new ECMR (as the Commission now has power to prohibit a merger which significantly impedes effective competition in the common market, even if it does not lead to the creation or strengthening of a dominant position), the ECMR cases on collective dominance remain of acute relevance to Article 82 and as it now seems clear that the concept is interpreted in the same way under both provisions. In *Gencor* the Court based its ruling upon the interpretation of the concept of collective dominance set out in the judgment of the CFI in *Flat Glass* (an Article 82 case).[357] Similarly, in *Irish Sugar plc* v. *Commission*[358] (an Article 82 case) the CFI relied on the ECJ's ruling in *France* v. *Commission, Société Commerciale des Potasses et de l'Azote* v. *Commission*[359] for its finding that:

a joint dominant position consists in a number of undertakings being able together, in particular because of factors giving rise to a connection between them, to adopt a common policy on the market and act to a considerable extent independently of their competitors, their customers, and ultimately consumers (Joined Cases C-68/94 and C-30/95 *France and Others* v. *Commission* [1998] ECR I-1375, paragraph 221).[360]

In both *Compagnie Maritime Belge* and *TACA* the ECJ and CFI respectively relied on the Court's ECMR ruling in *France* v. *Commission* when defining collective dominance for the purposes of Article 82. The *Compagnie Maritime Belge* judgment devotes a number of paragraphs to the meaning and means of establishing the existence of collective dominance.

Cases C-395 and 396/96 P, *Compagnie Maritime Belge Transports SA* v. *Commission* [2000] ECR I-1365, [2000] 4 CMLR 1076

Court of Justice

35. In terms of Article [82] of the Treaty, a dominant position may be held by several 'undertakings'. The Court of Justice has held, on many occasions, that the concept of 'undertaking' in the

---

[357] *Ibid.*, para. 273.

[358] In *Irish Sugar* [1997] OJ L258/1, [1997] 5 CMLR 666, the Commission fined Irish Sugar for a number of breaches of Article 82 of the Treaty. In particular, it found seven individual abuses by Irish Sugar on the market in granulated sugar intended for retail and for industry in Ireland. However, it found that for a period of 5 years some of the breaches had been of a collective dominant position held with a distributor. The decision imposed a fine of €8,800,000. The CFI upheld the finding of collective dominance: Case T-228/97, *Irish Sugar plc* v. *Commission* [1999] ECR II-2969, [1999] 5 CMLR 1300.

[359] Cases C-68/94 and C-30/95, [1998] ECR I-1375, [1998] 4 CMLR 829.

[360] Case T-228/97, *Irish Sugar plc* v. *Commission* [1999] ECR II-2969, [1999] 5 CMLR 1300, para. 46.

chapter of the Treaty devoted to the rules on competition presupposes the economic independence of the entity concerned (see, in particular, Case 22/71 *Béguelin Import* v. *G.L. Import Export* [1971] ECR 949).

36. It follows that the expression 'one or more undertakings, in Article [82] of the Treaty implies that a dominant position may be held by two or more economic entities legally independent of each other, provided that from an economic point of view they present themselves or act together on a particular market as a collective entity. That is how the expression 'collective dominant position', as used in the remainder of this judgment, should be understood.

37. However, a finding that an undertaking has a dominant position is not in itself a ground of criticism but simply means that, irrespective of the reasons for which it has such a dominant position, the undertaking concerned has a special responsibility not to allow its conduct to impair genuine undistorted competition on the common market (see *Michelin*, paragraph 57).

38. The same applies as regards undertakings which hold a collective dominant position. A finding that two or more undertakings hold a collective dominant position must, in principle, proceed upon an economic assessment of the position on the relevant market of the undertakings concerned, prior to any examination of the question whether those undertakings have abused their position on the market.

39. So, for the purposes of analysis under Article [82] of the Treaty, it is necessary to consider whether the undertakings concerned together constitute a collective entity *vis-à-vis* their competitors, their trading partners and consumers on a particular market. It is only where that question is answered in the affirmative that it is appropriate to consider whether that collective entity actually holds a dominant position and whether its conduct constitutes abuse.

40. In the contested judgment, the Court of First Instance was careful to examine separately those three elements, namely the collective position, the dominant position and the abuse of such a position.

41. In order to establish the existence of a collective entity as defined above, it is necessary to examine the economic links or factors which give rise to a connection between the undertakings concerned (see, *inter alia*, Case C-393/92 *Almelo* [1994] ECR I-1477, paragraph 43, and Joined Cases C-68/94 and C-30/95 *France and Others* v. *Commission* [1998] ECR I-1375, paragraph 221).

42. In particular, it must be ascertained whether economic links exist between the undertakings concerned which enable them to act together independently of their competitors, their customers and consumers (see *Michelin*).

43. The mere fact that two or more undertakings are linked by an agreement, a decision of associations of undertakings or a concerted practice within the meaning of Article [81](1) of the Treaty does not, of itself, constitute a sufficient basis for such a finding.

44. On the other hand, an agreement, decision or concerted practice (whether or not covered by an exemption under Article [81(3)] of the Treaty) may undoubtedly, where it is implemented, result in the undertakings concerned being so linked as to their conduct on a particular market that they present themselves on that market as a collective entity *vis-à-vis* their competitors, their trading partners and consumers.

45. The existence of a collective dominant position may therefore flow from the nature and terms of an agreement, from the way in which it is implemented and, consequently, from the links or factors which give rise to a connection between undertakings which result from it. Nevertheless, the existence of an agreement or of other links in law is not indispensable to a finding of a collective dominant position; such a finding may be based on other connecting factors and would depend on an economic assessment and, in particular, on an assessment of the structure of the market in question.

926 | EC COMPETITION LAW

Not only does this judgment follow the pattern of earlier cases of not distinguishing between cases on collective dominance decided under Article 82 and those decided under the ECMR, but it supports the view that, as in ECMR cases, formal links (e.g., contractual links) between the parties will be unnecessary to a finding of collective dominance.

The Court starts by spelling out that a dominant position within the meaning of Article 82 can be held by two or more undertakings provided that they *present themselves or act together on a particular market as a collective entity*. It then states that the proof of the existence of a collective dominant position involves a two-stage process: it is necessary first to establish the existence of a collective entity and then, where the position is established, to establish that the collective entity holds a dominant position.

It was when discussing the means of establishing the existence of a collective entity that the Court relied on the ruling in *Almelo* and its own ruling in the merger case, *France v. Commission*. These cases establish the necessity of 'economic links or factors which give rise to a connection between the undertakings concerned'. The Court held that such links could, but would not necessarily, be established by an agreement, decision, or concerted practice within the meaning of Article 81 concluded by the undertakings (even if exempted from the prohibition in Article 81(1) by Article 81(3)). The CEWAL agreement did in fact provide the requisite links. The Court stressed, however, in paragraph 45 that 'the existence of an agreement or of other links in law is not indispensable to a finding of a collective dominant position; such a finding may be based on other connecting factors and would depend on an economic assessment and, in particular, on an assessment of the structure of the market in question'. This indicates that, as the CFI held in both *Gencor* and *Airtours*,[361] undertakings which are able to engage in a parallel manner on a market by tacitly coordinating their behaviour, may be found collectively to hold a dominant position on a market.

This view receives support from the CFI judgments in *Atlantic Container Lines AB v. Commission* (TACA)[362] and *Laurent Piau v. Commission*.[363] In the *TACA* case there were again contractual links in place between the parties, and the CFI held that these links (a tariff, enforcement provisions and penalties, a secretariat and annual business plans of the TACA) were 'capable of justifying a collective assessment of the position on the relevant market of the members of that conference for the purposes of the application of Article [82] of the Treaty, in so far as those links are such as to allow them to adopt together, as a single entity which presents itself as such on the market vis-à-vis users and competitors, the same line of conduct on that market'.[364] However, it gave support for a broad view of the links required to establish a finding of collective dominance by relying on both ECMR and Article 82 cases. It concluded that for a collective dominant position to exist:[365]

the undertakings concerned must ... be sufficiently linked between themselves to adopt the same line of action on the market (*Centro Servizi Spediporto* ... , paragraph 33; *DIP and Others*, paragraph 26; Joined Cases C-68/94 and C-30/95 *France and Others* v. *Commission* (*Kali und Salz*) [1998] ECR I-1375, paragraph 221; Case C-309/99 *Wouters and Others* [2002] ECR I-1577, paragraph 113; and

---

361 *Supra* 923–4.

362 Cases T-191 and 214–216/98, *Atlantic Container Line AB v. Commission* [2003] ECR II-3275, [2005] 4 CMLR 20, para. 602.

363 Case T-193/02, *Laurent Piau v. Commission* [2005] ECR II-209, [2005] 5 CMLR 2.

364 Cases T-191 and 214–216, 198, [2003] ECR II-3275, [2005] 4 CMLR 20 para. 602.

365 *Ibid.*, para. 595. The Court also considered that the fact that the parties had not always adopted the same policy on the market did not negate the finding of collective dominance. There was 'no need to show that those undertakings have in fact all adopted that common policy in all circumstances', para. 631 relying on Case C-30/95, *France and others v. Commission* (*Kali und Salz*) [1998] ECR I-1375, para. 221.

CEWAL I . . . , paragraph 62). In that regard, it is necessary to examine the links or factors of economic correlation between the undertakings concerned and to ascertain whether those links or factors allow them to act together independently of their competitors, their customers and consumers (*Almelo*, cited at paragraph 594 above, paragraph 43; *Kali und Salz*, cited above, paragraph 221; Joined Cases C-395/96 P and C-396/96 P *Compagnie maritime belge transports and Others* v. *Commission (CEWAL II)* [2000] ECR I-1365, paragraphs 41 and 42; and *Wouters . . .* , paragraph 114).

More clearly the CFI in *Laurent Piau* stated in paragraph 111, relying on *Airtours*, that '[t]hree cumulative conditions must be met for a finding of collective dominance: first, each member of the dominant oligopoly must have the ability to know how the other members are behaving in order to monitor whether or not they are adopting the common policy; second, the situation of tacit coordination must be sustainable over time, that is to say, there must be an incentive not to depart from the common policy on the market; thirdly, the foreseeable reaction of current and future competitors, as well as of consumers, must not jeopardise the results expected from the common policy.' This approach is reinforced by the Commission in its Article 82 Discussion Paper on the application of Article 82 to exclusionary abuses.[366]

DG Competition Discussion Paper on the application of Article 82 of the Treaty to exclusionary abuses, December 2005

44. For collective dominance to exist under Article 82, two or more undertakings must from an economic point of view present themselves or act together on a particular market as a collective entity. It is not required that the undertakings concerned adopt identical conduct on the market in every respect. What matters is that they are able to adopt a common policy on the market and act to a considerable extent independently of their competitors, their customers, and also of consumers.

45. In order to establish the existence of such a collective entity on the market, it is necessary to examine the factors that giver rise to a connection between the undertakings concerned, Such factors may flow from the nature and terms of an agreement between the undertakings in question or from the way in which it is implemented, provided that the agreement leads the undertakings in question to present themselves or act together as a collective entity. This may, for instance, be the case if undertakings have concluded cooperation agreements that lead them to co-ordinate their conduct on the market. It may also be the case if ownership interests and other links in law lead the undertakings concerned to co-ordinate.

46. However, the existence of an agreement or of other links in law is not indispensable to a finding of a collective dominant position. Such a finding may be based on other connecting factors and depends on an economic assessment and, in particular, on an assessment of the structure of the market in question. It follows that the structure of the market and the way in which undertakings interact on the market may give rise to a finding of collective dominance.

47. Undertakings in oligopolistic markets may sometimes be able to raise prices substantially above the competitive level without having recourse to any explicit agreement or concerted practice. Coordination is more likely to emerge in markets where it is relatively simple to reach a common understanding on the terms of coordination. The simpler and more stable the economic environment, the easier it is for undertakings to reach a common understanding. Indeed, they may be able to coordinate their behaviour on the market by observing and reacting to each other's behaviour. In other words, they may be able to adopt a common strategy that allows them to present themselves or act together as a collective entity. Coordination may take various forms.

---

[366] See DG Competition Discussion Paper on the application of Article 82 of the Treaty to exclusionary abuses, December 2005, especially paras. 48–50 (which rely on *Airtours* and *Laurent Piau* for authority).

In some markets, the most likely coordination may involve directly coordinating on prices in order to keep them above the competitive level. In other markets, coordination may aim at limiting production or the amount of new capacity brought to the market. Firms may also coordinate by dividing the market, for instance by geographic area or other customer characteristics, or by allocating contracts in bidding markets. The ability to arrive at and sustain such co-ordination depends on a number of factors, the presence of which must be carefully examined in each case.

48. Firstly, each undertaking must be able to monitor whether or not the other undertakings are adhering to the common policy. It is not sufficient for each undertaking to be aware that inter-dependent market conduct is profitable for all of them, because each undertaking will be tempted to increase his share of the market by deviating from the common strategy. There must, therefore, be sufficient market transparency for all undertakings concerned to be aware, sufficiently precisely and quickly, of the market conduct of the others.

49. Secondly, the implementation of the common policy must be sustainable over time, which presupposes the existence of sufficient deterrent mechanisms, which are sufficiently severe to convince all the undertakings concerned that it is in their best interest to adhere to the common policy.

50. Finally, it must be established that competitive constraints do not jeopardise the implementation of the common strategy. As in the case of single dominance, it must be analysed what is the market position and strength of rivals that do not form part of the collective entity, what is the market position and strength of buyers and what is the potential for new entry as indicated by the height of entry barriers.

Although it now seems plain that the concept of collective dominance is the same for the purposes of both Articles 82 and the ECMR, it must be noted that an important difference between the provisions is, of course, that in Article 82 cases a collective dominant position must exist as a threshold matter (it prohibits only abuses of a dominant or collective dominant position not abuses that may lead to the creation of a collective dominant position) whilst in merger cases the Commission may act to prevent mergers which lead either to the creation of a collective dominant position *or* to the strengthening of a pre-existing collective dominant position. The CFI in *Independent Music Publishers and Labels Association (Impala)* v. *Commission* made it clear that this distinction is a material one and that the evidence required to establish the conditions of the ECMR have been met is affected by the question of whether the merger will lead to the creation of a collective dominant position or to the strengthening of a pre-existing one. Where the collective dominant position exists, the criteria set out in *Airtours* may be established by reference to evidence of market factors typical of the presence of a collective dominant position.

Independent Music Publishers and Labels Association (Impala) v. *Commission* [2006] ECR II-2289, [2006] 5 CMLR 19

249. It must be observed that, as is apparent from the very wording of those judgments, that case-law was developed in the context of the assessment of the risk that a concentration would create a collective dominant position and not, as in the context of the first part of the present plea, of the determination of the existence of a collective dominant position.

250. However, although when assessing the risk that such a dominant position will be created the Commission is required, *ex hypothesi*, to carry out a delicate prognosis as regards the probable development of the market and of the conditions of competition on the basis of a prospective

analysis, which entails complex economic assessments in respect of which the Commission has a wide discretion, the finding of the existence of a collective dominant position is itself supported by a concrete analysis of the situation existing at the time of adoption of the decision. The determination of the existence of a collective dominant position must be supported by a series of elements of established facts, past or present, which show that there is a significant impediment of competition on the market owing to the power acquired by certain undertakings to adopt together the same course of conduct on that market, to a significant extent, independently of their competitors, their customers and consumers.

251. It follows that, in the context of the assessment of the existence of a collective dominant position, although the three conditions defined by the Court of First Instance in *Airtours* v *Commission*, paragraph 45 above, which were inferred from a theoretical analysis of the concept of a collective dominant position, are indeed also necessary, they may, however, in the appropriate circumstances, be established indirectly on the basis of what may be a very mixed series of indicia and items of evidence relating to the signs, manifestations and phenomena inherent in the presence of a collective dominant position.

252. Thus, in particular, close alignment of prices over a long period, especially if they are above a competitive level, together with other factors typical of a collective dominant position, might, in the absence of an alternative reasonable explanation, suffice to demonstrate the existence of a collective dominant position, even where there is no firm direct evidence of strong market transparency, as such transparency may be presumed in such circumstances.

253. It follows that, in the present case, the alignment of prices, both gross and net, over the last six years, even though the products are not the same (each disc having a different content), and also the fact that they were maintained at such a stable level, and at a level seen as high in spite of a significant fall in demand, together with other factors (power of the undertakings in an oligopoly situation, stability of market shares, etc.), as established by the Commission in the Decision, might, in the absence of an alternative explanation, suggest, or constitute an indication, that the alignment of prices is not the result of the normal play of effective competition and that the market is sufficiently transparent in that it allowed tacit price coordination.

The judgment thus holds that where the allegation is that a collective dominant position is to be created, proof will inevitably have to be based on speculative evidence of how the market will probably develop, i.e. evidence that the merger is likely to create a market situation which is conducive to tacit collusion. Where, however, the allegation is that a collective dominant position exists, actual evidence of factors consistent with tacit collusion may be necessary or sufficient[367] to prove that the conditions that make the market conducive to collective dominance exist. This may mean that it is extremely hard to establish collective dominance in an Article 82 case where there are no contractual or other structural links existing between the parties.[368]

---

[367] The wording in paras. 250 and 251 seem to be inconsistent on this point. Para. 250 suggests that the *Airtour* criteria must be supported with past or present evidence whilst para. 251 suggest that the *Aitrours* criteria may alternatively be proved by evidence of the existence of a collective dominant position. R. O'Donoghue and A. J. Padilla, *The Law and Economics of Article 82* (Hart Publishing, 2006), para. 3.3.3.2 suggest that the assessment of a collective dominant position under Article 82 demands a higher standard of proof than that required in merger cases and proof that tacit collusion is taking place. This seems to impose an extremely onerous burden, however. Further, it is normal in antitrust cases for issues such as a restriction of competition or the holding of a single dominant position to be proved not directly, but indirectly from market analysis.

[368] See, e.g. R. O'Donoghue and A. J. Padilla, *The Law and Economics of Article 82* (Hart Publishing, 2006), para. 3.3.3.2 and see *supra* n. 367.

e. Summary

The concept of a collective dominant position is of enormous importance to Article 82 and has been of critical importance to the Merger Regulation. It now seems clear from the case law that:

(1) the concept of a collective dominant position is defined in the same way for the purposes of both the ECMR and Article 82;[369]

(2) independent economic entities may hold a collective dominant position provided that they are united by economic links which enable them that to present themselves as a collective entity and to adopt the same conduct on the market;

(3) the economic links may by contractual, structural (such as cross shareholdings or common directorships) or provided by the structure of the market which ensures parallelism of behaviour between firms on an oligopolistic market.[370]

(ii) Abuse of a Collective Dominant Position

Even if the applicability of Article 82 to undertakings which hold a collective dominant position seems settled, a further, perhaps more difficult, question arises for the future. What conduct may amount to an abuse of a collective dominant position? The development of the concept of collective dominance has *obviously been of critical* importance in the context of the Merger Regulation. It is important that the Commission should have the power to prevent mergers which will later lead to tacit collusion on a market.[371] A more difficult issue is what should be done if firms *are* already tacitly coordinating their behaviour on a market. Can such behaviour, or other behaviour, constitute an abuse of a collective dominant position?[372]

a. Flat glass

In *Flat Glass*, the Commission had concluded that the undertaking's communication of, for example, identical prices to customers and granting of identical discounts constituted abuses within the meaning of Article 82. However, the CFI criticized the Commission for simply having recycled the facts of the Article 81 infringement to present an infringement of Article 82. Since then the Commission has sought to spell out the relevant market for the purposes of Article 82, the position of the undertakings on the market, and the abuses in the context of the express provisions of Article 82.

---

[369] Obviously the assessments in each case will be different: in the case of Article 82 the examination determines whether or not there has been an abuse of an existing collective dominant position; in contrast an ECMR assessment is prospective in nature, to determine whether or not the merger (or concentration for the purposes of the Regulation) *will* lead to the creation of a collective dominant position or the strengthening of a pre-existing collective dominant position.

[370] See, e.g. J. Faull and A. Nikpay, *The EC Law of Competition* (2nd edn., Oxford University Press, 2007), paras. 4.109–4.126.

[371] The fear that a merger might alternatively result in 'non-coordinated' effects on the market, lead to the decision to alter the substantive test set out in the original Merger Regulation, Reg. 4064/89 [1989] OJ L395/1, as amended by Reg. 1310/97 [1997] OJ L180/1, see Reg. 139/2004 [2004] OJ L24/1, Art. 2(2) and (3).

[372] See, e.g., P. Fernandez, 'Increasing Powers and increasing Uncertainty: Collective Dominance and Pricing Abuses' [2000] 5 *ELRev* 645 and G. Monti, 'The scope of collective dominance under Article 82' (2001) 38 *CMLRev* 131.

The conduct alleged to be abusive in *French–West African Shipowners' Committee*[373] *CEWAL*,[374] and *TACA*[375] was nonetheless broadly the same as that which the Commission had already held to infringe Article 81 (the attempt by the members of the committee to eliminate effective competition from non-committee shipowners).[376]

b. Collective Abuses

In Chapter 7 it was seen that Article 82 has been used to condemn a range of conduct. It prohibits both exploitative practices (such as excessive pricing or inertia) and anti-competitive practices (such as predatory or discriminatory pricing, tying, refusals to supply, etc.). It is a crucial question whether or not these notions of abuse will be useful to control the behaviour of oligopolists that are not united together by virtue of contractual or other formal links.

In this chapter we have seen that where there is no explicit collusion, the key cause for concern in an oligopolistic market is that undertakings may engage in tacit collusion rather than price competition, setting their prices at a level which produces supra-competitive profits and restricts output.[377] A question which arises, therefore is could this behaviour be caught by Article 82, which expressly provides that an abuse may consist of directly or indirectly imposing 'unfair selling prices'? Professor Whish raises this question in clear terms in his book:

The economic theory around which the doctrine of collective dominance has developed under the ECMR is that in certain market conditions firms may be able to derive benefits from tacit coordination; and the very reason why the Commission might prohibit under the ECMR a concentration that would create or strengthen a collective dominant position is that it would make it easier for firms to benefit from this phenomenon. Does it follow from this that tacit coordination, when actually practiced, should be condemned as an abuse of a collective dominant position under Article 82? Is price parallelism in itself an abuse? To put the point another way, does symmetry require that, since predicted tacit coordination can be prevented through the prohibition of a concentration under the ECMR, actual coordination should be condemned under Article 82? If the answer to this question is no, what types of behaviour ought to be condemned under Article 82?[378]

Exploitative Behaviour and Excessive Pricing

It is seen in Chapter 7 that Article 82 has, in fact, rarely been used to condemn exploitative, unfair, or excessive prices. In practice it is very hard to establish that prices charged are excessive and in practice the Commission has not sought to do so but has preferred to avoid acting as price regulator.[379] Although it would thus seem possible, in principle, for the Commission to condemn oligopolists that have engaged in parallel pricing at a level that the Commission considers to be 'excessive' it seems extremely unlikely that it would attempt to do so. In addition, it is arguably perverse to prohibit conduct which is 'natural' in some oligopolies as abusive and, consequently, to render the relevant undertakings open to large fines by way of penalties and/or

---

[373] [1992] OJ L134/1.

[374] [1993] OJ L34/20.

[375] [1999] OJ L95/1, [1999] 4 CMLR 1415, fines annulled on appeal, Cases T-191 and 214–216/98, *Atlantic Container Line AB v. Commission* [2003] ECR II-3275, [2005] 4 CMLR 20.

[376] Although the Commission couched its analysis in terms of Article 82 and was careful not to recycle the facts, the fact remains that much of the conduct was anyway condemned under Article 81.

[377] Case IV/M524, *Airtours/First Choice* [2000] OJ L93/1, [2000] 5 CMLR 494, annulled on appeal Case T-342/99, *Airtours plc v. Commission* [2002] ECR II-2585, [2002] 5 CMLR 317, discussed *infra* Chap. 12.

[378] R. Whish, *Competition Law* (5th edn., Butterworths, 2003), 526–7.

[379] See Chap. 7. See also, e.g. *Attheraces Ltd v. British Horseracing Board Ltd* [2007] EWCA Civ 38.

to actions in national courts.[380] As 'the collusion is not such that it is capable of being addressed under Article 81, it would not be appropriate to do so 'through the back door' under Article 82. It is only when the tacit collusion results in the commission of an abuse that Article 82 can be applied'.[381]

Other Collective 'Anti-competitive' Abuses

In the liner conference cases discussed above the Commission condemned behaviour that was targeted at eliminating competitors seeking to compete outside of the liner conference. In *Compagnie Maritime Belge* the Court upheld the Commission's finding of abuse in *CEWAL*, including the finding that the putting on of fighting ships by the undertakings was an abuse for the purposes of Article 82.[382] In *TACA*[383] the Commission found that the members had abused their dominant position by (1) agreeing to place restrictions on the availability and content of service contracts[384] and (2) by altering the competitive structure of the market so as to reinforce TACA's dominant position (in particular, by trying to ensure that any potential competitors wishing to enter the market would do so only after it had become a party of the TACA). Although the existence of the first abuse was upheld on the appeal, the CFI found that on the facts the Commission had failed to demonstrate that the members had induced potential competitors to join the TACA by the measures referred to in the decision.[385]

It is hard to envisage what other abuses may be committed by undertakings indulging in non-collusive parallel behaviour. It would be difficult to explain collective decisions refusing to supply an undertaking, or targeting a new entrant to the market, on the grounds of mutual interdependence. However, it could be argued, for example, that an abuse will have been committed by collectively dominant undertakings which are inefficient or which refuse to innovate[386] or perhaps which all impose exclusive purchasing commitments on their distributors.[387]

c. Abuse by One of the Collectively Dominant Undertakings

In *Irish Sugar plc v. Commission*[388] the CFI held that an *individual* undertaking could engage in conduct which constitutes an abuse of its dominant position held collectively with one or more undertakings:

Whilst the existence of a joint dominant position may be deduced from the position which the economic entities concerned together hold on the market in question, the abuse does not necessarily have to

---

[380] See R. Whish and B. Sufrin, 'Oligopolistic Markets and EC Competition Law' [1992] YEL 59, 74–5. In condemning excessive prices of a monopolist, however, Article 82 in the same sense also condemns natural or rational behaviour by a monopolist. It is not therefore 'obvious that collectively dominant firms should enjoy an immunity from this offence which an individually dominant firm would not enjoy', R. Whish, *Competition Law* (5th edn., Butterworths, 2003), 527–8.

[381] J. Faull and A. Nikpay, *The EC Law of Competition* (2nd edn., Oxford University Press, 2007), para. 4.125.

[382] Cases C-395 and 396/96 P, *Compagnie Maritime Belge Transports SA v. Commission* [2000] ECR I-1365, [2000] 4 CMLR 1076.

[383] [1999] OJ L95/1, [1999] 4 CMLR 1415: on appeal, Case T-191/98 30 Sept. 2003.

[384] Contracts by which a shipper undertakes to provide a minimum quantity of cargo to be transported by the conference (conference service contracts) or by an individual carrier (individual service contracts) over a fixed period of time and the carrier or the conference commits to a certain rate or rate schedule as well as a defined service level.

[385] Cases T-191 and 212–214/98, *Atlantic Container Line v. Commission* [2003] ECR II-3275, [2005] 4 CMLR 20.

[386] See Chap. 7.

[387] Such conduct would be likely to be caught by Article 81(1) in any event, see Chap. 4.

[388] Case T-228/97, [1999] ECR II-2969, [1999] 5 CMLR 1300.

be the action of all the undertakings in question. It only has to be capable of being identified as one of the manifestations of such a joint dominant position being held. Therefore, undertakings occupying a joint dominant position may engage in joint or individual abusive conduct.[389]

This finding was made in the context of a dominant position held jointly by a dominant undertaking and its distributor (on a vertical level). In this case Irish Sugar had such a close relationship with its distributor that it seems possible that they actually formed a single economic unit. Had the Commission made such a finding, it would of course have been unnecessary to invoke the concept of collective dominance.[390] Further the parties were clearly acting to safeguard their collective dominant position on the market.[391]

In contrast, it is less easy to envisage what conduct which is traditionally seen as anti-competitive when indulged in by an individual dominant undertaking may also be found to be abusive when engaged in by one of a group of oligopolists. The granting of loyalty rebates, discriminatory pricing, or selective price-cutting by single dominant undertakings may be condemned (it may make it more difficult for competitors to gain access to the market).[392] On an oligopolistic market, however, the granting of rebates to customers, discriminatory pricing, or selective price-cutting by one of the undertakings may mean that price competition is in fact operating between the oligopolists.[393] Nonetheless it seems that the concept of an individual abuse of a dominant position could, perhaps, be useful to preclude behaviour targeted by one of the members at a new entrant with the objective of protecting the oligopoly generally or to prevent signalling its pricing preferences to other members of the oligopoly.[394] In addition, it could be used to prevent price cuts targeted at a price cutter that is destabilizing tacit collusion on a tight oligopolistic market.[395]

The implications of the *Irish Sugar* judgment are explored by G. Monti in the following extract from his article.

---

[389] *Ibid.*, para. 66.

[390] The various terms used in the contested decision to describe the applicant's position on the market before February 1990 are the result of the special nature of its links with SDL before that date. The Commission claims to have established the existence of infringements of Article [82] of the Treaty from 1985 to February 1990 committed by the applicant alone, by SDL alone, or by both together. Having accepted the applicant's argument that it did not control the management of SDL, despite holding 51% of SDH's capital, the Commission decided that even if it was not possible to regard the applicant and SDL as a single economic entity, they had, together at least, held a dominant position on the market in question. Para. 110 of the statement of objections confirms that that was the Commission's view: 'To defend its market [the applicant] had recourse to different forms of abusive conduct which were used alternatively or in combination with one another whenever it was felt necessary throughout the period from 1985. Some of the relevant practices were carried out by [the applicant] itself; others, on the retail sugar market, by SDL, the commercial subsidiary of [the applicant]': Case T-228/97, *Irish Sugar plc v. Commission* [1999] ECR II-2969, [1999] 5 CMLR 1300, para. 28.

[391] G. Monti, 'The Scope of Collective Dominance under Article 82' (2001) 38 *CMLRev* 131.

[392] See, e.g., Case 85/76, *Hoffmann-La Roche v. Commission* [1979] ECR 461, [1979] 3 CMLR 211.

[393] See *TACA* [1999] OJ L95/6, [1999] 4 CMLR 1415.

[394] G. Monti, 'The Scope of Collective Dominance under Article 82' (2001) 38 *CMLRev* 131, 146–9.

[395] In this case the predation may represent the 'punishment' mechanism which means that tacit collusion subsequently follows, see, e.g. the facts that arose in *Brooke Group Ltd. v. Brown & Williamson Tobacco Corp.* 509 US 209 (1993).

G. Monti, 'The Scope of Collective Dominance under Article 82 EC' [2001] 38 *CMLRev* 131, 143

This is an important conclusion, which could apply to a variety of situations, horizontal and vertical. On a horizontal level, it may be deployed to catch a scenario like this: say there are three companies that enjoy collective dominance (e.g. because of membership in an export cartel). Let us now say that a fourth competitor attempts to penetrate the market and one of the three engages in predatory pricing or other exclusionary tactics not forbidden by Article 81. In this scenario, the Commission is now empowered to find that undertaking liable under Article 82 for abusing the collective dominant position. It does not need to fine the other two undertakings. Moreover, and potentially more significantly, the *Irish Sugar* decision states that collective dominance can be held by undertakings in a vertical relationship, which entails that the a non-dominant distributor who has sufficiently strong links with a dominant manufacturer has the same degree of responsibility not to hinder competition that the manufacturer has, thus any attempt to protect his market position (e.g. terminating a retailer who sells competing goods) may be found to be an abuse.

This vastly extends the jurisdiction of the Commission under Article 82. While it is obviously a ruling which could be overturned by the ECJ, it is submitted that the reasoning of the CFI can be supported as consistent with well-established principles. Specifically, there is no need for a causal link between the dominant position and the abuse: the dominant position does not have to be used, so long as the conduct of a dominant firm has anti-competitive effects. This was established in *Continental Can* where the ECJ said that 'the strengthening of the position of an undertaking may be an abuse and prohibited under Article [82] of the Treaty, regardless of the means and procedure by which it is achieved' if it has anti-competitive effects. On this basis a contract clause that has an anti-competitive effects (e.g. SDL's product swap)[396] is a breach of Article 82 even if SDL is not individually dominant, because its effects was to consolidate the collective dominance by excluding potential competitors. This broad, effects-based application of Article 82 is in line with the 'special responsibility' imposed on dominant firms not to distort competition.

(iii) Remedies and Fines

In considering the appropriateness of Article 82 as a mechanism for dealing with oligopolistic markets it is also important to bear in mind the remedies available for a breach of Article 82. Under Regulation 1/2003, the Commission has power to require an undertaking to bring an infringement to an end (Article 7), and to impose fines on undertakings for any infringements committed (Article 15).[397] Article 7 is broad, enabling, for example, the Commission to order both behavioural and structural remedies where necessary to bring the infringement to an end. In theory the Commission could, therefore, in exceptional circumstances, order 'divestiture' where essential to improve the competitive structure of the market.[398] Although the Commission might be able to order price reductions were it to find abusive unfairly high

---

[396] One of the abuses of a collective dominant position found by the Commission was that SDL the distributor, had agreed with one retailer and one wholesaler to exchange its sugar for the sugar that the wholesaler and retailer had purchased from France.

[397] [1959–62] OJ Spec. Ed. 87. See *infra* Chap. 14.

[398] Structural remedies can, however, only be imposed where these is no equally effective behavioural remedy or where the behavioural remedy would be more burdensome, see Reg. 1/2003, recital 12. Further, the recital states that structural remedies will only be proportionate where there is a risk of lasting or repeated infringement which derives from the very structure of the undertaking, see Chaps. 5 and 14.

pricing, it could not engage in price control or look pragmatically for other problems causing price rigidity in the market and suggest solutions for resolving them.[399]

(iv) Conclusions

It appears that Article 82 may be applicable to independent undertakings that are not linked together by some agreement or other special relationship. Even if Article 82 is applied to oligopolists linked only by their mutual interdependence, it has been seen that the concept of abuse, developed in relation to individually dominant firms, is not a mechanism ideally equipped to control the behaviour of oligopolists. The idea that an 'individual' undertaking may commit an abuse of a collective dominant position may, however, render Article 82 more effective. Further, the action that the Commission may take under Regulation 1/2003 on the finding of an infringement may not be the most appropriate means of dealing with the problems posed. It is far from clear that imposing fines on undertakings for behaving in an economically rational way is logical. In addition, the power to order an undertaking to bring its infringement to an end may be an ineffective means of dealing with the oligopoly problem.

It is, however, perhaps the lack of any other effective method of dealing with oligopolies rather than the appropriateness of Article 82 itself that has led the Commission to persist in the development of the concept of an abuse of a collective perhaps dominant position.

C. ALTERNATIVE METHODS FOR DEALING WITH OLIGOPOLISTIC MARKETS UNDER EC LAW

(i) Merger Regulation

Given that oligopolistic markets often do not function as effectively as one in which free competition operates, and given the difficulties involved in applying either Article 81 or Article 82 to the conduct of undertakings operating on such markets, it may be that the Merger Regulation holds the key. It seems sensible to ensure that the ECMR is utilized to prevent mergers which create or strengthen a collective dominant position or which will lead to non-coordinated effects on an oligopolistic market. Prevention is better than a cure. If the Commission prohibits mergers causing market imperfections it will have to worry less frequently about corrective measures. This objective was extremely influential in the debate leading up to the eventual decision to change the substantive test for appraisal under the ECMR.

A strict merger policy may, therefore, reduce some of the difficulties that arise in attempting to control oligopolistic markets and markets on which one undertaking only is found to be dominant. Where a market is already an oligopolistic one the ECMR can obviously only be of use to ensure that the undertakings' positions on the market are not strengthened through merger. Other solutions may need to be found to deal with an oligopolistic market which already exists.

(ii) Sector Inquiries

Article 12(1) of Regulation 17 gave the Commission a wide discretion to conduct sector inquiries and to decide whether or not to investigate markets that it considers to be malfunctioning. To

---

[399] See *infra* 953–8.

conduct such an investigation the Commission did not have to have any evidence of, or even suspect, an infringement of either Article 81 or 82. Unfortunately the provision conferred no power on the Commission to take action to remedy any defects identified in an investigation and as such was, initially at least rarely used.

Whish and Sufrin argued that 'given the political will' the provision could form the:[400]

basis of a proper investigative system. Although there may be understandable concern about giving the Commission such large elements of discretion in respect of oligopolistic markets it is doubtful whether it is more worrying than the prospect of the Article [82] prohibition applied wholesale to the complex behaviour of oligopolies.

Article 17 Regulation 1/2003 amends Article 12 but does not give it the broad basis called for by Whish and Sufrin. It provides:

Regulation 1/2003, Article 17

Investigations into sectors of the economy and into types of agreement

1. Where the trend of trade between Member States, the rigidity of prices or other circumstances suggest that competition may be restricted or distorted within the common market, the Commission may conduct its inquiry into a particular sector of the economy or into a particular type of agreements across various sectors. In the course of that inquiry, the Commission may request undertakings or associations of undertakings concerned to supply the information necessary for giving effect to Articles 81 and 82 of the Treaty.

The Commission may in particular request the undertakings or associations of undertakings concerned to communicate to it all agreements, decisions and concerted practices.

The Commission may publish a report on the results of its inquiry into particular sectors of the economy or of particular types of agreements across various sectors and invite comments from interested parties.

Article 17(2) provides the Commission with the powers it needs to collect such information. The provision still does not, however, confer power on the Commission to adopt remedies following such a report. Although the provision may not provide great flexibility to tacit collusion on an oligopolistic market, it seems that the provision is useful for the investigation of sectors generally and the competition issues raised within them generally. Through such an inquiry the Commission can obtain a broader view of the sector than it would when concentrating on individual agreements concluded by firms operating on those market. Having done this it could then take further action, perhaps under the competition, or other Treaty, rules.

In 2004 the Commission used Article 12 of Regulation 17 for exactly this kind of purpose. In January 2004 it announced that it was launching a sector inquiry into the sale of sports rights to Internet companies and to providers of the third generation (3G) of mobile phones services.[401] In its press release the Commission stated that:

The purpose of the inquiry is to have as clear and wide a view as possible of the availability of audio-visual sports rights in the European Union. Sports rights and notably football rights are powerful

---

[400] R. Whish and B. Sufrin, 'Oligopolistic Markets and EC Competition Law' [1992] *YEL* 59, 83.

[401] IP/04/134.

drivers for the sale of pay-TV subscriptions but also for the roll-out of new media markets, such as enhanced Internet and UMTS services. In the interest of entrepreneurship, consumer choice and innovation, the Commission wants to make sure that access to this key premium content is not unduly restricted.

The decision to launch the sector inquiry was provoked partly from its experience of individual agreements which highlighted possible anti-competitive agreements across the whole industry, in particular through bundling of TV rights with new media/ UMTS rights and embargoes favouring either TV coverage over new types of coverage[402] or the purchase of new media/ UMTS rights on an exclusive basis.[403] The purpose of the broad inquiry is thus to develop a sector-wide approach, to provide guidance to both owners of rights and those willing to buy them and to discover whether current practice infringe Articles 81 or 82. In its note to the press release the Commission made the following observation about Article 12, Regulation 17 and Article 17, Regulation 1/2003:

Under Article 12 of its main procedural antitrust Regulation, the Commission may initiate general inquiries into those sectors of the economy where it believes competition might be restricted or distorted. The aim of this provision is to allow the Commission to investigate suspicious pricing structures or other practices indicating a possible anti-competitive situation across a whole industry.

Article 12 of Regulation 17/62 EC is particularly suitable for inquiries in established oligopolistic markets where the presence of a small number of important players incites concerted practices. It is also an appropriate instrument for inquiring into sectors where business practices are not yet established and competition is shaped through one shot big size agreements as in the New Media/3G content sector. Sector inquiries allow the Commission to investigate the agreements that shape now the future competitive environment in the sector.

In the framework of the new procedural Regulation 1/2003 which enters into force on 1 May 2004, sector inquiries provide a particularly appropriate instrument for investigating cross border market concerns and examining sector wide practices that do not normally fall within the scope of an individual case. Sector inquiries will allow the Commission to analyse allegedly anti-competitive practices in a systematic and transparent manner and will give the opportunity to national authorities to launch their own parallel national investigations on the basis of the Commission's findings.

The Commission has now concluded this inquiry and has warned market players that they should review their business practices and address anti-competitive behaviour. The Commission has also concluded inquiries in the energy[404] and retail banking sectors[405] and is conducting inquires in other areas, including with regard to access to local loop, mobile roaming charges and telecommunications leased line tariffs. The energy report, published in January 2007, identified a number of barriers to competition in the sector. The Commission has stated that it will pursue Article 81 and 82 proceedings, where appropriate to remedy anticompetitive practices identified (such as long-term downstream contracts, collusion between incumbents to share markets and lack of access to infrastructure), will consider competition and regulatory remedies to deal with other identified problems, will use the state aid rules where state subsidies contribute to maintenance of concentrated markets and prevent liberalisation from taking root, and will use the Merger Regulation to prevent increasing market concentration in this area. The Commission has also identified major barriers to competition in the retail banking sector and

---

[402] Since the 3G mobile phone market is still in its infancy the Commission is keen to ensure that it is not barred from key content.

[403] See, e.g., the discussion of the *European Champions League* case, *supra* 898 and *infra* Chap. 13.

[404] See http://ec.europa.eu/comm/competition/sectors/energy/inquiry/index.html.

[405] See http://ec.europa.eu/comm/competition/antitrust/others/sector_inquiries/financial_services/.

indicated that enforcement in the areas such as payment systems, credit registers, cooperation between banks and the setting of prices and policies might be necessary.

(iii) Cartels and Other Agreements

Many oligopolistic markets have characteristics which make them particularly prone to cartelization. The Commission is vigilant in these markets in case cartels are being operated. Further, it has been seen that other agreements, such as information sharing agreements, agreements on advertising or relating to trading terms and conditions and meeting competition provisions, may exacerbate the problems arising on oligopolistic markets, in particular by increasing transparency. Further, horizontal cooperation and vertical agreements concluded between and by players on oligopolistic markets may facilitate tacit collusion on markets.[406] Thus Community block exemptions do not, therefore, generally apply to agreements concluded between or by undertakings with large market shares and their benefit may be withdrawn where a market is affected by networks of agreements. In such cases, agreements need to be examined individually to ensure that they are not unduly restrictive of competition.

5. CONCLUSIONS

1. The Commission has wide investigative powers which it can use to unearth covertly operated cartels.

2. Where hardcore cartel activity (agreements to fix prices, restrict output, share markets and/or rig bids) is uncovered heavy fines will be imposed by the Commission on the undertakings involved.

3. A number of Member States treat cartel activity as a criminal offence.

4. The fight against cartels is now one of the, if not the, major priority of the Commission. Whistleblowers are encouraged and repeat offenders are punished particularly severely.

5. The Commission is trying to encourage consumers to seek compensation in the national courts from those engaged in hard-core cartel activity.

6. Article 81 also prohibits provisions designed to supplement and facilitate the operation of a cartel agreement.

7. Tacit collusion engaged in by firms operating on an oligopolistic market is not prohibited by Article 81(1). An agreement or some reciprocal direct or indirect contact between the undertakings operating on the market must be established. Article 81 may, however, prohibit practices such as exchange of information, meeting competition clauses or other clauses in vertical agreements which facilitate tacit collusion on a market. Further, the ECMR prohibits mergers which may lead to an increase in price through unilateral or coordinated effects on an oligopolistic market.

8. Article 82 may apply to oligopolists holding a collective dominant position on the market. Collective or individual actions designed to exclude new entrants into the market or to punish those deviating from the cooperative structure might constitute abuses of a collective dominant position.

9. Article 17 of Regulation 1/2003 is becoming an important mechanism for investigating concentrated markets. The Commission is using it to identify problems on a market which can

---

[406] See Chaps. 9 and 13.

later be addressed through use of its powers under Articles 81, 82, 86, the ECMR and/or the state aid rules.

10. In the UK, for example, the Enterprise Act[407] confers power on the Office of Fair Trading to refer markets to the Competition Commission for investigation where a feature or features of the market appear to prevent, restrict, or distort competition in the UK. The Competition Commission then investigates. Where it concludes that there is an adverse effect on competition it has power to impose remedies to deal with the problem or to recommend that others should take action. It may, for example, recommend the total or partial termination of an agreement; it may recommend that the prices to be charged for any specified goods or services on a market should be regulated; or recommend that any business, or part of a business, be disposed of (by the sale or any part of an undertaking or assets or otherwise).[408] It may also suggest or order measures should be taken by or against bodies other than the market players (e.g., where it considers that the market rigidity has been caused, partly at least, by advertising restrictions or other legal or regulatory barriers).

11. Resort to such draconian remedies as price control and divestiture may not always be a suitable means of dealing with the problems arising on oligopolistic markets. However, it can also be seen that a more flexible system may have advantages over one focusing exclusively on the abusive conduct, or the behaviour, of the undertakings on the market. Significant changes in the Community rules would need to be made before such a system could be operated by the Commission.

6. FURTHER READING

A. BOOKS

BISHOP, S., and WALKER, M., *The Economics of EC Competition Law: Concepts, Application and Measurement* (2nd edn., Sweet & Maxwell, 2002)

CLARKE, R., *Industrial Economics* (Blackwell, 1985), chap. 3

JEPHCOTT, M., and LÜBBIG, T., *Law of Cartels* (Jordans, 2003)

SCHERER, F. M., and MOSS, D., *Industrial Market Structure and Economic Performance* (3rd edn., Houghton Mifflin, 1990), chaps. 7 and 8

B. ARTICLES

ALBORS-LLORENS, A., 'Horizontal Agreements and Concerted Practices in EC Competition Law: Unlawful and Legitimate Contacts between Competitors' [2006] 51 *Ant Bull* 837

BISCOLLI, E. F., 'Trade Associations and Information Exchange under US and EC Competition Law [2000] 23(1) *World Competition* 29

BLACK, O., 'Communication, Concerted Practices and the Oligopoly Problem' [2006] *Euro CJ* 341

CARLE, J., and JOHNSSON, M., 'Benchmarking and EC Competition Law' [1998] *ECLR* 74

FRANZOSI, M., 'Oligopoly and the Prisoners' Dilemma: Concerted Practices and As If Behaviour' [1988] *ECLR* 385

JOLIET, R., 'La Notion de Pratique Concertée et l'Arrêt I.C.I. dans une perspective comparative' [1974] *CDE* 251

JONES, A., 'Wood Pulp: Concerted Practice and/or Conscious Parallelism' [1993] *ECLR* 273

KORAH, V., 'Concerted Practices' (1973) 36 *MLR* 260

—— '*Gencor* v. *Commission*: Collective Dominance' [1999] *ECLR* 337

---

[407] The Enterprise Act 2002 market investigation provisions (Part 4) repeal and replace the monopoly provisions of the Fair Trading Act 1973.

[408] See Enterprise Act 2002 1973, Sched. 8.

MONTI, G., 'The Scope of Collective Dominance under Article 82' (2001) 38 *CMLRev* 131

ROSHOWICZ, P. H., 'The Appropriateness of criminal Sanctions in the Enforcement of Competition Law' [2004] *ECLR* 12

VAN GERVEN, G., and VARONA, E. N. 'The Wool Pulp Case and the Future of Concerted Practices' (1994) 31 *CMLRev* 575

WERDEN, G. J and SIMON M. J., 'Why Price Fixers should go to Prison' (1987) 32 *Ant Bull* 917

WHISH, R., 'Collective Dominance' in D. O'Keefe and M. Andenas (eds.), *Liber Amicorum for Lord Slynn* (Kluwer, 2000)

—— and SUFRIN, B., 'Oligopolistic Markets and EC Competition Law' [1992] *YEL* 59

WILS, W., 'Does the Effective Enforcement of Articles 81 and 82 Required Not Only Fines on Undertakings But Also Individual Penalties, In Particular Imprisonment' in C. D. Ehlermann (ed.) *European Competition Law Annual 2001: Effective Private Enforcement of EC Antitrust Law* (Hart Publishing, 2002)

—— 'Is Criminalisation of EU Competition Law the Answer?' [2005] 28(2) *World Competition* 117.

12

MERGERS

1. CENTRAL ISSUES

1. Prior to 1990, the Commission had to rely on its power to apply Article 82, and Article 81, to prevent takeovers and acquisitions of shares in other undertakings.

2. In 1989 the Council adopted a European Merger Control Regulation (the 'ECMR') which seeks to regulate changes in market structure in the European Union. The Regulation came into force in 1990, was amended in 1997 and was amended again and consolidated into a new Regulation, Regulation 139/2004, in 2004.

3. The ECMR declares incompatible with the common market merger transactions, 'concentrations', with a 'Community dimension' which would significantly impede effective competition in the common market or a substantial part of it, in particular as a result of the creation or strengthening of a dominant position.

4. A 'concentration' occurs where two or more undertakings on a market 'merge' or where one or more undertakings acquire 'control' over another.

5. The concept of a Community dimension seeks to ensure that mergers creating structural changes which impact beyond the national borders of any one Member State are appraised by the Commission under the ECMR. It is a quantitative test based on the turnover of the undertakings concerned.

6. The general scheme of the ECMR is that, subject to certain limited exceptions:

  (a) concentrations with a Community dimension are appraised exclusively by the Commission under the provisions of the ECMR;

  (b) concentrations without a Community dimension are appraised exclusively at the national level.

7. Concentrations with a Community dimension must generally be notified to the Commission prior to completion and are suspended pending investigation.

8. Mergers are frequently motivated by the desire of the merging parties to increase efficiency.

9. Nonetheless, mergers may significantly impede effective competition on a market.

10. Horizontal mergers reduce the number of players on the market and increase the market share of the post-merger firm. Horizontal mergers may enable the post-merger firm to exercise market power either individually, or collectively, through tacit coordination with other firms operating on the market.

11. Non-horizontal mergers are less likely to cause competition concerns and provide greater scope for efficiencies. Nonetheless the Commission is concerned that where one of the parties to such a merger has market power in at least one market, vertical and conglomerate mergers may harm competition through:

  (a) foreclosure of a distinct upstream, downstream or related market; or

  (b) changing the structure of competition on a market in such a way that the firms operating on it are likely to coordinate their behaviour.

12. Merger analysis also requires assessment of factors which are likely to counteract the merged firm's ability to exercise market power, such as countervailing buyer power or new entry.

13. Efficiencies achieved by the merger may also offset any anticompetitive consequences.

14. Where one of the merging parties is failing the merger may not be the cause of any anticompetitive harm arising on the market.

2. INTRODUCTION

A. WHAT IS A MERGER?

A merger occurs where two or more formerly independent entities unite. A number of different transactions and agreements concluded by undertakings could result in a unification of the independent undertakings' decision-making process. Every jurisdiction needs, therefore, to adopt a definition of what constitutes a merger for the purposes of any merger control legislation. The European Community Merger Regulation (the 'ECMR')[1] applies to 'concentrations'.[2] Broadly, there is a concentration where two or more previously independent undertakings merge their businesses *or* where there is a change in control of an undertaking (sole or joint control of an undertaking being *acquired* by another undertaking or undertakings).[3]

B. THE PURPOSES OF MERGER CONTROL

The purpose of merger control is to enable competition authorities to regulate changes in market structure by deciding whether two or more commercial companies may merge, combine, or consolidate their businesses into one.[4] It has been seen that the Community authorities are hostile to anti-competitive agreements concluded between independent undertakings.[5] Mergers naturally create a more permanent and lasting change on the market than agreements. It might be expected, therefore, that many mergers, especially horizontal mergers, would be forbidden. Mergers may raise severe competition concerns. In particular, they may result in the undertakings acquiring or strengthening a position of market power and, consequently, in an increase in the market price of the products or services on the relevant market. However, mergers also give the owner of a business the opportunity to sell it. Without this possibility, entrepreneurs might be reluctant to start a business. Further, mergers provide many other efficiency opportunities.

The reasons for not making mergers unlawful per se or for not even coming anywhere near such a rule are plain. Widespread prohibition of mergers would impose serious, if not intolerable, burdens upon owners of businesses who wished to liquidate their holdings for irreproachable personal reasons. Moreover, economic welfare is significantly served by maintaining a good market for capital assets . . . Most importantly, a policy of free transferability of capital assets tends to put them in the hands of those who will use them to their utmost economic advantage, thus tending to maximize society's total output of goods and services.

Growth by merger . . . will often yield substantial economies of scale—in production, research, distribution, cost of capital and management. Entry by merger . . . may stimulate improved economic performance in an industry characterized by oligopolistic lethargy and inefficiency. Finally,

---

[1] Reg. 139/2004 [2004] OJ L24/1 ('ECMR'), this regulation replaced Reg. 4064/89 [1989] OJ L395/1, [1990] 4 CMLR 286, corrigendum [1990] OJ L257/1 (the ECMR) (amended by Reg. 1310/97 [1997] OJ L180/1, corrigendum [1998] OJ L40/17). Reg. 139/2004 came into force on 1 May 2004.

[2] In the UK, for example, the Enterprise Act 2002 applies to 'relevant merger situations', broadly where (a) one or more enterprises will or has ceased to be distinct, (b) the transaction meets the jurisdictional thresholds; and (c) either the merger has not taken place or took place within the last four months (ss. 23–5).

[3] ECMR, Art. 3. See discussion *infra* 958.

[4] For merger control to be effective, it is necessary to control both amicable agreements to merge and hostile takeovers.

[5] *Supra*, especially Chap. 11.

acquisition of diversified lines of business, by stabilizing profits, may minimize the risk of business failure and bankruptcy.[6]

The task of the competition authorities is to identify and to prohibit those mergers which have such an adverse impact on competition or society that any benefits resulting from them are outweighed or should be ignored. Although, therefore, the motives for, and benefits of, mergers are important, the key to effective merger control is to identify why and when a merger should be prohibited.

(i) The Motives for, and Advantages of, a Merger

a. Efficiency

In many cases the parties will state that the main motivation for their merger is that the merged entity will be more efficient. The entity may be able to exploit economies of scale in production (this argument will be strongest in the context of horizontal or, sometimes, vertical mergers where related operations are combined). Such economies will be of particular importance in a market in which the cost of production of a product is high in comparison to the size, or the anticipated size, of the market or where there is a minimum efficient scale of production.[7] The merger may also give rise to other operating efficiencies such as economies of scope,[8] marketing efficiencies (arising, for example, from broader product lines, streamlining of the sale force, the use of common advertising, etc.), efficiencies arising from integration of complementary activities or the ability to pool research and development skills (giving rise to the opportunity for greater innovation).

Mergers may, therefore, enable undertakings to increase these efficient levels of manufacture, research and development, and distribution more rapidly and more cheaply than they could by internal growth. They may also encourage management efficiency by ensuring that the most productive assets are managed by the most efficient managers (the merger may bring new and superior management to the business).[9]

b. Barriers to Exit

It has already been noted that few people would go to the trouble to set up a business if they could not sell it when they had had enough or when they wished to realize capital profits from it. In particular, many smaller business owners may wish to sell their business if no obvious successor is available.

c. Failing Undertakings and Unemployment

A merger may provide an escape route for a company facing an otherwise inevitable liquidation.[10] In a case such as this the possibility of selling the business to another may mean that productive

---

[6] D. Turner, 'Conglomerate Mergers and Section 7 of the Clayton Act' (1965) 78 *Harvard LR* 1313, 1317.

[7] *Supra* Chap. 1.

[8] Economies of scope occur where cost savings can be achieved by producing a greater variety of goods and/or services, for example, by using the same facilities and personnel to produce several products.

[9] The simple threat of a take-over may encourage the incumbent management of a company to strive for efficiency (rigid control of mergers will remove or greatly reduce this perceived threat). However, over-confident entrepreneurs may overestimate their ability to manage more complex undertakings or businesses in an unfamiliar field or market.

[10] See discussion *infra* 1047–52.

assets are kept in production and that creditors, owners, and employees are protected from the adverse consequences of the undertaking's failure.

d. Single Market Integration

Cross-border mergers may facilitate market integration. '[E]xternal growth by means of mergers and acquisitions can be a means of quickly realizing potential cost savings and integration gains offered by the internal market'.[11]

e. National or European Champions

The desire to increase the scale of national and European companies may be a goal of national, or European, industrial policy.[12] Mergers affect the structure of a market and questions of industrial policy inevitably arise. The ability to restructure or to create national or European champions may, for example, mean that the parties can, in combination, survive and compete more effectively on international markets, contribute to technical and economic progress, and/or facilitate cross-border trade.

(ii) The Adverse Consequence of Mergers

More important perhaps than focusing on the benefits of a merger is the answer to the question: why should mergers be prohibited?[13] When, and on what grounds, should a competition authority take steps to interfere with the market for corporate control? Failure to agree on this key issue was one of the factors which seriously delayed the introduction of any comprehensive system of merger control at the Community level. Should competition be the sole criterion relevant to a decision to clear or to prohibit a merger? Or should other wider policy issues, such as regional, industrial, or social policy, also be taken into account?

a. A Damaging Effect on the Competitive Structure of the Market

There is a danger that undertakings may wish to merge in order to achieve or to strengthen their market power.

In horizontal mergers, and especially in the massive consolidations that took place [in the US] around the turn of the century, the desire to achieve or strengthen monopoly power played a prominent role. Some 1887–1904 consolidations gained monopoly power by creating firms that dominated their industries. Others fell short of dominance, but transformed market structures sufficiently to curb the tendencies toward price competition toward which sellers gravitated in the rapidly changing market conditions of the time. As Thomas Edison remarked to a reporter concerning reasons for the formation of the General Electric Company in 1892:

> Recently there has been sharp rivalry between [Thomson-Houston and Edison General Electric], and prices have been cut so that there has been little profit in the manufacture of electrical machinery for anybody. The consolidation of the companies . . . will do away with competition

---

[11] 'Competition and Integration: Community Merger Policy' (1994) 57 *European Economy*, p. vii. The need for merger control at the Community level was, eventually, seen as a necessary complement to the 1992 single market programme: Commission's *XVIIIth and XIXth Reports on Competition Policy*, (Commission, 1988) and (Commission, 1989) and discussion *infra* 953.

[12] See *infra* 1070–2.

[13] It is not always necessary to show that a merger creates efficiencies. It should be sufficient that it does not create the power to restrict output: see R. H. Bork, *The Antitrust Paradox* (Basic Books, 1978, reprinted with a new Introduction and Epilogue, 1993), chaps. 9–11.

which has become so sharp that the product of the factories has been worth little more than ordinary hardware.

Those were days when businesspeople were not yet intimidated by the wrath of trustbusters or public opinion. Now they are more circumspect, and evidence of monopoly-creating intent is harder to find. Also, vigorous antitrust enforcement in the United States and, more recently, abroad has done much to curb competition-inhibiting mergers.[14]

Even if dominance or the acquisition of market power is not the motive for a merger, it may be its effect. A merger control system focusing exclusively on competition issues will adopt a strict policy against such mergers.

Horizontal Mergers

A horizontal merger is one which occurs between undertakings operating at the same level of the economy. As Hovenkamp points out, such mergers have two important implications for the market on which the merging firms operate:

Because the horizontal merger involves two firms in the same market, it produces two consequences that do not flow from vertical or conglomerate mergers: 1) after the merger the relevant market has one firm less than before; 2) the post-merger firm ordinarily has a larger market share than either of the partners had before the merger.[15]

The reduction in the number of firms active on the market and the increase in concentration may raise competition concerns. We have seen that markets dominated by a single undertaking may not deliver the same efficiencies as those achieved in a competitive market.[16] Further, that it is difficult for competition authorities to control the behaviour of a dominant undertaking and to detect abuse of market power. An active merger policy seeks to avoid these difficulties by precluding undertakings from merging where the parties will obtain or strengthen a dominant position or a position of individual market power which might be exploited at the expense of customers and protected by anti-competitive behaviour.[17]

A merger between two or more previously independent undertakings which does not lead to the creation of a dominant position may lead to a substantial increase in the concentration of a particular industry and enable the merging parties to raise price and restrict output, whether through explicit or tacit coordination of their behaviour with other firms operating on the market (coordinated effects) or through non-coordinated, unilateral effects.[18] Many competition authorities, therefore, adopt a merger policy which is wary of mergers occurring in an already concentrated market. A concern of US merger policy has been that 'horizontal mergers may facilitate express or tacit collusion or Cournot-style oligopoly behaviour':

Merger policy is the most powerful weapon available in the American antitrust arsenal for combating tacit collusion or Cournot style oligopoly. Since we cannot go after oligopoly directly under [section 1 Sherman Act], we do the next best thing. We try to prevent (taking efficiencies and other factors

---

[14] F. M. Scherer and D. Ross, *Industrial Market Structure and Economic Performance* (3rd edn., Houghton Mifflin, 1990), 160.

[15] H. Hovenkamp, *Federal Antitrust Policy: The Law of Competition and its Practice* (3rd edn., Thomson West, 2005), 12.1.b.

[16] See generally *supra* Chaps 5–7 and Chap. 11.

[17] The US antitrust authorities thus aim to prevent mergers which 'create or enhance market power or facilitate its exercise'. Horizontal Merger Guidelines, issued on 2 April 1992 (revised in 1997). The exercise of market power results in a misallocation of resources or a transfer of wealth from buyer to seller.

[18] See *supra* Chap. 11 and *infra* 1005 ff.

into account) the creation of market structures that tend to facilitate Cournot or collusion-like outcomes.[19]

In the EC, the extent to which the ECMR is, and has been, able to prevent mergers leading to coordinated or non-coordinated effects on oligopolistic markets has been controversial.[20]

Vertical Mergers

A vertical merger is one concluded between firms at different levels of production in the economy. The motive for vertical mergers is frequently to obtain a secure supply of a raw material or to secure an outlet for the sale of products. Vertical mergers may raise some competition concerns. The predominant fear is that where the merging firms have market power at one or more vertical level, vertical mergers may 'foreclose' the market or a source of supply to competitors.[21] For example, a merger between a manufacturer of a product and a supplier of an essential component for that product (backward integration) may have severe implications for competing manufacturers. The foreclosure effect will be acute where there are few or no other suppliers of the essential components. Similarly, the acquisition by a manufacturer of a distributor (forward integration) may make it more difficult for competitors to distribute their products. A vertical merger may also increase price transparency or facilitate collusion between firms operating on the market.

In the USA, the competition authorities have not frequently, in recent times, been interested in either vertical or conglomerate mergers since they consider that these mergers rarely lead to the increase of market power.[22] The Commission is sometime concerned about vertical mergers, however, and is in the process of preparing Guidelines on assessment on non-horizontal mergers.[23]

Conglomerate Mergers

Conglomerate mergers are concentrations which have no horizontal or vertical effect. As such mergers do not result in horizontal overlaps or vertical effects, they do not so obviously raise competition problems. Rather they may frequently be motivated by innocuous objectives from a competition perspective, such as the need for risk-reduction. An undertaking may, for example, wish to expand into another market where it is operating in a declining or cyclical industry or where it simply wishes to spread risk. However, where an undertaking is dominant in one market there may be concern that it will use its power in that market to foreclose competition in a neighbouring or related market, by engaging in tying or, by cross-subsidizing or predating in that market.[24] This may be more likely where the relevant markets are closely related and the merged undertakings will be able to offer a wide portfolio of products.[25] Alternatively there

---

[19] H. Hovenkamp, *Federal Antitrust Policy: The Law of Competition and its Practice* (3rd edn., Thomson West, 2005), 12.1b 502.

[20] See *infra* 1007–9 and 1018–37.

[21] See C. J. Cook and C. S. Kerse, *E.C. Merger Control* (3rd edn., Sweet & Maxwell, 2006), para. 7-020 and see discussion of vertical mergers *infra* 1054–9.

[22] Bork, in particular, has argued that antitrust laws should not be applied to prevent vertical or conglomerate mergers. They never put together rivals and do not, therefore, create or increase the ability to restrict output through an increase in market share. See R. H. Bork, *The Antitrust Paradox* (Basic Books, 1978, reprinted with a new Introduction and Epilogue, 1993), chaps. 11–12.

[23] See its draft Guidelines on the assessment of non-horizontal mergers, 13 February, 2007, available at http://ec.europa.eu/comm/competition/mergers/legislation/merger_guidelines.html.

[24] See *supra* Chap. 7.

[25] See *infra* 1059–70.

may be a fear that conglomeracy will lead to a loss of potential competition. A merger of firms operating in different product or geographic markets may cause a loss of potential competition. Any threat that they may enter each other's markets is eliminated. This may be of particular importance where the undertakings operate in the same product but a different geographic market or where they operate in neighbouring product markets.

These arguments against conglomeracy have been criticized by Bork:

the most common charges leveled against conglomerate mergers are that they may: (1) create a 'deep pocket' that enables a firm to devastate its less affluent rivals; (2) lower costs; (3) raise barriers to entry; (4) frighten smaller companies into less vigorous rivalry; (5) create the opportunity to engage in reciprocal dealing; and (6) eliminate potential competition. Of these alleged dangers, only the sixth, which is really a horizontal and not a conglomerate merger theory, has any possible validity, and that one will rarely be significant.[26]

In the EC, the elimination of a potential competitor is identified as a horizontal issue. In the Commission's Guidelines on the assessment of horizontal mergers under the Council Regulation on the control of concentrations between undertakings' (the 'Horizontal Merger Guidelines') it states:[27]

A merger with a potential competitor can generate horizontal anti-competitive effects, whether coordinated or non-coordinated, if the potential competitor significantly constrains the behaviour of the firms active in the market.

The European Commission has nonetheless displayed occasional concerns about purely conglomerate mergers.[28] A couple of these cases have been extremely high profile and controversial. Conglomerate mergers are also to be covered by Guidelines on assessment of non-horizontal mergers.[29]

Efficiency and/or Other Considerations?

A further matter of controversy is whether a finding that a merger has an adverse effect on competition should be final and fatal to the conclusion of the merger. It is arguable that, even where a position of market power is acquired or reinforced, a merger should be permitted if, for example: (1) it leads to greater efficiency (the cost savings resulting from the merger outweigh the detrimental impact of the merger on consumer welfare as a whole); (2) the merger will save a firm which, otherwise, faces an inevitable failure; or (3) the merger is supported as a matter of industrial or social or other policy. Whether or not these factors should be, or are, taken into account under the ECMR is considered below.

b. A Fear of Big Business

Mergers may cause other worries, apart from competition ones, for authorities. Most of the factors that will be discussed in this section and sections (c) and (d) below would not, however,

---

[26] R. H. Bork, *The Antitrust Paradox*, (Basic Books, 1978, reprinted with a new Introduction and Epilogue, 1993), 249. Bork concludes his chapter by stating: 'We have now examined all the major theories of the ways in which conglomerate mergers may injure competition and found that none of them (with a minor exception for a theory that is really horizontal) bears analysis. The conclusion must be, therefore, that conglomerate mergers should not be prohibited by judicial interpretation of Section 7 of the Clayton Act'.

[27] Guidelines on the assessment of horizontal mergers under the Council Regulation on the control of concentrations between undertakings (the Horizontal Merger Guidelines) [2004] OJ C31/5, para. 5.

[28] See *infra* 1054–70.

[29] See its draft Guidelines on the assessment of non-horizontal mergers, 13 February, 2007 available at http://ec.europa.eu/comm/competition/mergers/legislation/merger_guidelines.html.

cause concern on the ground of strict economic theory unless it could *also* be shown that consumer welfare was adversely affected by the merger.

Some commentators believe that conglomeracy, or mergers that would create large businesses, has implications for the freedom of society more generally. It is feared that too great economic concentration is anti-democratic and restricts individual freedom and enterprise or that it has an adverse effect on the distribution of wealth.

[O]ur concern for the maintenance of effective competition extends beyond purely economic considerations. Competition is one of the foundations of an open society . . . it is therefore necessary to weigh against the gains from industrial concentration the socio-political consequences of concentrations of private power, which could discredit property owning democracy.[30]

In Chapter 1 it was seen that it has been argued that one of the goals of European competition should be the diffusion of economic power and the protection of individual freedom.

Private power can cross economic boundaries and poses the threat of an 'extra market' power which can change the rules of the game in favour of the dominant corporations. In such a situation, where relationships between firms and their socio-economic environment constitute a mixture of market and non-market bonds, the authorities aim at the dispersion of private power. Even if this entails some loss of economic efficiency, such a choice would not necessarily be irrational, because such costs may be outweighed by social or political advantages.[31]

It is these sentiments which have led some authorities to utilize competition law as a tool to protect not only the process of competition but competitors (and the freedom of enterprise). In the US the Supreme Court concluded in *Brown Shoe Co* v. *US*[32] that a horizontal merger between competitors was illegal because, post-merger it would be able to undercut its competitors in price. The purpose of the competition rules was 'to promote competition through the protection of viable, small, locally owned businesses'. Although this might occasionally lead to higher prices at the time the court preferred decentralization.[33] It should be noted that this case does not reflect current US antitrust policy, however,

c. Special Sectors and Fear of Overseas Control

It may be believed that tighter control should be exercised over mergers which occur in particularly sensitive sectors. In these sectors it might be thought that a broader range of factors should be taken into account in determining whether or not a merger operates in the public interest. For example, interests of democracy may require the preservation of the 'plurality of the press' or national security may require that the ownership of certain industries such as oil and defence equipment does not pass overseas.

d. Unemployment

Mergers may mean asset-stripping, profits to shareholders, rationalization, and loss of jobs. Mergers which occur in depressed regions or in areas in which unemployment is already high may, therefore, cause concern.

---

[30] A. Caincross *et al.*, *Economic Policy for the European Community* (Macmillan, 1974).

[31] A. P. Jacquemin and H. W. de Jong, *European Industrial Organisation* (Macmillan, 1997), 198–9.

[32] See, e.g., *Brown Shoe Co* v. *United States* 370 US 294 (1962).

[33] *Ibid.*, 344.

C. THE HISTORY OF THE EUROPEAN MERGER CONTROL REGULATION

(i) The Initial Lacuna

The original EEC Treaty, unlike the ECSC Treaty,[34] did not contain any specific provision for controlling mergers. Articles 81 and 82 EC focus on the control of the behaviour of undertakings rather than mergers which affect a lasting change to the structure of the market. An explanation for the different approach set out in the ECSC and the EEC Treaties may be that the former was a *traité-loi* whilst the latter was a *traité-cadre* (a framework document, to be fleshed out by implementing legislation). However, it is more likely that other factors were responsible for the omission of merger control from the EEC Treaty.

In particular, it seems likely that it would have been easier to agree on a rule which would affect only the specific industries dealt with by the ECSC Treaty. Indeed, the ability to control mergers in these sectors was perceived to be of vital importance given their political and military significance.[35] In contrast, it would have been more difficult to agree on rules which were to affect all other undertakings generally. Further, at the time, it seems to have been considered that the objectives set out in Article 2 of the EEC Treaty of economic expansion might be achieved by concentrating economic power rather than prohibiting mergers.[36]

(ii) The Drive for Merger Control at the Community Level

The drive to introduce legislation at the Community level specifically focused on merger control was led by the Commission. In 1966 it first acknowledged, in its publication of its *Memorandum on the Concentration of Enterprises in the Common Market*,[37] that some form of EC merger control was necessary.[38] The Commission believed that its inability to control mergers inhibited its capability to operate effective competition control[39] and it adopted its first legislative proposal for a merger control regulation in 1973.[40]

Any regulation on merger control had to be passed unanimously by the Council.[41] For a long time there was no consensus amongst the Member States that merger control was necessary at all.[42] Those Member States that did recognize a need for merger control were reluctant to cede

[34] See Article 66(7) of the ECSC Treaty. The ECSC Treaty expired on 23 July 2002, see Chap. 2.

[35] The French in particular were keen to have in place rules which imposed constraints on the German war industry: S. Bulmer, 'Institutions and Policy Change: The Case of Merger Control' (1994) 72 *Public Administration* 423, 427–8.

[36] Undertakings might achieve industrial competitiveness by benefiting from economies of scale.

[37] EEC Competition Series Study No. 3.

[38] See C. Overbury, 'Politics or Policy? The Demystification of EC Merger Control' [1992] *Fordham Corp L Inst* 561.

[39] Prior to the adoption of the ECMR the Commission relied, where possible, on Articles 82 and 81 to prohibit some mergers. See in particular the discussion of Case 6/72, *Europemballage Corp and Continental Can Co Inc v. Commission* [1973] ECR 215, [1973] CMLR 199, *infra* 950–1.

[40] In the period between 1973 and 1989 a series of draft regulations was proposed and rejected by the Council: see [1973] OJ C92/1, [1982] OJ C36/3, [1984] OJ C51/8, [1988] OJ C130/4, [1989] OJ C22/141.

[41] The legal basis for the ECMR is Articles 83 (ex Art. 87) and 308 (ex Art. 235) of the Treaty. The latter is discussed *supra* Chap. 2 and see also discussion of significance of use of Art. 308 *infra* in the Addendum.

[42] The dangers posed by market dominance were apparent to a number of the European States (merger control was introduced in the UK in 1965 (although it was not then of course a Member State), in Germany in 1973, and in France in 1977).

power to the Commission and to relinquish their economic sovereignty. Many Member States wished to retain control over changes in industrial structure in their territories. In addition, early drafts of the Merger Regulation gave the Commission a broad discretion in assessing whether or not a merger was in the Community interest. Member States were divided on what substantive criteria should be used to appraise Community mergers. The UK, for example, was adamant, at least in later negotiations, that only the effects on competition should be taken into account, fearing perhaps that any exception to this strict approach would be used to allow social and industrial policy considerations in through the back door.[43] There were, therefore, two major sticking points:[44]

(i) *Jurisdiction*. Whether, and if so at what point, control should be relinquished by the Member States to the Commission and what the relationship between European and national law should be; and

(ii) *Appraisal criteria*. Should factors other than competition be taken into account in assessing whether a particular merger was compatible or incompatible with the common market?

(iii) The Catalyst for the ECMR

a. Articles 81 and 82 of the Treaty

Article 82

Frustrated by the lack of a specific provision enabling it to control mergers the Commission sought not only to persuade the Council to enact a specific merger control provision but it applied its existing tools to prevent them: it utilized Articles 82 and, subsequently, 81 of the Treaty to prevent takeovers and acquisitions of shareholdings in other undertakings.

In *Europemballage Corp and Continental Can Co Inc v. Commission*[45] the ECJ upheld the Commission's view that Article 82 could be used to prevent a dominant undertaking from abusing its dominant position by acquiring a competitor and thereby strengthening that dominant position.[46] In this case the Court of Justice confirmed that an abuse for the purpose of that Article does not have to be attributable to, or dependent on, the existing dominant position. Breach is not dependent upon use of the dominant position. Rather, an abuse occurs 'if an undertaking in a dominant position strengthens such a position in such a way that the degree of dominance reached substantially fetters competition'.[47] Because the Commission adopts a

---

[43] In the 1980s the decision in the UK whether or not to refer a merger for investigation to the UK's (then) Monopolies and Mergers Commission (now the Competition Commission) was predominantly determined by competition factors. The 'Tebbitt Guidelines' stressed that merger policy was an important part of the Government's policy of promoting competition within the economy in the interests of consumers. It was therefore rare for intervention to occur unless a merger potentially raised problems on competition grounds. The German authorities were reluctant to cede control over mergers which might have anti-competitive effects on its markets: see the discussion of the German clause *infra* 978–84.

[44] See B. E. Hawk and H. L. Huser, *European Community Merger Control A Practitioner's Guide* (Kluwer Law International, 1996), 2–3.

[45] Case 6/72, *Europemballage Corp & Continental Can Co Inc v. Commission* [1973] ECR 215, [1973] CMLR 199.

[46] See *supra* Chap. 5.

[47] Case 6/72, *Europemballage Corp & Continental Can Co Inc v. Commission* [1973] ECR 215, [1973] CMLR 199, para. 26. The abuse thus results from a limitation of competition in a market which it already dominates.

relatively low dominance threshold,[48] it appears that Article 82 was a reasonably effective weapon against mergers.[49] This view is expressed by Cook and Kerse in the extract below.

C. J. Cook and C. S. Kerse, *E.C. Merger Control* (4th edn., Sweet & Maxwell, 2006), 1-003

While the Commission's 1996 views on the use of Article 81 were to change its approach to the use of Article 82 to regulate concentrations remained fairly consistent. The Article was used on a number of occasions to exercise a significant measure of control, albeit often informal, over Community takeover activity. The European Court of Justice ("ECJ") bolstered the Commission's view when, in 1973, in *Continental Can*, . . . it found that the acquisition of a competitor could constitute an abuse of a dominant position falling within Article 82. It confirmed that Article 82 could apply to the acquisition of a competitor by a firm enjoying a dominant position:

> 'Abuse may . . . occur if an undertaking in a dominant position strengthens such a position in such a way that the degree of dominance reached substantially fetters competition, *i.e.* that only undertakings remain in the market whose behaviour depends on the dominant one.'
> [para. 26]

The test for intervention under Article 82 was a strict one, the virtual elimination of competition in the relevant product market being necessary. But *Continental Can* spurred the Commission to propose a form of prior control over concentrations, and, significantly, the Commission took the opportunity to consider, albeit informally, a number of mergers under Article 82. This achieved the results the Commission was looking for and prudent advisers tended increasingly to assess market concentration levels at Community and national level and, if the magic figure of 40 per cent was breached, to consider carefully at least informal approaches to the Competition Directorate. The latter part of the 1980s saw much greater use of such techniques as consortium bidding and financial leveraging to support a number of hostile acquisitions. The intervention of the Commission in a consortium bid for Irish Distillers showed the way for using the E.C. competition rules as a spoiling tactic.[50]

The use of Article 82 is, of course, limited by the fact that the acquiring company must have a dominant position before Article 82 can apply (abuses can only be committed by dominant firms). It does not, *prima facie*, apply where two or more undertakings merge to create a dominant position[51] or where a dominant undertaking is acquired by a non-dominant undertaking.

Article 81

The Commission initially appeared to accept that Article 81 would not be used to control mergers.[52] Indeed, Article 81 does not appear to be particularly suitable for the purpose. Because

---

[48] *Supra* Chap. 5–7.

[49] The extent to which Articles 81 and 82 can now be applied to 'concentrations' is discussed *infra* 992–4.

[50] Apart from its decision in *Continental Can* the Commission has, however, only once issued a decision prohibiting a merger transaction under Article 82, *Warner-Lambert/Gillette* [1993] OJ L116/21, [1993] 5 CMLR 559, especially paras. 22–32.

[51] '[O]nly the strengthening of dominant positions and not their creation can be controlled under Art. [82] of the Treaty': Case T-102/96, *Gencor Ltd* v. *Commission* [1999] ECR II-753, [1999] 4 CMLR 971, para. 155; and see Case 6/72, *Europemballage and Continental Can* v. *Commission* [1973] ECR 215, [1973] CMLR 864, para. 26.

[52] The Commission concluded in its *Memorandum on the Concentration of Enterprises in the Common Market*, EEC Competition Series Study No. 3 (published in 1966), para. 58, that Article 81 would not be applicable to agreements 'whose purpose is the acquisition of total or partial ownership of enterprises of the reorganization of the ownership of enterprises'.

the Article strikes principally at *agreements* between independent undertakings it would be artificial to try and deal with many types of mergers under its provisions (in particular, hostile takeovers which are opposed by the target undertaking).[53] Notwithstanding the early views expressed by the Commission, it later sought to apply Article 81 as a weapon against mergers. In *BAT and Reynolds v. Commission*[54] the ECJ confirmed that Article 81 might apply to the acquisition by an undertaking of a minority shareholding in another.

36. It should be recalled that the agreements prohibited by Article [81] are those which have as their object or effect the prevention, restriction or distortion of competition within the Common Market.

37. Although the acquisition by one company of an equity interest in a competitor does not in itself constitute conduct restricting competition, such an acquisition may nevertheless serve as an instrument for influencing the commercial conduct of the companies in question so as to restrict or distort competition on the market on which they carry on business.

38. That will be true in particular where, by the acquisition of a shareholding or through subsidiary clauses in the agreement, the investing company obtains legal or de facto control of the commercial conduct of the other company or where the agreement provides for commercial co-operation between the companies or creates a structure likely to be used for such co-operation.

39. That may also be the case where the agreement gives the investing company the possibility of reinforcing its position at a later stage and taking effective control of the other company. Account must be taken not only of the immediate effects of the agreement but also of its potential effects and of the possibility that the agreement may be part of a long-term plan.

This judgment indicated that agreed share transactions could fall within Article 81(1). The difficulties raised and the ambiguities left unresolved by the judgment (in particular whether or not Article 81 might be applied more broadly to mergers) led to widespread concern in industry which complained both to the Commission and to Member States. The ambiguities 'were fully exploited by the Commission and the resulting uncertainty was used skilfully, particularly by the then Competition Commissioner, Mr Peter Sutherland, to persuade Member States to return to the negotiating table on a new draft of a merger control regulation, first proposed by the Commission in 1973'.[55] Soon after this judgment the green light was given to the Commission to put forward another proposal for a merger regulation.

The subsequent adoption of the ECMR by Peter Sutherland's successor, Sir Leon Brittan, means that the question whether the acquisition of sole control is also caught by Article 81(1) is unlikely to be resolved. Where an undertaking acquires direct or indirect control of another a concentration is deemed to arise for the purposes of the ECMR.[56] The objective of the ECMR is that *it alone* shall apply to concentrations within the meaning of that Regulation and the Commission's powers to apply Articles 81 and 82 are disapplied.[57] The judgment will still be important, however, where direct or indirect control is not acquired so that the ECMR does not apply.[58] Article 81 also remains of relevance to 'joint ventures' which are not concentrations for the purposes of the ECMR.[59]

[53] Further, the sanction of nullity set out in Article 81(2) seems an inappropriate means of controlling and authorizing mergers.

[54] Cases 142 and 156/84, [1987] ECR 4487, [1988] 4 CMLR 24.

[55] C. J. Cook and C. S. Kerse, *E.C. Merger Control* (4th edn., Sweet & Maxwell, 2006), 1-003.

[56] ECMR, Art. 3, see discussion *infra* 958 ff.

[57] ECMR. Art. 21(1), but see discussion *infra* 992–4.

[58] See, e.g., *British Telecom-MCI* [1994] OJ L52/51, [1995] 5 CMLR 301 and. R. A. Struijlaart, 'Minority Share Acquisitions Below the Control Threshold of the EC Merger Regulation: An Economic and Legal Analysis' [2002] 25 *World Competition* 173.

[59] See *infra* 989.

The Residual Application of Articles 81 and 82

It is possible that irrespective of the existence of the ECMR the Commission itself, the national courts and/or the national competition authorities may in some circumstances still be empowered to act pursuant to the Treaty provisions. This possibility is discussed on pages 992–4 *infra*.

b. The Internal Market

The Commission's White Paper, *Completing the Internal Market*,[60] did not make any reference to merger control. However, business restructuring was a natural result of the programme. Commission data showed that an increasing number of mergers were completed in the lead-up to 1992,[61] many between companies in different EC countries or between EC companies and enterprises outside the Community. The need for some form of EC merger control thus became apparent and its absence anomalous. Industry, in particular, became keen to have a level playing field[62] and to have to comply with only *one* set of merger rules.

A combination of Commission support, pressure from industry, the single market programme and increasing numbers of mergers led to the eventual realization that a system of European merger control was inevitable.

(iv) The Original EC Merger Control Regulation—Council Regulation (EEC) 4064/89

The original Merger Control Regulation was adopted by the Council of Ministers on 21 December 1989.[63] It came into force nine months later on 21 September 1990. Its legal basis was Article 83 (ex Article 87) and Article 308 (ex Article 235) of the Treaty. The Regulation set out jurisdictional, procedural, and substantive rules. The procedural requirements were fleshed out by Regulation 447/98, which dealt with matters such as notification, time limits, and hearings.[64] Numerous Commission notices set out guidance on how the Commission interpreted various aspects of the Regulations.[65]

(v) The 1996 Green Paper and Council Regulation (EC) 1310/97

In 1996 the Commission issued its first Green Paper reviewing the ECMR.[66] The Paper looked at several areas of merger control which might be in need of change or reform. In particular, it noted that a number of mergers that significantly affected trade in the Member States escaped the ambit of the rules and it proposed improvements to the treatment of joint ventures.[67]

---

[60] COM(85)310.

[61] In 1982–3 there were 115 mergers, by 1988–9 the number had grown to 492 and to 622 in 1989–90: L. Tsoukalis, *The New European Economy Revisited* (2nd edn., Oxford University Press, 1993), 103.

[62] Some Member States did not have merger rules, whilst the rules in other Member States differed dramatically.

[63] Council Reg. (EEC) 4064/89 of 21 Dec. 1989 on the control of concentrations between undertakings [1989] OJ L395/1, corrigendum [1990] OJ LL257/14. See *supra* n. 41.

[64] Commission Reg. 447/98 [1998] OJ L61/1 of 1 March 1998 on the notifications, time limits, and hearings provided for in Council Reg. 4064/89 on the control of concentrations between undertakings [1998] OJ L61/1. It replaced Reg. 2367/90 (as amended by Reg. 3666/93).

[65] Although the notices do not have binding effect they are extremely useful indicators of the Commission's approach. The current Notices are listed *infra* 955.

[66] Community Merger Control, COM(96)19 final.

[67] See *infra* 962 ff.

In response to the Green Paper Council Regulation 1310/97,[68] which came into force on 1 March 1998, introduced some amendments to the ECMR. An additional (lower) jurisdictional threshold was introduced into the Regulation with the objective of reaching mergers which would otherwise have to be notified to three or more national competition authorities.[69] Many of the other Green Paper proposals were also introduced: for example, changes were introduced to the rules dealing with joint ventures and to the rules setting out when concentrations involving credit and other financial institutions have a Community dimension.[70]

(vi) The 2001 Green Paper

In 2000 the Commission had to report to the Council on the operation of the jurisdictional thresholds.[71] That Report concluded that an important number of transactions with significant cross-border effects remained outside the Community merger rules.[72] It considered, however, that a more in-depth analysis of the appropriate mechanisms for establishing jurisdiction was required and that other issues should be considered at the same time. It thus embarked on a comprehensive review of the Regulation. On 11 December 2001 the Commission published a Green Paper[73] mooting wide-ranging changes to jurisdictional, substantive and procedural matters set out in the ECMR. For example, the Green Paper invited discussion on issues as diverse as:

(i) How to deal with problem of mergers which do not have a Community dimension but which required multiple EU filings;

(ii) Whether to make provisions for referrals between the Commission and national competition authorities ('NCA's) (and vice versa) more flexible and to simplify the procedures;

(iii) Whether the substantive test for appraisal set out in the Regulation, the 'dominance' test, should be revised; and

(iv) Whether the timeframes should be revised or reorganized to make them more certain and, in particular, to leave sufficient time for the submission and discussion of commitments.

Following consultation on these issues, the Commission proposed a package of measures to reform the provisions and working of the ECMR which included a proposal for a new Council Regulation on the control of concentrations between undertakings (a consolidated replacement of Regulation 4064/89 rather than an amendment).[74] These proposals resulted in the adoption of the new ECMR, a new implementing Regulation, the adoption of Best Practice Guidelines, and various Commission interpretative notices.

---

[68] Council Reg. 1310/97 of 30 June 1997 [1997] OJ L180/1.

[69] See *infra* 958 ff.

[70] For a summary of the main changes see, e.g., C. Ahlborn and V. Turner, 'Expanding Success? Reform of the E.C. Merger Regulation' [1998] *ECLR* 249.

[71] The old ECMR, Art. 1(4).

[72] See the Report to the Council on the application of the Merger Regulation Thresholds, COM(2000) 399 final.

[73] 2001 Green Paper on the Review of Council Regulation (EEC) No. 4064/89, COM(2001) 745/6 final.

[74] COM(2002) 711 final, OJ [2003] C20/4. At the same time it also published a draft notice on the appraisal of horizontal mergers (Brussels, 11 Dec. 2002 COM(2002)) and a draft notice on best practices on the conduct of EC merger control proceedings (Draft Best Practices on the conduct of EC merger control proceedings, published on 19 Dec. 2003).

(vii) The Current Merger Control Regulation, Council Regulation (EC) 139/2004

After fairly intensive negotiation and discussion, political agreement for a new recast text of the ECMR was agreed by the Competitiveness Council on 27 November 2003. The new Regulation, Regulation 139/2004, was adopted and published in the Official Journal on 20 January 2004. The Regulation discussed in this chapter is, of course, unless otherwise stated, the current Regulation 139/2004, which incorporates elements of the original 1989 Regulation with amendments introduced in both 1997 and 2004. In the interest of legal certainty,[75] however, the Commission decided to recast the Regulation,[76] adopting a single legislative text to make the desired amendments.

The Regulation is supplemented by an implementing Regulation[77] and a number of Commission Notices which provide guidance as to the interpretation of various provisions of the ECMR. In particular, the following notices are of importance:[78]

(i)   Commission Consolidated Jurisdictional Notice[79] (replacing and consolidating into a single notice previous notices on the concept of a concentration,[80] on the concept of the undertakings concerned,[81] on the calculation of turnover,[82] and on the concept of full-function joint ventures[83])

(ii) Notice on simplified procedure for the treatment of certain concentrations[84]

(iii) Notice on remedies[85]

(iv) Notice on restrictions directly related and necessary to concentrations[86]

(v)   Notice on the appraisal of horizontal mergers[87]

(vi) Notice on case allocation under the referral rules of the Merger Regulation[88]

(vii) Notice on access to the file[89]

---

[75] The objective of this is to ensure that the legislation is both comprehensible and accessible The recasting procedure reproduces in one step what would otherwise require two steps, amendment and adoption of a codification measure, see 'Recasting of Council Regulation (EEC) No. 4064/89 on the control of concentrations between undertakings (The EC Merger Regulation), Some explanations regarding the formatting of the proposal for a new Council Regulation', European Commission (Brussels, 2003).

[76] In accordance with the Inter-institutional agreement of 28 Nov. 2001 on a more structured use of recasting technique for legal acts [2002] OJ C77/1.

[77] Reg. 802/2004, [2004] OJ L133/1.

[78] The Commission's notice on market definition is also of extreme importance, see *supra* Chap. 1.

[79] 10 July 2007.

[80] Notice on the concept of concentration [1998] OJ C66/5, [1998] 4 CMLR 586.

[81] Notice on the concept of undertakings concerned [1998] OJ C66/14, [1998] 4 CMLR 599.

[82] Notice on calculation of turnover [1998] OJ C66/25, [1998] 4 CMLR 613.

[83] Commission's Notice on the concept of full-function joint ventures [1998] OJ C66/1, [1998] 4 CMLR 581

[84] [2005] OJ C 56/32 replacing the 2000 Notice, [2000] OJ C217/32.

[85] [2001] OJ C68/3. See also the Commission's Merger Remedies Study, IP/05/327, available at http://ec.europa.eu/comm/competition/mergers/legislation/notices_on_substance.html#remedies and draft Remedies Notice discussed *infra* 1077 ff.

[86] [2005] OJ C56/24, replacing a 2001 Notice, [2001] OJ C188/5.

[87] [2004] OJ C31/5. See also draft Notice on the appraisal of non-horizontal mergers, *infra* n. 90.

[88] [2005] C56/2.

[89] [2005] OJ C325/7. The Commission has also published a decision on the terms of reference of hearing officers [2001] L 162/21.

The Commission has also published a draft Notice on the appraisal of non-horizontal (vertical and conglomerate) mergers,[90] Best Practice Guidelines on the conduct of EC Merger Regulation proceedings and model texts for divestiture commitments and trustee mandates.[91] The Best Practice Guidelines are designed to provide guidance to interested parties on the day-to-day conduct of EC merger control proceedings.

(viii) The Future

The ECMR provides for a mandatory review of the jurisdictional thresholds and provisions dealing with pre-notification reasoned submissions.[92] The review is to be carried out by 1 July 2009.[93] At this stage, the Commission may again decide to cast its review more broadly.

D. SCHEME OF THE ECMR

The ECMR applies to 'concentrations' with a 'Community dimension'. Both terms are defined in the Regulation itself.[94] The concept of a 'Community dimension' allocates responsibility over concentrations between the Commission and the Member States[95] and imposes an external limit of merger transactions caught within its jurisdiction.[96] Broadly, with certain limited exceptions, concentrations that do not have a Community dimension are assessed under any applicable national competition legislation (no Community law applies),[97] whilst concentrations with a Community dimension are assessed under the provisions of the ECMR.[98] In the latter case, the Commission's decision under the terms of the ECMR is decisive and, as a general rule, no other rule of national or Community competition law applies.[99] The basic scheme is, therefore, that concentrations with a Community dimension benefit from a 'one-stop shop'.[100]

Concentrations with a Community dimension must be notified to the Commission in accordance with the requirements set out in Form CO. On notification, the Commission is obliged to assess, within a period of 25–35 working days (WD), whether or not that concentration falls within the scope of the ECMR and, if so, whether it raises serious doubts about its compatibility with the common market (the Phase I investigation).[101] Approximately 85–90 per cent of mergers notified to the Commission are dealt with in first phase decisions (Phase I proceedings).[102]

---

[90] Published on 13 February 2007 and available at http://ec.europa.eu/comm/competition/mergers/legislation/merger_guidelines.html. The fact that such guidelines would be published was announced in 2002, see M. Monti, 'Merger control in the European Union: a radical reform', 7 Nov. 2002, Brussels (European Commission/IBA Conference on EU Merger Control),

[91] Available on DG Comp's web site at: http://ec.europa.eu/comm/competition/mergers/legislation/legislation.html.

[92] See *infra* 970 and 998.

[93] ECMR, Art. 1(4).

[94] See *infra* section 3.

[95] It is underpinned by the same principles as those which underlie the principle of subsidiarity.

[96] See discussion of its extraterritorial reach *infra* 1088–9 and Chap. 16.

[97] See *infra* 988 ff.

[98] See *infra* 975 ff.

[99] *Ibid.*

[100] It is recognized, however, that the concept of a 'Community dimension' does not always allocate jurisdiction correctly. See section on jurisdiction *infra*.

[101] ECMR, Art. 6(1)(a)–(c). The substantive test for appraisal is set out in Article 2, see *infra* section 5.

[102] See the merger statistics set out *infra* section 6.

Where the Commission believes that the concentration raises serious doubts about its compatibility with the common market a second-phase investigation will be launched to analyse whether or not this is the case. Phase II proceedings are initiated in only about five per cent of mergers notified to the Commission.[103] The Phase II investigation must normally be concluded within a period of 90–125 working days from the initiation of the Phase II proceedings.[104] In general, the operation of the concentration is suspended until the Commission's final decision.[105]

The procedures and tight legal time limits within which the Commission must act under the ECMR were critical to the adoption of the original ECMR[106] and have led to widespread respect for the system. At the time of their adoption these strict time periods were in stark contrast to those that then applied under Regulation 17 (there was no time limit within which an Article 81 or 82 decision had to be adopted and, in practice, such decisions were rare).[107] Under the new system set out in Regulation 1/2003, there is now generally no possibility of a clearance decision for transactions subject to Article 81. This disparity in treatment has led to particular concern in the sphere of joint ventures.[108]

There is a right of appeal from all Commission decisions to the CFI.[109] Despite the recognition of the need for speed in merger cases there is, however, only an expedited appeals procedure in straightforward cases.[110] It may, therefore, take up to three years before an appeal is heard against a Commission decision to prohibit, or clear, a merger.[111] This has led some to call for the creation of a specialist competition tribunal in the CFI.[112]

Section 3 below sets out more fully when the Commission has jurisdiction over mergers and the procedures it adopts in appraising such mergers. Section 4 deals with procedure whilst section 5 deals with substantive appraisal of mergers and the difficult question of how it is determined whether or not a merger is compatible with the common market. Section 6 sets out some merger statistics and appeals are dealt with in section 7. Section 8 deals with international issues and section 9 sets out some conclusions.

---

[103] See the merger statistics set out *infra* section 6.

[104] ECMR, Art. 10(3).

[105] ECMR, Art. 7, *infra* 998–9.

[106] In particular, Member States were anxious that delays should not hamper the flexibility of undertakings seeking to engage in industrial restructuring.

[107] See Chap. 14.

[108] See *infra* 989 ff.

[109] See *infra* 1084.

[110] See also Chap. 14. The judgment in Case T-464/04 *Independent Music Publishers and Labels Association (Impala) v. Commission* [2006] ECR II-2289, [2006] 5 CMLR 19, run under the expedited procedure, was still only handed down 19 months after the Commission's decision, see *infra* 1036.

[111] See *infra* 1086.

[112] A House of Lords select committee in the UK consulted on a proposal to establish a distinct competition court as a panel of the CFI. The UK's Confederation of British Industry considers the current merger review system to be fundamentally flawed, see e.g. D. Trapp, 'Competition court in the dock' 26 October 2006, *Legal Week* 21. On 24 April 2007, however, the Committee announced that it would not recommend either the creation of a separate competition court or a specialist competition chamber.

3. JURISDICTION

A. CONCENTRATIONS

(i) Definition

It has been explained that, subject to specified exceptions, the ECMR applies to 'concentrations' with a 'Community dimension'.[113] The ECMR seeks to govern operations resulting in 'a lasting change in the control of the undertakings concerned and therefore in the structure of the market'.[114] The term concentration is more specifically defined in Article 3 of the ECMR. Essentially, a concentration occurs where two or more undertakings merge their businesses *or* where there is an acquisition of sole or joint control of the whole or part of an existing undertaking or the creation of an autonomous full-function joint venture.[115]

Article 3(1) provides:

A concentration shall be deemed to arise where a change of control on a lasting basis results from:

(a) the merger of two or more previously independent undertakings or parts of undertakings, or

(b) the acquisition, by one or more persons already controlling at least one undertaking, or by one or more undertakings whether by purchase of securities or assets, by contract or by any other means, of direct or indirect control of the whole or parts of one or more other undertakings.

Article 3(4) provides:

The creation of a joint venture performing on a lasting basis all the functions of an autonomous economic entity shall constitute a concentration within the meaning of paragraph 3(1)(b).

A Commission Jurisdictional Notice provides guidance on how the Commission interprets the notion of a concentration.[116]

a. Article 3(1)(a)—Mergers between Previously Independent Undertakings

The Regulation does not define what is meant by the term 'merge'. The term is merely used to describe one type of concentration which falls within the ambit of the Regulation. It appears that the word is used 'narrowly'.

Were a very broad economically-oriented interpretation to the term 'merge' adopted, Article 3(1)(b) would be rendered otiose. The purpose of Article 3(1)(a) appears therefore to be to catch undertakings which have fused their businesses ('legal' mergers), that is where two or more undertakings amalgamate into one business and cease to exist as separate legal entities or where one undertaking acquires and completely absorbs another undertaking (which subsequently ceases to exist).[117] The distinction is important, as the question of whether there has been a merger or merely a change in control affects who must make the notification.[118]

---

[113] See generally, M. Broberg, *The European Commission's Jurisdiction to Scrutinise Mergers* (3rd edn., Kluwer, 2006).

[114] Recital 20.

[115] ECMR, Art. 3.

[116] The Commission Consolidated Jurisdictional Notice, 10 July 2007 replaces a previous notice on the concept of a concentration [1998] OJ C66/5, [1998] 4 CMLR 586 (replacing the notice set out in [1994] OJ C385/5).

[117] See C. J. Cook and C. S. Kerse, *E.C. Merger Control* (4th edn., Sweet & Maxwell, 2006), 2-009 and Commission Consolidated Jurisdictional Notice, 10 July 2007 para. 9. Para. 10 of the Notice states that a merger may also occur where, in the absence of a legal merger, the combining of the activities of previously independent undertakings results in the creation of a single economic unit.

[118] See *infra* 995.

b. Article 3(1)(b)—Acquisition of Control

Decisive Influence

Article 3(1)(b) applies where there is a change in control of an undertaking,[119] for example: where an undertaking acquires sole control of, or (sole) negative control over another on a legal or *de facto* basis, two or more undertakings acquire *joint* control of another,[120] or two or more undertakings establish a full function joint venture[121] in respect of which they exercise joint control. Control can therefore be acquired by one undertaking acting alone or by several undertakings acting jointly and there can be an acquisition of control where there is a change in the *quality* of control (where the acquiring company previously controlled or jointly controlled the company).[122] The acquisition of control is defined in Article 3(2):

Control shall be constituted by rights, contracts or any other means which, either separately or in combination and having regard to the considerations of fact or law involved, confer the possibility of exercising decisive influence on an undertaking, in particular by:

(a) ownership or the right to use all or part of the assets of an undertaking;

(b) rights or contracts which confer decisive influence on the composition, voting or decisions of the organs of an undertaking.

The Regulation is thus intended to catch transactions which lead to an undertaking or undertakings acquiring the ability to exercise *decisive influence* over another, the ability to control the strategic commercial behaviour of the undertakings concerned. This may be acquired through the acquisition of property rights, assets, through shareholders agreements or may result from economic dependence.[123]

Commission Consolidated Jurisdictional Notice, 10 July 2007

16. Control is defined by Article 3(2) of the Merger regulation as the possibility of exercising decisive influence on an undertaking. It is therefore not necessary to show that the decisive influence is or will be actually exercised; however, the possibility of exercising that influence must be effective. Article 3(2) further provides that the possibility of exercising decisive influence on an undertaking can exist on the basis of rights, contracts or any other means, either separately or in combination, and having regard to the considerations of fact and law involved. A concentration therefore may occur or a legal or a *de facto* basis, may take the form of sole or joint control, and extend to the whole or parts of one or more undertakings (cf. Article 3(1)(b)).

---

[119] It does not matter whether the direct or indirect acquisition of control was acquired in one, two or more stages or by means of one or more transactions, provided the end result constitutes a single concentration. Thus a concentration may be deemed to arise where a number of formally distinct legal transactions are interdependent so that none of them would be carried out without the others and the result consists in conferring on one or more undertakings direct or indirect economic control over the activities of another, see Case T-282/02 *Cementbouw Haniel & Industrie BV v. Commission* [2006] ECR II-319, [2006] 4 CMLR 26 paras. 104–109.

[120] Decisive influence exercised alone is substantially different from decisive influence exercised jointly.

[121] See discussion *infra* 962 ff and Chap. 13.

[122] Case IV/M.23, *ICI/Tioxide* [1991] 4 CMLR 792, Jurisdictional Notice, 10 July 2007 paras. 83–90 and see discussion of changes in quality of control *infra*.

[123] Legal control (a controlling interest) is not therefore necessary.

In its Jurisdictional Notice, the Commission distinguishes between sole control and joint control.

Sole Control

Sole control is acquired if one undertaking alone can exercise decisive influence on an undertaking. It can be acquired both where the solely controlling undertaking enjoys the power to determine strategic commercial decisions of the other or where a shareholder is able to veto strategic decisions in an undertaking but does not have the power to impose such decisions (so-called negative sole control. It can be acquired on a *de jure* or *de facto* basis. Sole control, or decisive influence, is ordinarily acquired on a legal basis through an acquisition of more than 50 per cent of the share capital and with it, more than 50 per cent of the voting rights of another undertaking. However, it will always be necessary to look at other factors. Even an undertaking with more than 50 per cent of the share capital will not acquire sole control if, for example, it does not have control of a majority of the voting rights or where a supermajority of voting rights is required for strategic decisions. In such circumstances the acquisition of a simple majority may lead to a scenario of negative or joint control.[124]

Sole control may also be gained where a share of considerably less than 50 per cent is acquired (a minority shareholding).[125] For example, sole control may be acquired on a legal basis where special rights are attached to the preferential shareholding (a majority of the voting rights are nonetheless conferred on the shareholder or the shareholder has power to appoint more than half of the management team). It may be acquired on a *de facto* basis where: the remainder of the shares are widely dispersed;[126] where the shareholder is likely to get a majority of votes at a shareholders' meeting;[127] or where an agreement confers an option to purchase shares in the near future.[128] The analysis in each case is very fact specific and it is important to consider a number of factors, including all shareholdings, special rights, and veto rights attached to the shareholding or set out in a management or shareholding agreement.

Negative sole control exists where a sole shareholder can veto strategic decisions in an undertaking, for example, where strategic decisions require a supermajority so that one shareholder has enough voting rights to veto all strategic decisions.[129] Such a shareholder does not have joint control as although it can block strategic decisions, no other shareholders enjoy the same level of influence and the shareholder exercising negative control does not necessarily have to cooperate with other shareholders in determining the strategic behaviour of the controlled undertaking.[130] Decisive influence and hence control is acquired because of the ability of the shareholder to produce a deadlock situation.

---

[124] Jurisdictional Notice, 10 July 2007, para. 56. In Case IV/M.17, *MBB/Aerospatiale* [1992] 4 CMLR M70, Aerospatiale and MBB formed a joint venture to carry out their helicopter businesses. Although Aerospatiale received 60% of equity (and MBB only 40%) the Commission found the parties had joint control of the joint venture. All strategic decisions for the joint venture required unanimous consent of both partners.

[125] See Jurisdictional Notice, 10 July 2007, para. 57 and Case IV/M.258, *CCIE/GTE*.

[126] See, e.g., Case IV/M.25, *Arjomari/Wiggins Teape* [1990] OJ C321/16 where a 39% shareholding was found to confer sole control because no other entity had more than a 4% shareholding.

[127] See, e.g., Case IV/M.343, *Société Générale de Belgique/Générale de Banque*.

[128] Case T-2/93, *Air France v. Commission* [1994] ECR II-323 and Jurisdictional Notice, 10 July 2007, paras. 59–60.

[129] See Jurisdictional Notice, 10 July 2007, paras. 54 and 57.

[130] *Ibid.*, para. 54.

Joint Control

The Commission explains joint control in its notice on Jurisdiction.[131]

Commission Jurisdictional Notice, 10 July 2007

62. Joint control exists where two or more undertakings or persons have the possibility of exercising decisive influence over another undertaking. Decisive influence in this sense normally means the power to block actions which determine the strategic commercial behaviour of an undertaking. Unlike sole control, which confers upon a specific shareholder the power to determine the strategic decisions in an undertaking, joint control is characterized by the possibility of a deadlock situation resulting from the power of two or more parent companies to reject proposed strategic decisions. It follows, therefore, that these shareholders must reach a common understanding in determining the commercial policy of the joint venture and that they are required to cooperate.

63. As in the case of sole control, the acquisition of joint control can also be established on a de jure or de facto basis. There is joint control if the shareholders (the parent companies) must reach agreement on major decisions concerning the controlled undertaking (the joint venture).

Joint control may be acquired where two parents hold the voting rights equally and also in the absence of equality (for example, where minority shareholders have additional rights which allow them to veto decisions which are essential for the strategic commercial behaviour of the joint venture). It is therefore necessary to consider not only the size of the undertakings' shareholdings but also factors such as the voting rights attached to the shareholdings and shareholder and management agreements, veto rights, and the ability of two or more undertakings to jointly exercise the majority of voting rights, etc.[132]

Changes in the Quality of Control

Not only does the Merger Regulation apply to transactions which lead to the acquisition of sole control, or joint control but it applies to operations leading to change in the quality of control[133] catching: transactions leading to a change from sole control to joint control; a change in joint control (by the entrance of a new shareholder, by replacement of an existing shareholder or possibly by a reduction in the number of jointly controlling shareholders); or by a change from joint control to sole control. It thus covers two categories: (1) an entrance of one or more new controlling shareholders irrespective of whether or not they replace existing controlling shareholders; and (2) a reduction of the number of controlling shareholders.[134]

---

[131] See also, in particular, the CFI's judgment in Case T-282/02 *Cementbouw Haniel & Industrie BV v. Commission* [2006] ECR II-319, [2006] 4 CMLR 26.

[132] Jurisdictional Notice, 10 July 2007, paras. 64–82.

[133] *Ibid.*, paras. 83–90.

[134] *Ibid.*, para. 84. In the draft Jurisdictional Notice the Commission stated that a change from (sole) negative control to sole control would constitute a concentration. It retreated from, and did not adopt, this position in the final Notice, however.

(ii) Joint Ventures

a. Introduction

It has been seen from the discussion above that a concentration may occur where two or more undertakings gain joint control over the whole or part of another firm which has a market presence (Article 3(1)(b)). It has also been seen that Article 3(4) of the ECMR provides that the creation of a 'full-function' joint venture constitutes a concentration, that is a joint venture performing on a lasting basis all of the functions of an autonomous economic entity. The full-functionality criterion therefore delineates the application of the ECMR for the creation of joint ventures by parties.

In EC law, joint ventures are thus dealt with under the merger rules only where they amount to a 'concentration' within the meaning of Article 3.[135] The definition of concentration with this regard is of critical importance, as the rules governing joint ventures under the ECMR and Article 81 respectively are, and have been, different. This has led to concern in industry about the difference in treatment. Broadly, joint ventures amounting to a 'concentration' for the purposes of the ECMR are perceived to receive significantly more favourable treatment. Apart from the fact that the substantive analysis conducted of the joint venture is different,[136] these joint ventures, for example, benefit from a *'one stop shop'* (national competition rules do not apply) where the concentration has a Community dimension and are not generally subject to EC competition law at all where the concentration does not have a Community dimension.[137] Further, decisions taken under the ECMR must be made within strict legal deadlines;[138] and clearance decisions are absolute and not limited in time.[139]

In contrast, where a joint venture falls to be assessed under Article 81 the application of national law (subject to Article 3 Regulation 1/2003)[140] is not precluded. In the past, Article 81 negative clearance or exemption decisions were rarely granted and any such decision did not have to be adopted within a specified time period. Currently, an Article 81 decision will be possible only if the Commission is prepared to grant an Article 10, finding of inapplicability, decision.[141]

---

[135] The difficulty with the concept of a 'joint venture' is that it covers a wide spectrum of activities, see *infra* Chap. 13 which includes an agreement to merge completely the activities of the partner companies on a particular market and to cease to operate in that market themselves, to an agreement to cooperate for particular functions such as R&D. This may make it difficult to know when these joint ventures should be dealt with under merger rules, which deal with transactions which lead to structural changes on a market, and when they should be dealt with under behavioural rules, such as Article 81, which focus on agreements concluded between undertakings operating on a particular market.

[136] The significant impediment to effective competition test applied in the ECMR (see Article 2 discussed *infra* 1005 ff) catches fewer transactions than the 'restriction of competition' test under Article 81.

[137] *Infra* ss. B–D.

[138] Most decisions are made within 25–35 working days of notification. The remainder are generally made within 115–150 working days, *infra* 994 ff.

[139] Although individual exemptions can no longer be granted (which were confined to a period of time) an agreement will still only avoid the prohibition of Article 81(1) for so long as the agreement does not infringe its provisions or for so long as the agreement meets the conditions set out in Article 81(3), see *supra* Chap. 4.

[140] See Chap. 14.

[141] Reg. 1/2003 [2004] OJ L1/1, Art. 10 (finding of inapplicability). Informal guidance (recital 38) may be available from the Commission in cases raising 'novel and unresolved' questions of law. The Commission Notice on informal guidance relating to novel questions concerning Articles 81 and 82 of the EC Treaty that arise in individual cases (guidance letters) [2004] OJ C101/78 specifically states that informal guidance may be available for non full-function joint ventures, see *infra* Chaps. 13 and 14. Although a negative clearance or exemption decision was possible under Reg. 17, in practice such decisions were rarely granted. The procedural restrictions were such that even though the Commission endeavoured to take a view of the compatibility of a joint venture with Article 81 within a period of 2 months it could do so only by administrative letter. No formal decision was possible in this time frame. An administrative letter did not give the parties the same degree of legal certainty as a formal decision, since it was not binding on either the national courts or national authorities of the Member States.

In addition, the joint venture agreement is valid only in so far as the agreement satisfies the conditions of Article 81 both at the time the agreement is concluded and in the future.[142]

The difficulties and inequalities perceived to exist in the past led to a number of changes in the treatment of joint ventures. The Commission sought to ameliorate the way in which it deals with joint ventures under Article 81.[143] Further, it adopted as broad as possible an interpretation of a 'concentration' for the purposes of the ECMR and in 1998 the definition of joint venture set out in the ECMR was expanded. Although there was a suggestion that more joint ventures might subsequently be brought within the scope of the ECMR, to ensure the retention of a prior authorization system for partial-function production joint ventures,[144] the Commission concluded in its 2001 Green Paper that there was no compelling reason to extend the scope of the ECMR to these joint ventures.

b. 'Full Function' Joint Ventures

Article 3(4)[145] makes it clear that the creation of a joint venture constitutes a concentration only if the joint venture is 'full function'. The full functionality criterion, which does *not* apply where joint control of an undertaking with market presence is *acquired* from a third party or parties,[146] requires that the joint venture is formed on a lasting basis to carry out the functions of an autonomous economic entity.

Joint Control

Joint ventures are undertakings jointly controlled by two or more undertakings. The meaning of joint control is explained above.

An Autonomous Economic Entity in Operational Respect

The Commission explains the concept of full-functionality in paragraphs 91–109 of the jurisdictional notice. It stresses the importance of the joint venture being autonomous from an operational point of view and hence having sufficient resources to operate independently on a market and being intended to operate on a lasting basis. The joint venture must therefore have 'a management dedicated to its day-to day operations and access to sufficient resources including finance, staff, and assets (tangible and intangible) in order to conduct on a lasting basis its business activities within the area provided for in the joint-venture agreement'.[147] Further, it seems that a joint venture is not full-function if it simply takes over one specific function for its parents.

Commission Jurisdictional Noice, 10 July 2007

95. A joint venture is not full-function if it only takes over one specific function within the parent companies' business activities without its own access to or presence on the market. This is the case, for example, for joint ventures limited to R&D or production. Such joint ventures are auxiliary to their parent companies' business activities. This is also the case where a joint venture is essentially

---

[142] In the past, any exemption decision granted was only for a specified period of time, see also supra n. 139.

[143] See *infra* Chap. 13.

[144] White Paper on modernisation of the rules implementing Articles 85 and 86 [now 81 and 82] of the EC Treaty [1999] OJ C132/1, [1999] OJ 5 CMLR 208, paras. 79–81.

[145] Article 3(2) of the old ECMR.

[146] Jurisdictional Notice, 10 July 2007, para. 94.

[147] *Ibid.*, para. 94.

limited to the distribution or sale of its parent companies' products and, therefore, acts principally as a sales agency. However, the fact that a joint venture makes use of the distribution network or outlet of one or more of its parent companies normally will not disqualify it as 'full-function' as long as the parent companies are acting only as agents of the joint venture.

96.   A frequent example where this question arises are joint ventures involved in the holding of real estate property, which are typically set up for tax and other financial reasons. As long as the purpose of the joint venture is limited to the acquisition and/or holding of certain real estate for the parents and based on financial resources provided by the parents, it will not usually be considered to be full-function as it lacks an autonomous, long term business activity on the market and will typically also lack the necessary resources to operate independently. This has to be distinguished from joint ventures that are actively managing a real estate portfolio and who act on their own behalf on the market, which typically indicates full-functionality.

Another relevant factor in the determination of full-functionality may be whether the parent companies make sales or purchases to or from the joint venture. Where sales are made to the parent companies, the main issue to be determined is whether, regardless of these sales, the joint venture can play an active role on the market and be considered economically autonomous from an operational viewpoint.[148] Further, a joint venture is unlikely to be full-function where it operates like a joint sales agency purchasing from its parents and adding little value to the products or services concerned.[149]

Commission Jurisdictional Notice, 10 July 2007

97.   The strong presence of the parent companies in upstream or downstream markets is a factor to be taken into consideration in assessing the full-function character of a joint venture where this presence results in substantial sales or purchases between the parent companies and the joint venture. The fact that for an initial start up period only, the joint venture relies almost entirely on sales to or purchases from its parent companies does not normally affect its full-function character. Such a start-up period may be necessary in order to establish the joint venture on a market. But the period will normally not exceed a period of three years, depending on the specific conditions of the market in question.

The jurisdictional notice also states that the fact that the agreement contains a clause providing for the dissolution of the joint venture, for example, on its failure or on disagreement between the parents, does not necessarily mean that the joint venture has not been established on a lasting basis. Further, a joint venture created for a finite period but long enough to affect the structure of the market will also be established on a lasting basis, but one established for a short finite period will not.

---

[148] Jurisdictional Notice, 10 July 2007, paras. 98–100.

[149] *Ibid*, para. 97.

Commission Jurisdictional Notice, 10 July 2007

103. Furthermore, the joint venture must be intended to operate on a lasting basis. The fact that the parent companies commit to the joint venture the resources described above normally demonstrates that this is the case. In addition, agreements setting up a joint venture often provide for certain contingencies, for example, the failure of the joint venture or fundamental disagreement as between the parent companies. This may be achieved by the incorporation of provisions for the eventual dissolution of the joint venture itself or the possibility for one or more parent companies to withdraw from the joint venture. This kind of provision does not prevent the joint venture from being considered as operating on a lasting basis. The same is normally true where the agreement specifies a period for the duration of the joint venture where this period is sufficiently long in order to bring about a lasting change in the structure of the undertakings concerned, or where the agreement provides for the possible continuation of the joint venture beyond this period.

104. By contrast, the joint venture will not be considered to operate on a lasting basis where it is established for a short finite duration. This would be the case, for example, where a joint venture is established in order to construct a specific project such as a power plant, but it will not be involved in the operation of the plant once its construction has been completed.

105. A joint venture also lacks the sufficient operations on a lasting basis at a stage where there are decisions of third parties outstanding that are of an essential core importance for starting the joint venture's business activity. Only decisions that go beyond mere formalities and the award of which is typically uncertain qualify for these scenarios. Examples are the award of a contract (e.g., in public tenders), licences (e.g., in the telecoms sector) or access rights to property (e.g., exploration rights for oil and gas). Pending the decision on such factors, it is unclear whether the joint venture will become operational at all. Thus, at that stage the joint venture cannot be consider to perform economic functions on a lasting basis and consequently does not qualify as full function. However, once a decision has been taken in favour of the joint venture in question, this criterion is fulfilled and a concentration arises.

The Notice deals at paragraphs 106–109 with the position if the parents enlarge the scope of the joint venture's activities in the course of its lifetime. It states that such enlargement may constitute a concentration requiring notification in particular, where the enlargement entails the acquisition of the whole or part of another undertaking from the parents that would, considered in isolation, quality as a concentration.

Some examples of joint ventures which are not full-function and which are consequently subject to Article 81 are set out in Chapter 13.

The Relevance of Coordination of Competitive Behaviour

The original ECMR provided that a joint venture which has as its object or effect the co-ordination of the competitive behaviour of undertakings which remain independent could not constitute a concentration. This *negative* condition was removed in 1997 so that the complex determination required by this condition no longer has to be made at the jurisdictional stage. It is still of importance to know whether a joint venture enables the coordination of the competitive behaviour of independent undertakings, however. First, a different *substantive* appraisal applies. Although the basic appraisal made in the case of each joint venture will be same, the coordinative aspects of joint ventures are assessed additionally for their compatibility with the common market in accordance with the criteria set out in Article 81 of the Treaty.[150] Secondly, in deroga-tion from the general rule, the Commission is able to apply Article 81 to a joint venture which enables the coordination of the competitive behaviour of independent undertakings but which does *not* have a Community dimension.[151]

(iii) Article 3(5)

Article 3(5) of the ECMR sets out several circumstances in which a concentration shall be deemed not to arise. These deal with shares held by financial institutions on a temporary basis, the acquisition of control by liquidators or other administrators, and operations carried out by financial holding companies. These are dealt with in paragraphs 110–116 of the jurisdictional notice.

(iv) Abandonment of a Concentration

If the Commission initiates Phase II proceedings following notification of a concentration to it, it must close the proceeding by means of a decision adopted under Article 8 of the ECMR 'unless the undertakings concerned have demonstrated to the satisfaction of the Commission that they have abandoned the concentration.'[152] The Commission's Notice on Jurisdiction sets out guid-ance as to how the parties may demonstrate that the transaction has been abandoned. General guidance, set out in paragraphs 119–120, is followed by specific guidance of the type of proof that is required depending upon whether the original concentration takes the form of a binding agreement, a good faith intention to conclude an agreement, a public announcement of a public bid or of the intention to make a public bid or an implemented concentration.

Commission Jurisdictional Notice, 10 July 2007

19. As a general principle, the requirements for the proof of the abandonment must corre-spond in terms of legal form intensity etc. to the initial act that was considered sufficient to make the concentration notifiable. In case the parties proceed from that initial act to a strengthening of their contractual links during the procedure, for example by concluding a binding agreement after the transaction was notified on the basis of a good faith intention, the requirements for the proof of the abandonment must correspond also to the nature of the latest act'.[153]

114. In line with this principle, in case of implementation of the concentration prior to a Commission decision, the re-establishment of the *status quo ante* has to be shown. The mere withdrawal of the notification is not considered as sufficient proof that the concentration has been abandoned in the sense of Article 6(1)(c). Likewise, minor modifications of a concentration which do not affect the change in control or the quality of that change, cannot be considered as an aban-donment of the original concentration.

---

[150] ECMR, Art. 2(4)(5), discussed *infra* 1072 ff.

[151] ECMR, Art. 21(1).

[152] ECMR, art 6(1)(c). See *infra* n. 352 and accompanying text. Prior to the initiation of Phase II proceedings, such requirements do not apply.

[153] Notice on Jurisdiction, para. 119. See also Commission's Information note on Article. 6(1)(c) 2nd sentence of Regulation 139/2004 (abandonment of concentrations).

B.COMMUNITY DIMENSION

(i) A Bright Line Jurisdictional Test

The ECMR aims to apply to concentrations which create significant structural changes the impact of which extend beyond the national borders of any one Member State.[154] It is concentrations with a *Community dimension* which fall for appraisal under the terms of the ECMR. Broadly, whether or not a merger has a Community dimension is assessed by reference to the *turnover* of the parties involved.[155] Since the notification of concentrations with a Community dimension is compulsory, and generally means that a notification cannot be made to the competition authorities of the Member States, the jurisdictional test incorporated within the ECMR is intended to be a bright line test which can be applied relatively simply, objectively and easily.[156] The corollary of having a simple quantitative jurisdictional test is that some mergers between non-EU undertakings whose business is principally carried on outside the EU may be caught by the regulation,[157] jurisdiction over European mergers is not always allocated appropriately as between the Commission and the Member States[158] and concentrations between undertakings which quite obviously do not significantly impede effective competition in the common market may be brought within the Regulation and be subject to mandatory notification. Thus mergers may be notifiable even if they have no effect on competition in the common market. The requirement that they should significantly impede effective competition in the common market is relevant only to the substantive assessment of whether or not the concentration is compatible with the common market.[159] The Commission is aware of the inconvenience and cost that this imposes and has taken steps to ameliorate the situation of undertakings in such a position. It has issued a Notice setting out a simplified procedure for the treatment of concentrations that do not raise competition concerns.[160] In such cases it may be possible to submit a short-form notification,[161] and where the Commission is satisfied that the concentration qualifies for the simplified procedure it normally adopts a short-form decision.[162]

The jurisdictional thresholds are set out in Article 1(2) and (3). Article 1(2) derives from the original ECMR, whilst Article 1(3) derives from an amendment made to the original Regulation by Regulation 1310/97. These thresholds were not revised in 2004 following the 2001 review.[163]

---

[154] ECMR, recital 8.

[155] 'Turnover is used as a proxy for the economic resources being combined in a concentration, and is allocated geographically in order to reflect the geographic distribution of those resources.' Jurisdictional Notice, 10 July 2007, para. 124.

[156] In some States, jurisdiction may be determined by reference to the market shares of parties, see, e.g., Greece, Spain, and Portugal. In these States even the question of whether the merger should be notified may be a complex one to determine.

[157] See *infra* 1088–9 and Chap. 16.

[158] See discussion *infra*.

[159] See infra 1005 ff.

[160] [2005] OJ C 56/32.

[161] See Short Form for the notification of a concentration pursuant to Regulation (EC) No. 139/2004, attached to Reg. 802/2004, [2004] OJ L133/1.

[162] Commission Notice on a simplified procedure for treatment of certain concentrations, [2005] OJ C 56/32, para. 17.

[163] See *infra* 970–1.

(ii) Article 1(2)

The primary test is that set out in Article 1(2). Only if this test is *not* satisfied is it necessary for an undertaking to consider whether or not the thresholds set out in Article 1(3) are satisfied.

Council Regulation (EC) No. 139/2004 of 20 January 2004 on the Control of Concentrations between Undertakings [2004] OJ L24/1, Article 1

1. Without prejudice to Article 4(5) and Article 22, this Regulation shall apply to all concentrations with a Community dimension as defined in this Article.

2. A concentration has a Community dimension where:
   (a) the combined aggregate worldwide turnover of all the undertakings concerned is more than EUR 5,000 million; and
   (b) the aggregate Community-wide turnover of each of at least two of the undertakings concerned is more than EUR 250 million.

   unless each of the undertakings concerned achieves more than two-thirds of its aggregate Community-wide turnover within one and the same Member State.

This test looks to the combined worldwide turnover of the undertakings concerned and the Community-wide turnover of at least two of the undertakings involved in the concentration (approximately £3,400 million and £170 million respectively).[164] Where the turnover requirements are not met the Article 1(2) test is obviously not satisfied. Even where the thresholds are met, jurisdiction is denied if the *proviso* applies. Where each of the undertakings concerned achieves more than two-thirds of its Community turnover within one and the same Member State there is no Community dimension. The purpose of the proviso is to exclude concentrations the effects of which are felt primarily in one Member State.[165] In 2006, Neelie Kroes expressed concern about the operation of the rule stating:

we have launched a review of the so-called "two/thirds rule" under the Merger Regulation. Recent experience in the energy sector suggests that it is debatable whether the two thirds rule still

---

[164] The thresholds are €5, 000 million and €250 million respectively.

[165] This does not necessarily mean that the relevant national merger control regime will apply (although it normally does). The application of this proviso can lead to peculiar results. For example, two competing bids made for the take-over of Midland Bank by Lloyds Bank and Hong Kong and Shanghai Bank respectively fell to be assessed under different merger regimes. The former bid did not have a Community dimension (and fell within the jurisdiction of the UK authorities. Although the bid was referred on 22 May 1992 to the (then) Monopolies and Mergers Commission for in-depth analysis, the reference was set aside when the bid was abandoned). The latter did have a Community dimension and fell to be assessed under the EC Merger rules, Case IV/M.213. The UK authorities could, however, have made use of Art. 22 ECMR (*infra* 989 ff) and requested the Commission to appraise the Lloyds Bank bid even though the concentration did not have a Community dimension. Alternatively, it could have requested (Art. 9) the referral of the Hong Kong and Shanghai Bank bid back to it: see e.g. *GEHE/Lloyds Chemists* where the Commission referred a case to the UK authorities which were already reviewing Unichem's bid for Lloyds, *infra* 978 ff. See also the bids for the Spanish electricity operator, Endesa. The bid by Spain's largest gas operator, Gas Natural, did not have a Community jurisdiction because of the two-thirds rule, see COMP/M.3986 and rejection of Endesa's appeal against the Commission's refusal to take jurisdiction, Case T-417/05 *Endesa v. Commission* [2006] ECR II-2533. In contrast E.On's bid did satisfy the Community threshold, was notified to and cleared unconditionally by the Commission, Case COMP/M.4110. See also *infra* n. 195 and accompanying text.

represents the best proxy for ensuring that cases with a cross-border impact should be dealt with in Brussels. We must be sure that mergers with significant cross-border effects are assessed consistently. The time is therefore ripe to have another look at the impact of the two thirds rule, and to consider the various options available.[166]

(iii) The 1996 Green Paper

The thresholds set in Article 1(2) are much higher than those originally proposed by the Commission to the Council in May 1989,[167] in the run up to the adoption of Regulation 4064/89. This was as a result of the reluctance of many of the Member States to relinquish merger control to the Commission. The Commission's fears that it would have no work if the turnovers were set at such unrealistic levels were not realized.[168] However, it held the view that significant mergers with cross-border effects fell outside the scope of the ECMR[169] so the thresholds were reviewed again in the 1996 Green Paper.[170] The Commission put forward a strong case in support of its proposal to lower both the worldwide and Community-wide thresholds. In particular, it stressed that many transnational mergers which did not meet the thresholds were likely to meet the notification requirements of more than one Member State and, consequently, would have to bear the additional costs and efforts of these notifications. These costs were compounded by the enormous differences between each of the national systems of merger control.[171] This situation meant undertakings restructuring within the Community did not have a level playing field. As a result of the problems caused by multiple notifications and multiple procedures, the Commission view gained support from much of European industry.

(iv) Article 1(3) of the ECMR

The solution eventually reached is set out in Article 1(3).[172] This provides that a concentration which satisfies lower worldwide and Community-wide turnovers then those set out in Article 1(2) may be caught if two additional criteria are satisfied. Broadly, these two factors aim to catch concentrations where the undertakings concerned, jointly and individually, have a minimum

---

[166] Speech 06/60 Speech before the EP Economic and Monetary Affairs Committee. 31 Jan 2006.

[167] It recommended that the worldwide turnover should be set at ECU 1,000 million, the Community-wide turnover at ECU 100 million, and that jurisdiction should then only be denied if more than *three-quarters* of the aggregate Community-wide turnover was achieved in one and the same Member State. The thresholds were originally expressed in ECU but were read as references to Euro from 1 Jan. 1999, Council Reg. 1103/97 [1997] OJ L162/1.

[168] The ECMR came into force almost at a peak of merger activity.

[169] Not only did it think that the actual thresholds excluded too many mergers which might have an important impact within the Community but the Commission believed that the two-thirds proviso enabled mergers with important cross-border effects to escape. At the time of the 1996 Green Paper the Commission noted that Siemens, for example, produced two-thirds of its turnover in one Member State but still had significant operations outside of its home market, see the Green Paper on Community Merger Control COM(96)19 final, para. 48.

[170] The original ECMR anticipated a review, and a lowering, of the thresholds by the end of 1993. Severe opposition from a number of Member States, including Germany, the UK, and France, meant that any such review was likely to be redundant. The Commissioner for Competition at the time, Karel van Miert, thus decided not to conduct a review at this stage.

[171] In some Member States notification is obligatory; in others (such as the UK) it is generally not obligatory; in one Member State there are no merger rules (Luxembourg). The jurisdictional thresholds triggering a notification or examination by the competent authorities vary from Member State to Member State and deadlines for investigating the impact of a merger vary. In some Member States the final decisions are taken by administrative or ministerial organizations, in others independent competition authorities. For a comparison of the different regimes see, e.g., 'Getting the Deal Through, Merger Control 2006' (*Global Competition Review*, 2006).

[172] On the passing of Council Regulation 1310/97.

level of activities in three or more Member States and which are therefore likely to be subject to the merger rules of those three or more Member States.[173] Like Article 1(2), paragraph 3 contains a proviso excluding concentrations where two-thirds of the Community-wide turnover of all of the undertakings involved is achieved in one and the same Member State.[174] It provides:

Council Regulation (EC) No. 139/2004 of 20 January 2004 on the Control of Concentrations between Undertakings [2004] OJ L24/1, Article 1(3)

A concentration that does not meet the thresholds laid down in paragraph 2 has a Community dimension where:

(a) the combined aggregate worldwide turnover of all the undertakings concerned is more than EUR 2 500 million;

(b) in each of at least three Member States, the combined aggregate turnover of all the undertakings concerned is more than EUR 100 million;

(c) in each of at least three Member States included for the purpose of point (b), the aggregate turnover of each of at least two of the undertakings concerned is more than EUR 25 million; and

(d) the aggregate Community-wide turnover of each of at least two of the undertakings concerned is more than EUR 100 million

unless each of the undertakings concerned achieves more than two-thirds of its aggregate Community-wide turnover within one and the same Member State.

(v) Review of the Thresholds

In 2000 the Commission had to report to the Council on the operation of these jurisdictional thresholds.[175] That Report concluded that, despite the introduction of Article 1(3), an important number of transactions with significant cross-border effects remained outside the Community merger rules.[176] In its 2001 Green Paper the Commission considered this problem in greater depth, and mooted the possibility of amending the Article 1(3) thresholds. It stressed its view that the provision had fallen short of achieving its underlying objective and that this factor led to great inconvenience for the companies concerned resulting from multiple filings in three or more Member States and difficulties, in terms of length of process, costs and legal certainty.[177]Although the Commission did put forward some conceivable options for amending Article 1,[178] for example, by providing for automatic community competence over cases subject to multiple filing requirements, the Commission ultimately recognized that these options were

---

[173] Reg. 1310/97 [1997] OJ L180/1, Art. 1(1)(a) and (b). The test was not set, however, by reference to the number of notifications which had to be made. It would have been excessively complicated to do it in this way, especially as some Member States do not have compulsory notification.

[174] But see *supra* n. 166

[175] The old ECMR, Art. 1(4).

[176] See the Report to the Council on the application of the Merger Regulation Thresholds, COM(2000) 399 final.

[177] Green Paper on the Review of Council Regulation (EEC) No. 4064/89 COM(2001) 745/6 Final, paras. 24–8 and see *supra* n. 171.

[178] It concluded that modifications to the Article 1(3) criteria would not provide the envisaged results.

unworkable. In the end, therefore, no amendment was made to the thresholds (although Article 1(4) provides for a review of the thresholds by 1 July 2009).[179] Instead, since it is accepted that Article 1 will not always allocate cases correctly as between the Commission and national competition authorities respectively, other provisions of the Regulation have been simplified and developed to provide an effective 'corrective' mechanism.[180]

(vi) Concentrations, Undertakings Concerned, and Calculation of Turnover

In order to apply the Articles 1(2) and (3) tests, it is first necessary to identify the number of concentrations involved. In simple cases, such as the acquisition of B by A, there will usually be only one. In more complex cases, such as the division of an existing joint venture company between its parents, there may however be more than one concentration.[181] Once the appropriate concentration, or concentrations, is identified it is necessary to determine (a) the undertakings concerned and (b) their turnover. Despite the aim of the Regulation to provide a clear, simple jurisdictional test these steps are not always straightforward.[182] The meaning of 'undertakings concerned' and 'turnover' is clarified in the jurisdictional notice.

The Notice seeks, guided by reference to cases previously notified to the Commission, to identify undertakings concerned in most typical situations. Paragraphs 134–153 provide detailed analysis of who the undertakings concerned are in acquisition of control cases (for example, acquisition of sole control, part or joint control change from joint to sole control or of controlling shareholders etc).

Commission Jurisdictional Notice 10 July 2007

2. MERGERS

132. In the case of a merger, the undertakings concerned are the merging undertakings.

3. ACQUISITION OF CONTROL

133. In the remaining cases, it is the concept of "acquiring control" that will determine which are the undertakings concerned. On the acquiring side, there can be one or more undertakings acquiring sole or joint control. On the acquired side, there can be one or more undertakings as a whole or parts thereof. As a general rule, each of these undertakings will be an undertaking concerned within the meaning of the Merger Regulation.

---

[179] Article 1(5) provides that the Council may review the thresholds acting by *qualified majority*.

[180] See ECMR, recital 22 and Articles 4(4)(5), 9, and 22. Article 4(5), in particular, allows parties to a concentration which does not have a Community dimension but which is capable of being reviewed under the national competition laws of a least three Member States to submit a reasoned submission to the Commission that it should review it. In the absence of disagreement by a competent Member State the transaction is deemed to have a Community dimension. See also ECMR Art 21(4) and Article 297EC.

[181] See, e.g., Case IV/M.197, *Solvay/LaPorte*, 30 Apr. 1992. In this case the parties jointly notified the division of their joint venture, the Interox group of companies, between themselves. The Commission concluded that this was two separate concentrations. The Solvay concentration had a Community dimension but did not raise serious doubt as to its compatibility with the common market. The Laporte concentration did not however, have a Community dimension so did not fall within the scope of the ECMR.

[182] See M. Broberg, *The European Commission's Jurisdiction to Scrutnise Mergers* (3rd edn., Kluwer, 2006), chaps. 2–6.

Once the undertakings concerned have been identified their turnover must be calculated. Article 5(1) defines turnover as 'the amount derived by the undertakings concerned in the previous financial year from the sale of products and provision of services falling within the undertaking's ordinary activities'.[183] Article 5(2) sets out rules which apply where only part of an undertaking is taken over or acquired. It provides that where the concentration consists of an acquisition of part or parts, of one or more undertakings, (such as a subsidiary or a division), only the turnover of the relevant parts which are the subject of the concentration shall be taken into account with regard to the seller or sellers.[184] Article 5(3) sets out special turnover rules which apply, for example, to credit and financial institutions and insurance undertakings. Article 5(4) provides that turnover is calculated not only by reference to those undertakings concerned but also to the turnover of all those entities which they control or by whom they are controlled, and to other connected undertakings. The operation of Article 5(4) is explained in the jurisdictional notice.

Commission Jurisdictional Notice, 10 July 2007

175. Where an undertaking concerned by a concentration belongs to a group, not only the turnover of the undertaking concerned is considered, but the Merger Regulation requires to also take into account the turnover of those undertaking with which the undertaking concerned has links consisting in the rights or powers listed in Article 5(4) in order to determine whether the thresholds contained in Article 1 of the Merger Regulation are met. The aim is again to capture the total volume of the economic resources that are being combined through the operation irrespective of whether the economic activities are carried out directly by the undertaking concerned or whether they are undertaken indirectly via companies and undertakings with which the undertaking concerned possessed the links described in Article 5(4).

176. The Merger Regulation does not delineate the concept of a group in a single abstract definition, but sets out in Article 5(4)(b) certain rights or powers. If an undertaking concerned directly or indirectly has such links with other companies, those are to be regarded as part of its group for purposes of turnover calculation under the Merger Regulation.

177. Article 5(4) of the Merger Regulation provides the following:

"Without prejudice to paragraph 2 [acquisition of parts], the aggregate turnover of an undertaking concerned within the meaning of Article 1(2) and (3) shall be calculated by adding together the respective turnovers of the following:

    (a) the undertakings concerned;

    (b) those undertakings in which the undertaking concerned directly or indirectly;

        (i)   owns more than half the capital of business assets, or

        (ii) has the power to exercise more than half the voting rights, or

        (iii) has the power to appoint more than half the members of the supervisory board, the administrative board or bodies legally representing the undertakings, or

        (vi) has the right to manage the undertaking's affairs;

    (c) those undertaking which have in an undertaking concerned the rights or powers listed in (b);

---

[183] Jurisdictional Notice, 10 July 2007 paras. 157–74.

[184] Acquisitions of parts between the same persons or undertakings in a series of transactions within a two-year period are treated as one and the same concentration, ECMR, Art. 5(2). The application of the ECMR cannot therefore be avoided through the acquisition of an undertaking in stages.

(d) those undertakings in which an undertaking as referred to in (c) has the rights or powers listed in (b);

(e) those undertakings in which two or more undertakings as referred to in (a) to (d) jointly have the rights or powers listed in (b)."

An undertaking which has in another undertaking the rights and powers mentioned in Article 5(4)(b) will be referred to as the "parent" of the latter in the present section of the Notice dealing with the calculation of turnover, whereas the latter is referred to as "subsidiary" of the former. In short, Article 5(4) therefore provides that the turnover of the undertaking concerned by the concentration (point (a)) should include its subsidiaries (point (b)), its parent companies (point (c)), the other subsidiaries of its parent undertakings (point (d)) and any other subsidiary jointly held by two or more of the undertakings identified under (a)-(d) (point (e)).

Note that with the aim of providing greater legal certainty, the definition of control in Article 5(4) is different from, and more tightly defined than, the definition of control set out in Article 3(2).[185] In general, the whole turnover of undertakings identified in Article 5 is taken into account. However, for joint ventures between two or more undertakings concerned, turnover of the joint ventures is apportioned equally amongst the undertakings concerned.[186] Further, in practice, the Commission allocates turnover for joint ventures between undertakings concerned and third parties on a per capita basis according to the number of undertakings exercising joint control.[187]

Examples

The following examples seek to clarify, through an examination of transactions carried out by entities within a larger group of companies, how Article 5 applies to identify the undertakings whose turnover is taken into account for the purposes of calculating Community dimension.

Group A

A is a wholly-owned subsidiary of W. A has two wholly-owned subsidiaries X and Y. Y and a third party, TP, jointly control Z.

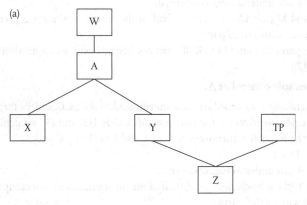

(a)

---

[185] Although the Commission invited comments as to whether the differences between the two meanings of control was problematic and whether it would be appropriate to harmonize the two provisions, no harmonization of the rules was in fact made, see 2001 Green Paper on the Review of Council Regulation (EEC) No. 4064/89, COM(2001) 745/6 final.

[186] ECMR, Art 5(5)(b).

[187] Jurisdictional Notice, 10 July 2007, para. 187.

Group B

B is company jointly owned by J and K. K has a wholly owned subsidiary L. B has a wholly-owned subsidiary M.

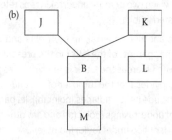

Group C

C is a company jointly controlled by D and E. E is a wholly-owned subsidiary of F.

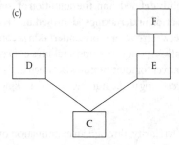

1. **A acquires B.**

   The undertakings concerned are A and B.

   The aggregate turnover for the purposes of Article 1(2) and (3) is calculated by adding together the respective turnovers of A, X, Y, Z(50%) and W in Group A and B and M (in Group B) That is:

   a. A and B (the undertakings concerned);

   b. X, Y and M (subsidiaries) and Z (half of the turnover, since it is a company jointly controlled with a third party);

   c. W (A's parent) but not J and K (B's parents, because only an acquisition of part of seller (Art 5(2)).

2. **C acquires sole control of A.**

   The undertakings concerned are the acquiring undertakings, C, and the target company, A. The aggregate turnover for the purposes of Article 1(2) and (3) is calculated by adding together the respective turnovers of C, D, E and F in Group C and A, X, Y and Z(50%) in Group A. That is:

   a. C and A (the undertakings concerned);

   b. X and Y (the subsidiaries) and Z (half of the turnover, since it is a company jointly controlled with a third party);

   c. D and E (C's parents) and F (C's parent's parent) but not W (A's parent because only an acquisition of part of seller (Art. 5(2)).

3. **J acquires sole control of B (a change from joint control with K to sole control by J).**

   The undertakings concerned are J and B. K, the existing shareholder (as seller) is not an undertaking concerned.

The aggregate turnover for the purposes of Article 1(2) and (3) is calculated by adding together the respective turnovers of J, B and M. That is:

a. J and B (the undertakings concerned);

b. M (B's subsidiary). To avoid double counting the turnover of J has to be calculated without the turnover of the joint venture, B.[188]

4. **A and B acquire joint control of C.**

The undertakings concerned are A and B (the undertakings acquiring joint control) and C (the pre-existing acquired undertaking).

The aggregate turnover for the purposes of Article 1(2) and (3) is calculated by adding together the respective turnovers of A, X, Y, Z (50%) and W in Group A; B, J, K and L in Group B; and C in Group C. That is:

a. A, B and C (the undertakings concerned);

b. X, Y and M (the subsidiaries) and Z (half of the turnover, since it is a company jointly controlled with a third party);

c. W, J and K, (A and B's parents) but not D, E or F (because only acquisition of part (Art. 5(2));

d. L (a subsidiary of B's parent K).

C. CONCENTRATIONS WITH A COMMUNITY DIMENSION: A ONE-STOP SHOP?

(i) Exclusive Competence of the Commission under the ECMR

Article 21(1)–(3) provides:

1. This Regulation alone shall apply to concentrations as defined in Article 3, and Council Regulations (EC) No 1/2003, (EEC) No 1017/68, (EEC) No 4056/86 and (EEC) No 3597/87[189] shall not apply, except in relation to joint ventures that do not have a Community dimension and which have as their object or effect the coordination of competitive behaviour of undertakings that remain independent.

2. Subject to review by the Court of Justice, the Commission shall have sole jurisdiction to take the decisions provided for in this Regulation.

3. No Member State shall apply its national legislation on competition to any concentration that has a Community dimension . . .

Article 21 thus indicates that no Community law applies to concentrations that do not have a Community dimension, the ECMR, but not national law, applies to concentrations with a Community dimension (parties to a concentration with a Community dimension benefit from a 'one-stop shop') and the Commission's decision under the ECMR is decisive. The one-stop shop held great appeal both to the Commission itself and the business community.

(ii) Case Allocation

Notwithstanding this basic starting point, there are circumstances in which a concentration with a Community dimension, or aspects of it, may be referred to a national authority for assessment under its domestic law at either a pre- or post-filing stage. Further, there may be

---

[188] The turnover of B's parents are not included. K's turnover is excluded because it is an acquisition of part and, to avoid double counting the turnover of the joint venture has to be taken without the turnover of the acquiring shareholder, J.

[189] Reg. 3597/87 has essentially been repealed by Reg. 411/2004 [2004] OJ L68/1.

circumstances where a concentration without a Community dimension may be referred to the Commission.[190] Several provisions in the Merger Regulation provide for the transfer of cases between the competent authorities of the Member States and the Commission on the initiative or invitation of the Commission, the Member States or the parties to the transaction themselves at a pre-notification stage.[191] The Commission has published a Notice on case allocation under the referral rules of the Merger Regulation (the 'Notice on case allocation')[192] which aims to describe the rationale underlying the case referral system and to provide practical guidance on the mechanics of the referral system.

The Notice on case allocation explicitly recognizes that although financial criteria relevant to the assessment of Community dimension generally serve as effective proxies for the category of transactions for which the Commission is the most appropriate authority, the jurisdictional mechanism should be flexible in some instances so that cases may have to be reattributed by the Commission to Member States and vice versa.[193] The 2004 revisions to the ECMR were designed to facilitate re-attribution of cases, consistently with the principle of subsidiarity, so that the most appropriate authority or authorities for carrying out a particular merger investigation should, where possible, deal with the case, whilst at the same time preserving the basic principle of the one-stop shop for Community mergers.[194] The Commission describes the guiding principles for this case allocation in its Notice and also provides more specific guidance on the legal requirements of each provision.

Commission Notice on Case Allocation Under the Referral Rules of the Merger Regulation [2005] OJ C56/2

Guiding principles

8. The system of merger control established by the Merger Regulation, including the mechanism for re-attributing cases between the Commission and Member States contained therein, is consistent with the principle of subsidiarity enshrined in the EC Treaty. Decisions taken with regard to the referral of cases should accordingly take due account of all aspects of the application of the principle of subsidiarity in this context, in particular the suitability of a concentration being examined by the authority more appropriate for carrying out the investigation, the benefits inherent in a 'one-stop-shop' system, and the importance of legal certainty with regard to jurisdiction. These factors are inter-linked and the respective weight placed upon each of them will depend upon the specificities of a particular case. Above all, in considering whether or not to exercise their discretion to make or accede to a referral, the Commission and Member States should bear in mind the need to ensure effective protection of competition in all markets affected by the transaction.

More appropriate authority

9. In principle, jurisdiction should only be re-attributed to another competition agency in circumstances where the latter is the more appropriate for dealing with a merger, having regard to the specific characteristics of the case as well as the tools and expertise available to the agency.

---

[190] And/or in which Articles 81 and 82 can be applied to a concentration by the Commission itself or by a national court or NCA.

[191] See discussion of Articles 4(4)(5), 9, 21(4) and 22 *infra*.

[192] [2005] OJ C56/2. See also P. Lowe 'The Interaction between the Commission and small Member States in Merger Review', Dublin 10 Oct. 2003.

[193] *Ibid.*, para. 3.

[194] *Ibid.*, para. 5.

Particular regard should be had to the likely locus of any impact on competition resulting from the merger. Regard may also be had to the implications, in terms of administrative effort, of any contemplated referral.

10. The case for re-attributing jurisdiction is likely to be more compelling where it appears that a particular transaction may have a significant impact on competition and thus may deserve careful scrutiny.

One-stop-shop

11. Decisions on the referral of cases should also have regard to the benefits inherent in a 'one-stop-shop' system, which is at the core of the Merger Regulation. The provision of a one-stop-shop is beneficial to competition authorities and businesses alike. The handling of a merger by a single competition agency normally increases administrative efficiency, avoiding duplication and fragmentation of enforcement effort as well as potentially incoherent treatment (regarding investigation, assessment and possible remedies) by multiple authorities. It normally also brings advantages to businesses, in particular to merging firms, by reducing the costs and burdens arising from multiple filing obligations and by eliminating the risk of conflicting decisions resulting from the concurrent assessment of the same transaction by a number of competition authorities under diverse legal regimes.

12. Fragmentation of cases through referral should therefore be avoided where possible, unless it appears that multiple authorities would be in a better position to ensure that competition in all markets affected by the transaction is effectively protected. Accordingly, while postal referrals are possible under Articles 4(4) and 9, it would normally be appropriate for the whole of a case (or at least all connected parts thereof) to be dealt with by a single authority.[195]

Legal certainty

13. Due account should also be taken of the importance of legal certainty regarding jurisdiction over a particular concentration, from the perspective of all concerned. Accordingly, referral should normally only be made when there is a compelling reason for departing from 'original jurisdiction' over the case in question, particularly at the post-notification stage. Similarly, if a referral has been made prior to notification, a post-notification referral in the same case should be avoided to the greatest extent possible.

14. The importance of legal certainty should also be borne in mind with regard to the legal criteria for referral, and particularly—given the tight deadlines—at the pre-notification stage. Accordingly, pre-filing referrals should in principle be confined to those cases where it is relatively straightforward to establish, from the outset, the scope of the geographic market and/or the existence of a possible competitive impact, so as to be able to promptly decide upon such requests.

Part III of the Notice on case allocation deals with the mechanics of the referral system, and cooperation within the network of competition authorities.[196] In particular the Notice reiterates the importance of cooperation and dialogue between the Commission and NCAs and the NCAs *inter se*.[197]

---

[195] This is consistent with the Commission's decision in Case COMP/M.2389, *Shell/DEA* and M.2533, *BP/E.ON* to refer to Germany all of the markets for downstream oil products. The Commission retained the parts of the cases involving upstream markets. Likewise, in M.2706, *P&O Princess/Carnival*, the Commission exercised its discretion not to refer a part of the case to the UK, because it wished to avoid a fragmentation of the case (See Commission press release of 11 Apr. 2002, IP/02/552).

[196] The specific ECMR provisions dealing with referral are set out *infra*.

[197] See Notice on case allocation, [2005] C56/2, especially part III 13.

Concentrations with a Community dimension, or aspects of such a concentration, may be dealt with by a NCA pursuant to Article 9 or Article 21(4) of the ECMR, Article 297 EC or following a reasoned submission by a party to a concentration that the concentration should be examined, in whole or in part, by a Member State.

(iii) Article 9—Distinct Markets

a. Objective of Article 9

Article 21(3) paragraph 2 states that the prohibition on a Member State applying its national competition legislation to a concentration with a Community dimension under the first paragraph (set out above) is 'without prejudice to any Member State's power to carry out any enquiries necessary for the application of Articles 4(4), 9(2) or after referral, pursuant to Article 9(3) first subparagraph, indent (b), or Article 9(5), to take the measures strictly necessary for the application of Article 9(8)'.

Article 9 of the ECMR was included at the particular insistence of Germany (hence it is often known as the 'German clause'). Germany was initially opposed to the introduction of EC merger control and, in particular, it feared that such rules would not be applied stringently enough. Article 9 was added at a late stage in the negotiations to meet the Germans' objections over loss of control. It provides for the referral, at the request of a national authority, of a merger, or aspects of a merger (i.e., total or partial referrals), to that authority where the concentration threatens competition in a 'distinct' market in that authority's State. It was designed to meet the fears that the Commission's action might be less rigorous than national merger control would be and that local or regional issues might not be sufficiently addressed by the criteria set out for the assessment of concentrations in Article 2 of the ECMR.[198]

Although Article 9 references were made reasonably frequently under the old ECMR[199] the Commission proposed, in conjunction with its review of the Article 1(3) thresholds in the 2001 Green Paper, that this provision could, along with Article 22,[200] be simplified to facilitate the exchange of cases between the authorities. Articles 9 and 22 thus operate as a corrective measure enabling the transfer of cases to achieve optimal allocation.

Council Regulation (EC) No. 139/2004 of 20 January 2004 on the Control of Concentrations between Undertakings [2004] OJ L24/1, Recital 11

(11) The rules governing the referral of concentrations from the Commission to Member States and from Member States to the Commission should operate as an effective corrective mechanism in the light of the principle of subsidiarity; these rules protect the competition interests of the Member Sates in an adequate manner and take due account of legal certainty and the 'one-stop shop' principle.

---

[198] Article 2 of the ECMR only permits the Commission to take action against concentrations which would impede competition in 'the common market or in a substantial part of it'.

[199] Although few referrals were made in the initial years, since 1997 there have been a number of referrals each year. A list of all Article 9 decisions are available on DG Comp's web site.

[200] Which allows competent authorities of the Member States to refer concentrations without a Community dimension to the Commission for appraisal, *infra* 989 ff.

The Notice on allocation recognizes that the objective of Article 9 is to ensure, subject to the principle of the one-stop shop and legal certainty, that a national competition authority should deal with a case when it is in the best position to do so.[201]

b. The Wording of Article 9

Council Regulation (EC) No. 139/2004 of 20 January 2004 on the Control of Concentrations between Undertakings [2004] OJ L24/1, Article 9

1. The Commission may, by means of a decision notified without delay to the undertakings concerned and the competent authorities of the other Member States, refer a notified concentration to the competent authorities of the Member State concerned in the following circumstances.

2. Within 15 working days of the date of receipt of the copy of the notification, a Member State, on its own initiative or upon the invitation of the Commission, may inform the Commission, which shall inform the undertakings concerned, that:

(a) a concentration threatens to affect significantly competition in a market within that Member State, which presents all the characteristics of a distinct market, or

(b) a concentration affects competition in a market within that Member State, which presents all the characteristics of a distinct market and which does not constitute a substantial part of the common market.

3. If the Commission considers that, having regard to the market for the products or services in question and the geographical reference market within the meaning of paragraph 7, there is such a distinct market and that such a threat exists, either:

(a) it shall itself deal with the case in accordance with this Regulation, or

(b) it shall refer the whole or part of the case to the competent authorities of the Member State concerned with a view to the application of that State's national competition law.

If, however, the Commission considers that such a distinct market or threat does not exist, it shall adopt a decision to that effect which it shall address to the Member State concerned, and shall itself deal with the case in accordance with the Regulation.

In cases where a Member State informs the Commission pursuant to paragraph 2(b) that a concentration affects competition in a distinct market within its territory that does not form a substantial part of the common market, the Commission shall refer the whole or part of the case relating to the distinct market concerned, if it considers that such a distinct market is affected.

---

c. Request

Article 9 is not triggered unless a Member State makes a request, either on its own initiative or on the invitation of the Commission,[202] for a reference back within 15 working days of receipt of the copy of the notification from the Commission.[203]

---

[201] Notice on case allocation, [2005] C56/2, paras. 9–13 and 37. Further, Article 4(4) provides that parties may request the possibility of a referral of a concentration with a Community dimension to a Member State *prior* to its notification to the Commission. Where it is agreed in such a situation that a case should be totally referred to a Member State, no notification to the Commission is required. Article 4 is discussed further in section 4 below.

[202] The provision that the Commission might invite a Member State to make a request was only added into the current Regulation. It does not, however, require a Member State to make the request.

[203] But see also Article. 4(4) *infra* 984 and 997.

Where the Commission receives a request from a Member State in accordance with Article 9(2)(a),[204] the Commission must determine whether the requesting State has *prima facie* demonstrated that (1) a distinct market exists and (2) the concentration threatens to affect significantly competition within that Member State.[205] Even where these conditions are satisfied, the Commission has a discretion to deal with the case itself *or* to make a total or partial[206] reference of the case to the competent national authority.[207]

37. Other than verification of the legal requirements, other factors should also be considered in assessing whether referral of a case is likely to be considered appropriate. This will involve an examination of the application of the guiding principles referred to above, and in particular whether the competition authority or authorities is/are in the best position to deal with the case. To this end, consideration should be given in turn both to the likely locus of the competitive effects of the transaction and to how well equipped the national competition authority would be to scrutinize the operation.

In Article 9(2)(b)[208] cases the Commission *must* refer the whole or part of the case relating to the distinct market, where the Member State has provided evidence to establish on a preliminary analysis that the concentration affects competition in a distinct market which does not constitute a substantial part of the common market (markets with a narrow geographic scope, within a Member State).[209]

Despite the background to the introduction of Article 9, the Article thus concedes little authority to the Member States. A Member State may express concern about the effect of a merger in its territory, but if the concentration has a Community dimension and potentially impedes effective competition in the common market or a substantial part of it, the ECMR provides that the Commission is the sole arbiter of whether or not the matter should be referred to the Member State under Article 9. In the recitals, however, the Regulation makes it clear that the Commission and competent authorities of the Member states will work together forming a 'network of public authorities' to ensure that their respective competences are applied in close cooperation, 'using efficient arrangements for information-sharing and consultation, with a view to ensuring that a case is dealt with by the most appropriate authority, in the light of the principle of subsidiarity and with a view to ensuring that multiple notifications of a given concentration are avoided to the greatest extent possible'.[210] The reality is, therefore, that in a great majority of cases a partial or full referral back is made following an Article 9 request.[211]

d. A Reference Back

The Commission's decision to refer or not to refer must generally be taken within 35 working days of notification or 65 working days where Phase II proceedings have been initiated.[212] If the Commission does make a reference to the national authority that authority must decide the

---

[204] See Commission Notice on Case Allocation, [2005] C56/2, paras. 34–7.

[205] Under the old ECMR the competent authority could only make a request where the concentration threatened to create or strengthen a dominant position.

[206] See Case IV/M.180, *Steetley plc/Tarmac* [1992] 4 CMLR 337 discussed *infra* 982.

[207] ECMR, Art. 9(3).

[208] Notice on case allocation, [2005] C56/2, paras. 38–41.

[209] The first Article 9(2)(b) reference made was in Case COMP/M.2446, *Govia/Connex South Central*. See also Case COMP M.2370, *Connex/DNVBVG* and Case COMP M.3130, *Arla Foods/Express Dairies* and case law under Article 82, *supra* Chap. 5.

[210] ECMR, recital 14.

[211] See the merger statistics set out *infra* section 6.

[212] ECMR Art 9(4) and 10(1). See Case IV/M.330, *McCormick/CPC/Ostmann*.

case 'without undue delay' and, in any event, must inform the undertakings concerned of the result of the preliminary competition assessment and what further action it proposes to take within 45 working days of the Commission's referral (or national notification if requested).[213]

In so far as a reference is made the Commission delegates power to investigate the aspects of the merger that affect competition in that distinct market. However, the Member State may only take 'measures strictly necessary to safeguard or restore effective competition on the market concerned'.[214]

e. Distinct Market

Whether a distinct market exists is determined with regard to the market for the products or services in question and, in particular, the geographical reference market. The meaning of a geographical reference market is set out in Article 9(7):

> 7. The geographical reference market shall consist of the area in which the undertakings concerned are involved in the supply and demand of products or services, in which the conditions of competition are sufficiently homogeneous and which can be distinguished from neighbouring areas because, in particular, conditions of competition are appreciably different in those areas. The assessment should take account in particular of the nature and characteristics of the products or services concerned, of the existence of entry barriers or of consumer preferences, of appreciable differences of the under-takings' market shares between the area concerned and neighbouring areas or of substantial price differences.

f. Success of Claims

Although the Commission may at first, perhaps, have been less willing to exercise its power to make references back under Article 9,[215] it has been seen that this provision now operates as an important corrective mechanism for reallocating appropriate cases to NCAs, for example where cases raise specific issues in a Member State[216] or regional[217] or local[218] markets. As the

---

[213] ECMR, Art. 9(6).

[214] ECMR, Art. 9(8).

[215] The Commission considered that the referral procedure should only apply in exceptional cases, see Commission and Council Notes on the 1989 Merger Regulation, Merger Control Law in the European Union, 1998 and e.g. Case IV/M.165, *Alcatel/AEG Kabel* [1992] OJ C6/23; Case IV/M.12, *Varta/Bosch* [1991] OJ L320/26, [1992] 5 CMLR M1; Case IV/M.222, *Mannesmann/Hoesch* [1993] OJ L114/34; and Case IV/M.238, *Siemens/Philips* (subsequently abandoned). In Case IV/M.330, *McCormick/CPC/Ostmann* a German request under Article 9 was finally successful. This was only on account of a Commission error, however! The German authorities wished to consider a concentration affecting the German herb and spice market. It considered that features of the distinct market meant that there would be no likely entrants onto the market, and that the merger threatened to create a dominant position as result of which competition would be significantly impeded. The Commission agreed that the German herb and spice market did constitute a distinct market within the meaning of Article 9 but intended to assess the merger itself. However, because of an error in the calculation of the time limits set out in Article 10(1) it was unable to launch a Phase II investigation (if the Commission fails to take a decision in accordance with the deadlines set out in Article 10(1) the concentration is 'deemed to have been declared compatible with the common market' (Art. 10(6)). The examination of the concentration would not, therefore, have been possible unless the notification had been referred to the German authorities. Soon after the reference the parties abandoned the concentration.

[216] See, e.g. *Compass/ Rail Gourmet/ Gourmet Nova*. But see e.g. *VEBA/VIAG* where the Commission declined to make a reference to Germany in the case of a merger in the energy sector, involving generation and distribution of electricity in Germany.

[217] See, e.g. Case IV/M.3373, *Accor/Barrière/Colony* and Case COMP/M.3905 *Tesco/Carrefour*.

[218] See, e.g. Case COMP/M.1388, *Total/PetroFina*, Case COMP/M.2533 *BP/E.ON*, Case COMP/M.2730 *Connex/DNVBVG*.

Commission is, however, currently very concerned about improving competition in the energy sector[219] and has indicated that it will use its ECMR powers to prevent increasing market concentration in this sector, an Article 9 reference may be particularly unlikely in an energy case.[220]

The first case in which the Commission agreed to make a reference back was *Steetley plc/Tarmac*.[221] In this case competing bids had been made for Steetley plc by Tarmac and Redland. Only the Tarmac bid had a Community dimension and the Redland bid fell to be assessed under domestic law.[222] The concentration between Steetley and Tarmac would have pooled the building material activities of the undertakings. In particular, the undertakings had very high market shares for bricks and clay tiles in some parts of England. The Commission agreed that the concentration would lead to particular local problems in the market for the manufacture and sale of bricks in the North East and South West of England and in relation to the manufacture of clay tiles throughout Great Britain.[223] The brick markets were regional (the cost of transporting such heavy products being high relative to the cost of the products) and trade flows in clay tiles between Great Britain and the rest of the Community were low (although the tiles were lighter and could be transported more easily throughout the country significant barriers to entry to the market remained—adequate clay reserves were necessary to manufacture the tiles). The economic implications were therefore substantially limited to the UK. The Commission issued a decision referring these aspects of the merger back to the UK to be assessed under the UK merger provisions.[224] On the same day it issued a decision finding that the remaining aspects of the concentration were compatible with the common market.[225]

In many cases a decision to make a reference to a national authority may cause concern to the notifying parties as the reference is unlikely to be requested unless the concentration is considered to pose particular risks for a distinct national market.[226] In *Interbrew/Bass*,[227] for example, the Commission cleared a merger between Interbrew and Bass but referred aspects of the case back to the UK authorities. In this case the parties closed the transaction following the Commission clearance, but the UK's Competition Commission subsequently recommended that the merger should be prohibited.[228] In judicial review proceedings before the English

---

[219] See its completed inquiry into the energy sector, available at http://ec.europa.eu/comm/competition/sectors/energy/inquiry/index.html (see *supra* Chap. 11).

[220] See e.g. *VEBA/VIAG* where the Commission declined to make an Article 9 reference to Germany in the case of a merger in the energy sector, involving generation and distribution of electricity in Germany. See also *supra* n. 166.

[221] Case IV/M.180, [1992] 4 CMLR 337. A number of Art 9 referrals have involved building or construction industries, see e.g. Case COMP/M.1030 *Redland/Lefarge* [1998] 4 CMLR 218, Case COMP/M.1779 *Anglo American/Tarmac*, Case COMP/M.2495 *Haniel/Fels* and Case COMP/M.2568 *Haniel/Ytong* and Case COMP/M.4298 *Aggregate Industries/Foster Yeoman*.

[222] Then the UK's Fair Trading Act 1973 (FTA). The FTA merger provisions have, however, now been repealed and replaced by Part 3 of the Enterprise Act 2002.

[223] The Commission also considered the fact that a competing bid was being assessed at the domestic level.

[224] For the powers of the UK authorities with respect to Article 9 see EEC Merger Regulation (Distinct Market Investigations) Regulations 1990 SI 1990/1715 (as amended by the EC Merger Control (Consequential Amendments) Regulations 2004 SI 2004/1079).

[225] Case IV/M.180.

[226] In Case IV/M.460, *Holdercim/Cedest*, however, the French authorities cleared aspects of a concentration which had been referred to it under Article 9. The remaining aspects were cleared by the Commission after a preliminary assessment under Art. 6(1)(b). See also Case COMP/M.3130, *Express Dairies/Arla Foods* cleared by the UK authorities (DTI Press Release, 15 Oct. 2003), Case COMP/M.4298 *Aggregate Industries/Foster Yeoman* (the OFT accepted undertakings from the parties in lieu of a reference to the Competition Commission) and discussion of *SEB/Moulinex infra*.

[227] Case IV/M.2044, [2000] OJ C293/11, IP/00/940.

[228] Interbrew SA and Bass plc: A report on the acquisition by Interbrew SA of the brewing interests of Bass plc, Cm. 5014, 2001.

courts, procedural errors were found to have been committed by the Competition Commission.[229] The court remitted the question of remedies back to the Secretary of State. Subsequently, it was agreed that the Competition Commission's concerns could be met by either the divestment of Bass Brewers or Carling Brewers.[230]

An Article 9 case which provides an illustration of the difficulties that can result from dual scrutiny in derogation of the one-stop shop principle, is *SEB/Moulinex*.[231] This case concerned a proposed concentration between two French companies. SEB put forward a proposal to purchase the small household electrical appliances business of Moulinex, which was in the midst of bankruptcy proceedings. SEB itself had a significant position in the small electrical household appliances market. The Commission appraised the concentration in so far as it affected fourteen countries, clearing the transaction subject to commitments in nine countries.[232] As the primary effects of the merger were to be felt in France, however, the Commission, at the same time, exercised its discretion to make a reference to the French authorities under Article 9(2)(a). The French authorities went on to unconditionally clear the merger, applying its 'failing firm' defence, even though the combined entity would achieve an average of 60–70 per cent market share on segments of the French small electrical household appliances market. The (Community) failing firm defence had been specifically rejected by the Commission.[233]

Two competitors of the parties, BaBybliss and Royal Philips, challenged both the Commission's decision (to clear the merger subject to commitments and to refer the French aspects of the merger back to the French authorities) and the French authority's decision.

The challenge to the Commission's appraisal of the aspects of the transaction it considered was successful[234] but the challenge to its decision to refer the concentration to the national authority was not. The CFI was not, of course, at liberty to rule on the compatibility of the French authority's decision with the Commission's approval decision (or with Community law) *only* on whether the Commission was entitled to refer the concentration to the French authorities, i.e., whether the conditions of Article 9(2)(a) were satisfied and, if so, whether the Commission had properly exercised its *discretion* whether or not to refer the merger back to the requesting authority. The Court held that the Commission was not entitled to make such a reference where the authority was not capable of acting so as to maintain or restore effective competition or if the reference would undermine the Commission's decision, including commitments, in respect of the parts not referred back. However, this determination had to be made at the time the reference back decision was made and not with the benefit of hindsight and the

[229] [2001] EWHC 367 (Admin) (Moses J).

[230] See DTI press releases, P/2001/495 and P/2002/045.

[231] Case COMP/M.2621, IP/02/22.

[232] *Ibid.* It initially cleared the transaction in Phase I proceedings subject to commitments. On appeal, however, the CFI annulled the Commission's decision in so far as it had cleared the concentration without commitments in five Member Sates on the grounds that it had not properly analysed the effects in those States, Case T-119/02, *Royal Philips Electronics v. Commission* [2003] ECR II-1433, [2003] 5 CMLR 53. The Commission subsequently reopened the case and after opening Phase II proceedings it again gave unconditional approval to the merger in Spain, Finland, Ireland, Italy, and the UK having carried out a new wide-ranging survey of the five countries concerned. The decision did not affect the 2002 decision as regards fulfilment by SEB of the commitments it had entered into in relation to the other nine countries considered by the Commission.

[233] Case COMP/M.2621, IP/02/22. For a discussion of the failing firm defence, see *infra* 1047–52. The next application for an Article 9 reference by the French authorities was rejected, see Case COMP/M.2978, *Lagardère/Natexis/VUP* IP/03/808. In this case the Commission took the view that most of the markets had a transnational element. Although some of the markets may have been national the Commission concluded that a single agency should examine the impact of the transaction as a whole. It also took account of Lagardère's preference to deal with one and not two agencies.

[234] See *supra* n. 232.

result of national proceedings. The fact that the referral fragmented the examination of the concentration and interfered with the one-stop shop principle did not affect the conclusion since 'a fragmented assessment undermining the "one-stop shop" principle is inherent in the referral procedure'.[235]

The surprising outcome in this case was therefore, that despite the objectives of Article 9 (to allow Member States to look at mergers where the effects are likely to be particularly acute in the national market), that 'in contrast to the Commission, which approved the concentration in question only after the commitments relating to the Moulinex trade market had been offered, the French competition authorities ... approved the concentration with respect to its effects on the relevant markets in France without imposing commitment's relying on the "failing firm" doctrine'.[236] Eventually, however, the French administrative Court (Conseil d'Etat)[237] annulled the French authority's authorization of the merger, holding that the failing firm conditions had not in fact been fulfilled.

g. Conclusions

The amendments made to Article 9 by the new ECMR make it easier for a Member State to request a referral from the Commission and are in fact designed to facilitate the transfer of a case to the most appropriate authority. In derogation of the one-stop shop principle, such mergers may therefore be subject to scrutiny both at the Community and national level. The Commission will, therefore, have to exercise its discretion carefully, if it is not to rob the one-stop shop principle of its substance[238] and to deny a coherent and uniform application of competition law in the Community, in cases which have cross border effects. The Commission's Notice on case allocation[239] indicates that decisions on referral of cases will have regard to the benefits inherent in the one-stop shop system, the core of the Merger Regulation, and to the principle of legal certainty.

(iv) Article 4(4) Request for Referral to a National Competition Authority

Article 4(4) allows notifying parties instead of notifying a concentration with a Community dimension to the Commission, to make a reasoned submission that a concentration may significantly affect competition in a distinct market in a Member State and should be examined in whole or in part by that Member State. In contrast, therefore, with an Article 9 request which is made by a Member State post notification of the transaction to the Commission, an Article 4(4) reasoned submission is lodged by the parties *prior* to notification. Article 4(4) is discussed in section 4 below.

---

[235] Case T-119/02, *Royal Philips Electronics v. Commission* [2003] ECR II-1433, [2003] 5 CMLR 53, para. 355. See also Cases T-346 and 347/02, *Cableuropa v. Commission*, [2005] ECR II-4251, [2004] 5 CMLR 25.

[236] Case T-119/02, *Royal Philips Electronics v. Commission* [2003] ECR II-1433, [2003] 5 CMLR 53, para. 345.

[237] No. 249627, 6 Feb. 2004.

[238] It has been suggested that the Commission's discretion to refer Article 9 distinct cases should be removed, see Pérez and Burnley, 'The Article 9 Referral Back Procedure: A Solution to the Jurisdictional Dilemma of the European Merger Regulation?' [2003] 8 *ECLR* 364.

[239] [2005] OJ C56/2.

(v) Article 21(4)—Legitimate Interests

Article 21(4) recognizes that there are some matters which are so sensitive to the national interest that the Member States should be entitled to retain control over them themselves.[240] Under Article 21(4), a Member State may take steps to protect 'legitimate interests' which are not protected under the ECMR itself:

> 4. Notwithstanding paragraphs 2 and 3, Member States may take appropriate measures to protect legitimate interests other than those taken into consideration by this Regulation and compatible with the general principles and other provisions of Community law.
>
> Public security, plurality of the media and prudential rules shall be regarded as legitimate interests within the meaning of the first subparagraph.
>
> Any other public interest must be communicated to the Commission by the Member State concerned and shall be recognised by the Commission after an assessment of its compatibility with the general principles and other provisions of Community law before the measures referred to above may be taken. The Commission shall inform the Member State concerned of its decision within 25 working days[241] of that communication.

This provision does *not* enable a Member State to clear a merger which the Commission has prohibited under the ECMR. It is defensive in nature. It enables a Member State to protect its legitimate interests by scrutinizing, and, if necessary, prohibiting mergers which may raise concerns other than pure competition ones (even were the Commission to consider that the merger was compatible with the common market).[242]

In *Newspaper Publishing*,[243] for example, although the proposed acquisition of Newspaper Publishing plc (publisher of the Independent) by Promotora de Informaciones SA, Editoriale l'Espresson SpA, and Mirror Group Newspapers plc fell within the scope of the ECMR, the UK was able to take steps to protect its legitimate interests, in this case the plurality of the media. The Commission cleared the merger but noted that the UK Secretary of State would also have to grant formal consent under the UK's merger rules.[244] The Commission made it clear that any measures adopted by the UK authorities would, however, have to be objectively the least restrictive to achieve the end pursued (they would, therefore, have to comply with the Community principle of proportionality). The UK is one of many States that consider that media ownership may require a different approach from that ordinarily applicable in domestic competition law.[245] In

---

[240] This was Article 21(3) under the old ECMR.

[241] Under the old ECMR the Commission had to inform the Member State concerned within one month of its decision.

[242] In that sense it is rather different from other provisions in Community law which recognize that Member States may wish to act to protect essential interests such as public policy or security or protection of the health and life of humans. Article 30 (ex Art. 36) of the Treaty, for example, permits the Member States, in specified circumstances, to derogate from the fundamental objective of creating an internal market characterized by the abolition of obstacles to the free movement of goods (Arts. 3(1)(c) (ex Art. 3(c)) and 28 (ex Art. 30) EC Treaty).

[243] Case IV/M.423.

[244] The merger provisions were then set out in the Fair Trading Act 1973. These have now been repealed and replaced by the Enterprise Act 2002.

[245] At the time the UK had special rules governing newspaper mergers: see ss. 57–62 of the Fair Trading Act 1973. Newspaper mergers have now been brought within the general regime for mergers set out in the Enterprise Act 2002 but they are now special cases in which the Secretary of State can intervene on public interest grounds, see e.g. reference of BSkyB's acquisition of 17.9 State in ITV plc to the Competition Commission, 24 May 2007.

Thomson CSF/Racal (II)[246] the UK authorities also stated an intention to consider the public security aspects of a concentration impacting on 'defence electronics' markets under Article 21(4) and in *Sun Alliance/Royal Insurance*[247] the Commission accepted that the UK authorities could apply UK insurance legislation to the transaction.

It is clear from the third paragraph of Article 22(4) that Member States may take steps to protect a 'public interest', other than those specifically referred to in the Article. In *Lyonnaise des Eaux SA/Northumbrian Water Group*[248] the Commission accepted that the regulation of the UK water industry constituted a legitimate interest. Following the privatization of the UK water industry, the water authority in the UK seeks to maintain competitive pressures on water suppliers (which enjoy a monopoly in the provision of local or regional services) by making comparisons of, for example, the relative operating and capital costs of the different water enterprises. In order to achieve this task a sufficient number of independent providers must be maintained. Thus mergers between water enterprises above a certain size are, in contrast to the general rule applying in the UK, automatically referable to the UK's Competition Commission. In accepting the legitimate interests of the UK the Commission held, however, that the UK authorities should not, in their scrutiny of the concentration, take account of factors which properly fell for assessment by the Commission:

the control exercised by the UK authorities is aimed at ensuring that the number of independently controlled water companies is sufficient to allow the Director General of Water Services to exercise his regulatory functions . . . in order not to go beyond the interest pursued by the UK regulatory legislation other issues in relation to mergers between water companies can only be taken into account to the extent that they affect the control regime set out above . . . [249]

The Commission has made it clear that where a Member State wishes to protect an interest not specifically referred to in Article 21(4) it must notify it to the Commission in accordance with paragraph 4.[250] In *BSCH/A.Champalimaud*,[251] for example, the Portuguese Minister of Finance opposed a concentration with a Community dimension which would give Banco Santander Central Hispano (BSCH) joint control of a group of companies, which included several insurance companies and Portuguese banks. The Portuguese authorities had not, however, communicated any public interest to the Commission that they considered it necessary to protect. The Commission considered that it had not been established that the measure was based on prudential rules and that neither the 'protection of national interest and strategic sectors' nor the 'violation of procedural rules' could constitute a legitimate interest within the meaning of the provision. It thus required the Republic of Portugal to suspend the measures adopted.

(vi) Article 296 of the EC Treaty—Essential Interests of Security

Article 296(1)(b) of the Treaty provides that nothing in the Treaty shall preclude the application by Member States of measures 'it considers necessary for the protection of the essential interests of its security which are connected with the production of or trade in arms, munitions and

---

[246] Case COMP/M.1858, IP/00/628. See also e.g. Case COMP/M.4561 *GE/Smiths Group* where the Commission approved GE's proposed acquisition of Smiths Group's aerospace division. The UK Secretary of State intervened under ECMR Art. 21(4), P/2007/60 but eventually accepted undertakings from the parties relating to the protection of sensitive information rather than referring it to the UK's Competition Commission.

[247] Case IV/M.759.

[248] Case IV/M.567, [1996] 4 CMLR 614. Contrast Case IV/M.1346, *EDF/London Electricity*.

[249] Case IV/M.567, [1996] 4 CMLR 614.

[250] Case IV/M.1616, *BSCH/A.Champaliaud*, para. 27.

[251] *Ibid*. See also Case COMP/M.2054, *Secit/Holderbank/Cimpor* and discussion of breach of ELMR Art. 21, *infra* 988.

war material'. Recital 19 to the ECMR makes it clear that the Regulation does not affect the Member States' ability to act under this Article. The ability of Member States to act under Article 296 is not, therefore, affected by the reference in Article 21(4) to matters of 'public security'. A Member State may request parties to a concentration not to notify military aspects of a merger to the Commission.

In the competing bids for VSEL plc (a builder of UK Trident submarines), for example, British Aerospace plc and GEC notified their competing bids (which amounted to concentrations) to the Commission only in so far as they related to the non-military activities of VSEL (only 2.5 per cent of the business). The UK, relying on Article 296(1)(b), had instructed the competitors not to notify the acquisition of the military activities. The Commission cleared the non-defence activities of the undertakings and stated that it was satisfied with the measures taken by the UK under Article 296. There was no need to take steps under Article 299 in order to ensure that the measures taken under Article 296 did not have the effect of distorting competition in the common market.[252] The UK authorities again invoked Article 296 to the military aspects of a proposed merger between Marconi Electronic Systems (a part of GEC) and British Aerospace plc. The Commission accepted that Article 296 applied and cleared the non-military aspects of the concentration.[253]

Case No IV/M. 1438—*British Aerospace/GEC Marconi*

III. Application of article 296(1)(b) of the EC treaty

7. As already stated in paragraph 2 of this decision, the government of the United Kingdom, relying upon Article 296(1)(b) the EC Treaty, has instructed BAe not to notify information which relates to the military aspects of the operation.

8. The Commission has considered the applicability of Article 296(1)(b) of the EC Treaty in the present case. In this context it has noted, on the basis of the information provided by the government of the United Kingdom, that:

— the part of the concentration which has not been notified only relates to the production of or trade in arms, munitions and war material which are mentioned in the list referred to in Article 296(2) EC;

— the measures taken by the United Kingdom are necessary for the protection of the essential interests of its security;

— the measures taken will have no spillover effects on the non-military products of BAe and MES.

9. Therefore, the Commission is satisfied that the measures taken by the United Kingdom fall within the scope of Article 296(1)b of the EC Treaty. To the extent that these measures do not have the effect of distorting the conditions of competition in the Common Market, the Commission sees no need to invoke Article 298 of the EC Treaty.

---

[252] See, e.g., Case IV/M.528 *British Aerospace/VSEL*. Ultimately the GEC bid prevailed even though on investigation the Monopolies and Mergers Commission recommended that the British Aerospace bid should be cleared but that the GEC bid would operate against the public interest, see *GEC/VSEL* Cm. 2852 (1995). The UK Secretary of State (who then made the final decision after the recommendations of the Competition Commission (formerly the Monopolies and Mergers Commission)) did not, however, accept opinion of majority and did not act to prevent the GEC bid. Merger decisions are generally now taken by the competition authorities in the UK and the Secretary of State retains a role only in public interest and special public interest cases, see Enterprise Act 2002.

[253] Case IV/M.1438, *British Aerospace/GEC Marconi* OJ [1999] C241/8, see also Case IV/M.820, *British Aerospace/Lagadère SCA* [1996] 5 CMLR 523.

In *Saab/Celsius*,[254] however, the Commission declined to accept an invocation of Article 296.[255] In this case the Swedish Government instructed the parties only to notify aspects of the merger that related to non-military or dual-use goods. The Commission, however, requested additional information from the parties to enable it to appraise *all* aspects of the concentration, including the impact of the concentration on competition with respect to defence products.

(vi) Breach of Article 21

The Commission will launch proceedings against Member States it considers to be violating the Treaty or the ECMR in relation to mergers. For example, the Commission opened an Article 226 EC infringement procedure against Spain for not lifting unlawful conditions imposed by the Spanish Energy Regulator on E.ON's bid for Spanish electricity operator, Endesa. The Commission considered that the imposition of the conditions was both in breach of the ECMR (Article 21) and the Community rules on freedom of establishment and free movement of capital.[256] Similarly, the Commission adopted a preliminary conclusion that Italy had violated Article 21 of the ECMR by imposing unjustified obstacles in the way of a concentration with a Community dimension, approved by the Commission,[257] between Abertis of Spain and Autostrade of Italy.[258] This matter was resolved, however, by Italy's removal of the obstacles.[259]

D. CONCENTRATIONS WITHOUT A COMMUNITY DIMENSION

(i) National Law Applies

Article 21(1) provides that the ECMR alone applies to 'concentrations' and disapplies Regulation 1/2003 and the other implementing regulations[260] that confer power on the Commission and national competition authorities to implement Articles 81 and 82. As these Regulations do not apply to concentrations, and because the general rule is that the ECMR applies only to concentrations which have a Community dimension,[261] the general principle is that national law *only* applies to concentrations which do not have a Community dimension.[262]

---

[254] Case COMP/M.1797, IP/00/118. See also, e.g. COMP/M.1080 *Thyssen/Krupp* and COMP/M.4191 *Thales/DCN* where mergers involving the defence sector were dealt with under the ordinary ECMR procedures.

[255] It has applied the ECMR to a number of concentrations relating to 'defence' products, see, e.g., Case COMP/M.1858, *Thomson CSF/Racal (II)* (in this case, however, the UK Government announced its intention to consider public security aspects of the case pursuant to Article 21(4) (then Article 21(3)) of the ECMR) and Case COMP/M.2308, *Northrop Grumman/Litton Industries* IP/01/438 where the Commission considered a concentration between 2 US companies active in the production and provision of a range of military and governmental high technology products.

[256] IP/06/1246. Despite the eventual relaxation of the conditions, E.ON's bid eventually failed. However, it reached a deal regarding the acquisition of assets with Enel and Acciona.

[257] Case COMP/M.4249, IP/06/1244.

[258] IP/06/1418. See also announcement of initiation of proceedings against Poland in relation to Case COMP/M.3894 *Unicredit/HVB* IP/06/277.

[259] MEMO/06/414.

[260] See *supra* Chap. 14.

[261] ECMR, Art. 1(1).

[262] The prohibition in Article 21(3) on a Member State applying its national legislation on competition applies only where the concentration has a Community dimension. But see discussion *infra* on the residual role of Articles 81 and 82 of the Treaty.

(ii) Joint Ventures

Article 21(1)[263] itself makes it clear that there is an exception to this general position.

It will be remembered that Regulation 1310/97 amended the definition of concentration in Article 3 of the original ECMR, bringing within its scope all full-function ventures, even those which might lead to the coordination of the competitive behaviour of independent undertakings.[264] Originally joint ventures with coordinative aspects would have been appraised under Article 81.[265] These joint ventures are now appraised under the ECMR if they have a Community dimension.[266] If they do not, however, the Commission is still able to apply Article 81 of the Treaty to the joint venture using its powers under Regulation 1/2003.

(iii) Article 22, Referrals to the Commission

a. Background

Article 22 has its origins in Art 22(3)–(5) of the old ECMR, which was known as the Dutch clause.[267] It also derogates from the general rule that concentrations without a Community dimension are appraised only at the national level. It provides:

> 1. One or more Member States may request the Commission to examine any concentration as defined in Article 3 that does not have a Community dimension within the meaning of Article 1 but affects trade between Member States and threatens to significantly affect competition within the territory of the Member State or States making the request.
>
> Such a request shall be made at most within 15 working days of the date on which the concentration was notified, of if no notification is required, otherwise made known to the Member State concerned.

The Article provides a mechanism by which a Member State can request the Commission to apply the provisions of the ECMR to a concentration which does not have a Community dimension but which, nonetheless, affects trade between Member States and where it has been *prima facie* established that the concentration significantly affects competition within the territory of the requesting State.[268] The original provision was included to enable Member States without merger control rules to refer particularly troublesome concentrations, from a competition perspective, to the Commission. Indeed three of the four first Article 22 references were made by Member States which did not have merger control rules and all three of these concentrations were prohibited by the Commission.[269] In *Kesko/Tuko*,[270] for example, the Finnish Office of Free

---

[263] Set out *supra* 975.

[264] See, *supra* 965–6.

[265] See *infra* Chap. 13.

[266] A different substantive test applies: *infra* 1072–5.

[267] The clause having been inserted at the request of the Dutch.

[268] Notice on case allocation, [2005] C56/2, paras. 42–5.

[269] See Case IV/M.553, *RTL/Veronica/Endemol* (upheld on appeal, Case T-221/95, *Enedmol Entertainment Holding BV v. Commission* [1999] ECR II-1299, [1999] 5 CMLR 611), Case IV/M.784, *Kesko/Tuko* (upheld on appeal Case T-22/99, *Kesko Oy v. Commission* [1999] ECR II-3775, [2000] 4 CMLR 335 and Case IV/M.890, *Blokker/Toys'R'Us*. The fourth was made by Belgium which wished the Commission to intervene in the *British Airways/Dan Air* merger (Case IV/M.278, [1993] 5 CMLR M61). The Belgian authorities did not have jurisdiction to preclude a merger between two UK companies. The Commission cleared the merger unconditionally.

[270] Case IV/M.784, [1997] OJ L174/47, *aff'd*, Case T-22/97, *Kesko Oy v. Commission* [1999] ECR II-3755, [2000] 4 CMLR 335.

Competition requested the Commission to examine the acquisition of Tuko Oy by Kesko Oy. Although the concentration did not have a Community dimension (both undertakings achieved more than two-thirds of their respective Community-wide turnover in Finland) the Commission found that the concentration affected trade between Member States within the meaning of Article 22. It could, therefore, assess the concentration following the Member State's request. The Commission ultimately prohibited the concentration. The acquisition having already taken place, the Commission ordered Kesko to divest itself of the Tuko business.[271]

As twenty-six of the twenty-seven Member States now have merger control rules, this type of reference is unlikely in the future.[272] A Member State could, however, make an Article 22 request where, for example, a competing bid has a Community dimension which will be considered by the Commission[273] or, critically, where the Member State considers that the case is one which is primarily of Community interest or which it could not adequately deal with under national law. In more recent years the provision has been used by Member States that do have national merger control rules but have considered that the Commission is better placed to review a particular concentration on account of its cross border effects. *Promatech SpA/Sulzer AG*[274] was the first case of a joint referral to the Commission made by the authorities of Spain, Italy, the UK, Germany, France, Portugal, and Austria. The Commission opened Phase II proceedings but ultimately approved the merger, subject to divestments. Other examples of joint referrals are *GEES/Unison,*[275] *GE/AGFA NDT*[276] and *Omya/Huber.*[277]

The new ECMR sought to simplify and clarify the Article 22 procedure (the previous provision had both procedural and operational weaknesses),[278] and to encourage and allow Member States to join in requests where the concentration does not have a Community dimension but has a clear impact on intra-Community trade.

Council Regulation (EC) No. 139/2004 of 20 January 2004 on the Control of Concentrations between Undertakings [2004] OJ L24/1, Recital 12

(12) Concentrations may qualify for examination under a number of national merger control systems if they fall below the turnover thresholds referred to in this Regulation. Multiple notification of the same transaction increases legal uncertainty, effort and cost for undertakings and may lead to conflicting assessments. The system whereby concentrations may be referred to the Commission by the Member states concerned should therefore be further developed.

---

[271] Kesko was required to find a purchaser which had to be a viable existing or prospective competitor, independent of and unrelated to the Kesko group, and with sufficient financial resources to enable it to maintain and develop the business as an active competitive force in competition with Kesko's business.

[272] The only Member State which does not have merger control rules now is Luxembourg.

[273] See *supra* n. 195 and accompanying text.

[274] Case COMP/M.2698.

[275] Case COMP/M.2738, *GEES/Unison.* The was the second joint referral to the Commission, where the Commission received referral requests from the authorities of Germany, France, Spain, Italy, the United Kingdom, and Greece on 14, 15, 27 February, and 15 March 2002 respectively. The joint referral request was published in Official Journal on 21 March 2002 and the merger was finally cleared by the Commission on 14 April 2002.

[276] Case COMP/M.3136, *GE/AGFA NDT* IP/03/1666 (Article 6 clearance subject to conditions and obligations).

[277] Case COMP/M.3796 IP/06/1017, Case T-275/06 *Omya v. Commission* (judgment pending).

[278] See 2001 Green Paper on the Review of Council Regulation (EEC) No. 4064/89, COM(2001) 745/6 final, 25–6.

The Commission has power to invite Member States to make an Article 22 request.[279] The Commission's Notice on case allocation[280] recognizes that care must be exercised, however, and that referrals should only be made where specific criteria are met.

> 45. As post-notification referrals to the Commission may entail additional cost and time delay for the merging parties, they should normally be limited to those cases which appear to present a real risk of negative effects on competition and trade between Member States, and where it appears that these would be best addressed at the Community level. The categories of cases normally most appropriate for referral to the Commission pursuant to Article 22 are accordingly the following:
>
> — Cases which give rise to serious competition concerns in a market/s which is/ are wider that national in geographic scope, or where some of the potentially affected markets are wider than national, and where the main economic impact of the concentration is connected to such markets.
>
> — Cases which give rise to serious competition concerns in a series of national or narrower than national markets located in a number of countries of the EU, in circumstances where coherent treatment (regarding possible remedies but also, in appropriate cases, the investigative efforts as such) is considered desirable, and where the main economic impact of the concentration is connected to such markets.

b. The Mechanics of Article 22

A Member State must make an Article 22 request, on its own initiative or at the invitation of the Commission,[281] within 15 working days of the date on which the concentration was notified, or otherwise made known,[282] to it. The procedure does not, therefore, prevent the parties from having to make national notifications (and perhaps multiple applications) prior to the request or requests being made.[283]

Where a request is made by a Member State under Article 22 the Commission must inform the competent authorities of all the Member States and the undertakings concerned of the request without delay.[284] At this time all applicable national time limits are suspended[285] and, to the extent that the concentration has not been implemented, the suspensory provisions in Article 7 apply.[286] Once such a notice is received the other Member States have 15 working days to decide if they would like to join the initial request.[287] If a Member State decides not to join the request and informs the Commission the suspension of its national time limit ends.[288]

Within 25 working days of informing the Member States and undertakings of the initial request, the Commission may decide to examine a concentration that affects trade between Member States and threatens to significantly affect competition with the territory of the requesting states (if it does not adopt a decision within this time period it is deemed to accept the request).[289]

---

[279] ECMR, Art. 22(5).

[280] July 2004.

[281] ECMR, Art. 22(5),

[282] In some jurisdictions, for example, the UK, there is no system of compulsory notification for mergers.

[283] Article 4(5), however, enables parties to make a reasoned submission to the Commission *prior* to notification at the national level indicating that a concentration which does not have a Community dimension but which is notifiable in three or more Member States should be examined by the Commission, see *infra* section 4.

[284] ECMR, Art. 22(2).

[285] *Ibid.*

[286] ECMR, Art. 22(4), the suspensory provisions are discussed *infra* 998–9.

[287] ECMR, Art. 22(2).

[288] *Ibid.*

[289] *Ibid.*, Art. 22(3).

If the Commission accepts the request the referring Member States retain no control over the Commission's investigation[290] and they may no longer apply their national competition rules (jurisdiction ceases).[291] The Commission may require notification from the parties. If so, the time periods set out in Article 10[292] run as usual from notification. Where notification is not required the time periods run from the working day after the Commission informs the undertakings that it has decided to examine the concentration.

The previous Regulation provided that in Article 22 cases the Commission was empowered only to take action to maintain or restore effective competition within the territory of the Member State or States at the request of which it intervenes.[293] Under the new Regulation, however, the Commission is empowered to proceed as if the merger itself had a Community dimension. Where therefore the concentration significantly impedes effective competition within the common market, or a substantial part of it, it may prohibit it. Where it does not, however, it may clear the transaction. In each case it is also possible that the transaction will be scrutinized at the national level, by Member States that decided not to join in the referral. A possibility of conflicting outcomes thus arises.

(iv) Article 4(5), Request for a Referral to the Commission

Article 4(5) provides a mechanism for parties to a concentration which does not have a Community dimension and which is capable of being reviewed under the national competition laws of at least three Member States, to make a reasoned submission that the Commission should examine the concentration. The submission may be filed with the Commission *prior* to national notification. Article 4(5) is discussed in section 4 below.

E. A RESIDUAL ROLE FOR ARTICLES 81 AND 82 OF THE TREATY

(i) The Relevance of Articles 81 and 82 of the Treaty

Prior to the enactment of the ECMR the Commission made use of both Articles 81 and 82 to prohibit transactions which would now amount to a 'concentration'.[294] Subject to the special provisions for coordinative full-function joint ventures,[295] Article 21(1) disapplies Regulation 1/2003 and the other implementing legislation and clearly intends, subject to the provisos discussed in sections C and D above, that the ECMR alone should apply to concentrations with a Community dimension and that national law alone should apply to concentrations which do not. The purpose is to exclude the possible application of Article 81 or 82 to *concentrations* altogether.

The difficulty is that the Regulation cannot disapply the application of Articles 81 and 82, which are Treaty provisions, but disapplies only the implementing legislation which delegates responsibility for the enforcement of the rules to the Commission.

---

[290] Case T-221/95, *Endemol Entertainment Holding BV v. Commission* [1999] ECR II-1299, [1999] 5 CMLR 611, para. 42.

[291] ECMR, Art. 22(3).

[292] See *infra* 999 ff.

[293] Old ECMR, Art. 22(5).

[294] See *supra* 950–3.

[295] See *supra* 989.

A question which arises is to what extent the national courts can apply Articles 81 and 82. Further, to what extent is the Commission, and/or national competition authority, authorized to intervene in 'concentration' cases by Articles 85 and 84 of the Treaty respectively?[296]

(ii) Application in the National Courts

Prior to 1 May 2004 the case law indicated that whilst Article 82 has direct effect and is applicable by national courts,[297] in contrast Article 81 was not directly effective, in the absence of implementing legislation. However, since Regulation 1/2003 came into force it now appears clear that both Articles 81 and 82 are directly effective in their entirety.[298] It is possible therefore that, in derogation of the one-stop shop principle and the principle that in the absence of a Community dimension Community law does not apply, a private individual might be able to challenge the compatibility of a concentration with Article 81 or Article 82 of the Treaty before a national court. This is possible unless the ECJ were to find that the provisions of the ECMR somehow deprived Articles 81 and 82 of their direct effect. In practice such a challenge would be most likely to occur where the concentration does not have a Community dimension.

(iii) The Commission and National Competition Authorities

It is also possible that both the Commission and the national competition authorities have power to apply Articles 81 and 82 using their residual powers set out in Article 85 and Article 84 of the Treaty respectively.[299]

Article 85 authorizes the Commission to investigate a breach of Article 81 or 82 on its own initiative or at the request of a Member State. Thus it could in theory investigate a breach of these provisions in respect of a concentration which does not have a Community dimension.[300] Because, however, the implementing regulations are suspended the Commission would have to operate without the powers set out therein, for example, the power to request information and the power to impose fines on those found to be in breach. It may, however, propose appropriate measures to bring an infringement to an end, and if the infringement is not brought to an end, it may issue a reasoned decision and authorize a Member State to take measures to remedy the situation. The Commission has never made use of Article 85 in this way and it seems unlikely that it would do so in the future.[301]

Article 84 also authorizes the competition authorities of the Member States to act when no implementing legislation applies.[302] Where a concentration does not have a Community dimension then neither the provisions of the ECMR nor of Regulation 1/2003 (save in the case of joint ventures with co-ordinative aspects)[303] apply.[304] Where, however, a concentration has a

---

[296] These provisions are discussed *supra* Chap. 2.

[297] Case 66/86, *Ahmed Saeed Flugreisen v. Zentrale zur Bekämpfung Unlauteren Wettbewerbs ev* [1989] ECR 803, [1990] 4 CMLR 102; see especially paras. 19–21, 30–3, and Cases 209–213/84, *Ministère Public v. Asjes (Nouvelles Frontières)* [1986] ECR 1425, [1986] 3 CMLR 173.

[298] See *supra* Chap. 2 and e.g. C.J. Cook and C. S. Kerse, *E.C. Merger Control* (3rd edn., Sweet & Maxwell, 2006), 1-021.

[299] These provisions are discussed *supra* Chap. 2.

[300] If the concentration does have a Community dimension it will in any event be examining the transaction under the provisions of the ECMR.

[301] See its statement at the time of the adoption of the original ECMR, [1990] 4 CMLR 314.

[302] The competent national authorities' power to apply Articles 81 and 82 of the Treaty by Reg. 1/2003, Art. 5 is disapplied.

[303] *Supra* 975.

[304] Consequently it seems that both Articles 81 and 82 could be applied.

Community dimension it seems that, since the parties are obliged to notify such concentrations to the Commission, the jurisdiction of the Member States is denied under Article 84.[305]

4. PROCEDURE

A. NOTIFICATION

The ECMR does not start with any presumption in favour of, or against, concentrations. It does require, however, to ensure effective control,[306] the notification of concentrations with a Community dimension.[307] Parties to a transaction may fear that news of their intentions will become public as a result of such notification. Although the Commission is obliged to publish the fact of notification, the Commission is bound to take account of the legitimate interest of the undertakings in the protection of their business secrets.[308] The Commission is bound by a general duty of confidentiality, set out in Article 286 (ex Article 213(b)) of the Treaty, and may not disclose business secrets.[309] Further, Article 17(2) of the ECMR specifically provides that, subject to specified limited exceptions, 'the Commission and the competent authorities of the Member States, their officials and other servants and other persons working under the supervision of these authorities as well as officials and civil servants of other authorities of the Member States shall not disclose information they have acquired through the application of this Regulation of the kind covered by the obligation of professional secrecy'.

Notifications must be made to the Commission within a time period set out in Article 4.

Council Regulation (EC) No. 139/2004 of 20 January 2004 on the Control of Concentrations between Undertakings [2004] OJ L24/1, Article 4

1. Concentrations with a Community dimension . . . shall be notified to the Commission prior to their implementation and following the conclusion of the agreement, the announcement of the public bid, or the acquisition of a controlling interest.

Notification may also be made where the undertakings concerned demonstrate to the Commission a good faith intention to conclude an agreement or, in the case of a public bid, where they have publicly announced an intention to make such a bid, provided that the intended agreement or bid would result in a concentration with a Community dimension.[310]

---

[305] *Supra* Chap. 2.

[306] ECMR, recital 17.

[307] But see *infra* 996 ff.

[308] ECMR, Art. 4(3).

[309] See *infra* Chap. 14.

[310] Until 1 May 2004 the ECMR provided that concentration had to be notified to the Commission 'not more than one week after the conclusion of the agreement, or the announcement of the public bid, or the acquisition of a controlling interest'. This deadline was tight in practice and was frequently waived by the Commission. The new provision provides greater flexibility permitting notification at any time prior to implementation. It also permits notification where an agreement or public bid is not yet binding but where the parties can show that they intend to proceed.

The parties may notify any time prior to implementation of an agreement, public bid or an acquisition of a controlling interest or where a good faith intention to conclude an agreement or make a public bid can be demonstrated. It is therefore possible to notify in circumstances where an agreement or public bid has not actually been made provided that it can be demonstrated 'that their plan for that proposed concentration is sufficiently concrete, for example on the basis of an agreement in principle, a memorandum of understanding, or a letter of intent signed by all undertakings concerned, or, in the case of a public bid, where they have publicly announced an intention to make such a bid'.[311]

Which parties to the concentration are obliged to notify is dependent on the type of transaction that occurs. Broadly, joint notification must be made by the merging parties in true merger cases or by those acquiring joint control in cases of joint control. In other cases, the undertaking acquiring control must notify.[312] The Implementing Regulation, Regulation 802/2004[313] and Form CO set out how notification should be made and the information and documents which must be furnished to the Commission.[314] Form CO is not a form but a pattern, divided into eleven sections, which prescribes how the information requested must be presented. A large amount of information is required (to enable the Commission to comply with the tight deadlines imposed on it). Thus the form requires a description of the concentration, information about the parties, details of the concentration, information about ownership and control, supporting documentation (which includes information bringing about the concentration and also copies of all analyses, reports, studies, surveys, and any comparable documents submitted to, or prepared by or for, any member(s) of the board of directors for the purposes of assessing or analysing the concentration with respect to market shares, competition condition, competitors, the rationale of the concentration, potential for sales growth),[315] information on market definitions and affected markets, overall market context and efficiencies, and cooperative effects of a joint venture. Section 11 requires the notification to be accompanied with a declaration signed by representatives of the undertakings.

It can be seen from this list that notification is costly and time-consuming to complete. Failure to recognize the time and effort involved in the notification could disrupt the completion of the deal between the merging undertakings. Further, if all the requisite information is not supplied the notification will be 'incomplete' and a decision from the Commission will be delayed.[316] Pre-notification discussions with the Commission are always possible and are ordinarily essential and play 'an important part of the whole review process'.[317] Pre-notification discussions may minimize the possibility of an incomplete notification and may lead to a reduction the amount of information that the parties are required to provide in a notification. The Commission's Best Practices on the Conduct of EC Merger Control Proceedings provide guidance on pre-notification contacts and the preparation of a draft and final Form CO. A Short

---

[311] ECMR, recital 34. See *supra* n. 310.

[312] ECMR, Art. 4(2).

[313] [2004] OJ L133/1.

[314] One original signed paper form must be submitted, together with five paper copies and 30 copies in CD or DVD-Rom format, see Reg. 802/2004, art. 3(2) and Commission Communication [2006] OJ C251/2.

[315] Form CO, section 5(4). This information can sometimes be damaging.

[316] The tight time limits imposed on the Commission for assessing the concentration do not start to run until notification is complete.

[317] DG Competition Best Practices on the conduct of EC merger control proceedings, para. 5. Section 3 deals with pre-notification.

Form, also attached to the implementing regulation, applies for certain concentrations that do not raise competition concerns.[318]

The Commission has power under Article 14(2)(a) of the ECMR to impose fines, not exceeding 10 per cent of the aggregate turnover of the undertakings concerned, on a party that, intentionally or negligently, fails to notify a concentration in accordance with Articles 4 and 22(3) prior to its implementation.[319] The Commission first imposed a fine of ECU 33,000 (at this time the amount of the fine could not exceed ECU 50,000)[320] on an undertaking, Samsung, which had failed to notify a concentration in due time. Samsung had acquired control over an American firm, AST Research Inc, without the Commission's authorization in breach of Community rules.[321] Fines have been imposed in subsequent cases and, now that the fining threshold has been significantly increased, it seems likely that fines may be greater in the future.[322] The fine may be larger the more serious the impact the non-notified concentration has on competition.

In *Gencor/Lonrho*[323] the Commission took the view that the parties' notification of the concentration to it meant that it had submitted to the Community jurisdiction.[324]

B. PRE-NOTIFICATION REASONED SUBMISSIONS

(i) Background

In the section dealing with jurisdiction above it has been explained that there has been a consistent concern as to whether the simple turnover thresholds set out in Article 1(2) and (3) are adequately able to identify concentrations with a Community dimension. It was also explained that in conducting its most recent review the Commission took the view that it would be difficult always to allocate jurisdiction appropriately between it and the competent authorities of the Member States through the application of numerical turnover thresholds. The solution afforded by Regulation 139/2004 is to accept that these thresholds might wrongly allocate jurisdiction in a limited number of cases but to provide flexible mechanisms for the transfer of such cases between the Commission and the national authorities. Articles 9 and 22 have been simplified and clarified in pursuit of this objective. In order to realize this goal, the Regulation also enables the parties to provide input into the determination of jurisdiction through the submission of reasoned submissions to the Commission *prior* to notification at the Community or national level (as relevant). Such submissions are made on Form RS, attached to the implementing regulation. The Commission's notice on case allocation[325] provides guidance on the

---

[318] Broadly where there are no horizontal overlaps or vertical or neighbouring market relationships or where these overlaps or relationships are small, see also the Commission notice on a simplified procedure for the treatment of certain concentrations [2005] OJ C 56/32.

[319] Unless the parties are authorized to do so by Art. 7, *infra* 998–9.

[320] The fines that can be imposed were significantly increased by Reg. 139/2004.

[321] Case IV/M.920, [1999] OJ L225/12, [1998] 4 CMLR 494. The Commission took into account the fact that the concentration had had no damaging effect on competition and that Samsung had recognized the breach and fully cooperated with the Commission. However, in the Commission's view a fine was necessary as a warning to other companies and because the notification was very late. Samsung was an important company with significant interests in Europe which would, undoubtedly, have been aware of the competition rules.

[322] In 1999, the Commission imposed a fine of Euro 219,000 on another firm, Case IV/M.969, *AP Moller*, [1999] OJ L183/29, [1999] 4 CMLR 392 for failing to notify three concentrations which it had effected. The breach had occurred prior to the Samsung decision, Moller had voluntarily informed the Commission of its breach and the concentrations were later cleared.

[323] Case IV/M.619, [1997] OJ L11/42, [1996] 4 CMLR 742.

[324] See discussion *infra* 1088–9 and *infra* Chap. 16.

[325] [2005] OJ C56/2.

system and practical guidance relating to the mechanics of the referral system, particularly the pre-notification referral mechanism provided for in Article 4(4) and (5).

In addition to enabling the parties to have input into the determination of jurisdiction, the procedure may enable them possibly to speed up the reference procedure and may, in some circumstances, preclude the need for a notification to an authority which is simply going to refer the case to another.

(ii) Article 4(4), Request for Referral to a National Competition Authority

Article 4(4) provides that where a concentration has a Community dimension the notifying parties may, prior to notification to the Commission, make a reasoned submission that a concentration may significantly affect competition in a distinct market in a Member State and should be examined in whole or in part by that Member State. Where such a submission is made the Commission must inform the relevant Member State without delay and the relevant Member State has a period of 15 working days to express agreement or disagreement with the request to refer the case.

Unless the Member State disagrees the Commission has a period of 25 working days from receiving the reasoned submission to determine whether or not to refer the case. If it fails to adopt a decision within this time period it is deemed to have adopted a decision to refer. In deciding whether or not to make a reference the Commission, other than verifying the legal requirements, will consider the guiding principles set out in its Notice[326] and in particular whether the authority or authorities to which they are contemplating requesting the referral of the case, is the most appropriate authority for dealing with the case. This will be dependent upon both the likely locus of the competitive effects and how appropriate the NCA would be for scrutinizing the transaction.[327]

Where the Commission decides to refer the whole of the case *no* notification to the Commission is required and national competition law applies, subject to the conditions set out in Article 9.[328] Article 4(4) requests may occur where, for example, the parties anticipate that an Article 9 request will be made by a Member State.

(iii) Article 4(5), Request for a Referral to the Commission

Article 4(5) provides that prior to national notifications parties to a concentration which does not have a Community dimension and which is capable of being reviewed under the national competition laws of at least three Member States, may make a reasoned submission that the concentration should be examined by the Commission. The parties may not implement the concentration while the Commission is considering it under Article 4(5).[329] The Commission must transmit such submissions to the Member States without delay. The Member States then have a period of 15 working days within which to express their disagreement with the procedure. The procedure is terminated if one Member State disagrees. Where, however, no Member State disagrees the concentration is deemed to have a Community dimension. It

---

[326] Notice on case allocation, [2005] C56/2, paras. 8–14 set out *supra* 976–7.

[327] *Ibid.*, paras. 19–23.

[328] See ECMR Arts. 9(6)–(9).

[329] See *infra* 998–9 ff.

becomes notifiable to the Commission and *no* Member State is permitted to apply its national competition law to the concentration.

The advantage of the Article 4(5) procedure is apparent: if no Member State objects the parties may be saved multiple notifications and the transaction may be deemed to have a Community dimension. The risks in it are also obvious: if just one Member State objects the procedure is terminated. This would mean that the parties may, having already made a reasoned submission, then have to make multiple notifications to the national authorities because one Member State has disagreed. Several of those Member States may then make an Article 22 reference to the Commission in which case a notification to the Commission, on form CO, may be required. The parties may then, having submitted a Form RS, national notifications and a Form CO, face an investigation both by the Commission *and* at the national level (by the Member State that refused to join in the Article 22 request). In order to minimize this risk and to encourage the use of Article 4(5) the Commission's notice on case allocation[330] provides guidance upon the question of when a referral of the case to the Commission is likely to be considered appropriate. Again, the Commission refers to the guiding principles and provides more specific guidance as to whether the Commission is the most appropriate authority for dealing with the case. A pre-notification Article 4(5) reasoned submission is likely to be particularly pertinent in cases where the transaction would affect competition beyond the territory of one Member State.[331]

(iv) Notice on Case Allocation

In order to encourage pre-filing referrals in appropriate cases it has been seen that the Commission's Notice on case allocation[332] provides guidance on the legal requirements of Article 4(4) and (5) and provides guidance as to when a referral is likely to be appropriate. Further, the notice stresses the dialogue and cooperation that occurs between the Commission and NCAs and the NCAs between themselves, which is aimed at ensuring that concentrations are referred in appropriate cases, the system of pre-filing referrals operates smoothly and that an early warning system is put in place with regard to post-notification requests. It also provides guidance for parties considering filing a Form RS. The system seems to be operating effectively as a corrective mechanism. At the end of March 2007, the Commission had received 31 Article 4(4) requests (27 of which led to a referral to a Member States and none of which were refused) and 101 Article 4(5) requests, 93 of which were accepted and only 2 of which were refused.[333]

(v) Review

The Commission is to report to the Council on the working of Article 4(4) and (5) by 1 July 2009, the same date for reporting on the operation of the jurisdictional thresholds set out in Articles 1(2) and (3).

C. SUSPENSION

It was a condition of German support of the ECMR initially that a concentration should be suspended pending investigation of the concentration. A suspensory period has thus been

---

[330] [2005] C56/2.

[331] Notice on case allocation, [2005] C56/2, paras. 25–32.

[332] [2005] C56/2.

[333] See merger statistics set out *infra* section 6. See also upto date statistics set out on the DG Comp's website.

incorporated since the original ECMR was adopted although Article 7 has been amended both in 1997 and again by the new ECMR.[334] Article 7(1) now provides that a concentration with a Community dimension or to be examined by the Commission pursuant to Article 4(5),[335] is not to be implemented 'either before its notification or until it has been declared compatible with the common market pursuant to a decision under Articles 6(1)(b), 8(1) or 8(2), or on the basis of a presumption according to Article 10(6)'. The Commission has power however to permit derogations from this suspensory effect following a request[336] and there is an automatic derogation for public bids[337] 'or a series of transactions in securities including those convertible into other securities admitted to trading on a market such as a stock exchange, by which control is acquired from various sellers, provided that'[338] the concentration is notified to the Commission and the acquirer does not exercise its voting rights or does so only to maintain the full value of its investments (based on an express derogation by the Commission).[339]

The Commission has power under Article 14(2)(b) to impose penalties not exceeding 10 per cent of the aggregate turnover on those, intentionally or negligently, breaching the suspensory provisions. Further, the validity of any such transaction is dependent upon a clearance decision of the Commission.[340] Undertakings which do not notify a concentration with a Community dimension to the Commission and/or which do not comply with the suspensory period risk having to reverse their concentration if the Commission later finds that the concentration is not compatible with the common market.[341]

D. PHASE I INVESTIGATION

The Commission must examine notifications as soon as they are received.[342] The time limits for initiating proceedings and decisions are set out in Article 10. The Implementing Regulation provides further information on the operation of the ECMR time-limits and compliance with them.[343]

---

[334] Article 7 of the ECMR originally provided for an automatic suspension period of three weeks. A concentration could not be put into effect 'before its notification or within the first three weeks following its notification'. Although the Commission used to be able to take a decision to extend this suspension period, it was a peculiar period to have adopted because the Commission has a period of one month, following notification, in which to make its preliminary assessment of the concentration's compatibility with the common market, see ECMR, Arts. 6(1) and 10(1). In practice, this meant that it had to make a firm assessment of whether it was likely to open stage two proceedings within three weeks, so that it could decide whether or not to extend the suspension period. Reg. 1310/97 [1997] OJ L180/1 amended Article 7 with the purpose of harmonizing the duration of the suspensory period with the duration of the investigation.

[335] See *supra* 949 ff.

[336] ECMR, Art. 7(3).

[337] *Ibid.*, Art. 7(2).

[338] This latter wording was added by the new ECMR, see 2001 Green Paper on the Review of Council Regulation (EEC) No. 4064/89, COM(2001) 745/6 final, paras. 187–9.

[339] In Case COMP/M.2282, *Schneider/Legrand* 10 Oct. 2001, for example, Schneider make a public exchange offer in respect of the shares held in Legrand and acquired 98.7% of the shares in Legrand prior to the Commission's final decision prohibiting the merger. The Commission consequently ordered the separation of Schneider and Legrand (see ECMR, Art. 8(4)(5) *infra*). The Commission's decision was annulled on appeal, Case T-310/01, *Schneider Electric SA v. Commission* [2002] ECR II-4071, [2003] 4 CMLR 768 and on 11th July 2007 the CFI ordered the commission to compensate Schneider in respect of some of the loss resulting from the Commission's manifest and grave disregard of the limits of its discretion, Case T-351/03 and see *infra* 1087.

[340] ECMR, Art. 7(4).

[341] *Ibid.*, Art. 8(4)(5).

[342] *Ibid.*, Art. 6(1).

[343] Reg. 802/2004, [2004] OJ L133/1, Arts. 7–10.

Phase I decisions must generally be taken within twenty-five working days following receipt of *complete* notification.[344] The period is extended to thirty-five working days in Article 9 cases or cases where commitments designed to render the concentration compatible with the common market are offered (so long as the commitments are offered within twenty working days of notification[345]).[346] Details of notification must be published in the Official Journal in order to give third parties the opportunity to react.[347]

At the end of the twenty-five or thirty-five working day period the Commission must adopt a decision under Article 6. This may take one of several forms.

(i) Article 6(1)(a)

Where the notified transaction does not in fact fall within the ECMR at all, it does not amount to a concentration with a Community dimension, the Commission may issue a decision to that effect.

(ii) Article 6(1)(b)

The Commission may declare the notified concentration to be compatible with the common market.[348] Alternatively, the Commission may declare the concentration to be compatible with the common market subject to the acceptance of commitments by the parties.[349] Such decisions are deemed to cover restrictions directly related and necessary to the implementation of the concentration.[350]

(iii) Article 6(1)(c)

Where the Commission has serious doubts about the concentration's compatibility with the common market it must issue a decision to that effect and initiate proceedings launching a second phase investigation. This is in fact a relatively rare occurrence as a great majority of cases (90–95 per cent) are dealt with in Phase I proceedings.[351]

Where such proceedings are launched, without prejudice to Article 9, then unless the undertakings can demonstrate to the satisfaction of the Commission that they have abandoned their concentration, the proceedings must be closed by virtue of an Article 8 decision[352] (see below).

---

[344] ECMR, Art. 10(1).

[345] Reg. 802/2004, [2004] OJ L133/1, Art. 19(1).

[346] ECMR, Art. 10(1).

[347] ECMR, Art. 4(3).

[348] The Commission can also make such a finding following modifications by the undertakings concerned to the transaction, ECMR, Art. 6(2).

[349] ECMR, Art. 6(2). See discussion of commitments, *infra* 1077 ff.

[350] See *infra* 1075–97.

[351] See statistics set out *infra* section 6.

[352] In Case COMP/M.1741, *MCI WorldCom/Sprint* the Commission issued a decision prohibiting the concentration even though the parties stated that they had abandoned the merger. In annulment proceedings before the CFI one of the allegations of the parties was that the Commission had no jurisdiction to adopt the decision, the transaction having been abandoned (the decision was also challenged on a number of other grounds, including procedural errors and errors in substantive appraisal), Case T-310/00 *MCI v. Commission* [2004] ECR II-3253; [2004] 5 CMLR 26. The CFI annulled the Commission's decision holding that the Commission had exceeded its powers by adopting a decision declaring a notified concentration incompatible with the common market when the notifying parties have formally withdrawn their notification and informed it of the abandonment of the concentration in the form envisaged in the notification. In the absence of a concentration agreement the Commission had no power to adopt a decision under Article 8(3).

In *Schneider v. Commission*[353] the CFI held that an Article 6(1)(c) decision initiating proceedings was not an appealable decision.

(iv) Article 10(6)

Where the Commission fails to adopt a decision within the prescribed periods the concentration 'shall be deemed to have been declared to be compatible with the common market'.

E. PHASE II

The Commission has a period of 90 working days from the day following the initiation of proceedings in which to make its assessment in Phase II proceedings.[354] This time period can be extended by fifteen working days where commitments are offered by the parties *after* the fifty fourth working day (commitments must generally be offered within sixty five working days).[355] Further, it is possible that the period can be extended up to a total of twenty working days either by the parties or at the request of the Commission with the consent of the parties.[356] This means that in complex cases the time period may be extended to a maximum of 125 working days.[357] Occasionally the Commission has also 'stopped the clock' on account of the parties failure to respond to requests for information by a stipulated time period.[358] Again, if no decision is taken within the prescribed period the concentration is deemed to be compatible with the common market.[359]

At the end of the proceedings the Commission may under Article 8 of the ECMR either:

(1) declare the concentration to be compatible with the common market;

(2) declare that the concentration, following modification, is compatible with the common market. Conditions and obligations can be attached to the decision to ensure that the undertakings concerned comply with the commitments they have entered into with a view to rendering the concentration compatible with the common market (the decision can subsequently be revoked if the parties breach the commitments);[360]

(3) declare the concentration to be *incompatible* with the common market.[361]

---

[353] Case T-48/03 [2006] ECR II-111.

[354] ECMR, Art. 10(3). This period can be extended in certain circumstances, e.g., to allow for information to be collected: Art. 10(4).

[355] Reg. 802/2004, [2004] OJ L133/1, Art. 19(2). This time period can be extended by the amount of days (up to a maximum of 20) that the total Phase II period has been extended either at the request of the parties or the Commission, *infra* n. 356.

[356] ECMR, Art. 10(3), second paragraph.

[357] The time period may go longer than this if the Commission 'stops the clock' because the parties have failed to respond to requests for information within a stipulated period.

[358] See, e.g., Case COMP/M.2282, *Schneider/Legrand* 10 Oct. 2001 where the Commission stopped the clock on account of the failure of the parties to respond to 322 questions within the 12 calendar days (5 working days) allowed by the Commission. On appeal, Case T-310/01, *Schneider Electric SA v. Commission* [2002] ECR II-4071, [2003] 4 CMLR 768, para. 100 the CFI held that a request for information by 18 April made on 6 April was reasonable given the circumstances of the case and the requirement for speed which characterizes the overall scheme of the ECMR.

[359] ECMR, Art. 10(6).

[360] *Ibid.*, Art. 8(6). It may also revoke decisions which are based on incorrect information.

[361] *Ibid.*, Art. 8(2). Commitments are discussed *infra* 1077–84.

In Article 8(1) and (2) cases the clearance decision is deemed to cover restrictions related and necessary to the concentration.[362] Where the concentration is declared incompatible with the common market and the parties have already completed the transaction the Commission has comprehensive powers, including the power to take interim measures or to take restorative measures.[363] These powers can also be exercised where a concentration is implemented in breach of a condition or obligation.

Council Regulation (EC) No. 139/2004 of 20 January 2004 on the Control of Concentrations between Undertakings [2004] OJ L24/1, Article 8

4. Where the Commission finds that a concentration:

(a) has already been implemented and that concentration has been declared incompatible with the common market, or

(b) has been implemented in contravention of a condition attached to a decision taken under paragraph 2, which found that, in the absence of the condition, the concentration would fulfil the criterion laid down in Article 2(3) or, in the cases referred to in Article 2(4), would not fulfill the criteria laid down in Article 81(3) of the Treaty, the Commission may:

— require the undertakings concerned to dissolve the concentration, in particular through the dissolution of the merger or the disposal of all the shares or assets acquired, so as to restore the situation prevailing prior to the implementation of the concentration; in circumstances where restoration of the situation prevailing before the implementation of the concentration is not possible through dissolution of the concentration, the Commission my take any other measure appropriate to achieve such restoration as far as possible,

— order any other appropriate measure to ensure that the undertakings concerned dissolve the concentration or take other restorative measures as required in its decision.

In cases falling within point (a) of the first subparagraph, the measures referred to in that subparagraph may be imposed either in a decision pursuant to paragraph 3 or by separate decision.

5. The Commission may take interim measures appropriate to restore or maintain conditions of effective competition where a concentration:

(a) has been implemented in contravention of Article 7, and a decision as to the compatibility of the concentration with the common market has not yet been taken;

(b) has been implemented in contravention of a condition attached to a decision under Article 6(1)(b) or paragraph 2 of this Article;

(c) has already been implemented and is declared incompatible with the common market.

---

[362] See infra 1075–7 ff.

[363] ECMR, Art. 8(4) and (5), see Cases COMP/M.2416, *Tetra Laval/Sidel*, COMP/M.2283, *Schneider/Legrand*, Case IV/M., *Blokker Toys 'R' Us* and IV/M.784, *Kesko/Tuko*. These powers have been expanded by Reg. 139/2004 [2004] OJ L24/1 since the powers under the old ECMR were considered to be inadequate.

F. CONDUCT OF MERGER INVESTIGATIONS

When making its assessment, within the short periods stipulated, the Commission has power under Articles 11 and 13 ECMR to obtain information from the parties, or third parties (such as customers, suppliers, or competitors), by means of a request, either by a simple request or decision,[364] or an inspection (including unannounced on the spot investigations).[365] Third parties play an important role in the merger proceedings. The investigation is ordinarily conducted in the form of written requests for information to customers, suppliers, or competitors but may also be addressed to the notifying parties. It may also seek the views of these parties orally. The Commission's powers of investigation were extended by the current Regulation to bring them more closely into line with the Commission's corresponding powers under Regulation 1/2003.

The Commission has power under Articles 14 and 15 to impose both fines, not exceeding 1 per cent of the aggregate turnover of the undertakings concerned, and periodic penalty payments for a number of offences, such as intentionally or negligently failing to respond to an Article 11 letter or supplying incorrect or misleading information in a notification or following a request for information.[366] In *BP/Erdölchemie*,[367] for example, the Commission issued a decision imposing a fine of €35,000 on Deutsche BP for having omitted to identify important information in its Form CO (the maximum fine was then €50,000 but is now 1 per cent of the turnover of the undertaking concerned). A decision adopted on the basis of incorrect information for which one of the undertakings is responsible may be revoked.[368]

State of play meetings are generally held during the process with the objective of contributing to the quality and efficiency of the decision-making process and of ensuring transparency and communication between DG Comp and the parties. If Phase II proceedings are initiated there are usually state of play meetings at five different points in the procedure. Occasionally, voluntary 'triangular' meetings involving the parties and third parties are held.

In the course of Phase II investigations a statement of objections (SO) is served on the notifying parties. This lets the parties know the Commission's objections to the concentration.[369] Parties then have an opportunity to respond to the statement in writing by a specified date (the Commission is not obliged to take account of comments received after the expiry of the specified time limit);[370] they have a right of access to the file[371] and to attend and speak at the oral hearing, which is conducted by the Hearing Officer in full independence.[372] Further, other involved parties[373] and third parties, including customers, suppliers, competitors, members of the administrative or management bodies of the undertakings concerned or the recognized representative of their employees, and consumer associations where the proposed concentration

---

[364] ECMR, Art. 11. The time limits for replying to such request for information are inevitably short since the Commission itself is complying with tight time constraints.

[365] *Ibid.*, Arts. 12 and 13. The power to carry out dawn raids is equivalent to those set out in Reg. 1/2003 [2003] OJ L1/1, discussed in Chap. 14. In practice, an inspection is unlikely, given the time constraints under which the Commission is operating.

[366] *Ibid.*, Art. 14(1), Case IV/29.895, *Telos* [1982] OJ L58/19, [1982] 1 CMLR 267.

[367] Case COMP/M.2624, [2004] OJ L91/40.

[368] ECMR, Arts. 6(3) and 8(6).

[369] *Ibid.*, Art. 18(1) and (2).

[370] *Ibid.* Art. 18(3), Reg. 802/2004, [2004] OJ L133/1, Art. 13(2)(3).

[371] *Ibid.* Art. 18(3), Reg. 802/2004, [2004] OJ L133/1, Art. 17(1).

[372] Reg. 802/2004, [2004] OJ L133/1, Arts. 14 and 15. Procedure and enforcement under Reg. 1/2003, which is similar, is discussed in detail *infra* Chap. 14.

[373] Parties to the transaction other than the notifying parties.

concerns products or services used by end consumers,[374] may have a right to receive the statement of objections, to respond to it, to have access to the file, to attend the oral hearing, and to speak at it. If disputes arise in the course of this procedure, the issue can be raised with the Hearing Officer.

The Court takes the procedural obligations of the Commission very seriously. In *Schneider Electric SA v. Commission*[375] the CFI was critical of the Commission's substantive analysis of the case[376] but annulled the decision on account of procedural irregularities committed by the Commission, in particular denial of the rights of defence. The CFI found that the SO had not adequately stated the Commission's case against the parties. In its final decision, the Commission took account of the conglomerate effects of the merger whilst the SO had identified only horizontal effects. The CFI held that although the Commission was able to add to or revise its arguments identified in the SO, the SO had to state objections in a sufficiently precise way to enable the parties to rebut the case against them and/or to devise or present remedies capable of saving the merger.[377]

Concentrations are initially investigated and appraised by merger units within DG Comp. These are located both in the merger policy unit in Directorate A, and within each sectoral units (B–E) (staff are referred to as the Merger Network).[378] In Phase II investigations an independent 'panel' is appointed with the task of scrutinizing the case team's conclusions with a fresh pair of eyes at key points of the enquiry (devil's advocate process).[379] This is designed to deal with the criticism that the case team was often convinced of their own arguments at the end of Phase I, and that this affected the outcome of the second phase investigations. The Advisory Committee on Concentrations must be consulted before a final decision is taken.[380] The final decision is made by the College of Commissioners[381] save, where delegated,[382] where it is adopted by a Commissioner (usually the Competition Commissioner).

---

[374] See, e.g., Reg. 802/2004, [2004] OJ L133/1, Art. 11(1)(b)(c). See also on the rights of third parties, Cases C-68/94 and C-30/95, *France v. Commission, Société Commerciale des Potasses et de l'Azote (SCPA) v. Commission* [1998] ECR I-1375, [1998] 4 CMLR 829.

[375] Case T-310/01, [2002] ECR II-4071, [2003] 4 CMLR 768.

[376] See *infra* 1017–8.

[377] In Case T-5/02, *Tetra Laval v. Commission* [2002] ECR II-4381, [2002] 5 CMLR 1182 the CFI rejected Tetra Laval's arguments that the Commission had failed to respect Tetra's rights to access to the file.

[378] The Merger Task Force has been dissolved, see organizational chart set out *supra* Chap. 2. There have been major reorganisations of the MTF designed to strengthen the rigour of analysis following the annulment by the CFI of three Commission decisions in 2001. The integration of the MTF into economic sectors brings its approach closer to that adopted by US and other European antitrust agencies.

[379] See M. Monti, 'Merger Control in the European Union: a radical reform' European Commission/ International Bar Association, Brussels 7 Nov. 2002, SPEECH/02/545. Representatives from the staff of the newly created Chief Competition Economist will participate in this panel.

[380] It must also be consulted, e.g., before a decision imposing a fine or penalty or ordering divestment is taken.

[381] In some particularly sensitive merger cases there is a fear that this factor allows political and other considerations to enter the decision-making process. This has led to some calls for the creation of an independent European cartel office or competition tribunal.

[382] e.g., Phase I decisions are usually delegated.

5. SUBSTANTIVE APPRAISAL OF CONCENTRATIONS UNDER THE EC MERGER REGULATION

A. BACKGROUND

The correct substantive test against which concentrations with a Community dimension should be appraised was controversial both at the time of the adoption of the original ECMR and, again, at the run up to the adoption of the recast Regulation.

At the time the original ECMR was adopted the disagreement between the Member States centred largely on the factors to be taken into account in assessing the compatibility of a merger with the common market and, in particular, on whether a strict competition-based approach should be adopted.[383] The *original* ECMR[384] adopted the 'dominance' test, providing in Article 2(2) and 2(3) that:

2. A concentration which does not create or strengthen a dominant position as a result of which effective competition would be significantly impeded in the common market or in a substantial part of it shall be declared compatible with the compatible.

3. A concentration which creates or strengthens a dominant position as a result of which effective competition would be significantly impeded in the common market or in a substantial part of it shall be declared incompatible with the common market.

In its 2001 Green Paper[385] the Commission discussed the merits of the dominance test, after 11 years of its application, and dealt with both procedural and substantive reasons that had been advanced for a re-evaluation of the test. In particular, it launched a debate as to whether there should be a move from the dominance standard to the 'substantial lessening of competition' ('SLC') test adopted in a number of other jurisdictions.

The Commission discussed both procedural and substantive arguments in favour of reform, The gist of the procedural argument in favour of reform was that alignment of the test with the SLC test used in a number of jurisdictions, including the US,[386] would lead to greater international convergence in the application of merger rules. The Commission was not entirely convinced by this argument partly because of the uncertainty that switching to a new substantive test for appraisal would create and partly because of the inconsistency it would cause at the European level where many Member and acceding States had modelled their merger rules on the EC dominance test.

The substantive reasons advanced hinged on the relative flexibility of the SLC test in particular when dealing with mergers in concentrated markets. It will be seen in the sections below[387] that despite initial doubt, it has been gradually established that the old ECMR applied not only to mergers leading to the creation or strengthening of a dominant position held by a single under-taking, but to mergers leading to the creation or strengthening of a collective dominant position

---

[383] The UK and Germany, in particular, were in favour of a test based solely on competition issues. See *supra* section 2.C.

[384] The substantive test was not amended by Reg. 1310/97 [1997] OJ L180/1.

[385] 2001 Green Paper on the Review of Council Regulation (EEC) No. 4064/89, COM(2001) 745/6 final, especially paras 160–7.

[386] The test is also used in Canada and Australia and has recently been adopted in the UK and Ireland.

[387] See also the discussion of collective dominance in Chap. 11.

(that is a dominant position held by the merging parties and another or other undertakings operating on the market).[388] Advocates of the adoption of the SLC test[389] took the view that in spite of this development, the dominance test was not broad enough to capture and prevent all problematic mergers occurring on a concentrated market. In particular concentrations could occur between undertakings on a concentrated market which would not lead to the creation or strengthening of a collective dominant position (*coordinated effects*) but which would nonetheless lead to higher prices on the market (*non-coordinated* or *unilateral effects*) without the creation of a single dominant position. For example, a merger between the second and third largest competitors on a market with only three players might not lead to the creation of a single dominant position, it might not lead to the coordination of the competitive behaviour of the two remaining firms on the market (arguably a necessary requirement for a finding of collective dominance),[390] but it might substantially lessen competition on the market by eliminating the rivalry between the merging firms and the competitive constraint that they had exercised both on each other and the market leader. The classic example given of this type of situation was the US 'baby food' case.[391] In this case Heinz, the third largest producer of baby food in the US, wished to acquire Milnot Holding Corporation, whose subsidiary, Beech-Nut, was the second largest producer of baby food in the US. Following the merger the parties would have acquired around 33 per cent of the relevant market, whilst Gerber, would have retained 65 per cent of the prepared baby food market. The merger clearly would not have given the merging parties a 'dominant' position and it was not clear that the merger would lead to coordinated effects on the market (e.g., tacit coordination of prices by the merged entity and Gerber). Nonetheless the US's Federal Trade Commission (FTC) considered that the merger would lead to a substantial lessening of competition on the market since the merging parties competed vigorously to be chosen as the number two supplier in supermarkets and in innovation in product development and differentiation. This competition also placed competitive pressure on Gerber with respect to both prices and innovation. Although the challenge to this merger led to its eventual abandonment in the US, it was argued that, had the same facts arisen in the EC, the EC authorities would have been powerless to prevent the merger under the dominance test. The ECMR was thus argued to include a 'blind spot'[392] or gap,[393] and did not cover all anti-competitive mergers of concern. In addition, there was a fear that the broadening of the concept of dominance set out in the ECMR was at the same time broadening the scope of dominance within the meaning of Article 82 and consequently curtailing the conduct of a broader category of undertakings.

In its Green Paper the Commission indicated that it was not convinced that there was such a gap, believing it to be more hypothetical than real. Nonetheless it was prepared to open a debate

---

[388] See also the discussion of collective dominance in Chap. 11.

[389] See, e.g., J. Vickers, 'Competition Economics and Policy' [2003] *ECLR* 95, R. Whish, 'Substantive Analysis under the EC Merger Regulation: should the dominance test be replaced by "substantial lessening of competition"' *EU Competition Law & Policy Developments & Priorities* (Hellenic Competition Commission, 2002), 45, Z. Biro and M. Parker, 'A New EC Merger Test? Dominance v. Substantial Lessening of Competition' [2002] 1 *Competition Law Journal* 157 and U. Böge and Muller, 'From the market dominance test to the SLC test: are there any reasons for change?' [2002] *ECLR* 495.

[390] See *infra* 1026 ff.

[391] *FTC v. HJ Heinz Co* 16 F Supp 2d 2000.

[392] S. Bishop and M. Walker, 'The Economics of EC Competition Law: Concepts, Application and Measurement' (2nd edn., Sweet & Maxwell, 2002), 310–11.

[393] J. Vickers, 'How to reform the EC merger test' A speech at the EC/IBA merger control conference, Brussels, 9 Nov. 2004.

which raged until the last moments before the text for the new ECMR was finally agreed. The UK[394] and Irish delegations[395] were, for example, in favour of introducing the SLC test into the ECMR whilst the German delegation,[396] for example, was in favour of retaining the dominance test which it considered to be adequate to catch all problematic mergers.[397]

B. REFORM AND THE NEW SUBSTANTIVE TEST

Given the need for unanimous agreement in the Council the end result of the reform process was a classic, yet ingenious, European 'compromise'.[398] The substantive test *was* altered but the SLC test was *not* adopted. The decision was made to utilize but to reorganize the wording of the original ECMR. The original ECMR provided that a concentration which creates or strengthens a dominant position as a result of which effective competition would be significantly impeded in the common market or in a substantial part of it shall be declared incompatible with the common market. Article 2(3) of the current Regulation states:

A concentration which would significantly impede effective competition in the common market or in a substantial part of it, in particular as a result of the creation or strengthening of a dominant position, shall be declared incompatible with the common market.

It can be seen from this that the new test seeks to meet the arguments of those in both the SLC and dominance camps. It is *broader* than the old test. The wording clearly establishes that a merger may be prohibited even if it does not create or strengthen a dominant position if a significant impediment to effective competition is established. By referring to the creation or strengthening of a dominant position, however, the ECMR preserves the previous decisional

---

[394] *Ibid.* and the submission of the DTI's to the Commission's 2001 Green Paper, available on DG Comp's web site. Sweden also supported a move to the SLC test.

[395] See the submission of the Irish Competition Authorities/Industry on the Commission's 2001 Green Paper, available on DG Comp's web site. The Irish delegation accepted that the dominance test had been a success, a useful body of precedent had developed, and that some took the view that the costs of switching exceeded any possible benefits and others took the view that 'If it ain't broke, don't fix it'. Nonetheless it took the view that the change was worth making: in particular because there were two categories of anti-competitive merger in oligopolistic markets that could not be controlled within the existing collective dominance label. 'One is the merger of two firms that produce differentiated or branded products that are close substitutes within a broader relevant market, and where the post merger market share is below the level for dominance (say 40 per cent), but competition is reduced because the brands are close substitutes within the relevant market. The other is where firms compete in output or capacities, often for a relatively homogenous product, and again in a situation where the post-merger market share is below the level of dominance. Such mergers are often described as 'unilateral effects' because welfare is reduced by a change in the competitive Nash equilibrium in which the merged firm will raise price unilaterally.' The Irish delegation thus considered that this is the single most compelling argument for a switch in the test, and that allowing the EU agency the flexibility to examine unilateral effects mergers in an open and transparent way, rather than shrouding them under an ever-expanding concept of collective dominance, far outweighs the once-off costs of switching. The delegation supported its arguments with four further points: first, the adoption of the SLC text would de-couple the concept of dominance in Article 82 from the ECMR test, this would be advantageous as *ex ante* merger control requires a fundamentally different standard and approach than *ex post* analysis under Article 82; secondly, the switching costs were not so great; thirdly the two EU Member States who most recently examined the question (Ireland and UK) had opted for the SLC test; and fourthly, the SLC test had an intuitively obvious or natural appeal.

[396] See the submission of the Bundeskartellamt on the Commission's 2001 Green Paper, available on DG Comp's web site. This view was also supported by Italy, The Netherlands, and the European Parliament. Some Member States (e.g., Portugal and Denmark) favoured a retention of the dominance test, but with a clarification of how the test applied on oligopolistic markets.

[397] But see the discussion of *T-Mobile/tele.ring infra* n. 497 and accompanying text and *Oracle/PeopleSoft infra* n. 571.

[398] France and Spain had supported a dual test combining features of the SLC and dominance test.

practice and case law of the ECJ. Indeed, the Commission takes the view 'it is expected that most cases of incompatibility of a concentration with the common market will continue to be based upon a finding of dominance'.[399] The Horizontal Merger Guidelines[400] have been adopted with the objective of clearly and comprehensively articulating the reasoning underlying the analytical approach to merger analysis.

The twin objectives, of broadening the test whilst at the same time preserving the dominance case law are explained in recitals 25 and 26 of the ECMR. In particular, recital 25 makes it crystal clear that the new substantive test is designed to catch mergers that will result in non-coordinated effects on an oligopolistic market even though a position of single of collective dominance may not be established.

(25) In view of the consequences that concentrations in oligopolistic market structures may have, it is all the more necessary to maintain effective competition in such markets. Many oligopolistic markets exhibit a healthy degree of competition. However, under certain circumstances, concentrations involving the elimination of important competitive constraints that the merging parties had exerted upon each other, as well as a reduction of competitive pressure on the remaining competitors, may, even in the absence of a likelihood of coordination between the members of the oligopoly, result in a significant impediment to effective competition. The Community courts have, however, not to date expressly interpreted Regulation (EEC) No 4064/89 as requiring concentrations giving rise to such non-coordinated effects to be declared incompatible with the common market. Therefore, in the interests of legal certainty, it should be made clear that this Regulation permits effective control of all such concentrations by providing that any concentration which would significantly impede effective competition, in the common market, or in a substantial part of it, should be declared incompatible with the common market. The notion of 'significant impediment to effective competition' in Article 2(2) and (3) should be interpreted as extending, beyond the concept of dominance, only to the anti-competitive effects of a concentration resulting from the non-coordinated behaviour of undertakings which would not have a dominant position on the market concerned.

(26) A significant impediment to effective competition generally results from the creation or strengthening of a dominant position. With a view to preserving the guidance that may be drawn from past judgments of the European courts and Commission decisions pursuant to Regulation (EEC) No 4064/89, while at the same time maintaining consistency with the standards of competitive harm which have been applied by the Commission and the Community courts regarding the compatibility of a concentration with the common market, this Regulation should accordingly establish the principle that a concentration with a Community dimension which would significantly impede effective competition, in the common market or a substantial part thereof, in particular as a result of the creation or strengthening of a dominant position, is to be declared incompatible with the common market.

Article 2(1) sets out the criteria to be used in appraising whether or not the concentration is compatible with the common market. This indicates that many factors are relevant to the Commission's appraisal.

Concentrations within the scope of this Regulation shall be appraised in accordance with the objectives of this Regulation and the following provisions with a view to establishing whether or not they are compatible with the common market.

In making this appraisal, the Commission shall take into account:

(a) the need to maintain and develop effective competition within the common market in view of, among other things, the structure of all the markets concerned and the actual or potential competition from undertakings located either within or outwith the Community;

---

[399] Horizontal Merger Guidelines [2004] OJ C31/5, para. 4.
[400] [2004] OJ C31/5, para. 5.

(b) the market position of the undertakings concerned and their economic and financial power, the alternatives available to suppliers and users, their access to supplies or markets, any legal or other barriers to entry, supply and demand trends for the relevant goods and services, the interests of the intermediate and ultimate consumers, and the development of technical and economic progress provided that it is to consumers' advantage and does not form an obstacle to competition.

Article 2(4) and (5) set out an additional test applying the criteria of Article 81(1) and 81(3) to the aspects of a full function joint venture that may appreciably restrict competition between undertakings that remain independent. This test is discussed in section E below.

The sections below examine how the Commission applies the substantive test for assessment.

C. BURDEN AND STANDARD OF PROOF AND COUNTERFACTUAL

In a merger case, it is for the Commission to demonstrate that a concentration cannot be declared compatible with the common market.[401] In determining whether a merger is likely to harm competition, the merger must be assessed in the context of the position that would exist were the merger not to be completed. This is necessary to demonstrate a causal link between completion of the merger and the competitive harm. The Commission explains this in its Horizontal Merger Guidelines.

9. In assessing the competitive effects of a merger, the Commission compares the competitive conditions that would result from the notified merger with the conditions that would have prevailed without the merger. In most cases, the competitive conditions existing at the time of the merger constitute the relevant comparison for evaluating the effects of a merger. However, in some circumstances, the Commission may take into account future changes to the market that can reasonably be predicted. It may, in particular, take account of the likely entry or exit of firms if the merger did not take place when considering what constitutes the relevant comparison.[402]

It seems clear that the standard of proof is the balance of probabilities.[403] In *Tetra Laval BV v. Commission*,[404] for example, the CFI held that it was not sufficient for the Commission to show the possibility of harm to competition. Rather, it had to show that it was likely to arise. In a series of cases it has been made clear that the CFI will rigorously review the Commission's decisions and, although it recognises that the Commission has a margin of discretion with regard to

---

[401] Case T-87/05, *EDP v. Commission* [2005] ECR II-3745, [2005] 5 CMLR 23, para. 61. See also discussion of Case T-464/04 *Independent Music Publishers and Labels Association (Impala) v. Commission* [2006] ECR II-2289, [2006] 5 CMLR 19and Case C-12/03 P *Commission v. Tetra Laval BV* [2005] ECR I-987, [2005] 4 CMLR 8 *infra*. The parties, however, may need to provide evidence which may be material to the decision and, for example, to support a view that there are few barriers to entry to the market, that one of the firms is failing or that the merger will achieve significant efficiencies, see *infra* and e.g. discussion in A. Lindsay, *The EC Merger Regulation: Substantive Issues* (2nd edn., Sweet & Maxwell, 2006), 2.5(a).

[402] See also discussion of failing firm defence and e.g. Case COMP/M.2810, *Deloitte & Touche/ Anderson (UK)* *infra* n. 645. The counterfactual may be complex where the Commission has to consider two proposed mergers on a relevant market. It appears that the assessment of the first merger must take account of the impact of proposed second merger even if it is being scrutinized separately by an NCA, see e.g. *BP/E.ON* and Case COMP/M.2389, *Shell/DEA*.

[403] Thus if there is appreciable uncertainty on the part of the Commission, it appears that the merger should be approved, Case C-12/03 P, *Commission v. Tetra Laval BV* [2005] ECR I-987, AG Tizzano, paras 76–77. See also e.g. C.J. Cook and C. S. Kerse, *E.C. Merger Control* (3rd edn., Sweet & Maxwell, 2006), para. 7–008 and A. Lindsay *The EC Merger Regulation: Substantive Issues* (2nd edn., Sweet & Maxwell, 2006), 2.5(b).

[404] Case T-5/02, [2002] ECR II-4381, [2002] 5 CMLR 28, paras. 153 and 251, *aff'd* Case C-12/03 P [2005] ECR I-987, [2005] 4 CMLR 8.

economic matters, it will consider whether the evidence relied upon by the Commission is correct, reliable, consistent, and is capable of substantiating the conclusions it has drawn. This imposes a particularly acute burden on the Commission, particularly in complex collective dominance and conglomerate cases where various chains of cause and effect must be a considered with a view of ascertaining which of them are the most likely. In *Tetra Laval BV v. Commission* the ECJ stated:[405]

39. Whilst the Court recognises that the Commission has a margin of discretion with regard to economic matters that does not mean that the Community Courts must refrain from reviewing the Commission's interpretation of the information of an economic nature. Not only must the Community Courts, *inter alia*, establish whether the evidence relied on its factually accurate, reliable and consistent but also whether that evidence contains all the information which must be taken into account in order to assess a complex situation and whether it is capable of substantiating the conclusions drawn from it. Such a review is all the more necessary in the case of a prospective analysis required when examining a planned merger with conglomerate effect.

40. Thus, the Court of First Instance was right to find, in paragraph 155 of the judgment under appeal, in reliance on, in particular, the judgment in *Kali und Salz* . . . , that the Commission's analysis of a merger producing a conglomerate effect is subject to requirements similar to those defined by the Court with regard to the creation of a situation of collective dominance and that it calls for a close examination of the circumstances which are relevant for an assessment of that effect on the conditions of competition on the reference market.

D. A SIGNIFICANT IMPEDIMENT TO EFFECTIVE COMPETITION, IN PARTICULAR BY THE CREATION OR STRENGTHENING OF A DOMINANT POSITION

(i) General

In order to assess whether or not the merger is compatible with the common market the Commission must determine whether or not it would significantly impede effective competition, that is whether the merger is the *cause* of the significant impediment to effective competition. 'The creation or the strengthening of a dominant position is a primary form of such competitive harm' and provides 'an important indication as to the standard of competitive harm that is applicable when determining whether a concentration is likely to impede effective competition to a significant degree.'[406] Decisional practice and Community case-law of course clarify when mergers will lead to the creation or strengthening of a dominant position. Further, the Commission has sought to clarify and explain its appraisal of when concentrations under the Regulation will significantly impede effective competition, through the publication of guidance.[407] The Commission's Horizontal Merger Guidelines are, therefore, intended to provide a sound economic framework for the assessment of horizontal concentrations with a view to determining whether or not they are likely to be declared compatible with the common market. Draft Guidelines seeking to identify the problems that may be arise from Non-Horizontal (Vertical and Conglomerate) Mergers have also been published.[408]

---

[405] C-12/03 P [2005] ECR I-987, [2005] 4 CMLR 8.

[406] Horizontal Merger Guidelines [2004] OJ C31/5, paras. 1 and 4.

[407] This is provided for, ECMR, recital 28.

[408] Available on DG Comp's website. The Commission commissioned and published on its website an Ex-post review of Merger Control Decisions, prepared by LEAR.

(ii) Market Definition

a. The Central Role of Market Definition

[A] proper definition of the relevant market is a necessary precondition for any assessment of the effect of a concentration on competition.[409]

An economic appraisal of the impact of the merger on the competitive process in order to determine whether or not it will significantly impede effective competition, in particular by the creation or strengthening of a dominant position,[410] requires, as a starting point, that the relevant market be defined. The definition of the market is crucial to enable the Commission to attain meaningful information regarding the market power that the merged parties will acquire, to understand how competition operates on the market and to make its competitive assessment. 'The main purpose of market definition is to identify in a systematic way the immediate competitive constraints facing the merged entity'.[411] It is not, therefore 'an end in itself but a tool to identify situations where there might be competition concerns'.[412] In some Phase I clearance decisions, the Commission does not make a final determination of the relevant market, however, because the merger will not be problematic, or because it will not affect the outcome of the case,[413] whichever way the market is defined.[414]

b. The Commission's Notice on Market Definition and Previous Decisional Practice

The Commission's Notice on the definition of the relevant market for the purpose of Community competition law[415] sets out how the Commission goes about determining the relevant market for the purposes of its merger decisions. In particular it stresses its use of the SSNIP test where possible 'postulating a hypothetical small, non-transitory change in relative prices and evaluating the likely reaction of customers to that increase'.[416] The test has greatest utility in the application of the merger rules since the practical problem presented by the *Cellophane fallacy* does not ordinarily apply.[417] The Notice and the SSNIP test were discussed in detail in Chapter 1.

An important initial point is that whilst market definition must be freshly addressed in every case (previous market definition is not binding upon the Commission),[418] there are now a

---

[409] Cases C-68/94 and C-30/95, *France v. Commission, Société Commerciale des Potasses et de l'Azote (SCPA) v. Commission* [1998] ECR I-1375, [1998] 4 CMLR 829, para. 143.

[410] The concept of dominance refers to 'a situation where one or more undertakings wield economic power which would enable them to prevent effective competition from being maintained in the relevant market by giving them the opportunity to act to a considerable extent independently of their competitors, their customers and, ultimately, of consumers' and requires first that the market be defined and that relevant undertaking's position on that market be appraised, Case T-102/96, *Gencor v. Commission* [1999] ECR II-753, [1999] 4 CMLR 971, para. 200. The key difference of course is that in Article 82 cases the analysis is retrospective in nature whilst in the context of the ECMR the analysis is forward-looking, i.e, prospective in nature.

[411] Horizontal Merger Guidelines [2004] OJ C31/5, para. 10. See also Chap. 1.

[412] M. Monti, 'Market Definition as a Cornerstone of EU Competition Policy' speech of 5 October, 2001.

[413] See Case IV/M.232, *PepsiCo/General Mills* [1992] 5 CMLR 203.

[414] See Case IV/M.833, *The Coca-Cola Company/Carlsberg A/S* [1998] OJ L145/41.

[415] [1997] OJ C372/5, discussed *supra* Chap. 1. For a comprehensive discussion of market definition in merger cases, see e.g. A. Lindsay *The EC Merger Regulation: Substantive Issues* (2nd edn., Sweet & Maxwell, 2006), Chap. 3.

[416] *Supra* Chap. 1.

[417] *Ibid.* The Commission's practice in defining markets for the purposes of the ECMR is the inspiration behind the SSNIP test set out in the Notice [1997] OJ C372/5.

[418] Cases T-125 and 127/97, *Coca-Cola v. Commission* [2000] ECR II-1733, [2000] 5 CMLR 467.

significant number of Article 82[419] and merger[420] decisions which provide useful precedence and guidance on market definition in most spheres.[421] In addition to being listed by case number, company name, date, and decision type, merger cases are also listed on DG Comp's web site by reference to NACE code (i.e., industry sector).[422] Earlier decisions adopted, and the market definitions utilized within them, in a particular industry may therefore be identified.

Form CO asks the parties to provide data relevant to the identification of any affected markets consisting of product markets in which there are horizontal, vertical, or neighbouring market relationships.[423]

c. Relevant Product Market

It will be remembered that '[a] relevant product market comprises all those products and/or services which are regarded as interchangeable or substitutable by the consumer, by reason of the products' characteristics their prices and their intended use'.[424] It will also be remembered that, in making its assessment, the Commission places most emphasis on demand-side substitution. This entails a determination of the range of products which are viewed as substitutes by the consumers. In addition, supply-side factors are relevant where suppliers can switch production to the relevant products in the short term without incurring significant additional costs or risks (where the effect is immediate).[425] As indicated in its Notice on market definition the Commission relies on a range of evidence in support of a particular definition of a market. Thus evidence of past behaviour, quantitative tests, the views of customers and competitors, consumer preference, physical characteristics, price and switching costs, etc. may be relevant.[426] As discussed in Chapter 1 market definition may be complicated by numerous factors such as chains of substitution, structure of supply and demand and questions such as whether there is a separate own label market, separate aftermarket, a new product market, or an innovation and/or technology market.

In many cases the parties to a merger may prefer a broad product market in which their market shares are lower. It will be much harder for the parties to persuade the Commission to clear a merger affecting a narrowly defined market in which they have, say, a 70 per cent market share than in a more broadly defined one in which they have, for example, a 30 per cent market share. On some occasions, however, a narrower product market definition may work to the parties' advantage, since this could result in a finding that there is no or less significant horizontal overlap in the products they produce.[427]

---

[419] In Case COMP/M. 2416 *Tetra Laval/Sidel*, for example, the market definition adopted in Case C-333/94 P, *Tetra Pak II* [1996] ECR I-5951, [1997] 4 CMLR 662 was followed.

[420] Between 1990 and the end of April 2004, 2,407 merger decisions were adopted, see *infra* section 6.

[421] Although only Phase II decisions are generally reported in the Official Journal the Phase I decisions are available, in the language of notification, from a number of sources, in particular, on the Competition Directorate's home page and on CELEX, http://europa.eu.int/comm/competition/index_en.html.

[422] Nomenclature générale des Activités économiques dans les Communautés Européennes.

[423] See sections 6 and 7 of Form CO.

[424] Commission Notice on the definition of the relevant market for the purposes of Community competition law [1997] OJ C372/5, para. 7 (this definition was adapted by reference to the definition set out in Form CO).

[425] See, e.g., Case IV/M.214, *ICI/Du Pont* [1992] OJ L7/13.

[426] The Commission has perhaps shown more sophistication in economic techniques and preparedness to rely on econometric techniques in merger analysis since the appointment of a Chief Economist, see, e.g. Case COMP/M.3216 *Oracle/PeopleSoft* and Case COMP/M.3625 *Blackstone/Acetex*.

[427] See, e.g., Case IV/M.1578, *Sanitec/Sphinx* [2000] OJ L294/1, [2001] 4 CMLR 507. In this case the parties argued that there were a series of individual markets for ceramic bathroom products, e.g., for wash basins, WCs, and WC cisterns, etc. The commission took the view, however, that ceramic sanitary ware constituted one single product market both from the demand-side and the supply-side points of view. It was not, however,

Emphasis on Demand-Side Factors

In many cases the Commission places emphasis on demand-side factors, which can involve a consideration of broader factors than just physical characteristics, price and intended use.

In *Aérospatiale-Alenia/de Havilland*[428] the Commission relied on the evidence of customers and competitors, in reaching its conclusion on the relevant product market.[429] The proposed concentration, by which Aérospatiale SNI and Alenia-Aeritalia e Selenia SpA would jointly acquire the de Havilland division from Boeing Company, affected the turbo-prop commuter aircraft market. The parties argued that there was one market for all aircraft of between twenty and seventy seats. The Commission concluded, however, that three separate markets were affected by the concentration. The turbo-prop commuter aircraft market was divided into three distinct markets, between commuters with twenty to thirty-nine seats; forty to forty-nine seats; and sixty seats and over, each of which attracted different categories of buyers.

Demand-side factors are often important in consumer product markets. In *Procter & Gamble/VP Schickedanz*[430] the Commission, in finding that separate markets exist for tampons and sanitary towels, placed much emphasis on consumer preferences and consumer behaviour which was affected by many factors other than price (such as cultural, psychological, and physical differences).

The structure of demand may also affect the definition of the relevant market. For example, in *CEAC/Magnetti Marelli*[431] the Commission concluded that there were two separate markets for starter batteries for cars: one for new cars and one for those used as replacements in cars. Despite being identical, the batteries were sold in different circumstances and on different terms to new car manufactures and dealers or garages stocking replacement batteries respectively.[432]

Supply-Side Factors

In some cases the ability of manufacturers easily to switch production to make a product will also be taken into account and may result in the product market being more broadly drawn than it would be from a purely demand-side oriented approach.[433]

In *Nestlé/Perrier*[434] the Commission relied on a wide range of factors in concluding that the relevant product market was that of bottled source water. The case concerned a public bid notified by Nestlé SA for 100 per cent of the shares of Source Perrier SA. The proposed concentration

necessary for the purpose of the decision to define exactly whether the relevant product market should comprise ceramic sanitary ware as a whole or, alternatively, individual products. The product market definition was left open as, on each alternative market definition, the operation would raise competition problems in the Nordic countries but no competition law problems in any of the national or regional markets in continental Europe. Such a finding will not necessarily result in a finding that the merger is compatible with the common market, however. The Commission has sometimes been concerned with mergers which do not result in horizontal overlaps but result in 'range' effects or portfolio power by increasing the range of products that the merged entity will produce, see discussion of conglomerate mergers *infra*.

[428] Case IV/M.53, [1991] OJ L334/42, [1992] 4 CMLR M2.

[429] It also considered supply-side factors in assessing whether or not potential competitors would exercise a restraining influence over the concentration (i.e., in assessing whether or not the high market shares which would be realized by the merger were indicative of market power).

[430] Case IV/M.430, [1994] OJ L354/32, [1994] 5 CMLR 146.

[431] Case IV/M.477, [1995] 4 CMLR 600.

[432] See also Chap. 6.

[433] See e.g. Case COMP/M.3197 *Candover/Cinven/Bertelsmann-Springer* which concerned academic publishing. From a demand side relevant markets would be very narrow and would not allow proper assessment of competition between the different publishers.

[434] Case IV/M.190, [1992] OJ L356/1, [1993] 4 CMLR M17.

primarily affected the business of bottling water originating from a natural spring or source ('source water').[435] Nestlé submitted that there was no separate market for bottled source water. Rather, the relevant market was non-alcoholic refreshment beverages, including both bottled source water and soft drinks.[436] The Commission, rejecting this conclusion, relied on price correlation analysis which suggested that consumers did not consider a number of soft drinks to be substitutable for bottled water. It relied, however on supply-side factors in support of its conclusion that it would be difficult to justify an exclusion of sparkling and flavoured source water from the relevant product market. Most companies marketing still and source water also marketed sparkling and flavoured source waters, and a bottler of sourced water could easily switch production to sparkling or flavoured source water. The Commission did not consider, however, that the assessment of the case would differ whether or not sparkling and flavoured waters were included or excluded from the market.[437]

In *Kali und Salz/MDK/Treuhand*[438] Kali und Salz and Mitteldeutsche Kali AG (MdK, owned by Treuhand) were to combine their potash and rock-salt activities. The Commission concentrated primarily on the effects of the concentration on the market for potash. Although there were two distinct categories of customers for the potash (producers that acquired the potash in powder form to make, in combination with other plant nutrients, compound fertilisers and farmers who purchased granulated potash for direct agricultural application) the Commission drew the market broadly. Irrespective of these different customer needs and irrespective of the fact that granulated potash was 10 per cent more expensive than the potash in its powder form it concluded that they were both part of the same market. Producers could make both forms of potash and could, without difficulty, change the balance of output of the two products.

'New Economy' Or 'Innovation' Markets

The definition of the relevant product market is particularly complex in new economy or 'innovation' markets.[439] In these cases, competition may be 'for' the market rather than 'in' it, competition may be predominately about innovation rather than price (so that the SSNIP test cannot be utilized) and, later when conducting the competitive assessment of the merger, market shares may not provide a good indication of the market strength of the merging parties. The extract from Bishop and Walker below explains the difficulties involved in appraising such mergers.

S. Bishop and M. Walker, *The Economics of EC Competition Law: Concepts, Application and Measurement* (2nd edn., Sweet & Maxwell, 2002), 202–3

7.90 Mergers in 'new economy' industries can raise some particular difficulties for the competitive assessment. In this section we use the phrase 'new economy' to refer to industries that are characterized by a high degree of new product innovation, usually based on large sunk research and

---

[435] Nestlé agreed that if it succeeded in acquiring control over Perrier it would sell the Volvic source of Perrier to BSN (the third major supplier on the French source water market).

[436] See the discussion of the case set out *supra* Chap. 6.

[437] Case IV/M.190, *Nestlé/Perrier* [1992] OJ L356/1, [1993] 4 CMLR M17.

[438] Case IV/M.308, [1994] OJ L186/30, [1994] 4 CMLR 526; on appeal Cases C-68/94 and C-30/95, *France v. Commission, Société Commerciale des Potasses et de l'Azote (SCPA) v. Commission* [1998] ECR I-1375, [1998] 4 CMLR 829.

[439] See *supra* Chaps. 1 and 6. See also M. Monti 'Competition and Information Technologies', Kangaroo Group Brussels, 18 Sept. 2000,

development costs, and which often exhibit demand-side 'network effects'. Demand-side network effects arise when the value of a particular product to a consumer is larger the more people that already use the product. An oft-cited example of a product that exhibits such network effects is computer software, where consumers often prefer to use the same software as the majority of other consumers also use. Another (hardly new) example is telecommunications: it is more valuable to a consumer to be on a telecoms network when there are already many others on the network than when there are few others. *Tipping* refers to the phenomenon whereby network effects can sometimes lead to the market being dominated by just one product (*e.g.*, Microsoft Windows).

Three questions are fundamental to the analysis of mergers in these 'high tech' industries. First, is competition best described as being 'in' the market or 'for' the market? Competition usually takes place 'in' the market, with a number of firms competing within the product market. However, sometime it takes place 'for' the market, with just one firm, or one standard, monopolizing the market. Where competition is for the market, it is common to see 'standards wars' in the early stages of the industry. Videos provide an example of this, with the standards war between Betamax and VHS ultimately being won by VHS. Where competition takes place for the market, traditional merger analysis concerns about high concentration are likely to be misplaced.

Secondly, what is the primary competitive focus: price or product innovation? Merger analysis has traditionally focused on pricing issues, but this may be inappropriate when firms compete primarily on the basis of product characteristics rather than price.

Thirdly, are current market positions likely to be good indicators of future market positions? Traditional merger analysis tends to assume that a high market share for a firm today will, *ceteris paribus*, be reflected in a high market share for that firm in the future as well. Where product innovation is extreme, this may be a poor assumption, with future market positions being largely independent of current market positions.

The Commission has shown itself to be aware of these difficulties. It has been prepared to analyse the impact of a merger on 'future' markets, for example in the pharmaceuticals industry[440] and has been wary of mergers that might make a market particularly prone to 'tipping'.[441] Some commentators have suggested that the Commission has taken a too pessimistic a view of competition in the new economy, consequently applying the merger rules too stringently.[442]

d. The Relevant Geographic Market

'The relevant geographic market comprises the area in which the undertakings concerned are involved in the supply and demand of products and services, in which the conditions of competition are sufficiently homogeneous and which can be distinguished from neighbouring areas because the conditions of competition are appreciably different in those areas'.[443] The objective of defining the market is to determine the area in which undertakings will genuinely be competitors of the concentration. Obviously, the geographic scope of the market can also have a critical impact on the outcome of the case.

[440] See, e.g., Case IV/M.737, *Ciba-Geigy/Sandoz*.

[441] See, e.g., Case IV/M.1069, *MCI/Worldcom (II)*.

[442] See, e.g., C. G. Veljanovski, 'EC Antitrust in the New Economy: Is the European Commission's View of the Network Economy Right?' [2001] *ECLR* 115, S. Liebowitz and S. E. Margolis, 'Network effects and externalities' *The New Palgrave Dictionary of Economics and Law* (Macmillan, 1998), Vol. 2, 671–5.

[443] Commission Notice on the definition of the relevant market for the purposes of Community competition law [1997] OJ C372/5, para. 8.

As in the assessment of the relevant product market, both demand and supply side substitution will be relevant in assessing the area comprising the geographic market: whether it is local/regional/national/EU/EEA, worldwide, or some other. The Commission has relied in its merger decisions on evidence such as current geographical pattern of purchases, price differences between areas,[444] past evidence of diversion of orders to other areas, basic demand characteristics, views of customers and competitors, trade-flows, patterns and barriers,[445] and switching costs when defining the geographic market. The Commission will also take account of the process of market integration in defining markets. In many cases this process may mean that in a short period the market may become wider than past figures suggest.[446]

It will frequently be the case that the parties will wish to argue for as wide a geographic market as possible in order to diminish their market shares. Even if, however, a more narrowly drawn geographic market will not result in horizontal overlaps the Commission may be prepared to characterize a merger between parties present on the same product market but in neighbouring geographic product markets, as having horizontal effects in consequence of their being 'potential' competitors.

A drawing of a broad 'worldwide' market is likely in the case of highly technical products involving significant research and development and large capital and manufacturing costs.[447] Further, a broad geographic market may be justified where product is very valuable, internationally traded and relatively cheap to transport. In *Gencor/Lonrho*,[448] for example, the Commission identified worldwide markets for various metal products, including platinum, which were traded on a global basis at publicly quoted prices. Further, in *Aérospatiale/Alenia/de Havilland*[449] the Commission concluded that the geographic market for the commuter aircraft was worldwide, excluding China and Eastern Europe. There were no tangible barriers to the importation of these aircraft into the Community and negligible costs of transportation.[450] In *Mannesmann/Vallourec/Ilva*,[451] however, the Commission rejected the parties' allegation that the market for seamless steel tubes was worldwide. The Commission did not consider that the parties' evidence, based on price correlations between Western Europe and the United States and figures establishing that more than 10 per cent of production was exported from Western Europe, established that the market was worldwide. Rather, it concluded that the market was Western Europe (the EC and EFTA countries). In this area there were no tariff barriers to trade, a high level of trade between the different countries, low transport costs, and similar structures of supply and demand.

In view of the single market project and the aim of breaking down barriers to trade between Member States, it is perhaps to be expected that many markets will be at least Community-wide rather than national. Nevertheless, particularly in consumer product markets, the market has often been found by the Commission to be national or even regional or local. National markets have been found where there are no legal barriers to entry and where it might not be anticipated that other barriers to entry would exist. In some markets technical barriers to entry may still

---

[444] Persistent price differences in different Member States which are not due to transport costs may be a strong indicator of separate geographic areas, Case COMP/M.3149 *Procter & Gamble/Wella*.

[445] In some cases regulatory policies may constitute a barrier to trade, e.g. in the pharmaceutical sector, see for example Case IV/M.737, *Ciba-Geigy/Sandoz*.

[446] Case IV/M.165, *Alcatel/AEG Kabel* [1992] OJ C6/23.

[447] See e.g. Case IV/M.269 *Shell/Montecatini* [1994] OJ L332/48.

[448] Case IV/M.619.

[449] Case IV/M.53, [1991] OJ 1334/42, [1992] 4 CMLR M2. See also Case IV/M.877 *Boeing/McDonnell Douglas* [1997] OJ L336/16, [1997] 5 CMLR 270.

[450] *Ibid.*, para. 20.

[451] Case IV/M.315, [1994] OJ L102/15, [1994] 4 CMLR 529.

exist.[452] In others the reason for a national market may be that transport costs are high relative to the cost of the product or due to consumer brand loyalty, national buying preferences, or a lack of effective cross-border distribution and marketing infrastructures. Markets may have evolved on national lines over a period of years and show little sign of change. In *Nestlé/Perrier*[453] a combination of factors led the Commission to conclude that the geographic market was France: water was a bulky product with relatively high transport costs and there were significant barriers to entry isolating the French market, in particular there was strong brand loyalty which made access to the retail market difficult and high (sunk) advertising costs would need to be expended if a new entrant wished to gain access to the market.[454]

Similarly in *Kali und Salz/MDK/Treuhand*[455] the Commission found that there were two relevant geographical potash markets. There was one market for Germany alone and another for the Community apart from Germany. The reasons for concluding that Germany constituted a separate market hinged on both historical factors (consumers had long-established supply relationships with German suppliers) and other factors (such as the relatively high transport cost within Germany).

The scope of the market was crucial in *Volvo/Scania*,[456] which involved a merger between two entities active on the heavy trucks market. The parties alleged that the market was a Community or EEA market. Such a finding would have considerably diluted the parties' market shares since they did not have such a significant presence on markets outside of the four Nordic countries (Denmark, Finland, Norway, and Sweden) and Ireland. The Commission concluded, however, that for these five countries the relevant geographic markets were still national in scope, in particular: the parties charged different prices and earned different profit margins in the different states; technical specifications varied and in some Member States regulatory barriers existed, purchasing tended to be done on a national basis and distribution and service networks acted as a severe barrier to entry to manufacturers who did not have a well-developed network.[457] This conclusion seriously affected the outcome of the case since the parties had market shares of approximately 90 per cent on the Swedish market and were the only significant competitors there.

National markets were also identified by the Commission in *Schneider/Legrand*.[458] The Commission prohibited Schneider's takeover of Legrand on the basis that the concentration would lead to the creation or strengthening of a dominant position on a number of identified electrical equipment markets[459] which existed in a number of distinct national geographic markets in the EEA. The conclusion that there were separate national markets for the products was founded on the fact that: there were significant differences between the products sold in the countries; prices were set at national level and the price varied considerably from country to country; the key factors in competition were dependent upon national factors; and there were significant barriers to entry and expansion between the countries. The Commission ordered

[452] See also discussion *supra* Chap. 6 and, e.g., Case IV/M.43, *CEAC/ Magneti Marelli* [1991] OJ L222/38, [1992] 4 CMLR M61.

[453] Case IV/M.190, [1992] OJ L356/1, [1993] 4 CMLR M17.

[454] Case IV/M.190, *Nestlé/Perrier* [1992] OJ L356/1, [1993] 4 CMLR M17, paras. 21–34.

[455] Case IV/M.308, [1994] OJ L186/30, [1994] 4 CMLR 526; on appeal Cases C-68/94 and C-30/95, *France v. Commission, Société Commerciale des Potasses et de l'Azote (SCPA) v. Commission* [1998] ECR I-1375, [1998] 4 CMLR 829.

[456] Case IV/M.1672, [2001] OJ L143/74.

[457] *Ibid.*, paras. 31–70.

[458] Case COMP/M.2283, IP/01/1393.

[459] Including distribution and final panel board components.

the reversal of the transaction which had already been put into effect. On appeal, the CFI[460] upheld the finding with respect to the French markets identified.[461] The CFI held, however, that the Commission had not proved dominance in the markets identified outside France.[462] In particular, the Commission had conducted a global analysis at the European level of the impact of the concentration and had not properly analysed the effects of the concentration on each national market identified. In order to identify effects on the individual national markets the analysis had to be based on each of those markets and transnational effects could be relied on only to supplement or support such analysis.[463]

In some cases the Commission will take account of the fact that barriers to entry into national markets are likely to be broken down. In *Alcatel/Telettra*[464] the Commission permitted Alcatel to acquire a controlling interest in Telettra even though the concentration would lead to the acquisition of an aggregate market share of 80 per cent of the Spanish market in the supply of microwave and line transmissions. The Commission took into account the fact that it was, at that time, taking steps to liberalize the telecommunications equipment market throughout the Community. This meant that in due course the Spanish monopsonistic purchaser, Telefonica, would be able to purchase products from both local and foreign sources.

(iii) Competitive Assessment of Horizontal Mergers

a. Introduction and Overview

The EC merger rules aim to preserve effective competition on a market, and to deliver benefits to consumers in the form of low prices, high quality products, a wide selection of goods, and services and innovation. By prohibiting mergers that will significantly impede effective competition the ECMR seeks to prevent mergers that would deprive customers of these benefits by significantly increasing the market power of firms.[465] 'By "increased market power" is meant the ability of one or more firms to profitably increase prices, reduce output, choice or quality of goods and services, diminish innovation, or otherwise influence the parameters of competition'.[466] Mergers between undertakings that are competitors, or potential competitors, on the same market eliminate a competitive restraint on the market, increase market concentration and may lead to the firms' gaining or enhancing their market power. In the context of horizontal relationships, Form CO thus requires the parties to provide data in relation to affected markets where 'two or more of the parties to the concentration are engaged in business activities in the same product market and where the concentration will lead to a combined market share of 15 per cent or more'.[467]

---

[460] Case T-310/01, *Schneider Electric SA v. Commission* [2002] ECR II-4071, [2003] 4 CMLR 768. This case was the first merger judgment to be given by the CFI under the fast-track appeals procedure. The Commission's decision was adopted on 10 October 2001 and the CFI's judgment was given on 22 October 2002, see *infra* 1086.

[461] Procedural irregularities with respect to the French market led to the annulment of the decision, however, see *supra* 1004.

[462] *Ibid.*, especially paras. 147–92.

[463] As the Commission had proved that competition would be impeded on the French market, the errors in the Commission's analysis on the other national markets were not sufficient to justify the annulment of the decision.

[464] Case IV/M.42, [1991] OJ L122/48, [1991] 4 CMLR 778.

[465] This inevitably involves a comparison of the existing competitive conditions with the conditions that will exist post-merger.

[466] Horizontal Merger Guidelines [2004] OJ C31/5, para. 8.

[467] Form CO, section 6 III.

The Commission outlines its analytical approach to the competitive assessment of a concentration with horizontal effects in its Horizontal Merger Guidelines.[468] Once it has identified the relevant market, it uses market share and concentration thresholds as a 'rule of thumb' to identify problematic mergers.[469] It then considers the likelihood that the merger will result in anti-competitive effects on the market, either through non-coordinated or coordinated effects, in the absence of countervailing factors.[470] It then considers whether or not countervailing factors, such as buyer power, new entry or efficiencies would counteract the potentially harmful effects identified.[471] It also considers that a concentration may be permitted where the anti-competitive effects result from the failure of a firm rather than the merger.[472]

b. Market Shares and Concentration Levels

Various methods have been adopted by competition authorities to explain the principles upon which they measure market power. Since 1982 the merger authorities in the USA have used a concentration index to make preliminary assessments of the legitimacy of a horizontal merger and the reduction in competition it will cause on a particular market. The Herfendahl–Hirschman index (the HHI) seeks to identify the concentration of a particular market by using numerical distinctions.[473] Its aim is to prevent acquisitions which are likely to create monopoly or oligopoly power. The HHI measures the concentration in a way which reflects both the concentration levels on the market generally and the degree to which larger firms are dominant in the market. It operates by adding together the squares of the market shares of each of the undertakings operating in the market.[474] The degree of concentration on the market is assessed by reference to the sum of those market shares (it thus gives greater weight proportionately to the market shares of the larger firms). Where the HHI is under 1,000, the market is not perceived to be concentrated: if it is between 1,000 and 1,800 the market is moderately concentrated; and over 1,800 the market is highly concentrated.

In the USA, in evaluating horizontal mergers, the market concentration (post-merger) and the increase in concentration resulting from the merger are assessed in order to create a presumption of the merger's legality or illegality:

(i)   There is an assumption that a merger does not raise any competition concerns if either the HHI is (post-merger) less than 1,000 or if the HHI is between 1,000 and 1,800 but the increase to the index is less than fifty;

(ii) Where (a) the HHI is above 1,800 and there is an increase of between fifty and 100 in the index or (b) where the HHI is between 1,000 and 1,800 and there is an increase in excess of 100 in the index, a challenge from the competition authorities is likely. The merger 'potentially raises significant competitive concerns';

(iii) Where the HHI is above 1,800 and the merger has led to an increase to the index in excess of 100 points the merger is presumed to be illegal.

---

468   [2004] OJ C31/5, para. 5.

469   Horizontal Merger Guidelines [2004] OJ C31/5, part III.

470   *Ibid.*, part IV.

471   *Ibid.*, parts V–VII.

472   *Ibid.*, part VIII.

473   The HHI has some drawbacks, see S. Bishop and M. Walker, *The Economics of EC Competition Law: Concepts, Application and Measurement* (2nd edn., Sweet & Maxwell, 2002), 3.29; F. Fishwick, *Making Sense of Competition Policy* (Kogan Page, 1993), 86.

474   The Commission states that '[a]lthough it is best to include all firms in the calculation, lack of information about very small firms may not be important because such firms do not affect the HHI significantly.' Horizontal Merger Guidelines, para. 16.

The Commission's Horizontal Merger Guidelines explain that it also relies on both market shares and concentration ratios to aid its *preliminary* assessment of a case. 'Market shares and concentration levels provide useful first indications of the market structure and of the competitive importance of both the merging parties and their competitors'.[475] For example, the Commission states that where the market share of the undertakings concerned does not exceed 25 per cent the merger is not liable to impede effective competition and is presumed to be compatible with the common market. Conversely, a market shares of over 50 per cent may in itself be evidence of the existence of a dominant market position.[476]

Horizontal Merger Guidelines [2004] OJ C31/7, paras. 17–18

Market share levels

17. According to well-established case-law, very large market shares—50 per cent or more—may in themselves be evidence of the existence of a dominant position. However, smaller competitors may act as a sufficient constraining influence if, for example, they have the ability and incentive to increase their supplies. A merger involving a firm whose market share will remain below 50 per cent after the merger may also raise competition concerns in view of other factors such as the strength and number of competitors, the presence of capacity constraints or the extent to which the products of the merging parties are close substitutes. The Commission has thus in several cases considered mergers resulting in firms holding market shares between 40 per cent and 50 per cent, and in come cases below 40 per cent, to lead to the creation or the strengthening of a dominant position.

18. Concentrations which, by reason of the limited market share of the undertakings concerned, are not liable to impede effective competition may be presumed to be compatible with the common market. Without prejudice to Articles 81 and 82 of the Treaty, an indication to this effect exists, in particular, where the market share of the undertakings concerned does not exceed 25 per cent either in the common market or in a substantial part of it.

Further, it believes that the overall concentration level in a market, often measured through the application of the HHI, provides useful information about the competitive situation and a useful indication of the market structure and of the competitive importance of the merging parties and their competitors.[477] Like market shares the HHI is used as an initial indicator of the absence of competition concerns. 'However, they do not give rise to a presumption of either the existence or the absence of such concerns'.[478] The Guidelines state that the Commission is *unlikely* to identify competition concerns in a market:[479]

- with a post-merger HHI below 1,000;

[475] Horizontal Merger Guidelines, para. 14.

[476] *Ibid.*, paras. 17–18. See also discussion of market shares and entry analysis *infra* and Case C-62/86, *AKZO Chemie BV v. Commission* [1991] ECR I-3359, [1993] 5 CMLR 215, para 60 where, in the context of an Article 82 case, the ECJ stated: 'With regard to market shares the Court has held that very large shares are in themselves, and save in exceptional circumstances, evidence of the existence of a dominant position (judgment in Case 85/76, *Hoffman-La Roche v Commission* [1979] ECR 461, [1979] 3 CMLR 211 paragraph 41). That is the situation where there is a market share of 50% such as that found to exist in this case.' This case is discussed further *supra* Chap. 6

[477] Horizontal Merger Guidelines, paras. 14–21.

[478] *Ibid.*, para. 21.

[479] *Ibid.*, paras. 19–21.

- with a post-merger HHI between 1,000–2,000, where the change in the HHI (the delta) is below 250

- with a post-merger HHI above 2,000, where the delta is below 150.

except where special circumstances exist, for example: one of the firms is a potential entrant or an important innovator; one of the firms is a maverick likely to disrupt coordinated conduct; one of the firms has a pre-merger market share of 50 per cent or more; cross-shareholdings exist between the market participants; or there is evidence of past coordination of facilitating practices on the market.

c. Possible Non-Coordinated Anti-Competitive Effects

Where a merger removes important competitive constraints on the merging firms those firms may acquire greater market power. The merged entity may then be able to increase price or reduce quality, choice or innovation irrespective of the response of its competitors.[480] Generally, such market power will be acquired, and the merger will give rise to non-coordinated effects, where the merger creates or strengthens the dominant position of a single firm which, typically, acquires a larger market share than the next competitor post-merger. The Horizontal Merger Guidelines also make it clear, however, that non-coordinated effects may arise outside this classic scenario where the merger occurs on an oligopolistic market.[481]

25. Generally, a merger giving rise to such non-coordinated effects would significantly impede effective competition by creating or strengthening the dominant position of a single firm, one which, typically, would have an appreciably larger market share than the next competitor post-merger. Furthermore, mergers in oligopolistic markets involving the elimination of important competitive constraints that the merging parties previously exerted on each other together with a reduction of competitive pressure on the remaining competitors may, even where there is little likelihood of coordination between the members of the oligopoly, also result in a significant impediment to competition. The Merger Regulation clarifies that all mergers giving rise to such non-coordinated effects shall also be declared incompatible with the common market.

The Guidelines set out a non-exhaustive list of factors that the Commission considers may influence its decision whether significant non-coordinated anti-competitive effects are likely to result from the merger:

The Market Shares held by the Merging Firms[482]

The larger the combined market shares and increase in market share the more likely it is that the merger will lead to a significant increase in market power.[483] The Commission recognizes, however, that high market shares cannot necessarily be equated with market power. An adverse finding may not result, for example, where market shares are volatile,[484] or where high market shares may be met by rigorous competition faced from another competitor on the market:

A market share as high as 90 per cent is, in itself, a very strong indicator of the existence of a dominant position. However, in certain rare circumstances even such a high market share may not necessarily

---

[480] If other firms on the market follow, then the anticompetitive effects will be felt throughout the market. In contrast with coordinated effects cases, however, the ability of the merged entity to increase price will not be dependent upon the reaction of other undertakings in the market.

[481] See also the discussion of *T-Mobile/tele.ring infra* n. 497 and accompanying text.

[482] Horizontal Merger Guidelines, para. 27.

[483] See the discussion of market shares, *supra* 1019–20.

[484] In Case IV/M.354, *American Cyanamid/Shell* [1993] OJ C273/6 the Commission considered that 'an analysis focusing on market shares alone is not particularly probative in a dynamic and R&D-intensive industry'. See also discussion of new economy markets, *supra* 1004–5.

result in dominance. In particular, if sufficient active competitors are present on the market, the company with the large market share may be prevented from acting to an appreciable extent independently of the pressure typical of a competitive market.[485]

High market shares may also be counteracted by the exercise of market power by a purchaser from the merged entity[486] or by new entry.[487]

The Closeness of Competition between the Merging Firms[488]

Where products are differentiated on a market, some will be closer substitutes for each other than others. A merger between firms which produce products that are closer substitutes, is more likely to produce anti-competitive consequences. The competition between firms may also be more intense the more proximately located the competitor.

S. Bishop and M. Walker, *The Economics of EC Competition Law: Concepts, Application and Measurement* (2nd edn., Sweet & Maxwell, 2002), 265–6

Mergers involving differentiated products

7.19 Where firms sell differentiated products, each product is not a perfect substitute for another and in consequence an increase in the relative price of one product does not necessarily result in that product losing all if its sales (as would be the case if products were homogeneous). Pre-merger if a firm were to impose a relative price increase, it would lose sales to other suppliers. But following a merger, some of these lost sales will be transferred to the other merging party. Hence, the impact of the price increase on profits is potentially smaller post-merger because some of the lost sales are recaptured in higher sales of the other merging party. This argument is symmetric in that it applies equally to the other merging party, so there may also be an incentive to increase the price of the product of the other merging party. In this manner, the elasticity of the firm's residual demand curve is reduced, permitting prices to be increased profitably. Moreover, and importantly for the assessment of mergers, in industries with differentiated products, the competitive constraints provided by different firms will vary and some firms will be 'closer' competitors to others. The concept of 'closeness' of competition is illustrated in the following example. Suppose there are four firms, A, B, C, and D, each with sales of 100. Suppose that if A raises its price by 5 per cent, it will lose 20 per cent, of its sales, which makes the price rise unprofitable. These sales will be picked up by the other three firms as shown in Table 7.1. Table 7.1 shows that B picks up 15 of the lost sales, C picks up 3 and D picks up 2. In this sense, B is a closer competitor to A than either C or D. If A and B were to merge, then the price rise by A would lead to the combined firm, AB losing only 5 sales. In consequence, increasing the price of A by 5 per cent may now be profitable.

---

[485] Case IV/M.68, *Tetra Pak/Alfa Laval* [1991] OJ L290/35, 38–9 [1992] 4 CMLR M81. Case IV/M.12, *Varta/Bosch* [1991] OJ L320/26, [1992] 5 CMLR M1 the merged entity held 44% of the German battery market. However, a competitor, with only 5–10% of the market would provide strong competition on account of its reputation and resources. Similarly, in Case IV/M.4, *Renault/Volvo* [1990] OJ C281/2 Renault would acquire 54% of the French market. Although Mercedes only had 18%, it had the reputation and resources to be able to exercise sufficient competitive restraint on Renault. However, some competitors may not provide effective competition and may be unlikely to do so in the future: Case IV/M.190, *Nestlé/Perrier.* [1992] OJ L356/1.

[486] See the discussion of Case IV/M.1225, *Enso/Stora infra* 1038.

[487] Case IV/M.42, *Alcatel/Telettra* [1991] OJ L122/48, [1991] 4 CMLR 778 and *infra* 1038.

[488] Horizontal Merger Guidelines, paras. 28–30.

Table 7.1 An illustration of unilateral effects

Firm	Sales at current prices	Sales if A raises price 5 per cent
A	100	80
B	100	115
C	100	103
D	100	102
AB	[2]00	195

This example illustrates that the degree to which a merger in a differentiated product market might result in a unilateral price increase depends on the relative 'closeness' of the merging firms to one another. In this case most of A's lost sales went to B, indicating that A and B are in some sense particularly close competitors.

The 'closeness of competition' can for instance be thought of in terms of product characteristics or geographical location. For example, a premium ice cream, say, is likely to face 'closer' competition from another supplier of a premium ice cream brand than from a supplier of an own-label product. Similarly, where transportation costs are important, a supplier is likely to face 'closer' competition from suppliers located nearby than from those located further away. A competitor will be said to be 'close' if following a relative price increase a significant proportion of the resulting lost sales would be gained by that competitor.

The Commission is thus more likely to be concerned with mergers between firms that produce products with a high degree of substitutability. In *Volvo/Scania*[489] the Commission, in assessing the effect of Volvo's acquisition of a controlling stake in Scania, was influenced by the fact that in various markets Volvo and Scania had similar market position and that their products were each other's closest substitutes. With respect to the Swedish heavy trucks market, for example, Volvo and Scania were each other's main competitors.[490] The loss of competition between them would significantly increase the merged entity's advantage over its competitors.[491] Similarly, in *Schneider/Legrand*[492] the Commission was influenced by the fact that the merger would, in some geographic markets, remove rivalry between the two firms which had provided the central element of competition. Although the CFI annulled the Commission's decision on appeal it did not 'doubt that the rivalry between the notifying parties was extremely significant on the French sectoral market to which the objections relate and that one effect of the merger will be to eliminate a key factor in competition there'.[493]

In *GE/Instrumentarium*[494] the Commission was concerned about the proposed acquisition by GE Medical Equipment of a Finnish-based company, Instrumentarium, which was a leading

[489] Case IV/M.1672, [2001] OJ L143/74.

[490] See *supra* 1017.

[491] *Ibid.*, para. 107.

[492] Case COMP/M. 2283, 11 Oct. 2001.

[493] Case T-310/01, *Schneider Electric SA v. Commission* [2002] ECR II-4071, [2003] 4 CMLR 768, para. 418.

[494] Case COMP/M.3083, IP/03/1193.

manufacturer of hospital equipment. The merger would bring together two of the four leading players in Europe in patient monitors, markets characterized by differentiated products with competition taking place through tenders. In particular, the Commission considered that the merger would lead to the merged entity acquiring high market shares in a number of national EU markets for perioperative monitors, used by anaesthesiologists to monitor patients during operations. The Commission conducted a series of statistical analyses and relied on bidding data and win-loss analysis[495] to establish that the parties were particularly close competitors, at least on some markets, so that the merger would significantly increase their market power.[496] Analysis showed that each of the parties was likely to charge a lower price where the other took place in a bidding contest. In the end the concentration was cleared subject to a package of remedies designed to remove the horizontal overlaps in the perioperative monitoring market.

In *T-Mobile/tele.ring*[497] the Commission considered a merger between the second (T-Mobile Austria) and fourth (tele.ring) players in the Austrian mobile telephony services market. Post-merger Mobilkom would remain the market leader so that, despite an increase in market shares, the merged entity would remain the number two player on the market. In its Phase II analysis, the Commission focused on the non-coordinated effects that would result from the merger.[498] In particular, the Commission was concerned about the removal of tele.ring from the extremely concentrated market. Although the Commission did not rely on the particular closeness of competition between the merging parties, it did consider that tele.ring had exerted significant competitive pressure on both Mobilkom and T-Mobile and that its removal from the market would significantly impede effective competition on the market. tele.ring was a relatively new entrant to the market which had quickly gained market share through vibrant competitive practices and the offering of low prices.[499] The Commission thus approved the merger only after specific remedies designed to strengthen the position of smaller players on the market were agreed.[500]

The Ability of Customers to Switch[501]

Customers unable to switch, for example, by the limited availability of alternative suppliers or by significant switching costs, are particularly vulnerable to price rises.

---

[495] The analysis considered the closeness of competition between the merging parties by analysing the ranking of the other party in contracts won by one of them. The analysis was used to dismiss concerns in some of the product markets identified but caused the Commission to conclude that the merger would remove a particularly close competition from the market in the case of perioperative monitors. Other mechanisms such as diversion rations, survey evidence, merger simulation, econometric techniques, shock analysis, internal documents may also be used to measure closeness of competition between the merging parties, see, e.g., A. Lindsay *The EC Merger Regulation: Substantive Issues* (2nd edn., Sweet & Maxwell, 2006), para. 7-006 and, e.g. Case COMP/M.3765 *Amer/Salomon* and Case COMP/M.3746 *Tetra Laval/SIG Simonazzi* and Case COMP/M.3658 *Noartis/Hexal*.

[496] Case COMP/M.3083, IP/03/1193, paras. 131 ff. But contrast, e.g. COMP/M.3765 *Amer/Salomon*

[497] Case COMP/M.3916

[498] The section 6(1)(c) document raised concerns about both coordinated and non-coordinated effects but the former were not pursued in the final decision.

[499] The Commission described tele,ring as a 'maverick', normally an important issue in coordinated (not non-coordinated) effects cases, see *infra* 1026 ff and Horizontal Merger Guidelines, para. 42.

[500] The merging parties agreed to divest UMTS frequencies and mobile telephony sites of to smaller players, such as Hutchison 3G. These commitments were designed to enable Hutchison 3G to expand its Austrian network all without being dependent on its current national roaming agreement with Mobilkom.

[501] Horizontal Merger Guidelines, para. 31.

The Likelihood that Competitors will Increase Supply[502]

If competitors cannot increase capacity then it may be easier for the merging firms to restrict output themselves and to benefit from price rises.[503] The ability of competitors to increase capacity in response to such a decision might be limited by capacity constraints, the cost of increasing capacity or 'barriers to expansion'.[504] Alternatively, the merging firms may themselves have the ability to hinder expansion by competitors,[505] for example, as a result of controlling or influencing the supply of essential inputs, access to distribution channels, access to intellectual property rights, or by giving the merged entity the ability and incentive to raise costs or decrease the quality of service to rivals in markets where interoperability between different infrastructures or platforms is important (e.g., in energy, telecommunications and communications industries).[506]

In *MCI Worldcom/Sprint*,[507] for example, the Commission prohibited a proposed merger of two global communications companies, MCI Worldcom Inc and Sprint Corporation. The Commission considered that the combination of the merged firms' extensive networks and customer base would lead to such a powerful force that both competitors and customers would have been dependent upon them to obtain Universal Internet connectivity. In particular, it would create a 'super Tier provider of global Internet connectivity. It will have an inherent strong position due to its absolute and relative size compared to its competitors. Given the size of the merged entity, it will be able to control the prices of its competitors and customers. It will also be in a position to control technical developments. The combined entity will be able to sustain such behaviour due to its capacity to discipline the market notably through the threat of selective degradation of its competitors Internet connectivity offering...and also through its essential ability to determine and agree any new technical development to enable advance Internet services...'.[508] In *GE/Instrumentarium*[509] the Commission also feared that the parties would be able to foreclose other preoperative monitor suppliers from the market by making its anaesthesia machines incompatible with rival monitors. This would, of course, have made it difficult for the competitors to respond to an increase in price by increasing capacity.

The Competitive Force Eliminated by the Merger[510]

The merger is more likely to cause concern where the merger is with a firm that is likely to change the competitive dynamics of a market more than its market share suggests, e.g., if the

---

[502] *Ibid.*, paras. 32–5.

[503] See, e.g. Case COMP/M.3637 *Total/Sasol/JV*.

[504] The inability of competitors to expand capacity is most likely to be problematic where products are homogenous, but it may also be important when suppliers produce differentiated products, Horizontal Merger Guidelines, para. 35.

[505] Horizontal Merger Guidelines, para. 36.

[506] The fact that such behaviour might constitute an abuse of a dominant position is one factor that must be taken into account, see *infra* 1056–9.

[507] Case COMP/M.1741. On appeal, Case T-310/00 *MCI v. Commission* [2004] ECR II-3253, [2004] 5 CMLR 26 however, the CFI annulled the Commission's decision, see *supra* n. 352.

[508] *Ibid.*, para. 146.

[509] Case COMP/M.3083, IP/03/1193.

[510] Horizontal Merger Guidelines, paras. 37–8.

merger involves a new entrant or an important innovator in the market (for example, where two companies have new competing products in the pipeline).

In *Boeing/McDonnell Douglas*[511] the Commission was concerned that the merger would strengthen Boeing's already dominant position in the markets for large commercial aircraft and for narrow-body and wide-body aircraft. Although McDonnell Douglas' market share had been declining responses from airlines indicated that, in the past, its competitive influence had been greater than that reflected in its market share. Its participation in the competitive process and influence on competition was of significant importance leading, it appeared, to a reduction of over 7 per cent in the realized price. Further, although it was not at the time a real force in the market the merger would enable Boeing to gain preferential access to McDonnell customers.[512] In the end the Commission cleared the merger subject to the parties complying with specified commitments.

d. Possible Coordinated Anti-Competitive Effects—Collective or Joint Dominance[513]

Background and the Position under the Old ECMR

It has been seen in Chapter 11 that some, but not all, oligopolistic markets are prone to both explicit collusion and tacit collusion or coordination. Undertakings operating on an oligopolistic market may agree to act in their own best interest. Even if they do not, undertakings may recognize their interdependence and that if they compete less vigorously they may be able to enjoy higher prices and profits. The undertakings may behave 'as if' they have colluded, with the consequent adverse impact on efficiency and consumer welfare as a whole (tacit collusion or coordination). Since such behaviour depends for its success on the cooperative responses of other players on the market it is known as coordinated effects.

It was also seen that a difficult problem for competition authorities is how they should control the behaviour of undertakings operating in such a way on a market. Since they have not actually colluded or concerted Article 81(1) does not prohibit the tacit collusion engaged in by the undertakings on the market. Further, although Article 82 has been interpreted to prohibit the abuse of a dominant position held collectively by one or more undertakings, Article 82 provides less than an ideal tool for controlling such behaviour.[514] Given this lacuna, it would seem critical that the ECMR should prevent mergers that would facilitate coordination on a market. A vigorous preventive merger control policy of course means that there will be less need for later control of a corrective nature. A system of merger control which did not allow it to prevent concentration, or the further concentration of an industry, would be seriously flawed.[515] The old ECMR only allowed the Commission to prohibit mergers leading to the creation or strengthening of a dominant position. In *Flat Glass*[516] the CFI confirmed that Article 82 applied to a situation in which a dominant position was held collectively by two or more independent entities united together by

---

[511] Case IV/M. 877 [1997] OJ L336/16, [1997] 5 CMLR 270.

[512] *Ibid.*, paras. 58–61.

[513] The terms collective, joint, and oligopolistic dominance have been used interchangeably. See generally R. Whish, 'Collective Dominance' in D. O'Keefe and M. Andenas (eds.), *Liber Amicorum for Lord Slynn* (Kluwer, 2000), i.

[514] See *supra* Chap. 11.

[515] If concentrations could be conducted which would result in highly concentrated markets, ripe for explicit or tacit collusion, there would be a serious gap in its ability effectively to apply a coherent system of antitrust enforcement. See Commission's *XVIth Report on Competition Policy* (Commission, 1986), 285.

[516] Cases T-68, 77–78/89, *Società Italiana Vetro (SIV) v. Commission* [1992] ECR II-1403, [1992] 5 CMLR 302.

'economic links'.[517] Even though the old ECMR provided *no* textual support the Commission took the view that the original ECMR[518] did, similarly, authorize it to act against concentrations which led to the creation or strengthening of a collective dominant position.[519] It recognized the difficulties of proof that would be involved,[520] but proceeded as a matter of expediency.[521] In a series of judgments the ECJ and CFI respectively, upheld the Commission's view. In *France* v. *Commission*[522] the ECJ confirmed that the ECMR did indeed apply to mergers which would create or strengthen a dominant position; and in *Gencor* v. *Commission*, [523] *Airtours plc* v. *Commission*[524] and *Independent Music Publishers and Labels Association (Impala)* v. *Commission*[525] the CFI clarified that a collective dominant position could be held by members of a 'tight oligopoly' economically linked together (only) by the market so that they could be expected to align their conduct on the market.

The ECJ's judgment in *France* v. *Commission*[526] arose from an appeal against the Commission's clearance decision in *Kali und Salz/MdK/Treuhand*.[527] In this case the Commission had found that the concentration created or led to the creation of a market-leading duopoly on the Community (except Germany) market for potash. Two entities would enjoy a dominant position: Kali und Salz (K+S)/MdK (the merging parties) and Société Commerciale des Potasses et de l'Azote (SCPA). To prevent the Commission from declaring the concentration to be incompatible with the common market, the parties offered the Commission commitments which affected not

---

[517] See *supra* Chap. 11.

[518] Although Article 82 refers to a dominant position held by 'one or more' undertakings, (see Chaps. 5 and 11) the old ECMR simply referred to concentrations which lead to the creation or strengthening of *a* dominant position. The main reason for doubting the ability of the ECMR to apply to such concentrations thus hinged on the wording of the Regulation itself. If it was intended that the Regulation should apply to prevent the creation or strengthening of a collective dominant position or a dominant position held by one or more independent undertakings why was this not spelt out in the legislation? See the arguments raised in Case T-102/96, *Gencor Ltd* v. *Commission* [1999] ECR II-753, [1999] 4 CMLR 971, report for the hearing, paras. 110–27. See, also e.g., D. Ridyard, 'Economic Analysis of Single Firm and Oligopolistic Dominance' [1994] *ECLR* 255, 258

[519] It first introduced the concept in Case IV/M.165, *Alcatel/AEG Kabel* [1992] OJ C6/23 but nonetheless cleared the merger.

[520] It cannot simply be assumed that an oligopolistic market will not operate competitively: Case IV/M.165, *Alcatel/AEG Kabel* [1992] OJ C6/23. In contrast, in Germany, for example, there is a (rebuttable) presumption that competition is threatened by collective dominance if the three largest firms have a combined market share of at least 50% or if the top five have a combined share of two-thirds of the market: Article 22(3) of the Gesetz gegen Wettbewerbsbeschrankungen (GWB, the German law against restrictions on competition).

[521] In *Nestlé/Perrier* [1992] OJ L356/1 the Commission first took commitments as a condition for clearing a concentration (between Nestlé and Perrier) which it considered would 'create a duopolistic dominant position which would significantly impede effective competition position on the French bottled water market'. There was insufficient competitive counterweight from local mineral and spring waters, retailers and wholesalers would become increasingly dependent on the portfolio of brands of Nestlé and BSN, and potential competition from newcomers would not provide effective price-constraint, para. 108. Nestlé and Perrier between them held 60% of the French bottled water market whilst another undertaking, BSN, had 22% of the market. The remainder of the market was shared by a number of much smaller companies. Price competition on the market was already weak, the price of bottled water was relatively inelastic, the reduction from three to two suppliers would make anti-competitive parallel behaviour leading to collective abuses much easier, the mineral water suppliers in France had developed instruments of transparency which facilitated a tacit coordination of pricing policies, and the reciprocal dependence of Nestlé and BSN would create a strong common interest and incentive to maximise profits by engaging in anti-competitive parallel behaviour.

[522] Cases C-68/94 and C-30/95, *France* v. *Commission, Société Commerciale des Potasses et de l'Azote (SCPA)* v. *Commission* [1998] ECR I-1375, [1998] 4 CMLR 829.

[523] Case T-102/96, *Gencor Limited* v. *Commission* [1999] ECR II-753, [1999] 4 CMLR 971.

[524] Case T-342/99, [2002] ECR II-2585, [2002] 5 CMLR 317.

[525] Case T-464/04 [2006] ECR II-2289, [2006] 5 CMLR 19, Case C-413/06 P (judgment pending).

[526] Cases C-68/94 and C-30/95, *France* v. *Commission, Société Commerciale des Potasses et de l'Azote (SCPA)* v. *Commission* [1998] ECR I-1375, [1998] 4 CMLR 829.

[527] Case IV/M.308, [1994] OJ L186/30; on appeal Cases C-68/94 and C-30/95, *France* v. *Commission, Société Commerciale des Potasses et de l'Azote (SCPA)* v. *Commission* [1998] ECR I-1375, [1998] 4 CMLR 829.

only themselves, but also SCPA. Their aim was broadly to bring to an end to the cooperation between K+S/MdK and SCPA.[528] Partly as a result of this the affected third party, SCPA, EMC (its parent company), and France brought actions for annulment, or partial annulment of the Commission's decision under Article 230 (then Article 173) of the Treaty.[529] On appeal, the ECJ annulled the Commission's decision, finding that the Commission had not established that the concentration would in fact give rise to a collective dominant position on the market.[530] Nonetheless, the judgment was of enormous significance since the ECJ held, applying an interpretation of the Regulation in accordance with 'its purpose and general structure', that 'collective dominant positions do not fall outside the scope of the Regulation'.[531]

In upholding a broad view of the ECMR the Court adopted, in its construction, a teleological approach which best reflected the Community's aims and objectives. The Court considered that a textual and historical examination of the Regulation was not conclusive on the question but that it was necessary to interpret the Regulation with reference to its purpose and general structure.[532] In particular, since the Regulation was intended to apply to all concentrations in so far as they were likely to prove incompatible with the system of undistorted competition envisaged by the Treaty, it was essential that concentrations which created or strengthened a dominant position on the part of parties concerned with an entity not involved in the concentration be prohibited by the Regulation.[533] Conversely, a narrow interpretation of the Regulation would have meant that competition in the common market could be distorted and that the Regulation would be deprived of much of its effect.[534]

Like *Flat Glass*[535] this judgment did not clarify whether or not the merger provisions would apply to the creation of oligopolistic dominance in the absence of links, such as contractual links, between the members of the oligopoly. The Court stressed that the key to collective dominance was the parties' ability to adopt a common policy on the market and to act independently of their competitors, customers, and consumers. Although this did not appear to limit a finding of collective dominance to a position where there were contractual or other arrangements between the parties, such as those in existence between K+S/MdK and SCPA, the Court did not expressly state what the position would have been had no such links existed.

The CFI's judgment in *Gencor Ltd v. Commission*[536] shed further light on this point. This case concerned a decision by two companies, Gencor Ltd (a South African company) and Lonrho Plc (a UK company), to merge their business activities in the platinum group metal ('PGM') sector. Although the platinum businesses were both based in South Africa (and the South African

---

[528] E.g., the parties agreed to withdraw from an export company in which SCPA was a shareholder and to terminate cooperation with SCPA as a distribution partner in France.

[529] Because one of the parties was a Member State the appeal was brought straight before the ECJ, see Chap. 14.

[530] This was the first case in which the ECJ annulled a Commission decision under the ECMR. Following the annulment, the Commission re-examined the concentration and cleared it following a Phase I investigation: see N. Hacker, 'The Kali+Salz Case—the Re-examination of a Merger after an Annulment by the Court' Commission's *Competition Policy Newsletter* 1998/3, 46.

[531] Cases C-68/94 and C-30/95, *France v. Commission, Société Commerciale des Potasses et de l'Azote (SCPA) v. Commission* [1998] ECR I-1375, [1998] 4 CMLR 829, para. 178.

[532] *Ibid.*, paras. 165–7. See also especially paras. 171–8.

[533] *Ibid.*, paras. 168–70.

[534] Neither the lack of procedural safeguards for third parties nor the argument based on the fifteenth recital, setting out a presumption that concentrations would be compatible with the common market if the undertakings concerned had a combined market share of less than 25 per cent, could cast doubt on the applicability of the regulation to cases of a collective dominant position. In particular, Community law required, irrespective of the provisions in the Regulation, that an individual whose interests would be adversely affected by proceedings had a right to be heard.

[535] Cases T-68, 77–8/89, *Società Italiana Vetro (SIV) v. Commission* [1992] ECR II-1403, [1992] 5 CMLR 302.

[536] Case T-102/96, *Gencor Limited v. Commission* [1999] ECR II-753, [1999] 4 CMLR 971.

Competition Board did not consider that the operation gave rise to competition policy concerns under South African law) the Commission nevertheless issued a decision prohibiting the merger. It considered that the merger would create a duopoly between the merged entity and Anglo American Corporation of South Africa Ltd ('AAC'), which, through its associated company, Amplats, was the remaining competitor on the market. Further, the anti-competitive effects of that duopoly would be felt on the relevant markets within the EU and EEA.[537] In this case no contractual or other structural links existed between the parties.

The applicant sought annulment of the Commission's decision. After reiterating that 'collective dominant positions do not fall outside the scope of the Regulation, as the Court of Justice indeed itself held ... in *France and Others* v. *E.C. Commission* (paragraph 178))' the Court rejected the applicant's claim that, in order that a finding of collective dominance be made, formal 'structural' links had to exist between the undertakings involved.

Case T-102/96, *Gencor Limited* v. *Commission* [1999] ECR II-753 [1999] 4 CMLR 971

Court of First Instance

273. In its judgment in the *Flat Glass* case, the Court referred to links of a structural nature only by way of example and did not lay down that such links must exist in order for a finding of collective dominance to be made.

274. It merely stated ... that there is nothing, in principle to prevent two or more independent economic entities from being united by economic links in a specific market and, by virtue of that fact, from together holding a dominant position *vis-à-vis* the other operators on the same market.

...

276. Furthermore, there is no reason whatsoever in legal or economic terms to exclude from the notion of economic links the relationship of interdependence existing between the parties to a tight oligopoly within which, in a market with the appropriate characteristics, in particular in terms of market concentration, transparency and product homogeneity, those parties are in a position to anticipate one another's behaviour and are therefore strongly encouraged to align their conduct in the market, in particular in such a way as to maximise their joint profits by restricting production with a view to increasing prices. In such a context, each trader is aware that highly competitive action on its part designed to increase its market share (for example a price cut) would provoke identical action by the others, so that it would derive no benefit from its initiative. All the traders would thus be affected by the reduction in price levels.

277. That conclusion is all the more pertinent with regard to the control of concentrations, whose objective is to prevent anti-competitive market structures from arising or being strengthened. Those structures may result from the existence of economic links in the strict sense argued by the applicant or from market structures of an oligopolistic kind where each undertaking may become aware of common interests and, in particular, cause prices to increase without having to enter into an agreement or resort to a concerted practice.

278. In the [present] case, therefore, the applicant's ground of challenge alleging that the Commission failed to establish the existence of structural links is misplaced.

279. The Commission was entitled to conclude, relying on the envisaged alteration in the structure of the market and on the similarity of the costs of Amplats and [Implats/LPD], that the proposed transaction would create a collective dominant position and lead in actual fact to a duopoly constituted by those two undertakings.

---

[537] See *infra* 1088–9 and Chap. 16.

The case is illuminating. By referring to *Flat Glass*[538] when considering the links required between undertakings before a finding of collective dominance can be made, the Court clearly indicates that the concept will be dealt with in the same way for the purposes of both Article 82 and the ECMR. For this reason, the Court's judgment is also of great importance when considering the scope of Article 82.[539]

In addition, the Court establishes that the contractual links given as examples of economic links in *Flat Glass* are not necessary to support a finding of collective dominance. Although the Court does not fully explain the difference between the 'structural' and 'economic links' it refers to in its judgment it is clear that the market structure itself (the relationship of interdependence existing between parties to a tight oligopoly) suffices to establish the economic links required for a finding of collective dominance. The key question now, therefore, is whether the links between the parties do or will facilitate collusion, tacit or explicit, between the members. If so, it does not matter whether the links are purely economic and provided by market structures of an oligopolistic kind or 'structural' provided by contracts or licences concluded between the undertakings or by shareholdings which one of the undertakings has in the other. If this is correct then the latter 'structural links' are just simply one type of link which may be used to establish the broader economic links essential to a finding of collective dominance.[540]

The next critical case in which the CFI ruled on the meaning of the concept of 'collective dominance' under the old ECMR arose from the Commission's decision in *Airtours/First Choice*.[541] Here the Commission adopted a controversial decision prohibiting the acquisition by Airtours of First Choice.[542] The Commission held that the concentration would lead to the creation or strengthening of a collective dominant position on the UK short-haul foreign package holiday (the 'FPH') market. The dominant position would be held by Airtours/First Choice (32 per cent), Thomson (27 per cent), and Thomas Cook (20 per cent). The remainder of the market was highly fragmented which meant that no effective restraint on the competitive conduct of the larger players would be exercised.

In reaching its decision the Commission appeared to expand the concept of collective dominance and to find its existence in circumstances beyond those which have so far been identified with collectively dominant positions. The Commission held at paragraph 54 of its decision that it was not necessarily essential to show that the parties would adopt a common policy on the market. Rather, it appeared to take the view that the ability to engage in explicit or tacit coordination is not essential. It was sufficient that each individual undertaking operating on the oligopolistic market had sufficient market power on that market to enable it to act independently.[543] Nonetheless the Commission did consider that tacit co-ordination between the parties would occur. That tacit coordination would, however, not occur in relation to price but

---

[538] Cases T-68, 77–8/89, *Società Italiana Vetro (SIV) v. Commission* [1992] ECR II-1403, [1992] 5 CMLR 302.

[539] See *supra* Chaps. 6 and 11. Similarly, in Case T-228/97, *Irish Sugar plc v. Commission* [1999] ECR II-2969, [1999] 5 CMLR 1300 (a case on the concept of dominant position within the context of Article 82) the CFI, para. 46, in upholding the Commission's finding of an abuse of a collective dominant position relied on the ECJ's ruling in *France v. Commission*, (a decision taken within the context of the ECMR) that 'a joint dominant position consists in a number of undertakings being able together, in particular because of factors giving rise to a connection between them, to adopt a common policy on the market and act to a considerable extent independently of their competitors, their customers, and ultimately consumers (Cases C-68/94 and C-30/95, *France v. Commission, Société Commerciale des Potasses et de l'Azote (SCPA) v. Commission* [1998] ECR I-1375, [1998] 4 CMLR 829, para. 221)'.

[540] See, e.g., J. Faull and A. Nikpay (eds.), *The EC Law of Competition* (2nd edn., Oxford University Press, 2007), 5.244.

[541] Case IV/M.1524, *Airtours/First Choice* [2000] OJ L93/1. The decision was annulled on appeal, Case T-342/00, *Airtours v. Commission* [2002] ECR II-2585, [2002] 5 CMLR 317.

[542] See proceedings by *My Travel* discussed *infra* n, 826 and accompanying text.

[543] Arguably, therefore, this was a classic 'gap' case, see especially para. 54 and discussion of non-coordinated effects and gap cases *supra*. Those in favour of retention of the dominance test argued that the concept of collective dominance was broad enough to catch such non-coordinated effects. This point will not now have

in relation to output or capacity on the market. For this reason perhaps the checklist of factors relied upon by the Commission to support its finding of collective dominance[544] was not perhaps as convincing as that relied upon in earlier cases.[545] Arguably, the characteristics of the UK's FPH market did not make the Commission's finding of collective dominance conclusive. Further, the Commission considered that it was not necessary for the undertakings to be able to punish those cheating or not conforming on the market.[546]

The parties argued that it was a requirement that collectively dominant undertakings should be able to adopt a common policy on the market, that the concentration would not facilitate tacit coordination on the FPH market, and that retaliation could not be taken against any undertaking which did not accede to the coordination. In their view a finding of collective dominance was, consequently, not possible.

On appeal the CFI annulled the Commission's decision in a judgment that was highly critical of the Commission's economic reasoning. Building upon the judgments in *France v. Commission*[547] and *Gencor v. Commission*[548] it set out three criteria necessary, including the need for a retaliatory mechanism, for a finding of a collective dominant position:

- Sufficient market transparency to enable each member of the dominant oligopoly to know how the other members are behaving and to monitor whether or not they are adopting a common policy;

- The ability to sustain the situation of tacit coordination over time, i.e., the existence of deterrents to ensure that there is a long-term incentive not to depart from the common policy; and

- The common policies must not be at risk from the foreseeable reaction of competitors or consumers.

The importance of establishing three criteria in collective dominance cases was re-iterated by the CFI in *Independent Music Publishers and Labels Association (Impala) v. Commission*[549] (discussed below).

Case T-342/99, *Airtours plc* v. *Commission* [2002] ECR II-2585, [2002] 5 CMLR 317

58. Where, for the purposes of applying Regulation No 4064/89, the Commission examines a possible collective dominant position, it must ascertain whether the concentration would have the direct and immediate effect of creating or strengthening a position of that kind, which is such as significantly and lastingly to impede competition in the relevant market (see, to that effect, *Gencor* v.

---

to be decided since the new ECMR and Horizontal Merger Guidelines make it clear that these mergers are in any event prohibited. Mergers in an oligopolistic market which reduce the competitive constraints exerted by the merging parties on one another together with a reduction of competitive pressure on the remaining competitors may, even if there is no likelihood of the members of the oligopoly coordinating their behaviour, result in a significant impediment to effective competition. ECMR, recital 25 and Horizontal Merger Guidelines, paras 5. 25.

[544] See especially para. 87 ff.

[545] Although the Commission stated, relying on its decisions in *Gencor/Lonrho* and *Price Waterhouse/Coopers & Lybrand*, in a footnote to para. 87 that '[t]he characteristics listed are substantially those employed in previous Commission Decisions in Merger Regulation cases where oligopoly ... was an issue.'

[546] Case IV/M.1524, *Airtours/First Choice* [2000] OJ L93/1, paras. 52–5.

[547] Cases C-68/94 and C-30/95, *France v. Commission, Société Commerciale des Potasses et de l'Azote (SCPA) v. Commission* [1998] ECR I-1375, [1998] 4 CMLR 829.

[548] Case T-102/96, *Gencor Limited v. Commission* [1999] ECR II-753, [1999] 4 CMLR 971.

[549] Case T-464/04 [2006] ECR II-2289, [2006] 5 CMLR 19, Case C-413/06 P (judgment pending).

Commission, paragraph 94). If there is no substantial alteration to competition as it stands, the merger must be approved (see, to that effect, Case T-2/93 *Air France* v. *Commission* [1994] ECR II-323, paragraphs 78 and 79, and *Gencor* v. *Commission*, paragraph 170, 180 and 193).

59. It is apparent from the case law that 'in the case of an alleged collective dominant position, the Commission is . . . obliged to assess, using a prospective analysis of the reference market, whether the concentration which has been referred to it leads to a situation in which effective competition in the relevant market is significantly impeded by the undertakings involved in the concentration and one or more other undertakings which together, in particular because of factors giving rise to a connection between them, are able to adopt a common policy on the market and act to a considerable extent independently of their competitors, their customers, and also of consumers' (*Kali & Salz*, cited above, paragraph 221, and *Gencor* v. *Commission*, paragraph 163).

60. The Court of First Instance has held that: 'There is no reason whatsoever in legal or economic terms to exclude from the notion of economic links the relationship of interdependence existing between the parties to a tight oligopoly within which, in a market with the appropriate characteristics, in particular in terms of market concentration, transparency and product homogeneity, those parties are in a position to anticipate one another's behaviour and are therefore strongly encouraged to align their conduct in the market, in particular in such a way as to maximise their joint profits by restricting production with a view to increasing prices. In such a context, each trader is aware that highly competitive action on its part designed to increase its market share (for example a price cut) would provoke identical action by the others, so that it would derive no benefit from its initiative. All the traders would thus be affected by the reduction in price levels.' (*Gencor* v. *Commission*, paragraph 276).

61. A collective dominant position significantly impeding effective competition in the common market or a substantial part of it may thus arise as the result of a concentration where, in view of the actual characteristics of the relevant market and of the alteration in its structure that the transaction would entail, the latter would make each member of the dominant oligopoly, as it becomes aware of common interests, consider it possible, economically rational, and hence preferable, to adopt on a lasting basis a common policy on the market with the aim of selling at above competitive prices, without having to enter into an agreement or resort to a concerted practice within the meaning of Article 81 EC (see, to that effect, *Gencor* v. *Commission*, paragraph 277) and without any actual or potential competitors, let alone customers or consumers, being able to react effectively.

62. As the applicant has argued and as the Commission has accepted in its pleadings, three conditions are necessary for a finding of collective dominance as defined:

— first, each member of the dominant oligopoly must have the ability to know how the other members are behaving in order to monitor whether or not they are adopting the common policy. As the Commission specifically acknowledges, it is not enough for each member of the dominant oligopoly to be aware that interdependent market conduct is profitable for all of them but each member must also have a means of knowing whether the other operators are adopting the same strategy and whether they are maintaining it. There must, therefore, be sufficient market transparency for all members of the dominant oligopoly to be aware, sufficiently precisely and quickly, of the way in which the other members' market conduct is evolving;

— second, the situation of tacit coordination must be sustainable over time, that is to say, there must be an incentive not to depart from the common policy on the market. As the Commission observes, it is only if all the members of the dominant oligopoly maintain the parallel conduct that all can benefit. The notion of retaliation in respect of conduct deviating from the common policy is thus inherent in this condition. In this instance, the parties concur that, for a situation of collective dominance to be viable, there must be adequate deterrents to ensure that there is a long-term incentive in not departing from the common policy, which means that each member of the dominant oligopoly must be aware that highly competitive action on its part designed to increase its market share would provoke identical action by the others, so that it would derive no benefit from its initiative (see, to that effect, *Gencor* v. *Commission*, paragraph 276);

— third, to prove the existence of a collective dominant position to the requisite legal standard, the Commission must also establish that the foreseeable reaction of current and future competitors, as well as of consumers, would not jeopardise the results expected from the common policy.

On the facts, the CFI concluded that the Commission's decision, far from basing its prospective analysis on cogent evidence, was vitiated by a series of errors of assessment as to factors fundamental to any assessment of whether a collective dominant position might be created.[550]

Coordinated Effects, Collective Dominance, and the new ECMR

The judgments in *Gencor*,[551] *Airtours*[552] and *Impala*[553] make it clear that mergers which create incentives for firms to develop a sustainable tacitly collusive arrangement on an oligopolistic market substantially impede effective competition through the creation or strengthening of a collective dominant position. [554]

The Horizontal Merger Guidelines[555] recognize the problem of tacit coordination.[556] The Guidelines deal separately with 'coordinated effects', effects resulting from a merger which may create or strengthen a *collective* dominant position because it increases the likelihood that firms are able to coordinate their behaviour and raise prices, limit production, divide markets or customers even without entering into an agreement or resorting to a concerted practice within the meaning of Article 81.[557] In making such an assessment the Commission states, relying on *Airtours plc v. Commission*,[558] that coordination is more likely to emerge in markets were it is relatively simple to reach a common understanding on terms of coordination and:

- The merging firms are able to monitor whether the terms of coordination are being adhered to;

---

[550] *Ibid.*, para. 294.

[551] Case T-102/96, *Gencor Limited v. Commission* [1999] ECR II-753, [1999] 4 CMLR 971.

[552] Case T-342/99, [2002] ECR II-2585, [2002] 5 CMLR 317.

[553] Case T-464/04 [2006] ECR II-2289, [2006] 5 CMLR 19.

[554] Arguably, these judgments confined the scope of collective dominance (and consequently the original ECMR) to mergers in which there was a risk of subsequent coordination on the market. If this was correct, the original regulation was not broad enough to prevent mergers that would lead to non-coordinated effects on an oligopolistic market where a position of single dominance was not created or strengthened. This led many to voice the opinion that the original substantive test set out in the ECMR was flawed since it would not prevent mergers on markets leading to non-coordinated effects, see *supra* 1005–9. The doctrine of 'non-coordinated' or 'unilateral' effects' predicts that such mergers, which produce no efficiency gains, may be detrimental leading to increases in prices. M. Motta, 'E.C. Merger Policy and the Airtours Case' [2000] 4 *ECLR* 199, 199–207. 'Consider for instance a situation where very few firms would be left in the industry after a merger, but none of them has enough market power to be considered dominant and it is also very unlikely that they will collude (i.e., they are not jointly dominant). In such a situation, economic theory suggests that, if there are no efficiency gains, the merging firms will unilaterally increase their prices, and that the merger will be detrimental . . .', 201. See *supra* n. 543.

[555] [2004] OJ C31/5, para. 5.

[556] I.e. that the structure of a market may be such that firms consider it possible, economically rational, and hence preferable to adopt a course of action on the market aimed at selling at increased prices.

[557] Horizontal Merger Guidelines, para. 39.

[558] Case T-342/99, [2002] ECR II-2585, [2002] 5 CMLR 317.

- There is some form of credible deterrent mechanism to ensure discipline; and

- The reaction of outsiders, customers or competitors will not jeopardize the results expected form the coordination.[559]

Factors facilitating coordination may be the simple reduction of firms on the market or, for example, the elimination of a maverick firm that has disrupted coordinated behaviour in the past.[560] Evidence of past coordination on the current or similar markets may also be relevant.[561]

Establishing Coordinated Effects or the Existence of a Collective Dominant Position

The Commission has an onerous burden to discharge to establish that that a collective dominant position has been created or strengthened and that coordinated effects on a market will significantly impede effective competition. In both *France* v. *Commission*[562] and *Airtours plc* v. *Commission*[563] the ECJ and CFI respectively annulled the Commission's decision on the ground that this burden had not been discharged.

In *France* v. *Commission*[564] the ECJ held that the Commission had not shown to the necessary legal standard that the concentration would give rise to a collective dominant position which was liable to impede significantly effective competition in the relevant market. In particular, a market share of 60 per cent (which would be held by K+S/MdK and SCPA after the concentration, they had 23 per cent and 37 per cent shares respectively) did not of itself point conclusively to the existence of a collective dominant position on the part of the undertakings. Further, the structural links between K+S and SCPA were not in fact as tight or binding as the Commission had sought to make out, and the Commission had not succeeded in showing that there was no effective competitive counterweight to the grouping allegedly formed by K+S/MdK and SCPA.

> 221. In the case of an alleged collective dominant position, the Commission is, therefore, obliged to assess, using a prospective analysis of the reference market, whether the concentration which has been referred to leads to a situation in which effective competition in the relevant market is significantly impeded by the undertakings involved in the concentration and one or more other undertakings which together, in particular because of factors giving rise to a connection between them, are able to adopt a common policy on the market and act to a considerable extent independently of their competitors, their customers, and also of consumers.

None of the other factors relied upon could be regarded as lending decisive support to the Commission's conclusion. Similarly, it has been seen that the CFI in *Airtours plc* v. *Commission*[565] held that the Commission had not presented cogent evidence in support of its analysis and conclusion. The foreign package holiday market involved in that case did not display the classic market characteristics deemed to facilitate tacit coordination.

---

[559] Horizontal Merger Guidelines, para. 41.

[560] *Ibid.*, para. 42.

[561] *Ibid.*, para. 43. For the relevance of past behaviour in strengthening of collective dominance cases, see *infra* 1037.

[562] Cases C-68/94 and C-30/95, *France* v. *Commission, Société Commerciale des Potasses et de l'Azote (SCPA)* v. *Commission* [1998] ECR I-1375, [1998] 4 CMLR 829. In this case the French Government and SCPA submitted that, if the regulation did apply to collective dominant positions, the Commission's reasoning concerning the alleged creation of a dominant duopoly had been based on an assessment which was wrong in fact or law and which was inadequate. The ECJ upheld this limb of the applicant's appeal, see in particular, paras. 179–250.

[563] Case T-342/99, [2002] ECR II-2585, [2002] 5 CMLR 317.

[564] Cases C-68/94 and C-30/95, *France* v. *Commission, Société Commerciale des Potasses et de l'Azote (SCPA)* v. *Commission* [1998] ECR I-1375, [1998] 4 CMLR 829.

[565] Case T-342/99, [2002] ECR II-2585, [2002] 5 CMLR 317.

These cases make it clear that a finding by the Commission of collective dominance or coordinated effects will have to be rigorously supported by evidence other than that relating to market shares.[566] In *Gencor/Lonrho* the Commission carefully set out the factors supporting its finding that a collective dominant position would be created on the platinum market. For example, it stated at paragraph 141 of its decision:

141. (a) on the demand side, there is moderate growth, inelastic demand and insignificant countervailing buyer power. Buyers are therefore highly vulnerable to a potential abuse;

(b) the supply side is highly concentrated with high market transparency for a homogenous product, mature production technology, high entry barriers (including high sunk costs) and suppliers with financial links and multi-market contacts. These supply side characteristics make it easy for suppliers to engage in parallel behaviour and provide them with incentives to do so, without any countervailing checks from the demand side.

On appeal[567] the CFI affirmed that these factors had been correctly relied upon and upheld the finding of collective dominance. Obviously the relevant factors may vary from market to market. This checklist, however, seems to 'be based upon the standard "textbook" characteristics which are thought to facilitate tacit collusion in a market'.[568] In its horizontal guidelines, the Commission devotes thirteen paragraphs[569] to the market features that are likely: (1) to enable the firms to reach terms of coordination; (2) to monitor deviation; (3) to provide a deterrent mechanism; and (4) to prevent outsiders jeopardizing the outcome of the expected coordination. These paragraphs will obviously provide critical guidance in cases involving mergers on oligopolistic markets.

Given the difficulties involved in proving collective dominance or the likelihood of coordinated effects, an interesting twist is the CFI's judgment *Independent Music Publishers and Labels Association (Impala) v. Commission*[570] in which the CFI annulled a Commission decision (taken under the old ECMR and hence the dominance test) unconditionally *clearing* a merger between two of the five music majors, Sony and BMG.[571] In its decision, the Commission despite indicating otherwise in

---

[566] In Case IV/M938, *Price Waterhouse/ Coopers & Lybrand* OJ [1997] L50/27, [1999] 4 CMLR 665 the Commission did not prohibit a merger between two of the (then) 'big six' firms of accountants on the grounds that there was no conclusive proof that the merger would create or strengthen a position of collective dominance. At the time of investigation, however, two of the other big six firms were also proposing to merge (KPMG and Ernst & Young) and had notified their concentration to the Commission. This of course would have led to a reduction from six to four firms rather than of six to five. If this had been the case it seems likely that both mergers would have been prohibited (in fact the negotiations between KPMG and Ernst & Young collapsed, Case IV/M938, OJ [1997] L50/27, [1999] 4 CMLR 665, para. 110). See also Case COMP/M.2389, *Shell/DEA* and J. M. Schmidt 'Spotting the Elephant in Parallel Mergers: First past the post, or combined assessment?' [2003] *ECLR* 183. See also now Case M.2810, *Deloitte & Touche/Andersen (UK)*, Case M. 2816, *Ernst & Young France/Andersen France* and Case M.2824, *Ernst & Young/Andersen Germany*.

[567] Case T-102/96, *Gencor Limited v. Commission* [1999] ECR II-753 [1999] 4 CMLR 971.

[568] The Lexecon *Competition Memo* of Nov. 1999. See *supra* Chap. 11.

[569] Horizontal Merger Guidelines, paras. 45–57.

[570] Case T-464/04 [2006] ECR II-2289, [2006] 5 CMLR 19, Case C-413/06 P (judgment pending).

[571] COMP/M. 3333. The CFI thus ordered the Commission to reconsider the merger and adopt a new decision in the light of current market conditions. The Commission initiated Phase II proceedings on 1 March 2007, see IP/07/272. In Case COMP/M.3126 *Oracle/PeopleSoft* (IP/04/1312) the Commission cleared Oracle Corp's proposed acquisition of PeopleSoft Inc, a rival maker of high function enterprise application software (a global market). Although the merger would lead to a reduction of the big players on the market from three to two, the Commission considered that the market remained competitive and rivals on the mid-market exercised a competitive constraint on the players in the market. The Commission considered the possibility of coordinated effects to be implausible on the market on account of the asymmetries in market share, the heterogeneity of the products and the lack of transparency in the market. In the US, the DOJ sought to enjoin the merger on account of its 'unilateral' (non-coordinated) effects. The District Court denied the injunction, however, as it was not convinced as to why other providers of enterprise application software would not constrain a small but significant non-transitory increase in price by Oracle/PeopleSoft, *US v. Oracle Corp* 331 F.Supp.2d 1098.

its statement of objections, made a fundamental U-turn concluding that the merger would not lead to the *strengthening* (or the creation) of a collective dominant position in the physical or digital recorded music markets.[572] With regard to the physical recorded music market, for example, the Commission found that there was no strengthening of a dominant position as the market was not characterised by features facilitating coordinated behaviour. Not only was there no evidence of parallel pricing, but the Commission considered the market was not transparent, the heterogeneity of the products made coordination unlikely and that there was no evidence of past cheating or retaliation against deviations from a collusive strategy. Further, there was nothing to suggest that a reduction in the number of players from five to four, would change the position such that a collective dominant position would be created. The CFI annulled the decision, on the grounds that the Commission's reasoning was inadequate and contained manifest errors of assessment.

When considering the concept of a collective dominant position, the CFI reaffirmed the previous ECMR judgments defining collective dominance and the conditions necessary to establish that collective dominance would be created.

Independent Music Publishers and Labels Association (Impala) v. *Commission* [2006] ECR II-2289, [2006] 5 CMLR 19

2. Concept of collective dominance

245. It follows from the case-law of the Court of Justice that in the case of an alleged collective dominant position, the Commission is obliged to assess, using a prospective analysis of the reference market, whether the concentration which has been referred to it leads to a situation in which effective competition in the relevant market is significantly impeded by the undertakings involved in the concentration and one or more other undertakings which together, in particular because of factors giving rise to a connection between them, are able to adopt a common policy on the market and act to a considerable extent independently of their competitors, their customers and, ultimately, of consumers (Joined Cases C-68/94 and C-30/95 *France and Others* v *Commission* (known as '*Kali und Salz*') [1998] ECR I-1375, paragraph 221).

246. The Court of First Instance has held that a situation of collective dominance which significantly impedes effective competition in the common market or a substantial part thereof may therefore arise following a concentration where, taking into account the actual characteristics of the relevant market and of the change to its structure brought about by the completion of the transaction, the concentration would have the consequence that, being aware of the common interests, each member of the dominant oligopoly would consider it possible, economically rational and therefore preferable to adopt the same policy on a lasting basis on the market with the aim of selling at above competitive prices, without having to conclude an agreement or resort to a concerted practice within the meaning of Article 81 EC, without actual or potential competitors, or customers and consumers, being able to react effectively (see, to that effect, Case T-102/96 *Gencor* v *Commission* [1999] ECR II-753, paragraph 276).

247. In *Airtours* v *Commission* . . . , paragraph 62, the Court of First Instance held, as stated at recital 68 to the Decision in the present case, that the three following conditions must be satisfied in order for collective dominance as defined to be created. First, the market must be sufficiently transparent for the undertakings which coordinate their conduct to be able to monitor sufficiently whether the rules of coordination are being observed. Second, the discipline requires that there be a form of deterrent mechanism in the event of deviant conduct. Third, the reactions of undertakings

---

[572] Case COMP/M.3333. See also e.g. Case COMP/M.3692 *Reuters/Telerate*.

which do not participate in the coordination, such as current or future competitors, and also the reactions of customers, should not be able to jeopardise the results expected from the coordination.

248. It follows from the case-law of the Court of Justice (*Kali und Salz*, paragraph 245 above, paragraph 222) and of the Court of First Instance (*Airtours v Commission*, paragraph 45 above, paragraph 63) that the prospective analysis which the Commission is required to carry out in the context of the control of concentrations, in the case of collective dominance, requires close examination of, in particular, the circumstances which, in each individual case, are relevant for assessing the effects of the concentration on competition in the reference market and that the Commission must provide solid evidence.

In analysing the Commission's decision the CFI concluded that the Commission had failed, applying the *Airtours* criteria to contain a sufficient statement of reasons for its finding that the market was not conducive to collective dominance. The Commission's finding that the market was not transparent was not supported and was vitiated by a failure to rely on data supporting the conclusion. Further, the reliance on the absence of previous instances of retaliation was vitiated by an error of law, or at the very least by manifest errors in the assessment.

In its assessment of whether a position of collective dominance existed, the Commission had focussed on the question of whether the *Airtours* conditions existed. It will be remembered from Chapter 11 that the CFI indicated that in the case of a strengthening of an *existing* dominant position, the Commission, instead of proving the *Airtours* criteria in the traditional way through recourse to theoretical analysis, could have established satisfaction of the *Airtours* criteria by reference to 'indicia and items of evidence relating to the signs, manifestations and phenomena inherent in the presence of a collective dominant position'.[573] When assessing whether a collective dominant position already exists, it may therefore be desirable for the Commission, instead of relying on prospective analysis of the probable development of the market or theoretical analysis, to determine, using past or present facts, that a number of undertakings have power to adopt the same course of conduct.

The CFI also quashed the Commission's finding that the merger would not lead to the *creation* of a collective dominant position on the basis that the examination carried out by the Commission were too 'succinct' and 'superficial' to satisfy its obligation to carry out a prospective analysis and to examine carefully the circumstances which may prove relevant for the purposes of assessing the effects of the concentration on competition in the reference market.[574]

(iv) Countervailing Buyer Power

The horizontal guidelines stress that a competitive constraint can be exercised over possible non-coordinated or coordinated anti-competitive effects identified not only by competitors (actual and potential) but by customers with countervailing buyer power. Such a buyer may have the incentive[575] to credibly threaten to find an alternative source of supplier, perhaps by changing supplier, vertically integrating or persuading/sponsoring new entry, were the supplier to increase price.[576] In such cases, the countervailing buyer power may neutralise the market power of the parties.[577]

---

[573] Case T-464/04, [2006] ECR II-2289, [2006] 5 CMLR 19, para. 251 and paras. 252–4 (set out *supra* Chap. 11).

[574] Case T-464/04, [2006] ECR II-2289, [2006] 5 CMLR 19, paras. 525–8.

[575] It may not if, for example, it can pass on the price increases to its customers, see e.g. Case IV/M.1225 *Enso/Stora* [1999] OJ L254/9, para. 91.

[576] *Ibid.*, para. 65.

[577] Case IV/M.833, *The Coca-Cola Company/Carlsberg A/S* [1998] OJ L145/41, [1997] 5 CMLR 564.

In *Enso/Stora*[578] the Commission considered that even though the merging parties would acquire a market share of 60 per cent in the market for liquid packaging board the merger would not be incompatible with the common market since they would face a very concentrated buying situation. In particular, Tetra Pak purchased 60 per cent of the packaging board and would be likely to set up an alternative source of supply if the new entity sought to exploit its position of market power.

Countervailing purchaser power was also relevant in *Alcatel/Telettra*.[579] In this case the Commission cleared a merger which gave the parties market shares of 83 per cent. The Commission considered that two main factors meant that the concentration would not be able to impede competition in the common market. Telefonica, the only purchaser, would be able to exert a downward pressure on prices.[580] Further, the Commission's initiative to erode barriers to cross-border trade in this sphere meant that Telefonica would seek products elsewhere if the concentration sought to charge excessive prices (high market shares in a market are unlikely to be significant in an opening market).

(v) Entry Analysis and Barriers to Entry

a. The Importance of Entry Analysis

The Commission will not be concerned with a horizontal merger if the parties' decision to raise prices and restrict output will be met by new entry into the market. Clear evidence that a position of market strength will only be temporary and will be quickly eroded because of a high probability of strong and timely market entry will thus lead to a finding that the concentration is compatible with the common market.[581] Even mergers involving firms with extremely high market shares have been cleared where new entry will be likely, timely and sufficient to frustrate an attempt by the merging firms to raise price or reduce quality, variety or innovation. In *HP/Compaq*,[582] for example, the Commission cleared a merger which the parties would gain market shares of between 85–95 percent as barriers to entry were low and competitors were likely to enter the market quickly.

The Commission stresses the importance of entry analysis in its Horizontal Merger Guidelines.

> 68. When entering a market is sufficiently easy, a merger is unlikely to pose any significant anti-competitive risk. Therefore, entry analysis constitutes an important element of the overall competitive assessment. For entry to be considered a sufficient competitive constraint on the merging parties, it must be shown to be likely, timely and sufficient to deter or defeat any potential anti-competitive effects of the merger.[583]

The Commission may also take account of constraining competition from manufacturers operating outside the geographic market.[584]

---

[578] Case IV/M.1225, [1999] OJ L254/9. See also, e.g., Case COMP/M.4057 *Körsnäs/AssiDomän Cartonboard*, especially paras. 57–64 (IP/06/610) and Case COMP/M. 16330, *Air Liquide/BOC* [2004] OJ L92/1.

[579] Case IV/M.42, [1991] OJ L122/48, [1991] 4 CMLR 778. See also, e.g. Case COMP/M.3732, *Procter & Gamble/Gillette* and Case COMP/M.3687, *Johnson & Johnson/Guidant*.

[580] See also Case IV/M.4, *Renault/Volvo* [1990] OJ C281/2 where the Commission found that large fleet buyers would exercise downward pressure on truck and bus prices.

[581] See, e.g., Case IV/M.477, *Mercedes-Benz/Kässbohrer* [1995] OJ L211/1, [1995] 4 CMLR 600; *cf.* Case IV/M.774, *Saint Gobain/Wacker-Chemie/NOM* [1997] OJ L247/1, [1997] 4 CMLR 25.

[582] Case COMP/M.2609.

[583] Horizontal Merger Guidelines, para. 68.

[584] Case IV/M.315, *Mannesmann/Vallourec/Ilva* [1994] OJ L102/15.

b. Likelihood of Entry

For entry to be likely it 'must be sufficiently profitable taking into account the price effects of injecting additional output into the market and the potential responses of the incumbents'.[585] Profitability of entry will be determined by entry risks and costs and barriers to entry. The Commission defines barriers to entry as 'specific features of the market, which give incumbent firms advantages over potential competitors'.[586] The Guidelines indicate the various forms that barriers to entry can take and stress that historical examples in an industry can provide useful information about the size of the barriers:

- Legal advantages encompass situations where regulatory barriers limit the number of market participants by, for example, restricting the number of licences. They also cover tariff and non-tariff trade barriers.

- The incumbents may also enjoy technical advantages, such as preferential access to essential facilities, natural resources. Innovation and R & D, or intellectual property rights, which make it difficult for any firm to compete successfully. For instance, in certain industries, it might be difficult to obtain essential input materials, or patents might protect products or processes. Other factors such as economies of scale and scope, distribution and sales networks, access to important technologies, may also constitute barriers to entry.

- Furthermore, barriers to entry may also exist because of the established position of the incumbent firms on the market. In particular, it may be difficult to enter a particular industry because experience or reputation is necessary to compete effectively, both of which may be difficult to obtain as an entrant. Factors such as consumer loyalty to a particular brand, the closeness of relationships between suppliers and customers, the importance of promotion advertising, or other advantages relating to reputation will be taken into account in this context. Barriers to entry also encompass situations where the incumbents have already committed to building large excess capacity,[587] or where the costs faced by customers in switching to a new supplier may inhibit entry.

A great variety of factors may, therefore, constitute barriers to entry and whether or not such barriers exist will be dependent upon a careful analysis of the market in each case. A legal or regulatory barrier, such as a restriction on the number of firms that will be licensed to operate on the market,[588] provides a clear example of a barrier to entry. Further, the ownership of patents or other intellectual property rights (IPRs) may prove to be a barrier to entry into a market, particularly in technology markets. The existence of IPRs may delay or postpone new entry by operators seeking to develop new technology or products that do not infringe them.[589] In *Tetra Pak/Alfa Laval*[590] the Commission relied on a number of factors, including Tetrapak's ownership of patents, to conclude that new entry was not likely in the market for aseptic carton packaging machines:[591] Tetra Pak's valuable patents were not available to competitors; purchasers were

[585] Horizontal Merger Guidelines, para. 69.

[586] *Ibid.*, para. 70. See also *supra* Chap. 1.

[587] See, e.g. Case IV/M.1157 *Skanska/Scancem* [1999] OJ L183/1, para. 140 where the Commission considered that the need for sunk costs and significant overcapacity in the market for production of ready mixed concrete was likely to deter new entrants to the market.

[588] See, e.g., Case IV/M.1430 *Vodafone/Airtouch* (the need for a licence to provide mobile telephony communications services).

[589] See, e.g., Case IV/M.269 *Shell/Montecatini* [1994] OJ L332/48, para. 32.

[590] Case IV/M.68 [1991] OJ L290/35, point 3.4.

[591] See also Chap. 6.

reluctant to purchase from a manufacturer without a proven track record; and specialized know-how and resources would need to be invested to enable new entry into the market. Other less technical factors may also inhibit entry, for example, the need to create a brand. In *The Coca-Cola Company/Carlsberg*[592] the Commission considered the impact of the merger on the carbonated soft drinks markets[593] in Denmark and Sweden. The Commission concluded that new entry into the market was not likely on account of severe barriers to entry which included access to brands, access to a distribution network, access to shelf space, the need for a sales and service network, brand image, customer loyalty, and (sunk) advertising costs.[594]

Factors such as the evolution of the market (entry is less likely to be profitable in a mature market than a dynamic one), scale economies, and network effects will also impact on the likelihood of entry.[595] In *Aérospatiale/Alenia/de Havilland*[596] the Commission held that countervailing factors would not prevent the anti-competitive effects that would result from the parties acquiring very large shares on the commuter aircraft market generally. The high risks involved in entering the market on account of the high sunk costs that would be required and the maturity of the market reduced the likelihood of new entry into the market.[597]

c. Timeliness

In looking at barriers to entry and the possibility of potential competition it seems that the Commission considers only potential competitors which are likely to enter the market within a relatively short time-frame. The Commission considers that what constitutes 'timelineness' is generally dependent upon the characteristics or dynamics of the market but that generally entry must occur within two years.[598] In *Aérospatiale/Alenia/de Havilland*[599] the Commission also considered that new entry into the commuter aircraft market was likely to occur only after a period of time and too late to catch an expected period of high demand.

d. Sufficiency

Any market entry must be on a sufficient scale to deter or defeat the anti-competitive effects of the merger.[600]

(vi) Efficiencies

a. An Efficiency Defence?

A merger which lead to efficiencies and, as such, increases competition between the merging parties and the other undertakings on the market, may not significantly impede competition at

---

[592] [1998] OJ L145/41, [1997] 5 CMLR 564.

[593] Although the Commission considered that the market could be defined more narrowly, to include different flavours of CSDs the exact definition did not affect the outcome of this case, *ibid.*, para. 43.

[594] *Ibid.*, paras. 72–5. The Commission took the view that it was very unlikely that anyone other than the existing international brand owners would be able to launch a new international CSD which would require heavy expenditure on advertising and promotion (sunk costs) in order to persuade brand-loyal consumers to switch away from their usual CSD brand. Consumer loyalty to the established brands would also make it difficult for a new supplier to persuade retail customers to change suppliers and would thus further hinder entry. A new entrant would also need access to a bottling and distribution system which would be expensive to set up and would have to have a costly sales and service network in order to obtain shelf space and to ensure its products were properly stocked and positioned.

[595] Horizontal Merger Guidelines, para. 73.

[596] Case IV/M.53, [1991] OJ L334/42, [1992] 4 CMLR M2, para. 53.

[597] D. Ridyard, 'Economic Analysis of Single Firm and Oligopolistic Dominance' [1994] *ECLR* 255, 256.

[598] Horizontal Merger Guidelines, para. 74.

[599] Case IV/M.53, [1991] OJ L334/42, [1992] 4 CMLR M2, paras. 53–7.

[600] Horizontal Merger Guidelines, para. 75 and e.g. Case IV/M.1157 *Skanska/Scancem* [1999] OJ L183/1, para. 184.

all. A further important question that has arisen is whether the ECMR admits, or should admit, an 'efficiency defence'. Such a defence would redeem a concentration which increases concentration and, prima facie significantly impedes effective competition, but which results in significant cost savings and economies of scale (which favour restructuring).

Horizontal mergers can create substantial efficiencies even as they facilitate collusion or enlarge market power. Courts and other policy makers have entertained three different positions concerning efficiency and the legality of mergers:

(1) mergers should be evaluated for their effect on market power or likelihood of collusion, and efficiency considerations should be largely irrelevant;

(2) mergers that create substantial efficiencies should be legal, or there should be at least a limited 'efficiency defense' in certain merger cases;

(3) mergers should be condemned because they create efficiencies, in order to protect competitors of the post-merger firm.[601]

In the USA the rule that mergers should be prohibited because they create efficiencies has been abandoned.[602] Instead the authorities are receptive to arguments based on the efficiencies and cost savings of a merger.[603] However, the onus of proving qualifying efficiencies rests on the parties to the merger.[604] The US Merger Guidelines[605] indicate that the defence may apply where (1) efficiencies relied upon are merger-specific (they will not be achieved in the absence of the merger); (2) the efficiencies are achieved in the same market as the market in which the anti-competitive effects of the merger are likely to be felt;[606] (3) the efficiencies are cognizable—they are verifiable and measurable; and finally that (4) the efficiencies outweigh or reverse the merger's potential harm to consumers in the relevant market by, for example, preventing price increases in that market. The guidelines indicate that the more anti-competitive the merger under the concentration analysis the stronger the evidence of efficiencies must be.

Such a defence is justifiable on grounds of strict economic theory, since the costs savings give rise to an increase in consumer welfare as a whole.

b. An Increase in Consumer Welfare

The argument raised in support of such a defence is outlined by Hovenkamp:

---

[601] H. Hovenkamp, *Federal Antitrust Policy: The Law of Competition and its Practice* (3rd edn., Thomson West, 2005), 12.2.

[602] This view was pursued for a period in the 1960s, see *Brown Shoe Co v. United States* 370 US 294 (1962).

[603] Efficiency defences have been recognized in Australia and Canada.

[604] Department of Justice and Federal Trade Commission Horizontal Merger Guidelines (1992, amended 1997).

[605] 1992 Guidelines (revised in 1997), para. 4.

[606] In some cases, merger efficiencies are "not strictly in the relevant market, but so inextricably linked with it that a partial divestiture or other remedy could not feasibly eliminate the anticompetitive effect in the relevant market without sacrificing the efficiencies in the other market(s)." 1992 Guidelines, para. 4 at n. 36. If out-of-market efficiencies are not inextricably linked to the relevant market, the Agencies often find an acceptable narrowly tailored remedy that preserves the efficiencies while preventing anticompetitive effects, see the DOJ/FTC Commentary on the horizontal merger guidelines (2006), available at http://www.usdoj.gov/atr/public/premerger.htm.

H. Hovenkamp, *Federal Antitrust Policy: The Law of Competition and its Practice* (3rd edn., Thomson West., 2005), 12.2b1

12.2b1 The Welfare 'Tradeoff' Model

The rule that mergers should be condemned because they create efficiency has been abandoned. The opposite position is that mergers should be legal when they create substantial efficiencies— or alternatively, that there should be an 'efficiency defense' in merger cases. Although the trail is still somewhat obscure, the courts are heading in the direction of adopting such a rule, and the government's Merger Guidelines explicitly recognize and define an 'efficiency defense.' Importantly, the rule comes into play *only* after the merger has been found presumptively anti-competitive by structural and behavioral analysis. If a merger poses no competitive threat to begin with, then analysis of possible efficiencies is unnecessary.

The argument for an 'efficiency defense' in merger cases is illustrated by the graph in Figure 1 ... The graph illustrates a merger that give the post-merger firm measurably more market power than it had before the merger. As a result, the firm reduces output from Q1 to Q2 on the graph, and increases price from P1 to P2. Triangle A1 represents the monopoly "deadweight loss" created by this increase in market power.

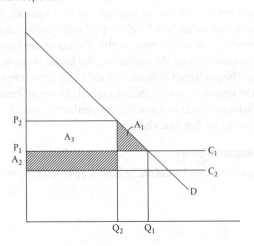

Figure 1

At the same time, the merger produces measurable economies, which show up as a reduction in the firm's costs from C1 to C2, Rectangle A2 represents efficiency gains that will result from these economies. If A2 is larger than A1 the merger produces a *net* efficiency gain, even though it permits the firm to raise its price above its marginal cost. Furthermore, A2 is often larger than A1. The efficiency gains illustrated by A2 are spread over the entire output of the post-merger firm. The deadweight losses in A1 are spread over only the reduction in output. If the post-merger firm reduced its output by 10%, each of the 90% of units still being produced would contribute to the efficiency gains; the deadweight loss, however, would accrue over only the 10% reduction.

Williamson concluded that in a market with average elasticities of demand and supply, a merger that produced "nontrivial" economies of 1.2% would be efficient even if it resulted in a price increase of 10%.[607]

---

[607] O. Williamson, 'Economies as an Antitrust Defense: the Welfare Trade-Offs', 58 *American Economic Review* 18 (1968), 22–3 and O. Williamson, 'Economies as an Antitrust Defense: Revisited' (1977) 125 *I Pa Law Rev* 699.

Williamson's analysis is vulnerable to some criticism. First, his description of triangle A1 in the figure as the efficiency costs of a merger probably understates the true social cost. Rectangles A2 plus A3 represent potential monopoly profits to the post-merger firm. A profit-maximizing firm will be willing to spend substantial resources in an effort to acquire or retain a certain amount of monopoly power. If a particular merger will give a firm $1,000, 000 in additional monopoly profits, the firm will spend up to $1,000,000 in order to accomplish the merger and then retain its monopoly position. It could spend this money in highly inefficient ways, such as espionage, predatory pricing against a potential take-over target, or vexatious litigation. At the extreme A2+A3 are not increased profits to the post-merger firm at all, but funds inefficiently spent in order to give the firm its market position. Importantly, the anti-competitive risk in the merger case is not increased likelihood of single-firm monopoly, but increased likelihood of collusion. The costs of managing a cartel or oligopoly can be quite high in relation to the profits that it produces. A cartel or oligopoly that occasions a price increase of 10% would very likely produce much smaller gains in profitability.

Another problem of the tradeoff model is that it apparently assumes a merger to monopoly. But most collusion facilitating mergers involve firms whose aggregate share is significantly less than 100%. For example, suppose a 20% firm should acquire a 10% firm, greatly increasing the extent of oligopoly performance. In that case, the increased coordination that results from the merger enables *both* the merging and the non-merging firms to increase their prices. However, gains are spread across only the output of the two merging firms, which account for only 30% of the market's output.

Broadly, Williamson establishes that in some cases mergers which enable the parties to acquire market power and, consequently, to restrict output and raise prices may nonetheless lead to an increase in consumer welfare. Although consumers lose output (and deadweight loss occurs) in some cases, where efficiency gains are large, that loss is offset by a greater gain in cost or resource savings. To determine whether or not this is the case a comparison must be made in each case of deadweight loss relative to cost savings.

Hovenkamp identifies a number of problems with the welfare trade-off model.[608] In the extract set out above it is explained that the theory may underestimate the social costs of the merger and does not work effectively when applied to mergers occurring on oligopolistic markets. In oligopolistic markets, however, the achievement of efficiencies may provoke more aggressive competition between the players on the market by destabilizing the tacit coordination. Further, Hovenkamp goes on to state that the theory can be criticized for treating all efficiency gains the same way no matter who gets the benefit: a merger which has an overall efficient effect (increasing total welfare) may nonetheless result in an actual output reduction and still lead to an increase in price for consumers (in such case the benefits accrue to the merging parties).[609] The US Merger Guidelines require that efficiencies are sufficient to reverse the harm to consumers, by preventing price increases in the market.[610] Hovenkamp also notes that it can be difficult to determine whether or not the efficiencies pleaded could be obtained by means other than merger, and that this explains why the defence has been successful so infrequently. A final problem identified is that courts are unable to make the measurements that its analysis would require. 'Our knowledge that mergers can produce both economies and monopoly pricing is fairly secure. However, quantifying either of these in a particular merger case is impossible. Most mergers found illegal under current law probably create efficiencies. They are

[608] H. Hovenkamp, *Federal Antitrust Policy: The Law of Competition and its Practice* (3rd edn., Thomson West, 2005), 12.2b 510.

[609] See the discussion of total welfare and consumer welfare, *supra* Chap. 1

[610] US Horizontal Merger Guidelines § 4.

condemned, however, because no court is capable of balancing the increase in market power of the potential for collusion against the economies achieved'.[611] As a result he concludes that '[M]ost of the courts that have considered the efficiency defense have been skeptical. Most have rejected evidence of efficiencies, while a few have recognized the defence'.[612] Others have suggested that even if the comparison could be made it should not be. Huge cost savings would be necessary to offset any associated price increases[613] and, in contrast, a rigorous merger policy would be more likely to bring about an increase in economic welfare. Public policy should thus concentrate on preserving and fostering competition for the ultimate benefit of consumers.

c. The ECMR

Arguably, the substantive test set out in Article 2 of the ECMR leaves little or no scope for the trade off of efficiencies where a concentration significantly impedes effective competition. Although there is no express provision for an efficiency defence, however, Article 2(1)(b) allows for 'technical and economic progress' to be taken into account as part of the appraisal 'provided it is to consumers' advantage and does not form an obstacle to competition'. Some commentators have argued that although efficiency considerations may lead to an increase in consumer welfare as a whole, it is hard to see how, as required by Article 2(1)(b), the technical and economic progress could be said to be to the consumers' advantage (the consumer would have to pay monopoly prices, post-merger) or that the merger would not form an obstacle to competition.[614] As the Commission has never applied the defence to authorize a merger which would otherwise have been declared incompatible with the common market,[615] it has remained questionable as to whether the defence can be invoked under the ECMR at all.[616]

Further and conversely, some commentators have alleged that the Commission's decisions have actually been reflective of an 'efficiency attack' or 'efficiency offense', a fear that mergers which would enable the parties to achieve significant economies of scale or scope may be more likely to result in a finding that the merger is incompatible with the common market as the parties will have even greater advantages over their nearest competitors.[617] In Aérospatiale-Alenia/de Havilland,[618] for example, the parties claim that efficiency gains arose from the merger arguably appeared, instead of acting as an offsetting factor to mitigate the adverse competitive effects of the merger, to have 'merely strengthened the Commission's view that the merged group would enjoy benefits that would be out of the reach of its competitors. If anything, the "efficiency defence" seems in this case to have reduced the chances of clearance for the deal'.[619]

[611] H. Hovenkamp, *Federal Antitrust Policy: The Law of Competition and its Practice* (2nd edn., Thomson West, 1999), 12.2b, 516.

[612] *Ibid.*, 505. See also, See R. H. Bork, *The Antitrust Paradox* (Basic Books, 1978, reprinted with a new Introduction and Epilogue, 1993).

[613] F. M. Scherer and D. Ross, *Industrial Market Structure and Economic Performance* (3rd edn., Houghton Mifflin, 1990), 174: statistical evidence supporting the hypotheses that profitability and efficiency increase following mergers is at best weak.

[614] See, e.g., A. Jacquemin, 'Mergers and European Policy' in P. H. Admiraal (ed.), *Merger and Competition Policy in the European Community* (Blackwell, 1990), 36.

[615] 'However, commentators have often suggested that the Commission is perfectly aware of the importance of efficiency gains, and that it has taken them into account *implicitly*, for instance at the stage of determination of market dominance': M. Motta, 'E.C. Merger Policy and the Airtours Case' [2000] *ECLR* 199, 203, relying on P. D. Camesasca, 'The Explicit Efficiency Defence in Merger Control: Does it Make the Difference?' [1999] *ECLR* 26–7. For cases in which efficiencies have been relevant, See *infra* 1047.

[616] See Case IV/M.1313, [2001] OJ L20/1, [2000] 5 CMLR 296, para. 198.

[617] See especially COMP/M.2220 GE/Honeywell *infra* 1045.

[618] Case IV/M.53, [1991] OJ L334/42, [1992] 4 CMLR M2.

[619] D. Ridyard, 'Economic Analysis of Single Firm and Oligopolistic Dominance' [1994] *ECLR* 255, 256–7.

In this case the Commission did not accept claims that significant efficiencies would result from the merger had been substantiated.[620] In some cases, involving conglomerate mergers, the Commission does seem to have accepted that efficiencies would result from a merger but that these efficiencies would enable the merging parties to offer their products at lower prices which would damage competitors. In *GE/Honeywell*[621] the Commission was particularly concerned that the merged entity would be able to offer low bundled prices for those that purchased both its aircraft engines and its avionics and non-avionics systems. The focus that the Commission placed on the harm that would result to the new entity's competitors led some commentators to take the view that the decision was indicative of a hostile approach to mergers that create efficiencies and as protective of competitors rather than competition.[622]

d. The Horizontal Merger Guidelines

In view of the confusion over the part played by efficiency considerations in EC merger cases, the Commission invited discussion of the proper role and scope that such considerations should play in its 2001 Green Paper.[623] Most respondents considered that, as part of a sound economics-based merger control policy, the Commission should take account of efficiencies in its analysis of the overall effects likely to be produced by a proposed merger. Further, that guidance should be produced on the proper scope of the defence. Recital 29 of the ECMR now provides that it 'is possible that the efficiencies brought forward by the concentration counteract the effects on competition, and in particular the potential harm to consumers, that it might otherwise have and that, as a consequence, the concentration would not significantly impede effective competition, in particular as a result of the creation or strengthening of a dominant position', The Commission now deals with efficiencies in its Horizontal Merger Guidelines.[624] In the Guidelines it is recognized that in making its substantive appraisal it takes account of Article 2(1) factors including the development of technical and economic progress provided that it is to the consumers' advantage and does not form an obstacle to competition,[625] and that 'efficiencies generated by the merger are likely to enhance the ability and incentive of the merged entity to act pro-competitively for the benefit of consumers, thereby counteracting the

---

[620] The Commission did not specifically state that efficiency considerations were relevant to the assessment, but considered the arguments 'without prejudice' to their relevance. The Commission concluded that the concentration would lead to the creation of a dominant position which would significantly impede effective competition within the common market and dismissed the efficiency arguments raised as negligent or unrelated to the merger. Similarly, in Case IV/M.126, *Accor/Wagon-Lits* [1992] OJ L204/1, [1993] 5 CMLR M13, the Commission indicated that efficiencies could not be taken into account unless it could be established that cost savings would be passed on to customers. On the facts there was, in any event, insufficient evidence of efficiencies. However, the Commission held that, even if there had been, it could not be established that the efficiencies would outweigh the anti-competitive effects of the concentration. The demand for motorway catering services was highly inelastic, so there was no indication that any benefits would be passed on to customers.

[621] Comp/M.2220, *aff'd* Cases T-209 and 210/01 *Honeywell v. Commission* and *General Electric Company v. Commission* [2005] ECR II-5527 and 5575. See the discussion of this case *infra* 1060–4. Mario Monti, then Commissioner for Competition, however, refuted the assertion that the Commission when dealing with conglomerate mergers was in fact applying an 'efficiency offence', see e.g. 'Antitrust in the US and Europe: a History of Convergence' 14 November 2001, available on DGComp's website.

[622] See *infra* 1060–4 and, e.g., S. Bishop and M. Walker, *The Economics of EC Competition Law: Concepts, Application and Measurement* (2nd edn., Sweet & Maxwell, London, 2002), 7.75–7.79 and 7.89.

[623] 2001 Green Paper on the Review of Council Regulation (EEC) No. 4064/89, COM(2001) 745/6 final. See also e.g. L.Roller, Stennek and Verboven 'Efficiency Gains from Mergers' The Research Institute of Industrial Economics, Working Paper No 543, 2000.

[624] [2004] OJ C31/5, para. 5. Form CO, also has a section on efficiency gains.

[625] Horizontal Merger Guidelines, para. 76.

adverse effects on competition which the merger might otherwise have'.[626] The Guidelines do not specifically state that the burden is on the parties to establish the efficiency defence. They make it clear, however, that the Commission will only take account of substantiated efficiency claims and that it is for the parties to provide the evidence to demonstrate the claimed efficiencies and that there are no less anti-competitive means of realizing those efficiencies.[627] The Commission will only take account of claimed efficiencies where they:[628] (1) benefit consumers;[629] (2) are merger specific;[630] and (3) are verifiable.[631]

Benefit to Consumers

It is a requirement that consumers should not be worse off as a result of the merger. The merger must thus bring timely efficiencies that will result, for example, in lower prices (perhaps through reduction in variable or marginal costs) or in new or improved products or services (e.g., from efficiency gains in the sphere of R&D). In the context of coordinated effects, efficiencies may lead to incentives to increase production and reduce output and disincentives to coordinate behaviour.

The Commission considers that the greater the market power acquired by the undertakings the more difficult it will be to show that benefits will result which will be passed on to consumers. Further, that those efficiencies should in principle benefit consumers in the market where the competition problems arise.[632]

Merger Specificity

Paragraph 85 of the Horizontal Guidelines explains the requirement of merger specificity.

Efficiencies are relevant to the competitive assessment when they are a direct consequence of the notified merger and cannot be achieved to a similar extent by less anti-competitive alternatives. In these circumstances, the efficiencies are deemed to be caused by the merger and thus, merger specific. It is for the parties to provide in due time all the relevant information necessary to demonstrate that there are no less anti-competitive, realistic and attainable alternatives of a non-concentrative nature (e.g., a licensing agreement, or a cooperative joint venture) or of a concentrative nature (e.g., a concentrative joint venture, or a differently structured merger) than the notified merger which preserve the claimed efficiencies. The Commission only considers alternatives that are reasonably practical in the business situation faced by the merging parties having regard to established business practices in the industry concerned.

Verifiability

A difficult task for the parties will be to verify the efficiencies 'such that the Commission can be reasonably certain that the efficiencies are likely to materialize, and be substantial enough to counteract a merger's potential harm to consumers'.[633] The Commission states that the parties

---

626 Horizontal Merger Guidelines, para. 77.

627 Ibid., paras. 77, 87, and 84 respectively.

628 Ibid., para. 78.

629 Ibid., paras. 79–84.

630 Ibid., para. 85.

631 Ibid., paras. 86–8.

632 Contrast the position in the US, see supra n. 606.

633 Horizontal Merger Guidelines, para. 85.

should quantify the efficiencies where possible or otherwise identify the positive impact on consumers.

Cases

Although efficiencies have not yet been given as a decisive factor for a merger clearance it was given as one of them in *Körsnäs/AssiDomän Cartonboard*.[634] In this case the Commission accepted that synergies resulting from the merger between two of the three main players active in the world-wide market for the production of liquid carton packaging board were likely to be passed on to consumers. The Commission also considered, however, that countervailing buyer power as well as competition from EnsoStora[635], suppliers outside of the EU and suppliers of other board materials, was likely to constrain the behavior of the merged parties.

(vii) The Failing Firm Defence or Rescue Mergers

The failing firm defence is well established in US antitrust case law and referred to in the US Horizontal Merger Guidelines.[636] The defence provides an escape route for a merger involving a firm facing an otherwise inevitable liquidation. Historically, it appears to have been adopted to ensure the protection of the creditors, owners, and/or employees of small businesses and as such was concerned not with efficiency but with distributive justice.[637] It appears, however, that a narrowly applied failing company 'could be efficient when it (1) enables a failing firm and its creditors to avoid the high administrative costs of bankruptcy; and (2) it keeps on the market productive assets that are worth keeping in production and would likely to be taken out of production were it not for the merger. Offsetting these is the social cost of any monopoly pricing that flows from the merger itself, less the social cost that would flow from any monopoly created if the failing firm simply went out of business'.[638]

In the US the defence may be raised where an undertaking can establish that the failing company will fail to meet its financial obligations in the future, will be unable to reorganize successfully, and has unsuccessfully sought reasonable, less anti-competitive alternative offers (i.e., an acquisition by a smaller competitor or non-competitor).[639] This position is broadly adopted by the 1992 Guidelines:

A merger is not likely to create or enhance market power or facilitate its exercise if the following circumstances are met: 1) the allegedly failing firm would be unable to meet its financial obligations in the near future; 2) it would be unable to reorganize successfully under Chapter 11 of the Bankruptcy Act; 3) it has made unsuccessful good-faith efforts to elicit reasonable alternative offers of acquisition of the assets of the failing firm that would both keep its tangible and intangible assets in the relevant

[634] Case COMP/M.4057, especially paras. 57–64 (IP/06/610). See also e.g. Case COMP/M.4187 *Metso/Aker Kvoerner* Case COMP/M.3732 *Procter & Gamble/Gillette*, Case COMP/M.3664 *Repsol Butano/Shell Gas* and Case COMP/M.3886 *Aster 2/Flint Ink* (efficiencies one factor in clearance) and Case COMP/M.4000 *Inco/Falconbridge* (the parties efficiencies claims were rejected) and e.g. P.Lowe, 'A more economic approach to competition law enforcement—making it operational' 15 December 2005.

[635] See *supra* n. 578 and accompanying text.

[636] 1992 Guidelines (revised in 1997). See also OECD, 'Failing Firm Defence' (1996), available at www.oecd.org.

[637] See H. Hovenkamp, *Federal Antitrust Policy: The Law of Competition and its Practice* (3rd edn., Thomson West, 20059), para. 12.9, 552. See also e.g. I. Kokkoris, 'Failing Firm Defence in the European Union: A Panacea for Mergers? [2006] *ECLR* 494.

[638] *Ibid.*, para. 12.9, 545.

[639] See, e.g., *Citizen Publishing Co. v. United States*, 394 US 131, 138, 89 S.Ct 927, 931 (1969).

market and pose a less severe danger to competition than does the proposed merger: and 4) absent the acquisition, the assets of the failing firm would exit the relevant market.[640]

It has also been accepted that there is room for a failing firm defence within the scheme of the ECMR where the deterioration of the competitive structure cannot be said to be *caused* by the merger, i.e., 'where the competitive structure would deteriorate to at least the same extent in the absence of the merger'.[641]

This principle was first recognized in *Kali und Salz/MdK/Treuhand*[642] which raised the question whether or not an undertaking with large market shares could combine activities with its only, or main, failing competitor. It has already been seen that the case concerned the combination of the potash and rock-salt activities of Kali und Salz and Mitteldeutsche Kali AG (MdK, owned by Treuhand). Although the Commission found that the concentration would acquire enormous shares on the potash market in Germany and the magnesium products market of 98 per cent and 100 per cent respectively, it concluded that the concentration did not lead to the creation or strengthening of a dominant position. It was not the merger that could be said to be the cause of the deterioration in the competitive structure. Even if the merger was prohibited, the acquiring undertaking would inevitably achieve or reinforce its dominant position to the same extent. The parties established (the onus being on them to do so) that:

- the acquired undertaking would in the near future be forced out of the market if not taken over by another undertaking (MdK, would have inevitably have been forced out of the market as it was in a critical economic position following the collapse of the relevant markets);

- the acquiring undertaking, Kali und Salz, would inevitably acquire the market share since it was the only other relevant participator on the respective markets; and

- no less anti-competitive purchase was possible (although tenders had been invited all other alternatives had practically been ruled out).

The Commission thus accepted that the failing company defence succeeded in that case. The French Government argued that the Commission had been wrong to use this defence to authorize a concentration leading to the creation of a monopoly without imposing conditions. The ECJ upheld the Commission's decision, however.[643] It held that the fact that the conditions relied on for concluding that there was no causal link between the concentration and the deterioration of the competitive structure did not coincide with the conditions applied in the US was not in itself a ground for invalidating the decision. Rather, to challenge it, it would have to be shown that the conditions set by the Commission were not capable of excluding the possibility that the concentration might be the cause of the deterioration in the competitive structure.

---

[640] 1992 Guidelines, (revised in 1997), para. 5.1. The Guidelines also recognize a failing division defence.

[641] Horizontal Mergers Guidelines, para. 89, relying on Case IV/M.1578 *Sanitec/Sphinx* [2000] OJ L294/1.

[642] Case IV/M.308, [1994] OJ L186/30, [1994] 4 CMLR 526; on appeal Cases C-68/94 and C-30/95, *France v. Commission, Société Commerciale des Potasses et de l'Azote (SCPA) v. Commission* [1998] ECR I-1375, [1998] 4 CMLR 829. See G. Monti and E. Rousseva 'Failing firms in the framework of the EC Merger Regulation' [1999] 24 ELRev 38.

[643] The Commission in para. 112 of its decision recognized that the conditions it set out in para. 111 were not identical to those set out in US law. It stated that it did not however wish simply to ape the US position. It has since then changed its approach, which is now the same as that adopted in the US, see *infra* 1052.

Cases C-68/94 and C-30/95, *France v. Commission, Société Commerciale des Potasses et de l'Azote (SCPA) v. Commission* [1998] ECR I-1375, [1998] 4 CMLR 829

Court of Justice

109. The Court observes at the outset that under Article 2(2) of the Regulation, a 'concentration which does not create or strengthen a dominant position as a result of which effective competition would be significantly impeded in the common market or in a substantial part of it shall be declared compatible with the common market'.

110. Thus if a concentration is not the cause of the creation or strengthening of a dominant position which has a significant impact on the competitive situation on the relevant market, it must be declared compatible with the common market.

111. It appears from point 71 of the contested decision that, in the Commission's opinion, a concentration which would normally be considered as leading to the creation or reinforcement of a dominant position on the part of the acquiring undertaking may be regarded as not being the cause of it if, even in the event of the concentration being prohibited, that undertaking would inevitably achieve or reinforce a dominant position. Point 71 goes on to state that, as a general matter, a concentration is not the cause of the deterioration of the competitive structure if it is clear that:

— the acquired undertaking would in the near future be forced out of the market if not taken over by another undertaking,

— the acquiring undertaking would gain the market share of the acquired undertaking if it were forced out of the market,

— there is no less anti-competitive alternative purchase.

112. It must be observed, first of all, that the fact that the conditions set by the Commission for concluding that there was no causal link between the concentration and the deterioration of the competitive structure do not entirely coincide with the conditions applied in connection with the United States 'failing company defence' is not in itself a ground of invalidity of the contested decision. Solely the fact that the conditions set by the Commission were not capable of excluding the possibility that a concentration might be the cause of the deterioration in the competitive structure of the market could constitute a ground of invalidity of the decision.

113. In the present case, the French Government disputes the relevance of the criterion that it must be verified that the acquiring undertaking would in any event obtain the acquired undertaking's share of the market if the latter were to be forced out of the market.

114. However, in the absence of that criterion, a concentration could, provided the other criteria were satisfied, be considered as not being the cause of the deterioration of the competitive structure of the market even though it appeared that, in the event of the concentration not proceeding, the acquiring undertaking would not gain the entire market share of the acquired undertaking. Thus, it would be possible to deny the existence of a causal link between the concentration and the deterioration of the competitive structure of the market even though the competitive structure of the market would deteriorate to a lesser extent if the concentration did not proceed.

115. The introduction of that criterion is intended to ensure that the existence of a causal link between the concentration and the deterioration of the competitive structure of the market can be excluded only if the competitive structure resulting from the concentration would deteriorate in similar fashion even if the concentration did not proceed.

116. The criterion of absorption of market shares, although not considered by the Commission as sufficient in itself to preclude any adverse effect of the concentration on competition, therefore helps to ensure the neutral effects of the concentration as regards the deterioration of the

competitive structure of the market. This is consistent with the concept of causal connection set out in Article 2(2) of the Regulation.

117. As to the criticism of the Commission that it failed to show that if the concentration did not proceed MdK would inevitably have been forced out of the market, it should be observed that the Commission stated in point 73 of the contested decision that, even though MdK had been restructured by 1 January 1993, that undertaking continued to make considerable losses in the first six months of the year. According to the Commission, MdK's serious economic situation was essentially a result of its obsolete operating structure and the crisis in sales attributable primarily to the collapse of markets in eastern Europe. MdK also lacked an efficient distribution system (see points 74 and 75 of the contested decision).

118. In point 76 of the contested decision, the Commission observed that MdK had been able to continue operating until now only because Treuhand had consistently covered its losses. The Commission added, however, that Treuhand could not cover MdK's losses in the long term from public aid, since that was in any case incompatible with the Treaty provisions on State aid.

119. In the light of the foregoing, the Commission cannot be criticised for finding that MdK was no longer economically viable and for considering that it was probable that, on its own, MdK would continue to accumulate losses even if Treuhand provided the funds envisaged for restructuring purposes in the proposed concentration.

120. In those circumstances, the Commission's forecast that MdK was highly likely to close down in the near future if it were not taken over by a private undertaking cannot be regarded as unsupported by a consistent body of evidence.

121. Finally, with respect to the condition concerning the absence of an alternative, less anti-competitive method of acquiring MdK, it should be noted that the French Government's complaint is that the Commission, because of the lack of transparency in the tendering procedure, failed to show that that condition was in fact satisfied.

122. Suffice it to note that the French Government has merely observed that the MdK trade unions pointed to a lack of transparency in the tendering procedure, without providing any details as to what constituted the alleged lack of transparency.

123. In the absence of any details of that complaint, it cannot be upheld.

124. It follows from the foregoing that the absence of a causal link between the concentration and the deterioration of the competitive structure of the German market has not been effectively called into question. Accordingly, it must be held that, so far as that market is concerned, the concentration appears to satisfy the criterion referred to in Article 2(2) of the Regulation, and could thus be declared compatible with the common market without being amended. Consequently, contrary to the French Government's assertion, it is not possible without contradicting that premiss to require the Commission, with respect to the German market, to attach any condition whatever to its declaration of the concentration's compatibility.

Since the *Kali and Salz* case the Commission has been prepared to apply the failing firm defence or the concept of the 'rescue merger' more broadly, and in line with the criteria set out in the US merger guidelines. The defence has been pleaded in a number of cases[644] and was successfully invoked by the parties in *BASF/Pantochim/Eurodial*.[645] This case involved BASF's proposed

[644] It has been rejected in a number of cases, see, e.g., Case IV/M.774, *Saint-Gobain/Wacker-Chemie-NOM* [1997] OJ L247/1, [1997] 4 CMLR 25, Case COMP/M.2621, *SEB/Moulinex*, Case COMP/M.2845, *Sogecable/Canalsatelite Digital/Via Digital* and Case IV/M.2876, *Newscorp/Telepiù* IP/03/478.

[645] Case IV/M.2314, IP/01/984. See also Case M.2810, *Deloitte & Touche/Andersen (UK)*, Case M. 2816, *Ernst & Young France/Andersen France* and Case M.2824, *Ernst & Young/Andersen Germany* and Case COMP/M.3910 *Rockwood/Süd-Chemie*. See K. Joergens, 'Anderson and the 'Failing Firm'' (2003) 26(3) *World Competition* 363 and I. Kokkoris, 'Failing Firm Defence in the European Union: A Panacea for Mergers? [2006] *ECLR* 494.

acquisition of Pantochim and Eurodiol from Sisal. The concentration was likely to lead to the acquisition of high market shares on certain base chemical markets. In applying the failing firm defence in this case the Commission stressed that the approach taken by the ECJ in its *Kali and Salz* judgment was wider than the criteria set out in the Commission's own decision in that case. The key requirement for a merger to be regarded as a rescue merger was that the competitive structure resulting from the concentration would deteriorate in a similar fashion even if the concentration did not proceed, i.e., even if the concentration was prohibited. Thus the essential conditions are that the undertaking to be acquired can be regarded as a 'failing firm' and that the merger will not be the *cause* of the deterioration of the competitive structure.

Case IV/M.2314, *BASF/Pantochim/Eurodiol*

(140) In general terms, the concept of the 'rescue merger' requires that the undertakings to be acquired can be regarded as 'failing firms' and that the merger is not the cause of the deterioration of the competitive structure. Thus, for the application of the rescue merger, two conditions must be satisfied:

(a) the acquired undertaking would in the near future be forced out of the market if not taken over by another undertaking; and

(b) there is no less anti-competitive alternative purchase.

(141) However, the application of these two criteria does not completely rule out the possibility of a takeover by third parties of the assets of the undertakings concerned in the event of their bankruptcy. If such assets were taken over by competitors in the course of bankruptcy proceedings, the economic effects would be similar to a takeover of the failing firms themselves by an alternative purchaser.

Thus it needs to be established in addition to the first two criteria, that the assets to be purchased would inevitably disappear from the market in the absence of the merger.

(142) Given this general framework, the Commission regards the following criteria as relevant for the application of the concept of the 'rescue merger':

(a) the acquired undertaking would in the near future be forced out of the market if not taken over by another undertaking;

(b) there is no less anti-competitive alternative purchase; and

(c) the assets to be acquired would inevitably exit the market if not taken over by another undertaking.

(143) In any event, the application of the concept of the 'rescue merger' requires that the deterioration of the competitive structure through the merger is at least no worse than in the absence of the merger.

The Commission thus does not require that the acquiring company would inevitably acquire the entire market share of the acquired undertaking if it were forced out of the market, but only that the acquired company's assets would inevitably exit the market were the firm not taken over.[646] The Commission explains the inevitability of the assets of the failing firm leaving the market in question as underlying, in the case of merger to monopoly, a finding that the market share of the failing firm would in any event accrue to the other merging party.[647] The approach

---

[646] It would seem to be inherent in the defence, however, that the acquiring firm would gain much or most of the market share.

[647] Horizontal Merger Guidelines, n. 111.

in *BASF/Pantochim/Eurodiol* was reiterated by the Commission in *Newscorp/Telepiù*[648] and is adopted by the Commission in its horizontal merger guidelines.

Guidelines on the assessment of horizontal mergers under the Council regulation on the control of concentrations between undertakings [2004] OJ C31/5

VIII. Failing firm

89. The Commission may decide that an otherwise problematic merger is nevertheless compatible with the common market if one of the merging parties is a failing firm. The basic requirement is that the deterioration of the competitive structure that follows the merger cannot be said to be caused by the merger. This will arise where the competitive structure of the market would deteriorate to at least the same extent in the absence of the merger.

90. The Commission considers the following three criteria to be especially relevant for the application of a 'failing firm defence'. First, the allegedly failing firm would in the near future be forced out of the market because of financial difficulties if not taken over by another undertaking. Second, there is no less anti-competitive alternative purchase than the notified merger. Third, in the absence of a merger, the assets of the failing firm would inevitably exit the market.

91. It is for the notifying parties to provide in due time all the relevant information necessary to demonstrate that the deterioration of the competitive structure that follows the merger is not caused by the merger.

Although the Commission has not ruled out the possibility of the defence applying where only part of the firm is failing, it appears that the defence, and lack of causality between the merger and the adverse effect on competition, will be much harder to establish in such cases.[649]

(viii) Competitive Assessment of Non-horizontal Mergers

a. The Draft Guidelines on the Assessment of Non-Horizontal Mergers

The Commission's merger decisions have over the year reflected concerns with significant impediments to effective competition resulting from horizontal, vertical and/or conglomerate mergers. Some of the cases dealing with vertical and conglomerate mergers have been extremely controversial. The Commission has now published, for discussion, draft guidance with the objective of eventually providing guidance as to how the Commission assesses, in the light of its evolving experience, concentrations where the undertakings concerned are active on distinct relevant markets.[650]

---

[648] Case IV/M.2876, IP/03/478. The rescue merger plea, raised only at the final stage of the investigation, was rejected in this case. The case involved a merger between Stream and Telepiù which would result in the parties acquiring very high shares in the Italian pay-TV market. Oddly in this case it was alleged that it was the acquiring company, Stream, that was failing. Although the Commission found that the strict legal requirements for the failing firm defence were not met it took account of the chronic financial difficulties faced by both companies in its decision and the disruption that the possible closure of Stream would cause to Italian pay-TV subscribers.

[649] See Case IV/M.1221, *Rewe/Mienl* [1999] OJ L274/1 and Case IV/M.2876, *Stream/Telepiù* IP/03/478.

[650] The draft Guidelines on the assessment of non-horizontal mergers are available on DG Comp's web site, http://ec.europa.eu/comm/competition/mergers/legislation/legislation.html. The consultation period closed on 12 May 2007. Comments are also available on DG Comp's web site. See also Report for DG Competition, European Commission prepared by Jeffrey Church (University of Calgary, Canada). September 2004, on The

The draft guidelines accept that non-horizontal mergers are generally less likely to create competition concerns than horizontal mergers since they do not entail the loss of direct competition between the merging parties and because the mergers provide substantial scope for efficiencies.[651]

11. Non-horizontal mergers are generally less likely to create competition concerns than horizontal mergers.

12. First, unlike horizontal mergers, vertical or conglomerate mergers do not entail the loss of direct competition between the merging firms in the same relevant market. As a result, the main source of anti-competitive effect in horizontal mergers is absent from vertical and conglomerate mergers.

13. Second, vertical and conglomerate mergers provide substantial scope for efficiencies. A characteristic of vertical mergers and certain conglomerate mergers is that the activities and/or the products of the companies involved are *complementary* to each other. The integration of complementary activities or products within a single firm may produce significant efficiencies and be pro-competitive. For instance, in vertical mergers, efforts to increase sales at one level (e.g. by lower price, or by stepping up innovation) will benefit sales at the other level. Depending on the market conditions, integration may increase the incentive to carry out such efforts. In particular, after the vertical integration, lowering the mark-up downstream may lead to increased sales not only downstream but also upstream and vice versa. This is often referred to as the "internalisation of double mark-ups."

14. Integration may also decrease transaction costs and allow for a better co-ordination in terms of product design, the organisation of the production process, and the way in which the products are sold. Similarly, mergers which involve products belonging to a range of products that are generally sold to the same set of customers (be they complementary products or not) may give rise to customer benefits such as one-stop shopping.

Nonetheless the Commission is concerned that both types of merger may give rise to both non-coordinated (principally through foreclosure) and coordinated effects (through changing the nature of competition so that the firms are significantly more likely to coordinate and raise prices) on a market. The draft Guidelines seek to set out the main sources of harm and efficiencies in the context of both vertical and conglomerate mergers.

b. Market Shares and Concentration Levels

As with horizontal mergers, the Commission indicates that the appraisal should begin with a consideration of market shares and concentration as non-horizontal mergers are unlikely to be problematic in the absence of the entity having 'market power' on at least one of the markets involved. Indeed, Form CO only requires the parties to provide data in relation to affected markets where 'one or more of the parties to the concentration are engaged in business activities in a product market, which is upstream or downstream of a product in which any other party to the concentration is engaged, and any of their individual or combined markets shares at either level is 25 per cent or more, regardless of whether there is or is not any existing supplier/ customer relationship between the parties to the concentration'[652] or where 'one or more of the parties to the concentration are engaged in business activities in a product market, which is a neighbouring market closely related to a product market in which any other party to the

Impact of Vertical and Conglomerate Mergers on Competition (available on DG Comp's web site at http://ec.europa.eu/ comm/competition/mergers/studies_reports/studies_reports.html.

[651] See also, e.g. RBB Economics, 'The Efficiency-Enhancing Effects of Non-Horizontal Mergers' Report for DG Enterprise, European Commission, 2005 available on DG Comp's website at, http://ec.europa.eu/comm/ competition/mergers/studies_reports/studies_reports.html.

[652] Form CO, s. 6 III.

concentration is engaged, where any of their individual or combined market shares in either market is 25 per cent or more. Product markets are closely related neighbouring markets when the products are complementary to each other or when they belong to a range of products that is generally purchased by the same set of customers for the same end use'.[653] The draft Guidelines indicate that market power in this context arises at a level below that required for dominance.[654]

23. Non-horizontal mergers pose no threat to effective competition unless the merged entity has market power in at least one of the markets concerned.

24. Market shares and concentration levels provide useful first indications of the market power and the competitive importance of both the merging parties and competitors.

The Commission is unlikely to find concern in non-horizontal mergers, be it of a coordinated or of a non-coordinated nature, where the market share post-merger of the new entity in each of the markets concerned is below [30%] and where the post-merger HHI is below [2000]. In practice, it will not extensively investigate such mergers, except where special circumstances such as, for instance, one or more of the following are present:

- a merger involves a company that is likely to expand significantly in the near future, e.g. because of a recent innovation;

- there are significant cross-shareholdings or cross-directorships among market participants;

- one of the merging firms is a firm with a high likelihood of disrupting coordinated conduct;

- indications of past or ongoing coordination, or facilitating practices, are present.

25. The Commission will use the above market share thresholds and HHI levels as an initial indicator of the absence of competition concerns. However, they do not give rise to a legal presumption. The Commission is of the opinion that presenting market share and concentration level above which there are competition concerns is less appropriate in this context. Indeed, market power in at least one of the markets concerned is a necessary condition for competitive harm, not a sufficient condition.

c. Assessment of Vertical Mergers

The key concerns resulting from vertical mergers identified in the draft non-horizontal merger guidelines are non-coordinated effects resulting from foreclosure and coordinated effects.

Non-Coordinated Effects: Foreclosure

The draft Guidelines state that a vertical merger may raise the cost of downstream rivals by restricting their access to an important input (input foreclosure) or foreclose upstream rivals by restricting their access to a sufficient customer base (customer foreclosure). In each case, however, the Commission will look to the ability of the merging parties to foreclose, their incentives to do so and the overall likely effect of such foreclosure on competition. [655] For example, in the context of input foreclosure, it seems unlikely that these conditions will be satisfied unless the input is sufficiently important, the firm has market power in the upstream market, the foreclosure will be profitable to the merged entity and foreclosure will significantly impede effective competition in the downstream market (through for example, increasing costs of downstream rivals and by raising barriers to entry to potential competitors). The Commission will also consider countervailing factors (such as buyer power and potential competition) and

---

[653] Form CO, s. 6 III.

[654] See *supra* Chap. 6.

[655] Draft non-horizontal merger guidelines, section IV.A.

assess efficiencies resulting from the merger (such as the internalisation of double mark-ups, better coordination of the production and distribution process and alignment of incentive of parties).

Draft Guidelines on the assessment of non-horizontal mergers

48. If there remain sufficient credible downstream competitors whose costs are not likely to be raised, for example because they are themselves vertically integrated or they are capable of switching to adequate alternative inputs, competition from those firms may constitutes a sufficient constraint on the merged entity and therefore prevent output prices from rising above pre-merger levels.

49. The effect on competition on the downstream market must also be assessed in light of countervailing factors such as the presence of buyer power or the likelihood that entry upstream would maintain effective competition.

50. Further, the effect on competition needs to be assessed in light of efficiencies identified and substantiated by the merging parties . . .

A number of cases focussed on by the Commission have raised vertical foreclosure concerns, including some involving mergers in the energy sector.[656] In *Skanska/Scancem*,[657] for example, the Commission considered the proposed acquisition by Skanska, a Swedish construction company active in building construction, production, and distribution of building materials and real estate management, of Scancem, a Swedish buildings materials group, primarily involved in the production and distribution of cement and other mineral-based materials. In particular, Scancem had 80–90 per cent of the Swedish market for the supply of cement and the merger would create vertical effects between cement and concrete/other mineral-based construction materials since cement (together with aggregates) constituted the main material for the production of the latter products. The Commission was thus concerned not only with the loss of competition on the cement market which would result from the acquisition but with vertical effects, for example, on the ready-mixed concrete market. With respect to this latter market the Commission concluded that there would be significant scope, given Scancem's dominant position in cement for the merged entity to raise the costs of its competitors on this market. Further, as a result of being the largest construction company in Sweden, it could affect the level of sales of competing ready-mixed producers by reducing or threatening to reduce purchases from them. The merger was therefore likely to create a dominant position on the Swedish market for ready-mixed concrete.[658]

The Commission has also been concerned with vertical effects with respect to mergers in the media-sector. *AOL/ Time Warner*,[659] for example, concerned a merger between Time Warner, a media and entertainment company and AOL, the leading Internet access provider in the US. The merger would create the first Internet vertically integrated content provider and would be

---

[656] See e.g. Case COMP/M.3440 *EDP/ENI/GDP* (*aff'd* Case T-87/05 *EDP v. Commission* [2005] ECR II-3745) and Case COMP/M.3696 *E.ON/MOL*. See also *supra* Chap 11, 935–8.

[657] Case IV/M.1157, [1999] OJ L183/1.

[658] In the end the Commission was, however, prepared to clear the merger subject to the divestment of all Scancem's assets used in the production, marketing, sale, and distribution of cement in Finland and divesting its entire shareholding in Scancem to a purchaser independent of and unconnected to Skanska

[659] Case COMP/M.1845, *Time-Warner/AOL* IP/00/1145.

able to distribute Time Warner content (music, news, and films) through AOL's Internet distribution network. AOL would also have access to Bertelsmann content in consequence of a joint venture it had with it in Europe. The Commission thus took the view that AOL would be able to dominate the emerging market for Internet music delivery on-line through its becoming the gatekeeper to the nascent market. In the end the Commission cleared the merger subject to a 'remedy package' which essentially required AOL to sever its links with Bertelsmann. This would leave Europe's largest media company free to compete and prevent the merged entity from dominating the market.

Incentive to Foreclose and Article 82

Vertical effects were also relevant in two controversial cases, *GE/Honeywell*[660] and *Tetra Laval/Sidel*,[661] which were principally concerned with conglomerate effects and the ability of the merged firm to foreclose related markets by offering their products at bundled prices to the detriment of their competitors.[662] Both, however, raised an important point, relevant to mergers involving vertical and/or conglomerate effects. The question arising was to what extent the existence of Article 82 can be expected to affect the incentive of the merged entity to engage in a course of conduct in breach of it? I.e. is the merger appraisal affected by the fact that foreclosure of the downstream, upstream or related market would, or might, constitute an abuse of a dominant position?

In *Tetra Laval* the CFI[663] stressed the importance of the Commission basing its analysis of the likelihood of engaging in anticompetitive behaviour in the future on sufficiently convincing, plausible and cogent evidence. It held that it could not be assumed that a dominant firm would automatically commit abuses of a dominant position and that its conduct would not be constrained by the existence of the competition rules. Rather, when the Commission sought, in assessing the likely affects of the merger, to rely on foreseeable conduct which was likely to constitute such an abuse, it was also required to assess whether, despite the prohibition, it was none the less likely that the entity would act in such a way or whether the illegal nature of the conduct and/or the risk of detection would make such a strategy unlikely. Although it was right to take into account the incentives to act illegally, therefore, the Commission should also have taken into account the extent to which the incentives would be eliminated, as a result of the illegality of the conduct, the likelihood of its detection, action taken by competent authorities, and the financial penalties which could ensue.

---

[660] Case COMP/M.2220, *aff'd* Cases T-209 and 210/01 *Honeywell v. Commission* and *General Electric Company v. Commission* [2005] ECR II-5527 and 5575. With regard to the vertical effects, however, the CFI considered that the Commission had committed a manifest error of assessment and had failed to prove that the practices would in fact create or strengthen a dominant position. In particular, the Commission had been concerned that the merged entity would have an incentive not to supply engine starters to rival manufacturers of jet engines.

[661] Case Comp/M.2416, annulled on appeal Case T-5/02, [2002] ECR II-4381, [2002] 5 CMLR 1182, *aff'd* Case C-12/03 [2005] ECR I-987, [2005] 4 CMLR 8.

[662] See *infra* 1060–4.

[663] Case T-5/02, [2002] ECR II-4381, [2002] 5 CMLR 1182.

Case T-5/02, *Tetra Laval BV* v. *Commission* [2002] ECR II-4381, [2002] 5 CMLR 1182

159. In this regard, it must be stated that, although the Regulation provides for the prohibition of a merger creating or strengthening a dominant position which has significant anti-competitive effects, these conditions do not require it to be demonstrated that the merged entity will, as a result of the merger, engage in abusive, and consequently unlawful, conduct. Although it cannot therefore be presumed that Community law will not be complied with by the parties to a conglomerate-type merger transaction, such a possibility cannot be excluded by the Commission when it carries out its control of mergers. Accordingly, when the Commission, in assessing the effects of such a merger, relies on foreseeable conduct which in itself is likely to constitute abuse of an existing dominant position, it is required to assess whether, despite the prohibition of such conduct, it is none the less likely that the entity resulting from the merger will act in such a manner or whether, on the contrary, the illegal nature of the conduct and/or the risk of detection will make such a strategy unlikely. While it is appropriate to take account, in its assessment, of incentives to engage in anti-competitive practices, such as those resulting in the present case for Tetra from the commercial advantages which may be foreseen on the PET equipment markets (recital 359), the Commission must also consider the extent to which those incentives would be reduced, or even eliminated, owing to the illegality of the conduct in question, the likelihood of its detection, action taken by the competent authorities, both at Community and national level, and the financial penalties which could ensue.

On appeal, the Commission alleged that such a burden would be impossible to comply with in practice. The ECJ[664] appeared to agree finding that although the Commission must make some assessment of the Article 82 position, the extent of the obligation imposed by the CFI was excessive. It held that although the likelihood of the merged entity engaging in a specific course had to be examined comprehensively, taking account of both the incentives to adopt such conduct and the factors liable to reduce or even eliminate those incentives, it would run counter to the purpose of the merger rules to require the Commission to examine in every merger case the extent to which the incentives to adopt anticompetitive conduct would be reduced or eliminated as a result of the unlawfulness of the conduct in question, the likelihood of its detection, the action taken by the competent authorities, both at Community and national level, and the financial penalties which could ensue.[665] Such an investigation would require too speculative an assessment about how Article 82 would apply to hypothetical future events.[666]

The enquiry demanded by the ECJ thus appears to be a pragmatic one, proportionate to the fact that the Commission is investigating a merger under constrained time limits.

---

[664] Case C-12/03 [2005] ECR I-987, [2005] 4 CMLR 8.

[665] *Ibid.*

[666] It also held that the Commission was required to take account of behavioural undertakings that would prevent that conduct , see discussion of remedies, *infra* 1083.

A. Lindsay *The EC Merger Regulation: Substantive Issues* (2nd edn., Sweet & Maxwell, 2006)

2–039 It appears therefore that the Commission is bound to take account of Art.82 when assessing whether a merged group has the incentive and the ability to adopt a particular course of conduct, but the inquiry must be a pragmatic one, proportionate to the fact that the Commission is investigating a merger under short time limits. On this reading, the European Court of Justice in *Tetra Laval* ruled that the Court of First Instance placed the Commission under an excessive and unrealistic burden in formulating the extent of the obligation to take account of Art.82 in merger control proceedings but, by stating that the Court of First Instance was correct to rule that the Commission had to consider the merged group's incentives to adopt a particular course of conduct, "including the possibility that the conduct is unlawful". It maintained a duty on the Commission to carry out a certain assessment of the position under Art.82. For example, if it can readily be established that Art.82 imposes an unambiguous obligation on the merged group not to adopt the conduct in question and that obligation is likely to be enforced in the case of breach, this ought to be taken into account in the merger control analysis. On the other hand, the Commission is not required to carry out a speculative assessment of the likelihood of enforcement by different authorities, predicting the likely penalty if infringements are found and determining whether the merged group would be likely to be deterred by these risks from adopting the course of conduct.

This interpretation gains some support from the judgment of the CFI in *General Electric v. Commission* which suggests that a summary not detailed analysis of this issue is required. The CFI does not, however, address the concern raised by the ECJ in *Tetra Laval* that this issue should not have an adverse impact on the ECMR's preventative function.

Case T-210/01, *General Electric Company* v. *Commission* [2005] ECR II-5575[667]

73. It follows from the foregoing that the Commission must, in principle, take into account the potentially unlawful, and thus sanctionable, nature of certain conduct as a factor which might diminish, or even eliminate, incentives for an undertaking to engage in particular conduct. That appraisal does not, however, require an exhaustive and detailed examination of the rules of the various legal orders which might be applicable and of the enforcement policy practised within them, given that an assessment intended to establish whether an infringement is likely and to ascertain that it will be penalised in several legal orders would be too speculative.

74. Thus, where the Commission, without undertaking a specific and detailed investigation into the matter, can identify the unlawful nature of the conduct in question, in the light of Article 82 EC or of other provisions of Community law which it is competent to enforce, it is its responsibility to make a finding to that effect and take account of it in its assessment of the likelihood that the merged entity will engage in such conduct (see, to that effect, *Commission v Tetra Laval*, paragraph 60 above, paragraph 74).

75. It follows that, although the Commission is entitled to take as its basis a summary analysis, based on the evidence available to it at the time when it adopts its merger-control decision, of the

---

[667] See also Case T-209/01 *Honeywell v. Commission* [2005] ECR II-5527, [2006] 4 CMLR 14.

lawfulness of the conduct in question and of the likelihood that it will be punished, it must none the less, in the course of its appraisal, identify the conduct foreseen and, where appropriate, evaluate and take into account the possible deterrent effect represented by the fact that the conduct would be clearly, or highly probably, unlawful under Community law.

The Commission seeks to synthesise the obligations imposed on it in these cases in its draft non-horizontal merger guideline when it states at paragraph 44.

44. In addition, when the adoption of a specific course of conduct by the merged entity is an essential step in foreclosure, the Commission examines both the incentives to adopt such conduct and the factors liable to reduce, or even eliminate, those incentives, including the possibility that the conduct is unlawful. Conduct may be unlawful *inter alia* because of competition rules or sector-specific rules at the EU or national levels. The appraisal, however, does not require an exhaustive and detailed examination of the rules of the various legal orders which might be applicable and of the enforcement policy practised within them. Moreover, the illegality of a conduct may be likely to provide significant disincentives for the merged entity to engage in such conduct only in certain circumstances. In particular, the Commission will consider, on the basis of a summary analysis: (i) the likelihood that the conduct would be clearly, or highly probably, unlawful under Community law, (ii) the likelihood that this illegal conduct could be detected, and (iii) penalties which could be imposed.

Other Non-Coordinated Effects and Coordinated Effects in Vertical Mergers

The Commission has not ordinarily been concerned with vertical mergers which have no foreclosure effects. However the draft non-horizontal merger guidelines state that the vertical mergers may also cause concern where the merged entity gains access to commercially sensitive information regarding the upstream or downstream activities of rivals through vertical integration, or where it changes the nature of competition in such a way that firms that previously were not coordinating their behaviour, are now significantly more likely to coordinate and raise prices or otherwise harm effective competition or to makes coordination easier, more stable or more effective.[668]

c. Assessment of Conglomerate Mergers

The Commission acknowledges in its draft non-horizontal merger guidelines that in the majority of circumstances conglomerate mergers will not lead to any competition problems. Nonetheless, it considers that they may harm competition through non-coordinated effects (principally through foreclosure) and through non-coordinated effects.

Non-Coordinated Effects—Foreclosure

The draft guidelines state that the main concern in the context of conglomerate mergers is foreclosure. 'The combination of products in related markets may confer on the merged entity the ability and incentive to leverage a strong market position from one market to another by means of tying or bundling or other exclusionary practices. Tying and bundling as such are common practices that often have no anticompetitive consequences. Companies engage in tying and bundling in order to provide their customers with better products or offerings in cost-effective ways. Nevertheless, in certain circumstances, these practices may lead to a reduction in actual or potential rivals' ability or incentive to compete. This may reduce the competitive pressure on

---

[668] Draft Guidelines on non-horizontal mergers, paras. 77–89.

the merged entity allowing it to increase prices'.[669] In order to determine whether this scenario is likely the Commission considers whether:

- the merged firm would have the ability to foreclose its rivals (unlikely unless, for example, the new entity has market power in one of the markets concerned, one of the products is viewed by many customers as important, there is a large common pool of customers for the individual products concerned);

- the merged firm would have the economic incentive to foreclose its rivals (this is dependent on the profitability of the strategy and the extent to which the incentives to adopt such conduct is reduced or eliminated by, for example, the possibility that the conduct is unlawful[670]); and

- a foreclosure strategy would have a significant detrimental effect on competition, causing harm to consumers.[671] The detriment on competition in this case is in the longer term since the tying or bundling will initially lead to a reduction in prices for the bundled/ tied products. The concern, however, is that this strategy will reduce sales by single-component rivals which will be unable or have reduced incentives to compete and deter entry by potential competitors. This in turn will allow the merged entity to acquire market power in the market for the tied or bundled goods and/or maintain market power in the market for the tying or leveraging goods.[672] The Commission accepts that the effect on competition needs to be assessed also in the light of countervailing factors such as the presence of buyer power, new entry and the efficiencies identified and substantiated by the merging parties.

The approach taken in the draft Guidelines is, no doubt, an attempt to meet the challenges set by the CFI and ECJ in appeals from the Commission's decisions in *GE/Honeywell*[673] and *Tetra Laval/Sidel*[674] respectively. In both of these cases the Commission prohibited mergers, principally on accounts of their conglomerate effects and on the basis that the mergers would create incentives for the merged firms to leverage market power between related markets. In both cases the courts were extremely critical of the Commission's analysis. The Commission's right to intervene in mergers resulting in conglomerate effects was, however, upheld.[675]

GE/Honeywell[676] was an extremely high profile case in which the Commission prohibited the proposed acquisition of Honeywell Inc by General Electric Co even though it had been cleared by the US antitrust authorities.[677] Essentially, the Commission was concerned that the $US 42

---

[669] Draft Guidelines on non-horizontal mergers, para. 92.

[670] See discussion *supra* 1056–9.

[671] Draft Guidelines on non-horizontal mergers, para. 93.

[672] See discussion of tying and bundling *supra* Chap. 7.

[673] Comp/M.2220, *aff'd* Cases T-209 and 210/01, *Honeywell v. Commission* and *General Electric Company v. Commission* [2005] ECR II-5527 and 5575.

[674] Case Comp/M.2416, annulled on appeal Case T-5/02, [2002] ECR II-4381, [2002] 5 CMLR 1182, *aff'd* Case C-12/03, [2005] ECR I-987, [2005] 4 CMLR 8. See also Case IV/M.794 *Coca-Cola Enterprises/Amalgamated Beverages*, Case IV/M.833, *The Coca-Cola Company/Carlsberg A/S* [1998] OJ L145/41; Case IV/M.938, *Guinness/Grand Metropolitan* [1998] OJ L288/24.

[675] See *infra*.

[676] Comp/M.2220, *aff'd* Cases T-209 and 210/01 *Honeywell, v. Commission* and *General Electric Company v. Commission* [2005] ECR II-5527 and 5575. See, e.g., G. Drauz, 'Unbundling GE/Honeywell' [2003] *ECLR* 115.

[677] See, e.g., F. D. Platt Majoras, 'GE-Honeywell: The US Decision', 29 Nov. 2001, Remarks before the Antitrust Law Section State Bar of Georgia, available on the US, DOJ Antitrust Division's web site. For the extraterritorial aspects of this decision see *infra* Chap. 16.

billion merger would strengthen GE's already dominant position in the markets for jet engines for large commercial aircraft and regional aircraft and create a dominant position in avionics, non-avionics, and corporate jet engines (Honeywell was the leading supplier of these products). In particular, the Commission considered that it would allow the merged entity to leverage its market power, thereby strengthening the dominant position in the large commercial jet engine market and creating a dominant position in the corporate jet engine market and avionics/non-avionics market.[678] The anticipated outcome of the bundling or strategic price costs was that competitors would be driven from the market, and that eventually prices could be expected to rise and product quality and service would reduce.[679] The speculative nature of this prediction triggered a 'firestorm of criticism', particularly in the US, 'not just from the US antitrust authorities, senior [US] administration officials, but also from the business community generally and from leading economists, antitrust legal scholars, and editorial writers'.[680]

The criticism centred on the notion that the EC authorities had prohibited a merger which was to lead to a reduction in prices and increase in output. The anti-competitive effect would only result if the other competitors could not match the merged firm's offerings. In the US, the authorities went out of their way to stress that they would not prohibit a merger which would make a firm more efficient, because of fears that it might force competitors from a market: antitrust laws 'protect competition, not competitors'.[681] Rather a competition authority should be very cautious about adopting a merger policy that sacrificed short-term efficiencies in the name of maintaining competition.[682]

W. J. Kolasky, 'Conglomerate Mergers and Range Effects: It's a long way from Chicago to Brussels' 9 November 2001, Address before George Mason University Symposium Washington, DC

At a minimum, before applying such a policy, we should make certain we have a high degree of confidence that the trade-off we are making will ultimately benefit consumers. This would require quantifying the efficiencies and determining the likely duration of the competitive round that will occur before less efficient rivals are forced from the market. It would also require a high degree of confidence that the rivals will in fact be forced from the market—that they will not be able to develop counter-strategies that will enable them to become more efficient themselves in order to

---

[678] It was also concerned that the aircraft financing arm of GE, GECAS, would specify Honeywell equipment in its aircraft purchases

[679] See D. Guikajis, L. Petit, G. Garnier, and P De Luyck 'General Electric/Honeywell—An Insight into the Commission's investigation and decision', Competition Policy Newsletter, October 2001, 5.

[680] See W. J. Kolasky, 'Conglomerate Mergers and Range Effects: It's a long way from Chicago to Brussels' 9 Nov. 2001, Address before George Mason University Symposium Washington, DC. See also A. Burnside 'GE, Honey, I sunk the merger' [2003] *ECLR* 107 and M. Pflanz and C. Caffarra, 'The Economics of GE/Honeywell' [2003] *ECLR* 115.

[681] The Commission denied it was acting to protect competitors rather than the competitive process. In its press release following its prohibition decision it specifically stated: 'The key test for assessing mergers in Europe is whether they create or strengthen a dominant position. European merger control is not about protecting competitors but about ensuring that markets remain sufficiently competitive in the long run so that consumers benefit from sufficient choice, innovation and competitive prices', IP/01939.

[682] See W. J. Kolasky, 'Conglomerate Mergers and Range Effects: It's a long way from Chicago to Brussels' 9 Nov. 2001, Address before George Mason University Symposium Washington, DC.

survive. Indeed, any business strategy that did not take into account competitive counter-strategies would fail the test for the Nash equilibrium . . . It would also require us to estimate the size of
the price increases likely to occur once the merged firm gains market power to determine
whether, taking into account the efficiencies, future prices to consumers are likely to be higher or
lower than they would be in a market populated by several less efficient firms. Finally we would
have to determine the likely duration for the monopoly period—which would be dependent on
entry conditions at the time the monopoly is finally achieved.

In the United States, we have very little confidence in our ability to make these judgments which
would necessarily involve predictions far out into the future. We believe . . . that we need to 'be
humble.' We have more confidence in the self-correcting nature of the markets. This confidence is
especially strong when the markets are populated by strong rivals and strong buyers, who will
usually find ways to protect themselves from an aspiring monopolist. Our strong belief in markets
and our humility in our predictive abilities lead us to be skeptical of claims by rivals that a merger
will lead to their ultimate demise and to demand strong empirical proof before we will accept such
claims.

In the appeal from the Commission's decision the CFI[683] upheld the Commission's decision but
only on the basis that its analysis of horizontal effects (the creation of a monopoly in market for
engines for large regional jets) provided sufficient basis to prohibit the merger. With regard to the
leveraging theory, the Court considered that the Commission had made a manifest error of
assessment and had failed to provide evidence to substantiate its claim that bundling between
engines and avionics/non-avionics was possible or feasible. The Commission had not established
that the merged entity had an economic incentive to bundle and consequently it had the burden of
putting forward other evidence to suggest that the merged entity would make the strategic decision to sacrifice profits in the short term with a view to reaping larger profits in the future. This
could be done, for example, through economic studies or the production of internal documents
showing that GE's directors had that objective on the launch of their bid for Honeywell.[684]

The CFI thus carefully scrutinised the Commission's decision to determine whether it had
been established that the merged entity would have the capability of engaging in the alleged
bundling practices, whether it was likely to do so and if, in consequence, anticompetitive harm
would occur (a dominant position would have been created or strengthened on one or more of
the relevant markets in the relatively near future[685]).

Case T-210/01, *General Electric Company* v. *Commission* [2005] ECR II-5575[686]

399. The Commission stated in essence in the contested decision that, following the merger,
the merged entity would have the ability, unlike its competitors, to offer its customers packages

---

[683] Cases T-209 and 210/01, *Honeywell* v. *Commission* and *General Electric Company* v. *Commission* [2005] ECR II-5527 and 5575. For a good summary of the case and the issues decided on appeal, see D. Howarth, 'The Court of First Instance in *GE/Honeywell*' [2006] *ECLR* 485.

[684] Case T-210/01, *General Electric Company* v. *Commission* [2005] ECR II-5575, [2006] 4 CMLR 15, para. 466.

[685] The case was decided under the old ECMR so the dominance not the significant impediment to effective competition test was applicable.

[686] See also Case T-209/01, *Honeywell* v. *Commission* [2005] ECR II-5527, [2006] 4 CMLR 15.

for large commercial aircraft, large regional aircraft and corporate aircraft, encompassing both engines and avionics and non-avionics products. It also held that such behaviour would clearly be in the commercial interests of the merged entity and would thus probably be engaged in after the merger had taken place (recitals 350 to 404, 412 to 416, 432 to 434, 443 and 444 and 445 to 458). As a consequence, a dominant position would have been created for Honeywell on the markets for avionics and non-avionics products and GE's dominant positions would have been strengthened, particularly on the market for large commercial jet aircraft engines (recital 458 of the contested decision).

400. The Commission's case is based on the fact that jet engines, on the one hand, and avionics and non-avionics products, on the other, are complementary, since all these products are indispensable in the construction of an aircraft. The final customer, the operator of the aircraft, must therefore purchase all of them, directly or indirectly, from their manufacturer. The Commission held in the contested decision that on the whole the customers are essentially the same for all those products and that the latter could therefore be bundled. The Commission also observes that the applicant's group is financially very strong, both compared with its main competitors on the engines markets and with its competitors on the markets for avionics and non-avionics products (see, as regards the latter, recitals 302 to 304, 323 and 324 of the contested decision; see also recital 398 et seq.). The merged entity would thus be in a position to reduce its profit margins on avionics and non-avionics products with a view to increasing its market share and making larger profits in the future.

401. It should be noted, as a preliminary point, that the way it is predicted that the merged entity will behave in the future is a vital aspect of the Commission's analysis of bundling in the present case. It follows from the fact that the applicant had no presence on the markets for avionics and non-avionics products prior to the merger, together with the fact that Honeywell had no presence on the market for large commercial jet aircraft engines before the merger, that the merger would have had no horizontal anti-competitive effect on those markets. Thus, the merger would, prima facie, have had no effect whatsoever on those markets.

402. Moreover, in so far as the Commission predicts, at recitals 443 and 444 of the contested decision, that bundling will have an impact on the market for engines for corporate jet aircraft, it should be noted that the applicant's pre-merger share of that market was only [10–20]%, in terms of the installed base, whilst Honeywell's was [40–50]%, and only [0–10]%, in terms of the installed base on those aircraft still in production, as compared with Honeywell's [40–50]% share (recital 88 of the contested decision). In those circumstances, even if it were shown that the merged entity would bundle those engines with avionics and non-avionics products after the merger, there would be no causal link between the merger and the bundled offers, except in the small minority of cases in which the engine was a product of the former GE. Moreover, it is not suggested in the contested decision that either of the parties to the merger manufactures engines for small regional aircraft. It follows that any bundling which might be engaged in by the merged entity on the market for regional aircraft would in any event concern only large regional aircraft.

403. The Commission held in the contested decision that each avionics product for regional and corporate aircraft constitutes a market in itself and that there is a market for each non-avionics product for all types of aircraft, including large commercial aircraft. Accordingly, its reasoning with regard to the creation, by means of bundling, of dominant positions on the markets for the different avionics products cannot be accepted in relation to the markets for each of the various avionics products for corporate and regional aircraft. Indeed, on the assumption that it actually becomes a reality after the transaction, any bundling attributable to the merger will affect only one segment of those markets, the large regional aircraft segment. In the same way, the Commission's reasoning is undermined (albeit to a lesser degree) in relation to non-avionics products, for which the Commission defined an individual market for each specific product, irrespective of the size and other features of the aircraft equipped.

404. It is therefore, in principle, in the sector for large commercial aircraft, for which the Commission has defined distinct markets both for jet engines and for each avionics product, that the Commission's case on bundling could conceivably be sustained.

405. In relation to the possible impact of the merger on (i) the markets for jet engines for large commercial aircraft and large regional aircraft, (ii) those for avionics products for large commercial aircraft and (iii) those for non-avionics products, the Court must determine whether the Commission has established that the merged entity would not only have the capability to engage in the bundling practices described in the contested decision but also, on the basis of convincing evidence, that it would have been likely to engage in those practices after the merger and that, in consequence, a dominant position would have been created or strengthened on one or more of the relevant markets in the relatively near future (*Tetra Laval* v *Commission*, paragraph 58 above, paragraphs 146 to 162).

Notwithstanding the general controversy the Commission's decision in *GE/Honeywell* provoked, in *Tetra Laval/Sidel*[687] the Commission prohibited another merger which it considered would enable the merged entity to leverage its market power in one market into another. This case concerned a public bid by Tetra Laval SA for shares in Sidel SA. Tetra, part of the Tetra Pak company, is the world market leader in the area of liquid food carton packaging. In contrast, Sidel is involved in the production of packaging equipment and systems and is a world-wide leader for the production and supply of stretch blow moulding machines (SBM), used in the production of polyethlylene terephthalate (PET) plastic bottles. The Commission considered that the merger would strengthen Tetra's dominant position in the market for aseptic carton packaging machines and cartons and create a dominant position in the market for PET packaging equipment. The Commission made findings of horizontal and vertical effects and held that the merger would enable the merged entity to exploit its dominant position on the carton markets by leveraging into the market for PET packaging equipment in order to dominate it. The Commission set out its reasons for concluding that the market structure was particularly conducive to leverage effects at paragraph 359 of its decision:

- There would be a common pool of customers requiring both carton and PET packaging systems to package sensitive liquids.

- Tetra has a particularly strong dominant position in aseptic carton packaging with more than [80–90 per cent] of the market and a dependent customer base.

- Tetra/Sidel would start from a strong, leading, position in PET packaging systems and in particular SBM machines with a market share in the region of [60–70 per cent].

- Tetra/Sidel would have the ability to target selectively specific customers or specific customer groups as the structure of the market enables price discrimination.

- Tetra/Sidel would have a strong economic incentive to engage in leveraging practices. As carton and PET are technical substitutes, when a customer switches to PET he/she is a lost customer on the carton side of the business either because he/she partially switched *from* carton or because he/she did not switch some of the production *to* carton from other packaging materials. This creates an added incentive to capture the customer on the PET

---

[687] Case COMP/M.2416. The Commission's decision in Case COMP/M.2283, *Schneider/Legrand* also relied on the conglomerate effects of the merger. In this case the CFI annulled the Commission's decision as the Commission had not identified its conglomeracy concerns in the SO, see *supra* 1004, Case T-310/01, *Schneider Electric SA* v. *Commission* [2002] ECR II-4071, [2003] 4 CMLR 768.

side of the business to recover the loss. Therefore, by leveraging its current market position in carton, Tetra/Sidel would not only enhance its market share on the PET side but defend or compensate its possible loss on the carton side.

- Competitors of Tetra/Sidel in both the carton and the PET equipment markets would be much smaller, with the largest competitor having no more than [10–20 per cent] share in the market for carton packaging machines or SBM machines.

The Commission considered that the leveraging would foreclose competitors from the rest of the SMB machine market and turn Sidel's leading position on the market into a dominant one. On appeal, the CFI annulled the Commission's decision finding the pleas alleging lack of horizontal, vertical and conglomerate anti-competitive effects were well founded.[688] The CFI's judgment was upheld by the ECJ on appeal.[689] The CFI devoted more than half of its judgment to the plea that the Commission had failed to establish foreseeable conglomerate effects,[690] concluding that the decision did not establish that the merger would give rise to significant anti-competitive conglomerate effects to the requisite legal standard.[691]

The CFI's accepted that the ECMR can apply to merger transactions having horizontal, vertical or conglomerate effects so long as the conditions set out in Article 2(3) are met[692] and drew a distinction between mergers where the conglomerate effects would be structural (arising directly from the economic structure created)[693] and those where they might be behavioural, in the sense that they arise only if the new entity created engages in certain commercial practices.[694] *Tetra Laval* was of the latter type. It was therefore necessary to determine whether the merger would have anti-competitive effects by, in all likelihood, allowing the new entity to obtain, in the relatively near future, a dominant position on a market in which one of the parties held a leading position, as a result of leveraging from a market in which the other party was already dominant.[695] In a case involving prospective analysis of conglomerate effects, the CFI stated that the Commission must establish that competition will be significantly impeded in the near future:[696] the parties must have both the ability and incentive to leverage and the consequences of leveraging must be particularly plausible and must in all likelihood occur in the very near future.

The judgment stressed the importance of the Commission basing its analysis of the likelihood of leveraging, and of the consequences of such leveraging, on sufficiently convincing, plausible and cogent evidence. Further, the CFI held that it could not be assumed that a dominant firm would automatically commit abuses of a dominant position (and that its conduct would not be constrained by the existence of the competition rules).[697]

---

[688] Case T-5/02, [2002] ECR II-4381, [2002] 5 CMLR 1182, *aff'd* Case C-12/03 P, [2005] ECR I-987, [2005] 4 CMLR 8. When the Commission re-examined the merger, it cleared it subject to a commitment that Tetra Laval license the new technology for making PET bottles to third parties.

[689] Case C-12/03 P, [2005] ECR I-987, [2005] 4 CMLR 8.

[690] Case T-5/02, [2002] ECR II-4381, [2002] 5 CMLR, paras. 142–336.

[691] *Ibid.*, para. 226.

[692] *Ibid.*, paras. 146–52.

[693] i.e., where the new entity would immediately and automatically create a second dominant position which the new entity could abuse.

[694] *Ibid.*, para. 147.

[695] *Ibid.*, para. 148.

[696] *Ibid.*, para. 153.

[697] See *supra* 1056–9.

Case T-5/02, *Tetra Laval BV* v. *Commission* [2002] ECR II-4381, [2002] 5 CMLR 1182

146. It should be observed, first, that the Regulation, particularly at Article 2(2) and (3), does not draw any distinction between, on the one hand, merger transactions having horizontal and vertical effects and, on the other hand, those having a conglomerate effect. It follows that, without distinction between those types of transactions, a merger can be prohibited only if the two conditions laid down in Article 2(3) are met (see paragraph 120 above). Consequently, a merger having a conglomerate effect must, like any other merger (see paragraph 120 above), be authorised by the Commission if it is not established that it creates or strengthens a dominant position in the common market or in a substantial part of it and that, as a result, effective competition will be significantly impeded.

...

155. The Commission's analysis of a merger producing a conglomerate effect is conditioned by requirements similar to those defined by the Court with regard to the creation of a situation of collective dominance (*Kali & Salz*, paragraph 222; and *Airtours* v. *Commission*, paragraph 63). Thus the Commission's analysis of a merger transaction which is expected to have an anti-competitive conglomerate effect calls for a particularly close examination of the circumstances which are relevant for an assessment of that effect on the conditions of competition in the reference market. As the Court has already held, where the Commission takes the view that a merger should be prohibited because it will create or strengthen a dominant position within a foreseeable period, it is incumbent upon it to produce convincing evidence thereof (*Airtours* v. *Commission*, paragraph 63). Since the effects of a conglomerate-type merger are generally considered to be neutral, or even beneficial, for competition on the markets concerned, as is recognised in the present case by the economic writings cited in the analyses annexed to the parties' written pleadings, the proof of anti-competitive conglomerate effects of such a merger calls for a precise examination, supported by convincing evidence, of the circumstances which allegedly produce those effects (see, by analogy, *Airtours* v. *Commission*, paragraph 63).

156. In the present case, the leveraging from the aseptic carton market, as described in the contested decision, would manifest itself—in addition to the possibility of the merged entity engaging in practices such as tying sales of carton packaging equipment and consumables to sales of PET packaging equipment and forced sales (recitals 345 and 365)—firstly, by the probability of predatory pricing by the merged entity (recital 364, cited in paragraph 49 above); secondly, by price wars; and, thirdly, by the granting of loyalty rebates. Engaging in these practices would enable the merged entity to ensure, as far as possible, that its customers on the carton markets obtain from Sidel any PET equipment they may require. The contested decision finds that Tetra holds a dominant position on the aseptic carton markets, that is to say, the markets for aseptic carton packaging systems and aseptic cartons (recital 231, see paragraph 40 above), a finding which is not disputed by the applicant.

157. It should be recalled that, according to settled case-law, where an undertaking is in a dominant position it is in consequence obliged, where appropriate, to modify its conduct so as not to impair effective competition on the market regardless of whether the Commission has adopted a decision to that effect (Case 322/81, *Michelin* v. *Commission* [1993] ECR 3461, paragraph 57; Case T-51/89 *Tetra Pak* v. *Commission* [1990] ECR II-309, paragraph 23; and Joined Cases T-125/97 and T-127/97 *Coca-Cola* v. *Commission* [2000] ECR II-1733, paragraph 80).

158. Moreover, in response to the questions put by the Court at the hearing, the Commission did not deny that leveraging by Tetra through the conduct described above could constitute abuse

of Tetra's pre-existing dominant position in the aseptic carton markets. This could also be the case, according to the concerns expressed by the Commission in its defence, in circumstances where the merged entity refused to participate in the installation and any necessary conversion of Sidel SBM machines, to provide after-sales service or to honour the guarantees for such machines when sold by converters. However, the Commission went on to state that the fact that a type of conduct may constitute an independent infringement of Article 82 EC does not preclude that conduct from being taken into account in the Commission's assessment of all forms of leveraging made possible by a merger transaction.

159. In this regard, it must be stated that, although the Regulation provides for the prohibition of a merger creating or strengthening a dominant position which has significant anti-competitive effects, these conditions do not require it to be demonstrated that the merged entity will, as a result of the merger, engage in abusive, and consequently unlawful, conduct. Although it cannot therefore be presumed that Community law will not be complied with by the parties to a conglomerate-type merger transaction, such a possibility cannot be excluded by the Commission when it carries out its control of mergers. Accordingly, when the Commission, in assessing the effects of such a merger, relies on foreseeable conduct which in itself is likely to constitute abuse of an existing dominant position, it is required to assess whether, despite the prohibition of such conduct, it is none the less likely that the entity resulting from the merger will act in such a manner or whether, on the contrary, the illegal nature of the conduct and/or the risk of detection will make such a strategy unlikely. While it is appropriate to take account, in its assessment, of incentives to engage in anti-competitive practices, such as those resulting in the present case for Tetra from the commercial advantages which may be foreseen on the PET equipment markets (recital 359), the Commission must also consider the extent to which those incentives would be reduced, or even eliminated, owing to the illegality of the conduct in question, the likelihood of its detection, action taken by the competent authorities, both at Community and national level, and the financial penalties which could ensue.

160. Since the Commission did not carry out such an assessment in the contested decision, it follows that, in so far as the Commission's assessment is based on the possibility, or even the probability, that Tetra will engage in such conduct in the aseptic carton markets, its findings in this respect cannot be upheld.

161. Moreover, the fact that the applicant offered commitments regarding its future conduct is also a factor which the Commission should have taken into account in assessing whether it was likely that the merged entity would act in a manner which could result in the creation of a dominant position on one or more of the relevant PET equipment markets. There is no indication in the contested decision that the Commission took account of the implications of those commitments when it assessed the creation of such a position in future through leveraging.

162. It follows from the foregoing that it is necessary to examine whether the Commission based its analysis of the likelihood of leveraging from the aseptic carton markets, and of the consequences of such leveraging by the merged entity, on sufficiently convincing evidence. In the course of that examination it is necessary, in the present case, to take account only of conduct which would, at least probably, not be illegal. In addition, since the anticipated dominant position would only emerge after a certain lapse of time, by 2005 according to the Commission, its analysis of the future position must, whilst allowing for a certain margin of discretion, be particularly plausible.

The ECJ rejected the Commission's appeal from this judgment in its entirety. Although it did find that the CFI had in some respects erred in the law, it held that these errors did not call into question the judgment in so far as it annulled the Commission's decision.[698] The judgment sheds light on a number of important issues, including the standard of proof of merger cases[699] and the impact that the illegality of the conduct has on the incentives of the merged entity to adopt any abusive conduct.[700] In particular, the ECJ stressed that the prospective analysis required in merger control, had to be carried out with great care: it required an analysis not of past events but of a prediction of the future, making it necessary to envisage various chains of cause and effect with a view to ascertaining which of them was most likely. The quality of evidence relied upon by the Commission in such circumstances is particularly important.

Case C-12/03 P, *Commission* v. *Tetra Laval BV* [2005] ECR I-987

42 A prospective analysis of the kind necessary in merger control must be carried out with great care since it does not entail the examination of past events—for which often many items of evidence are available which make it possible to understand the causes—or of current events, but rather a prediction of events which are more or less likely to occur in future if a decision prohibiting the planned concentration or laying down the conditions for it is not adopted.

43 Thus, the prospective analysis consists of an examination of how a concentration might alter the factors determining the state of competition on a given market in order to establish whether it would give rise to a serious impediment to effective competition. Such an analysis makes it necessary to envisage various chains of cause and effect with a view to ascertaining which of them are the most likely.

44 The analysis of a 'conglomerate-type' concentration is a prospective analysis in which, first, the consideration of a lengthy period of time in the future and, secondly, the leveraging necessary to give rise to a significant impediment to effective competition mean that the chains of cause and effect are dimly discernible, uncertain and difficult to establish. That being so, the quality of the evidence produced by the Commission in order to establish that it is necessary to adopt a decision declaring the concentration incompatible with the common market is particularly important, since that evidence must support the Commission's conclusion that, if such a decision were not adopted, the economic development envisaged by it would be plausible.

Portfolio Power and Foreclosure

In *Guinness/Grand Metropolitan*[701] the Commission had to examine a concentration which had an impact on certain separate spirits markets. Although there was some horizontal overlap in the relevant markets in which the parties operated, the merger also led to an extension of the complementary products and range of spirits offered. The Commission displayed concern about 'portfolio power'.

---

[698] Case C-12/03 P, [2005] ECR I-987. The Advocate General (Tizzano) took the view that the CFI was right to have declared that the Commission ought to have taken into consideration the various factors that might have influenced the likelihood of the merged entity behaving in such a way as to enable it to acquire the predicted dominant position on the PET market. '[T]he CFI correctly found that, just as the Commission had assessed the economic incentives for engaging in such conduct, so it ought to have taken into consideration the possible disincentives in that respect of the unlawful nature of the conduct in question ... or of the commitments into which that company had offered to enter', Opinion of 25 May 2004, para. 123.

[699] See *supra* 1009–10.

[700] See *supra* 1056–9.

[701] Case IV/M.938, [1998] OJ L288/24.

> ## Case IV/M.938, *Guinness/Grand Metropolitan* [1998] OJ L228/24
>
> 40. The holder of a portfolio of leading spirit brands may enjoy a number of advantages. In particular, his position in relation to his customers is stronger since he is able to provide a range of products and will account for a greater proportion of their business, he will have greater flexibility to structure his prices, promotions and discounts, he will have greater potential for tying, and he will be able to realize economies of scale and scope in his sales and marketing activities, Finally, the implicit (or explicit) threat of a refusal to supply is more potent.
>
> 41. The strength of these advantages, and their potential effect on the competitive structure of the market, depends on a number of factors, including whether the holder of the portfolio has the brand leader or one or more leading brands in a particular market; the market shares of the various brands, particular in relation to the shares of competitors; the relative importance of the individual markets in which the parties have significant shares and brands across the range of product markets in which the portfolio is held; and/or the number of markets in which the portfolio holder has a brand leader or leading brand.

The Commission concluded that the merger in that case would have portfolio effects. The effect was particularly acute on the Greek market where it would have a dominant position in the gin, brandy, and rum markets and where it would be able to supply the leading brands, with the exception of vodka. Through portfolio effects the dominant position in these markets would be reinforced.[702] This decision received criticism not for its adoption of the concept of portfolio power but for failing to identify with sufficient clarity what is wrong with an undertaking's acquisition of a wider portfolio of products. For example, some paragraphs, including paragraph 40, of the Commission's decision indicate that the Commission objected to the economies of scale and scope offered to the parties from the increased range of products that the merger allowed.[703] Such benefits would, however, not harm but benefit consumers and intervention on these grounds would give the Commission a broad discretion. An objection to portfolio power on the ground that it would give the merged entity greater power to tie products is less controversial.[704]

In the draft non-horizontal merger guidelines, the Commission clarify that it will be concerned about portfolio effects where they provide the opportunity for the merged parties to foreclose the market. 'However, the fact that the merged entity will have a broad range of products does not, as such, raise competition concerns'.[705]

Coordinated Effects

The Commission states in its draft non-horizontal merger guidelines that conglomerate mergers may 'in certain circumstance facilitate anticompetitive coordination in markets', for example, where the number of effective competitors is reduced, where foreclosed rivals choose not to

---

[702] *Ibid.*, paras. 90–118. The Commission permitted the merger only once the parties agreed to end its distribution arrangements for Bacardi rum in Greece even though the merger did not increase the parties' market shares on this market.

[703] [1998] OJ L288/24, para. 40.

[704] See e.g. S. Bishop and M. Walker, *The Economics of EC Competition Law: Concepts, Application and Measurement* (2nd edn., Sweet & Maxwell, 2002), 291–2.

[705] Draft Guidelines on non-horizontal mergers, para. 103.

contest the situation of coordination but prefer to live under the shelter of increased price level and/or where the extent and importance of multimarket competition is increased. 'Competitive interaction on several markets may increase the scope and effectiveness of disciplining mechanisms in ensuring that the terms of coordination are being adhered to'.[706]

(ix) Industrial, Social, and other Policy

a. General

A further question which arises is whether or not non-competition factors can, should or are/have been taken into account when appraising mergers under Article 2. Could, for example, the fact that a merger is advantageous from an industrial or social policy point of view be used to find that an otherwise problematic merger is nonetheless compatible with the common market? Alternatively, could non-competition factors be relied upon to prohibit a merger which is otherwise unproblematic from a competition perspective?

b. Other Policies as a Countervailing Factor

Industrial policy, for example, could support industrial restructuring where it is necessary for the undertakings to compete in a global market, to encourage cross-border concentration, to encourage technical progress, to protect certain industries, or to protect employment, even where a concentration might significantly impede effective competition. In the run up to the adoption of the original ECMR some Member States feared that EU industrial policy, aimed at safeguarding and ensuring 'the competitiveness of European industry', might support the creation of a Euro champion in circumstances where that Euro champion would be dominant and impede effective competition within the common market.[707] Although the ECMR allows technical and economic progress to be taken into account, this is just one factor to be taken into account in the overall appraisal. Recital 23 of the ECMR does, however, state that the Commission must place its appraisal within the general framework of the fundamental objectives set out in Article 2 of the EC Treaty and Article 2 of the Treaty of European Union.[708] Arguably, this permits broader Community policies to be taken into account in the appraisal process. In the view of the Commissioner responsible for competition at the time the original ECMR was passed, Sir Leon Brittan, however, the wording of Article 2(1) does not open the back door to industrial policy considerations, especially since it permits technical and economic progress to be taken into account only 'provided that it is to the consumers' advantage and does not form an obstacle to competition'.[709] Further, the Commission has been hostile to

---

[706] Draft Guidelines on non-horizontal mergers, paras. 117–19.

[707] An original draft of the ECMR gave the Commission power to exempt concentrations which led to the creation or strengthening of a dominant position but which resulted in technical and economic progress to the benefit of consumers. However, many Member States objected to the inclusion of such a defence on the ground that the Regulation would be used as an adjunct to industrial policy with the objective of supporting European winners. During the 1960s and 1970s industrial policy was applied by some Member States in a protectionist way.

[708] The 13th recital to the original ECMR also stated that the appraisal should be made within the general framework of the fundamental objectives referred to in Article 2 of the EC Treaty, but specified that this should include, the strengthening the Community's economic and social cohesion referred to in Article 157 (ex Article 130a) EC, see also Case T-12/93, *Comité Central d'Enterprise de la Société Anonyme Vittel v. Commission* [1995] ECR II-1247, paras. 38–40.

[709] See, e.g., IP/04/501 'The Commission puts industry center stage and reinforces competitiveness in an enlarged European Union'. The Commission believes that reform of EU competition law and a pro-active enforcement practice contributes to removing administrative burdens from business and its enforcement practice removes barriers to entry and impediments to effective competition that seriously harm competition in the internal market. See also, e.g., Case IV/M.469, *MSG Media Service GmbH* [1994] OJ L364/1, [1994] 5 CMLR 499.

attempts by Member States to protect or create national champions in breach of the ECMR rules.[710]

Similarly, Article 2 would not appear to permit other non-competition factors such as social policy to be taken into account as part of the appraisal process.[711] One factor that should not be overlooked, however, is that the final decision to clear or prohibit a concentration following a Phase II merger investigation is made by the College of Commissioners and not simply the Commissioner responsible for competition.[712] This means that in controversial or politically charged cases lobbying of the Commissioners takes place. This has led to concern that, even where DG Comp concentrates exclusively on competition criteria in its assessment, that these competition factors may be overridden by other policy considerations when the final decision is taken. Indeed, some high-profile merger cases appear to have caused a clash between proponents of industrial policy and supporters of a competition policy based strictly on competition factors alone.[713] The case of *Aérospatiale-Alenia/de Havilland*,[714] for example, appeared to cause considerable political controversy between those that supported the transaction from an industrial point of view,[715] and others, including the then Competition Commissioner, Sir Leon Brittan, that were opposed to the merger, believing that it would lead to the creation of a dominant position which would operate as a significant impediment to competition.[716] The Commission's eventual decision to prohibit the merger[717] was not a universally popular one and met with wide coverage in the media. The final decision to block the merger in *MSG/Media Services GmbH*[718] was also controversial and came under fierce attack for impeding the

In this case the Commission refused to clear a joint venture formed between two German media companies and the German State telecommunications company to operate in the pay-TV market. MSG was to provide administrative and technical services for the provision of pay-TV and multimedia and interactive services (services hitherto unavailable in the market place). The Commission rejected the argument that the creation of the joint venture would contribute to technical and economic development, the development of digital TV. It pointed out that the reference to technical and economic progress was subject to the reservation that no obstacle to competition be formed. In this case the concentration was likely to seal off the market and lead to an early creation of a dominant position. The concentration would therefore substantially hinder effective competition on the future market for pay-TV.

[710] See *supra* nn. 256 and 257 and accompanying text. Two mergers in the energy sector which would have created national energy champions were only cleared by the Commission subject to compliance with significant remedies, see Case COMP/M.3868 *DONG/Elsam/Energi E2* and Case COMP/M.4180 *Gaz de France/Suez*.

[711] Subject to a teleological interpretation being given to the provision, see *supra* Chaps. 2 and 4.

[712] See *supra* Chap. 2.

[713] This has led in the past to a call for an independent European Cartel Office to be created, which would be seen to operate independently and free from political constraints. Discussions in favour of an independent European Cartel Office (ECO) arose mainly out of fear that merger decisions would be taken not on competition grounds but on the grounds of short-term political considerations. The main support for the ECO has come from Germany. The former head of the German Bundeskartellamt, Wolfgang Kartte, was a strong supporter of an independent competition tribunal, e.g., it has been suggested that the ECO could be modelled on the German competition authority, the Bundeskartellamt. In view of the need for agreement from all Member States and for, amongst many other things, complicated Treaty amendments it seems unlikely that the ECO dream will ever by realized. See also *infra*, Chap. 14.

[714] Case IV/M.53, [1991] OJ L334/42, [1992] 4 CMLR M2.

[715] It seems that the French and Italian Governments, the (then) Commissioner for Industry, Martin Bangemann, and the then President of the Commission, Jacques Delors, supported the concentration.

[716] The concentration would not face effective competition from existing competitors and there was no realistic possibility of new competitors entering the market in the foreseeable future.

[717] The vote was only narrowly won, by 9–7 (one abstention).

[718] Case IV/M.469, [1994] OJ L364/1, [1994] 5 CMLR 499.

development of the European multi-media sector.[719] In *Mannesmann/Vallourec/Ilva*,[720] it appears that industrial considerations may have ultimately influenced the College of Commissioners' final decision to authorize a merger[721] but in *Volvo/Scania*[722] the Commission prohibited a merger that would create a leading European player in the market for trucks.

Although therefore DG Comp does not appear, overtly at least, to allow industrial criteria to prevail in merger policy, such criteria and other political factors may possibly arise at the final stage, the decision of the College of Commissioners.[723] Decisions of the Commission must, of course, be taken on legitimate grounds and be adequately justified and reasoned. A decision which is not so taken may be subject to judicial review proceedings before the court.[724]

c. Other Policy where the Concentration does not Significantly Impede Effective Competition

It is clear from the ECMR that a concentration which does not significantly impede effective competition must be declared to be compatible with the common market.[725] It has already been seen, however, that in such cases steps may nonetheless be taken by the authorities of the individual Member States to preclude the merger or aspects of the merger where necessary to protect their legitimate interests or essential interests of security.[726]

E. ARTICLE 2(4), (5), JOINT VENTURES[727]

The review of joint ventures[728] under the ECMR is potentially bi-partite. It is first necessary to determine whether or not the JV significantly impedes effective competition in the common market or a substantial part of it.[729] Secondly, it is necessary to determine whether the joint

[719] The Commission considered that the joint venture would create a durable dominant position in the market for administrative and technical services which would prevent future competition in this market and that this position would further strengthen the position of the parents in the markets for pay and cable TV. Again it seems that the Competition Commissioner faced strong opposition to the decision not only from, then, DGIII (Industry) but also from, then, DGXIII (Telecommunications, Information Market and Exploitation of Research). It was believed that the merger would lead to the creation of a European-based world telecommunications player.

[720] Case IV/M.315, [1994] OJ L102/15, [1994] 4 CMLR 529.

[721] In this case, it seems that the Merger Task Force wished to prohibit the merger which it considered would lead to the creation of a collective dominant position (held by the concentration, DMV, and its main competitor, Sandvik) on the Western European market for seamless steel tubes. A majority of the Advisory Committee on Concentrations agreed with the Commission's draft decision to this effect, [1994] OJ C111/6. However, the case caused political controversy and the deal was strongly supported by the Commissioner responsible for industry. The College of Commissioners was deadlocked. Since the Commission had not voted to prohibit the merger, the decision was rewritten to avoid clearance by default (which would have occurred had the Commissioners failed to deliver a formal decision in time).

[722] COMP/M.1672, see *supra* 1023.

[723] See, e.g., W. Sauter, *Competition Law and Industrial Policy in the EU* (Clarendon Press, 1997), 140.

[724] See *infra* 1084–8 and Chap. 14.

[725] ECMR, Art. 2(2).

[726] See *supra* 985–8.

[727] From 1998 to April 2002, Article 2(4) cases were designated as 'JV' cases and were often handled outside of the, then, MTF. Since April 2002 they are designated and have been handled like other merger cases within the merger network.

[728] All jointly controlled full-function joint ventures established on a lasting basis which have a Community dimension fall for assessment under the ECMR.

[729] ECMR, Art. 2(2) and (3). See G. A. Zonnekeyn, 'The treatment of joint ventures under the amended EC Merger Regulation' [1998] *ECLR* 414 and J. Temple Lang, 'International Joint Ventures under Community Law' [1999] *Fordham Corporate L Inst* 465.

venture will lead to the coordination of the competitive behaviour of undertakings which remain independent on any particular market (these joint ventures would previously have fallen for assessment not under the ECMR but under Article 81).[730] This may well occur if two or more of the parents compete in an upstream or downstream market or in the market of the JV itself. Where a joint venture does have such cooperative effects section 10 of Form CO requires that the parties should provide additional information about their activities in these markets.

If the object or effect of the joint venture is to co-ordinate the independent undertakings' behaviour Article 2(4) and (5) of the ECMR provides that these coordinative aspects of the joint venture will be appraised in accordance with criteria set out in Article 81(1) and (3):

4. To the extent that the creation of a joint venture constituting a concentration pursuant to Article 3 has as its object or effect the co-ordination of the competitive behaviour of undertakings that remain independent, such co-ordination shall be appraised in accordance with the criteria of Article 81(1) and (3) of the Treaty, with a view to establishing whether or not the operation is compatible with the common market.

5. In making this appraisal, the Commission shall take into account in particular:

— whether two or more parent companies retain, to a significant extent, activities in the same market as the joint venture or in a market which is downstream or upstream from that of the joint venture or in a neighbouring market closely related to this market,

— whether the co-ordination which is the direct consequence of the creation of the joint venture affords the undertakings concerned the possibility of eliminating competition in respect of a substantial part of the products or services in question.

These provisions thus require the Commission to consider whether two or more parents companies retain significant activities in the same market as the joint venture or in downstream, upstream or neighbouring market (the identification of candidate markets), and whether any coordination which is the direct consequence of the creation of the joint venture affords the undertakings concerned the possibility of eliminating competition in respect of a substantial part of the products or services in question. There must therefore be a causal link between the setting up of the joint venture and the appreciable restriction of competition on the market.[731]

There is no Commission guidance on the application of Article 2(4) and (5) to joint venture cases. For guidance it is therefore necessary to look at previous joint venture cases decided under the ECMR and relevant guidance on the application of Article 81 to horizontal cooperation agreements.[732] The Commission's decisions under the ECMR appear, perhaps, to display a more economically realistic approach than that which has been displayed in its Article 81 decisions.[733]

In *Telia/Telenor/Schibsted*[734] the Commission considered a joint venture for the provision of various Internet services. The Commission considered that the parents remained active on two markets in which co-ordinated behaviour might be possible. In particular both Telia and Telor remained present on the market to provide 'dial-up' internet access. Although the parents

---

[730] See *supra* 962 ff.

[731] See, e.g., Case IV/JV.2, *ENEL/DT/FT*. This case concerned a joint venture for fixed telephony in Italy. The Commission concluded that the likelihood of any coordination between the parents on the mobile market outside the joint venture (e.g., in France and Germany) would be due not to the joint venture at issue but to links and joint ventures previously concluded between the parties.

[732] Commission Guidelines on the application of Article 81 to horizontal cooperation agreements [2001] OJ C3/2, [2001] 4 CMLR 819, Commission Notice on agreements of minor importance which do not appreciably restrict competition under Article 81(1) [2001] OJ C368/13, [2002] 4 CMLR 699, the Commission's Guidelines on the application of Article 81(3) [2004] OJ C101/97.

[733] See *supra* Chap. 4 and *infra* Chap. 13.

[734] Case IV/JV.2, [1999] 4 CMLR 216.

already had joint market shares of between 35 per cent and 65 per cent of the market it was concluded that coordinated behaviour between the parents was not likely. These market shares were not significant on the growing market for dial up Internet access in Sweden. The market was characterized by high growth, low barriers to entry, and low switching costs. On the other market, the web site production market, the parent companies and the joint venture had less than 10 per cent of the market. Any coordination on such a market would not amount to appreciable restriction of competition.[735]

Nonetheless the Commission has, in some cases, accepted conditions and obligations to deal with coordination concerns. In *Fujitsu/Siemens*,[736] for example, the parties' agreement to create a joint venture to develop, manufacture, distribute, market and sell desktop computers did not have a significant impact on competition. The Commission did have concerns, however, about the effect that the merger would have on the parents' activities in a number of upstream and downstream markets. In particular, the Commission considered that the structure of the 'financial workstation'[737] market made coordination between the parents in financial workstations likely. The parties, however, proposed a remedy to resolve the problem identified and the Commission cleared the concentration subject to conditions and obligations.

Case IV/JV.22, *Fujitsu/Siemens*

63. For the reasons set forth below, the financial workstations market displays several structural characteristics, which make co-ordination between the parents in financial workstations likely. First, the market is highly concentrated with NCR, Siemens and Fujitsu accounting for a share of sales of approximately 70 per cent;. Second, NCR and Siemens together with Fujitsu have roughly symmetrical market shares. Third, the remaining competitors all have market shares, which do not exceed 10 per cent. Fourth, the technology for financial workstations is relatively mature, as the technology needed to operate financial workstations tends to be standard personal computer-based technology.

64. Any co-ordination between the parent companies would furthermore be appreciable. Both parties will jointly hold a share of sales of [20–40] per cent and will be the second biggest competitor next to NCR, which accounts for [30–40] per cent of the financial workstations market. In light of the almost symmetrical market shares of the two major groups in the financial workstations market and the resulting relationship of interdependence existing between NCR and Siemens/Fujitsu, taken as a group, any co-ordination between the parties appears likely to cause the elimination of competition in respect of a substantial part of the financial workstations market.

65. Co-ordination between the parent companies will also have an effect on trade between Member States. Both Siemens and Fujitsu are EEA-wide operators in financial workstations with activities covering all the major Member States of the EEA. Any alteration of their competitive behaviour would have an effect on intra-Community trade in financial workstations.

66. When these concerns were communicated to the parties, Siemens offered a remedy in order to remove the competitive concerns raised by the operation with regard to the EEA-wide financial workstations market.

---

[735] See *supra* Chap. 4 and *infra* Chap. 13.

[736] Case IV/JV.22.

[737] ATMs and cash dispensers.

> 67. In two letters dated 15 and 23 September 1999, respectively, Siemens undertakes the following:
>
> '(i) Siemens announced, in November 1998 its intention to sell off its retail and banking systems business. This will be done through the sale of all its shares in Siemens Nixdorf Retail and Banking Systems GmbH (based in Paderborn) and the sales of all respective business activities abroad to be carved out of regional legal entities (the "Retail and Banking System Business"); ...
>
>   Siemens commits itself to selling the Retail and Banking Systems Business ... '
>
> ...
>
> 69. The undertaking given by Siemens removes the Commission's concern that the creation of the JVC has as its effect the co-ordination of the competitive behaviour of Siemens and Fujitsu in the financial workstations market. The undertaking to divest Siemens' Retail and Banking Systems Business within ..., removes the incentive to co-ordinate its behaviour with that of Fujitsu [...]. After divestment ..., the financial workstation market will no longer be a candidate market for co-ordination within the meaning of Article 2(4) of the Merger Regulation.

In *BT/AT&T*[738] the coordinative aspects of a joint venture were also appraised by the Commission, this time in Phase II proceedings. Again, commitments were required to address the anti-competitive coordinative effects identified.

The methodology adopted by the Commission in these cases appears to be to consider (1) whether or not the creation of the joint venture has the object of coordinating the behaviour of the parents; and (2) it does not, whether or not this is its effect. In making this latter determination the Commission identifies candidate markets, considers whether coordination is likely on those markets, and whether the coordination would appreciably restrict competition and affect trade between Member States. The Commission did not consider Article 81(3) elements in *Fujitsu/Siemens* or *BT/AT&T* as in both cases the parties put forward remedies to deal with the Article 81(1) problems identified.

F. RESTRICTIONS DIRECTLY RELATED AND NECESSARY TO THE CONCENTRATION

Ancillary restraints are clauses the presence of which is vital to the particular concentration since the transaction, in its absence, would not take place. For example, it is usually a condition of a sale of a business that the vendor covenants not to compete with the business for a period of time. Otherwise the goodwill of the business may be rendered valueless.[739] Similarly, in joint ventures the parents may agree to license intellectual property rights to the joint venture and perhaps not to compete with the joint venture. Both the old and current ECMR have made it clear that restrictions directly related and necessary to the implementation of the concentration ('ancillary restraints') may be cleared along with the concentration.[740] To the extent that the restrictions are ancillary, the ECMR alone thus applies to them.[741] By contrast, Article 81 and 82 remain applicable to restrictions that cannot be considered to be ancillary.

---

[738] Case IV/JV.15.

[739] See also, e.g., the discussion of ancillary restraints *supra* Chap. 4.

[740] But see *infra* n. 1076.

[741] ECMR, Art. 21(1).

Prior to 2001 the Commission used to clear ancillary restraints concluded in agreements between undertakings in its decision to clear the concentration as a whole. It thus considered the concentration and ancillary restraints together.[742] In 2001 the Commission issued a replacement Notice regarding restrictions directly related and necessary to concentrations[743] which marked a significant change in practice by the Commission. Not only did it make it clear that Commission did not intend to make an assessment of restrictions directly related and necessary to the concentration in its merger decisions any longer, but it adopted a narrower view of when such restrictions could be considered to be ancillary to the concentration. Although the CFI held in *Lagadère SCA v. Canal+SA v. Commission*[744] that the practice of not assessing the restraints in individual cases was not consistent with the Commission's obligations under the original ECMR, the wording of the new ECMR has been altered to legitimize this practice. It now provides that Commission's clearance decisions (under both Phase I and II) 'shall be deemed to cover' restrictions directly related and necessary to the implementation of the concentration ('ancillary restraints').[745] The 2001 Notice was replaced by a new Notice in 2004.[746]

The Commission's Notices have been of critical importance since they provide guidance as to when ancillary restraints are automatically covered by the Commission's clearance decisions. Where the restraints do not fall within that permitted by the Notice the parties risk being unable to enforce the provision if it is subsequently found to be incompatible with Community law. If the notice does not provide guidance on a particular restraint and there is no other guidance to be found in decisional practice, the parties may apply to the Commission for individual assessment. The Commission may assess the ancillary restraints if the case presents 'novel and unresolved questions giving rise to genuine uncertainty'.[747]

The Commission's 2004 Notice set out both general principles[748] and principles applicable to commonly encountered restrictions in cases of acquisition of an undertaking,[749] and joint venture cases.[750] With regard to restrictions agreed in relation to the transfer of an undertaking the Commission states, for example, that non-competition obligations on the vendor are generally justified for periods of up to two or three years (three, where both goodwill and know-how are included in the transfer).[751] Non-competition clauses are not considered necessary when the transfer is limited to physical assets or to exclusive industrial and commercial property rights.[752] Any non-competition clause should ordinarily be limited to the products and services forming the economic activity of the undertaking transferred and the geographical area in

---

[742] ECMR, Art. 8(2). See also Article 6(1).

[743] [1990] OJ C203/5.

[744] Case T-251/00, [2002] ECR II-4825, [2003] 4 CMLR 965. See D. Sinclair, 'Ancillary Restraints under the Merger Regulation: The Commission's approach cast into doubt by the Court of First Instance' [2003] *ECLR* 315.

[745] ECMR Arts. 6(1)(b) and 8(1) and (2) and recital 21. The Commission states that '[t]his reflects the intention of the legislator not to oblige the Commission to assess and individually address ancillary restraints', July 2004, para. 2.

[746] [2005] OJ C56/24.

[747] ECMR, recital 21. See also the Commission's Notice on restrictions directly related and necessary to concentrations [2005] OJ C56/24, paras. 3–6.

[748] Commission Notice on restrictions directly related and necessary to concentrations, [2005] OJ C56/24 part II.

[749] *Ibid.*, part III.

[750] *Ibid.*, part IV.

[751] *Ibid.*, para. 20. The Commission evaluates non-solicitation and confidentiality clauses in the same way as non-competition clauses, para. 26.

[752] *Ibid.*, para. 21.

which the vendor offered them.[753] Licences of patents, similar rights, or know-how and purchase and supply obligations may also be considered necessary to the implementation of the concentration.[754] In the context of joint venture agreements, the Commission considers that non-competition obligations between the parent undertakings and a joint venture may be directly related and necessary to the concentration for the lifetime of the joint venture where the obligations correspond to the products, services and territories covered by the joint venture agreement or its by-laws.[755] Further, it may be legitimate for the parents to grant intellectual property right licences to the joint venture (whether granted exclusively, for a period of time, or whether a field of use restriction is incorporated), for licences to be granted by the joint venture to one of the parents, for cross-licences to be granted, or for purchase and supply agreements to be concluded by the parent undertakings and the joint venture. Licence agreements between the parents are not ancillary to the implementation of the joint venture.[756]

E. COMMITMENTS OR REMEDIES

(i) Legal Basis and Time Periods

In many cases where the Commission considers that a concentration will significantly impede effective competition and is in a position to demonstrate that the concentration cannot be declared compatible with the common market, the parties may propose modifications to the original concentration plan and offer commitments to the Commission. It is crucial, however, that the commitments offered are full and effective and satisfy the Commission that the remedies are sufficient to restore the conditions of effective competition in the common market on a permanent basis.[757] The legal basis for the acceptance of such commitments or remedies is set out in the ECMR itself. Recital 30 of the Regulation provides:

Where the undertakings concerned modify a notified concentration, in particular by offering commitments with a view to rendering the concentration compatible with the common market, the Commission should be able to declare the concentration, as modified, compatible with the common market. Such commitments should be proportionate to the competition problem and entirely eliminate it. It is also appropriate to accept commitments before the initiation of proceedings where the competition problem is readily identifiable and can easily be remedied. It should be expressly provided that the Commission may attach to its decision conditions and obligations in order to ensure that the undertakings concerned comply with their commitments in a timely and effective manner so as to render the concentration compatible with the common market. Transparency and effective consultation of Member States as well as of interested third parties should be ensured throughout this procedure.

More particularly, both Article 6(2) and 8(2) provide that the Commission may find, following modification, that the concentration is compatible with the common market and 'may attach to its decision ... conditions and obligations intended to ensure that the undertakings concerned comply with the commitments they have entered into vis-à-vis the Commission with a view to rendering the concentration compatible with the common market.'

---

[753] *Ibid.*, paras. 22–3.

[754] *Ibid.*, paras. 27–35.

[755] *Ibid.*, para. 36.

[756] *Ibid.*, paras. 42–3.

[757] The Commission does not, otherwise, have power to authorize a concentration which has been found to be incompatible with the common market.

Commitments may, therefore, be submitted and accepted both at Phase I, prior to initiation of proceedings, and in Phase II proceedings. 'However, given the fact that an in-depth market investigation is only carried out in phase II, commitments submitted to the Commission in phase I must be sufficient to clearly rule out "serious doubts" within the meaning of Article 6(1)(c)'.[758] Clearly, the Commission has significant bargaining power at this first stage of the proceedings, and the parties may have to be prepared to give up more at this stage if they wish to prevent the transaction being taken through to second phase proceedings. In contrast, in Phase II cases, the commitments must be sufficient to ensure that the concentration would not significantly impede effective competition. It is for the Commission, if it wants to reject the commitments, to demonstrate that the remedies offered do not resolve the competition concerns identified. It is not, therefore, for the parties to prove that their commitments eliminate the competition concerns identified.[759]

Commitments must be offered within specified periods of time, 20 working days of notification in Phase I proceedings and within 65 working days of the initiation of proceedings in Phase II proceedings.[760] Where commitments are submitted within the stipulated time frame, then, if offered in Phase I, the time period for examining the concentration is extended by 10 working days and, where offered in Phase II, the time period may be extended by 15 working days.[761] In very complex cases, a further extension of up to 20 working days may be agreed in Phase II.[762] The time periods for both submitting the remedies and for the Commission to make its decision are tight, which means that commitments should be considered very early on in the procedure and, generally, prior to notification.

The Commission tests the commitments submitted by taking them to the market.[763] Indeed, the Regulation specifically provides that transparency must be maintained and Member States and interested third parties should be consulted.[764] Third parties, competitors, suppliers, and customers are, therefore, heavily involved in the process. The Commission generally prefers to find a solution along these lines than to have to prohibit the merger outright.[765] The parties' ability to influence the outcome of the decision is, therefore, significant. In cases raising serious competition problems, however, the commitments may have to substantially modify the terms and conditions of the transaction.

(ii) The Commission's Notice on Remedies Acceptable under the ECMR

In 2001 the Commission issued a Notice on remedies acceptable ('the Remedies Notice),[766] which sets out the general principles applicable to remedies acceptable to the Commission and

---

[758] The Remedies Notices, [2001] OJ C6/3, para. 11.

[759] See e.g. Case T-87/05, *EDP v. Commission* [2005] ECR II-3745, paras. 65–69.

[760] Reg. 802/2004, [2004] OJ L13/1, Art. 19 (1) and (2). The latter period can be extended by up to a period of 20 working days where the time period for the investigation is so extended pursuant to Art. 10(3), see *supra* nn. 354 and 355 and accompanying text.

[761] Only if offered after the 54th working day.

[762] See *supra* nn. 345 and 346.

[763] An enforcement unit within the merger network advises on the acceptability and implementation of commitments.

[764] ECMR, recital 30. See also Cases C-68/94 and C-30/95, *France v. Commission, Société Commerciale des Potasses et de l'Azote (SCPA) v. Commission* [1998] ECR I-1375, [1998] 4 CMLR 829.

[765] See the statistics set out *infra* section 6.

[766] 'The Remedies Notice' [2001] OJ C6/3. See also the Commission's Merger Remedies Study, IP/05/327, available at http://ec.europa.eu/comm/competition/mergers/legislation/notices_on_substance.html#remedies

provides guidance on the types of commitments which may be suitable to resolve the competition concerns raised by a concentration, the procedure governing such commitments and the main requirements for implementation of commitments. The Notice reflects the Commission's experience regarding their assessment, acceptance, and implementation. Part II of the Notice sets out general principles, part III deals with types of remedy acceptable to the Commission, part IV sets out where remedies are difficult, if not impossible, part V deals with specific requirements for submission of commitments and part VI deals with implementation of commitments. Remedies may have to be implemented over a lengthy period (known as Phase III), particularly where behavioural remedies are involved.

In April 2007, the Commission launched a consultation on a draft revised Commission Notice on remedies acceptable under the ECMR.[767] The draft notice modifies the 2001 notice in the light of extensive study it published in 2005 on the implementation and effectiveness of remedies,[768] judgments of the ECMR and the provisions of the recast ECMR adopted in 2004.

(iii) Types of Commitments

Commitments concluded may relate to the *structure* of the concentration or to the *behaviour* of the parties, i.e., they may be structural or behavioural. A structural remedy ordinarily requires divestiture of the activities of an existing viable business that can operate on a stand-alone-basis. Alternatively, a commitment by the parties to terminate exclusive agreements which would otherwise have foreclosure effects, post-merger, or remedies to facilitate market entry through the grant to competitors of access to infrastructure, platforms, key technology, production or R&D facilities, or through the licensing of intellectual property rights might have a sufficient effect on the market to restore effective competition.

Although the Commission prefers structural remedies, the key requirement is that the commitments should ensure the effective competitive structure of the market and 'are capable of rendering the notified transaction compatible with the common market'.[769] In practice, a structural solution, such as a commitment to sell a subsidiary may be preferable, since the commitment may prevent the impediment to effective competition arising and it does not require medium or long-term monitoring measures.[770] Further, behavioural remedies may be extremely difficult to control and enforce.[771] It could also be that a structural remedy will be the only possible means of solving the structural problem caused by the creation of market power, which results in the significant impediment to effective competition.[772]

In some situations, no remedy may be adequate to deal with the adverse effects identified or may be so complex that the Commission cannot determine with the required degree of certainty that effective competition will be restored.[773] In *Schneider/Legrand*,[774] for example, the Commission prohibited concentrations even though the parties submitted commitments. In the latter case the parties twice submitted remedies which the Commission rejected, the second

---

[767] The draft Notice is available on DG Comp's web site, at http://ec.europa.eu/comm/competition/mergers/legislation/merger_remedies.html.

[768] IP/05/1327.

[769] Case T-10/96, *Gencor Ltd v. Commission* [1999] ECR II-753, [1999] 4 CMLR 971, para. 318.

[770] *Ibid.*, para. 319.

[771] See Case IV/M.490, *Nordic Satellite Distribution* [1990] OJ L53/21, [1995] CMLR 258 where the Commission rejected the undertakings offered by the parties on these grounds.

[772] See Case IV/M.469, *MSG Media Service GmbH* [1994] OJ L364/1, [1994] 5 CMLR 499, para. 99.

[773] The Remedies Notice [2001] OJ C68/3, paras. 31–2.

[774] Case COMP/M.2282.

time on the ground that they were too complex and did not address the Commission's concerns. On appeal, however, the CFI considered that the Commission had not clearly identified its concerns in its statement of objections. Consequently, the parties had been unable to put forward proposals for divestiture capable of rendering the concentration compatible with the common market. The effect of the Commission's irregularities was particularly serious as the Commission had made it clear that remedies were the only means of preventing the concentration falling under Article 2(3) of the Regulation and being declared incompatible. The decision was thus vitiated by the infringement of the rights of defence and annulled.[775]

(iv) Structural Remedies: Divestiture

The most effective means of restoring effective competition may be through divestiture of a subsidiary or production facilities and the creation of a new competitive entity. The divestiture gives a new or existing competitor the possibility of gaining access to the market.[776] In such cases the Commission will wish to ensure that the activities, consisting of a viable business which can operate on a stand-alone-basis and compete effectively with the merged entity on a lasting basis, are divested to a suitable purchaser within a specified time period. Sometimes the Commission may require the parties to find a buyer prior to completion of the notified operation (an upfront buyer or fix-it-first (where a buyer is identified and a binding agreement is concluded prior to the Commission's clearance decision)).[777] The sale of the entity may itself amount to a notifiable concentration. In some circumstances the Commission may also or alternatively require one of the parties to divest itself of a structural link which it has with another competitor on the market, perhaps through the operation of a joint venture.[778]

In *Nestlé/Perrier*[779] the Commission concluded that the proposed merger would create a dominant position as a result of which effective competition would be impeded in a substantial part of the common market. However, the commitments offered by Nestlé enabled the Commission to declare the concentration to be compatible with the common market. Broadly, Nestlé promised to sell several minor brands, not to BSN, but to a third party.[780] This was intended to facilitate the entry of a viable competitor with adequate resources in the bottled water market, or to increase the capacity of an existing competitor, so that such a competitor could effectively compete with Nestlé and BSN on the French bottled water market.[781] Behavioural remedies were also taken with the aim of reducing the transparency of the market. In *Totalfina/Elf Aquiatine*[782] a divestiture remedy was rejected on the grounds that it would not create an alternative competitor sufficient to address the competition concerns. Usually tight deadlines are set within which the divestiture must occur and the commitments will set out specific details and procedures relating to the Commission's oversight of the divestiture, in particular, approval of the trustee and approval of the purchaser and purchase agreement.[783]

---

[775] Case T-310/01, *Schneider Electric SA v. Commission* [2002] ECR II-4071, [2003] 4 CMLR 768, paras. 421–63.

[776] The Remedies Notice [2001] OJ C68/3, para. 13.

[777] See, e.g., Case COMP/M.2060, *Bosc/Rexroth*.

[778] See, e.g., Case COMP/M.1845, *Time Warner/AOL* I/00/1145.

[779] Case IV/M.190, [1992] OJ L35/1, [1993] 4 CMLR M17.

[780] See also, e.g., Case IV/M.430, *Procter and Gamble/ VP Schickedanz* [1994] OJ L356/32, [1994] 5 CMLR 499.

[781] [1992] OJ L356/1, [1993] 4 CMLR M17, paras. 136–8.

[782] Case IV/M.1628, *aff'd* on appeal, Case T-342/02, *Petrolessence and SGR2 v. Commission* [2002] ECR II-67, [2003] 5 CMLR 8.

[783] The Remedies Notice [2001] OJ C68/3, part IV deals with requirements for implementation of commitments. See also the Best Practice Guidelines which provide standard model texts for divestiture commitments and for trustee mandates.

The Commission sometimes accepts alternative remedies packages, recognizing that the parties' preferred divestiture option may be uncertain or difficult to complete. It may therefore accept the preferred divestiture package on condition that an alternative is available which is equally effective. The Commission explains alternative divestiture commitments and 'crown jewels' in its 2007 draft Remedies Notice.

1.4 Alternative Divestiture commitments: Crown Jewels

44. In certain cases, the implementation of the parties' preferred divestiture option (of a viable business solving the competition concerns) might be uncertain in view of third parties' pre-emption rights or uncertainty as to the transferability of key contracts, intellectual property rights, or the uncertainty to find a suitable purchaser. Nevertheless, the parties may consider that they would be able to divest this business to a suitable purchaser within a very short time period.

45. In such circumstances, the Commission cannot take the risk that, in the end, effective competition will not be maintained. Accordingly, the Commission will only accept such divestiture commitments under the following conditions; (a) absent the uncertainty, the first divestiture proposed in the commitments would consist of a viable business, and (b) the parties will have to propose a second alternative divestiture which the parties will be obliged to implement if they are not able to implement the first commitment. Such an alternative commitment normally has to be a "crown jewel", *i.e.*, it should be at least as good as the first proposed divestiture in terms of creating a viable competitor once implemented, it should not involve any uncertainties as to its implementation and it should be capable of being implemented quickly in order to avoid that the overall implementation period exceeds what would normally be regarded as acceptable in the conditions of the market in question. In order to limit the risk in the interim period, it is indispensable that interim preservation and holding separate measure apply to all assets included in both divestiture alternatives. Furthermore, the commitment has to establish clear criteria and a strict timetable as to how and when the alternative divestiture obligation will become effective and the Commission will require shorter periods for its implementation.

46. If there is uncertainty as to the implementation of the divestiture due to third party rights or as to finding a suitable purchaser crown jewel commitments and up-front buyers as discussed below in paragraphs 54 address the same concerns, and the parties may therefore choose between both structures.

Divestiture commitments may also be used for removing links between the parties and competitors where these links contribute to competitive concerns raised by the merger.[784]

(v) Other Remedies: Access Remedies, Behavioural Commitments and 'Remedy Packages'

It has already been seen that divestiture is not the only remedy acceptable to the Commission. The Commission deals with 'other' possible remedies in its Remedies Notice.

26. Whilst being the preferred remedy, divestiture is not the only remedy acceptable to the Commission. First, there may be situations where a divestiture of a business is impossible. Secondly, competition problems can also result from specific features, such as the existence of exclusive agreements, the combination of networks ('network effects') or the combination of key patents. In such circumstances, the Commission has to determine whether or not other types of remedy may have a sufficient effect on the market to restore effective competition.

27. The change in the market structure resulting from a proposed concentration can cause existing contractual arrangements to be inimical to effective competition. This is in particular true for exclusive long-term supply and distribution agreement if such agreement limit the market potential

---

[784] See e.g. Case IV/M.492 *VEBA/Degusa*, Case COMP/M.3653 *Siemens/VA Tech.*

available for competitors. Where the merged entity will have a considerable market share, the fore-closure effects resulting from **existing exclusive agreements** may contribute to the creation of a dominant position. In such circumstances, the termination of existing exclusive agreements may be considered appropriate to eliminate the competitive concerns if there is clearly no evidence that de facto exclusivity is being maintained.

28. The change in the market structure resulting from a proposed concentration can lead to major barriers or impediments to entry into the relevant market. Such barriers may arise from control over infrastructure, in particular networks, of key technology including patents, know-how or other intel-lectual property rights. In such circumstances, remedies may aim at facilitating market entry by ensuring that competitions will have **access to the necessary infrastructure** or **key technology**.

29. Where the competition problem is created by control over key technology, a divestiture of such technology is the preferable remedy as it eliminates a lasting relationship between the merged entity and its competitors. However, the Commission may accept licensing arrangements (preferably exclu-sive licences without any field-of-use restrictions on the licensee) as an alternative to divestiture where, for instance, a divestiture would have impeded efficient, on-going research. The Commission has pursued this approach in mergers involving, for example, the pharmaceutical industry.

30. Owing to the specifics of the competition problems raised by a given concentration in several markets, the parties may have to offer **remedy packages** which compromise a combination of divestiture remedies and other remedies that facilitate market entry by granting network access or access to specific content. Such packages may be appropriate to remedy specific foreclosure prob-lems arising, for instance, in concentrations in the telecommunication and media sectors. In addition, there may be transactions affecting mainly one product market where, however only a package including a variety of commitments will be able to remedy the competitive concerns raised by the specific concentration on an overall basis.

Other commitments are thus frequently offered and accepted, such as access remedies, change of long-term exclusive contracts and other behaviour commitments.[785] The thrust of such commitments is often aimed at opening market for competitors, for example, through giving access to infrastructure[786] or key technology. The parties may also have to make commitments as to 'interoperability'. In *GE/Instrumentarium*,[787] for example, the Commission was concerned about the effect of the merger in the perioperative monitors market and also that the parties could take steps to ensure that competitors' critical care and patient monitors could not inter-operate with its anaesthesia equipment. GE adopted a package of measures, divestiture of a company, and a series of supply agreement with its acquirer, to deal with the horizontal over-laps and to ensure the emergence of an effective competitor to the merged entity on the periop-erative monitors market. It also undertook to provide the electrical and mechanical interface for third parties' patient monitors to be able to interconnect with its own anaesthesia equipment.

Behavioural commitments may often be appropriate in cases involving the creation of a collective dominant position. In *Kali und Salz/Md/Treuhand*,[788] for example, the parties to the concentration offered to sever links with its main competitor, SCPA (which were considered to facilitate anti-competitive behaviour on the oligopolistic market).[789]

---

[785] Case IV/M.877, *Boeing/McDonnell Douglas* [1997] OJ L336/16, [1997] 5 CMLR 270. Further, the Commission also required Boeing to make some of its intellectual property rights available, through licences, to competitors.

[786] See, e.g., IV/JV.37, *BSkyB/Kirsch*.

[787] Case COMP/M.3083, IP/03/1193.

[788] Case IV/M.308, [1994] OJ L186/30; on appeal Cases C-68/94 and C-30/95, *France v. Commission, Société Commerciale des Potasses et de l'Azote (SCPA) v. Commission* [1998] ECR I-1375, [1998] 4 CMLR 829.

[789] Their imposition was one of the factors which caused SCPA and France to challenge, successfully, the legitimacy of the Commission's decision.

In *GE/Honeywell*[790] and *Laval/Sidel*[791] the parties offered commitments to abstain from certain commercial behaviour (e.g. bundling products) to deal with the Commission's concerns. The Commission rejected these on grounds that this was a pure promise and would involve excessive monitoring. In the *GE/Honeywell* appeals,[792] the CFI did not need to rule on the correctness of the Commission's actions in this regard as it considered that is competition assessment of the conglomerate effects contained manifest error of assessments. In *Commission v. Tetra Laval BV*,[793] however, the ECJ held that as the Commission had rejected the commitments as a matter of principle the CFI had been correct to find that this was a factor that the Commission should have taken into account when assessing the likelihood that the merged entity would act in such a way as to make it possible to create a dominant position on one of more of the relevant markets for PET equipment.

In the draft Remedies notice the Commission states 'non-structural types of remedies, such as promises by the parties to abstain from certain commercial behaviour (e.g. bundling products), will generally not eliminate the competition concerns resulting from horizontal overlaps. In any case, it may be difficult to achieve the required degree of effectiveness of such a remedy due to the absence of effective monitoring of its implementation ... Therefore, the Commission may examine other types of non-divesture remedies, such as behavioural promises, only exceptionally in specific circumstances, such as in respect of competition concerns arising in conglomerate structures'.

The broad range of packages accepted often requires the parties to be 'inventive' and to propose remedy packages which will resolve the competition problems identified by the Commission.

(vi) Other Cases

In some cases the Commission has accepted alternative remedies packages. For example, in *Nestlé/Ralston Purina*[794] the Commission accepted an 'alternative' remedy package. In particular, the Commission was concerned about the impact of the concentration in the Spanish markets for dry dog food, dry cat food and snacks and treats for cats and the Italian and Greek markets for dry cat food. With regard to Spain, the parties undertook to divest itself of its 'Friskies' brand, through the grant of exclusive licences for a substantial period and to divest itself of Spanish production plant or, if not implemented within a specified time period, alternatively, to remove the overlap in Spain by divesting itself of Ralston Purina's 50 per cent shareholding in the joint venture, Gallina Blanca Purina.

In some cases a concentration has been saved by a third party to the transaction. In *Alcatel/Telettra*,[795] for example, the Spanish telecommunications company, Telefonica, agreed to sell its interests in the parties to the concentration in order to persuade the Commission that the undertakings' potential market power would be counteracted by the countervailing exercise of monopolistic demand.

---

[790] Case COMP/M.2220.

[791] Case Comp/M.2416, annulled on appeal Case T-5/02, [2002] ECR II-4381, [2002] 5 CMLR 1182, *aff'd* Case C-12/03 [2005] ECR I-987, [2005] 4 CMLR 8.

[792] Cases T-209 and 210/01, *Honeywell v. Commission* and *General Electric Company v. Commission* [2005] ECR II-5527 and 5575.

[793] Case C-12/03, [2005] ECR I-987, [2005] 4 CMLR 8, paras. 85–9.

[794] Case IV/M.2337, IP/01/1136. See also *supra* 1081.

[795] Case IV/M.42, *Alcatel/Telettra* [1991] OJ L122/48, [1991] 4 CMLR 778.

(vii) Breach of a Condition or Obligations

Commitments consist of both 'conditions' and 'obligations'. The Commission may take a decision prohibiting the concentration where it finds that it has been implemented in contravention of a condition attached to a decision.[796] Further, the Commission may revoke a decision where the undertakings concerned commit a breach of an obligation, relating to the steps necessary to implement the commitment, attached to the decision.[797] In each case, fines may be imposed on the undertakings concerned. Further, the Commission may impose fines of up to 10 per cent of the aggregate turnover of the undertakings concerned that have failed to comply with conditions or obligations imposed[798] and periodic penalty payments on undertakings for delay caused by failure to comply with an obligation.[799]

6. ECMR STATISTICS

DG Comp produces statistics, which it updates monthly,[800] setting out what happens to merger notifications. The table below sets out the statistics up until 31 March 2007.

It can be seen from these statistics that between September 1990 and the end of March 2007 Phase II proceedings had been initiated in only 163 cases and there had, after sixteen and a half years application of the ECMR, only been nineteen prohibition decisions in total. In contrast, 3070 concentrations were cleared under Article 6.

7. APPEALS

The ECMR itself provides the Court of Justice with unlimited jurisdiction to review penalties imposed by the Commission and to cancel, reduce or increase any such fine imposed.[801] The ordinary provisions in the EC Treaty authorizing the review by the ECJ of Community acts and Community institutions' failure to act also apply.[802] A party to a concentration may, therefore, institute proceedings against a Commission merger decision under Article 230 of the Treaty. Appeals go initially to the CFI and subsequently, on points of law, to the ECJ.[803] Article 21(2) clearly envisages such a right of appeal. It provides:

Subject to review by the Court of Justice, the Commission shall have sole jurisdiction to take the decisions provided for in this Regulation.

Further, third parties, to whom a merger decision is not addressed, may appeal if it can be established that that the decision 'is of direct and individual concern to the third party'.[804] Thus a

---

[796] ECMR, Art. 8(7).

[797] *Ibid.*, Art. 6(3) and Art. 8(6).

[798] *Ibid.*, Art. 14(2)(d).

[799] *Ibid.*, Art. 15(1)(c).

[800] Available at: http://europa.eu.in/com/competitio/merger/case/stats.html.

[801] ECMR, Art. 16.

[802] See *infra* Chap. 14.

[803] But see *supra* n. 529 and accompanying text.

[804] No direct and individual concern was established in e.g. Case T-350/03, *Eirtschaftskammer Kärnten and best connect Ampere Strompool v. Commission*, 18 Sept. 2006.

European Merger Control—Council Regulation 139/2004—Statistics

21 September 1990 to 31 March 2007

I.) NOTIFICATIONS

	90	91	92	93	94	95	96	97	98	99	00	01	02	03	04	05	06	Mar 07	Total
Number of notified cases	11	64	59	59	95	110	131	168	224	276	330	335	277	211	247	313	356	102	3368
Cases withdrawn - Phase 1	0	0	3	1	6	4	5	9	5	7	8	8	3	0	3	6	7	1	76
Cases withdrawn - Phase 2	0	0	0	1	0	0	0	1	0	4	5	5	4	1	0	2	3	2	29

II.) REFERRALS

	90	91	92	93	94	95	96	97	98	99	00	01	02	03	04	05	06	Mar 07	Total
Art 4(4) request (Form RS)															2	14	13	2	31
Art 4(4) referral to Member State															2	11	13	1	27
Art 4(4) refusal of referral															0	0	0	0	0
Art 4(5) request (Form RS)															20	28	38	15	101
Art 4(5) referral accepted															16	24	39	14	93
Art 4(5) refusal of referral															2	0	0	0	2
Art 22 request	0	0	0	1	0	1	1	1	1	0	0	0	0	2	1	4	4	0	16
Art 22(3) referral (Art 22. 4 taken in conjunction with article 6 or 8 under Reg. 4064/89)	0	0	0	1	0	1	1	1	0	0	0	0	0	2	1	3	3	0	14
Art 22(3) refusal of referral																1	1	0	2
Art 9 request	0	1	1	1	1	0	3	7	4	9	4	9	8	10	4	7	6	2	77
Art 9.3 partial referral of Member State	0	0	1	0	1	0	0	6	3	2	3	6	7	1	1	3	1	1	36
Art 9.3 full referral	0	0	0	1	0	0	3	1	1	3	2	1	4	8	2	3	1	0	30
Art 9.3 refusal of referral	0	1	0	0	0	0	0	0	0	0	1	0	0	0	1	0	0	0	3

III.) FIRST PHASE DECISIONS

	90	91	92	93	94	95	96	97	98	99	00	01	02	03	04	05	06	Mar 07	Total
Art 6.1 (a) out of scope Merger Regulation	2	5	9	4	5	9	6	4	4	1	1	1	1	1	0	0	0	0	52
Art 6.1 (b) compatible	5	47	43	49	78	90	109	118	196	225	278	299	238	203	220	276	323	78	2875
Art 6.1 (b) compatible, under simplified procedure (figures included in 6.1 (b) compatible above)	0	0	0	0	0	0	0	0	0	0	41	141	103	110	137	167	207	48	954
Art 6.1 (b) in conjunction with Art 6.2 (compatible w. commitments	0	3	4	0	2	3	0	2	12	16	26	11	10	11	12	15	13	3	143

IV.) PHASE II PROCEEDINGS INITIATED

	90	91	92	93	94	95	96	97	98	99	00	01	02	03	04	05	06	Mar 07	Total
Art 6.1(c)	0	6	4	4	6	7	6	11	11	20	18	21	7	9	8	10	13	2	163

V.) SECOND PHASE DECISIONS

	90	91	92	93	94	95	96	97	98	99	00	01	02	03	04	05	06	Mar 07	Total
Art 8.1 compatible (8.2 under Reg. 4064/89)	0	1	1	1	2	2	1	1	3	0	3	5	2	2	2	2	4	0	32
Art 8.2 compatible with commitments	0	3	3	2	2	3	3	7	4	7	12	9	5	6	4	3	6	0	79
Art 8.3 prohibition	0	1	0	0	1	2	3	1	2	1	2	5	0	0	1	0	0	0	19
Art 8.4 restore effective competition	0	0	0	0	0	0	0	2	0	0	0	0	2	0	0	0	0	0	4

VI.) OTHER DECISIONS

	90	91	92	93	94	95	96	97	98	99	00	01	02	03	04	05	06	Mar 07	Total
Art 6.3 decision revoked	0	0	0	0	0	0	0	0	0	0	1	0	0	0	0	0	0	0	1
Art 8.6 decision revoked	0	0	0	0	0	0	0	0	0	0	0	0	0	0	0	0	0	0	0
Art 14 decision imposing fines	0	0	0	0	0	0	0	0	1	4	1	0	1	0	1	0	0	0	8
Art 7.3 derogation from suspension (7.4 under Reg. 4064/89)	1	1	2	3	3	2	4	5	13	7	4	7	14	8	10	6	2	0	92
Art 21	0	0	0	0	0	1	0	1	0	1	1	0	1	0	0	0	2	0	7

challenge to a merger decision may be commenced by a competitor of the merging parties,[805] or by a third party affected by commitments given in a merger decision even where the Commission clears a merger[806]

The appeals procedure is discussed more fully in Chapter 14. An important question which arises in merger cases, however, is whether there should be a fast-track procedure for appeals, as in Austria, for example. Although the Commission has to proceed within very tight time limits under the Regulation itself it may be years before a review of its decision is conducted by the Court. This, of course, puts the Commission in a powerful position.[807] Since 2001[808] an expedited procedure is available for cases (not limited to competition cases) capable of being resolved by abbreviated written procedures and a full oral procedure. The procedure, which ordinarily takes between nine to twelve months, was used, for example, in the *Philips*,[809] *Schneider*,[810] *Tetra Laval*[811] and *Impala*[812] appeals but is not available in all cases (only in straightforward cases).[813] Although the reform of the juridical procedures fell outside the scope of the 2001 ECMR review[814] the Commission is aware that the appeal process needs to be improved and speeded up.[815] It has discussed possible mechanisms for doing so, such as the introduction of a specialist competition judicial panel or merger chamber, with the CFI.[816] In the UK, a House of Lords select committee consulted on a proposal to establish a distinct competition court. It did not recommend either the creation of a separate competition court or a specialist competition chamber, however.[817]

[805] See e.g. Case T-2/93, *Air France* v. *Commission* [1994] ECR II-323, Case T-119/02, *Royal Philips Electronics* v. *Commission* [2003] ECR II-1433, [2003] 5 CMLR 53 and Case T-177/04, *easyJet Airline Co. Ltd* v. *Commission* [2006] ECR.

[806] See Cases C-68/94 and C-30/95, *France* v. *Commission, Société Commerciale des Potasses et de l'Azote (SCPA)* v. *Commission* [1998] ECR I-1375, [1998] 4 CMLR 829, paras. 173–5. See also Case T-464/04, *Independent Music Publishers and Labels Association (Impala)* v. *Commission* [2006] ECR II-2289, [2006] 5 CMLR 19, Case C-413/06 P (judgment pending).

[807] This fact may encourage the undertakings involved to give commitments to persuade the Commission to authorize the merger. Further, the parties will have to observe a prohibition or commitments imposed until the Commission's decision is suspended or annulled.

[808] [2000] OJ L322.

[809] Case T-119/02, *Royal Philips Electronics* v. *Commission* [2003] ECR II-1433, [2003] 5 CMLR 53. See also e.g. Case T-87/05 *EDP* v. *Commission* [2005] ECR II-3745.

[810] Case T-310/01, [2002] ECR II-4071, [2003] 4 CMLR 768.

[811] Case T-5/02, [2002] ECR II-4381, [2002] 5 CMLR 1182.

[812] Case T-464/04, *Independent Music Publishers and Labels Association (Impala)* v. *Commission* [2006] ECR II-2289, [2006] 5 CMLR 19, Case C-413/06 P (judgment pending). Although this case was run under the expedited procedure, judgment was not handed down until 19 months after the Commission's decision had passed. The CFI was critical of the way that Imapala had handled the case, having requested the expedited procedure and this fact was reflected in the costs order it made, see paras. 544–554.

[813] Schneider agreed to cut back its case so that the expedited procedure could be used. In both *Schneider* and *Tetra Laval* the CFI gave judgment within a period of about a year from the Commission's decision. See Chibnall, 'Expedited Treatment of Appeals against EC competition decisions under the EC Merger Control Regulation' [2002] 1 *Competition Law Journal* 327.

[814] 2001 Green Paper on the Review of Council Regulation (EEC) No. 406/89, COM(2001) 74/6 final, paras. 250–3.

[815] Where the procedure is not available appeals take around three years.

[816] See M. Monti, 'Merger Control in the European Union: a radical reform' European Commission/International Bar Association, Brussels 7 Nov. 2002, SPEECH/0/545.

[817] See recommendation of 24 April 2007.

The Court consistently stresses that when reviewing the Commission's decisions it takes full account of the wide discretion that the Regulation imposes upon the Commission and the complex economic assessments required.[818]

[I]t should be observed that the basic provisions of Regulation 4064/89,[819] in particular Article 2 thereof confer a discretion on the Commission, especially with respect to assessments of an economic nature. Consequently, review by the Community judicature of the exercise of that discretion, which is essential for defining the rules on concentrations, must take account of the discretionary margin implicit in the provisions of an economic nature which form part of the rules on concentrations (Joined Cases C68/94 and & 30/95 *France and Others* v. *EC Commission*: [1998] ECR 1375, [1998] 4 CMLR 829, paras. [223] and [224]).[820]

Despite this, in a series of cases, the Court has shown itself to be effective when reviewing the decisions adopted by the Commission. It has already been seen earlier in this chapter that in *Airtours plc* v. *Commission*,[821] *Schneider Electric SA* v. *Commission*,[822] *Tetra Laval* v. *Commission*,[823] and *Independent Music Publishers and Labels Association (Impala)* v. *Commission*[824] the CFI had no hesitation in annulling the Commission's decisions. In *Schneider* the decision was annulled on account of procedural flaws, and in many of the cases the CFI was critical of Commission findings and handling of the cases. The decisions were found to be inadequately reasoned and analysed, and not to be supported by sufficiently 'convincing' or 'cogent' evidence. Where a Commission decision is annulled, in whole or in part, the Commission has to examine the concentration 'afresh' in the light of current market conditions. This means that the parties must either put in a new notification, a supplement to the original notification, or where the notification has not become incomplete, a certification stating that there are no changes. The ordinary Phase I time procedure runs from the working day following the receipt of the new notification, supplementary notification or certification.[825]

In both My Travel (previously Airtours) and Schneider a new type of case has been commenced before the CFI. The claimants launched damages proceedings against the Commission in respect of the loss suffered in consequence of the wrongful prohibition of their proposed acquisitions.[826] In *Schneider* v. *Commission* the CFI awarded Schneider to damages in respect of two of the categories of loss claimed having found that some of the Commissions failures had manifestly and gravely disregarded the limit on its discretion.

---

[818] Cases C-68/94 and C-30/95, *France* v. *Commission, Société Commerciale des Potasses et de l'Azote (SCPA)* v. *Commission* [1998] ECR I-1375, [1998] 4 CMLR 829, paras. 223–4.

[819] Now Reg. 139/2004.

[820] Case T-221/95, *Endemol Entertainment Holding BV* v. *Commission* [1999] ECR II-1299 [1999] 5 CMLR 611.

[821] Case T-342/99, [2002] ECR II-2585, [2002] 5 CMLR 317.

[822] Case T-310/01, [2002] ECR II-4071, [2003] 4 CMLR 768

[823] Case T-5/02, [2002] ECR II-4381, [2002] 5 CMLR 1182.

[824] Case T-464/04 [2006] ECR II-2289, [2006] 5 CMLR 19, Case C-413/06 P (judgment pending).

[825] ECMR, Art. 10(5). See the discussion of the annulled decisions *supra*. For example, in the second investigation into the *Tetra Laval/Sidel* merger, Case COMP/M.2416, the merger was eventually cleared subject to commitments. Following a launch of a further Phase II investigation in the *Schneider* case, the merger was eventually abandoned, but see *infra* n. 826.

[826] Case T-212/03, *My Travel* v. *Commission* (judgment pending) and Case T-351/03, *Schneider* v. *Commission* 11 July 2007. These actions are brought under Article 288(2) EC, dealing with the non-contractual liability of the Community and raise the difficult of issue of what constitutes a serious enough error to justify a claim for compensation. For a discussion of Article 288 see, e.g., T. Hartley, *The Foundations of European Community Law* (5th edn., Oxford University Press, 2003), chap. 17.

8. INTERNATIONAL ISSUES

A. THE LONG ARM OF THE ECMR

The quantitative jurisdictional tests incorporated within the ECMR look not to the effect of the concentration on inter-State trade or on competition but to the size of the undertakings involved. So long as the Community-wide turnovers are satisfied, mergers between non-EU undertakings will be caught even though the undertakings' business is principally carried on outside the EU, even though the merger is completed outside the EU, a joint venture set up by non-EU parents has no activities in the EU,[827] the transaction has no or little impact on competition within the EU and even though the merger may have been cleared in another jurisdiction. As there is no exemption for mergers occurring outside the EU or any requirement that any of the undertakings involved is established or has substantial operations in any part of the EU,[828] the Commission's scrutiny of some mergers has been extremely politically sensitive in nature.

In 1997, for example, the Commission considered a merger announced in December 1996 between Boeing and McDonnell Douglas.[829] The merger was instigated with the encouragement of the US authorities (the Clinton administration) and had been approved by the US Federal Trade Commission in July 1997.[830] The concentration had a Community dimension and was notifiable to the Commission under EC rules irrespective of the fact that neither party had any facilities or assets in the Community. The Commission was hostile to the merger, believing that it would lead to the strengthening of Boeing's dominant position on the relevant market within the EU. In the end a political storm was saved by Boeing's offer of commitments to the Commission which resolved its competition concerns. Similarly, in *Genco/Lonrho*[831] a concentration concluded between a South African (Gencor) and UK (Lonrho) company merging business activities based in South Africa had a Community dimension and was notifiable under the EC merger rules. In this case the Commission actually prohibited the merger even though the South African Competition Board did not consider that the operation gave rise to competition concerns under South African law. Further, in *GE/Honeywell*[832], the Commission prohibited a merger which had been authorized by the US authorities.

It can be seen from these examples that a number of important issues arise in the application of the ECMR. The first is to what extent the Commission has *jurisdiction* to apply the ECMR extraterritorially to concentrations between foreign entities. The second relates to whether the provisions of the ECMR can be enforced against merging parties and third parties located

---

[827] If the parent companies, or other connected undertakings within the group, satisfy the worldwide and EU-wide turnover thresholds, the joint venture transaction will have a Community dimension and, accordingly, will require a notification to the Commission under the ECMR even if the joint venture created is not established in the EU, does not have activities in or make sales into the EU and it is not foreseeable that the joint venture will produce any direct and substantial effects in the EU.

[828] In earlier drafts of the ECMR it was a requirement that at least one of the undertakings was established in the Community and had substantial operations in one of the Member States: see Commission Proposal for a Regulation of the Council on the control of concentrations between undertakings, [1973] OJ C92/1, Art. 1(1), [1982] OJ C36/3, [1988] OJ C130/4.

[829] Case IV/M.877, [1997] OJ L336/16, [1997] 5 CMLR 270. The extraterritorial aspects of this case are discussed in greater detail *infra* in Chap. 16.

[830] The merger was cleared on 1 July 1997 without conditions: see US Federal Trade Commission Press Releases of 1 July 1997: *FTC Allows Merger of the Boeing Company and McDonnell Douglas Corporation*, 23 Sept. 1997.

[831] Case IV/M.619, [1997] OJ L11/30, [1996] 4 CMLR 742.

[832] Case COMP/M.2220, *aff'd* Cases T-209 and 210/01 *Honeywell v. Commission* and *General Electric Company v. Commission* [2005] ECR II-5527 and 5575.

outside of the EU.[833] The third relates to comity and cooperation and what steps the Community authorities have taken both to cooperate with the competition authorities of other States involved in the investigation of the same case and to avoid conflicting decisions being taken.

In *Gencor Ltd* v. *Commission*[834] the CFI had to deal with an argument which raised the right of the Commission to assert jurisdiction over the joint venture which Gencor alleged had no activities within the EU, was not implemented within the EU[835] and did not have an immediate, direct and substantial effect within the EU. The CFI, however, upheld the legality of the Commission's prohibition decision, ruling that the Commission's assertion of jurisdiction was not inconsistent with the ECMR, other Community case law or the rules of public international law.[836] Indeed, the CFI made it clear that even where there is doubt about the legality of the assertion of jurisdiction under the ECMR, compulsory notification of such transactions is justifiable, as the Commission must be in a position to assess whether or not a transaction falls within its purview.[837] These issues, and this aspect of the CFI's judgment in *Gencor*, are discussed in Chapter 16.

B. RECIPROCITY

Article 24 of the ECMR makes provision for the Member States to inform the Commission 'of any general difficulties encountered by their undertakings with concentrations...in a non-member country'. Further it provides for the Commission to draw up reports on this issue.

Where it appears that certain non-Member States do not permit or otherwise make it difficult for EU undertakings to carry out mergers in circumstances in which undertakings in that State would be permitted to carry out a merger in the EU, 'the Commission may submit proposals to the Council for an appropriate mandate for negotiation with a view to obtaining comparable treatment for Community undertakings'.[838]

9. CONCLUSIONS

1. In the seventeen-year period since the ECMR first came into force, the Commission has developed an effective and well-respected system of merger control.

2. During this period the Commission has not shied away from adopting decisions involving complex and difficult analysis within the stringent time periods prescribed by the ECMR.

3. The Commission has twice prompted a review of the operation and working of the ECMR and in 2004 wide-ranging changes were made to the ECMR. The objective of these changes was

---

[833] Neither the ECMR itself nor the implementing regulation explicitly deal with the limits of enforcement jurisdiction. Rather, the provisions apply broadly. Further, the Commission has in practice used the powers to request information from parties and even third parties located outside the EU and to prohibit, or clear subject to compliance with conditions or obligations, transactions between non-EU firms. See *infra* Chap. 16.

[834] Case T-102/96, *Gencor Ltd v Commission* [1999] ECR II-753, [1999] 4 CMLR 971.

[835] The ECMR is concerned with changes in structure of competition in the market. In contrast, an anti-competitive agreement concluded outside the EU may actually be implemented or operated within the EU. Arguably, as the structural changes in *Gencor* were not implemented within the EU, the implementation test expounded in *Woodpulp* had not been satisfied.

[836] Further, that the principles of non-interference or proportionality did not require the Commission to refrain from exercising jurisdiction where another authority had authorized but not required the transaction.

[837] The parties may be spared the inconvenience of a full notification in this situation as the short form notification and simplified procedure is likely to apply, see *supra* 967.

[838] ECMR, Art. 24(3).

to improve procedures and substantive analysis as well as tackling the complex jurisdictional problems that the ECMR provokes.

4. The challenge for the Commission remains to conduct the rigorous analysis demanded of it by the CFI, within the tight time periods set out in the ECMR.

10. FURTHER READING

A. BOOKS

BRITTAN, L., *Competition Policy and Merger Control in the Single European Market* (Hersh Lauterpacht Memorial Lectures) (Grotius, 1991)

BROBERG, M., *The European Commission's Jurisdiction to Scrutinise Mergers* (3rd edn., Kluwer, 2006)

CAMESASCA, D., *European Merger Control: Getting the Efficiencies Right* (Intersentia-Hart, 2000)

COOK, C. J., and KERSE, C. S., *EC Merger Control* (4th edn., Sweet & Maxwell, 2006)

HAWK, B. E., and HUSER, H. L., *European Community Merger Control, A Practitioner's Guide* (Kluwer Law International, 1996)

HOVENKAMP, H., *Federal Antitrust Policy: The Law of Competition and its Practice* (3rd edn., Thomson West, 2005)

JACQUIMIN, A., 'Mergers and European Policy' in P. H. Admiral (ed.), *Merger and Competition Policy in the European Community* (Blackwell, 1990)

LINDSAY, A., *The EC Merger Regulation: Substantive Issues* (2nd edn., Sweet & Maxwell, 2006)

SAUTER, W., *Competition Law and Industrial Policy in the EU* (Oxford University Press, 1997)

WHISH, R., 'Collective Dominance' in D. O'Keefe and M. Andenas (eds.), *Liber Amicorum for Lord Slynn* (Kluwer, 2000)

B. ARTICLES

BAILEY, D., 'Standard of Proof in EC Merger Proceedings: A Common Law Perspective' [2003] 40(4) *CMLRev* 845

BRIGHT, B., 'The European Merger Control Regulation: Do Member States still have an Independent Role in Merger Control?' [1991] *ECLR* 139

BRITTAN, L., 'The Law and Policy of Merger Control in the EEC' (1990) 15 *ELRev* 351

CAMESASCA, D., 'The Explicit Efficiency Defence in Merger Control: Does it Make the Difference?' [1999] *ECLR* 26

DOWNES, T. A., and MACDOUGALL, D. S., 'Significantly Impeding Effective Competition: Substantive Appraisal under the Merger Regulation' [1994] *ELR* 286

GOYDER, D., 'The Implementation of the Merger Control Regulation: New Wine in Old Bottles' [1992] *Current Legal Problems* 117

HACKER, N., 'The Kali+Salz Case—the Re-examination of a Merger after an Argument by the Court', Commission's *Competition Policy Newsletter* 1998/3, 40.

HOWARTH, D., 'The Court of First Instance in *GE/Honeywell*' [2006] *ECLR* 485

KOKKORIS, I., 'Failing Firm Defence in the European Union: A Panacea for Mergers? [2006] *ECLR* 494

MONTI, G., and ROUSSEVA, E., 'Failing firms in the framework of the EC Merger Regulation' [1999] 24 *ELRev* 38

MOTTA, M., 'EC Merger Policy and the Airtours Case' [2000] *ECLR* 199

RIDYARD, D., 'Economic Analysis of Single Firm and Oligopolistic Dominance' [1994] *ECLR* 255

SCHMIDT, J. M., 'Spotting the Elephant in Parallel Mergers: First past the post, or combined assessment?' [2003] *ECLR* 183

TURNER, D., 'Conglomerate Mergers and Section 7 of the Clayton Act' (1965) 78 *Harvard LR* 1313

VICKERS, J., 'Competition Economics and Policy' [2003] *ECLR* 95

WHISH, R., 'Substantive Analysis under the EC Merger Regulation: should the dominance test be replaced by "substantial lessening of competition" *EU Competition Law & Policy Developments & Priorities* (Hellenic Competition Commission, 2002)

13

JOINT VENTURES AND OTHER BENEFICIAL HORIZONTAL ARRANGEMENTS

1. CENTRAL ISSUES

1. Joint ventures and other horizontal cooperation agreements are often pro-competitive and bring benefits to consumers.

2. A joint venture is an arrangement by which two or more firms come together, pool their resources and integrate part of their operations to achieve particular commercial goals. Joint ventures which amount to a concentration are dealt with under the regime established by the ECMR, currently Regulation 139/2004.

3. The Commission's policy towards horizontal cooperation agreements which fall to be assessed under Article 81 has evolved, from a time when a wide range of essentially pro-competitive agreements were held to be caught by Article 81(1) but then exempted under Article 81(3) to the present position when a more effects-based assessment is made of whether the agreement is within Article 81(1) in the first place.

4. New block exemptions and Guidelines were adopted and issued in 2000. Since 2004 undertakings have had to self-assess as it is no longer possible to individually notify and gain an individual exemption. Horizontal cooperation must also be assessed in the light of the 2004 Guidelines on the application of Article 81(3).

5. The block exemptions cover research and development agreements and specialization agreements. They are 'new generation' type block exemptions, containing black clauses covering hard-core restrictions and market share thresholds.

6. The Guidelines deal with the treatment of six particular types of agreement: research and development, production (including specialisation), joint purchasing, commercialisation (including joint selling), standardisation and environmental.

2. INTRODUCTION

Cooperation between firms at the same level of the market is not necessarily anti-competitive. Outside the realm of hard-core cartel arrangements involving price-fixing, market-sharing, and quotas,[1] horizontal agreements may promote economic efficiency and integration. Cooperation may enable economies of scale to be achieved, new products or services to be brought onto the market, and/or new markets to be penetrated. Competition authorities will wish to allow or even encourage such beneficial arrangements while remaining steadfast against agreements and concerted practices which rig prices and markets.

---

[1] See Chap. 11.

Non-cartel-type cooperation between undertakings can take a wide variety of forms. It ranges from temporary arrangements at one level of activity, such as the research and development (R&D) stage, to what is in effect a merger uniting the undertakings' entire operations in a particular area of interest. Sometimes the parties to the arrangements are actual or potential competitors in the field in which they are cooperating, but sometimes they bring to the collaborative enterprise skills or resources which are complementary rather than parallel. Competition authorities, in judging whether the arrangements restrict competition, and if so whether they should be permitted, will be concerned not only with reductions of competition between the parties themselves but also with effects on third parties.

These types of cooperative arrangements are very common. Firms frequently look for 'partners' for particular operations, either in the short or long term. Notably, modern technological developments (and the liberalization of hitherto regulated markets) have led to an increase in collaborative arrangements as companies active in rapidly developing markets such as telecommunications, information technology, and the media decide to pool their resources and expertise in order to make the next leap forward feasible.

EC competition policy towards horizontal cooperation between undertakings has changed over the years, and one cannot assume that the same attitude towards a particular arrangement would be taken now as in the past. The Commission's thinking about what amounts to a 'restriction of competition' in this context has developed, and there have also been changes in the procedures dealing with cooperation between undertakings. In 1997[2] the Commission announced the launch of a review of its policy towards horizontal arrangements with the object of clarifying the instruments, such as regulations and notices, in this field. In 2000 the review culminated in a set of Guidelines on horizontal cooperation and new block exemptions for R&D agreements and specialization agreements.

This chapter considers first a particular *form* of horizontal arrangement, the joint venture. It then considers, in the light of the Guidelines and the block exemptions, how Article 81 applies to particular types of cooperation. It will be seen that in this area of competition law there are few judgments of the Court. This is because, on the whole, the Commission permitted the cooperation to take place, although sometimes after requiring that the plans be amended. Undertakings given the go-ahead therefore did not challenge the Commission in the Court, preferring to comply with the Commission's requirements if necessary and get on with the project. The result is that in this area of competition law the Commission has had an even freer hand than usual.[3]

Since 1 May 2004, when Regulation 1/2003 came into force, it has of course not been possible to individually notify horizontal cooperation agreements to the Commission. There is no longer any question of obtaining a negative clearance, individual exemption, or even a comfort letter. Undertakings (and their lawyers) have to make their own assessment of the agreement and hope that the Commission, national competition authorities and national courts would come to the same conclusion. However, horizontal cooperation arrangements are infinitely variable (vertical agreements tend to be more uniform) and may be extremely complex and

---

[2] Commission, *XXVIIth Report on Competition Policy* (Commission, 1997) parts 46 and 47. The review was provoked by the imminent expiry of the relevant block exemptions: see *infra* 1102.

[3] Cases which *have* reached the Court however, include Cases T-374, 375, 384, and 388/94, *European Night Services v. Commission* [1998] ECR II-3141, [1998] 5 CMLR 718, and a number of Article 234 references: Case C-250/92, *Gøttrup-Klim Grovvareforeninger v. Dansk Landburgs Grovvareselskab AmbA* [1994] ECR I-5641, [1996] 4 CMLR 191; Cases T-528, 542, 543, and 546/93, *Métropole Television SA v. Commission* [1996] ECR II-649, [1996] 5 CMLR 386; Case T-112/99, *Métropole Television (M6) v. Commission* [2001] ECR II-2459, [2001] 5 CMLR 1236; Cases T-185, 216, 299, and 300/00, *Métropole Television SA (M6) v. Commission* [2002] ECR II-3805, [2003] 4 CMLR 707.

involve enormous sums of money. The loss of (comparative) legal certainty arising from the repeal of Regulation 17 was therefore particularly serious in respect of these agreements. This was recognized in the Commission's White Paper on Modernisation,[4] which conceded that the new system might result in too much uncertainty for partial-function production joint ventures as 'operations of this kind generally require substantial investment and far reaching integration of operations, which makes it difficult to unravel them afterwards at the behest of a competition authority'.[5] It therefore proposed that such joint ventures should be subject to the European Community Merger Regulation (ECMR)[6] as full-function production joint ventures are,[7] if there was no applicable block exemption.[8] Partial-function production joint ventures would be subject to both the ECMR's Article 2(3) dominance test and the Article 81 test under Article 2(4).[9] In the event this proposal was dropped, and there is no special treatment for partial-function joint ventures in the modernized system.

There is the possibility, however, for the undertakings to seek a 'Guidance Letter' in accordance with the Commission's Notice on informal guidance.[10] Guidance letters are discussed in Chapter 14[11] but it should be noted here that one of the elements the Commission may take into account when deciding whether it is appropriate to issue a letter is 'the extent of the investments linked to the transaction in relation to the size of the companies concerned and the extent to which the transaction relates to a structural operation such as the creation of a non-full function joint venture'.[12] Furthermore, under Regulation 1/2003, Article 10, the Commission, acting on its own initiative, may adopt a decision finding that Article 81 is inapplicable to a particular agreement. This is, in effect, tantamount to an old-style negative clearance or exemption, but these decisions will only be taken where 'the Community public interest ... so requires' and it remains to be seen how willing the Commission will be to issue them.[13]

3. JOINT VENTURES

A. WHAT IS A JOINT VENTURE?

The term 'joint venture' could be used to describe virtually any commercial arrangement involving two or more firms.[14] It is normally used in competition law, however, to describe an

---

[4] White Paper on modernisation of the rules implementing Articles 85 and 86 [now 81 and 82] of the EC Treaty [1999] OJ C132/1.

[5] *Ibid.*, para. 79.

[6] Reg. 1309/2004 [2004] OJ L24/1, replacing Reg. 4064/89 [1989] OJ L395/1, [1990] 4 CMLR 286, corrigendum [1990] OJ L257/1, amended by Reg. 1310/97 [1997] OJ L180/1, corrigendum [1998] OJ L40/17.

[7] For the distinction between partial and full-function joint ventures and the significance of this, *see supra* Chap. 12 p. 962 ff and *infra* 1094.

[8] White Paper, para. 80.

[9] *Ibid.*, para. 81. For the application of the tests under the ECMR, now Reg. 139/2004 [2004] OJ L24/1, see *supra*, Chap. 12.

[10] Commission Notice on informal guidance relating to novel questions concerning Artciles 81 and 82 of the EC Treaty that arise in individual cases (guidance letters) [2004] OJ C101/78.

[11] *Infra* 1149.

[12] Notice on informal guidance, para. 8(b).

[13] See further *infra* Chap. 14, 1148.

[14] See J. Faull and A. Nikpay (eds.), *The EC Law of Competition* (2nd edn., Oxford University Press, 2007), para. 7.15.

arrangement by which two or more undertakings (the 'parents'), in order to achieve a particular commercial goal, integrate part of their operations, and put them under joint control.

According to the Commission's 1993 Notice on cooperative joint ventures[15] all joint ventures 'embody a special, institutionally fixed form of cooperation between undertakings. They are versatile instruments at the disposal of the parents, with the help of which different goals can be pursued and attained.' In the Notice on the concept of a full-function joint venture[16] the Commission said that joint ventures encompass a broad range of operations from merger-like operations to cooperation for particular functions such as R&D, production, and distribution. However, it identified the essential feature as joint control by two or more other undertakings. The entity set up by the parents may take the form of a jointly controlled subsidiary company, but it may only be a joint committee or a partnership. In every case, however, the parents each put resources into the enterprise: finance, intellectual property rights, know-how, personnel, premises, or equipment for example.

B. COMPETITION CONCERNS IN RESPECT OF JOINT VENTURES

The competition concerns over joint ventures are in respect of, first, the relations between the parents. A joint venture, unlike a full-scale merger, leaves the parents as economically independent undertakings. Their common links to the joint venture, however, may lead them to engage in collusion in matters outside the ambit of the joint venture, so-called 'spill-over effects'. If this happens the efficiency gains and other advantages derived from the activities of the joint venture may be offset by restrictions of competition in other respects. Secondly, there is the matter of a reduction of actual or potential competition between the parents or between the parents and the joint venture within the ambit of the joint venture. This needs to be weighed against the competitive gains from the new presence on the market. Thirdly, a joint venture may have the effect of foreclosing the market to competition. As in other areas of competition law, the question whether the undertakings concerned have market power plays an important part.

C. JOINT VENTURES AND THE MERGER REGULATION

As explained in Chapter 12,[17] since the system of European Community merger control came into force in 1990 some joint ventures have been dealt with under the ECMR rather than under Article 81. The criteria for deciding which joint ventures fall within the ambit of the ECMR have changed since 1990, but the current position is that under Article 3(4) the ECMR applies to joint ventures 'performing on a lasting basis all the functions of an autonomous economic entity', i.e., to 'full-function' joint ventures. This concept was elaborated upon in the Notice on the concept of full-function joint ventures, now replaced by the Consolidated Jurisdictional Notice.[18] Article 2(4) of the ECMR subjects the matter of the coordination of the competitive behaviour of the parents to appraisal in accordance with Article 81(1) and Article 81(3) but this is done within the ECMR procedure. The application of the ECMR to full-function joint ventures is discussed in Chapter 12.

---

[15] [1993] OJ C43/2, para. 1.

[16] [1998] OJ C66/1, para. 3 replaced by the Consolidated Jurisdictional Notice, *Infra* n. 18.

[17] *Supra* 962.

[18] Consolidated Jurisdictional Notice, 10 July 2007, paras 91–109; see *supra*, Chap. 12, 963.

D. THE COMMISSION'S APPROACH TO THE ASSESSMENT OF JOINT VENTURES UNDER ARTICLE 81 BEFORE 2000

(i) General

Despite more transactions being drawn within the scope of the ECMR there nevertheless remain many joint ventures which are not full-function. In respect of these the question is still whether they fall within Article 81(1) and, if so, whether they fulfil the Article 81(3) criteria. It must always be remembered that any restriction of competition arising from the joint venture must be *appreciable* under the normal criteria for the application of Article 81(1), and it was partly on the this point that the CFI annulled the Commission decision in *European Night Services*,[19] discussed below.

As explained below,[20] the Commission previously took a very interventionist approach to joint ventures based on a fear of coordination between the parents and on the loss of potential competition. However, the *XIIIth Competition Policy Report* signalled a change of policy which was applied in subsequent cases.

An early Notice on cooperation agreements in 1968[21] stated that there were certain forms of cooperation between undertakings which would not normally fall within Article 81(1). This was in effect incorporated into the Notice which the Commission issued in 1993. This Notice concerned the assessment of cooperative joint ventures pursuant to Article 81[22] and summarized the Commission's administrative practice to date in order to inform undertakings 'about both the legal, and economic criteria which will guide the Commission in the future application of Article [81(1)] and Article [81(3)] to cooperative joint ventures'.[23] In 1985 the Commission adopted two block exemption regulations relevant, *inter alia*, to joint ventures. These were Regulation 417/85 on specialization agreements,[24] and Regulation 418/85 on R&D agreements.[25] Both Regulations were of limited use because of their limited provisions. They were replaced in 2000 by Regulation 2658/2000 on specialization agreements[26] and Regulation 2659/2000 on research and development agreements.[27] As we see below, the Commission Guidelines on horizontal cooperation agreements do not deal with joint ventures as a separate species of agreement, but consider them according to their subject matter.

(ii) The Development of the Commission's Policy towards the Application of Article 81 to Joint Ventures

Until the early 1980s the Commission's practice was to hold that joint ventures were caught by Article 81(1), but then to exempt them under Article 81(3). It was invariably impressed by the

---

[19] Cases T-374–375, 384 and 388/94, *European Night Services v. Commission* [1998] 5 CMLR 718.

[20] See *infra* 1096 ff.

[21] [1968] OJ C75/3, rectified [1968] OJ C84/14.

[22] [1993] OJ C43/2.

[23] *Ibid.*, para. 7.

[24] [1985] OJ L53/1 as amended by Commission Reg. 151/93 [1993] OJ L21/8 and extended by Commission Reg. 2236/97 [1997] OJ L306/12.

[25] [1985] OJ L53/5 amended *ibid*.

[26] [2000] OJ L304/3.

[27] [2000] OJ L304/7.

benefits the joint venture offered, but considered that there was a restriction of competition involved which brought the joint venture within the prohibition. The concern about the loss of potential competition was vividly illustrated by the *Vacuum Interrupters* decision where the Commission found that the formation of a joint venture infringed Article 81(1) on the basis of the hypothetical possibility that despite all the evidence to the contrary the parents *might* each have proceeded alone, and *might* each have ultimately produced a commercial product which they could have sold in other Member States in competition with each other if a market had developed for it there.

AEI/Reyrolle Parsons re Vacuum Interrupters [1977] OJ L48/32, [1977] 1 CMLR D67

Two UK companies, AEI and Reyrolle Parsons, formed a jointly owned subsidiary company, Vacuum Interrupters Ltd, to develop, produce, and sell a particular type of vacuum interrupter, a product to be incorporated into circuit-breakers in switchgear apparatus. Both parents had been researching the product for ten years, but its construction and operation were complex and difficult and neither had been able to bring the product to the market. The agreement provided for the parents to cease independent work on the interrupter. As the Commission said (paragraph 10): 'Each of the companies found the cost of development was very substantial and each recognised that if vacuum interrupters were to be brought to commercial use at a price which would make them competitive with the conventional forms of switchgear, a collaboration and pooling of the resources available was essential in order that the heavy expenditure involved by the individual companies would be reduced'.

Commission

15. Prior to the signing of the agreement of 25 March 1970 neither Associated Electrical Industries Ltd nor Reyrolle Parsons Ltd were manufacturing vacuum interrupters. However, their experience in the field of heavy electrical equipment and their ability to manufacture components therefore, the extent and quality of their R&D work, some of which was concentrated in the field of vacuum interrupters, their skill in producing electrical equipment generally and the natural growth of their activities in the field of manufacture of electrical equipment might well have led them to extend their range of products to include vacuum interrupters, thereby making them direct competitors in the relevant product market. They must therefore be assumed to be potential competitors and the agreement of 25 March 1970 to have been concluded between potentially competing manufacturers.

16. The object and effect of the agreement is to restrict competition within the common market. There is not at present even one manufacturer of components for electrical equipment within the area of the common market which makes and sells vacuum interrupters. When two companies, each of which is a potential manufacturer and which are each within the common market, merge their activity in the fields of research, development, manufacture and sale by establishing a joint venture concerned with this one product on such terms that they deprive themselves of the possibility of developing and selling that product independently of and in competition with each other, there is a restriction of competition.

However, the joint venture scheme had obvious advantages and the Commission exempted it under Article 81(3):

22...

(1) The availability of vacuum interrupters enables switchgear manufacturers to design, develop and manufacture electric circuit breakers which have technical advantages over existing air and liquid apparatus.

(2) The agreement makes provision for the financial resources and technical support necessary to enable the R&D of vacuum interrupters to be carried out in depth.

(3) The users of switchgear incorporating vacuum interrupters receive benefits therefrom.

(4) The agreement enables the vacuum type interrupter to be developed, manufactured, and sold to consumers within the EEC on a competitive basis with those which will be available for import into the EEC from the United States and Japan when a market for the vacuum interrupter is established within the Member States of the EEC.

(5) The technical and financial effort required to produce the vacuum interrupter as a commercially viable product within a useful period of time would not have been achieved if both of the parties had relied solely on their own resources.

Decisions of this kind were subject to considerable criticism for finding restrictions of potential competition based on unrealistic assumptions. Further, exempting transactions like *Vacuum Interrupters* under Article 81(3) was theoretically inconsistent with their coming within Article 81(1) in the first place. One of the criteria for the application of Article 81(3) is that the agreement does not impose on undertakings restrictions which are not indispensable to the attainment of the agreement's (beneficial) objectives. Yet if the parents *were* able to enter the market independently, how could their coming together be indispensable?

The Commission re-evaluated its attitude towards the potential competition issue and in the Commission's *XIIIth Report on Competition Policy* (Commission, 1983) signalled a new approach. It set out a checklist of questions it would ask in future in gauging whether there really *was* a restriction of potential competition.

The result of this change of heart was seen in a number of subsequent decisions. *Optical Fibres* is considered to be the first manifestation of the new policy in practice.

Optical Fibres [1986] OJ L236/30

This concerned three joint ventures set up between a US company, Corning Glass Works, on the one hand and respectively BICC in the UK (a 50/50 unlimited partnership), Siemens in Germany (a joint venture company owned 50/50), and COFOCO in France (a joint venture company owned 40/60). The joint ventures were set up to develop, produce, and sell optical fibres and optical cables for use in the European telecommunications market. Corning had experience in optical fibre manufacture but none in cables and the European partners had no experience in optical fibres. There were no clauses restricting competition between Corning and the other parties and they were all free to do independent research and development in optical fibres although in reality there was no prospect of the European companies doing this.

Commission

46. The individual joint venture agreements do not as such restrict competition between Corning and its partners. When the agreements were concluded, the parties were not actual or potential competitors in the market for optical fibres or optical cables. The production of optical fibres and optical cables are different activities. Corning had no experience in cable manufacture, while Corning's partners had no experience in glass manufacture which could have led to an invention competitive with Corning's. In spite of the parties' considerable financial resources, the entry by

Corning into the optical cables market or by Corning's partners into the optical fibres market was not a natural and reasonably foreseeable extension of their respective business activities. The cooperation between Corning and its partners is rather of a complementary nature which does not give rise to restriction or distortion of competition at the level of the cooperating parties. Moreover, the agreements do not foreclose market access by third parties or have any other foreseeable anti-competitive impact on their activities. The various amendments made to the original agreements ensure that competition is maintained and that third parties do not suffer from discrimination or market partitioning. In addition, by virtue of the conditions and obligations attached to this Decision, competition is safe-guarded and the Commission is in a position to monitor future developments.

47. There is neither restriction nor distortion of competition between the parents and the joint venture. The agreements provide that the parents are free to engage in independent R&D of optical fibres. Furthermore, the individual joint venture agreements do not contain obligations which go beyond what would be admitted in simple licensing agreements between non-competitors. Thus the parties are free to engage in independent R&D of optical fibres, although in practice they depend on a continuous transfer of technology from Corning. In addition, there is no obligation on the joint ventures to grant exclusive licenses to Corning in respect of improvements or innovations.

48. The principal restrictions and distortions of competition in this case are to be found rather in the relationship between the joint ventures. The joint ventures have substantially the same business activity, namely the production and marketing of optical fibres. These joint ventures are therefore directly competing companies. The agreements taken together give rise to the creation of a network of inter-related joint ventures with a common technology provider in an oligopolistic market. Corning is one of the major producers and distributors of optical fibres in the world. Its partners are cable makers with large market shares in their respective home countries. The joint ventures therefore bring together companies with strong positions in the optical fibres and cables markets. Although the joint ventures are free to make active and passive sales into each other's territories, only passive sales are permitted in territories where Corning has an exclusive licensee. Corning has interests, whether through joint ventures, subsidiaries or licensees, in several Member States. Its financial stake and key technical and financial personnel representation in the joint ventures, the success of which depends on rapid access to Corning's technology, ensure that Corning is in a position to influence and coordinate the joint venture's conduct.

It can be seen from paragraphs 46 and 47 that the Commission did not consider that there was a restriction of competition between Corning and its partners. Neither side was able to develop and put on to the market the joint venture product without the collaboration of the other, and the individual joint venture agreements were therefore outside Article 81(1). What concerned the Commission was the setting up of the network of three joint ventures. This aspect of the operation *was* within Article 81(1) and needed exemption under Article 81(3). Exemption was given (for fifteen years) after modifications were made to the agreements to ensure competition between the joint ventures and to reduce Corning's control over them.[28]

In *ODIN*[29] however, the liberal policy led to a negative clearance. Metal Box (UK) and Elopak (Norway) set up a 50/50 jointly owned company called ODIN. Metal Box manufactured a range

---

[28] See also *Mitchell Cotts/Solfitra* [1987] OJ L41/31, [1988] 4 CMLR 111 (parents neither actual nor potential competitors, but the distribution arrangements brought it within Article 81(1) because they raised barriers to entry).

[29] *Metal Box/Elopak (ODIN)* [1990] OJ L209/15, [1991] 4 CMLR 832.

of metal, plastic, and polythene containers, bottles and other packaging, and various closures and seals. Elopak's expertise was in cartons for the dairy and food industries. The joint venture was to develop a new form of paperboard-based package with a separate laminated metal lid to be used for UHT-treated foods with a long shelf-life. The parties were not existing competitors and neither of them had all the technology required for the new product or the technical knowledge to develop it separately. The agreement did not contain ancillary restrictions[30] beyond those necessary to make the joint venture work. *Konsortium ECR 900*[31] concerned a cooperative joint venture between three undertakings for the development, manufacture, and distribution of a telecommunications system. It was held not to be caught by Article 81(1) because the undertakings could not have done it individually in the time required by the relevant tender deadline, the financial expenditure and staff resources required were too great for individual action, and as there were only fifteen potential customers the parties could not have borne the financial risk individually.

(iii) The 1993 Notice on the Assessment of Cooperative Joint Ventures

The Commission adopted the 1993 Notice in order to aid undertakings and their advisers by setting out its then current approach to the application of Article 81 to the assessment of joint ventures. In the Notice the Commission set out its policy of making a realistic economic analysis before finding that the joint venture restricts competition within Article 81(1).

(iv) The Application of Article 81(1) and (3) to Joint Ventures After 1993: Some Examples

Every cooperative joint venture is different and its assessment will turn on the individual facts. Despite the policy reflected in the 1993 Notice, the Commission sometimes still engaged in economic analysis under Article 81(3) rather than under Article 81(1). The judgment of the CFI in *European Night Services*,[32] however, showed that the Commission could not rely on granting exemption under Article 81(3) as a substitute for analysis under Article 81(1).

European Night Services was a significant case because the CFI annulled the Commission decision. The Commission found that a joint venture between four railway companies to provide overnight passenger rail services between the UK and the Continent through the Channel Tunnel restricted competition between the parents, between the parents and the joint venture, and *vis-à-vis* third parties and that these effects were exacerbated by a network of joint ventures set up by the parents. The joint venture was exempted, however, although subject to conditions unacceptable to the parties. The CFI held that the Commission had not shown why Article 81(1) applied. It had not identified the relevant market properly, had not applied the appreciability criteria properly, and had demonstrated insufficient economic reasoning: for example, the holding that potential competition was restricted was based on 'a hypothesis unsupported by any evidence or any analysis of the structures of the relevant market from which it might be concluded that it represented a real, concrete possibility'.[33] The exemption conditions were flawed as well,

---

[30] For ancillary restraints in mergers, see *infra* Chap. 12, 1075.

[31] [1990] OJ L228/31, [1992] 4 CMLR 54.

[32] Cases T-374–5, 384 and 388/94, *European Night Services v. Commission* [1998] ECR II-3141, [1998] 5 CMLR 718; see further *supra* Chap. 4.

[33] *Ibid.*, para. 142.

as the Commission had applied the essential facilities concept inappropriately[34] and had given the exemption for too short a time in view of the long-term investment required.

In *P&O/Stena*[35] P&O Ferries and Stena Lines formed a joint venture to provide cross channel ferry services on the Short French Sea[36] and the Belgian Strait.[37] There were two markets involved: that for tourist passenger services on the short sea routes and that for unitized freight services between England and mainland Europe. The Commission held that the joint venture was within Article 81(1) because the parties were actual competitors. There was, however, no appreciable risk of spill-over. The Commission then turned to Article 81(3). It held that the criteria were fulfilled in respect of the freight market. In respect of the tourist market the Commission had little difficulty in holding that the first three criteria were fulfilled. The problems lay in the fourth, that there should be no elimination of competition in respect of a substantial part of the products in question. The Commission's doubt was that the creation of the joint venture would lead to a duopolistic market structure between the joint venture and Eurotunnel. After analysing the situation it concluded that the joint venture and Eurotunnel were likely to compete rather than to act in parallel to raise prices. Given that the market conditions were likely to change, however, because of the abolition of duty-free sales in 1999 the Commission limited the duration of the exemption to three years.

P&O/Stena Line [1999] OJ L163/61, [1999] 5 CMLR 682

Commission

39. The formation of the joint venture constitutes a restriction of competition within the meaning of Article [81(1)] because the parties were actual competitors on the relevant markets on which the joint venture operates.

40. That restriction of competition is appreciable. The parties have a high combined market share (even if their combined market share on the Short Sea declined following the market entry of Eurotunnel). The joint venture is a full function joint venture which operates in the same freight transport market as its parents, and in a neighbouring passenger transport market to those in which its parents operate.

41. The formation of the joint venture has an effect on trade between Member States given the importance of the parties in the Short Sea tourist market and in the Anglo/Continental freight market; . . .

. . .

61. The first and second conditions of Article [81(3)] require an assessment of the efficiencies and other benefits that can be expected from merging the parties' separate ferry operations on the Short Sea, and the extent to which those efficiencies will benefit consumers.

62. The creation of the joint venture will bring about benefits, notably the improved frequency to be offered by the joint venture, continuous loading, and estimated cost savings of GPB [. . .] million. The overall positive benefits will arise even were the joint venture to decide to stop operating on the Newhaven/Dieppe route.

---

[34] See *supra* Chap. 7.

[35] [1999] OJ L163/61, [1999] 5 CMLR 682 (being in the maritime transport sector, notification was under Article 12 of Reg. 4056/86 [1986] OJ L378/4).

[36] Dover, Folkestone, Ramsgate, Newhaven/Calais, Dieppe, Boulogne, and Dunkirk.

[37] Ramsgate/Ostend.

7.2 Allowing consumers a fair share of the resulting benefit

63.   Customers can be expected to benefit from the improved frequency and continuous load-ing. Customers can be expected to benefit from the cost savings to the extent that the joint ven-ture will be faced by effective competition.

7.3 No restrictions which are not indispensable

64.   The third condition of Article [81(3)] requires consideration of whether less restrictive alter-natives are available to achieve the benefits of the proposed joint venture.

65.   The Commission considers that lesser forms of cooperation between P&O and Stena, such as joint scheduling, interlining or pooling, would be unlikely to lead to the benefits to be achieved by the joint venture. In particular, any form of cooperation less than a joint venture would not achieve the savings in administration and marketing, which represent a significant part (GPB [. . .] million) of the estimated GPB [. . .] million costs savings.

66.   Under the agreement, P&O and Stena undertake not to be involved directly or indirectly (other than through the joint venture) with the provision of ferry services calling at any port on the English coastline between (and including) Newhaven and (but excluding) Harwich or on the European mainland coastline between (and including) Dieppe and (but excluding) Zeebrugge. The joint venture's activities are limited to the provision of ferry services on the Dover/Calais, Dover/Zeebrugge and Newhaven/Dieppe routes. These restrictions can be regarded as necessary for the creation of the joint venture.

7.4 No elimination of competition in respect of a substantial part of the products in question

67.   The fourth condition of Article [81(3)] requires an assessment of whether the proposed joint venture can be expected to be faced with effective competition in the Short Sea tourist pas-senger market.

68.   In its 'letter of serious doubts' the Commission stated its concern that the creation of the joint venture could lead to a duopolistic market structure conducive to parallel behaviour of the joint venture and Eurotunnel. This issue is addressed in the following section.

. . .

127.   The Commission considers that characteristics of the market are such that the joint ven-ture and Eurotunnel can be expected to compete with each other rather than to act in parallel to raise prices. First, although a more concentrated market structure is brought about by the cre-ation of the joint venture, with Eurotunnel and the joint venture each having similar large market shares, market shares have not been stable in recent years. Secondly, Eurotunnel and the joint venture are unlikely both to face significant capacity restraints and they have different cost struc-tures. Thirdly, other ferry operators can, at least until 1999, be expected to provide competition. The proposed joint venture can therefore be expected to be faced with effective competition in the Short Sea tourist passenger market. The Commission therefore considers that the fourth con-dition of Article [81(3)] of the Treaty is fulfilled.

128.   An important change in market conditions will occur when duty-free concessions are abolished in mid-1999. The effects of the loss of revenue from duty-free sales is uncertain. It seems likely that ticket prices will rise . . . and some operators have stated that prices will be likely to rise in the order of 30 to 40 per cent . . . Price increases would, however, decrease the number of tourist passengers and operators have strong incentives to limit any price increases by reducing costs and to developing alternative sources of revenue.

129. The abolition of duty-free concessions may have knock-on effects on competition between the joint venture and Eurotunnel in one or more of the following ways. First, Eurotunnel might find its Le Shuttle tourist service capacity constrained if demand for cross-Channel travel were to increase more strongly than it has projected and notwithstanding possible price increases due to the loss of duty-free revenues. Secondly, to the extent that operators are not successful in developing revenue sources to replace duty-free sales, they will have less incentive to maximise load factors in order to increase revenues. Thirdly, the extent to which the other ferry operators will after 1999 be able to provide effective competition to the joint venture and Eurotunnel is uncertain.

130. The Commission therefore considers it appropriate in this case to limit the duration of the exemption to three years from the date of implementation of the agreement, that is from 10 March 1998. This will enable the Commission to assess the impact of the joint venture on the Short Sea tourist market after the 2000 summer season, by which time the full effects of the end of duty-free concessions on market conditions can be expected to be known.

In *ATLAS*[38] the Commission dealt with a joint venture between the French and German national telephone operators designed to provide a range of complex communications packages. The Commission granted an exemption to the joint venture despite the substantial elimination of competition between the parents which it involved. It considered that consumers would benefit from the earlier provision of improved technology and that the joint venture would enable better technical harmonization. The exemption was, however, made subject to stringent conditions and the Commission was described as granting the exemption 'in such a way as to use the leverage of the exemption request to forward its own policy priorities on the two governments concerned, thus possibly enabling liberalization of French and German telecommunications markets to occur more quickly than would otherwise be the case'.[39]

The Commission's more realistic application of Article 81(1) to a joint venture was shown in two cases in 1999 concerning telecommunications in France: *Re Cégétel: Vivendi/BT/Mannesmann/SBC International*[40] and *Re Telecom Développement: SNCF/Cégétel*.[41] The development of the Commission's policy towards Article 81(1) generally is considered in Chapter 4.[42]

4. RESEARCH AND DEVELOPMENT AGREEMENTS, SPECIALIZATION AGREEMENTS, AND THE 1985 BLOCK EXEMPTIONS

A. GENERAL

The Commission singled out two particular types of horizontal agreement for special treatment and in 1985 adopted two block exemptions, Regulations 417/85 on specialization

[38] [1996] OJ L239/29, [1997] 4 CMLR 89.
[39] D. Goyder, *EC Competition Law* (3rd edn., Oxford University Press, 1998), 456.
[40] [1999] OJ L218/14, [2000] 4 CMLR 106.
[41] [1999] OJ L218/24, [2000] 4 CMLR 124.
[42] See *supra* Chap. 4, 219ff.

agreements[43] and Regulation 418/85 on R&D agreements.[44] These were replaced in 2000 by Regulation 2658/2000[45] and 2659/2000[46] respectively, which are discussed below.[47] The Commission Guidelines on horizontal cooperation agreements of 2000 have sections devoted to these types of agreement.[48]

B. SPECIALIZATION AGREEMENTS

Specialization agreements are those by which the parties agree to specialize in manufacture by allocating the manufacture of certain products amongst themselves. Such agreements will normally involve a diminution of competition but they can contribute to efficiencies in that they may reduce costs and/or increase output. If competition on the market is not eliminated, in that competition from other manufacturers remains, they can often be exempted as they bring benefits to consumers.

There are various forms of specialization agreement. The classic example is *Jaz/Peter*.[49] Both parties manufactured clocks. Under the agreement Jaz in France was to continue making only electric clocks and domestic alarm clocks and Peter in Germany was to make large mechanical alarm clocks. They agreed that they would each supply the other with their products and spare parts, that they could both sell the whole range of the products in their respective territories, and that they would not buy the products covered by the agreement from third parties. The agreement was exempted: the rationalization of production would lead to lower prices.[50] *ACEC/Berliet*[51] was a different type of arrangement. The parties agreed to collaborate in bus manufacture, and the production and development of the individual components was divided between them. ACEC was to make the transmission systems and Berliet the basic bus structure. This agreement was also exempted.

Regulation 417/85[52] provided a block exemption for various types of specialization agreements, including the format in *Jaz/Peter* and *ACEC/Berliet*. It did not, however, cover arrangements of the kind in *Prym/Beka*[53] where one party gives up manufacture of a product altogether and agrees to obtain its future supplies of the product from the other, because there was a lack of mutuality. Although not as complex as the R&D exemption, Regulation 417/85 applied only where certain market share and turnover thresholds were not exceeded.[54]

---

[43] [1985] OJ L53/1 as amended by Commission Reg. 151/93 [1993] OJ L21/8 and extended by Commission Reg. 2236/97 [1997] OJ L306/12.

[44] [1985] OJ L53/5 as amended by Commission Reg. 151/93 [1993] OJ L21/8 and extended by Commission Reg. 2236/97 [1997] OJ L306/12.

[45] [2000] OJ L 304/3.

[46] [2000] OJ L 304/7.

[47] *Infra* 1112 ff and 1118 ff.

[48] [2001] OJ C 3/2. See *infra* 000 ff. and 000 ff.

[49] [1969] OJ L195/5, [1970] CMLR 129.

[50] The 10-year exemption was renewed in 1978: *Jaz-Peter (No. 2)* [1978] OJ L61/17, [1978] 2 CMLR 186.

[51] [1968] OJ L201/7, [1968] CMLR D35.

[52] [1985] OJ L53/1, as amended by Commission Reg. 151/93 [1993] OJ L21/8 and Commission Reg. 2236/97 [1997] OJ L306/12.

[53] [1973] OJ L296/24, [1973] CMLR D250.

[54] The products did not represent more than 20% of the market in the common market or a substantial part of it (but 10% if the parties, or a third party on their behalf were also entrusted with the distribution of the products) and the aggregate turnover of the parties concerned did not exceed €1,000 million.

C. RESEARCH AND DEVELOPMENT AGREEMENTS

R&D agreements may be structured in various ways and may or may not involve a joint venture. Some of the cases discussed above, for example *Konsortium ECR 900* and *ODIN*, were R&D agreements. They may be between companies but sometimes they involve a company cooperating with an academic institution or research institute. Faull and Nikpay explain why R&D arrangements are attractive to companies.

J. Faull and A. Nikpay (eds.), *The EC Law of Competition* (2nd edn., Oxford University Press, 2007), 685

7.107 In many industries a company's level of innovation may become a key competitive factor. From pharmaceuticals to computing and electronics it is not just price and quality that give firms a competitive edge but their technical know-how and ability to develop new products.

7.108 Cooperation at the level of research and development is therefore increasingly important to many companies. The costs and risks associated with R&D can be very high. Many companies choose therefore to co-operate to spread these risks. There are also potentially enormous benefits in avoiding expensive duplication of effort and in the cross-fertilization of ideas and experience that come from R&D cooperation. It is for these reasons that the Commission has taken a generally positive view of R&D cooperation.

7.109 Cooperation in R&D can take place at many levels. In some cases the cooperation is in fundamental research projects far from the market often in collaboration with universities or publicly funded research programmes. In other cases R&D constitutes basically no more than incremental improvements to existing products and may be an adjunct to a joint production arrangement.

Not only does the Commission have few problems with agreements simply limited to joint R&D, but the Community positively encourages cooperative projects through various research programmes.[55] Most of the difficulties arise when the parties wish to go beyond collaboration at the R&D stages and extend their cooperation into the stages of commercial exploitation and distribution.

The block exemption on R&D agreements, Regulation 418/85,[56] was little used. Overall, it contained detailed provisions with which few agreements complied. Further, it provided a limited exemption only for a very basic type of R&D, whereas most collaborative arrangements are more complex. Indeed, many R&D agreements which fell within the block exemption would not have been caught by Article 81(1) at all. In particular, there is only very limited exemption for cooperation in the distribution stage. Also, it applied only if certain preconditions were fulfilled, and it contained market share criteria.

---

[55] Article 163(2)) (ex Article 130(f)(2)) of the Treaty calls upon the Community to encourage undertakings, including small and medium sized undertakings, in their research and technological development activities of high quality, and to support their efforts to cooperate with one another. The Sixth Framework Programme for Research, Technological Development and Demonstration Activities was in force from 2002–2006 ([2002] OJ L232/1).

[56] [1985] OJ L53/5, as amended by Commission Reg. 151/93 [1993] OJ L21/8 and Commission Reg. 2236/97 [1997] OJ L306/12.

5. THE ASSESSMENT OF HORIZONTAL COOPERATION AGREEMENTS IN THE LIGHT OF THE COMMISSION GUIDELINES AND OF BLOCK EXEMPTIONS 2658/2000 AND 2659/2000

A. GENERAL

The review of the application of Article 81 to horizontal cooperation agreements upon which the Commission embarked in 1997[57] resulted in the adoption in November 2000 of a set of Guidelines, similar to those it had recently adopted on vertical restraints,[58] and two new block exemptions. The adoption of *two* block exemptions caused surprise in some quarters since it had been widely believed that the Commission intended to produce one 'umbrella' block exemption on horizontal agreements, in the same way that it had just produced an umbrella exemption for vertical agreements. The Guidelines replaced the 1968 Notice on cooperation agreements between enterprises and the 1993 Notice on the assessment of joint ventures.

The Guidelines are not limited to R&D and specialization. They deal with a number of types of agreement which 'potentially generate efficiency gains', i.e., R&D, production (which includes specialization), purchasing, commercialization, standardization, and environmental.[59] These types of agreement are dealt with in different sections, and where the agreement contains elements falling under more than one head the applicable section is to be determined according to the 'centre of gravity of the cooperation'.[60] However, the Guidelines do not cover 'more complex arrangements such as strategic alliances that combine a number of different areas and instruments of cooperation in varying ways'.[61] The Guidelines apply whether or not the transaction involves the formation of a joint venture, unless it is within the ECMR, and they apply to cooperation over both products and services.[62] The Guidelines do not apply to the extent that sector-specific rules apply.[63]

The purpose of the Guidelines is 'to provide an analytical framework for the most common types of horizontal cooperation'[64] and to 'complement' the new block exemptions.[65] After a statement of the scope of the Guidelines the Commission discusses the basic principles underlying the assessment of horizontal cooperation under Article 81. It then considers the application of Article 81 to the six specific types of horizontal agreement mentioned above. The application of Article 81(3) is discussed in the light of the block exemptions in respect of R&D

---

[57] See *supra* 1092.

[58] See *supra* Chap. 9.

[59] Guidelines [2001] OJ C3/2, para. 10. They do not deal with agreements on information exchanges or on minority shareholdings.

[60] *Ibid.*, para. 12.

[61] *Ibid.*

[62] *Ibid.*, para. 13.

[63] *Ibid.*, para. 13.

[64] *Ibid.*, para. 7.

[65] *Ibid.*, para. 8.

and specialization agreements.[66] The Commission illustrates the Guidelines with a number of examples, many of them based on agreements with which it has dealt in the past. Nevertheless, the Commission says that given the enormous variety in types and combinations of horizontal cooperation and market circumstances it is impossible to provide specific answers to every possible scenario.[67] For example, an important cooperation agreement not covered by the Guidelines is *Reims II*, in which the Commission renewed (for a further five years) the exemption given to the agreement between seventeen European postal operators with respect to the system of terminal dues (terminal dues are the remuneration postal operators pay to each other for the delivery of cross-border mail in the country of destination).[68] This was in effect a type of price fixing agreement. The general principles relating to Article 81(1) and Article 81(3), which are discussed in Chapters 3 and 4, apply to horizontal cooperation agreements and some of the cases and decisions discussed there are horizontal agreements of the kind which are the subject of this chapter.

It should be noted that the Guidelines were drawn up against the background of the Commission's proposals for modernizing the implementation of the competition rules.[69] As noted above, modernization puts more responsibility on undertakings to ensure that their agreements do comply with the rules. The Guidelines are therefore important in helping them to do this.[70] Agreements also have to be assessed in the light of the Commission's general Guidelines on the application of Article 81(3)[71] which in effect take precedence over the Horizontal Guidelines.[72]

B. THE POLICY OF THE HORIZONTAL GUIDELINES

The Guidelines should be seen as an integral part of the Commission's modernization process. They continue the Commission's policy of taking a realistic view of these agreements and looking at them in their legal and economic context to identify when there really is a threat to competition. In taking that approach the Commission is following in the vanguard of the Court. The Court may still take the view, however, that the Commission is not taking a sufficiently effects-based approach. In *O2 v. Commission*[73] the CFI annulled a decision of the Commission holding that roaming agreements between mobile telecommunications providers in Germany infringed Article 81(1) but satisfied Article 81(3).[74] The Commission considered that roaming agreements restrict competition 'by definition' and so are caught by Article 81(1). The CFI held that the Commission should have analysed what the competitive situation would have been in the *absence* of the agreements and should have demonstrated in concrete terms that they had restrictive effects on competition.

---

[66] See *infra* 1112 and 1118.

[67] *Ibid.*, para. 7.

[68] [2004] OJ L56/76.

[69] White Paper on modernization of the rules implementing Articles 85 and 86 [now 81 and 82] of the EC Treaty [1999] OJ C132/1.

[70] *Supra* 1093.

[71] [2004] OJ C101/97; see *supra* Chap. 4.

[72] Guidelines on Article 81(3), para. 5.

[73] Case T-328/03, *O2 v. Commission* [2006] ECR II-1231.

[74] The decision was taken under the Regulation 17 regime and the agreements had been notified, so the Commission decision granted an individual exemption.

In the Guidelines the Commission begins by recognizing the basic tension between the benefits of cooperation and the need to protect competition.

2. Horizontal cooperation may lead to competition problems. This is for example the case if the parties to a cooperation agree to fix prices or output, to share markets, or if the cooperation enables the parties to maintain, gain or increase market power and thereby causes negative market effects with respect to prices, output, innovation or the variety and quality of products.

3. On the other hand, horizontal cooperation can lead to substantial economic benefits. Companies need to respond to increasing competitive pressure and a changing market place driven by globalisation, the speed of technological progress and the generally more dynamic nature of markets. Cooperation can be a means to share risk, save costs, pool know how and launch innovation faster. In particular for small and medium sized enterprises cooperation is an important means to adapt to the changing market place.

4. The Commission, while recognising the economic benefits that can be generated by cooperation, has to ensure that effective competition is maintained. Article 81 provides the legal framework for a balanced assessment taking into account both anti-competitive effects as well as economic benefits.

The Commission states that as most horizontal cooperation agreements do not have as their *object* a restriction of competition it is necessary to analyse the agreement in its economic context. It considers that some agreements are not normally caught by Article 81(1):

24. Some categories of agreements do not fall under Article 81(1) because of their very nature. This is normally true for cooperation that does not imply a coordination of the parties' competitive behaviour in the market such as

— cooperation between non-competitors,
— cooperation between competing companies that cannot independently carry out the project or activity covered by the cooperation,
— cooperation concerning an activity which does not influence the relevant parameters of competition.

These categories of cooperation could only come under Article 81(1) if they involved firms with significant market power and are likely to cause foreclosure problems vis-à-vis third parties.

The Commission compares the above with agreements which usually do fall under Article 81(1):

25. Another category of agreements can be assessed from the outset as normally falling under Article 81(1). This concerns cooperation agreements that have the object to restrict competition by means of price fixing, output limitation or sharing of markets or customers. These restrictions are considered to be the most harmful, because they directly interfere with the outcome of the competitive process. Price fixing and output limitation directly lead to customers paying higher prices or not receiving the desired quantities. The sharing of markets or customers reduces the choice available to customers and therefore also leads to higher prices or reduced output. It can therefore be presumed that these restrictions have negative market effects. They are therefore almost always prohibited . . .

It will be noted that in paragraph 24 above the Commission refers to the possible anti-competitive effect of agreements involving firms with significant market power. The issue of market power is a central theme of the Guidelines. The market position of the parties is the major factor in determining whether or not the agreement falls within Article 81(1):

27. The starting point for the analysis is the position of the parties in the markets affected by the cooperation. This determines whether or not they are likely to maintain, gain or increase market power through the cooperation, i.e., have the ability to cause negative market effects as to prices,

output, innovation or the variety or quality of goods and services. To carry out this analysis the relevant market(s) have to be defined by using the methodology of the Commission's market definition notice. Where specific types of markets are concerned such as purchasing or technology markets, these Guidelines will provide additional guidance.

28. If the parties together have a low combined market share, a restrictive effect of the cooperation is unlikely and no further analysis normally is required. If one of just two parties has only an insignificant market share and if it does not possess important resources, even a high combined market share normally cannot be seen as indicating a restrictive effect on competition in the market . . . Given the variety of cooperation types and the different effects they may cause in different market situations, it is impossible to give a general market share threshold above which sufficient market power for causing restrictive effects can be assumed.

29. In addition to the market position of the parties and the addition of market shares, the market concentration, i.e., the position and number of competitors, may have to be taken into account as an additional factor to assess the impact of the cooperation on market competition. As an indicator the Herfindahl-Hirshman Index ('HHI'), which sums up the squares of the individual market shares of all competitors,[75] can be used: With an HHI below 1000 the market concentration can be characterized as low, 1000 and 1800 as moderate and above 1800 as high. Another possible indicator would be the leading firm concentration ratio, which sums up the individual market shares of the leading competitors . . .

Once an agreement is within Article 81(1) it is then a question, of course, of seeing whether it satisfies the exception in Article 81(3). The Commission rehearses the Article 81(3) criteria, and refers to the revised block exemptions for R&D and specialization agreements. It is able to adopt block exemptions for those categories because under certain conditions the criteria can be assumed to be fulfilled. The 'combination of complementary skills or assets can be the source of substantive efficiencies'.[76]

C. RESEARCH AND DEVELOPMENT AGREEMENTS

(i) General

The chapter in the Guidelines on R&D agreements[77] begins by explaining that it applies to all forms of such agreements (except those falling under the ECMR), including related agreements concerning the production or commercialization of the R&D results, provided that the cooperation's centre of gravity lies in R&D.

The Commission acknowledges that R&D agreements *may* cause competition problems but starts from the position that they can bring significant benefits:

40. Cooperation in R&D may reduce duplicative, unnecessary costs, lead to significant cross fertilisation of ideas and experience and thus result in products and technologies being developed more rapidly than would otherwise be the case. As a general rule R&D cooperation tends to increase overall R&D activities.

41. Small and Medium-sized Enterprises (SMEs) form a dynamic and heterogeneous community which is confronted by many challenges, including the growing demands of larger companies for

---

[75] A market consisting of four firms with shares of 30%, 25%, 25%, 20%, has a HHI of 2,550 (900 + 625 + 625 + 400) pre-cooperation. If the first two market leaders would cooperate, the HHI would change to 4,050 (3,025 + 625 + 400) post-cooperation. The HHI post-cooperation is decisive for the assessment of the possible market effects of a cooperation (Commission's own fn.).

[76] Guidelines [2001] OJ C3/2, para. 37.

[77] Paras. 39–77.

which they often work as sub-contractors. In R&D intensive sectors, fast growing SMEs, more often called 'start-up companies', also aim at becoming a leader in fast-developing market segments. To meet those challenges and to remain competitive, SMEs need constantly to innovate. Through R&D cooperation there is a likelihood that overall R&D by SMEs will increase and that they will be able to compete more vigorously with stronger market players.

(ii) Market Definition and Market Shares

Considerable attention is paid in the R&D chapter of the Guidelines to market definition and the calculation of market shares because of the particular problems that these issues pose in respect of R&D agreements. R&D may result in anything from slight improvements to existing products or technologies at one end of the spectrum to an entirely new product which creates its own new market at the other.[78] If only the improvement of existing products is concerned, the existing products and their close substitutes will form the relevant market.[79] However, where a significant change to an existing product or a new product replacing existing ones is concerned, the position is more complex:

45. If the R&D efforts aim at a significant change of an existing product or even at a new product replacing existing ones, substitution with the existing products may be imperfect or long-term. Consequently, the old and the potentially emerging new products are not likely to belong to the same relevant market. The market for existing products may nevertheless be concerned, if the pooling of R&D efforts is likely to result in the coordination of the parties' behaviour as suppliers of existing products. An exploitation of power in the existing market, however, is only possible if the parties together have a strong position with respect to both the existing product market and R&D efforts.

Where R&D cooperation concerns technology, and intellectual property rights are marketed separately from the products to which they relate, it will be necessary to define the 'relevant technology market'. This consists of the intellectual property that is licensed and its close substitutes, i.e., other technologies which customers could use as substitutes.[80] The methodology for defining technology markets follows the same principles as for defining product markets, i.e., that set out in the Commission Notice on market definition,[81] and market shares can be calculated by 'dividing the licensing income generated by the parties with the total licensing income of all sellers of substitutable technologies'.[82] However, the Commission recognizes that in technology markets particular emphasis must be put on potential competition.[83]

Furthermore, R&D cooperation may affect competition in innovation, the effects of which may not be able to be sufficiently assessed by analysing actual or potential competition in existing product or technology markets.[84] The Commission identifies two situations: where at an early stage it is possible to identify R&D poles and where it is not. An 'R&D pole' is an R&D effort directed at a certain new product or technology. Where credible competing R&D poles

[78] Guidelines, para. 43.

[79] Ibid., para. 44.

[80] Ibid., para. 47. The definition of technology markets is also an important factor in intellectual property licensing agreements, see Guidelines on the application of Article 81 to technology transfer agreements [2004] OJ C 101/2, discussed supra Chap. 10.

[81] [1997] OJ C 372/5, discussed supra Chap. 1, 63.

[82] Guidelines on horizontal cooperation agreements, para. 48. This is one method of calculation suggested in the Guidelines on technology transfer agreements (supra n. 80), para. 23, which sets out a fuller treatment of the subject: see supra Chap. 10, 814.

[83] Ibid., para. 49.

[84] Ibid., para. 50.

can be identified the Commission will take these into account.[85] Where they cannot, the Commission would limit its assessment to product and/or technology markets which are related to the R&D cooperation in question.[86]

The calculation of market shares is particularly important in relation to R&D agreements because of the market share thresholds contained in the block exemption. The Guidelines say on this:

53. The calculation of market shares, both for the purposes of the R&D block exemption Regulation and of these Guidelines, has to reflect the distinction between existing markets and competition in innovation. At the beginning of a cooperation the reference point is the market for products capable of being improved or replaced by the products under development. If the R&D agreement only aims at improving or refining existing products, this market includes the products directly concerned by the R&D. Market shares can thus be calculated on the basis of the sales value of the existing products. If the R&D aims at replacing an existing product, the new product will, if successful, become a substitute to the existing products. To assess the competitive position of the parties, it is again possible to calculate market shares on the basis of the sales value of the existing products. Consequently, the R&D block exemption Regulation bases its exemption of these situations on the market share in 'the relevant market for the products capable of being improved or replaced by the contract products'. For an automatic exemption, this market share may not exceed 25 per cent . . .

54. If the R&D aims at developing a product which will create a complete new demand, market shares based on sales cannot be calculated. Only an analysis of the effects of the agreement on competition in innovation is possible. Consequently, the R&D block exemption Regulation exempts these agreements irrespective of market share for a period of seven years after the product is first put on the market . . . However, the benefit of the block exemption may be withdrawn if the agreement would eliminate effective competition in innovation . . . After the seven year period, market shares based on sales value can be calculated, and the market share threshold of 25 per cent applies . . .

(iii) Substantive Assessement According to the Guidelines

The Guidelines distinguish between agreements that normally do not fall within Article 81(1), those almost always do, and those which may do.

The first category comprises agreements relating to cooperation in R&D 'at a rather theoretical stage, far removed from the marketing of possible results'[87] and agreements between non-competitors:

56. Moreover, R&D cooperation between non-competitors does generally not restrict competition. The competitive relationship between the parties has to be analysed in the context of affected existing markets and/or innovation. If the parties are not able to carry out the necessary R&D independently, there is no competition to be restricted. This can apply, for example, to firms bringing together complementary skills, technologies and other resources. The issue of potential competition has to be assessed on a realistic basis. For instance parties cannot be defined as potential competitors simply because the cooperation enables them to carry out the R&D activities. The decisive question is whether each party independently has the necessary means as to assets, know how and other resources.

Further, R&D cooperation 'which does not include the joint exploitation of possible results by means of licensing, production and/or marketing rarely falls under Article 81(1)'. It causes

---

[85] Guidelines, para. 51.

[86] Ibid., para. 52.

[87] Ibid., para. 55.

competition problems only if effective competition with respect to innovation is significantly reduced.[88]

The second category, agreements that almost always fall within Article 81(1), concerns cooperation which is a tool to engage in a disguised cartel.[89]

In the third category are agreements which cannot be assessed from the outset as non-restrictive of competition but have to be analysed in their economic context. The Guidelines specifically mention R&D cooperation set up at a stage close to the market launch and which is agreed between competitors.[90]

Turning to the question of market structure, the Guidelines state that the negative effects of R&D cooperation are likely to occur only where there is market power:

> 61. R&D cooperation can cause negative market effects in three respects: First, it may restrict innovation, secondly it may cause the coordination of the parties' behaviour in existing markets and thirdly, foreclosure problems may occur at the level of the exploitation of possible results. These types of negative market effects, however, are only likely to emerge when the parties to the cooperation have significant power on the existing markets and/or competition with respect to innovation is significantly reduced. Without market power there is no incentive to coordinate behaviour on existing markets or to reduce or slow down innovation. A foreclosure problem may only arise in the context of cooperation involving at least one player with significant market power for a key technology and the exclusive exploitation of results.

The Guidelines consider the application of Article 81(3) to R&D cooperation and say that the block exemption applies where there are no hard-core restrictions and only a limited degree of market power.

The Guidelines then set out how the Commission appraises the application of Article 81(3) to agreements which fall within Article 81(1) but are outside the block exemption because the market share thresholds are exceeded. The Guidelines distinguish between the improvement of existing products and the creation of new ones, but admit that most cases lie somewhere in between.

> 64. If the R&D is directed at the improvement or refinement of existing products/technology possible effects concern the relevant market(s) for these existing products/technology. Effects on prices, output and/or innovation in existing markets are, however, only likely if the parties together have a strong position, entry is difficult and few other innovation activities are identifiable. Furthermore, if the R&D only concerns a relatively minor input of a final product, effects as to competition in these final products are, if invariably, very limited. In general, a distinction has to be made between pure R&D agreements and more comprehensive cooperation involving different stages of the exploitation of results (i.e., licensing, production, marketing). As said above, pure R&D agreements rarely come under Article 81(1). This is in particular true for R&D directed towards a limited improvement of existing products/technology. If, in such a scenario, the R&D cooperation includes joint exploitation only by means of licensing, restrictive effects such as foreclosure problems are unlikely. If, however, joint production and/or marketing of the slightly improved products/technology are included, the cooperation has to be examined more closely. First, negative effects as to prices and output in existing markets are more likely if strong competitors are involved in such a situation. Secondly, the cooperation may come closer to a production agreement because the R&D activities may de facto not form the centre of gravity of such a collaboration.

---

[88] *Ibid.*, para. 58.

[89] *Ibid.*, para. 56.

[90] *Ibid.*, para. 57.

65. If the R&D is directed at an entirely new product (or technology) which creates its own new market, price and output effects on existing markets are rather unlikely. The analysis has to focus on possible restrictions of innovation concerning, for instance, the quality and variety of possible future products/technology or the speed of innovation. Those restrictive effects can arise where two or more of the few firms engaged in the development of such a new product, start to cooperate at a stage where they are each independently rather near to the launch of the product. In such a case, innovation may be restricted even by a pure R&D agreement. In general, however, R&D cooperation concerning entirely new products is pro-competitive. This principle does not change significantly if the joint exploitation of the results, even joint marketing, is involved. Indeed, the issue of joint exploitation in these situations is only relevant where foreclosure from key technologies plays a role. Those problems would, however, not arise where the parties grant licences to third parties.

66. Most R&D agreements will lie somewhere in between the two situations described above. They may therefore have effects on innovation as well as repercussions on existing markets. Consequently, both the existing market and the effect on innovation may be of relevance for the assessment with respect to the parties' combined positions, concentration ratios, number of players/innovators and entry conditions. In some cases there can be restrictive price/output effects on existing markets and a negative impact on innovation by means of slowing down the speed of development. For instance, if significant competitors on an existing technology market cooperate to develop a new technology which may one day replace existing products, this cooperation is likely to have restrictive effects if the parties have significant market power on the existing market (which would give an incentive to exploit it), and if they also have a strong position with respect to R&D. A similar effect can occur, if the major player in an existing market cooperates with a much smaller or even potential competitor who is just about to emerge with a new product/technology which may endanger the incumbent's position.

The Guidelines then turn to the application of Article 81(3) to R&D agreements. This is largely done with reference to the block exemption, discussed below. Although the application of the block exemption is limited to certain market share thresholds it is made clear that the provisions of the exemption are relevant to agreements which fall outside it because the thresholds are exceeded. For example, the 'black list' of hard core restrictions in Article 5 'will in most cases render an exemption impossible following an individual assessment too, and can therefore be regarded as a good indication of restrictions that are not indispensable to the cooperation'.[91]

The Guidelines then apply the principles set out in the R&D chapter to a number of example scenarios.

(iv) The Block Exemption Regulation on R&D Agreements, Regulation 2659/2000[92]

Like the Verticals Regulation,[93] the block exemption for R&D agreements, Regulation 2659/2000, which replaced Regulation 418/85, eschews a 'white list' of exempted clauses and concentrates instead on the 'black list' of restrictions or clauses which are not exempted. As in the case of the Verticals Regulation, the R&D exemption contains market share thresholds. It applies only to agreements where the participating undertakings' share of the relevant market is below a certain figure. The reason for this is explained in the recitals:

It is appropriate to move away from the approach of listing exempted clauses and to place greater emphasis on defining the categories of agreements which are exempted up to a certain level of

---

[91] Guidelines, para. 69. The phraseology in the Guidelines in respect of Article 81(3) reflects the fact that they date from 2000 when individual exemption under Reg. 17 was still possible.

[92] [2000] OJ L304/7.

[93] Reg. 2790/1999 [1999] OJ L336/21, discussed *supra* Chap. 9.

market power and on specifying the restrictions or clauses which are not to be contained in such agreements. This is consistent with an economics based approach which assesses the impact of agreements on the relevant market.[94]

In the Regulation market share is used as a proxy for market power.

Article 1 defines the scope of the exemption. It applies to three categories of agreements; joint R&D and joint exploitation of the results; joint exploitation of R&D previously carried out jointly; and joint R&D without joint exploitation. Under Article 1(2) ancillary provisions are exempted.

Article 1

Exemption

1. Pursuant to Article 81(3) of the Treaty and subject to the provisions of this Regulation, it is hereby declared that Article 81(1) shall not apply to agreements entered into between two or more undertakings (hereinafter referred to as 'the parties') which relate to the conditions under which those undertakings pursue:

   (a) joint research and development of products or processes and joint exploitation of the results of that research and development;

   (b) joint exploitation of the results of research and development of products or processes jointly carried out pursuant to a prior agreement between the same parties; or

   (c) joint research and development of products or processes excluding joint exploitation of the results.

This exemption shall apply to the extent that such agreements (hereinafter referred to as 'research and development agreements') contain restrictions of competition falling within the scope of Article 81(1).

2. The exemption provided for in paragraph 1 shall also apply to provisions contained in research and development agreements which do not constitute the primary object of such agreements, but are directly related to and necessary for their implementation, such as an obligation not to carry out, independently or together with third parties, research and development in the field to which the agreement relates or in a closely connected field during the execution of the agreement.

The first subparagraph does, however, not apply to provisions which have the same object as the restrictions of competition enumerated in Article 5(1).

'Exploitation of the results' is defined in Article 2(8) as meaning 'the production or distribution of the contract products or the application of the contract processes or the assignment or licensing of intellectual property rights or the communication of know-how required for such manufacture or application'.

Article 3 contains a list of conditions which must be fulfilled before the agreement may benefit from the block exemption. One of the conditions contained in the corresponding list in Regulation 418/85, that there had to be a framework programme defining the objectives of the work and the field in which it is to be carried out, has been deleted. It is specifically provided that academic or research bodies may agree to confine their use of the results of the work to further research.

---

[94] *Ibid.*, recital 7.

Article 3

Conditions for exemption

1. The exemption provided for in Article 1 shall apply subject to the conditions set out in paragraphs 2 to 5.

2. All the parties must have access to the results of the joint research and development for the purposes of further research or exploitation. However, research institutes, academic bodies, or undertakings which supply research and development as a commercial service without normally being active in the exploitation of results may agree to confine their use of the results for the purposes of further research.

3. Without prejudice to paragraph 2, where the research and development agreement provides only for joint research and development, each party must be free independently to exploit the results of the joint research and development and any pre-existing know-how necessary for the purposes of such exploitation. Such right to exploitation may be limited to one or more technical fields of application, where the parties are not competing undertakings at the time the research and development agreement is entered into.

4. Any joint exploitation must relate to results which are protected by intellectual property rights or constitute know-how, which substantially contribute to technical or economic progress and the results must be decisive for the manufacture of the contract products or the application of the contract processes.

5. Undertakings charged with manufacture by way of specialisation in production must be required to fulfil orders for supplies from all the parties, except where the research and development agreement also provides for joint distribution.

Article 4 provides that where the parties are not competing manufacturers of products capable of being improved or replaced by the contract products, the exemption can last for the duration of the R&D stage and, where the results are jointly exploited, for seven years from the time that the products concerned are put on the market in the common market. It can then *continue* to apply so long as the participating undertakings[95] do not attain a share of the relevant market which exceeds 25 per cent. If, however, the parties are competing manufacturers the exemption covers them only if their combined market share does not exceed 25 per cent at the time of the agreement. The rules for calculating the market share threshold are laid down in Article 6. The primary criterion is market sales value; if these data are not available recourse may be had to 'other reliable market information', including market sales volumes.[96]

Article 5 contains the blacklisted clauses. It is important to note that, by Article 5(2), it is permissible to set production targets for a production joint venture, and where a distribution joint venture is involved sales targets and sales prices may be fixed.

---

[95] As usual, 'participating undertakings' is defined in Article 2(2) as the undertakings party to the agreement and their respective connected undertakings. 'Connected undertakings' is defined in Article 2(3).

[96] Reg. 2659/2000, Art. 6(1)(a). Note that Article 6(2) and (3) contain some marginal relief in that where the agreement was originally within the threshold the 25% may be exceeded by 5% for up to 2 years without the benefit of the block exemption being lost, and by more than 5% for up to one year.

Article 5

Agreements not covered by the exemption

1. The exemption provided for in Article 1 shall not apply to research and development agreements which, directly or indirectly, in isolation or in combination with other factors under the control of the parties, have as their object:

    (a) the restriction of the freedom of the participating undertakings to carry out research and development independently or in cooperation with third parties in a field unconnected with that to which the research and development relates or, after its completion, in the field to which it relates or in a connected field;

    (b) the prohibition to challenge after completion of the research and development the validity of intellectual property rights which the parties hold in the common market and which are relevant to the research and development or, after the expiry of the research and development agreement, the validity of intellectual property rights which the parties hold in the common market and which protect the results of the research and development, without prejudice to the possibilty to provide for termination of the research and development agreement in the event of one of the parties challenging the validity of such intellectual property rights;

    (c) the limitation of output or sales;

    (d) the fixing of prices when selling the contract product to third parties;

    (e) the restriction of the customers that the participating undertakings may serve, after the end of seven years from the time the contract products are first put on the market within the common market;

    (f) the prohibition to make passive sales of the contract products in territories reserved for other parties;

    (g) the prohibition to put the contract products on the market or to pursue an active sales policy for them in territories within the common market that are reserved for other parties after the end of seven years from the time the contract products are first put on the market within the common market;

    (h) the requirement not to grant licences to third parties to manufacture the contract products or to apply the contract processes where the exploitation by at least one of the parties of the results of the joint research and development is not provided for or does not take place;

    (i) the requirement to refuse to meet demand from users or resellers in their respective territories who would market the contract products in other territories within the common market; or

    (j) the requirement to make it difficult for users or resellers to obtain the contract products from other resellers within the common market, and in particular to exercise intellectual property rights or take measures so as to prevent users or resellers from obtaining, or from putting on the market within the common market, products which have been lawfully put on the market within the Community by another party or with its consent.

2. Paragraph 1 shall not apply to:

    (a) the setting of production targets where the exploitation of the results includes the joint production of the contract products;

    (b) the setting of sales targets and the fixing of prices charged to immediate customers where the exploitation of the results includes the joint distribution of the contract products.

Provision is made in Article 7 for the Commission to withdraw the benefit of the exemption should it have effects incompatible with Article 81(3). The situations mentioned in particular are: the limitation of the scope for third parties to carry out R&D in the field because of limited research capacity elsewhere; the substantial restriction of the access of third parties to the market for the products; the failure of the parties to exploit the R&D for no objectively valid reason; lack of effective competition in respect of the products; and the elimination as a result of the existence of the agreement of effective competition in R&D on a particular market. However, Regulation 1/2003, Article 29 contains a general power for the Commission to withdraw the benefit of any block exemption in an individual case.[97]

The main differences between Regulation 2659/2000 and the previous block exemption, Regulation, 418/85,[98] can be summed up as:

- there is no white list of exempted clauses. The block exemption applies to all restrictions of competition except those listed in Article 5, provided the conditions in Article 3 are fulfilled;

- ancillary provisions are exempted;

- there is a single market share threshold of 25 per cent whether or not joint distribution is involved;

- production targets can be set for a production joint venture;

- sales targets and prices can be set for distribution joint ventures;

- there is no condition about setting a framework programme defining objectives;

- there is no opposition procedure (which is not relevant following the coming into force of Regulation 1/2003 anyway).[99]

D. PRODUCTION AGREEMENTS

(i) The Guidelines

'Production agreements' in this context means unilateral or reciprocal specialization,[100] joint production, and sub-contracting agreements. Subcontracting agreements are those whereby one party entrusts the production of a product to another party. They are vertical agreements and may be covered by the block exemption, Regulation 2790/1999,[101] unless they are between competitors, in which case the Horizontal Cooperation Guidelines apply. If they are between non-competitors and involve the transfer of know-how to the sub-contractor the 1979 Notice on sub-contracting agreements applies.[102] That states that sub-contracting agreements whereby the sub-contractor undertakes to produce certain products exclusively for the contractor generally fall outside Article 81(1) (although other restrictions, such as the obligation on the sub-contractor not to conduct or exploit its own R&D may be caught). A sub-contracting

---

[97] See *supra* Chap. 4, 288. It is also possible under Article 29 for a Member State to withdraw it in respect of its own territory in certain circumstances.

[98] [1985] OJ L53/5.

[99] For the opposition procedure before 1 May 2004, see *infra* Chap. 14.

[100] See *supra* 1103.

[101] [1999] OJ L336/21.

[102] [1979] OJ C1/2. This Notice remains applicable: see Guidelines on technology transfer agreements, [2004] OJ C101/2, para. 44.

agreement involving a licence of technology may be covered by the block exemption on technology tranfer agreements.[103]

The Guidelines state that production agreements between non-competitors are not normally caught by Article 81(1).[104] However, agreements between competitors are not necessarily caught either:

87. Even production agreements between competitors do not necessarily come under Article 81(1). First, cooperation between firms which compete on markets closely related to the market directly concerned by the cooperation, cannot be defined as restricting competition, if the cooperation is the only commercially justifiable possible way to enter a new market, to launch a new product or service or to carry out a specific project.

88. Secondly, an effect on the parties' competitive behaviour as market suppliers is highly unlikely if the parties have a small proportion of their total costs in common. For instance, a low degree of commonality in total costs can be assumed where two or more companies agree on specialisation/joint production of an intermediate product which only accounts for a small proportion of the production costs of the final product and, consequently, the total costs. The same applies to a subcontracting agreement between competitors where the input which one competitor purchases from another only accounts for a small proportion of the production costs of the final product. A low degree of commonality of total costs can also be assumed where the parties jointly manufacture a final product, but only a small proportion as compared to their total output of the final product. Even if a significant proportion is jointly manufactured, the degree of commonality of total costs may nevertheless be low or moderate, if the cooperation concerns heterogeneous products which require costly marketing.

As with R&D agreements, the Guidelines distinguish between agreements which almost always fall under Article 81(1) because they fix prices, limit output, or share customers[105] and those which have to be assessed in their economic context. Again, the Commission takes as the starting point for the analysis the position of the parties in the market as 'without market power the parties to a production agreement do not have an incentive to coordinate their competitive behaviour as suppliers'. Further, 'there is no effect on competition in the market without market power of the parties, even if the parties would coordinate their behaviour'.[106]

The block exemption, Regulation 2658/2000, as we see below, applies only to parties with a combined market share of below 20 per cent. For agreements caught by Article 81(1) but not covered by the block exemption the Guidelines state:

96. If the parties' combined market share is larger than 20 per cent, the likely impact of the production agreement on the market must be assessed. In this respect market concentration as well as market shares will be a significant factor. The higher the combined market share of the parties, the higher the concentration in the market concerned. However, a moderately higher market share than allowed for in the block exemption does not necessarily imply a high concentration ratio. Far instance, a combined market share of the parties of slightly more than 20 per cent may occur in a market with a moderate concentration (HHI below 1800). In such a scenario a restrictive effect is unlikely. In a more concentrated market, however, a market share of more than 20 per cent may, alongside other elements, lead to a restriction of competition (see also example 1 below). The picture may nevertheless change, if the market is very dynamic with new participants entering the market and market positions changing frequently.

---

[103] Reg. 772/2004 [2004] OJ L123/11, see *supra* Chap. 10.

[104] Guidelines [2001] OJ C3/2, para. 86.

[105] For the exceptions to this see *ibid.* para. 90.

[106] Guidelines [2001] OJ C3/2, para. 92.

97. For joint production, network effects, i.e., links between a significant number of competitors, can also play an important role. In a concentrated market the creation of an additional link may tip the balance and make collusion in this market likely, even if the parties have a significant, but still moderate, combined market share (see example 2 below).

98. Under specific circumstances a cooperation between potential competitors may also raise competition concerns. This is, however, limited to cases where a strong player in one market cooperates with a realistic potential entrant, for instance, with a strong supplier of the same product or service in a neighbouring geographic market. The reduction of potential competition creates particular problems if actual competition is already weak and threat of entry is a major source of competition.

The Guidelines also consider cooperation in upstream markets:

99. Joint production of an important component or other input to the parties' final product can cause negative market effects under certain circumstances:

— Foreclosure problems ... provided that the parties have a strong position on the relevant input market (non-captive use) and that switching between captive and non-captive use would not occur in the presence of a small but permanent relative price increase for the product in question.

— Spill-over effects ... provided that the input is an important component of costs and that the parties have a strong position in the downstream market for the final product.

Subcontracting agreements between competitors

100. Similar problems can arise if a competitor subcontracts an important component or other input to its final product from a competitor. This can also lead to:

— Foreclosure problems provided that the parties have a strong position as either suppliers or buyers on the relevant input market (non-captive use). Subcontracting could then either lead to other competitors not being able to obtain this input at a competitive price or to other suppliers not being able to supply the input competitively if they will be losing a large part of their demand.

— Spill-over effects provided that the input is an important component of costs and that the parties have a strong position in the downstream market for the final product.

As with R&D agreements, the Guidelines set out a number of hypothetical examples, showing how Article 81(3) would be applied to various situations.

(ii) The Block Exemption Regulation on Specialization Agreements, Regulation 2658/2000[107]

Like Regulation 2659/2000 on R&D agreements, the block exemption on specialization agreements contains does not contain a 'white list' of exempted clauses and applies only below certain thresholds. Recital 5, which explains this, is identical to recital 7 in 2659/2000 which is set out above.[108]

---

[107] [2000] OJ L304/3.
[108] *Supra* 1112.

Article 1 of Regulation 2658/2000 defines the type of agreement to which it relates:

Article 1

Exemption

1. Pursuant to Article 81(3) of the Treaty and subject to the provisions of this Regulation, it is hereby declared that Article 81(1) shall not apply to the following agreements entered into between two or more undertakings (hereinafter referred to as 'the parties') which relate to the conditions under which those undertakings specialise in the production of products (hereinafter referred to as 'specialisation agreements'):

   (a) unilateral specialisation agreements, by virtue of which one party agrees to cease production of certain products or to refrain from producing those products and to purchase them from a competing undertaking, while the competing undertaking agrees to produce and supply those products; or

   (b) reciprocal specialisation agreements, by virtue of which two or more parties on a reciprocal basis agree to cease or refrain from producing certain but different products and to purchase these products from the other parties, who agree to supply them; or

   (c) joint production agreements, by virtue of which two or more parties agree to produce certain products jointly.

This exemption shall apply to the extent that such specialisation agreements contain restrictions of competition falling within the scope of Article 81(1) of the Treaty.

2. The exemption provided for in paragraph 1 shall also apply to provisions contained in specialisation agreements, which do not constitute the primary object of such agreements, but are directly related to and necessary for their implementation, such as those concerning the assignment or use of intellectual property rights.

The first subparagraph does, however, not apply to provisions which have the same object as the restrictions of competition enumerated in Article 5(1).

The exemption therefore covers two types of specialization properly so called, unilateral specialization (the *Prym/Beka* situation which was not covered by Regulation 417/85)[109] and reciprocal specialization. It also covers agreements for joint production. Further, it encompasses ancillary provisions 'such as those concerning the assignment or use of intellectual property rights' which do not constitute the primary object of the agreement.[110] The two types of specialization, however, are exempted only if the agreement contains cross purchase and supply obligations. Recital 12 explains that this is to ensure that the benefits of specialization materialize without one party leaving the market downstream of production. Article 3(a) allows the related purchase and supply obligations to be exclusive,[111] and Article 3(b) provides exemption

---

[109] See *supra* 1103.

[110] If provisions concerning patents, know-how or software were the primary object of the agreement they might be covered by block exemption Reg. 772/2004 [2004] OJ L123/11, on technology transfer agreements.

[111] An 'exclusive supply obligation' is defined (Art. 2(8)) as an obligation not to supply a competing undertaking other than a party to the agreement with the product to which the specialization agreement relates. Note that this is different from the definition of exclusive supply obligation in the block exemption on vertical agreements, Reg. 2790/1999, Art. 1(c) of which provides that it means 'any direct or indirect obligation causing the supplier to sell the goods or services specified in the agreement only to one buyer inside the Community for the purposes of a specific use or for resale'.

for provisions whereby the parties arrange for joint distribution or for distribution by a (non-competitor) third party.

The 'products' referred to in Article 1 means goods or services, including intermediate and final goods and services, but does not include distribution or rental services.[112]

Article 4 provides that the block exemption applies only where the participating undertakings do not have a combined market share which exceeds 20 per cent of the relevant market.[113] The block exemption contains a market share threshold because the Commission considers, as it states in Recital 13, that '[i]t can be presumed that, where the participating undertakings' share of the relevant market does not exceed 20 per cent, specialisation agreements of the category defined in this Regulation will, as a general rule, give rise to economic benefits in the form of economies of scale or scope or better production technologies, while allowing consumers a fair share of the resulting benefits'.[114]

Article 5 contains the 'black list' of three hard-core restrictions, the presence of which in an agreement prevents the application of the block exemption:

Article 5

Agreements not covered by the exemption

1. The exemption provided for in Article 1 shall not apply to agreements which, directly or indirectly, in isolation or in combination with other factors under the control of the parties, have as their object:

    (a) the fixing of prices when selling the products to third parties;

    (b) the limitation of output or sales; or

    (c) the allocation of markets or customers.

2. Paragraph 1 shall not apply to:

    (a) provisions on the agreed amount of products in the context of unilateral or reciprocal specialisation agreements or the setting of the capacity and production volume of a production joint venture in the context of a joint production agreement;

    (b) the setting of sales targets and the fixing of prices that a production joint venture charges to its immediate customers in the context of point (b) of Article 3.

The proviso makes it clear that Article 5 does not outlaw provisions limiting the number of products subject to the specialization, or the amount to be produced by a production joint venture. It is also permissible to fix the prices charged by a production joint venture which also distributes the products.

As is the case with Regulation 2659/2000 the block exemption contains a provision allowing the Commission to withdraw the benefit of the block exemption from a particular agreement where it finds that the agreement's effects are incompatible with Article 81(3).[115]

---

[112] Reg. 2658/2000, Art. 2(4).

[113] Reg. 2658/2000, Art. 6, contains the same provisions about the calculation of market share as appear in Reg. 2659 on R&D (see *supra* 1114) except that the marginal relief, of course, starts from the base of 20% and not 25%.

[114] See also the importance accorded to market power in the Guidelines [2001] OJ C3/2, *supra* 1107.

[115] But note the provision in Reg. 1/2003 about withdrawal by the Commission and by Member States: see *supra* 1116.

The main differences between Regulation 2658/2000 and the previous block exemption are:

(i)   there is no white list of exempted clauses in 2658/2000. The block exemption applies to all restrictions of competition except those listed in Article 5;

(ii)   there is no turnover threshold, only the market share threshold of 20 per cent;

(iii)   the agreement must contain a cross supply obligation;

(iv)   exclusive supply and purchase obligations are permitted;

(v)   it applies to both products and services;

(vi)   it applies to unilateral as well as reciprocal specialization;

(vii)   a limit on capacity and production may be set;

(viii)   prices may be fixed where a production joint venture carries out distribution;

(ix)   ancillary provisions can be included.[116]

E. PURCHASING AGREEMENTS

Purchasing agreements concern the joint buying of products. Often, as the Guidelines say, they are concluded by small and medium sized enterprises:

115. This chapter focuses on agreements concerning the joint buying of products. Joint buying can be carried out by a jointly controlled company, by a company in which many firms hold a small stake, by a contractual arrangement or even looser form of cooperation.

116. Purchasing agreements are often concluded by small and medium-sized enterprises to achieve volumes and discounts similar to their bigger competitors. These agreements between small and medium-sized enterprises are therefore normally pro-competitive. Even if a moderate degree of market power is created, this may be outweighed by economies of scale provided the parties actually bundle volume.

Both horizontal and vertical agreements may be involved in joint purchasing. First, there will be horizontal agreements (assessed in accordance with these Guidelines) between the joint purchasers. If that is acceptable the vertical agreements between the joint purchasers and their suppliers and between the joint purchasers and individual members must be assessed (in accordance with the Guidelines on Vertical Restraints[117]).[118]

Moreover, joint purchasing agreements may affect two markets. First, the market(s) on which the joint purchasers buy (the purchasing, or procurement, market) and secondly, the downstream market(s) on which they sell.[119] The purchasing market will have to be defined from the supply side[120] and it is the alternatives for suppliers which are relevant.[121] The downstream selling market will be relevant if the joint purchasers are competitors there.[122]

Article 81(1) will rarely apply to purchasing agreements where the parties are not active on the same relevant market downstream unless they have a very strong position in the purchasing

---

[116] The Regulation also contains no opposition procedure, but see *supra* 1116 about this.

[117] [2000] OJ C291/1.

[118] Guidelines on horizontal cooperation agreements, para. 117.

[119] *Ibid.*, para. 119.

[120] In accordance with the Commission Notice on market definition [1997] OJ 372/5.

[121] Guidelines on horizontal cooperation agreements, para. 121.

[122] *Ibid.*, para. 122.

market, i.e., have buyer power.[123] Retailers forming a joint purchasing association to give themselves a better bargaining position *vis-à-vis* their suppliers may well be active in different geographic markets.

Purchasing agreements only come under Article 81(1) by their nature if they are in reality a disguised cartel.[124]

Most purchasing agreements, therefore, are in the category 'may fall under Article 81(1)' and have to be analysed in their legal and economic context. The starting point for this is the degree of the parties' buyer power. Buying power may be anti, rather than pro-competitive, for example where the parties have significant power on the selling market.

128. First, lower purchasing costs resulting from the exercise of buying power cannot be seen as pro-competitive, if the purchasers together have power on the selling markets. In this case, the cost savings are probably not passed on to consumers. The more combined power the parties have on their selling markets, the higher is the incentive for the parties to coordinate their behaviour as sellers. This may be facilitated if the parties achieve a high degree of commonality of costs through joint purchasing. For instance, if a group of large retailers buys a high proportion of their products together, they will have a high proportion of their total cost in common. The negative effects of joint buying can therefore be rather similar to joint production.

129. Secondly, power on the selling markets may be created or increased through buying power which is used to foreclose competitors or to raise rivals' costs. Significant buying power by one group of customers may lead to foreclosure of competing buyers by limiting their access to efficient suppliers. It can also cause cost increases for its competitors because suppliers will try to recover price reductions for one group of customers by increasing prices for other customers (e.g., rebate discrimination by suppliers of retailers). This is only possible if the suppliers of the purchasing markets also have a certain degree of market power. In both cases, competition in the selling markets can be further restricted by buying power.

The Commission takes a 15 per cent combined market share as the starting point. If the parties to the agreement have less than this on both purchasing and selling markets there is unlikely to be a market power problem.

130. There is no absolute threshold which indicates that a buying cooperation creates some degree of market power and thus falls under Article 81(1). However, in most cases, it is unlikely that market power exists if the parties to the agreement have a combined market share of below 15 per cent on the purchasing market(s) as well as a combined market share of below 15 per cent on the selling market(s). In any event, at that level of market share it is likely that the conditions of Article 81(3) explained below are fulfilled by the agreement in question.

131. A market share above this threshold does not automatically indicate that a negative market effect is caused by the cooperation but requires a more detailed assessment of the impact of a joint buying agreement on the market, involving factors such as the market concentration and possible countervailing power of strong suppliers. Joint buying that involves parties with a combined market share significantly above 15 per cent in a concentrated market is likely to come under Article 81(1), and efficiencies that may outweigh the restrictive effect have to be shown by the parties.

The Guidelines then set out how Article 81(3) applies to purchasing agreements which *do* fall within Article 81(1).

---

[123] Guidelines on horizontal cooperation agreements., para. 123.

[124] *Ibid.*, para. 124.

4.4.1. Economic benefits

132. Purchasing agreements can bring about economic benefits such as economies of scale in ordering or transportation which may outweigh restrictive effects. If the parties together have significant buying or selling power, the issue of efficiencies has to be examined carefully. Cost savings that are caused by the mere exercise of power and which do not benefit consumers cannot be taken into account.

4.4.2. Indispensability

133. Purchasing agreements cannot be exempted if they impose restrictions that are not indispensable to the attainment of the above mentioned benefits. An obligation to buy exclusively through the cooperation can in certain cases be indispensable to achieve the necessary volume for the realisation of economies of scale. However, such an obligation has to be assessed in the context of the individual case.

4.4.3. No elimination of competition

134. No exemption will be possible, if the parties are afforded the possibility of eliminating competition in respect of a substantial part of the products in question. This assessment has to cover buying and selling markets. The combined market shares of the parties can be regarded as a starting point. It then needs to be evaluated whether these market shares are indicative of a dominant position, and whether there are any mitigating factors, such as countervailing power of suppliers on the purchasing markets or potential for market entry in the selling markets. Where as a consequence of a purchasing agreement an undertaking is dominant or becoming dominant on either the buying or selling market, such an agreement which produces anti-competitive effects in the meaning of Article 81 can in principle not be exempted.

This is followed by a number of examples.

Gøttrup-Klim,[125] which is discussed in Chapter 4,[126] was a major case on joint purchasing. It will be recalled that there was a Danish cooperative association (DLG) which purchased farming supplies such as fertilizers on behalf of its members. The case arose because of a challenge to DLG's rules, which precluded its members from belonging to any competing cooperative. The Court held that the rules were not caught by Article 81(1) insofar as they were necessary to ensure the proper functioning of the cooperative. The Court recognized that the whole point of the cooperative was to present a significant counter-weight to the large, multi-national, suppliers.

In *Métropole Télévision*[127] the Commission dealt with a joint purchasing agreement in respect of television rights to sporting events. The European Broadcasting Union (EBU) is an association of radio and television organizations established in 1950. The main framework of the exchange of programmes amongst EBU members is Eurovsion. To become an active member a broadcasting organization must satisfy certain conditions, *inter alia*, as to its national coverage and the nature and financing of programmes. Métropole tried six times since 1987 to join the

---

[125] Case C-250/92, *Gøttrup-Klim Grovvareforeninger* v. *Dansk Landburgs Grovvareselskab AmbA* [1994] ECR I-5641, [1996] 4 CMLR 191.

[126] *Supra*, 251.

[127] Cases T-185/00, T-216/00, T-299/00 and T-300/00, *Métropole Télévision SA (M6) and others* v. *Commission* [2002] ECR II-3805, [2003] 4 CMLR 707.

EBU but was rejected each time. This led to an ongoing battle between Métropole and the EBU which has surfaced several times in the Community Courts. In the present case Métropole had complained about EBU practices concerning the acquisition of TV rights to sporting events. The original EBU rules on this were exempted by the Commission[128] but the decision was annulled on appeal by Métropole.[129] The Commission adopted a decision in May 2000 exempting revised rules.[130] This too was challenged by Métropole in the CFI.

Cases T-185/00, T-216/00, T-299/00 and T-300/00, *Métropole Télévision SA (M6) and others* v. *Commission* [2002] ECR II-3805, [2003] 4 CMLR 707

The rules in question concerned granting access to Eurovision rights for pay-TV. The rules provided a 'sub-licensing scheme' which granted access to Eurovision rights to major sporting events to third parties who were competitors of EBU members. The Commission exempted EBU's rules for the sharing of jointly acquired sports TV rights on the grounds that the sub-licensing scheme guaranteed access to the competitors and therefore avoided the elimination of competition in the market. The condition in Article 81(3) was therefore satisfied. Métropole claimed this was not so. The Commission did not settle on an exact definition of the market but contended that even on the basis of the narrowest possible definition (the acquisition of rights for a specific event such as the Football World Cup or the Summer Olympics) there was no elimination of competition. The CFI accepted that the Commission's assertion that the market could consist entirely of major sporting events did not affect the analysis of whether Article 81(3) was satisfied. It then turned to consider whether in making that analysis the Commission had made a manifest error of assessment.

Court of First Instance

63. As regards the effects of the Eurovision system on competition, the contested decision shows (paragraphs 71 to 80) that there are two types of restrictions. First, the joint acquisition of television rights to sporting events, their sharing and the exchange of signal restricts or even eliminates competition among EBU members which are competitors on both the upstream market, for the acquisition of rights, and for the downstream market, for televised transmission of sporting events. In addition, that system gives rise to restrictions on competition as regards third parties since those rights, as set out in paragraph 75 of the contested decision, are generally sold on an exclusive basis, so that EBU non-members would not in principle have access to them.

64. While it is true that the purchase of televised transmission rights for an event is not in itself a restriction on competition likely to fall under Article 81(1) EC and may be justified by particular characteristics of the product and the market in question, the exercise of those rights in a specific legal and economic context may none the less lead to such a restriction (see, by analogy, Case 262/81 Coditel v. Ciné-Vog Films [1982] ECR 3381, paragraphs 15 to 17).

65. In that vein, the Commission states, in paragraph 45 of the contested decision, that 'the acquisition of exclusive TV rights to certain major sporting events has a strong impact on the downstream television markets in which the sporting events are broadcast'.

66. In addition, it appears from the analysis of the documents in the case and the arguments of the parties that the acquisition of transmission rights to a major international sporting event such

---

[128] [1993] OJ L179/23, [1995] 4 CMLR 56

[129] Cases T-528, 542, 543 and 546/93, *Métropole Télévision SA* v. *Commission* [1996] ECR II-649, [1996] 5 CMLR 386.

[130] [2000] OJ L151/18, [2000] 5 CMLR 650.

as the Olympics or the football World Cup cannot fail to affect strongly the market in sponsorship and advertising, which is the main source of revenue for television channels which broadcast free-to-air, since those programmes attract a very wide audience.

67. Moreover, as pointed out by SIC, the effects which restrict competition for third parties as a result of the Eurovision system are accentuated, first, by the level of vertical integration of the EBU and its members, which are not merely purchasers of rights but also television operators which broadcast the rights purchased, and second, by the geographic extent of the EBU, whose members broadcast in all the countries of the European Union. As a result, when the EBU acquires transmission rights for an international sporting event, the access to that event is in principle auto-matically precluded for all non-member operators. By contrast, the situation appears to be differ-ent when the transmission rights for sporting events are acquired by an agency which buys those rights in order to resell them, or when they are bought by a media group which only has operators in certain Member States, since that group will tend to enter into negotiations with operators in other Member States in order to sell those rights. In that case, despite the exclusive purchase of the rights, other operators still have the opportunity to negotiate their acquisition for their respective markets.

68. In light of those facts—that is, the structure of the market, the position of the EBU in the market for certain international sporting events and the level of vertical integration of the EBU and its members—there is reason to determine whether the scheme for third-party access to the Eurovision system makes it possible to counterbalance the restrictions on competition affecting those third parties and thus to avoid their exclusion from competition.

73. However, even if it proves necessary, for reasons linked to exclusive transmission rights for sporting events and the guarantee of their economic value (see paragraph 60 above), for EBU members to reserve for themselves live transmission of the programmes acquired by the EBU, none of these reasons justifies their being able to extend that right to all the competitions which are part of the same event, even when they do not intend to broadcast all those competitions live.

. . .

83. All the information provided to the Court of First Instance thus goes to show that, contrary to what the Commission concludes in the contested decision, the sub-licensing scheme does not guarantee competitors of EBU members sufficient access to rights to transmit sporting events held by the latter on the basis of their participation in that purchasing association. Apart from a few exceptions, nothing in the rules or mode of implementation of the scheme enables competi-tors of EBU members to obtain sub-licences for the live broadcast of unused Eurovision rights. In reality, the scheme merely permits the acquisition of sub-licences to transmit roundups of com-petitions under extremely restrictive conditions.

The CFI therefore annulled the decision on the ground that the condition about no elimination of competition in Article 81(3) was not satisfied.

F. COMMERCIALIZATION AGREEMENTS

(i) General

Commercialization agreements are dealt with in paragraphs 139–58 of the Guidelines. They are described there as agreements involving cooperation between competitors in the selling, distri-bution or promotion of their products. This covers a wide spectrum of agreements.

139. . . . At one end of the spectrum, there is joint selling that leads to a joint determination of all commercial aspects related to the sale of the product including price. At the other end, there are

more limited agreements that only address one specific marketing function, such as distribution, service, or advertising.

Where the commercialization is in the context of another form of cooperation, e.g., joint production or purchasing, the agreement should be analysed in accordance with the section of the Guidelines relevant to that.[131]

Where the commercialization agreement deals solely with joint distribution, the Guidelines point out that (as will be recalled from Chapter 9)[132] the Verticals Regulation[133] only covers non-reciprocal agreements between competitors and then only if the conditions in Article 2(4) are met. In other cases the agreements must be analyzed in accordance with the horizontal cooperation Guidelines and if the horizontal aspects are acceptable the vertical aspects will be assessed under the Verticals Guidelines.[134]

Commercialization agreements between non-competitors do not infringe Article 81(1) in relation to their *horizontal* aspects, but may fall within Article 81(1) in respect of their *vertical* aspects. The Guidelines specifically say that there is no restriction of competition where undertakings submit a joint tender for projects for which they could not bid individually. The Commission states that in this situation the undertakings are not potential competitors for the tender.[135]

The Commission's main concern about about commercialization agreements between competitors is price fixing, and any agreement which has that object or effect will fall within Article 81(1).

5.3.1.2. Agreements that almost always fall under Article 81(1)

144. The principal competition concern about a commercialization agreement between competitors is price fixing. Agreements limited to joint selling have as a rule the object and effect of coordinating the pricing policy of competing manufacturers. In this case they not only eliminate price competition between the parties but also restrict the volume of products to be delivered by the participants within the framework of the system for allocating orders. They therefore restrict competition between the parties on the supply side and limit the choice of purchasers and fall under Article 81(1).

145. This appreciation does not change if the agreement is non-exclusive. Article 81(1) continues to apply even where the parties are free to sell outside the agreement, as long as it can be presumed that the agreement will lead to an overall coordination of the prices charged by the parties.

Where the cooperation does not involve joint selling the Commission is concerned with the exchange of sensitive commercial information and the opportunities for market partitioning.

---

[131] Guidelines, para. 141.
[132] See *supra* 746.
[133] Reg. 2790/1999 [1999] OJ L336/21.
[134] Horizontal Cooperation Guidelines, para. 140.
[135] *Ibid.*, para. 143.

5.3.1.3. Agreements that may fall under Article 81(1)

146. For commercialization arrangements that fall short of joint selling there will be two major concerns. The first is that the joint commercialization provides a clear opportunity for exchanges of sensitive commercial information particularly on marketing strategy and pricing. The second is that, depending on the cost structure of the commercialization, a significant input to the parties' final costs may be common. As a result the actual scope for price competition at the final sales level may be limited. Joint commercialization agreements therefore can fall under Article 81(1) if they either allow the exchange of sensitive commercial information, or if they influence a significant part of the parties' final cost.

147. A specific concern related to distribution arrangements between competitors which are active in different geographic markets is that they can lead to or be an instrument of market partitioning. In the case of reciprocal agreements to distribute each other's products, the parties to the agreement allocate markets or customers and eliminate competition between themselves. The key question in assessing an agreement of this type is if the agreement in question is objectively necessary for the parties to enter each other's market. If it is, the agreement does not create competition problems of a horizontal nature. However, the distribution agreement can fall under Article 81(1) if it contains vertical restraints, such as restrictions on passive sales, resale price maintenance, etc. If the agreement is not objectively necessary for the parties to enter each other's market, it falls under 81(1). If the agreement is not reciprocal, the risk of market partitioning is less pronounced. It needs however to be assessed if the non-reciprocal agreement constitutes the basis for a mutual understanding to not enter each other's market or is a means to control access to or competition on the 'importing' market.

As with other forms of horizontal cooperation, market power is the key issue. Cooperation agreements between competitors which do not involve price fixing are only subject to Article 81(1) if the parties have some degree of market power. Again, market power is said to be unlikely to exist if the parties have a combined market share below 15 per cent.[136] Where the agreement does fall to be assessed under Article 81(3) the Commission gives a general indication of how an agreement may fulfil the Article 81(3) criteria, and then gives examples.

5.4.1. Economic benefits

151. The efficiencies to be taken into account when assessing whether a joint commercialization agreement can be exempted will depend upon the nature of the activity. Price fixing can generally not be justified, unless it is indispensable for the integration of other marketing functions, and this integration will generate substantial efficiencies. The size of the efficiencies generated depends, *inter alia*, on the importance of the joint marketing activities for the overall cost structure of the product in question. Joint distribution is thus more likely to generate significant efficiencies for producers of widely distributed consumer products than for producers of industrial products which are only bought by a limited number of users.

152. In addition, the claimed efficiencies should not be savings which result only from the elimination of costs that are inherently part of competition, but must result from the integration of economic activities. A reduction of transport cost which is only a result of customer allocation without any integration of the logistical system can therefore not be regarded as an efficiency that would make an agreement exemptable.

---

[136] *Ibid.*, para. 149.

153. Claimed efficiency benefits must be demonstrated. An important element in this respect would be the contribution by both parties of significant capital, technology, or other assets. Cost savings through reduced duplication of resources and facilities can also be accepted. If, on the other hand, the joint commercialization represents no more than a sales agency with no investment, it is likely to be a disguised cartel and as such cannot fulfil the conditions of Article 81(3).

5.4.2. Indispensability

154. A commercialization agreement cannot be exempted if it imposes restrictions that are not indispensable to the attainment of the abovementioned benefits. As discussed above, the question of indispensability is especially important for those agreements involving price fixing or the allocation of markets.

5.4.3. No elimination of competition

155. No exemption will be possible, if the parties are afforded the possibility of eliminating competition in respect of a substantial part of the products in question. In making this assessment, the combined market shares of the parties can be regarded as a starting point. One then needs to evaluate whether these market shares are indicative of a dominant position, and whether there are any mitigating factors, such as the potential for market entry. Where as a consequence of a commercialization agreement an undertaking is dominant or becoming dominant, such an agreement which produces anti-competitive effects in the meaning of Article 81 can in principle not be exempted.

(ii) The Joint Selling of Football Rights

The Commission has been much concerned with the joint selling of commercial rights[137] to football, in particular the media rights. The rights to screen football matches, particularly live, are immensely valuable.

In most countries football is not only the driving force for the development of pay-TV services but is also an essential programme item for free-TV broadcasters. Joint selling of free-TV and pay-TV rights combined with wide exclusive terms therefore has significant effects on the structure of the TV broadcasting markets as it can enhance media concentration and hamper competition between broadcasters. If one broadcaster holds all or most of the relevant football TV rights in a Member State, it is extremely difficult for competing broadcasters to establish themselves successfully in that market.[138]

The selling arrangements amount to joint selling in as much as the media rights are not sold by the individual clubs, but collectively, through the league or association to which they belong. The Commission stated its basic position in the Helsinki Report on Sport in 1999:

Any exemptions granted in the case of the joint sale of broadcasting rights must take account of the benefits for consumers and of the proportional nature of the restriction on competition in relation to the legitimate objective pursued. In this context, there is also a need to examine the extent to which a link can be established between the joint sale of rights and financial solidarity between professional and amateur sport, the objectives of the training of young sportsmen and women and those of

---

[137] Media rights (radio, television, Internet, and UMTS), sponsorship, suppliership, licensing, and intellectual property rights.

[138] *Joint selling of the commercial rights of the UEFA Champions League* [2003] OJ L291/25, [2004] 4 CMLR 9 (UEFA), para. 20.

promoting sporting activities among the population. However, with regard to the sale of exclusive rights to broadcast sporting events, it is likely that any exclusivity which, by its duration and/or scope, resulted in the closing of the market, would be prohibited.[139]

A declaration on sport, based on the Helsinki Report, was pronounced at the European Council in Nice in December 2000. This proclaimed the Community's recognition of the social, educational, and cultural functions of sport and laid down principles with a view to preserving, *inter alia*, 'the cohesion and ties of solidarity that exist in sport at all levels' and fair competition. Of the sale of television rights it said:

As the sale of television broadcasting rights is one of the greatest sources of income for certain sports, the sharing of part of the corresponding revenue among the appropriate levels may be beneficial in order to preserve the principle of solidarity in sport.

In July 2003 the Commission granted an Article 81(3) exemption to the arrangements for selling the media rights to the UEFA Champions League.[140] UEFA[141] is an association of national football associations and the regulatory authority of European football. The Champions League is 'UEFA's most prestigious club competition'.[142] The exemption was the outcome of a lengthy negotiation. UEFA notified its new joint selling arrangements in 1999 but the Commission objected to them because UEFA wanted to sell all the television rights to the group and knockout phases of the Champions League[143] in one package to a single broadcaster on an exclusive basis for up to four years at a time. UEFA finally agreed to amend the selling arrangements. Under the exemption, which took effect in the 2003–4 season, the rights are split into different packages and offered for sale in a competitive bidding procedure open to all interested media operators. The main rights are in the Gold and Silver packages, which give the winning broadcasters the right to pick the best matches. The Bronze package is also initially offered by UEFA but if not sold the matches comprising it can be sold by the individual clubs. Furthermore, both UEFA and the clubs can offer Champions League content to Internet and mobile phone operators, and individual clubs can offer rights to their matches on a deferred basis and for video production. UEFA will sell the rights for no longer than three years at a time, and do it through a public tender procedure.

The Commission adopted a commitments decision in respect of the German Bundesliga's joint selling of broadcasting rights.[144] It accepted commitments which were essentially similar to those in the UEFA case. The Bundesligia were to make several packages available to broadcasters and exclusivity is not to last longer than three years at a time. This was the first commitments decision taken under Regulation 1/2003, Article 9.[145]

The exclusive rights to screen live English Football Association Premier League matches has been the engine which has driven the expansion of Sky in the UK. The rights are therefore extremely valuable to Sky, which is in consequence willing to pay extraordinarily large sums of

[139] Report from the Commission to the European Council with a view to safeguarding current sports structures and maintaining the social function of sport within the Community framework—*The Helsinki Report on Sport*, 10 Dec. 1999, para. 4.2.1.3.

[140] *Joint selling of the commercial rights of the UEFA Champions League* [2003] OJ L291/25, [2004] 4 CMLR 549; Commission Press Release, IP/03/2003.

[141] Union des Associations Européennes de Football.

[142] *UEFA*, para. 5. The Champions League is contested by the top clubs from the domestic leagues (based on their position at the end of the preceding season), although the rules on who 'gets into Europe' are somewhat arcane. There are 16 'automatic qualifiers'.

[143] The part of the competition which begins, with the final 32 clubs, in September each year.

[144] [2005] OJ L134/46.

[145] See *infra*, Chap. 14.

money to retain them. Those sums of money have, in turn, transformed English football. The Premier League was formed in 1992 and its revenues have increased sevenfold since then. The money has enabled English clubs to bring in star international players which makes Premier League matches even more attractive, outside as well as inside the UK. Not everyone is happy however. Free-to-air television has never been able to show live Premier League matches.[146] Non-subscribers to Sky cannot see the matches (in their own homes, at least), even though they have to pay the BBC licence fee to legally watch television at all. It is a factor which makes some viewers resentful of the licence fee. The commercial terrestrial stations lose out on valuable advertising rights, particularly as young males, who as a group otherwise watch comparatively little television,[147] can be reached during football coverage. There are also arguments (outside the remit of a book on competition law) that the money pumped into the Premier League has had a deleterious effect on English professional football as a whole.

The Commission was unhappy about the Premier League/Sky situation because it considered that the situation was disadvantageous to consumers. It saw what was in effect two monopolists coming to a cosy arrangement in which one party demands sums of money for its products which are so large that it knows only the other party can possibly afford to pay them. This is 'tantamount to price-fixing' according to the Commission.[148] The Commission (on its own initiative) opened an investigation in June 2001 into the sale of the Premier League rights. In June 2002 the Premier League notified its joint selling regulations to the Commission and requested clearance for them. The Commission sent a Statement of Objections to the Premier League in December 2002. It considered the arrangements anti-competitive.

In response the Premier League revised its arrangements with Sky. It had previously packaged its rights to live matches in two packages, both of which had been sold to Sky. The Premier League repackaged them into four lots and put these out to competitive tender in June 2003. Sky still ended up with all 138 games on offer, simply because it could bid so much more than any other broadcaster (£1.02 billion for a three year deal starting from the 2004–5 season). However, there were some other concessions.[149] The Commission was still not satisfied, and after six months of intense negotiation a compromise was reached in December 2003. Sky agreed that from the start of the 2004–5 season it would offer to sub-license a set of up to eight top quality Premier League matches each season to another broadcaster (so that for the first time it would be possible for live Premiership matches to appear on free-to-air television). Moreover, and more significantly, the Premier League had to agree to ensure that its tendering process would result in at least two broadcasters of live Premier League matches (the Single Buyer Rule):

... the Premier League will create balanced packages of matches showcasing the Premier League as a whole, and no one broadcaster will be allowed to buy all of the packages. The Premier League will also examine, jointly with the Commission, the way in which the auctions are conducted to ensure that they do not exclude potential competitors.[150]

---

[146] Indeed, before 1992 UK television could not show live Football League matches because the League considered that the club's gate receipts would fall as fans would not bother to attend if they could watch it on television. The Premier League/Sky arrangement has proved that wrong. Free-to-air television does carry (at least at the time of writing) other matches live, such as FA Cup matches.

[147] Surveys show that women over 55 years old watch the most.

[148] Commission Press Release IP/02/1951, issued when the Commission sent the Statement of Objections to the Premier League, 20 Dec. 2002.

[149] e.g., all matches not shown live would be shown later, and video clips could be delivered to mobile phones immediately, rather than after a delay. Internet and club television rights were also improved.

[150] Commission Press Release, IP/03/1748, 16 Dec. 2003. The Commission issued a Notice under Reg. 17, Art. 19(3) announcing its intention, once Reg. 1/2003 had become applicable, to adopt a decision under Reg. 1/2003, Art. 9 making the FAPL's commitments legally enforceable (see infra Chap. 14, 1207): [2004] OJ C115/3.

The Competition Commissioner, Mario Monti, said of the deal:

As consumer groups have argued, there are very real concerns with the way in which the Premier League has been treating football fans in the UK. I believe that the two-stage approach which has been agreed will safeguard the interests of these fans both now and in the future, while ensuring an orderly transition for the clubs.

By creating opportunities for broadcasters other than BSkyB now, and even greater opportunities in the future, the Commission is aiming to increase consumer choice in the UK. For the first time, there is a real opportunity for free to air broadcasters to provide their viewers with top flight Premier League action throughout the season.[151]

In the end no buyer was found for the sub-licence package agreed in December 2003.[152] Further negotiations resulted in a commitments decision in March 2006.[153] In this Decision the FAPL undertook commitments that were a strengthened version of those offered in December 2003. The FAPL agreed to offer live TV rights in six packages, more evenly balanced than previously, of which no single buyer may buy more than five; mobile phone rights will be made available during matches; increased radio rights will be made available; clubs can continue to exploit certain rights on a deferred basis; and the rights marketed by the FAPL will be sold to the highest stand-alone bidder. The decision applies until June 2013. The Competition Commissioner said in a press release at the time of the decision:

The solution we have reached will benefit football fans while allowing the Premier League to maintain its timetable for the sale of its rights.

However, the Commissioner may have been too sanguine over benefits to football fans. The rights packages for the 2007–2010 seasons have gone to BSkyB and another pay-TV company, Sentana. The BSkyB monopoly has been broken, but free to air television has not gained. BSkyB paid £1.3 billion for its rights, a figure way beyond the capacity of the BBC. The armchair football fan is now faced with having to pay two subscriptions to view the whole range of matches made available by the FAPL, instead on one.[154] The ideal for most football fans would be free to air coverage[155] but, given they have to pay, they were not concerned with the fact that until now BSkyB has had all the matches. The complaints were not from the viewers.[156] The result of the commitments decision is unlikely to be lower subscription fees.

The selling of media rights to football raises very sharply the issue of when competition authorities should intervene in markets to produce an outcome which is in some way more palatable to them than that which results from the free play of market forces. The reason why the June 2003 auction of the Premier League's rights failed to produce an outcome the Commission liked was that nothing could give the other broadcasters the money to match Sky. In effect there was only ever one possible purchaser. This was the free market economy in all its glory and the Premier League clubs found it difficult to understand why the Commission should be able to devalue its rights. In this area, however, there are matters of the sanctity of sport, as evinced in the

---

[151] *Ibid.*

[152] *The Times*, 13 May 2004. BSkyB had been allowed to set a reserve price and the bids received were too low.

[153] Case COMP/C-2/38.173, Joint selling of the media rights to the FA Premier League, 22 March 2006, [2006] 5 CMLR 1430.

[154] Unless to the two companies do some kind of deal.

[155] Although many *aficionados* currently consider Sky's football coverage superior to that of the terrestrial broadcasters.

[156] See the Ofcom report, 'Premier League Football. Research into viewing trends, stadium attendance, fans; preferences and behaviour, and the commercial market' (2005), available at http://ec.europa.eu/comm/competition/antitrust/cases/decisions/38173/en.pdf, which details the fans' overall satisfaction.

Council's Nice declaration, to consider. Moreover, the Commission is well aware of the central place which football plays in the life of Europe. While football rights continue to be sold collectively the Commission can deal with this matter as one of joint selling agreements, rather than grapple with any possible application of Article 82. As noted above, however, the Commission may itself decide that individual rather than joint selling would be preferable on competition grounds.[157] In January 2004 the Commission launched a broad investigation under Regulation 17, Article 12[158] into the sale of sports rights to Internet companies and to providers of third generation (3G) mobile phone services.[159] The report was published in September 2005.[160]

G. STANDARDIZATION AGREEMENTS

Standardization agreements are those which 'have as their primary objective the definition of technical or quality requirements with which current or future product, production processes or methods may comply'.[161] The Guidelines do not apply to the provision of professional services.[162]

Three relevant markets may be affected by a standardization agreement: that for the product(s) to which the standard(s) relate; the service market for standard setting (where a number of bodies may be active); and the market for testing and certification.[163]

Some standard setting will not fall within Article 81(1) at all.

163. Where participation in standard setting is unrestricted and transparent, standardisation agreements as defined above, which set no obligation to comply with the standard or which are parts of a wider agreement to ensure compatibility of products, do not restrict competition. This normally applies to standards adopted by the recognised standards bodies which are based on non-discriminatory, open and transparent procedures.

164. No appreciable restriction exists for those standards that have a negligible coverage of the relevant market, as long as it remains so. No appreciable restriction is found either in agreements which pool together SMEs to standardise access forms or conditions to collective tenders or those that standardise aspects such as minor product characteristics, forms and reports, which have an insignificant effect on the main factors affecting competition in the relevant markets.

On the other hand, where standard setting is in effect a means of excluding competitors, the agreement will fall within Article 81(3).[164]

Agreements may fall within Article 81(1) where they give the parties joint control over production and/or innovation. The Commission is concerned that scope should remain for the parties to develop alternative standards, or competing products which do not meet the standards (unless of course they are regulatory provisions, over safety for example).[165]

---

[157] It would also be open, of course, for a national competition authority apply the competition rules to their domestic league's agreements.

[158] See *Supra* Chap. 11,935. This provision is now Reg. 1/2003, Art. 17.

[159] Commission Press Release, 30 Jan. 2004, IP/04/134.

[160] See http://ec.europa.eu/comm/competition/antitrust/others/sector_inquiries/new_media/3g/final_report.pdf.

[161] *Ibid.*, para. 159. Standardization can range from the adoption of national consensus standards by the recognized European or national standards bodies, through consortia or fora, to agreements between single companies (Guidelines, n. 47).

[162] Guidelines, para. 160.

[163] *Ibid.*, para. 161.

[164] *Ibid.*, para. 165.

[165] *Ibid.*, para. 167.

In respect of standardization agreements the Commission does not have its usual concerns over market power and market shares. Rather, it is concerned that the standardization does not constitute a barrier to entry and foreclose third parties.

> 168. High market shares held by the parties in the market(s) affected will not necessarily be a concern for standardisation agreements. Their effectiveness is often proportional to the share of the industry involved in setting and/or applying the standard. On the other hand, standards that are not accessible to third parties may discriminate or foreclose third parties or segment markets according to their geographic scope of application. Thus, the assessment whether the agreement restricts competition will focus, necessarily on an individual basis, on the extent to which such barriers to entry are likely to be overcome.

In respect of a standardization agreement which does fall within Article 81(1), the Guidelines state that in order to fulfill the Article 81(3) conditions:

- The standardization must be available to those wishing to enter the market and an appreciable proportion of the industry must be involved in the setting of the standard in a transparent manner;[166]

- As standards will not include all possible specifications and technologies and it may be necessary in some cases to have only one solution, the standardization must be set on a non-discriminatory basis. Standardization should, ideally, be technology neutral. The parties must be able to justify the choice of one standard rather than another;[167]

- All competitors affected by the standard should have the possibility of being involved in setting the standard;[168]

- Normally there should be a clear distinction between setting the standard and its commercial exploitation;[169]

- If the agreement results in a de facto industry standard it must be as open as possible and applied in a non-discriminatory way. Third parties must have access on fair, reasonable, and non-discriminatory terms.[170] Competition must not be eliminated by foreclosing third parties.[171]

H. ENVIRONMENTAL AGREEMENTS

Environmental agreements are something quite specific. They are agreements by which the parties undertake to achieve pollution abatement as defined in environmental law, or environmental objectives, in particular those set out in Article 174 of the EC Treaty. The target or measures agreed upon have to be directly linked to reducing a pollutant or type of waste which is identified in the relevant regulations, and the agreement must not be one which merely triggers pollution abatement as a by-product of other measures.[172]

Agreements will not be caught by Article 81(1) if they do not put precise individual obligations on the parties, if they concern a loose contribution to a sector-wide environmental target[173] or if they do not appreciably affect product or production diversity.[174] Agreements

[166] *Ibid.*, para. 170.
[167] *Ibid.*, para. 171.
[168] *Ibid.*, para. 172.
[169] *Ibid.*, para. 173.
[170] *Ibid.*, para. 174.
[171] *Ibid.*, para. 175.
[172] *Ibid.*, para. 179.
[173] *Ibid.*, para. 185.
[174] *Ibid.*, para. 186.

which create new markets (such as recycling agreements) will not be caught if/so long as the parties could not do it individually and there are no other competitors.[175] On the other hand, agreements which are in effect a tool for disguising a cartel by limiting output, for example, will always be within Article 81(1).[176]

Where agreements fall within Article 81(1) because they restrict how or what the parties can produce, and perhaps affect third parties, it will be a question of applying Article 81(3). Not surprisingly, the Commission is sympathetic to environmental agreements. It is a particularly interesting example of the weighing up of benefits of the agreement against the restriction of competition.

---

192. The Commission takes a positive stance on the use of environmental agreements as a policy instrument to achieve the goals enshrined in Article 2 and Article 174 of the Treaty as well as in Community environmental action plans . . . , provided such agreements are compatible with competition rules . . .

193. Environmental agreements caught by Article 81(1) may attain economic benefits which, either at individual or aggregate consumer level, outweigh their negative effects on competition. To fulfil this condition, there must be net benefits in terms of reduced environmental pressure resulting from the agreement, as compared to a baseline where no action is taken. In other words, the expected economic benefits must outweigh the costs . . .

194. Such costs include the effects of lessened competition along with compliance costs for economic operators and/or effects on third parties. The benefits might be assessed in two stages. Where consumers individually have a positive rate of return from the agreement under reasonable payback periods, there is no need for the aggregate environmental benefits to be objectively established. Otherwise, a cost-benefit analysis may be necessary to assess whether net benefits for consumers in general are likely under reasonable assumptions.

7.4.2. Indispensability

195. The more objectively the economic efficiency of an environmental agreement is demonstrated, the more clearly each provision might be deemed indispensable to the attainment of the environmental goal within its economic context.

196. An objective evaluation of provisions which might 'prima facie' be deemed not to be indispensable must be supported with a cost-effectiveness analysis showing that alternative means of attaining the expected environmental benefits, would be more economically or financially costly, under reasonable assumptions. For instance, it should be very clearly demonstrated that a uniform fee, charged irrespective of individual costs for waste collection, is indispensable for the functioning of an industry-wide collection system.

7.4.3. No elimination of competition

197. Whatever the environmental and economic gains and the necessity of the intended provisions, the agreement must not eliminate competition in terms of product or process differentiation, technological innovation or market entry in the short or, where relevant, medium run. For instance, in the case of exclusive collection rights granted to a collection/recycling operator who has potential competitors, the duration of such rights should take into account the possible emergence of an alternative to the operator.

---

[175] Guidelines, para. 187. Negative clearance was given to a waste disposal scheme in France in *Eco-Emballages* [2001] OJ L 233/37.

[176] *Ibid.*, para. 188.

This all raises the interesting question, discussed elsewhere in this book,[177] about how far non-competition objectives should be pursued through the use of the competition provisions. For instance, one of the examples given in this section is of an agreement between washing-machine manufacturers not to manufacture or import into the EU products which do not comply with certain environmental criteria. This is clearly based on the exemption given in *European Council of Manufacturers of Domestic Appliances (CECED)*[178] to an agreement to this effect between virtually all the European producers and importers of washing-machines,[179] which is discussed in Chapter 4.[180] The Commission also gave an individual exemption in *DSD*[181] in respect of exclusive service agreements which facilitated the collection and disposal of waste packaging.

I. AGREEMENTS IN PARTICULAR SECTORS

The Commission has in the past cleared horizontal cooperation agreements in the insurance and banking sectors. For example, exemption under Article 81(3) was given in *Concordato Incendio* (fire insurance premiums),[182] *Uniform Eurocheques* (uniform commission charges),[183] *Nuovo CEGAM* (basic premiums of engineering insurers),[184] and *Dutch Banks* (uniform commission and exchange rates).[185] However, the Commission refused exemption in *Fire Insurance* to recommendations by German property insurers about an increase in fire insurance rates.[186] The Commission has issued a block exemption, Regulation 358/2003, in the insurance sector to deal with, *inter alia*, common risk premium tariffs, non-binding standard policy conditions, and the common coverage of certain risks.[187] Horizontal cooperation agreements have been allowed in the transport sector.[188]

6. CONCLUSIONS

1. The Commission's current policy towards horizontal cooperation agreements, as set out in the Guidelines, is to take a realistic view, based on economic analysis, of whether an agreement really does restrict competition in the first place, and to focus on market power as the main concern for the competition authorities.

---

[177] See *supra* Chap. 1 and Chap. 4.

[178] [2000] OJ L187/74, [2000] 5 CMLR 635. This was followed by approval of a similar agreement concerning dishwashers: see Commission Press Release IP/01/1659.

[179] Commission Press Release IP/00/148.

[180] *Supra* 276.

[181] [2001] OJ L319/1. An appeal by the undertaking against the obligations to which the exemption was subject was dismissed: Case T-289/01, *Der Grüne Punkt—Duales System Deutschland v. Commission*, 24 May 2007.

[182] [1990] OJ L15/25, [1991] 4 CMLR 199.

[183] [1985] OJ L35/43, [1985] 3 CMLR 434. However, the secret agreement to operate the Eurocheque scheme differently to the terms given exemption resulted in Commission proceedings and fines, Cases 39 and 40/92, *Groupement des Cartes Bancaires (Re the Eurocheque Helsinki Agreement)* [1994] ECR II-49.

[184] [1984] OJ L99/29, [1984] 2 CMLR 484.

[185] [1989] OJ L253/1, [1990] 4 CMLR 768.

[186] [1985] OJ L35/20, upheld by the ECJ, Case 45/85, *VdS v. Commission* [1987] ECR 405, [1988] 4 CMLR 264.

[187] [2003] OJ L53/8, replacing Reg. 3932/92.

[188] See *Butterworths Competition Law* (eds. B. Allan, M. Furse, B. Sufrin, looseleaf), Division IX, Chap. 3.

2. The abolition of individual notification under Regulation 1/2003 poses considerable problems for parties entering into cooperative arrangements in that the regime of 'self-assessment' applies to operations where the scale of the overall operation and the resources involved in it are very large indeed.

7. FURTHER READING

ARTICLES

BRODLEY, J., 'Joint Ventures and Antitrust Policy' (1982) 95 *Harvard LR* 1521

KATTAN, J., 'Antitrust Analysis of Technology Joint Ventures: Allocative Efficiency and the Rewards of Innovation' (1993) 61 *Antitrust LJ* 937

KITCH, E., 'The Antitrust Economics of Joint Ventures' (1987) 54 *Antitrust LJ* 957

MCCAULEY, D., 'Exclusively for All and Collectively for None: Refereeing Broadcasting Rights

Between the Premier League, the European Commission and BskyB' [2004] *ECLR* 370

NITSCHE, I., 'Collective Marketing of Broadcasting by Sports Associations in Europe' [2000] *ECLR* 208

WILBERT, S., 'Joint Selling of Bundesligia Media Rights—First Commission Decision Pursuant to Article 9 of Regulation 1/2003' (2005) 2 *EC Competition Policy Newsletter*, 44

14

PUBLIC ENFORCEMENT BY THE COMMISSION AND THE NATIONAL COMPETITION AUTHORITIES OF THE ANTITRUST PROVISIONS

1. CENTRAL ISSUES

1. The system for enforcing Articles 81 and 82 was fundamentally changed on 1 May 2004 when Regulation 1/2003 replaced Regulation 17 of 1962. Regulation 1/2003 rendered Article 81(3) directly applicable and 'decentralized' the enforcement of the antitrust provisions so that the Commission and the national competition authorities have parallel competence to apply the rules. The European Competition Network is the network of national competition authorities and the Commission working in close cooperation with one another.

2. The Commission's own powers of enforcement, previously contained in Regulation 17, are now set out in Regulation 1/2003 and in some respects are considerably strengthened. The Commission combines investigative, prosecutorial, and adjudicative functions in one body.

3. In investigating suspected breaches of the competition rules the Commission may require information and may carry out, *inter alia*, unannounced inspections at the premises of undertakings, and at private homes in certain situations. There are questions about the compatibility of some aspects of these procedures with the European Convention on Human Rights.

4. The Commission may take a number of decisions, including decisions ordering terminations of infringements, imposing fines, or accepting commitments. It can impose behavioural or strucural remedies. Commitments decisions are a new procedure introduced by Regulation 1/2003.

5. The Commission pursues an increasingly aggressive policy towards the detection and punishment of cartels. It operates a 'leniency policy' whereby participants in cartels are given immunity or a reduced penalty in exchange for providing the Commission with information about the cartel and their co-conspirators. The Commission imposes heavy fines on undertakings found to have committed serious breaches of the competition rules.

6. Commission decisions in competition cases are subject to judicial review by the Court.

7. Decentralization and the parallel enforcement competence of the NCAs means that there are complex procedures and arrangements within the ECN for, e.g. allocating cases and sharing information. Ultimately, the Commission is able to take a case on and thereby relieve the NCA of its competence in that matter.

8. Complaints about breaches of the competition rules play an important role. The Commission has no duty to pursue complaints but the Commission is obliged to make a formal rejection of complaints and these can be challenged before the Community Courts.

2. INTRODUCTION

It cannot have escaped the notice of the reader of this book that on 1 May 2004 the way in which the EC competition rules (other than merger control) are enforced fundamentally changed. From that day Council Regulation 1/2003[1] applied, and a new era began.

Regulation 1/2003 is the linchpin of the 'modernized' process. We have already seen that the modernization of EC competition law has included a more 'economic' approach to the substantive law[2] and a revised Merger Regulation (ECMR).[3] Regulation 1/2003 introduced fundamental changes to the way in which Articles 81 and 82 are enforced. The effects of this are far-reaching.

The previous implementing legislation, Regulation 17,[4] conferred the central role in the application and enforcement of EC competition law upon the Commission and the role of the national competition authorities (NCAs) and national courts was peripheral. Regulation 1/2003 'decentralized' application and enforcement and the NCAs were given a far greater role.[5] Furthermore, the reforms were designed to encourage more 'private' enforcement of EC competition law through litigation in the national courts of the Member States. 'Decentralization' therefore means decentralization to the national courts as well as to the NCAs. Public enforcement by the Commission and the NCAs is considered in this chapter.[6] Private enforcement through civil litigation in the national courts is discussed in Chapter 15.

In section 3 of this chapter we describe briefly the system, under Regulation 17, which applied before 1 May 2004. In sections 4 and 5 the reasons for, and salient features of, modernization are considered. In sections 4, 6 and 7 the powers of the Commission and the role of the Court is examined and in sections 8 and 9 we deal with enforcement by NCAs and the relationship between Community and national law. In section 10 we consider the possibility of sanctions against individuals and in 11 the position of those who 'complain' about the anti-competitive conduct of others is considered and some conclusions are set out in section 12.

It will be seen that a significant number of the articles of Regulation 1/2003 are identical in effect (if not in the exact wording) to articles in Regulation 17. In respect of these the previous case law of the Court applies to the new provisions as to the old. In 40 years of pronouncing on the Commission's powers under Regulation 17 the Court laid down and developed many important principles governing the exercise of the Commission's powers, for example on legal professional privilege[7] and on the right not to answer certain incriminating questions.[8] These also apply in the modernized system.

The extracts in this chapter contain references to articles in Regulation 17. The original numbers have been left intact and the corresponding articles in Regulation 1/2003 indicated.

---

[1] [2003] OJ L1/1.

[2] See in particular Chaps. 4, 9, and 13, and also 5–7 in respect of the proposals on Article 82.

[3] Reg. 139/2004, [2004], OJ L24/1, see *supra* Chap. 12.

[4] [1959–62] OJ Spec. Ed. 87.

[5] The position with regard to mergers is explained in Chap. 12. Some mergers can be dealt with *only* by the Commission (broadly, if they fall above certain turnover thresholds), and the others are left to be dealt with by the Member States.

[6] For a detailed treatment, reference should be had to practitioners' books. See, e.g., C. Kerse and N. Khan, *EC Antitrust Procedure* (5th edn., Sweet and Maxwell, 2005); L. Ortiz Blanco, *EC Competition Procedure* (2nd edn., Oxford University Press, 2006).

[7] Case 155/79, *AM&S Ltd* v. *Commission* [1982] ECR 1575, [1982] 2 CMLR 264.

[8] Case 374/87, *Orkem SA* v. *Commission* [1989] ECR 3283, [1991] 4 CMLR 502.

3. THE OLD ENFORCEMENT REGIME SET UP BY REGULATION 17

The most significant feature of Regulation 17[9] was that it set up a system whereby an agreement falling within Article 81(1) could only escape via Article 81(3) if it was 'exempted'. The granting of an exemption was a 'constitutive act'. There were two ways of obtaining exemption. First, the parties could bring their agreement within a 'block exemption' regulation. It is still possible to do this. Block exemptions are an important part of the system post 1 May 2004 and in various chapters of this book we examine the provisions of the current Regulations.[10] Secondly, the parties could obtain an individual exemption from the Commission. Article 9(1) of Regulation 17 conferred 'sole power' on the Commission 'to declare Article [81(1)] inapplicable pursuant to Article [81(3)] of the Treaty'. From this simple monopoly enormous consequences flowed.[11] Article 4(1) of Regulation 17 provided that parties to an agreement seeking an exemption had to notify it to the Commission. Until they did so, no decision pursuant to Article 81(3) could be taken. Only notification gave the possibility of exemption.[12] Agreements could also be notified for 'negative clearance', i.e., a decision finding that an agreement did not infringe Article 81(1) at all.[13] Article 15(5) of Regulation 17 provided those that notified with immunity from fines.[14]

When notifying an agreement it was necessary for the parties and the Commission to comply with the requisite procedure.[15] Notification had to be made in the format prescribed by Form A/B,[16] which required extensive information.[17] Following notification there were no time limits within which the Commission had to give a decision.[18]

Decisions granting individual exemption could only be issued for a specified period and could be made subject to conditions and obligations.[19] They had to specify the date from which they ran and the general rule was that this could not be earlier than the date of notification.[20]

---

[9] [1959–62] OJ Spec. Ed. 87.

[10] For block exemptions generally, see *supra* Chap. 4.

[11] See *infra* 1141.

[12] Certain agreements could be exempted retrospectively to the date that the agreement was concluded irrespective of whether they had or had not been notified. Non-notifiable agreements were defined in Reg. 17, Art. 4(2), as amended by Reg. 1216/99 [1999] OJ L148/5, to cover all vertical agreements.

[13] Reg 17, Art. 2. Negative clearance could also be sought in respect of Article 82.

[14] The immunity could be lifted under Reg. 17, Art. 15(6) following a preliminary examination of the agreement by the Commission.

[15] Antitrust Procedure (Applications and Notifications) Reg. 3385/94 [1994] OJ L377/28, [1995] 5 CMLR 507, replacing Reg. 27/62 [1959–62] OJ Spec. Ed. 132 as amended, in respect notifications under Reg. 17; Reg 2843/98 [1998] OJ L354/22 adopted a single form for notification of agreements within the transport sector.

[16] Set out in Reg. 3385/94. Some block exemptions contained an 'opposition procedure' whereby agreements not falling precisely within the terms of the block exemption could be notified to the Commission and allowed to benefit from the block exemption unless 'opposed' by the Commission within a specified time limit. For example, Reg. 240/96 on technology transfer agreements [1996] OJ L31/2, which was replaced on 1 May 2004 by Reg. 772/2004 [2004] OJ L123/11.

[17] Including the relevant market(s) on which the agreement was to operate, who were the competitors, the nature of demand for the products, and the largest customers of each of the parties.

[18] Except that in 1993 a 'fast-track' was introduced for the treatment of structural joint ventures: Reg. 3385/94, Form A/B, Introduction, Section D.

[19] Reg. 17, Art. 8(1). The parties could apply for it to be renewed (Reg. 17, Art. 8(2)). In certain circumstances they could be revoked or amended (Reg. 17, Art. 8(3)).

[20] Reg. 17, Art. 6(1). There was an exception to this in respect of 'non-notifiable' agreements under Article 4(2): see *supra* n. 12.

This meant that an agreement which infringed Article 81(1) but which had not been notified was void pursuant to Article 81(2) even if, had it been notified, the agreement would have merited exemption pursuant to Article 81(3).[21] Such an agreement was not, therefore, enforceable in a national court in respect of the period between the agreement coming into force and its notification. This was one reason for the large number of notifications the Commission received each year. In practice the Commission could not issue decisions granting an exemption or negative clearance to all the agreements notified to it. It granted a formal decision to a very small percentage of the notifications that it received.[22] The remainder were dealt with informally by administrative letter, a 'comfort letter'. The comfort letter enabled the Commission to deal with the numerous notifications it received whilst allowing it to give greater priority to cases which raised greater concern from the Community perspective. The system was far from satisfactory however.[23]

The use of comfort letters rather than formal decisions meant that for many years prior to 1 May 2004 the notification-and-exemption procedure did not operate in real life as had been intended by Regulation 17.

4. MODERNIZATION

A. THE REASONS FOR MODERNIZATION

In 1999 the Commission adopted a White Paper on modernisation of the rules implementing Articles 81 and 82.[24] The Commission had been considering the need for changes to the enforcement mechanisms for some time and had been promoting greater decentralization of enforcement through the national courts and competition authorities.[25] However, the Commission's

---

[21] *Ibid.*

[22] The Commission stated in its White Paper on modernisation of the rules implementing Articles 85 and 86 [now 81 and 82] of the EC Treaty [1999] OJ C132/1, [1999] 5 CMLR 208, para. 34, that 91% of cases (150–200 letters per year) were settled informally.

[23] A comfort letter took one of several forms. It could state the Commission's view that: (1) the agreement did not fall within Article 81(1) at all (a 'negative clearance comfort letter'); (2) the agreement was covered by a block exemption or by a Commission Notice; or (3) that the agreement was eligible for an Article 81(3) exemption. In the first two cases the parties were likely to feel fairly contented with the letter. However, the procedure was less satisfactory in situation (3). According to Article 81(2) an agreement which infringes Article 81 is void and in these circumstances no exemption had been granted. This type of comfort letter was thus the least comforting of the three. Although assuring the parties that the Commission would not pursue the matter further, the letter was *not* a decision which could be applied by the national courts and consequently did not give the parties the same degree of legal certainty as resulted from a decision. The letter was not binding on the national courts (or the Court of Justice or, for that matter, the Commission). In practice, however, parties accepted comfort letters as a matter of expediency. Further, if the question of the validity of the agreement was ever raised in national proceedings, the national court was likely to stay proceedings and ask the Commission to take a decision on the compatibility of the agreement with Article 81(1); the Notice on cooperation between national courts and the Commission [1993] OJ C39/5 gave guidance to national courts. Some administrative letters issued by the Commission were better described as 'discomfort letters'. These letters informed the parties that although the Commission did not intend to take a formal decision it considered that the notified agreement infringed the rules, and did not merit exemption.

[24] White Paper on modernisation of the rules implementing Articles 85 and 86 [now 81 and 82] of the EC Treaty [1999] OJ C132/1, [1999] 5 CMLR 208.

[25] The problems of the private enforcement of EC competition law are discussed *infra* Chap. 15, where it will be seen that modernization has by no means solved them all.

exclusive right to grant individual exemptions under Article 81(3) made it difficult for national courts and national competition authorities to participate in the enforcement process. Indeed, at the time of the White Paper only half of the NCAs had power under their domestic law to enforce the EC competition rules.[26] Further, the widespread perception that the Commission alone enforced the competition rules meant that undertakings preferred to complain to the Commission rather than bring private proceedings before the national courts.[27] The net result was that the Commission's limited resources were spent dealing with exemptions for essentially innocuous agreements leaving less available for the detection and prohibition of more serious violations of the rules. Moreover, the problem was likely to get worse in view of the imminent further expansion of the European Union.[28]

B. THE PROPOSALS IN THE WHITE PAPER

One obvious way of reforming the system, and one often urged upon the Commission, was to confer power on the NCAs to grant individual exemptions. The Commission had consistently resisted this idea. Unexpectedly, however, the White Paper proposed a far more radical and fundamental change. It proposed that the notification-and-exemption system should be abolished altogether. Instead, Article 81(3) should become a 'directly applicable exception'. The decision of whether or not an agreement fulfilled the criteria in Article 81(3) would no longer be taken by the Commission after notification of the agreement by the parties. Rather, the decision would be made by a national court if the matter were relevant to litigation before it, by a national competition authority, or by the Commission itself, but *not* after a notification. Undertakings would, therefore, be deprived of the comfort of being able to notify and receive assurance of the compatibility of their agreement with Article 81. Instead they would be left to judge for themselves the legitimacy of their arrangements.[29] In place of a prior authorization system there would be what the White Paper called 'intensified *ex post* control' which would include strengthening the Commission's powers of enquiry, and making it easier to lodge complaints.[30]

The proposals generated enormous controversy and debate in the competition law world.[31] One issue was whether Article 81(3) was able to be directly applied as an exception to the Article

---

[26] Austria, Denmark, Finland, Ireland, Luxembourg, Sweden, and the UK did not (although in the UK the EC Competition Law (Articles [84] and [85]) Enforcement Regulations 1996, SI 1996/2199, afterwards replaced by SI 2001/2916 as amended by SI 2002/42, gave the OFT power to enforce Articles 81 and 82 in respect of air transport between the UK and non-Member States as this was not covered by Reg. 17 or other implementing legislation).

[27] See *infra* Chap. 15.

[28] Which did, of course, come to pass with the accession of ten new Member States on 1 May 2004 and the accession of Bulgaria and Romania in January 2007.

[29] Unless the transaction was a partial-function production joint venture; *ibid.*, para. 79. This suggestion was ultimately abandoned: See *supra* Chap. 13, 1093 and *infra* 1150.

[30] White Paper on Modernization, para. 108.

[31] See R. Whish and B. Sufrin, 'Community Competition Law: Notification and Individual Exemption: Goodbye to All that' in D. Hayton (ed.) *Law's Future(s)* (Hart Publishing, 2000); C. D. Ehlermann and I. Atanasiu (eds.), *European Competition Law Annual 2000: The Modernisation of EC Antitrust Policy* (Hart Publishing, 2001); C. D. Ehlermann and I. Atanasiu (eds.), *European Competition Law Annual 2001: Effective Enforcement of EC Antitrust Law* (Hart Publishing, 2003); W. Wils, *The Optimal Enforcement of EC Antitrust Law* (Kluwer Law International, 2002); B. Hawk (ed.) *Fordham Corp L Inst* [2000]; B. Rodger, 'The Commission White Paper on on Modernisation of the Rules Implementing Articles 81 and 82 of the EC Treaty' (1999) 24 *ELRev* 653; R. Wesseling, 'The Commission White Paper on Modernisation of EC Antitrust: Unspoken Consequences and Incomplete Treatment of Alternative Options' [1999] *ECLR* 420; R. Wesseling, 'The Draft Regulation Modernising the Competition Rules: the Commission is Married to One Idea' (2001) 26 *ELRev* 357; D. Gerber, 'Modernising European Competition Law: A Developmental Perspective' [2001] *ECLR* 122.

81(1) prohibition (the doctrine *'de l'exception légale'*) or whether the wording of Article 81(3) *'may ... be declared inapplicable'* required a constitutive act of a public authority to lift the Article 81(1) prohibition.[32] Another was whether Article 81(3) was suitable for direct application in national courts. This point was bound up with the debate about whether in the application of Article 81(3) other factors than competition ones, such as social, cultural, industrial, and environmental considerations can be taken into account.[33]

The Commission recognized in the White Paper the critical importance of ensuring that the consistent and uniform application of the competition rules was maintained and not jeopardized. The great advantage of the system set up by Regulation 17 was that it had left the application and enforcement of the competition rules in the hands of one Community body (subject only to review by the Court) which, by maintaining its iron grip, had directed the development of competition policy and ensured that the law was applied uniformly across the Community. The limited private litigation in national courts at least meant that this uniformity was not significantly compromised. The Commission was determined that its proposal for decentralization should not be accompanied by divergent application among the various Member States. The White Paper thus proposed mechanisms and procedures to ensure continuing coherence and consistency.

The Commission recognized that its proposals, if adopted, would lead to less certainty for undertakings as, in the absence of the notification and authorization system, they would have to take greater responsibility for ensuring that they complied with the competition rules (acting, of course, on the advice of their lawyers). The Commission's official view was that 'undertakings are generally well placed to assess the legality of their actions in such a way as to enable them to take an informed decision on whether to go ahead with an agreement or practice and in what form'.[34] Measures were, however, put in place in the new system which allow for guidance to be granted in certain more exceptional cases, and these are discussed below.[35]

C. THE MODERNIZATION 'PACKAGE'

(i) Regulation 1/2003, the Implementing Regulation and the Modernization Notices

After much debate and an extensive consultation exercise the Commission's proposal to abolish notification, render Article 81(3) a directly applicable exception and decentralize the application and enforcement of the competition rules was accepted. The Council adopted Regulation 1/2003 on 16 December 2002[36] and it has applied since 1 May 2004.[37] In the intervening period much

---

[32] This was a fascinating debate. In the White Paper the Commission stated that the delegations from the original six future Member States who drafted the EC Treaty could not decide between a directly applicable system and an authorization system, as some favoured one and some the other. Article 81(3) was therefore deliberately drafted to allow for either possibility. It was only on the adoption of Regulation 17 that the Community legislator finally chose an authorization system. The main proponent of the view that Article 81(3) did not allow for a directly applicable exception was the German Government: see summary of observations on the White Paper, DG Comp. Doc. 29 Feb. 2000, para. 3.2. The arguments were set out in the submissions of the German Monopolkommission.

[33] See *supra* Chap. 4.

[34] Commission Notice on informal guidance relating to novel questions concerning Articles 81 and 82 that arise in individual cases (guidance letters) [2004] OJ C101/78, para. 3.

[35] 'Findings of inapplicability' under Reg.1/2003, Art. 10, and the possibility of 'guidance letters' under Commission Notice on informal guidance relating to novel questions, n. 34 *supra*, discussed *infra* 1149.

[36] [2003] OJ L1/1.

[37] It replaces Reg. 17.

thought was given to how the new system would actually operate in practice. The outcome of this was a new implementing Regulation (of the Commission) and a number of Notices which flesh out the bare bones of Regulation 1/2003. A major concern was to establish mechanisms and procedures for the cooperation between the Commission and the NCAs, without which the new decentralization could not work. The creation of the ECN has been of great importance in this respect.

The 'modernization package' thus consisted of the following:

(i)   Council Regulation 1/2003;

(ii)   Commission Regulation 773/2004 on the conduct of proceedings by the Commission pursuant to Articles 81 and 82 (the Implementation Regulation);[38]

(iii)   Commission Notice on cooperation within the network of competition authorities;[39]

(iv)   Commission Notice on cooperation between the Commission and the courts of the EU Member States in the application of Articles 81 and 82;[40]

(v)   Commission Notice on the handling of complaints;[41]

(vi)   Commission Notice on informal guidance relating to novel questions concerning Articles 81 and 82 that arise in individual cases (guidance letters);[42]

(vii)   Guidelines on the effect on trade concept contained in Articles 81 and 82;[43]

(viii) Guidelines on the application of Article 81(3).[44]

(ii) Regulation 1/2003

Broadly, Regulation 1/2003 deals with two matters. First, it renders Article 81(3) directly applicable and lays down the basic framework for the Commission, the NCAs, and the national courts to cooperate in the decentralized system. Secondly, it provides for and strengthens the powers and procedures of the Commission in the investigation of competition matters. It represents a shift from *ex ante* to *ex post* control in respect of non-cartel type agreements[45] and frees Commission resources to pursue those engaged in the most serious infringements of the rules.

Regulation 1/2003 contains eleven Chapters:

* Chapter I 'Principles' (Articles 1–3) deals with the direct applicability of Articles 81 and 82, the burden of proof in Article 81 and 82 proceedings, and the relationship between EC competition law and national competition laws.

* Chapter II 'Powers' (Articles 4–6) provides for the powers of the Commission, the NCAs and the national courts.

* Chapter III 'Commission Decisions' (Articles 7–10) provides for the Commission to take various types of decision: finding and termination of infringements; interim measures; commitments decisions; and findings of inapplicability decisions.

---

[38] [2004] OJ L123/18.

[39] [2004] OJ C101/43.

[40] [2004] OJ C101/54.

[41] [2004] OJ C101/65.

[42] [2004] OJ C101/78.

[43] [2004] OJ C101/81.

[44] [2004] OJ C101/96.

[45] That is, situations in which the parties are likely to be trying to comply with the competition rules.

- Chapter IV 'Cooperation' (Articles 11–16) deals with cooperation between the Commission, the NCAs and the national courts.
- Chapter V 'Powers of Investigation' (Articles 17–22) provides for the Commission's powers of investigation and for NCAs to carry out investigations on behalf of the Commission and other NCAs. Much of this Chapter corresponds to provisions in Regulation 17, although in significant respects the Commission's powers are expanded.
- Chapter VI 'Penalties' (Articles 23–24) provides for the fines and pecuniary penalties the Commission may impose. Again, this corresponds to provisions in Regulation 17.
- Chapter VII 'Limitation Periods' (Articles 25–26) provides for limitation periods in respect of the imposition and enforcement of penalties.
- Chapter VIII 'Hearings and Professional Secrecy' (Articles 27–8) provides for undertakings to be heard before certain decisions are taken, for the hearing of complainants and certain other parties, and for the confidentiality of information. Regulation 1/2003 does not provide for legal professional privilege. The position on this is to be found in the case law of the Court.[46] On the other hand, Article 27(2) does provide for the parties concerned to have access to the Commission's file, which was initially established in the case law.[47]
- Chapter IX 'Exemption Regulations' contains only one Article (Article 29) providing for the Commission (and in certain circumstances an NCA) to withdraw the benefit of a block exemption from an individual agreement.
- Chapter X 'General Provisions' (Articles 30–3) deals with the publication of decisions, review by the Court, matters excluded from the Regulation, and the power of the Commission to take further implementing measures in order to apply Regulation 1/2003.
- Chapter XI 'Transitional, Amending and Final Provisions' (Articles 34–45) is self-explanatory.

The table below summarizes the provision of Regulation 1/2003.

Regulation 1/2003	Summary of Article
Article 1	The application of Articles 81 and 82.
Article 2	Burden of proof.
Article 3	The relationship between Articles 81 and 82 and national competition laws.
Article 4	Statement that in applying Articles 81 and 82 the Commission has the powers provided for in this Regulation.
Article 5	Powers of the NCAs.
Article 6	Powers of the national courts.
Article 7	The Commission's power to order the termination of infringements and the types of remedy it can impose. Article 7(2) explains who can lodge a complaint with the Commission.
Article 8	The Commission's power to order interim measures.

---

[46] Case 155/79, AM&S Ltd v. Commission [1982] ECR 1575, [1982] 2 CMLR 264, see infra 1181.

[47] See infra 1191.

Regulation 1/2003	Summary of Article
Article 9	The Commission's power to make binding the commitments offered by undertakings.
Article 10	The Commission's power to make findings of inapplicability.
Article 11	Procedures for cooperation between the Commission and the NCAs.
Article 12	Exchanges of information between the Commission and the NCAs and between the NCAs *inter se*.
Article 13	The suspension or termination of proceedings.
Article 14	The Advisory Committee on Restrictive Practices and Dominant Positions.
Article 15	Cooperation with national courts.
Article 16	The uniform application of EC competition law (Commission decisions are binding on national courts).
Article 17	Investigations into sectors of the economy and into types of agreement.
Article 18	Requests for information.
Article 19	Power of the Commission to interview and take statements.
Article 20	The Commission's powers of inspection of undertakings.
Article 21	Commission power to inspect other premises, including the homes of the directors, managers, and staff of undertakings.
Article 22	Investigations (inspections) by NCAs.
Article 23	The Commission's power to fine.
Article 24	The Commission's power to impose periodic penalty payments.
Article 25	Limitation periods for the imposition of penalties.
Article 26	Limitation periods for the enforcement of penalties.
Article 27	Hearings before the Commission takes decisions. Article 27(2) gives a right of access to the file.
Article 28	Professional secrecy.
Article 29	General power of withdrawal of block exemptions in individual cases.
Article 30	The publication of decisions.
Article 31	Unlimited jurisdiction of the Court of Justice to review Commission decisions imposing fines or periodic penalty payments.
Article 32	Matters excluded from the scope of the Regulation.

Regulation 1/2003	Summary of Article
Article 33	Power of the Commission to take implementing measures.
Article 34	Transitional provisions.
Article 35	Designation by the Member States of the responsible competition authorities.
Articles 36–42	Amendment of other Regulations.
Article 43	Repeal of Regulation 17 (except for Article 8(3), which means that the Commission may revoke or amend an existing individual exemption decision until it expires) and Regulation 141.
Article 44	Commission shall report to the European Parliament and the Council on the application of Regulation 1/2003 after five years.
Article 45	Regulation 1/2003 to apply from 1 May 2004.

(iii) Regulation 773/2004

Regulation 773/2004[48] deals with the conduct of Commission proceedings in its application of the competition rules. It covers in more detail some of the matters provided for in Regulation 1/2003 (such as power to take statements, the handling of complaints, the exercise of the right of the parties and others to be heard[49] and the right of 'access to the file'). The provisions of Regulation 773/2004 are discussed in this chapter in the context of the matters to which they relate.

(iv) The Modernization Notices

The Commission's Modernization Notices have been discussed and referred to throughout this book. In this chapter, and Chapter 15, particular attention is focused on the Commission Notice on cooperation within the network of competition authorities,[50] the Commission Notice on cooperation between the Commission and the courts of the EU Member States in the application of Articles 81 and 82,[51] the Commission Notice on the handling of complaints,[52] and the Commission Notice on informal guidance relating to novel questions concerning Articles 81 and 82 that arise in individual cases (guidance letters).[53]

5. THE EUROPEAN COMPETITION NETWORK

The European Competition Network is the network of national competition authorities (NCAs) and the Commission who under Regulation 1/2003 share parallel competence to apply and

---

[48] [2004] OJ L123/18.

[49] Reg. 773/2004 replaces Reg. 2842/98 [1998] OJ L354/18 on the hearing of parties in certain proceedings under Articles 85 and 86 of the Treaty.

[50] [2004] OJ C101/43.

[51] [2004] OJ C101/54.

[52] [2004] OJ C101/65.

[53] [2004] OJ C101/78.

enforce Articles 81 and 82. The close cooperation of the authorities is crucial to the effective operation of the decentralized system. This is dealt with further in section 8.

6. ENFORCEMENT BY THE COMMISSION

A. GENERAL

(i) The Broad Powers of the Commission

In *Dansk Rørindustri*[54] the ECJ said:

The supervisory task conferred on the Commission by Articles [81(1)] and [82] of the EC Treaty . . . not only includes the duty to investigate and punish individual infringements but also encompasses the duty to pursue a general policy designed to apply, in competition matters, the principles laid down by the Treaty and to guide the conduct of undertakings in the light of those principles . . . .

The Commission may investigate infringements of the competition rules on its own initiative or acting on a complaint.[55] Complaints and the position of complainants are dealt with in section 7 below. In competition cases the Commission plays the part of law-maker, policeman, investigator, prosecutor, judge, and jury.[56] It performs the activities both of fact-finding and of legal evaluation. Inevitably, perhaps, this arrangement has long been subject to criticism,[57] and it is a notable that this position was not changed by modernization.[58] The Commission's exercise of its powers is, however, subject to judicial review by the Court, and many of the cases discussed in this chapter show how the Court has sought to reconcile human rights and the protection of those subject to the Commission's investigations and penalties with the tasks entrusted to the Commission.

The Court has held that the Commission has a margin of discretion to set priorities in enforcing the competition rules.[59] It has certain obligations when dealing with complaints[60] but otherwise can choose against whom, and when, to bring proceedings. In *British Airways* the CFI dismissed the airline's plea that the Commission had infringed the principle of non-discrimination by bringing an Article 82 action against it but not against other airlines.[61]

Although Regulation 1/2003 abolished the notification procedure, it is recognized that in some novel cases guidance as to the compatibility of an agreement or practice with the rules may be necessary, perhaps to provide legal certainty to the parties[62] and/or to aid the consistent application of the competition rules in the decentralized system.[63] Regulation 1/2003 thus

---

[54] Cases C-189/02 P, 202/02 P, 208/02 P and 213/02 P, *Dansk Rørindustri A/S and others v. Commission* [2005] ECR I-5425, [2005] 5 CMLR 796, para. 170, referring to Cases 100–103/80, *Musique Diffusion Française SA v. Commission (Pioneer)* [1983] ECR 1825, [1983] 3 CMLR 221, para. 105.

[55] This is clear from Reg. 1/2003, Art. 7 which gives the Commission power to take decisions when it has found an infringement: see *infra* 1202 ff for a general discussion of Article 7.

[56] This was also the case under the Reg. 17 system.

[57] See A. Pera and M. Todino, 'Enforcement of EC Competition Rules: Need for a Reform'? [1996] *Fordham Corporate Law Institute* 125, 144; F. Montag, 'The Case for Radical Reform of the Infringement Procedure under Regulation' [1998] *ECLR* 428.

[58] See W. Wils, 'The Combination of the Investigative and Prosecutorial Function and the Adjudicative Function in EC Antitrust Enforcement: A Legal and Economic Analysis' (2004) 27(2) *World Competition* 201.

[59] Case T-24/90, *Automec Srl v. Commission (Automec II)* [1992] ECR II-2223, [1992] 5 CMLR 431.

[60] See *infra* section 9.

[61] Case T-219/99, *British Airways v. Commission* [2003] ECR II-5917, [2004] 4 CMLR 1008.

[62] See Reg. 1/2003, recital 38.

[63] See Reg. 1/2003, recital 14 and Commission Notice on informal guidance, para. 2.

allows the Commission to adopt decisions of 'inapplicability'[64] and envisages that 'guidance letters' may be issued.[65]

(ii) Findings of Inapplicability and Guidance Letters

a. Findings of Inapplicability

Regulation 1/2003, Article 10

Finding of inapplicability

Where the Community public interest relating to the application of Articles 81 and 82 of the Treaty so requires, the Commission, acting on its own initiative, may by decision find that Article 81 of the Treaty is not applicable to an agreement, a decision by an association of undertakings or a concerted practice, either because the conditions of Article 81(1) of the Treaty are not fulfilled, or because the conditions of Article 81(3) of the Treaty are satisfied.

The Commission may likewise make such a finding with reference to Article 82 of the Treaty.

Article 10 provides that a finding of inapplicability will be made by decision and, as far as Article 81 is concerned, the finding may be that the conditions in Article 81(1) are not fulfilled (as was the case with a negative clearance) or that the conditions in Article 81(3) are satisfied (as was the case with an individual exemption). The Commission obviously needs sufficient information on which to come to a conclusion. This could be acquired through the fact-finding procedures discussed below[66] or through the parties supplying it voluntarily. Article 10 states that these declaratory decisions will be made when the *Community public interest* so requires and that the Commission will act *on its own initiative,* making it clear that the decisions are not intended (at least primarily) to be for the benefit of the parties. Regulation 1/2003, recital 14 says that Article 10 decisions will be adopted *in exceptional cases* 'with a view to clarifying the law and ensuring its consistent application throughout the Community, in particular with regard to new types of agreements or practices that have not been settled in the existing case-law and administrative practice'. Nevertheless, Article 10 decisions will clearly be greatly advantageous to the parties as they will be enforceable in national courts and give complete legal certainty . It will be interesting to see how far the distinction between the public interest and the parties' interests is maintained in practice, and how often 'exceptional circumstances' are found to arise. Article 10, however, leaves the Commission firmly in control.

It is anticipated that the Commission will use Article 10 as a way of laying down principles to be followed by the NCAs and national courts in the decentralized system.[67] Further, it may be used by the Commission to pre-empt a decision by an NCA since Article 11(6) of Regulation 1/2003 provides that if the Commission initiates proceedings NCAs are relieved of their competence to act

---

[64] Reg. 1/2003, Art. 10.

[65] Reg. 1/2003, recital 38 and Commission Notice on informal guidance relating to novel questions concerning Articles 81 and 82 that arise in individual cases (guidance letters) [2004] OJ C101/78.

[66] See *infra* 1152 ff.

[67] See *infra* section 8 for a discussion of the position of NCAs and Chap. 15 for that of national courts.

'under the same legal basis against the same agreement(s) or practice(s) by the same undertaking(s) on the same relevant geographic and product market'.[68]

b. Informal Guidance

Informal guidance letters have their genesis not in a specific article of Regulation 1/2003 but in a recital. Recital 38 states:

Legal certainty for undertakings operating under the Community competition rules contributes to the promotion of innovation and investment. Where cases give rise to genuine uncertainty because they present novel or unresolved questions for the application of these rules, individual undertakings may wish to seek informal guidance from the Commission. This Regulation is without prejudice to the ability of the Commission to issue such informal guidance . . .

The Commission set out in a Notice[69] the circumstances in which it may consider it appropriate to issue informal guidance. This stresses that the new enforcement system 'is designed to restore the focus on the primary task of effective enforcement' by rendering Article 81(3) directly applicable and doing away with notification[70] and that undertakings are best placed to assess the legality of their actions, given the block exemptions, notices, case law, and case practice which are available to assist them.[71] Nevertheless, it recognizes that in some situations this may not be adequate. It will therefore provide informal guidance to individual undertakings 'in so far as this is compatible with its enforcement priorities'.[72]

Commission Notice on Informal Guidance Relating to Novel Questions Concerning Articles 81 and 82 that Arise in Individual Cases (Guidance Letters) [2004] OJ C101/78

5. Where cases, despite the above elements, give rise to genuine uncertainty because they present novel or unresolved questions for the application of Articles 81 and 82, individual undertakings may wish to seek informal guidance from the Commission. . . . Where it considers it appropriate and subject to its enforcement priorities, the Commission may provide such guidance on novel questions concerning the interpretation of Articles 81 and/or 82 in a written statement (guidance letter). The present Notice sets out details of this instrument.

. . .

8. Subject to point 7, [the enforcement priorities of the Commission] the Commission, seized of a request for a guidance letter, will consider whether it is appropriate to process it. Issuing a guidance letter may only be considered if the following cumulative conditions are fulfilled:

(a) The substantive assessment of an agreement or practice with regard to Articles 81 and/or 82 of the Treaty, poses a question of application of the law for which there is no clarification in the existing EC legal framework including the case law of the Community Courts, nor

---

[68] Notice on cooperation within the Network of Competition Authorities [2004] OJ C101/43, para. 51. And see also para. 54(d).

[69] Commission Notice on informal guidance relating to novel questions concerning Articles 81 and 82 that arise in individual cases (guidance letters) [2004] OJ C101/78.

[70] *Ibid.,* para. 1.

[71] *Ibid.,* paras. 3 and 4.

[72] *Ibid.,* para. 7.

publicly available general guidance or precedent in decision-making practice or previous guidance letters.

(b) A prima facie evaluation of the specificities and background of the case suggests that the clarification of the novel question through a guidance letter is useful, taking into account the following elements:

  — the economic importance from the point of view of the consumer of the goods or services concerned by the agreement or practice, and/or

  — the extent to which the agreement or practice corresponds or is liable to correspond to more widely spread economic usage in the marketplace and/or

  — the extent of the investments linked to the transaction in relation to the size of the companies concerned and the extent to which the transaction relates to a structural operation such as the creation of a non-full function joint venture.

(c) It is possible to issue a guidance letter on the basis of the information provided, i.e., no further fact-finding is required.

The condition in paragraph 8(a) emphasizes that guidance will be given only in respect of 'novel' questions. The Commission will be the judge of the novelty. In respect of the second condition, the 'usefulness' of the guidance, the first two indents in 8(b) show that an element of 'public interest' is relevant. The third indent specifically indicates that guidance letters may be forthcoming in certain cases involving non-full function joint ventures.[73] The Commission will not issue a guidance letter if it would entail further fact-finding. It is entirely up to parties to provide the necessary information.[74]

Guidance letters will not be issued if the questions (identical or similar) are raised in a case pending before the ECJ or CFI, or the agreement or practice in issue is subject to proceedings before the Commission, an NCA, or a national court in a Member State.[75] They will not be issued in respect of hypothetical questions or agreements or practices that are no longer being implemented. They will, however, be considered in respect of an agreement or practice which is envisaged but not yet implemented, so long as it has reached a sufficiently advanced stage.[76] This is obviously useful in respect of agreements such as non-full function joint ventures. Guidance letters do not prevent the Commission opening proceedings under Regulation 1/2003 with regard to the same facts (although it will take the letter into account),[77] do not prejudge any assessment by the Court,[78] and do not bind the NCAs or national courts, although NCAs and national courts are entitled to take the Commission's views in the guidance letters into account 'in the context of a case'.[79] The letters will be posted on the Commission's web site[80] and will provide guidance on the Commission's thinking which may be useful to other

---

[73] In respect of which the abolition of notification was recognized in the White Paper as being particularly serious. For the original suggestion about this, see *supra* Chap. 13, 1093.

[74] *Ibid.*, para. 8(c). There is no form or format on or in which the information must be provided, but para. 14 lists the matters which the memorandum accompanying a request for a guidance letter should contain.

[75] *Ibid.*, para. 9.

[76] *Ibid.*, para. 10.

[77] *Ibid.*, paras. 11 and 24.

[78] *Ibid.*, para. 23.

[79] *Ibid.*, para. 24.

[80] *Ibid.*, para. 21.

undertakings as well as to NCAs and national courts. In that way they can help to achieve the consistency of application of the rules for which the Commission is striving.

In effect, guidance letters are the new comfort letters. Although not as valuable as Article 10 decisions their availability gives undertakings the possibility that they may still not have to assess their agreements on their own.

(iii) The Initiation of Proceedings

Another important matter to stress initially is the significance in the modernized system of the Commission 'initiating proceedings'. The initiation of proceedings by the Commission is a formal act[81] by which the Commission indicates its intention to adopt a decision under Regulation 1/2003.[82] Under Regulation 1/2003 the initiation of proceedings by the Commission relieves the NCAs of their competence to apply Articles 81 and 82 in the case.[83] National courts are not relieved of their competence, but they may not take a decision running counter to one adopted by the Commission.[84] Moreover, they must also avoid giving decisions which would conflict with a decision contemplated by the Commission.[85]

Regulation 773/2004, Article 2 provides that the Commission may publicize the initiation of proceedings, in any appropriate way,[86] having previously informed the parties. Article 2(1) states:

The Commission may decide to initiate proceedings with a view to adopting a decision pursuant to Chapter III of Regulation (EC) No 1/2003 at any point in time, but no later than the date on which it issues a preliminary assessment as referred to in Article 9(1) of that Regulation or a statement of objections or the date on which a notice pursuant to Article 27(4) of that Regulation is published, whichever is the earlier.[87]

It is not necessary for the Commission to initiate proceedings before rejecting a complaint.[88]

Regulation 773/2004, Article 2(3) states that the Commission may exercise its powers of investigation (the fact-finding procedures which are discussed below) before initiating proceedings. This is vital as until the Commission has carried out an investigation it may not be in a position to issue a statement of objections (SO).

---

[81] See Case 48/72, *SA Brasserie de Haecht v. Wilkin Janssen* [1973] ECR 77 para. 16: 'the initiation of a procedure . . . obviously concerns an authoritative act of the Commission, evidencing its intention to take a decision'.

[82] Notice on cooperation within the Network of Competition Authorities [2004] OJ C101/54, para. 52.

[83] Reg. 1/2003, Art. 11(6).

[84] Reg. 1/2003, Art. 16(1).

[85] See Chap. 15.

[86] It frequently does so by Press Release.

[87] The preliminary assessment in Reg. 1/2003, Art. 9(1) is the initial view of the Commission that an infringement has occurred, although it may accept from the undertakings commitments which meet its concerns and therefore decide to take no further action (see *infra* 1206). A statement of objections (SO) is the serving on the undertakings concerned of a notice setting out the Commission's case against them (see *infra* 1189). An Article 27(4) notice is the publication of a summary of the case and other details which must take place where the Commission intends to adopt a decision pursuant to Article 9 (decisions making commitments binding) or Article 10 (finding of applicability decision).

[88] Reg. 773/2004, Art. 2(4).

B. FACT-FINDING BY THE COMMISSION

(i) General

In fact-finding, the Commission has extensive investigatory powers under Regulation 1/2003, Articles 18 and 20 (which correspond respectively to Articles 11 and 14 of Regulation 17). These formal powers are crucial for obtaining information when undertakings do not provide it voluntarily.[89] The exercise of the powers is often hotly contested by the undertakings subjected to them. The rights of the parties have been spelt out in the case law of the Court when the Commission's actions have been challenged, often on the grounds that the Commission has acted in breach of the general principles of law or of fundamental rights.

Under Regulation 1/2003, Article 18, the Commission may request undertakings to supply it with information.[90] However, where the Commission investigates suspected infringements of the competition rules, either following a complaint or on its own initiative, it is frequently looking for information which the parties would rather not give it and which they may have taken active steps to conceal. Under Article 18 the Commission may turn to the undertakings under investigation and to other undertakings such as customers, competitors, or suppliers of the allegedly infringing firms and request them, and ultimately require them, to supply information.

Article 20 enables the Commission to conduct inspections on the undertakings' premises. It can exercise these powers immediately, and does not have to make a prior request for information under Article 20. The Court has emphasized that undertakings have an obligation to cooperate actively with the investigative measures.[91]

Under Regulation 1/2003, Article 19 the Commission has a new power to interview any natural or legal person who consents to be interviewed. Under Article 21 it has a new power to carry out inspections at non-business premises.

(ii) Article 18 Requests for Information

Article 18 provides that the Commission 'may, by simple request or by decision, require undertakings and associations of undertakings to provide all necessary information'.[92] Although Article 18 corresponds to Article 11 of Regulation 17 it differs from it in an important respect. Under Article 11 there was a two-stage process, an 'informal' one by which the Commission could just request information, and a 'formal' one by which it could demand it by decision.[93] The Commission had to go through the 'informal' stage first and only if the undertaking did not comply with the request could it proceed by decision. Under Regulation 1/2003, Article 18, however, the Commission can choose to demand information from undertakings by decision from the beginning. By Article 18(6) the governments of the Member States and the NCAs have to supply the Commission with all necessary information it requests.

---

[89] They will provide it voluntarily, for example, when they are seeking a decision under Reg. 1/2003, Art. 10, *supra* 1148 or taking advantage of the Leniency Notice, *infra* 1240.

[90] In the case of complaints complainants should provide the Commission with any relevant information they possess. See Form C (Annex to Regulation 773/2004) and *infra* section 11.

[91] Case 374/87, *Orkem SA v. Commission* [1989] ECR 3283, [1991] 4 CMLR 502, paras. 22 and 27.

[92] Reg. 1/2003, Art. 18(1).

[93] Reg. 17, Arts. 11(3) and 11(5) respectively.

The meaning of 'necessary information' was considered by the Court in *SEP*.[94] The CFI stated that the term 'necessary information'[95] must be interpreted by reference to the purposes for which the powers of investigation in question were conferred upon the Commission. The requirement for a correlation between the request for information and the presumed infringement is met if, at this stage of the procedure, the request can be legitimately considered to be related to the presumed infringement.[96] The ECJ upheld this.[97] Although it is not easy, therefore, to show that the information requested is outside the leeway allowed to the Commission, it does mean that the Commission cannot go on a complete 'fishing expedition' and that the Court would be prepared to hold in an appropriate case that it had exceeded its powers.[98]

Article 18(2) states what must be contained in a request for information:

2. When sending a simple request for information to an undertaking or association of undertakings, the Commission shall state the legal basis and the purpose of the request, specify what information is required and fix the time-limit within which the information is to be provided, and the penalties provided for in Article 23 for supplying incorrect or misleading information.

There is no *duty* to comply with the request, although the intentional or negligent provision of *incorrect* or *misleading* information can be penalized with a fine under Regulation 1/2003, Article 23(1)(a), and as will be noted, the undertakings are warned of this under Article 18(2). The level of fine for providing incorrect or misleading information used to be low[99] but has been raised by Regulation 1/2003, Article 23(1) to a maximum of 1 per cent of the undertaking's total turnover in the preceding business year.[100] A desire to cooperate with the Commission and not to make the situation worse is often also a spur to accuracy.

The fact that ultimately the Commission can demand the information by adopting a decision under Article 18(3) is another reason for complying with the Article 18(2) request. The *Scottish Football Association* case[101] demonstrates how undertakings served with a request are expected to cooperate if the Commission is not to proceed to a decision. There the Commission had received a complaint from the European Sports Network that the Scottish Football Association (SFA) was intending to prevent it from broadcasting Argentinian football matches in Scotland. The Commission asked the SFA certain specific questions about its correspondence with the Argentinian FA and communications with FIFA. The SFA wrote back expressing 'some surprise' at the letter, explaining in general terms its policy about broadcasts, and saying it was 'happy to meet you at any time to explain our views'. The Court did not think that this amounted to the required 'active cooperation' and said of the SFA's comment 'we honestly think that as to the Argentinian matter, the Commission need not be troubled about an exchange of correspondence between two fraternal associations…' that '[c]onsidered objectively, that remark constitutes a polite but explicit refusal to co-operate with the Commission in the matter'.[102]

---

[94] Case T-39/90, *SEP* v. *Commission* [1991] ECR II-1497, [1992] 5 CMLR 33.

[95] In Reg. 17, Art. 11, but it is the same under Regulation 1/2003.

[96] Ibid., para. 29.

[97] Case C-36/92 P, *SEP* v. *Commission* [1994] ECR I-1911.

[98] See also Case 155/79, *AM&S Ltd* v. *Commission* [1982] ECR 1575, [1982] 2 CMLR 264 and Case 374/87, *Orkem SA* v. *Commission* [1989] ECR 3283, [1991] 4 CMLR 502.

[99] €100 to 5,000 (Reg. 17, Art. 15(1)(b)) which was worth rather more in 1962, when it was set, than in 2004.

[100] For the calculation of turnover in respect of fines, see *infra* 1213.

[101] Case T-46/92, *The Scottish Football Association* v. *Commission* [1994] ECR II-1039.

[102] *Ibid.*, para. 33.

An Article 18 request is not precluded by the fact that the Commission has already carried out an Article 20 inspection and is using Article 18 to obtain documents which it failed to obtain during the inspection.[103]

A decision under Article 18(3) has to state, like a request, its legal basis and purpose, the information required and the time-limit. However, in addition to warning of Article 23 fines, it must also indicate or impose the periodic penalties under Article 24, whereby the Commission may impose periodic penalty payments of up to 5 per cent of the average daily turnover[104] in order to compel the production of *complete* and correct information.[105] Further, the decision must indicate that it can be reviewed by the Court of Justice.

Article 18(4) of Regulation 1/2003 provides that lawyers may supply the information on behalf of their clients, although the client remains fully responsible if the information is incorrect, incomplete, or misleading.

The Commission has to send a copy of the request or decision to the NCA of the Member State in whose territory the seat of the undertaking concerned is situated and to the NCA of the Member State whose territory is affected.[106]

The questions of when undertakings may withhold documents from the Commission on the ground that they are legally privileged, and to what extent they can refuse to supply information on grounds of self-incrimination are dealt with below.[107]

(iii) Article 20 Inspections

a. General

Article 20(1) gives the Commission powers to carry out 'all necessary inspections' of undertakings and associations of undertakings. This means investigations at the undertaking's premises. Inspections are carried out by officials and 'other accompanying persons authorized by the Commission'[108] such as IT experts. By Article 20(2) inspections involve the power:

(a) to enter any premises, land and means of transport of undertakings and associations of undertakings;

(b) to examine the books and other records related to the business, irrespective of the medium on which they are stored;

(c) to take or obtain in any form copies of or extracts from such books or records;

(d) to seal any business premises and books or records for the period and to the extent necessary for the inspection;

(e) to ask any representative or member of staff of the undertaking or association of undertakings for explanations on facts or documents relating to the subject-matter and purpose of the inspection and to record the answers.

Under Article 20(3) the Commission can carry out the inspection at the premises simply on production of a 'written authorization'.[109] The officials may either give advance notice of their

---

[103] Case 374/87, *Orkem SA v. Commission* [1989] ECR 3283, [1991] 4 CMLR 502, para. 14.

[104] See *infra* 1212.

[105] Art. 24(1)(d).

[106] Reg. 1/2003, Art. 18(5).

[107] See *infra* 1181 and 1173.

[108] Reg. 1/2003, Art. 20(3), (5), and (6).

[109] This must contain the same or equivalent matters as required in respect of requests for information under Article 18(2), see *supra* 1153.

arrival or come without warning (although they have to give notice 'in good time before the inspection' to the NCA of the Member State in whose territory the inspection is conducted). So long as they carry only the Article 20(3) 'authorization' an undertaking is under no legal obligation to submit to the inspection. Under Article 20(4), however, undertakings *must* submit to procedures ordered by decision of the Commission.[110] The undertaking must actively cooperate. In *Fabbrica Pisani* the Commission said:[111]

the obligation on undertakings to supply all documents required by Commission inspectors must be understood to mean not merely giving access to all files, but actually producing the specified documents required.

The most notorious form of Commission inspection is where the officials arrive without warning, armed with a decision. The ECJ held in *National Panasonic*[112] that they were entitled to do this under Regulation 17, Article 14(3), the precursor of Article 20(4), without going through the 'voluntary' (now Article 20(3)) procedure first. Although popularly known as 'dawn raids' unannounced inspections take place during normal business hours. There may, however, be simultaneous surprise arrivals at undertakings across the Community where, for example, the Commission suspects the existence of a hard-core cartel or abuses of a dominant position. The *Polypropylene* cartel investigation,[113] for example, involved ten simultaneous raids. Julian Joshua, at one time Deputy Head of the Cartel Unit in DG Comp, explained in 1983 why the apparently draconian powers of the Commission are necessary:[114]

More often, the most serious cartels are not modified at all. They are operated in conditions of strict secrecy. Communication between participants is kept to a minimum and knowledge of the arrangements confined to certain key employees. Meetings take place in safe countries or under the cover of a seemingly innocent trade association. There may even be emergency arrangements to shred documents and warn other participates by coded telex messages in the event of an investigation. Sometimes the cartel rules provide for members to deny all knowledge of documents or their contents even when these are found in the safe. In such circumstances resort to surprise must be a legitimate and essential precaution.[115]

Article 20(4) decisions can be taken by the Commissioner responsible for competition. This delegation by the College of Commissioners is valid as it does not involve a matter of principle.[116]

In *National Panasonic* an undertaking subjected to the first unannounced Regulation 17, Article 14(3) investigation claimed that the procedure infringed its fundamental rights. It relied in particular on Article 8 of the ECHR. It also claimed that in this case the principle of proportionality was infringed.

---

[110] Case 5/85, *AKZO v. Commission* [1986] ECR 2585, [1987] 3 CMLR 716; Cases 46/87 and 227/88, *Hoechst AG v. Commission* [1989] ECR 2859, [1991] 4 CMLR 410. The decision must contain the same or equivalent matters as required in respect of decisions under Article 18(3), *supra* 1154.

[111] [1980] OJ L75/30, [1980] 2 CMLR 354.

[112] Case 136/79, *National Panasonic v. Commission* [1980] ECR 2033, [1980] CMLR 169.

[113] *Polypropylene Cartel* [1986] OJ L230/1, [1988] 4 CMLR 347.

[114] J. M. Joshua: 'The Element of Surprise' (1983) 8 *ELRev* 3, 5.

[115] For a most instructive (and amusing) look at the inner workings of a cartel, see James M. Griffin, 'An Inside Look at a Cartel at Work: Common Characteristics of International Cartels' Speech of 6 April 2000, available on the US Department of Justice web site, http://www.usdoj.gov/atr/public/speeches/. This includes transcripts of cartel meetings caught on hidden microphones (obtaining which involved, *inter alia*, FBI agents disguised as hotel employees). The cartel concerned, the lysine (amino acids) cartel, also became the subject of an EC decision, [2001] OJ L 152/24, [2001] 5 CMLR 322, on appeal to the CFI, Case T-224/00, *Archer Daniels Midland v. Commission* [2003] ECR II-2597, [2003] 5 CMLR 561, *aff'd* by the ECJ, Case C-397/03 P, *Archer Daniels Midland v. Commission* [2006] ECR I-4429.

[116] Case 53/85, *AKZO v. Commission* [1986] ECR 2585, [1987] 3 CMLR 716.

Case 136/79, *National Panasonic* v. *Commission* [1980] ECR 2033, [1980] CMLR 169

Commission officials arrived at Panasonic's offices in Slough at 10.00 a.m. The directors asked if the inspection could be delayed to await the arrival of their solicitor, who was in Norwich. The officials waited until 10.45 a.m. and then began. The solicitor did not arrive until 1.45 p.m. and the inspection finished at 5.30 p.m. Panasonic subsequently challenged the validity of the decision ordering the inspection in the Court of Justice and asked that all the documents taken by the Commission should be returned or destroyed.

Court of Justice

17. The applicant then claims that by failing previously to communicate to it beforehand the decision ordering an investigation in question, the Commission has in this instance infringed fundamental rights of the applicant, in particular the right to receive advance notification of the intention to apply a decision regarding it, the right to be heard before a decision adversely affecting it is taken and the right to use the opportunity given to it under Article [242] of the Treaty to request a stay of execution of such a decision. The applicant relies in particular on Article 8 of the European Convention for the Protection of Human Rights and Fundamental Freedoms of 4 November 1950 whereby 'everyone has the right to respect for his private and family life, his home and his correspondence'. It considers that those guarantees must be provided *mutatis mutandis* also to legal persons.

18. As the Court stated in its judgment of 14 May 1974 in Case 4/73, *J. Nold, Kohlen-und Baustoffgrosshandlung* v. *Commission of the European Communities* [1974] ECR 491 at p. 507, fundamental rights form an integral part of the general principles of law, the observance of which the Court of Justice ensures, in accordance with constitutional traditions common to the Member States and with international treaties on which the Member States have collaborated or of which they are signatories.

19. In this respect it is necessary to point out that Article 8 (2) of the European Convention, in so far as it applies to legal persons, whilst stating the principle that public authorities should not interfere with the exercise of the rights referred to in Article 8(1), acknowledges that such interference is permissible to the extent to which it 'is in accordance with the law and is necessary in a democratic society in the interests of national security, public safety or the economic well-being of the country, for the prevention of disorder or crime, for the protection of health or morals, or for the protection of the rights and freedom of others.'

20. In this instance, as follows from the seventh and eighth recitals of the preamble to Regulation No 17, the aim of the powers given to the Commission by Article 14 of that regulation is to enable it to carry out its duty under the EEC Treaty of ensuring that the rules on competition are applied in the common market. The function of these rules is, as follows from the fourth recital of the preamble of the Treaty, Article 3[(1)(g)] and Articles [81] and [82], to prevent competition from being distorted to the detriment of the public interest, individual undertakings and consumers. The exercise of the powers given by the Commission by Regulation No 17 contributes to the maintenance of the system of competition intended by the Treaty which undertakings are absolutely bound to comply with. In these circumstances, it does not therefore appear that Regulation No 17, by giving the Commission powers to carry out investigations without previous notification, infringes the right invoked by the applicant.

21. Moreover, as regard more particularly the argument that the application was in this instance denied the right to be heard before a decision was taken regarding it, it is necessary to

state that the exercise of such a right of defence is chiefly incorporated in legal or administrative procedures for the termination of an infringement or for a declaration that an agreement, decision or concerted practice is incompatible with Article [81], such as the procedures referred to by Regulation No 99/63/EEC. On the other hand, the investigation procedure referred to in Article 14 of Regulation No 17 does not aim at terminating an infringement or declaring that an agreement, decision or concerted practice is incompatible with Article [81]; its sole objective is to enable the Commission to gather the necessary information to check that the actual existence and scope of a given factual and legal situation. Only if the Commission considers that the data for the appraisal thereof collected in this way justify the initiation of a procedure under Regulation No 99/63/EEC must the undertaking or association of undertakings concerned be heard before such a decision is taken pursuant to Article 19(1) of Regulation No 17 and to the provisions of Regulation No 99/63/EEC. Precisely this substantive difference between the decisions taken at the end of such a procedure and decisions ordering an investigation explains the wording of Article 19(1) which, in listing the decisions which the Commission cannot take before giving those concerned the opportunity of exercising their right of defence, does not mention that laid down in Article 14(3) of the same regulation.

22. Finally, the argument that the absence of previous information deprived the applicant of the opportunity of exercising its rights under Article [242] of the Treaty to request the Court for a stay of execution of the decision in question is contradicted by the very provisions of Article [242]. That article presupposes in fact that a decision has been adopted and that it is effective whereas the previous notification, which the applicant complains that the Commission did not send it, should have preceded the adoption of the contested decision and could not have been binding.

23. In view of these considerations, the second submission is not well founded.

(d) The violation of the principle of proportionality

28. The applicant points out in addition that the principle of proportionality, as established by the case-law of the Court of Justice, implies that a decision ordering an investigation adopted without the preliminary procedure may only be justified if the situation is very grave and where there is the greatest urgency and the need for complete secrecy before the investigation is carried out. It points out, finally, that the contested decision violates such a principle by not indicating in the statement of the reasons upon which it is based that any of those facts exists.

29. The Commission's choice between an investigation by straightforward authorization and an investigation ordered by a decision does not depend on the facts relied upon by the applicant but on the need for an appropriate inquiry, having regard to the special features of the case.

30. Considering that the contested decision aimed solely at enabling the Commission to collect the necessary information to appraise whether there was any infringement of the Treaty, it does not therefore appear that the Commission's action in this instance was disproportionate to the objective pursued and therefore violated the principle of proportionality.

31. For all these reasons, since the last submission cannot be accepted either, it is necessary to dismiss the application as unfounded.

The ECJ therefore rejected National Panasonic's claims and held that an unannounced Article 14(3) inspection did not infringe the inspected undertaking's fundamental rights.

The application of Article 8(1) of the ECHR was considered again in *Hoechst*. The position of undertakings faced with unannounced Article 14(3) inspections and the powers of the Commission in respect thereof were considered at length by the Court. The case arose from a dawn raid in the course of the Commission's investigations into the PVC and polyethylene cartels. Hoechst, unusually, simply refused to admit the Commission inspectors when they arrived.

Cases 46/87 and 227/88, *Hoechst AG* v. *Commission* [1989] ECR 2859, [1991] 4 CMLR 410

The Commission suspected the existence of cartel arrangements between certain suppliers and producers of polyethylene and PVC. On 15 January 1987 it adopted a decision providing for an Article 14(3) investigation into Hoechst. On 20 January the Commission inspectors arrived at Hoechst's offices but Hoechst refused to allow the investigation to go ahead. It claimed that the investigation was an unlawful search, and insisted that the inspectors noted its objections in writing. The inspectors tried twice more, on 22 and 23 January, but the same thing happened. The Commission sent Hoechst a telex calling upon it to submit to the investigation and setting a periodical penalty in the event of non-compliance of 1,000 ECUs per day, and on 3 February it adopted a decision imposing that penalty. The Commission had sought the assistance of the Bundeskartellamt (the Federal Cartel Office) under Regulation 17, Article 14(5) and (6) and the Bundeskartellamt applied to the local district court (the Amtsgericht, Frankfurt am Main) for a search warrant. On 12 February the Amtsgericht refused the warrant on the grounds that no facts had been put before it which justified the suspicions of the existence of a cartel. Hoechst applied to the Court of Justice for suspension of both the decision ordering the investigation and the decision imposing the periodic penalty but the President of the Court dismissed the application. The Bundeskartellamt applied to the Amtsgericht for a search warrant in the Commission's own name and this was granted on 31 March. The investigation was finally carried out at Hoechst's premises on 2 and 3 April. On 26 May the Commission adopted a decision fixing the definitive amount of the periodic penalty at 55,000 ECUs (i.e., 1,000 a day from 6 February to 1 April). Hoechst brought actions before the Court of Justice under Article 234 alleging that the decisions of 15 January, 3 February, and 26 May were all void. The following extract deals with the question of the decision of 15 January ordering the Article 14(3) investigation.

Court of Justice

12. It should be noted, before the nature and scope of the Commission's powers of investigation under Article 14 of Regulation No 17 are examined, that that article cannot be interpreted in such a way as to give rise to results which are incompatible with the general principles of Community law and in particular with fundamental rights.

13. The Court has consistently held that fundamental rights are an integral part of the general principles of law the observance of which the Court ensures, in accordance with constitutional traditions common to the Member States, and the international treaties on which the Member States have collaborated or of which they are signatories (see, in particular, the judgment of 14 May 1974 in Case 4/73 *Nold* v. *Commission* [1974] ECR 491). The European Convention for the Protection of Human Rights and Fundamental Freedoms of 4 November 1950 (hereinafter referred to as 'the European Convention on Human Rights') is of particular significance in that regard (see, in particular, the judgment of 15 May 1986 in Case 222/84 *Johnston* v. *Chief Constable of the Royal Ulster Constabulary* [1986] ECR 1651).

14. In interpreting Article 14 of Regulation No 17, regard must be had in particular to the rights of the defence, a principle whose fundamental nature had been stressed on numerous occasions in the Court's decisions (see, in particular, the judgment of 9 November 1983 in Case 322/81 *Michelin* v. *Commission* [1983] ECR 3461, paragraph 7).

15. In that judgment, the Court pointed out that the rights of the defence must be observed in administrative procedures which may lead to the imposition of penalties. But it is also necessary to prevent those rights from being irremediably impaired during the preliminary inquiry procedures

including, in particular, investigations which may be decisive in providing evidence of the unlawful nature of conduct engaged in by undertakings for which they may be liable.

16. Consequently, although certain rights of the defence relate only to the contentious proceedings which follow the delivery of the statement of objections, other rights, such as the right to legal representation and the privileged nature of correspondence between lawyer and client (recognized by the Court in the judgment of 18 May 1982 in Case 155/79 *AM & S* v. *Commission* [1982] ECR 1575) must be respected as from the preliminary-inquiry stage.

17. Since the application has also relied on the requirements stemming from the fundamental right to the inviolability of the home, it should be observed that, although the existence of such a right must be recognized in the Community legal order as a principle common to the laws of the Member States in regard to the private dwellings of natural persons, the same is not true in regard to undertakings, because there are not inconsiderable divergences between the legal systems of the Member States in regard to the nature and degree of protection afforded to business premises against intervention by the public authorities.

18. No other inference is to be drawn from Article 8(1) of the European Convention on Human Rights which provides that: 'Everyone has the right to respect for his private and family life, his home and his correspondence'. The protective scope of that article is concerned with the development of man's personal freedom and may not therefore be extended to business premises. Furthermore, it should be noted that there is no case-law of the European Court of Human Rights on that subject.

19. None the less, in all the legal systems of the Member States, any intervention by the public authorities in the sphere of private activities of any person, whether natural or legal, must have a legal basis and be justified on the grounds laid down by law, and, consequently, those systems provide, albeit in different forms, protection against arbitrary or disproportionate intervention. The need for such protection must be recognized as a general principle of Community law. In that regard, it should be pointed out that the Court has held that it has the power to determine whether measures of investigation taken by the Commission under the ECSC Treaty are excessive (judgment of 14 December 1962 in Joined Cases 5 to 11 and 13 to 15/62 *San Michele and Others* v. *Commission* [1962] ECR 449).

20. The nature and scope of the Commission's powers of investigation under Article 14 of Regulation No 17 should therefore be considered in the light of the general principles set out above.

21. Article 14(1) authorizes the Commission to undertake all necessary investigations into undertakings and associations of undertakings and provides that: 'To this end the officials authorized by the Commission are empowered:

(a) to examine the books and other business records;
(b) to take copies of or extracts from the books and business records;
(c) to ask for oral explanations on the spot;
(d) to enter any premises, land and means of transport of undertakings'.

22. Article 14(2) and (3) provide that investigations may be carried out upon production of an authorization in writing or of a decision requiring undertakings to submit to the investigation. As the Court has already decided, the Commission may choose between those two possibilities in the light of the special features of each case (judgment of 26 June 1980 in Case 1365/79 *National Panasonic* v. *Commission* [1980] ECR 2033). Both the written authorizations and the decisions must specify the subject-matter and purpose of the investigation. Whichever procedure is followed, the Commission is required to inform, in advance, the competent authority of the Member State in whose territory the investigation is to be carried out and, according to Article 14(4), that authority must be consulted before the decision ordering the investigation is adopted.

23. According to Article 14(5), the Commission's officials may be assisted in carrying out their duties by officials of the competent authority of the Member State in whose territory the investigation is to be made. Such assistance may be provided either at the request of that authority or of the Commission.

24. Finally, according to Article 14(6), the assistance of the national authorities is necessary for the carrying out of the investigation where it is opposed by an undertaking.

25. As the Court pointed out in the abovementioned judgment of 26 June 1980 (paragraph 20), it follows from the seventh and eighth recitals in the preamble to Regulation No 17 that the aim of the powers given to the Commission by Article 14 of that regulation is to enable it to carry out its under the EEC Treaty of ensuring that the rules on competition are applied in the common market. The function of those rules is, as follows from the fourth recital in the preamble to the Treaty, Article 3(1) and Articles [81] and [82], to prevent competition from being distorted to the detriment of the public interest, individual undertakings and consumers. The exercise of the powers given to the Commission by Regulation No 17 thus contributes to the maintenance of the system of competition intended by the Treaty with which undertakings are absolutely bound to comply. The eighth recital states that for that purpose the Commission must be empowered, throughout the common market, to require such information to be supplied and to undertake such investigations 'as are necessary' to bring to light any infringement of Articles [81] and [82].

26. Both the purpose of Regulation No 17 and the list of powers conferred on the Commission's officials by Article 14 thereof show that the scope of investigations may be very wide. In that regard, the right to enter any premises, land and means of transport of undertakings is of particular importance inasmuch as it is intended to permit the Commission to obtain evidence of infringements of the competition rules in the places in which such evidence is normally to be found, that is to say, on the business premises of undertakings.

27. That right of access would serve no useful purpose if the Commission's officials could do no more than ask for documents or files which they could identify precisely in advance. On the contrary, such a right implies the power to search for various items of information which are not already known or fully identified. Without such a power, it would be impossible for the Commission to obtain the information necessary to carry out the investigation if the undertakings concerned refused to co-operate or adopted an obstructive attitude.

28. Although Article 14 of Regulation No 17 thus confers wide powers of investigation on the Commission, the exercise of those powers is subject to conditions serving to ensure that the rights of the undertakings concerned are respected.

29. In that regard, it should be noted first that the Commission is required to specify that subject-matter and purpose of the investigation. That obligation is a fundamental requirement not merely in order to show that the investigation to be carried out on the premises of the undertakings concerned is justified but also to enable those undertakings to assess the scope of their duty to co-operate while at the same time safeguarding the rights of the defence.

30. It should also be pointed out that the conditions for the exercise of the Commission's investigative powers vary according to the procedure which the Commission has chosen, the attitude of the undertakings concerned and the intervention of the national authorities.

31. Article 14 of Regulation No 17 deals in the first place with investigations carried out with the co-operation of the undertakings concerned, either voluntarily, where there is a written authorization, or by virtue of an obligation arising under a decision ordering an investigation. In the latter case, which is the situation here, the Commission's officials have, *inter alia*, the power to have shown to them the documents they request, to enter such premises as they choose, and to have shown to them the contents of any piece of furniture which they indicate. On the other hand, they may not obtain access to premises of furniture by force or oblige the staff of the undertaking to give them such access, or carry out searches without the permission of the management of the undertaking.

32. The situation is completely different if the undertakings concerned oppose the Commission's investigation. In that case, the Commission's officials may, on the basis of Article 14(6) and without the co-operation of the undertakings, search for any information necessary for the investigation with the assistance of the national authorities, which are required to afford them the assistance necessary for the performance of their duties. Although such assistance is required only if the undertaking expresses its opposition, it may also be requested as a precautionary measure, in order to overcome any opposition on the part of the undertaking.

33. It follows from Article 14(6) that it is for each Member State to determine the conditions under which the national authorities will afford assistance to the Commission's officials. In that regard, the Member States are required to ensure that the Commission's action is effective, while respecting the general principles set out above. It follows that, within those limits, the appropriate procedural rules designed to ensure respect for undertakings' rights are those laid down by national law.

34. Consequently, if the Commission intends, with the assistance of the national authorities, to carry out an investigation other than with the co-operation of the undertakings concerned, it is required to respect the relevant procedural guarantees laid down by national law.

35. The Commission must make sure that the competent body under national law has all that it needs to exercise its own supervisory powers. It should be pointed out that that body, whether judicial or otherwise, cannot in this respect substitute its own assessment of the need for the investigations ordered for that of the Commission, the lawfulness of whose assessments of fact and law is subject only to review by the Court of Justice. On the other hand, it is within the powers of the national body, after satisfying itself that the decision ordering the investigation is authentic, to consider whether the measures of constraint envisaged are arbitrary or excessive having regard to the subject-matter of the investigation of those measures.

36. In the light of the foregoing, it must be held that the measures which the contested decision ordering the investigation permitted the Commission's officials to take did not exceed their powers under Article 14 of Regulation No 17. Article 1 of that decision merely requires the applicant 'to permit officials authorized by the Commission to enter its premises during normal office hours, to produce for inspection and to permit copies to be made of business documents related to the subject-matter of the enquiry which are requested by the said officials and to provide immediately any explanations which those officials may seek'.

It can be seen therefore that this judgment dealt with a number of issues:

- First, what powers the officials have during the inspection;
- Secondly, the role of national courts where the undertakings concerned are not willing to submit to the inspection;
- Thirdly, the question of the application of Article 8 of the ECHR and the principle of the inviolability of the home (the ECHR case law has developed subsequently to *Hoechst* and, moreover, Regulation 1/2003, Article 21 now gives the Commission a right to inspect homes as well as business premises);[117]
- Fourthly, the rights to legal representation and the legal privilege of correspondence between lawyer and client.

b. The Powers of the Inspectors

Of the five powers listed in Article 20(2), the power to seal any business premises or records did not appear in Regulation 17, and the power to ask for explanations on facts or

[117] *Infra*, 1171.

documents is wider than the power to ask for 'oral explanations on the spot' in Regulation 17, Article 14(1).

The Power to Enter any Premises, Land and Means of Transport (Article 20(2)(a))

The extent of this power was explained in *Hoechst* (paragraphs 31 and 32). If the undertakings are willing to cooperate, the Commission officials have power to have shown to them the documents they request, and to enter such premises they choose and have shown to them the contents of particular furniture they indicate. They are *not* entitled forcibly to enter premises or furniture or carry out searches without the undertaking's consent. If the undertaking does not submit to the investigation Regulation 20(6) comes into play and the Commission has to rely on the assistance of the Member State.[118]

The Power to Examine Books and Other Records (Article 20(2)(b))

Article 20(2)(b) elaborates upon the words of Regulation 17, Article 14(1)(a) to specify that the Commission may examine records 'irrespective of the medium on which they are stored'. This encompasses all forms of information technology.

The Power to Take or Obtain in any Form Copies of or Extracts from such Books or Records (Article 20(2)(c))

It is advisable for undertakings to make photocopying facilities available to the inspectors.

The Power to Seal any Business Premises and Books or Records for the Period and to the Extent Necessary for the Inspection (Article 20(2)(d))

This is a new power in Regulation 1/2003, although it was formerly the Commission's practice to do it if it thought it necessary. The difference is that the power is now expressly conferred on the Commission and the undertaking can be fined under Article 23(1)(e) for breaking the seals. Recital 25 says that seals should not normally be affixed for more than 72 hours.

The Power to Ask any Representative or Member of Staff of the Undertaking or Association of Undertakings for Explanations on Facts or Documents Relating to the Subject-matter and Purpose of the Inspection and to Record the Answers

The corresponding provision in Regulation 17 (Article 14(1)(c)) empowered the inspectors 'to ask for oral explanations on the spot' and there was a surprising lack of authority on what this covered.[119] The generally accepted view was that it encompassed asking questions directly arising from the books and records being examined and asking for explanations of such matters as the references, terms, and abbreviations appearing in them, but that it did not authorize a general interrogation of officers or employees of the undertaking. Article 14 did not specify who should answer the oral questions put to the undertaking but a failure by the undertaking to put forward a suitable person could be construed as a refusal to co-operate. These uncertainties have been remedied by Regulation 1/2003, Article 20(2)(e), which has expanded the Commission's powers to ask questions. The inspectors may now ask 'any representative or member of staff' for explanations on *facts* and documents relating to *the subject-matter and purpose*

---

[118] See *infra* 1163.

[119] As the Commission's guide, *Dealing with the Commission* (Commission, 1997), para. 5.6, recognized. There was some consideration of it in Case 136/79, *National Panasonic v. Commission* [1980] ECR 2033, [1980] CMLR 169 but no decisive ruling by the Court.

of the inspection. The answers can be recorded.[120] Article 23(1)(d) provides that the Commission may fine the undertaking up to 1 per cent of total turnover of the previous business year if:

in response to a question asked in accordance with Article 20(2)(e),

— they give an incorrect or misleading answer,

— they fail to rectify within a time-limit set by the Commission an incorrect, incomplete or misleading answer given by a member of staff, or

— they fail or refuse to provide a complete answer on facts relating to the subject-matter and purpose of an inspection ordered by a decision adopted pursuant to Article 20(4).

The 'they' in this paragraph refers to the undertaking, not to the individual member of staff. There are no powers under Regulation 1/2003 to impose fines on individuals.[121] It will be noted, however, that the fine is to be imposed for failure or refusal to rectify incomplete, incorrect or misleading answers. This is elaborated upon in Regulation 773/2004, Article 4(3) which provides:

In cases where a member of staff of an undertaking or of an association of undertakings who is not or was not authorized by the undertaking or by the association of undertakings to provide explanations on behalf of the undertaking or association of undertakings has been asked for explanations, the Commission shall set a time-limit within which the undertaking or the association of undertakings may communicate to the Commission any rectification, amendment or supplement to the explanations given by such member of staff. The rectification, amendment or supplement shall be added to the explanations as recorded pursuant to paragraph 1.[122]

This provision is unsatisfactory as it appears to relate only to staff 'not authorized by the undertaking to provide explanations'. Undertakings might also wish, however, to rectify or supplement answers given by staff who *are* 'authorized' (there is no definition of an 'authorized' member of staff) and it is submitted that it would be ungracious of the Commission not to allow them to do this without a fine, unless there was some evidence of bad faith on the part of the undertaking at the time that the misleading, etc. answer was given.

It should be noted that in addition to this wider power to ask for explanations during an inspection the Commission has a new power of interview under Regulation 1/2003, Article 19. This is discussed below.[123]

c. The Role of the NCAs, the Member States, and the National Courts in Article 20 Inspections

Regulation 1/2003, Article 20(5) provides that officials from the NCA on whose territory the inspection is conducted may actively assist the Commission officials (and have the Article 20(2) powers) if either the NCA or the Commission requests it. The role of the Member State becomes more important, however, if the undertaking does not submit to the investigation. The duty to submit to an Article 14(3) investigation was a continuing one, entailing both allowing the inspection to begin and cooperating thereafter, but the limited nature of the Commission officials'

---

[120] Under Reg. 773/2004, Art. 4(2) a copy of any recording made has to be made available to the undertaking after the inspection.

[121] The absence under EC law of liability on individuals is in contrast to the position in some Member States, including the UK.

[122] Under Reg. 773/2004, Art. 17(3) this has to be at least two weeks.

[123] *Infra* 1173.

powers, and their reliance on national authorities and national procedures, was sharply demonstrated in *Hoechst*. Article 20(6), replacing Regulation 17, Article 14(6) provides:

Where the officials and other accompanying persons authorised by the Commission find that an undertaking opposes an inspection ordered pursuant to this Article, the Member State concerned shall afford them the necessary assistance, requesting where appropriate the assistance of the police or of an equivalent enforcement authority, so as to enable them to conduct their inspection.

If the 'assistance' requires authorization, under national law, from a judicial authority (i.e., because national law requires a court to sanction coercive measures such as forcible entry) that must be applied for.[124] The powers and duties of the national court in this situation, which were not expressly mentioned under Regulation 17 but were spelt out in *Hoechst*, as seen above, were examined again in *Roquette Frères SA*, where the ECJ looked at the issue in the context of the general principles of Community law and the ECHR as developed since *Hoechst*.

Case C-94/00, *Roquette Frères SA* v. *Directeur Général de la Concurrence, de la Consommation et de la Répression des Fraudes* [2002] ECR I-9011, [2003] 4 CMLR 46

The Commission requested the assistance of the French Government over an inspection it wished to conduct at the premises of Roquette Frères SA (in connection with the investigation of the sodium gluconate cartel).[125] The French administrative authorities applied to the Tribunal de grande instance de Lille for authorization pursuant to the relevant French legislation and attached to the application a copy of the Commission decision ordering the investigation and a text of the *Hoechst* judgment. The Tribunal granted the authorization. Roquette Frères submitted, but later claimed in the French courts that the authorization should not have been made on the limited information placed before the Tribunal. The Cour de Cassation referred to the Court questions about the scope of the review to be carried out by the national court in this situation, and the information which the Commission should be required to produce.

Court of Justice

17. In the judgment making the reference, the Cour de cassation states that no information or evidence justifying any presumption of the existence of anti-competitive practices was put before the President of the Tribunal de grande instance de Lille, so that it was impossible for him to verify whether, in the specific circumstances, the application before him was justified. It further observes that, in the investigation decision of 10 September 1998, the Commission merely stated that it had information to the effect that Roquette Frères was engaging in the anti-competitive practices described by it, without however referring, even briefly, in its analysis to the information which it claimed to have and on which it based its assessment . . .

. . .

---

[124] Reg. 1/2003, Art. 20(7). At the time of *Hoechst* the enforcement of the Commission's powers in the UK was by way of application in the name of the Attorney-General to the High Court for an injunction, defiance of which would be a contempt of court. Under the Competition Act 1998, the OFT has power to enter premises with a warrant from the High Court in England and Wales or a Court of Session in Scotland using reasonable force as necessary.

[125] See IP/01/1355, re-issued 19 Mar. 2002.

22. As is apparent from the judgment making the reference, the Cour de cassation is uncertain as to the possible effect on the principles established by the Court in *Hoechst*, and hence on the answers to be given to its questions, of certain developments which have taken place in the field of the protection of human rights since delivery of the judgment in *Hoechst*.

23. According to settled case-law, fundamental rights form an integral part of the general principles of law observance of which the Court ensures. For that purpose, the Court draws inspiration from the constitutional traditions common to the Member States and from the guidelines supplied by international treaties for the protection of human rights on which the Member States have collaborated or to which they are signatories. The ECHR has special significance in that respect (see, in particular, *Hoechst*, paragraph 13, and Case C-274/99 P *Connolly* v *Commission* [2001] ECR I-1611, paragraph 37).

24. As the Court has also stated, the principles established by that case-law have been reaffirmed in the preamble to the Single European Act and in Article F.2 of the Treaty on European Union (Case C-415/93 *Bosman* [1995] ECR I-4921, paragraph 79). They are now set out in Article 6(2) EU (*Connolly* v *Commission*, cited above, paragraph 38).

25. In a different connection, the Court has likewise consistently held that, where national rules fall within the scope of Community law and reference is made to it for a preliminary ruling, it must provide all the criteria of interpretation needed by the national court to determine whether those rules are compatible with the fundamental rights the observance of which the Court ensures and which derive in particular from the ECHR (see, in particular, Case C-260/89 *ERT* [1991] ECR I-2925, paragraph 42, and Case C-159/90 *Society for the Protection of Unborn Children Ireland* [1991] ECR I-4685, paragraph 31).

26. Since the questions referred relate in essence to the scope of the review which may be carried out by a court of a Member State where that court is called upon to act on a request by the Commission for assistance pursuant to Article 14(6) of Regulation No 17, the Court of Justice is clearly competent to provide the referring court with all the criteria of interpretation needed by that court to determine whether the applicable national rules are compatible, for the purposes of such review, with Community law, including, as the case may be, the rights established by the ECHR as general principles of law observance of which is to be ensured by the Court of Justice.

27. It should be recalled in that regard that, in paragraph 19 of the judgment in *Hoechst*, the Court recognised that the need for protection against arbitrary or disproportionate intervention by public authorities in the sphere of the private activities of any person, whether natural or legal, constitutes a general principle of Community law.

28. The Court has likewise stated that the competent authorities of the Member States are required to respect that general principle when they are called upon to act in response to a request for assistance made by the Commission pursuant to Article 14(6) of Regulation No 17 (see *Hoechst*, paragraphs 19 and 33).

. . .

Review to ensure that the coercive measures are not arbitrary and the information which the Commission may be required to provide to that end

54. First, when conducting its review to ensure that there is nothing arbitrary about a coercive measure designed to permit implementation of an investigation ordered by the Commission, the competent national court is required, in essence, to satisfy itself that there exist reasonable grounds for suspecting an infringement of the competition rules by the undertaking concerned.

55. It is true that there is no fundamental difference between that review and the review which the Community judicature may be called upon to carry out for the purposes of ensuring that the investigation decision itself is in no way arbitrary, that is to say, that it has not been adopted in the absence of facts capable of justifying the investigation (Joined Cases 97/87 to 99/87 *Dow Chemical*

Ibérica and Others v. *Commission* [1989] ECR 3165, paragraph 52). It must be borne in mind in that regard that the investigations carried out by the Commission are intended to enable it to gather the necessary documentary evidence to check the actual existence and scope of a given factual and legal situation concerning which the Commission already possesses certain information (*National Panasonic* v. *Commission*, cited above, paragraphs 13 and 21).

56. However, that similarity in the nature of the review carried out by the Community judica-ture and that undertaken by the competent national body must not obscure the distinction between the objectives which those two types of review respectively seek to attain.

57. The investigatory powers conferred on the Commission by Article 14(1) of Regulation No 17 are limited to authorising its officials to enter such premises as they choose and to have shown to them the documents they request and the contents of any piece of furniture which they indicate (*Hoechst*, paragraph 31).

58. For their part, the coercive measures falling within the competence of the national author-ities entail the power to gain access to premises or furniture by force or to oblige the staff of the undertaking to give them such access, and to carry out searches without the permission of the management of the undertaking (*Hoechst*, paragraph 31).

59. Having regard to the invasion of privacy which they entail, recourse to such coercive meas-ures necessitates the ability of the competent national body autonomously to satisfy itself that they are not arbitrary.

60. In particular, such an examination of possible arbitrariness cannot be precluded on the ground that, in satisfying itself as to the existence of reasonable grounds for suspecting an infringement of the competition rules, the competent national body might, in accordance with paragraph 35 of the judgment in *Hoechst*, substitute its own assessment of the need for the inves-tigations ordered for that of the Commission and call in question the latter's assessments of fact and law.

61. It follows that, for the purposes of enabling the competent national court to satisfy itself that the coercive measures sought are not arbitrary, the Commission is required to provide that court with explanations showing, in a properly substantiated manner, that the Commission is in possession of information and evidence providing reasonable grounds for suspecting infringe-ment of the competition rules by the undertaking concerned.

62. On the other hand, the competent national court may not demand that it be provided with the information and evidence in the Commission's file on which the latter's suspicions are based.

63. In that regard, it is necessary to take into consideration the obligation of the Member States, pointed out in paragraph 35 of this judgment, to ensure that the Commission's action is effective.

64. First, as the Commission and the German and United Kingdom Governments have rightly observed, the Commission's ability to guarantee the anonymity of certain of its sources of infor-mation is of crucial importance with a view to ensuring the effective prevention of prohibited anti-competitive practices.

65. Clearly, if the Commission were obliged to send to the various national competition author-ities factual information and evidence revealing the identity of its sources of information, or enabling that identity to be deduced, that might well increase the risks to informants of disclosure of their identity to third parties, in view, particularly, of the procedural requirements of national law.

66. Second, it must also be borne in mind that the physical transmission to the competent national authorities of the various items of factual information and evidence held in the Commission's file could give rise to other risks as regards the effectiveness of the action taken by the Community, especially in cases involving parallel investigations to be carried out simultaneously in more than one Member State. Account must be taken of the uncertainties and delays that may affect such transmission and the different procedural rules with which they may have to comply under the

legal systems of the Member States concerned, as well as the time which the authorities in question may need to consider potentially complex and voluminous documents.

67. In the context of the allocation of competences in terms of Article 234 EC, it is in principle for the competent national court to assess whether, in a given case, the explanations referred to in paragraph 61 of this judgment have been properly provided and to carry out, on that basis, the review which it is required to undertake under Community law. In addition, where the national court is called upon to rule on a request for assistance submitted by the Commission pursuant to Article 14(6) of Regulation No 17, it must pay even greater heed to that allocation of competences, inasmuch as a reference for a preliminary ruling—unless made, as in the present case, after the investigations have been carried out—is apt to delay the decision of that court and may bring the request for assistance into the public domain, thereby creating a risk that the Commission's action may be paralysed and that any subsequent investigation may serve no useful purpose.

68. In the light of those considerations, the Court of Justice, when called upon to give a preliminary ruling, can provide the referring court with all the criteria of interpretation within the scope of Community law which may enable that court to determine the case before it.

69. As regards the main proceedings in the present case, it is clear from the reasons contained in the investigation decision of 10 September 1998, as reiterated in paragraph 11 of this judgment, that the Commission gave a very precise account of the suspicions harboured by it with regard to Roquette Frères and the other participants in the suspected cartel, providing detailed information as to the holding of regular secret meetings and as to what was discussed and agreed at those meetings.

70. Although the Commission has not indicated the nature of the evidence on which its suspicions are based, such as a complaint, testimony or documents exchanged between the participants in the suspected cartel, the mere fact that no such indication is given cannot suffice to cast doubt on the existence of reasonable grounds for those suspicions where, as in the main proceedings, the detailed account of the information held by the Commission concerning the specific subject-matter of the suspected cartel is such as to enable the competent national court to establish a firm basis for its conclusion that the Commission does indeed possess such evidence.

Review of the proportionality of the coercive measures to the subject-matter of the investigation and the information which the Commission may be required to provide to that end

71. Second, as regards the need to verify that the coercive measures are proportionate to the subject-matter of the investigation ordered by the Commission, it should be noted that this involves establishing that such measures are appropriate to ensure that the investigation can be carried out.

72. In that regard, it must be borne in mind, in particular, that Article 14(3) of Regulation No 17 requires the undertakings concerned to submit to investigations ordered by decision of the Commission and that Article 14(6) provides for Member States to afford assistance to the officials authorised by the Commission only in the event that an undertaking opposes such an investigation.

73. It is true that the Court has acknowledged that the assistance may be requested as a precautionary measure, in order to overcome any opposition on the part of the undertaking (*Hoechst*, paragraph 32).

74. However, coercive measures may be so requested on a precautionary basis only in so far as there are grounds for apprehending opposition to the investigation and/or attempts at concealing or disposing of evidence in the event that an investigation ordered pursuant to Article 14(3) of Regulation No 17 is notified to the undertaking concerned.

75. Consequently, it is for the Commission to provide the competent national court with the explanations needed by that court to satisfy itself that, if the Commission were unable to obtain,

as a precautionary measure, the requisite assistance in order to overcome any opposition on the part of the undertaking, it would be impossible, or very difficult, to establish the facts amounting to the infringement.

76. In addition, review of the proportionality of the coercive measures envisaged to the subject-matter of the investigation involves establishing that such measures do not constitute, in relation to the aim pursued by the investigation in question, a disproportionate and intolerable interference (Case C-331/88 *Fedesa and Others* [1990] ECR I-4023, paragraph 13; Joined Cases C-143/88 and C-92/89 *Zuckerfabrik Süderdithmarschen and Zuckerfabrik Soest* [1991] ECR I-415, paragraph 73; Case C-233/94 *Germany* v. *Parliament and Council* [1997] ECR I-2405, paragraph 57; and Case C-200/96 *Metronome Musik* [1998] ECR I-1953, paragraphs 21 and 26).

77. In that regard, it should certainly be kept in view that, in relation to the proportionality of the investigation measure itself, the Court has held that the Commission's choice between an investigation by straightforward authorisation and an investigation ordered by a decision does not depend on matters such as the particular seriousness of the situation, extreme urgency or the need for absolute discretion, but rather on the need for an appropriate inquiry, having regard to the special features of the case. The Court has concluded in that regard that, where an investigation decision is solely intended to enable the Commission to gather the information needed to assess whether the Treaty has been infringed, such a decision is not contrary to the principle of proportionality (*National Panasonic* v. *Commission*, cited above, paragraphs 28 to 30).

78. Similarly, it is in principle for the Commission to decide whether a particular item of information is necessary to enable it to bring to light an infringement of the competition rules (*AM & S Europe* v. *Commission*, paragraph 17; Case 374/87 *Orkem* v. *Commission* [1989] ECR 3283, paragraph 15). Even if it already has evidence, or indeed proof, of the existence of an infringement, the Commission may legitimately take the view that it is necessary to order further investigations enabling it to better define the scope of the infringement, to determine its duration or to identify the circle of undertakings involved (see to that effect, in relation to requests for additional information, *Orkem* v. *Commission*, cited above, paragraph 15).

79. However, if the scope of the review to be carried out by the competent national court is to be meaningful, and if proper account is to be taken of the invasion of privacy that recourse to law-enforcement authorities entails, it must be acknowledged, with regard to such a measure, that the national authority cannot carry out its review of proportionality without regard to factors such as the seriousness of the suspected infringement, the nature of the involvement of the undertaking concerned or the importance of the evidence sought.

80. Consequently, it must be open to the competent national court to refuse to grant the coercive measures applied for where the suspected impairment of competition is so minimal, the extent of the likely involvement of the undertaking concerned so limited, or the evidence sought so peripheral, that the intervention in the sphere of the private activities of a legal person which a search using law-enforcement authorities entails necessarily appears manifestly disproportionate and intolerable in the light of the objectives pursued by the investigation.

81. It follows that, in order for the competent national court to be able to carry out the review of proportionality which it is required to undertake, the Commission must in principle inform that court of the essential features of the suspected infringement, so as to enable it to assess their seriousness, by indicating the market thought to be affected, the nature of the suspected restrictions of competition and the supposed degree of involvement of the undertaking concerned.

82. On the other hand, as the Court has previously held in relation to the statement of reasons for investigation decisions themselves, it is not indispensable that the information communicated should precisely define the relevant market, set out the exact legal nature of the presumed infringements or indicate the period during which those infringements were committed (*Dow Benelux* v. *Commission*, cited above, paragraph 10).

83. The Commission is also obliged to indicate as precisely as possible the evidence sought and the matters to which the investigation must relate (*National Panasonic* v. *Commission*, cited above, paragraphs 26 and 27), as well as the powers conferred on the Community investigators.

84. However, the Commission cannot be required to limit its investigation to requesting the production of documents or files which it is able to identify precisely in advance. That would, in effect, render nugatory its right of access to such documents or files. On the contrary, as the Court has held, such a right implies the power to search for various items of information which are not already known or fully identified (*Hoechst*, paragraph 27).

85. As stated in paragraph 67 above, it is in principle for the competent national court to assess whether, in a given case, the information referred to in paragraphs 75, 81 and 83 above has been properly provided by the Commission and to carry out, on that basis, the review which it is required to undertake under Community law.

86. However, as is pointed out in paragraph 68 above, the Court of Justice is competent to provide all such criteria of interpretation within the scope of Community law as may enable the referring court to determine the case before it.

Regulation 1/2003, Article 20(8) now sets out the role of the national court. The provision enacts, in effect, the judgment of the Court in *Roquette Frères SA*.

Regulation 1/2003, Article 20(8)

Where authorisation as referred to in paragraph 7 is applied for, the national judicial authority shall control that the Commission decision is authentic and that the coercive measures envisaged are neither arbitrary nor excessive having regard to the subject matter of the inspection. In its control of the proportionality of the coercive measures, the national judicial authority may ask the Commission, directly or through the Member State competition authority, for detailed explanations in particular on the grounds the Commission has for suspecting infringement of Articles 81 and 82 of the Treaty, as well as on the seriousness of the suspected infringement and on the nature of the involvement of the undertaking concerned. However, the national judicial authority may not call into question the necessity for the inspection nor demand that it be provided with the information in the Commission's file. The lawfulness of the Commission decision shall be subject to review only by the Court of Justice.

Furthermore, the role of the national courts in the context of Commission inspections is spelt out again in the Notice on cooperation between the Commission and the courts of the EU Member States.[126]

d. The Application of Article 8 of the ECHR

It will be recalled from the extract from *Hoechst* above[127] that the Court stated (paragraph 18 of the judgment) that the principle of the inviolability of the home in Article 8(1) of the ECHR does not apply to commercial premises. However, the European Court of Human Rights (ECtHR) subsequently said in *Niemitz*[128] that the words 'private life' and 'home' in Article 8(1) included

---

[126] [2004] OJ C101/54, paras. 38–41.

[127] *Supra* 1159.

[128] *Niemitz* v. *Germany*, Series A, No. 251–B, (1993) 16 EHRR 97, para. 31.

certain professional or business activities or premises. In that case a lawyer's office was pro-tected. The ECtHR said this interpretation was necessary because otherwise unequal treatment could arise, in that self-employed persons may carry on professional activities at home and private activities at their place of work. In *PVC Cartel II*[129] the CFI said that the fact that the case law of the ECtHR had evolved since *Hoechst* had no direct impact on the merits of the solutions adopted in that case.[130] On appeal the ECJ did not find it necessary to rule on the matter.[131] In *Roquette Frères SA*, as seen above,[132] the ECJ was again concerned with compatibility with the principle of Community law that protects the private activities of natural or legal persons against the arbitrary or disproportionate intervention by public authorities. It said on this point:

29. For the purposes of determining the scope of that principle in relation to the protection of business premises, regard must be had to the case-law of the European Court of Human Rights sub-sequent to the judgment in *Hoechst*. According to that case-law, first, the protection of the home pro-vided for in Article 8 of the ECHR may in certain circumstances be extended to cover such premises (see, in particular, the judgment of 16 April 2002 in *Colas Est and Others v. France*, not yet published in the *Reports of Judgments and Decisions*, § 41) and, second, the right of interference established by Article 8(2) of the ECHR might well be more far-reaching where professional or business activities or premises were involved than would otherwise be the case (Niemietz v. Germany, cited above, § 31).[133]

The case referred to by the ECJ, *Colas Est*,[134] involved the French competition authority simultan-eously raiding fifty-six undertakings in the course of investigating suspected bid-rigging. Three of the undertakings challenged the legality of the raids on the grounds that the investigating officers had no warrant and were not accompanied by a police officer with judicial investigation powers. The ECtHR held that the rights guaranteed by Article 8 can apply to a company's head office, branch office, or place of business and that the inspections were disproportionate to the legitimate objectives being pursued. The French law at the time did not contain enough guaran-tees against abuse and Article 8 was violated. Although it was suggested at the time that in the light of this case Commission inspections do not comply with Article 8,[135] Commission offi-cials (speaking personally) have strongly argued that, particularly in the light of Article 20 of Regulation 1/2003, they do comply:[136]

When the Commission carries out an inspection, it cannot seize documents; nor is it empowered to copy the documents if the undertaking opposes such copying. It must in that event . . . turn to the NCA and ask for assistance. The opposition is noted in the minutes and triggers the assistance: . . . the undertakings know precisely when the coercion, if any, starts. The assistance is regulated by national law and most laws foresee a judicial authorisation beforehand . . . . When national powers are used to overcome the opposition, national law provides for safeguards of the rights of defence and for legal means to challenge the use of coercion before a judge . . . Finally, and most importantly, the

---

[129] Cases T-305–7, 313–16, 318, 325, 328–9 and 335/94, *Limburgse Vinyl Maatschappij NV v. Commission* [1999] ECR I-931 [1999] 5 CMLR 303.

[130] *Ibid.*, para. 420.

[131] Cases C-238, 244–5, 247, 250, 251–2 and 254/99, *Limburgse Vinyl Maatschappij NV v. Commission* [2002] ECR I-8375, [2003] 4 CMLR 397, para. 251.

[132] *Supra* 1164.

[133] The Advocate General considered the application of the ECHR at length, see in particular paras. 28–48 of his Opinion.

[134] Case No. 37971/97, Reports of Judgments and Decisions 2002-III.

[135] J. Temple Lang and C. Rizza, 'The *Ste Colas Est and Others v. France* case: European Court of Human Rights Case of 16 April 2002' [2002] *ECLR* 417.

[136] K. Dekeyser and C. Gauer, 'The New Enforcement System for Articles 81 and 82 and the Rights of Defence' 2004 *Fordham Corp L Inst* (B. Hawk, ed. 2005), 549, 556–7.

undertakings are able to contest the legality of the Commission decision before the Community Courts. Contrary to the French authority in the *Colas* case, the Commission is therefore not in a position to determine alone "*the expediency, number, length and scale of inspections*" (see point 49 of *Colas*). It acts under effective judicial control .

As will be seen below,[137] the Commission has a new power under Regulation 1/2003, Article 21 to carry out inspections at 'other premises' including the homes of directors, managers and other members of staff of undertakings and associations of undertakings.

e. Legal Advice

Article 20, like Regulation 17, Article 14 before it, says nothing about an undertaking's right to have legal advisers present during the investigation. The Court said in paragraph 16 of *Hoechst* that an undertaking has a right to legal representation in the investigation stage. When conducting the unannounced investigation in *National Panasonic*, however, the Commission was prepared to wait for some time for the undertakings' legal advisers to arrive, but after a while proceeded in their absence. The Court held that Panasonic's fundamental rights had not been infringed in the investigation, although it did not expressly avert to the legal adviser point. The Commission has a policy of allowing firms a reasonable time to secure the services of an in-house legal adviser or lawyer of its choice although it will not permit undue delay. During any wait the undertaking's management has to ensure that business records remain as they were on the officials' arrival and the officials have to be allowed to enter and remain in the offices of their choice. In other words, there must be no opportunity for the operation of the paper-shredder or the wiping of the hard-drive. Regulation 1/2003, Article 20(2)(d) now expressly provides for premises or books to be sealed, in order to ensure this.

The comments on the White Paper from industry and lawyers stressed the importance of the availability of legal advice to persons required to answer questions by Commission officials.[138]

f. Legal Privilege

The issue of the withholding of documents on the grounds of legal privilege is considered below.[139]

g. Self-incrimination

The issue of self-incrimination is considered below.[140]

(iv) Inspections on Private Premises Under Article 21

Regulation 1/2003 gives the Commission a new power to conduct inspections at private premises. In other words, dawn raids may be conducted at the homes (and on the private vehicles) of directors and employees. Article 21(1) states:

If a reasonable suspicion exists that books or other records related to the business and to the subject-matter of the inspection, which may be relevant to prove a serious violation of Article 81 or Article 82 of the Treaty, are being kept in any other premises, land and means of transport, including the homes of directors, managers and other members of staff of the undertakings and associations of

---

[137] *Infra.*

[138] Summary of observations on the White Paper on reform of Reg. 17, published by the Commission, 29 Feb. 2000, para. 7.4.

[139] *Infra* 1181.

[140] *Infra* 1173.

undertakings concerned, the Commission can by decision order an inspection to be conducted in such other premises, land and means of transport.

This provision has been introduced because, as the Commission says in Recital 26, '[e]xperience has shown that there are cases where business records are kept in the homes of directors or other people working for an undertaking'. In particular, the Commission is determined that its efforts to crack hard-core cartels are not frustrated by individuals keeping the incriminating evidence at home.[141] Obviously, the safeguards provided by Article 8 of the ECHR, discussed above in respect to Article 20 inspections,[142] apply *par excellence* to Article 21 inspections. Moreover, the inspection may only take place with prior authorization from the national judicial authority of the Member State concerned (so the Member State's courts become involved whether or not the inspection is opposed). The right of the national court to query the necessity for the inspection, however, is limited, similarly to the position under Article 20. Article 21(3) states:

A decision adopted pursuant to paragraph 1 cannot be executed without prior authorisation from the national judicial authority of the Member State concerned. The national judicial authority shall control that the Commission decision is authentic and that the coercive measures envisaged are neither arbitrary nor excessive having regard in particular to the seriousness of the suspected infringement, to the importance of the evidence sought, to the involvement of the undertaking concerned and to the reasonable likelihood that business books and records relating to the subject matter of the inspection are kept in the premises for which the authorisation is requested. The national judicial authority may ask the Commission, directly or through the Member State competition authority, for detailed explanations on those elements which are necessary to allow its control of the proportionality of the coercive measures envisaged.

However, the national judicial authority may not call into question the necessity for the inspection nor demand that it be provided with information in the Commission's file. The lawfulness of the Commission decision shall be subject to review only by the Court of Justice.

It will be noted that there are some safeguards additional to those in Article 20(8). The national court may consider the importance of the evidence sought and whether there is a reasonable likelihood that documents relating to the subject-matter of the inspection are kept at the premises concerned.[143] Moreover, there is no provision in Article 21 for sealing private premises, or for questioning the person whose premises are being searched. Regulation 1/2003 does not impose penalties for opposing the inspection: there is no provision in Article 23 for fining the undertaking concerned and nothing in Regulation 1/2003 puts any liability at all on individuals. However, the national court may be able to authorize entry by force.

(v) The Power to Take Statements

Regulation 1/2003, Article 19 gives the Commission a new power to 'take statements' by which it can conduct interviews with natural or legal persons. It can be exercised only with the consent

---

[141] See *SAS/Maersk* [2001] OJ L265/15, [2001] 5 CMLR 1119 for a case in which documents relating to a market-sharing agreement were kept at home, although they were voluntarily surrendered a few days after the Reg. 17, Art. 14(3) inspection. A note of one meeting recorded a Maersk representative as saying that 'all material on price agreements, market-sharing agreements and the like *had* to be destroyed before going home today. Anything that might be needed *had* to be taken home...' (*SAS/Maersk*, para. 89).

[142] *Supra* 1169.

[143] See also Notice on cooperation between the Commission and the courts of the EU Member States, [2004] OJ C101/54, para. 40.

of the person concerned, and only to collect information in relation to the subject matter of an investigation. Article 19 states:

1. In order to carry out the duties assigned to it by this Regulation, the Commission may interview any natural or legal person who consents to be interviewed for the purpose of collecting information relating to the subject-matter of an investigation.

2. Where an interview pursuant to paragraph 1 is conducted in the premises of an undertaking, the Commission shall inform the competition authority of the Member State in whose territory the interview takes place. If so requested by the competition authority of that Member State, its officials may assist the officials and other accompanying persons authorised by the Commission to conduct the interview.

Regulation 773/2004, Article 3 further provides:

Power to take statements

1. Where the Commission interviews a person with his consent in accordance with Article 19 of Regulation (EC) No 1/2003, it shall, at the beginning of the interview, state the legal basis and the purpose of the interview, and recall its voluntary nature. It shall also inform the person interviewed of its intention to make a record of the interview.

2. The interview may be conducted by any means including by telephone or electronic means.

3. The Commission may record the statements made by the persons interviewed in any form. A copy of any recording shall be made available to the person interviewed for approval. Where necessary, the Commission shall set a time-limit within which the person interviewed may communicate to it any correction to be made to the statement.[144]

The interviewee is free not to accept the Commission's invitation to be interviewed, and there is no sanction for refusing. During the interview the person concerned can refuse to answer questions, refuse to give reasons for the refusal and need not find documents, etc., again without sanction. There are no penalties for giving incorrect or misleading information under Article 19. As this is in sharp contrast to Article 20(2)(e) (explanations on facts) it may be essential for an undertaking to ascertain, when an inspection is taking place, whether an employee is being questioned under Article 19 or Article 20(2)(e). Undertakings may find it problematic that the Commission can now take statements from natural persons, such as unhappy employees, and yet the undertaking has no right to any copy of the record of the interview. Interviewees are entitled to be accompanied by lawyers and interviews may take place on or away from business premises. There appears to be no reason why an undertaking cannot instruct its employees not to accept invitations to interviews (or, e.g., not to do so without legal advice, away from the undertaking's premises, other than face-to face, etc.).

(vi) The Right not to Incriminate Oneself

The fact that the Commission has such wide powers to carry out inspections and ask for information under Regulation 1/2003, Articles 18, 20, and 21 raises the crucial issue of whether EC law recognizes a right not to incriminate oneself (or, in this context, the undertaking which one is representing). This again involves a consideration of the ECHR, this time Article 6 on the right

---

[144] The time-limit is at least two weeks, Reg. 773/2004, Art. 17(3).

to a fair trial. The case law of the Court on Regulation 17, Articles 11 and 14 is applied to the provisions of Regulation 1/2003.[145]

Orkem established that the duty actively to cooperate with the Commission does not mean that the undertaking has to incriminate itself by admitting to infringements of the competition rules. However, the Commission may ask questions, or demand the production of documents, by means of which it can *establish* an infringement.

Case 374/87, *Orkem SA v. Commission* [1989] ECR 3283, [1991] 4 CMLR 502

Like *Hoechst*,[146] this case arose out of the investigations conducted by the Commission into alleged cartels in the thermoplastics industry. The questions required to be answered asked for (1) factual information about a meeting, (2) clarification on 'every step or concerted measure which may have been envisaged or adopted to support such price initiatives', (3) the 'details of any system or method which made it possible to attribute sales or targets or quotas to the participants', and (4) 'details of any methods facilitating annual monitoring of compliance with any system of targets in terms of volumes or quotas'. The undertaking challenged the decision claiming that the Commission had infringed the general principle that no-one may be compelled to give evidence against himself, a principle which was part of Community law as it was recognized by the Member States, by Article 6 of the European Convention on Human Rights and by paragraph 3(g) of the International Covenant on Civil and Political Rights, 1966.

Court of First Instance

20. The rule necessary for the application of Articles [81] and [82], introduced by the Council, prescribe two successive but clearly separate procedures: first, a preparatory investigation procedure, and secondly, a procedure involving submissions by both parties initiated by the statement of objections.

21. The sole purpose of the preliminary investigation procedure is to enable the Commission to obtain the information and documentation necessary to check the actual existence and scope of a specific factual and legal situation (*National Panasonic* . . .).

22. For that purpose, Regulation 17 conferred on the Commission wide powers of investigation and imposed on undertakings the obligation to co-operate in the investigative measures.

23. Thus, Article 11(1) of Regulation 17 empowers the Commission to obtain all necessary information from undertakings and Article 11(5) authorizes it to require, by decision, that information be supplied to it where an undertaking does not supply the information requested, or supplies incomplete information.

24. If the Commission considers that the information thus obtained justifies such a course of action, it sends a statement of objections to the undertaking concerned, thus initiating the *inter partes* procedure governed by Commission Regulation 99/63 on the hearings provided for in Article 19(1) and (2) of Council Regulation 17.

25. For the purposes of the *inter partes* procedure, Article 19 of Regulation 17 and Regulation 99/63 provide in particular that the undertaking concerned is entitled to make known in writing and, if appropriate, orally its views on the objections raised against them (see also the judgments in Case 85/76, *Hoffmann-la Roche* v. *EC.Commission* . . . and Joined cases 10–103/80, *Musique*

---

[145] For a full discussion of the self-incrimination issue, see W. Wils, 'Self-incrimination in EC Antitrust Enforcement: A Legal and Economic Analysis' (2003) 26(4) *World Competition* 567.

[146] *Supra* 1158.

Diffusion Francasise And Others v. *E.C.Commission* . . . In any decision which the Commission might be prompted to adopt on conclusion of the procedure, it will be entitled to set out only those objections on which the undertaking concerned has had an opportunity of making known its views.

26. In the course of the preliminary investigation procedure, Regulation 17 expressly accords only certain guarantees to the undertaking under investigation. Thus, a decision requiring information to be supplied may be taken only after a prior request has proved unsuccessful. Similarly, a decision fixing the definitive amount of a fine or penalty payment, in a case where the undertaking concerned fails to supply the information required by the decision, may be adopted only after the undertaking in question has been given an opportunity to make its views known.

27. On the other hand, Regulation 17 does not give an undertaking under investigation any right to evade the investigation on the ground that the results thereof might provide evidence of an infringement by it of the competition rules. On the contrary, it imposes on the undertaking an obligation to co-operate actively, which implies that it must make available to the Commission all information relating to the subject-matter of the investigation.

28. In the absence of any right to remain silent expressly embodied in Regulation 17, it is appropriate to consider whether and to what extent the general principles of Community law, of which fundamental rights form an integral part and in the light of which all Community legislation must be interpreted, require, as the applicant claims, recognition of the right not to supply information capable of being used in order to establish against the person supplying it, the existence of an infringement of the competition rules.

29. In general, the laws of the Member-States grant the right not to give evidence against oneself only to a natural person charged with an offence in criminal proceedings. A comparative analysis of national law does not therefore indicate the existence of such a principle, common to the laws of the Member-States, which may be relied upon by legal persons in relation to infringements in the economic sphere, in particular infringements of competition law.

30. As far as Article 6 of the European Convention is concerned, although it may be relied upon by an undertaking subject to an investigation relating to competition law, it must be observed that neither the wording of that Article nor the decisions of European Court of Human Rights indicate that it upholds the right not to give evidence against oneself.

31. Article 14 of the International Covenant, which upholds, in addition to the presumption of innocence, the right (in paragraph 3(g)) not to give evidence against oneself or to confess guilt, relates only to persons accused of a criminal offence in court proceedings and thus has no bearing on investigations in the field of competition law.

32. It is necessary, however, to consider whether certain limitations on the Commission's powers of investigation are implied by the need to safeguard the rights of the defence which the Court has held to be fundamental principle of the Community order (Case 322/82, *Michelin* v. *E.C. Commission* . . .

33. In that connection, the court observed recently in its judgment in Joined Cases 46/87 and 227/88 *Hoechst* v. *E.C. Commission* . . . , that whilst it is true that the rights of the defence must be observed in administrative procedures which may lead to the imposition of penalties, it is necessary to prevent those rights from being irremediably impaired during preliminary inquiry procedures which may be decisive in providing evidence of the unlawful nature of conduct engaged in by undertakings and for which they may be liable. Consequently, although certain rights of the defence relate only to contentious proceedings which follow the delivery of the statement of objections, other rights must be respected even during the preliminary inquiry.

34. Accordingly, whilst the Commission is entitled, in order to preserve the useful effect of Article 11(2) and (5) of Regulation 17, to compel an undertaking to provide all necessary information concerning such facts as may be known to it and to disclose to it, if necessary, such documents

> relating thereto as are in its possession, even if the latter may be used to establish, against it or another undertaking, the existence of anti-competitive conduct, it may not, by means of a decision calling for information, undermine the rights of defence of the undertaking concerned.
>
> 35. Thus, the Commission may not compel an undertaking to provide it with answers which might involve an admission on its part of the existence of an infringement which it is incumbent upon the Commission to prove.

On this basis, the Court annulled the decision in respect of all the questions listed above except the first one. The Court drew a distinction (paragraphs 34 and 35) between a right to compel the undertaking to provide factual information which can be used to establish a breach of the rules, and a right to compel it to admit to the breach. The Commission has the former but not the latter right.

The problem is that this may not be in line with the interpretation by the European Court of Human Rights of Article 6 of the ECHR, which guarantees the right to a fair trial.[147] The Court denied in *Orkem* (see paragraph 30) that Article 6 included the right not to provide evidence against oneself. In *Funke*,[148] however, the European Court of Human Rights held that as a result of Article 6 anyone charged with a criminal offence within the meaning of that Article had the right 'to remain silent and not to contribute to incriminating himself'. This included the right not to produce incriminating documents. The basic question is whether competition infringements are criminal offences. Regulation 17, Article 15(4), expressly stated that fines under that Article 'shall not be of a criminal law nature', and in *Orkem* the Court considered that competition investigations do not involve a criminal offence (paragraph 31). However, it cannot be assumed that EC competition proceedings are not 'criminal' for the purposes of the ECHR. The definition of a 'criminal charge' is a matter of Convention law.[149] The competition rules are of general application and fines for breaches of the substantive rules can be considerable, running into many millions of Euros, and serve as both a sanction and a deterrent.[150] These are relevant factors in determining whether the matter is a 'criminal charge'.[151] Moreover, in *Société Stenuit v. France* the European Commission on Human Rights held in its Opinion that a fine imposed on undertakings by the French competition authorities was criminal in nature.[152]

In *Saunders v. United Kingdom*[153] the European Court of Human Rights held that the use in the case against Ernest Saunders in the *Guinness* criminal trial of incriminating statements obtained from him by DTI inspectors under their compulsory powers was oppressive, and impaired his

---

[147] See A. Riley, 'Saunders and the Power to Obtain Information in Community and United Kingdom Competition Law' (2000) 25 *ELRev* 264.

[148] *Funke* v. *France*, Series A, No. 256–A, (1993) 16 EHRR 297, para. 44.

[149] *Engel* v. *Netherlands* Series A, No. 22, (1979–80) 1 EHRR 647.

[150] See *infra* 1213 ff.

[151] See *Bendenoun* v. *France* Series A, No. 284, (1994) 18 EHRR 54. *Funke* involved possible infringements of French foreign currency regulations; *Benedenoun* involved possible infringements of French tax law.

[152] (1992) 14 EHRR 509: *Stenuit* did not proceed to a judgment by the European Court of Human Rights as the applicant and the French authorities settled the matter. See also Judge Vesterdorf (acting as Advocate-General) in Case T-1/89, *Rhône-Poulenc SA* v. *Commission* [1991] ECR II-867, 885, who wondered whether the penalties were criminal. The applicants raised *Stenuit* in Case T-348/94, *Enso Española* v. *Commission* [1998] ECR II-1875, but the CFI did not expressly deal with it. And see the CFI in Cases T-25/95, etc. *Cimenteries CBR SA* v. *Commission* [2000] ECR II-491, [2000] 5 CMLR 204, para. 718.

[153] *Saunders* v. *United Kingdom* (1997) 23 EHRR 313. This judgment would still allow procedures such as taking DNA samples or breath tests because they are not material which has an 'independence from the will' of the suspect.

ability to defend himself by undermining his right to remain silent. The result was an infringement of Article 6(1). However, the DTI inspectors were acting there under their compulsory powers, and the judgment suggested that compulsorily obtaining incriminating documents by a warrant would be justified.

The CFI reviewed the matter in *Mannesmannröhren-Werke AG* and restated the *Orkem* position.

Case T-112/98, *Mannesmannröhren-Werke AG* v. *Commission* [2001] ECR II-729, [2001] 5 CMLR 54

The Commission was conducting an investigating into an alleged cartel in the seamless tube industry.[154] Mannesmannröhren-Werke AG refused to reply to some requests for information the Commission made under Regulation 17, Article 11(4). The questions related to three sets of meetings. In respect of each of them the Commission asked for dates, places, names of participants, copies of all agendas, minutes and records relating to them and (by the last indent each time) 'in the case of meetings for which you are unable to find the relevant documents, please describe the purpose of the meeting, the decisions adopted and the type of documents received before and after the meeting'. The undertaking refused to answer the questions, claiming it was being asked to incriminate itself. Another set of questions related to four agreements. The undertaking was asked, *inter alia*, about the relationship of the agreements to another arrangement, and to what extent 'did the existence and implementation of these agreements influence the decisions adopted within the Europe-Japan Club and/or within the Special Circle?'. On the undertaking's refusal the Commission adopted a decision under Regulation 17, Article 11(5), demanding answers on pain of periodic penalty payments. Mannesmannröhren-Werke AG appealed against the decision.

Court of First Instance

59. It must be emphasised at the outset that the Court of First Instance has no jurisdiction to apply the Convention when reviewing an investigation under competition law, inasmuch as the Convention as such is not part of Community law (Case T-374/94 *Mayr-Melnhof* v. *Commission* [1998] ECR II-1751, paragraph 311).

60. However, it is settled case-law that fundamental rights form an integral part of the general principles of Community law whose observance is ensured by the Community judicature (see, in particular, Opinion 2/94 the Court of Justice of 28 March 1996 [1996] ECR I–1759, paragraph 33, and the judgment in *Kremzow*, [Case C-299/95, [1997] ECR I-2629] . . . , paragraph 14). For that purpose, the Court of Justice and the Court of First Instance draw inspiration from the constitutional traditions common to the Member States and from the guidelines supplied by international treaties for the protection of human rights on which the Member States have collaborated and to which they are signatories. The Convention has special significance in that respect (Case 222/84 *Johnston* [1986] ECR 1651, paragraph 18, and *Kremzow*, cited above, paragraph 14). Furthermore, paragraph 2 of Article F of the Treaty on European Union (now Article 6(2) EU) provides that the Union shall respect fundamental rights, as guaranteed by the [Convention] and as they result from the constitutional traditions common to the Member States, as general principles of Community law.

61. Next, it must be borne in mind that the purpose of the powers conferred on the Commission by Regulation No 17 is to enable that institution to fulfil its duty under the Treaty to ensure that the rules on competition within the common market are observed.

---

[154] This culminated in the *Seamless Steel Tubes* decision in 1999, [2003] OJ L14/1.

62. During the preliminary-investigation procedure, Regulation No 17 does not give an undertaking that is subjected to an investigative measure any right to avoid the application of that measure on the ground that the results thereof might provide evidence of an infringement by it of the competition rules. On the contrary, it places the undertaking under a duty of active cooperation, which means that it must be prepared to make available to the Commission any information relating to the subject-matter of the investigation (*Orkem*, paragraph 27, and *Société Générale*, [Case T-34/93, [1995] ECR II-545] . . . paragraph 72).

63. In the absence of any right to silence expressly provided for in Regulation No 17, it is necessary to consider whether certain limitations on the Commission's powers of investigation during a preliminary investigation are, however, implied by the need to safeguard the rights of defence (*Orkem*, paragraph 32).

64. In this respect, it is necessary to prevent the rights of defence from being irremediably impaired during preliminary-investigation procedures which may be decisive in providing evidence of the unlawful nature of conduct engaged in by undertakings (*Orkem*, paragraph 33, and *Société Générale*, paragraph 73).

65. However, it is settled case-law that, in order to ensure the effectiveness of Article 11(2) and (5) of Regulation No 17, the Commission is entitled to compel an undertaking to provide all necessary information concerning such facts as may be known to it and to disclose to the Commission, if necessary, such documents relating thereto as are in its possession, even if the latter may be used to establish, against it or another undertaking, the existence of anti-competitive conduct (*Orkem*, paragraph 34, and Case 27/88 *Solvay* v. *Commission* [1989] ECR 3355, summary publication, and *Société Générale*, paragraph 74).

66. To acknowledge the existence of an absolute right to silence, as claimed by the applicant, would go beyond what is necessary in order to preserve the rights of defence of undertakings, and would constitute an unjustified hindrance to the Commission's performance of its duty under Article 89 of the EC Treaty (now, after amendment, Article 85 EC) to ensure that the rules on competition within the common market are observed.

67. It follows that an undertaking in receipt of a request for information pursuant to Article 11(5) of Regulation No 17 can be recognised as having a right to silence only to the extent that it would be compelled to provide answers which might involve an admission on its part of the existence of an infringement which it is incumbent upon the Commission to prove (*Orkem*, paragraph 35).

Applying this, the CFI held that the last question in respect of each of the three sets of meetings asked the undertaking about the 'purpose' of meetings, and the 'decisions' adopted. This went beyond mere factual information: 'it follows that requests of this kind are such that they may compel the applicant to admit its participation in an unlawful agreement . . .'.[155] The decision was therefore annulled in respect of the three last questions. The decision was also annulled in respect of the whole question about the agreements as '[a]nswering this question would require the applicant to give its assessment of the nature of those decisions'.[156] The rest of the decision was upheld.

In *PVC Cartel II* the undertakings claimed that the ECHR jurisprudence since *Orkem* laid down a right to remain silent and 'in no way to contribute to one's own incrimination, without any distinction being made according to the type of information requested. That right precludes the situation in which an undertaking is itself required to provide evidence of infringements which

---

[155] *Mannesmannröhren-Werke AG*, para. 71.
[156] *Ibid.*, 74.

it has committed in any form, including documentary form'.[157] The ECJ stated that the developments in the ECHR jurisprudence since *Orkem* did not alter the established position in EC law.

Cases C-238, 244–245, 247, 250, 251–252 and 254/99 P, *Limburgse Vinyl Maatschappij NV and others* v. *Commission* [2002] ECR I-8375, [2003] 4 CMLR 397

Court of Justice

273. The *Orkem* judgment thus acknowledged as one of the general principles of Community law, of which fundamental rights are an integral part and in the light of which all Community laws must be interpreted, the right of undertakings not to be compelled by the Commission, under Article 11 of Regulation No 17, to admit their participation in an infringement (see *Orkem*, paragraphs 28, 38 in fine and 39). The protection of that right means that, in the event of a dispute as to the scope of a question, it must be determined whether an answer from the undertaking to which the question is addressed is in fact equivalent to the admission of an infringement, such as to undermine the rights of the defence.

274. The parties agree that, since *Orkem*, there have been further developments in the case-law of the European Court of Human Rights which the Community judicature must take into account when interpreting the fundamental rights, as introduced by the judgment in *Funke*, cited above, on which the appellants rely, and the judgments of 17 December 1996 in *Saunders* v. *United Kingdom* (Reports of Judgments and Decisions 1996-VI, p. 2044) and of 3 May 2001 in *J.B.* v. *Switzerland* (not yet published in the Reports of Judgments and Decisions).

275. However, both the *Orkem* judgment and the recent case-law of the European Court of Human Rights require, first, the exercise of coercion against the suspect in order to obtain information from him and, second, establishment of the existence of an actual interference with the right which they define.

276. Examined in the light of that finding and the specific circumstances of the present case, the ground of appeal alleging infringement of the privilege against self-incrimination does not permit annulment of the contested judgment on the basis of the developments in the case-law of the European Court of Human Rights.

In *Tokai Carbon* in 2004[158] the CFI, although appearing to consider that it was following settled case law, nonetheless held that the Commission's request for documents in respect of meetings such as the protocols, working documents, preparatory documents, hand-written notes, planning and discussion documents, etc. was tantamount to requiring that the undertaking admit its participation. The CFI reasoned that since, therefore, the undertaking concerned was not required to produce such documents on grounds of self-incrimination, if it *did* do so it must be regarded as doing so voluntarily and was thereby eligible for leniency under the Commission's leniency policy.[159] The Commission appealed against this part of the judgment to the ECJ,

---

[157] Cases C-238, 244–5, 247, 250, 251–2 and 254/99 P, *Limburgse Vinyl Maatschappij NV and others* v. *Commission* [2002] ECR I-8375, [2003] 4 CMLR 397, para. 259.

[158] Cases T-236/01, T-239/01, T-244/01 to T-246/01, T-251/01 and T-252/01 *Tokai Carbon Co. Ltd and others* v. *Commission* [2004] ECR II-1181, [2004] 5 CMLR 1465 (the appeal from the *Graphite Electrodes* cartel, [2002] OJ L100/1, [2002] 5 CMLR 829).

[159] *Ibid.*, paras. 408–9. For the leniency policy, see *infra*, 1240.

concerned that classifying the production of such documents as 'self-incrimination' could be a serious blow to the efficacy of inspections. The ECJ held that the CFI had erred in law, and that the CFI's judgment had weakened the principle that undertakings subject to an investigation have a duty to cooperate. It re-established the postion that undertakings cannot refuse to produce documents on grounds of self-incrimination.

Case C-301/04 P, *Commission* v. *SGL Carbon* [2006] ECR I-5915, [2006] 5 CMLR 877

39. It must be recalled first that, under Article 11(1) of Regulation No 17, in carrying out the duties assigned to it in the matter, the Commission may obtain all necessary information from the governments and competent authorities of the Member States and from undertakings and associations of undertakings. As set out in Article 11(4) thereof, the owners of the undertakings or their representatives and, in the case of legal persons, companies or firms, or of associations having no legal personality, the persons authorised to represent them by law or by their constitution are to supply the information requested.

40. As regards the Commission's powers to make such requests, it is important to note that, in paragraph 27 of the judgment in *Orkem* v *Commission*, the Court pointed out that Regulation No 17 does not give an undertaking which is being investigated under that regulation any right to evade the investigation and that, on the contrary, the undertaking in question is subject to an obligation to cooperate actively, which implies that it must make available to the Commission all information relating to the subject-matter of the investigation.

41. So far as concerns the question whether that obligation also applies to requests for information which could be used to establish, against the undertaking which provides the information, an infringement of the competition rules, the Court held, in paragraph 34 of that judgment that in order to ensure the effectiveness of Article 11(2) and (5) of Regulation No 17 the Commission is entitled to compel an undertaking, if necessary by adopting a decision, to provide all necessary information concerning such facts as may be known to it and to disclose to it, if necessary, such documents relating thereto as are in that undertaking's possession, even if the latter may be used to establish, against it or another undertaking, the existence of anti-competitive conduct.

42. By contrast, the situation is completely different where the Commission seeks to obtain answers from an undertaking which is being investigated by which that undertaking would be led to admit an infringement which it is incumbent upon the Commission to prove (see *Orkem* v *Commission*, paragraph 35).

43. It must be added that the Court of Justice, in paragraphs 274 to 276 of the judgment in *Limburgse Vinyl Maatschappij and Others* v *Commission*, observed that since the judgment in *Orkem* v *Commission* there have been further developments in the case-law of the European Court of Human Rights which the Community judicature must take into account when interpreting the fundamental rights. The Court of Justice stated however in that regard that those developments were not such as to put in question the statements of principle in *Orkem* v *Commission*.

44. It does not follow from that case-law that the Commission's powers of investigation have been limited as regards the production of documents in the possession of an undertaking which is subject to investigation. The undertaking concerned must therefore, if the Commission requests it, provide the Commission with documents which relate to the subject-matter of the investigation, even if those documents could be used by the Commission in order to establish the existence of an infringement.

45. It is important to point out also that the Court of First Instance itself, in paragraph 405 of the judgment under appeal, expressly referred to the principles stated in *Orkem* v *Commission* and to the fact that the Court of Justice has not reversed its previous case-law on the point.

46. The Court of First Instance found, however, in the course of its reasoning, that the Commission's request for information of 31 March 1999 was such as to require SGL Carbon to admit its participation in infringements of the Community competition rules.

47. That finding of the Court of First Instance misconstrues the scope of Article 11 of Regulation No 17, as interpreted by the Court of Justice, and therefore weakens the principle that undertakings subject to a Commission investigation must cooperate.

48. That obligation to cooperate means that the undertaking may not evade requests for production of documents on the ground that by complying with them it would be required to give evidence against itself.

49. In addition, as the Advocate General correctly observed in point 67 of his Opinion, while it is evident that the rights of the defence should be respected, the undertaking concerned is still able, either during the administrative procedure or in the proceedings before the Community Courts, to contend that the documents produced have a different meaning from that ascribed to them by the Commission.

50. Thus, the Court of First Instance made an error of law in holding that the conditions for a reduction in the fine by virtue of the Leniency Notice were fulfilled.

The privilege against self-incrimination is an important part of the 'rights of the defence' as is legal professional privilege, which is considered next.

(vii) Legal Privilege

The situation as regards legal privilege is set out in the case law of the Court. Regulation 1/2003, like Regulation 17, does not deal with the issue. Legal privilege is an established principle in English law. It means that confidential communications passing between lawyer and client with a view to giving or securing legal advice are privileged so far as the client is concerned, and protected from disclosure.[160] The leading case on this in EC law is AM&S, in which a UK undertaking argued that it was entitled to keep from the Commission correspondence with its legal advisers that would have been privileged under English law. The case raised two main issues: first, whether legal privilege does apply in EC competition cases, and if so, whether it is a *Community* principle or a matter of recognizing the rule in the Member State concerned; secondly, if legal privilege is recognized, how procedurally is it to be dealt with? It is not attractive to the investigated undertakings for the Commission inspectors to look at documents and then decide they are to be disregarded, whatever 'Chinese walls' the Commission erects internally between the inspectors and those deciding on the existence or otherwise of an infringement.

Case 155/79, *AM&S Ltd* v. *Commission* [1982] ECR 1575, [1982] 2 CMLR 264

On 20 February 1979 Commission officials arrived in the centre of Bristol at the offices of AM&S for an unannounced Article 14(2) investigation. The investigation proceeded for two days and at the end the Commission inspectors left with copies of about thirty-five documents, leaving behind a

---

[160] For a statutory formulation see, e.g., the Police and Criminal Evidence Act 1984, s. 10(1) and see the discussion of the concept in English law generally in Hodge M. Malek et al. (eds.), *Phipson on Evidence* (16th edn., Sweet & Maxwell, 2005), chap. 20.

written request for certain other documents to be supplied. The Managing Director in response to this sent a further seven files of documents on 26 March but with a letter saying that certain of the requested documents, set out in an appendix were not being produced because the undertaking's lawyers felt that they were covered by legal privilege. Without any further communication the Commission adopted a decision on 6 July under Article 14(3) demanding that the undertaking submit to an inspection and in particular produce the excluded documents. In the preamble to the decision the Commission stated that although Community competition law did not provide for protection for legal papers nonetheless it was willing not to use certain communications between the undertaking and its lawyers as evidence and that '[w]hen the Commission comes across such papers it does not copy them'. It was for the Commission, subject to review by the Court, to decide whether a given document should be used or not. The Commission inspectors arrived in Bristol and served the decision on 25 July and carried out a further investigation. The undertaking still refused to disclose all the disputed documents but finally, after further correspondence and a meeting with the Commission in Brussels, it disclosed all except one. On 4 October the undertaking commenced an action under Article 230 claiming that the decision of 6 July was void insofar as it required the disclosure of legally privileged documents.

The Court of Justice received evidence from several Member States and from the Consultative Committee of the Bars and Law Societies of the European Community. Advocate General Warner presented in his Opinion a survey of the position on legal privilege in all Member States.

Court of Justice

15. The purpose of Regulation No 17 of the Council which was adopted pursuant to the first subparagraph of Article [83(1)] of the Treaty, is, according to paragraph (2) (a) and (b) of that article, 'to ensure compliance with the prohibitions laid down in Article [81(1)] and in Article [82]' of the Treaty and 'to lay down detailed rules for the application of Article [81(3)]'. The regulation is thus intended to ensure that the aim stated in Article 3 (1)(g) of the Treaty is achieved. To that end it confers on the Commission wide powers of investigation and of obtaining information by providing in the eighth recital in its preamble that the Commission must be empowered, throughout the Common Market, to require such information to be supplied and to undertake such investigations 'as are necessary' to bring to light infringements of Articles [81] and [82] of the Treaty.

16. In Articles 11 and 14 of the regulation, therefore, it is provided that the Commission may obtain 'information' and undertake the 'necessary' investigations, for the purpose of proceedings in respect of infringements of the rules governing competition. Article 14(1) in particular empowers the Commission to require production of business records, that is to say, documents concerning the market activities of the undertaking, in particular as regards compliance with those rules. Written communications between lawyer and client fall, in so far as they have a bearing on such activities, within the category of documents referred to in Articles 11 and 14.

17. Furthermore since the documents which the Commission may demand are, as Article 14(1) confirms, those whose disclosure it considers 'necessary' in order that it may bring to light an infringement of the Treaty rules on competition, it is in principle for the Commission itself, and not the undertaking concerned or a third party, whether an expert or an arbitrator, to decide whether or not a document must be produced to it.

(b) Applicability of the protection of confidentiality in Community law

18. However, the above rules do not exclude the possibility of recognizing, subject to certain conditions, that certain business records are of a confidential nature. Community law, which derives from not only the economic but also the legal interpenetration of the Member States, must take into account the principles and concepts common to the laws of those States concerning the

observance of confidentiality, in particular, as regards certain communications between lawyer and client. That confidentiality serves the requirements, the importance of which is recognized in all of the Member States, that any person must be able, without constraint, to consult a lawyer whose profession entails the giving of independent legal advice to all those in need of it.

19. As far as the protection of written communications between lawyer and client is concerned, it is apparent from the legal systems of the Member States that, although the principle of such protection is generally recognized, its scope and the criteria for applying it vary, as has, indeed, been conceded both by the application and by the parties who have intervened in support of its conclusions.

20. Whilst in some of the Member States the protection against disclosure afforded to written communications between lawyer and client is based principally on a recognition of the very nature of the legal profession, inasmuch as it contributes towards the maintenance of the rule of law, in other Member States the same protection is justified by the more specific requirement (which, moreover, is also recognized in the first-mentioned States) that the rights of the defence must be respected.

21. Apart from these differences, however, there are to be found in the national laws of the Member States common criteria inasmuch as those law protect, in similar circumstances, the confidentiality of written communications between lawyer and client provided that, on the one hand, such communications are made for the purposes and in the interests of the client's rights of defence and, on the other hand, they emanate from independent lawyers, that is to say, lawyers who are not bound to the client by a relationship of employment.

22. Viewed in that context Regulation No 17 must be interpreted as protecting, in its turn, the confidentiality of written communications between lawyer and client subject to those two conditions, and thus incorporating such elements of that protection as are common to the laws of the Member States.

23. As far as the first of those two conditions is concerned, in Regulation No 17 itself, in particular in the eleventh recital in its preamble and in the provisions contained in Article 19, care is taken to ensure that the rights of the defence may be exercised to the full, and the protection of the confidentiality of written communications between lawyer and client is an essential corollary to those rights. In those circumstances, such protection must, if it is to be effective, be recognized as covering all written communications exchanged after the initiation of the administrative procedure under Regulation No 17 which may lead to a decision on the application of Articles [81] and [82] of the Treaty or to a decision imposing a pecuniary sanction on the undertaking. It must also be possible to extend it to earlier written communications which have a relationship to the subject-matter of that procedure.

24. As regards the second condition, it should be stated that the requirement as to the position and status as an independent lawyer, which must be fulfilled by the legal adviser from whom the written communications which may be protected emanate, is based on a conception of the lawyer's role as collaborating in the administration of justice by the courts and as being required to provide, in full independence, and in the overriding interests of that cause, such legal assistance as the client needs. The counterpart of that protection lies in the rules of professional ethics and discipline which are laid down and enforced in the general interest by institutions endowed with the requisite powers for that purpose. Such a conception reflects the legal traditions common to the Member States and is also to be found in legal order of the Community, as is demonstrated by Article 17 of the Protocols on the Statutes of the Court of Justice of the EEC and the EAEC, and also by Article 20 of the Protocol on the Statute of the Court of Justice of the ECSC.

25. Having regard to the principles of the Treaty concerning freedom of establishment and the freedom to provide services the protection thus afforded by Community law, in particular in the context of Regulation No 17, to written communications between lawyer and client must apply without distinction to any lawyer entitled to practice his profession in one of the Member States, regardless of the Member State in which the client lives.

26. Such protection may be not be extended beyond those limits which are determined by the scope of the common rules on the exercise of the legal profession as laid down in Council Directive 77/249/EEC of 22 March 1977 (OJ L 78, p. 17), which is based in its turn on the mutual recognition by all the Member States of the national legal concepts of each of them on this subject.

27. In view of all these factors it must therefore be concluded at although Regulation No 17, and in particular Article 14 thereof, interpreted in the light of its wording, structure and aims, and having regard to the laws of the Member States, empowers the Commission to require, in the course of an investigation within the meaning of that article, production of the business documents the disclosure of which it considers necessary including written communications between lawyer and client, for proceedings in respect of any infringements of Articles [81] and [82] of the Treaty, that power is, however, subject to a restriction imposed by the need to protect confidentiality, on the conditions defined above, and provided that the communications in question are exchanged between an independent lawyer, that is to say one who is not bound to his client by a relationship of employment, and his client.

28. Finally, it should be remarked that the principle of confidentiality does not prevent a lawyer's client from disclosing the written communications between them if he considers that it is in his interests to do so.

(c) The procedures relating to the application of the principle of confidentiality

29. If an undertaking which is the subject of an investigation under Article 14 of Regulation No 17 refuses, on the ground that it is entitled to protection of the confidentiality of information, to produce, among the business records demanded by the Commission, written communications between itself and its lawyer, it must nevertheless provide the Commission's authorised agents with relevant material of such a nature as to demonstrate that the communications fulfil the conditions for being granted legal protection as defined above, although it is not bound to reveal the contents of the communications in question.

30. Where the Commission is not satisfied that such evidence has been supplied, the appraisal of those conditions is not a matter which may be left to an arbitrator or to a national authority. Since this is a matter involving an appraisal and a decision which affect the conditions under which the Commission may act in a field as vital to the functioning of the Commission may act in a field as vital to the functioning of the common market as that of compliance with the rules on competition, the solution of disputes as to the application of the protection of the confidentiality of written communications between lawyer and client may be sought only at Community level.

31. In that case it is for the Commission to order, pursuant to Article 14(3) of Regulation No 17, production of the communications in question and, if necessary, to impose on the undertaking fines or periodic penalty payments under that regulation as a penalty for the undertaking's refusal either to supply such additional evidence as the Commission considers necessary or to produce the communications in question whose confidentiality, in the Commission's view, is not protected in law.

32. The fact that by virtue of Article [242] of the EEC Treaty any action brought by the undertaking concerned against such decisions does not have suspensory effect provides an answer to the Commission's concern as to the effect of the time taken by the procedure before the Court on the efficacy of the supervision which the Commission is called upon to exercise in regard to compliance with the Treaty rules on competition, whilst on the other hand the interests of the undertaking concerned are safeguarded by the possibility which exists under Articles [242] and [243] of the Treaty, as well as under Article 83 of the Rules and Procedure of the Court, of obtaining an order suspending the application of the decision which has been taken, or any other interim measure.

The Court thus held that EC law does recognize legal privilege. This judgment, holding that the Community legal order should recognize a principle contained in some form in nearly every Member State, is a famous example of the development of the jurisprudence on the general principles of law.[161] Legal privilege in EC law is, however, a *Community* concept and the Court held that in Community law it is subject to conditions: the communication must be with[162] an independent lawyer, not an in-house lawyer bound to the undertaking by an employment relationship; the lawyer must be entitled to practise in one of the Member States; and the documents must be made for the purposes and in the interests of the clients' rights of defence. That last condition (paragraphs 21 and 23) sounds restrictive, but the Court interpreted it broadly in *AM&S* itself, and in practice it has not caused difficulty, as the Commission accepts that earlier communications with a relationship to the subject-matter of the proceedings are also covered.

The limitation of privilege to external lawyers (paragraph 24) is grounded in the role of the lawyer as a collaborator in the administration of justice and the fact that in some Member States different rules of professional discipline apply once a lawyer is operating in an employment relationship. The limitation was softened by the CFI holding in *Hilti*[163] that a report made and circulated within the undertaking of the legal advice received from an external legal adviser is privileged. On the other hand, in *John Deere*[164] the Commission examined advice from in-house lawyers and concluded therefrom that the undertaking was aware that it was infringing Article 81. It took this into account when imposing the fine. Representations were made by in-house lawyers in submissions on the White Paper strongly arguing that privilege should be extended to them. In the system of non-notification brought in by Regulation 1/2003 undertakings are more heavily reliant on legal advice, and the lawyers said that such an extension would promote effective compliance with the competition rules.[165] They argued that all lawyers must act ethically as defined in the rules of professional ethics and discipline.[166] In a ruling in an application for interim relief in October 2003 the President of the CFI accepted that the position of written communications between in-house lawyer and employer merited re-examination. He ensured that the confidentiality of documents of this type (including e-mails) which were the subject of dispute between the Commission and AKZO Nobel would be preserved until the decision of the Court in the main proceedings.[167]

---

[161] J. Temple Lang, 'The *AM &S* Judgment' in M. Hoskins and W. Robinson, *A True European—Essays for Judge David* Edward (Hart Publishing, 2004), chap. 12. See generally, T. Tridimas, *The General Principles of EC Law* (2nd edn., Oxford University Press, 2006).

[162] The judgment is worded with reference to communications *from* the lawyer, but the right does encompass communications in both directions.

[163] Case T-30/89A, *Hilti AG v. Commission* [1990] 4 CMLR 602.

[164] [1985] OJ L35/58, [1985 2 CMLR 554.

[165] In Cases T-125/03 R and T-253/03 R, *Akzo Nobel Chemicals Ltd v. Commission* [2004] 4 CMLR 744, para. 91, the Commission disputed this. It argued that the fact that undertakings are required to undertake self-assessment of the compatibility of their activities with competition law pursuant to Regulation 1/2003 is unrelated to questions of professional privilege as self-assessment will be increasingly common in connection with the application of Article 81(3) (i.e., when undertakings are trying to comply with the rules), whereas questions associated with professional privilege arise usually in connection with the application of Article 81(1) (i.e., when the Commission is investigating hard-core cartels) and Article 82 EC.

[166] Summary of observations on the White Paper on reform of Reg. 17, published by the Commission, 29 Feb. 2000, para. 7.7.

[167] B. Vesterdorf, 'Legal Professional Privilege and the Privilege Against Self-Incrimination in EC Law: Recent Developments and Current Issues' 2004 *Fordham Corp L Inst* (B. Hawk, ed. 2005),107 is by the President of the CFI who made this order: the article also covers self-incrimination.

Cases T-125/03 R and T-253/03 R, *Akzo Nobel Chemicals Ltd* v. *Commission* [2004[OJ C 35/10, [2004] 4 CMLR 744

President of the Court of First Instance

117. It is necessary to examine, last, the two Set B e-mails between the General Manager of Akcros Chemicals and the Akzo Nobel's competition law coordinator.

118. In that regard, it should be pointed out that, in application of the principles laid down in *AM & S* v. *Commission*, ..., the protection afforded by Community law, especially in the context of Regulation No 17, to written communications between lawyer and client applies only in so far as those lawyers are independent, i.e., not bound to the client by a relationship of employment (*AM & S* v. *Commission* ..., paragraph 21).

119. In the present case, it is common ground that the e-mails in question were exchanged between the General Manager of Akcros Chemicals and a lawyer employed on a permanent basis by Akzo Nobel. Following *AM & S* v. *Commission* ..., those communications are therefore not in principle covered by professional privilege.

120. None the less, the President considers that the arguments put forward by the applicants and the interveners raise a question of principle which merits very special attention and which cannot be resolved in the present interim proceedings.

121. On the one hand, as the Commission emphasises, the Member States do not unanimously recognise the principle that written communications with in-house lawyers must be covered by professional privilege. Furthermore, as the Commission also points out, it is necessary to ensure that an extension of professional privilege cannot facilitate abuses which would enable evidence of an infringement of the Treaty competition rules to be concealed and thus prevent the Commission from carrying out its task of ensuring compliance with those rules.

122. On the other hand, however, the solution in *AM & S* v. *Commission* ..., is based, *inter alia*, on an interpretation of the principles common to the Member States dating from 1982. It is therefore necessary to determine whether, in the present case, the applicants and the interveners have adduced serious evidence of such a kind as to demonstrate that, taking into account developments in Community law and in the legal orders of the Member States since the judgment in *AM & S* v. *Commission* ..., it cannot be precluded that the protection of professional privilege should now also extend to written communications with a lawyer employed by an undertaking on a permanent basis.

123. The President considers that arguments to that effect have been submitted in the present case and that they are not wholly unfounded.

124. First, the applicants, the Algemene Raad van de Nederlandse Orde van Advocaten and ECLA have adduced evidence which indicates that, since 1982, a number of Member States have adopted rules designed to protect written communications with a lawyer employed by an undertaking on a permanent basis, provided that he is subject to certain rules of professional conduct. That appears to be the position, in particular, in Belgium and the Netherlands. At the hearing, ECLA further stated that in most Member States written communications with in-house lawyers subject to particular rules of professional conduct were protected by professional privilege. The Commission, on the other hand, contended in its observations that it was only in a minority of Member States that communications with in-house lawyers were covered by professional privilege.

125. Without its being possible at this stage to ascertain and to embark upon a thorough and detailed analysis of the evidence adduced by the applicants and the interveners, that evidence none the less appears prima facie to be capable of showing that the role assigned to independent lawyers of collaborating in the administration of justice by the courts, which proved decisive for the recognition of the protection of written communications to which they are parties (*AM & S* v.

Commission, cited at paragraph 66 above, paragraph 24), is now capable of being shared, to a certain degree, by certain categories of lawyers employed within undertakings on a permanent basis where they are subject to strict rules of professional conduct.

126. The evidence therefore tends to show that increasingly in the legal orders of the Member States and possibly, as a consequence, in the Community legal order, there is no presumption that the link of employment between a lawyer and an undertaking will always, and as a matter of principle, affect the independence necessary for the effective exercise of the role of collaborating in the administration of justice by the courts if, in addition, the lawyer is bound by strict rules of professional conduct, which where necessary require that he observe the particular duties commensurate with his status.

127. It must therefore be held that the applicants and the interveners have presented arguments which are not wholly unfounded and which are apt to justify raising again the complex question of the circumstances in which written communications with a lawyer employed by an undertaking on a permanent basis may possibly be protected by professional privilege, provided that the lawyer is subject to rules of professional conduct equivalent to those imposed on an independent lawyer. In the present case, the applicants maintained at the hearing, without being clearly contradicted on that point by the Commission, that the lawyer whom they employed on a permanent basis was in fact bound by professional rules equivalent to those governing independent lawyers of the Netherlands Bar.

128. Nor does that question of principle appear prima facie to have to be rejected at this stage as a result of the Commission's argument that recognition of professional privilege for written communications with lawyers employed on a permanent basis would give rise to different regimes within the European Union, depending on whether or not in-house lawyers are authorised by the Member States to be members of a Bar.

129. This complex question must be examined thoroughly, in particular as regards, first, the precise scope of the right which would then be recognised, second, the Community rules and national rules applicable to the professions of lawyer and in-house lawyer and, third, the legal and practical alternatives available to companies established in Member States which do not allow in-house lawyers to be members of a Bar.

130. It must therefore be concluded that, in the present case, the applicants have, by their second plea, raised a delicate question of principle, which requires a complex legal assessment and must be reserved for the Court when it adjudicates on the main application.[168]

In *AM&S* the Court reserved to itself the determination of whether any particular document is protected. The procedure is for the undertaking claiming that documents are privileged to provide the inspectors with proof of that fact without revealing their contents.[169] If the inspectors are not convinced the Commission may take a decision under Regulation 1/2003, Article 20(4), requiring the production of the document or further evidence of its status. Such a decision may be challenged by the undertaking under Article 230 of the Treaty (with an application for

[168] Ironically, shortly after the President of the CFI contemplated in *Akzo Nobel* that the EC rules on legal professional privilege might need widening, the English Court of Appeal suggested that the English rules should be re-examined because they might need narrowing: see *Three Rivers District Council and others v. The Governor and Company of the Bank of England* [2004] EWCA Civ 218 (1 March 2004). However, the House of Lords confirmed the previous position, *Three Rivers District Council and Others v. The Governor and Company of the Bank of England* [2004] UKHL 48.

[169] The fact that they emanated from an independent lawyer can be established by showing the inspectors the top of the headed notepaper.

interim measures under Articles 242 and 243 if appropriate) and so the Court will ultimately decide the matter.[170]

C. THE SECOND STAGE OF THE PROCEDURE

(i) General: The Right to be Heard

If the Commission finds evidence of an infringement it opens a formal procedure. Before taking Regulation 1/2003 decisions finding an infringement of the Treaty, taking interim measures, or imposing fines or periodic payments the Commission must, by Article 27(1),[171] grant the undertakings concerned the opportunity of being heard on matters to which the Commission has taken objection.[172] The ECJ has held that the right to a hearing means in the first place that parties must be told the case against them. It said in *Transocean Marine Paint*[173] that this is an application of the general rule that a person whose interests are perceptibly affected by a decision made by a public authority must be given the opportunity to make his views known, and to make his views known he must know the case against him. This case law is now embedded in Article 27(1) which provides that '[t]he Commission shall base its decisions only on objections on which the parties concerned have been able to comment'. The Commission satisfies this requirement by sending the undertakings a document called the statement of objections (SO). The undertakings may then make submissions in reply and are offered the opportunity of an oral hearing. The procedures are now set out in Commission Regulation 773/2004[174] (which replaced Regulation 2842/98[175]). If at the end of the proceedings the Commission finds that the competition rules have been infringed it may adopt a decision under Regulation 1/2003, Articles 7 or 8, and may impose a penalty under Article 23.

Considerable problems arise over the content of the rights of defence during these procedures, particularly where the rights of undertakings to know the case against them conflict with the Commission's duty to preserve the confidentiality of business secrets. Above all there is the pervasive problem of the Commission's multi-faceted role. Undertakings repeatedly appeal against Commission decisions on the ground that the competition procedures are contrary to Article 6 (1) of the ECHR which provides that 'in the determination of his civil rights and obligations or of any criminal charge against him, everyone is entitled to a fair and public hearing within a reasonable time by an independent and impartial tribunal'. The Court has held that the

---

[170] This procedure was set out again in *Akzo Nobel*, para. 132.

[171] The corresponding provision in Reg. 17 was Art. 19(1). Under that provision there was a right to a hearing before the Commission took a decision granting, refusing or revoking an exemption, which was one reason those decisions took such a long time.

[172] It also hears other natural or legal persons: see Reg. 1/2003, Art. 27(3). For the position of complainants, see *infra* 1293,. Note that in a case under Reg. 17 it was held that there is no duty to give parties a hearing where the Commission is simply replacing a decision ruled invalid for procedural defects at the final, authentication stage with another which relies on the same evidence as that which was annulled: see Cases C-238, 244–5, 247, 250, 251–2, and 254/99 P, *Limburgse Vinyl Maatschappij NV and others v. Commission* [2002] ECR I-8375, [2003] 4 CMLR 397.

[173] Case 17/74, *Transocean Marine Paint Association v. Commission (No. 2)* [1974] ECR 1063, [1974] 2 CMLR 459 where the decision concerned was an Article 81(3) exemption which was subject to conditions to which the addressee objected. The right to be heard, in all proceedings liable to culminate in a measure adversely affecting a particular person, is a fundamental principle of Community law: see Cases C-68/94 and 30/95, *France & SCPA v. Commission* [1998] ECR I-1375, [1998] 4 CMLR 829, para. 174.

[174] [2004] OJ L123/18.

[175] [1998] OJ L 354/18, the 'Hearing Regulation', which in turn replaced Regulation 99/63[1963–64] OJ Spec. Ed. 47.

Commission is not a tribunal within Article 6, as its decisions are those of an administrative authority.[176] However, it has also been held that the requirements of Article 6(1) are satisfied by the right of the parties to challenge Commission decisions in the Court. The CFI has held itself to be an independent and impartial court, established in order particularly to improve the judicial protection of individuals by making a close inspection of complex facts.[177]

In the following sections we consider the procedure from the sending of the SO to review by the Court. It should be noted, however, that some cases are settled *informally*[178] without the need for a formal procedure and decision.

(ii) The Statement of Objections

By Regulation 773/2004, Article 10(1)[179] 'the Commission shall inform the parties in writing of the objections raised against them'. By Article 11(2) Commission decisions can deal only with objections in respect of which the parties have been able to comment. The SO sets out the facts as understood by the Commission, a legal analysis explaining why it considers Article 81 or 82 to be infringed and any proposed remedy the Commission is contemplating adopting. It cannot fine parties unless it has expressed an intention to do so in the SO.[180] It must state the duration of the infringement.[181] The parties are invited to reply within a set time limit (Regulation 773/2004, Article 10(2)).[182] The Commission can send the parties fresh documents on which it intends to rely, after the initial SO, so long as it gives the necessary time for the parties to comment on them.[183]

In order for the parties to make their views known, the Commission must reveal the documents on which it intends to rely. The SO is therefore accompanied by annexes of such documents so that the addressees can see the evidence on which the Commission has based its case.[184] The Commission also supplies a CD–ROM detailing *all* the documents in the file. The addressees may then exercise there rights to inspect the file, at least insofar as the documents are 'accessible'.[185] The current practical arrangements for this are contained in the Commission's 2005 Notice on access to the file.[186] If the undertaking accompanies its reply to the SO by other

---

[176] Cases 209-215 and 218/78, *Van Landewyck v. Commission* [1980] ECR 3125, [1981] 3 CMLR 134 para. 81; *Musique Diffusion Française v. Commission* [1983] ECR 1823, [1983] 2 CMLR 221 at para. 7; Case T-11/89, *Shell v. Commission* [1992] ECR II-757, para. 39.

[177] Case T-348/94, *Enso Española v. Commission* [1998] ECR II-1875, paras. 57–63; Cases T-25/95 etc., *Cimenteries CBR SA v. Commission* [2000] ECR II-491, [2000] 5 CMLR 204, paras. 718–19. For the Court's exercise of judicial review, see *infra* 1252.

[178] See *infra* 1251.

[179] [2004] OJ L123/18.

[180] In Cases T-25/95 etc. *Cimenteries CBR SA v. Commission* [2000] ECR II-491, [2000] 5 CMLR 204 the CFI annulled the fines on associations of undertakings where the Commission had not announced in the SO its intention to fine the associations as distinct from their individual members. On the other hand, the ECJ annulled the fines on the individual members of a liner conference in Cases C-395 and 396/P, *Compagnie Maritime Belge and others v. Commission* [2000] ECR I-1365, [2000] 4 CMLR 1076, because the Commission had announced an intention to fine only the conference, not the individual shipping lines.

[181] Cases 100–103/80, *Musique Diffusion Française v. Commission (Pioneer)* [1983] ECR 1823, [1983] 2 CMLR 221.

[182] The minimum time set down in Reg. 773/20042004 is 4 weeks, but the period is usually 2 months and maybe 3: see Commissions *XXIIIrd Report on Competition Policy* (Commission, 1993), part 207.

[183] Case 107/82, *AEG-Telefunken v. Commission* [1983] ECR 3151, [1984] 3 CMLR 325; Cases T-305–307, 313–316, 318, 328–329, and 335/94, *Re the PVC Cartel II: Limburgse Vinyl Mij NV and others v. Commission* [1999] 5 CMLR 303, para. 497.

[184] For details, see Ortiz Blanco, n. 6 *supra*, 10.18.

[185] See *infra* 1198.

[186] [2005] OJ C325/7.

documents the Commission can subsequently rely on them even though they were not referred to in the SO.[187] The SO is not a reviewable act against which an action for annulment can be brought, as it is only a preparatory act and can be challenged in an action brought against the act concluding the proceedings.[188]

(iii) The Hearing Officer

In 1982 the Commission decided to meet some of the criticisms of its position as investigator, prosecutor, and judge, and of the lack of objectivity in its decision-making process by establishing the position of Hearing Officer.[189] Originally, his role was to preside over the oral hearing, but in 1994 it was extended to cover the whole of the Commission's administrative procedure.[190] His role and functions are now governed by Commission Decision 2001/462.[191] Since 1994 the Hearing Officer also has jurisdiction in relation to hearings provided for in the Merger Regulation.[192]

The rationale for creating the post in 1982 was to inject an element of disinterested objectivity into the Commission's decision-making process. He is attached, for administrative purposes, to the Competition Commissioner but the idea is that he is 'independent'.[193]

(iv) Access to the File

a. General

There is a problem about how far the parties are entitled to examine all the evidence in the Commission's 'file' on which the SO is based so that they may know the case against them. It appears from the judgment in *Hercules*[194] that 'access to the file' is an integral part of the right to be heard and not a right in itself:

> 75. . . . access to the file in competition cases is intended in particular to enable the addressees of Statements of Objections to acquaint themselves with the evidence in the Commission's file so that

---

[187] Case T-11/89, *Shell* v. *Commission* [1992] ECR II-757.

[188] Case 60/81, *IBM* v. *Commission* [1981] ECR 2639, [1981] 3 CMLR 635.

[189] See Commission's *XIth Report on Competition Policy* (Commission, 1981), paras. 26 and 27 and the *XIIth Report* (Commission, 1982), parts 36 and 37. The original terms of reference of the Hearing Officer, [1982] OJ C215/2, were reformulated in 1990 because of the need to take on board hearings in transport cases: see EC Commission *XXth Report on Competition Policy* (Commission, 1990), 312–14, and revised in 1994: Commission Decision 94/810 on the terms of reference of hearing officers in competition procedures before the Commission, [1994] OJ L330/67. See generally M. van der Woude, 'Hearing Officers and EC Antitrust Procedures; The Art of Making Subjective Procedures More Objective' (1996) 33 *CMLRev* 531.

[190] When the post was created in 1982 the rules on hearings were contained in Reg. 99/63 [1963–64] OJ Spec. Ed. 47 but this was replaced by Reg. 2842/98, which takes account of the 1994 terms of reference: see recital 2 of Reg. 2842/98 [1998] OJ L354/18.

[191] Commission Dec. 2001/462/EC on the terms of reference of hearing officers in certain competition proceedings (the Hearing Officer Mandate)[2001] OJ L162/21.

[192] Reg. 4064/89 [1989] OJ L395/1, now Reg. 139/2004 [2004] OJ L24/1. see the 2001 Terms of Reference, Art. 1.

[193] 2001 Terms of Reference. Recital 6 and Art. 2(2). It should be noted that the Hearing Officer does not appear on the chart of the organization of DG Comp on the web site, which is reproduced in Chap. 2.

[194] Case C-51/92 P, *Hercules Chemicals NV* v. *Commission (Polypropylene)* [1999] ECR I-4235, [1999] 5 CMLR 976 at paras. 75–6; see also Case C-185/95 P, *Baustahlgewebe GmbH* v. *Commission* [1999] 4 CMLR 1203 at para. 89 and Cases T-10–12, 14–15/92, *Cimenteries CBR SA* v. *Commission* [1992] ECR II-2667, [1992] 4 CMLR 243 at para. 38; note that the principles governing access to the Commission's file do not, as such, apply to Court proceedings, which are governed by the EC Statute of the ECJ and the Rules of Procedure of the CFI: see C-185/95 P, *Baustahlgewebe* at para. 90).

on the basis of that evidence they can express their views effectively on the conclusions reached by the Commission in its Statement of Objections . . .

76. Thus the general principles of Community law governing the right of access to the Commission's file are designed to ensure effective exercise of the rights of the defence, including the right to be heard provided for in Article 19(1) of Regulation 17 and Articles 3 and 7 to 9 of Commission Regulation 99/63 of 25 July 1963[195] on the hearings provided for in Article 19(1) and (2) of Regulation 17.

b. The Right of Parties to know the Case against them

The extent of the right of access to the file has changed over the years. Initially the Court expressed the right of the parties quite conservatively[196] but then began to insist on the parties being properly apprised of the details of the case against them.[197] In the *XXIIth Report* the Commission said it intended to 'go beyond the requirements laid down by the Court of Justice and improve the exercise of the rights of defence in the course of administrative procedures' and lay down a procedure for organizing the file and allowing undertakings to inspect it at the Commission's offices.[198] The CFI held in *Hercules*[199] that, although the Commission had imposed on itself rules exceeding the requirements laid down by the ECJ, it now had to follow them. Accordingly:

54. It follows that the Commission has an obligation to make available to the undertakings involved in Article [81(1)] proceedings all documents, whether in their favour or otherwise, which it has obtained in the course of the investigation, save where the business secrets of other undertakings, the internal documents of the Commission or other confidential information are involved.[200]

The right of access to the file is now set out in Regulation 1/2003, Article 27(2) and expanded upon in Regulation 773/2004.[201] The practical arrangements for access were revised and put into the 1997 Notice on access to the file.[202] The revision was made largely, as the Notice said, to ensure compatibility with the requirements laid down by the Court, particularly by the CFI in *Solvay* (the *Soda Ash* cases).[203] The Notice was further revised at the end of 2005.[204]

In *Solvay* the CFI annulled the Commission decisions because of the Commission's failure properly to disclose to the parties documents which might have been useful in their defence. The Court said that it is important that the undertakings have disclosed to them documents which tend to exonerate them (exculpatory documents) as well as those which tend to incriminate them (inculpatory). It is not for the Commission alone to decide what documents are

---

[195] Now Arts. 10–14 of Reg. 773/2004 [2004] OJ L123/18.

[196] See Cases 56 and 58, *Etablissements Consten SA & Grundig-Verkaufs-GmbH v. Commission* [1966] ECR 299, [1966] CMLR 418; Cases 43 and 63/82, *VBVB and VBBB v. Commission* [1984] ECR 19, [1985] 1 CMLR 27.

[197] See, e.g., Case C-185/95 P, *Baustahlgewebe GmbH v. Commission* [1998] ECR I-8471, [1999] 4 CMLR 1203, paras. 89–90, Case C-51/92 P, *Hercules Chemicals NV v. Commission (Polypropylene)* [1999] 5 CMLR 976, paras. 75–9.

[198] Commission' *XXIIth Report on Competition Policy* (Commission, 1982) parts 34 and 35.

[199] Case T-7/89, *Hercules v. Commission* [1991] ECR II-1711.

[200] *Ibid.*, para. 54.

[201] Arts. 15 and 16.

[202] Commission Notice on the internal rules of procedure for processing requests for access to the file [1997] OJ C23/3.

[203] Cases T-30/91, *Solvay SA v. Commission* [1995] ECR II-1775, [1996] 5 CMLR 57 and Case T-36/91, *ICI v. Commission* [1995] ECR II-1847, applied in Cases T-305–7, 313–16, 318, 328–9, and 335/94, *Re the PVC Cartel II: Limburgse Vinyl Mij NV and others v. Commission* [1999] ECR II-931, [1999] 5 CMLR 303.

[204] Commission Notice on the rules or access to the Commission file in cases pursuant to Articles 81 and 82 of the EC Treaty, Articles 53, 54, and 57 of the EEA Agreement and Council Regulation (EC) No. 139/2004, [2005] OJ C 325/7; see also IP/05/1581, 13 December 2005.

useful to the defence.[205] In the *Solvay* judgment the CFI introduced the 'general principle of equality of arms' between the Commission and the undertakings being investigated. This means that the undertakings' knowledge of the file used in the proceedings is the same as that of the Commission.

Cases T-30/91, *Solvay SA* v. *Commission* [1995] ECR II-1775, [1996] 5 CMLR 57

Court of First Instance

81. In that context the Commission observes that although its officials themselves examined and re-examined all the documents in its possession, they found no evidence which might exculpate the applicant, so that there was no point in disclosing them. In that regard, it should be stated that in the defended proceedings for which Regulation 17 provides it cannot be for the Commission alone to decide which documents are of use for the defence. Where, as in the present case, difficult and complex economic appraisals are to be made, the Commission must give the advisers of the undertaking concerned the opportunity to examine documents which may be relevant so that their probative value for the defence can be assessed.

82. That is particularly true where parallel conduct is concerned, which is characterised by a set of actions that are prima facie neutral, where documents may just as easily be interpreted in a way favourable to the undertakings concerned as in an unfavourable way. The Court considers that in such circumstances any error made by the Commission's officials in categorizing as 'neutral' a given document which, as an item of irrelevant evidence, will not then be disclosed to the undertakings, must not be allowed to impair their defence. The opposite view, for which the Commission contends, would mean that such an error could not be discovered in time, before adoption of the Commission's decision, except in the exceptional case where the undertakings concerned co-operated spontaneously, which would present unacceptable risks for the sound administration of justice . . .

83. Having regard to the general principle of equality of arms, which presupposes that in a competition case the knowledge which the undertaking concerned has of the file used in the proceeding is the same as that of the Commission, the Commission's view cannot be upheld. The Court considers that it is not acceptable for the Commission alone to have had available to it, when taking a decision on the infringement, the documents marked 'V', and for it therefore to be able to decide on its own whether or not to use them against the applicant, when the applicant had no access to them and was therefore unable likewise to decide whether or not it would use them in its defence. In such a situation, the rights of defence which the applicant enjoys during the administrative procedure would be excessively restricted in relation to the powers of the Commission, which would then act as both the authority notifying the objections and the deciding authority, while having more detailed knowledge of the case-file than the defence.

---

[205] *Solvay*, n. 203, para. 81.

The actual circumstances in *Solvay* were commented on by, *inter alia*, the former Director-General:

C. D. Ehlermann and B. J. Drijber, 'Legal Protection of Enterprises: Administrative Procedure, in Particular Access to the File and Confidentiality' [1996] 7 *ECLR* 375, 381

A first point concerns the attitude of the parties concerned in the course of the investigation and during the administrative procedure. ICI and Solvay had both requested confidential treatment of their documents *vis-à-vis* other producers. However, once it had received the statement of objections, ICI without lifting that claim of confidentiality asked for unrestricted access to the documents coming from other producers, including Solvay. It in fact asked a double standard to be applied. With the benefit of hindsight it may be easy to say that the Commission should have ignored ICI's and Solvay's general requests for confidential treatment, except for (an undefined category of) 'certain sensitive information' . . . But one easily understands the Commission's hesitations to concede to requests for disclosure from companies which themselves claimed that all their own material was (and is) highly confidential.

The procedural position of Solvay is even more striking. That company never made a request to see the Commission's file; it apparently felt it was sufficiently informed by the vast annexes to the statement of objections. Apart from some quibbles about the status of a limited number of documents produced at the oral hearing held in June 1990 (which Solvay had not thought worth attending), there had not been any procedural problems. In what may be seen as an attempt to ensure that the outcome of the two cases T–30/91 and T–36/91 would be the same, the CFI excused Solvay for not having requested access to the file at the appropriate moment by putting the blame on the Commission: such a request would have been futile anyhow since Solvay was aware that the Commission had already refused an identical request from ICI . . . In general, such reasoning is difficult to accept. It would potentially reward companies which intentionally fail to ask for access at the appropriate stage.

The CFI was generous to the applicants on yet another point. Its conclusion that the rights of the defence had been violated was to a large extent based on the link it construed between the Article [81] case and the two Article [82] cases. It is true that the other party's strength could be a plausible explanation for not selling outside one's 'own' territory. However obvious the argument may seem now, neither of the parties used it in their defence to the statement of objections or indeed in their application to the CFI. Significantly, at the oral hearing before the Commission, an expert witness explained that it was not economically feasible to ship soda ash across the Channel to France but that transport costs were no obstacle to making shipments to customers in Norway.

Another practical aspect relates to the meaning of the principle of 'equality of arms', as interpreted by the CFI . . . One may wonder whether a company is really put in a disadvantageous position if it has not been shown all the documents the Commission has it its possession. First, the Commission can hardly avoid gathering, during inspections, lots of paper which on examination prove to be devoid of any relevance for its case. The reason is very simple: due to time and other constraints, the number and the nature of the documents seized during an inspection are largely fortuitous. Much irrelevant material (although falling within the inspection mandate) will be seized, whereas potentially relevant material may be overlooked. Second, it is fair to assume that the companies themselves best know the industry, the market and their own behaviour in that market. For these obvious reasons, the companies are normally much better informed than the Commission. In a context so different from the traditional criminal law procedures, the argument derived from the principle of equality of arms should therefore be taken with a pinch of salt.

It is clear, however, that breach of the principle laid down in *Solvay* will not always lead to annulment of the decision. It will depend on whether, in the Court's view, the undertaking's ability to defend itself was prejudiced.[206]

The law on access to the file was restated by the ECJ in the final *Cement Cartel* appeals.

Cases C-204/00 P, C-205/00 P, C-211/00 P, C-213/00 P, C-217/00 P and C-219/00 P, *Aalborg Portland A/S and Others* v. *Commission* [2004] ECR I-123, [2005] 4 CMLR 251

Court of Justice

68. A corollary of the principle of respect for the rights of the defence, the right of access to the file means that the Commission must give the undertaking concerned the opportunity to examine all the documents in the investigation file which may be relevant for its defence (see, to that effect, Case T-30/91, *Solvay* v. *Commission* [1995] ECR II-1775, paragraph 81, and Case C-199/99 P *Corus UK* v. *Commission* [2003] ECR I-0000, paragraphs 125 to 128). Those documents include both incriminating evidence and exculpatory evidence, save where the business secrets of other undertakings, the internal documents of the Commission or other confidential information are involved (see Case 85/76, *Hoffmann-La Roche* v. *Commission* [1979] ECR 461, paragraphs 9 and 11; Case C-51/92 P, *Hercules Chemicals* v. *Commission* [1999] ECR I-4235, paragraph 75; and Joined Cases C-238/99 P, C-244/99 P, C-245/99 P, C-247/99 P, C-250/99 P to C-252/99 P and C-254/99 P, *Limburgse Vinyl Maatschappij and Others* v. *Commission* [2002] ECR I-8375, paragraph 315).

69. It may be that the undertaking draws the Commission's attention to documents capable of providing a different economic explanation for the overall economic assessment carried out by the Commission, in particular those describing the relevant market and the importance and the conduct of the undertakings acting on that market (see, to that effect, *Solvay* v. *Commission*, cited above, paragraphs 76 and 77).

70. The European Court of Human Rights has none the less held that, just like observance of the other procedural safeguards enshrined in Article 6(1) of the ECHR, compliance with the adversarial principle relates only to judicial proceedings before a tribunal and that there is no general, abstract principle that the parties must in all instances have the opportunity to attend the interviews carried out or to receive copies of all the documents taken into account in the case of other persons (see, to that effect, Euro. Court H.R., the *Kerojärvi* v. *Finland* judgment of 19 July 1995, Series A No 322, § 42, and the *Mantovanelli* v. *France* judgment of 18 March 1997, Reports of Judgments and Decisions 1997-II, § 33).

71. The failure to communicate a document constitutes a breach of the rights of the defence only if the undertaking concerned shows, first, that the Commission relied on that document to support its objection concerning the existence of an infringement (see, to that effect, Case 322/81, *Michelin* v. *Commission* [1983] ECR 3461, paragraphs 7 and 9) and, second, that the objection could be proved only by reference to that document (see Case 107/82 *AEG* v. *Commission* [1983] ECR 3151, paragraphs 24 to 30, and Solvay v. Commission, cited above, paragraph 58).

72. If there were other documentary evidence of which the parties were aware during the administrative procedure that specifically supported the Commission's findings, the fact that an

---

[206] See Cases T-305–7, 313–16, 318, 328–9, and 335/94, *Re the PVC Cartel II: Limburgse Vinyl Maatschappij NV and others v. Commission* [1999] ECR II-931, [1999] 5 CMLR 303, paras. 1011–22, confirmed by the ECJ Case Cases C-238, 244–5, 247, 250, 251–2, and 254/99 P, *Limburgse Vinyl Maatschappij NV and others v. Commission* [2002] ECR I-8375, [2003] 4 CMLR 397, paras. 315–28; Case C-51/92 P, *Hercules Chemicals NV v. Commission* [1999] ECR I-4235, [1999] 5 CMLR 976, paras. 75–81.

incriminating document not communicated to the person concerned was inadmissible as evidence would not affect the validity of the objections upheld in the contested decision (see, to that effect, *Musique Diffusion française and Others* v. *Commission*, cited above, paragraph 30, and *Solvay v. Commission*, cited above, paragraph 58).

73. It is thus for the undertaking concerned to show that the result at which the Commission arrived in its decision would have been different if a document which was not communicated to that undertaking and on which the Commission relied to make a finding of infringement against it had to be disallowed as evidence.

74. On the other hand, where an exculpatory document has not been communicated, the undertaking concerned must only establish that its non-disclosure was able to influence, to its disadvantage, the course of the proceedings and the content of the decision of the Commission (see *Solvay v. Commission*, paragraph 68).

75. It is sufficient for the undertaking to show that it would have been able to use the exculpatory documents in its defence (see *Hercules Chemicals* v. *Commission*. paragraph 81, and *Limburgse Vinyl Maatschappij and Others* v. *Commission*, paragraph 318), in the sense that, had it been able to rely on them during the administrative procedure, it would have been able to put forward evidence which did not agree with the findings made by the Commission at that stage and would therefore have been able to have some influence on the Commission's assessment in any decision it adopted, at least as regards the gravity and duration of the conduct of which it was accused and, accordingly, the level of the fine (see, to that effect, *Solvay v. Commission*, paragraph 98).

76. The possibility that a document which was not disclosed might have influenced the course of the proceedings and the content of the Commission's decision can be established only if a provisional examination of certain evidence shows that the documents not disclosed might—in the light of that evidence—have had a significance which ought not to have been disregarded (see *Solvay v. Commission*, paragraph 68).

77. In the context of that provisional analysis, it is for the Court of First Instance alone to assess the value which should be attached to the evidence produced to it (see order of 17 September 1996 in Case C–19/95 P, *San Marco* v. *Commission* [1996] ECR I-4435, paragraph 40). As stated at paragraph 49 of this judgment, its assessment of the facts does not, provided the evidence is not distorted, constitute a question of law which is subject, as such, to review by the Court of Justice.

c. Confidentiality

There is a fundamental tension between the rights of the parties to know the case against them and the Commission's obligation to preserve confidentiality. A general duty of confidentiality is laid down in the Treaty itself. Article 287 (ex Article 214) says:

The members of the institutions of the Community, the members of committees, and the officials and other servants of the Community shall be required, even after their duties have ceased, not to disclose information of the kind covered by the obligation of professional secrecy, in particular information about undertakings, their business relations or their cost components.

Regulation 1/2003, Article 28 is headed 'Professional Secrecy' and states that information collected pursuant to Articles 17–22 shall only be used for the purposes for which it is acquired. Article 28(2) addresses the matter of exchange of information within the network of competition authorities.[207]

---

[207] See Notice on cooperation within the Network of Competition Authorities [2004] OJ C101/54 and *infra* 1274. The Notice (para. 28(a)) states that 'professional secrecy' is a Community law concept.

Regulation 1/2003, Article 27(2) says that the parties' right to have access to the Commission's file is 'subject to the legitimate interest of undertakings in the protection their business secrets'. This is repeated in Regulation 773/2004, Article 15(2) which says that the right of access does not extend to 'business secrets or other confidential information'.[208] Nor does it extend to internal documents of the Commission or of the NCAs, or to correspondence between the Commission and the NCAs or between the NCAs *inter se* (insofar as this is in the Commission's file).[209] Further, Article 16(1) states:

Information, including documents, shall not be communicated or made accessible by the Commission in so far as it contains business secrets or other confidential information of any person.

Confidentiality is a significant issue in the context of competition proceedings because of the highly sensitive information which the Commission may obtain during an investigation. 'Business secrets' comprises information about an undertaking's business activity disclosure of which could result in serious harm to the undertaking.[210] 'Other confidential information' is information other than business secrets whose disclosure would significantly harm a person or undertaking.[211] This includes matters which would identify 'whistleblowers',[212] complainants, or other third parties who have a justified wish to remain anonymous. The 2005 Notice recognizes that the Community Courts have acknowledged that it is legitimate to refuse to reveal letters from an undertaking's customers which might expose the writers to retaliatory measures.[213]

The basic principle, laid down in *Hoffmann-La Roche*, is that the Commission cannot use to an undertaking's detriment facts or documents which it cannot disclose to it, where the absence of disclosure adversely affects the undertaking's opportunity to be heard:

---

[208] Reg. 1/2003, Art. 27(2), and Reg. 773/2004, Art. 15(2) also exclude from the right of access certain Commission and NCA documents.

[209] Reg. 1/2003, Art. 27(2), and Reg. 773/2004, Art. 15(2). For the exchange of information within the European Competition Network (ECN) of the Commission and the NCAs, see *infra* 000.

[210] 2005 Access to the file Notice, para. 18; Case T-353/94, *Postbank NV v. Commission*, [1996] ECR II-921, para. 87. Examples given in the 2005 Notice are technical and/or financial information relating to an undertaking's know-how, methods of assessing costs, production secrets and processes, supply sources, quantities produced and sold, market shares, customer and distributor lists, marketing plans, cost and price structure and sales strategy.

[211] 2005 Notice, para. 19.

[212] The Commission's notorious failure to conceal the identity of the whistleblower Stanley Adams from Hoffmann-La Roche rendered the Commission liable to him in damages under Art. 288(2) (ex Art. 215(2)): Case 145/83, *Adams v. Commission* [1985] ECR 3539, [1986] 1 CMLR 506.

[213] 2005 Notice, para. 19. In *BPB Industries and British Gympsum Ltd* [1995] ECR I-865, [1997] 4 CMLR 238 the Court accepted that the Commission was entitled to keep such correspondence confidential because of the fear of retaliation from the dominant firm in an Article 82 case. It has been argued (see M. Levitt, 'Commission Notice on Internal Rules of Procedure for Access to the File' [1997] *ECLR* 187) that whether the undertaking is in fact dominant may be one of the things which is in dispute and that the so-called 'economic or commercial pressure' may be no more than an unrealized fear of potential retaliation unrelated to the actual abuse allegation. In *Michelin II* (Case T-203/01 *Manufacture Française des Pneumatiques Michelin v. Commission* [2003] ECR II-4071, [2004] 4 CMLR 923, the CFI held that the Commission was justified, on account of the risk of retaliation, in withholding from Michelin the identity of the dealers who had answered its requests for information. Refusal by the Commission to reveal the identity of third parties has also been held justified in merger cases, see Case T-221/95, *Endemol v. Commission* [1999] ECR II-1299; Case T-5/02, *Tetra Laval v. Commission* [2002] ECR II-4381, [2002] 5 CMLR 1182.

Case 85/76, *Hoffmann-La Roche* v. *Commission* [1979] ECR 461, [1979] 3 CMLR 211

Court of Justice

14. The said Article 20 [of Regulation 17] by providing undertakings from whom information has been obtained with a guarantee that their interests which are closely connected with observance of professional secrecy, are not jeopardized enables the Commission to collect on the widest possible scale the requisite data for the fulfilment of the task conferred upon it by Articles [81] and [82] of the Treaty without the undertakings being able to prevent it from doing so, but it does not nevertheless allow it to use, to the detriment of the undertakings involved in a proceeding referred to in Regulation 17, facts, circumstances or documents which it cannot in its view disclose if such a refusal of disclosure adversely affects that undertaking's opportunity to make known effectively its views on the truth or implications of those circumstances on those documents or again on the conclusions drawn by the Commission from them.

Regulation 773/2004, Article 16 puts the onus on the parties to identify confidential material which they do not want disclosed.

Regulation 773/2004, Article 16

2. Any person which makes known its views pursuant to Article 6(1), Article 7(1), Article 10(2) and Article 13(1) and (3) or subsequently submits further information to the Commission in the course of the same procedure, shall clearly identify any material which it considers to be confidential, giving reasons, and provide a separate non-confidential version by the date set by the Commission for making its views known.

3. Without prejudice to paragraph 2 of this Article, the Commission may require undertakings and associations of undertakings which produce documents or statements pursuant to Regulation (EC) No 1/2003 to identify the documents or parts of documents which they consider to contain business secrets or other confidential information belonging to them and to identify the undertakings with regard to which such documents are to be considered confidential. The Commission may likewise require undertakings or associations of undertakings to identify any part of a statement of objections, a case summary drawn up pursuant to Article 27(4) of Regulation (EC) No 1/2003 or a decision adopted by the Commission which in their view contains business secrets.

The Commission may set a time-limit within which the undertakings and associations of undertakings are to:

(a) substantiate their claim for confidentiality with regard to each individual document or part of document, statement or part of statement;

(b) provide the Commission with a non-confidential version of the documents or statements, in which the confidential passages are deleted;

(c) provide a concise description of each piece of deleted information.

The 2005 Notice sets out the practical arrangements for giving access to the Commission's file while preserving confidentiality. The Notice clarifies that access to the file is granted only to addressees of statements of objections, and that other parties (complainants and other parties involved in merger cases) have a separate, more limited, right of access to specific documents

A distinction is made in the Notice between 'accessible' and 'non-accessible' documents.

The Hearing Officer has jurisdiction to determine whether or not particular documents fall within the protected category. As seen above, Article 16(2) and (3) provides for undertakings providing information to the Commission (voluntarily or not), and persons making their views known, to detail what they regard as confidential or business secrets and supply a non-confidential version.[214] Both business secrets and confidential information are 'non-accessible'. The Commission's internal documents are also 'non-accessible'... The Commission's rationale for the protection of internal documents is that they are not, by their nature, either incriminating or exculpatory and are not the sort of evidence on which the Commission can rely in its assessment of a case.[215] The 2005 Notice sets out in more detail than previously the procedure for resolving confidentiality and access to non-accessible information claims. In essence, if the Commission and the undertakings or other parties cannot agree, the matter is dealt with by the Hearing Officer.[216] Access to the file can be granted in one or more of several ways: electronically, paper copies sent by mail, or examination of the accessible file at the Commission's premises. The choice is the Commission's.[217]

In the Leniency Notice there is special provision for the protection of 'corporate statements' made by applicants for leniency. Access is granted only to the addressees of statements of objections, and then only under strict conditions which include being prohibited from making electronic or mechanical copies.[218]

d. Confidentiality and Complainants

It was held in *AKZO*,[219] that business secrets are accorded 'very special protection' and cannot be disclosed to third parties who have lodged complaints.[220] Otherwise, as the Court said, competitors could obtain access to other undertaking's secrets simply by lodging a complaint:

Case 53/85, *AKZO* v. *Commission* [1986] ECR 1965, [1987] 1 CMLR 231

ECS complained to the Commission about the alleged predatory pricing of AKZO. The Commission sent AKZO a Statement of Objections and a copy of it to ECS. ECS then asked the Commission for

---

[214] 2005 Notice, paras. 35–8.

[215] 2005 Notice, para. 12. Examples of internal documents given in the Notice are drafts, opinions, memos or notes from the Commission departments or other public authorities concerned. The Commission is under no obligation to take any minutes of any meetings with any person or undertaking, although if it does and they are agreed with the other parties, they may be made accessible (after deletion of confidential information and business secrets: see Notice, para. 13). The Commission's correspondence with other public authorities (including, *inter alia*, with the NCAs and with competition authorities of non-Member States) are non-accessible (para.15), although there are provisions for releasing non-confidential versions of some of these in exceptional circumstances (para. 16)

[216] 2005 Notice, paras. 42 and 47. Commission Decision 2001/462 on the terms of reference of hearing officers [2001] OJ L162/21, Art 9.

[217] 2005 Notice, para. 44.

[218] Commission Notice on Immunity from Fines and Reduction of Fines in Cartel Cases [2006] OJ C298/17, paras. 33–4, *infra* 1240.

[219] Case 53/85, AKZO v. *Commission* [1986] ECR 1965, [1987] 1 CMLR 231.

[220] For complaints generally, see *infra* 1287.

copies of the documents in the annexes to the Statement of Objections so that it could exercise its right to be heard under Regulation 17, Article 19(2). The Commission disclosed a number of documents to it. AKZO claimed that the Commission had breached its duty to preserve AKZO's business secrets.

Court of Justice

26. In the first place, it must be borne in mind that Article [287] of the Treaty requires the officials and other servants of the institutions of the Community not to disclose information in their possession of the kind covered by the obligation of professional secrecy. Article 20 of Regulation No 17/62 which implements that provision in regard to the rules applicable to undertakings, contains in paragraph (2) a special provision worded as follows: 'Without prejudice to the provisions of Articles 19 and 21, the Commission and the competent authorities of the Member States, their officials and other servants shall not disclose information acquired by them as a result of the application of this regulation and of the kind covered by the obligation of professional secrecy.'

27. The provisions of Articles 19 and 21, the application of which is thus reserved, deal with the Commission's obligations in regard to hearings and the publication of decisions. It follows that the obligation of professional secrecy laid down in Article 20(2) is mitigated in regard to third parties on whom Article 19(2) confers the right to be heard, that is to say in regard, in particular, to a third party who has made a complaint. The Commission may communicate to such a party certain information covered by the obligation of professional secrecy in so far as it is necessary to do so for the proper conduct of the investigation.

28. However, that power does not apply to all documents of the kind covered by the obligation of professional secrecy. Article 19(3) which provides for the publication of notices prior to the granting of negative clearance or exemptions, and Article 21 which provides for the publication of certain decisions, both require the Commission to have regard to the legitimate interest of undertakings in the protection of their business secrets. Business secrets are thus afforded very special protection. Although they deal with particular situations, those provisions must be regarded as the expression of a general principle which applies during the course of the administrative procedure. It follows that a third party who has submitted a complaint may not in any circumstances be given access to documents containing business secrets. Any other solution would lead to the unacceptable consequence that an undertaking might be inspired to lodge a complaint with the Commission solely in order to gain access to its competitors' business secrets.

29. It is undoubtedly for the Commission to assess whether or not a particular document contains business secrets. After giving an undertaking an opportunity to state its views, the Commission is required to adopt a decision in that connection which contains an adequate statement of the reasons on which it is based and which must be notified to the undertaking concerned. Having regard to the extremely serious damage which could result from improper communication of documents to a competitor, the Commission must, before implementing its decision, give the undertaking an opportunity to bring an action before the Court with a view to having the assessments made reviewed by it and to preventing disclosure of the documents in question.

30. In this case, the Commission gave the undertaking concerned an opportunity to make its position known and adopted a decision containing an adequate statement of the reasons on which it was based and concerning both the confidential nature of the documents at issue and the possibility of communicating them. At the same time, however, by an act which cannot be severed from that decision, the Commission decided to hand over the documents to the third party who had made the complaint even before it notified its findings to that undertaking. It thus made it impossible for the undertaking to avail itself of the means of redress provided by Article [230] in

> conjunction with Article [242] of the Treaty with the view to preventing the implementation of a contested decision.
>
> 31. That being the case, the decision which the Commission notified to the applicant by letter of 18 December 1984 must be declared void without there being any need to determine whether the documents communicated to the intervener did in fact contain business secrets.

The Court's order to the Commission to recover the documents meant that ECS was unable to rely on them in national proceedings.

It is clear from *AKZO* that complainants cannot have the same access to the file as alleged infringers. The rights of third parties (now laid down in Regulation 1/2003, Article 27) are limited to the right to participate in the administrative procedure. [221] This is embodied in paragraphs 30–31 of the 2005 Notice. A complainant who has been told of the intention to reject his complaint[222] may request access to the documents on which the Commission based the rejection but cannot have access to the confidential information or business secrets of the firm complained about, or of any third parties, which the Commission has acquired in the course of its investigations.

e. Confidentiality, NCAs, and National Proceedings

The issue of exchanges of information and confidentiality with regard to NCAs and national courts in the decentralized system of enforcement under Regulation 1/2003 is dealt with below and in Chapter 15.[223]

(v) The Oral Hearing

The right to be heard is primarily exercised in writing, but Regulation 773/2004, Article 12 gives the parties to whom a SO has been addressed the right to an oral hearing, if they request it in their written submissions. The oral hearing is controlled and supervised by the Hearing Officer.[224] Third parties such as complainants may be heard in addition to the parties.[225] The oral hearing is not a formal 'trial'. It may last anything from a day to two or three weeks, depending on the complexity of the case. It is not heard in public.[226] Regulation 773/2004, Article 14(5) provides that the persons being heard may be 'assisted by' their lawyers. It does not say 'represented by' because it is considered necessary that someone from the undertaking itself (although that can be an in-house lawyer) is present to provide relevant information about the organization.[227]

Regulation 773/2004, Article 14(8) provides that the statements made at the hearing shall be recorded and the record made available to the persons who attended the hearing, regard being

---

[221] Case T-17/93, *Matra Hachette SA v. Commission* [1994] ECR II-595.

[222] See *infra* 1294.

[223] *Infra* 1274.

[224] Terms of Reference [2001] OJ L162/21, Art. 12.

[225] Reg. 773/2004, Art. 13.

[226] Reg. 773/2004, Art. 14(6).

[227] See Case 49/69, *BASF v. Commission (Dyestuffs)* [1972] ECR 619, [1972] CMLR 557. Persons 'invited to attend' may be represented by legal representatives, Reg. 773/2004, Art. 14(4).

had for the protection of business secrets and confidential information. Business secrets and other confidential information are deleted.

The Hearing Officer is not a judge. It is not his function to come to a decision, but to report to the Competition Commissioner on the hearing and the conclusions to be drawn from it in respect of the right to be heard.[228] This report is not made available to the parties, who have no right to see it or comment on it. However, the Hearing Officer makes a final report which is attached to the draft decision submitted to the College of Commissioners[229] and which is made known to the addressees of the decision and is published in the Official Journal together with the decision.[230]

D. COMMISSION DECISIONS

(i) General

The Commission may take a final decision ordering the termination of infringements of the competition rules and may take procedural decisions during the course of its investigation, as seen in the sections above. It may also take interim measures in order to prevent irreparable damage occurring before it can come to a final decision. In addition it has two new powers under Regulation 1/2003: to take a decision making commitments binding but without making an infringement finding, and to take a 'positive' decision finding Article 81 or 82 inapplicable. It is usual to speak of 'the Commission' when discussing the conduct of EC competition policy, meaning the policy and actions of the Competition DG. However, it is important to remember that unless the taking of particular acts of management or administration has been delegated to a single Commissioner, decisions are collegiate acts of the whole Commission.[231] When the Commission adopts an infringement decision, therefore, the Commissioner responsible for competition lays the draft before the whole College at one of its meetings and the measure is adopted by the College.[232]

This section deals with the content of decisions other than the imposition of fines: fines are dealt with in Section E below.

---

[228] Terms of reference, Art. 13(1).

[229] *Ibid.*, Art. 16(1).

[230] *Ibid.*, Art. 16(3). However, the final report is often very short and simply records that the rights of the defence have been observed.

[231] This aspect of decisions was stressed by the CFI in the *Cement* appeal. Two of the applicants claimed a breach of the principle of impartiality, in that the same Commission official had carried out the investigation, acted as rapporteur, drawn up the Statement of Objections, and prepared the draft decision. The CFI held that the principle was not breached because the contested decision was actually taken by the College of Commissioners, not by the official: Joined Cases T-25/95, etc., *Cimenteries CBR SA v. Commission* [2000] ECR II-491, [2000] 5 CMLR 204 para. 721.

[232] The failure of the College to adopt an authenticated version of the decision was one reason for the annulment of the *PVC* decision in Case C-137/92 P, *Commission v. BASF and others* [1994] ECR I-2555: *infra* 1258.

(ii) Final Decisions

a. Termination of Infringements

Regulation 1/2003, Article 7[233] states:

> ### Finding and termination of infringement
>
> 1. Where the Commission, acting on a complaint or on its own initiative, finds that there is an infringement of Article 81 or of Article 82 of the Treaty, it may by decision require the undertakings and associations of undertakings concerned to bring such infringement to an end. For this purpose, it may impose on them any behavioural or structural remedies which are proportionate to the infringement committed and necessary to bring the infringement effectively to an end. Structural remedies can only be imposed either where there is no equally effective behavioural remedy or where any equally effective behavioural remedy would be more burdensome for the undertaking concerned than the structural remedy. If the Commission has a legitimate interest in doing so, it may also find that an infringement has been committed in the past.
>
> 2. Those entitled to lodge a complaint for the purposes of paragraph 1 are natural or legal persons who can show a legitimate interest and Member States.

A decision finding an infringement may therefore order undertakings to bring the infringement to an end where it has not definitely been terminated already. These are called 'cease and desist orders'. The decision may also contain a 'like effects order' whereby the parties are prohibited from entering into similar arrangements, as for example in *Welded Steel Mesh*, a cartel case, where Article 2 of the decision stated:[234]

The undertakings named in Article 1 which are still involved in the welded steel mesh sector in the Community shall forthwith bring the said infringements to an end (if they have not already done so) and shall henceforth refrain in relation to their welded steel mesh operations from any agreement or concerted practice which may have the same object or effect.

On the other hand, in *Langnese-Iglo*[235] the Court held that the Commission was not entitled to forbid the undertaking from entering into exclusive purchasing agreements *in the future*. It was an Article 81 proceeding, and whether or not an exclusive purchasing agreement is restrictive of competition and satisfies the Article 81(3) conditions depends on the circumstances and context.

The Court established in *Cementhandelaren*[236] that the Commission is justified in taking a decision after an infringement has terminated so that the decision is in effect only a declaration that the past conduct did infringe.

The corresponding provision to Article 7 in Regulation 17 was Article 3, which did not state whether the Commission could take decisions ordering the parties to take *positive* steps in order to bring the infringement to an end. The Court, however, held in *Commercial Solvents* that it

---

[233] Reg. 1/2003 [2003] OJ L1/1.

[234] [1989] OJ L260/1, [1991] 4 CMLR 13.

[235] Cases T-7 and 9/93, *Langnese-Iglo & Schöller Lebensmittel v. Commission* [1995] ECR II-1533, [1995] 5 CMLR 602, upheld by the ECJ in Case C-279/95 P, *Langnese-Iglo v. Commission* [1998] ECR I-5609, [1998] 5 CMLR 933.

[236] Case 8/72, *Cementhandelaren v. Commission* [1972] ECR 977, [1973] CMLR 7.

could:[237]

[Article 3] must be applied in relation to the infringement which has been established and may include an order to do certain acts or provide certain advantages which have been wrongfully withheld as well as prohibiting the continuation of certain actions, practices or situations which are contrary to the Treaty.

In *Commercial Solvents* the dominant undertaking was ordered to supply a certain amount of raw material to the complainant, which involved the parties entering into contractual relations. Many subsequent Article 82 cases on refusal to supply and essential facilities have involved ordering a dominant undertaking to supply or to share facilities.[238] Regulation 1/2003, Article 7(1) now expressly gives the Commission power to make positive orders by stating that it may impose 'any behavioural ... remedies which are proportionate to the infringement committed and necessary to bring the infringement effectively to an end'. Where infringements of *Article 81* are concerned, however, the CFI has said that the Commission does not have the power to order a party to enter into a contractual relationship where there are other ways of making the party end the infringement.

Case T-24/90, *Automec srl* v. *Commission (Automec II)* [1992] ECR II-2223, [1992] 5 CMLR 431

Automec was an Italian car dealer which had had a distributorship agreement with BMW. When BMW discontinued the agreement Automec brought an action in the Italian courts and lodged a complaint with the Commission, alleging that BMW's behaviour infringed Article 81 and asking the Commission for an injunction compelling BMW to resume supplies of its cars. The Commission rejected the complaint, *inter alia*, on the ground that it had no power to issue such an order under Article 81(1). Automec appealed to the Court of First Instance.

Court of First Instance[239]

51. As the freedom to contract must remain the rule, the Commission cannot in principle be acknowledged to possess, in the framework of its powers of injunction to put an end to infringements of Article [8(1)1], a power to order a party to enter into a contractual relationship where as a general rule the Commission has suitable means at its disposal for compelling an enterprise to end an infringement.

52. In particular there is no justification for any such restriction on the freedom to contract where several means exist for ending an infringement. This is the case with regard to infringements of Article [81(1)] arising from the application of a distribution system. Such infringements can also be discontinued by giving up or altering the distribution system. Under these circumstances the Commission undoubtedly has power to find the existence of the infringement and order the parties concerned to end it, but it is not for the Commission to impose upon the parties its own choice among the different potential courses of action which all conform to the Treaty.

53. In the circumstances of the particular case, therefore, it must be found that the Commission was not empowered to adopt specific injunctions compelling BMW to supply the applicant and to permit it to use BMW trade marks. It follows that the Commission has not broken Community law by refusing the application for the adoption of such injunctions on the ground that it had no power to do so.

---

[237] Cases 6, 7/73, *Istituto Chemioterapico Italiano Spa and Commercial Solvents Corp* v. *EC Commission* [1974] ECR 223, [1974] 1 CMLR 309, para. 45.

[238] See *supra* Chap. 7.

[239] For the other aspects of this case, see *infra* 1294.

54. The Commission's power to adopt a decision capable of producing practical effects equivalent to those of the injunctions sought by the applicant and the option, which was open to the Commission, of redefining Automec's application as an application for the adoption of such a decision are not such as to cast doubt on this conclusion. The Commission did not seek to rely on its lack of power to justify the rejection of the entire complaint, but only to justify the refusal to adopt the measures specifically requested. In so far the subject-matter of the complaint goes beyond this specific application, the question is not raised in the first part of the decision but the second.

In *Atlantic Container Line AB*[240] the Commission found that shipping companies had infringed Article 81(1) by an agreement which fixed prices and capacity. The decision, *inter alia*, required the parties to inform customers that they were entitled to renegotiate the terms of contracts concluded within the context of the agreement or to terminate them.[241] The CFI annulled that part of the decision as it went beyond what was required to terminate the infringement:

... the Commission may specify the scope of the obligations imposed on the undertakings concerned in order to bring an end to the infringements identified. That power must however be implemented according to the nature of the infringement declared (see, by analogy, *Istituto Chemioterapico Italiano and Commercial Solvents* v. *Commission*, paragraph 45; *RTE and ITP* v. *Commission*, paragraph 90; and Case C-279/95 P *Langnese-Iglo* v. *Commission* [1998] ECR I-5609, paragraph 74) and the obligations imposed must not exceed what is appropriate and necessary to attain the objective sought, namely re-establishment of compliance with the rules infringed (see *RTE and ITP* v. *Commission*, paragraph 93).[242]

The Commission may order an undertaking to amend its contractual terms and may restrict its future pricing policies (this is more likely to be to restrain predatory pricing than excessive pricing[243]). An example of this is the terms of the order in *Tetra Pak II*, where the dominant undertaking was found to have infringed Article 82 by predatory and discriminatory pricing and by imposing unfair terms on its customers.[244]

Tetra Pak II [1992] OJ L72/1, [1992] 4 CMLR 551

Article 3

In particular, Tetra Pak shall take the following measures:

1. Tetra Pak shall amend or where appropriate, delete from its machine purchase/lease contracts and carton supply contracts the clause listed under numbers (i) to (xxviii) so as to eliminate the aspects which have been found by the Commission to be abusive. The new contracts shall be submitted to the Commission;

2. Tetra Pak shall ensure that any differences between the prices charged for its products in the various member-States result solely from the specific market conditions. Any customer within the Community shall be supplied by any Tetra Pak subsidiary it chooses, and at the price it practices;

3. Tetra Pak shall not practise predatory or discriminatory prices and shall not grant to any customer any form of discount on its products or more favourable payment terms not justified by an

---

[240] Case T-395/94, *Atlantic Container Line AB v. Commission* [2002] ECR II-875, [2002] 4 CMLR 1008.

[241] *Trans-Atlantic Agreement* [1994] OJ L376/1, Art. 5.

[242] Case T-395/94, para. 410.

[243] See *supra* Chap. 7.

[244] For the substantive aspects of these case, see *supra* Chap. 7.

objective consideration. Thus, discounts on cartons should be granted solely according to the quantity of each order, and orders for different types of carton may not be aggregated for that purpose;

    4. Tetra Pak may not refuse orders, at prevailing prices, on the ground that the orderer is not an end-user of Tetra Pak products;

    5. Tetra Pak shall inform any customer purchasing or leasing a machine of the specifications which packaging cartons must meet in order to be used on its machines.

Article 4

During the period of five years beginning 1 January 1992, Tetra Pak shall, within the first six months of each year, give the Commission a report allowing it to establish if the actions taken by Tetra Pak pursuant to this Decision have indeed brought the infringements detailed in Article 1 to an end.

The problems of ensuring compliance with positive behavioural remedies are shown by the *Microsoft* case, in which in March 2004 the Commission ordered Microsoft to offer versions of Windows without Window Media Player incorporated (to remedy the abuse of tying) and to make available certain interoperability information (to remedy its refusal to supply).[245] The ensuing battle over Microsoft's (alleged) non-compliance with this decision, in failing to supply complete and accurate interoperability information, was still on-going in April 2007. Moreover, the battle has been fought out publicly, with the Commission issuing bellicose press releases at each stage.[246] Whether Microsoft has complied or not is a question of the monitoring trustee assessing the material that Microsoft is prepared to make available, in consultation with the potential licensees, a matter which is inherently liable to be highly contentious.[247]

    The power to order positive measures in appropriate cases in Regulation 17, Article 3(1) did not appear to include a general power to order divestiture. Article 82 is infringed by an abuse, not by the dominant position *per se* and Regulation 17, Article 3 provided only for the Commission to order the termination of the *infringement*. It did not give a power to restructure the market to prevent future abuses.[248] However, in *Continental Can*[249] the Commission decision held that an undertaking had

---

[245] *Microsoft*, 24 March 2004, COMP/C-3/37.792, [2005] 4 CMLR 965, on appeal Case T-201/04, *Microsoft* v. *Commission* (judgment pending).

[246] A monitoring trustee was appointed (Professor Neil Barrett, an internationally recognized computer scientist, assisted by two technical advisers, also professors of computer science), see IP/05/1215 and Commission Decision on the role of the Trustee in the *Microsoft* case, C(2005)2988 final, 28 July 2005; a Commission decision in November 2005 imposed periodic penalty payments if the required information was not made available by 15 December; and a Commission decision on 12 July 2006 (C(2006)4420 final) concluded that Microsoft was still not complying and imposed a penalty payment of €280.5 million (IP/06/979); on 19 July 2006 Microsoft submitted a revised system of technical documentation, but the Commission announced on 15 November 2006 (IP/06/430) that the technical documentation was still not complete.

[247] Indeed, on 1 March 2007 the Commission issued a Statement of Objections saying that Microsoft had not complied with the terms of the 2004 decision, in that it was charging unreasonably for the interoperability information it was providing as it contained insufficient innovation: see IP/07/269.

[248] See J. Faull and A. Nikpay (eds.), *The EC Law of Competition* (Oxford University Press, 1999), para. 3.350; C. S. Kerse, *EC Antitrust Procedure* (4th edn., Sweet & Maxwell, 1998), para. 6.19. In the UK the Secretary of State had power under the Fair Trading Act 1973, Sched. 8 Pt. II to order structural remedies, as does the Competition Commission under the Enterprise Act 2002, Sched. 8.

[249] Case 6/72, *Europemballage Corp & Continental Can Co Inc v. EC Commission* [1973] ECR 215, [1973] CMLR 199; see *supra* Chaps. 6, 7 and 12.

committed an abuse by acquiring another company and required the undertaking to dispose of it. The decision was annulled on substantive grounds, and so the order was never enforced. In this case, however, the order to divest related to the very subject-matter of the abuse. Regulation 1/2003, Article 7(1) now provides for the Commission to take any structural remedies 'which are proportionate to the infringement committed and necessary to bring the infringement to an end'. However, this power is hedged around with conditions. The structural remedy can only be imposed where no behavioural remedy would be equally effective or where the behavioural remedy would be more burdensome for the undertaking concerned. Recital 12 states that changes to the structure of an undertaking as it existed prior to the infringement would only be proportionate 'where there is a substantial risk of a lasting or repeated infringement that derives from the very structure of the undertaking'. The ability to impose a structural remedy, i.e., to order divestment or break up companies is a powerful weapon in the hands of a competition authority and not one to be used lightly.[250] However, in a speech when the Commission presented its report on its Regulation 1/2003, Article 17 enquiry into the European gas and energy sectors,[251] the Competition Commissioner stressed the powers of the Commission to impose structural remedies for breaches of Articles 81 and 82 (investigations into several energy companies having already begun).

b. Commitments Decisions

Regulation 1/2003 contains a new power whereby the Commission, without taking a final decision finding an infringement, may nevertheless render undertakings given by the parties binding upon them. The Commission may wish to do this where it has identified competition concerns but the parties are willing to give commitments to the Commission about their future conduct in order to avoid a finding of infringement. It is not suitable where the Commission intends to impose a fine and is unlikely to be used in cases of hard core cartels.

Article 9

1. Where the Commission intends to adopt a decision requiring that an infringement be brought to an end and the undertakings concerned offer commitments to meet the concerns expressed to them by the Commission in its preliminary assessment, the Commission may by decision make those commitments binding on the undertakings. Such a decision may be adopted for a specified period and shall conclude that there are no longer grounds for action by the Commission.

2. The Commission may, upon request or on its own initiative, reopen the proceedings:

(a) where there has been a material change in any of the facts on which the decision was based;

(b) where the undertakings concerned act contrary to their commitments; or

(c) where the decision was based on incomplete, incorrect or misleading information provided by the parties.

It will be noted that the power to take commitments decision arises *only* where the Commission otherwise intends to adopt a termination decision under Article 7. It is apparent from the Commission's practice so far, however, that this does not mean that it has to have sent an SO. It

---

[250] The consequences of a competition authority deciding to restructure an industry can be seen in the saga of the UK beer sector following the Monopolies and Mergers Commission Report in 1989: *The Supply of Beer* Cm. 651 (1989), The Supply of Beer (Loan Ties, Licensed Premises and Wholesale Prices) Order, SI 1989/2258 (revoked by SI 2003/52), and The Supply of Beer (Tied Estate) Order, SI 1989/2390 (revoked by SI 2002/3204). Under the Fair Trading Act 1973 the Orders were actually made by the Secretary of State rather than the Monopolies and Mergers Commission itself.

[251] Communication from the Commission COM(2006)851, 10 January 2007.

may have made its concerns known to the undertakings less formally: the requirement is that it has begun proceedings and that they are capable of leading to a finding of infringement.[252] The Commission does not usually put out a preliminary assessment in writing, but just waits to issue an SO, so if the parties wish to avoid the issue of an SO they have to offer commitments early on, and *then* the Commission may issue a preliminary assessment rather than an SO. There are a number of points about Article 9 decisions which are unclear.[253] For example, there is uncertainty as to what is meant by '…shall conclude that there are no longer grounds for action by the Commission' at the end of Article 9. These could mean that the Commission may to decide that it no longer wishes to pursue the case and is pragmatically satisfied with the position reached with the parties concerned[254] or that the Commission can definitively state that if the commitments are complied with there is no longer an infringement. Recital 13 of Regulation 1/2003, which explains Article 9, says that the decision is to be taken 'without concluding that there has been or still is an infringement' but that is different from finding that there will cease to be an infringement *in the future* if the commitments are carried out. However, the usefulness of Article 9 is likely to be severely compromised if the Commission has to make such a definitive finding. This may have implications, *inter alia*, in respect of possible actions by NCAs or in national courts.

It quickly became apparent after Regulation 1/2003 came into operation that commitment decisions are now a major instrument in the Commission's application of the competition rules. Up to the end of 2006 there were eight cases in which commitments had been offered under Article 9, six of which had been finalised and made binding. These were all in respect of cases in which investigations had been opened before (in some cases very long before) May 2004. Two of them, *Deutsche Bundesligia*,[255] and *FA Premier League*[256] concerned the collective selling of media rights to football matches.[257] Two concerned collecting societies and the licensing of online music.[258] *Austrian Airlines/SAS Cooperation Agreement*[259] concerned access to airport slots and access to frequent flyer programmes and *Repsol* was a move to open up the fuel distribution system in Spain.[260] There were two Article 9 decisions in respect of Article 82 infringements. In *Coca-Cola* the undertaking gave commitments in respect of its exclusivity arrangements, rebate policy, use of space in its coolers and using strong brands to sell less popular ones.[261] In *De Beers/ALROSA*[262] De Beers gave commitments to phase out between 2006 and 2008, and to cease

[252] Regulation 1/2003, recital 13, and see J. Temple Lang, 'Commitment Decisions and Settlements with Antitrust Authorities and Private Parties Under European Antitrust Law' 2005 *Fordham Corp L Inst.* 265 (B. Hawk, ed. 2006); C. Cook, 'Commitment Decisions: The Law and Practice under Article 9 (2006) 29(2) *World Competition* 209.

[253] Comprehensively discussed by J. Temple Lang, *op. cit.* n. 252.

[254] Case T-24/90, *Automec II* [1992] ECR II-2223, [1992] 5 CMLR 431 established that the Commission may set its own priorities and is no obligation to pursue proceedings at the behest of a complainant: see *infra* 1295.

[255] [2005] OJ L134/46, [2005] 5 CMLR 1715.

[256] [2006] 5 CMLR 1430.

[257] See *supra* Chap. 13. There is an arbitration clause, but no specific monitoring provisions in *Deutsche Bundesligia*. A monitoring trustee will monitor the auctions of the Premier League rights.

[258] *BUMA and SABAM* [2005] OJ C200/5 (Article 27(4) consultation notice) and *Cannes Extension Agreement* IP/06/1311.

[259] [2005] OJ C233/18 (Article 27(4) consultation notice).

[260] [2006] OJ L176/104. Repsol is to allow service stations to terminate their long-term supply agreements, will not conclude any new supply contracts for terms of more than five years, will not buy any independent service stations for two years and will allow its service stations more freedom in discounting. A monitoring trustee is to verify compliance and report annually to the Commission.

[261] [2005] OJ L253/21, see *supra* Chap. 7. Coca-Cola has to send the Commission annual reports to describe the steps taken to comply with the commitments and must confirm that a compliance programme has been implemented.

[262] [2006] OJ L205/24, see *supra* Chap. 7.

from 2009, all direct and indirect purchases of rough diamonds from ALROSA. ALROSA appealed against this decision, claiming a violation of its right to be heard; a violation of Article 9 in that the commitments which the decision (which was adopted for an unspecified period) made binding were made only by De Beers; and a violation of Article 82 EC, Article 9 and the principles of proportionality and freedom of contract. The CFI annulled it.[263]

It will be noted that Article 9(2) gives the Commission power to re-open the proceedings in certain circumstances.

c. Findings of Inapplicability

Under Regulation 1/2003, Article 10 the Commission is able to take 'positive' decisions finding that Articles 81 and 82 are inapplicable to particular agreements or practices. These decisions are discussed above.[264]

(iii) Procedural Decisions

As seen above, the Commission, in the course of its investigations, may take decisions about procedural matters. Thus, information may be demanded by decision under Regulation 1/2003, Article 18(3), and an inspection may be ordered under Regulation 1/2003, Article 20(4). Failure to comply with such decisions may be penalized by fines.[265] The question of the confidentiality of documents is settled by decision under Article 9 of Decision 2001/462.[266]

(iv) Interim Measures

Regulation 1/2003, Article 8 gives the Commission power to take decisions ordering interim measures.

Article 8

1. In cases of urgency due to the risk of serious and irreparable damage to competition, the Commission, acting on its own initiative may by decision, on the basis of a prima facie finding of infringement, order interim measures.

2. A decision under paragraph 1 shall apply for a specified period of time and may be renewed in so far this is necessary and appropriate.

This was a new provision in that Regulation 17 did not expressly provide powers for the Commission to take interim measures in relation to possible infringements of Articles 81 and 82. However, case law established that the Commission *did* have such powers. The Court recognized that otherwise there would be a serious lacuna, as Commission proceedings can be

[263] Case T-170/06, *ALROSA* v. *Commission*, 11 July 2007.

[264] *Supra* 1148.

[265] See *infra* 1152 ff.

[266] The terms of reference of hearing officers [2001] OJ L162/21. The jurisdiction of the Hearing Officer to take decisions in this respect means that the power to adopt a challengeable act has been delegated by the Commission to a single official. Such delegation is permitted where it does not involve a matter of principle: see Case T-450/93, *Listeral* [1994] ECR II-1177 and generally M. van der Woude, 'Hearing Officers and EC Antitrust Procedures; The Art of Making Subjective Procedures More Objective' (1996) 33 *CMLRev.* 531. *Cf.* the delegation of Reg. 1/2003, Art. 20(4) decisions to a single *Commissioner*: the validity of this in respect of Reg. 17, Art. 14(3) was confirmed in Case 53/85, *AKZO* v. *Commission* [1986] ECR 1965, [1987] 1 CMLR 231.

very protracted and irreparable damage might occur before it could take a final decision under Regulation 17, Article 3. The power to take interim measures was first established in *Camera Care*,[267] in a striking example of the Court's teleological interpretative technique, and developed in subsequent cases.[268] This case law, and the previous decisions of the Commission taking interim measures, are relevant to the application of Article 8.

Case 792/79 R, *Camera Care* v. *Commission* [1980] ECR 119, [1980] 1 CMLR 334

Camera Care sold and repaired cameras. It complained to the Commission, alleging that it was being denied supplies of Hasselblad cameras by Hasselblad and its distributors who were operating the distribution system in a way which hindered inter-Member State trade in Hasselblad equipment and maintained differential price levels. It asked the Commission to take interim measures to protect its position while the matter was being investigated, but the Commission considered it had no power to do so. Camera Care appealed to the Court of Justice against the Commission's decision refusing interim relief. The Court held that the Commission did have power to take interim measures, for otherwise the power in Article 3 to take final decisions might be 'ineffectual or illusory'. Having established the existence of the power it then turned to when and how it could be exercised.

Court of Justice

19. However, the Commission could not take such measures without having regard to the legitimate interests of the undertaking concerned by them. For this reason it is essential that interim measures be taken only in cases proved to be urgent in order to avoid a situation likely to cause serious and irreparable damage to the party seeking their adoption, or which is intolerable for the public interest. A further requirement is that these measures be of a temporary and con-servatory nature and restricted to what is required in the given situation. When adopting them the Commission is bound to maintain the essential safeguards guaranteed to the parties concerned by Regulation No 17, in particular by Article 19. Finally, the decisions must be made be made in such a form that an action may be brought upon them before the Court of Justice by any party who considers he has been injured.

20. As the President of the Court has indicated, in the context of the ECSC Treaty, in his inter-locutory order of 22 October 1975 in Case 109/75R (*National Carbonising Company*, [1975] ECR 1193), it is in accordance with the key principles of the Community that any interim measures which prove to be necessary should be taken by the Community institution which is given the task of receiving complaints by governments or individuals, of making enquiries and of taking decisions in regard to infringements which are found to exist, whilst the role of the Court of Justice consists in undertaking the legal review of the action taken by the Commission in these matters. In this regard, the rights of those concerned are safeguarded by the fact that if interim measures decided upon by the Commission adversely affect the legitimate interests of any party the person concerned may always obtain the revision of the decision made, by the appropriate judicial recourse, applying if necessary for emergency measures under Article [242] or Article [243] of the EEC Treaty.

---

[267] [1980] ECR 119, [1980] 1 CMLR 334.

[268] See also Cases 228–9/82 R, *Ford Werke AG* v. *Commission* [1982] ECR 3091, [1982] 3 CMLR 673; Case T-44/90, *La Cinq SA* v. *Commission* [1992] ECR II-1; the controversial *IMS* decision, *NDC Health/IMS: Interim Measures* [2002] OJ L59/18, [2002] 4 CMLR 111 was an interim decision, adopted because the Commission considered the competitors refused permission to use the dominant undertaking's copyright might otherwise not survive on the market.

The cases establish that certain conditions must be fulfilled before interim measures are taken:

- There must be a *prima facie* infringement of the competition rules;
- It must be a situation of proven urgency where there would otherwise be serious and irreparable damage to the party seeking the measures or damage which would be intolerable to the public interest; this includes damage such as the complainant suffering a long-term competitive disadvantage and is not limited to situations which are irremediable by the final Commission decision, such as where without the measures the complainant would go out of business;[269]
- The measures must be of a temporary and conservatory nature only and restricted to what is required in the particular situation to preserve the *status quo*; the measures have to accord, like all Community acts, with the principle of proportionality;
- The legitimate rights of the party on which the measures are being imposed must be observed and the 'essential guarantees' provided for by (now) Regulation 1/2003, especially Article 27 on the right to be heard, must be maintained;
- The measures must be in a form which is subject to review by the Court, i.e., in the form of a reasoned decision.

In *Boosey & Hawkes*[270] the complainant undertakings claimed that without interim measures they would be forced to cease trading. The interim measures therefore ordered the dominant undertaking to maintain supplies to them on the terms and conditions on which the parties had previously done business. In *Sealink/B&I*[271] Sealink was ordered to return to its previous published timetable. In *Sea Containers/Stena*[272] the Commission held that there was a *prima facie* case that the shipping company had abused its dominant position as controller of a port by refusing reasonable access to another ferry operator, but refused interim measures on the ground that there was not sufficient urgency. Since the initial application the complainant had been offered and had accepted an offer of access so there was no danger of serious and irreparable harm occurring. The Commission does not take interim measures lightly or often. Perhaps the most notorious case was the interim decision ordering an undertaking to license its copyright in *NDC Health/IMS: Interim Measures*.[273] The decision was suspended by interim measures ordered by the President of the CFI (confirmed by the President of the ECJ) and ultimately withdrawn without a final decision being taken.[274]

E. FINES AND PERIODIC PENALTY PAYMENTS

(i) General

Regulation 1/2003 empowers the Commission to take decisions to impose fines on undertakings and associations of undertakings both for substantive infringements of the competition

---

[269] Case T-44/90, *La Cinq supra* n. 268, paras. 78–83.

[270] *BBI/Boosey & Hawkes* [1987] OJ L286/36, [1988] 4 CMLR 67.

[271] *Sealink/B&I Holyhead: Interim Measures* [1992] 5 CMLR 255, where the decision ordering the interim measures contained the Commission's first explicit statement of the essential facilities doctrine in Community law (see *supra* Chap. 7): as in *Boosey & Hawkes* the case did not go to a final decision.

[272] [1994] OJ L15/8, [1995] 4 CMLR 84.

[273] [2002] OJ L59/18, [2002] 4 CMLR 111.

[274] Case T-184/01 R, and Case C-481/01 P(R), *IMS Health IMS Health v. Commission*, n. 268 *supra*. For the substantive issues in this case see *supra* Chap. 7, 563 ff. For the powers of the Court to order interim relief, see *infra* 1267.

rules (Article 23(2)) and for procedural infringements (Article 23(1)). The Commission may also impose periodic penalty payments, in order to compel undertakings to do what the Commission requires by penalizing defiance (Article 24). Regulation 1/2003 provides for fines and penalties to be levied only on *undertakings*: it does not impose liability on natural persons such as company directors and executives, unlike UK competition law and US antitrust law.[275]

The Commission's multiplicity of roles in the enforcement regime means that the prosecutor fixes the fine. However, Article 229 of the EC Treaty (ex Article 172) provides that regulations may give the ECJ 'unlimited jurisdiction with regard to the penalties provided for in such regulation'. Pursuant to this Regulation 1/2003, Article 31[276] states:

The Court of Justice shall have unlimited jurisdiction to review decisions whereby the Commission has fixed a fine or periodic penalty payment. It may cancel, reduce or increase the fine or periodic penalty payment imposed.

This jurisdiction is dealt with below.[277]

The limitation period for the imposition of penalties is provided for in Regulation 1/2003, Article 25. It is three years in respect of procedural infringements (in connection with requests for information and inspections) and five years in respect of all other infringements. Time runs from the day the infringement was committed or on the day it ended in the case of a repeated or continuous infringement. Under Article 26 the time limit for the enforcement of penalties is five years from the date of the decision.[278]

Note, in looking at past cases and decisions, that the units of account and ECUs in which the fines and penalties were expressed can be taken as equivalent to the sum in Euros. Regulation 17 expressed the monetary amounts of fines and penalties in units of account but these were read as referring to Euros after the introduction of the single currency (having previously become ECUs).[279] Regulation 1/2003 uses turnover percentages rather than objective monetary amounts in setting maximum fines.[280]

---

[275] See *infra* 1285.

[276] The corresponding provision in Reg. 17 was Article 17.

[277] See *infra* 1264.

[278] In Case T-153/04, *Ferriere Nord SpA v. Commission*, 27 September 2006, the Commission had failed to pursue payment of the outstanding balance of one of the fines imposed in the *Welded Steel Mesh cartel* [1989] OJ L260/1, after the decision was finally upheld by the ECJ, Case C-219/95P, *Ferriere Nord v. Commission* [1997] ECR I-4411. The undertaking had written to the Commission twice soon after the judgment asking it to reconsider the amount of the fine because of, *inter alia*, the severe devaluation of the lira. The Commission did not reply until 2004. The ECJ held that the enforcement of the balance was time-barred since 2002, despite the existence of a bank guarantee which could have been called in at any time (the provision concerned was Regulation 2988/74 on limitation periods, now replaced as regards competition proceedings, by Regulation 1/2003, Art. 26).

[279] Pursuant to Article 2(1) of Council Reg. 1103/97 [1997] OJ L162/1 on certain provisions relating to the introduction of the Euro. Previously to that fines were expressed in ECUs (and in the national currency most closely connected to the undertaking concerned as payment could not be made in ECUs). For the problems of expressing fines in ECUs, where the exchange rate with national currency fluctuated, see, e.g., Cases T-305–307, 313–16, 318, 328–9, and 335/94. *Re the PVC Cartel II: Limburgse Vinyl Mij NV and others v. Commission* [1999] 5 CMLR 303 at paras. 1225–35. Prior to 1980 the Community used units of account instead of ECUs. By Council Reg. 3368/80 [1980] OJ L345/1 all references to units of account in Community legal instruments were to read as references to ECUs.

[280] See *infra* 1212.

(ii) Fines for Procedural Infringements

Regulation 1/2003, Article 23(1) states:

The Commission may by decision impose on undertakings and associations of undertakings fines not exceeding 1 per cent of the total turnover in the preceding business year where, intentionally or negligently:

    (a) they supply incorrect or misleading information in response to a request made pursuant to Article 17 or Article 18(2);

    (b) in response to a request made by decision adopted pursuant to Article 17 or Article 18(3), they supply incorrect, incomplete or misleading information or do not supply information within the required time-limit;

    (c) they produce the required books or other records related to the business in incomplete form during inspections under Article 20 or refuse to submit to inspections ordered by a decision adopted pursuant to Article 20(4);

    (d) in response to a question asked in accordance with Article 20(2)(e),
       — they give an incorrect or misleading answer,
       — they fail to rectify within a time-limit set by the Commission an incorrect, incomplete or misleading answer given by a member of staff, or
       — they fail or refuse to provide a complete answer on facts relating to the subject-matter and purpose of an inspection ordered by a decision adopted pursuant to Article 20(4);

    (e) seals affixed in accordance with Article 20(2)(d) by officials or other accompanying persons authorised by the Commission have been broken.

Under this provision the Commission imposes fines for failure to cooperate with its investigations under Regulation 1/2003, Articles 17,[281] 18, and 20 or for supplying incorrect, incomplete, or misleading information. The maximum amount, 1 per cent of turnover, is a large increase on the maximum in Regulation 17, Article 15(1), which was €5,000.[282]

(iii) Periodic Penalty Payments

Periodic penalty payments may be imposed at a daily rate for defiance of the Commission. Regulation 1/2003, Article 24 states:

1. The Commission may, by decision, impose on undertakings or associations of undertakings periodic penalty payments not exceeding 5 per cent of the average daily turnover in the preceding business year per day and calculated from the date appointed by the decision, in order to compel them:

    (a) to put an end to an infringement of Article 81 or Article 82 of the Treaty, in accordance with a decision taken pursuant to Article 7;

    (b) to comply with a decision ordering interim measures taken pursuant to Article 8;

    (c) to comply with a commitment made binding by a decision pursuant to Article 9;

---

[281] The provision which provides for investigations into sectors of the economy and types of agreements: see *infra* 1251.

[282] Not a large amount in 1962, and derisory by 2004. The maximum procedural fines in the new ECMR, Council Reg. 139/2004 [2004] OJ L24/1, Art. 14 are the same as in Reg. 1/2003. This is also true with regard to the maximum amounts of periodic penalties.

(d) to supply complete and correct information which it has requested by decision taken pursuant to Article 17 or Article 18(3);

(e) to submit to an inspection which it has ordered by decision taken pursuant to Article 20(4).

2. Where the undertakings or associations of undertakings have satisfied the obligation which the periodic penalty payment was intended to enforce, the Commission may fix the definitive amount of the periodic penalty payment at a figure lower than that which would arise under the original decision. Article 23(4) shall apply correspondingly.

The maximum amount (5 per cent of average daily turnover) is an even bigger increase from Regulation 17 (Article 16(1) (a maximum of €1000) than that in respect of procedural fines. The penalty payment imposed on *Microsoft* in July 2006 was €280.5 million.[283]

(iv) Fines for Substantive Infringements

a. Broad Discretion Conferred on the Commission by Regulation 1/2003, Article 23(2)

Regulation 1/2003, Article 23(2), formerly Regulation 17, Article 15(2), provides for the imposition of fines for substantive infringements:

2. The Commission may by decision impose fines on undertakings and associations of undertakings where, either intentionally or negligently:

(a) they infringe Article 81 or Article 82 of the Treaty; or

(b) they contravene a decision ordering interim measures under Article 8; or

(c) they fail to comply with a commitment made binding by a decision pursuant to Article 9.

For each undertaking and association of undertakings participating in the infringement, the fine shall not exceed 10 per cent of its total turnover in the preceding business year.[284]

Where the infringement of an association relates to the activities of its members, the fine shall not exceed 10 per cent of the sum of the total turnover of each member active on the market affected by the infringement of the association.

3. In fixing the amount of the fine, regard shall be had both to the gravity and to the duration of the infringement.

4. When a fine is imposed on an association of undertakings taking account of the turnover of its members and the association is not solvent, the association is obliged to call for contributions from its members to cover the amount of the fine. Where such contributions have not been made to the association within a time-limit fixed by the Commission, the Commission may require payment of the fine directly by any of the undertakings whose representatives were members of the decision-making bodies concerned of the association.

After the Commission has required payment under the second subparagraph, where necessary to ensure full payment of the fine, the Commission may require payment of the balance by any of the members of the association which were active on the market on which the infringement occurred.

However, the Commission shall not require payment under the second or the third subparagraph from undertakings which show that they have not implemented the infringing decision of the association and either were not aware of its existence or have actively distanced themselves from it before the Commission started investigating the case.

---

[283] Commission Decision of 12 July 2006, C(2006)4420: see *supra* 1205.

[284] The 'preceding business year' to which the turnover relates means the last full business year of each of the undertakings concerned at the date of adoption of the decision. Cases T-25/95, etc., *Cimenteries CBR SA v. Commission* [2000] ECR II-491, [2000] 5 CMLR 204, para. 5009.

The financial liability of each undertaking in respect of the payment of the fine shall not exceed 10 per cent of its total turnover in the preceding business year.

5. Decisions taken pursuant to paragraphs 1 and 2 shall not be of a criminal law nature.

This crucial provision, which confers upon the Commission its power to punish violations of the competition rules, says four things (apart from the provisions about fining associations of undertakings in Article 23(4)):

- Fines can only be imposed for intentional or negligent infringements;
- The maximum fine is 10 per cent of turnover in the preceding business year[285] (although it does not specify what turnover is to be taken into account);
- In fixing the fine regard is to be had to both the gravity of the infringement and to its duration;
- Fines are not criminal penalties.

b. The Position of Trade Associations

Regulation 1/2003, Article 23 contains new provisions in respect of fines imposed on associations of undertakings. Regulation 17, Article 15 did not provide that the members are jointly and severally liable, and this could prevent collection of fines.[286] Article 23(4) provides that if the association is insolvent it must call upon its members for contributions to the fine. If that does not produce the fine within the time-limit imposed the Commission may fine the members directly (up to 10 per cent of that undertaking's turnover) but only those which were implicated in the infringement.

c. Intentional or Negligent Infringement

Article 23(2) provides that the Commission may impose a fine only where the infringement was intentional or negligent. An undertaking, however, can act only through human agency and the intentions and negligence in issue are in effect those of its human directors and employees. EC competition law has not concerned itself with theories of vicarious liability or become involved in the kind of agonizing over the imputation of the employees' conduct to the company which featured in UK cases under the Restrictive Trade Practices Act.[287] In EC law the undertaking is responsible for the conduct of its directors and employees and undertakings should have in place, and enforce, compliance programmes to prevent infractions of the rules.[288]

'Intentional' means an intention to restrict competition, not an intention to infringe the rules. In *PVC Cartel II* the CFI said:[289]

For an infringement of the competition rules of the Treaty to be regarded as having been committed intentionally, it is not necessary for an undertaking to have been aware that it was infringing those

---

[285] In Case T-33/02, *Britannia Alloys and Chemicals Ltd v. Commission* [2005] ECR II-4973, [2006] 4 CMLR 1047, para. 50, the CFI confirmed that the Commission was correct to use the undertaking's last 'full' business year.

[286] Commission's White Paper on Modernization [1999] OJ C132/1, paras. 127–8, and see Cases T-213/95 and T-18/96, *SCK and FNK v. Commission* [1997] ECR I-1739.

[287] *Director General of Fair Trading v. Pioneer Concrete (UK) (Ltd), Re Ready Mixed Concrete (Supply of) No. 2* [1995] 1 AC 456, [1995] 1 All ER 135.

[288] See W. Wils, 'The Undertaking as Subject of EC Competition Law and the Imputation of Infringements to Natural or Legal Persons' (2000) 25 *ELRev*. 99, 109–11. In Case C-338/00 P, *Volkswagen AG v. Commission* [2004] ECR I-9189, [2004] 4 CMLR 351, paras 94–8, the appellant argued that the Commission and CFI should have identified the persons who acted improperly and were therefore to be treated as responsible for the infringement. The ECJ held that this was unnecessary.

[289] Cases T-305–7, 313–16, 318, 328–9, and 335/94, *Re the PVC Cartel II: Limburgse Vinyl Mij NV and others v. Commission* [1999] 5 CMLR 303, para. 1111; see also Cases 100–103/80, *Musique Diffusion Française SA v. Commission (Pioneer)* [1983] ECR 1825, [1983] 3 CMLR 221, para. 221; Case T-65/89, *BPB Industries and British Gypsum Ltd v. Commission* [1993] ECR-II 389, [1993] 5 CMLR 32, paras. 165–6; Case T-143/89, *Ferriere Nord v. Commission* [1995] ECR II-917, para. 41.

rules; it is sufficient that it could not have been unaware that its conduct was aimed at restricting competition . . .

In *Miller International*[290] the undertaking claimed that it had not intentionally infringed Article 81(1) by prohibiting exports and that its lawyers had not pointed out the infringement. The Court dismissed this:[291]

17. The applicant has requested in the alternative that the fine of 70 000 u.a. should be annulled or reduced.

It has maintained that it did not intentionally commit the infringements of which it is accused and furthermore that those infringements were not serious. It claims that in adopting the clauses prohibiting exports it did not intentionally infringe the prohibitions contained in Article 81[(1)] of the Treaty.

This lack of awareness is said to be demonstrated by the opinion of a legal adviser consulted by the applicant concerning the drafting of its terms and conditions of sale, which opinion, produced as an annex to its reply, does not mention the fact that a clause prohibiting exports might be incompatible with Community law.

18. As is clear from the foregoing as a whole, the clauses in question were adopted or accepted by the applicant and the latter could not have been unaware that they had as their object the restriction of competition between its customers. Consequently, it is of little relevance to establish whether the applicant knew that it was infringing the prohibition contained in Article 81.

In this connection, the opinion of a legal adviser, on which it relies, is not a mitigating factor.

It must thus be held that the acts prohibited by the Treaty were undertaken intentionally and in disregard of the provisions of the Treaty.

Even if the infringement is not characterized as intentional it is likely to be held negligent. The Court has never defined negligence for this purpose but the Commission and the Court expect experienced commercial entities to understand what they are doing. Their attitude to claims of ignorance or inadvertence can be illustrated by *United Brands* and *Sandoz*. In *United Brands* the undertaking claimed that it did not know it was in a dominant position for the purposes of Article 82 and did not know its conduct constituted an abuse. The Court responded:[292]

298. The applicant submits that it did not know that it was in a dominant position, still less that it had abused it, especially as, according to the case-law of the Court to date, only undertakings which were pure monopolies or controlled an overwhelming share of the market have been held to be in a dominant position.

299. UBC is an undertaking which, having engaged for a very long time in international and national trade, has special knowledge of antitrust laws and has already experienced their severity.

300. UBC, by setting up a commercial system combining the prohibition of the sale of bananas while still green, discriminatory prices, deliveries less than the amounts ordered, all of which was to end in strict partitioning of national markets, adopted measures which it knew or ought to have known contravened the prohibition set out in Article [82] of the Treaty.

301. The Commission therefore had good reason to find that UBC's infringements were at the very least negligent.

In *Sandoz* the undertaking, a major pharmaceutical producer, sent invoices to its customers with 'export prohibited' printed on them. The company said it had used these invoices for many

---

[290] Case 19/77, *Miller International Schallplatten GmbH v. Commission* [1978] ECR 131, [1978] 2 CMLR 334.

[291] *Ibid.*

[292] Case 27/76, *United Brands v. Commission* [1978] ECR 207, [1978] 1 CMLR 429, paras. 298–301.

years, since before the inception of the Community, and had simply omitted to amend them. The Commission did not absolve it of liability.

Sandoz [1987] OJ L222/28, [1989] 4 CMLR 628[293]

Commission

34. . . . the invoices in question were adopted by Sandoz PF which could not have been unaware that the export ban had as its object the restriction of competition on trade between member-States. Consequently, it is of little relevance to establish whether or not Sandoz PF knew that it was infringing the prohibition contained in Article [81]. Therefore it can only be concluded that the acts prohibited by that Article were undertaken intentionally. However, even if Sandoz PF's thesis of a 'mere oversight' were to be accepted, this would not exclude its liability and would represent a grave form of negligence.

35. As explained above, Sandoz PF has stated that it was as a result of a 'mere oversight' that the invoice in question bore the words 'export prohibited', and that anyway the company had taken no steps to enforce the prohibition. However, on this point, it must be recalled that the words 'export prohibited' were found on the top right hand corner of the invoice in use until 31 December 1983, and were then moved to the bottom centre of the new invoice introduced from 1 January 1984, after the corporate name was changed. It is precisely because the words in question were moved that an actual recurrence of the 'mere oversight' is scarcely plausible. Indeed, it is rather difficult to imagine that the new invoice form, on which several significant changes were made compared to the earlier one, was examined and checked so superficially by the competent departments of Sandoz PF as to let slip an 'oversight' of such clear and evident commercial and legal importance, particularly to an important subsidiary of a multinational group.

36. As regards the Sandoz PF comment on the removal of the words 'export prohibited' which, at least up to 1970, still appeared on its drug packaging, it must first be stressed that, rather than strengthening the validity of the 'oversight' argument, the fact that the packaging was brought into line with the EEC rules is evidence of another occasion on which Sandoz PF should have brought the invoice into line with such rules. It must also be pointed out that even before 1970 it was clear that Community law did not permit undertakings to prohibit exports between the member-States. Therefore, the fact that Sandoz PF also retained this prohibition until the said date on the individual drugs packagings it distributed, as well as its invoices, is an aggravating and not an extenuating circumstance.

Since both intention and negligence produce liability to fines it may be unnecessary to decide into which category the infringement falls, except that intentional infringements tend to attract heavier fines.[294]

---

[293] Upheld by the ECJ, Case 277/87, *Sandoz Prodotti Farmaceutici SpA v. Commission* [1990] ECR I-45.

[294] It has been pointed out that the type of conduct which attracts fines rarely appears to be 'negligent', see H. de Broca, 'The Commission revises its Guidelines for setting fines in antitrust cases' (2006) 3 *EC Competition Policy Newsletter*, 1. Committing an infringement negligently is an attenuating circumstance under both the 1998 and 2006 Fining Guidelines, see *infra* 1231.

There are rare instances where ignorance has led to non-imposition of a fine[295] and the Commission may in particular consider that an undertaking has not been negligent where it condemns a practice as an infringement of the competition rules for the first time.[296]

d. Development of the Commission's Fining Policy

Regulation 17 contained no detailed provisions about the amount or purpose of fines. Like Regulation 1/2003, it merely gave a maximum amount (in the case of Regulation 17 this was €1 million, or 10 per cent of turnover in the preceding business year if greater),[297] said that gravity and duration should be taken into account, and stated that the fines are not of a criminal nature. To what turnover the 10 per cent figure related was not specified. There was no indication in the Regulation whether the purpose of of the fines was deterrence, punishment, ensuring that the offence does not pay, or some combination of these and perhaps other factors. In its *XIIIth Report on Competition Policy*, however, the Commission said that the purpose was twofold: 'to impose a pecuniary sanction on the undertaking for the infringement and prevent a repetition of the offence, and to make the prohibition in the Treaty more effective'.[298] The Commission's fining policy was developed in its decisional practice over the years (under the supervision of the Court) and set out in a Notice in 1998.[299] The 1998 Notice was replaced by a new one in 2006.[300]

The Commission first imposed a fine in 1969 in the *Quinine Cartel*.[301] The amount was 500,000 units of account. For the next ten years the level of fines was 'relatively light'.[302] Change came in 1979 when the Commission indicated in *Pioneer* that it intended to reinforce the deterrent effect of fines by raising their general level in cases of serious infringements. It fined one culprit over four million units of account.[303] The undertakings appealed and the Court confirmed the legality of the Commission's policy and strategy.

---

[295] See *Bayer Dental* [1990] OJ L351/46, [1992] 4 CMLR 61; *Stainless Steel* [1990] OJ L220/28 and the other cases discussed by L. Gyselen in 'The Commission's Fining Policy in Competition Cases— "Questo è il catalogo"' in P. Slot and A. McDonnell (eds), *Procedure and Enforcement in EC and US Competition Law* (Sweet & Maxwell, 1993), 63–75.

[296] See, e.g., *Vegetable Parchment* [1978] OJ L70/54, [1978] 2 CMLR 334. On the other hand, the arguable novelty of the developments in Article 82 did not save United Brands, (see *supra* 1215) or Hoffmann-La Roche in Case 85/76, *Hoffmann-La Roche v. Commission* [1979] ECR 461, [1979] 3 CMLR 211; nor did it save Tetra Pak in Case C-333/94 P, *Tetra Pak International SA v. Commission* [1996] ECR I-5951, [1997] 4 CMLR 662. The Commission did not, however, impose a fine on Van den Bergh Foods when it held for the first time that freezer exclusivity was contrary to Article 81 and an abuse under Article 82: *Van den Bergh Foods Ltd* [1998] OJ L246/1, [1998] 5 CMLR 530, discussed *supra* Chap. 7, 478 and Chap. 9, 721.

[297] Reg. 17, Art. 15(2) also provided a minimum, €1000.

[298] (Commission, 1983), para 62.

[299] Guidelines on the method of setting fines imposed pursuant to Reg. No. 17, Art. 15(2) and Art. 65(5) of the ECSC treaty [1998] OJ C9/3: see *infra* 1220.

[300] Guidelines on the method of setting fines imposed pursuant to Article 23(2)(a) of Regulation No 1/2003 [2006] OJ C210/2: see *infra* 1228.

[301] [1969] OJ L192/5, [1969] CMLR D241.

[302] According to the Commission in the *XIIIth Report on Competition Policy* (Commission, 1983), para 63.

[303] *Pioneer* [1980] OJ L60/21, [1980] 1 CMLR 457.

Cases 100–103/80, *Musique Diffusion Française SA* v. *Commission (Pioneer)* [1983] ECR 1825, [1983] 3 CMLR 221

Court of Justice

106. It follows that, in assessing the gravity of an infringement for the purpose of fixing the amount of the fine, the Commission must take into consideration not only the particular circumstances of the case but also the context in which the infringement occurs and must ensure that its action has the necessary deterrent effect, especially as regards those types of infringement which are particularly harmful to the attainment of the objectives of the Community.

107. From that point of view, the Commission was right to classify as very serious infringements prohibitions on exports and imports seeking artificially to maintain price differences between the markets of the various member-States. Such prohibitions jeopardize the freedom of intra-Community trade, which is a fundamental principle of the Treaty, and they prevent the attainment of one of its objectives, namely the creation of a single market.

108. It was also open to the Commission to have regard to the fact that practices of this nature, although they were established as being unlawful at the outset of Community competition policy, are still relatively frequent on account of the profit that certain of the undertakings concerned are able to derive from them and, consequently, it was open to the Commission to consider that it was appropriate to raise the level of fines so as to reinforce their deterrent effect.

109. For the same reasons, the fact that the Commission, in the past, imposed fines of a certain level for certain types of infringement does not mean that it is estopped from raising that level within the limits indicated in Regulation 17 if that is necessary to ensure the implementation of Community competition policy. On the contrary, the proper application of the Community competition rules requires that the Commission may at any time adjust the level of fines to the needs of that policy.

. . .

119. Thus the only express reference to the turnover of the undertaking concerns the upper limit of a fine exceeding 1 000 000 units of account. In such a case the limit seeks to prevent fines from being disproportionate in relation to the size of the undertaking and, since only the total turnover can effectively give an approximate indication of that size, the aforementioned percentage must, as the Commission has argued, be understood as referring to the total turnover. It follows that the Commission did not exceed the limit laid down in Article 15 of the Regulation.

120. In assessing the gravity of an infringement regard must be had to a large number of factors, the nature and importance of which vary according to the type of infringement in question and the particular circumstances of the case. Those factors may, depending on the circumstances, include the volume and value of the goods in respect of which the infringement was committed and the size and economic power of the undertaking and, consequently, the influence which the undertaking was able to exert on the market.

121. It follows that, on the one hand, it is permissible, for the purpose of fixing the fine, to have regard both to the total turnover of the undertaking, which gives an indication, albeit approximate and imperfect, of the size of the undertaking and of its economic power, and to the proportion of that turnover accounted for by the goods in respect of which the infringement was committed, which gives an indication of the scale of the infringement. On the other hand, it follows that it is important not to confer on one or the other of those figures an importance disproportionate in relation to the other factors and, consequently, that the fixing of an appropriate fine cannot be the result of a simple calculation based on the total turnover. That is particularly the case where the goods concerned account for only a small part of the figure. It is appropriate for the Court to bear in mind those considerations in its assessment, by virtue of its powers of unlimited jurisdiction, of the gravity of the infringements in question.

This confirmed that the Commission was justified in suddenly raising the level of fines and in using fines to deter other undertakings from infringing. It will be seen from paragraphs 120 and 121 that the Commission must take into account a number of factors, depending on the nature of the infringement and the circumstances of the case. In paragraph 119 the Court said that 'turnover' in Article 15(2) meant the *total* turnover of the undertaking or group, and not just that of the products in respect of which the infringement was committed.[304] On the other hand, the Commission should have regard to the latter turnover when fixing the fine, because it gives an indication of the scale of the infringement.[305] The total turnover means total *worldwide* turnover, not just that in the EU.[306] The Commission explained its policy in the light of its 'vindication' by the *Pioneer* judgment in the *XIIIth Report*:[307]

The Commission has discretion in fixing the size of fines, subject to the general power of judicial review by the Court of Justice. In assessing the fine, the Commission takes into account all relevant facts of the case as to the gravity and duration of the infringement and whether it was deliberate or merely negligent. It also endeavours to observe the principle of proportionality in its fining policy, i.e., to relate the fine to the infringement, the size of the undertaking concerned and its responsibility for the infringement.

The complexity of the factors to be weighed means that the assessment of fines, rather than being a mathematical exercise based on an abstract formula, involves a legal and economic appraisal of each case on the basis of the above principles.

It will be appreciated that this policy gave the Commission a very wide discretion, allowing it to 'individualize' the fine to each infringing undertaking.[308] The Commission increasingly took into account the Community turnover in the product concerned in the infringement and stated the importance of this factor in the *Cement Cartel* press release, where it said 'calculation is normally based on the Community turnover in the product concerned'.[309] In addition it took into account a number of other factors, either in mitigation or as aggravation, such as profits from the infringement in so far as these were calculable,[310] the economic circumstances faced by the undertakings,[311] the degree of cooperation with the Commission,[312] the knowledge and intention of the parties, the nature and gravity of the infringement,[313] the duration of the infringement,[314] the

---

[304] See also Case T-327/94, *SCA Holding v. Commission* [1998] ECR II-549, [1998] 5 CMLR 435, para. 176; Case T-23/99, *LR AF 1998 A/S v. Commission* [2002] ECR II-1705, [2002] 5 CMLR 571, paras. 278–80.

[305] *Ibid.*

[306] The CFI confirmed in Cases T-25/95, etc., *Cimenteries CBR SA v. Commission* [2000] ECR II-491, [2000] 5 CMLR 204, paras. 5022–3, that only total turnover gives an approximate indication of the undertaking's size and influence on the market and that Reg. 17, 15(2) (now Reg. 1/2003 Art. 23(2)) contained no territorial limit, so that the Commission could choose which turnover to take in terms of territory and products in order to determine the fine. See also Case C-289/04 P *Showa Denko v. Commission* [2006] 5 CMLR 840, paras 16–18, and the 2006 Fining Guidelines, para 18, discussed *infra* 1228 ff.

[307] *XIIIth Report on Competition Policy* (Commission, 1983), para 64.

[308] The CFI said in Case T-150/89, *Martinelli v. Commission* [1995] ECR II-1165, para. 69, that the Commission could not be expected to apply a precise mathematical formula to fining calculations. And see also Case 322/81, *Nederlandsche Banden-Industrie Michelin v. Commission* [1983] ECR 3461, [1985] 1 CMLR 282, paras. 17–21.

[309] Press release IP/1108 of 30 Nov. 1994.

[310] See, e.g. *Eurocheque: Helsinki Agreement* [1992] OJ L95/50.

[311] e.g., in *Polypropylene Cartel* [1986] OJ L230/1, [1988] 4 CMLR 347.

[312] *Ibid.*, in regard to ICI.

[313] Art. 15(2), like Reg. 1/2003, Art. 23(2) obliged the Commission to take gravity into account.

[314] Also stipulated in Art. 15(2), now Reg. 1/2003, Art. 15(2).

responsibility of each of the undertakings concerned where they are acting in concert, the actual effect of the infringement, uncertainty about the illegality of the conduct concerned, the adoption of a compliance programme,[315] and the willingness of the infringer to accept undertakings to remedy the situation.

In the *XX1st Competition Policy Report* the Commission said that in future it would continue to move closer to the maximum fine laid down in Regulation 17.[316] It also said that whenever it could ascertain the level of the ill-gotten gains from the infringement the calculation of the fine would have this as its starting point.[317] From the mid-1980s onwards the size of fines increased markedly. In 1992 a fine of 75 million ECUs, approximately 2.5 per cent of its overall turnover, was imposed on Tetra Pak for abuse of a dominant position[318] and forty-one participants in the *Cement Cartel* were fined a total of 248 million ECUs (including one fine of over 32 million ECUs) in 1994.[319] In 1996 the Commission, in pursuance of its desire to obtain hard evidence of the existence of cartels, introduced a Notice offering leniency over fines to cartel participants which informed on it to the Commission.[320]

e. The Commission's 1998 Guidelines on the Method of Setting Fines

The fining policy described above was criticized for its lack of transparency. It was often felt that the Commission plucked figures from the air in what could only be described as a lottery[321] and that the increasingly swingeing fines were based on no discernible methodology. The absence of a proper 'tariff', or to put it in the Commission's words, the rejection of 'a mathematical exercise based on an abstract formula' was contrasted unfavourably with the normal position in most national legal systems in relation to both civil damages and criminal sanctions. In the USA, the federal sentencing guidelines apply to criminal antitrust. The debate about the desirability of more certainty in fining practice involves, *inter alia*, assessing which is the best deterrent, certainty or uncertainty. If undertakings know what infringements will cost them, will they engage in a cost–benefit analysis and, deciding that they will on balance gain or lose, then act accordingly? Will they be deterred only if they face unknown amounts? Such questions are not, of course, unique to competition laws and there is a large literature on deterrence and criminal law and the economics of crime deterrence.[322]

Decisions levying fines can be challenged before the Court. As the Commission has to observe the normal general principles of Community law these decisions can be challenged on

---

[315] For whether these mitigate or aggravate the offence, see *infra* 1226, 1233.

[316] (Commission, 1992) at para 139.

[317] In Cases T-25/95, etc., *Cimenteries CBR SA v. Commission* [2000] ECR II-491,[2000] 5 CMLR 204, paras. 4884–5 the CFI explained that this did not mean that the Commission had taken it upon itself to establish in every case the financial advantage obtained, but merely that it would take it more into account where it could be assessed, albeit not precisely.

[318] *Tetra Pak II* [1992] OJ L/72/1, [1992] 4 CMLR 551, upheld on appeal Case T-83/91, *Tetra Pak Rausing* v. *Commission* [1994] ECR II-755, [1997] 4 CMLR 726 and Case C-333/94 P, *Tetra Pak International SA* v. *Commission* [1996] ECR I-5951, [1997] 4 CMLR 662: the fact that it was the first time that the Commission had held that an undertaking dominant on one market could abuse it by its conduct on the other did not reduce the size of the fine.

[319] Some of these fines were reduced on appeal where the Commission had not proved the length of the infringement it alleged: Cases T-25/95, etc., *Cimenteries CBR SA v. Commission* [2000] ECR II-491, [2000] 5 CMLR 204.

[320] See *infra* 1240.

[321] See I. Van Bael, 'Fining à la Carte: The Lottery of EU Competition Law' [1995] 4 *ECLR* 237.

[322] See W. P. J. Wils, 'EC Competition Fines: To Deter or Not to Deter' [1995] *Yearbook of European Law* 17 and the literature cited there.

grounds, *inter alia*, of lack of adequate reasoning, lack of proportionality, and discrimination[323] (the last is particularly relevant to the different treatment of cartel participants). A good example of the attitude of the CFI to fines is *Tréfilunion* in 1995.[324] There, one of the participants in the *Welded Steel Mesh Cartel*[325] claimed that the reasoning which led to the calculation of its fine was inadequate. The CFI accepted that it should not be necessary for an undertaking to have to bring court proceedings in order to ascertain how the fine was calculated, but still upheld the decision. It also upheld the Commission's decision in *PVC Cartel II*, where some undertakings argued that the decision contained no specific information explaining the level of fines imposed on each of them and that the Commission had failed to specify the objective standards used to assess the liability of the undertakings and their respective importance. The CFI held that in the light of the detailed account in the decision of the factual allegations made against the undertakings the decision did contain sufficient and relevant indications of the factors the Commission had taken into account.[326]

Nevertheless, conscious of the problems surrounding its fining policy the Commission published a Notice in January 1998, the Guidelines on the method of setting fines. The Commission did not thereby surrender its discretion. Rather it set out a methodology which still allowed a very wide margin of discretion. The Notice did not mean that fines could henceforth be precisely calculated with mathematical accuracy and much of it, in particular as regards aggravating and attenuating circumstances, reflected the previous practice of the Commission and the rulings of the Court.

The Guidelines went back to the two criteria stipulated in Regulation 17, gravity and duration, and based the calculation of fines on these. The Guidelines divided the gravity of infringements into 'minor',[327] 'serious'[328] and 'very serious'.[329] The fines for these were in the ranges €1,000 to €1 million, €1 million to €20 million, and above € 20 million respectively. The starting figure was then increased according to the duration of the infringement: short (generally less than a year), no increase; medium (generally one to five years), up to 50 per cent increase; long (generally more than five years), up to 10 per cent per year increase. The gravity plus duration calculation gave the basic amount of the fine, which could then be increased where there were 'aggravating circumstances'[330] or decreased where there were 'attenuating circumstances'.[331]

---

[323] See *infra* 1256 ff.

[324] Case T-148/89, etc., *Tréfilunion v. Commission* [1995] ECR II-1063.

[325] [1989] OJ L260/1, [1991] 4 CMLR 13.

[326] Cases T-305–7, 313–16, 318, 328–9, and 335/94, *Re the PVC Cartel II: Limburgse Vinyl Maatschappij NV and others v. Commission* [1999] ECR II-931 [1999] 5 CMLR 303, para. 1179.

[327] Trade restrictions, usually of a vertical nature, with a limited market impact and affecting only a substantial but relatively limited part of the Community market: 1998 Guidelines, para 1.

[328] Horizontal or vertical restrictions of the same type as 'minor' infringements, but more rigorously applied, with a wider market impact, and with effects in extensive areas of the common market; and some abuses of a dominant position: 1998 Guidelines, para 1.

[329] Horizontal restrictions such as price cartels and market-sharing quotas, or other practices jeopardizing the proper functioning of the single market, such as the partitioning of national markets and clear-cut abuse of a dominant position by undertakings holding a virtual monopoly: 1998 Guidelines, para 1. In Cases T-49/02 and 51/02, *Brasserie Nationale SA and others v. Commission* [2005] ECR II-3033 (the *Luxembourg Brewers* cartel), para. 178, the CFI appeared to consider that all horizontal cartels should be classified as 'very serious'.

[330] Repeated infringements, refusal to cooperate with or obstruction of the Commission, being the leader or instigator, taking retaliatory enforcement measures against other undertakings, a need to increase the penalty in order to exceed the ill-gotten gains (1998 Guidelines, section 2). The ECJ confirmed this in Case C-3/06 P, *Group Danone v. Commission*, 8 February 2007 para. 47.

[331] Playing only a passive role, not implementing the infringing agreements or practices, terminating the infringement as soon as the Commission intervened, the undertaking reasonably doubting that its conduct

The Commission confirmed its freedom to apply different fines to undertakings involved in the same infringing conduct to take into account the 'real impact' of each undertaking's behaviour. This was particularly relevant to cartels. The Commission also stressed the necessity of producing a sufficient deterrent effect[332] and of taking account of an undertaking's capacity to cause damage to others.

Although the Guidelines brought a more systematic approach to the calculation of fines it was still impossible for undertakings to compute their liability exactly. The Notice contained many variables and many matters which were a matter of discretionary assessment by the Commission,[333] and the language of the Notice was imprecise—full of 'might be', 'generally speaking', 'in general', 'particularly'. Above all, the base figure from which the calculation flowed was in the discretion of the Commission. The result of this uncertainty was a flood of appeals to the Community Courts against the calculation of the fines imposed in infringement decisions, particularly in cartel cases.

f. The Application of the 1998 Guidelines

In *Dansk Rørindustri*[334] the ECJ confirmed that the Commission was legally empowered to adopt fining Guidelines and had not exceeded its discretion in so doing. The criteria of gravity and duration used in the Guidelines were those referred to in Article 15(2) of Regulation 17 and the Guidelines were therefore in conformity with the legal framework of penalties set out there. The Commission was not required by Article 15(2) to calculate the fines on the basis of the turnover of the undertakings concerned, although it was permissible to take turnover into account in order to assess the gravity of the infringement. However, disproportionate importance should not be attributed to turnover in comparison with other relevant factors.[335]

In a number of cases the Commission imposed fines calculated in accordance with the principles in the 1998 Guidelines in respect of conduct that took place before they were adopted. In the leading case of *Dansk Rørindustri* the ECJ held that the principles of legitimate expectation and non-retroactivity were not thereby infringed. Echoing the *Musique Diffusion* judgment, it said that the Commission could at any time adjust fining levels in the light of the needs of competition policy.[336] The Commission had wide discretionary powers in the field of competition policy and the changes in fining policy were reasonably foreseeable at the time of the infringements.[337] In considering the principle of non-retroactivity the ECJ referred to the ECHR. It also made the point that although the legal basis of the fines was Article 15(2) rather than the Guidelines, the latter *were* relevant to the issue of retroactivity.

---

constituted an infringement, negligence or lack of intention, cooperation outside the scope of the Leniency Notice (1998 Guidelines, section 3. For the Leniency Notices, see *infra* 1240).

[332] The ECJ recognizes that the imposition of a 'deterrence multiplier' is justified, see e.g. Case C-289/04 P *Showa Denko v. Commission* [2006] 5 CMLR 840 (one of the *Graphite Electrodes Cartel* appeals), paras. 28–39. The deterrent effect means that the fact that an undertaking did not benefit from an infringement cannot preclude the imposition of fines, so the Commission is not required to establish that the undertaking concerned profited from the infringement: Case T-143/89, *Ferriere Nord v. Commission* [1995] ECR II-917; Cases T-25/95 etc., *Cimenteries CBR SA v. Commission* [2000] ECR II-491, [2000] 5 CMLR 204, para. 4881.

[333] See, e.g., the decision to add 20% for aggravating circumstances in *Volkswagen* [1998] OJ L124/60, [1998] 5 CMLR 33.

[334] Cases C-189/02 P, 202/02 P, 208/02 P and 213/02 P, *Dansk Rørindustri A/S and others v. Commission* [2005] ECR I-5425, [2005] 5 CMLR 796, the appeal from the judgments of the CFI in the *Pre-Insulated Pipes Cartel* case.

[335] *Ibid.*, paras. 250–8.

[336] See also Case C-3/06 P, *Group Danone v. Commission*, 8 February 2007, para. 90.

[337] This point is also relevant to the application of the 2006 Guidelines, see *infra* 1234.

Cases C-189/02 P, 202/02 P, 208/02 P and 213/02 P, *Dansk Rørindustri A/S and others* v. *Commission* [2005] ECR I-5425, [2005] 5 CMLR 796[338]

Court of Justice

169. . . . the Court of First Instance correctly observed that the fact that the Commission, in the past, imposed fines of a certain level for certain types of infringement does not mean that it is estopped from raising that level within the limits indicated in Regulation No 17 if that is necessary to ensure the implementation of Community competition policy. On the contrary, the proper application of the Community competition rules requires that the Commission may at any time adjust the level of fines to the needs of that policy (Joined Cases 100/80 to 103/80 *Musique Diffusion française and Others* v *Commission* [1983] ECR 1825, paragraph 109, and *Aristrain* v *Commission*, cited above, paragraph 81).

170. The supervisory task conferred on the Commission by Articles 85(1) and 86 of the EC Treaty (now Article 82 EC) not only includes the duty to investigate and punish individual infringements but also encompasses the duty to pursue a general policy designed to apply, in competition matters, the principles laid down by the Treaty and to guide the conduct of undertakings in the light of those principles (see *Musique Diffusion française and Others* v *Commission*, paragraph 105).

171. As the Court of First Instance appositely observed, traders cannot have a legitimate expectation that an existing situation which is capable of being altered by the Commission in the exercise of its discretionary power will be maintained (Case C-350/88 *Delacre and Others* v *Commission* [1990] ECR I-395, paragraph 33 and the case-law cited).

172. That principle clearly applies in the field of competition policy, which is characterised by a wide discretion on the part of the Commission, in particular as regards the determination of the amount of fines.

173. The Court of First Instance was also correct to infer that undertakings involved in an administrative procedure in which fines may be imposed cannot acquire a legitimate expectation in the fact that the Commission will not exceed the level of fines previously imposed, so that in the present case the applicants could not, in particular, found a legitimate expectation on the level of fines imposed in Commission Decision 94/601/EC of 13 July 1994 relating to a proceeding under Article 85 of the EC Treaty (IV/C/33.833—Cartonboard) (OJ 1994 L 243, p. 1). As the Commission observes, it follows that a legitimate expectation cannot be based on a method of calculating fines either.

. . .

213. The Court of First Instance was also correct to observe, at paragraph 418 of *HFB and Others* v *Commission* and paragraph 274 of *LR AF 1998* v *Commission*, that although the Guidelines do not constitute the legal basis of the contested decision, they determine, generally and abstractly, the method which the Commission has bound itself to use in assessing the fines imposed by the decision and, consequently, ensure legal certainty on the part of the undertakings.

214. Just as the admissibility of an objection of illegality raised against rules of conduct such as the Guidelines is not subject to the requirement that those rules constitute the legal basis of the act alleged to be illegal, the relevance of the Guidelines in the light of the principle of non-retroactivity does not presuppose that the Guidelines form the legal basis for the fines.

215. In that context, it is appropriate to refer to the case-law of the European Court of Human Rights on Article 7(1) of the ECHR, which, moreover, is cited by a number of the applicants (see, in

---

[338] See also Case C-397/03 P, *Archer Daniels Midland Company* v. *Commission* [2006] ECR I-4429, [2006] 5 CMLR 230.

particular, Eur. Court H.R., *S.W.* v *United Kingdom* and *C.R.* v *United Kingdom*, judgments of 22 November 1995, Series A Nos 335-B and 335-C, §§ 34 to 36 and §§ 32 to 34; *Cantoni* v *France*, judgment of 15 November 1996, *Reports of Judgments and Decisions*, 1996-V, §§ 29 to 32, and *Coëme and Others* v *Belgium*, judgment of 22 June 2000, *Reports*, 2000-VII, § 145).

216. It follows from that case-law that the concept of 'law' ('*droit*') for the purposes of Article 7(1) corresponds to 'law' ('*loi*') used in other provisions of the ECHR and encompasses both law of legislative origin and that deriving from case-law.

217. Although that provision, which enshrines in particular the principle that offences and punishments are to be strictly defined by law (*nullum crimen, nulla poena sine lege*), cannot be interpreted as prohibiting the gradual clarification of the rules of criminal liability, it may, according to that case-law, preclude the retroactive application of a new interpretation of a rule establishing an offence.

218. That is particularly true, according to that case-law, of a judicial interpretation which produces a result which was not reasonably foreseeable at the time when the offence was committed, especially in the light of the interpretation put on the provision in the case-law at the material time.

219. It follows from that case-law of the European Court of Human Rights that the scope of the notion of foreseeability depends to a considerable degree on the content of the text in issue, the field it is designed to cover and the number and status of those to whom it is addressed. A law may still satisfy the requirement of foreseeability even if the person concerned has to take appropriate legal advice to assess, to a degree that is reasonable in the circumstances, the consequences which a given action may entail. This is particularly true in relation to persons carrying on a professional activity, who are used to having to proceed with a high degree of caution when pursuing their occupation. They can on this account be expected to take special care in assessing the risks that such an activity entails (see *Cantoni* v *France*, cited above, § 35).

220. Those principles are also consistently reflected in the case-law of the Court to the effect that the obligation on the national court to refer to the content of the directive when interpreting the relevant rules of its national law is limited by the general principles of law which form part of Community law and in particular the principles of legal certainty and non-retroactivity (see Case 80/86 *Kolpinghuis Nijmegen* [1987] ECR 3969, paragraph 13).

221. According to that case-law, such an interpretation cannot lead to the imposition on an individual of an obligation laid down by a directive which has not been transposed or, a fortiori, have the effect of determining or aggravating, on the basis of the decision and in the absence of a law enacted for its implementation, the liability in criminal law of persons who act in contravention of that directive's provisions (see, in particular, *Kolpinghuis Nijmegen*, cited above, paragraph 14, and Case C-168/95 *Arcaro* [1996] ECR I-4705, paragraph 42).

222. Like that case-law on new developments in case-law, a change in an enforcement policy, in this instance the Commission's general competition policy in the matter of fines, especially where it comes about as a result of the adoption of rules of conduct such as the Guidelines, may have an impact from the aspect of the principle of non-retroactivity.

223. Having particular regard to their legal effects and to their general application, as indicated at paragraph 211 of this judgment, such rules of conduct come, in principle, within the principle of 'law' for the purposes of Article 7(1) of the ECHR.

224. As stated at paragraph 219 of this judgment, in order to ensure that the principle of non-retroactivity was observed, it is necessary to ascertain whether the change in question was reasonably foreseeable at the time when the infringements concerned were committed.

225. In that regard, it should be noted that, as a number of the appellants have pointed out, the main innovation in the Guidelines consisted in taking as a starting point for the calculation a basic amount, determined on the basis of brackets laid down for that purpose by the Guidelines;

those brackets reflect the various degrees of gravity of the infringements but, as such, bear no relation to the relevant turnover. The essential feature of that method is thus that fines are determined on a tariff basis, albeit one that is relative and flexible.

226. It is therefore necessary to consider whether that new method of calculating fines, on the assumption that it has the effect of increasing the level of fines imposed, was reasonably foreseeable at the time when the infringements concerned were committed.

227. As already stated at paragraph 169 of this judgment in connection with the pleas alleging breach of the principle of protection of legitimate expectations, it follows from the case-law of the Court that the fact that the Commission, in the past, imposed fines of a certain level for certain types of infringement does not mean that it is estopped from raising that level within the limits indicated in Regulation No 17 if that is necessary to ensure the implementation of Community competition policy. On the contrary, the proper application of the Community competition rules requires that the Commission may at any time adjust the level of fines to the needs of that policy.

228. It follows, as already held at paragraph 173 of this judgment, that undertakings involved in an administrative procedure in which fines may be imposed cannot acquire a legitimate expectation in the fact that the Commission will not exceed the level of fines previously imposed or in a method of calculating the fines.

229. Consequently, the undertakings in question must take account of the possibility that the Commission may decide at any time to raise the level of the fines by reference to that applied in the past.

230. That is true not only where the Commission raises the level of the amount of fines in imposing fines in individual decisions but also if that increase takes effect by the application, in particular cases, of rules of conduct of general application, such as the Guidelines.

231. It must be concluded that, particularly in the light of the case-law cited at paragraph 219 of this judgment, the Guidelines and, in particular, the new method of calculating fines contained therein, on the assumption that this new method had the effect of increasing the level of the fines imposed, were reasonably foreseeable for undertakings such as the appellants at the time when the infringements concerned were committed.

232. Accordingly, in applying the Guidelines in the contested decision to infringements committed before they were adopted, the Commission did not breach the principle of non-retroactivity.

It is beyond the scope of this book to consider in detail the fining practice of the Commission.[339] However, the application of the 1998 Guidelines can be illustrated by the following examples. In *British Sugar*[340] the fines totalled 50.2 million ECUs, including 39.6 million imposed on one undertaking. The case concerned concerted practices on the British sugar market aimed at price coordination between the two producers active there and two merchants. In view of what they were trying to do the infringement was categorized as intentional and 'serious'.[341] British Sugar, with the larger share of the market, was fined 18 million ECUs for gravity and Tate & Lyle ECU 10 million. The merchants, in a position of dependence on the producers, were fined ECU 1.5 millions each. The duration was 'medium' (four years) which resulted in another

[339] See generally, L. Ortiz Blanco, *EC Competition Procedure* (2nd edn., Oxford University Press, 2006), chap.11; C. Kerse and N. Khan, *EC Antitrust Procedure* (5th edn., Sweet & Maxwell, 2005), Chap. 7; D Geradin and D. Henry, 'EC Fining for Competition Law Violations: An Empirical Study of the Commission's Decisional Practice and the Community Courts' Judgments' (2005) 1 *European Competition Journal* 401.

[340] *British Sugar* [1999] OJ L76/1, [1999] 4 CMLR 1316.

[341] *British Sugar* [1999] OJ L76/1, [1999] 4 CMLR 1316, para. 193: while the Commission concluded that the collusion consisted in a 'collaborative strategy of higher pricing' it admitted that there was insufficient evidence to state that prices were jointly fixed.

ECU 7.2 millions for British Sugar, 4 million for Tate & Lyle and 0.5 million each for the merchants. British Sugar's fine was increased by 75 per cent (ECU 18.9 millions) for aggravating circumstances which included being the ringleader and, interestingly, for acting contrary to its own compliance programme, the adoption of which had been taken into account in mitigation when British Sugar's conduct was the subject of a previous Article 82 action.[342] The fact that this infringement overlapped with the earlier one and occurred on the same market also aggravated the offence. Tate & Lyle, on the other hand, was given a reduction of 50 per cent for cooperating with the Commission's investigation.[343]

In the *Pre-Insulated Pipe Cartel*[344] a fine of ECU 70 millions was imposed on one undertaking, ABB, (50 million for gravity and 20 million for duration) for the organization of the cartel 'conceived, approved and directed at a senior level of group management as were the measures to deny and conceal its existence and to continue its operation for nine months after the investigation'.[345] It would have been ECU 100 million had it not been given a 30 per cent reduction under the Leniency Notice for cooperating with the investigation.[346] A fine of ECU 8,900,000 was imposed on another undertaking, Løgstør, which represented a 30 per cent reduction under the Leniency Notice. Løgstør appealed claiming, *inter alia*, that the size of the fine threatened its very survival and that the Commission had failed to take into account its ability to pay the fine. The CFI held that the Commission was not obliged to take an undertaking's poor financial situation into account and pointed out that although the Guidelines stated that account should be taken of the 'real ability to pay in a specific social context', and the fines adjusted accordingly, this is subject to the proviso that it depends on the circumstances.[347] The ECJ upheld this, saying that an obligation to take an undertaking's poor financial situation into account would be tantamount to giving an unjustified competitive advantage to undertakings least well adapted to the market conditions.[348]

In the *Amino Acids (Lysine)Cartel*[349] the Commission imposed large fines on a number of undertakings found to be operating a hard-core cartel in the market for synthetic lysine (the principal amino acid used for nutritional purposes in animal feed). In respect of Archer Daniels Midland (ADM) the fine was €47.3 million. Thus was calculated as starting with a figure of €30 million for gravity, increasing it by 30 per cent for duration, then increasing it by 50 per cent for

---

[342] *Napier Brown-British Sugar* [1988] OJ L284/41, [19990] 4 CMLR 196: see *supra* Chap. 7.

[343] By analogy with the Notice on the non-imposition of fines in cartel cases [1996] OJ C207/4, as the events preceded the publication of that Notice. Tate & Lyle's reduction was increased by the CFI to 60%, Cases T-202/98, T-204/98, and T-207/98, *Tate & Lyle, British Sugar plc and Napier Brown plc v. Commission* [2001] ECR II-2035, [2001] 5 CMLR 859, but the fines were otherwise upheld and confirmed on appeal to the ECJ, Cases C-359/01 P, *British Sugar plc v. Commission*, [2004] ECR I-4933, [2004] 5 CMLR 329.

[344] [1999] OJ L24/1, [1999] 4 CMLR 402.

[345] *Ibid.*, para. 169.

[346] Notice on the non-imposition of fines in cartel cases [1996] OJ C207/4, replaced by [2002] OJ C45/3 and later by [2006] OJ C298/17.

[347] Case T-23/99, *LR AF 1998 A/S v. Commission* [2002] ECR II-1705, [2002] 5 CMLR 571, paras. 308 and 338.

[348] Cases C-189/02 P, 202/02 P, 208/02 P and 213/02 P, *Dansk Rørindustri A/S and others v. Commission* [2005] ECR I-5425, [2005] 5 CMLR 796, para. 327; see also Case C-308/04 P, *SGL Carbon v. Commission*, [2006] 5 CMLR 922 (the appeal from the Commission decision in *Graphite Electrodes* [2002] OJ L100/1) where the undertaking was appealing that the CFI should not have upheld the Commission's refusal to take into account that its ability to pay was significantly reduced by the heavy fines imposed by other competition authorities and by the heavy damages it had had to pay in non-Member States! Unusually, in *Speciality Graphite*, COMP/E-37.667, paras. 557–8, the Commission did make allowance for the fact that it had recently fined SGL for its participation in the Graphite Electrodes cartel. For the provision on this point in the 2006 Guidelines, see *infra* 1232.

[349] [2001] OJ L152/24, [2001] 5 CMLR 322.

aggravating circumstances (ADM had played a leading role). The sum was then reduced by 10 per cent for putting an end to the infringement as soon as a public authority had intervened (i.e. when the FBI searched its US premises) and by a further 10 per cent under Section D of the Leniency Notice. On appeal the CFI held that the correct way for the Commission to apply the Guidelines was to calculate any percentage increases or reductions to reflect aggravating or mitigating circumstances to the *basic* amount set by gravity and duration, not to any increase or reduction already applied. The CFI's recalculation in this case resulted in the fine being reduced to €43,875,000. The CFI was affirmed by the ECJ.[350]

On 24 March 2004 the Commission fined Microsoft €497,196,304 for abusing its dominant position by tying and refusing to supply, thereby infringing Article 82.[351] It was the largest fine ever imposed on a single undertaking. The figure was reached by starting with an initial amount to reflect gravity of €165,732,101, adjusted upwards by a factor of two in order to ensure a sufficient deterrent effect (given Microsoft's 'significant economic capacity') and increased by 50 per cent to take account of duration (five years five months).[352] There were no aggravating or mitigating circumstances. However, although €500 million might seem a large sum of money to most of us, Microsoft had $50 billion cash reserve alone at the time[353] and the fine amounted to nothing like 10 per cent of its worldwide turnover. It is difficult to identify the 'sufficient deterrent effect'. The real problem for Microsoft, of course, was not the *fine* imposed in the decision but the *remedies*—the requirement that it offer versions of Windows without Windows Media Player incorporated and make available interoperability information.[354]

The 1998 Guidelines have been replaced by new Guidelines, which are discussed below. However, they apply only to cases where the statement of objections is notified after their date of publication in the Official Journal, which was 1 September 2006.[355] There are therefore a number of cases in which the fines will still be calculated in accordance with the 1998 Guidelines.[356] In January 2007 the then largest fine ever imposed on a single cartel under the 1998 or 2002 Guidelines was issued in respect of the *Gas Insulated Switchgear* cartel.[357] Siemens was fined €397 million for its 'leadership' role and the total fines on the eleven undertakings involved were €751 million (one company escaped its €215 million fine by a grant of immunity under the 20002 Leniency Notice for revealing the cartel). The Commission had completed its investigation quickly[358] and this meant that the undertakings fell to be fined

---

[350] Case C-397/03 P, *Archer Daniels Midland Company* v. *Commission* [2006] ECR I-4429, [2006] 5 CMLR 230 affirming Case T-224/00, *Archer Daniels Midland Company* v. *Commission* [2003] ECR II-259.

[351] *Microsoft*, Case COMP/C-3/37.792, decision of 24 Mar. 2004, Case T-201/04 *Microsoft* v. *Commission* (appeal pending). For the substantive aspects, see *supra* Chaps. 7 and 10.

[352] *Ibid.*, paras. 1074–80.

[353] See *ibid.*, para. 1076, n. 1342, for Microsoft's financial situation.

[354] See *infra* Chap. 7. and *supra* 1205.

[355] [2006] OJ C210/5.

[356] And appeals from decisions applying the 1998 Guidelines will be coming before the Community Courts for some years.

[357] COMP/38.899, 24 January 2007. But on 21 February 2007 the Commission fined a cartel of lift and escalator suppliers €992 million. 'Between at least 1995 and 2004, these companies rigged bids for procurement contracts, fixed prices and allocated projects to each other, shared markets and exchanged commercially important and confidential information. The effects of this cartel may continue for twenty to fifty years as maintenance is often done by the companies that installed the equipment in the first place; by cartelising the installation, the companies distorted the markets for years to come'; IP/07/209. The Commission was particularly annoyed because the EU institutions in Brussels and Luxembourg were among the victims (perhaps not, in retrospect, a wise move by the cartel).

[358] Two and a half years from the dawn raid to the decision.

under the 1998 Guidelines rather than the more draconian 2006 Guidelines described below. This was, no doubt, greatly to the advantage of the cartelists.[359]

g. The 2006 Fining Guidelines

The Commission adopted new Guidelines on the method of setting fines in June 2006 to remedy some perceived shortcomings in the 1998 methodology, to reflect the Commission's most recent practice, and to take on board recent case law of the Community Courts.[360] The Commission was dissatisfied in particular with the classification of infringements into minor, serious, and very serious; recognized that the lump sum base figure provisions were widely criticized as vague and unsatisfactory; and wished to reinforce its fining policy with some more draconian elements. The 2006 Guidelines follow a similar two-step methodology to the 1998 Guidelines in providing first for a basic amount and secondly for an increase or decrease in the light of 'adjustment factors'—aggravating or attenuating circumstances. Those circumstances are much the same as under the 1998 Guidelines. They are repeat infringements, non-cooperation with the Commission, and being a leader, instigator or coercer on the one hand, and termination upon Commission intervention,[361] negligent infringement, limited involvement, cooperation with the Commission and national authorization of the anti-competitive conduct on the other.

The main features of the 2006 Guidelines are:

- *The basic amount is calculated on a proportion of the value of sales*

   The Commission has abandoned the use of categories of seriousness. Instead, the basic amount of the fine is calculated using the value of the undertaking's sales of goods or services to which the infringement directly or indirectly relates in the relevant geographic area within the EEA.[362] As a general rule the proportion of the value of the sales taken into account will be up to 30%.[363]

---

[359] It is thought that under the 2006 Guidelines the fines could have been four or five times higher (see Global Competition Review, News, 25 January 2007). The cartel concerned bid-rigging and market sharing in the energy market, and the Competition Commissioner described it as 'a cartel which has cheated public utility companies and consumers for more than sixteen years' (IP/07/80). The cartelists had tried to hide their tracks by using encrypted messages and anonymous email addresses. It appears that no undertaking, other than that given immunity, sought leniency.

[360] Guidelines on the method of setting fines imposed pursuant to Article 23(2)(a) of Regulation No. 1/2003 [2006] OJ C210/5; See Press Release, IP/06/857; Hubert de Broca, 'The Commission revises its Guidelines for setting fines in antitrust cases' (2006) 3 *EC Competition Policy Newsletter*, 1; Neelie Kroes, 'Delivering the crackdown: recent developments in the European Commission's campaign against cartels, Speech I Fiesole, 13 October 2006, http://europa.eu/rapid/pressReleasesAction.do?reference=SPEECH/06/595&format=HTML &aged=0&language=EN&guiLanguage=en; W.Wils, 'The European Commission's 2006 Guidelines on Antitrust Fines: A Legal and Economic Analysis' (2007) 30(2) *World Competition* 197.

[361] But note that by para. 29, first indent, of the 2006 Guidelines the 'termination of an infringement as soon as the Commission intervenes' as an attenuating circumstance is now said not to apply to secret agreements or practices such as cartels (otherwise undertakings can carry on a cartel and just desist when found out). The CFI said in Cases T-71/03, T-74/03, T-87/03 and T-91/03, *Tokai Carbon Co Ltd and others v. Commission* [2005] ECR II-10, para. 292 that 'the Commission is under no obligation in the exercise of its discretion ... to reduce a fine for the termination of a manifest infringement, whether that termination occurred before or after its investigation'.

[362] 2006 Guidelines, para. 13. 'Indirectly' encompasses situations such as horizontal price fixing where the price of the product concerned then serves as a basis for the price of lower or higher quality products (para. 13, n.1). In the case of worldwide cartels the Commission may take account of the value of sales in a relevant geographic area wider than the EEA (para. 18, relying on Cases T-236/01, T-239/01, T-244/01 to T-246/01, T-251/01 and T-252/01 *Tokai Carbon Co. Ltd and others v. Commission* [2004] ECR II-1181, [2004] 5 CMLR 1465, paras. 196–204 (*aff'd* by the ECJ on 29 July 2006, Case C-289/04P *Showa Denko v. Commission* [2006] 5 CMLR 840, paras 16–18)); Cases T-71/03, T-74/03, T-87/03 and T-91/03, *Tokai Carbon Co Ltd and others v, Commission* [2005] ECR II-10, para. 186).

[363] *Ibid.*, para. 21. In para. 37 the Commission reserves the right to depart from this limit in a particular case. The *Competition Policy Newsletter* (see *supra* n. 360) says this may be necessary, for instance, where no turnover figures are available at all.

- *The amount determined by the value of sales is multiplied by the number of years of participation in the infringement*[364]

Duration therefore plays a greater role in the determination of the basic amount than it did under the 1998 Guidelines. This provision alone would result in heavier fines than previously.

- *'Entry fees'*

In the case of horizontal price-fixing, market-sharing and output limitation agreements (i.e. cartels) the Commission *will* include as part of the basic amount of the fine a further sum of between 15 per cent and 25 per cent of the value of the sales simply as a punishment for having entered into the arrangement.[365] The purpose of this is to deter cartellists at the outset by making it expensive to participate for even a short time. The Commission *may* impose the entry fee in respect of other infringements too.

- *Repeat offenders heavily penalized*

It is expensive to be a repeat offender. One of the aggravating circumstances is for an undertaking to continue or repeat the same or similar infringements after having been found by the Commission or an NCA to have infringed previously. *Each* subsequent infringement will increase the basic amount of the fine by up to 100 per cent.

It must always be remembered that the final amount of the fine cannot exceed the 10 per cent of turnover in the preceding business year laid down in Regulation 1/2003, Article 23(2).[366]

Guidelines on the Method of Setting Fines Imposed Pursuant to Article 23(2)(A) of Regulation No. 1/2003 [200] OJ C210/2

13. In determining the basic amount of the fine to be imposed, the Commission will take the value of the undertaking's sales of goods or services to which the infringement directly or indirectly . . . relates in the relevant geographic area within the EEA. It will normally take the sales made by the undertaking during the last full business year of its participation in the infringement (hereafter "value of sales").

14. Where the infringement by an association of undertakings relates to the activities of its members, the value of sales will generally correspond to the sum of the value of sales by its members.

15. In determining the value of sales by an undertaking, the Commission will take that undertaking's best available figures.

16. Where the figures made available by an undertaking are incomplete or not reliable, the Commission may determine the value of its sales on the basis of the partial figures it has obtained and/or any other information which it regards as relevant and appropriate.

---

[364] *Ibid.*, para. 24. Less than six months counts as half a year, and six to twelve months counts as a full year.

[365] *Ibid.*, para. 25.

[366] And previously in Regulation 17, Art. 15(2). In the course of the calculation the Commission may exceed the 10 per cent, so long as the final sum imposed on the undertaking is below it. The 10 per cent does not therefore apply to the intermediate calculations: ; Cases C-189/02 P, 202/02 P, 208/02 P and 213/02 P, *Dansk Rørindustri A/S and others v. Commission* [2005] ECR I-5425, [2005] 5 CMLR 796, paras. 277–8.

17. The value of sales will be determined before VAT and other taxes directly related to the sales.

18. Where the geographic scope of an infringement extends beyond the EEA (e.g. worldwide cartels), the relevant sales of the undertakings within the EEA may not properly reflect the weight of each undertaking in the infringement. This may be the case in particular with worldwide market-sharing arrangements.

In such circumstances, in order to reflect both the aggregate size of the relevant sales within the EEA and the relative weight of each undertaking in the infringement, the Commission may assess the total value of the sales of goods or services to which the infringement relates in the relevant geographic area (wider than the EEA), may determine the share of the sales of each undertaking party to the infringement on that market and may apply this share to the aggregate sales within the EEA of the undertakings concerned. The result will be taken as the value of sales for the purpose of setting the basic amount of the fine.

B. Determination of the basic amount of the fine

19. The basic amount of the fine will be related to a proportion of the value of sales, depending on the degree of gravity of the infringement, multiplied by the number of years of infringement.

20. The assessment of gravity will be made on a case-by-case basis for all types of infringement, taking account of all the relevant circumstances of the case.

21. As a general rule, the proportion of the value of sales taken into account will be set at a level of up to 30 % of the value of sales.

22. In order to decide whether the proportion of the value of sales to be considered in a given case should be at the lower end or at the higher end of that scale, the Commission will have regard to a number of factors, such as the nature of the infringement, the combined market share of all the undertakings concerned, the geographic scope of the infringement and whether or not the infringement has been implemented.

23. Horizontal price-fixing, market-sharing and output-limitation agreements ..., which are usually secret, are, by their very nature, among the most harmful restrictions of competition. As a matter of policy, they will be heavily fined. Therefore, the proportion of the value of sales taken into account for such infringements will generally be set at the higher end of the scale.

24. In order to take fully into account the duration of the participation of each undertaking in the infringement, the amount determined on the basis of the value of sales (see points 20 to 23 above) will be multiplied by the number of years of participation in the infringement. Periods of less than six months will be counted as half a year; periods longer than six months but shorter than one year will be counted as a full year.

25. In addition, irrespective of the duration of the undertaking's participation in the infringement, the Commission will include in the basic amount a sum of between 15% and 25% of the value of sales as defined in Section A above in order to deter undertakings from even entering into horizontal price-fixing, market-sharing and output-limitation agreements. The Commission may also apply such an additional amount in the case of other infringements. For the purpose of deciding the proportion of the value of sales to be considered in a given case, the Commission will have regard to a number of factors, in particular those referred in point 22.

26. Where the value of sales by undertakings participating in the infringement is similar but not identical, the Commission may set for each of them an identical basic amount. Moreover, in determining the basic amount of the fine, the Commission will use rounded figures.

2. Adjustments to the basic amount

27. In setting the fine, the Commission may take into account circumstances that result in an increase or decrease in the basic amount as determined in Section 1 above. It will do so on the basis of an overall assessment which takes account of all the relevant circumstances.

A. Aggravating circumstances

28. The basic amount may be increased where the Commission finds that there are aggravating circumstances, such as:

— where an undertaking continues or repeats the same or a similar infringement after the Commission or a national competition authority has made a finding that the undertaking infringed Article 81 or 82: the basic amount will be increased by up to 100 % for each such infringement established;

— refusal to cooperate with or obstruction of the Commission in carrying out its investigations;

— role of leader in, or instigator of, the infringement; the Commission will also pay particular attention to any steps taken to coerce other undertakings to participate in the infringement and/or any retaliatory measures taken against other undertakings with a view to enforcing the practices constituting the infringement.

B. Mitigating circumstances

29. The basic amount may be reduced where the Commission finds that mitigating circumstances exist, such as:

— where the undertaking concerned provides evidence that it terminated the infringement as soon as the Commission intervened: this will not apply to secret agreements or practices (in particular, cartels);

— where the undertaking provides evidence that the infringement has been committed as a result of negligence;

— where the undertaking provides evidence that its involvement in the infringement is substantially limited and thus demonstrates that, during the period in which it was party to the offending agreement, it actually avoided applying it by adopting competitive conduct in the market: the mere fact that an undertaking participated in an infringement for a shorter duration than others will not be regarded as a mitigating circumstance since this will already be reflected in the basic amount;

— where the undertaking concerned has effectively cooperated with the Commission outside the scope of the Leniency Notice and beyond its legal obligation to do so;

— where the anti-competitive conduct of the undertaking has been authorized or encouraged by public authorities or by legislation.

C. Specific increase for deterrence

30. The Commission will pay particular attention to the need to ensure that fines have a sufficiently deterrent effect; to that end, it may increase the fine to be imposed on undertakings which have a particularly large turnover beyond the sales of goods or services to which the infringement relates.

31. The Commission will also take into account the need to increase the fine in order to exceed the amount of gains improperly made as a result of the infringement where it is possible to estimate that amount.

D. Legal maximum

32. The final amount of the fine shall not, in any event, exceed 10 % of the total turnover in the preceding business year of the undertaking or association of undertakings participating in the infringement, as laid down in Article 23(2) of Regulation No 1/2003.

33. Where an infringement by an association of undertakings relates to the activities of its members, the fine shall not exceed 10% of the sum of the total turnover of each member active on the market affected by that infringement.

E. Leniency Notice

34. The Commission will apply the leniency rules in line with the conditions set out in the applicable notice.

F. Ability to pay

35. In exceptional cases, the Commission may, upon request, take account of the undertaking's inability to pay in a specific social and economic context. It will not base any reduction granted for this reason in the fine on the mere finding of an adverse or loss-making financial situation. A reduction could be granted solely on the basis of objective evidence that imposition of the fine as provided for in these Guidelines would irretrievably jeopardise the economic viability of the undertaking concerned and cause its assets to lose all their value.

The Commission adopted the formula of value of sales multiplied by duration formula for the basic amount because it regards this as providing 'an appropriate proxy to reflect the economic importance of the infringement as well as the relative weight of each undertaking in the infringement'.[367] The 'entry fee' and the up to 100 per cent increase for repeat offenders also potentially make cartel participation much more expensive than hitherto. It will be noted that in paragraph 30 the Commission says that it may increase fines on undertakings which have a particularly large turnover beyond the value of sales to which the infringement relates in order to provide sufficient deterrence. This continues the 'deterrence multiplier' practice developed in the application of the 1998 Guidelines and approved by the ECJ. [368] Paragraph 31 says that the Commission may increase the fine in order to exceed the benefits of the infringement where it is possible to estimate them.[369] That provision was also in the 1998 Guidelines but among the 'aggravating factors' rather than under a separate deterrence head.[370] It is argued by economists that, in general, financial penalties should be based on the harm caused rather than the gain obtained,[371] but the practice of the Commission under the 1998 Guidelines did not appear to include any systematic attempt to gauge either the infringers' gains or the victims' losses[372] and it is not the purpose of paragraph 31 to force the Commission to make such an estimate of the

---

[367] 2006 Guidelines, para. 6.

[368] Case C-289/04 P *Showa Denko* v. *Commission* [2006] 5 CMLR 840, paras. 23–9. Note also the Commission's *Methylglucamine Cartel* decision, [2004] OJ L38/18, [2004] 4 CMLR 1591, para. 329 where the fine was increased as a deterrence measure, '[I]n order to ensure that the fine has a sufficient deterrent effect and takes account of the fact that large undertakings have legal and economic knowledge and infrastructures which enable them more easily to recognise that their conduct constitutes an infringement and be aware of the consequences stemming from it under competition law...'.

[369] *Ibid.*, para. 31.

[370] 1998 Guidelines, para. 2, fifth indent. The ECJ approved of raising the fine to exceed the improper gains in Cases C-189/02 P, 202/02 P, 208/02 P and 213/02 P, *Dansk Rørindustri A/S and others* v. *Commission* [2005] ECR I-5425, [2005] 5 CMLR 796, para 294, and see the remarks of the ECJ in Cases 100–103/80, *Musique Diffusion Française SA* v. *Commission (Pioneer)* [1983] ECR 1825, [1983] 3 CMLR 221, set out *supra* 1218.

[371] See W. Wils, 'The Commission's New Method for Calculating Fines in Antitrust Cases' (1998) 23 *ELRev* 252, 259; A. M. Polinsky and S. Shavell, 'Should Liability be Based on the Harm to the Victim or the Gain to the Injurer?' (1994) 10 *Journal of Law, Economics and Organization* 427. If the victims of competition law infringements want compensation for the harm they have suffered they have to bring private damages actions: see *infra* Chap. 15.

[372] 'See C. Veljanovski, 'Penalities for Price Fixers: An Analysis of Fines Imposed on 39 Cartels by the EU Commission' [2006] ECLR 510, and as a *Casenote* on the Case Associates web site, www.casecon.com, June 2006.

gains or suggest that the Commission should systematically try to do so.[373] Nevertheless, deterrence is the major theme of the Commission fining policy, in accordance with the duty identified back in 1983 in *Musique Diffusion*.[374] This encompasses not only specific deterrence (by sanctioning the undertaking concerned) but also general deterrence (deterring other undertakings).[375] The Competition Commissioner considered that the effect of the Guidelines would be to increase the amount of fines by a factor of three.[376] In fact, although the thrust of the 2006 Guidelines is to increase yet again the level of fines, the application of the leniency policy in cartel cases, discussed below, means that many infringers end up paying nothing, and others have greatly decreased fines. [377]

Amongst the aggravating and attenuating circumstances, the points of contention between undertakings and the Commission are likely to continue to be, as before, whether or not an undertaking played a leadership or instigation role[378] and whether or not it was merely 'passive' and therefore within the third indent of the paragraph 29. It will be noted that paragraph 29 does not list as a mitigating factor the adoption of a compliance programme[379] and the Commission's current practice is not to reduce the fine because the infringement was carried out in contravention of the undertaking's compliance programme. In *Nintendo*, where the undertaking had introduced a compliance programme after the infringement the Commission said that 'While the Commission does indeed welcome all steps taken by undertakings to raise awareness amongst their employees of existing competition rules, these initiatives cannot relieve the Commission of its duty to penalise their very serious infringement of competition rules'.[380]

Paragraph 35 of the 2006 Guidelines reflects the case law of the ECJ[381] that the Commission is not *required* to take into account the undertaking's ability to pay the fine, but *may* do so. 'Specific social context', according to the ECJ in *SGL Carbon*[382] interpreting the 1998 Guidelines, means the consequences which payment of a fine could have, in particular, by leading to an increase in

---

[373] According to Hubert de Broca, 'The Commission revises its Guidelines for setting fines in antitrust cases' (2006) 3 *EC Competition Policy Newsletter*, 1, 6.

[374] *Supra* 1218.

[375] 2006 Guidelines, para. 4.

[376] 'These innovations are likely to increase average fines, particularly for long lasting infringements in large markets, where fines could well increase by a factor of three. I think all this will make potential cartelists think twice!' Neelie Kroes, 'Delivering on the crackdown: recent developments in the European Commission's campaign against cartels', Speech at the European Institute 10th Annual Competition Conference, Fiesole, 13 October 2006.

[377] For an analysis of fines in cartel cases between 1998 and 2004, see C. Veljanovski, 'Penalties for Price Fixers: An Analysis of Fines Imposed on 39 Cartels by the EU Commission' [2006] *ECLR* 510.

[378] See, e.g. Case T-15/02, *BASF AG v. Commission*, [2006] ECR II-497 (an appeal from the *Vitamins Cartel* decision, [2003] LOJ 6/1) in which the CFI cancelled the 35 % increase in the basic amount imposed on BASF for being a leader of instigator or leader of the cartel in respect of two vitamins (C and D3) as the Commission had not sufficiently established this. The refusal of leniency under the 1996 Notice on the ground that it was not available to the leader or instigator therefore had to be re-examined too, but the CFI held that BASF still did not qualify.

[379] A compliance programme is a policy put in place by an undertaking to ensure that none of its staff breach the competition rules thereby imposing liability on the undertaking.

[380] [2003] OJ L255/33, [2004] 4 CMLR 421.

[381] See Cases 96–102, 104, 105, 108 and 110/82, *IAZ International Belgium v. Commission* [1983] ECR 3369, [1984] 3 CMLR 276, paras 54–5; Cases C-189/02 P, 202/02 P, 208/02 P and 213/02 P, *Dansk Rørindustri A/S and others v. Commission* [2005] ECR I-5425, [2005] 5 CMLR 796, para. 327; Case C-308/04 P, *SGL Carbon AG v. Commission* [2006] 5 CMLR 923, paras. 105–106.

[382] *Ibid.*, para. 106.

unemployment or deterioration in the economic sectors upstream and downstream of the undertakings concerned. The last sentence of paragraph 35, '... irretrievably jeopardise the economic viability...' sets 'a rather high standard'.[383]

As the 2006 Guidelines apply in cases where a statement of objections is notified after 1 September 2006[384] conduct which took place long before the Guidelines came into effect will be sanctioned in the light of the much harsher 2006 provisions. Such a result does not, according to *Dansk Rørindustri*,[385] infringe the principles of non-retroactivity or legitimate expectation.

h. The Legal Effect of Fining Guidelines

The Fining Guidelines of 1998 and 2006 are 'Notices'. As such they are not binding legislation within Article 249 of the EC Treaty, and are often described as 'soft law'.[386] However, the ECJ has held that by adopting Fining Guidelines the Commission imposes limits on its discretion, departure from which may involve a breach of the principles of equal treatment and legitimate expectation: '... whilst rules of conduct designed to produce external effects, as is the case of the Guidelines, which are aimed at traders, may not be regarded as rules of law which the administration is always bound to observe, they nevertheless form rules of practice from which the administration may not depart in an individual case without giving reasons that are compatible with the principle of equal treatment (see, to that effect, *Dansk Rørindustri and Others* v *Commission*, paragraphs 209 and 210)'.[387] In practice, appeals from Commission decisions imposing fines on cartel participants now often involve detailed arguments about whether the Commission correctly followed the its Guidelines (and the Leniency Notice[388]) more often than they involve arguments about whether or not there was an infringement in the first place.

i. General Principles of Law

In imposing fines, as in all other aspects of competition procedure, the Commission must abide by the general principles of Community law. As well as non-retroactivity and legitimate expectation the Commission must in setting fines particularly heed the principles of proportionality and equal treatment. As far as proportionality is concerned, the ECJ stated in *Musique Diffusion* that the upper limit on fines (10 per cent of turnover) was seeking to prevent fines from being disproportionate in relation to the size of the undertaking,[389] and the Commission recognizes

---

[383] H. de Broca, 'The Commission revises its Guidelines for setting fines in antitrust cases' (2006) *EC Competition Policy Newsletter*, 1, 6.

[384] 2006 Guidelines, para. 38. The fact that the Guidelines say 'a' statement means that these Guidelines will apply where a supplementary statement is notified after 1 September even if the first one was notified before, see H. de Broca, 'The Commission revises its Guidelines for setting fines in antitrust cases' (2006) 3 *EC Competition Policy Newsletter*, 1, 2.

[385] Cases C-189/02 P, 202/02 P, 208/02 P and 213/02 P, *Dansk Rørindustri A/S and others* v. *Commission* [2005] ECR I-5425, [2005] 5 CMLR 796, see *supra* 1223.

[386] See *supra* Chap. 2, 115.

[387] Case C-397/03 P, *Archer Daniels Midland Company* v. *Commission* [2006] ECR I-4429, [2006] 5 CMLR 230, para. 91. In that case the ECJ held that the CFI had erred in law in allowing the Commission to breach the 1998 Guidelines in the way in which it had dealt with the undertaking's turnover, but nevertheless upheld the judgment as the CFI, in an exercise of its unlimited jurisdiction (see *infra* 1264), had ascertained that the fine would not have been different had the Commission taken account of the correct turnover, see Case T-224/00, *Archer Daniels Midland Company* v. *Commission* [2003] ECR II-2597, [2003] 5 CMLR 583.

[388] *Infra* 1240.

[389] Cases 100–103/80, *Musique Diffusion Française SA* v. *Commission (Pioneer)* [1983] ECR 1825, [1983] 3 CMLR 221, paras. 119–20; see Case T-33/02, *Britannia Alloys and Chemicals Ltd* v. *Commission* [2006] 4 CMLR 1046, para. 43.

that in the imposition of fines it must be guided by the principle of proportionality.[390] Equal treatment means that comparable situations must be treated the same way and different situations treated differently, unless there is objective justification. Where a number of undertakings are involved in the same infringement—as in a cartel—the Commission applies weightings to reflect the differing impact of the undertakings' conduct. This may involve grouping the undertakings concerned.[391] The ECJ confirmed in *Dansk Rørindustri* that the Commission does not have to ensure that the final amounts of the fines resulting from its calculations reflect any distinctions between them in terms of their turnover.[392]

Appeals against fines on grounds of breach of the principles of proportionality and equal treatment are common. For example, in *Hoek Loos*[393] the undertaking pointed out the fine imposed on it in the Commission *Industrial Gases Cartel* decision[394] amounted to nearly 50 per cent of the total fines imposed in that case. It claimed that this was out of all proportion to its participation in the infringement or to its market share. The CFI rejected this argument, saying that the final amount of a fine is not, in principle, an appropriate factor in assessing the possible lack of proportionality of the fine as regards the importance of the participants in the cartel. That final amount was set, *inter alia*, on the basis of various factors linked to the individual conduct of the undertaking in question, such as the duration of the infringement, the aggravating or attenuating circumstances, and the degree to which the undertaking cooperated.[395] On the other hand, in *Degussa*[396] the CFI held that the Commission was wrong in applying the same deterrence multiplier to the applicant as to another of the cartelists (Aventis) despite the difference in the size of the two undertakings. It therefore reduced the fine from €118 million to €91,125 million.

j. Non Bis in Idem

The principle of *non bis in idem* (double jeopardy) means that a party cannot be prosecuted, tried, and convicted twice for the same (criminal) behaviour.[397] It is enshrined in Article 4 of Protocol 7 of the ECHR and in Article 50 of the EU Charter of Fundamental Rights[398] and is a fundamental principle of Community law.[399] In respect of competition cases it means that precludes, in competition matters, an undertaking from being found guilty or proceedings being brought against it a second time on the grounds of anti-competitive conduct in respect of which it has been penalized or declared not liable by a previous unappealable decision.[400] Under the system

---

[390] L. Ortiz Blanco, *EC Competition Procedure* (2nd edn., Oxford University Press, 2006), 11.23.

[391] *Ibid.*, 11.31.

[392] *Dansk Rørindustri*, para. 312.

[393] Case T-304/02, *Hoek Loos NV v. Commission*, [2006] ECR II-1887.

[394] [2003] OJ L84/1.

[395] Case T-304/02, para. 85.

[396] Case T-279/02, [2006] ECR II-897.

[397] For the issue of whether competition proceedings are civil or criminal, see *supra* 1176.

[398] See *supra* Chap. 2.

[399] Cases 18 and 35/65, *Gutmann v. Commission of the EAEC* [1966] ECR 149; Commission Green Paper 'On Conflicts of Jurisdiction and the Principle of *ne bis in idem* in Criminal Proceedings' COM(2005) 696 final; M. Wasmeier and N. Thwaites, 'The Development of ne bis in idem into a Transnational Fundamental Right in EU Law: Comments on Recent Developments (2006) 31 *ELRev* 565.

[400] Cases C-238, 244–5, 247, 250, 251–2, and 254/99, *Limburgse Vinyl Maatschappij NV v. Commission* [2002] ECR I-8375, [2003] 4 CMLR 397, para. 59. In that case the ECJ confirmed that the Commission could readopt a decision annulled on procedural grounds without going through all the unimpeached parts of the procedure again.

for the allocation of cases within the ECN several NCAs may investigate in parallel the same matter in respect of the same undertakings.[401] However, no NCA could impose a fine on an undertaking in respect of the same matter in the same market.[402] The question has also arisen in relation to situations where fines have already been imposed outside the EU. The principle here is technically a corollary of *non bis in idem*, as the undertakings are not pleading that the Commission had no right to take the proceedings, but only that it should have taken into account concurrent penalties concerning the same facts. The ECJ held in *Archer Daniels Midland*[403] that the Commission was justified in refusing to take into account when fixing the fine that the undertaking had already been sanctioned in the US for the same cartel, at least where it had not been proved that the actions complained of were identical.[404] In *Showa Denko* the ECJ explained more fully that in applying EC competition law the Commission is protecting specific Community interests, that the objective of deterrence which the Commission is entitled to pursue when setting the fine is to ensure compliance with the EC competition rules, and that consequently 'when assessing the deterrent nature of a fine to be imposed for infringement of those rules, the Commission is not required to take into account any penalties imposed on an undertaking for infringement of the competition rules of non-member States'.[405]

k. Liability for Fines

Difficulties may arise where an undertaking responsible for an infringement of the competition rules does not still exist (or does not still exist in an identical form) at the date of enforcement.[406]

Where one company acquires another by purchasing its shares there will normally be no problem. The purchaser will take over liability as the legal entity remains the same.[407] The difficulty is where a purchaser acquires the business of an infringer and the *assets* are transferred. In *Suiker Unie*[408] a new company took over the assets, rights, and obligations of four cooperatives, which were dissolved. The ECJ held the new company liable for the infringements the cooperatives had committed through their former coordinating body, as the new company had taken over the functions, premises, and personnel of that body. Similarly, in *CRAM v. Rheinzink*[409] the culprit had been dissolved and Rheinzink created in its place. The ECJ held that when 'from an economic point of view' the infringer and its successor are identical the new undertaking would be responsible for the past infringements. This principle is known as the 'economic continuity theory'. However, it normally applies only if the original undertaking has

[401] *Infra* 1371.

[402] L. Ortiz Blanco, *EC Competition Procedure* (2nd edn., Oxford University Press, 2006), 3.16–3.18, and see further W. Wils, 'Ne Bis In Idem in EC Antitrust Enforcement: A Legal and Economic Analysis' [2004] *World Competition–Law and Economics Review* 131 (142).

[403] Case C-397/03 P, *Archer Daniels Midland Company v. Commission* [2006] ECR I-4429, [2006] 5 CMLR 230, paras 46–53.

[404] ADM had paid US$70 million for its involvement in the lysine cartel in the US and Canadian $16 million for its involvement in lysine and citric acid cartels in Canada. Moreover, its executives had been jailed in the US.

[405] Case C-289/04 P, *Showa Denko v. Commission* [2006] 5 CMLR 840, para. 61.

[406] See K. Dykaer-Hansen and K. Høegh, 'Succession of Liability for Competition Law Infringements with Special Reference to Due Diligence and Warranty Claims' [2003] *ECLR* 203.

[407] Although there may be disputes between vendor and purchaser if, e.g., the possibility of competition law infringements was not disclosed at the time of sale and/or if there are questions over what is covered by warranties given on the sale.

[408] Cases 40–8, 50, and 54–6/73, *Re the European Sugar Cartel: Cooperatiëve Verniging 'Suiker Unie' UA v. Commission* [1975] ECR 1663, [1976] 1 CMLR 295.

[409] Cases 29 and 30/83, *Compagnie Royale Asturienne des Mines SA and Rheinzink GmbH v. Commission* [1984] ECR 1679, [1985] 1 CMLR 688.

ceased to exist. An undertaking which remains in existence retains its liability to the exclusion of the successor. In *PVC II*[410] the Commission clearly stated:

In a case where a producer has been subject to reorganization or has divested itself of its PVC activity the essential task is:

(i) to identify the undertaking which committed the infringement;

(ii) to determine whether that undertaking in its essential form is still in existence or whether it has been liquidated. The question of undertaking identity is one to be determined according to Community law and changes in organization under national company laws are not decisive.

It is thus irrelevant that an undertaking may have sold its PVC business to another: the purchaser does not thereby become liable for the participation of the seller in the cartel if the undertaking which committed the infringement continues in existence it remains responsible in spite of the transfer.

On the other hand, where the infringing undertaking itself is absorbed by another producer, its responsibility may follow it and attach to the new or merged entity.

It is not necessary that the acquirer be shown to have carried on or adopted the unlawful conduct as its own. The determining factor is whether there is a functional and economic continuity between the original infringer and the undertaking into which it was merged.[411]

The application of the principle that the 'economic continuity' should be applied only where the infringing undertaking no longer exists is not always straightforward. In *All Weather Sports Benelux BV v. Commission*[412] the Commission held liable an undertaking which had taken over the assets of a company which still existed, although only as a shell for tax purposes. The CFI annulled this finding on the grounds that the Commission had not adequately explained *why* it had fixed liability on the purchaser despite the continued existence of the infringer.

The basic principle was confirmed by the ECJ in *Anic*.[413] Anic had committed infringements of Article 81 (by participating in the polypropylene cartel). It claimed it was no longer liable for the infringement, as although it still legally existed it had sold its entire polypropylene business to another undertaking. The ECJ dismissed Anic's appeal against the judgment of the CFI holding that it was still liable:

In complaining that the Court of First Instance attributed responsibility for the infringement to it although it had transferred its polypropylene business to Monte, Anic is disregarding the principle of personal responsibility and neglecting the decisive factor, identifiable from the case-law of the Court of Justice (see to this effect *Suiker Unie and Others* v. *Commission*, . . . paragraphs 80 and 84), that the 'economic continuity' test can only apply where the legal person responsible for running the undertaking has ceased to exist in law after the infringement has been committed. It also follows that the application of these tests is not contrary in any way to the principle of legal certainty.[414]

In *Aalborg*[415] the economic activities of Aktieselskabet Aalborg Portland-Cement Fabrik (AAPC) had been transferred to Aalborg in 1990. AAPC became a holding company which

---

[410] *PVC Cartel (II)* [1994] OJ L239/14, para. 41. This replaced the previous decision, *PVC* [1989] OJ L74/1, [1990] 4 CMLR 345 (in which the corresponding paragraph was 43) which was annulled by the ECJ for procedural irregularities (see *infra* 1258).

[411] *Ibid.*, para. 41.

[412] Case T-38/92, [1994] ECR II-211, [1995] 4 CMLR 43.

[413] Case C-49/92 P, *Commission* v. *Anic* [1999] ECR I-4125, [2001] 4 CMLR 17.

[414] *Ibid.*, para. 145. See also Case C-279/98 P, *Cascades* v. *Commission* [2000] ECR I-9693, para. 78, and *Zinc Phosphate* [2003] OJ L153/1.

[415] Case C-204/00 P, *Aalborg Portland A/S* v. *Commission* (one of the *Cement Cartel* cases) [2004] ECR I-123, [2005] 4 CMLR 251.

held 50 per cent of the shares in Aalborg. The other 50 per cent were owned by Blue Circle. Aalborg argued that the Commission had, in holding it responsible for AACP's infringements, acted contrary to the case law establishing that 'the economic continuity test can apply only where the legal person responsible for running the undertaking has ceased to exist in law after the infringement has been committed'.[416] The ECJ rejected this claim holding:

357. When the Court of First Instance concluded...that Aalborg and Aktieselskabet Aalborg Portland-Cement Fabrik constituted the same economic entity for the purposes of applying Article [81(1)] of the Treaty, that finding must be taken to mean that the undertaking run by Aalborg from 1990 is the same as that previously run by Aktieselskabet Aalborg Portland-Cement Fabrik...

358. The fact that Aktieselskabet Aalborg Portland-Cement Fabrik still exists as a legal entity does not invalidate that finding and did not therefore in itself constitute a ground for annulling the Cement Decision in respect of Aalborg.

359. In that regard, it is true that in *Commission* v. *Anic* (paragraph 145) the Court held that there can be economic continuity only where the legal person responsible for running the undertaking has ceased to exist in law after the infringement has been committed. However, that case concerned two existing and functioning undertakings one of which had simply transferred part of its activities to the other and where there was no structural link between them. As is apparent from...this judgment, that is not the position in this case.

In this case there was a structural link between the two undertakings so that the *Anic* principle did not apply.

The continued existence of the infringer thus normally precludes the economic continuity test, unless the infringer and the purchaser are structurally related and, perhaps, where there are other exceptional circumstances. The overriding principle, however, is that some undertaking should be held responsible for past infringements whatever transfers and reorganizations have taken place in the meantime.

The way in which liability can be imposed on an 'innocent' company is demonstrated by *British Sugar*. British Sugar's management was replaced soon after the infringing events and the company was later acquired by another. This was irrelevant to the calculation of the fine and the Commission reiterated the principle that the purchaser of a company acquires its liabilities, including that arising from infringements of the competition rules.[417] This applies even where the acquired business was at the time of the infringement a subsidiary whose conduct could be imputed to a parent (see below) which still exists.[418]

As far as parents and subsidiaries are concerned, the position is that parent companies are liable for the infringements of their subsidiaries where they have decisive influence over them.[419] The Commission can generally assume that a wholly-owned subsidiary essentially follows the instructions given to it by its parent company without needing to check whether the parent company has in fact exercised that power.[420] In *Dansk Rørindustri*[421] the ECJ restated the

---

[416] Case C-204/00 P, *Aalborg Portland A/S* v. *Commission* (one of the *Cement Cartel* cases) [2004] ECR I-123, [2005] 4 CMLR 251, para. 347.

[417] *British Sugar* [1999] OJ L76/1, para. 211. And see W. Wils, 'The Undertaking as Subject of EC Competition Law and the Imputation of Infringements to Natural or Legal Persons' (2000) 25 ELRev 99, 114–16.

[418] Cases T-259/02–264/02 and T-271/02, *Raiffeisen Zentralbank Österreich AG* v. *Commission*, 14 December 2006. The reason is that the Commission can always choose whether it fines the original parent or the infringing subsidiary. If it chooses the latter the acquiring undertaking is liable for the fine.

[419] For the single economic entity doctrine, see *supra* Chap. 3.

[420] Case T-354/94, *Stora Kopparbergs Bergslags* v *Commission* [1998] ECR II-2111, para. 80, *aff'd* Case C-286/98 P *Stora Kopparbergs Bergslags* v *Commission* [2000] ECR I-9925, paras. 27–9; Cases T-71/03, T-74/03, T-87/03 and T-91/03, *Tokai Carbon Co. Ltd* v. *Commission* [2005] ECR II-10, para. 60.

[421] Cases C-189/02 P, 202/02 P, 208/02 P and 213/02 P, *Dansk Rørindustri A/S and others* v. *Commission* [2005] ECR I-5425, [2005] 5 CMLR 796; see also Case T-304/02, *Hoek Loos NV* v. *Commission*, [2006] ECR II-1887 para. 117.

basic principle and confirmed the judgment of the CFI where the latter had based liability not simply on the control of a company's share capital but on a number of other factors:

117. In that regard, it is settled case-law that the anti-competitive conduct of an undertaking can be attributed to another undertaking where it has not decided independently upon its own conduct on the market but carried out, in all material respects, the instructions given to it by that other undertaking, having regard in particular to the economic and legal links between them (see, in particular, Case C-294/98 P *Metsä-Serla and Others* v *Commission* [2000] ECR I-10065, paragraph 27).

118. It is true that the mere fact that the share capital of two separate commercial companies is held by the same person or the same family is insufficient, in itself, to establish that those companies are a single economic unit with the result that, under Community competition law, the actions of one company can be attributed to the other and that one can be held liable to pay the fine for the other (see Case C-196/99 P *Aristrain* v *Commission* [2003] ECR I-11005, paragraph 99).

119. However, in the present case the Court of First Instance did not infer the existence of the economic unit constituting the Henss/Isoplus group solely from the fact that the undertakings concerned were controlled from the viewpoint of their share capital by a single person, in this case Mr Henss.

120. It follows from paragraphs 56 to 64 of the judgment in *HFB and Others* v *Commission* that the Court of First Instance reached the conclusion that that economic unit existed on the basis of a series of elements which established that Mr Henss controlled the companies concerned, including, in addition to the fact that he or his wife held, directly or indirectly, all or virtually all the shares, the fact that Mr Henss held key functions within the management boards of those companies and also the fact that he represented the various undertakings at meetings of the directors' club, as indicated at paragraph 20 of this judgment, and that the undertakings were allocated a single quota by the cartel.

Both parents are normally liable for the conduct of a joint venture. In *Avebe*[422] the undertaking claimed that it was not liable for the behaviour of Glucona, its joint venture with Akzo in respect of Glucona's participation in the sodium gluconate cartel, as Akzo had been responsible for sales policy while Avebe was only involved in production and had not been active in managing the Glucona. The CFI held that according to Glucona's structure policy was decided jointly and that Avebe had not proved that, despite that legal situation, only Akzo was aware of and decided on Glucona's unlawful conduct.

l. The Payment and Collection of Fines

The payment of fines is enforceable pursuant to Article 256 (ex Article 192) of the Treaty which provides that enforcement of decisions of the Council or Commission which impose a pecuniary obligation on persons other than States shall be governed by the rules of civil procedure in force in the State in the territory of which it is carried out. Member States must designate a relevant national authority for enforcement purposes.[423] Decisions normally give the undertakings concerned three months in which to pay the fine and specify a bank account into which it is to be paid. They normally state that interest becomes payable after the specified time.[424] A challenge to the decision before the Court does not operate to suspend the payment of the fine but the Commission usually agrees to defer enforcing it pending the outcome of the appeal if the undertakings agree to pay interest on it and provide a bank guarantee. In the case

---

[422] Case T-314/01, *Coöperatieve Verkoop- en Productievereniging van Aardappelmeel en Derivaten Avebe BA*, v. *Commission* [2006] ECR II-3085, paras. 89–97.

[423] The UK has designated the High Court (the Court of Session in Scotland) pursuant to the European Communities (Enforcement of Community Judgments) Order SI 1972/1590. Fines are enforced as if they were judgments of the UK courts.

[424] The payment of interest was approved by the ECJ in Case 107/82, *AEG-Telefunken* v. *Commission* [1983] ECR 3151, [1984] 3 CMLR 325; see also the CFI in Case T-275/94, *Groupement des Cartes Bancaires CB* v. *Commission* [1995] ECR II-216.

of the *TACA* decision[425] one shipping line, which was fined €13,750,000, said that it was in such a parlous financial state that it could not obtain a bank guarantee. It therefore wanted the decision suspended but an appeal to the Court for interim measures[426] failed. It claimed that the refusal amounted to an infringement of its fundamental rights, contrary to Article 6 of the ECHR in that in effect it was deprived of judicial recourse and it brought an action (against the Member States) in the European Court of Human Rights.[427] The Commission did not try to collect the fine while these proceedings were current. In the event the *TACA* decision was annulled before the ECHR case was heard.[428]

m. The Leniency Policy in Cartel Cases

In 1996 the Commission published a Notice commonly called the 'Leniency Notice' (or sometimes the 'Whistleblower's' Notice')[429] stating that in the event of participants in cartels giving information to the Commission and cooperating with it in the investigation they could expect a reduction in the fine which would otherwise be imposed, or even no fine at all.

The Commission has serious problems in detecting cartels and in proving them to the standard required by the Court, particularly where oligopolistic industries are concerned and the participants plead the 'oligopoly defence'.[430] Although it has the inspection powers described above,[431] obtaining direct evidence of a cartel is much easier if some of the participants can be induced to turn 'Queen's evidence'. In *Cartonboard*, in 1994, one of the ringleaders 'spontaneously admitted' the infringement and provided detailed evidence to the Commission.[432] Its fine was reduced by two-thirds to ECU 11.25 million, representing 3 per cent of its turnover in the Community cartonboard market for the relevant year, rather than the 9 per cent suffered by the other ringleaders.[433] The 1996 Notice put such a practice on a systematic footing and offered undertakings involved in cartels certain specific degrees of leniency in return for cooperation at various stages of the investigation. It was an unabashed attempt to encourage 'whistleblowing' by appealing to undertakings' self-interest.

The Notice identified certain stages at which the undertaking could offer information and/or cooperation and stipulated what reduction in the fine could be expected at each stage and the conditions to be fulfilled. There were three levels of cooperation and consequent reduction. It was modelled on (although significantly different from) the US Department of Justice's Corporate Leniency Policy Notice.[434]

---

[425] [1999] OJ L95/1, [1999] 4 CMLR 1415.

[426] See *infra* 1267.

[427] *Senator Lines* v. *European Union*, Application 56672/00.

[428] Cases T-191/98 and T-212/98–214/98, *Atlantic Container Line* v. *Commission* [2003] ECR II-3275, [2005] 4 CMLR 1283.

[429] Commission Notice on the non-imposition or reduction of fines in cartel cases [1996] OJ C204/14.

[430] See *supra* Chap. 11.

[431] See *supra* 1152 ff.

[432] [1994] OJ L243/1, [1994] 5 CMLR 547, para. 171.

[433] See the discussion in the CFI judgments in the appeals from the decision, e.g., Case T-319/94, *Fiskeby Board AB* v. *Commission* [1998] ECR II-1331 paras. 86–104.

[434] 10 Aug. 1993. On 10 August 1994 the Department of Justice adopted an Individual Leniency Policy for individuals who come forward on their own behalf, rather than as part of a corporate confession. An individual given leniency pursuant to this is not charged criminally (in the US, as in the UK under the Enterprise Act 2002, but unlike the position in EC law, individuals can be criminally charged and imprisoned for antitrust offences). For the details of both the Corporate and Individual Leniency Policies, see the DOJ web site, http://www.usdoj.gov/atr/public/guidelines/lenind.htm.

The importance of the Commission's leniency policy in the fight against cartels was described in Chapter 11. The 1996 Notice was very successful. It resulted in more than 80 applications in six years.[435] Nevertheless it was unsatisfactory in several respects.[436] In particular, it provided that the first undertaking to come forward with information about the cartel before the Commission had undertaken an investigation ordered by decision 'will benefit from a reduction of at least 75 per cent of the fine or even from total exemption from the fine that would have been imposed if they had not co-operated'. It did not, however, *guarantee* full immunity (as did the US and Canadian policies[437]). Nor did it provide for the first undertaking to receive written confirmation that it would receive favourable treatment. Further, in order to qualify for the most favourable treatment the first undertaking had to adduce 'decisive evidence of the cartel's existence'.[438] 'Decisive evidence' was an uncertain concept. As far as undertakings which came forward later were concerned, the Commission had a wide discretion as to how they were treated.[439] A candidate for total immunity or for a 'substantial reduction' (50–75 per cent) was eligible only if it had not compelled another enterprise to take part in the cartel or 'acted as an instigator or played a determining role in the illegal activity'. The terms 'instigator' and 'determining role' proved too imprecise to satisfactorily apply, as the Commission itself recognized.[440] The Commission therefore reviewed the Notice and issued a new one in February 2002. The main features of the 2002 Notice[441] were:

• An undertaking was *guaranteed immunity* if it was the first to submit evidence sufficient either for the Commission to mount an Article 20(4) inspection (quite a low level to satisfy) or (if the dawn raid had already occurred) to enable the Commission to find an infringement. In addition the undertaking had to fulfil the conditions set out in paragraph 11 of the Notice (full, continuous and expeditious cooperation with the Commission,[442] end of its involvement in the cartel and no coercion of other undertakings to participate in the infringement);

• The Commission committed itself to giving conditional immunity in writing (conditional because of the undertaking's on-going requirement to cooperate);

• The position of undertakings which approached the Commission later was made clearer and more predictable. The first company which provided evidence of 'significant added value' received a 30–50 per cent reduction in the fine which would otherwise have been imposed, the second 30–20 per cent and subsequent ones up to 20 per cent;

---

[435] *Report on Competition Policy* (Commission, 2006), para. 175.

[436] See the comments by S. Hornsby and J. Hunter, 'New Incentives for "Whistleblowing": Will the EC Commissioners Notice Bear Fruit' [1997] *ECLR* 38.

[437] The US policy only grants immunity. Reductions of fines are dealt with under a plea-bargaining process, see *infra* 1249.

[438] Which the Commission would normally require to be in documentary form.

[439] For those providing the lowest level of co-operation, under Section D of the Notice, the reduction was between 10% and 50%, a huge variation when perhaps hundreds of millions of Euro are in issue.

[440] Commission Memorandum on the Leniency Policy, MEMO/02/23. And see the Commission's application of this provision in *Methylglucamine, supra* Chap. 11 n. 111.

[441] [2002] OJ C45/3. For comments on the Notice, see, e.g. N. Levy and R. O'Donoghue, 'The EU Leniency Programme Comes of Age', [2004] *World Competition- Law and Economics Review* 75–99 (92).

[442] In *Italian Raw Tobacco*, Comp/38.281, [2006] 4 CMLR 1766, on appeal, Case T-11/06 P, *Romana Tabacchi v. Commission* (judgment pending) one undertaking, Deltafina, applied for immunity under the 2002 Leniency Notice, only a few days after its adoption. It was the first undertaking to apply under the 2002 Notice. It was granted conditional immunity but a month later it revealed at a meeting with the other cartelists that it had confessed to the Commission and given it information about the cartel. This was before the Commission had mounted investigations under Regulation 17, Art. 14(3) at the premises of the other undertakings. The

- The reference to 'instigator' and 'determining role' was excised.[443] Immunity could be granted unless the undertaking concerned had positively coerced others.

These improvements did not remove all the problems about the degree of subjective evaluation which was left to the Commission, for example in assessing what 'in the Commission's view' enabled it to act or find an infringement, or what amounted to 'significant added value' in respect of the later undertakings. Nevertheless, the increased certainty it offered, in particular the guaranteed 100 per cent immunity, made it an outstandingly successful tool in the fight against cartels.[444] Guaranteed immunity set the scene for a race to the Commission's door. In less than four years it increased the number of applications to 165–86 for immunity and 79 for a reduction in fines.[445] Throughout 2006 there was a procession of new cartel decisions, in all of which the initial whistle-blower got 100 per cent immunity.[446] The Commission press release on the Synthetic Rubber Cartel on 29 November 2006 boasted that the fines so far imposed in 2006 totalled €1.843 billion, ' a new annual record for the Commission'.[447]

The Commission still considered that the Notice could be improved upon. Following public consultation a new Notice replacing the 2002 one was published in the Official Journal on 8 December 2006 and applied from that day in all cases in which no undertaking had already contacted the Commission in order to claim leniency.[448] The new Notice is consistent with the ECN Model Leniency Programme, published on 29 September 2006 to deal with the problems of divergences between national leniency policies.[449]

The 2006 Notice follows the same format as that of 2002, in that it provides both for guaranteed immunity for the first undertaking to come forward and for reductions for the subsequent applicants.

The main changes in the 2006 Notice are:[450]

- The immunity threshold has been clarified, and in some respects raised. The Notice sets out more explicitly what type of information and evidence applicants need to submit to qualify for immunity; it links the threshold for immunity to what the Commission needs in order to

Commission withdrew the conditional immunity on the grounds that Deltafina had failed to cooperate continuously and expeditiously as such cooperation included refraining from taking any step which could undermine the Commission's ability to investigate and/or find the infringement (para. 432).

[443] For the problems of deciding whether an undertaking is a leader or instigator, see Case T-15/02, *BASF* v. *Commission* [2006] ECR II-497. The concept remains in the 2006 Fining Guidelines, however, see *supra* 1231.

[444] See B. van Barlingen and M. Barennes, 'The European Commission's 2002 Leniency Notice in Practice', *Competition Policy Newsletter* Number 3, Autumn 2005, 6.

[445] *Report on Competition Policy* (Commission, 2006), para. 175.

[446] *Bleaching Chemicals* (hydrogen peroxide and perborate), IP/06/560, 3 May 2006, Degussa given immunity, fines on seven others totalled €388.128 million; *Acrylic Glass* (methacrylates) IP/06/698, 31 May 2006, Degussa given immunity, fines on others totalled €344.5 million (the cartel started with a meeting in a Dublin hotel room in 1999); *Road Bitumen in the Netherlands*, IP/06/1179, 13 September 2006, BP given immunity, fines totalling €266.717 on 14 others; *Synthetic Rubber*, IP/06/1647, 29 November 2006, Bayer given immunity, fines totalling €519 million on five other groups of companies; see also *Copper Fittings*, IP/06/1222, 20 September 2006, Mueller given 100 per cent reduction under the 1996 Notice, fines on 30 others totalled €314.7 million.

[447] IP/06/1647. It can be argued that the EC leniency policy has to be seen in its international context, and that applications for leniency in the EC often follow, or are contemporaneous with, applications for amnesty in other jurisdictions, in particular in the US where cartel participants are liable to criminal penalties: see M. Bloom, *Immunity/Leniency/Financial Incentives/Plea Bargaining* 11th EUI Competition Law and Policy Workshop, 2006.

[448] Except that the provisions on the protection of corporate statements (paras. 31–35, see *infra* 1248) applied to all pending applications as well.

[449] http://ec.europa.eu/comm/competition/ecn/model_leniency_en.pdf ; see *infra* 1279.

[450] For a summary, see the Commission's Press Release, IP/06/1705, 7 December 2006.

carry out a 'targeted inspection'; it clarifies what applicants are and are not required to produce in their initial application; and it states explicitly that applicants need to disclose their participation in the cartel;

• The conditions for immunity and the reduction of fines are made clearer. The Notice introduces flexibility over when applicants should terminate their participation in the cartel; it clarifies what genuine cooperation means in respect of providing information; and it extends the obligation not to destroy, falsify or conceal information to also cover the period when the applicant is 'contemplating making its application'; it states explicitly that applicants for reductions in fines have the same obligation of continuous cooperation with the Commission as immunity applicants.

• A discretionary 'marker system' is introduced whereby an applicant for immunity can reserve its place in the queue to be first by providing only limited information at first;

• A procedure has been devised for protecting the corporate statements made by undertakings applying for leniency from discovery procedures in civil actions for damages.

Commission Notice on Immunity from Fines and Reduction of Fines in Cartel Cases [2006] OJ C298/17

II. Immunity from Fines

A. Requirements to qualify for immunity from fines

(8) The Commission will grant immunity from any fine which would otherwise have been imposed to an undertaking disclosing its participation in an alleged cartel affecting the Community if that undertaking is the first to submit information and evidence which in the Commission's view will enable it to:

(a) carry out a targeted inspection in connection with the alleged cartel . . . ; or

(b) find an infringement of Article 81 EC in connection with the alleged cartel.

(9) For the Commission to be able to carry out a targeted inspection within the meaning of point (8)(a), the undertaking must provide the Commission with the information and evidence listed below, to the extent that this, in the Commission's view, would not jeopardize the inspections:

(a) A corporate statement . . . which includes, in so far as it is known to the applicant at the time of submission:

— A detailed description of the alleged cartel arrangement, including for instance its aims, activities and functioning; the product or service concerned, the geographic scope, the duration of and the estimated market volumes affected by the alleged cartel; the specific dates, locations, content of and participants in alleged cartel contacts, and all relevant explanations in connection with the pieces of evidence provided in support of the application.

— The name and address of the legal entity submitting the immunity application as well as the names and addresses of all the other undertakings that participate(d) in the alleged cartel;

— The names, positions, office locations and, where necessary, home addresses of all individuals who, to the applicant's knowledge, are or have been involved in the alleged cartel, including those individuals which have been involved on the applicant's behalf;

— Information on which other competition authorities, inside or outside the EU, have been approached or are intended to be approached in relation to the alleged cartel; and

(b) Other evidence relating to the alleged cartel in possession of the applicant or available to it at the time of the submission, including in particular any evidence contemporaneous to the infringement.

(10) Immunity pursuant to point (8)(a) will not be granted if, at the time of the submission, the Commission had already sufficient evidence to adopt a decision to carry out an inspection in connection with the alleged cartel or had already carried out such an inspection.

(11) Immunity pursuant to point (8)(b) will only be granted on the cumulative conditions that the Commission did not have, at the time of the submission, sufficient evidence to find an infringement of Article 81 EC in connection with the alleged cartel and that no undertaking had been granted conditional immunity from fines under point (8)(a) in connection with the alleged cartel. In order to qualify, an undertaking must be the first to provide contemporaneous, incriminating evidence of the alleged cartel as well as a corporate statement containing the kind of information specified in point (9)(a), which would enable the Commission to find an infringement of Article 81 EC.

(12) In addition to the conditions set out in points (8)(a), (9) and (10) or in points (8)(b) and 11, all the following conditions must be met in any case to qualify for any immunity from a fine:

(a) The undertaking cooperates genuinely, fully, on a continuous basis and expeditiously from the time it submits its application throughout the Commission's administrative procedure. This includes:

— providing the Commission promptly with all relevant information and evidence relating to the alleged cartel that comes into its possession or is available to it;

— remaining at the Commission's disposal to answer promptly to any request that may contribute to the establishment of the facts;

— making current (and, if possible, former) employees and directors available for interviews with the Commission;

— not destroying, falsifying or concealing relevant information or evidence relating to the alleged cartel; and

— not disclosing the fact or any of the content of its application before the Commission has issued a statement of objections in the case, unless otherwise agreed;

(b) The undertaking ended its involvement in the alleged cartel immediately following its application, except for what would, in the Commission's view, be reasonably necessary to preserve the integrity of the inspections;

(c) When contemplating making its application to the Commission, the undertaking must not have destroyed, falsified or concealed evidence of the alleged cartel nor disclosed the fact or any of the content of its contemplated application, except to other competition authorities.

(13) An undertaking which took steps to coerce other undertakings to join the cartel or to remain in it is not eligible for immunity from fines. It may still qualify for a reduction of fines if it fulfils the relevant requirements and meets all the conditions therefor.

It will be seen from the above that the threshold for immunity (para. 8) is information and evidence which enables the Commission to carry out a targeted inspection or to find an Article 81 infringement. 'Targeted' inspection is a new concept in the 2006 Notice and means that the Commission is able to carry out a more focussed Article 20 inspection with precise 'insider' information 'as to, for instance, what to look for and where in terms of evidence'.[451] This

---

[451] 'Competition: revised Leniency Notice—frequently asked questions', Commission MEMO/06/469, 7 December 2006, available at http://europa.eu/rapid/pressReleasesAction.do?reference=MEMO/06/469& format=HTML&aged=0&language=EN&guiLanguage=en. The quality of the applicant's submission is judged *ex ante*, and not in the light of what actually happens at the inspection.

appears to be a higher threshold than that under the 2002 Notice (which was simply that it enabled the Commission to adopt a decision to carry out 'an investigation' under Regulation 17, Article 14(3)) and may diverge from the requirements in other jurisdictions so that, possibly, evidence which could secure immunity in the US might not do so in the EU. The greatest problem for undertakings contemplating immunity applications is still that at the time of the submission the Commission must not already have sufficient evidence to carry out the inspection or find an infringement, and the undertaking has to be the first participant to provide it. So there is no immunity if the Commission has already gathered the necessary evidence, or if the undertaking has not got to the Commission first. The threshold for evidence required under paragraph 8(a) is lower than that under 8(b), to encourage undertakings to come forward early.

Paragraph 12 sets out more fully than the 2002 Notice (but in accordance with the case law) exactly what is involved in the required on-going cooperation. The third indent (making employees and directors available for interview with the Commission) is a reference to Regulation 1/2003, Article 19.[452] The Commission recognises that these individuals may not be keen on being interviewed, in the light of the criminal proceedings for cartel participation under the laws of some of the Member States,[453] but has said that the provisions in Regulation 1/2003, Article 12 on the exchange of information within the ECN[454] should be a sufficient safeguard for them.[455] The information the undertaking has to provide in its corporate statement—the confession which the leniency applicant has to make to the Commission—now has to include, where necessary and as far as the applicant knows them, the home addresses of implicated individuals. This reflects the powers of the Commission under Regulation 1/2003, Article 21, to carry out inspections at private premises.[456]

The 2006 Notice introduces a 'marker' system by which an undertaking may reserve its place in the queue for immunity (but not for fine reduction) by making an application which gives limited information. It is then given a period of time (set at the Commission's discretion[457]) to 'perfect' the application the additional evidence required to reach the immunity threshold

Commission Notice on Immunity from Fines and Reduction of Fines in Cartel Cases [2006] OJ C298/17

II. Immunity from Fines

(15) The Commission services may grant a marker protecting an immunity applicant's place in the queue for a period to be specified on a case-by-case basis in order to allow for the gathering of the necessary information and evidence. To be eligible to secure a marker, the applicant must provide the Commission with information concerning its name and address, the parties to the alleged

---

[452] See *supra* 1172.

[453] See *infra* 1285.

[454] See the discussion of Article 12, *infra* 1274.

[455] 'Competition: revised Leniency Notice—frequently asked questions', Commission MEMO/06/469. For the problems of the exchange of information within the ECN under Regulation 1/2003, Art. 12, see *infra* 1274 and A. Andreangeli, 'The Impact of the Modernisation Regulation on the Guarantees of Due Process in Competition Proceedings' (2006) 31 *ELRev* 342.

[456] See *supra* 1171.

[457] In 'Competition: revised Leniency Notice—frequently asked questions', Commission MEMO/06/469 the Commission expressly refrained from giving any indication about the length of time—' It 'will need to be decided based on the circumstances of each case'.

cartel, the affected products(s) and territory(-ies), the estimated duration of the alleged cartel and the nature of the cartel conduct. The applicant should also inform the Commission on other past or possible future leniency applications to other authorities in relation to the alleged cartel and justify its request for a marker. Where a marker is granted, the Commission services determine the period within which the applicant has to perfect the marker by submitting the information and evidence required to meet the relevant threshold for immunity. Undertakings which have been granted a marker cannot perfect it by making a formal application in hypothetical terms. If the applicant perfects the marker within the period set by the Commission services, the information and evidence provided will be deemed to have been submitted on the date when the marker was granted.

(16) An undertaking making a formal immunity application to the Commission must:

(a) provide the Commission with all information and evidence relating to the alleged cartel available to it, as specified in points (8) and (9), including corporate statements; or

(b) initially present this information and evidence in hypothetical terms, in which case the undertaking must present a detailed descriptive list of the evidence it proposes to disclose at a later agreed date. This list should accurately reflect the nature and content of the evidence, whilst safeguarding the hypothetical nature of its disclosure. Copies of documents, from which sensitive parts have been removed, may be used to illustrate the nature and content of the evidence. The name of the applying undertaking and of other undertakings involved in the alleged cartel need not be disclosed until the evidence described in its application is submitted. However, the product or service concerned by the alleged cartel, the geographic scope of the alleged cartel and the estimated duration must be clearly identified.

It will be noticed from the above that it is still possible to make a formal application in 'hypothetical terms' but a marker cannot be perfected by a hypothetical application. The difference between a marker and a formal application in hypothetical terms has been explained by the Commission as follows:[458]

A marker and a hypothetical application cannot be combined due to their different purposes and features. The hypothetical application is available to allow companies to ascertain whether the evidence in their possession would meet the immunity threshold before disclosing their identity or the infringement. In a hypothetical application, the company is supposed to actually show the evidence liable to meet the relevant immunity threshold, although it can be done by means of edited copies with the data that could identify the company and the cartel at that stage deleted.

In contrast, a marker is granted to protect the place in the queue of an applicant which has not yet gathered the evidence necessary to formalise an immunity application. In order to protect the place in the queue without obtaining the relevant evidence in exchange, the Commission must be in a position to ascertain whether it already has a previous immunity application for the same cartel and ensure that the company is seriously engaged to provide the evidence. Therefore, in order to obtain a marker, a company is expected to provide certain data listed in the Notice, which include the identity of the applicant and some details on the cartel, but not the rest of the evidence required to meet the immunity threshold. This can be submitted later within a specified timeframe.

[458] 'Competition: revised Leniency Notice—frequently asked questions', Commission MEMO/06/469. Hypothetical applications, which were introduced by the 2002 Notice, were often popularly referred to as 'markers', although this was misleading, see B. van Barlingen, 'The European Commission's 2002 Leniency Notice after one year of operation', *Competition Policy Newsletter* Number 2, Summer 2003, 16, 18 and Ortiz Blanco, *EC Competition Procedure* (2nd edn., Oxford University Press, 2006), 6.18. The 2006 Notice makes it clear that putting down a marker and making a hypothetical application are different things.

Undertakings which do not meet the criteria for immunity can still get a reduction of the fine. How much reduction depends on their position in the queue: the first gets 30–50 per cent, the second 20–30 per cent and the subsequent ones up to 20 per cent. They are required to produce information of 'significant added value' and comply with the same cooperation stipulations as are imposed on immunity applicants by paragraph 12. Obviously, the further down the queue an undertaking is, the more difficult it is to produce information of 'significant added value' to the Commission. There is no 'marker' system in respect of reductions.

Commission Notice on Immunity from Fines and Reduction of Fines in Cartel Cases [2006] OJ C298/17

III. Reduction of a Fine

A. Requirements to qualify for reduction of a fine

(23) Undertakings disclosing their participation in an alleged cartel affecting the Community that do not meet the conditions under section II above may be eligible to benefit from a reduction of any fine that would otherwise have been imposed.

(24) In order to qualify, an undertaking must provide the Commission with evidence of the alleged infringement which represents significant added value with respect to the evidence already in the Commission's possession and must meet the cumulative conditions set out in points 12(a) to 12(c) above.

(25) The concept of 'added value' refers to the extent to which the evidence provided strengthens, by its very nature and/or its level of detail, the Commission's ability to prove the alleged cartel. In this assessment, the Commission will generally consider written evidence originating from the period of time to which the facts pertain to have a greater value than evidence subsequently established. Incriminating evidence directly relevant to the facts in question will generally be considered to have a greater value than that with only indirect relevance. Similarly, the degree of corroboration from other sources required for the evidence submitted to be relied upon against undertakings involved in the case will have an impact on the value of that evidence, so that compelling evidence will be attributed a greater value than evidence such as statements which require corroboration if contested.

(26) The Commission will determine in any final decision adopted at the end of the administrative procedure the level of reduction an undertaking will benefit from, relative to the fine which would otherwise be imposed. For the:
— first undertaking to provide significant added value: a reduction of 30–50%,
— second undertaking to provide significant added value: a reduction of 20–30%,
— subsequent undertakings that provide significant added value: a reduction of up to 20%.

In order to determine the level of reduction within each of these bands, the Commission will take into account the time at which the evidence fulfilling the condition in point (24) was submitted and the extent to which it represents added value.

If the applicant for the reduction of a fine is the first to submit compelling evidence in the sense of point (25) which the Commission uses to establish additional facts increasing the gravity or the duration of the infringement, the Commission will not take such additional facts into account when setting any fine to be imposed on the undertaking which provided this evidence.

As the Commission points out in the Notice[459] nothing in the leniency programme can protect an undertaking in a civil action brought by injured third parties.[460] This is an important consideration for undertakings thinking of baring their souls to the Commission, especially as plaintiffs can rely on the Commission decisions before national courts in the EU.[461] It is possible that an increase in private damages actions in national courts may therefore serve in time as a disincentive to undertakings to take advantage of the leniency programme. The Commission is keen to encourage claims for damages in national courts against cartel participants,[462] but at the same time does not want private litigation to discourage leniency applicants. There is particular concern that leniency applicants should not be deterred by the fear that the corporate statements they make to the Commission[463] could be accessible to plaintiffs in later civil proceedings. Corporate statements become part of the Commission's file, access to which has to be made available. However, in jurisdictions with generous discovery procedures, plaintiffs may try to use discovery to force access to corporate statements and this has happened in a number of cases in the US courts.[464] In view of this problem the Commission started to allow leniency applicants to make oral corporate statements[465] of which only the Commission would retain a transcript. The 2006 now contains provisions which formalize this procedure. The Notice provides that a leniency applicant may make oral corporate statements at the Commission's premises which the Commission will record and transcribe, and which the applicant must then listen to and check.[466] The idea is that if the transcript is part of the Commission's file, and access limited only to addressees of a statement of objections in the same case[467] under strict conditions,[468] and the applicant itself does not retain a copy of the statement, third parties will not be able to use discovery procedures to obtain it. How far this will be a complete protection is uncertain.[469]

---

[459] Para. 31.

[460] For example, Aventis, given immunity in *Vitamins* was subsequently sued for compensation along with its fellow conspirators. See *infra* Chap. 15 for actions in national courts.

[461] See *infra* Chap. 15.

[462] See the Commission Green Paper on Damages Actions for Breach of EC Antitrust Rules, 19 December 2005 COM(2005) 672 final, *infra* Chap. 15, The Commission announced on 3 January 2007 that it was preparing a follow-up White Paper.

[463] *Supra* 1245.

[464] See *In re Vitamins Antitrust Litigation*, 217 F.R.D 229 (DDC 2002); *In re Methionine Antitrust Litigation*, 221 F.R.D. 1 (N.D.Cal.2002); *Intel Corp. v. Advanced Micro Device Inc.*, 542 U.S, S.Ct. 2466(2004), (the Commission intervened in these cases as *amicus curiae* to argue against discovery); K. Nordlander, 'Discovering Discovery—US Discovery of EC Leniency Statements' [2004] *ECLR* 646; M. Reynolds and D. Anderson, 'Immunity and Leniency in EU Cartel Cases: Current Issues' [2006] *ECLR* 82; M. Bloom *Immunity/Leniency/Financial Incentives/Plea Bargaining* 11th EUI Competition Law and Policy Workshop, 2006; Ortiz Blanco, *EC Competition Procedure* (Oxford University Press, 2006) 6.19; and see further *infra* Chaps 15 and 16.

[465] In the *Citric Acid Cartel* [2001] OJ L239/18 one undertaking for the first time obtained a 90 per cent reduction on the basis of an oral statement. In Cases T-236, 239, 244–246/01, *Tokai Carbon v. Commission* [2004] ECR II-1181, [2004] 5 CMLR 1465 and Case T-15/02, *BASF v. Commission*, [2006] ECR II-497, the CFI held that (under the 1996 Notice) statements could be made to the Commission orally.

[466] 2006 Notice, para. 32.

[467] Because of the rights of the defence: see Commission Notice on the rules for access to the Commission file [2005] OJ C325/7 and the discussion *supra* 1190 ff.

[468] The other parties and their lawyers may not make any copy by any mechanical or electronic means and may use the information only 'for the purpose of judicial or administrative proceedings for the application of Community competition rules at issue in the related administrative proceedings' under pain of doing otherwise being counted as lack of cooperation under the Notice, and of having their fine increased (in the case of undertakings) and of being reported to their professional body (in the case of external lawyers), 2006 Notice, para. 34.

[469] See C. S. Kerse and N. Khan, *EC Antitrust Procedure* (5th edn., Oxford University Press, 2005), 7-064, who point out that the fact that it is the Commission rather than the leniency applicant who creates it 'does not

The 2006 Notice does *not* contain a provision for what is known as 'Amnesty Plus' (or 'Leniency Plus'). This is a system by which an applicant for leniency in respect of one cartel is further rewarded if it reveals another cartel in the course of the proceedings. The argument for this is that undertakings which participate in cartels in one product or geographic market are likely to participate in others.[470] The UK's NCA, the Office of Fair Trading, operates an amnesty plus system,[471] as does the US. During the public consultation on the adoption of the 2006 Notice some respondents urged the Commission to put in the necessary provisions, but to no avail.[472]

Further, the Commission has not adopted a 'plea-bargaining' (or 'direct settlement') system, by which a cartel participant could reach a settlement with the Commission by pleading 'guilty' to an infringement and receiving immunity or a reduced fine without the Commission going through the long and detailed enforcement procedure leading to a fully reasoned decision. This is despite the Competition Commissioner seeming, in 2005, to favour the idea.[473] In the US plea-bargaining is the process by which undertakings subsequent to the one granted immunity receive reductions in the fine in return for cooperation, but plea-bargaining is not generally a feature of European criminal legal systems, whereas it is in the US. However, in March 2007 the Commissioner suggested in a speech that the direct settlement idea was being actively pursued by the Commission.[474]

The operation of the Commission's leniency policy has been complicated by the decentralized enforcement system. Regulation 1/2003 did not introduce a 'one-stop shop' for leniency applicants. This aspect of leniency is dealt with below in the context of the workings of the ECN.[475] It should be noted here, however, that some Member States do not (yet) have leniency policies. Leniency policies are sometimes viewed with distaste. Immunity enables wrong-doers to literally 'get away with it' in return for delivering their co-conspirators to the competition authorities,[476] and all idea of trying to recover the ill-gotten gains by a carefully formulated

---

necessarily remove the document from the scope of disclosure procedures. In England and Wales, for example, the duty of disclosure applies to all documents which are or have been in a party's "control", which is defined as including documents which a party "has or has had a right to inspect", a concept which arguably extends to the transcript of an oral statement which has been approved as accurate by the leniency applicant' (at n. 26). Margaret Bloom has argued that the concept of access to the file for the purposes of 'judicial or administrative proceedings for the application of the Community competition rules' may not be enough to exclude private damages actions, see *supra* n. 447.

[470] As any glance at the undertakings involved in EC cartel shows.

[471] Set out in OFT Guideline 423 *Guidance as to the appropriate amount of a penalty*, paras. 3.16–3.17.

[472] e.g., the solicitors' firm Clifford Chance said that it was 'surprising and disappointing' that the Commission was not proposing this. See 'Public Consultation on amendment of the Leniency Notice—comments received (October 2006), http://ec.europa.eu/comm/competition/cartels/legislation/leniency_consultation.html. See also D. McElwee, 'Should the European Commission adopt 'Amnesty Plus' in its Fight Against Hard-Core Cartels?' [2004] *ECLR* 558.

[473] Neelie Kroes, 'The First Hundred Days', Speech in Brussels, 7 April 2005, http://europa.eu/rapid/pressReleasesAction.do?reference=SPEECH/05/205&format=HTML&aged=0&language=EN&guiLanguage=en. See also her speech of 13 October 2006 in Fiesole 'Delivering on the crackdown: recent developments in the European Commission's campaign against cartels', http://europa.eu/rapid/pressReleasesAction.do?reference=SPEECH/06/595&format=HTML&aged=0&language=EN&guiLanguage=en.

[474] Neelie Kroes, 'Reinforcing the fight against cartels and developing private antitrust damage actions: two tools for a more competitive Europe', sppech at the Commission/IBA Joint Conference on EC Competition Policy, Brussels, 8 March 2007, available at http://europa.eu/rapid/pressReleasesAction.do?reference=SPEECH/07/128&format=HTML&aged=0&language=EN&guiLanguage=en .

[475] *Infra* 1276.

[476] In the US this can also entail delivering the individual directors and executives of the co-conspirators to the loving embrace of the US federal justice system. The UK also has criminal liability for individuals. Jurisdictions where criminal liability attaches to individuals also have to have leniency programmes for individuals. See further *infra* 1285.

fining policy flies out of the window.[477] It will be recollected from above[478] that under the 2006 Fining Guidelines repeat offenders are heavily punished for their recidivism[479] but under the EC system recidivists are not barred from either immunity or fine reduction and can, in theory, go on infringing and obtaining immunity time after time.[480] The point of leniency programmes, however, is not to maintain a morally defensible justice system but to provide a means of deterring, destabilizing and uncovering cartels, so that in the end they may cease as a phenomenon. Leniency policies are the carrot and the fining policy the stick, and the bigger the potential fines, the more attractive is leniency. Moreover, private actions for damages are not affected by the granting of leniency and although such actions are not yet frequent in Europe, they are increasing and are currently the subject of a major initiative by the Commission.[481] The true punishment for many of the cartel participants granted immunity from fines in Europe, however, is the damages actions for which they are liable in the US, given the international nature of many of the most serious cartels.

For an interesting illustration of the way in which leniency policies work, one can consider the fate of the participants in the *Fine Art Auction Houses Cartel*,[482] a fascinating and high-profile case of a cartel in the services sector.[483] Following a similar case against Sotheby's and Christie's, the world's two leading fine arts auction houses, by the DOJ in the US, the Commission found that they had colluded to fix commission fees and other trading terms between 1993 and early 2000. Evidence was first provided to the Commission (and to the DOJ) by Christie's (in fact by its former chief executive). The decision imposed a fine of €20.4 million on Sotheby's, which the Commission stated was 6 per cent of its worldwide turnover and represented a reduction of 40 per cent for co-operation with the investigation. Christie's on the other hand, received full leniency and was fined nothing. As violation of section 1 of the Sherman Act is a criminal offence in the US the billionaire chairman of Sotheby's, Alfred Taubman, ended up in jail in the US. The English chairman of Christie's, Sir Anthony Tennant, declined the invitation to go to the US. This was an extremely stark illustration of how the Leniency Notice results in a totally different treatment of equally guilty conspirators.[484]

---

[477] For an analysis of the outcome in 39 cartel cases handled by the Commission 1998–2004, see C. Veljanovski, 'Penalties for Price Fixers: An Analysis of Fines Imposed on 39 Cartels by the EU Commission' [2006] *ECLR* 510. Undertakings which have 'coerced' others are, not, however eligible for immunity under the Community leniency policy, see now 2006 Notice, para. 13.

[478] *Supra* 1231.

[479] 2006 Fining Guidelines, para. 28, provide for a 100 % increase on the basic amount of the fine for repeat offenders.

[480] Not quite a matter of *never* paying, but see for example Degussa AG, fined (with a reduction for cooperation, further reduced on appeal, Case T-279/02, *Degussa v. Commission*, 5 April 2006) in the *Methionine Cartel* [2003] OJ L255/1, and given immunity in *Bleaching Chemicals* (hydrogen peroxide and perborate), IP/06/560, 3 May 2006 and *Acrylic Glass* (methacrylates) IP/06/698, 31 May 2006.

[481] See *infra* Chap. 15.

[482] COMP/E-2/37.784, [2006] 4 CMLR 90 (30 October 2002).

[483] At the time of the action against the US action against the parties by the DOJ *The Observer*, 6 May 2001, said 'In London, Art World insiders say betrayal, revenge and desperation have brought the world's two most powerful auction houses to their knees.' For a journalist's colourful account of the collusion between Sotheby's and Christie's and the personalities involved, see C. Mason, *The Art of the Steal* (Putnam Publishing Group, 2004) and C. Mason, *Lords and Liars* (Gibson Square, 2005).

[484] At the time, cartel behaviour was not a (statutory) criminal offence under UK law, and extradition was not considered possible (see now the Enterprise Act 2002, ss. 188 and 191, and the discussion *infra* 1285).

F. INFORMAL SETTLEMENTS

(i) General

The Commission has sometimes not proceeded to a formal decision but terminated the matter informally. As explained above,[485] under the 'old' Regulation 17 regime notified agreements were often, and indeed usually, dealt with by way of comfort letter rather than by formal decision. Cases have also been terminated informally because the Commission and the parties have come to a settlement, usually because the companies had made enough concessions to satisfy the Commission, and the latter considered that nothing would be gained by pursuing a formal proceeding any further. The settlements were reached both before or after the statement of objections. Settlements often included the parties giving undertakings to the Commission. Several important cases were terminated in this way, such as *IBM*,[486] *Microsoft*,[487] *Digital*,[488] and *Deutsche Telekom Tariffs*.[489] One disadvantage to the development of the law was that it can mean that highly contentious matters were not fought out to the end and never reached the Court. *IBM*, for example, concerned access to technology, *Microsoft* concerned licensing terms, and the *Digital* settlement involved the assumption that Digital was not entitled to tie its software packages together, even though it was not dominant in the primary market.[490] Settlements were frequently publicized, in Commission press releases, in law reports, and in the Commission's annual reports, and inevitably they could attain the status of precedent. Clearly they were valuable guidance to other companies on what was acceptable to the Commission but of their nature they involved compromise and concession. Under Regulation 1/2003, Article 9 the Commission acquired a new power to take decisions which make commitments offered by companies binding upon them and it has made extensive use of this.[491] Although there is nothing in Regulation 1/2003 to prevent informal settlements, it is thought likely that given the existence of Article 9 they will now be rare.[492]

G. SECTOR INQUIRIES

As explained in Chapter 11[493] Regulation 1/2003, Article 17 provides for the Commission to conduct general inquiries into a sector of the economy. To this end the Commission has the powers to require information and carry out inspections contained in Articles 18, 19, and 20 (but not 21)[494] and to request the NCAs to carry out investigations under Article 22. It may

---

[485] *Supra* 1140.

[486] [1984] 3 CMLR 147.

[487] Commission Press Release IP(94)653 [1994] 5 CMLR 143.

[488] Commission Press Release IP/97/868.

[489] Commission's *XXVIIth Report on Competition Policy* (Commission, 1997), part 77.

[490] See the discussion of these cases *supra* in Chap. 7.

[491] *Supra* 1206.

[492] J. Temple Lang, 'Commitment Decisions and Settlements with Antitrust Authorities and Private Parties under European Antitrust Law' 2005 *Fordham Corp L Inst* (B. Hawk, ed. 2006), 265 (he suggests that informal settlements may still be used in 'small unimportant cases'); C. Kerse and N. Khan, *EC Antitrust Procedure* (5th edn., Sweet & Maxwell, 2005), 6.055; L. Ortiz Blanco, *EC Competition Procedure* (2nd edn., Oxford University Press, 2006), 4.14.

[493] *Supra* 936.

[494] The power to carry out inspections on non-business premises.

impose fines and penalties under Articles 23 and 24 (for example, to sanction the provision of incorrect information). It cannot, however, impose remedies.

7. PROCEEDINGS BEFORE THE COURT OF JUSTICE

A. JUDICIAL REVIEW

(i) General

Commission competition decisions can be challenged before the Court in an action for annulment under Article 230 (ex Article 173).[495] Although these actions are colloquially called 'appeals' they are in fact judicial review proceedings. The details of judicial review differ between EC law and national laws but the essence is the same: the legality of action taken by administrative authorities is determined by an independent, impartial judicial body. Being judicial review it is not the function of the Court to substitute its own judgment for that of the Commission but to ensure that the Commission keeps within the bounds of its powers and discretions and observes the law. It does not entail a rehearing. The question of the intensity of the review in which the Court engages in Article 230 actions is an issue across all areas of Community law but particularly so in competition law, where the delegation of powers by the Council to the Commission is so extensive. Since 1989 Article 230 actions in competition cases have gone first to the CFI with an appeal on a point of law to the ECJ. The CFI has examined the factual basis for the Commission's decisions with particular rigour. As the Commission is not a tribunal for the purposes of Article 6(1) of the ECHR the supervision by the Court must satisfy the requirement for a fair and public hearing before an independent and impartial tribunal if the competition proceedings are to comply with the Convention.[496]

Under Article 229 (ex Article 172) the Court has 'unlimited jurisdiction' in respect of fines and penalties imposed by the Commission in competition cases.

The review process before the Court is often protracted.[497] In cartel cases, for example, there may be numerous parties who appeal to the CFI, all claiming slightly different defects in the details of the Commission's procedure.[498] There is then an appeal to the ECJ. By the end the argument may be about events which took place 20 years earlier.[499] In *Cement Cartel*, for example, the Commission commenced its investigations in April 1989, and adopted the decision in 1994.[500] It found infringements going back to January 1983.[501] The judgment of the CFI,

---

[495] Article 232 (ex Art. 175), providing for an action for failure to act, is of limited application in competition law, as elsewhere, but can be relevant with regard to complainants: see further *infra* 1287 ff.

[496] See *supra* 1189.

[497] There is an expedited procedure for cases of urgency (Rules of Procedure of the Court of First Instance [1991] OJ L136/1, as amended, Art. 76a) but this is rarely applicable to this kind of appeal. For interim measures of the Court, see *infra* 1267.

[498] The cases are normally joined.

[499] Although Reg. 1/2003, Art. 25 lays down limitation periods, this only runs from the day the infringement ceases in the case of continued and repeated infringements.

[500] [1994] OJ L343/1, [1995] 4 CMLR 327.

[501] *Ibid.*, Art. 2.

which ran to over 5,000 paragraphs, was delivered in 2000[502] and, on appeal, the judgment of the ECJ was delivered in January 2004.[503]

In *Atlantic Container Line*[504] (which involved a liner conference, not a hidden cartel) the CFI stated that the amount of material presented to it amounted to an abuse and ordered the (successful) applicant to bear its own costs.

> 1646. In the present case, it is true that the contested decision is one of the longest ever adopted by the Commission in application of Articles [81] and [82] of the Treaty, that that decision raises relatively complex issues of fact and law in respect of which, when the actions were brought, there was no relevant case-law and that as Community law stands at present there is no provision limiting the length of the written pleadings or the number of documents lodged in support of an action for annulment under Article [230] of the Treaty. However, the four applications lodged by the applicants and the annexes thereto are unusually long—each application is some 500 pages long whilst the annexes make up approximately 100 files—and even if some of the pleas they contain have been upheld they are for the most part unfounded, and their number is so great as to amount to an abuse.
>
> 1647. In those circumstances, and notwithstanding the fact that some heads of the application have been upheld, since by their conduct the applicants have substantially added to the burden of dealing with this case, thus needlessly adding in particular to the costs of the Commission, the Court considers it fair, having regard to the circumstances of the case, to order each party to bear its own costs.

Not surprisingly, the lead solicitors in the case publicly protested, pointing out that although most of the grounds of appeal *were* dismissed, those which were upheld led to the annulment of the crucial parts of the decision and the quashing of the €273 fine for the abuse of a collective dominant position.[505]

(ii) Article 230 EC

Article 230 says:

The Court of Justice shall review the legality of acts adopted jointly by the European Parliament and the Council, of acts of the Council, of the Commission and of the ECB, other than recommendations and opinions, and of acts of the European Parliament intended to produce legal effects *vis-à-vis* third parties.

It shall for this purpose have jurisdiction in actions brought by a Member State, the Council or the Commission on grounds of lack of competence, infringement of an essential procedural requirement, infringement of this Treaty or of any rule of law relating to its application, or misuse of powers.

The Court of Justice shall have jurisdiction under the same conditions in actions brought by the European Parliament, by the Court of Auditors and by the ECB for the purpose of protecting their prerogatives.

---

[502] Cases T-25/95, etc. *Cimenteries CBR SA v. Commission* [2000] ECR II-25/95, etc., [2000] 5 CMLR 204.

[503] Cases C-204/00 P, C-205/00 P, C-211/00 P, C-213/00 P, C-217/00 P and C-219/00 P, *Aalborg Portland A/S and others v. Commission*, [2004] ECR I-1123, [2005] 4 CMLR 251.

[504] Cases T-191/98 and T-212/98–14/98, *Atlantic Container Line v. Commission* [2003] ECR II-3275, the appeal from *TACA* [1999] OJ L95/1, [1999] 4 CMLR 1415.

[505] The Commission, *inter alia*, had claimed that two companies were induced to join the alliance. The Court found that the relevant documents were inadmissible and that the evidence did not show coercion: see Chap. 7 581. The solicitors (Lovells) commented: 'Our clients wanted to leave no stone unturned in making the best possible case. The fact they won't get a contribution to their legal costs from the Commission is not the issue as far as they are concerned. They are just delighted not to be facing one of the highest fines imposed by the Commission'. (*Global Competition Review*, http://www.globalcompetitionreview.com/news/news, 13 Oct. 2003). In a new Practice Direction [2002] L87/51 the CFI laid down maxima for the normal length of pleadings.

Any natural or legal person may, under the same conditions, institute proceedings against a decision addressed to that person or against a decision which, although in the form of a regulation or a decision addressed to another person, is of direct and individual concern to the former.

The proceedings provided for in this Article shall be instituted within two months of the publication of the measure, or of its notification to the plaintiff, or, in the absence thereof, of the day on which it came to the knowledge of the latter, as the case may be.

The issues which arise from this provision are:

- Is there a challengeable act?
- Does the natural or legal person wishing to make the challenge have standing to do so?
- Are there grounds for annulling the act?

There is a short time limit (two months from publication or notification) for bringing an action. The limit is strictly applied. The position of addressees who do not appeal is illustrated by that of the undertakings in *Wood Pulp* which were not party to the challenge to the Commission's decision.[506]

(iii) Locus Standi—Who can Bring an Action?

The Member States and the Council and Commission are 'privileged applicants' who have standing to challenge any act.[507] Any other natural or legal person has limited standing, able only to challenge a decision actually addressed to it, or a decision which is of 'direct and individual concern' to it although in the form of a regulation or a decision addressed to *another* person.[508]

There is no problem about parties who seek to challenge acts of the Commission which are addressed to them. The problems arise concerning the rights of persons to challenge acts in the form of regulations or decisions addressed to other persons, and the issue has generated a large body of case law.[509] Competition cases do not usually involve the thorny question of when private persons may challenge regulations or challenge decisions addressed to Member States enabling the latter to take further action. They normally involve the simpler question when a person may challenge a decision addressed to another person, such as (in the past) the grant of an Article 81(3) exemption. The test formulated by the ECJ for deciding when a person is directly and individually concerned in a decision addressed to another is whether that decision 'affects them by reason of certain attributes which are peculiar to them or by reason of circumstances in which they are differentiated from all other persons and by virtue of these factors distinguishes them individually just as in the case of the person addressed'.[510]

The Court first allowed standing to a non-addressee of a decision in *Metro I*,[511] in respect of a party who had complained under Regulation 17, Article 3(2)(b), (which corresponds to Regulation 1/2003, Article 7(2)) and who objected to the granting of an exemption. In *Metro II*[512] it widened the 'complainant' category to cover a party who had not *formally* complained but who

---

[506] Case C-310/97 P, *Commission v. Assidomän Kraft Products AB and Others* [1999] ECR I-5363, [1999] 5 CMLR 1253: see *infra* 1263.

[507] Article 230(2). By para. 3 the Parliament, the Court of Auditors, and the European Central Bank may bring actions to protect their prerogatives.

[508] *Ibid.*, para. 4.

[509] See P. Craig and G. de Búrca, *EU Law: Text, Cases and Materials* (4th edn., Oxford University Press, 2007), Chap. 14.

[510] Case 25/62, *Plaumann & Co v. Commission* [1963] ECR 95, [1964] CMLR 29.

[511] Case 26/76, *Metro-SB-Grossmärkte GmbH v. Commission (No. 1)* [1977] ECR 1875, [1978] 2 CMLR 1.

[512] Case 75/84, *Metro-SB-Grossmärkte GmbH v. Commission (No. 2)* [1986] ECR 3021, [1987] 1 CMLR 118.

had taken part in the Commission's proceedings and been recognized by the Commission as having a 'legitimate interest'. The applicant in both *Metro* cases was a retailer who was excluded by the provisions of SABA's exempted selective distribution system from distributing SABA products. *Métropole*[513] shows how widely the CFI is prepared to cast the standing net. Antena 3, a TV service, was refused admission to the EBU as an active member before the Commission adopted a decision exempting the EBU's rules. Antena 3 brought an action to have the decision annulled. The Commission argued that it was not individually and directly concerned and had not submitted observations.[514] The CFI, however, held that taking part in the administrative proceedings was not a prerequisite for being accorded standing, and that its application to join the EBU distinguished Antena 3 in the same way as if it were an addressee of the decision.

On the other hand, in *Kruidvat*[515] the Commission denied standing to a retailer who wished to challenge the Article 81(3) exemption of Givenchy's selective distribution network. It had taken no part in the Commission proceedings, had not complained to the Commission, had not applied to become a member of Givenchy's network, and did not wish to be one.[516] It was simply a competitor of Givenchy's authorized distributors. The Commission said that to grant Kruidvat standing would be to 'allow a practically limitless number of actions from unforeseeable sources to be brought'. The CFI agreed and said that individual concern could not be established on the basis that the legality of the decision might affect indirectly related national proceedings. Although there are no individual exemption decisions under Regulation 1/2003, it is possible that a third party might wish to challenge a commitments decision under Article 9[517] or a 'finding of inapplicability' decision under Article 10.[518]

(iv) Which Acts can be Challenged?

It is not just formal decisions which can be challenged, but also other 'acts' taken by the Commission in the course of its procedures. The basic principle, laid down in *ERTA*,[519] is that Article 230 covers 'all measures adopted by the institutions which are intended to have legal force'. This was applied in *IBM*[520] where an undertaking wished to challenge the statement of objections. The Court said:

> 9. Any measure the legal effects of which are binding on, and capable of affecting the interests of, the applicant by bringing about a distinct change in his legal position is an act or decision which may be the object of an action under Article [230] for a declaration that it is void.

The test here is: does the act change the applicant's legal position? The statement of objections does not do so; it is merely a preparatory act and any irregularity can be dealt with in a challenge to the act which concludes the proceedings. Interim decisions can be challenged.[521] Where

---

[513] Cases T-528, 542, 543 and 546/93, *Métropole Télévision v. Commission* [1996] ECR II-652, [1996] 5 CMLR 386.

[514] Following the publication of the Reg. 17, Art. 19(3) notice.

[515] Case T-87/92, *BVBA Kruidvat v. Commission* [1996] ECR II-1851, [1997] 4 CMLR 1046.

[516] Its parent company was a member of a trade association which *had* participated, although the views of the association and of Kruidvat materially differed.

[517] *Supra* 1206.

[518] *Supra* 1146.

[519] Case 22/70, *Commission v. Council, Re ERTA* [1971] ECR 263, [1971] CMLR 335.

[520] Case 60/81, *IBM v. Commission* [1981] ECR 2639, [1981] 3 CMLR 635.

[521] As in the case of the *IMS* decision, Case T-184/01 R, *IMS Health v. Commission* [2001] ECR II-3193, [2002] 4 CMLR 58 (President of the CFI), confirmed Case C-481/01 P(R), *IMS Health v. Commission* [2002] ECR I-3401, [2002] 5 CMLR 44 (President of the ECJ): see *infra* 1268.

complaints are concerned, 'Article 6' letters cannot be challenged but the final rejection of the complaint can be, even if it is only in the form of a letter.[522]

(v) The Grounds of Review

a. General

Article 230 provides four grounds of challenge, although they are all really encompassed in the third one, the infringement of the Treaty or of any rule of law relating to its application. The fourth ground, misuse of powers (*détournement de pouvoir*) means that the Community institution has used its powers other than for the purpose for which they were conferred. A challenge on this ground very rarely succeeds as the burden on the applicant is a heavy one, and one has never succeeded in a competition case.[523] Given the large degree of overlap, the Court usually does not specify under which heading the reasons for an annulment fall.

b. Lack of Competence

This is the EC equivalent of the English concept, *ultra vires*. It covers: the lack of competence of the Community to act at all, because no Treaty provision has empowered it to do so; the lack of competence of the institutions to act under a particular empowering provision (incorrect legal basis); and the lack of competence of the particular institution or official to take the challenged act.

In the competition field the best example of the first situation is challenges made to the extraterritorial application of the competition rules. Undertakings outside the Community have argued that the Community could not apply its rules to them because they were outside the jurisdiction. These challenges have not succeeded.[524]

The second situation is exemplified in the challenges brought by Member States to directives adopted by the Commission on the basis of Article 86(3), where they claimed that the Commission should instead have used the harmonization of laws provisions, which would have involved going through the Council where the States could have influenced proceedings.[525] In *British Airways*[526] the CFI dismissed the undertaking's claim that the Commission had no competence to apply Regulation 17 to practices in the market for air travel agency services as it should have used Regulation 3975/87 on the air transport sector[527] instead.

The third situation has arisen in competition cases where parties have alleged that the power to take decisions was unlawfully delegated. The delegation to the Commissioner responsible for competition of the power to take decisions ordering 'dawn raid' inspections under Regulation 17, Article 14(3) was unsuccessfully challenged in *AKZO*,[528] and the delegation of the signing of documents such as statements of objections has likewise been upheld.[529] However, a challenge

---

[522] See *infra* 1298.

[523] Although it has been pleaded: see, e.g., Case 5/85, *AKZO Chemie BV v. Commission* [1986] ECR 2585, [1987] 3 CMLR 716; Case, T-5/93, *Roger Tremblay v. Commission* [1995] ECR II-185.

[524] See *infra* Chap. 16.

[525] See Case C-202/88, *France v. Commission (Telecommunications Equipment)* [1991] ECR I-1223; Cases C-271, 281, and 289/90, *Spain, Belgium & Italy v. Commission (Telecommunications Services)* [1992] ECR I-5833: see *supra* Chap. 8.

[526] Case T-219/99, *British Airways v. Commission* [2003] ECR II-5917, [2004] 4 CMLR 1008.

[527] [1987] OJ L374/1.

[528] Case 5/85, *AKZO Chemie BV v. Commission* [1986] ECR 2585, [1987] 3 CMLR 716.

[529] See Case 48/69, *ICI v. Commission (Dyestuffs)* [1972] ECR 619, [1972] CMLR 557.

to the adoption of a final decision finding an infringement by a single Commissioner succeeded in the *PVC cartel* case where a challenge to a decision on both competence and infringement of an essential procedural requirement grounds spectacularly succeeded.[530] A novel plea was made by British Airways when it claimed that the Commission had no competence to adopt the *Virgin/BA* decision of 14 July 1999[531] as, all the members of the Commission having resigned *en bloc* on 16 March 1999, they had authority only to deal with current business within the meaning of Article 201 of the Treaty pending their replacement in September. The CFI held that the Commissioners could exercise their normal powers until their resignations took effect on the date of their actual replacement.[532]

The issue of lack of competence is a matter of public interest and should therefore be raised by the Court of its on motion.[533]

c. Infringement of an Essential Procedural Requirement

Infringement of an essential procedural requirement covers situations where a measure has been passed without complying with the legislative process laid down by the Treaty,[534] or with the rules of procedure of the relevant institution,[535] or with a general principle of law concerned with procedure,[536] or where the measure does not contain an adequate statement of reasons contrary to Article 253 (ex Article 190). Inadequate statements of reasons and breaches of general principles of law guaranteeing procedural rights are also infringements of the Treaty or of any rule relating to its application but, as explained above, the Court is not concerned with categorization. The only issue is whether there is a defect which requires the act's annulment.

The Court annuls acts only for breach of an *essential* procedural requirement, and what amounts to such is a matter for the Court. A requirement is essential if the failure to observe it might have affected the final outcome of the act. On this basis the wrongful revelation of confidential material to the complainant in *AKZO*[537] was not a reason for annulling the Commission decision. An adequate statement of reasons is essential because it is necessary for the review process. As the ECJ said in *Germany v. Commission:*[538]

In imposing upon the Commission the obligation to state reasons for its decisions, Article [253] is not taking mere formal considerations into account but seeks to give an opportunity to the parties of defending their rights, to the Court of exercising its supervisory functions and to Member States and to all interested nationals of ascertaining the circumstances in which the Commission has applied the Treaty.

---

[530] Cases T-79/89, etc., *BASF and others v. Commission* [1992] ECR II-315, [1992] 4 CMLR 357, on appeal to the ECJ, Cases C-137/92 P, etc., *Commission v. BASF and others* [1994] ECR I-2555: see *infra* 1258.

[531] [2000] OJ L30/1, [2000] 4 CMLR 999.

[532] Case T-219/99, *British Airways v. Commission* [2003] ECR II-5917, [2004] 4 CMLR 1008, paras. 55–7. The resignation of the entire Santer Commission in March 1999 to avoid a motion of censure of Parliament was a situation not foreseen by the EC Treaty. Article 215 EC, which BA claimed prevented the resigned Commission transacting 'new' business, did not fit happily with what had happened in these rather extraordinary circumstances. Article 215 was amended by the Treaty of Nice.

[533] Cases T-79/89 etc., *BASF and others v. Commission* [1992] ECR II-315, [1992] 4 CMLR 357, para. 31.

[534] As where Parliament is not consulted: Case 138/79, *Roquette Frères v. Council* [1980] ECR 3333.

[535] Case 68/86, *United Kingdom v. Council* [1988] ECR 855, [1988] 2 CMLR 543, and note the application of this in the *PVC cartel* case: Cases C-137/92 P, *Commission v. BASF and others* [1994] ECR I-2555, discussed *infra* 1258.

[536] Such as the *audi alteram partem* rule giving parties a right to a hearing: Case 17/74, *Transocean Marine Paint v. Commission* [1974] ECR 1063, [1974] 2 CMLR 459: see the discussion *supra* 1191 ff.

[537] See *supra* 1198.

[538] Case 24/62, *Germany v. Commission* [1963] ECR 63, [1963] CMLR 347.

What amounts to adequate reasons depends on the context of the act. In an interlocking series of regulations the acts may refer to each other and the reasoning of the institutions may be deduced from them as a whole. In competition cases, where the Commission has wide discretion and a power of appraisal, the reasoning is of fundamental importance because in reviewing the decision the Court must be able to establish whether the factual and legal matters upon which the exercise of the power of appraisal depended were present.[539] The Commission has to deal properly with the parties' arguments. In the *Net Book Agreement* the Publishers' Association (PA) had argued that the resale price maintenance on books provided for in the Net Book Agreement should be allowed. It put forward as evidence the judgments of the UK Restrictive Practices Court (RPC) which permitted RPM on books in the UK and set out the benefits of such pricing. The ECJ annulled the decision because the Commission had not adequately dealt with this evidence.[540]

Challenges to competition decisions frequently plead procedural defects as grounds for annulment, as seen earlier in this chapter. The CFI annulled the *Soda-ash* decisions,[541] for example, on grounds that insufficient access to the Commission's file prejudiced the parties' right to be heard, and a significant part of the *TACA* decision[542] because the Commission had relied on an interpretation of number of inculpatory documents upon which the undertakings had been given no opportunity to comment.[543] The most celebrated case of annulment on procedural grounds (and of lack of competence), however, is the *PVC* case. There the CFI found differences in both the statement of reasons and the operative part of the decision between the version adopted by the College of Commissioners at its relevant meeting and the version notified to the undertakings concerned. The differences went beyond mere corrections of grammar and syntax. The Commission was unable to produce an authenticated version of the decision as adopted by the College. A draft in only three languages was available at the meeting, and the Competition Commissioner was authorized to adopt the measure in the other official Community languages, including those of undertakings to which the decision was addressed. Further, the Competition Commissioner whose signature appeared on the decision notified to all the addressees had left office some days before the notified version appeared to have been finalized. The CFI considered these procedural defects, including the breach of the principle of collegiate responsibility, so serious that it did not merely annul the decision, it declared it *non-existent*.[544] On appeal the ECJ held that the flaws were not so fundamental as to render the act non-existent. It put aside the judgment of the CFI, held that the decision existed, but annulled it.[545]

The Commission responded to the final annulment by adopting a new decision six weeks later. The undertakings again appealed, *inter alia*, on the grounds that this breached the principle of double jeopardy, *non bis in idem*, and that the Commission had denied them the right to be

---

[539] See K. Lenaerts and P. Van Nuffel, *Constitutional Law of the European Union* (Sweet & Maxwell, 1999), para. 14–085.

[540] Case C-360/92 P, *Publishers' Association v. Commission* [1995] ECR II-23, [1995] 5 CMLR 33 setting aside the CFI judgment, Case T-66/89, *Publishers' Association v. Commission* [1992] ECR II-1995, [1992] 5 CMLR 120.

[541] Cases T-30/91, *Solvay SA v. Commission* [1995] ECR II-1775, [1996] 5 CMLR 57.

[542] [1999] OJ L95/1, [1999] 4 CMLR 1415.

[543] Cases T-191/98 and T-212/98–214/98, *Atlantic Container Line v. Commission* [2003] ECR II-3275.

[544] Cases T-79/89, etc., *BASF v. Commission* [1992] ECR II-315, [1992] 4 CMLR 357.

[545] Cases C-137/92 P, *Commission v. BASF and others* [1994] ECR I-2555. The *LdPE* cartel (low-density polyethylene) decision [1989] OJ L74/21, [1990] 4 CMLR 382 was annulled on similar grounds in Cases T-80/89, etc., *BASF v. Commission* [1995] ECR II-729. After the *PVC* judgment two of the undertakings concerned in the *Polypropylene Cartel*, who were challenging that decision in an action before the CFI in which the oral proceedings had already been closed, asked the CFI to reopen those proceedings so that they could enter pleas based on the *PVC* arguments. They claimed that the CFI had wrongfully failed to raise those issues of its own motion. The

heard by not sending a new statement of objections and holding new hearings. The ECJ held that *non bis in idem* did not apply when the annulment was only on procedural grounds, and that given that the Court had not found any defects in the preparatory stages of the Commission's procedure, there was no need to repeat those stages. A right to be heard was necessary only in respect of matters which were not in the original decision.[546] The Commission's practice is, consequently, to re-adopt decisions annulled for procedural reasons.[547]

d. Infringement of the Treaty or any Rule of Law Relating to its Application

As noted above, this ground is so wide that it covers the other three grounds as well. 'The Treaty' means the Treaties establishing the Communities together with the Protocols, amending Treaties and Treaties and Acts of Accession. 'Any rule of law relating to its application' covers all the other binding provisions of the Community legal order, including the general principles of law and human rights developed in the Court's jurisprudence (and now embedded in the Charter of Fundamental Rights of the EU),[548] and provisions of international law, particularly principles of customary international law and agreements the Community itself has concluded.

The Court will therefore annul a decision where the Commission has misinterpreted the law or failed to abide by general principles of law such as proportionality, non-discrimination, legitimate expectation, the presumption of innocence, or legal certainty.[549] The rights to due process described in the sections above and the right to confidentiality are such principles. However, this ground of annulment goes beyond misinterpreting or misapplying the law: it also covers the Court finding that the Commission committed a 'manifest error of appraisal'[550] and that the evidence relied on or the facts established by the Commission do not support the finding of law. This is crucial in competition cases, for it means that the Court *does* look at the facts, not to rehear the case but to see whether the factual basis of the Commission decision was correct or sufficient and that the burden of proof was discharged. It annuls decisions where it finds that the Commission drew the wrong conclusions from the facts. The Court can play an active role by ordering measures of inquiry such as experts' reports.

CFI refused and this was upheld by the ECJ: see Case C-234/92 P, *Shell International Chemical Company Ltd* v. *Commission* [1999] 5 CMLR 1142 at paras. 66–8. The CFI did, however, annul a Commission decision in Cases T-31–2/91, *Solvay* v. *Commission* [1995] ECR II-1821 on non—authentication grounds. The applicants raised the plea after the close of the written procedure in the case, having read statements by Commission officials in the *Financial Times* and the *Wall Street Journal* that the Commission had been following the procedure condemned in the PVC case for the past 25 years. The annulment was upheld by the ECJ, Cases C-286–8/95 P, *Commission* v. *ICI* [2000] ECR I-2341, [2000] 5 CMLR 413. The Commission readopted the decisions eight months after the ECJ judgment, in December 2000, OJ [2003] L10/1.

[546] Cases C-238, 244–5, 247, 250, 251–2, and 254/99, *Limburgse Vinyl Maatschappij NV* v. *Commission* [2002] ECR I-8375, [2003] 4 CMLR 397, paras. 59–76, confirming Cases T-305–7, 313–16, 318, 328–9, and 335/94, *Re the PVC Cartel II: Limburgse Vinyl Maatschappij NV and others* v. *Commission* [1999] 5 CMLR 303.

[547] For two further examples of decisions re-adopted after annulments for procedural reasons, see *Steel Beams* COMP.38/907, 8 November 2006, undertaking fined €10 million (original decision (adopted under the ECSC Treaty) annulled in Case 176/99 P, *Arbed SA* v. *Commission* [2003] ECR I-10687 as the decision had not been addressed to the same addressee as the statement of objections) and *Alloy Surcharge* COMP 39/234, 20 December 2006, undertaking fined €3,168,000 (original decision annulled in Cases C-65/02 P and C-73/02 P, *ThyssenKrupp Stainless AG* v. *Commission* [2005] ECR I-6773 as ThyssenKrupp was fined without being explicitly invited to give its views of the cartel behaviour of Thyssen Stahl, who had merged with another company after the infringement to form ThyssenKrupp).

[548] Which will become legally binding (although with a UK opt-out) if and when the Reform Treaty comes into force: see *supra* Chap. 2 and the Addendum, *infra* 1399.

[549] Legal certainty was cited in the PVC judgments (*supra* 1258) as being infringed when the Commission did not follow its own rules of procedure and could not produce the authenticated decision.

[550] Case 42/84, *Remia & Nutricia* v. *Commission* [1985] ECR 2566, [1987] 1 CMLR 1, para. 34.

Continental Can was an early case where the Court annulled the decision because the Commission had failed to establish why a particular type of container should be considered a relevant market. This meant there was no basis for its finding of dominance and the application of Article 82, even though the Court confirmed the Commission's extensive interpretation of Article 82 to cover mergers.[551] In *Wood Pulp II*[552] the Court appointed experts to produce a report on parallelism of prices in the wood pulp industry, whether the documents relied on by the Commission justified their conclusions on the pricing and whether there was a distinction between the documents gathered before and after the statement of objections. A second experts' report into the structure and characteristics of the market was commissioned. These reports, particularly the finding that the market *was* oligopolistic, were crucial to the Court's judgment and it (largely) annulled the decision.

The CFI was established largely to relieve the ECJ of having to deal with complex issues of fact. In competition cases it has been assiduous in its examination of the factual basis of decisions. A leading example of this was its treatment of the *Italian Flat Glass* decision in *Società Italiana Vetro*[553] where the CFI subjected the Commission's documentary evidence to careful scrutiny and in the main found it seriously wanting. Two other striking examples of annulment are *Métropole*[554] and *European Night Services*.[555] In the former it annulled a decision because the Commission had not properly examined whether the fourth criterion for Article 81(3) exemption relating to the indispensability of restrictions was satisfied, and had taken into account the criteria in Article 86(2) (ex Article 90(2)) despite having decided that Article did not apply. The latter decision was annulled because the Commission had not analysed whether there *was* a restriction of competition, had applied the *de minimis* test in too mechanistic a manner, had unsatisfactorily defined the market, and had applied the essential facilities doctrine without explaining why the resources at issue could be considered essential facilities.[556]

On the other hand, the Court should not interfere with the exercise of the Commission's powers of appraisal of what are essentially matters of economic assessment. The ECJ stated again in *Aalborg* (the *Cement Cartel*) that '[E]xamination by the Community judicature of the complex economic assessments made by the Commission must necessarily be confined to verifying whether the rules on procedure and on the statement of reasons have been complied with, whether the facts have been accurately stated and whether there has been any manifest error of appraisal or misuse of powers'.[557] The CFI said the same thing in *Van den Bergh*[558] in respect of its function in reviewing the Commission's decision as to the application of both

---

[551] Case 6/72, *Europemballage Corp & Continental Can Co Inc v. EC Commission* [1973] ECR 215, [1973] CMLR 199.

[552] Cases C-89/85 etc., *A. Ahlström Oy v. Commission* [1993] ECR I-1307, [1993] 4 CMLR 407; see *supra* Chap. 11.

[553] Cases T-68/89, etc., *Società Italiana Vetro Spa v. EC Commission* [1992] ECR II-1403, [1992] 5 CMLR 302.

[554] Cases T-528, etc./93, *Métropole Télévision v. Commission* [1996] ECR II-652, [1996] 5 CMLR 386.

[555] Cases T-374–375, 384 and 388/94, *European Night Services v. Commission* [1998] 5 CMLR 718; see *supra* Chap. 4.

[556] The CFI has also been rigorous in its approach to Commission decisions under the Merger Regulation: see *supra* Chap. 12. So, also, was the ECJ in Cases C-68/94 and 30/95, *France & SCPA v. Commission* [1998] ECR I-1375, [1998] 4 CMLR 829 (where the case went straight to the ECJ because a Member State appealed against the decision: as Article 51 of the Statute of the Court has been amended by Council Decision 2004/407/EC, [2004] OJ L132/5, this would no longer be the case). The ECJ took the view that the Commission's analysis of the post-merger market did not stand up to examination and that its evidence of the structural links between the parties was unconvincing. It therefore quashed the decision.

[557] Cases C-204/00 P, C-205/00 P, C-211/00 P, C-213/00 P, C-217/00 P and C-219/00 P, *Aalborg Portland and others v. Commission* [2004] ECR I-123, [2005] 4 CMLR 251, echoing Case 42/84, *Remia v. Commission* [1985] ECR 2545, [1987] 1 CMLR 1.

[558] Case T-65/98, *Van den Bergh Foods Ltd. v. Commission* [2003] ECR II-4653, [2004] 4 CMLR 1.

Article 81(1) and Article 81(3).[559] It then proceeded to examine carefully the evidence on both matters before upholding the Commission.[560] It will be apparent from the cases discussed in other chapters of this book, however, that it comes down to what the Community Courts consider to be a 'manifest error of appraisal'.[561] Reference is often made to the Commission's 'discretion' or 'margin of discretion' in this respect but it has been cogently argued that it is a 'margin of appreciation' rather than discretion.[562] In *GlaxoSmithKline*, however, the CFI again referred to the Commission's 'margin of discretion' under Article 81(3) which was subject to a 'restricted judicial review',[563] suggesting that the Community Courts do indeed use the expressions 'appreciation' and 'discretion' interchangeably.[564]

GlaxoSmithKline is a good example of the difference between the Court second-guessing the Commission's economic assessment under Article 81(3) and judging whether the Commission has conducted the assessment properly. The Commission had held that GSK's general sales conditions had as their object and effect the restriction of competition in that they sought to limit parallel trade within the EU in certain pharmaceuticals. It refused an individual exemption under Article 81(3), giving very short shrift to GSK's argument that the first condition of Article 81(3) was satisfied in that limiting parallel trade produced efficiency gains by providing GSK with more profits to plough back into pharmaceutical research. The Commission therefore did not proceed to seriously examine the other three Article 81(3) conditions.[565] The CFI, having held that the provisions had the effect, though not the object of restricting competition, held that the Commission had failed in its duty to properly examine GSK's Article 81(3) arguments.

Case T-168/01, *Glaxo SmithKline Services Unlimited* [2006] 5 CMLR 1623

Court of First Instance

241. In that regard, the Court dealing with an application for annulment of a decision applying Article 81(3) EC carries out, in so far as it is faced with complex economic assessments, a review confined, as regards the merits, to verifying whether the facts have been accurately stated,

---

[559] *Ibid.*, paras. 80 and 135 respectively.

[560] In respect of Article 81(1) this meant confirming that the Commission was justified in holding that the agreements concerned were likely to significantly contribute to foreclosing the market (para. 118), and in respect of Article 81(3) that the agreements did not produce objective advantages to compensate for its anti-competitive effect (para. 141), see *supra* Chaps. 3 and 4. The ECJ upheld the CFI's judgment, Case C-552/03 P, *Unilever Bestfoods (Ireland) Ltd v. Commission* [2006] 5 CMLR 1494.

[561] The rigour of the CFI's review has particularly been so in respect of the CFI's treatment of appeals against Commission decisions under the ECMR, see *supra* Chap. 12. It can also be argued that the Community Courts' intensity of review of Commission antitrust decisions varies according to the provision concerned, and that in the past it has been more intense in respect of Article 81(1) than of Article 81(3), a matter which may change now that Article 81(3) is directly applicable, and firmly construed as an efficiency defence, see, e.g. C.-D. Ehlermann and I. Atansiu, 'The Modernisation of EC Antitrust Law: Consequences for the Future Role and Function of the EC Courts' [2002] *ECLR* 72.

[562] In that discretion involves choosing the standards according to which power is exercised or a decision made, while a margin of appreciation involves weighing up the evidence and assessing whether a given standard is reached, see O. Odudu, 'Article 81(3), Discretion and Direct Effect' [2002] *ECLR* 17; D. Bailey, 'Scope of Judicial Review Under Article 81 EC' (2004) 41 *CMLRev* 1327.

[563] Case T-168/01, *GlaxoSmithKlineServices Unlimited* [2006] 5 CMLR 1623, para. 244

[564] A. Schaub, 'Modernization of EC competition Law: Reform of Regulation No. 17' (2002) 23 *Fordham Inst LJ* 752, n.16; and see D. Bailey, *supra* n. 562.

[565] See *supra* Chap. 4.

whether there has been any manifest error of appraisal and whether the legal consequences deduced from those facts were accurate (*Consten and Grundig* v *Commission*, paragraph 110 above, p. 347; *Metro I*, paragraph 109 above, paragraph 25; *Remia and Others* v *Commission*, paragraph 57 above, paragraph 34; and *Aalborg Portland and Others* v *Commission*, paragraph 55 above, paragraph 279).

242. It is for the Court to establish not only whether the evidence relied on is factually accurate, reliable and consistent, but also whether it contains all the information which must be taken into account for the purpose of assessing a complex situation and whether it is capable of substantiating the conclusions drawn from it (Case C-12/03 P *Commission* v *Tetra Laval* [2005] ECR I-987, paragraph 39, and Case T-210/01 *General Electric* v *Commission* [2005] ECR II-0000, paragraphs 62 and 63).

243. On the other hand, it is not for the Court to substitute its own economic assessment for that of the institution which adopted the decision the legality of which it is requested to review.

244. The Commission has, in particular, a margin of discretion which is subject to a restricted judicial review, in the operation consisting, once it has been ascertained that one of the criteria on which Article 81(3) EC makes provision for an exemption was satisfied, in weighing up the advantages expected from the implementation of the agreement and the disadvantages which the agreement entails for the final consumer owing to its impact on competition, which takes the form of a balancing exercise carried out in the light of the general interest appraised at Community level.

. . .

275. However, the very structure of recitals 155 to 161 to the Decision shows that the Commission, after acknowledging the importance of competition by innovation in the relevant sector, failed to undertake a rigorous examination of the factual arguments and the evidence submitted by GSK concerning the nature of the investments in R&D, the characteristics of the financing of R&D, the impact of parallel trade on R&D and the applicable regulations, but confined itself, as indicated at recital 155 to the Decision, to observations which, to say the least, are fragmentary and, as GSK rightly claims, of limited relevance or value.

276. Such an omission is particularly serious where the Commission is required to determine whether the conditions for the application of Article 81(3) EC are satisfied in a legal and economic context, such as that characteristic of the pharmaceutical sector, where competition is distorted by the presence of national regulations. That circumstance obliges the Commission to examine with particular attention the arguments and evidence submitted to it by the person relying on Article 81(3) EC.

Review under Article 230 also entails ensuring that the Commission has properly interpreted the law. However, the Court is committed to interpreting Community law in a way which gives effect to the objectives of the Treaty. The great leaps forward which the Commission has made in the interpretation of the competition provisions have usually been confirmed by the Court: for example, the extension of the 'abuse' concept to cover mergers,[566] the development of the doctrine of collective dominance,[567] the idea that abuse and dominant position may be on

---

[566] Case 6/72, *Europemballage Corp & Continental Can Co Inc* v. *EC Commission* [1973] ECR 215, [1973] CMLR 199, although the decision was annulled because the Commission had not defined the market sufficiently, see *supra* Chap. 6.

[567] Cases T-68/89, etc., *Società Italiana Vetro Spa* v. *EC Commission* [1992] ECR II-1403, [1992] 5 CMLR 302; Cases C-68/94 and 30/95, *France & SCPA* v. *Commission* [1998] ECR I-1375, [1998] 4 CMLR 829; see *supra* Chaps. 11 and 12. In the merger appeal Case T-342/99, *Airtours* v. *Commission* [2002] ECR II-2585, [2002] 5 CMLR 317, however, the CFI narrowed the circumstances in which a collective dominant position can be held to exist,

different markets,[568] and the original finding that Article 81(1) applied equally to horizontal and vertical restraints.[569] On the other hand, the Court refused to accept that what was in reality unilateral behaviour by a non-dominant firm could be caught as an agreement under Article 81(1).[570]

(vi) The Effects of Annulment

Article 231 (ex Article 174) says that if the action is well-founded, the ECJ shall 'declare the act concerned to be void'. However, if articles of the decision are severable, the Court can declare some void and leave others. This is often done. The Court cannot, however, substitute its own decision for that of the Commission. So, in *European Night Services*[571] the CFI refused to annul the conditions which the Commission had attached to the Article 81(3) exemption and leave the applicants with an unconditional decision. It annulled the decision completely.[572]

Article 233 (ex Article 176) says:

The institution or institutions whose act has been declared void or whose failure to act has been declared contrary to this Treaty shall be required to take the necessary measures to comply with the judgment of the Court of Justice.

This does not, however, mean that the Commission has to refund the fine of parties who did *not* challenge a decision annulled at the suit of other addressees. Twenty-eight of the thirty-six addresses of the *Wood Pulp* decision[573] brought an action for annulment. The ECJ annulled or reduced the fines imposed on the applicants.[574] Subsequently the other addressees requested the Commission to refund to them the fines they had paid pursuant to the annulled articles. The Commission refused. The ECJ upheld this: a decision finding an infringement of the competition rules addressed to each undertaking concerned individually can be annulled only as regards the addressees who have successfully challenged it before the Court. The other addressees had not challenged the decision within the two-month time-limit and it continued to be valid and binding on them.[575]

---

contrary to the Commission's approach in its decision, *Airtours/First Choice* [2000] OJ L93/1, [2002] 5 CMLR 494. See further *supra* Chaps. 11 and 12.

[568] Case C-333/94 P, *Tetra Pak International SA v. Commission* [1996] ECR I-5951, [1997] 4 CMLR 662, see *supra* Chap. 7.

[569] Cases 56 and 58, *Etablissements Consten SA & Grundig-Verkaufs-GmbH v. Commission* [1966] ECR 299, [1966] CMLR 418; see *supra* Chap. 3.

[570] Cases C-2/01 P and 3/01 P, *Bundesverband der Arzneimittel-Importeure EV and the Commission v. Bayer AG* [2004] ECR I-23, [2004] 4 CMLR 653; Case C-74/04 P, *Commission v. Volkswagen* [2006] ECR I-6585.

[571] Cases T-374–375, 384 and 388/94, *European Night Services v. Commission* [2005] ECR II-3141, [1998] 5 CMLR 718.

[572] In Case T-168/01, *GlaxoSmithKlineServices Unlimited* [2006] 5 CMLR 1623, para. 320, the CFI annulled the part of the decision refusing GlaxoSmithKline's request for an individual exemption under Article 81(3) after that procedure had been abolished by Regulation 1/2003. The CFI told the Commission to rule on the request for exemption insofar as GSK was still requesting it, as the annulment had retrospective effect.

[573] [1985] OJ L85/1, [1985] 3 CMLR 474.

[574] Cases C-89/85, etc., *A. Ahlström Oy v. Commission* [1993] ECR I-1307, [1993] 4 CMLR 407.

[575] Case C-310/97 P, *Commission v. AssiDomän Kraft Products AB and Others* [1999] ECR I-5363, [1999] 5 CMLR 1253.

(vii) Appeals against Penalties: Article 229 EC

As discussed above[576] the Commission has a very wide discretion in setting fines under Regulation 1/2003, Article 23. Regulation 1/2003, Article 31 gives the Court a power to cancel, reduce, or increase the fines or periodic penalty pursuant to Article 229 EC.

The distinction between the Court's powers under Article 229 and under Article 230 is that under the former the Court may actually *change* the Commission's decision. It may cancel, increase, or reduce the fine (but not impose one where the Commission has not). Under Article 230, however, the Court is limited to reviewing the legality of the decision and annulling all or part of it on the grounds laid down in the Article but cannot substitute its own judgment for that of the Commission. Appeals against penalties go to the CFI, with an appeal to the ECJ.

The Court has been tolerant of the Commission's general approach to fining. The ECJ approved the change to higher fines for the sake of deterrence in *Pioneer*[577] and the Community Courts have not demurred from the ever higher level of fines imposed during the last twenty years.[578] The CFI will reduce the fine, however when it takes a different view to the Commission of the duration of an infringement[579] or of an undertaking's level of involvement in an infringement.[580] The Court demands that the Commission follow the methodology laid down in the Guidelines on Fines,[581] which create legitimate expectations.

As we have seen above[582] some of the most passionate arguments about fines before the CFI are now about the amount of reduction which the Commission accords cartel participants under the Leniency Notice. In *Graphite Electrodes* appeal the CFI *increased* the fine on an undertaking which, having been granted leniency for cooperation with the Commission, then argued about the facts before the CFI.[583]

(viii) Appeals from the Court of First Instance to the Court of Justice

An appeal lies from the CFI to the ECJ on a point of law. This means that the appeal is limited to the grounds of lack of competence of the CFI, a breach of procedure before it adversely affecting the interests of the applicant, or the infringement of Community law by the CFI.[584] The appellant has to state the errors alleged to have been made by the CFI. It is not sufficient for it simply to repeat the arguments it raised before the CFI[585] and it may not adduce new arguments. The

---

[576] See *supra* 1210 ff.

[577] Cases 100–103/80, *Musique Diffusion Française SA v. Commission (Pioneer)* [1983] ECR 1825, [1983] 3 CMLR 221.

[578] See the discussion on the level of fines, *supra* 1218 ff.

[579] See, e.g., the CFI judgment in the *Cement Cartel* cases, Cases T-25/95, etc. *Cimenteries CBR SA v. Commission* [2000] ECR II-25/95 etc., [2000] 5 CMLR 204.

[580] *Ibid.*, in respect of one undertaking's involvement in the white cement market cartel.

[581] *Supra* 1234.

[582] *Supra* 1240 ff.

[583] Cases T-236/01, 244–246/01, 251/01, and 252/01, *Tokai Carbon Co Ltd v. Commission* [2005] ECR II-10. It is difficult to reconcile this with earlier case law, see C. Kerse and N. Khan, *EC Antitrust Procedure* (5th edn., Sweet & Maxwell, 2005), 8-025; L. Ortiz Blanco, *EC Competition Procedure* (2nd edn., Oxford University Press, 2006), 15.22.

[584] Article 51 of the Statute of the ECJ.

[585] Case C-19/95 P, *San Marco v. Commission* [1996] ECR I-4435.

ECJ cannot be asked to review the facts found by the CFI, to raise matters of fact which were not found by the CFI, or to consider the assessment of evidence adduced before the CFI unless the CFI committed a manifest error which is apparent from the documents submitted to it.[586] The ECJ has explained the respective roles of the ECJ and the CFI on many occasions. The following extract is from the *Cement Cartel* appeal.[587]

Cases C-204/00 P, C-205/00 P, C-211/00 P, C-213/00 P, C-217/00 P and C-219/00 P, *Aalborg Portland A/S* v. *Commission* [2004] ECR I-123, [2005] 4 CMLR 251

The role of the Court in an appeal

47. In an appeal, the Court's task is limited to examining whether, in exercising its power of review, the Court of First Instance made an error of law. Under Article 225 EC and Article 51, first paragraph, of the EC Statute of the Court of Justice, an appeal must be limited to points of law and must lie on grounds of lack of competence of the Court of First Instance, a breach of procedure before it which adversely affects the interests of the applicant or infringement of Community law by the Court of First Instance.

48. An appeal may therefore be based only on grounds relating to the infringement of rules of law, to the exclusion of any appraisal of the facts. The Court of First Instance has exclusive jurisdiction, first, to establish the facts except where the substantive inaccuracy of its findings is apparent from the documents submitted to it and, second, to assess those facts (see, *inter alia*, Case C-284/98 P *Parliament* v. *Bieber* [2000] ECR I-1527, paragraph 31.

49. It follows that the appraisal of the facts by the Court of First Instance does not constitute, save where the clear sense of the evidence produced before it is distorted, a question of law which is subject, as such, to review by the Court of Justice (see, *inter alia*, Joined Cases C-280/99 P to C-282/99 P *Moccia Irme and Others* v. *Commission* [2001] ECR I–4717, paragraph 78).

50. Article 225 EC, Article 51, first paragraph, of the EC Statute of the Court of Justice and Article 112(1)(c) of the Rules of Procedure of the Court of Justice provide, in particular, that where the appellant alleges distortion of the evidence by the Court of First Instance, he must indicate precisely the evidence alleged to have been distorted by that Court and show the errors of appraisal which, in his view, led to that distortion.

51. The requirements resulting from those provisions are not satisfied by an appeal which, without even including an argument specifically identifying the error of law allegedly vitiating the judgment of the Court of First Instance, simply repeats or reproduces verbatim the pleas in law and arguments already put forward before that Court, including those which were based on facts expressly rejected by that Court. Such an appeal amounts in reality to no more than a request for re-examination of the application submitted to the Court of First Instance, which the Court of Justice does not have jurisdiction to undertake (see, *inter alia*, the order in Case C-317/97 P *Smanor and Others* v. *Commission* [1998] ECR I-4269, paragraph 21, and the judgment in Case C-352/98 P *Bergaderm and Goupil* v. *Commission* [2000] ECR I-5291, paragraph 35).

52. It is on the basis of those considerations, in particular, that the Court rejected at the outset as manifestly inadmissible certain of the pleas in law and arguments put forward by the appellants . . .

---

[586] Case C-53/92 P, *Hilti* v. *Commission* [1994] ECR I-666, [1994] 4 CMLR 614. In Case C-57/02 P, *Compañía española para la fabricación de aceros inoxidables SA (Acerinox)* v. *Commission* [2005] ECR I-6689, [2005] 4 CMLR 712, the ECJ annulled the part of the relating to the Spanish market as it held that the CFI had misrepresented the applicant's point of view and so the judgment contained an incorrect statement of reasons.

[587] See also, e.g., Cases C-7/95 P, *John Deere* v. *Commission* [1998] ECR I-3111, [1998] 5 CMLR 311; Case C-185/95 P, *Baustahlgewebe GmbH* v. *Commission* [1998] ECR I-8417, [1999] 4 CMLR 1203; Case C-199/92 P, *Hüls AG* v. *Commission (Polypropylene)* [1999] ECR II-4287, [1999] 5 CMLR 1016; C-238, 244–5, 247, 250, 251–2, and

The correction of a manifest error by the CFI was made in *Aalborg*. The CFI had included within the calculation of the fine to be imposed on one of the participants in the cement cartel the turnover of its Belgian subsidiary. However, at the time of the infringement the undertaking concerned had not yet assumed control of the Belgian company. This was apparent from the *Cement Cartel* decision itself.[588] The ECJ reduced the fine by nearly €3 million as it considered it had the necessary evidence to give judgment itself. It was entitled to do this because Article 61 of the Statute of the Court of Justice provides that if an appeal is well founded the ECJ must quash the CFI's decision and may either refer the matter back to the CFI or, 'where the state of proceedings so permits', itself give final judgment in the matter. The effect of this was nicely illustrated by ECJ's judgment in *PVC Cartel II*. It held that the CFI had wrongly refused to consider, on procedural grounds, Montedison's plea that its right of access to the file had been infringed, and its plea about the Commission's power to fine in the circumstances of the case.[589] The ECJ therefore partially annulled the CFI's decision. However, it decided that this was a case in which it could give final judgment itself. It therefore considered Montedison's pleas and rejected them, leaving Montedison in the same position as it was after the CFI judgment.[590] Article 61 was also applied in *Meca-Medina* where the ECJ set aside the CFI's judgment on the grounds that it had committed an error of law in holding that because purely sporting rules fell outside Articles 39 and 49 of the Treaty they were also excluded from the competition rules. The ECJ proceeded to decide whether the IOC's doping rules were in fact subject to Articles 81 and 82.[591] The ECJ does not always uphold the CFI's interpretation of the law.[592] Also, although upholding the CFI, the ECJ may phrase its own judgment in different terms. This happened in *Magill* where the CFI's attempts to struggle with the intellectual property rights/competition interface were side-stepped by the ECJ which gave a judgment in much narrower terms.[593]

There is an interesting question as to whether the ECJ could hold the CFI to have committed an 'error of law' in a case where the CFI has followed the previous case law of the ECJ but the ECJ wants to depart from that case law. The issue could arise in respect of the reform of Article 82.[594] It is submitted that the civilian conception of case law and precedent would allow the ECJ to find that the CFI *had* committed an error if the ECJ wished to reformulate the law.

In some cases applicants have claimed that proceedings before the CFI were of such an excessive length that their right to a fair trial within a reasonable period under article 6(1) of the

---

254/99, *Limburgse Vinyl Maatschappij NV v. Commission* [2002] ECR I-8375, [2003] 4 CMLR 397; Case C-359/01 P, *British Sugar plc v. Commission* [2004] ECR I-4933, [2004] 5 CMLR 329 .

[588] [1994] OJ L343/1, [1995] 4 CMLR 327.

[589] The peculiarities of the proceedings against the PVC Cartel, which resulted in a first annulled decision being replaced by a second one, are described 1258 *supra*.

[590] C-238, 244–5, 247, 250, 251–2, and 254/99, *Limburgse Vinyl Maatschappij NV v. Commission* [2002] ECR I-8375, [2003] 4 CMLR 397, paras. 355–79, 416–28, and 647–98.

[591] Case C-519/04 P, *Meca-Medina and Majcen v. Commission* [2006] 5 CMLR 1023, see *supra* Chap. 3. And see also Case C-57/02 P, *Compañía española para la fabricación de aceros inoxidables SA (Acerinox) v. Commission* [2005] ECR I-6689, [2005] 4 CMLR 712.

[592] e.g., it set aside the CFI's judgment upholding the Commission decision in the *Net Book Agreement* case, Case C-360/92 P, *Publishers' Association v. Commission* [1995] ECR II-23, [1995] 5 CMLR 33; replaced the CFI's finding of a non-existent act in *PVC I* with a finding of an act which should be annulled: Cases C-137/92 P, *Commission v. BASF and others* [1994] ECR I-2555; and set aside the CFI judgment against the Commission in Case C-51/92 P, *AssiDomän Kraft Products AB and others* [1999] ECR I-5363; [1999] 5 CMLR 1253.

[593] Cases T-69–70/89, 76/89, *RTE, ITP, BBC v. EC Commission* [1991] ECR II-485, [1991] 4 CMLR 586 and Cases C-241–241/91 P, *RTE & ITP v. Commission* [1995] ECR I-743, [1995] 4 CMLR 718: see *supra* Chap. 7.

[594] See *supra*, Chaps 5–7.

ECHR was infringed. The ECJ considers the length of the proceedings in the light of the complexity of the case.[595]

Where appeals against judgments of the CFI on fines are concerned, it is also necessary to distinguish between the functions of the ECJ and the CFI. The ECJ holds firmly that it is for the CFI to examine how the Commission assessed the gravity of the infringement and to decide whether the fine should be changed. The ECJ will not substitute its own assessment for that of the CFI. It stated in *Ferriere Nord*:[596]

31. As regards the allegedly unjust nature of the fine, it is important to point out that it is not for this Court, when ruling on questions of law in the context of an appeal, to substitute, on grounds of fairness, its own assessment for that of the Court of First Instance exercising its unlimited jurisdiction to rule on the amount of fines imposed on undertakings for infringements of Community law (Case C-310/93 P, *BPB Industries and British Gypsum* v. *E.C. Commission*...). In contrast, the Court of Justice does have jurisdiction to consider whether the Court of First Instance has responded to a sufficient legal standard to all the arguments raised by the appellant with a view to having the fine abolished or reduced.

(ix) Interim Measures by the Court under Article 242 EC

Bringing an Article 230 action for annulment does not automatically suspend the contested act. However, Article 242 (ex Article 185) states:

Actions brought before the Court of Justice shall not have suspensory effect. The Court of Justice may, however, if it considers that circumstances so require, order that application of the contested act be suspended.

Also, Article 243 (ex Article 186) provides that in any cases before it, the Court may prescribe any necessary measures. The President of the CFI normally hears applications for suspension. His or her decision may be appealed to the ECJ.[597]

In order for a decision to be suspended the applicants must show that the main action is admissible and that suspension is urgently needed to prevent them suffering irreparable damage which could not be remedied in the event of their winning the main action. On this basis suspension was ordered, *inter alia*, in *United Brands*,[598] *Magill*,[599] *Net Book Agreement*,[600]

---

[595] e.g. Case C-185/95 P, *Baustahlgewebe GmbH* v. *Commission* [1998] ECR I-8417, [1999] 4 CMLR 1203; Case C-194/99 P, *Thyssen Stahl AG* v. *Commission* [2003] ECR I-10821; Case C-403 and 405/04 P, *Sumitomo Metal Industries Ltd* v. *Commission*, 27 January 2007. In *Baustahlgewebe* the CFI had taken thirty-two months between the end of the written procedure and the decision to open the oral procedure and twenty-two months between the oral procedure and the judgment. The ECJ held the plea of excessive delay well-founded but as it had not prejudiced the outcome of the proceedings, the Court merely reduced the three million ECUs fine by 50,000 ECUs. In *Sumitomo* the case had lasted four years three months, but it involved seven undertakings and three languages and virtually all the facts forming the basis of the contested decision were disputed at first instance and therefore had to be verified. The ECJ therefore held the length of the case was justified.

[596] Case C-219/95, *Ferriere Nord* v. *Commission* [1997] ECR I-865; [1997] 5 CMLR 575; see also Case C-310/93 P, *BPB Industries and British Gypsum Ltd* v. *Commission* [1995] ECR I-865, [1997] 4 CMLR 238 at para. 34; Case C-185/95 P, *Baustahlgewebe GmbH* v. *Commission* [1999] 4 CMLR 1203 at paras. 128–9; Case C-359/01 P, *British Sugar* v. *Commission* [2004] ECR I-4933, [2004] 5 CMLR 329, paras. 47–8; Cases C-189/02 P, 202/02 P, 208/02 P and 213/02 P, *Dansk Rørindustri A/S and others* v. *Commission* [2005] ECR I-5425, [2005] 5 CMLR 796, paras. 244–6 and 302.

[597] The Commission appealed in *Atlantic Container Line* when the President suspended its decision: Case C-149/95 P(R), *Commission* v. *Atlantic Container Line and others* [1995] ECR I-2165.

[598] Case 27/76 R, *United Brands* v. *Commission* [1976] ECR 425, [1976] 2 CMLR 147.

[599] Cases 76–7 and 91/89 R, *RTE and others* v. *Commission* [1989] ECR 1141, [1989] 4 CMLR 749.

[600] Case 56/89 R, *Publishers' Association* v. *Commission* [1989] ECR 1693, [1989] 4 CMLR 816.

ADALAT,[601] *Atlantic Container Line*,[602] *Van den Bergh*,[603] and *IMS*.[604] Suspension was refused in *Microsoft* on the grounds that the undertaking had failed to show the likelihood of serious and irreparable damage.[605]

The President has to balance the harm to the applicant from non-suspension (foreseeable with a sufficient degree of probability)[606] with any harm which will be suffered by other parties if the suspension is granted. In *Adalat*, for example, the President considered that as a result of the order the applicant, Bayer, might be obliged to lower the prices of the drug in issue, risking major and irrecoverable losses of profit and that there was a risk that the pharmaceutical base of one subsidiary 'might be deprived of its economic basis, resulting in the dismissal of many employees'. He considered this would be disproportionate in relation to the interests of wholesalers in Spain and France in increasing their exports.[607] Moreover, he was concerned that the Commission's interpretation of the law (i.e., its view of what constitutes an 'agreement' for the purposes of Article 81) was questionable (as, indeed it proved to be).[608]

In *Van den Bergh* the Commission's decision prohibited a distribution system for impulse ice-cream which involved freezer exclusivity and which was the subject of proceedings before the Irish courts. The Irish High Court decided that the distribution system did not infringe but expressed its intention to seek an Article 234 ruling from the ECJ. Meanwhile the Commission's decision was appealed to the CFI. The President of the CFI said that the contradiction between the decision and the judgment was 'contrary to the general principle of legal certainty' and that in the circumstances the Commission's interest in having the infringement brought to an end could not prevail over the applicant's interest in not running the risk of jeopardizing its distribution system or over the interest in limiting the effects of a contradiction in the application of the provisions of the Treaty.[609] He therefore granted a suspension.[610]

The suspension in *IMS* was of an interim decision. Again, as with *Adalat*, the President of the CFI was concerned about the legal basis of the Commission's decision (which concerned the compulsory licensing of a copyright). The suspension was confirmed by the President of the ECJ.[611] The decision was ultimately withdrawn and a final decision not adopted.[612]

The CFI may suspend the obligation to give a bank guarantee ensuring payment of the fine but this is done only in very exceptional circumstances.[613] The CFI (and on appeal, the ECJ)

[601] Case T-41/96 R, *Bayer v. Commission* [1996] ECR II-407, [1996] 5 CMLR 290.

[602] See n. 597.

[603] Case T-65/98 R, *Van den Bergh Foods Ltd v. Commission* [1998] 5 CMLR 475.

[604] Case T-184/01 R, *IMS Health v. Commission* [2001] ECR II-3193, [2002] 4 CMLR 58 (President of the CFI). Case C-481/01 P(R), *IMS Health v. Commission* [2002] ECR I-3401, [2002] 5 CMLR 44 (President of the ECJ).

[605] Case T-201/04 R *Microsoft v EC Commission* [2004] ECR II-4463. See *supra* 1205 for the aftermath of the refusal to suspend the decision.

[606] Case C-280/93 R, *Commission v. Germany* [1993] ECR I-3667.

[607] [1996] ECR II-407 at paras. 59–60.

[608] The Commission's decision was annulled in Case T-41/96, *Bayer v. Commission* [2000] ECR II-3383, [2001] 4 CMLR 4, confirmed by the ECJ, Cases C-2/01 P and 3/01 P, *Bundesverband der Arzneimittel-Importeure EV and the Commission v. Bayer AG* [2004] ECR I-23; [2004] 4 CMLR 653, see *supra* Chap. 3.

[609] *Van den Bergh* at paras. 72–3.

[610] The Commission's decision was upheld by the CFI, Case T-65/98, *Van den Bergh Foods v. Commission* [2004] 4 CMLR 1, *aff'd* by the ECJ, Case C-552/03 P, *Unilever Bestfoods (Ireland) Ltd v EC Commission* [2006] 5 CMLR 1494.

[611] Case C-481/01 P(R), *IMS Health v. Commission* [2002] ECR I-3401, [2002] 5 CMLR 44 (President of the ECJ).

[612] See *supra* Chap. 7.

[613] See Case T-295/94 R, *Buchmann v. Commission* [1994] ECR II-1265 (one of several applications for such interim measures by the undertakings fined in the *Cartonboard Cartel* [1994] OJ L243/1, [1994] 5 CMLR 547).

refused to do it in respect of one of the shipping lines, DSR-Senator, fined in the *TACA* decision.[614]

B. ACTIONS FOR DAMAGES UNDER ARTICLE 288 EC

Article 288 of the Treaty provides for damages for non-contractual liability. The Community 'in accordance with the general principles common to the laws of the Member States' is to make good any damage caused by the institutions or by its servants in the performance of their duties. This raises the possibility that where a decision of the Commission is overturned by the Court the undertakings concerned may be able to sue the Commission for any damage caused to it by the defective decision.

Actions under Article 288 are notoriously difficult for plaintiffs to win.[615] The Community institution must have committed a sufficiently serious breach of a superior rule of law intended to confer rights on individuals, and the test for 'sufficiently serious' is whether the institution manifestly and gravely disregarded the limits on its discretion.[616] These conditions were held not to be fulfilled in *Holcim* where the CFI excused the Commission on the grounds, inter alia, of the difficulties it had faced in the case, which was one of the *Cement* Cartel appeals:

114. . . . regard being had to the fact that *Cement* was a particularly complex case, involving a very large number of undertakings and almost the entire European cement industry, to the fact that the structure of Cembureau made the investigation difficult owing to the existence of direct and indirect members, and to the fact that it was necessary to analyse a great number of documents, including in the applicant's specific situation, it must be held that the defendant was faced with complex situations to be regulated.

115. Last, it is necessary to take account of the difficulties in applying the provisions of the EC Treaty in matters relating to cartels . . . . Those practical difficulties were all the greater because the factual elements of the case in question, including in the part of the decision concerning the applicant, were numerous.[617]

Airtours (now MyTravel) commenced proceedings against the Commission in respect of the prohibition decision of its merger with First Choice which was annulled by the CFI,[618] as did Schneider Electric in respect of the Schneider/Legrand annulled merger decision.[619]

---

[614] Case T-191/98 R, *DSR-Senator Lines v. Commission* [1999] ECR II-2531, confirmed Case C-364/99 P(R), *DSR-Senator Lines v. Commission* [1999] ECR I-8733.

[615] See P. Craig and G. de Búrca, *EU Law: Text, Cases and Materials* (4th edn., Oxford University Press, 2007), chap. 16; T. Hartley, *The Foundations of European Community Law* (5th edn., Oxford University Press, 2003), 450–85.

[616] Case C-352/98 P, *Bergaderm and Goupil v Commission* [2000] ECR I-5291.

[617] Case T-28/03, *Holcim v. Commission* [2005] ECR II-1357, *aff'd* by the ECJ, Case C-252/05 P, *Holcim (Deutschland) AG v. Commission*, 19 April 2007. The undertaking was claiming damages in respect of the charges it had incurred in providing for the bank guarantee for the fine pending the appeal. The CFI held that the claim was, in any case, barred on limitation grounds, as it had not been brought within five years of the guarantee being provided. The five years did not run from the date that the CFI had annulled the decision.

[618] Case T-212/03 (pending), [2003] OJ C 200/28; see *supra* Chap. 12.

[619] Case T-351/03 judgment 11 July 2007. For the merger case, see *supra* Chap.12. The CFI held that the prohibition decision was vitiated by an infringement of Schneider's right to be heard which entailed an obligation on the part of the Community to pay compensation.

8. ENFORCEMENT BY THE NATIONAL COMPETITION AUTHORITIES WITHIN THE EUROPEAN COMPETITION NETWORK

A. GENERAL

The discussion above[620] explains the process of modernization and that the NCAs have, since 1 May 2004, played a much more significant role in the enforcement of the Treaty competition rules. Further, that Regulation 1/2003 creates a system of parallel competences in which the competition rules are enforced by a network of competition authorities (through the ECN), as well as by the national courts. Article 5 of Regulation 1/2003 provides that the 'competition authorities of the Member States shall have power to apply Articles 81 and 82' in individual cases.[621]

Regulation 1/2003, Article 5

Powers of the competent authorities of the Member States

The competition authorities for the Member States shall have the power to apply Articles 81 and 82 of the Treaty in individual cases. For the purpose, acting on their own initiative or on a complaint, they may take the following decisions:

— requiring that an infringement be brought to an end,

— ordering interim measures,

— accepting commitments,

— imposing fines, periodic penalty payments or any other penalty provided for in their national law.

Where on the basis of the information in their possession the conditions for prohibition are not met they may likewise decide that there are no grounds for action on their part.

The Regulation thus permits, and in some cases requires,[622] the NCAs to apply Articles 81 and 82 but leaves the Member State to determine which body will enforce the rules and what mechanisms for investigating infringements and enforcing decisions will apply. This is a notable feature of Regulation 1/2003. It does not demand any particular arrangement, so long as an NCA is designated[623] and the provisions of the Regulation can be complied with.[624] There is no further

---

[620] *Supra* 1142 ff and Chap. 2.

[621] The designation of the bodies responsible for the application of the rules is left to the Member States, Reg. 1/2003, Art. 35. In the UK, Articles 81 and 82 are enforced by the Office of Fair Trading (OFT) and the sectoral regulators have concurrent jurisdiction to enforce the rules in their sectors. The individual web sites of each NCA are accessible through a link from the Commission's web site, http://ec.europa.eu/comm/competition/ecn/news.html, some of them in more than one language. Twenty-one of them (including Ireland and the UK) are available there in English.

[622] See *infra* 1283.

[623] Reg. 1/2003, Art. 35, see *supra* n. 621.

[624] In Ireland, for example, the Competition Authority cannot rule on whether undertakings have breached competition law and cannot impose fines, as the Irish Constitution (Art. 34) reserves such functions for the

attempt at harmonization. Article 35 of Regulation 1/2003 provides that the designated authorities may include courts. It may be that experience with the decentralized system will show that some degree of harmonization is necessary to enable the ECN to function properly.[625]

The creation of a network of authorities responsible for enforcing the same rules obviously creates a number of potential difficulties, in particular, how work is to be allocated between the respective authorities,[626] whether information collected by one authority can be passed onto another, where an application for leniency should be made, whether one authority can conduct inspections on behalf of another and how a uniform and consistent approach in the interpretation and application of the provisions can be maintained. These, and other matters, are dealt with in Regulation 1/2003 itself (especially Articles 11–16) and more fully in the Commission's Notice on cooperation within the Network of Competition Authorities (the Cooperation Notice). Each NCA has signed a statement acknowledging the principles set out in the Notice and agreeing to abide by the principles.[627] The discussion in this chapter indicates, however, that these provisions do not by any means deal with all difficulties that are likely to arise.

B. DIVISION OF WORK

(i) Case Allocation—which Authority is Well Placed to Deal with a Case?

Chapter IV of Regulation 1/2003 deals with cooperation, including cooperation between the Commission and the competition authorities of the Member States. Further, a Joint Statement of the Council and the European Commission on the Functioning of the Network of Competition Authorities (the Joint Statement)[628] sets out the main principles governing the ECN, whilst the Commission's Cooperation Notice provides fuller and more specific detail of cooperation and division of work. Under the new system Article 81 and 82 cases can be dealt with by:

- A single NCA (possibly with the assistance of others);
- Several NCAs acting in parallel;[629] or
- The Commission.[630]

The basic principles[631] are that a case should be dealt with by the authority best placed to deal with it and able to restore or maintain competition in the market, and that cases should be allocated according to a predictable process and as soon as possible in the procedure.[632]

courts. The Irish Competition Authority investigates, but prosecution is in the hands of the Director of Public Prosecutions, and the case is heard in the ordinary courts. The Irish system is therefore similar to that in the US.

[625] The Commission's Notice on cooperation within the Network of Competition Authorities [2004] OJ C101/43 was deliberately left flexible and may well need to be revised.

[626] The principles on work allocation set out in this Notice are of critical importance to a complainant seeking to lodge its complaint with the authority best placed to deal with the case.

[627] This gives companies a legitimate expectation that the principles set out in the Notice will be adhered to.

[628] Available from the European Council's web site, at http://www.register.consilium.eu.int/pdf/en/02/st15/15435-a1en2.pdf.

[629] Cases should be dealt with by a single authority where possible.

[630] Cooperation Notice [2004] OJ C101/43, para. 5.

[631] Joint Statement of the European Council and the European Commission on the functioning of the network of competition authorities, 10 Dec. 2002, available at http://ec.europa.eu/comm/competition/ecn/joint_statement_en.pdf.

[632] *Ibid.*, paras. 11–14.

In order for an authority to be well placed, there must be a material link between the infringement and the territory of the authority (the conduct has substantial direct actual or foreseeable effects in the territory), the authority must be able to bring the entire infringement effectively to an end (either on its own or in parallel with another authority) and the authority be able to gather the evidence required (whether or not with the assistance of another authority).[633] Where two or more NCAs are well placed to act, then one NCA only should act where the action of one would be sufficient to bring the entire infringement to an end. If it would not, then two or more NCAs should act. The authorities should coordinate their action and where possible designate a lead authority for the case.[634] The guidance set out in Cooperation Notice with this respect is set out in the extract below. It can be seen from the extract that the guidance is relatively limited and does not deal with the question of what is to happen in the event of a dispute as to which NCA should act and/or which NCA should take the lead in an investigation.

The Commission is likely to be best placed to deal with an agreement or practice where: it has effects on competition in three or more Member States; the conduct is linked with other Community provisions which may be exclusively or more effectively applied by the Commission: or the Community interest requires it (to develop competition policy or to ensure effective enforcement).[635]

The determination as to which authority deals with the case may be of critical importance to the undertakings investigated, the complainant (if any) and the authorities themselves. Modernization did not entail harmonization of procedure, sanctions[636] or judicial review between the Member States or between the Member States and the Commission, and wide divergences on these matters still exist. Even where Regulation 1/2003 did make provision for the handling of certain matters within the ECN, problems remain.[637] The allocation principles discussed above are set out, with examples, in the Cooperation Notice.

Commission Notice on cooperation within the network of competition authorities [2004] OJ C101/43

8. An authority can be considered to be well placed to deal with a case if the following three cumulative conditions are met:

(1) the agreement or practice has substantial direct actual or foreseeable effects on competition within its territory, is implemented within or originates from its territory;

(2) the authority is able to effectively bring to an end the entire infringement, i.e., it can adopt a cease and desist order the effect of which will be sufficient to bring an end to the infringement and it can, where appropriate, sanction the infringement adequately;

(3) it can gather, possibly with the assistance of other authorities, the evidence required to prove the infringement.

---

[633] Where the effects of an infringement are felt outside the State of the investigating NCA, extraterritoriality issues may arise, see *infra* Chap. 16.

[634] Joint statement, *supra* n. 631, para. 18.

[635] *Ibid.*, para. 19.

[636] In the UK, the maximum level of fine was amended and harmonized with the EC maximum, see OFT Guideline 423 *Guidance as to the appropriate amount of a penalty*.

[637] See, e.g. R. Nazzini, *Concurrent Proceedings in Competition Law* (Oxford University Press, 2004); S. Brammer, 'Concurrent Jurisdiction under Regulation 1/2003 and the Issue of Case Allocation' (2005) 42 *CMLRev* 1383; A. Andreangeli, 'The Impact of the Modernisation Regulation on the Guarantees of Due Process in Competition Proceedings' (2006) 31 *ELRev* 342. For the question of leniency policies, see *infra* 1276.

9. The above criteria indicate that a material link between the infringement and the territory of a Member State must exist in order for that Member State's competition authority to be considered well placed. It can be expected that in most cases the authorities of those Member States where competition is substantially affected by an infringement will be well placed provided they are capable of effectively bringing the infringement to an end through either single or parallel action unless the Commission is better placed to act (see below paragraphs 14 and 15).

10. It follows that a single NCA is usually well placed to deal with agreements or practices that substantially affect competition mainly within its territory.

Example 1: Undertakings situated in Member State A are involved in a price fixing cartel on products that are mainly sold in Member State A.
The NCA in A is well placed to deal with the case.

11. Furthermore single action of an NCA might also be appropriate where, although more than one NCA can be regarded as well placed, the action of a single NCA is sufficient to bring the entire infringement to an end.

Example 2: Two undertakings have set up a joint venture in Member State A. The joint venture provides services in Member States A and B and gives rise to a competition problem. A cease and desist order is considered to be sufficient to deal with the case effectively because it can bring an end to the entire infringement. Evidence is located mainly at the offices of the joint venture in Member State A.
The NCAs in A and B are both well placed to deal with the case but single action by the NCA in A would be sufficient and more efficient than single action by NCA in B or parallel action by both NCAs.

12. Parallel action by two or three NCAs may be appropriate where an agreement or practice has substantial effects on competition mainly in their respective territories and the action of only one NCA would not be sufficient to bring the entire infringement to an end and/or to sanction it adequately.

Example 3: Two undertakings agree on a market sharing agreement, restricting the activity of the company located in Member State A to Member State A and the activity of the company located in Member State B to Member State B.
The NCAs in A and B are well placed to deal with the case in parallel, each one for its respective territory.

13. The authorities dealing with a case in parallel action will endeavour to coordinate their action to the extent possible. To that effect, they may find it useful to designate one of them as a lead authority and to delegate tasks to the lead authority such as for example the coordination of investigative measures, while each authority remains responsible for conducting its own proceedings.

14. The Commission is particularly well placed if one or several agreement(s) or practice(s), including networks of similar agreements or practices, have effects on competition in more than three Member States (cross-border markets covering more than three Member or several national markets).

Example 4: Two undertakings agree to share markets or fix prices for the whole territory of the Community. The Commission is well placed to deal with the case.

Example 5: An undertaking, dominant in four different national markets, abuses its position by imposing fidelity rebates on its distributor in all these markets. The Commission is well placed to deal with the case. It could also deal with one national market so as to create a 'leading' case and other national markets could be dealt with by NCAs, particularly if each national market requires a separate assessment.

15. Moreover, the Commission is particularly well placed to deal with a case if its is closely linked to other Community provisions which may be exclusively or more effectively applied by the Commission, or if the Community interest requires the adoption of a Commission decision to develop Community competition policy when a new competition issue arises or to ensure effective enforcement.

In order to ensure that allocation takes place as quickly as possible, and normally within a period of two months,[638] Article 11(3) of Regulation 1/2003 imposes an obligation on the NCAs to inform the Commission and other NCAs 'before or without delay after commencing the first formal investigative measure'.[639] Further, the Commission is obliged to transmit copies of documents to the NCAs that it has collected pursuant to its powers of investigation under Articles 18–21 of Regulation 1/2003. Once a case has been initially allocated the case should not ordinarily be re-allocated unless the facts known about the case change materially during the course of the proceedings.[640] Article 13 of Regulation 1/2003 specifically provides that an authority (the Commission or an NCA) may suspend proceedings or reject a case that is being, or has been, dealt with by another competition authority.[641]

It is possible that a decision by the Commission under Article 11(6) to remove a case from an NCA and deal with it itself is a challengeable act under Article 230 EC[642] although decisions of NCAs to terminate or open proceedings are challengeable only under their national laws.

(ii) Transfer of Information

Where an authority does suspend national proceedings or reject a complaint on the grounds that it is being dealt with by another authority, that authority is permitted to transfer information, including confidential information to the authority which is dealing with the case. Regulation 1/2003, Article 12(1) provides generally for the Commission and the NCAs to provide one another with and use in evidence 'any matter of fact or of law, including confidential information'.[643] In order to protect the interests of individuals and undertakings, safeguards exist against the use and exchange of this information in certain circumstances. In particular, the competition authorities are bound by an obligation of professional secrecy, the information transferred can be used only for the purposes of applying Articles 81 or 82 (and in certain circumstances national competition law) and in respect of the subject-matter for which it was collected,[644] and the information can only be used to impose sanctions on *natural* persons where the law of the transmitting authority foresees sanctions of a similar kind in relation to the infringement or the information has been collected in a way that affords the person the same level of protection of rights provided for under the rules of the receiving authorities. Thus an NCA which may not impose sanctions on individuals, may not transfer information to an NCA, such as the UK's OFT, which may, unless: (1) the information was collected in a way which respects the rights of defence afforded to the individuals by the rules of the receiving authority (but custodial sanctions can be imposed only where both the transmitting and the receiving authority can impose such a sanction); or (2) the receiving authority does not use the

---

[638] Cooperation Notice [2004] OJ C101/43, para. 18.

[639] In the UK this is after the use of powers of investigation set out in ss. 26–8 of the Competition Act 1998, see OFT 442 'Guideline on Modernisation', para. 7.7.

[640] *Ibid.*, para. 19.

[641] The Commission can also reject a complaint which lacks Community interest or which fails to substantiate an allegation, see *infra* 1294. National provisions may also provide an alternative basis for suspending a complaint.

[642] See *infra* 1280.

[643] The information must of course have been collected in a legal manner by the transmitting authority.

[644] Reg. 1/2003, Art. 12(2).

information in proceedings against an individual but only in proceedings against an undertaking. The safeguards are explained more fully in paragraph 28 of the Commission's Cooperation Notice.

Commission Notice on cooperation within the network of competition authorities [2004] OJ C101/43

28. The exchange and use of information contains in particular the following safeguards for undertakings and individuals

(a) First, Article 28 of the Council Regulation [Regulation 1/2003] states that 'the Commission and competition authorities of the Member States, their officials, servants and other persons working under the supervision of these authorities . . . shall not disclose information acquired or exchanged by them pursuant to the' Council Regulation which is 'of the kind covered by the obligation of professional secrecy'. However, the legitimate interest of undertakings in the protection of their business secrets may not prejudice the disclosure of information necessary to prove an infringement of Articles 81 and 82 of the Treaty. The term 'professional secrecy' used in Article 28 of the Council Regulation is a Community law concept and includes in particular business secrets and other confidential information. This will create a common minimum level of protection throughout the Community.

(b) The second safeguard given to undertakings relate to the use of information within the network. Under Article 12(2) of the Council Regulation, information so exchanged can only be used in evidence for the application of Articles 81 and 82 of the Treaty and for the subject matter for which it was collected. According to Article 12(2) of the Council Regulation, the information exchanged may also be used for the purpose of applying national competition law in parallel in the same case. This is, however, only possible if the application of national law does not lead to an outcome as regards the finding of an infringement different from that under Articles 81 and 82 of the Treaty.

(c) The third safeguard given by the Council Regulation relates to sanctions on individuals on the basis of information exchanged pursuant to Article 12(1). The Council Regulation only provides for sanctions on undertakings for violations of Articles 81 and 82 of the Treaty. Some national laws also provide for sanctions on individuals in connection with violations of Articles 81 and 82 of the Treaty. Individuals normally enjoy more extensive rights of defence (e.g., a right to remain silent compared to undertakings which may only refuse to answer questions which would lead them to admit that they have committed an infringement[645]). Article 12(3) of the Council Regulation ensures that information collected from undertakings cannot be used in a way which would circumvent the higher protection of individuals. This provision precludes sanctions being imposed on individuals on the basis of information exchanged pursuant to the Council Regulation if the laws of the transmitting and receiving authorities do not provide for sanctions of a similar kind in respect of individuals, unless the rights of the individual concerned as regards the collection of evidence have been respected by the transmitting authority to the same standard as they are guaranteed by the receiving authority. The qualification of the sanctions by national law ('administrative' or 'criminal') is not relevant for the purpose of applying Article 12(3) of the Council Regulation. The Council Regulation intends to create a distinction between sanctions which result in custody and other types of sanctions such as fines on individuals and other personal sanctions. If both the legal system of the transmitting state and that of the receiving authority provide for sanctions of similar kind (e.g., in both Member States fines can be imposed on a member of the

---

[645] See, e.g., Case 374/87, *Orkem* [1989] ECR 3282.

staff of an undertaking who has been involved in the violation of Article 81 or 82 of the Treaty), information exchanged pursuant to Article 12 of the Council Regulation can be used by the receiving authority. In that case, procedural safeguards in both systems are considered to be equivalent. If on the other hand, both legal systems do not provide for sanctions of a similar kind, the information can only be used if the same level of protection of the rights of the individual has been respected in the case at hand (see Article 12(3) of the Council Regulation). In the latter case however, custodial sanctions can only be imposed where both the transmitting and the receiving authority have the power to impose such a sanction.

It has been argued that, despite these provisions, serious doubts remain as to how well the rights of the defence are safeguarded by the exchange of information provided for by Article 12(1).[646] There is a particular problem, for instance, in the divergence between the Member States' legal systems in the protection given to certain classes of information, such as what is covered by legal professional privilege.[647] This could result in an NCA using information it would have been unable to collect under the rules of its own jurisdiction.[648]

(iii) Leniency Applications

In both Chapters 11 and above the importance of leniency regimes in the fight against cartels has been stressed, and the Commission's leniency regime discussed.[649] At the time of writing twenty-two Member States, including the UK, also operate leniency programmes.[650] Because, however, there is no EU-wide system 'an application for leniency to a given authority is not to be considered as an application for leniency to any other authority'.[651] An undertaking contemplating a leniency application will therefore have to consider making an application to *all* authorities which have competence to apply Article 81 in the territory affected by the infringement (which have leniency policies) and which are likely to be considered to be well placed to deal with the infringement (even if the infringement takes place in three or more Member States

---

[646] A. Andreangeli, 'The Impact of the Modernisation Regulation on the Guarantees of Due Process in Competition Proceedings' (2006) 31 *ELRev* 342.

[647] For the position on legal professional privilege in Community law, see *supra* 1181.

[648] A. Andreangeli, *supra* n. 646, 354–6; B. Vesterdof, 'Legal professional Privilege and the Privilege against Self-Incrimination in EC Law: Recent Developments and Current Issues' (2004) *Fordham Corp L Inst* 19 (B. Hawk, Ed. 2005); see for example the UK, where legal professional privilege extends to communications with in-house lawyers (c. f. the position in EC law, discussed *supra* 1181) and the OFT says: ' Whilst UK privilege rules would apply to cases being investigated in the UK by the OFT on its own behalf, the OFT could be sent the communications of in-house lawyers, or lawyers qualified outside the EU, by an NCA from another Member State where the communication of such lawyers are not privileged. Under those circumstances, the OFT may use the documentation received from the other NCA in its investigation' (OFT Guideline 404, *Powers of Investigation*, 6.3).

[649] *Supra* 1240.

[650] These are, at 1 February 2007: Austria (Bundeswettbewerbsbehörde), Belgium (Conseil de la Concurrence/Raad voor de Mededinging), Bulgaria (Commission for the Protection of Competition), Cyprus (Commission for the Protection of Competition-CPC), The Czech Republic (Office for the Protection of Competition), Estonia (Konkurentsiamet), Finland (Kilpailuvirasto), France (Conseil de la concurrence), Germany (Bundeskartellamt), Greece (Hellenic Competition Commission), Hungary (Gazdasági Versenyhivatal (GVH)), Ireland (The Competition Authority), Latvia (Konkurences padome), Lithuania (Lietuvos Respublikos konkurencijos taryba), Luxembourg (Ministère de l'Economie et du Commerce Extérieur), The Netherlands (Nederlandse Mededingingsautoriteit (NMa)), Poland (Urzad Ochrony Konkurencji i Konsumentów), Portugal (Autoridade da Concorrência), Romania (Consiliul Concurentei), Slovakia (Protimonopolný úrad Slovenskej republiky), Sweden (Konkurrensverket), The United Kingdom (Office of Fair Trading (OFT)) .

[651] Cooperation Notice [2004] OJ C 101/43, para. 37.

the applicants may not be sure that the Commission will take jurisdiction). In view of the importance of *timing* in leniency applications (totally immunity is usually available only to the first to come forward),[652] it will usually be advisable to make simultaneous applications. An authority considering opening an investigation as a result of a leniency application has a duty to inform other members of the ECN.[653] Information submitted to the network in this way may not, however, be used by the receiving authorities as a basis for starting an investigation on their own behalf. Further, information will, generally,[654] only be transmitted pursuant to Article 12 with the consent of the leniency applicant that has voluntary submitted the information voluntarily.[655]

Given the Commission's belief that leniency plays an important part in the fight against cartels, the inability for firms to file a single 'EU' leniency application was a notable omission from the Cooperation Notice. Even though not all Member States operate leniency programmes, it would have been possible, for example, to have established the Commission as the central recipient and co-ordinator of NCAs which do have such programmes or to have provided that NCAs may receive leniency applications on behalf of another NCA. The modernization programme did not make such provision, however. The Commission was anxious that the efficacy of leniency should not be undermined by decentralization[656] but the post May 2004 position had clear deficiencies from the view of both the competition authorities and the (potential) applicant.

C. Gauer and M. Jaspers, 'Designing a European Solution for a "One Stop Leniency Shop" ' (2006) *ECLR* 685, 686–687[657]

The current system has certain deficits both from the (potential) immunity applicant's . . . point of view and from the Competition Authorities' erspective. . . .

An applicant that has been involved in a cartel covering more than one jurisdiction may be faced with a number of potentially applicable leniency programmes with different rules and procedures that may even appear to be contradictory. . . .

This fact raises two different problems. First, certain discrepancies between the existing programmes (as well as the absence of programmes in certain jurisdictions) create what can be qualified as a "race to the top". An applicant will only be willing to come forward under any programme if it can qualify under the most restrictive programme and if it is satisfied with the lowest degree of legal certainty provided by the least beneficial programme. If, for example, an authority does not give any assurance to applicants before the very end of its proceedings, the potential applicant will balance that uncertainty before applying to any authority. Discrepancies not only make the assessment and the decision to report illegal activities more complex but some discrepancies may even deter applicants from reporting certain conduct at all.

---

[652] See *supra* 1243 And the provisions of the ECN Model Leniency Programme, *infra* 1279.

[653] Reg. 1/2003, Art. 11.

[654] But see Cooperation Notice [2004] OJ C101/43, para. 41.

[655] Cooperation Notice [2004] OJ C 101/43, paras. 39–42 and on the transfer of information, see *supra* 1274.

[656] S. Blake and D. Schnichels, 'Leniency Following Modernisation: Safeguarding Europe's Leniency Programmes' [2004] *ECLR* 765.

[657] The authors are officials in DG Comp, although the article is subject to the usual disclaimers. See also C. Gauer and M. Jaspers, 'The European Competition Network—Achievements and Challenges—a case in point: leniency' (2006) 1 *EC Competition Policy Newsletter*, 8.

> Secondly, multiple filing with a large number of authorities is often cumbersome, costly and difficult to organise within a very short period of time. In addition, applicants would normally be bound by a duty of co-operation vis-a-vis all these authorities, irrespective of whether the authorities would in the end investigate the case or not.
>
> The same deficits have also some unwanted consequences from the Competition Authorities' perspective. Primarily, the absence of leniency programmes in some jurisdictions and the "race to the top" created by the discrepancies between the existing programmes could have adverse effects on those programmes that offer a more favourable treatment to applicants and would seem to function well. It can result in potentially less applications to the authorities and to less cartel detection in the EU.
>
> Moreover, even if the current system ensures an efficient division of work between the authorities, processing leniency applications and granting immunity in cases where the authorities know that they will not take action is unnecessarily burdensome.
>
> Finally, the safeguards set out in the Network Notice create in a number of cases over protection of applicants. . . . This is in particular the case when two authorities with different immunity applicants for the same cartel wish to exchange information and need to abstain from imposing any fines on the other applicant in order to do so.

The Commission and the other members of the ECN were aware of these problems. In April 2005 the Competition Commissioner announced that she was consulting on the idea of a 'one-stop shop' for leniency applications.[658] In the event, ECN considered various ways of dealing with the difficulties.[659] First, a system of mutual recognition could have been established, by which immunity or a reduction of fines granted by one authority would be recognized by all other members of the ECN. This was rejected as impracticable as the authority receiving the application would have to check with all the others in order to see whether the applicant qualified (was it the first? did another authority already have sufficient information? etc) which would inevitably cause delays in a situation where speed is vital. Also, it would be unsatisfactory without some degree of harmonization between the policies. Secondly, a fully centralized 'one-stop shop' could have been established, by which all leniency applications would be made to the Commission: if the case was later allocated to an NCA (or NCAs) the leniency application would go with the allocation. That was also rejected as being impracticable as, again, the Commission would have to ensure that no NCA had sufficient information to act before granting immunity; participants in mainly national cartels might not apply if it meant becoming embroiled with the Commission; and it would deprive the NCA of direct contact with the applicant in the crucial period when the authority is preparing for an inspection by using the information provided. Thirdly, the ECN considered a system analogous to the regime established by the Merger Regulation,[660] whereby jurisdictional criteria would be developed for allocating cases between authorities and the applicants would approach those which would be dealing with their case. This solution was rejected because of the impossibility of formulating such criteria satisfactorily, as at the time the applicant was considering a leniency application it would not necessarily be aware of the extent and effects of the cartel, and different applicants might approach different authorities. Moreover, the Commission has power to take action against any cartel under Regulation 1/2003, Article 11(6).

---

[658] Neelie Kroes, 'The First Hundred Days', speech, Brussels, 7 April 2005, available on DG Comp's web site.

[659] C. Gauer and M. Jaspers, 'Designing a European Solution for a "One Stop Leniency Shop" ' (2006) *ECLR* 685.

[660] Regulation 139/2004 [2004] OJ L24/1, see *supra* Chap. 12.

The ECN turned instead to further harmonization. In September 2006 it adopted the ECN Model Leniency Programme. The aim was to produce a model setting out the minimum standards with which all ECN policies should be aligned.[661] It is without prejudice to an NCA adopting a more favourable stance towards applicants. The explanatory notes to the programme state:

8. While it is highly desirable to ensure that all Cas operate a leniency programme, the variety of legislative frameworks, procedures and sanctions across the EU makes it difficult to adopt one uniform system. The ECN Model Programme therefore sets out the principal elements which, after the soft harmonisation process has occurred, should be common to all leniency programmes across the ECN. This would be without prejudice to the possibility for a CA to add further detailed provisions which suit its own enforcement system or to provide for a more favourable treatment of its applicants if it considers it to be necessary in order to ensure effective enforcement.

The model provides for immunity (Type 1 applications: Type 1A is immunity before inspections, Type 1B is immunity after inspections, corresponding to paragraphs 8(a) and 8(b) of the Commission's 2006 Notice),[662] subject to conditions; and for a reduction in fines (Type 2 applications),[663] subject to conditions. It also contains procedural requirements, including a 'marker' system (as under the Commission's 2006 Notice[664]) and the acceptability of oral applications.[665] It provides for NCAs to accept 'summary applications' for Type 1A immunity, containing more limited information than normally required, where the applicant has, or is in the process of, filing an immunity application with the Commission.[666] The explanatory notes exhort those Member States which can impose sanctions on individuals to ensure that employees and directors of applicants for leniency are protected, in order to ensure the efficient working of the corporate programme.[667]

The Commission's 2006 Notice[668] is fully in line with the Model Programme.

C. CONSISTENT APPLICATION OF ARTICLES 81 AND 82

(i) General

It has been explained that, despite the creation of a network of authorities, the Commission has sought to retain its central role 'as the guardian of the Treaty' which 'has the ultimate but not the sole responsibility for developing policy and safeguarding consistency when it comes to the application of EC competition law'.[669]

---

[661] Or, in the case of Member State without a leniency programme, adopted and aligned. In some Member States the adoption of, or alterations to, a leniency programme requires legislation or some other form of law-making not under the control of the NCA, which means that the wish of the NCA to have such a programme is not definitive of the matter.

[662] ECN Model Leniency Programme, paras. 5–8.

[663] *Ibid.*, paras. 9–12.

[664] *Ibid.*, paras 16–18.

[665] *Ibid.*, paras 28–30.

[666] *Ibid.*, paras 22–5. The ECN page on the DG Comp web site contains a list of NCAs which accept summary applications, see http://ec.europa.eu/comm/competition/ecn/accepting_nca.pdf.

[667] *Ibid.*, Explanatory Notes, para. 15. For criminal sanctions, see *infra* 1285.

[668] *Supra* 1242 ff.

[669] Cooperation Notice, para. 43.

(ii) Mechanism of Cooperation

Article 11 of Regulation 1/2003 deals with cooperation between the Commission and the competition authorities of the Member States, providing that the NCAs and Commission should apply the Community competition rules in 'close cooperation'.[670] It has already been seen that it provides for: the Commission and NCAs respectively to inform each other when acting under Article 81 or 82,[671] and for the early allocation of cases. Article 11(4) also provides for the NCAs to inform the Commission[672] 30 days prior to the adoption of a decision applying Articles 81 or 82 and requiring that the infringement be brought to an end.[673] The Commission may then make written observations on the case before the adoption of the decision by the NCA, or may decide itself to initiate proceedings. Article 11(6) of Regulation 1/2003 provides that the initiation of proceedings by the Commission relieves the NCAs of their competence to apply Articles 81 and 82.[674] 'This means that once the Commission has opened proceedings, NCAs cannot act under the same legal basis against the same agreement(s) or practice(s) by the same undertaking(s) on the same relevant geographic and product market'.[675] The existence of Article 11(6) is thus a powerful weapon in the hands of the Commission and gives it considerable leverage over an NCA when it disapproves of the decision it is about to adopt. The Commission deals with the full consequence of its Article 11(6) power in its Cooperation Notice. The Notice indicates that it will only rarely initiate proceedings where a case has initially been allocated to another NCA.[676]

Commission Notice on cooperation within the network of competition authorities [2004] OJ C101/43

52. The initiation of proceedings by the Commission is a formal act by which the Commission indicates its intention to adopt a decision under Chapter III of the Council Regulation. It can occur at any stage of the investigation of the case by the Commission. The mere fact that the Commission has received a complaint is not in itself sufficient to relieve NCAs of their competence.

53. Two situations can arise. First, where the Commission is the first competition authority to initiate proceedings in a case for the adoption of a decision under the Council Regulation, national competition authorities may no longer deal with the case. Article 11(6) of the Council Regulation provides that once the Commission has initiated proceedings, the NCAs can no longer start their own procedure with a view to applying Articles 81 and 82 of the Treaty to the same agreement(s) or practice(s) by the same undertaking(s) on the same relevant geographic and product market.

---

[670] Reg. 1/2003, Art. 11(1).

[671] NCAs informed the Commission of 180 new case investigations in 2005 (Commission's *XXXVth Report on Competition Policy* (Commission, 2006), para. 210).

[672] The information may also be shared with the NCAs, Reg. 1/2003, Art. 11(4).

[673] Article 11(5) states that the NCAs may consult the Commission on any case involving the application of Community law. This may be useful, e.g., where the NCA wishes to adopt a decision rejecting a complaint or closing a procedure, etc.

[674] See *supra* 1274.

[675] Cooperation Notice [2004] OJ C101/43, para. 51.

[676] The Commission did not open proceedings in any of the 80 cases from 18 different NCAs in which it received information under Article 11(4) in 2005 (Commission's *XXXVth Report on Competition Policy* (Commission, 2006), paras. 216–17).

54. The second situation is where one or more NCAs have informed the network pursuant to Article 11(3) of the Council Regulation that they are acting on a given case. During the initial allocation period (indicative time period of two months, see paragraph 18 above), the Commission can initiate proceedings with the effects of Article 11(6) of the Council Regulation after having consulted the authorities concerned. After the allocation phase, the Commission will in principle only apply Article 11(6) of the Council Regulation if one of the following situations arises:

(a) Network members envisage conflicting decisions in the same case.

(b) Network members envisage a decision which is obviously in conflict with consolidated case law; the standards defined in the judgements of the Community courts and in previous decisions and regulations of the Commission should serve as a yardstick: concerning the assessment of the facts (e.g., market definition), only a significant divergence will trigger an intervention of the Commission;

(c) Network member(s) is (are) unduly drawing out proceedings in the case;

(d) There is a need to adopt a Commission decision to develop Community competition policy in particular when a similar competition issue arises in several Member States or to ensure effective enforcement;

(e) The NCA(s) concerned do not object.[677]

55. If an NCA is already acting on a case, the Commission will explain the reasons for the application of Article 11(6) of the Council Regulation in writing to the NCA concerned and to the other members of the Network.

56. The Commission will announce to the network its intention of applying Article 11(6) of the Council Regulation in due time, so that Network members will have the possibility of asking for a meeting of the Advisory Committee on the matter before the Commission initiates proceedings.

57. The Commission will normally not—and to the extent that Community interest is not at stake—adopt a decision which is in conflict with a decision of an NCA after proper information pursuant to both Article 11(3) and (4) of the Council Regulation has taken place and the Commission has not made use of Article 11(6) of the Council Regulation.

There are good grounds for arguing that the initiation of proceedings by the Commission which thereby removes the competence of an NCA to deal with the case under Article 11(6) is a challengeable act under Article 230 EC.[678] Although the initiation of proceedings is a 'preparatory act'[679] it is also a final decision to close the NCA's investigation and subjects the undertaking concerned to a new procedural regime, thus altering its legal position.[680]

---

[677] See also Joint Statement of the European Council and the European Commission on the functioning of the network of competition authorities, 10 Dec. 2002, *supra* n. 631 para. 21.

[678] See D. Geradin and N. Petit, 'Judicial Remedies under EC Competition Law: Complex Issues Arising from the "Modernisation" Process' 2005 *Fordham Corp L Inst* 393 (B. Hawk, ed. 2006); cf. C. Kerse and N. Khan, *EC Antitrust Procedure* (5th edn., Sweet & Maxwell, 2005), 2-079, L.Ortiz Blanco, *EC Competition Procedure* (2nd edn., Oxford University Press, 2006), 3.14.

[679] And thereby excluded from challenge, according to Case 60/81, *IBM* v. *Commission* [1981] ECR 2639, [1981] 3 CMLR 635.

[680] Further, an analogy can be drawn with Article 9 decisions under the ECMR, Regulation 139/2004 [2004] OJ L24/1, whereby the Commission refers a merger with a Community dimension back to a national authority (see *supra* Chap. 12). Article 9 decisions are challengeable, see Case T-112/02, *Royal Philips Electronics BV* v *Commission* [2003] ECR II-1433. The situation is, however, distinguishable from Article 11(6) as an Article 9 decision may subject the undertakings to different substantive law provisions, whereas the Commission and the NCAs are all supposed to applying the same provisions (Articles 81 and 82) in a uniform manner: see Geradin and Petit, *op.cit.*, n. 678 402–3.

D. EC AND NATIONAL COMPETITION LAW

National competition authorities are of course entrusted with the enforcement of their own domestic competition rules as well as the EC competition rules. The question of whether and when they may or must apply national rules, EC rules, or both to anti-competitive conduct and the relationship between EC and national competition law is dealt with below.

9. THE RELATIONSHIP BETWEEN EC AND NATIONAL COMPETITION LAW

It has always been the case that Articles 81 and 82 and the domestic competition rules of the Member States can be applied concurrently. The applicability of Articles 81 and 82 has not precluded the application of the national competition provisions.[681] The fact that the rules may apply concurrently obviously leads to the possibility that their joint application may not always achieve the same outcome. Important questions which have arisen therefore are whether an NCA or national court could, for example: (1) authorize an agreement or practice prohibited by Article 81 or 82; or (2) condemn conduct which is not prohibited by Community law (e.g., because an agreement does not infringe Article 81(1) or meets the criteria of Article 81(3)).

In the context of the ECMR, the allocation of jurisdiction over mergers between the Community and national authorities has always been defined by the regulation itself.[682] In contrast, Regulation 17 did not deal with this situation. Rather, case law developed which provided, in accordance with the principle of supremacy[683] and Article 10 EC,[684] that national law could be applied so long as its application did not 'prejudice the full and uniform application of Community law or the effects of measures taken or to be taken to implement it'.[685] The case law made it clear that a national authority could not authorize an agreement or conduct prohibited by Community law,[686] but was less clear on the question of whether, and if so when, national rules could be used to prohibit an agreement authorized at the Community level.[687] The position is now more clearly dealt with in Article 3 of Regulation 1/2003.

---

[681] Case 14/68, *Walt Wilhelm v. Bundeskartellamt* [1969] ECR 1, [1969] CMLR 100.

[682] This is dealt with in Chap. 12. A Notice on referrals deals with the circumstances in which jurisdiction may be passed by the Commission to the competent national authorities and *vice versa*.

[683] *Supra* Chap. 2.

[684] Article 10 of the Treaty provides that 'Member States shall take all appropriate measured...to ensure fulfilment of the obligations arising out of this Treaty or resulting from action taken by the institutions of the Community. They shall facilitate the achievement of the Community's tasks.' It thus imposes an obligation of solidarity on the national authorities in respect of the Community project.

[685] Case 14/68, *Walt Wilhelm v. Bundeskartellamt* [1969] ECR 1, [1969] CMLR 100, para. 9.

[686] *Ibid.* The fact that an agreement has been authorized at the national level does not preclude the Commission from subsequently finding that the agreement in fact infringes Article 81: see Case C-360/92 P, *Publishers' Association* [1995] ECR I-23, [1995] 5 CMLR 33.

[687] See, e.g., C. S. Kerse, *EC Antitrust Procedure* (4th edn., Sweet & Maxwell, 1998), para. 10.33.

Regulation 1/2003, Article 3

Relationship between Articles 81 and 82 of the Treaty and national competition laws

1. Where the competition authorities of the Member States or national courts apply national competition law to agreements, decisions by associations of undertakings or concerted practices within the meaning of Article 8(1) of the Treaty which may affect trade between Member States within the meaning of that provision, they shall also apply Article 81 of the Treaty to such agreements, decisions or concerted practices. Where the competition authorities of the Member States or national courts apply national competition law to any abuse prohibited by Article 82 of the Treaty, they shall also apply Article 82 of the Treaty.

2. The application of national competition law may not lead to the prohibition of agreements, decisions by associations of undertakings or concerted practices which may affect trade between Member States but which do not restrict competition within the meaning of Article 81(1) of the Treaty, or which fulfil the conditions of Article 81(3) of the Treaty or which are covered by a Regulation for the application of Article 81(3) of the Treaty. Member States shall not under this Regulation be precluded from adopting and applying on their territory stricter national laws which prohibit or sanction unilateral conduct engaged in by undertakings.

3. Without prejudice to general principles and other provisions of Community law, paragraphs 1 and 2 do not apply when the competition authorities and the courts of the Member States apply national merger control laws nor do they preclude the application of provisions of national law that predominantly pursue an objective different from that pursued by Articles 81 and 82 of the Treaty.

It can be seen from this that not only does Regulation 1/2003 make it clear that NCAs and national courts have the power to apply Articles 81 and 82, but Article 3(1) provides that where an NCA or national court applies national competition law to conduct which constitutes an agreement, decision, or concerted practice within the meaning of Article 81 or an abuse prohibited by Article 82, which affects trade between Member States,[688] it *shall* also apply Article 81 or Article 82.[689] National authorities are thus *obliged* when applying national law to agreements and abusive conduct that affect trade between Member states to also apply Community law.

In order to provide a level playing field,[690] Article 3(2) deals with the relationship between Community and national law and, specifically, with when national authorities may apply *stricter* national laws to agreements or conduct. The position differs depending upon whether Article 81 or 82 applies. If an agreement is authorized by Article 81, either because it does not restrict competition within the meaning of Article 81(1), it fulfils the criteria of Article 81(3), or satisfies the conditions of a block exemption, it cannot be prohibited by national law. The national authorities are, however, free to apply national competition laws which are stricter than Article 82 to unilateral conduct.[691] They may therefore prohibit or impose sanctions on unilateral conduct engaged in by undertakings which does not constitute an abuse of a dominant position.[692]

---

[688] For the meaning of an effect on trade between Member States, see *supra* Chap. 3.

[689] Reg. 1/2203, Art. 3(1).

[690] Reg. 1/2003, recital 8.

[691] In the UK such conduct may, therefore, be examined under the market investigation provisions of the Enterprise Act 2002.

[692] In the UK, the competition authorities may investigate a market and impose remedies under the Enterprise Act 2002. If the conduct amounts to an abuse of a dominant position under Article 82 the OFT

Article 3(2) does not deal with the position where conduct is prohibited by Article 81 or 82. However, the principle of supremacy of Community law means that such an agreement or conduct cannot be permitted under national law.

Article 3(3) makes it clear that neither Article 3(1) or (2) apply where the authority wishes to apply national merger control rules or national provisions that predominantly pursue a different objective to agreements or conduct. An NCA applying national merger rules to an acquisition or joint venture which is not a concentration with a Community dimension (or which has a Community dimension but has been referred back to the NCA) does not have to apply Article 81 or 82. Further, the Regulation does not preclude the implementation of more onerous 'national legislation, which protects other legitimate interests provided that such legislation is compatible with general principles and other provisions of Community law'.[693] This means that in the UK, for example, regulators, when applying sectoral powers which pursue a predominantly different objective to Articles 81 and 82, are not obliged to apply Article 81 or 82. To the extent that they are applying the UK competition rules or sectoral powers pursuing the same objective, however, they are obliged to apply Articles 81 and 82 and to comply with Article 3(2).

An interesting case dealing with the principle of supremacy of Community law and the relationship between Community and national law was CIF.[694] This case concerned Italian legislation, dating from 1923, which established a consortium of domestic match manufacturers, the CIF. The legislation had been altered over time but essentially conferred a monopoly on CIF over the right to manufacture and sell matches for consumption on the Italian match market. Complex rules governing the internal workings of the consortium set out production quotas for the different members of the consortium. The Italian competition authority investigated the market at the complaint of a German match manufacturer which was having trouble penetrating the Italian market. Although the Commission considered that some breaches of Article 81 had been committed by the undertakings acting 'autonomously',[695] it also declared the Italian legislation establishing and governing the CIF to be contrary to Article 81, read in conjunction with Articles 3(1)(g) and 10 EC.[696] CIF challenged both the assessment of the facts and the question of the whether the authority was competent to determine the validity of the national law with Community law. The Tribunale amministrativo regionale per il Lazio referred several questions to the ECJ for a preliminary ruling, including the question whether Article 81 requires or permits the national competition authority to disapply a national measure which requires or facilitates agreements contrary to Article 81 and to penalize the anti-competitive conduct of the undertakings or, in any event, to prohibit it for the future, and if so, with what legal consequences. In its judgment the ECJ stressed that the primacy of Community required any provision of national law which contravenes a Community rule to be disapplied and that the duty applied to all organs of the State, including administrative authorities.[697] It made no difference that the undertakings themselves could not be held accountable for infringements of

---

would be obliged to investigate taking into account the Enterprise Act remedies imposed. If the reference includes conduct that does not amount to an abuse, there would be no obligation to apply Article 82 and the UK authorities would be able to prohibit or sanction the conduct, see OFT 442, 'Guideline on Modernisation', para. 4.27.

[693] Reg. 1/2003, recital 9.

[694] Case C-198/01, *Consorzio Industrie Fiammiferi (CIF)* v. *Autorità Garante della Concorrenza e del Mercato* [2003] ECR I-8055; [2003] 5 CMLR 829.

[695] See also *supra* Chap. 3.

[696] See also *supra* Chap. 8.

[697] Case C-198/01, paras. 48–50.

Articles 81 or 82 required by national law:[698] the obligations of the Member State were distinct and the NCA remained duty bound to disapply the national legislation.[699] The ECJ thus gave the following answer to the first question referred by the Italian court:

> 58. In light of the foregoing considerations, the answer to be given to the first question referred for a preliminary ruling is that, where undertakings engage in conduct contrary to Article 81(1) EC and where that conduct is required or facilitated by national legislation which legitimises or reinforces the effects of the conduct, specifically with regard to price-fixing or market-sharing arrangements, a national competition authority, one of whose responsibilities is to ensure that Article 81 EC is observed:
>
> — has a duty to disapply the national legislation;
>
> — may not impose penalties in respect of past conduct on the undertakings concerned when the conduct was required by the national legislation;
>
> — may impose penalties on the undertakings concerned in respect of conduct subsequent to the decision to disapply the national legislation, once the decision has become definitive in their regard;
>
> — may impose penalties on the undertakings concerned in respect of past conduct where the conduct was merely facilitated or encouraged by the national legislation, whilst taking due account of the specific features of the legislative framework in which the undertakings acted.

Had the complaint been made to and brought before the Commission, it would not have had the power directly to disapply the national legislation that was incompatible with Community law.

10. SANCTIONS AGAINST INDIVIDUALS

EC competition law does not impose criminal liability or any type of sanction on natural persons i.e. it does not punish individuals. The conduct of employees, directors and officers by which an undertaking infringes the competition rules results in fines for the undertaking and not in penalties for those individuals.[700]

Some jurisdictions do impose criminal liability on individuals. The most notorious of these is the US, where the Sherman Act may be enforced by the Department of Justice through both civil and criminal processes.[701] In practice only clear, intentional violations, mostly cases of explicit price fixing or bid rigging are the subject of criminal proceedings,[702] but prosecutions in this type of case are pursued as a matter of determined and aggressive policy.[703] Individual

---

[698] There is a distinction national law which requires a breach of the rules and that which merely encourages or makes it easier for undertakings to engage in autonomous anti-competitive conduct, see *supra* Chap. 3, 000.

[699] Case C-198/01, para. 51. Generally such a step cannot expose the undertakings to sanctions in respect of actions taken before the disapplication, see paras. 52–5 and *supra* Chap. 3.

[700] See the discussion of fines, *supra* 1210 And where individuals, e.g give misleading or incorrect information in the course of an inspection under Article 20, the fine for the procedural offence is levied on the undertaking. Although the Commission now has power to conduct an inspection on the homes of individuals under Article 21, it is still only the undertaking that is responsible for what is found there. Of course, indulging in anti-competitive practices may amount to a breach of contract meriting dismissal, particularly if the undertaking has a proper compliance programme in place.

[701] The Federal Trade Commission, in contrast, has no criminal jurisdiction.

[702] H. Hovenkamp, *Federal Antitrust Policy: The Law of Competition and its Practice* (3rd edn., Thomson/West, 2005), 15.1a.

[703] Including pursuing individuals overseas by way of extradition proceedings, as in the *Norris* case, see *infra* and Chap. 16.

directors and executives are imprisoned.[704] The main argument in favour of criminalizing competition law infringements is that it has a deterrent effect way beyond that produced by sanctions against undertakings. There is evidence that the possibility of prison in the US leads some international cartels to 'carve out' the US, i.e. to collude in respect of the rest of the world but not the US.[705]

In the UK sanctions are also available against individuals involved in a breach of the competition rules. First, an individual who dishonestly engages in a hard-core cartel agreement may commit a statutory criminal offence under the Enterprise Act 2002,[706] punishable by imprisonment for up to five years and/or an unlimited fine.[707] Secondly, the OFT and sectoral regulators have power to seek a disqualification order against a director of a company that has committed a breach of the competition rules (which includes both Article 81 and 82 of the EC Treaty and their domestic equivalents[708]) and whose conduct makes him unfit to be concerned in the management of a company.[709] The statutory criminal offence applies only to conduct committed after the Enterprise Act came into force on 1 June 2003. However, the Administrative Court of England and Wales held at the beginning of 2007 that price fixing also amounts to a conspiracy to defraud at common law, which means that such conduct can be caught even if it took place prior to 2003. The issue was appealed to the House of Lords.[710]

---

[704] For example, Alfred Taubman, the billionaire who invented the shopping mall concept, spent nearly a year in prison as a result of the price fixing agreement between Sotheby's and Christie's, see *supra* 1250 and in 1999 executives from Archer Daniels Midland were convicted in connection with the lysine cartel and sentenced to prison terms of twenty-four to thirty months.

[705] M Bloom, *Immunity/Leniency/Financial Incentives/Plea Bargaining* 11th EUI Competition Law and Policy Workshop, 2006; S. Hammond (Deputy Assistant Attorney General for Criminal Enforcement, Antitrust Division, US DOJ), *Charting New Waters in International Cartel Prosecutions*, 2 March 2006, http://www.usdoj.gov/atr/public/speeches/214861.htm. Applications for immunity under the DOJ leniency programme are usually accompanied by leniency applications from the individuals implicated.

[706] Under s. 188(1) an individual is guilty of an offence if he 'dishonestly agrees' with one or more other person to engage in one of more of the cartel activities (such as price-fixing and limitation of supply) set out in s. 188(2). Prosecutions may be instituted by the Serious Fraud Office or by, or with the consent, of the OFT. Penalties may also be imposed on individuals for certain procedural offences under the Competition Act 1998, ss. 42–4.

[707] The OFT has power to issue 'no-action' letters to 'whistleblowers' confirming that an individual who meets certain stipulated conditions will not be prosecuted, Enterprise Act 2002, s. 190(4).

[708] Competition Act 1998, Chapter I and II prohibitions.

[709] Enterprise Act 2002, s. 204. The provisions amend the Company Directors Disqualification Act 1986.

[710] *Ian Norris v. Government of the United States of America* [2007] EWHC 71 (Admin), 25 January 2007. The case concerned a request from the US for the extradition of the former Chief Executive Officer of Morgan Crucible to face charges in the US over the carbon products cartel, see further Chap. 16. Extradition from the UK is possible only if the conduct in respect of which extradition is sought was also an offence under UK law at the time. The possibility of using the common law offence against cartels was mooted in an article by Sir Jeremy Lever QC and John Pike in 2005: J. Lever and J. Pike, 'Cartel Agreements, Criminal Conspiracy and the Statutory "Cartel Offence"' [2005] *ECLR* 70–7 and 164–72. The Administrative Court rejected the plea that it would amount to retrospective criminal liability, as the broad umbrella offence of conspiracy to defraud had been part of the law for a long time and the fact that it had not previously been applied to price fixing was irrelevant. On 13 March 2007 the High Court certified the question of whether conspiracy charges cover cartels as an issue of public importance, thereby giving Norris the right to appeal to the House of Lords. In April 2006 the Serious Fraud Office charged nine individuals and five companies with conspiracy to defraud in relation to the supply of drugs to the National Health Service: *R v. O'Neill* (Southwark Crown Court, T2006/7302, on-going at the time of writing).

Liability on individuals for breach of the EC competition rules could only be imposed across the EU by a harmonization measure which would entail each Member State making it an offence within its jurisdiction. Such a measure would need to go through the Council, but the Member States are not generally receptive to attempts to create new criminal offences in this way. EU-wide individual is therefore not an imminent prospect. In the meantime, the disparity between members of the ECN in matters of individual liability can lead to difficulties.[711]

11. COMPLAINTS

A. GENERAL

An entity which believes that another undertaking has committed, or is committing, a breach of Community competition law may wish to take action to ensure that the undertaking in breach complies and is punished in respect of that breach. In addition, it may hope to recover in respect of any loss suffered in consequence of the breach of the rules.

Such an entity essentially has two choices. It may complain to a public enforcer, the Commission or one of the NCAs, and hope that the authority acts on the complaint, perhaps by taking interim measures and/or by issuing a decision ordering the termination of a breach of the law. Alternatively, it may commence proceedings before a national court seeking a declaration that an agreement infringes the competition rules and is unenforceable, an injunction to prevent future breaches, and/or other remedies in respect of a breach. Both Articles 81 and 82 are directly applicable and confer rights on individuals that can be relied on before a national court.[712] Complainants thus play an important part in the enforcement process. Not only may they draw breaches of the competition rules to the attention of the competition authorities, but they may privately enforce the rules through civil litigation.

In many cases an aggrieved person may prefer to complain to the Commission or an NCA than to commence private proceedings. Such a step is of course the cheaper of the two options and causes least inconvenience to the individual. The Commission and many of the NCAs are, however, trying to encourage greater private enforcement of the competition rules at the national level. The Commission, in particular, wishes to preserve its resources for cases in which a point of particular 'Community' interest is raised (it has the resources to issue only a small number of decisions each year).[713] It may, therefore, decline to act on the complaint. Further, where the Commission finds an infringement of the rules it has power only to order a guilty undertaking to bring its infringement to an end[714] and to fine an undertaking in respect of any breach committed.[715] It does not have power to award damages or other compensation to those which have suffered as a result of the breach. Similarly, most NCAs only have power to impose fines, or other penalties on the undertaking in breach. It may be, therefore, that where an undertaking seeks compensation or another remedy a private action will be the only satisfactory option. Private enforcement of the competition rules through civil litigation is discussed in Chapter 15.[716]

---

[711] See B. Perrin, 'Challenges Facing the EU Network of Competition Authorities: Insights from a Comparative Criminal Law Perspective' (2006) 31 *ELRev* 540.

[712] See Chap. 15.

[713] See *supra* e.g. sections 2 and 3.

[714] Reg. 1/2003, Art. 7.

[715] *Ibid.*, Art. 23.

[716] An individual could of course commence private proceedings following proceedings by the Commission. The ability of that individual to rely on a Commission decision or other documents might

Regulation 1/2003 envisages that complaints may be made both to the Commission and to NCAs.[717] Article 7 provides that the Commission may, acting on a complaint or on its own initiative, find an infringement of Article 81 or 82 and that complaints may be lodged by 'natural or legal persons that can show a legitimate interest' and Member States. Further, Article 33 provides that the Commission shall be authorized to take measures as to the form, content, and other details of complaints lodged and of the procedure for rejecting complaints. In pursuit of this objective Chapter IV of the implementing Regulation, Regulation 773/2004,[718] deals with the handling of complaints and the Commission has issued a Notice on the handling of complaints that is intended to provide guidance to those seeking relief from infringements of the competition rules. Article 5 of Regulation 1/2003 provides that an NCA, acting on a complaint or its own initiative, may take decisions ordering an undertaking to bring an infringement of Article 81 or 82 to an end and Article 13 provides that the Commission and NCAs may reject a claim which is being, or has been, dealt with by another competition authority.

One of the difficulties of encouraging complaints is that, in many cases, they may be lodged by disgruntled entities losing out on the competitive process rather than by entities really suffering as a result of a breach of the EC competition rules. An authority must therefore take care to distinguish between legitimate and illegitimate complaints.

B. WHERE TO COMPLAIN

In the section above it was seen that complaints can be made both to the Commission and NCAs. An initial difficulty for a potential complainant is to decide who they should complain to, the Commission, one or more NCAs, or to all of these authorities?

The Commission's guidelines on the handling of complaints indicate that the complaint should be made to the 'authority most likely to be well placed to deal with their case'.[719] In determining who is best placed, guidance can be obtained from the Commission's Cooperation Notice,[720] which deals with work sharing between the Commission and NCAs inside the European Competition Network (ECN).[721] The authorities inform each other of investigations being made following a complaint, and members of the network seek to ensure that the correct authority is put in charge of the case.

---

facilitate those private proceedings. In the UK, for example, the specialist Competition Appeal Tribunal is empowered to award damages to claimants in cases where a competition law infringement (of EC or UK) law has been established by a public enforcer. In such proceedings, the infringement of the rule is assumed, but the claimant is required to establish causation and loss, see *infra* Chap. 15.

[717] Although Reg. 17 recognized that a complaint could be lodged with the Commission, the procedures governing complaints developed informally under this system. The Commission understood the importance of complaints which became an established part of the enforcement procedure. In its White Paper on Modernization, the Commission considered that complaints should play a fuller part in a directly applicable system. One of the objectives of the new rules is to encourage and facilitate the lodging of complaints and to draw the competition authorities' attention to serious infringements of the rules. Indeed, in its White Paper on Modernization the Commission estimated that almost 30% of new cases it dealt with resulted from complaints and that many of its own-initiative investigations began with information sent to the Commission informally, White Paper on modernisation of the rules implementing Articles 85 and 86 [now 81 and 82] of the EC Treaty [1999] OJ C132/1, [1999] 5 CMLR 208, para. 117.

[718] [2004] OJ 123/18.

[719] Commission Notice on the handling of complaints by the Commission under Articles 81 and 82 of the EC Treaty [2004] OJ C101/65, para. 21.

[720] [2004] OJ C101/54, especially points 8–15, set out *supra* 1272.

[721] Commission Notice on the handling of complaints by the Commission under Articles 81 and 82 of the EC Treaty [2004] OJ C101/65, paras. 19–25.

Commission Notice on the Handling of Complaints by the Commission under Article 81 and 82 of the EC Treaty [2004] OJ C101/65, paras. 23–5

23. Within the European Competition Network, information on cases that are being investigated following a complaint will be made available to the other members of the network before or without delay after commencing the first formal investigative measure. Where the same complaint has been lodged with several authorities or where a case has not been lodged with an authority that is well placed, the members of the network will endeavour to determine within an indicative time-limit of two months which authority or authorities should be in charge of the case.

24. Complainants themselves have an important role to play in further reducing the potential need for reallocation of a case originating from their complaint by referring to the orientations on worksharing in the network set out in the present chapter when deciding on where to lodge their complaint. If nonetheless a case if reallocated within the network, the undertakings concerned and the complainant(s) are informed as soon as possible by the competition authorities involved.

25. The Commission may reject a complaint in accordance with Article 13 of Regulation 1/2003, on the grounds that a Member State is dealing or has dealt with the case. When doing so the Commission must, in accordance with Article 9 of Regulation 773/2004 inform the complaint without delay of the national competition authority which is dealing or has already dealt with the case.

C. STANDING

Regulation 1/2003 provides that 'natural or legal persons who can show a legitimate interest' and Member States (which are deemed to have a legitimate interests for all complaints they lodge) have standing to complain about a breach of the competition rules.[722]

The requirement that an individual should have a legitimate interest does not ordinarily present a major obstacle to potential complainants. Any applicant who is directly and adversely affected, or will be so affected, as a result of the infringement will have standing. It has been held, for example, that an entity: which has been excluded, or threatened with exclusion, from a distribution network;[723] which believes that it was negotiating with members of a cartel;[724] or which believes itself to be a victim of abusive behaviour by a dominant undertaking,[725] has a legitimate interest within the meaning of Article 3(2). Further, in *BEMIM* v. *Commission*[726] the CFI held that a trade association had a legitimate interest where the conduct complained of was liable to affect adversely the interests of the members that it was entitled to represent. The Commission's Notice on the handling of complaints provides further guidance on this matter, providing examples of entities which would have a legitimate interest such as consumer associations.

[722] Art. 7(2). This is similar to the language previously used in Reg. 17, Art. 3.

[723] Case 210/81, *Demo-Studio Schmidt* v. *Commission* [1983] ECR 3045, [1984] 1 CMLR 63.

[724] See, e.g., *Building and Construction Industry in the Netherlands* [1992] OJ L92/1, [1993] 5 CMLR 135 (a complaint about collusive tendering lodged by a local authority).

[725] See, e.g., Cases 6 and 7/73, *Istituto Chemioterapico Italiano SpA and Commercial Solvents Corp* v. *Commission* [1974] ECR 223, [1974] 1 CMLR 309 (complaint by Zoja, *Zoja-CSC/ICI* [1972] OJ L299/51, [1973] CMLR D50); Case C-62/86, *AKZO Chemie BV* v. *Commission* [1991] ECR I-3359, [1993] 5 CMLR 215, complaint lodged by ECS; see *supra* Chaps. 6 and 7.

[726] Case T-144/92, [1995] ECR II-147, [1996] 4 CMLR 305; see in particular para. 28.

Commission Notice on the Handling of Complaints by the Commission under Article 81 and 82 of the EC Treaty [2004] OJ C101/65, paras. 35–40

35. The Court of First Instance had held that an association of undertakings may claim a legitimate interest in lodging a complaint regarding conduct concerning its members even if it not directly concerned, as an undertaking operating in the relevant market, by the conduct complained of, provided that, first, it is entitled to represent the interests of its members and secondly, the conduct complained of is liable to adversely affect the interests of its members.[727] Conversely, the Commission has been found to be entitled not to pursue the complaint of an association of undertakings whose members were not involved in the type of business transactions complained of.[728]

36. From this case law, it can be inferred that undertakings (themselves or through associations that are entitled to represent their interests) can claim a legitimate interest where they are operating in the relevant market or where the conduct complained of is liable to directly and adversely affect their interests. This confirms the established practice of the Commission which has accepted that a legitimate interest can, for instance, be claimed by the parties to the agreement or practice which is the subject of the complaint, by competitors whose interests have allegedly been damaged by the behaviour complained of or by undertakings excluded from a distribution system.

37. Consumer associations can equally lodge complaints with the Commission.[729] The Commission moreover holds the view that individual consumers whose economic interests are directly and adversely affected insofar as they are the buyers of goods or services that are the object of an infringement can be in a position to show a legitimate interest.[730]

38. However, the Commission does not consider as a legitimate interest within the meaning of Article 7(2) the interest of persons or organizations that wish to come forward on general interest considerations without showing that they or their members are liable to be directly and adversely affected by the infringement (pro bono publico).

39. Local or public authorities may be able to show a legitimate interest in their capacity as buyers or users of goods or services affected by the conduct complained of. Conversely, they cannot be considered as showing a legitimate interest within the meaning of Article 7(2) of Regulation 1/2002 to the extent that they bring to the attention of the Commission alleged infringements pro bono publico.

40. Complainants have to demonstrate their legitimate interest. Where a natural or legal person lodging a complaint is unable to demonstrate a legitimate interest, the Commission is entitled, without prejudice to its right to initiate proceedings of its own initiative, not to pursue the complaint. The Commission may ascertain whether this condition is met at any stage of the investigation.

In *Österreichische Postsparkasse* the CFI took a very broad view of those having a 'legitimate interest' under Article 3(2) of Regulation 17, the antecedent of Regulation 1/2003, Article 7(2). It extended this to any final consumer who can show that his economic interests have been

---

[727] See, e.g., Case T-114/92, *BEMIM v. Commission* [1995] ECR II-1427, para. 28.

[728] See, e.g., Cases T-133 and 204/95, *IECC v. Commission* [1998] ECR II-3645, paras. 79–83.

[729] See, e.g., *BEUC v. Commission* [1994] ECR II-285, para. 36.

[730] This point is currently raised in proceedings before the CFI, Cases T-213 and 214/01.

harmed. In this judgment the CFI made important statements about the objectives of the competition rules.[731]

Cases T-213/01 and 214/01, *Österreichische Postsparkasse v. Commission* [2006] ECR II-1601

The case was an appeal against two decisions of the Hearing Oficer to send to an Austrian political party (FPÖ) the non-confidential version of the statement of objections in the investigation which culminated in the *Lombard* Club decision.[732] The FPÖ complained to the Commission in June 1997 about certain practices of a group of Austrian banks. In February 1998 the Commission informed the FPÖ that it intended to reject its complaint, stating that it did not have a legitimate interest within Article 3(2) of Regulation 17. In fact, the Commission had already started an investigation on its own initiative in May 1997, before it had received the complaint. In due course the Commission sent the banks a statement of objections and informed them that it intended to send a non-confidential version to the FPÖ. The banks protested but the Hearing Officer overruled their objections.[733] The banks claimed that the FPÖ did not have sufficient 'legitimate interest' under Article 3(2) to merit receiving the statement of objections. The copy of the statement of objections was duly sent, and its contents was disclosed to the press.[734] The banks carried on with an appeal to the CFI, claiming, *inter alia*, that the FPÖ's status as a customer of banking services did not constitute a 'legitimate interest' under Article 3(2).

Court of First Instance

114. The Court of First Instance considers that there is nothing to prevent a final customer who purchases goods or services from being able to satisfy the notion of legitimate interest within the meaning of Article 3 of Regulation No 17. The Court considers that a final customer who shows that his economic interests have been harmed or are likely to be harmed as a result of the restriction of competition in question has a legitimate interest within the meaning of Article 3 of Regulation No 17 in making an application or a complaint in order to seek a declaration from the Commission that Articles 81 EC and 82 EC have been infringed.

115. It should be pointed out in this respect that the ultimate purpose of the rules that seek to ensure that competition is not distorted in the internal market is to increase the well-being of consumers. That purpose can be seen in particular from the wording of Article 81 EC. Whilst the prohibition laid down in Article 81(1) EC may be declared inapplicable in the case of cartels which contribute to improving the production or distribution of the goods in question or to promoting

---

[731] See *supra* Chap. 1.

[732] [2004] OJ L56/1, substantially upheld by the CFI in Cases T-259/02, T-264/02 and T-271/02, *Raiffeisen Zentralbank Österreich AG v. Commission*, 14 December 2006, an appeal case C-125/07 (judgment pending).

[733] In Case T-213/01 R, *Österreichische Postsparkasse v. Commission* [2001] ECR 3963 the President of the CFI rejected a request to suspend the Hearing Officer's decision ('In the present case, the Community interest in placing third parties whom the Commission has recognised as having a legitimate interest in applying under Article 3 of Regulation No 17 in a position to make appropriate observations on the objections raised by the Commission must take priority over that of the applicant to delay transmission of the statements of objections', para. 82).

[734] By the Governor of Carinthia, Jörg Haider, the leader of the FPÖ. The FPÖ, an extreme right-wing party, joined the Austrian government in a coalition in 2000, provoking a crisis for the EU. Article 7 of the Nice Treaty, which sets out how the EU should react when 'a clear danger exists of a Member State committing a serious breach of fundamental rights' was partly in response to this.

> technical or economic progress, that possibility, for which provision is made in Article 81(3) EC, is inter alia subject to the condition that a fair share of the resulting benefit is allowed for users of those products. Competition law and competition policy therefore have an undeniable impact on the specific economic interests of final customers who purchase goods or services. Recognition that such customers—who show that they have suffered economic damage as a result of an agreement or conduct liable to restrict or distort competition—have a legitimate interest in seeking from the Commission a declaration that Articles 81 EC and 82 EC have been infringed contributes to the attainment of the objectives of competition law.
>
> 116. Contrary to the claims made by the applicants, this finding does not effectively render the notion of legitimate interest meaningless by making it excessively broad or pave the way for an alleged 'actio popularis'. Acknowledging that a consumer who can show that his economic interests have been harmed as a result of a cartel complained of by him may have a legitimate interest in this regard within the meaning of Article 3(2) of Regulation No 17 is not the same as considering that any natural or legal person has such an interest.

An individual who does not have a legitimate interest within the meaning of Article 7(2) of Regulation 1/2003 even after *Österreichische Postsparkasse*, or for some reason does not want to make an official complaint, may draw the Commission's attention informally to market information which indicates that conduct may be in breach of the competition rules. 'For this purpose, the Commission has created a special web site to collect information from citizens and undertakings and their associations who wish to inform the Commission about suspected infringements'.[735] Once the conduct has been drawn to its intention the Commission is, of course, free to commence proceedings on its own initiative if it considers it appropriate to do so.

D. THE PROCEDURE

A complaint must be submitted in compliance with Form C[736] which is available on DG Comp's web site.[737] Form C requires the complainant to provide information regarding itself, details of the alleged infringement and evidence, an explanation of the findings sought from the Commission, the grounds on which a legitimate interest is claimed, and details of any approach made to another competition authority or lawsuits brought before a national court. In certain circumstances, the Commission may waive the need for submission of some of the comprehensive information and supporting documentation required.[738] The complainant must submit three paper copies, an electronic copy (if possible), and a non-confidential version of the complaint.

E. THE OBLIGATIONS ON THE COMMISSION

On receipt of a complaint the Commission is bound to collect information which enables it to determine whether it should reject the complaint or conduct an investigation.[739] During the

---

[735] Commission Notice on the handling of complaints by the Commission under Articles 81 and 82 of the EC Treaty [2004] OJ C101/65, para. 4. The informant may be concerned about their identity being disclosed.

[736] Reg. 773/2004 [2004] OJ L123/18, Art. 5.

[737] It is also set out as an annex to the Commission's Notice on the handling of complaints by the Commission under Articles 81 or 82 of the EC Treaty [2004] OJ C101/65.

[738] Reg. 773/2004 [2004] OJ L123/18, Art. 5(1).

[739] See *infra* and Commission's Notice on the handling of complaints by the Commission under Articles 81 or 82 of the EC Treaty [2004] OJ C101/65, para. 54.

first stage it will collect information from the complainant, give an initial reaction to the case and allow the complainant an opportunity to expand on its allegations.[740] During the second stage it investigates further to determine whether to initiate proceedings or to reject the complaint.[741] Before the Commission rejects a complaint, it must give the complainant an opportunity to make its views known within a specified time-limit.[742] The complainant may also be provided with access to non-confidential documents on which the Commission has based its provisional assessment. Taking cognizance of the views of the complainant the Commission, in the third stage, either initiates proceedings of rejects the complaint.[743]

If the Commission initiates proceedings and issues a statement of objections (SO) relating to a matter in respect of which it has received a complaint, it must provide a non-confidential version of the SO to the complainant and give it an opportunity to make its views known in writing. The complainant may also be given the opportunity to make oral submissions if it so requests.[744] In practice, the Commission seeks to keep the complainant fully informed.[745] In *BAT and Reynolds v. Commission*[746] the ECJ held that although the procedural rights of a complainant were not as extensive as those being investigated by the Commission, complainants had to 'be given the opportunity to defend their legitimate interests in the course of the administrative proceedings'. A complainant's right of access to the file is, however, much more limited than that of an undertaking complained of.[747] In *Matra Hachette v. Commission*[748] the CFI indicated that the right to full disclosure applied only to undertakings which were likely to be penalized by a Commission decision taken pursuant to Article 81 or 82. In contrast the right of third party complainants was simply to participate in the administrative procedure. In practice, however, complainants are informed of the contents of the file and given access to those documents which are not confidential[749] and kept informed of responses made by undertakings to the complaints lodged against them.[750]

Although the Commission considered introducing a time-period within which complaints should be handled this has not been done.[751] There is therefore no statutory time limit within which the Commission must deal with the complaint. Case law requires only that it should consider the complaint within a reasonable period.[752] 'What is a reasonable duration depends on

---

[740] Commission's Notice on the handling of complaints by the Commission under Articles 81 or 82 of the EC Treaty [2004] OJ C101/65, para. 55.

[741] *Ibid.*, para. 56.

[742] Reg. 773/2004 [2004] OJ L123/18, Art. 7(1).

[743] Commission's Notice on the handling of complaints by the Commission under Articles 81 or 82 of the EC Treaty [2004] OJ C101/65, para. 57.

[744] Reg. 773/2004 [2004] OJ L123/18, Art. 6. Commission's Notice on the handling of complaints by the Commission under Articles 81 or 82 of the EC Treaty [2004] OJ C101/65, paras. 64–7.

[745] Cases 142 and 156/84, *BAT and Reynolds v. Commission* [1987] ECR 4487, [1988] 4 CMLR 24.

[746] *Ibid.*, para. 20.

[747] See discussion *supra* 1191 ff.

[748] Case T-17/93, [1994] ECR II-595; see especially para. 34.

[749] The Commission's *XIIth Report on Competition Policy* (Commission, 1982), part 35.

[750] See, e.g., the Commission's *XIIIth Report on Competition Policy* (Commission, 1983), part 7.

[751] The Commission recognizes that this position may not be satisfactory for individuals who believe that they are being injured by a breach of the competition rules and need to know quickly whether or not the Commission will act upon their complaint. In its White Paper on Modernization the Commission proposed that a time limit of 4 months should be introduced within which it should be obliged to inform the complainant whether or not it intends to proceed. However, it also recognized that the procedures involved in rejecting a complaint are too cumbersome and should be simplified.

[752] Case C-282/95 P, *Guérin Automobiles v. Commission* [1997] ECR I-1503, para. 36. White Paper on Modernisation of the Rules Implementing Articles 85 and 86 [now 81 and 82] of the EC Treaty [1999] OJ C132/1, [1999] 5 CMLR 208, para. 120.

the circumstances of each case and in particular, its context, the various procedural steps followed by the Commission, the conduct of the parties in the course of the procedure, the complexity of the case and its importance for the various parties involved'.[753] The Commission states in its Notice on the handling of complaints, however, that it strives to inform complainants of the action it proposes to take within a period of four months of the receipt of the complaint.[754]

F. REJECTION OF THE COMPLAINT

(i) Introduction

The Commission may on investigation consider that no breach of the EC competition rules has occurred. Alternatively, it may consider that a breach might have occurred but that the case raises insufficient Community interest to warrant the time and resources that would be involved in investigation, or that another competition authority within the ECN would be better placed to deal with the case. Although the Commission has a duty 'to examine carefully the facts and points of law brought to its notice by the complainant in order to decide whether they disclose conduct liable to distort competition in the Common Market and affect trade between Member States'[755] it does not have a duty to proceed to final decision on the alleged breach of the rules. The Commission must, however, examine the case carefully in order to assess the Community interest in further investigation of the case.[756]

(ii) The Community Interest

In *Automec Srl* v. *Commission (Automec II)*[757] the CFI held that the Commission is entitled to prioritize cases before it. As a public enforcer it has a margin of discretion to set priorities in its enforcement activity. It may reject a complaint on the ground that it does not raise a sufficient Community interest. Save where the subject matter of the complaint falls within the exclusive purview of the Commission,[758] the rights conferred upon complainants do not, therefore, include a right to obtain a decision as regards the existence or otherwise of the alleged infringement. Rather, the Commission, in fulfilling its functions under the Treaty, is bound to apply different degrees of priority to the cases arising before it. The Commission is therefore entitled to assess whether the complaint raises sufficient Community interest to warrant an investigation.

---

[753] Commission Notice on the handling of complaints by the Commission under Articles 81 and 82 of the EC Treaty [2004] OJ C101/65, para. 60.

[754] *Ibid.*, paras. 61–3.

[755] Case T-575/93, *Koelman* v. *Commission* [1996] ECR II-1, [1996] 4 CMLR, para. 39.

[756] Notice on the handling of complaints by the Commission under Articles 82 or 82 of the EC Treaty [2004] OJ C101/65, para. 42.

[757] Case T-24/90, [1992] ECR II-2223, [1992] 5 CMLR 431.

[758] e.g., for the withdrawal of a block exemption in an individual case, see Reg. 1/2003, Art. 29.

Case T-24/90, *Automec Srl* v. *Commission (Automec II)* [1992] ECR II-2223, [1992] 5 CMLR 431

This case concerned a complaint lodged by Automec Srl, a private company, which had been a distributor of BMW vehicles for BMW Italia SpA in Treviso. On the expiry of its dealership in 1984, BMW Italia declined to renew the contract (although the applicant continued selling BMWs which it obtained from other BMW dealers). Automec brought proceedings before the national courts to compel BMW to continue the contractual relationship and subsequently, in 1988, lodged a complaint with the Commission under Article 3(2) of Regulation 17. In particular, it contended that since it met the qualitative criteria agreed by BMW with the Commission for the lawful operation of its selective distribution system[759] BMW was obliged to supply it with vehicles and spare parts on the terms applicable to other dealers. In 1988 the Commission sent Automec a letter stating that it had no power to grant its application. Automec commenced judicial review proceedings before the Court of First Instance seeking annulment of the letter and seeking damages from the Commission in respect of loss suffered in consequence of the Commission's failure to commence proceedings against BMW (*Automec I*). Subsequent to the commencement of these proceedings further letters were exchanged between the Commission and Automec. In February 1990 the Commissioner responsible for competition sent the applicant a letter rejecting the complaint. The letter stated that there was not a sufficient Community interest to justify examining the facts raised by the complaint. In 1990 the applicant brought further proceedings before the Court of First Instance seeking annulment of the February 1990 decision of the Directorate-General for Commission.

Court of First Instance

71. The Court considers that the question raised by this plea asks in substance what the Commission's obligations are when it receives an application under Article 3 of Regulation No 17 from a natural or legal person.

72. It is appropriate to point out that Regulations Nos 17 and 99/63 confer procedural rights on persons who have lodged a complaint with the Commission, such as the right to be informed of the reasons for which the Commission intends to reject their complaint and the right to submit observations in this connection. Thus the Community legislature has imposed certain specified obligations upon the Commission. However, neither Regulation No 17 nor Regulation No 99/63 contain express provisions relating to the action to be taken concerning the substance of a complaint and any obligations on the part of the Commission to carry out investigations.

73. In determining the Commission's obligations in this context, the first point to note is that the Commission is responsible for the implementation and orientation of Community competition policy (see the judgment of the Court of Justice in Case C-234/89 *Delimitis* v. *Henninger Bräu AG* [1991] ECR I-935, at I-991). For that reason, Article [85(1)] of the Treaty gave the Commission the task of ensuring that the principles laid down by Articles [81] and [82] were applied, and the provisions adopted pursuant to Article [83] have conferred wide powers upon it.

74. The scope of the Commission's obligations in the field of competition law must be examined in the light of Article [85(1)] of the Treaty, which, in this area, constitutes the specific expression of the general supervisory task entrusted to the Commission by Article [211] of the Treaty. However, as the Court of Justice has held with regard to Article [226] of the Treaty in Case 247/87 *Star Fruit* v. *Commission* [1989] ECR 291, at 301, that task does not mean that the Commission is

---

[759] *Bayerische Motoren Werke AG* [1975] OJ L29/1, [1975] 1 CMLR D44.

bound to commence proceedings seeking to establish the existence of any infringement of Community law.

75. In that regard, the Court observes that it appears from the case-law of the Court of Justice (judgment in *GEMA*, [Case 125/78, *GEMA* v. *Commission* [1979] ECR 3173] at 3189) that the rights conferred upon complainants by Regulations Nos 17 and 99/63 do not include a right to obtain a decision, within the meaning of Article [249] of the Treaty, as regards the existence or otherwise of the alleged infringement. It follows that the Commission cannot be required to give a decision in that connection unless the subject-matter of the complaint falls within its exclusive purview, as in the case of the withdrawal of an exemption granted under Article [81(3)] of the Treaty.

76. As the Commission is under no obligation to rule on the existence or otherwise of an infringement it cannot be compelled to carry out an investigation, because such investigation could have no purpose other than to seek evidence of the existence or otherwise of an infringement, which it is not required to establish. In that regard, it should be noted that, unlike the provision contained in the second sentence of Article [85(1)] in relation to applications by Member States, Regulations Nos 17 and 99/63 do not expressly oblige the Commission to investigate complaints submitted to it.

77. In that connection, it should be observed that, in the case of an authority entrusted with a public service task, the power to take all the organizational measures necessary for the performance of that task, including setting priorities within the limits prescribed by the law—where those priorities have not been determined by the legislature—is an inherent feature of administrative activity. This must be the case in particular where an authority has been entrusted with a supervisory and regulatory task as extensive and general as that which has been assigned to the Commission in the field of competition. Consequently, the fact that the Commission applies different degrees of priority to the cases submitted to it in the field of competition is compatible with the obligations imposed on it by Community law.

78. That assessment does not conflict with the judgments of the Court of Justice in *Demo-Studio Schmidt*, [Case 210/81 *Demo-Studio Schmidt* v. *Commission* [1983] ECR 3045], in Case 298/83 *CICCE* v. *Commission* [1985] ECR 1105 and in Joined Cases 142 and 156/84 *BAT and Reynolds* v. *Commission* [1987] ECR 4487. In the judgment in *Demo-Studio Schmidt*, the Court of Justice held that the Commission 'was under a duty to examine the facts put forward' by the complainant, without prejudging the question whether the Commission could refrain from investigating the complaint because, in that case, the Commission had examined the facts set out in the complaint and had rejected it on the ground that there was nothing to suggest the existence of an infringement. Likewise this question did not arise in the later cases of *CICCE* (cited above) and *BAT and Reynolds* (cited above).

79. However, although the Commission cannot be compelled to conduct an investigation, the procedural safeguards provided for by Article 3 of Regulation No 17 and Article 6 of Regulation No 99/63 oblige it nevertheless to examine carefully the factual and legal particulars brought to its notice by the complainant in order to decide whether they disclose conduct of such a kind as to distort competition in the common market and affect trade between Member States (see the judgments in *Demo-Studio Schmidt*, *CICCE* and *BAT and Reynolds*, cited above).

...

84. The next point to consider is whether it is legitimate, as the Commission has argued, to refer to the Community interest in a case as a priority criterion.

85. In this connection, it should be borne in mind that, unlike the civil courts, whose task is to safeguard the individual rights of private persons in their relations *inter se*, an administrative authority must act in the public interest. Consequently, the Commission is entitled to refer to the Community interest in order to determine the degree of priority to be applied to the various cases brought to its notice. This does not amount to removing action by the Commission from the scope

of judicial review, since, in view of the requirement to provide a statement of reasons laid down by Article [253] of the Treaty, the Commission cannot merely refer to the Community interest in the abstract. It must set out the legal and factual considerations which led it to conclude that there was insufficient Community interest to justify investigation of the case. It is therefore by reviewing the legality of those reasons that the Court can review the Commission's action.

86. In order to assess the Community interest in further investigation of a case, the Commission must take account of the circumstances of the case, and in particular of the legal and factual particulars set out in the complaint referred to it. The Commission should in particular balance the significance of the alleged infringement as regards the functioning of the common market, the probability of establishing the existence of the infringement and the scope of the investigation required in order to fulfil, under the best possible conditions, its task of ensuring that Articles [81] and [82] are complied with.

At paragraph 44 of its Notice on the handling of complaints,[760] the Commission sets out the criteria it uses to assess whether or not a particular case has a Community interest:[761]

— The Commission can reject a complaint on the ground that the complainant can bring an action to assert its rights before national courts.

— The Commission may not regard certain situations as excluded in principle from its purview under the task entrusted to it by the Treaty but is required to assess in each case how serious the alleged infringements are and how persistent their consequences are. This means in particular that it must take into account the duration and the extent of the infringements complained of and their effect on the competition situation in the Community.

— The Commission may have to balance the significance of the alleged infringement as regards the functioning of the common market, the probability of establishing the existence of the infringement and the scope of the investigation required in order to fulfil its task of ensuring that Articles 81 and 82 of the Treaty are complied with.

— While the Commission's discretion does not depend on how advanced the investigation of a case is, the stage of the investigation forms part of the circumstances of the case which the Commission may have to take into consideration.

— The Commission may decide that it is not appropriate to investigate a complaint where the practices in question have ceased. However, for this purpose, the Commission will have to ascertain whether anti-competitive effects persist and if the seriousness of the infringements or the persistence of their effects does not give the complaint a Community interest.

— The Commission may also decide that it is not appropriate to investigate a complaint where the undertakings concerned agree to change their conduct in such a way that it can consider that there is no longer a sufficient Community interest to intervene.

---

[760] [2004] OJ C101/65.

[761] After *Automec* the Commission dealt with the question of whether a particular case had a Community interest in its old 'Notice on cooperation between national courts and the Commission in applying Articles 85 and 86 [now 81 and 82] of the EEC [now EC] Treaty' [1993] OJ C39/6, [1993] 4 CMLR 12, see especially paras. 13–15. In that Notice (which has now been replaced by the Commission Notice on the cooperation between the Commission and the courts of the EU Member States in the application of Articles 81 and 82 EC) the Commission stressed that it would concentrate on cases with 'particular political, economic or legal significance for the Community' (para. 14) and that it would be unwilling to take action where the Community provisions could be enforced before the national courts.

(iii) Allegations not Substantiated

The Commission may also reject a complaint on the ground that it does not sufficiently sub-stantiate the allegations put forward, or on the ground that the conduct complained about does not infringe the EC competition rules.[762]

(iv) Investigation by Another Competition Authority

As already indicated, the Commission is entitled to reject a complaint on the grounds that an NCA is dealing, or has dealt, with the case.[763]

(v) The Commission is Obliged to Make a Formal Rejection of the Complaint

Where the Commission decides not to act on a complaint, has communicated this to the complainant and given it an opportunity to make its views known, the Commission is bound either to initiate a procedure or to reject the complaint by decision.[764]

Case T-186/94, *Guérin Automobiles* v. *Commission* [1995] ECR II-1753, [1996] 4 CMLR 685, para. 34

[I]t should be emphasized that, having submitted within the time stipulated in the letter of 13 June 1994 comments in response to the Article 6 notification, the applicant is henceforth entitled to obtain a definitive decision from the Commission on its complaint; and that decision may, if the applicant sees fit, be challenged in an action for annulment before this court . . .

Although, therefore, the Commission cannot be required in every case to proceed to a formal decision on the compatibility of the conduct complained of with the competition rules it must, if it is not going to investigate, formally reject the complaint by decision, stating reasons, before closing its file. This decision is subject to appeal before the Community Courts (see below).

G. ACTING ON A COMPLAINT

If the Commission considers it to be worthwhile to initiate proceedings, it may do so by issuing a Statement of Objections. The Commission's fact-finding powers and the opening of a formal procedure are discussed above. A few points of importance to a complainant will, however, be reiterated here. First, when acting on a complaint the Commission generally informs the under-takings being investigated of the allegations set out in the complaint. Since the Commission is

---

[762] Commission Notice on the handling of complaints by the Commission under Articles 81 and 82 of the EC Treaty [2004] OJ C101/65, para. 47.

[763] Reg. 1/2003, Art. 13.

[764] Reg. 773/2004 [2004] OJ L123/18, Art. 7(2). Case T-64/89, *Automec Srl v. Commission (Automec I)* [1990] ECR II-367, [1991] 4 CMLR 177.

bound by a general duty of confidentiality[765] the complainant should be sure to mark any business secrets or other confidential information which it does not wish the Commission to disclose. Secondly, the complainant has a right to be heard.[766] Thirdly, the complainant cannot specifically request that the Commission adopt interim measures. According to Article 8 of Regulation 1/2003 the Commission may order interim measures *on its own initiative* where there is the risk of serious and irreparable damage to *competition*. The Commission takes the view that requests for interim measures should be brought before the national courts which are better placed to decide on such measures.[767] Fourthly, if the Commission does find that an undertaking has infringed Article 81 or 82 it cannot compensate an entity which has suffered loss in consequence of a breach.[768]

H. JUDICIAL REVIEW PROCEEDINGS

(i) An Omission to Act

Where the Commission is in breach of an obligation to act it is possible, under Article 232 (ex Article 175) of the Treaty, to bring proceedings in respect of its failure to act.[769] Before such proceedings can be brought it is essential that the Commission should have been called upon to act and have failed to adopt a measure in relation to the complainant which that complainant was legally entitled to claim by virtue of the rules of Community law. Since a complainant cannot insist that the Commission should commence an investigation it cannot bring proceedings under Article 232 in respect of its failure to launch such an investigation. However, because the Commission is obliged to issue a formal rejection of a complaint, a complainant can bring Article 232 proceedings where such a final decision has not been taken. Once the Commission informs a complainant that it has decided to close its file and has formally rejected a complaint that complainant may, if it so wishes, bring judicial review proceedings under Article 230 (ex Article 173) EC challenging the validity of that decision (see below).

(ii) Review of Acts

a. Standing

A complainant may wish to bring proceedings to annul a Commission decision rejecting its complaint or any decision made subsequent to an investigation.[770] In the sphere of the competition rules the Court has taken a broad view of when individuals are directly and individually concerned within the meaning of Article 230 of the Treaty.[771] If an individual has standing to

---

[765] Article 287 of the Treaty and Reg. 1/2003, Art. 28 and 773/2004 [2004] OJ L123/18, Arts. 15 and 16.

[766] See *supra* 1293.

[767] Commission Notice on the handling of complaints by the Commission under Articles 81 and 82 of the EC Treaty [2004] OJ C101/65, para. 80. See Chap. 15.

[768] The fire goes into the Community coffers.

[769] See Craig and de Búrca op.cit. n. 509 *supra*.

[770] See *supra* 1253 ff.

[771] Contrast the position where an individual wishes to challenge the enactment of Regs. or decisions in other circumstances. In these cases the Community courts have taken an extremely strict approach to standing: see P. Craig and G. de Búrca, *EU Law: Text, Cases and Materials* (4th edn., Oxford University Press, 2007), Ch. 14.

complain to the Commission, it is considered that it will also have standing to institute proceedings where its complaint is rejected. In *Metro v. Commission* the ECJ held that it was essential
that a person with a legitimate interest 'should be able, if their request is not complied with
either wholly or in part, to institute proceedings in order to protect their legitimate interests. In
those circumstances, the applicant must be considered to be directly and individually concerned within the meaning of the second paragraph of Article [230], by the contested
decision'.[772]

b. A Reviewable Act

The formal rejection of a complaint is a reviewable act (a legally binding measure) within the
meaning of Article 230.[773] However, the Commission's initial letters and preliminary investigations are not and may not be challenged. In some cases it may be difficult to determine whether
or not the Commission has gone beyond the investigation procedure, which is not open to challenge, or whether the Commission has actually given a final decision which is susceptible to
challenge under Article 230.[774]

c. Grounds for Annulment

The grounds for annulment are the ordinary grounds set out in Article 230 of the Treaty itself,
lack of competence, infringement of an essential procedural requirement, infringement of the
Treaty, or any rule of law or misuse of power.[775]

In *Automec II* the CFI considered whether the Commission had been right to rule that the case
had insufficient Community interest to warrant further investigation.[776] This judgment makes
it clear that the Court will ensure that the Commission evaluates the factual and legal considerations with due care and that proper reasons are given for its rejection of a complaint. A complaint will, however, be legitimately rejected if the complainant can get effective protection of
his rights before a national court.

I. COMPLAINTS AND THE MERGER REGULATION

The rights of third parties under the EC Merger Regulation are dealt with in Chapter 12.

12. CONCLUSIONS

1. Regulation 1/2003 made dramatic changes to the way that Articles 81 and 82 are enforced
with the principal objective of strengthening enforcement of those rules. The changes are
far-reaching and have had significant effects on the Commission, NCAs, and undertakings.

---

[772] Case 26/76, *Metro SB-Grosmärtke GmbH & Co KG v. Commission* [1977] ECR 1875, [1978] 2 CMLR 1, para. 13.

[773] *Supra* 1255 ff.

[774] See also, e.g., Case T-37/92, *BEUC* [1995] ECR II-285, [1995] 4 CMLR 167 and Case C-39/93 P, *SFEI v. Commission* [1994] ECR I-2681.

[775] *Supra* 1256 ff.

[776] Case T-24/90, *Automec Srl v. Commission (Automec II)* [1992] ECR II-2223, [1992] 5 CMLR 431.

2. The Commission has gained new powers to facilitate it in its task of detecting and punishing breaches of Articles 81 and 82. It pursues an increasingly aggressive policy towards cartels, as demonstrated by the 2006 Leniency Notice and the 2006 Fining Guidelines.

3. The NCAs and national courts have gained the power to apply the competition provisions in their entirety. Regulation 1/2003 and the Commission's Modernization Notices seek to address some of the difficulties that might arise in the decentralised system. The operation of the ECN has so far been highly successful.

4. It remains to be seen whether the measures adopted are sufficient or whether further guidance and harmonization of the EC and domestic rules will be required.

13. FURTHER READING

A. BOOKS

AMATO, G., *Antitrust and the Bounds of Power* (Hart Publishing, 1997), chap. 8.

EHLERMANN, C.D., and ATANASIU, I. (eds.), *European Competition Law Annual 2000: The Modernisation of EC Antitrust Policy* (Hart Publishing, 2001)

—— (eds.), *European Competition Law Annual 2001: Effective Enforcement of EC Antitrust Law* (Hart Publishing, 2003)

FAULL, J., and NIKPAY, A., *The EC Law of Competition* (2nd edn., Oxford University Press, 2007), chap. 2

GYSELEN, L., 'The Commission's Fining Policy in Competition Cases— "Questo è il catalogo"' in P. J. Slot and A. McDonnell (eds.), *Procedure and Enforcement in EC and US Competition Law* (Sweet & Maxwell, 1993)

KERSE, C., and KHAN, N. *EC Antitrust Procedure* (5th edn., Sweet & Maxwell, 2005)

LAWSON, R., 'Confusion and Conflict? Diverging Interpretations of the European Convention on Human Rights in Strasbourg and Luxembourg' in R. Lawson and M. de Blois, *The Dynamics of the Protection of Human Rights in Europe: Essays in Honour of Henry G. Schermers* (Martinus Nijhoff, 1994)

NAZZINI, R., *Concurrent Proceedings in Competition Law* (Oxford University Press, 2004)

ORTIZ BLANCO, L., *EC Competition Procedure* (2nd edn., Oxford University Press, 2006)

TRIDIMAS, T., *The General Principles of EC Law* (2nd edn., Oxford University Press, 2006)

SPIELMAN, D., 'Human Rights Case Law in the Strasbourg and Luxembourg Courts: Conflicts, Inconsistencies, and Complementaries' in P. Alston (ed.), *The EU and Human Rights* (Oxford University Press, 1999)

WESSELING, R., *The Modernisation of EC Antitrust Law* (Hart Publishing, 2000)

WILS, W., *The Optimal Enforcement of EC Antitrust Law: Essays in Law and Economics* (Kluwer Law International, 2002)

B. ARTICLES

AMEYE, E., 'The Interplay Between Human Rights and Competition Law in the EU [2004] *ECLR* 332

ANDREANGELI, A., 'The Impact of the Modernisation Regulation on the Guarantees of Due Process in Competition Proceedings', (2006) 31 *ELRev* 342

BAILEY, D., 'Scope of Judicial Review Under Article 81 EC' (2004) 41 *CMLRev* 1327

BLAKE, S., and SCHNICHELS, D., Leniency Following Modernisation: Safeguarding Europe's Leniency Programmes [2004] *ECLR* 765

BRAMMER, S., 'Concurrent Jurisdiction under Regulation 1/2003 and the Issue of Case Allocation' (2005) 42 *CMLRev* 1383

COOK, C., Commitment Decisions: The Law and Practice under Article 9 (2006) 29(2) *World Competition* 209

DE BROCA, H. 'The Commission revises its Guidelines for setting fines in antitrust cases' (2006) 3 *EC Competition Policy Newsletter*, 1

DEKEYSER, K., and GAUER, C., 'The New Enforcement System for Articles 81 and 82 and the Rights of Defence' 2004 *Fordham Corp L Inst* (B. Hawk, ed. 2005), 549

EHLERMANN, C.-D., 'Reflections on a European Cartel Office' (1995) 32 *CMLRev* 471

GAUER, C., and JASPERS, M., 'Designing a European Solution for a "One Stop Leniency Shop' (2006) *ECLR* 685

GERADIN, D., and HENRY, D. 'EC Fining for Competition Law Violations: An Emprical Study of the Commission's Decisional Practice and the Community Courts' Judgments' (2005) 1 *European Competition Journal* 401

—— and PETIT, N. 'Judicial Remedies under EC Competition Law: Complex Issues Arising from the "Modernisation" Process' (2005) *Fordham Corp L Inst* 393 (B. Hawk, ed. 2006)

GERBER, D., 'Modernising European Competition Law: A Developmental Perspective' [2001] *ECLR* 122

JOSHUA, J., 'The Element of Surprise' (1983) 8 *ELRev* 3

LENAERTS, K., and VANHAMME J., 'Procedural Rights of Private Parties in the Community Administrative Process' (1997) 34 *CMLRev* 531

LEVER, J. and PIKE, J., 'Cartel Agreements, Criminal Conspiracy and the Statutory "Cartel Offence"' [2005] *ECLR* 70–7 and 164–72

LEVY, N. and O'DONOGHUE, R., 'The EU Leniency Programme Comes of Age' (2004) 27 *World Competition* 75

LEVITT, M., 'Commission Notice on Internal Rules of Procedure for Access to the File' [1997] *ECLR* 187

MONTAG, F., 'The Case for Radical Reform of the Infringement Procedure under Regulation' [1998] *ECLR* 428

ODUDU, O., 'Article 81(3), Discretion and Direct Effect' [2002] *ECLR* 17

RICHARDSON, R., 'Guidance Without Guidance—A European Revolution in Fining Policy? The Commission's New Guidelines on Fines' [1999] *ECLR* 360

RILEY, A., 'Saunders and the Power to Obtain Information in Community and United Kingdom Competition Law' (2000) 25 *ELRev* 264

—— 'EC Antitrust Modernisation: The Commission Does Very Nicely—Thank You! Part One: Regulation 1 and the Notification Burden' [2003] *ECLR* 604

—— 'EC Antitrust Modernisation: The Commission Does Very Nicely—Thank You! Part Two: Between the Idea and the Reality: Decentralisation under Regulation 1 [2003] *ECLR* 657

RIZZA, C., 'The Duty of National Competition Authorities to Disapply Anti-Competitive Domestic Legislation and the Resulting Limitations on the Availability of the State Action Defence (Case C-198/01 CIF)' [2004] *ECLR* 126

RODGER, B., 'The Commission White Paper on on Modernisation of the Rules Implementing Articles 81 and 82 of the EC Treaty' (1999) 24 *ELRev* 653

TEMPLE LANG, J. 'The *AM &S* Judgment' in M.Hoskins and W.Robinson, *A True European— Essays for Judge David* Edward (Hart Publishing, 2004), chap. 12

——, 'Commitment Decisions and Settlements with Antitrust Authorities and Private Parties Under European Antitrust Law' 2005 *Fordham Corp L Inst* 265 (B. Hawk, ed. 2006)

——, and RIZZA, C., 'The *Ste Colas Est and Others* v. *France* case: European Court of Human Rights Case of 16 April 2002' [2002] *ECLR* 417

TOTH, A. G., 'The European Union and Human Rights: The Way Forward' (1997) 34 *CMLRev* 491

VAN BARLINGEN, and BARENNES, M., 'The European Commission's 2002 Leniency Notice in Practice', *Competition Policy Newsletter* Number 3, Autumn 2005

VARONA, E. N., and DURÁTEZ, H. G., 'Interim Measures in Competition Cases Before the European Commission and the Courts' [2002] *ECLR* 512

—— 'The Undertaking as Subject of EC Competition Law and the Imputation of Infringements to Natural or Legal Persons' (2000) 25 *ELRev* 99

—— 'The Combination of the Investigative and Prosecutorial Function and the Adjudicative Function in EC Antitrust Enforcement: A Legal and Economic Analysis' (2004) 27 *World Competition* 201

VESTERDORF, B., ' Legal Professional Privilege and the Privilege Against Self-Incrimination in EC Law: Recent Developments and Current Issues' (2004) *Fordham Corp L Inst* (B. Hawk, ed. 2005)

WASMEIER, M., and THWAITES, N., 'The Development of ne bis in idem into a Transnational fundamental right in EU law: comments on recent developments (2006) 31 *ELRev* 565

WILS, W., 'Self-incrimination in EC Antitrust Enforcement: A Legal and Economic Analysis' (2003) 26(4) *World Competition*, 567

—— 'Ne Bis In Idem in EC Antitrust Enforcement: A Legal and Economic Analysis' [2004] *World Competition – Law and Economics Review* 131 (142)

WOUDE, M., VAN DER, 'Hearing Officers and EC Antitrust Procedures: The Art of Making Subjective Procedures more Objective' (1996) *CMLRev* 531

15

PROCEEDINGS IN THE NATIONAL COURTS

1. CENTRAL ISSUES

1. Individuals may 'privately' enforce the competition rules by raising Articles 81 or 82 either as a shield, or a sword, in civil proceedings before a national court.

2. Private proceedings may enable compensation for victims of breaches, relieve enforcement pressure on public enforcement agencies and may also deter violations of the rules.

3. National courts are bound to apply directly effective provisions of Community law. National rules of procedure, evidence and substance govern competition proceedings before the national courts subject to the overriding requirement that the rules must not be less favourable than those relating to similar claims of a domestic nature (the principle of equivalence or non-discrimination) and must not make it virtually impossible or excessively difficult to exercise the right that the national courts are obliged to protect (the principle of effectiveness).

4. Provisions in an agreement that contravene Article 81 or Article 82 are void and unenforceable. The entire agreement will be void if the prohibited provisions cannot be severed from the remainder of the agreement.

5. The ECJ has held that damages must, in principle, be available to those that have suffered loss in consequence of a breach of Article 81 or 82. Further, injunctions may need to be available to protect putative Community rights.

6. There has been relatively little antitrust litigation brought by private individuals before national courts.

7. The Commission has published a Green Paper which identifies key obstacles to damages claims in the Member States and sets out possible options for getting over these problems. A follow-up White Paper is anticipated at the end of 2007.

2. INTRODUCTION

A. GENERAL

In earlier chapters in this book the different mechanisms for enforcing the EC competition rules have been referred to. In the preceding chapter, public enforcement through the European competition network (the Commission and the National competition authorities ('NCA's)) was discussed. In this chapter we concentrate on private enforcement of the rules through claims made in the national courts and tribunals of the individual Member States.

B. DIRECT EFFECT AND THE PRINCIPLE OF NATIONAL PROCEDURAL AUTONOMY

It was explained in Chapter 2 that, as a result of the principles of direct effect and supremacy, private individuals can commence proceedings before the national courts against those that have infringed Articles 81 and 82 or may raise a violation of these provisions as a defence to a claim. The principle of direct effect allows and encourages proceedings at the national level in cases where the rules are breached. A litigant may question an agreement's or other conduct's compatibility with the competition rules.[1] Further, he may additionally, or alternatively, seek some form of redress in respect of a breach of the rules, perhaps damages to compensate him in respect of loss, restitution, or an injunction to put an immediate end to the violation and to prevent future breaches of the rules. National courts are bound to apply the directly effective provisions, to give them precedence over conflicting principles of national law and to protect the rights which individuals derive from Community law.

Where an individual seeks to vindicate or protect his Community rights before a national court, the general principle is that of 'national procedural autonomy', national law sets out the rules governing proceedings.

[I]n the absence of Community rules on this subject, it is for the domestic legal system of each Member State to designate the courts having jurisdiction and to determine the procedural conditions governing actions at law intended to ensure the protection of rights which citizens have from the direct effect of Community law . . . [2]

In principle, therefore, the protection given to Community rights, and the availability of any remedy for breach of the competition rules, is dependent on the procedural, evidential, and substantive rules applicable in each particular Member State. The law of each Member State, *prima facie*, determines the rules and remedies available to those injured by a breach of the competition rules. The position is not, however, in reality, that simple. The national courts are bound to respect the general principles of Community law and through their application, the ECJ has taken steps to ensure that national courts provide *real* protection of individuals' Community rights. Community law imposes limits on the national courts' freedom of action. National rules

(1) must not be less favourable than those relating to similar claims of a domestic nature (the principle of equivalence or non-discrimination); and

(2) must not make it virtually impossible or excessively difficult to exercise the right that the national courts are obliged to protect (the principle of effectiveness).[3]

---

[1] Articles 81 and 82 may thus be used as a shield to a contractual claim e.g. on the grounds that the agreement is in violation of the provisions and void. See discussion in section 3 *infra*. A violation of the competition rules may also be raised as a defence in proceedings for infringement of intellectual property rights, see, e.g., discussion of *Intel Corporation v. VIA Technologies* [2002] EWCA Civ 1905, [2002] All ER (D) 346 *infra* n. 259 and accompanying text and *Sirdar Ltd v. Les Fils de Louis Mulliez and Orsay Knitting Wools Ltd* [1975] FSR 309 (ChD), *British Leyland Motor Corp Ltd v. TI Silencers Ltd* [1981] FSR 213 (CA), *Integraph Corporation v. Solid Systems CAD Services Ltd* [1995] ECC 53 (ChD), *Pitney Bowes Inc. v. Francotyp-Postalia GmbH* [1991] FSR 72 (ChD) and *Philips Electronics NV v. Ingman Ltd* [1999] FSR 112 (ChD). For a detailed discussion of competition law litigation in the UK Courts see B. Rodger 'Competition Law Litigation in the UK Courts: A Study of All Cases to 2004'—Parts I, II and III [2006] *ECLR* 241–8, 279–92 and 341–50.

[2] Case 33/76, *Rewe-Zentral Finanz eG and Rewe-Zentral AG v. Landwirtschaftskammer für das Saarland* [1976] ECR 1989, [1997] 1 CMLR 533.

[3] *Ibid.* See discussion of damages claims brought by co-contractors, *infra* 1343–4.

The principle of effectiveness, in particular, imposes an important inhibition on the free application of the national rules. It has become clear that this obligation requires national courts to ensure real and effective judicial protection of the Community rights.[4] '[T]he full effectiveness of Community law would be impaired if individuals were unable to obtain redress when their rights were infringed by a breach of Community law'.[5] Although, therefore, the Court of Justice gives national courts freedom to apply the most appropriate measure or remedy to protect a Community right,[6] it has, stressing the duty imposed on Member States in Article 10 EC,[7] held that remedies granted by national courts must be adequate and must be such as to guarantee real and *effective* judicial protection for Community rights.[8] In some cases the requirement that a remedy must be adequate, real, and effective may leave a national court free to determine how best to protect those rights.[9] In some cases, it may leave the national court a choice between two or more possible remedies[10] and in others the requirement may mean that a national court must ensure that a specific remedy is available to remedy a specific wrong.[11]

For example, in certain circumstances it has been held that a Member State is obliged to compensate individuals who have been injured by its breach of Community law.[12] Further, that a Member State is required, in principle, to repay charges levied in breach of Community law.[13] Although national courts are not required to grant *new* remedies,[14] this obligation means that national rules may have to be adapted or extended to ensure that a remedy is available where it is required by Community law. National defences and procedural limitations to the claim will apply in so far as those rules comply with the Community principles of equivalence and effectiveness.[15]

The sections below consider the critical question of whether and in what circumstances the principle of effectiveness requires, within the sphere of competition law, that any Community remedies should be granted.

---

[4] Case 14/83, *Von Colson and Kamann v. Land Nordrhein-Westfalen* [1984] ECR 1891, [1986] 2 CMLR 430 especially para. 23. In accordance with the duty of cooperation, set out in Article 10 of the EC Treaty, see Case 33/76, *Rewe-Zentral Finanz eG and Rewe-Zentral AG v. Landswirtschaftskammer für das Saarland* [1976] ECR 1989, [1977] 1 CMLR 533, para. 5. Community law is thus capable of having a substantial impact on the Member States' national legal order and the rights of their citizens. 'By contrast with ordinary international treaties, the EEC Treaty has created its own legal system which ... became an integral part of the legal systems of the Member States and which their courts are bound to apply': Case 6/64, *Costa v. ENEL* [1964] ECR 585, 593–4, [1964] CMLR 425.

[5] Cases C-46 and 48/93, *Brasserie du Pêcheur SA v. Germany and R v. Secretary of State for Transport, ex parte Factortame Ltd* [1996] ECR I-1029, [1996] 1 CMLR 889, para. 20.

[6] Case 34/67, *Lück v. Hauptzollamt Köln* [1968] ECR 245.

[7] To take all appropriate measures to ensure the fulfillment of its obligations arising out of this Treaty.

[8] Case 14/83, *Von Colson and Kamann v. Land Nordrhein-Westfalen* [1984] ECR 1891 (especially para. 23 of the judgment).

[9] Case 34/67, *Lück v. Hauptzollamt Köln* [1968] ECR 245.

[10] See Case C-271/91, *Marshall v. Southampton and South-West Hampshire Area Health Authority (Teaching) (No. 2)* [1993] ECR I-4367, [1993] 3 CMLR 293.

[11] For example, in a series of cases the Court has held that charges levied by a public authority in breach of Community rules must, in principle, be repaid. In Case 199/82, *Ammistrazione delle Finanze dello Stato v. San Giorgio SpA* [1983] ECR 3595, [1985] 2 CMLR 658 the Court of Justice held that the applicant's right to restitution is a 'consequence of and an adjunct to' the rights conferred on that individual by Community law.

[12] See discussion of Cases C-6 and 9/90, *Francovich v. Italy* [1991] ECR I-5357, [1993] 2 CMLR 66. *infra* n. 149 and accompanying text.

[13] See e.g. Case C-242/95 *GT-Link A/S v. De Danske Statsbaner (DSB)* [1997] ECR I-4449, [1997] 5 CMLR 601.

[14] Case 158/80, *Rewe-Handelsgesellschaft Nord mbH v. Hauptzollamt Kiel* [1981] ECR 1805, [1981] 1 CMLR 449.

[15] For a fuller explanation of the relationship between the principles of national procedural autonomy and the principles of equivalence and effectiveness see, e.g., A. Jones, *Restitution and European Community Law* (LLP, 2000), 6–13.

C. A PAUCITY OF ANTITRUST LITIGATION IN EUROPE

Although it is clear that Article 81(1), Article 81(2), Article 82, and now Article 81(3) are directly effective, there has, within the European Union, been relatively little 'antitrust litigation' brought by private individuals before national courts to enforce the EC competition rules. This position is in stark contrast to that which exists in the US where there is a culture of antitrust litigation and approximately 90 per cent of competition cases are litigated privately.[16] Proceedings brought by private individuals enlists those closest to violations of the competition rules in the enforcement process, relieves enforcement pressure on public enforcement agencies, ensures compensation for victims of breaches (achieves corrective justice through compensation) and may deter violations of the rules. The Commission recognizes the significant advantages that would result, were greater private enforcement of the rules to be encouraged in Europe.[17] A number of factors have nonetheless deterred widespread use of such actions.

A key factor initially contributing to the dearth of litigation has undoubtedly been the way that Articles 81 and 82 were enforced prior to modernization. In particular, the Commission's exclusive right to grant exemptions under Article 81(3), coupled with its wide interpretation of Article 81(1) and its desire to mould competition policy, gave the Commission tight control over enforcement.[18] The monopoly over exemptions effectively excluded the national courts from 'what the legal system of the United States understands by antitrust analysis'[19] (the courts could apply only half of the Article 81 story). In its *Thirteenth Report on Competition Policy* the Commission complained about this 'widespread misconception on the part of the public in Europe that only the Commission can enforce Articles [81] and [82]'.[20] In contrast, 'the US

[16] White Paper on Competition Policy, 'World Class Competition Regime', Cm. 5233 (July 2001), para. 8.1. Arguably, this has contributed to the success of the US antitrust rules. Indeed, one commentator has suggested that 'no antitrust regulation system has any realistic chance of success without it. Government antitrust authorities will never have the resources to prosecute all infringements which should be pursued and should not be in the business of awarding compensation. My own experience in private antitrust litigation—mostly for the defence—has brought me to the belief that society, and even the best firms, benefit from the constraints on behaviour which exist and are perceived to exist from the presence of a viable private enforcement system. To those who believe that private enforcement is wasteful, I reply that this is sometimes true, but it is better than the alternative of inadequate private enforcement. If we are to have private antitrust laws, we should have effective ones which are enforced', C. A. Jones, *Private Enforcement of Antitrust Law in the EU, UK and USA* (Oxford University Press, 1999), p. xii. He also comments at p. xi. of the preface that he was prompted to write the book partly as a result of his astonishment to learn that 'antitrust litigation as known to most of the American antitrust bar essentially did not exist in Europe'. The purpose of his book is thus to 'encourage the private antitrust litigation in the UK and the EC' (p. xii). For the contrary view see, e.g., W. P. J. Wils, 'Should private antitrust enforcement be encouraged?' [2003] 26(3) *World Competition* 473 discussed *infra* n. 38 and accompanying text.

[17] In the USA, there has been some concern in more recent times that private litigation can be wasteful (encouraging settlement to avoid protracted litigation) or may even deter enforcement. In particular, there was a fear that private litigation deters whistleblowing and leniency applications, a key plank in the administration's cartel policy. In 2004 a new Act was introduced to reduce damages to 'single' damages from corporations participating in the amnesty programme, see Criminal Penalty Enhancement and Reform Act 2004 and *supra* Chap. 11, n. 118 and accompanying text. The detrebling provision was designed to address a major disincentive that confronts companies who are contemplating exposing cartel activity.

[18] See, e.g., M. Monti, 'Effective Private Enforcement of EC Antitrust Law' Sixth EU Competition Law and Policy Workshop Florence, 1–2 June 2001.

[19] C. A. Jones, *Private Enforcement of Antitrust Law in the EU, UK and USA* (Oxford University Press, 1999), 85; see also *supra* Chap. 4. In the USA this has not been possible since the prohibition of contracts in restraint of trade set out in section 1 of the Sherman Act 1890 can be applied in its entirety by the US courts. No part of it has ever been reserved exclusively to the US enforcement authorities.

[20] EC Commission, *XIIIth Report on Competition Policy* (Commission, 1983), part 217.

enforcement system was explicitly created with public-private pluralism in mind. The litigation-oriented US system has for decades relied on a ratio of private to public suits ranging from 10 to 1 to 20 to 1, and there has never been any expectation[21] that the Antitrust Division of the US Department of Justice would shape antitrust law in the manner of the Commission'.[22]

Private litigation seems also to have been deterred by a number of other obstacles confronting an individual considering action before a national court. These vary considerably from jurisdiction to jurisdiction but barriers include:[23]

• the cost and risk of litigation. This may well deter many potential claimants from acting, particularly when they have not suffered much loss individually (class or other consolidated actions and contingency fees are not widely available in Europe) and where unsuccessful claimants may have to pay a defendant's legal costs;[24]

• the difficulty of gathering the requisite evidence, especially where it is situated in another Member State or States. Discovery rules vary considerably between Member States and are generally much less favourable than those in the US and are unlikely to give access to the sort of information that might be uncovered in an investigation by a competition authority;[25]

• the fact that proceedings are likely to be lengthy and protracted;[26]

• the possibility that the defendant may invoke a privilege against self-incrimination;[27]

• the uncertainty whether, and if so when, the applicant may rely on Commission documents and Commission decisions in national proceedings;[28]

• the complex economic evidence which may have to be raised to establish a breach of the rules (most cases will require markets to be defined and may involve economic argument which arguably the national courts do not have the requisite expertise to deal with);[29]

• the need to establish a causal link between the damage suffered by the applicant and the infringement of the competition rules;[30]

• uncertainty over how national rules on damages and injunctions apply. For example, what type of damages are available in respect of a breach of the competition rules and how they should be quantified and in what circumstances a preliminary or permanent injunction is available;

---

[21] It is pointed out that one of the main purposes of the dual enforcement system in the USA was to prevent political and budgetary considerations from affecting enforcement resources and legal principles: C. A. Jones, *Private Enforcement of Antitrust Law in the EU, UK and USA* (Oxford University Press, 1999), 89.

[22] *Ibid.*, 85.

[23] See also discussion of obstacles identified by the Commission in its Green Paper: Damages Actions for Breach of the EC Antitrust Rules COM/2005/0672/final, *infra* 1313–4.

[24] See, e.g. J. Peysner 'Costs and Financing in Private Third Party Competition Damages Actions' *Competition Law Review* Volume 3, Issue 1, 97.

[25] In Case T-5/93 *Tremblay v. Commission* [1995] ECR II-185, the CFI acknowledged that difficulties would arise where a national court did not have sufficient powers to ensure all the evidence, whether situated locally or abroad, is gathered. In contrast, the Commission has wide powers to gather evidence and may unearth extremely useful evidence when conducting dawn raids (Reg. 1/2003, Art. 20). This breadth of information is unlikely to come to light when using the ordinary national civil disclosure rules.

[26] Especially if an Article 234 reference to the ECJ is necessary.

[27] The protection given to a defendant under English law (see *Rio Tinto Zinc v. Westinghouse Electric Corp.* [1978] AC 547) is greater than that granted to an undertaking being investigated by the Commission for a breach of one of the Treaty competition rules: see *supra* Chap. 14.

[28] But see now *infra* 1315–8.

[29] See *infra* n. 31.

[30] See *infra* 1325 ff.

- uncertainty over who may sue. For example, whether indirect and/or direct purchasers may recover damages from a firm in breach of the competition rules and/or whether a passing on defence is available where a direct purchaser has passed on its loss to a purchaser further down the chain;

  - uncertainty over issues such as how national limitation rules apply;

  and

- the fact that some national courts have limited experience dealing with antitrust arguments and may not, consequently, be the most appropriate or understanding forum for the hearing. Indeed, in a case before the English Court of Appeal in 2007, Mummery LJ remarked that the nature of the difficult issues arising in that case (access to essential facilities and legal curbs on excessive and discriminatory pricing) might:

be solved more satisfactorily by arbitration or by a specialist body equipped with appropriate expertise and flexible powers. The adversarial procedures of an ordinary private law action, the limited scope of expertise in the ordinary courts and the restricted scope of legal remedies available are not best suited to helping the parties out of a deadlocked negotiating position or to achieving a business-like result reflecting both their respective interests and the public interest. These are not, however, matters for decision by the court, which must do the best that it can with a complex piece of private law litigation.[31]

Further, a particular problem arises from the possibility of dual enforcement (public and private enforcement). National courts have an obligation to ensure that their decisions do not conflict with any decision given, or which might be given at the Community level, so national courts may in certain circumstances have to stay proceedings or take interim measures pending a Commission decision.[32]

In contrast it seems that the comparative success of private actions in the US has been founded on factors such as:

(1) specific legislative provisions providing for damages for those injured by reason of anything forbidden in the antitrust laws and injunctive relief against threatened loss or damage by a violation;[33]

(2) the availability of treble damages;[34]

(3) the existence of wide discovery powers;

(4) the statutory right for claimants to use judgments entered against the defendant as prima-facie evidence against that defendant;[35]

---

[31] *British Horseracing Board Limited v. Attheraces Limited* [2007] EWCA Civ 38, para 7.

[32] See *infra* 1315 ff.

[33] Clayton Act, ss 4 and 16.

[34] Clayton Act, s 4. 'It is thought by some in Europe that private antitrust actions under Community law will never be of importance due to the absence of the legislative provision for treble damages which so ubiquitously characterizes the remedy provisions of the Sherman Act. It is submitted that the perceived superiority of the treble damages provisions of US law over damages rules available in Europe is exaggerated. In fact, . . . other components of the damage system in the USA are such that "treble" damages under US law are essentially mythical and that comparable results are in fact obtainable in Europe, especially in the UK, without a treble damages multiplier': C. A. Jones, *Private Enforcement of Antitrust Law in the EU, UK and USA* (Oxford University Press, 1999), 199. That author also notes (at 35–6) that the model for the treble damages formula adopted in the USA was an English Statute of Monopolies 1623 (now repealed). He points out the irony in this 'in view of the distaste for US antitrust treble damages actions reflected in some British judgments and statutes' (see in particular *Midland Bank plc v. Laker Airways Ltd* [1986] 1 QB 689 and the Protection of Trading Interests Act 1980).

[35] Clayton Act, s 5(a).

(5) the ability of the successful plaintiff (claimant), contrary to ordinary rule in the US that each party bears its own cost, to recover costs, including reasonable attorney's fees;

(6) the ability to bring class actions under federal, and most state, laws;

(7) the availability of contingency fees;

(8) the fact that there is more of a 'litigation culture' in the US;

(9) the fact that most cases are tried by jury;

and

(10) the fact that the public authorities have not taken on such a central role in antitrust enforcement.

Although there is concern in the US that the rules are sometimes too litigation friendly and may encourage nuisance litigation, the prevailing view appears to be that the private enforcement is important from both a deterrence and compensatory point of view. Not only does private enforcement help to ensure that firms comply with the rules but it provides a remedy for those harmed by unlawful violations.

In the UK, the enforcement problems have been compounded by the general uncertainty that, until recently, surrounded the question of what remedies, if any, were available to compensate those which have suffered as a result of another's breach of the competition rules, the reluctance of the courts to grant interim relief, and, more generally, the far from enthusiastic response with which those pleading a breach of the competition rules have been met.[36]

Over the years the Commission has taken a number of steps designed to try and overcome these problems and to encourage private actions.[37]

D. REGULATION 1/2003, THE 2005 GREEN PAPER AND ENCOURAGEMENT OF PRIVATE ACTIONS

There is no doubt that greater private enforcement would have a significant effect on the application of the EC competition rules. In particular, it would mean that: (1) the enforcement of the rules is not left entirely to the Commission and NCAs which have limited resources; (2) the legal principles, in particular the interpretation of Article 81, would be more heavily influenced by the courts (national and, through Article 234 references, the ECJ) than has previously been the case; (3) victims would be able to obtain remedies, in particular compensation, in respect of breaches of the rules; and (4) the threat of private proceedings might also serve as an extra deterrent discouraging breaches of the rules which would work alongside public enforcement. The belief that private enforcement should be encouraged is not universal, however. Wouter Wils,[38] for example, has argued that private enforcement is unnecessary both as an additional mechanism for enforcement of the rules and as a mechanism for achieving corrective justice. Rather, he has argued that public enforcement provides a superior and less costly mechanism

---

[36] See e.g., the discussion of the background to the *Crehan* case, *infra* 1326 ff.

[37] e.g., pre-modernization, the Commission Notice on cooperation between the national courts and the Commission in applying Articles [81] and [82] [1993] OJ C39/6.

[38] See W. Wils, *Principles of European Antitrust Enforcement* (Hart Publishing, 2005), Chap. 4 and W. P. J. Wils 'Should private antitrust enforcement be encouraged?' [2003] 26(3) *World Competition* 473. The author argues that the paucity of private enforcement is desirable and that public antitrust enforcement is superior. Public enforcers have more effective investigative and sanctioning powers. Further private litigation is driven by private profit motives and is costly and wasteful. See also, e.g., F. G. Jacobs 'Civil Enforcement of EEC Antitrust Law' (1984) 82 *Mich. LR* 1364.

for ensuring that the competition rules are not violated and that corrective justice is unlikely to be served by such proceedings. Many others have warned that caution should be exercised in this area so that a litigation culture demonstrating the excesses of the US system is not unleashed.[39]

The Commission is aware of the dangers of putting in place a system that it too litigation friendly but accepts that increased enforcement at the national level will both heighten awareness of, and respect for, the Community provisions (create a culture of competition), provide an additional deterrent to anticompetitive behaviour, provide a complementary enforcement system to public enforcement and free the Commission's own resources for complex cases which raise new or difficult issues from a legal or economic point of view.[40] Further, that national proceedings will, frequently, provide a quicker and more efficient means of bringing infringements to an end than public enforcement.[41] In general the Commission will decline to act on a complaint where the complainant can assert its rights before a national court.[42] Indeed, the Commission's Notice on complaints stresses the advantages that may result to potential complainants if private proceedings are brought: the private litigant may be able to recover compensation in respect of loss; to obtain interim measures; to pursue remedies for breach of national law; and to recoup the costs of the proceedings.

Commission Notice on the Handling of Complaints by the Commission under Articles 81 and 82 of the EC Treaty [2004] OJ C101/65

B. The complementary roles of private and public enforcement

12. It has been consistently held by the Community Courts that national courts are called upon to safeguard the rights of individuals created by the direct effect of Articles 81(1) and 82.

13. National courts can decide upon the nullity or validity of contracts and only national courts can grant damages to an individual in case of an infringement of Articles 81 and 82. Under the case law of the Court of Justice, any individual can claim damages for loss caused to him by a contract or by conduct which restricts or distorts competition, in order to ensure the full effectiveness of the Community competition rules. Such actions for damages before the national courts can make a significant contribution to the maintenance of effective competition in the Community as they discourage undertakings from concluding or applying restrictive agreements or practices.

14. Regulation 1/2003 takes express account of the fact that national courts have an essential part to play in applying the EC competition rules. By extending the power to apply Article 81(3) to national courts it removes the possibility for undertakings to delay national court proceedings by

---

[39] See, e.g. the responses to the Commission's Green Paper: Damages Actions for Breach of the EC Antitrust Rules COM/2005/0672/final and D. Wilsher, 'The Public Aspects of Private Enforcement in EC Law: some Constitutional and Administrative Challenges of a Damages Culture' *Competition Law Review* Vol. 3, Issue 1, 27.

[40] It accepts that a balanced approach is needed that mitigates the unwanted social costs of encouraging private action, Staff Working Paper, Annex to the Commission's Green Paper: Damages Actions for Breach of the EC Antitrust Rules COM/2005/0672/final discussed *infra*, available on DGComp's web site, at http://ec.europa.eu/comm/competition/antitrust/actionsdamages/index.html.

[41] See the Commission's *XVth Report on Competition Policy* (Commission, 1985), part 39.

[42] Commission Notice on the handling of complaints [2004] OJ C101/65, paras. 17 and 44, *supra* Chap. 14. The Commission is also entitled to reject a complaint where an NCA is dealing, or has dealt, with the case, Reg. 1/2003, Art. 13.

a notification to the Commission and thus eliminates an obstacle for private litigation that existed under Regulation No. 17.

15. Without prejudice to the right or obligation of national courts to address a preliminary question to the Court of Justice in accordance with Article 234 EC, Article 15(1) of Regulation 1/2003 provides expressly that national courts may ask for opinions or information from the Commission. This provision aims at facilitating the application of Articles 81 and 82 by national courts.

16. Action before national courts has the following advantages for complainants:

— National courts may award damages for loss suffered as a result of the infringement of Articles 81 or 82.
— National courts may rule on claims for payment or contractual obligations based on an agreement that they examine under Article 81.
— It is for the national courts to apply the civil sanction of nullity of Article 81(2) in contractual relationship between individuals. They can in particular assess, in the light of the applicable national law, the scope and consequences of the nullity of certain contractual provisions under Article 81(2), with particular regard to all the other matters covered by the agreement.
— National courts are usually better placed than the Commission to adopt interim measures.
— Before national courts, it is possible to combine a claim under Community competition law with other claims under national law.
— Courts normally have the power to award legal costs to the successful applicant. This is never possible in an administrative procedure before the Commission.

The Commission has been in favour of, and has been seeking to encourage, greater private enforcement of Community competition law before the national courts for a number of years.[43] A key objective of Regulation 1/2003 was to decentralize the enforcement of EC competition law and to strengthen the possibility for individuals to seek and obtain effective relief before national courts.[44] In pursuit of this objective: [45]

• Article 1 provides that Articles 81 and 82 are directly effective in their entirety. This point is critical as, since 1 May 2004, the national courts have been able to apply Article 81(3). This means that proceedings can no longer be derailed by notifications to the Commission;

• Article 6 provides that national courts shall have the power to apply Articles 81 and 82 of the Treaty;

• Article 3 provides that the national courts shall apply Articles 81 and 82 to an agreement or abusive conduct which affects trade between Member states and which they are applying national competition law to and deals with the relationship between Community and national law;

[43] See, e.g. See the Commission's Thirteenth Report on Competition Policy, (1984) 147–149, Fourteenth Report on Competition Policy (1985) 59, Fifteenth Report on Competition Policy (1986), 52–55, the Commission's Answer to Written Question No 519/72, [1973] OJ C 67/54, and the answer given by Mr Andriessen on behalf of the Commission to Written Question No 1935/83, [1984] OJ C144/14, referred to by Van Gerven AG in Case C-128/92, *Banks & Co Ltd* v. *British Coal Corp* [1994], ECR I-1209, [1994] 5 CMLR 30, n. 112.

[44] See generally *supra* Chap. 14 and, e.g., Commission Notice on the handling of complaints by the Commission under Articles 81 and 82 of the EC Treaty [2004] OJ C101/65, para. 18.

[45] See also recital 7 which provides that national courts protect the subjective community rights of individuals when deciding disputes between them, for example, by awarding damages to the victims of infringements. In Case C-453/99, *Courage Ltd* v. *Crehan* [2001] ECR I-6297, [2001] 5 CMLR 28 the ECJ established that there is a Community right to damages in cases of breach of Article 81 or 82, see *infra* 1325 ff.

• Article 15 provides for cooperation between the Commission and the national courts; and

• Article 16(1) sets out provisions designed to ensure the uniform application of Community competition law.

The national courts thus have the power to apply Articles 81 and 82 and in some circumstances they are obliged to do so.[46] Further, they may be obliged to raise competition matters of their own motion.

Commission Notice on the Co-operation Between the Commission and the Courts of the EU Member States in the Application of Articles 81 and 82 EC [2004] OJ C101/54

3. To the extent that national courts have jurisdiction to deal with a case, they have the power to Articles 81 and 82 EC. Moreover, it should be remembered that Articles 81 and 82 EC are a matter of public policy and are essential to the accomplishment of the task entrusted to the Community, and, in particular, for the functioning of the internal market. According to the Court of Justice, where, by virtue of domestic law, national courts must raise of their own motion points of law based on binding domestic rules which have not been raised by the parties, such an obligation also exists where binding Community rules, such as the EC competition rules, are concerned. The position is the same if domestic law confers on national courts a discretion to apply of their own motion binding rules of law: national courts must apply the EC competition rules, even when the party with an interest in the application of those provisions has not relied on them, where domestic law allows such application by the national court. However, Community law does not require national courts to raise of their own motion an issue concerning the breach of provisions of Community law where examination of that issue would oblige them to abandon the passive role assigned to them by going beyond the ambit of the dispute defined by the parties themselves and relying on the facts and circumstances other than those on which the party with an interest in application of those provisions bases his claim.[47]

The Commission's Notice on the cooperation between the Commission and the courts of the EU Member States in the application of Articles 81 and 82 EC sets out general guidance for national courts dealing with cases which raise a point of Community competition law and addresses the cooperation between the Commission and the courts of the EU Member States, when the courts apply Articles 81 and 82.

Despite the steps taken in Regulation 1/2003 and the Commission's belief that private enforcement plays a key part in deterring anticompetitive practices and compensating those that suffer in consequence, the Commission accepts that the system of damages for infringements of competition law of the Member States 'presents a picture of "total underdevelopment"[48] and that the steps taken in Regulation 1/2003 will not be sufficient to stimulate private action. In its 2005

---

[46] In particular, where they apply national competition law to an agreement or practice that affects trade between Member States and where individuals seeks to protect their Community law rights before the courts.

[47] See Cases C-430 and 431/93, *Van Schijndel v. Stichting Pensioensfonds voor Fysiotherapeuten* [1995] ECR I-4705, [1996] 1 CMLR 801. See also Case C-312/93, *Peterbroek Van Campenhout & Cie v. Belgium* [1995] ECR I-4599, [1996] 1 CMLR 793.

[48] Green Paper: Damages actions for breach of the EC antitrust rules COM/2005/0672/final, 1.2. This view was based on a study prepared for DGComp by Ashurst on damages actions before national courts of the, then, 25 Member States see *infra* n. 92.

Green Paper on Damages actions for breach of the EC antitrust rules[49] it stated that '[s]ignificant obstacles exist in the different Member States to the effective operation of damages actions for infringement of Community antitrust law'.[50] The purpose of the Green Paper, and an accompanying Commission Staff Working Paper,[51] was therefore:

- 'to identify the main obstacles to a more efficient system of damages claims and to set out different options for further reflection and possible action to improve both follow-on actions (e.g. cases in which the civil action is brought after a competition authority has found an infringement) and stand-alone actions (that is to say actions which do not follow on from a prior finding by a competition authority of an infringement of competition law)'[52]; and

- to invite a discussion on obstacles identified and options formulated for getting over them and allowing a competition culture to develop.

The key issues identified for discussion were:

(1) access to evidence. In many Member States (particularly those with civil rather than common law systems) it is difficult to get access to relevant evidence held by the party committing the anti-competitive behaviour. The Discussion Paper thus invited discussion on issues such as whether special rules should be introduced on disclosure of documentary evidence in civil proceedings for damages under Articles 81 and 82 (and, if so, in which form) and whether there should be special rules regarding access to documents held by a competition authority;

(2) whether a damages action for breach of Articles 81 or 82 should require fault to be proven (often a requirement in tortious proceedings in the Member States (but not it seems in England & Wales)[53]) or whether proof of the infringement should be sufficient in all or some circumstances,

(3) uncertainty over the question of how damages should be defined and quantified. One option proposed is for the Commission to publish guidance on quantification of damages in competition cases;

(4) whether there should be rules on the admissibility and operation of the passing-on defence and whether indirect purchasers should have standing;

(5) how consumers' interests can be defended (especially those with small claims);

(6) whether cost rules operate as incentive or disincentives for bringing an action and whether special rules should be introduced to reduce the cost risk for the claimant;

(7) how public and private enforcement can be coordinated and, in particular, how it can be ensured that damages actions do not impact negatively on leniency programmes. With regard to the impact on leniency programmes, one option proposed is that, in general, participants in hardcore cartel activity should be liable to double damages. Liability could however be limited to single damages for successful leniency applicants and they could be exempted from joint and several liability;[54]

(8) which substantive law should be applicable to antitrust claims.

---

[49] COM/2005/0672/final.

[50] COM/2005/0672/final, 1.2.

[51] Commission Staff Working Paper, Annex to the Green Paper (available on DGComp's web site, at http://ec.europa.eu/comm/competition/antitrust/actionsdamages/index.html).

[52] Green Paper: Damages actions for breach of the EC antitrust rules COM/2005/0672/final, 1.3.

[53] See *infra* 1338–9.

[54] The Commission also accepts that leniency applications should not be disclosed in the course of discovery, see point (1) above.

Access to courts is also limited in some Member States by restrictive standing rules.

The intention of the Green Paper was thus to stimulate debate and elicit feedback on various options designed to facilitate private damages actions. To what extent these obstacles are in reality surmountable, whether through Community or national legislation[55] or Commission guidelines (changes required are likely to have implications which go beyond the scope of claims for damages in competition cases) is debatable and the project is undoubtedly an extremely ambitious one. Comments received by the Commission are available on its website. The Commission is now in the process of preparing a White Paper, due to be published toward the end of 2007/beginning of 2008. The White Paper will set out in more concrete terms ideas which followed from the Green Paper and the discussion it provoked.

E. UNIFORM AND CONCURRENT APPLICATION OF ARTICLES 81 AND 82

(i) Cooperation between the Commission and National Courts

In Chapter 14 it has been seen that a key concern is that decentralized enforcement of Articles 81 and 82 will lead to inconsistent interpretation and application of the rules by the Commission, the individual NCAs, and national courts respectively.

When applying Articles 81 and 82, the national courts are obviously bound to interpret those provisions in accordance with that adopted by the Court of Justice and to respect the principle of primacy of Community law. Article 234 provides an important mechanism for national courts struggling with the interpretation of Community law. Further, the ECJ has held that the duty of cooperation set out in Article 10 of the Treaty requires the Commission to assist national courts in their application of Community law and vice versa.[56] Both Regulation 1/2003 itself and the Commission's notice on cooperation between the Commission and the courts of the EU in the application of Articles 81 and 82 EC[57] explain how that cooperation may manifest itself.

Article 15 of Regulation 1/2003 envisages that the Commission should act as *amicus curiae* to the national courts. First, it provides that the national courts might request the Commission to provide information or an opinion on the application of the Community competition rules. The Commission seeks to provide information requested within one month and an opinion within four months of the request.[58] Any opinion given will deal with the economic, factual, or legal matter on which its opinion was sought but not with the merits of the case.[59] The Commission can request information from the court necessary to provide the opinion.

---

[55] The UK's Office of Fair Trading (the 'OFT') is also working to identify and overcome barriers to private actions and representative actions. The 2007 Budget Report discusses the Government's intention to work with the OFT on this issue, and on 18 April 2007 the OFT published a consultation paper designed to identify and consult on measures needed to overcome barriers to litigation without encouraging ill-founded claims.

[56] See, e.g., Case 234/89, *Delimitis v. Henninger Bräu* [1991] ECR I-935, [1992] 5 CMLR 210, para. 53.

[57] [2004] OJ C101/54.

[58] Commission Notice on cooperation between the Commission and the national courts [2004] OJ C101/54, paras. 22–33. The Commission will respect the rights of persons providing the information by upholding its obligation of professional secrecy

[59] *Ibid.*, para. 29.

Secondly, it provides that the Commission may, where 'the coherent application of Article 81 or Article 82 so requires',[60] submit written observations to the national courts and also, with their permission, make oral observations. NCAs are also entitled to submit written observations to the national courts of their Member State and oral observations with permission. The Commission and NCA may seek the transmission of documents from the courts which are necessary for its assessment of the case but these documents may only be used for the preparation of their observations.[61] Any opinion so provided is not binding on the courts although it is likely to have a persuasive impact. The procedural framework dealing with how the submissions should be provided, is governed by national law.[62]

Regulation 1/2003 also provides how the national courts must assist the Commission in the fulfillment of its tasks. In addition to providing the Commission and NCAs with the documents necessary for preparing written or oral observations to the courts, Member States must forward to the Commission 'a copy of any written judgment of national courts deciding on the application of Articles 81 or Article 82' without delay.[63] The Commission publishes these judgments on its web site according to the Member State of origin. This is obviously an immensely useful resource.[64]

(ii) Judgments Contrary to Decisions of the Commission

a. Article 16 Regulation 1/2003

The ECJ has held that the duty of cooperation set out in Article 10 requires a national court to follow a Commission decision dealing with the same parties and the same agreement in the same Member State.[65] Further, in order to ensure a uniform application of Articles 81 and 82 Article 16 of Regulation 1/2003 provides that the national courts must not adopt decisions contrary to a previous Commission decision and must avoid giving decisions that would conflict with a decision contemplated by the Commission.[66]

---

[60] Reg. 1/2003, Art. 15(3).

[61] *Ibid.*

[62] In the English courts there has traditionally been no procedure for submissions of amicus curiae briefs before the courts. It has yet to be determined whether such evidence will be admitted, e.g., as expert evidence of an expert witness, or in some other way. The OFT was, however, given leave to, and did, intervene in the proceedings before the House of Lords in *Inntrepreneur Pub Company v. Crehan* [2006] UKHL 38.

[63] Art. 15(2).

[64] The judgments are in chronological order, see the National Court Cases Database, http:// www. europa.eu.int/comm/competition/antitrust/national-courts/index_en.html. The utility of the resource is diminished by the fact the judgment is only available in the original language and contains only the name of the court and parties. A summary of the issues raised by the case in English/French would increase utility. The OFT publishes details of cases before the UK courts, and drawn to its attention, on its web site, see http://www. oft.gov.uk/Business/UK+competition+court+cases+database/default.htm. This part of the web site has not been kept up to day, however. There are now a number of journals, paper and on-line, which provide summaries of decisions/judgments adopted in the Member States and other international jurisdictions. The Commission will respect the rights of persons providing the information by upholding its obligation of professional secrecy, see *supra* Chap. 14.

[65] See, e.g. Case C-344/89, *Masterfoods* [2000] ECR I-11369 [2001] 4 CMLR 449 and Case 234/89, *Delimitis v. Henninger Bräu* [1991] ECR I-935, [1992] 5 CMLR 210.

[66] The risk of conflicting decisions being adopted by an EU court and the Commission respectively is in fact greater than the risk of a conflicting decisions being adopted by the Commission and a NCA. Unlike the position with NCAs, the initiation of proceedings by the Commission does not relieve the national courts of their jurisdiction to apply Articles 81 and 82. They may therefore apply EC competition law to conduct at the same time as the Commission or subsequent to the Commission.

Article 16

Uniform application of Community competition law

1. When national courts rule on agreements, decisions or practices under Article 81 or Article 82 of the Treaty which are already the subject of a Commission decision, they cannot take decisions running counter to the decision adopted by the Commission. They must also avoid giving decisions which would conflict with a decision contemplated by the Commission in proceedings it has initiated. To that effect, the national court may assess whether it is necessary to stay its proceedings. This obligation is without prejudice to the rights and obligations under Article 234 of the Treaty.

The Commission's Notice on the cooperation between the Commission and the courts of the EU Member States in the application of Articles 81 and 82 EC[67] provides further guidance on parallel or consecutive application of the EC competition rules by the Commission and national courts.[68]

b. Parallel Proceedings

Where the Commission has initiated proceedings but not determined a case, a national court must not adopt a decision which will conflict with that which will be adopted by the Commission. The Commission will provide the national court with information as to whether it has initiated proceedings, the progress of proceedings, and the likelihood of a decision. Unless the national court cannot doubt the Commission's contemplated decision or the Commission has already decided on a similar case, it should ordinarily stay the proceedings before it.[69] Where this occurs the Commission will endeavour to give the case priority.[70]

c. Consecutive Proceedings

Where the Commission has already decided on the case, the Commission's decision is binding on the national court, without prejudice to the interpretation of Community law by the Court of Justice.[71] If the national court does not agree with the decision of the Commission it must either await the outcome of an appeal, if any, from its decision, or refer the question to the Court of Justice for a preliminary ruling.[72]

Where the national court does stay proceedings in the context of parallel or consecutive proceedings, it should consider whether it should impose interim measures in order to safeguard the interests of the parties involved.[73]

---

[67] [2004] OJ C101/54.

[68] Commission Notice on the cooperation between the Commission and the courts of the EU Member States in the application of Articles 81 and 82 EC [2004] OJ C101/54, paras. 11–13.

[69] See, e.g., Case 234/89, *Delimitis v. Henninger Bräu* [1991] ECR I-935, [1992] 5 CMLR 210, para. 43–55. See the discussion of the *Pfizer* litigation, *AAH Pharmaceuticals Ltd and Others v. Pfizer Limited and Unichem Ltd* [2007] EWHC 565, *infra* n 266 and accompanying text.

[70] *Ibid.*, para. 11.

[71] Case 314/85, *Foto-Frost v. Haptzollamt Lübeck-Ort* [1987] ECR 4199, paras. 12–20.

[72] *Ibid.*, para. 12.

[73] Case C-344/89, *Masterfoods* [2000] ECR I-11369 [2001] 4 CMLR 449, para. 58, see discussion *infra* 1350 ff.

d. Consecutive Proceedings: Issues Arising in Proceedings between Different Parties

In *Inntrepreneur Pub Company* v. *Crehan*[74] the House of Lords adopted a narrow interpretation of the national court's duty of sincere cooperation and its obligation not to adopt decisions contrary to those in a previous Commission decision.

This ruling was the last in a saga which commenced in 1993 and saw the parties endure thirteen years of litigation before the High Court, the Court of Appeal, the ECJ, back to the High Court, the Court of Appeal and, finally, before the House of Lords. This case is discussed in greater detail in the sections below but, essentially, its outcome eventually turned upon the question of whether an English court was bound to adopt the same approach as the Commission had in similar cases, but involving different parties. The dispute centred around the compatibility of a beer tie agreement concluded by a UK brewer and a publican with Article 81(1). In a number of decisions, such as *Whitbread*, *Bass* and *Scottish & Newcastle*,[75] the Commission had held that extremely similar agreements concluded by other UK brewers foreclosed the UK market for the distribution of beer in on-licensed premises and violated Article 81(1). Further, although it did not actually adopt a decision, the Commission had indicated that the Inntrepreneur leases (the leases at issue) were also in breach of Article 81. Nonetheless, when the matter reverted to the High Court following a ruling of the ECJ,[76] Park J held that the beer tie agreements did not infringe Article 81(1).[77] Applying the test set out in *Delimitis*,[78] he considered that the first limb of the two part test was not satisfied. He held, contrary to the view of the Commission, that the UK market for the distribution of beer in on-licensed premises was not foreclosed.[79] Although Park J accepted that he should give the Commission decisions weight, he did not consider himself to be bound by them.[80]

In so ruling, the judge appeared to depart from the settled approach adopted not only by the European Commission,[81] but by the UK authorities,[82] and the English courts[83] in their analysis of beer tie agreements in the UK market. On appeal, the Court of Appeal held, noting that the judge was obliged to give greater deference to previous Commission decisional practice than he

---

[74] [2006] UKHL 38. For a discussion of this case see e.g. J. Temple Lang, 'Inntrepreneur and the Duties of National Courts under Article 10 EC' [2006] *Comp Law* 231.

[75] *Whitbread* [1999] OJ L88/26, [1999] 5 CMLR 118, *aff'd* Case T-133/99 *Shaw* v. *Commission* [2002] ECR II-2023, *Bass* [1999] OJ L186/1 and *Scottish and Newcastle* [199] OJ L 186/28.

[76] See *infra* 1325–9.

[77] *Crehan* v. *Inntrepreneur Pub Co* [2003] EWHC 1510 (Ch) In reaching such a conclusion the judgment arguably came to a decision inconsistent with the European Commission's decisional practice and the findings of the UK's OFT and CC, see *infra*.

[78] Case C-234/89, [1991] ECR I-935, [1992] 5 CMLR 210, discussed *supra* Chap. 4.

[79] Examining the leases in their economic and legal context, he concluded that it was not difficult for competitors to enter the market or to increase their market shares and to gain access to the national market for the distribution of beer in premises for the sale and consumption of beer. It was, therefore, unnecessary to go on to decide, as would have been required had the market been found to be foreclosed, whether or not Inntrepreneur's leases made a significant contribution the sealing-off effect brought about by the totality of agreements in their legal and economic context.

[80] If there had been a breach of Article 81(1), however, he considered that the block exemption did not apply, the high prices paid by Crehan had caused his business to fail and that he would have been entitled to recover damages for loss of profits up to the date of judgment and the value of the leases which he would still have owned had he been free of tie throughout.

[81] See the discussion *supra* Chaps. 4 and 9.

[82] See, e.g., The Supply of Beer: a report on the supply of beer for retail sale in the United Kingdom (Cm. 651, 1989).

[83] See *supra* section 2.

had been prepared to give,[84] that the judge had been wrong on this matter: the lease incorporating the beer tie, did infringe Article 81(1). The first Delimitis condition was satisfied and the agreements in question did contribute to the cumulative effect produced by the totality of similar contracts found on the market.

It is a striking feature of this case that, as Inntrepreneur very properly accepts, if the judge were right, the Commission has been consistently wrong for many years in its view of the foreclosure of the United Kingdom market. That view has been expressed not only in the decision and Art. 19(3) notices and comfort letters...but in other cases as well. The Commission in its XXIXth Report on Competition Policy 1999 described its decisions in Whitbread, Bass and Scottish and Newcastle as taken after 'an exhaustive examination by the Commission departments'.[85]

As the agreement did not meet the conditions of a block exemption and had not been granted an individual exemption, the Court concluded that Article 81(1) applied and the breach was established.[86]

The House of Lords, however, disagreed with the Court of Appeal holding that the judge was not bound by the Commission's assessment. No rule of Community law required the English court in this case to follow the Commission. The duty of sincere cooperation did not require the English court to accept the factual basis of a decision reached by a Community institution when considering an issue arising between different parties in respect of a different subject matter. A conflict would only exist when agreements, decisions or practices ruled on by the national court had been, or was about to be, the subject of a Commission decision. There was no conflict where a Commission decision related to other agreements, decisions, or practices in the same market. Lord Bingham of Cornhill thus considered that the judge was bound to consider the factual evidence presented to him and to analyse it giving particular attention to those points on which he differed from the Commission. To have done otherwise would have been an abdication of the judicial function. [87]

Had the Court of Appeal's opinion prevailed in this case, companies may have felt compelled to intervene in and challenge decisions addressed to other parties which may have affected their interest in the future. The House of Lords opinions, however, undoubtedly leave the slightly uncomfortable and unsatisfactory position that 'because the English courts did not ask the Commission for submissions, breweries to which Commission decisions were addressed now are in a different position from Inntrepreneur, and there is no obvious way of resolving this inconsistency'.[88]

---

[84] [2004] EWCA Civ 637, para. 97.

[85] *Ibid.*, para. 78.

[86] However, the Court awarded damages at a considerably lower rate than Park J would have, holding that the correct date of assessment was the date of loss (the date he lost the business on surrender of the pubs). Leave to appeal was granted (1) on the question of whether the beer tie agreements concluded between the parties infringed Article 81(1) (i.e. whether the Delimitis conditions were satisfied and/or whether the conditions of the block exemption, then Reg 1984/83, were satisfied); and (2) as to the type of damages recoverable (whether the loss was recoverable under English law and, if not, whether recovery would be required under the principle of effectiveness); (3) (in a cross-appeal) as to the measure of damages recoverable (was the Court of Appeal's assessment of the second head of damages correct?). The Opinions of the House of Lords dealt however essentially only with one question: whether the trial judge in this case should have treated the Commission's factual assessment of the UK beer market in its *Whitbread, Bass* and *Scottish and Newcastle* decisions as effectively binding upon him even if it was not formally binding.

[87] Lord Hoffmann also considered it would be pointless to make a reference to the ECJ asking whether Park J was obliged to follow the Commission decisions or, alternatively, whether in the light of the judge's finding of fact, the decision in *Whitbread* was valid. The House would either be asking about the validity of a decision about agreements between other parties or else asking the ECJ to decide a question of fact which was within the jurisdiction of the national court.

[88] J. Temple Lang, 'Inntrepreneur and the Duties of National Courts under Article 10 EC' [2006] *Comp Law* 231, 234.

F. CONCLUSION

There is a clear policy in favour of private enforcement in Europe. The Modernization package and Green Paper are designed to further encourage and stimulate civil litigation in the national courts. Nonetheless, there has to date been little private enforcement of the rules. Although Articles 81 and 82 have sometimes been used successfully as a shield in litigation, there are still very few cases in which damages have actually been awarded by a court of a Member State to compensate a claimant for loss resulting in consequence of an infringement of Article 81 or 82 of the Treaty.[89]

Modernization and the Commission's reluctance to deal with cases[90] it considers can be dealt with adequately in the national courts may mean that the number of such proceedings will increase. Proceedings may, however, continue to be deterred by other factors, for example, inadequate discovery rules and unavailability of class actions.[91] In recognition of the procedural impediments that may exist to civil litigation, the Commission's Green Paper is designed to look at additional ways to support such actions.[92] What steps might be proposed, in particular, whether any Community legislation harmonizing national rules should be adopted, will be revealed when the White Paper is published.

The sections below set out the difficulties confronting potential applicants and the issues that may have to be resolved if increased litigation is to become a reality. Section 3 deals with the enforceability of agreements infringing Articles 81 and 82 and Section 4 deals with claims for damages and other remedies before the courts, in particular, the question of whether there are any Community remedies for breach of the competition rules. Some conclusions are set out in section 5.

3. THE ENFORCEABILITY OF AGREEMENTS INFRINGING ARTICLES 81 OR 82

A. ARTICLE 81

(i) The Sanction of Nullity

Article 81(2) provides that agreements or decisions prohibited by Article 81(1) are void so long as the agreement does not satisfy the conditions of Article 81(3). Despite its wording, it has been held that the nullity provided for in Article 81(2) applies only to individual *clauses* in the agreement affected by the Article 81(1) prohibition.[93] The agreement as a whole is void only where those clauses are not severable from the remaining terms of the agreement. The invalidity of the agreement (or affected clauses) is absolute. An agreement which is null and void under Article

---

[89] See *infra* section 4.A.

[90] See also the UK OFT's decision to reprioritize its case work and to concentrate on high impact cases, announcement of 12 October 2006.

[91] See *supra*.

[92] At the end of 2003, it commissioned a study into the conditions of claims for damages in the, then, twenty-five Member States. The study regarding the conditions of claims for damages in case of infringement of EC competition rules was prepared by the law firm, Ashurst, 'Study on the conditions of claims for damages in case of infringement of EC Competition Rules', August 2004 (available on DGComp's web site).

[93] Case 56/65, *Société La Technique Minière v. Maschinenbau Ulm GmbH* [1966] ECR 234, 250, [1966] CMLR 357.

81(2) thus has no effect as between the contracting parties and cannot be invoked against third parties.[94] The incompatibility of a contract with Article 81 may be raised in national proceedings and national courts are obliged to apply Article 81 when applying national competition law to agreements, which may affect trade between Member States.[95] A plea that an agreement infringed Article 81 and was void often caused acute difficulties under the old Regulation 17 system. A national court could consider Article 81(1) and (2) and could apply the provisions of a block exemption but could not otherwise rule on the compatibility of the agreement with Article 81(3). If the agreement had been notified to the Commission the national courts' hands were tied and ordinarily they would have to stay proceedings pending the outcome of the Commission's investigation.[96] Since 1 May 2004 the position is simpler. Restrictive clauses in an agreement which infringes Article 81(1), and which does not benefit from an individual exemption,[97] meet the conditions of a block exemption, or satisfy the conditions of Article 81(3), are void. Further, the agreement as a whole is void if those clauses cannot be severed from the remaining provisions of the contract.[98]

The compatibility of an agreement, or clauses within it, with Article 81 has now been raised in a number of cases before the English courts. It would be fair to say, however, that such arguments have not been received with particular sympathy. Rather, the cases have been marked by an air of scepticism about the merits of the 'Euro-defence' and a reluctance to accept that Article 81 should be permitted to allow a party to wriggle out of a 'bad bargain'[99] and to avoid their contractual obligations.[100] In *Trent Taverns Ltd* v. *Sykes*, for example, Steel J stated that 'Article [81] is not concerned with furnishing a remedy for an improvident agreement'.[101] Despite this recalcitrance, it is crystal clear that should a national court find an infringement of Article 81, the sanction of nullity must be applied.[102]

[94] See Cases C-259–98/04 *Manfredi* v. *Lloyd Adriatico Assicurazioni SpA* [2006] ECR I-6619, [2006] 5 CMLR 17, para. 57.

[95] Reg. 1/2003, Art. 3(1), see *supra* Chap. 14.

[96] The duties of the national courts were dealt with in detail by the ECJ in Case 234/89, *Delimitis* v. *Henninger Bräu* [1991] ECR I-935, [1992] 5 CMLR 210. See also e.g., A. Jones and B. Sufrin, *EC Competition Law: Text, Cases and Materials* (Oxford University Press, 2001), chap. 15, especially 964–9. In *MTV Europe* v. *BMG Records* [1997] 1 CMLR 867, for example, the Court of Appeal granted a stay on proceedings brought by an independent third party against seven parties to an agreement. In this case the agreement had been notified to the Commission. Sir Thomas Bingham MR recognized the uncertainty which would be created were an inconsistent decision to be made by the Commission on the one hand and the national court on the other. The Court accepted, however, that some preparation of action for trial could be made in the meantime. See also *Williams* v. *Welsh Rugby Union* [1999] EuLR 195 and *Philips Electronics* v. *Ingman Ltd* [1998] 2 CMLR 839.

[97] Although it is not now possible to get an individual exemption, past individual exemption decisions are valid until their expiry or withdrawal, see *supra* Chap. 14.

[98] Case 56/65, *Société La Technique Minière* v. *Maschinêbau Ulm GmbH* [1966] ECR 234, [1966] CMLR 357; Case 319/82, *Société de Vente de Ciments et Bétons de l'Est SA* v. *Kerpen & Kerpen GmbH & Co KG* [1983] ECR 4173, [1985] 1 CMLR 511. See *supra* Chap. 3.

[99] In *Gibbs Mew plc* v. *Gemmell* [1999] 1 EGLR 43, 48, [1998] EuLR 588, Peter Gibson LJ expressed his 'clear view that Mr Gemmell did receive exactly what he bargained for, and is merely complaining of what he now sees as a bad bargain. Art. [81] provides no remedy for that'.

[100] In *Panayiotou* v. *Sony Music Entertainment (UK) Ltd* [1994] ECC 395, Park J did not have to rule on the compatibility of an agreement concluded between George Michael and Sony with Article 81, on the grounds that the agreement did not have an appreciable effect on trade. See also, e.g., *Society of Lloyd's* v. *Clementson* [1995] 1 CMLR 693; *Higgins* v. *Marchant & Eliot Underwriting Ltd* [1996] 3 CMLR 313; *Oakdale (Richmond) Ltd* v. *National Westminster Bank plc* [1997] EuLR 7, 40 *aff'd* [1997] 3 CMLR 815.

[101] [1999] EuLR 571, 578.

[102] See Case C-126/97, *Eco Swiss China Time Ltd* v. *Benetton* [1999] ECR I-3055, [2000] 5 CMLR 816. See also Case C-453/99, *Courage Ltd* v. *Crehan* [2001] ECR I-6297, [2001] 5 CMLR. 28, para. 21.

(ii) Severance

Although the effect of Article 81(2) has been spelt out by the ECJ, that court has held that the question whether the prohibited clauses can actually be severed from the remaining provisions in the contract is a matter for national, not Community, law. This approach has been criticized since it means that the enforceability of a contract will vary depending on which Member State's rules are applicable. Arguably, the impact of Article 81(2) should be uniform throughout the Community.[103]

Where the applicable law is English law,[104] English contractual rules on severance thus apply. Broadly, the English courts will sever parts of a contract where sufficient consideration remains to support the agreement and it is possible to sever by running a blue pencil through that offending part. The courts will not make a new contract or rewrite the contract for the parties, for example, by adding or re-arranging words. Nor will a court strike out words of a contract if so doing would leave a contract of an entirely different scope or intention.[105]

In *Chemidus Wavin Ltd* v. *TERI*[106] the Court of Appeal considered the severance rules in the context of a licence agreement containing clauses which, arguably, contravened Article 81(1). Buckley LJ stated that:

in applying Article [81] to an English contract, one may well have to consider whether, after the excisions required by the Article of the Treaty have been made from the contract, the contract could be said to fail for lack of consideration or on any other ground, or whether the contract would be so changed in its character as not to be the sort of contract that the parties intended to enter into at all.[107]

In England, the compatibility with Article 81(1) of beer supply agreements containing beer ties has been raised in a series of cases involving disputes between brewers and their publican tenants (the beer tie cases). In many of these cases it has been accepted that an exclusive commitment to purchase beer from a named supplier (a beer tie) within a tenancy agreement infringes Article 81(1).[108] The courts have, therefore, had to consider whether the rules allow the severance of the tie, if invalid, from the remainder of the agreement.[109] In addition, the cases have held that the contractual provisions prohibited by Article 81(1) are not only void but *also* illegal.

---

[103] See, e.g., R. Whish, 'The Enforceability of Agreements under EC and UK Competition Law' in F. Rose (ed.), *International Commercial Law* (LLP, 2000). The applicability of national rules may in some circumstances be constrained by the Community principle of effectiveness (discussed *supra* section 2.B).

[104] The applicable law should be determined by the Rome Convention on the Law Applicable to Contractual Obligations, 1980, consolidated version with First and Second Protocols [1998] OJ C27/31, but see the Commission proposal on the law-applicable to non-contractual obligations COM(2003) 427final. The Brussels Regulation, Reg. 44/2001 deals with the question of where litigation may take place and the recognition and enforcement of judgments in civil and commercial matters, see *infra*.

[105] See, e.g., *Goldsoll* v. *Goldman* [1914] 2 Chap. 603. In the Nordic countries, for example, the courts have more flexibility and have the power to adjust unenforceable contract clauses, see U. Bernitz, 'The Arlanda Terminal 2 Case: Substantial Damages Awarded on the Basis of Article 82 TEC' [2004] 1 *Competition Law Journal* 195.

[106] [1978] 3 CMLR 514.

[107] [1978] 3 CMLR 514, 520.

[108] But see the discussion of the *Crehan* case, [2006] UKHL 38, *supra* 1317–8.

[109] See *Inntrepreneur Estates Ltd* v. *Mason* [1993] 2 CMLR 293 and *Inntrepreneur Estates (GL) Ltd* v. *Boyes* [1993] 2 EGLR 112, See, in particular, *Gibbs Mew plc* v. *Gemmell* [1991] 1 EGLR 43, [1998] EuLR 588 and *Trent Taverns Ltd* v. *Sykes* [1998] EuLR 571, *aff'd* [1999] EuLR 492. But see also *Scottish Courage Ltd* v. *McCabe* [2007] EWHC 538 where the High Court had to consider an argument that a clause preventing McCabe from selling competing beers in

(iii) Nullity and Illegality

In *Gibbs Mew plc* v. *Gemmell*[110] the Court of Appeal considered that contractual provisions offending Article 81(1) are both void and illegal for the purposes of the (English) *in pari delicto* rule. Broadly, this rule is a principle of public policy which prevents a court from lending 'its aid to a man who founds his cause of action upon an immoral or illegal act'.[111] This finding caused the defeat of many claims for damages or restitution[112] brought by the tenant against the brewer in the beer tie cases. In *Courage Ltd* v. *Crehan*,[113] however, the ECJ make it clear that the illegality of the agreement could not operate as a general bar to damages' claims between parties to a prohibited agreement. The impact of the plea of illegality on the claims and its compatibility with Community law is discussed in greater detail below.[114]

(iv) Transient Nullity

An agreement infringes Article 81 only if all five of its elements of Article 81(1) are satisfied and the four conditions of Article 81(3) are not met.[115] It is possible that, as events change over a period of time, an agreement which does not infringe Article 81(1) will subsequently be found to infringe Article 81(1) and not to meet the Article 81(3) criteria and vice versa. Suppose, for example, a small, local undertaking concludes an agreement which does not infringe Article 81(1) on account of its minor importance. The undertaking has an extremely small share of the market.[116] Suppose, however, that that undertaking is subsequently taken over by a larger undertaking so that the agreement now does have an appreciable effect on competition and trade, does not meet the conditions of the block exemption[117] and does not fulfil the conditions of Article 81(3). The agreement which, previously, fell outside Article 81(1) now becomes subject to its prohibition. The agreement which was valid consequently becomes void. In *Passmore* v. *Morland plc* the reverse scenario occurred and the English Court of Appeal held that the reverse can occur: an agreement which was initially void can become valid (and possibly void again) as the agreement falls within and without the Article 81(1) prohibition.

---

an exclusive distribution agreement for certain beer products in Northern Ireland was in unreasonable restraint of trade, invalid and unenforceable. The Court considered that if the provision was in unreasonable restraint of trade it could not be severed as the fundamental nature of the agreement involved loyalty on both sides. The non-compete obligation was part and parcel of the exclusive right and duty to purchase from Scottish Courage and was directly connected with the exclusivity given to McCabe.

[110] [1999] 1 EGLR 43.

[111] *Holman* v. *Johnson* (1775) 1 Cowp. 341, 343, per Lord Mansfield. For a more detailed discussion of the rules see R. Goff and G. Jones, *The Law of Restitution* (7th edn., Sweet & Maxwell, 2006), Chap. 24.

[112] See *infra* n. 1326.

[113] Case C-453/99 [2001] ECR I-6297, [2001] 5 CMLR 28.

[114] See *infra* 1343–4.

[115] See *supra* Chaps. 3 and 4.

[116] Article 81(1) prohibits only agreements which have an appreciable effect on competition and trade; see *supra* Chap. 3.

[117] Most block exemptions are subject to a market share cap. For example, the Verticals block exemption, Regulation 2790/1999 [1999] OJ L336/21, [2000] 4 CMLR 398 is subject to a 30% market share cap, *supra* Chap. 9.

Passmore v. *Morland plc* [1999] 3 All ER 1005, 1014–15

This action concerned a beer tie case. It involved a tenancy agreement concluded initially between a brewer, Inntrepreneur Pub Co (IPC) (a relatively large brewer), and Passmore which imposed an obligation on Passmore to purchase all of his beer requirements from IPC. Later IPC sold the pub and the reversion of the lease was acquired by Morland, a much smaller brewer. The compatibility of the agreement with Article 81(1) was raised.

The claimant accepted that applying the test set out by the Court of Justice in *Delimitis* v. *Henninger Bräu*[118] it was likely that an agreement concluded *de novo* with Morland would have been compatible with Article 81(1).[119] It was argued, however, that since the agreement when concluded with IPC infringed Article 81(1) and was absolutely void it was not possible to assign that lease once it had been established that the lease was invalid.

The Court of Appeal disagreed. It held that the nullity set out in Article 81(2) was transient according to the agreement's compatibility with Article 81(1)

Court of Appeal

Chadwick LJ

[Article 81(1)] only prohibits agreements and concerted practices which have a particular offensive economic objective or effect; . . . in order to decide whether it is within the prohibition, each agreement, or clause in an agreement, has to be examined in the factual context in which it is to be operated . . .

It follows that an agreement which is not within Article [81(1)] at the time when it is entered into—because, in the circumstances prevailing in the relevant market at that time, it does not have the effect of preventing, restricting or distorting competition—may, subsequently and as the result of a change in those circumstances, come within Article [81(1)]—because, in the changed circumstances, it does have that effect . . .

It must follow, also, by a parity of reasoning, that an agreement which is within the prohibition in Article [81(1)] at the time when it is entered into—because, in the circumstances prevailing in the relevant market at that time, it does have the effect of preventing, restricting or distorting competition—may, subsequently and as the result of a change in those circumstances, fall outside the prohibition contained in that article—because, in the changed circumstances, it no longer has that effect.

The meaning and effect to be given to Article [81(2)]

Article [81(2)] has to be construed in conjunction with Article [81(1)]. In particular Article [81(2)] has to be construed in the light of an appreciation that the prohibition of Article [81(1)] is not an absolute prohibition; but rather a prohibition which arises when, and continues for so long as (and only for so long as), it is needed in order to promote the freedom of competition within the common market which is the stated objective of Article [81(1)]. The prohibition is temporaneous (or transient) rather than absolute; in the sense that it endures for a finite period of time—the period of time for which it is needed—rather than for all time . . .

---

[118] Case C-234/89, [1991] ECR I-935, [1992] 5 CMLR 210, *supra* Chap. 4.

[119] Morland owned relatively few pubs. Applying the test set out in Case 234/89, *Delimitis* v. *Henninger Bräu* [1991] ECR I-935, [1992] 5 CMLR 210 (set out *supra* Chap. 4), therefore, the agreement would escape the Article 81(1) prohibition. Although the market was foreclosed, the contribution of Morland's agreements to the foreclosure effect would be insignificant. See also the Commission's Notice on agreements of minor importance, *supra* Chap. 3.

B. ARTICLE 82

(i) Void and Unenforceable?

Article 82 contains no declaration of nullity equivalent to that set out in Article 81. This omission is not surprising, however, since Article 82 does not explicitly prohibit agreements but focuses on a much wider range of conduct than Article 81 (all aspects of a dominant undertaking's behaviour[120]). Nevertheless, the Article implicitly prohibits many contracts and contractual terms and the effect in relation to sanctioned agreements is, despite being couched in different terms, similar to that of Article 81. It is to be expected, therefore, that Article 82 should render a contract, or severable terms of a contract, affected by its prohibition void[121] or, at the very least, unenforceable.[122] The former view was taken by the High Court of England & Wales in *English Welsh & Scottish Railway Limited* v. *E.ON UK plc* [123] where it held that the effect of finding by a UK regulator (the Office of Rail Regulation, the 'ORR') that a contractual provision violated Article 82,[124] is that the offending contractual provision is illegal and void and the agreement as a whole is void if the prohibited clauses cannot be severed from the remaining terms of the agreement. Although Article 82 does not contain a declaration of nullity equivalent to that set out in Article 81, the court considered the effect to be the same.

(ii) Severance

In *English Welsh & Scottish Railway Limited* v. *E.ON UK plc* [125] the High Court went on to consider the effect of the nullity in relation to a Coal Carriage Agreement (the 'CCA') concluded between the claimant, EWS and E.ON. The ORR's decision had included a finding that EWS had abused its dominant position contrary to Article 82 by foreclosing the Great Britain coal haulage by rail market, including through entering into and maintaining exclusionary terms in the CCA.[126]

---

[120] The Article sets out a non-exhaustive list of abuses which may take many forms, e.g., refusing to supply, charging excessive, discriminatory or predatory prices, or imposing unfair trading terms on a business partner, see *supra* Chaps. 5 and 7.

[121] In *Scandinavian Airlines System (SAS)* v. *Swedish Board of Aviation* (unreported), the Swedish Court of Appeal considered that a contractual clause contravening Article 82 was void, see T. Pettersson, and J. Aswall, 'Discriminatory Pricing: Comments on a Swedish Case' [2003] *ECLR* 295, U. Bernitz, 'The Arlanda Terminal 2 case: Substantial Damages Awarded on the Basis of Article 82 TEC' [2004] 1 *Competition Law Journal* 195. See R. Whish, *Frontiers of Competition Law* (ed. Dr Julian Lonbay, Wiley, 1994) Chap. 5. In many cases an agreement concluded by a dominant undertaking which incorporates a contractual clause infringing Article 82, is likely to infringe Article 81(1) and not to meet the conditions of Article 81(3).

[122] Article 82 does not impose a multilateral prohibition against the parties entering into or implementing an agreement which offends the prohibition (as Article 81 does) but imposes only a unilateral prohibition against the abuse of a dominant position. Thus it is arguable that a clause in a contract concluded in contravention of Art. 82 is, in contrast to one included in an agreement contravening Article 81, not void but merely unenforceable. This was the argument raised by counsel for the claimant in *Gibbs Mew plc* v. *Gemmell* [1999] 1 EGLR 43, [1998] EuLR 588.

[123] [2007] EWHC 599.

[124] And the UK equivalent, Chapter II of the Competition Act 1998.

[125] [2007] EWHC 599.

[126] The ORR directed EWS and the other parties to the contracts to remove or modify the exclusionary aspects of the contract. The dispute in this case centred around the question of whether the exclusionary terms could be severed from the CCA contract so that EWS remained bound by the remainder of its terms or whether removal of these terms would leave a contract so changed in its character as not to be the sort of contract that the parties intended to enter and rendering the entire CCA contract void.

Field J held that the exclusionary aspects of the contract, being in breach of Article 82, had been illegal and void since execution. Further that as severance of the exclusionary terms would leave a contract of a fundamentally different nature, the effect of the ORR's decision was that the entire CCA was void and unenforceable.[127]

(iii) Illegality

The question whether a contract or contractual provision is illegal for the purposes of the English *in pari delicto* rule is more complex when dealing with Article 82, since Article 82 does not prohibit both parties from concluding the contract. However, even if the agreement is found to be illegal, that characterization should deny only a claim brought by the dominant undertaking. The rule should not prevent recovery where the applicant can establish that the parties were not *in pari delicto* (of equal fault). Rather, the duty of observing the law is placed squarely on the shoulders of the dominant party to the contract and is, in some circumstances at least, imposed to protect the other party from exploitation. The effect of the *in pari delicto* rule on damages claims is discussed below.

C. CONCLUSIONS

It is clear that contractual provisions offending the prohibition under Article 81(1) are void and unenforceable. Article 81 may, therefore, be used as a shield in national proceedings. Similarly, it seems that Article 82 can be used in an identical way. Up until 2000, however, it was unclear whether or not breach of Articles 81 or 82 could be used as a basis for a damages action. It has now been clarified that Articles 81 and 82 confer rights on individuals and that, in certain circumstances, breach of those rights demands a specific remedy to be granted.

4. REMEDIES: DAMAGES ACTIONS AND INJUNCTIONS

A. DAMAGES

(i) A Community Right to Damages

a. Introduction

The question of whether there is any Community right to damages fell to be decided by the ECJ following a reference to it of questions by the English Court of Appeal using the Article 234 procedure.

The English court made the reference in the course of hearing conjoined appeals in the case of *Courage Ltd v. Crehan* (see also discussion of case above).[128] The case concerned two leases of

---

[127] The court thus applied the same principles as those that would have been used where a contractual provision was void for being in restraint of trade or by reason of Article 81. The court also held that a clause in the contract providing that remaining provisions of the Agreement should not be affected or impaired by the illegality, invalidity or unenforceability of a provision within it was ineffective to allow severance where the resulting contract would not be the sort of contract that the parties intended to enter.

[128] The case was one in a series of cases that raised the compatibility of 'beer ties' with Article 81 of the Treaty, see also *supra* section 2.E and, e.g., the judgments of the Court of Appeal in *Gibbs Mew plc v. Gemmell* [1999] EGLR 43, [1998] EuLR 588 and *Trent Taversn v. Sykes* [1999] EuLR 492.

public houses that had been concluded between Inntrepreneur Estates (CPC) Ltd (owned equally by Grand Metropolitan plc and Courage Ltd) and Mr Crehan. The leases were Inntrepreneur standard form leases, granted for a period of twenty years. One of the terms of the lease required Mr Crehan to purchase minimum quantities of various beers for resale at the leased premises from Courage, and no other person. The proceedings involved an action brought by the brewers for the recovery of £15,266, alleged to be the price of beers sold and delivered to Mr Crehan. By way of defence Crehan alleged, amongst other things, that the beer tie in the lease was in breach of Article 81. He counterclaimed for damages and/or restitution.[129] The case thus raised the compatibility of the beer ties and the leases with Article 81 EC and the impact of any such incompatibility on the claims and counter-claims made by the parties.

b. Background to the Claim

Courage Ltd v. Crehan was one of a series of cases that had arisen before the English courts, raising the compatibility of leases containing beer ties with Article 81 and the ability for tenants to recover in respect of their loss suffered in consequence of the void beer tie (the actions were based on the brewer's breach of statutory duty)[130] or to recover the payments made pursuant to the void contract (the restitutionary claim).[131] By the time the *Crehan* case reached the Court of Appeal, authority established that the case must fail. The English courts had given short shrift to the claims which had been rejected as 'hopeless'. Although a whole host of different reasons had been given for the rejection of the claims,[132] the most significant obstacle to the actions had been that the claim were based on an illegal act. The English courts have generally refused to assist a claimant whose action is founded on an illegal act: *ex turpi causa non oritur actio*[133] and to allow a party to a prohibited contract either to enforce that contract or to bring any other action based upon it: *in pari delicto potior est conditio defendentis*.[134]

The objection, that a contract is immoral or illegal as between plaintiff and defendant . . . is founded in general principles of policy, which the defendant has the advantage of . . . as between him and the plaintiff . . . The principle of public policy is this: *ex dolo malo non oritur actio*. No Court will lend its aid to a man who founds his cause of action upon an immoral or an illegal act. If, from the plaintiff's own

---

[129] Broadly, in respect of excessive prices for his beer under the void beer tie and the consequential loss caused to his business. The restitutionary claim was eventually dropped.

[130] They have therefore claimed the difference between the contract price of the beer and its market value and other consequential loss.

[131] In many cases the restitutionary claims were eventually abandoned. The restitutionary claims were particularly problematic where the contract had been partly performed, and where payments and benefits had passed both ways under the contract. The restitutionary claims are discussed, e.g., in A. Jones, *Restitution and EC Law* (LLP, 2000), chap. 6 and A. Jones and B. Sufrin *EC Competition Law: Text, Cases and Materials* (Oxford University Press, 2001), Chap. 15, 991–1002.

[132] The courts questioned whether, in the context of a breach of Article 81, any tortious action for damages for breach of statutory duty lies at all. In *Inntrepreneur Estates (CPC) plc v. Milne*, unreported, 30 July 1993, Mitchell J considered the case of a breach of statutory duty only on the hypothesis that the duty existed. Further in *Matthew Brown plc v. Campbell* [1998] Eu LR 530 Michael Tugendhat QC, sitting as a Deputy High Court judge, felt that the existence of the statutory duty had not been accepted. It was also questioned whether, if available, any such statutory duty, is owed to a claimant/co-contractor. Some of the cases suggest any action for breach of statutory duty could not be brought by a party to a contract who was also in breach. A party to a contract would not be someone to whom the duty contemplated by the statute was owed (a requirement for establishing a breach of statutory duty). In *Courage Ltd v. Crehan* [1999] 2 EGLR 145, e.g., it was concluded that the contracts for the sale of beer were separate from the tenancy agreement which incorporated the beer tie and were, consequently, unaffected by the nullity.

[133] 'No court will lend its aid to a man who founds his action upon an immoral or illegal act.'

[134] 'Where both parties are equally wrongful the position of the defendant is stronger.'

stating or otherwise, the cause of action appears to arise *ex turpi causa*, or the transgression of a positive law of this country, there the Court says he has no right to be assisted.[135]

The term 'illegal' in English law developed broadly to discourage all contracts that are contrary to public policy. 'For an agreement to be illegal it need not be in breach of the criminal law'[136] but contracts which are, for example, immoral or expressly or implicitly forbidden by statute may also be characterized as illegal for the purposes of the rule. The fact that a breach of the EC competition rules does not attract criminal sanctions[137] has not, therefore, precluded the characterization of the contract as illegal for the purposes of the rule. In *Gibbs Mew plc* v. *Gemmel* Peter Gibson LJ specifically stated that 'English law does not allow a party to an illegal agreement to claim damages from the other party for loss caused to him by being a party to the illegal agreement'.[138]

Although the principles of illegality have developed differently in the context of tortious and restitutionary claims[139] a number of exceptions apply generally to the illegality rule.[140] One of the most important exceptions is that the principle does not apply if the claimant is a member of the vulnerable class for whose protection the illegality was created.[141]

In *Gibbs Mew* Peter Gibson LJ took the view that Article 81(1) was not intended, even partially, to protect parties to the contract and to ensure equality of bargaining power but was designed[142] to protect competition between the parties to the contract and third party competitors. It was concerned not with 'inequality of bargaining power between the parties to the illegal agreement but...the effect of the agreement on competition'.[143] Relying on the Court of Appeal's judgment in *Gibbs Mew*, Carnworth J, at first instance in *Courage Ltd* v. *Crehan*,[144] held that the tenant's claim failed. Morritt LJ, giving the judgment of the Court of Appeal[145] adopted a similar approach, agreeing that the vice of the tied house for the purposes of Article 81(1) was its foreclosing effect, in combination with other similar agreements, upon third party competitors. In his view the tenant benefited from the restriction of competition, rather than being its victim. Further, in his view English law would not afford a remedy of damages to a party to an agreement prohibited by Article 81:[146]

So far as English law is concerned, it is common ground that where a defendant is sued under an agreement that is prohibited under Article [81], he may rely on that prohibition as a defence, and that

---

[135] *Holman* v. *Johnson* (1775) 1 Cowp. 341, 343, per Lord Mansfield. The rule is a principle not of justice but of policy.

[136] *Gibbs Mew plc* v. *Gemmell* [1999] 1 EGLR 43, 49, [1998] EuLR 588.

[137] In some Member States the operation of a hard-core cartel is a criminal offence. This has been the case in the UK since 20 June 2003, see *supra* Chap. 3.

[138] [1999] 1 EGLR 43, 49.

[139] See, generally, N. Enonchong, *Illegal Transactions* (LLP, 1998). See also B. Rodger, 'The Interface between Competition Law and Private Law: Article 81, Illegality and Unjustified Enrichment' [2002] *Edinburgh LR* 217.

[140] See R. Goff and G. Jones, *The Law of Restitution* (7th edn., Sweet & Maxwell, 2006) chap. 24 and N. Enonchong, *Illegal Transactions* (LLP, 1998), Part III.

[141] 'Where contracts...are prohibited by positive statutes, for the sake of protecting one set of men from another set of men: the one, from their situation and condition, being liable to be oppressed or imposed upon by the other: then the parties are not in pari delicto; and in furtherance of those statutes the person injured after the transaction is finished and completed may bring his action and defeat the contract': *Browning* v. *Morris* (1778) 2 Cowp. 790, 792, per Lord Mansfield.

[142] In the context of vertical agreements at least.

[143] [1999] 1 EGLR 43, 50.

[144] Unreported.

[145] [1999] 2 EGLR 145, 149, [1999] EuLR 834.

[146] [1999] 2 EGLR 145, 151, [1999] EuLR 834.

a person who is not a party to a prohibited agreement may sue those who are parties to it for the damage caused to him by their operation of the agreement . . .

This court has ruled that 'English law does not allow a party to an illegal agreement to claim damages from the other party for loss caused to him by being a party to the illegal agreement. That is so whether the claim is for restitution or damages' [see *Gibbs Mew plc* v. *Gemmell* [1998] Eu. LR 588, 606]. That ruling was based on *Tinsley* v. *Milligan* [1994] 1 AC 340.

The English Court recognized, however, that there might be sound policy arguments in favour of accepting that a party to a prohibited agreement has a right to sue for damages. The Court referred to the ruling of the US Supreme Court in *Perma Life Mufflers Inc* v. *International Parts Corp*[147] In this case, the Supreme Court held that the illegality defence did not bar an action brought by a party to an anti-competitive agreement that was in an economically weaker position and not equally at fault (*in pari delicto*). It stressed the importance of private suits to antitrust enforcement and furthering the public policy in favour of competition. Such claims would be denied only where the plaintiff and defendant could be said to bear substantially equal responsibility for the injury resulting to one of them.

The Court of Appeal also accepted that there was an argument in favour of holding that a party to a prohibited agreement such as that before it, was given rights by virtue of Article 81 that were protected by Community law. If the tenant was not afforded a remedy by English law it was possible, therefore, that the principle of English law denying that right was incompatible with, and superseded by, Community law. Community law might require the court to protect rights conferred on a party to a contract prohibited by Article 81(1) and to award damages to an injured party.

The Court of Appeal thus made a reference to the ECJ requesting a preliminary ruling on four questions. Those questions sought to establish whether Article 81 conferred rights on a party to a (tied house) contract concluded in breach of that provision and, if so, whether such an individual should, in principle be entitled to damages. If damages should in principle be available it has asked whether, and if so when, the national court may nonetheless deny the claim on account of its illegality?[148] The Court accepted that even if a Community right to a specific remedy were recognized, it would not be absolute. Rather, in accordance with the traditions of the legal systems of the individual Member States, the Community right to a remedy might be limited or barred by the application of national rules complying with the Community principles of equivalence and effectiveness.

Courage Ltd v. *Crehan* [1999] 2 EGLR 145

Court of Appeal

1. Is Article 81 EC (ex Article 85) to be interpreted as meaning that a party to a prohibited tied house agreement may rely upon that article to seek relief from the courts from the other contracting party?

2. If the answer to question 1 is yes is the party claiming relief entitled to recover damages alleged to arise as a result of his adherence to the clause in the agreement which is prohibited under Article 81?

---

[147] 392 US 134 (1968). See also *Bateman, Eichler, Hill Richards, Inc* v. *Berner* 472 US 299.

[148] A restitutionary claim was raised but dismissed in *Crehan*. For this reason, the Court of Appeal did not ask the ECJ whether or not Community law required a party to restore benefits conferred under a contractual provision prohibited by Article 81 and whether any such right could be denied on account of the illegality of

3. Should a rule of national law which provides that Courts should not allow a person to plead and/or rely upon his own illegal actions as a necessary step to recovery of damages be allowed as consistent with Community law?

4. If the answer to Question 3 is that in some circumstances such a rule may be inconsistent with Community law what circumstances should the national court take into consideration.

c. The Case for a Community Right to Damages

Whether or not the English courts had, in denying the tenants' claims, acted in breach of their Community obligations was therefore dependent upon two questions: first, whether, as a matter of Community law, national courts were required *in principle* to ensure that an individual could recover in respect of loss caused by another's breach of Community law and; secondly, if they were, whether or not the application of the defence of illegality was compatible with the Community principle of effectiveness (since the rule is not discriminatory it complies with the Community principle of non-discrimination or equivalence). The possibility that Community law might require a right to damages essentially hinged on a series of cases, commencing with *Francovich v. Italy*.[149]

In *Francovich* the ECJ held that, where certain conditions are fulfilled, a Member State *must* make reparation for loss arising in consequence of its breach of Community law. Individuals have a right to seek compensation in national courts from a Member State for loss or damage caused by its breach of Community law where the requirements of Community law are satisfied. In this case the ECJ did not, therefore, leave the determination of the procedural and substantive rules to the national courts. Rather, it made clear that where the Community requirements were satisfied Community law *required* a remedy to be available. Compensation is obligatory as a matter of Community law.[150] Case law subsequent to *Francovich* clarified the conditions for liability under this principle. Of particular importance is the ECJ's ruling in *Brasserie du Pêcheur and Factortame*.[151]

Cases C-46 and C 48/93, *Brasserie du Pêcheur SA v. Germany and R v. Secretary of State for Transport, ex parte Factortame Ltd* [1996] ECR I-1029, [1996] 1 CMLR 889

27. Since the Treaty contains no provision expressly and specifically governing the consequences of breaches of Community law by Member States, it is for the Court, in pursuance of the task conferred on it by Article [220] of the Treaty of ensuring that in the interpretation and application of the Treaty the law is observed, to rule on such a question in accordance with generally accepted methods of interpretation, in particular by reference to the fundamental principles of the

---

the claim. It is regrettable that this reference was not made, since the nature of the two claims are distinct and the illegality defence might apply differently in the different contexts. For a further discussion of the restitutionary claim see, e.g., in A. Jones *Restitution and EC Law* (LLP, 2000), chap. 6 and A. Jones and B. Sufrin, *EC Competition Law: Text, Cases and Materials* (Oxford University Press, 2001), chap. 15, 991–1002.

[149] Cases C-6 and 9/90, [1991] ECR I-5357, [1993] 2 CMLR 66.

[150] C. A. Jones, *Private Enforcement of Antitrust Law in the EU, UK and USA* (Oxford University Press, 1999), 72.

[151] Cases C-46 and 48/93, *Brasserie du Pêcheur SA v. Germany and R v. Secretary of State for Transport, ex parte Factortame Ltd* [1996] ECR I-1029, [1996] 1 CMLR 889.

Community legal system and, where necessary, general principles common to the legal systems of the Member States.

. . .

51 . . . Community law confers a right to reparation where three conditions are met: the rule of law infringed must be intended to confer rights on individuals; the breach must be sufficiently serious; and there must be a direct causal link between the breach of the obligation resting on the State and the damage sustained by the injured parties.

These cases make it clear that where a Member State has acted in breach of Community law, Community law requires that State to make reparation in respect of its breach where the three substantive conditions set out in *Brasserie du Pêcheur and Factortame* are satisfied:[152]

(1) the Member State has infringed a rule of Community law which is intended to confer rights on an applicant;

(2) which is sufficiently serious; and

(3) in circumstances in which there is a direct causal link between its breach and the applicant's loss.

A question that followed was to what extent does this *Francovich* principle apply *horizontally* to cases where an *undertaking* which is not a State entity has committed a breach of the competition rules? Does a similar principle require such an undertaking to make reparation? Is a Community right to damages (similar to that set out by the Court in the series of cases commencing with *Francovich*) available in respect of breaches of the Community competition provisions? Many commentators argued that the *Francovich* principle *did* apply to all breaches of Community law, whether committed by a Member State or any other entity.[153] This view was supported both by the Opinion of the Advocate General in *Banks v. British Coal Corporation*[154] and the ECJ's judgment in *GT-Link A/S v. De Danske Statsbaner (DSB)*.[155] In the latter case the Court held that where the conditions set out in *Brasserie du Pêcheur and Factortame* are satisfied, an individual can claim reparation of loss caused by a state entity's or public undertaking's breach of Article 86 of the Treaty, read in conjunction with Article 82. In this case the public undertaking had levied charges from the applicant in breach of Article 82.[156] This case clearly establishes that the liability of a Member State to make reparation for its breaches of Community law applies where the breach has been of a Community provision which also has horizontal direct effect. Although in this case the Court was clearly dealing with the liability of the State, the Court also stressed the rights conferred upon the individual by Article 82.[157] This right not to have to pay

---

[152] The answer to the first two questions is a question of Community law, but the answer to the third is a question of national law.

[153] See, e.g., C. A. Jones, *Private Enforcement of Antitrust Law in the EU, UK and USA* (Oxford University Press, 1999), 75–8.

[154] Case C-128/92, [1994], ECR I-1209, [1994] 5 CMLR 30. In *Banks* the Advocate General explicitly stated his view that the *Francovich* principle should extend to horizontal actions between two private undertakings (see especially paras. 43–5). National courts should be required to ensure that damages are available to compensate victims of breaches of the competition provisions. The obligation to impose liability on those which had acted in breach of Community law is a natural extension of the principle developed by the ECJ in Cases C-6 and 9/90, *Francovich v. Italy* [1991] ECR I-5357, [1993] 2 CMLR 66.

[155] Case C-242/95, [1997] ECR I-4449, [1997] 5 CMLR 601.

[156] *Ibid.*, para. 60.

[157] *Ibid.*, para. 57.

unfair charges levied by a dominant undertaking in breach of Article 82 must be the same whether or not the charges had been levied by a State or non-State entity (the right not to be exploited by an undertaking in a dominant position).[158] Article 82 imposes obligations on both public and *private* entities.[159] It seemed natural, therefore, that the ruling should apply more broadly to breaches committed by private undertakings.[160]

d. The ECJ's Judgment in *Courage Ltd* v. *Crehan*

In *Courage Ltd* v. *Crehan*[161] the ECJ confirmed that there is a Community right to damages in cases of breach of the Treaty competition provisions. Damages must, in principle, be available to those that have suffered in consequence of a breach of Articles 81 or Article 82. In so concluding, the Court did not, however, rely on and extend the principle of State liability set out in *Francovich* and *Factorame*. The following extract sets out the key paragraphs of the ECJ's short judgment.

Case C-453/99 *Courage Ltd* v. *Crehan* [2001] ECR I-6297, [2001] 5 CMLR 28

19. It should be borne in mind, first of all, that the Treaty has created its own legal order, which is integrated into the legal systems of the Member States and which their courts are bound to apply. The subjects of that legal order are not only the Member States but also their nationals. Just as it imposes burdens on individuals, Community law is also intended to give rise to rights which become part of their legal assets. Those rights arise not only where they are expressly granted by the Treaty but also by virtue of obligations which the Treaty imposes in a clearly defined manner both on individuals and on the Member States and the Community institutions (see the judgments in Case 26/62 *Van Gend en Loos* [1963] ECR 1, Case 6/64 *Costa* [1964] ECR 585 and Joined Cases C-6/90 and C-9/90 *Francovich and Others* [1991] ECR I-5357, paragraph 31).

20. Secondly, according to Article 3(g) of the EC Treaty (now, after amendment, Article 3(1)(g) EC), Article [81] of the Treaty constitutes a fundamental provision which is essential for the accomplishment of the tasks entrusted to the Community and, in particular, for the functioning of the internal market (judgment in Case C-126/97 *Eco Swiss* [1999] ECR I-3055, paragraph 36).

21. Indeed, the importance of such a provision led the framers of the Treaty to provide expressly, in Article [81(2)] of the Treaty, that any agreements or decisions prohibited pursuant to that article are to be automatically void (judgment in *Eco Swiss*, cited above, paragraph 36).

22. That principle of automatic nullity can be relied on by anyone, and the courts are bound by it once the conditions for the application of Article [81(1)] are met and so long as the agreement concerned does not justify the grant of an exemption under Article [81(3)] of the Treaty (on the latter point, see, *inter alia*, Case 10/69 *Portelange* [1969] ECR 309, paragraph 10). Since the nullity

---

[158] Although dealing with duties demanded by a public undertaking, the Court, in reaching its conclusion that the charges should be repaid, clearly looked to and stressed the rights conferred on individuals by Article 82.

[159] It will be remembered that Articles 81 and 82 apply, broadly, to undertakings entity engaged in economic activities, see *supra* Chap. 3.

[160] Indeed the case suggests that, at least in the context of Article 82, it will do so. In particular, it would not seem satisfactory to draw a distinction between actions brought against State and non-State entities especially as the distinction between the two is 'so precarious and so difficult to employ' that it may be inadvisable to apply it: Opinion of Van Gerven AG in Cases C-128/92, *Banks & Co Ltd* v. *British Coal Corp* [1994] ECR I-1209, [1999] 5 CMLR 30, para. 41.

[161] Case C-453/99, [2001] ECR I-6297, [2001] 5 CMLR 28.

referred to in Article [81(2)] is absolute, an agreement which is null and void by virtue of this provision has no effect as between the contracting parties and cannot be set up against third parties (see the judgment in Case 22/71 *Béguelin* [1971] ECR 949, paragraph 29). Moreover, it is capable of having a bearing on all the effects, either past or future, of the agreement or decision concerned (see the judgment in Case 48/72 *Brasserie de Haecht II* [1973] ECR 77, paragraph 26).

23. Thirdly, it should be borne in mind that the Court has held that Article [81(1)] of the Treaty and Article 86 of the EC Treaty (now Article 82 EC) produce direct effects in relations between individuals and create rights for the individuals concerned which the national courts must safeguard (judgments in Case 127/73 *BRT and SABAM* [1974] ECR 51, paragraph 16, (*BRT I*) and Case C-282/95 P *Guérin Automobiles* v. *Commission* [1997] ECR I-1503, paragraph 39).

24. It follows from the foregoing considerations that any individual can rely on a breach of Article [81(1)] of the Treaty before a national court even where he is a party to a contract that is liable to restrict or distort competition within the meaning of that provision.

25. As regards the possibility of seeking compensation for loss caused by a contract or by conduct liable to restrict or distort competition, it should be remembered from the outset that, in accordance with settled case-law, the national courts whose task it is to apply the provisions of Community law in areas within their jurisdiction must ensure that those rules take full effect and must protect the rights which they confer on individuals (see, *inter alia*, the judgments in Case 106/77 *Simmenthal* [1978] ECR 629, paragraph 16, and in Case C-213/89 *Factortame* [1990] ECR I-2433, paragraph 19).

26. The full effectiveness of Article [81] of the Treaty and, in particular, the practical effect of the prohibition laid down in Article [81(1)] would be put at risk if it were not open to any individual to claim damages for loss caused to him by a contract or by conduct liable to restrict or distort competition.

27. Indeed, the existence of such a right strengthens the working of the Community competition rules and discourages agreements or practices, which are frequently covert, which are liable to restrict or distort competition. From that point of view, actions for damages before the national courts can make a significant contribution to the maintenance of effective competition in the Community.

28. There should not therefore be any absolute bar to such an action being brought by a party to a contract which would be held to violate the competition rules.

29. However, in the absence of Community rules governing the matter, it is for the domestic legal system of each Member State to designate the courts and tribunals having jurisdiction and to lay down the detailed procedural rules governing actions for safeguarding rights which individuals derive directly from Community law, provided that such rules are not less favourable than those governing similar domestic actions (principle of equivalence) and that they do not render practically impossible or excessively difficult the exercise of rights conferred by Community law (principle of effectiveness) (see Case C-261/95 *Palmisani* [1997] ECR I-4025, paragraph 27).

30. In that regard, the Court has held that Community law does not prevent national courts from taking steps to ensure that the protection of the rights guaranteed by Community law does not entail the unjust enrichment of those who enjoy them (see, in particular, Case 238/78 *Ireks-Arkady* v. *Council and Commission* [1979] ECR 2955, paragraph 14, Case 68/79 *Just* [1980] ECR 501, paragraph 26, and Joined Cases C-441/98 and C-442/98 *Michaïlidis* [2000] ECR I-7145, paragraph 31).

31. Similarly, provided that the principles of equivalence and effectiveness are respected (see *Palmisani*, cited above, paragraph 27), Community law does not preclude national law from denying a party who is found to bear significant responsibility for the distortion of competition the right to obtain damages from the other contracting party. Under a principle which is recognised in most

of the legal systems of the Member States and which the Court has applied in the past (see Case 39/72 *Commission* v. *Italy* [1973] ECR 101, paragraph 10), a litigant should not profit from his own unlawful conduct, where this is proven.

...

36. Having regard to all the foregoing considerations, the questions referred are to be answered as follows:

— a party to a contract liable to restrict or distort competition within the meaning of Article [81] of the Treaty can rely on the breach of that article to obtain relief from the other contracting party;

— Article [81] of the Treaty precludes a rule of national law under which a party to a contract liable to restrict or distort competition within the meaning of that provision is barred from claiming damages for loss caused by performance of that contract on the sole ground that the claimant is a party to that contract;

— Community law does not preclude a rule of national law barring a party to a contract liable to restrict or distort competition from relying on his own unlawful actions to obtain damages where it is established that that party bears significant responsibility for the distortion of competition.

It can be seen from this extract that the Court stresses the new legal order created by the Community, the rights the Treaty provisions confer on individuals, the centrality of the competition rules to the Community project, and the direct effect of Article 81(1). The Court did not hesitate to conclude that *any* individual is entitled to rely on a breach of Article 81(1) and the nullity set out in Article 81(2) before a national court, even a party to a prohibited contract.

The Court then goes on to stress the obligation of national courts to ensure that Community rules take full effect and to protect the Community rights those provisions conferred on individuals[162] and highlights the importance of private actions to the enforcement of the Community rules.[163] The Court thus concluded that there should be no absolute bar to a damages claim, even to one brought by a party to a contract violating the competition rules. In so far as the English principle of illegality provides an absolute bar to a claim for damages commenced under Article 81 EC it is therefore undoubtedly incompatible with Community law.

The Court then went on to deal with the question of when an application of the English illegality rule might be compatible with Community law. The Court indicated that so long as the Community principles of equivalence and effectiveness were respected, Community law did not preclude a national court from denying a party who is found to bear *significant responsibility* for the distortion of competition the right to obtain damages from the other contracting party.[164]

Although the Court did not speak in such explicit terms as it has done in the *Francovich* and *Factortame* line of case of a right to reparation, its judgment establishes that (1) Article 81 confers rights on individuals, even parties to a contract in breach; and (2) any breach of Article 81 is sufficiently serious to trigger a Community right to damages. Individuals must be entitled to claim

---

[162] Case C-453/99, [2001] ECR I-6297, [2001] 5 CMLR 28, para. 26.

[163] *Ibid.*, para. 27.

[164] Case C-453/99, paras. 31–5. In these circumstances the principle of Community law that a litigant should not profit from his own unlawful conduct would be respected, Case 39/72, *Commission v. Italy* [1973] ECR 101, para. 10.

damages for loss caused by an agreement or conduct that restricts competition.[165] The Court in *Crehan*[166] did not, however, as had been done in *Factortame*, specifically require that there be a direct causal link between the breach of the obligation resting on the defendant and the damage sustained by the injured party. In the absence of a ruling on this point, it seems that national rules on causation apply.[167]

e. A Community Right to Damages

The ruling in *Crehan*[168] sends out a clear message to the national courts of all Member States. What ever the position in national law, there must, in principle, a Community right to damages to compensate breaches of both Article 81 and 82.[169] The ruling is of significance to all damages claims, not just those involving co-contractors.

The ECJ reiterated this view in *Manfredi v. Lloyd Adriatico Assicurazioni SpA*[170] where it stated that the practical effect of the Article 81(1) prohibition would be put at risk if it were not open to any individual to claim damages for loss caused to him by a contract or by conduct liable to restrict or distort competition. 'It follows that any individual can claim compensation for the harm suffered where there is a causal relationship between that harm and an agreement or practice prohibited under Article 81'.[171] In this case, the Court was also asked whether Article 81 had to be interpreted as requiring national courts to award 'punitive' damages, greater than the advantage obtained by the offending operator, thereby deterring the adoption of prohibited agreements.[172] The ECJ stressed that the right to claim damages was designed to strengthen the working of the Community competition rules and to discourage prohibited agreements but that the question of whether to award punitive damages was, in the absence of Community rules governing the matter, for the domestic legal system of each Member State to determine, provided that the principles of equivalence and effectiveness are observed. It thus stated that

(1) it must be possible to award punitive damages if such damages may be awarded pursuant to similar actions founded on domestic law. However, Community law did not prevent national courts from taking steps to ensure that protection of Community rights does not entail unjust enrichment of those who enjoy them; and

(2) The right to seek compensation must include compensation not only for actual loss but also for loss of profit plus interest.[173]

f. Claims between Co-contractors

The ECJ's judgment in *Crehan* is of enormous importance for a national court adjudicating on a case involving co-contractors, parties to the same illegal contract. The Court makes it clear that

---

[165] This seems to indicate that in case of a breach of the competition rules, there is an automatic assumption that the first two conditions required by *Factorame* are established.

[166] Case C-453/99, [2001] ECR I-6297, [2001] 5 CMLR 28.

[167] In English law this means that the claimant will have to establish that the breach caused the loss complained of, i.e., that the damage would not have occurred but for the breach.

[168] Case C-453/99, [2001] ECR I-6297, [2001] 5 CMLR 28.

[169] Although the Court did not specifically deal with Article 82 it referred to the need to compensate those who have suffered loss caused to him by a contract *or* by conduct liable to restrict or distort competition.

[170] Case C-259–298/04 [2006] ECR I-6619, [2006] 5 CMLR 17, para. 60.

[171] *Ibid.*, para. 61.

[172] *Ibid.*, paras. 83–100.

[173] The Commission recognizes in its Notice on cooperation with the national courts the particular difficulties that may arise in consequence of the fact that there is no harmonization of procedures in the Member

the illegality of the agreement cannot operate as a general bar to claims brought between parties to a contract concluded in breach of Article 81(1). It can do so, however, where the claimant co-contractor can be said to bear 'significant responsibility' for the breach.[174] The ECJ deals with the meaning of significant responsibility in paragraphs 32–5 of its judgment.

Case C-453/99 *Courage Ltd* v. *Crehan* [2001] ECR I-6297, [2001] 5 CMLR 28

32. In that regard, the matters to be taken into account by the competent national court include the economic and legal context in which the parties find themselves and, as the United Kingdom Government rightly points out, the respective bargaining power and conduct of the two parties to the contract.

33. In particular, it is for the national court to ascertain whether the party who claims to have suffered loss through concluding a contract that is liable to restrict or distort competition found himself in a markedly weaker position than the other party, such as seriously to compromise or even eliminate his freedom to negotiate the terms of the contract and his capacity to avoid the loss or reduce its extent, in particular by availing himself in good time of all the legal remedies available to him.

34. Referring to the judgments in Case 23/67 *Brasserie de Haecht* [1967] ECR 127 and Case C-234/89 *Delimitis* [1991] ECR I-935, paragraphs 14 to 26, the Commission and the United Kingdom Government also rightly point out that a contract might prove to be contrary to Article [81(1)] of the Treaty for the sole reason that it is part of a network of similar contracts which have a cumulative effect on competition. In such a case, the party contracting with the person controlling the network cannot bear significant responsibility for the breach of Article [81], particularly where in practice the terms of the contract were imposed on him by the party controlling the network.

35. Contrary to the submission of Courage, making a distinction as to the extent of the parties' liability does not conflict with the case-law of the Court to the effect that it does not matter, for the purposes of the application of Article [81] of the Treaty, whether the parties to an agreement are on an equal footing as regards their economic position and function (see, *inter alia*, Joined Cases 56/64 and 58/64 *Consten and Grundig* v. *Commission* [1966] ECR 382). That case-law concerns the conditions for application of Article [81] of the Treaty while the questions put before the Court in the present case concern certain consequences in civil law of a breach of that provision.

When determining whether the claimant had significant responsibility for a breach a national court should, therefore, take account of factors, including: the economic and legal context within which parties found themselves; their respective bargaining position; and the conduct of the parties. It appears that parties who both encourage the agreement and the unlawful terms will be found to have significant responsibility for the breach. In contrast, a party in a markedly weaker position than the other, is unlikely to bear significant responsibility for the breach. In particular, the Court indicates that a party contracting with a person controlling a network will not bear significant responsibility of the breach where the person controlling the network of

---

States, see Commission Notice on the Cooperation Between the Commission and the Courts of the EU Member States in the Application of Articles 81 and 82 EC [2004] OJ C101/54, paras. 9–10.

[174] [2001] ECR I-6297, [2001] 5 CMLR 28, para. 31.

agreements imposed the terms of the contract.[175] This point was accepted and applied by the English judge when the case reverted to the English High Court.[176]

The significance of the judgment for actions between co-contractors is considered in more detail in the following extract from an article by Jones and Beard.

A. Jones and D. Beard, 'Co-contractors, Damages and Article 81: The ECJ Finally Speaks' [2002] *ECLR* 246, 252–3

The ruling of the Court of Justice in *Crehan* is also of course of critical significance to claims brought between co-contractors. The judgment undoubtedly means that the English courts will have to change their approach in such cases. The illegality principle cannot operate as a general bar to claims brought between parties to a contract concluded in breach of Article 81(1). Save where the claimant co-contractor can be said to bear significant responsibility for the breach a damages action should lie.

It is consequently vital to know what is meant by *significant responsibility*. The Court dealt with this matter in paragraphs 32–35 of its judgment, setting out the sorts of facts which a national court will have to take into account when making this assessment: the economic and legal context within which the parties found themselves, their respective bargaining power and the conduct of the parties. This suggests that both the bargaining position of the claimant and its conduct in negotiating the contract will be relevant to the determination of whether the claimant bears significant responsibility for the breach.

Parties who encourage both the agreement and the unlawful terms within it will therefore, it appears, be found to have significant responsibility for the breach. This seems to make it clear that a claim brought by a cartel member would not succeed. Take, for example, a price-fixing cartel operated by A and B. As a result, B's customers set up their own source of supply causing B acute loss. If B could sue A, claiming damages from A in respect of A's breach of Article 81(1), B might be encouraged to operate the cartel that that provision was designed to prevent. If the cartel is successful he will win, but if it fails he can recover his loss from A. The ruling in *Crehan* would prevent such a claim since it seems clear that B will have significant responsibility for the breach, having specifically sought the unlawful terms of the agreement.

In contrast, claims by distributors against manufacturers may not be so straight-forward. Although a distributor may be eager to become part of a distribution team it might not be keen to accept all of the terms of the contract proposed by the producer. In many cases a distributor may, for example, be unwilling to accept export bans, preventing it from selling outside of its territory, and increasing its sales in this way. In order to secure the contract, however, they may have to agree to clauses that are detrimental to their interest. In such cases the 'acquiescence' may have been 'necessary to obtain an otherwise attractive business activity'[177] but is not the same as seeking and encouraging the unlawful terms to the agreement.

In considering the relative bargaining position of the parties the Court in *Crehan* held that a national court should consider whether the claimant was in a markedly weaker position

---

[175] On remission of the case to the English Court, this factor led Park J and the Court of Appeal to hold that the tenant's claim could not be barred by the principle of illegality or significant responsibility, see *infra* 1343–4.

[176] *Ibid.*

[177] *Perma Mufflers v. Int'l Parts Corp* 392 US 134 (1968), at 139 per Black J.

than the other:

> such as seriously to compromise or even eliminate his freedom to negotiate the terms of the contract and his capacity to avoid the loss or reduce its extent, in particular by availing himself in good time of all the legal remedies available to him.[178]

Thus a party who has had to adhere to the standard terms of another or to other non-negotiable terms may be found to be in a weaker bargaining position.[179]

Assessment of relative bargaining positions will no doubt raise a number of difficulties for national courts. First, care needs to be exercised when determining whether a party that has adhered to another party's standard terms is truly in the weaker position. Many standard terms are adopted with the objective only of saving transaction costs. The wheels of commerce may be jammed if contracts have to be individually negotiated in order for the private parties to protect themselves from any future competition claims. Further, in English law the scrutiny of material relevant to the assessment of bargaining positions may also cause difficulties. This material will obviously be relevant to the question of whether an individual may be attributed with significant responsibility for the anti-competitive terms and to his entitlement to a remedy. English courts are not, however, entitled to scrutinize such information when interpreting the terms of a contract. A court would not, therefore, be entitled to consider this material when assessing the terms of the contract and determining whether the contract was anti-competitive, but would be bound to take it into account later when determining whether or not a remedy was available. This may mean that companies will have to be more careful about the information they exchange in negotiations leading up to the conclusion of a contract.

The Court also held that a party contracting with an undertaking controlling a network of contracts could not bear significant responsibility for the breach of Article 81, especially where in practice the terms of the contract were imposed on him by the other. In many cases, the very nature of a network of contracts means that they may only be concluded on standard terms dictated by the operator.

g. Limitation Rules and Other Bars to a Claim

Whether or not other national rules operating to limit or bar the claim (such as a limitation period[180] or a passing on defence[181]) can be applied will be dependent upon their being compatible with the Community principles of equivalence and effectiveness. In *Manfredi v. Lloyd Adriatico Assicurazioni SpA*[182] the ECJ was asked about the compatibility of a national limitation period with Community law. The relevant limitation period for seeking compensation for harm caused by an agreement or practice prohibited under Article 81 began to run from the day on which that prohibited agreement or practice was adopted. The ECJ held that such a national rule could make it practically impossible to exercise the right to seek compensation for the harm caused by that prohibited agreement or practice, particularly if that national rule also imposed a short limitation period which is not capable of being suspended. It noted that in case of continuous or repeated infringement, it was possible in these circumstances that the limitation period would expire even before the infringement is brought to an end.

---

[178] *Ibid.*, para. 33.

[179] The Court also makes it clear, however, that a claimant must act reasonably. It cannot wait indefinitely but must act in good time.

[180] Or, for example, a defence such as *volenti non fit injuria* or contributory negligence.

[181] See *infra* 1344–8.

[182] Case C-259–298/04 [2006] ECR I-6619, [2006] 5 CMLR 17.

h. Harmonization of National Rules

Although the ECJ has stated that damages must in principle be available to compensate breaches of Articles 81 and 82, the principle of national procedural autonomy still means that the success of the claim is very much dictated by the relevant national rules governing the claim. Irrespective of the principles of equivalence and effectiveness, national rules are left considerable freedom and this is likely to impact significantly on the likelihood of success or the failure for an antitrust claim. It is for this reason that the Commission is contemplating whether measures can or should be adopted to amend and/or harmonise national procedural and substantive rules e.g. on costs, access to evidence, standing, class or representative actions, fault and/or defences, such as the passing on defence.[183]

(ii) Damages Claims in the English Courts

a. A Tortious Claim

Now that the ECJ has finally settled that an individual, which has suffered loss as a result of breach by another undertaking or undertakings of Article 81 or 82, will be able to recover damages in respect of that loss, English law must supply the framework for such actions.

One of the factors which inhibited claims before the English courts prior to the ECJ's judgment in *Crehan* was that, for a long period of time, it was not settled that an undertaking which committed a breach of one of the directly effective competition provisions set out in the Treaty committed a wrong which was actionable in tortious proceedings. Nor was it clear, if damages were in principle available, whether the basis of the claim[184] was breach of statutory duty or some other tort, such as unlawful interference with trade,[185] *or* whether a new tort should be recognized to reflect the Community nature of the claim.[186]

Now that it is clear that an action must *prima facie* lie, the general consensus is[187] that the correct basis is breach of statutory duty,[188] the basis favoured, obiter, by Lord Diplock and three

---

[183] See the discussion of the Green Paper: Damages Actions for Breach of the EC Antitrust Rules COM/2005/0672/final *supra*.

[184] R. Whish, 'The Enforcement of EC Competition Law in the Domestic Courts of Member States' [1994] *ECLR* 60, 64–5.

[185] Some commentators questioned the suitability of breach of statutory duty as the correct cause of action. The broad objection is that liability should not be imposed strictly in respect of every breach of the competition rules which causes damage to another. An alternative solution is that the basis of the claim should be unlawful interference with trade or business. This tort would at least require the claimant to show that the defendant's unlawful act was specifically addressed to it or intended to harm it. See *Barretts & Baird (Wholesale)* v. *IPCS* [1987] IRLR 3, 6.

[186] It was suggested that, rather than trying to squeeze proceedings within one of the existing causes of action, it might be preferable to recognize a new tort which would reflect the Community basis of the claim. If necessary, such a tort could be moulded appropriately to comply with the requirements, if any, of Community law. In *Application des Gaz SA* v. *Falks Veritas Ltd* [1974] Ch 381 Lord Denning suggested that the English courts might recognize new torts where the competition provisions were breached, such as the tort of 'undue restriction of competition within the common market' and 'abuse of dominant position within the common market'. This view was not, however, favoured by Lord Diplock in *Garden Cottage Foods* and has had little support generally.

[187] In the beer tie cases the publican-tenants founded their action on the brewers' breach of statutory duty.

[188] In *R* v. *Secretary of State for Transport, ex parte Factortame* [1997] EuLR 475 the English courts appeared to accept that an individual who suffers loss as a result of the State's breach of Community law can bring an action for breach of statutory duty. It was recognized, however, that the action was *sui generis* since the substantive conditions of liability were determined primarily by Community, not national, law. The national court had to

other members of the House of Lords in *Garden Cottage Foods Ltd* v. *Milk Marketing Board*.[189] If this is correct, then a claimant must show that:

(1) the loss suffered is within the scope of the statute, i.e., that the statute imposes a duty for the benefit of the individual harmed;

(2) the statute gives rise to a civil cause of action;

(3) there has been a breach of statutory duty (generally liability is strict once the breach of duty is established so no proof of fault is required[190]); and

(4) the breach has caused the loss complained of.

These four requirements will of course have to be interpreted in such a way that liability is imposed where required by Community law. The action is thus to some extent *sui generis* since the substantive conditions of liability will be dictated, partially at least, by Community, not national, law. The judgment of the ECJ in *Crehan*[191] establishes that the first two requirements are satisfied in cases involving Articles 81 and 82, as it highlights the rights conferred on the individuals by the competition rules. It will, therefore, be necessary only to establish a breach of the rules and that the breach has caused the loss complained of.

Indeed, when the case of *Crehan*[192] reverted to the English High Court, Park J considered that the two questions of overriding importance were (1) whether the Inntrepreneur leases infringed Article 81; and if so (2) whether the failure of Mr Crehan's business was caused by the beer ties in the lease or other factors.[193] He specifically rejected Inntrepreneur's argument that as Mr Crehan was not an aspiring entrant to the market he was not the type of claimant and had not suffered the type of loss that Article 81 was designed to protect.[194] Such an argument would make the whole ECJ decision pointless.

---

ensure that damages were available where the conditions set out by the ECJ in Cases C-46/93 and 48/93, *Brasserie du Pêcheur SA* v. *Germany and R* v. *Secretary of State for Transport, ex parte Factortame Ltd* [1996] ECR I-1029, [1996] 1 CMLR 889 were satisfied. The decision of the Divisional Court was affirmed by both the Court of Appeal, [1998] 3 CMLR 192, and the House of Lords, [1999] 3 WLR 1062.

[189] [1984] AC 130. Lord Diplock (with whom three of the members of the House agreed) took the view that since Article 82 was directly effective it created rights in those suffering loss or damage in consequence of its breach which the English courts were bound to protect. Although he did not consider it to be totally clear that a breach of Article 82 gave rise to a civil cause of action, he considered that if it did, it should be a cause of action which sounded in damages. In his view the correct cause of action was breach of statutory duty (in this case Article 82 incorporated into UK law by virtue of s. 2 of the European Communities Act 1972). That prohibition was imposed not only for the purpose of promoting economic prosperity but also for the benefit of individuals to whom loss and damage is caused by a breach of that duty.

[190] See *supra* 1313, n. 53.

[191] Case C-453/99, [2001] ECR I-6297, [2001] 5 CMLR 28.

[192] *Crehan* v. *Inntrepreneur Pub Co* [2003] EWHC 1510 (Ch).

[193] The Court of Appeal, [2004] EWCA Civ 637 disagreed with the judge's findings that the beer ties did not infringe Article 81.

[194] The Court of Appeal, [2004] EWCA Civ 637 upheld the ruling on the High Court on this point. Although the Court considered that this argument was a formidable one as a matter of English law alone, it rejected it on the basis that the application of the English rule would be inconsistent with the Community principle of effectiveness, paras. 154–68, see also *infra* n. 222.

> ## *Crehan* v. *Inntrepreneur Pub Co* [2003] EWHC 1510 (Ch)
>
> 227. The CJEC was specifically considering whether a publican lessee (not, for example, a brewer based in another Member State) could have a claim for damages on the ground that his lessor's conduct infringed article 81. By giving the answer that he could the court must have taken it for granted that this particular defence being put forward by Inntrepreneur could not be maintained. Otherwise the court would have been wasting its time, and would have known it. No realistic case in which the court visualised that a lessee might have a claim for damages would be one in which the claimant lessee was both a publican in one Member State and a brewer or distributor in another Member State. The same comment can be made by reference to the decision in *Delimitis*. Mr Delimitis had a café business in Frankfurt. His landlord was seeking to retain a rent security deposit which he had made. The CJEC did not, of course, decide the result of the case—it never does, but limits itself to answering questions of Community law referred to it by national courts—but it clearly contemplated the possibility that Mr Delimitis might be able to succeed against his landlord if the German court, applying to the facts the legal guidance given by the CJEC, concluded that the tie provisions in the particular lease were in breach of article 81. *Mutatis mutandis*, Mr Crehan is in a similar position.

Similarly, in *Arkin* v. *Borchard Lines*[195] the basis of a claim made against undertakings that formed part of a liner conference, was breach of the defendant's duty under Articles 82 and 81 EC respectively.

Defendants under English law are jointly and severally liable.[196]

b. Proving a Breach

The burden is clearly on the claimant to establish a breach of Article 81(1) and/or Article 82.[197] In *Shearson Lehmann* v. *McLaine Watson*[198] Webster J, in the English High Court, held that a breach of Article 81 would have to be established to a high degree of probability (but less than the standard required in criminal matters). As the UK Competition Appeal Tribunal[199] has held, however, that the standard of proof in cases of public enforcement of the rules, which could lead to the imposition of a penalty (a criminal charges for the purpose of the European Convention of Humans Rights and Fundamental Freedoms), is the civil standard and not the criminal standard,[200] it now seems to be accepted that the former standard, the preponderance or balance of probabilities is the test to be applied in private litigation.[201]

---

[195] Case C-453/99, [2001] ECR I-6297, [2001] 5 CMLR 28.

[196] As a general rule there is a right to contribution under English law so that liability is apportioned by the court between the defendants in accordance with their responsibility for the loss.

[197] Once a breach of Article 81(1) has been established the burden shifts on to the parties, to establish that the conditions of Article 81(3) are satisfied, see Reg. 1/2003, Art. 1, *supra* Chap. 3.

[198] [1989] 2 Lloyd's Rep 570, 619L, [1989] 3 CMLR 429.

[199] Case 1001/1/1/01 *Napp* v. *DGFT* [2002] CAT 1, especially paras. 91–113.

[200] Proof beyond reasonable doubt.

[201] See *Arkin* v. *Borchard Lines Ltd* [2001] EuLR 232 (preliminary issues), [2003] EWHC 687 (Comm Ct) (final judgment) and *Crehan* v. *Inntrepreneur Pub Company* [2003] EWHC 1510 (Ch) (Park J), [2004] EWCA Civ 637 (CA). In *Masterfoods* v. *HB Ice Cream* [1992] 3 CMLR 830 the Irish High Court took the view that the requisite standard is balance of probabilities.

Follow on Actions

Obviously proving a breach will be easier to establish where a Commission or other NCA decision establishing a breach already exists. Where the Commission has previously ruled on a decision,[202] Article 10 EC and Article 16 of Regulation 1/2003 applies.[203]

In the UK the Competition Act 1998[204] also specifically allows 'follow-on' claims to be brought before the specialist Competition Appeal Tribunal (CAT) where a breach of Article 81 or 82 (or the UK domestic equivalent)[205] has been established in a public law decision (by the Commission or the UK's Office of Fair Trading (OFT)). Such claims may be brought both by individuals and by consumer organizations on behalf of wider groups of consumers (representative claims).[206] The entitlement to bring damages claims before the CAT subsists alongside, and does not affect, the ability to bring damages proceedings in the ordinary courts. In February 2004 the first such damages claim was commenced against Aventis SA, Rhodia Limited, Hoffman-La Roche AG, and Roche Products Limited. The claims were based on the Commission's *Vitamins*[207] decision but the claim was eventually settled. In *Healthcare at Home Ltd v. Genzyme,*[208] however, the CAT awarded the claimant, Healthcare at Home, an interim payment of £2 million in proceedings following on from an OFT decision holding that Genzyme had engaged in an abusive margin squeeze. Following this ruling the parties settled the proceedings so the CAT did not have the opportunity to rule on the amount of total damages to award (including the question of whether exemplary damages were available). In early 2007, two further follow-on actions were lodged before the CAT. In February 2007 the CAT gave notice of the receipt of a claim for damages brought by Emerson Electric Co and others against Morgan Crucible Co and others who had been found by the Commission to have participated in the carbon and graphite electrodes cartel. The claimants are direct purchasers from the cartel.[209] Further, on 5 March 2007 the CAT gave notice of the receipt of the very first representative claim by a specified

---

[202] It seems to be accepted by the English courts that a Commission decision cannot be challenged by the parties to an action, see, e.g., *Iberian UK Ltd v. BPB Industries plc* [1997] 4 CMLR 33. Further, it seems that litigants may rely on other Commission documents, such as a statement of objections, in national proceedings, see Case T-353/94, *Postbank v. Commission* [1996] ECR II-921, [1997] 4 CMLR 33 (subject to compliance with the *AKZO* procedure). *Cf.* the judgment in Case C-67/91, *Dirección General de Defensa de las Competencia v. Asociación España de Banca Privada (AEB) and others (Spanish Banks)* [1992] ECR I-4820.

[203] See *supra* section 2.E. The ECJ has held that it is not open to a national court to find that a decision of the Commission is invalid, that can only be done by the Court of Justice, Case 314/85 *Foto-Frost v. Haptzollamt Lübeck-Ort* [1987] ECR 4199.

[204] s. 47A introduced by Enterprise Act 2002, s. 18. See also e.g. s 33(4) of the German Competition Act which confers a binding effect on all Commission, Bundeskartellamt, and even other Member States' national competition atuhorities' decision, in follow-on civil litigation.

[205] Competition Act 1998, Chap. I and II prohibitions (modelled on Arts. 81 and 82 respectively).

[206] Competition Act 1998, ss. 47A and 47B, introduced by Enterprise Act 2002, s. 18. Section 16 EA also provides that the Lord Chancellor may, by statutory instrument, make a provision enabling the ordinary courts (High court and county court in England and Wales) to transfer matters relating to infringement issues (i.e., relating to the question of whether or not an infringement of Chapter I, II, Art. 81 or 82 has been committed) to the CAT.

[207] [2003] OJ L6/1, [2003] 4 CMLR 1030.

[208] [2006] CAT 29.

[209] A factor which is complicating these proceedings is that although the first defendant has not appealed the Commission's decision, the other defendants have appealed to the CFI seeking both annulment of the Commission's decision and/or a reduction in the levels of the fines. This has raised difficult questions as to how the CAT's two year limitation rule applies and whether the claimants need to apply for special permission to

consumer body. This case follows-on from the Office of Fair Trading's (the 'OFT') Replica Football Kit decision finding that JJB Sports and other had, along with other retailers and Umbro, fixed the retail price of replica Manchester and England football shirts.[210] The Consumers' Association is seeking compensatory, exemplary and/or restitutionary damages on behalf of some 130 customers listed in an appendix to the claim.

Other Actions

The claimant's position is obviously much more difficult where a breach has not previously been established. It has already been seen that this proved to be a particular problem for Mr Crehan. In this case although a number of other Commission decisions indicated that the beer tie agreements infringed Article 81(1) and the Commission had indicated that the Inntrepreneur leases were in breach of Article 81, there was no actual decision holding the leases in question to be in breach. When the matter reverted to the English courts following the ECJ's ruling, Mr Crehan therefore had to establish both that the agreements in question infringed Article 81 and that the breach caused the loss. In the end the House of Lords held that Park J had been correct to find that that the lease agreement did not infringe Article 81(1) at all.[211]

In *Arkin v. Borchard Lines*,[212] the claimant was also found to have failed to establish a breach of the competition rules. The claimant, a managing director of a liner company, sought to convince the court that it had been harmed by the anti-competitive conduct of the defendants, members of two liner conferences. He alleged that the defendants had committed abuses (predatory pricing, deployment of fighting ships, spreading rumours of insolvency) of their collective dominant positions and had concluded anti-competitive price fixing agreements contrary to Article 81. The judge found that the liner conferences did hold a collective dominant position, but that no abuse of that dominant position had been established. Further, breaches of Article 81 had not been proved. In *Attheraces Ltd v. British Horseracing Board*[213] the Court of Appeal also rejected a claim that the British Horseracing Board ('BHB') had abused its dominant position in the supply or pre-race data to broadcasters and bookmakers who require such information for their business on the grounds that no abuse had been established. Attheraces ('ATR') alleged that BHB had abused its dominant position by threatening to terminate supply of the pre-race data to ATR (an existing customer) and by charging excessive, unfair and discriminatory pricing for the data. In this case the Court, although uncomfortable with hearing the claim, accepted that there was no violation of Article 82, essentially as it had not been established that the alleged pricing behaviour would harm competition and consumers.

---

initiate a damages claim against the first defendant whilst an appeal as to the validity of the Commission's decision by another undertaking is still outstanding.

[210] See discussion of the case *supra* Chap. 3 and Case 1022/1/1/03 *JJB Sports plc v. Office of Fair Trading* [2004] CAT 17 (Judgment on Liability) *Argos Limited and Littlewoods Limited v. OFT, JJB Sports Plc v. OFT* [2006] EWCA Civ 1318

[211] See discussion of the case *supra* section 2.E.

[212] [2003] EWHC 687 (Comm Ct). This case is believed to be the first time an English court had to determine a claim for damages for breach of Articles 82 and/or 81 (it is understood that previous actions have been settled).

[213] [2007] EWCA Civ 38 (allowing the appeal). Subsequent to the appeal the parties announced that they had settled the matter between them and that Attheraces would not seek leave to appeal to the House of Lords. See discussion of excessive and discriminatory pricing, *supra* Chap. 7.

c. Causation

Before damages can be awarded in English law it must also be proved that the breach of the competition rules 'caused' the loss. The test is satisfied where the damage would not have occurred but for the breach. The burden is on the claimant to show that the breach caused the claimed loss. In both *Crehan* and *Arkin* the judges went on to consider the issue of causation in case their finding that there had not been a breach of the rules was subsequently found to be wrong.

In *Crehan*[214] the judge took the view that if a breach of Article 81(1) were established, then, on the balance of probabilities, the beer ties did cause the failure of Mr Crehan's business. The judge thus accepted Mr Crehan's view that if he had been free of the tie 'I would have succeeded and I would have been in my pubs today pulling beer'.[215]

In contrast, in *Arkin*,[216] Colman J took the view that even if a breach of Article 81 or Article 82 had been established, such a breach had not caused the loss suffered by the claimant. Rather the chain of causation between the breach and the losses suffered had been broken by the claimant's irrational and unjustified behaviour (reducing prices by up to 35 per cent and failing to withdraw at an earlier point from the market).

d. Claims between Co-contractors and the Illegality Defence

In *Crehan* v. *Inntrepreneur Pub Co*[217] Park J, on reversion of the case to him, accepted that if a breach of Article 81 could be established in principle, Mr Crehan would be able to recover damages in respect of the loss caused by the illegal beer ties. During the course of argument Inntrepreneur argued that responsibility for the beer tie provisions should be shared between Mr Crehan and Inntrepreneur to such an extent that the claim could not succeed.

With regard to shared responsibility, the judge accepted that the ECJ's judgment had left open the possibility for a 'shared illegality defence' in holding that a claimant could be denied responsibility if he bore a significant degree of responsibility for the illegality.[218] The judge declared, however, that the fact that Mr Crehan was a voluntary participant in the transaction was not determinative of the issue. Rather, as the leases in issue were standard form leases and that Inntrepreneur was not willing to take the beer ties out of the lease or to consider any variations to it, there was no equality of bargaining power.[219] He thus concluded that the defence could not apply in that case. The Court of Appeal upheld the view of the judge:

Crehan v. *Inntrepreneur Pub Company* [2004] EWCA Civ 1318

153. . . . The broad question of fact which [the judge] had to decide was whether it had been established that Mr. Crehan bore significant responsibility for the distortion of competition. The answer to that question was self-evidently: no. He was not of course compelled to enter into any agreement with Inntrepreneur. To that extent he had bargaining power. But he was dealing with the single largest tied house landlord in the United Kingdom who made it clear that the offending

---

[214] *Crehan* v. *Inntrepreneur Pub Co* [2003] EWHC 1510 (Ch).

[215] *Ibid.*, para. 234. The Court of Appeal, [2004] EWCA Civ 637 did not interfere with this finding, paras. 169–71.

[216] [2003] EWHC 687 (Comm Ct).

[217] [2003] EWHC 1510 (Ch).

[218] Case C-453/99, [2001] ECR I-6297, [2001] 5 CMLR 28, para. 31.

[219] Relying on the ECJ's judgment Case C-453/99, [2001] ECR I-6297, [2001] 5 CMLR 28, para. 34.

> tying terms in their agreement were not negotiable. There was no equality of bargaining power in any real sense. Mr. Crehan was in a markedly weaker position than Inntrepreneur: if he wanted to lease the pubs he had to agree to the tie. In practice Inntrepreneur imposed the tie on him. Looking at the way in which the ECJ analysed the position in paras. 32, 33 and 34 of its judgment there was, we think, only one answer to the question, which was the answer the judge gave.

e. Limitation Rules and Other Bars to a Claim

Whether or not other English rules operating to limit or bar the claim, such as a limitation period,[220] can be applied will be dependent upon their being compatible with the Community principles of equivalence and effectiveness.

f. Standing, Quantification of Loss and Other Issues

In *Crehan* Park J concluded that had a breach of Article 81 been established, the damages in this case would have had to be ascertained at the time of judgment. He calculated, under the first head, losses actually suffered by Mr Crehan and the profits which would have been made on a free of tie basis and, under the second head, the value of the leases, which he would still have owned had he been free of the tie throughout. The Court of Appeal assessed the damages at £131,336 (plus interest), considerably lower than that determined by Park J, holding that the correct date of assessment was the date of loss. The House of Lords did not consider the issue of damages as it upheld Park J's ruling that no breach of Article 81 had been established.

In this case the approach to damages was made in a relatively straightforward way.[221] The claimant was a co-contractor so no issue of remoteness arose. Further, the question whether the tenant had 'passed on' some or all of the higher price of the beer to his customers was not raised and no 'exemplary' damages were claimed. As damages claims emerge before the courts, difficult issues may arise such as whether a claimant must establish 'antitrust injury',[222] whether exemplary damages should be allowed,[223] whether account should be taken of the fact that a claimant may have 'passed-on' some of the injury that it has suffered to purchasers from it, and as to whether claimants who did not purchase directly from the claimant but who nonetheless claim to have suffered loss as a result of the infringement, should be able to bring proceedings. In the US, the Supreme Court has strictly limited the use of a pass-on theory both defensively and offensively. Some of these issues and the US law is considered in the extract from an article by Jones and Beard below. The problems that have resulted from the US case law in this area[224] are, however, likely to militate against a similar approach being adopted in England and/or in Europe. It seems unlikely, however, that a national court would apply a passing-on defence

---

[220] Or, for example, a defence such as *volenti non fit injuria* or contributory negligence.

[221] The loss of profits were agreed between the parties.

[222] In the US the claimant must have suffered injury of the type that the antitrust laws are designed to prevent, see, e.g.. *Brunswick Corp v, Pueblo Bowl-O-Mat Inc* 429 US 477 (1977), *Atlantic Richfield Co v. USA Petroleum Co.* 495 US 329 (1990). The argument that there was a similar requirement in English law was raised but rejected by the Court of Appeal in the *Crehan* case, [2004] EWCA Civ 637, para. 156. See also *supra* n. 000 and accompanying text.

[223] Exemplary damages were claimed in *Arkin*. As the judge found that there had been no breach of the rules and that, if there had been, any breach would not have caused the loss, he did not deal with quantification of damages in any detail. In Ireland the Supreme Court seems to have accepted that exemplary damages might be awarded, see *infra* n. 238 and accompanying text.

[224] See *infra* n. 228.

without making a reference to the ECJ raising the compatibility of such a rule with the Community principle of effectiveness.[225]

A. Jones and D. Beard, 'Co-contractors, Damages and Article 81: The ECJ Finally Speaks' [2002] *ECLR* 246, 253–5

Quantification of loss and other issues

The judgment in *Crehan* recognises that a Community right to damages should in principle be available to compensate breaches of Article 81 or Article 82 for two main reasons. First, to ensure that individuals are compensated in respect of loss caused by anti-competitive conduct ('the compensatory principle'). Secondly, to strengthen the working of the Community competition rules and to discourage anti-competitive practices- private actions contribute to the maintenance of effective competition in the Community ('the deterrence principle'). Both principles are closely linked to the need to ensure the effectiveness of the competition rules within the Community.

The recognition of a Community right to damages will mean that many national rules of procedure and substance may have to be tested for their compatibility with Community law. Two specific problems that are liable to arise in many damages actions are: who is entitled to claim? and how will loss be quantified? For example, take a cartel or monopolist that sells it goods at supra-competitive prices. A direct purchaser from the cartel or monopolist (say a wholesaler) will clearly suffer in consequence of paying a price that is in excess of the competitive price. However, the direct purchaser may be able to pass on some of the loss to the next purchaser in the chain, a retailer or a consumer. Ultimately, at least part of the inflated price may be passed on to the consumer. This leads to two related questions. First, if the direct purchaser brings a damages claim, should the national court take account into the fact that some of that loss has been passed on to other purchasers along the line? Second, should indirect purchasers, further down the chain, also be entitled to bring damages actions to compensate them in respect of their loss?

In the US the courts have already had to grapple with these, and other, difficult questions. In *Hanover Shoe Inc* v. *United Shoe Machine Corp* the Supreme Court held that the possibility that a claimant might have recouped some of an overcharge by passing it on to its customers is *not* relevant in the assessment of damages.[226] If such an allegation could be taken into account damages claims would become excessively complicated, private actions would be deterred and a wrongdoer in breach would be able to retain his unlawful profits and the fruits of his own illegality.

In symmetry with this conclusion, the Supreme Court in *Illinois Brick Co* v. *Illinois* stated that claims brought by *indirect* purchasers should generally be refused. If the fact that loss has been passed on by the purchaser may not be taken into account *defensively* in a claim between the seller and the purchaser, it should not be open to an indirect purchaser to use the passing on principle *offensively* in damages proceedings.[227] This latter rule has been subjected to criticism, principally on the grounds that it precludes claims by those who have suffered loss in consequence of anti-competitive activity.[228] However, advocates of the rule stress a number of

---

[225] But see e.g. decision of Turin Court of Appeals a wholesaler or retailer cannot claim antitrust damages in respect of loss it was able to pass on to final consumers (Appello Torino, 6 July 2000).

[226] *Hanover Shoe* v. *United Shoe Machinery Corp* 392 US 481 (1968).

[227] *Illinois Brick Co* v. *Illinois* 431 US 720 (1997). The Court did, however, suggest that there would be some exceptions to the rule. Further, many States permit indirect purchasers to recover under the antitrust rules, see *infra* n. 228.

[228] In practice, most states have adopted statutes to allow claims by indirect purchasers. 'As those state law arguments developed and were pursued, the consequences that the Supreme Court discussed in *Illinois Brick*

benefits it brings: (a) it precludes a multiplicity of claims and duplicate recovery from a defendant; (b) it prevents difficult issues of remoteness and tracing of injury from arising; (c) it prevents the process costs of litigation from increasing; (d) it prevents inconsistent judgments; (e) it sits sensibly with the conclusion set out above on the passing on allegation; and (f) it increases the effectiveness of the antitrust rules by encouraging those most likely to litigate to do so.

> The apportionment of recovery through the distribution chain would increase the overall costs of recovery by injecting extremely complex issues into the case; at the same time such an apportionment would reduce the benefits to each plaintiff by dividing the potential recovery among a much larger group. Added to the uncertainty of how much of an overcharge could be established at trial would be the uncertainty of how that overcharge would be apportioned among the various plaintiffs. This additional uncertainty would further reduce the incentive to sue. The combination of increasing the costs and diffusing the benefits of bringing a treble-damages action could seriously impair this important weapon of antitrust enforcement.[229]

A national court will not of course be bound by US case law. Rather it will instead have to reach its own conclusions, ensuring that the rules it applies are compatible with the Community principles of equivalence and effectiveness.

Passing on

At first sight, it would appear that the Community rules should not prevent a national court from taking into account the fact that loss has been passed on to another purchaser further down the line. The compensatory principle would, on its face, appear to suggest that a claimant should recover only that which he has lost in consequence of an infringement. Further, the Court of Justice has consistently held that Community law does not prevent national courts from ensuring that the protection of rights guaranteed by Community law does not entail the *unjust enrichment* of those who enjoyed them[230] and the Court specifically stated this in *Crehan*. Arguably, a claimant would be unjustly enriched if he could recover damages even though he had been able to pass some of the loss on to others.

However, the position is not quite so simple. First, even if it were accepted that theoretically the fact that losses have been passed on to customers should be taken into account, the quantification of loss then becomes fraught with difficulty. In many cases it will be difficult to determine whether or not the loss has actually been passed on. Even if this can be established, the cost of the

became manifest: multiple suits in different jurisdictions, the risk of duplicative recoveries, the risk of inconsistent verdicts, and complex and potentially speculative damage analyses.' Comments of the Section of Antitrust Law and the Section of International Law of the American Bar Association in Response to the Request for Public Comment of the Commission of the European Communities on Damage Actions for Breaches of EU Antitrust Rules, April 2006, 37, available on DGComp's web site at, http://ec.europa.eu/comm/competition/antitrust/others/actions_for_damages/gp_contributions.html http://ec.europa.eu/comm/competition/antitrust/others/actions_for_damages/gp_contributions.html. The difficulties and complications that may ensure from both federal and state actions has led the Antitrust Modernization Commission to conclude that direct and indirect purchaser litigation would be more efficient and more fair if it took place in one federal court for all purposes and did not result in duplicative recoveries, denial of recoveries to person to suffered injury, and windfall recoveries to persons who did not suffer injury. It thus has recommended that Congress should enact a comprehensive statute overruling both *Hanover Shoe* and *Illinois Brick* to the extent necessary to allow both direct and indirect purchasers to sue to recover for actual damages; allow removal of indirect purchaser actions brought under state antitrust law to federal court; allow consolidation of all direct and indirect purchaser actions in a single federal forum; allow for certification of classes of direct purchasers without regard to whether the injury alleged was passed on to customers of the direct purchasers.

229 *Illinois Brick Co* v. *Illinois* 431 US 720, 745 (1997). But see *supra* n. 228.

230 Case 68/79, *Just I/S* v. *Danish Ministry for Fiscal Affairs* [1980] ECR 501; Case 199/82, *Amministrazione delle Finanze dello Stato* v. *San Georgio SpA* [1983] ECR 3595.

increased price of the product can only be passed on through a price rise to customers. In most cases, this will mean a decline in sales. These types of difficulties have caused the English Court of Appeal to hold, in the context of a private claim for restitution, that a defence of passing on is not available.[231]

Secondly, the possibility that such arguments might be raised by a defendant and the complications involved in the assessment might deter private actions by direct purchasers. It may, therefore, interfere with the important of Community objective of encouraging private proceedings to strengthen the working of the competition rules. In other words, if the operation of compensatory principle enunciated by the Court in *Crehan* were invoked to justify the recognition of a passing on defence in national law, it may be argued that the rule would undermine the operation of the deterrence principle and the principle of effectiveness upon which the Court also relied.

Thirdly, the acceptance of a passing on argument would frequently allow the *wrongdoer* to benefit and to retain some of the fruits of its wrong since in a great majority of cases indirect purchasers, to whom some of the higher prices have been passed on, will not sue. In a case like *Crehan*, for example, the publican-tenants may have passed some of their loss down the chain to their customers. It seems unlikely, however, that even the most hardened drinkers would contemplate their losses being sufficient to make proceedings against the brewers worthwhile. In the UK the Government's proposals to facilitate damages actions on behalf of consumers might encourage claims by indirect purchasers. Nonetheless, the Government accepts that it will be an uphill struggle to encourage actions to be brought in intractable cases such as these.

Indirect purchasers

It has already been mentioned that the rule in *Illinois Brick*, precluding claims by indirect purchasers, has been subjected to considerable criticism in the US. In some states the rule has even been reversed through legislation. The most obvious argument in support of the rule is that it precludes duplicate recovery from a defendant (full recovery from the direct purchaser and recovery in respect of the part passed on by the indirect purchaser). Coupled with the *Hanover Shoe* rule, the *Illinois Brick* rule means that wrongdoers will face damages actions from those most directly affected by their conduct and will ensure that wrongdoers are stripped of the fruits of their wrongdoing (thus deterring anti-competitive behaviour).

However, it is clearly arguable that the application of such a rule by a national court would be inconsistent with direct effect of Articles 81 and 82 and would undermine the operation of the principle that an individual who has suffered loss in consequence of a breach of the competition rules is entitled to compensation. In some cases, the application of the rule may allow the direct purchaser to retain at least part of the fruits of the seller's wrongdoing whilst those further down the chain, who have also suffered loss, are not compensated.

Such potential outcomes might militate against the application in national, and EC, law of the *Illinois Brick* rule. Indeed, the UK's government's proposal to foster representative claims on behalf of consumers seems to indicate that it would not be in favour of the adoption of such a rule. Arguably, the risk of double recovery is outweighed by the public interest in ensuring that anti-competitive behaviour is deterred and that those who suffer loss as a result are properly compensated. In the following extract, Clifford Jones recognises that the Court of Justice will have some difficult policy decisions to make in the future.

[231] See *Kleinwort Benson Ltd v. Birmingham City Council* [1997] QB 380. In the context of restitutionary claims the application of the defence also raises theoretical difficulties. Since the claim is based on the principle of unjust enrichment, the enrichment unjustly received by the defendant is not affected by the fact that the claimant may have passed some of its loss onto another. For greater discussion of the difficulties of accepting a passing on defence in the context of restitutionary claims and the approach of the Court of Justice in this sphere, see A. Jones, *Restitution and European Community Law* (LLP, 2000), chaps. 2–4, sections on passing on.

The theoretical possibility of double recovery is inherent if defensive passing-on is not allowed but offensive passing-on is allowed. However, if defensive passing on is allowed and fewer than all indirect purchasers sue, then the wrongdoer retains at least some of the fruits of his violation. Both major alternatives have aspects which are unsatisfactory. At bottom, the ECJ will have to choose the approach which it considers best serves fair and effective Community law.

Specific legislative rules?

The policy difficulties inherent in these types of choices may mean that it would be preferable for the key principles governing the right to damages within the sphere of EC competition law to be set out in legislation. In the absence of such harmonizing legislation, there may be significant incentives for undertakings to engage in national forum shopping in order to secure the most advantageous conditions for the prosecution or defence of their damages claim.

g. Jurisdiction

The questions of which national court or courts have jurisdiction to hear an antitrust claim and what law is applicable are of fundamental importance. Community law provides a broad choice of jurisdictions from which a claimant may choose when deciding where to launch his action.[232] In *Provimi* v. *Aventis*[233] an important ruling was given by the English High Court. Provimi had purchased vitamins from members of the vitamin cartel across Europe. Both the European Commission and the US authorities had found the companies to have committed serious violations of the competition rules.[234] In this case the court confirmed that a European customer could bring a claim against a UK subsidiary which had participated in the infringement, even though it had not made a purchase from that subsidiary. The claimant wanted to bring a single claim in respect of all its losses in one jurisdiction and had selected a jurisdiction where favourable procedural rules[235] applied. The case clearly opens the door to forum- shopping in actions against members of a European wide cartel.

h. Settlement and Alternative Dispute Resolution

Many of the uncertain issues set out in the sections above have, perhaps, encouraged settlement of a number of the competition claims arising in private proceedings before the English courts. In addition, procedure in the commercial courts encourages alternative dispute resolution as a practical means of settling claims between the parties.[236]

---

[232] See Regulation 44/2001 on jurisdiction and the recognition and enforcement of judgment in civil and commercial matters [2001] OJ C189/2 (the Brussels Regulation) and Commission Staff Working Paper, Annex to the Green Paper (available on DGComp's web site, at http://ec.europa.eu/comm/competition/antitrust/actionsdamages/index.html, paras. 237–54. But see the English High Court judgment in *SanDisk Corporation* v. *Koninklijki Philips Electronics N.V.* [2007] EWHC 332 (Ch).

[233] [2003] EWHC 961. But see also *SanDisk Corporation* v. *Koninklijki Philips Electronics N.V.* [2007] EWHC 332 (Ch).

[234] See *supra* Chap. 11.

[235] e.g., the disclosure rules.

[236] See, e.g. The Admiralty and Commercial Courts Guide, section G (alternative dispute resolution) and the Chancery Guide, chap. 17.

(iii) Damages Claims in Other Member States

It has been seen that a number of obstacles have, to date, prevented wide spread use of damages actions before the English courts. It seems clear that obstacles, such as the fact that pre-trial discovery rules are not available, class actions are not available, restrictive limitation rules apply, the availability of a passing-on defence, also exist in other Member States so that there have been few successful antitrust actions in those jurisdictions.[237]

Two significant cases are *Dermot Donovan v. Electricity Supply Board*[238] and *Scandinavian Airlines System (SAS) v. Swedish Board of Aviation*,[239] judgments of the Irish Supreme Court and the Swedish Court of Appeal respectively. In the former case the Irish Supreme Court recognized that damages were available in respect of a breach of the Irish domestic equivalent of Article 82 (section 6 of its Competition Act 1991) and that damages were to be awarded on the same basis as in the case of any tort or civil wrong.[240] Similarly, in the *SAS* case the Swedish Court of Appeal gave a significant judgment awarding approximately €100,000,000 to SAS. It was found that the Aviation Board had abused dominant position (contrary to Article 82 and its Swedish counterpart) by applying discriminatory prices. It was thus obliged to repay approximately €60m Euros to SAS and SAS was relieved of its obligation of paying approximately €40m more to the Aviation Board.[241]

(iv) Damages Claims in the US

It has already been mentioned that private litigation, and damages actions, is more widespread in the US.[242] A vital issue which has arisen in recent years, is whether claimants that have suffered loss in consequence of a cartel operated worldwide or internationally, can pursue a US class action in respect of cartelized products purchased from the companies but delivered outside the United States. The US Court of Appeals[243] divided upon the question of whether US law[244] allows proceedings by claimants whose case does *not* arise from the *US effect* of the anti-competitive conduct and whether such claimants fall within the class of persons whom the

---

[237] See, e.g. the discussion of Case C-259–98/04 *Manfredi v. Lloyd Adriatico Assicurazioni SpA* [2006] ECR I-6619, [2006] 5 CMLR 17, para. 57, *supra* n 182 and accompanying text, the Ashurst Report (*supra* n. 92) and Getting the Deal Through, Private Antitrust Litigation, 2007, available at http://www.gettingthedealthrough.com/sector.php?id=50. Such claims are, however, increasingly becoming a reality. There is on-going litigation in a number of the Members States, see e.g. ongoing mobile operators case before the Paris Commercial court and litigation in Austria over the lift cartel (Chap 11, n. 217). Further, CDC, a Belgian company, has been created specifically to purchase and then bring actions in antitrust compensation cases.

[238] [1998] EuLR 212.

[239] Unreported. But see T. Pettersson, and J. Aswall, 'Discriminatory Pricing: Comments on a Swedish Case' [2003] *ECLR* 295, U. Bernitz, 'The Arlanda Terminal 2 case: Substantial Damages Awarded on the Basis of Article 82 TEC' [2004] 1 *Competition Law Journal*, 195.

[240] [1998] EuLR 212.

[241] See also *Euro Garage v. Renault*, 23 Mar. 1989 (Paris Court of Appeal), *Eco Systems v. Peugeot*, 22 October 1996 (Paris Court of Commerce), *Marbreries Lescarcelle v. OGF* 2004 (Paris Court of Appeal).

[242] See *supra* section 1.

[243] See *Den Norske Stas Oljeselskap As v. HeereMac Vof* 241 F.3d 420 (2001, 5th Cir) (the plaintiff's claim must arise from the US effect of the anti-competitive conduct) and *Kruman v. Christie's International plc* 284 F.3d 384, 400 (2002, 2nd Cir) (the claimant's injury does not need to arise from the domestic effect of the conspiracy, as long as the domestic effect violates the substantive provisions of the Sherman Act).

[244] The question is dependent upon the interpretation of the Foreign Trade Antitrust Improvements Act of 1982 which provides that the Sherman Act shall not apply to non-import foreign conduct unless it has a direct, substantial, and reasonably foreseeable effect on US commerce and that such effect gives rise to a claim under the Sherman Act (15 USC 6(a)(1) and (2)).

Sherman Act is designed to protect. In *F. Hoffmann-La Roche Ltd* v. *Empagran SA*[245] the DC Court of Appeals considered that for jurisdiction to exist it was only necessary that the conduct's harmful effect on US commerce would give rise to a claim by someone, even if not the foreign plaintiff before the Court. The Court considered that this view would maximize deterrence of international cartels by forcing the conspirator to internalize the full cost of its anti-competitive conduct.[246] The case went on appeal, however, before the Supreme Court. The US Department of Justice and Federal Trade Commission filed a brief before the Court, as *amicus curiae*, expressing their concern with the Court of Appeals' conclusion. In particular, they feared that the holding would substantially harm its ability to uncover and break up international cartels[247] and undermine law enforcement relationships between the US and its trading partners. The Supreme Court[248] reined in the extent to which foreign claimants can seek damages in the US. It held that they may *not* do so in respect of injuries flowing exclusively from foreign effects of allegedly anti-competitive global conduct, where the foreign effects are independent of, and not intertwined with, the US effects.[249] This case is discussed in further detail in Chapter 16. It is also, of course, of central importance to this chapter: where a European complainant is able to join class actions in the US (where the anti-competitive conduct also has had effects on the US market which are intertwined with the foreign effects), the incentives for litigation in Europe may be reduced.

(v) Conclusions and Issues Raised in the Green Paper

A whole myriad of factors have, in the past, deterred private litigation in Europe. Now that it is settled that damages must, in principle be available to compensate those that have suffered in consequence of a breach of the rules, national courts in Europe will have to grapple with the difficult questions of: who has standing to bring such claims; whether a breach of the competition rules has been established; whether the breach caused the loss suffered by the claimant; how any damages to be awarded should be quantified; and what rules may limit or bar such actions.

B. INTERIM INJUNCTIONS

(i) General

An individual suffering in consequence of a breach of the competition rules might request an injunction to prevent the undertaking or undertakings committing a breach of the rules in future. The injunction sought might be final or interim, pending resolution of the final dispute between the parties. The availability of an interim injunction will be of particular importance to an undertaking which believes that it is being driven out of the market, for example, by a dominant undertaking's predatory behaviour in breach of Article 82 or by a refusal to supply.

---

[245] 315 F.3d 338 (DC Cir. 2003).

[246] *Ibid.*, 24–32a.

[247] In particular, that it will deter leniency claims, see *supra* n. 54.

[248] 542 US 155(2004) (Justice Breyer delivered the opinion of the Court). See Chap. 14, 1365.

[249] On remand, the DC Circuit ruled for the defendants, 417 F.3d 1267 (D.C. Cir., 2005). See also, *In re Monosodium Glutamate Antitrust Litigation* 477 F.3d 535 (8th Cir. 2007).

(ii) A Community Right to an Injunction

The ECJ held in *R* v. *Secretary of State for Transport, ex parte Factortame Ltd*[250] that a national court must ensure that interim measures are available where necessary to protect putative Community rights:

19. In accordance with the case-law of the Court, it is for the national courts, in application of the principle of cooperation laid down in Article [10] of the [EC] Treaty, to ensure the legal protection which persons derive from the direct effect of provisions of Community law . . .

20. The Court has also held that any provision of a national legal system and any legislative, administrative or judicial practice which might impair the effectiveness of Community law by withholding from the national court having jurisdiction to apply such law the power to do everything necessary at the moment of its application to set aside national legislative provisions which might prevent, even temporarily, Community rules from having full force and effect are incompatible with those requirements, which are the very essence of Community law.

. . .

21. . . . the full effectiveness of Community law would be just as much impaired if a rule of national law could prevent a court seised of a dispute governed by Community law from granting interim relief in order to ensure the full effectiveness of the judgment to be given on the existence of the rights claimed under Community law. It follows that a court which in those circumstances would grant interim relief, if it were not for a rule of national law, is obliged to set aside that rule.

(iii) The Position in English Law

The English High Court has jurisdiction to grant both final and interim injunctions where the court considers it to be 'just and equitable' to do so.[251] Broadly, an interim injunction will be granted where the guidelines set out by the House of Lords in *American Cyanamid Co* v. *Ethicon*[252] are satisfied. The guidelines require the court to take account of the following factors:

(i) Whether or not the claimant's case is frivolous or vexatious, there must be a serious issue to be tried;

(ii) Whether damages would be an adequate remedy for either party. If the injunction is granted the claimant will usually be required to give a cross-undertaking in damages to the defendant;

(iii) Whether on the balance of convenience the injunction should be granted;

(iv) Whether there are other special factors.

The injunction will not be granted if, for example, it would result in summary judgment for the claimant.[253]

In the context of private claims the courts thus have jurisdiction to grant interim relief as long as it is satisfied, applying the *American Cyanamid* principles, that it is just and equitable to do so. An English court will have to take care when applying these principles in the context of a claim

---

[250] Case 213/89; [1990] ECR I-2433, [1990] 3 CMLR 1.

[251] The principles which govern a court's decision whether or not to grant an injunction differ depending upon whether the injunction sought is final or interim.

[252] [1975] AC 396.

[253] See, e.g., *Plessey Co plc* v. *General Electric Co plc* [1988] ECC 384, where the award of the interim injunction would have precluded any take-over bid.

alleging a breach of the Community competition rules, that it ensures that an interim injunction is granted where necessary to give effective protection to the claimant's Community rights. The principles set out in *American Cyanamid* should enable a court to do so. Indeed, they appear to impose less stringent requirements on a claimant than those which must be satisfied by a claimant seeking interim relief from the Commission.[254]

The English courts have refused interim relief in competition cases on a number of occasions,[255] In *Garden Cottage Foods v. Milk Marketing Board*[256] the court considered, but declined, to grant an interim injunction to prevent an alleged abuse of a dominant position on the grounds that damages would be an adequate remedy. Relief has however, been granted in a few cases. In *Cutsforth v. Mansfield Inns*[257] the claimant, a supplier of juke boxes, alleged that a clause in a tenancy agreement which obliged the defendant's tenants to use juke boxes only from specific suppliers was in breach of Article 81. The High Court held that there was a serious issue to be tried and that if the injunction was not granted the claimant would be likely to go out of business. Damages would not be an adequate remedy. Consequently, the balance of convenience favoured the grant of the injunction. In *Network Multimedia Television Ltd v. Jobserve Ltd*,[258] the court also granted an injunction, this time restraining implementation of a threat to refuse to supply. In essence, the claimant alleged that the defendant had abused its dominant position on the market for advertising IT recruitment agencies' job vacancies online, by threatening to exclude agencies that advertised on other sites. It was held that there were serious issues to be tried, damages would not be an adequate remedy (if the injunction was not continued, the claimant's IT recruitment web site would have to be closed down) and that, conversely, the defendant would not suffer damage that could not be compensated by an award of damages. The balance of convenience was thus found to lie in favour of the claimant.

Further, injunctions have been granted in *Intel Corporation v. VIA Technologies*[259] and *Adidas-Salomon v. Lawn Tennis Association and Others.*[260] In the *Intel* case the defendants, VIA, raised Articles 81 and 82 (and the UK domestic equivalents)[261] as a defence to a patent infringement action. VIA defended the patent infringement claim partly on the grounds that Intel's refusal to grant it a patent licence on reasonable lawful terms was in breach of Article 82 and the UK domestic equivalent.[262] The defendant relied on the controversial series of decisions and cases dealing with refusal to supply and licence, in particular *Magill.*[263] At first instance Lawrence Collins J granted Intel's claim for summary judgment. The Court of Appeal, however, allowed the appeal from summary judgment. With respect to the refusal to supply point the Court held

---

[254] See *supra* Chap. 14.

[255] *See, e.g., Claritas (UK) Ltd v. The Post Office* [2001] UKCLR 2, *Getmapping plc v. Ordnance Survey* [2002] UKCLR 410, *Suretrack Rail Services Ltd v. Infraco JNP Ltd* [2002] EWHC 316.

[256] [1984] AC 130. Parker J, at first instance, held that damages would be an adequate remedy for the claimant in that case were the breach to be established (the loss of profit could easily be calculated and the Milk Marketing Board could pay).

[257] [1986] I CMLR 1.

[258] Ch D (Peter Whiteman QC), judgment of 5 April 2001, appeal rejected by Court of Appeal, CA (Civ Div) (Mummery LJ, Longmore LJ, Harrison J), judgment of 21 Dec. 2001.

[259] [2002] EWCA Civ 1905, [2002] All ER (D) 346.

[260] [2006] EWHC 1318 (Ch).

[261] Competition Act 1998, Chaps. I and II prohibitions.

[262] The English courts have not generally been prepared to allow such a breach of the competition rules to be relied on as a defence to claim, unless the defendant can show that the claimant's exercise or assertion of its rights creates or buttresses the abuse, see *Chiron Corporation v. Organon Teknika Ltd* [1992] 3 CMLR 813.

[263] Cases C-241/99 P and C-242/91 P RTE and ITP v. Commission [1995] ECR I-743, [1995] 4 CMLR 718. See now also Case C-418/01, IMS v. NDC 29 April, 2004. Both cases are discussed *supra* Chap. 8.

that it was arguable that the facts pleaded by the defendant displayed 'exceptional circumstances' justifying a finding that a refusal to license constituted an abuse of a dominant position.[264] Consequently, it was considered that the point was one which should be disposed of at trial and not in summary proceedings.[265] In the *Adidas* case the Chancellor of the High Court granted an injunction against the defendants and ordered an expedited trial. This case concerned changes to the dress rules adopted by the grand slam tennis tournaments which Adidas alleged gave rise to exclusionary and discriminatory effects on the position of Adidas vis-a-vis its competitors contrary to Article 81. Adidas thus sought a declaration that the decision was unlawful and void and an order restraining the defendants from implementing them. The judge considered that Adidas had a real prospect of success in its claim and that the facts justified the grant of the interlocutory relief sought.

An interesting case, involving both a complaint to the UK's OFT and court proceedings is *AAH Pharmaceuticals Ltd and Others v. Pfizer Limited and Unichem Ltd.*[266] In this case the High Court declined to grant an interim injunction sought by the claimants against Pfizer Limited. The claim arose following a decision by Pfizer to stop supplying a number of full-line pharmaceutical wholesalers and instead to supply retail pharmacies and dispensing doctors direct through a single logistics service provider, UniChem Ltd. The new arrangement was announced in September 2006 and was due to take effect on 5 March 2007. The result of the new arrangement was that the claimants would be refused supply of Pfizer products and so would be unable to continue as a full-line wholesaler.[267] The claimants alleged that Pfizer's actions constituted an unlawful refusal to supply in breach of Article 82 and section 18 CA and that any understanding to that effect with UniChem breached Article 81 and section 2 CA. Further, that the new arrangement would cause them irreparable harm, leading to many of their customers switching to UniChem and making it extremely difficult to win the customers back again.

A complicating factor to the claim in this case was that the claimant had also sought interim measures from the OFT. In the end, the OFT did not adopt a decision either refusing or granting interim measures[268] but it was a result of waiting for the OFT to act that led to the High Court proceedings being heard 'at the last minute', on the last working day before the new arrangements were due to take effect. Although it understood the background, the High Court was extremely critical of the decision to leave such complex matters to be decided in an urgent decision and this was one of the factors that caused it to decline the injunction. The court considered it to be extraordinary for it to be faced with an application of this complexity in relation to proposals which have been well-known both publicly and to the claimants for several months. It is a strong thing for the court to interfere by interim injunction in the conduct of business,

---

[264] Sir Andrew Morritt V-C did not accept the claimant's argument that there could only be exceptional circumstances within the meaning of *Magill* if the refusal either excluded an entirely new product from the market or all competition to the patentee. Rather, he considered that there might be other circumstances in other cases, which might be regarded as exceptional. For further discussion of these difficult issues, see *supra* Chap. 8.

[265] In the end the actions were, on 7 April 2003, settled in six countries (including the UK). The terms of settlement included a licence to VIA to make chip sets that are compatible with a new faster technology that Intel was due to release later in the year.

[266] [2007] EWHC 565.

[267] Only UniChem would be able to supply pharmacists and dispensing doctors with the full range of prescription drugs.

[268] On 27 February 2007, it sent a letter to the claimant stating that it had not yet decided whether there were reasonable grounds to suspect an infringement of the competition rules, or if it should conduct an investigation, and that even if it were open to it to impose interim measures, it would not do so because there was insufficient evidence of irreparable harm.

particularly on the scale proposed. By depriving the defendants and the court of the proper opportunity of dealing with this application, the Court considered that the delay greatly increased the risk of injustice if an injunction is granted.

5. CONCLUSIONS

1. The Commission's modernization programme was designed to allow the Commission to refocus its scarce resources and to encourage greater enforcement of the rules at the national level. The Commission has not only sought to enlist the aid of NCAs in the enforcement of the rules, but is eager that private actions should be used more frequently to bolster public enforcement.

2. It is to be expected, therefore, that private actions in Europe will gradually become more commonplace. The abolition of the Commission's exclusive right to rule individually on the compatibility of an agreement with Article 81(3) has removed a fundamental impediment to the courts' participation in the enforcement process.

3. Further, the ECJ's ruling in *Courage Ltd* v. *Crehan* has given national courts clearer guidance on their obligations when hearing damages claims.

4. In the UK changes were introduced in 2003 to encourage private action, in particular by allowing claims, and representative claims, to be brought before the specialist competition tribunal.[269] The Office of Fair Trading is also consulting on facilitating private actions in competition law.

5. The national obstacles facing potential litigants in competition cases, and the question of whether national rules are compatible with the Community principles of non-discrimination and effectiveness may however continue to raise hurdles which prove too large to surmount.[270]

6. The Commission's proposals for further stimulating private enforcement are thus awaited with interest.[271]

6. FURTHER READING

A. BOOKS

BASEDOW, J., (ed.), *Private Enforcement of EC Competition Law* (Kluwer, 2007)

BREALEY, M., and HOSKINS, M., *Remedies in EC Law* (2nd edn., Sweet & Maxwell, 1998)

JONES, A., *Restitution and European Community Law* (LLP, 2000), Chapter 6

JONES, C. A., *Private Enforcement of Antitrust Law in the EU, UK and USA* (Oxford University Press, 1999)

SMITH, M., *Competition Law: Enforcement and Procedure* (Butterworths, 2001)

SLOT, P. J., and MACDONNELL, A., *Procedure and Enforcement in EC and US Competition Law* (Sweet & Maxwell, 1993)

WHISH, R., in LONBAY, J., (ed.), *Frontiers of Competition Law* (Wiley, 1994), Chapter 5

—— 'The Enforceability of Agreements under EC and UK Competition Law' in F. D. Rose (ed.), *Lex Mercatoria: Essays in International Commercial Law in Honour of Francis Reynolds* (LLP, 2000)

WILS, W., *Principles of European Antitrust Enforcement* (Hart Publishing, 2005), Chap. 4.

---

[269] See *supra* n. 204 and accompanying text.

[270] See the introduction *supra*.

[271] See *supra* 1314 and accompanying text.

B. ARTICLES

BAEL, I. van, 'The Role of the National Courts' [1994] *ECLR* 3

BREALEY, M., 'Adopt Perma Life but follow Hanover Shoe to Illinois? Who can sue for Damages for Breach of EC Competition Law' [2002] *Comp LJ* 1(2), 127

DRAKE, S., 'Scope of *Courage* and the Principle of "Individual Liability" for Damages: Further Development of the Principle of Effective Judicial Protection by the Court of Justice' (2006) 30 *ELRev* 841

JACOBS, F. G., 'Civil Enforcement of EEC Antitrust Law' (1984) 82 *Mich LR* 1364

JONES, A., and BEARD, D. 'Co-contractors, Damages and Article 81: The ECJ finally speaks' [2002] *ECLR* 246

MONTI, G. 'Anti-competitive Agreements: the Innocent Party's Right to Damages' (2002) 27 *ELRev* 282

ODUDU, O., and EDELMAN, J., 'Compensatory damages for breach of Article 81' (2002) 27 *ELRev* 327

RODGER. B., 'The Interface between Competition Law and Private Law: Article 81, Illegality and Unjustified Enrichment' [2002] *Edinburgh LR* 217

—— 'Competition Law Litigation in the UK Courts: A Study of All Cases to 2004'—Parts I, II and III [2006] *ECLR* 241–8, 279–92 and 341–50

—— and MACCULLOCH, A., 'Wielding the Blunt Sword: Interim Relief for Breaches of EC Competition Law before the UK Courts' [1996] *ECLR* 393.

TEMPLE LANG, J., 'Inntrepreneur and the Duties of National Courts under Article 10 EC' [2006] *Comp Law* 231

VAN GERVEN, W., 'Of Rights, remedies and Procedures' [2000] 37 *CMLRev* 501

WILS, W. P. J., 'Should private antitrust enforcement be encouraged?' [2003] 26(3) *World Competition* 473

16

EXTRATERRITORIALITY, INTERNATIONAL ASPECTS, AND GLOBALIZATION

1. CENTRAL ISSUES

1. Particularly in a globalized market-place, the effects of anti-competitive conduct can be felt far from where they originate and mergers frequently involve undertakings from different jurisdictions, or multi-national companies that operate world-wide.

2. It was the US which first developed concepts to try to deal with jurisdictional problems in competition law. The US formulated the 'effects doctrine' whereby US antitrust laws apply to conduct which has a direct, substantial and reasonably forseeable effect in the US.

3. The US can be an attractive jurisdiction to foreign plaintiffs. Damages actions for competition injury are more common in the US than in Europe and many aspects of US litigation are plaintiff friendly. Recent US cases, however, have limited the use of the US courts by foreign plaintiffs.

4. The EC's single economic entity doctrine has brought many foreign companies into its jurisdiction. The EC has also formulated an 'implementation' doctrine which is similar to the effects doctrine. The Merger Regulation takes jurisdiction over undertakings anywhere in the world on the basis of the amount of their turnover in the EU.

5. The EC has entered into bilateral cooperation agreements, particularly with the US. These have not prevented the occasional divergence over international mergers.

6. Plans for international competition regimes or rules, for instance within the WTO, have not progressed. However, there are very successful 'soft law' developments going on stemming from cooperation between competition agencies from around the world.

2. INTRODUCTION

Restrictions on competition and abusive conduct which affect trade between Member States may originate outside the Community. Foreign firms established outside the Community may, for example, fix prices in the Community or divide the common market between them. A firm established outside the Community may hold a dominant position in the common market and may engage in behaviour which is an abuse under Article 82. Further, concentrations involving non-EC undertakings may have consequences for competition inside the Community. It is important to know, therefore, to what extent the EC competition rules can be applied to undertakings established and acting outside its borders. How far does the jurisdiction of the EC competition authorities reach?

This issue is part of a broader debate about the rights of States to take jurisdiction outside their territory, i.e., *extraterritorially*. Extraterritoriality is a controversial topic of much complexity in international law.[1] International law usually distinguishes between two types of jurisdiction. On the one hand there is what is variously called prescriptive, legislative, or subject-matter jurisdiction: the right of States to make their laws applicable to persons, territory, or situations. On the other hand there is enforcement jurisdiction, which is the capacity to take executive action to enforce compliance with those laws.

While most States agree, at least officially, that murder, kidnap, and rape are criminal activities deserving of punishment, the belief that anti-competitive behaviour is also contrary to the public good depends on the acceptance of a certain set of economic and political beliefs.[2] Moreover, even in the States with competition law regimes, the detail of the laws may vary, or the authorities' application of them in a specific situation may differ. For example, in the case of the *Boeing/McDonnell Douglas*[3] and *GE/Honeywell*[4] mergers disputes the EC and US authorities had different views despite the close cooperation between the two jurisdictions in competition matters and the existence of similar laws. If States apply their competition laws extraterritorially undertakings may find themselves subject to a number of competing and irreconcilable actions, there may be conflict between national authorities, and other States may feel that their sovereignty is infringed.

Within the context of competition law the issue of extraterritoriality has become increasingly important as the 'globalization' of the world economy advances. It becomes more and more impossible to isolate the effects of transactions which take place on that global market. A company like Microsoft has a dominant position throughout the world. Consumers can be injured by global conspiracies and one issue of current concern is in which jurisdiction(s) the victims can sue for comenpsation. The two most pressing matters are dealing with multi-national mergers and international cartels, neither of which are confined within one jurisiction. A number of remedies have been proposed or put in place, including the conclusion of bilateral and multilateral international arrangements and dealing with competition policy within the framework of existing international organizations (such as the World Trade Organization (WTO)). The EU has been an enthusiastic proponent of international co-operation in competition law matters, in particular of using the WTO as a vehicle.[5]

In this chapter we consider first the question of competition law and extraterritoriality, particularly in respect of the EU and the US, and then look at the 'internationalization' of competition law and the moves which have been made towards dealing with competition issues on a global footing to match the global operations of undertakings on world markets.

3. THE POSITION IN US LAW

A. GENERAL

It is difficult to consider the question of extraterritoriality in EC competition law without first looking at the position in US law. The main US antitrust statute, the Sherman Act, is a criminal

---

[1] See *infra* 1369.

[2] See *supra* Chap. 1.

[3] [1997] OJ L336/16.

[4] Case No. COMP/M.2220.

[5] See, e.g., the yearly reports of the Commission on Competition Policy.

statute in that violations of it are criminal offences. However, it can also be enforced through private action. Because the Sherman Act dates from 1890 its extraterritorial reach inevitably became an issue before the EEC even existed.[6] The 'effects doctrine' propounded in the US courts has provided the central concept around which the discussion of extraterritoriality in competition law is usually conducted. The extraterritorial application of US antitrust law has long been controversial, not just as a matter of principle but because of the features of US antitrust litigation. US law, for example, provides that private individuals can recover 'treble damages' for breaches of the antitrust laws[7] and US law provides for far-ranging pre-trial discovery.[8] More recently the attractions to litigants of pursuing in US courts competition law claims with only an indirect connection to the US have led to a lively debate about the jurisdiction of US courts in antitrust cases.[9]

Two points about US law should be noted at the outset. First, there is a multiplicity of actors in US antitrust law. The two federal agencies, the Department of Justice (DOJ) and the Federal Trade Commission (FTC) are not decision-makers as is the European Commission as antitrust law is enforced in the ordinary courts. Different courts of equal authority can (and do) come to different conclusions on the same issues which can sometimes render it difficult to make general statements about US law.[10] Secondly, extraterritoriality in antitrust law is but one aspect of the long arm of US law which also encompasses legislation such as the Iran–Libya Sanctions Act 1996 and the Alien Tort Statute1789.[11]

B. THE EFFECTS DOCTRINE

In the first half-century following the enactment of the Sherman Act the US courts were diffident about applying the rules extraterritorially. In the *American Banana* case[12] Justice Oliver Wendell Holmes said in the Supreme Court that 'the general and almost universal rule is that the character of an act as lawful or unlawful must be determined wholly by the law of the country where the act is done'. Later cases retreated from this self-denying ordinance,[13] and in the *Alcoa* case[14] in 1945 Judge Learned Hand laid down what is known as the 'effects doctrine'. The case concerned a cartel of aluminium producers based in Switzerland which fixed production quotas to boost prices. The court (the Second Circuit Court of Appeals) held that the Sherman Act applied to a Canadian company which had participated in the cartel. Judge Learned Hand said that the Sherman Act *did* apply to agreements concluded outside the USA which were intended to affect US imports and did actually affect them.

Not surprisingly, the extraterritorial application of US antitrust laws met with hostility from other States.[15] The American courts have not been insensitive to this. In

---

[6] See R. Y. Jennings, 'Extraterritorial Jurisdiction and the United States Antitrust Laws' (1957) 33 BYIC, 146.

[7] Clayton Act, 15 USC Sec. 15. However, see the Antitrust Criminal Penalty Enhancement and Reform Act 2004, n. 51 *infra*.

[8] See *infra* 1363.

[9] See *F. Hoffmann-La Roche Ltd* v. *Empagran*, *infra* 1365.

[10] See the varying views of the different Circuits which culminated in the *Empagran* case, *infra* 1364.

[11] The Alien Torts Act was considered by the Supreme Court in *Sosa* v. *Alvarez-Machain*, 542 US 2004, a case in which an arrest was effected in Mexico by US Federal agents.

[12] *American Banana Co* v. *United Fruit Co*, 213 US 347, 356, 29 S.Ct 511, 512 (1909).

[13] See *United States* v. *Sisal Sales Corp*, 274 US 268, 47 S.Ct 592 (1927). The *American Banana* case has been limited to its facts and read in a limited way.

[14] *United States* v. *Aluminum Co of America*, 148 F.2d 416 (2d Cir. 1945).

[15] For the particular problems with regard to their enforcement, see *infra* 1362.

Timberlane[16] the Ninth Circuit Court of Appeals considered the notion of 'international comity' in this context. 'Comity' means living peacefully with other nations in mutual respect and accommodating their interests or, as one authority puts it, the 'rules of politeness, convenience and goodwill observed by States in their mutual intercourse without being legally bound by them'.[17] In *Timberlane* Judge Choy recognized the effects doctrine as laid down in *Alcoa*, but considered that its application had to be balanced against the interests of international comity. The case concerned an action by an American company alleging that the defendants in Honduras had conspired to exclude it from the Honduran lumber market, from where it planned to export to the USA (the allegations included claims that Honduran government officials had been bribed). Judge Choy said that three questions had to asked:

Timberlane Lumber Co. v. *Bank of America*, 549 F.2d 597 at 613 (9th Cir. 1976)

Judge Choy

Despite its description as 'settled law', ALCOA's assertion has been roundly disputed by many foreign commentators as being in conflict with international law, comity and good judgment. Nevertheless American courts have firmly concluded that there is some extra-territorial jurisdiction under the Sherman Act. Even among American courts and commentators, however, there is no consensus on how far the jurisdiction should extend . . .

There is no agreed black-letter rule articulating the Sherman Act's commerce coverage in the international context . . . The effects test by itself is incomplete because it fails to consider the other nation's interests; nor does it expressly take into account the full nature of the relationships between the actors and this country . . .

A tripartite analysis seems to be indicated. As acknowledged above, the antitrust laws require in the first instance that there be *some* effect—actual or intended—on American foreign commerce before the federal courts may legitimately exercise subject-matter jurisdiction under those statutes. Second, a greater showing of burden or restraint may be necessary to demonstrate that the effect is sufficiently large to present cognizable injury to the plaintiffs and therefore a civil violation of the antitrust laws . . . Third, there is the additional question, which is unique to the international setting, of whether the interests of and links to the United States, including the magnitude of the effect on American commerce, are sufficiently strong, *vis-à-vis* those of other nations, to justify an assertion of extra-territorial authority . . .

In answering this third question, which was necessary because 'at some point the interests of the United States are too weak and the foreign harmony incentive for restraint too strong to justify an extraterritorial assertion of jurisdiction', he said that the following factors should be taken into account:

the degree of conflict with foreign law or policy, the nationality or allegiance of the parties and the locations or principal places of business of corporations, the extent to which enforcement by either state can be expected to achieve compliance, the relative significance of effects on the United States as compared with those elsewhere, the extent to which there is explicit purpose to harm or affect

---

[16] *Timberlane Lumber Co v. Bank of America*, 549 F.2d 597 (9th Cir. 1976).

[17] Oppenheim's *International Law* (ed. R. Y. Jennings and A. Watts) (9th edn., Longman, 1992), i, 34 n. 1.

American commerce, the foreseeability of such effect, the relative importance to the violations charged of conduct within the United States as compared with conduct abroad.

The criteria were expanded in *Mannington Mills*,[18] where the plaintiff claimed that the defendant had infringed its export business by fraudulently obtaining foreign patents and the court added to the *Timberlane* list of factors to be brought into the balancing exercise.[19]

Timberlane and *Mannington Mills* do not *deny* jurisdiction to the US courts in the interests of comity, but merely hold that it should not be *exercised* where the interests of the USA in asserting jurisdiction are outweighed by the interests of comity.[20]

In 1982 the Foreign Trade Antitrust Improvements Act (FTAIA) amended the Sherman Act. The FTAIA stipulates that as regards foreign commerce *other than import commerce* the antitrust laws will not apply unless the conduct has a *direct, substantial, and reasonably foreseeable* effect on US commerce or on US exports and such effect gives rise to a claim under the Sherman Acts or FTC Acts. In other words, the FTAIA exempts export transactions from the Sherman Act unless they injure the American economy. This provision has inevitably come to be seen as a statutory formulation of the effects doctrine. The test it contains—direct, substantial, reasonably foreseeable—is very much like the *Alcoa* formula, except that it adds forseeability.[21] It does not address any *Timberlane*-type balancing exercise.

On the other hand, the American Law Institute's *Third Restatement of the Foreign Relations Law of the United States*[22] sets out the principles of extraterritorial jurisdiction in terms of the *Timberlane/Mannington Mills* balancing act.

In *Hartford Fire Insurance*[23] in 1993 the Supreme Court recognized the claims of comity, but took a robust approach to applying the effects doctrine. Re-insurers based in London were alleged to have agreed with parties in the USA to boycott certain types of insurers, which meant that some types of insurance cover were not available in the USA.[24] The Supreme Court, by a majority, held that the Sherman Act could be applied to the acts of the British insurers. Justice Souter, delivering the majority opinion, said that 'it is well established by now that the Sherman Act applies to foreign conduct that was meant to produce and did in fact produce some substantial effect in the United States'.[25] He looked to the FTAIA formulation as expressing the effects doctrine, and said that in the light of that the court should first decide whether it had jurisdiction. Then it could be determined whether jurisdiction should be declined on comity grounds. In this case there was no reason to decline it. He took the view that although the UK

[18] Accord *Mannington Mills Inc v. Congoleum Corp*, 595 F.2D 1287 (3rd Cir. 1979).

[19] The additional criteria were: the possible effect on foreign relations if the court exercises jurisdiction; if the relief is granted, whether a party will be put in the position of being forced to perform an act illegal in either country or be under conflicting requirements by both countries; whether an order for relief would be acceptable in the USA if made by a foreign nation under similar circumstances; whether a treaty with the affected nations has addressed the issue.

[20] Such a balancing act had earlier been advocated by Kingman Brewster, who called it a 'jurisdictional rule of reason' in *Antitrust and American Business Abroad* (McGraw-Hill, 1958). Note that in the *Timberlane* case itself the Court of Appeals said that, as there was no indication of a conflict with the law and policy of the Honduran government, the trial judge could not have dismissed the action on jurisdictional grounds. .

[21] Foreseeability indicates that the 'intent' in *Alcoa*, 274 US 268, 47 S. Ct 592 (1927) is objective rather than subjective.

[22] (American Law Institute, 1995) at s. 403. The American Law Institute is a private body, but the Restatements are accorded great respect.

[23] *Hartford Fire Insurance Co v. California*, 509 US 764, 113 S.Ct 2891 (1993).

[24] This stemmed from re-insurers' worries about certain long term risks, such as those arising from environmental pollution, where the claims could come up decades later.

[25] *Hartford Fire* at 796 (US).

allowed the conduct, it did not *compel* it.[26] There was therefore no conflict between British and American policy, and no reason for comity concerns to override the effects doctrine.

However, if international comity is only to prevent the USA taking jurisdiction in such narrowly drawn conflict situations it will rarely prevail. Further, it should be noted that when dealing with internal inconsistencies between federal antitrust law and the laws of US states, it is accepted that immunity from the former may sometimes arise as a consequence of the latter, even where the individual or undertaking concerned *could* comply with both.[27] The disregard of another jurisdiction which merely *permits* rather than *compels* conduct which is contrary to the first State's antitrust laws also arises in EC law. It is vividly demonstrated by the merger case, *Gencor*, discussed below.[28]

In *Hartford Fire Insurance* a strong dissent was voiced by Justice Scalia. His view was that comity is an integral part of determining whether the court has jurisdiction in the first place, rather than something to be taken into account when deciding whether to *exercise* jurisdiction.[29] Hovenkamp comments that antitrust law expresses the substantive economic policy of the United States and 'American "public" policy is entitled to be given as much weight by an American court as is the policy of a foreign sovereign, at least where American interests covered by the policy are substantially affected'.[30] F. A. Mann, writing in 1984,[31] disapproved of the 'balancing interests' idea. He considered that if a court has jurisdiction it must exercise it. If, on the other hand, international law says it has no jurisdiction that is the end of the matter. One cannot, however, have a court which has a discretion whether or not to exercise its own jurisdiction.

In 1995 the Department of Justice and the Federal Trade Commission issued a set of Antitrust Enforcement Guidelines for International Operations.[32] These explain, *inter alia*, that the agencies will take comity into account when deciding to bring an action or seek particular remedies. The Guidelines list a number of factors[33] that will be considered when making the decision. Once the decision is made, however, this represents 'a determination by the Executive Branch that the importance of antitrust enforcement outweighs any relevant foreign policy concerns'. The Guidelines warn that the courts should not 'second-guess' its judgment 'as to the proper role of comity concerns under these circumstances'. However, it should be remembered that in the USA, in contrast to the EC, the antitrust laws are predominantly enforced by private suits in the civil courts and not just by the antitrust authorities. The authorities do not have a strong influence over the courts or a claimant's decision to bring proceedings before the courts. The 1995 Guidelines state that the authorities will not bring an action unless they have weighed up the antitrust enforcement versus comity issues and decided that the former outweigh the latter but it is unlikely that a private plaintiff will go through the same process.

---

[26] The 'foreign sovereign compulsion defence' (the US courts do not hold private individuals liable for acts they were compelled to perform by a foreign sovereign on that sovereign's territory) therefore did not apply. (The USA also recognizes 'foreign sovereign immunity' whereby foreign governments have immunity in the courts, although this does not usually cover commercial activities).

[27] A. Robertson and M. Demetriou, 'But That was in Another Country ...': The Extraterritorial Application of US Antitrust Laws in the US Supreme Court (1994) 43 *ICLQ* 417, 421–2.

[28] Case T-102/96, *Gencor Ltd v. Commission* [1999] ECR II-753 [1999] 4 CMLR 971, discussed *infra* at 1378.

[29] See also the minority opinion by Judge Adams in *Mannington Mills*, 595 F.2d. 1287 (3d Cir. 1979).

[30] H. Hovenkamp, *Federal Antitrust Policy* (3rd edn., Thomson/West, 2005), 766.

[31] F. A. Mann, 'The Doctrine of International Jurisdiction Revisited After Twenty Years' (1984) 186 RdC 9, the sequel to the celebrated 1964 article, 'The Doctrine of Jurisdiction in International Law' (1964) 111 RdC 1.

[32] Antitrust and Trade Reg. Rep. (BNA), Special Supplement (6 Apr. 1995).

[33] Similar to those in *Timberlane* (*supra* 1359).

The effects doctrine was applied in *Nippon Paper*,[34] where the Antitrust Division of the Department of Justice commenced *criminal* proceedings under the Sherman Act against a Japanese company for a cartel fixing the price at which fax paper should be sold in the USA.[35] The conspirators were all Japanese and all the activities of the cartel—the meetings, monitoring, and the sales to distributors with instructions about the resale price in the USA—took place in Japan. In contrast to the position in *Hartford Fire Insurance* the conduct was *illegal* under Japanese law (although the Japanese government intervened in the case as an *amicus* on behalf of the defendant undertakings). The First Circuit Court of Appeals held that the US courts did have jurisdiction. The court said that *Hartford Fire* had 'stunted' the concept of comity in antitrust cases. It looked at the Restatement and the test of 'reasonableness' but considered that the Japanese undertakings should not, in these circumstances, be sheltered from prosecution by principles of comity:

> We see no tenable reason why principles of comity should shield [the Japanese undertakings] from prosecution. We live in an age of international commerce, where decisions reached in one corner of the world can reverberate around the globe in less time than it takes to tell the tale. Thus, a ruling in [the Japanese undertakings'] favor would create perverse incentives for those who would use nefarious means to influence markets in the United States, rewarding them for enacting as many territorial firewalls as possible between cause and effect.[36]

This was the first case in which extraterritorial *criminal* jurisdiction had been taken under the Sherman Act. It showed that the USA had lost none of its enthusiasm for the application of its antitrust laws beyond its borders.

C. ENFORCEMENT AND THE REACTIONS OF OTHER STATES

Other States have tended to react unfavourably to US claims of extraterritorial jurisdiction based on the effects doctrine.[37] Particular problems have arisen where the US has wished to take enforcement action extra-territorially. As has been shown in other chapters of this book[38] competition authorities need to investigate and gather information, and may ultimately wish to levy penalties and enforce orders remedying infringements of the competition rules. A stark example of the conflicts that can arise is *United States v. ICI Ltd.*[39] There a US court ordered, on the grounds of infringement of the Sherman Act, the cancellation of agreements between ICI and Du Pont, by which Du Pont assigned to ICI certain patents which were to be registered in the UK. ICI was ordered to reassign the patents to Du Pont. ICI, however, had already contracted to license the patents to British Nylon Spinners, a UK company. British Nylon Spinners sued in the English courts to enforce its rights under the contract. Danckwerts J granted a decree of specific

---

[34] *United States v. Nippon Paper Industries Co.*, 109 F.3d (1st Cir. 1997).

[35] See R. M. Reynolds, J. Sicilian, and P. S. Wellman, 'The Extraterritorial Application of the US Antitrust Laws to Criminal Conspiracies' [1998] *ECLR* 151; J. Griffin, 'Reactions to US Assertions of Extraterritorial Jurisdiction' [1998] *ECLR* 64, 68.

[36] *Nippon Paper*, at 9.

[37] There has also been opposition to the extraterritorial application of measures taken in pursuit of American foreign policy, *supra* n. 11.

[38] See particularly Chap. 14 *supra*.

[39] 105 F. Supp 215 (1952).

performance, saying that the US judge 'was applying an enactment of Congress, which has no application to the United Kingdom'.[40]

US pre-trial discovery confers wide-ranging powers on US plaintiffs wishing to search abroad for evidence of antitrust violations. In the UK the House of Lords reacted with hostility in *Rio Tinto Zinc*[41] to letters rogatory requesting the High Court to require directors and employees of a British company to give oral evidence before an examiner in London and to require the company to produce the documents contained in a lengthy schedule. The request was in connection with a private antitrust suit in Virginia. The House decided that the US court's request for assistance fell within the exceptions to the obligation to assist in requests for discovery by foreign courts contained in the Evidence (Proceedings in Other Jurisdictions) Act 1975, and consequently refused discovery.

The UK subsequently passed the Protection of Trading Interest Act 1980, to 'block' the enforcement of any foreign international trade laws, but largely directed in reality at US antitrust laws. First, the Act enables the Secretary of State to direct a person carrying on business in the UK not to comply with the orders of a foreign court or authority affecting international trade which threaten to damage the trading interests of the UK.[42] Section 2 of the Act empowers the Secretary of State to prohibit persons within the UK from complying with demands by foreign tribunals and authorities for commercial documents or information not located within the jurisdiction of the State concerned.[43] The Act also protects British defendants from the enforcement of punitive treble damages claims. Section 5 describes such awards as 'penal' and forbids their enforcement in UK courts under the usual reciprocal enforcement procedures.[44] Further, section 6 sets out a 'clawback' provision enabling British citizens or companies or persons carrying on business in the UK to bring an action in the UK courts to recover the non-compensatory part of any such damages they have paid. Other States have also passed such 'blocking' statutes.[45]

Violation of section 1 of the Sherman Act is a criminal offence, and individuals who participate in cartel arrangements are liable to criminal prosecution, fines and imprisonment. There is a great deal of disagreement as to whether or not the criminalization of cartel behaviour is appropriate or useful as a way of combating hard-core cartels, but the current view of the competition authorities in, *inter alia*, the US, the UK and Ireland is that it is.[46] Executives can escape US jails by lurking in countries which will not extradite to the US for antitrust offences. That was true of the UK until recently, but not any more. The Enterprise Act 2002, s. 191 introduced the 'cartel offence' into UK law.[47] The offence is extraditable[48] which means a person may be extradited to another country for an equivalent offence. Section 191 is not retrospective and so

---

[40] *British Nylon Spinners Ltd v. ICI Ltd* [1955] Ch 37.

[41] *Rio Tinto Zinc Corp v. Westinghouse Electric Corp* [1978] AC 547.

[42] Protection of Trading Interest Act 1980, s. 1.

[43] Note that in the current spirit of international cooperation the UK favours the ability to exchange information in order to further the enforcement of competition laws. The Enterprise Act 2002, s. 243 sets out the circumstances in which a UK public authority could disclose information to an overseas public authority, including a competition authority. In 2003 the OFT published draft guidance (for consultation) on how it proposed to exercise these powers (OFT 507) The UK/US Mutual Assistance Treaty now covers criminal infringements of competition law (UK/US Mutual Legal Assistance Treaty, 2001 (Cm. 5375)).

[44] See *supra* Chap. 15.

[45] See generally A. V. Lowe, *Extraterritorial Jurisdiction* (Grotius, 1983).

[46] Austria has had criminal sanctions for many years without anyone being imprisoned.

[47] Enterprise Act 2002, s. 188.

[48] *Ibid.*, s. 191.

does not apply to conduct prior to June 2003. However, in the context of an application by the US government to extradite Ian Norris, the ex-Chief Executive of Morgan Crucible, to face trial in the US for violation of the Sherman Act prior to 2003, the UK Administrative Court held that price fixing amounts to the common law offence of conspiracy to defraud and so applies to pre-2003 conduct. Norris's appeal is pending at the time of writing.[49]

D. FOREIGN PLAINTIFFS IN US COURTS

In Chapter 15 we saw that private litigation of antitrust cases is far more common in US courts than it is anywhere in Europe. As well as the differences in the systems of enforcement there are various features of the US legal system which make it easier or more attractive for plaintiffs in the US to bring actions. In brief, these are:

- very broad discovery rules;[50]
- class actions (in which, moreover, injured parties need not join in at the start of the case);
- contingent attorneys' fees;
- treble damages;[51]
- joint and several liability among the defendants.

Furthermore, in the US actions are heard before juries, which can be very generous in awarding damages to those they see as wronged by big corporations.

Overseas litigants look with envy and longing at the sight of US plaintiffs winning large damages awards in US courts in cartel cases. Some of these have been in respect of major international cartels which had effects in numerous countries. As explained in Chapter 15, overseas victims of international cartels recently started litigating in US courts in respect of harm suffered outside the US. At first sight these actions seemed unlikely to succeed: the FTAIA, as mentioned above,[52] states that as regards foreign commerce the antitrust laws will not apply unless the conduct has a direct, substantial and reasonably forseeable effect on US commerce. However, the US Court of Appeals differed in its reactions to claims over harm overseas.[53] The matter went to the Supreme Court in F. Hoffmann-La Roche Ltd v. Empagran.[54]

There were two strands of argument in Empagran. The first was a matter of statutory construction of the FTAIA in the light of international comity. The second was a matter of statutory

---

[49] Norris v. Government of the United States of America [2007] EWHC 71 (Admin) (25 January 2007). See Chap. 14, 1286. Moreover, as the US is designated as a 'category 2' country for the purposes of the Extradition Act 2003 it is not necessary 'to put before the court evidence sufficient to justify a committal or a case to answer if the conduct constituting the alleged offence had been committed in this country. It is enough for the requesting designated state to identify the conduct, for the court to consider whether it would, if proved, have constituted an offence in this country and, if so, whether the proposed extradition would be compatible with the individual's Convention rights, before sending the case to the Secretary of State for his decision' (Norris, para. 31, per Auld LJ).

[50] Although, as noted in Chap.15, the narrower discovery rules in European jurisdictions (very much narrower in some Member States) may be by-passed where the litigant is able to rely on the information laid out in a Commission decision (which may well have been uncovered by a Commission inspection under Reg. 1/2003, Art. 20).

[51] Note that on 23 June 2004 President Bush signed the Antitrust Criminal Penalty Enhancement and Reform Act 2004 which limits the damages recoverable from a corporate amnesty applicant, which also co-operates with private plaintiffs in their damages actions against remaining cartel members, to the damages actually inflicted by the amnesty applicant's conduct.

[52] Supra 1360.

[53] See supra Chap. 15, 1349.

[54] 542 US155 (2004).

construction in the light of its legislative history. The issue was whether the US could or should act as a kind of world policeman, welcoming litigants from all over the world who have been injured abroad by cartels which have also caused injury inside the US. *Empagran* itself was part of the saga of the worldwide vitamins cartel, punished in the US by fines of more than $800 million and jail sentences for some of the executives, and in the EC by swingeing fines, Hoffmann-La Roche alone being fined €462 million (after receiving leniency).[55] The plaintiffs were, *inter alia*, Ukrainian, Ecuadorean, and Panamanian buyers, while the defendant sellers were German and Swiss. The District of Columbia Court of Appeals held that they could seek damages in the US, as purchasers overseas who suffer losses from a cartel could sue in US courts provided similar claims could be brought in US courts in respect of the same cartel. One argument for the US courts taking jurisdiction was that global cartels do not really 'take place' in any particular territory. When foreign purchasers contract with a multi-national corporation the contract could be sourced anywhere, and there is no reason why a party's ability to recover should depend on how the multinational structures its transactions. Further it is argued that global cartels *do* harm US consumers, because in a globalized world there is no such thing as domestic price-fixing: the important thing to do is to deter cartel behaviour by making it too expensive (and allowing the victims to sue in US courts is one way to do this). The DOJ did not agree that US courts should take jurisdiction. It argued in its *amicus curiae* brief to the Supreme Court in *Empagran* that, in particular, the taking of jurisdiction by US courts would undermine the DOJ's leniency programme by expanding the scope of the cartellists potential civil liability, and would undermine cooperation with other competition authorities.

The Supreme Court held that the FTAIA excluded foreign plaintiffs from seeking damages in the US where the harm flowed exclusively from the foreign effects of the conduct which infringed the Sherman Act.

F. Hoffmann-La Roche Ltd v. Empagran SA, 542 US 155 (2004), 14 June 2004

Opinion of the Supreme Court

Justice Breyer

IV

We turn now to the basic question presented, that of the exception's application. Because the underlying antitrust action is complex, potentially raising questions not directly at issue here, we reemphasize that we base our decision upon the following: The price-fixing conduct significantly and adversely affects both customers outside the United States and customers within the United States, but the adverse foreign effect is independent of any adverse domestic effect. In these circumstances, we find that the FTAIA exception does not apply (and thus the Sherman Act does not apply) for two main reasons. *First*, this Court ordinarily construes ambiguous statutes to avoid unreasonable interference with the sovereign authority of other nations. See, *e.g.*, *McCulloch* v. *Sociedad Nacional de Marineros de Honduras*, 372 U.S. 10, 20–22 (1963) (application of National Labor Relations Act to foreign-flag vessels); *Romero* v. *International Terminal Operating Co.*, 358 U.S. 354, 382–383 (1959) (application of Jones Act in maritime case); *Lauritzen* v. *Larsen*, 345 U.S.

---

[55] *Vitamins* [2003] OJ L6/1, [2003] 4 CMLR 1030.

571, 578 (1953) (same). This rule of construction reflects principles of customary international law—law that (we must assume) Congress ordinarily seeks to follow. See Restatement (Third) of Foreign Relations Law of the United States §§403(1), 403(2) (1986) (hereinafter Restatement) (limiting the unreasonable exercise of prescriptive jurisdiction with respect to a person or activity having connections with another State); *Murray* v. *Schooner Charming Betsy*, 2 Cranch 64, 118 (1804) ('[A]n act of Congress ought never to be construed to violate the law of nations if any other possible construction remains'); *Hartford Fire Insurance Co.* v. *California*, 509 U.S. 764, 817 (1993) (SCALIA, J., dissenting) (identifying rule of construction as derived from the principle of 'prescriptive comity').

This rule of statutory construction cautions courts to assume that legislators take account of the legitimate sovereign interests of other nations when they write American laws. It thereby helps the potentially conflicting laws of different nations work together in harmony—a harmony particularly needed in today's highly interdependent commercial world.

No one denies that America's antitrust laws, when applied to foreign conduct, can interfere with a foreign nation's ability independently to regulate its own commercial affairs. But our courts have long held that application of our antitrust laws to foreign anti-competitive conduct is nonetheless reasonable, and hence consistent with principles of prescriptive comity, insofar as they reflect a legislative effort to redress domestic antitrust injury that foreign anti-competitive conduct has caused. See *United States* v. *Aluminum Co of America*, 148 F. 2d 416, 443–444 (CA2 1945) (L. Hand, J.); 1 P. Areeda & D. Turner, *Antitrust Law* ¶236 (1978).

But why is it reasonable to apply those laws to foreign conduct insofar as that conduct causes independent foreign harm and that foreign harm alone gives rise to the plain-tiff's claim? Like the former case, application of those laws creates a serious risk of interference with a foreign nation's ability independently to regulate its own commercial affairs. But, unlike the former case, the justi-fication for that interference seems insubstantial. See Restatement §403(2) (determining reason-ableness on basis of such factors as connections with regulating nation, harm to that nation's interests, extent to which other nations regulate, and the potential for conflict). Why should American law supplant, for example, Canada's or Great Britain's or Japan's own determination about how best to protect Canadian or British or Japanese customers from anti-competitive con-duct engaged in significant part by Canadian or British or Japanese or other foreign companies?

We recognize that principles of comity provide Congress greater leeway when it seeks to con-trol through legislation the actions of American companies, see Restatement §402; and some of the anti-competitive price-fixing conduct alleged here took place in America. But the higher for-eign prices of which the foreign plaintiffs here complain are not the consequence of any domestic anti-competitive conduct that Congress sought to forbid, for Congress did not seek to forbid any such conduct insofar as it is here relevant, i.e., insofar as it is intertwined with foreign conduct that causes independent foreign harm. Rather Congress sought to release domestic (and foreign) anti-competitive conduct from Sherman Act constraints when that conduct causes foreign harm. Congress, of course, did make an exception where that conduct also causes domestic harm. See House Report 13 (concerns about American firms' participation in international cartels addressed through 'domestic injury' exception). But any independent domestic harm the foreign conduct causes here has, by definition, little or nothing to do with the matter.

We thus repeat the basic question: Why is it reasonable to apply this law to conduct that is sig-nificantly foreign insofar as that conduct causes independent foreign harm and that foreign harm alone gives rise to the plaintiff's claim? We can find no good answer to the question . . .

    . . .

Respondents reply that many nations have adopted antitrust laws similar to our own, to the point where the practical likelihood of interference with the relevant interests of other nations is mini-mal. Leaving price fixing to the side, however, this Court has found to the contrary. See, e.g.,

Hartford Fire, 509 U.S. at 797–799 (noting that the alleged conduct in the London reinsurance market, while illegal under United States antitrust laws, was assumed to be perfectly consistent with British law and policy); see also, e.g., 2 W. Fugate, Foreign Commerce and the Antitrust Laws §16.6 (5th ed. 1996) (noting differences between European Union and United States law on vertical restraints).

Regardless, even where nations agree about primary conduct, say price fixing, they disagree dramatically about appropriate remedies. The application, for example, of American private treble-damages remedies to anti-competitive conduct taking place abroad has generated considerable controversy. See, e.g., 2 ABA Section of Antitrust Law, Antitrust Law Developments 1208–1209 (5th ed. 2002). And several foreign nations have filed briefs here arguing that to apply our remedies would unjustifiably permit their citizens to bypass their own less generous remedial schemes, thereby upsetting a balance of competing considerations that their own domestic antitrust laws embody . . .

These briefs add that a decision permitting independently injured foreign plaintiffs to pursue private treble-damages remedies would undermine foreign nations' own antitrust enforcement policies by diminishing foreign firms' incentive to cooperate with antitrust authorities in return for prosecutorial amnesty . . . Respondents alternatively argue that comity does not demand an interpretation of the FTAIA that would exclude independent foreign injury cases across the board. Rather, courts can take (and sometimes have taken) account of comity considerations case by case, abstaining where comity considerations so dictate. Cf., e.g., *Hartford Fire*, supra, at 797, n. 24; *United States* v. *Nippon Paper Industries Co.*, 109 F. 3d 1, 8 (CA1 1997); *Mannington Mills, Inc* v. *Congoleum Corp*, 595 F. 2d 1287, 1294–1295 (CA3 1979).

In our view, however, this approach is too complex to prove workable. The Sherman Act covers many different kinds of anti-competitive agreements. Courts would have to examine how foreign law, compared with American law, treats not only price fixing but also, say, information-sharing agreements, patent-licensing price conditions, territorial product resale limitations, and various forms of joint venture, in respect to both primary conduct and remedy. The legally and economically technical nature of that enterprise means lengthier proceedings, appeals, and more proceedings—to the point where procedural costs and delays could themselves threaten interference with a foreign nation's ability to maintain the integrity of its own antitrust enforcement system. Even in this relatively simple price-fixing case, for example, competing briefs tell us (1) that potential treble-damage liability would help enforce widespread anti-price-fixing norms (through added deterrence) and (2) the opposite, namely that such liability would hinder antitrust enforcement (by reducing incentives to enter amnesty programs). Compare, e.g., Brief for Certain Professors of Economics as Amici Curiae 2–4 with Brief for United States as Amicus Curiae 19–21. How could a court seriously interested in resolving so empirical a matter—a matter potentially related to impact on foreign interests—do so simply and expeditiously?

We conclude that principles of prescriptive comity counsel against the Court of Appeals' interpretation of the FTAIA. Where foreign anti-competitive conduct plays a significant role and where foreign injury is independent of domestic effects, Congress might have hoped that America's antitrust laws, so fundamental a component of our own economic system, would commend themselves to other nations as well. But, if America's antitrust policies could not win their own way in the international marketplace for such ideas, Congress, we must assume, would not have tried to impose them, in an act of legal imperialism, through legislative fiat.

The Supreme Court went on to consider the legislative history of the FTAIA and concluded that 'the FTAIA's language and history suggest that Congress designed the FTAIA to clarify, perhaps to limit, but not to expand in any significant way, the Sherman Act's scope as applied to foreign commerce'.

It will be noted that in the extract above the Supreme Court showed great sensitivity to the question of international comity. The effects doctrine is to 'redress domestic antitrust injury' and the court considered there is no justification for trespassing on the preserve of foreign sovereigns by taking action against purely foreign injury. Several foreign governments (including the UK) submitted briefs to the Supreme Court arguing against the US courts taking jurisdiction, and the Supreme Court took these views very seriously.[56]

Nevertheless, it is important to note exactly what the Supreme Court held. Because of the way in which the case was pleaded and argued it based its judgment on the assumption that the foreign effects of the cartel were quite independent of its effects in the US. It left open the question of what would be the position if the foreign and domestic effects could be shown to be intertwined e.g., if the prices abroad would have been lower had it not been for the effects in the US. However, in *Re Monosodium Glutamate Antitrust Litigation* the US Court of Appeals for the 8th Circuit upheld a ruling excluding foreign plaintiffs from bringing a class action against manufacturers involved in a cartel. The Court said that 'the domestic effects of the price fixing scheme—increased US prices—were not the direct cause of the appellants' injuries. Rather it was the foreign effects of the price fixing scheme—increased prices abroad.'[57] The Court set a high standard of proof for any effect on US commerce and rejected claims that a worldwide conspiracy in which prices must be inflated in every market (to avoid arbitrage) could satisfy the standard.

E. DISCOVERY IN US COURTS

In *Intel Corp v, Advanced Micro Devices Inc*[58] the Supreme Court delivered a judgment in a case in which a complainant to the EC Commission against the microprocessor firm, Intel, wanted production of documents that had surfaced in an action against Intel in the US. Federal district courts have authority to assist in the production of evidence for use in a 'foreign or international tribunal'. The Commission refused to ask the US courts for discovery. The Supreme Court held that although the CFI and ECJ did not themselves take proof, they did qualify as 'tribunals' which could review the decision of the Commission before which the documents could be used. This was sufficient for the Supreme Court to uphold the Court of Appeal's ruling[59] that discovery should be granted, despite the Commission's lack of support for AMD's request.

F. THE EFFECTS DOCTRINE AND FOREIGN CONDUCT AFFECTING EXPORTS

The FTAIA says that the Sherman Act only applies to export commerce where the conduct has a direct, substantial and reasonably foreseeable effect on US commerce. It can be argued, however, that if US exports are injured by being denied access to foreign markets there may be a disadvantageous effect on commerce inside the US. Taking jurisdiction where conduct of foreign actors abroad effects the US *export* trade is true extraterritoriality. Although the US agencies consider that they do in theory have jurisdiction over conduct abroad which affects exports,[60]

---

[56] On remand, the DC Circuit ruled for the defendants, 417 F.3d 1267 (D.C.Cir, 2005).

[57] 477 F.3d 535 (8th Cir 2007).

[58] 542 US 155 (2004).

[59] 292 F.3d 664 (2004).

[60] Antitrust Enforcement Guidelines for International Operations, para. 3.1222.

they do not usually take action against it.[61] Indeed, the practical enforcement problems are very great. In the *Fuji* case the US tried to use trade rather than competition law to advance the interests of its exporters. Kodak alleged that it was unable to penetrate the Japanese market because of anti-competitive activites there, in particular on the part of Fuji's distributors, despite the existence of Japanese anti-monopoly laws. Kodak brought a section 301 Trade Act 1974 petition in the US and the US Trade Representative referred the Japanese government's conduct in tolerating the anti-competitive behaviour to the WTO. Access to the WTO dispute resolution process is limited to governments. The WTO panel held that the WTO rules apply only to governments and that it is not open to governments to attack private measures in this way.[62] This showed that the WTO rules cannot be used to force open foreign markets which are obstructed by private conduct.

4. INTERNATIONAL LAW

Given the controversy the US effects doctrine has generated, it is interesting to consider whether or not it is in conformity with international law.[63] There is no clear answer to this. The US government considers that the effects doctrine, whereby it asserts jurisdiction based on 'direct, substantial, and reasonably foreseeable' effects within the United States is in accordance with international law. Other governments disagree.[64]

It is generally accepted that the two undoubted bases for criminal jurisdiction[65] in international law are nationality and territory. There are two aspects to territoriality: subjective and objective. Subjective territoriality gives a State jurisdiction over acts which originated within its territory but were completed abroad. Objective territoriality gives a State jurisdiction over acts which originated abroad but were completed, at least partially, within its own territory. Objective territoriality was recognized by the Permanent Court of International Justice in the *Lotus* case.[66] However, there is continuing uncertainty about what *Lotus* actually decided. It can be argued both that the effects doctrine is validly derived from the principle of objective territoriality recognized in *Lotus* and that it is an illegitimate extension which is

---

[61] But see *United States v. Pilkington* (1994–2) Trade Cases, para. 482.

[62] *Japan—Measures Affecting Consumer Photographic Film and Paper* WT/DS44/R, 31 Mar. 1998.

[63] There is an enormous literature on jurisdiction in international law, a complex issue of which the question of jurisdiction in competition law is but a small part. See, e.g., M. Akehurst, 'Jurisdiction in International Law' (1972–3) 46 *BYIL*, 145; F. A. Mann, 'The Doctrine of International Jurisdiction Revisited After Twenty Years' (1984) 156 *RdC* 9; F. A. Mann, 'The Doctrine of Jurisdiction in International Law' (1964) 111 *RdC* 3; D. W. Bowett, 'Jurisdiction: Changing Problems of Authority over Activities and Resources' (1982) 53 *BYIL*, R. Y. Jennings and A. D. Watts (eds.), *Oppenheim's International Law* (9th edn., Longman, 1992), i, 456; O. Schachter, *International Law in Theory and Practice* (Nijhoff, 1991) chap. XII; R. Higgins, *Problems and Process* (Oxford University Press, 1994), chap. 4. With particular reference to antitrust law, see K. M. Meessen, 'Antitrust Jurisdiction under Customary International Law' (1984) 78 *AJIL* 783; P. J. Slot and E. Grabandt, 'Extraterritoriality and Jurisdiction' (1986) 23 *CMLRev* 545; P. M. Roth, 'Reasonable Extraterritoriality: Correcting the "Balance of Interests"' (1992) 41 *ICLQ* 245.

[64] See J. Griffin, 'Reactions to US Assertions of Extraterritorial Jurisdiction' [1998] *ECLR* 64, 68.

[65] It is not clear whether there is any significant difference between jurisdiction in criminal, civil, and monetary matters: see, e.g., I. Brownlie, *Principles of Public International Law* (6th edn., Oxford University Press, 2003), 308; M. Akehurst, 'Jurisdiction in International Law' (1972–3) 46 *BYIL* 145, 177.

[66] (1927), PCIJ, Ser.A, No. 10, 23. The case arose from a collision on the high seas between a French ship and a Turkish ship which led to Turkey instituting criminal proceedings against the officers of the watch on the French ship when it put into a Turkish port. The PCIJ held that international law did not *prevent* Turkey instituting proceedings: it was not asked whether international law *authorized* it to do so. See J. Griffin, 'Reactions to US Assertions of Extraterritorial Jurisdiction' [1998] *ECLR* 64, 68.

inconsistent with the principle of the sovereignty of nations. The US position is, of course, the former.[67]

Further possible principles of jurisdiction are the passive personality principle, by which States claim jurisdiction over aliens who have committed acts abroad harmful to their nationals, and the protective or security principle[68] by which they claim jurisdiction over aliens for acts committed abroad which harm the security of the State. The latter principle is capable of indefinite expansion and could potentially be used to justify jurisdiction over economic acts.

It should be noted that private international law (conflict of laws), as well as public international law, is relevant to jurisdiction questions in competition cases. Private international law attempts to regulate whether a particular State has jurisdiction to try an issue and which law will be applied in determining it.

The problem for States in applying competition laws extraterritorially is that merely taking legislative (prescriptive) jurisdiction is not enough. As we saw above when discussing US law, it is essential that it has enforcement jurisdiction whereby its authorities can conduct investigations, collect evidence, serve proceedings and recover penalties abroad. The position in international law was surveyed by Advocate General Darmon in his opinion in the leading EC case, *Wood Pulp I*.[69] He recognized the distinction between prescriptive and enforcement jurisdiction and considered that the mere imposition of a pecuniary sanction is a matter of prescriptive jurisdiction, enforcement jurisdiction being involved only when steps are taken for its recovery, because only then is the State taking coercive measures in the territory of a foreign sovereign. He concluded that the effects doctrine was not contrary to international law and that it should be adopted by Community law:

57. . . . there is no rule of international law which is capable of being relied upon against the criterion of the direct, substantial and foreseeable effect. Nor does the concept of international comity, in view of its uncertain scope, militate against the criterion either.

58. In the absence of any such prohibitive rule and in the light of widespread State practice, I would therefore propose that in view of its appropriateness to the field of competition, it be adopted as a criterion for the jurisdiction of the Community.

As we shall see below, the ECJ considered that its taking of jurisdiction in *Wood Pulp* was 'covered by the territoriality principle as universally recognized in public international law'.[70] This may well be unduly sanguine. While there is undoubtedly a territoriality principle in international law, what it covers is far from certain. It appears, however, to be developing in the direction of a formulation which demands a 'substantial and genuine connection' between the subject matter and the source of the jurisdiction and an observance of the principle of non-intervention in the domestic or territorial jurisdiction of other States.[71]

---

[67] See the *Alcoa* case (*supra* n. 14) itself. F. A. Mann, 'The Doctrine of International Jurisdiction Revisited after Twenty Years', (1984) 186 *RdC* 9 concluded that although the effects doctrine is recognized by several countries, it does not seem to be regarded as a principle of international law.

[68] See the *Cutting* case (1886), J. B. Moore, Digest of International Law, Vol. II (1906). A further principle, not relevant here, is the universality principle, where jurisdiction is taken over aliens as a matter of international public policy for crimes such as piracy or aircraft hijacking. Jurisdiction over those who commit war crimes is sometimes seen as part of the universality principle, but may be a separate head of jurisdiction. see I. Brownlie, *Principles of Public International Law* (6th edn., Oxford University Press, 2003), 303.

[69] Cases 89, 104, 114, 116, 117, and 125–9/85, A. Ahlström Oy v. Commission [1988] ECR 5193, [1988] 4 CMLR 901 (*Wood Pulp I*), paras. 19–32 and 47–58 of the Opinion.

[70] *Ibid.*, para. 18.

[71] See, F. A. Mann, 'The Doctrine of Jurisdiction in International Law' (1964) III *RdC* 1; Brownlie, *supra* n. 68.

5. THE POSITION IN EC LAW

A. GENERAL

Articles 81 and 82 are silent on the question whether or not they apply extraterritorially. At first the development of the single economic entity doctrine[72] precluded the need for resolving the issue. However, the point finally had to be dealt with in *Wood Pulp*.[73] The Merger Regulation,[74] while not expressly addressing the extraterritoriality question, contains a jurisdiction threshold which may catch concentrations between undertakings based outside the EC so long as the EC turnover thresholds set out in the Regulation are satisfied.[75] The discussion below establishes that the CFI has dealt with the question of extraterritoriality in respect of mergers differently from the ECJ in respect of Articles 81 and 82.

B. THE *DYESTUFFS* CASE

In 1972 in *Béguelin*,[76] a case concerning a Japanese manufacturer whose distribution arrangements with its French distributor compartmentalized the common market on national lines the ECJ held that the agreement infringed Article 81(1). As one of the parties to the agreement was clearly within the Community, and in the context of the case the imposition of a penalty on the Japanese undertaking did not arise, jurisdiction could be asserted without the question of an effects doctrine having to be faced.

In the *Dyestuffs* case[77] the question whether EC law had an effects doctrine was raised for the first time. The Commission investigated an alleged cartel among the producers of aniline dyes. It found, *inter alia*, that ICI, a company incorporated and having its headquarters in the UK which was not at that time a member of the Community, had engaged in concerted practices contrary to Article 81(1) by virtue of the instructions it had given to its Belgian subsidiary. It imposed a fine of 50,000 units of account on ICI.[78] In paragraph 28 of the Decision the Commission said:

Under Article [81](1) of the Treaty instituting the [EC] all agreements between undertakings, all decisions by associations of undertakings and all concerted practices which may affect trade between Member States and the object or effect of which is to prevent, restrict or distort competition within the Common Market shall be prohibited as incompatible with the Common Market. The competition rules of the Treaty are, consequently, applicable to all restrictions of competition which produce within the Common Market effects set out in Article [81](1). There is therefore no need to examine whether the undertakings which are the cause of these restrictions of competition have their seat within or outside the Community.

It will be noted that here the Commission applied an 'effects' doctrine without any further amplification. The ICI appealed against the Commission decision, *inter alia*, on the jurisdiction

---

[72] See *supra* Chap. 3.

[73] Cases 89, 104, 114, 116, 117, and 125–9/85, *A. Ahlström Oy v. Commission* [1988] ECR 5193, [1988] 4 CMLR 901.

[74] Council Reg. 139/2004 [2004] L 24/1.

[75] For the Community dimension threshold generally, see *supra* Chap. 12.

[76] Case 22/71, *Béguelin Import Co v. GL Import Export* [1971] ECR 949, [1972] CMLR 81.

[77] Case 48/69, *ICI v. Commission (Dyestuffs)* [1972] ECR 619, [1972] CMLR 557. The case was also an important early decision on concerted practices: see *supra* Chap. 11.

[78] *Re the Cartel in Aniline Dyes* [1969] OJ L195/11, [1969] CMLR D23.

point. It claimed that the Commission had no power to apply the competition rules to an undertaking established outside the (then) EEC. In reply the Commission relied not just on an elaboration of the effects doctrine but also on the claim that, although the subsidiaries within the Community had separate legal personality in law, the reality was that they were merely carrying out the parent's orders, so that subsidiaries appeared 'as mere extensions of ICI in the Common Market'.[79]

Advocate General Mayras recommended that the Commission's decision should be upheld on the basis of the 'effects doctrine'. He reviewed the national laws of the Member States on this issue, the international law arguments, and, of course, US law. He said that the conditions necessary for taking extraterritorial jurisdiction were that the agreement or concerted practice must create a *direct and immediate* restriction of competition, that the effect of the conduct must be *reasonably foreseeable*, and that the effect produced on the territory must be *substantial*. The Advocate General justified this adoption of what amounted to an effects doctrine not just by reference to principle, but also on grounds of pragmatism.[80]

Just as it would be quite wrong to reduce the concept of a concerted practice to so narrow a meaning that it would no longer connote anything more than a particular expression of the concept of an agreement, the obvious risk being that Article [81](1) would not be given the effective scope intended by the authors of the Treaty, so—subject to a reservation concerning powers of enforcement—that article would be drained of a large part of its meaning and at any rate its force would be dissipated if the Community authorities were denied the use in relation to any undertaking outside the Common Market of the powers that that same Article [81] confers on them. Surely the Commission would be disarmed if, faced with a concerted practice the initiative for which was taken and the responsibility for which was assumed exclusively by undertakings outside the Common Market, it was deprived of the power to take any decision against them? This would also mean giving up a way of defending the Common Market and one necessary for bringing about the major objectives of the European Economic Community.

He drew a distinction, however, between prescriptive and enforcement jurisdiction. He considered that the *imposition* of fines is part of the legislative (prescriptive) jurisdiction, whereas their *recovery* (or other measures, such as the annulment of contracts) amounts to enforcement jurisdiction. He was prepared to accept that the decision taken by the Commission might not be capable of enforcement:[81]

the courts or administrative authorities of a State—and, *mutatis mutandis*, of the Community—are certainly not justified under international law in taking coercive measures or indeed any measure of inquiry, investigation or supervision outside their territorial jurisdiction where execution would inevitably infringe the internal sovereignty of the State on the territory of which they claimed to act.

In its judgment the ECJ did not take up its Advocate General's espousal of an effects doctrine. Instead it upheld the Commission's decision on the basis of what has become known as the single economic entity doctrine. It is explained in Chapter 3 that Community law has developed this doctrine by which parents and subsidiaries are considered to be one undertaking for the purposes of the application of the competition rules. In *Dyestuffs* the Court relied on this concept to impute the conduct of the subsidiary to the parent and to hold that the Commission did have jurisdiction over the UK company.

---

[79] Case 48/69, *ICI v. Commission (Dyestuffs)* [1972] ECR 619, 627.

[80] *Ibid.*, 696.

[81] *Ibid.*, 695.

Case 48/69, *ICI* v. *Commission (Dyestuffs)* [1972] ECR 619, [1972] CMLR 557

The Court of Justice

130. By making use of its power to control its subsidiaries established in the Community, the applicant was able to ensure that its decision was implemented on that market.

131. The applicant objects that this conduct is to be imputed to its subsidiaries and not to itself.

132. The fact that a subsidiary has separate legal personality is not sufficient to exclude the possibility of imputing its conduct to the parent company.

133. Such may be the case in particular where the subsidiary, although having separate legal personality, does not decide independently upon its own conduct on the market, but carries out, in all material respects, the instructions given to it by the parent company.

134. Where a subsidiary does not enjoy real autonomy in determining its course of action in the market, the prohibitions set out in Article [81(1)] may be considered inapplicable in the relationship between it and the parent company with which it forms one economic unit.

135. In view of the unity of the group thus formed, the actions of the subsidiaries may in certain circumstances be attributed to the parent company.

136. It is well-known that at the time the applicant held all or at any rate the majority of the shares in those subsidiaries.

137. The applicant was able to exercise decisive influence over the policy of the subsidiaries as regards selling prices in the Common Market and in fact used this power upon the occasion of the three price increases in question.

138. In effect the Telex messages relating to the 1964 increase, which the applicant sent to its subsidiaries in the Common Market, gave the addressees orders as to the prices which they were to charge and the other conditions of sale which they were to apply in dealing with their customers.

139. In the absence of evidence to the contrary, it must be assumed that on the occasion of the increases of 1965 and 1967 the applicant acted in a similar fashion in its relation with its subsidiaries established in the Common Market.

140. In the circumstances the formal separation between these companies, resulting from their separate legal personality, cannot outweight the unity of their conduct on the market for the purposes of applying the rules on competition.

141. It was in fact the applicant undertaking which brought the concerted practice into being within the Common Market.

142. The submission as to lack of jurisdiction raised by the applicant must therefore be declared to be unfounded.

The Court therefore held here that the subsidiary did not have 'real autonomy' but acted on its parent's instructions, so that the infringing conduct in the EEC could be treated as having been committed by the subsidiary as an agent of the parent.[82]

The application of the single economic entity doctrine to take what is in effect extraterritorial jurisdiction has its opponents. At the time of *Dyestuffs* the UK government disputed the disregarding of the legal separation between parent and subsidiary.

---

[82] F. A. Mann argued that the facts of the case did not support this conclusion: (1973) 22 *ICLQ* 35 and 'Reponsibility of Parent Companies for Foreign Subsidiaries' in C. Olmstead (ed.), *Extra-territorial Application of Laws and Responses Thereto* (ESC Publishing, 1984), 156.

The UK has, however, since dropped its hostility to this concept and the Competition Act 1998 receives it fully into UK law, along with the other jurisprudence of the Court on the competition rules.[83] However, it is worth noting that many countries continue to have particular concerns about the application of a similar concept in US law. As Griffin explains:[84]

Nearly all nations agree that nationality can be a valid basis for asserting extraterritorial jurisdiction. However, U.S. assertions of jurisdiction based upon the control exercised by an American parent over a subsidiary incorporated and operating abroad are not accepted as valid under international law by a number of nations. These nations contend that despite the American parent's majority ownership or its possession of effective working control, under international law nationality is properly determined by the place of incorporation ... Moreover, according to one knowledgeable British official,[85] 'even where nationality is a legitimate basis for extraterritorial jurisdiction it must remain subject to the primacy of the laws and policies of the territorial state.' ... U.S. officials typically respond to these contentions with the assertion that they cannot permit 'technicalities' such as the place of incorporation and inconsistent policies of host states to be used by American companies to evade their obligations under U.S. law ...

In *Dyestuffs* the ECJ neither approved nor disapproved the views of its Advocate General on the effects doctrine. It clearly preferred to proceed on the other available ground which was less controversial. Its silence on the point, however, encouraged the Commission's belief that Community law did recognize the effects doctrine.

C. THE *WOODPULP* CASE

Finally, a case came before the ECJ in which the existence or otherwise of an effects doctrine, or something similar, in EC law was addressed. This was *Wood Pulp I*, a leading case on cartels which is discussed in Chapter 11. The Commission investigated alleged price-fixing in the wood pulp industry. It found that a cartel existed, and held that forty-one producers and two trade associations (Finncell and KEA) had engaged in concerted practices contrary to Article 81(1). It imposed fines on thirty-six of the addressees.[86] All forty-three producers and trade associations concerned had their registered offices outside the EC. Most, if not all, of the producers had 'branches, subsidiaries, agencies or other establishments within the Community'.[87]

Many of the addressees appealed. There were two grounds: first that the Commission had no jurisdiction to apply its competition law to the addressees and, secondly, that they had not participated in concerted practices. The Court decided to hear the plea about the jurisdiction first.[88]

As already noted[89] Advocate General Darmon engaged in a lengthy survey of the relevant international and US law and the scholarly literature and concluded that the Community was

---

[83] Competition Act 1998, s. 60.

[84] J. Griffin, 'Reactions to US Assertions of Extraterritorial Jurisdiction' [1998] *ECLR* 64, 69.

[85] The reference is to William M. Knighton, *Nationality and Extraterritorial Jurisdiction: US Law Abroad*, Remarks before the International Law Institute of the Georgetown University Law Center 2, 13 Aug. 1981.

[86] *Wood Pulp* [1985] OJ L85/1, [1985] 3 CMLR 474.

[87] Only some of them did according to para. 79 of the Decision, [1988] OJ L85/1, but later, in its rejoinder before the Court, the Commission stated that all of them did: see W. van Gerven, 'EC Jurisdiction in Antitrust Matters: The Wood Pulp Judgment' [1989] *Fordham Corporate Law Institute* 451, 464.

[88] This is therefore colloquially known as *Wood Pulp I*. The judgment on the substantive issue is known as *Wood Pulp II*. Cases C-89/85, etc., A. *Ahlström Oy v. Commission* [1993] ECR I-1307, [1993] 4 CMLR 407.

[89] *Supra* 1370.

entitled to take, and should take, jurisdiction in this case on the basis of the effects doctrine. The Court, however, couched its judgment in slightly different terms:

Cases 89, 104, 114, 116, 117, and 125–9/85, *A. Ahlström Oy* v. *Commission* [1988] ECR 5193, [1988] 4 CMLR 901[90]

Court of Justice

11. In so far as the submission concerning the infringement of Article [81] of the Treaty itself is concerned, it should be recalled that that provision prohibits all agreements between undertakings and concerted practices which may affect trade between Member States and which have as their object or effect the restriction of competition within the Common Market.

12. It should be noted that the main sources of supply of wood pulp are outside the Community, in Canada, the United States, Sweden and Finland and that the market therefore has global dimensions. Where wood pulp producers established in those countries sell directly to purchasers established in the Community and engage in price competition in order to win orders from those customers, that constitutes competition within the Common Market.

13. It follows that where those producers concert on the prices to be charged to their customers in the Community and put that concertation into effect by selling at prices which are actually coordinated, they are taking part in concertation which has the object and effect of restricting competition within the Common Market within the meaning of Article [81] of the Treaty.

14. Accordingly, it must be concluded that by applying the competition rules in the Treaty in the circumstances of this case to undertakings whose registered offices are situated outside the Community, the Commission has not made an incorrect assessment of the territorial scope of Article [81].

15. The applicants have submitted that the decision is incompatible with public international law on the grounds that the application of the competition rules in this case was founded exclusively on the economic repercussions within the Common Market of conduct restricting competition which has adopted outside the Community.

16. It should be observed that an infringement of Article [81], such as the conclusion of an agreement which has had the effect of restricting competition within the Common Market, consists of conduct made up of two elements, the formation of the agreement, decision or concerted practice and the implementation thereof. If the applicability of prohibitions laid down under competition law were made to depend on the place where the agreement, decision or concerted practice was formed, the result would obviously be to give undertakings an easy means of evading those prohibitions. The decisive factor is therefore the place where it is implemented.

17. The producers in this case implemented their pricing agreement within the Common Market. It is immaterial in that respect whether or not they had recourse to subsidiaries, agents, sub-agents, or branches within the Community in order to make their contacts with purchasers within the Community.

18. Accordingly the Community's jurisdiction to apply its competition rules to such conduct is covered by the territoriality principle as universally recognized in public international law.

19. As regards the argument based on the infringement of the principle of non-interference, it should be pointed out that the applicants who are members of KEA have referred to a rule according to which where two States have jurisdiction to lay down and enforce rules and the effect of those rules is that a person finds himself subject to contradictory orders as to the conduct he must

---

[90] See generally W. van Gerven, 'EC Jurisdiction in Antitrust Matters: The Wood Pulp Judgment' [1989] *Fordham Corp L Inst* 451. Professor van Gerven was at the time of delivering this paper an AG at the ECJ.

adopt, each State is obliged to exercise its jurisdiction with moderation. The applicants have concluded that by disregarding that rule in applying its competition rules the Community has infringed the principle of non-interference.

20. There is no need to enquire into the existence in international law of such a rule since it suffices to observe that the conditions for its application are in any event not satisfied. There is not, in this case, any contradiction between the conduct required by the United States and that required by the Community since the Webb–Pomerene Act[91] merely exempts the conclusion of export cartels from the application of United States antitrust laws but does not require such cartels to be concluded.

21. It should further be pointed out that the United States authorities raised no objections regarding any conflict of jurisdiction when consulted by the Commission pursuant to the OECD Council Recommendation of 25 October 1979 concerning co-operation between Member Countries on Restrictive Business Practices affecting International Trade . . .

22. As regards the argument relating to disregard of international comity, it suffices to observe that it amounts to calling in question the Community's jurisdiction to apply its competition rules to conduct such as that found to exist in this case and that, as such, that argument has already been rejected.

23. Accordingly it must be concluded that the Commission's decision is not contrary to Article [81] of the Treaty or to the rules of public international law relied on by the applicants.

Significantly, this judgment avoided talking about 'effects'. Given the terms in which the Commission decision, the arguments before the Court, and the Advocate General's opinion had been couched, this avoidance of specific reference to the effects doctrine must have been deliberate. Instead, the Court talked about 'implementation' (paragraphs 16 and 17).

It will be noted that the judgment above (which comprises the entirety of the section on jurisdiction) falls into distinct parts. First, paragraphs 11–14 deal with whether or not the Commission infringed *the Treaty* by applying the competition rules to the individual undertakings.[92] The ECJ held that it had not, as it had correctly assessed the territorial scope of Article 81. Secondly, paragraphs 15–18 consider whether the Commission had infringed *international* law. The Court held that it had not done this either, as the taking of jurisdiction was covered by the 'universally recognized' territoriality principle (paragraph 18). Thirdly, paragraphs 19–22 reject the argument based on a possible 'non-interference' principle by saying that the US legislation did not *require* export cartels to be entered into, but merely tolerated them. This is the same position as that reached by the Supreme Court in *Hartford Fire* in respect of the UK legislation.

In paragraph 16 the Court divided the infringing conduct into two elements, the formation of the agreement and its implementation. It did not matter where the formation of the agreement took place: the decisive factor was the place where it was 'implemented'.

The crucial question is what is meant by 'implementation' and how, if at all, this differs from the effects doctrine? The first thing to note is that the Court said in paragraph 17 that it was immaterial whether or not the producers used subsidiaries, agents, sub-agents, or branches inside the Community. This means that 'implementation' covers *direct sales* to Community purchasers and does not depend on the sellers establishing some form of marketing organization

---

[91] The Webb-Pomerene Act 1918 is a US statute which allows American exporters to act together in export markets in ways which would otherwise violate the Sherman Act.

[92] As far as the applicant trade association, KEA, was concerned, the Court annulled the decision because it held that KEA had not played a separate role in the implementation of the price-fixing agreements: judgment [1988] ECR 5193 paras. 24–28).

within the Community. Jurisdiction is taken simply because of sales into the Community. Some commentators believe that this is not justified in international law. Van Gerven, for example, has argued:[93]

Accepting this type of conduct [i.e., setting up a marketing organisation and using it to give effect to a cartel] does not, I believe, unduly stretch the underlying strict territoriality and is, therefore, as indicated above, compatible with public international law. That cannot be said, however, of conduct which amounts to selling directly to purchasers within the Community, even when selling takes place through authorized but independent distributors or dealers that are doing business on their own behalf. Selling from abroad to purchasers and/or independent distributors or dealers within the regulating State cannot, I submit, reasonably be qualified as conduct of the 'parent' itself, or conduct imputable to it within the Common Market, because it does not constitute a sufficiently close and relevant link with the regulating State that is compelling enough to justify jurisdiction on its part. If the mere fact of selling directly in the territory (without requiring any permanent presence in the form of a sales organization, be it only a sales agent or sales representative) amounts to implementing conduct, then such a loose 'point of contact' can confer jurisdiction upon many States, thereby depriving the point of contact of its true content . . . The mere statement that the exercise of jurisdiction in such circumstances is permitted by the strict territoriality test, is of course, no proof of sufficient respect for that principle. It follows therefrom that I am not in a position to subscribe to the Court's statement in the *Wood Pulp* judgment that '[i]t is immaterial . . . whether or not [the undertakings] had recourse to subsidiaries, agents, sub-agents, or branches within the Community' . . .

A second point to note is that the preponderant view is that 'implementation' would *not* cover negative behaviour such as agreements concluded outside the Community by which undertakings agree not to sell within the Community, or agree not to purchase from Community producers.[94] However, such conduct could, it is argued, fall within the effects doctrine.[95]

In *Wood Pulp*, therefore, the Court confirmed that Article 81[96] could be applied extraterritorially, but did so by enunciating a Community concept of extraterritorial jurisdiction based on implementation rather than by adopting the effects doctrine as developed in US law. However, it is now necessary to consider the *Wood Pulp* judgment in the light of the case law under the ECMR.

D. THE MERGER REGULATION

(i) The Terms of the Merger Regulation

As is explained in Chapter 12, the EC Merger Regulation[97] provides that the Commission has sole jurisdiction[98] over concentrations with a 'Community dimension'.[99] The meaning of a

---

[93] W. van Gerven, 'EC Jurisdiction in Antitrust Matters: The Wood Pulp Judgment' [1989] *Fordham Corp L Inst* 451, 470.

[94] See, e.g., Griffin, *supra* n. 84; Van Gerven, *supra* n. 90. Van Gerven's view is also that any attempt to encompass such conduct within 'implementation' would be contrary to international law as there would not be a sufficiently close link to support jurisdiction.

[95] Griffin, *supra* n. 84.

[96] And presumably also Article 82.

[97] For the Merger Reg. 139/2004 [2004] L24/1 (replacing Reg. 4064/89 [1989] OJ 395/1) generally, see *supra* Chap. 12.

[98] Subject to certain exceptions, discussed in Chap. 12, such as Article 9 which allows for concentrations to be referred back to national authorities.

[99] For a full analysis of the 'Community dimension' see M. Broberg, *The European Commission's Jurisdiction to Scrutinise Mergers* (3rd edn., Kluwer, 2006).

'Community dimension' is set out in Article 1. Under Article 1(2) a concentration will have a Community dimension if the worldwide (€5,000 million) and Community-wide (€250 million) turnover thresholds are met. There is a proviso which excludes concentrations in which the undertakings concerned achieve at least two-thirds of the Community-wide turnover in the same Member State. An alternative set of thresholds is provided by Article 1(3).[100] Further, it should be noted that recital 10 of the Regulation states that a Community dimension exists where the thresholds are exceeded and 'that is the case irrespective of whether or not the undertakings have their seat or their principal fields of activity in the Community provided they have substantial operations there'.[101]

Article 1 does not, however, expressly say anything about where the undertakings concerned are incorporated, or carry on business, or whether the undertakings must have assets in the Community. Its criteria relate only to a worldwide turnover figure and a much smaller Community-wide turnover figure. Article 5, which deals with the calculation of turnover, says that '[t]urnover in the Community or in a Member State, shall comprise products sold and services provided to undertakings or consumers, in the Community or in that Member State as the case may be'.[102] The main reason for the orginal Merger Regulation not directly addressing the jurisdiction issue seems to be that the Council Working Group was dealing with the details of the Regulation at the time *Wood Pulp I* was before the Court. In the light of the problems raised in that case express references to jurisdiction were deleted from the final version.[103]

As a result of this jurisdictional test it was inevitable that undertakings established abroad would be drawn into the net of Community merger control by involvement in transactions with Community undertakings. The way that the Community dimension threshold is formulated, however, can also catch transactions which involve *only* undertakings located outside the Community with few assets inside it, and transactions which have minimal impact inside the Community. The broad jurisdiction is unlikely to cause great problems in most cases, in that the concentration concerned will clearly not be incompatible with the common market under the test in Article 2.[104] In a number of cases, involving for example Japanese banks, foreign undertakings have notified the Commission and duly got their Article 6(1) clearance within a month.[105] Even so, non-EC undertakings may object to the Commission's jurisdiction, particularly where the Commission is unhappy about a concentration.

(ii) The *Gencor* Case

In *Gencor/Lonrho* the Commission prohibited a merger in the South African platinum and rhodium industry,[106] on the ground that it would create a position of oligopolistic

---

[100] The object of this additional set of criteria is to provide for concentrations which do not reach the Article 1(2) thresholds and which might otherwise fall to be dealt with by several national merger authorities in the EC.

[101] The equivalent recital (11) in the old ECMR, Reg. 4064/89, was discussed in the *Gencor* judgment *infra* 1381: see Case T-102/96, *Gencor Ltd v. Commission* [1999] ECR II-753, [1999] 4 CMLR 971 at paras. 83–5.

[102] Merger Reg., Art. 5(1), second para.

[103] See C. J. Cook and C. S. Kerse, *EC Merger Control* (3rd edn., Sweet & Maxwell, 2000), 11–12.

[104] See Chap. 12.

[105] See, e.g., *Kyowa/Saitama Banks* [1992] 4 CMLR 1186; *Matsushita/MCA* [1992] 4 CMLR M36.

[106] Case IV/M 619, [1997] OJ L11/30, [1999] 4 CMLR 1076.

dominance.[107] One of the parties appealed, *inter alia*, on the ground that the Commission had no jurisdiction over the transaction.[108]

The case concerned a proposed merger between the platinum and rhodium mining interests in South Africa of Gencor and LPD. Both were companies incorporated in South Africa, although LPD was a subsidiary of Lonrho, which was incorporated in London. LPD's sales worldwide were made through Lonrho's Belgian subsidiary. Platinum group metal (PGM) is sold throughout the world, mainly in Japan (approximately 50 per cent of world demand), and North America and Western Europe (approximately 20 per cent each).[109] Approximately 70–75 per cent of the world supply of PGM comes from South Africa and 22–25 per cent from Russia[110] (although South Africa has 90 per cent of the world reserves). In South Africa the largest producer was Anglo-American, which was also incorporated there. The companies' sales figures were deleted from the published decision as business secrets, but it seems that Anglo-American probably had 35–50 per cent of world sales and LPD and Gencor 15–17 per cent each.[111]

All of Gencor's and LPD's production was in South Africa. The proposed merger was notified to the South African authorities, which found that there were no competition problems. The Deputy Foreign Minister told the Commission that he would not contest the Commission's policy, but that the South African government considered that two equally matched competitors (as Anglo-American and Gencor/Lonrho would be) were preferable to the prevailing situation of one dominant firm (Anglo-American).[112] The merger had a Community dimension because of the worldwide and Community-wide turnover of Gencor and Lonrho. The Commission found the merger to be incompatible with the common market on account of the effect which the creation of the dominant duopoly position would have on *sales* of PGM in the Community.

Gencor contested the Commission's assumption of jurisdiction before the CFI. It argued[113] that the Merger Regulation is applicable only if the activities forming the subject matter of the concentration are located within the Community. The location of the concentration was South Africa, and if the *Wood Pulp* test was applied the concentration was implemented in South Africa, not the Community. South Africa had approved the merger. Moreover, Gencor claimed, even if the test for jurisdiction *was* whether the merger had an immediate and substantial effect on competition within the Community, that test was not satisfied either: 'the Commission cannot claim jurisdiction in respect of a concentration on the basis of future and hypothetical behaviour in which undertakings in the relevant market might engage and which might or might not fall within its purview under the Treaty'.[114] The CFI, however,

---

[107] For this aspect of the case see *supra* Chap. 11 and 12.

[108] Once the Commission had blocked the merger there was no possibility of the transaction going ahead, since under the agreement between the parties it was a condition precedent that clearance from the Commission should be obtained by a certain date. The entire purchase agreement had therefore lapsed. Nevertheless, the CFI held that the action for annulment was still admissible since the applicant had an interest in having the legality of the decision addressed to it examined by the Community judicature: Case T-102/96, *Gencor Ltd* v. *Commission* [1999] ECR II-753, [1999] 4 CMLR 971, paras. 40–6.

[109] For the exact figures from 1991–5 see table 5 in, Case IV/M619, *Gencor/Lonrho* [1997] OJ L11/30, [1999] 4 CMLR 1076.

[110] *Ibid.*, table 2.

[111] See the figures extrapolated from the information in the decision in E. Fox, 'The Merger Regulation and its Territorial Reach', [1999] *ECLR* 334, 334.

[112] Para. 19 of the judgment.

[113] [1999] ECR II-753, 4 CMLR 971, paras. 48–63 of the judgment.

[114] *Ibid.*, para. 61.

upheld the Commission's decision.

Case T-102/96, *Gencor Ltd* v. *Commission* [1999] ECR II-753, [1999] 4 CMLR 971

Court of First Instance

78. The Regulation, in accordance with Article 1 thereof, applies to all concentrations with a Community dimension, that is to say to all concentrations between undertakings which do not each achieve more than two-thirds of their aggregate Community-wide turnover within one and the same Member State, where the combined aggregate worldwide turnover of those undertakings is more than ECU 5000 million and the aggregate Community-wide turnover of at least two of them is more than ECU 250 million.

79. Article 1 does not require that, in order for a concentration to be regarded as having a Community dimension, the undertakings in question must be established in the Community or that the production activities covered by the concentration must be carried out within Community territory.

80. With regard to the criterion of turnover, it must be stated that, as set out in paragraph 13 of the contested decision, the concentration at issue has a Community dimension within the meaning of Article 1(2) of the Regulation. The undertakings concerned have an aggregate world-wide turnover of more than ECU 10 000 million, above the ECU 5000 million threshold laid down by the Regulation. Gencor and Lonrho each had a Community-wide turnover of more than ECU 250 million in the latest financial year. Finally, they do not each achieve more than two-thirds of their aggregate Community-wide turnover within one and the same Member State.

81. The applicant's arguments to the effect that the legal bases for the Regulation and the wording of its preamble and substantive provisions preclude its application to the concentration at issue cannot be accepted.

82. The legal bases for the Regulation, namely Articles [83] and [308] of the Treaty, and more particularly the provisions to which they are intended to give effect, that is to say Articles 3[(1)(g)] and [81] and [82] of the Treaty, as well as the first to fifth, ninth and eleventh recitals in the preamble to the Regulation, merely point to the need to ensure that competition is not distorted in the common market, in particular by concentrations which result in the creation or strengthening of a dominant position. They in no way exclude from the Regulation's field of application concentrations which, while relating to mining and/or production activities outside the Community, have the effect of creating or strengthening a dominant position as a result of which effective competition in the common market is significantly impeded.

83. In particular, the applicant's view cannot be founded on the closing words of the 11th recital in the preamble to the Regulation.

84. That recital states that 'a concentration with a Community dimension exists . . . where the concentrations are effected by undertakings which do not have their principal fields of activities in the Community but which have substantial operations there'.

85. By that reference, in general terms, to the concept of substantial operations, the Regulation does not, for the purpose of defining its territorial scope, ascribe greater importance to production operations than to sales operations. On the contrary, by setting quantitative thresholds in Article 1 which are based on the worldwide and Community turnover of the undertakings concerned, it rather ascribes greater importance to sales operations within the common market as a factor linking the concentration to the Community. It is common ground that Gencor and Lonrho each carry out significant sales in the Community (valued in excess of ECU 250 million).

86. Nor is it borne out by either the 30th recital in the preamble to the Regulation or Article 24 thereof that the criterion based on the location of production activities is well founded. Far from laying down a criterion for defining the territorial scope of the Regulation, Article 24 merely regulates the procedures to be followed in order to deal with situations in which non-member countries do not grant Community undertakings treatment comparable to that accorded by the Community to undertakings from those non-member countries in relation to the control of concentrations.

87. The applicant cannot, by reference to the judgment in *Wood Pulp*, rely on the criterion as to the implementation of an agreement to support its interpretation of the territorial scope of the Regulation. Far from supporting the applicant's view, that criterion for assessing the link between an agreement and Community territory in fact precludes it. According to *Wood Pulp*, the criterion as to the implementation of an agreement is satisfied by mere sale within the Community, irrespective of the location of the sources of supply and the production plant. It is not disputed that Gencor and Lonrho carried out sales in the Community before the concentration and would have continued to do so thereafter.

88. Accordingly, the Commission did not err in its assessment of the territorial scope of the Regulation by applying it in this case to a proposed concentration notified by undertakings whose registered offices and mining and production operations are outside the Community.

2. Compatibility of the contested decision with public international law

89. Following the concentration agreement, the previously existing competitive relationship between Implats and LPD, in particular so far as concerns their sales in the Community, would have come to an end. That would have altered the competitive structure within the common market since, instead of three South African PGM suppliers, there would have remained only two. The implementation of the proposed concentration would have led to the merger not only of the parties' PGM mining and production operations in South Africa but also of their marketing operations throughout the world, particularly in the Community where Implats and LPD achieved significant sales.

90. Application of the Regulation is justified under public international law when it is foreseeable that a proposed concentration will have an immediate and substantial effect in the Community.

91. In that regard, the concentration would, according to the contested decision, have led to the creation of a dominant duopoly on the part of Amplats and Implats/LPD in the platinum and rhodium markets, as a result of which effective competition would have been significantly impeded in the common market within the meaning of Article 2(3) of the Regulation.

92. It is therefore necessary to verify whether the three criteria of immediate, substantial and foreseeable effect are satisfied in this case.

93. With regard, specifically, to the criterion of immediate effect, the words 'medium term' used in paragraphs 206 and 210 of the contested decision in relation to the creation of a dominant duopoly position are, contrary to the applicant's assertion, entirely unambiguous. They clearly refer to the time when it is envisaged that Russian stocks will be exhausted, enabling a dominant duopoly on the part of Amplats and Implats/LPD to be created on the world platinum and rhodium markets and, by the same token, in the Community as a substantial part of those world markets.

94. That dominant position would not be dependent, as the applicant asserts, on the future conduct of the undertaking arising from the concentration and of Amplats but would result, in particular, from the very characteristics of the market and the alteration of its structure. In referring to the future conduct of the parties to the duopoly, the applicant fails to distinguish between abuses of dominant position which those parties might commit in the near or more distant future, which might or might not be controlled by means of Articles [81] and/or [82] of the Treaty, and the

alteration to the structure of the undertakings and of the market to which the concentration would give rise. It is true that the concentration would not necessarily lead to abuses immediately, since that depends on decisions which the parties to the duopoly may or may not take in the future. However, the concentration would have had the direct and immediate effect of creating the conditions in which abuses were not only possible but economically rational, given that the concentration would have significantly impeded effective competition in the market by giving rise to a lasting alteration to the structure of the markets concerned.

95. Accordingly, the concentration would have had an immediate effect in the Community.

96. So far as concerns the criterion of substantial effect, it should be noted that, as held in paragraph 297 below, the Commission established to the requisite legal standard that the concentration would have created a lasting dominant duopoly position in the world platinum and rhodium markets.

97. The applicant cannot maintain that the concentration would not have a substantial effect in the Community in view of the low sales and small market share of the parties to the concentration in the EEA. While the level of sales in western Europe (20 per cent of world demand) and the Community market share of the entity arising from the concentration (. . .) per cent in respect of platinum) were already sufficient grounds for the Community to have jurisdiction in respect of the concentration, the potential impact of the concentration proved even higher than those figures suggested. Given that the concentration would have had the effect of creating a dominant duopoly position in the world platinum and rhodium markets, it is clear that the sales in the Community potentially affected by the concentration would have included not only those of the Implats/LPD undertaking but also those of Amplats (approximately 35 per cent to 50 per cent), which would have represented a more than substantial proportion of platinum and rhodium sales in western Europe and a much higher combined market share held by Implats/LPD and Amplats approximately (. . .) per cent to 65 per cent).

98. Finally, it is not possible to accept the applicant's argument that the creation of the dominant position referred to by the Commission in the contested decision is not of greater concern to the Community than to any other competent body and is even of less concern to it than to others. The fact that, in a world market, other parts of the world are affected by the concentration cannot prevent the Community from exercising its control over a concentration which substantially affects competition within the common market by creating a dominant position.

99. The arguments by which the applicant denies that the concentration would have a substantial effect in the Community must therefore be rejected.

100. As for the criterion of foreseeable effect, it follows from all of the foregoing that it was in fact foreseeable that the effect of creating a dominant duopoly position in a world market would also be to impede competition significantly in the Community, an integral part of that market.

101. It follows that the application of the Regulation to the proposed concentration was consistent with public international law.

102. It is necessary to examine next whether the Community violated a principle of non-interference or the principle of proportionality in exercising that jurisdiction.

103. The applicant's argument that, by virtue of a principle of non-interference, the Commission should have refrained from prohibiting the concentration in order to avoid a conflict of jurisdiction with the South African authorities must be rejected, without it being necessary to consider whether such a rule exists in international law. Suffice it to note that there was no conflict between the course of action required by the South African Government and that required by the Community given that, in their letter of 22 August 1995, the South African competition authorities simply concluded that the concentration agreement did not give rise to any competition policy concerns, without requiring that such an agreement be entered into (see, to that effect, *Wood Pulp*, paragraph 20).

104. In its letter of 19 April 1996 the South African Government, far from calling into question the Community's jurisdiction to rule on the concentration at issue, first simply expressed a general preference, having regard to the strategic importance of mineral exploitation in South Africa, for intervention in specific cases of collusion when they arose and did not specifically comment on the industrial or other merits of the concentration proposed by Gencor and Lonrho. It then merely expressed the view that the proposed concentration might not impede competition, having regard to the economic power of Amplats, the existence of other sources of supply of PGMs and the opportunities for other producers to enter the South African market through the grant of new mining concessions.

105. Finally, neither the applicant nor, indeed, the South African Government in its letter of 19 April 1996 have shown, beyond making mere statements of principle, in what way the proposed concentration would affect the vital economic and/or commercial interests of the Republic of South Africa.

106. As regards the argument that the Community cannot claim to have jurisdiction in respect of a concentration on the basis of future and hypothetical behaviour, namely parallel conduct on the part of the undertakings operating in the relevant market where that conduct might or might not fall within the competence of the Community under the Treaty, it must be stated, as pointed out above in connection with the question whether the concentration has an immediate effect, that, while the elimination of the risk of future abuses may be a legitimate concern of any competent competition authority, the main objective in exercising control over concentrations at Community level is to ensure that the restructuring of undertakings does not result in the creation of positions of economic power which may significantly impede effective competition in the common market. Community jurisdiction is therefore founded, first and foremost, on the need to avoid the establishment of market structures which may create or strengthen a dominant position, and not on the need to control directly possible abuses of a dominant position.

107. Consequently, it is unnecessary to rule on the question whether the letter of 22 August 1995 from the South African Competition Board constituted a definitive position on the concentration, on whether or not the South African Government was an authority responsible for competition matters and, finally, on the scope of South African competition law. There is accordingly no need to grant the application for measures of organisation of procedure or of inquiry made by the applicant in its letter of 3 December 1996.

108. In those circumstances, the contested decision is not inconsistent with either the Regulation or the rules of public international law relied on by the applicant.

109. For the same reasons, the objection, based on Article [241] of the Treaty, that the Regulation is unlawful because it confers upon the Commission competence in respect of the concentration between Gencor and Lonrho must be rejected.

110. As regards the reasoning in the contested decision justifying Community jurisdiction to apply the Regulation to the concentration, it must be held that the explanations contained in paragraphs 4, 13 to 18, 204 to 206, 210 and 213 of the contested decision satisfy the obligations incumbent on the Commission under Article [253] of the Treaty to give reasons for its decisions so as to enable the Community judicature to exercise its power of review, the parties to defend their rights and any interested party to ascertain the conditions in which the Commission applied the Treaty and its implementing legislation.

111. Accordingly, both pleas of annulment which have been examined must be rejected, without it being necessary to grant the application for measures of organisation of procedure or of inquiry made by the applicant in its letter of 3 December 1996.

It can be seen from the extract above, that in paragraphs 78–88 the CFI looked first at the Regulation itself. It concluded that it does not matter where the PGM *production* took place, because not only does Article 1 not require that the production should take place in the Community (paragraph 79), it actually accords *greater* importance to *sales*. Further, in the second half of paragraph 87 it returned to the *Wood Pulp* judgment and said that the criterion of the implementation of an agreement is satisfied by *mere sale in the Community*. This point answers the doubt raised in respect of the *Wood Pulp* judgment by Van Gerven, above:[115] mere selling *does* equal implementation.

In paragraphs 89–111, the CFI considered whether the decision was in accordance with public international law. It concluded that it was. In the most significant passage, paragraph 90, the CFI says, in words redolent of the effects doctrine, that the ECMR's application is justified in international law *'when it is foreseeable that a proposed concentration will have an immediate and substantial effect in the Community'*. The CFI did not expressly adopt the effects doctrine, but rather considered that the thresholds were an application of the *Wood Pulp* implementation principle. However, there is a problem[116] in that the ECMR demands prior notification of mergers which fall within its thresholds.[117] It does not follow that all mergers which do that have foreseeable immediate and substantial effects in the Community, and yet the ECMR imposes penalties for non-notification.[118]

Gencor is a striking demonstration of the implications of the effects/implementation doctrine. The EC forbade a merger involving producer undertakings in a non-member country because of the sales of the product (less than a quarter of the worldwide total) in the Community. The interests of South Africa did not come into the equation because South Africa did not *require* the transaction to take place. This raised the non-interference issue discussed in *Wood Pulp* (and in *Hartford Fire*). The CFI concluded that there is no conflict of jurisdiction between a State which prohibits something and a State which allows it (rather than requires it). The difficulty with this is that merger control invariably operates only to forbid certain concentrations, not to require them, and the prohibiting jurisdiction will always trump the other. As Fox argues in the passage below, the *Gencor* transaction between the mining companies was likely to have a more serious impact on the economy of South Africa than on consumers in the EC.

E. Fox, 'The Merger Regulation and its Territorial Reach' [1999] *ECLR* 334, 335–6

The market for platinum is a world market. If the concentration created a market structure that facilitated interdependence and thereby would produce higher prices, the price-raising effect would be equally felt in every country where platinum was sold. The E.U. was one of the three largest consuming regions; and the merging companies sold their platinum in the E.U. Moreover, if the merger was anti-competitive, South Africa might have profited from it, for consumption was predominantly abroad and the South African economy would probably have gained more than South African consumers would lose... A sound competition law system would certainly allow a directly and substantially harmed jurisdiction to reprehend an anti-competitive transaction, particularly where it is likely to escape condemnation at home and is not justified by considerations such as defence.

[115] See *supra* 90.

[116] See Y. van Gerven and L. Hoet, 'Gencor: Some Notes on Transnational Competition Law Issues' (2001) 28 *LIEI* 195.

[117] Reg. 139/2004, Art. 4.

[118] In *Samsung* [1999] OJ L 225/12, [1998] 4 CMLR 494 the non-EC undertaking was fined for failing to notify a merger which in the event raised no competition concerns.

Even so, there are remarkable aspects about this judgment. First, the Court of First Instance's expressed understanding of appropriate jurisdiction corresponds precisely with the United States' understanding of appropriate jurisdiction (and with the U.S. understanding of the effects test): that a jurisdiction may regulate conduct that has an immediate [or direct], substantial and foreseeable effect on the regulating jurisdiction's commerce . . . 'Immediate' is a concept with elasticity; it is enough that the structural conditions for harm have been set in place. Restraint in the exercise of jurisdiction may be required in the event of a direct conflict of the laws of two jurisdictions; but the home nation's permissive stance and the regulating nation's prohibitory stance are not such a conflict . . .

Second, as for E.C. law itself, the meaning of 'implemented' in *Woodpulp* has been an important undecided issue. Does the requirement that an offending act or agreement must be 'implemented' in the regulating jurisdiction add anything to the requirement that an act or agreement must have direct effects within the regulating jurisdiction? The Court of First Instance stated that 'implementation . . . is satisfied by mere sale within the Community . . .' If 'implementation' in a *merger* case is satisfied by mere sales in the jurisdiction of the merged firm's products, then implementation means effects, because the way that the anti-competitive nature of a merger is evidenced is through sales of the product of the merged firm.

To be sure, the worldwide sales subsidiary of the Lonrho parent was in Brussels; but if the consolidation of mining in South Africa were to trigger duopoly behaviour of Gencor/Lonrho with Anglo-American and thereby limit output in South Africa, this would be so no matter where the sales office was based. It is therefore unlikely that lack of a sales office in the Community would defeat the implementation requirement . . .

Third, challenging issues lurk beneath the surface. Was there really no conflict between E.C. law and South African law? . . . Should it count for anything that the home authority vetted the concentration and found that a strong number two firm would be better for competition than a clearly dominant firm? What if the South African Government had taken a strong stand in favour of 'its' merger, as did the U.S. Government in *Boeing/McDonnell Douglas*? Should the most prohibitory jurisdiction always prevail? . . . Should a big consuming jurisdiction prevail, in any event, where the home jurisdiction is not a major consuming market and the home country's producers stand to gain more than its consumers stand to lose if the merger is anti-competitive? On the other hand, if every consuming nation can abort a merger—and some may even err in good faith in their effort to predict competitive harm—are international mergers excessively vulnerable?

South Africa's diplomatic stance (*ie* no opposition) made resolution of the jurisdictional problem in *Gencor* an easy one—compared with what have been the case if South Africa had fought for 'its' merger.

The fact is, however, that we now live in a world of mutual, liberal extraterritoriality. Mutually expansive scope for national law will not always be frictionless. *Gencor*, combined with *Boeing*, the parallel U.S. initiatives, and the cases yet to come, will force us sooner or later to face the question: does the world need an international merger protocol?

(iii) The *Boeing/McDonnell Douglas* Case

The practical and diplomatic problems of taking jurisdiction over mergers involving undertakings established outside the Community were illustrated by *Boeing/McDonnell Douglas*.[119] Boeing and McDonnell Douglas (MDC) were both US aircraft manufacturers. In February 1997 the Commission received notification pursuant to the Merger Regulation of a concentration by

---

[119]   The Commission's final decision in this case is at [1997] OJ L336/16.

which Boeing would acquire control of MDC. The merger would create the world's largest aerospace manufacturer. The transaction clearly had a Community dimension within Article 1. The Commission had serious doubts about it and opened a Phase II investigation under Article 6(1)(c).[120] It was concerned that the number of large commercial jet aircraft manufacturers would be reduced from three to two (the other one being Airbus Industrie) and that Boeing's dominant position would be strengthened. It communicated its concerns to the US Federal Trade Commission pursuant to the EC-US Co-operation Agreement.[121] On 1 July 1997 the FTC cleared the merger (it considered the deal was not anti-competitive as Boeing already had a high market share and the addition of McDonnell Douglas's would not be significant) and on 13 July informed the Commission that, *inter alia*, a decision prohibiting the proposed merger could harm important US defence interests.[122] However, the Commission continued with its objections. At the last moment the Commission cleared the merger, after Boeing had given certain undertakings.[123] The undertakings related to the cessation of existing and future exclusive supply deals, the 'ring-fencing' of MDC's commercial aircraft activities, the licensing of patents to other jet aircraft manufacturers, commitments not to abuse relationships with customers and suppliers, and a commitment to report annually to the Commission.

The Commission issued a bullish Press Release, expressing satisfaction at this outcome:[124]

These commitments are considered adequate to resolve the identified competition problems, and the Commission has therefore decided to declare the operation compatible with the common market subject to conditions and obligations. The Commission has reached its decision after a rigorous analysis based on EU merger control law, and in accordance with its own past practice and the jurisprudence of the European Court. The Commission expects Boeing to comply fully with its decision, in particular as regards the commitments made by Boeing to resolve the competition problems identified by the Commission. The Commission will strictly monitor Boeing's compliance with these commitments. The EU Merger Regulation allows for appropriate measures to be taken by the Commission in the event of non-compliance by Boeing ... In arriving at this decision the Commission has taken into account concerns expressed by the U.S. Government relating to important US defence interests. The Commission took the US Government's concerns into consideration to the extent consistent with EU law, and has limited the scope of its action to the civil side of the operation, including the effects of the merger on the commercial jet aircraft market resulting from the combination of Boeing's and MDC's large defence and space interests.

In fact, the commitments were widely perceived in the Community as being weak and almost impossible to enforce, while US commentators and Boeing's lawyers claimed they were merely aimed at protecting and benefiting the European Airbus.[125] The Director General for Competition, writing in the aftermath of the affair, expressed general satisfaction that in dealing with the case 'the European Commission obtained positive results for European competition policy on the one hand and for our cooperation with the US on the other' but admitted that

---

[120] See *supra* Chap. 12 for Commission proceedings under the Merger Reg.

[121] Article VI. This agreement is discussed further, *infra* 1388.

[122] [1997] OJ L336/16, para. 12.

[123] *Ibid.*, paras. 115–19.

[124] IP (1997) 729 of 30 July 1997 [1997] 5 CMLR 271.

[125] See A. Kaczorowska, 'International Competition Law in the Context of Global Capitalism [2000] *ECLR* 117, 118. Bill Bishop, however, argues that there were very good reasons for blocking the merger, as it took the industry from three players to two, where there was evidence that the third player exerted a significant downward effect on prices. He concludes that 'the actual result was a compromise making little economic sense since customers were not protected by it at all. But by the light of international politics it was all too easy to understand the result': B. Bishop, 'Editorial, The Boeing/McDonnell Douglas Merger' [1997] *ECLR* 417.

'diverging approaches of the competition authorities in Brussels and Washington made it impossible to reach commonly accepted solutions'.[126]

The matter showed that, despite the existence of bilateral cooperation arrangements[127] between broadly like-minded competition authorities, clashes cannot always be avoided. It should be noted that the USA, the home of the effects doctrine, did *not* dispute the EC's assumption of extraterritorial jurisdiction, but expected that its assertions of the importance of the deal to its national interests would be deferred to by the Commission.[128]

(iv) The *GE/Honeywell* Case

In *GE/Honeywell*[129] the Commission prohibited a merger between two US companies which had been passed by the US authorities—not just *a* merger, but what would have been the biggest ever merger in US corporate history. The two corporate groups involved had a combined worldwide turnover of €180 billion. GE made aircraft engines. Honeywell made engines but, more significantly, avionics. GE had a leasing arm which was a purchaser of aircraft and therefore a downstream customer of both engines and avionics. The differences in the view of this merger lay largely in the different attitude of the Commission and the US authorities to conglomerate mergers,[130] to bundling and the possibility of leveraging. For present purposes, however, what is significant is that the prohibition happened[131] rather than why it happened. The whole affair was conducted under intense media interest and amid much political and diplomatic activity.[132] It was a dramatic illustration of the consequences of multi-national mergers being subjected to multiple jurisdictions with a slightly different 'take' on some matters. Nothing could have provided better ammunition for those who argue that the only way to deal with global transactions is through global competition mechanisms.

6. INTERNATIONAL COOPERATION

A. GENERAL

Faced with the globalization of the economy and with the problems of the application and enforcement of competition laws which are illustrated above, attention is increasingly turning to the desirability of international agreements as at least a partial solution. Agreements which are actually in place at the moment are mainly bilateral ones between major trading partners,

---

[126] A. Schaub, 'International Co-operation in Antitrust Matters: Making the Point in the Wake of the Boeing/MDD Proceedings' [1998] *Competition Policy Newsletter* No. 1, 2, 3–4.

[127] See *infra* 1388.

[128] See, generally, A. Bavasso, 'Boeing/McDonnell Douglas: Did the Commission Fly Too High? [1998] *ECLR* 243.

[129] Case No. COMP/M.2220.

[130] See *supra* Chap. 12.

[131] The Commission would, it appears have been willing to allow the merger to proceed if it had received satisfactory undertakings before its deadline. The decision was upheld by the CFI, Case T-210/01 *General Electric v Commission* [2005] ECR II-5575, [2006] 4 CMLR 686 because the CFI agreed with the Commission about the horizontal overlaps, but it was highly critical of the Commission's treatment of the conglomerate effects and bundling. See Chap. 12, 1062.

[132] See A. Burnside, 'GE, Honey I Sank the Merger' [2002] *ECLR* 107; D. Giotakos, L. Petit, G. Garnier and P. De Luyck, *GE/Honeywell*—An Insight into the Commission's Investigation and Decision (2001) *Competition Policy Newsletter* 3, 5.

but there has also been activity at the level of international organizations. The USA concluded bilateral agreements with Germany in 1976, Australia in 1982, and Canada in 1984 and 1995. These were all inspired by the OECD[133] Recommendation of (originally) 1967.[134] The 1991 Agreement between the USA and the EC, however, goes further than these agreements because it includes so-called 'positive comity' provisions.

B. BILATERAL AGREEMENTS

(i) The EC-US Cooperation Agreement

a. The Content of the 1991 and 1998 Agreements

In 1991 the Commission concluded an agreement with the US authorities about cooperation over the enforcement of their competition laws.[135] The authority of the Commission to enter into the agreement was subsequently challenged by France, supported by Spain and the Netherlands, and the ECJ found that the Commission did not have the power to conclude (as distinct from negotiate) agreements with foreign countries.[136] The agreement was finally approved by means of a joint decision of the Council and Commission in 1995.[137]

The Agreement provides for: the reciprocal notification of cases under investigation by either authority, where they may affect the important interests of the other party (Article II); exchanges of information and periodic meetings between competition officials from each country (Article III); and rendering each other assistance and coordinating their enforcement activities (Article IV). The most significant provisions, however, are Articles V and VI. Article V is the 'positive comity' Article, providing the possibility for one authority to request the other to take enforcement action, and Article VI provides for 'traditional' or 'negative' comity, i.e., for each authority to take into account the important interests of the other in the course of its enforcement activities. (This concept was introduced above, in the context of the US cases, and it should be noted that Article VI seems to be less restrictive than the version which appears in *Hartford Fire Insurance*.)

Agreement Between the Government of the USA and the Commission of the European Communities Regarding the Application of their Competition Laws, 1991

Article V

Cooperation regarding anti-competitive activities in the territory of one Party that adversely affect the interests of the other Party

 1. The Parties note that anti-competitive activities may occur within the territory of one Party that, in addition to violating that Party's competition laws, adversely affect important interests of

---

[133] Organization for Economic Cooperation and Development.

[134] See *infra* 1392.

[135] Agreement between the Government of the USA and the Commission of the European Communities regarding the application of their Competition Laws, 23 Sept. 1991 [1991] 4 CMLR 823, 30 *ILM* 1487.

[136] Case C-327/91, *France v. Commission* [1994] ECR I-3641, [1994] 5 CMLR 517.

[137] [1995] OJ L95/45.

the other Party. The Parties agree that it is in both their interests to address anti-competitive activities of this nature.

2. If a Party believes that anti-competitive activities carried out on the territory of the other Party are adversely affecting its important interests, the first Party may notify the other Party and may request that the other Party's competition authorities initiate appropriate enforcement activities. The notification shall be as specific as possible about the nature of the anti-competitive activities and their effects on the interests of the notifying Party, and shall include an offer of such further information and other cooperation as the notifying Party is able to provide.

3. Upon receipt of a notification under paragraph 2, and after such other discussion between the Parties as may be appropriate and useful in the circumstances, the competition authorities of the notified Party will consider whether or not to initiate enforcement activities, or to expand ongoing enforcement activities, with respect to the anti-competitive activities identified in the notification. The notified Party will advise the notifying Party of its decision. If enforcement activities are initiated, the notified Party will advise the notifying Party of their outcome and, to the extent possible, of significant interim developments.

4. Nothing in this Article limits the discretion of the notified Party under its competition laws and enforcement policies as to whether or not to undertake enforcement activities with respect to the notified anti-competitive activities, or precludes the notifying Party from undertaking enforcement activities with respect to such anti-competitive activities.

Article VI

Avoidance of conflicts over enforcement activities

Within the framework of its own laws and to the extent compatible with its important interests, each Party will seek, at all stages in its enforcement activities, to take into account the important interests of the other Party. Each Party shall consider important interests of the other Party in decisions as to whether or not to initiate an investigation or proceeding, the scope of an investigation or proceeding, the nature of the remedies or penalties sought, and in other ways, as appropriate. In considering one another's important interests in the course of their enforcement activities, the Parties will take account of, but will not be limited to, the following principles:

1. While an important interest of a Party may exist in the absence of official involvement by the Party with the activity in question, it is recognized that such interests would normally be reflected in antecedent laws, decisions or statements of policy by its competent authorities.

2. A Party's important interests may be affected at any stage of enforcement activity by the other Party. The Parties recognize, however, that as a general matter the potential for adverse impact on one Party's important interests arising from enforcement activity by the other Party is less at the investigative stage and greater at the stage at which conduct is prohibited or penalized, or at which other forms of remedial orders are imposed.

3. Where it appears that one Party's enforcement activities may adversely affect important interests of the other Party, the Parties will consider the following factors, in addition to any other factors that appear relevant in the circumstances, in seeking an appropriate accommodation of the competing interests:

(a) the relative significance to the anti-competitive activities involved of conduct within the enforcing Party's territory as compared to conduct within the other Party's territory;

(b) the presence or absence of a purpose on the part of those engaged in the anti-competitive activities to affect consumers, suppliers, or competitors within the enforcing Party's territory;

(c) the relative significance of the effects of the anti-competitive activities on the enforcing Party's interests as compared to the effects on the other Party's interests;

> (d) the existence or absence of reasonable expectations that would be furthered or defeated by the enforcement activities;
>
> (e) the degree of conflict or consistency between the enforcement activities and the other Party's laws or articulated economic policies; and
>
> (f) the extent to which enforcement activities of the other Party with respect to the same persons, including judgments or undertakings resulting from such activities, may be affected.

The Competition Commissioner, writing in the *XXVIIIth Report on Competition Policy* said that this amounted to 'a commitment by the EU and the USA to cooperate with respect to antitrust enforcement, and not to act unilaterally and extraterritorially unless the avenues provided by comity have been exhausted'.[138]

The successful operation of the Agreement persuaded the parties to strengthen the positive comity provisions. In 1998, therefore, they signed the EU–US Positive Comity Agreement[139] which entered into force on 4 June 1998. This spells out more clearly the circumstances in which a request for positive comity will be made and the manner in which such requests should be treated. Article III provides:

> ### Positive comity
>
> The competition authorities of a Requesting Party may request the competition authorities of a Requested Party to investigate and, if warranted, to remedy anti-competitive activities in accordance with the Requested Party's competition laws. Such a request may be made regardless of whether the activities also violate the Requesting Party's competition laws, and regardless of whether the competition authorities of the Requesting Party have commenced or contemplate taking enforcement activities under their own competition laws.

Article IV provides for investigations by the requesting party to be deferred or suspended in reliance on the requested party's enforcement. The effect of the 1998 Agreement is to create a presumption, as described by the Commission in its report on the application of the co-operation agreement for 1998:[140]

> The 1998 EC/US Positive Comity Agreement, like the 1991 Agreement, does not alter existing law, nor does it require any change in existing law. However, it does create a presumption that when anti-competitive activities occur in the whole or in a substantial part of the territory of one of the parties and affect the interests of the other party, the latter 'will normally defer or suspend its enforcement activities in favour of' the former. This is expected to happen particularly when these anti-competitive activities do not have a direct, substantial and reasonably foreseeable impact on consumers in the territory of the party deferring or suspending its activities.
>
> The presumption of deferral will only occur if the party in the territory of which the restrictive activities are occurring has jurisdiction over these activities and is prepared to deal actively and expeditiously with the matter. When dealing with the case that party will keep its counterpart closely informed of any developments in the procedure, within the limits of its internal rules protecting confidentiality.

---

[138] Commission's *XXVIIth Report on Competition Policy* (Commission, 1998), foreword, 5.

[139] [1998] OJ L173/28, [1999] 4 CMLR 502.

[140] At para. 3. See the *XXVIIIth Report on Competition Policy* (Commission, 1998), 315.

The new Agreement constitutes an important development, since it represents a commitment on the part of the European Union and the United States to cooperate with respect to antitrust enforcement in certain situations, rather than to seek to apply their antitrust laws extraterritorially.

It is important to note that because the EC merger rules do not allow for the deferral or suspension of action which the agreement envisages the EC merger rules are not within the 1998 agreement.[141]

b. The Application of the Agreements

Both the EC and US authorities consider that their cooperation works well and has made a very positive contribution to competition law enforcement. The EC and US authorities have a very close relationship. The 1991 procedures worked particularly successfully in respect of the investigation into Microsoft in 1994.[142] The US Department of Justice (DOJ) and the Commission actively cooperated. However, there is a major drawback in the operation of the agreement. Articles VII of the 1991 Agreement and V of the 1998 Agreement provide for the maintenance of the confidentiality of information acquired by the authorities in the course of their investigations. Further, Articles IX and VII, respectively, provide that nothing in the agreements is to be interpreted in a manner which is inconsistent with the parties' existing laws. This greatly limits the information which the authorities may exchange.[143] It is notable that in the 1994 investigation Microsoft, which was happy to have the US and EC investigations combined as it was easier for the company to deal with the two authorities together, agreed to waive its rights to confidentiality and to allow information exchanges between the Commission and the DOJ.[144]

The existence of the cooperation agreement did not, however, prevent the 1997 dispute over the *Boeing/McDonnell Douglas* merger or the *GE/Honeywell* row.[145] In *Boeing/McDonnell Douglas*, for instance, the authorities *did* consult each other. In accordance with the provisions of the agreement the Commission and the Federal Trade Commission carried out the necessary notifications and consultations, and the Commission took into account the US concerns over its defence interests. In the end, however, as the Director General recognized, '[p]rocedures of notification and consultation and the principles of traditional and positive comity allow us to bring our respective approaches closer in cases of common interest but there exist no mechanism for resolving conflicts in cases of substantial divergence of analysis'.[146]

(ii) Other Cooperation Agreements

Encouraged by the success of its agreement with the USA, the EC entered into a similar agreement with Canada which came into force on 29 April 1999. In particular, the Agreement contains (Articles V and VI), provisions similar to Articles V and VI of the 1991 Agreement including the principle of positive comity.[147] In June 2003 it entered into an agreement with

---

[141] Art. II(4)(a).

[142] Although because of the case brought by France (see *supra* n. 000) the agreement was not officially in force.

[143] See *supra* Chap. 14 for the question of confidentiality in EC competition procedure.

[144] See further C. Cocuzza and M. Montini, 'International Antitrust Co-operation in a Global Economy' [1998] *ECLR* 156; J. Parisi, 'Enforcement Co-operation Among Antitrust Authorities' [1999] *ECLR* 133.

[145] See *supra* 1387.

[146] Schaub, *supra* n. 126.

[147] [1999] OJ L175, [1999] 5 CMLR 713.

Japan. Again, the principal elements are mutual information, coordination of enforcement activities and exchange of non-confidential information. With Korea, the EC has established a permanent forum for consultation which shares experience and views on competition policy, as well as non-confidential information on enforcement. In respect of China the Commission has agreed on a structured dialogue to share experience and views on competition matters and provide technical and capacity-building assistance. The Commission cooperates with the competition authorities of other OECD member countries based on the 1995 OECD recommendation.

C. MULTILATERAL COOPERATION

(i) General

There have been initiatives within various international fora aimed at formulating mechanisms for increasing cooperation over competition laws and avoiding conflicts. These are briefly described here. We consider the problems inherent in such multilateral international arrangements and ask whether it is possible to envisage the creation of a multilateral international competition law mechanism at present.

(ii) UNCTAD and the OECD

The United Nations' Set of Multilaterally Agreed Equitable Principles and Rules for the Control of Restrictive Business Practices were adopted in 1980 under the auspices of UNCTAD[148] but provide only a voluntary, non-binding Code. In 1967 the OECD adopted a Recommendation that its member countries should cooperate with each other in the enforcement of their national competition laws.[149] This provides: for one country to notify another when the latter's important interests are affected by the former's investigation or enforcement; for countries to share information and to consult; for them to coordinate parallel investigations; for countries to assist one another in obtaining information inside each other's territory; and for countries to consider dealing with anti-competitive behaviour affecting their interests but occurring in another country's territory by requesting the latter's authorities to take action (positive comity). The bilateral agreements described in Section B above reflect these provisions but the 1991 EC-US Agreement was the first to include the 'positive comity' principle. In May 1998 the OECD (Committee of Competition Law and Policy) adopted a recommendation on hardcore cartels, aimed at strengthening the effectiveness and efficiency of the member countries' enforcement of their competition laws against such cartels. In 2006 the OECD issued a report *Competition Law and Policy in the EU*.[150]

(iii) The WTO

When the World Trade Organisation (WTO) was being negotiated in 1993 a Draft International Antitrust Code was drawn up by a group of experts at the Max Planck Institute. This would have

---

[148] The United Nations Conference on Trade and Development.

[149] Amended, *inter alia*, in 1995: OECD Doc. C(95)130/FINAL.

[150] Available on the Commission's website, http://ec.europa.eu/comm/competition/international/ multilateral/oecd.html, and on the OECD website, http://www.oecd.org/dataoecd/7/41/35908641.pdf

established an international antitrust regime.[151] The parties to the WTO did not agree to its adoption, however, and no agreement on international competition law was annexed to the WTO Charter. Promoted by the EU, the matter was later taken up at the First Ministerial Conference of the parties to the WTO in Singapore in 1996 and a Working Group on Trade and Competition Policy was set up in 1997. The first Chair of this Group was Professor Jenny of the French competition authority, Chair of the OECD Competition Law and Policy Committee.

In 1997 and 1998 the Working Group worked on a checklist of issues, of which the main elements were: the relationship between the objectives, principles, concepts, scope, and instruments of trade and competition policy and their relationship with development and economic growth; stocktaking and analysis of existing instruments, standards, and activities regarding trade and competition policy, including experience with their application; and the interaction between trade and competition policy. In 1999 the Group examined three further topics: the relevance of the fundamental WTO principles of national treatment, transparency, and most-favoured-nation treatment to competition policy and vice versa; approaches to promoting cooperation and communication among members, including in the field of technical cooperation; and the contribution of competition policy to achieving the objectives of the WTO, including the promotion of international trade.

Ultimately, the question which has to be addressed is whether a multilateral framework on competition policy should be set up under the auspices of the WTO. The US has been reluctant to go down that path whereas the EU has been a keen advocate of working through the WTO to achieve this. The EU's views were set out in a Discussion Document in March 1999, in preparation for the 1999 WTO Ministerial Conference in Seattle. The Document set out its objectives as:

a) The introduction of a competition law by significant trading partners which still lack one, and agreement that competition law should in principle cover all the sectors of the economy;

b) Ensuring that competition law, and its enforcement, are based on core principles of efficiency, transparency, non-discrimination, etc.;

c) Promoting a stricter enforcement policy in relation to anti-competitive practices with a significant impact on international trade and investment;

d) Promoting cooperation in the application of competition law to anti-competitive practices with an international dimension and limiting the risk of conflict arising from extraterritorial enforcement and fact-finding;

e) Reducing unnecessary costs and uncertainties for business arising from the application of different competition laws to the same international transactions.

In the event, the WTO meeting at Seattle collapsed. However, the US agreed to explore the idea of a multilateral framework within the WTO. The Fourth WTO Ministerial Conference at Doha in November 2001 adopted a Declaration which contained three paragraphs on competition policy. The Declaration recognized the case for a multilateral framework to enhance the contribution of competition policy to international trade and development and said that negotiations on trade and competition should take place after the Fifth Ministerial at Cancun in 2003. Until then the Working Group would work on formulating certain core principles on transparency, non-discrimination and procedural fairness; hard-core cartels; modalities of voluntary cooperation; and supporting the development of competition institutions in developing countries. Competition was one of the so-called 'Singapore Issues' (the others were trade facilitation, transparency in government procurement and the relationship between trade and investment).

---

[151] For the details, see C Cocuzza and M Montini, 'International Antitrust Co-operation in a Global Economy' [1998] *ECLR* 156, 160–1; E. U. Petersmann, 'International Competition Rules for Governments and for Private Business' (1996) 30 *J World Trade* 5.

The EU had high hopes for the meeting at Cancun but these were not fulfilled. The meeting was abruptly terminated amid much disagreement. Although there was certainly dispute over the 'Singapore Issues', including competition, many members of the WTO had grievances over a range of issues and the reasons for the collapse at Cancun are to do with a number of complex factors.[152] The agricultural subsidies offered by the EU and the US government to their home producers are a continuing cause of dissension and many developing countries have become unhappy with the concept of 'free trade' which seemed previously to have become universally accepted as the remedy for the world's ills. The WTO, like the World Bank, is seen in many quarters as part of the problem, not the remedy. The idea of a multilateral competition framework was a victim of the spirit of the times.[153] Moreover, in 2004 the General Council of the WTO abandoned any attempt to work on a set of antitrust rules.[154] It appears that this was due to the fears of the small or developing nations.[155]

(iv) The International Competition Network

While attempts to put competition on the map at the WTO run into difficulties competition authorities from around the world have quietly been getting on with setting up procedures and mechanisms through which they can cooperate. In October 2001 the International Competition Network was established. The impetus for this came from the US IPAC report (International Competition Policy Advisory Committee) in February 2000.[156] According to its web site[157] the ICN provides competition authorities with a specialized yet informal venue for maintaining contacts and addressing practical concerns. It facilitates procedural and substantive convergence in competition enforcement through a results-based and project-orientated working-groups. The ICN has already proved an useful and productive organization. It has a number of very active working groups: the Merger Working Group, which has adopted "guiding principles and recommended practices" which competition authorities should abide by when analysing mergers across several jurisdictions; the Cartels Working Group, which organizes an annual cartel workshop, has produced a number of reports on anti-cartel policy and has also drafted several chapters of a cartel enforcement manual, including a template for ICN member agencies to set out their rules governing cartel enforcement; and a Competition Policy Implementation Working Group, whose object is to 'identify key elements that contribute to successful capacity building and competition policy implementation in developing and transition economies'. This 'soft law' harmonization is highly effective.

(v) A Global Competition Law Regime?

The WTO remains the most obvious framework for the establishment of some type of international competition regime and its existing dispute settlement mechanism provides a possible

---

[152] See F. Jenny, 'Competition Trade and Development before and after Cancun' in B. Hawk (ed.) [2003] *Fordham Corp L Inst* 631.

[153] For an entertaining (yet with a serious message) account of Cancun, see F. Jenny, 'WTO Core Principles and Trade/Competition, Policies' in B. Hawk (ed.) [2003] *Fordham Corp L. Inst* 703, in which he tells the tale in the guise of the plot of the film *The Third Man* (with the EU Trade Commissioner as Holly Marten and 'Trade Consensus' as Harry Lime).

[154] Doha Work Programme Decision, 1 August 2004.

[155] See E. Elhauge and D. Geradin, *Global Competition Law and Economics* (Hart Publishing, 2007), 1107–12, for an explanation and criticism of this.

[156] US DOJ: available at http:www.usdoj.gov/atr/icpac/finalreport.htm.

[157] http://www.internationalcompetitionnetwork.org.

model. However, the problems currently facing the WTO vividly demonstrate how difficult it is to reach international consensus in the economic field when States are in such different stages of development and have such different interests. The requirement of the WTO is that all Member States, except the very poorest, subscribe to its rights and obligations in exchange for trade liberalization. Prominent among the organization's shortcomings, however, is that its rules do not sufficiently allow for socio-cultural and environmental criteria to be considered, and at least one voice has warned that it is essential to take account of socio-cultural divergences in any set of competition rules which are adopted at an international level.[158] Some developing countries have come to view the WTO as a 'rich man's club', run for the benefit of the world's most powerful trading blocs, although the bitterest disputes to date have been between the USA and the EC. Both caution and pragmatism would suggest that the present problems in the WTO need to be dealt with before a competition law element is added. However, more and more countries are adopting competition law regimes[159] and the capacity for conflict between them, should they all take extraterritorial jurisdiction, increases exponentially.

In the meantime, we live in what one EC official called a bipolar world, in which American antitrust is not the only show in town.[160] EC and US competition authorities have learned, despite the occasional high-profile disagreement, to cooperate closely and bilaterally to their mutual advantage. The EU, however, remains committed to the belief that competition policy can deliver benefits to the whole global economy and that international structures are essential to enable it fully to do this. At present though, it appears that soft law instruments, particularly within the ICN, are producing successful convergence and cooperation and spreading best practice between competition authorities from around the world. The EC is committed to these processes, which seem to hold out more promise than attempts to produce rules and regulations.

7. CONCLUSIONS

1. Traditional concepts of extra-territorial jurisdiction are not well-suited for use in international competition law situations.

2. Plaintiffs are understandably keen to sue in US courts when they have been victims of international cartels but the US courts are not welcoming at present and this may encourage the EC to develop better ways of facilitating damages actions in Europe.

3. Ideas for interntional competition regimes are unrealistic and over-ambitious. Bilateral agreements and friendly and cooperative relations between enforcers seem a better way ahead. While there are occasional high profile differences, much work has been done in building up an international consensus.

4. The international environment is not conducive at present to the imposition of rules. The best way forward is through soft law instruments.

---

[158] W. Pape, 'Socio-Cultural Differences and International Competition Law' (1999) 5 *ELJ* 438.

[159] The ICN had over eighty members in 2007.

[160] Jonathan Faull, speaking at the Fordham Corporate Law Institute, New York, 22–23 Oct. 1998.

8. FURTHER READING

A. BOOKS

BROWNLIE, I., *Principles of Public International Law* (6th edn., Oxford University Press, 2003)

DABBAH, M., *The Internationalisation of Antitrust Policy* (Cambridge University Press, 2003)

ELHAUGE, E., and GERADIN, D., *Global Competition Law and Economics* (Hart Publishing, 2007)

EPSTEIN, R., and GREVE, M. (eds.), *Competition Laws in Conflict: Antitrust Jurisdiction in a Global Economy* (AEI Press, 2004)

GAL, M., *'Competition Policy for Small Market Economies'* (Harvard University Press, 2003)

HIGGINS, R., *Problems and Process: International Law and How We Use It* (Clarendon Press, 1994)

JENNINGS, R. Y., and WATTS, A. (eds.), *Oppenheim's International Law* (9th edn., Longman, 1992)

JONES, C. A., and MATSUSHITA, M. (eds.), *Competition Policy in the Global Trading System* (Kluwer, 2002)

KENNEDY, K., *Competition Law and the World Trade Organization: The Limits of Multilateralism* (Sweet & Maxwell, 2001)

MANN, F. A. 'Responsibility of Parent Companies for Foreign Subsidiaries' in C. Olmstead (ed.), *Extra-territorial Application of Laws and Responses Thereto* (ESC Publishing, 1984), 156

SCHACHTER, O., *International Law in Theory and Practice* (Nijhoff, 1991), chap. XII

STIGLITZ, J., *Globalization and its Discontents* (Penguin, 2002)

SWAN, A. C., 'The Hartford Insurance Company Case; Antitrust in the Global Economy' in J. Bhandari and A. Sykes (eds.), *Economic Dimensions in International Law* (Cambridge University Press, 1997)

WOOD, D. P., 'The Trade Effects of Domestic Antitrust Enforcement' in J. Bhandari and A. Sykes (eds.), *Economic Dimensions in International Law* (Cambridge University Press, 1997)

ZANETTIN, B., *Cooperation Between Antitrust Agencies at the International Level* (Hart Publishing, 2002)

B. ARTICLES

AKEHURST, M., 'Jurisdiction in International Law' (1972–3) 46 *BYIL*, 145

BAVASSO, A., 'Boeing/McDonnell Douglas: Did the Commission Fly Too High?' [1998] *ECLR* 243

BISHOP, B., 'Editorial, The Boeing/McDonnell Douglas Merger' [1997] *ECLR* 417

BOWETT, D. W., 'Jurisdiction: Changing Problems of Authority over Activities and Resources' 1982 53 *BYIL* 1

BURNSIDE, A., 'GE, Honey I Sank the Merger' [2002] *ECLR* 107

COCUZZA C., and MONTINI, M., 'International Antitrust Co-operation in a Global Economy' [1998] *ECLR* 156

COLLINS, L., 'Blocking and Clawback Statutes' [1986] *JBL* 372

DURAND, B., FONT GALARZA, A., and MEHTA, K., 'The Interface Between Competition Policy and International Trade Liberalisation. Looking into the Future: Applying a New Virtual Anti-Trust Standard' (2004) 27 *World Competition* 3

FOX, E., 'Towards World Antitrust and Market Access' (1997) 91 *AJIL* 1

—— 'The Merger Regulation and its Territorial Reach' [1999] *ECLR* 334

GERVEN, VAN, W., 'EC Jurisdiction in Antitrust Matters: The Wood Pulp Judgment' [1989] *Fordham Corp L Inst* 451

GERVEN VAN, Y., and HOET, L., 'Gencor: Some Notes on Transnational Competition Law Issues' (2001) 28 *LIEI* 195

GREWLICH, A. S., 'Globalisation and Conflict in Competition Law' (2001) *Journal of World Competition* 367

GRIFFIN, J., 'Reactions to U.S. Assertions of Extraterritorial Jurisdiction' [1998] *ECLR* 64

GUZMAN, A., 'The Case for International Antitrust' (2004) *22 Berleley J Intl L* 355

JENNINGS, R. Y., 'Extraterritorial Jurisdiction and the United States Antitrust Laws' (1957) 33 *BYIL* 146

JENNY, F., 'Competition, Trade and Development Before and After Cancun' in B. Hawk, (ed.), [2003] *Fordham Corp L Inst* 631

—— 'Competition Law and Policy: Global Governance Issues' (2003) 26 *World Competition* 609.

KACZOROWSKA, A., 'International Competition Law in the Context of Global Capitalism' [2000] *ECLR* 117

LANGE D. F. G., and SANDAGE, J. B., 'The Wood Pulp Decision' (1989) 26 *CMLRev* 137

LIPSKY JR., A. B., 'Competition and the WTO: Beyond Cancun' in B. Hawk (ed.), [2003] *Fordham Corp L Inst* 657

MANN, F. A., 'The Doctrine of Jurisdiction in International Law' (1964) 111 RdC 1 'Casenote' (1973) 22 *ICLQ* 35

—— 'The Doctrine of International Jurisdiction Revisited After Twenty Years,' (1984) 186 RdC 9

MEESSEN, K. M., 'Antitrust Jurisdiction under Customary International Law' (1984) 78 *AJIL* 783

MITCHELL, A. D., 'Broadening the Vision of Trade Liberalisation' (2001) *Journal of World Competition* 367

PAPE, W., 'Socio-Cultural Differences and International Competition Law' (1999) 5 *ELJ* 438

PARISI, J., 'Enforcement Co-operation Among Antitrust Authorities' [1999] *ECLR* 133

PETERSMANN, E. U., 'International Competition Rules for Governments and for Private Business' (1996) 30 *Journal of World Trade Law* 5

PETERSMANN, E. U., 'WTO Core Principles and Trade/Competition' in in B. Hawk, (ed.), [2003] *Fordham Corp L Inst* 669

PITOFSKY, R., 'Competition Policy in a Global Economy' (1999) 3 *JIEL* 403

REYNOLDS, R. M., SICILIAN, J., and WELLMAN, P. S. 'The Extraterritorial Application of the US Antitrust Laws to Criminal Conspiracies' [1998] *ECLR* 151

ROBERTSON A., and DEMETRIOU, M., ' "But that was in Another Country" ': The Extraterritorial Application of US Antitrust Laws in the US Supreme Court' (1994) 43 *ICLQ* 417

ROTH, P. M., 'Reasonable Extraterritoriality: Correcting the "Balance of Interests" ' (1992) 41 *ICLQ* 245

SLOT P. J., and GRABANDI, E., 'Extraterritoriality and Jurisdiction' (1986) 23 *CMLRev* 545

TORREMANS, P., 'Extraterritorial Application of EC and US Competition Law' (1996) 21 *ELRev* 280

WOOD, D. P., 'Soft Harmonization Among Competition Laws: Track Record and Prospects' (2003) 48 *Antitrust Bull* 305.

ADDENDUM
THE BRUSSELS EUROPEAN COUNCIL,
21/22 JUNE 2007

INTRODUCTION

This Addendum outlines the outcome of the European Council Meeting of 21/22 June 2007, insofar as it affects matters discussed in this book. This material should, therefore, be read in conjunction with the chapters of this book, which make appropriate references to this Addendum.

BACKGROUND

Ratification of the Constitutional Treaty in the Member States faltered following rejection of the Treaty in referenda in France and the Netherlands in 2005. The European Council meeting of 21–22 June 2007, under the Presidency of Germany, focussed on the issue of how reform of the European Treaties could be resolved in the light of this failure.

CONCLUSIONS OF THE COUNCIL

The Council abandoned the idea of formally adopting a 'Constitution' but salvaged many of the elements of the Constitutional Treaty. After tense negotiations the Council agreed to convene an Intergovernmental Conference (IGC) in July 2007 to draw up an EU *Reform Treaty*.[1] The expected timetable is that the IGC completes its task by the end of 2007 and Member States should ratify the Reform Treaty by early 2009 in time for it to enter into force before European Parliamentary elections in June 2009. It is understood that despite the removal of the 'constitutional' elements, ratification in Ireland will still require a referendum. The position in respect of certain other Member States is less clear.

The Reform Treaty will contain two substantive clauses. One will amend the Treaty on European Union (TEU) and the other will amend the EC Treaty. The EC Treaty will be renamed the *Treaty on the Functioning of the Union* (TFU). The amendments to the two Treaties preserve much of the contents of the Constitutional Treaty but also reflect the compromises hammered out during the Council negotiations between Member States. In particular, some matters have now been enshrined in protocols, declarations and annexes rather than in Treaty articles.

There will therefore continue to be two Treaties and neither the TEU nor the TFU will have a constitutional character.[2] The Union will have a single legal personality and the European Community will cease to exist. The two Treaties will constitute the Treaties on which the Union

---

[1] Brussels European Council, 21/22 June 2007, Presidency Conclusions, doc. 11177/07, Brussels 23 June 2007. This Addendum reflects the draft of the Reform Treaty on which the IGC started work on 23 July 2007.

[2] *Ibid.*, Annex 1, para.3.

is founded and the Union will replace and succeed the Community.[3] The word 'Community' in the existing Treaties will therefore be replaced by 'Union'. EC Competition law therefore will finally become EU competition law.

General features of the new dispensation which may be relevant to the matters discussed in this book include the following:

- From 2014 the number of Commissioners will be reduced. The total number will be equal to two thirds of the number of the Member States and the Commissioners will be appointed pursuant to a rotation system. This means of course that at any one time not all Member States will have a Commissioner;

- The Court of First Instance will be renamed the 'General Court';

- There will be a cross-reference to the Charter of Fundamental Rights in the TEU. The Charter will be contained in an Annex to the Treaties. The TEU will specify that the Charter is legally binding on the EU institutions and in all Member States, except that the UK is to have an opt-out. Under the opt-out the UK itself may decide unilaterally on the Charter's application within the UK;

- A declaration on the primacy of Union law will be annexed to the Treaties. This will confirm the existing case law of the Court of Justice.

THE POSITION AS REGARDS COMPETITION POLICY

Unexpectedly, competition policy became a major issue during the Council negotiations.

As explained in Chapter 1, Article 3(1)(g) of the existing EC Treaty states that the activities of the Community shall include 'a system ensuring that competition in the internal market is not distorted'. This has been in the EC Treaty (the original wording has been slightly amended) since the inception of the EEC fifty years ago. In contrast, the list of the Union's objectives set out in Article 2 of the (existing) TEU does not mention competition.

The Constitutional Treaty would have contained an Article on 'The Union's Objectives' (Article I-3) which were to include the words 'The Union shall offer its citizens ... an internal market where competition is free and undistorted' (Article I-3(2)). Had the Constitutional Treaty come into force Article 3(1)(g) EC would have been repealed. Undistorted competition would have therefore become an *objective* and not simply an *activity* (although the use of Article 308 EC to pass the EC Merger Regulation indicates that competition had already been treated as an objective as Article 308 can only be used to attain one of the 'objectives of the Community').

During negotiations in the Council on 21 June 2007, when amendment to the TEU and the inclusion Article I-3 was under discussion, the recently elected President of France, Nicholas Sarkozy, proposed the removal of the reference to free and undistorted competition. The objectives of the TEU would therefore refer simply to the establishment of an internal market. During the course of 22 June, however, and after much lobbying by the competition community led by DG Competition, and (it is alleged) intervention by the British Prime Minister-in-waiting, Gordon Brown,[4] agreement

---

[3] Ibid., Annex 1, para.2.

[4] The Prime Minister, Tony Blair, attended the Council meeting but had announced that he was resigning as Prime Minister as from 27 June. Gordon Brown, the Chancellor of the Exchequer, had been elected leader of the Labour Party and was therefore about to become Prime Minister in his stead.

was reached for the annexation of a Protocol re-asserting the commitment of the Member States to competition policy.[5]

The outcome of these negotiations is that Article 3(3) of the TEU is to state:

'The Union shall establish an internal market' (Article 3).

The Protocol, however, will state:

Protocol on internal market and competition

The High Contracting Parties, considering that the internal market as set out in Article 3 of the Treaty of European Union includes a system ensuring that competition is not distorted Have agreed that, to this end, the Union shall, if necessary, take action under the provisions of the Treaties, including under Article 308 of the Treaty on the Functioning of the Union.[6]

Article 3(1)(g) EC will disappear. Article 3 TFU will state that the Union shall have exclusive competence in the area of 'the establishing of the competition rules necessary for the functioning of the internal market'.

IMPLICATIONS FOR COMPETITION POLICY

The absence of an explicit reference to 'free and undistorted competition' in the objectives of the Union laid down in Article 3 of the amended TEU may be no more than symbolic. Its practical effect will depend on any significance accorded to its absence by the Court of Justice. An important point to note, is that the provision to which the Court has consistently referred to in interpreting the competition provisions—Article 3(1)(g) EC—will not appear in the TFU. However, Article 3(3) TFU will be bolstered by the reference to undistorted competition in the Protocol. The references to competition elsewhere in the EC Treaty will also remain in place, and the text of the substantive competition articles are themselves to remain unchanged. In a letter to the *Financial Times* on 27 June 2007 the Director General of the European Commission Legal Service pointed out that since competition is not currently one of the objectives of the European Community set out in Article 2 EC, but an 'activity' in Article 3 EC, the decision to drop the disputed words merely brings us back to the present situation. As he says, 'Clearly an objective that does not exist cannot be lost!'

The wording of the Protocol is interesting. As well as including a paraphrase of Article 3(1)(g) it states that the Union shall, if necessary, take action under Article 308 TFU (currently Article 308 EC). As noted above, this article provides for action to be taken to attain one of the objectives of the Community (in future 'the Union'). The reference to Article 308 in the Protocol thus appears to reintroduce indirectly the concept of undistorted competition as an 'objective'.

Following the publication of the Presidency Conclusions, the Competition Commissioner, Neelie Kroes, put out a defiant press release which declared that events at the Council meeting would be no way affect DG Comp's work.

An Internal Market without competition rules would be an empty shell—nice words, but no concrete results.

The Protocol on Internal Market and Competition agreed at the European Council clearly repeats that competition policy is fundamental to the Internal Market. It retains the existing competition rules which have served us so well for 50 years. It re-confirms the European Commission's duties as the independent competition enforcement authority for Europe.

---

[5] The proposal was allegedly made by the UK Treasury.

[6] Brussels European Council, 21/22 June 2007, Presidency Conclusions, doc. 11177/07, Brussels 23 June 2007, Annex 1, n.16.

Now I would like to get back to the job. The Commission will continue to enforce Europe's competition rules firmly and fairly: to bust cartels and monopolies, to vet mergers, to control state subsidies. That is in the interests of our Internal Market. It is in the interests of European citizens and consumers, it is what Europe's business community quite rightly expects and deserves, and it is a firm foundation for Europe's prosperity, notably by ensuring fair conditions for international investment.[7]

It is, however, interesting to reflect a little more deeply on this crisis over competition policy. For the Commission, the competition community, and some Member States, the inclusion of free and undistorted competition among the Union's objectives was uncontroversial. It was not foreseen that it would operate as a sticking point. President Sarkozy was reported as saying during the meeting: 'Competition as an ideology, as a dogma: what has it done for Europe?'[8] It appears that he was reacting, in part at least, to the Commission's imminent action in the utilities markets following the sector investigation under Article 17 of Regulation1/2003,[9] to the Commission's aggressive stance towards Member States attempting to circumvent EC merger control in cases of take-overs of national utilities, and to on-going hostility to the Commission's State Aid policy.[10] In any event, President Sarkozy's intervention was a salutary reminder that for some Member States, and in some political arenas, the attachment to the social market model and even to protectionism is alive and well and that the concept of competition as a central organizing principle of European integration is still open to challenge.

SERVICES OF GENERAL ECONOMIC INTEREST

The treatment of services of economic interest under Articles 16 and 86(2) EC is dealt with in Chapter 8.

The Constitutional Treaty, Article III-122, would have contained an expanded and amended version of Article 16 EC. This will now appear in the TFU as an amended Article 14. It appears that it will state:

Without prejudice to [Article 4 TEU, Articles 73, 86, and 87 of the Treaty on the Functioning of the Union] , and given the place occupied by services of general economic interest as services to which all in the Union attribute value as well as their role in promoting its social and territorial cohesion, the Union and the Member States, each within their respective competences and within the scope of application of [this Treaty], shall take care that such services operate on the basis of principles and conditions, particularly economic and financial conditions, which enable them to fulfil their missions. The European Parliament and the Council, acting in accordance with the ordinary legislative

---

[7] Memo 07/250, 23 June 2007.

[8] *Financial Times*, 26 June 2007, p. 12.

[9] See *infra* Chapter 11.

[10] See the State Aids Chapter of this book in the Online Resource Centre. He was also, it is alleged, responding to the perceived concerns of part of the French electorate which were credited with contributing to the 'non' vote in the referendum on the Constitution. President Sarkozy's view of the outcome of the Council was given at a press conference on 23 June 2007: 'Sur le fond...nous avons obtenu une réorientation majeure des objectifs de l'Union. La concurrence n'est plus un objectif de l'Union ou une fin en soi, mais un moyen au service du marché intérieur. Un protocole confirme que les questions de concurrence relèvent de l'organisation du marché intérieur, c'est un point majeur' : see http://www.elysee.fr/elysee/elysee.fr/francais/interventions/2007/juin/conference_de_presse_finale_a_l_occasion_du_conseil_europeen_a_bruxelles.78925.html.

procedure shall establish these principles and set these conditions without prejudice to the competence of Member States, in compliance with these Treaties, to provide, to commission and to fund such services.

In addition, the Council agreed to annex the following Protocol to the Treaties:

Protocol on services of general interest

The High Contracting Parties, wishing to emphasise the importance of services of general interest have agreed upon the following interpretative provisions, which shall be annexed to the Treaty on European Union and to the Treaty on the Functioning of the Union:

Article 1

The shared values of the Union in respect of services of general economic interest within the meaning of [Article 14 TFU] include in particular:

— the essential role and the wide discretion of national, regional and local authorities in providing, commissioning and organizing services of general economic interest as closely as possible to the needs of the users;
— the diversity between various services of general economic interest and the differences in the needs and preferences of users that may result from different geographical, social or cultural situations;
— a high level of quality, safety and affordability, equal treatment and the promotion of universal access and of user rights;

Article 2

The provisions of the Treaties do not affect in any way the competence of Member States to provide, commission and organise non-economic services of general interest.

---

24 July 2007

INDEX